Biology

NINTH EDITION

ELDRA P. SOLOMON

former affiliations:

University of South Florida, Tampa
Hillsborough Community College

LINDA R. BERG

former affiliations:

University of Maryland, College Park
St. Petersburg College

DIANA W. MARTIN

Rutgers University

BROOKS/COLE
CENGAGE Learning

Australia • Brazil • Japan • Korea • Mexico • Singapore • Spain • United Kingdom • United States

BROOKS/COLE
CENGAGE Learning™

Biology, **Ninth Edition**
Eldra P. Solomon, Linda R. Berg, and Diana W. Martin

Publisher, Life Sciences: Yolanda Cossio

Developmental Editor: Christopher Delgado

Assistant Editor: Alexis Glubka

Editorial Assistant: Joshua W. Taylor

Media Editor: Lauren Oliveira

Marketing Manager: Tom Ziolkowski

Marketing Assistant: Elizabeth Wong

Marketing Communications Manager: Linda Yip

Content Project Manager: Hal Humphrey

Art Director: John Walker

Print Buyer: Judy Inouye

Rights Acquisitions Specialist, Text: Roberta Broyer

Rights Acquisitions Specialist, Image: Dean Dauphinais

Production Service: Joan Keyes, Dovetail Publishing Services

Text Designer: tani hasegawa

Photo Researcher: Tim Herzog, Bill Smith Group

Text Researcher: Sue C. Howard

Copy Editor: Susan M. Gall

Compositor: Thompson Type

Illustrator: Amanda Bickel, Precision Graphics

Cover Designer: John Walker

Cover Image: Leafy sea dragon (*Phycodurus eques*) in Southern Ocean; Michael Aw/Getty Images

The leafy sea dragon inhabits kelp-covered rocky reefs and seaweed beds in the waters off the southern and western coast of Australia. This fish lives in depths from about 3 m to 50 m. It feeds on plankton, mainly tiny crustaceans, and typically grows to a length of about 35 centimeters (14 inches). The leafy sea dragon, with its long leaflike extensions, blends with surrounding seaweed, a striking example of camouflage.

When the male leafy sea dragon is ready to mate, his tail becomes bright yellow. Females then deposit up to 250 bright pink eggs in a spongy brood patch on the underside of the male's tail. The eggs are fertilized during the transfer from the female to the male. The male incubates the eggs for four to six weeks. Then, miniature leafy sea dragons are released into the water.

Leafy sea dragon populations have decreased due to habitat loss, pollution, and collectors who sell them for aquariums. They are currently listed as "near threatened" in the International Union for Conservation of Nature's status list.

For product information and technology assistance, contact us at **Cengage Learning Customer & Sales Support, 1-800-354-9706.**

For permission to use material from this text or product, submit all requests online at **www.cengage.com/permissions**
Further permissions questions can be e-mailed to **permissionrequest@cengage.com**

Library of Congress Control Number: 2010931615

High School Edition:
ISBN-13: 978-0-538-49564-6
ISBN-10: 0-538-49564-2

Brooks/Cole
20 Davis Drive
Belmont, CA 94002-3098
USA

Cengage Learning is a leading provider of customized learning solutions with office locations around the globe, including Singapore, the United Kingdom, Australia, Mexico, Brazil and Japan. Locate your local office at **www.cengage.com/global**

Cengage Learning products are represented in Canada by Nelson Education, Ltd.

To learn more about Brooks/Cole, visit **www.cengage.com/ brookscole**

Printed in Canada
1 2 3 4 5 6 7 14 13 12 11 10

DEDICATION

To our families, friends, and colleagues who gave freely of their love, support, knowledge, and time as we prepared this ninth edition of *Biology*.

Especially to
Freda, Kathleen, Mical, Amy, and Belicia
Alan and Jennifer
Chuck and Margaret

ABOUT THE AUTHORS

ELDRA P. SOLOMON has written several leading college-level textbooks in biology and in human anatomy and physiology. Her books have been translated into more than 10 languages. Dr. Solomon earned an M.S. from the University of Florida and an M.A. and Ph.D. from the University of South Florida. Dr. Solomon taught biology and nursing students for more than 20 years.

In addition to being a biologist and science author, Dr. Solomon is a biopsychologist with a special interest in the neuro-physiology of traumatic experience. Her research has focused on the neurological, endocrine, and psychological effects of trauma, including Post-traumatic Stress Disorder and development of maladaptive coping strategies.

Dr. Solomon has presented her research at many national and international conferences, and her work has been published in leading professional journals. Dr. Solomon has been profiled more than 30 times in leading publications, including *Who's Who in America, Who's Who in Science and Engineering, Who's Who in Medicine and Healthcare, Who's Who in American Education, Who's Who of American Women,* and *Who's Who in the World.*

LINDA R. BERG is an award-winning teacher and textbook author. She received a B.S. in science education, an M.S. in botany, and a Ph.D. in plant physiology from the University of Maryland. Her research focused on the evolutionary implications of steroid biosynthetic pathways in various organisms.

Dr. Berg taught at the University of Maryland at College Park for 17 years and at St. Petersburg College in Florida for 8 years. During her career, she taught introductory courses in biology, botany, and environmental science to thousands of students. At the University of Maryland, she received numerous teaching and service awards. Dr. Berg is also the recipient of many national and regional awards, including the National Science Teachers Association Award for Innovations in College Science Teaching, the Nation's Capital Area Disabled Student Services Award, and the Washington Academy of Sciences Award in University Science Teaching.

During her career as a professional science writer, Dr. Berg has authored or co-authored several leading college science textbooks. Her writing reflects her teaching style and love of science.

DIANA W. MARTIN is the Director of General Biology, Division of Life Sciences, at Rutgers University, New Brunswick Campus. She received an M.S. at Florida State University, where she studied the chromosomes of related plant species to understand their evolutionary relationships. She earned a Ph.D. at the University of Texas at Austin, where she studied the genetics of the fruit fly, *Drosophila melanogaster,* and then conducted postdoctoral research at Princeton University. She has taught General Biology and other courses at Rutgers for more than 25 years and has been involved in writing textbooks since 1988. She is immensely grateful that her decision to study biology in college has led to a career that allows her many ways to share her excitement about all aspects of biology.

Brief Contents

Table of Contents

Part 7 STRUCTURE AND LIFE PROCESSES IN ANIMALS 821

Preface

This ninth edition of Solomon, Berg, Martin *Biology* conveys our vision of the dynamic science of biology and how it affects every aspect of our lives, from our health and behavior to the challenging environmental issues that confront us. New discoveries in the biological sciences continue to increase our understanding of both the unity and diversity of life's processes and adaptations. With this understanding, we become ever more aware of our interdependence with the vast diversity of organisms with which we share planet Earth.

BIOLOGY: THE STUDENT-FRIENDLY BIOLOGY BOOK

We want beginning students to experience learning biology as an exciting journey of discovery. In the ninth edition of *Biology*, we explore Earth's diverse organisms, their remarkable adaptations to the environment, and their evolutionary and ecological relationships. We present the workings of science and the contributions of scientists whose discoveries not only expand our knowledge of biology but also help shape and protect the future of our planet. *Biology* provides insight into what science is, how scientists work, what scientists have contributed, and how scientific knowledge affects daily life.

Since the first edition of *Biology*, we have worked to present the principles of biology in an integrated way that is accurate, interesting, and conceptually accessible to students. In this ninth edition of *Biology*, we continue this tradition. We also continue to present biology in an inquiry-based framework. Some professors interpret inquiry as a learning method that takes place in the laboratory as students perform experiments. Laboratory research is certainly an integral part of inquiry-based learning. But inquiry is also a way of learning in which the student actively pursues knowledge outside the laboratory. In *Biology*, we have always presented the history of scientific advances, including scientific debates, to help students understand that science is a process, that is, a field of investigative inquiry, as well as a body of knowledge (the product of inquiry). In the ninth edition of *Biology*, we make a concerted effort to further integrate inquiry-based learning into the textbook with the introduction of new features and the expansion of several others (discussed in the following sections).

Throughout the text, we stimulate interest by relating concepts to experiences within the student's frame of reference. By helping students make such connections, we facilitate their mastery of general concepts. We hope the combined effect of an engaging writing style and interesting features will motivate and excite students in their study of biology.

THE SOLOMON/BERG/MARTIN LEARNING SYSTEM

In the ninth edition, we have continued to refine our highly successful *Learning System*. This system provides the student with the learning strategies needed to integrate biological concepts and to demonstrate mastery of these concepts. Learning biology is challenging because the subject of biology is filled with so many new terms and so many facts that must be integrated into the framework of general biological principles. To help students focus on important principles and concepts, we provide *Learning Outcomes* for the course and *Learning Objectives* for each major section of every chapter. At the end of each section, we provide *Review Questions* based on the Learning Objectives so students can assess their level of understanding of the material presented in the section. At the end of each chapter, we include a *Summary: Focus on Learning Objectives* that is organized around the *Learning Objectives*. The *Summary* is followed by *Test Your Understanding* questions (including multiple-choice exercises and diagram labeling) and *Critical Thinking* questions.

Throughout the book, students are directed to CengageNOW, a powerful online diagnostic tool that helps students assess their study needs and master the chapter objectives. After taking a pretest on CengageNOW, students receive feedback based on their answers as well as a Personalized Study Plan with links to animations and other resources keyed to their specific learning needs. Selected illustrations in the text are also keyed to *Animated* figures in CengageNOW.

Pedagogical Features

Our *Learning System* includes numerous learning strategies that help students increase their success:

- ***NEW*** An updated and expanded *art program* reinforces concepts discussed in the text, and presents complex processes in clear steps. This edition expands the number of *Key Experiment* figures, which encourage students to evaluate investigative approaches that scientists have taken. *Key Experiment* figures emphasize the scientific process in both classic and modern research; examples include Figures 8-9, 20-13, 22-9, 27-11, and 52-21. Also expanded in this edition are *Key Point* figures, in which important concepts are stated in process diagrams of complex topics; examples include Figures 1-11, 6-6, 8-2, 29-4, and 32-7. Many of the *Key Point* figures have numbered parts that show sequences of events in biological processes or life cycles. Numerous photographs, both alone and combined with line art, help students grasp concepts by connecting the "real" to the "ideal." The line art uses features such as *orientation icons* to help the student put the detailed figures into the broader context. We use symbols and colors consistently throughout the book to help students connect concepts. For example, the same four colors and shapes are used throughout the book to identify guanine, cytosine, adenine, and thymine. Similarly, the same colors are used consistently in illustrations and tables to indicate specific clades of organisms.

- **NEW** *Research Method* figures describe why biologists use a particular method and explain how the method is executed. Examples include Figures 12-6, 15-5, and 23-11.

- **NEW** *Inquiring About* boxes explore issues of special relevance to students, such as the effects of smoking, how traumatic experiences affect the body, and breast cancer. These boxes also provide a forum for discussing some interesting topics in more detail, such as the smallest ancient humans, ancient plants and coal formation, hydrothermal vent communities, and declining amphibian populations.

- A list of *Key Concepts* at the beginning of each chapter provides a chapter overview and helps the student focus on important principles discussed in the chapter.

- *Learning Objectives* at the beginning of each major section in the chapter indicate, in behavioral terms, what the student must do to demonstrate mastery of the material in that section.

- Each major section of the chapter is followed by a series of *Review* questions that assess comprehension by asking the student to describe, explain, compare, contrast, or illustrate important concepts. The *Review* questions are based on the section Learning Objectives.

- *Concept Statement Subheads* introduce sections, previewing and summarizing the key idea or ideas to be discussed in that section.

- *Sequence Summaries* within the text simplify and summarize information presented in paragraph form. For example, paragraphs describing blood circulation through the body or the steps by which cells take in certain materials are followed by a *Sequence Summary* listing the sequence of structures or steps.

- Numerous *tables,* many illustrated, help the student organize and summarize material presented in the text. Many tables are color-coded.

- A *Summary: Focus on Learning Objectives* at the end of each chapter is organized around the chapter *Learning Objectives.* This summary provides a review of the material, and because selected key terms are boldfaced in the summary, students learn vocabulary words within the context of related concepts.

- End-of-chapter questions provide students with the opportunity to evaluate their understanding of the material in the chapter. *Test Your Understanding* consists of multiple-choice questions, some of which are based on the recall of important terms, whereas others challenge students to integrate their knowledge. Answers to the *Test Your Understanding* questions are provided in Appendix E. Thought-provoking *Critical Thinking* questions encourage the student to apply the concepts just learned to new situations or to make connections among important concepts. Each chapter has one or more *Evolution Link* questions in the *Critical Thinking* section. Many chapters contain one or more *Analyzing Data* questions that require students to actively interpret experimental data presented in the chapter.

- **NEW** Many *Critical Thinking* sections also include one or more *Science, Technology, and Society* questions.

- The *Glossary* at the end of the book, the most comprehensive glossary found in any biology text, provides precise definitions of terms. The *Glossary* is especially useful because it is extensively cross-referenced and includes pronunciations for many terms. The vertical blue bar along the margin facilitates rapid access to the *Glossary.* The companion website also includes glossary flash cards with audio pronunciations.

Course Learning Outcomes

At the end of a successful study of introductory biology, the student can demonstrate mastery of biological concepts by responding accurately to the following *Course Learning Outcomes:*

- Design an experiment to test a given hypothesis, using the procedure and terminology of the scientific method.

- Cite the cell theory, and relate the structure of organelles to their functions in both prokaryotic and eukaryotic cells.

- Describe the mechanisms of evolution, explain why evolution is the principal unifying concept in biology, and discuss natural selection as the primary agent of evolutionary change.

- Explain the role of genetic information in all species, and discuss applications of genetics that affect society.

- Describe several mechanisms by which cells and organisms transfer information, including the use of nucleic acids in genetic transmission of information, signal transduction, chemical signals (such as hormones and pheromones), electrical signals (for example, neural transmission), sounds, and visual displays.

- Argue for or against the classification of organisms in three domains and several kingdoms or supergroups, characterizing each of these clades; based on your knowledge of genetics and evolution, give specific examples of the unity and diversity of organisms in different domains and supergroups.

- Compare the structural adaptations, life processes, and life cycles of a prokaryote, protist, fungus, plant, and animal.

- Define *homeostasis,* and give examples of regulatory mechanisms, including feedback systems.

- Trace the flow of matter and energy through a photosynthetic cell and a nonphotosynthetic cell, and through the biosphere, comparing the roles of producers, consumers, and decomposers.

- Describe the study of ecology at the levels of an individual organism, a population, a community, and an ecosystem.

WHAT'S NEW: AN OVERVIEW OF *BIOLOGY*, NINTH EDITION

Three themes are interwoven throughout *Biology:* the evolution of life, the transmission of biological information, and the flow of energy through living systems. As we introduce the concepts of modern biology, we explain how these themes are connected and how life depends on them.

Educators present the major topics of an introductory biology course in a variety of orders. For this reason, we carefully designed the eight parts of this book so that they do not depend heavily on preceding chapters and parts. This flexible organization means that an instructor can present the 57 chapters in any number of sequences with pedagogical success. Chapter 1, which introduces the student to the major principles of biology, provides a comprehensive springboard for future discussions, whether the professor prefers a "top-down" or "bottom-up" approach.

In this edition, as in previous editions, we examined every line of every chapter for accuracy and currency, and we made a careful attempt to update every topic and verify all new material. The following brief summary provides a general overview of the organization of *Biology* and some changes made to the ninth edition.

Part 1 The Organization of Life

The six chapters that make up Part 1 provide basic principles of biology and the concepts of chemistry and cell biology that lay the foundation upon which the remaining parts of the book build. We begin Chapter 1 with a discussion of influenza pandemics and how scientists respond to new varieties of pathogens. We then introduce the main themes of the book—evolution, information transfer, and energy transfer. Chapter 1 examines several fundamental concepts in biology and the nature of the scientific process, including a discussion of systems biology. Chapters 2 and 3, which focus on the molecular level of organization, establish the foundations in chemistry necessary for understanding biological processes. Chapters 4, 5, and 6 focus on the cellular level of organization, including cell structure and function, cell membranes, and cell signaling. We have expanded coverage of signaling pathways and the evolution of cell communication. For example, we added a discussion of Ras pathways, as well as a *Key Experiment* on a Ras pathway that regulates reproduction in mammals.

Part 2 Energy Transfer through Living Systems

Because all living cells need energy for life processes, the flow of energy through living systems—that is, capturing energy and converting it to usable forms—is a basic theme of *Biology*. Chapter 7 examines how cells capture, transfer, store, and use energy. Chapters 8 and 9 discuss the metabolic adaptations by which organisms obtain and use energy through cellular respiration and photosynthesis. This section has a new *Key Experiment* figure on the evidence for chemiosmosis. Also, the concept of resonance has been included in the explanation for energy transfer within a photosystem.

Part 3 The Continuity of Life: Genetics

We have updated and expanded the eight chapters of Part 3 for the ninth edition. We begin this unit by discussing mitosis and meiosis in Chapter 10, which includes a new *Key Experiment* on using laser photobleaching to determine how chromosomes are transported toward the spindle poles during anaphase and a new figure on key checkpoints in the cell cycle. Chapter 11, which considers Mendelian genetics and related patterns of inheritance, has new paragraphs on nature versus nurture in human characters and on hydrangea flower color as an illustration of the influence of the environment on the phenotype. We then turn our attention to the structure and replication of DNA in Chapter 12. We include new photographs of Rosalind Franklin, Watson and Crick, phages, DNA replication in *E. coli,* and telomeres. Chapter 13 has a discussion of RNA and protein synthesis, including new information on the contributions of Roger Kornberg, transposons in the human genome, and the percentage of DNA coding for polypeptides versus the percentage of our genome that is expressed. Gene regulation is discussed in Chapter 14, which includes new material on eukaryotic promoters and enhancers and silencers, and on epigenetic inheritance. In Chapter 15, we focus on DNA technology and genomics, including an expanded discussion of engineered strains of *E. coli,* nucleic acid probes, Northern and Western blots, and molecular evolution. These chapters build the necessary foundation for exploring human genetics and the human genome in Chapter 16, which includes new sections on genomic imprinting and on genome-wide association (GWA) scans. In Chapter 17, we introduce the role of genes in development, emphasizing studies on specific model organisms that have led to spectacular advances in this field; changes include new material on induced pluripotent stem (iPS) cells.

Part 4 The Continuity of Life: Evolution

Although we explore evolution as the cornerstone of biology throughout the book, Part 4 discusses evolutionary concepts in depth. We provide the history behind the discovery of the scientific theory of evolution, the mechanisms by which it occurs, and the methods by which it is studied and tested. Chapter 18 introduces the Darwinian concept of evolution and presents several kinds of evidence that support the scientific theory of evolution. In Chapter 19, we examine evolution at the population level. Chapter 20 describes the evolution of new species and discusses aspects of macroevolution. Chapter 21 summarizes the evolutionary history of life on Earth. In Chapter 22, we recount the evolution of the primates, including humans. Many topics and examples have been added to the ninth edition, such as new material on genome sequencing, whale evolution, genetic polymorphism, cichlid evolution, hybrid zones, the metabolism-first hypothesis, and recent discoveries in human evolution, including new material on *Ardipithecus, Homo ergaster,* archaic humans (*H. antecessor* and *H. heidelbergensis*), and Neandertals.

Part 5 The Diversity of Life

Emphasizing the cladistic approach, we use an evolutionary framework to discuss each group of organisms. We present current hypotheses of how groups of organisms are related. Chapter 23 discusses *why* organisms are classified and provides insight into the scientific process of deciding *how* they are classified. New advances have enabled us to further clarify the connection between evolutionary history and systematics in the ninth edition. **NEW** Chapter 24 now focuses entirely on the viruses. We added a discussion of polydnaviruses, illustrated by a new *Key Experiment*. We also expanded the discussion of subviral agents. **NEW** Chapter 25 is now devoted to the prokaryotes. We added information on the archaea, including a brief discussion of their flagella. The discussion of antibiotic resistance was expanded, and an image of methicillin-resistant *Staphylococcus aureus* (MRSA) was added. Chapter 26, which describes the protists, was completely reorganized and updated to reflect recent evolutionary data; a new color-coded table summarizes the five "supergroups" of eukaryotes. Chapters 27 and 28 present the members of the plant kingdom; Chapter 28 includes new cladograms showing the evolution of land plants and the evolution of seedless vascular plants. Discussion of the origin and early evolution of angiosperms is included in Chapter 28. Chapter 29 describes the fungi. We have added a description of symbiotic relationships among fungi, grasses, and viruses and also a discussion of cell signaling in mycorrhizal fungi between fungi and root cells. In Chapters 30 through 32, we discuss the diversity of animals. We have reorganized some of the discussion and added several tables. We emphasize the cladistic approach, although we continue to include traditional phyla and classes.

Part 6 Structure and Life Processes in Plants

Part 6 introduces students to the fascinating plant world. It stresses relationships between structure and function in plant cells, tissues, organs, and individual organisms. In Chapter 33, we introduce plant structure, growth, and differentiation. Chapter 33 contains a new section on plant form that includes plant aspects of cell division, cell expansion, cell differentiation, tissue culture, morphogenesis, pattern formation, positional information, and *Arabidopsis* mutants. Chapters 34 through 36 discuss the structural and physiological adaptations of leaves, stems, and roots; these chapters include new discussion of the molecular control of plant leaf form, cotransport in phloem loading, and transcription factors that affect root hair development. Chapter 37 describes reproduction in flowering plants, including asexual reproduction, flowers, fruits, and seeds. New to this edition is a spread of photos and a table showing floral characteristics associated with various animal pollinators. Chapter 38 focuses on growth responses and regulation of growth. In the ninth edition, we present the latest findings generated by the continuing explosion of knowledge in plant biology, particularly at the molecular level. New topics include advances in auxin signaling, GA signaling, cytokinin signaling, ethylene signaling, and ABA receptors.

Part 7 Structure and Life Processes in Animals

In Part 7, we provide a strong emphasis on comparative animal physiology, showing the structural, functional, and behavioral adaptations that help animals meet environmental challenges. We use a comparative approach to examine how various animal groups have solved both similar and diverse problems. In Chapter 39, we discuss the basic tissues and organ systems of the animal body, homeostasis, and the ways that animals regulate their body temperature. Chapter 40 focuses on different types of body coverings, skeletons, and muscles, and discusses how they function. In Chapters 41 through 43, we discuss neural signaling, neural regulation, and sensory reception. In Chapters 44 through 51, we compare how different animal groups carry on life processes, such as internal transport, internal defense, gas exchange, digestion, reproduction, and development. Each chapter in this part considers the human adaptations for the life processes being discussed. Part 7 ends with a discussion of behavioral adaptations in Chapter 52. Reflecting recent research findings, we have revised or added new material on many topics, including neurotransmitters, learning, memory, sleep-wake cycles, coevolution of bats and moths, cardiovascular disease, Toll-like receptors, chronic inflammation, and certain hormones. The art program has been updated and improved, and many new photographs and photomicrographs have been added.

Part 8 The Interactions of Life: Ecology

Part 8 focuses on the dynamics of populations, communities, and ecosystems and on the application of ecological principles to disciplines such as conservation biology. Chapters 53 through 56 give the student an understanding of the ecology of populations, communities, ecosystems, and the biosphere, whereas Chapter 57 focuses on global environmental issues. Among the many new topics in this unit are correlations between lemming populations and climate change; a 2006 study by Peter and Rosemary Grant on character displacement in ground finches; evolution in scarlet king snakes away from their model, the coral snake; Paine's classic work with predatory Pisaster sea stars in rocky intertidal communities; ocean acidification; invasion of many of the world's grasslands by woody trees and shrubs; and data on climate change from the Fourth IPCC Assessment.

A COMPREHENSIVE PACKAGE FOR LEARNING AND TEACHING

A carefully designed supplement package is available to further facilitate learning. In addition to the usual print resources, we are pleased to present student multimedia tools that have been developed in conjunction with the text.

Resources for Students

Aplia is an online interactive homework solution that stimulates active learning by increasing student effort and engagement. *Aplia* enables students to optimize the time they spend devoted to coursework. *Aplia* courses are customized to fit with each instructor's syllabus, and provide automatically graded homework with detailed, immediate feedback on every question. *Aplia*'s interactive tools also serve to increase student engagement and understanding. The *Aplia* assignments allow students to apply what they learn in the text and in face-to-face instruction directly to their homework.

Aplia homework promotes active learning by:

- Leading students through the thought processes of doing science
- Helping students understand the scientific procedures that lead to scientific results covered in the textbook
- Connecting conceptual figures with scientific issues and problems

Aplia Gradebook Analytics show how each student is doing relative to peers in the class. This allows instructors to quickly and easily:

- Review progress student by student, and even drill down to the homework and question level
- Use graphs to monitor student, and class, performance
- Determine in what subject areas students are struggling and need more review

Straightforward language, a simple and intuitive user interface, and online material that reinforces the textbook all combine to make Aplia a solution that makes students think and helps students learn and retain knowledge.

CengageNOW. This updated and expanded online homework and learning tool helps students assess personal study needs and focus their time. By taking a pretest, they are provided with a Personalized Study Plan that directs them to text sections and narrated animations—many new to this edition—that they need to review. If they need to brush up on basic skills, the *How Do I Prepare?* feature walks them through tutorials on basic math, chemistry, study skills, and word roots. Homework and tests can be assigned through *CengageNOW,* with automatic grading for all multiple-choice and true/false questions.

Biology CourseMate. Cengage Learning's *Biology CourseMate* brings course concepts to life with interactive learning, study, and exam preparation tools that support the printed textbook. Watch student comprehension soar as the class works with the printed textbook and the textbook-specific website. *Biology CourseMate* includes:

- An interactive eBook
- Interactive teaching and learning tools including:
  - Quizzes
  - Videos
  - Animations
  - Flash cards
  - And more
- **Engagement Tracker,** a first-of-its-kind tool that monitors student engagement in the course

Go to www.cengagebrain.com to access these resources, and look for this icon ⬛CourseMate, which denotes a resource available within *CourseMate.*

Study Guide to accompany *Biology,* Ninth Edition, by Jennifer Aline Metzler of Ball State University and Robert Yost of Indiana University and Purdue University, Indianapolis. Updated for this edition, the study guide provides the student with many opportunities to review chapter concepts. Multiple-choice study questions, coloring-book exercises, vocabulary-building exercises, and

many other types of active-learning tools are provided to suit different cognitive learning styles.

A Problem-based Guide to Basic Genetics by Donald Cronkite of Hope College. This brief guide provides students with a systematic approach to solving genetics problems, along with numerous solved problems and practice problems.

Spanish Glossary. This Spanish glossary of biology terms is available to Spanish-speaking students.

Audio Study Tools. This edition of *Biology* is accompanied by useful study tools, which contain valuable information such as reviews of important concepts, key terms, questions, and study tips. Students can download the audio study tools.

Virtual Biology Laboratory 4.0. Now with an upgraded user interface, these 14 online laboratory experiments allow students to "do" science by acquiring data, performing simulated experiments, and using data to explain biological concepts. Assigned activities automatically flow to the instructor's grade book. Self-designed activities ask students to plan their procedures around an experimental question and write up their results.

Additional Resources for Instructors

The instructors' examination copy for this edition lists a comprehensive package of print and multimedia supplements, including online resources, available to qualified adopters. Please ask your local sales representative for details.

ACKNOWLEDGMENTS

The development and production of the ninth edition of *Biology* required extensive interaction and cooperation among the authors and many individuals in our family, social, and professional environments. We thank our editors, colleagues, students, family, and friends for their help and support. Preparing a book of this complexity is challenging and requires a cohesive, talented, and hardworking professional team. We appreciate the contributions of everyone on the editorial and production staff at Brooks/Cole–Cengage Learning who worked on this ninth edition of *Biology.* We thank our Publisher Yolanda Cossio for her commitment to *Biology* and for working closely with us throughout the entire process of development and production. We appreciate the help of our Developmental Editor, Christopher Delgado, who diligently kept us on track and coordinated many aspects of this complex project.

We thank Tom Ziolkowski, our Marketing Manager, whose expertise ensured that you would know about our new edition.

We appreciate the help of Senior Content Project Manager Hal Humphrey, who guided overall production of the project.

We thank Editorial Assistants Brandusa Radoias and Joshua Taylor for quickly providing us with resources whenever we needed them.

We thank Creative Director Rob Hugel, Art Director and Cover Designer John Walker, and Text Designer tani hasegawa. We also thank Jean Thompson for developing the instructor's preface.

We appreciate the work of Lauren Oliveira, Media Editor, who coordinated the many high-tech components of the computerized aspects of our *Learning System.* We thank Alexis Glubka, Assistant Editor, for coordinating the print supplements.

We are grateful to our Production Editor, Joan Keyes of Dovetail Publishing Services, for coordinating the many editors involved in the preparation of this edition and bringing together the thousands of complex pieces of the project to produce *Biology,* Ninth Edition. We value the careful work of our Copy Editor, Susan Gall, who patiently helped us maintain consistency and improve the manuscript. We thank Amanda Bickel of Precision Graphics for helping us greatly improve the art program for this book. We also appreciate the efforts of Photo Editor Tim Herzog of Bill Smith Group in helping us find excellent images. We appreciate the help, patience, and hard work of our production team. Our schedule for this project was very demanding. At times, it seemed like the team worked around the clock. When we sent an email at 11 P.M. or during the weekend, we often received an immediate response.

These dedicated professionals and many others on the Brooks/Cole team provided the skill, attention, patience, and good humor needed to produce *Biology,* Ninth Edition. We thank them for their help and support throughout this project.

We thank Dr. Susan Pross, University of South Florida, College of Medicine, for her helpful suggestions for updating the immunology chapter. We appreciate the help of obstetrician/gynecologist Dr. Amy Solomon for her input regarding pregnancy, childbirth, contraception, and sexually transmitted diseases. We appreciate the expert assistance of Mary Kay Hartung, Research and Information Specialist at Florida Gulf Coast University, who we counted on for help whenever we had difficulty finding needed research studies and other information. We thank doctoral student Lois Ball of the University of South Florida, who calculated scale bars for many of the photomicrographs. We are grateful to Mical Solomon for his computer help.

We thank our families and friends for their understanding, support, and encouragement as we struggled through many revisions and intense deadlines. We especially thank Dr. Kathleen M. Heide, Freda Brod, Alan Berg, Jennifer and Pat Roath, Dr. Charles Martin, and Margaret Martin for their support and input.

Our colleagues and students who have used our book have provided valuable input by sharing their responses to past editions of *Biology.* We thank them and ask again for their comments and suggestions as they use this new edition. We can be reached through the Internet via our website at www.CengageBrain.com or through our editors at Brooks/Cole, a division of Cengage Learning.

We express our thanks to the many biologists who have read the manuscript during various stages of its development and provided us with valuable suggestions for improving it. Ninth edition reviewers include the following:

Karl Aufderheide, Texas A & M University

Felicitas Avendano, Grand View College, Iowa

Brian Bagatto, University of Akron

Catherine Black, Idaho State University

Susan Boothe, Alabama Southern Community College

Mark Browning, Purdue University

Jill Buettner, Richland College

Doug Burks, Wilmington College, Ohio

David Byres, Florida Community College at Jacksonville

Geoffrey Church, Fairfield University

Reggie Cobb, Nash Community College

Barbara Collins, California Lutheran University

Karen Curto, University of Pittsburgh

Phillippa Drennan, Loyola Marymount University

James DuMond, Texas Southern University

Wayne Elisens, University of Oklahoma

Cheryld Emmons, Alfred University, New York

Suzanne Gollery, Sierra Nevada College

Jack Holt, Susquehanna University

Ursula Howson, Monmouth University

Ken Klemow, Wilkes University

Paula Lemons, Duke University

Diana Lipscomb, George Washington University

Christopher Loretz, University of Buffalo

Kathi Maleug, University of Colorado at Colorado Springs

Paul Manos, Duke University

Helen McDearman, University of Tennessee at Chattanooga

Virginia McDonough, Hope College

Betsy Morgan, Lonestar College

Dana Nayduch, Georgia Southern University

Onesimus Otieno, Oakwood University

Michael Pallidino, Monmouth College

Craig Peebles, University of Pittsburgh

Ed Perry, Faulkner State Community College

Eric Ribbens, Western Illinois University

Laurel Roberts, University of Pittsburgh

Darrin Rubino, Hanover College, Indiana

Timothy Schuh, St. Cloud State University

Sharon Thoma, University of Wisconsin

Joanne Tillotson, Purchase College, State University of New York

Timothy Tripp, Sam Houston State University

Paul Trombley, Florida State University

Mary Tyler, University of Maine

Fred Wasserman, Boston University

Susan Whittemore, Keene State College

Lawrence Williams, University of Houston

Steven Wilt, Bellarmine College, Kentucky

Robert Yost, Indiana University–Purdue University, Indianapolis

Wendy Zomlefer, University of Georgia

We would also like to thank the hundreds of previous edition reviewers, both professors and students, who are too numerous to mention. They asked thoughtful questions, provided new perspectives, offered alternative wordings to clarify difficult passages, and informed us of possible errors. We are truly indebted to their excellent feedback. Their suggestions have helped us improve each edition of *Biology.*

To the Student

Biology is a challenging subject. The thousands of students we have taught have differed in their life goals and learning styles. Some have had excellent backgrounds in science; others, poor ones. Regardless of their backgrounds, it is common for students taking their first college biology course to find that they must work harder than they expected.

The *Learning System* we use in this book is described in the Preface. Using the strategies of the *Learning System* will help you master the language and concepts of biology. You will also want to use the many online tools available to *Biology* students. These tools, also described in the Preface, include *Aplia, CengageNOW,* and *Biology CourseMate.* In addition to these learning strategies, you can make the task of learning biology easier by using approaches that have been successful to a broad range of our students over the years.

Make a Study Schedule

Many college professors suggest that students study 3 hours for every hour spent in class. This major investment in study time is one of the main differences between high school and college. To succeed academically, college students must learn to manage their time effectively. The actual number of hours you spend studying biology will vary depending on how quickly you learn the material, as well as on your course load and personal responsibilities, such as work schedules and family commitments.

The most successful students are often those who are best organized. At the beginning of the semester, make a detailed daily calendar. Mark off the hours you are in each class, along with travel time to and from class if you are a commuter. After you get your course syllabi, add to your calendar the dates of all exams, quizzes, papers, and reports. As a reminder, it also helps to add an entry for each major exam or assignment 1 week before the test or due date. Now add your work schedule and other personal commitments to your calendar. Using a calendar helps you find convenient study times.

Many of our successful biology students set aside 2 hours a day to study biology rather than depend on a weekly marathon session for 8 or 10 hours during the weekend (when that kind of session rarely happens). Put your study hours into your daily calendar, and stick to your schedule.

Determine Whether the Professor Emphasizes Text Material or Lecture Notes

Some professors test almost exclusively on material covered in lecture. Others rely on their students' learning most, or even all, of the content in assigned chapters. Find out what your professor's requirements are, because the way you study will vary accordingly.

How to study when professors test lecture material

If lectures are the main source of examination questions, make your lecture notes as complete and organized as possible. Before going to class, skim over the chapter, identifying key terms and examining the main figures, so that you can take effective lecture notes. Spend no more than 1 hour on this.

Within 24 hours after class, rewrite (or type) your notes. Before rewriting, however, read the notes and make marginal notes about anything that is not clear. Then read the corresponding material in your text. Highlight or underline any sections that clarify questions you had in your notes. Read the entire chapter, including parts that are not covered in lecture. This extra information will give you breadth of understanding and will help you grasp key concepts.

After reading the text, you are ready to rewrite your notes, incorporating relevant material from the text. It also helps to use the Glossary to find definitions for unfamiliar terms. Many students develop a set of flash cards of key terms and concepts as a way to study. Flash cards are a useful tool to help you learn scientific terminology. They are portable and can be used at times when other studying is not possible, for example, when riding a bus.

Flash cards are not effective when the student tries to second-guess the professor. ("She won't ask this, so I won't make a flash card of it.") Flash cards are also a hindrance when students rely on them exclusively. Studying flash cards instead of reading the text is a bit like reading the first page of each chapter in a mystery novel: it's hard to fill in the missing parts, because you are learning the facts in a disconnected way.

How to study when professors test material in the book

If the assigned readings in the text are going to be tested, you must use your text intensively. After reading the chapter introduction, read the list of Learning Objectives for the first section. These objectives are written in behavioral terms; that is, they ask you to "do" something in order to demonstrate mastery. The objectives give you a concrete set of goals for each section of the chapter. At the end of each section, you will find Review questions keyed to the Learning Objectives. Test yourself, going back over the material to check your responses.

Read each chapter section actively. Many students read and study passively. An active learner always has questions in mind and is constantly making connections. For example, there are many processes that must be understood in biology. Don't try to blindly memorize these; instead, think about causes and effects so that every process becomes a story. Eventually, you'll see that many processes are connected by common elements.

You will probably have to read each chapter two or three times before mastering the material. The second and third times through will be much easier than the first, because you'll be reinforcing concepts that you have already partially learned.

After reading the chapter, write a four- to six-page chapter outline by using the subheads as the body of the outline (first-level heads are boldface, in color, and all caps; second-level heads are in color and not all caps). Flesh out your outline by adding important concepts and boldface terms with definitions. Use this outline when preparing for the exam.

Now it is time to test yourself. Answer the Test Your Understanding questions, and check your answers. Write answers to each of the Critical Thinking questions. Finally, review the Learning Objectives in the Chapter Summary, and try to answer them before reading the summary provided. If your professor has told you that some or all of the exam will be short-answer or essay format, write out the answer for each Learning Objective. Remember that this is a self-test. If you do not know an answer to a question, find it in the text. If you can't find the answer, use the Index.

Learn the Vocabulary

One stumbling block for many students is learning the many terms that make up the language of biology. In fact, it would be much more difficult to learn and communicate if we did not have this terminology, because words are really tools for thinking. Learning terminology generally becomes easier if you realize that most biological terms are modular. They consist of mostly Latin and Greek roots; once you learn many of these, you will have a good idea of the meaning of a new word even before it is defined. For this reason, we have included Appendix C, Understanding Biological Terms. To be sure you understand the precise definition of a term, use the Index and Glossary. The more you use biological terms in speech and writing, the more comfortable you will be.

Form a Study Group

Active learning is facilitated if you do some of your studying in a small group. In a study group, the roles of teacher and learner can be interchanged: a good way to learn material is to teach. A study group lets you meet challenges in a nonthreatening environment and can provide some emotional support. Study groups are effective learning tools when combined with individual study of text and lecture notes. If, however, you and other members of your study group have not prepared for your meetings by studying individually in advance, the study session can be a waste of time.

Prepare for the Exam

Your calendar tells you it is now 1 week before your first biology exam. If you have been following these suggestions, you are well prepared and will need only some last-minute reviewing. No all-nighters will be required.

During the week prior to the exam, spend 2 hours each day actively studying your lecture notes or chapter outlines. It helps many students to read these notes out loud (most people listen to what they say!). Begin with the first lecture/chapter covered on the exam, and continue in the order on the lecture syllabus. Stop when you have reached the end of your 2-hour study period. The following day, begin where you stopped the previous day. When you reach the end of your notes, start at the beginning and study them a second time. The material should be very familiar to you by the second or third time around. At this stage, use your textbook only to answer questions or clarify important points.

The night before the exam, do a little light studying, eat a nutritious dinner, and get a full night's sleep. That way, you'll arrive in class on exam day with a well-rested body (and brain) and the self-confidence that goes with being well prepared.

Eldra P. Solomon
Linda R. Berg
Diana W. Martin

1 A View of Life

H1N1, the virus that causes H1N1 influenza (flu). H1N1 virus particles (blue) are visible on a cell (green). When this virus emerged, the human immune system was unfamiliar with its new combination of genes. As a result, the virus spread easily, causing a pandemic. The scanning electron micrograph (SEM) has been color-enhanced.

NIBSC/Science Photo Library

KEY CONCEPTS

1.1 Basic themes of biology include evolution, information transfer, and energy transfer.

1.2 Characteristics of life include cellular structure, growth and development, self-regulated metabolism, response to stimuli, and reproduction.

1.3 Biological organization is hierarchical and includes chemical, cell, tissue, organ, organ system, and organism levels; ecological organization includes population, community, ecosystem, and biosphere levels.

1.4 Information transfer includes DNA transfer of information from one generation to the next; chemical and electrical signals within and among the cells of every organism; and chemicals, visual displays, and sounds that allow organisms to communicate with one another and to interact with their environment.

1.5 Individual organisms and entire ecosystems depend on a continuous input of energy. Energy is transferred within cells and from one organism to another.

1.6 Evolution is the process by which populations of organisms change over time, adapting to changes in their environment; the tree of life includes three major branches, or domains.

1.7 Biologists ask questions, develop hypotheses, make predictions, and collect data by careful observation and experiment; based on their results, they come to conclusions.

The H1N1 influenza (flu) outbreak became the focus of attention in April 2009. Within a few months, more than 200 countries around the world had reported confirmed cases of this viral disease, and H1N1 had caused thousands of deaths. According to the U.S. Centers for Disease Control and Prevention (CDC), more than 200 known pathogens (disease-causing organisms) have the potential to strike globally. Historically, new viral strains have claimed many human lives. For example, in 1918 an influenza pandemic killed more than 20 million people throughout the world. Epidemiologists warn that even today an influenza pandemic could kill millions of people. Pandemics such as H1N1 have negative global impact. They affect many aspects of life, including the global economy, travel, tourism, and education.

Armed with new technology, biologists work closely with public health and other health-care professionals to prevent dangerous pandemics. When a new disease-causing agent emerges, biologists study its evolutionary relationships to known pathogens. For example, investigators have determined that the 1918 flu pandemic was caused by an influenza A (H1N1) virus that may have mutated and newly emerged from a swine or avian host. The H1N1 strain that was identified in 2009 was related to the 1918 pathogen.

Biologists determined that the 2009 H1N1 strain evolved from a combination of viruses that infected swine, birds, and humans. They found that this strain of H1N1 contains unique combinations of gene segments for which humans do not have preexisting immunity. Knowledge about a

1

virus's origins provides important clues to its structure and behavior, and suggests hypotheses for combating it. Scientists must then test their hypotheses in the laboratory. Researchers were able to determine the antigens (proteins) on the surface of H1N1. These antigens must combine with receptors on human cells in order to infect the cells. Based on careful studies of H1N1, a vaccine was quickly developed.

Pathogens can strike quickly and spread rapidly, and the continuous evolution of drug-resistant pathogens presents a major challenge. New varieties of H1N1 continue to emerge, and investigators must quickly characterize them and assess their potential virulence. Scientists predict that new varieties may show increased drug resistance and may be more virulent. In addition, recently developed vaccines may no longer be effective. Emerging diseases will be discussed further in Chapter 24.

This is an exciting time to study **biology,** the science of life. The remarkable new discoveries biologists are making almost daily affect every aspect of our lives, including our health, food, safety, relationships with humans and other organisms, and the environment of our planet. New knowledge provides new insights into the human species and the millions of other organisms with which we share this planet. Biology affects our personal, governmental, and societal decisions. For example, a combined effort at every level is necessary to provide the resources and knowledge to meet the challenges of global pandemics.

Whatever your college major or career goals, knowledge of biological concepts is a vital tool for understanding our world and for meeting many of the personal, societal, and global challenges that confront us. Among these challenges are the expanding human population, decreasing biological diversity, diminishing natural resources, global climate change, and prevention and cure of diseases, such as heart disease, cancer, diabetes, Alzheimer's disease, acquired immunodeficiency syndrome (AIDS), and influenza. Meeting these challenges will require the combined efforts of biologists and other scientists, health professionals, educators, politicians, and biologically informed citizens.

This book is a starting point for your exploration of biology. It will provide you with the basic knowledge and the tools to become a part of this fascinating science, as well as a more informed member of society.

1.1 THREE BASIC THEMES

◼ LEARNING OBJECTIVE

1   Describe three basic themes of biology.

In this first chapter we introduce three basic themes of biology. These themes are interconnected with one another and with almost every concept that we discuss in this book.

1. **Evolution.** Populations of organisms have evolved through time from earlier forms of life. Scientists have accumulated a wealth of evidence showing that the diverse life-forms on this planet are related and that populations have *evolved,* that is, have changed over time, from earlier forms of life. The process of *evolution* is the framework for the science of biology and is a major theme of this book.

2. **Information transfer.** Information must be transmitted within organisms and among organisms, and organisms must be able to receive information from their environment. The survival and function of every cell and every organism depend on the orderly transmission of information. Evolution depends on the transmission of genetic information from one generation to another.

3. **Energy transfer.** All life processes, including thousands of chemical transactions that maintain life's organization, require a continuous input of energy. Most of the energy for life comes from sunlight. Energy from the sun is transferred through living systems from producers to consumers; decomposers obtain energy as they feed on the dead bodies and wastes of both producers and consumers. Energy is also continuously transferred from one chemical compound to another within every cell.

Evolution, information transfer, and energy transfer are forces that give life its unique characteristics. We begin our study of biology by developing a more precise understanding of the fundamental characteristics of living systems.

Review

- Why are evolution, information transfer, and energy transfer considered basic to life?
- What does the term *evolution* mean as applied to populations of organisms?

1.2 CHARACTERISTICS OF LIFE

◼ LEARNING OBJECTIVE

2   Distinguish between living and nonliving things by describing the features that characterize living organisms.

We easily recognize that a pine tree, a butterfly, and a horse are living things, whereas a rock is not. Despite their diversity, the organisms that inhabit our planet share a common set of characteristics that distinguish them from nonliving things. These features include a precise kind of organization, growth and development, self-regulated metabolism, the ability to respond to stimuli, reproduction, and adaptation to environmental change.

Organisms are composed of cells

Although they vary greatly in size and appearance, all organisms consist of basic units called **cells.** New cells are formed only by the division of previously existing cells. As will be discussed in Chapter 4, these concepts are expressed in the **cell theory,** a fundamental unifying concept of biology.

Some of the simplest life-forms, such as protozoa, are **unicellular** organisms, meaning that each consists of a single cell (**FIG. 1-1**). In contrast, the body of a dog or a maple tree is made of billions of cells. In such complex **multicellular** organisms, life processes depend on the coordinated functions of component cells that may be organized to form tissues, organs, and organ systems.

Every cell is enveloped by a protective **plasma membrane** that separates it from the surrounding external environment. The plasma membrane regulates passage of materials between the cell and its environment. Cells have specialized molecules that contain genetic instructions and transmit genetic information. In most cells, the genetic instructions are encoded in deoxyribonucleic acid, more simply known as **DNA.** Cells typically have internal structures called **organelles** that are specialized to perform specific functions.

There are two fundamentally different types of cells: prokaryotic and eukaryotic. **Prokaryotic cells** are exclusive to bacteria and to microscopic organisms called *archaea*. All other organisms are characterized by their **eukaryotic cells.** These cells typically contain a variety of organelles enclosed by membranes, including a **nucleus,** which houses DNA. Prokaryotic cells are structurally simpler; they do not have a nucleus or other membrane-enclosed organelles.

Organisms grow and develop

Biological growth involves an increase in the size of individual cells of an organism, in the number of cells, or in both. Growth may be uniform in the various parts of an organism, or it may be greater in some parts than in others, causing the body proportions to change as growth occurs. Some organisms—most trees, for example—continue to grow throughout their lives. Many animals have a defined growth period that terminates when a characteristic adult size is reached. An intriguing aspect of the growth process is that each part of the organism typically continues to function as it grows.

Living organisms develop as well as grow. **Development** includes all the changes that take place during an organism's life. Like many other organisms, every human begins life as a fertilized egg that then grows and develops. The structures and body form that develop are exquisitely adapted to the functions the organism must perform.

Organisms regulate their metabolic processes

Within all organisms, chemical reactions and energy transformations occur that are essential to nutrition, the growth and repair of cells, and the conversion of energy into usable forms. The sum of all the chemical activities of the organism is its **metabolism.**

Metabolic processes occur continuously in every organism, and they must be carefully regulated to maintain **homeostasis,** an appropriate, balanced internal environment. When enough of a cell product has been made, its manufacture must be decreased or turned off. When a particular substance is required, cell processes that produce it must be turned on. These *homeostatic mechanisms* are self-regulating control systems that are remarkably sensitive and efficient.

250 μm

Mike Abbey/Visuals Unlimited, Inc.

(a) Unicellular organisms consist of one intricate cell that performs all the functions essential to life. Ciliates, such as this *Paramecium*, move about by beating their hairlike cilia.

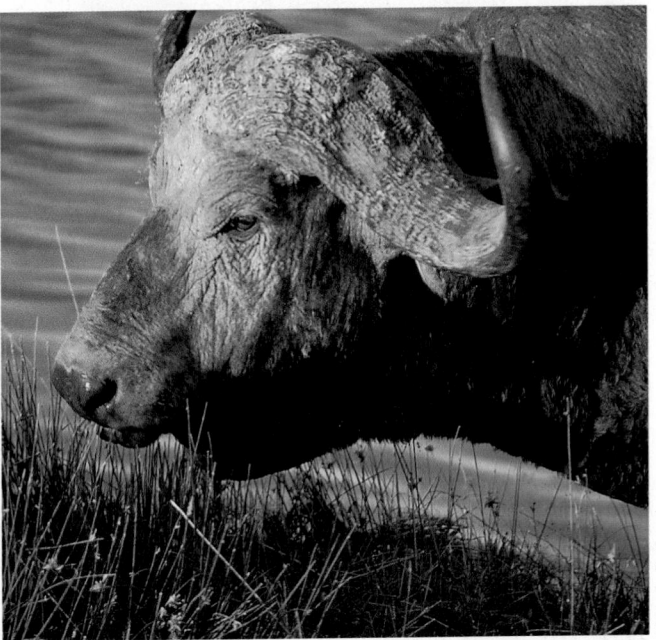

McMurray Photography

(b) Multicellular organisms, such as this African buffalo (*Syncerus caffer*) and the plants on which it grazes, may consist of billions of cells specialized to perform specific functions.

FIGURE 1-1 Unicellular and multicellular life-forms

The regulation of glucose (a simple sugar) concentration in the blood of complex animals is a good example of a homeostatic mechanism. Your cells require a constant supply of glucose molecules, which they break down to obtain energy. The circulatory system delivers glucose and other nutrients to all the cells. When the concentration of glucose in the blood rises above normal limits, glucose is stored in the liver and in muscle cells. When you have not eaten for a few hours, the glucose concentration begins to fall. Your body converts stored nutrients to glucose, bringing the glucose concentration in the blood back to normal levels. When the glucose concentration decreases, you also feel hungry and restore nutrients by eating.

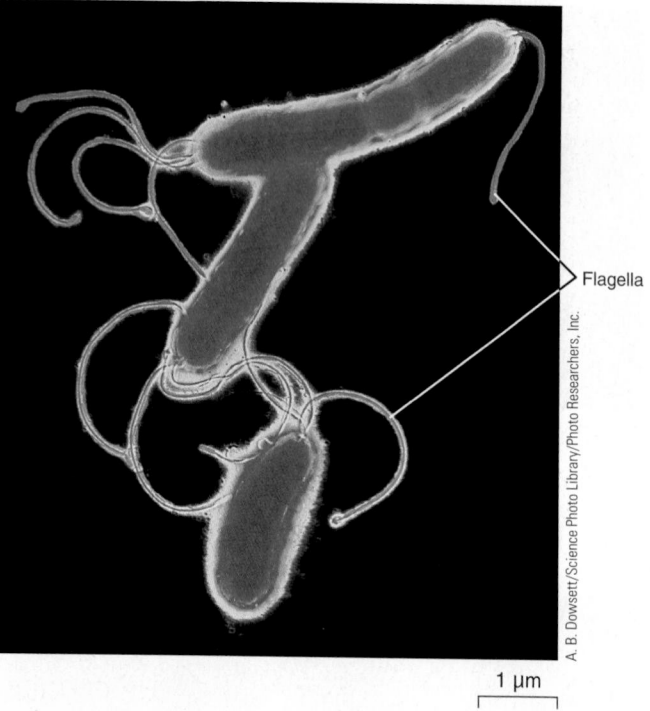

Flagella

1 μm

FIGURE 1-2 Biological movement

These bacteria (*Helicobacter pylori*), equipped with flagella for locomotion, have been linked to stomach ulcers. The photograph was taken using a scanning electron microscope. The bacteria are not really red and blue. Their color has been artificially enhanced.

Organisms respond to stimuli

All forms of life respond to **stimuli,** physical or chemical changes in their internal or external environment. Stimuli that evoke a response in most organisms are changes in the color, intensity, or direction of light; changes in temperature, pressure, or sound; and changes in the chemical composition of the surrounding soil, air, or water. Responding to stimuli involves movement, though not always locomotion (moving from one place to another).

In simple organisms, the entire individual may be sensitive to stimuli. Certain unicellular organisms, for example, respond to bright light by retreating. In some organisms, locomotion is achieved by the slow oozing of the cell, the process of *amoeboid movement.* Other organisms move by beating tiny, hairlike extensions of the cell called **cilia** or longer structures known as **flagella** (**FIG. 1-2**). Some bacteria move by rotating their flagella.

Most animals move very obviously. They wiggle, crawl, swim, run, or fly by contracting muscles. Sponges, corals, and oysters have free-swimming larval stages, but most are **sessile** as adults, meaning that they do not move from place to place. In fact, they may remain firmly attached to a surface, such as the sea bottom or a rock. Many sessile organisms have cilia or flagella that beat rhythmically, bringing them food and oxygen in the surrounding water. Complex animals, such as grasshoppers, lizards, and humans, have highly specialized cells that respond to specific types of stimuli. For example, cells in the retina of the vertebrate eye respond to light.

Although their responses may not be as obvious as those of animals, plants do respond to light, gravity, water, touch, and other stimuli. For example, plants orient their leaves to the sun and grow toward light. Many plant responses involve different growth rates of various parts of the plant body. A few plants, such as the Venus flytrap of the Carolina swamps, are very sensitive to touch and catch insects (**FIG. 1-3**). Their leaves are hinged along the midrib, and they have a scent that attracts insects. Trigger hairs on the leaf surface detect the arrival of an insect and stimulate the leaf to fold. When the edges come together, they interlock, preventing the insect's escape. The leaf then secretes enzymes that kill and digest the insect. The Venus flytrap usually grows in nitrogen-deficient soil. The plant obtains part of the nitrogen required for its growth from the insects it "eats."

(a) Hairs on the leaf surface of the Venus flytrap (*Dionaea muscipula*) detect the touch of an insect, and the leaf responds by folding.

(b) The edges of the leaf come together and interlock, preventing the fly's escape. The leaf then secretes enzymes that kill and digest the insect.

FIGURE 1-3 Plants respond to stimuli

Organisms reproduce

At one time, people thought worms arose spontaneously from horsehair in a water trough, maggots from decaying meat, and frogs from the mud

100 μm

(a) Asexual reproduction. One individual gives rise to two or more offspring that are similar to the parent. *Difflugia*, a unicellular amoeba, is shown dividing to form two amoebas.

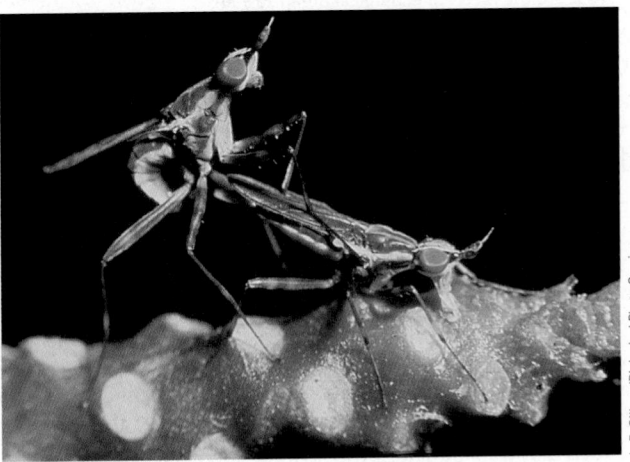

(b) Sexual reproduction. Typically, each of two parents contributes a gamete (sperm or egg). Gametes fuse to produce the offspring, which has a combination of the traits of both parents. A pair of tropical flies are shown mating.

FIGURE 1-4 Asexual and sexual reproduction

of the Nile. Thanks to the work of several scientists, including the Italian physician Francesco Redi in the 17th century and French chemist Louis Pasteur in the 19th century, we know that organisms arise only from previously existing organisms.

Simple organisms, such as amoebas, perpetuate themselves by **asexual reproduction** (**FIG. 1-4a**). When an amoeba has grown to a certain size, it reproduces by splitting in half to form two new amoebas. Before an amoeba divides, its hereditary material (set of *genes*) is duplicated, and one complete set is distributed to each new cell. Except for size, each new amoeba is similar to the parent cell. The only way that variation occurs among asexually reproducing organisms is by genetic *mutation,* a permanent change in the genes.

In most plants and animals, **sexual reproduction** is carried out by the fusion of an egg and a sperm cell to form a fertilized egg (**FIG. 1-4b**). The new organism develops from the fertilized egg. Offspring produced by sexual reproduction are the product of the interaction of various genes contributed by the mother and the fa-

FIGURE 1-5 Adaptations
These Burchell's zebras (*Equus burchelli*), photographed in Tanzania, are behaviorally adapted to position themselves to watch for lions and other predators. Stripes are thought to be an adaptation for visual protection against predators. They serve as camouflage or to break up form when spotted from a distance. The zebra stomach is adapted for feeding on coarse grass passed over by other grazers, an adaptation that helps the animal survive when food is scarce.

ther. This genetic variation is important in the vital processes of evolution and adaptation.

Populations evolve and become adapted to the environment

The ability of a population to evolve over many generations and adapt to its environment equips it to survive in a changing world. **Adaptations** are inherited characteristics that enhance an organism's ability to survive in a particular environment. The long, flexible tongue of the frog is an adaptation for catching insects, the feathers and lightweight bones of birds are adaptations for flying, and the thick fur coat of the polar bear is an adaptation for surviving frigid temperatures. Adaptations may be structural, physiological, biochemical, behavioral, or a combination of all four (**FIG. 1-5**). Every biologically successful organism is a complex collection of coordinated adaptations produced through evolutionary processes.

Review

- What characteristics distinguish a living organism from a nonliving object?
- What would be the consequences to an organism if its homeostatic mechanisms failed? Explain your answer.
- What do we mean by adaptations?

1.3 LEVELS OF BIOLOGICAL ORGANIZATION

■ LEARNING OBJECTIVE

3   Construct a hierarchy of biological organization, including levels characteristic of individual organisms and levels characteristic of ecological systems.

Whether we study a single organism or the world of life as a whole, we can identify a hierarchy of biological organization (**FIG. 1-6**). At every level, structure and function are precisely coordinated. One way to study a particular level is by looking at its components. Biologists can gain insights about cells by studying atoms and molecules. Learning about a structure by studying its parts is called **reductionism.** However, the whole is more than the sum of its parts. Each level has **emergent properties,** characteristics not found at lower levels. Populations of organisms have emergent properties such as population density, age structure, and birth and death rates. The *individuals* that make up a population do not have these characteristics. Consider also the human brain. The brain is composed of millions of neurons (nerve cells). However, we could study all of these individual neurons and have no clue about the functional capacities of the brain. Only when the neurons are wired together in precise fashion are the emergent properties, such as the capacity for thought, judgment, and motor coordination, evident.

Organisms have several levels of organization

The chemical level, the most basic level of organization, includes atoms and molecules. An **atom** is the smallest unit of a chemical element that retains the characteristic properties of that element. For example, an atom of iron is the smallest possible amount of iron. Atoms combine chemically to form **molecules.** Two atoms of hydrogen combine with one atom of oxygen to form a single molecule of water. Although composed of two types of atoms that are gases, water can exist as a liquid or solid. The properties of water are very different from those of its hydrogen and oxygen components, an example of emergent properties.

At the cellular level, many types of atoms and molecules associate with one another to form *cells.* However, a cell is much more than a heap of atoms and molecules. Its emergent properties make it the basic structural and functional unit of life, the simplest component of living matter that can carry on all the activities necessary for life.

During the evolution of multicellular organisms, cells associated to form **tissues.** For example, most animals have muscle tissue and nervous tissue. Plants have epidermis, a tissue that serves as a protective covering, and vascular tissues that move materials throughout the plant body. In most complex organisms, tissues organize into functional structures called **organs,** such as the heart and stomach in animals and roots and leaves in plants. In animals, each major group of biological functions is performed by a coordinated group of tissues and organs called an **organ system.** The circulatory and digestive systems are examples of organ systems. Functioning together with great precision, organ systems make up a complex, multicellular **organism.** Again, emergent properties are evident. An organism is much more than its component organ systems.

Several levels of ecological organization can be identified

Organisms interact to form still more complex levels of biological organization. All the members of one species living in the same geographic area at the same time make up a **population.** The populations of various types of organisms that inhabit a particular area and interact with one another form a **community.** A community can consist of hundreds of different types of organisms.

A community together with its nonliving environment is an **ecosystem.** An ecosystem can be as small as a pond (or even a puddle) or as vast as the Great Plains of North America or the Arctic tundra. All of Earth's ecosystems together are known as the **biosphere.** The biosphere includes all of Earth that is inhabited by living organisms—the atmosphere, the hydrosphere (water in any form), and the lithosphere (Earth's crust). The study of how organisms relate to one another and to their physical environment is called **ecology** (derived from the Greek *oikos,* meaning "house").

Review

- What are the levels of organization within an organism?
- What are the levels of ecological organization?

1.4 INFORMATION TRANSFER

■ LEARNING OBJECTIVE

4   Summarize the importance of information transfer within and between living systems, giving specific examples.

An organism inherits the information it needs to grow, develop, carry on self-regulated metabolism, respond to stimuli, and reproduce. Each organism must also have precise instructions for making the molecules necessary for its cells to communicate. The information an organism requires to carry on these life processes is coded and transmitted in the form of chemical substances and electrical impulses. Organisms must also communicate information to one another.

DNA transmits information from one generation to the next

Humans give birth only to human babies, not to giraffes or rosebushes. In organisms that reproduce sexually, each offspring is a combination of the traits of its parents. In 1953, James Watson and Francis Crick worked out the structure of DNA, the large molecule that makes up the **genes,** the units of hereditary material (**FIG. 1-7**). A DNA molecule consists of two chains of atoms twisted into a helix. As will be described in Chapter 2, each chain is made up of a sequence of chemical subunits called **nucleotides.** There are four types of nucleotides in DNA; and each sequence of three nucleotides is part of the genetic code.

Watson and Crick's work led to the understanding of this genetic code. The information coded in sequences of nucleotides in DNA transmits genetic information from generation to generation. The code works somewhat like an alphabet. The nucleotides can "spell" an amazing variety of instructions for making organisms as diverse as bacteria, frogs, and redwood trees. The genetic code is universal, that is, virtually identical in all organisms—a dramatic example of the unity of life.

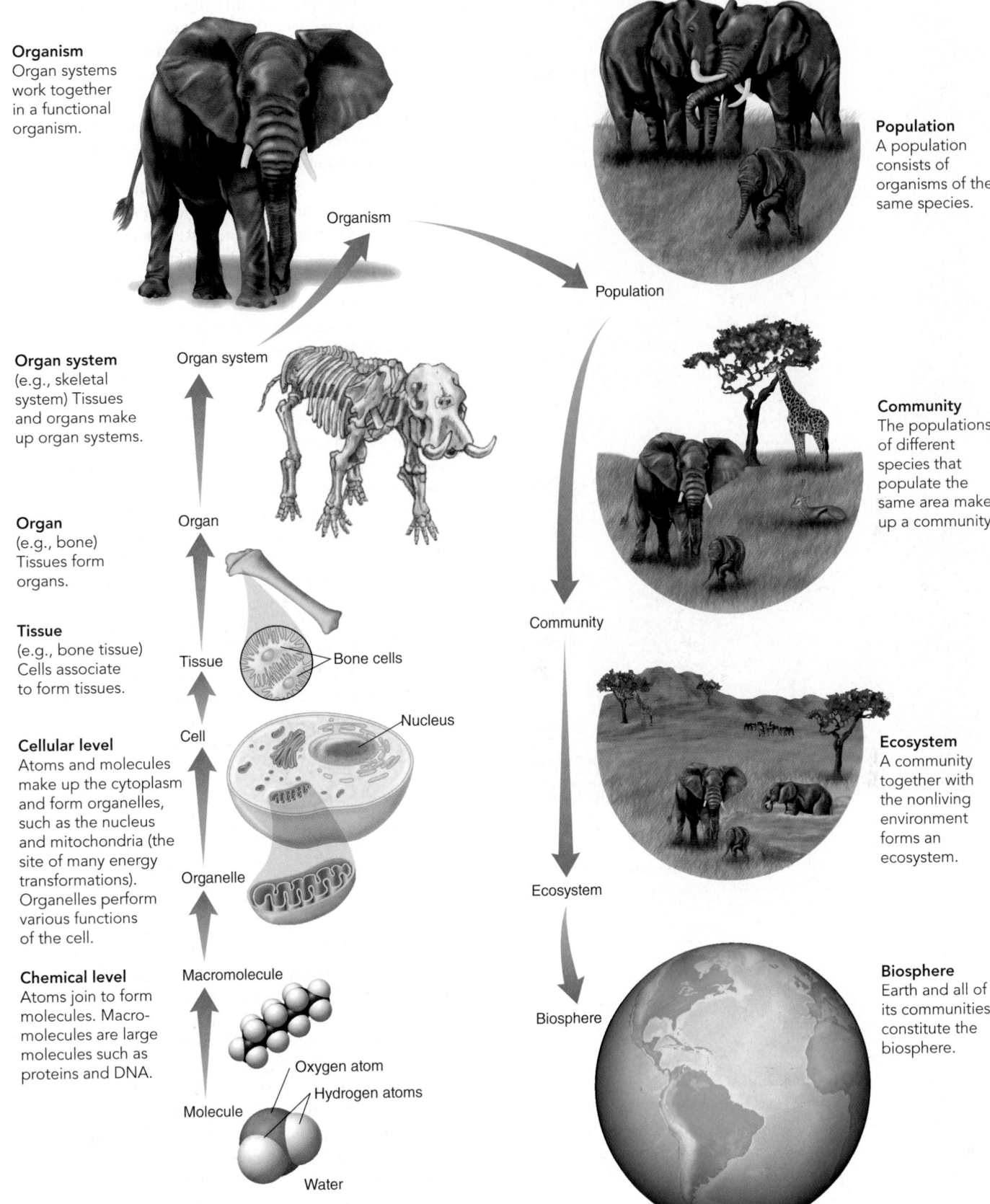

Organism
Organ systems work together in a functional organism.

Organism

Population
A population consists of organisms of the same species.

Population

Organ system
(e.g., skeletal system) Tissues and organs make up organ systems.

Organ system

Community
The populations of different species that populate the same area make up a community.

Community

Organ
(e.g., bone) Tissues form organs.

Organ

Tissue
(e.g., bone tissue) Cells associate to form tissues.

Tissue — Bone cells

Ecosystem
A community together with the nonliving environment forms an ecosystem.

Ecosystem

Cellular level
Atoms and molecules make up the cytoplasm and form organelles, such as the nucleus and mitochondria (the site of many energy transformations). Organelles perform various functions of the cell.

Cell — Nucleus

Organelle

Chemical level
Atoms join to form molecules. Macromolecules are large molecules such as proteins and DNA.

Macromolecule

Oxygen atom
Hydrogen atoms

Molecule

Water

Biosphere
Earth and all of its communities constitute the biosphere.

Biosphere

FIGURE 1-6 *Animated* The hierarchy of biological organization

FIGURE 1-7 DNA

DNA is the hereditary material that transmits information from one generation to the next. As shown in this model, DNA is a macromolecule that consists of two chains of atoms twisted into a helix. Each chain consists of subunits called nucleotides. The sequence of nucleotides makes up the genetic code.

Information is transmitted by chemical and electrical signals

Genes control the development and functioning of every organism. The DNA that makes up the genes contains the "recipes" for making all the proteins required by the organism. **Proteins** are large molecules important in determining the structure and function of cells and tissues. For example, brain cells differ from muscle cells in large part because they have different types of proteins. Some proteins are important in communication within and among cells. Certain proteins on the surface of a cell serve as markers so that other cells "recognize" them. Some cell-surface proteins serve as receptors that combine with chemical messengers.

Cells use proteins and many other types of molecules to communicate with one another. In a multicellular organism, cells produce chemical compounds, such as **hormones,** that signal other cells. Hormones and other chemical messengers can signal cells in distant organs to secrete a particular required substance or change some metabolic activity. In this way chemical signals help regulate growth, development, and metabolic processes. The mechanisms involved in **cell signaling** often involve complex biochemical processes.

Cell signaling is currently an area of intense research. A major focus has been the transfer of information among cells of the immune system. A better understanding of how cells communicate promises new insights into how the body protects itself against disease organisms. Learning to manipulate cell signaling may lead to new methods of delivering drugs into cells and new treatments for cancer and other diseases.

Some organisms use electrical signals to transmit information. Most animals have nervous systems that transmit information by way of both electrical impulses and chemical compounds known as **neurotransmitters.** Information transmitted from one part of the body to another is important in regulating life processes. In complex animals, the nervous system gives the animal information about its outside environment by transmitting signals from sensory receptors such as the eyes and ears to the brain.

Information must also be transmitted from one organism to another. Mechanisms for this type of communication include the release of chemicals, visual displays, and sounds. Typically, organisms use a combination of several types of communication signals. A dog may signal aggression by growling, using a particular facial expression, and laying its ears back. Many animals perform complex courtship rituals in which they display parts of their bodies, often elaborately decorated, to attract a mate.

Review

- What is the function of DNA?
- What are two examples of cell signaling?

1.5 THE ENERGY OF LIFE

LEARNING OBJECTIVE

5   Summarize the flow of energy through ecosystems and contrast the roles of producers, consumers, and decomposers.

Life depends on a continuous input of energy from the sun because every activity of a living cell or organism requires energy. Whenever energy is used to perform biological work, some is converted to heat and dispersed into the environment.

Recall that all the energy transformations and chemical processes that occur within an organism are referred to as its *metabolism.* Energy is necessary to carry on the metabolic activities essential for growth, repair, and maintenance. Each cell of an organism requires nutrients that contain energy. During **cellular respiration,** cells capture energy released by nutrient molecules through a series of carefully regulated chemical reactions (**FIG. 1-8**). The cell can use this energy to do work, including the synthesis of

Most of the energy for life is light energy from the sun, which is captured during photosynthesis; some of this energy is stored in the chemical bonds of glucose and other nutrients.

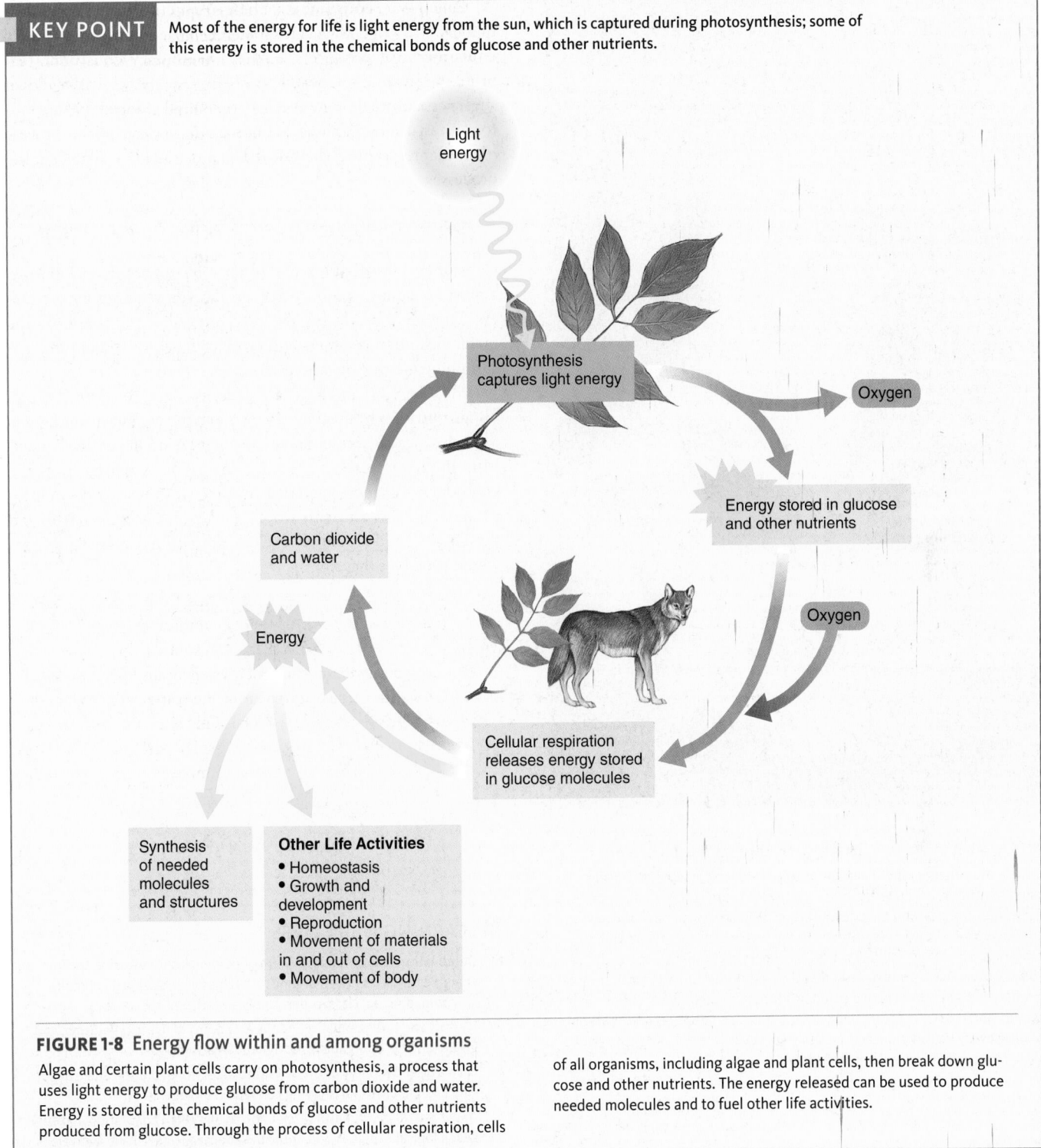

FIGURE 1-8 Energy flow within and among organisms

Algae and certain plant cells carry on photosynthesis, a process that uses light energy to produce glucose from carbon dioxide and water. Energy is stored in the chemical bonds of glucose and other nutrients produced from glucose. Through the process of cellular respiration, cells of all organisms, including algae and plant cells, then break down glucose and other nutrients. The energy released can be used to produce needed molecules and to fuel other life activities.

required materials, such as new cell components. Virtually all cells carry on cellular respiration.

Like individual organisms, ecosystems also depend on a continuous energy input. A self-sufficient ecosystem contains three types of organisms—producers, consumers, and decomposers—and includes a physical environment in which they can survive. These organisms depend on one another and on the environment for nutrients, energy, oxygen, and carbon dioxide. There is a one-way flow of energy through ecosystems. Organisms can neither create energy nor use it with complete efficiency. During every energy transaction, some energy disperses into the environment as heat and is no longer available to the organism (**FIG. 1-9**).

Plants, algae, and certain bacteria are producers, or **auto-trophs,** that produce their own food from simple raw materials.

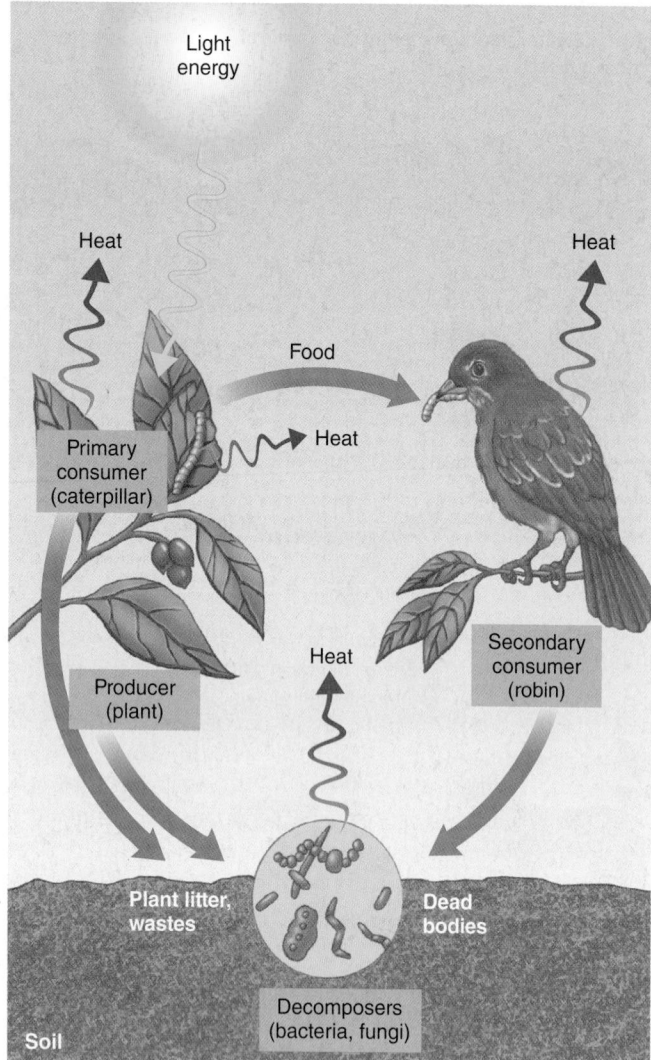

FIGURE 1-9 *Animated* **Energy flow through the biosphere**
Continuous energy input from the sun operates the biosphere. During photosynthesis, producers use the energy from sunlight to make complex molecules from carbon dioxide and water. Primary consumers, such as the caterpillar shown here, obtain energy, nutrients, and other required materials when they eat producers. Secondary consumers, such as the robin, obtain energy, nutrients, and other required materials when they eat primary consumers that have eaten producers. Decomposers obtain their energy and nutrients by breaking down wastes and dead organic material. During every energy transaction, some energy is lost to biological systems, dispersing into the environment as heat.

Most of these organisms use sunlight as an energy source and carry on **photosynthesis,** the process during which producers synthesize complex molecules such as glucose (a sugar) from carbon dioxide and water. The light energy is transformed into chemical energy, which is stored within the chemical bonds of the food molecules produced. Oxygen, which is required by the cells of most organisms including plant cells, is produced as a byproduct of photosynthesis:

$$\text{carbon dioxide} + \text{water} + \text{light energy} \longrightarrow \text{glucose} + \text{oxygen}$$

Animals are **consumers,** or **heterotrophs**—that is, organisms that depend on producers for food, energy, and oxygen. **Primary consumers** eat producers, whereas **secondary consumers** eat primary consumers. Consumers obtain energy by breaking down sugars and other food molecules originally produced during photosynthesis. When chemical bonds are broken during this process of cellular respiration, their stored energy is made available for life processes:

$$\text{glucose} + \text{oxygen} \longrightarrow \text{carbon dioxide} + \text{water} + \text{energy}$$

Consumers contribute to the balance of the ecosystem. For example, consumers produce carbon dioxide required by producers. (Note that producers also carry on cellular respiration.) The metabolism of consumers and producers helps maintain the life-sustaining mixture of gases in the atmosphere.

Most bacteria and fungi are **decomposers,** heterotrophs that obtain nutrients by breaking down nonliving organic material such as wastes, dead leaves and branches, and the bodies of dead organisms. In their process of obtaining energy, decomposers make the components of these materials available for reuse. If decomposers did not exist, nutrients would remain locked up in wastes and dead bodies, and the supply of elements required by living systems would soon be exhausted.

Review

- What components do you think a forest ecosystem might include?
- In what ways do consumers depend on producers? on decomposers? Include energy considerations in your answer.

1.6 EVOLUTION: THE BASIC UNIFYING CONCEPT OF BIOLOGY

▉ LEARNING OBJECTIVES

6   Demonstrate the binomial system of nomenclature by using specific examples and classify an organism (such as a human) in its domain, kingdom, phylum, class, order, family, genus, and species.
7   Identify the three domains and the kingdoms of living organisms, and give examples of organisms assigned to each group.
8   Give a brief overview of the scientific theory of evolution and explain why it is the principal unifying concept in biology.
9   Apply the theory of natural selection to any given adaptation and suggest a logical explanation of how the adaptation may have evolved.

Evolution is the process by which populations of organisms change over time. Evolutionary theory has become the most important unifying concept of biology. As we will discuss, evolution involves passing genes for new traits from one generation to another, leading to differences in populations. The evolutionary perspective is important in every specialized field within biology. Biologists try to understand the structure, function, and behavior of organisms and their interactions with one another by considering them in light of the long, continuing process of evolution. Although we discuss evolution in depth in Chapters 18 through 22, we present a brief overview here to give you the background necessary to understand other aspects of biology. First, we examine how biologists organize the millions of organisms that have evolved, and then we summarize some of the mechanisms that drive evolution.

Biologists use a binomial system for naming organisms

Biologists have identified about 1.8 million species of extant (currently living) organisms and estimate that several million more remain to be discovered. To study life, we need a system for organizing, naming, and classifying its myriad forms. **Systematics** is the field of biology that studies the diversity of organisms and their evolutionary relationships. **Taxonomy,** a subspecialty of systematics, is the science of naming and classifying organisms. In the 18th century, Carolus Linnaeus, a Swedish botanist, developed a hierarchical system of naming and classifying organisms. Biologists still use this system today, with some modification.

The **species** is a group of organisms with similar structure, function, and behavior. A species consists of one or more populations whose members are capable of breeding with one another; in nature, they do not breed with members of other species. Members of a population contribute to a common **gene pool** (all the genes present in the population) and share a common ancestry. Closely related species are grouped in the next broader category of classification, the **genus** (pl., *genera*).

The Linnaean system of naming species is known as the **binomial system of nomenclature** because each species is assigned a two-part name. The first part of the name is the genus, and the second part, the **specific epithet,** designates a particular species belonging to that genus. The specific epithet is often a descriptive word expressing some quality of the organism. It is always used together with the full or abbreviated generic name preceding it. The generic name is always capitalized; the specific epithet is generally not capitalized. Both names are always italicized or underlined. For example, the domestic dog, *Canis familiaris* (abbreviated *C. familiaris*), and the timber wolf, *Canis lupus* (*C. lupus*), belong to the same genus. The domestic cat, *Felis catus,* belongs to a different genus. The scientific name of the American white oak is *Quercus alba,* whereas the name of the European white oak is *Quercus robur.* Another tree, the white willow, *Salix alba,* belongs to a different genus. The scientific name for our own species is *Homo sapiens* ("wise man").

Taxonomic classification is hierarchical

Just as closely related species may be grouped in a common genus, related genera can be grouped in a more inclusive group, a **family.** Families are grouped into **orders,** orders into **classes,** and classes into **phyla** (sing., *phylum*). Phyla can be assigned to **kingdoms,** and kingdoms are grouped in **domains.** Each formal grouping at any given level is a **taxon** (pl., *taxa*). Note that each taxon is more inclusive than the taxon below it. Together they form a hierarchy ranging from species to domain (**TABLE 1-1** and **FIG. 1-10**).

Consider a specific example. The family Canidae, which includes all doglike carnivores (animals that eat mainly meat), consists of 12 genera and about 34 living species. Family Canidae, along with family Ursidae (bears), family Felidae (catlike animals), and several other families that eat mainly meat, are all placed in order Carnivora. Order Carnivora, order Primates (to which chimpanzees and humans belong), and several other orders belong to class Mammalia (mammals). Class Mammalia is grouped with several other classes that include fishes, amphibians, reptiles, and birds in subphylum Vertebrata. The vertebrates belong to phylum Chordata, which is part of kingdom Animalia. Animals are assigned to domain Eukarya.

The tree of life includes three domains and several kingdoms

Systematics has itself evolved as scientists have developed new techniques for inferring common ancestry among groups of organisms. As we will learn, biologists seek to classify organisms based on evolutionary relationships. These relationships are based on shared characteristics that distinguish a particular group. A group of organisms with a common ancestor is a **clade.** Systematists have developed a **tree of life,** a family tree showing proposed evolutionary relationships among organisms. These relationships are based on shared characteristics, including structural, developmental, behavioral, and molecular similarities, as well as on fossil evidence. **FIGURE 1-11** is a **cladogram,** a branching diagram that depicts the tree of life as it is currently understood. As researchers report new findings, the classification of organisms changes and the branches of the tree of life must be redrawn.

Although the tree of life is a work in progress, most biologists now assign organisms to three domains and to several kingdoms or clades. Bacteria have long been recognized as unicellular prokaryotic cells; they differ from all other organisms (except archaea) in that they are **prokaryotes.** Microbiologist Carl Woese (pronounced "woes") has been a pioneer in developing molecular approaches to systematics. Woese and his colleagues selected a molecule known as small subunit ribosomal RNA (rRNA) that functions in the process of manufacturing proteins in all organisms. Because its molecular structure differs somewhat in various organisms, Woese hypothesized that the molecular composition of rRNA in closely related organisms would be more similar than in distantly related organisms.

TABLE 1-1	Classification of the Cat, Human, and White Oak Tree		
Category	Cat	Human	White Oak
Domain	Eukarya	Eukarya	Eukarya
Kingdom	Animalia	Animalia	Plantae
Phylum	Chordata	Chordata	Anthophyta
Subphylum	Vertebrata	Vertebrata	None
Class	Mammalia	Mammalia	Eudicotyledones
Order	Carnivora	Primates	Fagales
Family	Felidae	Hominidae	Fagaceae
Genus	*Felis*	*Homo*	*Quercus*
Species	*Felis catus*	*Homo sapiens*	*Quercus alba*

Biologists use a hierarchical classification scheme with a series of taxonomic categories from species to domain; each category is more general and more inclusive than the one below it.

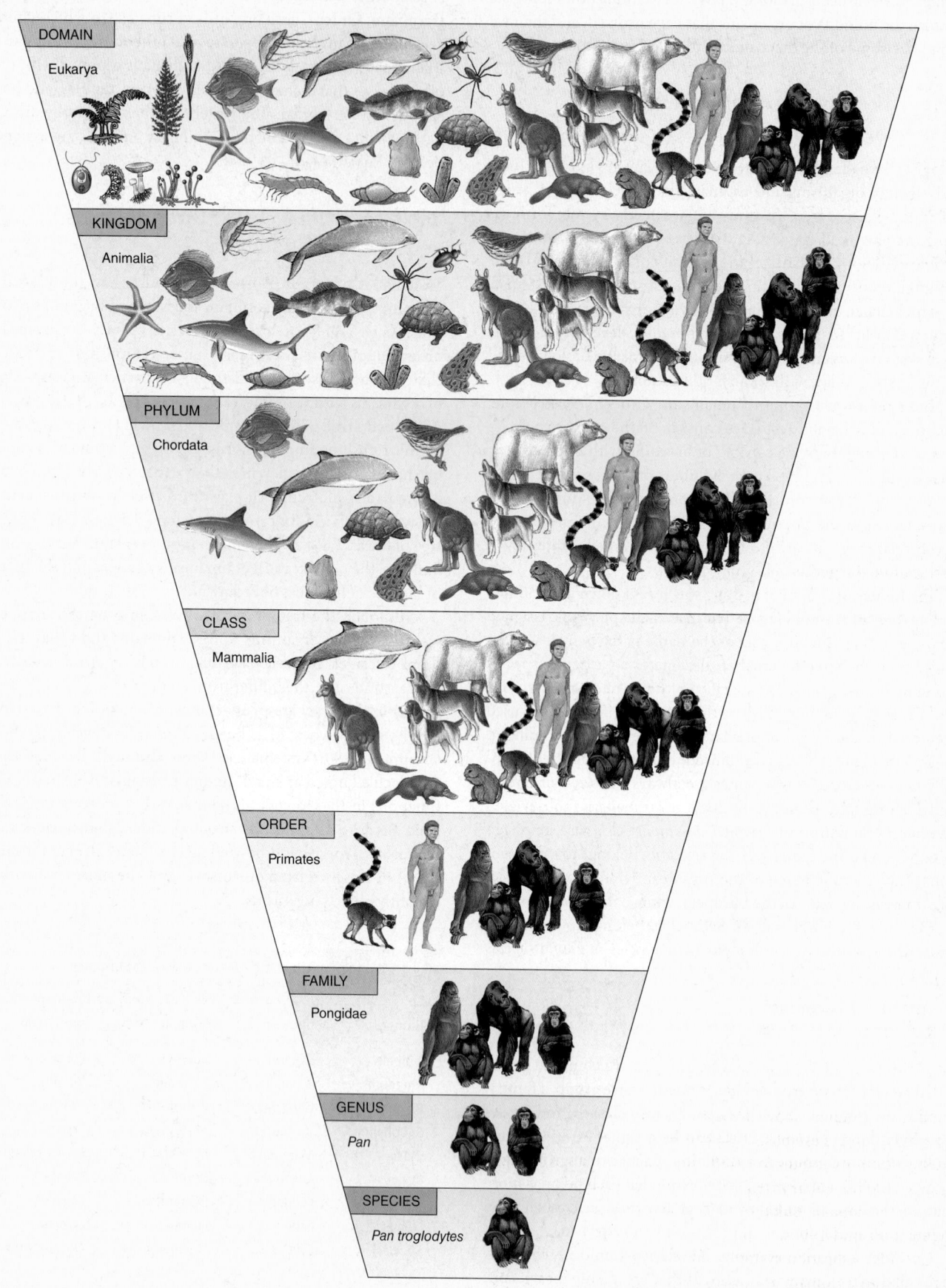

DOMAIN

Eukarya

KINGDOM

Animalia

PHYLUM

Chordata

CLASS

Mammalia

ORDER

Primates

FAMILY

Pongidae

GENUS

Pan

SPECIES

Pan troglodytes

FIGURE 1-10 Classification of the chimpanzee (*Pan troglodytes*)

This cladogram illustrates the evolutionary relationships among the three domains and among the major groups of organisms that belong to these domains.

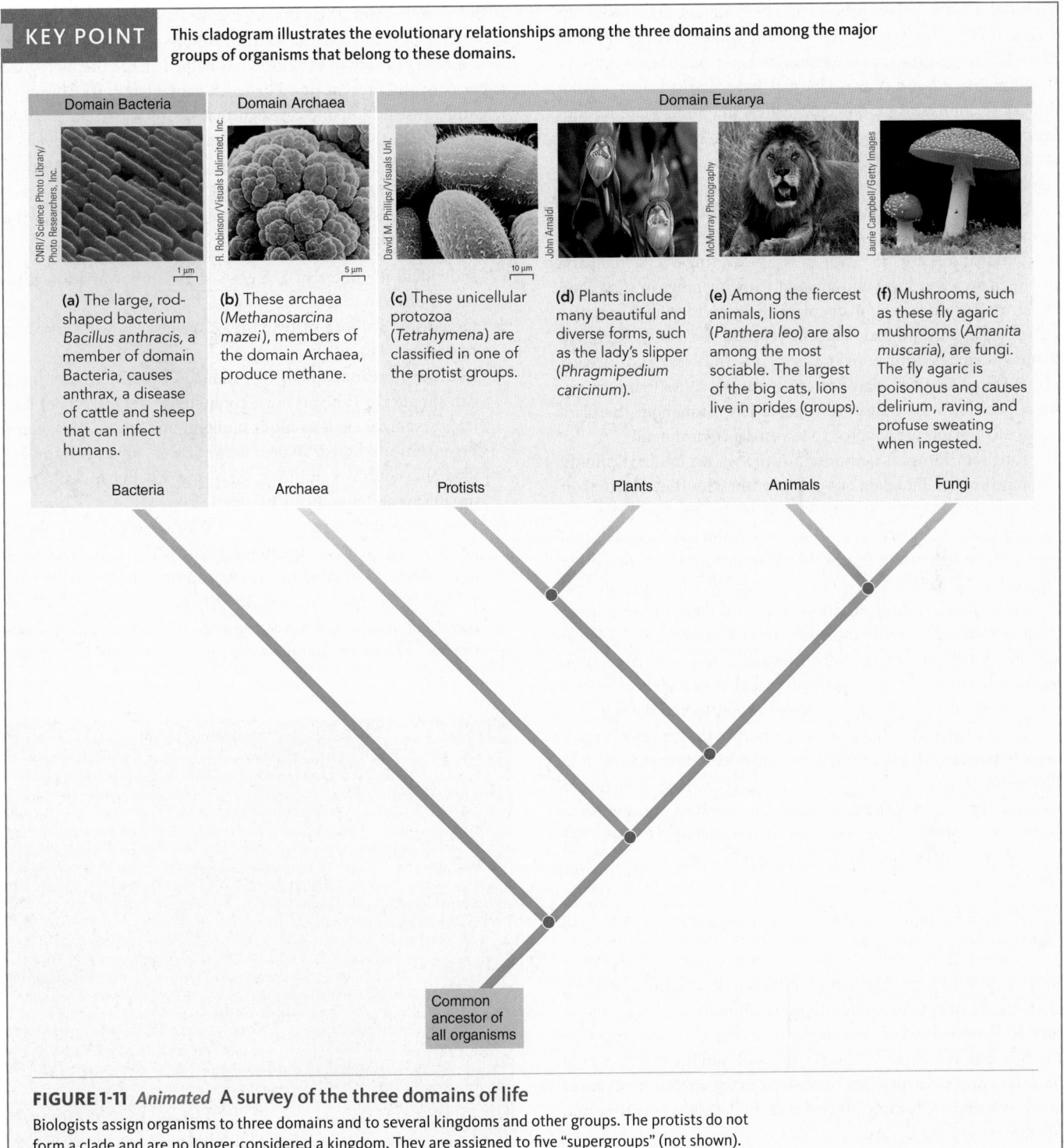

FIGURE 1-11 *Animated* **A survey of the three domains of life**

Biologists assign organisms to three domains and to several kingdoms and other groups. The protists do not form a clade and are no longer considered a kingdom. They are assigned to five "supergroups" (not shown).

Woese's findings showed that there are two distinct groups of prokaryotes. He established the domain level of taxonomy and assigned the prokaryotes to two domains: **Bacteria** and **Archaea** (ar′-key-ah). The **eukaryotes,** organisms with eukaryotic cells, are classified in domain **Eukarya.** Woese's work became widely accepted in the mid-1990s.

In the classification system used in this book, each organism is assigned to a domain and to a kingdom or "supergroup." Two

kingdoms correspond to the prokaryotic domains: kingdom Archaea corresponds to domain Archaea, and kingdom Bacteria corresponds to domain Bacteria. The remaining kingdoms and groups are assigned to domain Eukarya.

Protists (for example, algae, slime molds, amoebas, and ciliates) are unicellular, colonial, or simple multicellular organisms that have a eukaryotic cell organization. The word *protist*, from the Greek for "the very first," reflects the idea that protists were the first eukaryotes to evolve. Protists are primarily aquatic organisms with diverse body forms, types of reproduction, modes of nutrition, and lifestyles. Some protists are adapted to carry out photosynthesis. Based mainly on molecular data that have clarified many evolutionary relationships among eukaryotes, the protists are no longer considered a kingdom. As we will learn in Chapter 26, several clades of protists have been identified, and many biologists now classify protists into five "supergroups."

Members of kingdom **Plantae** are complex multicellular organisms adapted to carry out photosynthesis. Among characteristic plant features are the *cuticle* (a waxy covering over aerial parts that reduces water loss) and *stomata* (tiny openings in stems and leaves for gas exchange); many plants have multicellular *gametangia* (organs that protect developing reproductive cells). Kingdom Plantae includes both nonvascular plants (mosses) and vascular plants (ferns, conifers, and flowering plants), those that have tissues specialized for transporting materials throughout the plant body. Most plants are adapted to terrestrial environments.

Kingdom **Fungi** is composed of the yeasts, mildews, molds, and mushrooms. Fungi do not photosynthesize. They obtain their nutrients by secreting digestive enzymes into food and then absorbing the predigested food. Kingdom **Animalia** is made up of multicellular organisms that obtain their nutrition by eating other organisms. Most animals exhibit considerable cell and tissue specialization and body organization. These characters have evolved along with complex sense organs, nervous systems, and muscular systems. Most animals reproduce sexually; they have large, nonmotile (do not move from place to place) eggs and small sperm with flagella that propel them in their journey to find the egg.

We have provided an introduction here to the groups of organisms that make up the tree of life. We will refer to them throughout this book, as we consider the many kinds of challenges organisms face and the various adaptations that have evolved in response to them. We discuss the diversity of life in more detail in Chapters 23 through 32, and we summarize classification in Appendix B.

Species adapt in response to changes in their environment

Every organism is the product of numerous interactions between environmental conditions and the genes inherited from its ancestors. If all individuals of a species were exactly alike, any change in the environment might be disastrous to all, and the species would become extinct. Adaptations to changes in the environment occur as a result of evolutionary processes that take place over time and involve many generations.

Natural selection is an important mechanism by which evolution proceeds

Although philosophers and naturalists discussed the concept of evolution for centuries, Charles Darwin and Alfred Wallace first brought a theory of evolution to general attention and suggested a plausible mechanism, **natural selection,** to explain it. In his book *On the Origin of Species by Natural Selection*, published in 1859, Darwin synthesized many new findings in geology and biology. He presented a wealth of evidence supporting his hypothesis that present forms of life descended, with modifications, from previ-

ously existing forms. Darwin's book raised a storm of controversy in both religion and science, some of which still lingers.

Darwin's theory of evolution has helped shape the biological sciences to the present day. His work generated a great wave of scientific observation and research that has provided much additional evidence that evolution is responsible for the great diversity of organisms on our planet. Even today, the details of evolutionary processes are a major focus of investigation and discussion.

Darwin based his theory of natural selection on the following four observations:

1. Individual members of a species show some variation from one another.
2. Organisms produce many more offspring than will survive to reproduce (**FIG. 1-12**).
3. Because more individuals are produced than the environment can support, organisms must compete for necessary, but limited, resources such as food, sunlight, and space. Also, some organisms are killed by predators, disease organisms, or unfavorable natural conditions, such as weather changes. Which organisms are more likely to survive?
4. Individuals with characteristics that enable them to obtain and use resources, escape predators, resist disease organisms, and withstand changes in the environment are more likely to survive to reproductive maturity. The survivors that reproduce pass their adaptations for survival on to their offspring. Thus, the best-adapted individuals of a population leave, on average,

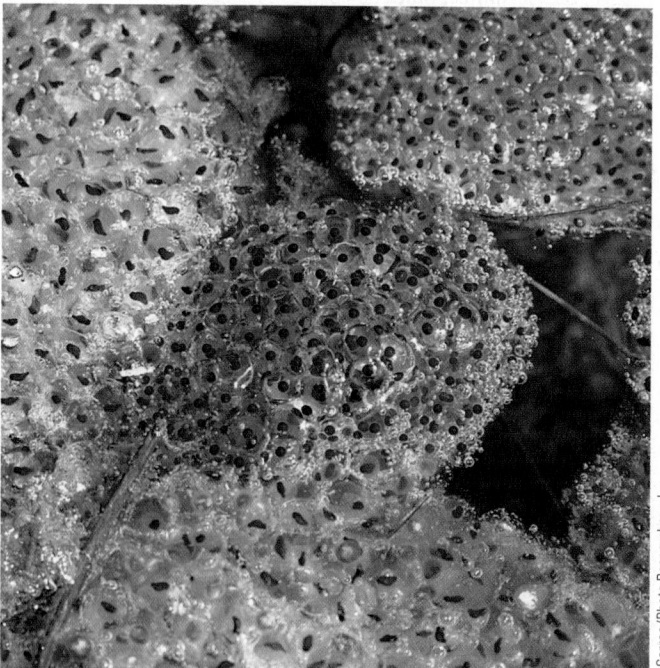

FIGURE 1-12 Egg masses of the wood frog (*Rana sylvatica*)
Many more eggs are produced than can possibly develop into adult frogs. Random events are largely responsible for determining which of these developing frogs will hatch, reach adulthood, and reproduce. However, certain traits of each organism also contribute to the probability for success in its environment. Not all organisms are as prolific as the frog, but the generalization that more organisms are produced than survive is true throughout the living world.

(a) The bill of this 'Akiapola'au male (*Hemignathus munroi*) is adapted for extracting insect larvae from bark. The lower mandible (jaw) is used to peck at and pull off bark, whereas the maxilla (upper jaw) and tongue remove the prey.

(b) 'I'iwi (*Vestiaria cocciniea*) in 'ohi'a blossoms. The bill is adapted for feeding on nectar in tubular flowers.

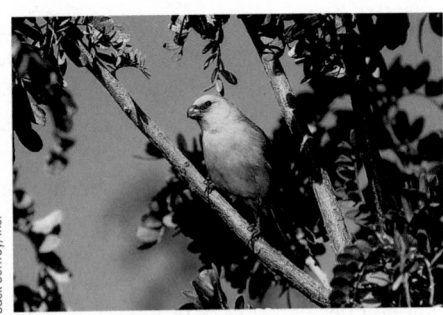

(c) Palila (*Loxiodes bailleui*) in mamane tree. This finch-billed honeycreeper feeds on immature seeds in pods of the mamane tree. It also eats insects, berries, and young leaves.

FIGURE 1-13 Adaptation and diversification in Hawaiian honeycreepers
All three species shown here are endangered, mainly because their habitats have been destroyed by humans or species introduced by humans.

more offspring than do other individuals. Because of this *differential reproduction,* a greater proportion of the population becomes adapted to the prevailing environmental conditions and challenges. The environment *selects* the best-adapted organisms for survival. Note that *adaptation involves changes in populations rather than in individual organisms.*

Darwin did not know about DNA or understand the mechanisms of inheritance. Scientists now understand that most variations among individuals are a result of different varieties of genes that code for each characteristic. The ultimate source of these variations is random **mutations,** chemical or physical changes in DNA that persist and can be inherited. *Mutations modify genes and by this process provide the raw material for evolution.*

Populations evolve as a result of selective pressures from changes in their environment

All the genes present in a population make up its **gene pool.** By virtue of its gene pool, a population is a reservoir of variation. Natural selection acts on individuals within a population. Selection favors individuals with genes specifying traits that allow them to respond effectively to pressures exerted by the environment. These organisms are most likely to survive and produce offspring. As successful organisms pass on their genetic recipe for survival, their traits become more widely distributed in the population. Over time, as populations continue to change (and as the environment itself changes, bringing different selective pressures), the members of the population become better adapted to their environment and less like their ancestors.

As a population adapts to environmental pressures and exploits new opportunities for finding food, maintaining safety, and avoiding predators, the population diversifies and new species may evolve. The Hawaiian honeycreepers, a group of related birds, are a good example. When honeycreeper ancestors first reached Hawaii, few other birds were present, so there was little competition. Genetic variation among honeycreepers allowed some to move into different food zones, and over time, species with various types of bills evolved (**FIG. 1-13**; see also Chapter 20 and Fig. 20-18). Some honeycreepers now have long, curved bills, adapted for feeding on nectar from tubular flowers. Others have short, thick bills for foraging for insects, and still others have adapted for eating seeds.

Review

■ What is the binomial system of nomenclature?

■ Biologists describe the tree of life as a work in progress. Why does the tree need to be modified?

■ How might you explain the sharp claws and teeth of tigers in terms of natural selection?

1.7 THE PROCESS OF SCIENCE

■ LEARNING OBJECTIVES

10 Design a study to test a given hypothesis, using the procedure and terminology of the scientific method.

11 Compare the reductionist and systems approaches to biological research.

Biology is a science. The word *science* comes from a Latin word meaning "to know." Science is a way of thinking and a method of investigating the natural world in a systematic manner. We test ideas, and based on our findings, we modify or reject these ideas. The **process of science** is investigative, dynamic, and often controversial. The observations made, the range of questions asked, and the design of experiments depend on the creativity of the individual scientist. Science, however, is influenced by cultural, social, historical, and technological contexts, so the process changes over time.

The **scientific method** involves a series of ordered steps. Using the scientific method, scientists make careful observations, ask critical questions, and develop *hypotheses,* which are tentative explanations. Using their hypotheses, scientists make predictions that can be tested by making further observations or by performing experiments. They gather **data,** information that they can analyze, often using computers and sophisticated statistical methods.

They interpret the results of their experiments and draw conclusions from them. As we will discuss, scientists pose many hypotheses that cannot be tested by using all of the steps of the scientific method in a rigid way. Scientists use the scientific method as a generalized framework or guide.

Biologists explore every imaginable aspect of life from the structure of viruses and bacteria to the interactions of the communities of our biosphere. Some biologists work mainly in laboratories, and others do their work in the field (**FIG. 1-14**). Perhaps you will decide to become a research biologist and help unravel the complexities of the human brain, discover new hormones that cause plants to flower, identify new species of animals or bacteria, or develop new stem cell strategies to treat cancer, AIDS, or heart disease. Applications of basic biological research have provided the technology to transplant kidneys, livers, and hearts; manipulate genes; treat many diseases; and increase world food production. Biology has been a powerful force in providing the quality of life that most of us enjoy. You may choose to enter an applied field of biology, such as environmental science, dentistry, medicine, pharmacology, or veterinary medicine. Many interesting careers in the biological sciences are discussed in the Careers section on our website.

Science requires systematic thought processes

Science is systematic. Scientists organize and often quantify knowledge, making it readily accessible to all who wish to build on its foundation. In this way, science is both a personal and a social endeavor. Science is not mysterious. Anyone who understands

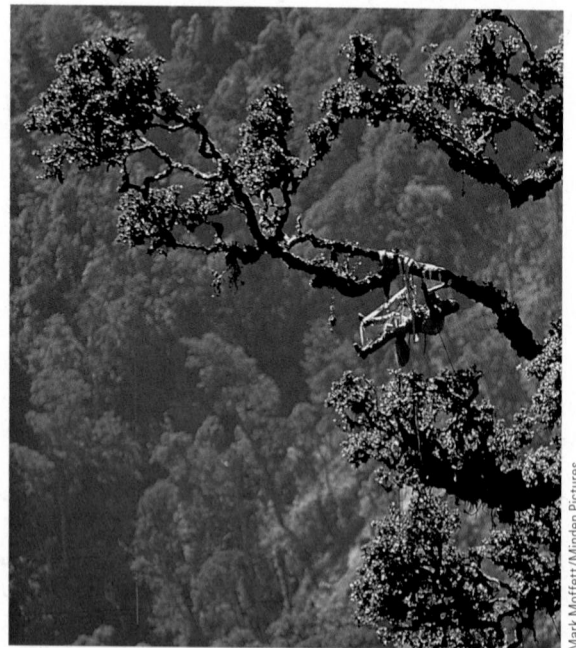

FIGURE 1-14 Biologist at work
This biologist studying the rainforest canopy in Costa Rica is part of an international effort to study and preserve tropical rain forests. Researchers study the interactions of organisms and the effects of human activities on the rain forests.

its rules and procedures can take on its challenges. What distinguishes science is its insistence on rigorous methods to examine a problem. Science seeks to give precise knowledge about the natural world; the supernatural is not accessible to scientific methods of inquiry. Science is not a replacement for philosophy, religion, or art. Being a scientist does not prevent one from participating in other fields of human endeavor, just as being an artist does not prevent one from practicing science.

Deductive reasoning begins with general principles

Scientists use two types of systematic thought processes: deduction and induction. With **deductive reasoning,** we begin with supplied information, called *premises,* and draw conclusions on the basis of that information. Deduction proceeds from general principles to specific conclusions. For example, if you accept the premise that all birds have wings and the second premise that sparrows are birds, you can conclude deductively that sparrows have wings. Deduction helps us discover relationships among known facts. A **fact** is information or knowledge based on evidence.

Inductive reasoning begins with specific observations

Inductive reasoning is the opposite of deduction. We begin with specific observations and draw a conclusion or discover a general principle. For example, you know that sparrows have wings, can fly, and are birds. You also know that robins, eagles, pigeons, and hawks have wings, can fly, and are birds. You might induce that all birds have wings and fly. In this way, you can use the inductive method to organize raw data into manageable categories by answering this question: What do all these facts have in common?

A weakness of inductive reasoning is that conclusions generalize the facts to all possible examples. When we formulate the general principle, we go from many observed examples to all possible examples. This is known as an *inductive leap.* Without it, we could not arrive at generalizations. However, we must be sensitive to exceptions and to the possibility that the conclusion is not valid. For example, the kiwi bird of New Zealand does *not* have functional wings (**FIG. 1-15**). We can never conclusively prove a universal generalization. The generalizations in inductive conclusions come from the creative insight of the human mind, and creativity, however admirable, is not infallible.

Scientists make careful observations and ask critical questions

In 1928, British bacteriologist Alexander Fleming observed that a blue mold had invaded one of his bacterial cultures. He almost discarded it, but then he noticed that the area contaminated by the mold was surrounded by a zone where bacterial colonies did not grow well. The bacteria were disease organisms of the genus *Staphylococcus,* which can cause boils and skin infections. Anything that could kill them was interesting! Fleming saved the mold, a variety of *Penicillium* (blue bread mold), and isolated the antibiotic penicillin from it. However, he had difficulty culturing it.

Even though Fleming recognized the potential practical benefit of penicillin, he did not develop the chemical techniques needed to purify it, and more than ten years passed before the drug was

FIGURE 1-15 Is this animal a bird?
The kiwi bird of New Zealand is about the size of a chicken. Its tiny 2-inch wings cannot be used for flight. The survivor of an ancient order of birds, the kiwi has bristly, hairlike feathers and other characteristics that qualify it as a bird.

put to significant use. In 1939, Sir Howard Florey and Ernst Boris Chain developed chemical procedures to extract and produce the active agent penicillin from the mold. Florey took the process to laboratories in the United States, and penicillin was first produced to treat wounded soldiers in World War II. In recognition of their work, Fleming, Florey, and Chain shared the 1945 Nobel Prize in Physiology or Medicine.

Chance often plays a role in scientific discovery

Fleming did not set out to discover penicillin. He benefited from the chance growth of a mold in one of his culture dishes. However, we may wonder how many times the same type of mold grew on the cultures of other bacteriologists who failed to make the connection and simply threw away their contaminated cultures. Fleming benefited from chance, but his mind was prepared to make observations and formulate critical questions, and his pen was prepared to publish them. Significant discoveries are usually made by those who are in the habit of looking critically at nature and recognizing a phenomenon or problem. Of course, the technology necessary for investigating the problem must also be available.

A hypothesis is a testable statement

Scientists make careful observations, ask critical questions, and develop hypotheses. A **hypothesis** is a tentative explanation for observations or phenomena. Hypotheses can be posed as "if . . . then . . ." statements. For example, *if* students taking introductory biology attend classes, *then* they will make a higher grade on the exam than students who do not attend classes.

In the early stages of an investigation, a scientist typically thinks of many possible hypotheses. A good hypothesis exhibits the following characteristics: (1) It is reasonably consistent with well-established facts. (2) It is capable of being tested; that is, it should generate definite predictions, whether the results are posi-

tive or negative. Test results should also be repeatable by independent observers. (3) It is falsifiable, which means it can be proven false, as we will discuss in the next section.

After generating hypotheses, the scientist decides which, if any, could and should be subjected to experimental test. Why not test them all? Time and money are important considerations in conducting research. Scientists must establish priority among the hypotheses to decide which to test first.

A falsifiable hypothesis can be tested

In science, a well-stated hypothesis can be tested. If no evidence is found to support it, the hypothesis is rejected. The hypothesis can be shown to be false. Even results that do not support the hypothesis may be valuable and may lead to new hypotheses. If the results do support a hypothesis, a scientist may use them to generate related hypotheses.

Let us consider a hypothesis that we can test by careful observation: female mammals (animals that have hair and produce milk for their young) bear live young. The hypothesis is based on the observations that dogs, cats, cows, lions, and humans all are mammals and all bear live young. Consider further that a new species, species X, is identified as a mammal based on its having hair and producing milk for its young. Biologists predict that females of species X will bear live young. (Is this inductive or deductive reasoning?) If a female of the new species gives birth to live offspring, the hypothesis is supported.

Before the Southern Hemisphere was explored, most people would probably have accepted the hypothesis without question because all known furry, milk-producing animals did, in fact, bear live young. But biologists discovered that two Australian animals (the duck-billed platypus and the spiny anteater) had fur and produced milk for their young—but laid eggs (**FIG. 1-16**). The hypothesis, as stated, was false no matter how many times it had previously been supported. As a result, biologists either had to consider the

FIGURE 1-16 Is this animal a mammal?
The duck-billed platypus (*Ornithorhynchus anatinus*) is classified as a mammal because it has fur and produces milk for its young. However, unlike most mammals, it lays eggs.

platypus and the spiny anteater as nonmammals or had to broaden their definition of mammals to include them. (They chose to do the latter.)

A hypothesis is not true just because some of its predictions (the ones people happen to have thought of or have thus far been able to test) have been shown to be true. After all, they could be true by coincidence. In fact, a hypothesis can be supported by data, but it cannot really be *proven* true.

An **unfalsifiable hypothesis** cannot be proven false; in fact, it cannot be scientifically investigated. Belief in an unfalsifiable hypothesis, such as the existence of invisible and undetectable elves, must be rationalized on grounds other than scientific ones.

Models are important in developing and testing hypotheses

Hypotheses have many potential sources, including direct observations or even computer simulations. Increasingly in biology, hypotheses may be derived from **models** that scientists have developed to provide a comprehensive explanation for a large number of observations. Examples of such testable models include the model of the structure of DNA and the model of the structure of the plasma membrane (discussed in Chapter 5).

The best design for an experiment can sometimes be established by performing computer simulations. Virtual testing and evaluation are undertaken before the experiment is performed in the laboratory or field. Modeling and computer simulation save time and money.

Many predictions can be tested by experiment

A hypothesis is an abstract idea, but based on their hypotheses, scientists can make predictions that can be tested. For example, we might predict that biology students who study for ten hours will do better on an exam than students who do not study. As used here, a **prediction** is a deductive, logical consequence of a hypothesis. It does not have to be a future event.

Some predictions can be tested by controlled experiments. Early biologists observed that the nucleus was the most prominent part of the cell, and they hypothesized that cells would be adversely affected if they lost their nuclei. Biologists predicted that if the nucleus were removed from the cell, then the cell would die. They then experimented by surgically removing the nucleus of a unicellular amoeba. The amoeba continued to live and move, but it did not grow, and after a few days it died. These results suggested

that the nucleus is necessary for the metabolic processes that provide for growth and cell reproduction.

But, the investigators asked, what if the operation itself, not the loss of the nucleus, caused the amoeba to die? They performed a controlled experiment, subjecting two groups of amoebas to the same operative trauma (**FIG. 1-17**). In the experimental group, the nucleus was removed; in the control group, it was not. Ideally, an **experimental group** differs from a control group only with respect to the variable being studied. In the **control group**, the researcher inserted a microloop into each amoeba and pushed it around inside the cell to simulate removal of the nucleus; then the instrument was withdrawn, leaving the nucleus inside.

Amoebas treated with such a sham operation recovered and subsequently grew and divided. This experiment showed that the removal of the nucleus, not simply the operation, caused the death

KEY EXPERIMENT

ASK CRITICAL QUESTIONS: Why is the nucleus so large? What is its importance?

DEVELOP HYPOTHESIS: Cells will be adversely affected if they lose their nuclei.

PERFORM EXPERIMENTS: Using a microloop, researchers removed the nucleus from each amoeba in the experimental group. Amoebas in the control group were subjected to the same surgical procedure, but their nuclei were not removed.

(a) Experimental group. When its nucleus is surgically removed with a microloop, the amoeba dies.

(b) Control group. A control amoeba subjected to similar surgical procedures (including insertion of a microloop), but without actual removal of the nucleus, does not die.

RESULTS: Amoebas without nuclei died. Amoebas in the control group lived.

CONCLUSION: Amoebas cannot live without their nuclei. The hypothesis is supported.

FIGURE 1-17 Testing a prediction regarding the importance of the nucleus
Scientists observed that the nucleus was the most prominent part of the cell. They asked critical questions about their observation and developed the hypothesis that cells would be adversely affected if they lost their nuclei. Based on their hypothesis, they made a prediction that could be tested: if the nucleus is removed from an amoeba, the amoeba will die. The investigators then performed experiments to test this prediction. They studied their results and concluded that their hypothesis was supported.

of the amoebas. The conclusion is that amoebas cannot live without their nuclei. The results support the hypothesis that if cells lose their nuclei, they are adversely affected. We can conclude that the nucleus is essential for the survival of the cell.

Researchers must avoid bias

In scientific studies, researchers must do their best to avoid bias or preconceived notions of what should happen. For example, to prevent bias, most medical experiments are carried out in a double-blind fashion. When a drug is tested, one group of patients receives the new medication, and a control group of matched patients receives a placebo (a harmless starch pill similar in size, shape, color, and taste to the pill being tested). This is a *double-blind study,* named so because neither the patient nor the physician knows who is getting the experimental drug and who is getting the placebo. The pills or treatments are coded in some way, and the code is broken only after the experiment is over and the results are recorded. Not all experiments can be so neatly designed; for example, it is often difficult to establish appropriate controls.

Scientists interpret the results of experiments and make conclusions

Scientists gather data in an experiment, interpret their results, and then draw conclusions from them. In the amoeba experiment described earlier, investigators concluded that the data supported the hypothesis that the nucleus is essential for the survival of the cell. When the results do support a hypothesis, scientists may use them to generate related hypotheses. Even results that do not support the hypothesis may be valuable and may lead to new hypotheses.

Let us discuss another experiment. Research teams studying chimpanzee populations in Africa have reported that chimpanzees appear to learn specific ways to use tools from one another. Behavior that is learned from others in a population and passed to future generations is what we call "culture." In the past, most biologists have thought that only humans had culture. It has been difficult to test this type of learning in the field, and the idea has been controversial.

Biologists have asked critical questions about whether chimpanzees learned how to use tools by observing one another. Investigators at Yerkes National Primate Research Center in Atlanta developed a hypothesis that chimpanzees can learn particular ways to use tools by observing other chimps. They predicted that if they taught one chimp to use a stick to obtain food from a dispenser, other chimps would learn the technique from the educated one (**FIG. 1-18**). These researchers divided chimpanzees into two experimental groups with 16 in each group. Then they taught a high-ranking female in each group to use a stick to obtain food from an apparatus. The two chimps were taught different methods. One chimp was taught to poke the stick inside the device to free the food. The other was taught to use the stick to lift a hook that removed a blockage, allowing the food to roll forward out of the device.

A third group served as a control group. The chimps in the control group were given access to the sticks and the apparatus with the food inside but none were taught how to use the sticks. All of the control-group chimps manipulated the apparatus with the stick, but none succeeded in releasing food.

When the chimps were returned to their groups, other chimps observed how the educated chimps used the stick, and a large majority began to use sticks in the same way. The chimps in each group learned the specific style of using the stick that their educated chimp had been taught. Most used the stick to obtain food at least 10 times. Two months later, the apparatus was reintroduced to the chimps. Again, most of the chimps used the learned technique for obtaining food. The results of the experiment supported the hypothesis. The researchers concluded that chimpanzees are capable of culturally transmitting learned technology.

Sampling error can lead to inaccurate conclusions

One reason for inaccurate conclusions is *sampling error.* Because not *all* cases of what is being studied can be observed or tested (scientists cannot study every amoeba or every chimpanzee population), scientists must be content with a sample. How can scientists know whether that sample is truly representative of whatever they are studying? If the sample is too small, it may not be representative because of random factors. A study with only two, or even nine, amoebas may not yield reliable data that can be generalized to other amoebas. If researchers test a large number of subjects, they are more likely to draw accurate scientific conclusions (**FIG. 1-19**). The scientist seeks to state with some level of confidence that any specific conclusion has a certain statistical probability of being correct.

Experiments must be repeatable

When researchers publish their findings in a scientific journal, they typically describe their methods and procedures in sufficient detail so that other scientists can repeat the experiments. When the findings are replicated, the conclusions are, of course, strengthened.

A theory is supported by tested hypotheses

Nonscientists often use the word *theory* incorrectly to refer to a hypothesis or even to some untestable idea they wish to promote. A **scientific theory** is actually an integrated explanation of some aspect of the natural world that is based on a number of hypotheses, each supported by consistent results from many observations or experiments. A scientific theory relates data that previously appeared unrelated. A good theory grows, building on additional facts as they become known. It predicts new facts and suggests new relationships among phenomena. It may even suggest practical applications.

A scientific theory, by showing the relationships among classes of facts, simplifies and clarifies our understanding of the natural world. As Einstein wrote, "In the whole history of science from Greek philosophy to modern physics, there have been constant attempts to reduce the apparent complexity of natural phenomena to simple, fundamental ideas and relations." Developing scientific theories is indeed a major goal of science.

Many hypotheses cannot be tested by direct experiment

Some well-accepted theories do not lend themselves to hypothesis testing by ordinary experiments. Often, these theories describe events that occurred in the distant past. We cannot directly observe

ASK CRITICAL QUESTIONS: Do chimpanzees learn how to use tools by observing one another?

DEVELOP HYPOTHESIS: Chimpanzees can learn particular ways to use tools by observing other chimps.

PERFORM EXPERIMENTS: One female in each of two groups of 16 chimps was educated in a specific way to use a stick to obtain food. The two educated chimps were then returned to their respective groups. Chimpanzees in a control group were not taught how to use a stick.

David Bygott

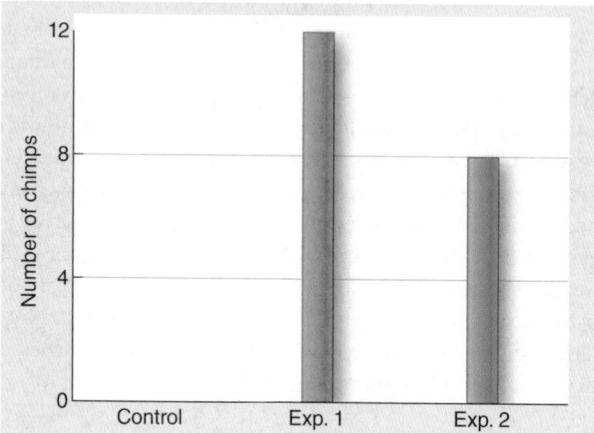

(a) Number of chimpanzees successfully employing specific method of tool use.

(b) Number of chimpanzees successfully employing learned method of tool use two months later.

FIGURE 1-18 Testing a prediction about learning in chimpanzee populations

In the photo, wild chimpanzees are shown observing a member of their group using a tool.

RESULTS: Chimpanzees in each experimental group observed the use of the stick by the educated chimp, and a majority began to use the stick in the same way. When tested two months later, many of the chimps in each group continued to use the stick. *The results presented here have been simplified and are based on the number of chimps observed to use the learned method at least 10 times.* All but one chimp in each group learned the technology, but a few used it only a few times. Some chimps taught themselves the alternative method and used that alternative. However, most conformed to the group's use of the method that the investigator taught to the educated chimp.

CONCLUSION: Chimpanzees learn specific ways to use tools by observing other chimps. The hypothesis was supported.

the origin of the universe from a very hot, dense state about 13.7 billion years ago (the Big Bang theory). However, physicists and cosmologists have been able to formulate many hypotheses related to the Big Bang and to test many of the predictions derived from these hypotheses.

Similarly, humans did not observe the evolution of major groups of organisms because that process took place over millions of years and occurred before humans had evolved. However, many hypotheses about evolution have been posed, and predictions

based on them have been tested. For example, if complex organisms evolved from simple life-forms, we would find the fossils of the simplest organisms in the oldest strata (rock layers). As we explore more recent strata, we would expect to find increasingly complex organisms. Indeed, scientists have found this progression of simple to complex fossils.

In addition to fossils, evidence for evolution comes from many sources, including physical and molecular similarities between organisms. Evidence also comes from recent and current studies

(a) Taking a single selection can result in sampling error. If the only marble selected is blue, we might assume all the marbles are blue.

(b) The greater the number of selections we take of an unknown, the more likely we can make valid assumptions about it.

FIGURE 1-19 *Animated* **Statistical probability**

of evolution in action. Many aspects of ongoing evolution can, in fact, be studied in the laboratory or in the field. The evidence for evolution is so compelling that virtually all scientists today accept evolutionary theory as an integral part of biology.

Paradigm shifts allow new discoveries

A **paradigm** is a set of assumptions or concepts that constitute a way of thinking about reality. For example, from the time of Aristotle to the mid-19th century, biologists thought that organisms were either plants (kingdom Plantae) or animals (kingdom Animalia). This concept was deeply entrenched. However, with the development of microscopes, investigators discovered tiny life-forms—bacteria and protists—that were neither plant nor animal. Biologists had to make a **paradigm shift,** that is, they changed their view of reality, to accommodate this new knowledge. They assigned these newly discovered organisms to new kingdoms. In a more recent paradigm shift, biologists have revised their idea that we are born with all of the brain cells we will ever have. We now understand that certain areas of the brain continue to produce new neurons throughout life.

Systems biology integrates different levels of information

In the *reductionist* approach to biology, researchers study the simplest components of biological processes. Their goal is to synthesize their knowledge of many small parts to understand the whole. Reductionism has been (and continues to be) important in biological research. However, as biologists and their tools have become increasingly sophisticated, huge amounts of data have been generated, bringing the science of biology to a different level.

Systems biology is a field of biology that builds on information provided by the reductionist approach and develops large data sets, typically generated by computers. Systems biology is also referred to as *integrative biology.* Reductionism and systems biology are complementary approaches. Using reductionism, biologists have discovered basic information about components, such as molecules, genes, cells, and organs. Systems biologists, who focus on systems as a whole rather than on individual components, need this basic knowledge to study, for example, the *interactions* among various parts and levels of an organism.

Systems biologists integrate data from various levels of complexity with the goal of understanding the big picture—how biological systems function. For example, systems biologists are developing models of different aspects of cell function. Normal cell function depends on the precise actions of hundreds of proteins that relay signals received from other cells. Proteins also relay signals from one part of the cell to another. Researchers are producing detailed maps of the molecular pathways that maintain cell function (**FIG. 1-20**).

One group of researchers has developed a model consisting of nearly 8000 chemical signals involved in a molecular network that leads to programmed cell death. By understanding cell communication, the interactions of genes and proteins in metabolic pathways, and physiological processes, systems biologists hope to eventually develop a model of the whole organism. Systems biology is increasingly used to study disease processes. For example, the interactions between the pathogen and the host cell can be mapped.

The development of systems biology was fueled by the huge amount of data generated by the Human Genome Project. Researchers working on this project identified the DNA sequences that make up the estimated 25,000 genes of the *human genome,* the complete set of genes that make up the human genetic material. Computer software developed for the Human Genome Project can analyze very large data sets. These programs are being used to integrate data about protein interactions and many other aspects of molecular biology. Systems biologists view biology in terms of information systems. Increasingly, they depend on mathematics, statistics, and engineering principles.

Hawoong Jeong, University of Notre Dame/Science Photo Library

FIGURE 1-20 Map showing protein interactions in a yeast cell (*Saccharomyces cerevisiae*)

Each dot represents one protein in this single-celled fungus. Lines connect proteins that interact with one another. Highly connected proteins are more critical to cell function. Many of these interactions have also been identified in human cells. Specific proteins were removed by removing the genes that coded for their production. The proteins have been color-coded according to the effect their removal has on the yeast cell: *red*, lethal; *green*, not lethal; *orange*, slower growth; *yellow*, unknown effects.

Science has ethical dimensions

Scientific investigation depends on a commitment to practical ideals, such as truthfulness and the obligation to communicate results. Honesty is particularly important in science. Consider the great (though temporary) damage done whenever an unprincipled or even desperate researcher, whose career may depend on the publication of a research study, knowingly disseminates false data. Until the deception is uncovered, researchers may devote thousands of dollars and hours of precious professional labor to futile lines of research inspired by erroneous reports. Deception can also be dangerous, especially in medical research. Fortunately, science tends to correct itself through consistent use of the scientific process. Sooner or later, someone's experimental results are sure to cast doubt on false data.

Science and technology continuously interact. As scientists doing basic research report new findings, engineers and other inventors develop new products. Many of those products contribute to our quality of life. New technology also provides scientists with more powerful tools for their research and increases the potential for new discoveries. For example, a few years ago determining the genome of any eukaryote required several rooms filled with machines that could sequence the genes. This endeavor also cost millions of dollars. New technologies have revolutionized gene sequencing, allowing complex genomes to be determined quickly, with less equipment, and at far less expense. Plans are under way to determine the genomes of 10,000 vertebrates.

Science and technology continue to change society, and these changes present new challenges. In addition to being ethical about their own work, scientists face many societal and political issues surrounding areas such as genetic research, stem cell research, cloning, and human and animal experimentation. For example, some stem cells that show great potential for treating human disease come from early embryos. The cells can be taken from five- or six-day-old human embryos and then cultured in laboratory glassware. At this stage, the embryo is a group of cells about 0.15 mm long (0.006 in). Such cells could be engineered to treat failing hearts or brains harmed by stroke, injury, Parkinson's disease, or Alzheimer's disease. They could save the lives of burn victims and perhaps be engineered to treat specific cancers. Scientists, and the larger society, will need to determine whether the potential benefits of any type of research outweigh its ethical risks.

The era of the genome brings with it many ethical concerns and responsibilities. How do people safeguard the privacy of genetic information? For example, suppose that you have a family history of breast cancer and learn from genetic testing that you have one of the BRCA mutations. These mutations increase risk for developing breast cancer and certain other cancers. How can you be certain that knowledge of your individual genetic code would not be used against you when you seek employment or health insurance? Scientists must be ethically responsible and must help educate people about their work, including its benefits relative to its risks. It is significant that at the very beginning of the Human Genome Project, part of its budget was allocated for research on the ethical, legal, and social implications of its findings.

Review

- What are the characteristics of a good hypothesis?
- What is meant by a "controlled" experiment?
- What is systems biology?

■ SUMMARY: FOCUS ON LEARNING OBJECTIVES

1.1 *(page 2)*

1 Describe three basic themes of biology.

- Three basic themes of biology are evolution, transfer of information, and energy transfer. The process of **evolution** results in populations changing over time and explains how the ancestry of organisms can be traced back to earlier forms of life. Information must be transmitted within cells, among cells, among organisms, and from one generation to the next. Life requires continuous input of energy from the sun.

1.2 *(page 2)*

2 Distinguish between living and nonliving things by describing the features that characterize living organisms.

- Every living organism is composed of one or more **cells.** Living things grow by increasing the size and/or number of their cells.
- **Metabolism** includes all the chemical activities that take place in the organism, including the chemical reactions essential to nutrition, growth and repair, and conversion of energy to usable forms. **Homeostasis** refers to the appropriate, balanced internal environment.

- Organisms respond to **stimuli,** physical or chemical changes in their external or internal environment. Responses typically involve movement.
- In **asexual reproduction,** offspring are typically identical to the single parent, except for size; in **sexual reproduction,** offspring are the product of the fusion of gametes, and genes are typically contributed by two parents.
- As populations evolve, they become adapted to their environment. **Adaptations** are traits that increase an organism's ability to survive in its environment.

1.3 *(page 5)*

3 Construct a hierarchy of biological organization, including levels characteristic of individual organisms and levels characteristic of ecological systems.

- Biological organization is hierarchical. A complex organism is organized at the chemical, cell, **tissue, organ, organ system,** and **organism** levels. Cells associate to form tissues that carry out specific functions. In most multicellular organisms, tissues organize to form functional structures called organs. An organized group of tissues and organs form an organ system. Functioning together, organ systems make up a complex, multicellular organism.

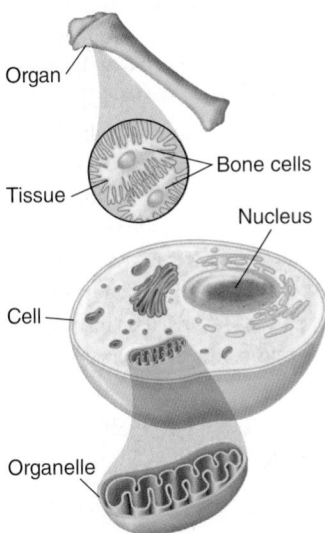

Organ
Tissue — Bone cells
Nucleus
Cell
Organelle

- The basic unit of ecological organization is the **population.** Various populations form **communities;** a community and its physical environment are an **ecosystem;** all of Earth's ecosystems together make up the **biosphere.**

CENGAGENOW™   Learn more about biological organization by clicking on the figure in CengageNOW.

1.4 *(page 7)*

4 Summarize the importance of information transfer within and between living systems, giving specific examples.

- Organisms transmit information chemically, electrically, and behaviorally.
- **DNA,** which makes up the **genes,** is the hereditary material. Information encoded in DNA is transmitted from one generation to the next. DNA contains the instructions for the development of an organism and for carrying out life processes. DNA codes for **proteins,** which are important in determining the structure and function of cells and tissues.
- **Hormones,** chemical messengers that transmit messages from one part of an organism to another, are important in **cell signaling.**
- Many organisms use electrical signals to transmit information; most animals have nervous systems that transmit electrical impulses and release **neurotransmitters.**

1.5 *(page 8)*

5 Summarize the flow of energy through ecosystems and contrast the roles of producers, consumers, and decomposers.

- Activities of living cells require energy. Life depends on continuous energy input from the sun. During **photosynthesis,** plants, algae, and certain bacteria use the energy of sunlight to synthesize complex molecules from carbon dioxide and water.
- Virtually all cells carry on **cellular respiration,** a biochemical process in which they capture the energy stored in nutrients by producers. Some of that energy is then used to synthesize required materials or to carry out other cell activities.
- A self-sufficient ecosystem includes **producers,** or **autotrophs,** which make their own food; **primary consumers,** which eat producers, and typically secondary consumers that eat primary consumers; and **decomposers,** which obtain energy by breaking down wastes and dead organisms. Consumers and decomposers are **heterotrophs,** organisms that depend on producers as an energy source and for food and oxygen.

CENGAGENOW™   Learn more about energy flow by clicking on the figure in CengageNOW.

1.6 *(page 10)*

6 Demonstrate the binomial system of nomenclature by using specific examples and classify an organism (such as a human) in its domain, kingdom, phylum, class, order, family, genus, and species.

- Millions of species have evolved. A **species** is a group of organisms with similar structure, function, and behavior that, in nature, breed only with one another. Members of a species contribute to a common **gene pool** and share a common ancestry.
- Biologists use a **binomial system of nomenclature** in which the name of each species includes a **genus** name and a **specific epithet.** Taxonomic classification is hierarchical; it includes species, genus, **family, order, class, phylum, kingdom,** and **domain.** Each grouping is referred to as a **taxon.** A group of organisms with a common ancestor is a **clade.**

7 Identify the three domains and the kingdoms of living organisms, and give examples of organisms assigned to each group.

- Bacteria and archaea have **prokaryotic cells;** all other organisms have **eukaryotic cells.** Prokaryotes make up two of the three domains.
- Organisms are classified in three domains: **Archaea, Bacteria,** and **Eukarya** and several kingdoms: **Archaea, Bacteria, Fungi** (e.g., molds and yeasts), **Plantae,** and **Animalia.** Protists (e.g., algae, water molds, slime molds, and amoebas) are now assigned to five "supergroups."

CENGAGENOW™   Learn more about life's diversity by clicking on the figure in CengageNOW.

8 Give a brief overview of the scientific theory of evolution and explain why it is the principal unifying concept in biology.

- **Evolution** is the process by which populations change over time in response to changes in the environment. Evolutionary theory explains how millions of species came to be and helps us understand the structure, function, behavior, and relationships of organisms.
- **Natural selection,** the major mechanism by which evolution proceeds, favors individuals with traits that enable them to cope with environmental changes. Charles Darwin based his theory of natural selection on his observations that individuals of a species vary; organisms produce more offspring than survive to reproduce; organisms must compete for limited resources; and individuals that are best adapted to their environment are more likely to survive and reproduce, and pass on their hereditary information. Their traits become more widely distributed in the population.
- The source of variation in a population is random **mutation.**

9 Apply the theory of natural selection to any given adaptation and suggest a logical explanation of how the adaptation may have evolved.

- When the ancestors of Hawaiian honeycreepers first reached Hawaii, few other birds were present, so there was little competition for food. Through many generations, honeycreepers with longer, more curved bills became adapted for feeding on nectar from tubular flowers. Perhaps those with the longest, most curved bills were best able to survive in this food zone and lived to transmit their genes to their offspring. Those with shorter, thicker bills were more successful foraging for insects and passed their genes to new generations of offspring. Eventually, different species evolved that were adapted to specific food zones.

1.7 *(page 15)*

10 Design a study to test a given hypothesis, using the procedure and terminology of the scientific method.

- The **process of science** is a dynamic approach to investigation. The **scientific method** is a general framework that scientists use in their work; it includes observing, recognizing a problem or stating a critical question, developing a hypothesis, making a prediction that can be tested, making further observations, performing experiments, interpreting results, and drawing conclusions that support or falsify the hypothesis.
- Deductive reasoning and inductive reasoning are two categories of systematic thought used in the scientific method. **Deductive reasoning** proceeds from general principles to specific conclusions and helps us discover relationships among known facts. **Inductive reasoning** begins with specific observations and draws conclusions from them. Inductive reasoning helps us discover general principles.
- A **hypothesis** is a tentative explanation for observations or phenomena. A hypothesis can be tested. If no evidence is found to support it, the hypothesis is rejected.
- A well-designed scientific experiment typically includes both a **control group** and an **experimental group** and must be as free as possible from bias. The control group should be as closely matched to the experimental group as possible. Ideally, the experimental group differs from the control group only with respect to the variable being studied.

  CENGAGENOW˜ Do your own random sampling by clicking on the figure in CengageNOW.

- A **scientific theory** is an integrated explanation of some aspect of the natural world that is based on a number of hypotheses, each supported by consistent results from many observations or experiments.

11 Compare the reductionist and systems approaches to biological research.

- Using reductionism, researchers study the simplest components of biological processes, for example, molecules or cells. **Systems biology** uses knowledge provided by reductionism. Systems biologists integrate data from various levels of complexity with the goal of understanding how biological systems function.

TEST YOUR UNDERSTANDING

1. Homeostasis (a) is the appropriate, balanced internal environment (b) is the sum of all the chemical activities of an organism (c) is the long-term response of organisms to changes in their environment (d) occurs at the ecosystem level, not in cells or organisms (e) may be sexual or asexual

2. An amoeba splits into two smaller amoebas. This is an example of (a) homeostasis (b) neurotransmission (c) asexual reproduction (d) sexual reproduction (e) metabolism

3. Cells (a) are the building blocks of living organisms (b) always have nuclei (c) are not found among the bacteria (d) a, b, and c (e) a and b

4. Which of the following is a correct sequence of levels of biological organization?
   1. organ system 2. chemical 3. tissue 4. organ 5. cell
   (a) 2, 3, 5, 4, 1 (b) 5, 3, 4, 1, 2 (c) 2, 5, 3, 1, 4 (d) 2, 5, 3, 4, 1 (e) 5, 2, 3, 4, 1

5. Which of the following is a correct sequence of levels of ecological organization?
   1. community 2. organism 3. ecosystem 4. population 5. biosphere
   (a) 5, 3, 1, 4, 2 (b) 2, 4, 1, 3, 5 (c) 2, 1, 4, 3, 5 (d) 4, 2, 1, 3, 5 (e) 2, 4, 3, 1, 5

6. DNA (a) is produced during cellular respiration (b) functions mainly to transmit information from one species to another (c) cannot be changed (d) is a neurotransmitter (e) makes up the genes

7. Cellular respiration (a) is a process whereby sunlight is used to synthesize cell components with the release of energy (b) occurs in heterotrophs only (c) is carried on by both autotrophs and heterotrophs (d) causes chemical changes in DNA (e) occurs in response to environmental changes

8. Fungi are assigned to domain (a) Protista (b) Archaea (c) Bacteria (d) Eukarya (e) Plantae

9. The scientific name for corn is *Zea mays. Zea* is the (a) specific epithet (b) genus (c) class (d) kingdom (e) phylum

10. Darwin suggested that evolution takes place by (a) mutation (b) changes in the individuals of a species (c) natural selection (d) interaction of hormones during competition for resources (e) homeostatic responses to each change in the environment

11. Ideally, an experimental group differs from a control group (a) only with respect to the hypothesis being tested (b) because its subjects are more reliable (c) in that it is less subject to bias (d) in that it is less vulnerable to sampling error (e) only with respect to the variable being studied

12. A systems biologist would most likely work on (a) better understanding the components of cells (b) developing a better system of classification of organisms (c) devising a new series of steps for the scientific method (d) researching a series of reactions that communicate information in the cell (e) identifying the connections and interactions of neurons in order to learn about brain function

13. Identify the domain and kingdoms by writing the name for each on the blank lines.

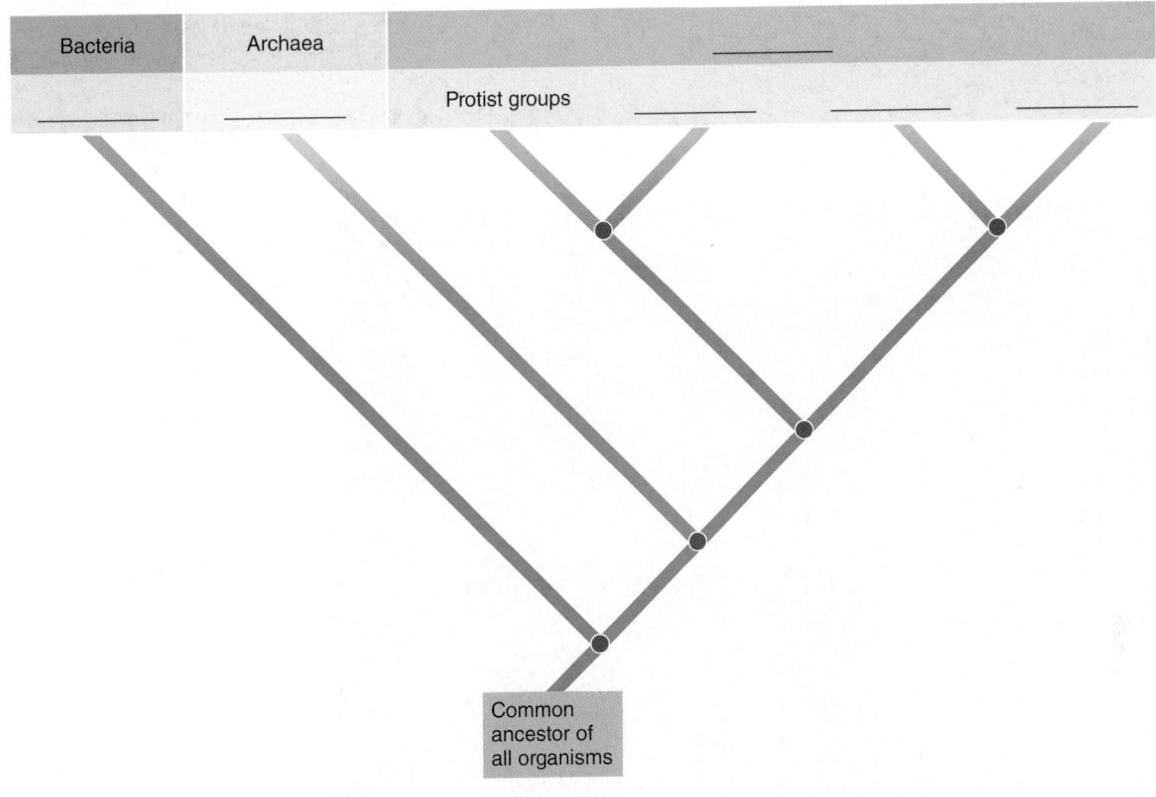

Bacteria   Archaea   _____

_____   _____   Protist groups   _____   _____   _____

Common ancestor of all organisms

CRITICAL THINKING

1. What would happen if a homeostatic mechanism failed? Describe a homeostatic mechanism at work in your body (other than the regulation of glucose cited in the chapter).

2. Contrast the reductionist approach with systems biology. How are the two approaches complementary? Which approach is more likely to consider emergent properties?

3. What are some characteristics of a good hypothesis? Give an example.

4. Make a prediction and devise a suitably controlled experiment to test each of the following hypotheses: (a) A type of mold found in your garden produces an effective antibiotic. (b) The growth rate of a bean seedling is affected by temperature. (c) Estrogen alleviates symptoms of Alzheimer's disease in elderly women.

5. **EVOLUTION LINK.** In what ways does evolution depend on transfer of information? In what ways does transfer of information depend on evolution?

6. **EVOLUTION LINK.** How might an understanding of evolutionary processes help a biologist doing research in (a) animal behavior, for example, the hunting behavior of lions? (b) the development of a new antibiotic to replace one to which bacteria have become resistant? (c) conservation of a specific plant in a rain forest?

7. **ANALYZING DATA.** Compare the two graphs in Figure 1-18. What information does the second graph illustrate? What possible explanation can you give for the differences shown in the two graphs?

8. **SCIENCE, TECHNOLOGY, AND SOCIETY.** New technology is allowing scientists to develop effective gene therapies to treat serious diseases. In the future gene therapy may be used to treat such conditions as addiction or bipolar disorder. What if gene therapy could be used to produce children with athletic ability, artistic ability, or high IQ? Do you have any ethical concerns about these possibilities? If so, where and how would you draw the line?

CENGAGENOW™   Additional questions are available in CengageNOW at www.cengage.com/login.

2

Atoms and Molecules: The Chemical Basis of Life

Water is a basic requirement for all life. A jaguar (*Panthera onca*), the largest cat in the Western Hemisphere, pauses to drink water from a rainforest stream.

Frans Lanting/Minden Pictures

KEY CONCEPTS

2.1 Carbon, hydrogen, oxygen, and nitrogen are the most abundant elements in living things.

2.2 The chemical properties of an atom are determined by its highest-energy electrons, known as valence electrons.

2.3 A molecule consists of atoms joined by covalent bonds. Other important chemical bonds include ionic bonds. Hydrogen bonds and van der Waals interactions are weak attractions.

2.4 The energy of an electron is transferred in a redox reaction.

2.5 Water molecules are polar, having regions of partial positive and partial negative charge that permit them to form hydrogen bonds with one another and with other charged substances.

2.6 Acids are hydrogen ion donors; bases are hydrogen ion acceptors. The pH scale is a convenient measure of the hydrogen ion concentration of a solution.

A knowledge of chemistry is essential for understanding organisms and how they function. This jaguar and the plants of the tropical rain forest, as well as abundant unseen insects and microorganisms, share fundamental similarities in their chemical composition and basic metabolic processes. These chemical similarities provide strong evidence for the evolution of all organisms from a common ancestor and explain why much of what biologists learn from studying bacteria or rats in laboratories can be applied to other organisms, including humans. Furthermore, the basic chemical and physical principles governing organisms are not unique to living things, for they apply to nonliving systems as well.

The success of the Human Genome Project and related studies has relied heavily on biochemistry and **molecular biology,** the chemistry and physics of the molecules that constitute living things. A biochemist may investigate the precise interactions among a cell's atoms and molecules that maintain the energy flow essential to life, and a molecular biologist may study how proteins interact with deoxyribonucleic acid (DNA) in ways that control the expression of certain genes. However, an understanding of chemistry is essential to *all* biologists. An evolutionary biologist may study evolutionary relationships by comparing the DNA of different types of organisms. An ecologist may study how energy is transferred among the organisms living in an estuary or monitor the biological effects of changes in the salinity of the water. A botanist may study unique compounds produced by plants and may even be a "chemical prospector," seeking new sources of medicinal agents.

In this chapter we lay a foundation for understanding how the structure of atoms determines the way they form chemical bonds to produce complex compounds. Most of our discussion focuses on small, simple substances known as **inorganic compounds.** Among the biologically important groups of inorganic compounds are water, many simple acids and bases, and simple salts. We pay particular attention to water, the most abundant substance in organisms and on Earth's surface, and we examine how its unique properties affect living things as well as their nonliving environment. In Chapter 3 we extend our discussion to **organic compounds,** carbon-containing compounds that are generally large and complex. In all but the simplest organic compounds, two or more carbon atoms are bonded to each other to form the backbone, or skeleton, of the molecule.

2.1 ELEMENTS AND ATOMS

■ LEARNING OBJECTIVES

1 Name the principal chemical elements in living things and provide an important function of each.

2 Compare the physical properties (mass and charge) and locations of electrons, protons, and neutrons. Distinguish between the atomic number and the mass number of an atom.

3 Define the terms *orbital* and *electron shell.* Relate electron shells to principal energy levels.

Elements are substances that cannot be broken down into simpler substances by ordinary chemical reactions. Each element has a **chemical symbol:** usually the first letter or first and second letters of the English or Latin name of the element. For example, O is the symbol for oxygen, C for carbon, H for hydrogen, N for nitrogen, and Na for sodium (from the Latin word *natrium*). Just four elements—oxygen, carbon, hydrogen, and nitrogen—are responsible for more than 96% of the mass of most organisms. Others, such as calcium, phosphorus, potassium, and magnesium, are also consistently present but in smaller quantities. Some elements, such as iodine and copper, are known as *trace elements* because they are required only in minute amounts. **TABLE 2-1** lists the elements that make up organisms and briefly explains the importance of each in typical plants and animals.

An **atom** is defined as the smallest portion of an element that retains its chemical properties. Atoms are much too small to be visible under a light microscope. However, by sophisticated techniques (such as scanning tunneling microscopy, with magnifications as great as 5 million times) researchers have been able to photograph the positions of some large atoms in molecules.

The components of atoms are tiny particles of **matter** (anything that has mass and takes up space) known as subatomic

particles. Physicists have discovered a number of subatomic particles, but for our purposes we need consider only three: electrons, protons, and neutrons. An **electron** is a particle that carries a unit of negative electric charge; a **proton** carries a unit of positive charge; and a **neutron** is an uncharged particle. In an electrically neutral atom, the number of electrons is equal to the number of protons.

Clustered together, protons and neutrons compose the **atomic nucleus.** Electrons, however, have no fixed locations and move rapidly through the mostly empty space surrounding the atomic nucleus.

An atom is uniquely identified by its number of protons

Every element has a fixed number of protons in the atomic nucleus, known as the **atomic number.** It is written as a subscript to the left of the chemical symbol. Thus, $_1H$ indicates that the hydrogen

TABLE 2-1	Functions of Elements in Organisms
Element* (chemical symbol)	**Functions**
Ⓞ Oxygen	Required for cellular respiration; present in most organic compounds; component of water
Ⓒ Carbon	Forms backbone of organic molecules; each carbon atom can form four bonds with other atoms
Ⓗ Hydrogen	Present in most organic compounds; component of water; hydrogen ion (H^+) is involved in some energy transfers
Ⓝ Nitrogen	Component of proteins and nucleic acids; component of chlorophyll in plants
Ⓒ Calcium	Structural component of bones and teeth; calcium ion (Ca^{2+}) is important in muscle contraction, conduction of nerve impulses, and blood clotting; associated with plant cell wall
Ⓟ Phosphorus	Component of nucleic acids and of phospholipids in membranes; important in energy transfer reactions; structural component of bone
Ⓚ Potassium	Potassium ion (K^+) is a principal positive ion (cation) in interstitial (tissue) fluid of animals; important in nerve function; affects muscle contraction; controls opening of stomata in plants
Ⓢ Sulfur	Component of most proteins
Ⓝⓐ Sodium	Sodium ion (Na^+) is a principal positive ion (cation) in interstitial (tissue) fluid of animals; important in fluid balance; essential for conduction of nerve impulses; important in photosynthesis in plants
Ⓜⓖ Magnesium	Needed in blood and other tissues of animals; activates many enzymes; component of chlorophyll in plants
Ⓒⓛ Chlorine	Chloride ion (Cl^-) is principal negative ion (anion) in interstitial (tissue) fluid of animals; important in water balance; essential for photosynthesis
Ⓕⓔ Iron	Component of hemoglobin in animals; activates certain enzymes

*Other elements found in very small (trace) amounts in animals, plants, or both include iodine (I), manganese (Mn), copper (Cu), zinc (Zn), cobalt (Co), fluorine (F), molybdenum (Mo), selenium (Se), boron (B), silicon (Si), and a few others.

nucleus contains 1 proton, and $_8O$ means that the oxygen nucleus contains 8 protons. The atomic number determines an atom's identity and defines the element.

The **periodic table** is a chart of the elements arranged in order by atomic number (**FIG. 2-1** and Appendix A). The periodic table is useful because it lets us simultaneously correlate many of the relationships among the various elements.

Figure 2-1 includes representations of the **electron configurations** of several elements important in organisms. These *Bohr models,* which show the electrons arranged in a series of concentric circles around the nucleus, are convenient to use, but inaccurate. The space outside the nucleus is actually extremely large compared

to the nucleus, and as you will see, electrons do not actually circle the nucleus in fixed concentric pathways.

Protons plus neutrons determine atomic mass

The mass of a subatomic particle is exceedingly small, much too small to be conveniently expressed in grams or even micrograms.[1] Such masses are expressed in terms of the **atomic mass unit (amu),** also called the **dalton** in honor of John Dalton, the English

---

[1] Tables of commonly used units of scientific measurement are printed inside the back cover of this text.

KEY POINT The periodic table provides information about the elements: their compositions, structures, and chemical behavior.

FIGURE 2-1 The periodic table

Note the Bohr models depicting the electron configuration of atoms of some biologically important elements, plus neon, which is unreactive, because its valence shell is full (to be discussed later in the chapter).

Although the Bohr model does not depict electron configurations accurately, it is commonly used because of its simplicity and convenience. A complete periodic table is given in Appendix A.

chemist who formulated an atomic theory in the early 1800s. One amu is equal to the approximate mass of a single proton or a single neutron. Protons and neutrons make up almost all the mass of an atom. The mass of a single electron is only about 1/1800 the mass of a proton or neutron.

The **atomic mass** of an atom is a number that indicates approximately how much matter it contains compared with another atom. This value is determined by adding the number of protons to the number of neutrons and expressing the result in atomic mass units or daltons.[2] The mass of the electrons is ignored because it is so small. The atomic mass number is indicated by a superscript to the left of the chemical symbol. The common form of the oxygen atom, with 8 protons and 8 neutrons in its nucleus, has an atomic number of 8 and a mass of 16 amu. It is indicated by the symbol $^{16}_{8}\text{O}$.

The characteristics of protons, electrons, and neutrons are summarized in the following table:

Particle	Charge	Approximate Mass	Location
Proton	Positive	1 amu	Nucleus
Neutron	Neutral	1 amu	Nucleus
Electron	Negative	Approx. 1/1800 amu	Outside nucleus

Isotopes of an element differ in number of neutrons

Most elements consist of a mixture of atoms with different numbers of neutrons and thus different masses. Such atoms are called **isotopes.** Isotopes of the same element have the same number of protons and electrons; only the number of neutrons varies. The three isotopes of hydrogen, $^{1}_{1}\text{H}$ (ordinary hydrogen), $^{2}_{1}\text{H}$ (deuterium), and $^{3}_{1}\text{H}$ (tritium), contain 0, 1, and 2 neutrons, respectively. **FIGURE 2-2** shows Bohr models of two isotopes of carbon, $^{12}_{6}\text{C}$ and $^{14}_{6}\text{C}$. The mass of an element is expressed as an average of the masses of its isotopes (weighted by their relative abundance in nature). For example, the atomic mass of hydrogen is not 1.0 amu, but 1.0079 amu, reflecting the natural occurrence of small amounts of deuterium and tritium in addition to the more abundant ordinary hydrogen.

Because they have the same number of electrons, all isotopes of a given element have essentially the same chemical characteristics. However, some isotopes are unstable and tend to break down, or decay, to a more stable isotope (usually becoming a different element); such **radioisotopes** emit radiation when they decay. For example, the radioactive decay of $^{14}_{6}\text{C}$ occurs as a neutron decomposes to form a proton and a fast-moving electron, which is emitted from the atom as a form of radiation known as a beta (β) particle. The resulting stable atom is the common form of nitrogen, $^{14}_{7}\text{N}$. Using sophisticated instruments, scientists can detect and measure β particles and other types of radiation. Radioactive decay can also be detected by a method known as **autoradiography,** in which radiation causes the appearance of dark silver grains in photographic film (**FIG. 2-3**).

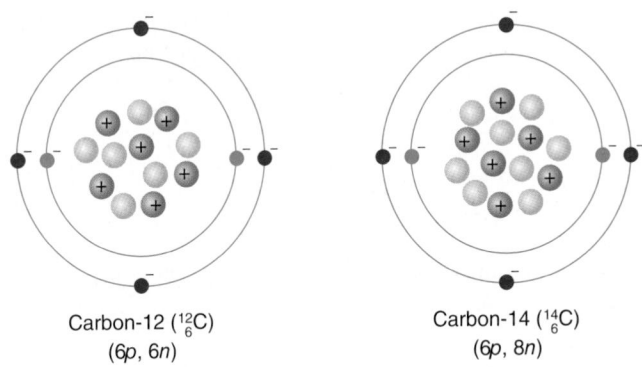

Carbon-12 ($^{12}_{6}\text{C}$)
(6p, 6n)

Carbon-14 ($^{14}_{6}\text{C}$)
(6p, 8n)

FIGURE 2-2 Isotopes

Carbon-12 ($^{12}_{6}\text{C}$) is the most common isotope of carbon. Its nucleus contains 6 protons and 6 neutrons, so its atomic mass is 12. Carbon-14 ($^{14}_{6}\text{C}$) is a rare radioactive carbon isotope. It contains 8 neutrons, so its atomic mass is 14.

Because the different isotopes of a given element have the same chemical characteristics, they are essentially interchangeable in molecules. Molecules containing radioisotopes are usually metabolized and/or localized in the organism in a similar way to their nonradioactive counterparts, and they can be substituted. For this reason, radioisotopes such as ^{3}H (tritium), ^{14}C, and ^{32}P are extremely valuable research tools used, for example, in dating fossils (see Fig. 18-10), tracing biochemical pathways, determining the sequence of genetic information in DNA (see Fig. 15-10), and understanding sugar transport in plants.

In medicine, radioisotopes are used for both diagnosis and treatment. The location and/or metabolism of a substance such as a hormone or drug can be followed in the body by labeling the substance with a radioisotope such as carbon-14 or tritium. Radioisotopes are used to test thyroid gland function, to provide images of blood flow in the arteries supplying the cardiac muscle, and to

Concentrated silver grains

50 µm

Peter J. Bryant/Biological Photo Service

FIGURE 2-3 Autoradiography

The chromosomes of the fruit fly, *Drosophila melanogaster*, shown in this light micrograph, have been covered with photographic film in which silver grains (*dark spots*) are produced when tritium (^{3}H) that has been incorporated into DNA undergoes radioactive decay. The concentrations of silver grains (*arrows*) mark the locations of specific DNA molecules.

---

[2]Unlike weight, mass is independent of the force of gravity. For convenience, however, we consider mass and weight equivalent. Atomic weight has the same numerical value as atomic mass, but it has no units.

study many other aspects of body function and chemistry. Because radiation can interfere with cell division, radioisotopes have been used therapeutically in treating cancer, a disease often characterized by rapidly dividing cells.

Electrons move in orbitals corresponding to energy levels

Electrons move through characteristic regions of 3-D space, or **orbitals.** Each orbital contains a maximum of 2 electrons. Because it is impossible to know an electron's position at any given time, orbitals are most accurately depicted as "electron clouds," shaded areas whose density is proportional to the probability that an electron is present there at any given instant. The energy of an electron depends on the orbital it occupies. Electrons in orbitals with similar energies, said to be at the same **principal energy level,** make up an **electron shell** (FIG. 2-4).

In general, electrons in a shell with a greater average distance from the nucleus have greater energy than those in a shell close to the nucleus. The reason is that energy is required to move a nega-

---

KEY POINT Electrons occupy orbitals corresponding to energy levels.

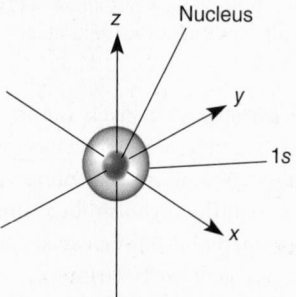

(a) The first principal energy level contains a maximum of 2 electrons, occupying a single spherical orbital (designated 1s). The electrons depicted in the diagram could be present anywhere in the blue area.

  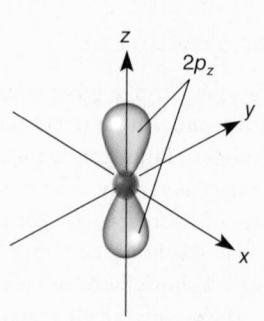

(b) The second principal energy level includes four orbitals, each with a maximum of 2 electrons: one spherical (2s) and three dumbbell-shaped (2p) orbitals at right angles to one another.

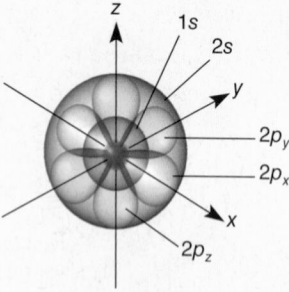

(c) Orbitals of the first and second principal energy levels of a neon atom are shown superimposed. Note that the single 2s orbital plus three 2p orbitals make up neon's full valence shell of 8 electrons. Compare this more realistic view of the atomic orbitals with the Bohr model of a neon atom at right.

(d) Neon atom (Bohr model)

FIGURE 2-4 *Animated* **Atomic orbitals**

Each orbital is represented as an "electron cloud." The arrows labeled *x*, *y*, and *z* establish the imaginary axes of the atom.

tively charged electron farther away from the positively charged nucleus. The most energetic electrons, known as valence electrons, are said to occupy the **valence shell.** The valence shell is represented as the outermost concentric ring in a Bohr model. As we will see in the next sections, it is these valence electrons that play a key role in chemical reactions.

An electron can move to an orbital farther from the nucleus by receiving more energy, or it can give up energy and sink to a lower energy level in an orbital nearer the nucleus. Changes in electron energy levels are important in energy conversions in organisms. For example, during photosynthesis, light energy absorbed by chlorophyll molecules causes electrons to move to a higher energy level (see Fig. 9-3).

Review

- Do all atoms of an element have the same atomic number? the same atomic mass?
- What is a radioisotope? What are some ways radioisotopes are used in biological research?
- How do electrons in different orbitals of the same electron shell compare with respect to their energy?

2.2 CHEMICAL REACTIONS

■ LEARNING OBJECTIVES

4 Explain how the number of valence electrons of an atom is related to its chemical properties.
5 Distinguish among simplest, molecular, and structural chemical formulas.
6 Explain why the mole concept is so useful to chemists.

The chemical behavior of an atom is determined primarily by the number and arrangement of its **valence electrons.** The valence shell of hydrogen or helium is full (stable) when it contains 2 electrons. The valence shell of any other atom is full when it contains 8 electrons. When the valence shell is not full, the atom tends to lose, gain, or share electrons to achieve a full outer shell. The valence shells of all isotopes of an element are identical; for this reason, they have similar chemical properties and can substitute for one another in chemical reactions (for example, tritium can substitute for ordinary hydrogen).

Elements in the same vertical column (belonging to the same *group*) of the periodic table have similar chemical properties because their valence shells have similar tendencies to lose, gain, or share electrons. For example, chlorine and bromine, included in a group commonly known as the *halogens,* are highly reactive. Because their valence shells have 7 electrons, they tend to gain an electron in chemical reactions. By contrast, hydrogen, sodium, and potassium each have a single valence electron, which they tend to give up or share with another atom. Helium (He) and neon (Ne) belong to a group referred to as the *noble gases.* They are quite unreactive because their valence shells are full. Notice in Figure 2-1 the incomplete valence shells of some of the elements important in organisms, including carbon, hydrogen, oxygen, and nitrogen, and compare them with the full valence shell of neon in Figure 2-4d.

Atoms form compounds and molecules

Two or more atoms may combine chemically. When atoms of *different* elements combine, the result is a chemical compound. A chemical **compound** consists of atoms of two or more different elements combined in a fixed ratio. For example, water is a chemical compound composed of hydrogen and oxygen in a ratio of 2:1. Common table salt, sodium chloride, is a chemical compound made up of sodium and chlorine in a 1:1 ratio.

Two or more atoms may become joined very strongly to form a stable particle called a **molecule.** For example, when two atoms of oxygen combine chemically, a molecule of oxygen is formed. Water is a molecular compound, with each molecule consisting of two atoms of hydrogen and one of oxygen. However, as you will see, not all compounds are made up of molecules. Sodium chloride (common table salt) is an example of a compound that is not molecular.

Simplest, molecular, and structural chemical formulas give different information

A **chemical formula** is a shorthand expression that describes the chemical composition of a substance. Chemical symbols indicate the types of atoms present, and subscript numbers indicate the ratios among the atoms. There are several types of chemical formulas, each providing specific kinds of information.

In a **simplest formula** (also known as an *empirical formula*), the subscripts give the smallest whole-number ratios for the atoms present in a compound. For example, the simplest formula for hydrazine is NH_2, indicating a 1:2 ratio of nitrogen to hydrogen. (Note that when a single atom of a type is present, the subscript number 1 is never written.)

In a **molecular formula,** the subscripts indicate the actual numbers of each type of atom per molecule. The molecular formula for hydrazine is N_2H_4, which indicates that each molecule of hydrazine consists of two atoms of nitrogen and four atoms of hydrogen. The molecular formula for water, H_2O, indicates that each molecule consists of two atoms of hydrogen and one atom of oxygen.

A **structural formula** shows not only the types and numbers of atoms in a molecule but also their arrangement. For example, the structural formula for water is H—O—H. As you will learn in Chapter 3, it is common for complex organic molecules with different structural formulas to share the same molecular formula.

One mole of any substance contains the same number of units

The molecular mass of a compound is the sum of the atomic masses of the component atoms of a single molecule; thus, the molecular mass of water, H_2O, is (hydrogen: 2×1 amu) + (oxygen: 1×16 amu), or 18 amu. (Because of the presence of isotopes, atomic mass values are not whole numbers, but for easy calculation each atomic mass value has been rounded off to a whole number.) Similarly, the molecular mass of glucose ($C_6H_{12}O_6$), a simple sugar that is a key compound in cell metabolism, is (carbon: 6×12 amu) + (hydrogen: 12×1 amu) + (oxygen: 6×16 amu), or 180 amu.

The amount of an element or compound whose mass in grams is equivalent to its atomic or molecular mass is **1 mole (mol).** Thus, 1 mol of water is 18 grams (g), and 1 mol of glucose has a mass of 180 g. The mole is an extremely useful concept because it lets us make meaningful comparisons between atoms and molecules of very different mass. The reason is that *1 mol of any substance always has exactly the same number of units,* whether those units are small atoms or large molecules. The very large number of units in a mole, 6.02×10^{23}, is known as **Avogadro's number,** named for the Italian physicist Amadeo Avogadro, who first calculated it. Thus, 1 mol (180 g) of glucose contains 6.02×10^{23} molecules, as does 1 mol (2 g) of molecular hydrogen (H_2). Although it is impossible to count atoms and molecules individually, a scientist can calculate them simply by weighing a sample. Molecular biologists usually deal with smaller values, either millimoles (mmol, one-thousandth of a mole) or micromoles (μmol, one-millionth of a mole).

The mole concept also lets us make useful comparisons among solutions. A 1 molar solution, represented by 1 M, contains 1 mol of that substance dissolved in a total volume of 1 liter (L). For example, we can compare 1 L of a 1 M solution of glucose with 1 L of a 1 M solution of sucrose (table sugar, a larger molecule). They differ in the mass of the dissolved sugar (180 g and 340 g, respectively), but they each contain 6.02×10^{23} sugar molecules.

Chemical equations describe chemical reactions

During any moment in the life of an organism—a bacterial cell, a mushroom, or a butterfly—many complex chemical reactions are taking place. Chemical reactions, such as the reaction between glucose and oxygen, can be described by means of chemical equations:

$$C_6H_{12}O_6 + 6\,O_2 \longrightarrow 6\,CO_2 + 6\,H_2O + \text{energy}$$
$$\text{Glucose} \qquad \text{Oxygen} \qquad \text{Carbon dioxide} \qquad \text{Water}$$

In a chemical equation, the **reactants,** the substances that participate in the reaction, are generally written on the left side, and the products, the substances formed by the reaction, are written on the right side. The arrow means "yields" and indicates the direction in which the reaction proceeds.

Chemical compounds react with one another in quantitatively precise ways. The numbers preceding the chemical symbols or formulas (known as *coefficients*) indicate the relative number of atoms or molecules reacting. For example, 1 mol of glucose burned in a fire or metabolized in a cell reacts with 6 mol of oxygen to form 6 mol of carbon dioxide and 6 mol of water.

Many reactions can proceed simultaneously in the reverse direction (to the left) and the forward direction (to the right). At **dynamic equilibrium,** the rates of the forward and reverse reactions are equal (see Chapter 7). Reversible reactions are indicated by double arrows:

$$CO_2 + H_2O \rightleftharpoons H_2CO_3$$
$$\text{Carbon dioxide} \qquad \text{Water} \qquad \text{Carbonic acid}$$

In this example, the arrows are drawn in different lengths to indicate that when the reaction reaches equilibrium, there will be more reactants (CO_2 and H_2O) than product (H_2CO_3).

Review

- Why is a radioisotope able to substitute for an ordinary (nonradioactive) atom of the same element in a molecule?
- Which kind of chemical formula provides the most information?
- How many particles would be included in 1 g of hydrogen atoms? in 2 g of hydrogen molecules?

2.3 CHEMICAL BONDS

◼ LEARNING OBJECTIVE

7 Distinguish among covalent bonds, ionic bonds, hydrogen bonds, and van der Waals interactions. Compare them in terms of the mechanisms by which they form and their relative strengths.

Atoms can be held together by forces of attraction called **chemical bonds.** Each bond represents a certain amount of chemical energy. **Bond energy** is the energy necessary to break a chemical bond. The valence electrons dictate how many bonds an atom can form. The two principal types of strong chemical bonds are covalent bonds and ionic bonds.

In covalent bonds electrons are shared

Covalent bonds involve the sharing of electrons between atoms in a way that results in each atom having a filled valence shell. A molecule consists of atoms joined by covalent bonds. A simple example of a covalent bond is the joining of two hydrogen atoms in a molecule of hydrogen gas, H_2. Each atom of hydrogen has 1 electron, but 2 electrons are required to complete its valence shell. The hydrogen atoms have equal capacities to attract electrons, so neither donates an electron to the other. Instead, the two hydrogen atoms share their single electrons so that the 2 electrons are attracted simultaneously to the 2 protons in the two hydrogen nuclei. The 2 electrons whirl around both atomic nuclei, thus forming the covalent bond that joins the two atoms. Similarly, unlike atoms can also be linked by covalent bonds to form molecules; the resulting compound is a **covalent compound.**

A simple way of representing the electrons in the valence shell of an atom is to use dots placed around the chemical symbol of the element. Such a representation is called the *Lewis structure* of the atom, named for G. N. Lewis, an American chemist who developed this type of notation. In a water molecule, two hydrogen atoms are covalently bonded to an oxygen atom:

$$H\cdot + H\cdot + \cdot\ddot{\underset{\cdot\cdot}{O}}\cdot \longrightarrow H\!:\!\ddot{\underset{\cdot\cdot}{O}}\!:\!H$$

Oxygen has 6 valence electrons; by sharing electrons with two hydrogen atoms, it completes its valence shell of 8. At the same time, each hydrogen atom obtains a complete valence shell of 2. (Note that in the structural formula H—O—H, each pair of shared electrons constitutes a covalent bond, represented by a solid line. Unshared electrons are usually omitted in a structural formula.)

The carbon atom has 4 electrons in its valence shell, all of which are available for covalent bonding:

When one carbon and four hydrogen atoms share electrons, a molecule of the covalent compound methane, CH_4, is formed:

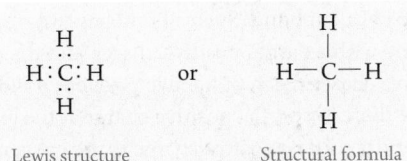

Lewis structure   Structural formula

The nitrogen atom has 5 electrons in its valence shell. Recall that each orbital can hold a maximum of 2 electrons. Usually, 2 electrons occupy one orbital, leaving 3 electrons available for sharing with other atoms:

When a nitrogen atom shares electrons with three hydrogen atoms, a molecule of the covalent compound ammonia, NH_3, is formed:

$$H:N:H \quad \text{or} \quad H-N-H$$

Lewis structure   Structural formula

When one pair of electrons is shared between two atoms, the covalent bond is called a **single covalent bond** (**FIG. 2-5a**). Two hydrogen atoms share a single pair of electrons. Two oxygen atoms

may achieve stability by forming covalent bonds with each other. Each oxygen atom has 6 electrons in its outer shell. To become stable, the two atoms share two pairs of electrons, forming molecular oxygen (**FIG. 2-5b**). When two pairs of electrons are shared in this way, the covalent bond is called a **double covalent bond,** which is represented by two parallel solid lines. Similarly, a **triple covalent bond** is formed when three pairs of electrons are shared between two atoms (represented by three parallel solid lines).

The number of covalent bonds usually formed by the atoms in biologically important molecules is summarized as follows:

Atom	Symbol	Covalent Bonds
Hydrogen	H	1
Oxygen	O	2
Carbon	C	4
Nitrogen	N	3
Phosphorus	P	5
Sulfur	S	2

The function of a molecule is related to its shape

In addition to being composed of atoms with certain properties, each kind of molecule has a characteristic size and a general overall shape. Although the shape of a molecule may change (within certain limits), the functions of molecules in living cells are dictated largely by their geometric shapes. A molecule that consists of two atoms is linear. Molecules composed of more than two atoms may

---

KEY POINT Covalent bonds form when atoms share electrons.

Hydrogen (H) + Hydrogen (H)   Molecular hydrogen (H_2)   or   H—H

(a) Single covalent bond formation. Two hydrogen atoms achieve stability by sharing a pair of electrons, thereby forming a molecule of hydrogen. In the structural formula on the right, the straight line between the hydrogen atoms represents a single covalent bond.

Oxygen (O) + Oxygen (O)   Molecular oxygen (O_2) (double bond is formed)   or   O=O

(b) Double covalent bond formation. In molecular oxygen, two oxygen atoms share two pairs of electrons, forming a double covalent bond. The parallel straight lines in the structural formula represent a double covalent bond.

FIGURE 2-5 Electron sharing in covalent compounds

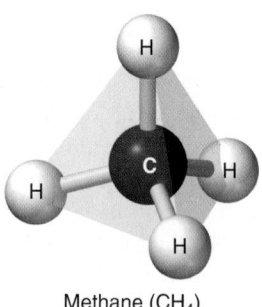

Methane (CH₄)

FIGURE 2-6 Orbital hybridization in methane
The four hydrogens are located at the corners of a tetrahedron because of hybridization of the valence shell orbitals of carbon.

have more complicated shapes. The geometric shape of a molecule provides the optimal distance between the atoms to counteract the repulsion of electron pairs.

When an atom forms covalent bonds with other atoms, the orbitals in the valence shell may become rearranged in a process known as **orbital hybridization,** thereby affecting the shape of the resulting molecule. For example, when four hydrogen atoms combine with a carbon atom to form a molecule of methane (CH_4), the hybridized valence shell orbitals of the carbon form a geometric structure known as a *tetrahedron*, with one hydrogen atom present at each of its four corners (**FIG. 2-6**; see also Fig. 3-2a).

We will explore the importance of molecular shape in more detail in Chapter 3 and in our discussion of the properties of water in this chapter.

Covalent bonds can be nonpolar or polar

Atoms of different elements vary in their affinity for electrons. **Electronegativity** is a measure of an atom's attraction for shared electrons in chemical bonds. Very electronegative atoms such as oxygen, nitrogen, fluorine, and chlorine are sometimes called "electron greedy." When covalently bonded atoms have similar electronegativities, the electrons are shared equally and the covalent bond is described as **nonpolar.** The covalent bond of the hydrogen molecule is nonpolar, as are the covalent bonds of molecular oxygen and methane.

In a covalent bond between two different elements, such as oxygen and hydrogen, the electronegativities of the atoms may be different. If so, electrons are pulled closer to the atomic nucleus of the element with the greater electron affinity (in this case, oxygen). A covalent bond between atoms that differ in electronegativity is called a **polar** covalent bond. Such a bond has two dissimilar ends (or poles), one with a partial positive charge and the other with a partial negative charge. Each of the two covalent bonds in water is polar because there is a partial positive charge at the hydrogen end of the bond and a partial negative charge at the oxygen end, where the "shared" electrons are more likely to be.

Covalent bonds differ in their degree of polarity, ranging from those in which the electrons are equally shared (as in the nonpolar hydrogen molecule) to those in which the electrons are much closer to one atom than to the other (as in water). Oxygen is quite electronegative and forms polar covalent bonds with carbon, hydrogen, and many other atoms. Nitrogen is also strongly electronegative, although less so than oxygen.

A molecule with one or more polar covalent bonds can be polar even though it is electrically neutral as a whole. The reason is that a **polar molecule** has one end with a partial positive charge and another end with a partial negative charge. One example is water (**FIG. 2-7**). The polar bonds between the hydrogens and the oxygen are arranged in a V shape, rather than linearly. The oxygen end constitutes the negative pole of the molecule, and the end with the two hydrogens is the positive pole.

Ionic bonds form between cations and anions

Some atoms or groups of atoms are not electrically neutral. A particle with 1 or more units of electric charge is called an ion. An atom becomes an ion if it gains or loses 1 or more electrons. An atom with 1, 2, or 3 electrons in its valence shell tends to lose electrons to other atoms. Such an atom then becomes positively charged because its nucleus contains more protons than the number of electrons orbiting around the nucleus. These positively charged ions are termed **cations.** Atoms with 5, 6, or 7 valence electrons tend to gain electrons from other atoms and become negatively charged **anions.**

The properties of ions are quite different from those of the electrically neutral atoms from which they were derived. For example, although chlorine gas is a poison, chloride ions (Cl^-) are

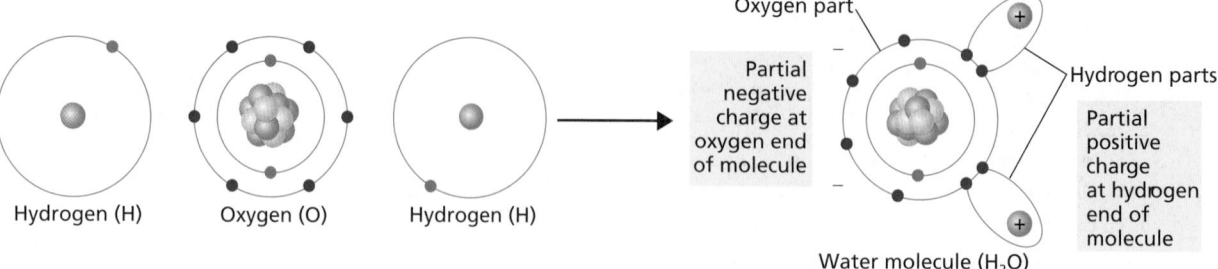

FIGURE 2-7 Water, a polar molecule
Note that the electrons tend to stay closer to the nucleus of the oxygen atom than to the hydrogen nuclei. This results in a partial negative charge on the oxygen portion of the molecule and a partial positive charge at the hydrogen end. Although the water molecule as a whole is electrically neutral, it is a polar covalent compound.

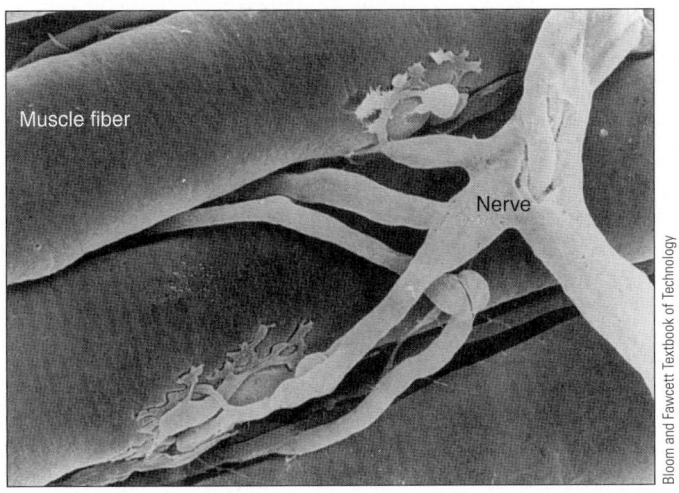

FIGURE 2-8 Ions and biological processes
Sodium, potassium, and chloride ions are essential for this nerve cell to stimulate these muscle fibers, initiating a muscle contraction. Calcium ions in the muscle cell are required for muscle contraction.

essential to life (see Table 2-1). Because their electric charges provide a basis for many interactions, cations and anions are involved in energy transformations within the cell, the transmission of nerve impulses, muscle contraction, and many other biological processes (**FIG. 2-8**).

A group of covalently bonded atoms can also become an ion (*polyatomic ion*). Unlike a single atom, a group of atoms can lose or gain protons (derived from hydrogen atoms) as well as electrons. Therefore, a group of atoms can become a cation if it loses 1 or more electrons or gains 1 or more protons. A group of atoms becomes an anion if it gains 1 or more electrons or loses 1 or more protons.

An **ionic bond** forms as a consequence of the attraction between the positive charge of a cation and the negative charge of an anion. An **ionic compound** is a substance consisting of anions and cations bonded by their opposite charges.

A good example of how ionic bonds are formed is the attraction between sodium ions and chloride ions. A sodium atom has 1 electron in its valence shell. It cannot fill its valence shell by obtaining 7 electrons from other atoms because it would then have a large unbalanced negative charge. Instead, it gives up its single valence electron to a very electronegative atom, such as chlorine, which acts as an electron acceptor (**FIG. 2-9**). Chlorine cannot give up the 7 electrons in its valence shell because it would then have a large positive charge. Instead, it strips an electron from an electron donor (sodium, in this example) to complete its valence shell.

When sodium reacts with chlorine, sodium's valence electron is transferred completely to chlorine. Sodium becomes a cation, with 1 unit of positive charge (Na^+). Chlorine becomes an anion, a chloride ion with 1 unit of negative charge (Cl^-). These ions attract each other as a result of their opposite charges. This electrical attraction in ionic bonds holds them together to form NaCl, sodium chloride, or common table salt.

Arrangement of atoms in a crystal of salt

FIGURE 2-9 *Animated* Ionic bonding
Sodium becomes a positively charged ion when it donates its single valence electron to chlorine, which has 7 valence electrons. With this additional electron, chlorine completes its valence shell and becomes a negatively charged chloride ion. These sodium and chloride ions are attracted to one another by their unlike electric charges, forming the ionic compound sodium chloride.

The term *molecule* does not adequately explain the properties of ionic compounds such as NaCl. When NaCl is in its solid crystal state, each ion is actually surrounded by six ions of opposite charge. The simplest formula, NaCl, indicates that sodium ions and chloride ions are present in a 1:1 ratio, but the actual crystal has no discrete molecules composed of one Na^+ and one Cl^- ion.

Compounds joined by ionic bonds, such as sodium chloride, have a tendency to *dissociate* (separate) into their individual ions when placed in water:

$$NaCl \xrightarrow{\text{in } H_2O} Na^+ + Cl^-$$

Sodium chloride   Sodium ion   Chloride ion

In the solid form of an ionic compound (that is, in the absence of water), ionic bonds are very strong. Water, however, is an excellent **solvent;** as a liquid it is capable of dissolving many substances, particularly those that are polar or ionic, because of the polarity of water molecules. The localized partial positive charge (on the hydrogen atoms) and partial negative charge (on the oxygen atom) on each water molecule attract and surround the anions and cations, respectively, on the surface of an ionic solid. As a result, the solid dissolves. A dissolved substance is referred to as a **solute.** In solution, each cation and anion of the ionic compound is surrounded by oppositely charged ends of the water molecules. This process is known as **hydration** (**FIG. 2-10**). Hydrated ions still interact with one another to some extent, but the transient ionic bonds formed are much weaker than those in a solid crystal.

Hydrogen bonds are weak attractions

Another type of bond important in organisms is the **hydrogen bond.** When hydrogen combines with oxygen (or with another relatively electronegative atom such as nitrogen), it acquires a partial positive charge because its electron spends more time closer to the electronegative atom. Hydrogen bonds tend to form between an atom with a partial negative charge and a hydrogen atom that is covalently bonded to oxygen or nitrogen (**FIG. 2-11**). The atoms involved may be in two parts of the same large molecule or in two different molecules. Water molecules interact with one another extensively through hydrogen bond formation.

FIGURE 2-10 *Animated* **Hydration of an ionic compound**
When the crystal of NaCl is added to water, the sodium and chloride ions are pulled apart. When the NaCl is dissolved, each Na^+ and Cl^- is surrounded by water molecules electrically attracted to it.

FIGURE 2-11 *Animated* **Hydrogen bonding**
A hydrogen bond (*dotted line*) can form between two molecules with regions of unlike partial charge. Here, the nitrogen atom of an ammonia molecule is joined by a hydrogen bond to a hydrogen atom of a water molecule.

Hydrogen bonds are readily formed and broken. Although individually relatively weak, hydrogen bonds are collectively strong when present in large numbers. Furthermore, they have a specific length and orientation. As you will see in Chapter 3, these features are very important in determining the 3-D structure of large molecules such as DNA and proteins.

van der Waals interactions are weak forces

Even electrically neutral, nonpolar molecules can develop transient regions of weak positive and negative charge. These slight charges develop as a consequence of the fact that electrons are in constant motion. A region with a temporary excess of electrons will have a weak negative charge, whereas one with an electron deficit will have a weak positive charge. Adjacent molecules may interact in regions of slight opposite charge. These attractive forces, called **van der Waals interactions,** operate over very short distances and are weaker and less specific than the other types of interactions we have considered. They are most important when they occur in large numbers and when the shapes of the molecules permit close contact between the atoms. Although a single interaction is very weak, the binding force of a large number of these interactions working together can be significant.

Review

- Are all compounds composed of molecules? Explain.
- What are the ways an atom or molecule can become an anion or a cation?
- How do ionic and covalent bonds differ?
- Under what circumstances can weak forces such as hydrogen bonds and van der Waals interactions play significant roles in biological systems?

2.4 REDOX REACTIONS

■ LEARNING OBJECTIVE

8 Distinguish between the terms *oxidation* and *reduction*, and relate these processes to the transfer of energy.

Many energy conversions that go on in a cell involve reactions in which an electron transfers from one substance to another. The reason is that the transfer of an electron also involves the transfer of the energy of that electron. Such an electron transfer is known as an oxidation–reduction, or **redox reaction.** Oxidation and reduction always occur together. **Oxidation** is a chemical process in which an atom, ion, or molecule *loses* one or more electrons. **Reduction** is a chemical process in which an atom, ion, or molecule *gains* one or more electrons. (The term refers to the fact that the gain of an electron results in the reduction of any positive charge that might be present.)

Rusting—the combining of iron (symbol Fe) with oxygen—is a simple illustration of oxidation and reduction:

$$4\,Fe + 3\,O_2 \longrightarrow 2\,Fe_2O_3$$
$$\text{Iron (III) oxide}$$

In rusting, each iron atom becomes oxidized as it loses 3 electrons.

$$4\,Fe \longrightarrow 4\,Fe^{3+} + 12e^-$$

The e^- represents an electron; the + superscript in Fe^{3+} represents an electron deficit. (When an atom loses an electron, it acquires 1 unit of positive charge from the excess of 1 proton. In our example, each iron atom loses 3 electrons and acquires 3 units of positive charge.) Recall that the oxygen atom is very electronegative, able to remove electrons from other atoms. In this reaction, oxygen becomes reduced when it accepts electrons from the iron.

$$3\,O_2 + 12e^- \longrightarrow 6\,O^{2-}$$

Redox reactions occur simultaneously because one substance must accept the electrons that are removed from the other. In a redox reaction, one component, the *oxidizing agent,* accepts 1 or more electrons and becomes reduced. Oxidizing agents other than oxygen are known, but oxygen is such a common one that its name was given to the process. Another reaction component, the *reducing agent,* gives up 1 or more electrons and becomes oxidized. In our example, there was a complete transfer of electrons from iron (the reducing agent) to oxygen (the oxidizing agent). Similarly, Figure 2-9 shows that an electron was transferred from sodium (the reducing agent) to chlorine (the oxidizing agent).

Electrons are not easily removed from covalent compounds unless an entire atom is removed. In cells, oxidation often involves the removal of a hydrogen atom (an electron plus a proton that "goes along for the ride") from a covalent compound; reduction often involves the addition of the equivalent of a hydrogen atom (see Chapter 7).

Review

- Why must oxidation and reduction occur simultaneously?
- Why are redox reactions important in some energy transfers?

2.5 WATER

■ **LEARNING OBJECTIVE**

9 Explain how hydrogen bonds between adjacent water molecules govern many of the properties of water.

A large part of the mass of most organisms is water. In human tissues the percentage of water ranges from 20% in bones to 85% in brain cells; about 70% of our total body weight is water. As much as 95% of a jellyfish and certain plants is water. Water is the source, through photosynthesis, of the oxygen in the air we breathe, and its hydrogen atoms become incorporated into many organic compounds. Water is also the solvent for most biological reactions and a reactant or product in many chemical reactions.

Water is important not only as an internal constituent of organisms but also as one of the principal environmental factors affecting them (**FIG. 2-12**). Many organisms live in the ocean or in freshwater rivers, lakes, or puddles. Water's unique combination of physical and chemical properties is considered to have been essential to the origin of life as well as to the continued survival and evolution of life on Earth.

Hydrogen bonds form between water molecules

As discussed, water molecules are polar; that is, one end of each molecule bears a partial positive charge and the other a partial negative charge (see Fig. 2-7). The water molecules in liquid water and in ice associate by hydrogen bonds. The hydrogen atom of one water molecule, with its partial positive charge, is attracted to the oxygen atom of a neighboring water molecule, with its partial negative charge, forming a hydrogen bond. An oxygen atom in a water molecule has two regions of partial negative charge, and each of the two hydrogen atoms has a partial positive charge. Each water molecule can therefore form hydrogen bonds with a maximum of four neighboring water molecules (**FIG. 2-13**).

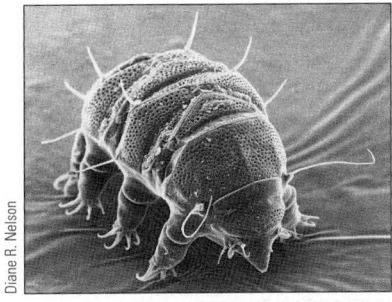

Diane R. Nelson

(a) Commonly known as "water bears," tardigrades, such as these members of the genus *Echiniscus*, are small animals (less than 1.2 mm long) that normally live in moist habitats, such as thin films of water on mosses.

100 μm

Robert O. Schuster, courtesy of Diane R. Nelson

(b) When subjected to desiccation (dried out), tardigrades assume a barrel-shaped form known as a *tun,* remaining in this state, motionless but alive, for as long as 100 years. When rehydrated, they assume their normal appearance and activities.

10 μm

FIGURE 2-12 The effects of water on an organism

FIGURE 2-13 Hydrogen bonding of water molecules
Each water molecule can form hydrogen bonds (*dotted lines*) with as many as four neighboring water molecules.

Water molecules have a strong tendency to stick to one another, a property known as **cohesion.** This is due to the hydrogen bonds among the molecules. Because of the cohesive nature of water molecules, any force exerted on part of a column of water is transmitted to the column as a whole. The major mechanism of water movement in plants (see Chapter 35) depends on the cohesive nature of water. Water molecules also display **adhesion,** the ability to stick to many other kinds of substances, most notably those with charged groups of atoms or molecules on their surfaces. These adhesive forces explain how water makes things wet.

A combination of adhesive and cohesive forces accounts for **capillary action,** which is the tendency of water to move in narrow tubes, even against the force of gravity (**FIG. 2-14**). For example, water moves through the microscopic spaces between soil particles to the roots of plants by capillary action.

FIGURE 2-14 Capillary action
(a) In a narrow tube, there is adhesion between the water molecules and the glass wall of the tube. Other water molecules inside the tube are then "pulled along" because of cohesion, which is due to hydrogen bonds between the water molecules. **(b)** In the wider tube, a smaller percentage of the water molecules line the glass wall. As a result, the adhesion is not strong enough to overcome the cohesion of the water molecules beneath the surface level of the container, and water in the tube rises only slightly.

FIGURE 2-15 Surface tension of water
Hydrogen bonding between water molecules is responsible for the surface tension of water, which causes a dimpled appearance of the surface as these water striders (*Gerris*) walk across it. Fine hairs at the ends of the legs of these insects create highly water-repellent "cushions" of air.

Water has a high degree of **surface tension** because of the cohesion of its molecules, which have a much greater attraction for one another than for molecules in the air. Thus, water molecules at the surface crowd together, producing a strong layer as they are pulled downward by the attraction of other water molecules beneath them (**FIG. 2-15**).

Water molecules interact with hydrophilic substances by hydrogen bonding

Because its molecules are polar, water is an excellent solvent, a liquid capable of dissolving many kinds of substances, especially polar and ionic compounds. Earlier we discussed how polar water molecules pull the ions of ionic compounds apart so that they dissociate (see Fig. 2-10). Because of its solvent properties and the tendency of the atoms in certain compounds to form ions in solution, water plays an important role in facilitating chemical reactions. Substances that interact readily with water are **hydrophilic** ("water-loving"). Examples include table sugar (sucrose, a polar compound) and table salt (NaCl, an ionic compound), which dissolve readily in water. Not all substances in organisms are hydrophilic, however. Many **hydrophobic** ("water-fearing") substances found in living things are especially important because of their ability to form associations or structures that are not disrupted. Hydrophobic interactions occur between groups of nonpolar molecules. Such molecules are insoluble in water and tend to cluster together. This is not due to formation of bonds between the nonpolar molecules but rather to the fact that the hydrogen-bonded water molecules exclude them and in a sense "drive them together." **Hydrophobic interactions** explain why oil tends to form globules when added to water. Examples of hydrophobic substances include fatty acids and cholesterol, discussed in Chapter 3.

Water helps maintain a stable temperature

Hydrogen bonding explains the way water responds to changes in temperature. Water exists in three forms, which differ in their degree of hydrogen bonding: gas (vapor), liquid, and ice, a crystalline

(a) Steam becoming water vapor (gas)

212°F — 100°C

50°C

(b) Water (liquid)

32°F — 0°C

(c) Ice (solid)

FIGURE 2-16 *Animated* Three forms of water

(a) When water boils, as in this hot spring at Yellowstone National Park, many hydrogen bonds are broken, causing steam, consisting of minuscule water droplets, to form. If most of the remaining hydrogen bonds break, the molecules move more freely as water vapor (a gas). **(b)** Water molecules in a liquid state continually form, break, and re-form hydrogen bonds with one another. **(c)** In ice, each water molecule participates in four hydrogen bonds with adjacent molecules, resulting in a regular, evenly distanced crystalline lattice structure.

solid (**FIG. 2-16**). Hydrogen bonds are formed or broken as water changes from one state to another.

Raising the temperature of a substance involves adding heat energy to make its molecules move faster, that is, to increase the energy of motion—**kinetic energy**—of the molecules (see Chapter 7). The term **heat** refers to the *total* amount of kinetic energy in a sample of a substance; **temperature** is a measure of the *average* kinetic energy of the particles. For the molecules to move more freely, some of the hydrogen bonds of water must be broken.

Much of the energy added to the system is used up in breaking the hydrogen bonds, and only a portion of the heat energy is available to speed the movement of the water molecules, thereby increasing the temperature of the water. Conversely, when liquid water changes to ice, additional hydrogen bonds must be formed, making the molecules less free to move and liberating a great deal of heat into the environment.

Heat of vaporization, the amount of heat energy required to change 1 g of a substance from the liquid phase to the vapor phase, is expressed in units called *calories*. A **calorie (cal)** is the amount of heat energy (equivalent to 4.184 joules [J]) required to raise the temperature of 1 g of water 1 degree Celsius (C). Water has a high heat of vaporization—540 cal—because its molecules are held together by hydrogen bonds. The heat of vaporization of most other common liquid substances is much less. As a sample of water is heated, some molecules are moving much faster than others (they have more heat). These faster-moving molecules are more likely to escape the liquid phase and enter the vapor phase (see Fig. 2-16a). When they do, they take their heat with them, lowering the temperature of the sample, a process called **evaporative cooling.** For this reason, the human body can dissipate excess heat as sweat evaporates from the skin, and a leaf can keep cool in the bright sunlight as water evaporates from its surface.

Hydrogen bonding is also responsible for water's high **specific heat;** that is, the amount of energy required to raise the temperature of water is quite large. The specific heat of water is 1 cal/g of water per degree Celsius. Most other common substances, such as metals, glass, and ethyl alcohol, have much lower specific heat values. The specific heat of ethyl alcohol, for example, is 0.59 cal/g/1°C (2.46 J/g/1°C).

Because so much heat input is required to raise the temperature of water (and so much heat is lost when the temperature is lowered), the ocean and other large bodies of water have relatively constant temperatures. Thus, many organisms living in the ocean are provided with a relatively constant environmental temperature. The properties of water are crucial in stabilizing temperatures on Earth's surface. Although surface water is only a thin film relative to Earth's volume, the quantity is enormous compared to the exposed landmass. This relatively large mass of water resists both the warming effect of heat and the cooling effect of low temperatures.

Hydrogen bonding causes ice to have unique properties with important environmental consequences. Liquid water expands as it freezes because the hydrogen bonds joining the water molecules in the crystalline lattice keep the molecules far enough apart to give ice a density about 10% less than the density of liquid water (see Fig. 2-16c). When ice has been heated enough to raise its temperature above 0°C (32°F), the hydrogen bonds are broken, freeing the molecules to slip closer together. The density of water is greatest at 4°C. Above that temperature water begins to expand again as the speed of its molecules increases. As a result, ice floats on the denser cold water.

This unusual property of water has been important to the evolution of life. If ice had a greater density than water, the ice would sink; eventually, all ponds, lakes, and even the ocean would freeze solid from the bottom to the surface, making life impossible. When a deep body of water cools, it becomes covered with floating ice. The ice insulates the liquid water below it, retarding freezing and permitting organisms to survive below the icy surface.

The high water content of organisms helps them maintain relatively constant internal temperatures. Such minimizing of temperature fluctuations is important because biological reactions can take place only within a relatively narrow temperature range.

Review

- Why does water form hydrogen bonds?

- What are some properties of water that result from hydrogen bonding? How do these properties contribute to the role of water as an essential component of organisms?
- How can weak forces, such as hydrogen bonds, have significant effects in organisms?

2.6 ACIDS, BASES, AND SALTS

LEARNING OBJECTIVES

10 Contrast acids and bases, and discuss their properties.
11 Convert the hydrogen ion concentration (moles per liter) of a solution to a pH value and describe how buffers help minimize changes in pH.
12 Describe the composition of a salt and explain why salts are important in organisms.

Water molecules have a slight tendency to ionize, that is, to dissociate into hydrogen ions (H^+) and hydroxide ions (OH^-). The H^+ immediately combines with a negatively charged region of a water molecule, forming a hydronium ion (H_3O^+). However, by convention, H^+, rather than the more accurate H_3O^+, is used. In pure water, a small number of water molecules ionize. This slight tendency of water to dissociate is reversible as hydrogen ions and hydroxide ions reunite to form water.

$$HOH \rightleftharpoons H^+ + OH^-$$

Because each water molecule splits into one hydrogen ion and one hydroxide ion, the concentrations of hydrogen ions and hydroxide ions in pure water are exactly equal (0.0000001 or 10^7 mol/L for each ion). Such a solution is said to be neutral, that is, neither acidic nor basic (alkaline).

An **acid** is a substance that dissociates in solution to yield hydrogen ions (H^+) and anions.

$$Acid \longrightarrow H^+ + anion$$

An acid is a proton *donor*. (Recall that a hydrogen ion, or H^+, is nothing more than a proton.) Hydrochloric acid (HCl) is a common inorganic acid.

A **base** is defined as a proton *acceptor*. Most bases are substances that dissociate to yield a hydroxide ion (OH^-) and a cation when dissolved in water.

$$NaOH \longrightarrow Na^+ + OH^-$$
$$OH^- + H^+ \longrightarrow H_2O$$

A hydroxide ion can act as a base by accepting a proton (H^+) to form water. Sodium hydroxide (NaOH) is a common inorganic base. Some bases do not dissociate to yield hydroxide ions directly. For example, ammonia (NH_3) acts as a base by accepting a proton from water, producing an ammonium ion (NH_4^+) and releasing a hydroxide ion.

$$NH_3 + H_2O \longrightarrow NH_4^+ + OH^-$$

pH is a convenient measure of acidity

The degree of a solution's acidity is generally expressed in terms of **pH,** defined as the negative logarithm (base 10) of the hydrogen ion concentration (expressed in moles per liter):

$$pH = -\log_{10}[H^+]$$

The brackets refer to concentration; therefore, the term $[H^+]$ means "the concentration of hydrogen ions," which is expressed in moles per liter because we are interested in the *number* of hydrogen ions per liter. Because the range of possible pH values is broad, a logarithmic scale (with a 10-fold difference between successive units) is more convenient than a linear scale.

Hydrogen ion concentrations are nearly always less than 1 mol/L. One gram of hydrogen ions dissolved in 1 L of water (a 1 *M* solution) may not sound impressive, but such a solution would be extremely acidic. The logarithm of a number less than 1 is a negative number; thus, the *negative* logarithm corresponds to a *positive* pH value. (Solutions with pH values less than zero can be produced but do not occur under biological conditions.)

Whole-number pH values are easy to calculate. For instance, consider our example of pure water, which has a hydrogen ion concentration of 0.0000001 (10^{-7}) mol/L. The logarithm is -7. The negative logarithm is 7; therefore, the pH is 7. **TABLE 2-2** shows how to calculate pH values from hydrogen ion concentrations, and the reverse. For comparison, the table also includes the hydroxide ion concentrations, which can be calculated because the product of the hydrogen ion concentration and the hydroxide ion concentration is 1×10^{-14}:

$$[H^+][OH^-] = 1 \times 10^{-14}$$

Pure water is an example of a **neutral solution;** with a pH of 7, it has equal concentrations of hydrogen ions and hydroxide ions (the concentration of each is 10^{-7} mol/L). An **acidic solution** has a hydrogen ion concentration that is higher than its hydroxide ion concentration and has a pH value of less than 7. For example, the hydrogen ion concentration of a solution with pH 1 is 10 times that of a solution with pH 2. A **basic solution** has a hydrogen ion concentration that is lower than its hydroxide ion concentration and has a pH greater than 7.

The pH values of some common substances are shown in **FIGURE 2-17**. Although some very acidic compartments exist within cells (see Chapter 4), most of the interior of an animal or plant cell is neither strongly acidic nor strongly basic but an essentially neutral mixture of acidic and basic substances. Certain bacteria are adapted to life in extremely acidic environments (discussed in Chapter 25), but a substantial change in pH is incompatible with life for most cells. The pH of most types of plant and animal cells (and their environment) ordinarily ranges from around 7.2 to 7.4.

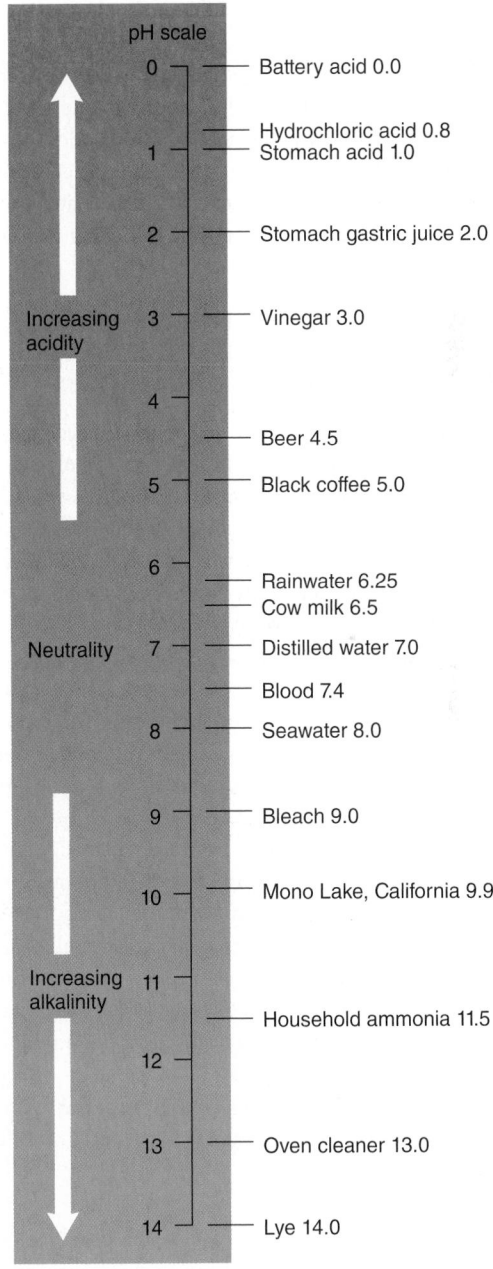

FIGURE 2-17 *Animated* pH values of some common solutions
A neutral solution (pH 7) has equal concentrations of H^+ and OH^-. Acidic solutions, which have a higher concentration of H^+ than OH^-, have pH values less than 7; pH values greater than 7 characterize basic solutions, which have an excess of OH^-.

TABLE 2-2	Calculating pH Values and Hydroxide Ion Concentrations from Hydrogen Ion Concentrations			
Substance	$[H^+]$*	$\log [H^+]$	pH	$[OH^-]$†
Gastric juice	$0.01, 10^{-2}$	-2	2	10^{-12}
Pure water, neutral solution	$0.0000001, 10^{-7}$	-7	7	10^{-7}
Household ammonia	$0.00000000001, 10^{-11}$	-11	11	10^{-3}

*$[H^+]$ = hydrogen ion concentration (mol/L)

†$[OH^-]$ = hydroxide ion concentration (mol/L)

Buffers minimize pH change

Many homeostatic mechanisms operate to maintain appropriate pH values. For example, the pH of human blood is about 7.4 and must be maintained within very narrow limits. If the blood becomes too acidic (for example, as a result of respiratory disease), coma and death may result. Excessive alkalinity can result in overexcitability of the nervous system and even convulsions. Organisms contain many natural buffers. A **buffer** is a substance or combination of substances that resists changes in pH when an acid or base is added. A buffering system includes a weak acid or a weak base. A weak acid or weak base does not ionize completely. At any given instant, only a fraction of the molecules are ionized; most are not dissociated.

One of the most common buffering systems functions in the blood of vertebrates (see Chapter 46). Carbon dioxide, produced as a waste product of cell metabolism, enters the blood, the main constituent of which is water. The carbon dioxide reacts with the water to form carbonic acid, a weak acid that dissociates to yield a hydrogen ion and a bicarbonate ion. The following expression describes the buffering system:

$$CO_2 + H_2O \rightleftharpoons H_2CO_3 \rightleftharpoons H^+ + HCO_3^-$$

Carbon dioxide   Water   Carbonic acid   Bicarbonate ion

As the double arrows indicate, all the reactions are reversible. Because carbonic acid is a weak acid, undissociated molecules are always present, as are all the other components of the system. The expression describes the system when it is at *dynamic equilibrium,* that is, when the rates of the forward and reverse reactions are equal and the relative concentrations of the components are not changing. A system at dynamic equilibrium tends to stay at equilibrium unless a stress is placed on it, which causes it to shift to reduce the stress until it attains a new dynamic equilibrium. A change in the concentration of any component is one such stress. Therefore, the system can be "shifted to the right" by adding reactants or removing products. Conversely, the system can be "shifted to the left" by adding products or removing reactants.

Hydrogen ions are the important products to consider in this system. The addition of excess hydrogen ions temporarily shifts the system to the left, as they combine with the bicarbonate ions to form carbonic acid. Eventually, a new dynamic equilibrium is established. At this point the hydrogen ion concentration is similar to the original concentration, and the product of the hydrogen ion and hydroxide ion concentrations is restored to the equilibrium value of 1×10^{-14}.

If hydroxide ions are added, they combine with the hydrogen ions to form water, effectively removing a product and thus shifting the system to the right. As this occurs, more carbonic acid ionizes, effectively replacing the hydrogen ions that were removed.

Organisms contain many weak acids and weak bases, which allows them to maintain an essential reserve of buffering capacity and helps them avoid pH extremes.

An acid and a base react to form a salt

When an acid and a base are mixed in water, the H^+ of the acid unites with the OH^- of the base to form a molecule of water. The remainder of the acid (an anion) combines with the remainder of the base (a cation) to form a salt. For example, hydrochloric acid reacts with sodium hydroxide to form water and sodium chloride:

$$HCl + NaOH \longrightarrow H_2O + NaCl$$

A **salt** is a compound in which the hydrogen ion of an acid is replaced by some other cation. Sodium chloride, NaCl, is a salt in which the hydrogen ion of HCl has been replaced by the cation Na^+.

When a salt, an acid, or a base is dissolved in water, its dissociated ions can conduct an electric current; these substances are called electrolytes. Sugars, alcohols, and many other substances do not form ions when dissolved in water; they do not conduct an electric current and are referred to as nonelectrolytes.

Cells and extracellular fluids (such as blood) of animals and plants contain a variety of dissolved salts that are the source of the many important mineral ions essential for fluid balance and acid–base balance. Nitrate and ammonium ions from the soil are the important nitrogen sources for plants. In animals, nerve and muscle function, blood clotting, bone formation, and many other aspects of body function depend on ions. Sodium, potassium, calcium, and magnesium are the chief cations present; chloride, bicarbonate, phosphate, and sulfate are important anions. The concentrations and relative amounts of the various cations and anions are kept remarkably constant. Any marked change results in impaired cell functions and may lead to death.

Review

- A solution has a hydrogen ion concentration of 0.01 mol/L. What is its pH? What is its hydroxide ion concentration? Is it acidic, basic, or neutral? How does this solution differ from one with a pH of 1?
- What would be the consequences of adding or removing a reactant or a product from a reversible reaction that is at dynamic equilibrium?
- Why are buffers important in organisms? Why can't strong acids or bases work as buffers?
- Why are acids, bases, and salts referred to as *electrolytes*?

■ SUMMARY: FOCUS ON LEARNING OBJECTIVES

2.1 *(page 27)*

1 Name the principal chemical elements in living things and provide an important function of each.

- An **element** is a substance that cannot be decomposed into simpler substances by normal chemical reactions. About 96% of an organism's mass consists of carbon, the backbone of organic molecules; hydrogen and oxygen, the components of water; and nitrogen, a component of proteins and nucleic acids.

2 Compare the physical properties (mass and charge) and locations of electrons, protons, and neutrons. Distinguish between the atomic number and the mass number of an atom.

- Each **atom** is composed of a nucleus containing positively charged protons and uncharged **neutrons.** Negatively charged **electrons** encircle the nucleus.
- An atom is identified as belonging to a particular element by its number of protons (**atomic number**). The **atomic mass** of an atom is equal to the sum of its protons and neutrons.
- A single proton or a single neutron each has a mass equivalent to one **atomic mass unit (amu).** The mass of a single electron is only about 1/1800 amu.

3 Define the terms *orbital* and *electron shell.* Relate electron shells to principal energy levels.

- In the space outside the nucleus, electrons move rapidly in electron **orbitals.** An **electron shell** consists of electrons in orbitals at the same **principal energy level.** Electrons in a shell distant from the nucleus have greater energy than those in a shell closer to the nucleus.

CENGAGENOW™ Learn more about atomic orbitals by clicking on the figure in CengageNOW.

2.2 *(page 31)*

4 Explain how the number of valence electrons of an atom is related to its chemical properties.

- The chemical properties of an atom are determined chiefly by the number and arrangement of its most energetic electrons, known as **valence electrons.** The valence shell of most atoms is full when it contains 8 electrons; that of hydrogen or helium is full when it contains 2. An atom tends to lose, gain, or share electrons to fill its valence shell.

5 Distinguish among simplest, molecular, and structural chemical formulas.

- Different atoms are joined by chemical bonds to form **compounds.** A **chemical formula** gives the types and relative numbers of atoms in a substance.
- A **simplest formula** gives the smallest whole-number ratio of the component atoms. A **molecular formula** gives the actual numbers of each type of atom in a molecule. A **structural formula** shows the arrangement of the atoms in a molecule.

6 Explain why the mole concept is so useful to chemists.

- One **mole** (the atomic or molecular mass in grams) of any substance contains 6.02×10^{23} atoms, molecules, or ions, enabling scientists to "count" particles by weighing a sample. This number is known as **Avogadro's number.**

2.3 *(page 32)*

7 Distinguish among covalent bonds, ionic bonds, hydrogen bonds, and van der Waals interactions. Compare them in terms of the mechanisms by which they form and their relative strengths.

- **Covalent bonds** are strong, stable bonds formed when atoms share valence electrons, forming molecules. When covalent bonds are formed, the orbitals of the valence electrons may become rearranged in a process known as **orbital hybridization.** Covalent bonds are **nonpolar** if the electrons are shared equally between the two atoms. Covalent bonds are **polar** if one atom is more **electronegative** (has a greater affinity for electrons) than the other.
- An **ionic bond** is formed between a positively charged **cation** and a negatively charged **anion.** Ionic bonds are strong in the absence of water but relatively weak in aqueous solution.

CENGAGENOW™ Learn more about ionic bonding by clicking on the figure in CengageNOW.

- **Hydrogen bonds** are relatively weak bonds formed when a hydrogen atom with a partial positive charge is attracted to an atom (usually oxygen or nitrogen) with a partial negative charge already bonded to another molecule or in another part of the same molecule.

Electronegative atoms

Hydrogen bond

CENGAGENOW™ Learn more about hydrogen bonding by clicking on the figure in CengageNOW.

- **van der Waals interactions** are weak forces based on fluctuating electric charges.

2.4 *(page 36)*

8 Distinguish between the terms *oxidation* and *reduction,* and relate these processes to the transfer of energy.

- **Oxidation** and **reduction** reactions (**redox reactions**) are chemical processes in which electrons (and their energy) are transferred from a reducing agent to an oxidizing agent. In oxidation, an atom, ion, or molecule loses electrons (and their energy). In reduction, an atom, ion, or molecule gains electrons (and their energy).

2.5 *(page 37)*

9 Explain how hydrogen bonds between adjacent water molecules govern many of the properties of water.

- Water is a **polar molecule** because one end has a partial positive charge and the other has a partial negative charge. Because its molecules are polar, water is an excellent **solvent** for ionic or polar **solutes.**
- Water molecules exhibit the property of **cohesion** because they form hydrogen bonds with one another; they also exhibit **adhesion** through hydrogen bonding to substances with ionic or polar regions.
- Water has a high **heat of vaporization.** Hydrogen bonds must be broken for molecules to enter the vapor phase. These molecules carry a great deal of heat, which accounts for **evaporative cooling.**
- Because hydrogen bonds must be broken to raise its temperature, water has a high **specific heat,** which helps organisms maintain a relatively constant internal temperature; this property also helps keep the ocean and other large bodies of water at a constant temperature.
- The hydrogen bonds between water molecules in ice cause it to be less dense than liquid water. The fact that ice floats makes the aquatic environment less extreme than it would be if ice sank to the bottom.

CENGAGENOW™ Learn more about the three forms of water by clicking on the figure in CengageNOW.

2.6 *(page 40)*

10 Contrast acids and bases, and discuss their properties.

- **Acids** are proton (hydrogen ion, H^+) donors; **bases** are proton acceptors. An acid dissociates in solution to yield H^+ and an anion. Many bases dissociate in solution to yield hydroxide ions (OH^-), which then accept protons to form water.

11 Convert the hydrogen ion concentration (moles per liter) of a solution to a pH value and describe how buffers help minimize changes in pH.

- **pH** is the negative log of the hydrogen ion concentration of a solution (expressed in moles per liter). A **neutral solution** with equal concentrations of H^+ and OH^- (10^{-7} mol/L) has a pH of 7, an **acidic solution** has a pH less than 7, and a **basic solution** has a pH greater than 7.

CENGAGENOW™ Learn more about the pH of common solutions by clicking on the figure in CengageNOW.

- A buffering system is based on a weak acid or a weak base. A **buffer** resists changes in the pH of a solution when acids or bases are added.

12 Describe the composition of a salt and explain why salts are important in organisms.

- A **salt** is a compound in which the hydrogen atom of an acid is replaced by some other cation. Salts provide the many mineral ions essential for life functions.

TEST YOUR UNDERSTANDING

1. Which of the following elements is *mismatched* with its properties or function? (a) carbon—forms the backbone of organic compounds (b) nitrogen—component of proteins (c) hydrogen—very electronegative (d) oxygen—can participate in hydrogen bonding (e) all of the above are correctly matched

2. $^{32}_{15}P$, a radioactive form of phosphorus, has (a) an atomic number of 32 (b) an atomic mass of 15 (c) an atomic mass of 47 (d) 32 electrons (e) 17 neutrons

3. Which of the following facts allows you to determine that atom A and atom B are isotopes of the same element? (a) they each have 6 protons (b) they each have 4 neutrons (c) the sum of the electrons and neutrons in each is 14 (d) they each have 4 valence electrons (e) they each have an atomic mass of 14

4. $^{1}_{1}H$ and $^{3}_{1}H$ have (a) different chemical properties because they have different atomic numbers (b) the same chemical properties because they have the same number of valence electrons (c) different chemical properties because they differ in their number of protons and electrons (d) the same chemical properties because they have the same atomic mass (e) the same chemical properties because they have the same number of protons, electrons, and neutrons

5. The orbitals composing an atom's valence electron shell (a) are arranged as concentric spheres (b) contain the atom's least energetic electrons (c) may change shape when covalent bonds are formed (d) never contain more than 1 electron each (e) more than one of the preceding is correct

6. Which of the following bonds and properties are correctly matched? (a) ionic bonds—are strong only if the participating ions are hydrated (b) hydrogen bonds—are responsible for bonding oxygen and hydrogen to form a single water molecule (c) polar covalent bonds—can occur between two atoms of the same element (d) covalent bonds—may be single, double, or triple (e) hydrogen bonds—are stronger than covalent bonds

7. In a redox reaction (a) energy is transferred from a reducing agent to an oxidizing agent (b) a reducing agent becomes oxidized as it accepts an electron (c) an oxidizing agent accepts a proton (d) a reducing agent donates a proton (e) the electrons in an atom move from its valence shell to a shell closer to its nucleus

8. Water has a high specific heat because (a) hydrogen bonds must be broken to raise its temperature (b) hydrogen bonds must be formed to raise its temperature (c) it is a poor insulator (d) it has low density considering the size of the molecule (e) it can ionize

9. A solution at pH 7 is considered neutral because (a) its hydrogen ion concentration is 0 mol/L (b) its hydroxide ion concentration is 0 mol/L (c) the product of its hydrogen ion concentration and its hydroxide ion concentration is 0 mol/L (d) its hydrogen ion concentration is equal to its hydroxide ion concentration (e) it is nonpolar

10. A solution with a pH of 2 has a hydrogen ion concentration that is _____ the hydrogen ion concentration of a solution with a pH of 4. (a) $\frac{1}{2}$ (b) $\frac{1}{100}$ (c) 2 times (d) 10 times (e) 100 times

11. Which of the following cannot function as a buffer? (a) phosphoric acid, a weak acid (b) sodium hydroxide, a strong base (c) sodium chloride, a salt that ionizes completely (d) a and c (e) b and c

12. Which of the following statements is true? (a) the number of individual particles (atoms, ions, or molecules) contained in one mole varies depending on the substance (b) Avogadro's number is the number of particles contained in one mole of a substance (c) Avogadro's number is 10^{23} particles (d) one mole of ^{12}C has a mass of 12 g (e) b and d

CRITICAL THINKING

1. Element A has 2 electrons in its valence shell (which is complete when it contains 8 electrons). Would you expect element A to share, donate, or accept electrons? What would you expect of element B, which has 4 valence electrons, and element C, which has 7?

  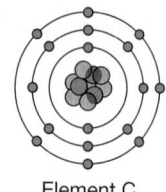

Element A   Element B   Element C

2. A hydrogen bond formed between two water molecules is only about $\frac{1}{20}$ as strong as a covalent bond between hydrogen and oxygen. In what ways would the physical properties of water be different if these hydrogen bonds were stronger (for example, $\frac{1}{10}$ the strength of covalent bonds)?

3. Consider the following reaction (in water).

$$HCl \longrightarrow H^+ + Cl^-$$

Name the reactant(s) and product(s). Does the expression indicate that the reaction is reversible? Could HCl be used as a buffer?

4. **ANALYZING DATA.** Could you safely immerse your hand in a solution containing 0.000,000,000,001 g of H^+ dissolved in 1 L of water?

5. **EVOLUTION LINK.** Initiatives designed to discover evidence for life (biosignatures or biomarkers) in the atmospheres of distant planets have been proposed by the U.S. National Aeronautics and Space Administration (NASA) and the European Space Agency (ESA). If implemented, both the Terrestrial Planet Finder project (NASA) and the Darwin project (ESA) will use special space telescopes to detect atmospheric water vapor, as well as oxygen and carbon dioxide. Which of these biosignatures would you consider the most fundamental indicator that life could have evolved on these planets? Why?

 Additional questions are available in CengageNOW at www.cengage.com/login.

3 The Chemistry of Life: Organic Compounds

Humans obtain organic molecules from food. This young girl is using a leaf to feed her baby brother.

KEY CONCEPTS

3.1 Carbon atoms join with one another or other atoms to form large molecules with a wide variety of shapes. Hydrocarbons are nonpolar, hydrophobic molecules; their properties can be altered by adding functional groups: hydroxyl and carbonyl groups (polar), carboxyl and phosphate groups (acidic), and amino groups (basic).

3.2 Carbohydrates are composed of sugar subunits (monosaccharides), which can be joined to form disaccharides, storage polysaccharides, and structural polysaccharides.

3.3 Lipids store energy (triacylglycerols) and are the main structural components of cell membranes (phospholipids).

3.4 Proteins have multiple levels of structure and are composed of amino acid subunits joined by peptide bonds.

3.5 Nucleic acids (DNA and RNA) are informational molecules composed of long chains of nucleotide subunits. ATP and some other nucleotides have a central role in energy metabolism.

3.6 Biological molecules have recognizable attributes that aid in their identification.

Both inorganic and organic forms of carbon occur widely in nature. Many types of organic compounds will become incorporated into the body of the baby in the photograph as he grows. Organic compounds are those in which carbon atoms are covalently bonded to one another to form the backbone of the molecule. Some very simple carbon compounds are considered inorganic if the carbon is not bonded to another carbon or to hydrogen. The carbon dioxide we exhale as a waste product from the breakdown of organic molecules to obtain energy is an example of an inorganic carbon compound. Organic compounds are so named because at one time it was thought that they could be produced only by living (organic) organisms. In 1828, the German chemist Friedrich Wühler synthesized urea, a metabolic waste product. Since that time, scientists have learned to synthesize many organic molecules and have discovered organic compounds not found in any organism.

Organic compounds are extraordinarily diverse; in fact, more than 5 million have been identified. There are many reasons for this diversity. Organic compounds can be produced in a wide variety of three-dimensional (3-D) shapes. Furthermore, the carbon atom forms bonds with a greater number of different elements than does any other type of atom. The addition of chemical groups containing atoms of other elements—especially oxygen, nitrogen, phosphorus, and sulfur—can profoundly change the properties of an organic molecule. Diversity also results from the fact that many organic compounds found in organisms are extremely large *macromolecules,* which cells construct from simpler modular subunits. For example, protein molecules are built from smaller compounds called *amino acids.*

As you study this chapter, you will develop an understanding of the major groups of organic compounds found in organisms, including carbohydrates, lipids, proteins, and nucleic acids (DNA and RNA). Why are these compounds of central importance to all living things? The answer to this question will become more obvious as you study subsequent chapters, in which we explore the evidence that all living things evolved from a common ancestor. Evolution provides a powerful explanation for the similarities of the molecules that constitute the structures of cells and tissues, participate in and regulate metabolic reactions, transmit information, and provide energy for life processes.

3.1 CARBON ATOMS AND ORGANIC MOLECULES

■ LEARNING OBJECTIVES

1 Describe the properties of carbon that make it the central component of organic compounds.
2 Define the term *isomer* and distinguish among the three principal isomer types.
3 Identify the major functional groups present in organic compounds and describe their properties.
4 Explain the relationship between polymers and macromolecules.

Carbon has unique properties that allow the formation of the carbon backbones of the large, complex molecules essential to life (**FIG. 3-1**). Because a carbon atom has 4 valence electrons, it can complete its valence shell by forming a total of four covalent bonds (see Fig. 2-2). Each bond can link it to another carbon atom or to an atom of a different element. Carbon is particularly well suited to serve as the backbone of a large molecule because carbon-to-carbon bonds are strong and not easily broken. However, they are not so strong that it would be impossible for cells to break them. Carbon-to-carbon bonds are not limited to single bonds (based

FIGURE 3-1 Organic molecules
Note that each carbon atom forms four covalent bonds, producing a wide variety of shapes.

on sharing one electron pair). Two carbon atoms can share two electron pairs with each other, forming double bonds:

$$\rangle C = C \langle$$

In some compounds, triple carbon-to-carbon bonds are formed:

$$-C \equiv C-$$

As shown in Figure 3-1, **hydrocarbons,** organic compounds consisting only of carbon and hydrogen, can exist as unbranched or branched chains, or as rings. Rings and chains are joined in some compounds.

The molecules in the cell are analogous to the components of a machine. Each component has a shape that allows it to fill certain roles and to interact with other components (often with a complementary shape). Similarly, the shape of a molecule is important in determining its biological properties and function. Carbon atoms can link to one another and to other atoms to produce a wide variety of 3-D molecular shapes because the four covalent bonds of carbon do not form in a single plane. Instead, as discussed in Chapter 2, the valence electron orbitals become elongated and project from the carbon atom toward the corners of a tetrahedron (**FIG. 3-2**). The structure is highly symmetrical, with an angle of about 109.5 degrees between any two of these bonds. Keep in mind that for simplicity, many of the figures in this book are drawn as two-dimensional (2-D) graphic representations of 3-D molecules. Even the simplest hydrocarbon chains, such as those in Figure 3-1, are not actually straight but have a 3-D zigzag structure.

Generally, there is freedom of rotation around each carbon-to-carbon single bond. This property permits organic molecules to be flexible and to assume a variety of shapes, depending on the extent to which each single bond is rotated. Double and triple bonds do not allow rotation, so regions of a molecule with such bonds tend to be inflexible.

(a) Carbon (C)   **(b)** Methane (CH_4)

(c) Carbon dioxide (CO_2)

FIGURE 3-2 Carbon bonding
(a) The 3-D arrangement of the bonds of a carbon atom is responsible for **(b)** the tetrahedral architecture of methane. **(c)** In carbon dioxide, oxygen atoms are joined linearly to a central carbon by polar double bonds.

Isomers have the same molecular formula but different structures

One reason for the great number of possible carbon-containing compounds is the fact that the same components usually can link in more than one pattern, generating an even wider variety of molecular shapes. Compounds with the same molecular formulas but different structures and thus different properties are called **isomers.** Isomers do not have identical physical or chemical properties and may have different common names. Cells can distinguish between isomers. Usually, one isomer is biologically active and the other is not. Three types of isomers are structural isomers, geometric isomers, and enantiomers.

Structural isomers are compounds that differ in the covalent arrangements of their atoms. For example, **FIGURE 3-3a** illustrates two structural isomers with the molecular formula C_2H_6O. Large compounds have more possible structural isomers. There can be up to 366,319 isomers of $C_{20}H_{42}$.

Geometric isomers are compounds that are identical in the arrangement of their covalent bonds but different in the spatial arrangement of atoms or groups of atoms. Geometric isomers are present in some compounds with carbon-to-carbon double bonds. Because double bonds are not flexible, as single bonds are, atoms joined to the carbons of a double bond cannot rotate freely about the axis of the bonds. These *cis–trans* isomers may be represented as shown in **FIGURE 3-3b**. The designation *cis* (Latin, "on this side") indicates that the two larger components are on the same side of the double bond. If they are on opposite sides of the double bond, the compound is designated a *trans* (Latin, "across") isomer.

Enantiomers are isomers that are mirror images of each other (**FIG. 3-3c**). Recall that the four groups bonded to a single carbon atom are arranged at the vertices of a tetrahedron. If the four bonded groups are all different, the central carbon is described as asymmetrical. Figure 3-3c illustrates that the four groups can be arranged around the asymmetrical carbon in two different ways that are mirror images of each other. The two molecules are enantiomers if they cannot be superimposed on each other no matter how they are rotated in space. Although enantiomers have similar chemical properties and most of their physical properties are identical, cells recognize the difference in shape, and usually only one form is found in organisms.

Functional groups change the properties of organic molecules

The existence of isomers is not the only source of variety among organic molecules. The addition of various combinations of atoms generates a vast array of molecules with different properties. Because covalent bonds between hydrogen and carbon are nonpolar, **hydrocarbons** lack distinct charged regions. For this reason, hydrocarbons are insoluble in water and tend to cluster together through **hydrophobic** interactions. "Water fearing," the literal meaning of the term *hydrophobic,* is somewhat misleading. Hydrocarbons interact with water, but much more weakly than the water molecules cohere to one another through hydrogen bonding.

Ethanol (C_2H_6O) Dimethyl ether (C_2H_6O)

(a) Structural isomers. Structural isomers differ in the covalent arrangement of their atoms.

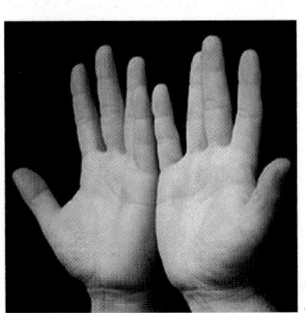

trans-2-butene *cis*-2-butene

(b) Geometric isomers. Geometric, or *cis–trans*, isomers have identical covalent bonds but differ in the order in which groups are arranged in space.

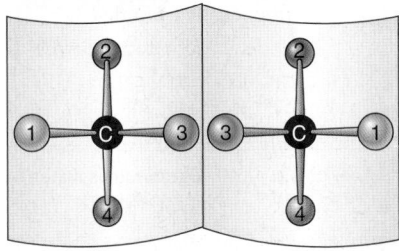

(c) Enantiomers. Enantiomers are isomers that are mirror images of each other. The central carbon is asymmetrical because it is bonded to four different groups. Because of their 3-D structure, the two figures cannot be superimposed no matter how they are rotated.

FIGURE 3-3 Isomers

Isomers have the same molecular formula, but their atoms are arranged differently.

Hydrocarbons interact weakly with one another, but the main reason for hydrophobic interactions is that they are driven together in a sense, having been excluded by the hydrogen-bonded water molecules.

However, the characteristics of an organic molecule can be changed dramatically by replacing one of the hydrogens with one or more **functional groups,** groups of atoms that determine the types of chemical reactions and associations in which the compound participates. Most functional groups readily form associations, such as ionic and hydrogen bonds, with other molecules. Polar and ionic functional groups are **hydrophilic** because they associate strongly with polar water molecules.

The properties of the major classes of biologically important organic compounds—carbohydrates, lipids, proteins, and nucleic acids—are largely a consequence of the types and arrangement of functional groups they contain. When we know what kinds of functional groups are present in an organic compound, we can predict its chemical behavior. Note that the symbol *R* is used to represent the *remainder* of the molecule of which each functional group is a part. For example, the **methyl group,** a common nonpolar hydrocarbon group, is abbreviated *R*—CH_3. As you read the rest of this section, refer to **TABLE 3-1** for the structural formulas of other important functional groups, as well as for additional information.

The **hydroxyl group** (abbreviated *R*—OH) is polar because of the presence of a strongly electronegative oxygen atom. Do not confuse it with the hydroxide ion, OH^-, discussed in Chapter 2. If a hydroxyl group replaces one hydrogen of a hydrocarbon, the resulting molecule can have significantly altered properties. For example, ethane (see Fig. 3-1a) is a hydrocarbon that is a gas at room temperature. If a hydroxyl group replaces a hydrogen atom, the resulting molecule is ethyl alcohol, or ethanol, which is found in alcoholic beverages (see Fig. 3-3a). Ethanol is somewhat cohesive because the polar hydroxyl groups of adjacent molecules interact; it is therefore liquid at room temperature. Unlike ethane, ethyl alcohol dissolves in water because the polar hydroxyl groups interact with the polar water molecules.

The **carbonyl group** consists of a carbon atom that has a double covalent bond with an oxygen atom. This double bond is polar because of the electronegativity of the oxygen; thus, the carbonyl group is hydrophilic. The position of the carbonyl group in the molecule determines the class to which the molecule belongs. An **aldehyde** has a carbonyl group positioned at the end of the carbon skeleton (abbreviated *R*—CHO); a **ketone** has an internal carbonyl group (abbreviated *R*—CO—*R*).

The **carboxyl group** (abbreviated *R*—COOH) in its non-ionized form consists of a carbon atom joined by a double covalent bond to an oxygen atom, and by a single covalent bond to another oxygen, which is in turn bonded to a hydrogen atom. Two electronegative oxygen atoms in such close proximity establish an extremely polarized condition, which can cause the hydrogen atom to be stripped of its electron and released as a hydrogen ion (H^+). The resulting ionized carboxyl group has 1 unit of negative charge (R—COO^-):

$$R - C \overset{\displaystyle O}{\underset{\displaystyle O-H}{\Big\langle}} \longrightarrow R - C \overset{\displaystyle O}{\underset{\displaystyle O^-}{\Big\langle}} + H^+$$

Carboxyl groups are weakly acidic; only a fraction of the molecules ionize in this way. This group therefore exists in one of

TABLE 3-1   Some Biologically Important Functional Groups

Functional Group and Description	Structural Formula	Class of Compound Characterized by Group
Hydroxyl Polar because electronegative oxygen attracts covalent electrons	R—OH	Alcohols Example, ethanol
Carbonyl **Aldehydes:** Carbonyl group carbon is bonded to at least one H atom; polar because electronegative oxygen attracts covalent electrons		Aldehydes Example, formaldehyde
Ketones: Carbonyl group carbon is bonded to two other carbons; polar because electronegative oxygen attracts covalent electrons		Ketones Example, acetone
Carboxyl Weakly acidic; can release an H^+	 Non-ionized Ionized	Carboxylic acids (organic acids) Example, amino acid
Amino Weakly basic; can accept an H^+	 Non-ionized Ionized	Amines Example, amino acid
Phosphate Weakly acidic; one or two H^+ can be released	 Non-ionized Ionized	Organic Phosphates Example, phosphate ester (as found in ATP)
Sulfhydryl Helps stabilize internal structure of proteins	R—SH	Thiols Example, cysteine

two hydrophilic states: ionic or polar. Carboxyl groups are essential constituents of amino acids.

An **amino group** (abbreviated R—NH_2) in its non-ionized form includes a nitrogen atom covalently bonded to two hydrogen atoms. Amino groups are weakly basic because they are able to ac-

cept a hydrogen ion (proton). The resulting ionized amino group has 1 unit of positive charge $(R$—$NH_3^+)$. Amino groups are components of amino acids and of nucleic acids.

A **phosphate group** (abbreviated R—PO_4H_2) is weakly acidic. The attraction of electrons by the oxygen atoms can result in

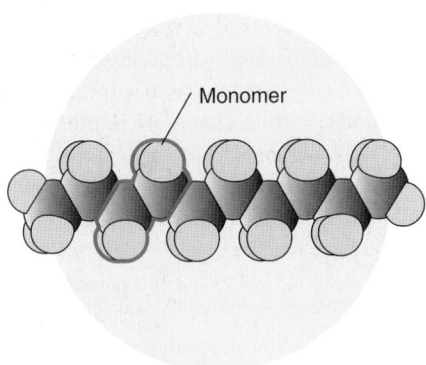

FIGURE 3-4 A simple polymer
This small polymer of polyethylene is formed by linking two-carbon ethylene (C_2H_4) monomers. One such monomer is outlined in red. The structure is represented by a space-filling model, which accurately depicts the 3-D shape of the molecule.

the release of one or two hydrogen ions, producing ionized forms with 1 or 2 units of negative charge. Phosphates are constituents of nucleic acids and certain lipids.

The **sulfhydryl group** (abbreviated *R*—SH), consisting of an atom of sulfur covalently bonded to a hydrogen atom, is found in molecules called *thiols*. As you will see, amino acids that contain a sulfhydryl group can make important contributions to the structure of proteins.

Many biological molecules are polymers

Many biological molecules such as proteins and nucleic acids are very large, consisting of thousands of atoms. Such giant molecules are known as **macromolecules.** Most macromolecules are **polymers,** produced by linking small organic compounds called **monomers** (**FIG. 3-4**). Just as all the words in this book have been written by arranging the 26 letters of the alphabet in various combinations, monomers can be grouped to form an almost infinite variety of larger molecules. The thousands of different complex organic compounds present in organisms are constructed from about 40 small, simple monomers. For example, the 20 monomers called *amino acids* can be linked end to end in countless ways to form the polymers known as *proteins.*

Polymers can be degraded to their component monomers by **hydrolysis reactions** ("to break with water"). In a reaction regulated by a specific enzyme (biological catalyst), a hydrogen from a water molecule attaches to one monomer, and a hydroxyl from water attaches to the adjacent monomer (**FIG. 3-5**).

Monomers become covalently linked by **condensation reactions.** Because the *equivalent* of a molecule of water is removed during the reactions that combine monomers, the term *dehydration synthesis* is sometimes used to describe condensation (see Fig. 3-5). However, in biological systems the synthesis of a polymer is not simply the reverse of hydrolysis, even though the net effect is the opposite of hydrolysis. Synthetic processes such as condensation require energy and are regulated by different enzymes.

In the following sections we examine carbohydrates, lipids, proteins, and nucleic acids. Our discussion begins with the smaller, simpler forms of these compounds and extends to the linking of these monomers to form macromolecules.

Review

- What are some of the ways that the features of carbon-to-carbon bonds influence the stability and 3-D structure of organic molecules?
- Draw pairs of simple sketches comparing two (1) structural isomers, (2) geometric isomers, and (3) enantiomers. Why are these differences biologically important?
- Sketch the following functional groups: methyl, amino, carbonyl, hydroxyl, carboxyl, and phosphate. Include both non-ionized and ionized forms for acidic and basic groups.
- How is the fact that a group is nonpolar, polar, acidic, or basic related to its hydrophilic or hydrophobic properties?
- Why is the equivalent of a water molecule important to both condensation reactions and hydrolysis reactions?

3.2 CARBOHYDRATES

◼ LEARNING OBJECTIVE

5   Distinguish among monosaccharides, disaccharides, and polysaccharides; compare storage polysaccharides with structural polysaccharides.

Sugars, starches, and cellulose are **carbohydrates.** Sugars and starches serve as energy sources for cells; cellulose is the main structural component of the walls that surround plant cells. Carbohydrates contain carbon, hydrogen, and oxygen atoms in a ratio of approximately one carbon to two hydrogens to one oxygen $(CH_2O)_n$. The term *carbohydrate,* meaning "hydrate (water) of

FIGURE 3-5 *Animated* **Condensation and hydrolysis reactions**
Joining two monomers yields a dimer; incorporating additional monomers produces a polymer. Note that condensation and hydrolysis reactions are catalyzed by different enzymes.

carbon," reflects the 2:1 ratio of hydrogen to oxygen, the same ratio found in water (H_2O). Carbohydrates contain one sugar unit (monosaccharides), two sugar units (disaccharides), or many sugar units (polysaccharides).

Monosaccharides are simple sugars

Monosaccharides typically contain from three to seven carbon atoms. In a monosaccharide, a hydroxyl group is bonded to each carbon except one; that carbon is double-bonded to an oxygen atom, forming a carbonyl group. If the carbonyl group is at the end of the chain, the monosaccharide is an aldehyde; if the carbonyl group is at any other position, the monosaccharide is a ketone. (By convention, the numbering of the carbon skeleton of a sugar begins with the carbon at or nearest the carbonyl end of the open chain.)

The large number of polar hydroxyl groups, plus the carbonyl group, gives a monosaccharide hydrophilic properties. **FIGURE 3-6** shows simplified, 2-D representations of some common monosaccharides. The simplest carbohydrates are the three-carbon sugars (trioses): glyceraldehyde and dihydroxyacetone. Ribose and deoxyribose are common pentoses, sugars that contain five carbons; they are components of nucleic acids (DNA, RNA, and related compounds). Glucose, fructose, galactose, and other six-carbon sugars are called hexoses. (Note that the names of carbohydrates typically end in -*ose*.)

Glucose ($C_6H_{12}O_6$), the most abundant monosaccharide, is used as an energy source in most organisms. During cellular respiration (see Chapter 8), cells oxidize glucose molecules, converting the stored energy to a form that can be readily used for cell work. Glucose is also used in the synthesis of other types of compounds

FIGURE 3-6 Monosaccharides

Shown are 2-D chain structures of **(a)** three-carbon trioses, **(b)** five-carbon pentoses, and **(c)** six-carbon hexoses. Although it is convenient to show monosaccharides in this form, the pentoses and hexoses are more accurately depicted as ring structures, as in Figure 3-7. The carbonyl group (*gray screen*) is terminal in aldehyde sugars and located in an internal position in ketones. Deoxyribose differs from ribose because deoxyribose has one less oxygen; a hydrogen (*white screen*) instead of a hydroxyl group (*blue screen*) is attached to carbon 2. Glucose and galactose differ in the arrangement of the hydroxyl group and hydrogen attached to carbon 4 (*red box*).

such as amino acids and fatty acids. Glucose is so important in metabolism that mechanisms have evolved to maintain its concentration at relatively constant levels in the blood of humans and other complex animals (see Chapter 49).

Glucose and fructose are structural isomers: they have identical molecular formulas, but their atoms are arranged differently. In fructose (a ketone) the double-bonded oxygen is linked to a carbon within the chain rather than to a terminal carbon as in glucose (an aldehyde). Because of these differences, the two sugars have different properties. For example, fructose, found in honey and some fruits, tastes sweeter than glucose.

Glucose and galactose are both hexoses and aldehydes. However, they differ in the arrangement of the atoms attached to asymmetrical carbon atom 4.

The linear formulas in Figure 3-6 give a clear but somewhat unrealistic picture of the structures of some common monosaccharides. As we have mentioned, molecules are not 2-D; in fact, the properties of each compound depend largely on its 3-D structure. Thus, 3-D formulas are helpful in understanding the relationship between molecular structure and biological function.

α-Glucose (ring form)   Formation of glucose ring   **β-Glucose** (ring form)

(a) When dissolved in water, glucose undergoes a rearrangement of its atoms, forming one of two possible ring structures: α-glucose or β-glucose. Although the drawing does not show the complete 3-D structure, the thick, tapered bonds in the lower portion of each ring represent the part of the molecule that would project out of the page toward you.

α-Glucose   **β-Glucose**

(b) The essential differences between α-glucose and β-glucose are more readily apparent in these simplified structures. By convention, a carbon atom is assumed to be present at each angle in the ring unless another atom is shown. Most hydrogen atoms have been omitted.

FIGURE 3-7 α and β forms of glucose

Molecules of glucose and other pentoses and hexoses in solution are actually rings rather than extended straight carbon chains.

Glucose in solution (as in the cell) typically exists as a ring of five carbons and one oxygen. It assumes this configuration when its atoms undergo a rearrangement, permitting a covalent bond to connect carbon 1 to the oxygen attached to carbon 5 (**FIG. 3-7**). When glucose forms a ring, two isomeric forms are possible, differing only in orientation of the hydroxyl (—OH) group attached to carbon 1. When this hydroxyl group is on the same side of the plane of the ring as the —CH₂OH side group, the glucose is designated beta glucose (β-glucose). When it is on the side (with respect to the plane of the ring) opposite the —CH₂OH side group, the compound is designated alpha glucose (α-glucose). Although the differences between these isomers may seem small, they have important consequences when the rings join to form polymers.

Disaccharides consist of two monosaccharide units

A **disaccharide** (two sugars) contains two monosaccharide rings joined by a glycosidic linkage, consisting of a central oxygen covalently bonded to two carbons, one in each ring (**FIG. 3-8**). The **glycosidic linkage** of a disaccharide generally forms between

carbon 1 of one molecule and carbon 4 of the other molecule. The disaccharide maltose (malt sugar) consists of two covalently linked α-glucose units. Sucrose, common table sugar, consists of a glucose unit combined with a fructose unit. Lactose (the sugar present in milk) consists of one molecule of glucose and one of galactose.

As shown in Figure 3-8, a disaccharide can be hydrolyzed, that is, split by the addition of water, into two monosaccharide units. During digestion, maltose is hydrolyzed to form two molecules of glucose:

maltose + water ⟶ glucose + glucose

Similarly, sucrose is hydrolyzed to form glucose and fructose:

sucrose + water ⟶ glucose + fructose

Polysaccharides can store energy or provide structure

A **polysaccharide** is a macromolecule consisting of repeating units of simple sugars, usually glucose. The polysaccharides are the most abundant carbohydrates and include starches, glycogen, and

(a) Maltose may be broken down (as during digestion) to form two molecules of glucose. The glycosidic linkage is broken in a hydrolysis reaction, which requires the addition of water.

(b) Sucrose can be hydrolyzed to yield a molecule of glucose and a molecule of fructose.

FIGURE 3-8 Hydrolysis of disaccharides
Note that an enzyme is needed to promote these reactions.

cellulose. Although the precise number of sugar units varies, thousands of units are typically present in a single molecule. A polysaccharide may be a single long chain or a branched chain.

Because they are composed of different isomers and because the units may be arranged differently, polysaccharides vary in their properties. Those that can be easily broken down to their subunits are well suited for energy storage, whereas the macromolecular 3-D architecture of others makes them particularly well suited to form stable structures.

Starch, the typical form of carbohydrate used for energy storage in plants, is a polymer consisting of α-glucose subunits. These monomers are joined by α 1—4 linkages, which means that carbon 1 of one glucose is linked to carbon 4 of the next glucose in the chain (**FIG. 3-9**). Starch occurs in two forms: amylose and amylopectin. Amylose, the simpler form, is unbranched. Amylopectin, the more common form, usually consists of about 1000 glucose units in a branched chain.

Plant cells store starch mainly as granules within specialized organelles called **amyloplasts** (see Fig. 3-9a); some cells, such as those of potatoes, are very rich in amyloplasts. When energy is needed for cell work, the plant hydrolyzes the starch, releasing the glucose subunits. Virtually all organisms, including humans and other animals, have enzymes that can break α 1—4 linkages.

Glycogen (sometimes referred to as *animal starch*) is the form in which glucose subunits, joined by α 1—4 linkages, are stored as an energy source in animal tissues. Glycogen is similar in structure to plant starch but more extensively branched and more water soluble. In vertebrates, glycogen is stored mainly in liver and muscle cells.

Carbohydrates are the most abundant group of organic compounds on Earth, and cellulose is the most abundant carbohydrate; it accounts for 50% or more of all the carbon in plants (**FIG. 3-10**). Cellulose is a structural carbohydrate. Wood is about half cellulose, and cotton is at least 90% cellulose. Plant cells are surrounded by strong supporting cell walls consisting mainly of cellulose.

Cellulose is an insoluble polysaccharide composed of many joined glucose molecules. The bonds joining these sugar units are different from those in starch. Recall that starch is composed of α-glucose subunits, joined by α 1—4 glycosidic linkages. Cellulose contains β-glucose monomers joined by β 1—4 linkages. These bonds cannot be split by the enzymes that hydrolyze the α linkages in starch. Because humans, like other animals, lack enzymes that digest cellulose, we cannot use it as a nutrient. The cellulose found in whole grains and vegetables remains fibrous and provides bulk that helps keep our digestive tract functioning properly.

Some microorganisms digest cellulose to glucose. In fact, cellulose-digesting bacteria live in the digestive systems of cows and sheep, enabling these grass-eating animals to obtain nourishment from cellulose. Similarly, the digestive systems of termites contain microorganisms that digest cellulose (see Fig. 26-4b).

Cellulose molecules are well suited for a structural role. The β-glucose subunits are joined in a way that allows extensive hydrogen bonding among different cellulose molecules, and they aggregate in long bundles of fibers (see Fig. 3-10a).

Some modified and complex carbohydrates have special roles

Many derivatives of monosaccharides are important biological molecules. Some form important structural components. The amino sugars galactosamine and glucosamine are compounds in which a hydroxyl group (—OH) is replaced by an amino group (—NH_2). Galactosamine is present in cartilage, a constituent of the skeletal system of vertebrates. *N*-acetyl glucosamine (NAG) subunits, joined by glycosidic bonds, compose **chitin**, a main component of the cell walls of fungi and of the external skeletons of insects, crayfish, and other arthropods (**FIG. 3-11**). Chitin forms very tough structures because, as in cellulose, its molecules interact through multiple hydrogen bonds. Some chitinous structures, such as the shell of a lobster, are further hardened by the addition of calcium carbonate ($CaCO_3$), an inorganic form of carbon.

Carbohydrates may also combine with proteins to form **glycoproteins,** compounds present on the outer surface of cells other than bacteria. Some of these carbohydrate chains allow cells to adhere to one another, whereas others provide protection. Most proteins secreted by cells are glycoproteins. These include the major components of mucus, a protective material secreted by the mucous membranes of the respiratory and digestive systems. Carbohydrates combine with lipids to form glycolipids, compounds on the surfaces of animal cells that allow cells to recognize and interact with one another.

Ed Reschke

100 μm

(a) Starch (*stained purple*) is stored in specialized organelles, called *amyloplasts,* in these cells of a buttercup root.

(b) Starch is composed of α-glucose molecules joined by glycosidic bonds. At the branch points are bonds between carbon 6 of the glucose in the straight chain and carbon 1 of the glucose in the branching chain.

(c) Starch consists of highly branched chains; the arrows indicate the branch points. Each chain is actually a coil or helix, stabilized by hydrogen bonds between the hydroxyl groups of the glucose subunits.

FIGURE 3-9 Starch, a storage polysaccharide

Review

- What features related to hydrogen bonding give storage polysaccharides, such as starch and glycogen, different properties from structural polysaccharides, such as cellulose and chitin?
- Why can't humans digest cellulose?

(a) **Cellulose fibers from a cell wall.** The fibers shown in this electron micrograph consist of bundles of cellulose molecules that interact through hydrogen bonds.

1 µm

Biophoto Associates/Photo Researchers, Inc.

(b) **The cellulose molecule is an unbranched polysaccharide.** It consists of about 10,000 β-glucose units joined by glycosidic bonds.

FIGURE 3-10 Cellulose, a structural polysaccharide

N-acetyl glucosamine

(a) **Chitin** is a polymer composed of *N*-acetyl glucosamine subunits.

FIGURE 3-11 Chitin, a structural polysaccharide

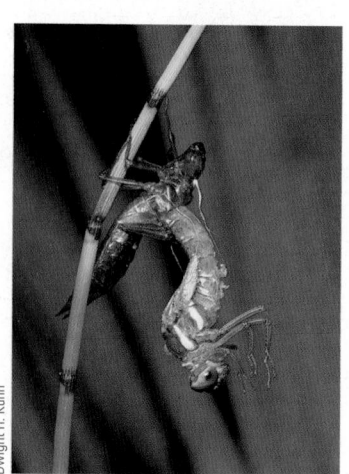

Dwight R. Kuhn

(b) Chitin is an important component of the exoskeleton (outer covering) this dragonfly is shedding.

3.3 LIPIDS

■ LEARNING OBJECTIVE

6 Distinguish among fats, phospholipids, and steroids, and describe the composition, characteristics, and biological functions of each.

Unlike carbohydrates, which are defined by their structure, **lipids** are a heterogeneous group of compounds that are categorized by the fact that they are soluble in nonpolar solvents (such as ether and chloroform) and are relatively insoluble in water. Lipid molecules have these properties because they consist mainly of carbon and hydrogen, with few oxygen-containing functional groups. Hydrophilic functional groups typically contain oxygen atoms; therefore, lipids, which have little oxygen, tend to be hydrophobic. Among the biologically important groups of lipids are fats, phospholipids, carotenoids (orange and yellow plant pigments), steroids, and waxes. Some lipids are used for energy storage, others serve as structural components of cell membranes, and some are important hormones.

Triacylglycerol is formed from glycerol and three fatty acids

The most abundant lipids in living organisms are **triacylglycerols.** These compounds, commonly known as *fats,* are an economical form of reserve fuel storage because, when metabolized, they yield more than twice as much energy per gram as do carbohydrates. Carbohydrates and proteins can be transformed by enzymes into fats and stored within the cells of adipose (fat) tissue of animals and in some seeds and fruits of plants.

A triacylglycerol molecule (also known as a *triglyceride*) consists of glycerol joined to three fatty acids (**FIG. 3-12**). **Glycerol** is a three-carbon alcohol that contains three hydroxyl (—OH) groups, and a **fatty acid** is a long, unbranched hydrocarbon chain with a carboxyl group (—COOH) at one end. A triacylglycerol molecule is formed by a series of three condensation reactions. In each reaction, the equivalent of a water molecule is removed as one of the glycerol's hydroxyl groups reacts with the carboxyl group of a fatty acid, resulting in the formation of a covalent linkage known as an **ester linkage** (see Fig. 3-12b). The first reaction yields a **monoacylglycerol** (*monoglyceride*); the second, a **diacylglycerol** (*diglyceride*); and the third, a triacylglycerol. During digestion, triacylglycerols are hydrolyzed to produce fatty acids and glycerol (see Chapter 47). Diacylglycerol is an important molecule for sending signals within the cell (see Chapters 6 and 49).

Saturated and unsaturated fatty acids differ in physical properties

About 30 different fatty acids are commonly found in lipids, and they typically have an even number of carbon atoms. For example, butyric acid, present in rancid butter, has four carbon atoms. Oleic acid, with 18 carbons, is the most widely distributed fatty acid in nature and is found in most animal and plant fats.

Saturated fatty acids contain the maximum possible number of hydrogen atoms. Palmitic acid, a 16-carbon fatty acid, is a common saturated fatty acid (see Fig. 3-12c). Fats high in saturated fatty acids, such as animal fat and solid vegetable shortening, tend to be solid at room temperature. The reason is that even electrically neutral, nonpolar molecules can develop transient regions of weak positive charge and weak negative charge. This occurs as the constant motion of their electrons causes some regions to have a temporary excess of electrons, whereas others have a temporary electron deficit. These slight opposite charges result in van der Waals interactions between adjacent molecules (see Chapter 2). Although van der Waals interactions are weak attractions, they are strong when many occur among long hydrocarbon chains. These van der Waals interactions tend to make a substance more solid by limiting the motion of its molecules.

Unsaturated fatty acids include one or more adjacent pairs of carbon atoms joined by a double bond. Therefore, they are not fully saturated with hydrogen. Fatty acids with one double bond are **monounsaturated fatty acids,** whereas those with more than one double bond are **polyunsaturated fatty acids.** Oleic acid is a monounsaturated fatty acid, and linoleic acid is a common polyunsaturated fatty acid (see Figs. 3-12d and e). Fats containing a high proportion of monounsaturated or polyunsaturated fatty acids tend to be liquid at room temperature. The reason is that each double bond produces a bend in the hydrocarbon chain that prevents it from aligning closely with an adjacent chain, thereby limiting van der Waals interactions and permitting freer molecular motion.

Glycerol   **Fatty acid**

(a)

(b)   **A triacylglycerol**

(c) Palmitic acid

(d) Oleic acid

(e) Linoleic acid

FIGURE 3-12 *Animated* Triacylglycerol, the main storage lipid
(a) Glycerol and fatty acids are the components of fats. **(b)** Glycerol is attached to fatty acids by ester linkages (*in gray*). The space-filling models show the actual shapes of the fatty acids. **(c)** Palmitic acid, a saturated fatty acid, is a straight chain. **(d)** Oleic acid (monounsaturated) and **(e)** linoleic acid (polyunsaturated) are bent or kinked wherever a carbon-to-carbon double bond appears.

Food manufacturers commonly hydrogenate or partially hydrogenate cooking oils to make margarine and other foodstuffs, converting unsaturated fatty acids to saturated fatty acids and making the fat more solid at room temperature. This process makes the fat less healthful because saturated fatty acids in the diet are known to increase the risk of cardiovascular disease (see Chapter 44). The hydrogenation process has yet another effect. Note that in the naturally occurring unsaturated fatty acids oleic acid and linoleic acid shown in Figure 3-12, the two hydrogens flanking each double bond are on the same side of the hydrocarbon chain (the *cis* configuration). When fatty acids are artificially hydrogenated, the double bonds can become rearranged, resulting in a *trans* configuration, analogous to the arrangement shown in Figure 3-3b. *Trans* fatty acids are technically unsaturated, but they mimic many of the properties of saturated fatty acids. Because the *trans* configuration does not produce a bend at the site of the double bond, *trans* fatty acids are more solid at room temperature; like saturated fatty acids, they increase the risk of cardiovascular disease.

At least two unsaturated fatty acids (linoleic acid and arachidonic acid) are essential nutrients that must be obtained from food because the human body cannot synthesize them. However, the amounts required are small, and deficiencies are rarely seen. There is no dietary requirement for saturated fatty acids.

Phospholipids are components of cell membranes

Phospholipids belong to a group of lipids called **amphipathic lipids,** in which one end of each molecule is hydrophilic and the other end is hydrophobic (**FIG. 3-13**). The two ends of a phospho-

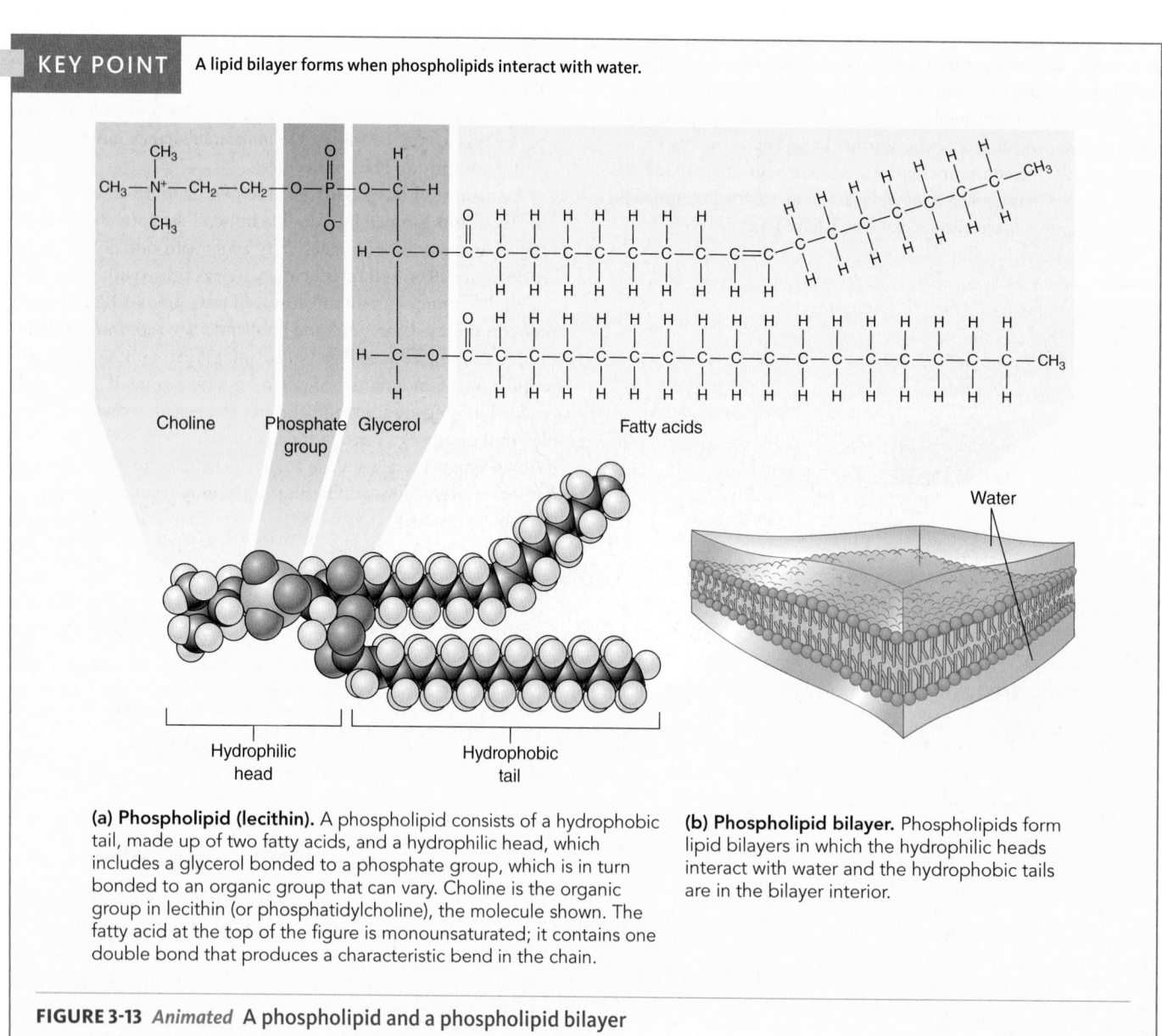

KEY POINT A lipid bilayer forms when phospholipids interact with water.

Choline   Phosphate group   Glycerol   Fatty acids

Hydrophilic head   Hydrophobic tail   Water

(a) Phospholipid (lecithin). A phospholipid consists of a hydrophobic tail, made up of two fatty acids, and a hydrophilic head, which includes a glycerol bonded to a phosphate group, which is in turn bonded to an organic group that can vary. Choline is the organic group in lecithin (or phosphatidylcholine), the molecule shown. The fatty acid at the top of the figure is monounsaturated; it contains one double bond that produces a characteristic bend in the chain.

(b) Phospholipid bilayer. Phospholipids form lipid bilayers in which the hydrophilic heads interact with water and the hydrophobic tails are in the bilayer interior.

FIGURE 3-13 *Animated* A phospholipid and a phospholipid bilayer lipid differ both physically and chemically. A **phospholipid** consists of a glycerol molecule attached at one end to two fatty acids and at the other end to a phosphate group linked to an organic compound such as choline. The organic compound usually contains nitrogen. (Note that phosphorus and nitrogen are absent in triacylglycerols, as shown in Figure 3-12b.) The fatty acid portion of the molecule (containing the two hydrocarbon "tails") is hydrophobic and not soluble in water. However, the portion composed of glycerol, phosphate, and the organic base (the "head" of the molecule) is ionized and readily water soluble. The amphipathic properties of phospholipids cause them to form lipid bilayers in aqueous (watery) solution. Thus, they are uniquely suited as the fundamental components of cell membranes (discussed in Chapter 5).

Carotenoids and many other pigments are derived from isoprene units

The orange and yellow plant pigments called **carotenoids** are classified with the lipids because they are insoluble in water and have an oily consistency. These pigments, found in the cells of plants, play a role in photosynthesis. Carotenoid molecules, such as β-carotene, and many other important pigments, consist of five-carbon hydrocarbon monomers known as **isoprene units** (FIG. 3-14).

Most animals convert carotenoids to vitamin A, which can then be converted to the visual pigment **retinal.** Three groups of animals—the mollusks, insects, and vertebrates—have eyes that use retinal in the process of light reception.

Notice that carotenoids, vitamin A, and retinal all have a pattern of double bonds alternating with single bonds. The electrons that make up these bonds can move about relatively easily when light strikes the molecule. Such molecules are *pigments*; they tend to be highly colored because the mobile electrons cause them to strongly absorb light of certain wavelengths and reflect light of other wavelengths.

Steroids contain four rings of carbon atoms

A **steroid** consists of carbon atoms arranged in four attached rings; three of the rings contain six carbon atoms, and the fourth contains five (FIG. 3-15). The length and structure of the side chains that extend from these rings distinguish one steroid from another. Like carotenoids, steroids are synthesized from isoprene units.

Among the steroids of biological importance are cholesterol, bile salts, reproductive hormones, and cortisol as well as other hormones secreted by the adrenal cortex. Cholesterol is an essential structural component of animal cell membranes, but when excess cholesterol in blood forms plaques on artery walls, the risk of cardiovascular disease increases (see Chapter 44).

Plant cell membranes contain molecules similar to cholesterol. Interestingly, some of these plant steroids block the intestine's absorption of cholesterol. Bile salts emulsify fats in the intestine so they can be enzymatically hydrolyzed. Steroid hormones regulate certain aspects of metabolism in a variety of animals and plants.

(a) Isoprene

(b) β-Carotene

(c) Vitamin A

(d) Retinal

FIGURE 3-14 Isoprene-derived compounds

(a) An isoprene subunit. (b) β-carotene, with dashed lines indicating the boundaries of the individual isoprene units within. The wavy line is the point at which most animals cleave the molecule to yield two molecules of (c) vitamin A. Vitamin A is converted to the visual pigment (d) retinal.

Some chemical mediators are lipids

Animal cells secrete chemicals to communicate with one another or to regulate their own activities. Some chemical mediators are produced by the modification of fatty acids that have been removed from membrane phospholipids. These include *prostaglandins,* which have varied roles, including promoting inflammation and smooth muscle contraction. Certain hormones, such as

(a) Cholesterol is an essential component of animal cell membranes.

(b) Cortisol is a steroid hormone secreted by the adrenal glands.

FIGURE 3-15 Steroids

Four attached rings—three six-carbon rings and one with five carbons—make up the fundamental structure of a steroid (*shown in green*). Note that some carbons are shared by two rings. In these simplified structures, a carbon atom is present at each angle of a ring; the hydrogen atoms attached directly to the carbon atoms have not been drawn. Steroids are mainly distinguished by their attached functional groups.

the juvenile hormone of insects, are also fatty acid derivatives (discussed in Chapter 49).

Review

- Why do saturated, unsaturated, and *trans* fatty acids differ in their properties?
- Why do phospholipids form lipid bilayers in aqueous conditions?

3.4 PROTEINS

■ LEARNING OBJECTIVES

7   Give an overall description of the structure and functions of proteins.

8   Describe the features that are shared by all amino acids and explain how amino acids are grouped into classes based on the characteristics of their side chains.

9   Distinguish among the four levels of organization of protein molecules.

TABLE 3-2	Major Classes of Proteins and Their Functions
Protein Class	Functions and Examples
Enzymes	Catalyze specific chemical reactions
Structural proteins	Strengthen and protect cells and tissues (e.g., collagen strengthens animal tissues)
Storage proteins	Store nutrients; particularly abundant in eggs (e.g., ovalbumin in egg white) and seeds (e.g., zein in corn kernels)
Transport proteins	Transport specific substances between cells (e.g., hemoglobin transports oxygen in red blood cells); move specific substances (e.g., ions, glucose, amino acids) across cell membranes
Regulatory proteins	Some are protein hormones (e.g., insulin); some control the expression of specific genes
Motile proteins	Participate in cellular movements (e.g., actin and myosin are essential for muscle contraction)
Protective proteins	Defend against foreign invaders (e.g., antibodies play a role in the immune system)

Proteins, macromolecules composed of amino acids, are the most versatile cell components. As will be discussed in Chapter 16, scientists have succeeded in sequencing virtually all the genetic information in a human cell, and the genetic information of many other organisms is being studied. Some people might think that the sequencing of genes is the end of the story, but it is actually only the beginning. Much genetic information is used to specify the structure of proteins, and biologists may devote most of the 21st century to understanding these extraordinarily multifaceted macromolecules that are of central importance in the chemistry of life. In a real sense, proteins are involved in virtually all aspects of metabolism because most **enzymes,** molecules that accelerate the thousands of different chemical reactions that take place in an organism, are proteins.

Proteins are assembled into a variety of shapes, allowing them to serve as major structural components of cells and tissues. For this reason, growth and repair, as well as maintenance of the organism, depend on proteins. As shown in **TABLE 3-2,** proteins perform many other functions. Each cell type contains characteristic forms, distributions, and amounts of protein that largely determine what the cell looks like and how it functions. A muscle cell contains large amounts of the proteins myosin and actin, which are responsible for its appearance as well as its ability to contract. The protein hemoglobin, found in red blood cells, is responsible for the specialized function of oxygen transport.

Amino acids are the subunits of proteins

Amino acids, the constituents of proteins, have an amino group (—NH$_2$) and a carboxyl group (—COOH) bonded to the same

FIGURE 3-16 An amino acid at pH 7

In living cells, amino acids exist mainly in their ionized form, as dipolar ions.

asymmetrical carbon atom, known as the **alpha carbon.** Amino acids in solution at neutral pH are mainly *dipolar ions;* that is, they possess a positive charge at one end and a negative charge at the opposite end. This is generally how amino acids exist at cell pH. Each carboxyl group (—COOH) donates a proton and becomes ionized (—COO⁻), whereas each amino group (—NH₂) accepts a proton and becomes —NH₃⁺ (**FIG. 3-16**). Because of the ability of their amino and carboxyl groups to accept and release protons, amino acids in solution resist changes in acidity and alkalinity and therefore are important biological buffers.

Twenty amino acids are commonly found in proteins, each identified by the variable side chain (R group) bonded to the α carbon (**FIG. 3-17**). Glycine, the simplest amino acid, has a hydrogen atom as its R group; alanine has a methyl (—CH₃) group. The amino acids are grouped in Figure 3-17 by the properties of their side chains. These broad groupings actually include amino acids with a fairly wide range of properties. Amino acids classified as having *nonpolar* side chains tend to have hydrophobic properties, whereas those classified as *polar* are more hydrophilic. An acidic amino acid has a side chain that contains a carboxyl group. At cell pH the carboxyl group is dissociated, giving the R group a negative charge. A basic amino acid becomes positively charged when the amino group in its side chain accepts a hydrogen ion. Acidic and basic side chains are ionic at cell pH and therefore hydrophilic.

Some proteins have unusual amino acids in addition to the 20 common ones. These rare amino acids are produced by the modification of common amino acids after they have become part of a protein. For example, after they have been incorporated into collagen, lysine and proline may be converted to hydroxylysine and hydroxyproline. These amino acids can form cross links between the peptide chains that make up collagen. Such cross links produce the firmness and great strength of the collagen molecule, which is a major component of cartilage, bone, and other connective tissues.

With some exceptions, prokaryotes and plants synthesize all their needed amino acids from simpler substances. If the proper raw materials are available, the cells of animals can manufacture some, but not all, of the biologically significant amino acids. **Essential amino acids** are those an animal cannot synthesize in amounts sufficient to meet its needs and must obtain from the diet. Animals differ in their biosynthetic capacities; what is an essential amino acid for one species may not be for another.

The essential amino acids for humans are isoleucine, leucine, lysine, methionine, phenylalanine, threonine, tryptophan, valine,

and histidine. Arginine is added to the list for children because they do not synthesize enough to support growth.

Peptide bonds join amino acids

Amino acids combine chemically with one another by a condensation reaction that bonds the carboxyl carbon of one molecule to the amino nitrogen of another (**FIG. 3-18**). The covalent carbon-to-nitrogen bond linking two amino acids is a **peptide bond.** When two amino acids combine, a **dipeptide** is formed; a longer chain of amino acids is a **polypeptide.** A protein consists of one or more polypeptide chains. Each polypeptide has a free amino group at one end and a free carboxyl group (belonging to the last amino acid added to the chain) at the opposite end. The other amino and carboxyl groups of the amino acid monomers (except those in side chains) are part of the peptide bonds. The process by which polypeptides are synthesized is discussed in Chapter 13.

A polypeptide may contain hundreds of amino acids joined in a specific linear order. The backbone of the polypeptide chain includes the repeating sequence

plus all other atoms *except those in the R groups.* The R groups of the amino acids extend from this backbone.

An almost infinite variety of protein molecules is possible, differing from one another in the number, types, and sequences of amino acids they contain. The 20 types of amino acids found in proteins may be thought of as letters of a protein alphabet; each protein is a very long sentence made up of amino acid letters.

Proteins have four levels of organization

The polypeptide chains making up a protein are twisted or folded to form a macromolecule with a specific *conformation,* or 3-D shape. Some polypeptide chains form long fibers. **Globular proteins** are tightly folded into compact, roughly spherical shapes. There is a close relationship between a protein's conformation and its function. For example, a typical enzyme is a globular protein with a unique shape that allows it to catalyze a specific chemical reaction. Similarly, the shape of a protein hormone enables it to combine with receptors on its target cell (the cell on which the hormone acts). Scientists recognize four main levels of protein organization: primary, secondary, tertiary, and quaternary.

Primary structure is the amino acid sequence

The sequence of amino acids, joined by peptide bonds, is the **primary structure** of a polypeptide chain. As discussed in Chapter 13, this sequence is specified by the instructions in a gene. Using analytical methods, investigators can determine the exact sequence of amino acids in a protein molecule. The primary structures of thousands of proteins are known. For example, glucagon, a hormone secreted by the pancreas, is a small polypeptide, consisting of only 29 amino acid units (**FIG. 3-19**).

Primary structure is always represented in a simple, linear, "beads-on-a-string" form. However, the overall conformation

(a) Nonpolar (hydrophobic)

Leucine (Leu, L)

Proline (Pro, P)

Alanine (Ala, A)

Valine (Val, V)

(b) Polar, uncharged

Threonine (Thr, T)

Serine (Ser, S)

Asparagine (Asn, N)

Glutamine (Gln, Q)

(c) Acidic

Aspartic acid (Asp, D)

Glutamic acid (Glu, E)

Methionine (Met, M)

Tryptophan (Trp, W)

Phenylalanine (Phe, F)

Isoleucine (Ile, I)

Glycine (Gly, G)

Cysteine (Cys, C)

Tyrosine (Tyr, Y)

Histidine (His, H)

(d) Basic

Lysine (Lys, K)

Arginine (Arg, R)

FIGURE 3-17 The 20 common amino acids

(a) Nonpolar amino acids have side chains that are relatively hydrophobic, whereas (b) polar amino acids have relatively hydrophilic side chains. Carboxyl groups and amino groups are electrically charged at cell pH; therefore, (c) acidic and (d) basic amino acids are hydrophilic. The standard three-letter and one-letter abbreviations appear beside the amino acid names.

63

FIGURE 3-18 *Animated* Peptide bonds

A dipeptide is formed by a condensation reaction, that is, by the removal of the equivalent of a water molecule from the carboxyl group of one amino acid and the amino group of another amino acid. The resulting peptide bond is a covalent, carbon-to-nitrogen bond. Note that the carbon is also part of a carbonyl group and that the nitrogen is also covalently bonded to a hydrogen. Additional amino acids can be added to form a long polypeptide chain with a free amino group at one end and a free carboxyl group at the other.

of a protein is far more complex, involving interactions among the various amino acids that make up the primary structure of the molecule. Therefore, the higher orders of structure—secondary, tertiary, and quaternary—ultimately derive from the specific amino acid sequence (the primary structure).

Secondary structure results from hydrogen bonding involving the backbone

Some regions of a polypeptide exhibit **secondary structure,** which is highly regular. The two most common types of secondary structure are the α-helix and the β-pleated sheet; the designations α and β refer simply to the order in which these two types of secondary structure were discovered. An **α-helix** is a region where a polypeptide chain forms a uniform helical coil (**FIG. 3-20a**). The helical structure is determined and maintained by the formation of hydrogen bonds between the backbones of the amino acids in successive turns of the spiral coil.

Each hydrogen bond forms between an oxygen with a partial negative charge and a hydrogen with a partial positive charge. The oxygen is part of the remnant of the carboxyl group of one amino acid; the hydrogen is part of the remnant of the amino group of the fourth amino acid down the chain. Thus, 3.6 amino acids are included in each complete turn of the helix. Every amino acid in an α-helix is hydrogen bonded in this way.

The α-helix is the basic structural unit of some fibrous proteins that make up wool, hair, skin, and nails. The elasticity of these fibers is due to a combination of physical factors (the helical shape) and chemical factors (hydrogen bonding). Although hydrogen bonds maintain the helical structure, these bonds can be broken, allowing the fibers to stretch under tension (like a telephone cord). When

the tension is released, the fibers recoil and hydrogen bonds reform. This explains why you can stretch the hairs on your head to some extent and they will snap back to their original length.

The hydrogen bonding in a **β-pleated sheet** takes place between different polypeptide chains, or different regions of a polypeptide chain that has turned back on itself (**FIG. 3-20b**). Each chain is fully extended; however, because each has a zigzag structure, the resulting "sheet" has an overall pleated conformation (much like a sheet of paper that has been folded to make a fan). Although the pleated sheet is strong and flexible, it is not elastic, because the distance between the pleats is fixed, determined by the strong covalent bonds of the polypeptide backbones. Fibroin, the protein of silk, is characterized by a β-pleated sheet structure, as are the cores of many globular proteins.

It is not uncommon for a single polypeptide chain to include both α-helical regions and regions with β-pleated sheet conformations. The properties of some biological materials result from such combinations. A spider's web is composed of a material that is extremely strong, flexible, and elastic. Once again we see function and structure working together, as these properties derive from the fact that spider silk is a composite of proteins with α-helical conformations (providing elasticity) and others with β-pleated sheet conformations (providing strength).

Tertiary structure depends on interactions among side chains

The **tertiary structure** of a protein molecule is the overall shape assumed by each individual polypeptide chain (**FIG. 3-21**). This 3-D structure is determined by four main factors that involve interactions among R groups (side chains) belonging to the same

^+H_3N—His—Ser—Gln—Gly—Thr—Phe—Thr—Ser—Asp—Tyr—Ser—Lys—Tyr—Leu—Asp—Ser—Arg—Arg—Ala—Gln—Asp—Phe—Val—Gln—Trp—Leu—Met—Asn—Thr—COO⁻
  1   2   3   4   5   6   7   8   9   10   11   12   13   14   15   16   17   18   19   20   21   22   23   24   25   26   27   28   29

FIGURE 3-19 Primary structure of a polypeptide

Glucagon is a very small polypeptide made up of 29 amino acids. The linear sequence of amino acids is indicated by ovals containing their abbreviated names (see Fig. 3-17).

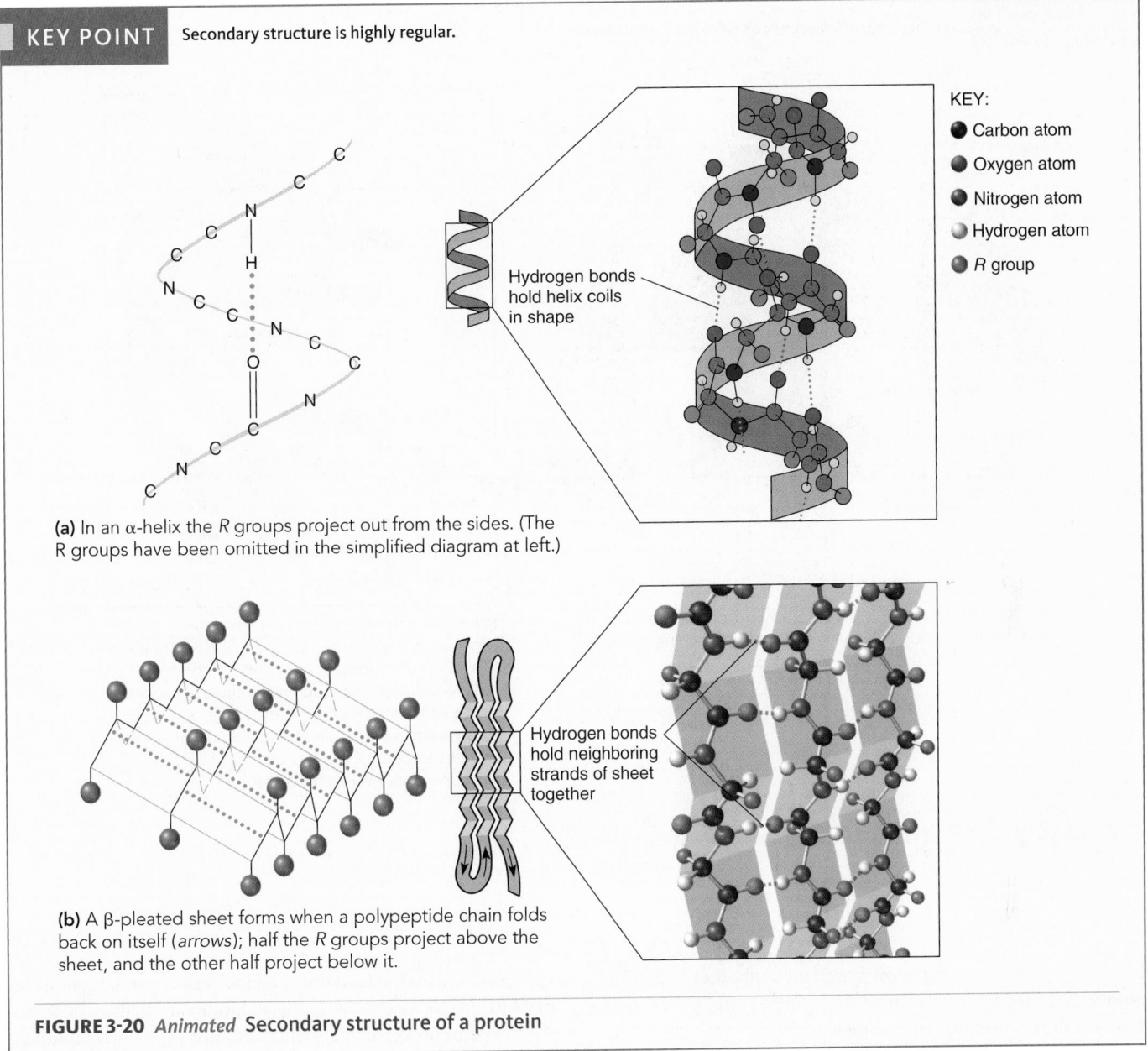

KEY:
- Carbon atom
- Oxygen atom
- Nitrogen atom
- Hydrogen atom
- *R* group

Hydrogen bonds hold helix coils in shape

(a) In an α-helix the *R* groups project out from the sides. (The *R* groups have been omitted in the simplified diagram at left.)

Hydrogen bonds hold neighboring strands of sheet together

(b) A β-pleated sheet forms when a polypeptide chain folds back on itself (*arrows*); half the *R* groups project above the sheet, and the other half project below it.

FIGURE 3-20 *Animated* Secondary structure of a protein

polypeptide chain. These include both weak interactions (hydrogen bonds, ionic bonds, and hydrophobic interactions) and strong covalent bonds.

1. Hydrogen bonds form between *R* groups of certain amino acid subunits.
2. An ionic bond can occur between an *R* group with a unit of positive charge and one with a unit of negative charge.
3. Hydrophobic interactions result from the tendency of nonpolar *R* groups to be excluded by the surrounding water and therefore to associate in the interior of the globular structure.
4. Covalent bonds known as *disulfide bonds* or *disulfide bridges* (—S—S—) may link the sulfur atoms of two cysteine subunits belonging to the same chain. A disulfide bridge forms when the sulfhydryl groups of two cysteines react; the two

hydrogens are removed, and the two sulfur atoms that remain become covalently linked.

Quaternary structure results from interactions among polypeptides

Many functional proteins are composed of two or more polypeptide chains, interacting in specific ways to form the biologically active molecule. **Quaternary structure** is the resulting 3-D structure. The same types of interactions that produce secondary and tertiary structure also contribute to quaternary structure; these include hydrogen bonding, ionic bonding, hydrophobic interactions, and disulfide bridges.

A functional antibody molecule, for example, consists of four polypeptide chains joined by disulfide bridges (see Chapter 45).

Tertiary structure depends on side chain interactions.

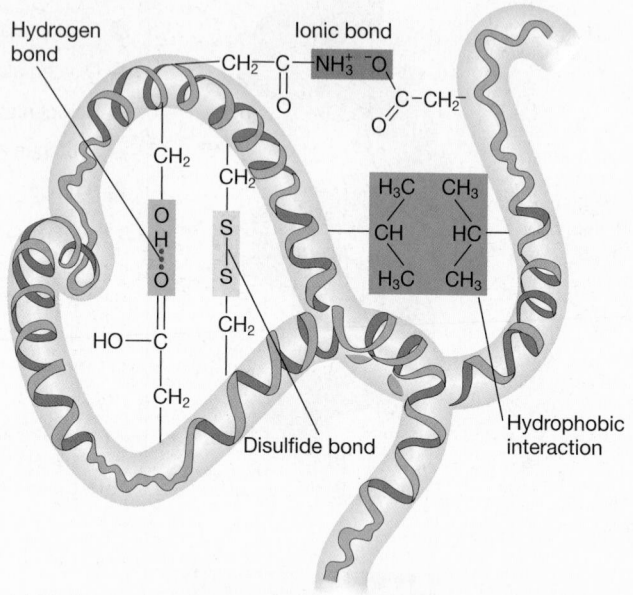

Hydrogen bond

Ionic bond

Disulfide bond

Hydrophobic interaction

(a) Hydrogen bonds, ionic bonds, hydrophobic interactions, and disulfide bridges between *R* groups hold the parts of the molecule in the designated shape.

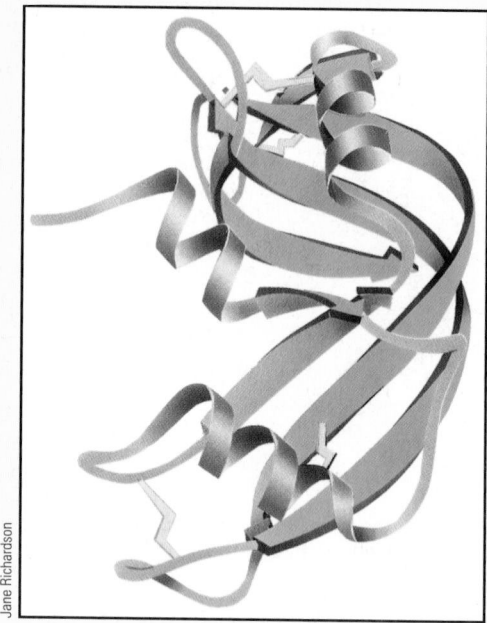

Jane Richardson

(b) In this drawing, α-helical regions are represented by purple coils, β-pleated sheets by broad green ribbons, and connecting regions by narrow tan ribbons. The interactions among *R* groups that stabilize the bends and foldbacks that give the molecule its overall conformation (tertiary structure) are represented in yellow. This protein is bovine ribonuclease a.

FIGURE 3-21 *Animated* Tertiary structure of a protein

Disulfide bridges are a common feature of antibodies and other proteins secreted from cells. These strong bonds stabilize the molecules in the extracellular environment.

Hemoglobin, the protein in red blood cells responsible for oxygen transport, is an example of a globular protein with a quaternary structure (**FIG. 3-22a**). Hemoglobin consists of 574 amino acids arranged in four polypeptide chains: two identical chains called *alpha chains* and two identical chains called *beta chains*.

Collagen, mentioned previously, has a fibrous type of quaternary structure that allows it to function as the major strengthener of animal tissues. It consists of three polypeptide chains wound about one another and bound by cross links between their amino acids (**FIG. 3-22b**).

The amino acid sequence of a protein determines its conformation

In 1972, U.S. researcher Christian B. Anfinsen was awarded the Nobel Prize in Chemistry for his studies on protein folding, which demonstrated that, at least under defined experimental conditions *in vitro* (outside a living cell), a polypeptide can spontaneously undergo folding processes that yield its normal, functional conformation. Since Anfinsen's pioneering work, many researchers studying various proteins and using a variety of highly sophisticated approaches have amassed evidence supporting the widely held conclusion that amino acid sequence is the ultimate determinant of protein conformation.

However, because conditions *in vivo* (in the cell) are quite different from defined laboratory conditions, proteins do not always fold spontaneously in the cell. On the contrary, scientists have learned that proteins known as **molecular chaperones** mediate the folding of other protein molecules. Molecular chaperones are thought to make the folding process more orderly and efficient and to prevent partially folded proteins from becoming inappropriately aggregated. However, there is no evidence that molecular chaperones actually dictate the folding pattern. For this reason, the existence of chaperones is not an argument against the idea that amino acid sequence determines conformation.

Proteins with two or more polypeptide chains have quaternary structure.

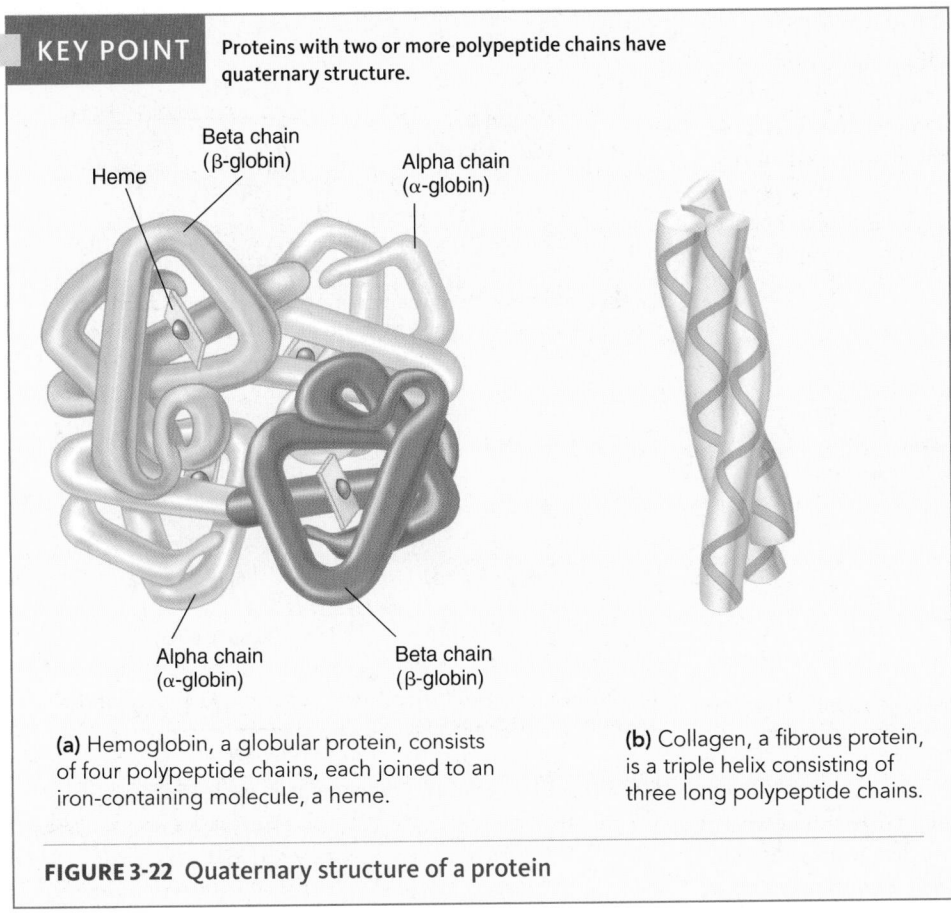

Heme
Beta chain (β-globin)
Alpha chain (α-globin)
Alpha chain (α-globin)
Beta chain (β-globin)

(a) Hemoglobin, a globular protein, consists of four polypeptide chains, each joined to an iron-containing molecule, a heme.

(b) Collagen, a fibrous protein, is a triple helix consisting of three long polypeptide chains.

FIGURE 3-22 Quaternary structure of a protein

Protein conformation determines function

The overall structure of a protein helps determine its biological activity. A single protein may have more than one distinct structural region, called a **domain,** each with its own function. Many proteins are modular, consisting of two or more globular domains, connected by less compact regions of the polypeptide chain.

Each domain may have a different function. For example, a protein may have one domain that attaches to a membrane and another that acts as an enzyme. The biological activity of a protein can be disrupted by a change in amino acid sequence that results in a change in conformation. For example, the genetic disease known as *sickle cell anemia* is due to a mutation that causes the substitution of the amino acid valine for glutamic acid at position 6 (the sixth amino acid from the amino end) in the beta chain of hemoglobin. The substitution of valine (which has a nonpolar side chain) for glutamic acid (which has a charged side chain) makes the hemoglobin less soluble and more likely to form crystal-like structures. This alteration of the hemoglobin affects the red blood cells, changing them to the crescent or sickle shapes that characterize this disease (see Fig. 16-8).

The biological activity of a protein may be affected by changes in its 3-D structure. When a protein is heated, subjected to significant pH changes, or treated with certain chemicals, its structure becomes disordered and the coiled peptide chains unfold, yielding a more random conformation. This unfolding, which is mainly due to the disruption of hydrogen bonds and ionic bonds, is typically accompanied by a loss of normal function. Such changes in shape and the accompanying loss of biological activity are termed *denaturation* of the protein.

For example, a denatured enzyme would lose its ability to catalyze a chemical reaction. An everyday example of denaturation occurs when we fry an egg. The consistency of the egg white protein, known as *albumin,* changes to a solid. Denaturation generally cannot be reversed (you cannot "unfry" an egg). However, under certain conditions, some proteins have been denatured and have returned to their original shape and biological activity when normal environmental conditions were restored.

Protein conformation is studied through a variety of methods

The architecture of a protein can be ascertained directly through various types of analysis, such as the X-ray diffraction studies discussed in Chapter 12. Because these studies are tedious and costly, researchers are developing alternative approaches, which rely heavily on the enormous databases generated by the Human Genome Project and related initiatives.

Today a protein's primary structure can be determined rapidly through the application of genetic engineering techniques (discussed in Chapter 15) or by the use of sophisticated technology such as mass spectrometry. Researchers use these amino acid sequence data to predict a protein's higher levels of structure. As you have seen, side chains interact in relatively predictable ways, such as through ionic and hydrogen bonds. In addition, regions with certain types of side chains are more likely to form α-helices or β-pleated sheets. Computer programs make such predictions, but these are often imprecise because of the many possible combinations of folding patterns.

Computers are an essential part of yet another strategy. Once the amino acid sequence of a polypeptide has been determined, researchers use computers to search databases to find polypeptides with similar sequences. If the conformations of any of those polypeptides or portions have already been determined directly by X-ray diffraction or other techniques, this information can be extrapolated to make similar correlations between amino acid sequence and 3-D structure for the protein under investigation. These predictions are increasingly reliable, as more information is added to the databases every day.

Misfolded proteins are implicated in human diseases

Studies on the mechanisms of protein folding, and on the relationship between the activity of a protein and its conformation, are increasingly of medical importance. For example, as discussed in Chapter 24, mad cow disease and related diseases in humans and other animals are caused by misfolded proteins called *prions*. Other serious diseases in which misfolded proteins play an important role include Alzheimer's disease (see Chapter 41) and Huntington's disease (see Chapter 16).

Review

- Draw the structural formula of a simple amino acid. What is the importance of the carboxyl group, amino group, and *R* group?
- How does the primary structure of a polypeptide influence its secondary and tertiary structures?

3.5 NUCLEIC ACIDS

■ LEARNING OBJECTIVE

10 Describe the components of a nucleotide. Name some nucleic acids and nucleotides, and discuss the importance of these compounds in living organisms.

Nucleic acids transmit hereditary information and determine what proteins a cell manufactures. Two classes of nucleic acids are found in cells: deoxyribonucleic acid and ribonucleic acid. **Deoxyribonucleic acid (DNA)** composes the genes, the hereditary material of the cell, and contains instructions for making all the proteins, as well as all the RNA the organism needs. **Ribonucleic acid (RNA)** participates in the process in which amino acids are linked to form polypeptides. Some types of RNA, known as **ribozymes,** can even act as specific biological catalysts. Like proteins, nucleic acids are large, complex molecules. The name *nucleic acid* reflects the fact that they are acidic and were first identified, by Swiss biochemist Friedrich Miescher in 1870, in the nuclei of pus cells.

Nucleic acids are polymers of **nucleotides,** molecular units that consist of (1) a five-carbon sugar, either **deoxyribose** (in DNA) or **ribose** (in RNA); (2) one or more phosphate groups, which make the molecule acidic; and (3) a nitrogenous base, a ring compound that contains nitrogen. The nitrogenous base may be either a double-ring **purine** or a single-ring **pyrimidine** (**FIG. 3-23**). DNA commonly contains the purines **adenine (A)** and **guanine (G),** the pyrimidines **cytosine (C)** and **thymine (T),** the sugar deoxyribose, and phosphate. RNA contains the purines adenine and guanine, and the pyrimidines cytosine and **uracil (U),** together with the sugar ribose, and phosphate. The molecules of nucleic acids are made of linear chains of nucleotides, which are joined by **phosphodiester linkages,** each consisting of a phosphate group and the covalent bonds that attach it to the sugars of adjacent nucleotides (**FIG. 3-24**). Note that each nucleotide is defined by its particular base and that nucleotides can be joined in any sequence. A nucleic acid molecule is uniquely defined by its specific sequence of nucleotides, which constitutes a kind of code (see

(a) Pyrimidines. The three major pyrimidine bases found in nucleotides are cytosine, thymine (in DNA only), and uracil (in RNA only).

(b) Purines. The two major purine bases found in nucleotides are adenine and guanine.

FIGURE 3-23 *Animated* **Components of nucleotides**
The hydrogens indicated by the white boxes are removed when the base is attached to a sugar.

Chapter 13). Whereas RNA is usually composed of one nucleotide chain, DNA consists of two nucleotide chains held together by hydrogen bonds and entwined around each other in a double helix (see Fig. 1-7).

Some nucleotides are important in energy transfers and other cell functions

In addition to their importance as subunits of DNA and RNA, nucleotides perform other vital functions in living cells. **Adenosine triphosphate (ATP),** composed of adenine, ribose, and three phosphates (see Fig. 7-5), is of major importance as the primary energy currency of all cells (see Chapter 7). The two terminal phosphate groups are joined to the nucleotide by covalent bonds. These are traditionally indicated by wavy lines, which indicate that ATP can transfer a phosphate group to another molecule, making that molecule more reactive. In this way ATP is able to donate some of its chemical energy. Most of the readily available chemical energy of the cell is associated with the phosphate groups of ATP. Like ATP, **guanosine triphosphate (GTP),** a nucleotide that contains the base guanine, can transfer energy by transferring a phosphate group and also has a role in cell signaling (see Chapter 6).

A nucleotide may be converted to an alternative form with specific cell functions. ATP, for example, is converted to **cyclic adenosine monophosphate (cyclic AMP, or cAMP)** by the enzyme adenylyl cyclase (**FIG. 3-25**). Cyclic AMP regulates certain

FIGURE 3-24 RNA, a nucleic acid

Nucleotides, each with a specific base, are joined by phosphodiester linkages.

Cyclic AMP

FIGURE 3-25 Cyclic adenosine monophosphate (cAMP)

The single phosphate is part of a ring connecting two regions of the ribose.

ter 7, **nicotinamide adenine dinucleotide** has a primary role in oxidation and reduction reactions in cells. It can exist in an oxidized form ($\mathbf{NAD^+}$) that is converted to a reduced form (**NADH**) when it accepts electrons (in association with hydrogen; see Fig. 7-7). These electrons, along with their energy, are transferred to other molecules.

Review

- How does the structure of a nucleotide relate to its function?

3.6 IDENTIFYING BIOLOGICAL MOLECULES

▪ LEARNING OBJECTIVE

11 Compare the functions and chemical compositions of the major groups of organic compounds: carbohydrates, lipids, proteins, and nucleic acids.

Although the classes of biological molecules may seem overwhelming at first, you will learn to distinguish them readily by understanding their chief attributes. These are summarized in **TABLE 3-3**.

Review

- How can you distinguish a pentose sugar from a hexose sugar? a disaccharide from a sterol? an amino acid from a monosaccharide? a phospholipid from a triacylglycerol? a protein from a polysaccharide? a nucleic acid from a protein?

cell functions, such as cell signaling, and is important in the mechanism by which some hormones act. A related molecule, **cyclic guanosine monophosphate (cGMP),** also plays a role in certain cell signaling processes.

Cells contain several dinucleotides, which are of great importance in metabolic processes. For example, as discussed in Chap-

TABLE 3-3   Classes of Biologically Important Organic Compounds

Class and Component Elements	Description	How to Recognize	Principal Function in Living Systems
Carbohydrates C, H, O	Contain approximately 1 C:2 H:1 O (but make allowance for loss of oxygen when sugar units as nucleic acids and glycoproteins are linked)	Count the carbons, hydrogens, and oxygens.	Cell fuel; energy storage; structural component of plant cell walls; component of other compounds such as nucleic acids and glycoproteins
	1. *Monosaccharides* (simple sugars). Mainly five-carbon (pentose) molecules such as ribose or six-carbon (hexose) molecules such as glucose and fructose	Look for the ring shapes:	Cell fuel; components of other compounds
	2. *Disaccharides.* Two sugar units linked by a glycosidic bond, e.g., maltose, sucrose	Count sugar units.	Components of other compounds; form of sugar transported in plants
	3. *Polysaccharides.* Many sugar units linked by glycosidic bonds, e.g., glycogen, cellulose	Count sugar units.	Energy storage; structural components of plant cell walls
Lipids C, H, O (sometimes N, P)	Contain much less oxygen relative to carbon and hydrogen than do carbohydrates		Energy storage; cellular fuel, components of cells; thermal insulation
	1. *Fats.* Combination of glycerol with one to three fatty acids. Monoacylglycerol contains one fatty acid; diacylglycerol contains two fatty acids; triacylglycerol contains three fatty acids. If fatty acids contain double carbon-to-carbon linkages (C=C), they are unsaturated; otherwise, they are saturated.	Look for glycerol at one end of molecule:	Cell fuel; energy storage
	2. *Phospholipids.* Composed of glycerol attached to one or two fatty acids and to an organic base containing phosphorus	Look for glycerol and side chain containing phosphorus and nitrogen.	Components of cell membranes
	3. *Steroids.* Complex molecules containing carbon atoms arranged in four attached rings (Three rings contain six carbon atoms each, and the fourth ring contains five.)	Look for four attached rings:	Some are hormones; others include cholesterol, bile salts, vitamin D; components of cell membranes
	4. *Carotenoids.* Orange and yellow pigments; consist of isoprene units	Look for isoprene units.	Converted to retinal (important in photoreception) and vitamin A
Proteins C, H, O, N (usually S)	One or more polypeptides (chains of amino acids) coiled or folded in characteristic shapes	Look for amino acid units joined by C—N bonds.	Serve as enzymes; structural components; muscle proteins; hemoglobin
Nucleic Acids C, H, O, N, P	Backbone composed of alternating pentose and phosphate groups, from which nitrogenous bases project. DNA contains the sugar deoxyribose and the bases guanine, cytosine, adenine, and thymine. RNA contains the sugar ribose and the bases guanine, cytosine, adenine, and uracil. Each molecular subunit, called a nucleotide, consists of a pentose, a phosphate, and a nitrogenous base.	Look for a pentose-phosphate backbone. DNA forms a double helix.	Storage, transmission, and expression of genetic information; some important in energy transfers, cell signaling, and other aspects of metabolism.

3.1 *(page 47)*

1 Describe the properties of carbon that make it the central component of organic compounds.

- Each carbon atom forms four covalent bonds with up to four other atoms; these bonds are single, double, or triple bonds. Carbon atoms form straight or branched chains or join into rings. Carbon forms covalent bonds with a greater number of different elements than does any other type of atom.

2 Define the term *isomer* and distinguish among the three principal isomer types.

- **Isomers** are compounds with the same molecular formula but different structures.
- **Structural isomers** differ in the covalent arrangements of their atoms. **Geometric isomers,** or *cis–trans* isomers, differ in the spatial arrangements of their atoms. **Enantiomers** are isomers that are mirror images of each other. Cells can distinguish between these configurations.

3 Identify the major functional groups present in organic compounds and describe their properties.

- **Hydrocarbons,** organic compounds consisting of only carbon and hydrogen, are nonpolar and **hydrophobic.** The **methyl group** is a hydrocarbon group.
- Polar and ionic functional groups interact with one another and are **hydrophilic.** Partial charges on atoms at opposite ends of a bond are responsible for the polar property of a functional group. **Hydroxyl** and **carbonyl groups** are polar.
- **Carboxyl** and **phosphate groups** are acidic, becoming negatively charged when they release hydrogen ions. The **amino group** is basic, becoming positively charged when it accepts a hydrogen ion.

4 Explain the relationship between polymers and macromolecules.

- Long chains of **monomers** (similar organic compounds) linked through **condensation reactions** are called **polymers.** Large polymers such as polysaccharides, proteins, and DNA are referred to as **macromolecules.** They can be broken down by **hydrolysis reactions.**

CENGAGENOW™ Learn more about condensation and hydrolysis reactions by clicking on the figure in CengageNOW.

3.2 *(page 51)*

5 Distinguish among monosaccharides, disaccharides, and polysaccharides. Compare storage polysaccharides with structural polysaccharides.

- **Carbohydrates** contain carbon, hydrogen, and oxygen in a ratio of approximately one carbon to two hydrogens to one oxygen. **Monosaccharides** are simple sugars such as glucose, fructose, and ribose. Two monosaccharides join by a **glycosidic linkage** to form a **disaccharide** such as maltose or sucrose.

- Most carbohydrates are **polysaccharides,** long chains of repeating units of a simple sugar. Carbohydrates are typically stored in plants as the polysaccharide **starch** and in animals as the polysaccharide

glycogen. The cell walls of plants are composed mainly of the structural polysaccharide **cellulose.**

CENGAGENOW™ Learn more about starch and cellulose by clicking on the figure in CengageNOW.

3.3 *(page 56)*

6 Distinguish among fats, phospholipids, and steroids, and describe the composition, characteristics, and biological functions of each.

- **Lipids** are composed mainly of hydrocarbon-containing regions, with few oxygen-containing (polar or ionic) functional groups. Lipids have a greasy or oily consistency and are relatively insoluble in water.
- **Triacylglycerol,** the main storage form of fat in organisms, consists of a molecule of **glycerol** combined with three **fatty acids. Monoacylglycerols** and **diacylglycerols** contain one and two fatty acids, respectively. A fatty acid can be either **saturated** with hydrogen or **unsaturated.**

- **Phospholipids** are structural components of cell membranes. A phospholipid consists of a glycerol molecule attached at one end to two fatty acids and at the other end to a phosphate group linked to an organic compound such as choline.
- **Steroid** molecules contain carbon atoms arranged in four attached rings. Cholesterol, bile salts, and certain hormones are important steroids.

CENGAGENOW™ Learn more about triacylglycerol and other lipids by clicking on the figures in CengageNOW.

3.4 *(page 60)*

7 Give an overall description of the structure and functions of proteins.

- **Proteins** are complex macromolecules made of simpler subunits, called **amino acids,** joined by **peptide bonds.** Two amino acids combine to form a **dipeptide.** A longer chain of amino acids is a **polypeptide.** Proteins are the most versatile class of biological molecules, serving a variety of functions, such as **enzymes,** structural components, and cell regulators.
- Proteins are composed of various linear sequences of 20 different amino acids.

CENGAGENOW™ Learn more about amino acids and peptide bonds by clicking on the figures in CengageNOW.

8 Describe the features that are shared by all amino acids and explain how amino acids are grouped into classes based on the characteristics of their side chains.

$$
\begin{array}{c}
COO^- \\
| \\
H_3N^+ - C - H \\
| \\
CH_3
\end{array}
$$

- All amino acids contain an amino group and a carboxyl group. Amino acids vary in their side chains, which dictate their chemical properties—nonpolar, polar, acidic, or basic. Amino acids generally exist as dipolar ions at cell pH and serve as important biological buffers.

9 Distinguish among the four levels of organization of protein molecules.

- **Primary structure** is the linear sequence of amino acids in the polypeptide chain.
- **Secondary structure** is a regular conformation, such as an **α-helix** or a **β-pleated sheet;** it is due to hydrogen bonding between elements of the backbones of the amino acids.
- **Tertiary structure** is the overall shape of the polypeptide chains, as dictated by chemical properties and interactions of the side chains of specific amino acids. Hydrogen bonds, ionic bonds, hydrophobic interactions, and disulfide bridges contribute to tertiary structure.
- **Quaternary structure** is determined by the association of two or more polypeptide chains.

    CENGAGENOW˜   Learn more about the structure of a protein by clicking on the figure in CengageNOW.

3.5 *(page 68)*

10 Describe the components of a nucleotide. Name some nucleic acids and nucleotides, and discuss the importance of these compounds in living organisms.

- The **nucleic acids DNA** and **RNA,** composed of long chains of nucleotide subunits, store and transfer information that specifies the sequence of amino acids in proteins and ultimately the structure and function of the organism.
- **Nucleotides** are composed of a two-ring **purine** or one-ring **pyrimidine** nitrogenous base, a five-carbon sugar (**ribose** or **deoxyribose**), and one or more phosphate groups.
- **ATP (adenosine triphosphate)** is a nucleotide of special significance in energy metabolism. **NAD$^+$** is also involved in energy metabolism through its role as an electron (hydrogen) acceptor in biological oxidation and reduction reactions.

3.6 *(page 69)*

11 Compare the functions and chemical compositions of the major groups of organic compounds: carbohydrates, lipids, proteins, and nucleic acids.

- Review Table 3-3.

TEST YOUR UNDERSTANDING

1. Carbon is particularly well suited to be the backbone of organic molecules because (a) it can form both covalent bonds and ionic bonds (b) its covalent bonds are very irregularly arranged in three-dimensional space (c) its covalent bonds are the strongest chemical bonds known (d) it can bond to atoms of a large number of other elements (e) all the bonds it forms are polar

2. The structures depicted are (a) enantiomers (b) different views of the same molecule (c) geometric (*cis–trans*) isomers (d) both geometric isomers and enantiomers (e) structural isomers

$$\begin{array}{ccc} CH_3 & CH_3 \\ | & | \\ H-C-C-H \\ | & | \\ H & H \end{array} \qquad \begin{array}{ccc} H & CH_3 \\ | & | \\ H-C-C-H \\ | & | \\ CH_3 & H \end{array}$$

3. Which of the following is a nonpolar molecule? (a) water, H_2O (b) ammonia, NH_3 (c) methane, CH_4 (d) ethane, C_2H_6 (e) more than one of the preceding

4. The synthetic process by which monomers are covalently linked is (a) hydrolysis (b) isomerization (c) condensation (d) glycosidic linkage (e) ester linkage

5. A monosaccharide designated as an aldehyde sugar contains (a) a terminal carboxyl group (b) an internal carboxyl group (c) a terminal carbonyl group (d) an internal carbonyl group (e) a terminal carboxyl group and an internal carbonyl group

6. Structural polysaccharides typically (a) have extensive hydrogen bonding between adjacent molecules (b) are much more hydrophilic than storage polysaccharides (c) have much stronger covalent bonds than do storage polysaccharides (d) consist of alternating α-glucose and β-glucose subunits (e) form helical structures in the cell

7. Saturated fatty acids are so named because they are saturated with (a) hydrogen (b) water (c) hydroxyl groups (d) glycerol (e) double bonds

8. Fatty acids in phospholipids and triacylglycerols interact with one another by (a) disulfide bridges (b) van der Waals interactions (c) covalent bonds (d) hydrogen bonds (e) fatty acids do not interact with one another

9. Which pair of amino acid side groups would be most likely to associate with each other by an ionic bond?
    1. $-CH_3$
    2. $-CH_2-COO^-$
    3. $-CH_2-CH_2-NH_3^+$
    4. $-CH_2-CH_2-COO^-$
    5. $-CH_2-OH$
    (a) 1 and 2 (b) 2 and 4 (c) 1 and 5 (d) 2 and 5 (e) 3 and 4

10. Which of the following levels of protein structure may be affected by hydrogen bonding? (a) primary and secondary (b) primary and tertiary (c) secondary, tertiary, and quaternary (d) primary, secondary, and tertiary (e) primary, secondary, tertiary, and quaternary

11. Which of the following associations between *R* groups are the strongest? (a) hydrophobic interactions (b) hydrogen bonds (c) ionic bonds (d) peptide bonds (e) disulfide bridges

12. Each phosphodiester linkage in DNA or RNA includes a phosphate joined by covalent bonds to (a) two bases (b) two sugars (c) two additional phosphates (d) a sugar, a base, and a phosphate (e) a sugar and a base

CRITICAL THINKING

1. Like oxygen, sulfur forms two covalent bonds. However, sulfur is far less electronegative. In fact, it is approximately as electronegative as carbon. How would the properties of the various classes of biological molecules be altered if you were to replace all the oxygen atoms with sulfur atoms?

2. Hydrogen bonds and van der Waals interactions are much weaker than covalent bonds, yet they are vital to organisms. Why?

3. **EVOLUTION LINK.** In what ways are all species alike biochemically? Why? Identify some ways in which species may differ from one another biochemically. Why?

4. **EVOLUTION LINK.** The total number of possible amino acid sequences in a polypeptide chain is staggering. Given that there are 20 amino acids, potentially there could be 20^{100} different amino acid sequences (an impossibly large number), just for polypeptides only 100 amino acids in length. However, the actual number of different polypeptides occurring in organisms is only a tiny fraction of this. Why?

5. **EVOLUTION LINK.** Each amino acid could potentially exist as one of two possible enantiomers, known as the D-form and the L-form (based on the arrangement of the groups attached to the asymmetric α carbon). However, in all organisms, only L-amino acids are found in proteins. What does this suggest about the evolution of proteins?

 Additional questions are available in CengageNOW at www.cengage.com/login.

4 Organization of the Cell

The cytoskeleton. The cell shown here was stained with fluorescent antibodies (specific proteins) that bind to proteins associated with DNA (*purple*) and to a protein (tubulin) in microtubules (*green*). Microfilaments (*red*) are also visible. This type of microscopy, known as confocal fluorescence microscopy, shows the extensive distribution of microtubules in this cell.

Jennifer C. Waters/Photo Researchers, Inc.

KEY CONCEPTS

4.1 The cell is the basic unit of life; its organization and size are critical in maintaining homeostasis, and its size and shape are adapted for its function.

4.2 Biologists study cells using microscopes and biochemical techniques such as cell fractionation.

4.3 Unlike prokaryotic cells, eukaryotic cells have internal membranes that divide the cell into compartments, allowing cells to conduct specialized activities within separate, small areas.

4.4 In eukaryotic cells, genetic information coded in DNA is located in the nucleus, which is typically the most prominent organelle in the cell.

4.5 Among the many organelles in the cytoplasm are ribosomes, which synthesize proteins; endoplasmic reticulum and Golgi complexes, which process proteins; and mitochondria and chloroplasts, which convert energy from one form to another.

4.6 The cytoskeleton is a dynamic internal framework that functions in various types of cell movement.

4.7 Most eukaryotic cells are surrounded by a cell coat; in addition, many animal cells are surrounded by an extracellular matrix; cells of most bacteria, archaea, fungi, and plants are surrounded by a cell wall.

The cell is the smallest unit that can carry out all activities we associate with life. When provided with essential nutrients and an appropriate environment, some cells can be kept alive and growing in the laboratory for many years. By contrast, no isolated part of a cell is capable of sustained survival. As you read this chapter, recall the discussion of systems biology in Chapter 1. Even as we describe individual components of cells, we discuss how these components work together, generating complex biological systems within the cell. The cell itself is a highly intricate biological system, and groups of cells make up tissues, organs, and organisms. Each of these is a biological system.

Most prokaryotes and many protists and fungi consist of a single cell. In contrast, most plants and animals are composed of millions of cells. Cells are the building blocks of complex multicellular organisms. Although they are basically similar, cells are also extraordinarily diverse and versatile. They are modified in a variety of ways to carry out specialized functions.

The cell is composed of a vast array of inorganic and organic ions and molecules, including water, salts, carbohydrates, lipids, proteins, and nucleic acids. These molecules are organized to form the structures within the cell and its biochemical pathways. Genetic information is stored in DNA molecules and is faithfully replicated. This information is passed to each new generation of cells during cell division. Information in DNA codes for specific proteins that, in turn, determine cell structure and function.

Cells exchange materials and energy with the environment. All living cells need one or more sources of energy, but a cell rarely obtains energy in a form that is immediately usable. Cells convert energy from one form to another, and that energy is used to carry out various activities, ranging from mechanical work to chemical synthesis. Cells convert energy to a convenient form, usually chemical energy stored in adenosine triphosphate, or ATP (see Chapter 3).

Both the chemical reactions that convert energy from one form to another and the mechanisms of information transfer are essentially the same in all cells, from those in bacteria to those of large, multicellular plants and animals. Such similarities suggest evolutionary relationships.

Thanks to advances in technology, cell biologists use increasingly sophisticated tools in their search to better understand the structure and function of cells. For example, investigation of the cytoskeleton (cell skeleton), currently an active and exciting area of research, has been greatly enhanced by advances in microscopy. In the photomicrograph, we see the extensive distribution of microtubules in cells. Microtubules are key components of the cytoskeleton. They help maintain cell shape, function in cell movement, and facilitate transport of materials within the cell.

4.1 THE CELL: BASIC UNIT OF LIFE

■ LEARNING OBJECTIVES

1 Describe the cell theory and relate it to the evolution of life.
2 Summarize the relationship between cell organization and homeostasis.
3 Explain the relationship between cell size and homeostasis.

Cells, the building blocks of organisms, are dramatic examples of the underlying unity of all living things.

The cell theory is a unifying concept in biology

Two German scientists, botanist Matthias Schleiden in 1838 and zoologist Theodor Schwann in 1839, used inductive reasoning to conclude that all plants and animals consist of cells. These investigators used their own observations and those of other scientists to reach their conclusions. Later, Rudolf Virchow, another German scientist, observed cells dividing and giving rise to daughter cells. In 1855, Virchow proposed that new cells form only by the division of previously existing cells. The work of Schleiden, Schwann, and Virchow contributed greatly to the development of the **cell theory,** the unifying concept that (1) cells are the basic living units of organization and function in all organisms and (2) that all cells come from other cells.

About 1880, another German biologist, August Weismann, added an important corollary to Virchow's concept by pointing out that the ancestry of all the cells alive today can be traced back to ancient times. Evidence that all living cells have a common origin is provided by the basic similarities in their structures and in the molecules of which they are made. When we examine a variety of diverse organisms, ranging from simple bacteria to the most complex plants and animals, we find striking similarities at the cellular level. Careful studies of shared cell characteristics help us trace the evolutionary history of various organisms and furnish powerful evidence that all organisms alive today had a common origin.

The organization of all cells is basically similar

The organization of cells and their small size allow them to maintain **homeostasis,** an appropriate internal environment. Cells experience constant changes in their environments, such as deviations in salt concentration, pH, and temperature. They must work continuously to restore and maintain the internal conditions that enable their biochemical mechanisms to function.

In order for the cell to maintain homeostasis, its contents must be separated from the external environment. The **plasma membrane** is a structurally distinctive surface membrane that surrounds all cells. By making the interior of the cell an enclosed compartment, the plasma membrane allows the chemical composition of the cell to be different from that outside the cell. The plasma membrane serves as a selective barrier between the cell contents and the outer environment. Cells exchange materials with the environment and can accumulate needed substances and energy stores.

Most cells have internal structures, called **organelles,** that are specialized to carry out metabolic activities, such as converting energy to usable forms, synthesizing needed compounds, and manufacturing structures necessary for functioning and reproduction. Each cell has genetic instructions coded in its DNA, which is concentrated in a limited region of the cell.

Cell size is limited

Although their sizes vary over a wide range (**FIG. 4-1**), most cells are microscopic and must be measured by very small units. The basic unit of linear measurement in the metric system (see inside back cover) is the meter (m), which is just a little longer than a yard. A millimeter (mm) is 1/1000 of a meter and is about as long as the bar enclosed in parentheses (-). The micrometer (μm) is the most convenient unit for measuring cells. A bar 1 μm long is 1/1,000,000 (one millionth) of a meter, or 1/1000 of a millimeter—far too short to be seen with the unaided eye. Most of us have difficulty thinking about units that are too small to see, but it is helpful to remember that a micrometer has the same relationship to a millimeter that a millimeter has to a meter (1/1000).

As small as it is, the micrometer is actually too large to measure most cell components. For this purpose biologists use the nanometer (nm), which is 1/1,000,000,000 (one billionth) of a meter, or 1/1000 of a micrometer. To mentally move down to the world of the nanometer, recall that a millimeter is 1/1000 of a meter, a micrometer is 1/1000 of a millimeter, and a nanometer is 1/1000 of a micrometer.

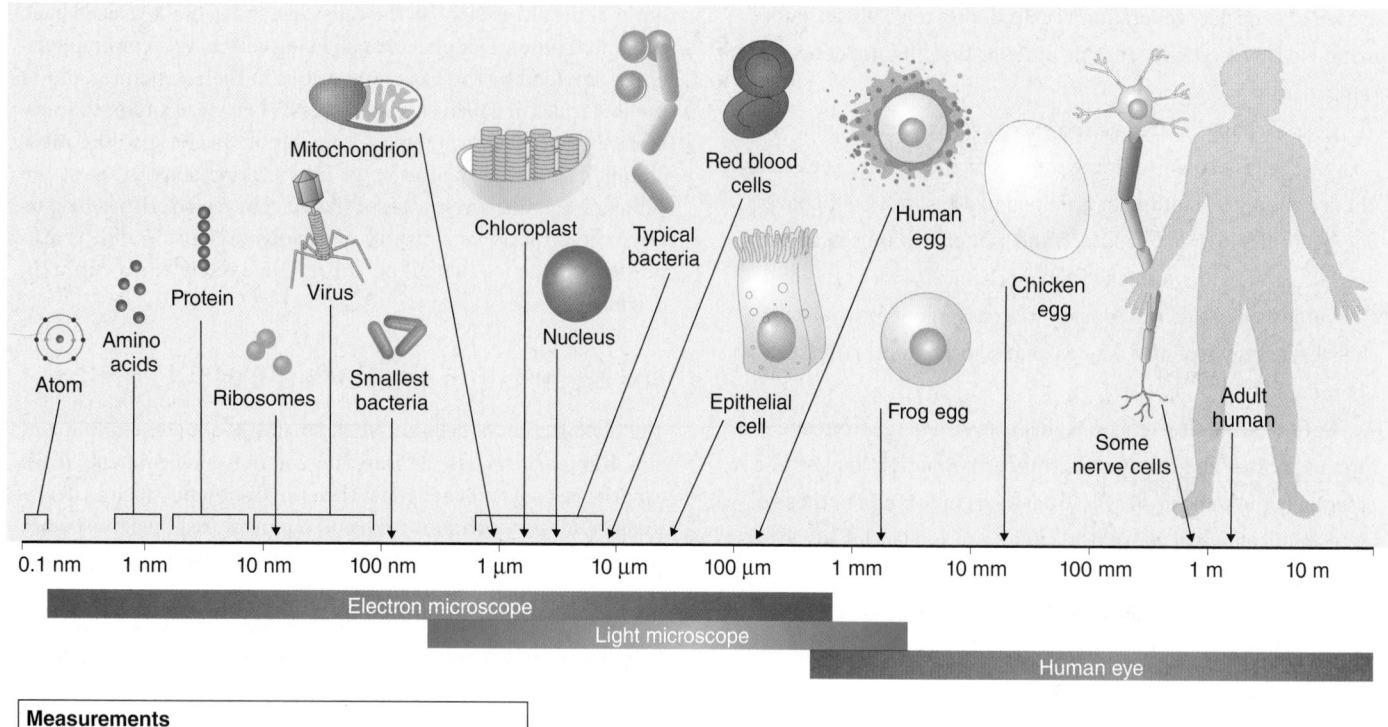

FIGURE 4-1 Biological size and cell diversity

We can compare relative size from the chemical level to the level of an entire organism by using a logarithmic scale (multiples of 10). The prokaryotic cells of most bacteria range in size from 1 to 10 μm long. Most eukaryotic cells are between 10 and 30 μm in diameter. Mitochondria are about the size of small bacteria, whereas chloroplasts are usually larger, about 5 μm long. Ova (egg cells) are among the largest cells. Although microscopic, some nerve cells are very long. The cells shown here are not drawn to scale.

A few specialized algae and animal cells are large enough to be seen with the naked eye. A human egg cell, for example, is about 130 μm in diameter, or approximately the size of the period at the end of this sentence. The largest cells are birds' eggs, but they are not typical cells because they include large amounts of food reserves—the yolk and the egg white. The functioning part of the cell is a small mass on the surface of the yolk.

Why are most cells so small? If you consider what a cell must do to maintain homeostasis and to grow, it may be easier to understand the reasons for its small size. A cell must take in food and other materials and must rid itself of waste products generated by metabolic reactions. Everything that enters or leaves a cell must pass through its plasma membrane. The plasma membrane contains specialized "pumps" and channels with "gates" that selectively regulate the passage of materials into and out of the cell. The plasma membrane must be large enough relative to the cell volume to keep up with the demands of regulating the passage of materials. Thus, a critical factor in determining cell size is the ratio of its surface area (the plasma membrane) to its volume (**FIG. 4-2**).

As a cell becomes larger, its volume increases at a greater rate than its surface area (its plasma membrane), which effectively places an upper limit on cell size. Above some critical size, the number of molecules required by the cell could not be transported into the cell fast enough to sustain its needs. In addition, the cell would not be able to regulate its concentration of various ions or efficiently export its wastes.

Of course, not all cells are spherical or cuboid. Because of their shapes, some very large cells have relatively favorable ratios of surface area to volume. In fact, some variations in cell shape represent a strategy for increasing the ratio of surface area to volume. For example, many large plant cells are long and thin, which increases their surface area–to-volume ratio. Some cells, such as epithelial cells lining the small intestine, have fingerlike projections of the plasma membrane, called **microvilli,** that significantly increase the surface area for absorbing nutrients and other materials (see Fig. 47-10).

Another reason for the small size of cells is that, once inside, molecules must be transported to the locations where they are converted into other forms. Because cells are small, the distances molecules travel within them are relatively short. Thus, molecules are rapidly available for cell activities.

Cell size and shape are adapted to function

The sizes and shapes of cells are adapted to the particular functions they perform. Some cells, such as amoebas and white blood

Surface Area (mm²)	Surface area = height × width × number of sides × number of cubes	24 (2 × 2 × 6 × 1)	48 (1 × 1 × 6 × 8)
Volume (mm³)	Volume = height × width × length × number of cubes	8 (2 × 2 × 2 × 1)	8 (1 × 1 × 1 × 8)
Surface Area/ Volume Ratio	Surface area/ volume	3 (24:8)	6 (48:8)

FIGURE 4-2 Surface area–to-volume ratio
The surface area of a cell must be large enough relative to its volume to allow adequate exchange of materials with the environment. Although their volumes are the same, eight small cells have a much greater surface area (plasma membrane) in relation to their total volume than one large cell does. In the example shown, the ratio of the total surface area to total volume of eight 1 mm cubes is double the surface area–to-volume ratio of the single large cube.

cells, change their shape as they move about. Sperm cells have long, whiplike tails, called *flagella,* for locomotion. Nerve cells have long, thin extensions that enable them to transmit messages over great distances. The extensions of some nerve cells in the human body may be as long as 1 meter! Certain epithelial cells are almost rectangular and are stacked much like building blocks to form sheetlike tissues. (Epithelial tissue covers the body and lines body cavities.)

Review

- How does the cell theory contribute to our understanding of the evolution of life?
- How does the plasma membrane help maintain homeostasis?
- Why is the relationship between surface area and volume of a cell important in determining cell-size limits?

4.2 METHODS FOR STUDYING CELLS

■ LEARNING OBJECTIVE

4 Describe methods that biologists use to study cells, including microscopy and cell fractionation.

One of the most important tools biologists use for studying cell structures is the microscope. Using a microscope he had made, Robert Hooke, an English scientist, first described cells in 1665 in his book *Micrographia.* Hooke examined a piece of cork and drew and described what he saw. Hooke chose the term *cell* because the tissue reminded him of the small rooms monks lived in. Interestingly, what

Hooke saw were not actually living cells but the walls of dead cork cells (**FIG. 4-3a**). Much later, scientists recognized that the interior enclosed by the walls is the important part of living cells.

A few years after Hooke's discovery and inspired by Hooke's work, the Dutch naturalist Antonie van Leeuwenhoek viewed living cells with small lenses that he made. Leeuwenhoek was highly skilled at grinding lenses and was able to magnify images more than 200 times. Among his important discoveries were bacteria, protists, blood cells, and sperm cells. Leeuwenhoek was among the first scientists to report cells in animals. Leeuwenhoek was a merchant and not formally trained as a scientist. However, his skill, curiosity, and diligence in sharing his discoveries with scientists at the Royal Society of London brought an awareness of microscopic life to the scientific world. Unfortunately, Leeuwenhoek did not share his techniques, and it was more than 100 years later, in the late 19th century, before microscopes were sufficiently developed for biologists to seriously focus their attention on the study of cells.

Light microscopes are used to study stained or living cells

The **light microscope (LM),** the type used by most students, consists of a tube with glass lenses at each end. Because it contains several lenses, the modern light microscope is referred to as a *compound microscope.* Visible light passes through the specimen being observed and through the lenses. Light is refracted (bent) by the lenses, magnifying the image. Images obtained with light microscopes are referred to as light micrographs, or **LMs.**

Two features of a microscope determine how clearly a small object can be viewed: magnification and resolving power. **Magnification** is the ratio of the size of the image seen with the microscope to the actual size of the object. The best light microscopes usually magnify an object no more than 2000 times. **Resolution,** or **resolving power,** is the capacity to distinguish fine detail in an image; it is defined as the minimum distance between two points at which they can both be seen separately rather than as a single, blurred point. Resolving power depends on the quality of the lenses and the wavelength of the illuminating light. As the wavelength decreases, the resolution increases.

The visible light used by light microscopes has wavelengths ranging from about 400 nm (violet) to 700 nm (red); this limits the resolution of the light microscope to details no smaller than the diameter of a small bacterial cell (about 0.2 μm). By the early 20th century, refined versions of the light microscope became available.

The interior of many cells is transparent and it is difficult to discern specific cell structures. Organic chemists have contributed greatly to light microscopy by developing biological stains that enhance contrast in the microscopic image. Staining has enabled biologists to discover the many different internal cell structures,

Cells are too small to be studied with the naked eye. Biologists use microscopes to view cells and structures inside cells. Many types of microscopes have been developed. Here we look at photomicrographs of *Paramecia* (a group of ciliated protists) made using several kinds of light microscopes.

(a) Robert Hooke's drawing of cork cells.

(b) Bright-field (stained).

(c) Dark-field.

(d) Phase contrast.

(e) Differential-interference-contrast (Nomarski).

(f) Confocal. Plasma membrane and contractile vacuoles are stained red. Proton pumps associated with the contractile vacuoles are stained yellow.

Using a crude microscope that he constructed, Robert Hooke looked at a thin slice of cork and drew what he saw. Biologists now view cells in more detail using the more sophisticated microscopes and techniques that have been developed. In the light microscope, a beam of light passes through the specimen being observed and through the lenses. The lenses refract the light, which magnifies the image. Bright-field microscopy can be enhanced by staining. The phase contrast and differential-interference-contrast microscopes enhance detail by increasing the differences in optical density in different regions of the cells.

FIGURE 4-3 *Animated* Using light microscopy

the organelles. Unfortunately, most methods used to prepare and stain cells for observation also kill them in the process.

Light microscopes with special optical systems now permit biologists to study living cells. In *bright-field microscopy,* an image is formed by transmitting light through a cell (or other specimen) (**FIG. 4-3b**). Because there is little contrast, the details of cell structure are not visible. In *dark-field microscopy,* rays of light are directed

from the side, and only light scattered by the specimen enters the lenses. The cell is seen as a bright image against a dark background (**FIG. 4-3c**). The specimen does not need to be stained.

Phase contrast microscopy and *Nomarski differential-interference-contrast microscopy* take advantage of variations in density within the cell (**FIG. 4-3d** and **e**). These variations in density cause differences in the way various regions of the cytoplasm refract (bend) light. Using these microscopes, scientists can observe living cells in action; they can view numerous internal structures that are constantly changing shape and location.

Cell biologists use the *fluorescence microscope* to detect the locations of specific molecules in cells. In the fluorescence microscope, filters transmit light that is emitted by fluorescently stained molecules. Fluorescent stains (like paints that glow under black light) are molecules that absorb light energy of one wavelength and then release some of that energy as light of a longer wavelength. These stains bind specifically to DNA or to specific protein molecules. The molecules absorb ultraviolet light and emit light of a different color. Cells can be stained, and the location of the labeled molecules can be determined, by observing the source of the fluorescent light within the cell. Biologists commonly use a fluorescent molecule known as green fluorescent protein (GFP) that occurs naturally in jellyfish. GFP has been valuable in observing specific proteins in living cells.

Some fluorescent stains chemically bond to *antibodies,* protein molecules important in internal defense. The antibody binds to a highly specific region of a molecule in the cell. A single type of antibody molecule binds to only one type of structure, such as a part of a specific protein or some of the sugars in a specific polysaccharide. Purified fluorescent antibodies known to bind to a specific protein are used to determine where that protein is located within the cell.

Confocal microscopy produces a sharper image than standard fluorescence microscopy (**FIG. 4-3f**). Living cells that have been labeled with fluorescent dye are mounted on a microscope slide. The confocal laser scanning microscope is a computerized microscope. A beam of ultraviolet light from a laser is focused at a specific depth within the cell. The fluorescent label emits visible light, and the investigator can visualize objects in a single plane of focus. The microscope produces optical sections (see the photomicrograph in the chapter introduction). A computer reassembles the images so that a series of optical sections from different planes of the cell can be used to construct a three-dimensional image. Powerful computer-imaging methods greatly improve the resolution of structures labeled by fluorescent dyes.

Electron microscopes provide a high-resolution image that can be greatly magnified

Even with improved microscopes and techniques for staining cells, ordinary light microscopes can distinguish only the gross details of many cell parts (**FIG. 4-4a**). In many cases, you can clearly see only the outline of an organelle. With the development of the **electron microscope (EM),** which came into wide use in the 1950s, researchers could begin to study the fine details, or **ultrastructure,** of cells.

The resolving power for the average human adult eye is about 100 μm. The best light microscopes have a resolving power of about 0.2 μm (200 nm). In comparison, some electron microscopes have resolving powers of just less than 1 nm. This is possible because electrons have very short wavelengths, on the order of about 0.1 to 0.2 nm. Although such resolution is difficult to achieve with biological material, researchers can approach that resolution when examining isolated molecules such as proteins and DNA. This high degree of resolution permits magnifications of more than 1 million

times as compared to typical magnifications of no more than 1500 to 2000 times in light microscopy.

The image formed by the electron microscope is not directly visible. The electron beam itself consists of energized electrons, which, because of their negative charge, can be focused by electromagnets just as images are focused by glass lenses in a light microscope (**FIG. 4-4b**). Two main types of electron microscopes are the **transmission electron microscope (TEM)** and the **scanning electron microscope (SEM).** The acronyms TEM and SEM also identify that a micrograph was prepared using a transmission or scanning EM. Electron micrographs are black and white. They are often colorized to highlight various structures.

In transmission electron microscopy, the specimen is embedded in plastic and then cut into extraordinarily thin sections (50 to 100 nm thick) with a glass or diamond knife. A section is then placed on a small metal grid. The electron beam passes through the specimen and then falls onto a photographic plate or a fluorescent screen. When you look at TEMs in this chapter (and elsewhere), keep in mind that each represents only a thin cross section of a cell.

Researchers detect certain specific molecules in electron microscope images by using antibody molecules to which very tiny gold particles are bound. The dense gold particles block the electron beam and identify the location of the proteins recognized by the antibodies as precise black spots on the electron micrograph.

In the scanning electron microscope, the electron beam does not pass through the specimen. Instead, the specimen is coated with a thin film of gold or some other metal. When the electron beam strikes various points on the surface of the specimen, secondary electrons are emitted whose intensity varies with the contour of the surface. The recorded emission patterns of the secondary electrons give a 3-D picture of the surface (**FIG. 4-4c**). The SEM provides information about the shape and external features of the specimen that cannot be obtained with the TEM.

Note that the LM, TEM, and SEM are focused by similar principles. A beam of light or an electron beam is directed by the condenser lens onto the specimen and is magnified by the objective lens and the eyepiece in the light microscope or by the objective lens and the projector lens in the TEM. The TEM image is focused onto a fluorescent screen, and the SEM image is viewed on a type of television screen. Lenses in electron microscopes are actually electromagnets that bend the beam of electrons.

Several other types of microscopes are now available, including two additional kinds of electron microscopes. Digital microscopes that use cameras to send a digital image to a monitor have also been developed.

Biologists use biochemical techniques to study cell components

The EM is a powerful tool for studying cell structure, but it has limitations. The methods used to prepare cells for electron microscopy kill them and may alter their structure. Furthermore, electron microscopy provides few clues about the functions of organelles and other cell components. To determine what organelles actually do, researchers use a variety of biochemical techniques.

Cell fractionation is a technique for separating (fractionating) different parts of cells so that they can be studied by physical and chemical methods. Generally, cells are broken apart in a

Electron microscopes have much greater resolving power than light microscopes. Electron microscopes can also magnify images to a much greater extent than light microscopes.

Light microscope

Light beam
Ocular lens

Objective lens
Specimen
Condenser lens
Light source

Transmission electron microscope

Electron gun
Electron beam
First condenser lens (electromagnet)
Specimen

Projector lens (electromagnetic)

Film or screen

Scanning electron microscope

Second condenser lens
Scanning coil
Final (objective) lens
Cathode ray tube synchronized with scanning coil

Secondary electrons
Specimen

Electron detector

Courtesy of T. K. Maugel, University of Maryland

100 μm

1 μm

100 μm

(a) A phase contrast light microscope can be used to view stained or living cells, but at relatively low resolution.

(b) The transmission electron microscope (TEM) produces a high-resolution image that can be greatly magnified. A small part of a thin slice through the *Paramecium* is shown.

(c) The scanning electron microscope (SEM) provides a clear view of surface features.

How Is It Done? In an electron microscope, a beam of electrons is focused on or through the specimen. Instead of glass lenses, electromagnetic lenses are used to form the image. Here we compare images of the protist *Paramecium* made using a phase contrast light microscope with images made using two types of electron microscopes. These three microscopes produce distinctive images of cells.

FIGURE 4-4 *Animated* **Using electron microscopes**

blender. The resulting mixture, called the **cell homogenate,** is subjected to centrifugal force by spinning in a **centrifuge** (**FIG. 4-5a**). The powerful ultracentrifuge can spin at speeds exceeding 100,000 revolutions per minute (rpm), generating a centrifugal force of $500,000 \times G$ (a G is equal to the force of gravity). Centrifugal force separates the extract into two fractions: a pellet and a supernatant. The *pellet* that forms at the bottom of the tube contains heavier materials, such as nuclei, packed together. The *supernatant,* the liquid above the pellet, contains lighter particles, dissolved molecules, and ions.

After the pellet is removed, the supernatant can be centrifuged again at a higher speed to obtain a pellet that contains the next-heaviest cell components, for example, mitochondria and chloroplasts. In **differential centrifugation,** the supernatant is spun at successively higher speeds, permitting various cell components to be separated on the basis of their different sizes and densities (**FIG. 4-5b**).

The pellets can be resuspended and their components can be further purified by **density gradient centrifugation.** In this procedure, the centrifuge tube is filled with a series of solutions of decreasing density. For example, sucrose solutions can be used. The concentration of sucrose is highest at the bottom of the tube and decreases gradually so that it is lowest at the top. The resuspended pellet is placed in a layer on top of the density gradient. Because the densities of organelles differ, each migrates during centrifugation. Each type of organelle forms a band at the position in the gradient where its own density equals that of the sucrose solution (**FIG. 4-5c**).

Why Is It Used? Cell fractionation is used to separate (fractionate) cell components according to their size and density.

(a) Centrifugation. Due to centrifugal force, large or very dense particles move toward the bottom of a tube and form a pellet.

(b) Differential centrifugation.

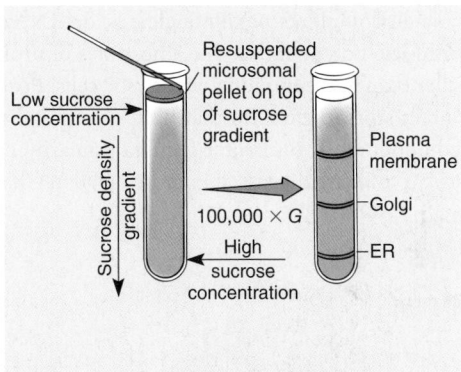

(c) Density gradient centrifugation.

How Is It Done? Cells are broken up in a blender. The cell homogenate (the resulting mixture) is then spun in a centrifuge. As a result of centrifugal force, the heaviest cell components, the nuclei, form a pellet at the bottom of the tube. The supernatant (the liquid above the pellet) can then be spun at a higher speed. The next heaviest component, the mitochondria and chloroplasts, form a pellet, and the supernatant can be spun at a higher speed. This process can be repeated several times. The pellet can be further purified by density gradient centrifugation (see text for further explanation).

FIGURE 4-5 Cell fractionation

Purified organelles can then be studied. For example, they can be examined to determine what kinds of proteins and other molecules they might contain, or what types of chemical reactions take place within them.

Review

- What is the main advantage of the electron microscope? Explain.
- What is cell fractionation? Describe the process.

4.3 PROKARYOTIC AND EUKARYOTIC CELLS

■ LEARNING OBJECTIVES

5   Compare and contrast the general characteristics of prokaryotic and eukaryotic cells, and contrast plant and animal cells.

6   Describe three functions of cell membranes.

Recall from Chapter 1 that two basic types of cells are known: **prokaryotic cells** and **eukaryotic cells.** Bacteria and archaea are prokaryotic cells. All other known organisms consist of eukaryotic cells.

Organelles of prokaryotic cells are not surrounded by membranes

Prokaryotic cells are typically smaller than eukaryotic cells. In fact, the average prokaryotic cell is only about 1/10 the diameter of the average eukaryotic cell. In prokaryotic cells, the DNA is typically located in a limited region of the cell called a **nuclear area,** or **nucleoid.** Unlike the nucleus of eukaryotic cells, the nuclear area is not enclosed by a membrane (**FIG. 4-6**). The term *prokaryotic,* meaning "before the nucleus," refers to this major difference between prokaryotic and eukaryotic cells. Other types of internal membrane–enclosed organelles are also absent in prokaryotic cells.

Like eukaryotic cells, prokaryotic cells have a plasma membrane that surrounds the cell. The plasma membrane confines the contents of the cell to an internal compartment. In some prokaryotic cells, the plasma membrane may be folded inward to form a complex of membranes along which many of the cell's metabolic reactions take place. Most prokaryotic cells have **cell walls,** which are extracellular structures that enclose the entire cell, including the plasma membrane.

Many prokaryotes have **flagella** (sing., *flagellum*), long fibers that project from the surface of the cell. Prokaryotic flagella, which operate like propellers, are important in locomotion. Their structure is different from that of flagella found in eukaryotic cells. Some prokaryotes also have hairlike projections called *fimbriae,* which are used to adhere to one another or to attach to cell surfaces of other organisms.

The dense internal material of the bacterial cell contains **ribosomes,** small complexes of ribonucleic acid (RNA) and protein that synthesize polypeptides. The ribosomes of prokaryotic cells are smaller than those found in eukaryotic cells. Prokaryotic cells also contain storage granules that hold glycogen, lipid, or phosphate compounds. This chapter focuses primarily on eukaryotic cells. Prokaryotes are discussed in more detail in Chapter 25.

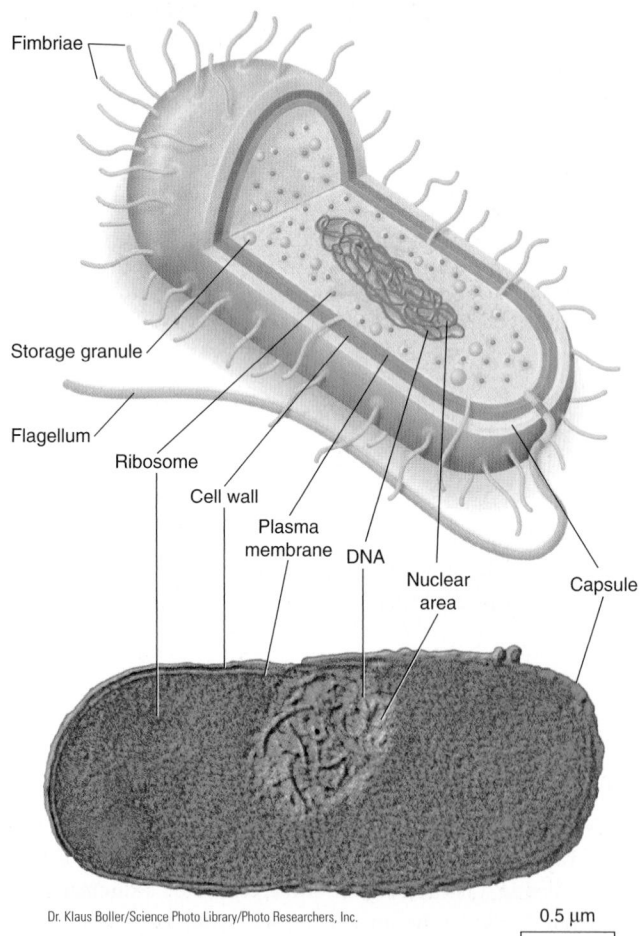

FIGURE 4-6 *Animated* Structure of a prokaryotic cell

This colorized TEM shows a thin lengthwise slice through an *Escherichia coli* bacterium. Note the prominent nuclear area containing the genetic material (DNA). *E. coli* is a normal inhabitant of the human intestine, but under certain conditions some strains can cause infections.

Dr. Klaus Boller/Science Photo Library/Photo Researchers, Inc.

0.5 μm

Membranes divide the eukaryotic cell into compartments

Eukaryotic cells are characterized by highly organized membrane-enclosed organelles, including a prominent *nucleus,* which contains DNA, the hereditary material. The term *eukaryotic* means "true nucleus." Early biologists thought cells consisted of a homogeneous jelly, which they called *protoplasm.* With the electron microscope and other modern research tools, perception of the environment within the cell has been greatly expanded. We now know that the cell is highly organized and complex (**FIGS. 4-7** through **4-10**). The eukaryotic cell has its own control center, internal transportation system, power plants, factories for making needed materials, packaging plants, and even a "self-destruct" system.

Biologists refer to the part of the cell outside the nucleus as **cytoplasm** and the part of the cell within the nucleus as **nucleoplasm.** Various organelles are suspended within the fluid component of the cytoplasm, which is called the **cytosol.** The term *cytoplasm* includes both the cytosol and all the organelles other than the nucleus.

The many specialized organelles of eukaryotic cells solve some of the problems associated with large size, so eukaryotic cells can be larger than prokaryotic cells. Eukaryotic cells also differ from prokaryotic cells in having a supporting framework, or cytoskeleton, important in maintaining shape and transporting materials within the cell.

Some organelles are present only in specific cells. For example, *chloroplasts,* structures that trap sunlight for energy conversion, are only in cells that carry on photosynthesis, such as certain plant or algal cells. Cells of fungi and plants are surrounded by a *cell wall* external to the plasma membrane. Plant cells also contain a large, membrane-enclosed *vacuole.* We discuss these and other differences among major types of cells throughout this chapter. Plant and animal cells are compared in Figures 4-7 and 4-8 and also in Figures 4-9 and 4-10.

Cell membranes have unique properties that enable membranous organelles to carry out a wide variety of functions. For example, cell membranes never have free ends. As a result, a membranous organelle always contains at least one enclosed internal space or compartment. These membrane-enclosed compartments allow certain cell activities to be localized within specific regions of the cell. Reactants located in only a small part of the total cell volume are far more likely to come in contact, dramatically increasing the rate of the reaction. On the other hand, membrane-enclosed compartments keep certain reactive compounds away from other parts of the cell that they might adversely affect. Compartmentalizing also allows many different activities to go on simultaneously.

Membranes serve as important work surfaces. For example, many chemical reactions in cells are carried out by enzymes that are bound to membranes. Because the enzymes that carry out successive steps of a series of reactions are organized close together on a membrane surface, certain series of chemical reactions occur more rapidly.

Membranes allow cells to store energy. The membrane serves as a barrier that is somewhat analogous to a dam on a river. As we will discuss in Chapter 5, there is both an electric charge difference and a concentration difference on the two sides of the membrane.

These differences constitute an *electrochemical gradient*. Such gradients store energy and so have *potential energy* (discussed in Chapter 7). As particles of a substance move across the membrane from the side of higher concentration to the side of lower concentration, the cell can convert some of this potential energy to the chemical energy of ATP molecules. This process of energy conversion (discussed in Chapters 7, 8, and 9) is a basic mechanism that cells use to capture and convert the energy necessary to sustain life.

In a eukaryotic cell, several types of membranes make up the internal membrane system, or **endomembrane system.** In Figures 4-7 and 4-8 (also see Figs. 4-9 and 4-10), notice how membranes divide the cell into many compartments: the nucleus, endoplasmic reticulum (ER), Golgi complex, lysosomes, vesicles, and vacuoles. Although it is not internal, the plasma membrane is also included because it participates in the activities of the endomembrane system. (Mitochondria and chloroplasts are also separate compartments but are not generally considered part of the endomembrane system because they function somewhat independently of other membranous organelles.)

Some organelles have direct connections between their membranes and other compartments. Others transport materials in **vesicles,** small, membrane-enclosed sacs formed by "budding" from

5 μm

Plasma membrane   Chromatin   Nucleolus   Nucleus

Golgi complex

Ribosomes

Rough endoplasmic reticulum

Zymogen granules

Mitochondria

Smooth endoplasmic reticulum

FIGURE 4-8 TEM of a human pancreas cell and an interpretive drawing

Most of the structures of a typical animal cell are present. However, like most cells, this one has certain structures associated with its specialized functions. Pancreas cells such as the one shown here secrete large amounts of digestive enzymes. The large, dark, circular bodies in the TEM and the corresponding structures in the drawing are zymogen granules, which contain inactive enzymes. When released from the cell, the enzymes catalyze chemical reactions such as the breakdown of peptide bonds of ingested proteins in the intestine. Most of the membranes visible in this section are part of the rough endoplasmic reticulum, an organelle specialized to manufacture protein. Can you label the TEM?

5 μm

Nucleus   Starch grain

Rough endoplasmic reticulum

Ribosome

Vacuole

Prolamellar body

Golgi complex

Plasma membrane

Intercellular space   Chloroplasts   Cell wall

FIGURE 4-7 TEM of a plant cell and an interpretive drawing

Most of this cross section of a cell from the leaf of a young bean plant (*Phaseolus vulgaris*) is dominated by a vacuole. Prolamellar bodies are membranous regions typically seen in developing chloroplasts. Can you label the TEM?

Cristae

Membranous
sacs

Golgi complex

Mitochondrion

Bloom and Fawcett Textbook of Histology

Bloom and Fawcett Textbook of Histology

Cell wall

Plasma membrane

Vacuole

Granum

Stroma

Smooth ER

Rough ER

Ribosomes

Nuclear
envelope

Nucleolus

Nuclear
pores

Chromatin

E. H. Newcomb and W. P. Wergin, Biological Photo Service

Bloom and Fawcett Textbook of Histology

Dr. Donald Fawcett/Visuals Unlimited, Inc.

Chloroplast

Rough and smooth endoplasmic
reticulum (ER)

Nucleus

FIGURE 4-9 *Animated* Composite diagram of a plant cell

Plant cells typically have a cell wall, chloroplasts, and prominent vacuoles. The TEMs show specific structures or areas of the cell. Some plant cells do not have all the organelles shown here. For example, leaf and stem cells that carry on photosynthesis contain chloroplasts, whereas root cells do not. Many of the organelles, such as the nucleus, mitochondria, and endoplasmic reticulum (ER), are characteristic of all eukaryotic cells.

Chromatin

Nuclear envelope

Nuclear pores

Nucleolus

Nucleus

Bloom and Fawcett Textbook of Histology

Membranous sacs of Golgi

Golgi complex

Bloom and Fawcett Textbook of Histology

Plasma membrane

Lysosome

Nuclear envelope

Cristae

Ribosomes

Rough ER

Smooth ER

Rough and smooth endoplastic reticulum (ER)

Dr. Donald Fawcett/Visuals Unlimited, Inc.

Centrioles

B. F. King, Biological Photo Service

Mitochondrion

Bloom and Fawcett Textbook of Histology

FIGURE 4-10 *Animated* **Composite diagram of an animal cell**

This generalized animal cell is shown in a realistic context surrounded by adjacent cells, which cause it to be slightly compressed. The TEMs show the structure of various organelles. Depending on the cell type, certain organelles may be more or less prominent.

the membrane of another organelle. Vesicles carry cargo from one organelle to another. A vesicle can form as a "bud" from the membrane of one organelle and then move to another organelle to which it fuses, thus delivering its contents into another compartment.

Review

- What are two important differences between prokaryotic and eukaryotic cells?
- What are three ways that a plant cell might differ from an animal cell?
- How do membrane-enclosed organelles facilitate cell metabolism?
- What organelles belong to the endomembrane system?

4.4 THE CELL NUCLEUS

■ LEARNING OBJECTIVE

7 Describe the structure and functions of the nucleus.

Typically, the **nucleus** is the most prominent organelle in the cell. It is usually spherical or oval in shape and averages 5 μm in diameter. Because of its size and the fact that it often occupies a relatively fixed position near the center of the cell, some early investigators guessed long before experimental evidence was available that the nucleus served as the control center of the cell. In the 19th century, biologists discovered that the marine alga *Acetabularia* consists of a single cell (**FIG. 4-11**). At up to 5 cm (2 in) in length, *Acetabularia* is small for a seaweed but gigantic for a cell. It consists of a rootlike holdfast; a long, cylindrical stalk; and a cuplike cap. The nucleus is in the holdfast, about as far away from the cap as it can be. Because it is a single giant cell, *Acetabularia* is easy for researchers to manipulate.

If the cap of *Acetabularia* is removed experimentally, another one grows after a few weeks. Such **regeneration** is common among

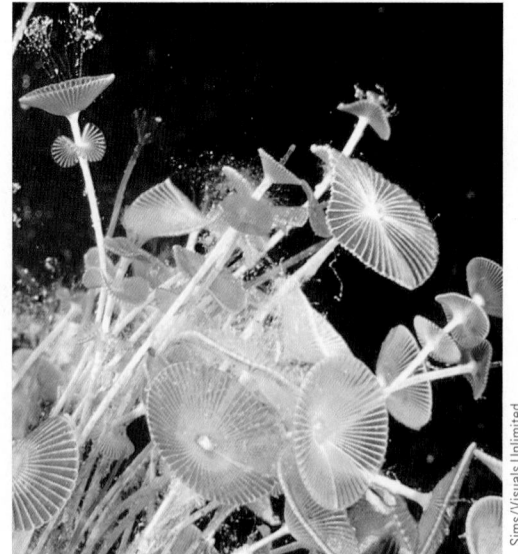

FIGURE 4-11 LM of *Acetabularia*
To the romantically inclined, the little seaweed *Acetabularia* resembles a mermaid's wineglass, although the literal translation of its name, "vinegar cup," is somewhat less elegant. *Acetabularia*, which consists of a single cell, has been a model organism for investigating the role of the nucleus.

L. Sims/Visuals Unlimited

KEY EXPERIMENTS

EXPERIMENT 1

QUESTION: What controls the shape of the cap in *Acetabularia*?

HYPOTHESIS: Something in the stalk or holdfast of *Acetabularia* controls the shape of the cap.

EXPERIMENT: Hämmerling removed the caps from *A. mediterranea* and *A. crenulata*. He then grafted together the two capless algae (**FIG. a**).

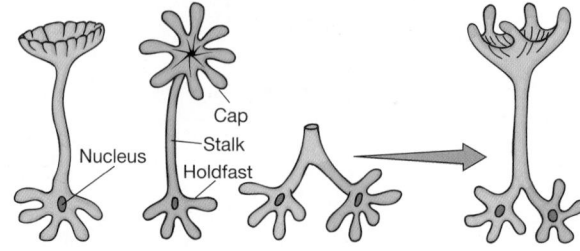

Cap
Stalk
Nucleus
Holdfast

A. mediterranea   *A. crenulata*

(a)

RESULTS AND CONCLUSION: The algae regenerated a common cap with characteristics intermediate between those of the two species involved. This experiment demonstrated that something in the stalk or holdfast controls cap shape.

FIGURE 4-12 *Acetabularia* and the control of cell activities
Biologist J. Hämmerling used two species of the single-celled seaweed *Acetabularia* for most of his experiments: *A. mediterranea*, which has a smooth cap, and *A. crenulata*, which has a cap divided into a series of fingerlike projections. When the cap is removed, the kind of cap that is regenerated depends on the species of *Acetabularia* used in the experiment. As you might expect, *A. crenulata* regenerates a "cren" cap, and *A. mediterranea* regenerates a "med" cap.

simple organisms. This fact attracted the attention of investigators, especially Danish biologist J. Hämmerling, who became interested in whether a relationship exists between the nucleus and the physical characteristics of the alga. Hämmerling (during the 1930s to 1950s) performed brilliant experiments that in many ways laid the foundation for much of our modern knowledge of the nucleus. Some of his experiments are summarized in **FIGURE 4-12**. Cell biologists extended these early findings as they developed our modern view of information flow and control in the cell. We now know that the cell stores information in the form of **DNA,** and most of the cell's DNA is located inside the nucleus.

The **nuclear envelope** consists of two concentric membranes that separate the nuclear contents from the surrounding cytoplasm (**FIG. 4-13**). These membranes are separated by about 20 to 40 nm. At intervals the membranes come together to form **nuclear pores.** Each nuclear pore consists of a molecular complex made up of many copies of about 30 different proteins. Nuclear pores regulate the passage of materials between nucleoplasm and cytoplasm.

A fibrous network of protein filaments, called the **nuclear lamina,** forms an inner lining for the nuclear envelope. The nuclear

EXPERIMENT 2

QUESTION: Does the stalk or the holdfast control the shape of the cap in *Acetabularia?*

HYPOTHESIS: Something in the holdfast of *Acetabularia* controls the shape of the cap.

EXPERIMENT: Hämmerling removed the caps from *A. mediterranea* and *A. crenulata.* Then he severed the stalks from the holdfasts. By telescoping the cell walls of the two species into each other, Hämmerling was able to attach a section of the stalk of one species to a holdfast of the other species (see **FIG. b**).

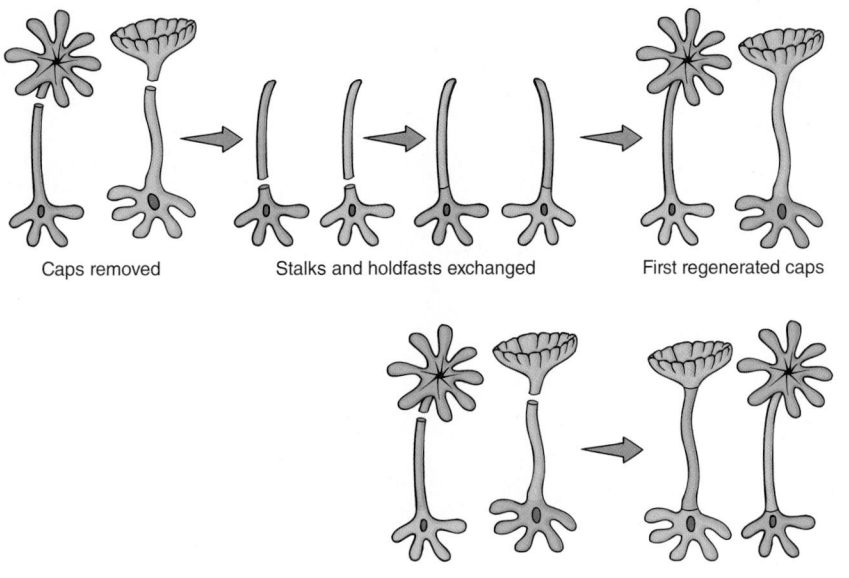

Caps removed   Stalks and holdfasts exchanged   First regenerated caps

(b)   Caps removed again   Second regenerated caps

RESULTS AND CONCLUSION: The results were surprising. The caps that regenerated were characteristic not of the species donating the hold-fasts but of those donating the stalks! However, when the caps were removed once again, this time the caps that regenerated were characteristic of the species that donated the holdfasts. This continued to be the case no matter how many more times the regenerated caps were removed.

From these results Hämmerling deduced that the ultimate control of the *Acetabularia* cell is associated with the holdfast. Because there is a time lag before the holdfast appears to take over, he hypothesized it produces some temporary cytoplasmic messenger substance whereby it exerts its control. Hämmerling further hypothesized that the grafted stalks initially contain enough of the substance from their former holdfasts to regenerate a cap of the former shape. But this still left the question of how the holdfast exerts its apparent control. An obvious suspect was the nucleus.

EXPERIMENT 3

QUESTION: Does the nucleus in the holdfast control the shape of the cap in *Acetabularia?*

HYPOTHESIS: The nucleus in the holdfast of *Acetabularia* controls the shape of the cap.

EXPERIMENT: Hämmerling removed the nucleus and cut off the cap of *Acetabularia* (**FIG. c**). A new cap typical of the species regenerated. *Acetabularia,* however, can usually regenerate only once without a nucleus. The researcher inserted a nucleus of another species and cut the cap off once again (**FIG. d**).

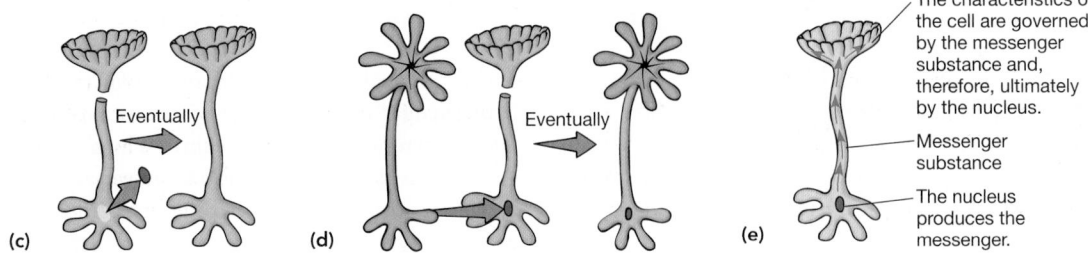

The characteristics of the cell are governed by the messenger substance and, therefore, ultimately by the nucleus.

Messenger substance

The nucleus produces the messenger.

RESULTS AND CONCLUSION: A new cap regenerated that was characteristic of the species of the nucleus. When two kinds of nuclei were inserted, the regenerated cap was intermediate in shape between those of the species that donated the nuclei.

As a result of these and other experiments, biologists began to develop some basic ideas about the control of cell activities. The holdfast controls the cell because the nucleus is located there. Further, the nucleus is the apparent source of some "messenger substance" that temporarily exerts control but is limited in quantity and cannot be produced without the nucleus (**FIG. e**). This information helped provide a starting point for research on the role of nucleic acids in the control of all cells. Much later, the "messenger substance" was characterized and named messenger RNA (mRNA).

FIGURE 4-13 *Animated* **The cell nucleus**

(a) The TEM and interpretive drawing show that the nuclear envelope, composed of two concentric membranes, is perforated by nuclear pores (*red arrows*). The outer membrane of the nuclear envelope is continuous with the membrane of the ER (endoplasmic reticulum). The nucleolus

is not bounded by a membrane. **(b)** TEM of nuclear pores. A technique known as freeze-fracture was used to split the membrane. **(c)** The nuclear pores, which are made up of proteins, form channels between the nucleoplasm and cytoplasm.

lamina supports the inner nuclear membrane and helps organize the nuclear contents. It also plays a role in DNA duplication and in regulating the cell cycle. Mutations in genes encoding proteins that make up the nuclear lamina are associated with several human genetic diseases, including muscular dystrophies and premature aging (progeria).

When a cell divides, the information stored in DNA must be reproduced and passed intact to the two daughter cells. DNA has the unique ability to make an exact duplicate of itself through a process called **replication.** DNA molecules include sequences of nucleotides called **genes,** which contain the chemically coded instructions for producing the proteins needed by the cell. The

nucleus controls protein synthesis by transcribing its information in **messenger RNA (mRNA)** molecules. Messenger RNA moves into the cytoplasm, where proteins are manufactured.

DNA is associated with RNA and certain proteins, forming a complex known as **chromatin.** This complex appears as a network of granules and strands in cells that are not dividing. Although chromatin appears disorganized, it is not. Because DNA molecules are extremely long and thin, they must be packed inside the nucleus in a regular fashion as part of structures called **chromosomes.** In dividing cells, the chromosomes become visible as distinct thread-like structures. If the DNA in the 46 chromosomes of one human cell could be stretched end to end, it would extend for 2 meters!

Most nuclei have one or more compact structures called **nucleoli** (sing., *nucleolus*). A nucleolus, which is *not* enclosed by a membrane, usually stains differently than the surrounding chromatin. Each nucleolus contains a **nucleolar organizer,** made up of chromosomal regions containing instructions for making the type of RNA in ribosomes. This **ribosomal RNA (rRNA)** is synthesized in the nucleolus. The proteins needed to make ribosomes are synthesized in the cytoplasm and imported into the nucleolus. Ribosomal RNA and proteins are then assembled into ribosomal subunits that leave the nucleus through the nuclear pores.

Review

- How does the nucleus store information?
- What is the function of the nuclear envelope?

4.5 ORGANELLES IN THE CYTOPLASM

■ LEARNING OBJECTIVES

8 Distinguish between smooth and rough endoplasmic reticulum in terms of both structure and function.

9 Trace the path of proteins synthesized in the rough endoplasmic reticulum as they are processed, modified, and sorted by the Golgi complex and then transported to specific destinations.

10 Describe the functions of lysosomes, vacuoles, and peroxisomes.

11 Compare the functions of mitochondria and chloroplasts, and discuss ATP synthesis by each of these organelles.

Cell biologists have identified many types of organelles in the cytoplasm of eukaryotic cells. Among them are the ribosomes, endoplasmic reticulum, Golgi complex, lysosomes, peroxisomes, vacuoles, mitochondria, and chloroplasts. **TABLE 4-1** summarizes eukaryotic cell structures and functions.

Ribosomes manufacture proteins

Ribosomes are tiny particles found free in the cytoplasm or attached to certain membranes. They consist of RNA and proteins and are synthesized by the nucleolus. Ribosomes contain the enzyme necessary to form peptide bonds, which join amino acids to produce polypeptides (see Chapter 3). Each ribosome has two main components: a large subunit and a small subunit. When the two ribosome subunits join, they function as manufacturing plants that assemble polypeptides. Cells that actively produce a lot of proteins may have millions of ribosomes, and the cell can change the number of ribosomes present to meet its metabolic needs. We will discuss much more about ribosomes in Chapter 13.

The endoplasmic reticulum is a network of internal membranes

One of the most prominent features in the electron micrographs in Figures 4-9 and 4-10 is a maze of parallel internal membranes that encircle the nucleus and extend into many regions of the cytoplasm. This complex of membranes, the **endoplasmic reticulum**

(ER), forms a network that makes up a significant part of the total volume of the cytoplasm in many cells. A higher-magnification TEM of the ER is shown in **FIGURE 4-14**. Remember that a TEM represents only a thin cross section of the cell, so there is a tendency to interpret the ER as a series of tubes. In fact, many ER membranes consist of a series of tightly packed and flattened, saclike structures that form interconnected compartments within the cytoplasm.

The internal space the membranes enclose is called the **ER lumen.** In most cells the ER lumen forms a single internal compartment that is continuous with the compartment formed between the outer and inner membranes of the nuclear envelope (see Fig. 4-13). The membranes of other organelles are not directly connected to the ER; they form distinct and separate compartments within the cytoplasm.

The ER membranes and lumen contain enzymes that catalyze many types of chemical reactions. In some cases the membranes serve as a framework for enzymes that carry out sequential biochemical reactions. The two surfaces of the membrane contain different sets of enzymes and represent regions of the cell with different synthetic capabilities, just as different regions of a factory make different parts of a particular product. Still other enzymes are located within the ER lumen.

Two distinct regions of the ER can be distinguished in TEMs: rough ER and smooth ER. Although these regions have different functions, their membranes are connected and their internal spaces are continuous.

Smooth ER synthesizes lipids

Smooth ER has a tubular appearance, and its outer membrane surfaces appear smooth. Enzymes in the membranes of the smooth ER catalyze the synthesis of many lipids and carbohydrates. The smooth ER is the primary site for the synthesis of phospholipids and cholesterol needed to make cell membranes. Smooth ER synthesizes steroid hormones, including reproductive hormones, from cholesterol. In liver cells, smooth ER is important in enzymatically breaking down stored glycogen. (The liver helps regulate the concentration of glucose in the blood.) Smooth ER also stores calcium ions.

Whereas smooth ER may be a minor membrane component in some cells, extensive amounts of smooth ER are present in others. For example, extensive smooth ER is present in human liver cells, where it synthesizes and processes cholesterol and other lipids and serves as a major detoxification site. Enzymes located along the smooth ER of liver cells break down toxic chemicals such as carcinogens (cancer-causing agents) and many drugs, including alcohol, amphetamines, and barbiturates. The cell then converts these compounds to water-soluble products that it excretes. Interestingly, alcohol and many other drugs stimulate liver cells to produce additional smooth ER, increasing the rate that these cells can detoxify the drugs. Alcohol abuse causes liver inflammation that can lead to cirrhosis and eventual liver failure.

Rough ER is important in protein synthesis

The outer surface of the **rough ER** is studded with ribosomes that appear as dark granules. Notice in Figure 4-14 that the lumen side

TABLE 4-1   Eukaryotic Cell Structures and Their Functions

Structure	Description	Function
Cell Nucleus		
Nucleus	Large structure surrounded by double membrane; contains nucleolus and chromosomes	Information in DNA is transcribed in RNA synthesis; specifies cell proteins
Nucleolus	Granular body within nucleus; consists of RNA and protein	Site of ribosomal RNA synthesis; ribosome subunit assembly
Chromosomes	Composed of chromatin, a complex of DNA and protein; condense during cell division, becoming visible as rodlike structures	Contain genes (units of hereditary information) that govern structure and activity of cell
Cytoplasmic Organelles		
Plasma membrane	Membrane boundary of cell	Encloses cell contents; regulates movement of materials in and out of cell; helps maintain cell shape; communicates with other cells (also present in prokaryotes)
Ribosomes	Granules composed of RNA and protein; some attached to ER, some free in cytosol	Synthesize polypeptides in both prokaryotes and eukaryotes
Endoplasmic reticulum (ER)	Network of internal membranes extending through cytoplasm	Synthesizes lipids and modifies many proteins; origin of intracellular transport vesicles that carry proteins
Smooth	Lacks ribosomes on outer surface	Lipid synthesis; drug detoxification; calcium ion storage
Rough	Ribosomes stud outer surface	Manufactures proteins
Golgi complex	Stacks of flattened membrane sacs	Modifies proteins; packages secreted proteins; sorts other proteins to vacuoles and other organelles
Lysosomes	Membranous sacs (in animals)	Contain enzymes that break down ingested materials; break down damaged or unneeded organelles and proteins
Vacuoles	Membranous sacs (mostly in plants, fungi, algae)	Store materials, wastes, water; maintain hydrostatic pressure
Peroxisomes	Membranous sacs containing a variety of enzymes	Site of many diverse metabolic reactions; e.g., break down fatty acids
Mitochondria	Sacs consisting of two membranes; inner membrane is folded to form cristae and encloses matrix	Site of most reactions of cellular respiration; transformation of energy originating from glucose or lipids into ATP energy
Plastids (e.g., chloroplasts)	Double-membrane structure enclosing internal thylakoid membrane; chloroplasts contain chlorophyll in thylakoid membrane	Chloroplasts are site of photosynthesis; chlorophyll captures light energy; ATP and other energy-rich compounds are produced and then used to convert CO_2 to carbohydrate
Cytoskeleton		
Microtubules	Hollow tubes made of subunits of tubulin protein	Provide structural support; have role in cell and organelle movement and cell division; components of cilia, flagella, centrioles, basal bodies
Microfilaments	Solid, rodlike structures consisting of actin protein	Provide structural support; play role in cell and organelle movement and cell division
Intermediate filaments	Tough fibers made of protein	Help strengthen cytoskeleton; stabilize cell shape
Centrioles	Pair of hollow cylinders located near nucleus; each centriole consists of nine microtubule triplets (9×3 structure)	Mitotic spindle forms between centrioles during animal cell division; may anchor and organize microtubule formation in animal cells; absent in most plant cells
Cilia	Relatively short projections extending from surface of cell; covered by plasma membrane; made of two central and nine pairs of peripheral microtubules ($9 + 2$ structure)	Movement of some unicellular organisms; used to move materials on surface of some tissues; important in cell signaling
Flagella	Long projections made of two central and nine pairs of peripheral microtubules ($9 + 2$ structure); extend from surface of cell; covered by plasma membrane	Cell locomotion by sperm cells and some unicellular organisms

of the rough ER appears bare, whereas the outer surface (the cytosolic side) looks rough. The ribosomes attached to the rough ER are known as *bound ribosomes; free ribosomes* are suspended in the cytosol.

The rough ER plays a central role in the synthesis and assembly of proteins. Many proteins that are exported from the cell (such as digestive enzymes), and proteins destined for other organelles, are synthesized on ribosomes bound to the ER membrane. The ribosome forms a tight seal with the ER membrane. A tunnel within the ribosome connects to an ER pore. Polypeptides are transported through the tunnel and the pore in the ER membrane into the ER lumen.

In the ER lumen, proteins are assembled and may be modified by enzymes that add carbohydrates or lipids to them. Other enzymes, called **molecular chaperones,** in the ER lumen catalyze the efficient folding of proteins into proper conformations. Pro-

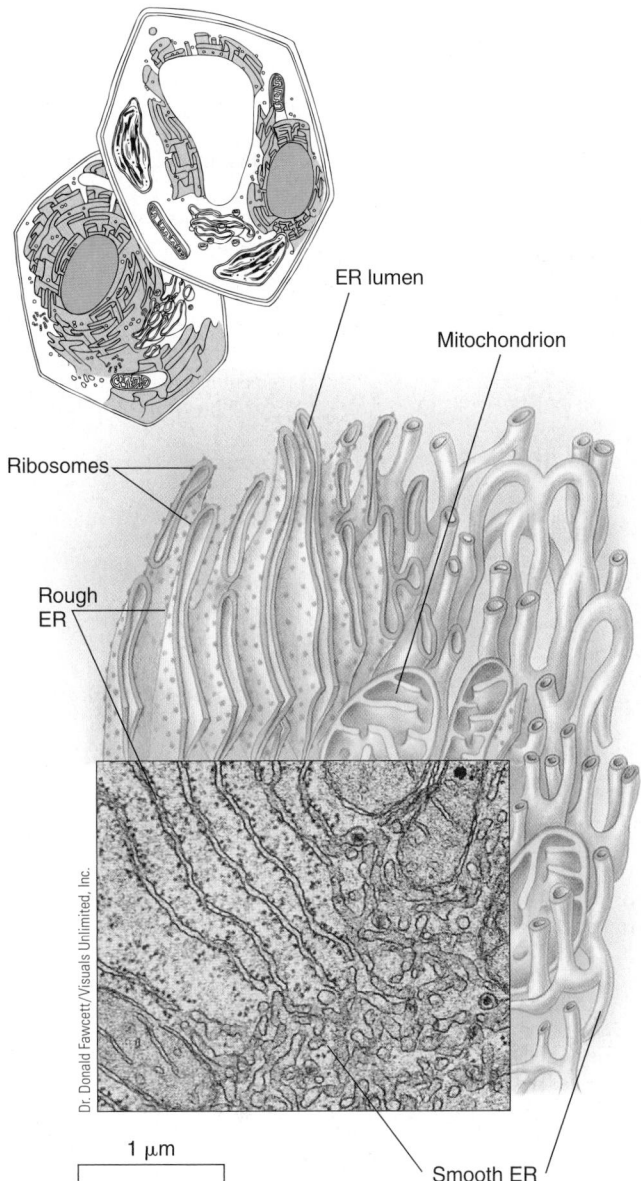

ER lumen

Mitochondrion

Ribosomes

Rough
ER

Smooth ER

Dr. Donald Fawcett/Visuals Unlimited, Inc.

1 μm

FIGURE 4-14 *Animated* **Endoplasmic reticulum (ER)**
The TEM shows both rough and smooth ER in a liver cell.

teins that are not processed correctly, for example, proteins that are misfolded, are transported to the cytosol. There, they are degraded by **proteasomes,** protein complexes in the cytosol that direct the destruction of defective proteins. Properly processed proteins are transferred to other compartments within the cell by small **transport vesicles,** which bud off the ER membrane and then fuse with the membrane of some target organelle.

The Golgi complex processes, sorts, and modifies proteins

The **Golgi complex** (also known as the *Golgi body* or *Golgi apparatus*) was first described in 1898 by the Italian microscopist Camillo Golgi, who found a way to specifically stain this organelle. However, many investigators thought the Golgi complex was an arti-

cis
face

trans
face

Golgi complex

Bloom and Fawcett Textbook of Histology

0.5 μm

FIGURE 4-15 TEM and an interpretive drawing of the Golgi complex

fact, and its legitimacy as a cell organelle was not confirmed until cells were studied with the electron microscope in the 1950s.

In many cells, the Golgi complex consists of stacks of flattened membranous sacs called **cisternae** (sing., *cisterna*). Each cisterna has an internal space, or lumen (**FIG. 4-15**). In certain regions, cisternae may be distended because they are filled with cell products. The Golgi complex contains a number of separate compartments, as well as some that are interconnected.

Each Golgi stack has three areas, referred to as the *cis face,* the *trans face,* and a *medial region* in between. Typically, the *cis* face (the entry surface) is located nearest the nucleus and receives materials from transport vesicles bringing molecules from the ER. The *trans* face (the exit surface) is closest to the plasma membrane. It packages molecules in vesicles and transports them out of the Golgi.

In a cross-sectional view like that in the TEM in Figure 4-15, many ends of the sheetlike layers of Golgi membranes are distended, an arrangement characteristic of well-developed Golgi complexes in many cells. In some animal cells, the Golgi complex lies at one side of the nucleus; other animal cells and plant cells have many Golgi complexes dispersed throughout the cell.

Cells that secrete large amounts of *glycoproteins* have many Golgi stacks. (Recall from Chapter 3 that a glycoprotein is a protein with a covalently attached carbohydrate.) Golgi complexes of plant cells produce extracellular polysaccharides that are used as components of the cell wall. In animal cells, the Golgi complex manufactures lysosomes.

The Golgi complex processes, sorts, and modifies proteins. Researchers have studied the function of the ER, Golgi complex,

① Polypeptides synthesized on ribosomes are inserted into ER lumen.

② Sugars are added, forming glycoproteins.

③ Transport vesicles deliver glycoproteins to *cis* face of Golgi.

④ Glycoproteins modified further in Golgi.

⑤ Glycoproteins move to *trans* face where they are packaged in transport vesicles.

⑥ Glycoproteins transported to plasma membrane (or other organelle).

⑦ Contents of transport vesicle released from cell.

Ribosomes

Rough ER

Glycoprotein

cis face

trans face

Golgi complex

Plasma membrane

FIGURE 4-16 *Animated* **Protein transport within the cell**

Glycoproteins are transported from ribosomes into the ER. They are then transported to the Golgi complex, where they are modified. This diagram shows the passage of glycoproteins through compartments of the endomembrane system of a mucus-secreting goblet cell from the lining of the intestine. Mucus consists of a complex mixture of covalently linked proteins and carbohydrates.

and other organelles by radioactively labeling newly manufactured molecules and observing their movement through the cell. The general pathway is from ribosomes to the lumen of the rough ER to the Golgi complex and then to some final destination (**FIG. 4-16**).

Proteins that are accurately assembled are transported from the rough ER to the *cis* face of the Golgi complex in small transport vesicles formed from the ER membrane. Transport vesicles fuse with one another to form clusters that move along microtubules (part of the cytoskeleton) to the Golgi complex. What happens to glycoprotein molecules released into the Golgi complex? One hypothesis holds that the glycoproteins are enclosed in new vesicles that shuttle them from one compartment to another within the Golgi complex. A competing hypothesis postulates that the cisternae themselves may move from *cis* to *trans* positions. Both hypotheses may be correct: glycoproteins may be transported by both methods.

Regardless of how proteins are moved through the Golgi complex, while there they are modified in different ways, resulting in the formation of complex biological molecules. For example, the carbohydrate part of a glycoprotein (first added to proteins in the rough ER) may be modified. In some cases the carbohydrate component may be a "sorting signal," a cellular zip code that tags the protein, routing it to a specific organelle.

Glycoproteins are packaged in transport vesicles in the *trans* face. These vesicles pinch off from the Golgi membrane and transport their contents to a specific destination. Vesicles transporting products for export from the cell fuse with the plasma membrane. The vesicle membrane becomes part of the plasma membrane, and the glycoproteins are secreted from the cell. Other vesicles may store glycoproteins for secretion at a later time, and still others are routed to various organelles of the endomembrane system. In summary, here is a typical sequence followed by a glycoprotein destined for secretion from the cell:

polypeptides synthesized on ribosomes ⟶ protein assembled and carbohydrate component added in lumen of ER ⟶ transport vesicles move glycoprotein to Golgi (*cis* face) ⟶ glycoprotein further modified in Golgi ⟶ in *trans* face, glycoproteins packaged in transport vesicles ⟶ glycoproteins transported to plasma membrane ⟶ contents released from cell

Lysosomes are compartments for digestion

Lysosomes are small sacs of digestive enzymes dispersed in the cytoplasm of most animal cells (**FIG. 4-17**). Researchers have identified about 40 different digestive enzymes in lysosomes.

Because lysosomal enzymes are active under rather acidic conditions, the lysosome maintains a pH of about 5 in its interior. The powerful enzymes and low pH that the lysosome maintains provide an excellent example of the importance of separating functions within the cell into different compartments. Under most normal conditions, the lysosome membrane confines its enzymes and their actions. However, some forms of tissue damage are related to "leaky" lysosomes.

Primary lysosomes are formed by budding from the Golgi complex. Their hydrolytic enzymes are synthesized in the rough ER. As these enzymes pass through the lumen of the ER, sugars attach to each molecule, identifying it as bound for a lysosome. This signal permits the Golgi complex to sort the enzyme to the lysosomes rather than to export it from the cell.

Bacteria (or debris) engulfed by scavenger cells are enclosed in a vesicle formed from part of the plasma membrane. One or more primary lysosomes fuse with the vesicle containing the ingested material, forming a larger vesicle called a *secondary lysosome.* Powerful enzymes in the secondary lysosome come in contact with the ingested molecules and degrade them into their components. Under some conditions, lysosomes break down organelles and allow their components to be recycled or used as an energy source.

In certain genetic diseases of humans, known as *lysosomal storage diseases,* one of the digestive enzymes normally present in lysosomes is absent. Its substrate (a substance the enzyme would normally break down) accumulates in the cell, which eventually interferes with cell activities. An example is Tay-Sachs disease, an inherited disease in which a normal lipid cannot be broken down (discussed in Chapter 16). The accumulation of this lipid in brain cells causes mental retardation, blindness, and death before age 4.

Vacuoles are large, fluid-filled sacs with a variety of functions

Although lysosomes have been identified in almost all kinds of animal cells, biologists have not identified them in plant and fungal cells. Many functions carried out in animal cells by lysosomes are performed in plant and fungal cells by a large, single, membrane-enclosed sac called a **vacuole.** The membrane of the vacuole, part of the endomembrane system, is called the **tonoplast.** The term *vacuole,* which means "empty," refers to the fact that these organelles have no internal structure. Although some biologists use the terms *vacuole* and *vesicle* interchangeably, vacuoles are usually larger structures, sometimes produced by the merging of many vesicles.

Vacuoles play a significant role in plant growth and development. Immature plant cells are generally small and contain numerous small vacuoles. As water accumulates in these vacuoles, they tend to coalesce, forming a large central vacuole. A plant cell increases in size mainly by adding water to this central vacuole. As much as 80% of the volume of a plant cell may be occupied by a large central vacuole containing water, stored food, salts, pigments, and metabolic wastes (see Figs. 4-7 and 4-9). The vacuole

Primary lysosome | Secondary lysosome | 5 μm

FIGURE 4-17 Lysosomes

The dark vesicles in this TEM are lysosomes, compartments that separate powerful digestive enzymes from the rest of the cell. Primary lysosomes bud off from the Golgi complex. After a lysosome takes in material to be digested, it is known as a secondary lysosome. The large vesicles shown here are secondary lysosomes containing various materials being digested.

may serve as a storage compartment for inorganic compounds. In seeds, vacuoles store molecules such as proteins.

Because the vacuole contains a high concentration of solutes (dissolved materials), it takes in water and pushes outward on the cell wall. This hydrostatic pressure, called *turgor pressure,* provides much of the mechanical strength of plant cells. The vacuole is important in maintaining homeostasis. For example, it helps maintain appropriate pH by taking in excess hydrogen ions.

Plants lack organ systems for disposing of toxic metabolic waste products. Plant vacuoles are like lysosomes in that they contain hydrolytic enzymes and break down wastes, as well as unneeded organelles and other cell components. Wastes may be recycled in the vacuole, or they may aggregate and form small crystals inside the vacuole. Compounds that are noxious to herbivores (animals that eat plants) may be stored in some plant vacuoles as a means of defense.

Vacuoles are also present in many types of animal cells and in unicellular protists such as protozoa. Most protozoa have **food vacuoles,** which fuse with lysosomes that digest the food (**FIG. 4-18**). Some protozoa also have **contractile vacuoles,** which remove excess water from the cell (discussed in Chapter 26).

Peroxisomes metabolize small organic compounds

Peroxisomes are membrane-enclosed organelles containing enzymes that catalyze an assortment of metabolic reactions in

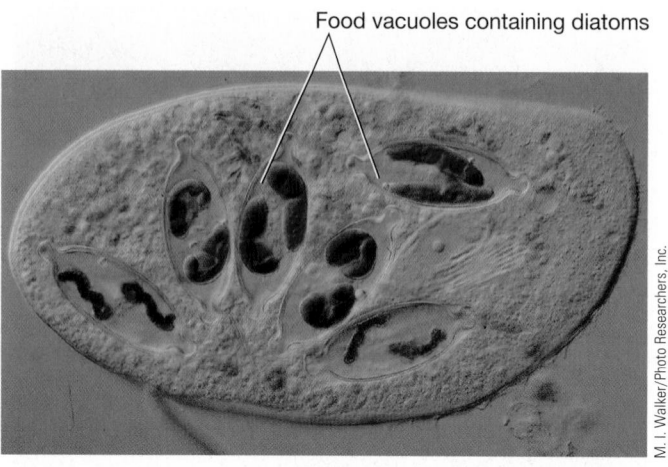

Food vacuoles containing diatoms

15 μm

M. I. Walker/Photo Researchers, Inc.

FIGURE 4-18 LM of food vacuoles

This protist, *Chilodonella*, has ingested many small, photosynthetic protists called diatoms (*dark areas*) that have been enclosed in food vacuoles. From the number of diatoms scattered about its cell, one might conclude that *Chilodonella* has a rather voracious appetite.

which hydrogen is transferred from various compounds to oxygen (**FIG. 4-19**). Peroxisomes get their name from the fact that during these oxidation reactions, they produce hydrogen peroxide (H_2O_2). Hydrogen peroxide detoxifies certain compounds; but if this compound were to escape from the peroxisome, it would damage other membranes in the cell. Peroxisomes contain the enzyme

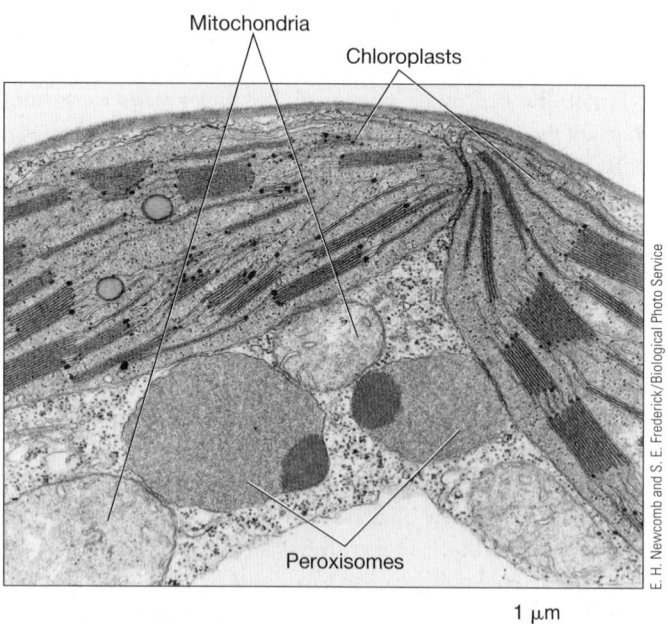

Mitochondria

Chloroplasts

Peroxisomes

1 μm

E. H. Newcomb and S. E. Frederick/Biological Photo Service

FIGURE 4-19 Peroxisomes

In this TEM of a tobacco (*Nicotiana tabacum*) leaf cell, peroxisomes are in close association with chloroplasts and mitochondria. These organelles may cooperate in carrying out some metabolic processes.

catalase, which rapidly splits excess hydrogen peroxide to water and oxygen, rendering it harmless.

Peroxisomes are found in large numbers in cells that synthesize, store, or degrade lipids. One of their main functions is to break down fatty acid molecules. Peroxisomes synthesize certain phospholipids that are components of the insulating covering of nerve cells. In fact, certain neurological disorders occur when peroxisomes do not perform this function. Mutations that cause synthesis of abnormal membrane lipids by peroxisomes are linked to some forms of mental retardation.

When yeast cells are grown in an alcohol-rich medium, they manufacture large peroxisomes containing an enzyme that degrades the alcohol. Peroxisomes in human liver and kidney cells detoxify certain toxic compounds, including ethanol, the alcohol in alcoholic beverages.

In plant seeds, specialized peroxisomes, called *glyoxysomes*, contain enzymes that convert stored fats to sugars. The sugars are used by the young plant as an energy source and as a component for synthesizing other compounds. Animal cells lack glyoxysomes and cannot convert fatty acids into sugars.

Mitochondria and chloroplasts are energy-converting organelles

The energy a cell obtains from its environment is usually in the form of chemical energy in food molecules (such as glucose) or in the form of light energy. These types of energy must be converted to forms that cells can use more conveniently. Some energy conversions occur in the cytosol, but other types take place in mitochondria and chloroplasts, organelles specialized to facilitate the conversion of energy from one form to another.

Chemical energy is most commonly stored in ATP. Recall from (Chapter 3) that the chemical energy of ATP can be used to drive a variety of chemical reactions in the cell. **FIGURE 4-20** summarizes the main activities that take place in mitochondria, found in almost all eukaryotic cells, and in chloroplasts, found only in algae and certain plant cells.

Mitochondria and chloroplasts grow and reproduce themselves. They contain small amounts of DNA that code for a small number of the proteins found in these organelles. These proteins are synthesized by mitochondrial or chloroplast ribosomes. Interestingly, these ribosomes are similar to the ribosomes of prokaryotes. The existence of a separate set of ribosomes and DNA molecules in mitochondria and chloroplasts and their similarity in size to many bacteria provide support for **serial endosymbiosis** (discussed in Chapters 21 and 26; see Figs. 21-8 and 26-2). According to this hypothesis, mitochondria and chloroplasts evolved from prokaryotes that took up residence inside larger eukaryotic cells. Eventually, these symbiotic prokaryotes lost the ability to function as autonomous organisms.

Mitochondria make ATP through cellular respiration

Virtually all eukaryotic cells (plant, animal, fungal, and protist) contain complex organelles called **mitochondria** (sing., *mito-*

Mitochondria and chloroplasts convert energy into forms that can be used by cells.

Aerobic respiration
Mitochondria (most eukaryotic cells)

Glucose + O_2 → ATP +

CO_2
H_2O

Photosynthesis
Chloroplasts (some plant and algal cells)

Light

CO_2
H_2O + ATP → O_2 + Glucose

FIGURE 4-20 Cellular respiration and photosynthesis

Cellular respiration takes place in the mitochondria of virtually all eukaryotic cells. In this process, some of the chemical energy in glucose is transferred to ATP. Photosynthesis, which is carried out in chloroplasts in some plant and algal cells, converts light energy to ATP and to other forms of chemical energy. This energy is used to synthesize glucose from carbon dioxide and water.

chondrion). These organelles are the site of **aerobic respiration,** an oxygen-requiring process that includes most of the reactions that convert the chemical energy present in certain foods to ATP (discussed in Chapter 8). During aerobic respiration, carbon and oxygen atoms are removed from food molecules, such as glucose, and converted to carbon dioxide and water.

Mitochondria are most numerous in cells that are very active and therefore have high energy requirements. More than 1000 mitochondria have been counted in a single liver cell! These organelles vary in size, ranging from 2 to 8 μm in length, and change size and shape rapidly. Mitochondria usually give rise to other mitochondria by growth and subsequent division.

Each mitochondrion is enclosed by a double membrane, which forms two *different* compartments within the organelle: the intermembrane space and the matrix (**FIG. 4-21;** we will provide more detailed descriptions of mitochondrial structure in Chapter 8). The **intermembrane space** is the compartment formed between the outer and inner mitochondrial membranes. The **matrix,** the compartment enclosed by the inner mitochondrial membrane, contains enzymes that break down food molecules and convert their energy to other forms of chemical energy.

The **outer mitochondrial membrane** is smooth and allows many small molecules to pass through it. By contrast, the **inner mitochondrial membrane** has numerous folds and strictly regulates the types of molecules that can move across it. The folds, called **cristae** (sing., *crista*), extend into the matrix. Cristae greatly increase the surface area of the inner mitochondrial membrane, providing a surface for the chemical reactions that transform the chemical energy in food molecules into the energy of ATP. The membrane contains the enzymes and other proteins needed for these reactions.

Mitochondria play an important role in programmed cell death, or **apoptosis.** Unlike **necrosis,** which is uncontrolled cell

Outer mitochondrial membrane

Inner mitochondrial membrane

Matrix

Cristae

Bloom and Fawcett Textbook of Histology

0.25 μm

FIGURE 4-21 *Animated* **Mitochondria**

Aerobic respiration takes place within mitochondria. Cristae are evident in the TEM as well as in the drawing. The drawing shows the relationship between the inner and outer mitochondrial membranes.

death that causes inflammation and damages other cells, apoptosis is a normal part of development and maintenance. For example, during the metamorphosis of a tadpole to a frog, the cells of the tadpole tail must die. The hand of a human embryo is webbed until apoptosis destroys the tissue between the fingers. Cell death also occurs in the adult. For example, cells that are no longer functional because they have aged or become damaged are destroyed and replaced by new cells.

Mitochondria initiate cell death in several different ways. For example, they can interfere with energy metabolism or activate enzymes that mediate cell destruction. When a mitochondrion is injured, large pores open in its membrane, and cytochrome *c*, a protein important in energy conversions, is released into the cytoplasm. Cytochrome *c* triggers apoptosis by activating enzymes known as **caspases,** which cut up vital compounds in the cell.

Inappropriate inhibition of apoptosis may contribute to a variety of diseases, including cancer. On the other hand, too much apoptosis may deplete needed cells and lead to death of brain cells associated with Alzheimer's disease, Parkinson's disease, and stroke. Mutations that promote apoptosis may be an important mechanism in mammalian aging. Pharmaceutical companies are developing drugs that block apoptosis. However, cell dynamics are extremely complex, and blocking apoptosis could lead to a worse fate, including necrosis.

Each mitochondrion in a mammalian cell has 5 to 10 identical, circular molecules of DNA, accounting for up to 1% of the total DNA in the cell. Mitochondrial DNA mutates far more frequently than nuclear DNA. Mutations in mitochondrial DNA have been associated with certain genetic diseases, including a form of young adult blindness, and certain types of progressive muscle degeneration. Mitochondria also affect health and aging by leaking electrons.

These electrons form **free radicals,** which are toxic, highly reactive compounds with unpaired electrons. The electrons bond with other compounds in the cell, interfering with normal function.

Chloroplasts convert light energy to chemical energy through photosynthesis

Certain plant and algal cells carry out **photosynthesis,** a set of reactions during which light energy is transformed into the chemical energy of glucose and other carbohydrates. **Chloroplasts** are organelles that contain **chlorophyll,** a green pigment that traps light energy for photosynthesis. Chloroplasts also contain a variety of light-absorbing yellow and orange pigments known as **carotenoids** (see Chapter 3). A unicellular alga may have only a single large chloroplast, whereas a leaf cell may have 20 to 100. Chloroplasts tend to be somewhat larger than mitochondria, with lengths usually ranging from about 5 to 10 μm or longer.

Chloroplasts are typically disc-shaped structures and, like mitochondria, have a system of folded membranes (**FIG. 4-22**; we will provide a more detailed description of chloroplast structure in Chapter 9). Two membranes enclose the chloroplast and separate it from the cytosol. The inner membrane encloses a fluid-filled space called the **stroma,** which contains enzymes. These enzymes produce carbohydrates from carbon dioxide and water, using energy trapped from sunlight. A system of internal membranes, which consists of an interconnected set of flat, disclike sacs called **thylakoids,** is suspended in the stroma. The thylakoids are arranged in stacks called **grana** (sing., *granum*).

The thylakoid membrane encloses the innermost compartments within the chloroplast, the **thylakoid lumen.** Chlorophyll is present in the thylakoid membrane, which like the inner mito-

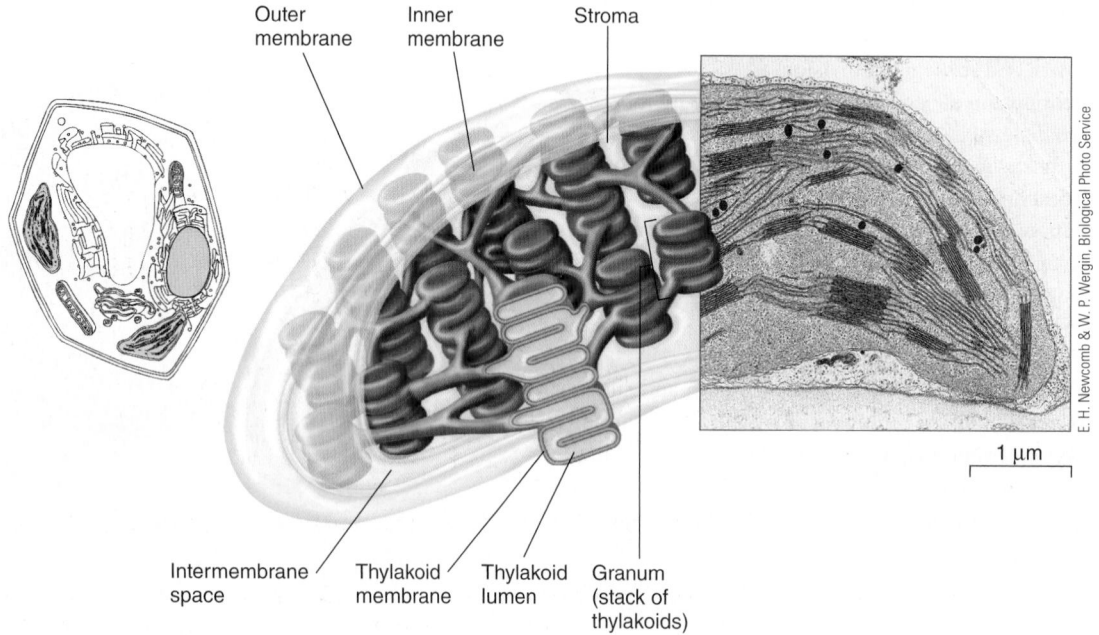

Outer membrane · Inner membrane · Stroma

Intermembrane space · Thylakoid membrane · Thylakoid lumen · Granum (stack of thylakoids)

1 µm

E. H. Newcomb & W. P. Wergin, Biological Photo Service

FIGURE 4-22 *Animated* A chloroplast, the organelle of photosynthesis

The TEM shows part of a chloroplast from a corn leaf cell. Chlorophyll and other photosynthetic pigments are in the thylakoid membranes. One granum is cut open to show the thylakoid lumen. The inner chloroplast membrane may or may not be continuous with the thylakoid membrane (*as shown*).

chondrial membranes, is involved in the formation of ATP. Energy absorbed from sunlight by the chlorophyll molecules excites electrons; the energy in these excited electrons is then used to produce ATP and other molecules that transfer chemical energy.

Chloroplasts belong to a group of organelles, known as **plastids,** that produce and store food materials in cells of plants and algae. All plastids develop from **proplastids,** precursor organelles found in less specialized plant cells, particularly in growing, undeveloped tissues. Depending on the specific functions a cell will eventually have, its proplastids can develop into a variety of specialized mature plastids. These are extremely versatile organelles; in fact, under certain conditions even mature plastids can convert from one form to another.

Chloroplasts are produced when proplastids are stimulated by exposure to light. **Chromoplasts** contain pigments that give certain flowers and fruits their characteristic colors; these colors attract animals that serve as pollinators or as seed dispersers. **Leukoplasts** are unpigmented plastids; they include **amyloplasts** (see Fig. 3-9), which store starch in the cells of many seeds, roots, and tubers (such as white potatoes).

Review

- How do the structure and function of rough ER differ from those of smooth ER?
- What are the functions of the Golgi complex?
- What sequence of events must take place for a protein to be manufactured and then secreted from the cell?
- How are chloroplasts like mitochondria? How are they different?
- Draw and label a chloroplast and a mitochondrion.

4.6 THE CYTOSKELETON

■ LEARNING OBJECTIVES

12 Describe the structure and functions of the cytoskeleton.

13 Compare cilia and flagella, and describe their functions.

Scientists watching cells growing in the laboratory see that they frequently change shape and that many types of cells move about. The **cytoskeleton,** a dense network of protein fibers, gives cells mechanical strength, shape, and their ability to move (**FIG. 4-23**). The cytoskeleton also functions in cell division and in the transport of materials within the cell.

The cytoskeleton is highly dynamic and constantly changing. Its framework is made of three types of protein filaments: microtubules, microfilaments, and intermediate filaments. Both microfilaments and microtubules are formed from beadlike, globular protein subunits, which can be rapidly assembled and disassembled. Intermediate filaments are made from fibrous protein subunits and are more stable than microtubules and microfilaments.

Microtubules are hollow cylinders

Microtubules, the thickest filaments of the cytoskeleton, are rigid, hollow rods about 25 nm in outside diameter and up to several micrometers in length. In addition to playing a structural role in the

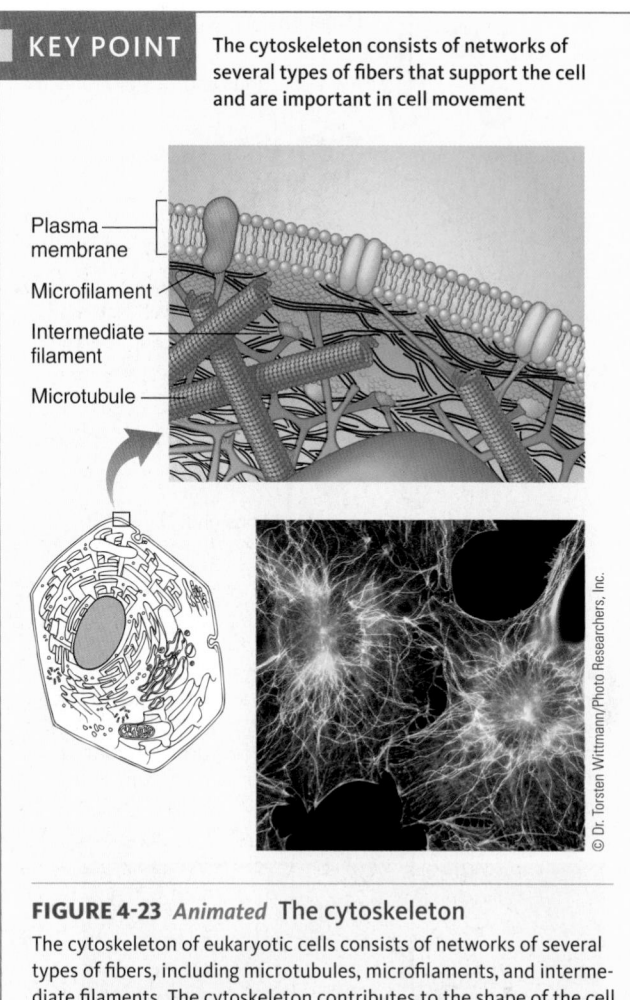

KEY POINT The cytoskeleton consists of networks of several types of fibers that support the cell and are important in cell movement

Plasma membrane

Microfilament

Intermediate filament

Microtubule

FIGURE 4-23 *Animated* **The cytoskeleton**

The cytoskeleton of eukaryotic cells consists of networks of several types of fibers, including microtubules, microfilaments, and intermediate filaments. The cytoskeleton contributes to the shape of the cell, anchors organelles, and sometimes rapidly changes shape during cell locomotion. This fluorescent LM shows the cytoskeleton of two fibroblast cells (microtubules, *yellow*; microfilaments, *blue*; nuclei, *green*).

cytoskeleton, these extremely adaptable structures are involved in the movement of chromosomes during cell division. They serve as tracks for several other kinds of intracellular movement and are the major structural components of cilia and flagella—specialized structures used in some cell movements.

Microtubules consist of two forms of the protein **tubulin:** α-tubulin and β-tubulin. These proteins combine to form a dimer. (Recall from Chapter 3 that a dimer forms from the association of two simpler units, referred to as monomers.) A microtubule elongates by the addition of tubulin dimers (**FIG. 4-24**). Microtubules are disassembled by the removal of dimers, which are recycled to form new microtubules. Each microtubule has polarity, and its two ends are referred to as *plus* and *minus*. The plus end elongates more rapidly.

Other proteins are important in microtubule function. **Microtubule-associated proteins (MAPs)** are classified into two groups: structural MAPs and motor MAPs. *Structural MAPs* may help regulate microtubule assembly, and they cross-link microtubules to other cytoskeletal polymers. *Motor MAPs* use ATP energy to produce movement.

Nancy Kedersha

50 μm

(a) Microtubules are manufactured in the cell by adding dimers of α-tubulin and β-tubulin to an end of the hollow cylinder. Notice that the cylinder has polarity. The end shown at the top of the figure is the fast-growing, or plus, end; the opposite end is the minus end. Each turn of the spiral requires 13 dimers.

(b) Fluorescent LM showing microtubules in green. A microtubule-organizing center (*pink dot*) is visible beside or over most of the cell nuclei (*blue*).

FIGURE 4-24 Organization of microtubules

What are the mechanisms by which organelles and other materials move within the cell? Nerve cells typically have long extensions called axons that transmit signals to other nerve cells, muscle cells, or cells that produce hormones. Because of the axon's length and accessibility and because other cells use similar transport mechanisms, researchers have used the axon as a model for studying the transport of organelles within the cell. They have found that many organelles, including mitochondria and transport and secretory vesicles, attach to microtubules. The microtubules serve as tracks along which organelles move to different cell locations.

One motor protein, **kinesin,** moves organelles toward the plus end of a microtubule (**FIG. 4-25**). **Dynein,** another motor protein, transports organelles in the opposite direction, toward the minus end. This dynein movement is referred to as *retrograde transport*. A protein complex called *dynactin* is also required for retrograde transport. Dynactin is an adapter protein that links dynein to the microtubule and the organelle. At times, for example, during peroxisome transport, kinesins and dyneins may work together.

Centrosomes and centrioles function in cell division

For microtubules to act as a structural framework or participate in cell movement, they must be anchored to other parts of the cell. In nondividing cells, the minus ends of microtubules appear to be anchored in regions called **microtubule-organizing centers (MTOCs).** In animal cells, the main MTOC is the cell center, or **centrosome,** a structure that is important in cell division.

In many cells, including almost all animal cells, the centrosome contains two structures called **centrioles** (**FIG. 4-26**). These structures are oriented within the centrosome at right angles to each other. They are known as *9 × 3 structures* because they consist of nine sets of three attached microtubules arranged to form a hollow cylinder. The centrioles are duplicated before cell division and may play a role in some types of microtubule assembly. Most plant cells and fungal cells have an MTOC but lack centrioles. This suggests that centrioles are not essential to most microtubule assembly processes and that alternative assembly mechanisms are present.

The ability of microtubules to assemble and disassemble rapidly is seen during cell division, when much of the cytoskeleton disassembles (discussed in Chapter 10). At that time tubulin subunits organize into a structure called the **mitotic spindle,** which serves as a framework for the orderly distribution of chromosomes during cell division.

Cilia and flagella are composed of microtubules

Thin, movable structures, important in cell movement, project from surfaces of many cells. If a cell has one, or only a few, of these appendages and if they are long (typically about 200 μm) relative to the size of the cell, they are called **flagella.** If the cell has many short (typically 2 to 10 μm long) appendages, they are called **cilia** (sing., *cilium*).

Cilia and flagella help unicellular and small multicellular organisms move through a watery environment. In animals and certain plants, flagella serve as the tails of sperm cells. In animals, cilia occur on the surfaces of cells that line internal ducts of the body (such as respiratory passageways). Cells use cilia to move liquids and particles across the cell surface. Investigators have shown that cilia also serve as the cell's antenna and play important roles in cell signaling.

Eukaryotic cilia and flagella are structurally alike (but different from bacterial flagella). Each consists of a slender, cylindrical stalk covered by an extension of the plasma membrane. The core

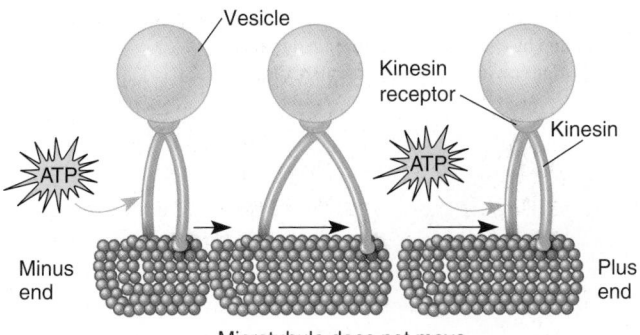

FIGURE 4-25 *Animated* **A model of a kinesin motor**
A kinesin molecule attaches to a specific receptor on the vesicle. Energy from ATP powers the kinesin molecule so that it changes its conformation and "walks" along the microtubule, carrying the vesicle along. (Size relationships are exaggerated for clarity.)

of the stalk contains a group of microtubules arranged so there are nine attached pairs of microtubules around the circumference and two unpaired microtubules in the center (**FIG. 4-27**). This *9 + 2 arrangement* of microtubules is characteristic of virtually all eukaryotic cilia and flagella.

The microtubules in cilia and flagella move by sliding in pairs past each other. The sliding force is generated by dynein proteins, powered by ATP. The dynein "feet" move the microtubule pairs by forming and breaking cross bridges on adjacent pairs of microtubules. Each microtubule pair "walks" along its neighbor. Flexible linking proteins between microtubule pairs prevent microtubules from sliding very far. As a result, the motor action causes the microtubules to bend, resulting in a beating motion (see Fig. 4-27e). Cilia typically move like the arms of a swimmer, alternating a power stroke in one direction with a recovery stroke in the opposite direction. They exert a force that is parallel to the cell surface. In contrast, a flagellum moves like a whip, exerting a force perpendicular to the cell surface.

Each cilium or flagellum is anchored in the cell by a **basal body,** which has nine sets of three attached microtubules in a cylindrical array (*9 × 3 structure*). The basal body appears to be the organizing structure for the cilium or flagellum when it first begins to form. However, experiments have shown that as growth proceeds, the tubulin subunits are added much faster to the tips of the microtubules than to the base.

Basal bodies and centrioles may be functionally related as well as structurally similar. In fact, centrioles are typically found in the cells of eukaryotic organisms that produce flagellated or ciliated cells; these include animals, certain protists, a few fungi, and a few plants. Both basal bodies and centrioles replicate themselves.

Almost every vertebrate cell has a **primary cilium,** a single cilium on the cell surface that serves as a cellular antenna. The primary cilium has receptors on its surface that bind with specific molecules outside the cell or on surfaces of other cells. Recent research indicates that primary cilia play important roles in many signaling pathways that regulate growth and specialization of cells during embryonic development. Primary cilia also help maintain healthy tissues. Malfunction of primary cilia has been associated

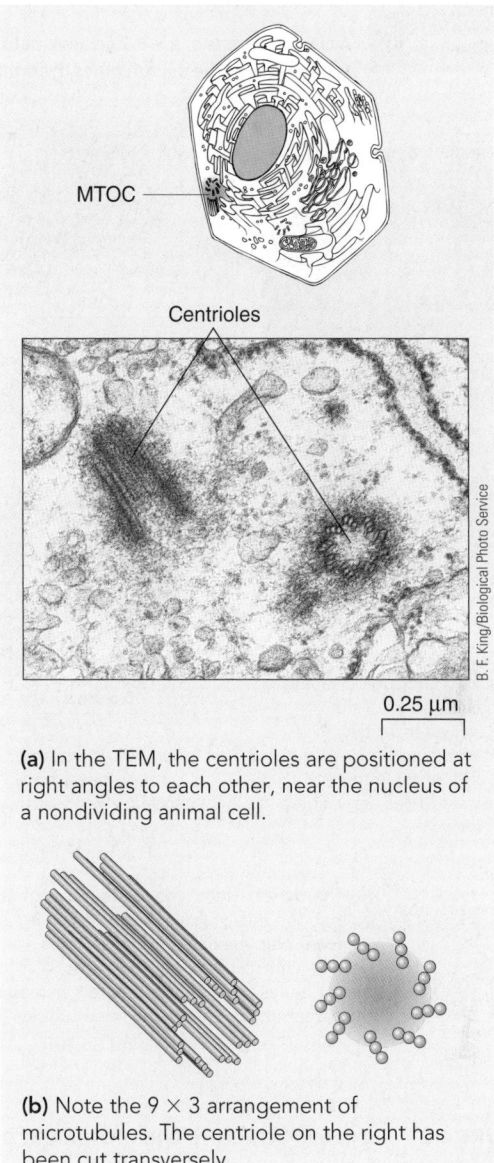

(a) In the TEM, the centrioles are positioned at right angles to each other, near the nucleus of a nondividing animal cell.

(b) Note the 9 × 3 arrangement of microtubules. The centriole on the right has been cut transversely.

FIGURE 4-26 Centrioles

with several human disorders, including developmental defects, degeneration of the retina, and polycystic kidney disease.

Microfilaments consist of intertwined strings of actin

Microfilaments, also called *actin filaments,* are flexible, solid fibers about 7 nm in diameter. Each microfilament consists of two intertwined polymer chains of beadlike **actin** molecules (**FIG. 4-28**). Microfilaments are linked with one another and with other proteins by linker proteins. They form bundles of fibers that provide mechanical support for various cell structures.

In many cells, a network of microfilaments is visible just inside the plasma membrane, a region called the **cell cortex.** Microfilaments give the cell cortex a gel-like consistency compared to the

A cilium consists of a 9 + 2 arrangement of microtubules surrounded by the plasma membrane; dynein proteins move the microtubules by forming and breaking cross bridges on adjacent pairs of microtubules.

0.5 μm

(b) TEM of cross sections through cilia showing 9 + 2 arrangement of microtubules.

0.5 μm

Dennis Kunkel

0.5 μm

(a) TEM of a longitudinal section through cilia and basal bodies of the freshwater protist *Paramecium*. Some of the interior microtubules are visible.

(c) TEM of cross section through basal body showing 9 × 3 structure.

Dr. David M. Phillips/ Visuals Unlimited

Outer pair of microtubules
Dynein
Plasma membrane
Central microtubules

(d) This 3-D representation shows nine attached microtubule pairs (doublets) arranged in a cylinder, with two unattached microtubules in the center. The dynein "feet," shown widely spaced for clarity, are actually much closer together along the longitudinal axis.

(e) The dynein "feet" move the microtubules so that one microtubule pair slides along an adjacent pair. Flexible linking proteins between microtubule pairs prevent microtubules from sliding very far. Instead, the motor action causes the microtubules to bend, resulting in a beating motion.

Microtubular bend

ATP

Linking proteins

Dynein

Pair of microtubules

FIGURE 4-27 *Animated* **Structure and movement of cilia**

more fluid state of the cytosol deeper inside the cell. The microfilaments in the cell cortex help determine the shape of the cell and are important in its movement.

Microfilaments themselves cannot contract, but they can generate movement by rapidly assembling and disassembling. Muscle cells have two types of specialized filaments, one composed mainly of the protein **myosin,** and another composed mainly of the protein actin. ATP bound to myosin provides energy for muscle contraction. When ATP is hydrolyzed to ADP, myosin binds to actin and causes the microfilament to slide. When thousands of filaments slide in this way, the muscle cell shortens. Thus, ATP, actin, and myosin generate the forces that contract muscles (discussed in Chapter 40).

In nonmuscle cells, actin also associates with myosin, forming contractile structures involved in various cell movements. For example, in animal cell division, contraction of a ring of actin asso-

ciated with myosin constricts the cell, forming two daughter cells (discussed in Chapter 10).

Some cells change their shape quickly in response to changes in the outside environment. Amoebas, human white blood cells, and cancer cells are among the many cell types that can creep along a surface, a process that includes changes in shape. Such responses depend on external signals that affect microfilament, as well as microtubule, assembly. Actin filaments push the plasma membrane outward, forming cytoplasm-filled bulges called **pseudopodia** ("false feet"). The pseudopodia adhere to the surface. Contractions of microfilaments at the opposite end of the cell force the cytoplasm forward in the direction of locomotion. Microtubules, myosin, and other proteins also appear necessary for cell creeping.

As mentioned earlier in the chapter, some types of cells have microvilli, projections of the plasma membrane that increase the surface area of the cell for transporting materials across the plasma

(a) A microfilament consists of two intertwined strings of beadlike actin molecules.

Nancy Kedersha

100 μm

(b) Many bundles of microfilaments (*green*) are evident in this fluorescent LM of fibroblasts, cells found in connective tissue.

FIGURE 4-28 Microfilaments

membrane. Composed of bundles of microfilaments, microvilli extend and retract as the microfilaments assemble and disassemble.

Intermediate filaments help stabilize cell shape

Intermediate filaments are tough, flexible fibers about 10 nm in diameter (**FIG. 4-29**). They provide mechanical strength and help stabilize cell shape. These filaments are abundant in regions of a cell that may be subject to mechanical stress applied from outside the cell. Intermediate filaments prevent the cell from stretching excessively in response to outside forces. Certain proteins cross-link intermediate filaments with other types of filaments and mediate interactions between them.

All eukaryotic cells have microtubules and microfilaments, but only some animal groups, including vertebrates, are known to have intermediate filaments. Even when present, intermediate filaments vary widely in protein composition and size among different cell types and different organisms. Examples of intermediate filaments are the keratins found in the epithelial cells of vertebrate skin and neurofilaments found in vertebrate nerve cells.

Certain mutations in genes coding for intermediate filaments weaken the cell and are associated with several diseases. For example, in the neurodegenerative disease amyotrophic lateral sclerosis (ALS, or Lou Gehrig's disease), abnormal neurofilaments have been identified in nerve cells that control muscles. This condition

Protofilament

Protein subunits

Intermediate filament

(a) Intermediate filaments are flexible rods about 10 nm in diameter. Each intermediate filament consists of components, called protofilaments, composed of coiled protein subunits.

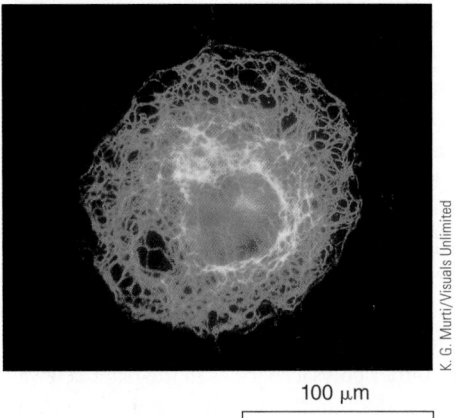

K. G. Murti/Visuals Unlimited

100 μm

(b) Intermediate filaments are stained green in this human cell isolated from a tissue culture.

FIGURE 4-29 Intermediate filaments

interferes with normal transport of materials in the nerve cells and leads to degeneration of the cells. The resulting loss of muscle function is typically fatal.

Review

- What are the main functions of the cytoskeleton?
- How are microfilaments and microtubules similar? How are they different?
- How are cilia and flagella similar? How are they different?

4.7 CELL COVERINGS

■ LEARNING OBJECTIVE

14 Describe the glycocalyx, extracellular matrix, and cell wall.

Many cells are surrounded by a **glycocalyx,** or **cell coat,** formed by polysaccharide side chains of proteins and lipids that are part of the plasma membrane. The glycocalyx protects the cell and may help keep other cells at a distance. Certain molecules of the glycocalyx enable cells to recognize one another, to make contact, and in some cases to form adhesive or communicating associations (discussed in Chapter 5). Other molecules of the cell coat contribute to the mechanical strength of multicellular tissues.

Many animal cells are also surrounded by an **extra-cellular matrix (ECM),** which they secrete. The ECM consists of a gel of carbohydrates and fibrous proteins (**FIG. 4-30**). The main structural protein in the ECM is *collagen,* a protein that forms very tough fibers (see Figure 3-22b). Certain glycoproteins of the ECM, called **fibronectins,** organize the matrix and help cells attach to it. Fibronectins bind to protein receptors that extend from the plasma membrane.

Integrins are receptor proteins in the plasma membrane. They maintain adhesion between the ECM and the intermediate filaments and microfilaments inside the cell. These proteins activate many cell signaling pathways that communicate information from the ECM, and they control signals inside the cell that regulate the differentiation and survival of the cell. When cells are not appropriately anchored, apoptosis is initiated. Integrins are also important in organizing the cytoskeleton so that cells assume a definite shape.

The cells of most bacteria, archaea, fungi, and plant cells are surrounded by a cell wall. Plant cells have thick cell walls that contain tiny fibers composed of the polysaccharide **cellulose** (see Fig. 3-10). Other polysaccharides in the plant cell wall form cross links between the bundles of cellulose fibers. Cell walls provide structural support, protect plant cells from disease-causing organisms, and keep excess water out of cells so they do not burst.

A growing plant cell secretes a thin, flexible *primary cell wall.* As the cell grows, the primary cell wall increases in size (**FIG. 4-31**). After the cell stops growing, either new wall material is secreted that thickens and solidifies the primary wall, or multiple layers of a *secondary cell wall* with a different chemical composition are formed between the primary wall and the plasma membrane. Wood is made mainly of secondary cell walls. The **middle lamella,** a layer of gluelike polysaccharides called *pectins,* lies between the primary cell walls of adjacent cells. The middle lamella causes the cells to adhere tightly to one another. (For more information on plant cell walls, see the discussion of the ground tissue system in Chapter 33.)

Review

- What are the functions of the glycocalyx?
- How do the functions of fibronectins and integrins differ?
- What is the main component of plant cell walls?
- How are plant cell walls formed?

FIGURE 4-30 The extracellular matrix (ECM)
Fibronectins, glycoproteins of the ECM, bind to integrins and other receptors in the plasma membrane.

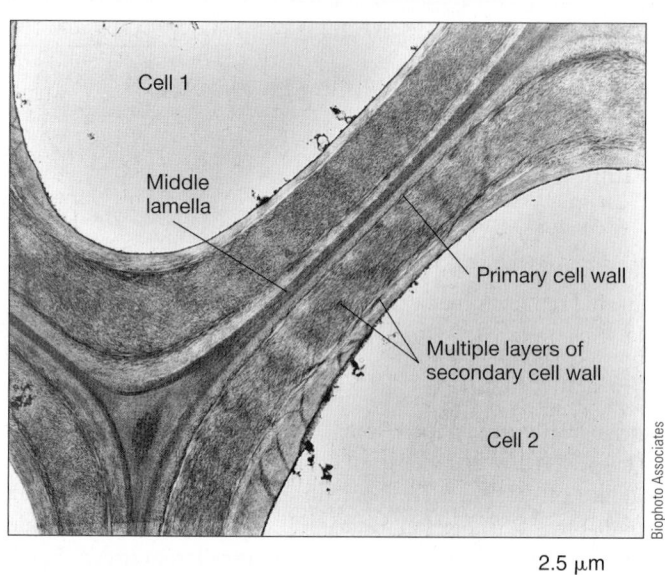

FIGURE 4-31 *Animated* Plant cell walls
The cell walls of two adjacent plant cells are labeled in this TEM. The cells are cemented together by the middle lamella, a layer of gluelike polysaccharides called pectins. A growing plant cell first secretes a thin primary wall that is flexible and can stretch as the cell grows. The thicker layers of the secondary wall are secreted inside the primary wall after the cell stops elongating.

■ SUMMARY: FOCUS ON LEARNING OBJECTIVES

4.1 *(page 75)*

1 Describe the cell theory and relate it to the evolution of life.

- The **cell theory** holds that (1) cells are the basic living units of organization and function in all organisms and (2) all cells come from

other cells. It explains that the ancestry of all the cells alive today can be traced back to ancient times. Evidence that all living cells have evolved from a common ancestor is supported by the basic similarities in their structures and in their molecular composition.

2 Summarize the relationship between cell organization and homeostasis.

- The organization of cells is important in maintaining **homeostasis,** an appropriate internal environment.
- Every cell is surrounded by a **plasma membrane** that separates it from its external environment. The plasma membrane allows the cell to maintain internal conditions that may be very different from those of the outer environment. The plasma membrane also allows the cell to exchange materials with its outer environment. Cells have many **organelles,** internal structures that carry out specific functions that help maintain homeostasis.

3 Explain the relationship between cell size and homeostasis.

- A critical factor in determining cell size is the ratio of the plasma membrane (surface area) to the cell's volume. The plasma membrane must be large enough relative to the cell volume to regulate the passage of materials into and out of the cell. For this reason, most cells are microscopic.
- Cell size and shape are related to function and are limited by the need to maintain homeostasis.

4.2 *(page 77)*

4 Describe methods that biologists use to study cells, including microscopy and cell fractionation.

- Biologists use **light microscopes, electron microscopes,** and a variety of chemical methods to study cells and learn about cell structure. The electron microscope has superior **resolving power,** enabling investigators to see details of cell structures not observable with conventional microscopes.
- Cell biologists use the technique of **cell fractionation** for purifying organelles to gain information about the function of cell structures.

4.3 *(page 81)*

5 Compare and contrast the general characteristics of prokaryotic and eukaryotic cells, and contrast plant and animal cells.

- **Prokaryotic cells** are enclosed by a plasma membrane but have little or no internal membrane organization. They have a **nuclear area** rather than a membrane-enclosed nucleus. Prokaryotic cells typically have a **cell wall** and **ribosomes** and may have propeller-like **flagella.**
- **Eukaryotic cells** have a membrane-enclosed nucleus, and their **cytoplasm** contains a variety of organelles; the fluid component of the cytoplasm is the **cytosol.**
- Plant cells differ from animal cells in that plant cells have rigid cell walls, plastids, and large vacuoles, which are important in plant growth and development. Cells of most plants lack centrioles.

CENGAGENOW™ Test yourself on the structure of prokaryotic and eukaryotic cells by clicking on the interaction in CengageNOW.

6 Describe three functions of cell membranes.

- Membranes divide the eukaryotic cell into compartments, allowing it to conduct specialized activities within small areas of the cytoplasm, concentrate reactants, and organize metabolic reactions. Small membrane-enclosed sacs, called **vesicles,** transport materials between compartments.
- Membranes are important in energy storage and conversion.
- A system of interacting membranes forms the **endomembrane system.**

CENGAGENOW™ Learn more about the endomembrane system by clicking on the figure in CengageNOW.

4.4 *(page 86)*

7 Describe the structure and functions of the nucleus.

- The **nucleus,** the control center of the eukaryotic cell, contains genetic information coded in DNA. The nucleus is bounded by a **nuclear envelope,** consisting of a double membrane perforated with **nuclear pores** that communicate with the cytoplasm.
- DNA in the nucleus associates with protein to form **chromatin,** which is organized into **chromosomes.** During cell division, the chromosomes condense and become visible as threadlike structures.
- The **nucleolus** is a region in the nucleus that is the site of ribosomal RNA synthesis and ribosome assembly.

4.5 *(page 89)*

8 Distinguish between smooth and rough endoplasmic reticulum in terms of both structure and function.

- The **endoplasmic reticulum (ER)** is a network of folded internal membranes in the cytosol. **Smooth ER** is the site of lipid synthesis, calcium ion storage, and detoxifying enzymes.
- **Rough ER** is studded along its outer surface with **ribosomes** that manufacture polypeptides. Polypeptides synthesized on rough ER may be moved into the ER lumen, where they are assembled into proteins and modified by the addition of a carbohydrate or lipid. These proteins may then be transferred to other compartments within the cell by small transport vesicles that bud off from the ER membrane.

9 Trace the path of proteins synthesized in the rough endoplasmic reticulum as they are processed, modified, and sorted by the Golgi complex and then transported to specific destinations.

- The **Golgi complex** consists of stacks of flattened membranous sacs called **cisternae** that process, sort, and modify proteins synthesized on the ER. The Golgi complex also manufactures lysosomes.
- Glycoproteins are transported from the ER to the *cis* face of the Golgi complex by transport vesicles, which are formed by membrane budding. The Golgi complex modifies carbohydrates and lipids that were added to proteins by the ER and packages them in vesicles.
- Glycoproteins exit the Golgi at its *trans* face. The Golgi routes some proteins to the plasma membrane for export from the cell. Others are transported to lysosomes or other organelles within the cytoplasm.

10 Describe the functions of lysosomes, vacuoles, and peroxisomes.

- **Lysosomes** contain enzymes that break down worn-out cell structures, bacteria, and debris taken into cells.
- **Vacuoles** store materials, water, and wastes. They maintain hydrostatic pressure in plant cells.
- **Peroxisomes** are important in lipid metabolism and detoxify harmful compounds such as ethanol. They produce hydrogen peroxide but contain the enzyme catalase, which degrades this toxic compound.

11 Compare the functions of mitochondria and chloroplasts, and discuss ATP synthesis by each of these organelles.

■ **Mitochondria,** organelles enclosed by a double membrane, are the sites of aerobic respiration. The inner membrane is folded, forming **cristae** that increase its surface area.

■ The cristae and the compartment enclosed by the inner membrane, the **matrix,** contain enzymes for the reactions of **aerobic respiration.** During aerobic respiration, nutrients are broken down in the presence of oxygen. Energy captured from nutrients is packaged in ATP, and carbon dioxide and water are produced as byproducts.

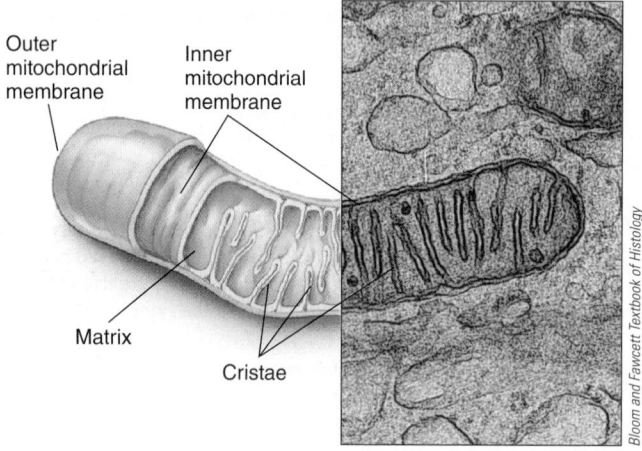

Outer mitochondrial membrane

Inner mitochondrial membrane

Matrix

Cristae

Bloom and Fawcett Textbook of Histology

0.25 μm

■ **Plastids** are organelles that produce and store food in the cells of plants and algae.

■ **Chloroplasts** are plastids that carry out **photosynthesis.**

■ The inner membrane of the chloroplast encloses a fluid-filled space, the **stroma.**

■ **Grana,** stacks of interconnected disclike membranous sacs called **thylakoids,** are suspended in the stroma.

■ During photosynthesis, **chlorophyll,** the green pigment found in the thylakoid membranes, traps light energy. This energy is converted to chemical energy in ATP and used to synthesize carbohydrates from carbon dioxide and water.

4.6 *(page 97)*

12 Describe the structure and functions of the cytoskeleton.

■ The **cytoskeleton** is a dynamic internal framework made of microtubules, microfilaments, and intermediate filaments. The cytoskeleton provides structural support and functions in various types of cell movement, including transport of materials in the cell.

■ **Microtubules** are hollow cylinders assembled from subunits of the protein **tubulin.** In cells that are not dividing, the minus ends of microtubules are anchored in **microtubule-organizing centers (MTOCs).** The main MTOC of animal cells is the **centrosome,** which usually contains two centrioles. Each centriole has a 9 × 3 arrangement of microtubules.

■ **Microfilaments,** or **actin** filaments, formed from subunits of the protein actin, are important in cell movement.

■ **Intermediate filaments** strengthen the cytoskeleton and stabilize cell shape.

CENGAGENOW™ Learn more about the cytoskeleton by clicking on the figure in CengageNOW.

13 Compare cilia and flagella, and describe their functions.

■ **Cilia** and **flagella** are thin, movable structures that project from the cell surface and function in movement. Each consists of a 9 + 2 arrangement of microtubules, and each is anchored in the cell by a basal body that has a 9 × 3 organization of microtubules. Cilia are short, and flagella are long.

4.7 *(page 101)*

14 Describe the glycocalyx, extracellular matrix, and cell wall.

■ Most cells are surrounded by a **glycocalyx,** or **cell coat,** formed by polysaccharides extending from the plasma membrane.

■ Many animal cells are also surrounded by an **extracellular matrix (ECM)** consisting of carbohydrates and protein. **Fibronectins** are glycoproteins of the ECM that bind to **integrins,** receptor proteins in the plasma membrane.

■ Cells of most bacteria, archaea, fungi, and plant cells are surrounded by a cell wall made mainly of carbohydrates. Plant cells secrete **cellulose** and other polysaccharides that form rigid cell walls.

TEST YOUR UNDERSTANDING

1. The ability of a microscope to reveal fine detail is known as (a) magnification (b) resolving power (c) cell fractionation (d) transmission microscopy (e) phase contrast

2. A plasma membrane is characteristic of (a) all cells (b) prokaryotic cells only (c) eukaryotic cells only (d) animal cells only (e) eukaryotic cells except plant cells

3. Detailed information about the shape and external features of a specimen can best be obtained by using a (a) differential centrifuge (b) fluorescence microscope (c) transmission electron microscope (d) scanning electron microscope (e) light microscope

4. Which of the following structures would *not* be found in prokaryotic cells? (a) cell wall (b) ribosomes (c) nuclear area (d) nucleus (e) propeller-like flagellum

5. Which of the following is/are most closely associated with protein synthesis? (a) ribosomes (b) smooth ER (c) mitochondria (d) microfilaments (e) lysosomes

6. Which of the following is/are most closely associated with the breakdown of ingested material? (a) ribosomes (b) smooth ER (c) mitochondria (d) microfilaments (e) lysosomes

7. Which of the following are most closely associated with photosynthesis? (a) basal bodies (b) smooth ER (c) cristae (d) thylakoids (e) MTOCs

8. Use the choices of numbered sequences to select the sequence that most accurately describes information flow in the eukaryotic cell. 1. DNA in nucleus 2. RNA 3. mitochondria 4. protein synthesis 5. ribosomes
(a) 1, 2, 5, 4 (b) 3, 2, 5, 1 (c) 5, 2, 3, 1 (d) 4, 3, 2, 1 (e) 1, 2, 3, 4

9. Use the choices of numbered sequences to select the sequence that most accurately describes glycoprotein processing in the eukaryotic cell.
   1. ER 2. ribosomes 3. *cis* face of Golgi 4. *trans* face of Golgi
   5. transport vesicle 6. grana
   (a) 1, 6, 2, 3, 4 (b) 2, 1, 3, 4, 5 (c) 1, 2, 4, 3, 5 (d) 2, 1, 4, 3, 5
   (e) 2, 1, 4, 5, 1

10. Which of the following organelles contain small amounts of DNA and convert energy? (a) microfilaments and microtubules (b) lysosomes and peroxisomes (c) ER and ribosomes (d) nucleus and ribosomes (e) mitochondria and chloroplasts

11. Which of the following function(s) in cell movement? (a) microtubules (b) nucleolus (c) grana (d) smooth ER (e) rough ER

12. Label the diagrams of the animal and plant cells. How is the structure of each organelle related to its function? Use Figures 4-9 and 4-10 to check your answers.

CRITICAL THINKING

1. Why does a eukaryotic cell need both membranous organelles and fibrous cytoskeletal components?

2. Describe a specific example of the correlation between cell structure and function. (*Hint:* Think of mitochondrial structure.)

3. The *Acetabularia* experiments described in this chapter suggest that DNA is much more stable in the cell than is messenger RNA. Is this advantageous or disadvantageous to the cell? Why? *Acetabularia* continues to live for a few days after its nucleus is removed. How can you explain this?

4. **EVOLUTION LINK.** What are the implications of the cell theory for the evolution of organisms?

5. **EVOLUTION LINK.** Biologists use similarities in cells to trace the evolutionary history of various groups of organisms. Explain their rationale. What do such similarities in cell structure and function tell biologists about the common origin of organisms? Explain.

 Additional questions are available in CengageNOW at www.cengage.com/login.

5 Biological Membranes

Cadherins. The human skin cells shown in this LM were grown in culture and stained with fluorescent antibodies. Cadherins, a group of membrane proteins, are seen as green belts around each cell in this sheet of cells. The nuclei appear as blue spheres; myosin in the cells appears red.

Nancy Kedersha

KEY CONCEPTS

5.1 Biological membranes are selectively permeable membranes that help maintain homeostasis in the cell; each cell membrane consists of a fluid bilayer composed of phospholipids in which a variety of proteins are embedded.

5.2 Membrane proteins, and thus membranes, have many functions, including transport of materials, enzymatic activity, transfer of information, and recognition of other cells.

5.3 Transport proteins move ions and small polar molecules through cell membranes.

5.4 Many ions and small molecules move through biological membranes by diffusion, the net movement of particles from a region of higher to a region of lower concentrations.

5.5 Because a cell requires many substances in higher concentrations than their concentrations outside the cell, substances must be actively transported against a concentration gradient; active transport requires a direct expenditure of energy.

5.6 Cells eject products by exocytosis and import materials by endocytosis; both processes require cells to expend energy.

5.7 Cells in close contact may form specialized junctions with one another.

The evolution of biological membranes that separate the cell from its external environment was an essential step in the origin of life. Later, these membranes made the evolution of complex cells possible. The extensive internal membranes of eukaryotic cells form multiple compartments with unique environments that allow highly specialized activities to take place.

Because membrane proteins are critical molecules in cell membrane activities, they are a major focus of cell membrane research. Some proteins associated with the plasma membrane transport materials, whereas others transmit information or serve as enzymes. Still others, known as *cell adhesion molecules,* are important in connecting cells to one another to form tissues. The principal cell adhesion molecules in vertebrates and in many invertebrates are **cadherins.**

The genes that code cadherins are found in choanoflagellates, the closest single-celled relatives of animals. These molecules were probably important in the evolution of animals because they provided a means for cells to adhere to one another and to communicate. Cadherins are responsible for adhesion between cells that form multicellular sheets. For example, these membrane proteins form cell junctions important in maintaining the structure of the epithelium that makes up human skin (see photograph). Cadherins are also important in signaling among cells. An absence of these membrane proteins is associated with the invasiveness of some malignant tumors.

In Chapter 4, we discussed a variety of cell organelles and how they interact to perform cell activities. In this chapter, we focus on the structure and functions of the plasma membrane that surrounds the cell, and on the biological membranes that surround many organelles. We first consider what is known about the composition and structure of biological membranes. Then we provide an overview of the many vital functions of cell membranes, including transport of materials and information transfer. We discuss how cells transport various materials, from ions to complex molecules and even bacteria, across membranes. Finally, we examine specialized structures that allow membranes of different cells to interact. Although much of our discussion centers on the structure and functions of plasma membranes, many of the concepts apply to other cell membranes.

5.1 THE STRUCTURE OF BIOLOGICAL MEMBRANES

▪ LEARNING OBJECTIVES

1 Evaluate the importance of membranes to the homeostasis of the cell, emphasizing their various functions.
2 Describe the fluid mosaic model of cell membrane structure.
3 Relate properties of the lipid bilayer to properties and functions of cell membranes.
4 Describe the ways that membrane proteins associate with the lipid bilayer.

To carry out the many chemical reactions necessary to sustain life, the cell must maintain an appropriate internal environment. Every cell is surrounded by a **plasma membrane** that physically separates it from the outside world and defines it as a distinct entity. By regulating passage of materials into and out of the cell, the plasma membrane helps maintain a life-supporting internal environment. As we discussed in Chapter 4, eukaryotic cells are characterized by numerous organelles that are surrounded by membranes. Some of these organelles—including the nuclear envelope, endoplasmic reticulum (ER), Golgi complex, lysosomes, vesicles, and vacuoles—form the endomembrane system, which extends throughout the cell.

Biological membranes are complex, dynamic structures made of lipid and protein molecules that are in constant motion. The properties of membranes allow them to perform many vital functions. They regulate the passage of materials, divide the cell into compartments, serve as surfaces for chemical reactions, adhere to and communicate with other cells, and transmit signals between the environment and the interior of the cell. Membranes are also an essential part of energy transfer and storage systems. How do the properties of cell membranes enable the cell to carry on such varied functions?

Long before the development of the electron microscope, scientists knew that membranes consist of both lipids and proteins. Work by researchers in the 1920s and 1930s had provided clues that the core of cell membranes consists of lipids, mostly phospholipids (see Chapter 3).

Phospholipids form bilayers in water

Phospholipids are primarily responsible for the physical properties of biological membranes, because certain phospholipids have unique attributes, including features that allow them to form bilayered structures. A phospholipid contains two fatty acid chains linked to two of the three carbons of a glycerol molecule (see Fig. 3-13). The fatty acid chains make up the nonpolar, *hydrophobic* ("water-fearing") portion of the phospholipid. Bonded to the third carbon of the glycerol is a negatively charged, *hydrophilic* ("water-loving") phosphate group, which in turn is linked to a polar, hydrophilic organic group. Molecules of this type, which have distinct hydrophobic and hydrophilic regions, are called **amphipathic molecules.** All lipids that make up the core of biological membranes have amphipathic characteristics.

Because one end of each phospholipid associates freely with water and the opposite end does not, the most stable orientation for them to assume in water results in the formation of a bilayer structure (**FIG. 5-1a**). This arrangement allows the hydrophilic heads of the phospholipids to be in contact with the aqueous medium while their oily tails, the hydrophobic fatty acid chains, are buried in the interior of the structure away from the water molecules.

Amphipathic properties alone do not predict the ability of lipids to associate as a bilayer. Shape is also important. Phospholipids tend to have uniform widths; their roughly cylindrical shapes, together with their amphipathic properties, are responsible for bilayer formation. In summary, phospholipids form bilayers because the molecules have (1) two distinct regions, one strongly hydrophobic and the other strongly hydrophilic (making them strongly amphipathic) and (2) cylindrical shapes that allow them to associate with water most easily as a bilayer.

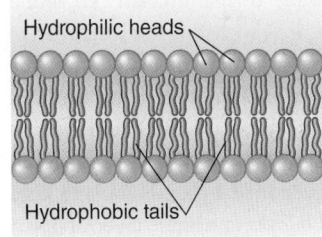

Hydrophilic heads
Hydrophobic tails

(a) Phospholipids in water. Phospholipids associate as bilayers in water because they are roughly cylindrical amphipathic molecules. The hydrophobic fatty acid chains are not exposed to water, whereas the hydrophilic phospholipid heads are in contact with water.

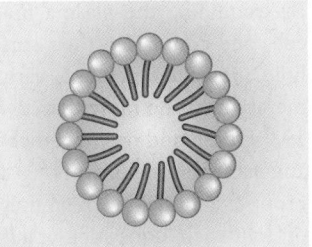

(b) Detergent in water. Detergent molecules are roughly cone-shaped amphipathic molecules that associate in water as spherical structures.

FIGURE 5-1 *Animated* **Properties of lipids in water**

The Davson–Danielli model was the accepted view until about 1970 when advances in biology and chemistry led to new findings about biological membranes that were incompatible with this model. The fluid mosaic model is supported by a large body of data.

(a) The Davson–Danielli model. According to this model, the membrane is a sandwich of phospholipids spread between two layers of protein. Although accepted for many years, this model was shown to be incorrect.

(b) Fluid mosaic model. According to this model, a cell membrane is a fluid lipid bilayer with a constantly changing "mosaic pattern" of associated proteins.

FIGURE 5-2 Two models of membrane structure

Do you know why detergents remove grease from your hands or from dirty dishes? Many common detergents are amphipathic molecules, each containing a single hydrocarbon chain (like a fatty acid) at one end and a hydrophilic region at the other. These molecules are roughly cone-shaped, with the hydrophilic end forming the broad base and the hydrocarbon tail leading to the point. Because of their shapes, these molecules do not associate as bilayers but instead tend to form spherical structures in water (**FIG. 5-1b**). Detergents can "solubilize" oil because the oil molecules associate with the hydrophobic interiors of the spheres.

The fluid mosaic model explains membrane structure

By examining the plasma membrane of mammalian red blood cells and comparing their surface area with the total number of lipid molecules per cell, early investigators calculated that the membrane is no more than two phospholipid molecules thick. In 1935, these findings, together with other data, led Hugh Davson and James Danielli, working at London's University College, to propose a model in which they envisioned a membrane as a kind of "sandwich" consisting of a *lipid bilayer* (a double layer of lipid) between two protein layers (**FIG. 5-2a**). This useful model had a great influence on the direction of membrane research for more than 20 years. Models are important in the scientific process; good ones not only explain the available data but are testable. Scientists use models to help them develop hypotheses that can be tested experimentally (see Chapter 1).

With the development of the electron microscope in the 1950s, cell biologists were able to see the plasma membrane for the first time. One of their most striking observations was how uniform and thin the membranes are. The plasma membrane is no more than 10 nm thick. The electron microscope revealed a three-

layered structure, something like a railroad track, with two dark layers separated by a lighter layer (**FIG. 5-3**). Their findings seemed to support the protein–lipid–protein sandwich model.

During the 1960s, a paradox emerged regarding the arrangement of the proteins. Biologists assumed membrane proteins were uniform and had shapes that would allow them to lie like thin sheets on the membrane surface. But when purified by cell fractionation, the proteins were far from uniform; in fact, they varied widely in composition and size. Some proteins are quite large. How could they fit within a surface layer of a membrane less than 10 nm thick?

FIGURE 5-3 TEM of the plasma membrane of a mammalian red blood cell

The plasma membrane separates the cytosol (*darker region*) from the external environment (*lighter region*). The hydrophilic heads of the phospholipids are the parallel dark lines, and the hydrophobic tails are the light zone between them.

At first, some researchers tried to answer this question by modifying the model with the hypothesis that the proteins on the membrane surfaces were a flattened, extended form, perhaps a β-pleated sheet (see Fig. 3-20b).

Other cell biologists found that instead of having sheetlike structures, many membrane proteins are rounded, or globular. Studies of many membrane proteins showed that one region (or domain) of the molecule could always be found on one side of the bilayer, whereas another part of the protein might be located on the opposite side. Rather than form a thin surface layer, many membrane proteins extended completely through the lipid bilayer. Thus, the evidence suggested that membranes contain different types of proteins of different shapes and sizes that are associated with the bilayer in a mosaic pattern.

In 1972, S. Jonathan Singer and Garth Nicolson of the University of California at San Diego proposed a model of membrane structure that represented a synthesis of the known properties of biological membranes. According to their **fluid mosaic model,** a cell membrane consists of a fluid bilayer of phospholipid molecules in which the proteins are embedded or otherwise associated, much like the tiles in a mosaic picture. This mosaic pattern is not static, however, because the positions of many of the proteins are constantly changing as they move about like icebergs in a fluid sea of phospholipids. This model has provided great impetus to research; it has been repeatedly tested and has been shown to accurately predict the properties of many kinds of cell membranes. **FIGURE 5-2b** depicts the plasma membrane of a eukaryotic cell according to the fluid mosaic model; prokaryotic plasma membranes are discussed in Chapter 25.

Biological membranes are two-dimensional fluids

An important physical property of phospholipid bilayers is that they behave like *liquid crystals*. The bilayers are crystal-like in that the lipid molecules form an ordered array with the heads on the outside and fatty acid chains on the inside; they are liquid-like in that despite the orderly arrangement of the molecules, their hydrocarbon chains are in constant motion. Thus, molecules are free to rotate and can move laterally within their single layer (**FIG. 5-4**). Such movement gives the bilayer the property of a *two-dimensional fluid.* Under normal conditions a single phospholipid molecule can travel laterally across the surface of a eukaryotic cell in seconds.

The fluid qualities of lipid bilayers also allow molecules embedded in

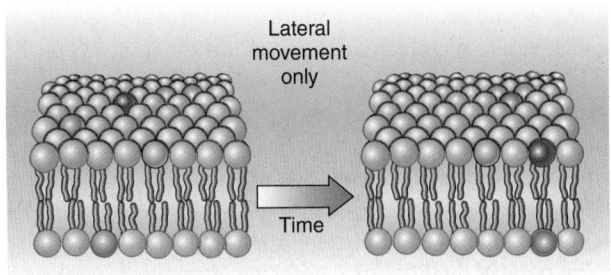

FIGURE 5-4 Membrane fluidity

The ordered arrangement of phospholipid molecules makes the cell membrane a liquid crystal. The hydrocarbon chains are in constant motion, allowing each molecule to move laterally on the same side of the bilayer.

them to move along the plane of the membrane (as long as they are not anchored in some way). David Frye and Michael Edidin elegantly demonstrated this in 1970. They conducted experiments in which they followed the movement of membrane proteins on the surface of two cells that had been joined (**FIG. 5-5**). When the plasma membranes of a mouse cell and a human cell are fused, within minutes at least some of the membrane proteins from each

KEY EXPERIMENT

QUESTION: Do proteins embedded in a biological membrane move about?

HYPOTHESIS: Proteins are able to move laterally in the plasma membrane.

EXPERIMENT: Larry Frye and Michael Edidin labeled membrane proteins of mouse and human cells using different-colored fluorescent dyes to distinguish between them. Then they fused mouse and human cells to produce hybrid cells.

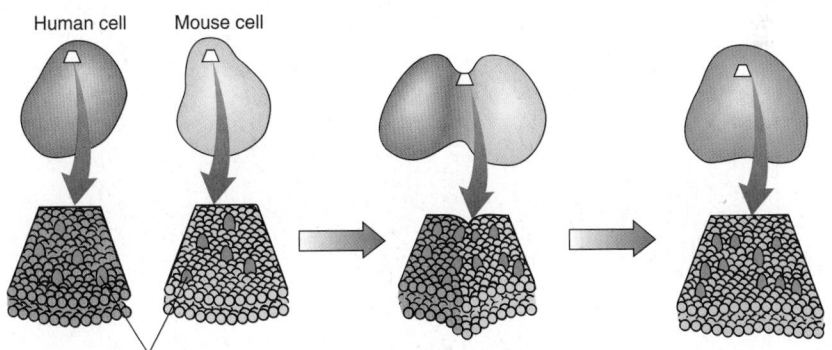

1 Labeled membrane proteins. Membrane proteins of mouse cells and human cells were labeled with fluorescent dye markers in two different colors.

2 Human-mouse hybrid cell forming. When plasma membranes of mouse cell and human cell were fused, mouse proteins migrated to the human side and human proteins to the mouse side.

3 Proteins randomly distributed. After a short time, mouse and human proteins became randomly distributed through the membrane.

RESULTS AND CONCLUSION: After a brief period of incubation, mouse and human cells intermixed over the surface of the hybrid cells. After about 40 minutes, the proteins of each species had become randomly distributed through the entire hybrid plasma membrane. This experiment demonstrated that proteins in the plasma membrane do move.

FIGURE 5-5 *Animated* Frye and Edidin's experiment

Source: Frye, L. D., and M. Edidin. "The rapid intermixing of cell surface antigens after formation of mouse-human heterokaryons." *Journal of Cell Science,* Vol. 7, 319–335, 1970.

cell migrate and become randomly distributed over the single, continuous plasma membrane that surrounds the joined cells. Frye and Edidin showed that the fluidity of the lipids in the membrane allows many of the proteins to move, producing an ever-changing configuration. Occasionally, with the help of enzymes in the cell membrane, phospholipid molecules flip-flop from one layer to the other.

For a membrane to function properly, its lipids must be in a state of optimal fluidity. The membrane's structure is weakened if its lipids are too fluid. However, many membrane functions, such as the transport of certain substances, are inhibited or cease if the lipid bilayer is too rigid. At normal temperatures, cell membranes are fluid, but at low temperatures the motion of the fatty acid chains is slowed. If the temperature decreases to a critical point, the membrane is converted to a more solid gel state.

Certain properties of membrane lipids have significant effects on the fluidity of the bilayer. Recall from Chapter 3 that molecules are free to rotate around single carbon-to-carbon covalent bonds. Because most of the bonds in hydrocarbon chains are single bonds, the chains themselves twist more and more rapidly as the temperature rises.

The fluid state of the membrane depends on its component lipids. You have probably noticed that when melted butter is left at room temperature it solidifies. Vegetable oils, however, remain liquid at room temperature. Recall from our discussion of lipids in Chapter 3 that animal fats such as butter are high in saturated fatty acids that lack double bonds. In contrast, a vegetable oil may be polyunsaturated, with most of its fatty acid chains having two or more double bonds. At each double bond there is a bend in the molecule that prevents the hydrocarbon chains from coming

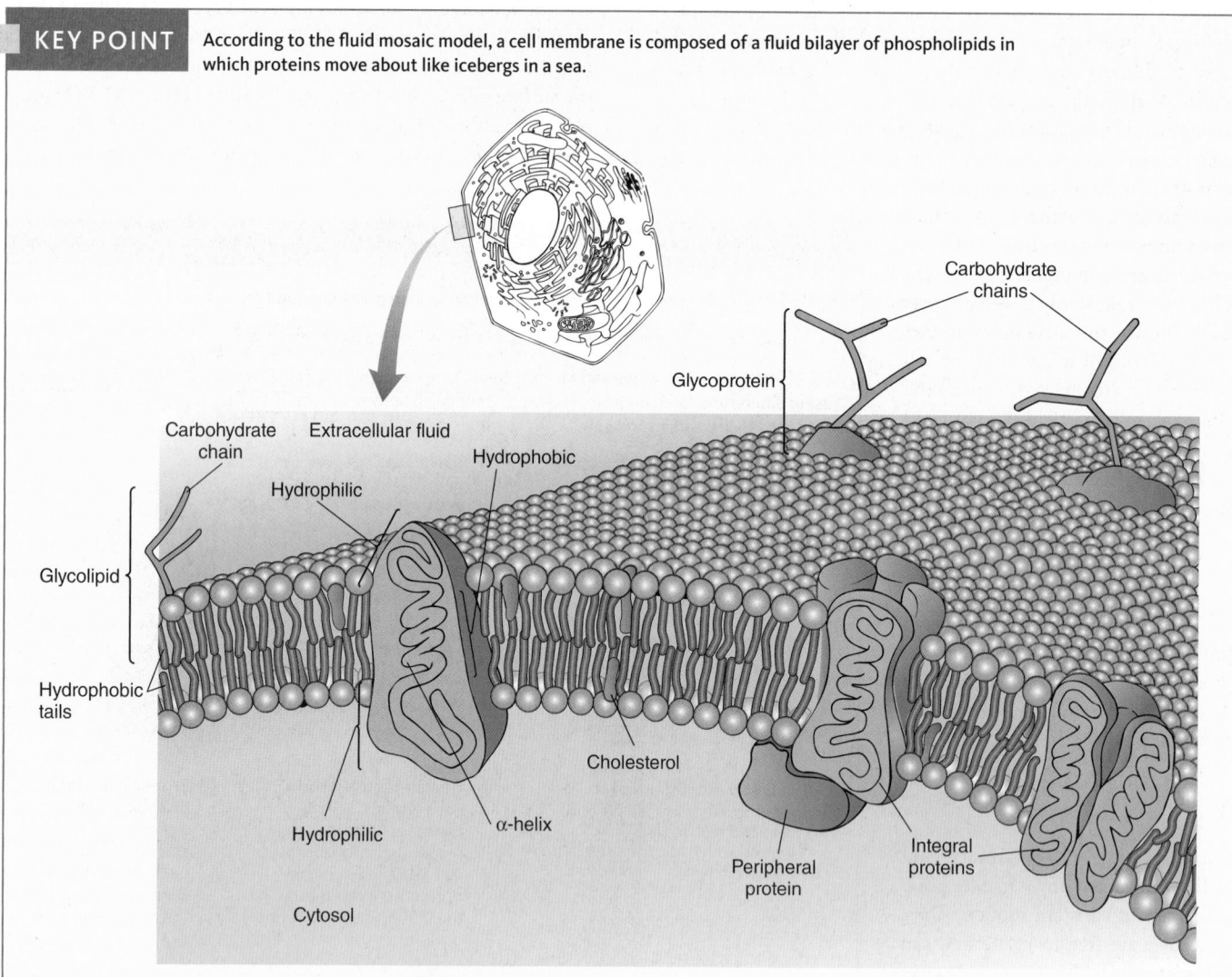

KEY POINT According to the fluid mosaic model, a cell membrane is composed of a fluid bilayer of phospholipids in which proteins move about like icebergs in a sea.

FIGURE 5-6 Detailed structure of the plasma membrane

Although the lipid bilayer consists mainly of phospholipids, other lipids, such as cholesterol and glycolipids, are present. Peripheral proteins are loosely associated with the bilayer, whereas integral proteins are tightly bound. The integral proteins shown here are transmembrane proteins that extend through the bilayer. They have hydrophilic regions on both sides of the bilayer, connected by a membrane-spanning α-helix. Glycolipids (carbohydrates attached to lipids) and glycoproteins (carbohydrates attached to proteins) are exposed on the extracellular surface; they play roles in cell recognition and adhesion to other cells.

close together and interacting through van der Waals interactions. In this way, unsaturated fats lower the temperature at which oil or membrane lipids solidify.

Many organisms have regulatory mechanisms for maintaining cell membranes in an optimally fluid state. Some organisms compensate for temperature changes by altering the fatty acid content of their membrane lipids. When the outside temperature is cold, the membrane lipids contain relatively high proportions of unsaturated fatty acids.

Some membrane lipids stabilize membrane fluidity within certain limits. One such "fluidity buffer" is cholesterol, a steroid found in animal cell membranes. A cholesterol molecule is largely hydrophobic but is slightly amphipathic because of the presence of a single hydroxyl group (see Fig. 3-15a). This hydroxyl group associates with the hydrophilic heads of the phospholipids; the hydrophobic remainder of the cholesterol molecule fits between the fatty acid hydrocarbon chains (**FIG. 5-6**).

At low temperatures cholesterol molecules act as "spacers" between the hydrocarbon chains, restricting van der Waals interactions that would promote solidifying. Cholesterol also helps prevent the membrane from becoming weakened or unstable at higher temperatures. The reason is that the cholesterol molecules interact strongly with the portions of the hydrocarbon chains closest to the phospholipid head. This interaction restricts motion in these regions. Plant cells have steroids other than cholesterol that carry out similar functions.

Biological membranes fuse and form closed vesicles

Lipid bilayers, particularly those in the liquid-crystalline state, have additional important physical properties. Bilayers tend to resist forming free ends; as a result, they are self-sealing and under most conditions spontaneously round up to form closed vesicles.

Lipid bilayers are also flexible, allowing cell membranes to change shape without breaking. Under appropriate conditions lipid bilayers fuse with other bilayers.

Membrane fusion is an important cell process. When a vesicle fuses with another membrane, both membrane bilayers and their compartments become continuous. Various transport vesicles form from, and also merge with, membranes of the ER and Golgi complex, facilitating the transfer of materials from one compartment to another. A vesicle fuses with the plasma membrane when a product is secreted from the cell.

Membrane proteins include integral and peripheral proteins

The two major classes of membrane proteins, integral proteins and peripheral proteins, are defined by how tightly they are associated with the lipid bilayer (**FIG. 5-7**). **Integral membrane proteins** are firmly bound to the membrane. Cell biologists usually can release them only by disrupting the bilayer with detergents. These proteins are amphipathic. Their hydrophilic regions extend out of the cell or into the cytoplasm, whereas their hydrophobic regions interact with the fatty acid tails of the membrane phospholipids.

Some integral proteins do not extend all the way through the membrane. Many others, called **transmembrane proteins,** extend completely through the membrane. Some span the membrane only once, whereas others wind back and forth as many as 24 times. The most common kind of transmembrane protein is an *a*-helix (see Chapter 3) with hydrophobic amino acid side chains projecting out from the helix into the hydrophobic region of the lipid bilayer. Some proteins span the membrane in the form of rolled-up β-pleated sheets. These protein formations are barrel-shaped and form pores through which water and other substances can pass.

Peripheral membrane proteins are not embedded in the lipid bilayer. They are located on the inner or outer surface of the plasma

(a) A single α-helix

(b) A protein consisting of several α-helices

(c) A rolled-up β-pleated sheet

(d) Peripheral protein bound to an integral protein

(e) Peripheral protein bound to an integral protein

FIGURE 5-7 *Animated* **Membrane proteins**

Three transmembrane proteins are shown in **(a), (b),** and **(c).** The rolled-up β-pleated sheet shown in **(c)** forms a pore through the membrane. Water molecules and ions pass through specific types of pores **(d, e).** Peripheral proteins are bound to integral proteins by noncovalent interactions.

Why Is It Used? The freeze-fracture method is used to split the lipid bilayer apart so that its components can be analyzed.

How Is It Done?

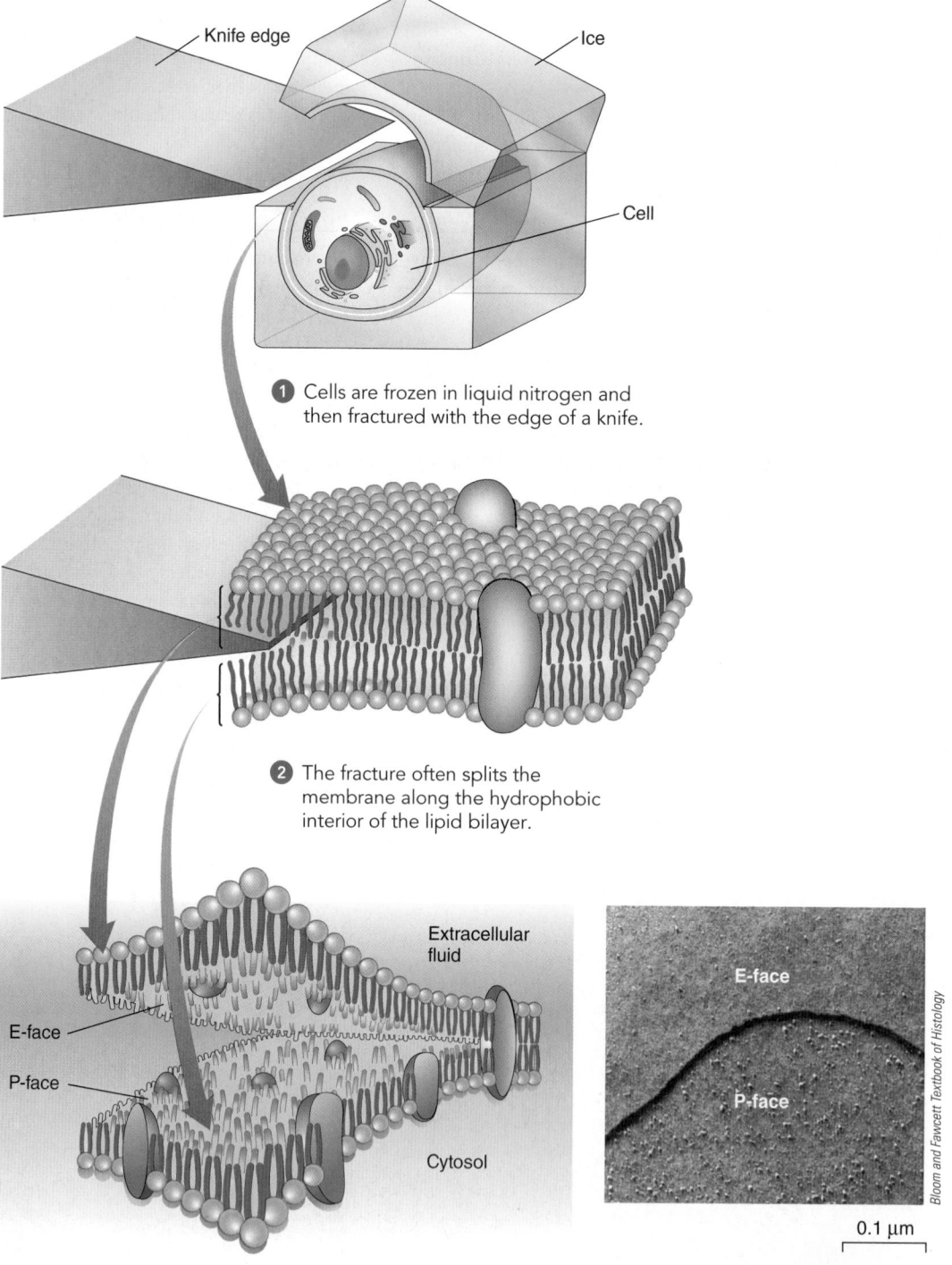

Knife edge

Ice

Cell

1 Cells are frozen in liquid nitrogen and then fractured with the edge of a knife.

2 The fracture often splits the membrane along the hydrophobic interior of the lipid bilayer.

Extracellular fluid

E-face

P-face

Cytosol

E-face

P-face

0.1 μm

Bloom and Fawcett Textbook of Histology

3 Two complementary fracture faces result. The inner half-membrane presents the P-face (or protoplasmic face), and the outer half-membrane presents the E-face (or external face). Integral proteins, including transmembrane proteins, are inserted through the lipid bilayer.

4 An electron microscope is used to view the interior surfaces (faces) of the two layers. In this TEM the particles (which appear as bumps) represent large integral proteins.

FIGURE 5-8 Freeze-fracture method

membrane, usually bound to exposed regions of integral proteins by noncovalent interactions. Peripheral proteins can be easily removed from the membrane without disrupting the structure of the bilayer.

Proteins are oriented asymmetrically across the bilayer

One of the most remarkable demonstrations that proteins are actually embedded in the lipid bilayer comes from *freeze–fracture* electron microscopy, a technique that splits the membrane into halves. The researcher can literally see the two halves of the membrane from "inside out." When cell biologists examine membranes in this way, they observe numerous particles on the fracture faces (**FIG. 5-8**). The particles are clearly integral membrane proteins, because researchers never see them in freeze-fractured artificial lipid bilayers. These findings profoundly influenced Singer and Nicolson in developing the fluid mosaic model.

Membrane protein molecules are *asymmetrically oriented*. The asymmetry is produced by the highly specific way in which each protein is inserted into the bilayer. Membrane proteins that will become part of the inner surface of the plasma membrane are manufactured by free ribosomes and move to the membrane through the cytoplasm. Membrane proteins that will be associated with the cell's outer surface are manufactured like proteins destined to be exported from the cell.

As discussed in Chapter 4, proteins destined for the cell's outer surface are initially manufactured by ribosomes on the rough ER. They pass through the ER membrane into the ER lumen, where sugars are added, making them **glycoproteins.** However, only a part of each protein passes through the ER membrane, so each completed protein has some regions that are located in the ER lumen and other regions that remain in the cytosol. Enzymes that attach the sugars to certain amino acids on the protein are found only in the lumen of the ER. Thus, carbohydrates can be added only to the parts of proteins located in that compartment.

In **FIGURE 5-9**, follow from top to bottom the vesicle budding and membrane fusion events that are part of the transport process. You can see that the same region of the protein that protruded into

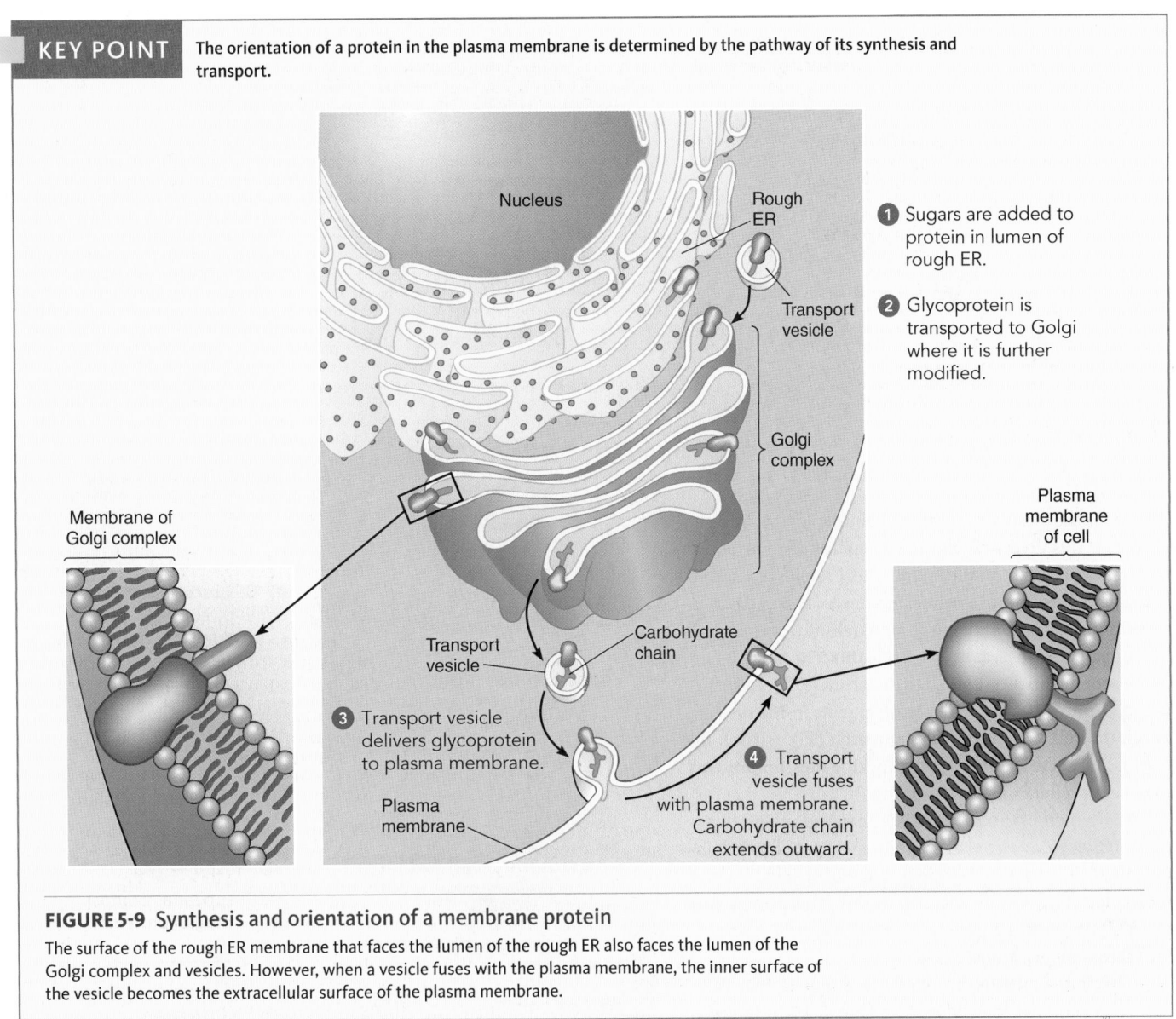

KEY POINT The orientation of a protein in the plasma membrane is determined by the pathway of its synthesis and transport.

Nucleus

Rough ER

Transport vesicle

Golgi complex

Membrane of Golgi complex

Transport vesicle

Carbohydrate chain

Plasma membrane of cell

① Sugars are added to protein in lumen of rough ER.

② Glycoprotein is transported to Golgi where it is further modified.

③ Transport vesicle delivers glycoprotein to plasma membrane.

Plasma membrane

④ Transport vesicle fuses with plasma membrane. Carbohydrate chain extends outward.

FIGURE 5-9 Synthesis and orientation of a membrane protein
The surface of the rough ER membrane that faces the lumen of the rough ER also faces the lumen of the Golgi complex and vesicles. However, when a vesicle fuses with the plasma membrane, the inner surface of the vesicle becomes the extracellular surface of the plasma membrane.

Biological Membranes   113

the ER lumen is also transported to the lumen of the Golgi complex. There additional enzymes further modify the carbohydrate chains. Within the Golgi complex, the glycoprotein is sorted and directed to the plasma membrane. The modified region of the protein remains inside the membrane compartment of a transport vesicle as it buds from the Golgi complex. Note that when the transport vesicle fuses with the plasma membrane, the inside layer of the transport vesicle becomes the outside layer of the plasma membrane. The carbohydrate chain extends to the exterior of the cell surface.

In summary, this is the sequence:

sugar added to protein in ER lumen ⟶ glycoprotein transported to Golgi complex, where it is further modified ⟶ glycoprotein transported to plasma membrane ⟶ transport vesicle fuses with plasma membrane (inside layer of transport vesicle becomes outer layer of plasma membrane)

Review

- What molecules are responsible for the physical properties of a cell membrane?
- How might a transmembrane protein be positioned in a lipid bilayer? How do the hydrophilic and hydrophobic regions of the protein affect its orientation?
- What is the pathway used by cells to place carbohydrates on plasma membrane proteins?

5.2 OVERVIEW OF MEMBRANE PROTEIN FUNCTIONS

◼ LEARNING OBJECTIVE

5   Summarize the functions of membrane proteins.

Why does the plasma membrane require so many different proteins? This diversity reflects the multitude of activities that take place in or on the membrane. Proteins associated with the membrane are essential for most of these activities. Generally, plasma membrane proteins fall into several broad functional categories, as shown in **FIGURE 5-10**. Some membrane proteins anchor the cell to its substrate. For example, *integrins,* proteins bound to microfilaments inside the cell, attach the cell to the extracellular matrix (Fig. 5-10a). Integrins also serve as receptors, or docking sites, for proteins of the extracellular matrix (see Fig. 4-30).

Many membrane proteins are involved in the transport of molecules across the membrane. Some form channels that selectively allow the passage of specific ions or molecules (Fig. 5-10b). Other proteins form pumps that use ATP, or other energy sources, to actively transport solutes across the membrane (Fig. 5-10c).

Certain membrane proteins are enzymes that catalyze reactions near the cell surface (Fig. 5-10d). In mito-

(a) Anchoring. Some membrane proteins, such as integrins, anchor the cell to the extracellular matrix; they also connect to microfilaments within the cell.

(b) Passive transport. Certain proteins form channels for selective passage of ions or molecules.

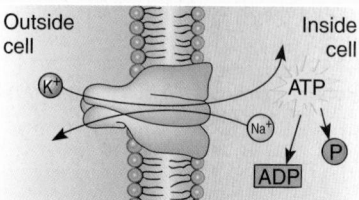

(c) Active transport. Some transport proteins pump solutes across the membrane, which requires a direct input of energy.

(d) Enzymatic activity. Many membrane-bound enzymes catalyze reactions that take place within or along the membrane surface.

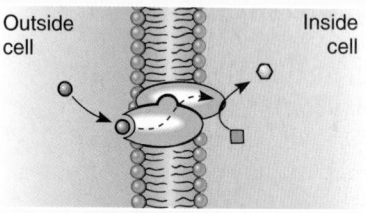

(e) Signal transduction. Some receptors bind with signal molecules such as hormones and transmit information into the cell.

(f) Cell recognition. Some glycoproteins function as identification tags. For example, bacterial cells have surface proteins, or antigens, that human cells recognize as foreign.

(g) Intercellular junction. Cell adhesion proteins attach membranes of adjacent cells.

FIGURE 5-10 Some functions of membrane proteins

chondrial or chloroplast membranes, enzymes are organized in sequences that allow the organelle to efficiently regulate series of reactions in cellular respiration or photosynthesis.

Some membrane proteins are receptors that receive information from other cells in the form of chemical or electrical signals. Most vertebrate cells have receptors for hormones released by endocrine glands. Information may be transmitted from proteins in the plasma membrane to the cell interior by *signal transduction* (discussed in Chapter 6; Fig. 5-10e).

Some membrane proteins serve as identification tags that other cells recognize. For example, certain cells recognize the surface proteins, or *antigens,* of bacterial cells as foreign. Antigens stimulate immune defenses that destroy the bacteria (Fig. 5-10f). When certain cells recognize one another, they connect to form tissues. Some membrane proteins form junctions between adjacent cells (Fig. 5-10g). These proteins may also serve as anchoring points for networks of cytoskeletal elements. In the remaining sections of this chapter, we will discuss the functions of cell membrane proteins in transporting material into and out of the cell, and we will discuss junctions between cells. We will discuss other functions of cell membranes in many of the chapters that follow.

Review

- How do proteins function in transporting materials into the cell?
- What role do membrane proteins play in cell recognition?

5.3 CELL MEMBRANE STRUCTURE AND PERMEABILITY

■ LEARNING OBJECTIVE

6   Describe the importance of selectively permeable membranes and compare the functions of carrier proteins and channel proteins.

A membrane is *permeable* to a given substance if it allows that substance to pass through and impermeable if it does not. The fluid mosaic structure of biological membranes allows them to function as **selectively permeable membranes**—they let some, but not all, substances pass through them. In response to varying environmental conditions or cell needs, a membrane may be a barrier to a particular substance at one time and actively promote its passage at another time. By regulating chemical traffic across its plasma membrane, a cell controls its volume and its internal ionic and molecular composition. This regulation allows the molecular composition of the cell to be quite different from that of its external environment.

Biological membranes present a barrier to polar molecules

In general, biological membranes are most permeable to small nonpolar (hydrophobic) molecules. Such molecules can pass through the hydrophobic lipid bilayer. Gases such as oxygen and carbon dioxide are small, nonpolar molecules that cross the lipid bilayer rapidly. Although they are polar, water molecules are small enough to pass through gaps that occur as a fatty acid chain momentarily moves out of the way. As a result, water molecules slowly cross the lipid bilayer.

The lipid bilayer of the plasma membrane is relatively impermeable to charged ions of any size, so ions and most large polar molecules pass through the bilayer slowly. Ions are important in cell signaling and many other physiological processes. For example, many cell processes, such as muscle contraction, depend on changes in the cytoplasmic concentration of calcium ions. Glucose, amino acids, and most other compounds required in metabolism are polar molecules that also pass through the lipid bilayer slowly. This is advantageous to cells because the impermeability of the plasma membrane prevents them from diffusing out. How then do cells obtain the ions and polar molecules they require?

Transport proteins transfer molecules across membranes

Systems of **transport proteins** that move ions, amino acids, sugars, and other needed polar molecules through membranes apparently evolved very early in the origin of cells. These transmembrane proteins have been found in all biological membranes. Two main types of membrane transport proteins are carrier proteins and channel proteins. Each type of transport protein transports a specific type of ion or molecule or a group of related substances.

Carrier proteins, also called **transporters,** bind the ion or molecule and undergo changes in shape, resulting in movement of the molecule across the membrane. Transfer of solutes by carrier proteins located within the membrane is called **carrier-mediated transport.** As we will discuss, the two forms of carrier-mediated transport—facilitated diffusion and carrier-mediated active transport—differ in their capabilities and energy sources.

ABC transporters make up a large, important group of carrier proteins. The acronym *ABC* stands for ATP-binding cassette. Found in the cell membranes of all species, ABC transporters use energy donated by ATP to transport certain ions, sugars, and polypeptides across cell membranes. Scientists have identified about 48 ABC transporters in human cells. Mutations in the genes encoding these proteins cause or contribute to many human disorders, including cystic fibrosis and certain neurological diseases. ABC transporters transport hydrophobic drugs out of the cell. This response can be a problem clinically because certain transporters remove antibiotics, antifungal drugs, and anticancer drugs.

Channel proteins form tunnels, called pores, through the membrane. Many of these channels are *gated,* which means that they can be opened and closed. Cells regulate the passage of materials through the channels by opening and closing the gates in response to electrical changes, chemical stimuli, or mechanical stimuli. Water and specific types of ions are transported through channels. There are numerous ion channels in every membrane of every cell.

Porins are transmembrane channel proteins that allow various solutes or water to pass through membranes. These channel proteins are rolled-up, barrel-shaped β-pleated sheets that form pores. Researchers Peter Agre of Johns Hopkins School of Medicine in Baltimore, Maryland, and Roderick MacKinnon of the Howard Hughes Medical Institute at Rockefeller University in New York shared the 2003 Nobel Prize in Chemistry for their work on transport proteins. Agre identified transmembrane proteins called **aquaporins** that function as gated water channels.

Aquaporins facilitate the rapid transport of water through the plasma membrane. About a billion water molecules per second can pass through an aquaporin! These channels are very selective and do not permit passage of ions and other small molecules. In some cells, such as those lining the kidney tubules of mammals, aquaporins respond to specific signals from hormones. Aquaporins help prevent dehydration by returning water from the kidney tubules into the blood.

Review

- What types of molecules pass easily through the plasma membrane?
- What are the two main types of transport proteins? What are their functions?
- What are aquaporins? What is their function?

5.4 PASSIVE TRANSPORT

◼ LEARNING OBJECTIVES

7 Contrast simple diffusion with facilitated diffusion.
8 Define *osmosis* and solve simple problems involving osmosis; for example, predict whether cells will swell or shrink under various osmotic conditions.

Passive transport does not require the cell to expend metabolic energy. Many ions and small molecules move through membranes by *diffusion*. Two types of diffusion are simple diffusion and facilitated diffusion.

Diffusion occurs down a concentration gradient

Some substances pass into or out of cells and move about within cells by **diffusion,** a physical process based on random motion. All atoms and molecules possess kinetic energy, or energy of motion, at temperatures above absolute zero ($0\,\text{K}$, $-273°\text{C}$, or $-459.4°\text{F}$). Matter may exist as a solid, liquid, or gas, depending on the freedom of movement of its constituent particles (atoms, ions, or molecules). The particles of a solid are closely packed, and the forces of attraction between them let them vibrate but not move around.

In a liquid the particles are farther apart; the intermolecular attractions are weaker, and the particles move about with considerable freedom. In a gas the particles are so far apart that intermolecular forces are negligible; molecular movement is restricted only by the walls of the container that encloses the gas. Atoms and molecules in liquids and gases move in a kind of "random walk," changing directions as they collide.

Although the movement of individual particles is undirected and unpredictable, we can nevertheless make predictions about the behavior of groups of particles. If the particles are not evenly distributed, then at least two regions exist: one with a higher concentration of particles and the other with a lower concentration. Such a difference in the concentration of a substance from one place to another establishes a **concentration gradient.**

In diffusion, the random motion of particles results in their net movement "down" their own concentration gradient, from the region of higher concentration to the one of lower concentration. This does not mean individual particles are prohibited from moving "against" the gradient. However, because there are initially more particles in the region of high concentration, it logically follows that more particles move randomly from there into the low-concentration region than the reverse (**FIG. 5-11**).

Thus, if a membrane is permeable to a substance, there is net movement from the side of the membrane where it is more highly concentrated to the side where it is less concentrated. Such a gradient across the membrane is a form of stored energy. Stored energy is *potential energy,* which is the capacity to do work as a result of position or state. The stored energy of the concentration gradient is released when ions or molecules move from a region of high concentration to one of low concentration. For this reason, movement down a concentration gradient is spontaneous. (Forms of energy and spontaneous processes are discussed in greater detail in Chapter 7.)

Diffusion occurs rapidly over very short distances. The rate of diffusion is determined by the movement of the particles, which in turn is a function of their size and shape, their electric charges, and the temperature. As the temperature rises, particles move faster and the rate of diffusion increases.

Particles of different substances in a mixture diffuse independently of one another. Diffusion moves solutes toward a state of equilibrium. If particles are not added to or removed from the system, a state of **dynamic equilibrium** is reached. In this condition, the particles are uniformly distributed and there is no net change in the system. Particles continue to move back and forth across the membrane, but they move at equal rates and in both directions.

In organisms, equilibrium is rarely attained. For example, human cells continually produce carbon dioxide as sugars and other molecules are metabolized during aerobic respiration. Carbon dioxide readily diffuses across the plasma

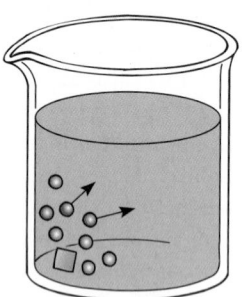

❶ When lump of sugar is dropped into beaker of pure water, sugar molecules begin to dissolve and diffuse through water.

❷ Sugar molecules continue to dissolve and diffuse through water.

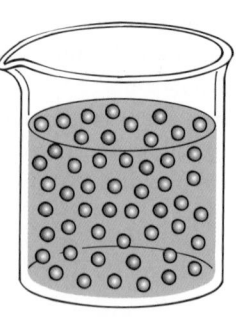

❸ Eventually, sugar molecules become distributed randomly throughout water.

FIGURE 5-11 Diffusion

membrane but then is rapidly removed by the blood. This limits the opportunity for the molecules to re-enter the cell, so a sharp concentration gradient of carbon dioxide molecules always exists across the plasma membrane.

In **simple diffusion** through a biological membrane, small, nonpolar (uncharged) solute molecules move directly through the membrane down their concentration gradient. Oxygen and carbon dioxide can rapidly diffuse through the membrane. The rate of simple diffusion is directly related to the concentration of the solute; the more concentrated the solute, the more rapid the diffusion.

Osmosis is diffusion of water across a selectively permeable membrane

Osmosis is a special kind of diffusion that involves the net movement of water (the principal *solvent* in biological systems) through a selectively permeable membrane from a region of higher concentration to a region of lower concentration. Water molecules pass freely in both directions, but as in all types of diffusion, *net* movement is from the region where the water molecules are more concentrated to the region where they are less concentrated. Most *solute molecules* (such as sugar and salt) cannot diffuse freely through the selectively permeable membranes of the cell.

The principles involved in osmosis can be illustrated using an apparatus called a U-tube (**FIG. 5-12**). The U-tube is divided into two sections by a selectively permeable membrane that allows solvent (water) molecules to pass freely but excludes solute molecules. A water/solute solution is placed on one side, and pure water is placed on the other. The side containing the solute has a lower effective concentration of water than the pure water side does. The reason is that the solute particles, which are charged (ionic) or polar, interact with the partial electric charges on the polar water molecules. Many of the water molecules are thus "bound up" and no longer free to diffuse across the membrane.

Because of the difference in effective water concentration, there is net movement of water molecules from the pure water side (with a high effective concentration of water) to the water/solute side (with a lower effective concentration of water). As a result, the fluid level drops on the pure water side and rises on the water/solute side. Because the solute molecules do not diffuse across the membrane, equilibrium is never attained. Net movement of water continues, and the fluid level rises on the side containing the solute. The weight of the rising column of fluid eventually exerts enough pressure to stop further changes in fluid levels, although water molecules continue to pass through the selectively permeable membrane in both directions.

We define the **osmotic pressure** of a solution as the pressure that must be exerted on the side of a selectively permeable membrane containing the higher concentration of solute to prevent the diffusion of water (by osmosis) from the side containing the lower solute concentration. In the U-tube example, you could measure the osmotic pressure by inserting a piston on the water/solute side of the tube and measuring how much pressure must be exerted

FIGURE 5-12 *Animated* Osmosis

The U-tube contains pure water on the right and water plus a solute on the left, separated by a selectively permeable membrane. Water molecules cross the membrane in both directions (*blue arrows*). Solute molecules cannot cross (*red arrows*). The fluid level would normally rise on the left and fall on the right because net movement of water would be to the left. However, the piston prevents the water from rising. The force that must be exerted by the piston to prevent the rise in fluid level is equal to the osmotic pressure of the solution.

by the piston to prevent the rise of fluid on that side of the tube. A solution with a high solute concentration has a low effective water concentration and a high osmotic pressure; conversely, a solution with a low solute concentration has a high effective water concentration and a low osmotic pressure.

Two solutions may be isotonic

Salts, sugars, and other substances are dissolved in the fluid compartment of every cell. These solutes give the cytosol a specific osmotic pressure. **TABLE 5-1** summarizes the movement of water into and out of a solution (or cell) depending on relative solute concentrations.

When a cell is placed in a fluid with exactly the same osmotic pressure, no net movement of water molecules occurs, either into

TABLE 5-1	Osmotic Terminology		
Solute Concentration in Solution A	Solute Concentration in Solution B	Tonicity	Direction of Net Movement of Water
Greater	Less	A hypertonic to B; B hypotonic to A	B to A
Less	Greater	B hypertonic to A; A hypotonic to B	A to B
Equal	Equal	A and B are isotonic to each other	No net movement

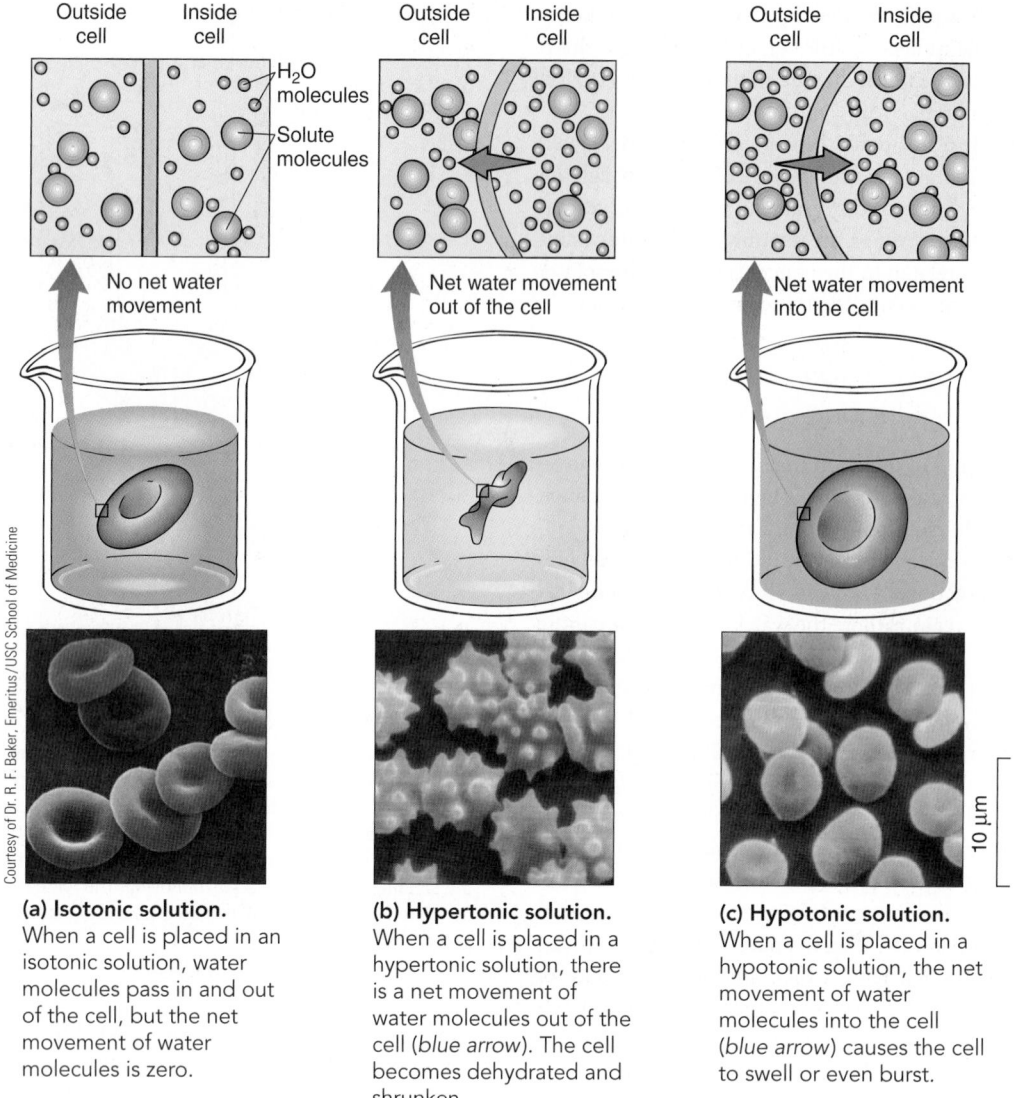

Outside cell   Inside cell   Outside cell   Inside cell   Outside cell   Inside cell

H_2O molecules

Solute molecules

No net water movement

Net water movement out of the cell

Net water movement into the cell

Courtesy of Dr. R. F. Baker, Emeritus/USC School of Medicine

10 μm

(a) Isotonic solution.
When a cell is placed in an isotonic solution, water molecules pass in and out of the cell, but the net movement of water molecules is zero.

(b) Hypertonic solution.
When a cell is placed in a hypertonic solution, there is a net movement of water molecules out of the cell (*blue arrow*). The cell becomes dehydrated and shrunken.

(c) Hypotonic solution.
When a cell is placed in a hypotonic solution, the net movement of water molecules into the cell (*blue arrow*) causes the cell to swell or even burst.

FIGURE 5-13 *Animated* The responses of animal cells to osmotic pressure differences

or out of the cell. The cell neither swells nor shrinks. Such a fluid is of equal solute concentration, or **isotonic,** to the fluid within the cell. Normally, your blood plasma (the fluid component of blood) and all your other body fluids are isotonic to your cells; they contain a concentration of water equal to that in the cells. A solution of 0.9% sodium chloride (sometimes called *physiological saline*) is isotonic to the cells of humans and other mammals. Human red blood cells placed in 0.9% sodium chloride neither shrink nor swell (**FIG. 5-13a**).

One solution may be hypertonic and the other hypotonic

If the surrounding fluid has a concentration of dissolved substances greater than the concentration within the cell, the fluid has a higher osmotic pressure than the cell and is said to be **hypertonic** to the cell. Because a hypertonic solution has a lower effective water concentration, a cell placed in such a solution shrinks as it loses water

by osmosis. Human red blood cells placed in a solution of 1.3% sodium chloride shrivel (**FIG. 5-13b**).

If the surrounding fluid contains a lower concentration of dissolved materials than does the cell, the fluid has a lower osmotic pressure and is said to be **hypotonic** to the cell; water then enters the cell and causes it to swell. Red blood cells placed in a solution of 0.6% sodium chloride gain water, swell (**FIG. 5-13c**), and may eventually burst. Many cells that normally live in hypotonic environments have adaptations to prevent excessive water accumulation. For example, *Paramecium* and certain other ciliates (members of the supergroup Chromalveolates) have contractile vacuoles that expel excess water (see Fig. 26-8).

Turgor pressure is the internal hydrostatic pressure usually present in walled cells

The cells of most prokaryotes, algae, plants, and fungi have relatively rigid cell walls. These cells can withstand, without bursting,

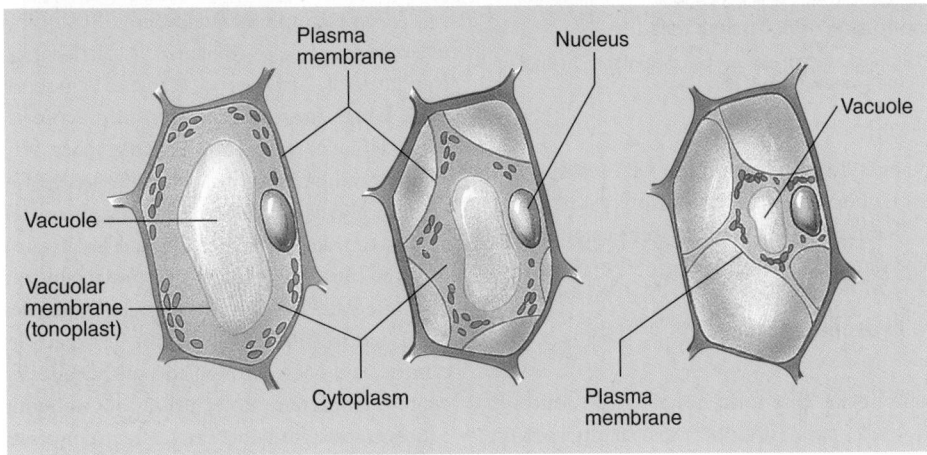

(a) In hypotonic surroundings, the vacuole of a plant cell fills with water, but the rigid cell walls prevent the cell from expanding. The cells of this healthy begonia plant are turgid.

(b) When the begonia plant is exposed to a hypertonic solution, its cells become plasmolyzed as they lose water.

(c) The plant wilts and eventually dies.

FIGURE 5-14 *Animated* Turgor pressure and plasmolysis

an external medium that is very dilute, containing only a very low concentration of solutes. Because of the substances dissolved in the cytoplasm, the cells are hypertonic to the outside medium (conversely, the outside medium is hypotonic to the cytoplasm).

Water moves into the cells by osmosis, filling their central vacuoles and distending the cells. The cells swell, building up **turgor pressure** against the rigid cell walls (**FIG. 5-14a**). The cell walls stretch only slightly, and a steady state is reached when their resistance to stretching prevents any further increase in cell size and thereby halts the *net movement* of water molecules into the cells. (Of course, molecules continue to move back and forth across the plasma membrane.) Turgor pressure in the cells is an important factor in supporting the body of nonwoody plants.

If a cell that has a cell wall is placed in a hypertonic medium, the cell loses water to its surroundings. Its contents shrink, and the plasma membrane separates from the cell wall, a process known as **plasmolysis** (**FIGS. 5-14b** and **14c**). Plasmolysis occurs in plants

when the soil or water around them contains high concentrations of salts or fertilizers. It also explains why lettuce becomes limp in a salty salad dressing and why a picked flower wilts from lack of water.

Facilitated diffusion occurs down a concentration gradient

In all processes in which substances move across membranes by diffusion, the net transfer of those molecules from one side to the other occurs as a result of a concentration gradient. We have seen that small, uncharged (nonpolar) solute molecules, such as oxygen and carbon dioxide, move directly through the membrane down their concentration gradient by simple diffusion. In **facilitated diffusion**, a specific transport protein makes the membrane permeable to a particular solute, such as a specific ion or polar molecule. A specific solute can be transported from inside the cell

FIGURE 5-15 Facilitated diffusion of potassium ions
In response to an electrical stimulus, the gate of the potassium ion channel opens, allowing potassium to diffuse out of the cell.

to the outside or from the outside to the inside, but net movement is always from a region of higher solute concentration to a region of lower concentration. Channel proteins and carrier proteins facilitate diffusion by different mechanisms.

Channel proteins form hydrophilic channels through membranes

Some channel proteins are porins that form rather large tunnels through which water and solutes pass. However, most channel proteins form narrow channels that transport specific ions down their gradients (**FIG. 5-15**). (As we will discuss, because ions are charged particles, these gradients are electrochemical gradients.) These *ion channels* are referred to as *gated channels* because they can open and close. As many as 100 million ions per second can pass through an open ion channel! Channels can facilitate transport only down a concentration gradient. They cannot actively transport ions from a region of lower concentration to a region of higher concentration.

Carrier proteins undergo a change in shape

Transport of solutes through carrier proteins is slower than through channel proteins. The carrier protein binds with one or more solute molecules on one side of the membrane. The protein then undergoes a conformational change (change in shape) that moves the solute to the other side of the membrane.

As an example of facilitated diffusion by a carrier protein, let us consider glucose transport. A carrier protein known as *glucose transporter 1*, or *GLUT 1*, transports glucose into red blood cells (**FIG. 5-16**). The concentration of glucose is higher in the blood plasma than in red blood cells, so glucose diffuses down its concentration gradient into these blood cells. The GLUT 1 transporter facilitates glucose diffusion, allowing glucose to enter the cell about 50,000 times as rapidly as it could by simple diffusion.

Red blood cells keep the internal concentration of glucose low by immediately adding a phosphate group to entering glucose molecules, converting them to highly charged glucose phosphates that cannot pass back through the membrane. Because glucose phosphate is a different molecule, it does not contribute to the glucose concentration gradient. Thus, a steep concentration gradient for glucose is continually maintained, and glucose rapidly diffuses into the

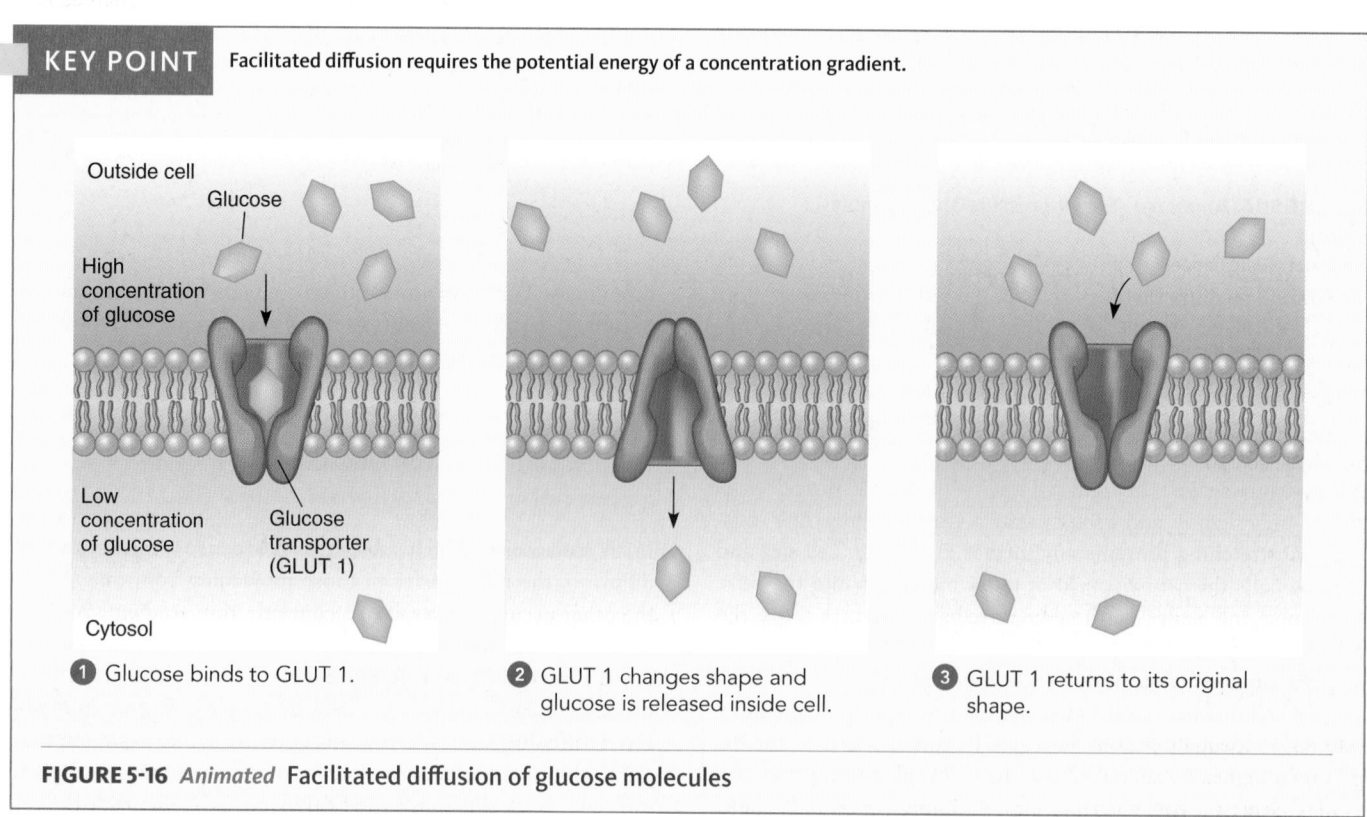

KEY POINT Facilitated diffusion requires the potential energy of a concentration gradient.

❶ Glucose binds to GLUT 1.

❷ GLUT 1 changes shape and glucose is released inside cell.

❸ GLUT 1 returns to its original shape.

FIGURE 5-16 *Animated* **Facilitated diffusion of glucose molecules**

cell, only to be immediately changed to the phosphorylated form. Facilitated diffusion is powered by the concentration gradient.

Researchers have studied facilitated diffusion of glucose using **liposomes,** artificial vesicles surrounded by phospholipid bilayers. The phospholipid membrane of a liposome does not allow the passage of glucose unless a glucose transporter is present in the liposome membrane. Glucose transporters and similar carrier proteins temporarily bind to the molecules they transport. This mechanism appears to be similar to the way an enzyme binds with its substrate, the molecule on which it acts (discussed in Chapter 7). In addition, as in enzyme action, binding apparently changes the shape of the carrier protein. This change allows the glucose molecule to be released on the inside of the cell. According to this model, when the glucose is released into the cytoplasm, the carrier protein reverts to its original shape and is available to bind another glucose molecule on the outside of the cell.

Another similarity to enzyme action is that carrier proteins become saturated when there is a high concentration of the molecule being transported. This saturation may occur because a finite number of carrier proteins are available and they operate at a defined maximum rate. When the concentration of solute molecules to be transported reaches a certain level, all the carrier proteins are working at their maximum rate.

It is a common misconception that diffusion, whether simple or facilitated, is somehow "free of cost" and that only active transport mechanisms require energy. Because diffusion always involves the net movement of a substance down its concentration gradient, we say that the concentration gradient "powers" the process. However, energy is required to do the work of establishing and maintaining the gradient. In our example of facilitated diffusion of glucose, the cell maintains a steep concentration gradient (high outside, low inside) by phosphorylating the glucose molecules once they enter the cell. One ATP molecule is spent for every glucose molecule phosphorylated, and there are additional costs, such as the energy required to make the enzymes that carry out the reaction.

Review

- What would happen if a plant cell were placed in an isotonic solution? a hypertonic environment? a hypotonic environment? How would you modify your predictions for an animal cell?
- What is the immediate source of energy for simple diffusion? For facilitated diffusion?
- In what direction do particles move along their concentration gradient? Would your answers be different for facilitated diffusion compared with simple diffusion?

5.5 ACTIVE TRANSPORT

■ LEARNING OBJECTIVE

9   Describe active transport, including cotransport.

Although adequate amounts of a few substances move across cell membranes by diffusion, cells must actively transport many solutes *against* a concentration gradient. The reason is that cells require many substances in higher concentrations than their concentration outside the cell.

Both diffusion and active transport require energy. The energy for diffusion is provided by a concentration gradient for the substance being transported. Active transport requires the cell to expend metabolic energy directly to power the process.

An **active transport** system can pump materials from a region of low concentration to a region of high concentration. The energy stored in the concentration gradient not only is unavailable to the system but actually works against it. For this reason, the cell needs some other source of energy. In many cases, cells use ATP energy directly. However, active transport may be coupled to ATP indirectly. In indirect active transport, a concentration gradient provides energy for the cotransport of some other substance, such as an ion.

Active transport systems "pump" substances against their concentration gradients

One of the most striking examples of an active transport mechanism is the **sodium–potassium pump** found in all animal cells (**FIG. 5-17**). The pump is an ABC transporter, a specific carrier protein in the plasma membrane. This transporter uses energy from ATP to pump sodium ions out of the cell and potassium ions into the cell. The exchange is unequal: usually only two potassium ions are imported for every three sodium ions exported. Because these particular concentration gradients involve ions, an electrical potential (separation of electric charges) is generated across the membrane; that is, the membrane is **polarized.**

Both sodium and potassium ions are positively charged, but because there are fewer potassium ions inside relative to the sodium ions outside, the inside of the cell is negatively charged relative to the outside. The unequal distribution of ions establishes an **electrical gradient** that drives ions across the plasma membrane. Sodium–potassium pumps help maintain a separation of charges across the plasma membrane. This separation is called a **membrane potential.** Because there is both an electric charge difference and a concentration difference on the two sides of the membrane, the gradient is called an **electrochemical gradient.** Such gradients store energy that is used to drive other transport systems. So important is the electrochemical gradient produced by these pumps that some cells (such as nerve cells) expend more than 25% of their total available energy just to power this one transport system.

Sodium–potassium pumps (as well as all other ATP-driven pumps) are transmembrane proteins that extend entirely through the membrane. By undergoing a series of conformational changes, the pumps exchange sodium for potassium across the plasma membrane. Unlike what occurs in facilitated diffusion, at least one of the conformational changes in the pump cycle requires energy, which is provided by ATP. The shape of the pump protein changes as a phosphate group from ATP first binds to it and is subsequently removed later in the pump cycle.

The use of electrochemical potentials for energy storage is not confined to the plasma membranes of animal cells. Cells of bacteria, fungi, and plants use carrier proteins, known as proton pumps, to actively transport hydrogen ions (which are protons) out of the cell. These ATP-driven membrane pumps transfer protons

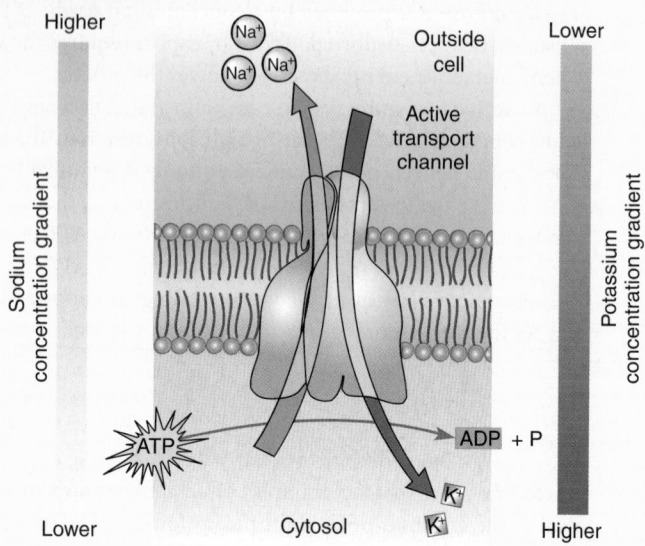

Higher

Outside
cell

Active
transport
channel

Lower

Na⁺

Na⁺ Na⁺

Sodium concentration gradient

Potassium concentration gradient

ATP

ADP + P

Lower

Cytosol

Higher

K⁺

K⁺

(a) The sodium–potassium pump is a carrier protein that requires energy from ATP. In each complete pumping cycle, the energy of one molecule of ATP is used to export three sodium ions (Na⁺) and import two potassium ions (K⁺).

ATP

Na⁺
Na⁺
P Na⁺

ADP

Na⁺ Na⁺

Na⁺

P

K⁺

K⁺

2 Phosphate group is transferred from ATP to carrier protein.

3 Phosphorylation causes carrier protein to change shape, releasing 3 Na⁺ outside cell.

Na⁺ Na⁺ Na⁺

1 Three Na⁺ bind to carrier protein.

P

4 Two K⁺ bind to carrier protein.

K⁺

K⁺

K⁺

K⁺

P

6 Phosphate release causes carrier protein to return to its original shape. Two K⁺ ions are released inside cell.

5 Phosphate is released.

(b) Follow the steps illustrating a model of active transport by the sodium–potassium pump.

FIGURE 5-17 *Animated* A model for the pumping cycle of the sodium–potassium pump from the cytosol to the outside (**FIG. 5-18**). Removal of positively charged protons from the cytoplasm of these cells results in a large difference in the concentration of protons between the outside and inside of the cell. The outside of the cells is positively charged relative to the inside of the plasma membrane. The energy stored in these electrochemical gradients can be used to do many kinds of cell work.

Other proton pumps are used in "reverse" to synthesize ATP. Bacteria, mitochondria, and chloroplasts use energy from food or sunlight to establish proton concentration gradients (discussed in Chapters 8 and 9). When the protons diffuse through the proton carriers from a region of high proton concentration to one of low concentration, ATP is synthesized. These electrochemical gradients form the basis for the major energy conversion systems in virtually all cells.

Ion pumps have other important roles. For example, they are instrumental in the ability of an animal cell to equalize the osmotic pressures of its cytoplasm and its external environment. If an animal cell does not control its internal osmotic pressure, its contents become hypertonic relative to the exterior. Water enters by osmosis, causing the cell to swell and possibly burst (see Fig. 5-13c). By controlling the ion distribution across the membrane, the cell indirectly controls the movement of water, because when ions are pumped out of the cell, water leaves by osmosis.

Carrier proteins can transport one or two solutes

You may have noticed that some carrier proteins, such as proton pumps, transport one type of substance in one direction. These carrier proteins are called **uniporters.** Other carrier proteins, **symporters,** move two types of substances in one direction. For example, a specific carrier protein transports both sodium and glucose into the cell. Still other carrier proteins, **antiporters,** move two substances in opposite directions. Sodium–potassium pumps transport sodium ions out of the cell and potassium ions into the cell. Both symporters and antiporters cotransport solutes.

Cotransport systems indirectly provide energy for active transport

A **cotransport system** moves solutes across a membrane by **indirect active transport.** Two solutes are transported at the same time. The movement of one solute down its concentration gradient provides energy for transport of some other solute up its concentration gradient. However, an energy source such as ATP is required to power the pump that produces the concentration gradient.

Sodium–potassium pumps (and other pumps) generate electrochemical concentration gradients. Sodium is pumped out of the cell and then diffuses back in by moving down its concentration gradient. This process generates sufficient energy to power the active transport of other essential substances. In these systems, a carrier protein *cotransports* a solute *against* its concentration gradient, while sodium, potassium, or hydrogen ions move *down* their gradient. Energy from ATP produces the ion gradient. Then the energy of this gradient drives the active transport of a required substance, such as glucose, against its gradient.

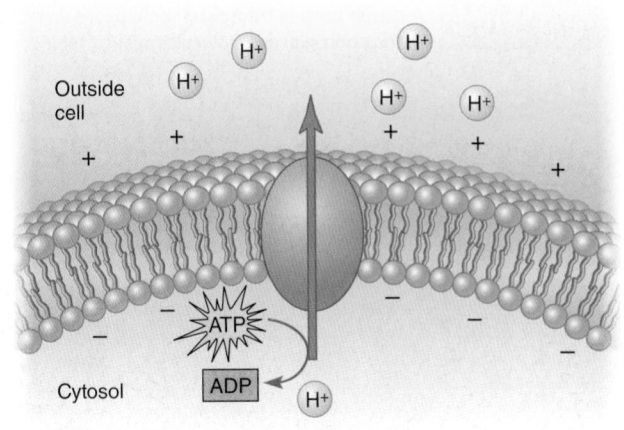

FIGURE 5-18 A model of a proton pump
Proton pumps use the energy of ATP to transport protons (hydrogen ions) across membranes. The energy of the electrochemical gradient established can then be used for other processes.

We have seen how glucose can be moved into the cell by facilitated diffusion. Glucose can also be cotransported into the cell. The sodium concentration inside the cell is kept low by the ATP-requiring sodium–potassium pumps that actively transport sodium ions out of the cell. In glucose cotransport, a carrier protein transports both sodium and glucose (**FIG. 5-19**). As sodium moves into the cell along its concentration gradient, the carrier protein captures the energy released and uses it to transport glucose into the cell. Thus, this indirect active transport system for glucose is "driven" by the cotransport of sodium.

Review

- What is the energy source for active transport?
- What is the energy source for cotransport?

5.6 EXOCYTOSIS AND ENDOCYTOSIS

■ LEARNING OBJECTIVE

10 Compare exocytotic and endocytotic transport mechanisms.

Individual molecules and ions pass through the plasma membrane by simple and facilitated diffusion and by carrier-mediated active transport. Some larger materials, such as large molecules, particles of food, and even small cells, are also moved into or out of cells. They are transported by exocytosis and endocytosis. Like active transport, these processes require cells to expend energy directly.

In exocytosis, vesicles export large molecules

In **exocytosis,** a cell ejects waste products, or specific products of secretion such as hormones, by the fusion of a vesicle with the

A carrier protein transports sodium ions down their concentration gradient and uses that energy to cotransport glucose molecules against their concentration gradient.

Outside cell   Na+

Carrier protein

Cytosol

1 Sodium ions and glucose bind to carrier protein.

Glucose

Lipid bilayer

Glucose concentration gradient

2 Carrier protein changes shape and releases sodium ions and glucose inside cell.

FIGURE 5-19 A model for the cotransport of glucose and sodium ions
Note that this carrier protein is a symporter.

1 Vesicle approaches plasma membrane,

2 fuses with it, and

3 releases its contents outside cell.

0.25 μm

Bloom and Fawcett Textbook of Histology

FIGURE 5-20 Exocytosis
The TEM shows exocytosis of the protein components of milk by a mammary gland cell.

1 Folds of plasma membrane surround particle to be ingested, forming small vacuole around it.

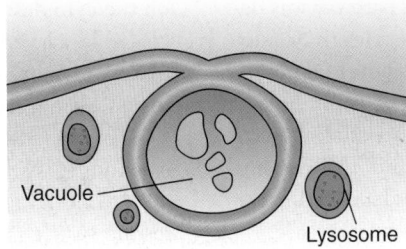

2 Vacuole then pinches off inside cell.

3 Lysosomes fuse with vacuole and pour potent hydrolytic enzymes onto ingested material.

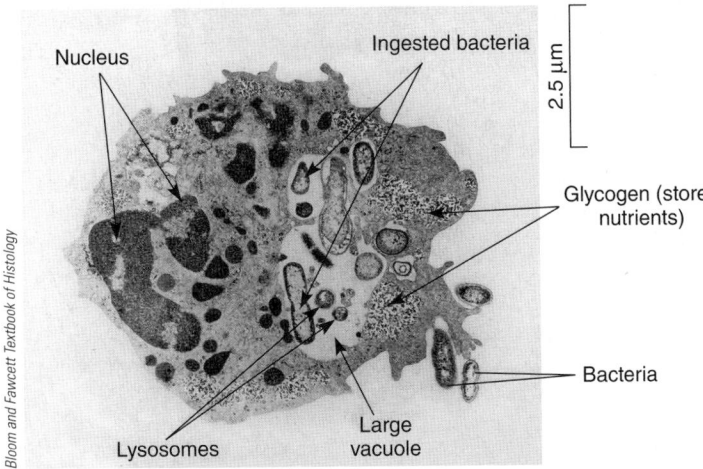

Bloom and Fawcett Textbook of Histology

FIGURE 5-21 *Animated* **Phagocytosis**

In this type of endocytosis, a cell ingests relatively large solid particles. The white blood cell (a neutrophil) shown in the TEM is phagocytizing bacteria. The vacuoles contain bacteria that have already been ingested. Lysosomes contain digestive enzymes that break down the ingested material. Other bacteria are visible outside the cell.

plasma membrane (**FIG. 5-20**). As the contents of the vesicle are released from the cell, the membrane of the secretory vesicle is incorporated into the plasma membrane. This is the primary mechanism by which plasma membranes grow larger.

In endocytosis, the cell imports materials

In **endocytosis,** materials are taken into the cell. Several types of endocytotic mechanisms operate in biological systems, including phagocytosis, pinocytosis, and receptor-mediated endocytosis.

In **phagocytosis** (literally, "cell eating"), the cell ingests large solid particles such as food or bacteria (**FIG. 5-21**). Certain protists ingest food by phagocytosis. Some types of vertebrate cells, including certain white blood cells, ingest bacteria and other particles by phagocytosis. During ingestion, folds of the plasma membrane enclose the cell or particle. When the membrane has encircled the particle, the membrane fuses at the point of contact, forming a vacuole. The vacuole may then fuse with lysosomes, which degrade the ingested material.

In **pinocytosis** ("cell drinking"), the cell takes in dissolved materials (**FIG. 5-22**). Tiny droplets of fluid are trapped by folds in the plasma membrane, which pinch off into the cytosol as tiny vesicles. As the liquid

contents of these vesicles are slowly transferred into the cytosol, the vesicles become progressively smaller.

In a third type of endocytosis, **receptor-mediated endocytosis,** specific molecules combine with receptor proteins in the plasma membrane. Receptor-mediated endocytosis is the main mechanism by which eukaryotic cells take in macromolecules. As an example, let us look at how mammalian cells take up cholesterol from the blood. Cells use cholesterol as a component of cell membranes and as a precursor of steroid hormones. Cholesterol is transported in the blood as part of particles called *low-density lipoproteins* (*LDLs;* popularly known as "bad cholesterol").

1 Tiny droplets of fluid are trapped by folds of plasma membrane.

2 These pinch off into cytosol as small fluid-filled vesicles.

3 Contents of these vesicles are then slowly transferred to cytosol.

FIGURE 5-22 Pinocytosis, or "cell drinking"

Much of the receptor-mediated endocytosis pathway was detailed through studies at the University of Texas Health Science Center by Michael Brown and Joseph Goldstein on the LDL receptor. These researchers were awarded the Nobel Prize in Physiology or Medicine in 1985 for their pioneering work. Their findings have important medical implications because cholesterol that remains in the blood instead of entering the cells can be deposited in the artery walls, which increases the risk of cardiovascular disease.

When it needs cholesterol, the cell makes LDL receptors. The receptors are concentrated in *coated pits,* depressed regions on the cytoplasmic surface of the plasma membrane. Each pit is coated by a layer of a protein, called *clathrin,* found just below the plasma membrane. A molecule that binds specifically to a receptor is called a **ligand.** In this case, LDL is the ligand. After the LDL binds with a receptor, the coated pit forms a *coated vesicle* by endocytosis.

FIGURE 5-23 shows the uptake of an LDL particle. Seconds after the vesicle moves into the cytoplasm, the coating dissociates from it, leaving an uncoated vesicle. The vesicles fuse with small compartments called *endosomes.* The LDL and LDL receptors sep-

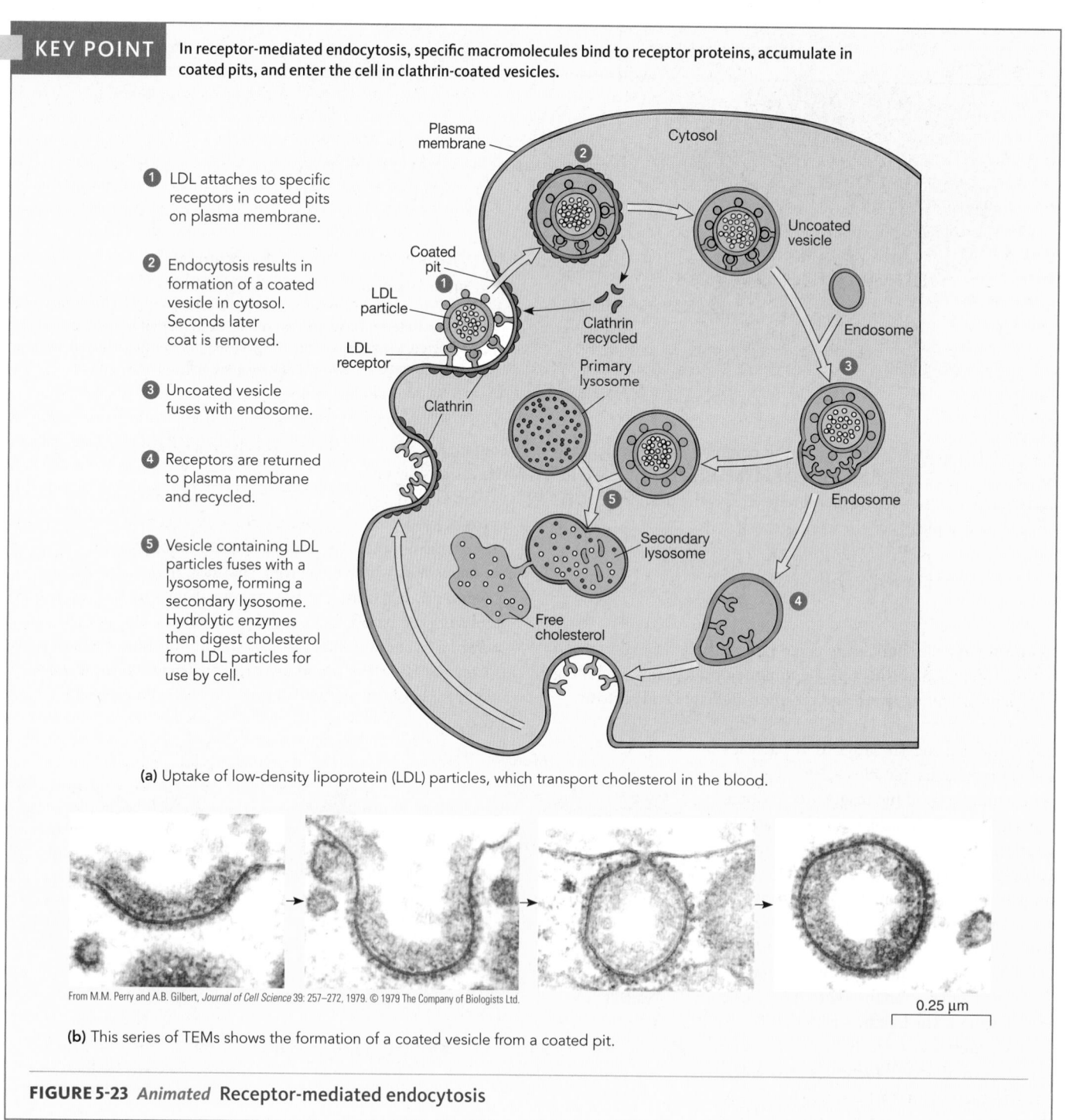

KEY POINT In receptor-mediated endocytosis, specific macromolecules bind to receptor proteins, accumulate in coated pits, and enter the cell in clathrin-coated vesicles.

1. LDL attaches to specific receptors in coated pits on plasma membrane.

2. Endocytosis results in formation of a coated vesicle in cytosol. Seconds later coat is removed.

3. Uncoated vesicle fuses with endosome.

4. Receptors are returned to plasma membrane and recycled.

5. Vesicle containing LDL particles fuses with a lysosome, forming a secondary lysosome. Hydrolytic enzymes then digest cholesterol from LDL particles for use by cell.

Plasma membrane • Cytosol • Coated pit • LDL particle • LDL receptor • Clathrin • Uncoated vesicle • Clathrin recycled • Endosome • Primary lysosome • Secondary lysosome • Free cholesterol • Endosome

(a) Uptake of low-density lipoprotein (LDL) particles, which transport cholesterol in the blood.

From M.M. Perry and A.B. Gilbert, *Journal of Cell Science* 39: 257–272, 1979. © 1979 The Company of Biologists Ltd.

0.25 μm

(b) This series of TEMs shows the formation of a coated vesicle from a coated pit.

FIGURE 5-23 *Animated* Receptor-mediated endocytosis

arate, and the receptors are transported to the plasma membrane, where they are recycled. LDL is transferred to a lysosome, where it is broken down. Cholesterol is released into the cytosol for use by the cell. A simplified summary of receptor-mediated endocytosis follows:

> ligand molecules bind to receptors in coated pits of plasma membrane ⟶ coated vesicle forms by endocytosis ⟶ coating detaches from vesicle ⟶ uncoated vesicle fuses with endosome ⟶ ligands separate from receptors which are recycled; endosome fuses with primary lysosome, forming secondary lysosome ⟶ contents of secondary lysosome are digested and released into the cytosol

The recycling of LDL receptors to the plasma membrane through vesicles causes a problem common to all cells that use endocytotic and exocytotic mechanisms: the plasma membrane changes size as the vesicles bud off from it or fuse with it. A type of phagocytic cell known as a *macrophage,* for example, ingests the equivalent of its entire plasma membrane in about 30 minutes, requiring an equivalent amount of recycling or new membrane synthesis for the cell to maintain its surface area. On the other hand, cells that are constantly involved in secretion must return an equivalent amount of membrane to the interior of the cell for each vesicle that fuses with the plasma membrane; if not, the cell surface would continue to expand even though the growth of the cell itself may be arrested.

Review

- How are exocytosis and endocytosis similar?
- How are the processes of phagocytosis and pinocytosis different?
- What is the sequence of events in receptor-mediated endocytosis?

5.7 CELL JUNCTIONS

◾ LEARNING OBJECTIVE

11 Compare the structures and functions of anchoring junctions, tight junctions, gap junctions, and plasmodesmata.

Cells in close contact with one another typically develop specialized intercellular junctions. These structures may allow neighboring cells to form strong connections with one another, prevent the passage of materials, or establish rapid communication between adjacent cells. Several types of junctions connect animal cells, including anchoring junctions, tight junctions, and gap junctions. Plant cells are connected by plasmodesmata.

Anchoring junctions connect cells of an epithelial sheet

Adjacent epithelial cells, such as those found in the outer layer of the mammalian skin, are so tightly bound to each other by **anchoring junctions** that strong mechanical forces are required to separate them. Cadherins, transmembrane proteins shown in the chapter opening photograph, are important components of an-

choring junctions. These junctions do not prevent the passage of materials between adjacent cells. Two common types of anchoring junctions are desmosomes and adhering junctions.

Desmosomes are points of attachment between cells (**FIG. 5-24**). They hold cells together at one point as a rivet or a spot weld does. Desmosomes allow cells to form strong sheets, and substances still pass freely through the spaces between the plasma membranes. Each desmosome is made up of regions of dense material associated with the cytosolic sides of the two plasma membranes, plus protein filaments that cross the narrow intercellular space between them. Desmosomes are anchored to systems of

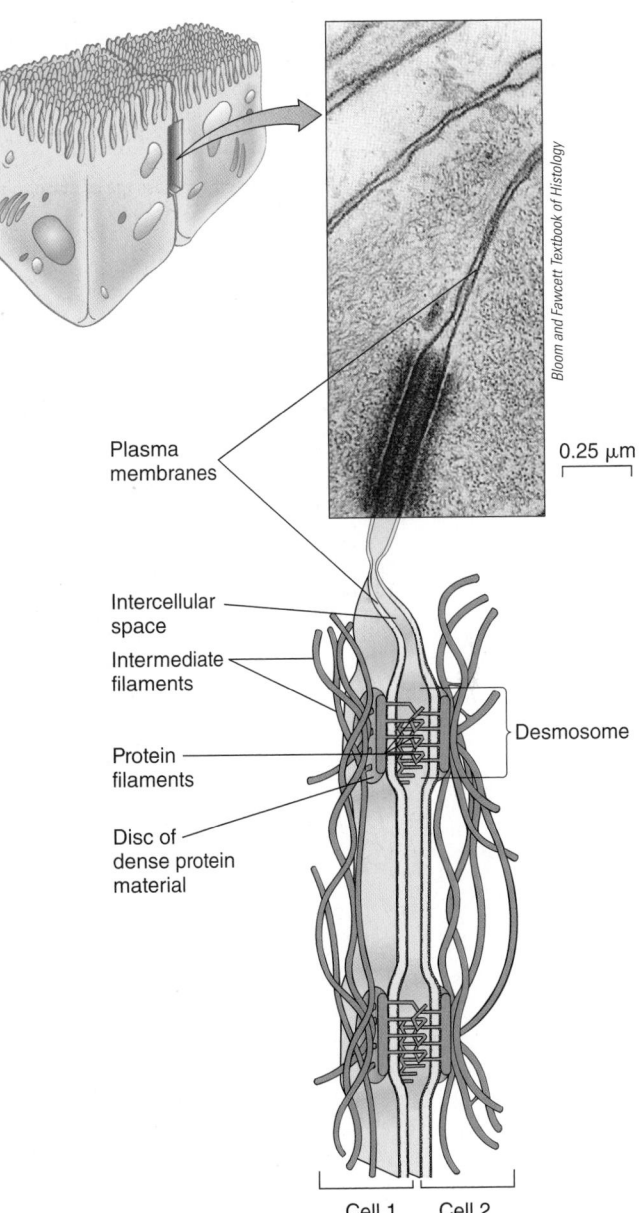

Bloom and Fawcett Textbook of Histology

0.25 μm

Plasma membranes

Intercellular space

Intermediate filaments

Protein filaments

Disc of dense protein material

Desmosome

Cell 1   Cell 2

FIGURE 5-24 Desmosomes
The dense structure in the TEM is a desmosome. Each desmosome consists of a pair of buttonlike discs associated with the plasma membranes of adjacent cells, plus the intercellular protein filaments that connect them. Intermediate filaments in the cells are attached to the discs and are connected to other desmosomes.

intermediate filaments inside the cells. Thus, the intermediate filament networks of adjacent cells are connected. As a result, mechanical stresses are distributed throughout the tissue.

Adhering junctions cement cells together. Cadherins form a continuous adhesion belt around each cell, binding the cell to neighboring cells. These junctions connect to microfilaments of the cytoskeleton. The cadherins of adhering junctions are a potential path for signals from the outside environment to be transmitted to the cytoplasm.

Tight junctions seal off intercellular spaces between some animal cells

Tight junctions are literally areas of tight connections between the membranes of adjacent cells. These connections are so tight that no space remains between the cells and substances cannot leak between them. TEMs of tight junctions show that in the region of the junction the plasma membranes of the two cells are held together by proteins in actual contact with each other. However, as shown in **FIGURE 5-25**, tight junctions are located intermittently. The plasma membranes of the two cells are not fused over their entire surface.

Cells connected by tight junctions seal off body cavities. For example, tight junctions between cells lining the intestine prevent substances in the intestine from passing between the cells and directly entering the blood. The sheet of cells thus acts as a selective barrier. Food substances must be transported across the plasma membranes and *through* the intestinal cells before they enter the blood. This arrangement helps prevent toxins and other unwanted materials from entering the blood and also prevents nutrients

KEY POINT Tight junctions prevent the passage of materials through spaces between cells.

Microvillus

Lumen of the intestine

Tight junction

Intercellular space

Cell 1   Cell 2

G. E. Palade

0.1 μm

Rows of tight junction proteins   Plasma membranes   Intercellular space

(a) This TEM shows points of fusion between plasma membranes of adjacent cells lining the intestine. One tight junction is marked by the box.

(b) A tight junction is formed by linkages between rows of proteins of adjacent cells. These proteins seal off the intercellular space, preventing passage of materials through spaces between cells.

FIGURE 5-25 *Animated* **Tight junctions**

from leaking out of the intestine. Tight junctions are also present between the cells that line capillaries in the brain. They form the *blood–brain barrier,* which prevents many substances in the blood from passing into the brain.

Gap junctions allow the transfer of small molecules and ions

A **gap junction** is like a desmosome in that it bridges the space between cells; however, the space it spans is somewhat narrower (**FIG. 5-26**). Gap junctions also differ in that they are communicating junctions. They not only connect the plasma membranes but also contain channels connecting the cytoplasm of adjacent cells.

Gap junctions are composed of *connexin,* an integral membrane protein. Groups of six connexin molecules cluster to form a cylinder that spans the plasma membrane. The connexin cylinders on adjacent cells become tightly joined. The two cylinders form a channel, about 1.5 nm in diameter. Small inorganic molecules (such as ions) and some regulatory molecules (such as cyclic AMP, which is illustrated in Figure 3-25) pass through the channels, but larger molecules are excluded. When a marker substance is in-

jected into one of a group of cells connected by gap junctions, the marker passes rapidly into the adjacent cells but does not enter the space between the cells.

Gap junctions provide for rapid chemical and electrical communication between cells. Cells control the passage of materials through gap junctions by opening and closing the channels (see Fig. 5-26d). Cells in the pancreas, for example, are linked by gap junctions in such a way that if one of a group of cells is stimulated to secrete insulin, the signal is passed through the junctions to the other cells in the cluster. This mechanism ensures a coordinated response to the initial signal. Gap junctions allow some nerve cells to be electrically coupled. Cardiac muscle cells are linked by gap junctions that permit the flow of ions necessary to synchronize contractions of the heart.

Plasmodesmata allow certain molecules and ions to move between plant cells

Because plant cells have walls, they do not need desmosomes for strength. Plant cells have connections that are functionally equivalent to the gap junctions of some animal cells. **Plasmodesmata**

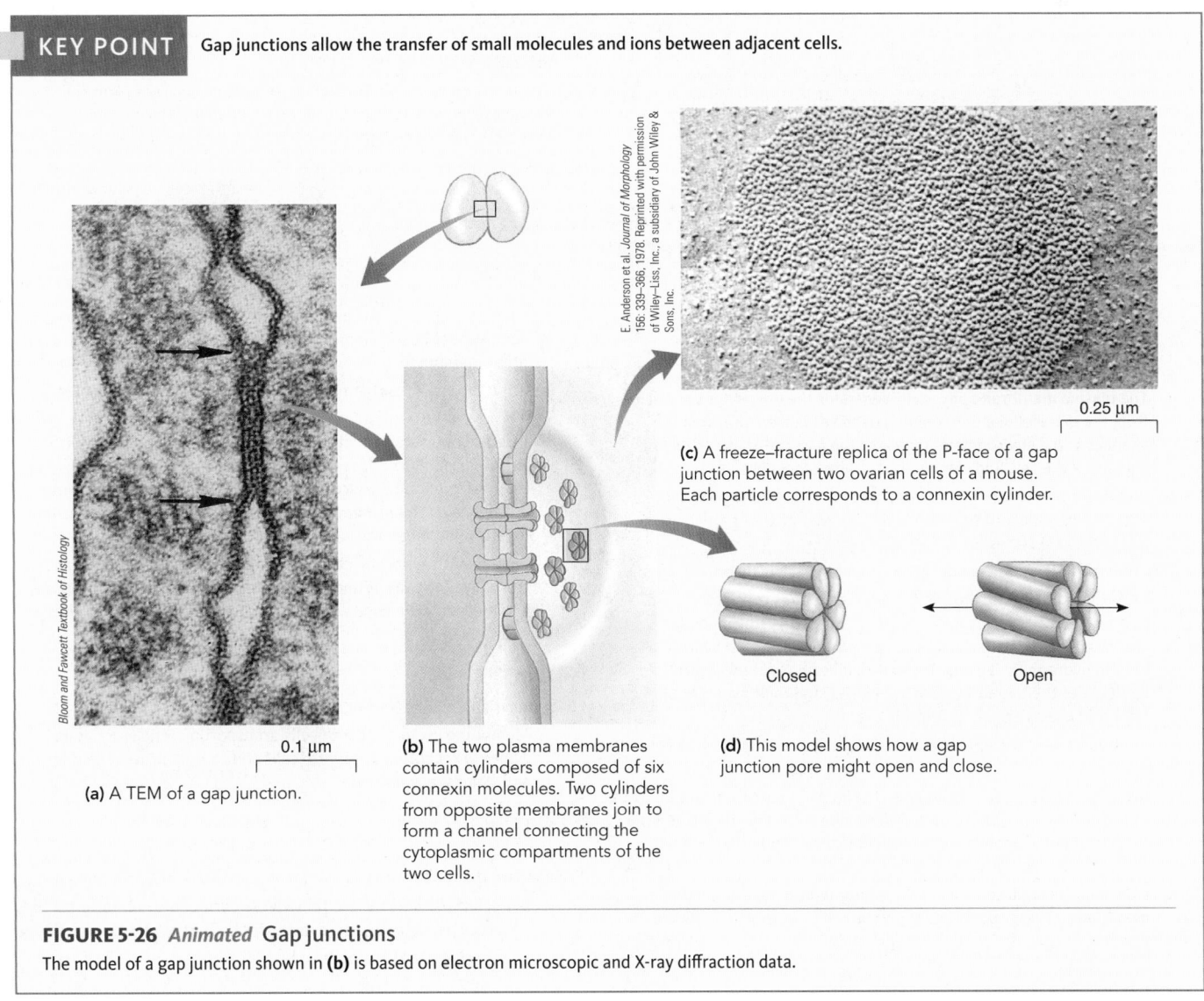

KEY POINT Gap junctions allow the transfer of small molecules and ions between adjacent cells.

E. Anderson et al. *Journal of Morphology* 156: 339–366, 1978. Reprinted with permission of Wiley-Liss, Inc., a subsidiary of John Wiley & Sons, Inc.

Bloom and Fawcett Textbook of Histology

0.1 μm

(a) A TEM of a gap junction.

(b) The two plasma membranes contain cylinders composed of six connexin molecules. Two cylinders from opposite membranes join to form a channel connecting the cytoplasmic compartments of the two cells.

0.25 μm

(c) A freeze–fracture replica of the P-face of a gap junction between two ovarian cells of a mouse. Each particle corresponds to a connexin cylinder.

Closed   Open

(d) This model shows how a gap junction pore might open and close.

FIGURE 5-26 *Animated* **Gap junctions**
The model of a gap junction shown in **(b)** is based on electron microscopic and X-ray diffraction data.

(sing., *plasmodesma*) are channels 20 to 40 nm wide that pass through the cell walls of adjacent plant cells, connecting the cytoplasm of neighboring cells (**FIG. 5-27**). The plasma membranes of adjacent cells are continuous with one another through the plasmodesmata. Most plasmodesmata contain a narrow cylindrical structure, called the **desmotubule**, which runs through the channel and connects the smooth ER of the two adjacent cells.

Plasmodesmata generally allow molecules and ions, but not organelles, to pass through the openings from cell to cell. The movement of ions through the plasmodesmata allows for a very slow type of electrical signaling in plants. Whereas the channels of gap junctions have a fixed diameter, plants cells can dilate the plasmodesmata channels. Certain proteins and RNA can pass through plasmodesmata. Some plant viruses spread infection by passing through these junctions.

Review

- How are desmosomes and tight junctions functionally similar? How do they differ?
- What is the justification for considering gap junctions and plasmodesmata to be functionally similar? How do they differ structurally?

KEY POINT Most plant cells have plasmodesmata that connect the cytoplasm of adjacent cells.

Cell walls — Cell 1
— Plasmodesmata
— Desmotubule
— Plasma membrane

Smooth ER

Cell 2

FIGURE 5-27 Plasmodesmata
Cytoplasmic channels through the cell walls of adjacent plant cells allow passage of water, ions, and small molecules. The channels are lined with the fused plasma membranes of the two adjacent cells.

■ SUMMARY: FOCUS ON LEARNING OBJECTIVES

5.1 *(page 107)*

1 Evaluate the importance of membranes to the homeostasis of the cell, emphasizing their various functions.

- The **plasma membrane** physically separates the interior of the cell from the extracellular environment, receives information about changes in the environment, regulates the passage of materials into and out of the cell, and communicates with other cells.
- Biological membranes form compartments within eukaryotic cells that allow a variety of separate functions. Membranes participate in and serve as surfaces for biochemical reactions.

2 Describe the fluid mosaic model of cell membrane structure.

- According to the **fluid mosaic model,** membranes consist of a fluid phospholipid bilayer in which a variety of proteins are embedded. The phospholipid molecules are **amphipathic:** they have hydrophobic and hydrophilic regions. The hydrophilic heads of the phospholipids are at the two surfaces of the bilayer, and their hydrophobic fatty acid chains are in the interior.

3 Relate properties of the lipid bilayer to properties and functions of cell membranes.

- In almost all biological membranes, the lipids of the bilayer are in a fluid or liquid-crystalline state, which allows the lipid molecules to move rapidly in the plane of the membrane. Proteins also move within the membrane.
- Lipid bilayers are flexible and self-sealing and can fuse with other membranes. These properties allow the cell to transport materials

from one region of the cell to another; materials are transported in vesicles that bud from one cell membrane and then fuse with some other membrane.

4 Describe the ways that membrane proteins associate with the lipid bilayer.

- **Integral membrane proteins** are embedded in the bilayer with their hydrophilic surfaces exposed to the aqueous environment and their hydrophobic surfaces in contact with the hydrophobic interior of the bilayer. **Transmembrane proteins** are integral proteins that extend completely through the membrane.
- **Peripheral membrane proteins** are associated with the surface of the bilayer, usually bound to exposed regions of integral proteins, and are easily removed without disrupting the structure of the membrane.

5.2 *(page 114)*

5 Summarize the functions of membrane proteins.

- Membrane proteins anchor cells, transport materials, act as enzymes or receptors, recognize cells and communicate with them, and structurally link cells.

5.3 *(page 115)*

6 Describe the importance of selectively permeable membranes and compare the functions of carrier proteins and channel proteins.

- Biological membranes are **selectively permeable membranes:** they allow the passage of some substances but not others. By regulating passage of molecules that enter and leave the cell and its compartments, the cell controls its volume and the internal composition of ions and molecules.

- Membrane **transport proteins** facilitate the passage of certain ions and molecules through biological membranes. **Carrier proteins** are transport proteins that undergo a series of conformational changes as they bind and transport a specific solute. **ABC transporters** are carrier proteins that use energy from ATP to transport solutes.

- **Channel proteins** are transport proteins that form passageways through which water and certain ions travel through the membrane. **Porins** are channel proteins that form relatively large pores through the membrane for passage of water and certain solutes.

CENGAGENOW™ Learn more about the plasma membrane and membrane proteins by clicking on the figures in CengageNOW.

5.4 *(page 116)*

7 Contrast simple diffusion with facilitated diffusion.

- **Diffusion** is the net movement of a substance down its **concentration gradient** from a region of greater concentration to one of lower concentration. Diffusion and osmosis are physical processes that do not require the cell to directly expend metabolic energy.

- In **simple diffusion** through a biological membrane, solute molecules or ions move directly through the membrane down their concentration gradient. **Facilitated diffusion** uses specific transport proteins to move solutes across a membrane. As in simple diffusion, net movement is always from a region of higher to a region of lower solute concentration. Facilitated diffusion cannot work against a concentration gradient.

8 Define *osmosis* and solve simple problems involving osmosis; for example, predict whether cells will swell or shrink under various osmotic conditions.

- **Osmosis** is a kind of diffusion in which molecules of water pass through a selectively permeable membrane from a region where water has a higher effective concentration to a region where its effective concentration is lower.

- The concentration of dissolved substances (solutes) in a solution determines its **osmotic pressure.** Cells regulate their internal osmotic pressures to prevent shrinking or bursting.

- An **isotonic** solution has an equal solute concentration compared to that of another fluid, for example, the fluid within the cell.

- When placed in a **hypertonic** solution, one that has a greater solute concentration than that of the cell, a cell loses water to its surroundings; plant cells undergo **plasmolysis**, a process in which the plasma membrane separates from the cell wall.

- When cells are placed in a **hypotonic** solution, one that has a lower solute concentration than the solute concentration of the cell, water enters the cells and causes them to swell.

- Plant cells withstand high internal hydrostatic pressure because their cell walls prevent them from expanding and bursting. Water moves into plant cells by osmosis and fills the central vacuoles. The cells swell, building up **turgor pressure** against the supportive cell walls.

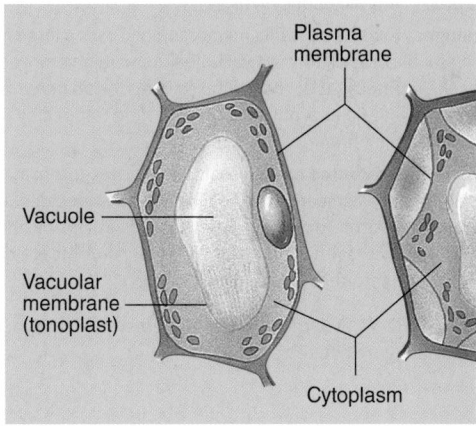

5.5 *(page 121)*

9 Describe active transport, including cotransport.

- In **active transport,** the cell expends metabolic energy to move ions or molecules across a membrane against a concentration gradient. For example, the **sodium–potassium pump** uses ATP to pump sodium ions out of the cell and potassium ions into the cell.

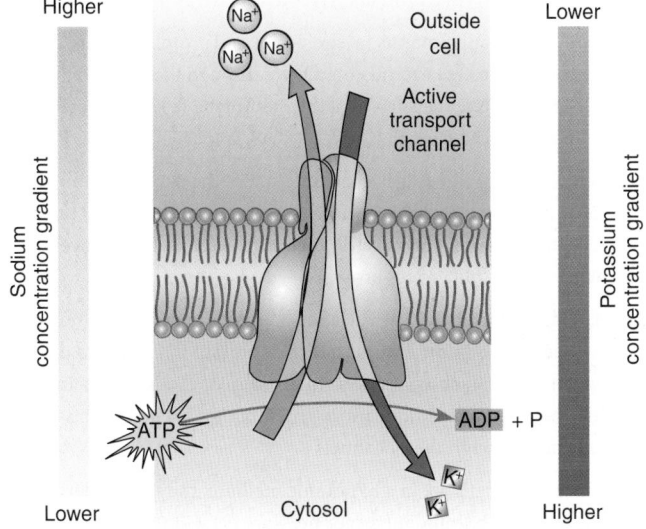

- In **cotransport,** also called **indirect active transport,** two solutes are transported at the same time. An ATP-powered pump maintains a concentration gradient. Then a carrier protein cotransports two solutes. It transports one solute down its concentration gradient and uses the energy released to move another solute against its concentration gradient.

5.6 *(page 123)*

10 Compare exocytotic and endocytotic transport mechanisms.

- The cell expends metabolic energy to carry on exocytosis and endocytosis. In **exocytosis,** the cell ejects waste products or secretes substances such as mucus by fusion of vesicles with the plasma membrane. This process increases the surface area of the plasma membrane.

- In **endocytosis,** materials such as food particles are moved into the cell. A portion of the plasma membrane envelops the material, enclosing it in a vesicle or vacuole that is then released inside the cell. This process decreases the surface area of the plasma membrane.
- Three types of endocytosis are phagocytosis, pinocytosis, and receptor-mediated endocytosis.
- In **phagocytosis,** the plasma membrane encloses a large particle such as a bacterium, forms a vacuole around it, and moves it into the cell. In **pinocytosis,** the cell takes in dissolved materials by forming tiny vesicles around droplets of fluid trapped by folds of the plasma membrane.
- In **receptor-mediated endocytosis,** specific receptors in coated pits along the plasma membrane bind **ligand molecules.** These pits, coated by the protein clathrin, form coated vesicles by endocytosis. The vesicles fuse with lysosomes, and their contents are digested and released into the cytosol.

CENGAGENOW™ Learn more about membrane transport by clicking on the figures in CengageNOW.

5.7 (page 127)

11 Compare the structures and functions of anchoring junctions, tight junctions, gap junctions, and plasmodesmata.

- Cells in close contact with one another may form intercellular junctions. **Anchoring junctions** include desmosomes and adhering junctions; they are found between cells that form a sheet of tissue. **Desmosomes** spot-weld adjacent animal cells together. **Adhering junctions** are formed by **cadherins, transmembrane proteins** that cement cells together.
- **Tight junctions** seal membranes of adjacent animal cells together, preventing substances from moving through the spaces between the cells.
- **Gap junctions,** composed of the protein connexin, form channels that allow communication between the cytoplasm of adjacent animal cells.
- **Plasmodesmata** are channels connecting adjacent plant cells. Openings in the cell walls allow the plasma membranes and cytosol to be continuous; certain molecules and ions can pass from cell to cell.

TEST YOUR UNDERSTANDING

1. According to the fluid mosaic model, membranes consist of (a) a lipid–protein sandwich (b) mainly phospholipids with scattered nucleic acids (c) a fluid phospholipid bilayer in which proteins are embedded (d) a fluid phospholipid bilayer in which carbohydrates are embedded (e) a protein bilayer that behaves as a liquid crystal

2. Transmembrane proteins (a) are peripheral proteins (b) are receptor proteins (c) extend completely through the membrane (d) extend along the surface of the membrane (e) are secreted from the cell

3. Which of the following is *not* a function of the plasma membrane? (a) transports materials (b) helps structurally link cells (c) has receptors that relay signals (d) anchors the cell to the extracellular matrix (e) manufactures proteins

4. ABC transporters (a) use the energy of ATP hydrolysis to transport certain ions and sugars (b) are important in facilitated diffusion of certain ions (c) are a small group of channel proteins (d) are found mainly in plant cell membranes (e) permit passive diffusion through their channels

5. When plant cells are in a hypotonic medium, they (a) undergo plasmolysis (b) build up turgor pressure (c) wilt (d) decrease pinocytosis (e) lose water to the environment

6. A laboratory technician accidentally places red blood cells in a hypertonic solution. What happens? (a) they undergo plasmolysis (b) they build up turgor pressure (c) they swell (d) they pump solutes out (e) they become dehydrated and shrunken

7. Which of the following processes requires the cell to expend metabolic energy directly (for example, from ATP)? (a) osmosis (b) facilitated diffusion (c) all forms of carrier-mediated transport (d) active transport (e) simple diffusion

8. Electrochemical gradients (a) power simple diffusion (b) are established by pinocytosis (c) are necessary for transport by aquaporins (d) are established by concentration gradients (e) are a result of both an electric charge difference and a concentration difference between the two sides of the membrane

9. In cotransport (indirect active transport) (a) a uniporter moves a solute across a membrane against its concentration gradient (b) the movement of one solute down its concentration gradient provides energy for transport of some other solute up its concentration gradient (c) a channel protein moves ions by facilitated diffusion (d) osmosis powers the movement of ions against their concentration gradient (e) sodium is directly transported in one direction, and potassium is indirectly transported in the same direction

10. A cell takes in dissolved materials by forming tiny vesicles around fluid droplets trapped by folds of the plasma membrane. This process is (a) indirect active transport (b) pinocytosis (c) receptor-mediated endocytosis (d) exocytosis (e) facilitated diffusion

11. Anchoring junctions that hold cells together at one point as a spot weld does are (a) tight junctions (b) adhering junctions (c) desmosomes (d) gap junctions (e) plasmodesmata

12. Junctions that permit the transfer of water, ions, and molecules between adjacent plant cells are (a) tight junctions (b) adhering junctions (c) desmosomes (d) gap junctions (e) plasmodesmata

13. Label the cell membrane. Consult Figure 5-6 to check your answers.

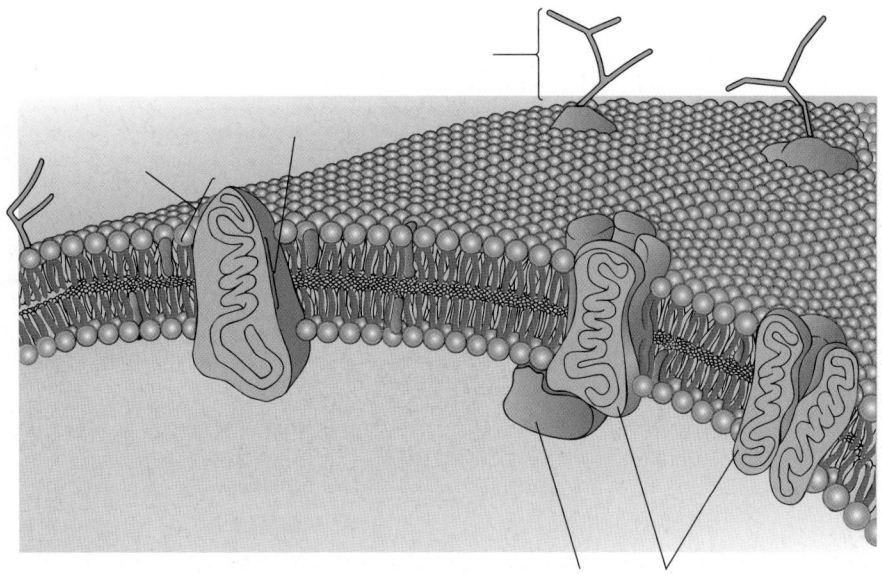

CRITICAL THINKING

1. Why can't larger polar molecules and ions diffuse through the plasma membrane? Would it be advantageous to the cell if they could? Explain.

2. Describe one way that an ion gradient can be established and maintained.

3. Most adjacent plant cells are connected by plasmodesmata, whereas only certain adjacent animal cells are associated through gap junctions. What might account for this difference?

4. **EVOLUTION LINK.** Hypothesis: the evolution of biological membranes was an essential step in the origin of life. Give arguments supporting (or challenging) this hypothesis.

5. **EVOLUTION LINK.** Transport proteins have been found in all biological membranes. What hypothesis could you make regarding whether these molecules evolved early or later in the history of cells? Argue in support of your hypothesis.

6. **SCIENCE, TECHNOLOGY, AND SOCIETY.** Biologists know quite a bit about the components that make up plant cell walls, but they do not have enough data to model the components of the cell wall as a system. Would you be in favor of investing government funds in the research and technology that would allow researchers to model the cell wall? Why or why not? Would your answer be different if you considered that a better understanding of the cell wall might allow biologists to manipulate plant growth, ripening of fruit, and the texture of certain foods?

 Additional questions are available in CengageNOW at www.cengage.com/login.

6 Cell Communication

From I. Joint et al., *Science* 298:1207

Cell-to-cell communication across the prokaryote–eukaryote boundary. Spores of the green seaweed *Enteromorpha* (Domain Eukarya) attach to biofilm-forming bacteria (Domain Bacteria) in response to chemical compounds released by the bacteria. The bacteria (*blue*) were stained and visualized with blue light. The spores appear red because of the fluorescence of chlorophyll within them.

KEY CONCEPTS

6.1 Cells communicate by signaling one another, a complex process that involves production of signaling molecules, reception of the signal, signal transduction, and a response.

6.2 Cells signal one another using chemical compounds such as neurotransmitters, hormones, and other signaling molecules.

6.3 A signaling molecule binds to a receptor molecule on the cell surface or inside the target cell.

6.4 In signal transduction, a cell converts an extracellular signal into an intracellular signal and relays the signal, leading to some change in the cell (the response).

6.5 The cell responds to signals by opening or closing ion channels; altering enzyme activity, which leads to metabolic changes and other alterations in cell activity; and by activating or inhibiting specific genes.

6.6 Similarities in cell communication among diverse organisms suggest that the molecules and mechanisms used in information transfer evolved long ago.

To maintain homeostasis, the cells of a multicellular organism must continuously communicate with one another. Many different mechanisms for transmitting information between cells, tissues, and organs have evolved, including electrical signaling and many types of chemical signaling. Organisms also communicate with other members of their species by secreting chemical signals. For example, bacteria release chemical signals that diffuse among nearby bacteria. As the population of bacteria increases, the concentration of the chemical signal increases. Through a process known as *quorum sensing,* the bacteria sense when a certain critical concentration of a signal molecule is reached. The bacteria respond by activating a specific biological process. For example, they may form a **biofilm,** a community of microorganisms attached to a solid surface. Forming a biofilm requires the coordinated activity of numerous bacteria.

Over billions of years, elaborate systems of cell signaling have evolved. Organisms of different species, and even different kingdoms and domains, communicate with one another. For example, the chemical signals released by bacteria can be intercepted by other organisms. During its life cycle, the green seaweed *Enteromorpha* produces spores that move about and temporarily attach to a surface. The spores sense a chemical signal released by bacteria that form biofilms. In response to the chemical signal, the spores move toward the biofilm and attach to individual bacteria that are part of the biofilm surface (see opening photograph).

Thousands of chemical reactions are involved in responding to signal molecules and regulating the communication among molecules necessary to maintain homeostasis. Many researchers are working on the molecular level to understand how proteins receive messages and relay signals. They are learning how proteins act as molecular switches, activating and deactivating molecules in complex signaling pathways.

Some cell biologists are using a systems biology approach to understand the intricate, dynamic interactions involved in cell communication. Biologists, biochemists, physicists, and scientists from many other disciplines are working together to understand how elaborate signaling systems within the cell interact to maintain homeostasis. They are studying how information is transferred between cells at the tissue and organ levels, and throughout the organism. Faulty signaling in cells and between cells can cause a variety of diseases, including cancer and diabetes.

In Chapter 1, we introduced three basic themes of biology. One of these, transmission of information, is the main focus of this chapter. In this chapter, we discuss how cells send and receive signals. We consider how information crosses the plasma membrane and is transmitted through signaling systems. We describe some of the responses that cells make. Finally, we discuss the evolution of cell communication. Increased understanding of the mechanisms of cell communication may suggest new strategies for preventing and treating diseases.

6.1 CELL COMMUNICATION: AN OVERVIEW

LEARNING OBJECTIVE

1   Describe the four main processes essential for cells to communicate.

When food is scarce, the amoeba-like cellular slime mold *Dictyostelium* secretes the compound **cyclic adenosine monophosphate (cAMP).** This chemical compound diffuses through the cell's environment and binds to *receptors* on the surfaces of nearby cells. The activated receptors send signals into the cells that result in movement toward the cAMP. Hundreds of slime molds come together and form a multicellular slug-shaped colony (**FIG. 6-1**; also see Fig. 26-20). (When conditions are favorable, the cells of the slug form a stalked fruiting body with spores at the top; when released, each spore gives rise to an amoeba-like cell.)

Even though they do not move from one place to another, plants also communicate with each other. For example, diseased maple trees send airborne chemical signals that are received by uninfected trees nearby. Cells of the uninfected trees respond by increasing their chemical defenses so that they are more resistant to the disease-causing organisms. Plants also send signals to insects. When tobacco plants are attacked by herbivorous insects, the

G. Gerisch et al./Max-Planck Institute

16.6 mm

FIGURE 6-1 Cell signaling in cellular slime molds
When food is scarce, the amoeba-like cellular slime mold *Dictyostelium* secretes the chemical compound cyclic AMP (cAMP). The slime molds respond to this chemical signal by aggregating. Converging streams of hundreds of individuals come together and form a multicellular colony.

plants release volatile chemicals. In response to these signals, the insects lay fewer eggs, thus reducing the number of insects feeding on the plants. Predator insects that eat the eggs of the herbivorous insects respond to the plant signals by eating more of the herbivorous insect eggs. Thus, natural selection has resulted in plant signals that herbivorous insects detect and avoid and that carnivorous insects detect and approach. This system of information transfer helps protect plants from herbivorous insects.

To survive, organisms must receive signals from the outside environment and effectively respond to them. In order to grow, develop, and function, the cells of a multicellular organism must also communicate with one another. In plants and animals, *hormones* and other regulatory molecules serve as important chemical signals between various cells and organs. In animals, neurons (nerve cells) transmit information electrically and chemically.

The term **cell signaling** refers to the mechanisms by which cells communicate with one another. If the cells are physically close to one another, a signaling molecule on one cell may combine with a *receptor* (a macromolecule that binds with signaling molecules) on another cell. Most commonly, cells communicate by sending chemical signals over some distance. As we will discuss, cell signaling must be precisely regulated. Cell signaling involves a sequence of four main processes (**FIG. 6-2**). We summarize them here and discuss them in more detail in the following sections of this chapter.

1.   **A cell must send a signal.** In chemical signaling, a cell must synthesize and release signaling molecules. For example, specialized cells in the vertebrate pancreas secrete the hormone insulin. If the **target cells,** the cells that can respond to the signal, are not in close proximity, the signal must be transported to them. The circulatory system transports insulin to target cells

throughout the body. Next, target cells must receive, relay, and respond to the information signaled.

2. **Reception.** Reception is the process of receiving an incoming signal. **Receptors** are large proteins or glycoproteins that bind with signaling molecules. Many types of signaling molecules do not actually enter the target cell. They bind to specific receptors on the surface of the target cell. Insulin, for example, binds to insulin receptors, which are transmembrane receptors.

3. **Signal transduction** is the process by which a cell converts an extracellular signal into an intracellular signal and relays the signal, leading to a cellular response. Signal transduction typically involves a chain of molecules that relay information. When insulin binds to an insulin receptor, the signal is relayed through several different signaling pathways.

4. **Response.** The final molecule in the signaling pathway converts the signal into a response that alters some cell process. For example, as we will discuss in Chapter 49, insulin stimulates cells to take up glucose from the blood. This response lowers the concentration of glucose in the blood. Insulin also helps regulate fat and protein metabolism. Many signaling molecules stimulate ion channels in the plasma membrane to open or close. Still other signaling molecules activate or inhibit specific genes in the nucleus. These responses can result in changes in cell division and other aspects of cell development.

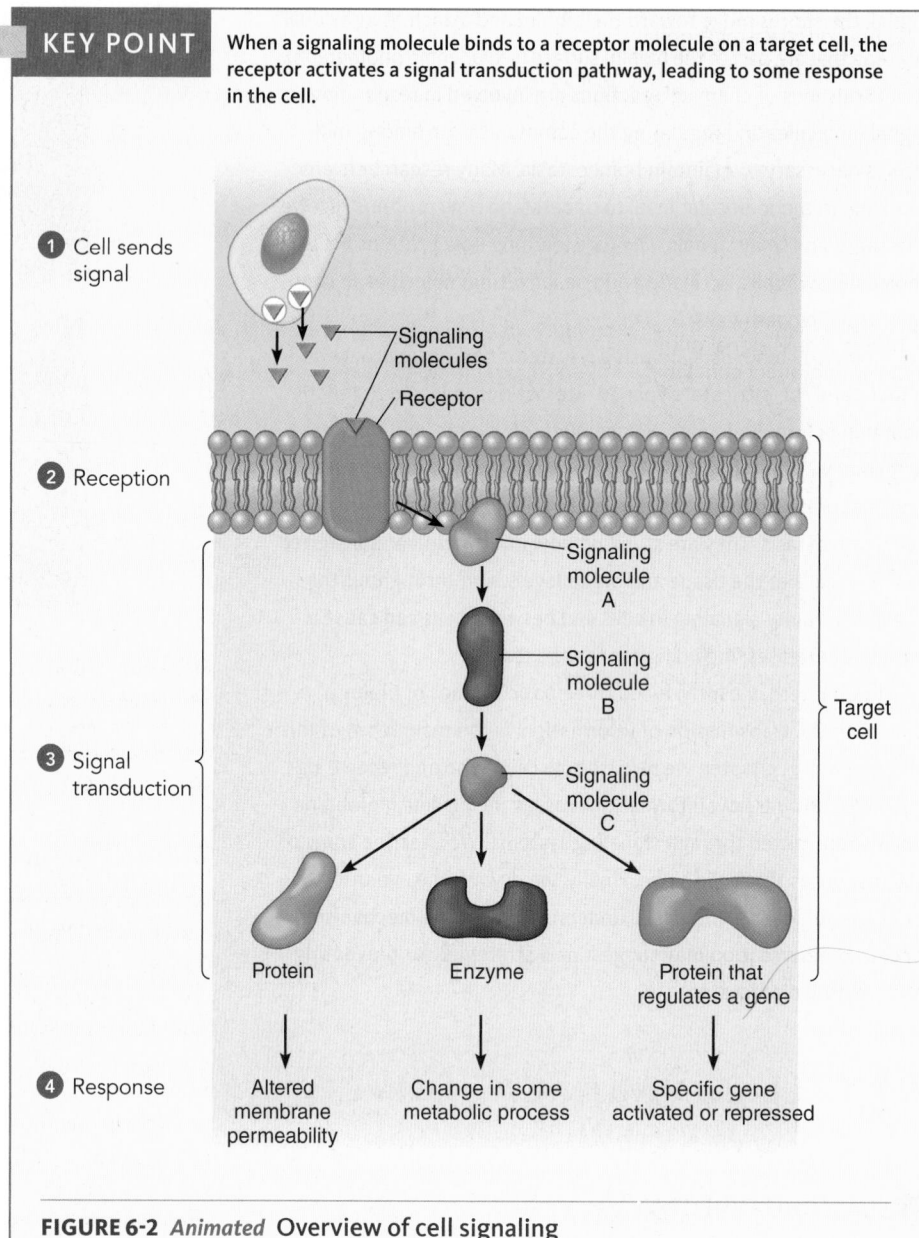

KEY POINT

When a signaling molecule binds to a receptor molecule on a target cell, the receptor activates a signal transduction pathway, leading to some response in the cell.

1. Cell sends signal

Signaling molecules

Receptor

2. Reception

Signaling molecule A

Signaling molecule B

3. Signal transduction

Signaling molecule C

Target cell

Protein

Enzyme

Protein that regulates a gene

4. Response

Altered membrane permeability

Change in some metabolic process

Specific gene activated or repressed

FIGURE 6-2 *Animated* **Overview of cell signaling**

After a signaling molecule has done its job, its action must be stopped, so during the signaling process, certain mechanisms operate to *terminate the signal.*

Review

- What is the sequence of events that takes place in cell signaling? Describe each process.

6.2 SENDING SIGNALS

■ LEARNING OBJECTIVE

2 Compare three types of signaling molecules: neurotransmitters, hormones, and local regulators.

Cells communicate in several ways, including directly through cell junctions, by way of electrical signals, temporary cell-to-cell contact, and chemical signals. Recall from Chapter 5 that gap junctions in animal cells allow rapid chemical and electrical communication between adjacent cells. For example, the gap junctions between cardiac muscle cells of the heart wall allow the rapid flow of ions necessary for synchronized contraction. Plasmodesmata between adjacent plant cells also allow signal molecules to pass quickly from one cell to another.

Cells that are not directly connected also communicate with one another. In animals, some neurons communicate with electrical signals. Most neurons, however, signal one another by releasing chemical compounds called **neurotransmitters** (FIG. 6-3a). Neurotransmitter molecules diffuse across *synapses,* tiny gaps between neurons. More than 60 different neurotransmitters have been

(a) Neurons transmit signals across synapses.

Signaling molecules

Receptor

Target neuron

Signaling neuron

(b) Some cells signal one another by making direct contact.

Receptor

Nucleus

Signaling cell

Target cell

(c) Many hormones are transported by the blood to target cells.

Signaling molecules (hormone)

Receptor

Endocrine cell

Hormone transported in blood

Target cell

(d) In paracrine regulation, a local regulator diffuses to target cells.

Signaling molecules (local regulator)

Receptor

Signaling cell

Target cell

FIGURE 6-3 Some types of cell signaling
Different types of cells may communicate in different ways.

hormones into the surrounding interstitial fluid. Typically, hormones diffuse into capillaries and are transported by the blood to target cells (**FIG. 6-3c**).

Some cells produce local regulators that signal cells in close proximity. A **local regulator** is a signaling molecule that diffuses through the **interstitial fluid,** the fluid surrounding the cells, and acts on nearby cells. This is called **paracrine regulation** (**FIG. 6-3d**). Some local regulators are considered hormones. Local regulators include local chemical mediators such as growth factors, histamine, nitric oxide, and prostaglandins. More than 50 **growth factors,** typically peptides, stimulate cell division and normal development in specific types of cells.

Histamine is a local regulator that is stored in certain cells of the immune system and is released in response to allergic reactions, injury, or infection. Histamine causes blood vessels to dilate and capillaries to become more permeable. **Nitric oxide (NO),** another local regulator, is a gas produced by many types of cells, including plant and animal cells. Nitric oxide released by cells lining blood vessels relaxes smooth muscle in the blood vessel walls. As a result, the blood vessels dilate, decreasing blood pressure.

Prostaglandins are local hormones that are paracrine regulators. Prostaglandins modify cAMP levels and interact with other signaling molecules to regulate metabolic activities. For example, some prostaglandins stimulate smooth muscle to contract.

identified, including acetylcholine, norepinephrine, dopamine, serotonin, and several amino acids and peptides.

Cells synthesize many different types of chemical signals and deliver them in various ways. In animals, certain cells in the immune system produce specific chemical compounds that are displayed on the cell surface. These cells recognize the chemical signals and communicate with one another by making direct contact (**FIG. 6-3b**).

Specialized cells in plants and animals produce signaling molecules called **hormones.** Hormones may be synthesized by neighboring cells or by specialized organs or tissues some distance from the target cells. In animals, many hormones are produced by **endocrine glands.** These glands have no ducts; they secrete their

Review

- What are neurotransmitters?
- How are hormones typically transported to target cells?
- What is paracrine regulation?

6.3 RECEPTION

LEARNING OBJECTIVES

3 Identify mechanisms that make reception a highly specific process.
4 Briefly compare ion channel–linked receptors, G protein–linked receptors, enzyme-linked receptors, and intracellular receptors.

Hundreds of different types of signaling molecules are present in the interstitial fluid, the tissue fluid that surrounds the cells of a multicellular organism. How do cells know which messages are for them? The answer is that each type of cell is genetically programmed to receive and respond to specific types of signals. Which signals a cell responds to depends on the specific receptors it is programmed to synthesize.

A signaling molecule, such as insulin, that binds to a specific receptor acts as a **ligand.** A ligand is a molecule, other than an enzyme, that binds specifically to a macromolecule (usually a protein), forming a macromolecule-ligand complex. The complex triggers a biological response. Most ligands are hydrophilic molecules that bind to protein receptors on the surface of target cells (**FIG. 6-4a**).

Some signaling molecules are small enough or sufficiently hydrophobic to move through the plasma membrane and enter the cell (**FIG. 6-4b**). These signaling molecules bind with intracellular receptors. Reception occurs when a signaling molecule binds to a specific receptor protein on the surface of, or inside, a target cell. The signaling molecule activates the receptor.

A receptor on the cell surface generally has at least three domains. Recall from Chapter 3 that in biochemistry, the term *domain* refers to a structural and functional region of a protein. The external domain is a docking site for a signaling molecule. A second domain extends through the plasma membrane, and a third domain is a "tail" that extends into the cytoplasm. The tail transmits the signal to a molecule inside the cell.

Reception is highly selective. Each type of receptor has a specific shape. The receptor binding site is somewhat like a lock, and signaling molecules are like different keys. Only the signaling molecule that fits the specific receptor can influence the metabolic machinery of the cell. Receptors are important in determining the specificity of cell communication.

Different types of cells can produce different types of receptors. Any one cell makes many different receptors. Furthermore, a cell may synthesize different kinds of receptors at different stages in its life cycle or in response to different conditions. Another consideration is that the same signal can have different meanings for various target cells.

Some receptors are specialized to respond to signals other than chemical signals. For example, in the vertebrate eye, a receptor called **rhodopsin** is activated by light. Rhodopsin is part of a signal transduction pathway that leads to vision in dim light. Plants and some algae have **phytochromes,** a family of blue-green pig-

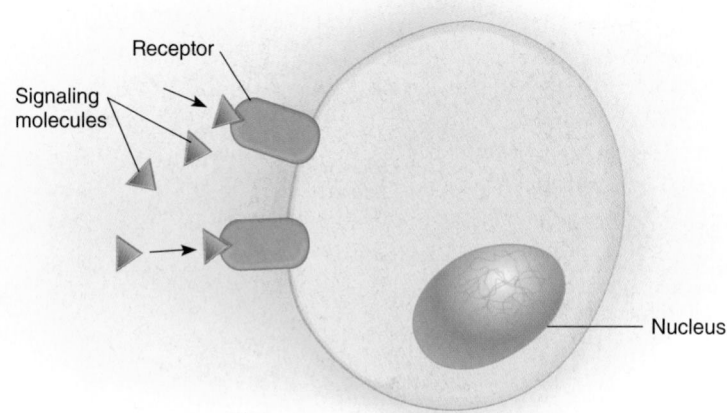

(a) Hydrophilic signaling molecules bind to receptors in the plasma membrane.

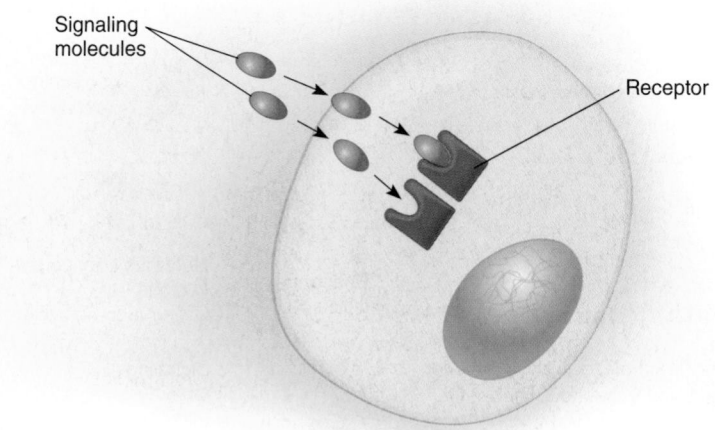

(b) Hydrophobic signaling molecules cross the plasma membrane and bind with receptors inside the cell.

FIGURE 6-4 Cell-surface and intracellular receptors
Hydrophilic (water-soluble) signaling molecules cannot pass through the plasma membrane. They bind to receptors on the cell surface. Hydrophobic (lipid-soluble) signaling molecules pass through the plasma membrane and bind with receptors in the cytosol or nucleus.

ment proteins that are activated by red light. Activation can lead to changes, such as flowering. Plants, some algae, and at least some animals have **cryptochromes,** pigments that absorb blue light. Cryptochromes play a role in biological rhythms.

Cells regulate reception

An important mechanism that cells use to regulate reception is increasing or decreasing the number of each type of receptor. Depending on the needs of the cell, receptors are synthesized or degraded. For example, when the concentration of the hormone insulin is too high for an extended period, cells decrease the number of their insulin receptors. This process is called **receptor down-regulation.** In the case of insulin, receptor down-regulation suppresses the sensitivity of target cells to the hormone. Insulin stimulates cells to take in glucose by facilitated diffusion, so receptor down-regulation decreases the ability of cells to take in glucose. Receptor down-regulation often involves transporting receptors to lysosomes, where they are destroyed.

Receptor up-regulation occurs in response to low hormone concentrations. A greater number of receptors are synthesized, and their increased numbers on the plasma membrane make it more likely that the signal will be received by a receptor on the cell. Receptor up-regulation thus *amplifies* the signaling molecule's effect on the cell. Receptor up-regulation and down-regulation are controlled in part by signals to genes that code for the receptors.

Three types of receptors occur on the cell surface

Three main types of receptors on the cell surface are ion channel–linked receptors, G protein–linked receptors, and enzyme-linked receptors.

Ion channel–linked receptors convert chemical signals into electrical signals

Ion channel–linked receptors are found in the plasma membrane. These receptors, which have been extensively studied in neurons and muscle cells, convert chemical signals into electrical signals (**FIG. 6-5a**). The receptor itself serves as a channel.

Ion channel–linked receptors are also called **ligand-gated channels,** which means that the ion channel opens or closes in response to the binding of the signaling molecule (ligand). Part of the receptor (protein) that makes up the channel forms the gate. The receptor responds to certain signals by changing its shape, opening or closing the gate. Typically, the gate of an ion channel remains closed until a ligand binds to the receptor.

Neurotransmitters released by neurons in the nervous system are signaling molecules. For example, **acetylcholine** is a neurotransmitter that binds to an acetylcholine receptor. This receptor is a ligand-gated sodium ion channel that is important in muscle contraction. When acetylcholine binds to the receptor, the channel opens, allowing sodium ions to enter the cell. The influx of sodium ions decreases the electric charge difference across the membrane (depolarization), which can lead to muscle contraction. After a brief time, the ligand dissociates from the receptor and the gate closes the channel. As we will discuss in Chapter 41, some ion channels, called voltage-activated channels, are regulated by electrical signals.

G protein–linked receptors link signaling molecules to signal transduction pathways

G protein–linked receptors (also called G protein–coupled receptors) are a large family of transmembrane proteins that loop back and forth through the plasma membrane seven times (**FIG. 6-5b**). The receptor consists of seven transmembrane alpha helices connected by loops that extend into the cytosol or outside the cell. G protein–linked receptors couple certain signaling molecules to various signal transduction pathways inside the cell. The outer part of the receptor has a binding site for a signaling molecule, and the part of the receptor that extends into the cytosol has a binding site for a specific **G protein.**

G proteins bind *guanine nucleotides.* When a signaling molecule binds with a G protein–linked receptor, the receptor changes shape. This change allows the G protein to associate with the receptor.

G protein–linked receptors are found in all eukaryotes. These receptors bind with hundreds of different signaling molecules. Some of the many critical processes that depend on G protein–linked receptors are vision, sense of smell, regulation of mood and behavior, and regulation of the immune system. As you might imagine, understanding how G protein–linked receptors work is medically important. About 60% of prescription medications currently in use act on these receptors. More than 900 G protein–linked receptors have been identified in mammals, and more than 400 of these receptors are potential targets for pharmaceutical interventions.

Enzyme-linked receptors function directly as enzymes or are linked to enzymes

Enzyme-linked receptors are transmembrane proteins with a binding site for a signaling molecule outside the cell and an enzyme component inside the cell. Recall from Chapter 3 that *enzymes* catalyze specific chemical reactions; most enzymes are proteins. Some enzyme-linked receptors do not have an enzyme component but have a binding site for an enzyme. Several groups of enzyme-linked receptors have been identified.

Proteins called *tyrosine kinases* make up a major group of enzyme-linked receptors. A **kinase** is an enzyme that transfers the terminal phosphate group from ATP to a *substrate* (the specific substance on which an enzyme acts). This process is called **phosphorylation.** A **tyrosine kinase** is an enzyme that catalyzes the transfer of phosphate groups from ATP to a specific *tyrosine* that is part of a protein. (Tyrosine is an amino acid.) The tyrosine kinase enzyme part of the receptor is the domain that extends into the cytosol. Tyrosine kinase receptors bind certain hormones, including insulin and *growth factors,* such as nerve growth factor. These receptors regulate many cellular processes and are important in development.

Before the tyrosine kinase can phosphorylate a signaling protein in the cell, it must first be activated. When signal molecules bind to two tyrosine kinase receptors, the receptors move closer together in the plasma membrane and pair, forming a *dimer.* A conformational change (change in shape) takes place, which allows the tyrosine kinase part of each receptor to add a phosphate from an ATP molecule to certain tyrosines on the other member of the dimer (**FIG. 6-5c**). Once activated, tyrosine kinase enzymes can phosphorylate signaling proteins inside the cell (discussed in the next section).

Many plant cell-surface receptors are enzyme-linked receptors. **Brassinosteroids (BRs),** a group of plant steroid hormones, regulate many plant processes, including cell division, cell elongation, and flower development (discussed in Chapter 38). Unlike animal steroid hormones, which typically bind with intracellular receptors, BRs bind with a protein kinase receptor in the plasma membrane. In plant protein kinase receptors, serine and threonine, rather than tyrosine, appear to be the amino acids that are phosphorylated.

The gas **ethylene** is a plant hormone that regulates a variety of processes, including seed germination and ripening of fruit. Ethylene is also important in plant responses to stressors. The ethylene receptor has two components. Each component has a domain that

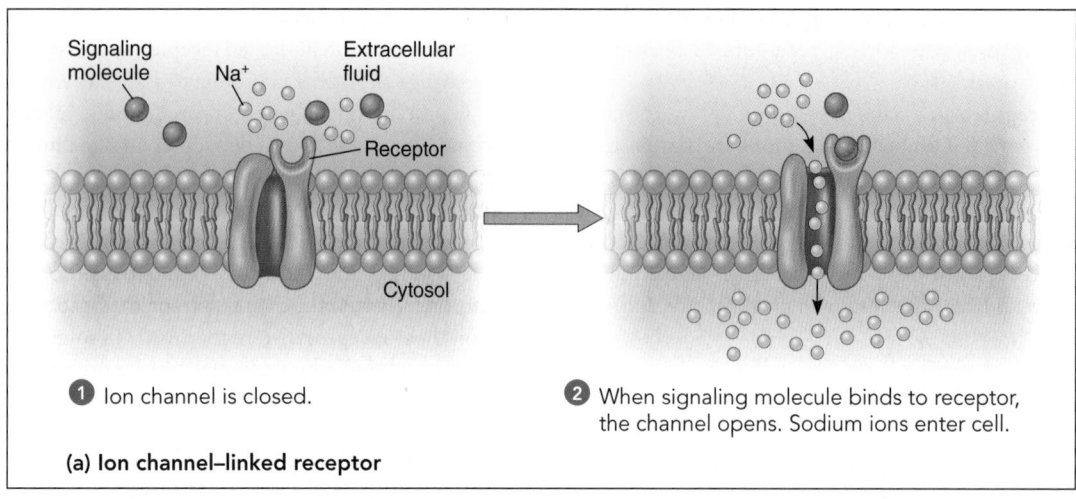

① Ion channel is closed.

② When signaling molecule binds to receptor, the channel opens. Sodium ions enter cell.

(a) Ion channel–linked receptor

① In inactive state, the three subunits of G protein are joined.

② When signaling molecule (ligand) binds to receptor, the ligand–receptor complex associates with G protein. This causes GDP to be replaced with GTP. One subunit of G protein then separates from the other two parts.

(b) G protein–linked receptor

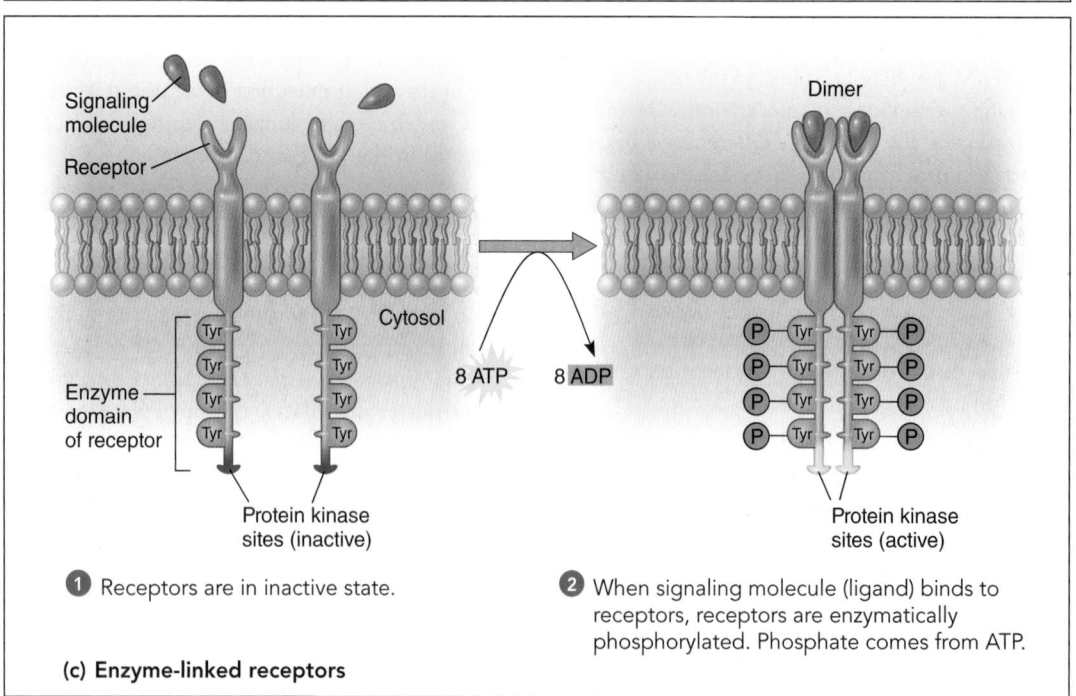

① Receptors are in inactive state.

② When signaling molecule (ligand) binds to receptors, receptors are enzymatically phosphorylated. Phosphate comes from ATP.

(c) Enzyme-linked receptors

FIGURE 6-5 Three types of cell-surface receptors

is an enzyme, a histidine kinase, that extends into the cell. Receptors with histidine kinase domains are also present in bacterial and yeast cells.

Some receptors are located inside the cell

Certain receptors are found in the cytosol or in the nucleus. Most of these **intracellular receptors** are **transcription factors,** proteins that regulate the expression of specific genes. The signaling molecules that bind with intracellular receptors are small, hydrophobic molecules that can diffuse across the membranes of target cells (see Fig. 6-4b).

In animal cells, most steroid hormones, such as the molting hormone *ecdysone* in insects and *cortisol* in vertebrates, enter target cells and combine with receptor molecules in the cytosol. Vitamins A and D and nitric oxide also bind with intracellular receptors. After binding, the ligand–receptor complex moves into the nucleus. *Thyroid hormones* (which are not steroids) bind to receptors already bound to DNA inside the nucleus.

Review

- How does a receptor "know" which signaling molecules to bind?
- Under what conditions might receptor up-regulation occur? receptor down-regulation?
- What are the three main types of cell-surface receptors? (Briefly describe each.)

6.4 SIGNAL TRANSDUCTION

◼ LEARNING OBJECTIVES

5 Compare the actions of the main types of receptors in signal transduction.

6 Trace the sequence of events in signal transduction for each of the following second messengers: cyclic AMP, inositol trisphosphate, diacylglycerol, and calcium ions.

As we have discussed, many regulatory molecules transmit information to the cell's interior without physically crossing the plasma membrane. Instead, they activate membrane proteins, which then *transduce* the signal. The first component in a signal transduction pathway is typically the receptor, which may be a transmembrane protein with a domain exposed on the extracellular surface. Each type of receptor activates a different signal transduction pathway.

In a typical signaling pathway, a signaling molecule binds with a cell-surface receptor and activates it by changing the shape of the receptor tail that extends into the cytoplasm. The signal may then be relayed through a sequence of proteins that are intracellular signaling molecules. Typically, the proteins in this chain are protein kinases. The chain of signaling molecules in the cell that relays a signal is called a **signaling pathway** or **signaling cascade.** During signal transduction, the original signal is amplified.

More than 3000 signaling proteins have been identified in the cells of mammals alone. Malfunctions in signal transduction pathways have been linked to major diseases, including cancer, heart disease, diabetes, and autoimmune diseases.

Signaling molecules can act as molecular switches

Each component in a signaling pathway acts as a molecular "switch," which can be in an active ("on") state or an inactive ("off") state. When an intracellular signaling molecule receives a signal, it is activated (turned on). Another process then occurs that inactivates (turns off) the signaling molecule. Every activated molecule in a signaling pathway must be inactivated in order to transmit a new signal. Molecular switches are typically regulated by the addition or removal of phosphate groups.

Each time a signal molecule binds to a receptor, a signaling pathway is turned on. As the signal is transmitted to each protein kinase in the chain, the protein is phosphorylated. Recall that in phosphorylation, an enzyme transfers phosphate groups from one molecule to another. As phosphate is transferred, the signal passes from protein kinase 1 to protein kinase 2 to protein kinase 3, and on down the chain (**FIG. 6-6**). Phosphorylation typically activates a protein kinase, although in some cases phosphorylation inhibits protein kinase activity. A signaling pathway in which a series of protein kinase molecules are phosphorylated is referred to as a **protein kinase cascade.** The last protein kinase in the cascade activates the target protein by phosphorylation. The target protein alters some process in the cell.

After the signal passes from protein kinase 1 to protein kinase 2, protein kinase 1 must be inactivated. Each molecule must be available to transmit a new signal. A **phosphatase** is an enzyme that catalyzes the removal of a phosphate group by hydrolysis; the process is called *dephosphorylation.* Protein phosphatases help regulate protein kinase cascades. Just as a cell contains hundreds of different protein kinases, it also contains many types of protein phosphatases. Rapid removal of phosphate groups by protein phosphatases is an important regulatory mechanism for protein kinase cascades. Such regulation ensures that these pathways operate only in response to the binding of a signal molecule to a receptor.

Ion channel–linked receptors open or close channels

The gates of many ion channels remain closed until a ligand binds to the receptor. For example, when the neurotransmitter acetylcholine binds to an acetylcholine receptor (which is an ion channel–linked receptor), the channel opens, allowing sodium ions to enter the cell (see Fig. 6-5a). Depending on the type of cell, the influx of sodium ions can result in transmission of a neural impulse or in muscle contraction.

Gamma-aminobutyric acid (GABA) is a neurotransmitter that binds to GABA receptors. One class of GABA receptors consists of ligand-gated chloride ion channels. When GABA binds to the receptor, the channel opens. Chloride ions, which are negatively charged, rush out of or into the neuron, depending on the conditions (electrochemical gradient) in the cell. Typically, chloride ions leave the cell, which inhibits transmission of neural impulses. Thus, GABA *inhibits* neural signaling. Barbiturates and benzodiazepine drugs such as Valium bind to GABA receptors. When this occurs, lower amounts of GABA are required to open the chloride channels and inhibit neural impulses. This action results in a tranquilizing effect. (Not all GABA receptors are *themselves* ion

Many signaling pathways are protein kinase cascades in which each protein kinase in the pathway is activated by the addition of a phosphate group.

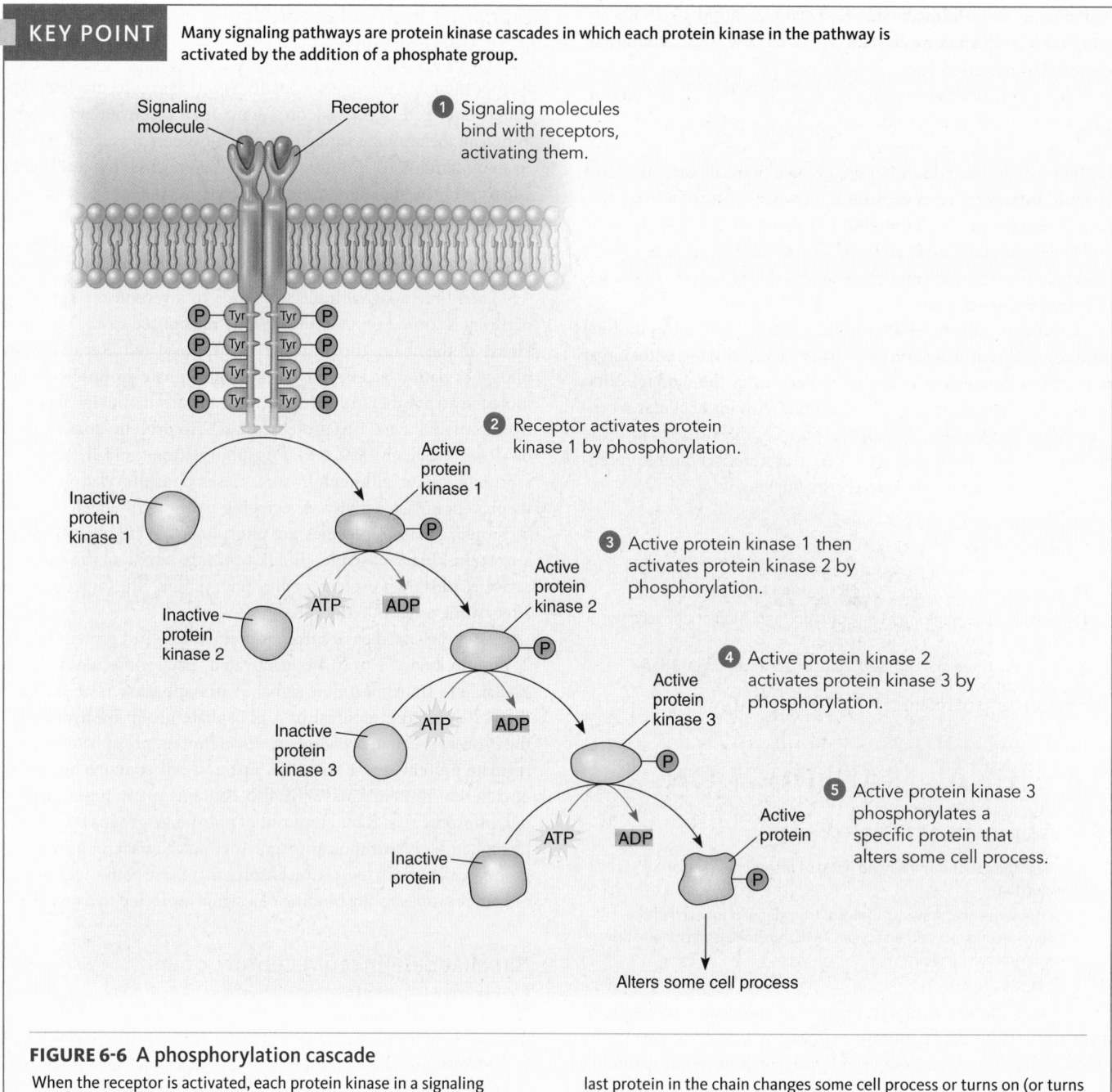

FIGURE 6-6 A phosphorylation cascade

When the receptor is activated, each protein kinase in a signaling pathway activates the next protein kinase in the pathway by phosphorylation. The phosphate group comes from ATP. Addition of a phosphate group typically changes the shape of the molecule. Activation of the last protein in the chain changes some cell process or turns on (or turns off) specific genes. (*P* represents phosphate.) Note that the number of protein kinases varies from pathway to pathway.

channels; some are G-protein–linked receptors or enzyme-linked receptors that trigger a series of reactions resulting in activation of other proteins that serve as ion channels.)

G protein–linked receptors initiate signal transduction

As discussed in the last section, G protein–linked receptors activate G proteins, a group of regulatory proteins important in many signal transduction pathways. These proteins are found in yeasts, protists, plants, and animals. They are involved in the action of

some plant and many animal hormones. Some G proteins regulate channels in the plasma membrane, allowing ions to enter or exit the cell. Other G proteins are involved in the perception of sight and smell. In 1994, Alfred G. Gilman of the University of Texas and Martin Rodbell of the National Institute of Environmental Health Sciences were awarded the Nobel Prize in Physiology or Medicine for their groundbreaking research on G proteins.

In its inactive state, the G protein consists of three subunits that are joined (see Fig. 6-5b). One subunit is linked to a molecule of **guanosine diphosphate (GDP),** a molecule similar to ADP but containing the base guanine instead of adenine. When a signaling molecule binds with the receptor, the GDP is released and is replaced by **guanosine triphosphate (GTP),** a nucleotide that, like ATP, functions in energy transactions.

The subunit of the G protein that is linked to the GTP separates from the other two subunits. The G protein subunit linked to the GTP is a GTPase, an enzyme that catalyzes the hydrolysis of GTP to GDP. This action, a process that releases energy, deactivates the G protein. Now in its inactive state, the G protein subunit rejoins the other two subunits.

When activated, a G protein initiates signal transduction by binding with a specific protein in the cell. In some cases, G proteins *directly* activate enzymes that catalyze changes in certain proteins. These changes lead to alterations in cell function. More commonly, the signaling molecule serves as the **first messenger,** and information is relayed by way of the G protein to a second messenger.

Second messengers are intracellular signaling agents

Second messengers are ions or small molecules that relay signals inside the cell. More than 15 second messengers have been identified in mammals. When receptors are activated, second messengers are produced in large quantities. Second messengers rapidly diffuse through the cell (or membrane), relaying the signal. Thus, second messengers amplify the signal.

Second messengers pass the signal along to other signaling proteins or target proteins. The signal typically passes through a chain of proteins and other molecules. The last molecule in the sequence activates the final response. Second messengers are not enzymes, but some regulate specific enzymes, such as protein kinases. Others bind to ion channels, opening or closing them.

Cyclic AMP is a second messenger

Most G proteins shuttle a signal between the receptor and a second messenger. In many signaling cascades in prokaryotic and animal cells, the second messenger is cyclic AMP (cAMP) (**FIG. 6-7**). Researcher Earl Sutherland identified cAMP as a second messenger in the 1960s and was awarded the 1971 Nobel Prize in Physiology or Medicine for his pioneering work.

When the G protein undergoes a conformational change (change in shape), it binds with and activates **adenylyl cyclase,** an enzyme on the cytoplasmic side of the plasma membrane. The type of G protein that activates adenylyl cyclase is known as a stimulatory G protein, or G_s. (Some G proteins, denoted as G_i, inhibit enzymes.) Note that the G protein couples the ligand–receptor complex to adenylyl cyclase action (see Fig. 6-7).

When activated, adenylyl cyclase catalyzes the production of cAMP from ATP (**FIG. 6-8**). By coupling the signaling molecule–receptor complex to an enzyme that generates a signal, G proteins amplify the effects of signaling molecules and many second-messenger molecules are rapidly produced. The pathway is regulated, in part, by **phosphodiesterase,** an enzyme that converts cAMP to adenosine monophosphate (AMP). This action is an off switch that rapidly inactivates cAMP when the receptor becomes inactive.

KEY POINT Cyclic AMP (cAMP), a second messenger, relays a signal from the plasma membrane to proteins in the cytosol.

1 Signaling molecule combines with G protein–linked receptor. G protein activates adenylyl cyclase, which then catalyzes formation of cAMP from ATP.

2 Signal is relayed by second messengers.

3 Response: Some cell process is altered.

Signaling molecule (first messenger)
Extracellular fluid
Receptor   G protein   Adenylyl cyclase
Plasma membrane
GTP
ATP
Cytosol
cAMP
cAMP   cAMP   cAMP   Second messenger
Protein   Protein   Protein
Alters metabolism   Affects gene activity   Opens or closes ion channels

FIGURE 6-7 Signal relay by a second messenger: An overview

FIGURE 6-8 Synthesis and inactivation of cyclic AMP

Cyclic AMP (cAMP) is a second messenger produced from ATP. The enzyme adenylyl cyclase catalyzes the reaction. Cyclic AMP is inactivated by the enzyme phosphodiesterase, which converts it to adenosine monophosphate (AMP).

FIGURE 6-9 illustrates in more detail the sequence of events in a signaling pathway involving G protein and cyclic AMP. Cyclic AMP activates certain protein kinase enzymes, particularly a group referred to as **protein kinase A.** Recall that protein kinases add phosphate groups to target proteins. When a protein is phosphorylated, its function is altered and it triggers a chain of reactions leading to some response in the cell, such as a metabolic change.

The **substrates,** the substances on which an enzyme acts, for protein kinases are different in various cell types. Consequently, the effect of the enzyme varies depending on the substrate. For example, in skeletal muscle cells, protein kinase A activates enzymes that break down glycogen to glucose, providing the muscle cells with energy. In certain neurons in the brain, the same enzyme acti-

① Signaling molecule binds with G protein–linked receptor in plasma membrane.

② Signal molecule–receptor complex activates G protein. GDP is replaced by GTP.

③ G protein activates adenylyl cyclase, which then catalyzes synthesis of cAMP. cAMP activates protein kinase A, which then phosphorylates specific proteins, leading to some response in cell.

FIGURE 6-9 Signal transduction involving a G protein and cyclic AMP

vates the reward system by regulating action of the neurotransmitter dopamine.

We can summarize the sequence of events beginning with the binding of the signaling molecule to the receptor and leading to a change in some cell function:

signaling molecule (first messenger) binds to G protein–linked receptor ⟶ activates G protein ⟶ activates adenylyl cyclase ⟶ catalyzes the formation of cAMP (second messenger) ⟶ activates protein kinase ⟶ phosphorylates proteins ⟶ response in cell

Some G proteins use phospholipids as second messengers

Certain signaling molecule–receptor complexes activate a G protein that then activates the membrane-bound enzyme **phospholipase C** (FIG. 6-10). This enzyme splits a membrane phospholipid, PIP_2 (phosphotidylinositol-4,5-bisphosphate), into two products, **inositol trisphosphate** (IP_3) and **diacylglycerol** (**DAG**). Both act as second messengers.

DAG remains in the plasma membrane, where in combination with calcium ions, it activates **protein kinase C** enzymes. Depending on the type of cell and the specific protein kinase C, the response of the cell can include growth, a change in cell pH,

---

KEY POINT When activated by a G protein, phospholipase C splits the phospholipid PIP_2, producing the second messengers DAG and IP_3.

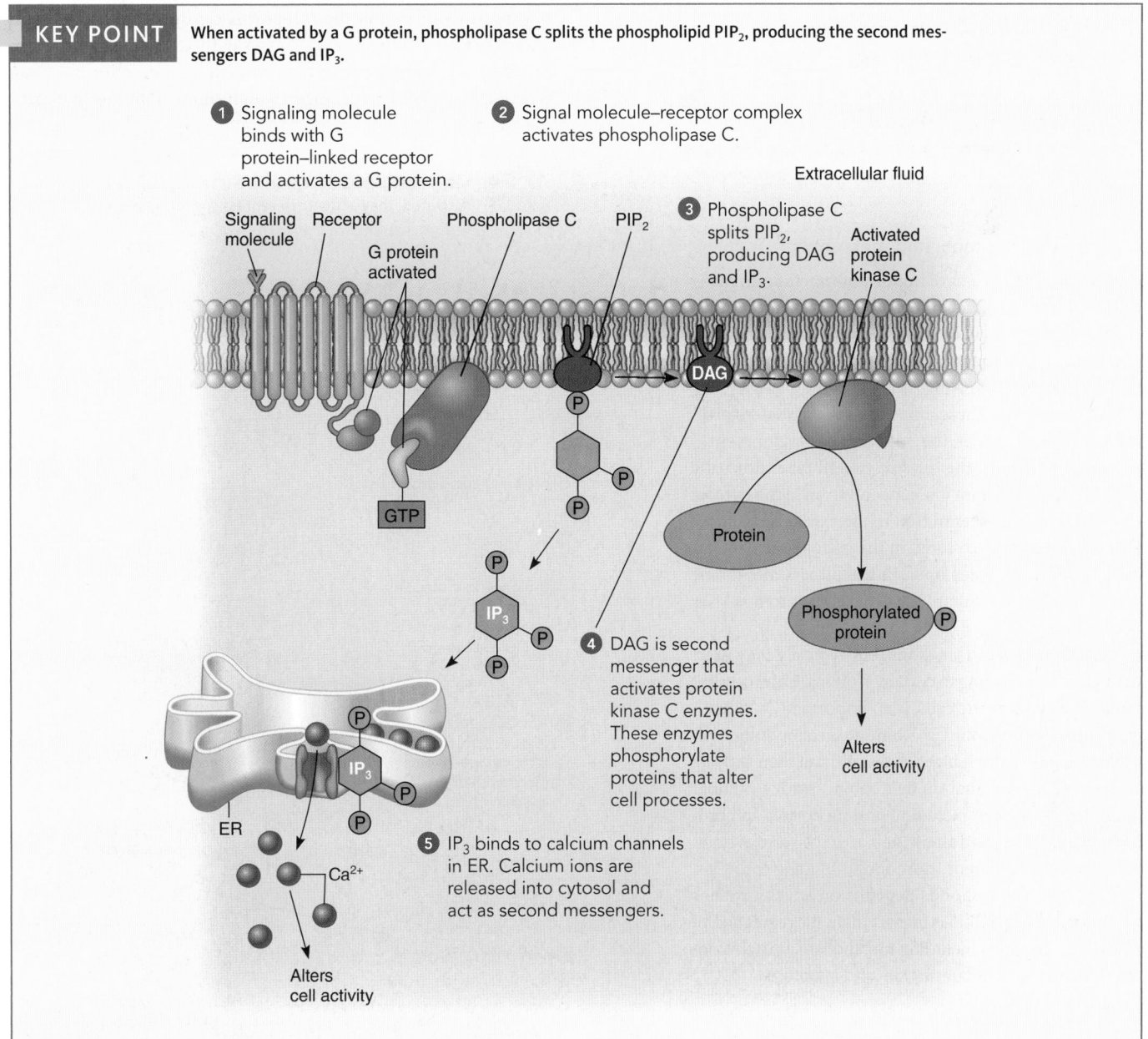

1 Signaling molecule binds with G protein–linked receptor and activates a G protein.

2 Signal molecule–receptor complex activates phospholipase C.

Extracellular fluid

Signaling molecule Receptor G protein activated Phospholipase C PIP_2

3 Phospholipase C splits PIP_2, producing DAG and IP_3. Activated protein kinase C

DAG

GTP

Protein

IP_3

Phosphorylated protein

4 DAG is second messenger that activates protein kinase C enzymes. These enzymes phosphorylate proteins that alter cell processes.

Alters cell activity

ER

IP_3

Ca^{2+}

5 IP_3 binds to calcium channels in ER. Calcium ions are released into cytosol and act as second messengers.

Alters cell activity

FIGURE 6-10 Phospholipid products as second messengers

An activated G protein activates phospholipase C. This enzyme splits PIP_2, producing two second messengers—IP_3 and DAG. IP_3 binds to calcium channels in the endoplasmic reticulum (ER); calcium ions are released into the cytosol and act as second messengers. DAG activates protein kinase C, a family of enzymes that activates signaling pathways by phosphorylating proteins; calcium ions are needed for the activation of protein kinase C.

or regulation of certain ion channels. Protein kinase C stimulates contraction of smooth muscle in the digestive system and in other organs of the body.

IP_3 is a member of a family of inositol phosphate messengers, some of which can donate phosphate groups to proteins. IP_3 binds to calcium channels in the endoplasmic reticulum (ER), causing them to open and release calcium ions into the cytosol. We can summarize this sequence of events as follows:

signaling molecule binds to G protein–linked receptor $\longrightarrow$ activates G protein $\longrightarrow$ activates phospholipase $\longrightarrow$ splits $PIP_2 \longrightarrow$ inositol trisphosphate (IP_3) + diacylglycerol (DAG)

DAG $\longrightarrow$ activates protein kinase enzymes $\longrightarrow$ phosphorylates proteins $\longrightarrow$ some response in cell

$IP_3 \longrightarrow$ binds to calcium channels in ER $\longrightarrow$ calcium ions released into the cytosol $\longrightarrow$ some response in the cell

Calcium ions are important messengers

Calcium ions (Ca^{2+}) have important functions in many cell processes, including microtubule disassembly, muscle contraction, blood clotting, secretion, and activation of certain cells in the immune system. Calcium ions are critical in neural signaling, including the pathways involved in learning. These ions are also essential in fertilization of an egg and in the initiation of development.

Ion pumps in the plasma membrane normally maintain a low calcium ion concentration in the cytosol compared to its concentration in the extracellular fluid. Calcium ions are also stored in the endoplasmic reticulum. When Ca^{2+} gates open in the plasma membrane or endoplasmic reticulum, the Ca^{2+} concentration rises in the cytosol.

Calcium ions can act alone, but typically they exert their effects by binding to certain proteins. **Calmodulin,** found in all eukaryotic cells, is an important Ca^{2+} binding protein. When four Ca^{2+} bind to a calmodulin molecule, the molecule changes shape and can then activate certain enzymes. Calmodulin combines with a number of different enzymes, including protein kinases and protein phosphatases, and alters their activity. Various types of cells have different calmodulin-binding proteins. How a target cell responds depends on which proteins are present. Calmodulin is important in the regulation of many key processes including metabolism, muscle contraction, memory, inflammation, and apoptosis.

Many enzyme-linked receptors activate protein kinase signaling pathways

Recall that many enzyme-linked receptors are tyrosine kinases, enzymes that phosphorylate the amino acid ty-

rosine in proteins (see Fig. 6-6). When a signaling molecule, such as a growth factor, binds to an enzyme-linked receptor, sites on the receptor are phosphorylated. Addition of the phosphates activates the enzyme part of the receptor. Once activated, tyrosine kinase enzymes can phosphorylate signaling proteins in the cell. Specific target proteins recognize the phosphorylated tyrosines on the tyrosine kinase receptor molecules. These signaling proteins bind to the phosphorylated sites on the receptor molecules. The signaling proteins are then phosphorylated and can activate specific signaling pathways.

Recall that in many signal transduction pathways, protein kinases form signaling cascades in which the protein kinases are phosphorylated one after another (see Fig. 6-6). Even when the amino acid phosphorylated in the receptor is tyrosine, the amino acids phosphorylated in the protein kinases in the signaling pathway can be serine or threonine, rather than tyrosine. Each reaction in a chain is dependent on the preceding one. Activation of the last protein in

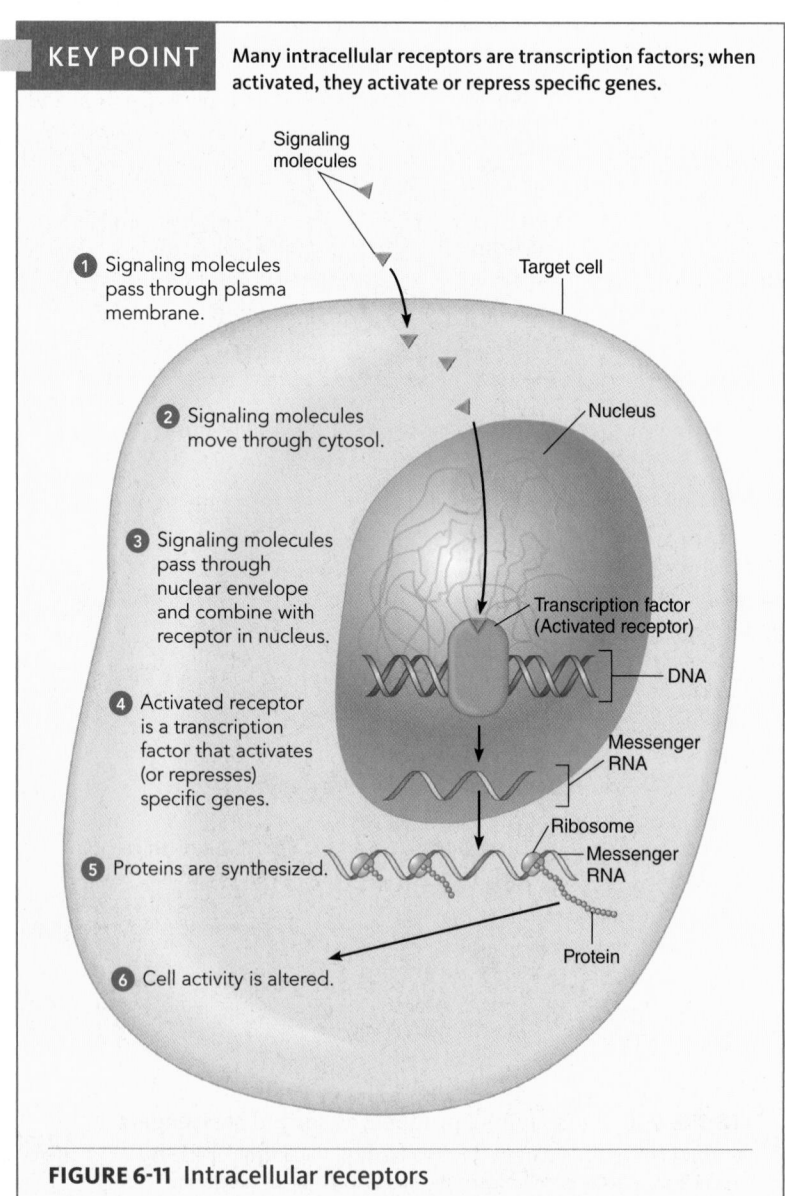

KEY POINT Many intracellular receptors are transcription factors; when activated, they activate or repress specific genes.

Signaling molecules

1 Signaling molecules pass through plasma membrane.

Target cell

2 Signaling molecules move through cytosol.

Nucleus

3 Signaling molecules pass through nuclear envelope and combine with receptor in nucleus.

Transcription factor (Activated receptor)

DNA

4 Activated receptor is a transcription factor that activates (or represses) specific genes.

Messenger RNA

Ribosome

5 Proteins are synthesized.

Messenger RNA

Protein

6 Cell activity is altered.

FIGURE 6-11 Intracellular receptors

the chain causes a specific cell response. Some cell process is altered.

Many activated intracellular receptors are transcription factors

Some hydrophobic signaling molecules diffuse across the membranes of target cells and bind with intracellular receptors in the cytosol or in the nucleus. For example, cortisol receptors are located in the cytosol. (Cortisol is a steroid hormone produced in the adrenal glands; its structure is shown in Figure 3-15b.) Thyroid hormones pass into the nucleus and bind with receptors that are bound to DNA in the nucleus. Many intracellular receptors are transcription factors that regulate the expression of specific genes. When a signaling molecule binds to a receptor, the receptor is activated. The ligand–receptor complex binds to a specific region of DNA and activates or represses specific genes (**FIG. 6-11**).

Gene activation can take place quickly—within about 30 minutes. Messenger RNA is produced and carries the code for synthesis of a particular protein into the cytoplasm. In combination with ribosomes, messenger RNA manufactures specific proteins that can alter cell activity.

Scaffold proteins increase efficiency

Signal transduction is a rapid, precise process. Enzymes must be organized so that they are available as needed for signaling pathways. **Scaffold proteins** organize groups of intracellular signaling molecules into signaling complexes (**FIG. 6-12**). These proteins position enzymes close to the proteins they regulate, increasing the probability that they will react with one another. At the same time, scaffold proteins decrease the chance that enzymes will be co-opted by other pathways. These organizing proteins guide interactions between molecules, reducing cross talk among different signaling pathways. Thus, scaffold proteins ensure that signals are relayed accurately, rapidly, and efficiently.

Scaffold proteins have been identified in many pathways, and similar scaffold proteins have been found in diverse organisms. Both yeasts and mammals have scaffold proteins that bind kinases in MAP kinase pathways (discussed in the next section).

Signals can be transmitted in more than one direction

Integrins, transmembrane proteins that connect the cell to the extracellular matrix, transduce signals in two directions. They transmit signals from outside the cell to the cell interior and also transmit information about the cell interior to the extracellular matrix.

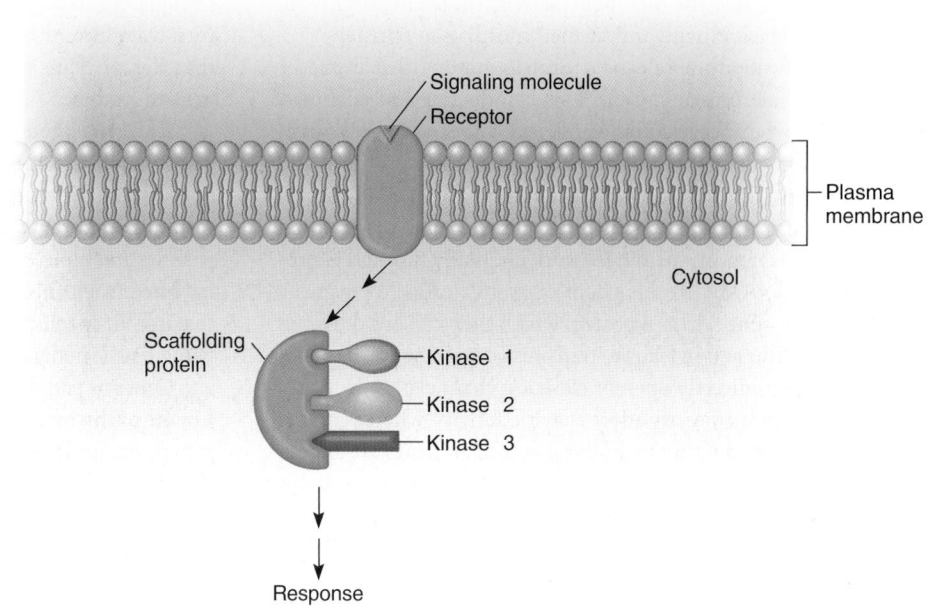

FIGURE 6-12 A scaffold protein

Scaffold proteins organize groups of signaling molecules into a signaling complex, making signal transduction faster, more precise, and more efficient.

Cell biologists have demonstrated that when certain signaling molecules bind to integrins in the plasma membrane, specific signal transduction pathways are activated. Interestingly, growth factors and certain molecules of the extracellular matrix may modulate one another's messages. Integrins also respond to information received from inside the cell. This *inside-out signaling* affects how selective integrins are with respect to the molecules to which they bind and how strongly they bind to them.

Review

- How is an extracellular signal converted to an intracellular signal in signal transduction? Give a specific example.
- What is the action of cyclic AMP? of DAG?
- What are the functions of scaffold proteins?

6.5 RESPONSES TO SIGNALS

■ LEARNING OBJECTIVES

7 Describe three types of responses that cells make to signaling molecules.
8 Contrast signal amplification with signal termination.

As we have learned, signaling molecules activate signal transduction pathways that bring about specific responses in the cell. Most of these responses fall into three categories: ion channels open or close; enzyme activity is altered, leading to metabolic changes and other effects; and specific gene activity may be turned on or off. Various mechanisms and pathways interact to produce specific actions that are responsible for the structure and function of the cell.

They are responsible for metabolic activity, movement, growth, cell division, development, and further information transfer.

In animals, neurons release neurotransmitters that excite or inhibit other neurons or muscle cells by affecting ion channels. For example, when acetylcholine binds with a receptor on a target neuron, an ion channel opens and allows passage of sodium and potassium ions. The resulting change in ion permeability can activate the neuron so that it transmits a neural impulse. Serotonin and some other neurotransmitters work indirectly through G proteins and cyclic AMP. In this chain of events, cAMP activates a kinase that phosphorylates a protein which then closes potassium ion channels. This action leads to transmission of a neural impulse. Some G proteins directly open or close ion channels.

Some receptors directly affect enzyme activity, whereas others initiate signal transduction pathways in which enzymes are altered by components of the pathway. When bacteria infect the body, they release certain peptides. Neutrophils, a type of white blood cell, have cell-surface receptors that detect these peptides. When the bacterial peptides bind to a neutrophil's receptors, enzymes are activated that lead to assembly of microfilaments (actin filaments) and microtubules. Contractions of microfilaments at the far end of the neutrophil force the cytoplasm forward. This action allows the neutrophil to move toward the invading bacteria and destroy them. Microtubules and a variety of proteins, including the contractile protein myosin, appear necessary for this movement.

Some signaling molecules affect gene activity. For example, some signaling molecules activate genes that lead to the manufacture of proteins needed for growth and cell division. In both plants and animals, steroid hormones regulate development by causing changes in the expression of specific genes. In animal cells, some steroid hormones bind to nuclear receptors and directly regulate expression of specific target genes. In plant cells, steroid hormones bind to receptors on the cell surface. The signal is then transmitted through a chain of molecules, eventually leading to changes in gene expression. Plant hormones will be discussed in greater detail in Chapter 38, and animal hormones are the focus of Chapter 49.

Ras pathways involve tyrosine kinase receptors and G proteins

Some tyrosine kinase receptors activate G proteins. For example, when growth factors bind to tyrosine kinase receptors, **ras proteins** are activated. Ras proteins are a group of small G proteins that, like other G proteins, are active when bound to GTP. Ras proteins are molecular switches that regulate signaling networks inside the cell. When activated, Ras triggers a cascade of reactions called the Ras pathway. In this pathway, a tyrosine in specific kinase proteins is phosphorylated, leading to critical cell responses.

Ras pathways are important in gene expression, cell division, cell movement, cell differentiation, cell adhesion, embryonic development, and apoptosis. For example, to initiate DNA synthesis, fibroblasts (a type of connective tissue cell) require the presence of two growth factors, epidermal growth factor and platelet-derived growth factor. In one study, investigators injected fibroblasts with antibodies that inactivate Ras proteins by binding to them. The fibroblasts no longer synthesized DNA in response to growth factors. Data from this and similar experiments led to the conclusion that Ras proteins are important in signal transduction involving growth factors.

Ras genes code for Ras proteins. Certain mutations in *Ras* genes result in mutant Ras proteins that bind GTP but cannot hydrolyze it. The mutant Ras proteins are stuck in the "on" state, resulting in unregulated cell division. This condition is associated with several types of human cancer. In fact, mutations in *Ras* genes have been identified in about one-third of all human cancers. Drugs that inhibit specific tyrosine kinase receptors and Ras pathways are being developed to treat cancer.

One Ras pathway that has been extensively studied is the **MAP kinase pathway,** also known as the **ERK pathway;** *MAP* is an acronym for "mitogen-activated protein" (mitogens induce mitosis, the nuclear division associated with eukaryotic cell division). *ERK* is an acronym for "extracellular signal-regulated kinases." Several distinct groups of MAP kinases have been described. The pathway illustrated in **FIGURE 6-13** shows three main MAP protein kinases: Raf, Mek, and ERK. Proteins in the MAP pathway phosphorylate a nuclear protein that combines with other proteins to form a transcription factor. When specific genes are activated, proteins needed for cell growth, cell division, and cell differentiation (specialization) are synthesized. The MAP kinase cascade is the main signaling pathway for cell division and differentiation. As illustrated in **FIGURE 6-14**, the signaling proteins ERK 1 and ERK 2 are important in fertility in mammals.

The response to a signal is amplified

Signaling molecules are typically present in very low concentrations, yet their effects on the cell are often profound. This is possible because the signal is *amplified,* as it is relayed through a signaling pathway. For example, let us examine how the action of a signaling molecule such as the hormone epinephrine is magnified as a signal passes through a series of proteins inside the cell. Epinephrine is released by the adrenal glands in response to danger or other stress. Among its many actions, epinephrine increases heart rate, blood flow to skeletal muscle, and glucose concentration in the blood.

Epinephrine binds to a G protein–linked receptor, causing the receptor to change shape and activate a G protein. A single molecule of a hormone such as epinephrine can activate many G proteins. Each G protein activates an adenylyl cyclase molecule and then returns to its inactive state. Before it becomes inactive, each adenylyl cyclase can catalyze the production of numerous cAMP molecules (**FIG. 6-15**). Then, each cAMP molecule can activate many molecules of a particular protein kinase. That protein kinase can phosphorylate many molecules of the next kinase in the pathway and so on down the cascade.

As a result of **signal amplification,** a single signaling molecule can lead to changes in millions of molecules at the end of a signaling cascade. The response is much greater than would be possible if each signaling molecule acted alone. This process of magnifying the strength of a signaling molecule explains how just a few signaling molecules can lead to major responses in the cell.

When growth factors bind to their receptors, they activate the G protein Ras; Ras activates a MAP-kinase signaling pathway, leading to activation (or repression) of specific genes, and ultimately to protein activity that affects some cell process.

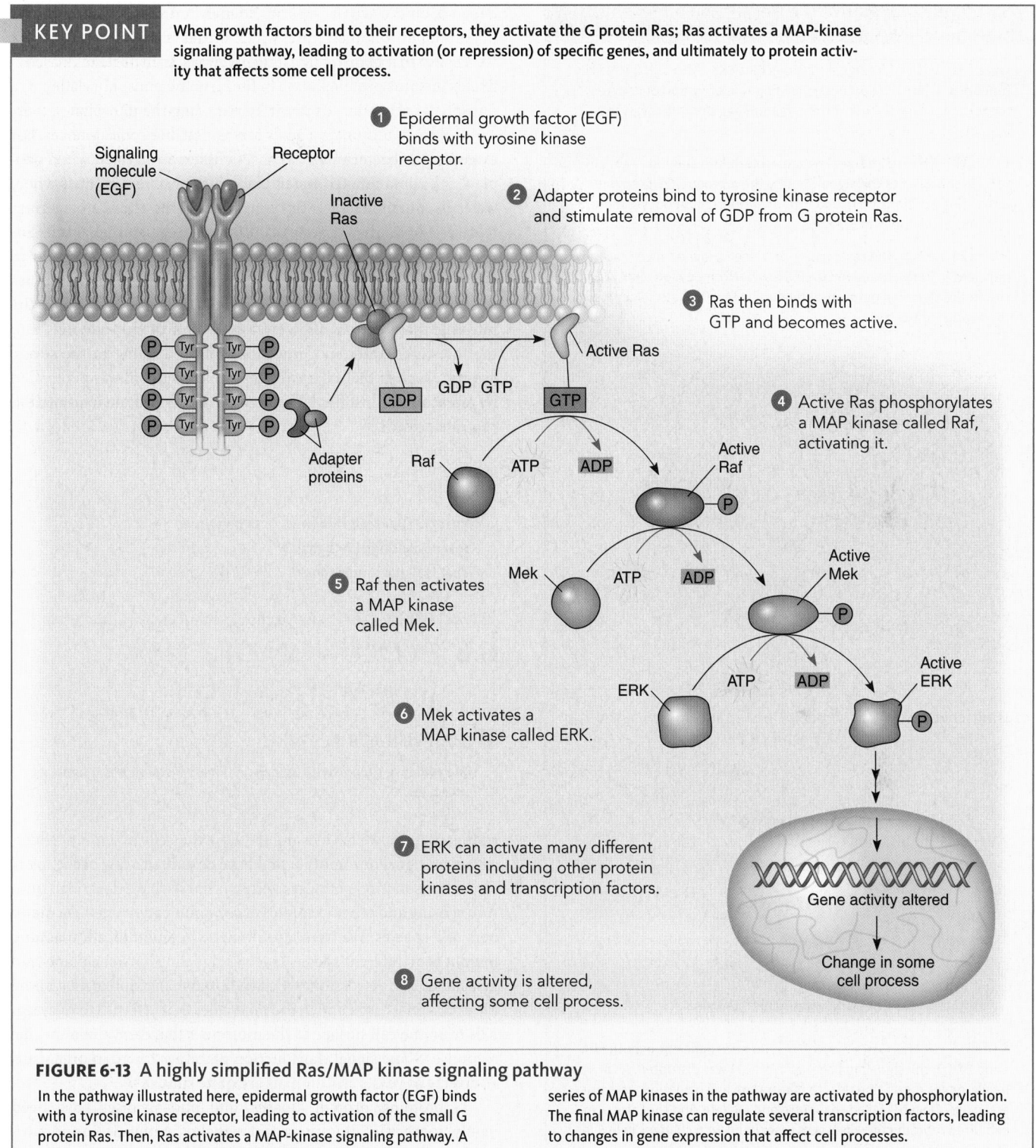

1 Epidermal growth factor (EGF) binds with tyrosine kinase receptor.

2 Adapter proteins bind to tyrosine kinase receptor and stimulate removal of GDP from G protein Ras.

3 Ras then binds with GTP and becomes active.

4 Active Ras phosphorylates a MAP kinase called Raf, activating it.

5 Raf then activates a MAP kinase called Mek.

6 Mek activates a MAP kinase called ERK.

7 ERK can activate many different proteins including other protein kinases and transcription factors.

8 Gene activity is altered, affecting some cell process.

Signaling molecule (EGF) Receptor Inactive Ras Active Ras

GDP GDP GTP GTP

Adapter proteins Raf ATP ADP Active Raf P

Mek ATP ADP Active Mek P

ERK ATP ADP Active ERK P

Gene activity altered

Change in some cell process

FIGURE 6-13 A highly simplified Ras/MAP kinase signaling pathway

In the pathway illustrated here, epidermal growth factor (EGF) binds with a tyrosine kinase receptor, leading to activation of the small G protein Ras. Then, Ras activates a MAP-kinase signaling pathway. A series of MAP kinases in the pathway are activated by phosphorylation. The final MAP kinase can regulate several transcription factors, leading to changes in gene expression that affect cell processes.

Signals must be terminated

Once a signal has done its job, it must be terminated. **Signal termination** returns the receptor and each of the components of the signal transduction pathway to their inactive states. This action allows the magnitude of the response to reflect the strength of the signal. Molecules in the system must also be ready to respond to new signals.

We have seen that after a G protein is activated, a subunit of the G protein, a GTPase, catalyzes the hydrolysis of GTP to GDP. This action inactivates the G protein. In the cyclic AMP pathway, any increase in cAMP concentration is temporary. Cyclic AMP is rapidly inactivated by a phosphodiesterase, which converts it to adenosine monophosphate (AMP). Thus, the concentration of cAMP

QUESTION: Do the signaling molecules ERK 1 and ERK 2 have key functions in signaling pathways leading to maturation of oocytes (eggs) and ovulation (release of a mature egg from the ovary) in mammals?

HYPOTHESIS: The signaling molecules ERK 1 and ERK 2 are key target molecules of the signal sent by the reproductive hormone, luteinizing hormone (LH), and thus are important in oocyte maturation and ovulation in mammals.

EXPERIMENT: The researchers produced a line of mice that were deficient in both ERK 1 and ERK 2. They performed biochemical analyses on the signaling pathway activated by LH. They also examined the ovaries of the mice.

RESULTS AND CONCUSIONS: In mice deficient in both ERK 1 and ERK 2, the signaling pathway from LH was disrupted. As a result, genes regulating oocyte maturation and ovulation were not activated. Oocytes failed to mature and ovulate, and the mice also exhibited reproductive disorders associated with changes in levels of reproductive hormones.

ERK 1 and ERK 2 are key molecules in a signaling pathway that regulates reproduction in mice. These results may lead to greater understanding of certain ovarian disorders that result in infertility in humans.

*EGF = epidermal growth factor

Source: Fan, H.-Y. et al., *Science*, Vol. 324, 938–941, 2009.

FIGURE 6-14 Identifying key molecules in a signaling pathway that regulates reproduction in mammals

depends on the activity of both adenylyl cyclase, which produces it, and of phosphodiesterase, which breaks it down (see Fig. 6-8). Recall also that in many signaling pathways, each protein kinase activates the next protein kinase in the chain by phosphorylating it; a phosphatase then inactivates it by removing the phosphate group.

Failure to terminate signals can lead to dire consequences. For example, the bacterium that causes cholera is ingested when people drink contaminated water. Cholera is prevalent in areas where water is contaminated with human feces. The cholera bacterium releases a toxin that activates G proteins in the epithelial cells lining the intestine. The toxin chemically changes the G protein so that it no longer switches off. As a result, the G protein continues to stimulate adenylyl cyclase to make cAMP. The cells lining the intestine malfunction, allowing a large flow of chloride ions into the intestine. Water and other ions follow, leading to the severe watery diarrhea that characterizes cholera. The disease is treated by replacing the lost fluid. If untreated, this G protein malfunction can cause death.

Review

- What are some cell responses to signals?
- How do cells amplify signals?
- What is signal termination?

6.6 EVOLUTION OF CELL COMMUNICATION

LEARNING OBJECTIVE

9   Cite evidence supporting a long evolutionary history for cell signaling molecules.

In this chapter, we have examined how the cells of a multicellular organism signal one another and have described a few of the many signal transduction pathways within cells. We have described quorum sensing and other examples of communication between members of a species. We have also discussed communication among members of different species, such as signaling between plants and insects. In our discussion, we have noted many similarities in the types of signals used and in the molecules that cells use to relay signals from the cell surface to the molecules that carry out a specific response. Some signal transduction pathways found in organisms as diverse as yeasts and animals are quite similar.

G proteins, protein kinases, and phosphatases have been highly conserved and are part of signaling pathways in most organisms. Certain disease-causing bacteria have signal transduction pathways similar to those found in eukaryotes. Bacteria may use some of these signal mechanisms to interfere with normal function in the eukaryotic cells they infect. Such similarities in many species suggest evolutionary relationships.

Similarities in cell signaling suggest that the molecules and mechanisms used in cell communication are very old. The evidence suggests that cell communication first evolved in prokaryotes and continued to change over time as new types of organisms evolved. However, the fact that some cell signaling molecules have not

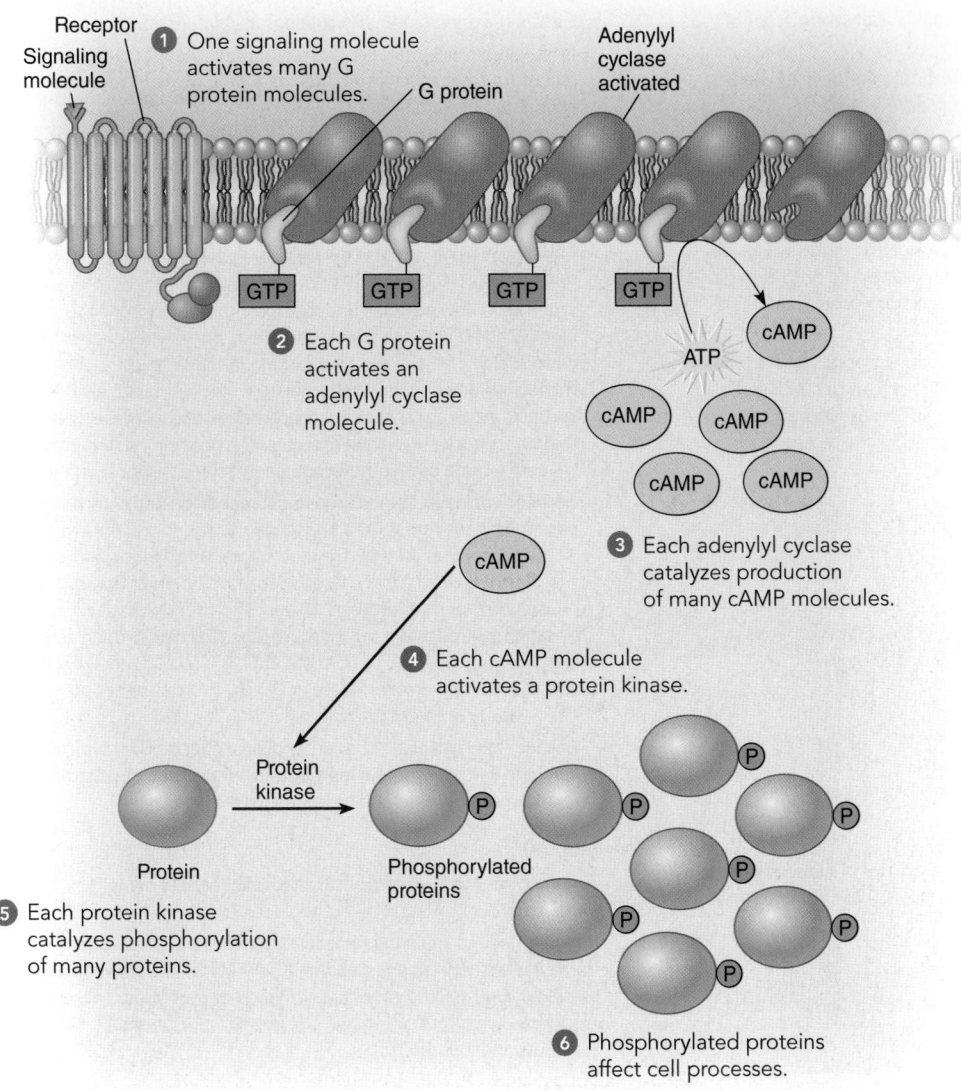

① One signaling molecule activates many G protein molecules.

Receptor

Signaling molecule

G protein

Adenylyl cyclase activated

② Each G protein activates an adenylyl cyclase molecule.

ATP

cAMP

cAMP   cAMP

cAMP   cAMP

③ Each adenylyl cyclase catalyzes production of many cAMP molecules.

cAMP

④ Each cAMP molecule activates a protein kinase.

Protein kinase

Protein

Phosphorylated proteins

⑤ Each protein kinase catalyzes phosphorylation of many proteins.

⑥ Phosphorylated proteins affect cell processes.

FIGURE 6-15 Signal amplification
The signal is amplified at each step in the pathway so that one activated receptor can give rise to thousands of final products (proteins at the end of the pathway). The response is far greater than what you might expect from a single receptor.

changed very much over time suggests that the importance of these pathways to cell survival has restricted any evolutionary changes that might have made them less effective. Thus, these pathways have weathered the demands of natural selection through millions of years of evolution.

Choanoflagellates, unicellular protists that are thought to be the most recent ancestors of animals, are used as models for studying the early evolution of animals. Choanoflagellates have many of the same proteins found in animals. These tiny organisms have protein kinases similar to those of animals, and a G protein–linked receptor has been identified. These findings indicate that important proteins necessary for cell communication in animals had evolved long before the evolution of animals. As we will discuss in later chapters, similarities and differences in basic molecules, such as G proteins, can be used to trace evolutionary pathways.

Review

■ Choanoflagellates and animals have similar protein kinases. What does that suggest about their cell signaling mechanisms?

■ SUMMARY: FOCUS ON LEARNING OBJECTIVES

6.1 *(page 135)*

1 Describe the four main processes essential for cells to communicate.

■ Cells communicate by **cell signaling,** which consists of four main processes: (1) synthesis, release, and transport of signaling molecules; (2) **reception** of information by **target cells;** (3) **signal transduction,** the process in which a receptor converts an extracellular signal into an intracellular signal and relays the signal, leading to a cellular response; and (4) **response** by the cell, for example, some metabolic process may be altered.

6.2 *(page 136)*

2 Compare three types of signaling molecules: neurotransmitters, hormones, and local regulators

■ Most neurons (nerve cells) signal one another by releasing chemical compounds called **neurotransmitters.**

■ **Hormones** are chemical messengers in plants and animals. In animals, they are secreted by **endocrine glands,** glands that have no ducts. Most hormones diffuse into capillaries and are transported by the blood to target cells.

■ **Local regulators** diffuse through the interstitial fluid and act on nearby cells. This is called **paracrine regulation.** Histamine, growth factors, **prostaglandins** (a type of local hormone), and **nitric oxide** (a gaseous signaling molecule that passes into target cells) are examples of local regulators.

6.3 *(page 137)*

3 Identify mechanisms that make reception a highly specific process.

■ Each type of receptor has a specific shape, and only the signaling molecule that fits the specific receptor can affect the cell. A cell can have many different types of receptors and can make different receptors at different stages in its life cycle or in response to different conditions. Different types of cells can have different types of receptors.

4 Briefly compare ion channel–linked receptors, G protein–linked receptors, enzyme-linked receptors, and intracellular receptors.

- When a signaling molecule binds to an **ion channel–linked receptor,** the ion channel opens or, in some cases, closes.

- **G protein–linked receptors** are transmembrane proteins that extend into the cytosol or outside the cell. These receptors couple specific signaling molecules to signal transduction pathways inside the cell. The tail of the receptor that extends into the cytosol has a binding site for a specific **G protein,** a regulatory protein that binds to GTP.

- **Enzyme-linked receptors** are transmembrane proteins with a binding site for a signaling molecule outside the cell and a binding site for an enzyme inside the cell. Many enzyme-linked receptors are **tyrosine kinases** in which the enzyme is part of the receptor.

- **Intracellular receptors** are located in the cytosol or in the nucleus. Their ligands are small, hydrophobic molecules that diffuse across the plasma membrane.

6.4 (page 141)

5 Compare the actions of the main types of receptors in signal transduction.

- Ion channel–linked receptors convert chemical signals into electrical signals. The gates of many ion channels remain closed until ligands bind to them.

- Many enzyme-linked receptors are tyrosine kinases, enzymes that phosphorylate proteins. Tyrosine kinase receptors activate several different signal transduction pathways. In a **protein kinase cascade,** each molecule in the signaling pathway is phosphorylated by the preceding protein kinase in the chain. The last protein kinase in the cascade activates the target protein by phosphorylation. The target protein alters some process in the cell.

- G protein–linked receptors activate G proteins. A G protein consists of three subunits. It is linked to a molecule of **guanosine diphosphate (GDP),** a molecule similar to ADP but containing the base guanine instead of adenine. When a ligand binds with the receptor, the GDP is released and is replaced by **guanosine triphosphate (GTP).** Then one subunit of the G protein separates from the other two subunits. The activated G protein may initiate a signal transduction pathway by binding with a specific protein in the cell.

Some G proteins directly activate enzymes that catalyze changes in certain proteins, leading to changes in cell function.

- Intracellular receptors are located in the cytosol or nucleus. These receptors are **transcription factors** that activate or repress the expression of specific genes.

6 Trace the sequence of events in signal transduction for each of the following second messengers: cyclic AMP, inositol trisphosphate, diacylglycerol, and calcium ions.

- In many signaling systems, the signaling molecule serves as the **first messenger.** Information is relayed by the G protein to a **second messenger,** an intracellular signaling molecule.

- When certain G proteins undergo a conformational change, they bind with and activate **adenylyl cyclase,** an enzyme on the cytoplasmic side of the plasma membrane. Adenylyl cyclase catalyzes the formation of **cyclic AMP (cAMP)** from ATP. Cyclic AMP is a second messenger that activates certain **protein kinase** enzymes that phosphorylate certain proteins. The phosphorylated protein triggers a chain of reactions that lead to some response in the cell.

- Certain G proteins activate the membrane-bound enzyme phospholipase C. This enzyme splits a phospholipid, PIP_2 (phosphotidylinositol-4,5-bisphosphate), into two products, **inositol trisphosphate (IP_3)** and **diacylglycerol (DAG).** IP_3 is a second messenger that can donate phosphate groups to proteins. IP_3 binds to calcium channels in the endoplasmic reticulum, which causes the channels to open and release calcium ions into the cytosol. DAG is a second messenger that activates certain protein kinase enzymes. These enzymes phosphorylate a variety of target proteins.

- Calcium ions can also act as second messengers. They typically combine with the protein **calmodulin,** which then affects the activity of protein kinases and protein phosphatases.

6.5 (page 147)

7 Describe three types of responses that cells make to signaling molecules.

- In response to signaling molecules: ion channels open or close; enzyme activity changes leading to metabolic changes and other effects; and specific genes are activated or repressed. These responses can affect cell shape, cell growth, cell division, cell differentiation, and metabolism.

8 Contrast signal amplification with signal termination.

- **Signal amplification** is the process of enhancing the cell's response to a signal as the signal is relayed through a signal transduction pathway. Before it becomes inactive, each enzyme can catalyze the production of numerous product molecules.

- **Signal termination** is the process of inactivating the receptor and each component of the signal transduction pathway once they have done their jobs. Signal termination allows molecules in the system to respond to new signals.

6.6 (page 150)

9 Cite evidence supporting a long evolutionary history for cell signaling molecules.

- Molecules important in cell signaling first evolved in prokaryotes. G proteins, protein kinases, and phosphatases have been highly conserved and are part of most signaling pathways.

TEST YOUR UNDERSTANDING

1. During signal transduction (a) the cell converts an extracellular signal into an intracellular signal that leads to a change in some cell process (b) a signaling molecule activates or represses several genes (c) each enzyme catalyzes production of one molecule of product (d) relay of the signal is regulated by paracrine regulation (e) the signal is terminated by prostaglandins

2. In paracrine regulation (a) endocrine glands release hormones that are transported by the blood (b) electrical signals are trans-

mitted (c) neurotransmitters signal growth factors (d) prosta-glandins terminate signals during signal transduction (e) a local regulator signals nearby cells

3. When a signaling molecule binds with a receptor (a) G proteins are inactivated (b) a third messenger is activated (c) cell signaling is terminated (d) the signaling cell is activated (e) the receptor is activated

4. G protein–linked receptors (a) inactivate G proteins (b) activate first messengers (c) consist of 18 transmembrane alpha helices (d) have a tail that extends into the cytosol and a binding site for a G protein (e) are located in the cytoplasm or nucleus

5. An enzyme-linked receptor (a) is an integral membrane protein (b) would not be found on plant cell surfaces (c) forms a dimer with another enzyme-linked receptor when a ligand binds to it (d) is typically an adenylyl cyclase molecule (e) typically activates ion channels

6. G proteins (a) relay a message from an activated receptor to an enzyme that activates a second messenger (b) are GTP molecules (c) terminate cell signaling (d) directly activate protein kinases (e) function as first messengers

7. Which is the correct sequence? 1. protein kinase activated 2. adenylyl cyclase activated 3. cAMP produced 4. proteins phosphorylated 5. G protein activated (a) 1, 2, 3, 5, 4 (b) 5, 3, 2, 1, 4 (c) 5, 2, 3, 4, 1 (d) 5, 2, 3, 1, 4 (e) 2, 3, 1, 4, 5

8. Which is the correct sequence? 1. phospholipase activated 2. G protein activated 3. PIP_2 split 4. proteins phosphorylated 5. DAG produced (a) 1, 2, 5, 3, 4 (b) 2, 1, 3, 5, 4 (c) 4, 2, 3, 1, 5 (d) 5, 2, 3, 1, 4 (e) 2, 3, 5, 4, 1

9. Calcium ions (a) can act as second messengers (b) split calmodulin (c) are kept at higher concentration in the cytosol than in the extracellular fluid (d) are produced in the ER by protein kinases and protein phosphatases (e) typically terminate signaling cascades

10. When growth hormone binds to an enzyme-linked receptor (a) G proteins form a cascade of molecules and are phosphorylated (b) the enzyme portion of the receptor is dephosphorylated (c) the receptor is activated and phorphorylates signaling proteins in the cell (d) an ion channel is opened (e) an immediate signal is sent into the nucleus and specific genes are activated or inhibited

11. Scaffold proteins (a) release kinases and phosphatases into the extracellular fluid (b) increase the probability that an enzyme can be used by several different pathways (c) increase accuracy but slow signaling cascades (d) organize groups of intracellular signaling molecules into signaling complexes (e) are transcription factors found mainly in plant cells

12. Each adenylyl cyclase molecule produces many cAMP molecules. This is an example of (a) receptor up-regulation (b) receptor down-regulation (c) signal amplification (d) scaffold (e) similarities produced by evolution

13. Label the following structures in the diagram: first messenger, G protein, ATP, cAMP (second messenger), protein, cell response. (Consult Fig. 6-7 to check your answers.)

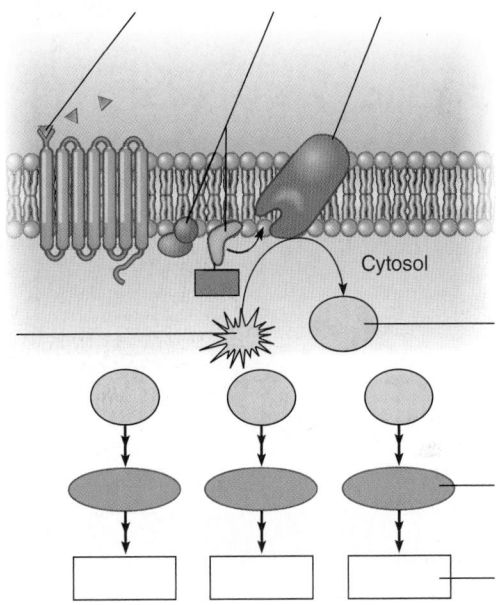

Cytosol

CRITICAL THINKING

1. In many instances, the pathway from signaling molecule to final response in the cell involves complex signaling cascades. Give an example of a complex signaling system, and explain why such complexity may have advantages.

2. More than 500 genes have been identified in the human genome that code for protein kinases. What does this imply regarding protein kinases? Explain your answer.

3. **EVOLUTION LINK.** Cell signaling in plant and animal cells is similar in some ways and different in others. Offer one or more hypotheses for these similarities and differences, and cite specific examples.

4. **EVOLUTION LINK.** Some of the same G protein–linked receptors and signal transduction pathways found in plants and animals have been identified in fungi and algae. What does this suggest

about the evolution of these molecules? What does it suggest about these molecules and pathways?

5. **SCIENCE, TECHNOLOGY, AND SOCIETY.** Mutant Ras proteins have been associated with many types of human cancer. Hundreds of millions of dollars are required for the basic research and development of each new drug. As a citizen are you willing to help fund development of new medications to treat cancer through government-sponsored research? Why or why not? If not, what alternatives do you propose?

 Additional questions are available in CengageNOW at www.cengage.com/login.

7 Energy and Metabolism

Giant panda (*Ailuropoda melanoleuca*). The chemical energy produced by photosynthesis and stored in bamboo leaves transfers to the panda as it eats.

Keren Su/Corbis

KEY CONCEPTS

7.1 Energy, the capacity to do work, can be kinetic energy (energy of motion) or potential energy (energy due to position or state).

7.2 Energy cannot be created or destroyed (the first law of thermodynamics), but the total amount of energy available to do work in a closed system decreases over time (the second law of thermodynamics). Organisms do not violate the laws of thermodynamics because, as open systems, they use energy obtained from their surroundings to do work.

7.3 In cells, energy-releasing (exergonic) processes drive energy-requiring (endergonic) processes.

7.4 ATP plays a central role in cell energy metabolism by linking exergonic and endergonic reactions. ATP transfers energy by transferring a phosphate group.

7.5 The transfer of electrons in redox reactions is another way that cells transfer energy.

7.6 As biological catalysts, enzymes increase the rate of specific chemical reactions. The activity of an enzyme is influenced by temperature, pH, the presence of cofactors, and inhibitors and/or activators.

All living things require energy to carry out life processes. It may seem obvious that cells need energy to grow and reproduce, but even nongrowing cells need energy simply to maintain themselves. Cells obtain energy in many forms, but that energy can seldom be used directly to power cell processes. For this reason, cells have mechanisms that convert energy from one form to another. The ordered systems of the cell provide the information that makes these energy transformations possible. Because most components of these energy conversion systems evolved very early in the history of life, many aspects of energy metabolism tend to be similar in a wide range of organisms.

The sun is the ultimate source of almost all the energy that powers life; this *radiant energy* flows from the sun as electromagnetic waves. Plants and other photosynthetic organisms capture about 0.02% of the sun's energy that reaches Earth. As discussed in Chapter 9, photosynthetic organisms convert radiant energy to *chemical energy* in the bonds of organic molecules. This chemical energy becomes available to plants, animals such as the giant panda shown in the photograph, and other organisms through the process of cellular respiration. In cellular respiration, discussed in Chapter 8, organic molecules are broken apart and their energy is converted to more immediately usable forms.

This chapter focuses on some of the basic principles that govern how cells capture, transfer, store, and use energy. We discuss the functions of adenosine triphosphate (ATP) and other molecules used in energy conversions, including those that transfer electrons in oxidation–reduction (redox) reactions. We also pay particular attention to the essential role of enzymes in cell energy dynamics. The flow of energy in ecosystems is discussed in Chapter 55.

7.1 BIOLOGICAL WORK

■ LEARNING OBJECTIVES

1 Define *energy*, emphasizing how it is related to work and to heat.
2 Use examples to contrast potential energy and kinetic energy.

Energy, one of the most important concepts in biology, can be understood in the context of **matter,** which is anything that has mass and takes up space. **Energy** is defined as the capacity to do work, which is any change in the state or motion of matter. Technically, mass is a form of energy, which is the basis behind the energy generated by the sun and other stars. More than 4 billion kilograms of matter per second are converted into energy in the sun.

Biologists generally express energy in units of work—**kilojoules (kJ).** It can also be expressed in units of *heat energy*—**kilocalories (kcal)**—thermal energy that flows from an object with a higher temperature to an object with a lower temperature. One kilocalorie is equal to 4.184 kJ. Heat energy cannot do cell work because a cell is too small to have regions that differ in temperature. For that reason, the unit most biologists prefer today is the kilojoule. However, we will use both units because references to the kilocalorie are common in the scientific literature.

Organisms carry out conversions between potential energy and kinetic energy

When an archer draws a bow, **kinetic energy,** the energy of motion, is used and work is performed (**FIG. 7-1**). The resulting tension in the bow and string represents stored, or potential, energy. **Potential energy** is the capacity to do work as a result of position or state. When the string is released, this potential energy is converted to kinetic energy in the motion of the bow, which propels the arrow.

Most actions of an organism involve a series of energy transformations that occur as kinetic energy is converted to potential energy or as potential energy is converted to kinetic energy. **Chemical energy,** potential energy stored in chemical bonds, is of particular importance to organisms. In our example, the chemical energy of food molecules is converted to kinetic energy in the muscle cells of the archer. The contraction of the archer's muscles, like many of the activities performed by an organism, is an example of *mechanical energy,* which performs work by moving matter.

Review

■ You exert tension on a spring and then release it. How do these actions relate to work, potential energy, and kinetic energy?

POTENTIAL
Energy of position

KINETIC
Energy of motion

FIGURE 7-1 Potential versus kinetic energy
The potential chemical energy released by cellular respiration is converted to kinetic energy in the muscles, which do the work of drawing the bow. The potential energy stored in the drawn bow is transformed into kinetic energy as the bowstring pushes the arrow toward its target.

7.2 THE LAWS OF THERMODYNAMICS

■ LEARNING OBJECTIVE

3 State the first and second laws of thermodynamics, and discuss the implications of these laws as they relate to organisms.

Thermodynamics, the study of energy and its transformations, governs all activities of the universe, from the life and death of cells to the life and death of stars. When considering thermodynamics, scientists use the term *system* to refer to an object that they are studying, whether a cell, an organism, or planet Earth. The rest of the universe other than the system being studied constitutes the *surroundings.* A **closed system** does not exchange energy with its surroundings, whereas an **open system** can exchange energy with its surroundings (**FIG. 7-2**). Biological systems are open systems. Two laws about energy apply to all things in the universe: the first and second laws of thermodynamics.

The total energy in the universe does not change

According to the **first law of thermodynamics,** energy cannot be created or destroyed, although it can be transferred or converted from one form to another, including conversions between matter

(a) A closed system does not exchange energy with its surroundings.

(b) An open system exchanges energy with its surroundings.

FIGURE 7-2 Closed and open systems

and energy. As far as we know, the total mass-energy present in the universe when it formed, almost 14 billion years ago, equals the amount of energy present in the universe today. This is all the energy that can ever be present in the universe. Similarly, the energy of any system plus its surroundings is constant. A system may absorb energy from its surroundings, or it may give up some energy to its surroundings, but the total energy content of that system plus its surroundings is always the same.

As specified by the first law of thermodynamics, organisms cannot create the energy they require in order to live. Instead, they must capture energy from the environment and transform it to a form that can be used for biological work.

The entropy of the universe is increasing

The **second law of thermodynamics** states that when energy is converted from one form to another, some usable energy—that is, energy available to do work—is converted into heat that disperses into the surroundings (see Fig. 55-1 for an illustration of energy flow through an ecosystem). As you learned in Chapter 2, **heat** is the kinetic energy of randomly moving particles. Unlike *heat energy,* which flows from an object with a higher temperature to one with a lower temperature, this random motion cannot perform work. As a result, the amount of usable energy available to do work in the universe decreases over time.

It is important to understand that the second law of thermodynamics is consistent with the first law; that is, the total amount of energy in the universe is *not* decreasing with time. However, the total amount of energy in the universe that is available to do work is decreasing over time.

Less-usable energy is more diffuse, or disorganized. **Entropy (S)** is a measure of this disorder, or randomness; organized, usable energy has a low entropy, whereas disorganized energy, such as heat, has a high entropy.

Entropy is continuously increasing in the universe in all natural processes. Maybe at some time, billions of years from now, all energy will exist as heat uniformly distributed throughout the universe. If that happens, the universe will cease to operate, because no work will be possible. Everything will be at the same temperature, so there will be no way to convert the thermal energy of the universe into usable mechanical energy.

As a consequence of the second law of thermodynamics, no process requiring an energy conversion is ever 100% efficient, because much of the energy is dispersed as heat, increasing entropy. For example, an automobile engine, which converts the chemical energy of gasoline to mechanical energy, is between 20% and 30% efficient. Thus, only 20% to 30% of the original energy stored in the chemical bonds of the gasoline molecules is actually transformed into mechanical energy; the other 70% to 80% dissipates as waste heat. Energy use in your cells is about 40% efficient, with the remaining energy given to the surroundings as heat.

Organisms have a high degree of organization, and at first glance they may appear to refute the second law of thermodynamics. As organisms grow and develop, they maintain a high level of order and do not appear to become more disorganized. However, organisms are open systems; they maintain their degree of order over time only with the constant input of energy from their surroundings. This is why plants must photosynthesize and animals must eat. Although the order within organisms may tend to increase temporarily, the total entropy of the universe (organisms plus surroundings) always increases over time.

Review

- What is the first law of thermodynamics? the second law?
- Life is sometimes described as a constant struggle against the second law of thermodynamics. How do organisms succeed in this struggle without violating the second law?

7.3 ENERGY AND METABOLISM

LEARNING OBJECTIVES

4 Discuss how changes in free energy in a reaction are related to changes in entropy and enthalpy.

5 Distinguish between exergonic and endergonic reactions, and give examples of how they may be coupled.

6 Compare the energy dynamics of a reaction at equilibrium with the dynamics of a reaction not at equilibrium.

The chemical reactions that enable an organism to carry on its activities—to grow, move, maintain and repair itself; reproduce; and respond to stimuli—together make up its metabolism. Recall from Chapter 1 that **metabolism** is the sum of all the chemical activities taking place in an organism. An organism's metabolism consists of many intersecting series of chemical reactions, or pathways. Two main types of metabolism are anabolism and catabolism. **Anabolism** includes the various pathways in which complex molecules are synthesized from simpler substances, such as in the linking of amino acids to form proteins. **Catabolism** includes the pathways in which larger molecules are broken down into smaller ones, such as in the degradation of starch to form monosaccharides.

As you will see, these changes involve not only alterations in the arrangement of atoms but also various energy transformations. Catabolism and anabolism are complementary processes; catabolic pathways involve an overall release of energy, some of which powers anabolic pathways, which have an overall energy requirement. In the following sections, we discuss how to predict whether a particular chemical reaction requires energy or releases it.

Enthalpy is the total potential energy of a system

In the course of any chemical reaction, including the metabolic reactions of a cell, chemical bonds break and new and different bonds may form. Every specific type of chemical bond has a certain amount of *bond energy*, defined as the energy required to break that bond. The total bond energy is essentially equivalent to the total potential energy of the system, a quantity known as **enthalpy (H).**

Free energy is available to do cell work

Entropy and enthalpy are related by a third type of energy, termed **free energy (G),** which is the amount of energy available to do work under the conditions of a biochemical reaction. (G, also known as "Gibbs free energy," is named for J. W. Gibbs, a Yale professor who was one of the founders of the science of thermodynamics.) Free energy, the only kind of energy that can do cell work, is the aspect of thermodynamics of greatest interest to a biologist. Enthalpy, free energy, and entropy are related by the following equation:

$$H = G + TS$$

in which H is enthalpy; G is free energy; T is the absolute temperature of the system, expressed in Kelvin units; and S is entropy. Disregarding temperature for the moment, enthalpy (the total energy of a system) is equal to free energy (the usable energy) plus entropy (the unusable energy).

A rearrangement of the equation shows that as entropy increases, the amount of free energy decreases:

$$G = H - TS$$

If we assume that entropy is zero, the free energy is simply equal to the total potential energy (enthalpy); an increase in entropy reduces the amount of free energy.

What is the significance of the temperature (T)? Remember that as the temperature increases, there is an increase in random molecular motion, which contributes to disorder and multiplies the effect of the entropy term.

Chemical reactions involve changes in free energy

Biologists analyze the role of energy in the many biochemical reactions of metabolism. Although the total free energy of a system (G) cannot be effectively measured, the equation $G = H - TS$ can be extended to predict whether a particular chemical reaction will release energy or require an input of energy. The reason is that *changes* in free energy can be measured. Scientists use the Greek capital letter delta (Δ) to denote any change that occurs in the system between its initial state before the reaction and its final state after the reaction. To express what happens with respect to energy in a chemical reaction, the equation becomes

$$\Delta G = \Delta H - T\Delta S$$

Notice that the temperature does not change; it is held constant during the reaction. Thus, the change in free energy (ΔG) during the reaction is equal to the change in enthalpy (ΔH) minus the product of the absolute temperature (T) in Kelvin units multiplied by the change in entropy (ΔS). Scientists express ΔG and ΔH in kilojoules or kilocalories per mole; they express ΔS in kilojoules or kilocalories per Kelvin unit.

Free energy decreases during an exergonic reaction

An **exergonic reaction** releases energy and is said to be a spontaneous or a "downhill" reaction, from higher to lower free energy (**FIG. 7-3a**). Because the total free energy in its final state is less than the total free energy in its initial state, ΔG is a negative number for exergonic reactions.

The term *spontaneous* may give the false impression that such reactions are always instantaneous. In fact, spontaneous reactions do not necessarily occur readily; some are extremely slow. The reason is that energy, known as *activation energy,* is required to initiate every reaction, even a spontaneous one. We discuss activation energy later in the chapter.

Free energy increases during an endergonic reaction

An **endergonic reaction** is a reaction in which there is a gain of free energy (**FIG. 7-3b**). Because the free energy of the products is greater than the free energy of the reactants, ΔG has a positive value. Such a reaction cannot take place in isolation. Instead, it must occur in such a way that energy can be supplied from the

(a) In an exergonic reaction, there is a net loss of free energy. The products have less free energy than was present in the reactants, and the reaction proceeds spontaneously.

(b) In an endergonic reaction, there is a net gain of free energy. The products have more free energy than was present in the reactants.

FIGURE 7-3 *Animated* **Exergonic and endergonic reactions**

Concentration gradient

Exergonic
(process occurs
spontaneously)

(a) A concentration gradient is a form of potential energy.

(b) When molecules are evenly distributed, they have high entropy.

FIGURE 7-4 Entropy and diffusion
The tendency of entropy to increase can be used to produce work, in this case, diffusion.

surroundings. Of course, many energy-requiring reactions take place in cells, and as you will see, metabolic mechanisms have evolved that supply the energy to "drive" these nonspontaneous cell reactions in a particular direction.

Diffusion is an exergonic process

In Chapter 5, you saw that randomly moving particles diffuse down their own concentration gradient (**FIG. 7-4**). Although the movements of the individual particles are random, net movement of the group of particles seems to be directional. What provides energy for this apparently directed process? A **concentration gradient**, with a region of higher concentration and another region of lower concentration, is an orderly state. A cell must expend energy to produce a concentration gradient. Because work is done to produce this order, a concentration gradient is a form of potential energy. As the particles move about randomly, the gradient becomes degraded. Thus, free energy decreases as entropy increases.

In cellular respiration and photosynthesis, the potential energy stored in a concentration gradient of hydrogen ions (H^+) is transformed into chemical energy in adenosine triphosphate (ATP) as the hydrogen ions pass through a membrane down their concentration gradient. This important concept, known as *chemiosmosis*, is discussed in detail in Chapters 8 and 9.

Free-energy changes depend on the concentrations of reactants and products

According to the second law of thermodynamics, any process that increases entropy can do work. As we have discussed, differences in the concentration of a substance, such as between two different parts of a cell, represent a more orderly state than that when the substance is diffused homogeneously throughout the cell. Free-energy changes in any chemical reaction depend mainly on the difference in bond energies (enthalpy, H) between reactants and products. Free energy also depends on *concentrations* of both reactants and products.

In most biochemical reactions there is little intrinsic free-energy difference between reactants and products. Such reactions are reversible, indicated by drawing double arrows:

$$A \rightleftharpoons B$$

At the beginning of a reaction, only the reactant molecules (A) may be present. As the reaction proceeds, the concentration of the reactant molecules decreases and the concentration of the product molecules (B) increases. As the concentration of the product molecules increases, they may have enough free energy to initiate the reverse reaction. The reaction thus proceeds in both directions simultaneously; if undisturbed, it eventually reaches a state of **dynamic equilibrium,** in which the rate of the reverse reaction equals the rate of the forward reaction. At equilibrium there is no net change in the system; a reverse reaction balances every forward reaction.

At a given temperature and pressure, each reaction has its own characteristic equilibrium. For any given reaction, chemists can perform experiments and calculations to determine the relative concentrations of reactants and products present at equilibrium. If the reactants have much greater intrinsic free energy than the products, the reaction goes almost to completion; that is, it reaches equilibrium at a point at which most of the reactants have been converted to products. Reactions in which the reactants have much less intrinsic free energy than the products reach equilibrium at a point where very few of the reactant molecules have been converted to products.

If you increase the initial concentration of A, then the reaction will "shift to the right," and more A will be converted to B. A similar effect can be obtained if B is removed from the reaction mixture. The reaction always shifts in the direction that reestablishes equilibrium so that the proportions of reactants and products characteristic of that reaction at equilibrium are restored. The opposite effect occurs if the concentration of B increases or if A is removed; here the system "shifts to the left." The actual free-energy change that occurs during a reaction is defined mathematically to include these effects, which stem from the relative initial concentrations of reactants and products. Cells use energy to manipulate the relative concentrations of reactants and products of almost every reaction. Cell reactions are virtually never at equilibrium. By displacing their reactions far from equilibrium, cells supply energy to endergonic reactions and direct their metabolism according to their needs.

Cells drive endergonic reactions by coupling them to exergonic reactions

Many metabolic reactions, such as protein synthesis, are anabolic and endergonic. Because an endergonic reaction cannot take place without an input of energy, endergonic reactions are coupled to exergonic reactions. In **coupled reactions,** the thermodynamically favorable exergonic reaction provides the energy required to drive the thermodynamically unfavorable endergonic reaction. The endergonic reaction proceeds only if it absorbs free energy released by the exergonic reaction to which it is coupled.

Consider the free-energy change, ΔG, in the following reaction:

(1) A $\longrightarrow$ B $\Delta G = +20.9$ kJ/mol ($+5$ kcal/mol)

Because ΔG has a positive value, you know that the product of this reaction has more free energy than the reactant. This is an endergonic reaction. It is not spontaneous and does not take place without an energy source.

By contrast, consider the following reaction:

$$(2)\ C \longrightarrow D \qquad \Delta G = -33.5\ kJ/mol\ (-8\ kcal/mol)$$

The negative value of ΔG tells you that the free energy of the reactant is greater than the free energy of the product. This exergonic reaction proceeds spontaneously.

You can sum up reactions 1 and 2 as follows:

$$(1)\ A \longrightarrow B \qquad \Delta G = +20.9\ kJ/mol\ (+5\ kcal/mol)$$
$$(2)\ C \longrightarrow D \qquad \Delta G = -33.5\ kJ/mol\ (-8\ kcal/mol)$$
$$\text{Overall} \qquad \Delta G = -12.6\ kJ/mol\ (-3\ kcal/mol)$$

Because thermodynamics considers the overall changes in these two reactions, which show a net negative value of ΔG, the two reactions taken together are exergonic.

The fact that scientists can write reactions this way is a useful bookkeeping device, but it does not mean that an exergonic reaction mysteriously transfers energy to an endergonic "bystander" reaction. However, these reactions are coupled if their pathways are altered so a common intermediate links them. Reactions 1 and 2 might be coupled by an intermediate (I) in the following way:

$$(3)\ A + C \longrightarrow I \qquad \Delta G = -8.4\ kJ/mol\ (-2\ kcal/mol)$$
$$(4)\ I \longrightarrow B + D \qquad \Delta G = -4.2\ kJ/mol\ (-1\ kcal/mol)$$
$$\text{Overall} \qquad \Delta G = -12.6\ kJ/mol\ (-3\ kcal/mol)$$

Note that reactions 3 and 4 are sequential. Thus, the reaction pathways have changed, but overall the reactants (A and C) and products (B and D) are the same, and the free-energy change is the same.

Generally, for each endergonic reaction occurring in a living cell there is a coupled exergonic reaction to drive it. Often the exergonic reaction involves the breakdown of ATP. Now let's examine specific examples of the role of ATP in energy coupling.

Review

- Consider the free-energy change in a reaction in which enthalpy decreases and entropy increases. Is ΔG zero, or does it have a positive value or a negative value? Is the reaction endergonic or exergonic?
- Why can't a reaction at equilibrium do work?

7.4 ATP, THE ENERGY CURRENCY OF THE CELL

◼ LEARNING OBJECTIVE

7 Explain how the chemical structure of ATP allows it to transfer a phosphate group and discuss the central role of ATP in the overall energy metabolism of the cell.

In all living cells, energy is temporarily packaged within a remarkable chemical compound called **adenosine triphosphate (ATP)**, which holds readily available energy for very short periods. We may think of ATP as the energy currency of the cell. When you work to earn money, you might say your energy is symbolically stored in the money you earn. The energy the cell requires for immediate use is temporarily stored in ATP, which is like cash. When you earn extra money, you may deposit some in the bank; similarly, a cell may deposit energy in the chemical bonds of lipids, starch, or glycogen. Moreover, just as you dare not make less money than you spend, the cell must avoid energy bankruptcy, which would mean its death. Finally, just as you probably do not keep money you earn very long, the cell continuously spends its ATP, which must be replaced immediately.

ATP is a nucleotide consisting of three main parts: adenine, a nitrogen-containing organic base; ribose, a five-carbon sugar; and three phosphate groups, identifiable as phosphorus atoms surrounded by oxygen atoms (**FIG. 7-5**). Notice that the phosphate

FIGURE 7-5 *Animated* ATP and ADP

ATP, the energy currency of all living things, consists of adenine, ribose, and three phosphate groups. The hydrolysis of ATP, an exergonic reaction, yields ADP and inorganic phosphate. (The black wavy lines indicate unstable bonds. These bonds allow the phosphates to be transferred to other molecules, making them more reactive.)

groups are bonded to the end of the molecule in a series, rather like three cars behind a locomotive, and, like the cars of a train, they can be attached and detached.

ATP donates energy through the transfer of a phosphate group

When the terminal phosphate is removed from ATP, the remaining molecule is adenosine diphosphate (ADP) (see Fig. 7-5). If the phosphate group is not transferred to another molecule, it is released as inorganic phosphate (P_i). This is an exergonic reaction with a relatively large negative value of ΔG. (Calculations of the free energy of ATP hydrolysis vary somewhat, but range between about -28 and -37 kJ/mol, or -6.8 to -8.7 kcal/mol.)

$$(5)\ ATP + H_2O \longrightarrow ADP + P_i$$
$$\Delta G = -32\ kJ/mol\ (or\ -7.6\ kcal/mol)$$

Reaction 5 can be coupled to endergonic reactions in cells. Consider the following endergonic reaction, in which two monosaccharides, glucose and fructose, form the disaccharide sucrose.

$$(6)\ glucose + fructose \longrightarrow sucrose + H_2O$$
$$\Delta G = +27\ kJ/mol\ (or\ +6.5\ kcal/mol)$$

With a free-energy change of -32 kJ/mol (-7.6 kcal/mol), the hydrolysis of ATP in reaction 5 can drive reaction 6, but only if the reactions are coupled through a common intermediate.

The following series of reactions is a simplified version of an alternative pathway that some bacteria use:

$$(7)\ glucose + ATP \longrightarrow glucose\text{-}P + ADP$$
$$(8)\ glucose\text{-}P + fructose \longrightarrow sucrose + P_i$$

Recall from Chapter 6 that a **phosphorylation reaction** is one in which a phosphate group is transferred to some other compound. In reaction 7 glucose becomes phosphorylated to form glucose phosphate (glucose-P), the intermediate that links the two reactions. Glucose-P, which corresponds to I in reactions 3 and 4, reacts exergonically with fructose to form sucrose. For energy coupling to work in this way, reactions 7 and 8 must occur in sequence. It is convenient to summarize the reactions thus:

$$(9)\ glucose + fructose + ATP \longrightarrow sucrose + ADP + P_i$$
$$\Delta G = -5\ kJ/mol\ (-1.2\ kcal/mol)$$

When you encounter an equation written in this way, remember that it is actually a summary of a series of reactions and that transitory intermediate products (in this case, glucose-P) are sometimes not shown.

ATP links exergonic and endergonic reactions

We have just discussed how the transfer of a phosphate group from ATP to some other compound is coupled to endergonic reactions in the cell. Conversely, adding a phosphate group to adenosine monophosphate, or AMP (forming ADP), or to ADP (forming ATP) requires coupling to exergonic reactions in the cell.

FIGURE 7-6 ATP links exergonic and endergonic reactions
Exergonic reactions in catabolic pathways (*top*) supply energy to drive the endergonic formation of ATP from ADP. Conversely, the exergonic hydrolysis of ATP supplies energy to endergonic reactions in anabolic pathways (*bottom*).

$$AMP + P_i + energy \longrightarrow ADP$$
$$ADP + P_i + energy \longrightarrow ATP$$

Thus, ATP occupies an intermediate position in the metabolism of the cell and is an important link between exergonic reactions, which are generally components of *catabolic pathways,* and endergonic reactions, which are generally part of *anabolic pathways* (**FIG. 7-6**).

The cell maintains a very high ratio of ATP to ADP

The cell maintains a ratio of ATP to ADP far from the equilibrium point. ATP constantly forms from ADP and inorganic phosphate as nutrients break down in cellular respiration or as photosynthesis traps the radiant energy of sunlight. At any time, a typical cell contains more than 10 ATP molecules for every ADP molecule. The fact that the cell maintains the ATP concentration at such a high level (relative to the concentration of ADP) makes its hydrolysis reaction even more strongly exergonic and more able to drive the endergonic reactions to which it is coupled.

Although the cell maintains a high ratio of ATP to ADP, the cell cannot store large quantities of ATP. The concentration of ATP is always very low, less than 1 mmol/L. In fact, studies suggest that a bacterial cell has no more than a 1-second supply of ATP. Thus, it uses ATP molecules almost as quickly as they are produced. A healthy adult human at rest uses about 45 kg (100 lb) of ATP each day, but the amount present in the body at any given moment is less than 1 g (0.035 oz). Every second in every cell, an estimated 10 million molecules of ATP are made from ADP and phosphate, and an equal number of ATPs transfer their phosphate groups, along with their energy, to whatever chemical reactions need them.

Review

- Why do coupled reactions typically have common intermediates?

- Give a generalized example of a coupled reaction involving ATP, distinguishing between the exergonic and endergonic reactions.
- Why is the ATP concentration in a cell about 10 times the concentration of ADP?

7.5 ENERGY TRANSFER IN REDOX REACTIONS

◼ LEARNING OBJECTIVE

8 Relate the transfer of electrons (or hydrogen atoms) to the transfer of energy.

You have seen that cells transfer energy through the transfer of a phosphate group from ATP. Energy is also transferred through the transfer of electrons. As discussed in Chapter 2, oxidation is the chemical process in which a substance loses electrons, whereas reduction is the complementary process in which a substance gains electrons. Because electrons released during an oxidation reaction cannot exist in the free state in living cells, every oxidation reaction must be accompanied by a reduction reaction in which the electrons are accepted by another atom, ion, or molecule. Oxidation and reduction reactions are often called redox reactions because they occur simultaneously. The substance that becomes oxidized gives up energy as it releases electrons, and the substance that becomes reduced receives energy as it gains electrons.

Redox reactions often occur in a series, as electrons are transferred from one molecule to another. These electron transfers, which are equivalent to energy transfers, are an essential part of cellular respiration, photosynthesis, and many other chemical pro-cesses. Redox reactions, for example, release the energy stored in food molecules so that ATP can be synthesized using that energy.

Most electron carriers transfer hydrogen atoms

Generally, it is not easy to remove one or more electrons from a covalent compound; it is much easier to remove a whole atom. For this reason, redox reactions in cells usually involve the transfer of a hydrogen atom rather than just an electron. A hydrogen atom contains an electron, plus a proton that does not participate in the oxidation–reduction reaction.

When an electron, either singly or as part of a hydrogen atom, is removed from an organic compound, it takes with it some of the energy stored in the chemical bond of which it was a part. That electron, along with its energy, is transferred to an acceptor molecule. An electron progressively loses free energy as it is transferred from one acceptor to another.

One of the most common acceptor molecules in cellular processes is **nicotinamide adenine dinucleotide** (**NAD$^+$**). When NAD$^+$ becomes reduced, it temporarily stores large amounts of free energy. Here is a generalized equation showing the transfer of hydrogen from a compound, which we call X, to NAD$^+$:

$$XH_2 + NAD^+ \longrightarrow X + NADH + H^+$$
$$\text{Oxidized} \qquad\qquad \text{Reduced}$$

Notice that the NAD$^+$ becomes reduced when it combines with hydrogen. NAD$^+$ is an ion with a net charge of $+1$. When 2 electrons and 1 proton are added, the charge is neutralized and the reduced form of the compound, **NADH,** is produced (**FIG. 7-7**). (Although the correct way to write the reduced form of NAD$^+$

FIGURE 7-7 NAD$^+$ and NADH

NAD$^+$ consists of two nucleotides, one with adenine and one with nicotinamide, that are joined at their phosphate groups. The oxidized form of the nicotinamide ring in NAD$^+$ (*left*) becomes the reduced form in NADH (*right*) by the transfer of 2 electrons and 1 proton from another organic compound (XH$_2$), which becomes oxidized (to X) in the process.

is NADH + H$^+$, for simplicity we present the reduced form as NADH in this book.) Some energy stored in the bonds holding the hydrogen atoms to molecule X has been transferred by this redox reaction and is temporarily held by NADH. When NADH transfers the electrons to some other molecule, some of their energy is transferred. This energy is usually then transferred through a series of reactions that ultimately result in the formation of ATP (discussed in Chapter 8).

Nicotinamide adenine dinucleotide phosphate (NADP$^+$) is a hydrogen acceptor that is chemically similar to NAD$^+$ but has an extra phosphate group. Unlike NADH, the reduced form of NADP$^+$, abbreviated **NADPH,** is not involved in ATP synthesis. Instead, the electrons of NADPH are used more directly to provide energy for certain reactions, including certain essential reactions of photosynthesis (discussed in Chapter 9).

Other important hydrogen acceptors or electron acceptors are FAD and the cytochromes. Flavin adenine dinucleotide (FAD) is a nucleotide that accepts hydrogen atoms and their electrons; its reduced form is FADH$_2$. The cytochromes are proteins that contain iron; the iron component accepts electrons from hydrogen atoms and then transfers these electrons to some other compound. Like NAD$^+$ and NADP$^+$, FAD and the cytochromes are electron transfer agents. Each exists in a *reduced state,* in which it has more free energy, or in an *oxidized state,* in which it has less. Each is an essential component of many redox reaction sequences in cells.

Review

- Which has the most energy, the oxidized form of a substance or its reduced form? Why?

7.6 ENZYMES

■ LEARNING OBJECTIVES

9 Explain how an enzyme lowers the required energy of activation for a reaction.

10 Describe specific ways enzymes are regulated.

The principles of thermodynamics help us predict whether a reaction can occur, but they tell us nothing about the speed of the reaction. The breakdown of glucose, for example, is an exergonic reaction, yet a glucose solution stays unchanged virtually indefinitely in a bottle if it is kept free of bacteria and molds and not subjected to high temperatures or strong acids or bases. Cells cannot wait for centuries for glucose to break down, nor can they use extreme conditions to cleave glucose molecules. Cells regulate the rates of chemical reactions with **enzymes,** which are biological **catalysts** that increase the speed of a chemical reaction without being consumed by the reaction. Although most enzymes are proteins, scientists have learned that some types of RNA molecules have catalytic activity as well (catalytic RNA is discussed in Chapter 13).

Cells require a steady release of energy, and they must regulate that release to meet metabolic energy requirements. Metabolic processes generally proceed by a series of steps such that a molecule may go through as many as 20 or 30 chemical transformations before it reaches some final state. Even then, the seemingly

completed molecule may enter yet another chemical pathway and become totally transformed or consumed to release energy. The changing needs of the cell require a system of flexible metabolic control. The key directors of this control system are enzymes.

The catalytic ability of some enzymes is truly impressive. For example, hydrogen peroxide (H$_2$O$_2$) breaks down extremely slowly if the reaction is uncatalyzed, but a single molecule of the enzyme **catalase** brings about the decomposition of 40 million molecules of hydrogen peroxide per second! Catalase has the highest catalytic rate known for any enzyme. It protects cells by destroying hydrogen peroxide, a poisonous substance produced as a byproduct of some cell reactions. The bombardier beetle uses the enzyme catalase as a defense mechanism (**FIG. 7-8**).

All reactions have a required energy of activation

All reactions, whether exergonic or endergonic, have an energy barrier known as the **energy of activation (E$_A$),** or **activation energy,** which is the energy required to break the existing bonds and begin the reaction. In a population of molecules of any kind, some have a relatively high kinetic energy, whereas others have a lower energy content. Only molecules with a relatively high kinetic energy are likely to react to form the product.

Even a strongly exergonic reaction, one that releases a substantial quantity of energy as it proceeds, may be prevented from proceeding by the activation energy required to begin the reaction. For example, molecular hydrogen and molecular oxygen can react explosively to form water:

$$2\,H_2 + O_2 \longrightarrow 2\,H_2O$$

Thomas Eisner and Daniel Aneshansley/Cornell University

FIGURE 7-8 Catalase as a defense mechanism

When threatened, a bombardier beetle (*Stenaptinus insignis*) uses the enzyme catalase to decompose hydrogen peroxide. The oxygen gas formed in the decomposition ejects water and other chemicals with explosive force. Because the reaction releases a great deal of heat, the water comes out as steam. (A wire attached by a drop of adhesive to the beetle's back immobilizes it. The researcher prodded its leg with the dissecting needle on the left to trigger the ejection.)

This reaction is spontaneous, yet hydrogen and oxygen can be safely mixed as long as all sparks are kept away because the required activation energy for this particular reaction is relatively high. A tiny spark provides the activation energy that allows a few molecules to react. Their reaction liberates so much heat that the rest react, producing an explosion. Such an explosion occurred on the space shuttle *Challenger* on January 28, 1986 (**FIG. 7-9**). The failure of a rubber O-ring to properly seal caused the liquid hydrogen in the tank attached to the shuttle to leak and start burning. When the hydrogen tank ruptured a few seconds later, the resulting force burst the nearby oxygen tank as well, mixing hydrogen and oxygen and igniting a huge explosion.

An enzyme lowers a reaction's activation energy

Like all catalysts, enzymes affect the rate of a reaction by lowering the activation energy (E_A) necessary to initiate a chemical reaction (**FIG. 7-10**). If molecules need less energy to react because the activation barrier is lowered, a larger fraction of the reactant molecules reacts at any one time. As a result, the reaction proceeds more quickly.

Although an enzyme lowers the activation energy for a reaction, it has no effect on the overall free-energy change; that is, an

FIGURE 7-9 The space shuttle *Challenger* explosion
This disaster resulted from an explosive exergonic reaction between hydrogen and oxygen. All seven crew members died in the accident on January 28, 1986.

KEY POINT An enzyme lowers the activation energy of a reaction but does not alter the free-energy change.

FIGURE 7-10 *Animated* **Activation energy and enzymes**
An enzyme speeds up a reaction by lowering its activation energy (E_A). In the presence of an enzyme, reacting molecules require less kinetic energy to complete a reaction.

enzyme can promote only a chemical reaction that could proceed without it. If the reaction goes to equilibrium, no catalyst can cause it to proceed in a thermodynamically unfavorable direction or can influence the final concentrations of reactants and products. Enzymes simply speed up reaction rates.

An enzyme works by forming an enzyme–substrate complex

An uncatalyzed reaction depends on random collisions among reactants. Because of its ordered structure, an enzyme reduces this reliance on random events and thereby controls the reaction. The enzyme accomplishes this by forming an unstable intermediate complex with the **substrate,** the substance on which it acts. When the **enzyme–substrate complex,** or **ES complex,** breaks up, the product is released; the original enzyme molecule is regenerated and is free to form a new ES complex:

$$\text{enzyme} + \text{substrate(s)} \longrightarrow \text{ES complex}$$
$$\text{ES complex} \longrightarrow \text{enzyme} + \text{product(s)}$$

The enzyme itself is not permanently altered or consumed by the reaction and can be reused.

As shown in **FIGURE 7-11a**, every enzyme contains one or more **active sites,** regions to which the substrate binds, to form the ES complex. The active sites of some enzymes are grooves or cavities in the enzyme molecule, formed by amino acid side chains. The active sites of most enzymes are located close to the surface. During

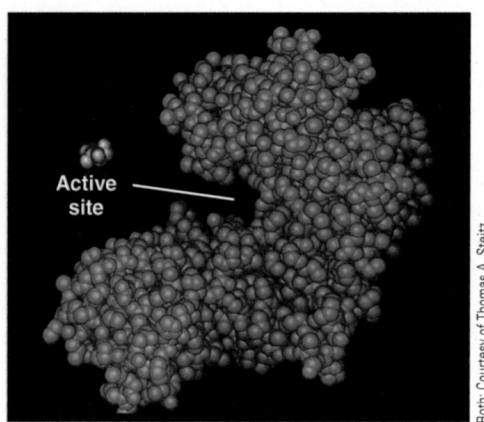

(a) Prior to forming an ES complex, the enzyme's active site is the furrow where the substrate will bind.

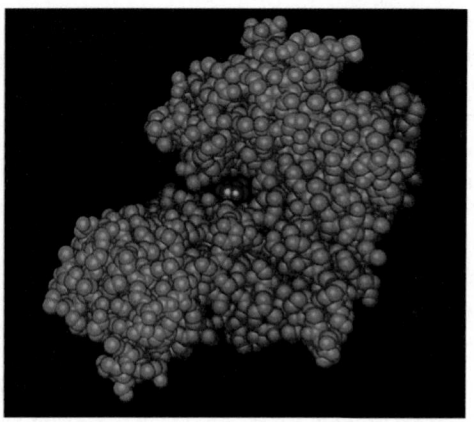

Both: Courtesy of Thomas A. Steitz

(b) The binding of the substrate to the active site induces a change in the conformation of the active site.

FIGURE 7-11 An enzyme–substrate complex
This computer graphic model shows the enzyme hexokinase (*blue*) and its substrate, glucose (*red*).

the course of a reaction, substrate molecules occupying these sites are brought close together and react with one another.

The shape of the enzyme does not seem exactly complementary to that of the substrate. The binding of the substrate to the enzyme molecule causes a change, known as **induced fit,** in the shape of the enzyme (**FIG. 7-11b**). Usually, the shape of the substrate also changes slightly, in a way that may distort its chemical bonds. The proximity and orientation of the reactants, together with strains in their chemical bonds, facilitate the breakage of old bonds and the formation of new ones. Thus, the substrate is changed into a product, which diffuses away from the enzyme. The enzyme is then free to catalyze the reaction of more substrate molecules to form more product molecules.

Enzymes are specific

Enzymes catalyze virtually every chemical reaction that takes place in an organism. Because the shape of the active site is closely related to the shape of the substrate, most enzymes are highly specific. Most catalyze only a few closely related chemical reactions or, in many cases, only one particular reaction. The enzyme urease, which decomposes urea to ammonia and carbon dioxide, attacks no other substrate. The enzyme sucrase splits only sucrose; it does not act on other disaccharides, such as maltose or lactose. A few enzymes are specific only to the extent that they require the substrate to have a certain kind of chemical bond. For example, lipase, secreted by the pancreas, splits the ester linkages connecting the glycerol and fatty acids of a wide variety of fats.

Scientists usually name enzymes by adding the suffix *-ase* to the name of the substrate. The enzyme sucrase, for example, splits sucrose into glucose and fructose. A few enzymes retain traditional names that do not end in *-ase*; some of these end in *-zyme*. For example, lysozyme (from the Greek *lysis,* "a loosening") is an enzyme found in tears and saliva; it breaks down bacterial cell walls. Other examples of enzymes with traditional names are pepsin and trypsin, which break peptide bonds in proteins.

Scientists classify enzymes that catalyze similar reactions into groups, although each particular enzyme in the group may catalyze only one specific reaction. **TABLE 7-1** describes the six classes of enzymes that biologists recognize. Each class is divided into many subclasses. For example, sucrase, mentioned earlier, is called a glycosidase because it cleaves a glycosidic linkage. Glycosidases are a subclass of the hydrolases (see Fig. 3-8b for the hydrolysis of sucrose). Phosphatases, enzymes that remove phosphate groups by hydrolysis, are also hydrolases. Kinases, enzymes that transfer phosphate groups to substrates, are transferases.

Many enzymes require cofactors

Some enzymes consist only of a protein. The enzyme pepsin, which is secreted by the animal stomach and digests dietary protein by breaking certain peptide bonds, is exclusively a protein molecule. Other enzymes have two components: a protein called the *apoenzyme* and an additional chemical component called a **cofactor.** Neither the apoenzyme nor the cofactor alone has catalytic activity; only when the two are combined does the enzyme function. A cofactor may be inorganic, or it may be an organic molecule.

Some enzymes require a specific metal ion as a cofactor. Two very common inorganic cofactors are magnesium ions and calcium ions. Most of the trace elements, such as iron, copper, zinc, and manganese, all of which organisms require in very small amounts, function as cofactors.

An organic, nonpolypeptide compound that binds to the apoenzyme and serves as a cofactor is called a coenzyme. Most coenzymes are carrier molecules that transfer electrons or part of a substrate from one molecule to another. We have already introduced some examples of coenzymes in this chapter. NADH, NADPH, and $FADH_2$ are coenzymes; they transfer electrons.

TABLE 7-1	Important Classes of Enzymes
Enzyme Class	**Function**
Oxidoreductases	Catalyze oxidation–reduction reactions
Transferases	Catalyze the transfer of a functional group from a donor molecule to an acceptor molecule
Hydrolases	Catalyze hydrolysis reactions
Isomerases	Catalyze conversion of a molecule from one isomeric form to another
Ligases	Catalyze certain reactions in which two molecules become joined in a process coupled to the hydrolysis of ATP
Lyases	Catalyze certain reactions in which double bonds form or break

ATP functions as a coenzyme; it is responsible for transferring phosphate groups. Yet another coenzyme, coenzyme A, is involved in the transfer of groups derived from organic acids. Most vitamins, which are organic compounds that an organism requires in small amounts but cannot synthesize itself, are coenzymes or components of coenzymes (see descriptions of vitamins in Table 47-3).

Enzymes are most effective at optimal conditions

Enzymes generally work best under certain narrowly defined conditions, such as appropriate temperature, pH (**FIG. 7-12**), and ion concentration. Any departure from optimal conditions adversely affects enzyme activity.

Each enzyme has an optimal temperature

Most enzymes have an optimal temperature, at which the rate of reaction is fastest. For human enzymes, the temperature optima are near the human body temperature (35°C to 40°C). Enzymatic

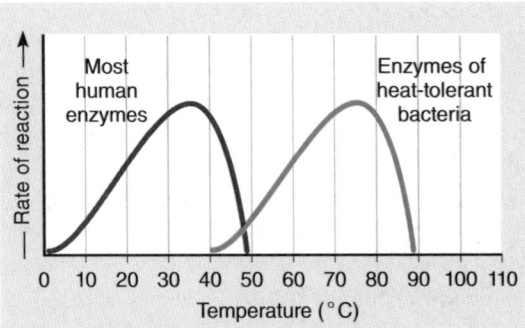

(a) Generalized curves for the effect of temperature on enzyme activity. As temperature increases, enzyme activity increases until it reaches an optimal temperature. Enzyme activity abruptly falls after it exceeds the optimal temperature because the enzyme, being a protein, denatures.

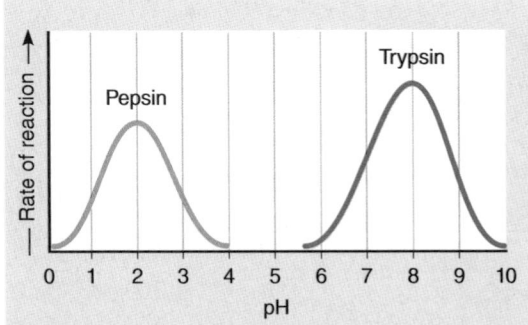

(b) Enzyme activity is very sensitive to pH. Pepsin is a protein-digesting enzyme in the very acidic stomach juice. Trypsin, secreted by the pancreas into the slightly basic small intestine, digests polypeptides.

FIGURE 7-12 *Animated* **The effects of temperature and pH on enzyme activity**

Substrate and enzyme concentrations are held constant in the reactions illustrated.

reactions occur slowly or not at all at low temperatures. As the temperature increases, molecular motion increases, resulting in more molecular collisions. The rates of most enzyme-controlled reactions therefore increase as the temperature increases, within limits (see Fig. 7-12a). High temperatures rapidly denature most enzymes. The molecular conformation (3-D shape) of the protein becomes altered as the hydrogen bonds responsible for its secondary, tertiary, and quaternary structures are broken. Because this inactivation is usually not reversible, activity is not regained when the enzyme is cooled.

Most organisms are killed by even a short exposure to high temperature; their enzymes are denatured, and they are unable to continue metabolism. There are a few stunning exceptions to this rule. Certain species of archaea (see Chapter 1 for a description of the archaea) can survive in the waters of hot springs, such as those in Yellowstone Park, where the temperature is almost 100°C; these organisms are responsible for the brilliant colors in the terraces of the hot springs (**FIG. 7-13**). Still other archaea live at temperatures much above that of boiling water, near deep-sea vents, where the extreme pressure keeps water in its liquid state (see Chapter 25 for a discussion of archaea that live in extreme habitats; see also Chapter 55, *Inquiring About: Life without the Sun*).

Each enzyme has an optimal pH

Most enzymes are active only over a narrow pH range and have an optimal pH, at which the rate of reaction is fastest. The optimal pH for most human enzymes is between 6 and 8. Recall from Chapter 2 that *buffers* minimize pH changes in cells so that the pH is maintained within a narrow limit. Pepsin, a protein-digesting enzyme secreted by cells lining the stomach, is an exception; it works only in a very acidic medium, optimally at pH 2 (see Fig. 7-12b). In contrast, trypsin, a protein-splitting enzyme secreted by the pancreas, functions best under the slightly basic conditions found in the small intestine.

FIGURE 7-13 **Grand Prismatic Spring in Yellowstone National Park**
The world's third-largest spring, about 61 m (200 ft) in diameter, the Grand Prismatic Spring teems with heat-tolerant archaea. The rings around the perimeter, where the water is slightly cooler, get their distinctive colors from the various kinds of archaea living there.

The activity of an enzyme may be markedly changed by any alteration in pH, which in turn alters electric charges on the enzyme. Changes in charge affect the ionic bonds that contribute to tertiary and quaternary structure, thereby changing the protein's conformation and activity. Many enzymes become inactive, and usually irreversibly denatured, when the medium is made very acidic or very basic.

Enzymes are organized into teams in metabolic pathways

Enzymes play an essential role in reaction coupling because they usually work in sequence, with the product of one enzyme-controlled reaction serving as the substrate for the next. You can picture the inside of a cell as a factory with many different assembly (and disassembly) lines operating simultaneously. An assembly line consists of a number of enzymes. Each enzyme carries out one step, such as changing molecule A into molecule B. Then molecule B is passed along to the next enzyme, which converts it into molecule C, and so on. Such a series of reactions is called a **metabolic pathway.**

$$\begin{array}{ccc} \text{Enzyme 1} & \text{Enzyme 2} \\ A \longrightarrow & B \longrightarrow & C \end{array}$$

Each of these reactions is reversible, despite the fact that an enzyme catalyzes it. An enzyme does not itself determine the direction of the reaction it catalyzes. However, the overall reaction sequence is portrayed as proceeding from left to right. Recall that if there is little intrinsic free-energy difference between the reactants and products for a particular reaction, the direction of the reaction is determined mainly by the relative concentrations of reactants and products.

In metabolic pathways, both intermediate and final products are often removed and converted to other chemical compounds. Such removal drives the sequence of reactions in a particular direction. Let us assume that reactant A is continually supplied and that its concentration remains constant. Enzyme 1 converts reactant A to product B. The concentration of B is always lower than the concentration of A because B is removed as it is converted to C in the reaction catalyzed by enzyme 2. If C is removed as quickly as it is formed (perhaps by leaving the cell), the entire reaction pathway is "pulled" toward C.

In some cases the enzymes of a metabolic pathway bind to one another to form a multienzyme complex that efficiently transfers intermediates in the pathway from one active site to another. An example of one such multienzyme complex, pyruvate dehydrogenase, is discussed in Chapter 8.

The cell regulates enzymatic activity

Enzymes regulate the chemistry of the cell, but what controls the enzymes? One regulatory mechanism involves controlling the amount of enzyme produced. A specific gene directs the synthesis of each type of enzyme. The gene, in turn, may be switched on by a signal from a hormone or by some other signal molecule. When the gene is switched on, the enzyme is synthesized. The total amount of enzyme present then influences the overall cell reaction rate.

If the pH and temperature are kept constant (as they are in most cells), the rate of the reaction can be affected by the substrate concentration or by the enzyme concentration. If an excess of substrate is present, the enzyme concentration is the rate-limiting factor. The initial rate of the reaction is then directly proportional to the enzyme concentration (**FIG. 7-14a**).

(a) In this example, the rate of reaction is measured at different enzyme concentrations, with an excess of substrate present. (Temperature and pH are constant.) The rate of the reaction is directly proportional to the enzyme concentration.

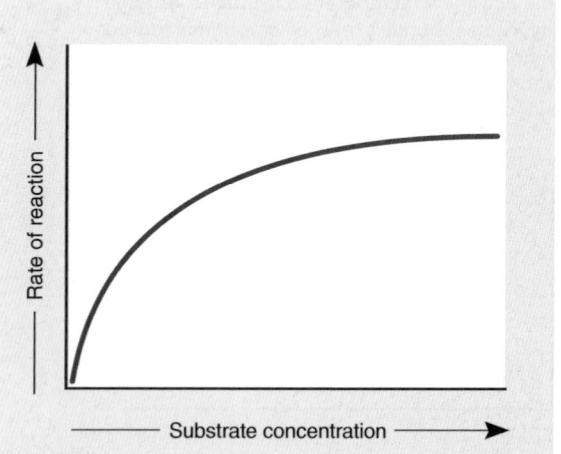

(b) In this example, the rate of the reaction is measured at different substrate concentrations, and enzyme concentration, temperature, and pH are constant. If the substrate concentration is relatively low, the reaction rate is directly proportional to substrate concentration. However, higher substrate concentrations do not increase the reaction rate because the enzymes become saturated with substrate.

FIGURE 7-14 The effects of enzyme concentration and substrate concentration on the rate of a reaction

If the enzyme concentration is kept constant, the rate of an enzymatic reaction is proportional to the concentration of substrate present. Substrate concentration is the rate-limiting factor at lower concentrations; the rate of the reaction is therefore directly proportional to the substrate concentration. However, at higher substrate concentrations, the enzyme molecules become saturated with substrate; that is, substrate molecules are bound to all available active sites of enzyme molecules. In this situation, increasing the substrate concentration does not increase the net reaction rate (FIG. 7-14b).

The product of one enzymatic reaction may control the activity of another enzyme, especially in a sequence of enzymatic reactions. For example, consider the following metabolic pathway:

$$\text{Enzyme 1} \quad \text{Enzyme 2} \quad \text{Enzyme 3} \quad \text{Enzyme 4}$$
$$A \longrightarrow B \longrightarrow C \longrightarrow D \longrightarrow E$$

A different enzyme catalyzes each step, and the final product E may inhibit the activity of enzyme 1. When the concentration of E is low, the sequence of reactions proceeds rapidly. However, an increasing concentration of E serves as a signal for enzyme 1 to slow down and eventually to stop functioning. Inhibition of enzyme 1 stops the entire reaction sequence. This type of enzyme regulation, in which the formation of a product inhibits an earlier reaction in the sequence, is called **feedback inhibition** (FIG. 7-15).

Another method of enzymatic control focuses on the activation of enzyme molecules. In their inactive form, the active sites of the enzyme are inappropriately shaped, so the substrates do not fit. Among the factors that influence the shape of the enzyme are pH, the concentration of certain ions, and the addition of phosphate groups to certain amino acids in the enzyme.

Some enzymes have a receptor site, called an **allosteric site,** on some region of the enzyme molecule other than the active site. (The word *allosteric* means "another space.") When a substance binds to an enzyme's allosteric site, the conformation of the enzyme's active site changes, thereby modifying the enzyme's activ-

FIGURE 7-15 *Animated* **Feedback inhibition**

Bacteria synthesize the amino acid isoleucine from the amino acid threonine. The isoleucine pathway involves five steps, each catalyzed by a different enzyme. When enough isoleucine accumulates in the cell, the isoleucine inhibits threonine deaminase, the enzyme that catalyzes the first step in this pathway.

ity. Substances that affect enzyme activity by binding to allosteric sites are called **allosteric regulators.** Some allosteric regulators are allosteric inhibitors that keep the enzyme in its inactive shape. Conversely, the activities of allosteric activators result in an enzyme with a functional active site.

The enzyme *cyclic AMP-dependent protein kinase* is an allosteric enzyme regulated by a protein that binds reversibly to the allosteric site and inactivates the enzyme. Protein kinase is in this inactive form most of the time (FIG. 7-16). When protein kinase activity is

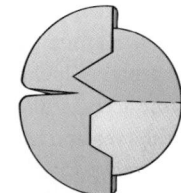

(a) Inactive form of the enzyme. The enzyme protein kinase is inhibited by a regulatory protein that binds reversibly to its allosteric site. When the enzyme is in this inactive form, the shape of the active site is modified so that the substrate cannot combine with it.

(b) Active form of the enzyme. Cyclic AMP removes the allosteric inhibitor and activates the enzyme.

(c) Enzyme–substrate complex. The substrate can then combine with the active site.

FIGURE 7-16 *Animated* **An allosteric enzyme**

needed, the compound cyclic AMP (cAMP; see Fig. 3-25 for the structure) contacts the enzyme-inhibitor complex and removes the inhibitory protein, thereby activating the protein kinase. Activation of protein kinases by cAMP is an important aspect of the mechanism of cell signaling, including the action of certain hormones (see Chapters 6 and 49 for discussions of cell signaling).

Enzymes are inhibited by certain chemical agents

Most enzymes are inhibited or even destroyed by certain chemical agents. Enzyme inhibition may be reversible or irreversible. **Reversible inhibition** occurs when an inhibitor forms weak chemical bonds with the enzyme. Reversible inhibition can be competitive or noncompetitive.

In **competitive inhibition,** the inhibitor competes with the normal substrate for binding to the active site of the enzyme (**FIG. 7-17a**). Usually, a competitive inhibitor is structurally similar to the normal substrate and fits into the active site and combines with the enzyme. However, it is not similar enough to substitute fully for the normal substrate in the chemical reaction, and the enzyme cannot convert it to product molecules. A competitive inhibitor occupies the active site only temporarily and does not permanently damage the enzyme. In competitive inhibition, an active site is occupied by the inhibitor part of the time and by the normal substrate part of the time. If the concentration of the substrate is increased relative to the concentration of the inhibitor, the active site is usually occupied by the substrate. Biochemists demonstrate competitive inhibition experimentally by showing that increasing the substrate concentration reverses competitive inhibition.

In **noncompetitive inhibition,** the inhibitor binds with the enzyme at a site other than the active site (**FIG. 7-17b**). Such an inhibitor inactivates the enzyme by altering its shape so that the active site cannot bind with the substrate. Many important noncompetitive inhibitors are metabolic substances that regulate enzyme activity by combining reversibly with the enzyme. Allosteric inhibition, discussed previously, is a type of noncompetitive inhibition in which the inhibitor binds to a special site, the allosteric site.

In **irreversible inhibition,** an inhibitor permanently inactivates or destroys an enzyme when the inhibitor combines with one of the enzyme's functional groups, either at the active site or elsewhere. Many poisons are irreversible enzyme inhibitors. For example, heavy metals such as mercury and lead bind irreversibly to and denature many proteins, including enzymes. Certain nerve gases poison the enzyme acetylcholinesterase, which is important for the functioning of nerves and muscles. Cytochrome oxidase, one of the enzymes that transports electrons in cellular respiration, is especially sensitive to cyanide. Death results from cyanide poisoning because cytochrome oxidase is irreversibly inhibited and no longer transfers electrons from its substrate to oxygen.

Some drugs are enzyme inhibitors

Physicians treat many bacterial infections with drugs that directly or indirectly inhibit bacterial enzyme activity. For example, sulfa drugs have a chemical structure similar to that of the nutrient

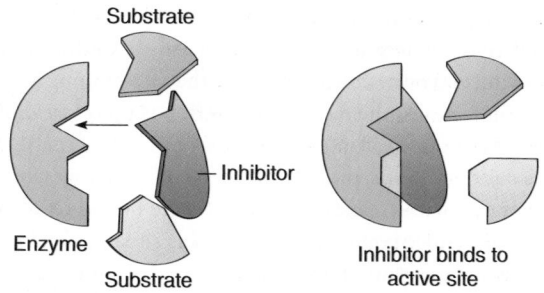

(a) Competitive inhibition. The inhibitor competes with the normal substrate for the active site of the enzyme. A competitive inhibitor occupies the active site only temporarily.

(b) Noncompetitive inhibition. The inhibitor binds with the enzyme at a site other than the active site, altering the shape of the enzyme and thereby inactivating it.

FIGURE 7-17 *Animated* **Competitive and noncompetitive inhibition**

para-aminobenzoic acid (PABA) (**FIG. 7-18**). When PABA is available, microorganisms can synthesize the vitamin *folic acid,* which is necessary for growth. Humans do not synthesize folic acid from PABA. For this reason, sulfa drugs selectively affect bacteria. When a sulfa drug is present, the drug competes with PABA for the active site of the bacterial enzyme. When bacteria use the sulfa drug in-

FIGURE 7-18 **Para-aminobenzoic acid and sulfonamides**

Sulfa drugs inhibit an enzyme in bacteria necessary for the synthesis of folic acid, an important vitamin required for growth. (Note the unusual structure of the sulfonamide molecule; sulfur, which commonly forms two covalent bonds, forms six instead.)

stead of PABA, they synthesize a compound that cannot be used to make folic acid. Therefore, the bacterial cells are unable to grow.

Penicillin and related antibiotics irreversibly inhibit a bacterial enzyme called *transpeptidase*. This enzyme establishes some of the chemical linkages in the bacterial cell wall. Bacteria susceptible to these antibiotics cannot produce properly constructed cell walls and are prevented from multiplying effectively. Human cells do not have cell walls and therefore do not use this enzyme. Thus, except for individuals allergic to it, penicillin is harmless to humans. Unfortunately, during the years since it was introduced, resistance to penicillin has evolved in many bacterial strains. The resistant bacteria fight back with an enzyme of their own, penicillinase, which breaks down the penicillin and renders it ineffective. Because bacteria evolve at such a rapid rate, drug resistance is a growing problem in medical practice.

Review

- What effect does an enzyme have on the required activation energy of a reaction?
- How does the function of the active site of an enzyme differ from that of an allosteric site?
- How are temperature and pH optima of an enzyme related to its structure and function?
- Is allosteric inhibition competitive or noncompetitive?

■ SUMMARY: FOCUS ON LEARNING OBJECTIVES

7.1 *(page 155)*

1 Define *energy*, emphasizing how it is related to work and to heat.
- **Energy** is the capacity to do work (expressed in **kilojoules, kJ**). Energy can be conveniently measured as **heat energy,** thermal energy that flows from an object with a higher temperature to an object with a lower temperature; the unit of heat energy is the **kilocalorie (kcal),** which is equal to 4.184 kJ. Heat energy cannot do cell work.

2 Use examples to contrast potential energy and kinetic energy.
- **Potential energy** is stored energy; **kinetic energy** is energy of motion.
- All forms of energy are interconvertible. For example, photosynthetic organisms capture radiant energy and convert some of it to **chemical energy,** a form of potential energy that powers many life processes, such as muscle contraction.

7.2 *(page 155)*

3 State the first and second laws of thermodynamics, and discuss the implications of these laws as they relate to organisms.
- A **closed system** does not exchange energy with its surroundings. Organisms are **open systems** that do exchange energy with their surroundings.
- The **first law of thermodynamics** states that energy cannot be created or destroyed but can be transferred and changed in form. The first law explains why organisms cannot produce energy; but as open systems, they continuously capture it from the surroundings.
- The **second law of thermodynamics** states that disorder (entropy) in the universe, a closed system, is continuously increasing. No energy transfer is 100% efficient; some energy is dissipated as **heat,** random motion that contributes to **entropy (S),** or disorder. As open systems, organisms maintain their ordered states at the expense of their surroundings.

7.3 *(page 156)*

4 Discuss how changes in free energy in a reaction are related to changes in entropy and enthalpy.
- As entropy increases, the amount of **free energy** decreases, as shown in the equation $G = H - TS$, in which G is the free energy, H is the **enthalpy** (total potential energy of the system), T is the absolute temperature (expressed in Kelvin units), and S is entropy.
- The equation $\Delta G = \Delta H - T\Delta S$ indicates that the change in free energy (ΔG) during a chemical reaction is equal to the change in enthalpy (ΔH) minus the product of the absolute temperature (T) multiplied by the change in entropy (ΔS).

5 Distinguish between exergonic and endergonic reactions, and give examples of how they may be coupled.
- An **exergonic reaction** has a negative value of ΔG; that is, free energy decreases. Such a reaction is spontaneous; it releases free energy that can perform work.
- Free energy increases in an **endergonic reaction.** Such a reaction has a positive value of ΔG and is nonspontaneous. In a **coupled reaction,** the input of free energy required to drive an endergonic reaction is supplied by an exergonic reaction.

  CENGAGENOW™ Learn more about exergonic and endergonic reactions by clicking on the figure in CengageNOW.

6 Compare the energy dynamics of a reaction at equilibrium with the dynamics of a reaction not at equilibrium.
- When a chemical reaction is in a state of **dynamic equilibrium,** the rate of change in one direction is exactly the same as the rate of change in the opposite direction; the system can do no work because the free-energy difference between the reactants and products is zero.
- When the concentration of reactant molecules is increased, the reaction shifts to the right and more product molecules are formed until equilibrium is re-established.

7.4 *(page 159)*

7 Explain how the chemical structure of ATP allows it to transfer a phosphate group and discuss the central role of ATP in the overall energy metabolism of the cell.
- **Adenosine triphosphate (ATP)** is the immediate energy currency of the cell. It donates energy by means of its terminal phosphate group, which is easily transferred to an acceptor molecule. ATP is formed by the **phosphorylation** of **adenosine diphosphate (ADP),** an endergonic process that requires an input of energy.
- ATP is the common link between exergonic and endergonic reactions and between **catabolism** (degradation of large complex molecules into smaller, simpler molecules) and **anabolism** (synthesis of complex molecules from simpler molecules).

7.5 *(page 161)*

8 Relate the transfer of electrons (or hydrogen atoms) to the transfer of energy.
- Energy is transferred in **oxidation–reduction (redox) reactions.** A substance becomes oxidized as it gives up one or more electrons to another substance, which becomes reduced in the process. Electrons are commonly transferred as part of hydrogen atoms.

- NAD$^+$ and NADP$^+$ accept electrons as part of hydrogen atoms and become reduced to form **NADH** and **NADPH,** respectively. These electrons (along with some of their energy) can be transferred to other acceptors.

7.6 *(page 162)*

9 Explain how an enzyme lowers the required energy of activation for a reaction.

- An **enzyme** is a biological **catalyst;** it greatly increases the speed of a chemical reaction without being consumed.

- An enzyme works by lowering the **activation energy (E$_A$),** the energy necessary to get a reaction going. The **active site** of an enzyme is a 3-D region where **substrates** come into close contact and thereby react more readily. When a substrate binds to an active site, an **enzyme–substrate complex** forms in which the shapes of the enzyme and substrate change slightly. This **induced fit** facilitates the breaking of bonds and formation of new ones.

CENGAGENOW™ Learn more about activation energy by clicking on the figure in CengageNOW.

10 Describe specific ways enzymes are regulated.

- Enzymes work best at specific temperature and pH conditions.
- A cell can regulate enzymatic activity by controlling the amount of enzyme produced and by regulating metabolic conditions that influence the shape of the enzyme.
- Some enzymes have **allosteric sites,** noncatalytic sites to which an **allosteric regulator** binds, changing the enzyme's activity. Some allosteric enzymes are subject to **feedback inhibition,** in which the formation of an end product inhibits an earlier reaction in the metabolic pathway.
- **Reversible inhibition** occurs when an inhibitor forms weak chemical bonds with the enzyme. Reversible inhibition may be **competitive,** in which the inhibitor competes with the substrate for the active site, or **noncompetitive,** in which the inhibitor binds with the enzyme at a site other than the active site. **Irreversible inhibition** occurs when an inhibitor combines with an enzyme and permanently inactivates it.

CENGAGENOW™ Learn more about enzymes by clicking on the figures in CengageNOW.

TEST YOUR UNDERSTANDING

1. Which of the following can do work in a cell? (a) entropy (b) heat (c) heat energy (d) all of the above (e) none of the above

2. In a chemical reaction occurring in a cell, free energy is equivalent to (a) heat energy (b) heat (c) disorder (d) potential energy (e) more than one of the above is true

3. Cells are able to function because they (a) are subject to the laws of thermodynamics (b) have mechanisms that transform energy from the environment into useful forms (c) can use enzymes to convert endergonic reactions into spontaneous reactions (d) all of the above

4. Diffusion is an (a) endergonic process because free energy increases (b) endergonic process because free energy decreases (c) exergonic process because entropy increases (d) exergonic process because entropy decreases (e) more than one of the above

5. A spontaneous reaction is one in which the change in free energy (ΔG) has a _____ value. (a) positive (b) negative (c) positive or negative (d) none of these (ΔG has no measurable value)

6. Healthy living cells maintain (a) ATP and ADP at equilibrium (b) equal concentrations of ATP and ADP (c) an ATP/ADP ratio of at least 10:1 (d) an ATP/ADP ratio of no more than 1:10 (e) most of the cell's stored energy in the form of ATP

7. Which of the following reactions could be coupled to an endergonic reaction with $\Delta G = +3.56$ kJ/mol?

(a) A $\longrightarrow$ B, $\Delta G = +6.08$ kJ/mol
(b) C $\longrightarrow$ D, $\Delta G = +3.56$ kJ/mol
(c) E $\longrightarrow$ F, $\Delta G = 0$ kJ/mol
(d) G $\longrightarrow$ H, $\Delta G = -1.22$ kJ/mol
(e) I $\longrightarrow$ J, $\Delta G = -5.91$ kJ/mol

8. Consider this reaction: glucose + 6 O$_2$ $\longrightarrow$ 6 CO$_2$ + 6 H$_2$O ($\Delta G = -2880$ kJ/mol). Which of the following statements about this reaction is *not* true? (a) the reaction is spontaneous in a thermodynamic sense (b) a small amount of energy (activation energy) must be supplied to start the reaction, which then proceeds with a release of energy (c) the reaction is exergonic (d) the reaction can be coupled to an endergonic reaction (e) the reaction must be coupled to an exergonic reaction

9. The required energy of activation of a reaction (a) is fixed, and cannot be altered (b) can be lowered by a specific enzyme (c) can be raised by a specific enzyme (d) b or c, depending on the enzyme (e) none of the above

10. "Induced fit" means that when a substrate binds to an enzyme's active site (a) it fits perfectly, like a key in a lock (b) the substrate and enzyme undergo conformational changes (c) a site other than the active site undergoes a conformational change (d) the substrate and the enzyme become irreversibly bound to each other (e) c and d

11. The function of a biochemical pathway is to (a) supply energy to reactions (b) drive a sequence of reactions in a particular direc-

tion (c) maintain chemical equilibrium (d) make energy available to endergonic reactions (e) any of the above, depending on the pathway

12. In the following reaction series, which enzyme(s) is/are most likely to have an allosteric site to which the end product E binds?

(a) enzyme 1 (b) enzyme 2 (c) enzyme 3 (d) enzyme 4 (e) enzymes 3 and 4

Enzyme 1   Enzyme 2   Enzyme 3   Enzyme 4

A ⟶ B ⟶ C ⟶ D ⟶ E

CRITICAL THINKING

1. Given what you have learned in this chapter, explain why an extremely high fever (body temperature above 40°C, or 105°F) can be fatal.

2. **EVOLUTION LINK.** What does the fact that all organisms use ATP/ADP as central links between exergonic and endergonic reactions suggest about the evolution of energy metabolism?

3. **EVOLUTION LINK.** Some have argued that "evolution is impossible because the second law of thermodynamics states that entropy always increases; therefore natural processes cannot give rise to greater complexity." In what ways is this statement a misunderstanding of the laws of thermodynamics?

4. **ANALYZING DATA.** Does the figure illustrate an exergonic reaction or an endergonic reaction? How do you know?

5. **ANALYZING DATA.** Reactions 1 and 2 happen to have the same standard free-energy change: $\Delta G - 41.8$ kJ/mol (-10 kcal/mol). Reaction 1 is at equilibrium, but reaction 2 is far from equilibrium. Is either reaction capable of performing work? If so, which one?

6. **ANALYZING DATA.** You are performing an experiment in which you are measuring the rate at which succinate is converted to fumarate by the enzyme succinic dehydrogenase. You decide to add a little malonate to make things interesting. You observe that the reaction rate slows markedly and hypothesize that malonate is inhibiting the reaction. Design an experiment that will help you decide whether malonate is acting as a competitive inhibitor or a noncompetitive inhibitor.

 Additional questions are available in CengageNOW at www.cengage.com/login.

8

How Cells Make ATP: Energy-Releasing Pathways

Grizzly bear (*Ursus arctos*). This grizzly, shown attempting to eat a jumping salmon, may also eat fruit, nuts, roots, insects, and small vertebrates such as mice and ground squirrels.

Digital Vision/Getty Images

KEY CONCEPTS

8.1 Aerobic respiration is an exergonic redox process in which glucose becomes oxidized, oxygen becomes reduced, and energy is captured to make ATP.

8.2 Aerobic respiration consists of four stages: glycolysis, formation of acetyl coenzyme A, the citric acid cycle, and the electron transport chain and chemiosmosis.

8.3 Nutrients other than glucose, including many carbohydrates, lipids, and amino acids, can be oxidized by aerobic respiration.

8.4 Anaerobic respiration and fermentation are ATP-yielding redox processes in which glucose becomes oxidized, but oxygen does not become reduced. Instead, these processes involve the reduction of inorganic substances (in anaerobic respiration) or organic substances (in fermentation).

Cells are tiny factories that process materials on the molecular level, through thousands of metabolic reactions. Cells exist in a dynamic state and are continuously building up and breaking down the many different cell constituents. As you learned in Chapter 7, metabolism has two complementary components: **catabolism,** which releases energy by splitting complex molecules into smaller components, and **anabolism,** the synthesis of complex molecules from simpler building blocks. Anabolic reactions produce proteins, nucleic acids, lipids, polysaccharides, and other molecules that help maintain the cell or the organism. Most anabolic reactions are endergonic and require ATP or some other energy source to drive them.

Every organism must extract energy from food molecules that it either manufactures by photosynthesis or obtains from the environment. Grizzly bears, such as the one in the photograph, obtain organic molecules from their varied plant and animal diets. How do they obtain energy from these organic molecules? First, the food molecules are broken down by digestion into simpler components that are absorbed into the blood and transported to all the cells. The catabolic processes that convert the energy in the chemical bonds of nutrients to chemical energy stored in ATP then occur inside cells, usually through a process known as **cellular respiration.**

Cellular respiration may be either aerobic or anaerobic. *Aerobic respiration* requires oxygen, whereas *anaerobic pathways,* which include anaerobic respiration and fermentation, do not require oxygen. In the process of *organismal respiration* (discussed in Chapter 46), your lungs provide a steady supply of oxygen that enables your cells to capture energy through aerobic respiration, which is by far the most common pathway and the main subject of this chapter. All three pathways—aerobic respiration, anaerobic respiration, and fermentation—are exergonic and release free energy that can be captured by the cell.

8.1 REDOX REACTIONS

■ LEARNING OBJECTIVE

1   Write a summary reaction for aerobic respiration that shows which reactant becomes oxidized and which becomes reduced.

Most eukaryotes and prokaryotes carry out **aerobic respiration,** a form of cellular respiration requiring molecular oxygen (O_2). During aerobic respiration, nutrients are catabolized to carbon dioxide and water. Most cells use aerobic respiration to obtain energy from glucose, which enters the cell through a specific transport protein in the plasma membrane (see discussion of facilitated diffusion in Chapter 5). The overall reaction pathway for the aerobic respiration of glucose is summarized as follows:

$$C_6H_{12}O_6 + 6\,O_2 + 6\,H_2O \longrightarrow$$
$$6\,CO_2 + 12\,H_2O + energy \text{ (in the chemical bonds of ATP)}$$

Note that water is shown on both sides of the equation because it is a reactant in some reactions and a product in others. For purposes of discussion, the equation for aerobic respiration can be simplified to indicate that there is a net yield of water:

$$\overset{\overbrace{\qquad\text{Oxidation}\qquad}}{C_6H_{12}O_6} + 6\,O_2 \rightarrow 6\,CO_2 + 6\,H_2O + energy \text{ (in the chemical bonds of ATP)}$$
$$\underset{\underbrace{\qquad\text{Reduction}\qquad}}{}$$

If we analyze this summary reaction, it appears that CO_2 is produced by the removal of hydrogen atoms from glucose. Conversely, water seems to be formed as oxygen accepts the hydrogen atoms. Because the transfer of hydrogen atoms is equivalent to the transfer of electrons, this is a **redox reaction** in which glucose becomes **oxidized** and oxygen becomes **reduced** (see discussion of redox reactions in Chapters 2 and 7).

The products of the reaction would be the same if the glucose were simply placed in a test tube and burned in the presence of oxygen. However, if a cell were to burn glucose, its energy would be released all at once as heat, which not only would be unavailable to the cell but also would actually destroy it. For this reason, cells do not transfer hydrogen atoms directly from glucose to oxygen. Aerobic respiration includes a series of redox reactions in which electrons associated with the hydrogen atoms in glucose are transferred to oxygen in a series of steps (**FIG. 8-1**). During this process, the free energy of the electrons is coupled to ATP synthesis.

Review

■   In the overall reaction of aerobic respiration, which reactant becomes oxidized and which becomes reduced?
■   What is the specific role of oxygen in most cells?

8.2 THE FOUR STAGES OF AEROBIC RESPIRATION

■ LEARNING OBJECTIVES

2   List and give a brief overview of the four stages of aerobic respiration.
3   Indicate where each stage of aerobic respiration takes place in a eukaryotic cell.

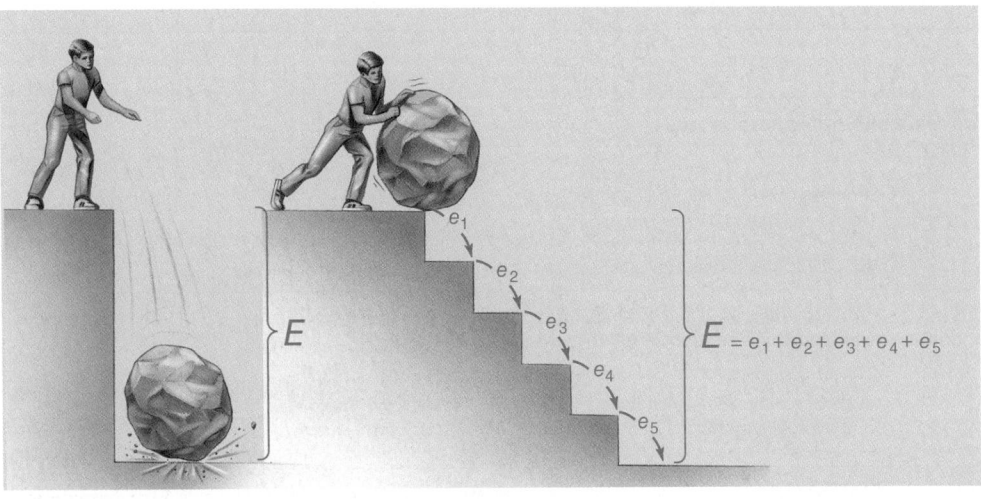

FIGURE 8-1 Changes in free energy
The release of energy from a glucose molecule is analogous to the liberation of energy by a falling object.
The total energy released (*E*) is the same whether it occurs all at once or in a series of steps.

4   Add up the energy captured (as ATP, NADH, and FADH₂) in each stage of aerobic respiration.

5   Define *chemiosmosis* and explain how a gradient of protons is established across the inner mitochondrial membrane.

6   Describe the process by which the proton gradient drives ATP synthesis in chemiosmosis.

The chemical reactions of the aerobic respiration of glucose are grouped into four stages (**FIG. 8-2** and **TABLE 8-1**; see also the summary equations at the end of the chapter). In eukaryotes, the first stage (glycolysis) takes place in the cytosol, and the remaining stages take place inside mitochondria. Most bacteria and archaea also carry out these processes, but because prokaryotic cells lack mitochondria, the reactions of aerobic respiration occur in the cytosol and in association with the plasma membrane.

1. *Glycolysis.* A six-carbon glucose molecule is converted to two three-carbon molecules of pyruvate.[1] Some of the energy of glucose is captured with the formation of two kinds of energy

---

[1]Pyruvate and many other compounds in cellular respiration exist as anions at the pH found in the cell. They sometimes associate with H^+ to form acids. For example, pyruvate forms pyruvic acid. In some textbooks these compounds are presented in the acid form.

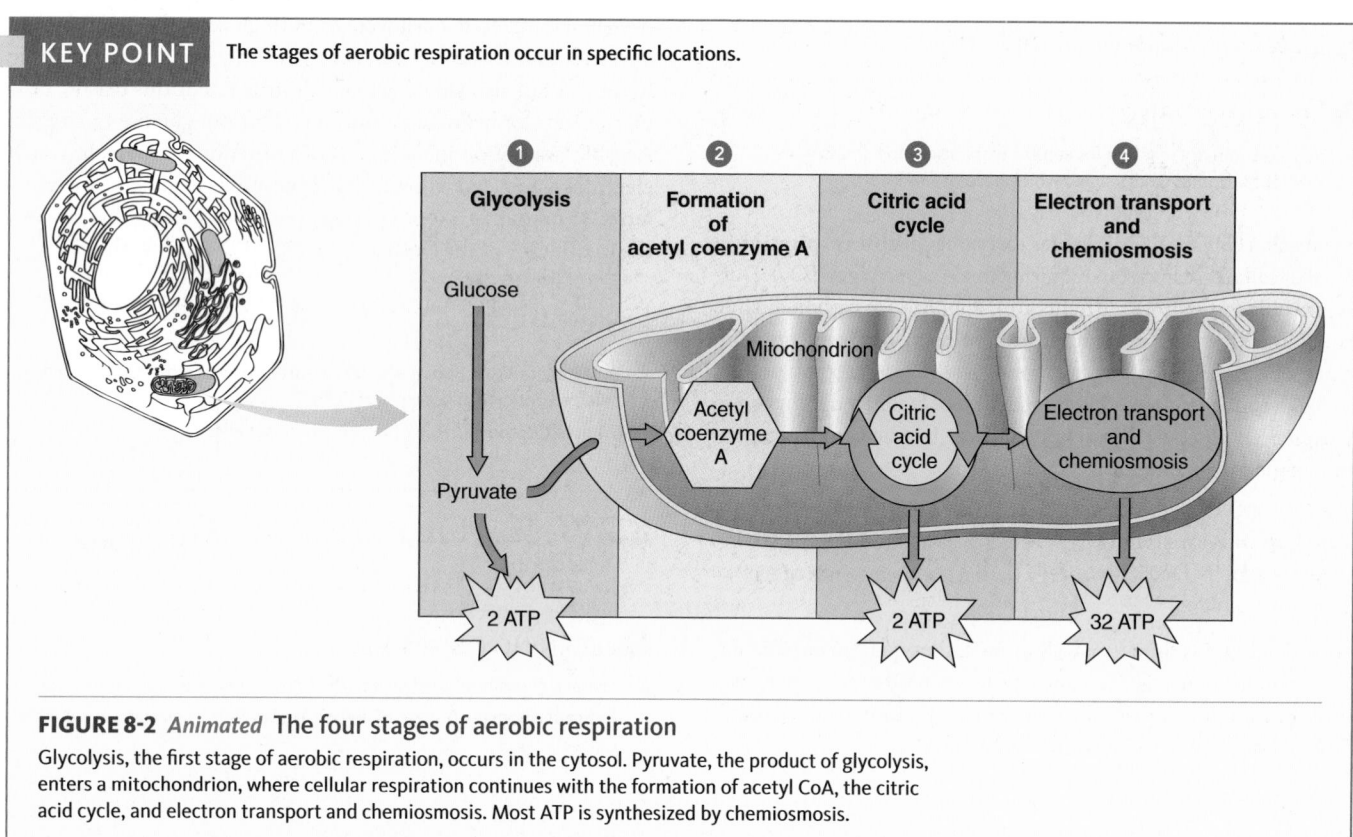

KEY POINT The stages of aerobic respiration occur in specific locations.

FIGURE 8-2 *Animated* **The four stages of aerobic respiration**

Glycolysis, the first stage of aerobic respiration, occurs in the cytosol. Pyruvate, the product of glycolysis, enters a mitochondrion, where cellular respiration continues with the formation of acetyl CoA, the citric acid cycle, and electron transport and chemiosmosis. Most ATP is synthesized by chemiosmosis.

TABLE 8-1	Summary of Aerobic Respiration		
Stage	Summary	Some Starting Materials	Some End Products
1. Glycolysis (in cytosol)	Series of reactions in which glucose is degraded to pyruvate; net profit of 2 ATPs; hydrogen atoms are transferred to carriers; can proceed anaerobically	Glucose, ATP, NAD^+, ADP, P_i	Pyruvate, ATP, NADH
2. Formation of acetyl CoA (in mitochondria)	Pyruvate is degraded and combined with coenzyme A to form acetyl CoA; hydrogen atoms are transferred to carriers; CO_2 is released	Pyruvate, coenzyme A, NAD^+	Acetyl CoA, CO_2, NADH
3. Citric acid cycle (in mitochondria)	Series of reactions in which the acetyl portion of acetyl CoA is degraded to CO_2; hydrogen atoms are transferred to carriers; ATP is synthesized	Acetyl CoA, H_2O, NAD^+, FAD, ADP, P_i	CO_2, NADH, $FADH_2$, ATP
4. Electron transport and chemiosmosis (in mitochondria)	Chain of several electron transport molecules; electrons are passed along chain; released energy is used to form a proton gradient; ATP is synthesized as protons diffuse down the gradient; oxygen is final electron acceptor	NADH, $FADH_2$, O_2, ADP, P_i	ATP, H_2O, NAD^+, FAD

carriers, ATP and NADH.[2] See Chapter 7 to review how ATP transfers energy by transferring a phosphate group (see Figs. 7-5 and 7-6). NADH is a reduced molecule that transfers energy by transferring electrons as part of a hydrogen atom (see Fig. 7-7).

2. *Formation of acetyl coenzyme A.* Each pyruvate enters a mitochondrion and is oxidized to a two-carbon group (acetate) that combines with coenzyme A, forming acetyl coenzyme A. NADH is produced, and carbon dioxide is released as a waste product.

3. *The citric acid cycle.* The acetate group of acetyl coenzyme A combines with a four-carbon molecule (oxaloacetate) to form a six-carbon molecule (citrate). In the course of the cycle, citrate is recycled to oxaloacetate, and carbon dioxide is released as a waste product. Energy is captured as ATP and the reduced, high-energy compounds NADH and $FADH_2$ (see Chapter 7 to review $FADH_2$).

4. *Electron transport and chemiosmosis.* The electrons removed from glucose during the preceding stages are transferred from NADH and $FADH_2$ to a chain of electron acceptor compounds. As the electrons are passed from one electron acceptor to another, some of their energy is used to transport hydrogen ions (protons) across the inner mitochondrial membrane, forming a proton gradient. In a process known as *chemiosmosis* (described later), the energy of this proton gradient is used to produce ATP.

Most reactions involved in aerobic respiration are one of three types: dehydrogenations, decarboxylations, and those we informally categorize as preparation reactions. **Dehydrogenations** are reactions in which two hydrogen atoms (actually, 2 electrons plus 1 or 2 protons) are removed from the substrate and transferred to NAD^+ or FAD. **Decarboxylations** are reactions in which part of a carboxyl group (—COOH) is removed from the substrate as a molecule of CO_2. The carbon dioxide you exhale with each breath is derived from decarboxylations that occur in your cells. The rest of the reactions are preparation reactions in which molecules undergo rearrangements and other changes so that they can undergo further dehydrogenations or decarboxylations. As you examine the individual reactions of aerobic respiration, you will encounter these three basic types.

In following the reactions of aerobic respiration, it helps to do some bookkeeping as you go along. Because glucose is the starting material, it is useful to express changes on a per glucose basis. We will pay particular attention to changes in the number of carbon atoms per molecule and to steps in which some type of energy transfer takes place.

In glycolysis, glucose yields two pyruvates

The word *glycolysis* comes from Greek words meaning "sugar splitting," which refers to the fact that the sugar glucose is metabolized. Glycolysis does not require oxygen and proceeds under aerobic or anaerobic conditions. **FIGURE 8-3** shows a simplified overview of glycolysis, in which a glucose molecule consisting of six carbons is

converted to two molecules of **pyruvate,** a three-carbon molecule. Some of the energy in the glucose is captured; there is a net yield of two ATP molecules and two NADH molecules. The reactions of glycolysis take place in the cytosol, where the necessary reactants, such as ADP, NAD^+, and inorganic phosphate, float freely and are used as needed.

The glycolysis pathway consists of a series of reactions, each of which is catalyzed by a specific enzyme (**FIG. 8-4**, pages 178 and 179). Glycolysis is divided into two major phases: the first includes endergonic reactions that require ATP, and the second includes exergonic reactions that yield ATP and NADH.

The first phase of glycolysis requires an investment of ATP

The first phase of glycolysis is sometimes called the "energy investment phase" (see Fig. 8-4, steps 1 to 5). Glucose is a relatively stable molecule and is not easily broken down. In two separate **phosphorylation reactions,** a phosphate group is transferred from ATP to the sugar. The resulting phosphorylated sugar (fructose-1,6-bisphosphate) is less stable and is broken enzymatically into two three-carbon molecules, dihydroxyacetone phosphate and glyceraldehyde-3-phosphate (G3P). The dihydroxyacetone phosphate is enzymatically converted to G3P, so the products at this point in glycolysis are two molecules of G3P per glucose. We can summarize this portion of glycolysis as follows:

$$\underset{\substack{\text{Six-carbon}\\\text{compound}}}{\text{glucose}} + 2\,\text{ATP} \longrightarrow \underset{\substack{\text{Three-}\\\text{carbon}\\\text{compound}}}{2\,\text{G3P}} + 2\,\text{ADP}$$

The second phase of glycolysis yields NADH and ATP

The second phase of glycolysis is sometimes called the "energy capture phase" (see Fig. 8-4, steps 6 to 10). Each G3P is converted to pyruvate. In the first step of this process, each G3P is oxidized by the removal of 2 electrons (as part of two hydrogen atoms). These immediately combine with the hydrogen carrier molecule, NAD^+:

$$\underset{\text{Oxidized}}{NAD^+} + \underset{\text{(From G3P)}}{2\,\text{H}} \longrightarrow \underset{\text{Reduced}}{NADH} + H^+$$

Because there are two G3P molecules for every glucose, two NADH are formed. The energy of the electrons carried by NADH is used to form ATP later. This process is discussed in conjunction with the electron transport chain.

In two of the reactions leading to the formation of pyruvate, ATP forms when a phosphate group is transferred to ADP from a phosphorylated intermediate (see Fig. 8-4, steps 7 and 10). This process is called **substrate-level phosphorylation.** Note that in the energy investment phase of glycolysis two molecules of ATP are consumed, but in the energy capture phase four molecules of ATP are produced. Thus, glycolysis yields a net energy profit of *two* ATPs per glucose.

We can summarize the energy capture phase of glycolysis as follows:

$$2\,\text{G3P} + 2\,NAD^+ + 4\,\text{ADP} \longrightarrow$$
$$2\,\text{pyruvate} + 2\,\text{NADH} + 4\,\text{ATP}$$

---

[2]Although the correct way to write the reduced form of NAD^+ is $NADH + H^+$, for simplicity we present the reduced form as NADH throughout the book.

Glycolysis includes both energy investment and energy capture.

FIGURE 8-3 *Animated* An overview of glycolysis

The black spheres represent carbon atoms. The energy investment phase of glycolysis leads to the splitting of sugar; ATP and NADH are produced during the energy capture phase. During glycolysis, each glucose molecule is converted to two pyruvates, with a net yield of two ATP molecules and two NADH molecules.

Pyruvate is converted to acetyl CoA

In eukaryotes, the pyruvate molecules formed in glycolysis enter the mitochondria, where they are converted to **acetyl coenzyme A (acetyl CoA).** These reactions occur in the cytosol of aerobic prokaryotes. In this series of reactions, pyruvate undergoes a process known as **oxidative decarboxylation.** First, a carboxyl group is removed as carbon dioxide, which diffuses out of the cell (**FIG. 8-5**). Then the remaining two-carbon fragment becomes oxidized, and NAD^+ accepts the electrons removed during the oxidation. Finally, the oxidized two-carbon fragment, an acetyl group, becomes attached to **coenzyme A,** yielding acetyl CoA. *Pyruvate dehydrogenase,* the enzyme that catalyzes these reactions, is an enormous multienzyme complex consisting of 72 polypeptide chains! Recall from Chapter 7 that coenzyme A transfers groups derived from organic acids. In this case, coenzyme A transfers an acetyl group, which is related to acetic acid. Coenzyme A is manufactured in the cell from one of the B vitamins, pantothenic acid.

The overall reaction for the formation of acetyl coenzyme A is:

$$2 \text{ pyruvate} + 2\,NAD^+ + 2\,CoA \longrightarrow$$
$$2 \text{ acetyl CoA} + 2\,NADH + 2\,CO_2$$

Note that the original glucose molecule has now been partially oxidized, yielding two acetyl groups and two CO_2 molecules. The electrons removed have reduced NAD^+ to NADH. At this point in aerobic respiration, four NADH molecules have been formed as a result of the catabolism of a single glucose molecule: two during glycolysis and two during the formation of acetyl CoA from pyruvate. Keep in mind that these NADH molecules will be used later (during electron transport) to form additional ATP molecules.

The citric acid cycle oxidizes acetyl CoA

The **citric acid cycle** is also known as the **tricarboxylic acid (TCA) cycle** and the **Krebs cycle,** after Hans Krebs, the German biochemist who assembled the accumulated contributions of many scientists and worked out the details of the cycle in the 1930s. He received a Nobel Prize in Physiology or Medicine in 1953 for this contribution. A simplified overview of the citric acid cycle, which takes place in the matrix of the mitochondria, is given in **FIGURE 8-6**, page 180. The eight steps of the citric acid cycle are shown in **FIGURE 8-7**, page 181. A specific enzyme catalyzes each reaction.

The first reaction of the cycle occurs when acetyl CoA transfers its two-carbon acetyl group to the four-carbon acceptor compound **oxaloacetate,** forming **citrate,** a six-carbon compound.

oxaloacetate	+	acetyl CoA	$\longrightarrow$	citrate	+	CoA
Four-carbon compound		Two-carbon compound		Six-carbon compound		

The citrate then goes through a series of chemical transformations, losing first one and then a second carboxyl group as CO_2. One ATP is formed (per acetyl group) by substrate-level phosphorylation. Most of the energy made available by the oxidative steps of the cycle is transferred as energy-rich electrons to NAD^+, forming NADH. For each acetyl group that enters the citric acid cycle, three molecules of NADH are produced (steps 3, 4, and 8). Electrons are also transferred to the electron acceptor FAD, forming $FADH_2$.

In the course of the citric acid cycle, two molecules of CO_2 and the equivalent of eight hydrogen atoms (8 protons and 8 electrons) are removed, forming three NADH and one $FADH_2$. You may wonder why more hydrogen equivalents are generated by these reactions than entered the cycle with the acetyl CoA molecule. These hydrogen atoms come from water molecules that are added during the reactions of the cycle. The CO_2 produced accounts for the two carbon atoms of the acetyl group that entered the citric acid cycle. At the end of each cycle, the four-carbon oxaloacetate has been regenerated, and the cycle continues.

Because two acetyl CoA molecules are produced from each glucose molecule, two cycles are required per glucose molecule. After two turns of the cycle, the original glucose has lost all its carbons and may be regarded as having been completely consumed. To summarize, the citric acid cycle yields four CO_2, six NADH, two $FADH_2$, and two ATPs per glucose molecule.

At this point in aerobic respiration, only four molecules of ATP have been formed per glucose by substrate-level phosphorylation: two during glycolysis and two during the citric acid cycle. Most of the energy of the original glucose molecule is in the form of high-energy electrons in NADH and $FADH_2$. Their energy will be used to synthesize additional ATP through the electron transport chain and chemiosmosis.

The electron transport chain is coupled to ATP synthesis

Let us consider the fate of all the electrons removed from a molecule of glucose during glycolysis, acetyl CoA formation, and the citric acid cycle. Recall that these electrons were transferred as part of hydrogen atoms to the acceptors NAD^+ and FAD, forming NADH and $FADH_2$. These reduced compounds now enter the **electron transport chain,** where the high-energy electrons of their hydrogen atoms are shuttled from one acceptor to another. As the electrons are passed along in a series of exergonic redox reactions, some of their energy is used to drive the synthesis of ATP, which is an endergonic process. Because ATP synthesis (by phosphorylation of ADP) is coupled to the redox reactions in the electron transport chain, the entire process is known as **oxidative phosphorylation.**

The electron transport chain transfers electrons from NADH and $FADH_2$ to oxygen

The electron transport chain is a series of electron carriers embedded in the inner mitochondrial membrane of eukaryotes and in the plasma membrane of aerobic prokaryotes. Like NADH and $FADH_2$, each carrier exists in an oxidized form or a reduced form. Electrons pass down the electron transport chain in a series of redox reactions that works much like a bucket brigade, the old-time chain of people who passed buckets of water from a stream to one another, to a building that was on fire. In the electron transport chain, each acceptor molecule becomes alternately reduced as it accepts electrons and oxidized as it gives them up. The electrons entering the electron transport chain have a relatively high energy content. They lose some of their energy at each step as they pass along the chain of electron carriers (just as some of the water spills out of the bucket as it is passed from one person to another).

FIGURE 8-4
A detailed look at glycolysis

A specific enzyme catalyzes each of the reactions in glycolysis. Note the net yield of two ATP molecules and two NADH molecules. (The black wavy lines indicate bonds that permit the phosphates to be readily transferred to other molecules; in this case, ADP.)

Energy investment phase and splitting of glucose
Two ATPs invested per glucose

1 Glycolysis begins with preparation reaction in which glucose receives phosphate group from ATP molecule. ATP serves as source of both phosphate and energy needed to attach phosphate to glucose molecule. (Once ATP is spent, it becomes ADP and joins ADP pool of cell until turned into ATP again.) Phosphorylated glucose is known as glucose-6-phosphate. (Note phosphate attached to its carbon atom 6.) Phosphorylation of glucose makes it more chemically reactive.

2 Glucose-6-phosphate undergoes another preparation reaction, rearrangement of its hydrogen and oxygen atoms. In this reaction glucose-6-phosphate is converted to its isomer, fructose-6-phosphate.

3 Next, another ATP donates phosphate to molecule, forming fructose-1,6-bisphosphate. So far, two ATP molecules have been invested in process without any being produced. Phosphate groups are now bound at carbons 1 and 6, and molecule is ready to be split.

4 Fructose-1,6-bisphosphate is then split into two 3-carbon sugars, glyceraldehyde-3-phosphate (G3P) and dihydroxyacetone phosphate.

5 Dihydroxyacetone phosphate is enzymatically converted to its isomer, glyceraldehyde-3-phosphate, for further metabolism in glycolysis.

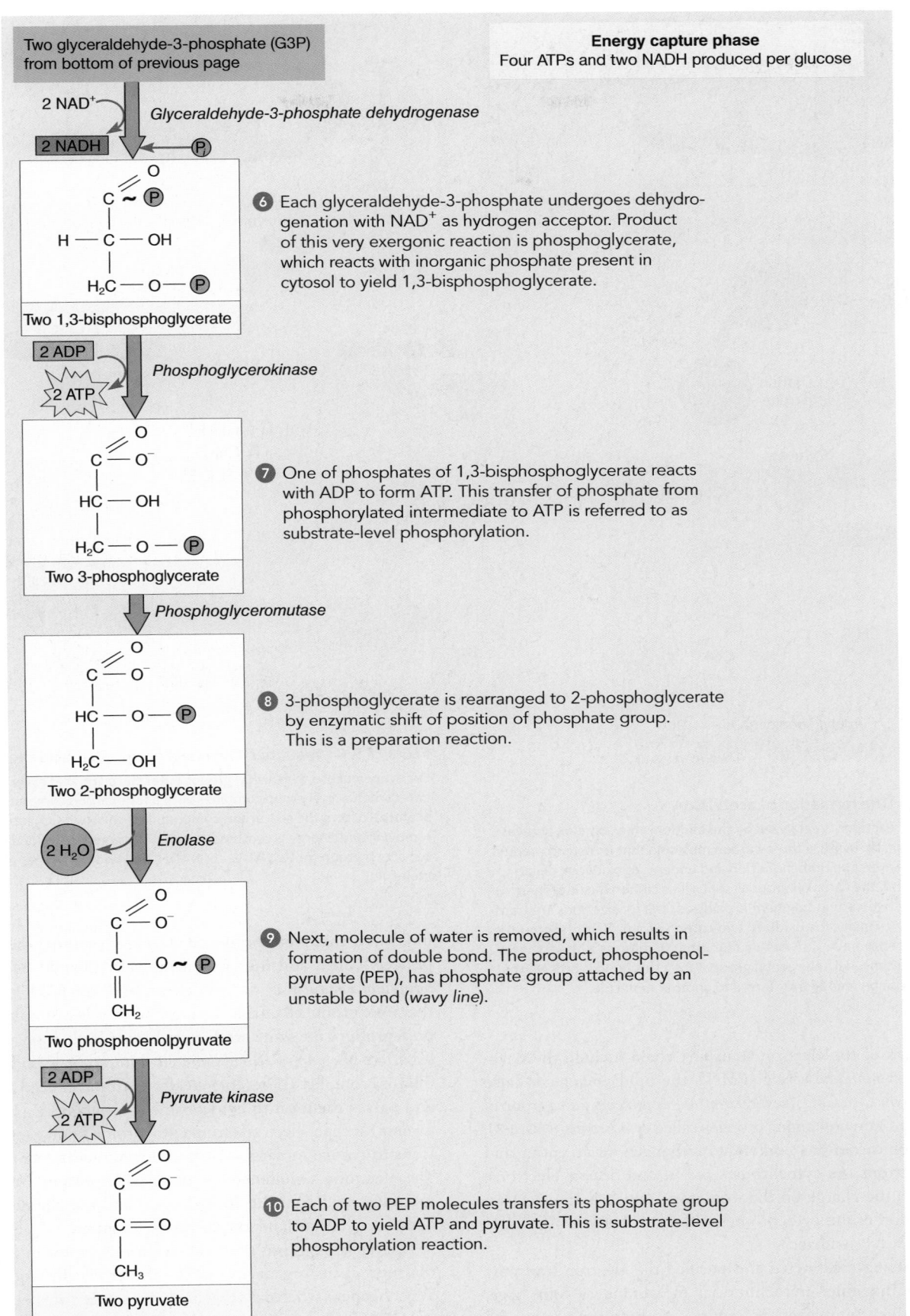

Two glyceraldehyde-3-phosphate (G3P) from bottom of previous page

2 NAD⁺

Glyceraldehyde-3-phosphate dehydrogenase

2 NADH   Pᵢ

Two 1,3-bisphosphoglycerate

6 Each glyceraldehyde-3-phosphate undergoes dehydrogenation with NAD⁺ as hydrogen acceptor. Product of this very exergonic reaction is phosphoglycerate, which reacts with inorganic phosphate present in cytosol to yield 1,3-bisphosphoglycerate.

2 ADP

2 ATP

Phosphoglycerokinase

Two 3-phosphoglycerate

7 One of phosphates of 1,3-bisphosphoglycerate reacts with ADP to form ATP. This transfer of phosphate from phosphorylated intermediate to ATP is referred to as substrate-level phosphorylation.

Phosphoglyceromutase

Two 2-phosphoglycerate

8 3-phosphoglycerate is rearranged to 2-phosphoglycerate by enzymatic shift of position of phosphate group. This is a preparation reaction.

2 H₂O   *Enolase*

Two phosphoenolpyruvate

9 Next, molecule of water is removed, which results in formation of double bond. The product, phosphoenolpyruvate (PEP), has phosphate group attached by an unstable bond (*wavy line*).

2 ADP

2 ATP

Pyruvate kinase

Two pyruvate

10 Each of two PEP molecules transfers its phosphate group to ADP to yield ATP and pyruvate. This is substrate-level phosphorylation reaction.

FIGURE 8-5 The formation of acetyl CoA

This series of reactions is catalyzed by the multienzyme complex pyruvate dehydrogenase. Pyruvate, a three-carbon molecule that is the end product of glycolysis, enters the mitochondrion and undergoes oxidative decarboxylation. First, the carboxyl group is split off as carbon dioxide. Then, the remaining two-carbon fragment is oxidized, and its electrons are transferred to NAD^+. Finally, the oxidized two-carbon group, an acetyl group, is attached to coenzyme A. CoA has a sulfur atom that forms a bond, shown as a black wavy line, with the acetyl group. When this bond is broken, the acetyl group can be readily transferred to another molecule.

Members of the electron transport chain include the flavo-protein *flavin mononucleotide (FMN)*, the lipid *ubiquinone* (also called *coenzyme* Q or *CoQ*), several *iron–sulfur proteins,* and a group of closely related iron-containing proteins called *cytochromes* (**FIG. 8-8**). Each electron carrier has a different mechanism for accepting and passing electrons. As cytochromes accept and donate electrons, for example, the charge on the iron atom, which is the electron carrier portion of the cytochromes, alternates between Fe^{2+} (reduced) and Fe^{3+} (oxidized).

Scientists have extracted and purified the electron transport chain from the inner mitochondrial membrane as four large, distinct protein complexes, or groups, of acceptors. *Complex I (NADH–ubiquinone oxidoreductase)* accepts electrons from NADH

FIGURE 8-6 *Animated* **Overview of the citric acid cycle**

For every glucose, two acetyl groups enter the citric acid cycle (*top*). Each two-carbon acetyl group combines with a four-carbon compound, oxalo-acetate, to form the six-carbon compound citrate. Two CO_2 molecules are removed, and energy is captured as one ATP, three NADH, and one $FADH_2$ per acetyl group (or two ATPs, six NADH, and two $FADH_2$ per glucose molecule).

molecules that were produced during glycolysis, the formation of acetyl CoA, and the citric acid cycle. *Complex II (succinate–ubiquinone reductase)* accepts electrons from $FADH_2$ molecules that were produced during the citric acid cycle. Complexes I and II both produce the same product, reduced ubiquinone, which is the substrate of *complex III (ubiquinone–cytochrome c oxidoreductase).* That is, complex III accepts electrons from reduced ubiquinone and passes them on to cytochrome *c. Complex IV (cytochrome c oxidase)* accepts electrons from cytochrome *c* and uses these electrons to reduce molecular oxygen, forming water in the process. The electrons simultaneously unite with protons from the surrounding medium to form hydrogen, and the chemical reaction between hydrogen and oxygen produces water.

Because oxygen is the final electron acceptor in the electron transport chain, organisms that respire aerobically require oxygen. What happens when cells that are strict aerobes are deprived of oxygen? The last cytochrome in the chain retains its electrons when no oxygen is available to accept them. When that occurs, each

FIGURE 8-7 A detailed look at the citric acid cycle

Begin with step 1, in the upper right corner, where acetyl coenzyme A attaches to oxaloacetate. Follow the steps in the citric acid cycle to see that the entry of a two-carbon acetyl group is balanced by the release of two molecules of CO_2. Electrons are transferred to NAD^+ or FAD, yielding NADH and $FADH_2$, respectively, and ATP is formed by substrate-level phosphorylation.

① Unstable bond attaching acetyl group to coenzyme A breaks. 2-carbon acetyl group becomes attached to 4-carbon oxaloacetate molecule, forming citrate, 6-carbon molecule with three carboxyl groups. Coenzyme A is free to combine with another 2-carbon group and repeat process.

⑧ Malate is dehydrogenated, forming oxaloacetate. Two hydrogens removed are transferred to NAD^+. Oxaloacetate can now combine with another molecule of acetyl coenzyme A, beginning new cycle.

⑦ With addition of water, fumarate is converted to malate.

⑥ Succinate is oxidized when two of its hydrogens are transferred to FAD, forming $FADH_2$. Resulting compound is fumarate.

⑤ Succinyl coenzyme A is converted to succinate, and substrate-level phosphorylation takes place. Bond attaching coenzyme A to succinate (~S) is unstable. Breakdown of succinyl coenzyme A is coupled to phosphorylation of GDP to form GTP (compound similar to ATP). GTP transfers its phosphate to ADP, yielding ATP.

② Atoms of citrate are rearranged by two preparation reactions: first, molecule of water is removed, and then molecule of water is added. Through these reactions citrate is converted to its isomer, isocitrate.

③ Isocitrate undergoes dehydrogenation and decarboxylation to yield 5-carbon compound α-ketoglutarate.

④ Next α-ketoglutarate undergoes decarboxylation and dehydrogenation to form 4-carbon compound succinyl coenzyme A. Reaction is catalyzed by multienzyme complex similar to complex that catalyzes conversion of pyruvate to acetyl coenzyme A.

CITRIC ACID CYCLE

Glucose   Fatty acids

Acetyl coenzyme A

Citrate synthase → Coenzyme A

Oxaloacetate

Malate dehydrogenase

NADH / NAD^+

Malate

Fumarase / H_2O

Fumarate

Succinate dehydrogenase

$FADH_2$ / FAD

Succinate

GTP / ADP / GDP / ATP

Succinyl CoA synthetase

Coenzyme A

Succinyl coenzyme A

Citrate

Aconitase / H_2O / H_2O

Isocitrate

Isocitrate dehydrogenase

NAD^+ / NADH / CO_2

α-Ketoglutarate

α-Ketoglutarate dehydrogenase

NAD^+ / NADH / Coenzyme A / CO_2

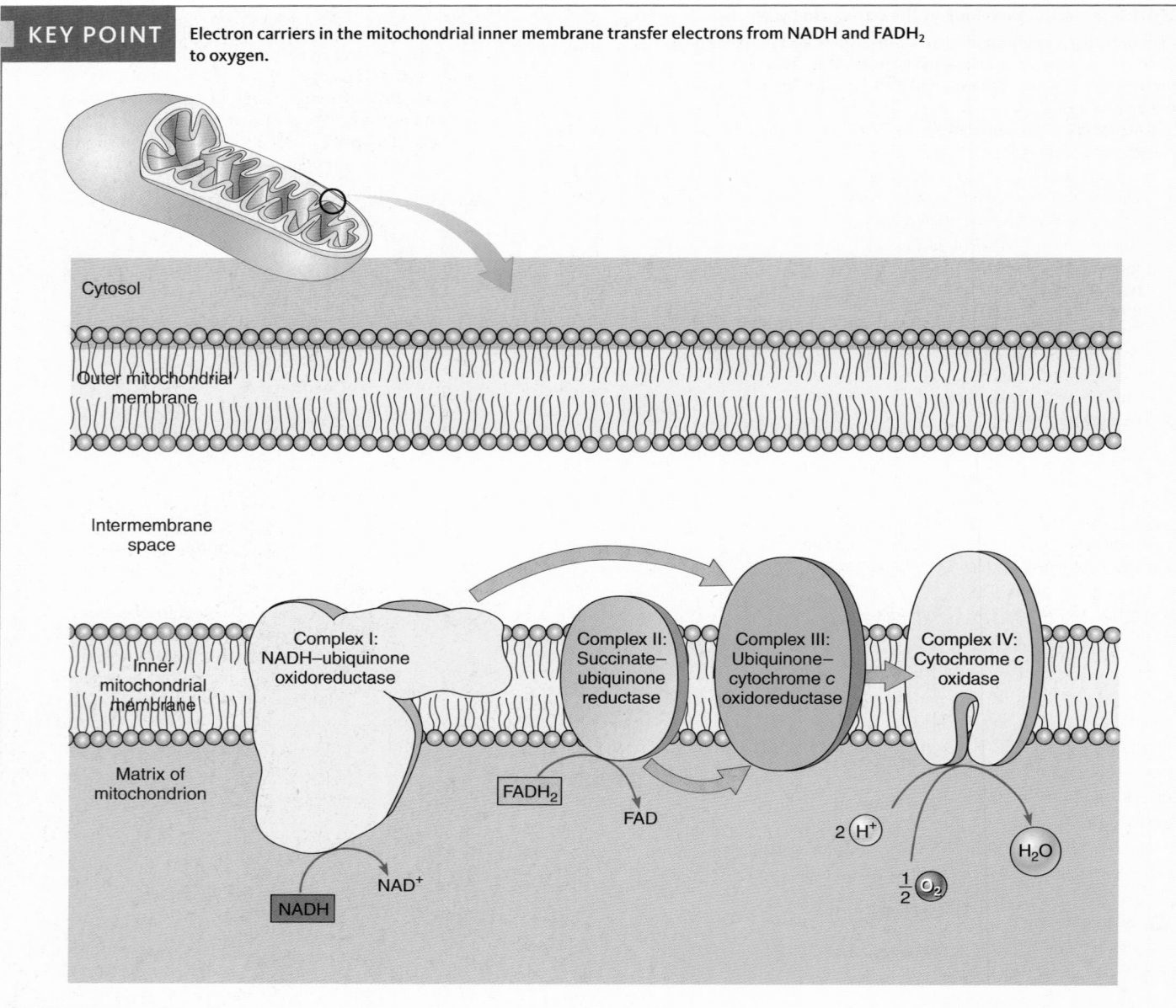

Electron carriers in the mitochondrial inner membrane transfer electrons from NADH and FADH$_2$ to oxygen.

Cytosol

Outer mitochondrial membrane

Intermembrane space

Inner mitochondrial membrane

Complex I: NADH–ubiquinone oxidoreductase

Complex II: Succinate–ubiquinone reductase

Complex III: Ubiquinone–cytochrome c oxidoreductase

Complex IV: Cytochrome c oxidase

Matrix of mitochondrion

FADH$_2$

FAD

$2\,H^+$

H$_2$O

$\frac{1}{2}O_2$

NADH

NAD$^+$

FIGURE 8-8 *Animated* **An overview of the electron transport chain**

Electrons fall to successively lower energy levels as they are passed along the four complexes of the electron transport chain located in the inner mitochondrial membrane. (The orange arrows indicate the pathway of electrons.) The carriers within each complex become alternately reduced and oxidized as they accept and donate electrons. The terminal acceptor is oxygen; one of the two atoms of an oxygen molecule (written as $\frac{1}{2}O_2$) accepts 2 electrons, which are added to 2 protons from the surrounding medium to produce water.

acceptor molecule in the chain retains its electrons (each remains in its reduced state), and the entire chain is blocked all the way back to NADH. Because oxidative phosphorylation is coupled to electron transport, no additional ATP is produced by way of the electron transport chain. Most cells of multicellular organisms cannot live long without oxygen because the small amount of ATP they produce by glycolysis alone is insufficient to sustain life processes.

Lack of oxygen is not the only factor that interferes with the electron transport chain. Some poisons, including cyanide, inhibit the normal activity of the cytochromes. Cyanide binds tightly to the iron in the last cytochrome in the electron transport chain, making it unable to transport electrons to oxygen. This blocks the

further passage of electrons through the chain, and ATP production ceases.

Although the flow of electrons in electron transport is usually tightly coupled to the production of ATP, some organisms uncouple the two processes to produce heat (see *Inquiring About: Electron Transport and Heat*).

The chemiosmotic model explains the coupling of ATP synthesis to electron transport in aerobic respiration

For decades, scientists were aware that oxidative phosphorylation occurs in mitochondria, and many experiments had shown that the transfer of 2 electrons from each NADH to oxygen (via the

ELECTRON TRANSPORT AND HEAT

What is the source of our body heat? Essentially, it is a byproduct of various exergonic reactions, especially those involving the electron transport chains in our mitochondria. Some cold-adapted animals, hibernating animals, and newborn animals produce unusually large amounts of heat by uncoupling electron transport from ATP production. These animals have adipose tissue (tissue in which fat is stored) that is brown. The brown color comes from the large number of mitochondria found in the brown adipose tissue cells. The inner mitochondrial membranes of these mitochondria contain an uncoupling protein that produces a passive proton channel through which protons flow into the mitochondrial matrix. As a consequence, most of the energy of glucose is converted to heat rather than to chemical energy in ATP.

Certain plants, which are not generally considered "warm" organisms, also have the ability to produce large amounts of heat. Skunk cabbage (*Symplocarpus foetidus*), for example, lives in North American swamps and wet woodlands and generally flowers during February and March when the ground is still covered with snow (see figure). Its uncoupled mitochondria generate large amounts of heat, enabling the plant to melt the snow and attract insect pollinators by vaporizing certain odiferous molecules into the surrounding air. The flower temperature of skunk cabbage is 15° to 22°C (59° to 72°F) when the air surrounding it is −15° to 10°C (5° to 50°F). Skunk cabbage flowers maintain this temperature for two weeks or more. Other plants, such as split leaf philodendron (*Philodendron selloum*) and sacred lotus (*Nelumbo nucifera*), also generate heat when they bloom and maintain their temperatures within precise limits.

Some plants generate as much or more heat per gram of tissue than animals in flight, which have long been considered the greatest heat producers in the living world. The European plant lords-and-ladies (*Arum maculatum*), for example, produces 0.4 J (0.1 cal) of heat per second per gram of tissue, whereas a hummingbird in flight

Leonard Lee Rue III/Animals Animals

Skunk cabbage (*Symplocarpus foetidus*)
This plant not only produces a significant amount of heat when it flowers but also regulates its temperature within a specific range.

produces 0.24 J (0.06 cal) per second per gram of tissue.

---

electron transport chain) usually results in the production of up to three ATP molecules. However, for a long time, the connection between ATP synthesis and electron transport remained a mystery.

In 1961, Peter Mitchell, a British biochemist, proposed the *chemiosmotic model,* which was based on his experiments and on theoretical considerations. One type of experiment involved using bacteria as a model system (**FIG. 8-9**). Because the respiratory electron transport chain is located in the plasma membrane of an aerobic bacterial cell, the bacterial plasma membrane can be considered comparable to the inner mitochondrial membrane. Mitchell demonstrated that if bacterial cells were placed in an acidic environment (that is, an environment with a high hydrogen ion, or proton, concentration), the cells synthesized ATP even if electron transport was not taking place. On the basis of these and other experiments, Mitchell proposed that electron transport and ATP synthesis are coupled by means of a proton gradient across the inner mitochondrial membrane in eukaryotes (or across the plasma membrane in bacteria). His model was so radical that it was not immediately accepted, but by 1978, so much evidence had accumulated in support of **chemiosmosis** that Peter Mitchell was awarded a Nobel Prize in Chemistry.

The electron transport chain establishes the proton gradient; some of the energy released as electrons pass down the electron transport chain is used to move protons (H^+) across a membrane. In eukaryotes the protons are moved across the inner mitochondrial membrane into the intermembrane space (**FIG. 8-10**). Hence, the inner mitochondrial

KEY EXPERIMENT

QUESTION: What is the mechanism of oxidative phosphorylation?

HYPOTHESIS: Peter Mitchell proposed that the cell uses energy released during electron transport to create a proton gradient across a membrane. The potential energy inherent in that gradient then drives the synthesis of ATP.

EXPERIMENT: Aerobic bacteria were placed in an acid (high H^+ concentration) environment, thus creating a proton gradient across the plasma membrane. This was done under conditions in which no electron transport was occurring.

RESULTS AND CONCLUSION: The bacteria synthesized ATP in the absence of aerobic respiration. These results supported Mitchell's view that a proton gradient across a membrane is an essential link in the conversion of the electrical energy of the electron transport chain to chemical energy in ATP.

FIGURE 8-9 Evidence for chemiosmosis

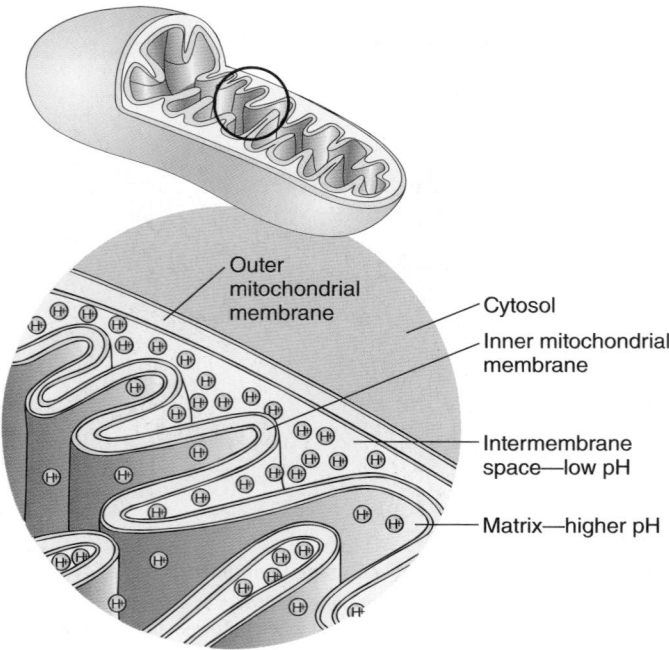

Outer
mitochondrial
membrane

Cytosol

Inner mitochondrial
membrane

Intermembrane
space—low pH

Matrix—higher pH

FIGURE 8-10 The accumulation of protons (H^+) within the intermembrane space

As electrons move down the electron transport chain, the electron transport complexes move protons (H^+) from the matrix to the intermembrane space, creating a proton gradient. The high concentration of H^+ in the intermembrane space lowers the pH.

membrane separates a space with a higher concentration of protons (the intermembrane space) from a space with a lower concentration of protons (the mitochondrial matrix).

Protons are moved across the inner mitochondrial membrane by three of the four electron transport complexes (complexes I, III, and IV) (**FIG. 8-11a**). Like water behind a dam, the resulting proton gradient is a form of potential energy that can be harnessed to provide the energy for ATP synthesis.

Diffusion of protons from the intermembrane space, where they are highly concentrated, through the inner mitochondrial membrane to the matrix of the mitochondrion is limited to specific channels formed by a fifth enzyme complex, **ATP synthase,** a transmembrane protein. Portions of these complexes project from the inner surface of the membrane (the surface that faces the matrix) and are visible by electron microscopy (**FIG. 8-11b**). Diffusion of the protons down their gradient, through the ATP synthase complex, is exergonic because the entropy of the system increases. This exergonic process provides the energy for ATP production, although the exact mechanism by which ATP synthase catalyzes the phosphorylation of ADP is still not completely understood.

In 1997, Paul Boyer of the University of California at Los Angeles and John Walker of the Medical Research Council Laboratory of Molecular Biology, Cambridge, England, shared the Nobel Prize in Chemistry for the discovery that ATP synthase functions in an unusual way. Experimental evidence strongly suggests that ATP synthase acts like a highly efficient molecular motor: During the production of ATP from ADP and inorganic phosphate, a central structure of ATP synthase rotates, possibly in response to the

force of protons moving through the enzyme complex. The rotation apparently alters the conformation of the catalytic subunits in a way that drives ATP synthesis.

Chemiosmosis is a fundamental mechanism of energy coupling in cells; it allows exergonic redox reactions to drive the endergonic reaction in which ATP is produced by phosphorylating ADP. In photosynthesis (discussed in Chapter 9), ATP is produced by a comparable process.

Aerobic respiration of one glucose yields a maximum of 36 to 38 ATPs

Let us now review where biologically useful energy is captured in aerobic respiration and calculate the total energy yield from the complete oxidation of glucose. **FIGURE 8-12** summarizes the arithmetic involved.

1. In glycolysis, glucose is activated by the addition of phosphates from 2 ATP molecules and converted ultimately to 2 pyruvates + 2 NADH + 4 ATPs, yielding a net profit of 2 ATPs.
2. The 2 pyruvates are metabolized to 2 acetyl CoA + 2 CO_2 + 2 NADH.
3. In the citric acid cycle, the 2 acetyl CoA molecules are metabolized to 4 CO_2 + 6 NADH + 2 $FADH_2$ + 2 ATPs.

Because the oxidation of NADH in the electron transport chain yields up to 3 ATPs per molecule, the total of 10 NADH molecules can yield up to 30 ATPs. The 2 NADH molecules from glycolysis, however, yield either 2 or 3 ATPs each. The reason is that certain types of eukaryotic cells must expend energy to shuttle the NADH produced by glycolysis across the mitochondrial membrane (to be discussed shortly). Prokaryotic cells lack mitochondria; hence, they have no need to shuttle NADH molecules. For this reason, bacteria are able to generate 3 ATPs for every NADH, even those produced during glycolysis. Thus, the maximum number of ATPs formed using the energy from NADH is 28 to 30.

The oxidation of $FADH_2$ yields 2 ATPs per molecule (recall that electrons from $FADH_2$ enter the electron transport chain at a different location than those from NADH), so the 2 $FADH_2$ molecules produced in the citric acid cycle yield 4 ATPs.

4. Summing all the ATPs (2 from glycolysis, 2 from the citric acid cycle, and 32 to 34 from electron transport and chemiosmosis), you can see that the complete aerobic metabolism of one molecule of glucose yields a maximum of 36 to 38 ATPs. Most ATP is generated by oxidative phosphorylation, which involves the electron transport chain and chemiosmosis. Only 4 ATPs are formed by substrate-level phosphorylation in glycolysis and the citric acid cycle.

We can analyze the efficiency of the overall process of aerobic respiration by comparing the free energy captured as ATP to the total free energy in a glucose molecule. Recall from Chapter 6 that although heat energy cannot power biological reactions, it is convenient to measure energy as heat. This is done through the use of a calorimeter, an instrument that measures the heat of a reaction. A sample is placed in a compartment surrounded by a chamber of water. As the sample burns (becomes oxidized), the temperature of the water rises, providing a measure of the heat released during the reaction.

The electron transport chain forms a concentration gradient for H^+, which diffuses through ATP synthase complexes, producing ATP.

(a) The electron transport chain in the inner mitochondrial membrane includes three proton pumps that are located in three of the four electron transport complexes. (The orange arrows indicate the pathway of electrons; and the black arrows, the pathway of protons.) The energy released during electron transport is used to transport protons (H^+) from the mitochondrial matrix to the intermembrane space, where a high concentration of protons accumulates. The protons cannot diffuse back into the matrix except through special channels in ATP synthase in the inner membrane. The flow of the protons through ATP synthase provides the energy for generating ATP from ADP and inorganic phosphate (P_i). In the process, the inner part of ATP synthase rotates (thick red arrows) like a motor.

R. Bhatnagar/Visuals Unlimited, Inc.

250 nm

(b) This TEM shows hundreds of projections of ATP synthase complexes along the surface of the inner mitochondrial membrane.

FIGURE 8-11 A detailed look at electron transport and chemiosmosis

Most ATP is produced by electron transport and chemiosmosis (oxidative phosphorylation)

FIGURE 8-12 Energy yield from the complete oxidation of glucose by aerobic respiration

are transferred to the electron transport chain in the inner mitochondrial membrane, and up to three molecules of ATP are produced per pair of electrons.

In skeletal muscle, brain, and some other types of cells, another type of shuttle operates. Because this shuttle requires more energy than the shuttle in liver, kidney, and heart cells, the electrons are at a lower energy level when they enter the electron transport chain. They are accepted by ubiquinone rather than by NAD^+ and so generate a maximum of 2 ATP molecules per pair of electrons. For this reason, the number of ATPs produced by aerobic respiration of 1 molecule of glucose in skeletal muscle cells is 36 rather than 38.

Cells regulate aerobic respiration

Aerobic respiration requires a steady input of fuel molecules and oxygen. Under normal conditions these materials are adequately provided and do not affect the rate of respiration. Instead, the rate of aerobic respiration is regulated by how much ADP and phosphate are available, with ATP synthesis continuing until most of the ADP has been converted to ATP. At this point oxidative phosphorylation slows considerably, which in turn slows down the citric acid cycle.

Glycolysis is partly controlled by feedback regulation (see Fig. 7-15 for an illustration of feedback regulation) exerted on the enzyme phosphofructokinase, which catalyzes an early reaction of glycolysis (see Fig. 8-4). The active site of phosphofructokinase binds ATP and fructose-6-phosphate. However, the enzyme has two allosteric sites: an inhibitor site to which ATP binds when present at very high levels, and an activator site to which AMP (adenosine monophosphate, a molecule formed when two phosphates are removed from ATP) binds. Therefore, this enzyme is inactivated when ATP levels are high and activated when they are low. Respiration proceeds when the enzyme becomes activated, thus generating more ATP.

Review

- How much ATP is made available to the cell from a single glucose molecule by the operation of (1) glycolysis, (2) the formation of acetyl CoA, (3) the citric acid cycle, and (4) the electron transport chain and chemiosmosis?
- Why is each of the following essential to chemiosmotic ATP synthesis: (1) electron transport chain, (2) proton gradient, and (3) ATP synthase complex?
- What are the roles of NAD^+, FAD, and oxygen in aerobic respiration?
- What are some of the ways aerobic respiration is controlled?

When 1 mol of glucose is burned in a calorimeter, some 686 kcal (2870 kJ) are released as heat. The free energy temporarily held in the phosphate bonds of ATP is about 7.6 kcal (31.8 kJ) per mole. When 36 to 38 ATPs are generated during the aerobic respiration of glucose, the free energy trapped in ATP amounts to 7.6 kcal/mol × 36, or about 274 kcal (1146 kJ) per mole. Thus, the efficiency of aerobic respiration is 274/686, or about 40%. (By comparison, a steam power plant has an efficiency of 35% to 36% in converting its fuel energy into electricity.) The remainder of the energy in the glucose is released as heat.

Mitochondrial shuttle systems harvest the electrons of NADH produced in the cytosol

The inner mitochondrial membrane is not permeable to NADH, which is a large molecule. Therefore, the NADH molecules produced in the cytosol during glycolysis cannot diffuse into the mitochondria to transfer their electrons to the electron transport chain. Unlike ATP and ADP, NADH does not have a carrier protein to transport it across the membrane. Instead, several systems have evolved to transfer just the *electrons* of NADH, not the NADH molecules themselves, into the mitochondria.

In liver, kidney, and heart cells, a special shuttle system transfers the electrons from NADH through the inner mitochondrial membrane to an NAD^+ molecule in the matrix. These electrons

8.3 ENERGY YIELD OF NUTRIENTS OTHER THAN GLUCOSE

◼ LEARNING OBJECTIVE

7 Summarize how the products of protein and lipid catabolism enter the same metabolic pathway that oxidizes glucose.

Many organisms, including humans, depend on nutrients other than glucose as a source of energy. In fact, you usually obtain more of your energy by oxidizing fatty acids than by oxidizing glucose. Amino acids derived from protein digestion are also used as fuel molecules. Such nutrients are transformed into one of the metabolic intermediates that are fed into glycolysis or the citric acid cycle (FIG. 8-13).

Amino acids are metabolized by reactions in which the amino group (—NH₂) is first removed, a process called **deamination.** In mammals and some other animals, the amino group is converted to urea (see Fig. 48-1 for the biochemical pathway) and excreted, but the carbon chain is metabolized and eventually is used as a reactant in one of the steps of aerobic respiration. The amino acid alanine, for example, undergoes deamination to become pyruvate, the amino acid glutamate is converted to α-ketoglutarate, and the amino acid aspartate yields oxaloacetate. Pyruvate enters aerobic respiration as the end product of glycolysis, and α-ketoglutarate and oxaloacetate both enter aerobic respiration as intermediates in the citric acid cycle. Ultimately, the carbon chains of all the amino acids are metabolized in this way.

FIGURE 8-13 *Animated* **Energy from proteins, carbohydrates, and fats**

Products of the catabolism of proteins, carbohydrates, and fats enter glycolysis or the citric acid cycle at various points. This diagram is greatly simplified and illustrates only a few of the principal catabolic pathways.

Each gram of lipid in the diet contains 9 kcal (38 kJ), more than twice as much energy as 1 g of glucose or amino acids, which have about 4 kcal (17 kJ) per gram. Lipids are rich in energy because they are highly reduced; that is, they have many hydrogen atoms and few oxygen atoms. When completely oxidized in aerobic respiration, a molecule of a six-carbon fatty acid generates up to 44 ATPs (compared with 36 to 38 ATPs for a molecule of glucose, which also has six carbons).

Both the glycerol and fatty acid components of a triacylglycerol (see Figure 3-12 for structures) are used as fuel; phosphate is added to glycerol, converting it to G3P or another compound that enters glycolysis. Fatty acids are oxidized and split enzymatically into two-carbon acetyl groups that are bound to coenzyme A; that is, fatty acids are converted to acetyl CoA. This process, which occurs in the mitochondrial matrix, is called **β-oxidation** (beta-oxidation). Acetyl CoA molecules formed by β-oxidation enter the citric acid cycle.

Review

- How can a person obtain energy from a low-carbohydrate diet?
- What process must occur before amino acids enter the aerobic respiratory pathway?
- Where do fatty acids enter the aerobic respiratory pathway?

8.4 ANAEROBIC RESPIRATION AND FERMENTATION

■ LEARNING OBJECTIVE

8 Compare and contrast anaerobic respiration and fermentation. Include the mechanism of ATP formation, the final electron acceptor, and the end products.

Anaerobic respiration, which does not use oxygen as the final electron acceptor, is performed by some prokaryotes that live in anaerobic environments, such as waterlogged soil, stagnant ponds, and animal intestines. As in aerobic respiration, electrons are transferred in anaerobic respiration from glucose to NADH; they then pass down an electron transport chain that is coupled to ATP synthesis by chemiosmosis. However, an inorganic substance such as nitrate (NO_3^-) or sulfate (SO_4^{2-}) replaces molecular oxygen as the terminal electron acceptor. The end products of this type of anaerobic respiration are carbon dioxide, one or more reduced inorganic substances, and ATP. The following equation summarizes one representative type of anaerobic respiration, which is part of the biogeochemical cycle known as the **nitrogen cycle** (discussed in Chapter 55).

$$C_6H_{12}O_6 + 12\ KNO_3 \longrightarrow$$
Potassium
nitrate

$$6\ CO_2 + 6\ H_2O + 12\ KNO_2 + \text{energy}$$
Potassium   (in the chemical
nitrite   bonds of ATP)

TABLE 8-2	A Comparison of Aerobic Respiration, Anaerobic Respiration, and Fermentation		
	Aerobic Respiration	Anaerobic Respiration	Fermentation
Immediate fate of electrons in NADH	Transferred to electron transport chain	Transferred to electron transport chain	Transferred to organic molecule
Terminal electron acceptor of electron transport chain	O_2	Inorganic substances such as NO_3^- or SO_4^{2-}	No electron transport chain
Reduced product(s) formed	Water	Relatively reduced inorganic substances	Relatively reduced organic compounds (commonly, alcohol or lactate)
Mechanism of ATP synthesis	Oxidative phosphorylation/chemiosmosis; also substrate-level phosphorylation	Oxidative phosphorylation/chemiosmosis; also substrate-level phosphorylation	Substrate-level phosphorylation only (during glycolysis)

Certain other bacteria, as well as some fungi, regularly use **fermentation,** an anaerobic pathway that does not involve an electron transport chain. During fermentation only two ATPs are formed per glucose (by substrate-level phosphorylation during glycolysis). One might expect that a cell that obtains energy from glycolysis would produce pyruvate, the end product of glycolysis. However, this cannot happen because every cell has a limited supply of NAD^+, and NAD^+ is required for glycolysis to continue. If virtually all NAD^+ becomes reduced to NADH during glycolysis, then glycolysis stops and no more ATP is produced.

In fermentation, NADH molecules transfer their hydrogen atoms to organic molecules, thus regenerating the NAD^+ needed to keep glycolysis going. The resulting relatively reduced organic molecules (commonly, alcohol or lactate) tend to be toxic to the cells and are essentially waste products.

TABLE 8-2 compares aerobic respiration, anaerobic respiration, and fermentation.

Alcohol fermentation and lactate fermentation are inefficient

Yeasts are **facultative anaerobes** that carry out aerobic respiration when oxygen is available but switch to **alcohol fermentation** when deprived of oxygen (**FIG. 8-14a**). These eukaryotic, unicellular fungi have enzymes that decarboxylate pyruvate, releasing carbon dioxide and forming a two-carbon compound called *acetaldehyde.* NADH produced during glycolysis transfers hydrogen atoms to acetaldehyde, reducing it to *ethyl alcohol* (**FIG. 8-14b**). Alcohol fermentation is the basis for the production of beer, wine, and other alcoholic beverages. Yeast cells are also used in baking to

KEY POINT Fermentation regenerates NAD^+ needed for glycosis.

(a) Yeast cells

(b) Alcohol fermentation

(c) Lactate fermentation

FIGURE 8-14 *Animated* **Fermentation**

(a) Light micrograph of live brewer's yeast (*Saccharomyces cerevisiae*). Yeast cells have mitochondria and carry on aerobic respiration when O_2 is present. In the absence of O_2, yeasts carry on alcohol fermentation. **(b, c)** Glycolysis is the first part of fermentation pathways. In alcohol fermentation **(b)**, CO_2 is split off, and the two-carbon compound ethyl alcohol is the end product. In lactate fermentation **(c)**, the final product is the three-carbon compound lactate. In both alcohol and lactate fermentation, there is a net gain of only two ATPs per molecule of glucose. Note that the NAD^+ used during glycolysis is regenerated during both alcohol fermentation and lactate fermentation.

produce the carbon dioxide that causes dough to rise; the alcohol evaporates during baking.

Certain fungi and bacteria perform **lactate (lactic acid) fermentation.** In this alternative pathway, NADH produced during glycolysis transfers hydrogen atoms to pyruvate, reducing it to *lactate* (**FIG. 8-14c**). The ability of some bacteria to produce lactate is exploited by humans, who use these bacteria to make yogurt and to ferment cabbage for sauerkraut.

Vertebrate muscle cells also produce lactate. Exercise can cause fatigue and muscle cramps possibly due to insufficient oxygen, the depletion of fuel molecules, and the accumulation of lactate during strenuous activity. This buildup of lactate occurs because muscle cells shift briefly to lactate fermentation if the amount of oxygen delivered to muscle cells is insufficient to support aerobic respiration. The shift is only temporary, however, and oxygen is required for sustained work. About 80% of the lactate is eventually exported to the liver, where it is used to regenerate more glucose for the muscle cells. The remaining 20% of the lactate is metabolized in muscle cells in the presence of oxygen. For this reason, you continue to breathe heavily after you have stopped exercising: the additional oxygen is needed to oxidize lactate, thereby restoring the muscle cells to their normal state.

Although humans use lactate fermentation to produce ATP for only a few minutes, a few animals can live without oxygen for much longer periods. The red-eared slider, a freshwater turtle, remains underwater for as long as two weeks. During this time, it is relatively inactive and therefore does not expend a great deal of energy. It relies on lactate fermentation for ATP production.

Both alcohol fermentation and lactate fermentation are highly inefficient because the fuel is only partially oxidized. Alcohol, the end product of fermentation by yeast cells, can be burned and is even used as automobile fuel; obviously, it contains a great deal of energy that the yeast cells cannot extract using anaerobic methods. Lactate, a three-carbon compound, contains even more energy than the two-carbon alcohol. In contrast, all available energy is removed during aerobic respiration because the fuel molecules become completely oxidized to CO_2. A net profit of only 2 ATPs is produced by the fermentation of one molecule of glucose, compared with up to 36 to 38 ATPs when oxygen is available.

The inefficiency of fermentation necessitates a large supply of fuel. To perform the same amount of work, a cell engaged in fermentation must consume up to 20 times as much glucose or other carbohydrate per second as a cell using aerobic respiration. For this reason, your skeletal muscle cells store large quantities of glucose in the form of glycogen, which enables them to metabolize anaerobically for short periods.

Review

- What is the fate of hydrogen atoms removed from glucose during glycolysis when oxygen is present in muscle cells? How does this compare to the fate of hydrogen atoms removed from glucose when the amount of available oxygen is insufficient to support aerobic respiration?
- Why is the ATP yield of fermentation only a tiny fraction of the yield from aerobic respiration?

■ SUMMARY: FOCUS ON LEARNING OBJECTIVES

8.1 (page 173)

1 Write a summary reaction for aerobic respiration that shows which reactant becomes oxidized and which becomes reduced.

$$C_6H_{12}O_6 + 6\ O_2 \xrightarrow{\quad\quad} 6\ CO_2 + 6\ H_2O + \text{energy}$$

(with Oxidation bracket over $C_6H_{12}O_6$ to $6\ CO_2$, and Reduction bracket from $6\ O_2$ to $6\ H_2O$)

- **Aerobic respiration** is a catabolic process in which a fuel molecule such as glucose is broken down to form carbon dioxide and water. It includes **redox reactions** that result in the transfer of electrons from glucose (which becomes **oxidized**) to oxygen (which becomes **reduced**).
- Energy released during aerobic respiration is used to produce up to 36 to 38 ATPs per molecule of glucose.

8.2 (page 173)

2 List and give a brief overview of the four stages of aerobic respiration.

- The chemical reactions of aerobic respiration occur in four stages: glycolysis, formation of acetyl CoA, the citric acid cycle, and the electron transport chain and chemiosmosis.
- During **glycolysis,** a molecule of glucose is degraded to two molecules of **pyruvate.** Two ATP molecules (net) are produced by **substrate-level phosphorylation** during glycolysis. Four hydrogen atoms are removed and used to produce two NADH.

CENGAGENOW⁻ See the process of glycolysis unfold by clicking on the figure in CengageNOW.

- During the formation of **acetyl CoA,** the two pyruvate molecules each lose a molecule of carbon dioxide, and the remaining acetyl groups each combine with **coenzyme A,** producing two molecules of acetyl CoA; one NADH is produced per pyruvate.
- Each acetyl CoA enters the **citric acid cycle** by combining with a four-carbon compound, **oxaloacetate,** to form **citrate,** a six-carbon compound. Two acetyl CoA molecules enter the cycle for every glucose molecule. For every two carbons that enter the cycle as part of an acetyl CoA molecule, two leave as carbon dioxide. For every acetyl CoA, hydrogen atoms are transferred to three NAD^+ and one FAD; only one ATP is produced by substrate-level phosphorylation.

CENGAGENOW⁻ Interact with the citric acid cycle by clicking on the figure in CengageNOW.

- Hydrogen atoms (or their electrons) removed from fuel molecules are transferred from one electron acceptor to another down an **electron transport chain** located in the mitochondrial inner membrane; ultimately, these electrons reduce molecular oxygen, forming water. In **oxidative phosphorylation,** the redox reactions in the electron transport chain are coupled to synthesis of ATP through the mechanism of **chemiosmosis.**

CENGAGENOW⁻ See the electron transport chain in action by clicking on the figure in CengageNOW.

3 Indicate where each stage of aerobic respiration takes place in a eukaryotic cell.

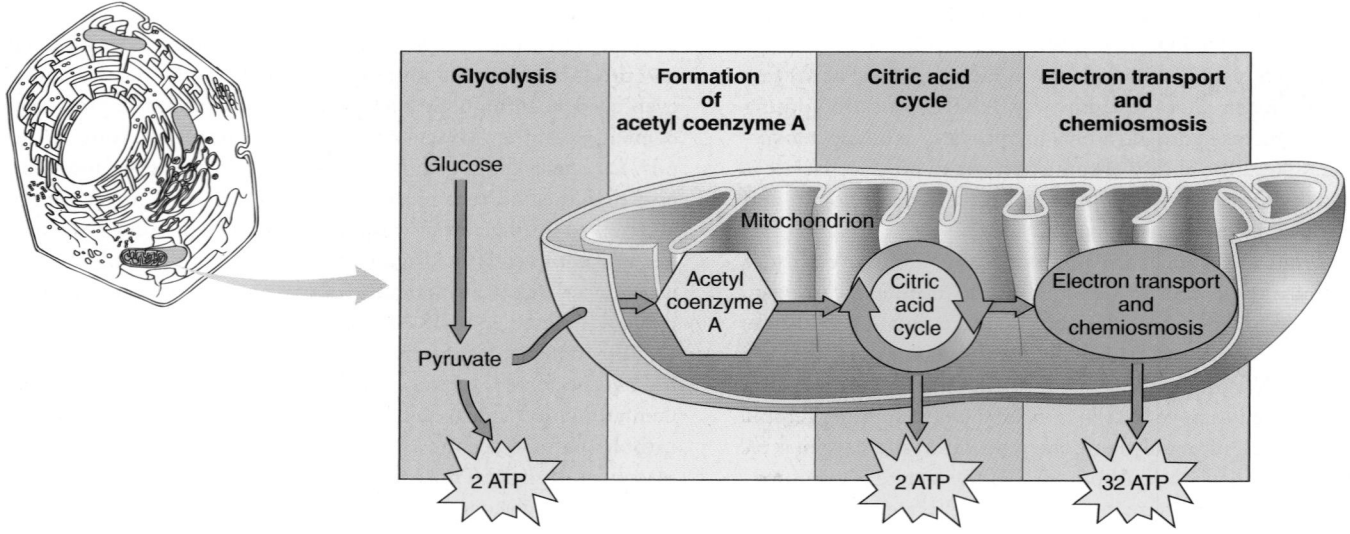

| Glycolysis | Formation of acetyl coenzyme A | Citric acid cycle | Electron transport and chemiosmosis |

Glucose

Mitochondrion

Acetyl coenzyme A

Citric acid cycle

Electron transport and chemiosmosis

Pyruvate

2 ATP

2 ATP

32 ATP

- Glycolysis occurs in the cytosol, and the remaining stages of aerobic respiration take place in the mitochondria.

4 Add up the energy captured (as ATP, NADH, and FADH$_2$) in each stage of aerobic respiration.

- In glycolysis, each glucose molecule produces 2 NADH and 2 ATPs (net). The conversion of 2 pyruvates to acetyl CoA results in the formation of 2 NADH. In the citric acid cycle, the 2 acetyl CoA molecules are metabolized to form 6 NADH, 2 FADH$_2$, and 2 ATPs. To summarize, we have 4 ATPs, 10 NADH, and 2 FADH$_2$.

- When electrons donated by the 10 NADH and 2 FADH$_2$ pass through the electron transport chain, 32 to 34 ATPs are produced by chemiosmosis. Therefore, each glucose molecule yields a total of up to 36 to 38 ATPs.

5 Define *chemiosmosis* and explain how a gradient of protons is established across the inner mitochondrial membrane.

- In chemiosmosis, some of the energy of the electrons in the electron transport chain is used to pump protons across the inner mitochondrial membrane into the intermembrane space. This pumping establishes a proton gradient across the inner mitochondrial membrane. Protons (H$^+$) accumulate within the intermembrane space, lowering the pH.

6 Describe the process by which the proton gradient drives ATP synthesis in chemiosmosis.

- The diffusion of protons through channels formed by the enzyme **ATP synthase,** which extends through the inner mitochondrial membrane from the intermembrane space to the mitochondrial matrix, provides the energy to synthesize ATP.

8.3 *(page 186)*

7 Summarize how the products of protein and lipid catabolism enter the same metabolic pathway that oxidizes glucose.

- Amino acids undergo **deamination,** and their carbon skeletons are converted to metabolic intermediates of aerobic respiration.

- Both the glycerol and fatty acid components of lipids are oxidized as fuel. Fatty acids are converted to acetyl CoA molecules by the process of *β***-oxidation.**

8.4 *(page 187)*

8 Compare and contrast anaerobic respiration and fermentation. Include the mechanism of ATP formation, the final electron acceptor, and the end products.

- In **anaerobic respiration,** electrons are transferred from fuel molecules to an electron transport chain that is coupled to ATP synthesis by chemiosmosis; the final electron acceptor is an inorganic substance such as nitrate or sulfate, not molecular oxygen.

- **Fermentation** is an anaerobic process that does not use an electron transport chain. There is a net gain of only two ATPs per glucose; these are produced by substrate-level phosphorylation during glycolysis. To maintain the supply of NAD$^+$ essential for glycolysis, hydrogen atoms are transferred from NADH to an organic compound derived from the initial nutrient.

- Yeast cells carry out **alcohol fermentation,** in which ethyl alcohol and carbon dioxide are the final waste products.

- Certain fungi, prokaryotes, and animal cells carry out **lactate (lactic acid) fermentation,** in which hydrogen atoms are added to pyruvate to form lactate, a waste product.

CENGAGENOW™ Learn more about fermentation by clicking on the figure in CengageNOW.

Summary Reactions for Aerobic Respiration

Summary reaction for the complete oxidation of glucose:

$$C_6H_{12}O_6 + 6\,O_2 + 6\,H_2O \longrightarrow 6\,CO_2 + 12\,H_2O + \text{energy (36 to 38 ATP)}$$

Summary reaction for glycolysis:

$$C_6H_{12}O_6 + 2\,ATP + 2\,ADP + 2\,P_i + 2\,NAD^+ \longrightarrow$$
$$2\,\text{pyruvate} + 4\,ATP + 2\,NADH + H_2O$$

Summary reaction for the conversion of pyruvate to acetyl CoA:

$$2\,\text{pyruvate} + 2\,\text{coenzyme A} + 2\,NAD^+ \longrightarrow$$
$$2\,\text{acetyl CoA} + 2\,CO_2 + 2\,NADH$$

Summary reaction for the citric acid cycle:

$$2\,\text{acetyl CoA} + 6\,NAD^+ + 2\,FAD + 2\,ADP + 2\,P_i + 2\,H_2O \longrightarrow$$
$$4\,CO_2 + 6\,NADH + 2\,FADH_2 + 2\,ATP + 2\,CoA$$

Summary reactions for the processing of the hydrogen atoms of NADH and $FADH_2$ in the electron transport chain:

$$NADH + 3\ ADP + 3\ P_i + \tfrac{1}{2}O_2 \longrightarrow NAD^+ + 3\ ATP + H_2O$$

$$FADH_2 + 2\ ADP + 2\ P_i + \tfrac{1}{2}O_2 \longrightarrow FAD^+ + 2\ ATP + H_2O$$

Summary Reactions for Fermentation

Summary reaction for lactate fermentation:

$$C_6H_{12}O_6 \longrightarrow 2\ \text{lactate} + \text{energy (2 ATP)}$$

Summary reaction for alcohol fermentation:

$$C_6H_{12}O_6 \longrightarrow 2\ CO_2 + 2\ \text{ethyl alcohol} + \text{energy (2 ATP)}$$

TEST YOUR UNDERSTANDING

1. A chemical process during which a substance gains electrons and energy is called (a) oxidation (b) oxidative phosphorylation (c) deamination (d) reduction (e) dehydrogenation

2. Which of the following is a correct ranking of molecules with respect to their energy value in glycolysis (*note:* > means "greater than")? (a) two pyruvates > one glucose (b) one glucose > one fructose-1,6-bisphosphate (c) two glyceraldehyde-3-phosphates (G3P) > one glucose (d) two pyruvates > one fructose-1,6-bisphosphate (e) two pyruvates > two glyceraldehyde-3-phosphates (G3P)

3. The reactions of _____ take place within the cytosol of eukaryotic cells. (a) glycolysis (b) oxidation of pyruvate (c) the citric acid cycle (d) chemiosmosis (e) the electron transport chain

4. Before pyruvate enters the citric acid cycle, it is decarboxylated, oxidized, and combined with coenzyme A, forming acetyl CoA, carbon dioxide, and one molecule of (a) NADH (b) $FADH_2$ (c) ATP (d) ADP (e) $C_6H_{12}O_6$

5. In the first step of the citric acid cycle, acetyl CoA reacts with oxaloacetate to form (a) pyruvate (b) citrate (c) NADH (d) ATP (e) CO_2

6. Which of the following is the major source of electrons that flow through the mitochondrial electron transport chain? (a) H_2O (b) ATP (c) NADH (d) ATP synthase (e) coenzyme A

7. The "aerobic" part of aerobic cellular respiration occurs during (a) glycolysis (b) the conversion of pyruvate to acetyl CoA (c) the citric acid cycle (d) electron transport (e) all of the above are aerobic processes

8. Substrate-level phosphorylation (a) occurs through a chemiosmotic mechanism (b) accounts for most of the ATP formed during aerobic cellular respiration (c) occurs during the conversion of pyruvate to acetyl CoA (d) occurs during glycolysis and the citric acid cycle (e) requires high energy electrons from NADH

9. Which of the following is a correct ranking of molecules, according to their energy value in oxidative phosphorylation (*note:* > means "greater than")? (a) ATP = NADH (b) NAD^+ > NADH (c) FAD > $FADH_2$ (d) NADH > ATP

10. A net profit of only 2 ATPs can be produced anaerobically from the _____ of one molecule of glucose, compared with a maximum of 38 ATPs produced in _____. (a) fermentation; anaerobic respiration (b) aerobic respiration; fermentation (c) aerobic respiration; anaerobic respiration (d) dehydrogenation; decarboxylation (e) fermentation; aerobic respiration

11. When deprived of oxygen, yeast cells obtain energy by fermentation, producing carbon dioxide, ATP, and (a) acetyl CoA (b) ethyl alcohol (c) lactate (d) pyruvate (e) citrate

12. Label the figure. Use Figure 8-10 to check your answers.

CRITICAL THINKING

1. How are the endergonic reactions of the first phase of glycolysis coupled to the hydrolysis of ATP, which is exergonic? How are the exergonic reactions of the second phase of glycolysis coupled to the endergonic synthesis of ATP and NADH?

2. In what ways is the inner mitochondrial membrane essential to the coupling of electron transport and ATP synthesis? Could the membrane carry out its function if its lipid bilayer were readily permeable to hydrogen ions (protons)?

3. Based on what you have learned in this chapter, explain why a schoolchild can run 17 miles per hour in a 100-yard dash, but a trained athlete can run only about 11.5 miles per hour in a 26-mile marathon.

4. When you lose weight, where does it go?

5. **EVOLUTION LINK.** The reactions of glycolysis are identical in *all* organisms—prokaryotes, protists, fungi, plants, and animals—that obtain energy from glucose catabolism. What does this universality suggest about the evolution of glycolysis?

6. **EVOLUTION LINK.** Molecular oxygen is so reactive that it would not exist in Earth's atmosphere today if it were not constantly replenished by organisms that release oxygen as a waste product of photosynthesis. What does that fact suggest about the evolution of aerobic respiration and oxygen-releasing photosynthetic processes?

 Additional questions are available in CengageNOW at www.cengage.com/login.

9 Photosynthesis: Capturing Light Energy

Photosynthesis. These trees use light energy to power the processes that incorporate CO_2 into organic molecules.

© tbkmedia.de/Alamy

Look at all the living things that surround you—the trees, your pet goldfish, your own body. Most of that biomass is made up of carbon-based biological molecules. What is the ultimate source of all that carbon? Surprising to some, the source is carbon dioxide from the air. Your cells cannot take carbon dioxide from the air and incorporate it into organic molecules—but some plant cells can. They do this through **photosynthesis,** the sequence of events by which light energy is converted into the stored chemical energy of organic molecules. Photosynthesis is the first step in the flow of energy through most of the living world, capturing the vast majority of the energy that living organisms use. Photosynthesis not only sustains plants (see photograph) and other photosynthetic organisms such as algae and photosynthetic bacteria but also indirectly supports most nonphotosynthetic organisms such as animals, fungi, protozoa, and most bacteria.

Each year photosynthetic organisms convert CO_2 into billions of tons of organic molecules. These molecules have two important roles in both photosynthetic and nonphotosynthetic organisms: they are both the building blocks of cells and, as we saw in Chapter 8, a source of chemical energy that fuels the metabolic reactions that sustain almost all life. Photosynthesis also releases O_2, which is essential to aerobic cellular respiration, the process by which plants, animals, and most other organisms convert this chemical energy to ATP to power cellular processes.

193

In this chapter we first examine how light energy is used in the synthesis of ATP and other molecules that temporarily hold chemical energy but are unstable and cannot be stockpiled in the cell. We then see how their energy powers the anabolic pathway by which a photosynthetic cell synthesizes stable organic molecules from the simple inorganic compounds CO_2 and water. Finally, we explore the role of photosynthesis in plants and in Earth's environment.

9.1 LIGHT AND PHOTOSYNTHESIS

■ LEARNING OBJECTIVE

1   Describe the physical properties of light and explain the relationship between a wavelength of light and its energy.

Because most life on this planet depends on light, either directly or indirectly, it is important to understand the nature of light and its essential role in photosynthesis. Visible light represents a very small portion of a vast, continuous range of radiation called the *electromagnetic spectrum* (**FIG. 9-1**). All radiation in this spectrum travels as waves. A **wavelength** is the distance from one wave peak to the next.

At one end of the electromagnetic spectrum are gamma rays, which have very short wavelengths measured in fractions of nanometers, or nm (1 nanometer equals 10^{-9} m, one-billionth of a meter). At the other end of the spectrum are radio waves, with wavelengths so long they can be measured in kilometers. The portion of the electromagnetic spectrum from 380 to 760 nm is called the *visible spectrum* because we humans can see it. The visible spectrum includes all the colors of the rainbow (**FIG. 9-2**); violet has the shortest wavelength, and red has the longest.

Light is composed of small particles, or packets, of energy called **photons.** The energy of a photon is inversely proportional to its wavelength: shorter-wavelength light has more energy per photon than longer-wavelength light.

Why does photosynthesis depend on light detectable by the human eye (visible light) rather than on some other wavelength of radiation? We can only speculate about the answer. Perhaps the reason is that radiation within the visible-light portion of the spectrum excites certain types of biological molecules, moving electrons into higher energy levels. Radiation with wavelengths longer than those of visible light does not have enough energy to excite these biological molecules. Radiation with wavelengths shorter than those of visible light is so energetic that it disrupts the bonds of many biological molecules. Thus, visible light has just the right amount of energy to cause the kinds of reversible changes in molecules that are useful in photosynthesis.

When a molecule absorbs a photon of light energy, one of its electrons becomes energized, which means that the electron shifts from a lower-energy atomic orbital to a high-energy orbital that is more distant from the atomic nucleus. One of two things then happens to the energized electron, depending on the atom and its

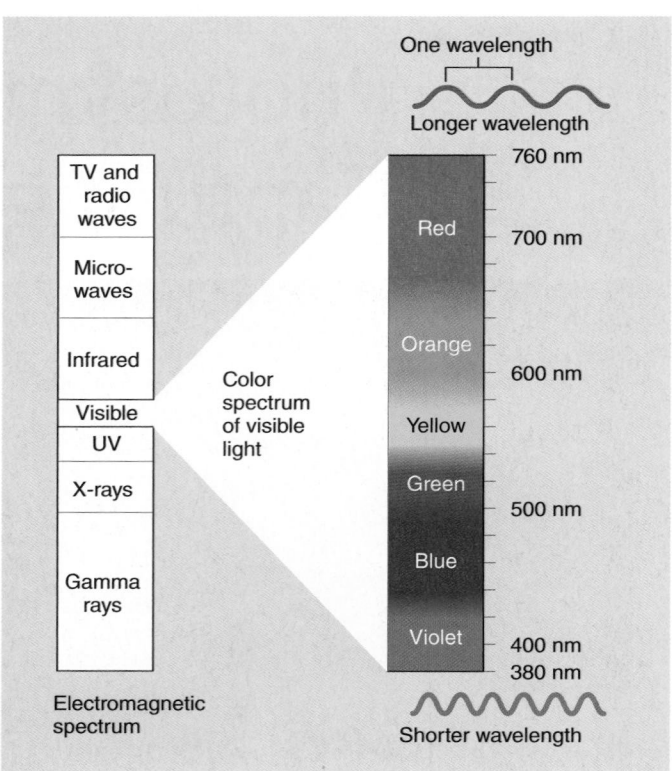

FIGURE 9-1 *Animated* **The electromagnetic spectrum**

Waves in the electromagnetic spectrum have similar properties but different wavelengths. Radio waves are the longest (and least energetic) waves, with wavelengths as long as 20 km. Gamma rays are the shortest (and most energetic) waves. Visible light represents a small fraction of the electromagnetic spectrum and consists of a mixture of wavelengths ranging from about 380 to 760 nm. The energy from visible light is used in photosynthesis.

surroundings (**FIG. 9-3**). The atom may return to its **ground state,** which is the condition in which all its electrons are in their normal, lowest-energy levels. When an electron returns to its ground state, its energy dissipates as heat or as an emission of light of a longer wavelength than the absorbed light; this emission of light is called **fluorescence.** Alternatively, the energized electron may leave the atom and be accepted by an electron acceptor molecule,

FIGURE 9-2 **Visible radiation emitted from the sun**

Electromagnetic radiation from the sun includes ultraviolet radiation and visible light of varying colors and wavelengths.

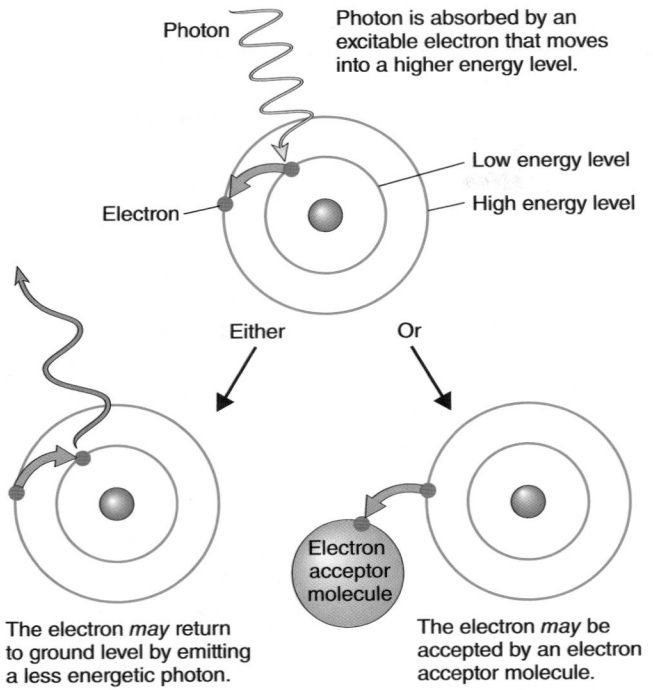

Photon

Photon is absorbed by an excitable electron that moves into a higher energy level.

Low energy level

High energy level

Electron

Either

Or

Electron acceptor molecule

The electron *may* return to ground level by emitting a less energetic photon.

The electron *may* be accepted by an electron acceptor molecule.

FIGURE 9-3 Interactions between light and atoms or molecules

(*Top*) When a photon of light energy strikes an atom or a molecule of which the atom is a part, the energy of the photon may push an electron to an orbital farther from the nucleus (that is, into a higher energy level). (*Lower left*) If the electron returns to the lower, more stable energy level, the energy may be released as a less energetic, longer-wavelength photon, known as fluorescence (*shown*), or as heat. (*Lower right*) If the appropriate electron acceptors are available, the electron may leave the atom. During photosynthesis, an electron acceptor captures the energetic electron and passes it to a chain of acceptors.

which becomes reduced in the process; this is what occurs in photosynthesis.

Now that you understand some of the properties of light, let us consider the organelles that use light for photosynthesis.

Review

- Why does photosynthesis require visible light?
- Which color of light has the longer wavelength, violet or red?
- Which color of light has the higher energy per photon, violet or red?

9.2 CHLOROPLASTS

■ LEARNING OBJECTIVES

2   Diagram the internal structure of a chloroplast and explain how its components interact and facilitate the process of photosynthesis.

3   Describe what happens to an electron in a biological molecule such as chlorophyll when a photon of light energy is absorbed.

If you examine a section of leaf tissue in a microscope, you see that the green pigment, chlorophyll, is not uniformly distributed in the cell but is confined to organelles called chloroplasts. In plants, **chloroplasts** lie mainly inside the leaf in the cells of the **mesophyll,** a layer with many air spaces and a very high concentration of water vapor (**FIG. 9-4a**). The interior of the leaf exchanges gases with the outside through microscopic pores, called **stomata** (sing., *stoma*). Each mesophyll cell has 20 to 100 chloroplasts.

The chloroplast, like the mitochondrion, is enclosed by outer and inner membranes (**FIG. 9-4b**). The inner membrane encloses a fluid-filled region called the **stroma,** which contains most of the enzymes required to produce carbohydrate molecules. Suspended in the stroma is a third system of membranes that forms an interconnected set of flat, disclike sacs called **thylakoids.**

The thylakoid membrane encloses a fluid-filled interior space, the **thylakoid lumen.** In some regions of the chloroplast, thylakoid sacs are arranged in stacks called **grana** (sing., *granum*). Each granum looks something like a stack of coins, with each "coin" being a thylakoid. Some thylakoid membranes extend from one granum to another. Thylakoid membranes, like the inner mitochondrial membrane (see Chapter 8), are involved in ATP synthesis. (Photosynthetic prokaryotes have no chloroplasts, but thylakoid membranes are often arranged around the periphery of the cell as infoldings of the plasma membrane.)

Chlorophyll is found in the thylakoid membrane

Thylakoid membranes contain several kinds of *pigments,* which are substances that absorb visible light. Different pigments absorb light of different wavelengths. **Chlorophyll,** the main pigment of photosynthesis, absorbs light primarily in the blue and red regions of the visible spectrum. Green light is not appreciably absorbed by chlorophyll. Plants usually appear green because some of the green light that strikes them is scattered or reflected.

A chlorophyll molecule has two main parts, a complex ring and a long side chain (**FIG. 9-5**). The ring structure, called a *porphyrin ring,* is made up of joined smaller rings composed of carbon and nitrogen atoms; the porphyrin ring absorbs light energy. The porphyrin ring of chlorophyll is strikingly similar to the heme portion of the red pigment hemoglobin in red blood cells. However, unlike heme, which contains an atom of iron in the center of the ring, chlorophyll contains an atom of magnesium in that position. The chlorophyll molecule also contains a long, hydrocarbon side chain that makes the molecule extremely nonpolar and anchors the chlorophyll in the membrane.

All chlorophyll molecules in the thylakoid membrane are associated with specific *chlorophyll-binding proteins;* biologists have identified about 15 different kinds. Each thylakoid membrane is filled with precisely oriented chlorophyll molecules and chlorophyll-binding proteins that facilitate the transfer of energy from one molecule to another.

There are several kinds of chlorophyll. The most important is **chlorophyll *a*,** the pigment that initiates the light-dependent reactions of photosynthesis. **Chlorophyll *b*** is an accessory pigment that also participates in photosynthesis. It differs from chlorophyll *a* only in a functional group on the porphyrin ring: the methyl group (—CH_3) in chlorophyll *a* is replaced in chlorophyll *b* by a terminal carbonyl group (—CHO). This difference shifts the wavelengths of light absorbed and reflected by chlorophyll *b*, making it appear yellow-green, whereas chlorophyll *a* appears bright green.

Chloroplasts have other accessory photosynthetic pigments, such as **carotenoids,** which are yellow and orange (see Fig. 3-14). Carotenoids absorb different wavelengths of light than chlorophyll, thereby expanding the spectrum of light that provides energy for photosynthesis. Chlorophyll may be excited by light directly by energy passed to it from the light source, or indirectly by energy passed to it from accessory pigments that have become excited by light. When a carotenoid molecule is excited, its energy can be transferred to chlorophyll *a*. In addition, carotenoids are antioxidants that inactivate highly reactive forms of oxygen generated in the chloroplasts.

Chlorophyll is the main photosynthetic pigment

As you have seen, the thylakoid membrane contains more than one kind of pigment. An instrument called a *spectrophotometer* measures the relative abilities of different pigments to absorb different wavelengths of light. The **absorption spectrum** of a pigment is a plot of its absorption of light of different wavelengths. **FIGURE 9-6a** shows the absorption spectra for chlorophylls *a* and *b*.

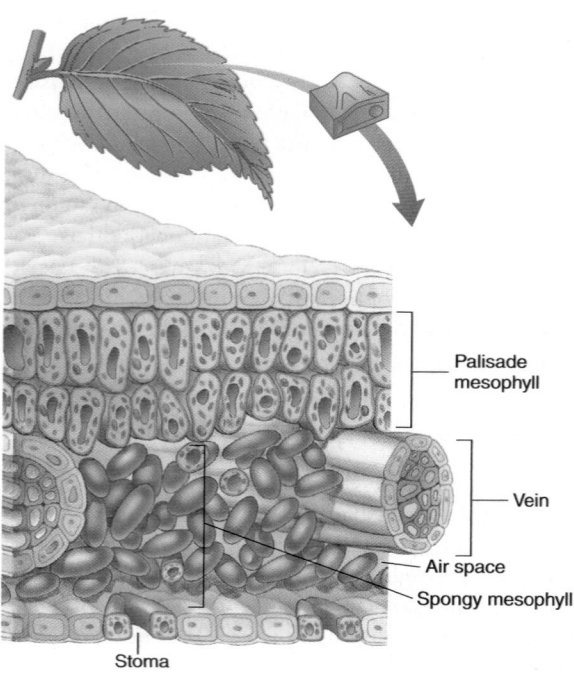

(a) This leaf cross section reveals that the mesophyll is the photosynthetic tissue. CO_2 enters the leaf through tiny pores or stomata, and H_2O is carried to the mesophyll in veins.

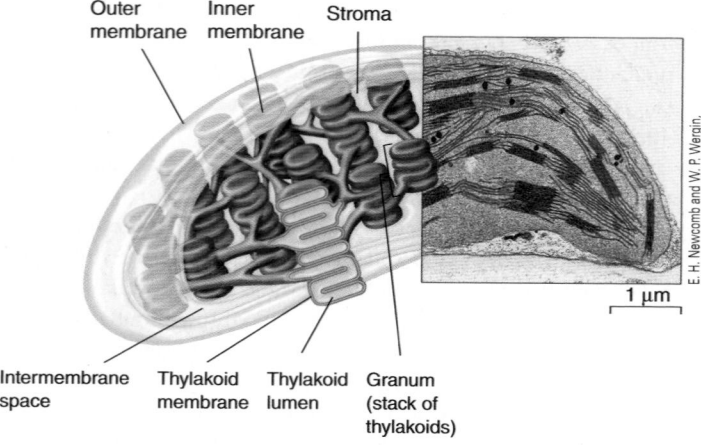

(b) In the chloroplast, pigments necessary for the light-capturing reactions of photosynthesis are part of thylakoid membranes, whereas the enzymes for the synthesis of carbohydrate molecules are in the stroma.

FIGURE 9-4 *Animated* **The site of photosynthesis**

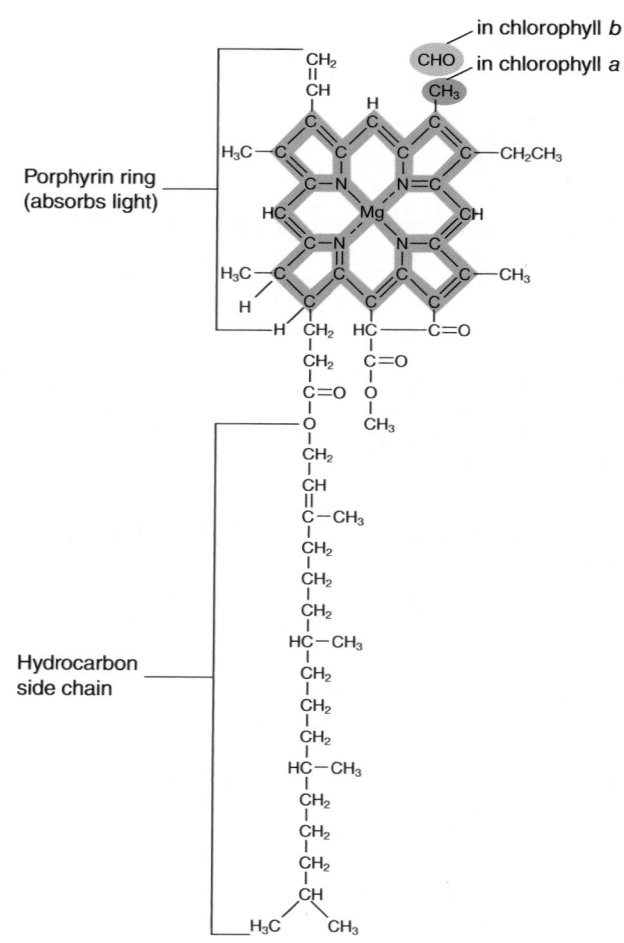

FIGURE 9-5 **The structure of chlorophyll**
Chlorophyll consists of a porphyrin ring and a hydrocarbon side chain. The porphyrin ring, with a magnesium atom in its center, contains a system of alternating double and single bonds; these are commonly found in molecules that strongly absorb certain wavelengths of visible light and reflect others (chlorophyll reflects green). Notice that at the top right corner of the diagram, the methyl group (—CH₃) distinguishes chlorophyll *a* from chlorophyll *b*, which has a carbonyl group (—CHO) in this position. The hydrophobic hydrocarbon side chain anchors chlorophyll to the thylakoid membrane.

An **action spectrum** of photosynthesis is a graph of the relative effectiveness of different wavelengths of light. To obtain an action spectrum, scientists measure the rate of photosynthesis at each wavelength for leaf cells or tissues exposed to monochromatic light (light of one wavelength) (**FIG. 9-6b**).

In a classic biology experiment, the German biologist T. W. Engelmann obtained the first action spectrum in 1883. Engelmann's experiment, described in **FIGURE 9-7**, took advantage of the shape of the chloroplast in a species of the green alga *Spirogyra*. Its long, filamentous strands are found in freshwater habitats, especially slow-moving or still waters. *Spirogyra* cells each contain a long, spiral-shaped, emerald-green chloroplast embedded in the cyto-

plasm. Engelmann exposed these cells to a color spectrum produced by passing light through a prism. He hypothesized that if chlorophyll were indeed responsible for photosynthesis, the process would take place most rapidly in the areas where the chloroplast was illuminated by the colors most strongly absorbed by chlorophyll.

(a) Chlorophylls *a* and *b* absorb light mainly in the blue (422 to 492 nm) and red (647 to 760 nm) regions.

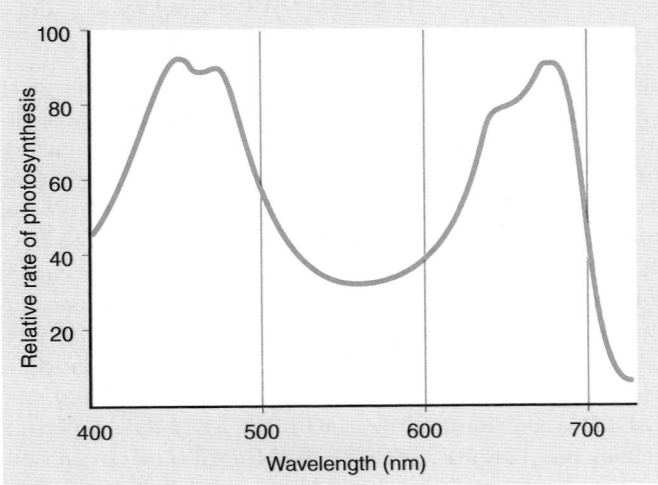

(b) The action spectrum of photosynthesis indicates the effectiveness of various wavelengths of light in powering photosynthesis. Many plant species have action spectra for photosynthesis that resemble the generalized action spectrum shown here.

FIGURE 9-6 A comparison of the absorption spectra for chlorophylls *a* and *b* with the action spectrum for photosynthesis

KEY EXPERIMENT

QUESTION: Is a pigment in the chloroplast responsible for photosynthesis?

HYPOTHESIS: Engelmann hypothesized that chlorophyll was the main photosynthetic pigment. Accordingly, he predicted that he would observe differences in the amount of photosynthesis, as measured by the amount of oxygen produced, depending on the wavelengths of light used, and that these wavelengths would be consistent with the known absorption spectrum of chlorophyll.

EXPERIMENT: The photograph (a) shows cells of the filamentous alga *Spirogyra*, which has a long spiral-shaped chloroplast. The drawing (b) shows how Engelmann used a prism to expose the cells to light that had been separated into various wavelengths. He estimated the formation of oxygen (which he knew was a product of photosynthesis) by exploiting the fact that certain aerobic bacteria would be attracted to the oxygen. As a control (*not shown*), he also exposed the bacteria to the spectrum of light in the absence of *Spirogyra* cells.

RESULTS AND CONCLUSION: Although the bacteria alone (*control*) showed no preference for any particular wavelength, large numbers were attracted to the photosynthesizing cells in red or blue light, wavelengths that are strongly absorbed by chlorophyll (see Fig. 9-6). Thus, Engelmann concluded that chlorophyll is responsible for photosynthesis.

FIGURE 9-7 *Animated* The first action spectrum of photosynthesis

Yet how could photosynthesis be measured in those technologically unsophisticated days? Engelmann knew that photosynthesis produces oxygen and that certain motile bacteria are attracted to areas of high oxygen concentration. He determined the action spectrum of photosynthesis by observing that the bacteria swam toward the parts of the *Spirogyra* filaments in the blue and red regions of the spectrum. How did Engelmann know bacteria were not simply attracted to blue or red light? Engelmann exposed bacteria to the spectrum of visible light in the absence of *Spirogyra* as a control. The bacteria showed no preference for any particular wavelength of light. Because the action spectrum of photosynthesis closely matched the absorption spectrum of chlorophyll, Engelmann concluded that chlorophyll in the chloroplasts (and not another compound in another organelle) is responsible for photosynthesis. Numerous studies using sophisticated instruments have since confirmed Engelmann's conclusions.

If you examine Figure 9-6 closely, you will observe that the action spectrum of photosynthesis does not parallel the absorption spectrum of chlorophyll exactly. This difference occurs because accessory pigments, such as carotenoids, transfer some of the energy of excitation produced by green light to chlorophyll molecules. The presence of these accessory photosynthetic pigments can be demonstrated by chemical analysis of almost any leaf, although it is obvious in temperate climates when leaves change color in the fall. Toward the end of the growing season, chlorophyll breaks down (and its magnesium is stored in the permanent tissues of the tree), leaving orange and yellow accessory pigments in the leaves.

Review

- What chloroplast membrane is most important in photosynthesis? What two compartments does it separate?
- What is the significance of the fact that the combined absorption spectra of chlorophylls *a* and *b* roughly match the action spectrum of photosynthesis? Why do they not coincide exactly?
- Does fluorescence play a role in photosynthesis?

9.3 OVERVIEW OF PHOTOSYNTHESIS

LEARNING OBJECTIVES

4 Describe photosynthesis as a redox process.
5 Distinguish between the light-dependent reactions and carbon fixation reactions of photosynthesis.

During photosynthesis, a cell uses light energy captured by chlorophyll to power the synthesis of carbohydrates. The overall reaction of photosynthesis can be summarized as follows:

$$6\ CO_2 + 12\ H_2O \xrightarrow[\text{Chlorophyll}]{\text{Light energy}} C_6H_{12}O_6 + 6\ O_2 + 6\ H_2O$$

Carbon dioxide   Water   Glucose   Oxygen   Water

The equation is typically written in the form just given, with H_2O on both sides, because water is a reactant in some reactions and a product in others. Furthermore, all the oxygen produced comes from water, so 12 water molecules are required to produce 12 oxygen atoms. However, because there is no net yield of H_2O, we can simplify the summary equation of photosynthesis for purposes of discussion:

$$6\ CO_2 + 6\ H_2O \xrightarrow[\text{Chlorophyll}]{\text{Light}} C_6H_{12}O_6 + 6\ O_2$$

When you analyze this process, it appears that hydrogen atoms are transferred from H_2O to CO_2 to form carbohydrate, so you can recognize it as a redox reaction. Recall from Chapter 7 that in a redox reaction one or more electrons, usually as part of one or more hydrogen atoms, are transferred from an electron donor (a reducing agent) to an electron acceptor (an oxidizing agent).

$$6\ CO_2 + 6\ H_2O \xrightarrow[\text{Chlorophyll}]{\text{Light}} C_6H_{12}O_6 + 6\ O_2$$

(diagram: Reduction arrow from $6\ CO_2$ to $C_6H_{12}O_6$; Oxidation arrow from $6\ H_2O$ to $6\ O_2$)

When the electrons are transferred, some of their energy is transferred as well. However, the summary equation of photosynthesis is somewhat misleading because no direct transfer of hydrogen atoms actually occurs. The summary equation describes *what* happens but not *how* it happens. The *how* is more complex and involves multiple steps, many of which are redox reactions.

The reactions of photosynthesis are divided into two phases: the light-dependent reactions (the *photo* part of photosynthesis) and the carbon fixation reactions (the *synthesis* part of photosynthesis). Each set of reactions occurs in a different part of the chloroplast: the light-dependent reactions in association with the thylakoids, and the carbon fixation reactions in the stroma (**FIG. 9-8**).

ATP and NADPH are the products of the light-dependent reactions: An overview

Light energy is converted to chemical energy in the **light-dependent reactions,** which are associated with the thylakoids. The light-dependent reactions begin as chlorophyll captures light energy, which causes one of its electrons to move to a higher energy state. The energized electron is transferred to an acceptor molecule and is replaced by an electron from H_2O. When this happens, H_2O is split and molecular oxygen is released (**FIG. 9-9**). Some energy of the energized electrons is used to phosphorylate **adenosine diphosphate (ADP),** forming **adenosine triphosphate (ATP).** In addition, the coenzyme **nicotinamide adenine dinucleotide phosphate (NADP⁺)** becomes reduced, forming **NADPH.**[1] NADPH is a hydrogen carrier similar to NADH, differing by the addition of a phosphate group. Unlike NADH, which is generally associated with catabolic pathways like aerobic cellular respiration, NADPH has the ability to provide high-energy electrons to power

---

[1]Although the correct way to write the reduced form of NADP⁺ is NADPH + H⁺, for simplicity's sake we present the reduced form as NADPH throughout the book.

KEY POINT The light-dependent reactions in the thylakoids capture energy as ATP and NADPH, which power the carbon fixation reactions in the stroma.

FIGURE 9-8 *Animated* An overview of photosynthesis

certain reactions in anabolic pathways, such as the carbon fixation reactions of photosynthesis. Thus, the products of the light-dependent reactions, ATP and NADPH, are both needed in the energy-requiring carbon fixation reactions.

Carbohydrates are produced during the carbon fixation reactions: An overview

The ATP and NADPH molecules produced during the light-dependent phase are suited for transferring chemical energy but not for long-term energy storage. For this reason, some of their energy is transferred to chemical bonds in carbohydrates, which can be produced in large quantities and stored for future use. Known

as **carbon fixation,** these reactions "fix" carbon atoms from CO_2 to existing skeletons of organic molecules. Because the carbon fixation reactions have no direct requirement for light, they were previously referred to as the "dark" reactions. However, they do not require darkness; in fact, many of the enzymes involved in carbon fixation are much more active in the light than in the dark. Furthermore, carbon fixation reactions depend on the products of the light-dependent reactions. Carbon fixation reactions take place in the stroma of the chloroplast.

Now that we have presented an overview of photosynthesis, let us examine the entire process more closely.

Review

- Which is more oxidized, oxygen that is part of a water molecule or molecular oxygen?
- In what ways do the carbon fixation reactions depend on the light-dependent reactions?

FIGURE 9-9 Oxygen produced by photosynthesis
On sunny days, the oxygen released by aquatic plants is sometimes visible as bubbles in the water. This plant (*Elodea*) is actively carrying on photosynthesis.

Bernard Wittich/Visuals Unlimited

9.4 THE LIGHT-DEPENDENT REACTIONS

LEARNING OBJECTIVES

6 Describe the flow of electrons through photosystems I and II in the noncyclic electron transport pathway and the products produced. Contrast this with cyclic electron transport.

7 Explain how a proton (H^+) gradient is established across the thylakoid membrane and how this gradient functions in ATP synthesis.

In the light-dependent reactions, the radiant energy from sunlight phosphorylates ADP, producing ATP, and reduces $NADP^+$, forming NADPH. The light energy that chlorophyll captures is temporarily stored in these two compounds. The light-dependent reactions are summarized as follows:

$$12\,H_2O + 12\,NADP^+ + 18\,ADP + 18\,P_i \xrightarrow[\text{Chlorophyll}]{\text{Light}} 6\,O_2 + 12\,NADPH + 18\,ATP$$

Photosystems I and II each consist of a reaction center and multiple antenna complexes

The light-dependent reactions of photosynthesis begin when chlorophyll *a* and/or accessory pigments absorb light. According to the currently accepted model, chlorophylls *a* and *b* and accessory pigment molecules are organized with pigment-binding proteins in the thylakoid membrane into units called **antenna complexes.** The pigments and associated proteins are arranged as highly ordered groups of about 250 chlorophyll molecules associated with specific enzymes and other proteins. Each antenna complex absorbs light energy and transfers it to the **reaction center,** which consists of chlorophyll molecules and proteins, including electron transfer components, that participate directly in photosynthesis (**FIG. 9-10**). Light energy is converted to chemical energy in the reaction centers by a series of electron transfer reactions.

Two types of photosynthetic units, designated photosystem I and photosystem II, are involved in photosynthesis. Their reaction centers are distinguishable because they are associated with proteins in a way that causes a slight shift in their absorption spectra. Ordinary chlorophyll *a* has a strong absorption peak at about 660

FIGURE 9-10 *Animated* **Schematic view of a photosystem**
Chlorophyll molecules (*green circles*) and accessory pigments (*not shown*) are arranged in light-harvesting arrays, or antenna complexes. A portion of one such complex within a photosystem is depicted. Each complex consists of several hundred pigment molecules, in association with special proteins (*not shown*). These proteins hold the pigments in a highly ordered spatial array, such that when a molecule in an antenna complex absorbs a photon, energy derived from that photon is readily passed from one pigment molecule to another (*black arrow*). When this energy reaches one of the two chlorophyll molecules in the reaction center (*green diamonds*), an electron becomes energized and is accepted by a primary electron acceptor.

nm. In contrast, the reaction center of **photosystem I** consists of a pair of chlorophyll *a* molecules with an absorption peak at 700 nm and is referred to as **P700.** The reaction center of **photosystem II** is made up of a pair of chlorophyll *a* molecules with an absorption peak of about 680 nm and is referred to as **P680.**

When a pigment molecule absorbs light energy, that energy is passed, through a process known as *resonance,* directly from one pigment molecule to another within the antenna complex until it reaches the reaction center. When the energy reaches a molecule of P700 (in a photosystem I reaction center) or P680 (in a photosystem II reaction center), an electron is then raised to a higher energy level. As we explain in the next section, this energized electron can be donated to an electron acceptor that becomes reduced in the process.

Noncyclic electron transport produces ATP and NADPH

Let us begin our discussion of **noncyclic electron transport** with the events associated with photosystem I (**FIG. 9-11**). A pigment molecule in an antenna complex associated with photosystem I absorbs a photon of light. The absorbed energy is transferred from one pigment molecule to another until it reaches the reaction center, where it excites an electron in a molecule of P700. This energized electron is transferred to a primary electron acceptor, a special molecule of chlorophyll *a,* which is the first of several electron acceptors in a series. The energized electron is passed along an **electron transport chain** from one electron acceptor to another, until it is passed to *ferredoxin,* an iron-containing protein. Ferredoxin transfers the electron to $NADP^+$ in the presence of the enzyme *ferredoxin–NADP$^+$ reductase.*

When $NADP^+$ accepts two electrons, they unite with a proton (H^+); thus, the reduced form of $NADP^+$ is NADPH, which is released into the stroma. P700 becomes positively charged when it gives up an electron to the primary electron acceptor; the missing electron is replaced by one donated by photosystem II.

As in photosystem I, photosystem II becomes activated when a pigment molecule in an antenna complex absorbs a photon of light energy. The energy is transferred to the reaction center, where it causes an electron in a molecule of P680 to move to a higher energy level. This energized electron is accepted by a primary electron acceptor (a highly modified chlorophyll molecule known as *pheophytin*) and then passes along an electron transport chain until it is donated to P700 in photosystem I.

How is the electron that has been donated to the electron transport chain replaced? This occurs through **photolysis** (light splitting) of water, a process that not only yields electrons but also is the source of almost all the oxygen in Earth's atmosphere. A molecule of P680 that has given up an energized electron to the primary electron acceptor is positively charged ($P680^+$). $P680^+$ is an oxidizing agent so strong that it pulls electrons away from an oxygen atom that is part of an H_2O molecule. In a reaction catalyzed by a unique, manganese-containing enzyme, water is broken into its components: two electrons, two protons, and oxygen. Each electron is donated to a P680 molecule, which then loses its positive charge; the protons are released into the thylakoid lumen. Because oxygen does not exist in atomic form, the oxygen produced

Noncyclic electron transport converts light energy to chemical energy in ATP and NADPH.

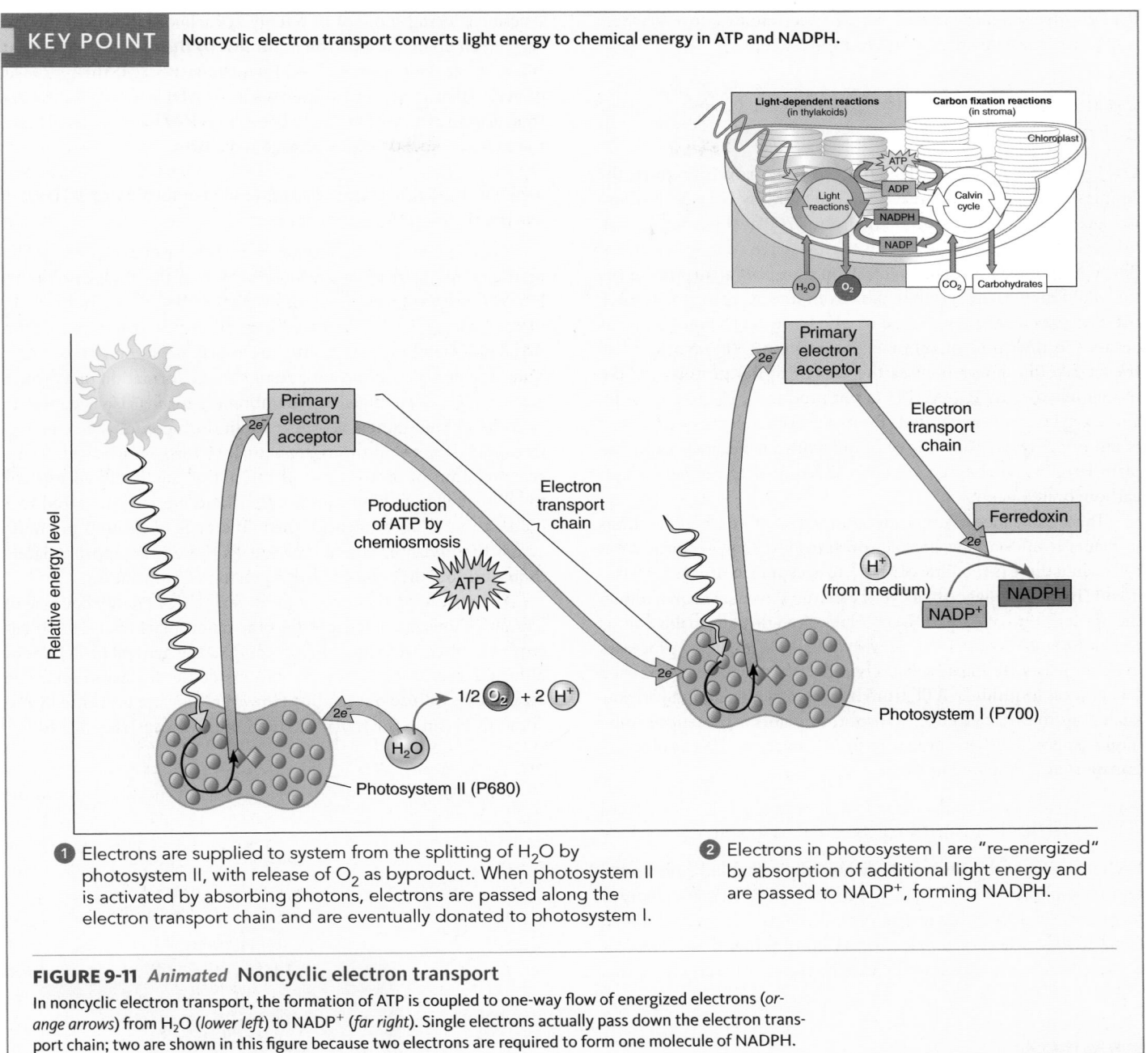

① Electrons are supplied to system from the splitting of H_2O by photosystem II, with release of O_2 as byproduct. When photosystem II is activated by absorbing photons, electrons are passed along the electron transport chain and are eventually donated to photosystem I.

② Electrons in photosystem I are "re-energized" by absorption of additional light energy and are passed to $NADP^+$, forming NADPH.

FIGURE 9-11 *Animated* **Noncyclic electron transport**

In noncyclic electron transport, the formation of ATP is coupled to one-way flow of energized electrons (*orange arrows*) from H_2O (*lower left*) to $NADP^+$ (*far right*). Single electrons actually pass down the electron transport chain; two are shown in this figure because two electrons are required to form one molecule of NADPH.

by splitting one H_2O molecule is written $\frac{1}{2} O_2$. Two water molecules must be split to yield one oxygen molecule. The photolysis of water is a remarkable reaction, but its name is somewhat misleading because it implies that water is broken by light. Actually, light splits water indirectly by causing P680 to become oxidized.

Noncyclic electron transport is a continuous linear process

In the presence of light, there is a continuous, one-way flow of electrons from the ultimate electron source, H_2O, to the terminal electron acceptor, $NADP^+$. Water undergoes enzymatically catalyzed photolysis to replace energized electrons donated to the electron

transport chain by molecules of P680 in photosystem II. These electrons travel down the electron transport chain that connects photosystem II with photosystem I. Thus, they provide a continuous supply of replacements for energized electrons that have been given up by P700.

As electrons are transferred along the electron transport chain that connects photosystem II with photosystem I, they lose energy. Some of the energy released is used to pump protons across the thylakoid membrane, from the stroma to the thylakoid lumen, producing a proton gradient. The energy of this proton gradient is harnessed to produce ATP from ADP by *chemiosmosis,* which we discuss later in the chapter. ATP and NADPH, the products of the light-dependent reactions, are released into the stroma, where both are required by the carbon fixation reactions.

Cyclic electron transport produces ATP but no NADPH

Only photosystem I is involved in **cyclic electron transport,** the simplest light-dependent reaction. The pathway is cyclic because energized electrons that originate from P700 at the reaction center eventually return to P700. In the presence of light, electrons flow continuously through an electron transport chain within the thylakoid membrane. As they pass from one acceptor to another, the electrons lose energy, some of which is used to pump protons across the thylakoid membrane. An enzyme (ATP synthase) in the thylakoid membrane uses the energy of the proton gradient to manufacture ATP. NADPH is not produced, H_2O is not split, and oxygen is not generated. By itself, cyclic electron transport could not serve as the basis of photosynthesis because, as we explain later in the chapter, NADPH is required to reduce CO_2 to carbohydrate.

The significance of cyclic electron transport to photosynthesis in plants is unclear. Cyclic electron transport may occur in plant cells when there is too little $NADP^+$ to accept electrons from ferredoxin. There is evidence that cyclic electron flow may help maintain the optimal ratio of ATP to NADPH required for carbon fixation, as well as provide extra ATP to power other ATP-requiring processes in chloroplasts. Biologists generally agree that ancient bacteria used this process to produce ATP from light energy. A reaction pathway analogous to cyclic electron transport in plants is present in some modern photosynthetic prokaryotes. Noncyclic and cyclic electron transport are compared in **TABLE 9-1.**

ATP synthesis occurs by chemiosmosis

Each member of the electron transport chain that links photosystem II to photosystem I can exist in an oxidized (lower-energy) form and a reduced (higher-energy) form. The electron accepted from P680 by the primary electron acceptor is highly energized; it is passed from one carrier to the next in a series of exergonic redox

reactions, losing some of its energy at each step. Some of the energy given up by the electron is not lost by the system, however; it is used to provide energy for ATP synthesis. Because the synthesis of ATP (that is, the phosphorylation of ADP) is coupled to the transport of electrons that have been energized by photons of light, the process is called **photophosphorylation.**

The chemiosmotic model explains the coupling of ATP synthesis and electron transport

As discussed earlier, the pigments and electron acceptors of the light-dependent reactions are embedded in the thylakoid membrane. Energy released from electrons traveling through the chain of acceptors is used to pump protons from the stroma, across the thylakoid membrane, and into the thylakoid lumen (**FIG. 9-12**). Thus, the pumping of protons results in the formation of a proton gradient across the thylakoid membrane. Protons also accumulate in the thylakoid lumen as water is split during noncyclic electron transport. Because protons are actually hydrogen ions (H^+), the accumulation of protons causes the pH of the thylakoid interior to fall to a pH of about 5 in the thylakoid lumen, compared to a pH of about 8 in the stroma. This difference of about 3 pH units across the thylakoid membrane means there is an approximately thousand-fold difference in hydrogen ion concentration.

The proton gradient has a great deal of free energy because of its state of low entropy. How does the chloroplast convert that energy to a more useful form? According to the general principles of diffusion, the concentrated protons inside the thylakoid might be expected to diffuse out readily. However, they are prevented from doing so because the thylakoid membrane is impermeable to H^+

	Noncyclic Electron Transport	Cyclic Electron Transport
Electron source	H_2O	None—electrons cycle through the system
Oxygen released?	Yes (from H_2O)	No
Terminal electron acceptor	$NADP^+$	None—electrons cycle through the system
Form in which energy is temporarily captured	ATP (by chemiosmosis); NADPH	ATP (by chemiosmosis)
Photosystem(s) required	PS I (P700) and PS II (P680)	PS I (P700) only

TABLE 9-1 A Comparison of Noncyclic and Cyclic Electron Transport

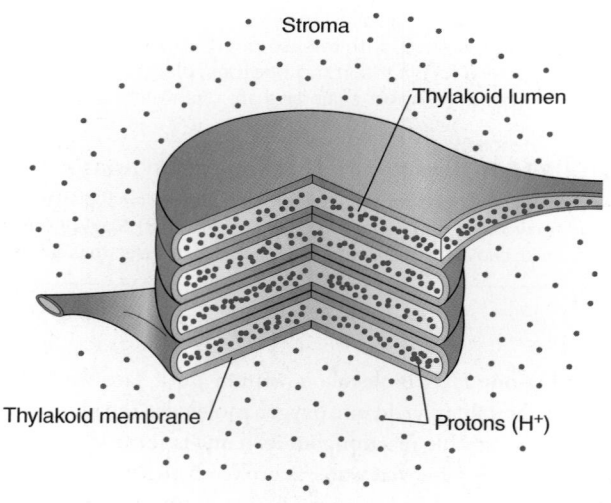

FIGURE 9-12 The accumulation of protons in the thylakoid lumen

As electrons move down the electron transport chain, protons (H^+) move from the stroma to the thylakoid lumen, creating a proton gradient. The greater concentration of H^+ in the thylakoid lumen lowers the pH.

except through certain channels formed by the enzyme **ATP synthase.** This enzyme, a transmembrane protein also found in mitochondria, forms complexes so large they can be seen in electron micrographs (see Fig. 8-11b). ATP synthase complexes project into the stroma. As the protons diffuse through an ATP synthase complex, free energy decreases as a consequence of an increase in entropy. Each ATP synthase complex couples this exergonic process of diffusion down a concentration gradient to the endergonic process of phosphorylation of ADP to form ATP, which is released

into the stroma (**FIG. 9-13**). The movement of protons through ATP synthase is thought to induce changes in the conformation of the enzyme that are necessary for the synthesis of ATP. It is estimated that for every four protons that move through ATP synthase, one ATP molecule is synthesized.

The mechanism by which the phosphorylation of ADP is coupled to diffusion down a proton gradient is called **chemiosmosis.** As the essential connection between the electron transport chain and the phosphorylation of ADP, chemiosmosis is a basic

KEY POINT Electron carriers associated with the thylakoid membrane transfer energized electrons from water to NADP⁺, forming NADPH. ATP is generated by chemiosmosis.

❶ Orange arrows indicate pathway of electrons along electron transport chain in thylakoid membrane. Electron carriers within membrane become alternately reduced and oxidized as they accept and donate electrons.

❷ Energy released during electron transport is used to transport H^+ from the stroma to the thylakoid lumen, where a high concentration of H^+ accumulates.

❸ H^+ are prevented from diffusing back into stroma except through special channels in ATP synthase in the thylakoid membrane.

❹ H^+ flows through ATP synthase, generating ATP.

FIGURE 9-13 A detailed look at electron transport and chemiosmosis

TABLE 9-2 A Comparison of Photosynthesis and Aerobic Respiration

	Photosynthesis	Aerobic Respiration
Type of metabolic reaction	Anabolism	Catabolism
Raw materials	CO_2, H_2O	$C_6H_{12}O_6$, O_2
End products	$C_6H_{12}O_6$, O_2	CO_2, H_2O
Which cells have these processes?	Cells that contain chlorophyll (certain cells of plants, algae, and some bacteria)	Every actively metabolizing cell has aerobic respiration or some other energy-releasing pathway
Sites involved (in eukaryotic cells)	Chloroplasts	Cytosol (glycolysis); mitochondria
ATP production	By photophosphorylation (a chemiosmotic process)	By substrate-level phosphorylation and by oxidative phosphorylation (a chemiosmotic process)
Principal electron transfer compound	$NADP^+$ is reduced to form NADPH*	NAD^+ is reduced to form NADH*
Location of electron transport chain	Thylakoid membrane	Mitochondrial inner membrane (cristae)
Source of electrons for electron transport chain	In noncyclic electron transport: H_2O (undergoes photolysis to yield electrons, protons, and oxygen)	Immediate source: NADH, $FADH_2$ Ultimate source: glucose or other carbohydrate
Terminal electron acceptor for electron transport chain	In noncyclic electron transport: $NADP^+$ (becomes reduced to form NADPH)	O_2 (becomes reduced to form H_2O)

*NADPH and NADH are very similar hydrogen (i.e., electron) carriers, differing only in a single phosphate group. However, NADPH generally works with enzymes in anabolic pathways, such as photosynthesis. NADH is associated with catabolic pathways, such as cellular respiration.

mechanism of energy coupling in cells. You may recall from Chapter 8 that chemiosmosis also occurs in aerobic respiration (see **TABLE 9-2**).

Review

- Why is molecular oxygen a necessary byproduct of photosynthesis?
- What process is the actual mechanism of photophosphorylation?
- Why are both photosystems I and II required for photosynthesis? Can cyclic phosphorylation alone support photosynthesis? Explain your answer.

9.5 THE CARBON FIXATION REACTIONS

LEARNING OBJECTIVES

8 Summarize the three phases of the Calvin cycle and indicate the roles of ATP and NADPH in the process.
9 Discuss how photorespiration reduces photosynthetic efficiency.
10 Compare the C_4 and CAM pathways.

In carbon fixation, the energy of ATP and NADPH is used in the formation of organic molecules from CO_2. The carbon fixation reactions may be summarized as follows:

$$12\,NADPH + 18\,ATP + 6\,CO_2 \longrightarrow$$
$$C_6H_{12}O_6 + 12\,NADP^+ + 18\,ADP + 18\,P_i + 6\,H_2O$$

Most plants use the Calvin cycle to fix carbon

Carbon fixation occurs in the stroma through a sequence of 13 reactions known as the **Calvin cycle.** During the 1950s, University of California researchers Melvin Calvin, Andrew Benson, and oth-

ers elucidated the details of this cycle. Calvin was awarded a Nobel Prize in Chemistry in 1961.

The 13 reactions of the Calvin cycle are divided into three phases: CO_2 uptake, carbon reduction, and RuBP regeneration (**FIG. 9-14**). All 13 enzymes that catalyze steps in the Calvin cycle are located in the stroma of the chloroplast. Ten of the enzymes also participate in glycolysis (see Chapter 8). These enzymes catalyze reversible reactions, degrading carbohydrate molecules in cellular respiration and synthesizing carbohydrate molecules in photosynthesis.

1. *CO_2 uptake.* The first phase of the Calvin cycle consists of a single reaction in which a molecule of CO_2 reacts with a phosphorylated five-carbon compound, **ribulose bisphosphate (RuBP).** This reaction is catalyzed by the enzyme *ribulose bisphosphate carboxylase/oxygenase,* also known as **rubisco.** The chloroplast contains more rubisco enzyme than any other protein, and rubisco may be one of the most abundant proteins in the biosphere. The product of this reaction is an unstable six-carbon intermediate, which immediately breaks down into two molecules of **phosphoglycerate (PGA)** with three carbons each.

   The carbon that was originally part of a CO_2 molecule is now part of a carbon skeleton; the carbon has been "fixed." The Calvin cycle is also known as the C_3 **pathway** because the product of the initial carbon fixation reaction is a three-carbon compound. Plants that initially fix carbon in this way are called C_3 **plants.**

2. *Carbon reduction.* The second phase of the Calvin cycle consists of two steps in which the energy and reducing power from ATP and NADPH (both produced in the light-dependent reactions) are used to convert the PGA molecules to **glyceraldehyde-3-phosphate (G3P).** As shown in Figure 9-14, for every six carbons that enter the cycle as CO_2, six carbons can leave the system as two molecules of G3P, to be used in car-

ATP and NADPH provide the energy that drives carbon fixation in the Calvin cycle.

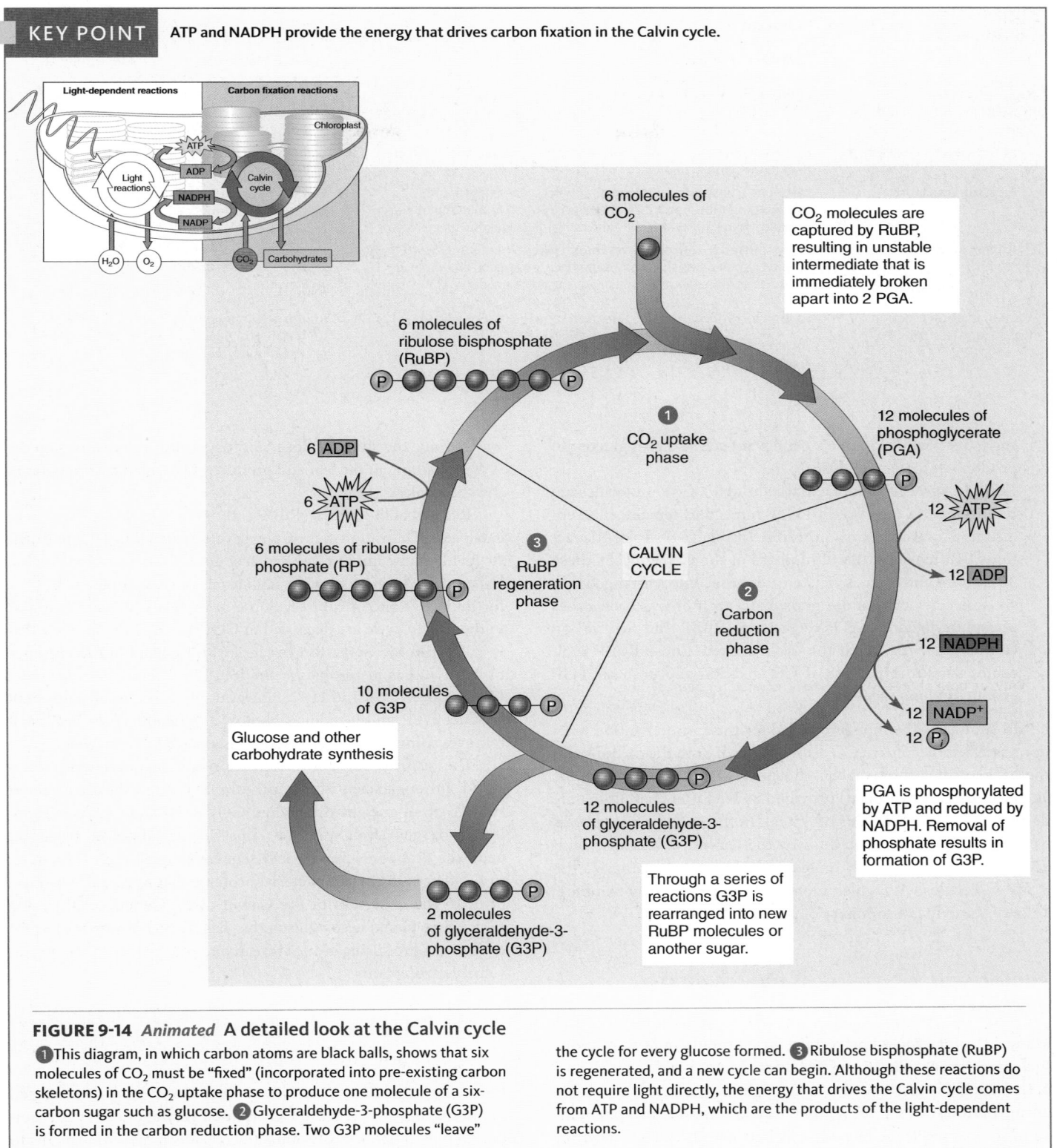

FIGURE 9-14 *Animated* **A detailed look at the Calvin cycle**

① This diagram, in which carbon atoms are black balls, shows that six molecules of CO_2 must be "fixed" (incorporated into pre-existing carbon skeletons) in the CO_2 uptake phase to produce one molecule of a six-carbon sugar such as glucose. ② Glyceraldehyde-3-phosphate (G3P) is formed in the carbon reduction phase. Two G3P molecules "leave" the cycle for every glucose formed. ③ Ribulose bisphosphate (RuBP) is regenerated, and a new cycle can begin. Although these reactions do not require light directly, the energy that drives the Calvin cycle comes from ATP and NADPH, which are the products of the light-dependent reactions.

bohydrate synthesis. Each of these three-carbon molecules of G3P is essentially half a hexose (six-carbon sugar) molecule. (In fact, you may recall that G3P is a key intermediate in the splitting of sugar in glycolysis; see Figs. 8-3 and 8-4.)

The reaction of two molecules of G3P is exergonic and leads to the formation of glucose or fructose. In some plants, glucose and fructose are then joined to produce sucrose (common table sugar). (Sucrose can be harvested from sugarcane,

TABLE 9-3	Summary of Photosynthesis		
Reaction Series	Summary of Process	Needed Materials	End Products
Light-dependent reactions (take place in thylakoid membranes)	Energy from sunlight used to split water, manufacture ATP, and reduce $NADP^+$		
Photochemical reactions	Chlorophyll-activated; reaction center gives up photoexcited electron to electron acceptor	Light energy; pigments (chlorophyll)	Electrons
Electron transport	Electrons transported along chain of electron acceptors in thylakoid membranes; electrons reduce $NADP^+$; splitting of water provides some H^+ that accumulates inside thylakoid space	Electrons, $NADP^+$, H_2O, electron acceptors	NADPH, O_2
Chemiosmosis	H^+ permitted to diffuse across the thylakoid membrane down their gradient; they cross the membrane through special channels in ATP synthase complex; energy released is used to produce ATP	Proton gradient, ADP + P_i, ATP synthase	ATP
Carbon fixation reactions (take place in stroma)	Carbon fixation: carbon dioxide used to make carbohydrate	Ribulose bisphosphate, CO_2, ATP, NADPH, necessary enzymes	Carbohydrates, ADP + P_i, $NADP^+$

sugar beets, and maple sap.) The plant cell also uses glucose to produce starch or cellulose.

3. *RuBP regeneration.* Notice that although 2 G3P molecules are removed from the cycle, 10 G3P molecules remain; this represents a total of 30 carbon atoms. Through a series of 10 reactions that make up the third phase of the Calvin cycle, these 30 carbons and their associated atoms become rearranged into six molecules of ribulose phosphate, each of which becomes phosphorylated by ATP to produce RuBP, the five-carbon compound with which the cycle started. These RuBP molecules begin the process of CO_2 fixation and eventual G3P production once again.

In summary, the inputs required for the carbon fixation reactions are six molecules of CO_2 (the source of both the carbons and the oxygens in carbohydrate), phosphates transferred from ATP, and electrons (as hydrogen) provided by NADPH (but ultimately derived from the photolysis of water). In the end, the six carbons from the CO_2 are accounted for by the harvest of a hexose molecule. The remaining G3P molecules are used to synthesize the RuBP molecules with which more CO_2 molecules may combine. **TABLE 9-3** provides a summary of photosynthesis.

Photorespiration reduces photosynthetic efficiency

Many C_3 plants, including certain agriculturally important crops such as soybeans, wheat, and potatoes, do not yield as much carbohydrate from photosynthesis as might be expected, especially during periods of very hot temperature in summer. This phenomenon is a consequence of trade-offs between the plant's need for CO_2 and its need to prevent water loss. Recall that most photosynthesis occurs in mesophyll cells inside the leaf and that the entry and exit of gases from the interior of the leaf are regulated by stomata, tiny pores concentrated on the underside of the leaf (see Fig. 9-4a). On hot, dry days, plants close their stomata to conserve

water. Once the stomata close, photosynthesis rapidly uses up the CO_2 remaining in the leaf and produces O_2, which accumulates in the chloroplasts.

Recall that the enzyme RuBP carboxylase/oxygenase (rubisco) catalyzes CO_2 fixation in the Calvin cycle by attaching CO_2 to RuBP. As its full name implies, rubisco acts not only as a carboxylase but also as an oxygenase because high levels of O_2 compete with CO_2 for the active site of rubisco. Some of the intermediates involved in the Calvin cycle are degraded to CO_2 and H_2O in a process that is called **photorespiration** because (1) it occurs in the presence of light; and as in aerobic respiration, (2) it requires oxygen and (3) produces CO_2 and H_2O. However, photorespiration does not produce ATP, and it reduces photosynthetic efficiency because it removes some of the intermediates used in the Calvin cycle.

The reasons for photorespiration are incompletely understood, although scientists hypothesize that it reflects the origin of rubisco at an ancient time when CO_2 levels were high and molecular oxygen levels were low. This view is supported by recent evidence that some amino acid sequences in rubisco are similar to sequences in certain bacterial proteins that apparently evolved prior to the evolution of the Calvin cycle. Genetic engineering to produce plants with rubisco that has a much lower affinity for oxygen is a promising area of research to improve yields of certain valuable crop plants.

The initial carbon fixation step differs in C_4 plants and in CAM plants

Photorespiration is not the only problem faced by plants engaged in photosynthesis. Because CO_2 is not a very abundant gas (composing only 0.038% of the atmosphere), it is not easy for plants to obtain the CO_2 they need. As you have learned, when conditions are hot and dry, the stomata close to reduce the loss of water vapor, greatly diminishing the supply of CO_2. Ironically, CO_2 is potentially less available at the very times when maximum sunlight is available to power the light-dependent reactions.

Many plant species living in hot, dry environments have adaptations that facilitate carbon fixation. **C$_4$ plants** first fix CO_2 into a four-carbon compound, **oxaloacetate. CAM plants** initially fix carbon at night through the formation of oxaloacetate. These special pathways found in C$_4$ and CAM plants precede the Calvin cycle (C$_3$ pathway); they do not replace it.

The C$_4$ pathway efficiently fixes CO_2 at low concentrations

The **C$_4$ pathway,** in which CO_2 is fixed through the formation of oxaloacetate, occurs not only before the C$_3$ pathway but also in different cells. Leaf anatomy is usually distinctive in C$_4$ plants. The photosynthetic mesophyll cells are closely associated with prominent, chloroplast-containing **bundle sheath cells,** which tightly encircle the veins of the leaf (**FIG. 9-15**). The C$_4$ pathway occurs in the mesophyll cells, whereas the Calvin cycle takes place within the bundle sheath cells.

The key component of the C$_4$ pathway is a remarkable enzyme that has an extremely high affinity for CO_2, binding it effectively even at unusually low concentrations. This enzyme, **PEP carboxylase,** catalyzes the reaction by which CO_2 reacts with the three-carbon compound **phosphoenolpyruvate (PEP),** forming oxaloacetate (**FIG. 9-16**).

In a step that requires NADPH, oxaloacetate is converted to some other four-carbon compound, usually malate. The malate then passes to chloroplasts within bundle sheath cells, where a different enzyme catalyzes the decarboxylation of malate to yield pyruvate (which has three carbons) and CO_2. NADPH is formed, replacing the one used earlier.

$$malate + NADP^+ \longrightarrow pyruvate + CO_2 + NADPH$$

The CO_2 released in the bundle sheath cell combines with ribulose bisphosphate in a reaction catalyzed by rubisco and goes through the Calvin cycle in the usual manner. The pyruvate formed in the decarboxylation reaction returns to the mesophyll cell, where it reacts with ATP to regenerate phosphoenolpyruvate.

Because the C$_4$ pathway captures CO_2 and provides it to the bundle sheath cells so efficiently, CO_2 concentration within the bundle sheath cells is about 10 to 60 times as great as its concentration in the mesophyll cells of plants having only the C$_3$ pathway. Photorespiration is negligible in C$_4$ plants such as crabgrass because the concentration of CO_2 in bundle sheath cells (where rubisco is present) is always high.

The combined C$_3$–C$_4$ pathway involves the expenditure of 30 ATPs per hexose, rather than the 18 ATPs used by the C$_3$ pathway alone. The extra energy expense required to regenerate PEP from pyruvate is worthwhile at high light intensities because it ensures a high concentration of CO_2 in the bundle sheath cells and permits them to carry on photosynthesis at a rapid rate. At lower light intensities and temperatures, C$_3$ plants are favored. For example, winter rye, a C$_3$ plant, grows lavishly in cool weather, when crabgrass cannot because it requires more energy to fix CO_2.

CAM plants fix CO_2 at night

Plants living in dry, or *xeric,* conditions have a number of structural adaptations that enable them to survive. Many xeric plants have physiological adaptations as well, including a special carbon fixation pathway, the **crassulacean acid metabolism (CAM) pathway.** The name comes from the stonecrop plant family (the Crassulaceae), which uses the CAM pathway, although the pathway has evolved

Upper epidermis
Palisade mesophyll
Bundle sheath cells of veins
Mesophyll
Spongy mesophyll
Chloroplasts

(a) In C$_3$ plants, the Calvin cycle takes place in the mesophyll cells and the bundle sheath cells are nonphotosynthetic.

(b) In C$_4$ plants, reactions that fix CO_2 into four-carbon compounds take place in the mesophyll cells. The four-carbon compounds are transferred from the mesophyll cells to the photosynthetic bundle sheath cells, where the Calvin cycle takes place.

FIGURE 9-15 C$_3$ and C$_4$ plant structure compared

FIGURE 9-16 *Animated* **Summary of the C₄ pathway**

CO_2 combines with phosphoenolpyruvate (PEP) in the chloroplasts of mesophyll cells, forming a four-carbon compound that is converted to malate. Malate goes to the chloroplasts of bundle sheath cells, where it is decarboxylated. The CO_2 released in the bundle sheath cell is used to make carbohydrate by way of the Calvin cycle.

FIGURE 9-17 A typical CAM plant

Prickly pear cactus (*Opuntia*) is a CAM plant. The more than 200 species of *Opuntia* living today originated in various xeric habitats in North and South America.

independently in some members of more than 25 other plant families, including the cactus family (Cactaceae), the lily family (Liliaceae), and the orchid family (Orchidaceae) (**FIG. 9-17**).

Unlike most plants, CAM plants open their stomata at night, admitting CO_2 while minimizing water loss. They use the enzyme PEP carboxylase to fix CO_2, forming oxaloacetate, which is converted to malate and stored in cell vacuoles. During the day, when stomata are closed and gas exchange cannot occur between the plant and the atmosphere, CO_2 is removed from malate by a decarboxylation reaction. Now the CO_2 is available within the leaf tissue to be fixed into sugar by the Calvin cycle (C_3 pathway).

The CAM pathway is very similar to the C_4 pathway but with important differences. C_4 plants initially fix CO_2 into four-carbon organic acids in mesophyll cells. The acids are later decarboxylated to produce CO_2, which is fixed by the C_3 pathway in the bundle sheath cells. In other words, the C_4 and C_3 pathways occur in *different locations* within the leaf of a C_4 plant. In CAM plants, the initial fixation of CO_2 occurs at night. Decarboxylation of malate and subsequent production of sugar from CO_2 by the normal C_3 photosynthetic pathway occur during the day. In other words, the CAM and C_3 pathways occur at *different times* within the same cell of a CAM plant.

Although it does not promote rapid growth the way that the C_4 pathway does, the CAM pathway is a very successful adaptation to xeric conditions. CAM plants can exchange gases for photosynthesis and reduce water loss significantly. Plants with CAM photosynthesis survive in deserts where neither C_3 nor C_4 plants can.

Review

- What are the three phases of the Calvin cycle?
- Which phase of the Calvin cycle requires both ATP and NADPH?
- In what ways does photorespiration differ from aerobic respiration?
- Do C_3, C_4, and CAM plants all have rubisco? PEP carboxylase?

9.6 METABOLIC DIVERSITY

◼ LEARNING OBJECTIVE

11 Contrast photoautotrophs and chemoheterotrophs with respect to their energy and carbon sources.

Land plants, algae, and certain prokaryotes are known as **photoautotrophs.** They are **phototrophs** because they use light energy to make ATP and NADPH, which temporarily hold chemical energy but are unstable and cannot be stockpiled in the cell. They are **autotrophs** (from the Greek *auto,* which means "self," and *trophos,* which means "nourishing") that synthesize complex organic compounds from simpler, inorganic raw materials. The chemical energy of ATP and NADPH then drives carbon fixation, the anabolic pathway in which stable organic molecules are synthesized from CO_2 and water. These organic compounds are used not only as starting materials to synthesize all the other organic compounds the photosynthetic organism needs (such as complex carbohydrates, amino acids, and lipids) but also for energy storage. Glucose and other carbohydrates produced during photosynthesis are relatively reduced compounds that can be subsequently oxidized by aerobic respiration or by some other catabolic pathway (see Chapter 8).

In contrast, animals, fungi, and most bacteria are known as **chemoheterotrophs.** They are **chemotrophs** because they obtain energy from chemicals, typically by redox reactions (see Chapters 7 and 8). They are **heterotrophs** (from the Greek *heter,* which means "other," and *trophos,* which means "nourishing") because they cannot fix carbon; they use organic molecules produced by *other* organisms as the building blocks from which they synthesize the carbon compounds they need.

We are so familiar with plants as photoautotrophs and animals such as ourselves as chemoheterotrophs that we tend to think that all organisms should fit in these two "mainstream" categories. Two other types of nutrition are found in certain bacteria. A few bacteria, known as nonsulfur purple bacteria, are **photoheterotrophs,** able to use light energy but unable to carry out carbon fixation, so they must obtain carbon from organic compounds. Some other bacteria are **chemoautotrophs,** which obtain their energy from the oxidation of reduced inorganic molecules such as hydrogen sulfide (H_2S), nitrite (NO_2^-), or ammonia (NH_3). Some of this captured energy is subsequently used to carry out carbon fixation.

Review

- How does a green plant obtain energy? carbon? How does your body obtain these things?

9.7 PHOTOSYNTHESIS IN PLANTS AND IN THE ENVIRONMENT

■ LEARNING OBJECTIVE

12 State the importance of photosynthesis both in a plant and to other organisms.

Although we characterize plants as photoautotrophs, not all plant cells carry out photosynthesis, and even cells with chloroplasts also possess mitochondria and carry out aerobic respiration. In fact, respiration utilizing the organic molecules the plant has made for itself is the direct source of ATP needed for most plant metabolism.

Several mechanisms regulate the relative activities of photosynthesis and aerobic respiration in plants. Although the enzymes of the Calvin cycle do not require light to function, they are actually regulated by light. As a consequence of the light-requiring reactions, the stroma becomes more basic (approximately pH 8), activating rubisco and other Calvin cycle enzymes. In contrast, light tends to inhibit the enzymes of glycolysis in the cytosol. Hence photosynthesis, not aerobic respiration, is favored in the light. When light is very dim, at a point known as the *light compensation point,* photosynthesis still occurs, but it is not evident because the rate of CO_2 fixation by photosynthesis is equal to the rate of CO_2 release through aerobic respiration. On the other hand, when light is very bright, photorespiration can significantly diminish photosynthetic yields.

As we have seen in this chapter, the reactions of the Calvin cycle provide a net yield of the three-carbon phosphorylated sugar, G3P. What are the various fates of G3P in the plant? Consider a leaf cell actively conducting photosynthesis. A series of enzymes may convert some of the G3P to glucose and then to starch. This starch is stored in starch granules that form inside chloroplasts. It has been recently shown that when this starch is broken down, the disaccharide maltose is typically formed (see Fig. 3-8a). Maltose is transported out of the chloroplast and then cleaved in the cytosol, providing glucose for aerobic respiration. Not all G3P ends up as carbohydrate; some is ultimately converted to amino acids, fatty acids, and other organic molecules needed by the photosynthetic cell.

Some of the G3P is exported to the cytosol, where enzymes convert it to the disaccharide sucrose (see Fig. 3-8b). Sucrose is then actively transported out of the cell, moves through the vascular system of the plant (see Chapter 35 for a discussion of plant transport), and is actively transported into the various cells. Sucrose can be broken down to glucose and fructose, which are used in aerobic respiration or as starting points for the synthesis of the various organic molecules the cells need, such as amino acids, lipids, and carbohydrates. Important carbohydrates include cellulose for cell walls (see Fig. 3-10) and starch, particularly in starch-storing structures such as roots (see Fig. 3-9a) and developing seeds and tubers (such as potatoes).

The benefits of photosynthesis in the environment are staggering. Of course, by fixing carbon, photoautotrophs are the ultimate source of virtually all organic molecules used as energy and carbon sources by chemoheterotrophs such as ourselves (for an exception, see *Inquiring About: Life without the Sun* in Chapter 55). In carrying out carbon fixation, photoautotrophs remove CO_2 from the atmosphere, thereby slowing global warming (see Chapter 57). Also of prime importance is the fact that photolysis of water by photosystem II releases the O_2 that all aerobic organisms require for aerobic respiration. Molecular oxygen is so reactive that it could not be maintained in the atmosphere if it were not constantly replenished in this way.

As discussed in Chapter 21, the evolution of oxygen-producing photosynthesis was a critical event in the history of life on Earth, which not only permitted the evolution of aerobic organisms, but also made terrestrial life possible because in the stratosphere O_2 is converted to ozone (O_3), which shields the planet from damaging ultraviolet light.

Review

- How does a root cell obtain energy? organic molecules?
- What is the source of molecular oxygen in Earth's atmosphere?

9.1 *(page 194)*

1 Describe the physical properties of light and explain the relationship between a wavelength of light and its energy.

- Light consists of particles called **photons** that move as waves.
- Photons with shorter **wavelengths** have more energy than those with longer wavelengths.

9.2 *(page 195)*

2 Diagram the internal structure of a chloroplast and explain how its components interact and facilitate the process of photosynthesis.

- In plants, **photosynthesis** occurs in chloroplasts, which are located mainly within **mesophyll** cells inside the leaf.
- **Chloroplasts** are organelles enclosed by a double membrane; the inner membrane encloses the **stroma** in which membranous, saclike **thylakoids** are suspended. Thylakoids enclose the **thylakoid lumen.** Thylakoids arranged in stacks are called **grana.**
- **Chlorophyll *a*, chlorophyll *b*, carotenoids,** and other photosynthetic pigments are components of the thylakoid membranes of chloroplasts.

3 Describe what happens to an electron in a biological molecule such as chlorophyll when a photon of light energy is absorbed.

- Photons excite biological molecules such as chlorophyll and other photosynthetic pigments, causing one or more electrons to become energized. These energized electrons may be accepted by electron acceptor compounds.
- The combined **absorption spectra** of chlorophylls *a* and *b* are similar to the **action spectrum** for photosynthesis.

9.3 *(page 198)*

4 Describe photosynthesis as a redox process.

- During photosynthesis, light energy is captured and converted to the chemical energy of carbohydrates; hydrogens from water are used to reduce carbon, and oxygen derived from water becomes oxidized, forming molecular oxygen.

5 Distinguish between the light-dependent reactions and carbon fixation reactions of photosynthesis.

- In the **light-dependent reactions,** electrons energized by light are used to generate **ATP** and **NADPH;** these compounds provide energy for the formation of carbohydrates during the **carbon fixation reactions.**

CENGAGENOW™ Learn more about photosynthesis in plants by clicking on the figures in CengageNOW.

9.4 *(page 199)*

6 Describe the flow of electrons through photosystems I and II in the noncyclic electron transport pathway and the products produced. Contrast this with cyclic electron transport.

- **Photosystems I** and **II** are the two types of photosynthetic units involved in photosynthesis. Each photosystem includes chlorophyll

molecules and accessory pigments organized with pigment-binding proteins into **antenna complexes.**

- Only a special pair of chlorophyll *a* molecules in the **reaction center** of an antenna complex give up energized electrons to a nearby electron acceptor. **P700** is in the reaction center for photosystem I; **P680** is in the reaction center for photosystem II.
- During the noncyclic light-dependent reactions, known as **noncyclic electron transport,** ATP and NADPH are formed.
- Electrons in photosystem I are energized by the absorption of light and passed through an **electron transport chain** to NADP$^+$, forming NADPH. Electrons given up by P700 in photosystem I are replaced by electrons from P680 in photosystem II.
- A series of redox reactions takes place as energized electrons are passed along the electron transport chain from photosystem II to photosystem I. Electrons given up by P680 in photosystem II are replaced by electrons made available by the **photolysis** of H$_2$O; oxygen is released in the process.
- During **cyclic electron transport,** electrons from photosystem I are eventually returned to photosystem I. ATP is produced by **chemiosmosis,** but no NADPH or oxygen is generated.

CENGAGENOW™ Experience the process of noncyclic electron transport by clicking on the figure in CengageNOW.

7 Explain how a proton (H$^+$) gradient is established across the thylakoid membrane and how this gradient functions in ATP synthesis.

- **Photophosphorylation** is the synthesis of ATP coupled to the transport of electrons energized by photons of light. Some of the energy of the electrons is used to pump protons across the thylakoid membrane, providing the energy to generate ATP by chemiosmosis.
- As protons diffuse through **ATP synthase,** an enzyme complex in the thylakoid membrane, ADP is phosphorylated to form ATP.

9.5 *(page 204)*

8 Summarize the three phases of the Calvin cycle and indicate the roles of ATP and NADPH in the process.

- The carbon fixation reactions proceed by way of the **Calvin cycle,** also known as the **C$_3$ pathway.**
- In the CO$_2$ uptake phase of the Calvin cycle, CO$_2$ is combined with **ribulose bisphosphate (RuBP),** a five-carbon sugar, by the enzyme ribulose bisphosphate carboxylase/oxygenase, commonly known as **rubisco,** forming the three-carbon molecule **phosphoglycerate (PGA).**
- In the carbon reduction phase of the Calvin cycle, the energy and reducing power of ATP and NADPH are used to convert PGA molecules to **glyceraldehyde-3-phosphate (G3P).** For every 6 CO$_2$ molecules fixed, 12 molecules of G3P are produced, and 2 molecules of G3P leave the cycle to produce the equivalent of 1 molecule of glucose.
- In the RuBP regeneration phase of the Calvin cycle, the remaining G3P molecules are modified to regenerate RuBP.

CENGAGENOW™ See the Calvin cycle in action by clicking on the figure in CengageNOW.

9 Discuss how photorespiration reduces photosynthetic efficiency.

- In **photorespiration,** C$_3$ plants consume oxygen and generate CO$_2$ by degrading Calvin cycle intermediates but do not produce ATP. Photorespiration is significant on bright, hot, dry days when plants close their stomata, conserving water but preventing the passage of CO$_2$ into the leaf.

10 Compare the C_4 and CAM pathways.

- In the **C_4 pathway,** the enzyme **PEP carboxylase** binds CO_2 effectively, even when CO_2 is at a low concentration. C_4 reactions take place within mesophyll cells. The CO_2 is fixed in oxaloacetate, which is then converted to malate. The malate moves into a **bundle sheath cell,** and CO_2 is removed from it. The released CO_2 then enters the Calvin cycle.

- The **crassulacean acid metabolism (CAM)** pathway is similar to the C_4 pathway. PEP carboxylase fixes carbon at night in the mesophyll cells, and the Calvin cycle occurs during the day in the same cells.

    CENGAGENOW™ See a comparison of the C_3 and C_4 pathways by clicking on the figure in CengageNOW.

9.6 *(page 208)*

11 Contrast photoautotrophs and chemoheterotrophs with respect to their energy and carbon sources.

- **Photoautotrophs** use light as an energy source and are able to incorporate atmospheric CO_2 into preexisting carbon skeletons.
- **Chemoheterotrophs** obtain energy by oxidizing chemicals and obtain carbon as organic molecules from other organisms.

9.7 *(page 209)*

12 State the importance of photosynthesis both in a plant and to other organisms.

- Photosynthesis is the ultimate source of all chemical energy and organic molecules available to photoautotrophs, such as plants, and to virtually all other organisms as well. It also constantly replenishes the supply of oxygen in the atmosphere, vital to all aerobic organisms.

Summary Reactions for Photosynthesis

The light-dependent reactions (noncyclic electron transport):

$$12\ H_2O + 12\ NADP^+ + 18\ ADP + 18\ P_i \xrightarrow[\text{Chlorophyll}]{\text{Light}}$$
$$6\ O_2 + 12\ NADPH + 18\ ATP$$

The carbon fixation reactions (Calvin cycle):

$$12\ NADPH + 18\ ATP + 6\ CO_2 \longrightarrow$$
$$C_6H_{12}O_6 + 12\ NADP^+ + 18\ ADP + 18\ P_i + 6\ H_2O$$

By canceling out the common items on opposite sides of the arrows in these two coupled equations, we obtain the simplified overall equation for photosynthesis:

$$6\ CO_2 + H_2O \xrightarrow[\text{Chlorophyll}]{\text{Light energy}} C_6H_{12}O_6 + O_2 + 6\ H_2O$$

Carbon dioxide   Water   Glucose   Oxygen   Water

TEST YOUR UNDERSTANDING

1. Where is chlorophyll located in the chloroplast? (a) thylakoid membranes (b) stroma (c) matrix (d) thylakoid lumen (e) between the inner and outer membranes

2. In photolysis, some of the energy captured by chlorophyll is used to split (a) CO_2 (b) ATP (c) NADPH (d) H_2O (e) both b and c

3. Light is composed of particles of energy called (a) carotenoids (b) reaction centers (c) photons (d) antenna complexes (e) photosystems

4. The relative effectiveness of different wavelengths of light in photosynthesis is demonstrated by (a) an action spectrum (b) photolysis (c) carbon fixation reactions (d) photoheterotrophs (e) an absorption spectrum

5. In plants, the final electron acceptor in noncyclic electron flow is (a) $NADP^+$ (b) CO_2 (c) H_2O (d) O_2 (e) G3P

6. In _____, electrons that have been energized by light contribute their energy to add phosphate to ADP, producing ATP. (a) crassulacean acid metabolism (b) the Calvin cycle (c) photorespiration (d) C_4 pathways (e) photophosphorylation

7. The mechanism by which electron transport is coupled to ATP production by means of a proton gradient is called (a) chemiosmosis (b) crassulacean acid metabolism (c) fluorescence (d) the C_3 pathway (e) the C_4 pathway

8. The Calvin cycle begins when CO_2 reacts with (a) phosphoenolpyruvate (b) glyceraldehyde-3-phosphate (c) ribulose bisphosphate (d) oxaloacetate (e) phosphoglycerate

9. The enzyme directly responsible for almost all carbon fixation on Earth is (a) rubisco (b) PEP carboxylase (c) ATP synthase (d) phosphofructokinase (e) ligase

10. In C_4 plants, C_4 and C_3 pathways occur at different _____; whereas in CAM plants, CAM and C_3 pathways occur at different _____. (a) times of day; locations within the leaf (b) seasons; locations (c) locations; times of day (d) locations; seasons (e) times of day; seasons

11. An organism characterized as a photoautotroph obtains energy from _____ and carbon from _____. (a) light; organic molecules (b) light; CO_2 (c) organic molecules; organic molecules (d) organic molecules; CO_2 (e) O_2; CO_2

12. Label the figure. Use Figure 9-8 to check your answers.

CRITICAL THINKING

1. Must all autotrophs use light energy? Explain.

2. Only some plant cells have chloroplasts, but all actively metabolizing plant cells have mitochondria. Why?

3. Explain why the proton gradient formed during chemiosmosis represents a state of low entropy. (You may wish to refer to the discussion of entropy in Chapter 7.)

4. The electrons in glucose have relatively high free energies. How did they become so energetic?

5. **SCIENCE, TECHNOLOGY, AND SOCIETY.** What strategies may be employed in the future to increase world food supply? Base your answer on your knowledge of photosynthesis and related processes.

6. What would life be like for photoautotrophs if there were no chemoheterotrophs? For chemoheterotrophs if there were no photoautotrophs?

7. What might you suspect if scientists learned that a distant planet has an atmosphere that is 15% molecular oxygen?

8. **EVOLUTION LINK.** Propose an explanation for the fact that bacteria, chloroplasts, and mitochondria all have ATP synthase complexes.

9. **ANALYZING DATA.** The figure depicts the absorption spectrum of a plant pigment. What colors/wavelengths does it absorb? What is the color of this pigment?

 Additional questions are available in CengageNOW at www.cengage.com/login.

10 Chromosomes, Mitosis, and Meiosis

Fluorescence LM of a cultured newt lung cell in mitosis (early prometaphase). The nuclear envelope has broken down, and the microtubules of the mitotic spindle (*green*) now interact with the chromosomes (*blue*).

Alexey Khodjakov, Wadsworth Center, Albany, NY

KEY CONCEPTS

10.1 In eukaryotic cells, DNA is wound around specific proteins to form chromatin, which in turn is folded and packaged to make individual chromosomes.

10.2 In mitosis, duplicated chromosomes separate (split apart) and are evenly distributed into two daughter nuclei. Mitosis is an important part of the cell cycle, which consists of the successive stages through which a cell passes.

10.3 An internal genetic program interacts with external signals to regulate the cell cycle.

10.4 Meiosis, which reduces the number of chromosome sets from diploid to haploid, is necessary to maintain the normal chromosome number when two cells join during sexual reproduction. Meiosis helps to increase genetic variation among offspring.

10.5 Meiosis and gamete production precede fertilization in the life cycles of sexually reproducing organisms.

Pre-existing cells divide to form new cells. This remarkable process enables an organism to grow, repair damaged parts, and reproduce. Cells serve as the essential link between generations. Even the simplest cell contains a large amount of precisely coded genetic information in the form of deoxyribonucleic acid (DNA). An individual's DNA is organized into informational units called *genes,* which control the activities of the cell and are passed on to its descendants. When a cell divides, the information contained in the DNA must be faithfully replicated and the copies then transmitted to each daughter cell through a precisely choreographed series of steps (see photograph).

DNA is a very long, thin molecule that could easily become tangled and broken, and a eukaryotic cell's nucleus contains a huge amount of DNA. In this chapter we consider how eukaryotes accommodate the genetic material by packaging each DNA molecule with proteins to form a structure called a *chromosome,* each of which contains hundreds or thousands of genes.

We then consider *mitosis,* the highly regimented process that ensures a parent cell transmits one copy of every chromosome to each of its two daughter cells. In this way, the chromosome number is preserved through successive mitotic divisions. Most *somatic cells* (body cells) of eukaryotes divide by mitosis. Mitosis is an active area of biological research, and for good reason: errors in mitosis can result in a host of disorders and diseases

213

such as cancer, a disease condition in which cells divide at an uncontrolled rate and become invasive. Thus, a clearer understanding of mitosis has the potential to improve our treatment of many diseases.

Finally, we discuss *meiosis*, a process that reduces the chromosome number by half. Sexual life cycles in eukaryotes require meiosis. Sexual reproduction involves the fusion of two sex cells, or *gametes*, to form a fertilized egg called a *zygote*. Meiosis makes it possible for each gamete to contain only half the number of chromosomes in the parent cell, thereby preventing the zygotes from having twice as many chromosomes as the parents.

10.1 EUKARYOTIC CHROMOSOMES

■ LEARNING OBJECTIVES

1   Discuss the significance of chromosomes in terms of their information content.

2   Explain how DNA is packed into chromosomes in eukaryotic cells.

The major carriers of genetic information in eukaryotes are the **chromosomes,** which lie within the cell nucleus. Although *chromosome* means "colored body," chromosomes are virtually colorless; the term refers to their ability to be stained by certain dyes. In the 1880s, light microscopes had been improved to the point that scientists such as the German biologist Walther Fleming began to observe chromosomes during cell division. In 1903, American biologist Walter Sutton and German biologist Theodor Boveri noted independently that chromosomes were the physical carriers of genes, the genetic factors Gregor Mendel discovered in the 19th century (discussed in Chapter 11).

Chromosomes are made of **chromatin,** a material consisting of DNA and associated proteins. When a cell is not dividing, the chromosomes are present but in an extended, partially unraveled form. Chromatin consists of long, thin threads that are somewhat aggregated, giving them a granular appearance when viewed with the electron microscope (see Fig. 4-13). During cell division, the chromatin fibers condense and the chromosomes become visible as distinct structures (**FIG. 10-1**).

DNA is organized into informational units called genes

An organism may have thousands of genes. For example, humans have about 20,000 genes that code for proteins. As you will see in later chapters, the concept of the gene has changed considerably since the science of genetics began, but our definitions have always centered on the gene as an informational unit. By providing information needed to carry out one or more specific cell functions, a gene affects some characteristic of the organism. For example, genes govern eye color in humans, wing length in flies, and seed color in peas.

10 μm

FIGURE 10-1 Chromosomes

Human chromosomes from an unidentified cell are shown in this fluorescence LM.

DNA is packaged in a highly organized way in chromosomes

Prokaryotic and eukaryotic cells differ markedly in their DNA content as well as in the organization of DNA molecules. The bacterium *Escherichia coli* normally contains about 4×10^6 base pairs (almost 1.35 mm) of DNA in its single, circular DNA molecule. In fact, the total length of its DNA is about 1000 times as long as the length of the cell itself. Therefore, the DNA molecule is, with the help of proteins, twisted and folded compactly to fit inside the bacterial cell (see Fig. 25-2).

A typical eukaryotic cell contains much more DNA than a bacterium does, and it is organized in the nucleus as multiple chromosomes; these vary widely in size and number among different species. Although a human nucleus is about the size of a large bacterial cell, it contains more than 1000 times the amount of DNA found in *E. coli*. The DNA content of a human sperm cell is about 3×10^9 base pairs; stretched end to end, it would measure almost 1 m long. Remarkably, this DNA fits into a nucleus with a diameter of only 10 μm.

How does a eukaryotic cell pack its DNA into the chromosomes? Chromosome packaging is facilitated by certain proteins known as **histones.**[1] Histones have a positive charge because they have a high proportion of amino acids with basic side chains (see Chapter 3). The positively charged histones associate with DNA, which has a negative charge because of its phosphate groups, to form structures called **nucleosomes.** The fundamental unit of each nucleosome consists of a beadlike structure with 146 base pairs of DNA wrapped around a disc-shaped core of eight histone molecules (two each of four different histone types) (**FIG. 10-2**).

---

[1] A few types of eukaryotic cells lack histones. Conversely, histones occur in one group of prokaryotes, the archaea (see Chapter 25).

DNA wound
around a cluster
of histone
molecules

Histone tails

Linker DNA

Nucleosome
(10 nm diameter)

100 nm

D. E. Olins and A. L. Olins

(a) A model for the structure of a nucleosome. Each nucleosome bead contains a set of eight histone molecules, forming a protein core around which the double-stranded DNA winds. The DNA surrounding the histones consists of 146 nucleotide pairs; another segment of DNA, about 60 nucleotide pairs long, links nucleosome beads.

(b) TEM of nucleosomes from the nucleus of a chicken cell. Normally, nucleosomes are packed more closely together, but the preparation procedure has spread them apart, revealing the DNA linkers.

FIGURE 10-2 Nucleosomes

Although the nucleosome was originally defined as a bead plus a DNA segment that links it to an adjacent bead, today the term more commonly refers only to the bead itself (that is, the eight histones and the DNA wrapped around them).

Nucleosomes function like tiny spools, preventing DNA from becoming tangled. You can see the importance of this role in **FIGURE 10-3**, which illustrates the enormous length of DNA that unravels from a mouse chromosome after researchers have removed the histones. The role of histones is more than simply structural because their arrangement also affects the activity of the DNA with which they are associated. Histones are increasingly viewed as an important part of the regulation of gene expression—that is, whether genes are turned off or on. We discuss gene regulation by histones in Chapter 14.

The wrapping of DNA into nucleosomes represents the first level of chromosome structure. **FIGURE 10-4** shows the higher-order structures of chromatin leading to the formation of a condensed chromosome. The nucleosomes themselves are 10 nm in diameter. The packed nucleosome state occurs when a fifth type of histone, known as *histone H1*, associates with the linker DNA, packing adjacent nucleosomes together to form a compacted 30 nm chromatin fiber. In extended chromatin, these fibers form large, coiled loops held together by **scaffolding proteins,** nonhistone proteins that help maintain chromosome structure. The loops then interact to form the condensed chromatin found in a chromosome. Cell biologists have identified a group of proteins, collectively called **condensin,** required for chromosome compaction. Condensin binds to DNA and wraps it into coiled loops that are compacted into a mitotic or meiotic chromosome.

DNA loops

Scaffolding proteins

Courtesy of U. Laemmli, from *Cell* 12:817, 1988. Copyright by Cell Press

2 μm

FIGURE 10-3 TEM of a mouse chromosome depleted of histones
Notice how densely packed the DNA strands are, even though they have been released from the histone proteins that organize them into tightly coiled structures.

Chromosome number and informational content differ among species

Every individual of a given species has a characteristic number of chromosomes in the nuclei of its somatic (body) cells. However, it is not the number of chromosomes that makes each species unique but

When a cell prepares to divide, its chromosomes become thicker and shorter as their long chromatin fibers are compacted.

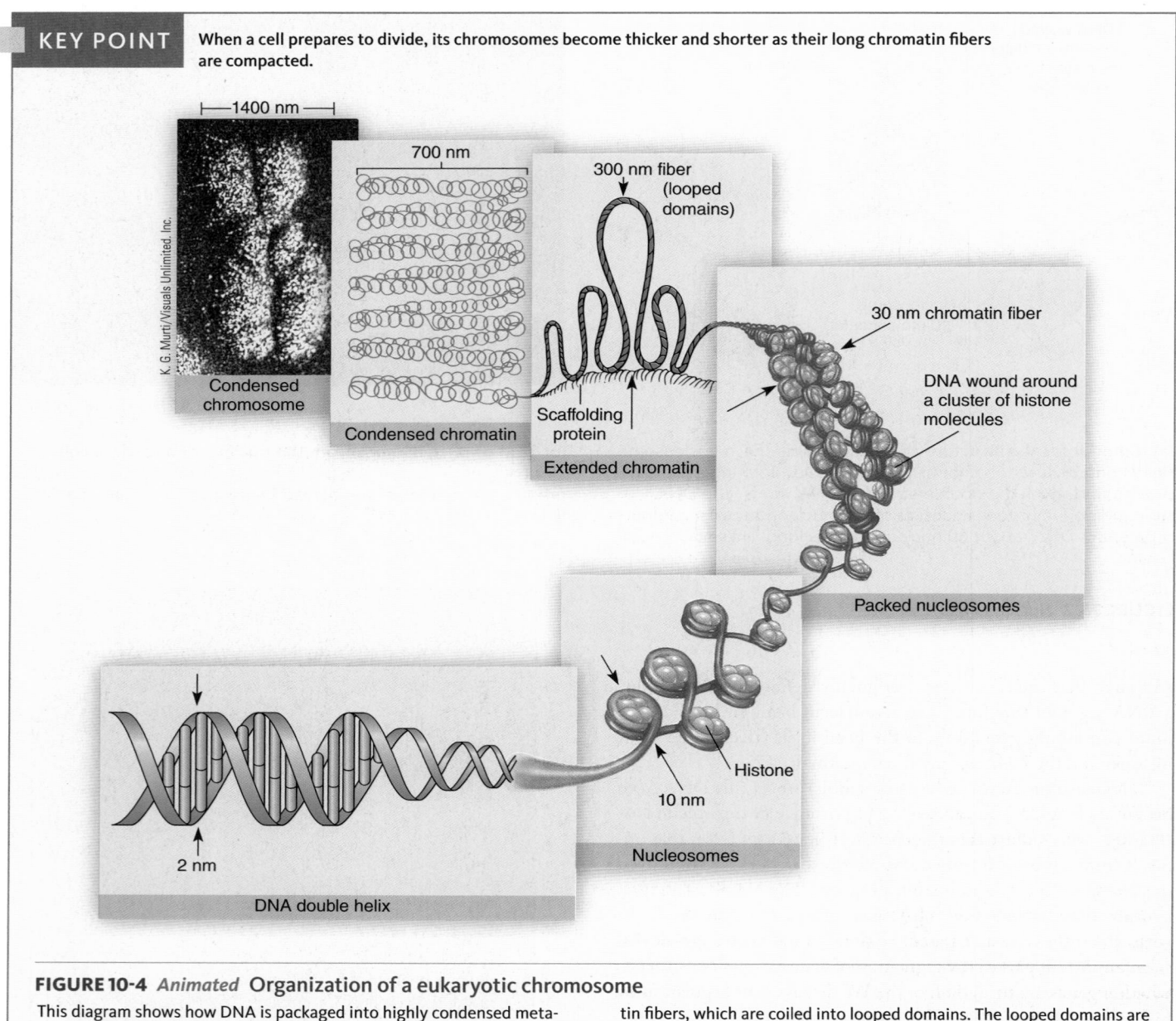

K. G. Murti/Visuals Unlimited, Inc.

├─1400 nm─┤

Condensed chromosome

700 nm

Condensed chromatin

300 nm fiber (looped domains)

Scaffolding protein

Extended chromatin

30 nm chromatin fiber

DNA wound around a cluster of histone molecules

Packed nucleosomes

Histone

10 nm

Nucleosomes

2 nm

DNA double helix

FIGURE 10-4 *Animated* Organization of a eukaryotic chromosome

This diagram shows how DNA is packaged into highly condensed metaphase chromosomes. First, DNA is wrapped around histone proteins to form nucleosomes. Then, the nucleosomes are compacted into chromatin fibers, which are coiled into looped domains. The looped domains are compacted, ultimately forming chromosomes.

the information the genes specify. Most human somatic cells have exactly 46 chromosomes, but humans are not humans merely because we have 46 chromosomes. Some other species—the olive tree, for example—also have 46. Some humans have an abnormal chromosome composition with more or fewer than 46 (see Fig. 16-4).

Other species have different chromosome numbers. A certain species of roundworm has only 2 chromosomes in each cell, whereas some crabs have as many as 200, and some ferns have more than 1000. Most animal and plant species have between 8 and 50 chromosomes per somatic cell. Numbers above and below

these are uncommon. The number of chromosomes a species has does not indicate the species' complexity or its status within a particular domain or kingdom.

Review

■ What are the informational units on chromosomes called? Of what do these informational units consist?

■ How is the large discrepancy between DNA length and nucleus size addressed in eukaryotic cells?

10.2 THE CELL CYCLE AND MITOSIS

LEARNING OBJECTIVES

3 Identify the stages in the eukaryotic cell cycle and describe their principal events.

4 Describe the structure of a duplicated chromosome, including the sister chromatids, centromeres, and kinetochores.

5 Explain the significance of mitosis and describe the process.

When cells reach a certain size, they usually either stop growing or divide. Not all cells divide; some, such as skeletal muscle and red blood cells, do not normally divide once they are mature. Other cells undergo a sequence of activities required for growth and cell division.

The stages through which a cell passes from one cell division to the next are collectively referred to as the **cell cycle.** Timing of the cell cycle varies widely, but in actively growing plant and animal cells, it is about 8 to 20 hours. The cell cycle consists of two main phases, interphase and M phase, both of which can be distinguished under a light microscope (**FIG. 10-5**).

Chromosomes duplicate during interphase

Most of a cell's life is spent in **interphase,** the time when no cell division is occurring. A cell is metabolically active during interphase, synthesizing needed materials (proteins, lipids, and other biologically important molecules) and growing. Here is the sequence of interphase and M phase in the eukaryotic cell cycle:

The time between the end of mitosis and the beginning of the S phase is termed the G_1 **phase** (G stands for *gap*, an interval during which no DNA synthesis occurs). Growth and normal metabolism take place during the G_1 phase, which is typically the longest phase. Cells that are not dividing usually become arrested in this part of the cell cycle and are said to be in a state called G_0. Toward the end of G_1, the enzymes required for DNA synthesis become more active. Synthesis of these enzymes, along with proteins needed to initiate cell division (discussed later in the chapter), enable the cell to enter the S phase.

During the **synthesis phase,** or **S phase,** DNA replicates and histone proteins are synthesized so that the cell can make duplicate copies of its chromosomes. How did researchers identify the S phase of the cell cycle? In the early 1950s, researchers demonstrated that cells preparing to divide duplicate their chromosomes at a relatively restricted time interval during interphase and not during early mitosis, as previously hypothesized. These investigators used isotopes, such as ^3H, to synthesize radioactive thymidine, a nucleotide that is incorporated specifically into DNA as it is synthesized. After radioactive thymidine was supplied for a

The cell cycle is the successive series of events in the life of a cell.

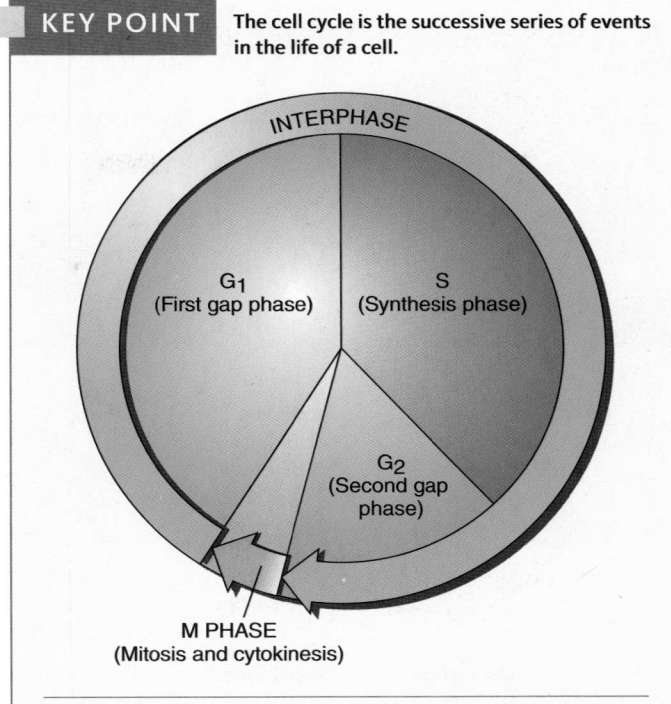

FIGURE 10-5 *Animated* The eukaryotic cell cycle

The cell cycle includes interphase (G_1, S, and G_2) and M phase (mitosis and cytokinesis). Proportionate amounts of time spent at each stage vary among species, cell types, and growth conditions. If the cell cycle were a period of 12 hours, G_1 would be about 5 hours, S would be 4.5 hours, G_2 would be 2 hours, and M phase would be 30 minutes.

brief period (such as 30 minutes) to actively growing cells, *autoradiography* (see Fig. 2-3) on exposed film showed that a fraction of the cells had silver grains over their chromosomes. The nuclei of these cells were radioactive because during the experiment DNA had replicated. DNA replication was not occurring in the cells that did not have radioactively labeled chromosomes. Researchers therefore inferred that the proportion of labeled cells out of the total number of cells provides a rough estimate of the length of the S phase relative to the rest of the cell cycle.

After it completes the S phase, the cell enters a second gap phase, the G_2 **phase.** At this time, increased protein synthesis occurs, as the final steps in the cell's preparation for division take place. For many cells, the G_2 phase is short relative to the G_1 and S phases.

M phase involves two main processes, mitosis and cytokinesis. **Mitosis,** the nuclear division that produces two nuclei containing chromosomes identical to the parental nucleus, begins at the end of the G_2 phase. Cytokinesis, which generally begins before mitosis is complete, is the division of the cell cytoplasm to form two cells.

Mitosis is a continuous process, but for descriptive purposes, it is divided into five stages:

prophase ⟶ prometaphase ⟶ metaphase ⟶ anaphase ⟶ telophase

INTERPHASE

PROPHASE

PROMETAPHASE

Chromatin   Nucleolus

Nucleus

Fragments
of nuclear
envelope

Nuclear
envelope

Plasma
membrane

Centrioles

Sister chromatids
of duplicated
chromosome

Developing
mitotic spindle

Kinetochore

Spindle
microtubule

(a) Cell carries out normal life activities. Chromosomes become duplicated.

(b) Long fibers of chromatin condense as compact mitotic chromosomes, each consisting of two chromatids attached at their centromeres. Cytoskeleton is disassembled, and mitotic spindle forms between centrioles, which have moved to poles of cell. Nuclear envelope begins to disassemble.

(c) Spindle microtubules attach to kinetochores of chromosomes. Chromosomes begin to move toward cell's midplane.

FIGURE 10-6 *Animated* **Interphase and the stages of mitosis**
The LMs show plant cells, which lack centrioles. The drawings depict generalized animal cells with a diploid chromosome number of four; the sizes of the nuclei and chromosomes are exaggerated to show the structures more clearly.

Study **FIGURE 10-6** while you read the following descriptions of these stages as they occur in a typical plant or animal cell.

During prophase, duplicated chromosomes become visible with the microscope

The first stage of mitosis, **prophase,** begins with chromosome compaction, when the long chromatin fibers that make up the chromosomes begin a coiling process that makes them shorter and thicker. The compacted chromatin can then be distributed to the daughter cells with less likelihood of tangling.

When stained with certain dyes and viewed through the light microscope, chromosomes become visible as darkly stained bodies as prophase progresses. It is now apparent that each chromosome was duplicated during the preceding S phase and consists of a pair of **sister chromatids,** which contain identical, double-stranded DNA sequences. Each chromatid includes a constricted region called the **centromere.** Sister chromatids are tightly associated in the vicinity of their centromeres (**FIG. 10-7**). The chemical basis for this close association at the centromeres consists of precise DNA sequences that are tightly bound to specific proteins.

For example, sister chromatids are physically linked by a ring-shaped protein complex called **cohesin.** Cohesins extend along the length of the sister chromatid arms and are particularly concentrated at the centromere (**FIG. 10-8**). These cohesins, which hold the replicated chromosomes together from their synthesis in S phase onward, help to ensure accurate chromosome segregation during mitosis.

Attached to each centromere is a **kinetochore,** a multiprotein complex to which **microtubules** can bind. These microtubules function in chromosome distribution during mitosis, in which one copy of each chromosome is delivered to each daughter cell.

A dividing cell can be described as a globe, with an equator that determines the midplane (equatorial plane) and two opposite poles. This terminology is used for all cells regardless of their actual shape. Microtubules radiate from each pole, and some of these protein fibers elongate toward the chromosomes, forming the **mitotic spindle,** a structure that separates the duplicated chromosomes

METAPHASE

ANAPHASE

TELOPHASE

25 μm

Spindle

Centriole pair at spindle pole

Cell's midplane (metaphase plate)

Cleavage furrow

Daughter chromosomes

Re-forming nuclear envelope

(d) Chromosomes line up along cell's midplane. Spindle microtubules attach each chromosome to both poles.

(e) Sister chromatids separate at their centromeres. One group of chromosomes moves toward each pole of cell. Spindle poles move farther apart.

(f) Chromosomes are grouped at poles. Chromosomes decondense, and nuclear envelopes begin to form. Cytokinesis produces two daughter cells.

▲ **FIGURE 10-6** Continued

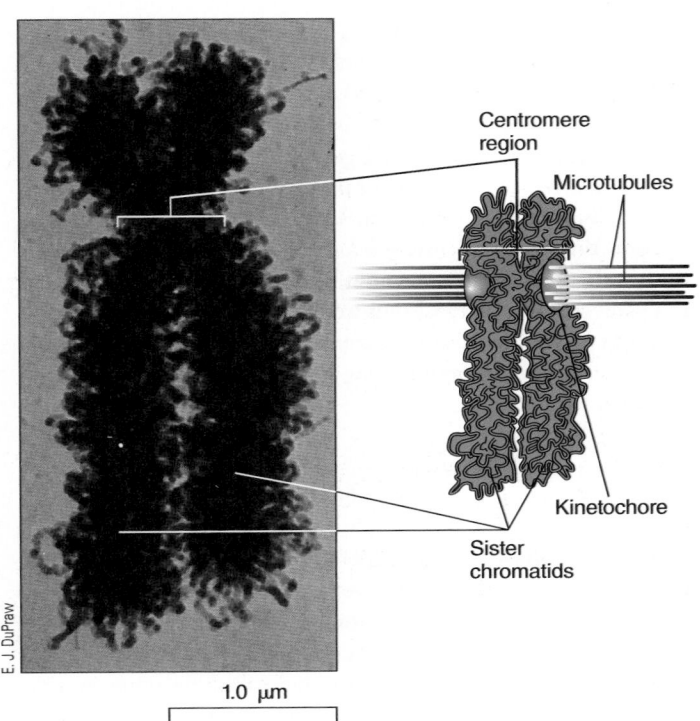

Centromere region

Microtubules

Kinetochore

Sister chromatids

E. J. DuPraw

1.0 μm

◀ **FIGURE 10-7 Sister chromatids and centromeres**
The sister chromatids, each consisting of tightly coiled chromatin fibers, are tightly associated at their centromere regions, indicated by the brackets. Associated with each centromere is a kinetochore, which serves as a microtubule attachment site. Kinetochores and microtubules are not visible in this TEM of a metaphase chromosome.

during anaphase (**FIG. 10-9**). The *minus* ends of these microtubules are at the poles, and the *plus* ends extend to the cell's midplane. It might be helpful to review Figure 4-24, which shows the organization of microtubules as linear polymers of the protein *tubulin*. The organization and function of the spindle require the presence of motor proteins and a variety of signaling molecules.

Animal cells differ from plant cells in the details of mitotic spindle formation. In both types of dividing cells, each pole contains a region, the **microtubule-organizing center,** from which extend the microtubules that form the mitotic spindle. The electron microscope shows that microtubule-organizing centers in certain plant cells consist of fibrils with little or no discernible structure.

In contrast, animal cells have a pair of **centrioles** in the middle of each microtubule-organizing center (see Fig. 4-26). The centrioles are surrounded by fibrils that make up the **pericentriolar**

Sister chromatids of duplicated chromosome

Kinetochore

Cohesin complexes

Prophase

1 As mitosis progresses, cohesins dissociate from the duplicated chromosome arms.

Cohesin complexes in centromere region

Spindle microtubule

Metaphase

2 Cohesins then dissociate at the centromere, allowing the daughter chromosomes to separate during anaphase.

Daughter chromosomes

Anaphase

FIGURE 10-8 Cohesins

material. The spindle microtubules terminate in the pericentriolar material, but they do not actually touch the centrioles. Although cell biologists once thought spindle formation in animal cells required centrioles, their involvement is probably coincidental. Current evidence suggests that centrioles organize the pericentriolar material and ensure its duplication when the centrioles duplicate.

Each of the two centrioles is duplicated during the S phase of interphase, yielding two centriole pairs. Late in prophase, microtubules radiate from the pericentriolar material surrounding the centrioles; these clusters of microtubules are called asters. The two asters migrate to opposite sides of the nucleus, establishing the two poles of the mitotic spindle.

Prometaphase begins when the nuclear envelope breaks down

During **prometaphase** the nuclear envelope fragments so that the spindle microtubules come into contact with the chromosomes; units of the disassembled nuclear envelope are sequestered in vesicles to be used later, to assemble nuclear envelopes for the daughter cells. The nucleolus shrinks and usually disappears, and the mitotic spindle is completely assembled. At the start of prometaphase, the duplicated chromosomes are scattered throughout the nuclear region (see the chapter introduction photograph, which shows early prometaphase). The spindle microtubules grow and shrink as they move toward the center of the cell in a "search and capture" process. Their random, dynamic movements give the appearance that they are "searching" for the chromosomes. If a microtubule comes near a centromere, one of the kinetochores of a duplicated chromosome "captures" it. As the now-tethered chromosome continues moving toward the cell's midplane, the unattached kinetochore of its sister chromatid becomes connected to a spindle microtubule from the cell's other pole.

During the chromosomes' movements toward the cell's midplane, long microtubules are shortened by the removal of tubulin subunits, and the short microtubules are lengthened by the addition of tubulin subunits. Evidence indicates that shortening and lengthening occurs at the kinetochore end (the plus end) of the microtubule, not at the spindle pole end (the minus end). This shortening or lengthening occurs while the spindle microtubule remains firmly tethered to the kinetochore. Motor proteins located at the kinetochores may be involved in this tethering of the spindle microtubule. These motor proteins may work in a similar fashion to the kinesin motor shown in Figure 4-25.

To summarize the events of prometaphase, sister chromatids of each duplicated chromosome become attached at their kinetochores to spindle microtubules extending from opposite poles of the cell, and the chromosomes begin to move toward the cell's midplane. As the cell transitions from prometaphase to metaphase, cohesins dissociate from the sister chromatid arms, freeing them from one another, although some cohesins remain in the vicinity of the centromere.

Duplicated chromosomes line up on the midplane during metaphase

During **metaphase,** all the cell's chromosomes align at the cell's midplane, or **metaphase plate.** As already mentioned, one of the two sister chromatids of each chromosome is attached by its kinetochore to microtubules from one pole, and its sister chromatid is attached by its kinetochore to microtubules from the opposite pole.

The mitotic spindle has three types of microtubules: polar microtubules, kinetochore microtubules, and astral microtubules

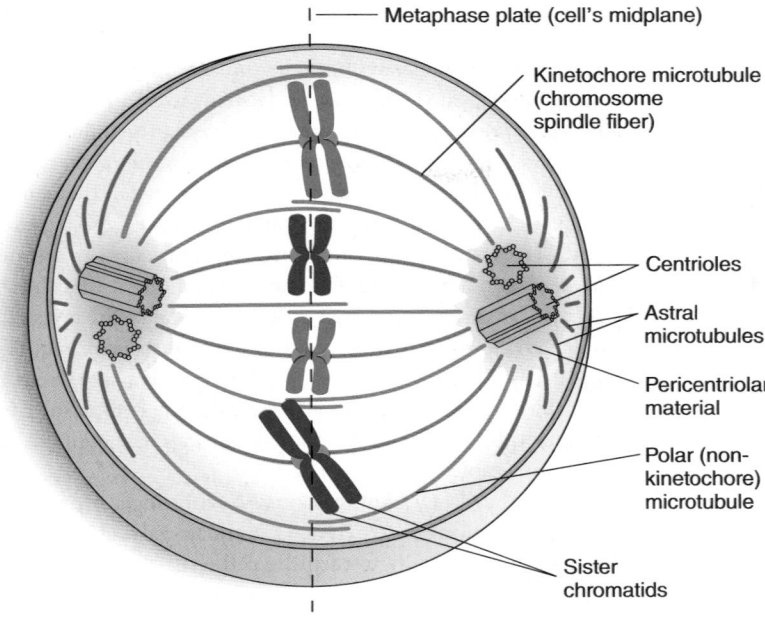

Metaphase plate (cell's midplane)

Kinetochore microtubule (chromosome spindle fiber)

Centrioles

Astral microtubules

Pericentriolar material

Polar (non-kinetochore) microtubule

Sister chromatids

(a) One end of each microtubule of this animal cell is associated with one of the poles. Astral microtubules (*green*) radiate in all directions, forming the aster. Kinetochore microtubules (*red*) connect the kinetochores to the poles, and polar (nonkinetochore) microtubules (*blue*) overlap at the midplane.

10 μm

CNRI/Phototake, NYC

(b) This fluorescence LM of an animal cell at metaphase shows a well-defined spindle and asters (chromosomes, *orange*; microtubules, *green*).

FIGURE 10-9 The mitotic spindle

(see Fig. 10-9). **Polar microtubules,** also known as *nonkinetochore microtubules,* extend from each pole to the equatorial region, where they overlap and interact with nonkinetochore microtubules from the opposite pole. **Kinetochore microtubules** extend from each pole and attach to chromosomes at their kinetochores. **Astral microtubules** are the short microtubules that form asters at each pole.

Each chromatid is completely condensed and appears distinct during metaphase. Because individual chromosomes are more obvious at metaphase than at any other time, the **karyotype,** or chromosome composition, is usually checked at this stage for chromosome abnormalities (see Chapter 16). As the mitotic cell transitions from metaphase to anaphase, the remaining cohesin proteins joining the sister chromatids at their centromere dissociate.

During anaphase, chromosomes move toward the poles

Anaphase begins as the sister chromatids separate. Once the chromatids are no longer attached to their duplicates, each chromatid is called a *chromosome.* The now-separate chromosomes move to opposite poles, using the spindle microtubules as tracks. The kinetochores, still attached to kinetochore microtubules, lead the way, with the chromosome arms trailing behind. Anaphase ends when all the chromosomes have reached the poles.

Cell biologists are making significant progress in understanding the overall mechanism of chromosome movement in anaphase. Chromosome movements are studied in several ways. The

number of microtubules at a particular stage or after certain treatments is determined by carefully analyzing electron micrographs. Researchers also physically perturb living cells that are dividing, using microlaser beams or mechanical devices known as *micromanipulators*. A skilled researcher can move chromosomes, break their connections to microtubules, and even remove them from the cell entirely.

Microtubules lack elastic or contractile properties. Then how do the chromosomes move apart? Are they pushed or pulled, or do other forces operate? Microtubules are dynamic structures, with *tubulin* subunits constantly being removed from their ends and others being added. Evidence indicates that during anaphase, kinetochore microtubules shorten, or *depolymerize,* at their *plus* ends, that is, closest toward the midplane of the cell (**FIG. 10-10**). This shortening mechanism pulls the chromosomes toward the poles.

A second mechanism also plays a role in chromosome separation. During anaphase the spindle as a whole elongates, at least partly because polar microtubules originating at opposite poles are associated with motors that let them slide past one another at the midplane. The sliding decreases the degree of overlap, thereby "pushing" the poles apart. This mechanism indirectly causes the chromosomes to move apart because they are attached to the poles by kinetochore microtubules.

During telophase, two separate nuclei form

During the final stage of mitosis, **telophase,** chromosomes arrive at the poles and there is a return to interphase-like conditions. The

QUESTION: Do spindle microtubules move chromosomes by a shortening (that is, depolymerization) of microtubules at the spindle poles or at the kinetochore ends?

HYPOTHESIS: Spindle microtubules move chromosomes toward the spindle poles by a mechanism in which the spindle microtubules are shortened at their kinetochore ends.

EXPERIMENT: Microtubules in pig kidney cells in early anaphase were labeled with a fluorescent dye that specifically attaches to microtubules.

The researchers marked the microtubules by using a laser microbeam to bleach the dye while keeping the microtubules intact.

RESULTS AND CONCLUSION: The chromosomes moved toward the bleached areas of the spindle microtubules, indicating a shortening of the microtubules on the kinetochore side. The microtubules on the polar ends did not shorten.

Chromosomes moved poleward because they remained anchored to the kinetochore microtubules as tubulin subunits were removed at the kinetochore ends of the microtubules.

FIGURE 10-10 *Animated* Using laser photobleaching to determine how chromosomes are transported toward the spindle poles during anaphase

chromosomes decondense by partially uncoiling. A new nuclear envelope forms around each set of chromosomes, made at least in part from small vesicles and other components derived from the old nuclear envelope. The spindle microtubules disappear, and the nucleoli reorganize.

Cytokinesis forms two separate daughter cells

Cytokinesis, the division of the cytoplasm to yield two daughter cells, is the last step in M phase and usually overlaps mitosis, generally beginning during telophase. Cytokinesis of an animal or fungal cell (yeast, for example) begins as an *actomyosin contractile ring* is assembled and attached to the plasma membrane. The contractile ring encircles the cell in the equatorial region, at right angles to the spindle (**FIG. 10-11a**). The contractile ring consists of an association between actin and myosin filaments; it is thought that the motor activity of myosin moves actin filaments to cause the constriction, similar to the way actin and myosin cause muscle contraction (see Fig. 40-10). The ring contracts, producing a **cleavage furrow** that gradually deepens and eventually separates the cytoplasm into two daughter cells, each with a complete nucleus. The contractile ring then disassembles.

In plant cells, cytokinesis occurs by forming a **cell plate** (**FIG. 10-11b**), a partition constructed in the equatorial region of the spindle that grows laterally toward the cell wall. The cell plate forms as a line of vesicles originating in the *Golgi complex.* The vesicles contain materials to construct both a primary cell wall for each daughter cell and a middle lamella that cements the primary cell walls together. The vesicle membranes fuse to become the plasma membrane of each daughter cell.

Multinucleated cells form if mitosis is not followed by cytokinesis; this is a normal condition for certain cell types. For example, the body of plasmodial slime molds consists of a multinucleate mass of cytoplasm (see Fig. 26-19a).

Mitosis produces two cells genetically identical to the parent cell

The remarkable regularity of the process of cell division ensures that each daughter nucleus receives exactly the same number and kinds of chromosomes that the parent cell had. Thus, with a few exceptions, every cell of a multicellular organism has the same genetic makeup. If a cell receives more or fewer than the characteristic number of chromosomes through some malfunction of the cell division process, the resulting cell may show marked abnormalities and often cannot survive.

Mitosis provides for the orderly distribution of chromosomes (and of centrioles, if present), but what about the various cytoplasmic organelles? For example, all eukaryotic cells, including plant cells, require mitochondria. Likewise, photosynthetic plant cells cannot carry out photosynthesis without chloroplasts. These organelles contain their own DNA and appear to form by the division of previously existing mitochondria or plastids or their precursors. This nonmitotic division process is similar to prokaryotic cell division (discussed in the next section) and generally occurs during interphase. Because many copies of each organelle are present in each cell, organelles are apportioned with the cytoplasm that each daughter cell receives during cytokinesis.

Lacking nuclei, prokaryotes divide by binary fission

Bacteria and archaea contain much less DNA than do most eukaryotic cells, but precise distribution of the genetic material into two daughter cells is still a formidable process. Prokaryotic DNA usually consists of a single, circular chromosome that is packaged with associated proteins. Although the distribution of genetic material in dividing prokaryotic cells is a simpler process than mitosis, it nevertheless is very precise, to ensure that the daughter cells are genetically identical to the parent cell.

Prokaryotes reproduce asexually, generally by **binary fission,** a process in which one cell divides into two daughter cells (**FIG. 10-12**). The circular DNA molecule replicates, resulting in two identical chromosomes. DNA replication begins at a single site on the bacterial chromosome, termed the *origin of replication.* DNA synthesis proceeds from that point in both directions until they eventually meet (see Fig. 12-16a).

Following replication, the daughter chromosomes separate and move to opposite ends of the elongating cell. Cytokinesis between the daughter chromosomes is controlled by the **Z ring,** a

protein scaffold that holds about 10 different proteins around the cell's midsection. There the plasma membrane grows inward between the two DNA copies, dividing the cell's cytoplasm in half, and a new transverse cell wall is synthesized between the two cells. (Bacterial reproduction is described further in Chapter 25.)

Review

- What are the stages of the cell cycle? During which stage does DNA replicate?
- What are the stages of mitosis and what happens in each stage?

10.3 REGULATION OF THE CELL CYCLE

◼ LEARNING OBJECTIVE

6　Explain some ways in which the cell cycle is controlled.

When conditions are optimal, some prokaryotic cells can divide every 20 minutes. The generation times of eukaryotic cells are generally much longer, although the frequency of cell division varies widely among different species and among different tissues of the same species. Some skeletal muscle cells usually stop dividing after the first few months of life, whereas blood-forming cells, digestive tract cells, and skin cells divide frequently throughout the life of the organism. Under optimal conditions of nutrition, temperature, and pH, the length of the eukaryotic cell cycle is constant for any given cell type. Under less favorable conditions, however, the generation time may be longer.

Certain regulatory molecules that control the cell cycle are common to all eukaryotes. Genetically programmed in the cell's

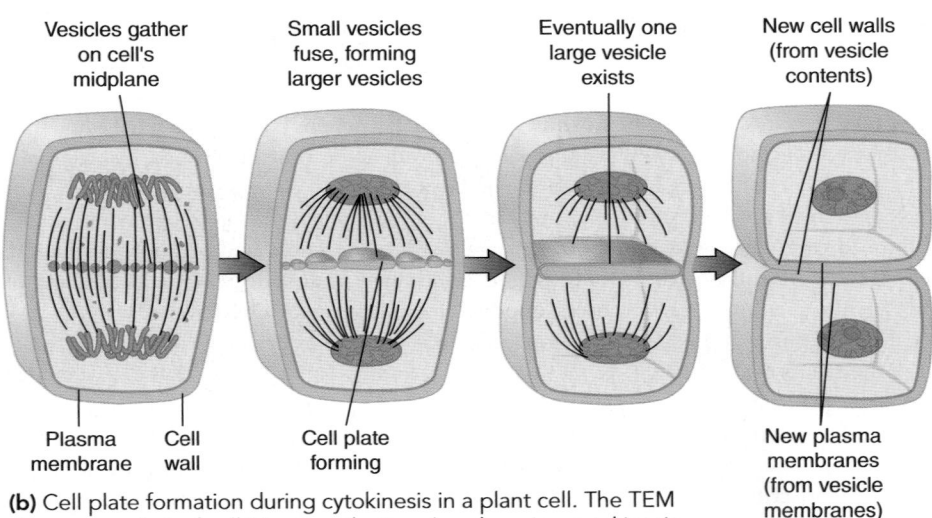

(a) TEM of the equatorial region of a cultured animal cell undergoing cytokinesis. Note the cleavage furrow. Dividing fungal cells also have a contractile ring that causes cytokinesis.

(b) Cell plate formation during cytokinesis in a plant cell. The TEM shows a maple leaf cell (*Acer saccharinum*) undergoing cytokinesis.

FIGURE 10-11 *Animated* **Cytokinesis in animal and plant cells**
The nuclei in both TEMs are in telophase. The drawings show 3-D relationships.

Binary fission is a precisely orchestrated sequence of events that ensures each bacterial daughter cell has identical genetic material.

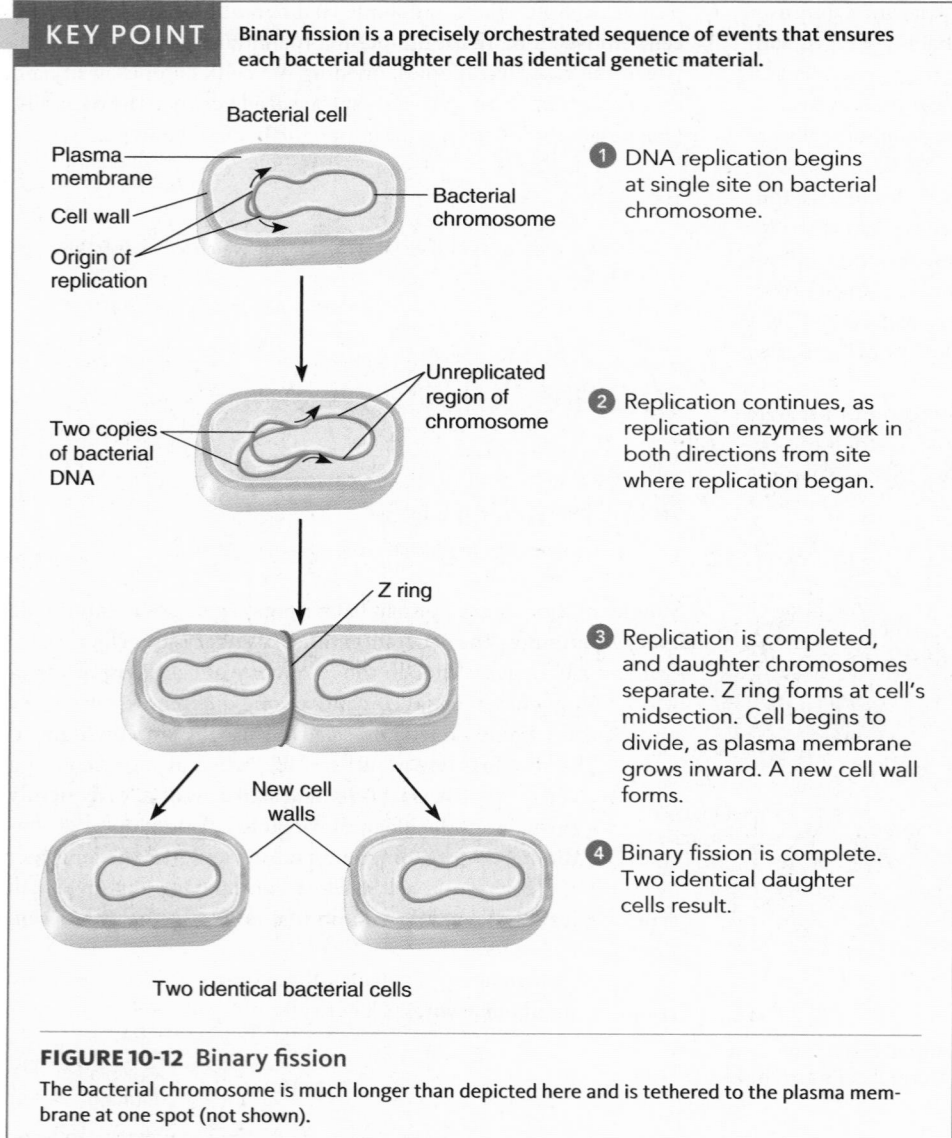

Bacterial cell

Plasma membrane

Cell wall

Origin of replication

Bacterial chromosome

1 DNA replication begins at single site on bacterial chromosome.

Unreplicated region of chromosome

Two copies of bacterial DNA

2 Replication continues, as replication enzymes work in both directions from site where replication began.

Z ring

3 Replication is completed, and daughter chromosomes separate. Z ring forms at cell's midsection. Cell begins to divide, as plasma membrane grows inward. A new cell wall forms.

New cell walls

4 Binary fission is complete. Two identical daughter cells result.

Two identical bacterial cells

FIGURE 10-12 Binary fission

The bacterial chromosome is much longer than depicted here and is tethered to the plasma membrane at one spot (not shown).

nucleus, these regulatory molecules are components of the *cell cycle control system* found in organisms as diverse as yeast, clams, frogs, humans, and plants. Regulatory molecules trigger a specific sequence of events during the cell cycle.

Because the cell cycle consists of hundreds of sequential events that proceed in an orderly manner, a failure to carefully control these events can have disastrous consequences. Control mechanisms in the genetic program, called **cell-cycle checkpoints,** temporarily block key events from being initiated during the cell cycle. Cell-cycle checkpoints ensure that all the events of a particular stage have been completed before the next stage begins (**FIG. 10-13**). The checkpoints are inactivated after they have done their job so the cell cycle can proceed.

Genes that encode molecules involved in checkpoints are critically important to the cell cycle. If a checkpoint gene is defective, it can result in cancer or other serious diseases. Consider what might happen if the metaphase-anaphase checkpoint molecules were nonfunctional. In this case, anaphase might be initiated too early, before all chromosomes were properly attached to spindle fibers.

The resulting daughter cells might have too few or too many chromosomes. An abnormal number of chromosomes is associated with Down syndrome as well as many cancers.

FIGURE 10-14 shows some of the key molecules involved in regulating the cell cycle. Among them are **protein kinases,** enzymes that activate or inactivate other proteins by *phosphorylating* (adding phosphate groups to) them. The protein kinases involved in controlling the cell cycle are **cyclin-dependent kinases (Cdks).** The activity of various Cdks increases and then decreases as the cell moves through the cell cycle. Cdks are active only when they bind tightly to regulatory proteins called **cyclins.** The cyclins are so named because their levels fluctuate predictably during the cell cycle (that is, they "cycle," or are alternately synthesized and degraded as part of the cell cycle).

Three scientists who began their research in the 1970s and 1980s on the roles of protein kinases and cyclins in the cell cycle (Leland Hartwell from the United States, and Paul Nurse and Tim Hunt from Great Britain) were awarded the Nobel Prize in Physiology or Medicine in 2001. Their discoveries were cited as important not only in working out the details of the fundamental cell process of mitosis but also in understanding why cancer cells divide when they should not. For example, cyclin levels are often higher than normal in human cancer cells.

When a specific Cdk associates with a specific cyclin, it forms a **cyclin–Cdk complex.** Cyclin–Cdk complexes phosphorylate enzymes and other proteins. Some of these proteins become activated when they are phosphorylated, and others become inactivated. For example, phosphorylation of the protein **p27,** known to be a major inhibitor of cell division, is thought to initiate degradation of the protein. As various enzymes are activated or inactivated by phosphorylation, the activities of the cell change. Thus, a decrease in a cell's level of p27 causes a nondividing cell to resume division.

Eukaryotic cells form four major cyclin–Cdk complexes: G_1-Cdk, G_1/S-Cdk, S-Cdk, and M-Cdk. Each cyclin–Cdk complex phosphorylates a different group of proteins. G_1-Cdk prepares the cell to pass from the G_1 phase to the S phase, and then G_1/S-Cdk commits the cell to undergo DNA replication. S-Cdk initiates DNA replication. M-Cdk promotes the events of mitosis, including chromosome condensation, nuclear envelope breakdown, and mitotic spindle formation.

M-Cdk also activates another enzyme complex, the **anaphase-promoting complex (APC),** toward the end of metaphase. APC initiates anaphase by allowing degradation of the cohesins and

When a cell has not completed the steps leading to a cell-cycle checkpoint, the checkpoint is active and halts the cell cycle. When the necessary steps are completed, the checkpoint is inactivated, and the cell cycle proceeds.

1 **G_1-S checkpoint:** The first key checkpoint ensures that the cell has the necessary growth factors, nutrients, and enzymes to synthesize DNA. Without the proper signals that the cell is ready to proceed, the checkpoint will not let DNA synthesis begin.

G_1 (First gap phase)

S (Synthesis phase)

G_2 (Second gap phase)

3 **Metaphase-anaphase checkpoint:** Sometimes called the *spindle checkpoint*, this checkpoint occurs at the end of metaphase and prevents anaphase from occurring until all kinetochores are properly attached to spindle fibers along the cell's midplane.

2 **G_2-M checkpoint:** This cell-cycle checkpoint ensures that DNA replication is finished before the cell begins mitosis. If a cell has damaged or unreplicated DNA, the checkpoint will not let the cell undergo mitosis.

FIGURE 10-13 Key checkpoints in the cell cycle

The cell cycle consists of hundreds of sequential events. The red bars show three important checkpoints that determine that previous steps are completed so that the next steps may proceed. Each checkpoint is inactivated after it has performed its function, allowing the cell cycle to continue.

other proteins that hold the sister chromatids together during metaphase. As a result, the sister chromatids separate as two daughter chromosomes. At this point, cyclin is degraded to negligible levels and M-Cdk activity drops, allowing the mitotic spindle to disassemble and the cell to exit mitosis.

Certain drugs can stop the cell cycle at a specific checkpoint. Some of these prevent DNA synthesis, whereas others inhibit the synthesis of proteins that control the cycle or inhibit the synthesis of structural proteins that contribute to the mitotic spindle. Because one of the distinguishing features of most cancer cells is their high rate of cell division relative to that of most normal somatic cells, cancer cells are greatly affected by these drugs. Many side effects of certain anticancer drugs (such as nausea and hair loss) are due to the drugs' effects on normal cells that divide rapidly in the digestive system and hair follicles.

In plant cells, certain hormones stimulate mitosis. These include the **cytokinins,** a group of plant hormones that promote mitosis both in normal growth and in wound healing (see Chapter 38). Similarly, animal hormones, such as certain steroids, stimulate growth and mitosis (see Chapter 49).

Protein **growth factors,** which are active at extremely low concentrations, stimulate mitosis in some animal cells. Of the approximately 50 protein growth factors known, some act only on specific types of cells, whereas others act on a broad range of cell types. For example, the effects of the growth factor *erythropoietin* are limited to cells that will develop into red blood cells, but *epidermal growth factor* stimulates many cell types to divide. Many types of cancer cells divide in the absence of growth factors.

Review

- What are cell-cycle checkpoints?
- What are two molecular controls that trigger the onset of different stages of the cell cycle?

10.4 SEXUAL REPRODUCTION AND MEIOSIS

■ LEARNING OBJECTIVES

7 Differentiate between asexual and sexual reproduction.
8 Distinguish between haploid and diploid cells, and define *homologous chromosomes.*
9 Explain the significance of meiosis and describe the process.
10 Contrast mitosis and meiosis, emphasizing the different outcomes.

Cyclin-dependent kinases (Cdks) control the phosphorylation of other proteins, thereby regulating the transitions between phases of the cell cycle.

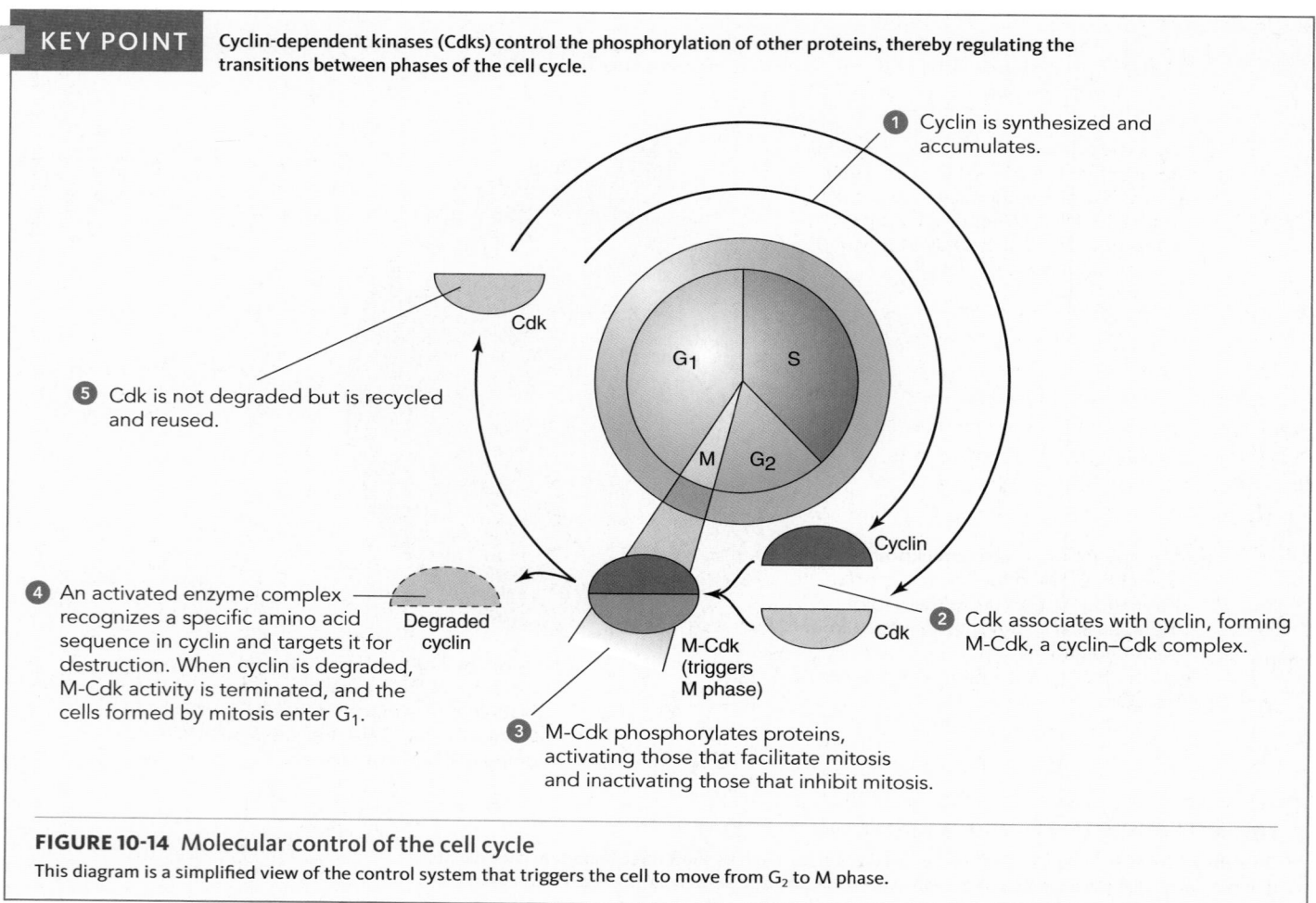

1 Cyclin is synthesized and accumulates.

5 Cdk is not degraded but is recycled and reused.

Cdk

G₁

S

M G₂

Cyclin

4 An activated enzyme complex recognizes a specific amino acid sequence in cyclin and targets it for destruction. When cyclin is degraded, M-Cdk activity is terminated, and the cells formed by mitosis enter G₁.

Degraded cyclin

Cdk

2 Cdk associates with cyclin, forming M-Cdk, a cyclin–Cdk complex.

M-Cdk (triggers M phase)

3 M-Cdk phosphorylates proteins, activating those that facilitate mitosis and inactivating those that inhibit mitosis.

FIGURE 10-14 Molecular control of the cell cycle
This diagram is a simplified view of the control system that triggers the cell to move from G_2 to M phase.

Although the details of the reproductive process vary greatly among different kinds of eukaryotes, biologists distinguish two basic types of reproduction: asexual and sexual. In **asexual reproduction** a single parent splits, buds, or fragments to produce two or more individuals. In most kinds of eukaryotic asexual reproduction, all the cells are the result of mitotic divisions, so their genes and inherited traits are like those of the parent. Such a group of genetically identical organisms is called a **clone.** In asexual reproduction, organisms that are well adapted to their environment produce new generations of similarly adapted organisms. Asexual reproduction occurs rapidly and efficiently, partly because the organism does not need to expend time and energy finding a mate.

In contrast, **sexual reproduction** involves the union of two sex cells, or **gametes,** to form a single cell called a **zygote.** Usually two different parents contribute the gametes, but in some cases a single parent furnishes both gametes. In the case of animals and plants, the egg and sperm cells are the gametes, and the fertilized egg is the zygote.

Sexual reproduction results in genetic variation among the offspring. (*How* this genetic variation arises is discussed later in this chapter and in Chapter 11.) Because the offspring produced by sexual reproduction are not genetically identical to their parents or to each other, some offspring may be able to survive environmental

changes better than either parent does. However, one disadvantage of sexual reproduction is that some offspring with a different combination of traits may be less likely to survive than their parents.

There is a potential problem in eukaryotic sexual reproduction: if each gamete had the same number of chromosomes as the parent cell that produced it, then the zygote would have twice as many chromosomes. This doubling would occur generation after generation. How do organisms avoid producing zygotes with ever-increasing chromosome numbers? To answer this question, we need more information about the types of chromosomes found in cells.

Each chromosome in a somatic cell of a plant or animal normally has a partner chromosome. The two partners, known as **homologous chromosomes,** are similar in size, shape, and the position of their centromeres. Furthermore, special chromosome-staining procedures produce a characteristic pattern of bands evident in the members of each chromosome pair. In most species, chromosomes vary enough in their structure that cell biologists can distinguish the different chromosomes and match up the homologous pairs. The 46 chromosomes in human cells constitute 23 homologous pairs.

The most important feature of homologous chromosomes is that they carry information about the same genetic traits, although this information is not necessarily identical. For example, each member of a homologous pair may carry a gene that specifies hemoglobin structure. But one member may have the information for the normal hemoglobin β chain (see Fig. 3-22a), whereas the other may specify the abnormal form of hemoglobin associated with sickle cell anemia (see Chapter 16). Homologous chromosomes can therefore be contrasted with the two members of a pair of sister chromatids, which are precisely identical to each other.

A set of chromosomes has one of each kind of chromosome; in other words, it contains one member of each homologous pair. If a cell or nucleus contains two sets of chromosomes, it is said to have a **diploid** chromosome number. If it has only a single set of chromosomes, it has the **haploid** number.

In humans, the diploid chromosome number is 46 and the haploid number is 23. When a sperm and egg fuse at fertilization, each gamete is haploid, contributing one set of chromosomes; the diploid number is thereby restored in the fertilized egg (zygote). When the zygote divides by mitosis to form the first two cells of the embryo, each daughter cell receives the diploid number of chromosomes, and subsequent mitotic divisions repeat this. Thus, somatic cells are diploid.

An individual whose cells have three or more sets of chromosomes is **polyploid.** Polyploidy is relatively rare among animals but common among plants (see Chapter 20). In fact, polyploidy has been an important mechanism of plant evolution. As many as 80% of all flowering plants are polyploid. Polyploid plants are often larger and hardier than diploid members of the same group. Many commercially important plants, such as wheat and cotton, are polyploid.

The chromosome number found in the gametes of a particular species is represented as n, and the zygotic chromosome number is represented as $2n$. If the organism is not polyploid, the haploid chromosome number is equal to n, and the diploid number is equal to $2n$; thus, in humans, $n = 23$ and $2n = 46$. For simplicity, in the rest of this chapter, the organisms used as examples are not polyploid. We use diploid and $2n$ interchangeably, and haploid and n interchangeably, although the terms are not strictly synonymous.

Meiosis produces haploid cells with unique gene combinations

A cell division that reduces chromosome number is called **meiosis.** The term *meiosis* means "to make smaller," and the chromosome number is reduced by one-half. In meiosis a diploid cell undergoes two cell divisions, potentially yielding four haploid cells. It is important to note that haploid cells do not contain just any combination of chromosomes, but one member of each homologous pair.

The events of meiosis are similar to the events of mitosis, with four important differences:

1. Meiosis involves two successive nuclear and cytoplasmic divisions, producing up to four cells.
2. Despite two successive nuclear divisions, the DNA and other chromosome components duplicate only once—during the interphase preceding the first meiotic division.
3. Each of the four cells produced by meiosis contains the haploid chromosome number, that is, only one chromosome set containing only one representative of each homologous pair.
4. During meiosis, each homologous chromosome pair is shuffled, so the resulting haploid cells each have a virtually unique combination of genes.

Four haploid (n) cells, each with two unduplicated chromosomes

FIGURE 10-15 Overview of meiosis

This figure begins with a diploid cell with four unduplicated chromosomes. The chromosomes derived from one parent are shown in blue, and those from the other parent are red. Homologous pairs are similar in size and shape.

Meiosis typically consists of two nuclear and cytoplasmic divisions, designated the *first* and *second meiotic divisions,* or simply **meiosis I** and **meiosis II** (FIG. 10-15). Each includes prophase, metaphase, anaphase, and telophase stages. During meiosis I, the partner homologous chromosomes pair and then separate and move into different nuclei. In meiosis II, the sister chromatids that make up each duplicated chromosome separate from each other and are distributed to two different nuclei. The following discussion describes meiosis in an organism with a diploid chromosome number of 4. Refer to **FIGURE 10-16** as you read.

INTERPHASE

MEIOSIS I

Mid-prophase I

Late prophase I

Clare Hasenkampf/Biological Photo Service

Nucleolus
Nuclear envelope
Chromatin
Centrioles

Homologous chromosomes
Developing meiotic spindle

Interphase preceding meiosis; DNA replicates.

Homologous chromosomes synapse and exchange segments by crossing over; nuclear envelope breaks down.

MEIOSIS II

Prophase II

Metaphase II

Anaphase II

Daughter chromosomes

Chromosomes condense again following brief period of interkinesis. DNA does *not* replicate again.

Chromosomes line up along cell's midplane.

Sister chromatids separate, and chromosomes move to opposite poles.

FIGURE 10-16 *Animated* **Interphase and the stages of meiosis**

Meiosis consists of two nuclear divisions, meiosis I (*top row*) and meiosis II (*bottom row*). The LMs show sectioned plant cells, which lack centrioles. The drawings depict generalized animal cells with a diploid chromosome number of 4; the sizes of the nuclei and chromosomes are exaggerated to show the structures more clearly.

Metaphase I

Microtubule attached to kinetochore

Sister chromatids

Tetrads line up on cell's midplane. Tetrads held together at chiasmata (sites of prior crossing-over).

Anaphase I

Separation of homologous chromosomes

Homologous chromosomes separate and move to opposite poles. Note that sister chromatids remain attached at their centromeres.

Telophase I

Cleavage furrow

One of each pair of homologous chromosomes is at each pole. Cytokinesis occurs.

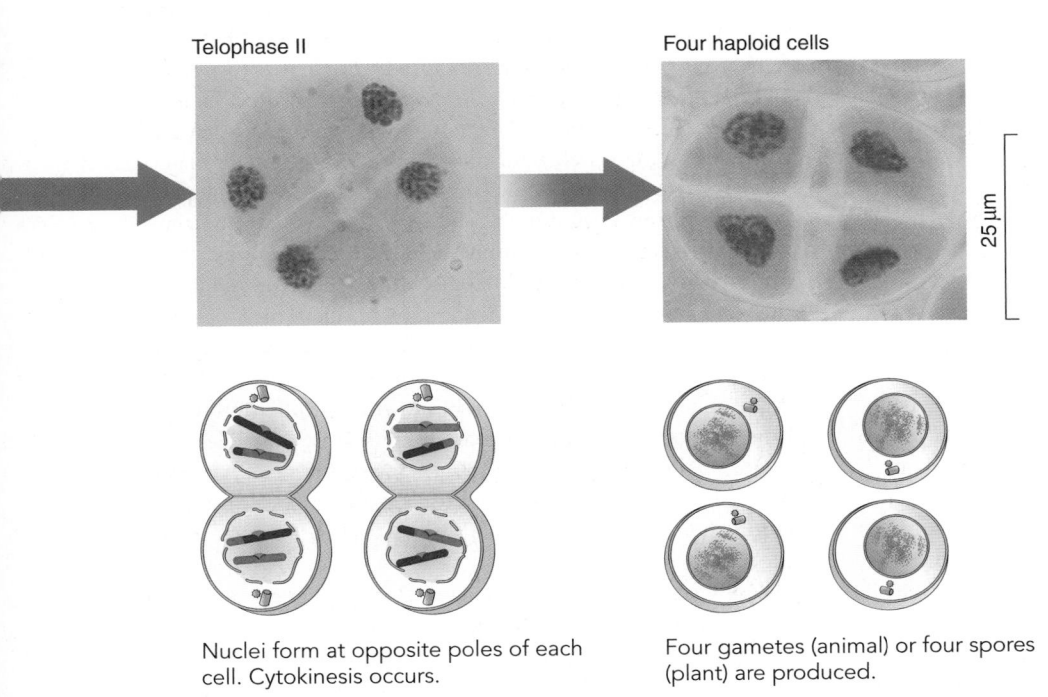

Telophase II

Nuclei form at opposite poles of each cell. Cytokinesis occurs.

Four haploid cells

25 μm

Four gametes (animal) or four spores (plant) are produced.

FIGURE 10-16 Continued

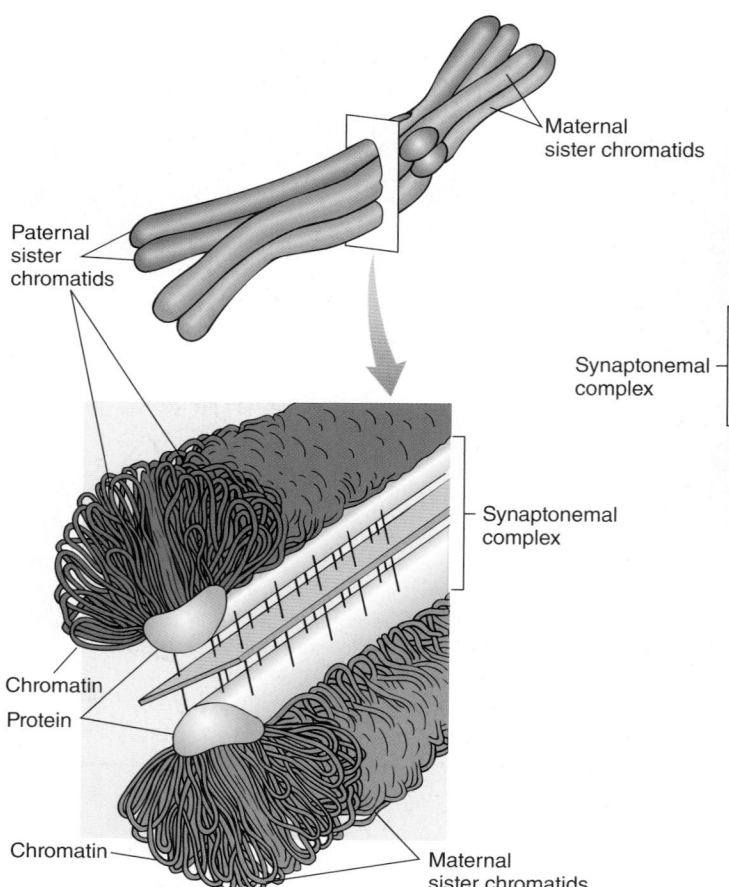

(a) A 3-D model of a tetrad with a complete synaptonemal complex.

FIGURE 10-17 A synaptonemal complex

Synapsing homologous chromosomes in meiotic prophase I are held together by a synaptonemal complex, composed mainly of protein.

0.5 μm

(b) TEM of a synaptonemal complex.

Prophase I includes synapsis and crossing-over

As occurs during mitosis, the chromosomes duplicate in the S phase of interphase, before the complex movements of meiosis actually begin. Each duplicated chromosome consists of two chromatids, which are linked by cohesins. During **prophase I,** while the chromatids are still elongated and thin, the homologous chromosomes come to lie lengthwise side by side. This process is called **synapsis,** which means "fastening together." For example, in an animal cell with a diploid number of four, synapsis results in two homologous pairs.

One member of each homologous pair is called the **maternal homologue** because it was originally inherited from the female parent; the other member of a homologous pair is the **paternal homologue** because it was inherited from the male parent. Because each chromosome duplicated during interphase and now consists of two chromatids, synapsis results in the association of four chromatids. The resulting association is a **tetrad.** The number of tetrads per prophase I cell is equal to the haploid chromosome number. In an animal cell with a diploid number of 4, there are 2

tetrads (and a total of 8 chromatids); in a human cell at prophase I, there are 23 tetrads (and a total of 92 chromatids).

Homologous chromosomes become closely associated during synapsis. Electron microscopic observations reveal that a characteristic structure, the **synaptonemal complex,** forms along the entire length of the synapsed homologues (**FIG. 10-17**). This proteinaceous structure holds the synapsed homologues together and is thought to play a role in chromosome **crossing-over,** a process in which enzymes break and rejoin DNA molecules, allowing paired homologous chromosomes to exchange genetic material. Crossing-over produces new combinations of genes. The **genetic recombination** from crossing-over greatly enhances the genetic variation—that is, new combinations of traits—among sexually produced offspring. Some biologists think that recombination is the main reason for sexual reproduction in eukaryotes.

In addition to the unique processes of synapsis and crossing-over, events similar to those in mitotic prophase also occur during prophase I. A spindle forms, consisting of microtubules and other components. In animal cells, one pair of centrioles moves to each pole, and astral microtubules form. The nuclear envelope disappears in late prophase I, and in cells with large and distinct chromosomes, the structure of the tetrads can be seen clearly with the microscope.

The sister chromatids remain closely aligned along their lengths. However, the centromeres (and kinetochores) of the homologous chromosomes become separated from one another. In late prophase I, the homologous chromosomes are held together only at specific regions, termed **chiasmata** (sing., *chiasma*). Each chiasma originates at a crossing-over site, that is, a site at which homologous chromatids exchanged genetic material and rejoined, producing an X-shaped configuration (**FIG. 10-18**). At the chiasmata, cohesins hold homologous chromosomes together after the synaptonemal complex has been disassembled. Later, the cohesins dissociate from the chiasmata, freeing the homologous chromo-

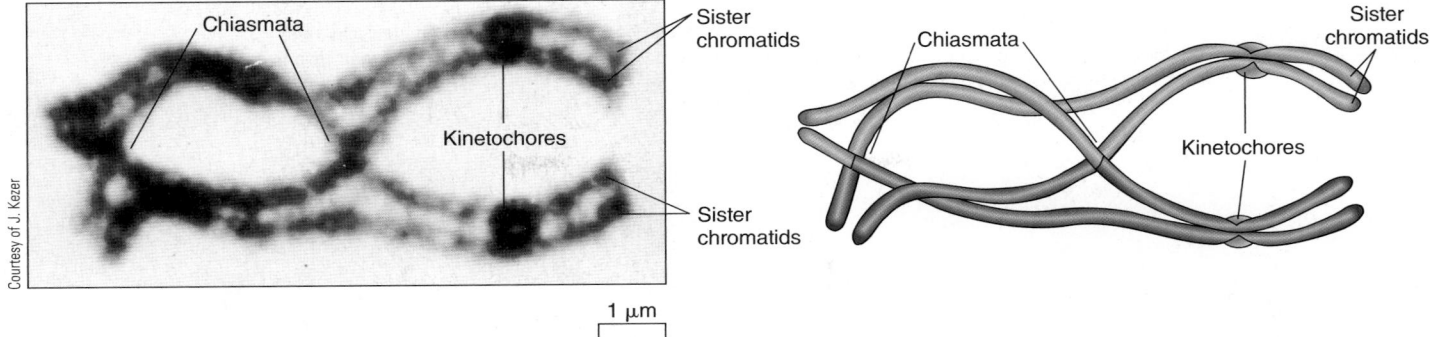

(a) LM of a tetrad during late prophase I of a male meiotic cell (spermatocyte) from a salamander.

(b) A drawing showing the structure of the tetrad. The paternal chromatids are blue, and the maternal chromatids are red.

FIGURE 10-18 A meiotic tetrad with two chiasmata
The two chiasmata are the result of separate crossing-over events.

some arms from one another. The consequences of crossing-over and genetic recombination are discussed in Chapter 11 (for example, see Fig. 11-12).

During meiosis I, homologous chromosomes separate

Metaphase I occurs when the tetrads align on the midplane. Both sister kinetochores of one duplicated chromosome are attached by spindle fibers to the same pole, and both sister kinetochores of the other duplicated homologous chromosome are attached to the opposite pole. (By contrast, sister kinetochores of each duplicated chromosome are attached to opposite poles in mitosis.)

During **anaphase I,** the paired homologous chromosomes separate, or disjoin, and move toward opposite poles. Each pole receives a random combination of maternal and paternal chromosomes, but only one member of each homologous pair is present at each pole. The sister chromatids remain united at their centromere regions. Again, this differs from mitotic anaphase, in which the sister chromatids separate and move to opposite poles.

During **telophase I,** the chromatids generally decondense somewhat, the nuclear envelope may reorganize, and cytokinesis may take place. Each telophase I nucleus contains the haploid number of chromosomes, but each chromosome is a duplicated chromosome (it consists of a pair of chromatids). In our example, 2 duplicated chromosomes lie at each pole, for a total of 4 chromatids; humans have 23 duplicated chromosomes (46 chromatids) at each pole.

An interphase-like stage called **interkinesis** usually follows. Interkinesis is not a true interphase: there is no S phase and therefore no DNA replication. Interkinesis is brief in most organisms and absent in some.

Chromatids separate in meiosis II

Because the chromosomes usually remain partially condensed between divisions, the prophase of the second meiotic division is brief.

Prophase II is similar to mitotic prophase in many respects. There is no pairing of homologous chromosomes (indeed, only one member of each pair is present in each nucleus) and no crossing-over.

During **metaphase II** the chromosomes line up on the midplanes of their cells. You can easily distinguish the first and second metaphases in diagrams; at metaphase I the chromatids are arranged in bundles of four (tetrads), and at metaphase II they are in groups of two (as in mitotic metaphase). This is not always so obvious in living cells.

During **anaphase II** the chromatids, attached to spindle fibers at their kinetochores, separate and move to opposite poles, just as they would at mitotic anaphase. As in mitosis, each former chromatid is now referred to as a *chromosome.* Thus, at **telophase II** there is one representative for each homologous pair at each pole. Each is an unduplicated (single) chromosome. Nuclear envelopes re-form, the chromosomes gradually elongate to form chromatin fibers, and cytokinesis occurs.

The two successive divisions of meiosis yield four haploid nuclei, each containing *one* of each kind of chromosome. Each resulting haploid cell has a different combination of genes. This genetic variation has two sources: (1) DNA segments are exchanged between maternal and paternal homologues during crossing-over. (2) During meiosis, the maternal and paternal chromosomes of homologous pairs separate independently. The chromosomes are "shuffled" so that each member of a pair becomes randomly distributed to one of the poles at anaphase I.

Mitosis and meiosis lead to contrasting outcomes

Although mitosis and meiosis share many similar features, specific distinctions between these processes result in the formation of different types of cells. Mitosis is a single nuclear division in which sister chromatids separate from each other and are distributed to the two daughter cells, which are genetically identical to each other and to the original cell. A diploid cell that undergoes mitosis produces two diploid cells. Similarly, a haploid cell that

Each species has a characteristic number of chromosomes that does not change. In each life cycle, the doubling of chromosomes that occurs during fertilization is compensated for by the reduction in chromosome number that occurs during meiosis.

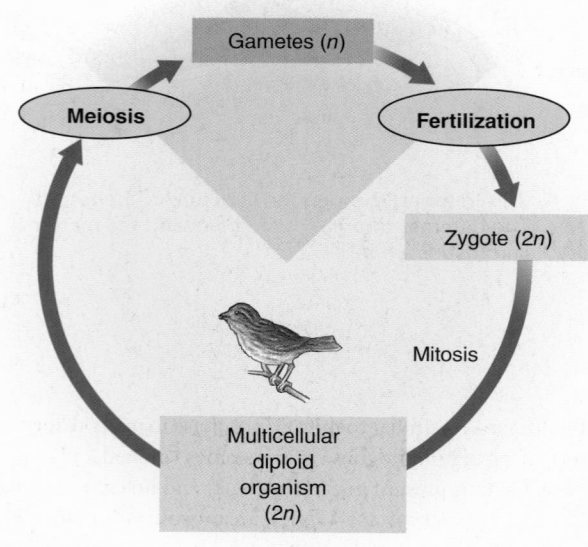

Gametes (*n*)

Meiosis

Fertilization

Zygote (2*n*)

Mitosis

Multicellular diploid organism (2*n*)

(a) Animals

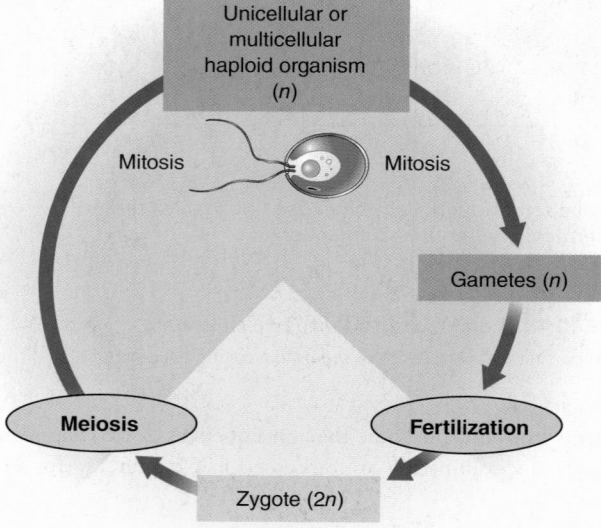

Unicellular or multicellular haploid organism (*n*)

Mitosis Mitosis

Gametes (*n*)

Meiosis Fertilization

Zygote (2*n*)

(b) Most fungi and many protists

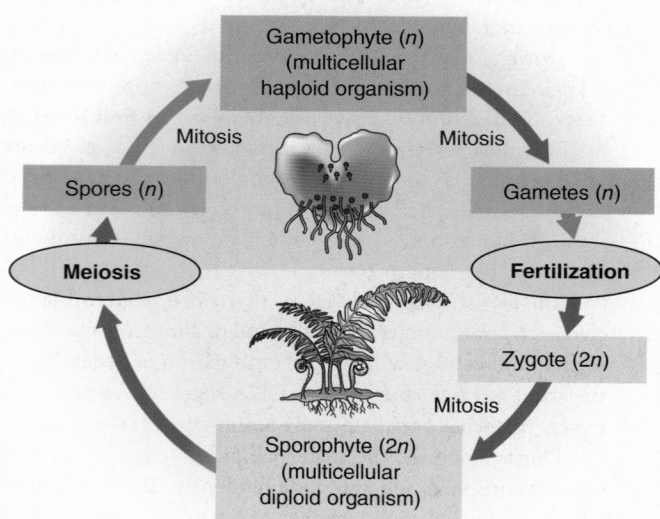

Gametophyte (*n*) (multicellular haploid organism)

Mitosis Mitosis

Spores (*n*) Gametes (*n*)

Meiosis Fertilization

Zygote (2*n*)

Mitosis

Sporophyte (2*n*) (multicellular diploid organism)

(c) Plants, some algae, and some fungi

FIGURE 10-19 Representative life cycles

The color code and design here is used throughout the rest of the book. For example, in all life cycles the haploid (*n*) generation is shown in purple, and the diploid (2*n*) generation is gold. The processes of meiosis and fertilization always link the haploid and diploid generations.

undergoes mitosis produces two haploid cells. (Some eukaryotic organisms—certain yeasts, for example—are haploid, as are plants at certain stages of their life cycles.) Homologous chromosomes do not associate physically at any time in mitosis.

In meiosis, a diploid cell undergoes two successive nuclear divisions, meiosis I and meiosis II. In prophase I of meiosis, the homologous chromosomes undergo synapsis to form tetrads. Homologous chromosomes separate during meiosis I, and sister chromatids separate during meiosis II. Meiosis ends with the formation of four genetically different, haploid daughter cells. The fates of these cells depend on the type of life cycle; in animals they differentiate as gametes, whereas in plants they become spores.

Review

- Are homologous chromosome pairs present in a diploid cell? Are they present in a haploid cell?
- How does the outcome of meiosis differ from the outcome of mitosis?
- Can haploid cells divide by mitosis? by meiosis?

10.5 SEXUAL LIFE CYCLES

■ LEARNING OBJECTIVE

11 Compare the roles of mitosis and meiosis in various generalized life cycles.

Because sexual reproduction is characterized by the fusion of two haploid sex cells to form a diploid zygote, it follows that in a sexual life cycle, meiosis must occur before gametes can form. The timing of meiosis in the life cycle varies among species.

In animals and a few other organisms, meiosis leads directly to gamete production (**FIG. 10-19a** on facing page). An organism's somatic cells multiply by mitosis and are diploid; the only haploid cells produced are the gametes. Gametes develop when **germ line cells,** which give rise to the next generation, undergo meiosis.

The formation of gametes is known as **gametogenesis.** Male gametogenesis, termed **spermatogenesis,** forms four haploid

sperm cells for each cell that enters meiosis. (See Chapter 50 and Fig. 50-5 for a detailed description of spermatogenesis.)

In contrast, female gametogenesis, called **oogenesis,** forms a single egg cell, or *ovum,* for every cell that enters meiosis. In this process, most of the cytoplasm goes to only one of the two cells produced during each meiotic division. At the end of meiosis I, one nucleus is retained and the other, called the first *polar body,* often degenerates. Similarly, at the end of meiosis II, one nucleus becomes another polar body and the other nucleus survives. In this way, one haploid nucleus receives most of the accumulated cytoplasm and nutrients from the original meiotic cell. (See Chapter 50 and Fig. 50-11 for a detailed description of oogenesis.)

Although meiosis occurs at some point in a sexual life cycle, it does not always *immediately* precede gamete formation. Many eukaryotes, including most fungi and many protists, remain haploid (their cells dividing mitotically) throughout most of their life cycles, with individuals being unicellular or multicellular. Two haploid gametes (produced by mitosis) fuse to form a diploid zygote that undergoes meiosis to restore the haploid state (**FIG. 10-19b**). Examples of these types of life cycles are found in Figures 26-16 and 29-9.

Plants and some algae and fungi have complicated life cycles (**FIG. 10-19c**). These life cycles, characterized by an **alternation of generations,** consist of a multicellular diploid stage, the **sporophyte generation,** and a multicellular haploid stage, the **gametophyte generation.** Sporophyte cells undergo meiosis to form haploid spores, each of which may divide mitotically to produce a multicellular haploid gametophyte. Gametophytes produce gametes by mitosis. The female and male gametes (egg and sperm cells) fuse to form a diploid zygote that divides mitotically to form a multicellular sporophyte. You can find more detailed descriptions of alternation of generations in plants in Chapters 27 and 28.

Review

- In animals, which cells are produced by mitosis? by meiosis?
- Assuming a sexually reproducing organism is haploid, how do meiosis and fertilization maintain the normal chromosome number?

■ SUMMARY: FOCUS ON LEARNING OBJECTIVES

10.1 *(page 214)*

1 Discuss the significance of chromosomes in terms of their information content.
- Genes, the cell's informational units, are made of DNA. In eukaryotes, DNA associates with protein to form the **chromatin** fibers that make up **chromosomes.**

2 Explain how DNA is packed into chromosomes in eukaryotic cells.
- The organization of eukaryotic DNA into chromosomes allows the DNA to be accurately replicated and sorted into daughter cells without tangling. In eukaryotic cells DNA is associated with **histones** (basic proteins) to form **nucleosomes,** each of which consists of a histone bead with DNA wrapped around it. Nucleosomes are organized into large, coiled loops held together by nonhistone **scaffolding proteins.**

10.2 *(page 217)*

3 Identify the stages in the eukaryotic cell cycle and describe their principal events.

- The eukaryotic **cell cycle** is the period from the beginning of one division to the beginning of the next. The cell cycle consists of interphase and M phase.

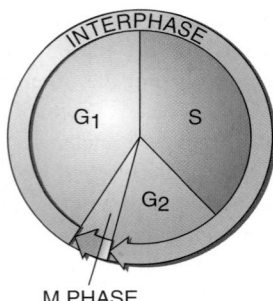

M PHASE

- **Interphase** consists of the first gap phase (G_1), the synthesis phase (S), and the second gap phase (G_2). During the **G_1 phase,** the cell grows and prepares for the S phase. During the **S phase,** DNA and the chromosome proteins are synthesized, and chromosome duplication occurs. During the **G_2 phase,** protein synthesis increases in preparation for cell division.
- **M phase** consists of **mitosis,** the nuclear division that produces two nuclei identical to the parental nucleus, and **cytokinesis,** the division of the cytoplasm to yield two daughter cells.

  CENGAGENOW˜ Learn more about the cell cycle by clicking on the figure in CengageNOW.

4 Describe the structure of a duplicated chromosome, including the sister chromatids, centromeres, and kinetochores.

- A duplicated chromosome consists of a pair of **sister chromatids,** which contain identical DNA sequences. Each chromatid includes a constricted region called a **centromere.** Sister chromatids are tightly associated in the region of their centromeres. Attached to each centromere is a **kinetochore,** a protein structure to which microtubules can bind.

5 Explain the significance of mitosis and describe the process.

- Mitosis assures that the chromosome number is preserved when one eukaryotic cell divides to form two. In mitosis, identical chromosomes are distributed to each pole of the cell, and a nuclear envelope forms around each set.
- During **prophase,** the structure of the duplicated chromosomes becomes apparent as the chromatin condenses; each is composed of a pair of identical sister chromatids. The nuclear envelope begins to disassemble, and the **mitotic spindle** begins to form.
- During **prometaphase,** spindle microtubules attach to kinetochores of chromosomes, and chromosomes begin to move toward the cell's midplane.
- During **metaphase,** the chromosomes are aligned on the cell's midplane, or **metaphase plate;** the mitotic spindle is complete, and the kinetochores of the sister chromatids are attached by microtubules to opposite poles of the cell.
- During **anaphase,** the sister chromatids separate and move to opposite poles. Each former chromatid is now a chromosome.
- During **telophase,** a nuclear envelope re-forms around each set of chromosomes, nucleoli become apparent, the chromosomes uncoil, and the spindle disappears. Cytokinesis generally begins in telophase.

  CENGAGENOW˜ Walk step-by-step through the stages of mitosis by clicking on the figure in CengageNOW.

CENGAGENOW˜ Watch cytokinesis unfold by clicking on the figure in CengageNOW.

10.3 *(page 223)*

6 Explain some ways in which the cell cycle is controlled.

- Control mechanisms, called **cell-cycle checkpoints,** temporarily block key events from being initiated during the cell cycle. **Cyclin-dependent kinases (Cdks)** are **protein kinases** involved in regulating the cell cycle. Cdks are active only when they bind tightly to regulatory proteins called **cyclins.** Cyclin levels fluctuate predictably during the cell cycle.

10.4 *(page 225)*

7 Differentiate between asexual and sexual reproduction.

- Offspring produced by **asexual reproduction** usually have hereditary traits identical to those of the single parent. Mitosis is the basis for asexual reproduction in eukaryotic organisms.
- In **sexual reproduction,** two haploid sex cells, or **gametes,** fuse to form a single diploid **zygote.** In a sexual life cycle, meiosis must occur before gametes can be produced.

8 Distinguish between haploid and diploid cells, and define *homologous chromosomes.*

- A **diploid** cell has a characteristic number of chromosome pairs per cell. The members of each pair, called **homologous chromosomes,** are similar in length, shape, and other features and carry genes affecting the same kinds of attributes of the organism.
- A **haploid** cell contains only one member of each homologous chromosome pair.

9 Explain the significance of meiosis and describe the process.

- A diploid cell undergoing **meiosis** completes two successive cell divisions, yielding four haploid cells. Sexual life cycles in eukaryotes require meiosis, which makes it possible for each gamete to contain only half the number of chromosomes in the parent cell.
- **Meiosis I** begins with **prophase I,** in which the members of a homologous pair of chromosomes physically join by the process of **synapsis. Crossing-over** is a process of **genetic recombination** during which homologous (nonsister) chromatids exchange segments of DNA strands.
- At **metaphase I, tetrads**—each consisting of a pair of homologous chromosomes held together by one or more **chiasmata**—line up on the metaphase plate. The members of each pair of homologous chromosomes separate during meiotic **anaphase I** and are distributed to different nuclei. Each nucleus contains the haploid number of chromosomes; each chromosome consists of two chromatids.
- During **meiosis II,** the two chromatids of each chromosome separate, and one is distributed to each daughter cell. Each former chromatid is now a chromosome.

  CENGAGENOW˜ Walk step-by-step through the stages of meiosis by clicking on the figure in CengageNOW.

10 Contrast mitosis and meiosis, emphasizing the different outcomes.

- Mitosis involves a single nuclear division in which the two daughter cells formed are genetically identical to each other and to the original cell. Synapsis of homologous chromosomes does not occur during mitosis.
- Meiosis involves two successive nuclear divisions and forms four haploid cells. Synapsis of homologous chromosomes occurs during prophase I of meiosis.

  CENGAGENOW˜ Watch a movie that features living cells undergoing mitosis and meiosis in CengageNOW.

11 Compare the roles of mitosis and meiosis in various generalized life cycles.

- Somatic cells of animals are diploid and are produced by mitosis. The only haploid cells are gametes, produced by **gametogenesis,** which in animals occurs by meiosis.

- Most fungi and many protists are haploid and are produced by mitosis. The only diploid stage is the zygote, which undergoes meiosis to restore the haploid state.

- The life cycle of plants, some algae, and some fungi includes an **alternation of generations.** The multicellular diploid **sporophyte generation** forms haploid spores by meiosis. Each spore divides mitotically to form a multicellular haploid **gametophyte generation,** which produces gametes by mitosis. Two haploid gametes then fuse to form a diploid zygote, which divides mitotically to produce a new sporophyte generation.

TEST YOUR UNDERSTANDING

1. Chromatin fibers include (a) DNA and structural polysaccharides (b) RNA and phospholipids (c) protein and carbohydrate (d) DNA and protein (e) triacylglycerol and steroids

2. A nucleosome consists of (a) DNA and scaffolding proteins (b) scaffolding proteins and histones (c) DNA and histones (d) DNA, histones, and scaffolding proteins (e) histones only

3. The term *S phase* refers to (a) DNA synthesis during interphase (b) synthesis of chromosome proteins during prophase (c) gametogenesis in animal cells (d) synapsis of homologous chromosomes (e) fusion of gametes in sexual reproduction

4. At which of the following stages do human skin cell nuclei have the same DNA content? (a) early mitotic prophase and late mitotic telophase (b) G_1 and G_2 (c) G_1 and early mitotic prophase (d) G_1 and late mitotic telophase (e) G_2 and late mitotic telophase

5. In a cell at _____, each chromosome consists of a pair of attached chromatids. (a) mitotic prophase (b) meiotic prophase II (c) meiotic prophase I (d) meiotic anaphase I (e) all of the preceding

6. The molecular tether that links sister chromatids of a duplicated chromosome to each other is (a) condensin (b) actin (c) myosin (d) cohesin (e) actomyosin

7. In an animal cell at mitotic metaphase, you would expect to find (a) two pairs of centrioles located on the metaphase plate (b) a pair of centrioles inside the nucleus (c) a pair of centrioles within each microtubule-organizing center (d) a centriole within each centromere (e) no centrioles

8. Cell plate formation usually begins during (a) telophase in a plant cell (b) telophase in an animal cell (c) G_2 in a plant cell (d) G_2 in an animal cell (e) a and b

9. A diploid nucleus at early mitotic prophase has _____ set(s) of chromosomes; a diploid nucleus at mitotic telophase has _____ set(s) of chromosomes. (a) 1; 1 (b) 1; 2 (c) 2; 2 (d) 2; 1 (e) not enough information has been given

10. You would expect to find a synaptonemal complex in a cell at (a) mitotic prophase (b) meiotic prophase I (c) meiotic prophase II (d) meiotic anaphase I (e) meiotic anaphase II

11. A chiasma links a pair of (a) homologous chromosomes at prophase II (b) homologous chromosomes at late prophase I (c) sister chromatids at metaphase II (d) sister chromatids at mitotic metaphase (e) sister chromatids at metaphase I

12. Match the following descriptions (a–e) to the steps of meiosis (1–5) in the following figure. (a) haploid cells with unduplicated chromosomes (b) haploid cells with duplicated chromosomes (c) synapsis of homologous chromosomes to form tetrads (d) sister chromatids move to opposite poles (e) homologous chromosomes move to opposite poles

CRITICAL THINKING

1. How can two species have the same chromosome number yet have very different attributes?

2. How does the DNA content of the cell change from the beginning of interphase to the end of interphase? Does the number of chromatids change? Explain. Does the number of chromosomes change? Explain.

In questions 3–4, decide whether each is an example of sexual or asexual reproduction, and state why.

3. A diploid queen honeybee produces haploid eggs by meiosis. Some of these eggs are never fertilized and develop into haploid male honeybees (drones).

4. Seeds develop after a flower has been pollinated with pollen from the same plant.

5. **ANALYZING DATA.** In the experiment with spindle microtubules during anaphase (see Fig. 10-10), how would the spindle mi-crotubules have looked during anaphase if they had disassembled at their polar ends instead of their kinetochore ends?

6. **EVOLUTION LINK.** How does mitosis provide evidence for relationships among eukaryotes as diverse as mammals and seaweeds?

7. **EVOLUTION LINK.** Some organisms—for example, certain fungi—reproduce asexually when the environment is favorable and sexually when the environment becomes unfavorable. What might be the evolutionary advantage of sexual reproduction with the associated process of meiosis during unfavorable conditions?

 Additional questions are available in CengageNOW at www.cengage.com/login.

11 The Basic Principles of Heredity

Gregor Mendel. This painting shows Mendel with his pea plants in the monastery garden at Brünn, Austria (now Brüno, Czech Republic).

© Science Source/Photo Researchers, Inc.

KEY CONCEPTS

11.1 The experiments of Gregor Mendel, a pioneer in the field of genetics, revealed the basic principles of inheritance. In Mendel's principle of segregation, members of a gene pair segregate (separate) from one another prior to gamete formation. In the principle of independent assortment, members of different gene pairs assort independently (randomly) into gametes.

11.2 You can use probability to predict Mendelian inheritance: the product rule shows how to combine the probabilities of independent events, and the sum rule shows how to combine the probabilities of mutually exclusive events.

11.3 Chromosome behavior during meiosis helps explain Mendel's principles of inheritance.

11.4 Distinctive inheritance patterns (that is, "extensions" to Mendel's principles) characterize some traits.

Human characters such as eye color and hair color, along with a multitude of other characteristics, are passed on from one generation to another. **Heredity,** the transmission of genetic information from parent to offspring, generally follows predictable patterns in organisms as diverse as humans, penguins, baker's yeast, and sunflowers. **Genetics,** the science of heredity, studies both genetic similarities and **genetic variation,** the differences between parents and offspring or among individuals of a population.

The study of inheritance as a modern branch of science began in the mid-19th century with the work of Gregor Mendel (1822–1884), a monk who bred pea plants (see picture). Mendel was the first scientist to effectively apply quantitative methods to the study of inheritance. He did not merely describe his observations; he planned his experiments carefully, recorded the data, and analyzed the results mathematically. Although unappreciated during his lifetime, his work was rediscovered in 1900.

During the decades following the rediscovery of Mendel's findings, geneticists extended Mendel's principles by correlating the transmission of genetic information from generation to generation with the behavior of chromosomes during *meiosis*. By studying a variety of organisms, geneticists verified Mendel's findings and added a growing list of so-called exceptions to his principles.

Geneticists study not only the transmission of genes but also the expression of genetic information. As you will see in this chapter and those that follow, understanding the relationships between an organism's genes and its characteristics has become increasingly sophisticated as biologists have learned more about the orderly transmission of information in cells from one generation to another.

11.1 MENDEL'S PRINCIPLES OF INHERITANCE

◼ LEARNING OBJECTIVES

1 Define the terms *phenotype, genotype, locus, allele, dominant allele, recessive allele, homozygous,* and *heterozygous.*
2 Describe Mendel's principles of segregation and independent assortment.
3 Distinguish among monohybrid, dihybrid, and test crosses.
4 Explain Mendel's principles of segregation and independent assortment, given what scientists now know about genes and chromosomes.

Gregor Mendel was not the first plant breeder. At the time he began his work, breeders had long recognized the existence of **hybrid** plants and animals, the offspring of two genetically dissimilar parents. When Mendel began his breeding experiments in 1856, two

---

RESEARCH METHOD

Why Is It Used? Garden peas normally self-fertilize during reproduction, that is, the male and female gametes are from the same flower. Because pea petals completely enclose the reproductive parts, there is little chance of natural cross-pollination between separate flowers. Cross-pollination enables the researcher to study various patterns of inheritance in peas.

How Is It Done?

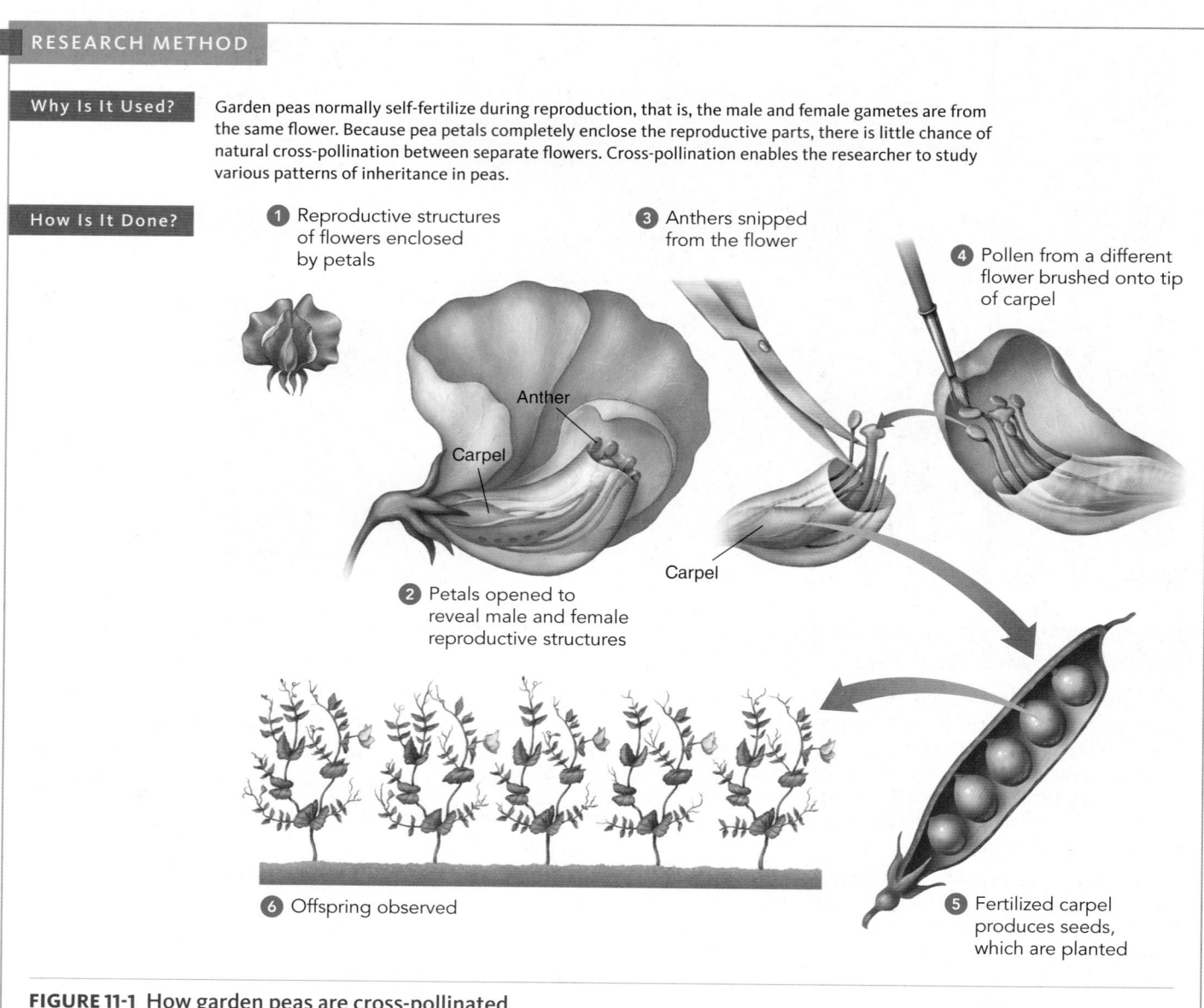

❶ Reproductive structures of flowers enclosed by petals

❷ Petals opened to reveal male and female reproductive structures

Anther

Carpel

❸ Anthers snipped from the flower

❹ Pollen from a different flower brushed onto tip of carpel

Carpel

❺ Fertilized carpel produces seeds, which are planted

❻ Offspring observed

FIGURE 11-1 How garden peas are cross-pollinated

---

main concepts about inheritance were widely accepted: (1) All hybrid plants that are the offspring of genetically pure, or **true-breeding,** parents are similar in appearance. (2) When these hybrids mate with each other, they do not breed true; their offspring show a mixture of traits. Some look like their parents, and some have features like those of their grandparents.

Mendel's genius lay in his ability to recognize a pattern in the way the parental traits reappear in the offspring of hybrids. Before Mendel, no one had categorized and counted the offspring and analyzed these regular patterns over several generations to the extent he did. Just as geneticists do today, Mendel chose the organism for his experiments very carefully. The garden pea, *Pisum sativum,* had several advantages. Pea plants are easy to grow, and many varieties were commercially available. Another advantage of pea plants is that controlled pollinations are relatively easy to conduct. Pea flowers have both male and female parts and naturally self-pollinate. However, the anthers (the male parts of the flower that produce pollen) can be removed to prevent self-fertilization (**FIG. 11-1**). Pollen from a different source can then be applied to the stigma (the receptive surface of the carpel, or female part). Pea flowers are easily protected from other sources of pollen because the petals completely enclose the reproductive structures.

Mendel obtained his original pea seeds from commercial sources and did some important preliminary work before starting his actual experiments. For two years he verified that the varieties were true-breeding lines for various inherited features. Today, scientists use the term **phenotype** to refer to the physical appearance of an organism and **genotype** to refer to the genetic makeup for that organism, which is most often expressed in symbols. A true-breeding line produces only offspring expressing the same phenotype (for example, round seeds or tall plants) generation after generation. During this time Mendel apparently chose those traits of his pea strains that he could study most easily. He probably made the initial observations that later formed the basis of his hypotheses.

Mendel eventually chose strains representing seven **characters,** the attributes (such as seed color) for which heritable differences, or **traits,** are known (such as yellow seeds and green seeds). The characters Mendel selected had clearly contrasting phenotypes (**FIG. 11-2**). Mendel's results were easy to analyze because he chose easily distinguishable phenotypes and limited the genetic variation studied in each experiment.

Mendel began his experiments by crossing plants from two different true-breeding lines with contrasting phenotypes; these genetically pure individuals constituted the **parental generation, or P generation.** In every case, the members of the first generation of offspring all looked alike and resembled one of the two parents. For example, when he crossed tall plants with short plants, all the

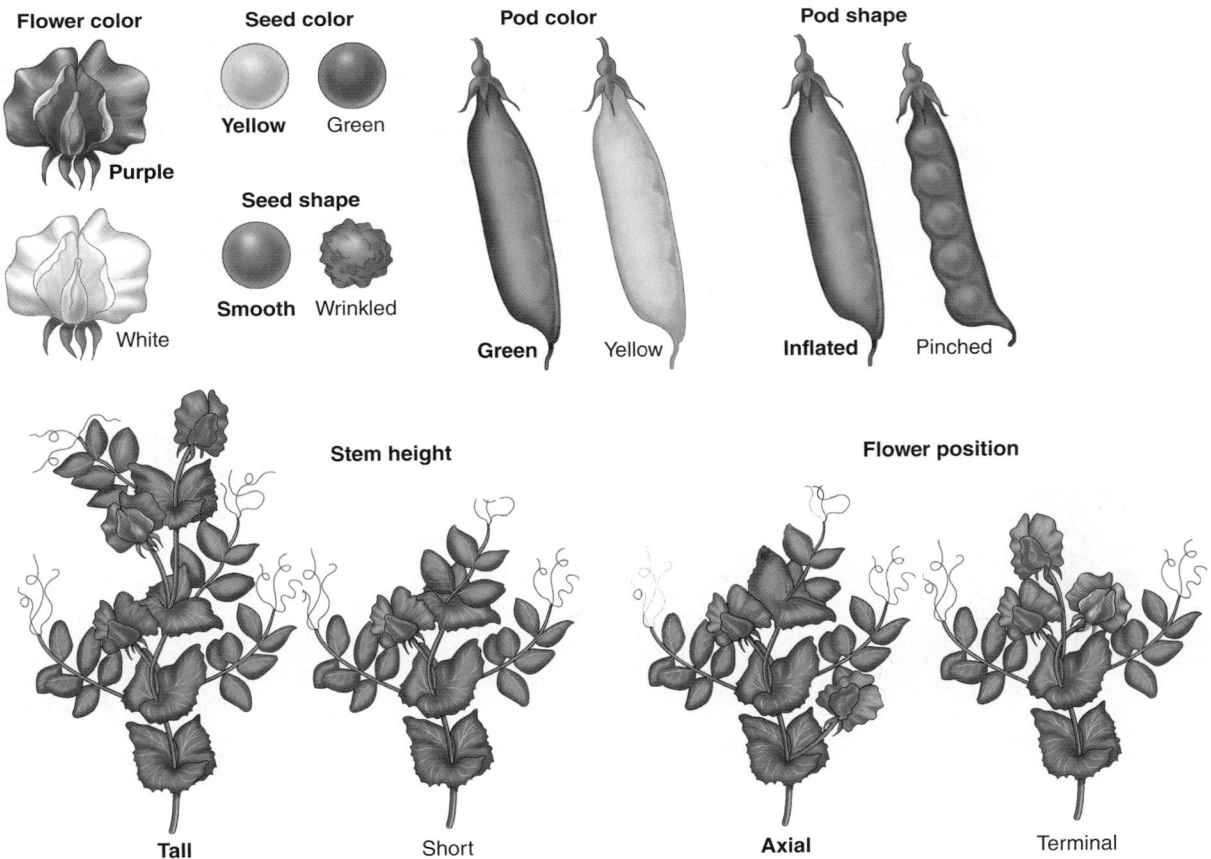

FIGURE 11-2 Seven characters in Mendel's study of pea plants
Each character had two clearly distinguishable phenotypes; the dominant phenotype is boldface.

QUESTION: When the F$_1$ generation of tall pea plants is self-pollinated, what phenotypes appear in the F$_2$ generation?

HYPOTHESIS: Although only the "factor" (gene) for tall height is expressed in the F$_1$ generation, Mendel hypothesized that the factor for short height is not lost. He predicted that the short phenotype would reappear in the F$_2$ generation.

EXPERIMENT: Mendel crossed true-breeding tall pea plants with true-breeding short pea plants, yielding only tall offspring in the F$_1$ generation. He then allowed these F$_1$ individuals to self-pollinate to yield the F$_2$ generation.

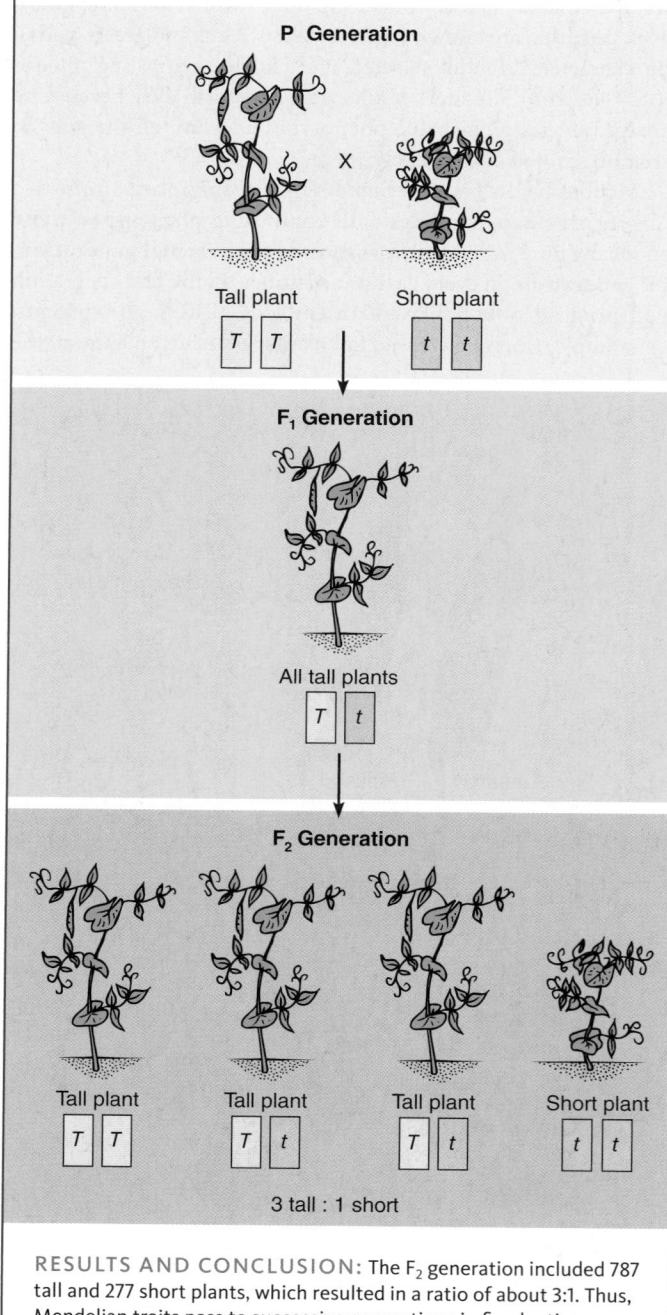

RESULTS AND CONCLUSION: The F$_2$ generation included 787 tall and 277 short plants, which resulted in a ratio of about 3:1. Thus, Mendelian traits pass to successive generations in fixed ratios.

FIGURE 11-3 *Animated* One of Mendel's pea crosses

offspring were tall (**FIG. 11-3**). These offspring were the first filial generation, or the **F$_1$ generation** (*filial* is from the Latin for "sons and daughters"). The second filial generation, or **F$_2$ generation,** resulted from a cross between F$_1$ individuals or by self-pollination of F$_1$ individuals. Mendel's F$_2$ generation in this experiment included 787 tall plants and 277 short plants. **TABLE 11-1** shows Mendel's experimental results for all seven pea characters.

Most breeders in Mendel's time thought that inheritance involved the blending of traits. In *blending inheritance,* male and female gametes supposedly contained fluids that blended together during reproduction to produce hybrid offspring with features intermediate between those of the mother and father. In fact, some plant breeders had obtained such hybrids.

Although Mendel observed some intermediate types of hybrids, he chose for further study those F$_1$ hybrids in which "hereditary factors" (as he called them) from one of the parents apparently masked the expression of those factors from the other parent. Other breeders had also observed these types of hybrids, but they had not explained them. Using modern terms, we say that the factor expressed in the F$_1$ generation (tallness, in our example) is **dominant;** the one hidden in the F$_1$ (shortness) is **recessive.** Dominant traits mask recessive ones when both are present in the same individual. Although scientists know today that dominance is not always observed, the fact that dominance can occur was not consistent with the notion of blending inheritance.

Mendel's results were inconsistent with the hypothesis of blending inheritance in a more compelling way. Once two fluids have blended, it is very difficult to imagine how they can separate. However, in the preceding example, in the F$_1$ generation the hereditary factor(s) that controlled shortness clearly was not lost or blended inseparably with the hereditary factor(s) that controlled tallness because shortness reappeared in the F$_2$ generation. Mendel was very comfortable with the theoretical side of biology because he was also a student of physics and mathematics. He therefore proposed that each kind of inherited feature of an organism is controlled by two factors that behave like discrete particles and are present in every individual.

To Mendel these hereditary factors were abstractions—he knew nothing about chromosomes and DNA. These factors are essentially what scientists today call **genes**—units of heredity that affect an organism's traits. At the molecular level, a gene is a DNA sequence that contains the information to make an RNA or pro-

TABLE 11-1	Mendel's Experimental Results for Seven Characters				

Characters and Traits in Peas				F$_2$ Generation	
Character	Dominant Trait	×	Recessive Trait	Dominant: Recessive	Ratio
Stem height	Tall	×	Short	787:277	2.84:1
Flower color	Purple	×	White	705:224	3.15:1
Flower position	Axial	×	Terminal	651:207	3.14:1
Pod color	Green	×	Yellow	428:152	2.82:1
Pod shape	Inflated	×	Pinched	882:299	2.95:1
Seed color	Yellow	×	Green	6022:2001	3.01:1
Seed shape	Smooth	×	Wrinkled	5474:1850	2.96:1

tein product with a specific function. (Chapter 13 traces the development of ideas regarding the nature of genes.)

Mendel's experiments led to his discovery and explanation of the major principles of heredity, which we now know as the principles of segregation and independent assortment (see **TABLE 11-2** for a summary of Mendel's model of inheritance). We discuss the first principle next and the second later in the chapter.

Alleles separate before gametes are formed: the principle of segregation

Alternative forms of a gene are called **alleles.** In the example in Figure 11-3, each F_1 generation tall plant had two different alleles that control plant height: a **dominant allele** for tallness (which we designate T) and a **recessive allele** for shortness (designated t). Because the tall allele was dominant, these plants were tall. To explain his experimental results, Mendel proposed an idea now known as the **principle of segregation.** Using modern terminology, the principle of segregation states that before sexual reproduction occurs, the two alleles carried by an individual parent must become separated (that is, segregated).

Recall that during meiosis, homologous chromosomes, and therefore the alleles that reside on them, separate. (You may want to review meiosis in Figure 10-16.) As a result, each sex cell (egg or sperm) formed contains only one allele of each pair. (Later, at the time of fertilization, each haploid gamete contributes one chromosome from each homologous pair and therefore one allele for each gene pair.) An essential feature of meiosis is that the alleles remain

intact (one does not mix with or eliminate the other); thus, recessive alleles are not lost and can reappear in the F_2 generation. In our example, before the F_1 plants formed gametes, the allele for tallness segregated from the allele for shortness; so half the gametes contained a T allele, and the other half, a t allele (**FIG. 11-4**).

The random process of fertilization led to three possible combinations of alleles in the F_2 offspring: one-fourth with two tallness alleles (TT), one-fourth with two shortness alleles (tt), and one-half with one allele for tallness and one for shortness (Tt). Because both TT and Tt plants are tall, Mendel expected approximately three-fourths (787 of the 1064 plants he obtained) to express the phenotype of the dominant allele (tall) and about one-fourth (277/1064) to express the phenotype of the recessive allele (short). We will explain the mathematical reasoning behind these predictions later in the chapter.

TABLE 11-2	Mendel's Model of Inheritance

1. **Alternative forms of a "factor" (what we now call a *gene*) account for variations in inherited traits.**

   Although Mendel observed only two forms (what we now call *alleles*) for each factor he studied, we now know that many genes have more than two alleles.

2. **Inherited traits pass from parents to offspring as unmodified factors.**

   Mendel did not observe offspring of intermediate appearance, as a hypothesis of blending inheritance would have predicted. Exceptions to this concept are known today.

3. **Each individual has two sets of factors, one of each pair inherited from the mother and one from the father.**

   It does not matter which parent contributes which set of factors.

4. **The paired factors separate during the formation of reproductive cells (the principle of segregation).**

   Because of *meiosis*, which was discovered after Mendel's time, each parent passes one set of factors to each offspring.

5. **Factors may be expressed or hidden in a given generation, but they are never lost.**

   For example, factors not expressed in the F_1 generation reappear in some F_2 individuals.

6. **Each factor is passed to the next generation independently from all other factors (the principle of independent assortment).**

   Research since Mendel's time has revealed that there are exceptions to this principle.

KEY POINT Mendel's principle of segregation is related to the events of meiosis: the separation of homologous chromosomes during meiosis results in the segregation of alleles.

Homologous chromosomes

METAPHASE I

METAPHASE II

T-carrying gametes t-carrying gametes

FIGURE 11-4 *Animated* **Chromosomes and segregation**
Note that half of the gametes carry T and half carry t.

Alleles occupy corresponding loci on homologous chromosomes

Today scientists know that each unduplicated chromosome consists of one long, linear DNA molecule and that each gene is actually a segment of that DNA molecule. We also know that homologous chromosomes not only are similar in size and shape but also usually have the same genes (often with different alleles) located in corresponding positions. The term **locus** (pl., *loci*) originally designated the location of a particular gene on the chromosome (**FIG. 11-5**). We are actually referring to a segment of the DNA that has the information for controlling some aspect of the structure or function of the organism. One locus may govern seed color, another seed shape, another shape of the pods, and so on. Traditional genetic methods can infer the existence of a particular locus only if at least two allelic variants of that locus, producing contrasting phenotypes (for example, yellow peas versus green peas), are available for study. In the simplest cases, an individual can express one (yellow) or the other (green) but not both.

Alleles are, therefore, genes that govern variations of the same character (yellow versus green seed color) and occupy corresponding loci on homologous chromosomes. Geneticists assign each allele of a locus a single letter or group of letters as its symbol.[1]

Although geneticists often use more complicated forms of notation, it is customary when working simple genetics problems to indicate a dominant allele with a capital letter and a recessive allele with the same letter in lowercase.

Remember that the term *locus* designates not only a position on a chromosome but also a type of gene controlling a particular character; thus, Y (yellow) and y (green) represent a specific pair of alleles of a locus involved in determining seed color in peas. Although you may initially be uncomfortable with the fact that geneticists sometimes use the term *gene* to specify a locus and at other times to specify one of the alleles of that locus, the meaning is usually clear from the context.

A monohybrid cross involves individuals with different alleles of a given locus

The basic principles of genetics and the use of genetics terms are best illustrated by examples. In the simplest case, a **monohybrid cross,** the inheritance of two different alleles of a single locus, is studied. **FIGURE 11-6** illustrates a monohybrid cross featuring a locus that governs coat color in guinea pigs. The female comes from

---

[1]Early geneticists developed their own symbols to represent genes and alleles. Later, groups of scientists met and decided on specific symbols for a given research organism, such as the fruit fly, but each research group had its own rules for assigning symbols. Universally accepted rules for assigning symbols for genes and alleles still do not exist.

A gamete has one set of chromosomes, the *n* number. It carries *one* chromosome of *each* homologous pair. A given gamete can have only *one* gene of any particular pair of alleles.

When the gametes fuse, the resulting zygote is diploid (2*n*) and has homologous pairs of chromosomes. For purposes of illustration, these are shown physically paired.

(a) One member of each pair of homologous chromosomes is of maternal origin (*red*), and the other is paternal (*blue*).

Gene loci

(b) These chromosomes are nonhomologous. Each chromosome is made up of hundreds or thousands of genes. A locus is the specific place on a chromosome where a gene is located.

A pair of alleles

These genes are not allelic to one another

(c) These chromosomes are homologous. Alleles are members of a gene pair that occupy corresponding loci on homologous chromosomes.

Alleles controlling fur color:
Black   Brown

Alleles controlling fur length:
Long   Short

(d) Alleles govern the same character but do not necessarily contain the same information.

FIGURE 11-5 *Animated* Gene loci and their alleles

a true-breeding line of black guinea pigs. We say she is **homozygous** for black because the two alleles she carries for this locus are identical. The brown male is also from a true-breeding line and is homozygous for brown. What color would you expect the F$_1$ offspring to be? Actually, it is impossible to make such a prediction without more information.

In this particular case, the F$_1$ offspring are black, but they are **heterozygous,** meaning they carry two different alleles for this locus. The brown allele determines coat color only in a homozygous brown individual; it is a recessive allele. The black allele influences coat color in both homozygous black and heterozygous individuals; it is a dominant allele. On the basis of this information, we can use symbols to designate the dominant black allele *B* and the recessive brown allele *b*.

During meiosis in the female parent (*BB*), the two *B* alleles separate according to Mendel's principle of segregation, so each egg has only one *B* allele. In the male (*bb*) the two *b* alleles sepa-

rate, so each sperm has only one *b* allele. The fertilization of each *B* egg by a *b* sperm results in heterozygous F$_1$ offspring, each *Bb*; that is, each individual has one allele for brown coat and one for black coat. Because this is the only possible combination of alleles present in the eggs and sperm, all the F$_1$ offspring are *Bb*. Also, note that it does not make any difference whether the offspring receive the dominant allele from the mother or father guinea pig.

A Punnett square predicts the ratios of the various offspring of a cross

During meiosis in heterozygous black guinea pigs (*Bb*), the chromosome containing the *B* allele becomes separated from its homologue (the chromosome containing the *b* allele), so each normal sperm or egg contains *B* or *b* but never both. Heterozygous *Bb* individuals form gametes containing *B* alleles and gametes containing *b* alleles in equal numbers. Because no special attraction or repulsion occurs between an egg and a sperm containing the same allele, fertilization is a random process.

As you can see in Figure 11-6, the possible combinations of eggs and sperm at fertilization can be represented in the form of a grid, or **Punnett square,** devised by the early English geneticist Sir Reginald Punnett. The types of gametes (and their expected frequencies) from one parent are listed across the top, and those from the other parent are listed along the left side. The squares are then filled in with the resulting F$_2$ combinations. Three-fourths of all F$_2$ offspring have the genetic constitution *BB* or *Bb* and are phenotypically black; one-fourth have the genetic constitution *bb* and are phenotypically brown. The genetic mechanism that governs the approximate 3:1 F$_2$ ratios obtained by Mendel in his pea-breeding experiments is again evident. These ratios are called *monohybrid F$_2$ phenotypic ratios.*

The phenotype of an individual does not always reveal its genotype

As mentioned earlier, an organism's phenotype is its appearance with respect to a certain inherited trait. However, because some alleles may be dominant and others recessive, we cannot always determine, simply by examining its phenotype, which alleles are carried by an organism. In the cross we have been considering, the genotype of the female parent is homozygous dominant, *BB*, and her phenotype is black. The genotype of the male parent is homozygous recessive, *bb*, and his phenotype is brown. The genotype of all the F$_1$ offspring is heterozygous, *Bb*, and their phenotype is black. To prevent confusion, we always indicate the genotype of a heterozygous individual by writing the symbol for the dominant allele first and the recessive allele second (always *Bb*, never *bB*). The expression of dominance partly explains why an individual may resemble one parent more than the other, even though the two parents contribute equally to their offspring's genetic constitution.

Dominance is not predictable—that is, dominance is not an intrinsic part of an allele but is the property of an allele relative to other alleles. Dominance is produced by the mechanism of gene expression and can be determined only by experiment. In one species of animal, black coat may be dominant to brown; in another species, brown may be dominant to black. In a population, the dominant phenotype is not necessarily more common than the recessive phenotype.

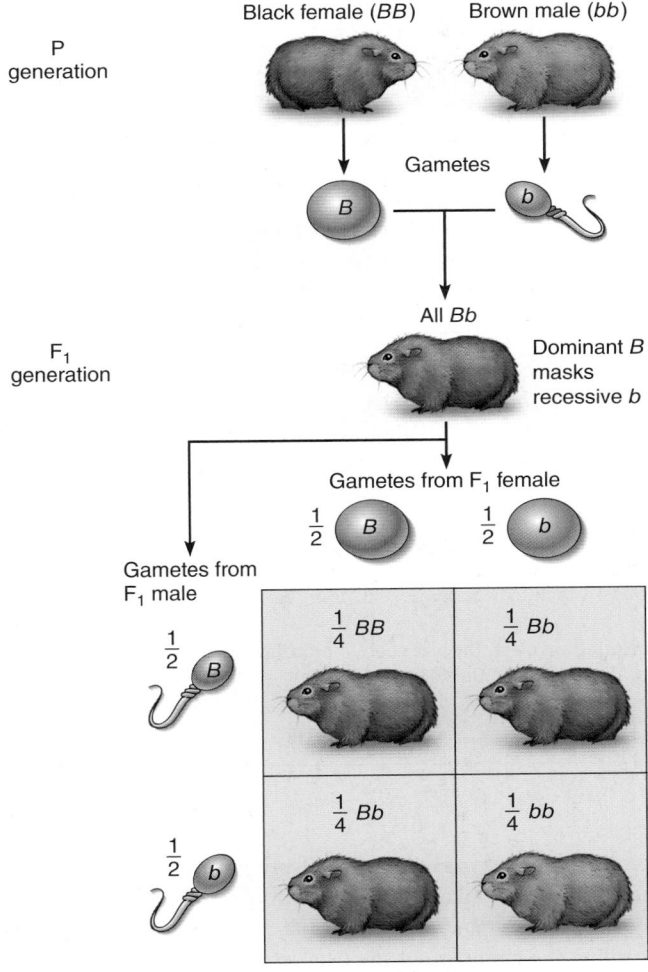

FIGURE 11-6 *Animated* **A monohybrid cross in guinea pigs**

In this example, a homozygous black guinea pig is mated with a homozygous brown guinea pig. The F$_1$ generation includes only black individuals. However, the mating of two of these F$_1$ offspring yields F$_2$ generation offspring in the expected ratio of 3 black to 1 brown, indicating that the F$_1$ individuals are heterozygous.

QUESTION: How do you determine the genotype of an individual with a dominant phenotype?

HYPOTHESIS: A test cross between an individual with a dominant phenotype but unknown genotype and an individual that is homozygous recessive for the gene in question yields offspring that provide insight into the genotype of the dominant individual.

EXPERIMENT: Cross a black guinea pig of unknown genotype with a brown guinea pig, which is known to be homozygous recessive.

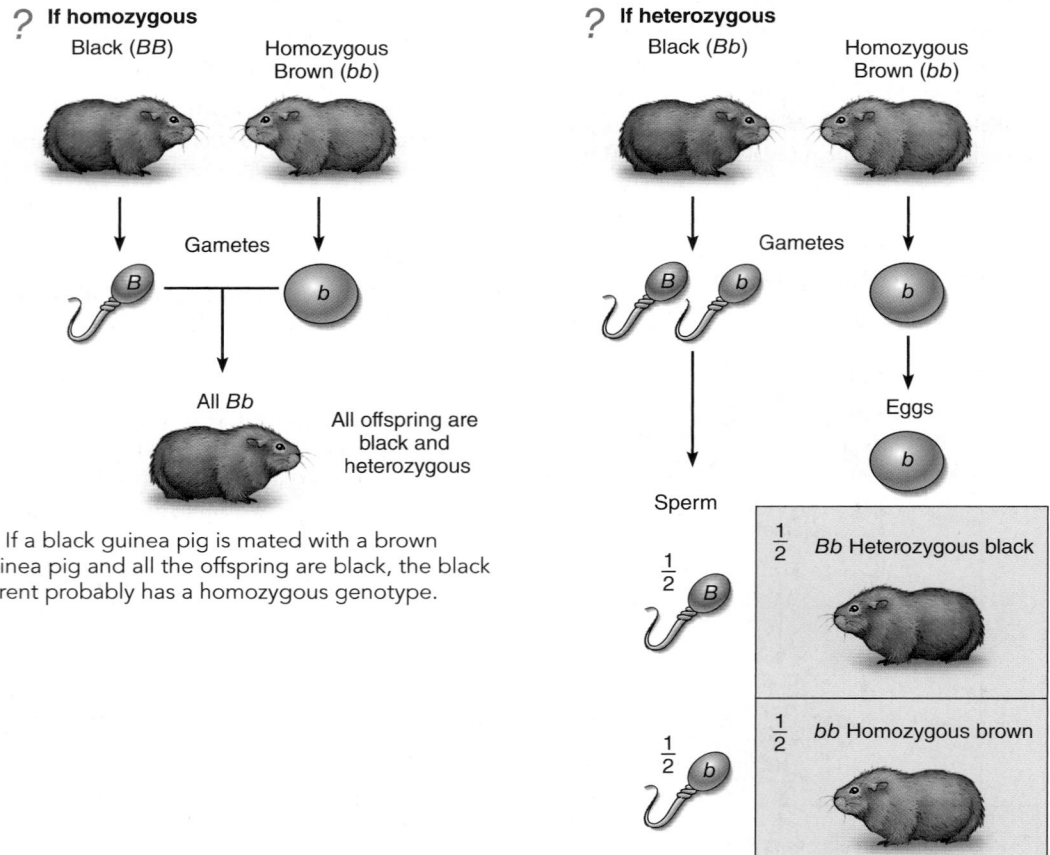

(a) If a black guinea pig is mated with a brown guinea pig and all the offspring are black, the black parent probably has a homozygous genotype.

(b) If any of the offspring is brown, the black guinea pig must be heterozygous. The expected phenotypic ratio is 1 black to 1 brown.

RESULTS AND CONCLUSION: There are two possible outcomes. If all the offspring are black, the black parent probably has a homozygous genotype. If any of the offspring are brown, the black parent must be heterozygous. The expected ratio is 1 black: 1 brown.

FIGURE 11-7 *Animated* A test cross in guinea pigs

A test cross can detect heterozygosity

Guinea pigs with the genotypes *BB* and *Bb* are alike phenotypically; they both have black coats. How, then, can we know the genotype of a black guinea pig? Geneticists accomplish this by performing an experimental cross known as a **test cross,** in which an individual of unknown genotype is crossed with a recessive individual (**FIG. 11-7**). In a test cross, the alleles carried by the gametes from the parent of unknown genotype are never "hidden" in the offspring by dominant alleles contributed by the other parent. Therefore, you can deduce the genotypes of all offspring directly

from their phenotypes. If all the offspring were black, what inference would you make about the genotype of the black parent? If any of the offspring were brown, what conclusion would you draw regarding the genotype of the black parent? Would you be more certain about one of these inferences than about the other?[2]

---

[2]If any of the offspring were brown, the black parent must be heterozygous, *Bb*. If all the offspring were black, you could infer that the black parent is *probably* homozygous, *BB*. (For example, statisticians calculate that if the black parent is heterozygous, the probability of four black offspring, and no brown, is only $\frac{1}{16}$.)

Mendel conducted several test crosses; for example, he bred F₁ (tall) pea plants with homozygous recessive (*tt*) short ones. He reasoned that the F₁ individuals were heterozygous (*Tt*) and would be expected to produce equal numbers of *T* and *t* gametes. Because the homozygous short parents (*tt*) were expected to produce only *t* gametes, Mendel hypothesized that he would obtain equal numbers of tall (*Tt*) and short (*tt*) offspring. His results agreed with his hypothesis, providing additional evidence for the hypothesis that there is 1:1 segregation of the alleles of a heterozygous parent. Thus, Mendel's principle of segregation not only explained the known facts, such as the 3:1 monohybrid F₂ phenotypic ratio, but also let him successfully anticipate the results of other experiments—in this case, the 1:1 test-cross phenotypic ratio.

A dihybrid cross involves individuals that have different alleles at two loci

Monohybrid crosses involve a pair of alleles of a single locus. Mendel also analyzed crosses involving alleles of two or more loci. A mating between individuals with different alleles at two loci is called a **dihybrid cross.** Consider the case of two pairs of alleles carried on nonhomologous chromosomes (that is, one pair of alleles is in one pair of homologous chromosomes, and the other pair of alleles is in a different pair of homologous chromosomes). Each pair of alleles is inherited independently; that is, each pair segregates during meiosis independently of the other.

An example of a dihybrid cross carried through the F₂ generation is shown in **FIGURE 11-8.** In this example, black is dominant to brown, and short hair is dominant to long hair. When a homozygous, black, short-haired guinea pig (*BBSS*) and a homozygous, brown, long-haired guinea pig (*bbss*) are mated, the *BBSS* animal produces gametes that are all *BS,* and the *bbss* individual produces gametes that are all *bs.* Each gamete contains one allele for each of the two loci. The union of the *BS* and *bs* gametes yields only individuals with the genotype *BbSs.* All these F₁ offspring are heterozygous for hair color and for hair length, and all are phenotypically black and short-haired.

Each F₁ guinea pig produces four kinds of gametes with equal probability: *BS, Bs, bS,* and *bs.* Hence, the Punnett square has 16 (that is, 4²) squares representing the F₂ offspring, some of which are genotypically or phenotypically alike. There are 9 chances in 16 of obtaining a black, short-haired individual; 3 chances in 16 of obtaining a black, long-haired individual; 3 chances in 16 of obtaining a brown, short-haired individual; and 1 chance in 16 of obtaining a brown, long-haired individual. This 9:3:3:1 phenotypic ratio is expected in a dihybrid F₂ if the hair color and hair length loci are on nonhomologous chromosomes.

Alleles on nonhomologous chromosomes are randomly distributed into gametes: the principle of independent assortment

On the basis of results similar to the guinea pig example, Mendel formulated the principle of inheritance, now known as Mendel's **principle of independent assortment,** which states that members of any gene pair segregate from one another independently of the

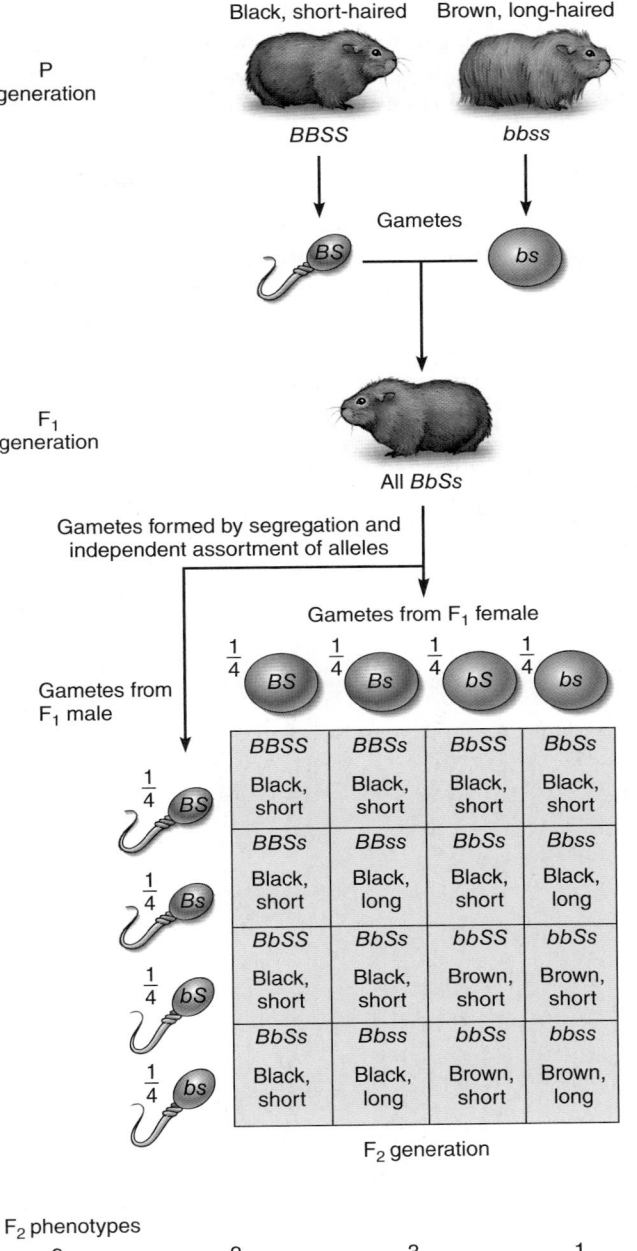

FIGURE 11-8 *Animated* **A dihybrid cross in guinea pigs**

When a black, short-haired guinea pig is crossed with a brown, long-haired one, all the offspring are black and have short hair. However, when two members of the F₁ generation are crossed, the ratio of phenotypes is 9:3:3:1.

members of the other gene pairs. This mechanism occurs in a regular way to ensure that each gamete contains one allele for each locus, but the alleles of different loci are assorted at random with respect to each other in the gametes. The independent assortment of these alleles can result in **genetic recombination** (or simply **recombination**), the process of assorting and passing alleles to offspring in new combinations that are different from those in the parents.

Today we recognize that independent assortment is related to the events of meiosis. It occurs because two pairs of homologous chromosomes can be arranged in two different ways at metaphase I of meiosis (**FIG. 11-9**). These arrangements occur randomly, with approximately half the meiotic cells oriented one way and half oriented the opposite way. The orientation of the homologous chromosomes on the metaphase plate then determines the way they subsequently separate and disperse into the haploid cells. (As you will soon see, however, independent assortment does not always occur.)

Recognition of Mendel's work came during the early 20th century

Mendel reported his findings at a meeting of the Brünn Society for the Study of Natural Science (in what is now the Czech Republic); he published his results in the society's report in 1866. At that time biology was largely a descriptive science, and biologists had little interest in applying quantitative and experimental methods such as those Mendel had used. Other biologists of the time did not appreciate the importance of his results nor his interpretations of those results. For 34 years his findings were largely neglected.

In 1900, Hugo DeVries in Holland, Carl Correns in Germany, and Erich von Tschermak in Austria recognized Mendel's princi-

KEY POINT Mendel's principle of independent assortment—that factors for different characteristics separate independently of one another prior to gamete formation—is a direct consequence of the events of meiosis.

METAPHASE I

METAPHASE II

bs

BS

bS

Bs

FIGURE 11-9 *Animated* **Meiosis and independent assortment**

Two different pairs of homologous chromosomes can line up two different ways at metaphase I and be subsequently distributed. A cell with the orientation shown at the left produces half *BS* and half *bs* gametes.

Conversely, the cell at the right produces half *Bs* and half *bS* gametes. Because approximately half of the meiotic cells at metaphase I are of each type, the ratio of the four possible types of gametes is 1:1:1:1.

ples in their own experiments; they later discovered Mendel's paper and found that it explained their own research observations. By this time biologists had a much greater appreciation of the value of quantitative experimental methods. Correns gave credit to Mendel by naming the basic laws of inheritance after him.

Although gametes and fertilization were known at the time Mendel carried out his research, mitosis and meiosis had not yet been discovered. It is truly remarkable that Mendel formulated his ideas mainly on the basis of mathematical abstractions. Today his principles are much easier to understand because we relate the transmission of genes to the behavior of chromosomes.

The details of mitosis and meiosis were described during the late 19th century, and in 1902, American biologist Walter Sutton and German biologist Theodor Boveri independently pointed out the connection between Mendel's segregation of alleles and the separation of homologous chromosomes during meiosis. This connection developed into the **chromosome theory of inheritance,** or the *Sutton–Boveri theory,* which stated that inheritance can be explained by assuming that genes are linearly arranged in specific locations along the chromosomes.

The chromosome theory of inheritance was initially controversial, because at that time there was no direct evidence that genes are found on chromosomes. However, new research provided the findings necessary for wider acceptance and extension of these ideas and their implications. For example, the work of American geneticist Thomas Hunt Morgan in 1910 provided evidence for the location of a particular gene (white eye color) on a specific chromosome (the X chromosome) in fruit flies. Morgan and his graduate students also provided insight into the way genes are organized on chromosomes; we discuss some of Morgan's research contributions later in the chapter.

Review

- What are the relationships among loci, genes, and alleles?
- What is Mendel's principle of segregation?
- What is Mendel's principle of independent assortment?

11.2 USING PROBABILITY TO PREDICT MENDELIAN INHERITANCE

LEARNING OBJECTIVE

5   Apply the product rule and sum rule appropriately when predicting the outcomes of genetic crosses.

All genetic ratios are properly expressed in terms of probabilities. In monohybrid crosses, the expected ratio of the dominant and recessive phenotypes is 3:1. The probability of an event is its expected frequency. Therefore, we can say there are 3 chances in 4 (or $\frac{3}{4}$) that any particular individual offspring of two heterozygous individuals will express the dominant phenotype and 1 chance in 4 (or $\frac{1}{4}$) that it will express the recessive phenotype. Although we sometimes speak in terms of percentages, probabilities are calcu-

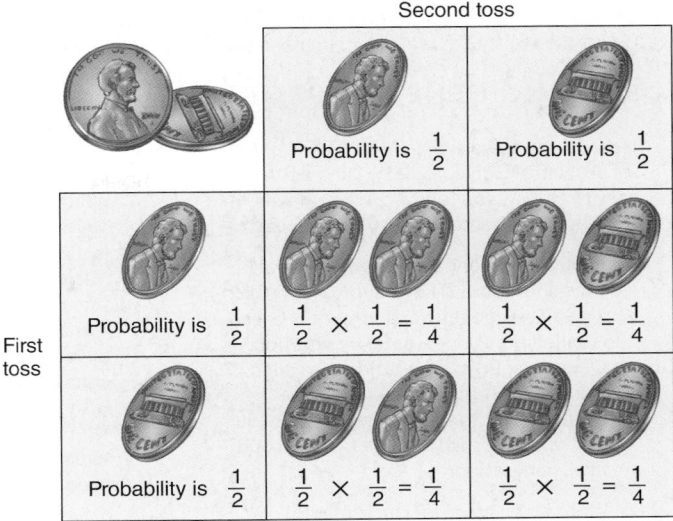

FIGURE 11-10 The rules of probability

For each coin toss, the probability of heads is $\frac{1}{2}$, and the probability of tails is also $\frac{1}{2}$. Because the outcome of the first toss is independent of the outcome of the second, the combined probabilities of the outcomes of successive tosses are calculated by multiplying their individual probabilities (according to the product rule: $\frac{1}{2} \times \frac{1}{2} = \frac{1}{4}$). These same rules of probability predict genetic events.

lated as fractions (such as $\frac{3}{4}$) or decimal fractions (such as 0.75). If an event is certain to occur, its probability is 1; if it is certain *not* to occur, its probability is 0. A probability can be 0, 1, or some number between 0 and 1.

The Punnett square lets you combine two or more probabilities. When you use a Punnett square, you are following two important statistical principles known as the product rule and the sum rule. The **product rule** predicts the combined probabilities of independent events. Events are *independent* if the occurrence of one does not affect the probability that the other will occur. For example, the probability of obtaining heads on the first toss of a coin is $\frac{1}{2}$; the probability of obtaining heads on the second toss (an independent event) is also $\frac{1}{2}$. If two or more events are independent of each other, the probability of both occurring is the product of their individual probabilities. If this seems strange, keep in mind that when we multiply two numbers that are less than 1, the product is a smaller number. Therefore, the probability of obtaining heads two times in a row is $\frac{1}{2} \times \frac{1}{2} = \frac{1}{4}$, or 1 chance in 4 (**FIG. 11-10**).

Similarly, we can apply the product rule to genetic events. If both parents are *Bb*, what is the probability they will produce a child who is *bb*? For the child to be *bb*, he or she must receive a *b* gamete from each parent. The probability of a *b* egg is $\frac{1}{2}$, and the probability of a *b* sperm is also $\frac{1}{2}$. Like the outcomes of the coin tosses, these probabilities are independent, so we combine them by the product rule ($\frac{1}{2} \times \frac{1}{2} = \frac{1}{4}$). You might like to check this result using a Punnett square.

The **sum rule** predicts the combined probabilities of *mutually exclusive* events. In some cases, there is more than one way to obtain a specific outcome. These different ways are mutually exclusive; if one occurs, the other(s) cannot. For example, if both parents are

SOLVING GENETICS PROBLEMS

How do you solve simple Mendelian genetics problems? Such problems can be fun and easy to work if you follow certain conventions and are methodical in your approach.

1. Always use standard designations for the generations. The generation in which a particular genetic experiment is begun is called the P, or parental, generation. Offspring of this generation are called the F_1, or first filial, generation. The offspring resulting when two F_1 individuals are bred constitute the F_2, or second filial, generation.

2. Write down a key for the symbols you are using for the allelic variants of each locus. Use an uppercase letter to designate a dominant allele and a lowercase letter to designate a recessive allele. Use the same letter of the alphabet to designate both alleles of a particular locus. If you are not told which allele is dominant and which is recessive, the phenotype of the F_1 generation is a good clue.

3. Determine the genotypes of the parents of each cross by using the following types of evidence:

   • Are they from true-breeding lines? If so, they should be homozygous.

   • Can their genotypes be reliably deduced from their phenotypes? This is usually true if they express the recessive phenotype.

   • Do the phenotypes of their offspring provide any information? Exactly how this is done is discussed shortly.

4. Indicate the possible kinds of gametes formed by each of the parents. It is helpful to draw a circle around the symbols for each kind of gamete.

   • If it is a monohybrid cross, we apply the principle of segregation; that is, a heterozygote *Aa* forms two kinds of gametes, *A* and *a*. A homozygote, such as *aa*, forms only one kind of gamete, *a*.

   • If it is a dihybrid cross, we apply the principles of segregation and independent assortment. For example, an individual heterozygous for two loci would have the genotype *AaBb*. Allele *A* segregates from *a*, and *B* segregates from *b*. The assortment of *A* and *a* into gametes is independent of the assortment of *B* and *b*. *A* is equally likely to end up in a gamete with *B* or *b*. The same is true for *a*. Thus, an individual with the genotype *AaBb* produces four kinds of gametes in equal amounts: *AB, Ab, aB,* and *ab*.

5. Set up a Punnett square, placing the possible types of gametes from one parent down the left side and the possible types from the other parent across the top.

6. Fill in the Punnett square. Avoid confusion by consistently placing the dominant allele first and the recessive allele second in heterozygotes (*Aa*, never *aA*). If it is a dihybrid cross, always write the two alleles of one locus first and the two alleles of the other locus second. It does not matter which locus you choose to write first, but once you have decided on the order, it is crucial to maintain it consistently. This means that if the individual is heterozygous for both loci, you will always use the form *AaBb*. Writing this particular genotype as *aBbA*, or even as *BbAa*, would cause confusion.

7. If you do not need to know the frequencies of all the expected genotypes and phenotypes, you can use the rules of probability as a shortcut instead of making a Punnett square. For example, if both parents are *AaBb*, what is the probability of an *AABB* offspring? To be *AA*, the offspring must receive an *A* gamete from each parent. The probability that a given gamete is *A* is $\frac{1}{2}$, and each gamete represents an independent event, so combine their probabilities by multiplying ($\frac{1}{2} \times \frac{1}{2} = \frac{1}{4}$). The probability

of *BB* is calculated similarly and is also $\frac{1}{4}$. The probability of *AA* is independent of the probability of *BB*, so again, use the product rule to obtain their combined probabilities ($\frac{1}{4} \times \frac{1}{4} = \frac{1}{16}$).

8. Very often the genotypes of the parents can be deduced from the phenotypes of their offspring. In peas, for example, the allele for yellow seeds (*Y*) is dominant to the allele for green seeds (*y*). Suppose plant breeders cross two plants with yellow seeds, but you don't know whether the yellow-seeded plants are homozygous or heterozygous. You can designate the cross as: *Y_* × *Y_*. The offspring of the cross are allowed to germinate and grow, and their seeds are examined. Of the offspring, 74 produce yellow seeds, and 26 produce green seeds. Knowing that green-seeded plants are recessive, *yy*, the answer is obvious: Each parent contributed a *y* allele to the green-seeded offspring, so the parents' genotypes must have been *Yy* × *Yy*.

   Sometimes it is impossible to determine from the data given whether an individual is homozygous dominant or heterozygous. For example, suppose a cross between a yellow-seeded plant and a green-seeded plant yields offspring that all produce yellow seeds. From the information given about the parents, you can designate the cross as: *Y_* × *yy*. Because all the offspring have yellow seeds, they have the genotype *Yy*. You can deduce this because each parent contributes one allele. (The offspring have yellow seeds, so they must have at least one *Y* allele; however, the green-seeded parent can contribute only a *y* allele to the offspring.) Therefore, the cross is most likely (*YY* × *yy*), but you cannot be absolutely certain about the genotype of the yellow-seeded parent. Further crosses would be necessary to determine this.

Bb, what is the probability that their first child will also have the *Bb* genotype? There are two different ways these parents can have a *Bb* child: either a *B* egg combines with a *b* sperm (probability $\frac{1}{4}$), or a *b* egg combines with a *B* sperm (probability $\frac{1}{4}$).

Naturally, if there is more than one way to get a result, the chances of its being obtained improve; we therefore combine the probabilities of mutually exclusive events by summing (adding) their individual probabilities. The probability of obtaining a *Bb* child in our example is therefore $\frac{1}{4} + \frac{1}{4} = \frac{1}{2}$. (Because there is only

one way these heterozygous parents can produce a homozygous recessive child, *bb*, that probability is only $\frac{1}{4}$. The probability of a homozygous dominant child, *BB*, is likewise $\frac{1}{4}$.)

The rules of probability can be applied to a variety of calculations

The rules of probability have wide applications. For example, what are the probabilities that a family with two (and only two) children will have two girls, two boys, or one girl and one boy? For purposes of discussion, let's assume male and female births are equally probable. The probability of having a girl first is $\frac{1}{2}$, and the probability of having a girl second is also $\frac{1}{2}$. These are independent events, so we combine their probabilities by multiplying: $\frac{1}{2} \times \frac{1}{2} = \frac{1}{4}$. Similarly, the probability of having two boys is $\frac{1}{4}$.

In families with both a girl and a boy, the girl can be born first or the boy can be born first. The probability that a girl will be born first is $\frac{1}{2}$, and the probability that a boy will be born second is also $\frac{1}{2}$. We use the product rule to combine the probabilities of these two independent events: $\frac{1}{2} \times \frac{1}{2} = \frac{1}{4}$. Similarly, the probability that a boy will be born first and a girl second is $\frac{1}{4}$. These two kinds of families represent mutually exclusive outcomes, that is, two different ways of obtaining a family with one boy and one girl. Having two different ways of obtaining the desired result improves our chances, so we use the sum rule to combine the probabilities: $\frac{1}{4} + \frac{1}{4} = \frac{1}{2}$.

In working with probabilities, keep in mind a point that many gamblers forget: Chance has no memory. If events are truly independent, past events have no influence on the probability of the occurrence of future events. Probability only has predictive value in the long run, over many trials. (Recall that Mendel counted hundreds of offspring for each cross, and this was one of the reasons for his success.) When working probability problems, common sense is more important than blindly memorizing rules. Examine your results to see whether they appear reasonable; if they don't, re-evaluate your assumptions. (See *Inquiring About: Solving Genetics Problems* for procedures to solve genetics problems, including when to use the rules of probability.)

Review

- Use the rules of probability to answer the following question: In a cross between homozygous pea plants with yellow, round seeds (*YYRR*) and homozygous pea plants with green, wrinkled seeds (*yyrr*), what is the probability of an F$_2$ plant having yellow, round seeds?

- In the previous question, did you use the product rule or the sum rule? Why?

11.3 INHERITANCE AND CHROMOSOMES

■ LEARNING OBJECTIVES

6 Define *linkage* and relate it to specific events in meiosis.

7 Show how data from a test cross involving alleles of two loci can be used to distinguish between independent assortment and linkage.

8 Discuss the genetic determination of sex and the inheritance of X-linked genes in mammals.

It is a measure of Mendel's genius that he worked out the principles of segregation and independent assortment without knowing anything about meiosis or the chromosome theory of inheritance. The chromosome theory of inheritance also helps explain certain apparent exceptions to Mendelian inheritance. One of these so-called exceptions involves linked genes.

Linked genes do not assort independently

Beginning around 1910, the research of geneticist Thomas Hunt Morgan and his graduate students extended the concept of the chromosome theory of inheritance. Morgan's research organism was the fruit fly (*Drosophila melanogaster*). Just as the garden pea was an excellent model research organism for Mendel's studies, the fruit fly was perfect for extending general knowledge about inheritance. Fruit flies have a short life cycle—just 14 days—and their small size means that thousands can be kept in a research lab. The large number of individuals increases the chance of identifying mutants. Also, fruit flies have just four pairs of chromosomes, one of which is a pair of sex chromosomes.

By carefully analyzing the results of crosses involving fruit flies, Morgan and his students demonstrated that genes are arranged in a linear order on each chromosome. Morgan also showed that independent assortment does not apply if the two loci lie close together in the same pair of homologous chromosomes. In fruit flies there is a locus controlling wing shape: the dominant allele *V* for normal wings and the recessive allele *v* for abnormally short, or vestigial, wings. Another locus controls body color: the dominant allele *B* for gray body and the recessive allele *b* for black body. If a homozygous *BBVV* fly is crossed with a homozygous *bbvv* fly, the F$_1$ flies all have gray bodies and normal wings, and their genotype is *BbVv*.

Because these loci happen to lie close to each other in the *same pair* of homologous chromosomes, their alleles do not assort independently; instead, they are **linked genes** that tend to be inherited together. **Linkage** is the tendency for a group of genes on the same chromosome to be inherited together in successive generations. You can readily observe linkage in the results of a test cross in which heterozygous F$_1$ flies (*BbVv*) are mated with homozygous recessive (*bbvv*) flies (**FIG. 11-11**). Because heterozygous individuals are mated to homozygous recessive individuals, this test cross is similar to the test cross described earlier. However, it is called a **two-point test cross** because alleles of two loci are involved.

If the loci governing these traits were unlinked—that is, on different chromosomes—the heterozygous parent in a test cross would produce four kinds of gametes (*BV*, *Bv*, *bV*, and *bv*) in equal numbers. This independent assortment would produce offspring with new gene combinations not present in the parental generation. Recall that any process that leads to new allele combinations is called genetic recombination. In our example, gametes *Bv* and *bV* are **recombinant types.** The other two kinds of gametes, *BV* and *bv*, are **parental types** because they are identical to the gametes produced by the P generation.

Of course, the homozygous recessive parent produces only one kind of gamete, *bv*. Thus, if independent assortment were to occur in the F$_1$ flies, approximately 25% of the test-cross offspring would be gray-bodied and normal-winged (*BbVv*), 25% black-bodied and normal-winged (*bbVv*), 25% gray-bodied and vestigial-winged (*Bbvv*), and 25% black-bodied and vestigial-winged (*bbvv*). Notice that the two-point test cross lets us determine the genotypes of the offspring directly from their phenotypes.

By contrast, the alleles of the loci in our example do not undergo independent assortment because they are linked. Alleles at different loci but close to one another on a given chromosome

QUESTION: How can linkage be recognized in fruit flies?

HYPOTHESIS: Linkage can be recognized when an excess of parental-type offspring and a deficiency of recombinant-type offspring are produced in a two-point test cross.

EXPERIMENT: Fruit flies with gray, normal wings (*BbVv*) are crossed with flies that have black, vestigial wings (*bbvv*). If the alleles for color and wing shape are not linked (i.e., the alleles assort independently), the offspring will consist of an equal number of each of four phenotypes (*bottom row*).

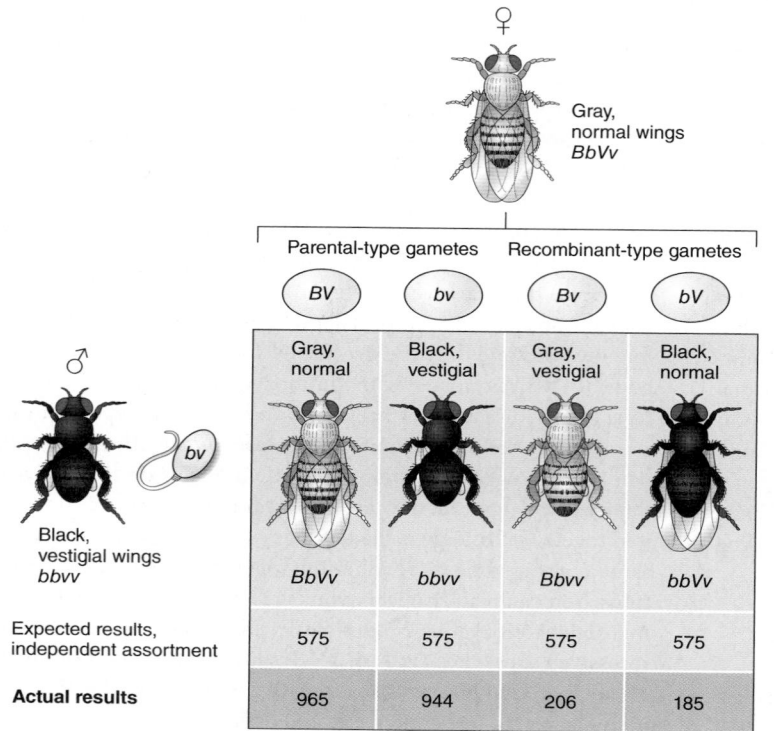

	Parental-type gametes		Recombinant-type gametes	
	BV	bv	Bv	bV
	Gray, normal	Black, vestigial	Gray, vestigial	Black, normal
	BbVv	*bbvv*	*Bbvv*	*bbVv*
Expected results, independent assortment	575	575	575	575
Actual results	965	944	206	185

RESULTS AND CONCLUSION: In the 2300 offspring (*bottom row*) of an actual cross, about 1909 of the offspring belong to each of the two parental types (83% total), and 391 belong to each of the two recombinant types (17% total). Thus, loci for wing length and body color are linked on a homologous chromosome pair.

FIGURE 11-11 A two-point test cross to detect linkage in fruit flies

arose by **crossing-over** between these loci in a meiotic cell of a heterozygous female fly. (Fruit flies are unusual in that crossing-over occurs only in females and not in males; it is far more common for crossing-over to occur in both sexes of a species.) When chromosomes pair and undergo synapsis, crossing-over occurs as homologous (nonsister) chromatids exchange segments of chromosome material by a process of breakage and rejoining catalyzed by enzymes (**FIG. 11-12**). Also see the discussion of prophase I in Chapter 10, Section 10.4.

Calculating the frequency of crossing-over reveals the linear order of linked genes on a chromosome

In our fruit fly example (see Fig. 11-11), 391 of the offspring are recombinant types: gray flies with vestigial wings, *Bbvv* (206 of the total); and black flies with normal wings, *bbVv* (185 of the total). The remaining 1909 offspring are parental types. These data can be used to calculate the percentage of crossing-over between the loci (**TABLE 11-3**). You do this by adding the number of individuals in the two recombinant types of offspring, dividing by the *total number of offspring,* and multiplying by 100: $391 \div 2300 = 0.17$; $0.17 \times 100 = 17\%$. Thus, the *V* locus and the *B* locus have 17% recombination between them.

During a single meiotic division, crossing-over may occur at several different points along the length of each homologous chromosome pair. In general, crossing-over is more likely to occur between two loci if they lie far apart on the chromosome and less likely to occur if they lie close together. Because of this rough correlation between the frequency of recombination of two loci and the linear distance between them, a genetic map of the chromosome can be generated by converting the percentage of recombination to **map units.** By convention, 1% recombination between two loci equals a distance of 1 map unit, so the loci in our example are 17 map units apart.

tend to be inherited together; because chromosomes pair and separate during meiosis as units, the alleles at different loci on a given chromosome tend to be inherited as units. If linkage were complete, only parental-type flies would be produced, with approximately 50% having gray bodies and normal wings (*BbVv*) and 50% having black bodies and vestigial wings (*bbvv*).

However, in our example, the offspring also include some gray-bodied, vestigial-winged flies and some black-bodied, normal-winged flies. These are recombinant flies, having received a recombinant-type gamete from the heterozygous F₁ parent. Each recombinant-type gamete

TABLE 11-3	How to Determine Recombination Frequency from a Two-Point Test Cross			
	Test-Cross Results (from Fig. 11-11)			
Type of Offspring	Parental Type		Recombinant Type	
Phenotype	Gray, normal	Black, vestigial	Gray, vestigial	Black, normal
Genotype	*BbVv*	*bbvv*	*Bbvv*	*bbVv*
Number of offspring	965	944	206	185
Calculations of recombination frequency	1. Number of parental-type offspring = 1909 2. Number of recombinant-type offspring = 391 3. Total number of offspring = 1909 + 391 = 2300 4. Recombination frequency = 391/2300 × 100 = 17%			

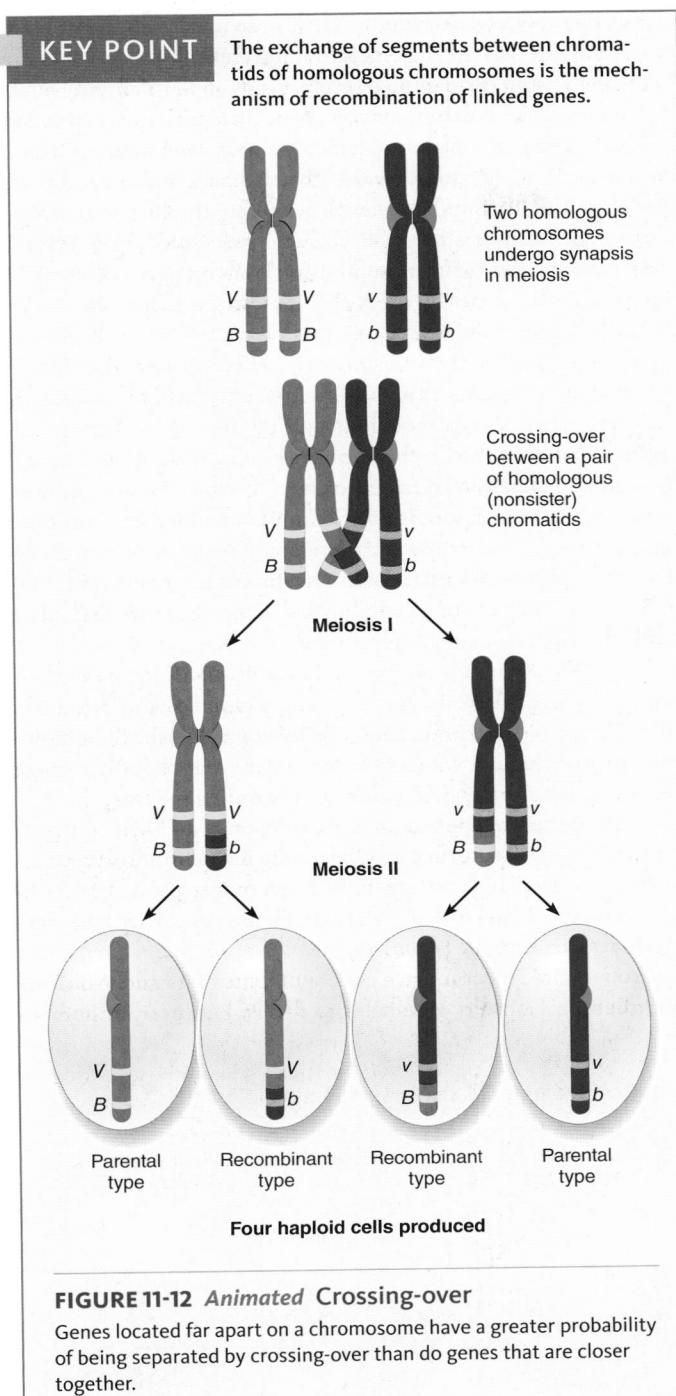

KEY POINT The exchange of segments between chromatids of homologous chromosomes is the mechanism of recombination of linked genes.

Two homologous chromosomes undergo synapsis in meiosis

Crossing-over between a pair of homologous (nonsister) chromatids

Meiosis I

Meiosis II

Parental type | Recombinant type | Recombinant type | Parental type

Four haploid cells produced

FIGURE 11-12 *Animated* **Crossing-over**

Genes located far apart on a chromosome have a greater probability of being separated by crossing-over than do genes that are closer together.

(a) If the recombination between A and C is 8% (8 map units), then B must be in the middle.

(b) If the recombination between A and C is 2%, then C must be in the middle.

FIGURE 11-13 Gene mapping

Gene order (that is, which locus lies between the other two) is determined by the percentage of recombination between each of the possible pairs. In this hypothetical example, the percentage of recombination between locus A and locus B is 5% (corresponding to 5 map units) and that between B and C is 3% (3 map units). There are two alternatives for the linear order of these alleles.

many plants, especially those that are important crops. In addition, researchers have used genetic methods to develop a detailed map for *Escherichia coli,* a bacterium with a single, circular DNA molecule, and many other prokaryotes and viruses. They have made much more sophisticated maps of chromosomes of various species by means of recombinant DNA technology (discussed in Chapter 15). Using these techniques, the *Human Genome Project* has produced detailed maps of human chromosomes (discussed in Chapter 16).

Sex is generally determined by sex chromosomes

In some species, environmental factors exert a large control over an individual's sex. However, genes are the most important sex determinants in most eukaryotic organisms. The major sex-determining genes of mammals, birds, and many insects are carried by **sex chromosomes.** Typically, members of one sex have a pair of similar sex chromosomes and produce gametes that are all identical in sex chromosome constitution. The members of the other sex have two different sex chromosomes and produce two kinds of gametes, each bearing a single kind of sex chromosome.

The cells of female mammals, including humans, contain two **X chromosomes.** In contrast, the males have a single X chromosome and a smaller **Y chromosome** that bears only a few active genes (**FIG. 11-14**). For example, human females have 22 pairs of **autosomes,** which are chromosomes other than the sex chromosomes, plus a pair of X chromosomes; males have 22 pairs of autosomes plus one X chromosome and one Y chromosome. Domestic

Scientists have determined the frequencies of recombination between specific linked loci in many species. All the experimental results are consistent with the hypothesis that genes are present in a linear order in the chromosomes. **FIGURE 11-13** illustrates the traditional method for determining the linear order of genes in a chromosome.

By putting together the results of numerous crosses, scientists have developed detailed linkage maps for many eukaryotes, including the fruit fly, the mouse, yeast, *Neurospora* (a fungus), and

FIGURE 11-14 SEM of human Y chromosome (left) and X chromosome (right)

Each chromosome is in the duplicated state and consists of two identical chromatids.

cats have 19 pairs of autosomes, to which are added a pair of X chromosomes in females, or an X plus a Y in males. In contrast, sex determination is based on different chromosome systems in animals other than mammals (**TABLE 11-4**).

The Y chromosome determines male sex in most species of mammals

Do male humans have a male phenotype because they have only one X chromosome, or because they have a Y chromosome? Much of the traditional evidence bearing on this question comes from studies of people with abnormal sex chromosome constitutions (see discussion in Chapter 16). A person with an XXY constitution is a nearly normal male in external appearance, although his testes are underdeveloped (Klinefelter syndrome). A person with one X but no Y chromosome has the overall appearance of a female but has defects such as short stature and undeveloped ovaries (Turner syndrome). An embryo with a Y but no X does not survive. Based on these and other obser-

vations, biologists concluded that all individuals require at least one X, and the Y is the male-determining chromosome.

Geneticists have identified several genes on the Y chromosome that are involved in determination of the male sex. The *sex reversal on Y (SRY) gene,* the major male-determining gene on the Y chromosome, acts as a "genetic switch" that causes testes to develop in the fetus. The developing testes then secrete the hormone *testosterone,* which causes other male characteristics to develop. Several other genes on the Y chromosome also play a role in sex determination, as do many genes on the X chromosome, which explains why an XXY individual does not have a completely normal male phenotype. Some genes on the autosomes also affect sex development.

Evidence suggests that the X and Y chromosomes of mammals originated as a homologous pair of autosomes. During the evolution of the X and Y chromosomes, almost all of the original functional genes were retained on the X chromosome and lost from the Y chromosome. Today, about 95% of the Y chromosome is male-specific. Either the Y chromosome retained certain genes that coded for proteins that determine maleness, or perhaps mutations occurred in existing genes on the Y chromosome that made it the male-determining chromosome.

Thus, the sex chromosomes are not truly homologous in their present forms because they are not similar in size, shape, or genetic constitution. Nevertheless, the Y chromosome has short, homologous "pairing regions" at its tips that lets it synapse and exchange genetic material with the X chromosome during meiosis.

Half the sperm contain an X chromosome, and half contain a Y chromosome. All normal eggs bear a single X chromosome. Fertilization of an X-bearing egg by an X-bearing sperm results in an XX (female) zygote, or fertilized egg; fertilization by a Y-bearing sperm results in an XY (male) zygote.

You might expect to have equal numbers of X- and Y-bearing sperm and a 1:1 ratio of females to males. However, in humans

TABLE 11-4 Representative Examples of Sex Determination in Animals

X-Y system Mammals, including humans	X-O system Certain insects	Z-W system Birds, fishes, and some insects	Haplo-diploid system Most bees and ants
Male XY Occurs when sperm cell contains a Y chromosome	**Male XO** Occurs when sperm cell contains no sex chromosome	**Male ZW** Occurs when an egg cell contains a W chromosome	**Male Haploid** No sex chromosomes; male develops from unfertilized egg
Female XX Occurs when sperm cell contains an X chromosome	**Female XX** Occurs when sperm cell contains an X chromosome	**Female ZZ** Occurs when an egg cell contains a Z chromosome	**Female Diploid** No sex chromosomes; female develops from fertilized egg

more males are conceived than females, and more males die before birth. Even at birth the ratio is not 1:1; about 106 boys are born for every 100 girls. The Y-bearing sperm appear to have a selective advantage, possibly because sperm containing the Y chromosome are smaller and have less mass than sperm containing the X chromosome; it is hypothesized that, on average, the sperm carrying the Y chromosome can swim slightly faster than X-bearing sperm to reach the egg.

X-linked genes have unusual inheritance patterns

The human X chromosome contains many loci that are required in both sexes. Genes located in the X chromosome, such as those governing color perception and blood clotting, are sometimes called *sex-linked genes*. It is more appropriate, however, to refer to them as **X-linked genes** because they follow the transmission pattern of the X chromosome and, strictly speaking, are not linked to the sex of the organism.

A female receives one X from her mother and one X from her father. A male receives his Y chromosome, which makes him male, from his father. From his mother he inherits a single X chromosome and therefore all his X-linked genes. In the male, every allele present on the X chromosome is expressed, whether that allele was dominant or recessive in the female parent.

A male is neither homozygous nor heterozygous for his X-linked alleles; instead, he is always **hemizygous**—that is, he has only one copy of each X-linked gene. The significance of hemizygosity in males, including human males, is that rare, recessive X-linked genes are expressed, making males more likely to be affected by the many genetic disorders associated with the X chromosome. In comparison only a few genes are located exclusively on the Y chromosome. X and Y chromosomes also have short areas where they carry the same genes, enabling the X and Y to pair during meiosis I.

We will use a simple system of notation for problems involving X linkage, indicating the X chromosome and incorporating specific alleles as superscripts. For example, the symbol X^e signifies a recessive X-linked allele for color blindness and X^E the dominant X-linked allele for normal color vision. The Y chromosome is written without superscripts because it does not carry the locus of interest. Two recessive X-linked alleles must be present in a female for the abnormal phenotype to be expressed (X^eX^e), whereas in the hemizygous male a single recessive allele (X^eY) causes the abnormal phenotype. As a consequence, these abnormal alleles are much more frequently expressed in male offspring. A heterozygous female may be a *carrier*, an individual who possesses one copy of a mutant recessive allele but does not express it in the phenotype (X^EX^e).

To be expressed in a female, a recessive X-linked allele must be inherited from both parents. A color-blind female, for example, must have a color-blind father and a mother who is homozygous or heterozygous for a recessive allele for color blindness (**FIG. 11-15**).

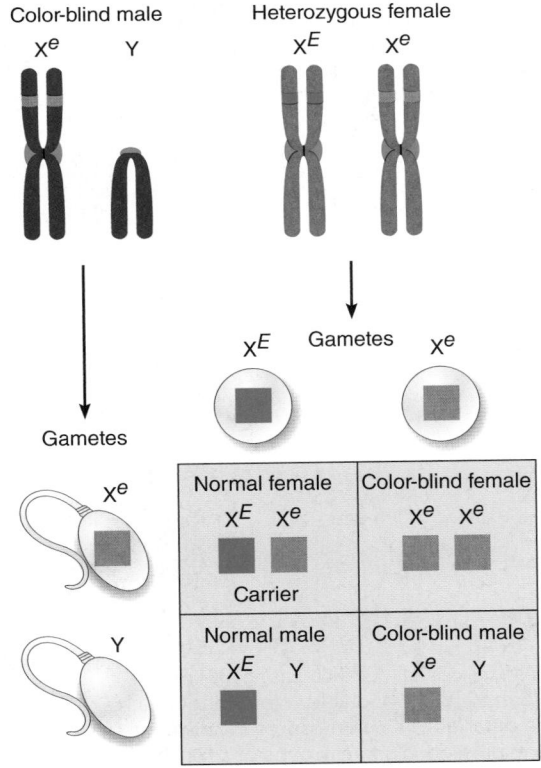

(a) To be color-blind, a female must inherit alleles for color blindness from both parents.

(b) If a normal male mates with a carrier (heterozygous) female, half of their sons would be expected to be color-blind and half of their daughters would be expected to be carriers.

FIGURE 11-15 *Animated* X-linked red–green color blindness
Note that the Y chromosome does not carry a gene for color vision.

The homozygous combination is unusual because the frequency of alleles for color blindness is relatively low. In contrast, a color-blind male need only have a mother who is heterozygous for color blindness; his father can have normal vision. Therefore, X-linked recessive traits are generally much more common in males than in females, a fact that may partially explain why human male embryos are more likely to die.

Dosage compensation equalizes the expression of X-linked genes in males and females

The X chromosome contains numerous genes required by both sexes, yet a normal female has two copies ("doses") for each locus, whereas a normal male has only one. **Dosage compensation** is a mechanism that makes equivalent the two doses in the female and the single dose in the male. Because of dosage compensation,

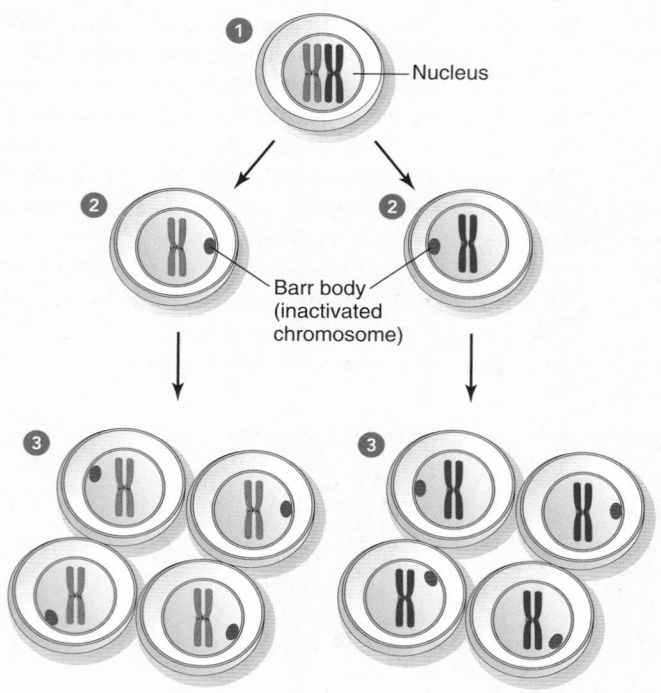

KEY POINT In female mammals, one of the two X chromosomes is randomly inactivated during early development, equalizing the level of expression of genes at loci on the X chromosome in males and females.

— Nucleus

Barr body (inactivated chromosome)

1 The zygote and early embryonic cells have two X chromosomes, one from each parent.

2 Random inactivation of one X chromosome occurs early in development. Roughly half the cells inactivate one X chromosome (*left cell*), and the other half inactivate the second X chromosome (*right cell*). The inactive X chromosome is visible as a Barr body near the nuclear envelope.

3 Chromosome inactivation persists through subsequent mitotic divisions, resulting in patches of cells in the adult body.

(a) Inactivation of one X chromosome in female cells.

Eunice Percy/Animals Animals

(b) Persian calico cat. A calico cat has X-linked genes for both black and yellow (or orange) fur. Because of random X chromosome inactivation, black is expressed in some groups of cells and orange is expressed in others. (The patches of white fur are due to the presence of other genes that affect fur color.)

FIGURE 11-16 *Animated* Dosage compensation in female mammals males and females produce the same amounts of proteins coded by X-linked genes. Male fruit flies accomplish this by making their single X chromosome more active. In most fly tissues, the metabolic activity of a single male X chromosome is equal to the combined metabolic activity of the two X chromosomes present in the female.

Our understanding of dosage compensation in humans and other mammals is incomplete, but the process generally involves the random inactivation of one of the two X chromosomes in the female (**FIG. 11-16a**). During interphase, a dark spot of chromatin is visible at the edge of the nucleus of each female mammalian cell when stained and observed with a microscope. This dark spot, a **Barr body,** is a dense, metabolically inactive X chromosome. The other X chromosome resembles the metabolically active autosomes; during interphase, it is a greatly extended thread that is not evident in light microscopy. From this and other evidence, the British geneticist Mary Lyon hypothesized in 1961 that in most cells of a female mammal, only one of the two X chromosomes is active; the other is inactive and is condensed as a Barr body. Actually, however, X chromosome inactivation is never complete; as many as 25% of the genes on the inactive chromosome are expressed to some degree.

X chromosome inactivation is a random event in each somatic (body) cell of the female embryo. A female mammal that is heterozygous at an X-linked locus expresses one of the alleles in about half her cells, and the other allele in the other half. X chromosome inactivation is sometimes evident in the phenotype. Mice and cats have several X-linked genes for certain coat colors. Females that are heterozygous for such genes may show patches of one coat color in the middle of areas of the other coat color. This phenomenon, termed **variegation,** is evident in tortoiseshell and calico cats (**FIG. 11-16b**). Early in development, when relatively few cells are present, X chromosome inactivation occurs randomly in each cell. X inactivation is then maintained during all subsequent divisions of that cell line. When any one of these cells divides by mitosis, the cells of the resulting *clone* (a group of genetically identical cells) all have the same active X chromosome, and therefore a patch develops of cells that all express the same color.

You might wonder why variegation is not always apparent in females heterozygous at X-linked loci. The answer is that, although variegation usually occurs, we may need to use special techniques to observe it. For example, color blindness is caused by a defect involving the pigments in the cone cells in the retina of the eye. In at least one type of red–green color blindness, the retina of a heterozygous female actually contains patches of abnormal cones, but the patches of normal cones are enough to provide normal color vision. Variegation can be very hard to observe in cases where cell products become mixed in bodily fluids. For instance, in females heterozygous for the allele that causes hemophilia, only half the cells responsible for producing a specific blood-clotting factor do so, but they produce enough to ensure that the blood clots normally.

Review

- What are linked genes?
- How do geneticists use a two-point test cross to detect linkage?

- Which chromosome determines the male sex in humans and other mammals?
- What is dosage compensation, and what does it generally involve in mammals?

11.4 EXTENSIONS OF MENDELIAN GENETICS

LEARNING OBJECTIVES

9 Explain some of the ways genes may interact to affect the phenotype; discuss how a single gene can affect many features of the organism simultaneously.
10 Distinguish among incomplete dominance, codominance, multiple alleles, epistasis, and polygenic inheritance.
11 Describe *norm of reaction* and give an example.

The relationship between a given locus and the trait it controls may or may not be simple. A single pair of alleles of a locus may regulate the appearance of a single trait (such as tall versus short in garden peas). Alternatively, a pair of alleles may participate in the control of several traits, or alleles of many loci may interact to affect the phenotypic expression of a single character. Not surprisingly, these more complex relationships are quite common.

You can assess the phenotype on one or many levels. It may be a morphological trait, such as shape, size, or color. It may be a physiological trait or even a biochemical trait, such as the presence or absence of a specific enzyme required for the metabolism of some specific molecule. In addition, changes in the environmental conditions under which the organism develops may alter the phenotypic expression of genes.

Dominance is not always complete

Studies of the inheritance of many traits in a wide variety of organisms have shown that one member of a pair of alleles may not be completely dominant over the other. In such instances, it is inaccurate to use the terms *dominant* and *recessive*.

The plants commonly called four o'clocks (*Mirabilis jalapa*) may have red or white flowers. Each color breeds true when these plants are self-pollinated. What flower color might you expect in the offspring of a cross between a red-flowering plant and a white-flowering one? Without knowing which is dominant, you might predict that all would have red flowers or all would have white flowers. German botanist Carl Correns, one of the rediscoverers of Mendel's work, first performed this cross and found that all F_1 offspring have pink flowers!

Does this result in any way indicate that the principles of inheritance that Mendel deduced are wrong? Did the parental traits blend inseparably in the offspring? Quite the contrary, for when two of these pink-flowered plants are crossed, red-flowered, pink-flowered, and white-flowered offspring appear in a ratio of 1:2:1 (**FIG. 11-17**). In this instance, as in all other aspects of the scientific process, results that differ from those hypothesized prompt scientists to re-examine and modify their hypotheses to account for the exceptional results. The pink-flowered plants are clearly the heterozygous individuals, and neither the red allele nor the white

In incomplete dominance, an F₁ heterozygote has a phenotype intermediate between its parents.

FIGURE 11-17 *Animated* **Incomplete dominance in four o'clocks**

Two incompletely dominant alleles, R^1 and R^2, are responsible for red, white, and pink flower colors. Red-flowered plants are R^1R^1, white-flowered plants are R^2R^2, and heterozygotes (R^1R^2) are pink. Note that uppercase letters are used for both alleles because neither is recessive to the other.

allele is completely dominant. When the heterozygote has a phenotype intermediate between those of its two parents, the genes show **incomplete dominance.** In these crosses, the genotypic and phenotypic ratios are identical.

Incomplete dominance is not unique to four o'clocks, and additional examples of incomplete dominance are known in both plants and animals. For example, true-breeding white chickens and true-breeding black chickens produce bluish gray offspring, or Andalusian blues, when crossed.

In both cattle and horses, reddish coat color is not completely dominant to white coat color. Heterozygous individuals have a mixture of reddish hairs and white hairs, which is called *roan*. If you saw a white mare nursing a roan foal, what would you guess was the coat color of the foal's father? Because the reddish and white colors are expressed independently (hair by hair) in the roan heterozygote, scientists sometimes refer to this as a case of **codominance.** Strictly speaking, the term *incomplete dominance* refers to instances in which the heterozygote is intermediate in phenotype, and *codominance* refers to instances in which the heterozygote simultaneously expresses the phenotypes of both types of homozygotes.

TABLE 11-5	ABO Blood Types		
Phenotype (blood type)	Genotype	Surface Antigen on RBC	Serum Antibodies to A or B Antigens
A	I^AI^A or I^Ai	A	Anti-B
B	I^BI^B or I^Bi	B	Anti-A
AB	I^AI^B	A, B	None
O	ii	None	Anti-A, anti-B

*This table and the discussion of the ABO system have been simplified somewhat. Note that the body produces antibodies against the antigens *lacking* on its own red blood cells (RBCs). Because of their specificity for the corresponding antigens, these antibodies are used in standard tests to determine blood types.

Humans have four blood types (A, B, AB, and O), collectively called the **ABO blood group.** The human ABO blood group is an excellent example of codominant alleles. Blood types A, B, AB, and O are controlled by three alleles representing a single locus (**TABLE 11-5**). Allele I^A codes for the synthesis of a specific glycoprotein, antigen A, which is expressed on the surface of red blood cells. (Immune responses are discussed in Chapter 45.) *Antigens* are substances capable of stimulating an immune response. Allele I^B leads to the production of antigen B, a different but related glycoprotein. Allele i is allelic to I^A and I^B, but it does not code for an antigen.

Individuals with the genotype I^AI^A or I^Ai have blood type A. People with genotype I^BI^B or I^Bi have blood type B. Those with genotype I^AI^B have blood type AB, whereas those with genotype ii have blood type O. These results show that neither allele I^A nor allele I^B is dominant to the other. Both alleles are expressed phenotypically in the heterozygote and are therefore codominant to each other, although each is dominant to allele i.

At one time, determining blood types was used to settle cases of disputed parentage. Although blood-type tests can *exclude* someone as a possible parent of a particular child, they can never prove a certain person is the parent; they only determine he or she *could* be. Could a man with blood type AB be the father of a child with blood type O? Could a woman with blood type O be the mother of a child with blood type AB? Could a type B child with a type A mother have a type A father or a type O father?[3]

Multiple alleles for a locus may exist in a population

Most of our examples so far have dealt with situations in which each locus was represented by a maximum of two allelic variants (three in the example of blood types). It is true that a single diploid individual has a maximum of two different alleles for a particular locus and that a haploid gamete has only one allele for each locus. However, if you survey a population, you may find more than two alleles for a particular locus, as you saw with the ABO blood group (see Table 11-5). If three or more alleles for a given locus exist within the population, that locus has **multiple alleles.**

Research has shown that many loci have multiple alleles. Some alleles can be identified by the activity of a certain enzyme or by

---

[3]The answer to all these questions is no.

some other biochemical feature but do not produce an obvious phenotype. Others produce a readily recognizable phenotype, and certain patterns of dominance can be discerned when the alleles are combined in various ways. In other series of multiple alleles, certain alleles may be codominant and others incompletely dominant. In such cases, the heterozygotes commonly have phenotypes intermediate between those of their parents.

A single gene may affect multiple aspects of the phenotype

In our examples, the relationship between a gene and its phenotype has been direct, precise, and exact, and the loci have controlled the appearance of single traits. However, the relationship of gene to trait may not have such a simple genetic basis. Most genes affect several different characters. The ability of a single gene to have multiple effects is known as **pleiotropy.** Most cases of pleiotropy can be traced to a single fundamental cause. For example, a defective enzyme may affect the functioning of many types of cells. Pleiotropy is evident in many genetic diseases in which a single pair of alleles causes multiple symptoms. For example, people who are homozygous for the recessive allele that causes cystic fibrosis produce abnormally thick mucus in many parts of the body, including the respiratory, digestive, and reproductive systems (cystic fibrosis is discussed in Chapter 16).

Alleles of different loci may interact to produce a phenotype

Several pairs of alleles may interact to affect a single phenotype, or one pair may inhibit or reverse the effect of another pair. One example of gene interaction is illustrated by the inheritance of combs in chickens, where two genes may interact to produce a novel phenotype (**FIG. 11-18**). The allele for a rose comb, *R*, is dominant to that for a single comb, *r*. A second, unlinked pair of alleles governs the inheritance of a pea comb, *P*, versus a single comb, *p*. A single-comb chicken is homozygous for the recessive allele at both loci (*pprr*). A rose comb chicken is either *ppRR* or *ppRr*, and a pea comb chicken is either *PPrr* or *Pprr*. When an *R* and *P* occur in the same individual, the phenotype is neither pea nor rose comb but a completely different type, a walnut comb. The walnut comb phenotype is produced whenever a chicken has one or two *R* alleles, plus one or two *P* alleles (that is, *PPRR*, *PpRR*, *PPRr*, or *PpRr*). What would you hypothesize about the types of combs among the offspring of two heterozygous walnut comb chickens, *PpRr*? How does this form of gene interaction affect the ratio of phenotypes in the F$_2$ generation? Is it the typical Mendelian 9:3:3:1 ratio?[4]

Epistasis is a common type of gene interaction in which the presence of certain alleles of one locus can prevent or mask the expression of alleles of a different locus and express their own pheno-

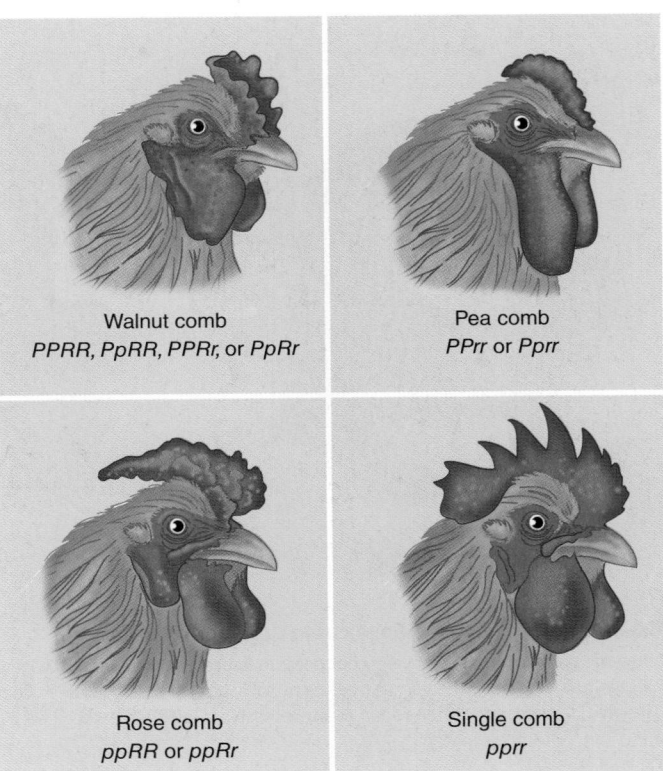

FIGURE 11-18 *Animated* **Gene interaction in chickens**
Two gene pairs govern four chicken comb phenotypes. Chickens with walnut combs have the genotype *P_R_*. Chickens with pea combs have the genotype *P_rr*, and those with rose combs have the genotype *ppR_*. Chickens that are homozygous recessive for both loci, *pprr*, have a single comb. (The blanks represent either dominant or recessive alleles.)

type instead. (The term *epistasis* means "standing on.") Unlike the chicken example, no novel phenotypes are produced in epistasis.

Coat color in Labrador retrievers is an example of epistasis that involves a gene for pigment and a gene for depositing color in the coat (**FIG. 11-19**). The two alleles for the pigment gene are *B* for black coat and its recessive counterpart, *b*, for brown coat. The gene for depositing color in the coat has two alleles, *E* for the expression of black and brown coats and *e*, which is epistatic and blocks the expression of the *B/b* gene. The epistatic allele is recessive and therefore is expressed as a yellow coat only in the homozygous condition (*ee*), regardless of the combination of *B* and *b* alleles in the genotype.

In polygenic inheritance, the offspring exhibit a continuous variation in phenotypes

Many human characters—such as height, body form, and skin pigmentation—are not inherited through alleles at a single locus. The same holds true for many commercially important characters in domestic plants and animals, such as milk and egg production. Alleles at several, perhaps many, loci affect each character. The term **polygenic inheritance** is applied when multiple independent pairs of genes have similar and additive effects on the same character.

As many as 60 loci account for the inheritance of skin pigmentation in humans. To keep things simple in this example, we

---

[4]The offspring of two heterozygous walnut comb chickens will have four genotypes in what appears to be a Mendelian 9:3:3:1 ratio: 9 walnut comb, 3 pea comb, 3 rose comb, and 1 single comb. This example is not a typical Mendelian 9:3:3:1 ratio because it involves a single character (comb shape) coded by alleles at two different loci. In Mendelian inheritance, the 9:3:3:1 ratio involves *two* characters (such as seed color and seed shape) coded by alleles at two loci.

Black
BBEE, BbEE, BBEe or BbEe

Yellow
BBee, Bbee or bbee

Chocolate
bbEE or bbEe

Renee Stockdale/Animals Animals

FIGURE 11-19 *Animated* **Epistasis in Labrador retrievers**
Two gene pairs interact to govern coat color in Labrador retrievers. Black Labs have the genotype *B_E_*; yellow Labs have the genotype *B_ee* or *bbee*; and chocolate Labs have the genotype *bbE_*. (The blanks represent either dominant or recessive alleles.)

illustrate the principle of polygenic inheritance in human skin pigmentation with pairs of alleles at three unlinked loci. These can be designated *A* and *a, B* and *b,* and *C* and *c.* The capital letters represent incompletely dominant alleles producing dark skin. The more capital letters, the darker the skin because the alleles affect skin pigmentation in an additive fashion. A person with the darkest skin possible would have the genotype *AABBCC,* and a person with the lightest skin possible would have the genotype *aabbcc.* The F_1 offspring of an *aabbcc* person and an *AABBCC* person are all *AaBbCc* and have an intermediate skin color. The F_2 offspring of two such triple heterozygotes (*AaBbCc* × *AaBbCc*) would have skin pigmentation ranging from very dark to very light (**FIG. 11-20**).

Polygenic inheritance is characterized by an F_1 generation that is intermediate between the two completely homozygous parents and by an F_2 generation that shows wide variation between the two parental types. When the number of individuals in a population is plotted against the amount of skin pigmentation and the points are connected, the result is a bell-shaped curve, a *normal distribution curve.* Most of the F_2 generation individuals have one of the intermediate phenotypes; only a few show the extreme phenotypes of the original P generation (that is, the grandparents). On average, only 1 of 64 is as dark as the very dark grandparent, and only 1 of 64 is as light as the very light grandparent. The alleles *A, B,* and *C* each produce about the same amount of darkening of the skin; hence, the genotypes *AaBbCc , AABbcc, AAbbCc, AaBBcc, aaBBCc, AabbCC,* and *aaBbCC* all produce similar intermediate phenotypes.

Genes interact with the environment to shape phenotype

Hydrangeas are shrubs grown for their attractive flowers. The color of certain hydrangea flowers ranges from blue to purple to pink

depending on the level of aluminum in the soil before the flowers begin to develop. It is easy to manipulate the level of aluminum by adding alum or aluminum sulfate to the soil or by lowering the soil pH (in acidic soils, aluminum is more soluble). Under these conditions, hydrangea flowers are blue. In alkaline soils (made by adding limestone to the soil), aluminum is less soluble, and the flowers are pink (**FIG. 11-21**).

Another example of the effect of environment on gene expression involves Himalayan rabbits. The phenotype of these rabbits is white fur except for dark patches on the ears, nose, and paws. The local surface temperature of a rabbit's ears, nose, and paws is colder in the rabbit's natural environment, and this temperature difference causes the production of dark fur. If you raise rabbits with the Himalayan genotype at a warm temperature

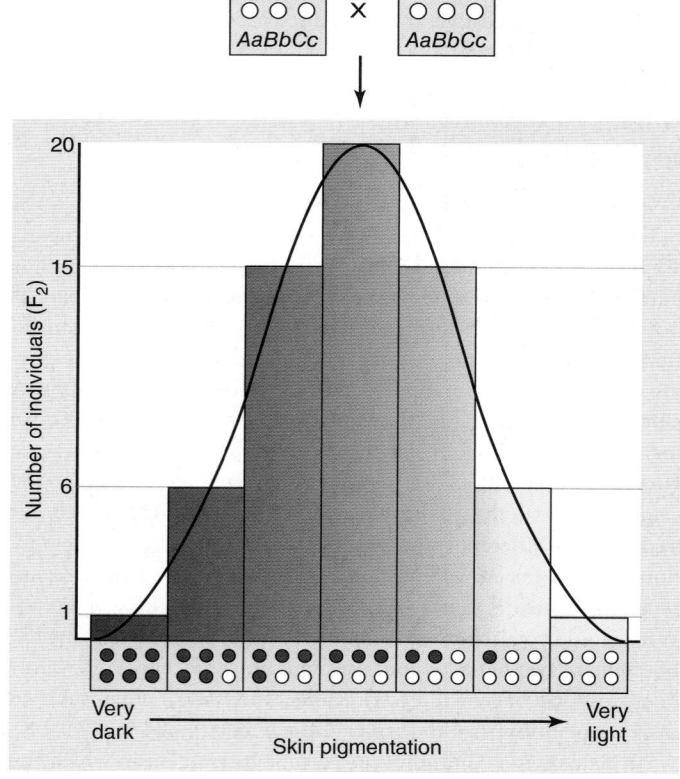

FIGURE 11-20 Polygenic inheritance in human skin pigmentation
This simplified example assumes that skin pigmentation in humans is governed by alleles of three unlinked loci. The alleles producing dark skin (*A, B,* and *C*) are represented by capital letters, but they are not dominant. Instead, their effects are additive. The number of dark dots, each signifying an allele producing dark skin, is counted to determine the phenotype. A wide range of phenotypes is possible when individuals of intermediate phenotype mate and have offspring (*AaBbCc* × *AaBbCc*). The expected distribution of phenotypes is consistent with the superimposed normal distribution curve.

FIGURE 11-21 Influence of the environment on hydrangea flower color
Hydrangea flowers vary in color depending on availability of aluminum, which in turn is dependent on soil pH. Blue flowers develop in a soil pH of 5.5 or less, purple flowers in a soil pH of 5.6 to 6.4, and pink flowers in a soil pH of 6.5 to 7.0.

(30°C), the rabbits are completely white, with no dark patches on the ears, nose, or paws (**FIG. 11-22a**). If you raise Himalayan rabbits at a cooler temperature (25°C), however, they develop the characteristic dark patches of fur (**FIG. 11-22b**). Thus, genes can function differently in different environments.

Now let's examine a human example—height—in the context of genes and the environment. The inheritance of height in humans is polygenic and involves alleles representing ten or more loci. Because many genes are involved and because height is modified by a variety of environmental conditions, such as diet and general health, the height of most adults ranges from 4 ft 2 in (1.25 m) to 7 ft 2 in (2.15 m). The genes that affect height set limits for the phenotype—no human is 12 ft tall, for example—but the environment shapes the phenotype within its genetic limits. The range of phenotypic possibilities that can develop from a single genotype under different environmental conditions is known as the **norm of reaction.** In certain genotypes the norm of reaction is quite limited. In other genotypes, such as those involved in human height, the norm of reaction is quite broad.

Although interactions between genes and the environment influence the phenotypes of many characters, it is difficult to de-

termine the exact contributions of genes and the environment to a given phenotype. In some cases the environment regulates the activity of certain genes, turning them on in some environmental conditions and off in others. Investigators argued for years about

(a) The Himalayan genotype at warm temperatures.

(b) The Himalayan genotype at cold temperatures.

FIGURE 11-22 *Animated* **Influence of the environment on rabbit coat color**
These rabbits have the same genotype for coat color, but have been exposed to different temperatures.

the relative importance of *nature* (genetics/biology) versus *nurture* (environmental influences) regarding such human characters as intelligence, depression, bipolar disorder, and schizophrenia. Studies with identical twins raised in different environments indicate that individuals may inherit genetic potential or vulnerabilities, but environmental conditions may influence the expression of the genotype. Thus, phenotypic expression depends on a combination of nature *and* nuture.

Review

- What is incomplete dominance? codominance?
- What is the difference between multiple alleles and polygenic inheritance?
- What is pleiotropy? epistasis?
- What is a norm of reaction?

■ SUMMARY: FOCUS ON LEARNING OBJECTIVES

11.1 *(page 238)*

1 Define the terms *phenotype, genotype, locus, allele, dominant allele, recessive allele, homozygous,* and *heterozygous.*

- **Genes** are in chromosomes; the site a gene occupies in the chromosome is its **locus.** Different forms of a particular gene are **alleles;** they occupy corresponding loci on homologous chromosomes.
- An individual that carries two identical alleles is **homozygous** for that locus. If the two alleles are different, that individual is **heterozygous** for that locus.
- One allele, the **dominant allele,** may mask the expression of the other allele, the **recessive allele,** in a heterozygous individual. For this reason two individuals with the same appearance, or **phenotype,** may differ from each other in their genetic makeup (that is, their combination of alleles), or **genotype.**

2 Describe Mendel's principles of segregation and independent assortment.

- According to Mendel's **principle of segregation,** during meiosis the alleles for each locus separate, or segregate, from each other. When haploid gametes are formed, each contains only one allele for each locus.
- According to Mendel's **principle of independent assortment,** alleles of different loci are distributed randomly into gametes. This can result in **genetic recombination,** the production of new allele combinations that were not present in the **parental (P) generation.**

CENGAGENOW™ Learn more about independent assortment by clicking on the figure in CengageNOW.

3 Distinguish among monohybrid, dihybrid, and test crosses.

- A cross between homozygous parents (P generation) that differ from each other with respect to their alleles at one locus is called a **monohybrid cross;** if they differ at two loci, it is called a **dihybrid cross.** The first generation of offspring, called the **F₁ generation,** is heterozygous; the generation produced by a cross of two F₁ individuals is the **F₂ generation.**
- A **test cross** between an individual of unknown genotype and a recessive individual helps determine the unknown genotype.

CENGAGENOW™ Learn more about monohybrid, dihybrid, and test crosses by clicking on the figures in CengageNOW.

4 Explain Mendel's principles of segregation and independent assortment, given what scientists now know about genes and chromosomes.

- Segregation of alleles is a direct result of homologous chromosomes separating during meiosis.
- Independent assortment occurs because there are two ways in which two pairs of homologous chromosomes can be arranged at metaphase I of meiosis. The orientation of homologous chromosomes on the metaphase plate determines the way chromosomes are distributed into haploid cells.

11.2 *(page 247)*

5 Apply the product rule and sum rule appropriately when predicting the outcomes of genetic crosses.

- According to the **product rule,** the probability of two independent events occurring together can be calculated by multiplying the probabilities of each event occurring separately.
- According to the **sum rule,** the probability of an outcome that can be obtained in more than one way can be calculated by adding the separate probabilities.

11.3 *(page 249)*

6 Define *linkage* and relate it to specific events in meiosis.

- **Linkage** is the tendency for a group of genes on the same chromosome to be inherited together. Independent assortment does not apply if two loci are linked close together on the same pair of homologous chromosomes.
- Recombination of linked genes can result from **crossing-over** (breaking and rejoining of homologous chromatids) in meiotic prophase I. (Recall from **Section 11.1** that recombination can also result from independent assortment of unlinked genes.)

7 Show how data from a test cross involving alleles of two loci can be used to distinguish between independent assortment and linkage.

- To distinguish between independent assortment of unlinked genes and linked genes, perform a **two-point test cross** between an individual that is heterozygous at both loci and an individual that is homozygous recessive for both.
- Linkage is recognized when an excess of parental-type offspring and a deficiency of recombinant-type offspring are produced in a two-point test cross.

8 Discuss the genetic determination of sex and the inheritance of X-linked genes in mammals.

- The sex of humans and other mammals is determined by the **X** and **Y chromosomes.** Normal female mammals have two X chromosomes; normal males have one X and one Y. The fertilization of an X-bearing egg by an X-bearing sperm results in a female (XX) zygote. The fertilization of an X-bearing egg by a Y-bearing sperm results in a male (XY) zygote.
- The Y chromosome determines male sex in mammals. The X chromosome contains many important genes unrelated to sex determination that are required by both males and females. A male receives all his **X-linked genes** from his mother. A female receives X-linked genes from both parents.

9 Explain some of the ways genes may interact to affect the phenotype; discuss how a single gene can affect many features of the organism simultaneously.

- **Pleiotropy** is the ability of one gene to have several effects on different characters. Most cases of pleiotropy can be traced to a single cause, such as a defective enzyme. Alternatively, alleles of many loci may interact to affect the phenotypic expression of a single character.

10 Distinguish among incomplete dominance, codominance, multiple alleles, epistasis, and polygenic inheritance.

- Dominance does not always apply; some alleles demonstrate **incomplete dominance**, in which the heterozygote is intermediate in phenotype, or **codominance**, in which the heterozygote simultaneously expresses the phenotypes of both homozygotes.
- **Multiple alleles,** three or more alleles that can potentially occupy a particular locus, may exist in a population. A diploid individual has any two of the alleles; a haploid individual or gamete has only one.

- In **epistasis,** an allele of one locus can mask the expression of alleles of a different locus.
- In **polygenic inheritance,** multiple independent pairs of genes may have similar and additive effects on the phenotype.

11 Describe *norm of reaction* and give an example.

- The range of phenotypic possibilities that can develop from a single genotype under different environmental conditions is known as the **norm of reaction.**
- Many genes are involved in the inheritance of height in humans. Also, height is modified by a variety of environmental conditions, such as diet and general health. The genes that affect height set the norm of reaction—that is, the limits—for the phenotype, and the environment molds the phenotype within its norm of reaction.

TEST YOUR UNDERSTANDING

1. One of the autosomal loci controlling eye color in fruit flies has two alleles, one for brown eyes and the other for red eyes. Fruit flies from a true-breeding line with brown eyes were crossed with flies from a true-breeding line with red eyes. The F_1 flies had red eyes. What conclusion can be drawn from this experiment? (a) these alleles underwent independent assortment (b) these alleles underwent segregation (c) these genes are X-linked (d) the allele for red eyes is dominant to the allele for brown eyes (e) all of the preceding are true

2. The F_1 flies described in question 1 were mated with brown-eyed flies from a true-breeding line. What phenotypes would you expect the offspring to have? (a) all red eyes (b) all brown eyes (c) half red eyes and half brown eyes (d) red-eyed females and brown-eyed males (e) brown-eyed females and red-eyed males

3. The type of cross described in question 2 is (a) an F_2 cross (b) a dihybrid cross (c) a test cross (d) a two-point test cross (e) none of these

4. Individuals of genotype *AaBb* were crossed with *aabb* individuals. Approximately equal numbers of the following classes of offspring were produced: *AaBb, Aabb, aaBb,* and *aabb.* These results illustrate Mendel's principle(s) of (a) linkage (b) independent assortment (c) segregation (d) a and c (e) b and c

5. Assume that the ratio of females to males is 1:1. A couple already has two daughters and no sons. If they plan to have a total of six children, what is the probability they will have four more girls? (a) $\frac{1}{4}$ (b) $\frac{1}{8}$ (c) $\frac{1}{16}$ (d) $\frac{1}{32}$ (e) $\frac{1}{64}$

6. Red–green color blindness is an X-linked recessive disorder in humans. Your friend is the daughter of a color-blind father. Her mother had normal color vision, but her maternal grandfather was color-blind. What is the probability your friend is color-blind? (a) 1 (b) $\frac{1}{2}$ (c) $\frac{1}{4}$ (d) $\frac{3}{4}$ (e) 0

7. When two long-winged flies were mated, the offspring included 77 with long wings and 24 with short wings. Is the short-winged condition dominant or recessive? What are the genotypes of the parents?

8. The long hair of Persian cats is recessive to the short hair of Siamese cats, but the black coat color of Persians is dominant to the brown-and-tan coat color of Siamese. Make up appropriate symbols for the alleles of these two unlinked loci. If a pure black, long-haired Persian is mated to a pure brown-and-tan, short-haired Siamese, what will be the appearance of the F_1 offspring? If two of these F_1 cats are mated, what is the chance that a long-haired, brown-and-tan cat will be produced in the F_2 generation? (Use the shortcut probability method to obtain your answer; then, check it with a Punnett square.)

9. Mr. and Mrs. Smith are concerned because their own blood types are A and B, respectively, but their new son, Richard, is blood type O. Could Richard be the child of these parents?

10. A walnut comb rooster is mated to three hens. Hen A, which has a walnut comb, has offspring in the ratio of 3 walnut to 1 rose. Hen B, which has a pea comb, has offspring in the ratio of 3 walnut to 3 pea to 1 rose to 1 single. Hen C, which has a walnut comb, has only walnut comb offspring. What are the genotypes of the rooster and the three hens?

11. Individuals of genotype *AaBb* were mated to individuals of genotype *aabb.* One thousand offspring were counted, with the following results: 474 *Aabb,* 480 *aaBb,* 20 *AaBb,* and 26 *aabb.* What type of cross is this? Are these loci linked? What are the two parental classes and the two recombinant classes of offspring? What is the percentage of recombination between these two loci? How many map units apart are they?

12. Genes *A* and *B* are 6 map units apart, and *A* and *C* are 4 map units apart. Which gene is in the middle if *B* and *C* are 10 map units apart? Which is in the middle if *B* and *C* are 2 map units apart?

CRITICAL THINKING

1. Sketch a series of diagrams showing each of the following, making sure to end each series with haploid gametes:
   (a) How a pair of alleles for a single locus segregate in meiosis
   (b) How the alleles of two unlinked loci assort independently in meiosis
   (c) How the alleles of two linked loci undergo genetic recombination

2. Can you always ascertain an organism's genotype for a particular locus if you know its phenotype? Conversely, if you are given an organism's genotype for a locus, can you always reliably predict its phenotype? Explain.

3. Compare the mechanisms of genetic recombination in linked and unlinked genes.

4. **EVOLUTION LINK.** Darwin's theory of evolution by natural selection is based on four observations about the natural world. One of these is that each individual has a combination of traits that makes it uniquely different. Darwin recognized that much of this variation among individuals must be inherited, but he did not know about Mendel's mechanism of inheritance. Based on what you have learned in this chapter, briefly explain the variation among individuals that Darwin observed.

5. **ANALYZING DATA.** Using the graph in Figure 11-20, determine how many offspring were involved in the hypothetical cross studying skin color. What percentage had the lightest skin possible? the darkest skin?

6. **ANALYZING DATA.** The following figure shows a cross between a homozygous black and a homozygous yellow Labrador retriever. What is the phenotype of the F_1 generation? What are the phenotypes and the phenotypic ratio of the F_2 generation? Inheritance of coat color in Labrador retrievers is an example of what type of inheritance pattern?

Homozygous parents:

F_1 puppies:

BbEe

Allele combinations possible among F_2 puppies:

	BE	Be	bE	be
BE	BBEE	BBEe	BbEE	BbEe
Be	BBEe	BBee	BbEe	Bbee
bE	BbEE	BbEe	bbEE	bbEe
be	BbEe	Bbee	bbEe	bbee

 CENGAGENOW™ Additional questions are available in CengageNOW at www.cengage.com/login.

12 DNA: The Carrier of Genetic Information

Electron micrograph of DNA replication. During replication, two DNA molecules are synthesized from the original parent molecule. Replication is occurring at the Y-shaped structure, which is called a *replication fork.*

Dr. Gopal Murti/Visuals Unlimited

KEY CONCEPTS

12.1 Starting in the 1920s, evidence began to accumulate that DNA is the hereditary material.

12.2 The DNA molecule consists of two strands that wrap around each other to form a double helix; the order of its building blocks provides for the storage of genetic information. The DNA building blocks consist of four different nucleotide subunits, designated T, C, A, and G. The pairing of nucleotide subunits occurs based on precise pairing rules: T pairs with A, and C pairs with G.

12.3 DNA replication, which results in two identical double-stranded DNA molecules, provides the molecular mechanism for passing genetic information from one generation to the next.

After the rediscovery of Mendel's principles in 1900, geneticists conducted experiments to learn how genes are arranged in chromosomes and how they are transmitted from generation to generation. However, basic questions remained unanswered through most of the first half of the 20th century: What are genes made of? How do genes work? The studies of inheritance patterns described in Chapter 11 did not answer these questions. However, they provided a foundation of knowledge that enabled scientists to make predictions about the molecular (chemical) nature of genes and how genes function.

Scientists generally agreed that genes would have to store information in a form that the cell could retrieve and use. But scientists also had to account for other properties of genes. For example, experiments on a variety of organisms had demonstrated that genes are usually stable and passed unchanged from generation to generation. However, occasionally a gene converted to a different form; such genetic changes, called *mutations,* were then transmitted unchanged to future generations.

As the science of genetics was developing, biochemists were making a growing effort to correlate the known properties of genes with the nature of various biological molecules. What kind of molecule could store information? How could that information be retrieved and used to direct cell functions? What kind of molecule could be relatively stable but have the capacity to change, resulting in a mutation, under certain conditions?

As they learned more about the central role of proteins in virtually every aspect of cell structure and metabolism, some scientists considered proteins the prime candidates for the genetic material. However, protein did not turn out to be the molecule that governs inheritance. In this chapter we discuss how researchers discovered that **deoxyribonucleic acid (DNA),** a nucleic acid once thought unremarkable, is the molecular basis of inheritance. We explore the unique features of DNA, including its structure and replication (see photograph), that enable it to carry out this role.

12.1 EVIDENCE OF DNA AS THE HEREDITARY MATERIAL

◼ LEARNING OBJECTIVES

1 Summarize the evidence that accumulated during the 1940s and early 1950s demonstrating that DNA is the genetic material.

2 State the questions that these classic experiments addressed: Griffith's transformation experiment, Avery's contribution to Griffith's work, and the Hershey–Chase experiments.

During the 1930s and early 1940s, most geneticists paid little attention to DNA, convinced that the genetic material must be protein. Given the accumulating evidence that genes control production of proteins (discussed in Chapter 13), it certainly seemed likely that genes themselves must also be proteins. Scientists knew proteins consisted of more than 20 different kinds of amino acids in many different combinations, which conferred unique properties on each type of protein. Given their complexity and diversity compared with other molecules, proteins seemed to be the "stuff" of which genes are made.

In contrast, scientists had established that DNA and other nucleic acids were made of only four nucleotides, and what was known about their arrangement made them relatively uninteresting to most researchers. For this reason, several early clues to the role of DNA were not widely noticed.

DNA is the transforming principle in bacteria

One of these clues had its origin in 1928, when Frederick Griffith, a British medical officer, made a curious observation concerning two strains of pneumococcus bacteria (**FIG. 12-1**). A smooth (S) strain, named for its formation of smooth colonies on a solid growth medium, exhibited **virulence,**

KEY EXPERIMENTS

QUESTION: Can a genetic trait be transmitted from one bacterial strain to another?

HYPOTHESIS: The ability of pneumococcus bacteria to cause disease can be transmitted from the virulent strain (smooth, or S cells) to the avirulent strain (rough, or R cells).

EXPERIMENT: Griffith performed four experiments on mice, using the two strains of pneumococci: (1) injection of mice with live rough cells, (2) injection with live smooth cells, (3) injection with heat-killed smooth cells, and (4) injection with both live rough cells and heat-killed smooth cells.

Experiment 1	Experiment 2	Experiment 3	Experiment 4
R cells injected	S cells injected	Heat-killed S cells injected	R cells and heat-killed S cells injected
Mouse lives	**Mouse dies**	**Mouse lives**	**Mouse dies**

RESULTS AND CONCLUSION: Although neither the rough strain nor the heat-killed smooth strain could kill a mouse, a combination of the two did. Autopsy of the dead mouse showed the presence of living S-strain pneumococci. These results indicated that some substance in the heat-killed S cells had transformed the living R cells into a virulent form.

FIGURE 12-1 *Animated* Griffith's transformation experiments

Griffith was trying to develop a vaccine against pneumonia when he serendipitously discovered the phenomenon of transformation.

the ability to cause disease, and often death, in its host. When living cells of this strain were injected into mice, the animals contracted pneumonia and died. Not surprisingly, the injected animals survived if the cells were first killed with heat. A related rough (R) strain of bacteria, which forms colonies with a rough surface, exhibited **avirulence,** or inability to produce pathogenic effects; mice injected with either living or heat-killed cells of this strain survived. However, when Griffith injected mice with a mixture of *heat-killed* virulent S cells and *live* avirulent R cells, a high proportion of the mice died. Griffith then isolated living S cells from the dead mice.

Because neither the heat-killed S strain nor the living R strain could be converted to the living virulent form when injected by itself in the control experiments, it seemed that something in the heat-killed cells converted the avirulent cells to the lethal form. This type of permanent genetic change in which the properties of one strain of dead cells are conferred on a different strain of living cells is called **transformation.** Scientists hypothesized that some chemical substance (a *transforming principle,* or *factor*) was transferred from the dead bacteria to the living cells and caused transformation.

In 1944, Oswald T. Avery and his colleagues Colin M. MacLeod and Maclyn McCarty chemically identified Griffith's transforming factor as DNA. They did this through a series of careful experiments in which they lysed (split open) S cells and separated the cell contents into several fractions: lipids, proteins, polysaccharides, and nucleic acids (DNA and RNA). They tested each fraction to see if it could transform living R cells into S cells. The experiments using lipids, polysaccharides, and proteins did not cause transformation. However, when Avery treated living R cells with nucleic acids extracted from S cells, the R cells were transformed into S cells.

Although today scientists consider these results to be the first definitive demonstration that DNA is the genetic material, not all scientists of the time were convinced. Many thought the findings might apply only to bacteria and might not have any relevance for the genetics of eukaryotes. During the next few years, new evidence accumulated that the haploid nuclei of pollen grains and gametes such as sperm contain only half the amount of DNA found in diploid somatic cells of the same species. (*Somatic cells* are body cells and never become gametes.) Because scientists generally accepted that genes are located on chromosomes, these findings correlating DNA content with chromosome number provided strong circumstantial evidence for DNA's importance in eukaryotic inheritance.

DNA is the genetic material in certain viruses

In 1952, geneticists Alfred Hershey and Martha Chase performed a series of elegant experiments on the reproduction of viruses that infect bacteria, known as **bacteriophages** or **phages** (discussed in Chapter 24). When they planned their experiments, they knew that phages reproduce inside a bacterial cell, eventually causing the cell to break open and release large numbers of new viruses. Because electron microscopic studies had shown that only part of an infecting phage actually enters the cell, they reasoned that the genetic material should be included in that portion (**FIG. 12-2**).

FIGURE 12-2 Bacteriophages on a bacterial cell

This colorized TEM shows several phages attached to the bacterium *Escherichia coli*. Note the viral genetic material being injected into the bacterium.

As shown in **FIGURE 12-3**, they labeled the viral protein of one sample of phages with ^{35}S, a radioactive isotope of sulfur, and the viral DNA of a second sample with ^{32}P, a radioactive isotope of phosphorus. Recall from Chapter 3 that proteins contain sulfur as part of the amino acids cysteine and methionine and that nucleic acids contain phosphate groups. The phages in each sample attached to bacteria, and the researchers shook the phages off by agitating the sample in a blender. Then they centrifuged the samples.

In the sample in which they had labeled the proteins with ^{35}S, they subsequently found radioactivity in the supernatant, indicating that the protein had not entered the cells. In the sample in which they had labeled the DNA with ^{32}P, they found radioactivity associated with the bacterial cells (in the pellet): DNA had actually entered the cells. Hershey and Chase concluded that phages inject their DNA into bacterial cells, leaving most of their protein on the outside. This finding emphasized the significance of DNA in viral reproduction, and many scientists saw it as an important demonstration of DNA's role as the hereditary material.

Review

- How did the experiments of Avery and his colleagues point to DNA as the essential genetic material?
- How did the Hershey–Chase experiments establish that DNA is the genetic material in bacteriophages?

12.2 THE STRUCTURE OF DNA

■ LEARNING OBJECTIVES

3   Explain how nucleotide subunits link to form a single DNA strand.

4   Describe how the two strands of DNA are oriented with respect to each other.

5   State the base-pairing rules for DNA and describe how complementary bases bind to each other.

QUESTION: Is DNA or protein the genetic material in bacterial viruses (phages)?

HYPOTHESIS: DNA is the genetic material in bacterial viruses.

EXPERIMENT: Hershey and Chase produced phage populations with either radioactively labeled DNA or radioactively labeled protein. In both cases, they infected bacteria with the phages and then determined whether DNA or protein was injected into bacterial cells to direct the formation of new viral particles.

① Radioactively labeled phages infect bacterial cells.

② Cells agitated in blender and centrifuged. Bacteria, which are heavier, settle into pellet. Phages and phage parts, which are lighter, remain in supernatant.

③ Pellets and supernatants tested for radioactivity.

^{35}S

Experiment A, phages with ^{35}S-labeled protein coat (green)

^{35}S-labeled protein in supernatant

Bacteria in pellet do not contain ^{35}S label.

Phages from pellet inject bacteria into genetic material.

No radioactively labeled protein enters cell.

^{32}P

Experiment B, phages with ^{32}P-labeled DNA (red)

Phages from pellet inject genetic material.

^{32}P

Bacteria in pellet contain ^{32}P-labeled DNA.

Some newly assembled viruses have radioactively labeled DNA.

RESULTS AND CONCLUSION: The researchers could separate phage protein coats labeled with the radioactive isotope ^{35}S from infected bacterial cells without affecting viral reproduction. However, they could not separate viral DNA labeled with the radioactive isotope ^{32}P from infected bacterial cells. This demonstrated that viral DNA enters the bacterial cells and is required for the synthesis of new viral particles. Thus, DNA is the genetic material in phages.

FIGURE 12-3 *Animated* The Hershey–Chase experiments

Scientists did not generally accept DNA as the genetic material until 1953, when American scientist James Watson and British scientist Francis Crick, both working in England, proposed a model for its structure that had extraordinary explanatory power. The story of how the structure of DNA was figured out is one of the most remarkable chapters in the history of modern biology (**TABLE 12-1**).

As you will see in the following discussion, scientists already knew a great deal about DNA's physical and chemical properties when Watson and Crick became interested in the problem; in fact, they did not conduct any experiments or gather any new data. Their all-important contribution was to integrate all the available information into a model that demonstrated how the molecule can both

Date	Discovery
1871	**Friedrich Miescher** reports discovery of new substance, *nuclein,* from cell nuclei. Nuclein is now known to be a mixture of DNA, RNA, and proteins.
1928	**Frederick Griffith** finds a substance in heat-killed bacteria that "transforms" living bacteria.
1944	**Oswald Avery, Colin MacLeod,** and **Maclyn McCarty** chemically identify Griffith's transforming principle as DNA.
1949	**Erwin Chargaff** reports relationships among DNA bases that provide a clue to the structure of DNA.
1952	**Alfred Hershey** and **Martha Chase** demonstrate that DNA, not protein, is involved in viral reproduction.
1952	**Rosalind Franklin** produces X-ray diffraction images of DNA.
1953	**James Watson** and **Francis Crick** propose a model of the structure of DNA; this contribution is widely considered the start of a revolution in molecular biology that continues to the present.
1958	**Matthew Meselson** and **Franklin Stahl** demonstrate that DNA replication is semiconservative.
1962	**James Watson, Francis Crick,** and **Maurice Wilkins** are awarded the Nobel Prize in Medicine for discoveries about the molecular structure of nucleic acids.*
1969	**Alfred Hershey** is awarded the Nobel Prize in Medicine for discovering the replication mechanism and genetic structure of viruses.

*Rosalind Franklin could not share the prize because she was deceased.

FIGURE 12-4 The nucleotide subunits of DNA

A single strand of DNA consists of a backbone (*superimposed on blue screen*) of phosphate groups alternating with the sugar deoxyribose (*green*). Phosphodiester linkages (*pink*) join sugars of adjacent nucleotides. Linked to the 1′ carbon of each sugar is one of four nitrogenous bases (*top to bottom*): thymine, adenine, cytosine, and guanine. (*The nucleotide containing the base adenine is highlighted yellow.*) Note the polarity of the polynucleotide chain, with the 5′ end at the top of the figure and the 3′ end at the bottom.

carry information for making proteins and serve as its own **template** (pattern or guide) for its duplication.

Nucleotides can be covalently linked in any order to form long polymers

As discussed in Chapter 3, each DNA building block is a **nucleotide** consisting of the pentose sugar **deoxyribose,** a phosphate, and one of four nitrogenous bases (**FIG. 12-4**). It is conventional to number the atoms in a molecule using a system devised by organic chemists. Accordingly, in nucleic acid chemistry the individual carbons in each sugar and each base are numbered. The carbons in a base are designated by numerals, but the carbons in a sugar are distinguished from those in the base by prime symbols, such as 2′. The nitrogenous base is attached to the 1′ carbon of the sugar, and the phosphate is attached to the 5′ carbon. The bases include two **purines, adenine (A)** and **guanine (G),** and two **pyrimidines, thymine (T)** and **cytosine (C).**

The nucleotides are linked by covalent bonds to form an alternating sugar–phosphate backbone. The 3′ carbon of one sugar is bonded to the 5′ phosphate of the adjacent sugar to form a 3′, 5′ **phosphodiester linkage.** The result is a polymer of indefinite length, with the nucleotides linked in any order. Scientists now know that most DNA molecules found in cells are millions of bases long. Figure 12-4 also shows that a single polynucleotide chain is directional. No matter how long the chain may be, one end, the **5′ end,** has a 5′ carbon attached to a phosphate and the other, the **3′ end,** has a 3′ carbon attached to a hydroxyl group.

In 1949, Erwin Chargaff and his colleagues at Columbia University had determined the base composition of DNA from several organisms and tissues. They found a simple relationship among the bases that turned out to be an important clue to the structure of DNA. Regardless of the source of the DNA, in Chargaff's words the "ratios of purines to pyrimidines and also of adenine to thymine and of guanine to cytosine were not far from 1" (**TABLE 12-2**).

TABLE 12-2	Base Compositions in DNA from Selected Organisms

	Percentage of DNA Bases				Ratios	
Source of DNA	A	T	G	C	A/T	G/C
E. coli	26.1	23.9	24.9	25.1	1.09	0.99
Yeast	31.3	32.9	18.7	17.1	0.95	1.09
Sea urchin sperm	32.5	31.8	17.5	18.2	1.02	0.96
Herring sperm	27.8	27.5	22.2	22.6	1.01	0.98
Human liver	30.3	30.3	19.5	19.9	1.00	0.98
Corn (*Zea mays*)	25.6	25.3	24.5	24.6	1.01	1.00

In other words, in double-stranded DNA molecules, the number of purines equals the number of pyrimidines, the number of adenines equals the number of thymines (A equals T), and the number of guanines equals the number of cytosines (G equals C). These equalities are called **Chargaff's rules.**

DNA is made of two polynucleotide chains intertwined to form a double helix

Key information about the structure of DNA came from X-ray diffraction studies on crystals of purified DNA, carried out by British scientist Rosalind Franklin at King's College from 1951 to 1953 (**FIG. 12-5**).

X-ray diffraction, a powerful method for determining the 3-D structure of a molecule, can determine the distances between the atoms of molecules arranged in a regular, repeating crystalline structure (**FIG. 12-6**). X-rays have such short wavelengths that they can be scattered by the electrons surrounding the atoms in a molecule. Atoms with dense electron clouds (such as phosphorus and oxygen) tend to deflect electrons more strongly than atoms with lower atomic numbers. Exposing a crystal to an intense beam of X-rays causes the regular arrangement of its atoms to diffract, or scatter,

FIGURE 12-5 Rosalind Franklin

Franklin was a gifted scientist whose contributions helped elucidate the double helix structure of DNA.

© Science Source/Photo Researchers, Inc.

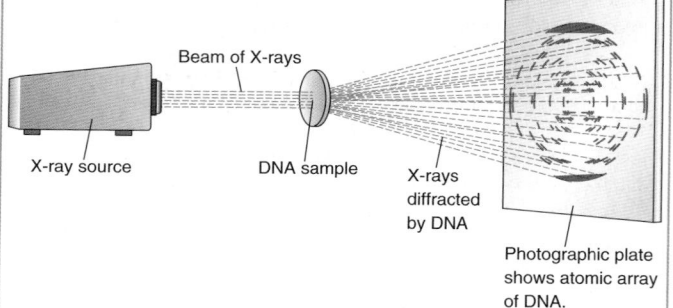
Why Is It Used?   X-ray diffraction can be used to determine the regular array of atoms in a crystalline sample of, for example, DNA. Because each type of crystal has its own characteristic pattern, the three-dimensional structure of the molecule being studied can be deduced.

How Is It Done?   ❶ Researchers direct a narrow beam of X-rays at a single crystal of DNA. X-rays are diffracted (bent) at specific angles based on the density of electrons of different atoms. Important clues about DNA structure are provided by detailed mathematical analysis of measurements of the spots, which are formed by X-rays hitting the photographic plate

Beam of X-rays

X-ray source   DNA sample   X-rays
diffracted
by DNA

Photographic plate
shows atomic array
of DNA.

❷ X-ray diffraction image of DNA. This diagonal pattern of spots stretching from 11 to 5 and from 1 to 7 (as on a clock face) provides evidence for the helical structure of DNA. The elongated horizontal patterns at the top and bottom indicate that the purine and pyrimidine bases are stacked 0.34 nm apart and are perpendicular to the axis of the DNA molecule.

Dr. S. Dover, Division of Biomolecular Sciences, Kings College, London

FIGURE 12-6 How X-ray diffraction works

the X-rays in specific ways. The pattern of diffracted X-rays appears on photographic film as dark spots. Mathematical analysis of the pattern and distances between the spots yields the precise distances between atoms and their orientation within the molecules.

Franklin had already produced X-ray crystallographic films of DNA patterns when Watson and Crick began to pursue the problem of DNA structure. Her pictures clearly showed that DNA has a type of helical structure, and three major types of regular, repeating patterns in the molecule (with the dimensions 0.34 nm, 3.4 nm, and 2.0 nm) were evident. Franklin and colleague Maurice Wilkins had inferred from these patterns that the nucleotide bases (which are flat molecules) are stacked like the rungs of a ladder. Using this information, Watson and Crick began to build scale models of the DNA components and then fit them together to correlate with the experimental data (**FIG. 12-7**).

After several trials, they worked out a model that fit the existing data (**FIG. 12-8**). The nucleotide chains conformed to the dimensions of the X-ray data only if each DNA molecule consisted of *two* polynucleotide chains arranged in a coiled **double helix.** In their model, the sugar–phosphate backbones of the two chains form the outside of the helix. The bases belonging to the two chains associate as pairs along the central axis of the helix. The reasons for the repeating patterns of 0.34 nm and 3.4 nm measurements are readily apparent from the model: each pair of bases is exactly 0.34 nm from the adjacent pairs above and below. Because exactly 10 base pairs are present in each full turn of the helix, each turn constitutes 3.4 nm of length. To fit the data, the two chains must run in opposite directions; therefore, each end of the double helix must have an exposed 5′ phosphate on one strand and an exposed 3′ hydroxyl

group (—OH) on the other. Because the two strands run in opposite directions, they are **antiparallel** to each other (**FIG. 12-9a**).

In double-stranded DNA, hydrogen bonds form between A and T and between G and C

Other features of the Watson and Crick model integrated critical information about the chemical composition of DNA with the

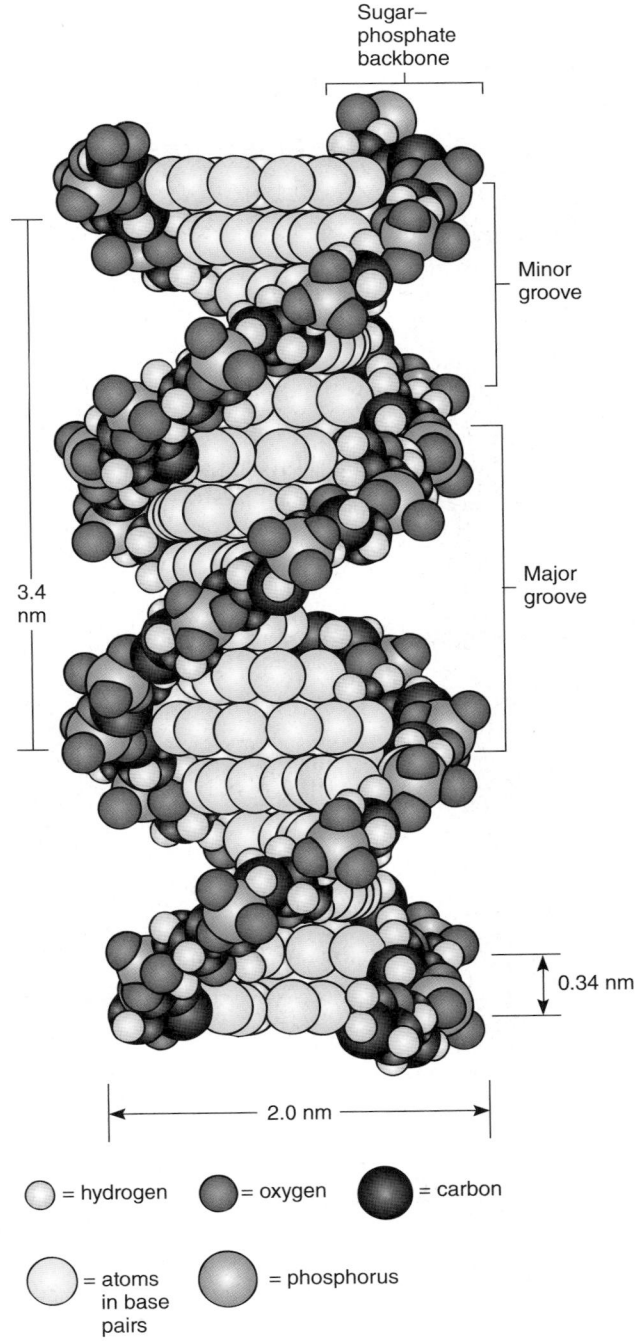

Sugar–phosphate backbone

Minor groove

Major groove

3.4 nm

0.34 nm

2.0 nm

○ = hydrogen ● = oxygen ● = carbon

○ = atoms in base pairs ○ = phosphorus

FIGURE 12-8 *Animated* **A three-dimensional model of the DNA double helix**

The measurements match those derived from X-ray diffraction images.

FIGURE 12-7 James Watson and Francis Crick

Watson (left) and Crick (right) are shown with their model of DNA's double helix.

Base pairing and the sequence of bases in DNA provide a foundation for understanding both DNA replication and the inheritance of genetic material.

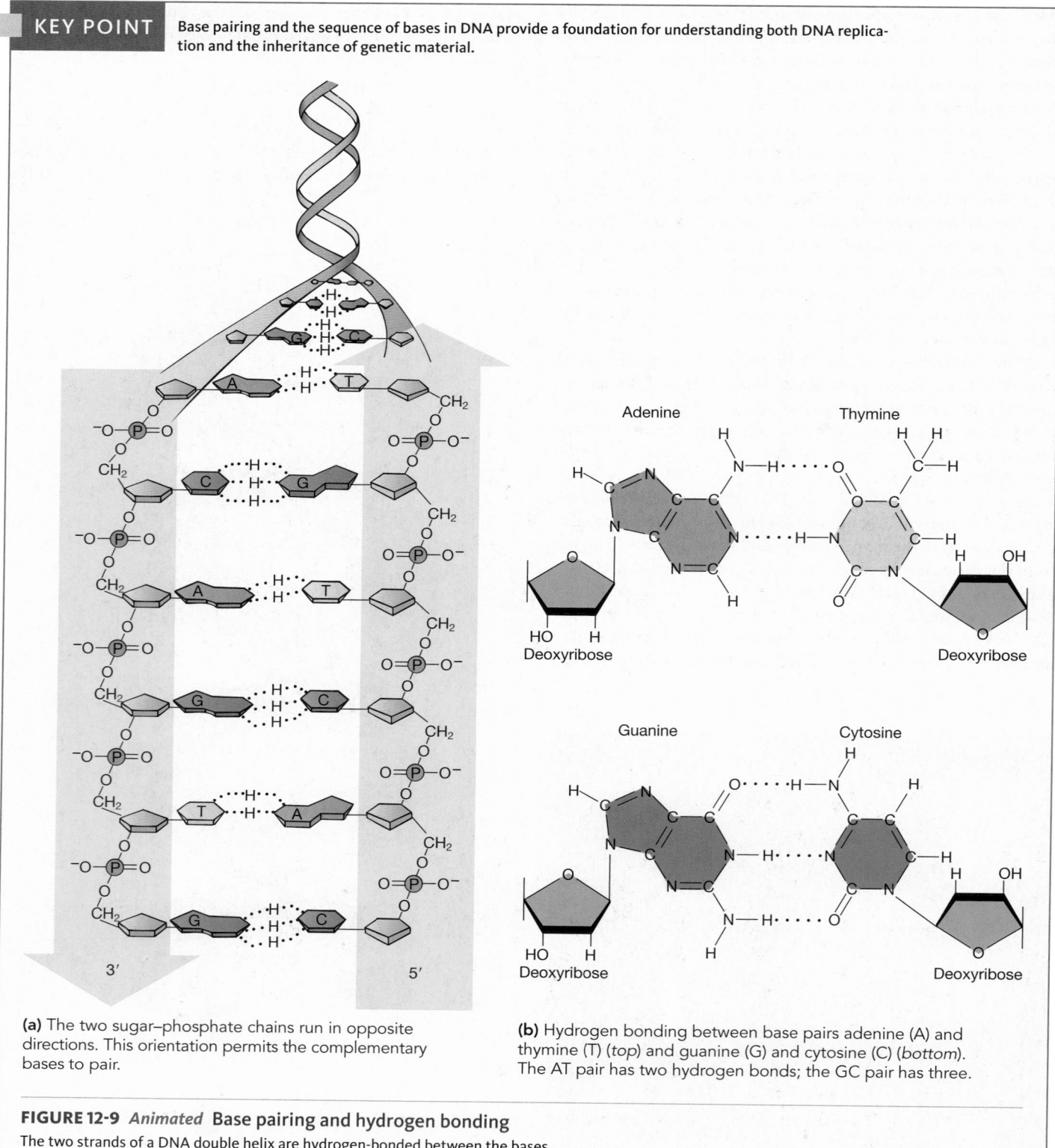

(a) The two sugar–phosphate chains run in opposite directions. This orientation permits the complementary bases to pair.

(b) Hydrogen bonding between base pairs adenine (A) and thymine (T) (*top*) and guanine (G) and cytosine (C) (*bottom*). The AT pair has two hydrogen bonds; the GC pair has three.

FIGURE 12-9 *Animated* **Base pairing and hydrogen bonding**
The two strands of a DNA double helix are hydrogen-bonded between the bases.

X-ray diffraction data. The X-ray diffraction studies indicated that the double helix has a precise and constant width, as shown by the 2.0 nm measurements. This finding is actually consistent with Chargaff's rules. As Figure 12-4 shows, each pyrimidine (cytosine or thymine) contains only one ring of atoms, whereas each purine (guanine or adenine) contains two rings. Study of the models made it clear to Watson and Crick that if each rung of the ladder contained one purine and one pyrimidine, the width of the helix at each base pair would be exactly 2.0 nm. By contrast, the combination of two purines (each of which is 1.2 nm wide) would be wider than 2.0 nm and that of two pyrimidines would be narrower, so the diameter would not be constant. Further examination of the model showed that adenine can pair with thymine (and guanine with cytosine) in such a way that hydrogen bonds form between them; the opposite combinations, cytosine with adenine and guanine with thymine, do not lead to favorable hydrogen bonding.

The nature of the hydrogen bonding between adenine and thymine and between guanine and cytosine is shown in **FIGURE 12-9b**. Two hydrogen bonds form between adenine and thymine, and three between guanine and cytosine. This concept of specific base pairing neatly explains Chargaff's rules. The amount of cytosine must equal the amount of guanine because every cytosine in one chain must have a paired guanine in the other chain. Similarly, every adenine in the first chain must have a thymine in the second chain. The sequences of bases in the two chains exhibit **complementary base pairing**—that is, the sequence of nucleotides in one chain dictates the complementary sequence of nucleotides in the other. For example, if one strand has this sequence,

$$3'\text{—AGCTAC—}5'$$

then the other strand has the complementary sequence:

$$5'\text{—TCGATG—}3'$$

The double-helix model strongly suggested that the sequence of bases in DNA provides for the storage of genetic information and that this sequence ultimately relates to the sequences of amino acids in proteins. Although restrictions limit how the bases on opposite strands pair with each other, the number of possible linear sequences of bases in a strand is virtually unlimited. Because a DNA molecule in a cell can be millions of nucleotides long, it can store enormous amounts of information, usually consisting of hundreds of genes.

Review

- What types of subunits make up a single strand of DNA? How are the subunits linked?
- What is the structure of double-stranded DNA, as determined by Watson and Crick?
- How do Chargaff's rules relate to the structure of DNA?

12.3 DNA REPLICATION

■ LEARNING OBJECTIVES

6 Cite evidence from Meselson and Stahl's experiment that enabled scientists to differentiate between semiconservative replication of DNA and alternative models.

7 Summarize how DNA replicates and identify some unique features of the process.

8 Explain the complexities of DNA replication that make it (a) bidirectional and (b) continuous in one strand and discontinuous in the other.

9 Discuss how enzymes proofread and repair errors in DNA.

10 Define *telomere*, and describe the possible connections between telomerase and cell aging and between telomerase and cancer.

Two immediately apparent and distinctive features of the Watson–Crick model made it seem plausible that DNA is the genetic mate-

rial. We have already mentioned that the sequence of bases in DNA can carry coded information. The model also suggested a way in which the sequence of nucleotides in DNA could be precisely copied, a process known as **DNA replication.**

The connection between DNA replication and the behavior of chromosomes in mitosis was obvious to Watson and Crick. A chromosome becomes duplicated so that it consists of two identical sister chromatids that later separate at anaphase; the genetic material must be precisely duplicated and distributed to the daughter cells. They noted, in a classic and now famous understatement at the end of their first brief paper, "It has not escaped our notice that the specific pairing we have postulated immediately suggests a possible copying mechanism for the genetic material."

The model suggested that because the nucleotides pair with each other in complementary fashion, each strand of the DNA molecule could serve as a template for synthesizing the opposite strand. It would simply be necessary for the hydrogen bonds between the two strands to break (recall from Chapter 2 that hydrogen bonds are relatively weak) and the two chains to separate. Each strand of the double helix could then pair with new complementary nucleotides to replace its missing partner. The result would be two DNA double helices, each identical to the original one and consisting of one original strand from the parent molecule and one newly synthesized complementary strand. This type of information copying is called **semiconservative replication** (**FIG. 12-10a**).

Meselson and Stahl verified the mechanism of semiconservative replication

Although the semiconservative replication mechanism suggested by Watson and Crick was (and is) a simple and compelling model, experimental proof was needed to establish that DNA in fact replicates in that manner. Researchers first needed to rule out other possibilities. With *conservative replication,* both parent (or old) strands would remain together, and the two newly synthesized strands would form a second double helix (**FIG. 12-10b**). As a third hypothesis, the parental and newly synthesized strands might become randomly mixed during the replication process—that is, *dispersive replication* (**FIG. 12-10c**). To discriminate among semiconservative replication and the other models, investigators had to distinguish between old and newly synthesized strands of DNA.

One technique is to use a heavy isotope of nitrogen, ^{15}N (ordinary nitrogen is ^{14}N), to label the bases of the DNA strands, making them more dense. Using **density gradient centrifugation,** scientists can separate large molecules such as DNA on the basis of differences in their density (see Fig. 4-5). When DNA is mixed with a solution containing cesium chloride (CsCl) and centrifuged at high speed, the solution forms a density gradient in the centrifuge tube, ranging from a region of lowest density at the top to one of highest density at the bottom. During centrifugation, the DNA molecules migrate to the region of the gradient identical to their own density.

In 1958, Matthew Meselson and Franklin Stahl at the California Institute of Technology grew the bacterium *Escherichia coli* on a medium that contained ^{15}N in the form of ammonium chloride (NH$_4$Cl). The cells used the ^{15}N to synthesize bases, which then became incorporated into DNA (**FIG. 12-11**). The resulting DNA molecules, which contained heavy nitrogen, were extracted from some of the cells. When the researchers subjected them to density

(a) Hypothesis 1: Semiconservative replication

Parental DNA   First generation   Second generation

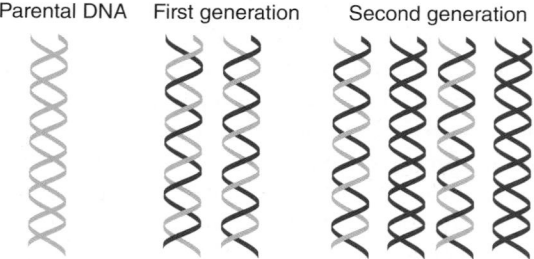

(b) Hypothesis 2: Conservative replication

Parental DNA   First generation   Second generation

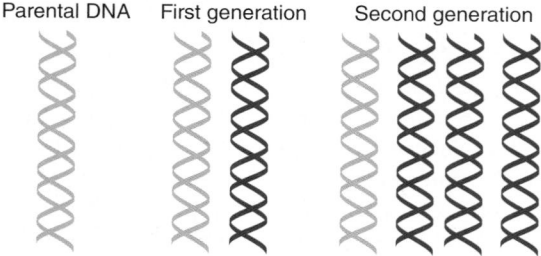

(c) Hypothesis 3: Dispersive replication

Parental DNA   First generation   Second generation

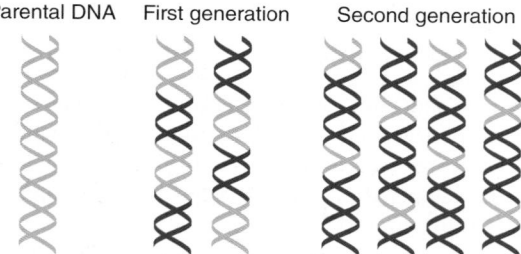

FIGURE 12-10 Alternative models of DNA replication
The hypothesized arrangement of old (*light blue*) and newly synthesized (*dark blue*) DNA strands after one and two generations, according to **(a)** the semiconservative model, **(b)** the conservative model, and **(c)** the dispersive model.

KEY EXPERIMENT

QUESTION: What is the mechanism of DNA replication?

HYPOTHESIS: Figure 12-10 depicts three hypotheses of DNA replication and predicts the arrangement of old and newly synthesized DNA strands after one or two generations according to each hypothesis.

EXPERIMENT: Meselson and Stahl grew bacteria (*E. coli*) in heavy nitrogen (^{15}N) growth medium for many generations so that all the DNA strands would be heavy. Then they transferred some of the cells to light nitrogen (^{14}N) medium so that the newly synthesized strands would be light. They isolated DNA from bacterial cells after 20 minutes (one generation) and 40 minutes (two generations) and centrifuged it to separate DNA into bands based on density.

In density gradient centrifugation, the concentration of CsCl is highest at the bottom of the tube and lowest at the top. DNA molecules move to positions where their density equals that of the CsCl solution in which they are centrifuged.

RESULTS AND CONCLUSION: Based on the observed density of the DNA molecules in each generation, Meselson and Stahl concluded that the semiconservative model accurately predicts the mechanism of DNA replication.

The location of DNA molecules within the centrifuge tube can be determined by UV optics. DNA solutions absorb strongly at 260 nm.

FIGURE 12-11 The Meselson–Stahl experiment

---

gradient centrifugation, they accumulated in the high-density region of the gradient. The team transferred the rest of the bacteria (which also contained ^{15}N-labeled DNA) to a different growth medium in which the NH_4Cl contained the naturally abundant, lighter ^{14}N isotope and then allowed them to undergo additional cell divisions.

Meselson and Stahl expected the newly synthesized DNA strands to be less dense because they incorporated bases containing the lighter ^{14}N isotope. Indeed, double-stranded DNA from cells isolated after one generation had an intermediate density, indicating they contained half as many ^{15}N atoms as the "parent" DNA. This finding supported the semiconservative replication model, which predicted that each double helix would contain a previously synthesized strand (heavy in this case) and a newly synthesized strand (light in this case). It was also consistent with the disper-

sive model, which would also yield one class of molecules, all with intermediate density. It was inconsistent with the conservative model, which predicted two classes of double-stranded molecules, those with two heavy strands and those with two light strands.

After another cycle of cell division in the medium with the lighter ^{14}N isotope, two types of DNA appeared in the density gradient, exactly as predicted by the semiconservative replication model. One consisted of DNA with a density intermediate between ^{15}N-labeled DNA and ^{14}N-labeled DNA, whereas the other contained only DNA with a density of ^{14}N-labeled DNA. This finding refuted the dispersive model, which predicted that all strands would have an intermediate density.

Semiconservative replication explains the perpetuation of mutations

The recognition that DNA could be copied by a semiconservative mechanism suggested how DNA could explain a third essential characteristic of genetic material—the ability to mutate. It was long known that **mutations,** or genetic changes, could arise in genes and then be transmitted faithfully to succeeding generations. For example, a mutation in the fruit fly (*Drosophila melanogaster*) produces vestigial wings.

When the double-helix model was proposed, it seemed plausible that mutations could represent a change in the sequence of bases in the DNA. You could predict that if DNA is copied by a mechanism involving complementary base pairing, any change in the sequence of bases on one strand would produce a new sequence of complementary bases during the next replication cycle. The new base sequence would then transfer to daughter molecules by the same mechanism used to copy the original genetic material, as if no change had occurred.

For the example in **FIGURE 12-12**, an adenine base in one of the DNA strands has been changed to guanine. This could occur by a rare error in DNA replication or by one of several other known mechanisms. As discussed later, certain enzymes correct errors when they occur, but not all errors are corrected properly. By one estimate, the rate of uncorrected errors that occur during DNA replication is equal to about one nucleotide in a billion. When the DNA molecule containing an error replicates (left side of Fig. 12-12), one of the strands gives rise to a molecule exactly like its parent strand; the other (mutated) strand gives rise to a molecule with a new combination of bases that is transmitted generation after generation.

DNA replication requires protein "machinery"

Although semiconservative replication by base pairing appears simple and straightforward, the actual process is highly regulated and requires a "replication machine" containing many types of protein and enzyme molecules. Many essential features of DNA replication are common to all organisms, although prokaryotes and eukaryotes differ somewhat because their DNA is organized differently. In most bacterial cells, such as *E. coli,* most or all the DNA is in the form of a single, *circular,* double-stranded DNA molecule. In contrast, each unreplicated eukaryotic chromosome contains a single, *linear,* double-stranded molecule associated with at least as much protein (by mass) as DNA.

We now present DNA replication, based on the current understanding of the process. Although scientists know much about DNA replication, many aspects of the process remain unclear. For example, in the unicellular yeast *Saccharomyces cerevisiae,* which is considered a relatively "simple" eukaryote, 88 genes are involved in DNA replication! Determining the roles and interactions of all those genes will require the efforts of many scientists over a long period.

DNA strands must be unwound during replication

DNA replication begins at specific sites on the DNA molecule, called **origins of replication,** where small sections of the double helix unwind. **DNA helicases** are helix-destabilizing enzymes

FIGURE 12-12 The perpetuation of a mutation
The process of DNA replication can stabilize a mutation (*bright yellow*) so that it is transmitted to future generations.

(several have been identified) that bind to DNA at the origin of replication and break hydrogen bonds, thereby separating the two strands (**TABLE 12-3**). Both DNA strands replicate at the same time at the junction between the separated strands, which is a Y-shaped structure called the **replication fork** (see chapter opener photograph). Helicase travels along the helix, opening the double helix like a zipper during movement of the replication fork.

Once DNA helicases separate the strands, **single-strand binding (SSB) proteins** bind to single DNA strands and stabilize them; this prevents the double helix from re-forming until the strands are replicated. SSB proteins also prevent the hydrolysis of the single-strand regions by other enzymes (*nucleases;* as we discuss later in the chapter, nucleases are involved in DNA repair).

Watson and Crick recognized that in their double-helix model, the two DNA strands wrap around each other like the strands of a rope. If you try to pull the strands apart, the rope must either rotate or twist into tighter coils. You could expect similar results when complementary DNA strands are separated for replication. As the DNA strands unwind to open for replication, torsional strain from supercoiling (excessive twisting) occurs in another part of the DNA molecule. Enzymes called **topoisomerases** produce breaks in the DNA molecules and then rejoin the strands, relieving strain and effectively preventing supercoiling and knot formation during replication. There are two ways that topoisomerases reduce supercoiling. Some topoisomerases produce a temporary break in the polynucleotide backbone of a single strand of DNA, pass that strand through the excessively twisted part, and then reseal the break. Other topoisomerases break both DNA strands, pass some of the helix between the cut ends, and then reseal the break.

TABLE 12-3	Proteins Involved in DNA Replication	
	Enzyme	Function
	Helicase	Opens the double helix at replication forks by disrupting the hydrogen bonds that hold the two strands together.
	Single-strand binding (SSB) protein	Binds to single strands of DNA and prevents the helix from re-forming before it can be used as a template for replication.
	Topoisomerase	Breaks one or both DNA strands, preventing excessive coiling during replication, and then rejoins them in a more relaxed configuration.
	DNA polymerase	Links nucleotide subunits to form a new DNA strand from a DNA template.
	DNA primase	Synthesizes short RNA primers on the lagging strand. Begins replication of the leading strand.
	DNA ligase	Links Okazaki fragments by joining the 3′ end of the new DNA fragment to the 5′ end of the adjoining DNA.

need additional energy. Because the polynucleotide chain is elongated by the linkage of the 5′ phosphate group of the next nucleotide subunit to the 3′ hydroxyl group of the sugar at the end of the existing strand, the new strand of DNA always grows in the 5′ ⟶ 3′ direction. Some DNA polymerases are very efficient in joining nucleotides to the growing polypeptide chain. **DNA Pol III,** which is one of five DNA polymerases that have been identified in the bacterium *E. coli,* can join 1200 nucleotides per minute.

Regardless of their modes of action, topoisomerases give replicating DNA a more relaxed configuration.

DNA synthesis always proceeds in a 5′ ⟶ 3′ direction

The enzymes that catalyze the linking of successive nucleotide subunits are called **DNA polymerases.** They add nucleotides only to the 3′ end of a growing polynucleotide strand, and this strand must be paired with the DNA template strand (**FIG. 12-13**). Nucleotides with three phosphate groups are substrates for the polymerization reaction. As the nucleotides become linked, two of the phosphates are removed. These reactions are strongly exergonic and do not

DNA synthesis requires an RNA primer

As mentioned, DNA polymerases add nucleotides only to the 3′ end of an *existing* polynucleotide strand. Then, how is DNA synthesis initiated once the two strands are separated? The answer is that first a short piece of RNA (5 to 14 nucleotides) called an **RNA primer** is synthesized at the point where replication begins (**FIG. 12-14**).

RNA, or **ribonucleic acid** (see Chapters 3 and 13), is a nucleic acid polymer consisting of nucleotide subunits that can associate by complementary base pairing with the single-strand DNA template. The RNA primer is synthesized by **DNA primase,** an enzyme that starts a new strand of RNA opposite a short stretch

FIGURE 12-13 *Animated* **A simplified view of DNA replication**
One nucleotide at a time is added to the 3′ end of a growing chain.

DNA replication requires several steps and involves several enzymes, proteins, and RNA primers.

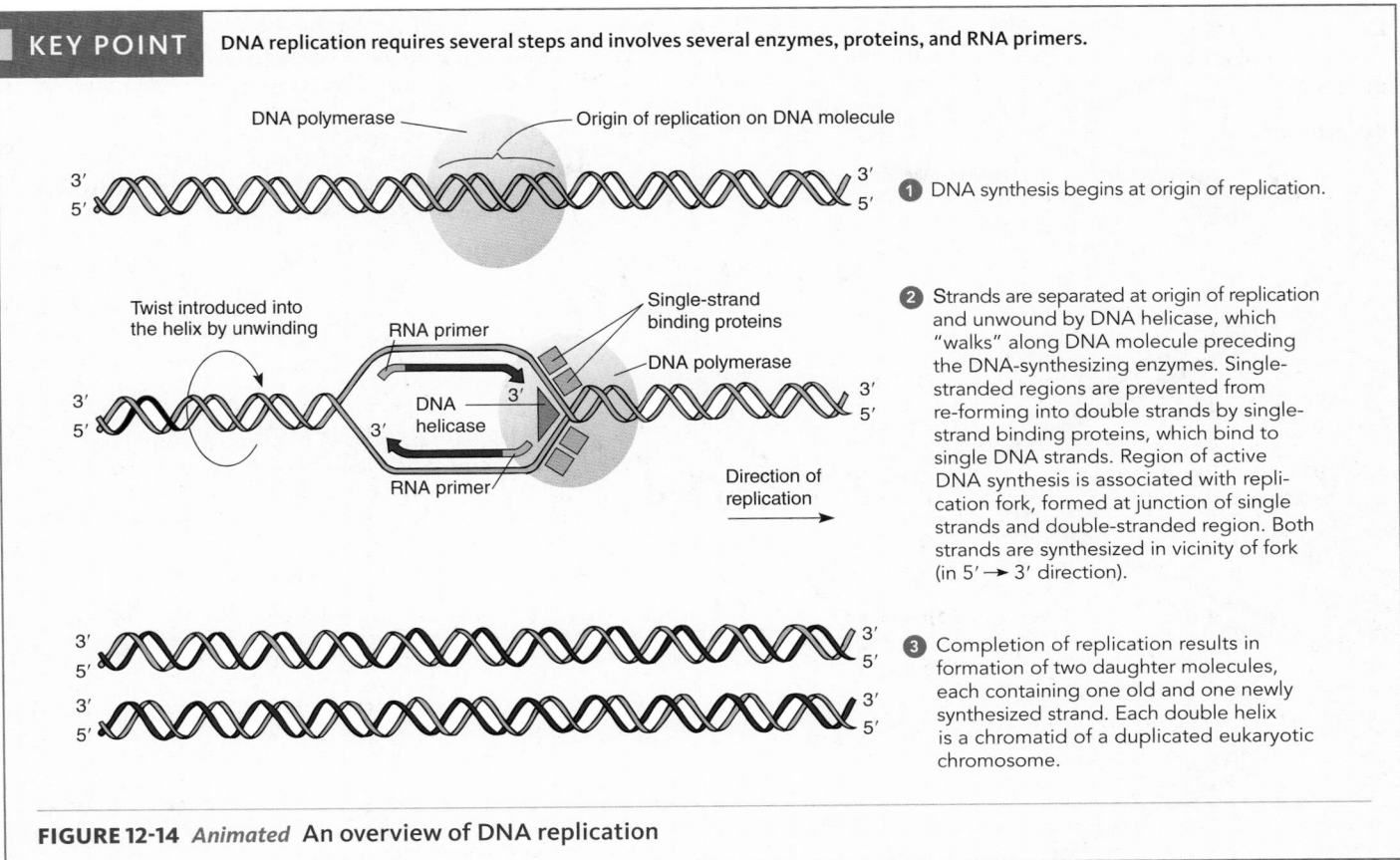

FIGURE 12-14 *Animated* An overview of DNA replication

1 DNA synthesis begins at origin of replication.

2 Strands are separated at origin of replication and unwound by DNA helicase, which "walks" along DNA molecule preceding the DNA-synthesizing enzymes. Single-stranded regions are prevented from re-forming into double strands by single-strand binding proteins, which bind to single DNA strands. Region of active DNA synthesis is associated with replication fork, formed at junction of single strands and double-stranded region. Both strands are synthesized in vicinity of fork (in 5′ → 3′ direction).

3 Completion of replication results in formation of two daughter molecules, each containing one old and one newly synthesized strand. Each double helix is a chromatid of a duplicated eukaryotic chromosome.

of the DNA template strand. After a few nucleotides have been added, DNA polymerase displaces the primase and subsequently adds subunits to the 3′ end of the short RNA primer. Specific enzymes later degrade the primer (discussed in the next section), and the space fills in with DNA.

DNA replication is discontinuous in one strand and continuous in the other

We mentioned earlier that the complementary DNA strands are antiparallel. DNA synthesis proceeds only in the 5′ ⟶ 3′ direction, which means that the strand being copied is being read in the 3′ ⟶ 5′ direction. Thus, it may seem necessary to copy one of the strands starting at one end of the double helix and the other strand starting at the opposite end. Some viruses replicate their DNA in this way, but this replication method is not workable in the extremely long DNA molecules in eukaryotic chromosomes.

Instead, as previously mentioned, DNA replication begins at origins of replication, and both strands replicate at the same time at a replication fork (**FIG. 12-15**). The position of the replication fork is constantly moving as replication proceeds. Two identical DNA polymerase molecules catalyze replication. One of these adds nucleotides to the 3′ end of the new strand that is always growing *toward* the replication fork. Because this strand is synthesized smoothly and continuously, it is called the **leading strand.**

A separate DNA polymerase molecule adds nucleotides to the 3′ end of the other new strand. Called the **lagging strand,** it is al-

ways growing *away* from the replication fork. Only short pieces can be synthesized, because if the DNA polymerase were to add continuously to the 3′ end of that strand, it would need to move far from the replication fork. These 100- to 2000-nucleotide pieces are called **Okazaki fragments** after their discoverer, Japanese molecular biologist Reiji Okazaki.

DNA primase periodically catalyzes the synthesis of an RNA primer on the lagging strand. A separate RNA primer initiates each Okazaki fragment, which DNA polymerase then extends toward the 5′ end of the previously synthesized fragment. When the RNA primer of the previously synthesized fragment is reached, DNA polymerase degrades and replaces the primer with DNA. The fragments are then joined by **DNA ligase,** an enzyme that links the 3′ hydroxyl of one Okazaki fragment to the 5′ phosphate of the DNA immediately next to it, forming a phosphodiester linkage. (As you will see later in the chapter, DNA ligase also rejoins broken phosphodiester bonds during DNA repair.)

DNA synthesis is bidirectional

When double-stranded DNA separates, two replication forks form, and the molecule replicates in both directions from the origin of replication. In bacteria, each circular DNA molecule usually has only one origin of replication, so the two replication forks proceed around the circle and eventually meet at the other side to complete the formation of two new DNA molecules. **FIGURE 12-16a** shows a replicating bacterial plasmid. **Plasmids** are small, circular DNA

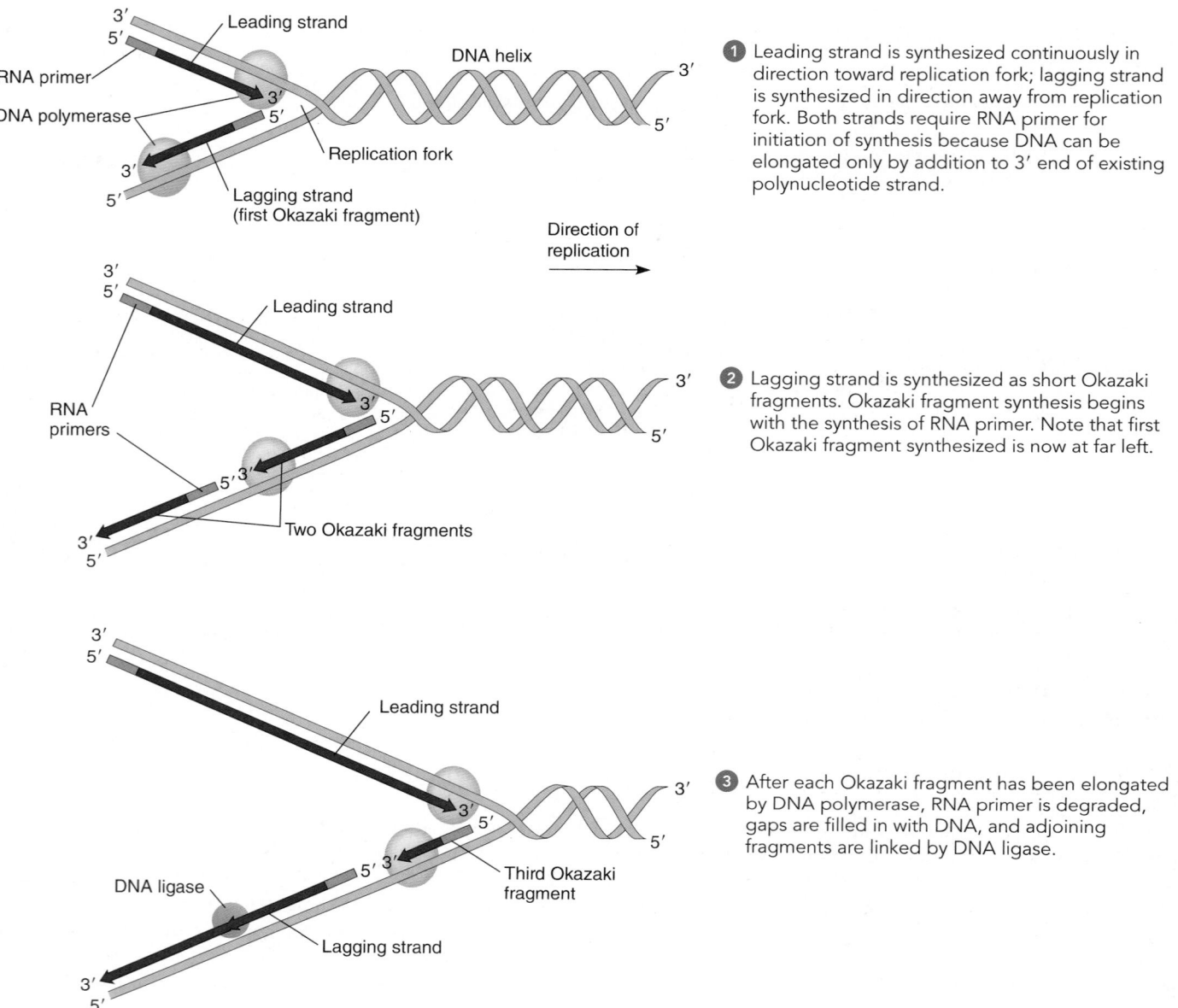

FIGURE 12-15 Leading and lagging DNA strands

The figure contains the following labels and callouts:

Top diagram:
3′, 5′, Leading strand, RNA primer, DNA polymerase, DNA helix, 3′, Replication fork, Lagging strand (first Okazaki fragment), 3′, 5′, 3′, 5′, 3′, 5′

1 Leading strand is synthesized continuously in direction toward replication fork; lagging strand is synthesized in direction away from replication fork. Both strands require RNA primer for initiation of synthesis because DNA can be elongated only by addition to 3′ end of existing polynucleotide strand.

Direction of replication →

3′, 5′, Leading strand, RNA primers, 3′, 5′, 5′ 3′, Two Okazaki fragments, 3′, 5′, 3′, 5′

2 Lagging strand is synthesized as short Okazaki fragments. Okazaki fragment synthesis begins with the synthesis of RNA primer. Note that first Okazaki fragment synthesized is now at far left.

3′, 5′, Leading strand, 3′, 5′, 5′ 3′, DNA ligase, Third Okazaki fragment, Lagging strand, 3′, 5′, 3′, 5′

3 After each Okazaki fragment has been elongated by DNA polymerase, RNA primer is degraded, gaps are filled in with DNA, and adjoining fragments are linked by DNA ligase.

molecules that carry genes separate from those on a bacterial chromosome. Because plasmids are so small compared to the circular bacterial chromosome, they are possible to clearly photograph during replication.

A eukaryotic chromosome consists of one long, linear DNA molecule, so having multiple origins of replication expedites the replication process (**FIG. 12-16b**). Synthesis continues at each replication fork until it meets a newly synthesized strand coming from the opposite direction. This results in a chromosome containing two DNA double helices, each corresponding to a chromatid.

Enzymes proofread and repair errors in DNA

DNA replication occurs only once during each cell generation, and it is important that the process be as accurate as possible to avoid harmful, or possibly even lethal, mutations. Although base pairing during DNA replication is very accurate, errors do occur. Mechanisms have evolved that ensure that errors in replication are corrected. During replication, DNA polymerases proofread each newly added nucleotide against its template nucleotide. When an error in base pairing is found, DNA polymerase immediately removes the incorrect nucleotide and inserts the correct one. A few uncorrected mutations still occur, but they are very infrequent—on the order of one error for every 10^9 or 10^{10} base pairs.

When errors have been left uncorrected by the normal repair activities of DNA polymerase during DNA replication, cells make use of other repair mechanisms (although exactly *how* DNA repair enzymes identify these rare, often-subtle errors in the vast amount of normal DNA is not well understood). In **mismatch repair**, special enzymes recognize the incorrectly paired nucleotides and

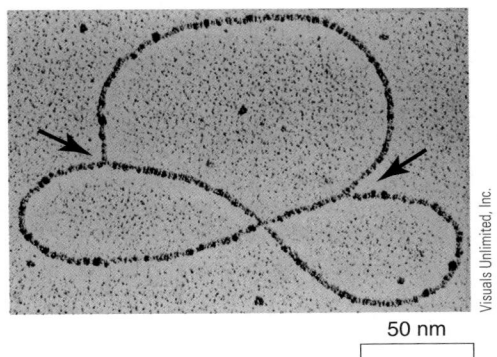

50 nm

Visuals Unlimited, Inc.

Template DNA (light blue) New DNA (dark blue)

(a) TEM (above left) of a replicating plasmid of *E. coli*. Most bacterial plasmids and chromosomes have only one origin of replication. Because DNA synthesis proceeds from that point in both directions, two replication forks form (*black arrows*), travel around the circle, and eventually meet.

340 nm

H. J. Kriegstein and D. S. Hogness, *Proc. Nat. Acad. Sci. USA* 71 : 135–139, 1974

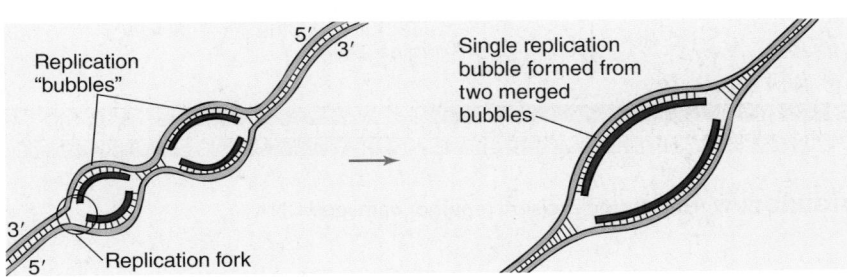

Replication "bubbles"

Single replication bubble formed from two merged bubbles

Replication fork

(b) TEM (left) of two replication forks (black arrows) in a segment of a eukaryotic chromosome that has partly replicated. Eukaryotic chromosome DNA contains multiple origins of replication. DNA synthesis proceeds in both directions from each origin until adjacent replication "bubbles" eventually merge.

FIGURE 12-16 Bidirectional DNA replication in bacteria and eukaryotes
The illustrations do not show leading strands and lagging strands.

remove them; DNA polymerases then fill in the missing nucleotides. The observation that individuals with a hereditary defect in a mismatch repair enzyme are likely to develop a type of colon cancer demonstrates the crucial role of mismatch repair enzymes in ensuring the fidelity of DNA replication from one generation to the next.

In Chapter 13 you will discover that some types of radiation and chemicals, both in the environment and within the cells themselves, cause mutations in DNA. These mutations are almost always harmful, and cells usually correct mutations by using one or more DNA repair enzymes. About 100 kinds of repair enzymes in the bacterium *E. coli* and 130 kinds in human cells have been discovered so far.

One type of DNA repair—**nucleotide excision repair**—is commonly used to repair DNA lesions (deformed DNA) caused by the sun's ultraviolet radiation or by harmful chemicals (**FIG. 12-17**). Three enzymes are involved in nucleotide excision repair—a nuclease to cut out the damaged DNA, a DNA polymerase

to add the correct nucleotides, and DNA ligase to close the breaks in the sugar–phosphate backbone. Individuals suffering from the disease *xeroderma pigmentosum* have an inherited defect in a nucleotide excision repair enzyme. Affected individuals develop many skin cancers at an early age because DNA lesions caused by ultraviolet radiation are not repaired.

Telomeres cap eukaryotic chromosome ends

Unlike bacterial DNA, which is circular, eukaryotic chromosomes have free ends. Because DNA replication is discontinuous in the lagging strand, DNA polymerases do not complete replication of the strand neatly. At the end of the DNA, a small portion is left unreplicated, and a small, single-strand segment of the DNA is lost with each cell cycle (**FIG. 12-18a**).

The important genetic information is retained because chromosomes have protective end caps, or telomeres, that do not contain protein-coding genes. **Telomeres** consist of short,

① A nuclease cuts out a piece of DNA, including the damaged part.

DNA polymerase
DNA ligase

② DNA polymerase and DNA ligase complete the repair by synthesizing the removed part and sealing the new DNA to the original DNA.

New DNA

FIGURE 12-17 Nucleotide excision repair of damaged DNA

noncoding, guanine-rich DNA sequences that repeat many times (**FIG. 12-18b**). For example, in human sperm and egg cells, the sequence 5′—TTAGGG—3′ is repeated more than 1000 times at the ends of each chromosome. Therefore, although a small amount of telomeric DNA fails to replicate each time the cell divides, a cell can divide many times before it starts losing essential genetic information.

Telomerase, a special DNA replication enzyme, can lengthen telomeric DNA by adding repetitive nucleotide sequences to the ends of eukaryotic chromosomes. This enzyme, which researchers discovered in 1984, is typically present in cells that divide an unlimited number of times, including protozoa and other unicellular eukaryotes, and most types of **cancer cells.** In humans and other mammals, active telomerase is usually present in germ line cells (which give rise to eggs and sperm) and rapidly dividing cells (such as blood cells, cells lining the intestine, and skin cells) but not in most somatic cells of adult tissues.

When most cells divide for repair or replacement, their chromosome ends shorten. Researchers have demonstrated that in cancer cells of the prostate and pancreas, telomeres are abnormally short: they shorten to a critical point, at which time telomerase is reactivated, which may explain the ability of cancer cells to proliferate in a rapid and uncontrolled manner. Telomere shortening has also been demonstrated in precancerous lesions from the bladder, breast, colon, esophagus, mouth, and cervix.

Research evidence suggests that the shortening of telomeres may contribute to **cell aging** and **apoptosis,** which is programmed

cell death. Scientists have analyzed cell aging since the 1960s, following the pioneering studies of American biologist Leonard Hayflick, who showed that when normal somatic cells of the human body are grown in culture, they lose their ability to divide after a limited number of cell divisions. Furthermore, the number of cell divisions is determined by the age of the individual from whom the cells were taken. Cells from a 70-year-old can divide only 20 to 30 times, compared with those from an infant, which can divide 80 to 90 times.

Many investigators have observed correlations between telomerase activity and the ability of cells to undergo unlimited divisions without showing signs of the aging process. However, they could not find evidence of a causal relationship until the early 2000s, when scientists at the Geron Corporation and the University of Texas Southwestern Medical Center conducted a direct test. Using recombinant DNA technology (see Chapter 15), they infected cultured normal human cells with a virus that carried the genetic information coding for the catalytic subunit of telomerase. The infected cells not only produced active telomerase, which elongated the telomeres significantly, but also continued to divide long past the point at which cell divisions would normally cease.

Telomeres and telomerase are an active focus of current research, for both scientific and practical reasons. The ability to give somatic cells telomerase so they can divide many times more than they ordinarily would has many potential therapeutic applications, especially if lost or injured cells must be replaced. However, giving such cells the property of unlimited cell division also has potentially serious consequences. For example, if transplanted into the body, cells with active telomerase might behave like cancer cells.

Cancer cells have the ability to divide hundreds of times in culture; in fact, they are virtually immortal. Most cancer cells, including human cancers of the breast, lung, colon, prostate gland, and pancreas, have telomerase, which allows them to maintain telomere length and possibly to resist apoptosis. Research is underway to develop anticancer drugs that inhibit telomerase activity. An alternative treatment for cancer is also under study—directing the body's immune system to recognize and attack cancer cells that contain telomerase.

Review

- How did Meselson and Stahl verify that DNA replication is semiconservative?
- Why is DNA replication continuous for one strand but discontinuous for the other?
- How does mismatch repair of DNA compare with nucleotide excision repair?

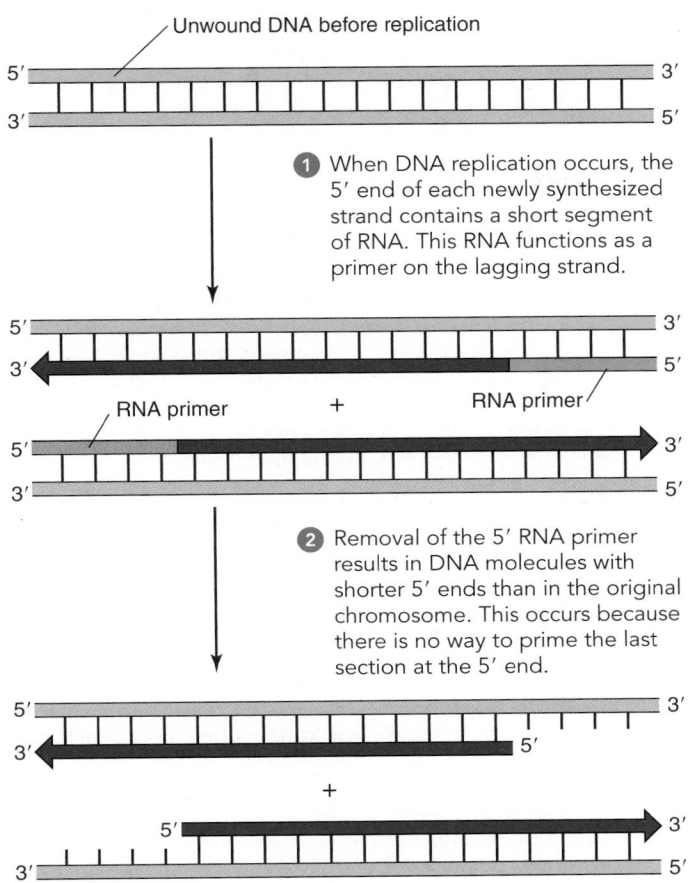

Unwound DNA before replication

5′ 3′
3′ 5′

1 When DNA replication occurs, the 5′ end of each newly synthesized strand contains a short segment of RNA. This RNA functions as a primer on the lagging strand.

5′ 3′
3′ 5′

RNA primer   +   RNA primer

5′ 3′
3′ 5′

2 Removal of the 5′ RNA primer results in DNA molecules with shorter 5′ ends than in the original chromosome. This occurs because there is no way to prime the last section at the 5′ end.

5′ 3′
3′   5′

+

5′   3′
3′   5′

(a) Why one strand of DNA is shorter than that of the preceding generation.

Peter Lansdorp/Visuals Unlimited, Inc.

10 μm

(b) LM of duplicated human chromosomes with fluorescent-tagged telomeres (*yellow*).

FIGURE 12-18 Telomeres

SUMMARY: FOCUS ON LEARNING OBJECTIVES

12.1 *(page 264)*

1 Summarize the evidence that accumulated during the 1940s and early 1950s demonstrating that DNA is the genetic material.

- Many early geneticists thought genes were made of proteins. They knew proteins were complex and variable, whereas they thought nucleic acids were simple molecules with a limited ability to store information.

- Several lines of evidence supported the idea that **DNA (deoxyribonucleic acid)** is the genetic material. In **transformation** experiments, the DNA of one strain of bacteria can endow related bacteria with new genetic characteristics.

- When a bacterial cell becomes infected with a **bacteriophage** (virus), only the DNA from the virus enters the cell; this DNA is sufficient for the virus to reproduce and form new viral particles.

2 State the questions that these classic experiments addressed: Griffith's transformation experiment, Avery's contribution to Griffith's work, and the Hershey–Chase experiments.

- Griffith's transformation experiment addressed this question: Can a genetic trait be transmitted from one bacterial strain to another? (The answer is yes.)

- Avery's experiments addressed this question: What molecule is responsible for bacterial transformation? (The answer is DNA.)

- The Hershey–Chase experiments addressed this question: Is DNA or protein the genetic material in bacterial viruses (phages)? (The answer is DNA.)

12.2 *(page 265)*

3 Explain how nucleotide subunits link to form a single DNA strand.

- Watson and Crick's model of the structure of DNA demonstrated how information can be stored in the molecule's structure and how DNA molecules can serve as **templates** for their own replication.

- DNA is a polymer of **nucleotides.** Each nucleotide subunit contains a nitrogenous base, which may be one of the **purines** (**adenine** or **guanine**) or one of the **pyrimidines** (**thymine** or **cytosine**). Each base covalently links to a pentose sugar, **deoxyribose,** which covalently bonds to a phosphate group.

- The backbone of each single DNA chain is formed by alternating sugar and phosphate groups, joined by covalent phosphodiester linkages. Each phosphate group attaches to the 5′ carbon of one deoxyribose and to the 3′ carbon of the neighboring deoxyribose.

4 Describe how the two strands of DNA are oriented with respect to each other.

- Each DNA molecule consists of two polynucleotide chains that associate as a **double helix.** The two chains are **antiparallel** (running in opposite directions); at each end of the DNA molecule, one chain has a phosphate attached to a 5′ deoxyribose carbon, the **5′ end,** and the other has a hydroxyl group attached to a 3′ deoxyribose carbon, the **3′ end.**

CENGAGENOW™   Interact with the structure of the DNA double helix by clicking on the figures in CengageNOW.

5 State the base-pairing rules for DNA and describe how complementary bases bind to each other.

■ Hydrogen bonding between specific base pairs holds together the two chains of the helix. Adenine (A) forms two hydrogen bonds with thymine (T); guanine (G) forms three hydrogen bonds with cytosine (C).

■ **Complementary base pairing** between A and T and between G and C is the basis of Chargaff's rules, which state that A equals T and that G equals C.

■ Because complementary base pairing holds together the two strands of DNA, it is possible to predict the base sequence of one strand if you know the base sequence of the other strand.

12.3 *(page 271)*

6 Cite evidence from Meselson and Stahl's experiment that enabled scientists to differentiate between semiconservative replication of DNA and alternative models.

■ When *E. coli* cells are grown for many generations in a medium containing heavy nitrogen (^{15}N), they incorporate the ^{15}N into their DNA. When researchers transfer cells from a ^{15}N medium to a ^{14}N medium and isolate them after either one or two generations, the density of the DNA in each group is what would be expected if DNA replication were semiconservative. In **semiconservative replication,** each daughter double helix consists of an original strand from the parent molecule and a newly synthesized complementary strand.

7 Summarize how DNA replicates and identify some unique features of the process.

■ During **DNA replication,** the two strands of the double helix unwind. Each strand serves as a template for forming a new, complementary strand. Replication is initiated as **DNA primase**

synthesizes a short **RNA primer. DNA polymerase** then adds new nucleotide subunits to the growing DNA strand.

■ Additional enzymes and other proteins are required to unwind and stabilize the separated DNA helix. **DNA helicases** open the double helix, and **topoisomerases** prevent tangling and knotting.

8 Explain the complexities of DNA replication that make it (a) bidirectional and (b) continuous in one strand and discontinuous in the other.

■ DNA replication is bidirectional, starting at the **origin of replication** and proceeding in both directions from that point. A eukaryotic chromosome may have multiple origins of replication and may be replicating at many points along its length at any one time.

■ DNA synthesis always proceeds in a 5′ $\longrightarrow$ 3′ direction. This requires that one DNA strand, the **lagging strand,** be synthesized discontinuously, as short **Okazaki fragments.** DNA primase synthesizes short RNA primers on the lagging strand, and **DNA ligase** links Okazaki fragments of newly synthesized DNA. The opposite strand, the **leading strand,** is synthesized continuously.

CENGAGENOW™   Watch the process of replication by clicking on the figure in CengageNOW.

9 Discuss how enzymes proofread and repair errors in DNA.

■ During replication, DNA polymerases proofread each newly added nucleotide against its template nucleotide. When an error in base pairing is found, DNA polymerase immediately removes the incorrect nucleotide and inserts the correct one.

■ In **mismatch repair,** enzymes recognize incorrectly paired nucleotides and remove them; DNA polymerases then fill in the missing nucleotides.

■ **Nucleotide excision repair** is commonly used to repair DNA lesions caused by the sun's ultraviolet radiation or by harmful chemicals. Three enzymes are involved: a nuclease to cut out the damaged DNA, a DNA polymerase to add the correct nucleotides, and DNA ligase to close the breaks in the sugar–phosphate backbone.

10 Define *telomere,* and describe the possible connections between telomerase and cell aging and between telomerase and cancer.

■ Eukaryotic chromosome ends, called **telomeres,** are short, noncoding, repetitive DNA sequences. Telomeres shorten slightly with each cell cycle but can be extended by the enzyme **telomerase.**

■ The absence of telomerase activity in certain cells may be a cause of **cell aging,** in which cells lose their ability to divide after a limited number of cell divisions.

■ Most **cancer cells,** including human cancers of the breast, lung, colon, prostate gland, and pancreas, have telomerase to maintain telomere length and possibly to resist **apoptosis.**

TEST YOUR UNDERSTANDING

1. When Griffith injected mice with a combination of live rough-strain and heat-killed smooth-strain pneumococci, he discovered that (a) the mice were unharmed (b) the dead mice contained living rough-strain bacteria (c) the dead mice contained living smooth-strain bacteria (d) DNA had been transferred from the smooth-strain bacteria to the mice (e) DNA had been transferred from the rough-strain bacteria to the smooth-strain bacteria

2. Which of the following inspired Avery and his colleagues to perform the experiments demonstrating that the transforming factor in bacteria is DNA? (a) the fact that A is equal to T, and G is equal to C (b) Watson and Crick's model of DNA structure (c) Meselson and Stahl's studies on DNA replication in *E. coli* (d) Griffith's experiments on smooth and rough strains of pneu-

mococci (e) Hershey and Chase's experiments on the reproduction of bacteriophages

3. In the Hershey–Chase experiment with bacteriophages, (a) harmless bacterial cells permanently transformed into virulent cells (b) DNA was shown to be the transforming factor of earlier bacterial transformation experiments (c) the replication of DNA was conclusively shown to be semiconservative (d) viral DNA was shown to enter bacterial cells and cause the production of new viruses within the bacteria (e) viruses injected their proteins, not their DNA, into bacterial cells

4. The two complementary strands of the DNA double helix are held to each other by (a) ionic bonds between deoxyribose molecules (b) ionic bonds between phosphate groups (c) covalent bonds be-

tween nucleotide bases (d) covalent bonds between deoxyribose molecules (e) hydrogen bonds between nucleotide bases

5. If a segment of DNA is 5′—CATTAC—3′, the complementary DNA strand is (a) 3′—CATTAC—5′ (b) 3′—GTAATG—5′ (c) 5′—CATTAC—3′ (d) 5′—GTAATG—3′ (e) 5′—CATTAC—5′

6. Each DNA strand has a backbone that consists of alternating (a) purines and pyrimidines (b) nucleotide bases (c) hydrogen bonds and phosphodiester linkages (d) deoxyribose and phosphate (e) phosphate and phosphodiester linkages

7. The experiments in which Meselson and Stahl grew bacteria in heavy nitrogen conclusively demonstrated that DNA (a) is a double helix (b) replicates semiconservatively (c) consists of repeating nucleotide subunits (d) has complementary base pairing (e) is always synthesized in the 5′ ⟶ 3′ direction

8. The statement "DNA replicates by a semiconservative mechanism" means that (a) only one DNA strand is copied (b) first one DNA strand is copied, and then the other strand is copied (c) the two strands of a double helix have identical base sequences (d) some portions of a single DNA strand are old, and other portions are newly synthesized (e) each double helix consists of one old and one newly synthesized strand

9. Topoisomerases (a) synthesize DNA (b) synthesize RNA primers (c) join Okazaki fragments (d) break and rejoin DNA to reduce torsional strain (e) prevent single DNA strands from joining to form a double helix

10. A lagging strand forms by (a) joining primers (b) joining Okazaki fragments (c) joining leading strands (d) breaking up a leading strand (e) joining primers, Okazaki fragments, and leading strands

11. The immediate source of energy for DNA replication is (a) the hydrolysis of nucleotides with three phosphate groups (b) the oxidation of NADPH (c) the hydrolysis of ATP (d) electron transport (e) the breaking of hydrogen bonds

12. Which of the following statements about eukaryotic chromosomes is *false*? (a) eukaryotic chromosomes have free ends (b) telomeres contain protein-coding genes (c) telomerase lengthens telomeric DNA (d) telomere shortening may contribute to cell aging (e) cells with active telomerase may undergo many cell divisions

CRITICAL THINKING

1. What characteristics must a molecule have to function as genetic material?

2. What important features of the structure of DNA are consistent with its role as the chemical basis of heredity?

3. What do telomeres on the ends of chromosomes protect against?

4. **ANALYZING DATA.** In the Hershey–Chase experiment, the radioactive label ^{32}P was present inside bacterial cells (i.e., in the pellet), whereas the radioactive label ^{35}S was present outside bacterial cells (in the supernatant). What would the researchers have concluded had the reverse been true—that is, if the radioactive label ^{35}S was inside the cells and the radioactive label ^{32}P was outside the cells?

5. **ANALYZING DATA.** In the following diagram of DNA replication, label the 3′ and 5′ ends of the leading strand, lagging strand, and the two strands of the DNA double helix.

6. **EVOLUTION LINK.** How does the fact that DNA is the universal molecule of inheritance in all cells support evolutionary theory?

CENGAGENOW™ Additional questions are available in CengageNOW at www.cengage.com/login.

Leading strand

RNA primer

DNA polymerase

DNA helix

Replication fork

Lagging strand (first Okazaki fragment)

Direction of replication

13 Gene Expression

Visualizing transcription. In this TEM, RNA molecules (*lateral strands*) are synthesized as complementary copies of a DNA template (*central axis*).

Professor Oscar Miller/Science Photo Library/Photo Researchers, Inc.

KEY CONCEPTS

13.1 Beadle and Tatum demonstrated the relationship between genes and proteins in the 1940s.

13.2 The transmission of information in cells is typically from DNA to RNA to polypeptide.

13.3 A sequence of DNA base triplets is transcribed into mRNA codons.

13.4 A sequence of mRNA codons is translated into a sequence of amino acids in a polypeptide.

13.5 Bacterial and eukaryotic cells differ in certain details of gene expression.

13.6 Mutations can cause changes in phenotype.

In Chapter 12, we discussed how the cell accurately replicates the nucleotide sequence in DNA to pass the genetic material unaltered to the next generation. Watson and Crick originally described the basic features of the DNA double helix, which scientists now know to be the same in all cells studied to date—from the simplest bacterial cells to intricate human cells.

By the mid-1950s, researchers had determined that the sequence of bases in DNA contains the information that specifies all the proteins the cell needs. However, more than a decade of intense investigation by many scientists preceded a fundamental understanding of how cells convert DNA information into the amino acid sequences of proteins. Much of that understanding came from studying the functions of bacterial genes. After Watson and Crick discovered the structure of DNA, researchers chose bacterial cells as the organisms for these studies because bacteria grow quickly and easily and because they contain the minimal amount of DNA needed for growth and reproduction. As researchers learned that all organisms have fundamental genetic similarities, the validity, as well as the utility, of this approach was repeatedly confirmed.

In this chapter we examine the evidence that accumulated in the first half of the 20th century indicating that most genes specify the structure of proteins. We then consider how DNA affects the phenotype of the organism at the molecular level through the process of gene expression. **Gene expression** involves a series of steps in which the information in the sequence of bases in DNA specifies the makeup of the cell's proteins. The proteins affect the phenotype in some way; these effects range from readily observable physical traits to subtle changes detectable only at the biochemical level. The first major step of gene expression is *transcription*, the synthesis of RNA molecules complementary to the DNA (see photograph). The second major step is *translation*, in which RNA becomes a coded template to direct polypeptide synthesis.

13.1 DISCOVERY OF THE GENE–PROTEIN RELATIONSHIP

■ LEARNING OBJECTIVES

1 Summarize the early evidence indicating that most genes specify the structure of proteins.
2 Describe Beadle and Tatum's experiments with *Neurospora*.

The idea that genes and proteins are connected originated early in the 20th century, shortly after scientists rediscovered Mendel's principles. In the first edition of his book, *Inborn Errors of Metabolism* (1908), Archibald Garrod, a physician and biochemist, discussed a rare genetic disease called **alkaptonuria,** which scientists hypothesized had a simple recessive inheritance pattern. The condition involves the metabolic pathway that breaks down the amino acid tyrosine, ultimately converting it to carbon dioxide and water. An intermediate in this pathway, homogentisic acid, accumulates in the urine of affected people, turning it black when exposed to air (**FIG. 13-1**). Other symptoms of alkaptonuria include the later development of arthritis and, in men, stones in the prostate gland.

In Garrod's time, scientists knew about enzymes but did not recognize they were proteins. Garrod hypothesized that people with alkaptonuria lack the enzyme that normally oxidizes homogentisic acid. Before the second edition of his book had been published, in 1923, researchers found that affected people do indeed lack the enzyme that oxidizes homogentisic acid. Garrod's hypothesis was correct: a mutation in this gene is associated with the absence of a specific enzyme. Shortly thereafter, in 1926, U.S. biochemist James Sumner purified a different enzyme, urease, and showed it to be a protein. This was the first clear identification of an enzyme as a protein. In 1946, Sumner was awarded the Nobel Prize in Chemistry for being the first to crystallize an enzyme.

FIGURE 13-1 An "inborn error of metabolism"
Garrod proposed that alkaptonuria is a genetic disease caused by the absence of the enzyme homogentisic acid oxidase, which normally converts homogentisic acid to maleylacetoacetate. Thus, the acid accumulates in the blood and is excreted in the urine, which turns black on contact with the air.

Beadle and Tatum proposed the one-gene, one-enzyme hypothesis

A major advance in understanding the relationship between genes and enzymes came in the early 1940s, when U.S. geneticists George Beadle and Edward Tatum and their associates developed a new approach to the problem. Most efforts until that time had focused on studying known phenotypes, such as eye color in *Drosophila* or pigments in plants, and seeking to determine what biochemical reactions they affected. Researchers found that a series of biosynthetic reactions controls specific phenotypes, but it was not clear whether the genes themselves were acting as enzymes or whether they controlled the workings of enzymes in some indirect way.

Beadle and Tatum decided to take the opposite approach. Rather than try to identify the enzymes affected by single genes, they decided to look for mutations interfering with known metabolic reactions that produce essential molecules, such as amino acids and vitamins. They chose as an experimental organism a fungus, the pink-orange bread mold *Neurospora*, for several important reasons. Wild-type *Neurospora* is easy to grow in culture. (The adjective **wild-type** refers to an individual with the normal phenotype.) *Neurospora* manufactures all its essential biological molecules when grown on a simple growth medium (minimal medium) containing only sugar, salts, and the vitamin biotin. However, a mutant *Neurospora* strain that cannot make a substance such as an amino acid can still grow if that substance is added to the growth medium.

Neurospora is also an ideal experimental organism because it grows primarily as a haploid organism. The haploid condition allows a researcher to immediately identify a recessive mutant allele; there is no homologous chromosome that might carry a dominant allele that would mask its expression.

Beadle and Tatum began by exposing thousands of haploid wild-type *Neurospora* asexual spores to X-rays or ultraviolet radiation to produce mutant strains. They first grew each irradiated strain on a complete growth medium, which contained all the amino acids and vitamins normally made by *Neurospora*. Then they tested each strain on the minimal medium described previously. About 1% to 2% of the strains that grew on the complete medium failed to grow after transfer to the minimal medium. Beadle and Tatum reasoned that such strains carried a mutation that prevented the fungus from producing a chemical essential for growth. Further testing of the mutant strain on media containing different combinations of amino acids, vitamins, and other nutrients enabled the investigators to determine the exact compound required (**FIG. 13-2**).

The work on *Neurospora* revealed that each mutant strain had a mutation in only one gene and that each gene affected only one enzyme. Beadle and Tatum stated this one-to-one correspondence between genes and enzymes as the *one-gene, one-enzyme hypothesis*. In 1958, they received the Nobel Prize in Physiology or Medicine for discovering that genes regulate specific chemical events. The work of Beadle, Tatum, and others led to a more precise understanding of what a gene is and to additional predictions about the chemical nature of genes. The idea that a gene encodes the information to produce a single enzyme held for almost a decade, until additional findings required a modification of this definition.

In the late 1940s, researchers began to understand that genes control not only enzymes but other proteins as well. The U.S. chemist Linus Pauling and his colleagues demonstrated in 1949 that a mutation of a single gene alters the structure of hemoglobin. This particular mutant form of hemoglobin is associated with the genetic disease sickle cell anemia (discussed in Chapter 16). British biochemist Vernon Ingram extended Pauling's research in 1957 when he determined that sickle cell hemoglobin and normal hemoglobin differ by only one amino acid.

Studies by other scientists showed that many proteins are constructed from two or more polypeptide chains, each of which is under the control of a different locus. For example, hemoglobin contains two types of polypeptide chains, the α and β subunits. See the structure of hemoglobin in Figure 3-22a. Sickle cell anemia results from a mutation affecting the β subunits.

Scientists therefore extended the definition of a gene to include that one gene is responsible for one polypeptide chain. Even this definition has proved only partially correct, although as you will see later in this chapter, scientists still define a gene in terms of its product.

Although the elegant work of Beadle and Tatum and others demonstrated that genes are expressed in the form of proteins, the mechanism of gene expression was completely unknown. After Watson and Crick's discovery of the structure of DNA, many scientists worked to understand exactly how gene expression takes place. We begin with an overview of gene expression and then consider the various steps in more detail.

Review

- What is the one-gene, one-enzyme hypothesis?
- What were the contributions of each of the following scientists—Garrod, Beadle and Tatum, and Pauling—to our understanding of the relationship between genes and proteins?

KEY EXPERIMENT

QUESTION: Can genes code for enzymes?

HYPOTHESIS: Mutations induced in *Neurospora*, a type of bread mold, correspond to the absence of functional enzymes.

EXPERIMENT: Beadle and Tatum irradiated *Neurospora* spores to induce mutations. They grew cultures derived from these spores on complete growth medium containing all amino acids, vitamins, and other nutrients that *Neurospora* normally makes for itself. They identified nutritional requirements in mutant strains by testing for growth on minimal media supplemented with individual vitamins or amino acids.

Expose *Neurospora* spores to UV light or X-rays.

Fungal growth (mycelium)

Each irradiated spore is used to establish culture on complete growth medium (minimal medium plus amino acids, vitamins, etc.).

RESULTS AND CONCLUSION: They transferred some fungal cells to each of three tubes: one with minimal medium plus vitamins; one with minimal medium plus amino acids; and one with minimal medium (the control). In this example the mutant fungus grew on the minimal medium only if it was supplemented with amino acids.

Transfer cells to minimal medium plus vitamins.

Transfer cells to minimal medium plus amino acids.

Transfer cells to minimal medium (control).

To determine which amino acid the mutant fungus had lost the ability to synthesize, they transferred the mutant fungus to tubes containing minimal medium and one amino acid only.

| Minimal medium plus arginine | Minimal medium plus tryptophan | Minimal medium plus lysine | Minimal medium plus leucine | Minimal medium plus other amino acids |

In this example, only the medium containing the amino acid arginine supported growth, indicating that the mutation affected some part of arginine's biosynthetic pathway. Beadle and Tatum then identified the enzyme-catalyzed step that was blocked in the synthesis of arginine. On the basis of many similar experiments, they concluded that each gene controls the production of a single enzyme.

FIGURE 13-2 The Beadle–Tatum experiments

13.2 INFORMATION FLOW FROM DNA TO PROTEIN: AN OVERVIEW

3 Outline the flow of genetic information in cells, from DNA to RNA to polypeptide.

4 Compare the structures of DNA and RNA.

5 Explain why the genetic code is said to be redundant and virtually universal, and discuss how these features may reflect its evolutionary history.

Although the sequence of bases in DNA determines the sequence of amino acids in polypeptides, cells do not use the information in DNA directly. Instead, a related nucleic acid, **ribonucleic acid (RNA),** links DNA and protein. When a gene that codes for a protein is expressed, first an RNA copy is made of the information in the DNA. It is this RNA copy that provides the information that directs polypeptide synthesis.

Like DNA, RNA is a polymer of nucleotides, but it has some important differences (**FIG. 13-3**). RNA is usually single-stranded, although internal regions of some RNA molecules may have complementary sequences that allow the strand to fold back and pair to form short, double-stranded segments. As shown in Figure 13-3, the sugar in RNA is **ribose,** which is similar to deoxyribose of DNA but has a hydroxyl group at the 2′ position. (Compare ribose with the deoxyribose of DNA, shown in Figure 12-4, which has a hydrogen at the 2′ position.) The base **uracil** substitutes for thymine and, like thymine, is a pyrimidine that can form two hydrogen bonds with adenine. Hence, uracil and adenine are a complementary pair.

DNA is transcribed to form RNA

The process by which RNA is synthesized resembles DNA replication in that the sequence of bases in the RNA strand is determined by complementary base pairing with one of the DNA strands, the **template strand** (**FIG. 13-4**). Because RNA synthesis takes the information in one kind of nucleic acid (DNA) and copies it as another nucleic acid (RNA), this process is called **transcription** ("copying").

Three main kinds of RNA molecules are transcribed: messenger RNA, transfer RNA, and ribosomal RNA. **Messenger RNA (mRNA)** is a single strand of RNA that carries the information for making a protein. Each of the 45 or so kinds of **transfer RNAs (tRNAs)** is a single strand of RNA that folds back on itself to form a specific shape. Each kind of tRNA bonds with only one kind of amino acid and carries it to the *ribosome.* (Because there are more kinds of tRNA molecules than there are amino acids, many amino acids are carried by two or more kinds of tRNA molecules.) **Ribosomal RNA (rRNA),** which is in a globular form, is an important part of the structure of ribosomes and has catalytic functions needed during protein synthesis.

RNA is translated to form a polypeptide

Following transcription, the transcribed information in the mRNA is used to specify the amino acid sequence of a polypeptide (see

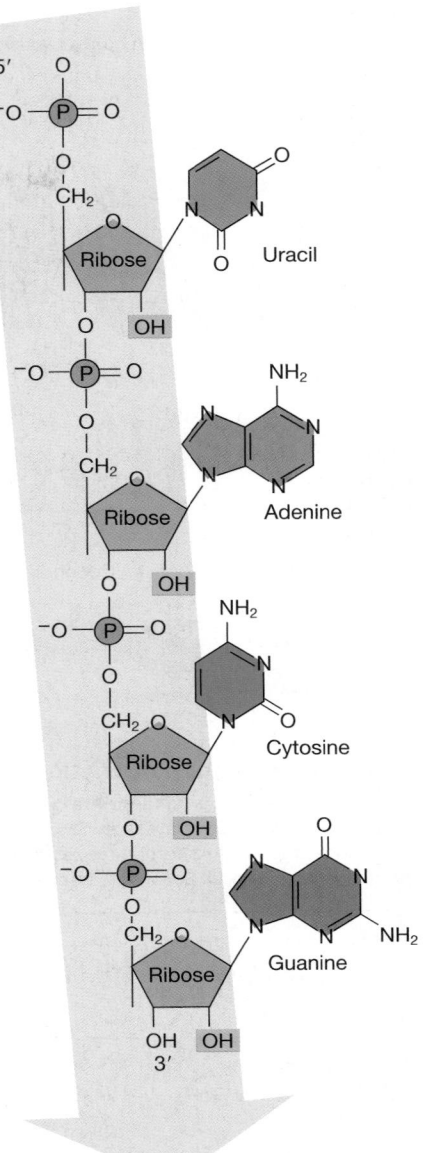

FIGURE 13-3 The nucleotide structure of RNA

The nucleotide subunits of RNA are joined by 5′ ⟶ 3′ phosphodiester linkages, like those found in DNA. Adenine, guanine, and cytosine are present, as in DNA, but the base uracil replaces thymine. All four nucleotide types contain the five-carbon sugar ribose, which has a hydroxyl group (*blue*) on its 2′ carbon atom.

Fig. 13-4). This process is called **translation** because it involves conversion of the "nucleic acid language" in the mRNA molecule into the "amino acid language" of protein.

In translation of the genetic instructions to form a polypeptide, a sequence of three consecutive bases in mRNA, called a **codon,** specifies one amino acid. For example, one codon that corresponds to the amino acid phenylalanine is 5′—UUC—3′. Because each codon consists of three nucleotides, the code is described as a **triplet code.** The assignments of codons for amino acids and for start and stop signals are collectively named the **genetic code** (**FIG. 13-5**).

Protein synthesis requires two major steps: DNA $\xrightarrow{\text{transcription}}$ RNA $\xrightarrow{\text{translation}}$ protein

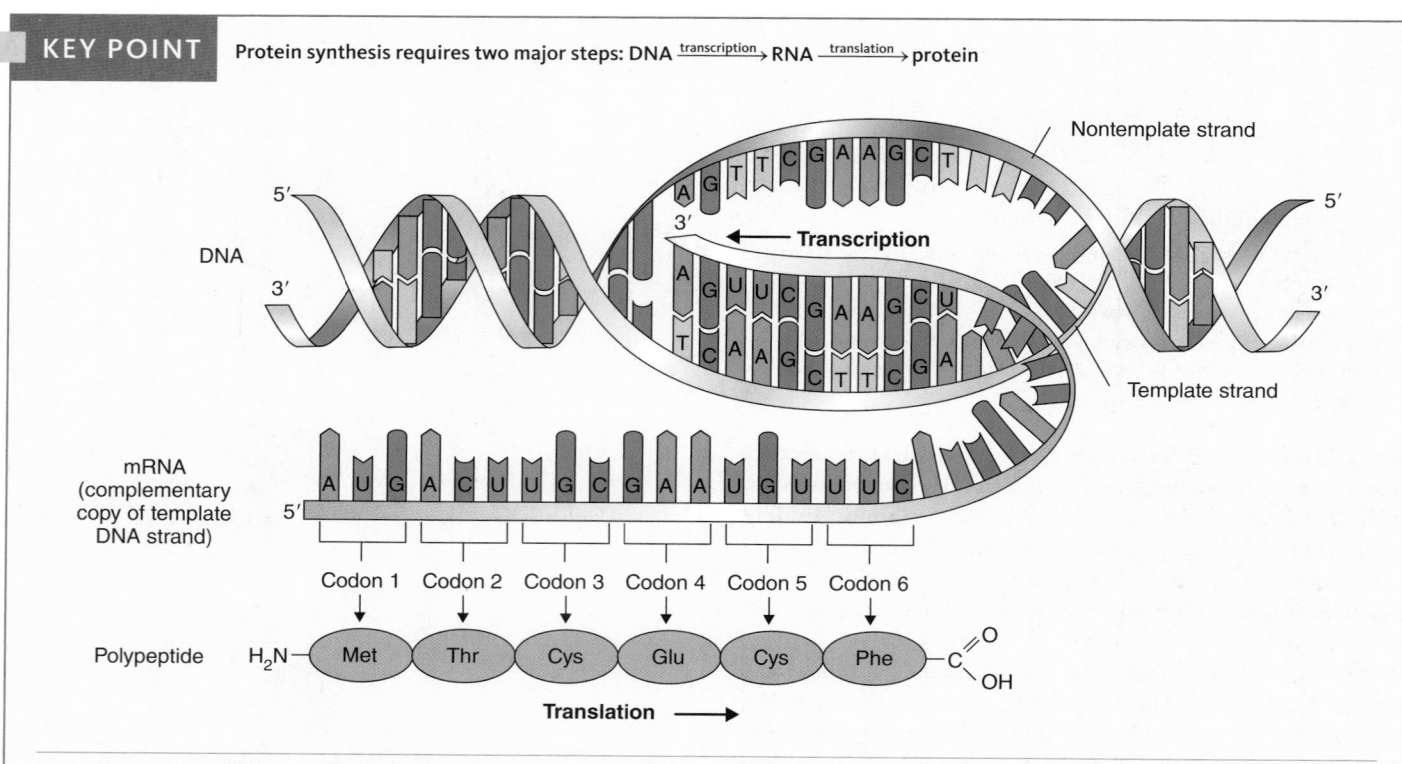

FIGURE 13-4 An overview of transcription and translation

In transcription, messenger RNA is synthesized as a complementary copy of one of the DNA strands, the template strand. Messenger RNA carries genetic information in the form of sets of three bases, or codons, each of which specifies one amino acid. Codons are translated consecutively, thus specifying the linear sequence of amino acids in the polypeptide chain. Translation requires tRNA and ribosomes (*not shown*). The figure depicts transcription and translation in bacteria. In eukaryotes, transcription takes place in the nucleus and translation occurs in the cytosol.

Transfer RNAs are crucial parts of the decoding machinery because they act as "adapters" that connect amino acids and nucleic acids. This mechanism is possible because each tRNA can (1) link with a specific amino acid and (2) recognize the appropriate mRNA codon for that particular amino acid (**FIG. 13-6**). A particular tRNA can recognize a particular codon because it has a sequence of three bases, called the **anticodon,** that hydrogen-bonds with the mRNA codon by complementary base pairing. The exact anticodon that is complementary to the codon for phenylalanine in our example is 3'—AAG—5'.

Translation requires that each tRNA anticodon be hydrogen-bonded to the complementary mRNA codon and that the amino acids carried by the tRNAs be linked in the order specified by the sequence of codons in the mRNA. **Ribosomes,** the site of translation, are organelles composed of two different subunits, each containing protein and rRNA. (The structure and function of ribosomes were introduced in Chapter 4.) Ribosomes attach to the 5'

◀ **FIGURE 13-5 The genetic code**

The genetic code specifies all possible combinations of the three bases that compose codons in mRNA. Of the 64 possible codons, 61 specify amino acids (see Fig. 3-17 for an explanation of abbreviations). The codon AUG specifies the amino acid methionine and also signals the ribosome to initiate translation ("start"). Three codons—UAA, UGA, and UAG—do not specify amino acids; they terminate polypeptide synthesis ("stop").

Second letter

	U	C	A	G	
U	UUU Phe / UUC Phe / UUA Leu / UUG Leu	UCU / UCC / UCA / UCG Ser	UAU Tyr / UAC Tyr / UAA Stop / UAG Stop	UGU Cys / UGC Cys / UGA Stop / UGG Trp	U C A G
C	CUU / CUC / CUA / CUG Leu	CCU / CCC / CCA / CCG Pro	CAU His / CAC His / CAA Gln / CAG Gln	CGU / CGC / CGA / CGG Arg	U C A G
A	AUU / AUC Ile / AUA / AUG Met or start	ACU / ACC / ACA / ACG Thr	AAU Asn / AAC Asn / AAA Lys / AAG Lys	AGU Ser / AGC Ser / AGA Arg / AGG Arg	U C A G
G	GUU / GUC / GUA / GUG Val	GCU / GCC / GCA / GCG Ala	GAU Asp / GAC Asp / GAA Glu / GAG Glu	GGU / GGC / GGA / GGG Gly	U C A G

(First letter (5' end) / Third letter (3' end))

▯ = Stop codon

▮ = Start codon

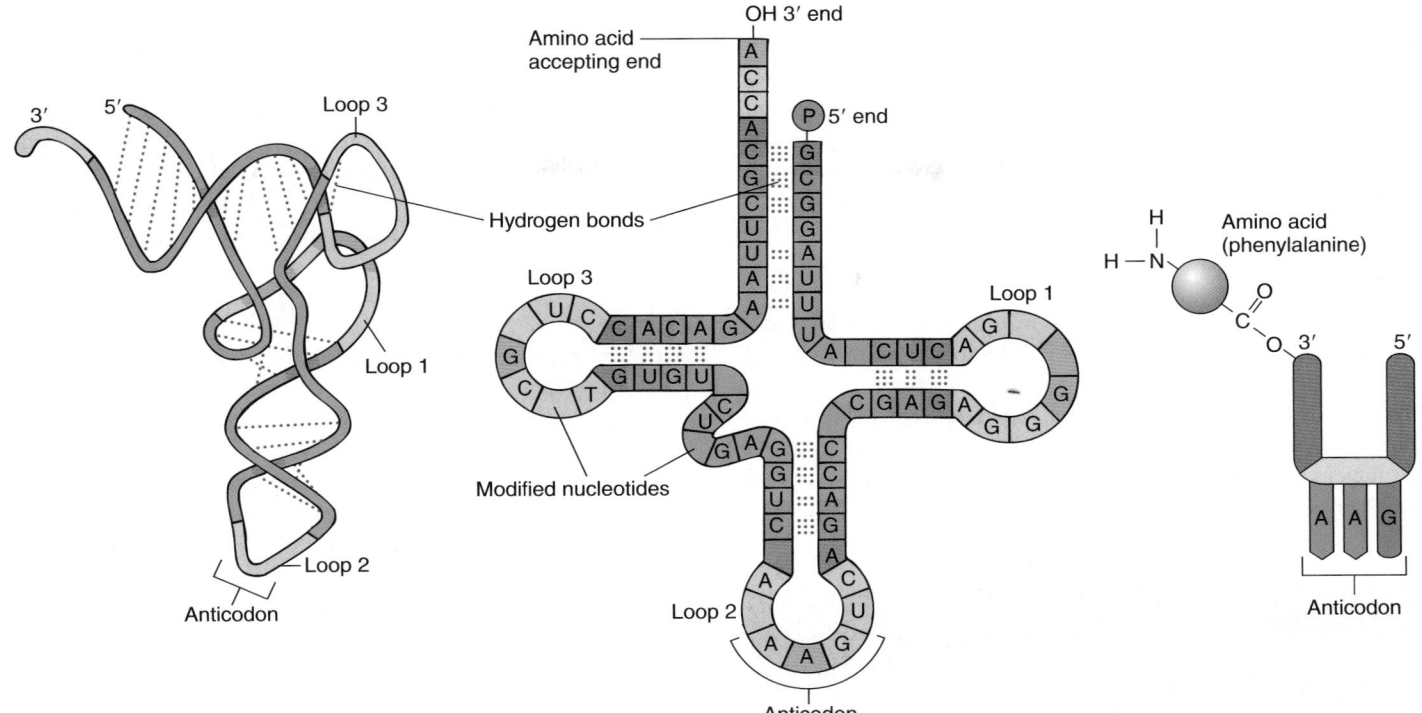

(a) The 3-D shape of a tRNA molecule is determined by hydrogen bonds formed between complementary bases.

(b) One loop contains the anticodon; these unpaired bases pair with a complementary mRNA codon. The amino acid attaches to the terminal nucleotide at the hydroxyl (OH) 3′ end.

(c) This stylized diagram of an aminoacyl-tRNA shows that the amino acid attaches to tRNA by its carboxyl group, leaving its amino group exposed for peptide bond formation.

FIGURE 13-6 Three representations of a tRNA molecule

end of the mRNA and travel along it, allowing the tRNAs to attach sequentially to the codons of mRNA. In this way the amino acids carried by the tRNAs take up the proper position to be joined by *peptide bonds* in the correct sequence to form a polypeptide.

Biologists cracked the genetic code in the 1960s

Before the genetic code was deciphered, scientists had become interested in how a genetic code might work. The Watson and Crick model of DNA showed it to be a linear sequence of four different nucleotides. If each nucleotide coded for a single amino acid, the genetic code could specify only 4 amino acids, not the 20 found in the vast variety of proteins in the cell.

Scientists saw that the DNA bases could serve as a four-letter "alphabet" and hypothesized that three-letter combinations of the four bases would make it possible to form a total of 64 "words," more than enough to specify all the naturally occurring amino acids. In 1961, Crick and British scientist Sydney Brenner concluded from experimental evidence that the code used nonoverlapping triplets of bases. They predicted that the code is read, one triplet at a time, from a fixed starting point that establishes the **reading frame** for the genetic message.

Marshall Nirenberg, a U.S. biochemist, and his postdoctoral researcher, Heinrich Matthaei, studied protein synthesis outside living cells in purified *cell-free systems* derived from the bacterium

Escherichia coli. Nirenberg and Matthaei obtained the first experimental evidence indicating the assignment of triplets to specific amino acids. By constructing artificial mRNA molecules with known base sequences, they determined which amino acids would be incorporated into protein. For example, when they added the synthetic mRNA polyuridylic acid (UUUUUUUUU . . .) to a mixture of purified ribosomes, aminoacyl-tRNAs (amino acids linked to their respective tRNAs), and essential cofactors needed to synthesize polypeptide, only phenylalanine was incorporated into the resulting polypeptide chain. The inference was inescapable that the UUU triplet codes for phenylalanine. Similar experiments showed that polyadenylic acid (AAAAAAAAA . . .) codes for a polypeptide of lysine and that polycytidylic acid (CCCCCCCCC . . .) codes for a polypeptide of proline.

By using mixed nucleotide polymers (such as a random polymer of A and C) as artificial messengers, researchers such as H. Gobind Khorana, then at the University of Wisconsin, assigned the other codons to specific amino acids. However, three of the codons—UAA, UGA, and UAG—did not specify any amino acids. These codons are now known to be the signals that terminate the coding sequence for a polypeptide chain. By 1967, the genetic code was completely "cracked," and scientists had identified the coding assignments of all 64 possible codons shown in Figure 13-5. In 1968, Nirenberg and Khorana received the Nobel Prize in Physiology or Medicine for their work in deciphering the genetic code.

Remember that the genetic code is an mRNA code. The tRNA anticodon sequences, as well as the DNA sequence from which the message is transcribed, are complementary to the sequences in Figure 13-5. For example, the mRNA codon for the amino acid methionine is 5′—AUG—3′. It is transcribed from the DNA base sequence 3′—TAC—5′, and the corresponding tRNA anticodon is 3′—UAC—5′.

The genetic code is virtually universal

Perhaps the single most remarkable feature of the code is that it is essentially universal. Over the years, biologists have examined the genetic code in a diverse array of species and found it the same in organisms as different as bacteria, redwood trees, jellyfish, and humans (**FIG. 13-7**). These findings strongly suggest that the code is an ancient legacy that evolved early in the history of life (discussed in Chapter 21).

FIGURE 13-7 Genetically engineered tobacco plant

This plant glows as it expresses the luciferase gene from a firefly. Luciferase is an enzyme that catalyzes a reaction that produces a flash of light. This classic experiment indicated that animal genes can be expressed in plants.

Scientists have discovered some minor exceptions to the universality of the genetic code. In several unicellular protozoa, UAA and UGA code for the amino acid glutamine instead of functioning as stop signals. Other exceptions are found in mitochondria, which contain their own DNA and protein synthesis machinery for some genes. These slight coding differences vary with the organism, but keep in mind that in each case, all the other coding assignments are identical to those of the standard genetic code.

The genetic code is redundant

Given 64 possible codons and only 20 common amino acids, it is not surprising that more than one codon specifies certain amino acids. This redundancy in the genetic code has certain characteristic patterns. The codons CCU, CCC, CCA, and CCG are "synonymous" in that they all code for the amino acid proline. The only difference among the 4 codons involves the nucleotide at the 3′ end of the triplet. Although the code may be read three nucleotides at a time, only the first two nucleotides seem to contain specific information for proline. A similar pattern can be seen for several other amino acids. Only methionine and tryptophan are specified by single codons. Each of the other amino acids is specified by 2 to 6 different codons.

Crick first proposed this apparent breach of the base-pairing rules as the **wobble hypothesis.** He reasoned that the third nucleotide of a tRNA anticodon (which is the 5′ base of the anticodon sequence) may sometimes form hydrogen bonds with more than one kind of third nucleotide (the 3′ base) of a codon. Investigators later established this experimentally by determining the anticodon sequences of tRNA molecules and testing their specificities in artificial systems. Some tRNAs bond exclusively to one codon, but other tRNA molecules pair with as many as three separate codons that differ in their third nucleotide but that specify the same amino acid. Thus, the wobble hypothesis accounts for the possible variation in base pairing between the third base of a codon and the corresponding base in its anticodon. "Wobble" results in several acceptable forms of base pairing between mRNA and tRNA.

Review

- Sketch a simple flow diagram that shows the relationships among the following: RNA, translation, DNA, transcription, and polypeptide.
- How are the structures of DNA and RNA similar? How are they different?

13.3 TRANSCRIPTION

LEARNING OBJECTIVES

6 Compare the processes of transcription and DNA replication, identifying both similarities and differences.

7 Compare bacterial and eukaryotic mRNAs, and explain the functional significance of their structural differences.

Now that we have presented an overview of information flow from DNA to RNA to polypeptide, let us examine the entire process more closely. The first stage in the flow of information from DNA to polypeptide is the transcription of a DNA nucleotide sequence into an RNA nucleotide sequence. Stanford University biologist Roger Kornberg painstakingly worked out the details of transcription, for which he was awarded the 2006 Nobel Prize in Chemistry.

In eukaryotic transcription, most RNA synthesis requires one of three **RNA polymerases,** enzymes present in all cells. The three RNA polymerases differ in the kinds of RNA synthesis they catalyze. *RNA polymerase I* catalyzes the synthesis of several kinds of rRNA molecules that are components of the ribosome; *RNA polymerase II* catalyzes the production of the protein-coding mRNA; and *RNA polymerase III* catalyzes the synthesis of tRNA and one of the rRNA molecules.

RNA polymerases require DNA as a template and have many similarities to the DNA polymerases discussed in Chapter 12. Like DNA polymerases, RNA polymerases carry out synthesis in the $5' \longrightarrow 3'$ direction; that is, they begin at the $5'$ end of the RNA molecule being synthesized and then continue to add nucleotides at the $3'$ end until the molecule is complete (**FIG. 13-8**). RNA polymerases use nucleotides with three phosphate groups (for example, ATP and GTP) as substrates for the polymerization reaction. As the nucleotides link to the $3'$ end of the RNA, two of the phosphates are removed. These reactions are strongly exergonic and do not need the input of additional energy.

Recall from Chapter 12 that whenever nucleic acid molecules associate by complementary base pairing, the two strands are **antiparallel.** Just as the two paired strands of DNA are antiparallel, the template strand of the DNA and the complementary RNA strand are also antiparallel. Therefore, when transcription takes place, as RNA is synthesized in its $5' \longrightarrow 3'$ direction, the DNA template is read in its $3' \longrightarrow 5'$ direction.

Scientists conventionally refer to a sequence of bases in a gene or the mRNA sequence transcribed from it as upstream or downstream from some reference point. *Upstream* is toward the $5'$ end of the mRNA sequence or the $3'$ end of the template DNA strand. *Downstream* is toward the $3'$ end of the RNA or the $5'$ end of the template DNA strand.

Upstream		Downstream
	5′—A—T—G—A—C—T—3′	nontemplate DNA strand
	3′—T—A—C—T—G—A—5′	template DNA strand
	Direction of transcription $\longrightarrow$	
	5′—A—U—G—A—C—U—3′	RNA

The synthesis of mRNA includes initiation, elongation, and termination

In both bacteria and eukaryotes, the nucleotide sequence in DNA to which RNA polymerase and associated proteins initially bind is called the **promoter.** Because the promoter is not transcribed, RNA polymerase moves past the promoter to begin transcription of the protein-coding sequence of DNA. Different genes may have

FIGURE 13-8 *Animated* **A molecular view of transcription**
Incoming nucleotides with three phosphates pair with complementary bases on the template DNA strand (*right*). RNA polymerase cleaves two phosphates (*not shown*) from each nucleotide and covalently links the remaining phosphate to the $3'$ end of the growing RNA chain. Thus, RNA, like DNA, is synthesized in the $5' \longrightarrow 3'$ direction.

slightly different promoter sequences, so the cell can direct which genes are transcribed at any one time. Bacterial promoters are usually about 40 bases long and lie in the DNA just upstream of the point at which transcription will begin. Once RNA polymerase has recognized the correct promoter, it unwinds the DNA double helix and *initiates* transcription (**FIG. 13-9**). Unlike DNA synthesis, RNA synthesis does not require a primer. However, transcription requires several proteins in addition to RNA polymerase; we discuss these in Chapter 14.

The first nucleotide at the $5'$ end of a new mRNA chain initially retains its triphosphate group (see Fig. 13-8). However, during the *elongation* stage of transcription, as each additional nucleotide is incorporated at the $3'$ end of the growing RNA molecule, two of its phosphates are removed in an exergonic reaction that leaves the remaining phosphate to become part of the sugar–phosphate backbone (as in DNA replication). The last nucleotide to be incorporated has an exposed $3'$-hydroxyl group.

Elongation of RNA continues until *termination*, when RNA polymerase recognizes a termination sequence consisting of a

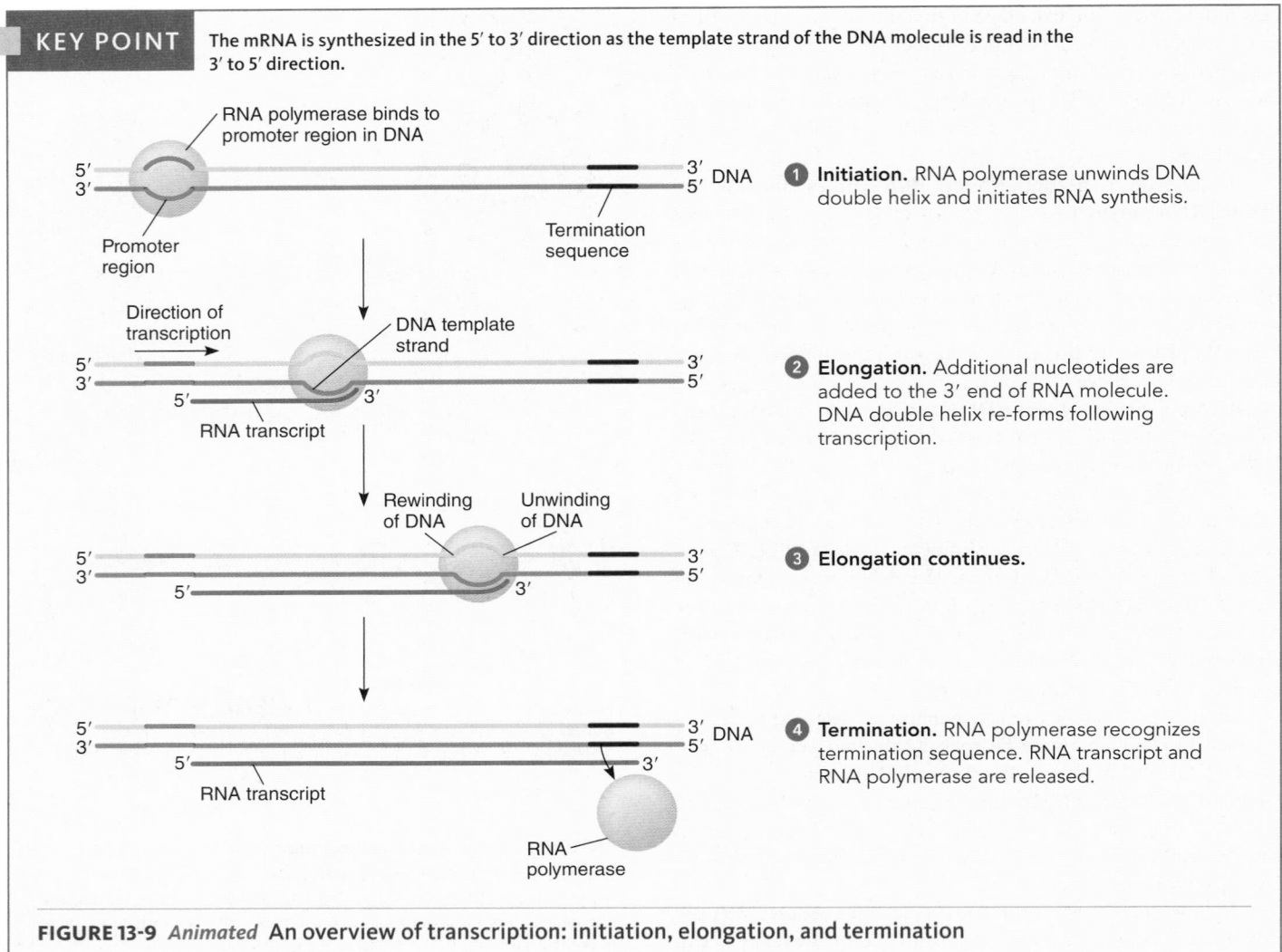

KEY POINT The mRNA is synthesized in the 5' to 3' direction as the template strand of the DNA molecule is read in the 3' to 5' direction.

RNA polymerase binds to promoter region in DNA

5'
3' DNA

Promoter region

Termination sequence

1 Initiation. RNA polymerase unwinds DNA double helix and initiates RNA synthesis.

Direction of transcription

DNA template strand

5'
3'

5'   3'

RNA transcript

3'
5'

2 Elongation. Additional nucleotides are added to the 3' end of RNA molecule. DNA double helix re-forms following transcription.

Rewinding of DNA   Unwinding of DNA

5'
3'

5'   3'

3'
5'

3 Elongation continues.

5'
3' DNA

5'   3'

RNA transcript

3'
5'

RNA polymerase

4 Termination. RNA polymerase recognizes termination sequence. RNA transcript and RNA polymerase are released.

FIGURE 13-9 *Animated* **An overview of transcription: initiation, elongation, and termination**

specific sequence of bases in the DNA template. This signal leads to a separation of RNA polymerase from the template DNA and the newly synthesized RNA.

Termination of transcription occurs by different mechanisms in bacteria and eukaryotes. In bacteria, transcription stops at the end of the termination sequence. When RNA polymerase comes to the termination sequence, it releases the DNA template and the new RNA strand. In eukaryotic cells, RNA polymerase adds nucleotides to the mRNA molecule after it passes the termination sequence. The 3' end of the mRNA becomes separated from RNA polymerase about 10 to 35 nucleotides past the termination sequence.

Only one strand in a protein-coding region of DNA is used as a template. For example, consider a segment of DNA that contains the following DNA base sequence in the template strand:

3'—TAACGGTCT—5'

If the complementary DNA strand

5'—ATTGCCAGA—3'

were used as a template, a message would be produced specifying an entirely different (and probably nonfunctional) protein. However, just because one strand is transcribed for a given gene does not mean the same DNA strand is always the template for all genes throughout the length of a chromosome-sized DNA molecule. Instead, a particular strand may serve as the template strand for some genes and the nontemplate strand for others (**FIG. 13-10**).

Messenger RNA contains base sequences that do not directly code for protein

A completed mRNA molecule contains more than the nucleotide sequence that codes for a protein. **FIGURE 13-11** shows a typical bacterial mRNA. (The unique features of eukaryotic mRNA are discussed in the next section.) In both bacteria and eukaryotes, RNA polymerase starts transcription of a gene upstream of the protein-coding DNA sequence. As a result, the mRNA has a noncoding **leader sequence** at its 5' end. The leader has recognition sites for ribosome binding, which properly position the ribosomes to translate the message. The **start codon** follows the leader sequence and signals the beginning of the **coding sequence** that contains the

FIGURE 13-10 The template strand for one gene may be the nontemplate strand for another gene
Only one of the two strands is transcribed for a given gene, but the opposite strand may be transcribed for a neighboring gene. Each transcript starts at its own promoter region (*orange*). The orange arrow associated with each promoter region indicates the direction of transcription.

actual message for the polypeptide. Unlike coding in eukaryotic cells, in bacterial cells it is common for more than one polypeptide to be encoded by a single mRNA molecule (see Chapter 14). At the end of each coding sequence, a **stop codon** signals the end of the protein. The stop codons—UAA, UGA, and UAG—end both bacterial and eukaryotic messages. They are followed by noncoding 3′ **trailing sequences,** which vary in length.

Eukaryotic mRNA is modified after transcription and before translation

Other differences exist between bacterial and eukaryotic mRNA. Bacterial mRNAs are used immediately after transcription, without further processing. In eukaryotes, the original transcript, called **precursor mRNA,** or **pre-mRNA,** is modified in several ways while it is still in the nucleus. These *posttranscriptional modification and processing* activities produce mature mRNA for transport and translation.

Modification of the eukaryotic message begins when the growing RNA transcript is about 20 to 30 nucleotides long. At that point, enzymes add a **5′ cap** to the 5′ end of the mRNA chain (**FIG. 13-12**).

The cap is in the form of an unusual nucleotide, 7-methylguanosine, which is linked to the mRNA transcript by three phosphate groups. Eukaryotic ribosomes cannot bind to an uncapped message.

Capping may also protect the mRNA from certain types of degradation and may therefore partially explain why eukaryotic mRNAs are much more stable than bacterial mRNAs. Eukaryotic mRNAs have half-lives ranging from 30 minutes to as long as 24 hours. The average half-life of an mRNA molecule in a mammalian cell is about 10 hours compared with 2 minutes in a bacterial cell.

A second modification of eukaryotic mRNA, known as **polyadenylation,** may occur at the 3′ end of the molecule. Near the 3′ end of a completed message usually lies a sequence of bases that serves as a signal for adding many adenine-containing nucleotides, known as a **poly-A tail** (for *polyadenylated*). Enzymes in the nucleus recognize the signal for the poly-A tail and cut the mRNA molecule at that site. This process is followed by the enzymatic addition of a string of 100 to 250 adenine nucleotides to the 3′ end. Polyadenylation appears to have several functions: it helps export the mRNA from the nucleus, stabilizes some mRNAs against degradation in the cytosol (the longer the poly-A tail, the longer

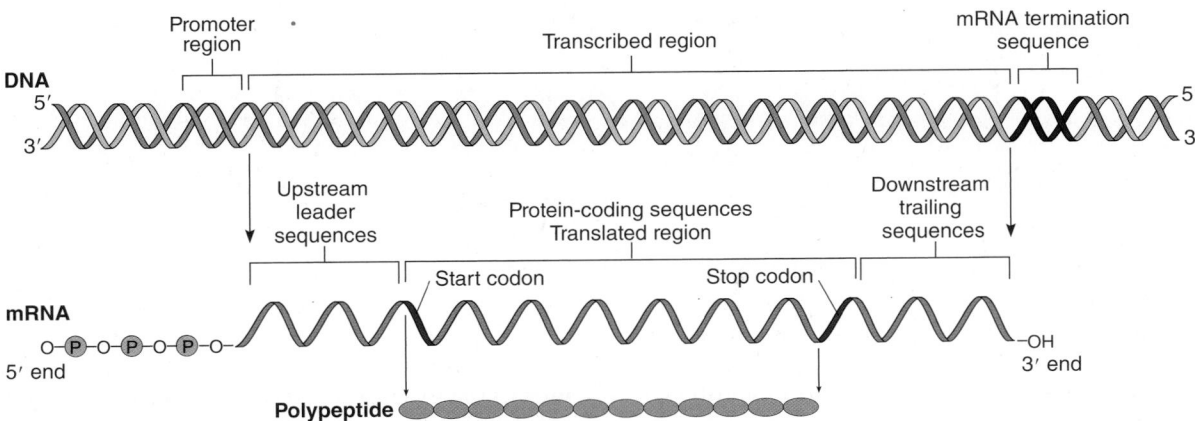

FIGURE 13-11 Bacterial mRNA
This figure compares a bacterial mRNA with the region of DNA from which it was transcribed. RNA polymerase recognizes, but does not transcribe, promoter sequences in the DNA. Initiation of RNA synthesis occurs five to eight bases downstream from the promoter. Ribosome recognition sites are located in the 5′ mRNA upstream leader sequences. Protein-coding sequences begin at a start codon, which follows the leader sequences, and end at a downstream stop codon near the 3′ end of the mRNA molecule. Downstream trailing sequences, which vary in length, follow the polypeptide-coding sequences.

After transcription in eukaryotes, pre-mRNA undergoes extensive modification to produce mature, functional mRNA.

FIGURE 13-12 *Animated* Posttranscriptional modification of eukaryotic messenger RNA

the molecule persists in the cytosol), and facilitates initiation of translation by helping ribosomes recognize the mRNA.

Both noncoding and coding sequences are transcribed from eukaryotic genes

One of the greatest surprises in the history of molecular biology was the finding that most eukaryotic genes have **interrupted coding sequences:** long sequences of bases within the protein-coding sequences of the gene do not code for amino acids in the final polypeptide product. The noncoding regions within the gene are called

introns (*in*tervening sequences), as opposed to **exons** (*ex*pressed sequences), which are parts of the protein-coding sequence.

A typical eukaryotic gene may have multiple exons and introns, although the number varies. For example, the human β-globin gene, which produces one component of hemoglobin, contains 2 introns and 3 exons; the human gene for albumin contains 14 introns and 15 exons; and the human gene for titin, the largest protein known, found in muscle cells, contains 233 introns and 234 exons. In many cases, the combined lengths of the intron sequences are much greater than the combined lengths of the exons. For instance, the ovalbumin gene contains about 7700 base pairs, whereas the total of all the exon sequences is only 1859 base pairs.

When a gene that contains introns is transcribed, the entire gene is copied as a large RNA transcript, the pre-mRNA. A pre-mRNA molecule contains both intron and exon sequences. (Note that *intron* and *exon* refer to corresponding nucleotide sequences in both DNA and RNA.) For the pre-mRNA to be made into a functional message, it must be capped and have a poly-A tail added, and the introns must be removed and the exons spliced together to form a continuous protein-coding message.

Splicing itself occurs by several different mechanisms, depending on which type of RNA is involved. In many instances, splicing involves the association of several **small nuclear ribonucleoprotein complexes** (**snRNPs,** pronounced "snurps") to form a large ribonucleoprotein complex called a **spliceosome.** Spliceosomes, which are similar in size to ribosomes, catalyze the reactions that remove introns from pre-mRNA. In other instances the RNA within the intron acts as an RNA catalyst, or **ribozyme,** splicing itself without the use of a spliceosome or protein enzymes.

Posttranscriptional modification in eukaryotes is summarized as follows:

pre-mRNA containing introns and exons ⟶ 5′ end of pre-mRNA capped with modified nucleotide ⟶ poly-A tail added to 3′ end ⟶ introns removed and exons spliced together ⟶ mature mRNA transported into cytosol ⟶ translation at ribosome

Following pre-mRNA processing, the mature mRNA is transported through a nuclear pore into the cytosol to be translated by a ribosome.

Review

- In what ways are DNA polymerase and RNA polymerase similar? How do they differ?
- A certain template DNA strand has the following nucleotide sequence:

3′—TACTGCATAATGATT—5′

What would be the sequence of codons in the mRNA transcribed from this strand? What would be the nucleotide sequence of the complementary nontemplate DNA strand?

- What features do mature eukaryotic mRNA molecules have that bacterial mRNAs lack?

13.4 TRANSLATION

LEARNING OBJECTIVES

8 Identify the features of tRNA that are important in decoding genetic information and converting it into "protein language."

9 Explain how ribosomes function in polypeptide synthesis.

10 Describe the processes of initiation, elongation, and termination in polypeptide synthesis.

Translation adds another level of complexity to the process of information transfer because it involves conversion of the triplet nucleic acid code to the 20–amino acid alphabet of polypeptides. Translation requires the coordinated functioning of more than 100 kinds of macromolecules, including the protein and RNA components of the ribosomes, mRNA, and amino acids linked to tRNAs.

Amino acids are joined by *peptide bonds* to form proteins. (See the formation of a peptide bond in Figure 3-18.) This joining links the amino and carboxyl groups of adjacent amino acids. The translation process ensures both that peptide bonds form and that the amino acids link in the correct sequence specified by the codons in the mRNA.

An amino acid is attached to tRNA before incorporation into a polypeptide

How do the amino acids align in the proper sequence so they can link? Crick proposed that a molecule was needed to bridge the gap between mRNA and proteins. This molecule was determined to be tRNA. DNA contains genes that are transcribed to form the tRNAs. Each kind of tRNA molecule binds to a specific amino acid. Amino acids are covalently linked to their respective tRNA molecules by enzymes, called **aminoacyl–tRNA synthetases,** which use ATP as an energy source (**FIG. 13-13**). The resulting complexes, called

FIGURE 13-13 Linkage of a specific amino acid to the appropriate tRNA
Amino acids are covalently linked to their respective tRNA molecules by aminoacyl–tRNA synthetases, which use ATP as an energy source.

aminoacyl–tRNAs, bind to the mRNA coding sequence to align the amino acids in the correct order to form the polypeptide chain.

The tRNAs are polynucleotide chains 70 to 80 nucleotides long, each with several unique base sequences as well as some sequences that are common to all. Although considerably smaller than mRNA or rRNA molecules, tRNA molecules have an intricate structure. A tRNA molecule has several properties essential to its function: (1) it has an anticodon, a complementary binding sequence for the correct mRNA codon; (2) it is recognized by an aminoacyl–tRNA synthetase that adds the correct amino acid; (3) it has an attachment site for the specific amino acid specified by the anticodon (the site lies about 180 degrees from the anticodon); and (4) it is recognized by ribosomes.

Complementary base pairing within each tRNA molecule causes it to be doubled back and folded. Three or more loops of unpaired nucleotides are formed, one of which contains the anticodon. The amino acid–binding site is at the 3' end of the molecule. The carboxyl group of the amino acid is covalently bound to the exposed 3' hydroxyl group of the terminal nucleotide, leaving the amino group of the amino acid free to participate in peptide bond formation. The pattern of folding in tRNAs keeps a constant distance between the anticodon and amino acid, allowing precise positioning of the amino acids during translation.

The components of the translational machinery come together at the ribosomes

The importance of ribosomes and of protein synthesis in cell metabolism is exemplified by a rapidly growing *E. coli* cell, which contains some 15,000 ribosomes—nearly one-third of the total mass of the cell. Although bacterial and eukaryotic ribosomes are not identical, ribosomes from all organisms share many fundamental features and basically work in the same way. Ribosomes consist of two subunits, both made up of protein (about 40% by weight) and rRNA (about 60% by weight). Unlike mRNA and tRNA, rRNA has catalytic functions and does not transfer information. The ribosomal proteins do not appear to be catalytic but instead contribute to the overall structure and stability of the ribosome.

Researchers have isolated each ribosomal subunit intact in the laboratory, then separated each into its RNA and protein constituents. In bacteria, the smaller of these subunits contains 21 proteins and one rRNA molecule, and the larger subunit contains 34 proteins and two rRNA molecules. Under certain conditions researchers can reassemble each subunit into a functional form by adding each component in its correct order. Using this approach, together with sophisticated electron microscopic studies, researchers have determined the 3-D structure of the ribosome (**FIG. 13-14a**), as well as the way it is assembled in the living cell. The large subunit contains a depression on one surface into which the small subunit fits. During translation, the mRNA fits in a groove between the contact surfaces of the two subunits.

The ribosome has four binding sites, one for mRNA and three for tRNAs. Thus, the ribosome holds the mRNA template, the aminoacyl–tRNA molecules, and the growing polypeptide chain in the correct orientation so the genetic code can be read and the next peptide bond formed. Transfer RNA molecules attach to three depressions on the ribosome, the A, P, and E binding sites

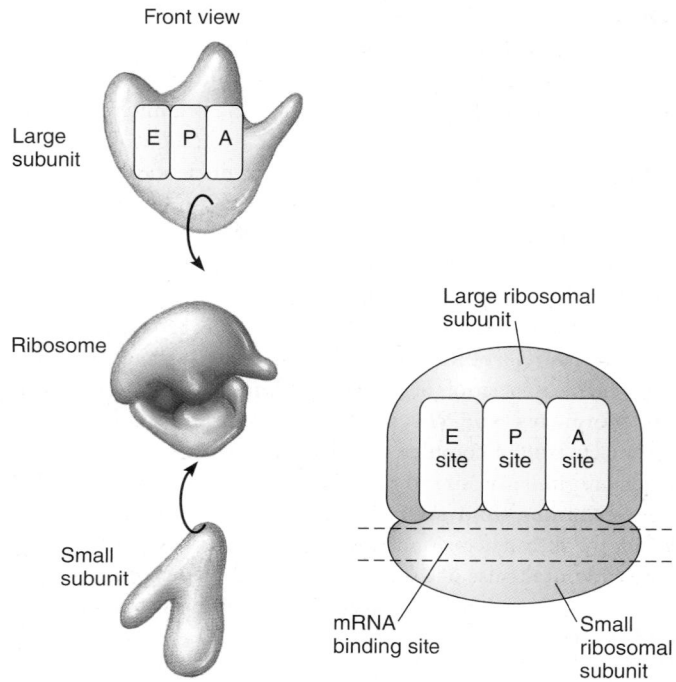

(a) A ribosome consists of two subunits, one large and one small. This model of a ribosome is based on a 3-D reconstruction of electron microscopic images.

(b) The mRNA passes through a groove between the two ribosomal subunits. Each ribosome contains three binding sites for tRNA molecules.

FIGURE 13-14 *Animated* Ribosome structure

(**FIG. 13-14b**). The **P site,** or peptidyl site, is so named because the tRNA holding the growing polypeptide chain occupies the P site. The **A site** is named the aminoacyl site because the aminoacyl–tRNA delivering the next amino acid in the sequence binds at this location. The **E site** (for *exit*) is where tRNAs that have delivered their amino acids to the growing polypeptide chain exit the ribosome.

Translation begins with the formation of an initiation complex

The process of protein synthesis has three distinct stages: initiation, repeating cycles of elongation, and termination. Initiation of protein synthesis is essentially the same in all organisms. Here we describe initiation in bacteria and then briefly discuss some differences between bacterial and eukaryotic initiation.

The **initiation** of translation uses proteins called **initiation factors,** which become attached to the small ribosomal subunit. In bacteria, three different initiation factors attach to the small subunit, which then binds to the mRNA molecule in the region of the AUG start codon (**FIG. 13-15**). A leader sequence upstream (toward the 5' end) of the AUG helps the ribosome identify the AUG sequence that signals the beginning of the mRNA code for a protein.

The tRNA that bears the first amino acid of the polypeptide is the **initiator tRNA.** The amino acid methionine is bound to the initiator tRNA, and as a result, the first amino acid on new poly-

Initiation in bacteria involves a ribosome, an mRNA, an initiator tRNA to which formylated methionine (fMet) is bound, and several protein initiation factors.

1 The small ribosomal subunit binds to the mRNA at the AUG start codon. The leader sequence upstream of the AUG sequence helps the ribosome identify the AUG sequence.

2 The initiator tRNA binds to the start codon, and one of the initiation factors is released.

3 When the large ribosomal subunit binds to the small subunit and the remaining initiation factors are released, the initiation complex is complete.

FIGURE 13-15 The initiation of translation in bacteria

peptides is methionine. (Quite often, the methionine is removed later.) In bacteria, the initiator methionine is modified by the addition of a one-carbon group derived from formic acid and is designated *fMet* for *N*-formylmethionine. The fMet–initiator tRNA, which has the anticodon 3'—UAC—5', binds to the AUG start codon, releasing one of the initiation factors in the process. The **initiation complex** is complete when the large ribosomal subunit binds to the small subunit and the remaining initiation factors are released.

In eukaryotes, initiation of translation differs in three respects. First, the methionine of the initiator tRNA is unmodified. Second, instead of a leader sequence to help identify the start codon on mRNA, the start codon is embedded within a short sequence (such as ACCAUGG) that indicates the site (the underlined AUG) of translation initiation. Third, the initiation complex, which contains perhaps 10 protein factors, is different from that of bacteria.

During elongation, amino acids are added to the growing polypeptide chain

FIGURE 13-16 outlines the four steps in a cycle of **elongation,** the stage of translation in which amino acids are added one by one to the growing polypeptide chain. Elongation is essentially the same in bacteria and eukaryotes. The appropriate aminoacyl–tRNA recognizes the codon in the A site and binds there by base pairing of its anticodon with the complementary mRNA codon. This binding step requires several proteins called **elongation factors.** It also requires energy from **guanosine triphosphate (GTP),** an energy transfer molecule similar to ATP.

The amino group of the amino acid at the A site is now aligned with the carboxyl group of the preceding amino acid attached to

the growing polypeptide chain at the P site. A peptide bond forms between the amino group of the new amino acid and the carboxyl group of the preceding amino acid. In this way, the polypeptide is released from tRNA at the P site and attaches to the aminoacyl–tRNA at the A site. This reaction is spontaneous (it does not require additional energy) because ATP transferred energy during formation of the aminoacyl–tRNA. Peptide bond formation does, however, require the enzyme **peptidyl transferase.** Remarkably, this enzyme is not a protein but a ribozyme that is an RNA component of the large ribosomal subunit. Two biochemists, American Thomas Cech (University of Colorado) and Canadian Sidney Altman (Yale University), received a Nobel Prize in Chemistry in 1989 for their independent discovery of ribozymes.

Recall from Chapter 3 that polypeptide chains have direction, or polarity. The amino acid on one end of the polypeptide chain has a free amino group (the amino end), and the amino acid at the other end has a free carboxyl group (the carboxyl end). Protein synthesis always proceeds from the amino end to the carboxyl end of the growing polypeptide chain:

In **translocation,** the ribosome moves down the mRNA by one codon. As a result, the mRNA codon specifying the next amino acid in the polypeptide chain becomes positioned in the unoccupied A site. The translocation process requires energy, which again GTP supplies. The uncharged tRNA—that is, the tRNA without an attached amino acid—is moved from the P site

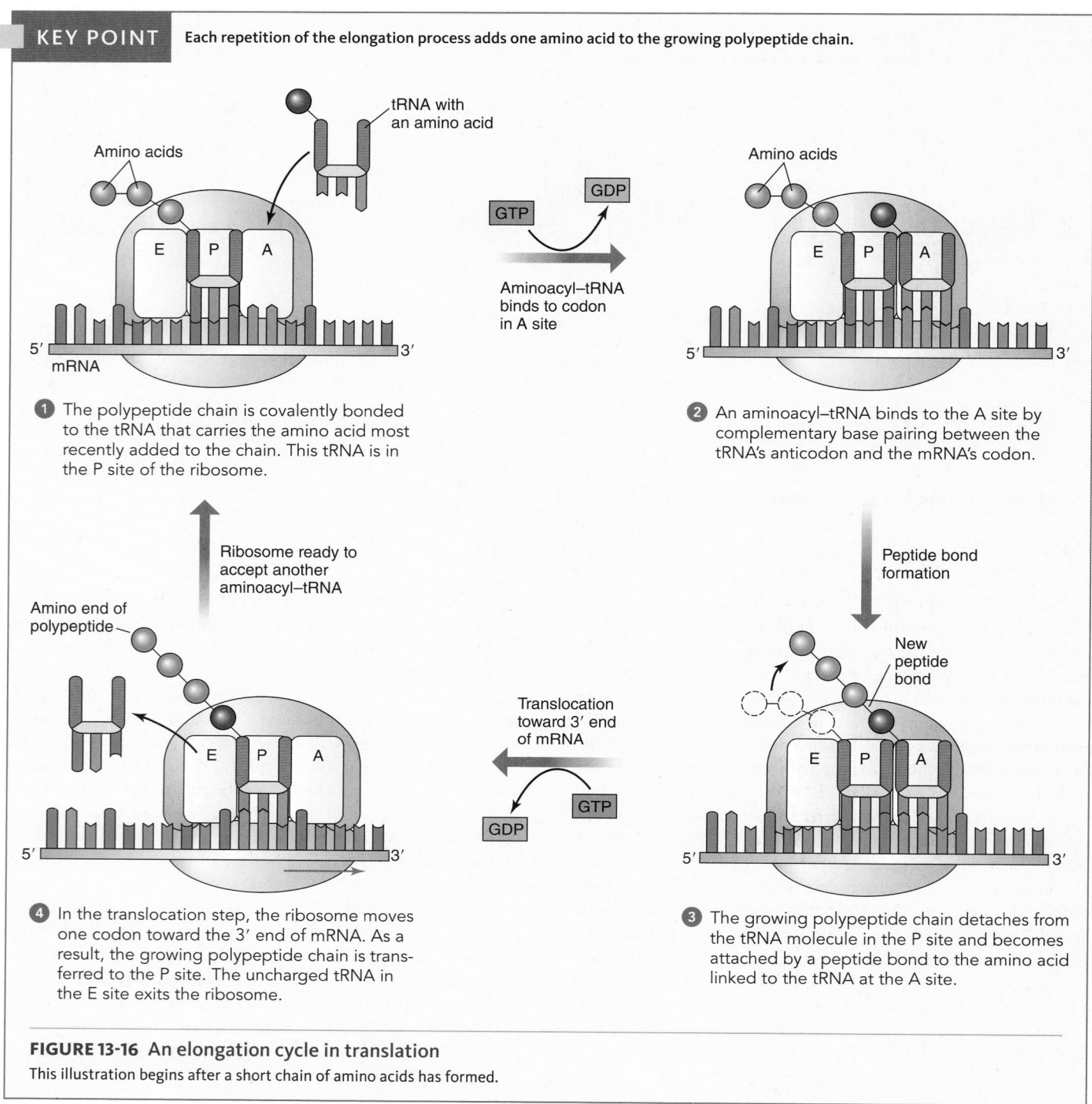

KEY POINT   Each repetition of the elongation process adds one amino acid to the growing polypeptide chain.

tRNA with
an amino acid

Amino acids

GTP → GDP

Aminoacyl–tRNA
binds to codon
in A site

Amino acids

E P A

5′ mRNA 3′

1 The polypeptide chain is covalently bonded to the tRNA that carries the amino acid most recently added to the chain. This tRNA is in the P site of the ribosome.

E P A

5′ 3′

2 An aminoacyl–tRNA binds to the A site by complementary base pairing between the tRNA's anticodon and the mRNA's codon.

Ribosome ready to
accept another
aminoacyl–tRNA

Peptide bond
formation

Amino end of
polypeptide

New
peptide
bond

Translocation
toward 3′ end
of mRNA

E P A

GDP ← GTP

5′ 3′

4 In the translocation step, the ribosome moves one codon toward the 3′ end of mRNA. As a result, the growing polypeptide chain is transferred to the P site. The uncharged tRNA in the E site exits the ribosome.

E P A

5′ 3′

3 The growing polypeptide chain detaches from the tRNA molecule in the P site and becomes attached by a peptide bond to the amino acid linked to the tRNA at the A site.

FIGURE 13-16 An elongation cycle in translation
This illustration begins after a short chain of amino acids has formed.

to the E site. From there it exits the ribosome and joins the cytosolic pool of tRNAs.

Because translocation involves movement of the ribosome in the 3′ direction along the mRNA molecule, translation always proceeds in the 5′ ⟶ 3′ direction. Each peptide bond forms in a fraction of a second; by repeating the elongation cycle, an average-sized protein of about 360 amino acids is assembled by a bacterium in approximately 18 seconds and by a eukaryotic cell in a little more than 1 minute.

One of three stop codons signals the termination of translation

Termination is the final stage of translation. In termination, the synthesis of the polypeptide chain is terminated by a **release factor,** a protein that recognizes the stop codon at the end of the coding sequence. (Because no tRNA molecule binds to a stop codon, the codon is available for binding by the release factor.) When the release factor binds to the A site, the bond between the tRNA in

A stop signal terminates polypeptide synthesis, because no tRNA molecules exist with an anticodon complementary to a stop codon.

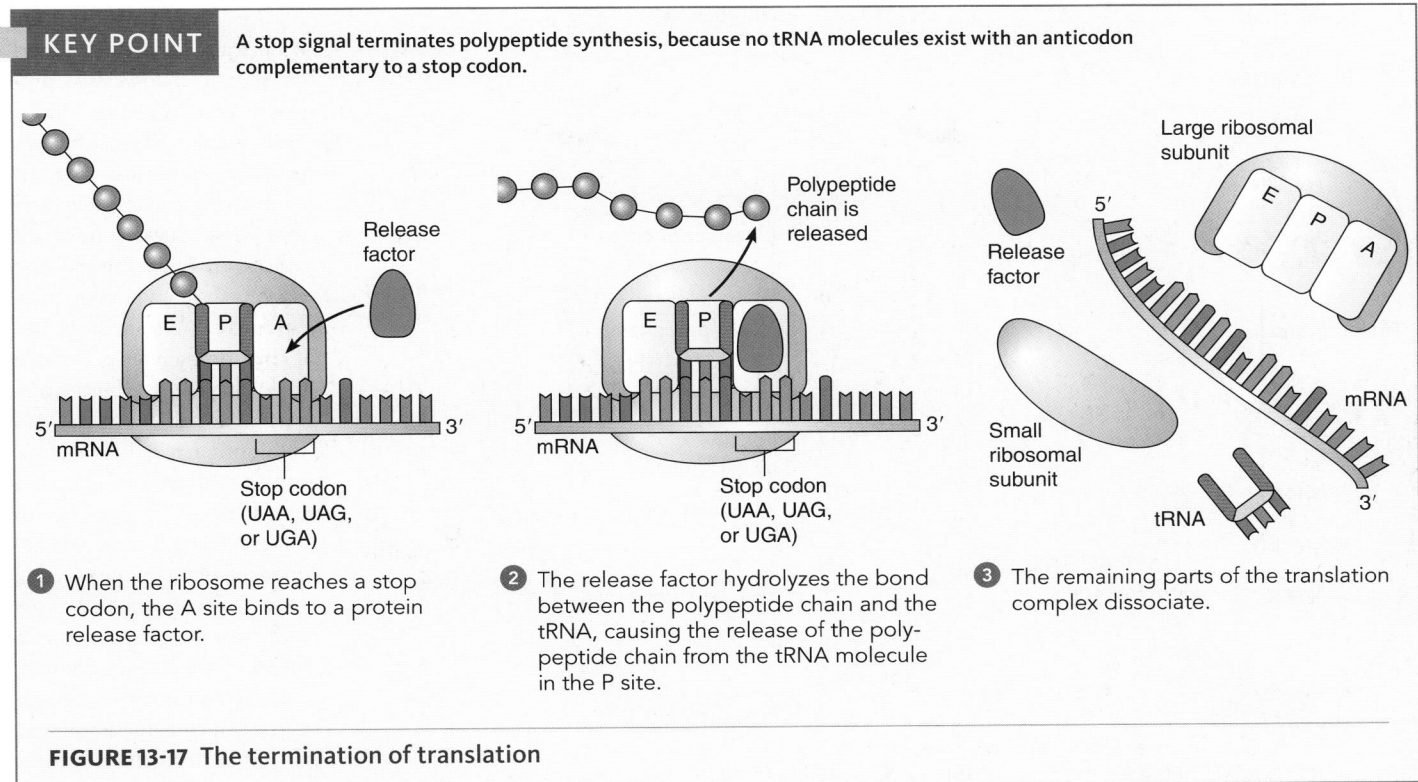

① When the ribosome reaches a stop codon, the A site binds to a protein release factor.

② The release factor hydrolyzes the bond between the polypeptide chain and the tRNA, causing the release of the polypeptide chain from the tRNA molecule in the P site.

③ The remaining parts of the translation complex dissociate.

FIGURE 13-17 The termination of translation

the P site and the last amino acid of the polypeptide chain breaks (**FIG. 13-17**). This hydrolysis reaction frees the newly synthesized polypeptide and also separates the translation complex into its parts: the mRNA molecule, the release factor, the tRNA molecule in the P site, and the large and small ribosomal subunits. The two ribosomal subunits can be used to form a new initiation complex with another mRNA molecule. Each mRNA is translated only a limited number of times before it is destroyed.

Specialized ribosome-associated proteins, called **molecular chaperones,** assist in the folding of the newly synthesized polypeptide chain into its three-dimensional active shape (see Chapter 3). The sequence of amino acids in the polypeptide chain dictates the shape that it ultimately forms. However, without the molecular chaperone's help, interactions among the various regions of the amino acid chain might prevent the proper folding process from occurring.

Review

- What are ribosomes made of? Do ribosomes carry information to specify the amino acid sequence of proteins?
- What happens in each stage of polypeptide synthesis: initiation, elongation, and termination?
- A certain mRNA strand has the following nucleotide sequence:

  5′—AUG—ACG—UAU—AAC—UUU—3′

  What is the anticodon for each codon? What is the amino acid sequence of the polypeptide? (Use Fig. 13-5 to help answer this question.)

13.5 VARIATIONS IN GENE EXPRESSION

■ LEARNING OBJECTIVES

11 Describe a polyribosome in bacterial cells.

12 Briefly discuss RNA interference.

13 Describe retroviruses and the enzyme reverse transcriptase.

You have seen that the basic mechanisms of transcription and translation are quite similar in all organisms. Some significant differences exist between bacteria and eukaryotes (**FIG. 13-18**). Some of these differences result from bacterial versus eukaryotic cell structure. Bacteria lack a nucleus, whereas eukaryotic chromosomes are confined to the cell nucleus and protein synthesis takes place in the cytosol. In eukaryotes, mRNA must move from the nucleus (the site of transcription) to the cytosol (the site of translation, or polypeptide synthesis). Also, as we discussed earlier in the chapter, extensive mRNA processing occurs in eukaryotic cells before translation.

Transcription and translation are coupled in bacteria

In *E. coli* and other bacteria, translation begins very soon after transcription, and several ribosomes are attached to the same mRNA (**FIG. 13-19**). The end of the mRNA molecule synthesized first during transcription is also the first to be translated to form a polypeptide.

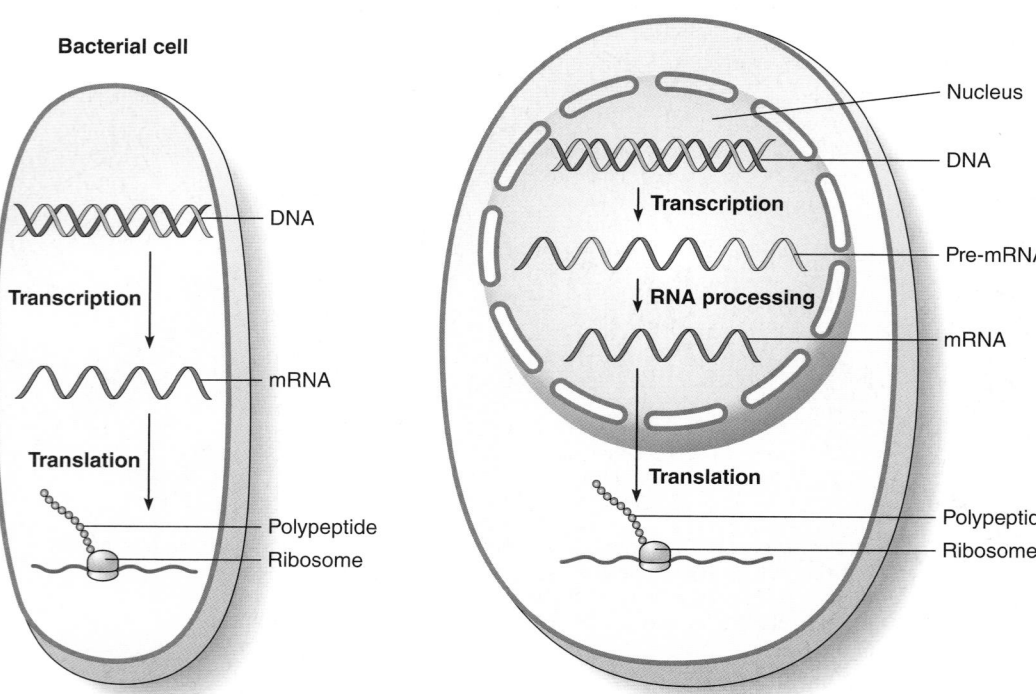

Bacterial cell

DNA

Transcription

mRNA

Translation

Polypeptide
Ribosome

(a) In a bacterial cell, mRNA is immediately ready for translation by ribosomes.

Eukaryotic cell

Nucleus

DNA

Transcription

Pre-mRNA

RNA processing

mRNA

Translation

Polypeptide
Ribosome

(b) In a eukaryotic cell, RNA processing occurs in the nucleus before the mRNA exits the nucleus for translation.

FIGURE 13-18 Summary: the flow of genetic information in bacteria and eukaryotes

Ribosomes bind to the 5′ end of the growing mRNA and initiate translation long before the message is fully synthesized. As many as 15 ribosomes may bind to a single mRNA. An mRNA molecule that is bound to clusters of ribosomes constitutes a **polyribosome,** or *polysome.* Polyribosomes also occur in eukaryotic cells, but not while transcription is still occurring.

Although many polypeptide chains can be actively synthesized on a single mRNA at any one time, the half-life of mRNA molecules in bacterial cells is only about 2 minutes. (Half-life is the time it takes for half the molecules to be degraded.) Usually, degradation of the 5′ end of the mRNA begins even before the first polypeptide is complete. Once the ribosome recognition sequences at the 5′ end of the mRNA have been degraded, no more ribosomes attach and initiate protein synthesis.

Biologists debate the evolution of eukaryotic gene structure

The reason for the intricate structure of eukaryotic genes is a matter of ongoing discussion among molecular biologists. Why do introns occur in most eukaryotic nuclear genes but not in the genes of most bacteria (or of mitochondria and chloroplasts)? How did this remarkable genetic system with interrupted coding sequences ("split genes") evolve, and why has it survived? It seems incredible that as much as 75% of the original transcript of a eukaryotic nuclear gene must be *removed* to make a working message.

In the early 1980s, American Walter Gilbert of Harvard University proposed that exons are nucleotide sequences that code for **protein domains,** regions of protein tertiary structure that may have important functions. For example, the active site of an enzyme may compose one domain. A different domain may enable that enzyme to bind to a particular cell structure, and yet another may be a site involved in allosteric regulation (see Chapter 7). Analyses of the DNA and amino acid sequences of many eukaryotic genes have shown that most exons are too small to code for an entire protein domain, although a block of several exons can code for a domain.

Gilbert further postulated that new proteins with new functions emerge rapidly when genetic recombination produces novel combinations of exons that code for different proteins. This hypothesis has become known as *evolution by exon shuffling.* It has been supported by examples such as the low-density lipoprotein (LDL) receptor protein, a protein found on the surface of human cells that binds to cholesterol transport molecules (see Chapter 5). The LDL receptor protein has domains that are related to parts of other proteins with totally different functions. However, many other genes and their corresponding proteins show no evidence of exon shuffling.

After introns were discovered in a few genes in archaea and bacteria, some biologists hypothesized that introns are relics from the ancient ancestors of all organisms living today. Through billions of years of evolution, the pressure in prokaryotic organisms, which are unicellular, to have a streamlined set of genes may have caused them to lose most of their introns.

Regardless of how split genes originated, intron excision provides one of many ways in which present-day eukaryotes regulate expression of their genes (see Chapter 14). This opportunity for control, together with the fact that eukaryotic RNAs are far more stable than those of bacteria, may balance the energy cost of maintaining a large load of noncoding DNA.

Several kinds of eukaryotic RNA have a role in gene expression

In addition to mRNA, rRNA, and tRNA, eukaryotic cells contain several other kinds of RNA that are an essential part of the complex system that results in protein synthesis (**TABLE 13-1**). **Small**

(a) This TEM shows two strands of *E. coli* DNA, one inactive and the other actively producing mRNA. Protein synthesis begins while the mRNA is being completed.

(b) A sequence (*left to right*) of coupled transcription and translation. Note that several ribosomes translate each mRNA molecule simultaneously.

FIGURE 13-19 Coupled transcription and translation in bacteria

nuclear RNA (snRNA) molecules bind to specific proteins to form a small nuclear ribonucleoprotein complex (snRNP), which in turn combines with other snRNPs to form a spliceosome. (Recall from the discussion earlier in the chapter that a spliceosome catalyzes intron removal.)

Some polypeptides enter the endoplasmic reticulum (ER) as they are being synthesized. **Signal-recognition particle RNA (SRP RNA),** in combination with proteins, directs the ribosome–mRNA–polypeptide complex to the rough ER shortly after translation begins. Translation continues after the complex binds to an integral protein in the ER membrane, and the newly synthesized protein is then distributed to its destination within the cell or outside the cell (for example, as a secretion).

A special group of RNA molecules, known as **small nucleolar RNAs (snoRNAs),** processes pre-rRNA molecules in the nucleolus during ribosome subunit formation. Small nucleolar RNAs bind to complementary regions of pre-rRNA and target sites for cleavage or methylation. A pre-rRNA molecule is larger than the combined size of the three rRNA molecules made from it. In mammalian cells, about 48% of the pre-rRNA molecule is removed during the cleavage steps. Pre-rRNA may have methyl groups added to regions that are to be saved during processing.

The discovery that RNA has the ability to regulate gene expression made big news in biology, both because this phenomenon, known as **RNA interference (RNAi),** is found in many organisms and because it has great potential as a research and medical tool (see Chapters 15 and 17). In RNAi, certain small RNA molecules

TABLE 13-1	Selected Kinds of RNA in Eukaryotic Cells
Kind of RNA	**Function**
Messenger RNA (mRNA)	Specifies the amino acid sequence of a protein
Transfer RNA (tRNA)	Binds to specific amino acid and serves as adapter molecule when amino acids are incorporated into growing polypeptide chain
Ribosomal RNA (rRNA)	Has both structural and catalytic (ribozyme) roles in ribosome
Small nuclear RNA (snRNA)	Involved in intron removal and regulation of transcription; part of spliceosome particles
Signal-recognition particle RNA (SRP RNA)	Helps direct the ribosome–mRNA–polypeptide complex to the rough ER shortly after translation begins
Small nucleolar RNA (snoRNA)	Processes pre-rRNA in nucleolus during formation of ribosome subunits
Small interfering RNA (siRNA)	Controls transposons and fights viral infections
MicroRNA (miRNA)	Controls expression of genes involved in growth and development by inhibiting the translation of mRNA; involved in several diseases, including prevention of cancer

interfere with the expression of genes or their RNA transcripts. RNA interference involves small interfering RNAs, microRNAs, and a few other kinds of short RNA molecules.

Small interfering RNAs (siRNAs) are double-stranded molecules that are 20 to 25 nucleotides in length. These RNA molecules help control damage from transposons (discussed later in the chapter) and viral infections; they also regulate gene expression of protein-coding genes.

MicroRNAs (miRNAs) are single-stranded RNA molecules 20 to 25 nucleotides long that inhibit the translation of mRNAs involved in many biological processes, such as growth and development (**FIG. 13-20**). MicroRNAs are transcribed from genes and then shortened before they are combined with proteins to form a complex that inhibits the expression of mRNA molecules with sequences complementary to the miRNA. More than 200 distinct miRNA genes have been identified in the human genome, but the specifics of how they regulate gene expression by degrading mRNAs and/or preventing mRNAs from being translated into polypeptides are not yet clear. Biologists now recognize that miRNAs have an important role in preventing cancer: cancer cells have measurably lower levels of miRNAs than noncancer cells. A breakdown in miRNA function has also been implicated in heart disease and possibly Parkinson's disease.

The definition of a gene has evolved as biologists have learned more about genes

At the beginning of this chapter, we traced the development of ideas regarding the nature of the gene. For a time scientists found it useful to define a *gene* as "a sequence of nucleotides that codes for one polypeptide chain." However, as we have learned more about the human genome, research teams have determined that DNA coding for polypeptides makes up about 2% of our genome, whereas about 80% of our genome is expressed; many genes are transcribed to produce the various kinds of RNA molecules (see Table 13-1). Further, as you will see in Chapter 14, studies have shown that in eukaryotic cells, a single gene may produce more than one polypeptide chain by modifications in the way the mRNA is processed.

It is perhaps most useful to define a gene in terms of its product: a **gene** is a DNA nucleotide sequence that carries the information needed to produce a specific RNA or polypeptide product.

The usual direction of information flow has exceptions

For several decades, a central premise of molecular biology was that genetic information always flows from DNA to RNA to protein. Through his studies of viruses, U.S. biologist Howard Temin discovered an important exception to this rule in 1964. Although viruses are not cellular organisms, they contain a single type of nucleic acid and reproduce in a host cell. Temin was studying unusual, cancer-causing tumor viruses that have RNA, rather than DNA, as their genetic material. He found that infection of a host cell by one of these viruses is blocked by inhibitors of DNA synthesis and also by inhibitors of transcription. These findings suggested

Javier F. Palatnik and Detlef Weigel

FIGURE 13-20 The effect of an miRNA molecule on plant growth
A normal *Arabidopsis* plant (*top view, leaf, and side view of seedling*) is shown on the left and serves as a control. Biologists modified an miRNA molecule in the plant on the right, and as a result, it exhibits severe developmental abnormalities, such as curly leaves.

that DNA synthesis and transcription are required for RNA tumor viruses to multiply and that there must be a way for information to flow in the "reverse" direction—from RNA to DNA.

Temin proposed that a **DNA provirus** forms as an intermediary in the replication of RNA tumor viruses. This hypothesis required a new kind of enzyme that would synthesize DNA using RNA as a template. In 1970, Temin and U.S. biologist David Baltimore discovered just such an enzyme, and they shared the Nobel Prize in Physiology or Medicine in 1975 for their discovery. This RNA-directed DNA polymerase, also known as **reverse transcriptase,** is found in all RNA tumor viruses. (Some RNA viruses that do not produce tumors, however, replicate without using a DNA intermediate.) **FIGURE 13-21** shows the steps of RNA tumor virus reproduction. Because they reverse the usual direction of information flow, viruses that require reverse transcriptase are called **retroviruses.** HIV-1, the virus that causes AIDS, is the most widely known retrovirus. As you will see in Chapter 15, the reverse transcriptase enzyme has become an important research tool for molecular biologists.

Review

- What is RNA interference?
- What is a gene?
- How do retroviruses use the enzyme reverse transcriptase?

13.6 MUTATIONS

LEARNING OBJECTIVE

14 Give examples of the different classes of mutations that affect the base sequence of DNA and explain the effects that each has on the polypeptide produced.

One of the first major discoveries about genes was that they undergo **mutations,** changes in the nucleotide sequence of the DNA. However, the overall mutation rate is much higher than the frequency of damage to DNA because all organisms have systems of enzymes that repair certain kinds of DNA damage.

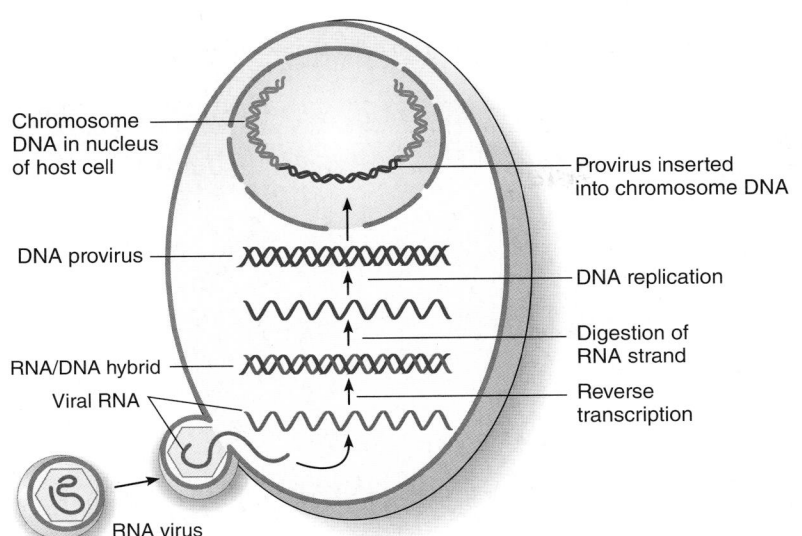

(a) After an RNA tumor virus enters the host cell, the viral enzyme reverse transcriptase synthesizes a DNA strand that is complementary to the viral RNA. Next, the RNA strand is degraded and a complementary DNA strand is synthesized, thus completing the double-stranded DNA provirus, which is then integrated into the host cell's DNA.

(b) The provirus DNA is transcribed, and the resulting viral mRNA is translated to form viral proteins. Additional viral RNA molecules are produced and then incorporated into mature viral particles enclosed by protein coats.

FIGURE 13-21 The infection cycle of an RNA tumor virus

If a DNA sequence has been changed and not corrected, DNA replication copies the altered sequence just as it would copy a normal sequence, making the mutation stable over an indefinite number of generations. In most cases, the mutant allele has no greater tendency than the original allele to mutate again.

Although most uncorrected mutations are either *silent* (and have no discernible effect) or harmful (such as those that cause inherited diseases and cancer), a few are useful. Because they can be passed to the next generation in cell lines that give rise to gametes, mutations are of vital importance in evolution. Mutations provide the variation among individuals that evolutionary forces act on. Mutations are also useful in research (recall Beadle and Tatum's work with mutations) because they provide the diversity of genetic material that enables researchers to study inheritance and the molecular nature of genes. Scientists now determine where a particular mutation occurs in a gene by using recombinant DNA methods to isolate the gene and determine its sequence of bases (see Chapter 15).

Base-pair substitution mutations result from the replacement of one base pair by another

Mutations can alter genes in several ways. The simplest type of mutation, called a **base-pair substitution,** involves a change in only one pair of nucleotides. Often these mutations result from errors in base pairing during the replication process. For example, a GC, CG, or TA pair might replace an AT base pair. Such a mutation may cause the altered DNA to be transcribed as an altered mRNA. The altered mRNA may then be translated into a polypeptide chain with only one amino acid different from the normal sequence.

Silent mutations are base-pair substitutions that have no discernible effect—as, for example, a mutation in a protein-coding gene that does not alter the amino acid sequence (**FIGS. 13-22a, b**). Base-pair substitutions that result in replacement of one amino acid by another are sometimes called **missense mutations** (**FIG. 13-22c**). Missense mutations have a wide range of effects. If the amino acid substitution occurs at or near the active site of an enzyme, the activity of the altered protein may decrease or even be destroyed. Some missense mutations involve a change in an amino acid that is not part of the active site. Others may result in the substitution of a closely related amino acid (one with very similar chemical characteristics). Such mutations have no effect on the function of a gene product and may be undetectable. Because these mutations occur relatively frequently, the true number of mutations in an organism is much greater than is actually observed.

Nonsense mutations are base-pair substitutions that convert an amino acid–specifying codon to a stop codon (**FIG. 13-22d**). A nonsense mutation usually destroys the function of the gene product; in the case of a protein-specifying gene, the part of the polypeptide chain that follows the mutant stop codon is missing.

Frameshift mutations result from the insertion or deletion of base pairs

In **frameshift mutations,** one or two nucleotide pairs are inserted into or deleted from the molecule, altering the reading frame. As a result, codons downstream of the insertion or deletion site specify an entirely new sequence of amino acids. Depending on where the insertion or deletion occurs in the gene, different effects are generated. Frameshift mutations may produce a stop

(a) Normal DNA sequence

DNA template strand

mRNA (normal sequence)

Polypeptide (normal sequence)

(b) Base-pair substitution (silent mutation)

(c) Base-pair substitution (missense)

(d) Base-pair substitution (nonsense)

(e) Frameshift (nonsense)

(f) Frameshift (altered amino acid sequence)

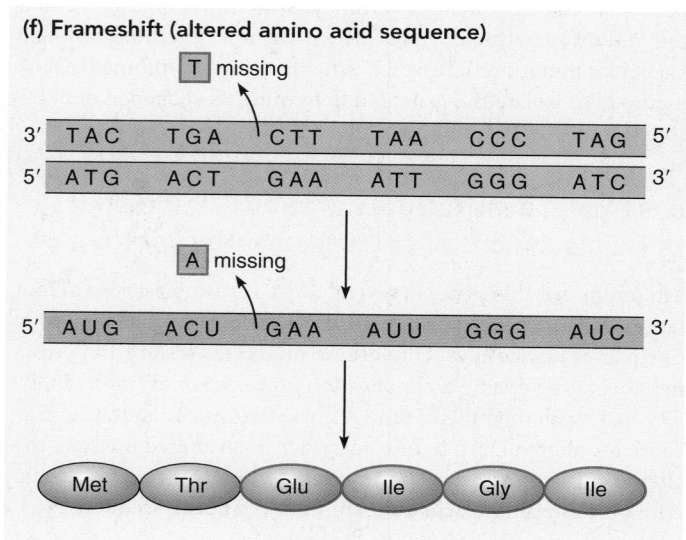

codon within a short distance of the mutation (**FIG. 13-22e**). This codon terminates the already altered polypeptide chain. In addition to producing a stop codon, frameshift mutations can result in an altered amino acid sequence immediately after the change (**FIG. 13-22f**). A frameshift mutation in a gene specifying an enzyme usually results in a complete loss of enzyme activity.

Some mutations involve mobile genetic elements

One type of mutation is caused by DNA sequences that "jump" into the middle of a gene. These movable sequences of DNA are known as **mobile genetic elements,** or **transposons.** Mobile genetic elements not only disrupt the functions of some genes but also inactivate some previously active genes. Transposons were discovered in maize (corn) by the U.S. geneticist Barbara McClintock in the 1950s (**FIG. 13-23**). She observed that certain genes appeared to be turned off and on spontaneously. She deduced that the mechanism involved a segment of DNA that moved from one region of a chromosome to another, where it would inactivate a gene. In recognition of her insightful findings, McClintock was awarded the Nobel Prize in Physiology or Medicine in 1983.

Biologists did not appreciate the significance of transposons until the development of recombinant DNA methods and the discovery of transposons in a wide variety of organisms, including humans. We now know that transposons are segments of DNA that range from a few hundred to several thousand bases. In humans, almost half of our genome consists of transposons.

Several kinds of mobile genetic elements have been identified. One of these, called a **DNA transposon,** moves genetic material from one site to another using a "cut-and-paste" method. DNA transposons are common in bacteria and animals, including humans.

Many mobile genetic elements are **retrotransposons,** which replicate by forming an RNA intermediate. Reverse transcriptase converts them into their original DNA sequence before they jump into a gene. Many retrotransposons enlist a host cell's gene expression machinery to produce reverse transcriptase encoded by the retrotransposon. Because retrotransposons use reverse transcriptase, some biologists hypothesize that certain retrotransposons may have evolved from retroviruses, or vice versa. Scientists think that human cells have fewer than 100 retrotransposons actively jumping around. Nevertheless, retrotransposons are extremely important agents of mutation and therefore increase an organism's ability to evolve. By one estimate, retrotransposons are responsible for about 10% of naturally occurring mutations that cause noticeable phenotypic changes.

Mutations have various causes

Most types of mutations occur infrequently but spontaneously from mistakes in DNA replication or defects in the mitotic or meiotic separation of chromosomes. Some regions of DNA, known as *mutational hot spots,* are much more likely than others to undergo mutation. An example is a short stretch of repeated nucleotides, which can cause DNA polymerase to "slip" while reading the template during replication.

Mutations in certain genes increase the overall mutation rate. For example, a mutation in a gene coding for DNA polymerase may make DNA replication less precise, or a mutation in a gene coding for a repair enzyme may allow more mutations to arise as a result of unrepaired DNA damage.

Not all mutations occur spontaneously. **Mutagens,** which cause many of the types of mutations discussed previously, include various types of radiation—such as X-rays, gamma rays, cosmic rays, and ultraviolet rays—and certain chemicals. Some chemical mutagens react with and modify bases in the DNA, leading to mistakes in complementary base pairing when the DNA molecule is replicated. Other chemical mutagens cause nucleotide pairs to be inserted into or deleted from the DNA molecule, changing the normal reading frame during replication.

Despite the presence of enzymes that repair damage to DNA, some new mutations do arise. In fact, each of us has some mutant alleles that neither of our parents had. Although

Jerome Wexler/Visuals Unlimited

FIGURE 13-23 Transposons in maize

The white lines and streaks in these kernels are caused by transposons that have moved from one location to another, turning off pigment production in certain cells. The number of cell divisions during the development of the kernel since the transposon turned off the gene determines how much pigment is produced. Some kernels are colorless (unpigmented) because the pigment-producing genes were turned off very early in development.

some of these mutations alter the phenotype, most are not noticeable because they are recessive.

Mutations that occur in the cells of the body (somatic cells) are not passed on to offspring. However, these mutations are of concern because somatic mutations and cancer are closely related. Many mutagens are also **carcinogens,** agents that cause cancer.

Review

- What are the main types of mutations?
- What effects does each type of mutation have on the polypeptide product produced?

■ SUMMARY: FOCUS ON LEARNING OBJECTIVES

13.1 (page 283)

1 Summarize the early evidence indicating that most genes specify the structure of proteins.
- Garrod's work on inborn errors of metabolism provided evidence that genes specify proteins. Garrod studied a rare genetic disease called **alkaptonuria** and hypothesized that people with alkaptonuria lack the enzyme that normally oxidizes homogentisic acid.

2 Describe Beadle and Tatum's experiments with *Neurospora*.
- Beadle and Tatum exposed *Neurospora* spores to X-rays or ultraviolet radiation to induce mutant strains, and then identified strains that carried a mutation preventing the fungus from producing a chemical essential for growth. Their work revealed that each mutant strain had a mutation in only one gene and that each gene affected only one enzyme.

13.2 (page 285)

3 Outline the flow of genetic information in cells, from DNA to RNA to polypeptide.
- The process by which information encoded in DNA specifies the sequences of amino acids in proteins involves transcription and translation. During **transcription,** an RNA molecule complementary to the template DNA strand is synthesized. **Messenger RNA (mRNA)** molecules contain information that specifies the amino acid sequences of polypeptide chains.
- During **translation,** a polypeptide chain specified by the mRNA is synthesized. Each sequence of three nucleotide bases in the mRNA constitutes a **codon,** which specifies one amino acid in the polypeptide chain, or a start or stop signal. Translation requires tRNAs and cell machinery, including ribosomes.

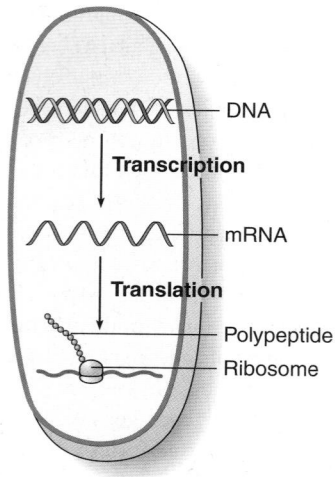

4 Compare the structures of DNA and RNA.
- Like DNA, RNA is formed from nucleotide subunits. However, in RNA each subunit contains the sugar **ribose,** a base (**uracil,** ad-

enine, guanine, or cytosine), and three phosphates. Like DNA, RNA subunits are covalently joined by 5′—3′ linkages to form an alternating sugar–phosphate backbone.

5 Explain why the genetic code is said to be redundant and virtually universal, and discuss how these features may reflect its evolutionary history.
- The **genetic code** is read from mRNA as a series of codons that specify a single sequence of amino acids. The genetic code is redundant because some amino acids are specified by more than one codon. Only a few minor variations are exceptions to the genetic code found in all organisms, strongly suggesting that all organisms are descended from a common ancestor.

13.3 (page 288)

6 Compare the processes of transcription and DNA replication, identifying both similarities and differences.
- **RNA polymerases,** involved in RNA synthesis, have many similarities to DNA polymerases involved in DNA replication. Both enzymes carry out synthesis in the 5′ ⟶ 3′ direction. Both use nucleotides with three phosphate groups as substrates, removing two of the phosphates as the nucleotides are covalently linked to the 3′ end of the newly synthesized strand.
- Just as the paired strands of DNA are **antiparallel,** the template strand of the DNA and its complementary RNA strand are antiparallel. As a result, the DNA template strand is read in its 3′ ⟶ 5′ direction as RNA is synthesized in its 5′ ⟶ 3′ direction.
- The same base-pairing rules are followed as in DNA replication, except that uracil is substituted for thymine.

CENGAGENOW™ Watch transcription unfold by clicking on the figure in CengageNOW.

7 Compare bacterial and eukaryotic mRNAs, and explain the functional significance of their structural differences.
- Eukaryotic genes and their mRNA molecules are more complicated than those of bacteria. After transcription, a **5′ cap** (a modified guanosine triphosphate) is added to the 5′ end of a eukaryotic mRNA molecule. The molecule also has a **poly-A** tail of adenine-containing nucleotides added at the 3′ end. These modifications may protect eukaryotic mRNA molecules from degradation, giving them a longer lifespan than bacterial mRNA.
- In many eukaryotic genes, the coding regions, called **exons,** are interrupted by noncoding regions, called **introns.** Both exons and introns are transcribed, but the introns are later removed from the original **pre-mRNA,** and the exons are spliced together to produce a continuous polypeptide-coding sequence.

13.4 (page 293)

8 Identify the features of tRNA that are important in decoding genetic information and converting it into "protein language."
- **Transfer RNAs (tRNAs)** are the "decoding" molecules in the translation process. Each tRNA molecule is specific for only one amino acid. One part of the tRNA molecule contains an **anticodon** that is

complementary to a codon of mRNA. Attached to one end of the tRNA molecule is the amino acid specified by the complementary mRNA codon.

9 Explain how ribosomes function in polypeptide synthesis.

■ Each **ribosome** is made of a large and a small subunit; each subunit contains **ribosomal RNA (rRNA)** and many proteins. Ribosomes couple the tRNAs to their proper codons on the mRNA, catalyze the formation of peptide bonds between amino acids, and translocate the mRNA so the next codon can be read.

    CENGAGENOW™ Learn more about the structure of ribosomes by clicking on the figure in CengageNOW.

10 Describe the processes of initiation, elongation, and termination in polypeptide synthesis.

■ **Initiation** is the first stage of translation. **Initiation factors** bind to the small ribosomal subunit, which then binds to mRNA in the region of AUG, the **start codon.** The **initiator tRNA** binds to the start codon, followed by binding of the large ribosomal subunit.

■ **Elongation** is a cyclic process in which amino acids are added one by one to the growing polypeptide chain. Elongation proceeds in the 5′ ⟶ 3′ direction along the mRNA.

■ **Termination,** the final stage of translation, occurs when the ribosome reaches one of three **stop codons.** The A site binds to a **release factor,** which triggers the release of the completed polypeptide chain and dissociation of the translation complex.

    CENGAGENOW™ Learn more about protein synthesis by clicking on the figure in CengageNOW.

13.5 *(page 297)*

11 Describe a polyribosome in bacterial cells.

■ Unlike the processes in eukaryotic cells, transcription and translation are coupled in bacterial cells. Bacterial ribosomes bind to the 5′ end of the growing mRNA and initiate translation before the message is fully synthesized. As many as 15 ribosomes may bind to a single mRNA, forming a **polyribosome.**

12 Briefly discuss RNA interference.

■ **RNA interference (RNAi)** occurs when small RNA molecules, such as **small interfering RNAs (siRNAs)** and **microRNAs (miRNAs)** interfere with the expression of genes or their RNA transcripts.

13 Describe retroviruses and the enzyme reverse transcriptase.

■ **Retroviruses** are viruses that synthesize DNA from an RNA template. In retroviruses the flow of genetic information is reversed by the enzyme **reverse transcriptase.** HIV-1, the virus that causes AIDS, is a retrovirus.

13.6 *(page 300)*

14 Give examples of the different classes of mutations that affect the base sequence of DNA and explain the effects that each has on the polypeptide produced.

■ A **base-pair substitution** is a **mutation** that may alter or destroy the function of a protein if a codon changes so that it specifies a different amino acid (a **missense mutation**) or becomes a stop codon (a **nonsense mutation**).

■ The insertion or deletion of one or two base pairs in a gene invariably destroys the function of that protein because it results in a **frameshift mutation,** which changes the codon sequences downstream from the mutation.

■ One type of mutation is caused by movable DNA sequences, known as **transposons,** that "jump" into the middle of a gene. Many transposons are **retrotransposons,** which replicate by forming an RNA intermediate; **reverse transcriptase** converts them to their original DNA sequence before they jump into a gene.

    CENGAGENOW™ Learn more about mutations by clicking on the figure in CengageNOW.

TEST YOUR UNDERSTANDING

1. Beadle and Tatum (a) predicted that tRNA molecules would have anticodons (b) discovered the genetic disease alkaptonuria (c) showed that the genetic disease sickle cell anemia is caused by a change in a single amino acid in a hemoglobin polypeptide chain (d) worked out the genetic code (e) studied the relationship between genes and enzymes in *Neurospora*

2. What is the correct order of information flow in bacterial and eukaryotic cells? (a) DNA ⟶ mRNA ⟶ protein (b) protein ⟶ mRNA ⟶ DNA (c) DNA ⟶ protein ⟶ mRNA (d) protein ⟶ DNA ⟶ mRNA (e) mRNA ⟶ protein ⟶ DNA

3. During transcription, how many RNA nucleotide bases would usually be encoded by a sequence of 99 DNA nucleotide bases? (a) 297 (b) 99 (c) 33 (d) 11 (e) answer is impossible to determine with the information given

4. The genetic code is defined as a series of _____ in _____. (a) anticodons; tRNA (b) codons; DNA (c) anticodons; mRNA (d) codons; mRNA (e) codons and anticodons; rRNA

5. RNA differs from DNA in that the base _____ is substituted for _____. (a) adenine; uracil (b) uracil; thymine (c) guanine; uracil (d) cytosine; guanine (e) guanine; adenine

6. RNA grows in the _____ direction, as RNA polymerase moves along the template DNA strand in the _____ direction. (a) 5′ ⟶ 3′; 3′ ⟶ 5′ (b) 3′ ⟶ 5′; 3′ ⟶ 5′ (c) 5′ ⟶ 3′; 5′ ⟶ 3′ (d) 3′ ⟶ 3′; 5′ ⟶ 5′ (e) 5′ ⟶ 5′; 3′ ⟶ 3′

7. Which of the following is/are *not* found in a bacterial mRNA molecule? (a) stop codon (b) upstream leader sequences (c) downstream trailing sequences (d) start codon (e) promoter sequences

8. Which of the following is/are typically removed from pre-mRNA during nuclear processing in eukaryotes? (a) upstream leader sequences (b) poly-A tail (c) introns (d) exons (e) all the preceding

9. The role of tRNA is to transport (a) amino acids to the ribosome (b) amino acids to the nucleus (c) initiation factors to the ribosome (d) mRNA to the ribosome (e) release factors to the ribosome

10. Suppose you mix the following components of protein synthesis in a test tube: amino acids from a rabbit; ribosomes from a dog; tRNAs from a mouse; mRNA from a chimpanzee; and necessary enzymes plus an energy source from a giraffe. If protein synthesis occurs, which animal's protein will be made? (a) rabbit (b) dog (c) mouse (d) chimpanzee (e) giraffe

11. The _____ catalyzes the excision of introns from pre-mRNA. (a) ribosome (b) spliceosome (c) RNA polymerase enzyme (d) aminoacyl–tRNA synthetase enzyme (e) reverse transcriptase enzyme

12. A nonsense mutation (a) causes one amino acid to be substituted for another in a polypeptide chain (b) results from the deletion of one or two bases, leading to a shift in the reading frame (c) results from the insertion of one or two bases, leading to a shift in the reading frame (d) results from the insertion of a transposon (e) usually results in the formation of an abnormally short polypeptide chain

CRITICAL THINKING

1. Compare and contrast the formation of mRNA in bacterial and eukaryotic cells. How do the differences affect the way in which each type of mRNA is translated? Does one system have any obvious advantage in terms of energy cost? Which system offers greater opportunities for control of gene expression?

2. Biologists hypothesize that transposons eventually lose the ability to replicate and therefore remain embedded in DNA without moving around. Based on what you have learned in this chapter, suggest a possible reason for this loss.

3. How was the genetic code deciphered?

4. Draw an arrow on this figure to show where reverse transcription, catalyzed by the enzyme reverse transcriptase, occurs. Also, show where the enzymes DNA polymerase, RNA polymerase, and peptidyl transferase are involved.

5. **ANALYZING DATA.** You are repeating Beadle and Tatum's classic experiment in biology lab. First, you expose *Neurospora* spores to X-rays, establish a culture from an irradiated spore, and then grow it on (1) a minimal medium plus vitamins, (2) a minimal medium plus amino acids, and (3) a minimal medium. Interpret your results if the fungus grows in *all three* media. Interpret your results if the fungus doesn't grow in *any* of the media.

6. **EVOLUTION LINK.** Because introns are present in all eukaryotes and a few prokaryotes, biologists hypothesize that introns evolved very early in the history of life. If that is true, suggest why the majority of prokaryotes living today lost most of their introns during the course of evolution.

 Additional questions are available in CengageNOW at www.cengage.com/login.

14 Gene Regulation

Specific gene expression in a mouse embryo. This 13.5-day-old mouse embryo has been genetically engineered so that cells that transcribe and express the myogenin gene stain blue. The myogenin gene is expressed only in those cells of the embryo that will give rise to muscle tissue. (The gestation period for a mouse is 18 to 20 days.)

KEY CONCEPTS

14.1 Cells regulate which genes will be expressed and when. Gene regulation in bacteria is primarily in response to stimuli in the environment; gene regulation in eukaryotes helps to maintain homeostasis.

14.2 Gene regulation in bacteria occurs primarily at the level of transcription; regulation of transcription can be either positive or negative.

14.3 Gene regulation in eukaryotes occurs at the levels of transcription, posttranscription, translation, and posttranslation.

Each type of cell in a multicellular organism has a characteristic shape, carries out very specific activities, and makes a distinct set of proteins. Yet with few exceptions, all cells in an organism contain the same genetic information. Why, then, aren't cells identical in structure, molecular composition, and function? Cells differ because gene expression is regulated, and only certain subsets of the total genetic information are expressed in any given cell (see photograph).

What mechanisms control gene expression? Consider a gene coding for a protein that is an enzyme. Expressing that gene involves three basic steps: transcribing the gene to form messenger RNA (mRNA), translating the mRNA into protein, and activating the protein so it can catalyze a specific reaction in the cell. Thus, gene expression results from a series of processes, each of which is regulated in many ways. The control mechanisms use various signals, some originating within the cell and others coming from other cells or from the environment. These signals interact with DNA, RNA, or protein.

Mechanisms that regulate gene expression include control of the amount of mRNA transcribed, of the rate of translation of mRNA, and of the activity of the protein product. These controls are accomplished in several ways. For example, the rate of transcription and the rate of mRNA degradation both control the amount of available mRNA.

Although bacteria are not multicellular, regulation of gene expression is also essential for their survival. Gene regulation in bacteria often involves controlling the transcription of genes whose products are involved in resource use. In eukaryotes, by contrast, fine-tuning the control systems occurs at *all* levels of gene regulation. Involving all levels of gene regulation is consistent with the greater complexity of eukaryotic cells and the need for developmental controls in multicellular organisms.

14.1 GENE REGULATION IN BACTERIA AND EUKARYOTES: AN OVERVIEW

■ LEARNING OBJECTIVE

1 Explain why bacterial and eukaryotic cells have different mechanisms of gene regulation.

Bacterial and eukaryotic cells use distinctly different mechanisms of gene regulation, based on the specific requirements of the organism. Bacterial cells can exist independently, and each cell performs all its own essential functions. Because they grow rapidly and have relatively short times between cell division events, bacteria carry fewer chemical components.

Expression of bacterial genes occurs when it helps bacteria adjust to their environment, including any food that might be present in the surroundings. The primary requirement of bacterial gene regulation is the production of enzymes and other proteins when needed, and **transcriptional-level control** is the most efficient mechanism.

The organization of related genes into groups that are rapidly turned on and off as units allows the synthesis of only the gene products needed at any particular time. This type of regulation requires rapid turnover of mRNA molecules to prevent messages from accumulating and continuing to be translated when they are not needed. Bacteria rarely regulate enzyme levels by degrading proteins. Once the synthesis of a protein ends, the previously synthesized protein molecules are diluted so rapidly in subsequent cell divisions that breaking them down is usually not necessary. Only when cells are starved or deprived of essential amino acids do

protein-digesting enzymes recycle amino acids by breaking down proteins no longer needed for survival.

Eukaryotic cells have different regulatory requirements. Although transcriptional-level control predominates, control at other levels of gene expression is also very important, especially in multicellular organisms, in which groups of cells cooperate with one another in a division of labor. Because a single gene is regulated in different ways in different types of cells, eukaryotic gene regulation is complex.

Eukaryotic cells usually have a long lifespan during which they may need to maintain homeostasis while responding to many different stimuli. New enzymes are not necessarily synthesized each time the cells respond to a stimulus; instead, in many instances pre-formed enzymes and other proteins are rapidly converted from an inactive to an active state. Some cells have a large store of inactive messenger RNA; for example, the mRNA of an egg cell becomes activated when the egg is fertilized.

Much gene regulation in multicellular organisms is focused on the differential expression of genes in the cells in various tissues. Each type of cell has certain genes that are active and other genes that may never be used. For example, developing red blood cells produce the oxygen transport protein hemoglobin, whereas muscle cells never produce hemoglobin but instead produce myoglobin, a related protein coded for by a different gene that stores oxygen in muscle tissues. Apparently, the selective advantages of cell cooperation in multicellular eukaryotes far outweigh the detrimental effects of carrying a load of inactive genes through many cell divisions.

The domesticated pig provides another example of how gene regulation in multicellular organisms affects expression in different tissues. In 2003, biologists reported details of a genetic mutation in pigs that makes them develop more muscle tissue (**FIG. 14-1**). The mutation is in a gene, designated **insulin-like growth factor**

FIGURE 14-1 A lean pig with a mutation in the *IGF2* gene
Years ago, farmers discovered a pig with more muscle and less fat. They selectively bred this pig, and today most commercial pig populations have the mutation that confers this trait. The mutation, which was recently identified as a substitution of a guanine nucleotide for an adenine nucleotide, occurs in a nonprotein-coding region of the *IGF2* gene.

2 (IGF2), which codes for a protein produced by both muscle and liver tissues. The biologists found that a *base-substitution mutation* (see Chapter 13) in the *IGF2* gene makes the gene 3 times more active in pig muscles, resulting in leaner meat. However, the mutation does not change expression of the gene in liver cells. Interestingly, this mutation is not in the protein-coding portion of the gene but in a nonprotein-coding, and presumably regulatory, region.

Review

- What is the most efficient mechanism of gene regulation in bacteria?
- How would you contrast gene regulation in prokaryotes with that in eukaryotes?

14.2 GENE REGULATION IN BACTERIA

■ LEARNING OBJECTIVES

2 Define *operon* and explain the functions of the operator and promoter regions.
3 Distinguish among inducible, repressible, and constitutive genes.
4 Differentiate between positive and negative control, and show how both types of control operate in regulating the *lac* operon.
5 Describe the types of posttranscriptional control in bacteria.

The *Escherichia coli* bacterium is common in the intestines of humans and other mammals. It has 4288 genes that code for proteins, approximately 60% of which have known functions. Some of these genes encode proteins that are always needed (such as enzymes involved in glycolysis). These genes, which are constantly transcribed, are **constitutive genes,** and biologists describe them as *constitutively expressed.* Other proteins are needed only when the bacterium is growing under certain conditions.

For instance, bacteria living in the colon of an adult cow are not normally exposed to the milk sugar lactose, a disaccharide. If those cells ended up in the colon of a calf, however, they would have lactose available as a source of energy. This situation presents a dilemma. Should a bacterial cell invest energy and materials to produce lactose-metabolizing enzymes just in case it ends up in the digestive system of a calf? Yet if *E. coli* cells could not produce those enzymes, they might starve in the middle of an abundant food supply. Thus, *E. coli* functions by regulating many enzymes to efficiently use available organic molecules.

Cell metabolic activity is controlled in two ways: by regulating the *activity* of certain enzymes (how effectively an enzyme molecule works) and/or by regulating the *number* of enzyme molecules present in each cell. Some enzymes are regulated in both ways.

An *E. coli* cell growing on glucose needs about 800 different enzymes. Some are present in large numbers, whereas only a few molecules of others are required. For the cell to function properly, the quantity of each enzyme must be efficiently controlled.

Bacteria respond to changing environmental conditions. If lactose is added to a culture of *E. coli* cells, they rapidly synthesize the three enzymes needed to metabolize lactose. Bacteria respond so efficiently because functionally related genes—such as the three

genes involved in lactose metabolism—are regulated together in gene complexes called *operons.*

Operons in bacteria facilitate the coordinated control of functionally related genes

The French researchers François Jacob and Jacques Monod are credited with the first demonstration, in 1961, of gene regulation at the biochemical level through their elegant studies on the genes that code for the enzymes that metabolize lactose. In 1965, they received the Nobel Prize in Physiology or Medicine for their discoveries relating to genetic control of enzymes.

To use lactose as an energy source, *E. coli* cells first cleave the sugar into the monosaccharides glucose and galactose, using the enzyme β-galactosidase. Another enzyme converts galactose to glucose, and enzymes in the glycolysis pathway further break down the resulting two glucose molecules (see Chapter 8).

E. coli cells growing on glucose produce very little β-galactosidase enzyme. However, each cell grown on lactose as the sole carbon source has several thousand β-galactosidase molecules, accounting for about 3% of the cell's total protein. Amounts of two other enzymes, lactose permease and galactoside transacetylase, also increase when the cells are grown on lactose. The cell needs permease to transport lactose efficiently across the bacterial plasma membrane; without it, only small amounts of lactose enter the cell. The transacetylase may function in a minor aspect of lactose metabolism, although its role is not clear.

Jacob and Monod identified mutant strains of *E. coli* in which a single genetic defect wiped out all three enzymes. This finding, along with other information, led the researchers to conclude that the DNA coding sequences for all three enzymes are linked as a unit on the bacterial DNA and are controlled by a common mechanism. Each enzyme-coding sequence is a **structural gene.** Jacob and Monod coined the term **operon** for a gene complex consisting of a group of structural genes with related functions plus the closely linked DNA sequences responsible for controlling them. The structural genes of the *lac* operon (lactose operon)—*lacZ, lacY,* and *lacA*—code for β-galactosidase, lactose permease, and transacetylase, respectively (**FIG. 14-2**).

Transcription of the *lac* operon begins as RNA polymerase binds to a single **promoter** region *upstream* from the coding sequences. It then proceeds to transcribe the DNA, forming a single mRNA molecule that contains the coding information for all three enzymes. Each enzyme-coding sequence on this mRNA contains its own start and stop codons; thus, the mRNA is translated to form three separate polypeptides. Because all three enzymes are translated from the same mRNA molecule, their synthesis is coordinated by turning a single molecular "switch" on or off.

The switch that controls mRNA synthesis is the **operator,** which is a sequence of bases upstream from the first structural gene in the operon. In the absence of lactose, a **repressor protein** called the **lactose repressor** binds tightly to the operator. RNA polymerase binds to the promoter but is blocked from transcribing the protein-coding genes of the *lac* operon.

The lactose repressor protein is encoded by a **repressor gene,** which in this case is an adjacent structural gene located upstream

The structural genes of the *lac* operon are coordinately controlled and transcribed as a single mRNA.

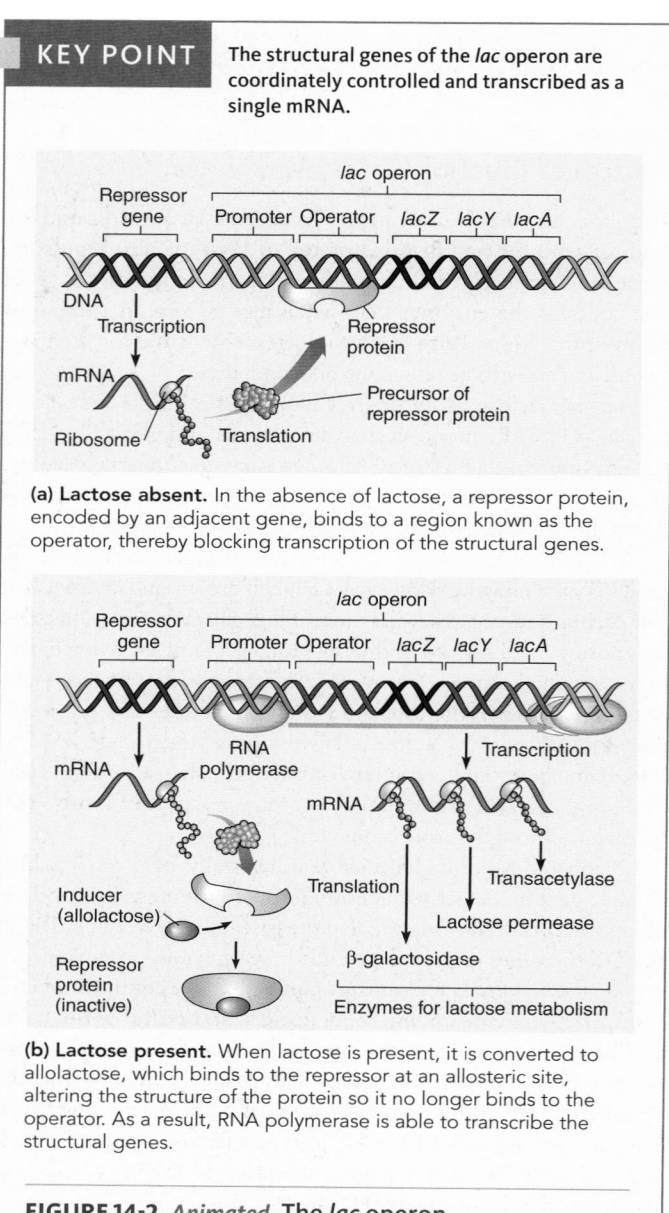

(a) Lactose absent. In the absence of lactose, a repressor protein, encoded by an adjacent gene, binds to a region known as the operator, thereby blocking transcription of the structural genes.

(b) Lactose present. When lactose is present, it is converted to allolactose, which binds to the repressor at an allosteric site, altering the structure of the protein so it no longer binds to the operator. As a result, RNA polymerase is able to transcribe the structural genes.

FIGURE 14-2 *Animated* The *lac* operon

from the promoter site. Unlike the *lac* operon genes, the repressor gene is constitutively expressed and is therefore constantly transcribed; the cell continuously produces small amounts of the repressor protein.

The repressor protein binds specifically to the *lac* operator sequence. When cells grow in the absence of lactose, a repressor molecule nearly always occupies the operator site. When the operator site is briefly free of the repressor, the cell synthesizes a small amount of mRNA. However, the cell synthesizes very few enzyme molecules because *E. coli* mRNA is degraded rapidly (it has a half-life of about 2 to 4 minutes).

Lactose "turns on," or *induces,* the transcription of the *lac* operon because the lactose repressor protein contains a second functional region (an *allosteric site;* see Chapter 7) separate from its DNA-binding site. This allosteric site binds to allolactose, a struc-

tural isomer made from lactose. If lactose is in the growth medium, a few molecules enter the cell and are converted to allolactose by the few β-galactosidase molecules present. The binding of a molecule of allolactose to the repressor alters the shape of the protein so that its DNA-binding site no longer recognizes the operator. When the repressor molecules have allolactose bound to them and are therefore inactivated, RNA polymerase actively transcribes the structural genes of the operon.

The *E. coli* cell continues to produce β-galactosidase and the other *lac* operon enzymes until it uses up virtually all the lactose. When the intracellular level of lactose drops, so too does the concentration of allolactose. Therefore, allolactose dissociates from the repressor protein, which then assumes a shape that lets the repressor bind to the operator region and shut down transcription of the operon.

Jacob and Monod isolated genetic mutants to study the *lac* operon

How did Jacob and Monod elucidate the functioning of the *lac* operon? Their approach involved the use of mutant strains, which even today are an essential tool of researchers trying to unravel the components of various regulatory systems. Genetic crosses of mutant strains allow investigators to determine the *map positions* (linear order) of the genes on the DNA and to infer normal gene functions by studying what happens when they are missing or altered. Researchers usually combine this information with the results of direct biochemical studies.

Jacob and Monod divided their mutant strains into two groups, based on whether a particular mutation affected only one enzyme or all three (**FIG. 14-3**). In one group, only one enzyme of the three—β-galactosidase, lactose permease, or galactoside transacetylase—was affected. Subsequent gene-mapping studies showed these were mutations in structural genes located next to each other in a linear sequence.

Jacob and Monod also studied regulatory mutants in which a single mutation affected the expression of all three enzymes. Some of the regulatory mutants transcribed the structural genes of the *lac* operon at a significant rate, even in the absence of lactose, causing the cell to waste energy in producing unneeded enzymes. One group of these gene mutations had map positions just outside the *lac* operon. Jacob and Monod hypothesized the existence of a repressor gene that codes for a repressor molecule (later found to be a protein). Although the specific defect may vary, the members of this group of mutants produce defective repressors; hence, no binding to the *lac* operator and promoter takes place, and the *lac* operon is constitutively expressed.

In contrast, some regulatory mutants failed to transcribe the *lac* operon even when lactose was present. Researchers eventually found that each of these abnormal genes coded for a repressor with an abnormal binding site that prevented allolactose from binding, although the repressor could still bind to the operator. Once bound to the operator, such a mutant repressor remained bound, keeping the operon "turned off."

The genes responsible for another group of regulatory mutants had map positions within the *lac* operon but did not directly involve any of the three structural genes. Jacob and Monod hypothesized that the members of this group produced normal repressor mol-

FIGURE 14-3 Genetic and biochemical characterization of the *lac* operon
The diagram shows how Jacob and Monod inferred conclusions based on their experimental results.

ecules but had abnormal operator sequences incapable of binding to the repressor.

An inducible gene is not transcribed unless a specific inducer inactivates its repressor

Geneticists call the *lac* operon an **inducible operon.** A repressor usually controls an inducible gene or operon by keeping it "turned off." The presence of an **inducer** (in this case, allolactose) inactivates the repressor, permitting the gene or operon to be transcribed. Inducible genes or operons usually code for enzymes that are part of catabolic pathways, which break down molecules to provide both energy and components for anabolic reactions. This type of regulatory system lets the cell save the energy cost of making enzymes when no substrates are available on which they can act.

A repressible gene is transcribed unless a specific repressor–corepressor complex is bound to the DNA

Another type of gene regulation system in bacteria is associated mainly with anabolic pathways such as those in which cells synthesize amino acids, nucleotides, and other essential biological molecules from simpler materials. Enzymes coded by repressible genes normally regulate these pathways.

Repressible operons and genes are usually "turned on"; they are turned off only under certain conditions. In most cases the mo-

lecular signal for regulating these genes is the end product of the anabolic pathway. When the supply of the end product (such as an amino acid) becomes low, all enzymes in the pathway are actively synthesized. When intracellular levels of the end product rise, enzyme synthesis is repressed. Because the growing cell continuously needs compounds such as amino acids, the most effective mechanism for the cell is to keep the genes that control their production turned on, except when a large supply of the amino acid is available. The ability to turn the genes off prevents cells from overproducing amino acids and other molecules that are essential but expensive to make in terms of energy.

The *trp* operon (tryptophan operon) is an example of a repressible system. In both *E. coli* and a related bacterium, *Salmonella*, the *trp* operon consists of five structural genes that code for the enzymes that the cell needs to synthesize the amino acid tryptophan; these genes are clustered as a transcriptional unit with a single promoter and a single operator (**FIG. 14-4a**). A distant repressor gene codes for a diffusible repressor protein, which differs from the lactose repressor in that the cell synthesizes it in an inactive form that cannot bind to the operator region of the *trp* operon.

The DNA-binding site of the repressor becomes effective only when tryptophan, its **corepressor,** binds to an allosteric site on the repressor (**FIG. 14-4b**). When intracellular tryptophan levels are low, the repressor protein is inactive and cannot bind to the operator region of the DNA. The enzymes required for tryptophan

Structural genes coding for enzymes that synthesize the amino acid tryptophan are organized in a repressible operon.

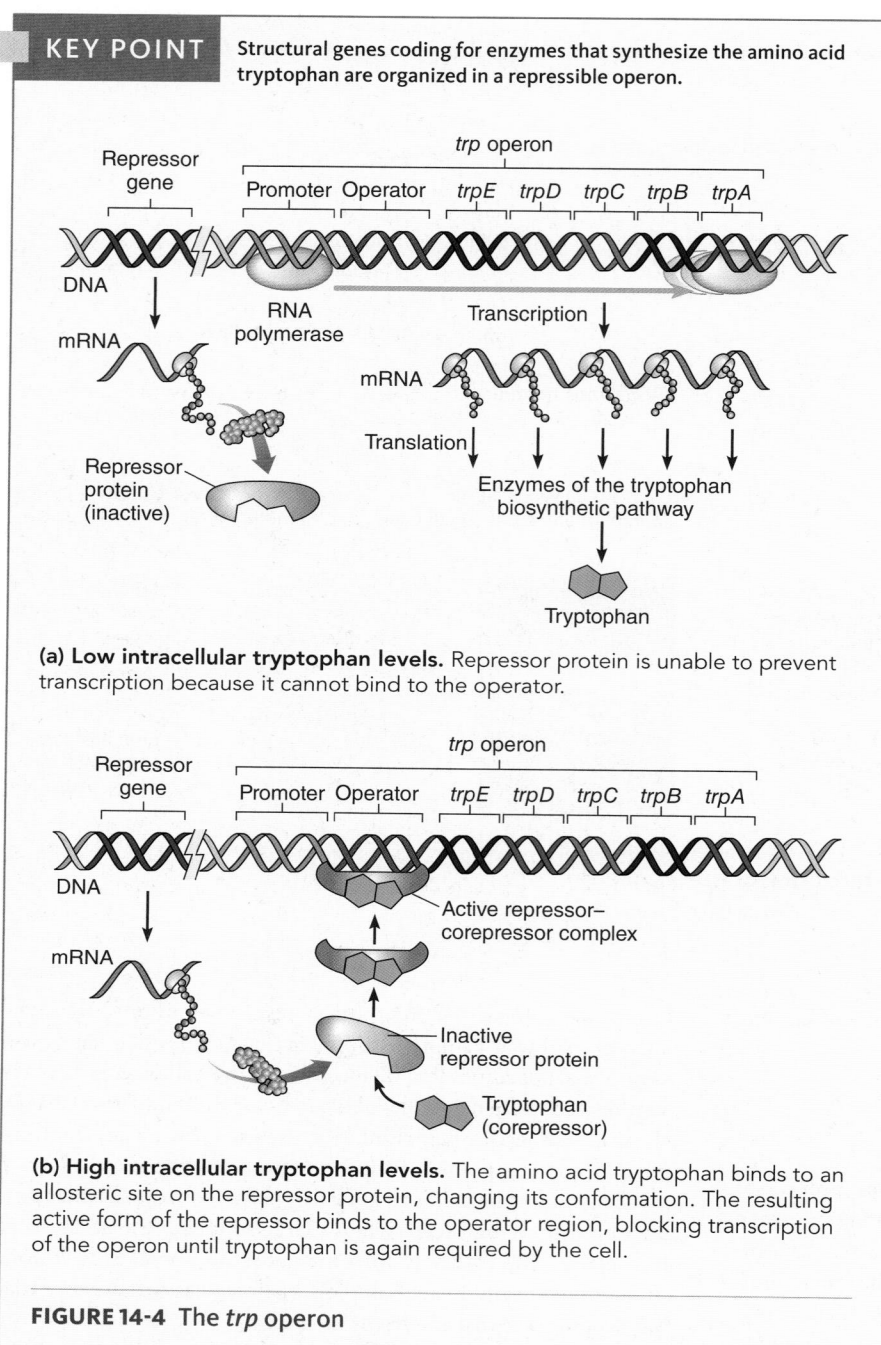

(a) Low intracellular tryptophan levels. Repressor protein is unable to prevent transcription because it cannot bind to the operator.

(b) High intracellular tryptophan levels. The amino acid tryptophan binds to an allosteric site on the repressor protein, changing its conformation. The resulting active form of the repressor binds to the operator region, blocking transcription of the operon until tryptophan is again required by the cell.

FIGURE 14-4 The *trp* operon

synthesis are produced, and the intracellular concentration of tryptophan increases. Some of it binds to the repressor, altering the repressor's shape so it binds tightly to the operator. This switches the operon off, thereby blocking transcription.

Negative regulators inhibit transcription; positive regulators stimulate transcription

The features of the *lac* and *trp* operons we have described so far are examples of **negative control,** a regulatory mechanism in which the DNA binding regulatory protein is a repressor that turns off transcription of the gene. **Positive control** is regulation by acti-

vator proteins that bind to DNA and thereby stimulate the transcription of a gene. The *lac* operon is controlled by both a negative regulator (the lactose repressor) and a positively acting activator protein.

Positive control of the *lac* operon requires the cell to recognize the absence of the sugar glucose, which is the initial substrate in the glycolysis pathway. Lactose, like glucose, undergoes stepwise breakdown to yield energy. However, because glucose is a product of the catabolic hydrolysis of lactose, it is most efficient for *E. coli* cells to use the available supply of glucose first, sparing the cell the considerable energy cost of making additional enzymes such as β-galactosidase (**FIG. 14-5a**).

The *lac* operon has a very inefficient promoter element—that is, it has a low affinity for RNA polymerase, even when the repressor protein is inactivated. However, a DNA sequence adjacent to the promoter site is a binding site for another regulatory protein, the **catabolite activator protein (CAP).** When activated, CAP stimulates transcription of the *lac* operon and several other bacterial operons.

In its active form, CAP is bound by an allosteric site to **cyclic AMP,** or **cAMP,** an alternative form of adenosine monophosphate. Examine Figure 3-25 to see the chemical structure of cAMP. As the cells become depleted of glucose, cAMP levels increase (**FIG. 14-5b**). After the cAMP molecules bind to CAP, the resulting active complex then binds to the CAP-binding site near the *lac* operon promoter. This binding of active CAP bends DNA's double helix (**FIG. 14-6**), strengthening the affinity of the promoter region for RNA polymerase so that the rate of transcriptional initiation accelerates in the presence of lactose. Thus, the *lac* operon is fully active only if lactose is available and intracellular glucose levels are low. **TABLE 14-1** summarizes negative and positive controls in bacteria.

Constitutive genes are transcribed at different rates

Many gene products encoded by *E. coli* DNA are needed only under certain environmental or nutritional conditions. As you have seen, these genes are generally regulated at the level of transcription. They are turned on and off as metabolic and environmental conditions change. By contrast, constitutive genes are continuously transcribed, but they are not necessarily transcribed (or their mRNAs translated) at the same rate. Some enzymes work more effectively or are more stable than others and thus are present in smaller amounts. Constitutive genes that encode proteins required in large amounts generally have greater expression—that is, are transcribed more rapidly—than genes coding for proteins re-

The lactose promoter by itself is weak and binds RNA polymerase inefficiently even when the lactose repressor is inactive.

(a) Lactose high, glucose high, cAMP low. When glucose levels are high, cAMP is low. CAP is in an inactive form and cannot stimulate transcription. Transcription occurs at a low level or not at all.

(b) Lactose high, glucose low, cAMP high. When glucose concentrations are low, each CAP polypeptide has cAMP bound to its allosteric site. The active form of CAP binds to the DNA sequence, and transcription becomes activated.

FIGURE 14-5 Positive control of the *lac* operon

◄ **FIGURE 14-6 The binding of CAP to DNA**

This computer-generated image shows the bend formed in the DNA double helix when it binds to CAP. CAP is a dimer consisting of two identical polypeptide chains, each of which binds one molecule of cAMP.

quired in smaller amounts. The promoter elements of these genes control their transcriptional rate. Constitutive genes with efficient ("strong") promoters bind RNA polymerase more frequently and consequently transcribe more mRNA molecules than those with inefficient ("weak") promoters.

Genes coding for repressor or activator proteins that regulate metabolic enzymes are usually constitutive and produce their protein products constantly. Because each cell usually needs relatively few molecules of any specific repressor or activator protein, promoters for those genes tend to be relatively weak.

Some posttranscriptional regulation occurs in bacteria

As you have seen, much of the variability in protein levels in *E. coli* is determined by transcriptional-level control. However, regulatory mechanisms after transcription, known as **posttranscriptional controls,** also occur at various levels of gene expression.

Translational controls are posttranscriptional controls that regulate the rate at which an mRNA molecule is translated. Because the lifespan of an mRNA molecule in a bacterial cell is very short, one that is translated rapidly produces more proteins than one that is translated slowly. Some mRNA molecules in *E. coli* are translated as much as 1000 times faster than other mRNAs. Most of the differences appear to be due to the rate at which ribosomes attach to the mRNA and begin translation.

Posttranslational controls act as switches that activate or inactivate one or more existing enzymes, thereby letting the cell respond to changes in the intracellular concentrations of essential molecules, such as amino acids. A common posttranslational control adjusts the rate of synthesis in a metabolic pathway through **feedback inhibition.** An example of feedback inhibition is diagrammed in Figure 7-15. The end product of a metabolic pathway binds to an allosteric site on the first enzyme in the pathway, temporarily inactivating the enzyme. When the first enzyme in the pathway does not function, all the succeeding enzymes are deprived of substrates. Notice that feedback inhibition differs from the repression caused by tryptophan discussed previously. In that case, the end product of the pathway (tryptophan) prevented the formation of *new* enzymes. Feedback inhibition acts as a fine-tuning mechanism that regulates the activity of the *existing* enzymes in a metabolic pathway.

TABLE 14-1 Transcriptional Control in Bacteria*

Negative Control	Result
Inducible genes	
Repressor protein alone	Active repressor turns off regulated gene(s)
Lactose repressor alone	*lac* operon not transcribed
Repressor protein + inducer	Inactive repressor–inducer complex fails to turn off regulated gene(s)
Lactose repressor + allolactose	*lac* operon transcribed
Repressible genes	
Repressor protein alone	Inactive repressor fails to turn off regulated gene(s)
Tryptophan repressor alone	*trp* operon transcribed
Repressor protein + corepressor	Active repressor–corepressor complex turns off regulated gene(s)
Tryptophan repressor + tryptophan	*trp* operon not transcribed

Positive Control	Result
Activator protein alone	Activator alone cannot stimulate transcription of regulated gene(s)
CAP alone	Transcription of *lac* operon not stimulated
Activator complex	Functional activator complex stimulates transcription of regulated gene(s)
CAP + cAMP	Transcription of *lac* operon stimulated

*A general description of each type is followed by a specific example.

Review

- What is the function of each of the parts of the *lac* operon (promoter, operator, and structural genes)?
- What structural features does the *trp* operon share with the *lac* operon?
- Why do scientists define the *trp* operon as repressible and the *lac* operon as inducible?
- How is glucose involved in positive control of the *lac* operon?

14.3 GENE REGULATION IN EUKARYOTIC CELLS

■ LEARNING OBJECTIVES

6 Discuss the structure of a typical eukaryotic gene and the DNA elements involved in regulating that gene.

7 Give examples of some of the ways eukaryotic DNA-binding proteins bind to DNA.

8 Illustrate how a change in chromosome structure may affect the activity of a gene.

9 Explain how a gene in a multicellular organism may produce different products in different types of cells.

10 Identify some of the types of regulatory controls that operate in eukaryotes after mature mRNA is formed.

Like bacterial cells, eukaryotic cells respond to changes in their environment. In addition, multicellular eukaryotes require regulation modes that let individual cells commit to specialized roles and let groups of cells organize into tissues and organs. These processes are accomplished mainly by regulating transcription, but posttranscriptional, translational, and posttranslational controls are also important. In Chapters 12 and 13, we observed that in eukaryotes all aspects of information transfer—including replication, transcription, and translation—are more complicated than in prokaryotes. Not surprisingly, this complexity offers more ways to control gene expression.

Unlike many bacterial genes, eukaryotic genes are not typically arranged in operon-like clusters. (A notable exception is the nematodes, or roundworms, in which some genes are organized into operons.) However, each eukaryotic gene has specific regulatory sequences that are essential in controlling transcription.

Many "housekeeping" enzymes (those needed by virtually all cells) are encoded by constitutive genes, which are expressed in all cells at all times. Some inducible genes have also been found; these respond to environmental threats or stimuli, such as heavy-metal ingestion, viral infection, and heat shock. For example, when a cell is exposed to high temperature, many proteins fail to fold properly. These unfolded proteins elicit a survival response in which *heat-shock genes* are transcribed and heat-shock proteins are synthesized. Although the functions of most heat-shock proteins in eukaryotic cells are unknown, some are **molecular chaperones** that help newly synthesized proteins fold into their proper shape (discussed in Chapters 3 and 13).

Some genes are inducible only during certain periods in the life of the organism; they are controlled by **temporal regulation.** Finally, some genes are under **tissue-specific regulation.** For example, a gene involved in production of a particular enzyme may be regulated by one stimulus (such as a hormone) in muscle tissue, by an entirely different stimulus in pancreatic cells, and by a third stimulus in liver cells. We explore these types of regulation in more detail in Chapters 17 and 49.

FIGURE 14-7 summarizes the regulation of gene expression in eukaryotes. You may want to refer to it as you read the following discussion.

Eukaryotic transcription is controlled at many sites and by many regulatory molecules

Like bacterial genes, most genes of multicellular eukaryotes are controlled at the transcriptional level. As you will see, various base sequences in the DNA are important in transcriptional control. In addition, regulatory proteins and the way the DNA is organized in the chromosome affect the rate of transcription.

Chromosome organization affects the expression of some genes

A chromosome is not only a bearer of genes. Various arrangements of a chromosome's ordered components increase or decrease expression of the genes it contains. Figure 10-4 shows the organization of a eukaryotic chromosome. In multicellular eukaryotes, only a subset of the genes in a cell is active at any one time. The inactivated genes differ among cell types and in many cases are irreversibly dormant.

Some of the inactive genes lie in highly compacted chromatin, visible microscopically as densely stained regions of chromosomes during cell division. These regions of chromatin remain tightly coiled and bound to chromosome proteins throughout the cell cycle; even during interphase, they are visible as darkly stained fibers called **heterochromatin** (**FIG. 14-8a**). Evidence suggests that most of the heterochromatin DNA is not transcribed. For example, most of the inactive X chromosome of the two X chromosomes in female mammals is heterochromatic and appears as a *Barr body* (see Fig. 11-16).

Active genes are associated with a more loosely packed chromatin structure called **euchromatin** (**FIG. 14-8b**). The exposure of the DNA in euchromatin lets it interact with *transcription factors* (discussed later in the chapter) and other regulatory proteins.

Cells may have several ways to change chromatin structure from heterochromatin to euchromatin. One way is to chemically modify **histones,** the proteins that associate with DNA to form **nucleosomes.** Each histone molecule has a so-called tail, a string of amino acids that extends from the DNA-wrapped nucleosome (see Fig. 10-2). Methyl groups, acetyl groups, sugars, and even proteins chemically attach to the histone tail and may expose or hide genes, turning them on or off.

Such chemical modifications of histones are the focus of active research because they appear to influence gene expression and therefore offer promise of new approaches to treat cancer and other diseases with a genetic component. Biologists have found general correlations between gene activity and certain chemical groups attached to or absent from histone tails. For

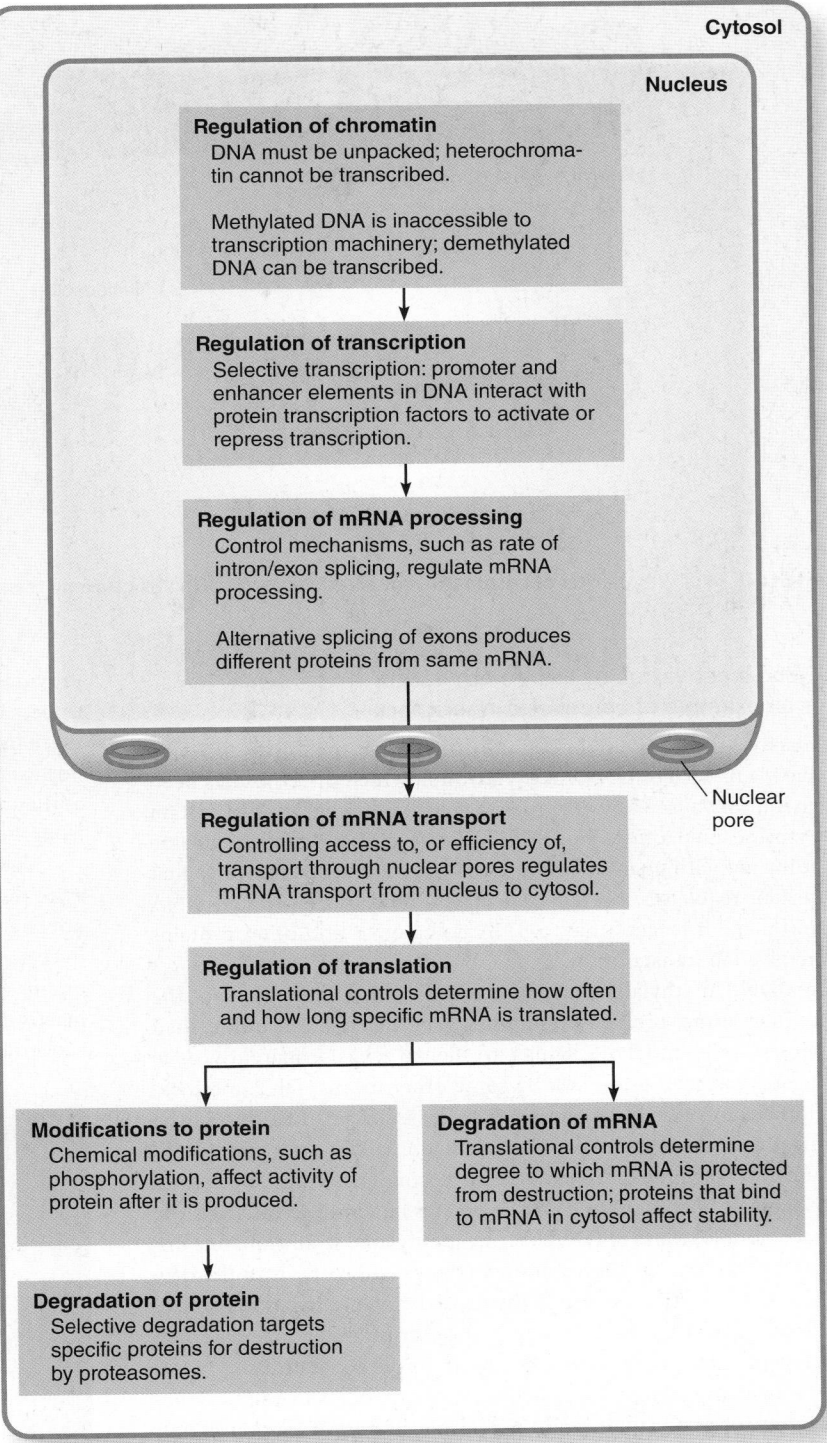

FIGURE 14-7 Gene regulation in eukaryotic cells

example, the genes on DNA in nucleosomes where histone tails are flagged with acetyl groups generally tend to be expressed. Biologists are now trying to determine if specific histone modifications are associated with the activity or inactivity of specific genes within a cell.

(a) Inactive region of DNA.
Heterochromatin is organized into tightly associated nucleosomes.

Heterochromatin: genes silent

Chromatin decondensation

Nucleosome

Histones

DNA

(b) Active region of DNA.
Active genes are found in decondensed chromatin called euchromatin. Euchromatin increases the accessibility to RNA polymerase required for transcription. The histones are physically removed from the DNA in the region where transcription occurs.

Transcribed region

Euchromatin: genes active

FIGURE 14-8 Regulation of chromatin: the effect of chromatin structure on transcription

Gene inactivation by DNA methylation is an example of epigenetic inheritance

Inactive genes of vertebrates and some other organisms typically show a pattern of **DNA methylation** in which the DNA has been chemically altered by enzymes that add methyl groups to certain cytosine nucleotides in DNA. (The resulting 5-methylcytosine still pairs with guanine in the usual way.) Evidence indicates that certain regulatory proteins selectively bind to methylated DNA and make it inaccessible to RNA polymerase and other proteins involved in transcription.

DNA methylation, which is found in inactive regions of the cell's genome, probably reinforces gene inactivation rather than serves as the initial mechanism to silence genes. Apparently, once a gene has been turned off by some other means, DNA methylation ensures it will remain inactive. For example, the DNA of the inactive X chromosome of a female mammal becomes methylated after the chromosome has become a condensed Barr body (see Chapter 11). When the DNA replicates in a mitotic cell division, each double strand of DNA has one methylated strand and one unmethylated strand. Methylation enzymes add methyls to the new strand, thereby perpetuating the pre-existing methylation pattern. Hence, the DNA continues to be transcriptionally inactive in all descendants of these cells, often for multiple generations.

In mammals, DNA methylation maintained in this way accounts for **genomic imprinting** (also called *parental imprinting*), in which the phenotypic expression of certain genes is determined by whether a particular allele is inherited from the female or the male parent. Genomic imprinting is associated with some human genetic diseases, such as *Prader–Willi syndrome* and *Angelman syndrome* (both discussed in Chapter 16).

Genomic imprinting is an example of epigenetics. **Epigenetic inheritance** involves changes in how a gene is expressed. In contrast, *genetic inheritance* involves changes in a gene's nucleotide sequence. Because DNA methylation patterns tend to be passed to successive cell generations during cell division, methylation

provides a mechanism for epigenetic inheritance. Evidence continues to accumulate that epigenetic inheritance is an important mechanism of gene regulation over the lifetime of an individual. For example, the methylation of genes increases in many people as they age, and decreases in others, perhaps in response to signals from the environment.

New phenotypic traits can arise from epigenetic changes despite the fact that the nucleotide sequence of the gene itself has not changed (**FIG. 14-9**). Epigenetic changes have also been linked to certain human diseases, such as cancer. For example, *tumor suppressor genes* that inhibit cell division (and cancer) are sometimes inactivated epigenetically, resulting in cancer. Chapter 17 discusses cancer and tumor suppressor genes. Thus, some inherited charac-

FIGURE 14-9 Epigenetic variation in the *agouti* gene in mice
The DNA of these mice is almost identical, yet their coat colors and body shapes vary significantly. These mice differ in the presence or absence of epigenetic "marks," such as methyl groups on DNA in the region of a gene known as *agouti*.

© Randy Jirtle/Duke University

Drosophila chorion gene

Gene amplification by repeated DNA replication of chorion gene region

Chorion gene in ovarian cell

FIGURE 14-10 Regulation of transcription: gene amplification

In *Drosophila*, multiple replications of a small region of the chromosome amplify the chorion (eggshell) protein genes. Replication is initiated at a discrete chromosome origin of replication (*top pink box*) for each copy of the gene that is produced. Replication is randomly terminated, resulting in a series of forked structures in the chromosome.

teristics do not depend exclusively on the sequence of nucleotides in DNA.

Gene amplification increases the number of copies of a gene

A single gene cannot always provide enough copies of its mRNA to meet the cell's needs. The requirement for high levels of certain products is met if multiple copies of the genes that encode them are present in the chromosome. Genes of this type, whose products are essential for all cells, may occur as multiple copies arranged one after another along the chromosome, in **tandemly repeated gene sequences.** Histone genes are usually present as multiple copies of 50 to 500 genes in cells of multicellular organisms. Similarly, multiple copies (150 to 450) of genes for rRNA and tRNA are present in cells.

Other genes, which are required only by a small group of cells, are selectively replicated in those cells in a process called **gene amplification.** For example, the *Drosophila* chorion (eggshell) gene product is a protein made specifically in cells of the female insect's reproductive tract. These cells make massive amounts of the protein that envelops and protects the zygote. Amplifying the chorion protein gene by DNA replication meets the demand for chorion mRNA. In other words, the DNA in that small region of the chromosome is copied many times (**FIG. 14-10**). In other cells

of the insect body, however, the gene exists as a single copy in the chromosome.

Eukaryotic promoters vary in efficiency, depending on the presence of functional promoter elements

In eukaryotic as well as bacterial cells, the transcription of any gene requires a base pair where transcription begins, known as the **transcription initiation site,** or *start site,* plus a sequence of bases, the *promoter,* to which RNA polymerase binds. The promoter is a relatively short DNA sequence located adjacent to the gene it regulates.

In almost all multicellular eukaryotes, the promoter contains an element called the TATA box. The **TATA box,** which consists of a sequence of DNA nucleotides such as TATAAA is located about 25 to 30 base pairs upstream from the transcription initiation site (**FIG. 14-11**). Studies show that mutations in the TATA box reduce the rate of transcription.

Some eukaryotic genes have promoter elements in addition to the TATA box. Like the TATA box, these promoter elements have a regulatory function and facilitate the expression of the gene. Many eukaryotic promoters have a promoter element of one or more sequences of nucleotide bases located within a short distance (for example, 80 base pairs) upstream of the RNA polymerase–binding site. Mutations in these elements, like mutations in the TATA box, lower the basic level of transcription.

Enhancers increase the rate of transcription, whereas silencers decrease the rate of transcription

Regulated eukaryotic genes commonly have DNA sequences called **enhancers** that help form an active transcription initiation complex. In this way, enhancers increase the rate of RNA synthesis, often by several orders of magnitude.

Enhancers are remarkable in many ways. Although they are present in all cells, a particular enhancer is functional only in certain types of cells. An enhancer regulates a gene on the same DNA molecule from very long distances—up to thousands of base pairs away from the promoter—and is either upstream or downstream of the promoter it regulates. Furthermore, if an enhancer element is experimentally cut out of the DNA and inverted, it still regulates the gene it normally controls.

Many eukaryotic genes are associated with **silencers,** DNA sequences that can decrease transcription. Like enhancers, silencers are often located long distances from the genes they regulate. As you will see, enhancers and silencers work by interacting with DNA-binding proteins that regulate transcription.

FIGURE 14-11 Regulation of transcription: eukaryotic elements

Eukaryotic regulatory elements include the promoter and various enhancers and silencers. The promoter elements help determine the basic level of transcription that normally occurs, whereas the enhancers (and silencers) have the potential to greatly increase (or decrease) that rate of transcription. (For simplicity, the DNA double helix is represented as a rod.)

Transcription factors are regulatory proteins with several functional domains

We previously discussed some DNA-binding proteins that regulate transcription in bacteria. These included the lactose repressor, the tryptophan repressor, and the catabolite activator protein (CAP). Researchers have identified many more DNA-binding proteins that regulate transcription in eukaryotes than in bacteria; these eukaryotic proteins are collectively known as **transcription factors.** Researchers have identified more than 2000 transcription factors in humans.

It is useful to compare regulatory proteins in bacteria and eukaryotes. Many regulatory proteins are modular molecules; that is, they have more than one **domain,** a region with its own tertiary structure and function. Each eukaryotic transcription factor, like the regulatory proteins of bacteria, has a DNA-binding domain plus at least one other domain that is either an activator or a repressor of transcription for a given gene.

Many transcription factors in eukaryotes (and regulatory proteins in bacteria) have similar DNA-binding domains. One example is the *helix-turn-helix* arrangement, consisting of two α-helical segments. One of these, the recognition helix, inserts into the major groove of the DNA without unwinding the double helix. The other helps hold the first one in place (**FIG. 14-12a**). The "turn" in the helix-turn-helix is a sequence of amino acids that forms a sharp bend in the molecule.

Other transcription factors have DNA-binding domains with multiple "zinc fingers," loops of amino acids held together by zinc ions. Each loop includes an α-helix that fits into a groove of the DNA (**FIG. 14-12b**). Certain amino acid functional groups ex-posed in each finger have been shown to recognize specific DNA sequences.

Many transcription factors have DNA-binding domains that function only as pairs, or *dimers.* Many of these transcription factors are known as **leucine zipper proteins** because they are held together by the side chains of leucine and other hydrophobic amino acids (**FIG. 14-12c**). In some cases the two polypeptides that make up the dimer are identical and form a *homodimer.* In other instances they are different, and the resulting *heterodimer* may have very different regulatory properties from those of a homodimer. For a simple and speculative example, let us assume that three regulatory proteins—A, B, and C—are involved in controlling a particular set of genes. These three proteins might associate as dimers in six different ways: three kinds of homodimers (AA, BB, and CC) and three kinds of heterodimers (AB, AC, and BC). Such multiple combinations of regulatory proteins greatly increase the number of possible ways that transcription is controlled.

Transcription in eukaryotes requires multiple regulatory proteins that are bound to different parts of the promoter. The *general transcriptional machinery* is a protein complex that binds to the TATA box of the promoter near the transcription initiation site. That complex is required for RNA polymerase to bind, thereby initiating transcription.

Both enhancers and silencers become functional when specific transcription factors bind to them. **FIGURE 14-13** shows interactions involving an enhancer and a transcription factor that acts as an **activator.** Each activator has at least two functional domains: a DNA recognition site that usually binds to an enhancer and a gene activation site that contacts the target in the general transcriptional machinery. The DNA between the enhancer and promoter

(a) Helix-turn-helix. This portion of a transcription factor (*purple*) contains the helix-turn-helix arrangement. The recognition helix is inserted into the groove of the DNA and is connected to a second helix that helps hold it in place by a sequence of amino acids that form a sharp bend.

(b) Zinc fingers. Regions of certain transcription factors form projections known as "zinc fingers," which insert into the grooves of the DNA and bind to specific base sequences.

(c) Leucine zipper. This leucine zipper protein is a dimer, held together by hydrophobic interactions involving side chains of leucine and other amino acids.

FIGURE 14-12 Regulation of transcription: regulatory proteins

In these illustrations, cylinders represent α-helical regions of regulatory proteins and ribbons represent β-pleated sheets.

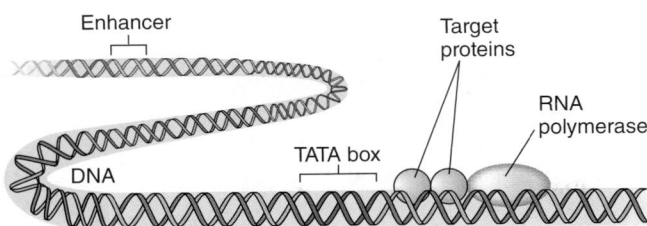

(a) **Low rate of transcription.** This gene is transcribed at a basic level when the general transcriptional machinery, including RNA polymerase, is bound to the promoter.

(b) **High rate of transcription.** A transcription factor that functions as an activator binds to an enhancer. The intervening DNA forms a loop, allowing the transcription factor to contact one or more target proteins in the general transcriptional machinery, thereby increasing the rate of transcription. This diagram is highly simplified, and many more target proteins than the two shown are involved.

FIGURE 14-13 Regulation of transcription: the stimulation of transcription by an enhancer

elements forms a loop that lets an activator bound to an enhancer come in contact with the target proteins associated with the general transcriptional machinery. When this contact occurs, the rate of transcription increases.

The mRNAs of eukaryotes have many types of posttranscriptional control

The half-life of bacterial mRNA is usually minutes long; eukaryotic mRNA, even when it turns over rapidly, is far more stable. Bacterial mRNA is transcribed in a form that is translated immediately. In contrast, eukaryotic mRNA molecules undergo further modification and processing before they are used in protein synthesis. The message is capped, polyadenylated, spliced, and then transported from the nucleus to the cytoplasm to initiate translation (see Fig. 13-12). These events represent potential control points for translation of the message and the production of its encoded protein.

The addition of a **poly-A tail** to eukaryotic mRNA, for example, appears necessary to initiate translation. Researchers have shown that mRNAs with long poly-A tails are efficiently translated, whereas mRNAs with short poly-A tails are essentially dormant. *Polyadenylation,*

which commonly occurs in the nucleus, can also take place in the cytosol. When the short poly-A tail of an mRNA is elongated, the mRNA becomes activated and is then translated.

Some pre-mRNAs are processed in more than one way

Investigators have discovered several forms of regulation involving mRNA processing. In some instances, the same gene produces one type of protein in one tissue and a related but somewhat different type of protein in another tissue. This is possible because many genes produce pre-mRNA molecules that have **alternative splicing** patterns; that is, they are spliced in different ways depending on the tissue.

Typically, such a gene includes at least one segment that can be either an **intron** or an **exon** (see Chapter 13). As an intron, the sequence is removed, but as an exon, it is retained. Through alternative splicing, the cells in each tissue produce their own version of mRNA corresponding to the particular gene (**FIG. 14-14**). For example, this mechanism produces different forms of troponin, a protein that regulates muscle contraction, in different muscle tissues.

The stability of mRNA molecules varies

Controlling the lifespan of a particular kind of mRNA molecule permits control over the number of protein molecules translated from it. In some cases, mRNA stability is under hormonal control. This is true for mRNA that codes for vitellogenin, a protein synthesized in the liver of certain female animals, such as frogs and chickens. Vitellogenin is transported to the oviduct, where it is used in forming egg yolk proteins.

The hormone estradiol regulates vitellogenin synthesis. When estradiol levels are high, the half-life of vitellogenin mRNA in frog liver is about 500 hours. When researchers deprive cells of estradiol, the half-life of the mRNA drops rapidly, to less than 165 hours. This quickly lowers cell vitellogenin mRNA levels and decreases synthesis of the vitellogenin protein. In addition to affecting mRNA stability, the hormone seems to control the rate at which the mRNA is synthesized.

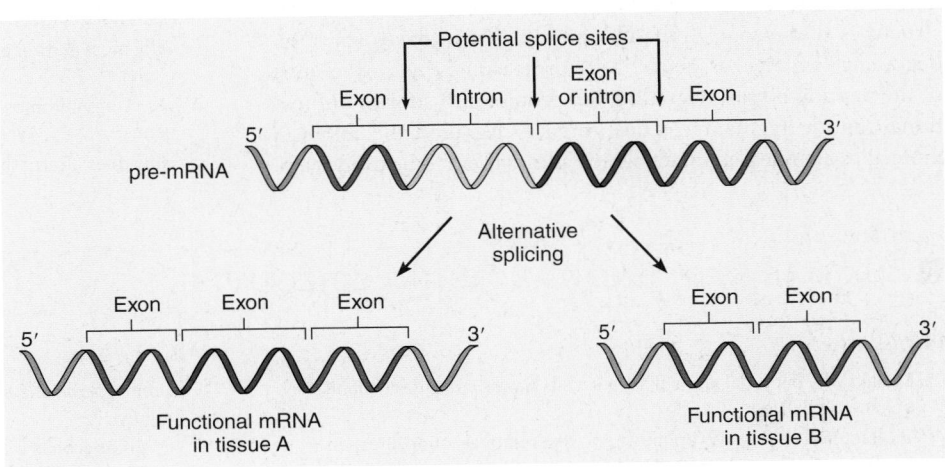

FIGURE 14-14 Regulation of mRNA processing: alternative splicing

In some cases, a pre-mRNA molecule is processed in more than one way to yield two or more mature mRNAs, each of which encodes a related, but different, protein. In this generalized example, the gene contains a segment that can be an exon in tissue A (*left*) but an intron in tissue B (*right*).

Posttranslational chemical modifications may alter the activity of eukaryotic proteins

Another way to control gene expression is by regulating the activity of the gene product. Many metabolic pathways in eukaryotes, as in bacteria, contain allosteric enzymes regulated through feedback inhibition. In addition, after they are synthesized, many eukaryotic proteins are extensively modified.

In **proteolytic processing,** proteins are synthesized as inactive precursors, which are converted to an active form by the removal of a portion of the polypeptide chain. For example, proinsulin contains 86 amino acids. Removing 35 amino acids yields the hormone insulin, which consists of two polypeptide chains containing 30 and 21 amino acids, respectively, linked by disulfide bridges.

Chemical modification, by adding or removing functional groups, reversibly alters the activity of an enzyme. One common way to modify the activity of an enzyme or other protein is to add or remove phosphate groups. Enzymes that add phosphate groups are called **kinases;** those that remove them are **phosphatases.** For example, the cyclin-dependent kinases discussed in Chapter 10 help control the cell cycle by adding phosphate groups to certain key proteins, causing them to become activated or inactivated. Chemical modifications such as protein phosphorylation also let the cell respond rapidly to certain hormones, or to fast-changing environmental or nutritional conditions.

Posttranslational control of gene expression can also involve **protein degradation.** The amino acid found at the amino end of a protein correlates with whether the protein is long-lived or short-lived. Some proteins, for example, have a 50% turnover of synthesis and degradation every 3 days. Other proteins, such as proteins in the lens of the human eye, may persist for the entire life of the individual.

Proteins that are selectively targeted for destruction are covalently bonded to **ubiquitin,** a small polypeptide tag that contains 76 amino acids. Additional molecules of ubiquitin are added, forming short chains attached to the soon-to-be degraded protein (**FIG. 14-15**). A protein tagged by ubiquitin is targeted for degradation in a proteasome. **Proteasomes** are large macromolecular structures that recognize the ubiquitin tags. **Proteases** (protein-degrading enzymes) associated with proteasomes hydrolyze some of the peptide bonds, degrading the protein into short, nonfunctional peptide fragments. As the protein is degraded, the ubiquitin molecules are released intact, which allows them to be used again.

① Ubiquitin molecules attach to protein targeted for degradation.

② Protein enters proteasome.

③ Ubiquitins are released and available for reuse. Protein is degraded into peptide fragments.

FIGURE 14-15 Degradation of protein: ubiquitin and proteasomes

Review

- How does regulation of eukaryotic genes differ from regulation of bacterial genes?
- Why must certain genes in eukaryotic cells be present in multiple copies?
- How does chromosome structure affect the activity of some eukaryotic genes?
- How does alternative splicing give rise to different proteins?

■ SUMMARY: FOCUS ON LEARNING OBJECTIVES

14.1 *(page 308)*

1 Explain why bacterial and eukaryotic cells have different mechanisms of gene regulation.

- Bacterial cells grow rapidly and have a relatively short lifespan. **Transcriptional-level control** is the most common way for the prokaryotic cell to regulate gene expression.
- Eukaryotic cells usually have a relatively long lifespan, during which they must maintain homeostasis in response to many different stimuli. Although transcriptional-level control predominates, control at other levels of gene expression is also important.

14.2 *(page 309)*

2 Define *operon* and explain the functions of the operator and promoter regions.

- An **operon** is a gene complex consisting of a group of **structural genes** with related functions plus the closely linked DNA sequences responsible for controlling them.
- Each operon has a single **promoter** region upstream from the protein-coding regions; the promoter is where RNA polymerase first binds to DNA before transcription begins.

- The **operator** serves as the regulatory switch for transcriptional-level control of the operon. The binding of a **repressor protein** to the operator sequence prevents transcription; although RNA polymerase binds to the promoter, it is blocked from transcribing the structural genes. When the repressor is not bound to the operator, transcription proceeds.

3 Distinguish among inducible, repressible, and constitutive genes.
- An **inducible operon,** such as the *lac* operon, is normally turned off. The repressor protein is synthesized in an active form that binds to the operator. If lactose is present, it is converted to allolactose, the **inducer,** which binds to the repressor protein. The altered repressor cannot bind to the operator, and the operon is turned on.

  CENGAGENOW™ Watch the lactose operon in action by clicking on the figure in CengageNOW.

- A **repressible operon,** such as the *trp* operon, is normally turned on. The repressor protein is synthesized in an inactive form that cannot bind to the operator. A metabolite (usually the end product of a metabolic pathway) acts as a **corepressor.** When corepressor levels are high, a corepressor molecule binds to the repressor, which can now bind to the operator and turn off transcription of the operon.
- **Constitutive genes** are neither inducible nor repressible; they are active at all times. The activity of constitutive genes is controlled by how efficiently RNA polymerase binds to their promoter regions.

4 Differentiate between positive and negative control, and show how both types of control operate in regulating the *lac* operon.
- Repressible and inducible operons are under **negative control.** When the repressor protein binds to the operator, transcription of the operon is turned off.
- Some inducible operons are also under **positive control,** in which an activator protein binds to the DNA and stimulates transcription of the gene. **Catabolite activator protein (CAP)** activates the *lac* operon; CAP binds to the promoter region, stimulating transcription by binding RNA polymerase tightly. To bind, CAP requires **cyclic AMP (cAMP),** which increases in the cell as glucose decreases.

5 Describe the types of posttranscriptional control in bacteria.
- Some **posttranscriptional controls** operate in bacteria. A **translational control** is a posttranscriptional control that regulates the rate of translation of a particular mRNA. **Posttranslational controls** include **feedback inhibition** of key enzymes in some metabolic pathways.

14.3 *(page 314)*

6 Discuss the structure of a typical eukaryotic gene and the DNA elements involved in regulating that gene.
- Eukaryotic genes are not normally organized into operons. Regulation of eukaryotic genes occurs at the levels of transcription, mRNA processing, translation, and modifications of the protein product.
- Transcription of a gene requires a **transcription initiation site,** where transcription begins, plus a promoter to which RNA polymerase binds. In almost all multicellular eukaryotes, the promoter contains an element called the **TATA box** that has a regulatory function and facilitates expression of the gene.

- Some eukaryotic genes have **enhancers** and **silencers** located thousands of bases away from the promoter. These regulatory elements increase or decrease the rate of transcription.

7 Give examples of some of the ways eukaryotic DNA-binding proteins bind to DNA.
- Eukaryotic genes are controlled by DNA-binding proteins called **transcription factors.** Many are transcriptional activators; others are transcriptional repressors.
- Each transcription factor has a DNA-binding **domain.** Some transcription factors have a helix-turn-helix arrangement and insert one of the helices into the DNA. Other transcription factors have loops of amino acids held together by zinc ions; each loop includes an α-helix that fits into the DNA. Some transcription factors are **leucine zipper proteins** that associate as dimers that insert into the DNA.

8 Illustrate how a change in chromosome structure may affect the activity of a gene.
- Densely packed regions of chromosomes, called **heterochromatin,** contain inactive genes. Active genes are associated with a loosely packed chromatin structure called **euchromatin.** Methyl groups, acetyl groups, sugars, and proteins may chemically attach to the **histone** tail, a string of amino acids that extends from the DNA-wrapped **nucleosome,** and may expose or hide genes, turning them on or off.
- **DNA methylation** perpetuates gene inactivation. **Epigenetic inheritance** is an important mechanism of gene regulation that involves changes in how a gene is expressed. Because DNA methylation patterns tend to be repeated in successive cell generations, they provide a mechanism for epigenetic inheritance.
- Some genes whose products are required in large amounts exist as multiple copies in the chromosome. In the process of **gene amplification,** some cells selectively amplify genes by DNA replication.

9 Explain how a gene in a multicellular organism may produce different products in different types of cells.
- As a result of **alternative splicing,** a single gene produces different forms of a protein in different tissues, depending on how the pre-mRNA is spliced. Typically, such a gene contains a segment that can be either an intron or an exon. As an intron, the sequence is removed, and as an exon, the sequence is retained.

10 Identify some of the types of regulatory controls that operate in eukaryotes after mature mRNA is formed.
- Certain regulatory mechanisms increase the stability of mRNA, allowing more protein molecules to be synthesized before mRNA degradation. Sometimes mRNA stability is under hormonal control.
- Posttranslational control of eukaryotic genes occurs by feedback inhibition or by modification of the protein structure. The function of a protein is changed by **kinases** adding phosphate groups or by **phosphatases** removing phosphates.
- Posttranslational control of gene expression also involves **protein degradation.** Proteins targeted for destruction are covalently bonded to **ubiquitin,** which tags it for degradation in a **proteasome,** a large macromolecular structure. **Proteases** associated with proteasomes degrade the protein into short peptide fragments.

TEST YOUR UNDERSTANDING

1. The regulation of most bacterial genes occurs at the level of (a) transcription (b) translation (c) replication (d) posttranslation (e) postreplication

2. The operator of an operon (a) encodes information for the repressor protein (b) is the binding site for the inducer (c) is the binding site for the repressor protein (d) is the binding site for RNA polymerase (e) encodes the information for the CAP

3. A mutation that inactivates the repressor gene of the *lac* operon results in (a) the continuous transcription of the structural genes (b) no transcription of the structural genes (c) the binding of the repressor to the operator (d) no production of RNA polymerase (e) no difference in the rate of transcription

4. A repressible operon codes for the enzymes of the following pathway.

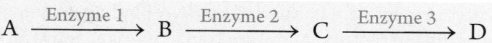

Which component of the pathway is most likely to be the corepressor for that operon? (a) substance A (b) substance B or C (c) substance D (d) enzyme 1 (e) enzyme 3

5. Feedback inhibition is an example of control at the level of (a) transcription (b) translation (c) posttranslation (d) replication (e) all the preceding

6. Which of the following is an example of positive control? (a) transcription occurs when a repressor binds to an inducer (b) transcription cannot occur when a repressor binds to a corepressor (c) transcription is stimulated when an activator protein binds to DNA (d) a and b (e) a and c

7. The "zipper" of a leucine zipper protein attaches (a) specific amino acids to specific DNA base pairs (b) two polypeptide chains to

each other (c) one DNA region to another DNA region (d) amino acids to zinc atoms (e) RNA polymerase to the operator

8. Inactive genes tend to be found in (a) highly condensed chromatin, known as euchromatin (b) decondensed chromatin, known as euchromatin (c) highly condensed chromatin, known as heterochromatin (d) decondensed chromatin, known as heterochromatin (e) chromatin that is not organized as nucleosomes

9. Which of the following is characteristic of genes and gene regulation in bacteria, but *not* in eukaryotes? (a) presence of enhancers (b) capping of mRNAs (c) many chromosomes per cell (d) binding of DNA to regulatory proteins (e) no requirement for exon splicing

10. Which of the following is characteristic of genes and gene regulation in *both* bacteria and eukaryotes? (a) promoters (b) noncoding DNA within coding sequences (c) enhancers (d) operons (e) DNA located in a nucleus

11. Through alternative splicing, eukaryotes (a) reinforce gene inactivation (b) prevent transcription of heterochromatin (c) produce related but different proteins in different tissues (d) amplify genes to meet the requirement of high levels of a gene product (e) bind transcription factors to enhancers to activate transcription

CRITICAL THINKING

1. Compare the types of bacterial genes associated with inducible operons, those associated with repressible operons, and those that are constitutive. Predict the category into which each of the following would most likely fit: (a) a gene that codes for RNA polymerase, (b) a gene that codes for an enzyme required to break down maltose, (c) a gene that codes for an enzyme used in the synthesis of adenine.

2. The regulatory gene that codes for the tryptophan repressor is not tightly linked to the *trp* operon. Would it be advantageous if it were? Explain your answer.

3. **EVOLUTION LINK.** Suggest why evolution resulted in multiple levels of gene regulation in multicellular eukaryotes.

4. **EVOLUTION LINK.** Comparing DNA sequences in different species indicates that more DNA segments that do not code for protein have been conserved (unchanged) than protein-coding regions. These nonprotein-coding regions are interpreted as gene regulatory elements. Suggest why gene regulatory elements have not undergone many changes during the course of evolution.

5. **ANALYZING DATA.** Develop a simple hypothesis that would explain the behavior of each of the following types of mutants in *E. coli*:

Mutant a: The map position of this mutation is in the *trp* operon. The mutant cells are constitutive; that is, they produce all the enzymes coded for by the *trp* operon, even if large amounts of tryptophan are present in the growth medium.

Mutant b: The map position of this mutation is in the *trp* operon. The mutant cells do not produce any enzymes coded for by the *trp* operon under any conditions.

Mutant c: The map position of this mutation is some distance from the *trp* operon. The mutant cells are constitutive; that is, they produce all the enzymes coded for by the *trp* operon, even if the growth medium contains large amounts of tryptophan.

6. **ANALYZING DATA.** You are studying the rate of transcription of a particular eukaryotic gene. When the DNA located several thousand bases upstream of the gene is removed, the transcription rate of the gene decreases dramatically. How would you interpret these results?

 Additional questions are available in CengageNOW at www.cengage.com/login.

15 DNA Technology and Genomics

Transgenic fish (GloFish®). These aquarium fish glow green, red, or yellow because researchers inserted a foreign gene encoding a fluorescent protein from either jellyfish or sea corals.

Courtesy of GloFish®

Beginning in the mid-1970s, the development of new ways to study DNA led to radically new research approaches, such as **recombinant DNA technology,** in which researchers splice together DNA from different organisms in the laboratory. One goal of this technology is to enable scientists to obtain many copies of a specific DNA segment for the purpose of studying it. Because new methods to analyze DNA are continually emerging, we do not attempt to explore them all here. Instead, we discuss some of the major approaches that have provided a foundation for the technologies commonly used by molecular geneticists.

We then consider how studies of DNA sequences have helped scientists understand the organization of genes and the relationship between genes and their products. In fact, most of our current knowledge of the structure and control of eukaryotic genes, and of the roles of genes in development, comes from applying these methods. DNA sequencing has also revolutionized systematics by helping to clarify evolutionary relationships.

This chapter also explores some of the practical applications of DNA technologies. One of the rapidly advancing areas of study is **molecular modification**—altering the DNA of an organism to produce new genes with new traits. Molecular modification, also called *genetic engineering,* can take many forms, ranging from basic research to the production of strains of bacteria that manufacture useful protein products, to the development of plants and animals that express foreign genes (see photograph).

The development of DNA cloning, molecular modification, and related techniques have transformed people's view of **biotechnology,** which is the commercial or industrial use of cells or organisms. Today, biotechnology includes numerous applications in such diverse areas as medicine, foods and agriculture, and forensic science.

15.1 DNA CLONING

■ LEARNING OBJECTIVES

1 Explain how a typical restriction enzyme cuts DNA molecules and give examples of the ways in which these enzymes are used in recombinant DNA technology.

2 Distinguish among a genomic DNA library, a chromosome library, and a complementary DNA (cDNA) library; explain why one would clone the same eukaryotic gene from both a genomic DNA library and a cDNA library.

3 Explain how researchers use a DNA probe.

4 Describe how the polymerase chain reaction amplifies DNA in vitro.

Recombinant DNA technology was not developed quickly. It actually had its roots in the 1940s with genetic studies of bacteria and **bacteriophages** ("bacteria eaters"), the viruses that infect them. (See Figure 12-2, which shows bacteriophages on the bacterium *Escherichia coli.*) Molecular biologist Paul Berg was the first investigator to construct a recombinant DNA molecule; in 1980, he shared the Nobel Prize in Chemistry for his contributions to recombinant DNA technology. After decades of basic research and the accumulation of extensive knowledge, the technology became feasible and available to the many scientists who now use these methods.

In recombinant DNA technology, scientists use **restriction enzymes** from bacteria to cut DNA molecules only in specific places. Restriction enzymes enable researchers to cut DNA into manageable segments. Each fragment is then incorporated into a suitable **vector** molecule, a carrier capable of transporting the DNA fragment into a cell.

Bacteriophages and DNA molecules called plasmids are two examples of vectors. Bacterial DNA is generally circular; most **plasmids** are separate, much smaller, circular DNA molecules that may be present and replicate inside a bacterial cell, such as *E. coli.* Researchers introduce plasmids into bacterial cells by a method called **transformation,** the uptake of foreign DNA by cells (see Chapter 12). For transformation to be efficient, the researcher alters the cells chemically or by *electroporation*—delivering an electric shock—to make the plasma membrane permeable to the plasmid DNA molecules. Once a plasmid enters a cell, it is replicated and distributed to daughter cells during cell division. When a *recombinant plasmid*—one that has foreign DNA spliced into it—replicates in this way, many identical copies of the foreign DNA are made; in other words, the foreign DNA is **cloned.**

Transposons are an efficient vector for transferring genes into mice and other research organisms. Recall from Chapter 13 that a transposon is a mobile genetic element that can cut itself out of one location in a cell's genome and insert itself into a different location.

Restriction enzymes are "molecular scissors"

Discovering **restriction enzymes** was a major breakthrough in developing recombinant DNA technology. Today, large numbers of different types of restriction enzymes, each with its own characteristics, are readily available to researchers. For example, a restriction enzyme known as *Hind*III searches a DNA molecule for the restriction site 5′—AAGCTT—3′, and when it finds that site, it cuts the DNA. (A *restriction site* is a DNA sequence containing the cleavage site that is cut by a particular restriction enzyme.) The sequence 5′—GAATTC—3′ is cut by another restriction enzyme, known as *Eco*RI. The names of restriction enzymes are generally derived from the names of the bacteria from which they were originally isolated. Thus, *Hind*III and *Eco*RI are derived from *Hemophilus influenzae* and *E. coli,* respectively.

Why do bacteria produce such enzymes? During infection, a bacteriophage injects its DNA into a bacterial cell. The bacterium can defend itself if it has restriction enzymes that can attack the bacteriophage DNA. The bacterial cell protects its own DNA from breakdown by modifying it after replication. An enzyme adds a methyl group to one or more bases in each restriction site so that the restriction enzyme does not recognize and cut the bacterial DNA.

Restriction enzymes enable scientists to cut DNA from chromosomes into shorter fragments in a controlled way. Many of the restriction enzymes used for recombinant DNA studies cut **palindromic sequences,** which means the base sequence of one strand reads the same as its complement when both are read in the 5′ ⟶ 3′ direction. Thus, in our *Hind*III example, both strands read 5′—AAGCTT—3′, which as a double-stranded molecule is diagrammed as follows:

> 5′—AAGCTT—3′
> 3′—TTCGAA—5′

By cutting both strands of the DNA, but in a staggered fashion, these enzymes produce fragments with identical, complementary, single-stranded ends:

> 5′—A   AGCTT—3′
> 3′—TTCGA   A—5′

These ends are called *sticky ends* because they pair by hydrogen bonding with the complementary, single-stranded ends of other DNA molecules that have been cut with the same enzyme (**FIG. 15-1**). Once the sticky ends of two molecules have been joined in this way, they are treated with **DNA ligase,** an enzyme that covalently links the two DNA fragments to form a stable recombinant DNA molecule. (DNA ligase was discussed in the section on DNA replication in Chapter 12.)

Recombinant DNA forms when DNA is spliced into a vector

In recombinant DNA technology, geneticists cut both the DNA to be cloned and plasmid DNA with the same restriction enzyme. The two DNA samples are then mixed under conditions that facilitate hydrogen bonding between the complementary bases of the sticky ends, and the nicks in the resulting recombinant DNA are sealed by DNA ligase (**FIG. 15-2**).

FIGURE 15-1 *Animated* Cutting DNA with a restriction enzyme

Many restriction enzymes, such as *Hind*III, cut DNA at sequences that are palindromic, producing complementary sticky ends. The small black arrows designate the enzyme's cleavage sites.

RESEARCH METHOD

Why Is It Used? A plasmid carries foreign DNA into a host bacterial cell, where many copies of the gene of interest are made as the bacterial cell divides. These copies are used in many types of research, for example, to make the gene product encoded by the foreign DNA.

How Is It Done?

Plasmid from a bacterium

DNA of interest from another organism

1 Plasmid and DNA from another organism are cut by the same restriction enzyme (in this example, *Hind*III). This produces molecules with complementary single-stranded ends.

Clonable DNA fragment

2 Mix two types of molecules so their sticky ends pair. DNA ligase then forms covalent bonds at junctions, linking fragments.

Recombinant DNA

3 Transfer recombinant DNA molecule to host cell, where it is copied and transcribed to produce gene product.

FIGURE 15-2 Splicing foreign DNA (gene of interest) into a cloning vector (in this example, a bacterial plasmid) to make recombinant DNA

(b) The relative sizes of a plasmid and the main DNA of a bacterium.

(a) This plasmid vector has many useful features. Researchers constructed it from DNA fragments they had isolated from plasmids, *E. coli* genes, and yeast genes. The two origins of replication, one for *E. coli* and one for yeast, *Saccharomyces cerevisiae*, let it replicate independently in either type of cell. Letters on the outer circle designate sites for restriction enzymes that cut the plasmid only at that position. Resistance genes for the antibiotics ampicillin and tetracycline and the yeast *URA-3* gene are also shown. The *URA-3* gene is useful when transforming yeast cells lacking an enzyme required for uracil synthesis. Cells that take up the plasmid grow on a uracil-deficient medium.

FIGURE 15-3 Plasmids

The plasmids now used in recombinant DNA work have been extensively manipulated in the laboratory to include features helpful in isolating and analyzing cloned DNA (**FIG. 15-3**). Among these are an origin of replication (see Chapter 12), one or more restriction sites, and genes that let researchers select cells transformed by recombinant plasmids. These genes allow transformed cells to grow under specified conditions that do not allow untransformed cells to grow. In this way, the researchers use features that are also common in naturally occurring plasmids. Typically, plasmids do not contain genes essential to the bacterial cells under normal conditions. However, they often carry genes that are useful under specific environmental conditions, such as genes that confer resistance to particular antibiotics or that let the cells use a specific nutrient. For example, cells transformed with a plasmid that includes a gene for resistance to the antibiotic tetracycline can grow in a medium that contains tetracycline, whereas untransformed cells cannot.

A limiting property of any vector is the size of the DNA fragment it can effectively carry. The size of a DNA segment is often given in kilobases (kb), with 1 kb being equal to 1000 base pairs. Fragments that are smaller than 10 kb are usually inserted into plasmids for use in *E. coli*. However, larger fragments require the use of bacteriophage vectors, which can handle up to 23 kb of DNA. Other vectors are **cosmid cloning vectors,** which are combination vectors with features from both bacteriophages and plasmids, and **bacterial artificial chromosomes (BACs),** which accommodate much larger fragments of DNA. A single BAC can include up

to about 200 kb of extra DNA, a feature that made BACs especially useful in the *Human Genome Project,* which is discussed later in the chapter.

Recombinant DNA can also be introduced into cells of eukaryotic organisms. For example, geneticists use modified viruses as vectors in mammal cells. These viruses are disabled so they do not kill the cells they infect. Instead, the viral DNA molecules, as well as any foreign DNA they carry, become incorporated into the cell's chromosomes after infection. As discussed later, other methods do not require a biological vector.

DNA can be cloned inside cells

Because a single gene is only a small part of the total DNA in an organism, isolating the piece of DNA containing that particular gene is like finding a needle in a haystack: a powerful detector is needed. Today, many methods enable biologists to isolate a specific nucleotide sequence from an organism. We start by discussing methods in which DNA is cloned inside bacterial cells. We use the cloning of human DNA as an example, although the procedure is applicable for any organism.

A genomic DNA library contains fragments of all DNA in the genome

The total DNA in a cell is called its **genome.** For example, if DNA is extracted from human cells, we refer to it as human genomic DNA. A **genomic DNA library** is a collection of thousands of DNA fragments that represent all of the DNA in the genome. Each fragment is inserted into a plasmid, which is usually incorporated into a bacterial cell. Thus, a human genomic DNA library is stored in a collection of recombinant bacteria, each with a different fragment of human DNA. Scientists use genomic DNA libraries to isolate and study specific genes. In addition, genomic DNA libraries contain a huge number of sequences that do not code for protein.

Individual chromosomes can also be isolated to make a **chromosome library** containing all the DNA fragments in that specific chromosome. If a gene of interest is known to be associated with a particular chromosome, it is easier to isolate that gene from a chromosome library than from a genomic DNA library.

The basic cloning methods just described are used to make genomic DNA or chromosome libraries. First, the DNA is cut with a restriction enzyme, generating a population of DNA fragments (**FIG. 15-4**). These fragments vary in size and in the genetic information they carry, but they all have identical sticky ends. Ge-

A genomic library is a collection of all the DNA fragments in an organism's genome; a chromosome library is a collection of all the DNA fragments in a specific chromosome. Each DNA fragment is "stored" in a clone of recombinant bacterial cells. Scientists use genomic and chromosome libraries to isolate and study genes.

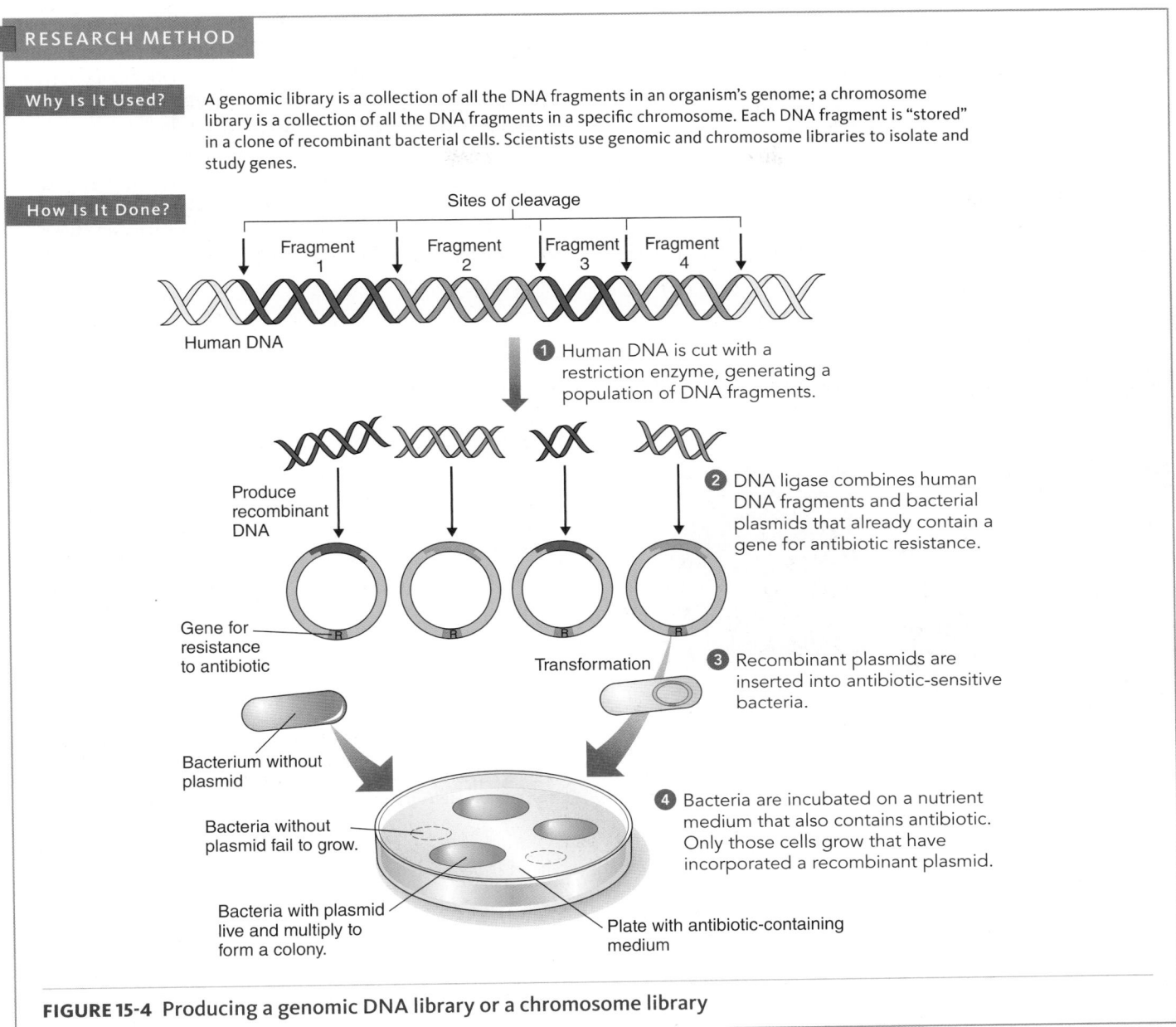

Sites of cleavage

Fragment 1 Fragment 2 Fragment 3 Fragment 4

Human DNA

① Human DNA is cut with a restriction enzyme, generating a population of DNA fragments.

Produce recombinant DNA

② DNA ligase combines human DNA fragments and bacterial plasmids that already contain a gene for antibiotic resistance.

Gene for resistance to antibiotic

Transformation

③ Recombinant plasmids are inserted into antibiotic-sensitive bacteria.

Bacterium without plasmid

Bacteria without plasmid fail to grow.

④ Bacteria are incubated on a nutrient medium that also contains antibiotic. Only those cells grow that have incorporated a recombinant plasmid.

Bacteria with plasmid live and multiply to form a colony.

Plate with antibiotic-containing medium

FIGURE 15-4 Producing a genomic DNA library or a chromosome library

neticists treat plasmid DNA that will be used as a vector with the same restriction enzyme, which converts the circular plasmids into linear molecules with sticky ends complementary to those of the human DNA fragments. Recombinant plasmids are produced by mixing the two kinds of DNA (human and plasmid) under conditions that promote hydrogen bonding of complementary bases. Then, DNA ligase is used to covalently bond the paired ends of the plasmid and human DNA, forming recombinant DNA. Unavoidably, nonrecombinant plasmids also form (*not shown in figure*) because some plasmids revert to their original circular shape without incorporating foreign DNA.

The geneticists insert plasmids into antibiotic-sensitive bacterial cells by transformation. Because the ratio of plasmids to cells is kept very low, it is rare for a cell to receive more than one plasmid molecule, and not all cells receive a plasmid. The researchers incubate normally antibiotic-sensitive cells on a nutrient medium that includes antibiotics; the only cells that are able to grow have incorporated a plasmid that contains a gene for antibiotic resistance. In addition, the plasmid has usually been modified in ways that enable researchers to identify those cells containing recombinant plasmids.

Genomic DNA and chromosome libraries contain redundancies; that is, certain human DNA sequences have been inserted into plasmids more than once, purely by chance. However, each individual recombinant plasmid—analogous to a book in the library—contains only a single fragment of the total human genome.

To identify a plasmid containing a sequence of interest, the researcher clones each plasmid until there are millions of copies to work with. This process occurs as the bacterial cells grow and divide. A dilute sample of the bacterial culture is spread on solid growth medium (agar plates), so the cells are widely separated. Each cell divides many times, yielding a visible **colony,** which is a clone of genetically identical cells originating from a single cell.

All the cells of a particular colony contain the same recombinant plasmid, so during this process a specific sequence of human DNA is also cloned. The major task is to determine which colony out of thousands contains a cloned fragment of interest. Specific DNA sequences are identified in various ways.

A complementary DNA probe detects a specific DNA sequence

Suppose a researcher wishes to screen the thousands of recombinant DNA molecules in bacterial cells to find the specific DNA sequence of interest. A common approach to detecting a specific DNA sequence involves using a **DNA probe,** which is a segment of DNA that is homologous to part of the sequence of interest. The DNA probe is usually a radioactively labeled segment of single-stranded DNA that can **hybridize**—attach by base pairing—to complementary base sequences in the target DNA.

To find a specific DNA, biologists transfer the genomic library to a nitrocellulose or nylon membrane (**FIG. 15-5**). They treat the cells on the membrane chemically to lyse them, releasing the DNA and making the DNA single-stranded. (Single-stranded DNA

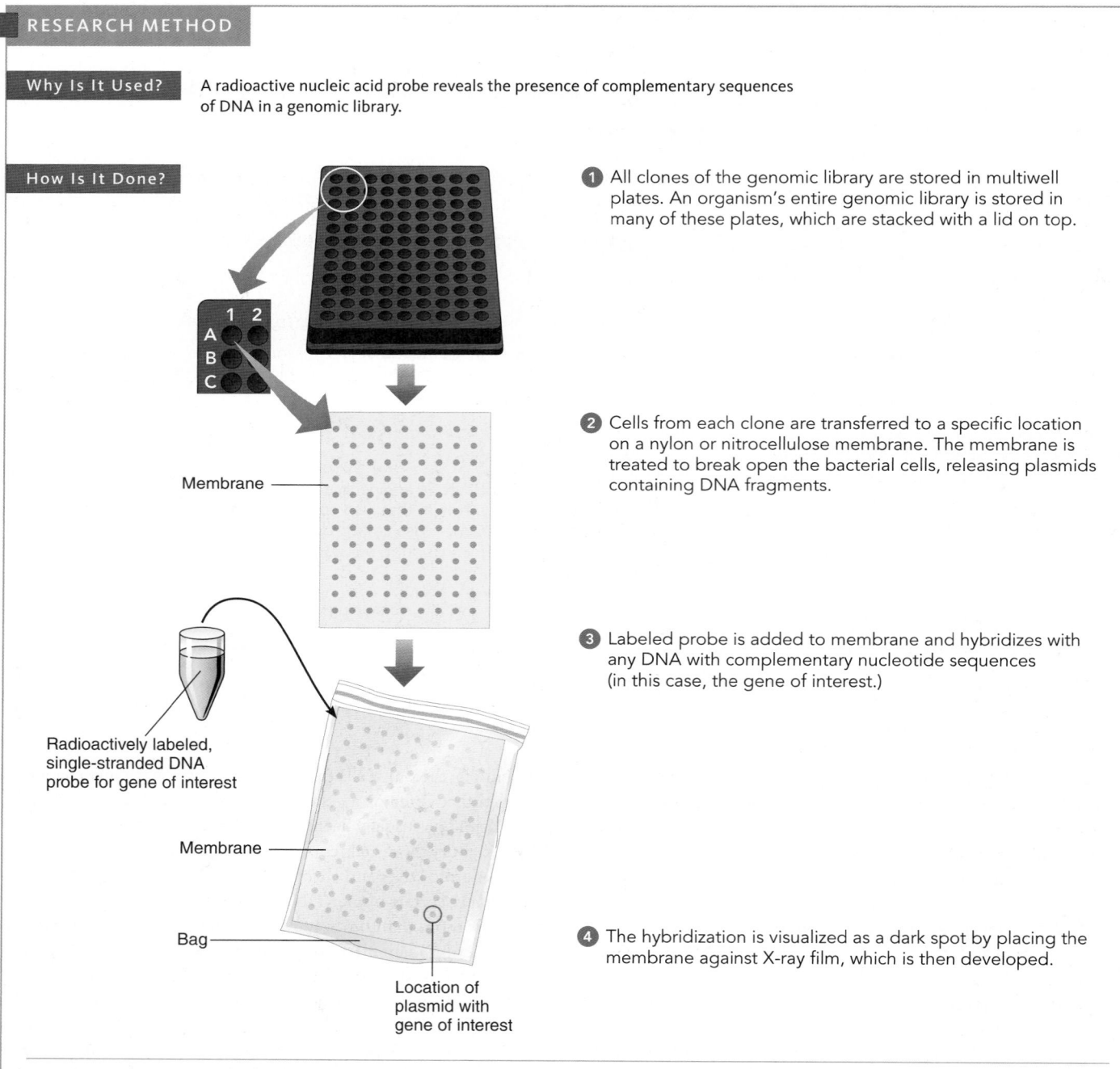

RESEARCH METHOD

Why Is It Used?   A radioactive nucleic acid probe reveals the presence of complementary sequences of DNA in a genomic library.

How Is It Done?

1 2
A
B
C

Membrane

Radioactively labeled, single-stranded DNA probe for gene of interest

Membrane

Bag

Location of plasmid with gene of interest

1 All clones of the genomic library are stored in multiwell plates. An organism's entire genomic library is stored in many of these plates, which are stacked with a lid on top.

2 Cells from each clone are transferred to a specific location on a nylon or nitrocellulose membrane. The membrane is treated to break open the bacterial cells, releasing plasmids containing DNA fragments.

3 Labeled probe is added to membrane and hybridizes with any DNA with complementary nucleotide sequences (in this case, the gene of interest.)

4 The hybridization is visualized as a dark spot by placing the membrane against X-ray film, which is then developed.

FIGURE 15-5 Identifying a specific DNA sequence in a genomic library by hybridization with a nucleic acid probe binds to the membrane.) Then they incubate the membrane with the radioactive probe mixture to let the probes hybridize with any complementary strands of DNA that may be present. Each spot on the membrane containing DNA that is complementary to that particular probe becomes radioactive and is detected by *autoradiography* (see Chapter 2), using X-ray film. Each spot on the film therefore identifies a colony containing a plasmid that includes the DNA of interest. The biologist then returns to the genomic library and removes cells that contain the cloned sequence of interest. These cells are then grown in culture to produce millions of new bacteria, all containing the recombinant DNA of interest.

A cDNA library is complementary to mRNA and does not contain introns

Researchers frequently wish to clone intact genes while avoiding **introns,** which are regions of eukaryotic genes that do not code for proteins. Scientists also may wish to clone only genes that are expressed in a particular cell type. In such cases, they construct libraries of DNA copies of mature mRNA from which introns have been removed. The copies, known as **complementary DNA (cDNA)** because they are complementary to mRNA, also lack introns. The researchers use the enzyme **reverse transcriptase** (see Chapter 13) to synthesize single-stranded cDNA. DNA polymerase is then used to make the cDNA double-stranded (**FIG. 15-6**). A **cDNA library** is formed using mRNA from a single cell type as the starting material. The double-stranded cDNA molecules are inserted into plasmid or virus vectors, which then multiply in bacterial cells.

Analyzing cDNA clones lets investigators determine certain characteristics of the protein encoded by the gene, including its amino acid sequence. They can also study the structure of the mature mRNA. Because the cDNA copy of the mRNA does not contain intron sequences, comparing the DNA base sequences in cDNA and the DNA in genomic DNA or chromosome libraries reveals the locations of intron and exon coding sequences in the gene.

Cloned cDNA sequences are also useful when geneticists want to produce a eukaryotic protein in bacteria. When they introduce an intron-containing human gene, such as the gene for human growth hormone, into a bacterium, it cannot remove the introns from the transcribed RNA to make a functional mRNA for producing its protein product. If they insert a cDNA clone of the gene into the bacterium, however, its transcript contains an uninterrupted coding region. A functional protein is synthesized if the geneticist inserts the gene downstream of an appropriate bacterial promoter and if he or she places the appropriate bacterial translation initiation sequences in it.

The polymerase chain reaction amplifies DNA in vitro

The methods just described for amplifying, or making multiple copies of, a specific DNA sequence involve cloning DNA in cells, usually those of bacteria. These processes are time consuming and require an adequate DNA sample as the starting material. The **polymerase chain reaction (PCR),** which biochemist Kary Mullis developed in 1985, lets researchers amplify a tiny sample

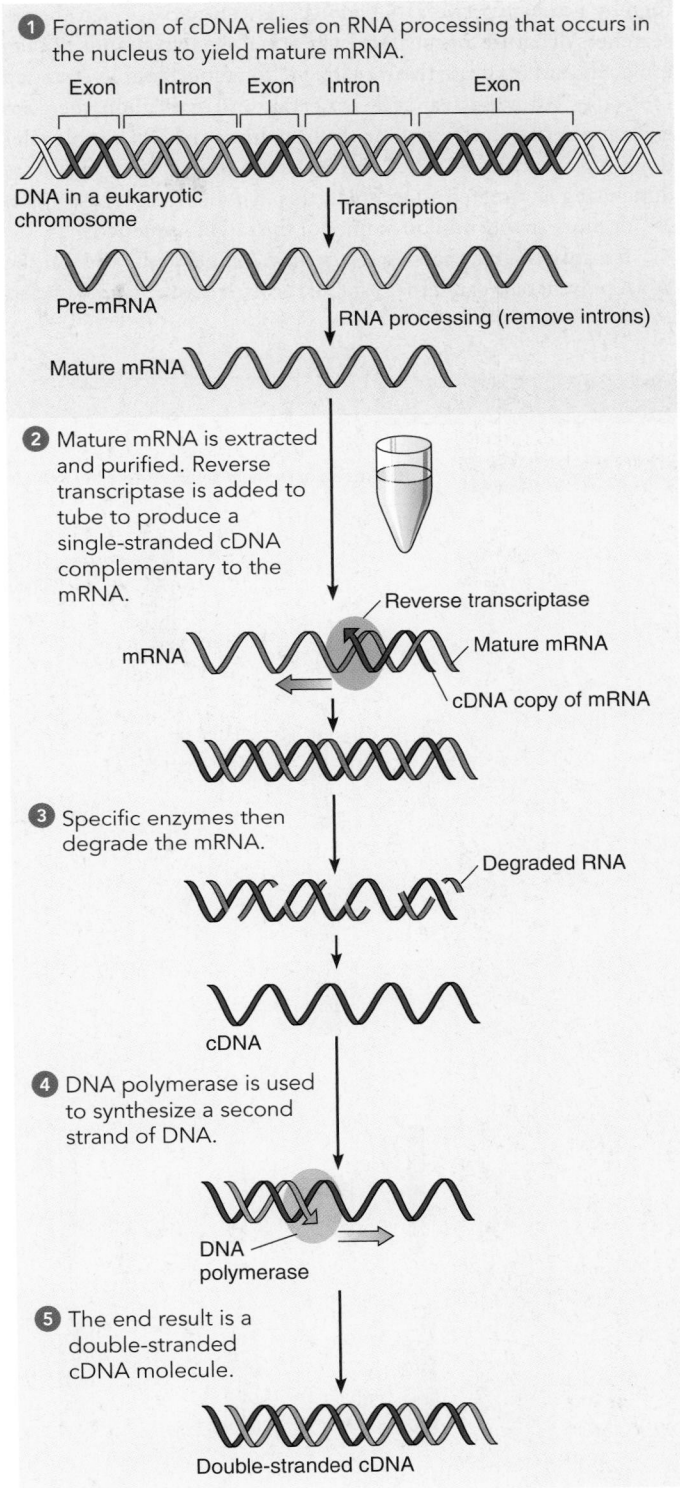

① Formation of cDNA relies on RNA processing that occurs in the nucleus to yield mature mRNA.

Exon Intron Exon Intron Exon

DNA in a eukaryotic chromosome

Transcription

Pre-mRNA

RNA processing (remove introns)

Mature mRNA

② Mature mRNA is extracted and purified. Reverse transcriptase is added to tube to produce a single-stranded cDNA complementary to the mRNA.

Reverse transcriptase

mRNA

Mature mRNA

cDNA copy of mRNA

③ Specific enzymes then degrade the mRNA.

Degraded RNA

cDNA

④ DNA polymerase is used to synthesize a second strand of DNA.

DNA polymerase

⑤ The end result is a double-stranded cDNA molecule.

Double-stranded cDNA

FIGURE 15-6 *Animated* The formation of cDNA

of DNA *without cloning in a cell.* The DNA is amplified millions of times in a few hours. In 1993, Mullis received the Nobel Prize in Chemistry for his work.

In PCR, DNA polymerase uses nucleotides and primers to replicate a DNA sequence in vitro (outside a living organism), thereby producing two DNA molecules (**FIG. 15-7**). Then the researchers denature, or separate by heating, the two strands of each molecule and replicate them again, yielding four double-stranded molecules. After the next cycle of heating and replication, there are eight molecules, and so on, with the number of DNA molecules doubling in each cycle. After only 20 heating and cooling cycles are done using automated equipment, this exponential process yields 2^{20}, or more than 1 million, copies of the target sequence!

Because the reaction can be carried out efficiently only if the DNA polymerase can remain stable through many heating cycles, researchers use a heat-resistant DNA polymerase, known as *Taq* polymerase. The name of this enzyme reflects its source, *Thermus aquaticus,* a bacterium that lives in hot springs in Yellowstone National Park. Because the water in this environment is close to the boiling point, all enzymes in *T. aquaticus* have evolved to be stable at high temperatures. (Recall from Chapter 3 that, when heated, most proteins are irreversibly denatured—they change their overall shape and lose their biological activity.) Bacteria living in deep-sea thermal vents have evolved similar heat-resistant enzymes.

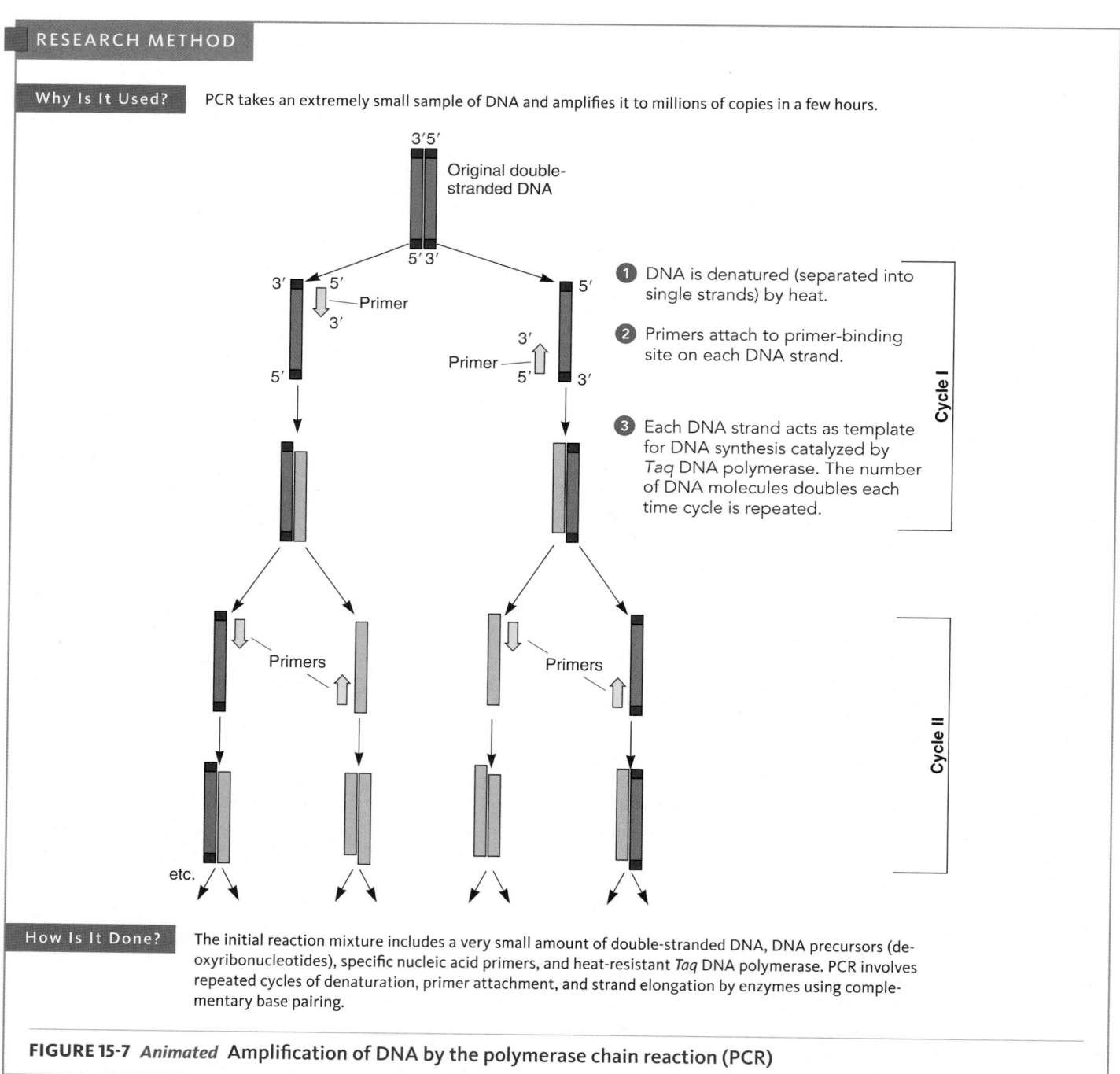

RESEARCH METHOD

Why Is It Used? PCR takes an extremely small sample of DNA and amplifies it to millions of copies in a few hours.

Original double-stranded DNA

1. DNA is denatured (separated into single strands) by heat.

2. Primers attach to primer-binding site on each DNA strand.

3. Each DNA strand acts as template for DNA synthesis catalyzed by *Taq* DNA polymerase. The number of DNA molecules doubles each time cycle is repeated.

Cycle I

Primers

Primers

Cycle II

etc.

How Is It Done? The initial reaction mixture includes a very small amount of double-stranded DNA, DNA precursors (deoxyribonucleotides), specific nucleic acid primers, and heat-resistant *Taq* DNA polymerase. PCR involves repeated cycles of denaturation, primer attachment, and strand elongation by enzymes using complementary base pairing.

FIGURE 15-7 *Animated* **Amplification of DNA by the polymerase chain reaction (PCR)**

The PCR technique has virtually limitless applications. It makes cloning easier. It enables researchers to amplify and analyze tiny DNA samples from a variety of sources, ranging from crime scenes to archaeological remains. For example, investigators have used PCR to analyze mitochondrial DNA obtained from the bones of Neandertals (see Chapter 22). Some of the Neandertal genome was sequenced in 2006, enabling researchers to compare it to equivalent parts of the human genome.

A limitation of the PCR technique is that it is almost too sensitive. Even a tiny amount of contaminant DNA in a sample may become amplified if it includes a DNA sequence complementary to the primers, potentially leading to an erroneous conclusion. Researchers take appropriate precautions to avoid this and other technical pitfalls.

Review

- What are restriction enzymes? How are they used in recombinant DNA research?
- What are the relative merits of genomic DNA libraries, chromosome libraries, and cDNA libraries?
- How are DNA probes used?
- Why is the PCR technique valuable?

15.2 DNA ANALYSIS

◼ LEARNING OBJECTIVES

5 Distinguish among DNA, RNA, and protein blotting.
6 Describe the chain termination method of DNA sequencing.

DNA cloning in cells and the PCR technique have had major impacts on genetic analysis because they provide enough genetic material to address certain fundamental questions about specific genes and their RNA or protein products. For example, when—and how—is a gene expressed? Is a given gene identical from one individual to the next? Is it different from one species to the next? Where is the gene found within the genome? In this and the following section, we consider various techniques that help address these questions. We then examine some of the practical applications of DNA technology in the final section of the chapter.

Gel electrophoresis is used for separating macromolecules

Mixtures of certain macromolecules—proteins, polypeptides, DNA fragments, or RNA—are separated by **gel electrophoresis,** a method that exploits the fact that these molecules carry charged groups that cause them to migrate in an electrical field. **FIGURE 15-8** illustrates gel electrophoresis of DNA molecules. Nucleic acids migrate through the gel toward the positive pole of the electric field because they are negatively charged due to their phosphate groups. Because the gel slows down the large molecules more than the small molecules, the DNA is separated by size. Including DNA fragments of known size as standards ensures accurate measurements of the molecular weights of the unknown fragments. The gel is stained after the DNA fragments are separated to show their number and location.

DNA, RNA, and protein blots detect specific fragments

Geneticists can identify specific DNA fragments that hybridize with a complementary DNA probe. However, it is impossible to hybridize a probe to DNA fragments contained in a gel. For this reason the DNA is usually denatured and then transferred to a nitrocellulose or nylon membrane, which picks up the DNA like a blotter picks up ink. The resulting blot, which is essentially a replica of the gel, is incubated with a DNA probe, which hybridizes with any complementary DNA fragments. If the probe is radioactive, the blot is subjected to autoradiography. The resulting spots on the X-ray film correspond to the locations of the fragments in the gel that are complementary to the probe. Today, many probes are detected by chemical luminescence, which is analyzed by computer scanners, eliminating the need for autoradiography.

This method of detecting DNA fragments—separating them by gel electrophoresis and then transferring them to a nitrocellulose or nylon membrane—is called a **Southern blot,** named for its inventor, Edward M. Southern of Edinburgh University in Scotland (**FIG. 15-9**). The procedure has widespread applications, such as being used to diagnose certain types of genetic disorders. For example, in some cases the DNA of a mutant allele is detected because it migrates differently in the gel than the DNA of its normal counterpart does.

Similar blotting techniques are used to study RNA and proteins. When RNA molecules separated by electrophoresis are transferred to a membrane and detected using a nucleic acid probe, the result is called a **Northern blot** (as a pun on Southern's name being associated with his technique). In the same spirit, the term **Western blot** is applied to a blot consisting of proteins or polypeptides previously separated by gel electrophoresis. (So far, no one has invented a type of blot that could be called an Eastern blot.) In the case of Western blotting, scientists recognize the polypeptides of interest by labeled antibody molecules that bind to them specifically. For example, Western blotting is used diagnostically to detect the presence of proteins specific to HIV-1, the AIDS virus.

Restriction fragment length polymorphisms are a measure of genetic relationships

The variability of genes within a population can be studied in several ways. A traditional approach is based on the premise that no two individuals have the exact same number or position of restriction enzyme cutting sites in the genome: random DNA mutations and recombination may result in individuals with different lengths of fragments produced by a given restriction enzyme. Such **restriction fragment length polymorphisms,** commonly known as **RFLPs,** or "riflips," can be used to determine how closely related different members of a population are. (The term *polymorphism* means "many forms" and refers to inherited differences found within a population.) A **genetic polymorphism** exists if individuals of two or more discrete types, or "morphs," are found in a population.

Gel electrophoresis separates molecules such as nucleic acids based on their size and charge as they migrate through an electrical field.

1 A researcher sets up an electrical field in a gel material, consisting of agarose or polyacrylamide, which is poured as a thin slab on a glass or Plexiglas holder. After the gel has solidified, the researcher loads samples containing a mixture of macromolecules (in this case, DNA fragments of different sizes) in wells formed at one end of the gel.

2 When an electrical current is applied, the negatively charged DNA molecules move from the negative pole to the positive pole. The smallest DNA fragments travel the longest distance. The DNA bands are invisible at this point.

Standards of known sizes placed in well

Direction of movement

Mixtures placed in well

Gel

Buffer solution

Anode

Longer molecules

Shorter molecules

Cathode

3 This gel contains separated DNA fragments. The gel is stained with ethidium bromide, a dye that binds to DNA and is fluorescent under UV light.

Eurelios/Photo Researchers, Inc.

FIGURE 15-8 Gel electrophoresis

Restriction enzymes are used to cut the DNA from two or more individuals, and the fragments are separated by gel electrophoresis, with the DNA from each individual in a separate lane; shorter fragments migrate farther than longer fragments. To visualize the fragments, researchers make a Southern blot of the DNA on the gel, which is then denatured and allowed to hybridize with a DNA probe. The resulting pattern of bands can then be compared.

RFLP analysis has been used when conducting paternity testing and when analyzing evidence found at crime scenes. RFLP analysis has also been used to help map the exact location of gene mutations, such as the mutation that causes cystic fibrosis. Although the RFLP technique has provided useful information in many areas of biology, it is rapidly being replaced by newer methods, such as automated DNA sequencing (discussed in the next section).

Why Is It Used? The Southern blotting technique allows DNA separated by electrophoresis to be transferred to a filter in the same location as it was on the gel. It can then be hybridized with radioactive complementary probes.

How Is It Done?

① Digest DNA with restriction enzymes.

DNA

DNA fragments

② Load DNA fragments on gel and separate by electrophoresis.

Buffer solution   Agarose gel

③ Visualize DNA fragments using UV light.

Longer DNA fragments

Shorter DNA fragments

④ In blotting, buffer solution moves upward, transferring DNA fragments to a DNA-binding filter.

Weight
Absorbent paper
Nitrocellulose filter
Gel
Wick
Buffer

⑤ DNA fragments on filter are in same location as those on gel.

⑥ Place filter and radioactively labeled probe together in sealed bag so it can hybridize.

Radioactive probe solution

⑦ Wash filter to remove excess probe and then expose filter to X-ray film; resulting autoradiograph shows hybridized DNA fragments.

FIGURE 15-9 The Southern blotting technique

Methods to rapidly sequence DNA have been developed

One way to characterize DNA is to determine its sequence of nucleotides. Investigators use a cloned piece of DNA as a research tool for many different applications. For example, they may clone a gene to obtain the encoded protein for some industrial or medical process. Regardless of the particular application, researchers must know a great deal about the gene and how it functions. They usually start by determining the sequence of nucleotides.

In the 1990s, the advent of automated **DNA-sequencing** machines connected to powerful computers let scientists sequence huge amounts of DNA quickly and reliably. Automated DNA sequencing relies on the **chain termination method** that British biochemist Fred Sanger developed in 1974. In 1980, Sanger shared the Nobel Prize in Chemistry for this contribution. This was Sanger's second Nobel Prize; his first was for his work on the structure of the protein insulin. Although DNA sequencing is now fully automated, many of the automated techniques are still based on Sanger's chain termination method (**FIG. 15-10**).

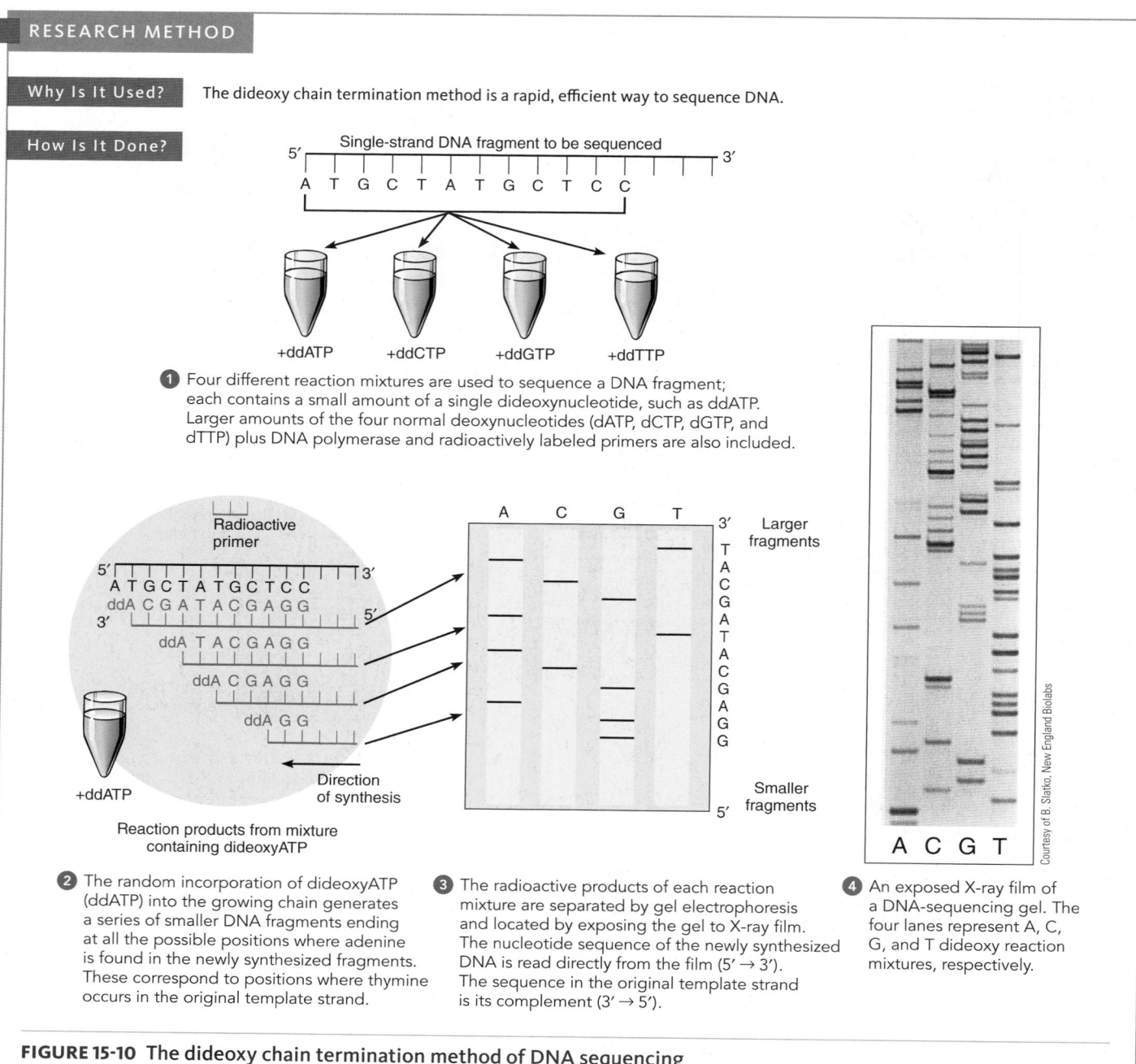

The dideoxy chain termination method is a rapid, efficient way to sequence DNA.

Single-strand DNA fragment to be sequenced

5′ A T G C T A T G C T C C 3′

+ddATP   +ddCTP   +ddGTP   +ddTTP

1 Four different reaction mixtures are used to sequence a DNA fragment; each contains a small amount of a single dideoxynucleotide, such as ddATP. Larger amounts of the four normal deoxynucleotides (dATP, dCTP, dGTP, and dTTP) plus DNA polymerase and radioactively labeled primers are also included.

Radioactive primer

5′ A T G C T A T G C T C C 3′
ddA C G A T A C G A G G 5′
3′

ddA T A C G A G G

ddA C G A G G

ddA G G

+ddATP

Direction of synthesis

Reaction products from mixture containing dideoxyATP

A C G T

3′ T A C G A T A C G A G G 5′

Larger fragments

Smaller fragments

A C G T

Courtesy of B. Slatko, New England Biolabs

2 The random incorporation of dideoxyATP (ddATP) into the growing chain generates a series of smaller DNA fragments ending at all the possible positions where adenine is found in the newly synthesized fragments. These correspond to positions where thymine occurs in the original template strand.

3 The radioactive products of each reaction mixture are separated by gel electrophoresis and located by exposing the gel to X-ray film. The nucleotide sequence of the newly synthesized DNA is read directly from the film (5′ → 3′). The sequence in the original template strand is its complement (3′ → 5′).

4 An exposed X-ray film of a DNA-sequencing gel. The four lanes represent A, C, G, and T dideoxy reaction mixtures, respectively.

FIGURE 15-10 The dideoxy chain termination method of DNA sequencing

The chain termination method of DNA sequencing is based on the fact that a replicating DNA strand that has incorporated a modified synthetic nucleotide, known as a *dideoxynucleotide,* cannot elongate beyond that point. Unlike a "normal" deoxynucleotide, which has a hydroxyl group on its 3′ carbon, a dideoxynucleotide lacks a hydroxyl group on its 3′ carbon. (Recall from Chapter 12 that a 3′ hydroxyl group reacts each time a phosphodiester linkage is formed.) Thus, dideoxynucleotides terminate elongation during DNA replication.

The researcher prepares four different reaction mixtures. Each contains multiple identical single-stranded copies of the DNA to be sequenced; DNA polymerase; appropriate radioactively la-

beled primers; and all four deoxynucleotides needed to synthesize DNA—dATP, dCTP, dGTP, and dTTP. Each mixture also includes a small amount of only one of the four dideoxynucleotides: ddATP, ddCTP, ddGTP, or ddTTP. The prefix "dd" refers to dideoxynucleotides, to distinguish them from deoxynucleotides, which are designated "d."

Here's how the reaction proceeds in the mixture that includes ddATP. At each site where adenine is specified, occasionally a growing strand incorporates a ddATP, halting elongation so DNA fragments of varying lengths form in the reaction mixture. Each fragment that contains a ddATP marks a specific location where adenine would normally be found in the newly synthesized strand.

Similarly, in the reaction mixture that includes ddCTP, each fragment that contains ddCTP marks the position of a cytosine in the newly synthesized strand, and so on.

The radioactive fragments from each reaction are denatured and then separated by gel electrophoresis, with each reaction mixture, corresponding to A, T, G, or C, occupying its own lane in the gel. The positions of the newly synthesized fragments in the gel can then be determined by autoradiography. Because the high resolution of the gel makes it possible to distinguish between fragments that differ in length by only a single nucleotide, the researcher can read off the sequence in the newly synthesized DNA one base at a time.

The chain termination method is still used in many automated DNA-sequencing machines. However, the method of detection has changed in that the nucleotide sequence is no longer visualized by radioactivity. Instead, researchers label the primer or each of the four ddNTPs with a different-colored fluorescent dye. The computer uses a laser to read the fluorescence of the dye markers as the bases emerge from the end of a lane of electrophoresis medium (**FIG. 15-11**).

Entire genomes have been sequenced using automated DNA sequencing

Sequencing machines today are very powerful and can decode about 1.5 million bases in a 24-hour period. These advances in sequencing technology have made it possible for researchers to study the nucleotide sequences of entire genomes in a wide variety of bacteria, archaea, and eukaryotic organisms.

Much of this research received its initial impetus from the **Human Genome Project**, which began in 1990. The sequencing of the 3 billion base pairs of the human genome was essentially completed in 2001. The genomes of about 800 organisms have been sequenced now, and several hundred more are in various stages of planning or completion. We are in the middle of an extraordinary explosion of gene sequence data, largely due to automated sequencing methods.

DNA sequence information is now kept in large computer databases, many of which are accessed through the Internet. Examples are databases maintained by the National Center for Biotechnology Information and by the Human Genome Organization (HUGO). Geneticists use these databases to compare newly discovered sequences with those already known to identify genes and to access many other kinds of information. By searching for DNA or amino acid sequences in a database, researchers can gain a great deal of insight into the function and structure of the gene product, the evolutionary relationships among genes, and the variability among gene sequences within a population. DNA sequencing of species has added much new information in support of evolution (see Chapter 18).

Review

- What is a Southern blot?
- What technique does automated DNA sequencing use? Outline the basic steps of this method.

15.3 GENOMICS

■ LEARNING OBJECTIVES

7 Describe three important areas of research in genomics.

8 Explain what a DNA microarray does and give an example of its research and medical potential.

9 Define *pharmacogenetics* and *proteomics*.

Now that we have sequenced the genomes of humans and several hundred other species, what do we do with that information? **Genomics** is the emerging field of biology that studies the entire DNA sequence of an organism's genome to identify all the genes, determine their RNA or protein products, and ascertain how the genes are regulated. As you will see, genomics has important practical applications in addition to answering scientific questions.

The science of genomics has several research areas, including structural genomics, functional genomics, comparative genomics, and metagenomics. *Structural genomics* is concerned with mapping and sequencing genomes. *Functional genomics* deals with the functions of genes and nongene sequences in genomes. *Comparative genomics* involves comparing the genomes of different species to determine what changes in DNA have occurred during the course of evolution. This knowledge furthers our understanding of evolutionary relationships because genes with little or no variation among species are functionally important in the species in which they are found. *Metagenomics* uses the techniques of genomics to analyze communities of microorganisms instead of individual organisms. Metagenomics enables researchers to identify and study all the genes in a community at the same time.

FIGURE 15-11 *Animated* A small segment of the printout of automated DNA-sequencing results

The computer produces the series of peaks shown as it reads the fluorescing bands on the electrophoresis gel. The nucleotide base adenine is shown in green, guanine in black, cytosine in blue, and thymine in red. The DNA sequence assigned by the computer appears at the top of the printout.

© Mark Harmel/Alamy

Identifying protein-coding genes is useful for research and for medical applications

The majority of the human genome contains DNA sequences that do not code for proteins. Although the entire genome is of interest to biologists, the protein-coding regions are of particular interest to medical researchers. Scientists have compiled tens of thousands of short (25 to 30 nucleotides) cDNA sequences, known as **expressed sequence tags (ESTs),** that can help identify protein-coding genes.

A large data set containing thousands of human ESTs is available to scientists via the Internet. Using gene-hunting software, biologists working on a particular DNA sequence can access the data set and match their DNA sequence to a known EST sequence.

Many ESTs in the data set have been identified by comparing them to known DNA sequences from other species. For example, the human telomerase gene *TRT* was identified by matching its human EST sequence to that of a known yeast telomerase sequence. (Recall from Chapter 12 that telomerase adds repetitive nucleotide sequences to the ends, or telomeres, of eukaryotic chromosomes.)

One way to study gene function is to silence genes one at a time

RNA interference (RNAi), first discovered in the mid-1990s, can be used to quickly determine the function of a specific gene. You may recall from Chapter 13 that RNAi is caused by small RNA molecules that interfere with the expression of genes or, more precisely, their mature mRNA transcripts. RNA interference involves small interfering RNAs, microRNAs, and a few other kinds of short RNA molecules. Biologists hypothesize that RNAi, which occurs in many eukaryotic organisms, originally evolved in nature because it protected cells against viruses that have double-stranded RNA molecules.

After a protein-coding gene is identified, perhaps by using ESTs, the function of that gene can be studied by using RNA interference to inactivate the gene. To do this, biologists synthesize a short stretch of RNA that is complementary to part of the DNA sequence of the gene being examined. The RNA is put into cells, and after the gene is silenced, biologists observe any changes in the phenotype to help determine the function of the missing protein.

Gene targeting also reveals gene function

Another research tool that reveals gene function is **gene targeting,** a procedure in which the researcher chooses and "knocks out," or inactivates, a single gene in an organism. *Knockout mice* have been particularly useful in studying the roles of orthologous genes with unknown functions in mammals, including humans. **Orthologous genes** are homologous genes found in different species because they were inherited from a common ancestor. The roles of the inactivated gene are determined by observing the phenotype of the mice bearing the knockout gene. If the gene codes for a protein, for example, studying individuals who lack that protein helps the researcher identify the function of the protein. Because 98% to 99% of the loci of mice are orthologous to human loci, information about knockout genes in mice also provides details about human genes.

Unlike RNA interference, gene targeting is a lengthy procedure. It takes about a year for scientists to develop a new strain of knockout mice through gene targeting. A nonfunctional, or knockout, gene is cloned and introduced into mouse **embryonic stem cells (ES cells)** (also see Chapters 1 and 17). Once inside the ES cells, genes are relatively easy to handle because, like cancer cells, ES cells grow in culture indefinitely. Most important, if placed in a mouse embryo, ES cells divide and produce all the cell types normally found in the mouse. In a tiny fraction of these ES cells, the introduced knockout gene becomes physically associated with the corresponding gene in a chromosome. If this occurs, the gene on the chromosome and the knockout gene tend to exchange DNA segments in a process called *homologous recombination*. In this way, the knockout allele replaces the normal allele in the mouse chromosome.

Researchers inject into early mouse embryos ES cells they think are likely to carry a knockout gene and let the mice develop to maturity. The researchers generally study animals that carry the knockout gene in every cell. However, because many genes are essential to life, researchers have modified the knockout technique to develop strains in which a specific gene is selectively inactivated in only one cell type. Research laboratories around the world have developed thousands of different strains of knockout mice, each displaying its own characteristic phenotype, and the number continues to grow.

Gene targeting in mice is providing answers to basic biological questions relating to the development of embryos, the development of the nervous system, and the normal functioning of the immune system. This technique has great potential for revealing more about various human diseases, especially because many diseases have a genetic component. Geneticists are using gene targeting to study cancer, heart disease, sickle cell anemia, respiratory diseases such as cystic fibrosis, and other disorders.

Mutagenesis screening reveals the genes involved in a particular phenotype

Many large-scale mutagenesis screening projects in mice and other organisms are currently underway. In **mutagenesis screening,** researchers treat male mice with chemical *mutagens* that cause mutations in DNA. They then breed the males with normal females and screen their offspring for unusual phenotypes. Unlike gene targeting, mutagenesis does not necessarily disable a gene completely; instead, it usually causes small, random mutations that change the properties of the proteins that the DNA encodes. The scale of mutagenesis screening is enormous; one screening project in Germany has screened some 28,000 different mouse mutants for changes in phenotypes.

DNA microarrays are a powerful tool for studying gene expression

DNA microarrays provide a way to study patterns of gene expression in a variety of organisms. Each spot in a DNA microarray consists of a single-stranded probe placed on a glass slide or chip (**FIG. 15-12**). First, a mechanical robot prepares the microarray. It spots each location on the grid with thousands to millions of copies of a specific complementary DNA (cDNA) strand. Each spot, known as a *microdot*, contains many copies of a specific single-stranded cDNA molecule. These were synthesized to make a complementary copy of a specific mRNA, which was then amplified by PCR.

Why Is It Used? DNA microarray analysis indicates gene expression levels of hundreds or even thousands of specific genes in different cell types. This technique helps scientists understand which genes are active (or inactive) in untreated (control) cells as well as in cells treated with a specific drug.

How Is It Done?

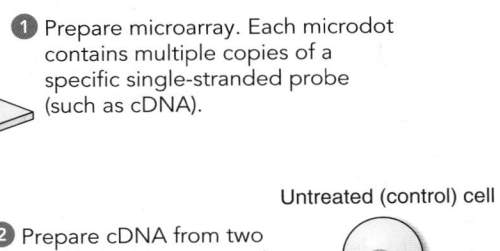

① Prepare microarray. Each microdot contains multiple copies of a specific single-stranded probe (such as cDNA).

Treated cell

Untreated (control) cell

② Prepare cDNA from two cell populations (treated and control).

Mature mRNA — Reverse transcriptase

cDNA copy of mRNA

③ Tag each cDNA with different fluorescent dye.

Mature mRNA — Reverse transcriptase

cDNA copy of mRNA

cDNA   mRNA (discard)

cDNA   mRNA (discard)

④ Hybridize two cDNA populations to array.

Laser 1

Laser 2

⑤ Scan array to identify fluorescence where hybridization has occurred.

Emissions

⑥ Computer analysis produces color-coded readout.

● Gene in treated cell that increased activity, compared to control

● Gene in treated cell that decreased activity, compared to control

○ Gene that was active in both treated and untreated cells

○ Gene that was inactive in both treated and untreated cells

FIGURE 15-12 DNA microarray analysis

Researchers then isolate mature mRNA molecules from two cell populations—for example, liver cells treated with a newly developed drug and control liver cells not treated with the drug. Liver cells are often tested because the liver produces many enzymes that metabolize foreign molecules, including drug molecules. Drugs the liver cannot metabolize, or metabolizes weakly, may be too toxic to be used.

Researchers use the isolated mRNA molecules to prepare cDNA molecules for each cell population, which are then tagged with different-colored fluorescent dyes. For example, the treated cells' cDNA molecules might be labeled with red dye and the untreated cells' cDNA molecules with green dye. Then researchers add the two cDNA populations to the array, and some of the cDNA subsequently hybridizes (forms base pairs with) the cDNA on the array.

After washing it to remove any cDNA that has not hybridized to the array, investigators scan the array with lasers to identify red and green fluorescence where hybridization has occurred. Computer analysis of the ratio of red to green fluorescence at each spot in the array produces a color-coded readout that researchers can further analyze. For example, a medical researcher might compare the overall pattern of gene activity in cells treated with an experimental drug with that of cells exposed to known drugs and toxins. If the pattern of gene activity for the treated cells matches that of cells treated with a toxin that damages the liver, the drug will probably not go into clinical trials.

DNA microarrays enable researchers to compare the activities of thousands of genes in cell types from various tissue samples and in normal and diseased cells. Because cancer and other diseases exhibit altered patterns of gene expression, DNA microarrays have the potential to identify disease-causing genes or the proteins they code for, which can then be targeted by therapeutic drugs.

Here's an example of the application. Diffuse large B-cell lymphoma is a cancer of white blood cells that has different subtypes. In 2002, researchers used microarrays to identify 17 genes that are active in various combinations for each subtype. Using DNA microarrays, researchers determined which combination of those 17 genes is active in each subtype of this form of cancer. Armed with the knowledge of which cancer subtype a patient has, physicians can choose the treatment that will probably be most effective for that patient. Examining patterns of gene activity with DNA microarrays also helps medical scientists identify which patients will probably remain free of cancer after treatment and which will probably relapse.

The Human Genome Project stimulated studies of genome sequencing for other species

To aid in analyzing the human genome, investigators carried out comparative genomics by sequencing and mapping studies simultaneously on the mouse and rat genomes. Mice and rats were obvious choices for DNA sequencing because they have been studied for almost a century and much is known about their biology. Mice and rats are sufficiently different from humans that any conserved (that is, identical) sequences found in both rodents and humans are probably functionally important.

In addition, mice are similar enough to humans that both share many physiological traits, including some of the same diseases. To demonstrate the shared similarity between the mouse and human genomes, a consortium of scientists published a study in 2002 that compared the mouse chromosome 16 with the human genome. Only 14 of the 731 known genes on the mouse chromosome had no human counterpart; the remaining 717 genes appeared in one form or another in the human genome.

Comparison of the DNA sequences and chromosome organization of related genes from different species is a powerful tool for identifying the elements essential for their functions. If a human gene has an unknown function, researchers can often deduce clues about its role by studying the equivalent gene in another species, such as a mouse or rat.

Investigators have also sequenced the genomes of other model vertebrate organisms, such as the zebrafish and pufferfish. Biologists have used the zebrafish for many years as a model of vertebrate development because its embryonic stages are transparent and therefore convenient to examine. The pufferfish has the smallest known genome of all vertebrates. By comparing the human genome to that of the pufferfish, researchers have identified shared sequences that have not changed in several hundred million years. Because these sequences have resisted the selective forces of evolution, they may be genes or regulatory elements that direct vertebrate development and are essential in all vertebrates.

Genome analysis of commercially important organisms, such as salmon, chickens, pigs, and rice, is also a priority. For example, scientists have published the rice genome, the genome of the parasite that causes malaria, and the genome of the parasite that causes African sleeping sickness.

One of the most significant genome-sequencing efforts from an evolutionary perspective focuses on nonhuman primates, such as the chimpanzee (whose sequence data were published in 2005). Comparing the DNA sequences of humans and our closest living relatives is helping biologists understand the genetic changes that occurred during human evolution, including which genes govern mental and linguistic capabilities.

Several scientific fields—bioinformatics, pharmacogenetics, and proteomics— have emerged

We have already mentioned that the amount of genomic data now available requires that it be evaluated using powerful computers. The discipline known as **bioinformatics,** or *biological computing,* includes the storage, retrieval, and comparison of nucleotide or amino acid sequences within a given species and among different species. Bioinformatics uses powerful computers and sophisticated software to store, manage, and analyze large amounts of data generated by sequencing and other technologies. For example, as researchers determine new DNA sequences, automated computer programs scan the sequences for patterns typically found in genes. Through comparison of the databases of DNA sequences from different organisms, bioinformatics has already led to insights about gene identification, gene function, and evolutionary relationships.

The new science of gene-based medicine known as **pharmacogenetics** studies how genetic variation among patients affects the action of drugs in individuals. The goal of pharmacogenetics is to customize drugs to match an individual's genetic makeup. Currently, a physician does not know in advance whether a particular medication will benefit a patient or cause severe side effects. An individual's genes, especially those that code for drug-metabolizing enzymes, largely determine that person's response to a specific drug. Pharmacogenetics takes into account the subtle genetic differences among individuals. In as few as 5 to 10 years, patients may take routine genetic screening tests before a physician prescribes a drug.

Pharmacogenetics, like other fields in human genetics, presents difficult ethical questions. The genetic testing that will become an everyday part of pharmacogenetics raises issues of privacy, genetic bias, and potential discrimination. We consider these issues in Chapter 16. Individualized genetic testing may cause people to worry unnecessarily about a genetic disease for which they may never develop symptoms. Most common diseases result from a complex interplay between multiple genes and nongenetic, or environmental, factors. (Recall from Chapter 11 that the environment is an important factor influencing gene expression.) In humans, healthy environmental factors include proper diet, adequate exercise, and not smoking.

The study of all the proteins expressed by a cell at a given time is known as **proteomics.** For example, scientists have identified all the proteins made by a given kind of cell, but the process is much more complicated than sequencing the human genome. Some genes, for example, encode several different proteins. (See Figure 14-14 for an example of alternative splicing.) Also, every somatic cell in the human body has essentially the same genome, but cells in different tissues vary greatly in the kinds of proteins they produce (recall the earlier discussion of DNA microarrays). Protein expression patterns vary not only in different tissues but also at different stages in the development of a single cell.

Scientists want to understand the role of each protein in a cell, the way the various proteins interact, the 3-D structure for each protein, how proteins are spatially arranged within the cell's cytosol and organelles, and protein profiles in diseased cells. While advancing biological knowledge, these goals also promise advances in medicine. If they know the shape of a protein associated with a type of cancer or other disease, scientists may be able to develop drugs that bind to active sites on that protein, turning its activity off. Today, the pharmaceutical industry has drugs that target about 500 proteins in the cell. However, researchers estimate proteomics may yield 10,000 to 20,000 additional protein targets.

Review

- How would you distinguish among structural, functional, and comparative genomics?
- What is a DNA microarray?
- What is pharmacogenetics? proteomics?

15.4 APPLICATIONS OF DNA TECHNOLOGIES

■ LEARNING OBJECTIVE

10 Describe at least one important application of recombinant DNA technology in each of the following fields: medicine, DNA fingerprinting, and transgenic organisms.

Recombinant DNA technology has provided both a new and unique set of tools for examining fundamental questions about cells and new approaches to applied problems in many other fields.

In some areas, the production of genetically modified proteins and organisms has begun to have considerable impact on our lives. The most striking of these has been in medicine.

DNA technology has revolutionized medicine

In increasing numbers of cases, doctors perform **genetic tests** to determine whether an individual has a particular genetic mutation associated with such disorders as Huntington's disease, hemophilia, cystic fibrosis, Tay-Sachs disease, breast cancer, and sickle cell anemia. **Gene therapy,** the use of specific DNA to treat a genetic disease by correcting the genetic problem, is another application of DNA technology that is currently in its infancy. Because genetic testing and gene therapy focus almost exclusively on humans, these applications of DNA technology are discussed in Chapter 16. We focus our discussion here on the use of DNA technology to produce medical products.

Human *insulin* produced by *E. coli* became one of the first genetically modified proteins approved for use by humans. Before the use of recombinant DNA techniques to generate genetically altered bacteria capable of producing the human hormone, insulin was derived exclusively from other animals. Many diabetic patients become allergic to the insulin from animal sources because its amino acid sequence differs slightly from that of human insulin. The ability to produce the human hormone by recombinant DNA methods has resulted in significant medical benefits to insulin-dependent diabetics.

Genetically modified human *growth hormone (GH)* is available to children who need it to overcome growth deficiencies, specifically pituitary dwarfism (see Chapter 49). In the past, human GH was obtainable only from cadavers. Only small amounts were available, and evidence suggested that some of the preparations from human cadavers were contaminated with infectious agents similar to those that cause bovine spongiform encephalopathy, or mad cow disease (discussed in Chapter 24).

The list of products produced by molecular modification is continually growing. For example, *tissue plasminogen activator (TPA),* a protein that prevents or dissolves blood clots, is used to treat cardiovascular disease. If administered shortly after a heart attack, TPA reduces the risk of a subsequent attack. *Tissue growth factor-beta (TGF-β)* promotes the growth of blood vessels and skin, and is used in wound and burn healing. Researchers also use TGF-*β* in tissue engineering, a developing technology to meet the pressing need for human tissues and, eventually, organs for transplantation by growing them from cell cultures.

The U.S. Food and Drug Administration (FDA) has approved tissue-engineered skin grafts for individuals who have been badly burned, and tissue-engineered cartilage is used for joint repairs. Researchers are investigating the development and use of cardiac cells from ES cells; these cells could be used to repair the heart following heart attacks. Work is also being done on building organs such as bladders and hearts.

Hemophilia A is treated with *human clotting factor VIII*. Before the development of recombinant DNA techniques, factor VIII was available only from human or animal-derived blood, which posed a risk of transmitting infectious agents, such as HIV. *Dornase Alpha (DNase)* improves respiratory function (it helps to liquefy and thin sticky mucus) in people with cystic fibrosis.

Recombinant DNA technology is increasingly used to produce vaccines that provide safe and effective immunity against infectious diseases in humans and animals. One way to develop a recombinant vaccine is to clone a gene for a surface protein produced by the disease-causing agent, or pathogen; the researcher then introduces the gene into a nondisease-causing vector. The vaccine, when delivered into the human or animal host, stimulates an immune response to the surface-exposed protein. As a result, if the pathogen carrying that specific surface protein is encountered, the immune system targets it for destruction. Human examples of antiviral recombinant vaccines include vaccines for influenza A, hepatitis B, and polio.

Recombinant vaccines are also being developed against certain bacterial diseases and human cancers. For example, in 2006 the Food and Drug Administration approved a recombinant vaccine against several types of human papillomavirus (HPV). The vaccine, which is administered to females ages 9 to 26, protects against the 70% of cervical cancers caused by HPV.

DNA fingerprinting has numerous applications

The analysis of DNA fragments extracted from an individual, which is unique to that individual, is known as **DNA fingerprinting.** DNA fingerprinting has many applications in humans and other organisms, as in the following examples:

1. Analyzing evidence found at crime scenes (forensic analysis) (**FIG. 15-13**)
2. Identifying mass disaster victims
3. Proving parentage in dogs for pedigree registration purposes
4. Identifying human cancer cell lines
5. Studying endangered species in conservation biology
6. Tracking tainted foods
7. Studying the genetic ancestry of human populations
8. Clarifying disputed parentage
9. Exonerating prisoners wrongfully convicted of a crime

Historically, DNA fingerprinting relied on RFLPs (discussed earlier). Today, many techniques for DNA fingerprinting rely on PCR amplification, restriction enzyme digestion, and Southern blot hybridization to detect molecular markers. The most useful molecular markers are highly polymorphic within the human population (recall our earlier discussion of *polymorphism*). **Short tandem repeats (STRs)** are molecular markers that are short sequences of repetitive DNA—up to 200 nucleotide bases with a simple repeat pattern such as GTGTGTGTGT or CAGCAGCAG-CAG. Because they vary in length from one individual to another, STRs are highly polymorphic. This characteristic makes them useful with a high degree of certainty in identifying individuals.

If enough markers are compared, the odds that two people taken at random from the general population would have identical DNA profiles may be as low as one in several billion. The FBI uses a set of STRs from 13 different markers to establish a unique DNA profile for an individual. Such a profile distinguishes that person from every other individual in the United States, except an identical twin.

Recall that DNA is also found in the cell's mitochondria. Whereas nuclear DNA occurs in two copies per cell—one on each of the homologous chromosomes—mitochondrial DNA has as

① ② ③ From blood at crime scene ④ ⑤ ⑥ ⑦

Cellmark Diagnostics, Abingdon, U.K.

FIGURE 15-13 *Animated* DNA fingerprinting

These DNA fingerprints show DNA from a crime scene (*in middle*), along with the DNA profiles of seven suspects. Can you pick the suspect whose DNA profile matches blood from the crime scene?

many as 100,000 copies per cell. Therefore, mitochondrial DNA is the molecule of choice for DNA fingerprinting in which biological samples have been damaged—identifying exhumed human remains, for example.

DNA fingerprinting has revolutionized law enforcement. In 1990, the FBI established the Combined DNA Index System (CODIS), consisting of DNA databases from all 50 states. A DNA profile of an unknown suspect can be compared to millions of DNA profiles of convicted offenders in the database, often resulting in identification of the suspect. The DNA from the unknown suspect may come from blood, semen, bones, teeth, hair, saliva, urine, or feces left at the crime scene. Tiny amounts of human DNA have even been extracted from cigarette butts, licked envelopes or postage stamps, dandruff, fingerprints, razor blades, chewing gum, wristwatches, earwax, debris from under fingernails, and toothbrushes.

If applied properly, DNA fingerprinting has the power to identify the guilty and exonerate the innocent. Hundreds of convicted individuals have won new trials and have been subsequently released from incarceration based on correlating DNA profiles with physical evidence from the crime scene. One limitation arises from the fact that the DNA samples are usually small and may have been degraded. Obviously, great care must be taken to prevent contamination of the samples. This is especially crucial if the PCR technique is used to amplify DNA.

Transgenic organisms have foreign DNA incorporated into their cells

Plants and animals in which foreign genes have been incorporated are called **transgenic organisms.** Researchers use varied approaches to insert foreign genes into plant or animal cells. They often use viruses as vectors, although other methods, such as the direct injection of DNA into cells, have also been applied.

Transgenic animals are valuable in research

Transgenic animals are usually produced by injecting the DNA of a particular gene into the nucleus of a fertilized egg cell or of ES cells. The researcher then implants the eggs into the uterus of a female and lets them develop. Alternatively, the researcher injects genetically modified ES cells into isolated *blastocysts,* an early stage in embryonic development, and then implants them into a foster mother.

Injecting DNA into cells is not the only way to produce transgenic animals. Researchers may use viruses as recombinant DNA vectors. RNA viruses called **retroviruses** make DNA copies of themselves by reverse transcription. Sometimes the DNA copies become integrated into the host chromosomes, where they are replicated along with host DNA.

Transgenic animals provide valuable applications over a wide range of research areas, such as regulation of gene expression, immune system function, genetic diseases, viral diseases, and genes involved in the development of cancer. The laboratory mouse is a particularly important model organism for these studies.

In a classic study of the control of gene expression, University of Pennsylvania geneticist Ralph L. Brinster in 1983 produced transgenic mice carrying a gene for rat growth hormone (see Fig. 17-18). Brinster and his coworkers wanted to understand the controls that let certain genes be expressed in some tissues and not in others. The pituitary gland of a mouse normally produces small amounts of GH, and these researchers reasoned that other tissues might also be capable of producing the hormone. First they isolated the GH gene from a library of genomic rat DNA. They combined it with the promoter region of a mouse gene that normally produces metallothionein, a protein that is active in the liver and whose synthesis is stimulated by the presence of toxic amounts of heavy metals such as zinc. The researchers used metallothionein regulatory sequences as a switch to turn the production of rat GH on and off at will. After injecting the modified gene into mouse embryo cells, they implanted the embryos into the uterus of a mouse and let them develop.

Because of the difficulty in manipulating the embryos without damaging them, the gene transplant succeeded in only a small percentage of the animals. When exposed to small amounts of zinc, these transgenic mice produced large amounts of growth hormone because the liver is a much larger organ than the pituitary gland. The mice grew rapidly, and one mouse, which developed from an embryo that had received two copies of the GH gene, grew to more than double the normal size (**FIG. 15-14**). As might be expected, such mice often transmit their increased growth capability to their offspring.

Transgenic animals can produce genetically modified proteins

Certain transgenic animal strains produce milk containing foreign proteins of therapeutic or commercial importance. For example, researchers have introduced into sheep the gene for the human protein tissue plasminogen activator (TPA). Producing transgenic livestock (such as pigs, sheep, cows, and goats) that secrete foreign proteins in their milk is known informally as "pharming," a combination of "pharmaceuticals" and "farming" (**FIG. 15-15**).

In pharming, recombinant genes are fused to the regulatory sequences of the milk protein genes, and such genes are therefore activated only in mammary tissues involved in milk production. The advantages of obtaining a protein drug from milk are that

R. L. Brinster, University of Pennsylvania Medical School

FIGURE 15-14 A transgenic mouse
The mouse on the right is normal, whereas the mouse on the left is a transgenic animal that expresses rat growth hormone in large amounts.

Pentti Vänskä, Helsingin Sanomat International Edition

FIGURE 15-15 Transgenic "pharm" cows
These cows contain a human gene that codes for lactoferrin, a protein found in human mothers' milk and in secretions such as tears, saliva, bile, and pancreatic fluids. Lactoferrin is one of the immune system's lines of defense against disease-causing organisms. The cows secrete human lactoferrin in their milk.

potentially it can be produced in large quantities and that it can be harvested simply by milking the animal. The protein is then purified from the milk. The introduction of the gene does not harm the animals, and because the offspring of the transgenic animal usually produce the recombinant protein, transgenic strains are established.

Transgenic plants are increasingly important in agriculture

People have selectively bred plants for thousands of years. The success of such efforts depends on desirable traits in the variety of plant selected or in closely related wild or domesticated plants whose traits are transferred by crossbreeding. Local varieties or closely related species of cultivated plants often have traits, such as disease resistance, that agriculturalists could advantageously introduce into varieties more useful to modern human needs. If genes are introduced into plants from strains or species with which they do not ordinarily interbreed, the possibilities for improvement increase greatly.

The most widely used vector system for introducing recombinant genes into many types of plant cells is the crown gall bacterium, *Agrobacterium tumefaciens*. This bacterium normally produces plant tumors by introducing a plasmid, called the *Ti plasmid,* into the cells of its host; *Ti* stands for "tumor-inducing." The Ti plasmid induces abnormal growth by forcing the plant cells to produce elevated levels of a plant growth hormone called *cytokinin* (discussed in Chapter 38).

Geneticists "disarm" the Ti plasmid so that it does not induce tumor formation and then use it as a vector to insert genes into plant cells. The cells into which the altered plasmid is introduced are essentially normal except for the inserted genes. Genes placed in the plant genome in this fashion may be transmitted sexually, via seeds, to the next generation, but they can also be propagated asexually, for example, by taking cuttings.

Unfortunately, not all plants take up DNA readily, particularly the cereal grains that are a major food source for humans. One useful approach has been the development of a genetic "shotgun." Researchers coat microscopic gold or tungsten fragments with DNA and then shoot them into plant cells, penetrating the cell walls. Some of the cells retain the DNA, which transforms them. Those cells can then be cultured and used to regenerate an entire plant (see Fig. 17-2). Geneticists have successfully used such an approach to transfer a gene for resistance to a bacterial disease into cultivated rice from one of its wild relatives.

An additional complication of plant genetic modification is that about 120 plant genes lie in the DNA of the chloroplasts; the other 3000 or so genes that plants require to function are in the nucleus. Chloroplasts are essential in photosynthesis, which is the basis for plant productivity. Because great agricultural potential hinges on improving the productivity of photosynthesis, developing methods for changing the part of the plant's DNA within the chloroplast is desirable. Dozens of labs are currently studying methods of chloroplast engineering, although progress has been slow. In 2001, Australian plant physiologists reported that they had altered **rubisco,** the key carbon-fixing enzyme of photosynthesis (see Chapter 9), by changing one of the genes in the chloroplast genome.

The United States is the world's top producer of transgenic crops, also known as **genetically modified (GM) crops.** In 2007,

U.S. farmers planted 57.7 hectares (143 million acres) of GM crops. Globally, 51% of the soybean crop, 31% of corn, 13% of cotton, and 5% of canola are GM crops.

Selected Applications of Transgenic Plants Agricultural geneticists are developing GM plants that are resistant to insect pests, viral and fungal diseases, heat, cold, herbicides, salty or acidic soil, and drought. For example, genetically modified papaya trees, which are resistant to the ringspot virus, have been grown in Hawaii for more than 10 years. A variety of corn that has been genetically modified to be resistant to drought is currently being tested in field trials (**FIG. 15-16**).

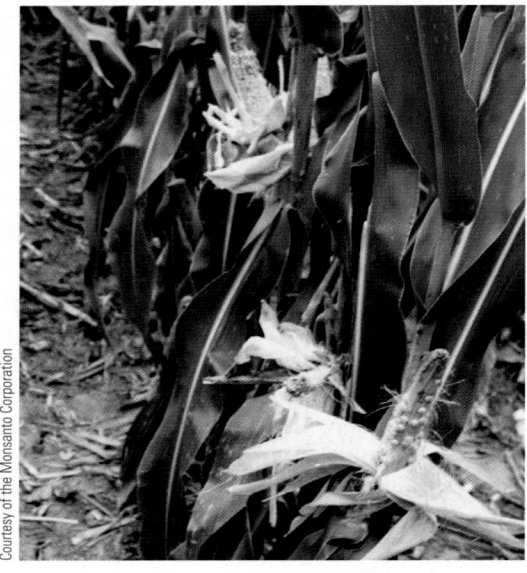

(a) Note the poor yield in genetically unmodified corn plants used as a control.

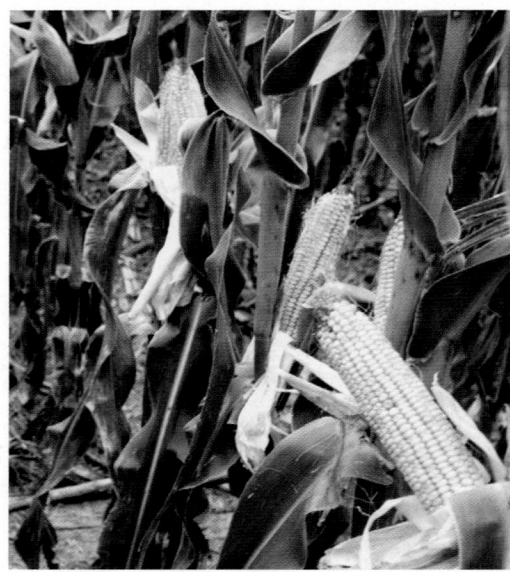

(b) Genetically modified corn plants withstood drought better than the unmodified corn.

FIGURE 15-16 *Animated* **Field test of transgenic corn with resistance to drought**

Corn has also been genetically modified to contain the *Bt* gene, a bacterial gene that codes for a protein with insecticidal properties; *Bt* stands for the bacterium's scientific name, *Bacillus thuringiensis*. *Bt* corn, introduced in the United States in 1996, does not need periodic sprays of chemical insecticides to control the European corn borer, the most damaging insect pest of corn in the United States and Canada.

DNA technology also has the potential to develop crops that are more nutritious. For example, in the 1990s geneticists modified rice to produce high quantities of β-carotene, which the human body uses to make vitamin A. In developing countries, vitamin A deficiency is a leading cause of irreversible blindness in children. Vitamin A deficiency also makes children more susceptible to measles and other infectious diseases. Because rice is the staple diet in many countries with vitamin A deficiency, the widespread use of GM rice with β-carotene could help prevent blindness in many of the world's children. However, GM rice is not yet approved for human consumption.

Like some transgenic animals, certain transgenic plants can potentially be "pharmed" to produce large quantities of medically important proteins. Examples include antibodies against the herpes virus and a patient-specific vaccine for lymphoma, a type of cancer.

Some people are concerned about the health effects of consuming foods derived from GM crops and think that such foods should be restricted. For example, critics say that some consumers may develop food allergies. Scientists also recognize this concern and routinely screen new GM crops for allergenicity. There is also an ongoing controversy as to whether GM foods should be labeled. The FDA and most scientists think such labeling would be counterproductive because it would increase public anxiety over a technology that is as safe as traditional breeding methods. In 1996, the U.S. Court of Appeals upheld the FDA position that labeling should not be required.

Review

- In what way has the production of human insulin by recombinant DNA methods had significant medical advantages for diabetics?
- What are short tandem repeats (STRs), and why are they so useful in DNA fingerprinting?
- Why do gene targeting and mutagenesis screening in mice have potential benefits for humans?

15.5 DNA TECHNOLOGY HAS RAISED SAFETY CONCERNS

■ LEARNING OBJECTIVE

11 Describe at least two safety issues associated with recombinant DNA technology and explain how these issues are being addressed.

When recombinant DNA technology was introduced in the early 1970s, many scientists considered the potential misuses at least as significant as the possible benefits. The possibility that an organism with undesirable environmental effects might be accidentally produced was of great concern. Scientists feared that new strains of bacteria or other organisms, with which the world has no previous experience, might be difficult to control. The scientists who developed the recombinant DNA methods insisted on stringent guidelines for making the new technology safe.

Experiments in thousands of university and industry laboratories over more than 35 years have shown that recombinant DNA manipulations can be carried out safely. Geneticists have produced strains of *E. coli* that cannot survive outside of the laboratory. Researchers carry out experiments that might present unusual risks in facilities designed to hold pathogenic organisms; this precaution ensures that researchers can work with them safely. So far, no evidence suggests that researchers have accidentally cloned hazardous genes or have released dangerous organisms into the environment. However, malicious *intentional* manipulation of dangerous genes certainly remains a concern.

As the safety of the experiments has been established, scientists have relaxed many of the restrictive guidelines for using recombinant DNA. Stringent restrictions still exist, however, in certain areas of recombinant DNA research where there are known dangers or where questions about possible effects on the environment are still unanswered.

These restrictions are most evident in research that proposes to introduce transgenic organisms into the wild, such as agricultural strains of plants whose seeds or pollen might spread in an uncontrolled manner. A great deal of research now focuses on determining the effects of introducing transgenic organisms into a natural environment. Carefully conducted tests have shown that transgenic organisms are not dangerous to the environment simply because they are transgenic.

It is, however, important to assess the risks of each new recombinant organism. Scientists determine whether the organism has characteristics that might cause it to be environmentally hazardous under certain conditions. For example, if geneticists have modified a transgenic crop plant to resist an herbicide, could that gene be transferred, via pollen or some other route, to that plant's weedy relatives, generating herbicide-resistant "superweeds"? In 2003, ecologists at the University of Tennessee, Knoxville, announced the crossing of transgenic oilseed rape plants that contained the *Bt* gene with their wild relative, which is a weed. They crossed the resulting hybrids with the wild relative again and then tested its ability to compete with other weeds in a field of wheat. The transgenic weed was a poor competitor and had less effect on wheat production than its wild relatives in a control field. These results, although encouraging, must be interpreted with care. Scientists must evaluate each transgenic crop plant individually to see if there is gene flow to wild relatives, and if so, what effects might result.

Other concerns relate to plants modified to produce pesticides, such as the *Bt* toxin. The future of the *Bt* toxin in transgenic crops is not secure because low levels of the insecticide could potentially provide ideal conditions for selection for resistant individuals in the insect population. It appears certain insects may evolve genetic resistance to the *Bt* toxin in transgenic plants in the same way they evolve genetic resistance to chemical insecticides.

Another concern is that nonpest species could be harmed. For example, people paid a great deal of attention to the finding that monarch butterfly larvae raised in the laboratory are harmed if they are fed pollen from *Bt* corn plants. However, more recent studies suggest that monarch larvae living in a natural environment do not consume enough pollen to cause damage. Also, evidence indicates that the harm to nonpest species from spraying pesticides is far greater than any harm from transgenic crops.

Environmental concerns about transgenic animals also exist. Several countries are in the process of developing fast-growing transgenic fish, usually by inserting a gene that codes for a growth hormone. Transgenic Atlantic salmon, for example, grow up to six times as fast as nontransgenic salmon grown for human consumption. The transgenic fish do not grow larger than other fish, just faster. The benefits of such genetically enhanced fish include reduced pressure on wild fisheries and less pollution from fish farms. However, if the transgenic fish escaped from the fish farm, what effect would they have on wild relatives? To address this concern, the researchers are developing only nonreproducing female transgenic salmon.

To summarize, DNA technology in agriculture offers many potential benefits, including higher yields by providing disease resistance, more nutritious foods, and the reduced use of chemical pesticides. However, like other kinds of technology, molecular modification poses some risks, such as the risk that genetically modified plants and animals could pass their foreign genes to wild relatives, causing unknown environmental problems. The science of **risk assessment,** which uses statistical methods to quantify risks so they can be compared and contrasted, will help society decide whether to ignore, reduce, or eliminate specific risks of molecularly modified organisms.

Review

- What are some of the environmental concerns regarding transgenic organisms? What kinds of information does society need to determine if these concerns are valid?

■ SUMMARY: FOCUS ON LEARNING OBJECTIVES

15.1 *(page 324)*

1 Explain how a typical restriction enzyme cuts DNA molecules and give examples of the ways in which these enzymes are used in recombinant DNA technology.

- **Recombinant DNA technology** isolates and amplifies specific sequences of DNA by incorporating them into **vector** DNA molecules. Researchers then **clone**—propagate and amplify—the resulting recombinant DNA in organisms such as *E. coli.*

- Researchers use **restriction enzymes** to cut DNA into specific fragments. Each type of restriction enzyme recognizes and cuts DNA at a highly specific base sequence. Many restriction enzymes cleave DNA sequences to produce complementary, single-stranded sticky ends.

  CENGAGENOW™ Learn more about restriction enzymes by clicking on the figure in CengageNOW.

- Geneticists often construct recombinant DNA molecules by allowing the ends of a DNA fragment and a vector, both cut with the same restriction enzyme, to associate by complementary base pairing. Then **DNA ligase** covalently links the DNA strands to form a stable recombinant molecule.

  CENGAGENOW™ Learn more about the formation of recombinant DNA by clicking on the figure in CengageNOW.

2 Distinguish among a genomic DNA library, a chromosome library, and a complementary DNA (cDNA) library; explain why one would clone the same eukaryotic gene from both a genomic DNA library and a cDNA library.

- A **genomic DNA library** contains thousands of DNA fragments that represent the total DNA of an organism. A **chromosome library** contains all the DNA fragments from a specific chromosome. Each DNA fragment of a genomic DNA or chromosome library is stored in a specific bacterial strain.

- A **cDNA library** is produced using **reverse transcriptase** to make DNA copies of mature mRNA isolated from eukaryotic cells. These copies, known as **complementary DNA (cDNA),** are then incorporated into recombinant DNA vectors.

  CENGAGENOW™ Learn more about the formation of cDNA by clicking on the figure in CengageNOW.

- Genes present in genomic DNA and chromosome libraries from eukaryotes contain **introns,** regions that do not code for protein. Those genes can be amplified in bacteria, but the protein is not properly expressed. Because introns have been removed from mature mRNA molecules, eukaryotic genes in cDNA libraries can be expressed in bacteria to produce functional protein products.

3 Explain how researchers use a DNA probe.

- Researchers use a radioactive DNA sequence as a **DNA probe** to screen thousands of recombinant DNA molecules in bacterial cells to find the colony that contains the DNA of interest.

  CENGAGENOW™ Watch the process for using a DNA probe to find bacterial cells with a specific recombinant DNA molecule by clicking on the figure in CengageNOW.

4 Describe how the polymerase chain reaction amplifies DNA in vitro.

- The **polymerase chain reaction (PCR)** is a widely used, automated, in vitro technique in which researchers use specific primers to target a particular DNA sequence and then clone it using a heat-resistant DNA polymerase.

- Using PCR, scientists amplify and analyze tiny DNA samples taken from various sites, from crime scenes to archaeological remains.

  CENGAGENOW™ Watch the amplification of DNA by PCR by clicking on the figure in CengageNOW.

15.2 *(page 331)*

5 Distinguish among DNA, RNA, and protein blotting.

- A **Southern blot** detects DNA fragments by separating them using gel electrophoresis and then transferring them to a nitrocellulose or nylon membrane. A probe is then **hybridized** by complementary base pairing to the DNA bound to the membrane, and the band or bands of DNA are identified by autoradiography or chemical luminescence.

- When RNA molecules that are separated by electrophoresis are transferred to a membrane, the result is a **Northern blot.**

- A **Western blot** consists of proteins or polypeptides previously separated by gel electrophoresis.

6 Describe the chain termination method of DNA sequencing.

- **DNA sequencing** yields information about the structure of a gene and the probable amino acid sequence of its encoded proteins.

- Automated DNA sequencing is based on the **chain termination method,** which uses dideoxynucleotides, each tagged with a different-colored fluorescent dye, to terminate elongation during DNA replication. Gel electrophoresis separates the resulting fragments, and a laser identifies the nucleotide sequence.

  CENGAGENOW™ Learn more about automated DNA sequencing by clicking on the figure in CengageNOW.

15.3 *(page 335)*

7 Describe three important areas of research in genomics.

- **Genomics** is the emerging field of biology that studies the entire DNA sequence of an organism's **genome.** Structural genomics is concerned with mapping and sequencing genomes. Functional genomics deals with the functions of genes and nongene sequences in genomes. Comparative genomics involves comparing the genomes of different species to further our understanding of evolutionary relationships.

8 Explain what a DNA microarray does and give an example of its research and medical potential.

- Many diagnostic tests involve **DNA microarrays,** in which hundreds of different DNA molecules are placed on a glass slide or chip. DNA microarrays enable researchers to compare the activities of thousands of genes in normal and diseased cells from tissue samples. Because cancer and other diseases exhibit altered patterns of gene expression, DNA microarrays have the potential to identify disease-causing genes or the proteins they code for, which can then be targeted by therapeutic drugs.

9 Define *pharmacogenetics* and *proteomics.*

- **Pharmacogenetics,** the new science of gene-based medicine, takes into account the subtle genetic differences among individuals and customizes drugs to match a patient's genetic makeup.

- The study of all the proteins encoded by the human genome and produced in a person's cells and tissues is **proteomics.** Scientists want to identify all the proteins made by a given kind of cell, but the process is much more complicated than sequencing the human genome.

15.4 *(page 339)*

10 Describe at least one important application of recombinant DNA technology in each of the following fields: medicine, DNA fingerprinting, and transgenic organisms.

- Genetically altered bacteria produce many important human protein products, including insulin, growth hormone, tissue plasminogen activator (TPA), tissue growth factor-beta (TGF-β), clotting factor VIII, and Dornase Alpha (DNase).

- **DNA fingerprinting** is the analysis of an individual's DNA. It is based on a variety of **short tandem repeats (STRs),** molecular markers that are highly **polymorphic** within the human population. DNA fingerprinting has applications in areas such as law enforcement, issues of disputed parentage, and tracking tainted foods.

  CENGAGENOW™ Solve a murder case with DNA fingerprinting by clicking on the figure in CengageNOW.

- **Transgenic organisms** have foreign DNA incorporated into their genetic material. Transgenic livestock produce foreign proteins in their milk. Transgenic plants have great potential in agriculture.

15.5 *(page 343)*

11 Describe at least two safety issues associated with recombinant DNA technology and explain how these issues are being addressed.

- Some people are concerned about the safety of molecularly modified organisms. To address these concerns, scientists carry out recombinant DNA technology under specific safety guidelines.

- The introduction of transgenic plants and animals into the natural environment, where they may spread in an uncontrolled manner, is an ongoing concern.

TEST YOUR UNDERSTANDING

1. A plasmid (a) can be used as a DNA vector (b) is a type of bacteriophage (c) is a type of cDNA (d) is a retrovirus (e) b and c

2. DNA molecules with complementary sticky ends associate by (a) covalent bonds (b) hydrogen bonds (c) ionic bonds (d) disulfide bonds (e) phosphodiester linkages

3. Human DNA and a particular plasmid both have sites that are cut by the restriction enzymes *Hin*dIII and *Eco*RI. To make recombinant DNA, the scientist should (a) cut the plasmid with *Eco*RI and the human DNA with *Hin*dIII (b) use *Eco*RI to cut both the plasmid and the human DNA (c) use *Hin*dIII to cut both the plasmid and the human DNA (d) a or b (e) b or c

4. Which technique rapidly replicates specific DNA fragments without cloning in cells? (a) gel electrophoresis (b) cDNA libraries (c) DNA probe (d) restriction fragment length polymorphism (e) polymerase chain reaction

5. The PCR technique uses (a) heat-resistant DNA polymerase (b) reverse transcriptase (c) DNA ligase (d) restriction enzymes (e) b and c

6. A cDNA clone contains (a) introns (b) exons (c) anticodons (d) a and b (e) b and c

7. The dideoxynucleotides ddATP, ddTTP, ddGTP, and ddCTP are important in DNA sequencing because they (a) cause premature termination of a growing DNA strand (b) are used as primers (c) cause the DNA fragments that contain them to migrate more slowly through a sequencing gel (d) are not affected by high temperatures (e) have more energy than deoxynucleotides

8. In the Southern blot technique, _____ is/are transferred from a gel to a nitrocellulose or nylon membrane. (a) protein (b) RNA (c) DNA (d) bacterial colonies (e) reverse transcriptase

9. Gel electrophoresis separates nucleic acids on the basis of differences in (a) length (molecular weight) (b) charge (c) nucleotide sequence (d) relative proportions of adenine and guanine (e) relative proportions of thymine and cytosine

10. A genomic DNA library (a) represents all the DNA in a specific chromosome (b) is made using reverse transcriptase (c) is stored in a collection of recombinant bacteria (d) is a DNA copy of mature mRNAs (e) allows researchers to amplify a tiny sample of DNA

11. Tissue growth factor-beta (a) is a DNA probe for recombinant plasmids (b) is a product of DNA technology used in tissue engineering (c) is necessary to make a cDNA library (d) cannot be synthesized without a heat-resistant DNA polymerase (e) is isolated by the Southern blot technique

12. These highly polymorphic molecular markers are useful in DNA fingerprinting: (a) cosmid cloning vectors (b) cloned DNA sequences (c) palindromic DNA sequences (d) short tandem repeats (e) complementary DNAs

CRITICAL THINKING

1. What are some of the problems that might arise if you were trying to produce a eukaryotic protein in a bacterium? How might using transgenic plants or animals help solve some of these problems?

2. Would molecular modification be possible if we did not know a great deal about the genetics of bacteria? Explain.

3. How is proteomics related to functional genomics?

4. **ANALYZING DATA.** RFLP analysis was performed on blood from a crime scene as well as from two suspects. The crime scene DNA is marked E(vs). Which suspect is probably guilty? Which suspect is definitely innocent?

Leonard Lessin/Peter Arnold, Inc.

5. **EVOLUTION LINK.** DNA technology, such as the production of transgenic animals, is possible only because widely different organisms have essentially identical genetic systems (DNA $\longrightarrow$ RNA $\longrightarrow$ protein). What is the evolutionary significance of the universality of genetic systems in organisms as diverse as bacteria and pigs?

6. **SCIENCE, TECHNOLOGY, AND SOCIETY.** What are some ways that recent DNA technologies might affect you personally?

 Additional questions are available in CengageNOW at www.cengage.com/login.

16 Human Genetics and the Human Genome

78E1	
91A2	
81G1	
87G10	
98D7	
58C11	
101C7	
29F6	
106H5	
51H2	
60D11	
66E12	
911D9	
858H7	
932F11	
937A6	

Rapid chromosome mapping. This fluorescent LM of human chromosome 10 (*left*) has different-colored fluorescent probes attached to specific DNA sequences. (Loci and key are at *right*.) This technique allows researchers to efficiently determine certain chromosome rearrangements and abnormalities.

© Regents of the University of California 2005/Dr. Uli Weier/Photo Researchers, Inc.

KEY CONCEPTS

16.1 Pedigree analysis and karyotype analysis are traditional methods to study human genetics; molecular aspects of the human genome, including genome-wide association scans and comparative genomics, are increasingly used today.

16.2 Chromosome abnormalities such as aneuploidies—the presence or absence of a single chromosome—can cause serious medical conditions.

16.3 Mutations in single genes can produce genetic disorders.

16.4 Researchers are developing gene therapy methods that could potentially correct certain genetic disorders.

16.5 Genetic testing and counseling help individuals make reproductive decisions.

16.6 Certain advances in human genetics raise ethical questions.

The principles of genetics apply to all organisms, including humans. However, important differences separate genetic research on humans and genetic research on other organisms. To study inheritance in other species, geneticists may conduct controlled matings between individuals and raise the offspring under carefully controlled conditions. Of course, setting up experimental matings in humans is unethical and illegal.

An important difference between genetic research in humans and other organisms is that organisms used in genetic research generally produce many offspring and have short generation times between reproductive periods. In contrast, most human families are small, and 20 to 30 years or more elapse between generations.

Despite the inherent difficulties of studying inheritance in humans, **human genetics,** the science of inherited variation in humans, is progressing rapidly (see figure). Researchers conduct population studies of large extended families. Also, the medical attention given to human genetic diseases has expanded our knowledge of human genetics. Genetic studies of other organisms have provided invaluable insights: many human inheritance questions have been explained using model organisms, such as bacteria, yeasts, worms, fruit flies, and mice.

More recently, the **human genome,** which represents the totality of genetic information in human cells, has been mapped and sequenced. In **DNA sequencing,** researchers identify the order of nucleotides in DNA to understand the genetic basis of human similarities and differences.

In this chapter we first examine the methods of human genetics, including new research directions that are developing as a result of the Human Genome Project. Then we discuss a variety of human genetic disorders. We explore the use of gene therapy for some of these disorders, as well as the application of genetic testing, screening, and counseling for families at risk. The chapter concludes with a discussion of ethical issues related to human genetics.

16.1 STUDYING HUMAN GENETICS

■ LEARNING OBJECTIVES

1 Distinguish between karyotyping and pedigree analysis.
2 Discuss the implications of the Human Genome Project.
3 Discuss the mouse model for studying cystic fibrosis.

Human geneticists use a variety of methods that enable them to help identify genetic defects and to make inferences about a trait's mode of inheritance. We consider three of these methods—the identification of chromosomes by karyotyping, the analysis of family inheritance patterns using pedigrees, and DNA sequencing and mapping of genes by genome projects. Investigators often study human inheritance most effectively by combining these and other approaches.

Human chromosomes are studied by karyotyping

Like Mendel and his pea plants, researchers working with simpler organisms have discovered many of the basic principles of genetics. In such organisms, it is often possible to relate genetic data to the number and structure of specific chromosomes. Some organisms used in genetics, such as the fruit fly *Drosophila melanogaster,* have very few chromosomes; the fruit fly has only four pairs. In *Drosophila* larval salivary glands, the chromosomes are large enough that their structural details are readily evident. (Note the detail shown in the light micrograph of *Drosophila* chromosomes in Figure 2-3.) This organism, therefore, has provided unique opportunities for correlating certain inherited phenotypic changes with alterations in chromosome structure.

The normal number of chromosomes for the human species is 46: 44 **autosomes** (22 pairs) and 2 sex chromosomes (1 pair). A **karyotype** (from Greek, meaning "nucleus") is an individual's chromosome composition, both chromosome number and large structural defects in a chromosome. Until the mid-1950s, when biologists adopted modern methods of karyotyping, the accepted

number of chromosomes for the human species was 48, based on a study of human chromosomes published in 1923. The reason researchers counted 48 human chromosomes was the difficulty in separating the chromosomes so they could be accurately counted.

In 1952, University of Texas cell biologist T. C. Hsu treated cells with a hypotonic salt solution by mistake; this caused the cells to swell and the chromosomes to spread apart, thereby making them easier to count. Other techniques were also developed, and in 1956 researchers Joe Hin Tjio and Albert Levan, working in Sweden, reported that humans have 46 chromosomes, not 48. Other researchers subsequently verified this report. The story of the human chromosome number is a valuable example of the "self-correcting" nature of science (although such corrections may take time). The re-evaluation of established facts and ideas, often by using improved techniques or new methods, is an essential part of the scientific process.

Human chromosomes are visible only in dividing cells (see Chapter 10), and it is difficult to obtain dividing cells directly from the human body. Researchers typically use blood because white blood cells can be induced to divide in a culture medium by treating them with certain chemicals. Other sources of dividing cells include skin and, for prenatal chromosome studies, chorionic villi or fetal cells shed into the amniotic fluid (discussed later in the chapter).

In karyotyping, biologists culture dividing human cells and then treat them with the drug *colchicine,* which arrests the cells at mitotic metaphase or late prophase, when the chromosomes are most highly condensed. Next, the researchers put the cells into a hypotonic solution; the cells swell, and the chromosomes spread out so they are easily observed. The investigators then flatten the cells on microscope slides and stain the chromosomes to reveal the patterns of bands, which are unique for each homologous pair. After the microscopic image has been scanned into a computer, the homologous pairs are electronically matched and placed together (**FIG. 16-1**).

By convention, geneticists identify chromosomes by length; position of the centromere; banding patterns, which are produced by staining chromosomes with dyes that produce dark and light crossbands of varying widths; and other features such as *satellites,* tiny knobs of chromosome material at the tips of certain chromosomes. With the exception of the sex chromosomes, all chromosomes but chromosome 21, which is smaller than chromosome 22, are numbered and lined up in order of size. The largest human chromosome (chromosome 1) is about five times as long as the smallest one (chromosome 21), but there are only slight size differences among some of the intermediate-sized chromosomes. The X and Y chromosomes of a normal male are homologous only at their tips; normal females have two X chromosomes and no Y chromosome. Differences from the normal karyotype—that is, deviations in chromosome number or structure—are associated with certain disorders such as Down syndrome (discussed later in the chapter).

Another way to distinguish chromosomes in a karyotype is by **fluorescent in situ hybridization (FISH).** A geneticist tags a DNA strand complementary to DNA in a specific chromosome with a fluorescent dye. The DNA in the chromosome is denatured—that is, the two strands are separated—so the tagged strand can bind to it. A different dye is used for each chromosome, "painting" each with a different color (see karyotype in Fig. 16-1). A chromosome that is multicolored (*not shown*) indicates breakage and fusion of chromosomes, an abnormality associated with certain genetic diseases and many types of cancer.

RESEARCH METHOD

Why Is It Used? Researchers use karyotypes to screen individuals for chromosome abnormalities.

How Is It Done? Karyotypes are commonly prepared from cultures of white blood cells. Researchers place prepared cells on a slide, and the chromosomes spill out of the ruptured nuclei. The light microscope under which the slide is viewed is connected to a computer with image analysis software, which helps the biologist match homologous chromosomes and organize them by size. Before computers were used, researchers cut and pasted chromosomes from photographs.

SIU/Peter Arnold, Inc.

These chromosomes have been "painted" by different-colored fluorescent dyes that hybridize to specific pairs of homologous chromosomes. Painting helps the researcher identify chromosomes. A normal human male karyotype is shown.

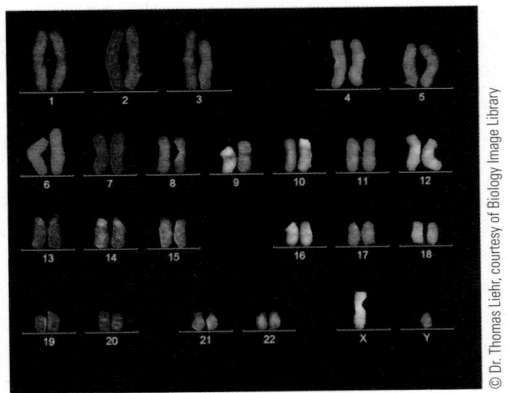

© Dr. Thomas Liehr, courtesy of Biology Image Library

FIGURE 16-1 Karyotyping

Family pedigrees help identify certain inherited conditions

Early studies of human genetics usually dealt with readily identified pairs of contrasting traits and their distribution among members of a family. A "family tree" that shows inheritance patterns, the transmission of genetic traits within a family over several generations, is known as a **pedigree.** Pedigree analysis remains widely used, even in today's world of powerful molecular genetic techniques, because it helps molecular geneticists determine the exact interrelationships of the DNA molecules they analyze from related individuals. Pedigree analysis is also an important tool of genetic counselors and clinicians. However, because human families tend to be small and information about certain family members, particularly deceased relatives, may not be available, pedigree analysis has limitations.

Pedigrees are produced using standardized symbols. Examine **FIGURE 16-2**, which shows a pedigree for **albinism,** a lack of the pigment melanin in the skin, hair, and eyes. Each horizontal row represents a separate generation, with the earliest generation (Roman numeral I) at the top and the most recent generation at the bottom. Within a given generation, the individuals are usually numbered consecutively, from left to right, using Arabic numerals. A horizontal line connects two parents, and a vertical line drops from the parents to their children. For example, individuals II-3 and II-4 are parents of four offspring (III-1, III-2, III-3, and III-4). Note that individuals in a given generation can be genetically unrelated. For example, II-1, II-2, and II-3 are unrelated to II-4 and II-5. Within a group of siblings, the oldest is on the left, and the youngest is on the right.

The allele for albinism cannot be dominant; if it were, at least one of female III-2's parents would have been an albino. This pedigree is explained if albinism is inherited as an autosomal (not carried on a sex chromosome) recessive allele. In such cases, two phenotypically normal parents could produce an albino offspring because they are heterozygotes and could each transmit a recessive allele.

Studying pedigrees enables human geneticists to predict how phenotypic traits that are governed by the genotype at a single locus are inherited. About 10,000 traits have been described in humans. Pedigree analysis most often identifies three modes of single-locus inheritance: autosomal dominant, autosomal recessive, and X-linked recessive. We define and discuss examples of these inheritance modes later in the chapter.

The Human Genome Project sequenced the DNA on all human chromosomes

Scientists working on the **Human Genome Project** sequenced the DNA in the entire nuclear human genome—about 2.9 billion base pairs. (The human mitochondrial genome was sequenced in 1981.) This international undertaking, based on the DNA from 6 to 10 anonymous individuals, was essentially completed in 2001 by hundreds of researchers working in two independent teams, the government-funded International Human Genome Sequencing Consortium and the privately funded company Celera Genomics. The completion of the Human Genome Project in 2003 was a significant milestone in genetics (**TABLE 16-1**).

(a) An albino Cuna Indian girl plays with her friends. Albinism is common among the Cuna people living on the San Blas Islands of Panama.

Key:

○ Normal female

□ Normal male

● Albino female

■ Albino male

□—○ Mating

(siblings diagram) Siblings produced by mating

(b) By studying family histories, a researcher can determine the genetic mechanism of an inherited trait. In this example, III-2 represents an albino girl with two phenotypically normal parents, II-3 and II-4.

FIGURE 16-2 *Animated* A pedigree for albinism

TABLE 16-1	Selected Milestones in Genetics
Year	Scientific Advance
1866	Mendel proposed existence of hereditary factors now known as genes
1871	Nucleic acids discovered
1879	Chromosomes identified and observed during cell division
1929	Chemical nature of nucleotides characterized
1953	Double-helix structure of DNA determined
1960s	Genetic code explained (how proteins are made from DNA)
1972	First recombinant DNA molecule produced
1977	DNA sequencing began
1986	DNA sequencing automated
1995	Sequencing of first prokaryotic genome (bacterium *Haemophilus influenzae*) completed
1996	Sequencing of first eukaryotic genome (yeast *Saccharomyces cerevisiae*) completed
1998	Sequencing of first multicellular eukaryotic genome (nematode worm *Caenorhabditis elegans*) completed
2001	Draft sequence of entire human genome published; discovered that 95% of genome is noncoding
2003	Completion of DNA sequencing of human genome

Gene identification represents a formidable challenge. How do you identify a gene in a DNA sequence if you know nothing about it? The human genome is extremely complex. It includes the DNA content of both the nucleus and the mitochondria. However, nuclear DNA accounts for almost all the genetic information in the human genome. Like genomes of other eukaryotic organisms, some (in humans, only about 2%) of the human genome specifies the synthesis of polypeptides, whereas some other segments code only for RNA products.

Most of the human genome consists of noncoding regulatory elements, repetitive sequences (multiple copies) of DNA, and gene segments whose functions remain unknown. Sometimes genes overlap one another, and in other cases a single gene codes for multiple proteins. Relating specific genes to the RNAs and proteins they code for and determining the roles these RNAs and proteins play in the body are some of the avenues of human genetic research that scientists are currently pursuing.

In human chromosome 22, for example, computers scanned DNA sequences for identifying markers such as promoter elements that are typically associated with genes. Using this approach, researchers identified 545 genes. Many of these are "potential" genes in that their messenger RNAs (mRNAs) and protein products have not yet been isolated. Other genes were identified because they code for proteins similar to those previously identified in humans or other organisms. Despite the difficulties, scientists are making

Scientists hope to eventually identify where all the genes are located in the sequenced DNA. In 2001, the National Human Genome Research Institute (NHGRI) estimated there were 35,000 to 45,000 protein-coding genes in the human genome, but by the end of the decade the estimate had been lowered to 20,000 to 25,000.

progress, and mapping studies will help scientists understand the physical and functional relationships among genes and groups of genes as revealed by their order on the chromosomes.

Now that the human genome has been sequenced, researchers will be busy for many decades analyzing the growing body of human molecular data. In addition to identifying genes, scientists want to understand what each gene's role is, how each gene interacts with other genes, and how the expression of each gene is regulated in different tissues. Eventually, all the thousands of proteins produced in human cells will be identified, their 3-D structures determined, and their properties and functions evaluated.

Genome-wide association scans demonstrate the genetic complexity of major human diseases

Researchers have begun to study sequence variations within the human genome to elucidate differences that might be related to susceptibility to illness or disease. The potential medical applications of the Human Genome Project are extremely promising. Genes on human chromosome 22, for example, are associated with at least 27 diseases known to have a genetic component. The causative genes of many of these disorders have not yet been identified. For example, a gene involved in schizophrenia is strongly linked to human chromosome 22, but scientists do not know its exact location or function.

Genome-wide association (GWA) scans compare the genomes of individuals with a particular disease to healthy individuals without that disease. In 2007, for example, researchers scanned the genomes of more than 16,000 British people to compare genetic patterns in healthy people with those in people with one of seven common diseases: bipolar disorder, coronary artery disease, Crohn's disease, hypertension, rheumatoid arthritis, type 1 diabetes, and type 2 diabetes. These disease phenotypes exhibit complex inheritance patterns, with many different genes contributing to susceptibility. In this particular study, scientists found 24 variations associated with an increased risk of one or more of these diseases. The functions of most of these GWA variations have not yet been determined, but knowing their locations on particular chromosomes will make it easier for researchers to study the genetics of many common human diseases.

Comparative genomics has revealed DNA identical in both mouse and human genomes

About 500 DNA segments longer than 200 base pairs are known to be 100% conserved (that is, identical) between the mouse and human genomes. This remarkable degree of conservation has interesting evolutionary implications because it means that these segments have not mutated during the past 75 million years that mice and humans have shared a common ancestor. During this time, other DNA sections underwent considerable mutation and selection, allowing mice and humans to diverge to their present states. Although the functions of these unchanged elements are not yet determined, they clearly have a vital role. (If they were not essential in their present form, they would have undergone mutation and selection.) Many highly conserved segments appear to contain nonprotein-coding elements that may regulate the expression of other genes.

Researchers use mouse models to study human genetic diseases

Many questions relating to human genetic diseases are difficult to answer because of the ethical issues involved in using humans as test subjects. However, research on any disease is greatly facilitated if an animal model is used for experimentation. A good example is *cystic fibrosis,* a genetic disease caused by a single gene mutation inherited as a recessive allele. In 1994, researchers used **gene targeting** to produce strains of mice that were either homozygous or heterozygous for cystic fibrosis.

The allele that causes cystic fibrosis is a mutant form of a locus involved in controlling the body's water and electrolyte balance. Geneticists have cloned this gene and found that it codes for a protein, the *CFTR protein,* that serves as a chloride ion channel in the plasma membrane. (*CFTR* stands for *cystic fibrosis transmembrane conductance regulator.*) This ion channel transports chloride ions out of the cells lining the digestive tract and the respiratory system. When the chloride ions leave the cells, water follows by osmosis. Thus, the normal secretions of these cells are relatively watery. Because the cells of individuals with cystic fibrosis lack normal chloride ion channels, the individuals' secretions have a low water content and their sweat is very salty. Cells of heterozygous individuals have only half the usual number of functional CFTR ion channels, but these are enough to maintain the normal fluidity of their secretions.

Some researchers are now focusing on understanding the way in which the CFTR channel is activated or inactivated in mice. They hope to use this information to design drugs that enhance chloride transport through the CFTR channels. Such drugs have the potential to treat cystic fibrosis in humans by activating the mutant channels.

Review

- What kinds of information can a human karyotype provide?
- What is pedigree analysis?
- What are two possible benefits scientists hope to obtain by further study of the human genome?
- How does using a mouse model for a genetic disease overcome some of the difficulties in studying human inheritance?

16.2 ABNORMALITIES IN CHROMOSOME NUMBER AND STRUCTURE

■ LEARNING OBJECTIVES

4 Explain how nondisjunction in meiosis is responsible for chromosome abnormalities such as Down syndrome, Klinefelter syndrome, and Turner syndrome.

5 Distinguish among the following structural abnormalities in chromosomes: translocations, deletions, and fragile sites.

Polyploidy, the presence of multiple sets of chromosomes, is common in plants but rare in animals. It may arise from the failure of chromosomes to separate during meiosis or from the fertilization of an egg by more than one sperm. When it occurs in all the cells of the body, polyploidy is lethal in humans and many other animals. For example, *triploidy* (3*n*) is sometimes found in human embryos that have been spontaneously aborted in early pregnancy.

Abnormalities caused by the presence of a single extra chromosome or the absence of a chromosome—called **aneuploidies**—are more common than polyploidy. **Disomy** is the normal state: two of each kind of chromosome in a cell or individual. In **trisomy,** a cell or individual has two copies of each chromosome except for one, which has three copies; a trisomic chromosome number is designated 2*n* + 1. In **monosomy,** an individual lacks one member of a pair of chromosomes; a monosomic chromosome number is designated 2*n* − 1. **TABLE 16-2** summarizes some disorders that aneuploidies produce.

Aneuploidies generally arise as a result of an abnormal meiotic (or, rarely, mitotic) division in which chromosomes fail to separate at anaphase. This phenomenon, called **nondisjunction,** can occur with the autosomes or with the sex chromosomes. In meiosis, chromosome nondisjunction may occur during the first or second meiotic division (or both). For example, two X chromosomes that fail to separate at either the first or the second meiotic division may both enter the egg nucleus. Alternatively, the two joined X chromosomes may go into a *polar body,* leaving the egg with no X chromosome. (Recall from Chapter 10 that a polar body is a nonfunctional haploid cell produced during oogenesis; also see Fig. 50-11.)

Nondisjunction of the XY pair during the first meiotic division in the male may lead to the formation of a sperm with both X and Y chromosomes or a sperm with neither an X nor a Y chromosome (**FIG. 16-3**). Similarly, nondisjunction at the second meiotic division can produce sperm with two Xs or two Ys. When an abnormal gamete unites with a normal one, the resulting zygote has a chromosome abnormality that will be present in every cell of the body.

Meiotic nondisjunction results in an abnormal chromosome number at the zygote stage of development, so all cells in the individual have an abnormal chromosome number. In contrast, nondisjunction during a mitotic division occurs sometime later in development and leads to the establishment of a clone of abnormal cells in an otherwise normal individual. Such a mixture of cells with different chromosome numbers may or may not affect somatic (body) or germ line (reproductive) tissues.

Different numbers of chromosomes are common in many cancer cells, particularly those in solid tumors. Whether aneuploidy is a cause or a consequence of cancer, however, is not yet clear.

Recognizable chromosome abnormalities are seen in less than 1% of all live births, but substantial evidence suggests the rate at conception is much higher. At least 17% of pregnancies recognized at 8 weeks will end in spontaneous abortion (miscarriage). Approximately half of these spontaneously aborted embryos have major chromosome abnormalities, including autosomal trisomies (such as trisomy 21), triploidy, tetraploidy, and Turner syndrome (X0), in which the 0 refers to the absence of a second sex chromosome. Autosomal monosomies are exceedingly rare, possibly because they induce a spontaneous abortion very early in the pregnancy, before a woman is even aware she is pregnant. Some investigators give surprisingly high estimates (50% or more) for the loss rate of very early embryos. Chromosome abnormalities probably induce many of these spontaneous abortions.

Down syndrome is usually caused by trisomy 21

Down syndrome is one of the most common chromosome abnormalities in humans. (The term *syndrome* refers to a set of symptoms that usually occur together in a particular disorder.) It was named after J. Langdon Down, the British physician who in 1866 first described the condition. Affected individuals have abnormalities of the face, eyelids, tongue, hands, and other parts of the body and are mentally retarded (**FIG. 16-4a**). They are also unusually susceptible to certain diseases, such as leukemia and Alzheimer's disease.

TABLE 16-2	Chromosome Abnormalities: Disorders Produced by Aneuploidies	
Karyotype	Common Name	Clinical Description
Trisomy 13	Patau syndrome	Multiple defects, with death typically by age 3 months
Trisomy 18	Edwards syndrome	Ear deformities, heart defects, spasticity, and other damage; death typically by age 1 year, but some survive much longer
Trisomy 21	Down syndrome	Overall frequency is about 1 in 800 live births. Most conceptions involving true trisomy occur in older (age 35+) mothers, but translocation resulting in the equivalent of trisomy is not age-related. Trisomy 21 is characterized by a fold of skin above the eye, varying degrees of mental retardation, short stature, protruding furrowed tongue, transverse palmar crease, cardiac deformities, and increased risk of leukemia and Alzheimer's disease.
X0	Turner syndrome	Short stature, webbed neck, sometimes slight mental retardation; ovaries degenerate in late embryonic life, leading to rudimentary sexual characteristics; gender is female; no Barr bodies
XXY	Klinefelter syndrome	Male with slowly degenerating testes, enlarged breasts; one Barr body per cell
XYY	XYY karotype	Many males have no unusual symptoms; others are unusually tall, with heavy acne, and some tendency to mild mental retardation
XXX	Triplo-X	Despite three X chromosomes, usually fertile females with normal intelligence; two Barr bodies per cell

Aneuploidy may occur by meiotic nondisjunction, the abnormal segregation of chromosomes during meiosis.

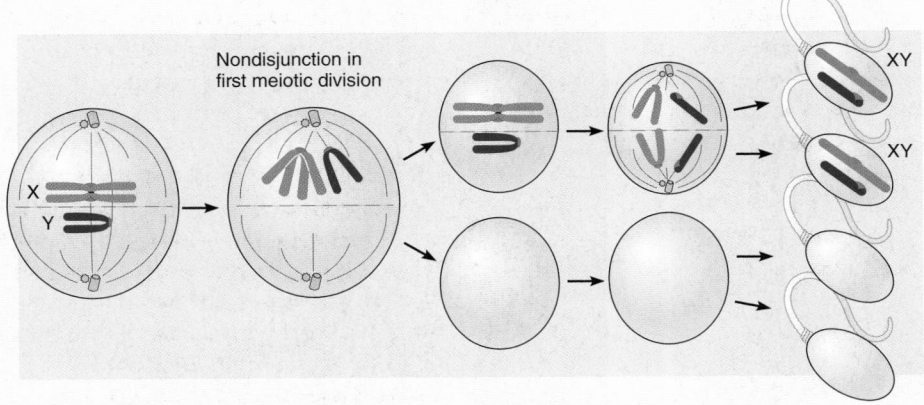

(a) First meiotic division nondisjunction results in two XY sperm and two sperm with neither an X nor a Y.

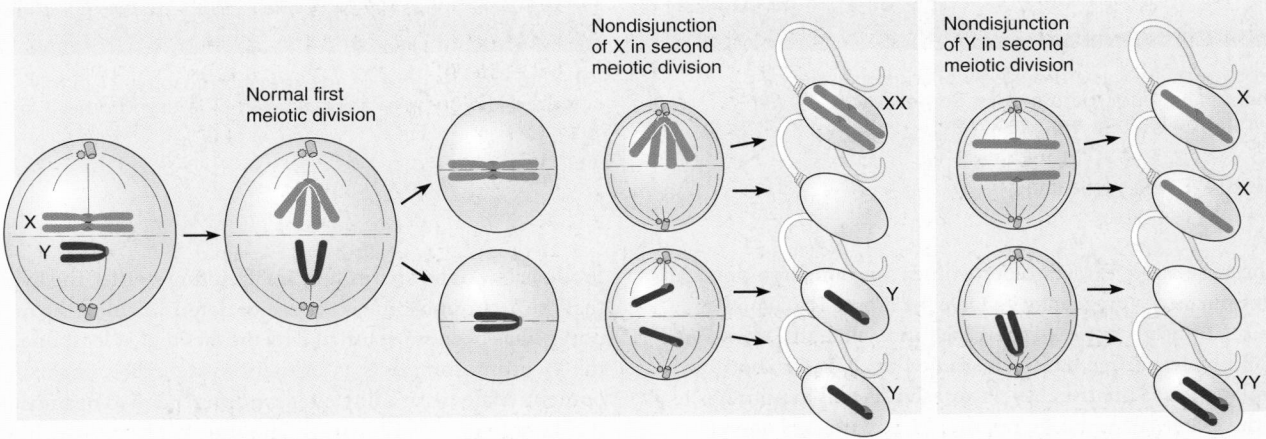

(b) Second meiotic division nondisjunction of the X chromosome results in one sperm with two X chromosomes, two with one Y each, and one with no sex chromosomes. Nondisjunction of the Y chromosome results in one sperm with two Y chromosomes, two with one X each, and one with no sex chromosome (*box on right*).

FIGURE 16-3 Meiotic nondisjunction

In these examples of nondisjunction of the sex chromosomes in the human male, only the X (*purple*) and Y (*blue*) chromosomes are shown. (The positions of the metaphase chromosomes have been modified to save space.)

Genetic studies have revealed that most people with Down syndrome have 47 chromosomes because of *autosomal trisomy:* this condition is known as **trisomy 21** (**FIG. 16-4b**). Nondisjunction during meiosis is responsible for the presence of the extra chromosome. Although no genetic information is missing in these individuals, the extra copies of chromosome 21 genes bring about some type of genetic imbalance that causes abnormal physical and mental development. Down syndrome is quite variable in expression, with some individuals far more severely affected than others. Researchers are using DNA technologies to pinpoint genes on chromosome 21 that affect mental development, as well as possible *oncogenes* (cancer-causing genes) and genes that may be involved in Alzheimer's disease. (Like many human conditions, cancer and Alzheimer's disease have both genetic and environmental components.)

Down syndrome occurs in all ethnic groups in about 1 out of 800 live births. Its incidence increases markedly with increasing maternal age. The occurrence of Down syndrome is not affected by the father's age (although other disorders are, including schizophrenia and achondroplasia, the most common form of dwarfism). Down syndrome is 68 times as likely in the offspring of mothers of age 45 than in the offspring of mothers age 20. However, most babies with Down syndrome in the United States are born to mothers younger than 35, in part because these greatly outnumber older mothers, and

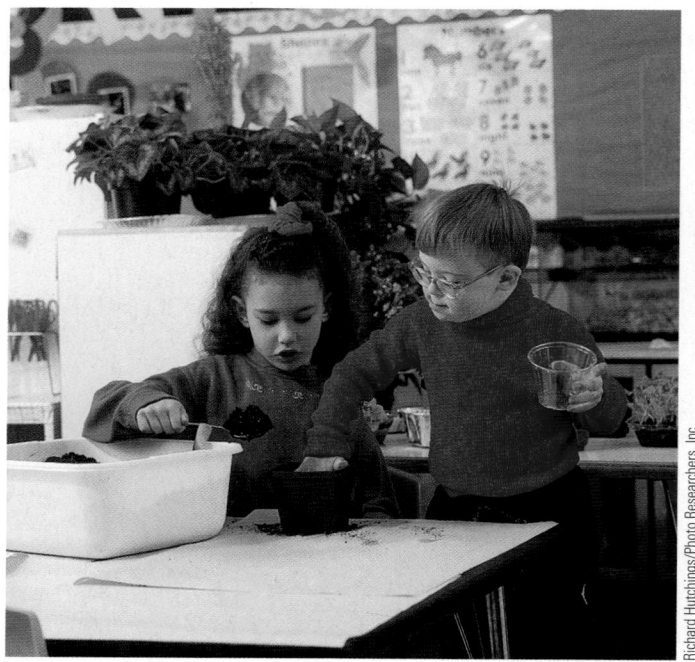

(a) This boy with Down syndrome is working on a science experiment in his kindergarten class. Some individuals with Down syndrome learn to read and write.

(b) Note the presence of an extra chromosome 21 in this colorized karyotype of a female with Down syndrome.

FIGURE 16-4 Down syndrome

in part because about 90% of older women who undergo prenatal testing terminate the pregnancy if Down syndrome is diagnosed.

The relationship between increased incidence in Down syndrome and maternal age has been studied for decades, but there is no explanation. Scientists have proposed several hypotheses to explain the maternal age effect, but none are supported unequivocally. One explanation is that older women have held eggs in suspended meiosis too long, leading to a deterioration of the meiotic spindle apparatus. (A woman is born with all the oocytes she will ever have; these oocytes remain in prophase I of meiosis until ovulation.) Another possibility is that an aging uterus is less likely to reject an abnormal fetus.

Most sex chromosome aneuploidies are less severe than autosomal aneuploidies

Sex chromosome aneuploidies are tolerated relatively well (see Table 16-2) This is true, at least in part because of the mechanism of **dosage compensation:** mammalian cells compensate for extra X chromosome material by rendering all but one X chromosome inactive. The inactive X is seen as a **Barr body**, a region of darkly stained, condensed chromatin next to the nuclear envelope of an interphase nucleus (see Fig. 11-16). Investigators have used the presence of the Barr body in the cells of normal females as an initial screen to determine whether an individual is genetically female or male. However, as you will see shortly in the context of sex chromosome aneuploidies, the Barr body test has limitations.

Individuals with **Klinefelter syndrome** are males with 47 chromosomes, including two Xs and one Y. They have small testes,

produce few or no sperm, and are therefore sterile. The hypothesis that the Y chromosome is the major determinant of the male phenotype has been substantiated by the fact that at least one gene on the Y chromosome acts as a genetic switch, directing male development. Males with Klinefelter syndrome tend to be unusually tall and have female-like breast development. About half show some mental retardation, but many live relatively normal lives. However, each of their cells has one Barr body. On the basis of such a test, they would be erroneously classified as females. About 1 in 1000 live-born males has Klinefelter syndrome.

The sex chromosome composition for **Turner syndrome,** in which an individual has only one sex chromosome, an X chromosome, is designated X0. Because they lack the male-determining effect of the Y chromosome, individuals with Turner syndrome develop as females. However, both their internal and their external genital structures are underdeveloped, and they are sterile. Apparently, a second X chromosome is necessary for normal development of ovaries in a female embryo. Examination of the cells of these individuals reveals no Barr bodies because there is no extra X chromosome to be inactivated. Using the standards of the Barr body test, such an individual would be classified erroneously as a male. About 1 in 2500 live-born females has Turner syndrome.

People with an X chromosome plus two Y chromosomes are phenotypically males, and they are fertile. Other characteristics of these individuals (tall, often with severe acne) hardly qualify as a syndrome; hence the designation **XYY karyotype.** Some years ago, several widely publicized studies suggested that males with this condition are more likely to display criminal tendencies and thus to be imprisoned. However, these studies were flawed because they were based on small numbers of XYY males, without adequate or well-matched control studies of XY males. The prevailing opinion in medical genetics today is that there are many undiagnosed XYY males in the general population who do not have overly aggressive or criminal behaviors and are unlikely to be incarcerated.

Abnormalities in chromosome structure cause certain disorders

Chromosome abnormalities are caused not only by changes in chromosome number but also by distinct changes in the structure of one or more chromosomes. The breakage and rejoining of chromosome parts result in four structural changes within or between chromosomes: duplications, inversions, deletions, and translocations (**FIG. 16-5**). Breaks in chromosomes are the result of errors in replication or recombination. In a **duplication,** a segment of the chromosome is repeated one or more times; these repeats often appear in tandem with one another. The orientation of a chromosome segment is reversed in an **inversion.** In a **deletion,** breakage causes loss of part of a chromosome, along with the genes on that segment. A deletion can occur at the end of a chromosome or on an internal part of the chromosome. In some cases of **translocation,** a chromosome fragment breaks off and attaches to a nonhomologous chromosome. In a **reciprocal translocation,** two nonhomologous chromosomes exchange segments.

Here we consider three simple examples of chromosomal structural changes that result in abnormal phenotypes: translocations, deletions, and *fragile sites,* which are chromosome sites that are susceptible to breakage.

Translocation is the attachment of part of one chromosome to another

The consequences of translocations vary considerably. They include deletions, in which some genes are missing, and duplications, in which extra copies of certain genes are present. In about 4% of individuals with Down syndrome, only 46 chromosomes are present, but one is abnormal. The large arm of chromosome 21 has been translocated to the large arm of another chromosome, usually chromosome 14. Individuals with **translocation Down syndrome** have one chromosome 14, one combined 14/21 chromosome, and two normal copies of chromosome 21. All or part of the genetic material from chromosome 21 is thus present in triplicate. When studying the karyotypes of the parents in such cases, geneticists usually find that either the mother or the father has only 45 chromosomes, although she or he is generally phenotypically normal. The parent with 45 chromosomes has one chromosome 14, one combined 14/21 chromosome, and one chromosome 21; although the karyotype is abnormal, there is no extra genetic material. In contrast to trisomy 21, translocation Down syndrome can run in families, and its incidence is not related to maternal age.

A deletion is the loss of part of a chromosome

Sometimes chromosomes break and fail to rejoin. Such breaks result in deletions of as little as a few base pairs to as much as an entire chromosome arm. As you might expect, large deletions are generally lethal, whereas small deletions may have no effect or may cause recognizable human disorders.

One deletion disorder (1 in 50,000 live births) is **cri du chat syndrome,** in which part of the short arm of chromosome 5 is

(a) A **duplication** is a repeated segment of a chromosome. In this example, segment A is repeated.

(b) An **inversion** is a chromosome segment with a reversed orientation. An inversion does not change the amount of genetic material in the chromosome, only its arrangement.

(c) A **deletion** is the loss of a chromosome segment. A deletion can occur at the tip (shown) or within the chromosome.

(d) A **reciprocal translocation** occurs when two nonhomologous chromosomes exchange segments.

FIGURE 16-5 *Animated* Common abnormalities of chromosome structure deleted. As in most deletions, the exact point of breakage in chromosome 5 varies from one individual to another; some cases of cri du chat involve a small loss, whereas others involve a more substantial deletion of base pairs. Infants born with cri du chat syndrome typically have a small head with altered features described as a "moon face" and a distinctive cry that sounds like a kitten mewing. (The name literally means "cry of the cat" in French.) Affected individuals usually survive beyond childhood but exhibit severe mental retardation.

Fragile sites are weak points at specific locations in chromatids

A **fragile site** is a place where part of a chromatid appears to be attached to the rest of the chromosome by a thin thread of DNA. Fragile sites occur at corresponding locations on both chromatids of a chromosome. They have been identified on the X chromosome as well as on certain autosomes. The location of a fragile site is exactly the same in all of an individual's cells, as well as in cells of other family members. Scientists report growing evidence that cancer cells may have breaks at these fragile sites. Whether cancer destabilizes the fragile sites, leading to breakage, or the fragile sites themselves contain genes that contribute to cancer is unknown at this time.

In **fragile X syndrome,** also known as **Martin–Bell syndrome,** a fragile site occurs near the tip of the X chromosome, where the fragile X gene contains a nucleotide triplet CGG that repeats from 200 to more than 1000 times (**FIG. 16-6**). In a normal chromosome, CGG repeats up to 50 times.

Fragile X syndrome is the most common cause of inherited mental retardation. The effects of fragile X syndrome, which are more pronounced in males than in females, range from mild learning and attention deficit disorders to severe mental retardation and hyperactivity. According to the National Fragile X Foundation, about 80% of boys and 35% of girls with fragile X syndrome are at least mildly mentally retarded. Females with fragile X syndrome are usually heterozygous (because their other X chromosome is normal) and are therefore more likely to have normal intelligence.

The discovery of the fragile X gene in 1991 and the development of the first fragile X mouse model in 1994 have provided researchers with ways to develop and test potential treatments, including gene therapy. At the microscopic level, the nerve cells of individuals with fragile X syndrome have malformed dendrites (the part of the nerve cell that receives nerve impulses from other nerve cells). At the molecular level, the triplet repeats associated with fragile X syndrome disrupt the functioning of a gene that codes for a certain protein, designated *fragile X mental retardation protein (FMRP)*. In normal cells, FMRP binds to dozens of different mRNA molecules (exactly why it binds is not yet understood), but in cells of individuals with fragile X syndrome the mutated allele does not produce functional FMRP.

Genomic imprinting is determined by whether inheritance is from the male or female parent

Some traits are the result of **genomic** or **parental imprinting,** in which the expression of a gene in a given tissue or developmental stage is based on its parental origin—that is, whether the indi-

1 μm

Science/Visuals Unlimited

Fragile site

CGG repeats
(200 to more than
1000 times)

CGG repeats
(up to 50 times)

(a) The defective allele at the tips of both chromatids of the X chromosome.

(b) The normal allele.

FIGURE 16-6 Fragile X syndrome
This colorized SEM shows an X chromosome with a fragile site and a normal X chromosome.

vidual inherits the gene from the male or female parent. For some imprinted genes, the paternally inherited allele is always repressed (not expressed); for other imprinted genes, the maternally inherited allele is always repressed. Thus, maternal and paternal genomes have different imprints that result in differential gene expression in the embryo. As discussed in Chapter 14, **epigenetic inheritance** refers to changes in how a gene is expressed without any change in the coding of the DNA bases. Epigenetic inheritance may cause genomic imprinting.

Two rare genetic disorders provide a fascinating demonstration of genomic imprinting. In *Prader-Willi syndrome (PWS)*, individuals become compulsive overeaters and obese; they are also short in stature and mildly to moderately retarded. In *Angelman syndrome (AS)*, affected individuals are hyperactive, mentally retarded, and unable to speak, and they suffer from seizures. A small *deletion* of several loci from the same region of chromosome 15 causes both PWS and AS (**FIG. 16-7a**). One of these deleted loci is responsible for PWS, another for AS.

Pedigree analysis has shown that when the person inherits the deletion from the father, PWS occurs, whereas when the person inherits the deletion from the mother, AS occurs. This inheritance pattern suggests that the normal PWS gene is expressed only in the paternal chromosome and the normal AS gene is expressed only in the maternal chromosome. PWS occurs because the repressed

(a) Homologous chromosome 15, showing (left) close proximity of the PWS and AS genes and (right) site of deletion that includes both PWS and AS loci.

(b) This individual has Prader-Willi syndrome because the sperm contributed a chromosome 15 in which the PWS gene had been deleted. The chromosome with the repressed (imprinted) PWS gene from the egg is unable to compensate for the deletion.

(c) This individual has Angelman syndrome because the egg contributed a chromosome 15 in which the AS gene had been deleted. The chromosome with the repressed (imprinted) AS gene from the sperm is unable to compensate for the deletion.

FIGURE 16-7 Genomic imprinting and development of Prader-Willi syndrome (PWS) and Angelman syndrome (AS)

The PWS gene is active in the male gamete and repressed (imprinted) in the female gamete. Conversely, the AS gene is active in the female gamete and repressed (imprinted) in the male gamete.

(imprinted) PWS gene from the mother cannot make up for the absent PWS gene in the paternal chromosome (**FIG. 16-7b**). Similarly, AS occurs because the repressed (imprinted) AS gene from the father cannot make up for the absent AS gene in the maternal chromosome (**FIG. 16-7c**).

Review

- What are the specific chromosome abnormalities in Down syndrome, Klinefelter syndrome, and Turner syndrome?
- What is the chromosome abnormality in cri du chat syndrome?
- What is the chromosome abnormality in fragile X syndrome?

16.3 GENETIC DISEASES CAUSED BY SINGLE-GENE MUTATIONS

◼ LEARNING OBJECTIVE

6   State whether each of the following genetic defects is inherited as an autosomal recessive, autosomal dominant, or X-linked recessive: phenylketonuria (PKU), sickle cell anemia, cystic fibrosis, Tay-Sachs disease, Huntington's disease, and hemophilia A.

You have seen that several human disorders involve chromosome abnormalities. Hundreds of human disorders, however, involve enzyme defects caused by mutations of single genes. *Phenylketonuria (PKU)* and *alkaptonuria* (discussed in Chapter 13) are examples of these disorders, each of which is sometimes referred to as an **inborn error of metabolism,** a metabolic disorder caused by the mutation of a gene that codes for an enzyme needed in a biochemical pathway. Both PKU and alkaptonuria involve blocks in the metabolism of specific amino acids.

Many genetic diseases are inherited as autosomal recessive traits

Many human genetic diseases have a simple autosomal recessive inheritance pattern and therefore are expressed only in the homozygous state. Why are these traits recessive? Most recessive mutations result in a mutant allele that encodes a product that no longer works (either there is not enough gene product, or it is a defective gene product). In the heterozygous state, there is one functional copy of the gene and one mutated, nonfunctional copy. The normal copy of the gene generally produces enough protein to meet the cell's needs. In homozygous recessive individuals, *both* alleles of the gene are nonfunctional, and the cell's needs are not met. As a result, the person shows symptoms of disease.

Phenylketonuria results from an enzyme deficiency

Phenylketonuria (PKU), which is most common in individuals of western European descent, is an autosomal recessive disease caused by a defect of amino acid metabolism. It affects about 1 in 10,000 live births in North America. Homozygous recessive individuals lack an enzyme that converts the amino acid phe-

nylalanine to another amino acid, tyrosine. These individuals accumulate high levels of phenylalanine, phenylpyruvic acid, and similar compounds.

The accumulating phenylalanine is converted to phenylketones, which damage the central nervous system, including the brain, in children. The ultimate result in untreated cases is severe mental retardation. An infant with PKU is usually healthy at birth because its mother, who is heterozygous, breaks down excess phenylalanine for both herself and her fetus. However, during infancy and early childhood the accumulation of toxic products eventually causes irreversible damage to the central nervous system.

Beginning in the 1950s, infants with PKU have been identified early and placed on a low-phenylalanine diet, dramatically alleviating their symptoms. The diet is difficult to adhere to because it contains no meat, fish, dairy products, breads, or nuts. Also, individuals with PKU should not consume the sugar substitute aspartame, found in many diet drinks and foods, because it contains phenylalanine. Biochemical tests for PKU have been developed, and screening of newborns through a simple blood test is required in the United States. Because of these screening programs and the availability of effective treatment, thousands of PKU-diagnosed children have not developed severe mental retardation. Most must continue the diet through at least adolescence. Doctors now recommend that patients stay on the diet throughout life because some adults who have discontinued the low-phenylalanine diet experience certain mental problems, such as difficulty in concentration and short-term memory loss.

Ironically, the success of PKU treatment in childhood presents a new challenge today. If a homozygous female who has discontinued the special diet becomes pregnant, the high phenylalanine levels in her blood can damage the brain of the fetus she is carrying, even though that fetus is heterozygous. Therefore, she must resume the diet, preferably before becoming pregnant. This procedure is usually (although not always) successful in preventing the effects of **maternal PKU.** It is especially important for women with PKU to be aware of maternal PKU and to obtain appropriate counseling and medical treatment during pregnancy.

Sickle cell anemia results from a hemoglobin defect

Sickle cell anemia is inherited as an autosomal recessive trait. The disease is most common in people of African descent (approximately 1 in 500 African Americans), and about 1 in 12 African Americans is heterozygous. Under low oxygen conditions, the red blood cells of an individual with sickle cell anemia are shaped like sickles, or half-moons, whereas normal red blood cells are biconcave discs.

The mutation that causes sickle cell anemia was first identified in 1957. The sickled cells contain abnormal hemoglobin molecules, which have the amino acid valine instead of glutamic acid at position 6 (the sixth amino acid from the amino terminal end) in the β-globin chain (see Fig. 3-22a). The substitution of valine for glutamic acid makes the hemoglobin molecules stick to one another to form fiberlike structures that change the shape of some of the red blood cells. This sickling occurs in the veins after the oxygen has been released from the hemoglobin. The blood cells' abnormal sickled shape slows blood flow and blocks small blood vessels (**FIG. 16-8**), resulting in tissue damage from lack of oxygen and essential nutrients and in episodes of pain. Because sickled red blood cells also have a shorter lifespan than normal red blood cells, many affected individuals have severe anemia.

Treatments for sickle cell anemia include pain-relief measures, transfusions, and, more recently, medicines such as hydroxyurea, which activates the gene for the production of normal fetal hemoglobin (this gene is generally not expressed after birth). The presence of normal fetal hemoglobin in the red blood cells dilutes the sickle cell hemoglobin, thereby minimizing the painful episodes and reducing the need for blood transfusions. The long-term effects of hydroxyurea are not known at this time, but there are concerns that it may induce tumor formation.

Ongoing research is directed toward providing gene therapy for sickle cell anemia. The development of a mouse model for studying sickle cell anemia has enabled researchers to test gene therapy. The first gene therapy treatments in mice used a mouse retrovirus as a **vector,** a carrier that transfers the genetic information. However, the retrovirus did not effectively transport the normal gene for hemoglobin into the bone marrow, where stem cells produce new blood cells. In 2001, researchers cured sickle cell anemia in mice using a modified HIV as a vector. Before this treatment can be tested in humans, however, researchers must demonstrate that the HIV vector is safe. Bone marrow transplants are also a promising future treatment for seriously ill individuals.

The reason the sickle cell allele occurs at a higher frequency in parts of Africa and Asia is well established. Individuals who are heterozygous ($Hb^A Hb^S$) and carry alleles for both normal hemoglobin (Hb^A) and sickle cell hemoglobin (Hb^S) are more resistant to the malarial parasite, *Plasmodium falciparum,* which causes a severe, often fatal, form of malaria. The malarial parasite, which spends part of its life cycle inside red blood cells, does not thrive when sickle cell hemoglobin is present. (An individual heterozygous for sickle cell anemia produces both normal and sickle cell hemoglobin.) Areas in Africa where *falciparum* malaria occurs correlate well with areas in which the frequency of the sickle cell allele is more common in the human population. Thus, $Hb^A Hb^S$ individuals, possessing one copy of the mutant sickle cell allele, have a selective advantage over both types of homozygous individuals, $Hb^A Hb^A$ (who may die of malaria) and $Hb^S Hb^S$ (who may die of sickle cell anemia). This phenomenon, known as **heterozygote advantage,** is discussed further in Chapter 19 (see Fig. 19-7).

Cystic fibrosis results from defective ion transport

Cystic fibrosis is the most common autosomal recessive disorder in children of European descent (1 in 2500 births). About 1 in 25 individuals in the United States is a heterozygous carrier of the mutant cystic fibrosis allele. Abnormal secretions characterize this disorder. The most severe effect is on the respiratory system, where abnormally viscous mucus clogs the airways. The cilia that line the bronchi cannot easily remove the mucus, and it becomes a growth medium for dangerous bacteria. These bacteria or their toxins attack the surrounding tissues, leading to recurring pneumonia and other complications. The heavy mucus also occurs elsewhere in the body, causing digestive difficulties and other effects.

As discussed earlier, the gene responsible for cystic fibrosis codes for CFTR, the protein that regulates the transport of chloride ions across cell membranes. The defective protein, found in plasma membranes of epithelial cells lining the passageways of the lungs, intestines, pancreas, liver, sweat glands, and reproductive organs, results in the production of an unusually thick mucus that eventually leads to tissue damage. Although many forms of cystic fibrosis exist that vary somewhat in the severity of symptoms, the disease is almost always serious.

Antibiotics are used to control bacterial infections, and daily physical therapy is required to clear mucus from the respiratory system (**FIG. 16-9**). Treatment with *Dornase Alpha (DNase),* an enzyme produced by recombinant DNA technology, helps break down the mucus. Without treatment, death would occur in infancy. With treatment, the average life expectancy for individuals with cystic fibrosis is about 38 years. Because of the serious limitations of available treatments, gene therapy for cystic fibrosis is under development.

The most severe mutant allele for cystic fibrosis predominates in northern Europe, and another, somewhat less serious, mutant allele is more prevalent in southern Europe. Presumably, these mutant alleles are independent mutations that have been maintained by natural selection. Some experimental evidence supports the

Dr. Stanley Flegler/ Visuals Unlimited

Capillary (small blood vessel)

Sickled red blood cells

Normal red blood cells

10 μm

FIGURE 16-8 Sickle cell anemia
Sickled red blood cells do not pass through small blood vessels as easily as unsickled red blood cells do. The sickled cells can cause blockages that prevent oxygen from being delivered to tissues.

FIGURE 16-9 Treating cystic fibrosis

One traditional treatment for cystic fibrosis is chest percussion, or gentle pounding on the chest, to clear mucus from clogged airways in the lungs. This technique is typically done after nebulizer therapy, which loosens the mucus.

hypothesis that heterozygous individuals are less likely to die from infectious diseases that cause severe diarrhea, such as cholera, another possible example of heterozygote advantage.

Tay-Sachs disease results from abnormal lipid metabolism in the brain

Tay-Sachs disease is an autosomal recessive disease that affects the central nervous system and results in blindness and severe mental retardation. The symptoms begin within the first year of life and result in death before the age of 5 years. Because of the absence of an enzyme, a normal membrane lipid in brain cells fails to break down properly and accumulates in intracellular organelles called *lysosomes* (discussed in Chapter 4). The lysosomes swell and cause nerve cells to malfunction. Although research is ongoing, no effective treatment for Tay-Sachs disease is available at this time. However, an effective treatment strategy in a mouse model was reported in 1997: oral administration of an inhibitor reduced the synthesis of the lipid that accumulates in the lysosomes. This treatment offers the hope of future breakthroughs to deal more effectively with Tay-Sachs disease in humans.

The abnormal allele is especially common in the United States among Jewish individuals whose ancestors came from eastern and central Europe (Ashkenazi Jews). In contrast, Jewish individuals whose ancestors came from the Mediterranean region (Sephardic Jews) have a very low frequency of the allele.

Some genetic diseases are inherited as autosomal dominant traits

Huntington's disease (HD), named after George Huntington, the U.S. physician who first described it in 1872, is caused by a rare autosomal dominant allele that affects the central nervous system. The disease causes severe mental and physical deterioration, uncontrollable muscle spasms, and personality changes; death ultimately results. No effective treatment has been found. Every child of an affected individual has a 50% chance of also being affected (and, if affected, of passing the abnormal allele to his or her offspring). Ordinarily, we would expect a dominant allele with such devastating effects to occur only as a new mutation and not to be transmitted to future generations. Because HD symptoms typically do not appear until relatively late in life (most people do not develop the disease until they are in their forties), affected individuals are likely to produce children before the disease develops (**FIG. 16-10**). In North America, HD occurs in 1 in 20,000 live births.

The gene responsible for HD is located on the short end of chromosome 4. The mutation is a nucleotide triplet (CAG) that is repeated many times; the normal allele repeats CAG from 6 to 35 times, whereas the mutant allele repeats CAG from 40 to more than 150 times. Because CAG codes for the amino acid glutamine, the resulting protein, called "huntingtin," has a long strand of glutamines. The number of nucleotide triplet repeats seems to be important in determining the age of onset and the severity of the disease; larger numbers of repeats correlate with an earlier age of onset and greater severity.

Much research now focuses on how the mutation is linked to neurodegeneration in the brain. A mouse model of HD is providing valuable clues about the development of the disease. Using this model, researchers have demonstrated that the defective version of huntingtin binds to enzymes called *acetyltransferases* in brain cells,

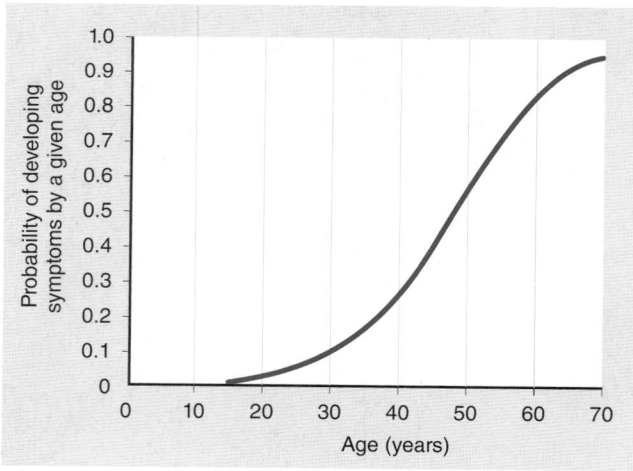

FIGURE 16-10 Age of onset of Huntington's disease

The graph shows the cumulative probability that an individual carrying a Huntington's disease allele will have developed symptoms at a given age. (Adapted from Harper, P. S., *Genetic Counseling*, 5th ed., Butterworth-Heinemann, Oxford, 1998.)

blocking their action. Acetyltransferases are involved in turning genes on for expression, so in the brain cells of HD individuals, much of normal transcription cannot occur. Once neurologists better understand HD's mechanism of action on nerve cells, it may be possible to develop effective treatments to slow the progression of the disease.

Cloning of the HD allele became the basis for tests that allow those at risk to learn presymptomatically if they carry the allele. The decision to be tested for any genetic disease is understandably a highly personal one. The information is, of course, invaluable for those who must decide whether or not to have children. However, someone who tests positive for the HD allele must then live with the virtual certainty of eventually developing this devastating and incurable disease. Researchers hope that information from affected individuals who choose to be identified before the onset of symptoms may ultimately contribute to the development of effective treatments.

Some genetic diseases are inherited as X-linked recessive traits

Hemophilia A was once referred to as a disease of royalty because of its high incidence among male descendants of Queen Victoria, but it is also found in many nonroyal pedigrees. Caused by the absence of a blood-clotting protein called factor VIII, hemophilia A is characterized by severe internal bleeding in the head, joints, and other areas from even a slight wound. The mode of inheritance is X-linked recessive. Thus, affected individuals are almost exclusively male, having inherited the abnormal allele on the X chromosome from their heterozygous carrier mothers. (For a female to be affected by an X-linked trait, she would have to inherit the defective allele from both parents, whereas an affected male need only inherit one defective allele from his mother.)

Treatments for hemophilia A consist of blood transfusions and the administration of clotting factor VIII (the missing gene product) by injection. Unfortunately, these treatments are costly. During the 1980s, many clotting factor VIII preparations made from human plasma were unknowingly contaminated with HIV, and many men with hemophilia subsequently died from AIDS. Since 1992, virus-free clotting factor VIII has been available from both human plasma and recombinant DNA technology.

Geneticists are beginning to unravel X-linked genes affecting intelligence

The X chromosome contains a disproportionate number of the more than 200 genes identified so far that affect cognitive abilities, for example, by coding for proteins required for the brain to function normally. Not surprisingly, many kinds of mental impairment are linked to defects in genes on the X chromosome. By one count, the human X chromosome contains less than 4% of the human genome, yet 10% of the genes in which defects are known to cause some form of mental retardation are found on the X chromosome. Because males have only one X chromosome, more boys than girls have some form of mental impairment, a fact that has been observed for more than a century.

Review

- Which of the following genetic diseases is/are inherited as an autosomal recessive: phenylketonuria, Huntington's disease, Tay-Sachs disease?
- Which of the following genetic diseases is/are inherited as an autosomal dominant: sickle cell anemia, hemophilia A, Huntington's disease?
- Which of the following genetic diseases is/are inherited as an X-linked recessive: hemophilia A, cystic fibrosis, Tay-Sachs disease?

16.4 GENE THERAPY

▪ LEARNING OBJECTIVE

7 Briefly discuss the process of gene therapy, including some of its technical challenges.

Because serious genetic diseases are difficult to treat, scientists have dreamed of developing actual cures. Today, advances in genetics are bringing these dreams closer to reality. One strategy is **gene therapy,** which aims to compensate for a defective, mutant allele by adding a normal, therapeutic allele (and its expressed protein) to certain cells. The rationale is that although a particular allele may be present in all cells, it is expressed only in some. Expression of the normal allele in only the cells that require it may be sufficient to yield a normal phenotype (**FIG. 16-11**).

This approach presents several technical problems. The solutions to these problems must be tailored to the nature of the gene itself, as well as to its product and the types of cells in which it is expressed. First, the gene is cloned and the DNA is introduced into the appropriate cells.

One of the most successful techniques is packaging the normal allele in a viral vector, a virus that moves the normal allele into target cells that currently have a mutant allele. Ideally, the virus should infect a high percentage of the cells. Most important, the virus should do no harm, especially over the long term. Early gene therapy trials used an adenovirus, which causes the common cold. However, some individuals had a strong immune reaction to the virus, so many current trials use an adeno-associated virus that does not cause side effects.

To date, gene therapy has had a greater than 90% success rate in restoring the immune systems of 30 children with *severe combined immunodeficiency (SCID)*. (SCID is a group of inherited disorders that seriously compromise the immune system.) This success rate is significantly better than the 50% success rate of the older therapy involving bone marrow transplants.

Although many obstacles must be overcome, gene therapies for several other genetic diseases are under development or are being tested on individuals in clinical trials. Scientists are currently addressing some of the unique problems presented by each disease.

Gene therapy programs are carefully scrutinized

Until recently, major technical advances caused the number of clinical studies involving gene therapy to grow dramatically. However, the death of a young man in a gene therapy trial in 1999, and five more recent cases of cancer (leukemia) in children, one of whom

Why Is It Used? Mice are a model system for the development of gene therapy, the use of normal genes to correct or alleviate the symptoms of a genetic disease caused by defective copies of a particular gene. This procedure is performed on humans for certain types of genetic disease.

How Is It Done?

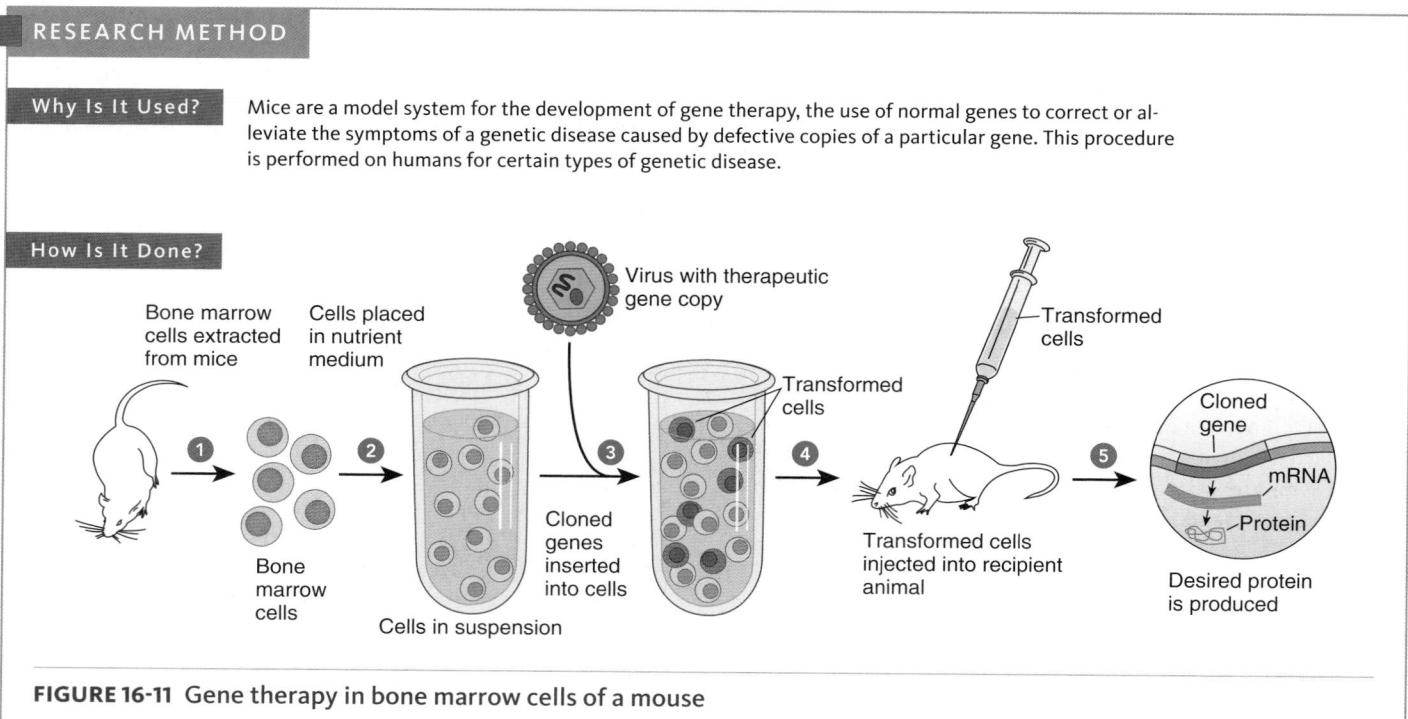

Virus with therapeutic gene copy

Transformed cells

Bone marrow cells extracted from mice

Cells placed in nutrient medium

Bone marrow cells

Cells in suspension

Cloned genes inserted into cells

Transformed cells

Transformed cells injected into recipient animal

Cloned gene

mRNA

Protein

Desired protein is produced

FIGURE 16-11 Gene therapy in bone marrow cells of a mouse

died, led to a shutdown of many trials, pending the outcome of investigations about health risks. The main safety concern in these inquiries is the potential toxicity of viral vectors. The vector used in the young man who died was an adenovirus that was required in large doses to transfer enough copies of the normal alleles for effective therapy. Unfortunately, the high viral doses triggered a fatal immune response in the patient's body. The children who developed leukemia were being treated for SCID. The vector in these cases was a retrovirus that inserted itself into and activated an oncogene that can cause childhood leukemia.

Performing clinical trials on humans always has inherent risks. Researchers carefully select patients and thoroughly explain the potential benefits and risks, as far as they are known, so the patient—or, in the case of children, the parents—can give informed consent for the procedure. However, the problems in gene therapy trials in recent years have researchers busy developing safer alternatives to viral vectors.

Review

- How are viruses used in human gene therapy?
- Why are viral vectors of potential concern in human gene therapy?

16.5 GENETIC TESTING AND COUNSELING

LEARNING OBJECTIVES

8 State the relative advantages and disadvantages of amniocentesis, chorionic villus sampling, and preimplantation genetic diagnosis in the prenatal diagnosis of human genetic abnormalities.

9 Distinguish between genetic screening programs for newborns and adults, and discuss the scope and implications of genetic counseling.

Geneticists have made many advances in detecting genetic disorders in individuals in recent years, including in prenatal diagnosis and genetic screening. With these advances comes increased information for couples at risk of having children with genetic diseases. Helping couples understand and deal with the genetic information now available is part of the rapidly expanding field of genetic counseling.

Prenatal diagnosis detects chromosome abnormalities and gene defects

Health-care professionals are increasingly successful at diagnosing genetic diseases prenatally. In the diagnostic technique called **amniocentesis,** a physician obtains a sample of the *amniotic fluid* surrounding the fetus by inserting a needle through the pregnant woman's abdomen, into the uterus, and then into the amniotic sac surrounding the fetus. Some of the amniotic fluid is withdrawn from the amniotic cavity into a syringe (**FIG. 16-12**). The fetus is normally safe from needle injuries because **ultrasound imaging** helps determine the positions of the fetus, placenta, and the needle. (Figure 51-18 shows an ultrasound of a human fetus.) However, there is a 0.5%, or 1 in 200, chance that amniocentesis will induce a miscarriage.

Amniotic fluid contains living cells sloughed off the body of the fetus and hence genetically identical to the cells of the fetus. After cells grow for about 2 weeks in culture in the lab, technicians karyotype dividing cells to detect chromosome abnormalities. Other DNA tests have also been developed to identify most chromosome abnormalities. Amniocentesis, which has been per-

KEY POINT In amniocentesis, the fluid surrounding the developing fetus is sampled, usually during the 16th week of pregnancy, to detect genetic and developmental disorders.

16-week fetus

Ultrasound probe determines position of fetus

Uterine wall

Amniotic cavity

Placenta

1 About 20 mL of amniotic fluid containing cells sloughed off from fetus is removed through mother's abdomen.

2 Fluid is centrifuged.

3 Amniotic fluid is analyzed.

4 Fetal cells are checked to determine sex, and purified DNA is analyzed.

5 Some cells are grown for 2 weeks in culture medium.

6 Karyotype is analyzed for sex chromosomes or any chromosome abnormality.

7 Cells are analyzed biochemically for presence of about 40 metabolic disorders.

FIGURE 16-12 *Animated* **Amniocentesis**
Certain genetic diseases and other abnormal conditions are diagnosed prenatally by amniocentesis.

of a normally occurring protein, *α-fetoprotein,* in the amniotic fluid. Some of this protein crosses the placenta into the mother's blood, which is tested for *maternal serum α-fetoprotein (MSAFP)* as a screen for spinal cord defects. If an elevated level of MSAFP is detected, the physician performs diagnostic tests, such as ultrasound imaging and amniocentesis. (Interestingly, abnormally *low* levels of MSAFP are associated with Down syndrome and other trisomies.)

One problem with amniocentesis is that most of the conditions it detects are unpreventable and incurable, and the results are generally not obtained until well into the second trimester, when terminating the pregnancy is both psychologically and medically more difficult than earlier. Therefore, researchers have developed tests that yield results earlier in the pregnancy. **Chorionic villus sampling (CVS)** involves removing and studying cells that will form the fetal contribution to the placenta (**FIG. 16-13**). CVS, which has been performed in the United States since about 1983, is associated with a slightly greater risk of infection or miscarriage than amniocentesis, but its advantage is that results are obtained earlier in the pregnancy than in amniocentesis, usually within the first trimester.

A relatively new embryo-screening process, known as **preimplantation genetic diagnosis (PGD),** is available for couples who carry alleles for Tay-Sachs disease, hemophilia, sickle cell anemia, and dozens of other inherited genetic conditions. PGD is an adjunct to assisted reproductive technology. Conception is by **in vitro fertilization (IVF),** in which gametes are collected, eggs are fertilized in a dish in the laboratory, and the resulting embryo is then implanted in the uterus for development (see *Inquiring About: Novel Origins,* in Chapter 50). Prior to implantation, the physician screens single cells of early embryos for one or more genetic diseases before placing a healthy embryo into the woman's uterus. PGD differs from amniocentesis and CVS in that the test is performed *before* a woman is pregnant, so it eliminates the decision of whether or not to terminate the pregnancy if an embryo has a genetic abnormality. However, PGD is not as accurate as amniocentesis or CVS, and it is more expensive. Moreover, PGD is sometimes controversial because some couples use it to choose the gender of their offspring, not to screen for genetic diseases.

formed since the 1960s, is routinely offered for pregnant women older than age 35 because their fetuses have a higher-than-normal risk of Down syndrome.

Researchers have developed prenatal tests to detect many genetic disorders with a simple inheritance pattern, but these disorders are rare enough that physicians usually order the tests performed only if they suspect a particular problem. Enzyme deficiencies can often be detected by incubating cells recovered from amniotic fluid with the appropriate substrate and measuring the product; this technique has been useful in prenatal diagnosis of disorders such as Tay-Sachs disease. The tests for several other diseases, including sickle cell anemia, Huntington's disease, and cystic fibrosis, involve directly testing the individual's DNA for the mutant allele.

Amniocentesis is also useful in detecting a condition known as *spina bifida,* in which the spinal cord does not close properly during development. A relatively common malformation (about 1 in 300 births), this birth defect is associated with abnormally high levels

KEY POINT In chorionic villus sampling, chorionic cells genetically identical to the embryo are sampled, usually during the eighth or ninth week of pregnancy, to detect genetic disorders.

Transabdominal sampling technique

Withdrawn chorionic villi cells

Ultrasound probe

Cervical sampling technique

Catheter

Syringe

Withdrawn chorionic villi cells

or

Chorionic villi   Catheter

Cells are cultured; biochemical tests and karyotyping are performed

FIGURE 16-13 Chorionic villus sampling (CVS)

This test allows the early diagnosis of some genetic abnormalities. Samples may be obtained by inserting a needle through the uterine wall or the cervical opening.

Although using amniocentesis, CVS, and PGD can help physicians diagnose certain genetic disorders with a high degree of accuracy, the tests are not foolproof, and many disorders cannot be diagnosed at all. Therefore, the lack of an abnormal finding is no guarantee of a normal baby.

Genetic screening searches for genotypes or karyotypes

Genetic screening is a systematic search through a population for individuals with a genotype or karyotype that might cause a serious genetic disease in themselves or their offspring. There are two main types of genetic screening, for newborns and for adults, and each serves a different purpose. Newborns are screened primarily as the first step in preventive medicine, and adults are screened to help them make informed reproductive decisions.

Newborns are screened to detect and treat certain genetic diseases before the onset of serious symptoms. The routine screening of infants for PKU began in 1962 in Massachusetts. Laws in all 50 states of the United States, as well as in many other countries, currently require PKU screening. Sickle cell anemia is also more effectively treated with early diagnosis. Screening newborns for sickle

cell anemia reduces infant mortality by about 15% because doctors can administer daily doses of antibiotics, thereby preventing bacterial infections common to newborns with the disease. The number of genetic disorders that can be screened in newborns is rapidly increasing, and the March of Dimes currently recommends screening newborns for 29 disorders, most of which are genetic.

Genetic screening of adults identifies carriers (heterozygotes) of recessive genetic disorders. If both prospective parents are heterozygous, the carriers are counseled about the risks involved in having children. Since the 1970s, about 1 million young Jewish adults in the United States, Israel, and other countries have been screened voluntarily for Tay-Sachs disease, and about 1 in 30 has been identified as a carrier. Tay-Sachs screening programs have reduced the incidence of Tay-Sachs disease to almost zero.

Genetic counselors educate people about genetic diseases

Couples who are concerned about the risk of abnormality in their children, because they have either an abnormal child or a relative affected by a hereditary disease, may seek **genetic counseling** for medical and genetic information as well as support and guidance. Genetic clinics, available in most major metropolitan centers, are usually affiliated with medical schools.

Genetic counselors, who have received training in counseling, medicine, and human genetics, provide people with the information they need to make reproductive decisions. They offer advice, tempered with respect and sensitivity, in terms of risk estimates—that is, the *probability* that any given offspring will inherit a particular condition. The counselor uses the complete family histories of both the man and the woman, and a clinical geneticist (a physician who specializes in genetics) may screen for the detection of heterozygous carriers of certain conditions.

When a disease involves only a single gene locus, probabilities can usually be easily calculated. For example, if one prospective parent is affected with a trait that is inherited as an autosomal dominant disorder, such as Huntington's disease, the probability that any given child will have the disease is 0.5, or 50%. The birth to phenotypically normal parents of a child affected with an autosomal recessive trait, such as albinism or PKU, establishes that both parents are heterozygous carriers, and the probability that any subsequent child will be affected is therefore 0.25, or 25%. For a disease inherited through a recessive allele on the X chromosome, such as hemophilia A, a normal woman and an affected man will have daughters who are carriers and sons who are normal. The probability that the son of a carrier mother and a normal father will be affected is 0.5, or 50%; the probability that their daughter will be a carrier is also 0.5, or 50%.

It is important for identified carriers to receive appropriate genetic counseling. A genetic counselor is trained not only to provide information pertaining to reproductive decisions but also to help individuals understand their situation and avoid feeling stigmatized.

Review

- What are the relative advantages and disadvantages of amniocentesis, chorionic villus sampling, and preimplantation genetic diagnosis?
- What is the purpose of genetic screening for newborns?
- What is the purpose of genetic screening for adults?

16.6 HUMAN GENETICS, SOCIETY, AND ETHICS

◼ LEARNING OBJECTIVE

10 Discuss the controversies of genetic discrimination.

Many misconceptions exist about genetic diseases and their effects on society. Some people erroneously think of certain individuals or populations as genetically unfit and thus responsible for many of society's ills. They argue, for example, that medical treatment of people affected with genetic diseases, especially those who reproduce, increases the frequency of abnormal alleles in the population. However, such notions are incorrect. Genetic disorders are so rare that modern medical treatments will have only a negligible effect on their incidence.

Recessive mutant alleles are present in *all* individuals and *all* ethnic groups; no one is exempt. According to one estimate, each of us is heterozygous for several (3 to 15) harmful recessive alleles, any of which could cause debilitating illness or death in the homozygous state. Why, then, are genetic diseases relatively uncommon? Each of us has many thousands of essential genes, any of which can be mutated. It is very unlikely that the abnormal alleles that one individual carries are also carried by that individual's mate. Of course, this possibility is more likely if the harmful allele is a relatively common one, such as the one responsible for cystic fibrosis.

Relatives are more likely than nonrelatives to carry the same harmful alleles, having inherited them from a common ancestor. A greater-than-normal frequency of a particular genetic disease among offspring of **consanguineous matings,** matings between genetically related individuals, is often the first clue that the mode of inheritance is autosomal recessive. The offspring of consanguineous matings have a small but significantly increased risk of genetic disease. In fact, they account for a disproportionately high percentage of those individuals in the population with autosomal recessive disorders. Because of this perceived social cost, marriages of close relatives, including first cousins, are prohibited by about half the

states in the United States. However, consanguineous marriages are still relatively common in many other countries.

Genetic discrimination provokes heated debate

One of the fastest-growing areas of medical diagnostics is genetic screening and testing, and new genetic tests that screen for diseases such as cystic fibrosis, sickle cell anemia, Huntington's disease, colon cancer, and breast cancer increase each year. However, genetic testing raises many social, ethical, and legal issues that we as a society must address.

One of the most difficult issues is whether genetic information should be available to health insurance and life insurance companies. Many people think genetic information should not be given to insurance companies, but others, including employers, insurers, and many organizations representing people affected by genetic disorders, say such a view is unrealistic. If people use genetic tests to help them decide when to buy insurance and how much, then insurers insist they should also have access to this information. Insurers say they need access to genetic data to help calculate equitable premiums (insurance companies average risks over a large population). However, some are concerned that insurers might use the results of genetic tests to discriminate against people with genetic diseases or to deny them coverage.

Physicians argue that people at risk for a particular genetic disease might delay being tested because they fear genetic discrimination from insurers and employers. **Genetic discrimination** is discrimination against an individual or family members because of differences from the "normal" genome in that individual. The perception of genetic discrimination already exists in society. A 1996 study found that 25% of 332 people with family histories of one or more genetic disorders thought they had been refused life insurance, 22% thought they had been refused health insurance, and 13% thought they had been denied employment because of genetic discrimination. In a 1998 survey by the National Center for Genetic Resources, 63% of respondents said they probably or definitely would not take a genetic test if the results could be disclosed to either their employers or insurers.

Complicating the issue even more, genetic tests are sometimes difficult to interpret, in part because of the many complex interactions between genes and the environment. If a woman tests positive for an allele that has been linked to breast cancer, for example, she is at significant risk, but testing positive does not necessarily mean she will develop breast cancer. These uncertainties also make it hard to decide what form of medical intervention, from frequent mammograms to surgical removal of healthy breasts, is appropriate.

The Ethical, Legal, and Social Implications (ELSI) Research Program of the National Human Genome Research Institute has developed principles designed to protect individuals against genetic discrimination. In 2008 the **Genetic Information Nondiscrimination Act (GINA)** extended significant protection against workplace and health discrimination. This law prohibits employers and insurance companies from discriminating on the basis of information derived from genetic tests. For example, neither employers nor insurance companies are permitted to request a genetic test. Employers cannot base employment decisions on genetic information. Also, insurance companies cannot cancel or deny coverage or increase the price of premiums based on genetic information.

Many ethical issues related to human genetics must be addressed

Genetic discrimination is only one example of ethical issues arising from our expanding knowledge of human genetics. Consider the following questions, all of which deal with the broad ethical issue of individual rights: What is the youngest age at which genetic testing should be permitted for adult-onset diseases, such as Huntington's disease? What are the emotional and psychological effects on individuals who are told they have tested positive for an incurable genetic disease? Should testing be performed when some family members want testing and others do not? Should parents be able to test their minor children? Should access to genetic test data be

permitted in cases of paternity or kinship testing? Should states be able to collect genetic data on their residents? Should school administrators or law enforcement agencies have access to genetic data? These questions are only a sample of the many issues that both ethicists and society must consider now and in the future. As human genetics assumes an increasingly important role in society, issues of genetic privacy and the confidentiality of genetic information must be addressed.

Review

- Why is it incorrect to assume that certain individuals or populations carry most of the abnormal alleles found in humans?
- To be expressed, an autosomal recessive genetic disease must be homozygous. What relationship does this fact have to consanguineous matings?
- Why do health and life insurance companies want genetic information about their clients?

■ SUMMARY: FOCUS ON LEARNING OBJECTIVES

16.1 (page 348)

1 Distinguish between karyotyping and pedigree analysis.

- Studies of an individual's **karyotype,** the number and kinds of chromosomes present in the nucleus, enable researchers to identify various chromosome abnormalities.

- A **pedigree** is a "family tree" that shows the transmission of genetic traits within a family over several generations. Pedigree analysis is useful in detecting autosomal dominant mutations, autosomal recessive mutations, X-linked recessive mutations, and defects due to **genomic imprinting,** which is the expression of a gene based on its parental origin.

  CENGAGENOW™ Learn more about pedigrees by clicking on the figure in CengageNOW.

2 Discuss the implications of the Human Genome Project.

- The **human genome** is the total genetic information in human cells. The **Human Genome Project** sequenced the DNA in the nuclear human genome. Now that the human genome has been sequenced, researchers will be busy for decades identifying genes and understanding what each gene's role is, how each gene interacts with other genes, and how the expression of each gene is regulated in different tissues. For example, researchers have begun to use **genome-wide association (GWA) scans** to identify genetic variations associated with complex human diseases.

3 Discuss the mouse model for studying cystic fibrosis.

- The use of animal models greatly helps researchers investigate human disease. Researchers used **gene targeting** to produce strains of mice that are either homozygous or heterozygous for cystic fibrosis. Results from these studies may yield more effective drugs for treating the disease.

16.2 (page 351)

4 Explain how nondisjunction in meiosis is responsible for chromosome abnormalities such as Down syndrome, Klinefelter syndrome, and Turner syndrome.

- In **aneuploidy,** there are either missing or extra copies of certain chromosomes. Aneuploidies include **trisomy,** in which an individual's cells contain an extra chromosome, and **monosomy,** in which one member of a pair of chromosomes is missing.

- **Trisomy 21,** the most common form of **Down syndrome,** and **Klinefelter syndrome** (XXY) are examples of trisomy. **Turner syndrome** (X0) is an example of monosomy.

- Trisomy and monosomy are caused by meiotic **nondisjunction,** in which sister chromatids or homologous chromosomes fail to move apart properly during meiosis.

  CENGAGENOW™ Learn more about karyotypes by clicking on the figure in CengageNOW.

5 Distinguish among the following structural abnormalities in chromosomes: translocations, deletions, and fragile sites.

- In a **translocation,** part of one chromosome becomes attached to another. About 4% of individuals with Down syndrome have a translocation in which the long arm of chromosome 21 is attached to the long arm of one of the larger chromosomes, such as chromosome 14.

- A **deletion** can result in chromosome breaks that fail to rejoin. The deletion may range in size from a few base pairs to an entire chromosome arm. One deletion disorder in humans is **cri du chat syndrome,** in which part of the short arm of chromosome 5 is deleted.

- **Fragile sites** may occur at specific locations on both chromatids of a chromosome. In **fragile X syndrome,** a fragile site occurs near the tip on the X chromosome, where the nucleotide triplet CGG is repeated many more times than is normal. Fragile X syndrome is the most common cause of inherited mental retardation.

16.3 *(page 358)*

6 State whether each of the following genetic defects is inherited as an autosomal recessive, autosomal dominant, or X-linked recessive: phenylketonuria (PKU), sickle cell anemia, cystic fibrosis, Tay-Sachs disease, Huntington's disease, and hemophilia A.

- Most human genetic diseases that show a simple inheritance pattern are transmitted as autosomal recessive traits. **Phenylketonuria (PKU)** is an autosomal recessive disorder in which toxic phenylketones damage the developing nervous system. **Sickle cell anemia** is an autosomal recessive disorder in which abnormal hemoglobin (the protein that transports oxygen in the blood) is produced. **Cystic fibrosis** is an autosomal recessive disorder in which abnormal secretions are produced primarily in organs of the respiratory and digestive systems. **Tay-Sachs disease** is an autosomal recessive disorder caused by abnormal lipid metabolism in the brain.
- **Huntington's disease** is an autosomal dominant inheritance pattern that results in mental and physical deterioration, usually beginning in adulthood.
- **Hemophilia A** is an X-linked recessive disorder that results in a defect in a blood component required for clotting.

16.4 *(page 361)*

7 Briefly discuss the process of gene therapy, including some of its technical challenges.

- In **gene therapy,** the normal allele is cloned and the DNA is introduced into certain human cells where its expression may be sufficient to yield a normal phenotype.
- One technical challenge in gene therapy is finding a safe, effective **vector,** usually a virus, to deliver the gene of interest into the cells.

16.5 *(page 362)*

8 State the relative advantages and disadvantages of amniocentesis, chorionic villus sampling, and preimplantation genetic diagnosis in the prenatal diagnosis of human genetic abnormalities.

- In **amniocentesis,** a physician samples the amniotic fluid surrounding the fetus and cultures and screens the fetal cells suspended in the fluid for genetic defects. Amniocentesis provides results in the second trimester of pregnancy.

  CENGAGENOW¯ Learn more about amniocentesis by clicking on the figure in CengageNOW.

- In **chorionic villus sampling (CVS),** a physician removes and studies some of the fetal cells. CVS provides results in the first trimester of pregnancy but is associated with a slightly greater risk of infection and miscarriage than amniocentesis.
- Couples who conceive by in vitro fertilization may elect to have **preimplantation genetic diagnosis (PGD).** A physician screens the embryos for one or more genetic diseases before placing a healthy embryo into the woman's uterus. PGD is not as accurate as amniocentesis or CVS, and it is more expensive.

9 Distinguish between genetic screening programs for newborns and adults, and discuss the scope and implications of genetic counseling.

- **Genetic screening** identifies individuals who might carry a serious genetic disease. Screening of newborns is the first step in preventive medicine, and screening of adults helps them make informed reproductive decisions.
- Couples who are concerned about the risk of abnormality in their children may seek **genetic counseling.** A genetic counselor provides medical and genetic information pertaining to reproductive decisions and helps individuals understand their situation and avoid feeling stigmatized.

16.6 *(page 365)*

10 Discuss the controversies of genetic discrimination.

- **Genetic discrimination** is discrimination against an individual or family member because of differences from the "normal" genome in that individual.
- One of the most difficult issues in avoiding genetic discrimination is whether genetic information should be available to employers and to health and life insurance companies. The **Genetic Information Nondiscrimination Act (GINA)** prohibits employers and insurance companies from discriminating on the basis of information derived from genetic tests.

TEST YOUR UNDERSTANDING

1. A diagram of a pedigree shows (a) controlled matings between members of different true-breeding strains (b) the total genetic information in human cells (c) a comparison of DNA sequences among genomes of humans and other species (d) the subtle genetic differences among unrelated people (e) the expression of genetic traits in the members of two or more generations of a family

2. Which pattern of inheritance is associated with a trait that (1) is not usually expressed in the parents, (2) is expressed in about one-fourth of the children, and (3) is expressed in both male and female children? (a) autosomal recessive (b) autosomal dominant (c) X-linked recessive (d) X-linked dominant (e) Y-linked

3. An abnormality in which there is one more or one fewer than the normal number of chromosomes is called (a) a karyotype (b) a fragile site (c) an aneuploidy (d) trisomy (e) a translocation

4. The failure of chromosomes to separate normally during cell division is called (a) a fragile site (b) an inborn error of metabolism (c) a satellite knob (d) a translocation (e) nondisjunction

5. The chromosome composition of an individual or cell is called its (a) karyotype (b) nucleotide triplet repeat (c) pedigree (d) DNA microarray (e) translocation

6. An inherited disorder caused by a defective or absent enzyme is called (a) a karyotype (b) trisomy (c) a reciprocal translocation (d) an inborn error of metabolism (e) an aneuploidy

7. In _____, a genetic mutation codes for an abnormal hemoglobin molecule that is less soluble than usual and more likely than normal to deform the shape of the red blood cell. (a) Down syndrome (b) Tay-Sachs disease (c) sickle cell anemia (d) PKU (e) hemophilia A

8. During this procedure, a sample of the fluid that surrounds the fetus is obtained by inserting a needle through the walls of the abdomen and uterus. (a) DNA marking (b) chorionic villus sampling (c) ultrasound imaging (d) preimplantation genetic diagnosis (e) amniocentesis

9–11. Examine the following pedigrees and decide on the most likely mode of inheritance of each disorder. (a) autosomal recessive (b) autosomal dominant (c) X-linked recessive (d) a, b, or c (e) a or c

9.   10.   11.

CRITICAL THINKING

1. **SCIENCE, TECHNOLOGY, AND SOCIETY.** Imagine that you are a genetic counselor. What advice or suggestions might you give in the following situations?

   a. A couple has come for advice because the woman had a sister who died of Tay-Sachs disease.

   b. A young man and woman who are not related are engaged to be married. However, they have learned that the man's parents are first cousins, and they are worried about the possibility of increased risk of genetic defects in their own children.

   c. A young woman's paternal uncle (her father's brother) has hemophilia A. Her father is free of the disease, and there has never been a case of hemophilia A in her mother's family. Should she be concerned about the possibility of hemophilia A in her own children?

   d. A 20-year-old man is seeking counseling because his father was recently diagnosed with Huntington's disease.

   e. A 45-year-old woman has just been diagnosed with Huntington's disease. She says she will not tell her college-age sons because of the burden it will place on them. Given that the woman, not her sons, is your client, do you have a duty to inform the sons? Explain your reasoning.

2. A common belief about human genetics is that an individual's genes alone determine his or her destiny. Explain why this is a misconception.

3. Is a chromosome deletion equivalent to a frameshift mutation (discussed in Chapter 13)? Why or why not?

4. **EVOLUTION LINK.** Explain some of the evolutionary implications that one can conclude from the fact that mice and humans have about 500 DNA segments that are completely identical.

5. **ANALYZING DATA.** Examine Figure 16-10, and estimate the age at which half of individuals carrying a Huntington's disease allele will have developed symptoms. At what age will three-fourths of these individuals have symptoms?

 Additional questions are available in CengageNOW at www.cengage.com/login.

17 Developmental Genetics

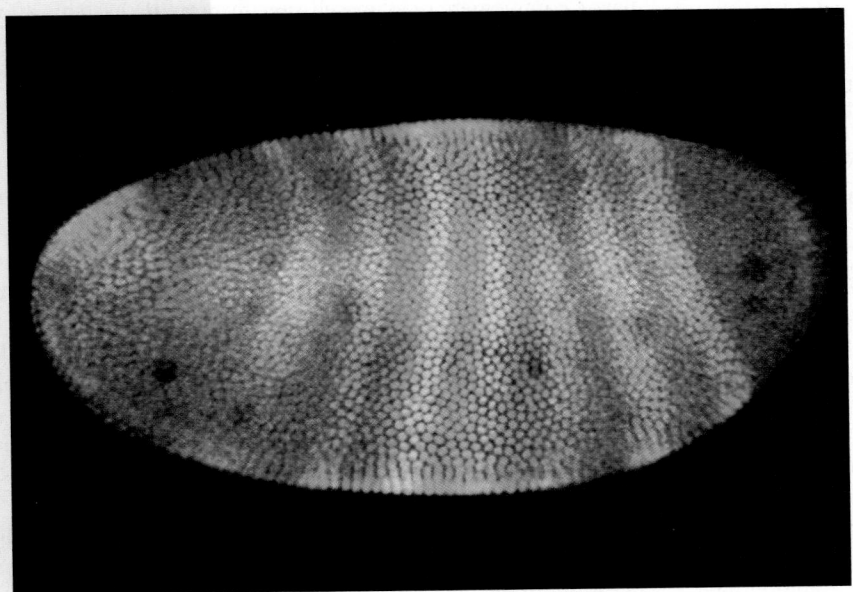

Differential gene expression in the model organism *Drosophila melanogaster.*

Stephen W. Paddock

Developmental genetics is the study of the genes involved in cell differentiation and development of an organism. Until the late 1970s, biologists knew little about how genes interact to control development. Unraveling the genetic interactions that take place during development was an intractable problem using traditional methods. However, rapid progress in recombinant DNA research led scientists to search for developmental mutants and to apply sophisticated techniques to study them. (A *mutant* is an individual with an abnormal phenotype caused by a gene mutation.)

The organism in the photograph is a developing embryo of the fruit fly *Drosophila melanogaster.* Geneticists used **immunofluorescence,** in which a fluorescent dye is joined to an antibody that binds to a specific protein to localize the protein. In this case researchers bound three different antibodies—one red, one blue, and one yellow—to three specific proteins. The patterns of colored bands indicate that different cells of the embryo have *differential gene expression*—that is, different genes are active at the same time.

Work with *Drosophila* and other organisms has profound implications for understanding both normal human development (including aging) and malfunctions that lead to birth defects and cancer. Striking similarities among genes that govern development in widely different species suggest that developmentally important genetic mechanisms are deeply rooted in the evolutionary history of multicellular organisms. There are also differences in species' developmental patterns that reflect their separate evolutionary paths. As you will learn in Chapter 18, developmental genes have played a role in reshaping organisms during the course of their evolution.

Biologists are now studying how genes are activated, inactivated, and modified to control development. Eventually, scientists expect to understand how a single cell—a fertilized egg—develops into a multicellular organism as complex as a human.

17.1 CELL DIFFERENTIATION AND NUCLEAR EQUIVALENCE

◼ LEARNING OBJECTIVES

1 Distinguish between cell determination and cell differentiation, and between nuclear equivalence and totipotency.
2 Describe the classic experiments of Steward, Gurdon, and Wilmut.
3 Define *stem cells*, distinguish between embryonic stem cells and pluripotent stem cells, and describe some of the promising areas of research involving stem cells.

The study of **development,** broadly defined as all the changes that occur in the life of an individual, encompasses some of the most fascinating and difficult problems in biology today. Of particular interest is the process by which cells specialize and organize into a complex organism. During the many cell divisions required for a single cell to develop into a multicellular organism, groups of cells become gradually committed to specific patterns of gene activity through the process of **cell determination.** As cell determination proceeds, it restricts an embryonic cell's developmental pathway so that its fate becomes more and more limited. The final step leading to cell specialization is **cell differentiation.** A differentiated cell, which has a characteristic appearance and characteristic activities, appears to be irreversibly committed to its fate.

Another intriguing part of the developmental puzzle is the building of the body. In **morphogenesis,** the development of form, cells in specific locations differentiate and become spatially organized into recognizable structures. Morphogenesis proceeds through the multistep process of **pattern formation,** the organization of cells into three-dimensional structures. Pattern formation includes signaling between cells, changes in cell shapes, and cell migrations. Depending on their location, cells are exposed to different concentrations of signaling molecules that specify positional information. Thus, *where* a given cell is located often determines *what* it will become when it matures.

The human body, like that of other vertebrates, contains about 250 recognizably different types of cells (**FIG. 17-1**). Combinations of these specialized cells, known as **differentiated cells,** are organized into diverse and complex structures—such as the eye, hand, and brain—each capable of carrying out many sophisticated activities. Most remarkable of all is the fact that all the structures of the body and the different cells within them descend from a unicellular **zygote,** a fertilized egg.

All multicellular organisms undergo complex patterns of development. The root cells of plants, for example, have structures and functions very different from those of the various types of cells located in leaves. Diversity is also found at the molecular level; most strikingly, each type of plant or animal cell makes a highly specific set of proteins. In some cases, such as the protein hemoglobin in red blood cells, one cell-specific protein may make up more than 90% of the cell's total mass of protein. Other cells may have a complement of many cell-specific proteins, each of which is present in small amounts but still plays an essential role. However, because certain proteins are required in every type of cell (all cells, for example, require the same enzymes for glycolysis), cell-specific proteins usually make up only a fraction of the total number of different kinds of proteins.

When researchers first discovered that each type of differentiated cell makes a unique set of proteins, some scientists hypothesized that each group of cells loses the genes it does not need and retains only those required. However, this does not generally seem true. According to the principle of **nuclear equivalence,** the nuclei of essentially all differentiated adult cells of an individual are genetically (though not necessarily metabolically) identical to one another and to the nucleus of the zygote from which they descended. This means that virtually all *somatic cells* in an adult have the same genes. However, different cells express different subsets of these genes.

Somatic cells are all the cells of the body other than **germ line cells,** which ultimately give rise to a new generation. In animals, germ line cells—whose descendants ultimately undergo meiosis and differentiate into gametes—are generally set aside early in development. In plants, the difference between somatic cells and germ line cells is not as distinct, and the determination that certain cells undergo meiosis is made much later in development.

The evidence for nuclear equivalence comes from cases in which differentiated cells or their nuclei have been found to retain the potential of directing the development of the entire organism. Such cells or nuclei are said to exhibit **totipotency.**

Most cell differences are due to differential gene expression

Because genes do not seem to be lost regularly during development (and thus nuclear equivalence is present in different cell types), differences in the molecular composition of cells must be regulated by the activities of different genes. The process of developmental gene regulation is often referred to as **differential gene expression.**

As discussed in Chapter 14, the expression of eukaryotic genes is regulated in many ways and at many levels. For example, a particular enzyme may be produced in an inactive form and then be activated later. However, much of the regulation that is important in development occurs at the transcriptional level. The transcription of certain sets of genes is repressed, whereas that of other sets is activated. Even the expression of genes that are *constitutive*—that is, constantly transcribed—is regulated during development so that the *quantity* of each product varies from one tissue type to another.

As development proceeds, somatic cells that previously had the potential to develop into a variety of cells become increasingly committed to a specific fate.

FIGURE 17-1 Vertebrate cell lineages

Repeated divisions of the fertilized egg (*bottom*) result in the establishment of tissues containing groups of specialized cells. Germ line cells (cells that produce the gametes) are set aside early in development.

Somatic cells progress along various developmental pathways undergoing a series of commitments that progressively determine their fates.

We can think of differentiation as a series of pathways leading from a single cell to cells in each of the different specialized tissues, arranged in an appropriate pattern. At times a cell makes genetic commitments to the developmental path its descendants will follow. These commitments gradually restrict the development of the descendants to a limited set of final tissue types. Determination, then, is a progressive fixation of the fate of a cell's descendants.

As the development of a cell becomes determined along a differentiation pathway, its physical appearance may or may not change significantly. Nevertheless, when a stage of determination is complete, the changes in the cell usually become self-perpetuating and are not easily reversed. Cell differentiation is usually the last stage in the developmental process. At this stage, a precursor cell becomes structurally and functionally recognizable as a bone cell, for example, and its pattern of gene activity differs from that of a neuron (nerve cell) or any other cell type.

A totipotent nucleus contains all the instructions for development

In plants, some differentiated cells can be induced to become the equivalent of embryonic cells. Biologists use *tissue culture techniques* to isolate individual cells from certain plants and to allow them to grow in a nutrient medium.

In the 1950s, F. C. Steward and his coworkers at Cornell University conducted some of the first experiments investigating cell totipotency in plants (**FIG. 17-2**). **Totipotent cells** have the potential to give rise to all parts of an organism because they contain a complete set of genetic instructions required to direct the normal development of an entire organism. Steward and his colleagues induced root cells from a carrot to divide in a liquid nutrient medium, forming groups of cells called *embryoid* (embryo-like) *bodies*. These clumps of dividing cells were then transferred to an agar medium, which provided nutrients and a solid supporting structure for the developing plant cells. Some of the cells of the embryoid bodies gave rise to roots, stems, and leaves. The resulting small plants, called *plantlets* to distinguish them from true seedlings, were then transplanted to soil, where they ultimately developed into adult plants capable of producing flowers and viable seeds.

Because these plants are all derived from the same parent plant, they are genetically alike and therefore constitute a clone. As mentioned in Chapter 15, a **clone** consists of individual organisms, cells, or DNA molecules that are genetically identical to another individual, cell, or DNA molecule, from which it was derived. The methods of plant tissue culture are now extensively used to produce genetically engineered plants because they enable researchers to regenerate whole plants from individual cells that have incorporated recombinant DNA molecules (see Chapter 38).

In the 1950s, researchers began testing whether steps in the process of determination are reversible in animal cells by transplanting the *nucleus* of a cell in a relatively late stage of development into an egg cell that had been *enucleated* (that is, its own nucleus had been destroyed). Robert Briggs and Thomas J. King of the Institute for Cancer Research in Pennsylvania pioneered *nuclear transplantation experiments*. They transplanted nuclei from frog cells at different stages of development into egg cells whose nuclei had been removed. Some of the transplants proceeded normally through several developmental stages, and a few even developed into normal tadpoles. As a rule, the nuclei transplanted from cells at earlier stages were most likely to support development to the tadpole stage. As the fate of the cells became more and more determined, the probability quickly declined that a transplanted nucleus could control normal development.

British biologist John B. Gurdon carried out experiments on nuclear transplantation in frogs during the 1960s. In a few cases he demonstrated that nuclei isolated from the intestinal epithelial cells of a tadpole directed development up to the tadpole stage (**FIG. 17-3**). This result occurred infrequently (about 1.5% of the time); however, in these kinds of experiments success counts more

KEY EXPERIMENT

QUESTION: Are differentiated somatic plant cells totipotent?

HYPOTHESIS: Differentiated somatic carrot cells can be induced to develop into an entire plant.

EXPERIMENT: F. C. Steward and his coworkers cultured carrot root tissues in a liquid nutrient medium. These cells divided to form clumps of undifferentiated cells. The clumps were then transferred to a solid growth medium.

Mature plant

❸ When transferred to soil, plantlets grow into mature plants.

❶ Carrot root tissues are cut into discs and cultured in a liquid nutrient medium. Cells divide, forming mass of undifferentiated cells.

❷ If transferred to solid medium, some of clumps form tiny plantlets.

RESULTS AND CONCLUSION: The development of a complete carrot plant from differentiated somatic cells demonstrated the totipotency of these cells.

Source: Shantz, E. M., and F. C. Steward. "Investigations on Growth and Metabolism of Plant Cells VII: Sources of Nitrogen for Tissue Cultures under Optimal Conditions for Their Growth." *Annals of Botany,* Vol. 23, 371–390, 1959. By permission of Oxford University Press.

FIGURE 17-2 Steward's experiment on cell totipotency in carrots

than failure. Therefore, he could safely conclude that at least some nuclei of differentiated animal cells are in fact totipotent.

For many years, because these successes with frogs could not be repeated with mammalian embryos, many developmental biologists concluded that some fundamental feature of mammalian reproductive biology might be an impenetrable barrier to mammalian cloning. This perception changed markedly in 1996 and 1997 with the first reports of the birth of cloned mammals.

QUESTION: Are nuclei in differentiated animal cells totipotent?

HYPOTHESIS: Nuclei from differentiated cells contain the information required for normal development.

EXPERIMENT: John Gurdon injected the nuclei of differentiated cells (tadpole intestinal cells) into eggs whose own nuclei were destroyed by ultraviolet radiation.

RESULTS AND CONCLUSION: Normal development proceeded to the tadpole stage in about 1.5% of trials, indicating that the genes for programming development up to that point were still present and could be appropriately activated.

Source: Gurdon, J. B. "The Developmental Capacity of Nuclei Taken from Intestinal Epithelium Cells of Feeding Tadpoles." *Journal of Embryology and Experimental Morphology* Vol. 10, Dec. 1962.

FIGURE 17-3 Gurdon's experiment on nuclear totipotency in frogs

The first cloned mammal was a sheep

In 1996, Ian Wilmut, Keith Campbell, and their coworkers at the Roslin Institute in Edinburgh, Scotland, reported that they had succeeded in cloning sheep by using nuclei from an early stage of sheep embryos (the *blastocyst* stage; see Chapter 51). These scientists received worldwide attention in early 1997 when they announced the birth of a lamb named Dolly (after the singer Dolly Parton). Dolly's genetic material was derived from a cultured sheep mammary gland cell that was fused with an enucleated sheep's egg. The resulting cell divided and developed into an embryo that was then cultured in vitro until it reached a stage at which it could be transferred to a host mother (**FIG. 17-4**). Not surprisingly, the overall success rate was low: of 277 fused cells, only 29 developed into embryos that could be transferred, and Dolly was the only live lamb produced.

Why did Wilmut's team succeed when so many other researchers had failed? Applying the basic principles of cell biology, they recognized that the **cell cycles** (see Chapter 10) of the egg cytoplasm and the donor nucleus were not synchronous. The egg cell is arrested at metaphase II of meiosis, whereas the actively growing donor somatic cell is usually in the DNA synthesis phase (S), or in G_2. By withholding certain nutrients from the mammary gland cells used as donors, the researchers caused these cells to enter a nondividing state referred to as G_0. This had the effect of synchronizing the cell cycles of the donor nucleus and the egg. They then used an electric shock to fuse the donor cell with the egg and initiate embryo development.

Although an extremely high level of technical expertise is required, these and other researchers have modified and extended these techniques to produce cloned calves, pigs, horses, rats, mice, dogs, and cats, among others. The list of mammalian species suc-

cessfully cloned continues to grow. However, the success rate for each set of trials is low, around 1% to 2%, and the incidence of genetic defects is high. Dolly was euthanized at age 6 because she was suffering from a virus-induced lung cancer that infected several sheep where she was housed. However, she developed arthritis at 5½ years, which is relatively young for a sheep to have this degenerative disease. Some biologists speculate that using adult genetic material to produce a clone might produce an animal with prematurely old cells (see discussion of telomeres and cell aging in Chapter 12). Further research may provide some answers to this potential problem.

The main focus of cloning research is the production of **transgenic** organisms, in which foreign genes have been incorporated (see Chapter 15). Researchers are actively pursuing new techniques to improve the efficiency of the cloning process. Only then will it be possible to produce large numbers of cloned transgenic animals for a variety of uses, such as increasing the populations of endangered species. For example, the first healthy clone of an endangered species, a wild relative of cattle known as a *banteng*, was born in 2003. The nucleus for this clone came from a frozen skin cell of a banteng that died in 1980 at the San Diego Zoo.

Stem cells divide and give rise to differentiated cells

Stem cells are undifferentiated cells that can divide to produce differentiated descendants yet retain the ability to divide to maintain the stem cell population. When a stem cell divides, its daughter cells can remain stem cells or differentiate into specialized cells such as muscle cells, neurons, or blood cells. What happens depends on the presence or absence of an array of biochemical signals. One of

KEY EXPERIMENT

QUESTION: Are nuclei in differentiated mammalian cells totipotent?

HYPOTHESIS: The nucleus of a differentiated cell from an adult mammal fused with an enucleated egg can provide the genetic information to direct normal development.

EXPERIMENT: Ian Wilmut and his colleagues produced a sheep embryo by fusing a cultured adult sheep mammary cell with an enucleated sheep's egg. He then implanted the embryo into the uterus of a host mother.

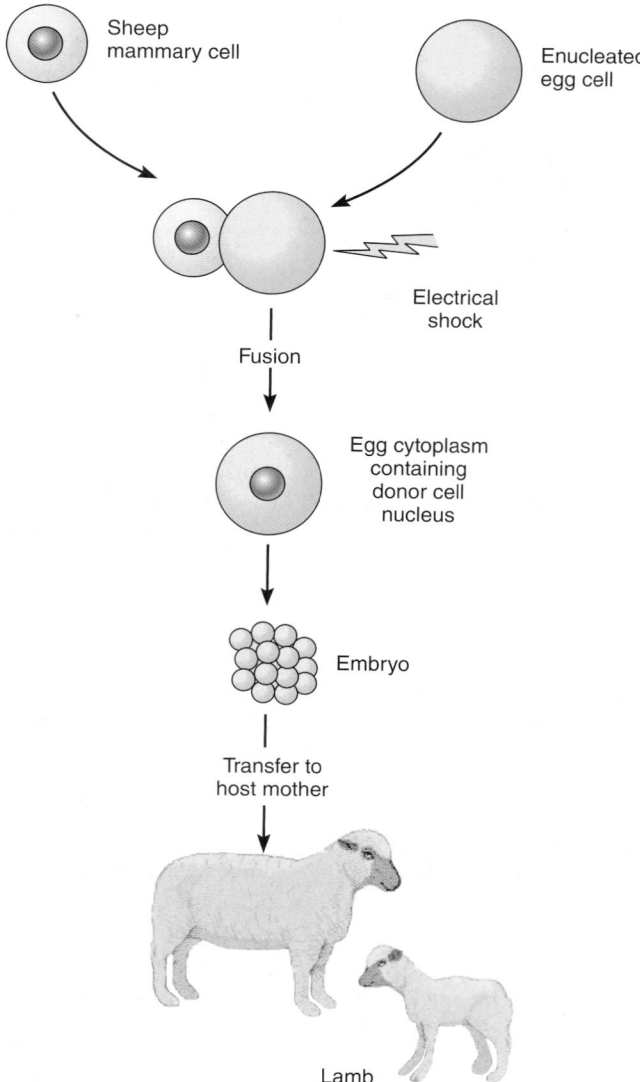

RESULTS AND CONCLUSION: Normal development proceeded, and a female lamb—the world's first cloned mammal—was born. To provide additional evidence that the cloned sheep was fully functioning, when she matured, she was bred and gave birth to a normal offspring.

Source: Campbell, K. H., J. McWhir, W. A. Ritchie, and I. Wilmut. "Sheep Cloned by Nuclear Transfer from a Cultured Cell Line." *Nature*, Vol. 380, 1996.

FIGURE 17-4 *Animated* Wilmut's experiment on mammalian cloning

the most challenging areas of stem cell research today involves determining the identity, order, and amounts of the chemical signals that will result in a specific type of cell differentiation.

The most versatile stem cells—zygotes—are totipotent and have the potential to give rise to all tissues of the body and placenta. Stem cells can also be derived from embryos or adult cells. (The term *adult* is somewhat misleading because **adult stem cells** can be harvested from umbilical cord tissue, infants, and children as well as adults.) Embryonic and adult stem cells are known as **pluripotent stem cells** because they can give rise to many, but not all, of the types of cells in an organism. **Embryonic stem cells (ES cells),** formed after a zygote has undergone several rounds of cell division to form a 5- or 6-day-old blastocyst, are more versatile than adult stem cells (**FIG. 17-5**). For example, ES cells are pluripotent and have the potential to develop into any type of cell in the body; ES cells are not totipotent because they cannot form cells of the placenta.

Adult stem cells have been found in the human brain, retina, heart, bone marrow, dental pulp, intestines, and other sites. Adult neural stem cells in the brain are pluripotent and differentiate to form neurons and glial cells. Adult stem cells in the bone marrow form both red blood cells and the various types of white blood cells of the immune system. The range of cells that adult stem cells can differentiate into is more limited than that of ES cells. However, recent studies suggest that even specialized stem cells may be more versatile than once thought. For example, adult neural stem cells form blood cells when transplanted into bone marrow.

Stem cells are potential sources for cell transplantation into patients to treat serious degenerative conditions. For example, Parkinson's disease results from a progressive loss of cells that produce the neurotransmitter dopamine in a specific region of the brain. Transplantation of stem cells that have been induced to differentiate as dopamine-producing cells holds great promise as an effective long-term treatment. Similarly, stem cells may become a source of insulin-producing cells for transplantation into the pancreas of individuals with diabetes mellitus. Stem cells might also provide replacement neurons in people with spinal cord injury or other types of neurological damage.

Researchers ultimately hope to establish lines of human pluripotent stem cells that can grow indefinitely in culture, be induced to differentiate under controlled conditions and stably maintain their differentiated state, and be manipulated genetically. They particularly want to develop ES cell lines from patients with cancer, diabetes, cardiovascular disease, and neurogenerative disorders (such as Parkinson's disease); such cell lines would be invaluable in research on these disorders. Although work on stem cells in mice and other mammals has been conducted for many years, similar studies in humans have progressed slowly, despite the great promise of stem cells as a therapeutic tool.

Thus far, the only known source of ES cells is early human embryos left over from **in vitro fertilization** (see Chapter 50). Some countries have government restrictions on public funding due to ethical considerations related to the origins of ES cells. Other countries, notably some Asian countries, have no restrictions on this type of research. In the United States, the Obama administration lifted restrictions on stem cell research that were established during the George W. Bush administration, and public funding became available in 2009.

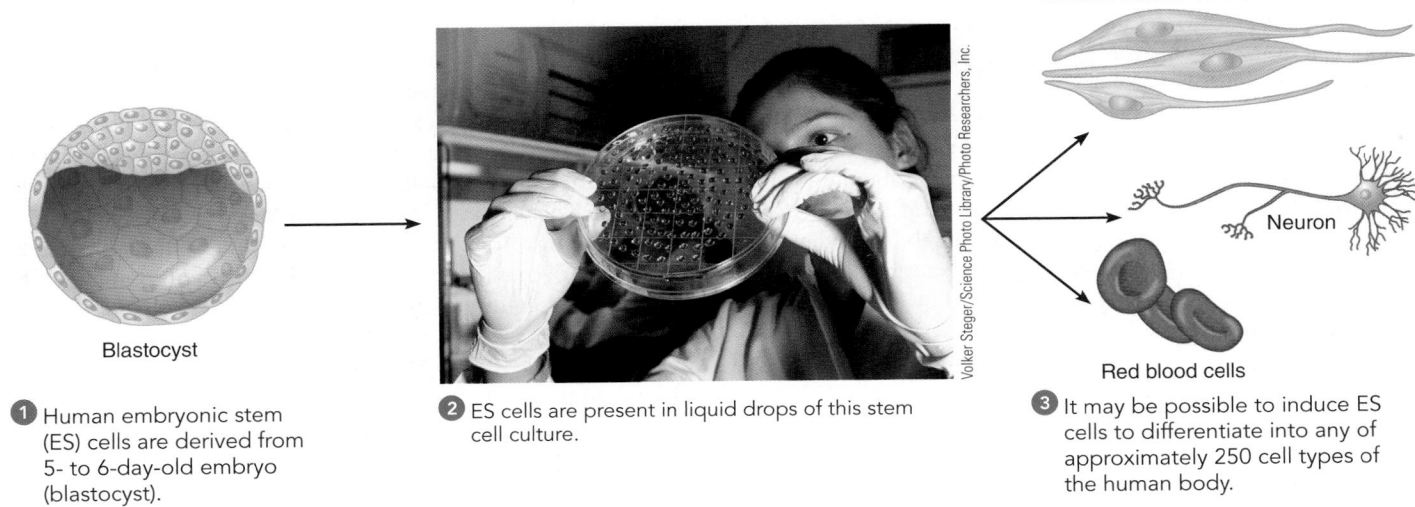

① Human embryonic stem (ES) cells are derived from 5- to 6-day-old embryo (blastocyst).

Blastocyst

② ES cells are present in liquid drops of this stem cell culture.

③ It may be possible to induce ES cells to differentiate into any of approximately 250 cell types of the human body.

Smooth muscle cells

Neuron

Red blood cells

Volker Steger/Science Photo Library/Photo Researchers, Inc.

FIGURE 17-5 Human embryonic stem (ES) cells

Induced pluripotent stem (iPS) cells may eventually replace ES cells

In 2007 and 2008, scientists at several research labs were able to produce **induced pluripotent stem (iPS) cells** by introducing a few key **transcription factors** into mature mouse and human cells such as fibroblasts and skin cells. (Recall from Chapter 14 that transcription factors are DNA-binding proteins that regulate gene transcription in eukaryotic cells.)

The transcription factors reprogrammed the developmental state of the mature cells so they became pluripotent embryonic cells, but the mechanism by which they accomplished this is currently unknown. The transcription factors may have removed methyl groups from key genes that are normally turned off in adult cells but turned on in embryonic cells. (Recall from Chapter 14 that epigenetic inheritance consists of gene inactivation, for example, by DNA methylation.) For genes that are inactivated by methylation, removing the methyl groups would reactivate the genes.

Scientists must learn more about iPS cells before they can be used to replace embryonic stem cells in research. It does not appear that there is any difference between iPS cells and ES cells. If this is the case, then the ethical concerns that make ES cells controversial (discussed in the next section) may soon not matter because scientists will not need to use ES cells.

Ethical questions exist relating to human cloning

Cloning research continues to fuel an ongoing debate regarding the potential for human cloning and its ethical and religious implications. In the United States, the National Bioethics Advisory Commission has been established to study this and other questions. In considering these issues, it is important to recognize that *cloning* is a broad term that includes several different processes involved in producing biological cells, tissues, organs, or organisms.

Human reproductive cloning has the goal of producing a newborn human that is genetically identical to another, usually adult, human. It would involve placing a human embryo produced by a process other than fertilization into a woman's body. Many countries are opposed to human reproductive cloning.

In contrast, **human therapeutic cloning** would involve duplication of human ES cells or iPS cells for scientific study or medical purposes; no newborn human would develop. These cells would provide a supply of replacement tissues, such as heart muscle or nervous tissue, for revolutionary medical procedures.

Many people support research in therapeutic cloning because of the potential benefits in curing disease. Other people have ethical or religious objections if ES cells are used.

Review

- What lines of evidence support the principle of nuclear equivalence?
- Why was Wilmut's team successful in mammalian cloning where others had failed?
- What are stem cells?

17.2 THE GENETIC CONTROL OF DEVELOPMENT

■ LEARNING OBJECTIVES

4 Indicate the features of *Drosophila melanogaster*, *Caenorhabditis elegans*, *Mus musculus*, and *Arabidopsis thaliana* that have made these organisms valuable models in developmental genetics.

5 Distinguish among maternal effect genes, segmentation genes, and homeotic genes in *Drosophila*.

6 Explain the relationship between transcription factors and genes that control development.

7 Define *induction* and *apoptosis*, and give examples of the roles they play in development.

Development has been an important area of research for many years, and biologists have spent considerable time studying the development of invertebrate and vertebrate animals. By investigating patterns of morphogenesis in different species, researchers have identified both similarities and differences in the basic plan of development from a zygote to an adult in organisms ranging from the sea urchin to mammals (see Chapter 51).

In addition to descriptive studies, many classic experiments have demonstrated how groups of cells differentiate and undergo pattern formation. Researchers have developed elaborate screening programs to detect mutations that let them identify many developmental genes in both plants and animals. They then use molecular genetic techniques and other sophisticated methodologies to determine how those genes work and how they interact to coordinate developmental processes.

A variety of model organisms provide insights into basic biological processes

In studies of the genetic control of development, the choice of organism to use as an experimental model is important. A **model organism** is a species chosen for biological studies because it has characteristics that allow for the efficient analysis of biological processes. Because most model organisms are small organisms with short generation times, they are easy to grow and study under controlled conditions. For example, mice are a better model organism than kangaroos.

One of the most powerful approaches in developmental genetics involves isolating mutants of a model organism with abnormal development. Not all organisms have useful characteristics that allow researchers to isolate and maintain developmental mutants for future study. Geneticists so thoroughly understand the genetics of the fruit fly, *Drosophila melanogaster,* that this organism has become one of the most important systems for such studies. Other organisms—the yeast *Saccharomyces cerevisiae;* the nematode worm, *Caenorhabditis elegans;* the zebrafish, *Danio rerio;* the laboratory mouse, *Mus musculus;* and certain plants, including *Arabidopsis thaliana,* a tiny weed—have also become important models in developmental genetics. Each of these organisms has attributes that make it particularly useful for examining certain aspects of development (**FIG. 17-6**).

In the 1990s, developmental geneticists working on *C. elegans* discovered RNA interference, which has become a powerful research tool. In **RNA interference (RNAi)** certain small RNA molecules interfere with the expression of genes or their RNA transcripts (see Chapter 13). One way these molecules work is to silence genes by selectively cleaving mRNA molecules that have base sequences complementary to the small RNA molecules. The use of RNAi makes it possible to knock out the expression of a specific gene in an organism during its development, thereby deducing the purpose of the gene.

Many genes that control development have been identified in the fruit fly

The fruit fly (*Drosophila*) genome sequence, which was completed in late 1999, includes about 13,600 protein-coding genes. At least 1200 of these are essential for embryonic development.

Two of the traditional advantages of *Drosophila* as a research organism are the abundance of mutant alleles, including those of

developmental genes, available for study and the relative ease with which a new mutation is mapped on the chromosomes. U.S. biologist Edward B. Lewis (1918–2004), a pioneering developmental geneticist, began working with *Drosophila* mutants in the 1940s. The work of German researcher Christiane Nüsslein-Volhard and American Eric Wieschaus extended our understanding of development in fruit flies. Lewis, Nüsslein-Volhard, and Wieschaus shared the 1995 Nobel Prize in Physiology or Medicine for their decades of painstaking research on the genetics of *Drosophila* development. Many of the genes they discovered in the fruit fly are now known to be important in the growth and development of all animals.

The *Drosophila* life cycle includes egg, larval, pupal, and adult stages

Development in *Drosophila* consists of several distinct stages (**FIG. 17-7**). After the egg is fertilized, a period of embryogenesis occurs during which the zygote develops into a sexually immature form known as a **larva** (pl., *larvae*). After hatching from the egg, each larva undergoes several molts (shedding of the external covering, or cuticle). The periods between molts are called *instars*. Each molt results in a size increase until the larva is ready to become a **pupa.** Pupation involves a molt and the hardening of the new external cuticle so that the pupa is completely encased. The insect then undergoes **metamorphosis,** a complete change in form. During that time, most of the larval tissues degenerate and other tissues differentiate to form the body parts of the sexually mature adult fly.

The larvae are wormlike in appearance and look nothing like the adult flies. However, very early in embryogenesis of the developing larvae, precursor cells of many of the adult structures are organized as relatively undifferentiated, paired structures called **imaginal discs.** The name comes from *imago,* the adult form of the insect. Each imaginal disc occupies a definite position in the larva and will form a specific structure, such as a wing or a leg, in the adult body (**FIG. 17-8**). The discs are formed by the time embryogenesis is complete and the larva is ready to begin feeding. In some respects the larva is a developmental stage that feeds and nurtures the precursor cells that give rise to the adult fly, which is the only form that reproduces.

The organization of the precursors of the adult structures, including the imaginal discs, is under genetic control. Thus far, more than 50 genes have been identified that specify the formation of the imaginal discs, their positions within the larva, and their ultimate functions within the adult fly. Those genes were identified through mutations that either prevent certain discs from forming or alter their structure or ultimate fate.

Drosophila developmental mutations affect the body plan

Scientists have identified many developmental mutations in *Drosophila*. Researchers have examined their effects on development in various combinations and have studied them extensively at the molecular level. In our discussion we pay particular attention to mutations that affect the segmented body plan of the organism, in both the larva and the adult.

FIGURE 17-6 Model organisms in developmental genetics ▶

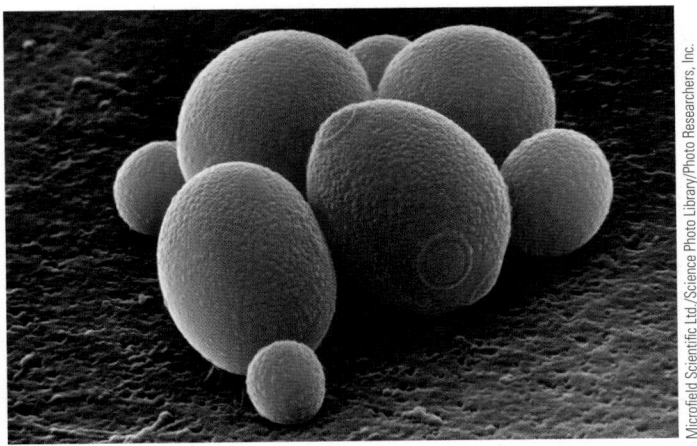

5 μm

(a) Yeast (*Saccharomyces cerevisiae*) is a model organism for studying developmental genetics in haploid, unicellular eukaryotes.

(b) Fruit fly (*Drosophila melanogaster*) development involves an anterior-posterior body plan that is common to many invertebrates and vertebrates.

0.25 mm

(c) The **nematode (*Caenorhabditis elegans*)** adult body consists of only 959 cells, and its transparency allows researchers to trace the development of each cell.

(d) Zebrafish (*Danio rerio*) are small (2 to 4 cm long) and easy to grow, providing an ideal organism for studying the genetic basis of development in vertebrates.

(e) Mouse (*Mus musculus*) is a model organism for studying developmental genetics, including the genetics of cancer, in mammals.

(f) Mouse-ear cress (*Arabidopsis thaliana*) is a small plant with a small genome that is used to study development in flowering plants.

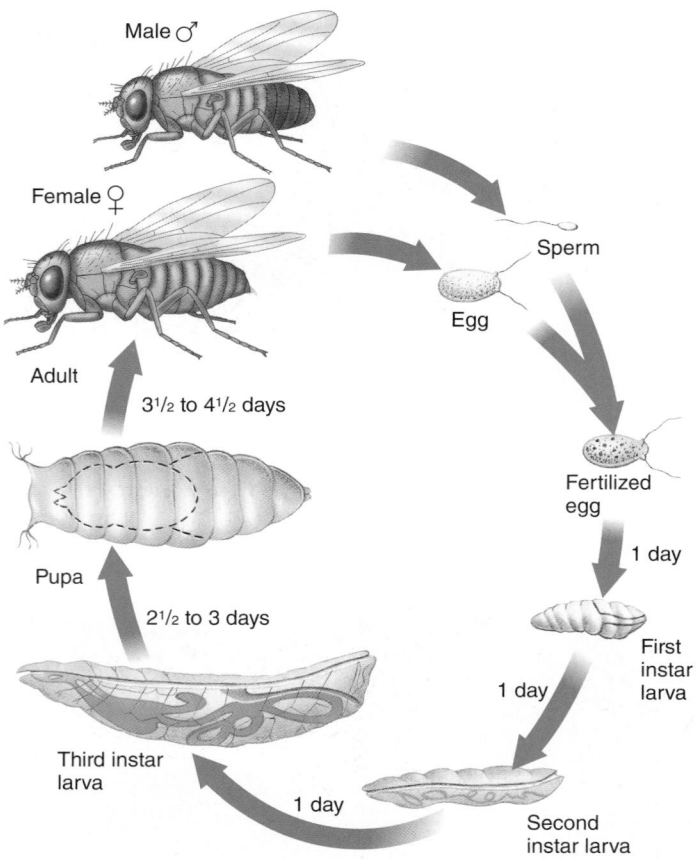

FIGURE 17-7 The life cycle of *Drosophila*

As it develops from a zygote to a sexually mature adult fly, a fruit fly passes through several stages. It takes about 12 days, at 25°C, to complete the life cycle. The dotted lines within the pupa represent the animal undergoing metamorphosis.

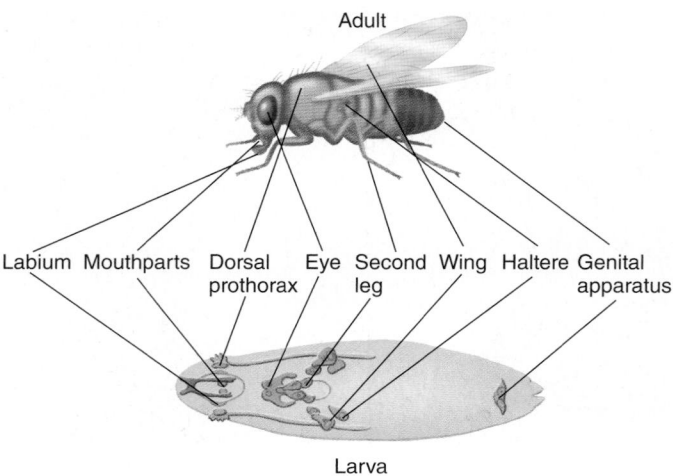

FIGURE 17-8 The location of imaginal discs

Each pair of discs in a *Drosophila* larva (*bottom*) develops into a specific pair of structures in the adult fly.

In early development of *Drosophila,* the structure of the egg becomes organized as it develops in the ovary of the female. Stores of mRNA, along with yolk proteins and other cytoplasmic molecules, pass from the surrounding maternal cells into the egg. Immediately after fertilization, the zygote nucleus divides, beginning a series of 13 mitotic divisions.

Each division takes only 5 or 10 minutes, which means that the DNA in the nuclei replicates constantly and at a very rapid rate. During that time, the nuclei do not synthesize RNA. Cytokinesis does not take place, and the nuclei produced by the first seven divisions remain at the center of the embryo until the eighth division occurs. At that time, most of the nuclei migrate out from the center and become localized at the periphery of the embryo. This is known as the *syncytial blastoderm* stage because the nuclei are not surrounded by individual plasma membranes. (A *syncytium* is a structure containing many nuclei residing in a common cytoplasm.) Subsequently, plasma membranes form, and the embryo becomes known as a *cellular blastoderm.*

Maternal Effect Genes The genes that organize the structure of the egg cell are called **maternal effect genes.** These genes in the surrounding maternal tissues are transcribed to produce mRNA molecules that are transported into the developing egg. Analysis of

mutant flies with defective maternal effect genes has revealed that many of these genes are involved in establishing the polarity of the embryo—such as which part of the embryo will become the head. Polarity dictates those parts of the egg that are dorsal or ventral and those that are anterior or posterior (see Chapter 30); thus, these genes are known as *egg polarity genes.*

FIGURE 17-9a illustrates concentration gradients for two specific maternal mRNA molecules in the very early embryo. These mRNA transcripts of some of the maternal effect genes are identified by their ability to hybridize with radioactive DNA probes derived from cloned genes (discussed in Chapter 15). Alternatively, researchers use fluorescently tagged antibodies (as in the chapter opening photograph) to bind to specific protein products of the maternal effect genes. These protein gradients organize the early pattern of development in the embryo by determining anterior and posterior regions.

A combination of protein gradients may provide positional information that specifies the fate—that is, the developmental path—of each nucleus within the embryo. For example, mutations in certain maternal effect genes result in an embryo with two heads or two posterior ends.

In many cases, injecting normal maternal mRNA into the mutant embryo reverses the phenotype associated with a mutation in a given maternal effect gene. The fly subsequently develops normally, indicating that the gene product is needed only for a short time in the earliest stages of development.

Segmentation Genes As the nuclei start to migrate to the periphery of the embryo, **segmentation genes** in those nuclei begin to produce embryonic mRNA. Thus far, geneticists have identified at least 24 segmentation genes that are responsible for generating a repeating pattern of body segments within the embryo and adult fly. Based on the study of mutant phenotypes, researchers group the segmentation genes into three classes—gap genes, pair–rule genes, and segment polarity genes.

Gap genes are the first set of segmentation genes to act. These genes interpret the maternal anterior-posterior information in the

Stage of development

Anterior   Posterior

Gene activity

Anterior   Posterior

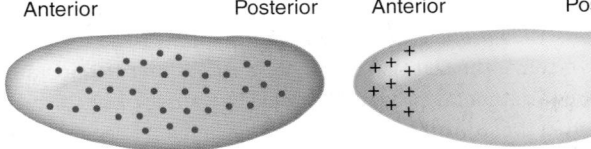

(a) At 1.25 hours after fertilization, the embryo consists of a common cytoplasm with about 128 nuclei (*purple circles*). Maternal effect genes divide the embryo into anterior and posterior sections. The crosses in the anterior region represent mRNA molecules transcribed from one maternal effect gene. The pink shading represents a different maternal mRNA molecule that is more concentrated in the anterior region.

(b) At 2 hours after fertilization, about 1500 nuclei have migrated into the periphery of the embryo and started to make their own mRNA molecules. The gap genes divide the embryo into anterior, middle, and posterior sections. The maternal RNA (shown in pink) is now transcribed from segmentation genes (*crosses*) in nuclei in the anterior region. The mRNA from another gap gene is transcribed in the middle of the embryo (*black region*).

FIGURE 17-9 Early development in *Drosophila*

Longitudinal sections on the left show two early stages of development of the *Drosophila* embryo. These are matched with the simplified patterns of gene activity at each stage on the right. (Adapted from Akam, M. E., "The Molecular Basis for Metameric Pattern in the Drosophila Embryo," *Development*, Vol. 101, 1987.)

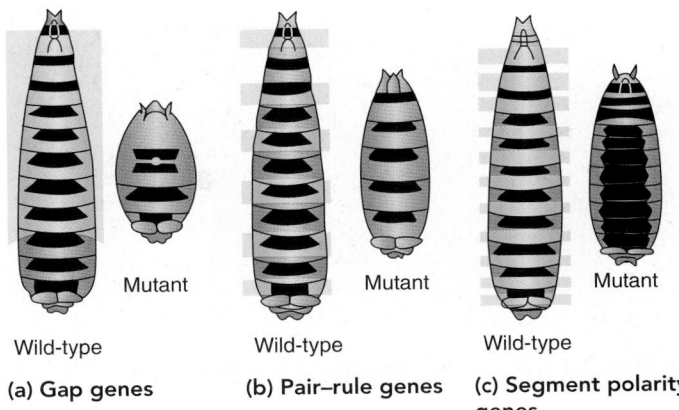

Mutant   Mutant   Mutant

Wild-type   Wild-type   Wild-type

(a) Gap genes   **(b) Pair–rule genes**   **(c) Segment polarity genes**

FIGURE 17-10 A comparison of mutations in *Drosophila* segmentation genes

Gap genes, pair–rule genes, and segment polarity genes control the pattern of body segments in a *Drosophila* embryo. The blue bands mark the regions in which the protein products of these genes are normally expressed in wild-type embryos. These same regions are absent in embryos in which the gene is mutated—that is, the mutant lacks the blue-shaded parts. The resulting phenotype is characteristic of the class to which the gene belongs. (Adapted from Nusslein-Volhard, C., and E. Wieschaus, "Mutations Affecting Segment Number and Polarity in Drosophila," *Nature*, Vol. 287, 1980.)

egg and begin organization of the body into anterior, middle, and posterior regions (**FIG. 17-9b**). A mutation in one of the gap genes usually causes the absence of one or more body segments in an embryo (**FIG. 17-10a**).

The other two classes of segmentation genes do not act on small groups of body segments; instead, they affect all segments. Mutations in **pair–rule genes** delete every other segment, producing a larva with half the normal number of segments (**FIG. 17-10b**

and **FIG. 17-11**). Mutations in **segment polarity genes** produce segments in which one part is missing and the remaining part is duplicated as a mirror image (**FIG. 17-10c**). The effects of the different classes of mutants are summarized in **TABLE 17-1**.

Each segmentation gene has distinctive times and places in the embryo in which it is most active. The observed pattern of expression of maternal effect genes and segmentation genes indicates that a progressive series of developmental events determines cells destined to form adult structures. First, maternal effect genes that form gradients of morphogens in the egg determine the anterior-posterior (head-to-tail) axis and the dorsal and ventral regions of the embryo. A **morphogen** is a chemical agent that affects the differentiation of cells and the development of form. Morphogen gradients are signals that help cells determine their location within the embryo and promote their eventual differentiation into specialized tissues and organs.

TABLE 17-1	Classes of Genes Involved in Establishing Segmented Body Plan in *Drosophila*	
Class of Gene	Site of Gene Activity	Functions of Genes
Maternal effect genes	Maternal tissues surrounding egg	Initiate anterior-posterior regions in embryo and regulate expression of segmentation genes
Segmentation genes		
Gap genes	Embryo	Divide embryo into broad regions and influence activity of pair–rule genes
Pair–rule genes	Embryo	Divide embryo into strips, each about two segments wide, and influence activity of segment polarity genes
Segment polarity genes	Embryo	Define all segments of body, and divide each segment into anterior and posterior halves
Homeotic genes	Embryo	Control identities of segments; expression of homeotic gene is controlled by segmentation genes

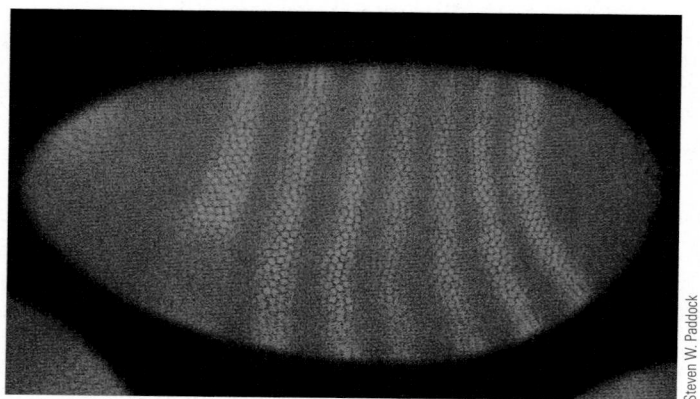

50 μm

Steven W. Paddock

FIGURE 17-11 Segmentation gene activity

The bright bands in this fluorescence LM reveal the presence of mRNA transcribed from one of the pair–rule genes known as *fushi tarazu* (Japanese for "not enough segments"). When this locus is mutated, the segments of the larva that are normally derived from these bands are absent.

Next, segmentation genes respond to the morphogens at each location to regulate the production of segments from the head to the posterior region. Within each segment, other genes are then activated to specify which body part that segment will become. Every cell's position is further specified with a specific "address" designated by combinations of the activities of the regulatory genes.

The segmentation genes act in sequence, with the gap genes acting first, then the pair–rule genes, and finally the segment polarity genes. In addition, the genes of the three groups interact. Each time a new group of genes acts, cells for that group become more determined in their development. As the embryo develops, each region is progressively subdivided into smaller regions.

Most segmentation genes code for transcription factors. For example, some segmentation genes code for a "zinc-finger" type of DNA-binding regulatory protein. (See Figure 14-12b to review zinc fingers.) *Homeotic genes,* discussed next, also code for transcription factors. The fact that many of the genes involved in controlling developmental processes code for transcription factors indicates that those proteins act as genetic switches to regulate the expression of other genes.

Once researchers have identified proteins that function as transcription factors, they can use the purified proteins to determine the DNA target sequences to which the proteins bind. This approach has been increasingly useful in identifying additional parts of the regulatory pathway involved in different stages of development. Transcription factors also play a role in cancer (discussed later in the chapter).

Homeotic Genes After segmentation genes have established the basic pattern of segments in the fly body, **homeotic genes** specify the developmental plan for each segment. Mutations in homeotic genes cause one body part to be substituted for another and therefore produce some peculiar changes in the adult. A striking example is the *Antennapedia* mutant fly, which has legs that grow from the head where the antennae would normally be (**FIG. 17-12**).

Homeotic genes in *Drosophila* were originally identified by the altered phenotypes produced by mutant alleles. When geneticists

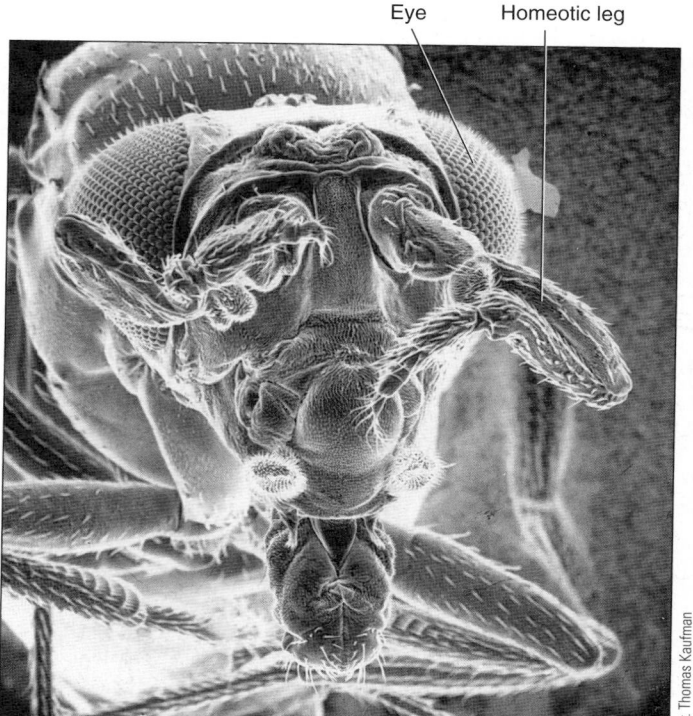

Eye   Homeotic leg

Dr. Thomas Kaufman

(b) SEM of the head of a fly with an *Antennapedia* mutation.

250 μm

Antenna

Eye

Mouthparts

Normal adult fly

Homeotic leg

Homeotic *Antennapedia* mutant

(a) The head of a normal fly and a fly with an *Antennapedia* mutation.

FIGURE 17-12 The *Antennapedia* locus

Antennapedia mutations cause homeotic transformations in *Drosophila* in which legs or parts of legs replace the antennae.

analyzed the DNA sequences of several homeotic genes, they discovered a short DNA sequence of approximately 180 base pairs, which characterizes many homeotic genes as well as some other genes that play a role in development. This DNA sequence is called the **homeobox.** Each homeobox codes for a protein functional region called a **homeodomain,** consisting of 60 amino acids that form four α-helices. One of these serves as a recognition helix that binds to specific DNA sequences and thereby affects transcription. Thus, the products of homeotic genes, like those of the earlier-acting segmentation genes, are transcription factors. In fact, some segmentation genes also contain homeoboxes.

Studies of **Hox genes,** clusters of homeobox-containing genes that specify the anterior-posterior axis during development, provide insights about evolutionary relationships. *Hox* genes were initially discovered in *Drosophila,* where they are arranged in two adjacent groups on the chromosome: the *Antennapedia complex* and the *bithorax complex.* As *Hox* genes have been identified in other animals, such as other arthropods, sea anemones, annelids (segmented worms), roundworms, and vertebrates, researchers have found that these genes are also clustered and that their organization is remarkably similar to that in *Drosophila.*

FIGURE 17-13 compares the organization of the *Hox* gene clusters of the fruit fly and mouse. The fruit fly and mouse *Hox* genes are located in the same order along the chromosome. Moreover, the linear order of the genes on the chromosome reflects the order of the corresponding regions they control, from anterior to posterior, in the animal. This organization apparently reflects the need for these genes to be transcribed in a specific temporal sequence.

Drosophila has only one *Antennapedia–bithorax* complex. However, mice, humans, and many other vertebrates have four similar *Hox* gene clusters, each located in a different chromosome. These complexes probably arose through gene duplication. The fact that extra copies of these genes are present helps explain why mutations causing homeotic-like transformations are seldom seen in vertebrate animals. One does not see an extra eye growing where a mouse leg should be, for example. However, one particular type of *Hox* mutation that has been described in both mice and humans causes abnormalities in the limbs and genitalia. The involvement of the genitalia provides a further explanation for the rarity of these mutant alleles because affected individuals are unlikely to reproduce.

The fact that very similar developmental controls are seen in organisms as diverse as insects and vertebrates (including humans) indicates that the basic mechanism evolved early and has been highly conserved in all animals that have an anterior-posterior axis, even those that are not segmented. Clearly, once a successful way of regulating groups of genes and integrating their activities evolved, it was retained, although it has apparently been modified to provide alterations of the body plan.

The finding of homeobox-like genes in plants suggests these genes originated early during eukaryotic evolution. With further investigations, researchers hope to develop an overall model of how the rudiments of morphogenesis are controlled in all multicellular eukaryotes. These systems of master genes that regulate development are a rich source of "molecular fossils" that are illuminating evolutionary history in new and exciting ways. These kinds of studies have led to an ongoing synthesis of evolution and developmental biology that has come to be known as **Evo Devo.**

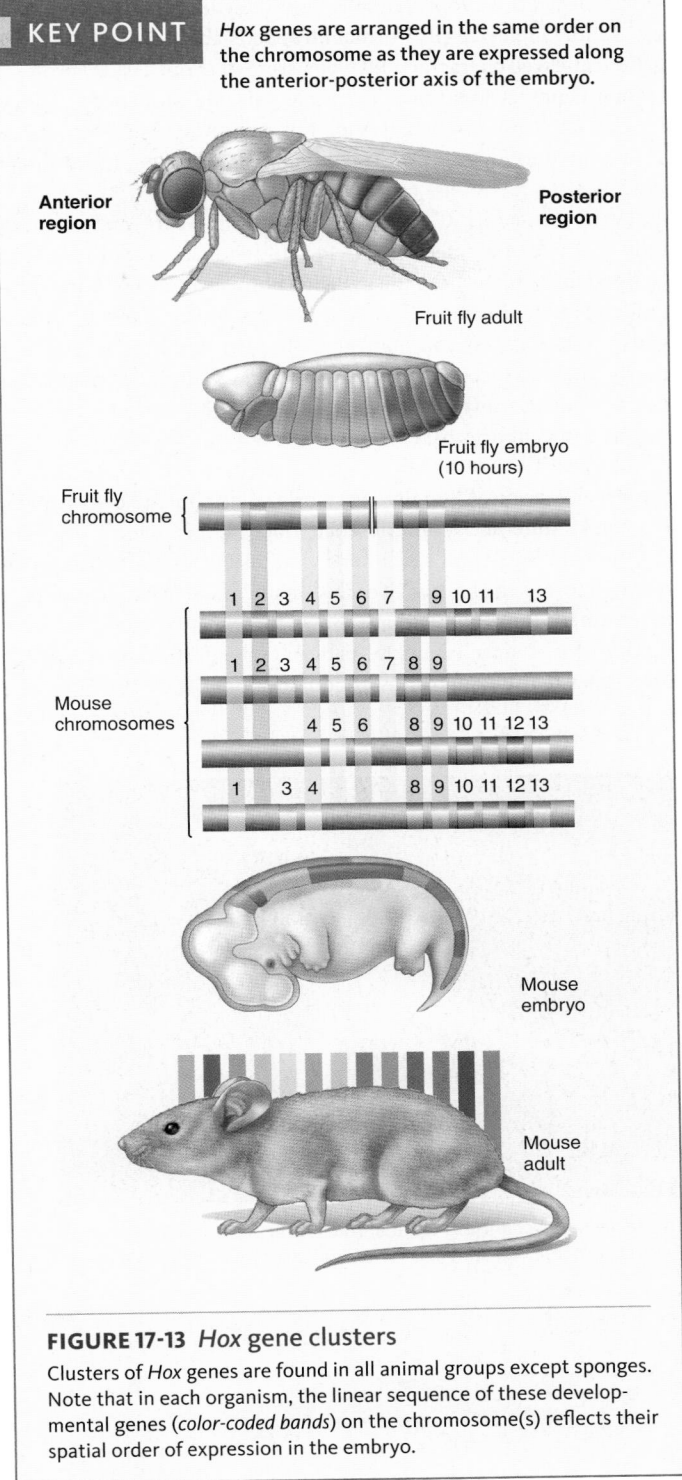

KEY POINT *Hox* genes are arranged in the same order on the chromosome as they are expressed along the anterior-posterior axis of the embryo.

Anterior region

Posterior region

Fruit fly adult

Fruit fly embryo (10 hours)

Fruit fly chromosome

Mouse chromosomes

Mouse embryo

Mouse adult

FIGURE 17-13 *Hox* gene clusters

Clusters of *Hox* genes are found in all animal groups except sponges. Note that in each organism, the linear sequence of these developmental genes (*color-coded bands*) on the chromosome(s) reflects their spatial order of expression in the embryo.

Caenorhabditis elegans has a relatively rigid developmental pattern

The nematode worm *C. elegans* is an ideal model organism because its system for the genetic control of development is relatively easy to study. Sydney Brenner, a British molecular geneticist, began studying molecular development in this animal at Cambridge

University in the 1960s. He selected *C. elegans* because it is small, has a short life cycle (its normal lifespan is about 3 weeks), and is genetically well characterized. Consisting of about 19,700 protein-coding genes, it was the first animal genome sequenced. Today, *C. elegans* is an important tool for answering basic questions about the development of individual cells within a multicellular organism.

When an adult, *C. elegans* is only 1.5 mm long and contains only 959 somatic cells (**FIG. 17-14**). Individuals are either males or **hermaphrodites,** organisms with both sexes in the same individual. Hermaphroditic *C. elegans* are capable of self-fertilization, which makes it easy to obtain offspring that are homozygous for newly induced recessive mutations. The availability of males that can reproduce sexually with the hermaphrodites makes it possible to perform genetic crosses as well.

Because the worm's body is transparent, researchers can follow the development of literally every one of its somatic cells using a Nomarski differential interference microscope, which provides contrast in transparent specimens. As a result of efforts by several research teams, the lineage of each somatic cell in the adult has been determined. Those studies have shown that the nematode has a very rigid, or fixed, developmental pattern. After fertilization, the egg undergoes repeated divisions, producing about 550 cells that make up the small, sexually immature larva. After the larva hatches from the egg case, further cell divisions give rise to the adult worm.

The lineage of each somatic cell in the adult can be traced to a single cell in a small group of **founder cells,** which are formed early in development (**FIG. 17-15a**). If a particular founder cell is destroyed or removed, the adult structures that would normally develop from that cell are missing. Such a rigid developmental pattern, in which the fates of the cells become restricted early in development, is referred to as **mosaic development.** Each cell has a specific fate in the embryo, just as each tile in a mosaic design forms part of the pattern.

Scientists initially hypothesized that every organ system in *C. elegans* might be derived from only one founder cell. Detailed analysis of cell lineages, however, reveals that many of the structures found in the adult, such as the nervous system and the musculature, are in fact derived from more than one founder cell (**FIG. 17-15b**). A few lineages have been identified in which a neuron and a muscle cell are derived from the division of a single cell.

A researcher who uses microscopic laser beams small enough to destroy individual cells can determine the influence one cell has on the development of a neighboring cell. Consistent with the rigid pattern of cell lineages, the destruction of an individual cell in *C. elegans* results, in most cases, in the absence of all of the structures derived from that cell but with the normal differentiation of all the neighboring somatic cells. This observation suggests that development in each cell is regulated through its own internal program.

However, the developmental pattern of *C. elegans* is not entirely mosaic. In some cases, cell differentiation is influenced by interactions with particular neighboring cells, a phenomenon known as **induction.** One example is the formation of the vulva (pl., *vulvae*), the reproductive structure through which the eggs are laid. A single nondividing cell, called the *anchor cell,* is a part of the ovary, the structure in which the germ line cells undergo meiosis to produce the eggs. The anchor cell attaches to the ovary and to a point on the outer surface of the animal, triggering the formation of a passage through which the eggs pass to the outside. When the anchor cell is present, it induces cells on the surface to form the vulva and its opening. If the anchor cell is destroyed by a laser beam, however, the vulva does not form, and the cells that would normally form the vulva remain as surface cells (**FIG. 17-16**).

The analysis of worm mutations has contributed to our understanding of inductive interactions. For example, several types of mutations cause more than one vulva to form. In such mutant animals, multiple vulvae form even if the anchor cell is destroyed. Thus, the mutant cells do not require an inductive signal from an anchor cell to form a vulva. Evidently, in these mutants the gene or genes responsible for vulva formation are constitutive. Conversely, mutants lacking a vulva are also known. In some of these, the cells that would normally form the vulva apparently do not respond to the inducing signal from the anchor cell.

C. elegans is a model system to study apoptosis

During normal development in *C. elegans,* there are instances in which cells are destined to die shortly after they are produced. **Apoptosis,** or genetically programmed cell death, has been observed in a wide variety of organisms, both plant and animal. For example, the human hand is formed as a webbed structure, but

James King-Holmes/Photo Researchers, Inc.

0.3 mm

(a) False-color scanning optical micrograph of adult hermaphrodite nematodes. The oval structures are eggs.

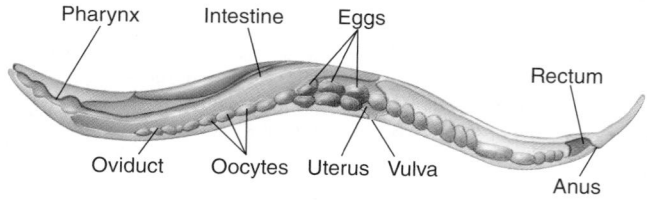

Pharynx   Intestine   Eggs

Rectum

Oviduct   Oocytes   Uterus   Vulva

Anus

(b) Structures in the adult hermaphrodite. The sperm-producing structures are not shown.

FIGURE 17-14 *Caenorhabditis elegans*

This transparent organism has a fixed number of somatic cells. (Part **b** adapted from Fig. 22-6a in V. Walbot and N. Holder, *Developmental Biology.* © 1987. Used with permission from McGraw-Hill companies.)

The nematode worm *C. elegans* has a fixed developmental pattern in which the fate of each adult cell can be traced to one of several founder cells in the embryo.

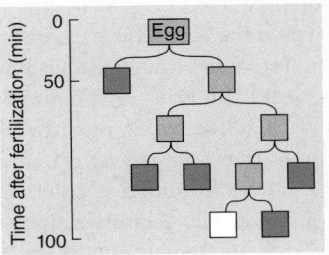

(a) All somatic cells of *C. elegans* are derived from five somatic founder cells (*shown in blue*) produced during the early cell divisions of the embryo. The cell shown in white gives rise to germ line cells.

(b) The nervous system, hypodermis, and musculature derive from several founder cells. This lineage map traces the development of the cells that form the intestine. (The dashed lines represent many cell divisions of a particular lineage.)

FIGURE 17-15 Cell lineages of *Caenorhabditis elegans*

the fingers become individualized when the cells between them undergo apoptosis. In *C. elegans,* as in other organisms, apoptosis is under genetic control. The worm embryos undergo mitosis to produce a total of 1090 cells, but 131 of these undergo apoptosis during development, resulting in adult worms with 959 cells.

In 1986, U.S. molecular geneticist Robert Horvitz discovered several mutant worms that were defective in some way relating to apoptosis. He characterized the mutations and the genes responsible for them at the molecular level. For example, one of the genes codes for a protein that regulates the release from mitochondria of molecules that trigger apoptosis (mitochondria are now known to have a crucial role in apoptosis in animals ranging from *C. elegans* to humans). Other genes were identified that code for a family of proteins known as **caspases,** proteolytic enzymes active in the early stages of apoptosis. Homologous genes were subsequently identified in other organisms, including humans; some of these loci in mammals also code for caspases. The molecular events that trigger apoptosis remain an area of intense research interest, the results of which will shed considerable light on the general processes of cell aging and cancer.

Robert Horvitz and British scientists Sydney Brenner and John Sulston shared the Nobel Prize in Physiology or Medicine in 2002 for their work on the genetic regulation of organ development and apoptosis in *C. elegans.* Sulston was one of Brenner's

FIGURE 17-16 Induction ▶

A single anchor cell induces neighboring cells to form the vulva in *C. elegans.* This diagram shows how laser destruction of single cells or groups of cells influences neighboring cells.

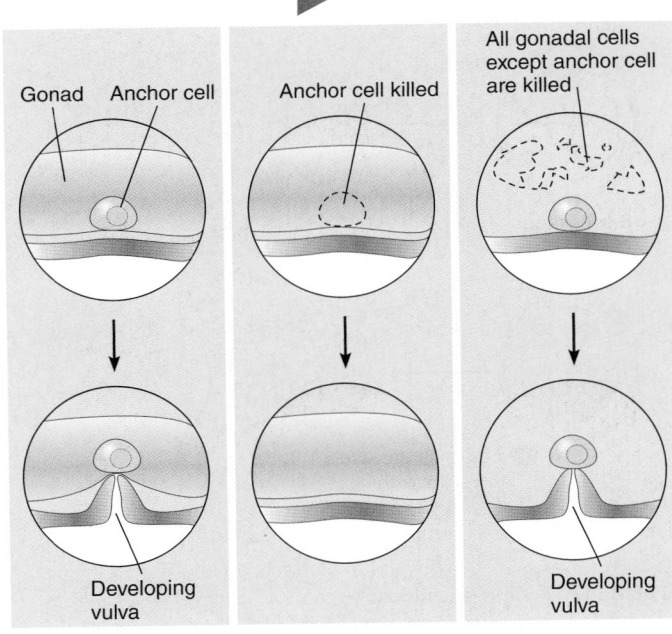

(a) Normal development of vulva

(b) No vulva develops

(c) Normal development of vulva

students. He traced the lineage of how a single zygote gives rise to the 959 cells in the nematode adult and also observed that some cells die during normal development. Continuing Sulston's work on apoptosis, Horvitz, as mentioned earlier, was the first to discover genes involved in apoptosis.

The mouse is a model for mammalian development

Mammalian embryos develop in markedly different ways from the embryos of *Drosophila* and *C. elegans*. The laboratory mouse, *Mus musculus,* is the best-studied example of mammalian development. Researchers have identified numerous genes affecting development in the mouse. The mouse genome sequence, which was published in 2002, contains 27,000 to 30,000 genes, similar to the number of protein-coding genes in the human genome. Indeed, 99% of the genes in the mouse have counterparts in humans.

The early development of the mouse and other mammals is similar in many ways to human development. During the early developmental period, the embryo lives free in the reproductive tract of the female. It then implants in the wall of the uterus, after which the mother meets its nutritional and respiratory needs. Consequently, mammalian eggs are very small and contain little in the way of food reserves. Almost all research on mouse development has concentrated on the stages leading to implantation because in those stages the embryo is free-living and can be experimentally manipulated. During that period, developmental commitments that have a significant effect on the future organization of the embryo take place.

After fertilization, a series of cell divisions gives rise to a loosely packed group of cells. Research shows that all cells are equivalent in the very early mouse embryo. For example, at the two-cell stage of mouse embryogenesis, if researchers destroy one cell and implant the remaining cell into the uterus of a surrogate mother, a normal mouse usually develops.

Conversely, if two embryos at the eight-cell stage of development are fused and implanted into a surrogate mother, a normal-sized mouse develops (**FIG. 17-17**). By using two embryos with different genetic characters, such as coat color, researchers demonstrated that the resulting mouse has four genetic parents. These chimeric mice have fur with patches of different colors derived from clusters of genetically different cells. A **chimera** is an organism containing two or more kinds of genetically dissimilar cells arising from different zygotes. (The term is derived from the name of a mythical beast that was said to have the head of a lion, the body of a goat, and a snakelike tail.) Chimeras let researchers use genetically marked cells to trace the fates of certain cells during development.

The responses of mouse embryos to such manipulations contrast with the mosaic or predetermined nature of early *C. elegans* development, in which destroying one of the founder cells results in the loss of a significant portion of the embryo. For this reason, biologists say that the mouse has highly **regulative development**—the early embryo acts as a self-regulating whole that accommodates missing or extra parts.

Transgenic mice are used in studies of developmental regulation

In transformation experiments, foreign DNA injected into fertilized mouse eggs is incorporated into the chromosomes and expressed (**FIG. 17-18**). (Also see Figure 15-14 for an example of a transgenic mouse.) The resulting transgenic mice provide insights

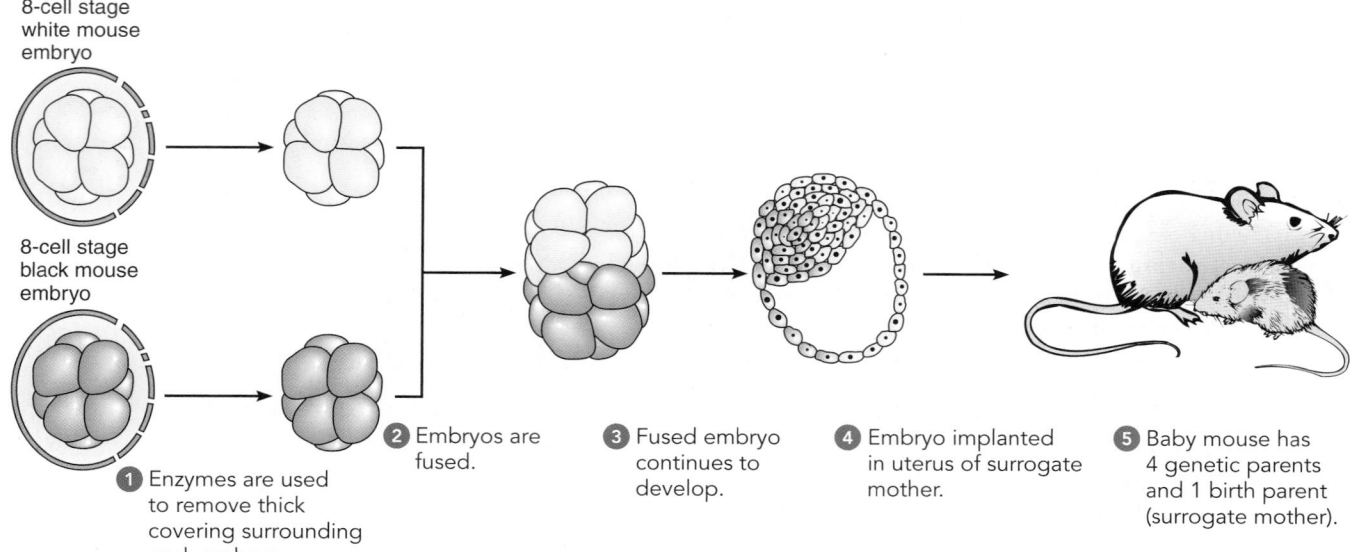

FIGURE 17-17 Chimeric mouse

Researchers remove embryos from females of two different strains and combine the cells in vitro. The resulting aggregate embryo continues to develop and is implanted in the uterus of a surrogate mother. The offspring has four different genetic parents. Although the surrogate mother is the birth mother, she is not genetically related.

into how genes are activated during development. Scientists can identify a *transgene* (foreign gene) that has been introduced into a mouse and determine whether it is active by marking the gene in several ways. Sometimes a similar gene from a different species is used; its protein is distinguished from the mouse protein by specific antibodies.

It is also possible to construct a hybrid gene consisting of the regulatory elements of a mouse gene and part of another, non-mouse, gene that codes for a "reporter" protein. For example, the reporter protein could be an enzyme not normally found in

Why Is It Used? This method is used to establish a transgenic line of mice that contain genes with useful traits for scientific and medical research.

How Is It Done?

Fertile

♀ × ♂

1. Collect fertilized eggs.

2. Inject cloned DNA fragment into nucleus.

3. Implant injected embryos into female.

Surrogate mother

4. Test for transgene in offspring of surrogate mother.

Transgenic offspring

5. Breed transgenic animals.

Fetal/neonatal   Pup   Adult

FIGURE 17-18 Producing a transgenic mouse

mice. Such studies have been important in showing which DNA sequences of a mouse homeobox gene determine where the gene is expressed in the embryo.

Many developmentally controlled genes introduced into mice have yielded important information about gene regulation. When researchers introduce developmentally controlled genes from other species, such as humans or rats, into mice, the genes are regulated the same way they normally are in the donor animal. When introduced into the mouse, for example, human genes encoding insulin, globin, and crystallin—which are normally expressed in cells of the pancreas, blood, and eye lens, respectively—are expressed only in those same tissues in the mouse. That these genes are correctly expressed in their appropriate tissues indicates that the signals for tissue-specific gene expression are highly conserved through evolution. Information on the regulation of genes controlling development in one organism can have valuable applications to other organisms, including humans.

Mice and other model organisms are providing insights into the aging process

Aging, which is defined as a progressive decline in the performance of various parts of the body, is an important field of developmental biology. The study of aging has great practical potential because age-related diseases represent one of the biggest challenges of biomedical research today. Scientists have demonstrated that many environmental factors influence aging. For example, severe calorie restriction in rodents and other mammals delays aging. However, how the human genome interacts with the cell environment during the aging process is not well understood.

Researchers working with model organisms, such as *Drosophila* and *C. elegans,* have found that more than 1000 protein-coding genes affect aging to variable degrees. In the nematode worm *C. elegans,* most aging genes are under the control of three genes (ELT-3, ELT-5, and ELT-6), all of which code for transcription factors.

Many of the genes that slow aging in organisms as diverse as yeasts, nematodes, and mammals are associated with cells' responses to nutrients. Dietary restrictions are known to extend lifespan for many organisms, from yeasts to dogs and possibly even to primates. Two genes (the PHA-4 gene and the SKN-1 gene) that extend survival in *C. elegans* code for transcription factors.

One of the most potent lifespan-extending genes, present in *C. elegans,* codes for a protein similar to the membrane receptor that allows cells to respond to the peptide **insulin-like growth factor (IGF)** in humans and other mammals. The binding of IGF to its receptor triggers **signal transduction** within the cell, which regulates the expression of many genes.

Researchers wondered if the IGF receptor influences aging in mammals, including humans. To test this hypothesis, they produced *knockout mice* with an inactivated gene for the insulin-like growth factor receptor (IGF-1R). (Knockout mice were first discussed in Chapter 15.) Because mice are diploid organisms, they have two copies of the gene, designated *igf1r.* When both alleles of *igf1r* are inactivated, the mice develop many abnormalities and die at birth. However, when one allele of *igf1r* is inactivated and the other is left in its normal state, the mice thrive and live about 25% longer than control mice. In all other respects, the heterozygous mice are normal. They are virtually indistinguishable from control mice in their rate of development, metabolic rate, ability to reproduce, and body size. Mice heterozygous at the *igf1r* locus produce fewer IGF receptors, and therefore the cells are not exposed to as much signaling from IGF.

Research on the IGF receptor and aging in mice suggests that some of the hundreds of other mutant genes associated with aging in *C. elegans* may also be involved in mammalian aging. Thus, the genetic control of mammalian aging has enough research topics to occupy molecular geneticists for many years.

Arabidopsis is a model for studying plant development, including transcription factors

Mouse-ear cress (*Arabidopsis thaliana*), the organism most widely used to study the genetic control of development in plants, is a member of the mustard family. Although *Arabidopsis* itself is a weed of no economic importance, it has several advantages for research. The plant completes its life cycle in just a few weeks and is small enough to be grown in a petri dish, yielding thousands of individuals in limited space. Botanists use chemical mutagens to produce mutant strains and have isolated many developmental mutants. When they insert cloned foreign genes into *Arabidopsis* cells, the genes integrate into the chromosomes and are expressed. The researchers then induce these transformed cells to differentiate into transgenic plants.

In 2000, the *Arabidopsis* genome became the first plant genome sequenced. Although its genome is relatively small (the rice genome is about four times larger), it includes about 26,000 protein-coding genes. In comparison, *Drosophila* has about 13,600 genes and *C. elegans* about 19,700. Many genes in *Arabidopsis* are functionally equivalent to genes in *Drosophila, C. elegans,* and other animal species.

Of particular importance to development are the more than 1500 genes that code for transcription factors in *Arabidopsis* (compared to 635 at last count for *Drosophila*). Not surprisingly, many genes known to specify identities of parts of the *Arabidopsis* flower code for transcription factors. During the development of *Arabidopsis* flowers, four distinct flower parts differentiate: sepals, petals, stamens, and carpels (**FIG. 17-19a**; also see Fig. 33-1). Sepals cover and protect the flower when it is a bud, petals help attract animal pollinators to the flower, stamens produce pollen grains, and the carpel produces ovules, which develop into seeds following fertilization (discussed in Chapter 28).

The **ABC model** explains how three classes of homeotic genes control the development of the four floral organs; this model may help explain the thousands of different forms of flowers that have evolved. Class *A* genes are needed to specify sepals; both *A* and *B* genes are needed to specify petals; both *B* and *C* genes are needed to specify stamens; and class *C* genes are needed to specify the carpel. Mutations in the *A, B,* or *C* organ-identity genes, all of which code for transcription factors, cause one flower part to be substituted for another. For example, class *C* homeotic mutants (which have an inactive *C* gene) have petals in place of stamens and sepals in place of the carpel. Therefore, the entire flower consists of only sepals and petals. **FIGURES 17-19b, c,** and **d** shows three homeotic mutants of *Arabidopsis.*

The ABC model is not the entire explanation for floral development. Another class of genes, designated *SEPALLATA*, interacts with the *B* and *C* genes to specify the development of petals, stamens, and carpels. Remarkably, when *SEPALLATA* genes are turned on permanently in *Arabidopsis*, the resulting plants have white petals growing where the leaves should be. (Because these plants do not photosynthesize, they are grown on a nutrient medium.)

These findings in *Arabidopsis* vastly increase the number of molecular probes available in plants. Researchers use these probes to identify other genes that control development in various plant species and to compare them with genes from a wide range of organisms. The success of the *Arabidopsis* sequencing project led to an international initiative by plant biologists to understand the functions of all genes in *Arabidopsis*. This functional genomic information will lead to a far deeper understanding of plant development and evolutionary history.

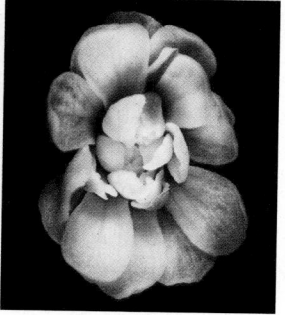

Photos courtesy of Jose Luis Reichmann and Elliot Meyerowitz

(a) A normal *Arabidopsis* flower has four outer leafy green sepals, four white petals, six stamens (the male reproductive structures), and a central carpel (the female reproductive structure).

(b) This homeotic mutant is missing petals.

(c) This homeotic mutant has only sepals and carpels.

(d) This homeotic mutant has sepals and petals but no other floral structures.

FIGURE 17-19 Homeotic mutants in *Arabidopsis* flowers

Review

- What are the relative merits of *Drosophila*, *C. elegans*, *M. musculus*, and *Arabidopsis* as model organisms for the study of development?
- What are transcription factors, and how do they influence development?
- What role does induction play in development?
- What is apoptosis?

17.3 CANCER AND CELL DEVELOPMENT

■ LEARNING OBJECTIVE

8 Discuss the relationship between cancer and mutations that affect cell developmental processes.

Cancer cells lack normal biological inhibitions. Normal cells are tightly regulated by control mechanisms that prompt them to divide when necessary and prevent them from growing and dividing inappropriately. Cells of many tissues in the adult are normally prevented from dividing; they reproduce only to replace a neighboring cell that has died or become damaged. Cancer cells have escaped such controls and can divide continuously.

As a consequence of their abnormal growth pattern, some cancer cells eventually form a mass of tissue called a **tumor,** or *neoplasm.* If the tumor remains at the spot where it originated, it can usually be removed by surgery. One of the major problems with certain forms of cancer is that the cells can escape from the controls that maintain them in one location. **Metastasis** is the spreading of cancer cells to different parts of the body. Cancer cells invade other tissues and form multiple tumors. Lung cancer, for example, is particularly deadly because its cells are highly metastatic; they enter the bloodstream, spread, and form tumors in other parts of the lungs and in other organs, such as the liver and the brain.

Biologists now know that cancer is caused by the altered expression of specific genes critical for cell division. Using recombinant DNA methods, researchers have identified many of the genes that when functioning abnormally transform normal cells into cancer cells. The traits of each kind of cancer cell come from at least one, and probably several, **oncogenes,** or cancer-causing genes. Oncogenes arise from changes in the expression of certain genes called **proto-oncogenes,** which are *normal* genes found in all cells and are involved in the control of growth and development.

Investigators first discovered oncogenes in viruses that infect mammalian cells and transform them into cancer cells, in a process known as *malignant transformation.* Such viruses have oncogenes as part of their genomes. When these viruses infect a cell, the viral oncogenes are expressed, causing the cell to divide.

A proto-oncogene in a cell that has not been infected by a virus can also mutate and become an oncogene. One of the first oncogenes researchers identified was isolated from a tumor in a human urinary bladder. In the cell that gave rise to the tumor, a proto-oncogene had undergone a single base-pair mutation; the result was that the amino acid valine replaced the amino acid glycine in the protein product of the gene. This subtle change was apparently a critical factor in converting the normal cell into a cancer cell.

Some of the control mechanisms of cell growth are illustrated in greatly simplified form in **FIGURE 17-20**. One or more external signal molecules trigger the growth and division of cells. Some of these substances are **growth factors** that bind to specific **growth factor receptors** associated with the cell surface, initiating a cascade of events inside the cell. Often the growth factor receptor complex acts as a **protein kinase,** an enzyme that phosphorylates proteins, which then phosphorylate specific amino acids of several cytoplasmic proteins. This posttranslational modification usually results in the activation of previously inactive enzymes. These activated enzymes then catalyze the activation of certain nuclear proteins, many of which are transcription factors. Activated transcription factors bind to their DNA targets and stimulate the transcription of specific sets of genes that initiate growth and cell division.

Even in the simplified scenario presented in the figure, it is evident that multiple steps are required to control cell proliferation. Researchers have identified the proto-oncogenes that encode the products responsible for many of these steps. The current list

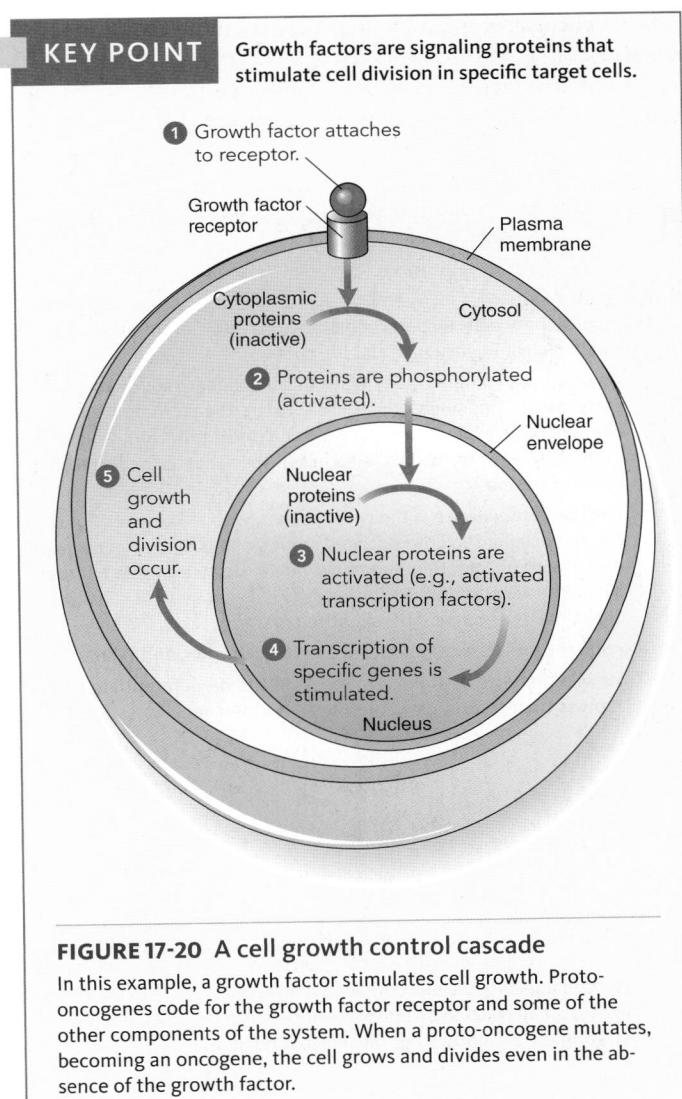

KEY POINT Growth factors are signaling proteins that stimulate cell division in specific target cells.

1. Growth factor attaches to receptor.

Growth factor receptor

Plasma membrane

Cytoplasmic proteins (inactive)

Cytosol

2. Proteins are phosphorylated (activated).

Nuclear envelope

5. Cell growth and division occur.

Nuclear proteins (inactive)

3. Nuclear proteins are activated (e.g., activated transcription factors).

4. Transcription of specific genes is stimulated.

Nucleus

FIGURE 17-20 A cell growth control cascade

In this example, a growth factor stimulates cell growth. Proto-oncogenes code for the growth factor receptor and some of the other components of the system. When a proto-oncogene mutates, becoming an oncogene, the cell grows and divides even in the absence of the growth factor.

of known proto-oncogenes includes genes that code for various growth factors or growth factor receptors and genes that respond to stimulation by growth factors, including many transcription factors. When a proto-oncogene mutates or is expressed inappropriately (i.e., when it becomes an oncogene), the cell may misinterpret the signal and respond by growing and dividing. For example, in some cases a proto-oncogene encoding a growth factor receptor mutates in a way that compromises regulation of the receptor. It is always switched "on," even in the absence of the growth factor that normally controls it.

Not all genes that cause cancer when mutated are proto-oncogenes. About half of all cancers are caused by a mutation in a **tumor suppressor gene.** These genes, also known as *anti-oncogenes,* normally interact with growth-inhibiting factors to block cell division. When mutated, they lose their ability to "put on the brakes," and uncontrolled growth ensues.

Currently, more than 100 oncogenes and 15 tumor suppressor genes have been identified, and many more probably remain to be identified. A change in a single proto-oncogene is usually insufficient to cause a cell to become malignant. The development of cancer is usually a multistep process involving both mutations that activate oncogenes and mutations that inactivate tumor suppressor genes.

Additional factors, such as chromosome translocations (see Chapter 16) or the inappropriate activation of the enzyme respon-sible for the maintenance of telomeres (see Chapter 12), may also play a role in the development of cancer. The Cancer Genome Project, a long-term international initiative based in Great Britain, is currently examining every human gene for cancer-related mutations. As more of these genes are discovered and their interactions are unraveled, we will gain a fuller understanding of the control of growth and development. This understanding will improve the diagnosis and treatments of various types of cancer.

Some researchers view cancer as a stem cell disease because cancer cells are propagated by a small number of cells that have many properties of stem cells. However, the propagation of normal stem cells is tightly regulated, so the question that some biologists are pursuing is how cell mechanisms that regulate stem cell self-renewal are changed to cause cancer cell proliferation. It is possible that the relatively long life of stem cells allows them to accumulate mutations that cause the cells to proliferate in an uncontrolled fashion. Although this line of research is promising, it should be emphasized that the validity of cancer as a stem cell disease remains to be demonstrated for most kinds of cancer.

Review

- How are oncogenes and tumor suppressor genes related to genes involved in the control of normal growth and development?
- How is a growth factor involved in a typical growth control cascade?

■ SUMMARY: FOCUS ON LEARNING OBJECTIVES

17.1 *(page 370)*

1 Distinguish between cell determination and cell differentiation, and between nuclear equivalence and totipotency.

- An organism contains many types of cells that are specialized to carry out specific functions. These cells are the product of a process of gradual commitment, called **cell determination,** which ultimately leads to the final step in cell specialization, called **cell differentiation.**
- **Nuclear equivalence** is the concept that, with a few exceptions, all the nuclei of the differentiated **somatic cells** of an organism are identical to one another and to the nucleus of the single cell from which they descended. **Totipotency** is the capability of cells to direct the development of an entire organism.

2 Describe the classic experiments of Steward, Gurdon, and Wilmut.

- Steward induced mature carrot root cells to de-differentiate and express their totipotency, forming an entire plant.

- Gurdon injected nuclei from tadpole intestinal cells into enucleated eggs; a small fraction of these developed into tadpoles, demonstrating the totipotency of the injected nucleus.

- Wilmut fused a differentiated cell from an adult sheep cell with an enucleated egg and implanted it into the uterus of a host mother, where it developed into a normal lamb.

CENGAGENOW™ Learn more about sheep cloning by clicking on the figure in CengageNOW.

3 Define *stem cells,* distinguish between embryonic stem cells and pluripotent stem cells, and describe some of the promising areas of research involving stem cells.

- **Stem cells** can divide to produce differentiated descendants yet retain the ability to divide to maintain the stem cell population. Totipotent stem cells give rise to all cell types of the body and placenta, whereas **pluripotent stem cells** give rise to many, but not all, types of cells in an organism.
- **Embryonic stem (ES) cells,** formed after a zygote has undergone several rounds of cell division to become a 5- or 6-day-old blastocyst, are pluripotent and have the potential to develop into any type of cell in the body; ES cells are not totipotent because they cannot form cells of the placenta.
- Stem cells show promise in treating diseases, such as Parkinson's disease and diabetes mellitus.

17.2 *(page 375)*

4 Indicate the features of *Drosophila melanogaster, Caenorhabditis elegans, Mus musculus,* and *Arabidopsis thaliana* that have made these organisms valuable models in developmental genetics.

- Developmental mutations have been identified in the fruit fly, *Drosophila,* many of which affect the organism's segmented body plan. Many developmental genes discovered in the fruit fly are now known to be important in the growth and development of all animals.

- C. elegans is a roundworm with **mosaic development,** a rigid developmental pattern in which the fates of cells are restricted early in development. The lineage of every somatic cell in the adult is known, and each can be traced to a single **founder cell** in the early embryo.
- The laboratory mouse, *M. musculus,* is extensively used in studies of mammalian development. The mouse shows **regulative development;** the very early embryo is a self-regulating whole and can develop normally even if it has extra or missing cells. **Transgenic** mice, in which foreign genes have been incorporated, have helped researchers determine how genes are activated and regulated during development.
- Genes affecting development have also been identified in certain plants, such as *A. thaliana.* The **ABC model** of interactions among three kinds of genes hypothesizes how floral organs develop in *Arabidopsis.* Mutations in these homeotic genes cause one flower part to be substituted for another.

5 Distinguish among maternal effect genes, segmentation genes, and homeotic genes in *Drosophila.*

- The earliest developmental events to operate in the egg are established by **maternal effect genes** in the surrounding maternal tissues, which are active prior to fertilization. Some produce gradients of **morphogens,** chemical agents that affect the differentiation and development of form. Maternal effect genes establish polarity in the embryo.
- **Segmentation genes** generate a repeating pattern of body segments within the embryo. **Gap genes** are segmentation genes that begin organizing the body into anterior, middle, and posterior regions; **pair–rule genes** and **segment polarity genes** affect all segments.

- The later-acting **homeotic genes** are responsible for specifying the identity of each segment.

6 Explain the relationship between transcription factors and genes that control development.

- **Transcription factors** are DNA-binding proteins that regulate transcription in eukaryotes. Some genes that code for transcription factors contain a DNA sequence called a **homeobox,** which codes for a protein with a DNA-binding region called a **homeodomain.**
- Some homeobox genes are organized into complexes that appear to be systems of master genes specifying an organism's body plan. Parallels exist between the homeobox complexes of *Drosophila* and those of other animals.

7 Define *induction* and *apoptosis,* and give examples of the roles they play in development.

- **Induction** is developmental interactions with neighboring cells. During development in *C. elegans,* the anchor cell induces cells on the surface to organize to form the vulva, the structure through which the eggs are laid.
- **Apoptosis** is programmed cell death. During human development, the human hand forms as a webbed structure, but the fingers become individualized when the cells between them die.

17.3 *(page 387)*

8 Discuss the relationship between cancer and mutations that affect cell developmental processes.

- The traits of cancer cells are due to cancer-causing **oncogenes.** Oncogenes arise from changes in the expression of normal genes called **proto-oncogenes,** which exist in all cells and are involved in the control of growth and development.
- Known proto-oncogenes include genes that code for various **growth factors** or **growth factor receptors** and genes that respond to stimulation by growth factors, including many transcription factors. When a proto-oncogene is expressed inappropriately (i.e., becomes an oncogene), the cell may misinterpret the signal and respond by growing and dividing.
- **Tumor suppressor genes** normally interact with growth-inhibiting factors to block cell division. A mutation in a tumor suppressor gene may inactivate it and thereby lead to cancer.

TEST YOUR UNDERSTANDING

1. Morphogenesis occurs through the multistep process of (a) differentiation (b) determination (c) pattern formation (d) totipotency (e) selection

2. The cloning experiments carried out on frogs demonstrated that (a) all differentiated frog cells are totipotent (b) some differentiated frog cells are totipotent (c) all nuclei from differentiated frog cells are totipotent (d) some nuclei from differentiated frog cells are totipotent (e) cell differentiation always requires the loss of certain genes

3. The anterior-posterior axis of a *Drosophila* embryo is first established by certain (a) homeotic genes (b) maternal effect genes (c) segmentation genes (d) proto-oncogenes (e) pair–rule genes

4. You discover a new *Drosophila* mutant in which mouth parts are located where the antennae are normally found. You predict that the mutated gene is most likely a (a) homeotic gene (b) gap gene (c) pair–rule gene (d) maternal effect gene (e) segment polarity gene

5. Most segmentation genes code for (a) transfer RNAs (b) enzymes (c) transcription factors (d) histones (e) transport proteins

6. Homeobox genes (a) are found in fruit flies but no other animals (b) tend to be expressed in the order that they appear on a chromosome (c) contain a characteristic DNA sequence (d) b and c (e) a, b, and c

7. The developmental pattern of *C. elegans* is said to be mosaic because (a) development is controlled by gradients of morphogens (b) part of the embryo fails to develop if a founder cell is destroyed (c) some individuals are self-fertilizing hermaphrodites (d) all development is controlled by maternal effect genes (e) apoptosis never occurs

8. Which of the following illustrates the regulative nature of early mouse development? (a) the mouse embryo is free-living prior to implantation in the uterus (b) it is possible to produce a transgenic mouse (c) it is possible to produce a mouse in which a specific gene has been knocked out (d) genes related to *Drosophila* homeotic genes have been identified in mice (e) a chimeric mouse can be produced by fusing two mouse embryos

9. *Arabidopsis* is useful as a model organism for the study of plant development because (a) it is of great economic importance (b) it has a very long generation time (c) many developmental mutants have been isolated (d) it contains a large amount of DNA per cell (e) it has a rigid developmental pattern

10. Pluripotent stem cells (a) lose genetic material during development (b) give rise to many, but not all, types of cells in an organism (c) organize into recognizable structures through pattern formation (d) cannot grow in tissue culture (e) have been used to clone a sheep and several other mammals

11. Which of the following statements about cancer is *false*? (a) oncogenes arise from mutations in proto-oncogenes (b) tumor suppressor genes normally interact with growth-inhibiting factors to block cell division (c) more than 100 oncogenes and 15 tumor suppressor genes have been identified (d) oncogenes were first discovered in mouse models for cancer (e) the development of cancer is usually a multistep process involving both oncogenes and mutated tumor suppressor genes

12. Proto-oncogenes code for (a) morphogens (b) antibodies for immune responses (c) growth factor receptors and other components of the growth control cascade (d) enzymes such as reverse transcriptase (e) ES cells

CRITICAL THINKING

1. Why is an understanding of gene regulation in eukaryotes crucial to an understanding of developmental processes?

2. Why do scientists study development in more than one type of organism?

3. Could a gene be involved in the growth of both stem cells and some kinds of cancer? Explain your answer.

4. **EVOLUTION LINK.** How are the striking similarities among genes that govern development in widely differing species strong evidence for evolution?

5. **EVOLUTION LINK.** What is the common ground between evolutionary biologists and developmental biologists who have adopted the perspective known as Evo Devo?

6. **ANALYZING DATA.** Flower parts are arranged in four concentric circles: sepals, petals, stamens, and carpel. According to the ABC model of floral organ development in *Arabidopsis*, class *A* genes are needed to specify sepals, the *A* and *B* genes to specify petals, the *B* and *C* genes to specify stamens, and class *C* genes to specify the carpel. If a mutation occurs in one of the *B* genes, rendering it inactive, what will the resulting flowers consist of?

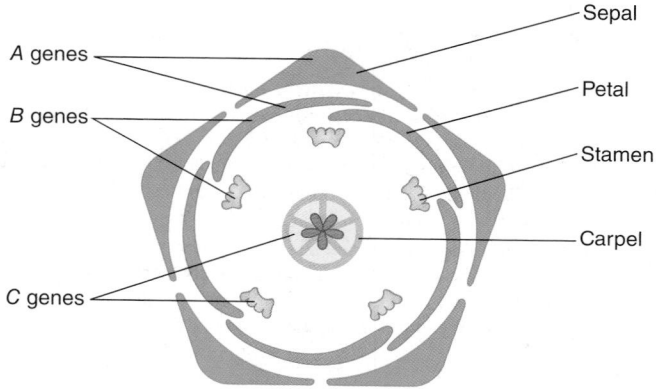

CENGAGENOW™ Additional questions are available in CengageNOW at www.cengage.com/login.

18 Introduction to Darwinian Evolution

Charles Darwin. This portrait was made shortly after Darwin returned to England from his voyage around the world.

Science Source/Photo Researchers, Inc.

18.1 Evolution is the accumulation of inherited changes within populations over time.

18.2 Ideas about evolution originated long before Darwin's time.

18.3 Darwin's scientific theory of evolution, natural selection, explained how natural forces in the environment could cause evolution. Natural selection occurs because individuals with traits that make them better adapted to local conditions are more likely to survive and produce offspring than are individuals that are not as well adapted. The modern synthesis combines Darwin's theory with genetics.

18.4 The evidence that evolution has taken place and is still occurring is overwhelming. This evidence includes fossils, biogeography, comparative anatomy, molecular biology, developmental biology, and evolutionary experiments with living organisms.

A great deal of evidence suggests that the biological diversity represented by the millions of species currently living on our planet evolved from a single ancestor during Earth's long history. Thus, organisms that are radically different from one another are in fact distantly related, linked through numerous intermediate ancestors to a single, common ancestor. The British naturalist Charles Darwin (1809–1882) developed a simple, scientifically testable mechanism to explain the relationship among Earth's diversity of organisms. He argued persuasively that all the species that exist today, as well as the countless extinct species that existed in the past, arose from earlier ones by a process of gradual *divergence* (splitting into separate evolutionary pathways), or *evolution*.

The concept of evolution is the cornerstone of biology because it links all fields of the life sciences into a unified body of knowledge. As stated by U.S. geneticist Theodosius Dobzhansky, "Nothing in biology makes sense except in the light of evolution."[1] Biologists seek to understand both the remarkable variety and the fundamental similarities of organisms within the context of evolution. The science of evolution allows biologists to

[1]*American Biology Teacher,* Vol. 35, No. 125 (1973).

compare common threads among organisms as seemingly different as bacteria, whales, lilies, slime molds, and tapeworms. Animal behavior, developmental biology, genetics, evolutionary ecology, systematics, and molecular evolution are examples of some of the biological disciplines that are grounded in evolution.

This chapter discusses Charles Darwin and the development of his evolutionary theory by natural selection. It also presents evidence that supports evolution, including fossils, biogeography, comparative anatomy, molecular biology, developmental biology, and experimental studies of ongoing evolutionary change in both the laboratory and nature.

18.1 WHAT IS EVOLUTION?

■ LEARNING OBJECTIVE

1 Define *evolution*.

In beginning our study of evolution, we define **evolution** as the accumulation of genetic changes within populations over time. A **population** is a group of individuals of one species that live in the same geographic area at the same time. Just as the definition of a *gene* changed as you studied genetics, you will find that the definition of *evolution* will become more precise in later chapters.

The term *evolution* does not refer to changes that occur in an individual within its lifetime. Instead, it refers to changes in the characteristics of populations over the course of generations. These changes may be so small that they are difficult to detect or so great that the population differs markedly from its ancestral population.

Eventually, two populations may diverge to such a degree that we refer to them as different species. The concept of species is developed extensively in Chapter 20. For now, a simple working definition is that a **species** is a group of organisms, with similar structure, function, and behavior, that are capable of interbreeding with one another.

Evolution has two main perspectives—the minor evolutionary changes of populations usually viewed over a few generations (*microevolution,* discussed in Chapter 19) and the major evolutionary events usually viewed over a long period, such as formation of different species from common ancestors (*macroevolution,* discussed in Chapter 20).

Evolution has important practical applications. Agriculture must deal with the evolution of pesticide resistance in insects and other pests. Likewise, medicine must respond to the rapid evolutionary potential of disease-causing organisms such as bacteria and viruses (**FIG. 18-1**). (Significant evolutionary change occurs in a very short time period in insects, bacteria, and other organisms with short lifespans.) Medical researchers use evolutionary principles to predict which flu strains are evolving more quickly, information that scientists need to make the next year's flu vaccine. Also, researchers developing effective treatment strategies for the human immunodeficiency virus (HIV) must understand its evolution, both within and among hosts.

The conservation management of rare and endangered species makes use of the evolutionary principles of population genetics. The rapid evolution of bacteria and fungi in polluted soils is used in the

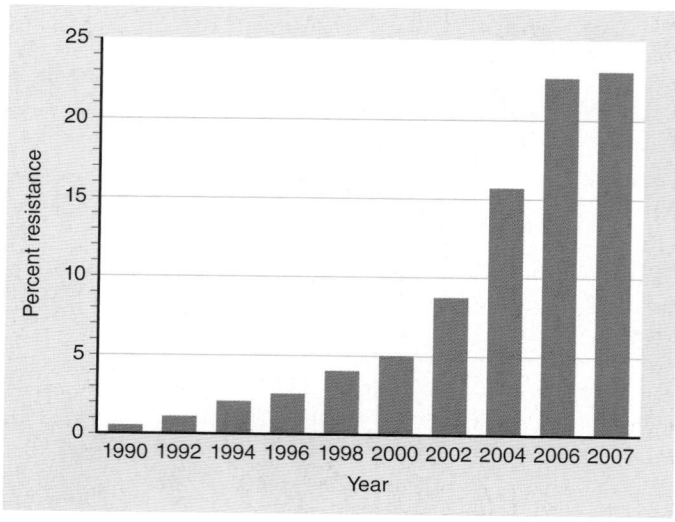

FIGURE 18-1 Evolution of antibiotic resistance to ciprofloxacin in *E. coli*

These data show an increasing resistance to *E. coli* in patients with blood and cerebrospinal infections in England, Wales, and Northern Ireland, 1990 to 2007. (Source: Livermore, D. "Zietgeist of Resistance." *The Journal of Antimicrobial Chemotherapy,* Vol. 60, i59–i61, 2007. By permission of Oxford University Press.)

field of **bioremediation,** in which microorganisms are employed to clean up hazardous-waste sites. Evolution even has applications beyond biology. For example, certain computer applications make use of algorithms that mimic natural selection in biological systems.

Review

- What is evolution?
- Do individuals evolve? Explain your answer.

18.2 PRE-DARWINIAN IDEAS ABOUT EVOLUTION

■ LEARNING OBJECTIVE

2 Discuss the historical development of evolutionary theory.

Although Darwin is universally associated with evolution, ideas of evolution predate Darwin by centuries. Aristotle (384–322 BCE) saw much evidence of natural affinities among organisms. This led him to arrange all the organisms he knew in a "scale of nature" that extended from the exceedingly simple to the most complex. Aristotle visualized organisms as being imperfect but "moving toward a more perfect state." Some scientific historians have interpreted this idea as the forerunner of evolutionary theory, but Aristotle was vague on the nature of this "movement toward perfection" and certainly did not propose that natural processes drove the process of evolution. Furthermore, modern evolutionary theory now recognizes that evolution does not move toward more "perfect" states or even necessarily toward greater complexity.

Long before Darwin's time, fossils had been discovered embedded in rocks. Some of these corresponded to parts of familiar species, but others were strangely unlike any known species. Fossils were often found in unexpected contexts; for example, marine invertebrates (sea animals without backbones) were sometimes discovered in rocks high on mountains. Leonardo da Vinci (1452–1519) was among the first to correctly interpret these unusual finds as the remains of animals that had existed in previous ages but had become extinct.

The French naturalist Jean Baptiste de Lamarck (1744–1829) was the first scientist to propose that organisms undergo change over time as a result of some natural phenomenon rather than divine intervention. According to Lamarck, a changing environment caused an organism to alter its behavior, thereby using some organs or body parts more and others less. Over several generations, a given organ or body part would increase in size if it was used a lot, or shrink and possibly disappear if it was used less. His hypothesis required that organisms pass traits they acquired during their lifetimes to their offspring. For example, Lamarck suggested that the long neck of the giraffe developed when a short-necked ancestor stretched its neck to browse on the leaves of trees. Its offspring inherited the longer neck, which stretched still further as they ate. This process, repeated over many generations, resulted in the long necks of modern giraffes. Lamarck also thought that all organisms were endowed with a vital force that drove them to change toward greater complexity and "perfection" over time.

Lamarck's proposed mechanism of evolution is quite different from the mechanism later proposed by Darwin. However, Lamarck's hypothesis remained a reasonable explanation for evolution until Mendel's basis of heredity was rediscovered at the beginning of the 20th century. At that time, Lamarck's ideas were largely discredited.

Review

- Why is Aristotle linked to early evolutionary thought?
- What were Jean Baptiste de Lamarck's ideas concerning evolution?

18.3 DARWIN AND EVOLUTION

LEARNING OBJECTIVES

3 Explain the four premises of evolution by natural selection as proposed by Charles Darwin.

4 Compare the modern synthesis with Darwin's original evolutionary theory.

Darwin, the son of a prominent physician, was sent at the age of 15 to study medicine at the University of Edinburgh. Finding himself unsuited for medicine, he transferred to Cambridge University to study theology. During that time, he became the protégé of the Reverend John Henslow, who was a professor of botany. Henslow encouraged Darwin's interest in the natural world. Shortly after receiving his degree, Darwin embarked on the HMS *Beagle*, which was taking a 5-year exploratory cruise around the world to prepare navigation charts for the British navy.

The *Beagle* left Plymouth, England, in 1831 and cruised along the east and west coasts of South America (**FIG. 18-2**). While other members of the crew mapped the coasts and harbors, Darwin spent many weeks ashore studying the animals, plants, fossils, and geologic formations of both coastal and inland regions, areas that had not been extensively explored. He collected and cataloged thousands of plant and animal specimens and kept notes of his observations, information that became essential in the development of his theory.

The *Beagle* spent almost 2 months at the Galápagos Islands, 965 km (600 mi) west of Ecuador, where Darwin continued his observations and collections. He compared the animals and plants of the Galápagos with those of the South American mainland. He was particularly impressed by their similarities and wondered why the organisms of the Galápagos should resemble those from South America more than those from other islands in different parts of the world. Moreover, although there were similarities between Galápagos and South American species, there were also distinct

FIGURE 18-2 *Animated* The voyage of HMS *Beagle*
The 5-year voyage began in Plymouth, England (*star*), in 1831. Observations made in the Galápagos Islands (*bull's-eye*) off the western coast of South America helped Darwin develop a satisfactory mechanism to explain how a population of organisms could change over time.

differences. There were even recognizable differences in the reptiles and birds from one island to the next. Darwin wondered why these remote islands should have such biological diversity. After he returned home, Darwin pondered these observations and attempted to develop a satisfactory explanation for the distribution of species among the islands.

Darwin drew on several lines of evidence when considering how species might have originated. Despite the work of Lamarck, the general notion in the mid-1800s was that Earth was too young for organisms to have changed significantly since they had first appeared. During the early 19th century, however, geologists advanced the idea that mountains, valleys, and other physical features of Earth's surface did not originate in their present forms. Instead, these features developed slowly over long periods by the geologic processes of volcanic activity, uplift, erosion, and glaciation. On his voyage Darwin took with him *Principles of Geology,* published by English geologist Charles Lyell in 1830, and studied it carefully. Lyell provided an important concept for Darwin—that the slow pace of geologic processes, which still occur today, indicated that Earth was extremely old.

Other important evidence that influenced Darwin was the fact that breeders and farmers could develop many varieties of domesticated animals in just a few generations. They did so by choosing certain traits and breeding only individuals that exhibited the desired traits, a procedure known as **artificial selection.** Breeders, for example, have produced numerous dog varieties—such as bloodhounds, dalmatians, Airedales, border collies, and Pekinese—by artificial selection.

Many plant varieties were also produced by artificial selection. For example, cabbage, broccoli, brussels sprouts, cauliflower, collard greens, kale, and kohlrabi are distinct vegetable crops that are all members of the same species, *Brassica oleracea* (**FIG. 18-3**). Selective breeding of the colewort, or wild cabbage, a leafy plant native to Europe and Asia, produced all seven vegetables. Beginning more than 4000 years ago, some farmers artificially selected wild cabbage plants that formed overlapping leaves. Over time, these leaves became so prominent that the plants, which resembled modern cabbages, became recognized as separate and distinct from their wild cabbage ancestor. Other farmers selected different features of the wild cabbage, giving rise to the other modifications. For example, kohlrabi was produced by selection for an enlarged storage stem, and brussels sprouts by selection for enlarged axillary buds. Thus, humans are responsible for the evolution of *B. oleracea* into seven distinct vegetable crops. Darwin was impressed by the changes induced by artificial selection and hypothesized that a similar selective process occurred in nature. Darwin therefore used artificial selection as a model when he developed the concept of natural selection.

The ideas of Thomas Malthus (1766–1834), a British clergyman and economist, were another important influence on Darwin. In *An Essay on the Principle of Population as It Affects the Future Improvement of Society,* published in 1798, Malthus noted that population growth is not always desirable—a view contrary to the beliefs of his day. He observed that populations have the capacity to increase geometrically ($1 \longrightarrow 2 \longrightarrow 4 \longrightarrow 8 \longrightarrow 16$) and thus outstrip the food supply, which only has the capacity to increase arithmetically ($1 \longrightarrow 2 \longrightarrow 3 \longrightarrow 4 \longrightarrow 5$). In the case of humans, Malthus suggested that the conflict between pop-

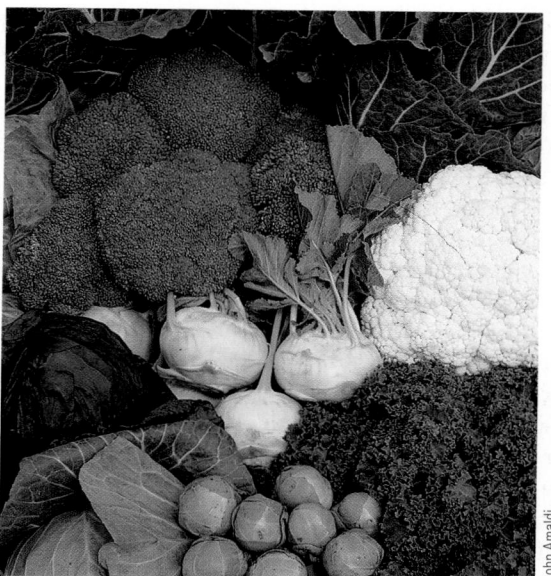

John Arnaldi

FIGURE 18-3 Artificial selection in *Brassica oleracea*

An enlarged terminal bud (the "head") was selected in cabbage (*lower left*), flower clusters in broccoli (*upper left*) and cauliflower (*middle right*), axillary buds in brussels sprouts (*bottom middle*), leaves in collards (*upper right*) and kale (*lower right*), and stems in kohlrabi (*middle*).

ulation growth and food supply generates famine, disease, and war, which serve as inevitable brakes on population growth.

Malthus's idea that there is a strong and constant check on human population growth strongly influenced Darwin's explanation of evolution. Darwin's years of observing the habits of animals and plants had introduced him to the struggle for existence described by Malthus. It occurred to Darwin that in this struggle, inherited variations favorable to survival would tend to be preserved, whereas unfavorable ones would be eliminated.

The result would be **adaptation,** an evolutionary modification that improves the chances of survival and reproductive success in a given environment. Eventually, the accumulation of modifications might result in a new species. Time was the only thing required for new species to originate, and the geologists of the era, including Lyell, had supplied evidence that Earth was indeed old enough to provide adequate time.

Darwin had at last developed a workable scientific explanation of evolution, that of **natural selection,** in which better adapted organisms are more likely to survive and become the parents of the next generation. As a result of natural selection, the population changes over time; the frequency of favorable traits increases in successive generations, whereas less favorable traits become scarce or disappear. Darwin spent the next 20 years formulating his arguments for natural selection, accumulating an immense body of evidence to support his theory, and corresponding with other scientists.

As Darwin was pondering his ideas, Alfred Russel Wallace (1823–1913), a British naturalist who studied the plants and animals of the Malay Archipelago for 8 years, was similarly struck by the diversity of species and the peculiarities of their distribution. He wrote a brief essay on this subject and sent it to Darwin, by then a world-renowned biologist, asking his opinion. Darwin recognized his own theory and realized Wallace had independently arrived at the same conclusion—that evolution occurs by natural selection. Darwin's colleagues persuaded him to present Wallace's manuscript along with an abstract of his own work, which he had prepared and circulated to a few friends several years earlier. Both papers were presented in July 1858 at a London meeting of the Linnaean Society. Darwin's monumental book, *On the Origin of Species by Natural Selection; or, The Preservation of Favored Races in the Struggle for Life,* was published in 1859. In 1870, Wallace's book, *Contributions to the Theory of Natural Selection,* was published, 8 years after he returned from the Malay Archipelago.

Darwin proposed that evolution occurs by natural selection

Darwin's mechanism of evolution by natural selection consists of observations on four aspects of the natural world: variation; overproduction; limits on population growth, or a struggle for existence; and differential reproductive success.

1. *Variation.* The individuals in a population exhibit variation (**FIG. 18-4**). Each individual has a unique combination of traits, such as size, color, ability to tolerate harsh environmental conditions, and resistance to certain parasites or infections. Some traits improve an individual's chances of survival and reproductive success, whereas others do not. Remember that the variation necessary for evolution by natural selection must be inherited. Although Darwin recognized the importance to evolution of inherited variation, he did not know the mechanism of inheritance.

2. *Overproduction.* The reproductive ability of each species has the potential to cause its population to geometrically increase over time. A female frog lays about 10,000 eggs, and a female cod produces perhaps 40 million eggs! In each case, however, only about two offspring survive to reproduce. Thus, in every generation each species has the capacity to produce more offspring than can survive.

3. *Limits on population growth, or a struggle for existence.* There is only so much food, water, light, growing space, and other resources available to a population, so organisms compete with one another for these limited resources. Because there are more individuals than the environment can support, not all survive to reproduce. Other limits on population growth include predators, disease organisms, and unfavorable weather conditions.

4. *Differential reproductive success.* Those individuals that have the most favorable combination of characteristics (those that make individuals better adapted to their environment) are more likely to survive and reproduce. Offspring tend to resemble their parents because the next generation inherits the parents' genetically based traits. Successful reproduction is the key to natural selection: the best-adapted individuals produce the most offspring, whereas individuals that are less well adapted die prematurely or produce fewer or inferior offspring.

Over time, enough changes may accumulate in geographically separated populations (often with slightly different environments) to produce new species. Darwin noted that the Galápagos finches appeared to have evolved in this way. The 14 species are closely related. All descended from a common ancestor—a single species that found its way from the South American mainland 2 million to 3 million years ago. (The closest genetic relatives of the Galápagos finches are small seed-eating birds known as grassquits that live in western South America.)

During this 2-million to 3-million year period, the number of islands increased, the climate changed, and the plant life and food supply changed. The different islands of the Galápagos kept the finches isolated from one another, thereby allowing them to diverge into separate species in response to varying conditions (**FIG. 18-5**).

Peter Grant, Rosemary Grant, and colleagues have documented natural selection in the Galápagos finches in their natural environment since the early 1970s. As an example of the evolutionary process in action, consider the sharp-beaked ground finch (*Geospiza difficilis*). This species lives on several different islands, and each population has evolved different beak shapes and sizes depending on the diet available on the island where it lives.

We revisit the Galápagos finches in later chapters. Some long-term research by Peter Grant, Rosemary Grant, and colleagues on the microevolution of Galápagos finches when droughts affect the food supply is described in Chapter 19; these studies have demonstrated that environmental change can drive natural selection. *Character displacement*, an aspect of evolutionary ecology, is described in Galápagos finches in Chapter 54.

The modern synthesis combines Darwin's theory with genetics

One of the premises on which Darwin based his scientific theory of evolution by natural selection is that individuals transmit traits to the next generation. However, Darwin was unable to explain *how* this occurs or *why* individuals vary within a population. As discussed in Chapter 11, Gregor Mendel elucidated the basic patterns of inheritance. Darwin, who was a contemporary of Mendel, was apparently not acquainted with Mendel's work. Indeed, the scientific community did not recognize Mendel's work until the early part of the 20th century.

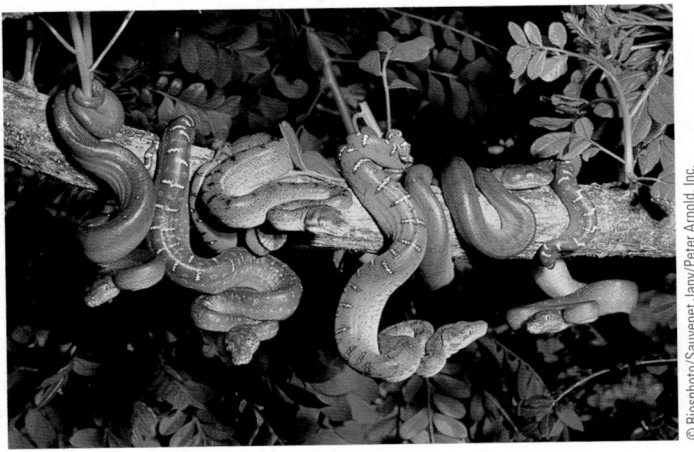

© Biosphoto/Sauvenet Jany/Peter Arnold, Inc.

FIGURE 18-4 Genetic variation in emerald tree boas
These snakes, all of the same species (*Corallus caninus*), were caught in a small section of forest in French Guiana. Many snake species exhibit considerable variation in their coloration and patterns.

(a) The cactus finch (*Geospiza scandens*), which feeds on the fleshy parts of cacti, such as their flowers, has a long, pointed beak.

(b) The large ground finch (*Geospiza magnirostris*) has an extremely heavy, nutcracker-type beak adapted for eating thick, hard-walled seeds.

(c) The warbler finch (*Certhidia olivacea*) has a slender beak for eating insects.

(d) The woodpecker finch (*Camarhynchus pallidus*) digs insects out of bark and crevices by using spines, twigs, or even dead leaves.

FIGURE 18-5 *Animated* Galápagos finches

Darwin inferred that these birds are derived from a common ancestral population of seed-eating birds from South America. Variation in their beaks is the result of adaptation to the availability of different kinds of food.

Beginning in the 1930s and 1940s, biologists experienced a conceptual breakthrough when they combined the principles of Mendelian inheritance with Darwin's theory of natural selection. The result was a unified explanation of evolution known as the **modern synthesis.** In this context, *synthesis* refers to combining parts of several theories to form a unified whole. Some of the founders of the modern synthesis were U.S. geneticist Theodosius Dobzhansky, British geneticist and statistician Ronald Fisher, British geneticist J. B. S. Haldane, British biologist Julian Huxley, U.S. biologist Ernst Mayr, U.S. paleontologist George Gaylord Simpson, U.S. botanist G. Ledyard Stebbins, and U.S. geneticist Sewell Wright.

Today, the modern synthesis incorporates our expanding knowledge in genetics, which on its own makes an irrefutable case for evolution, systematics, paleontology, developmental biology, behavior, and ecology. The modern synthesis explains Darwin's observation of variation among offspring in terms of **mutation,** or changes in DNA, such as nucleotide substitutions. Mutations provide the genetic variability on which natural selection acts during evolution. The modern synthesis, which emphasizes the genetics of populations as the central focus of evolution, has held up well since it was developed. It has dominated the thinking and research of biologists working in many areas and has resulted in an enormous accumulation of new discoveries that validate evolution by natural selection.

Most biologists not only accept the basic principles of the modern synthesis but also try to better understand the causal processes of evolution. For example, what is the role of chance in evolution? How rapidly do new species evolve? These and other questions have arisen in part from a re-evaluation of the fossil record and in part from new discoveries in molecular aspects of inheritance. Such critical analyses are an integral part of the scientific process because they stimulate additional observation and experimentation, along with re-examination of previous evidence. Science is an ongoing process, and information obtained in the future may require modifications to certain parts of the modern synthesis.

We now consider one of the many evolutionary questions currently being addressed by biologists: the relative effects of chance and natural selection on evolution.

Biologists study the effect of chance on evolution

Biologists have wondered whether we would get the same results if we were able to repeat evolution by starting with similar organisms exposed to similar environmental conditions. That is, would the same kinds of changes evolve, as a result of natural selection? Or would the organisms be quite different as a result of random events? Several recently reported examples of evolution in action suggest that chance may not be as important as natural selection, at least at the population level.

A fruit fly species (*Drosophila subobscura*) native to Europe inhabits areas from Denmark to Spain. Biologists noted that the northern flies have larger wings than southern flies (**FIG. 18-6**). The same fly species was accidentally introduced to North America in the late 1970s. Ten years after its introduction, biologists determined that no statistically significant changes in wing size had occurred in the different regions of North America. However, 20 years after its introduction, the fruit flies in North America exhibited the same type of north–south wing changes as in Europe. (It is not known why larger wings evolve in northern areas and smaller wings in southern climates.)

A study of the evolution of fishes known as *sticklebacks* in three coastal lakes of western Canada yielded intriguingly similar results to the fruit fly study. Molecular evidence indicates that when the lakes first formed several thousand years ago, they were populated with the same ancestral species. (Analysis of the mitochondrial DNA of sticklebacks in the three lakes supports the hypothesis of a common ancestor.) In each lake, the same two species have evolved from the common ancestral fish. One species is large and consumes invertebrates along the bottom of the lake, whereas the other species is smaller and consumes plankton at the lake's surface.

FIGURE 18-6 Wing size in female fruit flies

In Europe, female fruit flies (*Drosophila subobscura*) in northern countries have larger wings than flies in southern countries. Shown are two flies: one from Denmark (*right*) and the other from Spain (*left*). The same evolutionary pattern emerged in North America after the accidental introduction of *D. subobscura* to the Americas.

George Gilchrist

Members of the two species within a single lake do not interbreed with each other, but individuals of the larger species from one lake interbreed in captivity with individuals of the larger species from the other lakes. Similarly, smaller individuals from one lake interbreed in captivity with smaller individuals from the other lakes.

In these examples, natural selection appears to be a more important agent of evolutionary change than chance. If chance were the most important factor influencing the direction of evolution, then fruit fly evolution would not have proceeded the same way on two different continents, and stickleback evolution would not have proceeded the same way in three different lakes. However, just because we have many examples of the importance of natural selection in evolution, it does not necessarily follow that random events should be discounted as a factor in directing evolutionary change. Proponents of the role of chance think that chance is more important in the evolution of major taxonomic groups (macroevolution) than in the evolution of populations (microevolution). It also may be that random events take place but their effects on evolution are harder to demonstrate than natural selection.

Review

- What is natural selection?
- Why are only inherited variations important in the evolutionary process?
- What part of Darwin's theory was he unable to explain? How does the modern synthesis fill this gap?

18.4 EVIDENCE FOR EVOLUTION

◼ LEARNING OBJECTIVES

5   Summarize the evidence for evolution obtained from the fossil record.

6   Define *biogeography* and describe how the distribution of organisms supports evolution.

7   Describe the evidence for evolution derived from comparative anatomy.

8   Briefly explain how molecular biology and developmental biology provide insights into the evolutionary process.

9   Give an example of how evolutionary hypotheses are tested experimentally.

A vast body of scientific evidence supports evolution, including observations from the fossil record, biogeography, comparative anatomy, molecular biology, and developmental biology. In addition, evolutionary hypotheses are increasingly being tested experimentally. Taken together, this evidence confirms the scientific theory that life unfolded on Earth by the process of evolution.

The fossil record provides strong evidence for evolution

Perhaps the most direct evidence for evolution comes from the discovery, identification, and interpretation of **fossils,** which are the remains or traces typically left in sedimentary rock by previously existing organisms. (The term *fossil* comes from the Latin word *fossilis,* meaning "something dug up.") Sedimentary rock forms by the accumulation and solidification of particles (pebbles, sand, silt, or clay) produced by the weathering of older rocks, such as volcanic rocks. The sediment particles, which are usually deposited on a riverbed, lake bottom, or the ocean floor, accumulate over time and exhibit distinct layers (**FIG. 18-7**). In an undisturbed rock sequence, the oldest layer is at the bottom, and upper layers are successively younger. The study of sedimentary rock layers, including their composition, arrangement, and similarity from one location to another, enables geologists to place events recorded in rocks in their correct sequence.

The fossil record shows a progression from the earliest unicellular organisms to the many unicellular and multicellular organisms living today (see Table 21-1). The fossil record therefore demonstrates that life has evolved through time. To date, paleontologists (scientists who study extinct species) have described and named about 300,000 fossil species, and others are still being discovered.

Although most fossils are preserved in sedimentary rock, some more recent remains have been exceptionally well preserved in bogs, tar, amber (ancient tree resin), or ice (**FIG. 18-8**). For example, the remains of a woolly mammoth deep-frozen in Siberian ice for more than 25,000 years were so well preserved that part of its DNA could be analyzed.

Few organisms that die become fossils. The formation and preservation of a fossil require that an organism be buried under conditions that slow or prevent the decay process. This is most likely to occur if an organism's remains are covered quickly by a sediment of fine soil particles suspended in water. In this way the remains of aquatic organisms may be trapped in bogs, mudflats, sandbars, or deltas. Remains of terrestrial organisms that lived on a floodplain may also be covered by waterborne sediments or, if the organism lived in an arid region, by windblown sand. Over time, the sediments harden to form sedimentary rock, and minerals usually replace the organism's remains so that many details of its structure, even cellular details, are preserved.

The fossil record is not a random sample of past life but instead is biased toward aquatic organisms and those living in the

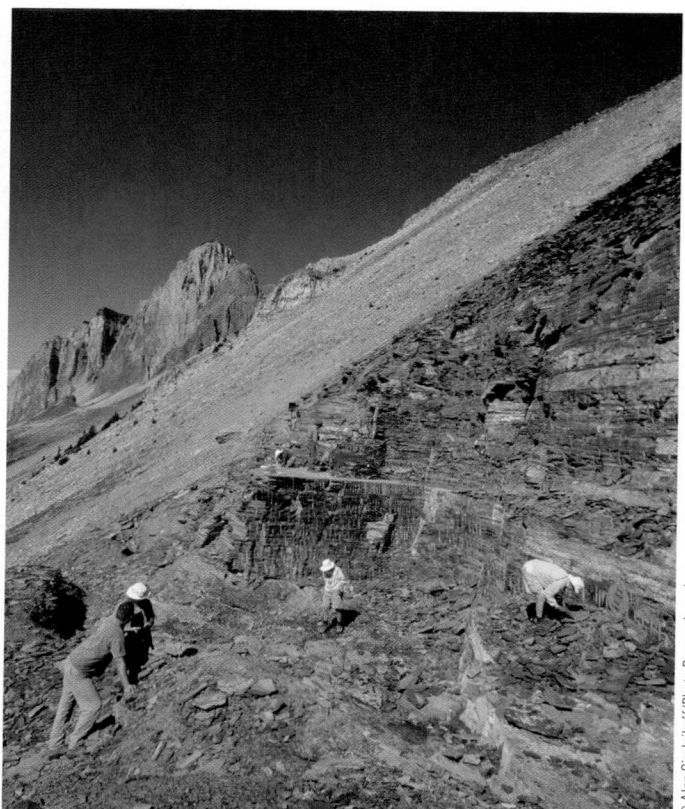

FIGURE 18-7 Exposed layers of sedimentary rock at the Burgess shale fossil bed

This site, located in the Canadian Rockies, was formed about 500 million years ago when an avalanche of mud buried and preserved diverse and unusual marine animals.

© Alan Sirulnikoff/Photo Researchers, Inc.

few terrestrial habitats conducive to fossil formation. Relatively few fossils of tropical rainforest organisms have been found, for example, because their remains decay extremely rapidly on the forest floor, before fossils can develop. Another reason for bias in the fossil record is that organisms with hard body parts such as bones and shells are more likely to form fossils than are those with soft body parts. Also, rocks of different ages are unequally exposed at Earth's surface; some rocks of certain ages are more accessible to paleontologists for fossil study than are rocks of other ages.

Because of the nature of the scientific process, each fossil discovery represents a separate "test" of evolutionary theory. If any of the tests fail, the theory would have to be modified to fit the existing evidence. The verifiable discovery, for example, of fossil remains of modern humans (*Homo sapiens*) in Precambrian rocks, which are more than 570 million years old, would falsify evolutionary theory as currently proposed. However, Precambrian rocks examined to date contain only fossils of simple organisms, such as algae and small, soft-bodied animals, that evolved early in the history of life. The earliest fossils of *H. sapiens* with anatomically modern features do not appear in the fossil record until approximately 195,000 years ago (see Chapter 22).

Fossils provide a record of ancient organisms and some understanding of where and when they lived. Using fossils of organisms from different geologic ages, scientists can sometimes infer the lines of descent (evolutionary relationships) that gave rise to modern-day organisms. In many instances, fossils provide direct evidence of the origin of new species from pre-existing species, including many transitional forms.

Transitional fossils document whale evolution

Over the past century, biologists have found evidence suggesting that whales and other cetaceans (an order of marine mammals) evolved from land-dwelling mammals. During the 1980s and 1990s, paleontologists discovered several fossil intermediates in whale evolution that help document the whales' transition from land to water.

Fossils of *Ambulocetus natans,* a 50-million-year-old transitional form discovered in Pakistan, have many features of modern whales but also possess hind limbs and feet (**FIG. 18-9a**). (Modern whales do not have hind limbs, although *vestigial* pelvic and hind-limb bones persist. Vestigial structures are discussed later in the chapter.) The vertebrae of *Ambulocetus's* lower back were very flexible, allowing the back to move dorsoventrally (up and down) during swimming and diving, as with modern whales. This ancient whale could swim but also moved about on land, perhaps as sea lions do today.

Rodhocetus is a fossil whale found in more recent rocks in Pakistan (**FIG. 18-9b**). The vertebrae of *Rodhocetus* were even more flexible than those found in *Ambulocetus*. The flexible vertebrae allowed *Rodhocetus* a more powerful dorsoventral movement during swimming. *Rodhocetus* may have been totally aquatic.

By 40 million years ago (mya), the whale transition from land to ocean was almost complete. Egyptian fossils of *Basilosaurus* show a whale with a streamlined body and front flippers for steering, like those of modern-day whales (**FIG. 18-9c**). *Basilosaurus* retained vestiges of its land-dwelling ancestors—a pair of reduced hind limbs that were disjointed from the backbone and probably not used in locomotion. Reduction in the hind limbs continued to the present. The modern blue whale has vestigial pelvis and femur bones embedded in its body (**FIG. 18-9d**).

Various methods determine the age of fossils

Because layers of sedimentary rock occur naturally in the sequence of their deposition, with the more recent layers on top of the older, earlier ones, most fossils are dated by their relative position in sedimentary rock. However, geologic events occurring after the rocks were initially formed have occasionally changed the relationships of some rock layers. Geologists identify specific sedimentary rocks not only by their positions in layers but also by features such as mineral content and by the fossilized remains of certain organisms, known as **index fossils,** that characterize a specific layer over large geographic areas. Index fossils are fossils of organisms that existed for a relatively short geologic time but were preserved as fossils in large numbers. With this information, geologists can arrange rock layers and the fossils they contain in chronological order and identify comparable layers in widely separated locations.

Radioactive isotopes, also called **radioisotopes,** present in a rock provide a means to accurately measure its age (see Chapter 2). Radioisotopes emit invisible radiations. As radiation is emitted, the nucleus of a radioisotope changes into the nucleus of a different element; this process is known as **radioactive decay.** The radioactive nucleus of uranium-235, for example, decays into lead-207.

Each radioisotope has its own characteristic rate of decay. The time required for one half of the atoms of a radioisotope to change into a different atom is known as its **half-life** (**FIG. 18-10**). Radioisotopes differ significantly in their half-lives. For example,

(a) Although some fossils contain traces of organic matter, all that remains in this fossil of a 500-million-year-old jellyfish is an impression, or imprint, in the rock.

(b) Petrified wood from the Petrified Forest National Park in Arizona consists of trees that were buried and infiltrated with minerals. The logs were exposed by erosion of the mudstone layers in which they were buried.

(c) A 2-million-year-old insect fossil (a midge) was embedded in amber.

(d) A cast fossil of ancient echinoderms called *crinoids* formed when the crinoids decomposed, leaving a mold that later filled with dissolved minerals that hardened.

(e) Dinosaur footprints, each 75 to 90 cm (2.5 to 3 ft) in length, provide clues about the posture, gait, and behavior of these extinct animals.

FIGURE 18-8 Fossils develop in different ways

(a) *Ambulocetus natans*, a transitional form between modern whale descendants and their terrestrial ancestors, possessed several recognizable whale features. It retained the hind limbs of its four-legged ancestors, however.

(b) The more recent *Rodhocetus* had flexible vertebrae that permitted a powerful dorsoventral movement during swimming.

(c) *Basilosaurus* was more streamlined and possessed tiny nonfunctional hind limbs.

(d) *Balaenoptera*, the modern blue whale, contains vestiges of pelvis and leg bones embedded in its body.

FIGURE 18-9 Fossil intermediates in whale evolution

Biologists hypothesize that the ancestors of whales had four legs, as shown in these reconstructions of whale intermediates based on fossil evidence. Fossils indicate that ankle bones in whale intermediates match those found in present-day hippos, cows, pigs, and camels. Figures are not drawn to scale. (**a–c:** Adapted with permission from Futuyma, D. J., *Science on Trial: The Case for Evolution*, Fig. 2, pp. 260–261, Sinauer Associates, Sunderland, MA, 1995.)

the half-life of iodine-132 is only 2.4 hours, whereas the half-life of uranium-235 is 704 million years. The half-life of a particular radioisotope is constant and does not vary with temperature, pressure, or any other environmental factor.

The age of a fossil in sedimentary rock is usually estimated by measuring the relative proportions of the original radioisotope and its decay product in volcanic rock intrusions that penetrate the sediments. For example, the half-life of potassium-40 is 1.3 billion years, meaning that in 1.3 billion years half of the radioactive potassium will have decayed into its decay product, argon-40. The

FIGURE 18-10 *Animated* Radioisotope decay

At time zero, the sample is composed entirely of the radioisotope and the radioactive clock begins ticking. After one half-life, only 50% of the original radioisotope remains. During each succeeding half-life, half of the remaining radioisotope is converted to decay product(s).

radioactive clock begins ticking when the magma solidifies into volcanic rock. The rock initially contains some potassium but no argon. Because argon is a gas, it escapes from hot rock as soon as it forms, but when potassium decays in rock that has cooled and solidified, the argon accumulates in the crystalline structure of the rock. If the ratio of potassium-40 to argon-40 in the rock being tested is 1:1, the rock is 1.3 billion years old.

Several radioisotopes are commonly used to date fossils. Three of these are potassium-40 (half-life 1.3 billion years), uranium-235 (half-life 704 million years), and carbon-14 (half-life 5730 years). Radioisotopes other than carbon-14 are used to date the *rock* in which fossils are found, whereas carbon-14 is used to date the *carbon remains* of anything that was once living, such as wood, bones, and shells. Whenever possible, the age of a fossil is independently verified using two or more different radioisotopes.

Carbon-14, which is continuously produced in the atmosphere from nitrogen-14 (by cosmic radiation), subsequently decays to nitrogen-14. Because the formation and the decay of carbon-14 occur at constant rates, the ratio of carbon-14 to carbon-12 (a more abundant, stable isotope of carbon) is constant in the atmosphere. Organisms absorb carbon from the atmosphere either directly (by photosynthesis) or indirectly (by consuming photosynthetic organisms). Because each organism absorbs carbon from the atmosphere, its ratio of carbon-14 to carbon-12 is the same as that in the atmosphere. When an organism dies, however, it no longer absorbs carbon, and the proportion of carbon-14 in its remains declines as carbon-14 decays to nitrogen-14. Because of its relatively short half-life, carbon-14 is useful for dating fossils that are 50,000 years old or less. It is particularly useful for dating archaeological sites.

The distribution of plants and animals supports evolution

The study of the past and present geographic distribution of organisms is called **biogeography.** The geographic distribution of organisms affects their evolution. Darwin was interested in biogeography, and he considered why the species found on ocean islands tend to resemble species of the nearest mainland, even if the environment is different. He also observed that species on ocean islands do not tend to resemble species on islands with similar environments in other parts of the world.

Darwin studied the plants and animals of two sets of arid islands—the Cape Verde Islands, nearly 640 km (400 mi) off western Africa, and the Galápagos Islands, about 960 km (600 mi) west of Ecuador, South America. On each group of islands, the plants and terrestrial animals were indigenous (native), but those of the Cape Verde Islands resembled African species and those of the Galápagos resembled South American species. The similarities of Galápagos species to South American species were particularly striking considering that the Galápagos Islands are dry and rocky and the nearest part of South America is humid and has a lush tropical rain forest. Darwin concluded that species from the neighboring continent migrated or were carried to the islands, where they subsequently adapted to the new environment and, in the process, evolved into new species.

If evolution were not a factor in the distribution of species, we would expect to find a given species everywhere that it could survive. However, the actual geographic distribution of organisms makes sense in the context of evolution. For example, Aus-

tralia, which has been a separate landmass for millions of years, has distinctive organisms. Australia has populations of egg-laying mammals (monotremes) and pouched mammals (marsupials) not found anywhere else. Two hundred million years ago, Australia and the other continents were joined in a major landmass. Over the course of millions of years, the Australian continent gradually separated from the others. The monotremes and marsupials in Australia continued to thrive and diversify. The isolation of Australia also prevented placental mammals, which arose elsewhere at a later time, from competing with its monotremes and marsupials. In other areas of the world where placental mammals evolved, most monotremes and marsupials became extinct.

We now consider how Earth's dynamic geology has affected biogeography and evolution.

Biogeography and evolution are related to Earth's geologic history

In 1915, the German scientist Alfred Wegener, who had noted a correspondence between the geographic shapes of South America and Africa, proposed that all the landmasses had at one time been joined into one huge supercontinent, which he called Pangaea (**FIG. 18-11a**). He further suggested that Pangaea had subsequently broken apart and that the various landmasses had separated in a process known as **continental drift.** Wegener did not know of any

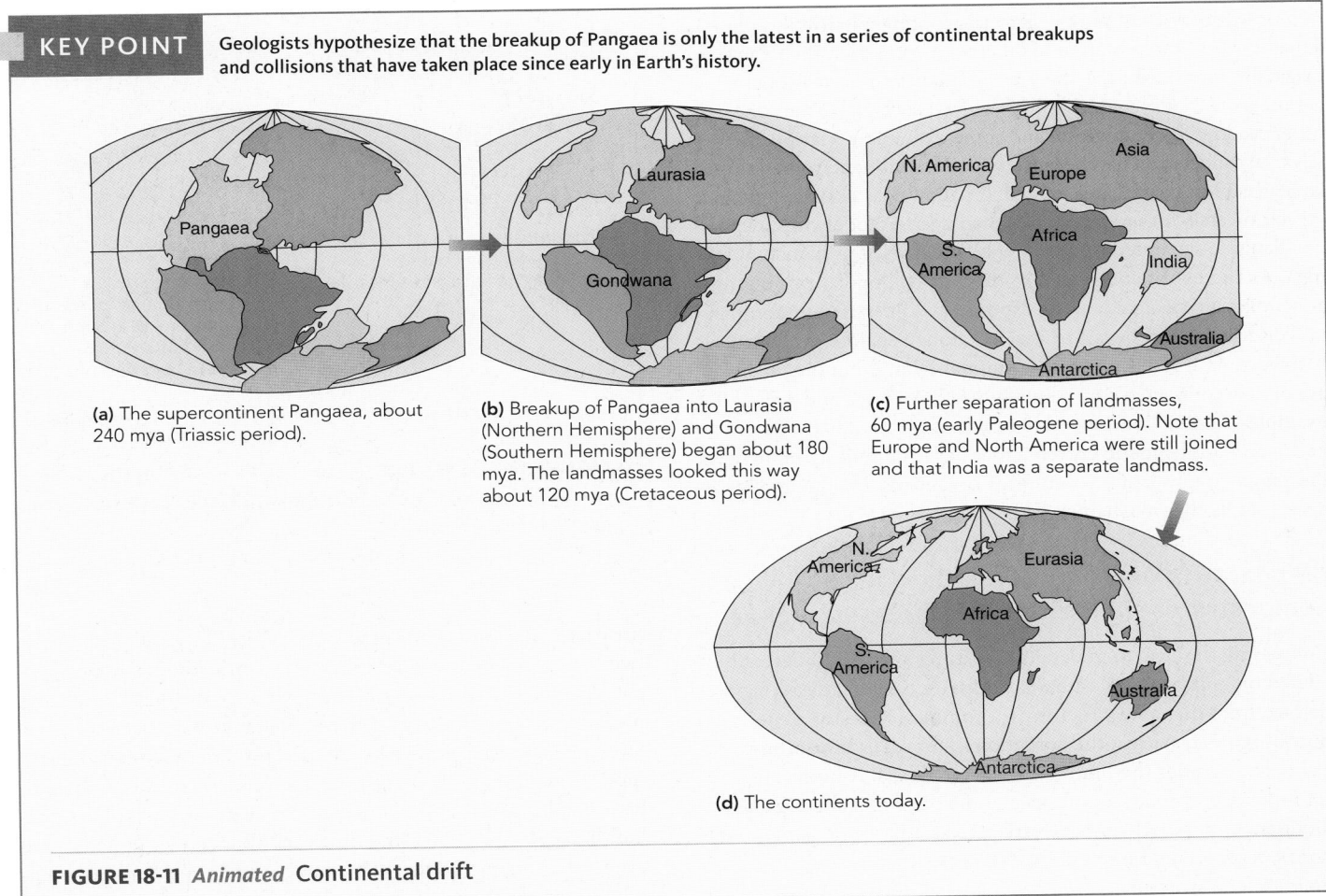

KEY POINT Geologists hypothesize that the breakup of Pangaea is only the latest in a series of continental breakups and collisions that have taken place since early in Earth's history.

(a) The supercontinent Pangaea, about 240 mya (Triassic period).

(b) Breakup of Pangaea into Laurasia (Northern Hemisphere) and Gondwana (Southern Hemisphere) began about 180 mya. The landmasses looked this way about 120 mya (Cretaceous period).

(c) Further separation of landmasses, 60 mya (early Paleogene period). Note that Europe and North America were still joined and that India was a separate landmass.

(d) The continents today.

FIGURE 18-11 *Animated* **Continental drift**

mechanism that could have caused continental drift, so his idea, although debated initially, was largely ignored.

In the 1960s, scientific evidence provided the explanation for continental drift. Earth's crust is composed of seven large plates (plus a few smaller ones) that float on the mantle, which is the mostly solid layer of Earth lying beneath the crust and above the core. (Because of its hotter temperature, the solid rock of the mantle is more plastic than the solid rock of the crust above it.)

The landmasses are situated on some of these plates. As the plates move, the continents change their relative positions (**FIGS. 18-11b, c,** and **d**). The movement of the crustal plates is termed **plate tectonics.**

Any area where two plates meet is a site of intense geologic activity. Earthquakes and volcanoes are common in such a region. Both San Francisco, noted for its earthquakes, and the Mount Saint Helens volcano are situated where two plates meet. If landmasses lie on the edges of two adjacent plates, mountains may form. The Himalayas formed when the plate carrying India rammed into the plate carrying Asia. When two plates grind together, one of them is sometimes buried under the other in a process known as *subduction.* When two plates move apart, a ridge of lava forms between them. The Atlantic Ocean is increasing in size because of the expanding zone of lava along the Mid-Atlantic Ridge, where two plates are separating.

Knowledge that the continents were at one time connected and have since drifted apart is useful in explaining certain aspects of biogeography (**FIG. 18-12**). Likewise, continental drift has played a major role in the evolution of different organisms. When Pangaea originally formed during the late Permian period, it brought together terrestrial species that had evolved separately from one another, leading to competition and some extinction. Marine life was adversely affected, in part because, with the continents joined as one large mass, less coastal area existed. (Shallow coastal areas contain a greater diversity of marine species than deep-water environments.)

Pangaea separated into several landmasses approximately 180 mya. As the continents began to drift apart, populations became geographically isolated, were exposed to different environmental conditions, and began to diverge along separate evolutionary pathways. As a result, the plants, animals, and other organisms of previously connected continents—South America and Africa, for example—differ. Continental drift also caused gradual changes in ocean and atmospheric currents that have profoundly influenced the biogeography and evolution of organisms. (Biogeography is discussed further in Chapter 56.)

Comparative anatomy of related species demonstrates similarities in their structures

Comparing the structural details of features found in different but related organisms reveals a basic similarity. Such features that are derived from the same structure in a common ancestor are termed **homologous features;** the condition is known as **homology.** For example, consider the limb bones of mammals. A human arm, a cat forelimb, a whale front flipper, and a bat wing, although quite different in appearance, have strikingly similar arrangements of bones, muscles, and nerves. **FIGURE 18-13** shows a comparison of their skeletal structures. Each has a single bone (the humerus) in

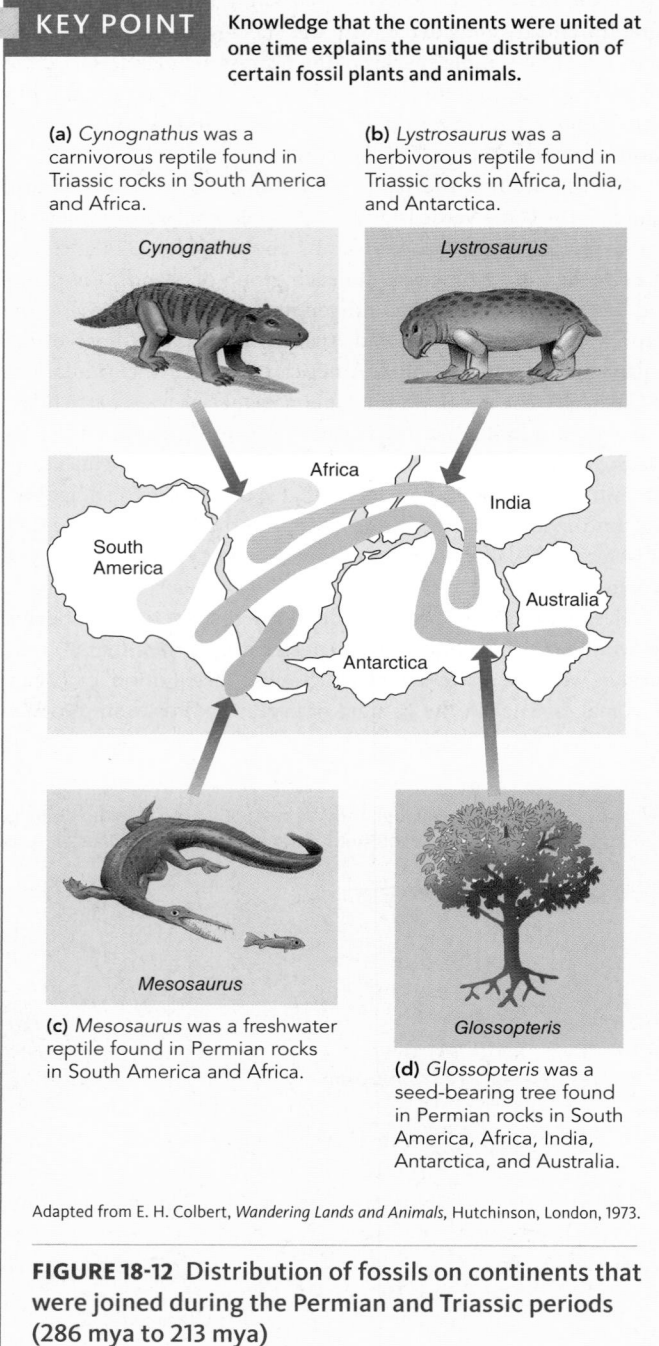

KEY POINT Knowledge that the continents were united at one time explains the unique distribution of certain fossil plants and animals.

(a) *Cynognathus* was a carnivorous reptile found in Triassic rocks in South America and Africa.

(b) *Lystrosaurus* was a herbivorous reptile found in Triassic rocks in Africa, India, and Antarctica.

(c) *Mesosaurus* was a freshwater reptile found in Permian rocks in South America and Africa.

(d) *Glossopteris* was a seed-bearing tree found in Permian rocks in South America, Africa, India, Antarctica, and Australia.

Adapted from E. H. Colbert, *Wandering Lands and Animals*, Hutchinson, London, 1973.

FIGURE 18-12 Distribution of fossils on continents that were joined during the Permian and Triassic periods (286 mya to 213 mya)

the part of the limb nearest the trunk of the body, followed by the two bones (radius and ulna) of the forearm, a group of bones (carpals) in the wrist, and a variable number of digits (metacarpals and phalanges). This similarity is particularly striking because arms, forelimbs, flippers, and wings are used for different types of locomotion, and there is no overriding mechanical reason for them to be so similar structurally. Similar arrangements of parts of the forelimb are evident in ancestral birds, reptiles, and amphibians and even in the first fishes that came out of water onto land hundreds of millions of years ago (see Fig. 32-17).

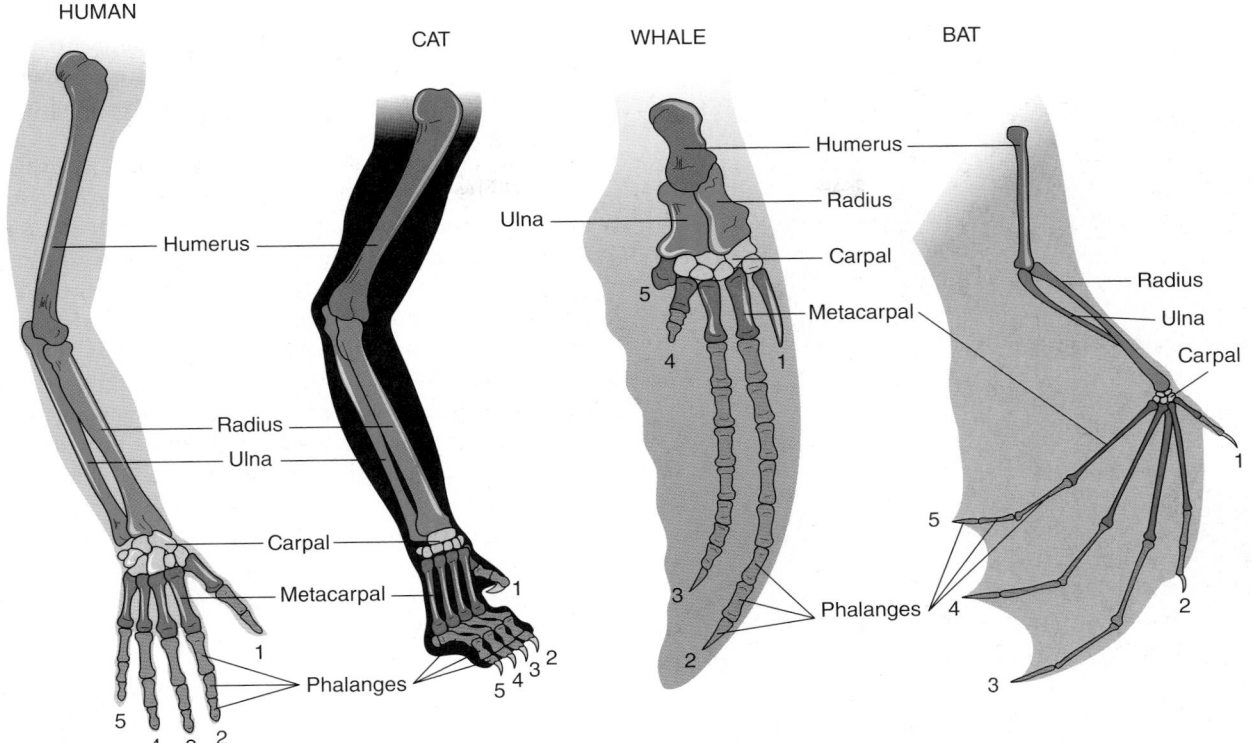

FIGURE 18-13 *Animated* **Structural homology in vertebrates**

The human arm, cat forelimb, whale flipper, and bat wing have a basic underlying similarity of structure because they are derived from a common ancestor. The five digits are numbered in each drawing.

Leaves provide an example of homology in plants. In many plant species, leaves have been modified for functions other than photosynthesis. A cactus spine and a pea tendril, although quite different in appearance, are homologous because both are modified leaves (**FIG. 18-14**). The spine protects the succulent stem tissue of the cactus, whereas the tendril, which winds around a small object once it makes contact, helps support the climbing stem of the pea plant. Such modifications in organs used in different ways are the expected outcome of a common evolutionary origin. The basic structure present in a common ancestor was modified in different ways for different functions as various descendants subsequently evolved.

Not all species with "similar" features have descended from a recent common ancestor, however. Sometimes similar environmental conditions result in the evolution of similar adaptations. Such independent evolution of similar structures in distantly related organisms is known as **convergent evolution.** Aardvarks, anteaters, and pangolins are an excellent example of convergent evolution (**FIG. 18-15**). They resemble one another in lifestyle and certain structural features. All have strong, sharp claws to dig open ant and termite mounds and elongated snouts with long, sticky tongues to catch these insects. Yet aardvarks, anteaters, and pangolins evolved from three distantly related orders of mammals. (See Figure 32-28, which shows several examples of convergent evolution in placental and marsupial mammals.)

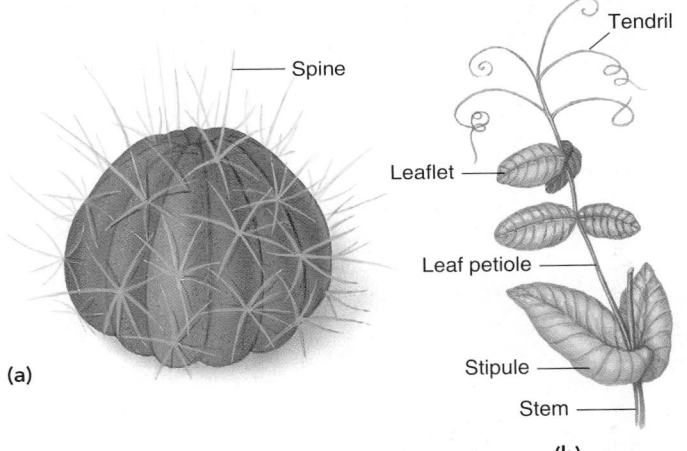

(a)

(b)

FIGURE 18-14 Homology in plants

(a) The spines of the fishhook cactus (*Ferocactus wislizenii*) are modified leaves, as are **(b)** the tendrils of the garden pea (*Pisum sativum*). Leaves of the garden pea are compound, that is, they are divided into smaller components called leaflets. The terminal leaflets are modified into tendrils that are frequently branched.

Structurally similar features that are not homologous but have similar functions that evolved independently in distantly related organisms are said to be **homoplastic features.** Such similarities in different species that are independently acquired by convergent evolution and not by common descent are called **homoplasy.**[2]

---

[2]An older, less precise term that some biologists still use for nonhomologous features with similar functions is *analogy.*

(a) The aardvark (*Orycteropus afer*) is native to central, southern, and eastern Africa.

(b) A giant anteater (*Myrmecophaga tridactyla*) at a termite mound. The anteater is native to Latin America, from southern Mexico to northern Argentina.

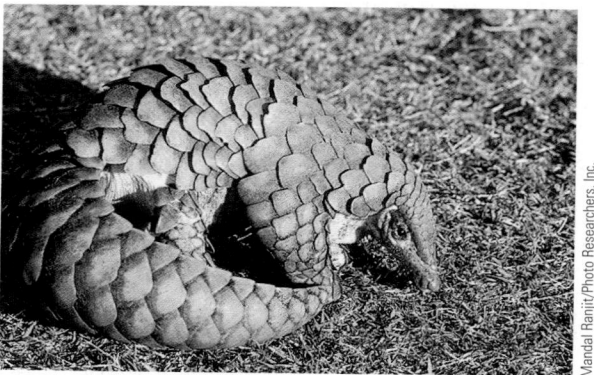

(c) The pangolin (*Manis crassicaudata*) is native to Africa and to southern and southeastern Asia.

FIGURE 18-15 Convergent evolution

Three distantly related mammals adapted independently to eat ants and termites in similar grassland/forest environments in different parts of the world.

For example, the wings of various distantly related flying animals, such as insects and birds, resemble one another superficially; they are homoplastic features that evolved over time to meet the common function of flight, although they differ in more fundamental aspects. Bird wings are modified forelimbs supported by bones, whereas insect wings may have evolved from gill-like appendages present in the aquatic ancestors of insects.

Spines, which are modified leaves, and thorns, which are modified stems, are an example of homoplasy in plants. Spines and thorns resemble one another superficially but are homoplastic features that evolved independently to solve the common need for protection from herbivores (**FIG. 18-16**).

Like homology, homoplasy offers crucial evidence of evolution. Homoplastic features are of evolutionary interest because they demonstrate that organisms with separate ancestries may adapt in similar ways to similar environmental demands.

Comparative anatomy also reveals the existence of **vestigial structures.** Many organisms contain organs or parts of organs that are seemingly nonfunctional and degenerate, often undersized or lacking some essential part. Vestigial structures are remnants of more developed structures that were present and functional in ancestral organisms. In the human body, more than 100 structures are considered vestigial, including the coccyx (fused tailbones), third molars (wisdom teeth), and the muscles that move our ears. Whales and pythons have vestigial hind-limb bones (**FIG. 18-17**); pigs have vestigial toes that do not touch the ground; wingless birds such as the kiwi have vestigial wing bones; and many blind, burrowing, or cave-dwelling animals have nonfunctioning, vestigial eyes.

The occasional presence of a vestigial structure is to be expected as a species adapts to a changing mode of life. Some structures become much less important for survival and may end up as vestiges. When a structure no longer confers a selective advantage, it may become smaller and lose much or all of its function with the passage of time. Because the presence of the vestigial structure is usually not harmful to the organism, however, selective pressure for completely eliminating it is weak, and the vestigial structure is found in many subsequent generations.

Molecular comparisons among organisms provide evidence for evolution

Fossils, biogeography, and comparative anatomy provided Darwin with important clues about the evolutionary history of life. Today, similarities and differences in the biochemistry and molecular biology of various organisms provide additional compelling evidence for evolutionary relationships. Molecular evidence for evolution includes the universal genetic code and the conserved sequences of amino acids in proteins and of nucleotides in DNA.

The genetic code is virtually universal

Organisms owe their characteristics to the types of proteins they possess, which in turn are determined by the sequence of nucleotides in their messenger ribonucleic acid (mRNA), as specified by the order of nucleotides in their DNA. Evidence that all life is related comes from the fact that all organisms use a genetic code that is virtually identical. (There is some minor variation in the genetic code. For example, some mitochondria have several deviations from the standard code.)

Recall from Chapter 13 that the genetic code specifies a triplet (a sequence of three nucleotides in DNA) that codes for a particular codon (a sequence of three nucleotides in mRNA). The codon then codes for a particular amino acid in a polypeptide chain. For example, "AAA" in DNA codes for "UUU" in mRNA, which codes for the amino acid phenylalanine in organisms as diverse as

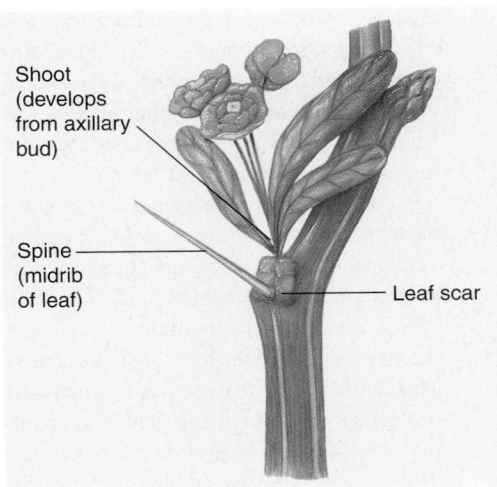

Shoot (develops from axillary bud)

Spine (midrib of leaf)

Leaf scar

Thorn (develops from axillary bud)

(a) A spine of Japanese barberry (*Berberis thunbergii*) is a modified leaf. (In this example, the spine is actually the midrib of the original leaf, which has been shed.)

(b) Thorns of downy hawthorn (*Crataegus mollis*) are modified stems that develop from axillary buds.

FIGURE 18-16 Homoplasy in plants

shrimp, humans, bacteria, and tulips. In fact, "AAA" codes for phenylalanine in all organisms examined to date.

The universality of the genetic code—no other code has been found in any organism—is convincing evidence that all organisms arose from a common ancestor. The genetic code has been maintained and transmitted through all branches of the evolutionary tree since its origin in some extremely early (and successful) organism.

Proteins and DNA contain a record of evolutionary change

Researchers have carried out thousands of comparisons of protein and DNA sequences from various species during the past 30 years

E. R. Degginger/Animals Animals

J. D. Cunningham/Visuals Unlimited

(a) An African rock python (*Python sebae*).

(b) Close-up of part of a python skeleton showing the hind-limb bones.

FIGURE 18-17 Vestigial structures

All pythons have remnants of hind-limb bones embedded in their bodies.

or so. Moreover, the recent explosion in DNA sequencing information (more than 1000 species have now had their genomes sequenced) is beginning to provide a wealth of evolutionary data as these genomes are compared. Sequence-based relationships generally agree with earlier studies, which based evolutionary relationships on similarities in structure among living organisms and on fossil data of extinct organisms.

Investigations of the sequence of amino acids in proteins that play the same roles in many species have revealed both great similarities and certain specific differences. Even organisms that are only remotely related share some proteins, such as cytochrome *c*, which is part of the electron transport chain in aerobic respiration. To survive, all aerobic organisms need a respiratory protein with the same basic structure and function as the cytochrome *c* of their common ancestor. Consequently, not all amino acids that confer the structural and functional features of cytochrome *c* are free to change. Any mutations that changed the amino acid sequence at structurally important sites of the cytochrome *c* molecule would have been harmful, and natural selection would have prevented such mutations from being passed to future generations. However, in the course of the long, independent evolution of different organisms, mutations have resulted in the substitution of many amino acids at less important locations in the cytochrome *c* molecule. The greater the differences in the amino acid sequences of their cytochrome *c* molecules, the longer it has been since two species diverged.

Because a protein's amino acid sequences are coded in DNA, the differences in amino acid sequences indirectly reflect the nature and number of underlying DNA base-pair changes that must have occurred during evolution. Of course, not all DNA codes for proteins (witness introns and transfer RNA genes). **DNA sequencing**—that is, determining the order of nucleotide bases in DNA—of both protein-coding DNA and nonprotein-coding DNA—is useful in determining evolutionary relationships.

Generally, the more closely species are considered related on the basis of other scientific evidence, the greater the percentage of nucleotide sequences that their DNA molecules have in common. By using the DNA sequence data in **FIGURE 18-18**, for example, you can conclude that the closest living relative of humans is the chimpanzee (because its DNA has the lowest percentage of differences in the sequence examined). (Primate evolution is discussed in Chapter 22.)

In some cases, molecular evidence challenges traditional evolutionary ideas that were based on structural comparisons among living species and/or on studies of fossil skeletons. Consider even-toed hoofed mammals such as pigs, camels, deer, antelope, cattle, and hippos. Whales lack toes and were traditionally not classified as close relatives of hoofed mammals.

Introduction to Darwinian Evolution

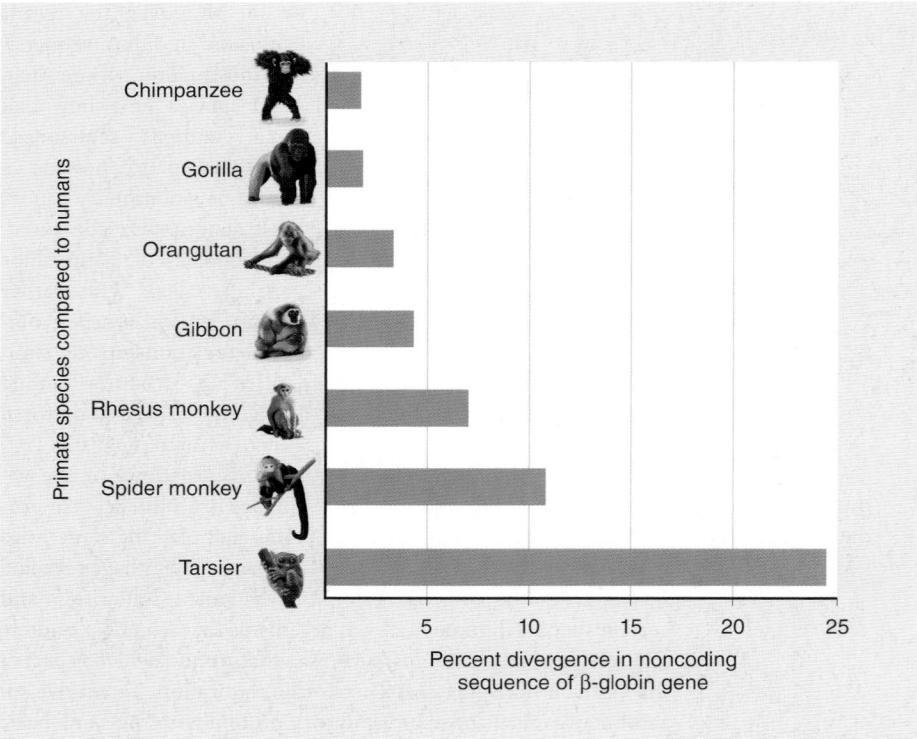

FIGURE 18-18 Differences in DNA nucleotide sequences as evidence of evolutionary relationships

Comparing the same gene in different organisms provides a window into evolution. Here the differences in the noncoding region of the β-globin gene are compared between humans and other primates. Evolutionary biologists are beginning to expand such studies from comparing one or several genes to comparing entire genomes.

FIGURE 18-19 depicts a **cladogram,** or **phylogenetic tree,** based on molecular data for whales and selected hoofed mammals. Such cladograms—diagrams showing lines of descent—can be derived from differences in a given DNA nucleotide sequence. This diagram indicates that whales are more closely related to hippos than to any other hoofed mammal. The branches representing whales and hippos probably diverged relatively recently because of the close similarity of DNA sequences in these species. In contrast, camels, which have DNA sequences that are less similar to those of whales, diverged much earlier. The molecular evidence indicates that whales and hippos share a recent common ancestor.

The molecular evidence linking whales and even-toed hoofed mammals has led to a reexamination of early fossil whales. Like today's hoofed mammals, early fossil whales had an even number of toes on their appendages. Fossil whales also had the same type of specialized ankle bone (called a double pulley) as hippos and other hoofed mammals.

Developmental biology helps unravel evolutionary patterns

As early as 1975, biologists were suggesting that regulatory changes in gene expression, particularly of genes involved in development, were responsible for many differences between closely related species. Today much evidence supports the idea that regulatory changes—how genes are switched on and off during development—help explain the diversity of form in species with similar genes. Mutations in genes that regulate development often result in dramatically different structures (see Fig. 17-12).

Increasingly, developmental biology, particularly at the molecular level, is providing answers to such questions as how snakes became elongated and lost their limbs. In many cases, evolutionary changes such as the loss of limbs in snakes occur as a result of changes in genes that regulate the orderly sequence of events that occurs during development. In pythons, for example, the loss of forelimbs and elongation of the body are linked to mutations in several *Hox* genes that affect the expression of body patterns and limb formation in a wide variety of animals. (See the discussion of *Hox* gene clusters in Chapter 17.) The hind limbs may not develop because python embryonic tissue does not respond to internal signals that trigger leg elongation.

Developmental geneticists at Harvard Medical School and Princeton University are studying the developmental basis for the different beak shapes of the Galápagos finches. They have determined that a gene that codes for an important signaling molecule, bone morphogenic protein 4 (BMP4), affects the development of the birds' craniofacial skeletons. The gene for BMP4 is turned on earlier in development and has a higher level of expression in finch species with larger, thicker beaks than in finches with smaller beaks.

Scientific evidence overwhelmingly demonstrates that development in different animals is controlled by the same kinds of genes; these genetic similarities in a wide variety of organisms reflect a shared evolutionary history. For example, vertebrates have similar patterns of embryological development that indicate they share a common ancestor. All vertebrate embryos have segmented muscles, pharyngeal (throat) pouches, a tubular heart without left and right sides, a system of arteries known as *aortic arches* in the pharyngeal region, and many other shared features. All these structures are necessary and functional in the developing fish. The small, segmented muscles of the fish embryo give rise to the segmented muscles used by the adult fish in swimming. The pharyngeal pouches break through to the surface as gill slits. The adult fish heart remains undivided and pumps blood forward to the gills that develop in association with the aortic arches.

Because none of these embryonic features persists in the adults of reptiles, birds, or mammals, why are these fishlike structures present in their embryos? Evolution is a conservative process, and natural selection builds on what has come before rather than starting from scratch. The evolution of new features often does not require the evolution of new developmental genes but instead depends on a modification in developmental genes that already exist (see discussion of pre-adaptations in Chapter 20). Terrestrial ver-

This branching diagram, called a *cladogram*, shows hypothetical evolutionary relationships. The organisms depicted here share a common ancestor.

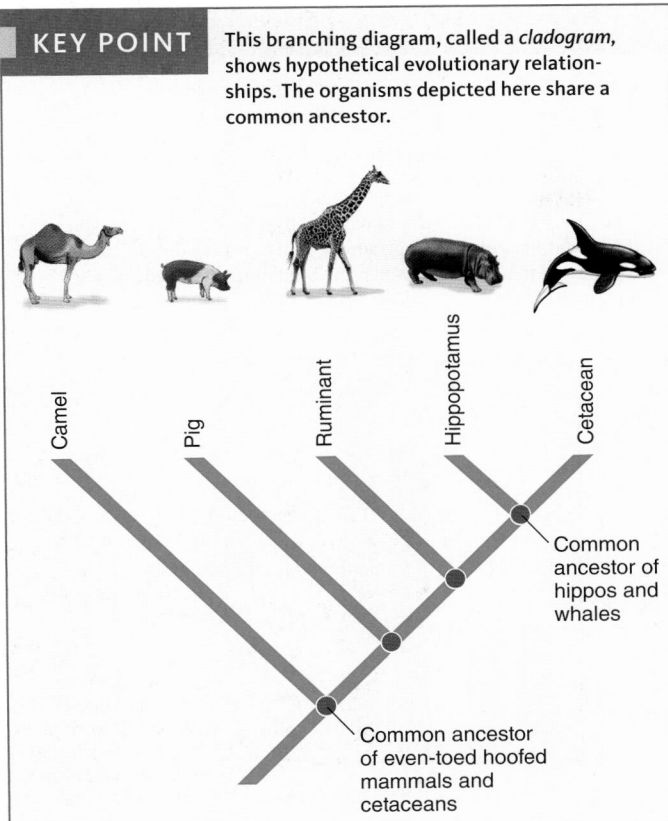

Camel

Pig

Ruminant

Hippopotamus

Cetacean

Common ancestor of hippos and whales

Common ancestor of even-toed hoofed mammals and cetaceans

Adapted from Nikaido, M., et al., "Phylogenetic Relationships among Cetartiodactyls Based on Insertions of Short and Long Interspersed Elements: Hippopotamuses Are the Closest Extant Relatives of Whales," *Proceedings of the National Academy of Sciences*, Vol. 96, Aug. 31, 1999.

FIGURE 18-19 Cladogram of whales and their closest living relatives

DNA sequence differences among selected mammals suggest that hoofed mammals such as hippos and giraffes are the closest living relatives of whales. The hippopotamus is probably the closest living relative of whales and other cetaceans. The nodes (*circles*) represent branch points where a species splits into two or more lineages. (Ruminants are mammals such as cows, sheep, and giraffes that have a multichambered stomach and chew regurgitated plant material to make it more digestible.)

Fish

Chicken

Human

1 day

3 days

32 days

3 days

12 days

56 days

John Burgoyne/National Geographic Image Collection

FIGURE 18-20 Development of fish fins, chicken wings, and human limbs

Fish, chickens, and humans are vertebrates with strikingly similar genes. Although the early embryos of these organisms are much alike, the areas colored orange follow different developmental pathways, resulting in fins, wings, or limbs. (Figures are not to scale.)

tebrates are thought to have evolved from fishlike ancestors; therefore, they share some of the early stages of development still found in fishes today. The accumulation of genetic changes over time in these vertebrates has modified the basic body plan laid out in fish development (**FIG. 18-20**).

Evolutionary hypotheses are tested experimentally

Increasingly, biologists are designing imaginative experiments, often in natural settings, to test evolutionary hypotheses. David Reznick from the University of California at Santa Barbara and John Endler from James Cook University in Australia have studied evolution in guppy populations in Venezuela and in Trinidad, a small island in the southern Caribbean.

Reznick and Endler observed that different streams have different kinds and numbers of fishes that prey on guppies. Predatory fishes that prey on larger guppies are present in all streams at lower elevations; these areas of intense predation pressure are known as *high-predation habitats*. Predators are often excluded from tributaries or upstream areas by rapids and waterfalls. The areas above such barriers are known as *low-predation habitats* because they contain only one species of small predatory fish that occasionally eats smaller guppies.

Differences in predation are correlated with many differences in the guppies, such as male coloration, behavior, and attributes known as *life history traits* (discussed in more detail in Chapter 53). These traits include age and size at sexual maturity, the number of offspring per reproductive event, the size of the offspring, and the frequency of reproduction. For example, guppy adults are larger in streams found at higher elevations and smaller in streams found at lower elevations.

Do predators actually cause these differences to evolve? Reznick and colleagues tested this evolutionary hypothesis by conducting field experiments in Trinidad. Taking advantage of waterfalls that prevent the upstream movement of guppies, guppy predators, or both, they moved either guppies or guppy predators over such barriers. For example, guppies from a high-predation habitat were introduced into a low-predation habitat by moving them over a barrier waterfall into a section of stream that was free of guppies and large predators. The only fish species that lived in this section of stream before the introduction was the small predatory fish.

Eleven years later, the researchers captured adult females from the introduction site (low-predation habitat) and the control site below the barrier waterfall (high-predation habitat). They bred these females in their laboratory and compared the life history traits of succeeding generations. The descendants of guppies introduced into the low-predation habitat matured at a larger size than did the descendants of guppies from the control site below the waterfall (**FIG. 18-21**). They also produced fewer, but larger, offspring. The introduced fish populations had evolved to have life histories similar to those of fishes typically found in such low-predation habitats. Similar studies have demonstrated that predators have played an active role in the evolution of other traits, such as the average number of offspring produced during the lifetime of an individual female (fecundity), male coloration, and behavior.

Rapid evolution on a scale of years has also been observed in organisms as diverse as marine snails, mussels, soapberry bugs, mayflies, anole lizards, 'i'iwis (scarlet honeycreepers), and wild rabbits. These and other experiments and observations demonstrate not only that evolution is real but also that it is occurring now, driven by selective environmental forces, such as predation, that can be experimentally manipulated. Darwin incorrectly assumed evolution to be so gradual that humans cannot observe it. As Jonathan Weiner, author of *The Beak of the Finch: A Story of Evolution in Our Time,* notes, "Darwin did not know the strength of his own theory. He vastly underestimated the power of natural selection. Its action is neither rare nor slow. It leads to evolution daily and hourly, all around us, and we can watch."

Review

- How do scientists date fossils?
- How can we explain that fossils of *Mesosaurus*, an extinct reptile that could not swim across open water, are found in the southern parts of both Africa and South America?
- How do homologous and homoplastic features provide evidence of evolution?
- How does developmental biology provide evidence of a common ancestry for vertebrates as diverse as reptiles, birds, pigs, and humans?
- How do predator preferences drive the evolution of size in guppies?

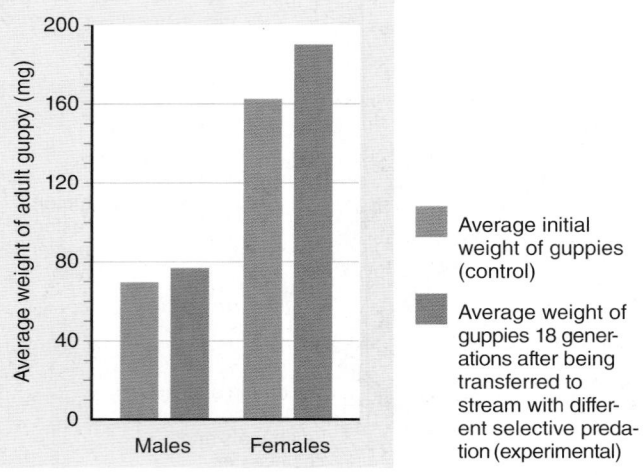

KEY EXPERIMENT

QUESTION: Can natural selection be observed in a natural population?

HYPOTHESIS: A natural population will respond adaptively to environmental change.

EXPERIMENT: Male and female guppies from a stream in which the predators preferred large adult guppies as prey (*brown bars*) were transferred to a stream in which the predators preferred juveniles and small adults.

Legend:
- Average initial weight of guppies (control)
- Average weight of guppies 18 generations after being transferred to stream with different selective predation (experimental)

RESULTS AND CONCLUSION: After 11 years, the descendants of the transferred guppies (*pink bars*) were measurably larger than their ancestors, indicating that larger guppies had a selective advantage in the new environment.

Data used with permission from Reznick, D. N., et al., "Evaluation of the Rate of Evolution in Natural Populations of Guppies [*Poecilia reticulata*]," *Science,* Vol. 275, Mar. 28, 1997.

FIGURE 18-21 D. N. Reznick's experiment in guppy evolution

▪ SUMMARY: FOCUS ON LEARNING OBJECTIVES

18.1 *(page 392)*

1 Define *evolution.*

- **Evolution** is the accumulation of inherited changes within a **population** over time. Evolution is the unifying concept of biology because it links all fields of the life sciences into a coherent body of knowledge.

18.2 *(page 392)*

2 Discuss the historical development of evolutionary theory.

- Jean Baptiste de Lamarck was the first scientist to propose that organisms undergo change over time as a result of some natural phenomenon rather than divine intervention. Lamarck thought organisms were endowed with a vital force that drove them to change toward greater complexity over time. He thought organisms could pass traits acquired during their lifetimes to their offspring.

- Charles Darwin's observations while voyaging on the HMS *Beagle* were the basis for his evolutionary theory. Darwin tried to explain the similarities between animals and plants of the arid Galápagos Islands and the humid South American mainland.

- Darwin was influenced by **artificial selection,** in which breeders develop many varieties of domesticated plants and animals in just a few generations. Darwin applied Thomas Malthus's ideas on the natural increase in human populations to natural populations. Darwin was influenced by the idea that Earth was extremely old, an idea promoted by Charles Lyell and other geologists.

18.3 *(page 393)*

3 Explain the four premises of evolution by natural selection as proposed by Charles Darwin.

- Charles Darwin and Alfred Wallace independently proposed evolution by **natural selection,** which is based on four observations.

First, genetic variation exists among the individuals in a population. Second, the reproductive ability of each species causes its populations to have the potential to geometrically increase in number over time. Third, organisms compete with one another for the resources needed for life, such as food, living space, water, and light. Fourth, offspring with the most favorable combination of inherited characteristics are most likely to survive and reproduce, passing those genetic characteristics to the next generation.

■ Natural selection results in **adaptations,** evolutionary modifications that improve the chances of survival and reproductive success in a particular environment. Over time, enough changes may accumulate in geographically separated populations to produce new species.

CENGAGENOW™ Learn more about the Galápagos Islands and the Galápagos Island finches by clicking on the figures in CengageNOW.

4 Compare the modern synthesis with Darwin's original evolutionary theory.

■ The **modern synthesis** combines Darwin's evolutionary theory by natural selection with modern genetics to explain why individuals in a population vary and how species adapt to their environment.

■ **Mutation** provides the genetic variability that natural selection acts on during evolution.

18.4 *(page 397)*

5 Summarize the evidence for evolution obtained from the fossil record.

■ Direct evidence of evolution comes from **fossils,** the remains or traces of ancient organisms. Layers of sedimentary rock normally occur in their sequence of deposition, with the more recent layers on top of the older, earlier ones. **Index fossils** characterize a specific layer over large geographic areas. **Radioisotopes** present in a rock provide a way to accurately measure the rock's age.

CENGAGENOW™ Learn more about fossil intermediates by clicking on the figure in CengageNOW.

6 Define *biogeography* and describe how the distribution of organisms supports evolution.

■ **Biogeography,** the geographic distribution of organisms, affects their evolution. Areas that have been separated from the rest of the world for a long time contain organisms that have evolved in isolation and are therefore unique to those areas.

■ At one time the continents were joined to form a supercontinent. **Continental drift,** which caused the various landmasses to break apart and separate, has played a major role in evolution.

CENGAGENOW™ Watch continental drift by clicking on the figure in CengageNOW.

7 Describe the evidence for evolution derived from comparative anatomy.

■ **Homologous features** have basic structural similarities, even though the structures may be used in different ways because ho-

mologous features derive from the same structure in a common ancestor. Evolutionary affinities exist among the organisms that have homologous features.

■ **Homoplastic features** evolved independently to have similar functions in distantly related organisms. Homoplastic features demonstrate **convergent evolution,** in which organisms with separate ancestries adapt in similar ways to comparable environmental demands.

■ **Vestigial structures** are nonfunctional or degenerate remnants of structures that were present and functional in ancestral organisms. Structures occasionally become vestigial as species adapt to different modes of life.

CENGAGENOW™ Learn more about vestigial structures by clicking on the figure in CengageNOW.

8 Briefly explain how molecular biology and developmental biology provide insights into the evolutionary process.

■ Molecular evidence for evolution includes the universal genetic code and the conserved sequences of amino acids in proteins and of nucleotides in DNA.

■ Evolutionary changes are often the result of mutations in genes that affect the orderly sequence of events during development. Development in different animals is controlled by the same kinds of genes, which indicates these animals have a shared evolutionary history.

■ The accumulation of genetic changes since organisms diverged, or took separate evolutionary pathways, has modified the pattern of development in more complex vertebrate embryos.

9 Give an example of how evolutionary hypotheses are tested experimentally.

■ Reznick and Endler have studied the effects of predation intensity on the evolution of guppy populations in the laboratory and in nature. Such experiments are a powerful way for investigators to test the underlying processes of natural selection.

TEST YOUR UNDERSTANDING

1. Evolution is based on which of the following concepts? (a) organisms share a common origin (b) over time, organisms have diverged from a common ancestor (c) an animal's body parts can change over its lifetime, and these acquired changes are passed to the next generation (d) a and b (e) a, b, and c

2. Evolution is the accumulation of genetic changes within _____ over time. (a) individuals (b) populations (c) communities (d) a and b (e) a and c

3. Charles Darwin proposed that evolution could be explained by the differential reproductive success of organisms that resulted from their naturally occurring variation. Darwin called this process (a) coevolution (b) convergent evolution (c) natural selection (d) artificial selection (e) homoplasy

4. Which of the following is *not* part of Darwin's mechanism of evolution? (a) differential reproductive success (b) variation

in a population (c) inheritance of acquired (nongenetic) traits (d) overproduction of offspring (e) struggle for existence

5. The modern synthesis (a) is based on the sequence of fossils in rock layers (b) uses genetics to explain the source of hereditary variation that is essential to natural selection (c) was first proposed by ancient Greek scholars (d) considers the influence of the geographic distribution of organisms on their evolution (e) is reinforced by homologies that are explained by common descent

6. The evolution of beak size in the various species of Galápagos finches is associated with their (a) songs (b) diets (c) body sizes (d) predators (e) none of the preceding

7. The fossil record (a) usually occurs in sedimentary rock (b) sometimes appears fragmentary (c) is relatively complete for tropical rainforest organisms but incomplete for aquatic organisms (d) a and b (e) a, b, and c

8. In _____, the selecting agent is the environment, whereas in _____, the selecting agent is humans. (a) natural selection; con-

vergent evolution (b) mutation; artificial selection (c) homoplasy; homology (d) artificial selection; natural selection (e) natural selection; artificial selection

9. Aardvarks, anteaters, and pangolins are only distantly related but are similar in structure and form as a result of (a) homology (b) convergent evolution (c) biogeography (d) vestigial structures (e) artificial selection

10. The species of the Galápagos Islands (a) are similar to those on other islands at the same latitude (b) are similar to those on the South American mainland (c) are identical to those on other islands at the same latitude (d) are identical to those on the South American mainland (e) are similar to those on both the African and South American mainlands

11. Changes in just a few genes that regulate _____ are often responsible for the evolution of new anatomical features in a population. (a) fossil formation (b) vestigial structures (c) development (d) biogeography (e) adaptation

CRITICAL THINKING

1. **EVOLUTION LINK.** The use of model organisms such as the mouse for research and biomedical testing of human diseases is based on the assumption that all organisms share a common ancestor. On what evidence is this assumption based?

2. **EVOLUTION LINK.** What adaptations must an animal possess to swim in the ocean? Why are such genetically different organisms as porpoises, which are mammals, and sharks, which are fish, so similar in form?

3. **EVOLUTION LINK.** The human fetus grows a coat of fine hair (the lanugo) that is shed before or shortly after birth. Fetuses of chimpanzees and other primates also grow coats of hair, but they are not shed. Explain these observations based on what you have learned in this chapter.

4. **EVOLUTION LINK.** Charles Darwin once said, "It is not the strongest of the species that survive, nor the most intelligent, but the one most responsive to change." Explain what he meant.

5. **EVOLUTION LINK.** Write short paragraphs explaining each of the following statements:

   a. Natural selection chooses from among the individuals in a population those most suited to *current* environmental conditions. It does not guarantee survival under future conditions.

   b. Individuals do not evolve, but populations do.

   c. The organisms that exist today do so because their ancestors had traits that allowed them and their offspring to thrive.

   d. At the molecular level, evolution can take place by the replacement of one nucleotide by another.

   e. Evolution is said to have occurred within a population when measurable genetic changes are detected.

6. **EVOLUTION LINK.** Although most salamanders have four legs, a few species that live in shallow water lack hind limbs and have extremely tiny forelimbs (*see photograph*). Develop a hypothesis to

The narrow-striped dwarf siren (*Pseudobranchus striatus axanthus*) is an aquatic salamander that resembles an eel. It is native to Florida.

explain how limbless salamanders came about according to Darwin's mechanism of evolution by natural selection. How could you test your hypothesis?

7. **ANALYZING DATA.** Which of the primates in Figure 18-18 is the most distantly related to humans? Explain your answer.

8. **SCIENCE, TECHNOLOGY, AND SOCIETY.** Farmers often face a predicament, known as the pesticide treadmill, in which the cost of applying pesticides increases because the pesticides have to be applied more frequently or in larger doses, while their effectiveness decreases. Based on what you have learned in this chapter, offer an explanation for why the pesticides lose their effectiveness.

 Additional questions are available in CengageNOW at www.cengage.com/login.

19 Evolutionary Change in Populations

Genetic variation in snail shells. Shown are the shell patterns and colors in a single snail species (*Cepaea nemoralis*), native to Scotland. Variation in shell color may have adaptive value in these snails because some colors predominate in cooler environments whereas other colors are more common in warmer habitats.

G. I. Bernard/Animals Animals

KEY CONCEPTS

19.1 The genotype, phenotype, and allele frequencies of a population's gene pool (all alleles of all loci) can be calculated.

19.2 The Hardy–Weinberg principle predicts allele and genotype frequencies for a population that is not evolving.

19.3 Natural selection, as well as nonrandom mating, mutation, genetic drift, and gene flow are forces that drive changes in a population's gene pool over successive generations (microevolution). Modes of natural selection include stabilizing selection, directional selection, and disruptive selection.

19.4 Populations typically exhibit genetic variation, which may include genetic polymorphism, balanced polymorphism, or geographic variation.

As you learned in Chapter 18, evolution occurs in populations, not individuals. Although natural selection acts on individuals, causing differential survival and reproduction, individuals themselves do not evolve during their lifetimes. Evolutionary change, which includes modifications in structure, physiology, ecology, and behavior, is inherited from one generation to the next. Although Darwin recognized that evolution occurs in populations, he did not understand how the attributes of organisms are passed to successive generations. One of the most significant advances in biology since Darwin's time has been the demonstration of the genetic basis of evolution.

Recall from Chapter 18 that a **population** consists of all individuals of the same species that live in a particular place at the same time. Individuals within a population vary in many recognizable characters. A population of snails, for example, may vary in shell size, weight, or color (see photograph). Some of this variation is due to heredity, and some is due to environment (nonheritable variation), such as the individual differences observed in the pink color of flamingos, which is partly attributable to differences in diet.

Biologists study variation in a particular character (characteristic) by taking measurements of that character in a population. By comparing the character in parents and offspring, it is possible to estimate the amount of observed variation that is genetic, as represented by the number, frequency, and kinds of alleles in a population. (Recall from

Chapter 11 that an **allele** is one of two or more alternate forms of a gene. Alleles occupy corresponding positions, or **loci,** on homologous chromosomes.)

This chapter will help you develop an understanding of the importance of genetic variation as the raw material for evolution and of the basic concepts of **population genetics,** the study of genetic variability within a population and of the evolutionary forces that act on it. Population genetics represents an extension of Gregor Mendel's principles of inheritance (see Chapter 11). You will learn how to distinguish genetic equilibrium from evolutionary change and to assess the roles of the five factors responsible for evolutionary change: nonrandom mating, mutation, genetic drift, gene flow, and natural selection.

19.1 GENOTYPE, PHENOTYPE, AND ALLELE FREQUENCIES

■ LEARNING OBJECTIVES

1   Define what is meant by a population's gene pool.
2   Distinguish among genotype, phenotype, and allele frequencies.

Each population possesses a **gene pool,** which includes all the alleles for all the loci present in the population. Because diploid organisms have a maximum of two different alleles at each genetic locus, a single individual typically has only a small fraction of the alleles present in a population's gene pool. The genetic variation that is evident among individuals in a given population indicates that each individual has a different subset of the alleles in the gene pool.

The evolution of populations is best understood in terms of genotype, phenotype, and allele frequencies. Suppose, for example, that all 1000 individuals of a hypothetical population have their genotypes tested, with the following results:

Genotype	Number	Genotype Frequency
AA	490	0.49
Aa	420	0.42
aa	90	0.09
Total	1000	1.00

Each **genotype frequency** is the proportion of a particular genotype in the population. Genotype frequency is usually expressed as a decimal fraction, and the sum of all genotype frequencies is 1.0 (somewhat like probabilities, which were discussed in Chapter 11). For example, the genotype frequency for the *Aa* genotype is 420 ÷ 1000 = 0.42.

A **phenotype frequency** is the proportion of a particular phenotype in the population. If each genotype corresponds to a specific phenotype, then the phenotype and genotype frequencies are the same. If allele *A* is dominant over allele *a,* however, the phenotype frequencies in our hypothetical population would be the following:

Phenotype	Number	Phenotype Frequency
Dominant	910	0.91
Recessive	90	0.09
Total	1000	1.00

In this example, the dominant phenotype is the sum of two genotypes, *AA* and *Aa,* so the number 910 is obtained by adding 490 + 420.

An **allele frequency** is the proportion of a specific allele (that is, of *A* or *a*) in a particular population. As mentioned earlier, each individual, being diploid, has two alleles at each genetic locus. Because we started with a population of 1000 individuals, we must account for a total of 2000 alleles. The 490 *AA* individuals have 980 *A* alleles, whereas the 420 *Aa* individuals have 420 *A* alleles, making a total of 1400 *A* alleles in the population. The total number of *a* alleles in the population is 420 + 90 + 90 = 600. Now it is easy to calculate allele frequencies:

Allele	Number	Allele Frequency
A	1400	0.7
a	600	0.3
Total	2000	1.0

Review

- Does the term *gene pool* apply to individuals, populations, or both?
- Can the frequencies of all genotypes in a population be determined directly with respect to a locus that has only two alleles, one dominant and the other recessive?
- In a human population of 1000, 840 are tongue rollers (*TT* or *Tt*), and 160 are not tongue rollers (*tt*). What is the frequency of the dominant allele (*T*) in the population?

19.2 THE HARDY–WEINBERG PRINCIPLE

■ LEARNING OBJECTIVES

3   Discuss the significance of the Hardy–Weinberg principle as it relates to evolution and list the five conditions required for genetic equilibrium.
4   Use the Hardy–Weinberg principle to solve problems involving populations.

In the example just discussed, we observe that only 90 of the 1000 individuals in the population exhibit the recessive phenotype characteristic of the genotype *aa.* The remaining 910 individuals exhibit the dominant phenotype and are either *AA* or *Aa.* You might assume that after many generations, genetic recombination during sexual reproduction would cause the dominant allele to become more common in the population. You might also assume that the recessive allele would eventually disappear altogether. These were common assumptions of many biologists early in the 20th century. However, these assumptions are incorrect because the frequencies of alleles and genotypes do not change from generation to generation unless influenced by outside factors (discussed later in the chapter).

A population whose allele and genotype frequencies do not change from generation to generation is said to be at **genetic equilibrium.** Such a population, with no net change in allele or genotype frequencies over time, is not undergoing evolutionary change. A population that is at genetic equilibrium is not evolving with respect to the locus being studied. However, if allele frequencies change over successive generations, evolution is occurring.

The explanation for the stability of successive generations in populations at genetic equilibrium was provided independently by Godfrey Hardy, an English mathematician, and Wilhelm Weinberg, a German physician, in 1908. They pointed out that the expected frequencies of various genotypes in a population can be described mathematically. The resulting **Hardy–Weinberg principle** shows that if the population is large, the process of inheritance does not by itself cause changes in allele frequencies. It also explains why dominant alleles are not necessarily more common than recessive ones. The Hardy–Weinberg principle represents an ideal situation that seldom occurs in the natural world. However, it is useful because it provides a model to help us understand the real world. Knowledge of the Hardy–Weinberg principle is essential to understanding the mechanisms of evolutionary change in sexually reproducing populations.

We now expand our original example to illustrate the Hardy–Weinberg principle. Keep in mind as we go through these calculations that in most cases we know only the phenotype frequencies. When alleles are dominant and recessive, it is usually impossible to visually distinguish heterozygous individuals from homozygous dominant individuals. The Hardy–Weinberg principle lets us use phenotype frequencies to calculate the expected genotype frequencies and allele frequencies, assuming we have a clear understanding of the genetic basis for the character under study.

As mentioned earlier, the frequency of either allele, A or a, is represented by a number that ranges from 0 to 1. An allele that is totally absent from the population has a frequency of zero. If all the alleles of a given locus are the same in the population, then the frequency of that allele is 1.

Because only two alleles, A and a, exist at the locus in our example, the sum of their frequencies must equal 1. If we let p represent the frequency of the dominant (A) allele in the population, and q the frequency of the recessive (a) allele, then we can summarize their relationship with a simple binomial equation, $p + q = 1$. When we know the value of either p or q, we can calculate the value of the other: $p = 1 - q$, and $q = 1 - p$.

Squaring both sides of $p + q = 1$ results in $(p + q)^2 = 1$. This equation can be expanded to describe the relationship of the allele frequencies to the genotypes in the population. When it is expanded, we obtain the frequency of the offspring genotypes:

p^2	+	$2pq$	+	q^2	=	1
Frequency of AA		Frequency of Aa		Frequency of aa		All individuals in the population

We always begin Hardy–Weinberg calculations by determining the frequency of the homozygous recessive genotype. From the fact that we had 90 homozygous recessive individuals in our population of 1000, we infer that the frequency of the aa genotype, q^2,

Genotypes	AA	Aa	aa
Frequency of genotypes in population	0.49	0.42 (0.21 + 0.21)	0.09
Frequency of alleles in gametes	$A = 0.49 + 0.21$ $= 0.7$		$a = 0.21 + 0.09$ $= 0.3$

(a) Genotype and allele frequencies. The figure illustrates how to calculate frequencies of the alleles A and a in the gametes produced by each genotype.

(b) Segregation of alleles and random fertilization. When eggs and sperm containing A or a alleles unite randomly, the frequency of each of the possible genotypes (AA, Aa, aa) among the offspring is calculated by multiplying the frequencies of the alleles A and a in eggs and sperm.

FIGURE 19-1 *Animated* The Hardy–Weinberg principle

is 90/1000, or 0.09. Because q^2 equals 0.09, q (the frequency of the recessive a allele) is equal to the square root of 0.09, or 0.3. From the relationship between p and q, we conclude that the frequency of the dominant A allele, p, equals $1 - q = 1 - 0.3 = 0.7$.

Given this information, we can calculate the frequency of homozygous dominant (AA) individuals: $p^2 = 0.7 \times 0.7 = 0.49$ (**FIG. 19-1**). The expected frequency of heterozygous individuals (Aa) would be $2pq = 2 \times 0.7 \times 0.3 = 0.42$. Thus, approximately 490 individuals are expected to be homozygous dominant, and 420 are expected to be heterozygous. Note that the sum of homozygous dominant and heterozygous individuals equals 910, the number of individuals showing the dominant phenotype with which we started.

Any population in which the distribution of genotypes conforms to the relation $p^2 + 2pq + q^2 = 1$, whatever the absolute values for p and q may be, is at genetic equilibrium. The Hardy–Weinberg principle allows biologists to calculate allele frequencies in a given population if we know the genotype frequencies, and vice versa. These values provide a basis of comparison with a population's allele or genotype frequencies in succeeding generations. During that time, if the allele or genotype frequencies deviate from the values predicted by the Hardy–Weinberg principle, then the population is evolving.

Genetic equilibrium occurs if certain conditions are met

The Hardy–Weinberg principle of genetic equilibrium tells us what to expect when a sexually reproducing population is not evolving. The relative proportions of alleles and genotypes in successive generations will always be the same, provided the following five conditions are met:

1. *Random mating.* In unrestricted random mating, each individual in a population has an equal chance of mating with any individual of the opposite sex. In our example, the individuals represented by the genotypes *AA, Aa,* and *aa* must mate with one another at random and must not select their mates on the basis of genotype or any other factors that result in nonrandom mating.

2. *No net mutations.* There must be no mutations that convert *A* into *a,* or vice versa. That is, the frequencies of *A* and *a* in the population must not change because of mutations.

3. *Large population size.* Allele frequencies in a small population are more likely to change by random fluctuations (that is, by genetic drift, which is discussed later) than are allele frequencies in a large population.

4. *No migration.* There can be no exchange of alleles with other populations that might have different allele frequencies. In other words, there can be no migration of individuals into or out of a population.[1]

5. *No natural selection.* If natural selection is occurring, certain phenotypes (and their corresponding genotypes) are favored over others. These more successful genotypes are said to have greater **fitness,** which is the relative ability to make a genetic contribution to subsequent generations. Consequently, the allele frequencies will change, and the population will evolve.

Human MN blood groups are a valuable illustration of the Hardy–Weinberg principle

Humans have dozens of antigens on the surfaces of their blood cells. (An *antigen* is a molecule, usually a protein or carbohydrate, that is recognized as foreign by cells of another organism's immune system.) One group of antigens, designated the MN blood group, stimulates the production of antibodies when injected into rabbits or guinea pigs. However, humans do not produce antibodies for M and N, so the MN blood group is not medically important, for example, when giving blood transfusions. (Recall the discussion of the medically important ABO alleles in Chapter 11.) The MN

---

[1]Note that evolutionary biologists use the term *migration,* not in its ordinary sense of periodic or seasonal movement of individuals from one location to another but in reference to a movement of individuals that results in a transfer of alleles from one population to another.

blood group is of interest to population geneticists because the alleles for the MN blood group, usually designated *M* and *N,* are codominant (genotype *MM* produces antigen M only, genotype *NN* produces antigen N only, and the heterozygous genotype *MN* produces both antigens). This allows population geneticists to directly observe all three possible genotype frequencies and compare them with calculated frequencies. The following data are typical of the MN blood group in people in the United States:

Genotype	Observed
MM	320
MN	480
NN	200
Total	1000

Because 1000 diploid individuals are in the sample, there are a total of 2000 alleles. The frequency of *M* alleles in the population $= p = (2 \times 320 + 480) \div 2000 = 0.56$. The frequency of *N* alleles in the population $= q = (2 \times 200 + 480) \div 2000 = 0.44$. As a quick check, the sum of the frequencies should equal 1. Does it?

If this population is in genetic equilibrium, then the expected *MM* genotype frequency $= p^2 = (0.56)^2 = 0.31$. The expected *MN* genotype frequency $= 2pq = 2 \times 0.56 \times 0.44 = 0.49$. The expected *NN* genotype frequency $= q^2 = (0.44)^2 = 0.19$. As a quick check, the sum of the three genotype frequencies should equal 1. Does it? You can use the calculated genotype frequencies to determine how many individuals in a population of 1000 should have the expected genotype frequencies. By comparing the expected numbers with the actual results observed, you see how closely the population is to genetic equilibrium. Simply multiply each genotype frequency by 1000:

Genotype	Observed	Expected
MM	320	313.6
MN	480	492.8
NN	200	193.6
Total	1000	1000.0

The expected numbers closely match the observed numbers, indicating that the *MN* blood groups in the human population are almost at genetic equilibrium. This is not surprising because the lack of medical significance suggests that the *MN* characteristic is not subject to natural selection and that it does not produce a visible phenotype that might affect random mating.

Review

- In a population at genetic equilibrium, the frequency of the homozygous recessive genotype (*tt*) is 0.16. What are the allele frequencies of *T* and *t,* and what are the expected frequencies of the *TT* and *Tt* genotypes?

- In a population at genetic equilibrium, the frequency of the dominant phenotype is 0.96. What are the frequencies of the dominant (*A*) and recessive (*a*) alleles, and what are the expected frequencies of the *AA, Aa,* and *aa* genotypes?

- The genotype frequencies of a population are determined to be 0.6 *BB,* 0.0 *Bb,* and 0.4 *bb.* Is it likely that this population meets all the conditions required for genetic equilibrium?

19.3 MICROEVOLUTION

LEARNING OBJECTIVES

5   Define *microevolution*.

6   Discuss how each of the following microevolutionary forces alters allele frequencies in populations: nonrandom mating, mutation, genetic drift, gene flow, and natural selection.

7   Distinguish among stabilizing selection, directional selection, and disruptive selection.

Evolution represents a departure from the Hardy–Weinberg principle of genetic equilibrium. The degree of departure between the observed allele or genotype frequencies and those expected by the Hardy–Weinberg principle indicates the amount of evolutionary change. This type of evolution—generation-to-generation changes in allele or genotype frequencies *within* a population—is sometimes referred to as **microevolution** because it often involves relatively small or minor changes, usually over a few generations.

Changes in the allele frequencies of a population result from five microevolutionary processes: nonrandom mating, mutation, genetic drift, gene flow, and natural selection. These microevolutionary processes are the opposite of the conditions that must be met if a population is in genetic equilibrium. When one or more of these processes acts on a population, allele or genotype frequencies change from one generation to the next.

Nonrandom mating changes genotype frequencies

When individuals select mates on the basis of phenotype (thereby selecting the corresponding genotype), they bring about evolutionary change in the population. Two examples of nonrandom mating are inbreeding and assortative mating.

In many populations, individuals mate more often with close neighbors than with more distant members of the population. As a result, neighbors tend to be more closely related—that is, genetically similar—to one another. The mating of genetically similar individuals who are more closely related than if they had been chosen at random from the entire population is known as **inbreeding.** Although inbreeding does not change the overall allele frequency, the frequency of homozygous genotypes increases with each successive generation of inbreeding. The most extreme example of inbreeding is self-fertilization, which is particularly common in certain plants.

Inbreeding does not appear to be detrimental in some populations, but in others it causes **inbreeding depression,** in which inbred individuals have lower fitness than those not inbred. **Fitness** is usually measured as the average number of surviving offspring of one genotype compared to the average number of surviving offspring of competing genotypes. Inbreeding depression, as evidenced by fertility declines and high juvenile mortality, is thought to be caused by the expression of harmful recessive alleles as homozygosity increases with inbreeding.

Several studies in the 1990s provided direct evidence of the deleterious consequences of inbreeding in nature. For example,

white-footed mice (*Peromyscus leucopus*) were taken from a field and used to develop both inbred and non-inbred populations in the laboratory. When these laboratory-bred populations were returned to nature, their survivorship was estimated from release–recapture data. The non-inbred mice had a statistically significant higher rate of survival (**FIG. 19-2**). It is not known why the inbred mice had a lower survival rate. Some possibilities include higher disease susceptibility, poorer ability to evade predators, less ability to find food, and less ability to win fights with other white-footed mice.

Assortative mating, in which individuals select mates by their phenotypes, is another example of nonrandom mating. For example, biologists selected two phenotypes—high bristle number and low bristle number—in a fruit fly (*Drosophila melanogaster*) population. Although the researchers made no effort to control mating, they observed that the flies preferentially mated with those of similar phenotypes. Females with high bristle number tended to mate with males with high bristle number, and females with low bristle number tended to mate with males with low bristle number. Such

KEY EXPERIMENT

QUESTION: Does inbreeding affect survival?

HYPOTHESIS: Non-inbred white-footed mice (*Peromyscus leucopus*) will have a survival advantage over inbred mice in a natural environment.

EXPERIMENT: Field-captured mice were used to establish inbred and non-inbred laboratory populations. The mice were marked and then released back into the field population. The population was then sampled by capturing mice, noting the number of inbred and non-inbred mice, and re-releasing the mice. The *x*-axis represents the 10-week period during which the samples were collected. Values on the *y*-axis are the estimated proportion of mice that survived from one week to the next. For example, the value of 0.2 in week 3 for the inbred mice means that 20% of the inbred mice that were alive at the beginning of the week survived through that week.

RESULTS AND CONCLUSION: Non-inbred mice (*red*) had a consistently higher survival rate than inbred mice (*blue*). Thus, inbreeding had a negative effect on survival in this species in nature.

Adapted with permission from Jiménez, J. A., et al., "An Experimental Study of Inbreeding Depression in a Natural Habitat," *Science*, Vol. 266, Oct. 14, 1994. Copyright © 1994 American Association for the Advancement of Science.

FIGURE 19-2 Survival of inbred and non-inbred mice

selection of mates with the same phenotype is known as *positive assortative mating* (as opposed to the less common phenomenon, *negative assortative mating,* in which mates with opposite phenotypes are selected).

Positive assortative mating is practiced in many human societies, in which men and women tend to marry individuals like themselves in such characteristics as height or intelligence. Like inbreeding, assortative mating usually increases homozygosity at the expense of heterozygosity in the population and does not change the overall allele frequencies in the population. However, assortative mating changes genotype frequencies only at the loci involved in mate choice, whereas inbreeding affects genotype frequencies in the entire genome.

Mutation increases variation within a population

Variation is introduced into a population through **mutation,** which is an unpredictable change in deoxyribonucleic acid (DNA). As discussed in Chapter 13, mutations, which are the source of all new alleles, result from (1) a change in the nucleotide base pairs of a gene, (2) a rearrangement of genes within chromosomes so that their interactions produce different effects, or (3) a change in chromosome structure. Mutations occur unpredictably and spontaneously. A particular locus may have a DNA sequence that causes certain types of mutations to occur more frequently than others. The rate of mutation appears relatively constant for a particular locus but may vary by several orders of magnitude among genes within a single species and among different species.

Not all mutations pass from one generation to the next. Those occurring in somatic (body) cells are not inherited. When an individual with such a mutation dies, the mutation is lost. Some mutations, however, occur in reproductive cells. These mutations may or may not overtly affect the offspring because most of the DNA in a cell is "silent" and does not code for specific polypeptides or proteins that are responsible for physical characteristics. Even if a mutation occurs in the DNA that codes for a polypeptide, it may still have little effect on the structure or function of that polypeptide (we discuss such *neutral variation* later in the chapter). However, when a polypeptide is sufficiently altered to change its function, the mutation is usually harmful. By acting against seriously abnormal phenotypes, natural selection eliminates or reduces to low frequencies the most harmful mutations. Mutations with small phenotypic effects, even if slightly harmful, have a better chance of being incorporated into the population, where at some later time, under different environmental conditions, they may produce phenotypes that are useful or adaptive.

The "needs" of a population do not determine what mutations will occur. Consider a population living in an increasingly dry environment. A mutation producing a new allele that helps an individual adapt to dry conditions is no more likely to occur than one for adapting to wet conditions or one with no relationship to the changing environment. The production of new mutations simply increases the genetic variability that is acted on by natural selection and, therefore, increases the potential for new adaptations.

Mutation by itself causes small deviations in allele frequencies from those predicted by the Hardy–Weinberg principle. Although allele frequencies may be changed by mutation, these changes are typically several orders of magnitude smaller than changes caused by other evolutionary forces, such as genetic drift. Mutation is usually negligible as an evolutionary force, but it is essential to the evolutionary process because it is the ultimate source of genetic variation.

In genetic drift, random events change allele frequencies

The size of a population has important effects on allele frequencies because random events, or chance, tend to cause changes of relatively greater magnitude in a small population. If a population consists of only a few individuals, an allele present at a low frequency in the population could be completely lost by chance. Such an event would be unlikely in a large population. For example, consider two populations, one with 10,000 individuals and one with 10 individuals. If an uncommon allele occurs at a frequency of 10%, or 0.1, in both populations, then 1900 individuals in the large population have the allele.[2] That same frequency, 0.1, in the smaller population means that only about 2 individuals have the allele.[3] From this exercise, it is easy to see that there is a greater likelihood of losing the rare allele from the smaller population than from the larger one. Predators, for example, might happen to kill one or two individuals possessing the uncommon allele in the smaller population purely by chance, so these individuals would leave no offspring.

The production of random evolutionary changes in small breeding populations is known as **genetic drift.** Genetic drift results in changes in allele frequencies in a population from one generation to another. One allele may be eliminated from the population purely by chance, regardless of whether that allele is beneficial, harmful, or of no particular advantage or disadvantage. Thus, genetic drift decreases genetic variation *within* a population, although it tends to increase genetic differences *among* different populations.

When bottlenecks occur, genetic drift becomes a major evolutionary force

Because of fluctuations in the environment, such as depletion in food supply or an outbreak of disease, a population may rapidly and markedly decrease from time to time. The population is said to go through a bottleneck during which genetic drift can occur in the small population of survivors. As the population again increases in size, many allele frequencies may be quite different from those in the population preceding the decline.

Scientists hypothesize that genetic variation in the cheetah was considerably reduced by a bottleneck at the end of the last Ice Age, some 10,000 years ago (see Fig. 52-9). Cheetahs nearly became extinct, perhaps from overhunting by humans. The few surviving cheetahs had greatly reduced genetic variability, and as a result, the cheetah population today is so genetically uniform that unrelated cheetahs can accept skin grafts from one another. (Normally, only identical twins accept skin grafts so readily.)

---

[2] $2pq + q^2 = 2(0.9)(0.1) + (0.1)^2 = 0.18 + 0.01 = 0.19; 0.19 \times 10,000 = 1900$

[3] $0.19 \times 10 = 1.9$

The founder effect occurs when a few "founders" establish a new colony

When one or a few individuals from a large population establish, or found, a colony (as when a few birds separate from the rest of the flock and fly to a new area), they bring with them only a small fraction of the genetic variation present in the original population. As a result, the only alleles among their descendants will be those of the colonizers. Typically, the allele frequencies in the newly founded population are quite different from those of the parent population. The genetic drift that results when a small number of individuals from a large population found a new colony is called the **founder effect.**

The Finnish people may illustrate the founder effect (**FIG. 19-3**). Geneticists who sampled DNA from Finns and from the European population at large found that Finns exhibit considerably less genetic variation than other Europeans. This evidence supports the hypothesis that Finns are descended from a small group of people who settled about 4000 years ago in the area that is now Finland and, because of the geography, remained separate from other European societies for centuries. The subpopulation in eastern Finland is especially homogeneous because it existed in relative isolation after being established by only several hundred founders in the 1500s.

The founder effect and population bottlenecks have also apparently affected the genetic composition of the population of Iceland. Iceland's 275,000 citizens are descended from a small group of Norse and Celtic people who settled that island in the ninth century. Isolation and population bottlenecks due to disease and natural disasters have contributed to the relative genetic homogeneity of the Icelandic people.

The founder effect can be of medical importance. For example, by chance one of the approximately 200 founders of the Amish population of Pennsylvania carried a recessive allele that, when homozygous, is responsible for a form of dwarfism, Ellis–van Creveld syndrome. Although this allele is rare in the general population (frequency about 0.001), today it is relatively common in the Amish population (frequency about 0.07).

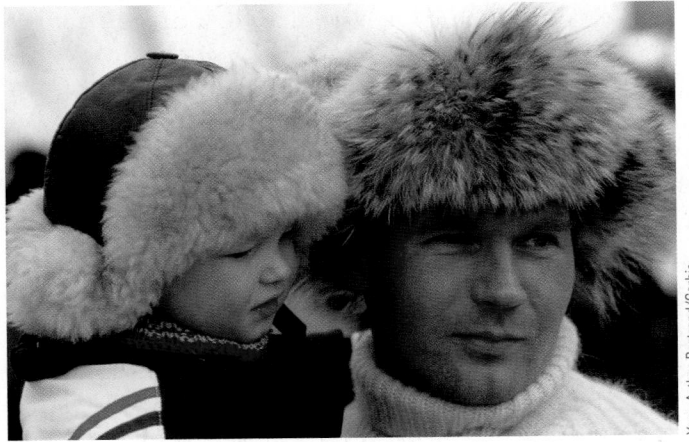

FIGURE 19-3 Finns and the founder effect
The Finnish people are thought to have descended from a small founding population that remained separate from the rest of Europe for centuries.

The Finnish and Icelandic populations, as well as certain Amish populations, are being studied by researchers in the quest to identify genetic contributions to a large number of diseases. The task is simplified in these studies because confounding factors such as variability in the rest of the genome and differences in such environmental factors as nutrition, access to medical care, and exposure to pollutants are relatively controlled.

Gene flow generally increases variation within a population

Individuals of a species tend to be distributed in local populations that are genetically isolated to some degree from other populations. For example, the bullfrogs of one pond form a population separated from those in an adjacent pond. Some exchanges occur by migration between ponds, but the frogs in one pond are much more likely to mate with those in the same pond. Because each population is isolated to some extent from other populations, each has distinct genetic traits and gene pools.

The migration of breeding individuals between populations causes a corresponding movement of alleles, or **gene flow,** that has significant evolutionary consequences. As alleles flow from one population to another, they usually increase the amount of genetic variability within the recipient population. If sufficient gene flow occurs between two populations, they become more similar genetically. Because gene flow reduces the amount of variation between two populations, it tends to counteract the effects of natural selection and genetic drift, both of which often cause populations to become increasingly distinct.

If migration by members of a population is considerable and if populations differ in their allele frequencies, then significant genetic changes occur in local populations. For example, by 10,000 years ago modern humans occupied almost all of Earth's major land areas except a few islands. Because the population density was low in most locations, the small, isolated human populations underwent random genetic drift and natural selection. More recently (during the past 300 years or so), major migrations have increased gene flow, significantly altering allele frequencies within previously isolated human populations.

Natural selection changes allele frequencies in a way that increases adaptation

Natural selection is the mechanism of evolution first proposed by Darwin in which members of a population that are more successfully adapted to the environment have greater fitness—that is, they are more likely to survive and reproduce (see Chapter 18). Over successive generations, the proportion of favorable alleles increases in the population. In contrast with other microevolutionary processes (nonrandom mating, mutation, genetic drift, and gene flow), natural selection leads to adaptive evolutionary change. Natural selection not only explains why organisms are well adapted to the environments in which they live but also helps account for the remarkable diversity of life. Natural selection enables populations to change, thereby adapting to different environments and different ways of life.

Natural selection results in the differential reproduction of individuals with different traits, or phenotypes (and therefore different genotypes), in response to the environment. Natural selection preserves individuals with favorable phenotypes and eliminates those with unfavorable phenotypes. Individuals that survive and produce fertile offspring have a selective advantage.

The mechanism of natural selection does not develop a "perfect" organism. Rather, it weeds out those individuals whose phenotypes are less adapted to environmental challenges, while allowing better-adapted individuals to survive and pass their alleles to their offspring. By reducing the frequency of alleles that result in the expression of less favorable traits, the probability is increased that favorable alleles responsible for an adaptation will come together in the offspring.

Natural selection operates on an organism's phenotype

Natural selection does not act directly on an organism's genotype. Instead, it acts on the phenotype, which is, at least in part, an expression of the genotype. The phenotype represents an interaction between the environment and all the alleles in the organism's genotype. It is rare that alleles of a single locus determine the phenotype, as Mendel originally observed in garden peas. Much more common is the interaction of alleles of several loci for the expression of a single phenotype. Many plant and animal characteristics are under this type of *polygenic* control (see Chapter 11).

When characters are under polygenic control (as is human height), a range of phenotypes occurs, with most of the population located in the median range and fewer at either extreme. This

is a normal distribution or standard bell curve (**FIG. 19-4a**; see also Fig. 11-20). Three kinds of selection cause changes in the normal distribution of phenotypes in a population: stabilizing, directional, and disruptive selection. Although we consider each process separately, in nature their influences generally overlap.

Stabilizing Selection The process of natural selection associated with a population well adapted to its environment is known as **stabilizing selection.** Most populations are probably influenced by stabilizing forces most of the time. Stabilizing selection selects against phenotypic extremes. In other words, individuals with average, or intermediate, phenotypes are favored.

Because stabilizing selection tends to decrease variation by favoring individuals near the mean of the normal distribution at the expense of those at either extreme, the bell curve narrows (**FIG. 19-4b**). Although stabilizing selection decreases the amount of variation in a population, variation is rarely eliminated by this process because other microevolutionary processes act against a decrease in variation. For example, mutation is slowly but continually adding to the genetic variation within a population.

One of the most widely studied cases of stabilizing selection involves human birth weight, which is under polygenic control and is also influenced by environmental factors. Extensive data from hospitals have shown that infants born with intermediate weights are most likely to survive (**FIG. 19-5**). Infants at either extreme (too small or too large) have higher rates of mortality. When newborn infants are too small, their body systems are immature, and when they are too large, they have difficult deliveries because they cannot pass as easily through the cervix and vagina. Stabilizing selec-

---

KEY POINT   Stabilizing, directional, and disruptive selection can change the distribution of phenotypes in a population.

No selection	Stabilizing selection	Directional selection	Disruptive selection
			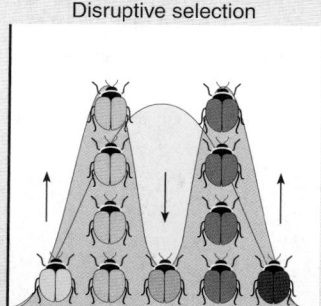

(a) A character that is under polygenic control (in this example, wing colors in a hypothetical population of beetles) exhibits a normal distribution of phenotypes in the absence of selection.

(b) As a result of stabilizing selection, which trims off extreme phenotypes, variation about the mean is reduced.

(c) Directional selection shifts the curve in one direction, changing the average value of the character.

(d) Disruptive selection, which trims off intermediate phenotypes, results in two or more peaks.

FIGURE 19-4 *Animated* **Modes of selection**

The blue screen represents the distribution of individuals by phenotype (in this example, color variation) in the original population. The purple screen represents the distribution by phenotype in the evolved population. The arrows represent the pressure of natural selection on the phenotypes.

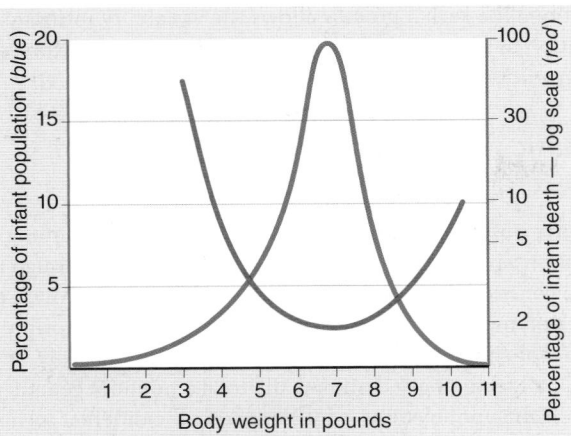

FIGURE 19-5 Stabilizing selection
The blue curve shows the distribution of birth weights in a sample of 13,730 infants. The red curve shows mortality (death) at each birth weight. Infants with very low or very high birth weights have higher death rates than infants of average weight. The optimum birth weight, that is, the one with the lowest mortality, is close to the average birth weight (about 7 lb). (Adapted from Cavalli-Sforza, L. L., and W. F. Bodmer, *The Genetics of Human Populations*, W. H. Freeman and Company, San Francisco, 1971.)

tion operates to reduce variability in birth weight so it is close to the weight with the minimum mortality rate.

Directional Selection If an environment changes over time, **directional selection** may favor phenotypes at one of the extremes of the normal distribution (**FIG. 19-4c**). Over successive generations, one phenotype gradually replaces another. So, for example, if greater size is advantageous in a new environment, larger individuals will become increasingly common in the population. However, directional selection occurs only if alleles favored under the new circumstances are already present in the population.

Darwin's Galápagos finches provide an excellent example of directional selection. Since 1973, Peter Grant and Rosemary Grant of Princeton University have studied the Galápagos finches. The Grants did a meticulous analysis of finch eating habits and beak sizes on Isla Daphne Major during three extended droughts (1977–1978, 1980, and 1982), one of which was followed by an extremely wet El Niño event (1983). During the droughts, the number of insects and small seeds declined, and large, heavy seeds became the finches' primary food source.

Many finches died during this time, and most of the survivors were larger birds whose beaks were larger and deeper. In a few generations, these larger birds became more common in the population (**TABLE 19-1**). After the El Niño event, however, smaller seeds became the primary food source, and smaller finches with average-sized beaks were favored. In this example, natural selection is directional: during the drought, natural selection operated in favor of the larger phenotype; whereas after the wet period, selection occurred in the opposite direction, favoring the smaller phenotype. The guppy populations studied in Venezuela and Trinidad (see Chapter 18) are another example of directional selection.

Directional selection by hunters has been observed in bighorn sheep (*Ovis canadensis*) in Canada. Sport hunters target large rams with rapidly growing horns for their trophy value (**FIG. 19-6**).

Character	Average before Drought (634)*	Average after Drought (135)*	Difference
Weight (g)	16.06	17.13	+1.07
Wing length (mm)	67.88	68.87	+0.99
Tarsus (leg, just above the foot) length (mm)	19.08	19.29	+0.21
Bill length (mm)	10.63	10.95	+0.32
Bill depth (mm)	9.21	9.70	+0.49
Bill width (mm)	8.58	8.83	+0.25

TABLE 19-1 Population Changes in *Geospiza fortis* before and after the 1976–1977 Drought

From P. R. Grant and B. R. Grant, "Predicting Microevolutionary Responses to Directional Selection on Heritable Variation," *Evolution*, Vol. 49, 1995.

*Number of birds in sample.

FIGURE 19-6 Bighorn sheep
This ram exhibits the massive horns that characterize this species.

Because these rams are typically killed prior to reaching their full reproductive potential, they contribute less to the gene pool; the result has been a 25% decline in average ram weight and horn length over a period of 30 years. Paradoxically, the rams that would normally have the greatest fitness because of their size and ability to use their horns in competition with other males for mates become less fit when these attributes cause them to be singled out by hunters.

Disruptive Selection Sometimes extreme changes in the environment may favor two or more different phenotypes at the expense of the mean. That is, more than one phenotype may be favored in the new environment. **Disruptive selection** is a special type of directional selection in which there is a trend in several directions rather than just one (**FIG. 19-4d**). It results in a divergence, or splitting apart, of distinct groups of individuals within a population. Disruptive selection, which is relatively rare, selects against the average, or intermediate, phenotype.

Limited food supply during a severe drought caused a population of finches on another island in the Galápagos to experience disruptive selection. The finch population initially exhibited a variety of beak sizes and shapes. Because the only foods available on this island during the drought were wood-boring insects and seeds from cactus fruits, natural selection favored birds with beaks suitable for obtaining these types of food. Finches with longer beaks survived because they could open cactus fruits, and those with wider beaks survived because they could strip off tree bark to expose insects. However, finches with intermediate beaks could not use either food source efficiently and had a lower survival rate.

Natural selection induces change in the types and frequencies of alleles in populations only if there is pre-existing inherited variation. Genetic variation is the raw material for evolutionary change because it provides the diversity on which natural selection acts. Without genetic variation, evolution cannot occur. In the next section we explore the genetic basis for variation that is acted on by natural selection.

Review

- Which microevolutionary force leads to adaptive changes in allele frequencies?
- Why is mutation important to evolution if it is the microevolutionary force that generally has the smallest effect on allele frequencies?
- Which microevolutionary forces are most associated with an increase in variation within a population? among populations?
- Which microevolutionary force typically changes genotype frequencies without changing allele frequencies? Explain.

19.4 GENETIC VARIATION IN POPULATIONS

◼ LEARNING OBJECTIVE

8 Describe the nature and extent of genetic variation, including genetic polymorphism, balanced polymorphism, neutral variation, and geographic variation.

Populations contain abundant genetic variation that was originally introduced by mutation. Sexual reproduction, with its associated crossing-over, independent assortment of chromosomes during meiosis, and random union of gametes, also contributes to genetic variation. The sexual process allows the variability introduced by mutation to be combined in new ways, which may be expressed as new phenotypes.

Genetic polymorphism can be studied in several ways

Genetic polymorphism, which is genetic variation among individuals in a population, is extensive in populations, although many of the genetic variants are present at low frequencies. Much of genetic polymorphism is not evident because it does not produce distinct phenotypes.

One way biologists estimate the total amount of genetic polymorphism in populations is by comparing the different forms of a particular protein. Each form consists of a slightly different amino acid sequence that is coded for by a different allele. For example, tissue extracts containing a particular enzyme may be analyzed for different individuals by gel electrophoresis. In *gel electrophoresis,* the enzymes are placed in slots on an agarose gel and an electric current is applied, causing each enzyme to migrate across the gel (see Fig. 15-8). Slight variations in amino acid sequences in the different forms of a particular enzyme cause each to migrate at a different rate, which can be detected using special stains or radioactive labels. Depending on the species studied, the percentage of enzymes that are polymorphic can range from about 15% to as much as 70%. In general, polymorphism of enzyme-coding loci tends to be greater in plants than in animals.

Determining the sequence of nucleotides in DNA from individuals in a population provides a *direct* estimate of genetic polymorphism that is sensitive enough to detect alleles that differ by only one nucleotide (**single nucleotide polymorphisms, SNPs**). (DNA sequencing is shown in Figures 15-10 and 15-11.) DNA sequencing of specific alleles in an increasing number of organisms, including humans, indicates that SNPs are common in most populations.

Recent studies have revealed that genetic changes in which segments of DNA have been gained or lost (compared to a reference genome) are common in model organisms such as mice and *Drosophila,* as well as humans. These **copy number variations,** or **CNVs,** can involve DNA segments that range from as few as 500 to 1000 base pairs up to about two million base pairs. It is currently estimated that the average human may have a dozen or more CNVs in their genome. In most cases, there does not appear to be an associated phenotype, or the phenotype is benign, such as an effect on eye color. However, as more sophisticated technologies have been developed to support ongoing research, evidence is accumulating that links specific CNVs to increased risk for certain medically important conditions, such as autism, Alzheimer's disease, and susceptibility to HIV infection.

Balanced polymorphism exists for long periods

Balanced polymorphism is a special type of genetic polymorphism in which two or more alleles persist in a population over many generations as a result of natural selection. Heterozygote advantage and frequency-dependent selection are mechanisms that preserve balanced polymorphism.

Genetic variation may be maintained by heterozygote advantage

We have seen that natural selection often eliminates unfavorable alleles from a population, whereas favorable alleles are retained. However, natural selection sometimes helps maintain genetic diversity. In some cases natural selection may even maintain a population's alleles that are unfavorable in the homozygous state. This happens, for example, when the heterozygote *Aa* has a higher degree of fitness than either homozygote *AA* or *aa*. This phenomenon, known as **heterozygote advantage,** is demonstrated in humans by the selective advantage of heterozygous carriers of the sickle cell allele.

The mutant allele (Hb^S) for sickle cell anemia produces an altered hemoglobin that deforms or sickles the red blood cells, making them more likely to form dangerous blockages in capillaries and to be destroyed in the liver, spleen, or bone marrow (discussed in Chapter 16). People who are homozygous for the sickle cell allele ($Hb^S Hb^S$) usually die at an early age if medical treatment is not available.

Heterozygous individuals carry alleles for both normal (Hb^A) and sickle cell hemoglobin. The heterozygous condition ($Hb^A Hb^S$) makes a person more resistant to a type of severe malaria (caused by the parasite *Plasmodium falciparum*) than people who are homozygous for the normal hemoglobin allele ($Hb^A Hb^A$). In a heterozygous individual, each allele produces its own specific kind of hemoglobin, and the red blood cells contain the two kinds in roughly equivalent amounts. Such cells sickle much less readily than cells containing only the Hb^S allele. They are more resistant to infection by the malaria-causing parasite, which lives in red blood cells, than are the red blood cells containing only normal hemoglobin.

Where malaria is a problem, each of the two types of homozygous individuals is at a disadvantage. Those homozygous for the sickle cell allele are likely to die of sickle cell anemia, whereas those homozygous for the normal allele may die of malaria. The heterozygote is therefore more fit than either homozygote. In parts of Africa, the Middle East, and southern Asia where falciparum malaria is prevalent, heterozygous individuals survive in greater numbers than either homozygote (**FIG. 19-7**). The Hb^S allele is maintained at a high frequency in the population, even though the homozygous recessive condition is almost always lethal.

What happens to the frequency of Hb^S alleles in Africans and others who possess it when they migrate to the United States and other countries with few cases of malaria? As might be expected, the frequency of the Hb^S allele gradually declines in such populations, possibly because it confers a selective disadvantage by causing sickle cell anemia in homozygous individuals but no longer confers a selective advantage by preventing malaria in heterozygous individuals. The Hb^S allele never disappears from the population, however, because it is "hidden" from selection in heterozygous individuals and because it is reintroduced into the population by gene flow from the African population.

Genetic variation may be maintained by frequency-dependent selection

Thus far in our discussion of natural selection, we have assumed that the fitness of particular phenotypes (and their corresponding genotypes) is independent of their frequency in the population. However, in cases of **frequency-dependent selection,** the fitness of a particular phenotype depends on how frequently it appears in the population. Often a phenotype has a greater selective value when rare than when common in the population. Such phenotypes lose their selective advantage as they become more common.

Frequency-dependent selection often acts to maintain genetic variation in populations of prey species. In this case, the predator catches and consumes the more common phenotype but may ignore the rarer phenotypes. Consequently, the less common phenotype produces more offspring and therefore makes a greater relative contribution to the next generation.

Frequency-dependent selection is demonstrated in scale-eating fish (cichlids of the species *Perissodus microlepis*) from Lake

(a) The geographic distribution of falciparum malaria (*green*).

(b) The distribution of the sickle cell anemia allele (*red and orange*).

Frequency of Hb^S allele
- 1–10%
- 10–20%

FIGURE 19-7 Heterozygote advantage

Over large geographic areas, the distribution of individuals heterozygous for the sickle cell (Hb^s) allele is similar to the distribution of falciparum malaria. This evidence for greater fitness of heterozygous individuals in malarial regions supports the hypothesis of heterozygote advantage. (Adapted from Allison, A. C., "Protection Afforded by Sickle-Cell Traits against Subtertian Malarial Infection," *British Medical Journal*, Vol. 1, 1954.)

Tanganyika in Africa (**FIG. 19-8**). The scale-eating fish, which obtain food by biting scales off other fish, have either left-pointing or right-pointing mouths. A single locus with two alleles determines this characteristic; the allele for right-pointing mouth is dominant over the allele for left-pointing mouth. These fish attack their prey from behind and from a single direction, depending on mouth morphology. Those with left-pointing mouths always attack the right flanks of their prey, whereas those with right-pointing mouths always attack the left flanks.

The prey species are more successful at evading attacks from the more common form of scale-eating fish. For example, if the cichlids with right-pointing mouths are more common than those with left-pointing mouths, the prey are attacked more often on their left flanks. They therefore become more wary against such attacks, conferring a selective advantage to the less common cichlids with left-pointing mouths. The cichlids with left-pointing mouths would be more successful at obtaining food and would therefore have more offspring. Over time, the frequency of fish with left-pointing mouths would increase in the population, until their abundance causes frequency-dependent selection to work against them and confer an advantage on the now less common fish with right-pointing mouths. Thus, frequency-dependent selection maintains both populations of fish at approximately equal numbers.

Neutral variation may give no selective advantage or disadvantage

Some of the genetic variation observed in a population may confer no apparent selective advantage or disadvantage in a particular environment. For example, random changes in DNA that do not alter protein structure usually do not affect the phenotype. Variation that does not alter the ability of an individual to survive and reproduce and is, therefore, not adaptive is called **neutral variation.**

The extent of neutral variation in organisms is difficult to determine. It is relatively easy to demonstrate that an allele is beneficial or harmful if its effect is observable. But the variation in alleles that involves only slight differences in the proteins they code for may or may not be neutral. These alleles may be influencing the organism in subtle ways that are difficult to measure or assess. Also, an allele that is neutral in one environment may be beneficial or harmful in another.

Populations in different geographic areas often exhibit genetic adaptations to local environments

In addition to the genetic variation among individuals within a population, genetic differences often exist among different populations within the same species, a phenomenon known as **geographic variation.** One type of geographic variation is a **cline,** which is a gradual change in a species's phenotype and genotype frequencies through a series of geographically separate populations as a result of an environmental gradient. A cline exhibits variation in the expression of such attributes as color, size, shape, physiology, or behavior. Clines are common among species with continuous ranges over large geographic areas. For example, the body sizes of many widely distributed birds and mammals increase gradually as the latitude increases, presumably because larger animals are better able to withstand the colder temperatures of winter.

The common yarrow (*Achillea millefolium*), a wildflower that grows in a variety of North American habitats from lowlands to

---

KEY EXPERIMENT

QUESTION: Can evidence for frequency-dependent selection be found in natural populations?

HYPOTHESIS: Equal proportions of scale-eating cichlids with right-pointing mouths vs. left-pointing mouths in a population are maintained by frequency-dependent selection.

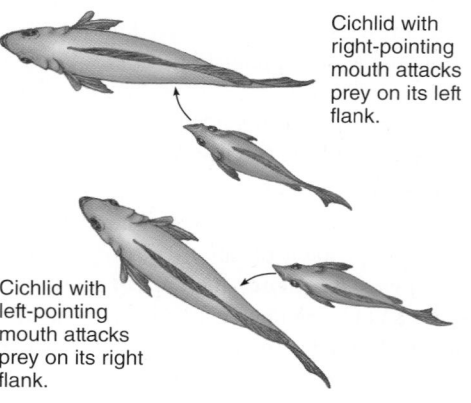

Cichlid with right-pointing mouth attacks prey on its left flank.

Cichlid with left-pointing mouth attacks prey on its right flank.

EXPERIMENT: The relative frequencies of scale-eating cichlids with left-pointing and right-pointing mouths in Lake Tanganyika in Africa were monitored over a 10-year period.

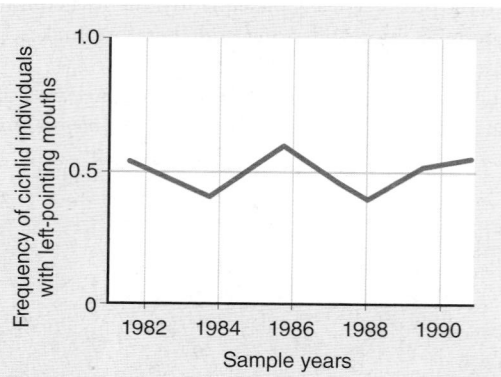

RESULTS AND CONCLUSION: Relative frequencies of left-pointing and right-pointing cichlids varied slightly from year to year, but remained close to 0.5. This approximate 1:1 ratio is consistent with frequency-dependent selection because prey fish become especially wary to attacks by the cichlid type that is currently most common; therefore either type is at a selective disadvantage if its frequency rises above 0.5.

FIGURE 19-8 Frequency-dependent selection in scale-eating cichlids

(Adapted with permission from Hori, M., "Frequency-Dependent Natural Selection in the Handedness of Scale-Eating Cichlid Fish," *Science*, Vol. 260, April 9, 1993. Copyright © 1993 American Association for the Advancement of Science.)

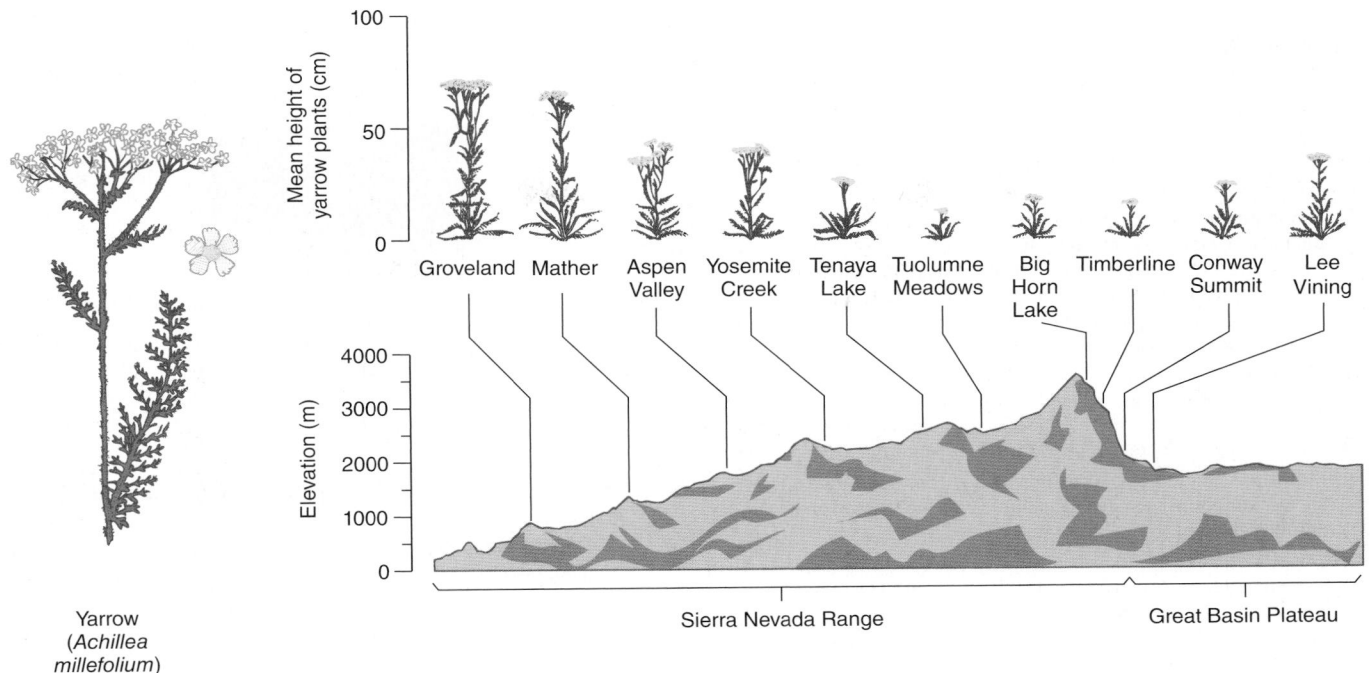

FIGURE 19-9 Clinal variation in yarrow (*Achillea millefolium*)
(After J. Clausen, D. D. Keck, and W. M. Hiesey, "Experimental Studies on the Nature of Species: III. Environmental Responses of Climatic Races of *Achillea*," Carnegie Institute Washington Publication, Vol. 58, 1948.)

mountain highlands, exhibits clinal variation in height in response to different climates at different elevations. Although substantial variation exists among individuals within each population, individuals in populations at higher elevations are, on average, shorter than those at lower elevations. The genetic basis of these clinal differences was experimentally demonstrated in a set of classical experiments in which series of populations from different geographic areas were grown in the same environment (**FIG. 19-9**). Despite being exposed to identical environmental conditions, each experimental population exhibited the traits characteristic of the elevation from which it was collected.

Review

- How does the sickle cell allele illustrate heterozygote advantage?
- How does frequency-dependent selection affect genetic variation within a population over time?
- How can researchers test the hypothesis that clinal variation among populations of a particular species has a genetic basis?

■ SUMMARY: FOCUS ON LEARNING OBJECTIVES

19.1 *(page 412)*

1 Define what is meant by a population's gene pool.

- All the individuals that live in a particular place at the same time make up a **population.** Each population has a **gene pool,** which includes all the **alleles** for all the **loci** present in the population.
- **Population genetics** is the study of genetic variability within a population and of the forces that act on it.

2 Distinguish among genotype, phenotype, and allele frequencies.

- A **genotype frequency** is the proportion of a particular genotype in the population. A **phenotype frequency** is the proportion of a particular phenotype in the population. An **allele frequency** is the proportion of a specific allele of a given genetic locus in the population.

19.2 *(page 412)*

3 Discuss the significance of the Hardy–Weinberg principle as it relates to evolution and list the five conditions required for genetic equilibrium.

- The **Hardy–Weinberg principle** states that allele and genotype frequencies do not change from generation to generation (no evolution is occurring) in a population at **genetic equilibrium.**
- The Hardy–Weinberg principle applies only if mating is random in the population, there are no net mutations that change the allele frequencies, the population is large, individuals do not migrate between populations, and natural selection does not occur.

4 Use the Hardy–Weinberg principle to solve problems involving populations.

- In the Hardy–Weinberg equation, p = the frequency of the dominant allele, q = the frequency of the recessive allele: $p + q = 1$.
- The genotype frequencies of a population are described by the relationship $p^2 + 2pq + q^2 = 1$, where p^2 is the frequency of the homozygous dominant genotype, $2pq$ is the frequency of the heterozygous genotype, and q^2 is the frequency of the homozygous recessive genotype.

CENGAGENOW™ Interact with the Hardy–Weinberg principle by clicking on the figure in CengageNOW.

5 Define *microevolution*.

■ **Microevolution** is a change in allele or genotype frequencies within a population over successive generations.

6 Discuss how each of the following microevolutionary forces alters allele frequencies in populations: nonrandom mating, mutation, genetic drift, gene flow, and natural selection.

■ In nonrandom mating, individuals select mates on the basis of phenotype, indirectly selecting the corresponding genotype(s). **Inbreeding** is the mating of genetically similar individuals that are more closely related than if they had been chosen at random from the entire population. Inbreeding in some populations causes **inbreeding depression,** in which inbred individuals have lower **fitness** (relative ability to make a genetic contribution to the next generation) than non-inbred individuals. In **assortative mating** individuals select mates by their phenotypes. Both inbreeding and assortative mating increase the frequency of homozygous genotypes.

■ **Mutations,** unpredictable changes in DNA, are the source of new alleles. Mutations increase the genetic variability acted on by natural selection.

■ **Genetic drift** is a random change in the allele frequencies of a small population. Genetic drift decreases genetic variation within a population, and the changes caused by genetic drift are usually not adaptive. A sudden decrease in population size caused by adverse environmental factors is known as a bottleneck. The **founder effect** is genetic drift that occurs when a small population colonizes a new area.

■ **Gene flow,** a movement of alleles caused by the migration of individuals between populations, causes changes in allele frequencies.

■ **Natural selection** causes changes in allele frequencies that lead to adaptation. Natural selection operates on an organism's phenotype, but it changes the genetic composition of a population in a favorable direction for a particular environment.

7 Distinguish among stabilizing selection, directional selection, and disruptive selection.

■ **Stabilizing selection** favors the mean at the expense of phenotypic extremes. **Directional selection** favors one phenotypic extreme over another, causing a shift in the phenotypic mean. **Disruptive selection** favors two or more phenotypic extremes.

Harry Engels, Photo Researchers, Inc.

CENGAGENOW™   Watch natural selection in action by clicking on the figure in CengageNOW.

8 Describe the nature and extent of genetic variation, including genetic polymorphism, balanced polymorphism, neutral variation, and geographic variation.

■ **Genetic polymorphism** is the presence of genetic variation within a population.

■ **Balanced polymorphism** is a special type of genetic polymorphism in which two or more alleles persist in a population over many generations as a result of natural selection.

■ **Heterozygote advantage** occurs when the heterozygote exhibits greater fitness than either homozygote. In **frequency-dependent selection,** a genotype's selective value varies with its frequency of occurrence.

■ **Neutral variation** is genetic variation that confers no detectable selective advantage.

■ **Geographic variation** is genetic variation that exists among different populations within the same species. A **cline** is a gradual change in a species's phenotype and genotype frequencies through a series of geographically separate populations.

TEST YOUR UNDERSTANDING

1. The genetic description of an individual is its genotype, whereas the genetic description of a population is its (a) phenotype (b) gene pool (c) genetic drift (d) founder effect (e) changes in allele frequencies

2. In a diploid species, each individual possesses (a) one allele for each locus (b) two alleles for each locus (c) three or more alleles for each locus (d) all the alleles found in the gene pool (e) half of the alleles found in the gene pool

3. The MN blood group is of interest to population geneticists because (a) people with genotype *MN* cannot receive blood transfusions from either *MM* or *NN* people (b) the *MM, MN,* and *NN* genotype frequencies can be observed directly and compared with calculated expected frequencies (c) the *M* allele is dominant to the *N* allele (d) people with the *MN* genotype exhibit frequency-dependent selection (e) people with the *MN* genotype exhibit heterozygote advantage

4. If all copies of a given locus have the same allele throughout the population, then the allele frequency is (a) 0 (b) 0.1 (c) 0.5 (d) 1.0 (e) 10.0

5. If a population's allele and genotype frequencies remain constant from generation to generation, (a) the population is undergoing evolutionary change (b) the population is said to be at genetic equilibrium (c) microevolution has taken place (d) directional selection is occurring, but only for a few generations (e) genetic drift is a significant evolutionary force

6. Analysis of DNA sequences for a particular locus among individuals within a population provides biologists with one way to estimate (a) genetic drift (b) genetic polymorphism (c) gene flow (d) heterozygote advantage (e) frequency-dependent selection

7. The continued presence of the allele that causes sickle cell anemia in areas where falciparum malaria is prevalent demonstrates which of the following phenomena? (a) inbreeding depression (b) frequency-dependent selection (c) heterozygote advantage (d) genetic drift (e) a genetic bottleneck

8. According to the Hardy–Weinberg principle, (a) allele frequencies are not dependent on dominance or recessiveness but remain essentially unchanged from generation to generation (b) the sum of allele frequencies for a given locus is always greater than 1 (c) if a

locus has only one allele, the frequency of that allele is zero (d) allele frequencies change from generation to generation (e) the process of inheritance, by itself, causes changes in allele frequencies

9. The Hardy–Weinberg principle may be applicable if (a) population size is small (b) migration occurs only at the beginning of the breeding season (c) mutations occur at a constant rate (d) matings occur exclusively between individuals of the same genotype (e) natural selection does not occur

10. Mutation (a) leads to adaptive evolutionary change (b) adds to the genetic variation of a population (c) is the result of genetic drift (d) almost always benefits the organism (e) a and b

11. Which of the following is *not* true of natural selection? (a) natural selection acts to preserve favorable traits and eliminate unfavorable traits (b) the offspring of individuals that are better adapted to the environment will make up a larger proportion of the next generation (c) natural selection directs the course of evolution

by preserving the traits acquired during an individual's lifetime (d) natural selection acts on a population's genetic variability, which arises through mutation (e) natural selection may result in changes in allele frequencies in a population

12. The distribution of phenotypes shown in the figure is most consistent with (a) no selection (b) stabilizing selection (c) directional selection (d) disruptive selection (e) genetic equilibrium

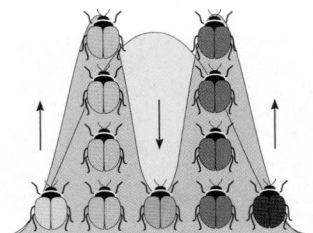

CRITICAL THINKING

1. **EVOLUTION LINK.** Why are mutations almost always neutral or harmful? If this is true, why are mutations nevertheless essential to evolution?

2. **EVOLUTION LINK.** Explain this apparent paradox: scientists discuss evolution in terms of *genotype* fitness (the selective advantage that a particular genotype confers on an individual), yet natural selection acts on an organism's *phenotype*.

3. **EVOLUTION LINK.** Why is it easier for researchers to study the genetic contribution to disease in the populations of Finland or Iceland, as opposed to those of the United States?

4. **EVOLUTION LINK.** Evolution is sometimes characterized as "survival of the fittest." Is this consistent with an evolutionary biologist's definitions of *fitness* and *natural selection*? Is this a good way to think about evolution, or a poor one?

5. **ANALYZING DATA.** Recall that the allele for right-pointing mouth in cichlids (*A*) is dominant over that for left-pointing mouth (*a*). Use the Hardy–Weinberg principle to calculate the allele frequencies that would correspond to equal frequencies of the two phenotypes. Which allele has the higher frequency? Why? How are these scale-eating fish an example of balanced polymorphism?

6. **ANALYZING DATA.** The recessive allele that causes Ellis–van Creveld syndrome when homozygous has a frequency of about 0.07 in the Amish population of Pennsylvania, although its fre-

quency is only about 0.001 in the general population. How many persons out of 1000 in the Amish population would be expected to have the disease? How many out of a million in the general population?

7. **ANALYZING DATA.** You study males in populations of a certain species of minnows in a series of lakes at different latitudes. You find that they exhibit clinal variation in average weight at maturity and hypothesize that the weight differences are due to genetic factors. You predict that the average weights at maturity of representatives of each population reared in aquaria will differ in ways that are consistent with the differences you observed among the wild populations. However, when you conduct the experiment, you find no differences among the population averages. What is your conclusion?

8. **SCIENCE, TECHNOLOGY, AND SOCIETY.** Automated techniques are being developed that will provide new information on the extent of genetic polymorphism among humans, particularly with respect to single nucleotide polymorphisms (SNPs) and copy number variations (CNVs). In what ways might this information prove useful? In what ways might it present challenges?

 Additional questions are available in CengageNOW at www.cengage.com/login.

20 Speciation and Macroevolution

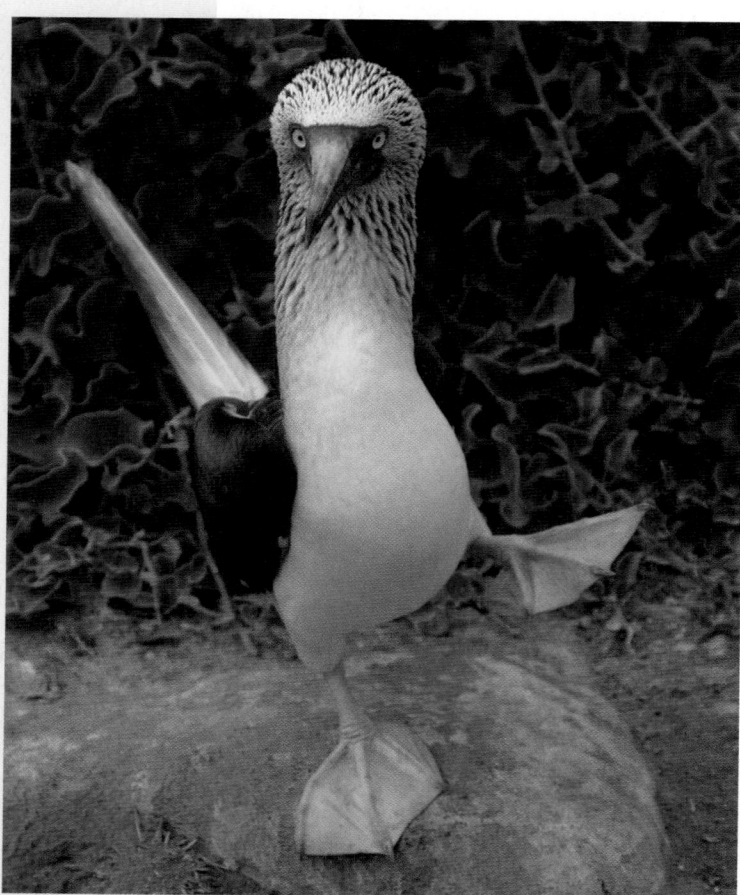

Blue-footed booby. Blue-footed boobies are large sea birds that nest on the Galápagos Islands and several other arid islands in the eastern Pacific Ocean. Male and female pairs are monogamous and typically nest on black lava. The largest blue-footed booby breeding population is found in the Galápagos Islands.

© iStockphoto.com/Mariko Yuki

KEY CONCEPTS

20.1 According to the biological species concept, a species consists of individuals that can successfully interbreed with one another but not with individuals from other species.

20.2 The evolution of different species begins with reproductive isolation, in which two populations are no longer able to interbreed successfully.

20.3 In allopatric speciation, populations diverge into different species due to geographic isolation, or physical separation. In sympatric speciation, populations become reproductively isolated from one another despite living in the same geographic area.

20.4 Speciation may require millions of years but sometimes occurs much more quickly.

20.5 The evolution of species and higher taxa is known as macroevolution.

A Brazilian rain forest contains thousands of species of insects, amphibians, reptiles, birds, and mammals. The Great Barrier Reef off the coast of Australia has thousands of species of sponges, corals, mollusks, crustaceans, sea stars, and fishes. The various environments on Earth abound in rich assemblages of species. Scientists have currently named about 1.8 million species.

We do not know exactly how many species exist today, but many biologists estimate the number to be on the order of 4 million to 100 million! Often this diversity has been portrayed as many twig tips on a "tree of life." As one follows the twigs from the tips toward the main body of the tree, they form connections that represent common ancestors that are now extinct. Indeed, more than 99.9% of all species that ever existed are now extinct. Tracing the branches of the tree of life to larger and larger connections eventually leads to a single trunk that represents the few simple unicellular organisms that evolved early in Earth's history and became the ancestors of all species living today.

Thus, life today is the product of 3 billion to 4 billion years of evolution. How did all these species diversify throughout Earth's history? Darwin's studies led him to conclude that the Galápagos Islands were the birthplace of many new species (see photograph). Our understanding of how species evolve has advanced significantly since Darwin published *On the Origin of Species*.

In this chapter we consider the reproductive barriers that isolate species from one another and the possible evolutionary mechanisms that explain how the millions of species that live today or lived in the past originated from ancestral species. We then examine the rate of evolutionary change and the evolution of higher taxonomic categories (species, genus, family, order, class, and phylum), which is the focus of macroevolution.

20.1 WHAT IS A SPECIES?

◼ LEARNING OBJECTIVE

1   Describe the biological species concept and list two potential problems with the concept.

The concept of distinct kinds of organisms, known as **species** (from Latin, meaning "kind"), is not new. However, there are several different definitions of species, and every definition has some sort of limitation. Linnaeus was the 18th-century biologist who founded modern taxonomy—the science of naming, describing, and classifying organisms. He classified plants and other organisms into separate species based on their visible structural differences, such as feathers or number of flower parts. This method, known as the *morphological species concept,* is still used to help characterize species, but structural differences alone are not adequate to explain what constitutes a species.

The biological species concept is based on reproductive isolation

Population genetics did much to clarify the concept of species. According to the **biological species concept,** first expressed by evolutionary biologist Ernst Mayr in 1942, a species consists of one or more populations whose members interbreed in nature to produce fertile offspring and do not interbreed with—that is, are reproductively isolated from—members of different species. Gene flow occurs between individuals of a given species when they mate, but reproductive barriers restrict individuals of one species from interbreeding, or exchanging genes, with members of other species. As a result, reproductive barriers keep a given species genetically distinct from other species. An extension of the biological species concept holds that new species evolve when formerly interbreeding populations become reproductively isolated from one another.

The biological species concept is currently the most widely accepted definition of species, but it has several shortcomings. One problem with the biological species concept is that it applies only to sexually reproducing organisms. Bacteria reproduce asexually,

Wim van Egmond/Visuals Unlimited, Inc.

150 μm

FIGURE 20-1 Bdelloid rotifer (*Philodina roseola*)

Bdelloid rotifers are all females. Because they do not reproduce sexually, it is difficult to classify these small marine animals as species under the biological species concept.

although they may have considerable exchange of genetic material by means of *horizontal gene transfer* among bacterial individuals that are classified as different species. Thus, reproductive isolation is not a good criterion for defining species of bacteria.

Small marine organisms known as bdelloid rotifers are an example of animals that reproduce asexually (**FIG. 20-1**). All bdelloid rotifers are females, and they produce offspring without needing males. These organisms and also extinct organisms must be classified based on their structural and biochemical characteristics; the biological species concept does not apply to them.

Another potential problem with the biological species concept is that although individuals assigned to different species do not normally interbreed, they may *sometimes* successfully interbreed. For example, where their ranges overlap, some coyotes have been known to mate with wolves. As a result, some wolves carry coyote genes and vice versa. Yet, most biologists agree that wolves and coyotes are separate species.

The phylogenetic species concept defines species based on such evidence as molecular sequencing

Some biologists prefer the **phylogenetic species concept**, also called the *evolutionary species concept,* in which a population is declared a separate species if it has undergone evolution long enough for statistically significant differences in diagnostic traits to emerge. If a population has a unique diagnostic trait—a set of spines running down the back, for example—that can be demonstrated to be inherited, then this population is considered a separate species. This approach has the advantage of being testable by comparing gene sequences between two groups. However, many biologists do not want to abandon the biological species concept, in part because the phylogenetic species concept cannot be applied if the evolutionary history (as determined by DNA sequencing) of a taxonomic group has not been carefully studied; most groups have not been rigorously analyzed. Also, if the phylogenetic species concept were universally embraced, the number of named species would probably double. This increase would occur because many closely related populations that are classified as **subspecies** (a taxonomic subdivision of a species) under the biological species concept would fit the requirements of separate species under the phylogenetic species concept.

Thus, the exact definition of a species remains fuzzy. Unless we clearly state otherwise, when we mention *species* in this text, we are referring to the biological species concept.

Review

- What is a species, according to the biological species concept? What are some of the limitations of this definition?

20.2 REPRODUCTIVE ISOLATION

■ LEARNING OBJECTIVE

2 Explain the significance of reproductive isolating mechanisms and distinguish among the various prezygotic and postzygotic barriers.

Various **reproductive isolating mechanisms** prevent interbreeding between two different species whose *ranges* (areas where each lives) overlap. These mechanisms preserve the genetic integrity of each species because gene flow between the two species is prevented.

Most species have two or more mechanisms that block a chance occurrence of individuals from two closely related species overcoming a single reproductive isolating mechanism. Although most mechanisms operate before mating or fertilization occurs (*prezygotic*), others work after fertilization has taken place (*postzygotic*).

Prezygotic barriers interfere with fertilization

Prezygotic barriers are reproductive isolating mechanisms that prevent fertilization from taking place. Because male and female gametes never come into contact, an *interspecific zygote*—that is, a fertilized egg formed by the union of an egg from one species and a sperm from another species—is never produced. Prezygotic barriers include temporal isolation, habitat isolation, behavioral isolation, mechanical isolation, and gametic isolation.

Sometimes genetic exchange between two groups is prevented because they reproduce at different times of the day, season, or year. Such examples demonstrate **temporal isolation.** For example, two very similar species of fruit flies, *Drosophila pseudoobscura* and *D. persimilis,* have ranges that overlap to a great extent, but they do not interbreed. *Drosophila pseudoobscura* is sexually active only in the afternoon; and *D. persimilis,* only in the morning. Similarly, two frog species have overlapping ranges in eastern Canada and the United States. The wood frog (*Rana sylvatica*) usually mates in late March or early April, when the water temperature is about 7.2°C (45°F), whereas the northern leopard frog (*R. pipiens*) usually mates in mid-April, when the water temperature is 12.8°C (55°F) (**FIG. 20-2**).

Although two closely related species may be found in the same geographic area, they usually live and breed in different habitats in that area. This provides **habitat isolation** between the two species. For example, the five species of small birds known as flycatchers are nearly identical in appearance and have overlapping ranges in the eastern part of North America. They exhibit habitat isolation because during the breeding season, each species stays in a particular habitat within its range, so potential mates from different species do not meet. The least flycatcher (*Empidonax minimus*)

(a) The wood frog (*Rana sylvatica*) mates in early spring, often before the ice has completely melted in the ponds.

(b) The leopard frog (*Rana pipiens*) typically mates a few weeks later.

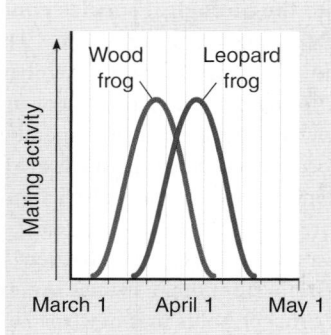

(c) Graph of peak mating activity in wood and leopard frogs. In nature, wood and leopard frogs do not interbreed.

FIGURE 20-2 *Animated* Temporal isolation in wood and leopard frogs

R. Brown/VIREO

FIGURE 20-3 Behavioral isolation in bowerbirds
Each bowerbird species has highly specialized courtship patterns that prevent its mating with another species. The male satin bowerbird (*Ptilonorhynchus violacens*) constructs an enclosed place, or bower, of twigs to attract a female. (The bower is the dark "tunnel" on the left.) Note the white flowers and blue decorations, including human-made objects such as bottle caps, that he has arranged at the entrance to his bower.

frequents open woods, farms, and orchards; whereas the acadian flycatcher (*E. virescens*) is found in deciduous forests, particularly in beech trees, and swampy woods. The alder flycatcher (*E. alnorum*) prefers wet thickets of alders, the yellow-bellied flycatcher (*E. flaviventris*) nests in conifer woods, and the willow flycatcher (*E. traillii*) frequents brushy pastures and willow thickets.

Many animal species exchange a distinctive series of signals before mating. Such courtship behaviors illustrate **behavioral isolation** (also known as **sexual isolation**). Bowerbirds, for example, exhibit species-specific courtship patterns. The male satin bowerbird of Australia constructs an elaborate bower of twigs, adding decorative blue parrot feathers and white flowers at the entrance (**FIG. 20-3**). When a female approaches the bower, the male dances around her, holding a particularly eye-catching decoration in his beak. While dancing, he puffs his feathers, extends his wings, and sings a courtship song that consists of a variety of sounds, including loud buzzes and hoots. These specific courtship behaviors keep closely related bird species reproductively isolated from the satin bowerbird. If a male and female of two different bowerbird species begin courtship, it stops when one member does not recognize or respond to the signals of the other.

Another example of behavioral isolation involves the wood frogs and northern leopard frogs just discussed as an example of temporal isolation. Males of these two species have very specific vocalizations to attract females of their species for breeding. These vocalizations reinforce each species's reproductive isolation.

Sometimes members of different species court and even attempt copulation, but the incompatible structures of their genital organs prevent successful mating. Structural differences that inhibit mating between species produce **mechanical isolation.** For example, many flowering plant species have physical differences in their flower parts that help them maintain their reproductive isolation from one another. In such plants, the flower parts are adapted for specific insect pollinators. Two species of sage, for example, have overlapping ranges in southern California. Black sage (*Salvia mellifera*), which is pollinated by small bees, has a floral structure different from that of white sage (*S. apiana*), which is pollinated by large carpenter bees (**FIG. 20-4**). Interestingly, black sage and white sage are also prevented from mating by a temporal barrier: black sage flowers in early spring, and white sage flowers in late spring and early summer. Presumably, mechanical isolation prevents insects from cross-pollinating the two species should they happen to flower at the same time.

If mating takes place between two species, their gametes may still not combine. Molecular and chemical differences between species cause **gametic isolation,** in which the egg and sperm of different species are incompatible. In aquatic animals that release their eggs and sperm into the surrounding water simultaneously, interspecific fertilization is extremely rare. The surface of the egg contains specific proteins that bind only to complementary molecules on the surface of sperm cells of the same species (see Chapter 51). A similar type of molecular recognition often occurs between pollen grains and the stigma (receptive surface of the

(a) The petal of the black sage functions as a landing platform for small bees. Large bees cannot fit on this platform.

(b) The larger landing platform and longer stamens of white sage allow pollination by larger California carpenter bees (a different species). If smaller bees land on white sage, their bodies do not brush against the stamens. (In the figure, the upper part of the white sage flower has been removed.)

FIGURE 20-4 Mechanical isolation in black sage and white sage
The differences in their floral structures allow black sage and white sage to be pollinated by different insects. Because the two species exploit different pollinators, they cannot interbreed.

female part of the flower) so that pollen does not germinate on the stigma of a different plant species.

Postzygotic barriers prevent gene flow when fertilization occurs

Fertilization sometimes occurs between gametes of two closely related species despite the existence of prezygotic barriers. When this happens, **postzygotic barriers** that increase the likelihood of reproductive failure come into play. Generally, the embryo of an interspecific hybrid spontaneously aborts. **Development,** the orderly sequence of events that occurs as an organism grows and matures, is a complex process requiring the precise interaction and coordination of many genes. Apparently, the genes from parents belonging to different species do not interact properly in regulating the mechanisms for normal development. In this case, reproductive isolation occurs by **hybrid inviability.** For example, in crosses between different species of irises the embryos die before reaching maturity. Similarly, nearly all the hybrids die in the embryonic stage when the eggs of a bullfrog are fertilized artificially with sperm from a leopard frog.

If an interspecific hybrid does live, it may not reproduce, for several reasons. Hybrid animals may exhibit courtship behaviors incompatible with those of either parental species, and as a result they will not mate. More often, **hybrid sterility** occurs when problems during meiosis cause the gametes of an interspecific hybrid to be abnormal. Hybrid sterility is particularly common if the two parental species have different chromosome numbers. For example, a mule is the offspring of a female horse ($2n = 64$) and a male donkey ($2n = 62$) (**FIG. 20-5**). This type of union almost always results in sterile offspring ($2n = 63$) because synapsis (the pairing of homologous chromosomes during meiosis) and segregation of chromosomes cannot occur properly.

Occasionally, a mating between two F_1 hybrids produces a second hybrid generation (F_2). The F_2 hybrid may exhibit **hybrid breakdown,** the inability of a hybrid to reproduce because of some defect. For example, hybrid breakdown in the F_2 generation

of a cross between two sunflower species was 80%. In other words, 80% of the F_2 generation were defective in some way and could not reproduce successfully. Hybrid breakdown also occurs in the F_3 and later generations.

TABLE 20-1 summarizes the various prezygotic and postzygotic barriers that prevent interbreeding between two species.

Biologists are discovering genes responsible for reproductive isolating mechanisms

Progress has been made in identifying some of the genes involved in reproductive isolation. For example, scientists have determined the genetic basis for prezygotic isolation in species of abalone, large mollusks found along the Pacific coast of North America. In abalone, the fertilization of eggs by sperm requires *lysin,* a sperm protein that attaches to a lysin receptor protein located on the egg envelope. After attachment, the lysin produces a hole in the egg envelope that permits the sperm to penetrate the egg. Scientists cloned the lysin receptor gene and demonstrated that this gene varies among abalone species. Differences in the lysin receptor protein in various abalone species determine sperm compatibility with the egg. Sperm of one abalone species do not attach to a lysin receptor protein of an egg of a different abalone species.

Other genes related to reproductive isolating mechanisms—loosely referred to as "speciation genes"—have been identified in a diverse group of organisms, such as Florida beach mice, cactus finches, fruit fly (*Drosophila*) species, and flycatcher birds in the South Pacific.

Review

- What barriers prevent wood frogs and leopard frogs from interbreeding in nature?
- How is temporal isolation different from behavioral isolation?
- How is mechanical isolation different from gametic isolation?
- Of which postzygotic barrier is the mule an example?

FIGURE 20-5 Hybrid sterility in mules
Mules are interspecific hybrids formed by mating a female horse (*left*) with a male donkey (*right*). Although the mule (*center*) exhibits valuable characteristics of each of its parents, it is sterile.

John Eastcott/Yva Momatiuk/Earth Scenes/Animals Animals

20.3 SPECIATION

■ LEARNING OBJECTIVES

3 Explain the mechanism of allopatric speciation and give an example.
4 Explain the mechanisms of sympatric speciation and give both plant and animal examples.

We are now ready to consider how entirely new species may arise from previously existing ones. The evolution of a new species is called **speciation.** The formation of two species from a single species occurs when a population becomes reproductively isolated from other populations of the species and the **gene pools** of the two separated populations begin to diverge in genetic composition. When a population is sufficiently different from its ancestral species that there is no genetic exchange between them, we consider speciation to have occurred. Speciation happens in two ways: allopatric speciation and sympatric speciation.

TABLE 20-1	*Animated*	Reproductive Isolating Mechanisms
Mechanism	How It Works	Example

Prezygotic barriers prevent fertilization

Temporal isolation	Similar species reproduce at different times		Two species of fruit flies of the genus *Drosophila* live in the same geographic area, but one is sexually active only in the afternoon and the other only in the morning.
Habitat isolation	Similar species reproduce in different habitats		Several flycatcher species of the genus *Empidonax* live in the same geographic area but in different habitats; for example, the least flycatcher in open woods, farms, and orchards, and the acadian flycatcher in deciduous forests and swampy woods.
Behavioral isolation	Similar species have distinctive courtship behaviors		The male satin bowerbird of Australia constructs an elaborate bower, dances around the female, and sings a specific courtship song that keeps closely related bowerbird species reproductively isolated from the satin bowerbird.
Mechanical isolation	Similar species have structural differences in their reproductive organs		Black sage (genus *Salvia*) is pollinated by small bees, whereas white sage is pollinated by large carpenter bees. Because of differences in the flower structures, neither type of bee can successfully pollinate the other sage species.
Gametic isolation	Gametes of similar species are chemically incompatible		In aquatic animals such as sponges that release their eggs and sperm into the water simultaneously, interspecific fertilization rarely occurs because the egg surface is compatible only with the sperm surface of the same species.

Postzygotic barriers reduce viability or fertility of hybrid

Hybrid inviability	Interspecific hybrid dies at early stage of embryonic development		In crosses between different species of irises (genus *Iris*), fertilization occurs but the embryos in the seeds die before reaching maturity.
Hybrid sterility	Interspecific hybrid survives to adulthood but is unable to reproduce successfully		A mule, the offspring of a female horse and a male donkey, has sterile offspring because synapsis and segregation of chromosomes do not occur properly during gamete formation.
Hybrid breakdown	Offspring of interspecific hybrid are unable to reproduce successfully		In a cross between two sunflower species, most of the F_2 generation are defective in some way and cannot reproduce successfully. Hybrid breakdown also occurs in later generations.

Long physical isolation and different selective pressures result in allopatric speciation

Speciation that occurs when one population becomes geographically separated from the rest of the species and subsequently evolves by natural selection and/or genetic drift is known as **allopatric speciation** (from the Greek *allo*, "different," and *patri*, "native land"). Recall from Chapter 18 that *natural selection* occurs as individuals that possess favorable adaptations to the environment survive and become parents of the next generation. *Genetic drift* is a random change in allele frequency resulting from the effects of chance on the survival and reproductive success of individuals in a small breeding population (see Chapter 19). Both natural selection and genetic drift result in changes in allele frequencies in a population, but only in natural selection is the change in allele frequency adaptive.

Allopatric speciation is the most common method of speciation and accounts for almost all evolution of new animal species. The geographic isolation required for allopatric speciation may occur in several ways. Earth's surface is in a constant state of change. Such change includes rivers shifting their courses; glaciers migrating; mountain ranges forming; land bridges forming that separate previously united aquatic populations; and large lakes diminishing into several smaller, geographically separated pools.

What may be an imposing geographic barrier to one species may be of no consequence to another. Birds and cattails, for example, do not become isolated when a lake subsides into smaller pools; birds easily fly from one pool to another, and cattails disperse their pollen and fruits by air currents. Fishes, in contrast, usually cannot cross the land barriers between the pools and so become reproductively isolated.

In the Death Valley region of California and Nevada, large interconnected lakes formed during wetter climates of the last Ice Age. These lakes were populated by one or several species of pupfishes. Over time, the climate became drier, and the large lakes dried up, leaving isolated pools. Presumably, each pool contained a small population of pupfish that gradually diverged from the common ancestral species by genetic drift and natural selection in response to habitat differences—the high temperatures, high salt concentrations, and low oxygen levels characteristic of desert springs. Today, there are 20 or so distinct species, subspecies, and populations in the area of Death Valley, California, and Ash Meadows, Nevada (**FIG. 20-6**). Many, such as the Devil's Hole pupfish and the Owens pupfish, are restricted to one or two isolated springs.

Allopatric speciation also occurs when a small population migrates or is dispersed (such as by a chance storm) and colonizes a new area away from the range of the original species. This colony is geographically isolated from its parental species, and the small *microevolutionary* changes that accumulate in the isolated gene pool over many generations may eventually be sufficient to form a new species. Because islands provide the geographic isolation required for allopatric speciation, they offer excellent opportunities to study this evolutionary mechanism. A few individuals of a few species probably colonized the Galápagos Islands and the Hawaiian Islands, for example. The hundreds of unique species presently found on each island presumably descended from these original colonizers (**FIG. 20-7**).

Speciation is more likely to occur if the original isolated population is small. Recall from Chapter 19 that genetic drift, including the founder effect, is more consequential in small populations. Genetic drift tends to result in rapid changes in allele frequencies in a small, isolated population. The different selective pressures of the new environment to which the population is exposed further accentuate the divergence caused by genetic drift.

The Kaibab squirrel is an example of allopatric speciation in progress

About 10,000 years ago, when the American Southwest was less arid, the ponderosa pine forests in the area supported a tree squir-

(a) Devil's Hole pupfish (*Cyprinodon diabolis*), photographed at Devil's Hole, Ash Meadows National Wildlife Refuge, Nevada.

(b) Ash Meadows pupfish (*Cyprinodon nevadensis ssp. mionectes*), photographed at Point of Rocks Springs, Ash Meadows National Wildlife Refuge, Nevada.

FIGURE 20-6 Allopatric speciation of pupfishes (*Cyprinodon*)
Shown are two pupfish species that evolved when larger lakes in southern Nevada dried up about 10,000 years ago, leaving behind small, isolated desert pools fed by springs. The pupfish's short, stubby body is characteristic of fish that live in springs; fish that live in larger bodies of water are more streamlined.

FIGURE 20-7 Allopatric speciation of the Hawaiian goose (the nene)

Nene (pronounced "nay-nay"; *Branta sandvicensis*) are geese originally found only on volcanic mountains on the geographically isolated islands of Hawaii and Maui, which are some 4200 km (2600 mi) from the nearest continent. Compared with those of other geese, the feet of Hawaiian geese are not completely webbed, their toenails are longer and stronger, and their foot pads are thicker; these adaptations enable Hawaiian geese to walk easily on lava flows. Nenes probably evolved from a small population of geese that originated in North America. Photographed in Hawaii Volcanoes National Park, Hawaii.

rel with conspicuous tufts of hair sprouting from its ears. A small tree squirrel population living on the Kaibab Plateau of the Grand Canyon became geographically isolated when the climate changed, thus causing areas to the north, west, and east to become desert. Just a few miles to the south lived the rest of the squirrels, which we know as Abert squirrels, but the two groups were separated by the Grand Canyon. With changes over time in both its appearance and its ecology, the Kaibab squirrel is on its way to becoming a new species.

During its many years of geographic isolation, the small population of Kaibab squirrels has diverged from the widely distributed Abert squirrels in several ways. Perhaps most evident are changes in fur color. The Kaibab squirrel now has a white tail and a gray belly, in contrast to the gray tail and white belly of the Abert squirrel (**FIG. 20-8**). Biologists think these striking changes arose in Kaibab squirrels as a result of genetic drift.

Scientists have not reached a consensus about whether the two squirrel populations are separate species, and most biologists today consider the Kaibab squirrel (*Sciurus aberti ssp. kaibabensis*) and the Abert squirrel (*Sciurus aberti*) as distinct subspecies. Because the Kaibab and Abert squirrels remain reproductively isolated from each other, it is assumed that they will continue to evolve into separate species.

Porto Santo rabbits diverged rapidly from European rabbits

Allopatric speciation has the potential to occur quite rapidly. Early in the 15th century, a small population of rabbits was released on Porto Santo, a small island off the coast of Portugal. Because there were no other rabbits or competitors and no predators on the island, the rabbits thrived. By the 19th century, these rabbits were markedly different from their European ancestors. They were only half as large (weighing slightly more than 500 g, or 1.1 lb), with a different color pattern and a more nocturnal lifestyle. More significant, attempts to mate Porto Santo rabbits with mainland European rabbits failed. Many biologists concluded that within 400 years, an extremely brief period in evolutionary history, a new species of rabbit had evolved.

Not all biologists agree that the Porto Santo rabbit is a new species. The objection stems from a more recent breeding experiment and is based on biologists' lack of a consensus about the definition of a species. In the experiment, foster mothers of the wild Mediterranean rabbit raised newborn Porto Santo rabbits. When they reached adulthood, these Porto Santo rabbits mated successfully with Mediterranean rabbits to produce healthy, fertile offspring. To some biologists, this experiment clearly demonstrated that Porto Santo rabbits are not a separate species but a subspecies. These biologists cite the Porto Santo rabbits as an example of speciation in progress, much like the Kaibab squirrels just discussed.

Many other biologists think the Porto Santo rabbit is a separate species because it does not interbreed with the other rabbits under natural conditions. They point out that the breeding experiment was successful only after the baby Porto Santo rabbits were raised under artificial conditions that probably modified their natural behavior.

(a) The Kaibab squirrel, with its white tail and gray belly, is found north of the Grand Canyon.

(b) The Abert squirrel, with its gray tail and white belly, is found south of the Grand Canyon.

FIGURE 20-8 *Animated* **Allopatric speciation in progress**

Two populations diverge in the same physical location by sympatric speciation

Although geographic isolation is an important factor in many cases of evolution, it is not an absolute requirement. In **sympatric speciation** (from the Greek *sym*, "together," and *patri*, "native land"), a new species evolves within the same geographic region as the parental species. The divergence of two populations in the same geographic range occurs when reproductive isolating mechanisms evolve at the *start* of the speciation process. Sympatric speciation is especially common in plants. The role of sympatric speciation in animal evolution is probably much less important than allopatric speciation; until recently, sympatric speciation in animals has been difficult to demonstrate in nature.

Sympatric speciation occurs in at least two ways: a change in **ploidy** (the number of chromosome sets making up an organism's genome) and a change in ecology. We now examine each of these mechanisms.

Allopolyploidy is an important mechanism of sympatric speciation in plants

As a result of reproductive isolating mechanisms discussed earlier, the union of two gametes from different species rarely forms viable offspring; if offspring are produced, they are usually sterile. Synapsis cannot usually occur in interspecific hybrid offspring because not all the chromosomes are homologous. However, if the chromosome number doubles *before* meiosis, then homologous chromosomes can undergo synapsis. Although not common, this spontaneous doubling of chromosomes has been documented in a variety of plants and a few animals. It produces nuclei with multiple sets of chromosomes.

Polyploidy, the possession of more than two sets of chromosomes, is a major factor in plant evolution. Reproductive isolation occurs in a single generation when a polyploid species with multiple sets of chromosomes arises from diploid parents. There are two kinds of polyploidy: autopolyploidy and allopolyploidy. An **autopolyploid** contains multiple sets of chromosomes from a single species, and an **allopolyploid** contains multiple sets of chromosomes from two or more species. We discuss only allopolyploidy because it is much more common in nature.

Allopolyploidy occurs in conjunction with **hybridization,** which is sexual reproduction between individuals from closely related species. Allopolyploidy produces a fertile interspecific hybrid because the polyploid condition provides the homologous chromosome pairs necessary for synapsis during meiosis. As a result, gametes may be viable (**FIG. 20-9**). An allopolyploid—that is, an interspecific hybrid produced by allopolyploidy—reproduces with itself (self-fertilization) or with a similar individual. However, allopolyploids are reproductively isolated from both parents because their gametes have a different number of chromosomes from those of either parent.

If a population of allopolyploids (that is, a new species) becomes established, selective pressures cause one of three outcomes. First, the new species may not compete successfully against species that are already established, so it becomes extinct. Second, the allopolyploid individuals may assume a new role in the environment and so coexist with both parental species. Third, the new species

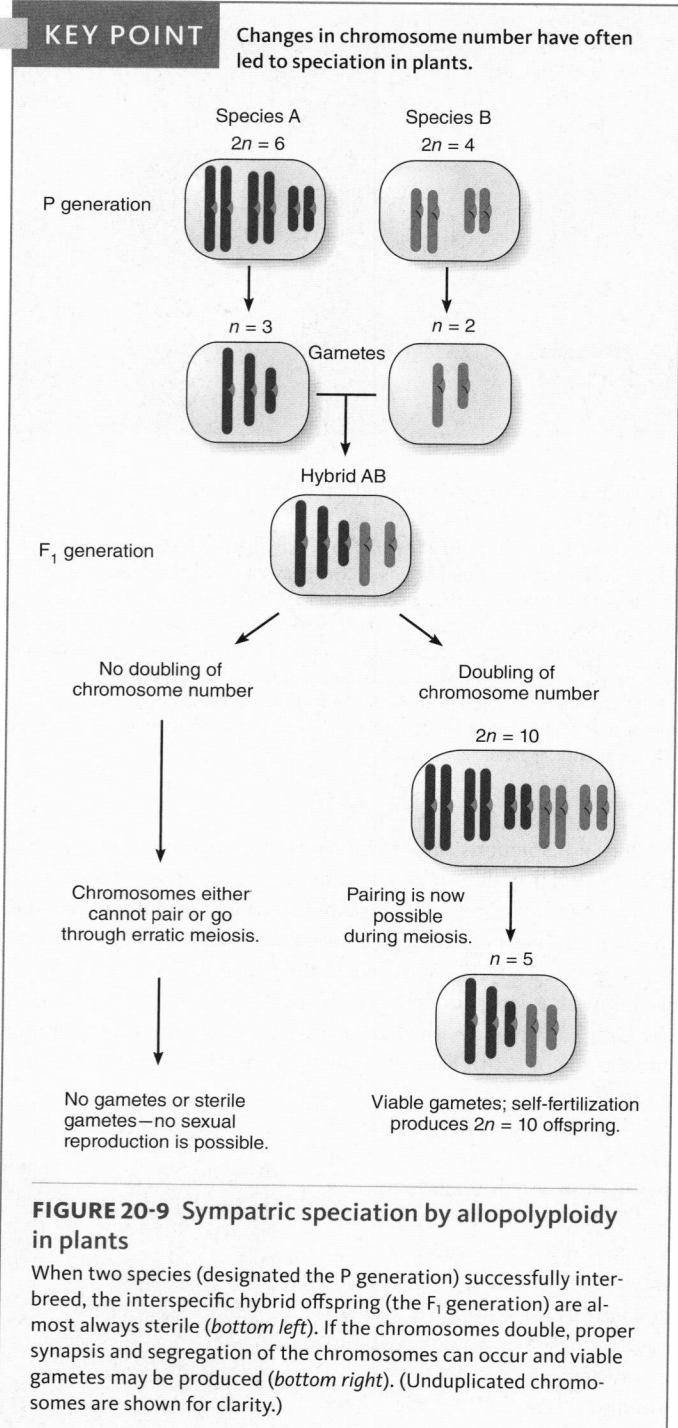

KEY POINT Changes in chromosome number have often led to speciation in plants.

FIGURE 20-9 Sympatric speciation by allopolyploidy in plants

When two species (designated the P generation) successfully interbreed, the interspecific hybrid offspring (the F_1 generation) are almost always sterile (*bottom left*). If the chromosomes double, proper synapsis and segregation of the chromosomes can occur and viable gametes may be produced (*bottom right*). (Unduplicated chromosomes are shown for clarity.)

may successfully compete with either or both of its parental species. If it has a combination of traits that confers greater fitness than one or both parental species for all or part of the original range of the parent(s), the hybrid species may replace the parent(s).

Although allopolyploidy is extremely rare in animals, it is significant in the evolution of flowering plant species. As many as 80% of all flowering plant species are polyploids, and most of these are allopolyploids. Moreover, allopolyploidy provides a mechanism for extremely rapid speciation. A single generation is all that is needed to form a new, reproductively isolated species. Allopolyploidy may explain the rapid appearance of many flowering plant species in the fossil record and their remarkable diversity today (at least 300,000 species).

The kew primrose (*Primula kewensis*) is an example of sympatric speciation that was documented at the Royal Botanic Gardens at Kew, England, in 1898 (**FIG. 20-10**). Plant breeders developed *P. kewensis* as an interspecific hybrid of two primrose species, *P. floribunda* ($2n = 18$) and *P. verticillata* ($2n = 18$). *Primula kewensis* had a chromosome number of 18 but was sterile. Then, at three different times, it was reported to have spontaneously formed a fertile branch, which was an allopolyploid ($2n = 36$) that produced viable seeds of *P. kewensis*.

The mechanism of sympatric speciation has been experimentally verified for many plant species. One example is a group of species, collectively called *hemp nettles,* that occur in temperate parts of Europe and Asia. One hemp nettle, *Galeopsis tetrahit* ($2n = 32$), is a naturally occurring allopolyploid hypothesized to have formed by the hybridization of two species, *G. pubescens* ($2n = 16$) and *G. speciosa* ($2n = 16$). This process occurred in nature but was experimentally reproduced. *Galeopsis pubescens* and *G. speciosa* were crossed to produce F_1 hybrids, most of which were sterile. Nevertheless, both F_2 and F_3 generations were produced. The F_3 generation included a polyploid plant with $2n = 32$ that self-fertilized to yield fertile F_4 offspring that could not mate with either of the parental species. These allopolyploid plants had the same appearance and chromosome number as the naturally occurring *G. tetrahit*. When the experimentally produced plants were crossed with the naturally occurring *G. tetrahit,* a fertile F_1 generation was formed. Thus, the experiment duplicated the speciation process that occurred in nature.

Changing ecology causes sympatric speciation in animals

Biologists have observed the occurrence of sympatric speciation in animals, but its significance—how often it happens and under what conditions—is still debated. Many examples of sympatric speciation in animals involve parasitic insects and rely on genetic mechanisms other than polyploidy. For example, in the 1860s in the Hudson River Valley of New York, a population of fruit maggot flies (*Rhagoletis pomonella*) parasitic on the small red fruits of native hawthorn trees was documented to have switched to a new host, domestic apples, which had been introduced from Europe. Although the sister populations (hawthorn maggot flies and apple maggot flies) continue to occupy the same geographic area, no gene flow occurs between them because they eat, mate, and lay their eggs on different hosts (**FIG. 20-11**). In other words, because the hawthorn and apple maggot flies have diverged and are reproductively isolated from each other, they have effectively become separate species. Most entomologists, however, still recognize hawthorn and apple maggot flies as a single species because their appearance is virtually identical.

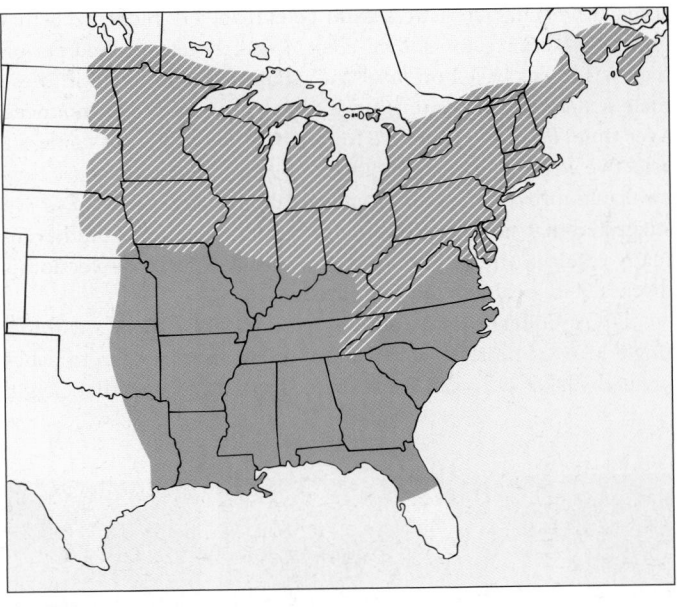

■ Hawthorn maggot fly range

▨ Apple maggot fly and hawthorn maggot fly range

FIGURE 20-11 Ranges of apple and hawthorn maggot flies

Apple and hawthorn maggot flies are sympatric throughout the northern half of the hawthorn maggot fly's range. (Adapted from G. L. Bush, "Sympatric Host Race Formation and Speciation in Frugivorous Flies of the Genus *Rhagoletis* [Diptera, Tephritidae]," *Evolution*, Vol. 23, No. 2, June 1969.)

| *Primula floribunda* | *Primula kewensis* | *Primula verticillata* |

FIGURE 20-10 *Animated* **Sympatric speciation of a primrose**

A new species of primrose, *Primula kewensis*, arose in 1898 as an allopolyploid derived from the interspecific hybridization of *P. floribunda* and *P. verticillata*. Today, *P. kewensis* is a popular houseplant.

In situations such as that of the fruit maggot flies, a mutation arises in an individual and spreads through a small group of insects by sexual reproduction. The particular mutation leads to *disruptive selection* (see Chapter 19), in which both the old and new phenotypes are favored. Selection is disruptive because the original population is still favored when it parasitizes the original host, and the mutants are favored by a new ecological opportunity—in this case, to parasitize a different host species. Additional mutations may occur that cause the sister populations to diverge even further.

Cichlids in East Africa intrigue evolutionary biologists

Biologists have studied the speciation of colorful fishes known as *cichlids* (pronounced "sik-lids") in several East African lakes. The different species of cichlids in a given lake have remarkably different eating habits, which are reflected in the shapes of their jaws and teeth. Some graze on algae; some consume dead organic material at the bottom of the lake; and others are predatory and eat plankton (microscopic aquatic organisms), insect larvae, the scales off fish, or even other cichlid species. In some cichlids, food preferences are related to size (smaller cichlids consume plankton), which in turn is related to mating preference (small, plankton-eating cichlids mate only with other small, plankton-eating cichlids).

In other cichlids, related species do not differ in size but only in color and mating habits. Each species has a distinct male coloration, which matches the preferences of females of that species in choosing mates (**FIG. 20-12**).

Charles Darwin called choosing a mate based on its color or some other characteristic **sexual selection.** He recognized that female preference for showy colors or elaborate ornaments on males, if it was based on *inherited* variation, could result in these male sexual traits becoming more common and more pronounced over time. Female preference for a particular male trait confers a selective advantage to the males exhibiting that trait because they have an improved chance to mate and pass on their genes. Darwin suggested that sexual selection, like natural selection, could eventually result in the evolution of new species. (Sexual selection is discussed in greater detail in Chapter 52.)

DNA sequence data indicate that the cichlid species within a single lake are more closely related to one another than to fishes in nearby lakes or rivers. These molecular data suggest that cichlid species evolved sympatrically, or at least within the confines of a lake, rather than by repeated colonizations by fish populations in nearby rivers.

How rapidly did sympatric speciation occur in cichlids? Seismic and drill core data provide evidence that Lake Victoria dried up completely during the Late Pleistocene, when much of north and equatorial Africa was arid. The diverse cichlid species may have arisen after the climate became wetter and Lake Victoria refilled. Further, the more than 500 **endemic** (found nowhere else) cichlid species in Lake Victoria may have evolved from one or a few common ancestors in a remarkably short period—as little as 12,000 years. Other biologists have offered competing hypotheses about the timing and geographic origin of Lake Victoria's cichlids. Regardless of the uncertainties of certain details, Lake Victoria's cichlids are widely recognized as exemplifying the fastest rate of evolution known for such a large group of vertebrate species.

Loss of Cichlid Diversity in Lake Victoria. In recent years, many of the cichlid species living in Lake Victoria have become extinct. The Nile perch, a voracious predator that was deliberately introduced into the lake in 1960 to stimulate the local fishing economy and whose population exploded in the 1980s, has been blamed for the extinction of most of the cichlid species that have disappeared.

Biologists from the University of Leiden in the Netherlands observed, however, that species were also disappearing in habitats in the lake where the Nile perch is known to have little or no impact. Ole Seehausen and his colleagues measured environmental features at 22 localities with such habitats and found strong correlations between bright and diverse male colors and clear, well-lit water. Each species has its own distinct male coloration, which is used by females of that species to choose mates. In clear water, members of each species do not interbreed with members of other species.

As nearby forests have been cut, soil erosion has made the water of Lake Victoria more turbid (cloudy). Agricultural practices in the area have also contributed fertilizer and sediment pollution. Seehausen demonstrated that as the water became more turbid from pollution, light could not penetrate effectively. He hypothesized that as a result, females could not distinguish males of their own species from males of closely related species.

As already discussed, cichlids have evolved during the past 12,000 years. Their relative youth as species means they may not

(a) *Pundamilia pundamilia* males have bluish-silver bodies.

(b) *Pundamilia nyererei* males have red backs.

(c) *Pundamilia* "red head" males have a red "chest." (The "red head" species has not yet been scientifically named.)

a–c: Ole Seehausen, University of Bern

FIGURE 20-12 Color variation in Lake Victoria cichlids
Some evidence suggests that changes in male coloration may be the first step in speciation of Lake Victoria cichlids. Later, other traits, including ecological characteristics, diverge. Female cichlids generally have cryptic coloration; their drab colors help them blend into their surroundings.

yet have evolved additional reproductive isolating mechanisms other than mate preference based on color. It also means that closely related species can be expected to interbreed without loss of fertility. With increasing turbidity, males lose their bright colors because they are no longer favored by sexual selection, and females have mated with males of other species (**FIGURE 20-13**). Thus, many species are being replaced with a few hybrids.

The study of hybrid zones has made important contributions to what is known about speciation

When two populations have significantly diverged as a result of geographic separation, there is no easy way to determine if the speciation process is complete (recall the disagreement about whether Porto Santo rabbits are a separate species or a subspecies). If such populations, subspecies, or species come into secondary contact before strong prezygotic isolating mechanisms have evolved, they may hybridize, producing fertile offspring, where they meet. A **hybrid zone** is an area of overlap between two recently diverged populations in which interbreeding takes place and hybrid offspring are common. Hybrid zones are typically narrow, presumably because the hybrids are not well adapted for either parental environment. The hybrid population is typically very small compared with the parental populations.

On the Great Plains of North America, red-shafted and yellow-shafted flickers (types of woodpeckers) meet and interbreed. The red-shafted flicker, named for the male's red underwings and tail, is found in the western part of North America, from the Great Plains to the Pacific Ocean. Yellow-shafted flicker males, which have yellow underwings and tails, range east of the Rock-

ies. Hybrid flickers, which form a stable hybrid zone from Texas to southern Alaska, are varied in appearance, although many have orange underwings and tails.

According to the biological species concept, if red-shafted and yellow-shafted flickers are two species, they should maintain their reproductive isolation. Because a hybrid zone has formed, most biologists think the red-shafted and yellow-shafted flickers are geographic subspecies instead of separate species; red-shafted, yellow-shafted, and hybrid flickers are collectively called northern flickers.

Three evolutionary processes may occur in hybrid zones

When two diverging populations or closely related species come into contact and form a hybrid zone, one of three possibilities can occur: reinforcement, which helps maintain two separate species; fusion of the two species into one; or stability of the hybrid zone (**FIG. 20-14**). **Reinforcement** occurs when the hybrids in the hybrid zone are less fit than the two parental populations. Reinforcement is the increase in reproductive isolation that often occurs over time in a hybrid zone—that is, natural selection strengthens and increases the number of prezygotic barriers between the two species. As a result, fewer and fewer hybrids are formed, and the hybrid zone gradually disappears.

In **fusion,** the hybrids in a hybrid zone are as fit as either of the parental populations. Over time, differences in the reproductive barriers between the two parental populations weaken, and the hybrid zone enlarges. The eventual result is a fusing of two species (or subspecies) into one. Hybridization of the Lake Victoria cichlids (discussed earlier in the chapter) is an example of species loss due to fusion.

KEY EXPERIMENT

QUESTION: Why is cichlid diversity declining in Lake Victoria?

HYPOTHESIS: Cichlids are disappearing from Lake Victoria because of changes in their habitat.

EXPERIMENT: Seehausen and colleagues took field measurements in 22 different locations in Lake Victoria and later verified these field observations with laboratory experiments in which two cichlid species were placed in aquaria that were either well-lit or not.

RESULTS AND CONCLUSION: When aquaria were well-lit (left), females of two closely related cichlid species (one red, the other blue) consistently chose mates of their own species (circled area) over those of other species. When light was blocked to simulate turbid conditions found in parts of Lake Victoria (right), females often chose males of other species.

Thus, increasing turbidity of Lake Victoria's water is preventing females of cichlid species from using color to select mates of their own species. As a result, females are interbreeding with males of other species, and the number of cichlid species is declining as the distinctive gene pools of different species are merging.

Source: Seehausen, O., et al. "Speciation through Sensory Drive in Cichlid Fish." *Nature*, Vol. 455, October 2, 2008.

FIGURE 20-13 Explaining the rapid loss of cichlid diversity in Lake Victoria

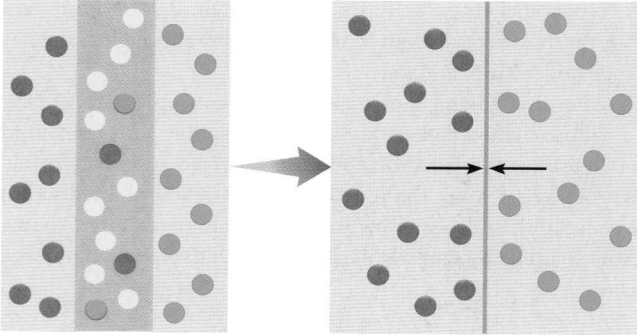

(a) Reinforcement. Hybrids are not as fit as the parents. Over time, the differences between the two parental populations increase, and hybrids are no longer produced. As the hybrid zone shrinks, the resulting outcome is two species.

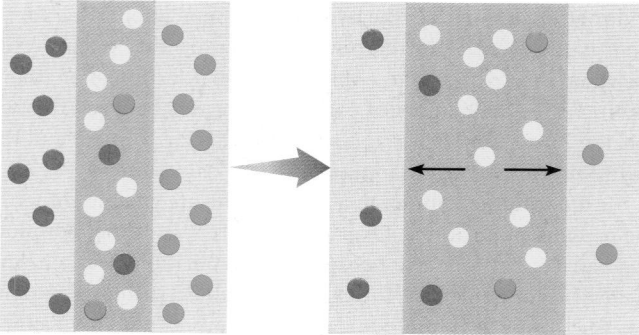

(b) Fusion. Hybrids are as fit as the two parental populations. Over time, differences between the two parental populations weaken and the hybrid zone enlarges. The essential result is a single species.

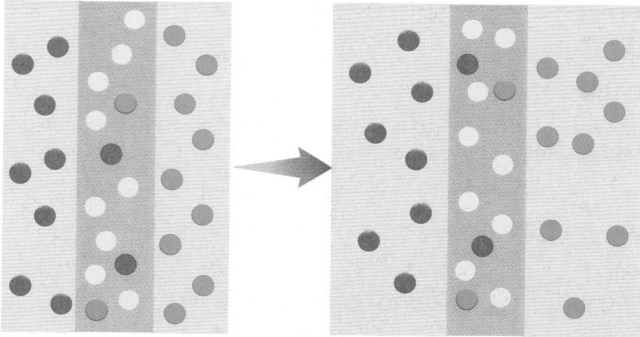

(c) Stability. Hybrids are more fit than either parental population. The fitness of the hybrids results in a stable hybrid zone. Eventually, a third species may form in the hybrid zone.

FIGURE 20-14 How hybrid zones between two closely related species or diverging populations can change over time

Stability is an evolutionary process in which the hybrids are more fit than either parental population. Hybrids continue to be formed, resulting in a stable hybrid zone. Stable hybrid zones often occur in **ecotones,** areas of transition between two different envi-

ronments. In this case, the two incipient species are adapted to two different communities, and the hybrids' combination of characters from both parental populations allows them to flourish in the ecotone. Eventually, a third species may form in such a hybrid zone. (Ecotones are discussed further in Chapter 56.)

In the example of the flicker hybrid zone, reinforcement does not appear to be occurring. At the same time, the two kinds of flickers are not fusing together into one distinct group. The flicker hybrid zone has not expanded; the two types of flickers have maintained their distinctiveness and have not rejoined into a single, freely interbreeding population. Thus, at this time, flicker hybrids have formed a stable hybrid zone.

Review

- What are five geographic barriers that might lead to allopatric speciation?
- How do hybridization and polyploidy cause a new plant species to form in as little as one generation?
- What is the likely mechanism of speciation for pupfishes? for cichlids?

20.4 THE RATE OF EVOLUTIONARY CHANGE

■ LEARNING OBJECTIVE

5 Discuss the pace of evolution by describing punctuated equilibrium and phyletic gradualism.

We have seen that speciation is hard for us to directly observe as it occurs. Does the fossil record provide clues about how rapidly new species arise? Biologists have long recognized that the fossil record lacks many transitional forms; the starting points (ancestral species) and the end points (new species) are present, but the intermediate stages in the evolution from one species to another are often lacking. This observation has traditionally been explained by the incompleteness of the fossil record, although scientists have sometimes made new fossil discoveries that fill in the missing parts.

Two different models—punctuated equilibrium and phyletic gradualism—explain evolution as observed in the fossil record (**FIG. 20-15**). The **punctuated equilibrium** model was proposed by paleontologists who questioned whether the fossil record really is as incomplete as it initially appeared. In the history of a species, long periods of **stasis** (little or no evolutionary change) appeared to be punctuated, or interrupted, by short periods of rapid speciation that were perhaps triggered by changes in the environment—that is, periods of great evolutionary stress. Thus, speciation proceeded in "spurts." These relatively short periods of active evolution (perhaps 100,000 years) were followed by long periods (perhaps 2 million years) of stability.

Punctuated equilibrium accounts for the abrupt appearance of a new species in the fossil record, with little or no evidence of intermediate forms. Proponents hypothesize that few transitional forms appear in the fossil record because few transitional forms occurred during speciation.

Punctuated equilibrium and phyletic gradualism represent opposite ends of a spectrum of speciation patterns. Speciation often proceeds in an intermediate or mixed pattern.

(a) In **punctuated equilibrium**, long periods of stasis are interrupted by short periods of rapid speciation.

(b) In **phyletic gradualism**, a slow, steady change in species occurs over time.

FIGURE 20-15 Punctuated equilibrium and gradualism
In this figure, structural changes in the lizards are represented by changes in skin color.

In contrast, the traditional Darwinian view of evolution espouses the **phyletic gradualism** model, in which evolution proceeded continuously over long periods. Gradualism is rarely observed in the fossil record because the record is incomplete. (Recall from Chapter 18 that precise conditions are required for fossil formation. Most organisms leave no trace of their existence because they decompose when they die.) Occasionally, a complete fossil record of transitional forms has been discovered and cited as a strong case for gradualism. The gradualism model maintains that populations slowly diverge from one another by the gradual accumulation of adaptive characteristics within each population. These adaptive characteristics accumulate as a result of different selective pressures encountered in different environments.

Scientists supporting phyletic gradualism maintain that any periods of stasis evident in the fossil record are the result of *stabilizing selection* (see Chapter 19). They also emphasize that stasis in fossils is deceptive because fossils do not reveal all aspects of evolution. Although fossils display changes in external structure and skeletal structure, other genetic changes—in physiology, internal structure, resistance to infection, and behavior—all of which also represent evolution, are not evident. Gradualists recognize rapid evolution only when strong *directional selection* occurs.

Many biologists today embrace both models to explain the fossil record. They contend that the pace of evolution may be abrupt in certain instances and gradual in others and that neither punctuated equilibrium nor gradualism exclusively characterizes the changes associated with evolution. Many biologists do not view the distinction between punctuated equilibrium and phyletic gradualism as real. They suggest that genetic changes occur gradually and at a roughly constant pace and that the majority of these mutations do not cause speciation. When the mutations that do cause speciation occur, they are dramatic and produce a pattern consistent with the punctuated equilibrium model.

Review

- Are the phyletic gradualism and punctuated equilibrium models mutually exclusive? Explain your answer.

20.5 MACROEVOLUTION

■ LEARNING OBJECTIVES

6 Define *macroevolution*.
7 Discuss macroevolution in the context of novel features, including preadaptations, allometric growth, and paedomorphosis.
8 Discuss the macroevolutionary significance of adaptive radiation and extinction.

Macroevolution is large-scale phenotypic changes in populations that generally warrant their placement in taxonomic groups at the species level and higher—that is, new species, genera, families, orders, classes, and even phyla, kingdoms, and domains. One concern of macroevolution is to explain evolutionary novelties, which are large phenotypic changes such as the appearance of jointed limbs during the evolution of arthropods (crustaceans, insects, and spiders). These phenotypic changes are so great that the new species possessing them are assigned to different genera or higher taxonomic categories. Studies of macroevolution also seek to discover and explain major changes in species diversity through time such as occur during *adaptive radiation,* when many species appear, and *mass extinction,* when many species disappear. Thus, evolutionary novelties, adaptive radiation, and mass extinction are important aspects of macroevolution.

Evolutionary novelties originate through modifications of pre-existing structures

New designs arise from structures already in existence. A change in the basic pattern of an organism produces something unique, such as wings on insects, flowers on plants, and feathered wings on birds. Usually, these evolutionary novelties are variations of some pre-existing structures, called **preadaptations,** that originally fulfilled one role but subsequently changed in a way that was adaptive for a different role. Feathers, which evolved from reptilian scales and may have originally provided thermal insulation in primitive birds and some dinosaurs, represent a preadaptation for flight. With gradual modification, feathers evolved to function in flight as well as to fulfill their original thermoregulatory role. (Interestingly, a few feather-footed bird species exist; this phenotype is the result of a change in gene regulation that alters scales, normally found on bird feet, into feathers.)

How do such evolutionary novelties originate? Many are probably due to changes during development. *Regulatory genes* exert control over hundreds of other genes during development, and very slight genetic changes in regulatory genes could ultimately cause major structural changes in the organism (see Chapters 17 and 18).

For example, during development most organisms exhibit varied rates of growth for different parts of the body, known as **allometric growth** (from the Greek *allo,* "different," and *metr,* "measure"). The size of the head in human newborns is large in proportion to the rest of the body. As a human grows and matures, the torso, hands, and legs grow more rapidly than the head. Allometric growth is found in many organisms, including the male fiddler crab with its single, oversized claw, and the ocean sunfish with its enlarged tail (**FIG. 20-16**). If growth rates are altered even slightly, drastic changes in the shape of an organism may result, changes that may or may not be adaptive. For example, allometric growth may help explain the extremely small and relatively useless forelegs of the dinosaur *Tyrannosaurus rex,* compared with those of its ancestors.

Sometimes novel evolutionary changes occur when a species undergoes changes in the *timing* of development. Consider, for example, the changes that would occur if juvenile characteristics were retained in the adult stage, a phenomenon known as **paedomorphosis** (from the Greek *paed,* "child," and *morph,* "form"). Adults of some salamander species have external gills and tail fins, features found only in the larval (immature) stages of other salamanders.

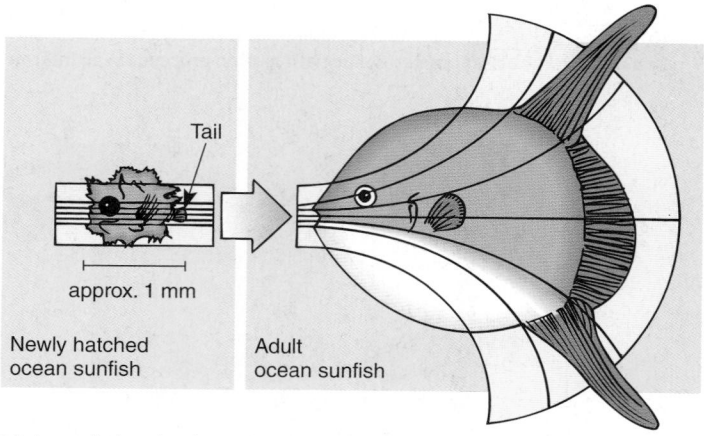

(a) A newly hatched ocean sunfish, only 1 mm long, has an extremely small tail.

(b) This allometric transformation is visualized by drawing rectangular coordinate lines through a picture of the juvenile fish and then changing the coordinate lines mathematically.

Richard Herrmann

(c) An ocean sunfish swims off the coast of southern California. The adult ocean sunfish may reach 4 m (13 ft) and weigh about 1500 kg (3300 lb).

FIGURE 20-16 Allometric growth in the ocean sunfish

The tail end of an ocean sunfish (*Mola mola*) grows faster than the head end, resulting in the unique shape of the adult.

Retention of external gills and tail fins throughout life obviously alters the salamander's behavioral and ecological characteristics (**FIG. 20-17**). Perhaps such salamanders succeeded because they had a selective advantage over "normal" adult salamanders; that is, by remaining aquatic, they did not have to compete for food with the terrestrial adult forms of related species. The paedomorphic forms also escaped the typical predators of terrestrial salamanders (although they had other predators in their aquatic environment). Studies suggest that paedomorphosis in salamanders is probably the result of mutations in genes that block the production of hormones that stimulate metamorphic changes. When paedomorphic salamanders receive hormone injections, they develop into adults lacking external gills and tail fins.

FIGURE 20-17 Paedomorphosis in a salamander

An adult axolotl salamander (*Ambystoma mexicanum*) retains the juvenile characteristics of external gills (feathery structures protruding from the neck) and a tail fin (*not visible*). Paedomorphosis allows the axolotl to remain permanently aquatic and to reproduce without developing typical adult characteristics.

Adaptive radiation is the diversification of an ancestral species into many species

Some ancestral species have given rise to far more species than have other evolutionary lineages. **Adaptive radiation** is the evolutionary diversification of many related species from one or a few ancestral species in a relatively short period.

Evolutionary innovations such as those we considered in the last section may trigger an adaptive radiation. Alternatively, an adaptive radiation may occur because the ancestral species happens to have been in the right place at the right time to exploit numerous ecological opportunities.

Biologists developed the concept of adaptive zones to help explain this type of adaptive radiation. **Adaptive zones** are new ecological opportunities that were not exploited by an ancestral organism. At the species level, an adaptive zone is essentially identical to one or more similar *ecological niches* (the functional roles of species within a community; see Chapter 54). Examples of adaptive zones include nocturnal flying to catch small insects, grazing on grass while migrating across a savanna, and swimming at the ocean's surface to filter out plankton. When many adaptive zones are empty, as they were in Lake Victoria when it refilled some 12,000 years ago (discussed earlier in the chapter), colonizing species such as the cichlids may rapidly diversify and exploit them.

Because islands have fewer species than do mainland areas of similar size, latitude, and topography, vacant adaptive zones are more common on islands than on continents. Consider the Hawaiian honeycreepers, a group of related birds found in the Hawaiian Islands. When the honeycreeper ancestors reached Hawaii, few other birds were present. The succeeding generations of honeycreepers quickly diversified into many new species and, in the process, occupied the many available adaptive zones that on the mainland are occupied by finches, honeyeaters, treecreepers, and woodpeckers. The diversity of their bills is a particularly good illus-

tration of adaptive radiation (**FIG. 20-18**). Some honeycreeper bills are curved to extract nectar out of tubular flowers, whereas others are short and thick for ripping away bark in search of insects.

Another example of vacant adaptive zones involves the Hawaiian silverswords, 28 species of closely related plants found only in the Hawaiian Islands. When the silversword ancestor, a California plant related to daisies, reached the Hawaiian Islands, many diverse environments, such as cool, arid mountains; exposed lava flows; dry woodlands; shady, moist forests; and wet bogs were present and more or less unoccupied. The succeeding generations of silverswords quickly diversified in structure and physiology to occupy the many adaptive zones available to them. The diversity in their leaves, which changed during the course of natural selection as different populations adapted to various levels of light and moisture, is a particularly good illustration of adaptive radiation (**FIG. 20-19**). Leaves of silverswords that are adapted to shady, moist forests are large, for example, whereas those of silverswords living in arid areas are small. The leaves of silverswords living on exposed volcanic slopes are covered with dense, silvery hairs that may reflect some of the intense ultraviolet radiation off the plant.

Adaptive radiation appears more common during periods of major environmental change, but it is difficult to determine how these changes are related to adaptive radiation. It is possible that major environmental change indirectly affects adaptive radiation by increasing the extinction rate. Extinction produces empty adaptive zones, which provide new opportunities for species that remain. Mammals, for example, diversified and exploited a variety of adaptive zones relatively soon after the dinosaurs' extinction. Flying bats, running gazelles, burrowing moles, and swimming whales all originated from early mammals that had coexisted with reptiles for millions of years.

Extinction is an important aspect of evolution

Extinction, the end of a lineage, occurs when the last individual of a species dies. The loss is permanent, for once a species is extinct, it never reappears. Extinctions have occurred continually since the origin of life; by one estimate, only 1 species is alive today for every 2000 that have become extinct. Extinction is the eventual fate of all species, in the same way that death is the eventual fate of all individual organisms.

Although extinction has a negative short-term impact on the number of species, it facilitates evolution over a period of thousands to millions of years. As mentioned previously, when species become extinct, their adaptive zones become vacant. Consequently, surviving species are presented with new evolutionary opportunities and may diverge, filling in some of the unoccupied zones. In other words, the extinct species may eventually be replaced by new species.

During the long history of life, extinction appears to have occurred at two different rates. The continuous, low-level extinction of species is sometimes called **background extinction.** In contrast, five or possibly six times during Earth's history, **mass extinctions** of numerous species and higher taxonomic groups have taken place in both terrestrial and marine environments. The most recent mass extinction, which occurred about 65 million years ago (mya), killed off many marine organisms, terrestrial plants, and

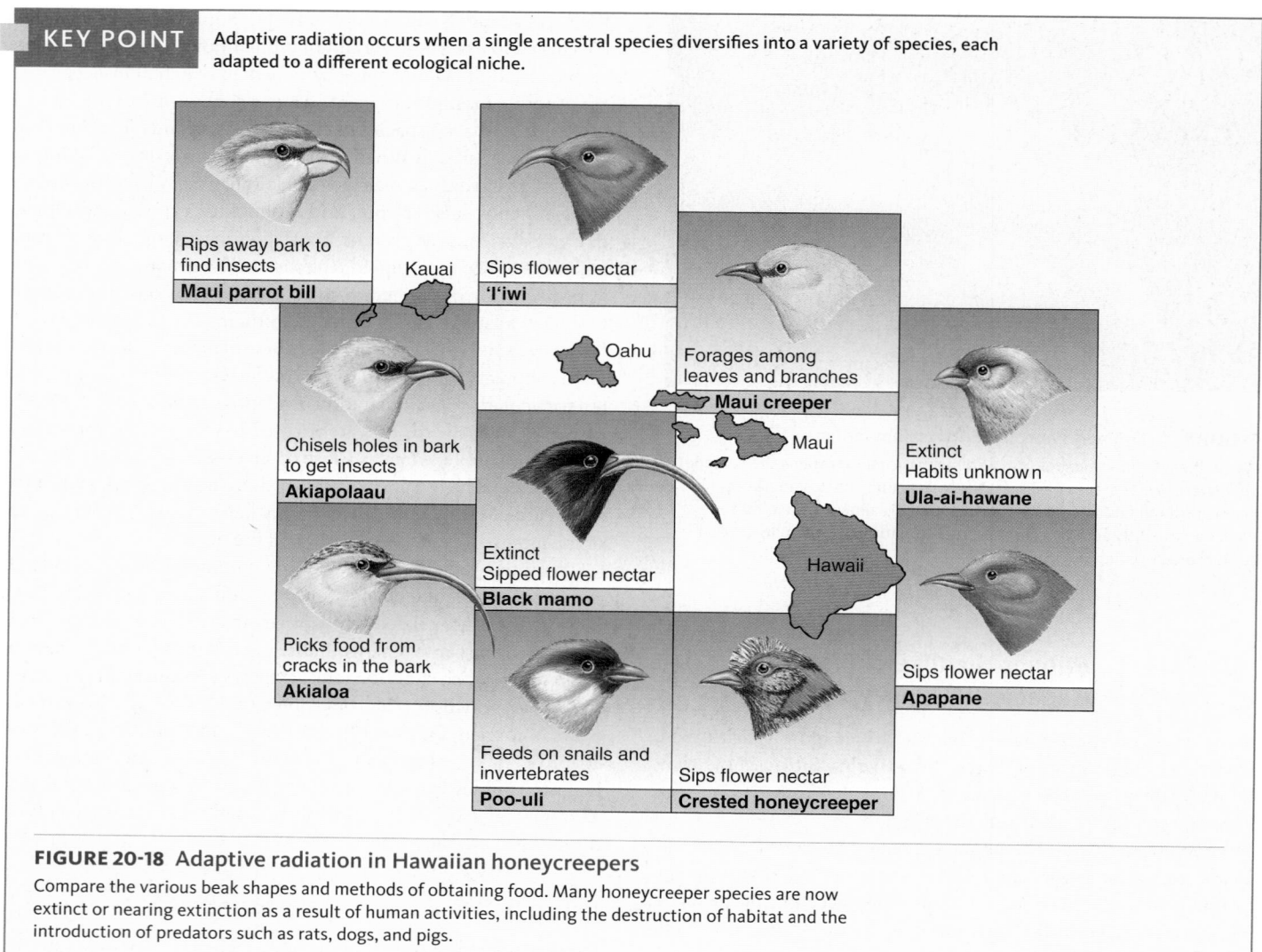

Adaptive radiation occurs when a single ancestral species diversifies into a variety of species, each adapted to a different ecological niche.

Rips away bark to find insects
Maui parrot bill

Kauai

Sips flower nectar
ʻIʻiwi

Oahu

Forages among leaves and branches
Maui creeper

Maui

Extinct
Habits unknown
Ula-ai-hawane

Chisels holes in bark to get insects
Akiapolaau

Extinct
Sipped flower nectar
Black mamo

Hawaii

Picks food from cracks in the bark
Akialoa

Sips flower nectar
Apapane

Feeds on snails and invertebrates
Poo-uli

Sips flower nectar
Crested honeycreeper

FIGURE 20-18 Adaptive radiation in Hawaiian honeycreepers

Compare the various beak shapes and methods of obtaining food. Many honeycreeper species are now extinct or nearing extinction as a result of human activities, including the destruction of habitat and the introduction of predators such as rats, dogs, and pigs.

vertebrates, including the last of the dinosaurs. The time span over which a mass extinction occurs may be several million years, but that is relatively short compared with the 3.5 billion years or so of Earth's history of life. Each period of mass extinction has been followed by a period of adaptive radiation of some of the surviving groups.

The causes of past episodes of mass extinction are not well understood. Both environmental and biological factors seem to have been involved. Major changes in climate could have adversely affected those plants and animals that lacked the genetic flexibility to adapt. Marine organisms, in particular, are adapted to a steady, unchanging climate. If Earth's temperature were to increase or decrease by just a few degrees overall, many marine species would probably perish.

It is also possible that past mass extinctions were due to changes in the environment induced by catastrophes. If a large comet or small asteroid collided with Earth, the dust ejected into the atmosphere on impact could have blocked much of the sunlight. In addition to disrupting the food chain by killing many plants (and

therefore terrestrial animals), this event would have lowered Earth's temperature, leading to the death of many marine organisms. Evidence exists that the extinction of dinosaurs was caused by an extraterrestrial object's collision with Earth (see Chapter 21).

Biological factors also trigger extinction. Competition among species may lead to the extinction of species that cannot compete effectively. The human species, in particular, has had a profound impact on the rate of extinction. The habitats of many animal and plant species have been altered or destroyed by humans, and habitat destruction can result in a species's extinction. Some biologists think we have entered the greatest mass extinction episode in Earth's history. (Extinction is discussed further in Chapter 57.)

Is microevolution related to speciation and macroevolution?

The concepts presented in Chapters 18 and 19 represent the **modern synthesis,** in which mutation provides the genetic variation on which natural selection acts. The modern synthesis combines

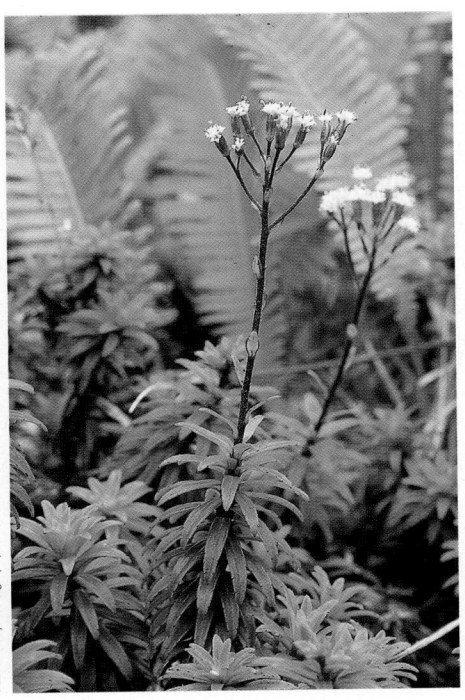

(a) The Haleakala silversword (*Argyroxyphium sandwicense ssp. macrocephalum*) is found only in the cinders on the upper slope of Haleakala Crater on the island of Maui. This plant is adapted to low precipitation and high levels of ultraviolet radiation.

(b) This silversword species (*Wilkesia gymnoxiphium*), which superficially resembles a yucca, is found only along the slopes of Waimea Canyon on the island of Kauai.

(c) *Daubautia scabra* is a small, herbaceous silversword found in moist to wet environments on several Hawaiian islands. (The fern fronds in the background give an idea of the small size of *D. scabra*.)

FIGURE 20-19 Adaptive radiation in Hawaiian silverswords
The 28 silversword species, which are classified in three closely related genera, live in a variety of habitats.

Darwin's theory with important aspects of genetics. Many aspects of the modern synthesis have been tested and verified at the population and subspecies levels. Many biologists contend that microevolutionary processes explain macroevolution. They assert that natural selection, mutation, genetic drift, and gene flow account for not only the genetic variation within populations but also the origin of new species and higher taxa as well.

A considerable body of data from many fields supports the modern synthesis as it relates to speciation and macroevolution. Consider, for example, the *fish–tetrapod transition* (the evolution of four-legged amphibians from fishes), which was a major macroevolutionary event in the history of vertebrates (see Chapter 32). The fish–tetrapod transition is well documented in the fossil record. Studies of fossil intermediates show that the transition from aquatic fishes to terrestrial amphibians occurred as evolutionary novelties, such as changes in the limbs and skull roof, were added. These novelties accumulated as a succession of small changes over a period of 9 million to 14 million years. This time scale is sufficient to have allowed natural selection and other microevolutionary processes to produce the novel characters.

Although few biologists doubt the role of natural selection and microevolution in generating specific adaptations, some question the *extent* of microevolution's role in the overall pattern of life's history. These biologists ask whether speciation and macroevolution have been dominated by microevolutionary processes or by external, chance events, such as an impact by an asteroid. Chance events do not "care" about adaptive superiority but instead lead to the random extinction or survival of species. In the case of an asteroid impact, for example, certain species may survive because they were "lucky" enough to be in a protected environment at the time of impact. If chance events have been the overriding factor during life's history, then microevolution cannot be the exclusive explanation for the biological diversity present today (see discussion of the role of chance in evolution in Chapter 18).

Review

- Why are evolutionary novelties important to scientists studying macroevolution?
- What is a preadaptation? What is paedomorphosis?
- What roles do extinction and adaptive radiation play in macroevolution?

20.1 *(page 427)*

1 Describe the biological species concept and list two potential problems with the concept.

- According to the **biological species concept,** a species consists of one or more populations whose members interbreed in nature to produce fertile offspring and do not interbreed with members of different species.

- One problem with the biological species concept is that it applies only to sexually reproducing organisms. Also, although individuals assigned to different species do not normally interbreed, they may occasionally successfully interbreed.

20.2 *(page 428)*

2 Explain the significance of reproductive isolating mechanisms and distinguish among the various prezygotic and postzygotic barriers.

- **Reproductive isolating mechanisms** restrict gene flow between species.

- **Prezygotic barriers** are reproductive isolating mechanisms that prevent fertilization from taking place. **Temporal isolation** occurs when two species reproduce at different times of the day, season, or year. In **habitat isolation,** two closely related species live and breed in different habitats in the same geographic area. In **behavioral isolation,** distinctive courtship behaviors prevent mating between species. **Mechanical isolation** is due to incompatible structural differences in the reproductive organs of similar species. In **gametic isolation,** gametes from different species are incompatible because of molecular and chemical differences.

- **Postzygotic barriers** are reproductive isolating mechanisms that prevent gene flow after fertilization has taken place. **Hybrid inviability** is the death of interspecific embryos during development. **Hybrid sterility** prevents interspecific hybrids that survive to adulthood from reproducing successfully. **Hybrid breakdown** prevents the offspring of hybrids that survive to adulthood and successfully reproduce from reproducing beyond one or a few generations.

  CENGAGENOW™   Explore reproductive isolation by clicking on the figures in CengageNOW.

20.3 *(page 430)*

3 Explain the mechanism of allopatric speciation and give an example.

- **Speciation** is the evolution of a new species from an ancestral population. **Allopatric speciation** (for example, in Death Valley pupfishes) occurs when one population becomes geographically isolated from the rest of the species and subsequently diverges. Speciation is more likely to occur if the original isolated population is small because genetic drift is more significant in small populations.

  CENGAGENOW™   Explore allopatric speciation by clicking on the figures in CengageNOW.

4 Explain the mechanisms of sympatric speciation and give both plant and animal examples.

- **Sympatric speciation** does not require geographic isolation. In plants, sympatric speciation can result from **allopolyploidy,** in

which a **polyploid** individual (one with more than two sets of chromosomes) is a hybrid derived from two species. One example of sympatric speciation by allopolyploidy is the hemp nettle.

- Sympatric speciation occurs in animals, such as fruit maggot flies and cichlids, but how often it occurs and under what conditions remain to be determined.

  CENGAGENOW™   Explore sympatric speciation by clicking on the figure in CengageNOW.

20.4 *(page 438)*

5 Discuss the pace of evolution by describing punctuated equilibrium and phyletic gradualism.

- According to the **punctuated equilibrium** model, evolution of species proceeds in spurts. Short periods of active speciation are interspersed with long periods of **stasis.** According to the **phyletic gradualism** model, populations slowly diverge from one another by the accumulation of adaptive characteristics within a population.

20.5 *(page 439)*

6 Define *macroevolution.*

- **Macroevolution** is large-scale phenotypic changes in populations that typically warrant the placement of the populations in taxonomic groups at the species level and higher—that is, new species, genera, families, orders, classes, and even phyla, kingdoms, and domains.

7 Discuss macroevolution in the context of novel features, including preadaptations, allometric growth, and paedomorphosis.

- Evolutionary novelties may be due to changes during **development,** the orderly sequence of events that occurs as an organism grows and matures. Slight genetic changes in regulatory genes could cause major structural changes in an organism.

- Evolutionary novelties may originate from **preadaptations,** structures that originally fulfilled one role but changed in a way that was adaptive for a different role. Feathers are an example of a preadaptation.

- **Allometric growth,** varied rates of growth for different parts of the body, results in overall changes in the shape of an organism. Examples include the expanded tail region of the ocean sunfish and the enlarged claw of the male fiddler crab.

- **Paedomorphosis,** the retention of juvenile characteristics in the adult, occurs because of changes in the timing of development. Adult axolotl salamanders, with external gills and tail fins, are an example of paedomorphosis.

8 Discuss the macroevolutionary significance of adaptive radiation and extinction.

- **Adaptive radiation** is the process of diversification of an ancestral species into many new species. **Adaptive zones** are new ecological opportunities that were not exploited by an ancestral organism. When many adaptive zones are empty, colonizing species may rapidly diversify and exploit them. Hawaiian honeycreepers and silverswords both underwent adaptive radiation after their ancestors colonized the Hawaiian Islands.

- **Extinction** is the death of a species. When species become extinct, the adaptive zones that they occupied become vacant, allowing other species to evolve and fill those zones. **Background extinction** is the continuous, low-level extinction of species. **Mass extinction** is the extinction of numerous species and higher taxonomic groups in both terrestrial and marine environments.

TEST YOUR UNDERSTANDING

1. A prezygotic barrier prevents (a) the union of egg and sperm (b) reproductive success by an interspecific hybrid (c) the development of the zygote into an embryo (d) allopolyploidy from occurring (e) changes in allometric growth

2. The reproductive isolating mechanism in which two closely related species live in the same geographic area but reproduce at different times is (a) temporal isolation (b) behavioral isolation (c) mechanical isolation (d) gametic isolation (e) hybrid inviability

3. Interspecific hybrids, if they survive, are (a) always sterile (b) always fertile (c) usually sterile (d) usually fertile (e) never sterile

4. The first step leading to allopatric speciation is (a) hybrid inviability (b) hybrid breakdown (c) adaptive radiation (d) geographic isolation (e) paedomorphosis

5. The pupfishes in the Death Valley region are an example of which evolutionary process? (a) background extinction (b) allopatric speciation (c) sympatric speciation (d) allopolyploidy (e) paedomorphosis

6. Which of the following evolutionary processes is associated with allopolyploidy? (a) gradualism (b) allometric growth (c) sympatric speciation (d) mass extinction (e) preadaptation

7. According to the punctuated equilibrium model, (a) populations slowly diverge from one another (b) the evolution of species occurs in spurts interspersed with long periods of stasis (c) evolutionary novelties originate from preadaptations (d) reproductive isolating mechanisms restrict gene flow between species (e) the fossil record, being incomplete, does not accurately reflect evolution as it actually occurred

8. The evolutionary conversion of reptilian scales into feathers is an example of (a) allometric growth (b) paedomorphosis (c) gradualism (d) hybrid breakdown (e) a preadaptation

9. Adaptive radiation is common following a period of mass extinction, probably because (a) the survivors of a mass extinction are remarkably well adapted to their environment (b) the unchanging environment following a mass extinction drives the evolutionary process (c) many adaptive zones are empty (d) many ecological niches are filled (e) the environment induces changes in the timing of development for many species

10. The Hawaiian silverswords are an excellent example of which evolutionary process? (a) allometry (b) preadaptation (c) microevolution (d) adaptive radiation (e) extinction

CRITICAL THINKING

1. **EVOLUTION LINK.** Why is allopatric speciation more likely to occur if the original isolated population is small?

2. **EVOLUTION LINK.** The photograph shows a "zebrass," a sterile hybrid produced on a Texas ranch by a cross between a zebra and a donkey. Based on what you have learned about prezygotic and postzygotic isolating mechanisms, which reproductive isolating mechanism(s) would you say is/are probably at work here? How would you test your hypothesis?

Harry Engels/Photo Researchers, Inc.

3. **EVOLUTION LINK.** Could hawthorn and apple maggot flies be considered an example of assortative mating, which was discussed in Chapter 19? Explain your answer.

4. **EVOLUTION LINK.** Because mass extinction is a natural process that may facilitate evolution during the period of thousands to millions of years that follow it, should humans be concerned about the current mass extinction that we are causing? Why or why not?

5. **ANALYZING DATA.** Examine Figure 20-2c, and predict which date is likeliest for researchers to have collected wood and leopard frogs and interbred them in the lab: March 10, April 1, or April 15. Explain your answer.

 Additional questions are available in CengageNOW at www.cengage.com/login.

21 The Origin and Evolutionary History of Life

Fossil of an Early Permian reptile. This well-preserved fossil of *Orobates pabsti* was matched to well-preserved fossil footprints found nearby. Although the limbs are spread out in death, *Orobates* walked with an upright gait with its limbs under its body. Discovered and photographed in Germany.

© Phil Degginger/Carnegie Museum/Alamy

KEY CONCEPTS

21.1 Although there is no direct fossil evidence of the origin of life, biochemical experiments have demonstrated how the complex organic molecules that are found in all living organisms may have formed.

21.2 The first cells were probably heterotrophic, anaerobic, and prokaryotic. Photosynthesis, aerobic respiration, and eukaryotic cell structure represent several major advances that occurred during the early history of life.

21.3 The fossil record tells us much of what we know about the history of life, such as what kinds of organisms existed and where and when they lived. Scientists identify and demonstrate relationships among fossils in rock layers from different periods of geologic time.

The preceding three chapters were concerned with biological evolution. However, we have not dealt with what many regard as a fundamental question: How did life begin? Although biologists generally accept the hypothesis that life developed from nonliving matter, exactly how this process, called **chemical evolution,** occurred is not certain. Current models suggest that small organic molecules first formed spontaneously and accumulated over time. Large organic macromolecules such as proteins and nucleic acids could have then assembled from the smaller molecules.

The macromolecules interacted, combining into more complicated structures that could eventually metabolize and replicate, passing their genetic information on to their descendants, which eventually became the first true cells. After the first cells originated, they diverged over several billion years into the rich biological diversity that characterizes our planet today.

Initially, unicellular prokaryotes (archaea and bacteria) predominated, followed by unicellular eukaryotes. The first multicellular eukaryotes were soft-bodied marine animals that did not leave many fossils.

Shelled animals and other marine invertebrates (animals without backbones) appeared next, as exemplified by trilobites, primitive aquatic arthropods. Marine invertebrates were followed by the first vertebrates (animals with backbones). The first fishes with jaws appeared and diversified. Some of these gave rise to amphibians, the first vertebrates with limbs that were capable of moving about on land. Amphibians gave rise to reptiles, which diversified and populated the land (see photograph). Reptiles, in turn, gave rise independently to birds and to mammals. Plants underwent a comparable evolutionary history and diversification.

In this chapter we survey life over a vast span of time, starting when our planet was relatively young. We first examine proposed models about how life began and then trace life's long evolutionary history.

21.1 CHEMICAL EVOLUTION ON EARLY EARTH

◼ LEARNING OBJECTIVES

1 Describe the conditions that scientists think existed on early Earth.
2 Contrast the prebiotic soup hypothesis and the iron–sulfur world hypothesis.

Scientists generally agree that life's beginnings occurred under environmental conditions quite different from those of today. Therefore,

we must examine the conditions of early Earth to understand the origin of life. Evidence from many sources provides us with clues that help us formulate plausible scenarios of the steps in which life originated. Study of the origin of life is an active area of scientific research today, and many important contributions are adding to our understanding of how life began.

Astrophysicists and geologists estimate that Earth is about 4.6 billion years old. The atmosphere of early Earth apparently included carbon dioxide (CO_2), water vapor (H_2O), carbon monoxide (CO), and nitrogen (N_2). It may also have contained some ammonia (NH_3), hydrogen sulfide (H_2S), and methane (CH_4), although ultraviolet radiation from the sun most likely broke these reduced molecules down rapidly. The early atmosphere probably contained little or no free oxygen (O_2).

Four requirements must have existed for the chemical evolution of life: little or no free oxygen, a source of energy, the availability of chemical building blocks, and time. First, life could have begun only in the absence of free oxygen. Oxygen is quite reactive and would have oxidized the organic molecules that are necessary building blocks in the origin of life. Earth's early atmosphere was probably strongly reducing, which means that any free oxygen would have reacted with other elements to form oxides. Thus, oxygen would have been tied up in compounds.

The origin of life would also have required energy to do the work of building biological molecules from simple inorganic chemicals. Early Earth was a place of high energy with violent thunderstorms; widespread volcanic activity; bombardment from meteorites and other extraterrestrial objects; and intense radiation, including ultraviolet radiation from the sun (**FIG. 21-1**). The young

FIGURE 21-1 Conditions on early Earth
Volcanoes erupted, spewing gases that contributed to the atmosphere, and violent thunderstorms triggered torrential rainfall that washed molecules out of the atmosphere and eroded the land. Meteorites and other extraterrestrial objects bombarded Earth, cataclysmically changing the crust, ocean, and atmosphere. Deep-sea thermal vents, heated by Earth's internal heat, spewed forth chemicals. High-energy radiation from cosmic and ultraviolet rays blasted the planet.

sun probably produced more ultraviolet radiation than it does today, and ancient Earth had no protective ozone layer to filter it.

A third requirement would have been the presence of the chemical building blocks needed for chemical evolution. These included water, dissolved inorganic minerals (present as ions), and the gases present in the early atmosphere. A final requirement for the origin of life was time for molecules to accumulate and react with one another. Earth is approximately 4.6 billion years old, and evidence suggests that life arose early in Earth's history.

Organic molecules formed on primitive Earth

Because organic molecules are the building materials for organisms, it is reasonable to first consider how they may have originated. Two main models seek to explain how the organic precursors of life originated: the **prebiotic soup hypothesis** proposes that these molecules formed near Earth's surface, whereas the **iron–sulfur world hypothesis** proposes that organic precursors formed at cracks in the ocean's floor.

Organic molecules may have been produced at Earth's surface

The concept that simple organic molecules such as sugars, nucleotide bases, and amino acids could form spontaneously from simpler raw materials was first advanced in the 1920s by two scientists working independently: A. I. Oparin, a Russian biochemist, and J. B. S. Haldane, a Scottish physiologist and geneticist.

Their hypothesis was tested in the 1950s by U.S. biochemists Stanley Miller and Harold Urey, who designed a closed apparatus that simulated conditions that presumably existed on early Earth (**FIG. 21-2**). They exposed an atmosphere rich in H_2, CH_4, H_2O, and NH_3 to an electric discharge that simulated lightning. Their analysis of the chemicals produced during one week revealed that amino acids and other organic molecules had formed. Although more recent data suggest that Earth's early atmosphere was not rich in methane, ammonia, or hydrogen, similar experiments using different combinations of gases have produced a wide variety of organic molecules that are important in contemporary organisms. These include all 20 amino acids, several sugars, lipids, the nucleotide bases of RNA and DNA, and ATP (when phosphate is present). Thus, before life began, its chemical building blocks were probably accumulating as a necessary step in chemical evolution.

Oparin envisioned that the organic molecules would, over vast spans of time, accumulate in the shallow seas to form a "sea of organic soup." He envisioned smaller organic molecules (monomers) combining to form larger ones (polymers) under such conditions. Evidence gathered since Oparin's time indicates that organic polymers may have formed and accumulated on rock or clay surfaces rather than in the primordial seas. Clay, which consists of microscopic particles of weathered rock, is particularly intriguing as a possible site for early polymerizations because it binds organic monomers and contains zinc and iron ions that may have served as catalysts. Laboratory experiments have confirmed that organic polymers form spontaneously from monomers on hot rock or clay surfaces.

Organic molecules may have formed at hydrothermal vents

Some biologists hypothesize that early polymerizations leading to the origin of life may have occurred in cracks in the deep-ocean floor where hot water, carbon monoxide, and minerals such as sulfides of iron and nickel spew forth—the iron–sulfur world hypothesis. Such **hydrothermal vents** would have been better protected than Earth's surface from the catastrophic effects of meteorite bombardment.

Today, these anaerobic hot springs produce precursors of biological molecules and of energy-rich "food," including the highly reduced compounds hydrogen sulfide and methane. These chemicals support a diverse community of microorganisms, clams, crabs, tube worms, and other animals (see *Inquiring About: Life without the Sun,* in Chapter 55).

Testing the iron–sulfur world hypothesis at hydrothermal vents is difficult, but laboratory experiments simulating the high pressures and temperatures at the vents have yielded intriguing results. For example, iron and nickel sulfides catalyze reactions between carbon monoxide and hydrogen sulfide, producing acetic acid and other simple organic compounds. Also, experiments show that ammonia, one of the precursors of proteins and nucleic acids, is produced in abundance, suggesting that vents were ammonia-rich environments in the prebiotic world and that the earliest organisms could have formed in this seemingly inhospitable environment.

Review

- What are the four requirements for chemical evolution, and why is each essential?
- What is the prebiotic soup hypothesis?
- How does the iron–sulfur world hypothesis differ from the prebiotic soup hypothesis?

21.2 THE FIRST CELLS

◼ LEARNING OBJECTIVES

3 Outline the major steps hypothesized to have occurred in the origin of cells.

4 Explain how the evolution of photosynthetic autotrophs affected both the atmosphere and other organisms.

5 Describe the hypothesis of serial endosymbiosis.

After the first polymers formed, could they have assembled spontaneously into more complex structures with an outer membranous boundary? Scientists have synthesized several different **protobionts,** which are vesicle-like assemblages of abiotically produced (that is, not produced by organisms) organic polymers. These protobionts resemble living cells in several ways, thus providing clues as to how aggregations of complex nonliving molecules took that "giant leap" and became living cells. These protobionts exhibit many functional and structural attributes of living cells. They often divide in half (binary fission) after they have sufficiently "grown." Protobionts maintain an internal chemical environment that is different from the external environment (homeostasis), and some of them show the beginnings of metabolism (catalytic activity). They are highly organized, considering their relatively simple composition.

Microspheres are a type of protobiont formed by adding water to abiotically formed polypeptides (**FIG. 21-3**). Some microspheres are excitable: they produce an electrical potential across their surfaces, reminiscent of electrochemical gradients in cells. Microspheres can also absorb materials from their surroundings

2 μm

FIGURE 21-3 Microspheres
These tiny protobionts exhibit some of the properties of life.

(selective permeability) and respond to changes in osmotic pressure as though membranes enveloped them, even though they contain no lipid.

In 2008, scientists constructed protobionts in which membranes of fatty acids and monoglycerides surround larger DNA-like molecules. These protobionts are impermeable to the genetic molecules but allow smaller organic molecules—that is, "nutrients"—to enter. This study is significant because it suggests how early cells could have held on to their "genes" and absorbed needed nutrients from their environment without the sophisticated membrane structure associated with contemporary cells.

The study of protobionts shows that relatively simple nonliving structures have some of the properties of life. However, it is a major step (or several steps) to go from simple molecular aggregates such as protobionts to living cells.

The origin of a simple metabolism within a membrane boundary may have occurred early in the evolution of cells

Although we have learned many things about how organic molecules may have formed on primitive Earth, the problem of how pre-cells evolved into living cells remains to be solved. Let's examine one possible scenario—the **metabolism first hypothesis**—supported by chemist Robert Shapiro at New York University and many others. Shapiro envisions life beginning as a self-sustaining, organized system consisting of chemical reactions between simple molecules that are enclosed within a boundary—that is, separated from the external environment (**FIG. 21-4a**).

A source of energy must be available to drive these chemical reactions (thereby maintaining an internal organization different from the external environment). To be self-sustaining, the energy source must be coupled to the chemical reaction sequence (**FIG. 21-4B**). (Recall how ATP links exergonic and endergonic reactions, shown in Figure 7-6.)

(a) Within a membranous boundary, chemical reactions occur among simple molecules.

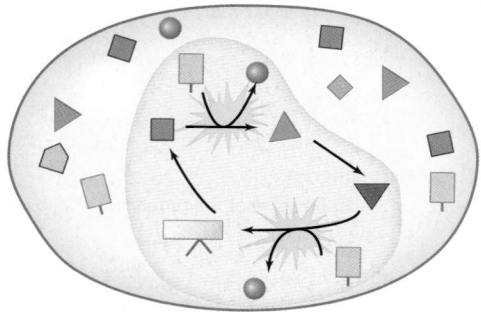

(b) A source of energy is coupled to the chemical reaction sequence.

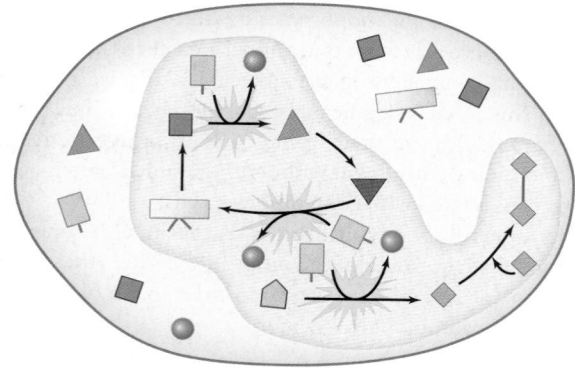

(c) As the pre-cell system continues to evolve, its size and organization increase.

(d) The pre-cell system develops the ability to reproduce.

FIGURE 21-4 Origin of life: the metabolism first scenario

As the pre-cells continue to evolve, their organization increases (**FIG. 21-4c**). Finally, to survive, the pre-cell system must grow and reproduce. One of the most significant parts of the origin of living cells from pre-cells was the evolution of molecular reproduction (**FIG. 21-4d**).

Molecular reproduction was a crucial step in the origin of cells

In living cells, genetic information is stored in the nucleic acid DNA, which is transcribed into messenger RNA (mRNA), which in turn is translated into the proper amino acid sequence in proteins. All three macromolecules in the DNA ⟶ RNA ⟶ protein sequence contain precise information. Of these, only DNA and RNA are capable of self-replication (although only in the presence of the proper enzymes in cells today). Because both RNA and DNA can form spontaneously on clay in much the same way that other organic polymers do, the question becomes, which molecule, DNA or RNA, first appeared in the prebiotic world?

Many scientists have suggested that RNA was the first informational molecule to evolve in the progression toward a self-sustaining, self-reproducing cell and that proteins and DNA came along later. According to a model known as the **RNA world,** the chemistry of prebiotic Earth gave rise to self-replicating RNA molecules that functioned as both enzymes and substrates for their own replication. We represent the replication of RNA in the RNA world scenario as a circular arrow:

RNA often has catalytic properties; such enzymatic RNAs are called **ribozymes.** Before the evolution of true cells, ribozymes may have catalyzed their own replication in the clays, shallow rock pools, or hydrothermal vents where life originated. When RNA strands are added to a test tube containing RNA nucleotides but no enzymes, the nucleotides combine to form short RNA molecules.

The occurrence of an RNA world early in the history of life can never be proven, but experiments with **in vitro evolution,** also called **directed evolution,** have shown it is feasible. These experiments address an important question about the RNA world, namely, could RNA molecules have catalyzed the many different chemical reactions needed for life? In directed evolution, a large pool of RNA molecules with different sequences is mixed, and molecules are selected for their ability to catalyze a single biologically important reaction (**FIG. 21-5**). Those molecules that have at least some catalytic ability are selected by researchers, who then amplify them into many copies. The researchers use certain chemicals to cause mutations, and then expose the molecules to another round of selection. After this cycle is repeated several times, the RNA molecules at the end of the selection process function efficiently as catalysts for the reaction. In vitro evolution studies have shown that RNA has a large functional repertoire—that is, RNA can catalyze a variety of biologically important reactions.

Biologists hypothesize that in the RNA world, ribozymes initially catalyzed protein synthesis and other important biological reactions; only later did protein enzymes catalyze these reactions.

QUESTION: Can in vitro natural selection result in chemical evolution of catalysts?

HYPOTHESIS: Self-replicating RNA molecules can undergo changes that make them more efficient catalysts.

EXPERIMENT: RNA molecules are selected from a large pool, based on their ability to catalyze a specific reaction, then amplified and mutated (*see figure*). This process is repeated 7 to 20 additional times.

Large pool of RNA molecules

Selection for ability to catalyze a chemical reaction

Molecules with some ability to catalyze the reaction

Amplification and mutation to create large pool of similar RNA molecules

Repeat the selection → amplification → mutation process

Molecules with best ability to catalyze the reaction

RESULTS AND CONCLUSION: The final group of RNA molecules is the most efficient at catalyzing the chemical reaction selected for. Scientists have developed more than two dozen synthetic RNA catalysts by in vitro evolution.

FIGURE 21-5 In vitro evolution of RNA molecules

Interestingly, in test tube experiments, RNA molecules have evolved that direct protein synthesis by catalyzing peptide bond formation. Some single-stranded RNA molecules fold back on themselves as a result of interactions among the nucleotides composing the RNA strand. Sometimes the conformation (shape) of the folded RNA molecule is such that it weakly binds to an amino acid (see discussion of peptidyl transferase in Chapter 13). Amino acids held close to one another by RNA molecules may bond, forming a polypeptide.

We have considered how the evolution of informational molecules may have given rise to RNA and later to proteins. If a self-replicating RNA capable of coding for proteins appeared prior to DNA, how did DNA, the universal molecule of heredity in cells, become involved? Perhaps RNA made double-stranded copies of itself that eventually evolved into DNA.

$$DNA \longleftarrow RNA \longrightarrow protein$$

The incorporation of DNA into the information transfer system was advantageous because the double helix of DNA is more stable (less reactive) than the single strand of RNA. Such stability in a molecule that stores genetic information would have provided a decided advantage in the prebiotic world (as it does today).

Thus, in the DNA/RNA/protein world, DNA became the information storage molecule, RNA remained involved in protein synthesis, and protein enzymes catalyzed most cell reactions, including DNA replication and RNA synthesis.

$$DNA \rightarrow RNA \rightarrow protein$$

RNA is still a necessary component of the information transfer system because DNA is not catalytic. Thus, natural selection at the molecular level favored the DNA ⟶ RNA ⟶ protein information sequence. Once DNA was incorporated into this sequence, RNA molecules assumed their present role as an intermediary in the transfer of genetic information.

Several additional steps had to occur before a true living cell could evolve from macromolecular aggregations. For example, the self-replicating genetic code must have arisen extremely early in the prebiotic world because all organisms possess it—but how did it originate? Also, how did an encapsulating membrane of lipid and protein evolve? These kinds of questions remain for scientists to address.

Biological evolution began with the first cells

No one knows exactly when or where the first cells appeared on Earth. Did they live at hydrothermal vents or at Earth's surface? Were they bacteria? We cannot answer these questions, in part because no fossils exist that trace the transition from nonlife to life. Nonfossil evidence—isotopic "fingerprints" of organic carbon in ancient rocks in Greenland—suggest to some researchers that life existed as early as 3.8 billion years ago (bya). However, other scientists vigorously debate this conclusion.

Microfossils, ancient remains of microscopic life, suggest that cells may have been thriving as long as 3.5 bya. Rich deposits of microfossils appear to exist in the Pilbara rocks of northwestern Australia and the Barberton rocks in South Africa; both of these deposits are about 3.3 billion to 3.5 billion years old. However, some scientists have challenged the interpretation of the oldest

Fred Bavendam/Peter Arnold, Inc.

(a) These living stromatolites at Hamlin Pool in Western Australia consist of mats of cyanobacteria (unicellular photosynthetic prokaryotes) and minerals such as calcium carbonate. They are several thousand years old.

Stanley M. Awramik/Biological Photo Service

(b) Cutaway view of a fossil stromatolite showing the layers of microorganisms and sediments that accumulated over time. This stromatolite, also from Western Australia, is about 3.5 billion years old.

FIGURE 21-6 Stromatolites

carbon-rich "squiggles" in ancient rocks as microfossils of prokaryotic organisms. They suggest that microfossils are not fossils at all but are formed by natural geologic processes.

Evidence suggests that the earliest cells were prokaryotic. **Stromatolites,** another type of fossil evidence of the earliest cells, are rocklike columns composed of many minute layers of prokaryotic cells—that is, microbial biofilms (**FIG. 21-6**). Over time, sediment collects around the cells and mineralizes. Meanwhile, a new layer of living cells grows over the older, dead cells. Fossil stromatolite reefs are found in several places in the world, including Great Slave Lake in Canada and the Gunflint Iron Formations along Lake Superior in the United States. Some fossil stromatolites are extremely ancient. One group in Western Australia, for example, has been dated at more than 3 billion years.

Living stromatolite reefs are rare but are found in certain hot springs and warm, shallow pools of fresh and salt water. Interestingly, in 2008 scientists reported that the microorganisms inhabiting living stromatolite communities are strikingly different from microorganisms in all other ecosystems studied to date; this discovery suggests that the microorganisms living in today's stromatolites may have evolved from microorganisms living in the ancient stromatolite ecosystems.

The first cells were probably heterotrophic

The earliest cells probably did not synthesize the organic molecules they needed but instead obtained them from the environment. These primitive **heterotrophs** may have consumed many types of organic molecules that had formed spontaneously—for example, sugars, nucleotides, and amino acids. By fermenting these organic compounds, they obtained the energy they needed to support life. *Fermentation* is, of course, an anaerobic process (performed in the absence of oxygen), and the first cells were almost certainly **anaerobes.**

When the supply of spontaneously generated organic molecules gradually declined, only certain organisms could survive. Mutations had probably already occurred that permitted some cells to obtain energy directly from sunlight, perhaps by using sunlight to make ATP. These cells, which did not require the energy-rich organic compounds that were now in short supply in the environment, had a distinct selective advantage.

Photosynthesis requires both light energy and a source of electrons, which are used to reduce CO_2 to form organic molecules such as glucose. (Recall the discussion of photosynthesis in Chapter 9.) Most likely, the first photosynthetic **autotrophs**—organisms that produce their own food from simple raw materials—used the energy of sunlight to split hydrogen-rich molecules such as H_2S, releasing elemental sulfur (not oxygen) in the process. Splitting H_2S is energetically much easier than splitting H_2O because sulfur is not electronegative like oxygen (see Chapter 9). Indeed, the green sulfur bacteria and the purple sulfur bacteria still use H_2S as a hydrogen (electron) source for photosynthesis. (Members of a third bacterial group, the purple nonsulfur bacteria, use other organic molecules or hydrogen gas as a hydrogen source.)

The first photosynthetic autotrophs to obtain hydrogen electrons by splitting *water* were the **cyanobacteria.** Water was quite abundant on early Earth, as it is today, and the selective advantage of splitting water allowed cyanobacteria to thrive. The process of splitting water released oxygen as a gas (O_2). Initially, the oxygen released during photosynthesis oxidized minerals in the ocean and in Earth's crust, and oxygen did not begin to accumulate in the atmosphere for a long time. Eventually, however, oxygen levels increased in the ocean and the atmosphere.

Scientists estimate the timing of the events just described on the basis of geologic and fossil evidence. Fossils from that period, which include rocks containing traces of chlorophyll, as well as the fossil stromatolites discussed earlier, indicate that the first photosynthetic organisms may have appeared as early as 3.5 bya.

This evidence suggests that heterotrophic forms may have existed even earlier.

Aerobes appeared after oxygen increased in the atmosphere

Based on sulfur isotope data from ancient rocks in South Africa, it appears that cyanobacteria had produced enough oxygen to begin significantly changing the composition of the atmosphere by 2.4 bya. This date may be changed as more data accumulate: in 2009 geoscientists at Pennsylvania State University found strong isotopic evidence in Australia that oxygen was present in the oceans as early as 3.46 bya. Scientists are now looking for the same kind of evidence at other sedimentary layers known to be older than 2.4 bya.

The increase in atmospheric oxygen affected life profoundly. The oxygen poisoned *obligate anaerobes* (organisms that cannot use oxygen for cellular respiration), and many species undoubtedly perished. Some anaerobes, however, survived in environments where oxygen did not penetrate; adaptations evolved in others that neutralized the oxygen so it could not harm them. In some organisms, called **aerobes,** a respiratory pathway evolved that *used* oxygen to extract more energy from food. Aerobic respiration was joined with the existing anaerobic process of glycolysis.

The evolution of organisms that could use oxygen in their metabolism had several consequences. Organisms that respire aerobically gain much more energy from a single molecule of glucose than anaerobes gain by fermentation. (Recall the comparison of fermentation and aerobic respiration in Table 8.2.) As a result, the newly evolved aerobic organisms were more efficient and more competitive than anaerobes. Coupled with the poisonous nature of oxygen to many anaerobes, the efficiency of aerobes forced anaerobes into relatively minor roles. Today, the vast majority of organisms, including plants, animals, and most fungi, protists, archaea, and bacteria, use aerobic respiration; only a few archaea and bacteria and even fewer protists and fungi are anaerobic.

The evolution of aerobic respiration stabilized both oxygen and carbon dioxide levels in the biosphere. Photosynthetic organisms used carbon dioxide as a source of carbon for synthesizing organic compounds. This raw material would have been depleted from the atmosphere in a relatively brief period without the advent of aerobic respiration, which released carbon dioxide as a waste product from the complete breakdown of organic molecules. Carbon thus started cycling in the biosphere, moving from the nonliving physical environment, to photosynthetic organisms, to heterotrophs that ate the photosynthetic organisms (see Chapter 55). Aerobic respiration released carbon back into the physical environment as carbon dioxide, and the carbon cycle continued. In a similar manner, molecular oxygen was produced by photosynthesis and used during aerobic respiration.

Another significant consequence of photosynthesis occurred in the upper atmosphere, where molecular oxygen reacted to form **ozone (O_3)** (**FIG. 21-7**). A layer of ozone eventually blanketed Earth, preventing much of the sun's ultraviolet radiation from penetrating to the surface. With the ozone layer's protection from the mutagenic effect of ultraviolet radiation, organisms could live closer to the surface in aquatic environments and eventually move

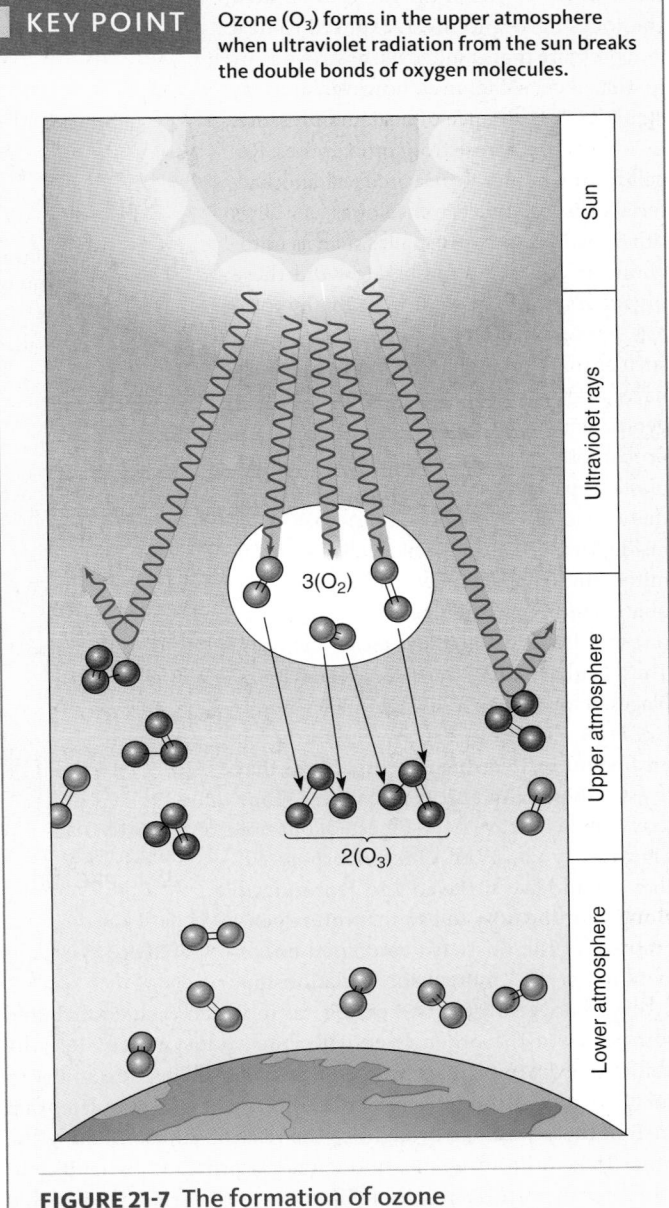

Sun

Ultraviolet rays

$3(O_2)$

$2(O_3)$

Upper atmosphere

Lower atmosphere

FIGURE 21-7 The formation of ozone

onto land. Because the energy in ultraviolet radiation may have been necessary to form organic molecules, however, their abiotic synthesis decreased.

Eukaryotic cells descended from prokaryotic cells

Eukaryotes may have appeared in the fossil record as early as 2.2 bya, and geochemical evidence suggests that eukaryotes were present much earlier. *Steranes,* molecules derived from steroids, have been discovered in Australian rocks dated at 2.7 billion years old. Because bacteria are not known to produce steroids, the steranes may be biomarkers for eukaryotes. These ancient rocks lack fossil traces of ancient organisms because the rocks have since been exposed to heat and pressure that would have destroyed any fossilized cells. Steranes, however, are very stable in the presence of heat and pressure.

Eukaryotes arose from prokaryotes. Recall from Chapter 4 that archaeal and bacterial cells lack nuclear envelopes as well as other membranous organelles such as mitochondria and chloroplasts. How did these organelles arise? According to the hypothesis of **serial endosymbiosis,** organelles such as mitochondria and chloroplasts may have originated from mutually advantageous symbiotic relationships between two prokaryotic organisms (**FIG. 21-8**). Chloroplasts apparently evolved from photosynthetic bacteria (cyanobacteria) that lived inside larger heterotrophic cells, whereas mitochondria presumably evolved from aerobic bacteria (perhaps ancient purple bacteria) that lived inside larger anaerobic cells. Thus, early eukaryotic cells were assemblages of formerly free-living prokaryotes.

How did these bacteria come to be **endosymbionts,** which are organisms that live symbiotically inside a host cell? They may originally have been ingested, but not digested, by a host cell. Once incorporated, they could have survived and reproduced along with the host cell so that future generations of the host also contained endosymbionts. A mutualistic relationship evolved between these two organisms in which each contributed something to the other. Eventually, the endosymbiont lost the ability to exist outside its host, and the host cell lost the ability to survive without its endosymbionts. This hypothesis stipulates that each of these partners brought to the relationship something the other lacked. For example, mitochondria provided the ability to carry out the aerobic respiration lacking in the original anaerobic host cell. Chloroplasts provided the ability to use a simple carbon source (CO_2) to produce needed organic molecules. The host cell provided endosymbionts with a safe environment and raw materials or nutrients.

The principal evidence in favor of serial endosymbiosis is that mitochondria and chloroplasts possess some (although not all) of their own genetic material and translational components. They have their own DNA (as a circular molecule similar to that of archaea and bacteria; discussed in Chapter 25) and their own ribosomes (which resemble bacterial rather than eukaryotic ribosomes). Mitochondria and chloroplasts also possess some of the machinery for protein synthesis, including tRNA molecules, and conduct protein synthesis on a limited scale independent of the nucleus. Furthermore, it is possible to poison mitochondria and chloroplasts with an antibiotic that affects bacteria but not eukaryotic cells. As discussed in Chapter 4, double membranes envelope

ORIGINAL PROKARYOTIC HOST CELL

DNA

Aerobic bacteria

Multiple invaginations of the plasma membrane

Aerobic bacteria become mitochondria

Endoplasmic reticulum and nuclear envelope form from the plasma membrane invaginations (not part of serial endosymbiosis)

Photosynthetic bacteria become chloroplasts

EUKARYOTIC CELLS: PLANTS, SOME PROTISTS

EUKARYOTIC CELLS: ANIMALS, FUNGI, SOME PROTISTS

FIGURE 21-8 *Animated* Serial endosymbiosis

mitochondria and chloroplasts. The outer membrane apparently developed from the invagination (infolding) of the host cell's plasma membrane, whereas the inner membrane is derived from the endosymbiont's plasma membrane. (Serial endosymbiosis is discussed in greater detail in Chapter 26.)

Many endosymbiotic relationships exist today. Many corals have algae living as endosymbionts within their cells (see Fig. 54-12). Protozoa (*Myxotricha paradoxa*) live symbiotically in the gut of termites; in turn, several different endosymbionts, including spirochete bacteria, attach to the protozoa and function as whiplike flagella, allowing the protozoa to move.

Although much evidence supports serial endosymbiosis, it does not completely explain the evolution of eukaryotic cells from prokaryotes. For example, serial endosymbiosis does not currently explain how a double membranous envelope came to surround the genetic material in the nucleus.

Review

- What major steps probably occurred in the origin of cells?
- How did the presence of molecular oxygen in the atmosphere affect early life?
- What kinds of evidence support serial endosymbiosis?

21.3 THE HISTORY OF LIFE

◼ LEARNING OBJECTIVE

6   Briefly describe the distinguishing organisms and major biological events of the Ediacaran period and the Paleozoic, Mesozoic, and Cenozoic eras.

The sequence of biological, climate, and geologic events that make up the history of life is recorded in rocks and fossils. The sediments of Earth's crust consist of five major rock strata (layers), each subdivided into minor strata, lying one on top of the other. Very few places on Earth show all layers, but the strata present typically occur in the correct order, with younger rocks on top of older ones. These sheets of rock formed from the accumulation of mud and sand at the bottoms of the ocean, seas, and lakes. Each layer contains certain characteristic **index fossils** that identify deposits made at about the same time in different parts of the world.

Geologists divide Earth's history into units of time based on major geologic, climate, and biological events. **Eons** are the largest divisions of the geologic time scale. Eons are divided into **eras**; where fossil evidence exists, these divisions are based primarily on organisms that characterized each era. Eras are subdivided into **periods,** which in turn are composed of **epochs.**

Relatively little is known about Earth from its beginnings approximately 4.6 bya up to 2.5 bya, a time known as the **Archaean eon** (TABLE 21-1). Life originated on Earth during the Archaean eon. Signs of life date as early as 3.5 bya. Not much physical evidence is available because the rocks of the Archaean eon, being extremely ancient, are deeply buried in most parts of the world. Ancient rocks are exposed in a few places, including the bottom of the Grand Canyon and along the shores of Lake Superior. Many Archaean rock formations have revealed what appear to be microfossils of cyanobacteria and other bacteria.

Rocks from the Ediacaran period contain fossils of cells and simple animals

That part of time from 2500 mya to 542 mya is known as the **Proterozoic eon.** This enormous span of time is easier to study than the preceding Archaean eon because the rocks are less altered by heat and pressure. Life at the beginning of the Proterozoic eon consisted of prokaryotes such as cyanobacteria. Stromatolites were abundant. About 2.2 bya the first eukaryotic cells appeared. By the end of the Proterozoic eon, multicellularity was evident in the abundant fossils of small, soft-bodied, invertebrate animals.

The **Ediacaran period** (pronounced "ee-dee-ack'-uh-run"), from 600 mya to 542 mya, is the last (most recent) period of the Proterozoic eon. It is named for the fossil deposits in the Ediacara Hills in South Australia, although Ediacaran fossils are also found in Newfoundland, the Mackenzie Mountains of northwestern Canada, the Doushantuo Formation of China, and other locations. Currently, more than 270 Ediacaran species have been identified and described.

Ediacaran fossils are the oldest known fossils of multicellular animals (**FIG. 21-9**). Experts have not yet identified all the

FIGURE 21-9 Reconstruction of life in an Ediacaran sea
The organisms shown here are based on fossils from the Ediacara Hills of South Australia, although similar associations have been found in Ediacaran rocks from every continent except Antarctica. Shown are organisms that some scientists have interpreted as jellyfish, flatworms, algae, and paddle-shaped organisms similar in appearance to soft corals.

simple, soft-bodied animals found in the Ediacara Hills and at other sites. Some paleontologists interpret many of these fossils as early sponges, jellyfish, corals, and comb jellies; however, other scientists think that the Ediacaran animals were not ancestral to modern-day species but instead became extinct at the end of the Ediacaran period.

A diversity of organisms evolved during the Paleozoic era

The **Paleozoic era** began approximately 542 mya and lasted about 291 million years. It is divided into six periods: Cambrian, Ordovician, Silurian, Devonian, Carboniferous, and Permian.

Rocks rich in fossils represent the oldest subdivision of the Paleozoic era, the **Cambrian period.** For about 40 million years, evolution was in such high gear, with the sudden appearance of many new animal body plans, that this period is called the **Cambrian Radiation,** or more informally, *Cambrian explosion.* Fossils of all contemporary animal phyla are present, along with many bizarre, extinct phyla, in marine sediments. The seafloor was covered with sponges, corals, sea lilies, sea stars, snails, clamlike bivalves, primitive squidlike cephalopods, lamp shells (brachiopods), and trilobites (see Fig. 31-26). In addition, small vertebrates—cartilaginous fishes—became established in the marine environment.

Scientists have not determined the factors responsible for the Cambrian Radiation, a period unmatched in the evolutionary history of life. There is some evidence that oxygen concentrations, which had continued to gradually increase in the atmosphere, passed some critical threshold late in the Proterozoic eon. Scientists who advocate the *oxygen enrichment hypothesis* note that until late in the Proterozoic eon, Earth did not have enough oxygen to support larger animals. The most important fossil sites that document the Cambrian Radiation are the **Chengjiang site** in China (for Early Cambrian fossils) and the **Burgess Shale** in British Columbia (for Middle Cambrian fossils) (**FIG. 21-10**).

TABLE 21-1			Some Important Biological Events in Geologic Time			

Eon	Era	Period	Epoch	Time*	Some Important Biological Events
Phanerozoic eon	Cenozoic era	Quaternary period	Holocene epoch	0.01 (10,000 years ago)	Decline of some woody plants; rise of herbaceous plants; age of *Homo sapiens*
			Pleistocene epoch	2.6 mya	Extinction of some plant species; extinction of many large mammals at end
		Neogene period	Pliocene epoch	5 mya	Expansion of grasslands and deserts; many grazing animals
			Miocene epoch	23 mya	Flowering plants continue to diversify; diversity of songbirds and grazing mammals
		Paleogene period	Oligocene epoch	34 mya	Spread of forests; apes appear; present mammalian families are represented
			Eocene epoch	56 mya	Flowering plants dominant; modern mammalian orders appear and diversify; modern bird orders appear
			Paleocene epoch	66 mya	Semitropical vegetation (flowering plants and conifers) widespread; primitive mammals diversify
	Mesozoic era	Cretaceous period		146 mya	Rise of flowering plants; dinosaurs reach peak, then become extinct at end; toothed birds become extinct
		Jurassic period		200 mya	Gymnosperms common; large dinosaurs; first toothed birds
		Triassic period		251 mya	Gymnosperms dominant; ferns common; first dinosaurs; first mammals
	Paleozoic era	Permian period		299 mya	Conifers diversify; cycads appear; modern insects appear; mammal-like reptiles; extinction of many invertebrates and vertebrates at end of Permian
		Carboniferous period		359 mya	Forests of ferns, club mosses, horsetails, and gymnosperms; many insect forms; spread of ancient amphibians; first reptiles
		Devonian period		416 mya	First forests; gymnosperms appear; many trilobites; wingless insects appear; fishes with jaws appear and diversify; amphibians appear
		Silurian period		444 mya	Vascular plants appear; coral reefs common; jawless fishes diversify; terrestrial arthropods
		Ordovician period		488 mya	Fossil spores of terrestrial plants (bryophytes?); invertebrates dominant; coral reefs appear; first fishes appear
		Cambrian period		542 mya	Bacteria and cyanobacteria; algae; fungi; age of marine invertebrates; first chordates
Proterozoic eon		Ediacaran period		600 mya	Algae and soft-bodied invertebrates diversify
		Early Proterozoic period		2500 mya	Eukaryotes evolve
Archaean eon				4600 mya	Oldest known rocks; prokaryotes evolve; atmospheric oxygen begins to increase

*Time from beginning of eon, period, or epoch to present (millions of years).

(a) *Marrella splendens* was a small arthropod with 26 body segments. It is the most abundant fossil arthropod found in the Burgess Shale.

(b) *Wiwaxia* was a bristle-covered marine worm that was distantly related to earthworms. It had scaly armor and needlelike spines for protection.

FIGURE 21-10 Fossils from the Cambrian Radiation
These fossils were discovered in the Burgess Shale in the Canadian Rockies of British Columbia.

According to geologists, seas gradually flooded the continents during the Cambrian period. In the **Ordovician period,** much land was covered by shallow seas, in which there was another burst of evolutionary diversification, although not as dramatic as the Cambrian Radiation. The Ordovician seas were inhabited by giant cephalopods, squidlike animals with straight shells 5 to 7 m (16 to 23 ft) long and 30 cm (12 in) in diameter. Coral reefs first appeared during this period, as did small, jawless, bony-armored fishes called *ostracoderms* (**FIG. 21-11**). Lacking jaws, these fishes typically had round or slitlike mouth openings that may have sucked in small food particles from the water or scooped up organic debris from the bottom. Ordovician deposits also contain fossil spores of terrestrial (land-dwelling) plants, suggesting the colonization of land had begun.

During the **Silurian period,** jawless fishes diversified considerably, and jawed fishes first appeared. Definitive evidence of two life-forms of great biological significance appeared in the Silurian period: terrestrial plants and air-breathing animals. The evolution of plants allowed animals to colonize the land because plants provided the first terrestrial animals with food and shelter. All air-breathing land animals discovered in Silurian rocks were arthropods—millipedes, spiderlike arthropods, and possibly centipedes. From an ecological perspective, the energy flow from plants to animals probably occurred via detritus, which is organic debris from decomposing organisms, rather than directly from living plant material. Millipedes eat plant detritus today, and spiders and centipedes prey on millipedes and other animals.

The **Devonian period** is frequently called the Age of Fishes. This period witnessed the explosive radiation of fishes with jaws, an adaptation that lets a vertebrate chew and bite. Armored *placoderms*, an extinct group of jawed fishes, diversified to exploit varied lifestyles (see Fig. 32-10). Appearing in Devonian deposits are sharks and the two predominant types of bony fishes: lobe-finned fishes and ray-finned fishes, which gave rise to the major orders of modern fishes (see Chapter 31).

Tiktaalik was a transitional form between fishes and *tetrapods,* which are vertebrates with four limbs (see Fig. 32-17). *Tiktaalik* is considered a fish because it had scales and fins. Like tetrapods, however, *Tiktaalik* had a movable neck and ribs that enclosed lungs. Upper (more recent) Devonian sediments contain fossil remains of salamander-like amphibians (*labyrinthodonts*) that were often quite large, with short necks and heavy, muscular tails. Wingless insects also originated in the Late Devonian period.

The early vascular plants (plants with specialized tissue to conduct water and nutrients) diversified during the Devonian period in a burst of evolution that rivaled that of animals during the Cambrian Radiation. With the exception of flowering plants, all major plant groups appeared during the Devonian period. Forests of ferns, club mosses, horsetails, and seed ferns (an extinct group of ancient plants that had fernlike foliage but reproduced by forming seeds) flourished.

The **Carboniferous period** is named for the great swamp forests whose remains persist today as major coal deposits. Much of the land during this time was covered with low swamps filled with horsetails, club mosses, ferns, seed ferns, and gymnosperms, which are seed-bearing plants such as conifers (**FIG. 21-12**). Amphibians, which underwent an **adaptive radiation** and exploited both aquatic and terrestrial ecosystems, were the dominant terrestrial carnivores of the Carboniferous period. Reptiles first appeared and diverged to form two major lines at this time. One line consisted of mostly small and mid-sized insectivorous (insect-eating) lizards; this line later led to lizards, snakes, crocodiles, dinosaurs, and birds. The other reptilian line led to a diverse group of Permian and Early Mesozoic mammal-like reptiles. Two groups of winged insects, cockroaches and dragonflies, appeared in the Carboniferous period.

(b) *Pterapsis*

(c) *Jamoytius*

(a) *Thelodus*

FIGURE 21-11 Ostracoderms
Ostracoderms, primitive jawless fishes that lived in the Ordovician, Silurian, and Devonian periods, ranged from 10 to 50 cm (4 to 20 in) in length.

FIGURE 21-12 Reconstruction of a Carboniferous forest
Plants of this period included giant ferns, horsetails, club mosses, seed ferns, and early gymnosperms.

Amphibians continued in importance during the **Permian period,** but they were no longer the dominant carnivores in terrestrial ecosystems. During the Permian period, reptiles diversified and dominated both carnivorous and herbivorous terrestrial lifestyles. One important group of mammal-like reptiles, originating in the Permian and extending into the Mesozoic era, were the *therapsids,* a group that included the ancestor of mammals (see Fig. 32-24). During the Permian period, seed plants diversified and dominated most plant communities. Cone-bearing conifers were widespread, and cycads (plants with crowns of fernlike leaves and large, seed-containing cones) and ginkgoes (trees with fan-shaped leaves and exposed, fleshy seeds) appeared.

The greatest **mass extinction** of all time occurred at the end of the Paleozoic era, between the Permian and Triassic periods, 251 mya. More than 90% of all existing marine species became extinct at this time, as did more than 70% of the vertebrate genera living on land. There is also evidence of a major extinction of plants. Many causes for the Late Permian mass extinction have been suggested, from meteor impacts to global warming to changes in ocean chemistry. Regardless of cause, evidence suggests that the extinction occurred globally in a very compressed period, within a few hundred thousand years. This is an extremely short period in the geologic time scale and suggests that some sort of catastrophic event caused the mass extinction.

Dinosaurs and other reptiles dominated the Mesozoic era

The **Mesozoic era** began about 251 mya and lasted some 185 million years. It is divided into the Triassic, Jurassic, and Cretaceous periods. Fossil deposits from the Mesozoic era occur worldwide.

Notable sites include the **Yixian Formation** in northeastern China, the Solnhofen Limestone in Germany, northwestern Patagonia in Argentina, the Sahara in central Niger, the Badlands in South Dakota, and other sites in western North America.

The outstanding feature of the Mesozoic era was the origin, differentiation, and ultimately the extinction of a large variety of reptiles. For this reason, the Mesozoic era is commonly called the Age of Reptiles. Most of the modern orders of insects appeared during the Mesozoic era. Snails and bivalves (clams and their relatives) increased in number and diversity, and sea urchins reached their peak diversity. From a botanical viewpoint, the Mesozoic era was dominated by gymnosperms until the Mid-Cretaceous period, when the flowering plants first diversified.

During the **Triassic period,** reptiles underwent an adaptive radiation leading to the formation of many groups. On land, the dominant Triassic groups were the mammal-like therapsids, which ranged from small-sized insectivores (insect-eating reptiles) to moderately large herbivores (plant-eating reptiles), and a diverse group of *thecodonts,* early "ruling reptiles," that were primarily carnivores. Thecodonts are the ancestral reptiles that gave rise to crocodilians, flying reptiles, dinosaurs, and birds.

In the ocean, several important marine reptile groups, the plesiosaurs and ichthyosaurs, appeared in the Triassic period. *Plesiosaurs* had bodies up to 15 m (about 49 ft) long and paddlelike fins. *Ichthyosaurs* had body forms superficially resembling those of sharks or porpoises, with short necks, large dorsal fins, and shark-type tails (**FIG. 21-13**). Ichthyosaurs had very large eyes, which may have helped them see at diving depths of 500 m (1650 ft) or more.

Pterosaurs, the first flying reptiles, appeared and underwent considerable diversification during the Mesozoic era (**FIG. 21-14**). This group produced some quite spectacular forms, most notably

FIGURE 21-13 Ichthyosaurs

Brachypterygius (also known by the genus *Grendelius*) was an ichthyosaur that superficially resembled a shark or porpoise. It had large teeth and strong jaws and was about 4 m (13 ft) long.

FIGURE 21-14 Pterosaurs

Shown are *Peteinosaurus* (*left*), with a wingspan of 60 cm (2 ft), and *Eudimorphodon* (*right foreground*), with a wingspan of 75 cm (2.5 ft). Both species had long, sharp teeth for catching insects or fishes while flying.

the giant *Quetzalcoatlus,* known from fragmentary Cretaceous fossils in Texas to have had a wingspan of 11 to 15 m (36 to 49 ft). Pterosaur wings were leathery membranes of skin that were supported by an elongated fourth finger bone. Claws extended from the other finger bones.

The first mammals to appear in the Triassic period were small insectivores that evolved from the mammal-like therapsids. Mammals diversified into a variety of mostly small, nocturnal insectivores during the remainder of the Mesozoic era, with marsupial and placental mammals appearing later in the Mesozoic.

During the **Jurassic** and **Cretaceous periods,** crocodiles, lizards, snakes, and birds appeared, and the dinosaurs diversified dramatically (**FIG. 21-15**). The *mosasaurs,* one group of lizards, were large, voracious marine predators during the Late Cretaceous

FIGURE 21-15 Dinosaurs

Three *Deinonychus* dinosaurs attack a larger *Tenontosaurus*. The name *Deinonychus* means "terrible claw" and refers to the enlarged, sharp claw on the second digit of its hind feet. *Deinonychus* dinosaurs were small (3 m, or 10 ft in length) but fearsome predators that hunted in packs. *Tenontosaurus* adults were as long as 7.5 m (24 ft).

period. The mosasaurs, which are now extinct, attained lengths of 10 m (33 ft) or more.

The evolutionary radiation of the dinosaurs expanded from one lineage to several dozen that ecologically filled a variety of adaptive zones. Dinosaurs are placed in two main groups based on their pelvic bone structure: the *saurischians* and the *ornithischians* (**FIG. 21-16**). Some saurischians were fast, bipedal (walking on two feet) forms ranging from those the size of a dog to the ultimate representatives of this group, the gigantic carnivores of the Cretaceous period—*Tyrannosaurus, Giganotosaurus,* and *Carcharodontosaurus.* Other saurischians were huge, quadrupedal (walking on four feet) dinosaurs that ate plants. Some of these were the largest terrestrial animals that have ever lived, including *Argentinosaurus,* with an estimated length of 30 m (98 ft) and an estimated weight of 72 to 90 metric tons (80 to 100 tons).

The other group of dinosaurs, the ornithischians, was entirely herbivorous. Although some ornithischians were bipedal, most were quadrupedal. Some had no front teeth and possessed stout, horny, birdlike beaks. In some species these beaks were broad and ducklike, hence the common name *duck-billed dinosaurs.* Other ornithischians had great armor plates, possibly as protection against carnivorous saurischians. *Ankylosaurus,* for example, had a broad, flat body covered with armor plates (actually bony scales embedded in the skin) and large, laterally projecting spikes.

Over the past few decades, scientists have reconsidered many traditional ideas about dinosaurs and no longer think they were all cold-blooded, slow-moving monsters living in swamps. Recent evidence suggests that at least some dinosaurs were warm-blooded, agile, and able to move extremely fast. Many dinosaurs appear to have had complex social behaviors, including courtship rituals and parental nurturing of their young. Some species lived in social groups and hunted in packs.

Birds appeared by the Late Jurassic period, and fossil evidence indicates they evolved directly from saurischian dinosaurs (see *Inquiring About: The Origin of Flight in Birds*). *Archaeopteryx,* the oldest known bird in the fossil record, lived about 150 mya (see Fig. 32-22b). It was about the size of a pigeon and had rather feeble wings that it used to glide rather than actively fly. Although *Archaeopteryx* is considered a bird, it had many reptilian features, including a mouthful of teeth and a long, bony tail.

Thousands of well-preserved bird fossils have been found in Early Cretaceous deposits in China. These include *Sinornis,* a 135-million-year-old sparrow-sized bird capable of perching, and the magpie-sized *Confuciusornis,* the earliest known bird with a toothless beak. *Confuciusornis* may date back as far as 142 mya.

At the end of the Cretaceous period, 66 mya, dinosaurs, pterosaurs, and many other animals abruptly became extinct. Many gymnosperms, with the exception of conifers, also perished. Evidence suggests that a catastrophic collision of a large extraterrestrial body with Earth dramatically changed the climate at the end of the Cretaceous period. Part of the evidence is a thin band of dark clay, with a high concentration of iridium, located between Mesozoic and Cenozoic sediments at more than 200 sites around the world. Iridium is rare on Earth but abundant in meteorites. The force of the impact would have driven the iridium into the atmosphere, to be deposited later on the land by precipitation.

The Chicxulub crater, buried under the Yucatán Peninsula in

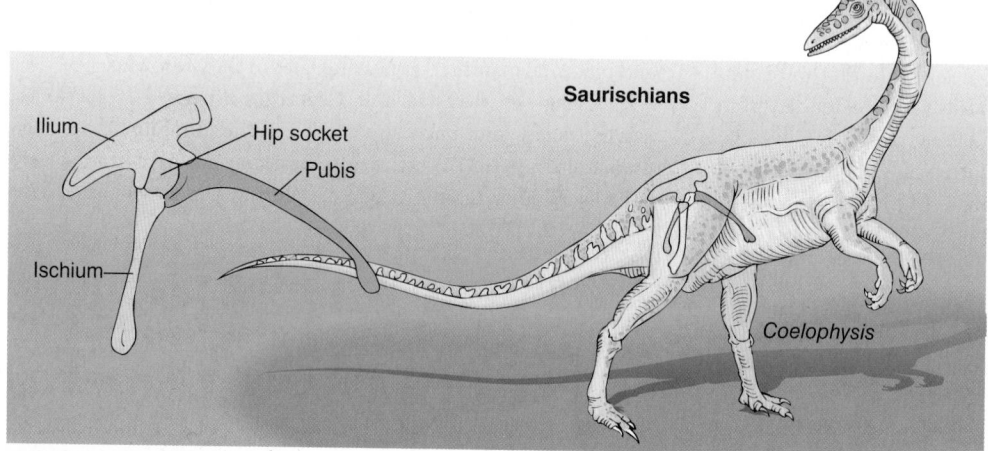

(a) **The saurischian pelvis.** Note the opening (hip socket), a trait possessed by no quadrupedal vertebrates other than dinosaurs.

(b) **The ornithischian pelvis.** Note that it has the hole in the hip socket but differs from the saurischian pelvis in that it has a backward-directed extension of the pubis.

FIGURE 21-16 Saurischian and ornithischian dinosaurs
In each dinosaur figure, the pale yellow femur is shown relative to the pelvic bone.

THE ORIGIN OF FLIGHT IN BIRDS

Do we know how birds evolved? The evolution of birds is arguably one of the most interesting chapters in Earth's history of life. Given the substantial fossil evidence, most paleontologists have concluded that the ancestors of birds were dinosaurs, specifically the *dromaeosaurs,* a group of ground-dwelling, bipedal theropods (carnivorous saurischians). Beginning in 1997, paleontologists made several discoveries of fossil dinosaurs with feathers, indicating that feathers appeared before birds. Scientists think that feathers evolved as one or a series of evolutionary novelties, or **preadaptations** (see Chapter 20). The first feathers may have provided thermal insulation but were subsequently modified for flight.

Once dinosaurs and early birds had feathers, how did they fly? Did tree-dwelling animals glide as an intermediate step in bird flight, or did ground-dwelling animals flap their wings and run to provide thrust and lift for a takeoff? The question about how flight originated in birds has intrigued biologists for more than a century. In 1915, U.S. zoologist William Beebe hypothesized that the ancestors of birds were probably tree-dwelling gliders that had feathers on all four limbs.[1] Because no fossil evidence supported his suggestion, scientists did not consider it seriously at the time.

Almost a century later, in 2003, a group of Chinese paleontologists announced the discovery of two nearly complete fossils of the organisms that Beebe had hypothesized.[2] The fossils of a small, feathered dromaeosaur dinosaur were found in Liaoning Province in northeastern China. The dinosaur, *Microraptor gui,* had feathers on both forelimbs and hind limbs as well as on its long tail (see figure). It was small—77 cm (about 30 inches) in length, including the tail—and appeared to be adapted to life in the trees. The feathers on *M. gui* were similar to those of modern-day birds. Downy feathers covered the body, and each limb had about 12 "primary" flight feathers and about 18 shorter, "secondary" feathers. *Microraptor gui*'s flight feathers were asymmetrical, a characteristic associated with flight or gliding in modern birds. The primary and secondary feathers followed a similar pattern on both the forelimbs and hind limbs, and this pattern resembles that on modern birds. In part because *M. gui*'s breastbone was not structured to attach large flight muscles, the dinosaur probably glided rather than flapped its wings.

Portia Sloan

Microraptor gui, which is about 126 million years old, is not a direct ancestor of birds. Birds had already evolved when *M. gui* existed. The earliest known bird, *Archaeopteryx,* lived about 150 mya and therefore predates *M. gui* by about 25 million years. *Microraptor gui* is considered to have evolved from a *basal member*—that is, an earlier evolutionary branch—of the most recent ancestor of *Archaeopteryx* and other birds. Like *M. gui,* earlier feathered dinosaurs may have been four-winged organisms that lived and glided in the trees.

During the course of bird evolution, the feathered hind limbs may have become reduced and eventually lost. However, an alternative hypothesis is that feathered hind limbs may have been a failed evolutionary experiment restricted to dromaeosaurs and not important as an intermediate step in bird evolution. Further analysis of *M. gui* and future discoveries of earlier dromaeosaur fossils may shed some light on the importance of feathered hind limbs.

Microraptor gui has given paleontologists and biologists much to consider in the evolutionary transition from dinosaurs to birds. Scientists will continue to study and debate the evolution of flight in birds for many years.

[1]Beebe, W. H. "A Tetrapteryx Stage in the Ancestry of Birds." *Zoologica,* Vol. 2, 1915.

[2]Xu, X., Z. Zhou, X. Wang, X. Kuang, F. Zhang, and X. Du. "Four-Winged Dinosaurs from China." *Nature,* Vol. 421, Jan. 23, 2003.

Mexico, is the apparent site of this collision. The impact produced giant tsunamis (tidal waves) that deposited materials from the extraterrestrial body around the perimeter of the Gulf of Mexico, from Alabama to Guatemala. It may have caused global forest fires and giant smoke and dust clouds that lowered global temperatures for many years.

Although scientists widely accept that a collision with an extraterrestrial body occurred 66 mya, they have reached no consensus about the effects of such an impact on organisms. The extinction of many marine organisms at or immediately after the time of the impact was probably the result of the environmental upheaval that the collision produced. However, many clam species associated with the mass extinction at the end of the Cretaceous period seem to have gone extinct *before* the impact, suggesting that other factors caused some of the massive extinctions occurring then.

The Cenozoic era is the age of mammals

With equal justice the **Cenozoic era** could be called the Age of Mammals, the Age of Birds, the Age of Insects, or the Age of Flowering Plants. This era is marked by the appearance of all these forms in great variety and numbers of species. The Cenozoic era extends from 66 mya to the present. It is subdivided into three periods: the **Paleogene period,** encompassing some 43 million years, the **Neogene period,** which was 20.4 million years in length, and the **Quaternary period,** which covers the last 2.6 million years. The Paleogene period is subdivided into three epochs, named from earliest to latest: Paleocene, Eocene, and Oligocene. The Neogene period is subdivided into two epochs: the Miocene and Pliocene. The Quaternary period is subdivided into the Pleistocene and Holocene epochs.

Flowering plants, which arose during the Cretaceous period, continued to diversify during the Cenozoic era. During the Paleocene and Eocene epochs, fossils indicate that tropical and semitropical plant communities extended to relatively high latitudes. Palms, for example, are found in Eocene deposits in Wyoming. Later in the Cenozoic era, there is evidence of more open habitats. Grasslands and savannas spread throughout much of North America during the Miocene epoch, with deserts developing later in the Pliocene and Pleistocene epochs. During the Pleistocene epoch, plant communities changed dynamically in response to the fluctuating climates associated with the multiple advances and retreats of continental glaciers.

During the Eocene epoch, there was an explosive radiation of birds, which acquired adaptations for different habitats. Paleontologists hypothesize that the jaws and beak of the flightless giant bird *Diatryma*, for example, may have been adapted primarily for crushing and slicing vegetation in Eocene forests, marshes, and grasslands. Other paleontologists hypothesize that these giant birds were carnivores that killed or scavenged mammals and other vertebrates (**FIG. 21-17**).

During the Paleocene epoch, an explosive radiation of primitive mammals occurred. Most of these were small forest dwellers that are not closely related to modern mammals. During the Eocene epoch, mammals continued to diverge, and all the modern orders first appeared. Again, many of the mammals were small, but there were also some larger herbivores.

During the Oligocene epoch, many modern families of mammals evolved, including the first apes in Africa. Many lineages showed adaptations that suggest a more open type of habitat, such as grassland or savanna. Many mammals were larger and had longer legs for running, specialized teeth for chewing coarse vegetation or for preying on animals, and increases in their relative brain

© John Sibbick

FIGURE 21-18 A mammal from the Oligocene epoch
Paraceratherium was an indricothere, a hornless relative of the rhinoceros. This huge land mammal was about 8 m (26 ft) long and weighed about 15 to 20 tons. It probably ate leaves and branches of deciduous trees, much as a modern-day giraffe does.

sizes. The *indricotheres*, for example, are extinct relatives of the rhinoceros. These mammals, which lived on the grassless plains of Eurasia, became progressively larger during the Oligocene epoch (**FIG. 21-18**).

Human ancestors appeared in Africa during the Late Miocene and Early Pliocene epochs. *Homo*, the genus to which humans belong, appeared approximately 2.5 mya. (Primate evolution, including human evolution, is discussed in Chapter 22.)

The Pliocene and Pleistocene epochs witnessed the introduction of spectacular North and South American large-mammal fauna, including mastodons, saber-toothed cats, camels, giant ground sloths, and giant armadillos. However, many of the large mammals became extinct at the end of the Pleistocene epoch. This extinction was possibly due to climate change—the Pleistocene epoch was marked by several ice ages—or to the influence of humans, which had spread from Africa to Europe and Asia, and later to North and South America by crossing a land bridge between Siberia and Alaska. Archaeological evidence indicates that this mass extinction event was concurrent with the appearance of human hunters.

© John Sibbick

FIGURE 21-17 A bird from the Eocene epoch
The flightless bird *Diatryma*, which stood 2.1 m (7 ft) tall and weighed about 175 kg (385 lb), may have been an herbivore or a formidable predator. In this picture, *Diatryma* has captured a small, horselike perissodactyl.

Review

- What is the correct order of appearance in the fossil record, starting with the earliest: eukaryotic cells, multicellular organisms, prokaryotic cells?
- What is the correct order of appearance in the fossil record, starting with the earliest: reptiles, mammals, amphibians, fishes?
- What is the correct order of appearance in the fossil record, starting with the earliest: flowering plants, ferns, gymnosperms?

21.1 *(page 447)*

1 Describe the conditions that scientists think existed on early Earth.

■ Biologists generally agree that life originated from nonliving matter by **chemical evolution.** Hypotheses about chemical evolution are testable.

■ Four requirements for chemical evolution are (1) the absence of oxygen, which would have reacted with and oxidized abiotically produced organic molecules; (2) energy to form organic molecules; (3) chemical building blocks, including water, minerals, and gases present in the atmosphere; and (4) sufficient time for molecules to accumulate and react.

CENGAGENOW™ Learn more about conditions on early Earth by clicking on the figure in CengageNOW.

2 Contrast the prebiotic soup hypothesis and the iron–sulfur world hypothesis.

■ During chemical evolution, small organic molecules formed spontaneously and accumulated. The **prebiotic soup hypothesis** proposes that organic molecules formed near Earth's surface in a "sea of organic soup" or on rock or clay surfaces. The **iron–sulfur world hypothesis** suggests that organic molecules were produced at **hydrothermal vents,** cracks in the deep-ocean floor.

CENGAGENOW™ See the Miller–Urey experiment unfold by clicking on the figure in CengageNOW.

21.2 *(page 449)*

3 Outline the major steps hypothesized to have occurred in the origin of cells.

■ After small organic molecules formed and accumulated, macromolecules assembled from the small organic molecules. Macromolecular assemblages called **protobionts** formed from macromolecules. Cells arose from the protobionts.

■ According to a model known as the **RNA world,** RNA was the first informational molecule to evolve in the progression toward a self-sustaining, self-reproducing cell. Natural selection at the molecular level eventually resulted in the information sequence DNA ⟶ RNA ⟶ protein.

4 Explain how the evolution of photosynthetic autotrophs affected both the atmosphere and other organisms.

■ The first cells were prokaryotic **heterotrophs** that obtained organic molecules from the environment. They were almost certainly **anaerobes.** Later, **autotrophs**—organisms that produce their own organic molecules by photosynthesis—evolved.

■ The evolution of oxygen-generating photosynthesis ultimately changed early life. The accumulation of molecular oxygen in the atmosphere permitted the evolution of **aerobes,** organisms that could use oxygen for a more efficient type of cellular respiration.

5 Describe the hypothesis of serial endosymbiosis.

■ Eukaryotic cells arose from prokaryotic cells. According to the hypothesis of **serial endosymbiosis,** certain eukaryotic organelles (mitochondria and chloroplasts) evolved from prokaryotic **endo-symbionts** incorporated within larger prokaryotic hosts.

CENGAGENOW™ Learn more about serial endosymbiosis by clicking on the figure in CengageNOW.

21.3 *(page 455)*

6 Briefly describe the distinguishing organisms and major biological events of the Ediacaran period and the Paleozoic, Mesozoic, and Cenozoic eras.

■ Life at the beginning of the **Proterozoic eon** (2500 mya to 542 mya) consisted of prokaryotes. About 2.2 bya the first eukaryotic cells appeared. The **Ediacaran period,** from 600 mya to 542 mya, is the last period of the Proterozoic eon. Ediacaran fossils are the oldest known fossils of multicellular animals. Ediacaran fauna were small, soft-bodied invertebrates.

■ During the **Paleozoic era,** which began about 542 mya and lasted approximately 291 million years, all major groups of plants, except flowering plants, and all animal phyla appeared. Fishes and amphibians flourished, and reptiles appeared. The greatest mass extinction of all time occurred at the end of the Paleozoic era, 251 mya. More than 90% of marine species and 70% of land-dwelling vertebrate genera became extinct, as well as many plant species.

■ The **Mesozoic era** began about 251 mya and lasted some 185 million years. Flowering plants appeared, and reptiles diversified. Dinosaurs, which descended from early reptiles, dominated. Insects flourished, and birds and early mammals appeared. At the end of the Cretaceous period, 66 mya, many species abruptly became extinct. A collision of a large extraterrestrial body with Earth may have resulted in dramatic climate changes that played a role in this mass extinction.

■ In the **Cenozoic era,** which extends from 66 mya to the present, flowering plants, birds, insects, and mammals diversified greatly. Human ancestors appeared in Africa during the Late Miocene and Early Pliocene epochs.

TEST YOUR UNDERSTANDING

1. Energy, the absence of oxygen, chemical building blocks, and time were the requirements for (a) chemical evolution (b) biological evolution (c) the Cambrian Radiation (d) the mass extinction episode at the end of the Cretaceous period (e) directed evolution

2. Many scientists think that _____ was the first information molecule to evolve. (a) DNA (b) RNA (c) a protein (d) an amino acid (e) a lipid

3. The first cells were probably (a) heterotrophs (b) autotrophs (c) anaerobes (d) a and c (e) b and c

4. According to the hypothesis of serial endosymbiosis, (a) life originated from nonliving matter (b) the pace of evolution quickened at the start of the Cambrian period (c) chloroplasts, mitochondria, and possibly other organelles originated from intimate relationships among prokaryotic cells (d) banded iron formations reflect the buildup of sufficient oxygen in the atmosphere to oxidize iron at Earth's surface (e) the first photosynthetic organisms appeared 3.1 bya to 3.5 bya

5. During the Early _____, life consisted of prokaryotic cells, but by the end of this geologic time span, multicellular eukaryotic organisms had evolved. (a) Cenozoic era (b) Paleozoic era (c) Mesozoic era (d) Archaean eon (e) Proterozoic eon

6. Geologists divide the eons into (a) periods (b) epochs (c) eras (d) millennia (e) none of the preceding

7. Ediacaran fossils (a) are the oldest known fossils of multicellular animals (b) come from the Burgess Shale in British Columbia (c) contain remains of large salamander-like organisms (d) are the oldest fossils of early vascular plants (e) contain a high concentration of iridium

8. The time of greatest evolutionary diversification in the history of life occurred during the (a) Cambrian period (b) Ordovician period (c) Silurian period (d) Carboniferous period (e) Permian period

9. The greatest mass extinction episode in the history of life occurred at what boundary? (a) Pliocene–Pleistocene (b) Permian–Triassic (c) Mesozoic–Cenozoic (d) Cambrian–Ordovician (e) Triassic–Jurassic

10. The Age of Reptiles corresponds to the (a) Paleozoic era (b) Mesozoic era (c) Cenozoic era (d) Pleistocene epoch (e) Permian period

11. Evidence exists that a catastrophic collision between Earth and a large extraterrestrial body occurred 66 mya, resulting in the extinction of (a) worms, mollusks, and soft-bodied arthropods (b) jawless ostracoderms and jawed placoderms (c) dinosaurs, pterosaurs, and many gymnosperm species (d) mastodons, saber-toothed cats, and giant ground sloths (e) ferns, horsetails, and club mosses

12. Flowering plants and mammals diversified and became dominant during the (a) Paleozoic era (b) Mesozoic era (c) Cenozoic era (d) Devonian period (e) Cambrian period

CRITICAL THINKING

1. **EVOLUTION LINK.** If you were studying how protobionts evolved into cells and you developed a protobiont that was capable of self-replication, would you consider it a living cell? Why or why not?

2. **EVOLUTION LINK.** If living cells were produced in a test tube from nonbiological components by chemical processes, would this accomplishment prove that life evolved in a similar manner billions of years ago? Why or why not?

3. **EVOLUTION LINK.** Why did the evolution of multicellular organisms such as plants and animals have to be preceded by the evolution of oxygen-producing photosynthesis?

4. **ANALYZING DATA.** Evidence for the oldest cyanobacterial fossils (stromatolites) dates to about 2 billion years, but molecular evidence inferred from lipids in ancient rocks puts the date for living cyanobacteria and eukaryotes at 2.7 billion years. Develop two opposing hypotheses to explain the discrepancy between the dates.

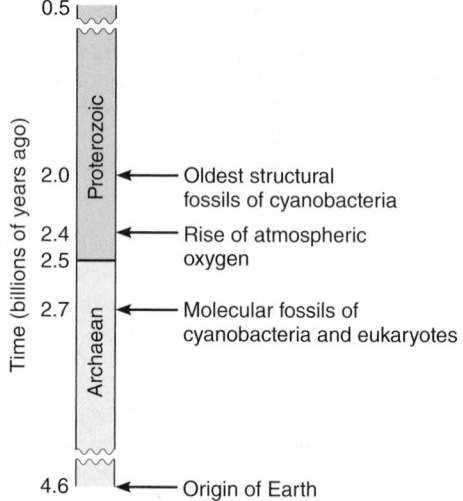

CENGAGENOW™ Additional questions are available in CengageNOW at www.cengage.com/login.

22 The Evolution of Primates

Studying human evolution. The late Drs. Mary and Louis Leakey studied fossil teeth from *Australopithecus boisei,* an early hominin (human) that lived in Africa. This photo was taken in Olduvai Gorge in Tanzania. The Leakey family has contributed much of what we know about human evolution. Son Richard, daughter-in-law Meave, and granddaughter Louise have followed in the footsteps of Mary and Louis.

Des Bartlett/Photo Researchers, Inc.

KEY CONCEPTS

22.1 Humans are classified in the order Primates, along with lemurs, tarsiers, monkeys, and apes. This classification is based on close evolutionary ties.

22.2 The study of living primates provides clues to help scientists reconstruct the adaptations and lifestyles of early primates, some of which were ancestors of humans.

22.3 Fossil evidence indicates that the earliest human ancestors arose in Africa and shared many features with their apelike ancestors. The human brain did not begin to enlarge to its present size and complexity until long after human ancestors had evolved bipedal locomotion.

22.4 Human culture began when human ancestors started making stone tools.

Twelve years after Darwin wrote *On the Origin of Species by Natural Selection,* he published another controversial book, *The Descent of Man,* which addressed human evolution. In this book, Darwin hypothesized that humans and apes share a common ancestry. For nearly a century after Darwin's studies, fossil evidence of human ancestry remained fairly incomplete. However, research during the last several decades, especially in Africa, has yielded a rapidly accumulating set of fossils that gives an increasingly clear answer to the question, "Where did we come from?" (see photograph).

Fossil evidence from **paleoanthropology,** the study of human evolution, has allowed scientists to infer not only the structure but also the habits of early humans and other primates. Teeth and bones are the main fossil evidence that paleoanthropologists study. Much information can be obtained by studying teeth, which have changed dramatically during the course of primate and human evolution. Because tooth enamel is more mineralized (harder) than bone, teeth are more likely to fossilize. The teeth of each primate species, living or extinct, are distinctive enough to identify the species, approximate age, diet, and even sex of the individual.

Based on fossil evidence, paleontologists hypothesize that the first primates descended from small, shrewlike **placental mammals** that lived in trees and ate insects. (Placental mammals are the largest and most successful group of mammals. They have a *placenta*, an organ that exchanges materials between the mother and the embryo/fetus developing in the uterus.) Many traits of the 233 living primate species are related to their **arboreal** (tree-dwelling) past. This chapter focuses on humans and their ancestors, who differ from most other primates because they did not remain in the trees but instead adapted to a terrestrial way of life.

22.1 PRIMATE ADAPTATIONS

■ LEARNING OBJECTIVE

1   Describe the structural adaptations that primates have for life in treetops.

Humans and other **primates**—including lemurs, tarsiers, monkeys, and apes—are mammals that share such traits as flexible hands and feet with five digits, a strong social organization, and front-facing eyes, which permit depth perception. Mammals (class Mammalia) evolved from mammal-like reptiles known as *therapsids* more than 200 million years ago (mya), during the Mesozoic era (see Fig. 32-24). These early mammals remained a minor component of life on Earth for almost 150 million years and then rapidly diversified during the Cenozoic era (from 66 mya to the present).

Fossil evidence indicates that the first primates with traits characteristic of modern primates appeared by the Early Eocene epoch about 56 mya. These early primates had digits with nails, and their eyes were directed somewhat forward on the head.

Several novel adaptations evolved in early primates that allowed them to live in trees. One of the most significant primate features is that each limb has five highly flexible digits: four lateral digits (fingers) plus a partially or fully opposable first digit (thumb and, in many primates, big toe; **FIG. 22-1**). An **opposable thumb** positions the fingers opposite the thumb, enabling primates to grasp objects such as tree branches with precision. Nails (instead of claws) provide a protective covering for the tips of the digits, and the fleshy pads at the ends of the digits are sensitive to touch. Another arboreal feature is long, slender limbs that rotate freely at the hips and shoulders, giving primates full mobility to climb and search for food in the treetops.

Having eyes located in the front of the head lets primates integrate visual information from both eyes simultaneously;

they have *stereoscopic* (three-dimensional) vision, which is important in judging distance and in depth perception. Stereoscopic vision is vital in an arboreal environment, especially for species that leap from branch to branch, because an error in depth perception may cause a fatal fall. In addition to having sharp sight, primates hear acutely.

Primates share several other characteristics, including a relatively large brain. Biologists have suggested that the increased sensory input associated with primates' sharp vision and greater agility favored the evolution of larger brains. Primates are generally very social and intelligent animals that reach sexual maturity relatively late in life. They typically have long lifespans. Females usually bear one offspring at a time; the baby is helpless and requires a long period of nurturing and protection.

Review

- How are primate hands and feet adapted to an arboreal existence?
- Why is the location of primate eyes in the front of the head an important adaptation for an arboreal life?

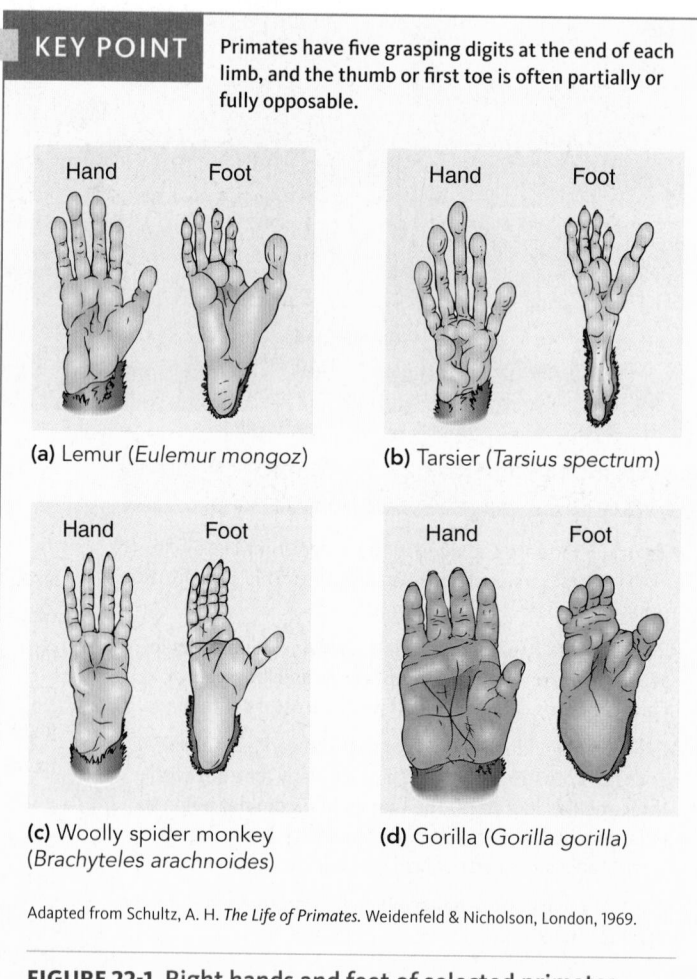

KEY POINT   Primates have five grasping digits at the end of each limb, and the thumb or first toe is often partially or fully opposable.

(a) Lemur (*Eulemur mongoz*)

(b) Tarsier (*Tarsius spectrum*)

(c) Woolly spider monkey (*Brachyteles arachnoides*)

(d) Gorilla (*Gorilla gorilla*)

Adapted from Schultz, A. H. *The Life of Primates*. Weidenfeld & Nicholson, London, 1969.

FIGURE 22-1 Right hands and feet of selected primates
Figures not drawn to scale.

22.2 PRIMATE CLASSIFICATION

LEARNING OBJECTIVES

2 List the three suborders of primates and give representative examples of each.

3 Distinguish among anthropoids, hominoids, and hominins.

Now that we have surveyed the general characteristics of primates, let us look at how they are classified. Many biologists currently divide the order Primates into three groups, or suborders (**FIG. 22-2**). The suborder Prosimii includes lemurs, galagos, and lorises; the suborder Tarsiiformes includes tarsiers; and the suborder Anthropoidea includes **anthropoids** (monkeys, apes, and humans).

All lemurs are restricted to the island of Madagascar off the coast of Africa. Because of extensive habitat destruction and hunt-

ing, they are very endangered. Lorises, which live in tropical areas of Southeast Asia and Africa, resemble lemurs in many respects, as do galagos, which live in sub-Saharan Africa. Lemurs, lorises, and galagos have retained several early mammalian features, such as elongated, pointed faces.

Tarsiers are found in rain forests of Indonesia and the Philippines (**FIG. 22-3**). They are small primates (about the size of a small rat) and are very adept leapers. These nocturnal primates resemble anthropoids in several ways, including their shortened snouts and forward-pointing eyes.

Suborder Anthropoidea includes monkeys, apes, and humans

Anthropoid primates arose during the Middle Eocene epoch, at least 45 mya. Several different fossil anthropoids have been

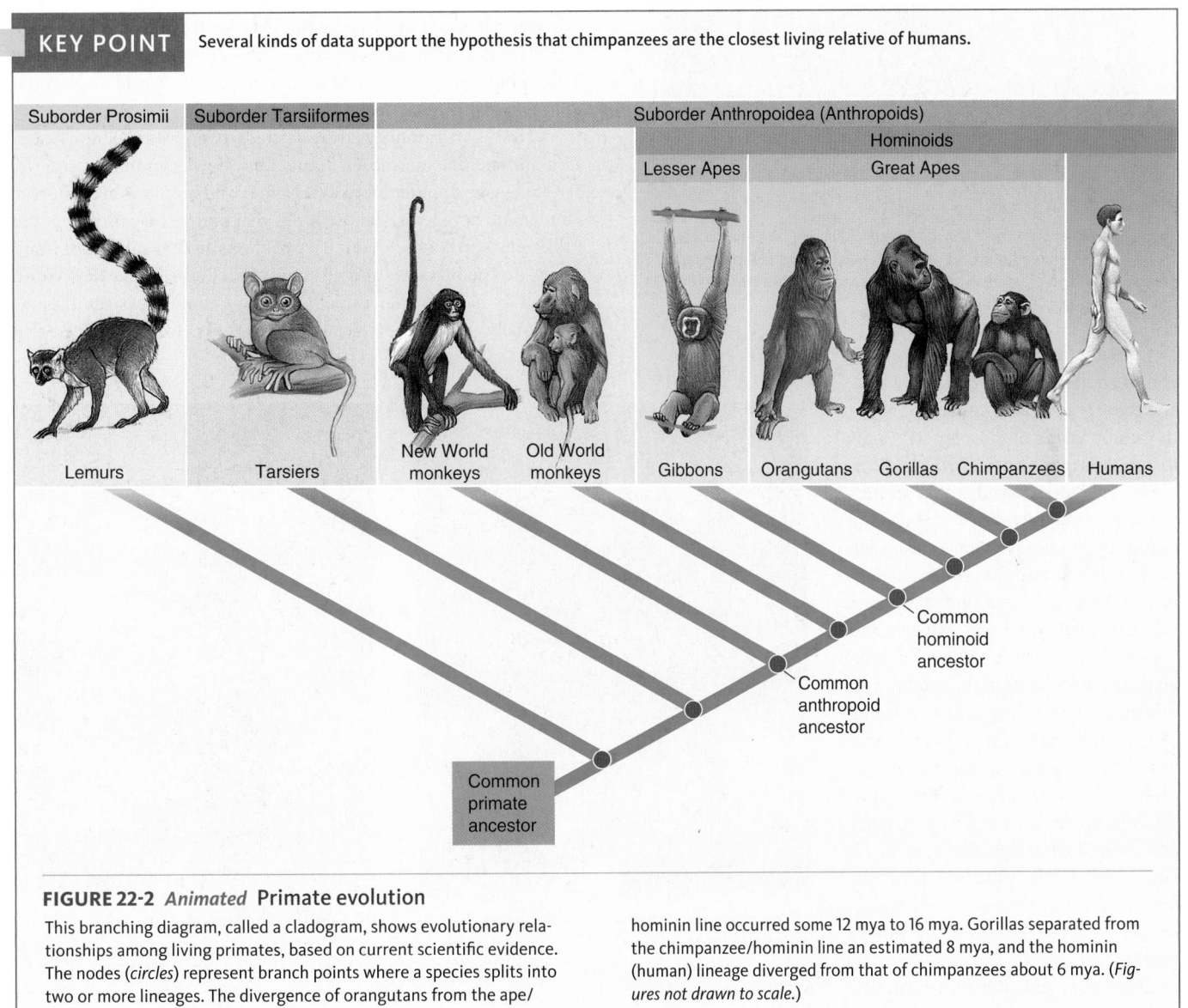

KEY POINT Several kinds of data support the hypothesis that chimpanzees are the closest living relative of humans.

FIGURE 22-2 *Animated* **Primate evolution**

This branching diagram, called a cladogram, shows evolutionary relationships among living primates, based on current scientific evidence. The nodes (*circles*) represent branch points where a species splits into two or more lineages. The divergence of orangutans from the ape/ hominin line occurred some 12 mya to 16 mya. Gorillas separated from the chimpanzee/hominin line an estimated 8 mya, and the hominin (human) lineage diverged from that of chimpanzees about 6 mya. (*Figures not drawn to scale.*)

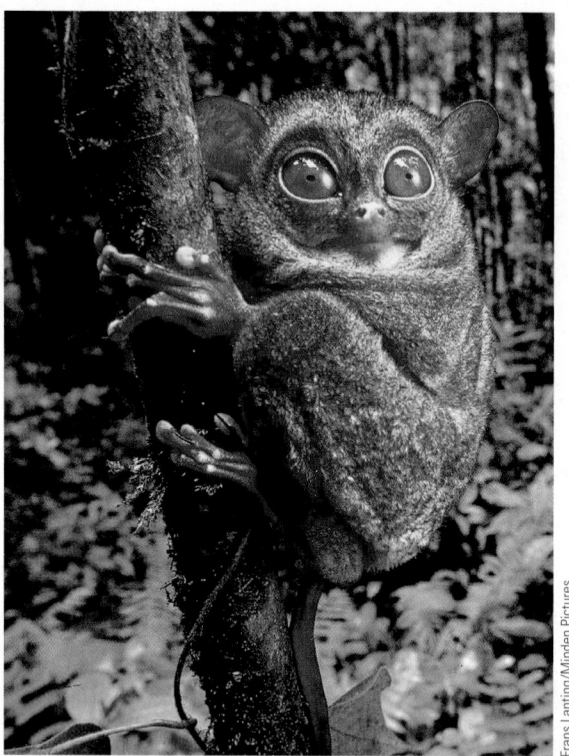

FIGURE 22-3 A tarsier

The huge eyes of the tarsier (*Tarsius bancanus*) help it find insects, lizards, and other prey when it hunts at night. When a tarsier sees an insect, it pounces on it and grasps the prey with its hands. Tarsiers live in the rain forests of Indonesia and the Philippines.

particular, is more developed in monkeys, apes, and humans, where it functions as a highly complex center for learning, voluntary movement, and interpretation of sensation.

Monkeys are generally diurnal (active during the day) tree dwellers. They tend to eat fruit and leaves, with nuts, seeds, buds, insects, spiders, birds' eggs, and even small vertebrates playing a smaller part in their diets. The two main groups of monkeys, New World monkeys and Old World monkeys, are named for the hemispheres where they diversified. Monkeys in South and Central America are called New World monkeys, whereas monkeys in Africa, Asia, and Europe are called Old World monkeys. New and Old World monkeys have been evolving separately for tens of millions of years.

One of the most important and interesting questions in anthropoid evolution concerns *how* monkeys arrived in South America. Africa and South America had already drifted apart. (Continental drift is presented in Figure 18-11.) The ancestors of New World monkeys may have rafted from Africa to South America on floating masses of vegetation. The South Atlantic Ocean would have been about half as wide as it is today, and islands could have provided "stepping stones." Once established in the New World, these monkeys rapidly diversified.

New World monkeys are restricted to Central and South America and include marmosets, capuchins, howler monkeys, squirrel monkeys, and spider monkeys. New World monkeys are arboreal, and some have long, slender limbs that permit easy movement in the trees (**FIG. 22-4a**). A few have **prehensile tails** capable of wrapping around branches and serving as fifth limbs. Some New World monkeys have shorter thumbs, and in certain cases the thumbs are totally absent. Their facial anatomy differs from that of the Old

identified, from Asia and North Africa, and there is a growing consensus about the relationships of these fossil groups to one another and to living anthropoids. Evidence indicates that anthropoids originated in Africa or Asia. The oldest known anthropoid fossils, such as 42-million-year-old *Eosimias,* have been found in China and Myanmar. Given details about their dentition and the few bones that have been discovered, scientists infer that *Eosimias* and other ancestral anthropoids were small, insect-eating arboreal primates that were active during the day. Once they evolved, anthropoids quickly spread throughout Europe, Asia, and Africa and arrived in South America much later. (Paleoanthropologists date the oldest known South American primate, *Branisella,* from Bolivia, at 26 million years old.)

One significant difference between anthropoids and other primates is the size of their brains. The cerebrum, in

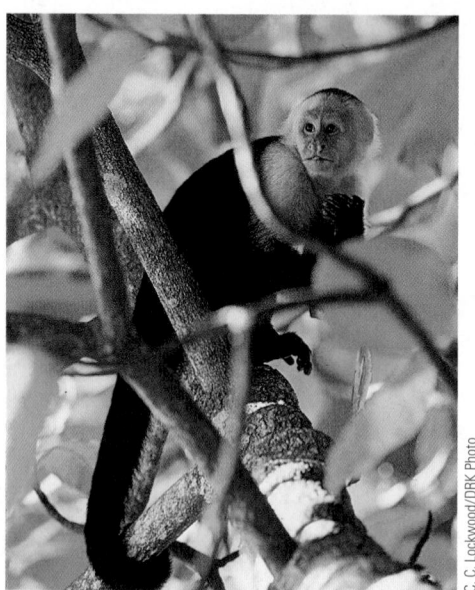

(a) New World monkey. The white-faced monkey (*Cebus capucinus*) has a prehensile tail and a flattened nose with nostrils directed to the side.

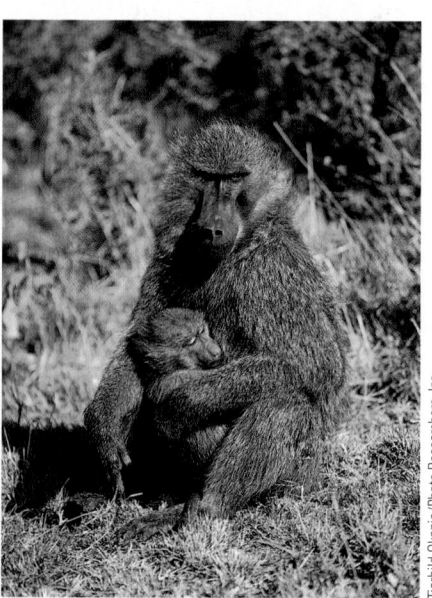

(b) Old World monkey. The Anubis baboon (*Papio anubis*) is native to Africa. Note that its nostrils are directed downward.

FIGURE 22-4 New World and Old World monkeys

World monkeys; New World monkeys have flattened noses with the nostrils opening to the side. They live in groups and engage in complex social behaviors.

Old World monkeys are distributed in tropical parts of Africa and Asia. In addition to baboons and macaques (pronounced "muh-kacks'"), the Old World group includes guenons, mangabeys, langurs, and colobus monkeys. Most Old World monkeys are arboreal, although some, such as baboons and macaques, spend much of their time on the ground (**FIG. 22-4b**). The ground dwellers, which are **quadrupedal** (four footed; they walk on all fours), arose from arboreal monkeys. None of the Old World monkeys has a prehensile tail, and some have extremely short tails. They have a fully opposable thumb, and unlike the New World monkeys, their nostrils are closer together and directed downward. Old World monkeys are intensely social animals.

Apes are our closest living relatives

Old World monkeys shared a common ancestor with the **hominoids,** a group composed of apes and **hominins** (humans and their ancestors; also called *hominids*). A fairly primitive anthropoid, discovered in Egypt, was named *Aegyptopithecus* (**FIG. 22-5a**). A cat-sized, forest-dwelling arboreal monkey with a few apelike characteristics, *Aegyptopithecus* lived during the Oligocene epoch, approximately 34 mya.

Fossil evidence indicates that apes and Old World monkeys had diverged between 25 mya and 23 mya, although a 2004 genetic analysis of living apes and monkeys suggests that this divergence may have occurred even earlier. During the Miocene epoch, as many as 100 species of apes lived in Africa, Asia, and Europe.

Paleoanthropologists have discovered the oldest fossils with hominoid features in East Africa, mostly in Kenya. *Proconsul,* for example, appeared early in the Miocene epoch, about 20 mya (**FIG. 22-5b**). It had a larger brain than that of monkeys, apelike teeth and diet (fruits), but a monkeylike body. At least 30 other early hominoid species lived during the Miocene epoch, but most of them became extinct and were not the common ancestor of modern apes and humans.

Miocene fossils of forest-dwelling, chimpanzee-sized apes called **dryopithecines,** which lived about 15 mya, are of special interest because this hominoid lineage may have given rise to modern apes as well as to humans (**FIG. 22-5c**). The dryopithecines, such as *Dryopithecus, Kenyapithecus,* and *Morotopithecus,* were distributed widely across Europe, Africa, and Asia. As the climate gradually cooled and became drier, their range became more limited. These apes had highly modified bodies for swinging through the branches of trees, although there is also evidence that some of them may have left the treetops for the ground as dense forest gradually changed into open woodland. Many questions about the relationships among the various early apes have been generated by the discovery of these and other Miocene hominoids. As future fossil finds are evaluated, they may lead to a rearrangement of ancestors in the hominoid family tree.

Five genera of hominoids exist today: gibbons (*Hylobates*), orangutans (*Pongo*), gorillas (*Gorilla*), chimpanzees (*Pan*), and humans (*Homo*). Gibbons are known informally as lesser apes; orangutans, gorillas, and chimpanzees are known as great apes. Molecular evidence indicates a close relationship between humans and the great apes, particularly chimpanzees.

(a) Fossils of *Aegyptopithecus*, a fairly primitive anthropoid, were discovered in Egypt.

(c) *Dryopithecus*, a more advanced ape, may have been ancestral to modern hominoids.

(b) Skeletal reconstruction of *Proconsul*. (The reconstructed parts are white.) This anthropoid had the limbs and body proportions of a monkey but lacked a tail, like all apes.

FIGURE 22-5 Ape evolution
(*Figures not drawn to scale.*)

Gibbons are natural acrobats that can **brachiate,** or arm-swing, with their weight supported by one arm at a time (**FIG. 22-6a**). Orangutans are also tree dwellers, but chimpanzees and especially gorillas have adapted to life on the ground (**FIG. 22-6b–d**). Gorillas and chimpanzees have retained long arms typical of brachiating primates but use these to assist in quadrupedal walking, sometimes known as **knuckle walking** because of the way they fold (flex) their digits when moving. Like humans, apes lack tails, a characteristic that makes them easy to distinguish from monkeys. They are generally much larger than monkeys, although gibbons are a notable exception.

Molecular data provide clues about evolution of anthropoid primates

Evidence of the close relatedness of orangutans, gorillas, chimpanzees, and humans is abundant at the molecular level. The amino acid sequence of the chimpanzee's hemoglobin is identical to that of the human; hemoglobin molecules of the gorilla and rhesus monkey differ from the human's by 2 and 15 amino acids, respectively. DNA sequence analyses indicate that chimpanzees are likely to be our nearest living relatives among the apes. (Figure 18-18 shows the percent divergence in a noncoding sequence on the β-globin gene between various primates, including the apes, and humans.)

Researchers plan to sequence the genomes of many primates, including all of the apes. The chimpanzee genome was sequenced in 2005, and the macaque (an Old World monkey) in 2007. Macaques are thought to have split from the anthropoid lineage about 25 mya, so comparing their genome to those of chimpanzees and humans helps researchers identify the genetic changes that evolved only in the anthropoid lineage.

Molecular evidence suggests that orangutans may have diverged from the gorilla, chimpanzee, and hominin lines about 14 mya. Gorillas may have diverged from the chimpanzee and hominin lines some 8 mya, whereas chimpanzee and hominin lines probably separated about 6 mya to 7 mya.

(a) A mother white-handed gibbon (*Hylobates lar*) nurses her baby. Gibbons are extremely acrobatic and often move through the trees by brachiation.

(b) An orangutan (*Pongo pygmaeus*) mother and baby. Orangutan anatomy is adapted to living in trees.

(c) A young lowland gorilla (*Gorilla gorilla*) in knuckle-walking stance. Gorillas spend most of the day eating plants.

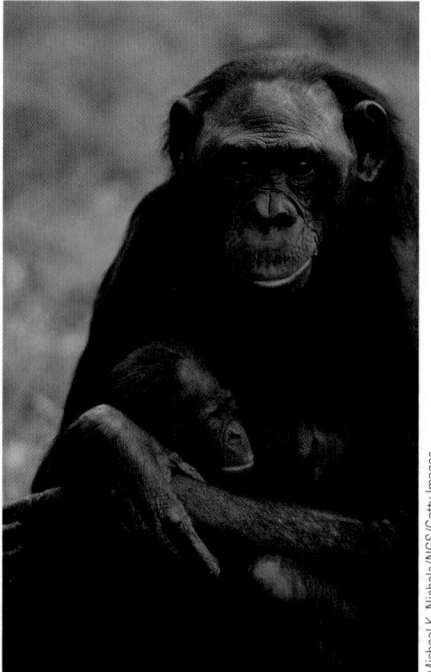

(d) A mother bonobo chimpanzee (*Pan paniscus*) holds her sleeping baby. Bonobos are endemic to a single country, the Democratic Republic of Congo.

FIGURE 22-6 Apes

Review

- What are the three suborders of primates?
- How can you distinguish between anthropoids and hominoids?

22.3 HOMININ EVOLUTION

LEARNING OBJECTIVES

4   Describe skeletal and skull differences between apes and hominins.
5   Briefly describe the following early hominins: *Orrorin*, *Ardipithecus*, and *Australopithecus anamensis*, *A. afarensis*, and *A. africanus*.
6   Distinguish among the following members of genus *Homo*: *H. habilis*, *H. ergaster*, *H. erectus*, *H. antecessor*, *H. heidelbergensis*, *H. neanderthalensis*, and *H. sapiens*.
7   Discuss the origin of modern humans.

Scientists have a growing storehouse of hundreds of hominin fossils, which provide useful data about general trends in the body design, appearance, and behavior of ancestral humans. For example, before their brains enlarged, early hominins clearly adopted a **bipedal** (two-footed) posture. Despite the wealth of fossil evidence, scientists continue to vigorously debate interpretations of hominin characteristics, classification, and evolution, and new discoveries raise new questions. As in other scientific fields, ideas about hominin evolution are influenced by the different perspectives of the various workers studying it. The lack of scientific consensus regarding certain aspects of hominin evolution is, therefore, an expected part of the scientific process.

Evolutionary changes from the earliest hominins to modern humans are evident in some of the characteristics of the skeleton and skull. Compared with the ape skeleton, the human skeleton shows distinct differences that reflect humans' ability to stand erect and walk on two feet (**FIG. 22-7**). These differences also reflect the habitat change for early hominins, from an arboreal existence in the forest to a life spent at least partly on the ground.

The curvature of the human spine provides better balance and weight distribution for bipedal locomotion. The human pelvis is shorter and broader than the ape pelvis, allowing better attachment of muscles used for upright walking. (The shape of the human pelvis also allows the birth of offspring with large brains.) In apes the **foramen magnum,** the hole in the base of the skull for the spinal cord, is located in the rear of the skull. In contrast, the

FIGURE 22-7 Gorilla and human skeletons
When gorilla and human skeletons are compared, the skeletal adaptations for bipedalism in humans become apparent.

human foramen magnum is centered in the skull base, positioning the head for erect walking. An increase in the length of the legs relative to the arms, and alignment of the first toe with the rest of the toes, further adapted the early hominins for bipedalism.

Another major trend in hominin evolution was an increase in brain size relative to body size (**FIG. 22-8**). The ape skull has prominent **supraorbital ridges** above the eye sockets, whereas modern human skulls lack these ridges. Human faces are flatter than those of apes, and the jaws are different. The arrangement of teeth in the ape jaw is somewhat rectangular, compared with a rounded, or U-shaped, arrangement in humans. Apes have larger front teeth (canines and incisors) than do humans, and their canines are especially large. Gorillas and orangutans also have larger back teeth (premolars and molars) than do humans.

We now examine some of the increasing number of fossil hominins in the human lineage. As you read the following descriptions of human evolution, keep in mind that much of what is discussed is open to reinterpretation and major revision as additional discoveries are made. Although we present human evolution in a somewhat linear fashion, from ancient hominins to anatomically and behaviorally modern humans, the human family tree is not a single trunk

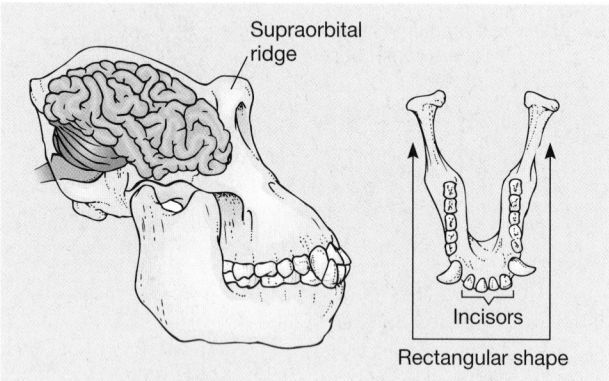

(a) The ape skull has a pronounced supraorbital ridge.

(b) The human skull is flatter in the front and has a pronounced chin. The human brain, particularly the cerebrum (*purple*), is larger than that of an ape, and the human jaw is structured so that the teeth are arranged in a U shape. Human canines and incisors are also smaller than those of apes.

FIGURE 22-8 Gorilla and human heads

but has several branches (**FIG. 22-9**). Perhaps it is most useful to think of the known hominin fossils as a sampling of human evolution instead of a continuous sequence.

Homo sapiens is the only species of hominin in existence today, but more than one hominin species coexisted at any given time for most of the past 4 million years. In addition, do not make the mistake of thinking that your smaller-brained ancestors were inferior to yourself. Ancestral hominins were evolutionarily successful in that they were well adapted to their environment and survived for millions of years.

The earliest hominins may have lived 6 mya to 7 mya

Hominin evolution began in Africa. Although most hominin fossils have been discovered in Ethiopia and Kenya, in 2002 French paleontologist Michel Brunet and an international team made a stunning discovery in a dry lake bed in Chad, which is in central Africa. The fossil, which has been reliably dated at 6 million to 7 million years old, may be the earliest known hominin. Viewed from the back, the skull of **Sahelanthropus,** with its small braincase, resembles that of a chimpanzee. However, viewed from the front, the face and teeth have many characteristics of larger-brained human ancestors. Most paleoanthropologists place *Sahelanthropus* close to the base of the human family tree—that is, close to when genetic analyses suggest the last common ancestor of hominins and chimpanzees existed. The discovery of *Sahelanthropus* is important in its own right, but it is also significant because it shows that early hominins exhibited more variation and lived over a larger area of Africa than had been originally hypothesized.

Orrorin, discovered in 2000 in Kenya, may also represent one of the earliest known hominins. The sediments in which fossils of *Orrorin* were found have been reliably dated at 6 million years old. In 2008, researchers studying the fossil leg bones of *Orrorin* concluded that it walked upright and was bipedal.

As with many aspects of human evolution, scientists have differing interpretations of *Sahelanthropus* and *Orrorin*. For example, some paleoanthropologists hypothesize that *Sahelanthropus* was a forerunner of modern apes, specifically the gorilla, and not one of the earliest humans. Other researchers think the similar features of *Sahelanthropus, Orrorin,* and *Ardipithecus* (discussed in the next section) fossils mean that they are all members of the same genus, *Ardipithecus*. This point remains controversial, largely because there are currently no skeletal bones (leg, pelvis, and foot bones) to indicate if *Sahelanthropus* walked upright, a hallmark characteristic of hominins. (A 2005 reconstruction of the skull has features that strongly suggest *Sahelanthropus* was bipedal.) Future fossil discoveries and additional analyses of existing fossils should help clarify the evolutionary relationships among *Sahelanthropus, Orrorin,* and *Ardipithecus*.

Ardipithecus, Australopithecus, and *Paranthropus* are australopithecines, or "southern man apes"

After *Sahelanthropus* and *Orrorin,* the next-oldest hominin belongs to the genus **Ardipithecus,** which lived in eastern Africa between

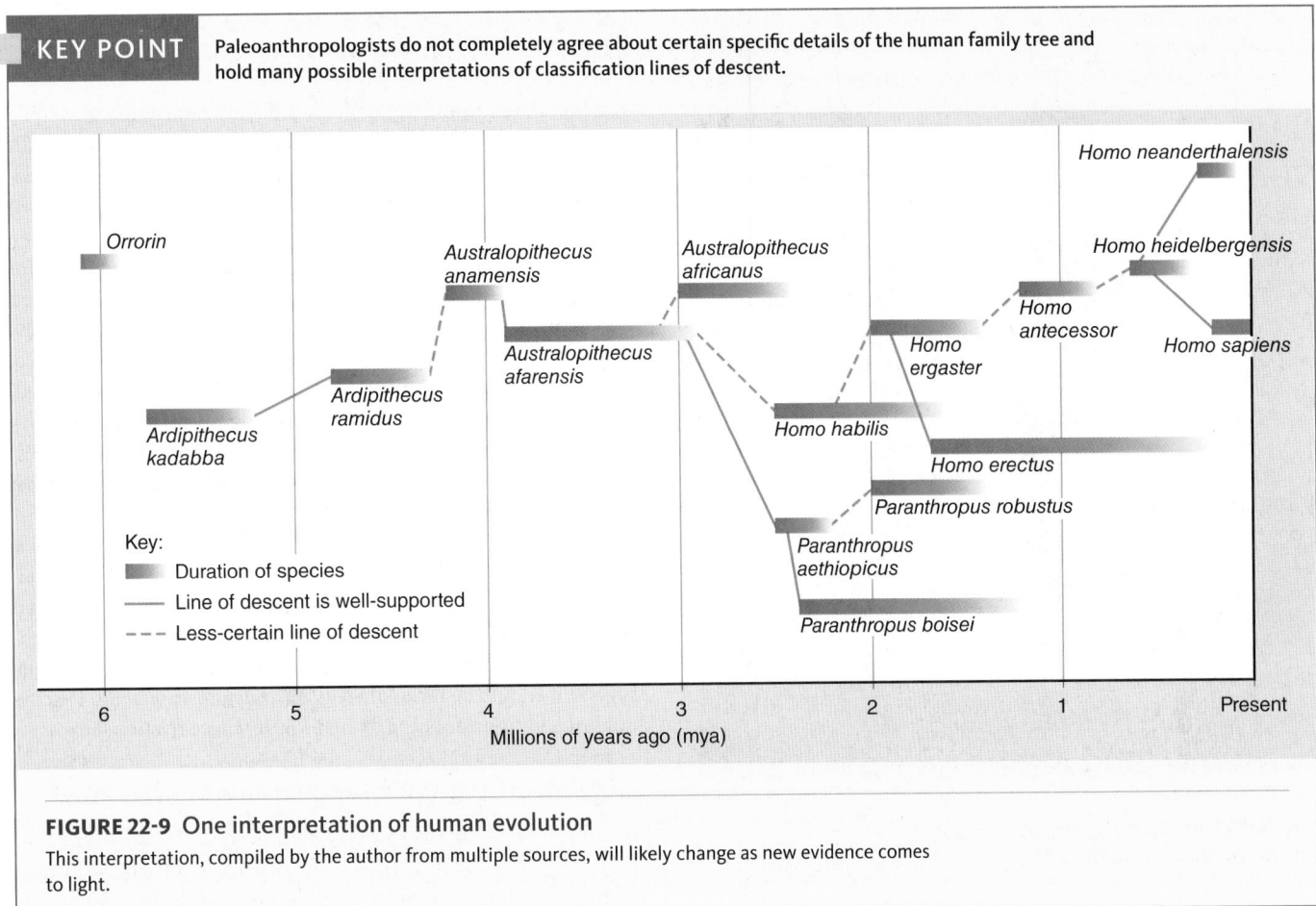

FIGURE 22-9 One interpretation of human evolution
This interpretation, compiled by the author from multiple sources, will likely change as new evidence comes to light.

4 mya and 6 mya. Although not as primitive as *Sahelanthropus, Ardipithecus* is close to the "root" of the human family tree. The shape of the toe bones suggests that *Ardipithecus* walked upright.

Two species of *Ardipithecus* have been described. The canine teeth of the earliest species, *A. kadabba,* have certain primitive features similar to those of *Sahelanthropus* and *Orrorin.* The specific epithet *kadabba* comes from Afar words meaning "basal family ancestor." *Ardipithecus ramidus* appeared about 4.8 mya. A remarkably complete fossil of a female *A. ramidus,* named Ardi, was scientifically described in 2009.

Ardipithecus gave rise to **Australopithecus,** a genus that includes several species that lived between 4 mya and 1 mya. Both *Ardipithecus* and *Australopithecus* had longer arms, shorter legs, and smaller brains relative to those of modern humans.

Hominins that existed between 4.2 mya and 3.9 mya are assigned to the species **Australopithecus anamensis,** first named by paleoanthropologist Meave Leakey and her co-workers in 1995 from fossils discovered in eastern Africa. This hominin species, which has a mixture of apelike and humanlike features, presumably evolved from *Ardipithecus ramidus.* A comparison of male and female *Australopithecus anamensis* body sizes and canine teeth reveals **sexual dimorphism,** marked phenotypic differences between the two sexes of the same species. (The modern-day gorilla is sexually dimorphic.) The back teeth and jaws of *A. anamensis* are

larger than those of modern chimpanzees, whereas the front teeth are smaller and more like those of later hominins. A fossil leg bone, the tibia, indicates that *A. anamensis* had an upright posture and was bipedal, although it also may have foraged in the trees. Thus, bipedalism occurred early in human evolution and appears to have been the first human adaptation.

Australopithecus afarensis, another primitive hominin, probably evolved directly from *A. anamensis.* Many fossils of *A. afarensis* skeletal remains have been discovered in Africa, including a remarkably complete 3.2-million-year-old skeleton, nicknamed Lucy, found in Ethiopia in 1974 by a team led by U.S. paleoanthropologist Donald Johanson (**FIG. 22-10**). In 1978, British paleoanthropologist Mary Leakey and co-workers discovered beautifully preserved fossil footprints of three *A. afarensis* individuals who walked more than 3.6 mya. In 1994, paleoanthropologists found the first adult skull of *A. afarensis.* The skull, characterized by a relatively small brain, pronounced supraorbital ridges, a jutting jaw, and large canine teeth, is an estimated 3 million years old. It is probable that *A. afarensis* did not construct tools or make fires because no evidence of tools or fire has been found at fossil sites.

Many paleoanthropologists think that *A. afarensis* gave rise to several **australopithecine** species, including **Australopithecus africanus,** which may have appeared as early as 3 mya. The first *A. africanus* fossil was discovered in South Africa in 1924, and since

FIGURE 22-10 *Australopithecus afarensis*
This artist's rendition of a female australopithecine and child is based on the fossils of Lucy, discovered in 1974.

Homo habilis is the oldest member of genus *Homo*

The first hominin to have enough uniquely human features to be placed in the same genus as modern humans is **Homo habilis.** It was first discovered in the early 1960s at Olduvai Gorge in Tanzania. Since then, paleoanthropologists have discovered other fossils of *H. habilis* in eastern and southern Africa. *Homo habilis* was a small hominin with a larger brain and smaller premolars and molars than those of the australopithecines. This hominin appeared approximately 2.5 mya and persisted for about 0.9 million years. Fossils of *H. habilis* have been found in numerous areas in Africa. These sites contain primitive tools, stones that had been chipped, cracked, or hammered to make sharp edges for cutting or scraping. *Oldowan* pebble choppers and flakes, for example, were probably used to cut through animal hides to obtain meat and to break bones for their nutritious marrow.

The relationship between the australopithecines and *H. habilis* is not clear. Using physical characteristics of their fossilized skeletons as evidence, many paleoanthropologists have inferred that the australopithecines were ancestors of *H. habilis*. Some researchers do not think that *H. habilis* belongs in the genus *Homo*, and they suggest it should be reclassified as *Australopithecus habilis*. Discoveries of additional fossils may help clarify these relationships.

Homo ergaster may have arisen from *H. habilis*

Initially, fossils that are now classified as *Homo ergaster* were considered by some scientists as early *H. erectus* (discussed in next section). With the discovery of additional fossils, however, many scientists hypothesized that the fossils classified as *H. erectus* really represent two species, **Homo ergaster,** an earlier African species, and *H. erectus*, a later eastern Asian offshoot. The best-known fossils of *H. ergaster*, which existed from 2.0 to 1.4 mya, come from the Lake Turkana region in Kenya. Researchers who support the split speculate that *H. ergaster* may be the direct ancestor of later humans, whereas *H. erectus* may be an evolutionary dead end.

Homo erectus probably evolved from *H. ergaster*

Investigators found the first fossil evidence of **Homo erectus** in Indonesia in the 1890s. Since then, searchers have found numerous fossils of *H. erectus* throughout Africa and Asia. Paleoanthropologists think that *H. erectus* originated in Africa about 1.7 mya and then spread to Europe and Asia. Peking man and Java man, discovered in Asia, were later examples of *H. erectus*, which existed until at least 200,000 years ago; some populations of *H. erectus* may have persisted more recently.

Homo erectus was taller than *H. habilis*. Its brain, which was larger than that of *H. habilis*, got progressively larger during the course of its evolution. Its skull, although larger, did not possess totally modern features, retaining the heavy supraorbital ridge and projecting face that are more characteristic of its ape ancestors (**FIG. 22-11**). *Homo erectus* is the first hominin to have fewer differences between the sexes.

The increased intelligence associated with a larger brain enabled these early humans to make more advanced stone tools, known as *Acheulean* tools, including hand axes and other imple-

then hundreds have been found. This hominin walked erect and possessed hands and teeth that were distinctly humanlike. Given the characteristics of the teeth, paleoanthropologists think that *A. africanus* ate both plants and animals. Like *A. afarensis*, it had a small brain, more like that of its primate ancestors than of present-day humans.

Three australopithecine species (*Paranthropus robustus* from South Africa, and *P. aethiopicus* and *P. boisei*, both from East Africa) were larger than *A. africanus* and had extremely large molars, very powerful jaws, relatively small brains, and bony skull crests. Most females lacked the skull crests and had substantially smaller jaws, another example of sexual dimorphism in early hominins. The teeth and jaws suggest a diet, perhaps of tough roots, nuts, and seeds, that would require powerful grinding. (However, a 2008 study of fossil teeth of *P. boisei* found that the wear on the teeth suggested a softer diet, such as fruits. *P. boisei* apparently ate soft food during times of plenty but could eat hard items during food shortages.) These so-called *robust australopithecines* may or may not be closely related but are generally thought to represent evolutionary offshoots, or side branches, of human evolution. The first robust australopithecine, *P. aethiopicus*, appeared about 2.5 mya.

The actual number of australopithecine species for which fossil evidence has been found is under debate. In some cases, differences in the relatively few skeletal fragments could indicate either variation among individuals within a species or evidence of separate species.

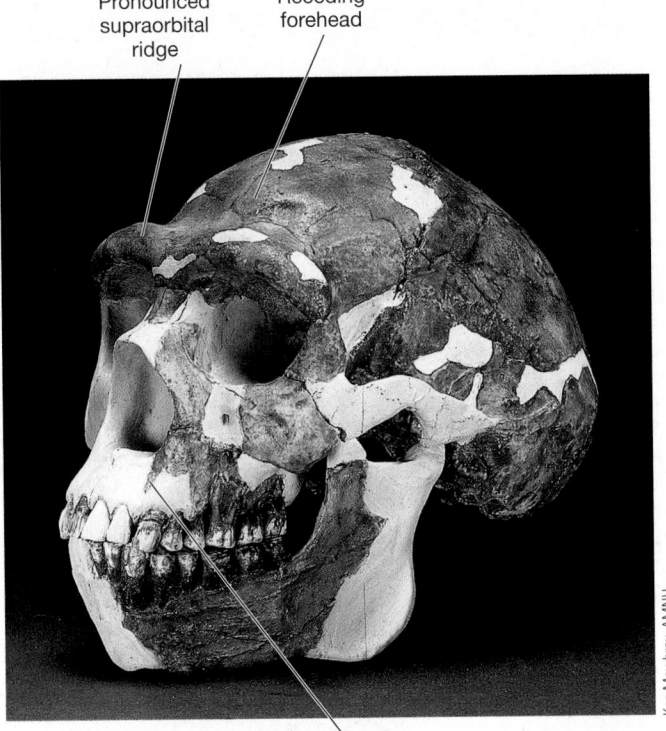

Pronounced supraorbital ridge

Receding forehead

Projecting face/jaws

Ken Mowbray, AMNH

FIGURE 22-11 *Homo erectus* skull from China

The reconstructed parts are white. Note the receding forehead, pronounced supraorbital ridge, and projecting face and jaws.

© Javier Trueba/Madrid Scientific Films/Photo Researchers, Inc.

FIGURE 22-12 Acheulean tool

This stone tool is a typical Acheulean tool. It was made about 800,000 years ago by striking both sides of the biface (shown) to make a teardrop shape. The tool was found with other fossils and tools in Gran Dolina, Sierra de Atapuerca, Spain.

ments that scientists have interpreted as choppers, borers, and scrapers (**FIG. 22-12**). Their intelligence also allowed these humans to survive in cold areas. *Homo erectus* obtained food by hunting or scavenging and may have worn clothing, built fires, and lived in caves or shelters. Evidence of weapons (spears) has been unearthed at *H. erectus* sites in Europe. (For the remarkable story of an evolutionary offshoot from *H. erectus,* see *Inquiring About: The Smallest Humans.*)

Archaic humans date from about 1.2 mya to 200,000 years ago

Archaic humans are regionally diverse descendants of *H. ergaster* that lived in Africa, Asia, and Europe from about 1.2 mya to 200,000 years ago. The brains of archaic humans were essentially the same size as our brains, although their skulls retained some ancestral characters. Populations of archaic humans had rich and varied cultures (learned traditions) that included making many kinds of tools and objects with symbolic and ceremonial meaning.

Some researchers classify the oldest archaic human fossils discovered in Europe (in Spain) as ***Homo antecessor.*** *Homo antecessor* existed from about 1.2 mya to 800,000 years ago. Sites where *H. antecessor* fossils have been found show numerous cuts on human bones that suggest these early humans practiced cannibalism.

Homo heidelbergensis, which appeared about 600,000 years ago and existed until about 300,000 years ago, may have descended

from *H. antecessor.* Fossils of *H. heidelbergensis* were first discovered in Germany about 100 years ago. This extinct hominin had a larger brain—similar in size to that of modern humans—than *H. ergaster* or *H. antecessor.*

Some scientists do not recognize *H. antecessor* and suggest *H. antecessor* fossils should be classified as *H. heidelbergensis.* Classification of *H. heidelbergensis* is also controversial because many (but not all) of the scientists studying its fossil remains think that both Neandertals and modern humans descended from it.

Neandertals appeared approximately 250,000 years ago

Fossils of **Neandertals** were first discovered in the Neander Valley in Germany.[1] They lived throughout Europe and western Asia from about 250,000 to 28,000 years ago. Although at one time many scientists considered Neandertals as a subspecies of *H. sapiens,* increasing evidence suggests Neandertals were a separate species from modern humans, ***Homo neanderthalensis.***

---

[1]*Neandertal* was formerly spelled *Neanderthal.* The silent *h* has been dropped in modern German but not in the scientific name.

THE SMALLEST HUMANS

Evolutionarily speaking, what are "hobbits"? In 2004, paleoanthropologists reported a startling discovery—fossils of seven humans in a cave on the Indonesian island of Flores. The finding was completely unexpected because the fossil bones and teeth were from adult humans that were about 1 m (about 3 ft) tall.

The tiny humans, which have been dubbed "hobbits" by the media, may represent a new species, *Homo floresiensis*. Although these hominins had small, ape-sized brains, sophisticated stone tools, fireplaces, and charred bones found with the fossils indicate that *H. floresiensis* was capable of complex thinking and activities. The charred bones were primarily from pygmy elephants (*Stegodon*) and Flores giant rats (*Papagomys*) and provide clues about the food that *H. floresiensis* hunted and killed (see figure). Based on several dating methods, *H. floresiensis* is thought to have existed from about 38,000 years ago to as recently as 12,000 years ago, when it went extinct.

Detailed studies of the *H. floresiensis* braincase, published in 2005, revealed that it was similar in many ways to the larger brain of *H. erectus*, which is known to have lived on nearby islands. Many researchers have concluded from this and other evidence that *H. floresiensis* was an evolutionary offshoot of *H. erectus*.

Why was *H. floresiensis* so small? Biologists have often observed two evolutionary trends of mammals living on remote islands: large mammals tend to evolve into much smaller species, and small mammals tend to evolve into much larger species. It is not unreasonable to assume that the small population of *H. erectus* ancestors that colonized Flores, perhaps by rafting to the island on a log, underwent evolutionary dwarfing over the thousands of years they were isolated on Flores. (If *H. erectus* had been a frequent visitor to Flores, gene flow between the indigenous population and the visitors would have prevented the indigenous population from becoming measurably smaller.)

Not everyone agrees with the hypothesis that *H. floresiensis* is a separate species of tiny humans. Some researchers think the fossils have not been identified properly. In a study published in 2006, these researchers suggest that the fossils are from *H. sapiens* individuals suffering from a rare genetic defect (microcephaly) that causes small brains and bodies.

The research team that unearthed the fossils has returned to the cave and will continue excavations. It is anticipated that future discoveries will help scientists answer the many questions we have about Earth's smallest humans. Meanwhile, the debate about the origin of *H. floresiensis* continues.

These early humans had short, sturdy builds. Their faces projected slightly, their chins and foreheads receded, they had heavy supraorbital ridges and jawbones, and their brains and front teeth were larger than those of modern humans. They had large nasal cavities and receding cheekbones. Scientists have suggested that the large noses provided larger surface areas in Neandertal sinuses, enabling them to better warm the cold air of Ice Age Eurasia as inhaled air traveled through the head to the lungs.

Neandertal tools, known as *Mousterian* tools, were more sophisticated than those of *H. erectus* (**FIG. 22-13**). Studies of Neandertal sites indicate that Neandertals hunted large animals. The existence of skeletons of elderly Neandertals and of some with healed fractures may demonstrate that Neandertals cared for the aged and the sick, an indication of advanced social cooperation. They apparently had rituals, possibly of religious significance, and sometimes buried their dead.

The disappearance of the Neandertals about 28,000 years ago is a mystery that has sparked debate among paleoanthropologists. Other groups of *H. sapiens* with more modern features coexisted with the Neandertals for several thousand years. Perhaps the other humans outcompeted or exterminated the Neandertals, leading to their extinction. It is also possible that the Neandertals interbred with these humans, diluting their features beyond recognition.

Analysis of **mitochondrial DNA (mtDNA)** contributes useful data for such controversies. Each of the several hundred mitochondria within a cell has about 10 copies of a small loop of DNA that codes for transfer RNAs, ribosomal RNAs, and certain respiratory enzymes. The mtDNA is transmitted only through the maternal line because eggs, not sperm, contribute mitochondria. Because mtDNA mutates more rapidly than nuclear DNA, mtDNA is a sensitive indicator of evolution. Researchers have extracted and evaluated the mtDNA from seven separate Neandertals. Its sequence differs significantly from all modern human mtDNA sequences, although it is more similar to human than to chimpanzee mtDNA. This finding suggests that Neandertals are an evolutionary dead end that did not interbreed appreciably with more modern humans. However, the amount of interbreeding that may have occurred between Neandertals and anatomically modern humans remains controversial.

Scientists have reached a near consensus on the origin of modern *Homo sapiens*

Homo sapiens with anatomically modern features existed in Africa about 195,000 years ago. As these anatomically modern humans dispersed around the world, they displaced other hominins such as *H. erectus* and *H. neanderthalensis*. By about 30,000 years ago, anatomically modern humans were the only members of genus *Homo* remaining, excluding small, isolated populations.

Both recent fossil finds and extensive molecular analyses have promoted the **(recent) out-of-Africa model** (also called *Recent*

FIGURE 22-13 Mousterian tool

Mousterian tools are named after a Neandertal site in Le Moustier, France. Mousterian tools include a variety of skillfully made stone tools; this tool, with its sharp edges, was probably used to scrape hides and/or to form the point of a spear. Although Neandertals had spears, they did not develop bows and arrows and so had to get close to their prey when hunting.

Africa Origin, or *RAO*) as the main explanation for the origin of modern humans living around the world. New data include the discovery of the earliest fossilized remains of modern *H. sapiens* in Africa and analyses of DNA from mitochondria, the Y chromosome, and autosomes. In 2005, fossils of the earliest known modern *H. sapiens* were reliably dated at 195,000 years old; these fossils were found in southern Ethiopia. No *H. sapiens* fossils of comparable age have been found in Europe or Asia. The earliest fossils of anatomically modern *H. sapiens* in Europe and most parts of Asia date to 45,000 to 40,000 years ago. One exception is in Israel, where *H. sapiens* fossils have been dated at 100,000 years before present.

Molecular anthropology, the comparison of biological molecules from present-day individuals of regional human populations, provides clues that help scientists unravel the origin of modern humans and trace human migrations. A series of recent genetic studies of mtDNA, Y chromosome, and autosomal DNA has strengthened the case for Africa as the birthplace of modern humans (**FIG. 22-14**). These studies provide detailed comparisons of DNA in present-day populations around the world as well as ancient DNA extracted from Neandertal and early *H. sapiens* remains.

Review

- How do the skulls of apes and humans differ?
- How does an ape skeleton differ from a human skeleton?
- How do australopithecines and *Homo* differ?
- How can you distinguish between *H. habilis* and *H. erectus*?
- How do *H. neanderthalensis* and *H. sapiens* differ?

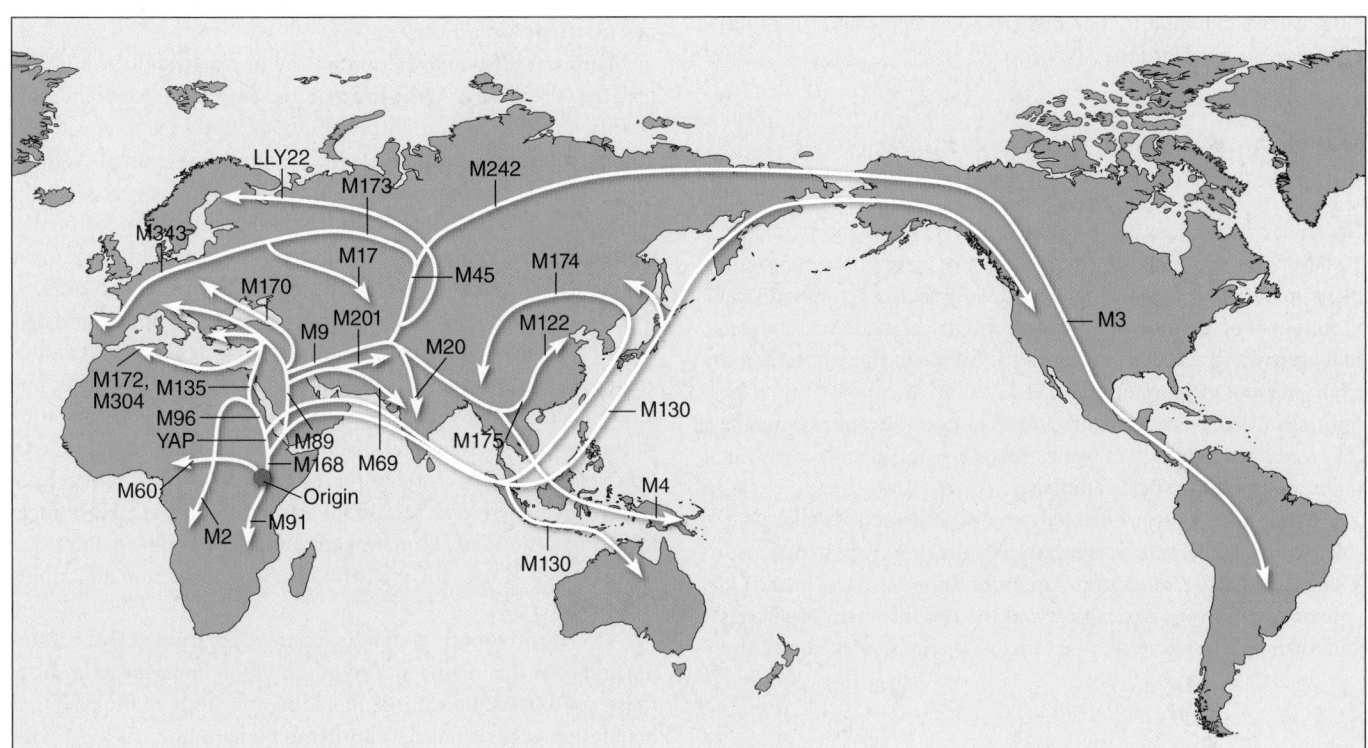

FIGURE 22-14 The path of human migrations, based on Y chromosome data

Homo sapiens originated in eastern Africa and migrated from there throughout the world.

(Source: Stix, G. "Traces of a Distant Past." *Scientific American*, p. 59, July 2008. Author credits information in *National Geographic* maps.)

22.4 CULTURAL CHANGE

■ LEARNING OBJECTIVE

8   Describe the impact of human culture on the biosphere.

Genetically speaking, humans are not very different from other primates. At the level of our DNA sequences, we are roughly 98% identical to gorillas and 99% identical to chimpanzees. Our relatively few genetic differences, however, give rise to several important distinguishing features, such as greater intelligence and the ability to capitalize on it by transmitting knowledge from one generation to the next. Human culture is not inherited in the biological sense but instead is learned, largely through the medium of language.[2] Human culture is dynamic and is modified as people obtain new knowledge. Human culture is generally divided into three stages: (1) the development of hunter–gatherer societies, (2) the development of agriculture, and (3) the Industrial Revolution.

Early humans were hunters and gatherers who relied on what was available in their immediate environment. They were nomadic, and as the resources in a given area were exhausted or as the population increased, they migrated to a different area. These societies required a division of labor and the ability to make tools and weapons, which were needed to kill game, scrape hides, dig up roots and tubers, and cook food. Although scientists are not certain when hunting was incorporated into human society, they do know it declined in importance approximately 15,000 years ago. This may have been due to a decrease in the abundance of large animals, triggered in part by overhunting. A few isolated groups of hunter–gatherer societies, such as the Inuit of the northern polar region and the Mbuti of Africa, survived into the 21st century.

Development of agriculture resulted in a more dependable food supply

Evidence that humans had begun to cultivate crops approximately 10,000 years ago includes the presence of agricultural tools and plant material at archaeological sites. Agriculture resulted in a more dependable food supply. Archaeological evidence suggests that agriculture arose in several steps. Although there is variation from one site to another, plant cultivation, in combination with hunting, usually occurred first. Animal domestication generally followed later, although in some areas, such as Australia, early humans did not domesticate animals.

Agriculture, in turn, often led to more permanent dwellings because considerable time was invested in growing crops in one area. Villages and cities often grew up around the farmlands, but the connection between agriculture and the establishment of villages and towns is complicated by certain discoveries. For example, Abu

---

[2]Humans are not the only animals to have culture. Chimpanzees have primitive cultures that include tool-using techniques, hunting methods, and social behaviors that vary from one population to another. These cultural traditions are passed to the next generation by teaching and imitation; see Figures 1-18 and 52-13b.

Hureyra in Syria was a village founded *before* agriculture arose. The villagers subsisted on the rich plant life of the area and the migrating herds of gazelle. Once people turned to agriculture, however, they seldom went back to hunting and gathering to obtain food.

Other advances in agriculture include the domestication of animals, which people kept to supply food, milk, and hides. Archaeological evidence indicates that wild goats and sheep were probably the first animals to be domesticated in southwestern Turkey, northern Iraq, and Iran. In the Old World, people also used animals to prepare fields for planting. Another major advance in agriculture was irrigation, which began more than 5000 years ago in Egypt.

Producing food agriculturally was more time-consuming than hunting and gathering, but it was also more productive. In hunter–gatherer societies, everyone shares the responsibility for obtaining food. In agricultural societies, fewer people are needed to provide food for everyone. Thus, agriculture freed some people to pursue other endeavors, including religion, art, and various crafts.

Human culture has had a profound impact on the biosphere

Human culture has had far-reaching effects on both human society and on other organisms. The Industrial Revolution, which began in the 18th century, drew populations to concentrate in urban areas near centers of manufacturing. Advances in agriculture encouraged urbanization because fewer and fewer people were needed in rural areas to produce food for everyone. The spread of industrialization increased the demand for natural resources to supply the raw materials for industry.

Human culture has permitted the human population, which reached 6.8 billion in 2009, to expand so dramatically that there are serious questions about Earth's ability to support so many people indefinitely (see Chapter 53). According to the United Nations' *2008 State of Food Insecurity*, 923 million people lack access to the food needed to be healthy and lead productive lives. To further compound the problem, the UN projects that 2.6 billion *additional* people will be added to the world population by the year 2050.

Human culture has resulted in large-scale disruption and degradation of the environment. Tropical rain forests and other natural environments are rapidly being eliminated. Soil, water, and air pollution occur in many places. Since World War II, soil degradation caused by poor agricultural practices, overgrazing, and deforestation has occurred in an area equal to 17% of Earth's total vegetated surface area. Many species cannot adapt to the rapid environmental changes caused by humans and thus are becoming extinct. The decrease in biological diversity from species extinction is alarming (see Chapter 57).

On a positive note, people are aware of the damage we are causing and have the intelligence to modify their behavior to improve these conditions. Education, including the study of biology, may help future generations develop greater environmental sensitivity.

Review

■   How has human culture affected planet Earth?

22.1 *(page 466)*

1 Describe the structural adaptations that primates have for life in treetops.

- **Primates** are **placental mammals** that arose from small, arboreal (tree-dwelling), shrewlike mammals. Primates possess five grasping digits, including an **opposable thumb** or toe; long, slender limbs that move freely at the hips and shoulders; and eyes located in front of the head.

22.2 *(page 467)*

2 List the three suborders of primates and give representative examples of each.

- Primates are divided into three suborders. The suborder Prosimii includes lemurs, galagos, and lorises. The suborder Tarsiiformes includes tarsiers. The suborder Anthropoidea includes anthropoids—monkeys, apes, and humans.

  CENGAGENOW™   Learn more about primate evolution by clicking on the figure in CengageNOW.

3 Distinguish among anthropoids, hominoids, and hominins.

- **Anthropoids** include monkeys, apes, and humans. Early anthropoids branched into two groups: New World monkeys and Old World monkeys.

- **Hominoids** include apes and humans. Hominoids arose from the Old World monkey lineage. There are four modern genera of apes: gibbons, orangutans, gorillas, and chimpanzees.

- The **hominin** line consists of humans and their ancestors.

22.3 *(page 471)*

4 Describe skeletal and skull differences between apes and hominins.

- Unlike ape skeletons, hominin skeletons have adaptations that reflect the ability to stand erect and walk on two feet. These adaptations include a complex curvature of the spine; a shorter, broader pelvis; repositioning of the **foramen magnum** to the base of the skull; and a first toe that is aligned with the other toes.

- The human skull lacks a pronounced **supraorbital ridge,** is flatter than ape skulls in the front, and has a pronounced chin. The human brain is larger than ape brains, and the jaw is structured so that the teeth are arranged in a U shape.

CENGAGENOW™   Learn more about monkey, gorilla, and human skeletons by clicking on the figure in CengageNOW.

5 Briefly describe the following early hominins: *Orrorin, Ardipithecus,* and *Australopithecus anamensis, A. afarensis,* and *A. africanus.*

- **Orrorin** is an early hominin that arose about 6 mya. Researchers studying the fossil leg bones of *Orrorin* think that it walked upright and was **bipedal** (walked on two feet).

- *Ardipithecus, Australopithecus,* and *Paranthropus* species are often referred to as **australopithecines.** Australopithecines were bipedal,

a hominin feature. The first **Ardipithecus** species, **A. kadabba,** appeared about 5.8 mya. **Ardipithecus ramidus,** which appeared about 4.8 mya, may have given rise to **Australopithecus anamensis,** which in turn probably gave rise to another primitive hominin, **Australopithecus afarensis.** Many paleoanthropologists think that *A. afarensis* gave rise to several australopithecine species, including **Australopithecus africanus,** *Paranthropus* spp., and possibly *Homo habilis.*

6 Distinguish among the following members of genus *Homo: H. habilis, H. ergaster, H. erectus, H. antecessor, H. heidelbergensis, H. neanderthalensis,* and *H. sapiens.*

- **Homo habilis** was the earliest known hominin with some of the human features lacking in the australopithecines, including a slightly larger brain. *Homo habilis* fashioned crude tools from stone.

- The best-known fossils of **H. ergaster,** which existed from 2.0 to 1.4 mya, come from Kenya. *Homo ergaster* may be the direct ancestor of later humans.

- **Homo erectus** had a larger brain than *H. habilis;* made more sophisticated tools; and may have worn clothing, built fires, and lived in caves or shelters. *Homo erectus,* which is probably a later Asian offshoot of *H. ergaster,* appears to be an evolutionary dead end.

- Archaic humans are regionally diverse descendants of *H. ergaster* that lived in Africa, Asia, and Europe from about 1.2 mya to 200,000 years ago. The brains of archaic humans were essentially the same size as our brains, although their skulls retained some ancestral characters, and they had rich and varied cultures.

- Some researchers classify the oldest archaic human fossils discovered in Europe (in Spain) as **Homo antecessor.** *Homo antecessor* existed from about 1.2 mya to 800,000 years ago.

- **Homo heidelbergensis,** which appeared about 600,000 years ago and existed until about 300,000 years ago, may have descended from *H. antecessor.* This extinct hominin had a larger brain—similar in size to that of modern humans—than either *H. ergaster* or *H. antecessor.* Many scientists studying *H. heidelbergensis* think that both Neandertals and modern humans descended from it.

- **Neandertals** lived from about 250,000 to 30,000 years ago. Neandertals had short, sturdy builds; receding chins and foreheads; heavy supraorbital ridges and jawbones; larger front teeth; and nasal cavities with unusual triangular bony projections. Many scientists think that Neandertals were a separate species, **Homo neanderthalensis.**

- **Homo sapiens,** anatomically modern humans, existed in Africa about 195,000 years ago. By about 30,000 years ago, anatomically modern humans were the only members of genus *Homo* remaining, excluding small, isolated populations.

  CENGAGENOW™   Learn more about *Homo* skulls by clicking on the figure in CengageNOW.

7 Discuss the origin of modern humans.

- Recent fossil finds and extensive molecular analyses have promoted the **(recent) out-of-Africa model** as the main explanation for the origin of modern humans living around the world. New data include the discovery of the earliest fossilized remains of modern *H. sapiens* in Africa and analyses of DNA from mitochondria, the Y chromosome, and autosomes.

22.4 *(page 478)*

8 Describe the impact of human culture on the biosphere.

- Large human brain size makes possible the transmission of knowledge from one generation to the next. Two significant advances in human culture were the development of agriculture and the Industrial Revolution.

TEST YOUR UNDERSTANDING

1. The first primates evolved from (a) shrewlike monotremes (b) therapsids (c) shrewlike placental mammals (d) tarsiers (e) shrewlike marsupials

2. The anthropoids are more closely related to _____ than to _____. (a) tarsiers; lemurs (b) lemurs; monkeys (c) tree shrews; tarsiers (d) lemurs; tarsiers (e) tree shrews; monkeys

3. With what group do hominoids share the most recent common ancestor? (a) Old World monkeys (b) New World monkeys (c) tarsiers (d) lemurs (e) lorises and galagos

4. The _____ in humans is centered at the base of the skull, positioning the head for erect walking. (a) supraorbital ridge (b) foramen magnum (c) pelvis (d) bony skull crest (e) femur

5. Scientists collectively call humans and their *immediate* ancestors (a) mammals (b) primates (c) anthropoids (d) hominoids (e) hominins

6. The earliest hominin that scientists placed in the genus *Homo* is (a) *H. habilis* (b) *H. ergaster* (c) *H. erectus* (d) *H. heidelbergensis* (e) *H. neanderthalensis*

7. Some scientists now think that fossils identified as *Homo erectus* represent which two different species? (a) *H. habilis* and *H. erectus* (b) *H. ergaster* and *H. erectus* (c) *H. heidelbergensis* and *H. ergaster* (d) *H. neanderthalensis* and *H. erectus* (e) *H. neanderthalensis* and *H. sapiens*

8. Archaic humans appeared as early as _____ years ago. (a) 5 million (b) 1.2 mya (c) 250,000 (d) 100,000 (e) 5000

9. _____ were an early group of humans with short, sturdy builds and heavy supraorbital ridges that lived throughout Europe and western Asia from about 250,000 to 30,000 years ago. (a) Australopithecines (b) Dryopithecines (c) Archaic humans (d) Neandertals (e) Cro-Magnons

10. The modern human skull *lacks* (a) small canines (b) a foramen magnum centered in the base of the skull (c) pronounced supraorbital ridges (d) a U-shaped arrangement of teeth on the jaw (e) a large cranium (braincase)

11. The comparison of genetic material from individuals of regional populations of humans, used to help unravel the origin and migration of modern humans, is known as (a) paleoarchaeology (b) cultural anthropology (c) molecular anthropology (d) cytogenetics (e) genetic dimorphism

12. Place the following hominins in chronological order of appearance in the fossil record, beginning with the earliest: 1. *H. ergaster* 2. *H. sapiens* 3. *H. neanderthalensis* 4. *H. erectus* (a) 1, 4, 2, 3 (b) 4, 1, 2, 3 (c) 4, 1, 3, 2 (d) 3, 1, 4, 2 (e) 1, 4, 3, 2

CRITICAL THINKING

1. If you were evaluating whether other early humans exterminated the Neandertals, what kinds of archaeological evidence might you look for?

2. The remains of *H. sapiens* have been found in southern Europe alongside reindeer bones, but reindeer currently exist only in northern Europe and Asia. Explain the apparent discrepancy.

3. **EVOLUTION LINK.** What was the common ancestor of chimpanzees and humans—a chimpanzee, a human, or neither? Explain your answer.

4. **EVOLUTION LINK.** Some scientists say that modern medicine and better sanitation are slowing down or altering the course of human evolution in highly developed countries today. As a result, evolution in humans today has gone from survival of the fittest to survival of almost everyone. Do you think this is a valid idea? Why or why not?

5. **ANALYZING DATA.** If you were to add *H. floresiensis* to Figure 22-9, where would you put it? Justify your answer.

6. **ANALYZING DATA.** Using the information in Figure 22-9, draw a simple cladogram that represents a reasonable hypothesis of human evolution at the genus level. (*Hint:* Your diagram will have three branches.)

7. **ANALYZING DATA.** The four chromosomes depicted below are Y chromosomes from men in different parts of the world. The purple bands represent specific genes that are identical in all four men. The red bands represent genetic mutations (M) that appeared at different times; M168 appeared about 50,000 years ago, M9 about 40,000 years ago, and M3 about 10,000 years ago. Based on what you have learned in this chapter, identify the geographic source of men carrying each of these chromosomes: African, Eurasian, Amerindian, and first migrants out of Africa. (You may wish to refer back to Figure 22-14.)

 Additional questions are available in CengageNOW at www.cengage.com/login.

23 Understanding Diversity: Systematics

Pink iguana. Based on genetic analysis, this pink iguana was identified as a new species in 2009. The iguana inhabits the Wolf volcano on Isabela, one of the Galapagos Islands.

AP Images

KEY CONCEPTS

23.1 Traditionally, biologists have named organisms using a binomial system (in which each species has a genus name followed by a specific epithet) and have classified organisms in taxonomic categories arranged in a hierarchy from most inclusive (domain) to least inclusive (species).

23.2 Based on current knowledge, the three main branches of the tree of life are the three domains: Bacteria, Archaea, and Eukarya.

23.3 Modern systematics seeks to reconstruct phylogeny (evolutionary history of a group of species) based on common ancestry inferred from shared characters (characteristics), including structural, developmental, behavioral, and molecular similarities, as well as from fossil evidence.

23.4 Cladograms (a type of phylogenetic tree) are diagrams of hypothetical evolutionary relationships; they are constructed by analyzing shared derived characters.

The total number of living species is estimated to be between 4 million and 100 million, but only about 1.8 million species have been described. Biologists estimate that to date they have identified less than 10% of bacteria, about 10% of fungi, only about 2% of nematode (roundworm) species, and less than 20% of insect species. Many regions on our planet have not yet been carefully inventoried, including the forest canopy, soil, and the deep regions of the ocean.

Biologists discover thousands of new species each year. For example, in 2009, researchers described a pink iguana that inhabits the Galapagos Islands as a newly identified species (see photo). The research team performed genetic analyses indicating that this iguana split off from other iguanas about five million years ago.

The variety of living organisms and the ecosystems they are part of are referred to as **biological diversity,** or **biodiversity.** The totality of life on Earth represents our biological heritage, and the quality of life for all

481

organisms depends on the health and balance of this worldwide web of life-forms. For example, we depend on organisms to maintain the life-sustaining composition of gases in the atmosphere, form soil, break down wastes, recycle nutrients, and provide food for one another. We humans exploit many species for economic benefit. One very anthropocentric (human-centered) example of the practical importance of biodiversity is that more than 40% of the prescriptions that pharmacists dispense in the United States derive from living organisms. Investigators are just learning how to effectively screen organisms for potential drugs. Unfortunately, human activity is seriously reducing biodiversity, and species are becoming extinct faster than researchers can study them. (See the discussion on declining biodiversity in Chapter 57.)

Alarmed by these extinctions, biologists are mobilizing to more rapidly identify new species and to conserve biodiversity. Many biologists agree that describing and classifying all the surviving species of the world should be a major scientific goal of the 21st century. Important steps toward this goal are being taken by such international research endeavors as the *Catalogue of Life* and the *Encyclopedia of Life*. The *Catalogue of Life* is the work of a collaborative international research team that manages a comprehensive global database made available on the Internet. The *Catalogue of Life* categorizes and lists all of the world's known species. The *Encyclopedia of Life (EOL)*, a project launched in 2007, is an electronic database that will include a home page for each species. Data will include alternative names for each organism, classification, habitat, distribution, and diet. The Convention on Biological Diversity is an international treaty made up of 190 countries committed to reducing the "rate of loss of biodiversity." This convention is committed to developing strategies for the conservation and sustainable use of Earth's biological diversity.

In this chapter, we learn more about evolution and information transfer, two of the basic themes of life introduced in Chapter 1. We explore some of the approaches and methods used by biologists to classify organisms and to infer their evolutionary history and relationships. Information comes from many sources, including fossils, biogeography, patterns of development, and structural and behavioral characteristics. Advances in DNA sequencing have generated huge amounts of data about molecular similarities and differences.

Systematists organize information about organisms they are studying into large databases and manipulate them using computer algorithms to generate hypotheses regarding evolutionary relationships. From these data, biologists are constructing a "tree of life." As more sophisticated molecular methods and discovery of new fossils provide new data, old data are reinterpreted. As we gain greater understanding of how organisms are related, we revise the way we classify organisms, and the structure of the tree of life changes.

23.1 CLASSIFYING ORGANISMS

■ LEARNING OBJECTIVES

1 State two justifications for the use of scientific names and classifications of organisms.
2 Describe the binomial system of naming organisms and arrange the Linnaean categories in hierarchical fashion from most inclusive to least inclusive.

The scientific study of the diversity of organisms and their evolutionary relationships is called **systematics.** Recall from earlier chapters (for example, see Chapter 18) that **evolution** is the accumulation of inherited changes within populations over time. An important aspect of systematics is **taxonomy,** the science of naming, describing, and classifying organisms. In biology, the term **classification** means arranging organisms into groups based on similarities that reflect evolutionary relationships among lineages.

Organisms are named using a binomial system

Because there are millions of kinds of organisms, scientists need a system for accurately identifying them. Imagine that you were going to develop a classification system. How would you use what you already know about living things to assign them to categories? Would you place insects, bats, and birds in one category because they all have wings and fly? And would you, perhaps, place squid, whales, fish, penguins, and Olympic backstroke champions in another category because they all swim? Or would you classify organisms according to a culinary scheme, placing lobsters and tuna in the same part of the menu, perhaps identifying them as "seafood"? Any of these schemes might be valid, depending on your purpose. Similar methods have been used throughout history. St. Augustine in the 4th century classified animals as useful, harmful, or superfluous—to humans. During the Renaissance, scholars began to develop categories based on the characteristics of the organisms themselves.

Of the many classification systems that were developed, the one designed by Carolus Linnaeus in the mid-18th century has survived with some modification to the present day. Linnaeus grouped organisms according to their similarities, mainly structural similarities.

Before the mid-18th century, each species had a lengthy descriptive name, sometimes consisting of ten or more Latin words! Linnaeus simplified scientific classification, developing a **binomial system of nomenclature** in which each species is assigned a unique two-part name. The first part of a binomial scientific name is a noun that designates the **genus** (pl., *genera*), and the second part, an adjective modifying that noun, is called the **specific epithet.**

The genus name is always capitalized, whereas the specific epithet is usually not. Both names are underlined or italicized. The genus, or generic, name can be used alone to designate all species in the genus (for example, the genus *Quercus* includes all oak species). Note that the specific epithet alone is *not* the species's name. In fact, the same specific epithet can be used as the second name of species in different genera. For example, *Quercus alba* is the scientific species name for the white oak, and *Salix alba* is the species name for the white willow (*alba* comes from a Latin word meaning "white"). Thus, both parts of the name must be used to accurately identify the species. The specific epithet is never used alone; it must always follow the full or abbreviated genus name, for example, *Quercus alba* or *Q. alba*.

Scientific names are generally derived from Greek or Latin roots or from Latinized versions of the names of persons, places, or characteristics. For example, the generic name for the bacterium *Escherichia coli* is based on the name of the scientist, Theodor Escherich, who first described it. The specific epithet *coli* reminds us that *E. coli* lives in the colon (large intestine).

Most areas of biology depend on scientific names and classification. For example, to study the effects of pollution on an aquatic community, biologists must be able to accurately record the relative numbers of each type of organism present and changes in their populations over time. This requires that all investigators identify each species accurately by name.

Scientific names permit biology to be a truly international science. Even though the common names of an organism may vary in different locations and languages, an organism can be universally identified by its scientific name. A researcher in Puerto Rico knows exactly which organisms were used in a study published by a Russian scientist and therefore can repeat or extend the Russian's experiments using the same species.

Each taxonomic level is more general than the one below it

Linnaeus devised a system for assigning species to a hierarchy of increasingly broader groups. As you move up the hierarchy, each group is more inclusive, that is, it includes the groups below it. When he set up his system, Linnaeus did not have a theory of evolution in mind. Nor did he have any idea of the vast number of extant (living) and extinct organisms that would later be discovered. Yet his system has proved remarkably flexible and adaptable to new biological knowledge and theory. Very few other 18th-century inventions survive today in a form that would still be recognizable to their originators.

The range of taxonomic categories from species to domain forms a hierarchy (**FIG. 23-1** and **TABLE 23-1**). Closely related species are assigned to the same genus, and closely related genera are grouped in a single **family.** Families are grouped into **orders,** orders into **classes,** classes into **phyla,** phyla into **kingdoms** (some biologists use the term *division* for this category in plants), and kingdoms into **domains.** A species is considered a true biological entity, but taxonomic categories above the species level, at least until recently, have been artificial constructs used to conveniently catalogue the diverse life-forms on Earth. As we will discuss in this chapter, the modern systematists work to validate taxonomic groups.

A **taxon** (pl., *taxa*) is a formal grouping of organisms at any given level, such as species, genus, or phylum. For example, class Mammalia is a taxon that includes many different orders. A taxon can be separated into subgroupings, such as subphyla or superclasses. Subphylum Vertebrata, a subgroup of phylum Chordata, is a taxon that contains several classes, including Amphibia and Mammalia.

TABLE 23-1	Classification of Corn
Domain	Eukarya
	Organisms that have nuclei and other membrane-enclosed organelles
Kingdom	Plantae
	Terrestrial, multicellular, photosynthetic organisms
Phylum	Anthophyta
	Vascular plants with flowers, fruits, and seeds
Class	Monocotyledones
	Monocots: Flowering plants with one seed leaf (cotyledon) and flower parts in threes
Order	Commelinales
	Monocots with reduced flower parts, elongated leaves, and dry 1-seeded fruits
Family	Poaceae
	Grasses with hollow stems; fruit is a grain; and abundant endosperm in seed
Genus	*Zea*
	Tall annual grass with separate female and male flowers
Species	*Zea mays*
	Corn

Review

- What are the key features of the binomial system of nomenclature?
- What are the advantages to using scientific, rather than common, names for organisms?
- Classify the domestic cat, using taxa from domain to species.

23.2 DETERMINING THE MAJOR BRANCHES IN THE TREE OF LIFE

LEARNING OBJECTIVES

3 Describe the three domains and argue for and against classifying organisms in the domains. (Compare this approach with using kingdoms as the main rank of classification.)

4 Interpret a cladogram, describing the meaning of its specific nodes and branches.

The history of taxonomy at the kingdom and domain levels is a good example of the process of science. In this section we will review some highlights of this process.

Systematics is an evolving science

From the time of Aristotle to the mid-19th century, biologists divided organisms into two kingdoms: **Plantae** and **Animalia.** After the development of microscopes, it became increasingly obvious that many organisms could not be easily assigned to either the

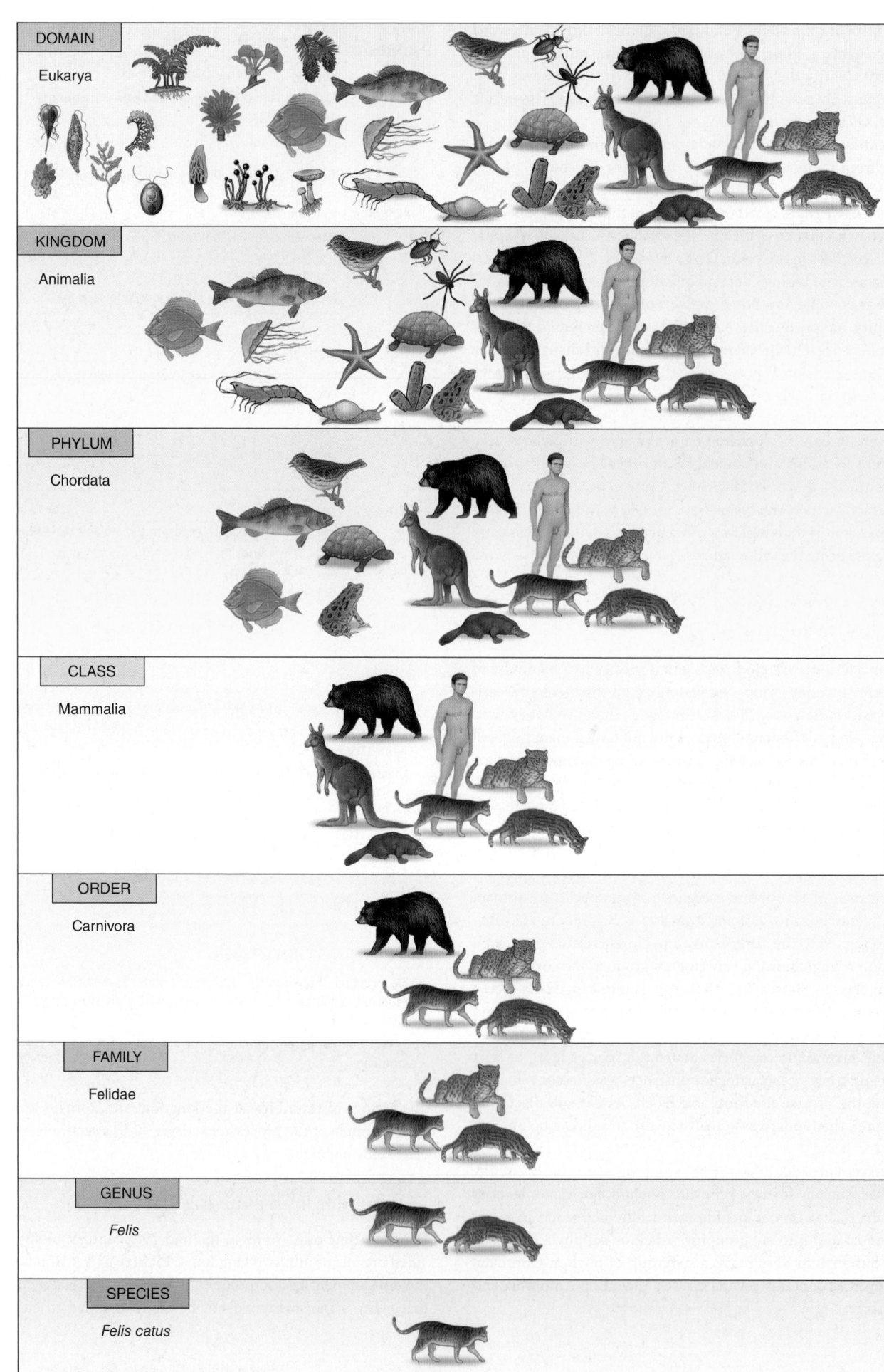

DOMAIN	Eukarya
KINGDOM	Animalia
PHYLUM	Chordata
CLASS	Mammalia
ORDER	Carnivora
FAMILY	Felidae
GENUS	*Felis*
SPECIES	*Felis catus*

The domestic cat (*Felis catus*) is classified here to illustrate the hierarchical organization of the Linnaean taxonomic system. Each level is more inclusive than the one below it, meaning that it includes more groups of organisms.

plant or the animal kingdom. For example, the unicellular organism *Euglena* has been classified at various times in the plant kingdom and in the animal kingdom, but did not really fit in either kingdom. *Euglena* carries on photosynthesis in the light, but in the dark, it uses its flagellum to move about in search of food (see Fig. 26-5). In 1866, a German biologist, Ernst Haeckel, proposed that a third kingdom, **Protista,** be established to accommodate bacteria and other microorganisms. However, biologists largely ignored this kingdom for about a hundred years.

In 1937, the French marine biologist Edouard Chatton suggested the term *procariotique* ("before nucleus") to describe bacteria and the term *eucariotique* ("true nucleus") to describe all other cells. This dichotomy between prokaryotes and eukaryotes is now universally accepted by biologists as a fundamental evolutionary divergence.

In the 1960s, advances in electron microscopy and biochemical techniques revealed further cell differences that inspired many new proposals for classifying organisms. In 1969, R. H. Whittaker proposed a five-kingdom classification based mainly on cell structure and the way that organisms derive nutrition from their environment. (Although Whittaker is generally credited, the concept of five kingdoms was actually first proposed in 1949 by T. L. Jahn and F. Jahn in their book *How to Know the Protozoa.*)

Whittaker suggested that the fungi (which include the mushrooms, molds, and yeasts) be removed from the plant kingdom and classified in their own kingdom, **Fungi.** After all, fungi are not photosynthetic and must absorb nutrients produced by other organisms. Fungi also differ from plants in the composition of their cell walls, in their body structures, and in their modes of reproduction. Kingdom **Prokaryotae** was established to accommodate the bacteria, which are fundamentally different from all other organisms in that they do not have distinct nuclei and other membranous organelles and do not undergo mitotic division (see Fig. 4-6).

In the late 1970s, Carl Woese (pronounced "woes"), of the University of Illinois, and his colleagues began to study the evolutionary relationships among organisms by analyzing their 16S rRNA. Using sequence analysis, Woese used variations in this universal molecule to challenge the long-held view that all prokaryotes were closely related and very similar to one another. He showed that there are two fundamentally different groups of prokaryotes, archaea and bacteria. Woese argued that the prokaryotes account for two of the three major branches of organisms.

Woese's hypothesis gained support in 1996 when Carol J. Bult of the Institute for Genomic Research in Rockville, Maryland, reported in the journal *Science* that she and her colleagues had sequenced the complete genome of a methane-producing archaea, *Methanococcus jannaschii.* When these researchers compared gene sequences with those of two previously sequenced bacteria, they found that fewer than half of the genes matched. Gene sequencing indicates that the archaea have a combination of bacteria-like and eukaryote-like genes. Biologists have identified other important differences between bacteria and archaea. For example, bacteria are characterized by the presence of a compound called peptidoglycan in their cell walls, whereas this compound is not present in

archaea. Based on molecular evidence, biologists now divide the prokaryotes into two major groups: **Bacteria** and **Archaea.**

Kingdom Protista has had an interesting history. Biologists placed *Euglena,* along with other unicellular organisms traditionally referred to as protozoa, in kingdom Protista. At various times, they have also assigned algae (including multicellular forms), water molds, and slime molds to kingdom Protista. Thus, this kingdom became a diverse group of mainly unicellular, mainly aquatic eukaryotic organisms. During the past few years, systematists have established that the protist groups did not descend from one recent common ancestor. As we will discuss in Chapter 26, many biologists have abandoned kingdom Protista (as well as a kingdom classification for plants and animals) and now assign the eukaryotes to five "supergroups" based on molecular data.

The three domains form the three main branches of the tree of life

Based on fundamental molecular differences among the bacteria, archaea, and eukaryotes, biologists now classify organisms in three domains: **Archaea, Bacteria,** and **Eukarya** (eukaryotes). Systematists have inferred that the three domains are the three main branches of the tree of life (**FIG. 23-2**). In Chapter 25 we will discuss characters that distinguish these domains. As we will discuss in Chapter 24, the viruses are a special case and are not classified in any of the three domains.

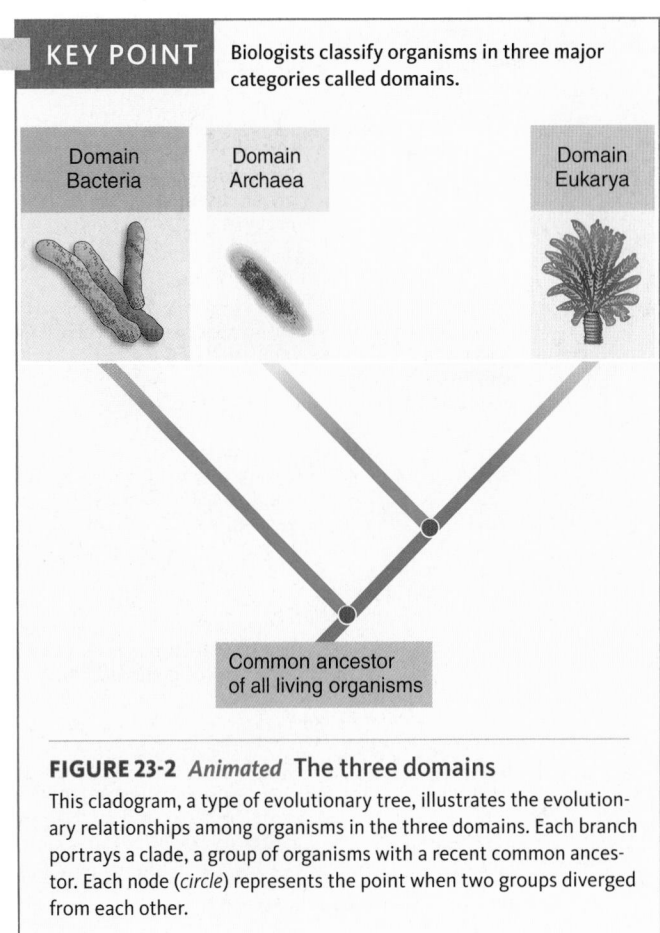

KEY POINT Biologists classify organisms in three major categories called domains.

Domain Bacteria   Domain Archaea   Domain Eukarya

Common ancestor of all living organisms

FIGURE 23-2 *Animated* **The three domains**
This cladogram, a type of evolutionary tree, illustrates the evolutionary relationships among organisms in the three domains. Each branch portrays a clade, a group of organisms with a recent common ancestor. Each node (*circle*) represents the point when two groups diverged from each other.

Some biologists are moving away from Linnaean categories

Most biologists now classify organisms into the three domains. Some continue to classify organisms into kingdoms: Bacteria, Archaea, Fungi, Plantae, and Animalia, but many systematists no longer recognize "kingdom Protista." (See **TABLE 23-2**.) Instead, they assign protists to a number of "supergroups" that more accurately reflect evolutionary relationships.

Many systematists argue that the traditional hierarchical Linnaean categories are limiting and do not fit well with recent findings. They maintain that using kingdoms, classes, and other ranks are cumbersome and that classification using these ranks must be frequently modified as researchers gather more data. The former kingdom Protista is a good example of the need to continuously re-evaluate and change classification.

Some systematists prefer classifying organisms into clades. A **clade** is defined as a group of organisms that share *characters* (characteristics) inherited from a common ancestor. These systematists prefer to identify clades and classify them in one of the three domains, rather than using the traditional hierarchical system.

Some biologists use an approach to classification known as **PhyloCode**, in which organisms are grouped into clades based on evolutionary relationships. A species is defined as a segment of a population lineage. In this system, taxonomic ranks are not required. Advocates of PhyloCode argue that this system avoids the problem of changing names when discoveries of new species require shifts in ranks. The system also makes it easier to name clades one at a time as they are discovered.

In this edition of *Biology,* we classify organisms using the three domains and also classify them using traditional taxonomy. We remind our readers frequently that the traditional ranks are categories developed for convenience, and classification changes as new data are analyzed. Taxonomists must reclassify organisms as they adjust hypotheses about relationships among organisms.

Phylogenetic trees show hypothesized evolutionary relationships

Systematists use **phylogenetic trees** to graphically represent hypothesized evolutionary relationships among organisms that have a common ancestor. In Figure 23-2 we use a phylogenetic tree to illustrate the relationship of the three domains, and the phylogenetic tree in **FIGURE 23-3** illustrates the main branches that make up each of the three domains. This tree is one of the current versions of the tree of life.

TABLE 23-2	Domains and Kingdoms		
Domain	Kingdom	Characteristics	Ecological Role and Comments
Bacteria	Bacteria	Prokaryotes (lack distinct nuclei and other membranous organelles); unicellular; microscopic; cell walls generally composed of peptidoglycan.	Most are decomposers; some parasitic (and pathogenic); some chemosynthetic autotrophs; some photosynthetic; important in recycling nitrogen and other elements; some used in industrial processes.
Archaea	Archaea	Prokaryotes; unicellular; microscopic; peptidoglycan absent in cell walls; differ biochemically from bacteria.	Methanogens are anaerobes that inhabit sewage, swamps, and animal digestive tracts; extreme halophiles inhabit salty environments; extreme thermophiles inhabit hot, sometimes acidic environments.
Eukarya*	Protists formerly classified in kingdom Protista; now assigned to a number of "supergroups"	Eukaryotes; mainly unicellular or simple multicellular.	Protozoa are an important part of zooplankton. Algae are important producers, especially in marine and freshwater ecosystems; important oxygen source. Some protists cause diseases, for example, malaria.
	Plantae	Eukaryotes; multicellular; photosynthetic; possess multicellular reproductive organs; alternation of generations; cell walls of cellulose.	Terrestrial biosphere depends on plants in their role as primary producers; important source of oxygen in Earth's atmosphere.
	Fungi	Eukaryotes; heterotrophic; absorb nutrients; do not photosynthesize; body composed of threadlike hyphae that form tangled masses that infiltrate food or habitat; cell walls of chitin.	Decomposers; some parasitic (and pathogenic); some form important symbiotic relationships with plant roots (mycorrhizae) or algae (lichens); some used as food; yeast used in making bread and alcoholic beverages; some used to make industrial chemicals or antibiotics; responsible for much spoilage and crop loss.
	Animalia	Eukaryotes; multicellular heterotrophs; many exhibit tissue differentiation and complex organ systems; most able to move about by muscular contraction; nervous tissue coordinates responses to stimuli.	Consumers; some specialized as herbivores, carnivores, or detritus feeders.

*For another approach to classification of eukarya, see Figure 23-3.

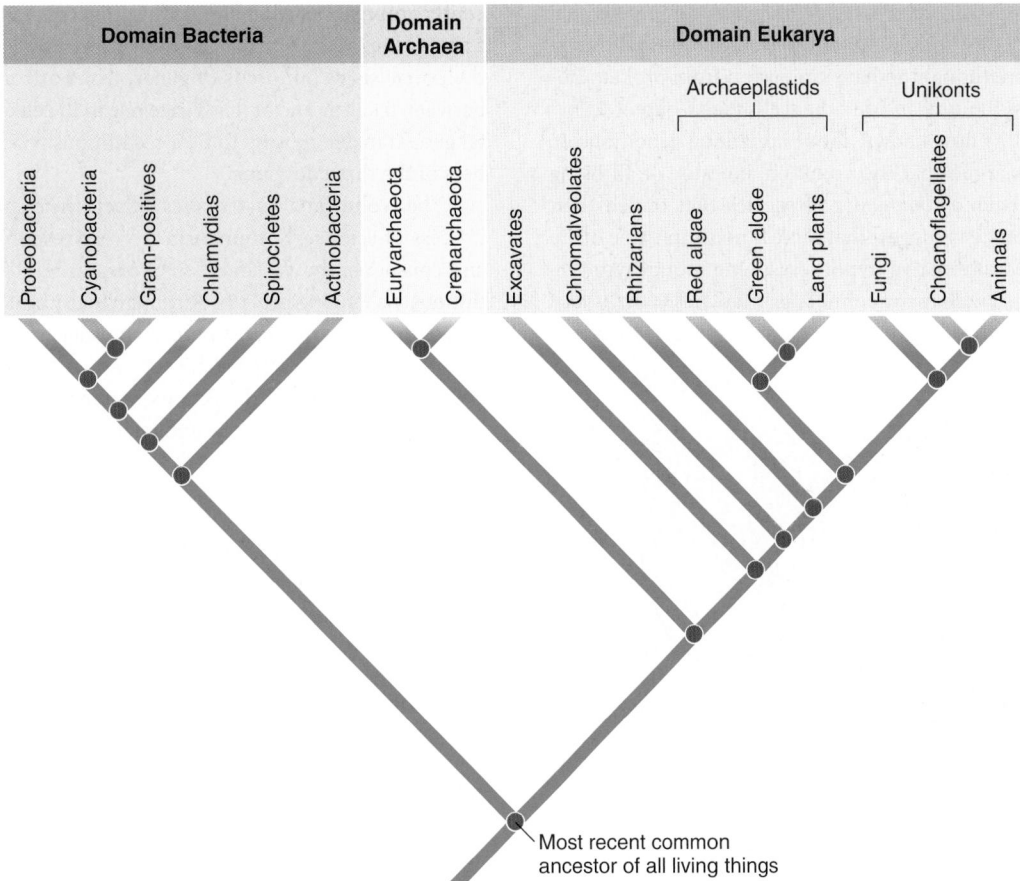

Domain Bacteria

- Proteobacteria
- Cyanobacteria
- Gram-positives
- Chlamydias
- Spirochetes
- Actinobacteria

Domain Archaea

- Euryarchaeota
- Crenarchaeota

Domain Eukarya

Archaeplastids

Unikonts

- Excavates
- Chromalveolates
- Rhizarians
- Red algae
- Green algae
- Land plants
- Fungi
- Choanoflagellates
- Animals

Most recent common ancestor of all living things

FIGURE 23-3 The tree of life, a work in progress

Some major branches of each of the three domains are shown. As new data are analyzed, the relationships of some of the branches will change.

The type of phylogenetic tree we use in this book is called a **cladogram.** Each **branch** in a cladogram represents a clade, a group of organisms with a common ancestor. Each branching point, referred to as a **node** (depicted by a circle), represents the divergence, or splitting, of two or more new groups from a common ancestor. Thus, the node represents the *most recent common ancestor* of each clade depicted by the branches. In this way, a cladogram uses the positions of branch points to illustrate the hypothesized evolutionary relationships among taxa. Each branch represents one or more characteristics shared by the clade, but not found in the ancestors of the clade. (*Shared derived characters* are discussed in the next section). These shared characteristics can be indicated by labels or by bars across the branches.

Cladograms are rooted if the most recent common ancestor is known. The **root,** or node at the base of the cladogram, represents the most recent common ancestor of all of the clades depicted in the tree. We will discuss more about constructing cladograms as we proceed through this chapter.

Although a cladogram depicts the evolutionary relationships of each group through time, the *lengths* of the branches do not tell us *when* a particular species evolved. Other types of phylogenetic trees, for example, *phylograms,* can be constructed to indicate time, or rate of evolution, as well as to indicate the relationships among

taxa. In a phylogram, the length of the branches is proportional to the amount of inferred change in characteristics.

Systematists continue to consider other hypotheses

When we think of how organisms acquire their genes, we think of **vertical gene transfer** in which genes are transmitted from parent to offspring within the same species. As biologists continue to investigate the origin and relationships of the domains, they have discovered that evolution is not always linear. During the course of evolution, genes not only were passed down "vertically" from one generation to the next but were also exchanged laterally. Such gene swapping between organisms in one taxon and unrelated organisms in another taxon is called **horizontal gene transfer,** or *lateral gene transfer.* In this process, genes move from one species to another species in the same generation.

Horizontal gene transfer can occur in several ways, such as by exchange of DNA among different populations or species of bacteria, or by interbreeding between closely related groups. In eukaryotes, horizontal gene transfer has occurred by endosymbiosis, a process in which one organism lives inside the cell of another organism, and the two become a single functional organism. In fact, eukaryotic cells most likely evolved from prokaryotic cells that lived symbiotically one within another. Recall that mitochondria and chloroplasts are thought to have originated from prokaryotes that lived as endosymbionts inside other cells (see Chapter 21).

Based on what is now known about horizontal gene transfer, some systematists argue that the common ancestor of all living things may have been a *community* of species that traded their genes. Some systematists suggest that there is no simple tree of life and have proposed alternative hypotheses. One group hypothesizes a complex bush with many connecting branches (**FIG. 23-4a**). Researchers at the University of California at Los Angeles, have re-

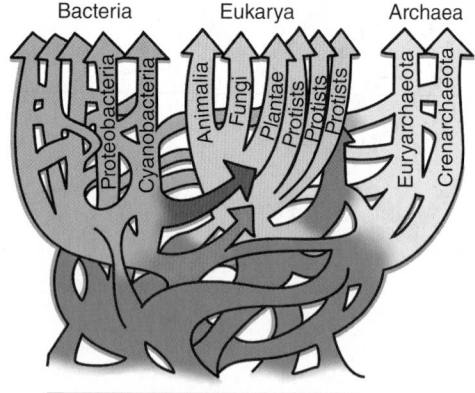

(a) The three-domain approach drawn to show horizontal gene transfer as a continuous process between domains and also among groups within each domain. Only some of the branches are labeled. The diagonal brown arrow represents mitochondrial endosymbiosis; the diagonal green arrow represents chloroplast endosymbiosis.

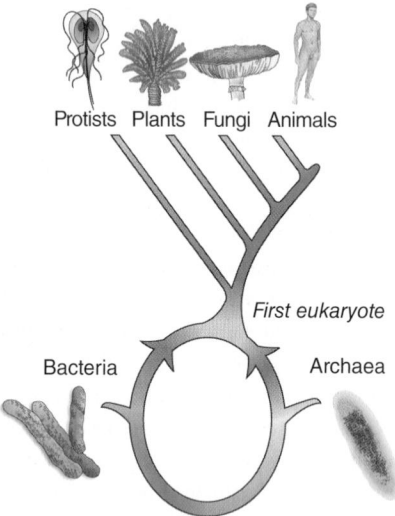

(b) The ring of life is based on the hypothesis that lateral gene transfer between bacteria and archaea gave rise to the eukaryotes.

FIGURE 23-4 Other ways to represent the tree of life
(Part **a** based on Doolittle, W. F., *Science*, Vol. 284, pp. 2124–2128, 1999; part **b** based on Rivera, M. C., and J. A. Lake. *Nature*, Vol. 431, pp. 152–155, Sept. 9, 2004.)

cently proposed another approach—the tree of life may actually be a ring of life (**FIG. 23-4b**). These systematists hypothesize, based on their analysis of hundreds of genes, that horizontal gene transfer between bacteria and archaea gave rise to the eukaryotes. Horizontal gene transfer appears to be a continuous process among members of the three domains.

The evolution of systematics reflects the creative and dynamic process of science. Systematists are very responsive to new data, and consequently, classification of organisms at all levels is a continuously changing process. Although many biologists are moving away from a hierarchical system, some suggest adding new groups so that the classical approach keeps up with new findings. Whatever approach is used, the goal of systematics is to base classification on evolutionary change and relationships.

Review

- What are some of the defining characteristics of each of the three domains? of kingdom Fungi?
- In which domain and kingdom would you classify each of the following: white willow, the bacterium *Escherichia coli*, tapeworm, and black bread mold?
- What does each branch represent in a cladogram? each node?

23.3 RECONSTRUCTING EVOLUTIONARY HISTORY

LEARNING OBJECTIVES

5 Critically review the difficulties encountered in choosing taxonomic criteria.
6 Apply the concept of shared derived characters to the classification of organisms.
7 Describe how analyses of molecular homologies contribute to the science of systematics.
8 Contrast monophyletic, paraphyletic, and polyphyletic taxa.

Modern taxonomy is based on evolution. The goal is to reconstruct **phylogeny** (literally, "production of phyla"), the evolutionary history of a group of organisms from a common ancestor. As systematists determine evolutionary relationships among species and between species and higher taxa, they build classifications based on common ancestry. Consequently, systematics reflects the integration of all evolutionary processes and evolutionary evidence. Systematics is at the center of how we understand and explain the nonrandom occurrence and relationships of life-forms on Earth.

Once phylogenies are established, they help answer other questions in biology. For example, phylogenies help us understand evolutionary patterns that might provide clues to the origin and spread of HIV and other pathogens. Phylogenies also help biologists identify new species and predict their characteristics. Systematists may classify a new species based on specific characters that it shares with other organisms in a particular taxon. They may then infer that the new species shares other characters with organisms in that group.

As you read the following sections, remember that phylogenies are testable hypotheses. They are supported or falsified by the available data. Systematics proceeds by constantly re-evaluating data, hypotheses, and theoretical constructs. As new data are discovered and old data are reinterpreted, systematists modify their hypotheses. As a result, our understanding of how organisms are related and the way we classify organisms are continuously being revised. Systematics is a dynamic science that changes as biologists discover new species and use ever more sophisticated techniques to investigate the evolutionary relationships among organisms.

Recall that a **population** is made up of all the individuals of the same species that live in a particular area. A population has a dimension in space—its geographic range—and also a dimension in time. Each population extends backward in time. Somewhat like branches of a tree, a population may diverge from other populations enough to become a new species (which may be depicted by a new tree branch; see Chapters 19 and 20). Species have various degrees of evolutionary relationships with one another, depending on the degree of genetic divergence since their populations branched from a common ancestor.

Homologous structures are important in determining evolutionary relationships

Just how to determine phylogeny and how to group species into higher taxa—genera, families, orders, classes, or phyla—can be difficult decisions. Biologists base their judgments about the degree of relationship on the extent of similarity among species. They examine structural, physiological, developmental, behavioral, and molecular traits, as well as fossil evidence. When examining these traits, they look for homologies among different organisms. Recall from Chapter 18 that **homology** refers to the presence, in two or more species, of a structure derived from a recent common ancestor. For example, the bones in the wing of a bat, the paw of a dog, and the hand of a human are homologous. As we will discuss, identifying homologous traits is very important in inferring phylogeny.

It is often difficult to determine whether traits are similar as a result of homology. Although the wings of a butterfly are adapted for flight, their structure is different from bird wings, and these animals do not share a common winged ancestor. Similar structures sometimes evolve when unrelated or distantly related species become adapted to similar environmental conditions. Thus, wings may occur in two or more species not derived from a recent common ancestor. Recall from Chapter 18 that independent evolution of similar structures in distantly related organisms is known as **convergent evolution.** Sharks and dolphins have similar, but independently derived, body forms because they have become adapted to similar environments (aquatic) and lifestyles (predatory). Sometimes it is obvious that convergent evolution has occurred. In other cases, researchers must test their hypotheses using all available data.

Another challenge in deciding on homology is **reversal,** in which a trait reverts to its ancestral state. A reversal removes a similarity that had evolved. A characteristic that superficially appears homologous but is actually independently acquired by convergent evolution or reversal is described as exhibiting **homoplasy.** Distinguishing between homology and homoplasy can be challenging.

Shared derived characters provide clues about phylogeny

Determining which traits indicate evolutionary relationships is extremely important. How does a systematist interpret the significance of similarities between organisms? In making decisions about taxonomic relationships, the systematist first examines the characteristics in the largest group (such as phylum or class) of organisms being studied and interprets them as indicating the most *remote* common ancestry. These **shared ancestral characters,** or *plesiomorphies,* are features that were present in an ancestral species and remain present in all groups descended from that ancestor. For example, the vertebral column, present in all vertebrates, is an ancestral character for study of classes within the subphylum Vertebrata. Studying the presence or absence of the vertebral column does not help us discriminate among various classes of vertebrates (for example, between amphibians and mammals) because all individuals in these classes have a vertebral column.

When two populations become separated and begin to evolve independently, some of their homologous traits change as a result of mutation, natural selection, and genetic drift. The novel traits that evolve are referred to as **shared derived characters,** or *synapomorphies.* Note that shared derived characters originate in a *recent* common ancestor and are present in its descendants. Species that share derived characters form a clade. Systematists use shared derived characters to identify points where groups diverged from one another. A trait viewed as a *derived character* in a more inclusive (broader) taxon may also be considered an *ancestral character* in a less inclusive (narrower) taxon.

More recent common ancestry is indicated by classification into less and less inclusive taxonomic groups with more and more specific shared derived characters. For example, the three small bones in the middle ear are useful in identifying a branch point between reptiles and mammals. The evolution of this derived character was a unique event, and only mammals have these bones. However, if we compare mammals with one another, the three ear bones are a shared ancestral character because all mammals have them. Consequently, they have no value in distinguishing among mammalian taxa. Other characters must be used to establish branch points among the mammals.

If we compare dogs, goats, and dolphins (all of which are mammals), we find that dogs and goats have abundant hair whereas dolphins do not. Hair is an ancestral trait in mammals and therefore cannot be used as evidence that dogs and goats share a more recent common ancestor. In contrast, the virtual absence of hair in mature dolphins is a derived character within mammals. When we compare dogs, dolphins, and whales, we find that dolphins and whales share this derived character, providing evidence that these animals evolved from a common ancestor not shared by dogs.

Biologists carefully choose taxonomic criteria

Both fishes and dolphins have streamlined body forms, but this characteristic is homoplastic and does not indicate close evolutionary relationships. In contrast, dolphins share important homologous derived characters (synapomorphies) with mammals:

mammary glands, which produce milk for the young; three small bones in the middle ear; and a muscular diaphragm that helps move air into and out of the lungs. Thus, we classify the dolphin as a mammal.

Although dolphins have more shared *derived* characters in common with humans than with fishes, some characters are shared by all three. Among these shared *ancestral* characters are a dorsal tubular nerve cord, and during embryonic development, a notochord (skeletal rod) and rudimentary gill slits. These shared ancestral characters (plesiomorphies) indicate a common ancestry and serve as a basis for classification. The ancestry is more remote between the dolphin and the fish than between the dolphin and the human. Therefore, although fishes, humans, and dolphins are grouped in a more inclusive taxon, the phylum Chordata, humans and dolphins are also classified in class Mammalia, a less inclusive taxon within phylum Chordata, indicating that they are more closely related.

Determining which traits best illustrate evolutionary relationships can be challenging. What, for example, are the most important taxonomic characteristics of a bird? We might list feathers, beak, wings, absence of teeth, egg laying, and *endothermy* (an endothermic animal uses metabolic heat to maintain a constant body temperature despite variations in surrounding temperature). The duck-billed platypus and a few other mammals (members of a group called monotremes) have many of these same characteristics: beaks, absence of teeth, egg laying, and endothermy. Yet we do not classify them as birds (**FIG. 23-5**). No mammal, however, has feathers. Is this trait absolutely diagnostic of birds? According to the conventional taxonomic wisdom, the presence or absence of feathers determines what is and is not a bird. As we will discuss

later, though, birds evolved from a group of dinosaurs whose fossils bear impressions of feathers! The presence of feathers in some dinosaurs and in birds is a shared derived character that shows that they are closely related. Many biologists now classify birds as part of the reptile clade.

Organisms are typically classified on the basis of a combination of traits rather than on any single trait. The significance of these combinations is determined inductively, that is, by integrating and interpreting the data. Such induction is a necessary part of the process of science. Systematists may hypothesize that all birds should have beaks, feathers, no teeth, and so forth. Then they re-examine the living world and observe whether any organisms might reasonably be called birds that do not fit the current definition of "birdness." If not, the definition stands. If too many exceptions emerge, the definition may be modified or abandoned. Sometimes the systematist determines that an apparent exception—the bat, for instance—resembles a bird only superficially and should not be considered one. The bat has all the basic characteristics of a mammal, such as hair and mammary glands that produce milk for the young.

Molecular homologies help clarify phylogeny

When a new species evolves, it does not always exhibit obvious phenotypic differences when compared to closely related species. For example, two distinct species of fruit flies may appear identical. Some of their DNA, proteins, and other molecules, however, are different. Such variations in the structure of specific macromolecules among species, just like differences in anatomical structure, result from mutations. Advances in molecular biology have provided the tools for biologists to compare the macromolecules of various organisms. In fact, organisms can now be identified by their molecular structure.

In 2003, scientists at the University of Guelph in Canada proposed in the British *Proceedings of the Royal Society* that we identify all living things by their unique sequences of DNA or RNA, rather than by their physical structure. The molecular sequence selected can be used as a genetic marker, or **barcode,** to identify organisms, much like the barcodes on grocery store items. This method can be used to distinguish among species that look alike. For example, until recently the African elephant and the Indian elephant were the only two species of living elephants recognized. Using molecular methods, biologists demonstrated that there are at least two distinct species of African elephants. Each species has its own distinctive DNA barcode. Biologists can use barcodes to identify the species of an organism in any stage of life, even as an egg or seed.

The science of **molecular systematics** focuses on molecular structure to clarify evolutionary relationships. DNA, RNA, and amino acid sequencing are used to compare the macromolecules of organisms being studied. Macromolecules that are functionally similar in two different types of organisms are considered homologous if their subunit sequence is similar. Such comparisons provide systematists with valuable information about the degree of relatedness among organisms. The more subunit sequences of two species correspond, the more closely related the species are considered to be. The number of differences in certain DNA or RNA nucleotide

FIGURE 23-5 Is this animal a bird?
A few mammals, such as the duck-billed platypus, lay eggs, have beaks, and lack teeth. However, the platypus does not have feathers, and it nourishes its young with milk secreted from mammary glands.

sequences or in amino acid sequences in two groups of organisms may reflect how much time has passed since the groups branched from a common ancestor. (This can be true only if the molecular changes occur at a steady rate.) Thus, specific macromolecules can be used as **molecular clocks.**

Many systematists look to ribosomal RNA structure to help determine phylogenies. All known organisms have ribosomes that function in protein synthesis, and certain ribosomal RNA nucleotide sequences have been highly conserved in evolution. Recall that the division of organisms into three domains was based, in large part, on the comparison of ribosomal RNA by Carl Woese and his research team.

The ribosomes of archaea and bacteria contain three types of RNA, named in order of increasing size: 5S, 16S, and 23S. (These numbers are sedimentation coefficients, measures of relative size, used to characterize behavior of a particle when centrifuged.) The 5S and 16S RNAs have been extensively used to determine evolutionary relationships among bacteria. These rRNA gene sequences are useful because the number of base pairs is manageable and because these molecules are transcribed from highly conserved regions of DNA. Also, these gene sequences contain variable regions that are species-specific for various types of bacteria and archaea.

Researchers have also used comparison of ribosomal RNA sequences to challenge the once widely accepted idea that fungi are closely related to plants. According to ribosomal RNA analysis, fungi are more closely related to animals than to plants; that is, animals and fungi share a more recent common ancestor, perhaps a flagellate.

Because genes can evolve at different rates, researchers now typically compare subunit sequences from many different genes of the organisms under study. Molecular sequence data have been sampled from more than 10% of all known species. The very precise tools provided by molecular biology have put systematics on the cutting edge of biological research.

Scientists at Broad's Genome Sequencing and Analysis program at MIT and Harvard recently provided another example of applied molecular systematics (**FIG. 23-6**). They sequenced the genome of the domestic dog and compared coding regions of more than 13,000 dog genes with human and mouse genes. Then, they selected exons and introns and compared their nucleotide sequences in 30 living canids (members of the family Canidae to which the dog belongs). The data they gathered enabled these investigators to construct a cladogram of the phylogenetic relationships of canids. They confirmed earlier research showing that the dog's closest relative is the gray wolf. These nucleotide data are being used to identify genes responsible for specific diseases, and can be compared to the human genome in an effort to better understand the many diseases that canids have in common with humans.

Taxa are grouped based on their evolutionary relationships

Most known organisms were classified by biologists before the days of phylogenetics. Modern systematists use phylogenetic analysis to test these hypothesized relationships among groups of organisms. Based increasingly on molecular data, they either

QUESTION: How is the dog related to other canids?

HYPOTHESIS: Analysis of molecular data from a variety of canids will clarify the evolutionary relationships of canids.

EXPERIMENT: Researcher Kerstin Lindblad-Toh and her colleagues sequenced the genome of the domestic dog. They compared coding regions of more than 13,000 dog genes with corresponding human and mouse genes. Then they selected 12 exons and 4 introns and sequenced them in 30 out of 34 living canids.

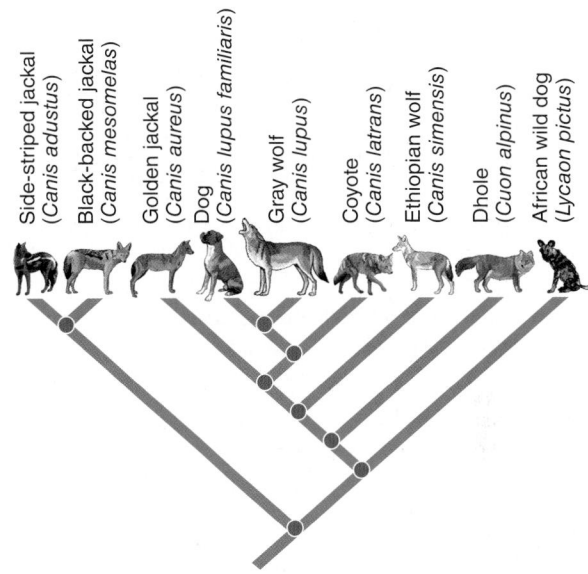

RESULTS AND CONCLUSION: Analysis of the comparisons of exon and intron nucleotide sequences allowed these researchers to build a cladogram of Canidae species. The data indicated that the dog is most closely related to the gray wolf. (Sequence divergence of nuclear exon and intron sequences is 0.04% and 0.21, respectively.) The two African jackals (branch at left) are the sister group of this clade, suggesting an African origin for the canids.

Lindblad-Toh, K., et al. "Genome Sequence, Comparative Analysis and Haplotype Structure of the Domestic Dog." *Nature*, Vol. 438, Dec. 8, 2005.

FIGURE 23-6 Molecular phylogeny

Molecular similarities indicate that the dog is closely related to the gray wolf. Note that some biologists list the scientific name for the domestic dog as *Canis familiaris* and others, including the Smithsonian Institution and the American Society of Mammalogists, consider the dog a subspecies of the gray wolf and list its name as *Canis lupus familiaris*.

confirm or modify the work of earlier biologists. Using their data, systematists construct cladograms to reflect relationships among clades. Cladograms show three types of taxonomic relationships: monophyletic, paraphyletic, and polyphyletic.

A **monophyletic group** includes an ancestral species and all its descendants (**FIG. 23-7a**). It is defined by shared derived characters. Mammals, for example, have mammary glands that produce milk for the young, three small bones in the middle ear, and a muscular diaphragm. All mammals are thought to have evolved from a common ancestral mammal that had these shared derived

Groups of organisms can be described as monophyletic, paraphyletic, or polyphyletic. Only monophyletic groups are considered clades.

(a) Group I and group II are monophyletic groups, or clades. Each includes a common ancestor and all its descendants.

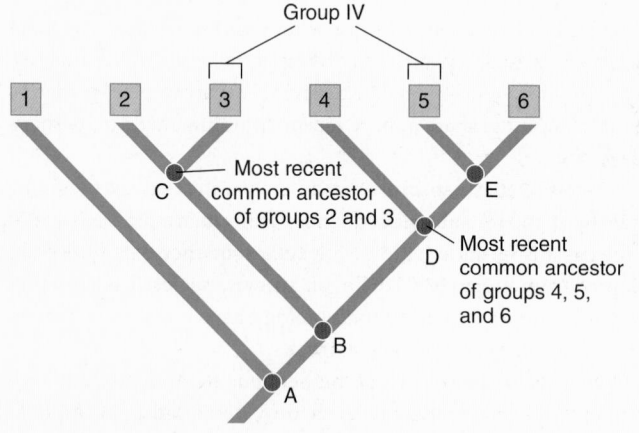

(b) Group III is paraphyletic. It includes some, but not all of the descendants of the recent common ancestor indicated at node D.

FIGURE 23-7 *Animated* **Evolutionary relationships**

In all three figures, the branch point at node A represents the common ancestor of all groups shown. Node B represents the common ancestor of groups 2 through 6. Node C represents the common ancestor of groups 2 and 3. Node D represents the common ancestor of groups 4, 5, and 6. Node E represents the common ancestor of groups 5 and 6. Common ancestry is the basis for making decisions about classification.

(c) Group IV is polyphyletic. Members of this group do not share the same recent common ancestor.

characters, and all descendants of this ancestor are mammals. Monophyletic taxa are called clades. They are natural groupings because they represent true evolutionary relationships and include all close relatives. **Sister taxa,** or sister groups, share a more recent common ancestor with one another than either taxon does with any other group shown on a cladogram. In Figure 23-7, taxa 2 and 3 are sister taxa; taxa 5 and 6 are also sister taxa.

A **paraphyletic group** is a group that contains a common ancestor and some, but not all, of its descendants (**FIG. 23-7b**). Members of the group share ancestral characters. As discussed later in this chapter, the class Reptilia is paraphyletic because it does not include all descendants of the most recent common ancestor of reptiles. Birds share a recent common ancestor with reptiles.

A **polyphyletic group** consists of several evolutionary lines that do not share the same recent common ancestor (**FIG. 23-7c**).

Biologists might have mistakenly classified the members of such a group together because these organisms share similar (homoplastic) features arising from convergent evolution. Systematists avoid constructing polyphyletic taxa because they are unnatural and misrepresent evolutionary relationships. Polyphyletic taxa are sometimes accepted temporarily until research provides additional data.

Review

- How are shared ancestral characters and shared derived characters different?
- Why don't shared ancestral characters provide evidence for relationships between organisms within a taxon that has those traits? Give an example.
- How is molecular biology contributing to the science of systematics?
- Why do systematists prefer monophyletic taxa to polyphyletic taxa?
- Why do representations of the tree of life constantly change?

23.4 CONSTRUCTING PHYLOGENETIC TREES

LEARNING OBJECTIVES

9 Contrast the classification of reptiles and birds by a cladist and by an evolutionary systematist.

10 Describe the construction of a cladogram by using outgroup analysis.

11 Apply the principle of parsimony to cladogram construction.

In determining the relationships among organisms, systematists use a variety of data and methods. How data are analyzed and interpreted depends on the systematist's approach. In the **phenetic approach,** also known as numerical taxonomy, classification is based on the number of shared characters. This approach does not distinguish between shared ancestral characters and shared derived characters.

Phenetic techniques are currently used with molecular data. For example, each amino acid in a protein can be considered a character. Then, amino acid sequences of various animals can be determined in the laboratory and compared by computer. The information about differences in amino acid sequences can be used to construct phylogenetic diagrams. Species are placed at relative distances from one another, reflecting the extent of difference in amino acid sequence. Thus, systematists using a phenetic approach define phylogenetic relationships by statistics, such as genetic distances, which summarize overall similarities among taxa based on collected data. A researcher can compare the base sequences of a given gene or coding region to arrive at an average percentage of difference between the taxa being analyzed. A computer program then compares these values and generates trees that cluster similar taxa and place divergent taxa on more distant branches.

Cladistics (also known as *phylogenetic systematics*) is an approach in which organisms are classified based on recent common ancestry. Shared derived characters are analyzed and used to infer evolutionary relationships. Cladists emphasize common ancestry rather than phenotypic similarity as the basis for classification. They base their assessment on shared derived characters that can be structural, behavioral, physiological, or molecular. The characters must be homologous. Cladists typically do not use a hierarchy of taxa, for example, order, class, family.

According to cladistics, dolphins are classified with mammals rather than with fishes because dolphins and mammals share derived characters not present in fishes. Their shared derived characters indicate that dolphins and mammals share a more recent common ancestor. Cladists use shared derived characters to reconstruct evolutionary relationships of organisms, and they express them in *cladograms.*

Consider the grouping of mammals, lizards, snakes, crocodiles, dinosaurs, and birds. Birds, along with dinosaurs, are thought to share a recent common ancestor with modern crocodiles and alligators (node D in **FIG. 23-8a**). Crocodiles, dinosaurs, and birds, then, constitute a monophyletic group, or clade. Similarly, snakes and lizards form a clade that is the closest group to birds, dinosaurs, and crocodiles. Mammals make up a different clade.

Biologists who use the traditional **evolutionary systematic approach** use phenotypic similarity and a combination of shared ancestral characters and shared derived characters to establish evolutionary relationships and build classifications. Although most of the taxa that they currently recognize are monophyletic, evolutionary systematists recognize paraphyletic taxa as well. (Recall that paraphyletic groups include some, but not all, subgroups of organisms that share the same most recent common ancestor.)

In contrast to cladists, evolutionary systematists recognize class Reptilia as a valid group containing snakes, lizards, crocodiles, dinosaurs, and turtles, even though this class is paraphyletic; it does not include all subgroups, such as birds, that evolved from the ancestral reptile (**FIG. 23-8b**). Evolutionary systematists assign birds to a separate class because birds have diverged markedly from the reptiles.

Outgroup analysis is used in constructing and interpreting cladograms

A crucial step in most cladistic analyses is **outgroup analysis,** a research method for estimating which attributes are shared derived characters in a given group of organisms (**FIG. 23-9**). An **outgroup** is a taxon that is considered to have branched off earlier than the taxa under investigation, the **ingroups.** An ideal outgroup is the closest relative of the group being studied, its sister taxon, and has not been highly modified since its origin. Recall that sister taxa evolved from the same recent common ancestor. Systematists argue that an outgroup is likely to retain the ancestral state for characters being used in the analysis, allowing the researchers to identify the evolutionary changes leading to derived characters. To help you understand outgroup analysis, we describe the specific example illustrated in Figure 23-9.

The first step in constructing a cladogram is to select the taxa, which may consist of individuals, species, genera, or other taxonomic levels. Here we use a representative group of eight chordates: the lancelet, lamprey, sunfish, frog, lizard, bear, chimpanzee, and human. The next step is to select the homologous characters to be analyzed. In our example, we use seven characters. For each character, we must define all the different conditions, or states, as they exist in our taxa. For simplicity, we consider our characters to have only two different states: *present* or *absent*. Keep in mind that many characters used in cladistics have more than two states. For example, black, brown, yellow, and red may be only a few of the many possible states for the character of hair color.

The last, and often the most difficult, step in preparing the data is to organize the character states into their correct evolutionary order. For this step, we use outgroup analysis. In our example, the lancelet, a small marine chordate with a fishlike appearance, is the chosen outgroup. It belongs to a taxon that is considered to have diverged earlier than any of the other taxa under investigation but to be closely related to vertebrates; thus, the lancelet represents an approximation of the ancestral condition for vertebrates. Therefore, the character state "absent" for a particular character state such as vertebrae is the ancestral (plesiomorphic) condition, and the character state "present" is the derived condition for the characters in Figure 23-9.

Many biologists prefer the cladistic approach, shown in (a), because it recognizes reptiles and birds as a monophyletic group.

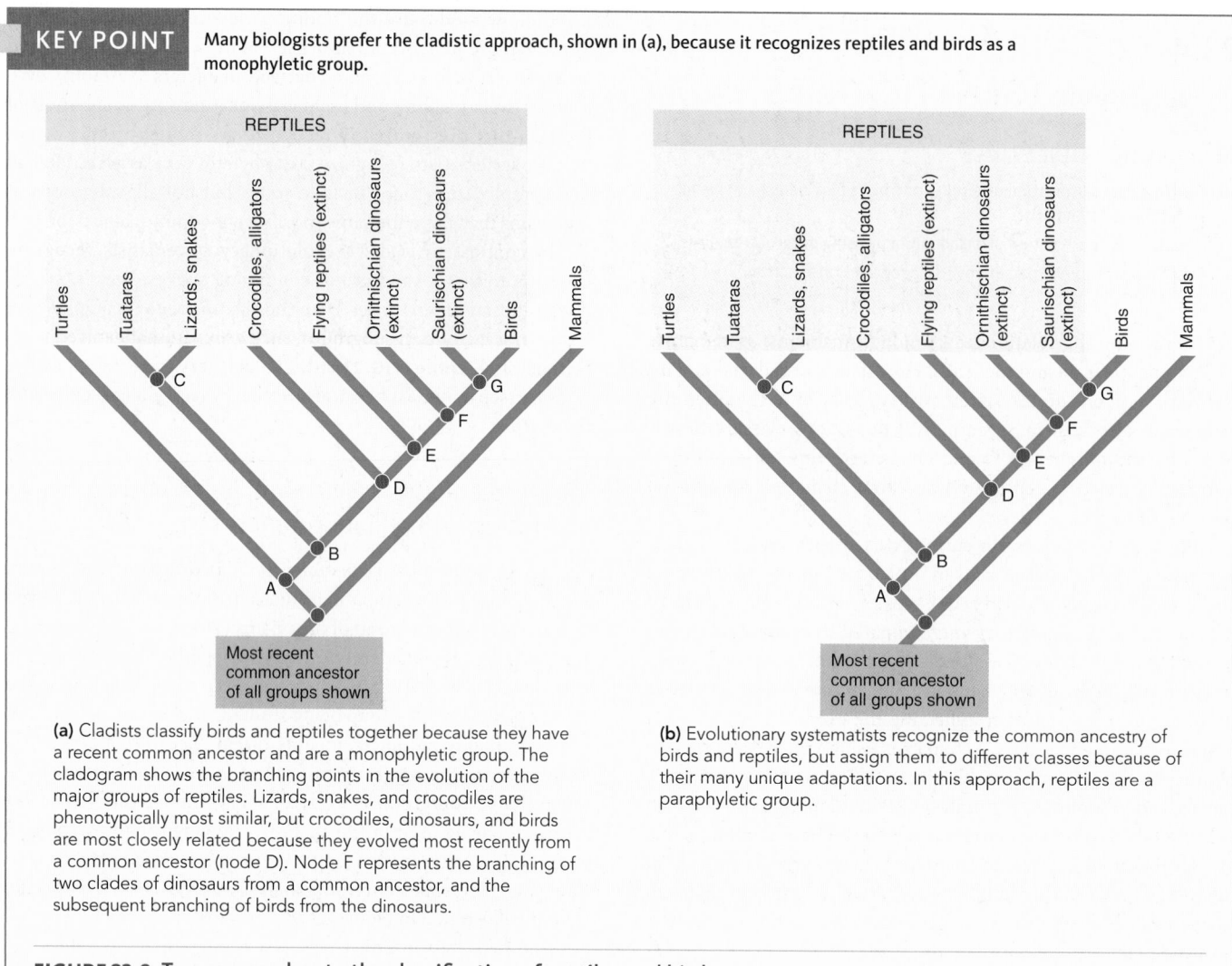

(a) Cladists classify birds and reptiles together because they have a recent common ancestor and are a monophyletic group. The cladogram shows the branching points in the evolution of the major groups of reptiles. Lizards, snakes, and crocodiles are phenotypically most similar, but crocodiles, dinosaurs, and birds are most closely related because they evolved most recently from a common ancestor (node D). Node F represents the branching of two clades of dinosaurs from a common ancestor, and the subsequent branching of birds from the dinosaurs.

(b) Evolutionary systematists recognize the common ancestry of birds and reptiles, but assign them to different classes because of their many unique adaptations. In this approach, reptiles are a paraphyletic group.

FIGURE 23-8 Two approaches to the classification of reptiles and birds

A cladogram is constructed by considering shared derived characters

Our objective is to construct a cladogram that requires the fewest number of evolutionary changes in the characters. Taxa are grouped by the presence of shared derived characters. To form a valid monophyletic group, all members must share at least one derived character. Membership in a clade cannot be established by shared ancestral characters (plesiomorphies).

In our example, notice that all taxa, except the outgroup lancelet, have vertebrae. We can therefore conclude that these seven vertebrate taxa form a valid clade. Next, among the seven vertebrate taxa, note that jaws are present in all groups except lampreys (a group of jawless vertebrates). Using these data, we construct a preliminary cladogram (see **FIG. 23-9a**).

Recall that the root, or base, of the cladogram represents the common ancestor for all taxa being analyzed. In Figure 23-9a, node A represents the common chordate ancestor from which the outgroup (lancelet) and the seven vertebrate taxa evolved. Similarly, node B represents the common ancestor of the vertebrates; and node C, the common ancestor of the jawed vertebrates. Con-

tinuing with this procedure, notice that among the six-jawed taxa, all but sunfish are tetrapods (animals with four limbs) (see **FIG. 23-9b**). Among the five tetrapods, all but frogs have amniotic eggs in which the embryo is surrounded by a fluid-filled sac called an "amnion" (see **FIG. 23-9c**). The branching process is continued, using the data in the table in the top center of the figure, until all clades are established (see **FIG. 23-9d**).

In a cladogram each branch point represents a major evolutionary step

Notice that humans and chimpanzees share a recent common ancestor at node G in Figure 23-9d. This hypothesis is supported by the derived characters they share (synapomorphies). In the same way, bears are more closely related to the human–chimpanzee clade than to any other clade considered in our example, as indicated by the common ancestor at node F.

Note that shared derived characters are nested. As you trace the tree from its root to its tips, each branch reflects the addition of one or more shared derived characters. When we compare the nodes, the order of divergence (branching) is indicated by relative

Why Is It Used?   Outgroup analysis is used to organize character states into their evolutionary order, that is, to reconstruct phylogeny.

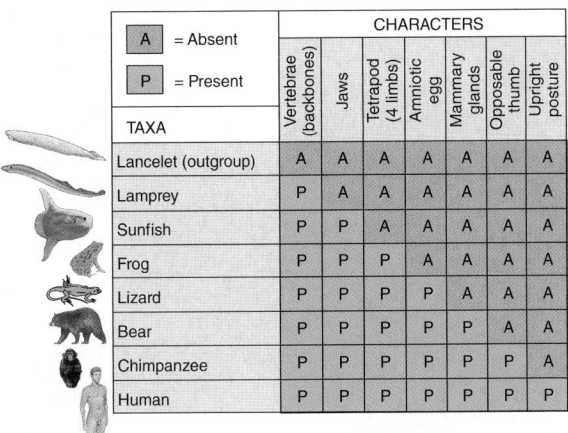

		CHARACTERS						
A = Absent P = Present		Vertebrae (backbones)	Jaws	Tetrapod (4 limbs)	Amniotic egg	Mammary glands	Opposable thumb	Upright posture
TAXA								
Lancelet (outgroup)		A	A	A	A	A	A	A
Lamprey		P	A	A	A	A	A	A
Sunfish		P	P	A	A	A	A	A
Frog		P	P	P	A	A	A	A
Lizard		P	P	P	P	A	A	A
Bear		P	P	P	P	P	A	A
Chimpanzee		P	P	P	P	P	P	A
Human		P	P	P	P	P	P	P

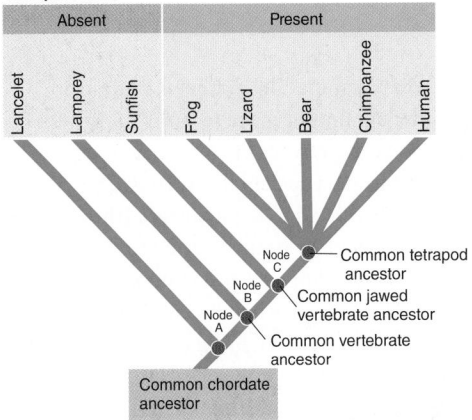

(a) All of the seven vertebrate taxa shown here have jaws, except the lamprey. Jaws are a shared derived character for these six taxa.

(b) Tetrapod limbs are a shared derived character for all vertebrate taxa shown here except the lamprey and sunfish.

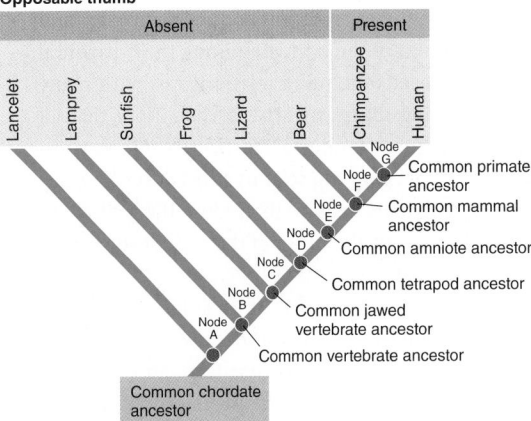

(c) The taxa represented by lizard, bear, chimpanzee, and human are amniotes. They share the derived character amniotic egg.

(d) Of the vertebrate taxa shown here, only the chimpanzee and human share the derived character opposable thumb.

How Is It Done?
1 Select the taxa of interest and the homologous characters to be analyzed.
2 Define the possible conditions, for example, present (P) or absent (A).
3 Here, the lancelet is selected as the outgroup, a taxon that diverged earlier than any of the other taxa being considered. The lancelet represents an approximation of the ancestral condition.
4 Refer to the table as you follow steps (a) through (d) to build a cladogram.

FIGURE 23-9 *Animated* Constructing a cladogram

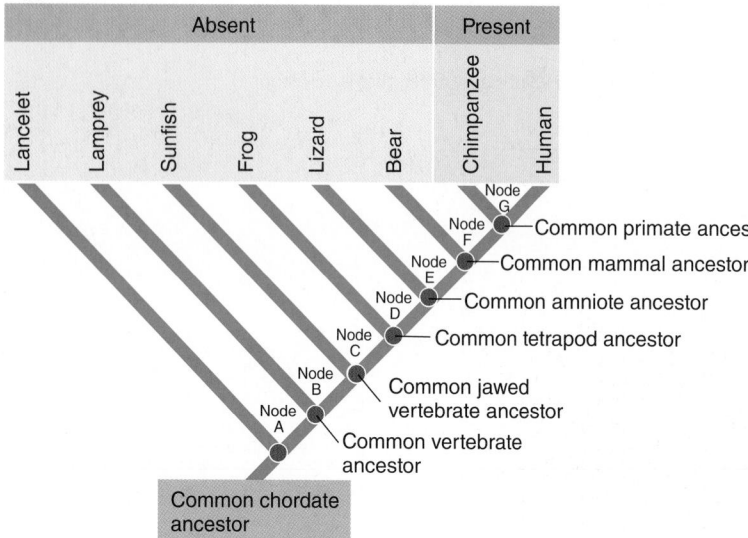

Opposable thumb

(a) This cladogram, the style used in this book, has diagonal branches.

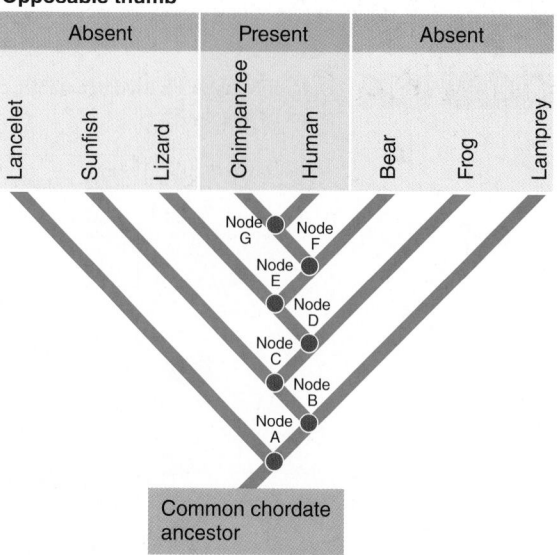

Opposable thumb

(b) This is another way to depict the same relationships shown in (a).

distance from the base of the diagram. The farther a node is located from the base of the cladogram, the more recently the group diverged. In our example, node G represents the most recent divergence, and node A represents the most ancient divergence. Thus, in our example, humans are closely related to chimpanzees (through node G) but more distantly related to bears (through node F). Therefore, classical biologists assign humans and chimpanzees to a less inclusive taxon (order Primates), whereas humans, chimpanzees, and bears are assigned to a broader, more inclusive taxon (class Mammalia). In addition, the cladogram reveals that lizards are more closely related to the mammal clade than to frog, sunfish, or any other clade. Can you explain why?

Two important concepts guide interpretation of cladograms. First, the relationships among taxa are determined only by tracing along the branches back to the most recent common ancestor and *not* by the relative placement of the branches along the horizontal axis. It is possible to represent the same relationships with many different types of branching diagrams (**FIG. 23-10**). Note that all three cladograms in this figure are equivalent. (Verify this by comparing the nodes and by checking the relationships described earlier.) Thus, a tree can be rotated around its nodes. The branching relationships are important, not the order of the taxa or the size of the branches.

A second important concept is that the cladogram tells us which taxa shared a common ancestor and how recently they shared a common ancestor. The ancestor itself remains unspecified. The cladogram does not establish direct ancestor–descendant relationships among taxa. In other words, a cladogram does not suggest that a taxon gave rise to any other taxon.

Systematists use the principles of parsimony and maximum likelihood to make decisions

When systematists consider the evolutionary relationships of organisms, they must choose between multiple, competing clado-

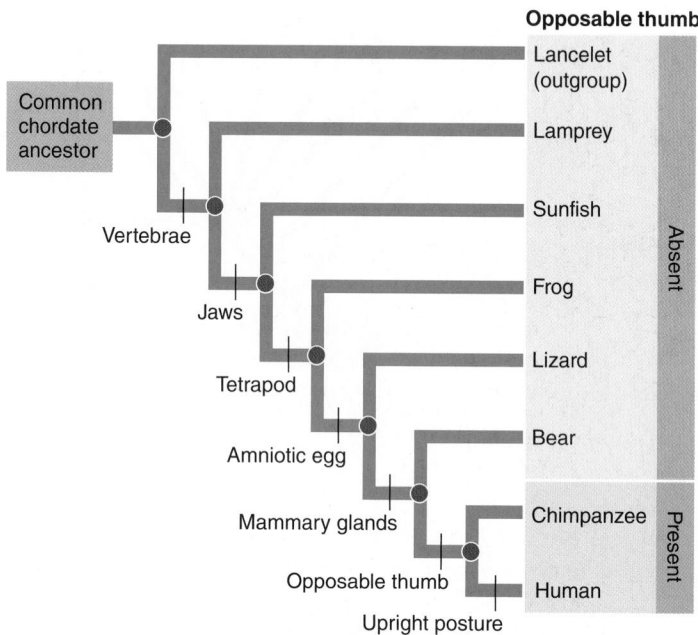

(c) This cladogram has rectangular branches and is rotated 90 degrees. However, it illustrates the same relationships as the cladograms in (a) and (b).

FIGURE 23-10 Cladogram styles
These three cladograms look very different, but they depict the same relationships. Remember that the relationships are depicted by which groups branch at the nodes. The length of the branches is not important.

grams. How do they choose the most accurate branching pattern? The most common criterion is the principle of **parsimony**—they choose the simplest explanation to interpret the data. Parsimony, a guiding principle in many areas of research, is based on the experience that the simplest explanation is probably the correct one. Applied to choice of cladograms, parsimony requires that the clad-

Applying the principle of parsimony to cladogram construction

Why Is It Used? Cladogram construction is used to choose between alternative hypotheses of evolutionary relationships by selecting the most accurate branching pattern.

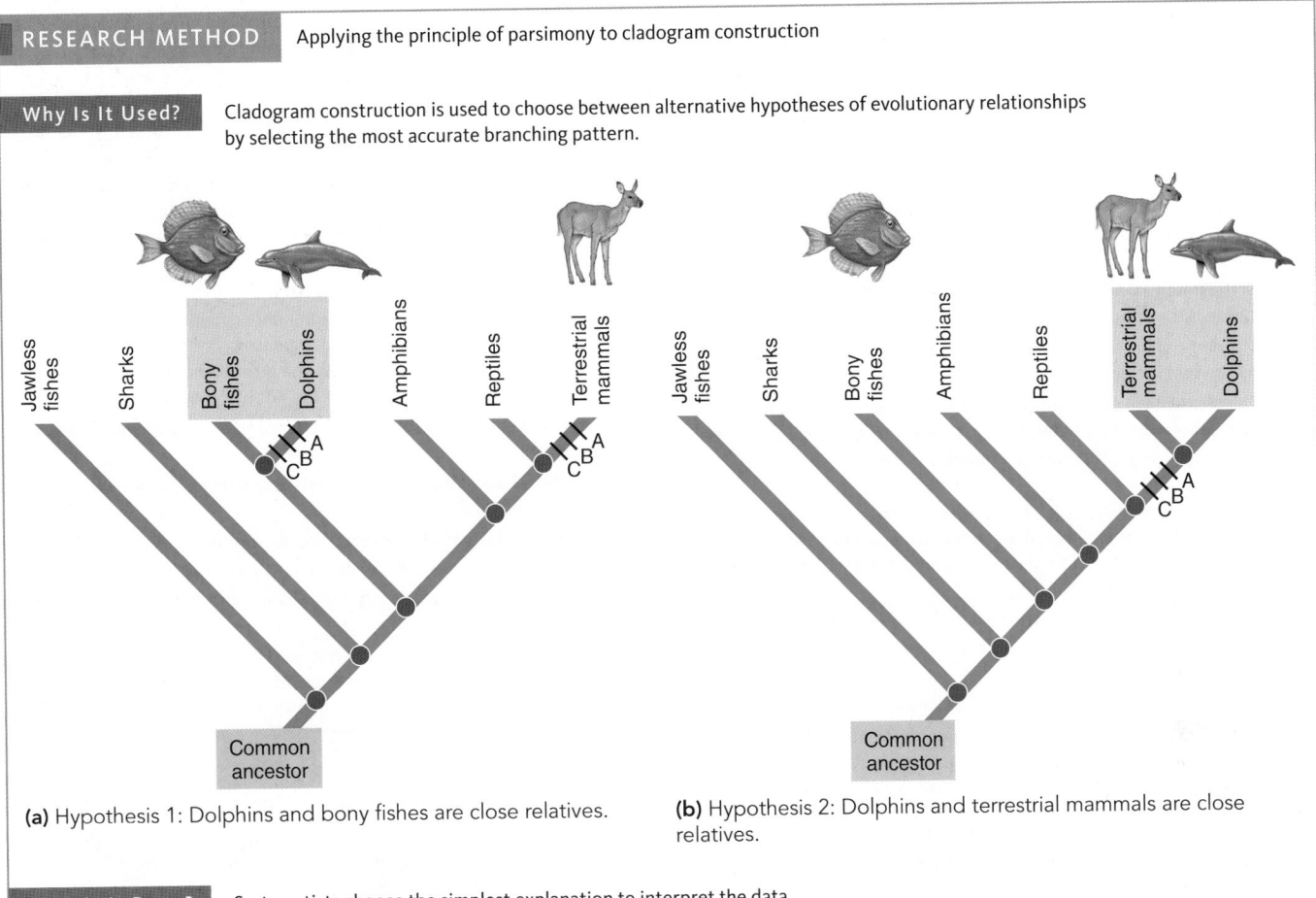

(a) Hypothesis 1: Dolphins and bony fishes are close relatives.

(b) Hypothesis 2: Dolphins and terrestrial mammals are close relatives.

How Is It Done? Systematists choose the simplest explanation to interpret the data.
1 Draw the possible cladograms.
2 Examine the relevant characters. In this example, character A = hair; B = mammary glands; C = middle ear bones.
3 Note that in the first cladogram (hypothesis 1), all three characters examined had to evolve independently twice.
4 Hypothesis 2 is chosen because it requires that each character evolve only once.

FIGURE 23-11 Biologists use the principle of parsimony to choose between alternative hypotheses of evolutionary relationships

ogram with the fewest changes in characters (the one with the fewest homoplasies) be accepted as most probable (**FIG. 23-11**). In actual practice it is often possible to generate several cladograms that are equally parsimonious. The excluded choices are those with more homoplasies because shared derived characters are more likely than homoplasies.

Systematists also use **maximum likelihood** to make decisions, especially when analyzing molecular data. Maximum likelihood is a statistical method that depends on probability, for example, the probability that nucleotide sequences in DNA and RNA change at a constant rate over time. Complex computer programs analyze large data sets and report the probability of a particular tree.

Many evolutionary questions remain. New hypotheses about how organisms are related suggest new taxonomic schemes. Systematics offers tools to help us test these hypotheses. In Chapters 24 through 32, we explore many evolutionary puzzles and discuss current hypotheses about relationships and classifications of organisms.

Review

- In what way do cladists use shared derived characters in their work?
- What is outgroup analysis?
- How do systematists apply the principle of parsimony?

■ SUMMARY: FOCUS ON LEARNING OBJECTIVES

23.1 (page 482)

1 State two justifications for the use of scientific names and classifications of organisms.

- **Systematics** is the scientific study of the diversity of organisms and their evolutionary relationships. **Taxonomy** is the branch of systematics devoted to naming, describing, and classifying organisms.

Classification is the process of arranging organisms into groups based on similarities that reflect evolutionary relationships.

- Scientific names allow biologists from different countries with different languages to communicate about organisms. Biologists in distant locations must know with certainty that they are studying the same (or different) organisms.
- Classifications help biologists organize their knowledge.

2 Describe the binomial system of naming organisms and arrange the Linnaean categories in hierarchical fashion from most inclusive to least inclusive.

- In the **binomial system of nomenclature,** the basic unit of classification is the **species.**
- The name of each species has two parts: the **genus** name followed by the **specific epithet.**
- The hierarchical system of classification includes **domain, kingdom, phylum, class, order, family, genus,** and **species.** Each formal grouping at any given level is a **taxon.**

23.2 *(page 483)*

3 Describe the three domains and argue for and against classifying organisms in the domains. (Compare this approach with using kingdoms as the main rank of classification.)

- The three-domain classification system assigns organisms to domains **Archaea, Bacteria,** or **Eukarya.** The domain classification is based on molecular data.
- Domain Eukarya includes the fungi, plants, animals, and protists.
- Some systematists recognize the kingdoms **Archaea, Bacteria, Fungi, Plantae,** and **Animalia.** Several "supergroups" composed of mainly unicellular, mainly aquatic eukaryotic organisms were formerly classified as kingdom Protista. Members of Archaea and Bacteria are prokaryotes. The fungi, which include molds, yeasts, and mushrooms, absorb nutrients produced by other organisms. Kingdoms Plantae and Animalia both consist of multicellular eukaryotes. For additional characteristics of the kingdoms, refer to Table 23-2. As new data are interpreted, organisms assigned to these kingdoms often must be reclassified.

CENGAGENOW™ Explore the tree of life by clicking on the figures in CengageNOW.

4 Interpret a cladogram, describing the meaning of its specific nodes and branches.

- In a **cladogram,** each **branch** represents a **clade,** a group of organisms with a common ancestor. Each **node,** or branching point, represents the splitting of two or more new groups from a common ancestor. The node represents the *most recent common ancestor* of the clade represented by the branches. The **root** represents the most recent common ancestor of all the clades shown in the tree.
- We can determine the relationships among taxa by tracing along the branches back to the nodes. The cladogram indicates which

taxa shared a recent common ancestor and how recently they shared that ancestor compared to other groups.

23.3 *(page 488)*

5 Critically review the difficulties encountered in choosing taxonomic criteria.

- Systematists seek to determine evolutionary relationships, or **phylogeny,** based on shared characteristics. **Homology,** the presence in two or more species of a trait derived from a recent common ancestor, implies evolution from a common ancestor.
- Some seemingly homologous characters are acquired independently by **convergent evolution,** independent evolution of similar structures in distantly related organisms, or by **reversal,** reversion of a trait to its ancestral state. The term **homoplasy** refers to superficially similar characters that are not homologous.

6 Apply the concept of shared derived characters to the classification of organisms.

- **Shared ancestral characters** (plesiomorphies) suggest a distant common ancestor.
- **Shared derived characters** (synapomorphies) indicate a more recent common ancestor and can be used as taxonomic criteria.

7 Describe how analyses of molecular homologies contribute to the science of systematics.

- **Molecular systematics** depends on molecular structure to clarify phylogeny. Comparisons of nucleotide sequences in DNA and RNA, and of amino acid sequences in proteins, provide important information about how closely organisms are related

8 Contrast monophyletic, paraphyletic, and polyphyletic taxa.

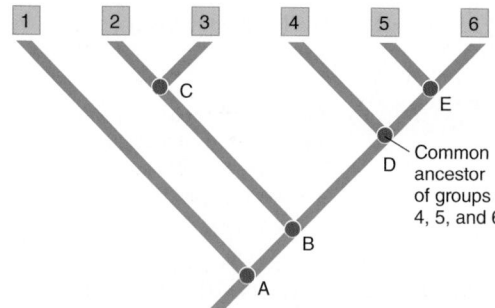

- A **monophyletic group,** or clade, includes all the descendants of the most recent common ancestor.
- A **paraphyletic group** consists of a common ancestor and some, but not all, of its descendants.
- A **polyphyletic group** consists of organisms that evolved from different recent ancestors.

23.4 *(page 493)*

9 Contrast the classification of reptiles and birds by a cladist and by an evolutionary systematist.

- Scientists applying the principles of **cladistics** insist that taxa be monophyletic. Each monophyletic group consists of a common ancestor and all its descendants. Cladists use shared derived characters to determine these relationships. Cladists classify reptiles and birds in a single clade.
- Biologists using an **evolutionary systematics approach** classify reptiles and birds in separate classes even though these classes are paraphyletic groups. Evolutionary systematics is based on shared ancestral characters as well as shared derived characters.

10 Describe the construction of a cladogram by using outgroup analysis.

- Cladists use shared derived characters to reconstruct evolutionary relationships and diagram these relationships in cladograms. They

- use **outgroup analysis** to determine which characters in a given group of taxa are ancestral and which are derived.

  - An **outgroup** is a taxon that diverged earlier than any of the other taxa being investigated.

11 Apply the principle of parsimony to cladogram construction.

- In using the principle of **parsimony,** cladists choose the simplest explanation to interpret the data.

  CENGAGENOW™ Learn more about interpreting and constructing cladograms by clicking on the figures in CengageNOW.

TEST YOUR UNDERSTANDING

1. The science of describing, naming, and classifying organisms is (a) systematics (b) taxonomy (c) cladistics (phylogenetic systematics) (d) phenetics (e) evolutionary systematics

2. The mold that produces penicillin is *Penicillium notatum. Penicillium* is the name of its (a) genus (b) order (c) family (d) species (e) specific epithet

3. Decomposers such as molds and mushrooms belong to which domain and kingdom? (a) Eukarya, Plantae (b) Bacteria, Archaea (c) Archaea, Fungi (d) Eukarya, Archaea (e) Eukarya, Fungi

4. Each branching point in a cladogram (a) is called a root (b) represents a clade (c) represents the divergence of two or more groups from a common ancestor (d) represents horizontal gene transfer (e) marks the divergence of two kingdoms

5. The presence of homologous structures in two different groups of organisms suggests that (a) the organisms evolved from a common ancestor (b) convergent evolution has occurred (c) they belong to a polyphyletic group (d) homoplasy has occurred (e) independently acquired characters may evolve when organisms inhabit similar environments

6. The dolphin and the human both have the ability to nurse their young, whereas the less closely related fish does not. The ability to nurse their young is a (a) shared derived character of mammals (b) shared ancestral character of all vertebrates (c) shared derived character of fish and mammals (d) homologous behavior (e) homoplasy

7. Using specific regions of DNA as a molecular barcode (a) is effective only with bacteria (b) is possible because of similarities in sugars (c) could cause major mistakes in distinguishing among closely related species (d) is an effective way to identify vertical

gene transfer (e) could help taxonomists identify and describe new species

8. A group of organisms that includes a recent common ancestor and all its descendants is (a) polyphyletic (b) paraphyletic (c) monophyletic (d) an example of horizontal gene transfer (e) a sister group

9. Some systematists classify crocodiles and birds in the same taxon because they are contained within a monophyletic group. These systematists follow which approach? (a) phyletic (b) cladistic (c) evolutionary systematic (d) polyphyletic (e) both cladistic and evolutionary systematic

10. In cladistic analysis (a) ancestral characters are used to reconstruct phylogenies (b) characters must be homoplastic (c) polyphyletic groups are preferred (d) the method called maximum likelihood is rarely used (e) outgroup analysis is used to determine a taxon that diverged earlier than the other taxa being studied

11. In interpreting a cladogram (a) we can identify the ancestor of each group by tracing each branch back to the node closest to the root (b) we can identify the taxa to which each group gave rise (c) we must study the relative placement of smaller branches along the main axis of the tree (d) we can determine the relationships by tracing along the branches back to the most recent common ancestor (e) we must identify horizontal gene transfer

12. When cladists apply the principle of parsimony, they (a) choose the cladogram that requires the fewest changes in characters as the most probable explanation to interpret the data (b) select multiple hypotheses to explain each relationship (c) do not use outgroups (d) typically use a polyphyletic approach (e) hypothesize that the most complex explanation is most probably the correct one

CRITICAL THINKING

1. What are the advantages of PhyloCode? of barcoding organisms?

2. What are some of the criteria/tools biologists might use to assign the protists to monophyletic groups?

3. **EVOLUTION LINK.** Explain why evolution is not always linear.

4. **EVOLUTION LINK.** Are members of a clade similar because they share a common ancestor, or do they belong to the same clade because they are similar? How might your answer vary depending on which approach to systematics you are following?

5. **EVOLUTION LINK.** The TATA-binding protein (TBP) is thought to be necessary for transcription in all eukaryotic cell nuclei. Studies show that archaea, but not bacteria, have a pro-

tein structurally and functionally similar to TBP. What does this similarity suggest regarding the evolution of archaea, bacteria, and eukaryotes? How might knowledge of this similarity affect how systematists classify these organisms?

6. **ANALYZING DATA.** Construct a cladogram based on the following data. Mosses are plants with no vascular tissue. Horsetails, ferns, gymnosperms (pines and other plants with naked seeds), and angiosperms (flowering plants) are all vascular plants. Seeds are absent in all but the gymnosperms and angiosperms. Angiosperms are the only seed plants with flowers. (*Hint:* To help you construct the cladogram, draw a simple table showing which characters are present in each group. See Figure 23-9.)

7. **ANALYZING DATA.** In the illustration, what kind of grouping is represented by the bracketed area? What type of group is formed by 2 and 3? What type of group is formed by 2, 4, and 6?

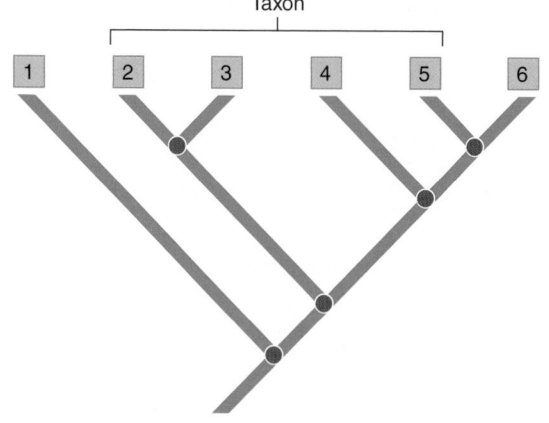

8. **SCIENCE, TECHNOLOGY, AND SOCIETY.** A nurse and two patients in the same hospital die from an unknown bacterial infection that does not respond to penicillin. How would you go about determining the phylogeny of this bacterium? (Consider strategies learned in this chapter.) How might knowing its phylogeny be helpful in this situation?

CENGAGENOW™   Additional questions are available in CengageNOW at www.cengage.com/login.

24 Viruses and Subviral Agents

This colorized SEM shows human immunodeficiency virus (HIV; *red*) infecting a T helper cell (an immune system cell; *green*).

NIBSC/Science Photo Library/Photo Researchers, Inc.

During the late 1800s, botanists searched for the cause of tobacco mosaic disease, which stunts the growth of tobacco plants and gives the infected tobacco leaves a spotted, mosaic appearance. They found they could transmit this disease to healthy plants by daubing their leaves with the sap of diseased plants. In 1892, Dmitri Ivanowsky, a Russian botanist, showed that the sap was still infective after it had been passed through porcelain filters designed to filter out all known bacteria. A few years later, in 1898, Martinus Beijerinck, a Dutch microbiologist, provided evidence that the agent that caused tobacco mosaic disease had many characteristics of a living organism. However, it appeared that the infective agent could reproduce only within a living cell. Beijerinck named the infective agent, *virus* (from the Latin word *virus*, which means "poison"). Tobacco mosaic virus was the first virus to be recognized.

Early in the 20th century, scientists discovered other infective agents, like those responsible for tobacco mosaic disease, that could cause disease in animals or kill bacteria. These pathogens were so small that they could not be seen with the light microscope. They also passed through filters that removed all known bacteria. Curiously, they could not be grown

501

in laboratory cultures unless living cells were present. The development of the electron microscope in the 1930s made it possible to see viruses for the first time.

Most of the viruses that infect animals, plants, and bacteria were identified during the second half of the 20th century. Viruses cause many plant diseases and are responsible for billions of dollars in crop losses each year. You may be familiar with some of the many human viral diseases, including influenza. smallpox, rubella (German measles), mumps, rabies, polio, herpes, and acquired human immunodeficiency syndrome (AIDS; see figure).

Viruses are the most numerous microorganisms on Earth, and they influence many ecological processes. For example, viruses kill large amounts of marine biomass each day, contributing significantly to the recycling of nutrients. Viruses adapt to their environments through evolution. They also influence the biodiversity of other organisms. Viruses can transfer their own genes into the genetic material of their hosts. They can also transfer eukaryotic genes from one organism to another, crossing species boundaries.

In this chapter we examine the characteristics and diversity of viruses, and the smaller subviral agents, viroids and prions. We include viruses in the diversity unit of *Biology* because they have some characteristics of living things and because they impact all living organisms.

24.1 THE STATUS AND STRUCTURE OF VIRUSES

■ LEARNING OBJECTIVES

1 Contrast a virus with a cellular organism.
2 Describe the structure of a virus.

A **virus** is a very small infective agent that consists of a core of nucleic acid and is dependent on a living host. The study of viruses is called **virology,** and biologists who study viruses are **virologists.** Most biologists view viruses as nonliving particles because they are not composed of cells and they cannot carry on metabolic activities or reproduce on their own. They do not have the components necessary to carry on cellular respiration or to synthesize proteins and other molecules.

Viruses do contain the nucleic acids necessary to make copies of themselves. They replicate by invading living cells and commandeering their metabolic machinery. In order to multiply, a virus must *infect* a cell in which it can replicate. Thus, viruses are **obligate intracellular parasites;** they survive only by using the resources of a **host cell,** the cell the virus invades. Viruses infect all types of organisms, including bacteria, archaea, protists, plants, fungi, and animals. Some viruses even infect other viruses. Interestingly, viruses evolve by natural selection. For these reasons, most biologists view viruses as being at the edge of life, although a few argue that they are very simple life-forms.

Viruses are very small

As early investigators reported, viruses are indeed very small. Most range in size from 20 to 300 nm. (A nanometer is one-thousandth of a micrometer.) The poliovirus is about 30 nm in diameter (about the size of a ribosome). If we could line these viruses up end to end, it would take almost a million of them to span one inch! A larger virus, such as the poxvirus that causes smallpox, can measure up to 300 nm long and 200 nm wide. The largest known virus is Mimivirus, with a diameter of about 400 nm, the size of a small bacterium (mycoplasma). Mimivirus, which was discovered in 2003, infects amoebas.

A virus consists of nucleic acid surrounded by a protein coat

The nucleic acid core of the virus is surrounded by a protein coat called a **capsid.** Microbiologists use the term *virion* to refer to the complete virus particle that is outside a **host cell.** The virion is the form in which the virus moves from the cell in which it was produced to a new host cell in which it can replicate its genome. However, here we will use the term *virus* in a broad sense, even when referring to virions.

A typical virus contains *either* deoxyribonucleic acid (DNA) or ribonucleic acid (RNA), not both. The nucleic acid can be single-stranded or double-stranded. Thus, a virus can have single-stranded (ss) DNA, double-stranded (ds) DNA, ssRNA, or dsRNA. As we will discuss, the type of nucleic acid is important in classifying viruses. The virus genome typically consists of 5000 to more than 100,000 bases or base pairs (depending on whether it is single-stranded or double-stranded). Again, Mimivirus is an exception. Investigators have sequenced the genome of Mimivirus and reported that this large double-stranded DNA virus has more than one million base pairs. Mimivirus also has six transfer RNAs.

The capsid is a protective protein coat

The capsid consists of protein subunits, called *capsomers.* The capsomers determine the shape of the virus. Capsids generally are either helical or polyhedral, or a combination of both shapes. Helical viruses, such as the tobacco mosaic virus (TMV), appear as long rods or threads (**FIG. 24-1a**). Its capsid is a hollow cylinder made up of proteins that form a groove into which the RNA fits.

Polyhedral viruses, such as the adenoviruses (which cause a number of human illnesses, including some respiratory infections), appear somewhat spherical (**FIG. 24-1b**). Its capsomers are organized in equilateral triangles. The capsid of a large virus can consist of several hundred capsomers. The most common polyhedral structure is an *icosahedron,* a structure with 20 identical surface faces (each face is a triangle). The human immunodeficiency virus (HIV) that causes acquired immunodeficiency syndrome (AIDS) is an enveloped virus. Proteins in the envelope extend outward like spikes (**FIG. 24-1c**).

Some viruses have both helical and polyhedral components. Viruses that infect bacteria are called *bacteriophages,* or simply *phages* (**FIG. 24-1d**). The T4 phage that infects the bacterium *Esch-*

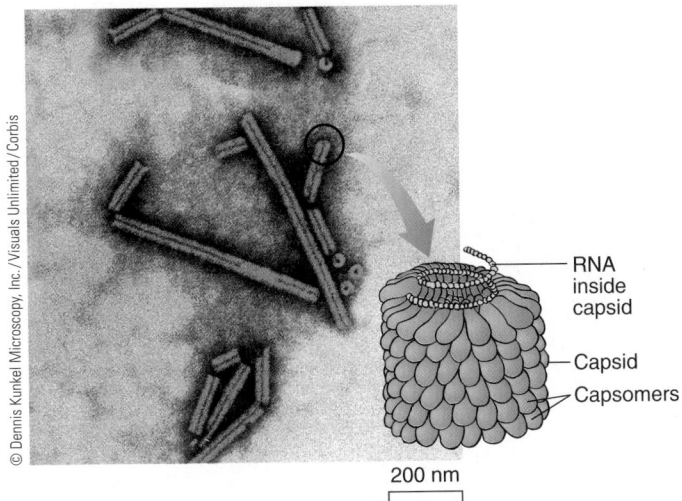

(a) **TEM of tobacco mosaic virus.** This virus is rod-shaped with a helical arrangement of capsid proteins.

RNA inside capsid

Capsid

Capsomers

200 nm

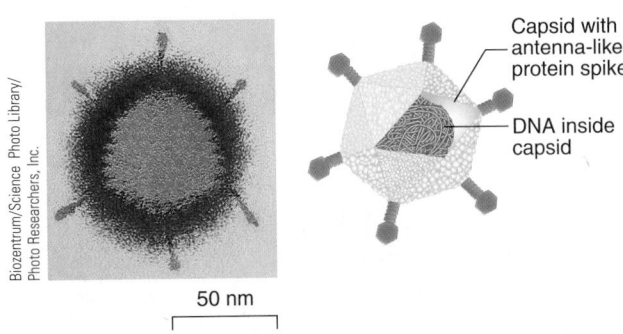

50 nm

Capsid with antenna-like protein spikes

DNA inside capsid

(b) **Color-enhanced TEM of an adenovirus.** The capsid is composed of 252 subunits (visible as tiny ovals) arranged into a 20-sided polyhedron. Twelve of the subunits have projecting protein spikes that permit the virus to recognize host cells.

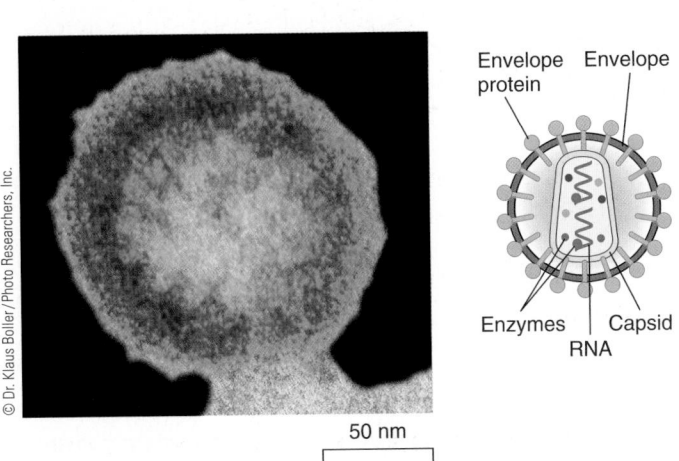

Envelope protein Envelope

Enzymes Capsid

RNA

(c) **Color-enhanced TEM of HIV, the virus that causes AIDS.** The virus is leaving a host cell (*pink*). The virus is enclosed in an envelope (*green*) derived from the host's plasma membrane. Viral proteins project from the envelope. The capsid of the virus is shown in yellow.

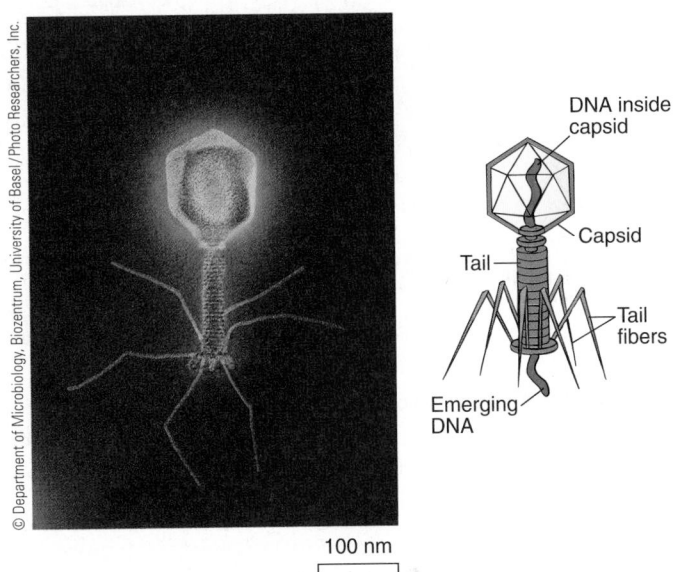

DNA inside capsid

Capsid

Tail

Tail fibers

Emerging DNA

100 nm

(d) **Color-enhanced TEM of T4 bacteriophage.** This virus has a polyhedral head and a helical tail. The virus attaches to the cell wall of the bacterial host by its tail fibers.

FIGURE 24-1 *Animated* **The structure of a virus**

A virus consists of a DNA or RNA core surrounded by a protein coat called a capsid. The capsid is made up of protein subunits called capsomers. Some viruses have an outer membranous envelope surrounding the capsid.

erichia coli consists of a polyhedral "head" attached to a helical "tail." Many phages have this shape. Many phages also have tail fibers that attach to the host cell.

Some viruses are surrounded by an envelope

Some viruses, called *enveloped viruses,* have an outer membranous envelope that surrounds the capsid. Typically, the virus acquires the envelope from the host cell's plasma membrane as it leaves the host cell (**FIG. 24-2**). Interestingly, while inside the host cell, the virus synthesizes certain proteins and inserts them into the host's

plasma membrane. Thus, the viral envelope consists of phospholipids and proteins of the host's plasma membrane, as well as distinctive proteins produced by the virus itself. Some viruses produce envelope proteins that extend out from the envelope as spikes. As we will discuss, these spikes can be very important in the virus's interaction with the host cell.

Review

- What characteristics of life are absent in a virus?
- What are the structural components of a virus?

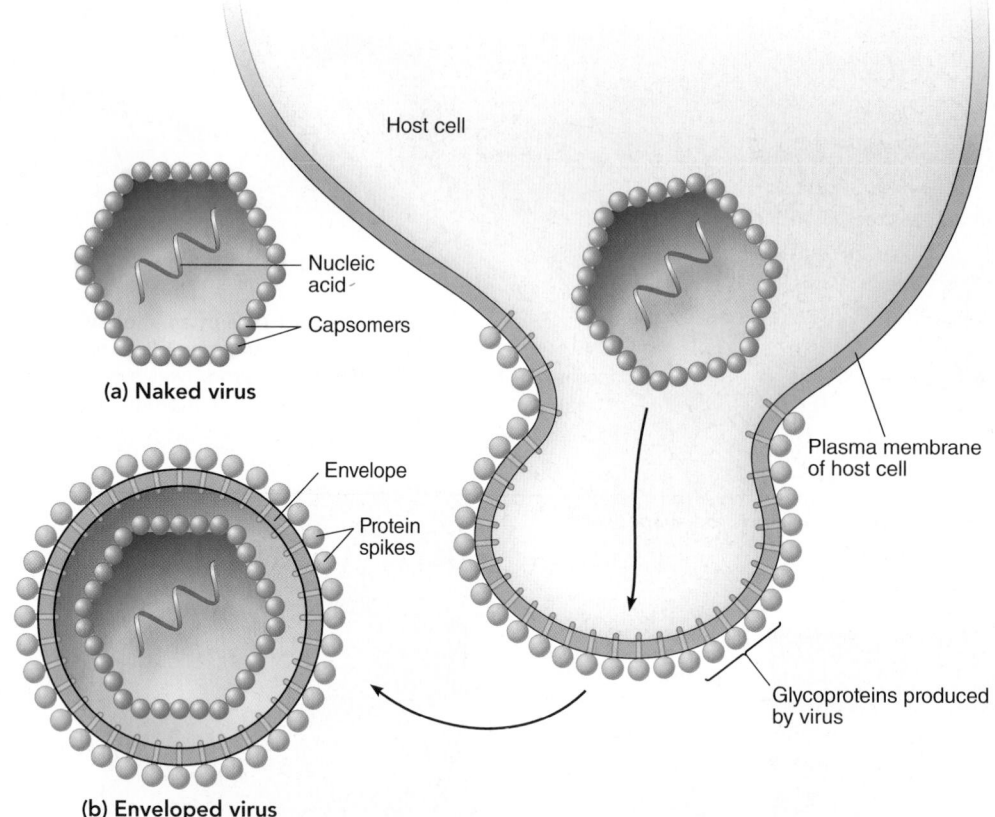

FIGURE 24-2 Comparison of naked and enveloped viruses
As the virus leaves the host cell, the host's plasma membrane wraps around the virus, forming the envelope. The envelope contains proteins produced by the virus.

**Labels on figure:**
Host cell
Nucleic acid
Capsomers
(a) Naked virus
Envelope
Protein spikes
(b) Enveloped virus
Plasma membrane of host cell
Glycoproteins produced by virus

24.2 CLASSIFICATION OF VIRUSES

■ LEARNING OBJECTIVE

3 Identify three characteristics used to classify viruses.

Viruses present a taxonomic challenge to biologists because they do not have the characteristics that define living organisms (see Chapter 1). They are acellular, do not carry on metabolic activities, and reproduce only by taking over the reproductive machinery of other cells. Viruses do not manufacture proteins and so do not have distinctive rRNA. For these reasons, viruses are not classified in any of the three domains.

Viruses can be classified based on their **host range,** the types of organisms they infect. They may be referred to as plant viruses, animal viruses, bacterial viruses, and so on. Viruses are more formally classified into taxa from species to orders. The International Committee on Taxonomy of Viruses (ICTV), a group of virologists, decides on specific criteria for classifying and naming viruses. Recently, based on host range and other characteristics, the ICTV classified viruses into 5 orders, 84 families, 307 genera, and more than 2000 species. Virus family names include the suffix *-viridae.* Note that this classification system is not a tra-ditional Linnaean system; it does not assign viruses to domains, kingdoms, or phyla.

The Baltimore classification system classifies viruses based on the type of nucleic acid the virus contains, whether the nucleic acid is single-stranded or double-stranded, and on how mRNA is produced. Other traits considered in viral classification are the size and shape of the virus, the presence of an envelope, and the method by which the virus is transmitted from host to host.

Review

■ What are three characteristics used to classify viruses?

24.3 VIRAL REPLICATION

■ LEARNING OBJECTIVES

4 Characterize bacteriophages.
5 Contrast a lytic cycle with a lysogenic cycle.

As we have discussed, viruses reproduce, but only within the complex environment of the living host cells they infect. Viruses use their genetic information to force their host cells to replicate their viral nucleic acid and to make the proteins they need. They take over the transcriptional and translational mechanisms of the host cell.

Bacteriophages infect bacteria

Much of our knowledge of viruses has come from studying **bacteriophages** ("bacteria eaters"), more simply referred to as **phages.** These viruses can be cultured easily within living bacteria in the laboratory. Microbiologists have identified more than 2000 phages. Bacteriophages are among the most complex viruses (see Fig. 24-1d). Their most common structure consists of a long nucleic acid molecule (usually dsDNA) coiled within a polyhedral head. Most have a tail, which may be contractile and may function in penetration of the host cell.

Before the age of sulfa drugs and antibiotics, phages were used clinically to treat infection. In the 1940s, they were abandoned (at least in Western countries) in favor of antibiotics, which were more dependable and easier to use. Now, with the widespread and growing problem of bacterial resistance to antibiotics, these bacteria-killing viruses are once again the focus of research. With new knowledge of phages and sophisticated technology, several research groups are investigating phages to determine which ones kill which species of bacteria. Scientists are genetically engineering phages so that bacteria will be slower to evolve resistance to them.

Phages can also be used to improve food safety. For example, certain phages can kill deadly strains of *E. coli* in cattle. These bacteria do not appear to make cattle ill but can cause illness and death in people who eat contaminated, undercooked hamburgers.

Viruses replicate inside host cells

Viruses infect bacterial, plant, and animal cells in basically similar ways. We will focus on phage infection of bacteria because this process is best understood. The reproductive cycle of viruses begins with a virus coming into contact with a host cell. The virus typically attaches to the surface of the host cell. The viral nucleic acid must enter the host cell and synthesize the components it needs to reproduce itself. Then, viral components are assembled and viruses are released from the cell—ready to invade other cells. Two types of viral reproductive cycles are lytic and lysogenic cycles.

Lytic reproductive cycles destroy host cells

In a **lytic cycle,** the virus lyses (destroys) the host cell. When the virus infects a susceptible host cell, it forces the host to use its metabolic machinery to replicate viral particles. Viruses that have only a lytic cycle are described as **virulent,** which means that they cause disease, and often death.

Five steps are typical in lytic viral reproduction (**FIG. 24-3**):

1. **Attachment (or adsorption).** The virus attaches to specific receptors on the host cell. This process ensures that the virus infects only its specific host.
2. **Penetration.** The virus penetrates the host plasma membrane and moves into the cytoplasm. Many viruses that infect animal cells enter the host cell intact. Some phages inject only their nucleic acid into the cytoplasm of the host cell; the capsid remains on the outside.

KEY POINT Viruses reproduce by seizing control of the metabolic machinery of a host cell. The host cell is destroyed in a lytic infection.

Phages

Bacterium

1 **Attachment.** Phage attaches to cell surface of bacterium.

Bacterial DNA

2 **Penetration.** Phage DNA enters bacterial cell.

Phage protein
Phage DNA

3 **Replication and synthesis.** Phage DNA is replicated. Phage proteins are synthesized.

4 **Assembly.** Phage components are assembled into new viruses.

5 **Release.** Bacterial cell lyses and releases many phages that can then infect other cells.

(a) The sequence of events in a lytic infection.

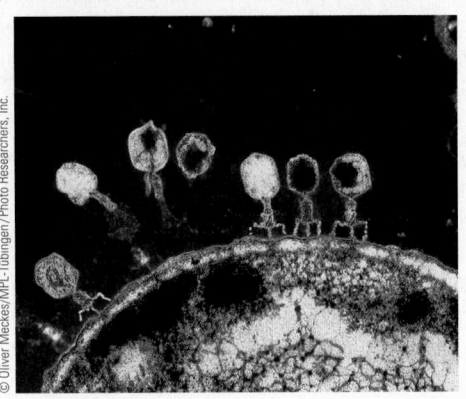

© Oliver Meckes/MPL-Tübingen / Photo Researchers, Inc.

80 nm

(b) Color-enhanced TEM of phages infecting a bacterium, *Escherichia coli*.

FIGURE 24-3 *Animated* **Lytic cycle**
In a lytic cycle, the virus destroys the host cell.

3. **Replication and synthesis.** The viral genome contains all the information necessary to produce new viruses. Once inside, the virus degrades the host-cell nucleic acid and uses the molecular machinery of the host cell to replicate its own nucleic acid and to produce viral proteins. Many antiviral drugs interfere with replication of viral nucleic acid.
4. **Assembly.** The newly synthesized viral components are assembled into new viruses.
5. **Release.** Assembled viruses are released from the cell. Generally, lytic enzymes, produced by the phage late in the replication process, destroy the host plasma membrane. Phage release typically occurs all at once and results in rapid cell lysis. In contrast, animal viruses are often released slowly or bud off from the plasma membrane.

Once released, the viruses infect other cells, and the process begins anew. The time required for viral reproduction, from attachment to the release of new viruses, varies from less than 20 minutes to more than an hour.

How do bacteria protect themselves from phage infection? You may recall from Chapter 15 that bacteria produce **restriction enzymes,** enzymes that cut up the foreign DNA of the phage; this prevents the phage DNA from duplicating. The bacterial cell protects its own DNA by slightly modifying it after replication so that the restriction enzyme does not recognize the sites it would cut.

In lysogenic cycles, temperate viruses integrate into the host DNA

Temperate viruses do not always destroy their hosts. In a **lysogenic cycle,** the viral genome usually becomes integrated into the host bacterial DNA. The integrated virus is called a **prophage** or **provirus.** When the bacterial DNA replicates, the prophage also replicates (**FIG. 24-4**). The viral genes that code for viral structural proteins may be repressed indefinitely. Bacterial cells carrying prophages are called *lysogenic cells.* Certain external conditions (such as ultraviolet light and X-rays) cause temperate viruses to revert to a lytic cycle and then destroy their host. Sometimes temperate viruses become lytic spontaneously.

Bacterial cells containing certain temperate viruses may exhibit new properties. This change is called **lysogenic conversion.** An interesting example involves the bacterium *Corynebacterium diphtheriae,* which causes diphtheria. Two strains of this species exist, one that produces a toxin (and causes diphtheria) and one that does not. The only difference between these two strains is that the toxin-producing bacteria are infected by a specific temperate phage. The phage DNA codes for the powerful toxin that causes the symptoms of diphtheria. Similarly, the bacterium *Clostridium botulinum,* which causes botulism, a serious form of food poisoning, is harmless unless it contains certain prophage DNA that induces synthesis of the toxin.

Review

- What are the steps in a lytic cycle? Draw diagrams to illustrate your answer.
- How is a lysogenic cycle different from a lytic cycle?

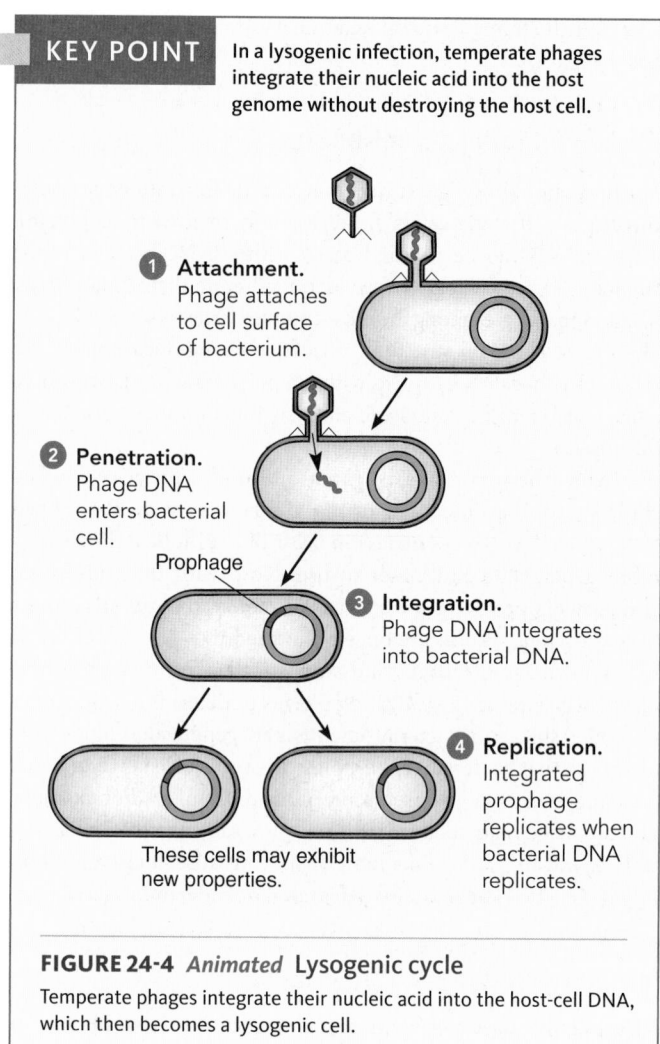

KEY POINT In a lysogenic infection, temperate phages integrate their nucleic acid into the host genome without destroying the host cell.

1 **Attachment.** Phage attaches to cell surface of bacterium.

2 **Penetration.** Phage DNA enters bacterial cell.

Prophage

3 **Integration.** Phage DNA integrates into bacterial DNA.

4 **Replication.** Integrated prophage replicates when bacterial DNA replicates.

These cells may exhibit new properties.

FIGURE 24-4 *Animated* Lysogenic cycle
Temperate phages integrate their nucleic acid into the host-cell DNA, which then becomes a lysogenic cell.

24.4 VIRAL DISEASES

LEARNING OBJECTIVES

6 Contrast viral infection of plants and animals, and identify specific diseases caused by viruses.
7 Describe the reproductive cycle of a retrovirus, such as human immunodeficiency virus (HIV).

Sir Peter Medawar, 1960 Nobel laureate in Medicine, defined a *virus* as "a piece of bad news wrapped in protein." Viruses that are **pathogens** are responsible for some very serious diseases, including smallpox, rabies, influenza (flu), and AIDS. However, although viruses must infect cells in order to reproduce, most known viruses do *not* cause disease. Here we focus on viral infection of plants and animals.

Viruses cause serious plant diseases

Viruses cause many important plant diseases and are responsible for billions of dollars in agricultural losses and lower crop quality worldwide each year. Infected crops almost always produce lower yields.

Viral infections do not usually kill plants, but they do stunt their growth, cause changes in the shape of the foliage, and may cause spots, streaks, or mottled patterns on leaves, flowers, or fruits (**FIG. 24-5**). Most plant viruses have capsids, but do not have envelopes. The genome of most plant viruses consists of single-stranded RNA. Plant viruses are typically named according to the type of plant they infect and by their effects on the plant. Tobacco mosaic virus was the first virus ever discovered.

Insects are important vectors of plant disease. As they feed on plant tissues, aphids, leaf-hoppers, and many other insects spread viral diseases among plants. Because of plants' thick cell walls, viruses cannot penetrate plant cells unless the cells are damaged. Plant viruses can also be transmitted from one generation to the next through infected seeds or by asexual propagation. Once a plant is infected, the virus spreads through the plant body by passing through plasmodesmata (cytoplasmic connections) that penetrate the walls between adjacent cells (see Fig. 5-27).

There are no known cures for most viral diseases of plants, so infected plants are commonly burned. Many agricultural scientists are focusing their efforts on preventing viral disease by developing virus-resistant strains of important crop plants.

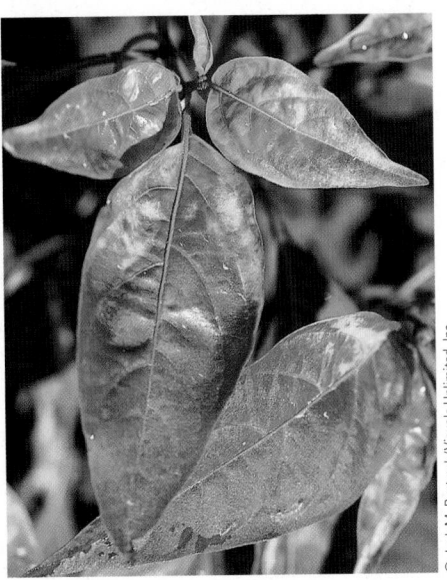

(a) **Virus-streaked tulip.** The virus that causes this relatively harmless disease affects pigment formation in the petals.

(b) **Pepper leaves infected with tobacco mosaic virus.** The leaf is characteristically mottled with light green areas.

FIGURE 24-5 Plant diseases caused by viruses

Viruses cause serious diseases in animals

Hundreds of different viruses infect animals, including humans. Animal viruses cause hog cholera, foot-and-mouth disease, canine distemper, influenza, and certain types of cancer (such as feline leukemia and cervical cancer). Viruses cause chickenpox, herpes simplex (one type causes genital herpes), mumps, rubella (German measles), rubeola (measles), rabies, warts, infectious mononucleosis, influenza, viral hepatitis, and AIDS (**TABLE 24-1** and *Inquiring About: Influenza and Other Emerging Diseases*). Most humans suffer from two to six viral infections each year, including common colds.

As discussed in Chapter 1, the outbreak of H1N1 influenza in 2009 was met by rapid responses from the World Health Organization (WHO), U.S. Centers for Disease Control and Prevention (CDC), and other public health agencies throughout the world. Careful surveillance and willingness of countries to rapidly share information helped minimize the spread of this pandemic. Effective vaccines and treatment protocols were quickly developed.

Human activity, including social factors such as urbanization, global travel, and war, contributes to epidemics of infectious dis-

ease. Living conditions, including sanitation, nutrition, physical stress, level of health care, and sexual practices, are important factors in the spread of disease. In the United States and other highly developed countries, infectious disease accounts for about 4% to 8% of deaths compared with death rates of 30% to 50% in developing regions. Even at the level of our current knowledge about viruses and epidemiology, just how prepared are we to contain a particularly virulent virus? How well are we containing HIV (the virus that causes AIDS), which continues to infect and kill millions of people worldwide every year?

Since the September 11, 2001, terrorist attacks in the United States, bioterrorism has become a critical concern worldwide. **Bioterrorism** is the intentional use of microorganisms or toxins derived from living organisms to cause death or disease in humans, animals, or plants on which humans depend. Terrorists could conceivably initiate epidemics of smallpox, anthrax, plague, and other potentially fatal diseases. (Note that anthrax and plague are caused by bacteria; see Table 25-5 in Chapter 25.) The quest for effective treatments and vaccines for these diseases has taken on new urgency.

Many animal viruses have lytic reproductive cycles

Most viruses cannot survive very long outside a living host cell, so their survival depends on their being transmitted from one animal to another. However, their host range may be quite limited because attachment to a host cell is very specific. The type of attachment proteins on the surface of a virus determines what type of cell it can infect. Receptors typically vary with each species and sometimes with each type of tissue. Thus, many human viruses can infect only humans because the viral attachment proteins combine only with receptor sites found on human cell surfaces. The measles virus and poxviruses infect many types of human

TABLE 24-1 Some Viruses That Infect Vertebrates

Group	Diseases Caused	Characteristics
DNA Viruses with Envelope		
Poxviruses	Smallpox, cowpox,* monkeypox, and economically important diseases of domestic fowl	dsDNA; large, complex viruses; replicate in the cytoplasm of the host cell
Herpesviruses	Cold sores (herpes simplex virus type 1); genital herpes, a sexually transmitted disease (herpes simplex virus type 2); chickenpox and shingles (herpes varicella–zoster virus); infectious mononucleosis and Burkitt's lymphoma (Epstein–Barr virus)	dsDNA; medium to large, enveloped viruses; replicate in the host nucleus[†]
DNA Viruses with No Envelope		
Adenoviruses	Respiratory tract disorders (e.g., sore throat, tonsillitis), conjunctivitis, and gastrointestinal disorders are caused by more than 40 types of adenoviruses in humans; other varieties infect other animals	dsDNA; replicate in the host nucleus
Papovaviruses[‡]	Human warts and some degenerative brain diseases; some cancers, including cervical cancer	dsDNA
Parvoviruses	Infections in dogs, swine, arthropods, rodents; gastroenteritis in humans (transmitted by consumption of infected shellfish)	ssDNA; some require a helper virus in order to multiply
RNA Viruses with Envelope		
Togaviruses	Rubella (German measles)	ssRNA that can serve as mRNA; large diverse group of medium-sized, enveloped viruses; many transmitted by arthropods
Orthomyxoviruses	Influenza (flu) in humans and other animals	ssRNA that serves as template for mRNA synthesis; medium-sized viruses that often exhibit projecting spikes
Paramyxoviruses	Rubeola (measles) and mumps in humans; distemper in dogs	ssRNA; resemble orthomyxoviruses but somewhat larger
Rhabdoviruses	Rabies	ssRNA
Coronaviruses	Upper respiratory infections; SARS	ssRNA; largest known RNA virus
Flaviviruses	Yellow fever; West Nile virus; hepatitis C (the most common reason for liver transplants in the United States)	ssRNA
Filoviruses	Hemorrhagic fever, including that caused by the Ebola virus	ssRNA
Bunyaviruses	St. Louis encephalitis; hantavirus pulmonary syndrome (caused by Sin Nombre virus, a hantavirus)	ssRNA
Retroviruses	AIDS; some types of cancer	ssRNA viruses that contain reverse transcriptase for transcribing the RNA genome into DNA; two identical molecules of ssRNA
RNA Viruses with No Envelope		
Picornaviruses	Polio (poliovirus); hepatitis A (hepatitis A virus); intestinal disorders (enteroviruses); common cold (rhinoviruses); aseptic meningitis (coxsackievirus, echovirus)	ssRNA that can serve as mRNA; diverse group of small viruses
Reoviruses	Vomiting and diarrhea; encephalitis	dsRNA

*The vaccinia (cowpox) virus is used to produce genetically engineered vaccines.

[†]These viruses frequently cause latent infections; some cause tumors.

[‡]The virus SV40 has been used as a vector to transport genes into cells.

tissue because their attachment proteins combine with receptor sites on a variety of cells. In contrast, the poliovirus attaches to specific types of human cells, such as those that line the digestive tract and motor neurons of the brain and spinal cord.

Some viruses, such as the adenoviruses, have fibers that project from the capsid and adhere to complementary receptors on the host cell. Other viruses, such as those that cause herpes and rabies, are surrounded by a lipoprotein envelope with projecting glycoprotein spikes that attach to a host cell. The influenza virus has rodlike spikes that project from its envelope. The glycoprotein spikes bind with specific receptors present only on cells lining the

respiratory tract of certain vertebrates, including wild and domestic birds, horses, pigs, and humans. Influenza vaccine prevents attachment by stimulating the host's antibodies to cover the spikes projecting from the virus.

Viruses have several ways to penetrate animal cells (**FIG. 24-6**). After attachment to a host-cell receptor, some enveloped viruses fuse with the animal cell's plasma membrane. The entire virus, including the capsid and nucleic acid, is released into the animal cell. Other viruses enter the host cell by *endocytosis*. In this process, the plasma membrane of the animal cell invaginates to form a membrane-enclosed vesicle that contains the virus. Endocytosis is

INFLUENZA AND OTHER EMERGING DISEASES

How do new strains of the influenza virus re-emerge? **Emerging diseases,** those new to the human population—such as AIDS, severe acute respiratory syndrome (SARS), Ebola, eastern equine encephalitis, and West Nile virus—often appear suddenly. Many new, continual, or re-emerging pathogens have the potential to strike globally. **Re-emerging diseases** are those that have been almost eradicated and then strike unpredictably, causing an epidemic, sometimes in a new geographic area. Many familiar diseases, such as influenza, malaria, tuberculosis, and bacterial pneumonias, continue to infect large numbers of people and increasingly reappear in forms that are resistant to drug treatments. Drug-resistant pathogens are a major challenge to public health and other health-care professionals.

Historically, new viral strains have claimed many human lives. For example, in 1918 an influenza (flu) pandemic killed more than 20 million people throughout the world. Flu pandemics also occurred in 1957 and 1968. Each year new strains of influenza virus evolve and become infectious. If the new combination of viral genes is unfamiliar to the human immune system, it may spread easily, resulting in a pandemic. According to the U.S. Centers for Disease Control and Prevention (CDC), influenza kills about 36,000 individuals in the United States every year.

New strains of influenza are thought to infect one species, such as a species of birds. At first, they are not able to spread among mammals. However, a virus of the avian strain can mutate and become virulent. The avian virus can also exchange RNA with a virus that has the genetic material necessary to spread among swine or other mammals. Swine can be susceptible to both avian and human strains of the virus. Inside a swine's body, the viruses can exchange bits of RNA and develop the ability to infect humans. Such reassortment can also occur inside a human host and produce a viral strain that can spread from person to person (see figure). H1N1 influenza evolved in this way.

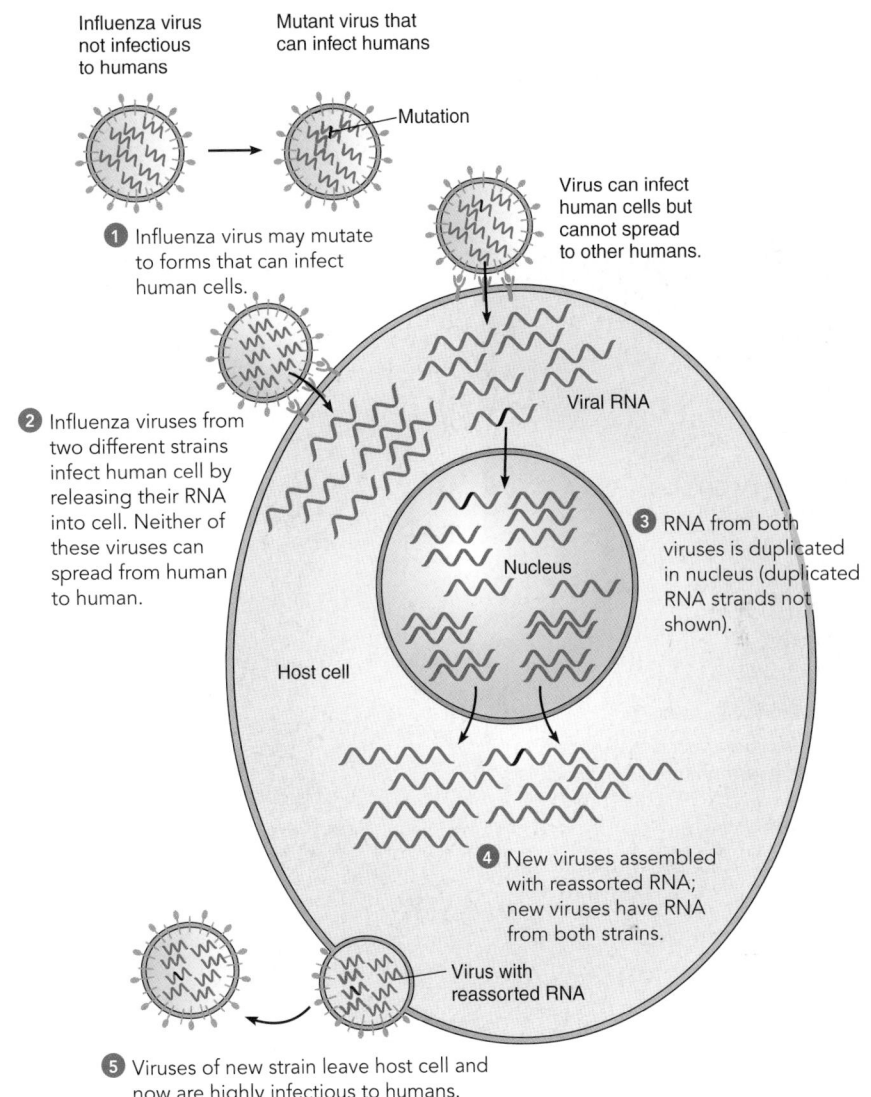

1 Influenza virus may mutate to forms that can infect human cells.

2 Influenza viruses from two different strains infect human cell by releasing their RNA into cell. Neither of these viruses can spread from human to human.

3 RNA from both viruses is duplicated in nucleus (duplicated RNA strands not shown).

4 New viruses assembled with reassorted RNA; new viruses have RNA from both strains.

5 Viruses of new strain leave host cell and now are highly infectious to humans.

An influenza virus such as H1N1 evolves as it mutates and its RNA reassorts in the bodies of birds, swine, and humans. Eventually, it becomes virulent.

---

advantageous to the virus because the endocytotic vesicle delivers the virus deep into the cytosol.

In DNA animal viruses, replication of viral DNA and protein synthesis are similar to the processes by which the host cell would normally carry out its own DNA replication and protein synthesis. In most RNA viruses, RNA synthesis takes place with the help of an RNA-dependent RNA polymerase.

Retroviruses are RNA viruses that have a DNA polymerase called **reverse transcriptase,** which transcribes the RNA genome into a DNA intermediate (**FIG. 24-7**). This DNA becomes integrated into the host DNA by an enzyme also carried by the virus. Copies of the viral RNA are synthesized as the incorporated DNA is transcribed by host RNA polymerases. The **human immunodeficiency virus (HIV)** that causes acquired immunodeficiency syndrome (AIDS) is a retrovirus. Certain cancer-causing viruses are also retroviruses.

After viral genes are transcribed, the viral structural proteins are synthesized. The capsid is produced, and then assembly of new virus

Viruses enter animal cells by membrane fusion or by endocytosis.

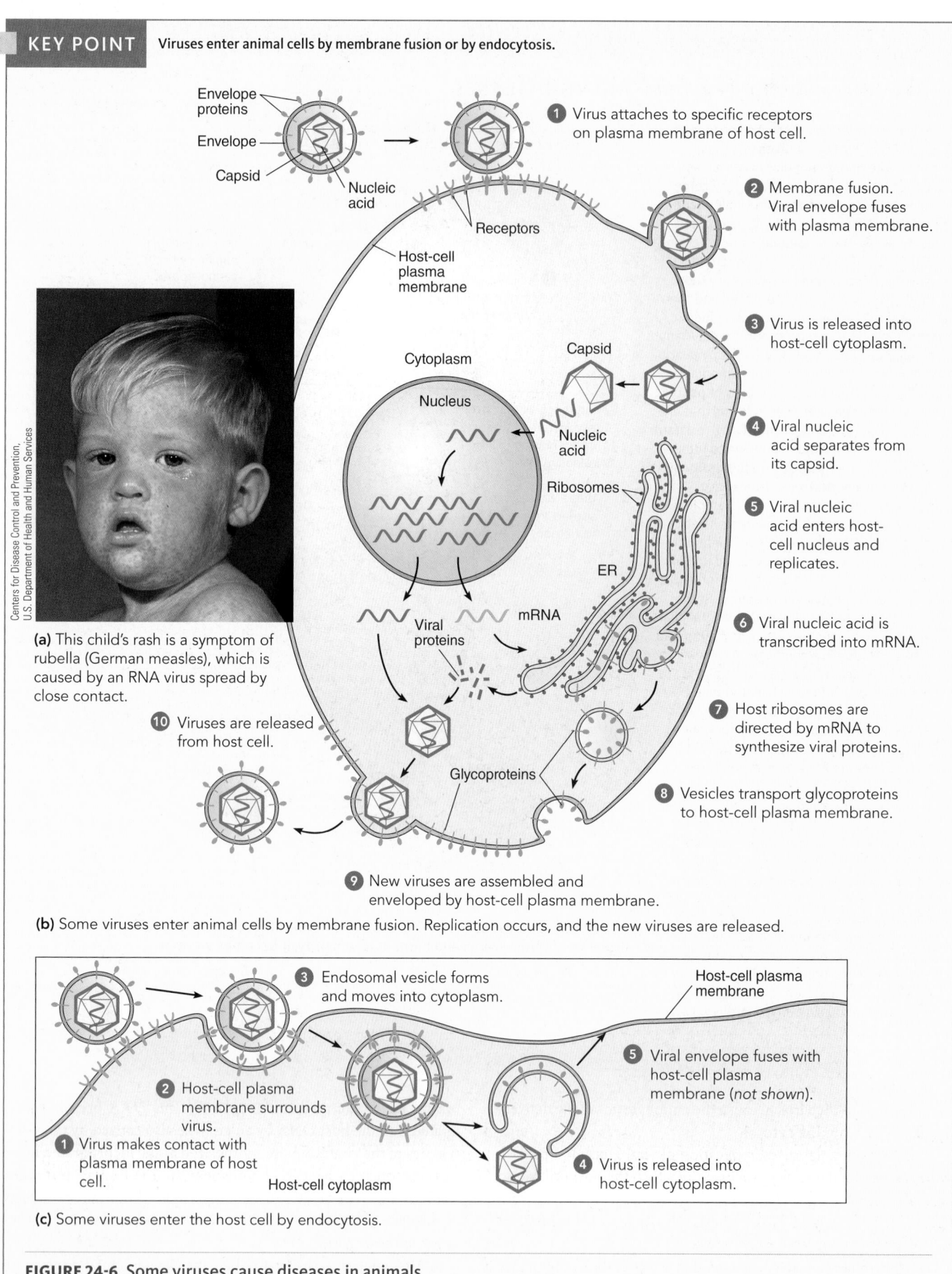

Envelope proteins

Envelope

Capsid

Nucleic acid

Receptors

Host-cell plasma membrane

Cytoplasm

Nucleus

Capsid

Nucleic acid

Ribosomes

ER

Viral proteins

mRNA

Glycoproteins

① Virus attaches to specific receptors on plasma membrane of host cell.

② Membrane fusion. Viral envelope fuses with plasma membrane.

③ Virus is released into host-cell cytoplasm.

④ Viral nucleic acid separates from its capsid.

⑤ Viral nucleic acid enters host-cell nucleus and replicates.

⑥ Viral nucleic acid is transcribed into mRNA.

⑦ Host ribosomes are directed by mRNA to synthesize viral proteins.

⑧ Vesicles transport glycoproteins to host-cell plasma membrane.

⑨ New viruses are assembled and enveloped by host-cell plasma membrane.

⑩ Viruses are released from host cell.

Centers for Disease Control and Prevention, U.S. Department of Health and Human Services

(a) This child's rash is a symptom of rubella (German measles), which is caused by an RNA virus spread by close contact.

(b) Some viruses enter animal cells by membrane fusion. Replication occurs, and the new viruses are released.

③ Endosomal vesicle forms and moves into cytoplasm.

Host-cell plasma membrane

⑤ Viral envelope fuses with host-cell plasma membrane (*not shown*).

② Host-cell plasma membrane surrounds virus.

① Virus makes contact with plasma membrane of host cell.

④ Virus is released into host-cell cytoplasm.

Host-cell cytoplasm

(c) Some viruses enter the host cell by endocytosis.

FIGURE 24-6 Some viruses cause diseases in animals

Retroviruses use reverse transcriptase to transcribe their RNA into DNA; the viral DNA becomes part of the host DNA. When activated, viral DNA uses host enzymes to transcribe viral RNA.

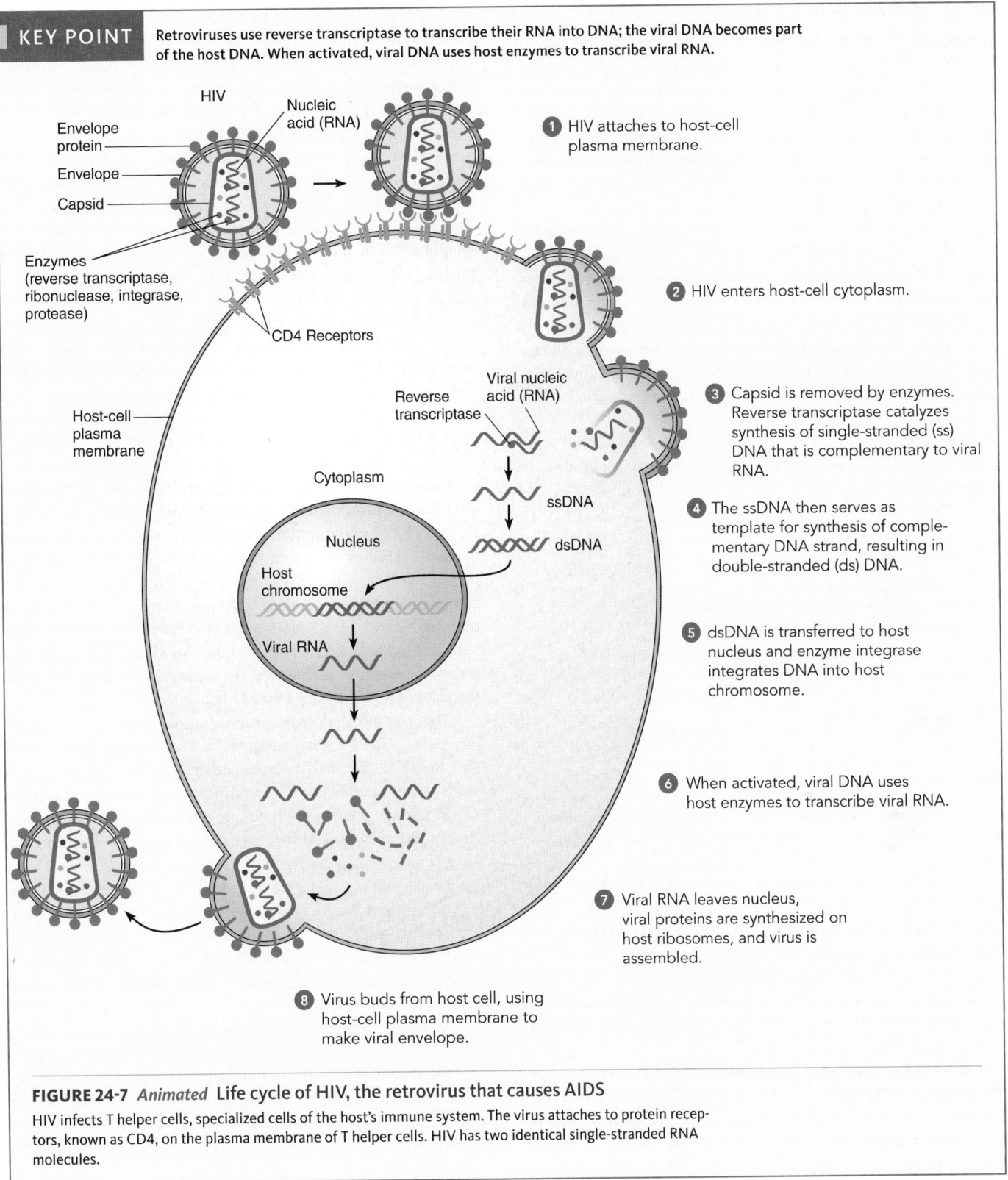

HIV

Envelope protein

Envelope

Capsid

Nucleic acid (RNA)

Enzymes (reverse transcriptase, ribonuclease, integrase, protease)

CD4 Receptors

Host-cell plasma membrane

Reverse transcriptase

Viral nucleic acid (RNA)

Cytoplasm

Nucleus

Host chromosome

Viral RNA

ssDNA

dsDNA

1 HIV attaches to host-cell plasma membrane.

2 HIV enters host-cell cytoplasm.

3 Capsid is removed by enzymes. Reverse transcriptase catalyzes synthesis of single-stranded (ss) DNA that is complementary to viral RNA.

4 The ssDNA then serves as template for synthesis of complementary DNA strand, resulting in double-stranded (ds) DNA.

5 dsDNA is transferred to host nucleus and enzyme integrase integrates DNA into host chromosome.

6 When activated, viral DNA uses host enzymes to transcribe viral RNA.

7 Viral RNA leaves nucleus, viral proteins are synthesized on host ribosomes, and virus is assembled.

8 Virus buds from host cell, using host-cell plasma membrane to make viral envelope.

FIGURE 24-7 *Animated* **Life cycle of HIV, the retrovirus that causes AIDS**

HIV infects T helper cells, specialized cells of the host's immune system. The virus attaches to protein receptors, known as CD4, on the plasma membrane of T helper cells. HIV has two identical single-stranded RNA molecules.

particles takes place. Finally, release occurs. Viruses that do not have an outer envelope exit by cell lysis. The plasma membrane ruptures, releasing many new viral particles. Enveloped viruses obtain their lipoprotein envelopes by picking up a fragment of the host plasma membrane as they leave the infected cell (see Figs. 24-6b and 24-7).

Viral proteins damage the host cell in several ways. These proteins may alter the permeability of the plasma membrane or may inhibit synthesis of host nucleic acids or proteins. Viruses sometimes damage or kill their host cells by their sheer numbers. A poliovirus can produce 100,000 new viruses within a single host cell!

Viruses quickly become resistant to antiviral drugs

Antibiotics are specific for fighting bacteria; they do not kill viruses. However, researchers have developed several antiviral drugs. Most of these drugs inhibit the replication of many RNA and DNA viruses. Amantadine has been used mainly to treat patients with influenza. The drug inhibits penetration or uncoating of viral nucleic acids. However, recent strains of influenza virus have become resistant to Amantadine, perhaps as a result of using the drug in poultry feed in certain areas of Asia.

A newer type of antiviral drug, including Tamiflu, inhibits neuraminidase, a viral enzyme necessary for the virus to leave the host cell. However, viruses are quickly becoming resistant to Tamiflu. In 2008, the Centers for Disease Control and Prevention found that about 11% of individuals with the most common type of influenza had Tamiflu-resistant strains. In 2009, 99% of individuals with this influenza had Tamiflu-resistant strains! It is thought that a single mutation that occurs spontaneously is responsible for this resistance.

Other antiviral drugs are in clinical trials. Some inhibit viral attachment to host cells, and others interfere with replication of viral nucleic acid.

Review

- How do viruses infect plant cells?
- What are the mechanisms by which viruses enter animal cells?
- How do viruses damage animal cells?
- How do retroviruses such as HIV make copies of themselves?

24.5 EVOLUTION OF VIRUSES

◼ LEARNING OBJECTIVE

8   Trace the evolutionary origin of viruses according to current hypotheses and describe recent research regarding the evolution of polydnaviruses.

Where did viruses come from? The most widely held hypothesis is that viruses derive from bits of nucleic acid that "escaped" from cellular organisms. According to this **cellular origin hypothesis,** viruses may have originated as mobile genetic elements such as *transposons* (see Chapter 13) or *plasmids* (small, circular DNA fragments discussed in Chapter 15 and Chapter 25). Such fragments could have moved from one cell and entered another through damaged cell membranes.

According to this hypothesis, some viruses may trace their origin to animal cells, others to plant cells or to bacterial cells. Their multiple origins may explain why many viruses are species specific; perhaps they infect only those species that are closely related to the organisms from which they originated. This hypothesis is supported by the genetic similarity between some viruses and their host cells—a closer similarity than exists between one type of virus and another.

According to the *coevolution hypothesis,* viruses appeared early in the history of life, even before the three domains diverged. Evidence for this hypothesis comes from similarities found in the protein structures of some viral capsids and in genetic similarities between some viruses that infect archaea and some that infect bacteria. Molecular biologists studying this hypothesis consider it improbable that these similarities evolved independently. This evidence suggests that viruses diverged very early. However, viruses are parasites, dependent on their hosts. How could they have existed before their hosts evolved?

According to the *regressive hypothesis,* viruses evolved from small, independent cells that were parasites in larger cells. Genes that they did not need, like those for protein synthesis, were gradually lost through evolution. This hypothesis is supported by certain bacteria (chlamydia and rickettsia) that are able to reproduce only inside the cells of their hosts (see Table 25-4). The regressive hypothesis is also supported by the Mimivirus. The investigators who sequenced the Mimivirus genome reported that its genome is larger than the genomes of 20 different bacteria and archaea. Also unlike other viruses, Mimivirus has genes that encode components for protein translation. These researchers suggest that this giant virus evolved from a more complex cellular ancestor and gradually lost some of the genes necessary for protein synthesis. This hypothesis explains how viruses could have existed before their present-day hosts evolved.

Recent studies on the origin of polydnaviruses contribute to our understanding of viral evolution. **Polydnaviruses** are particles that consist of multiple circles of double-stranded DNA encased in capsid proteins and an envelope. Each circle of DNA contains part of the virus genome. These viruses are found in ovary cells of many species of parasitic wasps. The polydnaviruses are unusual in that their circular DNA does not have genes for making the proteins needed to replicate and produce new viruses. Genes needed for viral replication are found in the wasp genome; the viruses can replicate only in the wasp ovary cells.

The wasp injects polydnaviruses along with her eggs into certain caterpillars. The polydnaviruses express toxins that interfere with the caterpillar's immune defenses and development. The wasp eggs hatch and develop inside the caterpillar, feeding on the caterpillar.

Biologists wondered whether the polydnaviruses were really viruses. Were the polydnaviruses simply particles derived from wasp genes? An alternative hypothesis was that millions of years ago a particular virus infected wasps. The virus genome became integrated into the wasp genome and lost the capacity to enter virus particles. Instead, wasp DNA was incorporated into the particles. Read the Key Experiment, **FIGURE 24-8,** to learn which hypothesis is supported by the recent research of Jean-Michel Drezen, Annie Bézier, and their colleagues.

No matter how viruses came to be and how they continue to evolve, they are here in large numbers and are important players in evolution. They mutate constantly, producing many new alleles. They replicate rapidly, and some of their genes are incorporated into the genomes of host cells, an example of horizontal gene transfer. In fact, viruses may be a major source of new genes for their host cells.

Review

- Which of the hypotheses presented do you think best explains the origin of viruses? Why?
- In what way are polydnaviruses mutualistic partners with certain wasps?

24.6 SUBVIRAL AGENTS

LEARNING OBJECTIVE

9 Compare and contrast satellites, viroids, and prions.

Subviral agents are infective agents that are smaller and simpler than viruses. Subviral agents include satellites, viroids, and prions.

Satellites depend on helper viruses

Satellites are subviral agents that depend on co-infection of a host cell with a helper virus. The satellite, which consists of either DNA or RNA, cannot reproduce without the helper virus. After a satellite encodes the protein for its protein coat, it is called a satellite virus. The agent that causes hepatitis D is a satellite that can reproduce only when the hepatitis B virus is also present.

Sputnik is a satellite that infects the Mimivirus, which in turn infects an amoeba. Sputnik is dependent on the replication and assembly machinery set up by Mimivirus. Some researchers now refer to Sputnik as a *virophage*.

Viroids are the smallest known pathogens

In 1971, Theodor Otto Diener, a plant pathologist, discovered an infective agent in potatoes that he named a **viroid**. Since that time, more than 30 species have been identified. Smaller than a virus, a viroid consists of a very short, circular, single strand of naked RNA (only 250 to 400 nucleotides). The viroid has no protective protein coat and no associated proteins to assist in duplication. Its RNA serves as a template that is copied by host RNA polymerases. Viroids are extremely hardy and resist heat and ultraviolet radiation because of the condensed folding of their RNA.

Many viroids have been identified that cause plant diseases, including potato spindle tuber viroid, apple scar skin viroid, avocado sunblotch viroid, and tomato chlorotic dwarf viroid. Viroids cause stunted or distorted growth and sometimes kill the plant. For example, cadang-cadang disease has killed more than 30 million coconut palms trees in the Philippines. Viroids are transmitted by infected pollen or seeds.

Viroids are generally found within the host-cell nucleus and appear to interfere with gene regulation. Molecular biologists have hypothesized that viroids mirror gene sequences in their hosts and silence critically important host genes. The viroid's single-stranded RNA replicates, forming double-stranded RNA. The plant's defense response cleaves this viroid RNA, producing small interfering RNAs (siRNAs); discussed in Chapter 13. However, the viroid siRNAs then cause host ribonucleases to selectively cleave host mRNAs with complementary base sequences. This action inactivates host mRNA and silences specific host genes. The viroids, themselves, are resistant to RNA silencing.

Prions are protein particles

Stanley Prusiner, professor of neurology and biochemistry at the University of California School of Medicine, San Francisco, began his studies of prions in the early 1970s, motivated by the death

KEY EXPERIMENT

QUESTION: What is the origin of polydnaviruses?

HYPOTHESIS: Polydnaviruses evolved from ancient viruses that infected wasps.

EXPERIMENT: Annie Bézier, Jean-Michel Drezen, and their colleagues searched for virus-related genes in the wasp genome. The team analyzed DNA from three different wasp species. They compared nucleotide sequences with sequences of public databases containing sequences of all organisms and viruses studied.

Polydnavirus particles

Juline Herbinière

250 nm

RESULTS AND CONCLUSION: The researchers identified 22 genes in wasp ovaries where viral particles are produced. These genes are present in the wasp genome and resemble key genes of nudiviruses, a family of insect viruses. The investigators found that many of these genes code for proteins that are part of the polydnavirus particles. These genes were conserved in several different wasp families that have polydnaviruses.

The research team concluded that the polydnavirus evolved from a nudivirus that infected wasps millions of years ago. In time, the virus genome became incorporated into the wasp genome. Proteins needed for viral replication are now part of the wasp's DNA, and the virus can replicate only in the wasp's ovaries. At the same time, the wasps depend on the virus because the virus depresses the caterpillar's immune defenses, allowing the wasp larvae to develop in the caterpillar. Thus, a mutualistic relationship has evolved between the wasp and the polydnavirus.

The investigators suggested that the polydnavirus acts as a gene vector, transporting large chunks of DNA to the caterpillar. Might learning more about this mechanism have clinical applications?

Source: Bézier, Annie, et al., "Polydnaviruses of Braconid Wasps Derive from an Ancestral Nudivirus." *Science*, Vol. 323, No. 5916, Feb. 13, 2009, pp. 926–930.

FIGURE 24-8 Exploring the evolution of polydnaviruses
The TEM shows polydnavirus particles in the nucleus of a cell in a wasp ovary. The polydnavirus particles are located at the periphery of an electron-dense region thought to be a "viral factory."

of a patient from Creutzfeldt–Jakob disease (CJD), a degenerative brain disease. Prusiner discovered that the infective agent was not affected by radiation (which typically mutates nucleic acids), and he could not find DNA or RNA in the particles. In 1982, he named the infective agent **prion,** for "proteinaceous infectious particle."

Pruisner's hypothesis that an infectious agent could cause disease without nucleic acids was not readily accepted because there was no known mechanism by which this could occur. However,

Pruisner and other researchers continued to study prions and discovered how they can cause cells to malfunction. In 1997, Prusiner was awarded the Nobel Prize in Physiology or Medicine for his discovery of prions—a new biological principle of infection.

Prusiner and others have shown that animals have a gene that encodes a normally harmless protein known as PrP. Normal forms of the protein are found on the surfaces of brain cells and many other types of cells. The PrP protein, which consists of 208 amino acids, helps neurons transport copper and may play a role in the sense of smell in animals. Recently, researchers have discovered that normal prion proteins interact with the peptides associated with Alzheimer's disease.

Sometimes, the PrP protein folds into a different shape, an insoluble form that can cause disease. This misfolded protein is the prion. Mutations in the gene that encodes the PrP protein increase the risk that the protein will misfold and become a prion. The prion then somehow induces other PrP molecules to misfold into the pathogenic form (**FIG. 24-9**). Prions apparently can aggregate and accumulate in the brain and in certain other tissues and cause serious damage.

Prions are found in the brains of patients with **transmissible spongiform encephalopathies (TSEs).** This group of fatal degenerative brain diseases has been identified in birds and mammals. These diseases are called TSEs because when infected, the brain appears to develop holes and becomes somewhat spongelike. The TSEs are in some ways like viral illnesses. However, there is a long latency period (about 5 years in cows and up to 10 years in humans) between contracting the infection and developing symptoms of the illness. Also, the TSEs have proven very difficult to treat. Genetically engineered mice that lack the prion protein gene are immune to TSE infection.

The oldest known prion disease is *scrapie* in sheep and goats. When infected, animals lose coordination, become irritable, and itch so severely that they scrape off their wool or hair. Bovine spongiform encephalopathy (BSE) is a related prion disease popularly referred to as "mad cow disease" because some diseased cattle become aggressive. BSE became epidemic in cattle in the United Kingdom in the 1990s.

More than 150 people have died from a human variety of BSE, providing evidence that the disease is transmissible from cow to human. The human disease is called vCJD because it is a variant of CJD, which is caused by the transformation of PrP proteins into prions. The infectious agent of vCJD has been recovered from infected human neural tissue and appears similar to the prion that causes scrapie in sheep. New regulations have been instituted in several countries to safeguard the food supply. Human-to-human transmission of vCJD has been associated with tissue and organ transplants and transfusion with contaminated blood.

Chronic wasting disease, an illness related to mad cow disease, has spread among deer and elk populations in North America.

1 Prion induces normal PrP to misfold, forming another prion.

2 Each prion can induce additional PrP proteins to misfold.

3 Proteins aggregate.

FIGURE 24-9 A model for how prion populations expand
Prions contact normal PrP proteins and induce them to misfold and become prions. Each new prion can then contact additional PrP molecules and induce them to misfold, thus expanding the prion population. Prions can form clumps by aggregating.

Studies are under way to determine whether this disease can infect livestock or humans. A disease that is killing up to 70% of cheetahs in captivity also appears to be a prion disease. In this disease, large deposits of a misfolded protein accumulate in the liver and spleen.

Like viruses, prions exhibit variability. There are different strains of prions that may differ from one another in the conformation of their proteins, in their properties, and in the diseases they cause. Prions are different from viruses in that they can arise spontaneously, most likely as a result of mutation. Researchers are studying ways to block prions from forming. They are also looking for ways to stimulate cells to destroy prions. Early diagnosis is critical, and the search is on for a blood test that would detect prion disease.

Review

- How do viroids differ from prions?
- How do viroids and prions differ from viruses?

24.1 (*page 502*)

1 Contrast a virus with a cellular organism.

■ A **virus** is a very small infective agent that consists of a core of nucleic acid and is dependent on a living host. Viruses contain the nucleic acids necessary to make copies of themselves, but in order to reproduce they must invade living cells and commandeer their metabolic machinery.

2 Describe the structure of a virus.

■ A **virus** is a subcellular particle consisting of a DNA or RNA genome surrounded by a protein coat, which is called a **"capsid."** Some viruses are surrounded by an outer envelope.

CENGAGENOW˙ Learn more about virus structure by clicking on the figure in CengageNOW.

24.2 (*page 504*)

3 Identify three characteristics used to classify viruses.

■ Viruses are classified based on **host range,** the types of organisms they infect; the type of nucleic acid they contain; and whether the nucleic acid is single-stranded or double-stranded. Other factors used to classify viruses include size and shape, presence of an envelope, and method of transmission from host to host.

24.3 (*page 504*)

4 Characterize bacteriophages.

■ **Bacteriophages,** or **phages,** are complex viruses that infect bacteria. They typically consist of a long molecule of dsDNA coiled within a polyhedral head.

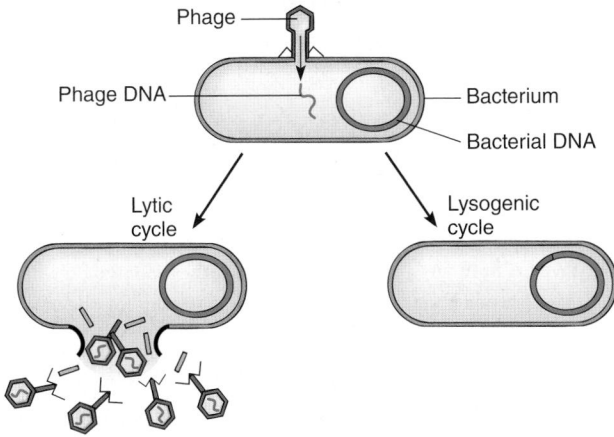

5 Contrast a lytic cycle with a lysogenic cycle.

■ In a **lytic cycle,** the virus destroys the host cell. There are five steps in a lytic cycle: **attachment** to the host cell; **penetration** of viral nucleic acid into the host cell; **replication** of the viral nucleic acid; **assembly** of newly synthesized components into new viruses; and **release** from the host cell.

■ The genome of a **temperate virus** can be replicated along with replication of the host's DNA without causing death of the host cell. This is a **lysogenic cycle.**

■ The nucleic acid of some phages becomes integrated into the bacterial DNA and is then called a **prophage.** Bacterial cells that carry prophages are lysogenic cells. In **lysogenic conversion,** bacterial cells containing certain temperate viruses exhibit new properties.

CENGAGENOW˙ Watch the lytic and lysogenic cycles by clicking on the figure in CengageNOW.

24.4 (*page 506*)

6 Contrast viral infection of plants and animals, and identify specific diseases caused by viruses.

■ Most plant viruses are ssRNA viruses that do not have envelopes. Plant viruses can be spread among plants by insect vectors. Viruses spread through the plant via plasmodesmata.

■ Viruses enter animal cells by membrane fusion or by endocytosis. Viral nucleic acid is replicated within the host cell, proteins are synthesized, and new viruses are assembled and released from the cell. Among the diseases caused by DNA viruses are smallpox, herpes, respiratory infections, and gastrointestinal disorders. RNA viruses cause influenza, upper respiratory infections, AIDS, and some types of cancer.

7 Describe the reproductive cycle of a retrovirus, such as human immunodeficiency virus (HIV).

■ **Retroviruses,** such as HIV, use **reverse transcriptase** to transcribe their RNA genome into a DNA intermediate that becomes integrated into the host DNA. Copies of the viral RNA are then synthesized.

CENGAGENOW˙ Watch the HIV life cycle by clicking on the figure in CengageNOW.

24.5 (*page 512*)

8 Trace the evolutionary origin of viruses according to current hypotheses and describe recent research regarding the evolution of polydnaviruses.

■ According to the **cellular origin** hypothesis, viruses may be bits of nucleic acid that originally "escaped" from cellular organisms.

■ According to the coevolution hypothesis, viruses evolved before the three domains diverged; biologists who support this hypothesis think it unlikely that the similarities between viruses that infect archaea and those that infect bacteria evolved twice.

■ According to the regressive hypothesis, viruses evolved from independent cells that were parasites of larger cells.

■ Recent research suggests that **polydnaviruses** evolved from viruses that infected wasps. They have become mutualistic partners with their wasp hosts.

24.6 (*page 513*)

9 Compare and contrast satellites, viroids, and prions.

■ Satellites, viroids, and prions are smaller than viruses. Satellites reproduce only with the help of a helper virus. A **viroid** consists of a short strand of RNA with no protein coat. Many viroids cause plant diseases. A **prion** consists only of protein. Prions cause **transmissible spongiform encephalopathies (TSEs).**

TEST YOUR UNDERSTANDING

1. The genome of a virus consists of (a) DNA (b) RNA (c) prions (d) DNA and RNA (e) DNA or RNA

2. The capsid of a virus consists of (a) protein subunits (b) nucleic acid (c) helical lipids (d) a carbohydrate envelope (e) RNA and lipid

3. Viruses that kill host cells are (a) lysogenic (b) lytic (c) viroids (d) prophages (e) temperate

4. Arrange the following list into the correct sequence for viral reproduction.
   1. penetration 2. assembly 3. replication 4. attachment 5. release
   (a) 1, 2, 3, 4, 5 (b) 5, 2, 3, 4, 1 (c) 4, 1, 3, 2, 5 (d) 4, 1, 2, 3, 5 (e) 3, 1, 2, 4, 5

5. In lysogenic conversion (a) bacterial cells may exhibit new properties (b) the host cell dies (c) prions sometimes convert to viroids (d) reverse transcriptase transcribes DNA into RNA (e) lytic viruses become temperate

6. The types of organisms a particular virus can infect are referred to as its (a) assembly (b) commensal cohort (c) host range (d) prophage range (e) restriction cycle

7. Plant viruses (a) typically cause rapid death of infected plants (b) are mainly retroviruses (c) are killed with antibiotics (d) are transmitted throughout the plant body by insects (e) can be transmitted from one generation to the next through infected seeds

8. When a virus enters an animal cell by membrane fusion (a) the viral envelope fuses with the host plasma membrane (b) the capsid remains intact until the virus is released from the cell (c) an endo- somal vesicle forms (d) viral DNA replicates in the host cytoplasm (e) the viral envelope fuses with the host nuclear membrane

9. Arrange the following list into the correct sequence for part of the cycle of a retrovirus.
   1. dsDNA integrated into host DNA 2. viral proteins synthesized on host ribosomes 3. viral DNA uses host enzymes to transcribe viral RNA 4. reverse transcriptase catalyzes synthesis of ssDNA 5. synthesis of complementary DNA strand
   (a) 5, 2, 1, 3, 4 (b) 5, 2, 3, 4, 1 (c) 4, 5, 1, 3, 2 (d) 4, 1, 2, 3, 5 (e) 2, 1, 3, 4, 5

10. According to the cellular origin hypothesis, viruses (a) appeared before the three domains diverged (b) came from mobile genetic elements and had multiple origins (c) evolved from early plant cells (d) are bits of nucleic acid that escaped from cellular organisms (e) evolved from cells that were parasites in larger cells

11. Prions (a) consist of RNA with no protein coat (b) are misfolded proteins (c) cause several important plant diseases (d) are the cause of several important emerging diseases (e) consist of proteins that stimulate host RNA to produce DNA

12. What does this diagram illustrate? Complete the labels.

CRITICAL THINKING

1. How are viral genomes different from those of plant or animal cells?

2. How do viroids and prions differ? In what ways are both different from viruses?

3. **EVOLUTION LINK.** Discuss the coevolution of organisms that are mutualistic partners. *Hint:* You may want to use the example of polydnaviruses. (See discussion and Key Experiment on polydnaviruses.)

4. **EVOLUTION LINK.** Historically, biologists thought that viruses, because of their simple structure, evolved before cellular organisms. Later, the hypothesis that viruses escaped from cells gained favor. A third view is the regressive hypothesis. Based on what you have learned about viruses, present an argument for one of these hypotheses.

5. **SCIENCE, TECHNOLOGY, AND SOCIETY.** What is the continuous challenge that influenza virus presents to scientists and public health officials? How can they meet this challenge?

 Additional questions are available in CengageNOW at www.cengage.com/ login.

25 Bacteria and Archaea

Color-enhanced TEM of a bacterium (*Streptococcus pyogenes*) dividing by binary fission. This bacterium, a pathogen that inhabits the human nose and throat, can cause scarlet fever and inflammation of the heart tissue. The strain shown here is resistant to antibiotics, and infection can be fatal.

K. Lounatmaa/Photo Researchers, Inc.

KEY CONCEPTS

25.1 Bacteria and archaea are single-celled organisms that, in contrast to eukaryotic cells, do not have membrane-enclosed organelles; most have a cell wall that surrounds the plasma membrane, and have a single, circular DNA molecule.

25.2 Evolution occurs rapidly in prokaryotes; natural selection acts on the genetic variation provided by mutations and genetic recombination, and is facilitated by rapid reproduction.

25.3 The great diversity that has evolved in their metabolism and mode of nutrition allows prokaryotes to thrive in all kinds of habitats.

25.4 Prokaryotes make up two of the three domains: Bacteria and Archaea.

25.5 Prokaryotes play critical roles in ecology, commerce, and technology.

25.6 The many adaptations that have evolved in pathogenic bacteria contribute to their great success.

In this chapter, we examine the diversity and characteristics of bacteria and archaea, two of the three main branches of the tree of life. These organisms, informally called prokaryotes, have inhabited our planet for more than 3.5 billion years—much longer than eukaryotes, which evolved about 2.2 billion years ago. Although prokaryotes are microscopic, they are so numerous that they, together with the fungi, account for approximately half of Earth's biomass, the mass of living material. In contrast, plants account for about 35% and animals for about 15% of the biomass of our planet.

The Dutch microscopist Anton van Leeuwenhoek discovered bacteria and other microorganisms in 1674 when he looked at a drop of lake water through a glass lens. During the late 1800s, many microorganisms, including some bacteria, fungi, and protozoa, were identified as **pathogens,** agents that cause disease (see photograph). Bacteria cause many diseases, for example, tuberculosis, tetanus, respiratory infections, and food poisoning in humans. However, only a small minority of bacterial species are pathogens. In fact, bacteria play essential roles in the biosphere. As decomposers, they break down organic molecules into their components.

Along with fungi, prokaryotes are nature's chief recyclers. Without these microorganisms, elements such as carbon, nitrogen, phosphorus, and sulfur would remain locked up in the wastes and dead bodies of plants, animals, and other organisms and would be unavailable for the synthesis of new cells and organisms.

Some prokaryotes are producers that carry on photosynthesis. Others convert atmospheric nitrogen to ammonia and then to nitrates, forms that are used by plants (see Fig. 55-8). This conversion enables plants and animals (because they eat plants) to manufacture essential nitrogen-containing compounds such as proteins and nucleic acids.

We begin this chapter with a description of the structure of bacteria and archaea, and then discuss prokaryote reproduction and evolution. We outline some of the nutritional and metabolic adaptations of these organisms, and then describe the phylogeny of the two prokaryote domains. We present an overview of the impact of prokaryotes on ecology, technology, and commerce, and end the chapter with a discussion of bacteria and disease.

25.1 THE STRUCTURE OF BACTERIA AND ARCHAEA

■ LEARNING OBJECTIVES

1   Describe the structure and common shapes of prokaryotic cells.
2   Contrast the bacterial cell wall in gram-positive and gram-negative bacteria.
3   Describe movement in prokaryotes, and describe the structure of the bacterial flagellum.

In contrast to viruses, viroids, and prions, which consist only of nucleic acid and/or protein, **prokaryotes** are cellular organisms. (Recall from Chapters 4 and 23 that the cell structure of prokary-

otes is fundamentally different from that of the eukaryotic cells of other living organisms.) Microbiologists assign prokaryotes to two domains: Archaea and Bacteria.

Most prokaryotic cells are very small. Typically, their diameter ranges from 0.5 to 1.0 μm, and their length, from 1.0 to 5.0 μm. Their cell volume is only about one-thousandth that of small eukaryotic cells, and their length is only about one-tenth. Most prokaryotes are unicellular, but some form colonies or filaments containing specialized cells.

Prokaryotes have several common shapes

Two basic prokaryote shapes are spherical and rod-shaped. Spherical prokaryotes, known as **cocci** (sing., *coccus*), occur singly in some species and in groups of independent cells in others (**FIG. 25-1a**). Cells may be grouped in twos (*diplococci*), in long chains (*streptococci*), or in irregular clumps that look like bunches of grapes (*staphylococci*). Rod-shaped prokaryotes, called **bacilli** (sing., *bacillus*), may occur as single rods or as long chains of rods (**FIG. 25-1b**). Some prokaryotes form spirals. If the spiral-shaped cell is flexible, it is a **spirochete;** if rigid, it is a **spirillum** (pl., *spirilla*) (**FIG. 25-1c**). A spirillum shaped like a comma is called a **vibrio.** Some archaea have unusual shapes, such as triangular or square-shaped cells.

Prokaryotic cells do not have membrane-enclosed organelles

In contrast to eukaryotic cells, prokaryotic cells do not have a nucleus or other membrane-enclosed organelles (**FIG. 25-2**; see Chapter 4). Although the prokaryotic cell does not have a membrane-enclosed nucleus, it does have a **nuclear area,** also referred to as the **nucleoid,** which contains DNA.

The dense cytoplasm of the prokaryotic cell contains ribosomes (smaller than those found in eukaryotic cells) and storage granules that hold glycogen, lipid, and phosphate compounds. Enzymes needed for metabolic activities may be located in the cytoplasm. Although the membranous organelles of eukaryotic

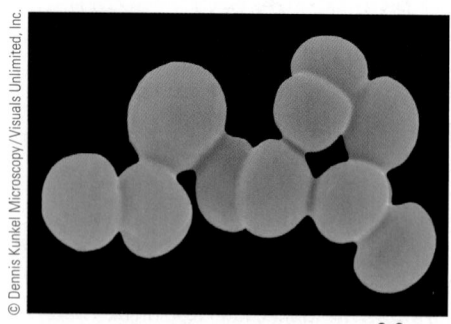

0.6 µm

(a) Cocci bacteria. Colorized SEM of *Staphylococcus aureus*. These bacteria cause skin and wound infections, food poisoning, and toxic shock syndrome.

3 µm

(b) Bacilli bacteria. Colorized SEM of *Salmonella*. These bacilli cause food poisoning.

12 µm

(c) Spirochete bacteria. Colorized SEM of *Borrelia burgdorferi*. These spirochetes cause Lyme disease, transmitted by infected deer ticks.

FIGURE 25-1 Common shapes of prokaryotes

In contrast to eukaryotic cells, prokaryotic cells do not have a nucleus or other organelles enclosed by membranes. They typically have a nuclear area with a single, circular DNA molecule.

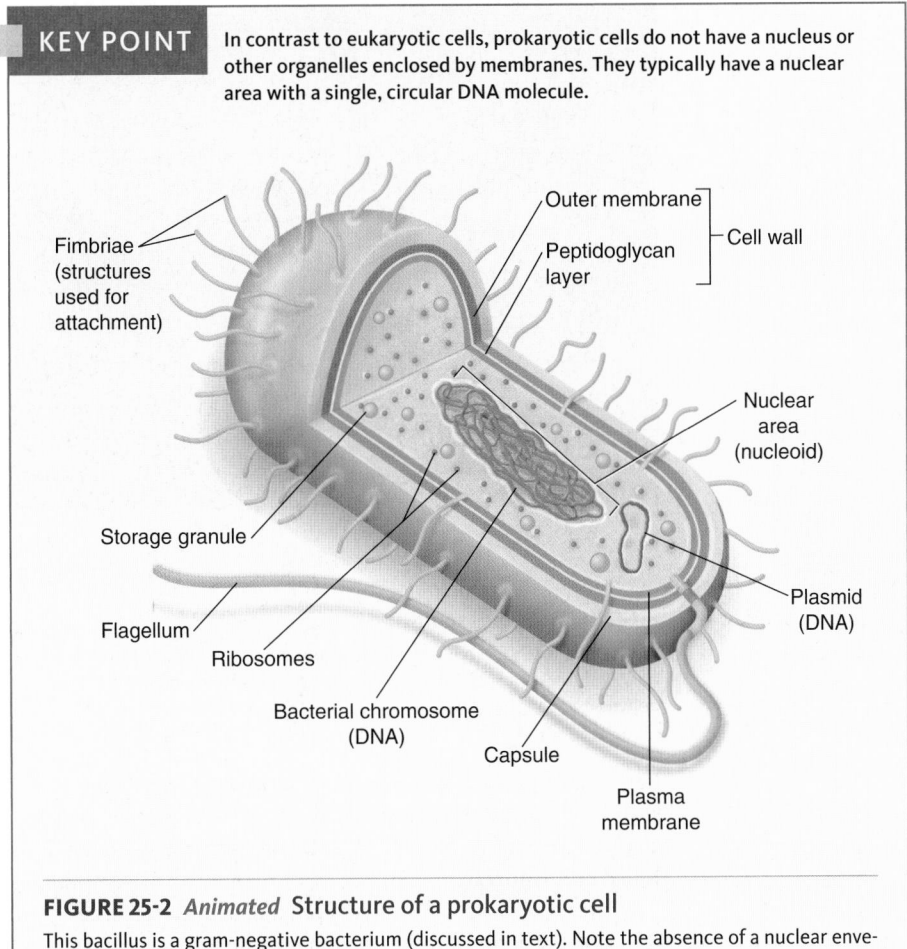

FIGURE 25-2 *Animated* Structure of a prokaryotic cell

This bacillus is a gram-negative bacterium (discussed in text). Note the absence of a nuclear envelope surrounding the bacterial DNA.

are joined to form a single macromolecule that surrounds the entire plasma membrane. Peptidoglycan is absent in the archaean cell wall.

Differences in bacterial cell wall composition are of great interest to microbiologists and are important clinically. In 1888, the Danish physician Christian Gram developed the Gram staining procedure. Bacteria that absorb and retain crystal violet stain in the laboratory are referred to as **gram-positive,** whereas those that do not retain the stain when rinsed with alcohol are **gram-negative.** The cell walls of gram-positive bacteria are very thick and consist primarily of peptidoglycan. The cell walls of gram-negative bacteria have two layers: a thin peptidoglycan layer and a thick outer membrane. The outer membrane resembles the plasma membrane but contains polysaccharides bonded to lipids (**FIG. 25-3**).

Distinguishing between gram-positive and gram-negative bacteria is important in treating certain diseases. For example, the antibiotic penicillin interferes with peptidoglycan synthesis, ultimately resulting in a fragile cell wall that cannot protect the cell (see Chapter 7 discussion of drugs that are enzyme inhibitors). Predictably, penicillin works most effectively against gram-positive bacteria.

cells are absent, in some prokaryotic cells the plasma membrane is extensively folded inward. Enzymes needed for cellular respiration and photosynthesis may be associated with the plasma membrane or its folds.

A cell wall protects most prokaryotes

Most prokaryotic cells have a **cell wall** surrounding the plasma membrane. The cell wall provides a rigid framework that supports the cell and maintains its shape. Bacterial cells have a high concentration of dissolved solutes. The cell wall keeps the cell from bursting under hypotonic conditions (see Chapter 5). Thus, most bacteria are adapted to hypotonic surroundings. When wall-less forms of bacteria are produced experimentally, they must be maintained in isotonic solutions to keep them from bursting. However, cell walls are of little help when a bacterium is in a hypertonic environment, as in food preserved by a high sugar or salt content. For this reason, most bacteria grow poorly in jellies, jams, salted fish, and other foods preserved in these ways.

The bacterial cell wall includes **peptidoglycan,** a complex polymer that consists of two unusual types of sugars (amino sugars) linked with short polypeptides. The sugars and polypeptides

Some bacteria produce capsules or slime layers

Many prokaryote species produce a **capsule** or **slime layer** that surrounds the cell wall. A slime layer is more loosely attached to the cell wall than a capsule. These outer layers are made of polysaccharide or protein.

In free-living species, the outer covering may provide the cell with added protection against phagocytosis (engulfment; see Chapter 5) by other microorganisms. In disease-causing bacteria, a capsule or slime layer may protect against phagocytosis by the host's white blood cells. The ability of *Streptococcus pneumoniae* to cause bacterial pneumonia depends on its capsule. A strain of *S. pneumoniae* that lacks a capsule does not cause the disease. Bacteria also use their capsules to attach to surfaces such as rocks, plant roots, or human teeth (where they cause dental plaque).

Some prokaryotes have fimbriae or pili

Some prokaryotes have hundreds of hairlike appendages called **fimbriae** (sing., *fimbria*). Fimbriae, which are made of protein, are shorter than flagella. **Pili** (sing., *pilus*) are usually longer than fimbriae. There are typically fewer pili on the cell surface than fimbriae. Bacteria use fimbriae and pili to attach to cell surfaces,

(a) **Gram-positive cell wall.** A thick layer of peptidoglycan molecules is held together by amino acids.

Cell wall

Thick peptidoglycan layer

Plasma membrane

Transport protein

(b) **Gram-negative cell wall.** A thin layer of peptidoglycan is covered by an outer membrane.

Polysaccharides

Lipoprotein

Cell wall

Outer membrane

Thin peptidoglycan layer

Plasma membrane

Transport protein

FIGURE 25-3 Bacterial cell walls

including the surfaces of cells they infect. These protein structures also help bacteria adhere to one another. Some elongated pili, called *sex pili,* are important in transmitting DNA between bacteria.

Some bacteria survive unfavorable conditions by forming endospores

When the environment becomes unfavorable, for example, when nutrients are limited or the environment becomes very dry or

2 µm

Endospores

FIGURE 25-4 Endospores

Color-enhanced TEM of *Clostridium tetani,* the bacterium that causes tetanus. Each bacterial cell (*blue*) contains one endospore (*orange*), a resistant, dehydrated cell that develops within the original cell.

hot, some types of bacteria become dormant. The cell loses water, shrinks slightly, and remains inactive until water is again available. Certain types of bacteria form dormant, extremely durable cells called **endospores.**

After an endospore forms, the cell wall of the original cell lyses, releasing the endospore. Formation of endospores is not a type of reproduction in bacteria; endospores are not comparable to the reproductive spores of fungi and plants. Only one endospore is formed per original cell, so the total number of individuals does not increase. Archaea do not form endospores; these prokaryotes produce unique enzymes on the cell surface that protect them from cold, heat, and desiccation.

Endospores survive in very dry, hot, or frozen environments or at times when food is scarce (**FIG. 25-4**). Some endospores are so resistant that they can survive an hour or more of boiling or centuries of freezing. When environmental conditions are again suitable for growth, the endospore germinates, forming an active, growing bacterial cell.

Several types of bacteria that form endospores cause disease. The endospore of *Bacillus anthracis,* the bacterium that causes anthrax, is so hardy that this pathogen has become a concern as an agent of biological warfare. The bacteria (*Clostridium tetani*) that cause tetanus and the bacteria (*C. perfringens*) that cause gas gangrene typically enter the body with soil when a person suffers a deep cut or puncture wound. Patients may also be exposed to these serious diseases when surgical instruments are not effectively sterilized, allowing endospores to survive.

Many types of prokaryotes are motile

Can you imagine trying to swim through molasses? Water has the same relative viscosity to prokaryotes that molasses has to humans. Most motile prokaryotes manage to move by means of rotating

flagella. The number and location of flagella are important in classifying some bacterial species.

Unlike eukaryotic flagella, prokaryotic flagella do not consist of microtubules (see Chapter 4). A bacterial flagellum is a long, thin appendage, consisting of three parts: a basal body, a hook, and a single filament (**FIG. 25-5**). The basal body is a complex structure that anchors the flagellum into the cell wall by disc-shaped plates. The curved hook connects the basal body to the long, hollow filament that extends into the outside environment.

The basal body is a motor, somewhat like the propeller of a boat motor. The bacterium uses energy from ATP to pump protons out of the cell. Diffusion of these protons back into the cell powers the motor that spins the flagellum. The rotary motion produced pushes the cell much like a propeller pushes a ship through the water. The flagellum rotates counterclockwise, pushing the cell forward.

Archaea also have flagella. These flagella are thinner than those of bacteria. Biologists do not yet know the structure of the motor in the archaeal flagellum. Some prokaryotes that lack flagella move by gliding.

Many prokaryotes exhibit **chemotaxis,** movement in response to chemicals in the environment. For example, bacteria move toward food. Certain bacteria also move toward one another. However, bacteria move away from certain harmful chemicals.

Review

- In what ways do prokaryotic cells differ from eukaryotic cells?
- How do gram-positive and gram-negative bacteria differ? Why is this important?
- How does a bacterial flagellum differ from a eukaryotic flagellum?

25.2 PROKARYOTE REPRODUCTION AND EVOLUTION

◼ LEARNING OBJECTIVES

4 Describe asexual reproduction in prokaryotes, and summarize three mechanisms (transformation, transduction, and conjugation) that may lead to genetic recombination.

5 State specific factors that contribute to the rapid evolution of bacteria.

The genetic material of a prokaryote lies in the nuclear area, but is not surrounded by a nuclear envelope. In most species, the genetic material is contained in a single, circular DNA molecule. If stretched out to its full length, this molecule would be about 1000 times as long as the cell itself. Unlike the DNA in eukaryotic chromosomes, prokaryote DNA has little protein associated with it.

In addition to their genomic DNA, most bacteria have one or more **plasmids,** smaller circular fragments of DNA. Bacterial plasmids often have genes that code for catabolic enzymes, for genetic exchange, or for resistance to antibiotics. Plasmids replicate independently of the genomic DNA or become integrated into it (see Chapter 15).

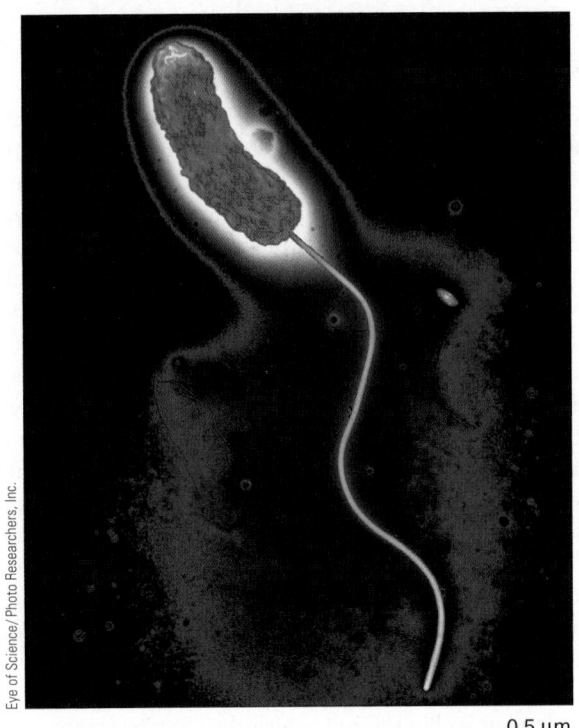

Eye of Science/Photo Researchers, Inc.

0.5 µm

(a) Color-enhanced TEM of *Vibrio cholerae*. This flagellate bacterium causes cholera in humans.

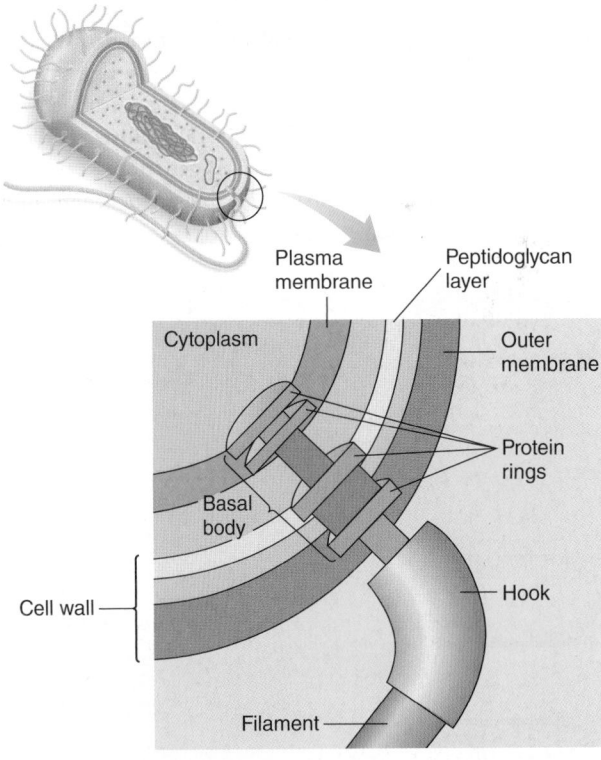

Plasma membrane

Peptidoglycan layer

Cytoplasm

Outer membrane

Protein rings

Basal body

Cell wall

Hook

Filament

(b) Structure of a bacterial flagellum. The basal body is the motor. It consists of a series of disc-shaped plates that anchor the flagellum to the cell wall and plasma membrane. These plates spin the hook and filament of the flagellum.

FIGURE 25-5 Bacterial flagella

Rapid reproduction contributes to prokaryote success

Prokaryotes are extremely successful organisms in terms of their numbers and distribution. Their success is in large part due to their remarkable ability to reproduce rapidly. Prokaryotes reproduce asexually, generally by **binary fission,** a process in which one cell divides into two similar cells, as in the chapter opening photograph (also see Fig. 10-12). First, the circular DNA replicates; and then an ingrowth of both the plasma membrane and the cell wall forms a transverse wall.

Binary fission occurs with remarkable speed. Under ideal conditions, some bacterial species divide in less than 20 minutes. At this rate, if nothing interfered, one bacterium could give rise to more than one billion bacteria within 10 hours! Fortunately, bacteria cannot reproduce at this rate for very long before lack of food or the accumulation of waste products slows their population expansion.

A less common form of asexual reproduction among bacteria is **budding.** In budding, a cell develops a bulge, or bud, that enlarges, matures, and eventually separates from the mother cell. A few species of bacteria (actinomycetes) divide by **fragmentation.** Walls develop within the cell, which then separates into several new cells.

Prokaryotes transfer genetic information

Although sexual reproduction involving the fusion of gametes does not occur in prokaryotes, genetic material can be exchanged among bacteria and among archaea. Such exchange of genes, or **gene transfer,** results in genetic recombination. **Horizontal gene transfer** occurs when an organism transfers genetic material to another organism that is not its offspring. (Transfer of genetic mate-

rial from parent to offspring is called *vertical gene transfer.*) Gene transfer among bacteria takes place by three different mechanisms: transformation, transduction, and conjugation.

1. When bacteria die, they release DNA that can be taken in by certain other bacteria. In **transformation,** a bacterial cell takes up fragments of foreign DNA (or RNA) released by another bacterium. The DNA must bind to DNA-binding proteins on the surface of the bacterium. Once it enters the bacterial cell, some of the DNA is incorporated into the host's

FIGURE 25-7 Transduction

In transduction, a phage transfers bacterial DNA from one bacterium to another, resulting in genetic recombination. Transduction is an important means of horizontal gene transfer.

① Bacterium dies and releases DNA.

② Fragments of foreign DNA bind to proteins on surface of living bacterium.

③ DNA enters cell, and some DNA is incorporated into host cell by reciprocal recombination.

DNA exchanged

FIGURE 25-6 Transformation

In transformation, foreign DNA from a bacterium that has died enters a host bacterium. Some DNA is exchanged, resulting in a recombinant cell.

own genome by reciprocal recombination (the DNA is exchanged) between the new DNA and the host chromosome (**FIG. 25-6**). Recall from Chapter 12 that Oswald T. Avery and his colleagues identified DNA as the agent that transformed bacterial cells experimentally and showed that DNA is the chemical basis of heredity.

Foreign DNA can also be taken up as plasmids. When this occurs, DNA does not undergo recombination; it remains as a plasmid separate from the bacterial chromosome.

2. In a different process of horizontal gene transfer, **transduction,** a phage carries bacterial genes from one bacterial cell into another (**FIG. 25-7**). Normally, a phage contains only its own DNA. However, sometimes a phage incorporates some of the bacterial DNA of its host. Then, when the phage infects another bacterium, it transfers that DNA to its new host. The bacterial chromosome of this new host then becomes a recombination of its own original DNA and the DNA from another bacterium.

3. In **conjugation,** two cells of different mating types come together, and genetic material is transferred from one to the other (**FIG. 25-8**). In contrast to transformation and transduction, conjugation involves contact between two cells.

Conjugation has been most extensively studied in the bacterium *Escherichia coli.* In the *E. coli* population, there are **donor cells,** or **F⁺ cells,** which have DNA that can be transmitted to **recipient cells,** or **F⁻ cells.** F⁺ cells have a DNA sequence known as the **F factor** (F stands for fertility) that is necessary for a bacterium to serve as a donor during conjugation. The F factor can be in the form of a plasmid, or it can be part of the DNA in the bacterial chromosome.

F genes encode enzymes essential for transferring DNA. Certain F genes encode **sex pili,** long, hairlike extensions that project from the cell surface. The sex pilus of an F⁺ cell recognizes and binds to the surface of an F⁻ cell, forming a cytoplasmic conjugation bridge between the two cells. The F plasmid replicates itself, and DNA is transferred from donor to recipient bacterium through the conjugation bridge. F plasmids may also have other types of genes, including those that determine resistance to antibiotics.

Evolution proceeds rapidly in bacterial populations

Because bacteria reproduce rapidly by binary fission, mutations are quickly passed on to new generations. Mutations that confer some advantage

Conjugation, a mechanism of horizontal gene transfer, results in genetic recombination.

Sex pilus

0.5 μm

© Dennis Kunkel Microscopy, Inc./Phototake/Alamy

(a) Color-enhanced SEM of *E. coli* bacteria conjugating. The bacteria are connected by a sex pilus. When stimulated by the contact, the cells pull close together and form a conjugation bridge between donor and recipient cells (*not shown*).

F⁺ (donor) cell

F⁻ (recipient) cell

Bacterial chromosome   F plasmid

1 F⁺ (donor) cell produces sex pilus.

2 Sex pilus develops into conjugation bridge.

3 Single strand of F plasmid DNA is transferred from F⁺ cell to F⁻ cell.

4 DNA replicates. Both bacterial cells now contain double-stranded F plasmid. The F⁻ cell has been converted to an F⁺ cell.

(b) The process of conjugation.

FIGURE 25-8 *Animated* **Conjugation**

In conjugation, a donor bacterium transfers plasmid DNA to a recipient bacterium. Conjugation requires cell-to-cell contact.

spread through the population, and the effects of natural selection are quickly evident.

Horizontal gene transfer greatly contributes to the rapid evolution that takes place in prokaryotes. Acquisition of new DNA and genetic recombination are important sources of the genetic variation required for diversification and adaptation. New DNA introduced into a bacterium's genome represents raw material for evolution. New genes are subject to mutation and are acted on by the forces of natural selection. The changes in the genetic material are passed to succeeding generations by binary fission. Changes that result in adaptation can quickly spread through future bacterial populations. Genetic recombination is also an important mechanism in the evolution of archaea.

Review

- How do prokaryotes reproduce? What mechanisms result in gene transfer?
- How does transduction contribute to the rapid evolution of bacterial populations?
- What are the steps that take place during conjugation?

25.3 NUTRITIONAL AND METABOLIC ADAPTATIONS

LEARNING OBJECTIVE

6   Describe the principal modes by which prokaryotes carry on nutrition and energy capture, and compare their requirements for oxygen.

Based on the *two main ways of obtaining nutrition,* prokaryotes are classified as autotrophs (*-troph* comes from a Greek word that means "nutrition") or heterotrophs. **Autotrophs** are able to use inorganic compounds, such as carbon dioxide, as a source of carbon for manufacturing their organic molecules. Most prokaryotes are **heterotrophs** that obtain carbon atoms from the organic compounds of other organisms.

Based on *two principal ways of capturing energy,* autotrophs are classified as chemotrophs and autotrophs. **Chemotrophs** obtain their energy from chemical compounds. **Phototrophs** capture energy from light. More than three billion years ago, early bacteria developed the ability to use the sun as an energy source. These early phototrophs used hydrogen sulfide to reduce carbon dioxide. They released sulfur as a waste product. About 2.7 billion years ago, the ability to use water, rather than hydrogen sulfide, to reduce carbon dioxide evolved in early cyanobacteria. Oxygen was released as a waste product. When we consider the source of carbon *and* the source of energy, we can classify prokaryotes into four main groups (**TABLE 25-1**):

1. **Photoautotrophs,** such as cyanobacteria, use the energy from sunlight to synthesize organic compounds from carbon dioxide and other inorganic compounds.
2. **Chemoautotrophs** also use carbon dioxide as a carbon source, but they do not use sunlight as their energy source. Instead, they obtain energy by oxidizing inorganic chemical substances such as ammonia (NH_3) and hydrogen sulfide (H_2S).
3. **Photoheterotrophs,** such as the purple nonsulfur bacteria, obtain their carbon from other organisms but use chlorophyll and other photosynthetic pigments to trap energy from sunlight.
4. The majority of prokaryotes are **chemoheterotrophs.** They depend on organic molecules for both their carbon and energy. Many bacterial chemoheterotrophs are free-living **decomposers** that obtain their carbon and energy from dead organic matter. These bacteria are sometimes called *saprotrophs.* Some chemoheterotrophs are pathogens, which obtain their nourishment from the organisms they infect. They harm their hosts by causing diseases. Other heterotrophic bacteria benefit their hosts. For example, some of the bacteria that inhabit the human large intestine produce vitamin K and certain B vitamins for their hosts.

Most prokaryotes require oxygen

Whether they are heterotrophs or autotrophs, most bacterial cells are **aerobic** and require oxygen for cellular respiration. Many are **facultative anaerobes** that use oxygen for cellular respiration if it is available but can carry on metabolism anaerobically when necessary. Other bacteria are **obligate anaerobes** that carry out anaerobic respiration; they respire with terminal electron acceptors other than oxygen, for example, sulfate (SO_4^{2-}), nitrate (NO_3^-), or iron (Fe^{2+}). Some obligate anaerobes, including certain archaea, are actually killed by even low concentrations of oxygen.

TABLE 25-1	Modes of Nutrition and Energy Capture		
Mode of Nutrition	Energy Source	Carbon Source	Examples of Organisms
Autotroph			
Photoautotroph	Sunlight	CO_2	Cyanobacteria; purple sulfur bacteria
Chemoautotroph	Inorganic chemicals (e.g., NH_3, H_2S, Fe^{2+})	CO_2	Certain proteobacteria; most archaea, e.g., methanogens, extreme halophiles
Heterotroph			
Photoheterotroph	Sunlight	Organic compounds	Purple and green nonsulfur bacteria
Chemoheterotroph	Organic compounds	Organic compounds	Free-living decomposers; most bacterial pathogens

Some prokaryotes fix and metabolize nitrogen

All organisms require nitrogen in order to manufacture amino acids and nucleic acids. Some bacteria (for example, certain cyanobacteria) and archaea (for example, methanogens) can reduce nitrogen in the atmosphere to ammonia. This process is called **nitrogen fixation.** Ammonia produced by nitrogen fixation is converted to ammonium ions (NH_4^+). Nitrogen-fixing bacteria can use these simple forms of nitrogen to produce organic compounds.

Certain bacteria convert ammonia or ammonium ions to nitrite (NO_2^-), and others convert nitrite to nitrate (NO_3^-). This process, called **nitrification,** converts nitrogen to a form that can be used by plants and fungi. Animals obtain nitrogen from organic compounds when they eat other organisms. As we will discuss in a later section, all other organisms ultimately depend on nitrogen fixation and nitrification by prokaryotes for their survival (see Chapter 55).

Review

- How do chemoheterotrophs obtain energy?
- How do facultative anaerobes differ from obligate anaerobes? How do they differ from aerobes?
- How do bacteria obtain nitrogen needed to produce amino acids and nucleic acids?

25.4 THE PHYLOGENY OF THE TWO PROKARYOTE DOMAINS

■ LEARNING OBJECTIVES

7 Compare characteristics of the three domains: Archaea, Bacteria, and Eukarya.
8 Distinguish between the two main groups of archaea and identify specific types of archaea belonging to each group.
9 Describe the main groups of bacteria discussed in this chapter (see Table 25-4).

Under a microscope, most prokaryotes appear rather similar in size and form. However, using sequence analysis of small subunit 16S ribosomal RNA (SSU rRNA), Carl Woese and his co-workers demonstrated that there are two fundamentally different groups of prokaryotes (see Chapter 23). Each group has **signature sequences,** regions of SSU rRNA that have unique nucleotide sequences. The explanation is that after they diverged, prokaryote populations diversified and mutations occurred that affect RNA sequences. Using such analyses, Woese hypothesized that ancient prokaryotes split into two lineages early in the history of life.

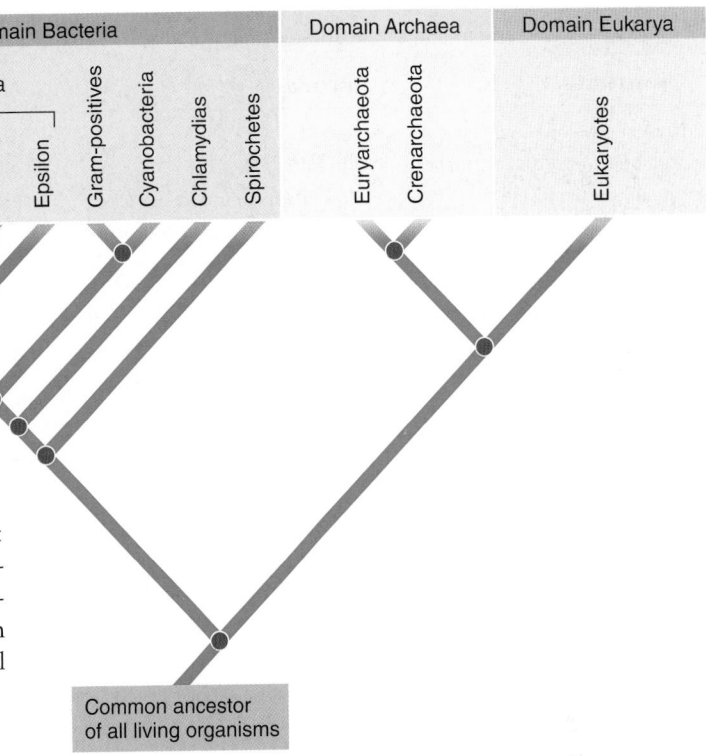

FIGURE 25-9 Three domains

This highly simplified diagram depicts some representative taxa of domain Bacteria and domain Archaea. The relationships illustrated are based on analyses of ribosomal RNA gene sequences. As taxonomists consider additional data, these relationships will be modified.

Based on Woese's work and on other recent data, systematists now classify the modern descendants of these two ancient lines in two domains: **Archaea** and **Bacteria** (**FIG. 25-9**). These groups are thought to have diverged from a common ancestor about four billion years ago. Archaea and bacteria were the only living organisms on our planet for about two billion years. Thus, archaea and bacteria have had a very long time to evolve and adapt to all types of environments. Their diversity is staggering. Horizontal gene transfer has also contributed to the diversity of these organisms. As a result of gene transfer, sometimes from distantly related species, the genomes of archaea and bacteria are actually a mix of genes from many prokaryotes.

Key characters distinguish the three domains

Several key characters distinguish archaea from bacteria. In contrast to bacteria, archaea do not have peptidoglycan in their cell walls. Although their plasma membranes are structurally similar, they are chemically unique. In the plasma membranes of bacteria and eukaryotes, straight-chain fatty acids are linked to glycerol molecules by *ester linkages*. In contrast, fatty acid components are not found in archaea. Instead, branched-chain hydrocarbons (synthesized from isoprene units) are bonded to glycerol by *ether linkages* (**TABLE 25-2**).

TABLE 25-2 Comparison of the Three Domains

Characteristic	Bacteria	Archaea	Eukarya
Nuclear envelope	Absent	Absent	Present
Membrane-enclosed organelles	Absent	Absent	Present
Circular chromosome	Present (linear in some species)	Present	Absent
Number of chromosomes	Typically one (may also have plasmid)	Typically one (may also have plasmid)	Typically many
Histones associated with DNA	Absent	Present	Present
Peptidoglycan in cell wall	Present	Absent	Absent
Structure of lipids in plasma membrane	Straight-chain fatty acids bonded to glycerol by ester linkages	Branched-chain hydrocarbons linked to glycerol by ether linkages	Straight-chain fatty acids bonded to glycerol by ester linkages
Size of ribosomes	70S*	70S	80S except in mitochondria and chloroplasts
RNA polymerase	One relatively simple RNA polymerase	One relatively complex RNA polymerase	Several relatively complex RNA polymerases
Translation	Begins with formylmethionine	Begins with methionine	Begins with methionine
Growth above 70°C	Yes	Yes	No

*The numbers 70S and 80S refer to the sedimentation coefficient (a measure of relative size) when centrifuged.

Ester linkage **Ether linkage**

The absence of a second electronegative oxygen atom makes ether linkages stronger than ester linkages. This unique membrane structure may contribute to the ability of the archaea to survive and thrive in harsh environments.

In some ways, archaea are more like eukaryotes than like bacteria. For example, archaea do not have the simple RNA polymerase found in bacteria. Like eukaryotes, their translation process begins with methionine, whereas in bacteria, translation begins with formylmethionine (see Chapter 13). In addition, several antibiotics that affect bacteria do not affect archaea or eukaryotes.

Bacteria also share some characters (that are absent in archaea) with eukaryotes. For example, as stated above, bacteria and eukarya both have ester-linked membrane lipids, whereas archaea have ether-linked membrane lipids. Some microbiologists hypothesize that eukaryotes are a product of fusion between an archaean, which contributed components for transcription and translation, and a bacterium, which contributed enzymes necessary for energy metabolism.

Taxonomy of archaea and bacteria continuously changes

Prokaryote taxonomy is now based largely on molecular data, mainly RNA sequencing, and more recently, on sequencing entire genomes. Groups that branched off earlier had more time to accumulate mutations in their SSU rRNA. Their nucleotide sequences are less similar than those of groups that diverged more recently.

Microbiologists who are developing phylogenetic trees based on sequencing entire genomes argue that there may be 1000 genes that code proteins for every 1 gene that codes an rRNA. These researchers prefer to consider the proportions of genes (or proteins) that genomes of various groups have in common. Taxonomy of archaea and bacteria continuously changes as systematists study new molecular data that provide new clues to the phylogeny of these groups.

Although prokaryotic taxonomy is controversial and continuously changing, about 7000 species of prokaryotes have been classified. Hundreds of thousands of additional species are thought to exist. The editors of *Bergey's Manual of Systematic Bacteriology*, considered the definitive reference text by microbiologists, have divided archaea into 2 phyla and bacteria into about 20 phyla based on 16S rRNA analyses.

Many archaea inhabit harsh environments

Domain Archaea consists of two major groups (phyla): *Crenarchaeota* and *Euryarchaeota* (**TABLE 25-3**). This phylogeny is based on 16S rRNA and on sequencing of entire genomes. Systematists have not yet determined whether these two groups represent phyla or higher level taxa. If they are higher level taxa, the branches of each group may represent phyla.

The **Crenarchaeota** consist mainly of extreme thermophiles, archaea that require a very high temperature or very low temperature for growth. The optimum temperature for many is greater than 80°C (176°F). These archaea inhabit very hot, sometimes acidic, environments. One species is found in the hot sulfur springs of Yellowstone Park at temperatures near 80°C and pH values of 1 to 2, the pH of concentrated sulfuric acid (**FIG. 25-10a**). Others inhabit volcanic areas under the sea. One species, found near deep-sea hydrothermal vents on the seafloor of the Pacific Ocean, lives at temperatures ranging from 80°C to 120°C. In contrast, some Crenarchaeota live in very cold environments (below 15°C).

(a) **Extreme thermophiles.** Orange and yellow colonies of extreme thermophiles thrive in the Grand Prismatic Spring in Yellowstone National Park in Wyoming, USA.

FIGURE 25-10 Archaea that inhabit extreme environments

(b) **Extreme halophiles.** These seawater evaporating ponds near San Francisco Bay are colored pink, orange, and yellow from the large number of extreme halophiles that inhabit them. The colors are a result of pigments in the cell membranes. These bacteria are harmless, and the ponds are used to produce salt commercially.

Some of these archaea drift in the ocean and are an important part of the plankton.

The **Euryarchaeota** also include many archaea that inhabit extreme environments. This group includes methanogens, extreme halophiles, and extreme thermophiles. The **methanogens** (methane producers) are a large, diverse group that inhabit oxygen-free environments in sewage, swamps, and the digestive tracts of humans and other animals. They are obligate anaerobes that produce methane gas from simple carbon compounds. The methanogens are important in recycling components of organic products of organisms that inhabit swamps. Methanogens that inhabit the digestive tracts of cows and other grazing animals produce methane, which is belched out by the animals. Methanogens produce more than 80% of the methane (more than two billion tons each year) in Earth's atmosphere. Methane is an important greenhouse gas.

Extreme halophiles are heterotrophs that require large amounts of Na^+ for their growth. They live in saturated brine solutions such as salt ponds, the Dead Sea, and Great Salt Lake (**FIG. 25-10b**). The extreme halophiles use aerobic respiration to make ATP. However, they also carry out a form of photosynthesis in which they capture the energy of sunlight using a purple pigment (*bacteriorhodopsin*). This pigment is very similar to the pigment rhodopsin involved in animal vision.

Nanoarchaeum is a very small (400 nm) anaerobic, extreme thermophile that is now classified as a euryarchaeote. This microbe is one of the smallest cellular organisms identified to date. It also has one of the smallest genomes (less than 500,000 nucleotides). *Nanoarchaeum* lives attached to another archaean and depends on its host for many of its metabolic needs.

Many archaea inhabit less extreme conditions. For example, nonextreme archaea are abundant in the soil and in the cold ocean surface waters near Antarctica. Microbiologists have suggested that the archaea may be important in biogeochemical cycles and in marine food chains. No pathogenic archaea have been identified.

Bacteria are the most familiar prokaryotes

The bacteria are widely distributed in the environment and are better known to microbiologists than are the archaea. Five major groups are considered here: proteobacteria (gram-negative), cyanobacteria (gram-negative), gram-positive bacteria, chlamydias (gram-negative), and spirochetes (gram-negative). These groups are summarized in **TABLE 25-4**.

Review

- What are two types of archaeans that inhabit extreme environments? What are methanogens?
- How do these bacteria differ (described in Table 25-4): (1) proteobacteria, (2) cyanobacteria, and (3) chlamydias?

TABLE 25-3   Two Groups of Archaea

Crenarchaeota

1 μm

Eye of Science / Photo Researchers, Inc.

Some extremely thermophilic (thrive at 70°C, and some thrive at temperatures greater than 100°C); others can live at temperatures below 15°C. Many are chemoautotrophs. Important part of plankton in cold, oxygen-rich seas.

SEM of *Pyrococcus furiosus*, an anaerobe that inhabits marine sand
This methanogen is highly resistant to heat; its optimum temperature is 100°C. *Pyrococcus* grows on sugars and small peptides, which serve as electron donors. DNA polymerase from *P. furiosus* is used in PCR (polymerase chain reaction) DNA amplification process because it is stable at high temperatures and is highly accurate.

Euryarchaeota

1 μm

Dr. Kari Lounatmaa / Science Photo Library / Photo Researchers, Inc.

Includes methanogens, halophiles (not all extreme), and acidophiles. Some extreme thermophiles included in this phylum.

TEM of a methanogen (*Methanospirillum hungatii*) undergoing cell division
Two other archaea are visible in cross section. When not dividing, these archaea are spiral shaped.

TABLE 25-4   Major Groups of Bacteria

Proteobacteria (Gram-negative)

2 μm

Science Photo Library

SEM of *Escherichia coli* colony
E. coli are Gamma Proteobacteria.

50 μm

© Phototake, Inc. / PhototakeUSA.com

SEM of fruiting body of the myxobacterium *Stigmatella aurantiaca*
Protective resting cells within the fruiting bodies are very resistant to heat and drying. Myxobacteria are Delta Proteobacteria.

A large, very diverse group of gram-negative bacteria. Based on rRNA sequences, the group is divided into five subgroups designated as alpha, beta, gamma, delta, and epsilon.

Alpha Proteobacteria
Includes many symbionts of plants and animals, and some pathogens. *Rhizobium* species live symbiotically in root nodules of legumes (e.g., beans) and convert atmospheric nitrogen to a form usable by plants (nitrogen fixation). **Rickettsias** are very small, rod-shaped bacteria. A few species are pathogenic to humans and other animals; transmitted by arthropods through bites or through contact with their excretions. Among these are typhus (transmitted by fleas and lice) and Rocky Mountain spotted fever (transmitted by ticks).

Beta Proteobacteria
Several diverse groups, including *Nitrosomonas*, which oxidizes ammonia. Pathogenic bacteria in this group include *Neisseria gonorrhoeae*, which causes gonorrhea.

Gamma Proteobacteria
Includes the **enterobacteria,** decomposers that live on decaying plant matter, pathogens, and a variety of bacteria that inhabit humans. Although *Escherichia coli* is a normal inhabitant of the animal intestinal tract, certain strains can cause moderate to severe diarrhea. One species of *Salmonella* infects food and produces a toxin that causes a form of food poisoning; another species causes typhoid fever.

Vibrios are mainly marine; some are bioluminescent. *Vibrio cholerae* causes cholera.

Pseudomonads are heterotrophs that produce nonphotosynthetic pigments; cause disease in plants and animals, including humans.

Purple sulfur bacteria are photoautotrophs that do not produce oxygen.

Delta Proteobacteria
Includes the **myxobacteria** (slime bacteria), which secrete slime and glide or creep along. When nutrients are exhausted, these bacteria aggregate into stalked, multicellular reproductive structures called fruiting bodies. Bacterial cells within the fruiting body enter a resting stage. When conditions are favorable, resting cells become active.

Epsilon Proteobacteria
A small group of bacteria that inhabit the animal digestive tract. *Helicobacter* can cause peptic ulcers.

(continued)

TABLE 25-4   Major Groups of Bacteria (continued)

Cyanobacteria (Gram-negative)

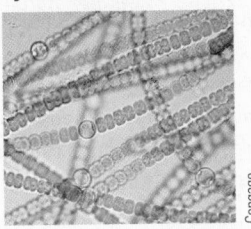

20 μm

Cengage

LM of *Anabaena,* a filamentous cyanobacterium that fixes nitrogen
Nitrogen fixation takes place in the rounded cells, called *heterocysts.*

Cyanobacteria contain chlorophyll *a* and are the only prokaryotes, which, like plants and algae, carry on photosynthesis that generates oxygen. Cyanobacteria were the first organisms that carried on oxygen-generating photosynthesis; considered very important in the evolution of life-forms because their photosynthesis changed the early reducing atmosphere on Earth to an oxidizing atmosphere. Chloroplasts are thought to have evolved from endosymbiotic cyanobacteria. Inhabit ponds, lakes, swimming pools, moist soil, dead logs, tree bark. Some form filaments; other species are solitary. As primary producers, they are an important source of food for marine and freshwater organisms. Some species have special structures that fix nitrogen.

Gram-positive Bacteria

10 μm

© David Scharf / Science Faction / Corbis

SEM of *Actinomycetes naeslundi,* a soil-dwelling bacterium that forms filamentous colonies

5 μm

© David M. Phillips / Visuals Unlimited, Inc.

SEM of *Mycoplasma* on fibroblast cells

An extremely diverse group. A few examples follow.

Actinomycetes superficially resemble fungi. However, they have peptidoglycan in their cell walls, lack nuclear envelopes, and have other prokaryotic characteristics. Most actinomycetes are saprotrophs that decompose organic materials in soil. Some are anaerobic. Several species of the genus *Streptomyces* produce antibiotics such as streptomycin, erythromycin, chloramphenicol, and the tetracyclines. Some actinomycetes cause serious lung disease and other infections in humans and other animals.

Lactic acid bacteria ferment sugar, producing lactic acid as the main end product. Inhabit decomposing plant material, milk, and other dairy products; responsible for the characteristic taste of yogurt, pickles, sauerkraut, and green olives. Among the normal inhabitants of the human mouth and vagina.

Mycobacteria are slender, irregular rods; contain a waxy substance in their cell walls. One species causes tuberculosis; another causes leprosy.

Streptococci inhabit the mouth and digestive tract of humans and some other animals. Among the harmful species are those that cause "strep throat," dental caries, a form of pneumonia, scarlet fever, and rheumatic fever (see chapter opener).

Staphylococci normally live in the nose and on skin. Opportunistic pathogens that cause disease when the immunity of the host is lowered. *Staphylococcus aureus* causes boils and skin infections (some extremely serious); may infect wounds. Certain strains of *S. aureus* cause a form of food poisoning; other strains cause toxic shock syndrome (see Fig. 25-14).

Clostridia are anaerobic. One species causes tetanus; another causes gas gangrene. *Clostridium botulinum* can cause botulism, an often fatal type of food poisoning.

The **mycoplasmas** are a group of very small bacteria that lack cell walls. They may have evolved from bacteria with gram-positive cell walls. They inhabit soil and sewage; some are parasitic on plants or animals. Some inhabit human mucous membranes but do not generally cause disease; one species causes a mild type of bacterial pneumonia in humans.

Chlamydias (Gram-negative)

1 μm

© David M. Phillips / Visuals Unlimited, Inc.

TEM of *Chlamydia trachomatis* in human oviduct cell

Chlamydias lack peptidoglycan in their cell walls. They are energy parasites, completely dependent on their hosts for ATP. Infect almost every species of bird and mammal. A strain of *Chlamydia* causes trachoma, the leading cause of blindness in the world. Sexually transmitted chlamydias are the major cause of pelvic inflammatory disease (PID) in women.

Spirochetes (Gram-negative)

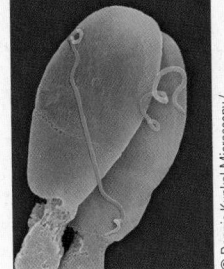

5 μm

© Dennis Kunkel Microscopy / Visuals Unlimited, Inc.

LM of *Treponema pallidum,* the spirochete that causes syphilis

Spirochetes are spiral-shaped bacteria with flexible cell walls; move by means of unique internal flagella called *axial filaments.* Some species are free-living, whereas others form symbiotic associations; a few are parasitic. The spirochete of greatest medical importance is *Treponema pallidum,* which causes syphilis.

25.5 IMPACT ON ECOLOGY, TECHNOLOGY, AND COMMERCE

LEARNING OBJECTIVES

10 Identify the critical ecological roles played by prokaryotes.
11 Describe some of the important roles played by prokaryotes in commerce and technology.

Prokaryotes inhabit virtually every environment on Earth and are vital members of the biosphere. They affect other organisms directly and by the ecological roles they play. Prokaryotes produce nitrogen in forms usable by other organisms, and they are a reservoir for nutrients. These microscopic organisms recycle nutrients and are key players in biogeochemical cycles.

Prokaryotes form intimate relationships with other organisms

Prokaryotes interact with other organisms in both beneficial and harmful ways. An intimate relationship between members of two or more species is called **symbiosis.** The partners in a symbiotic relationship are called **symbionts.** Symbiotic relationships arise by coevolution. Three forms of symbiosis are mutualism, commensalism, and parasitism.

Mutualism is a symbiotic relationship in which both partners benefit. Cows and other ruminants (cud-chewing animals) have mutualistic relationships with bacteria that inhabit their digestive tracts. Ruminants lack enzymes for digesting cellulose. They provide the bacteria with a nutrient-rich home, and the bacteria digest the cellulose for them.

Trillions of bacteria inhabit the nutrient-rich human intestine. Some of these are mutualistic bacteria. For example, in exchange for nutrients and a place to live, *Bacteroides* break down indigestible complex carbohydrates into sugars that their human host can absorb. These bacteria also produce certain vitamins that their host absorbs and uses. In addition, *Bacteroides* promote proliferation of blood vessels that improve intestinal function. Investigators have reported that these bacteria can turn on specific genes in cells of the host's intestine; apparently, they can induce synthesis of a compound that may kill competing bacteria.

In **commensalism,** one partner benefits and the other is neither harmed nor helped. Many bacteria that inhabit the human intestine are commensals that live on unused food. In **parasitism,** one partner lives on or in the other. The **parasite** benefits and the **host** is harmed. Disease-causing bacteria are usually not considered obligate parasites because these **pathogens** typically can survive in other ways.

Some types of bacteria may influence evolution of other species

The proteobacteria *Wolbachia* infect many invertebrates, including insects, spiders, crustaceans, and nematodes (roundworms). *Wolbachia* are transmitted from generation to generation in the eggs of their hosts, so male hosts are not useful to them. Consequently,

these parasites limit or eradicate males from the population. In some insect species, infected males can reproduce only when they mate with infected females carrying the same *Wolbachia* strain. In other species, these parasites convert male insects into females. In some wasp species, *Wolbachia* induces *parthenogenesis,* development of unfertilized eggs into adult organisms. Because they affect reproduction in their hosts, *Wolbachia* and other reproductive parasites may influence evolutionary divergence and even extinction in some species. *Wolbachia* may also affect evolution by horizontal gene transfer.

Many bacteria form biofilms

Many types of bacteria that inhabit watery environments form dense films called **biofilms** that attach to solid surfaces. The bacteria in a biofilm form layers up to 200 μm thick. The bacteria secrete a slimy, gluelike substance rich in polysaccharides and become embedded in this matrix. Biofilms are communities of microorganisms. Most biofilms consist of many species of bacteria and may include other types of organisms, such as archaea, fungi, and protozoa. Scientists have found evidence of ancient biofilms in sediments from coastal marine environments 3.5 billion years old.

The dental plaque that forms on teeth is a familiar example of a biofilm (**FIG. 25-11**). Dental plaque consists of several hundred different types of bacteria and archaea. Biofilms also commonly form on the surfaces of contact lenses and catheters. They sometimes develop on surgical implants such as pacemakers and joint replacements.

Prokaryotes play key ecological roles

Bacteria, especially actinomycetes and myxobacteria, are the most numerous inhabitants of soil. As described earlier in this chapter, many prokaryotes are essential decomposers, chemoheterotrophs

10 μm

FIGURE 25-11 A familiar biofilm: dental plaque
Colorized SEM of dental plaque, which consists of a film of bacteria (*red*) embedded in a matrix of glycoprotein (*blue*). Bacteria in the plaque can produce acids that erode tooth enamel, leading to tooth decay.

that break down dead organic matter and wastes. They use the products of decomposition as an energy source. When prokaryotes break down organic compounds, many of their components, including nitrogen, oxygen, carbon, phosphorus, sulfur, and certain trace elements, are recycled. (The roles of bacteria in biogeochemical cycles, particularly the nitrogen cycle, are discussed in Chapter 55.)

Nitrogen is constantly removed from the soil by plants and other natural processes, as well as by human activities, such as agriculture. Plant growth depends on the availability of usable nitrogen, so it must be continually added to the soil. Several types of bacteria, including cyanobacteria, transform atmospheric nitrogen to forms that can be used by plants (see Table 25-4). Some marine crenarchaeotes also carry on nitrification and may be important in the ocean nitrogen cycle.

Rhizobial bacteria, a type of motile bacteria that inhabit the soil, form mutualistic relationships with the roots of legumes, a large family of plants that includes important crops such as beans, peas, and peanuts. The infected plant cells form tumorlike nodules in which the bacteria reside and fix nitrogen (see Fig. 55-9). The bacteria supply the plant with the nitrogen it requires, and the plant provides the bacteria with organic compounds, including sugar needed for cellular respiration. Because many soils are deficient in nitrogen, legumes that have formed mutualistic associations with rhizobial bacteria have a decided advantage over other plants. When the legumes die and are decomposed, the fixed nitrogen is released and enriches the soil.

Many prokaryotes, such as the cyanobacteria, carry out photosynthesis, using water as the electron source and generating oxygen. During this process, they fix huge amounts of carbon dioxide into organic molecules.

Microbiologists are only beginning to unravel the mysteries of prokaryote ecology. For example, proteobacteria in the SAR11 clade are among the most successful organisms on Earth. Although they are one of the most abundant organisms in the Atlantic Ocean, they were not successfully cultured until 2002, and very little is known about their ecological role. There is some evidence that they are important in cycling carbon, nitrogen, and sulfur in the ocean.

Prokaryotes are important in many commercial processes and in technology

Some microorganisms produce *antibiotics*. These compounds limit competition for nutrients by inhibiting or destroying other microorganisms. By the 1950s, antibiotics had become important clinical tools that transformed the treatment of infectious disease. Today, about 100 clinically useful antibiotics are available, and literally tons of antibiotics are produced annually. Pharmaceutical companies obtain most antibiotics from three groups of microorganisms: a large group of gram-positive soil bacteria, the *actinomycetes*; gram-positive bacteria of the genus *Bacillus*; and molds (eukaryotes belonging to kingdom Fungi).

Because of their prolific reproduction rates, bacteria are ideal "factories" for the production of biomolecules. Microbiologists have genetically engineered bacteria to produce certain vaccines, human growth hormone, insulin, and many other clinically im-

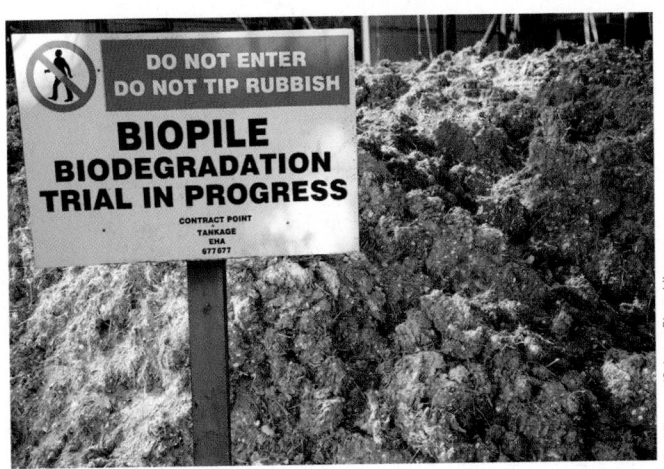

FIGURE 25-12 Bioremediation

As they feed on the gasoline and certain other waste products in contaminated soil, certain microorganisms convert hydrocarbons in these pollutants to carbon dioxide and water. Photographed at an oil refinery and chemical plant in the United Kingdom.

portant compounds (see Chapter 15). Researchers are developing genetically engineered bacteria for production of many other medically and agriculturally useful products.

Microbial fermentation helps produce many foods and beverages. Lactic acid bacteria are used in producing acidophilus milk, yogurt, pickles, olives, and sauerkraut. Several types of bacteria are used in the production of cheese. Bacteria are involved in making fermented meats such as salami and in producing vinegar, soy sauce, chocolate, certain B vitamins (B_{12} and riboflavin), and citric acid, a compound added to candy and to most soft drinks.

Bacteria are used in **bioremediation,** the process of using microorganisms (and sometimes other organisms) to detoxify or remove oil, gasoline, and other pollutants or toxic chemicals from the environment. Microorganisms break down certain toxins, leaving behind harmless metabolic byproducts such as carbon dioxide and chlorides (**FIG. 25-12**). More than 1000 different species of bacteria and fungi have been used to clean up various forms of pollution, and microbiologists are searching for others. For example, bacteria and other microorganisms are used in oil spills to break down oil, oxidizing it to CO_2. Microorganisms are also used in sewage treatment and to break down solid wastes in landfills.

Archaea are also economically important. Archaea that are adapted to high temperatures or extremely acidic conditions, for example, are a source of enzymes that can be used under these extreme conditions. Archaeal enzymes have been added to laundry and industrial detergents to increase their performance at higher temperatures and pH levels. Another archaeal enzyme has been useful in the food industry to convert cornstarch to dextrins.

Review

- In what ways do bacteria form relationships with other organisms?
- What is the composition of a biofilm?
- What are three ways that prokaryotes are ecologically important?
- What is bioremediation?

25.6 BACTERIA AND DISEASE

Some prokaryote species have coevolved with eukaryotes and are interdependent with them. All plants and animals harbor a population of microorganisms that are considered normal **microbiota** (also referred to as microflora)—harmless symbiotic prokaryotes. An estimated 700 trillion bacteria normally inhabit the human body! This number greatly exceeds the number of the body's own cells (about 70 trillion). The presence of certain bacterial populations prevents harmful microorganisms (including other bacteria) from flourishing.

A small percentage of bacterial species are important pathogens of plants and animals. Some of the normal bacterial inhabitants are opportunistic pathogens that cause disease only under certain conditions. For example, when the immune system is compromised, opportunistic bacteria increase in number and cause disease. Some important bacterial diseases and the pathogens that cause them are listed in **TABLE 25-5**. To date, no archaea have been shown to cause specific diseases.

Many scientists have contributed to our understanding of infectious disease

The idea that some unknown agent caused disease was debated long before Leeuwenhoek discovered microorganisms with his microscope in the late 1600s. However, not until much later did scientists develop the tools or the methods needed to accurately understand the relationships between bacteria and disease. During the late 19th century, several physicians, microbiologists, and chemists working independently laid the foundations for the science of microbiology. French chemist Louis Pasteur disproved the prevailing views of spontaneous generation by demonstrating that sterilization of a sugar and protein culture prevented bacterial growth. Pasteur also developed a rabies vaccine, showing that people can be stimulated to develop immunity to disease.

The German physician Robert Koch was the first to clearly demonstrate that bacteria cause infectious disease. In 1876, he showed that *Bacillus anthracis* caused anthrax. Using a microscope, Koch observed the bacteria in the blood and spleens of dead sheep. When he inoculated mice with the infected sheep blood, he was able to identify *B. anthracis* in the blood of the mice. He also cultured *B. anthracis* and showed that when he injected the bacteria into healthy mice they developed anthrax.

Koch proposed a set of guidelines, now known as **Koch's postulates,** that are still used to demonstrate that a specific pathogen causes specific disease symptoms: (1) the pathogen must be present in every individual with the disease, (2) a sample of the microorganism taken from the diseased host can be grown in pure culture, (3) a sample of the pure culture causes the same disease when injected into a healthy host, and (4) the microorganism can be recovered from the experimentally infected host.

Many adaptations contribute to pathogen success

Pathogenic microorganisms can enter the body in food, dust, or droplets or through wounds. Many diseases are transmitted by insect or animal bites. To cause disease, a pathogen must adhere to a specific cell type, multiply, and produce toxic substances. Adherence and multiplication occur only when the pathogen competes successfully with the normal microbiota and counteracts the host's defenses against invasion.

Helicobacter pylori, the most common cause of peptic ulcers (ulcers of the stomach and duodenum), is an extremely successful pathogen (**FIG. 25-13**). It is also associated with chronic gastritis (stomach inflammation) and with stomach cancer, the second most common type of cancer in the world. *Helicobacter pylori* inhabits the intestinal tracts of an estimated 40% of adults in developed countries and 80% of adults in developing countries. Among its many adaptations is its ability to produce an alkaline shield around itself that protects it from stomach acid. Also contributing

2 μm

(a) SEM of *Helicobacter pylori* attached to the epithelial lining of the stomach.

FIGURE 25-13 *Helicobacter pylori* **causes peptic ulcers**

TABLE 25-5   Important Bacterial Diseases and Their Causative Agents

Disease	Pathogen	Epidemiology/Comments
Anthrax	*Bacillus anthracis*	Most commonly occurs in domestic animals such as cattle. Can be transmitted to humans from infected animals or animal products. Endospores can live in soil for many years. Anthrax is not spread from person to person. Infection can occur in three forms: cutaneous, by inhalation, and gastrointestinal.
Botulism	*Clostridium botulinum*	Contracted by eating foods that contain the endotoxin or from infected wound. Infant botulism is caused by ingesting endospores. Causes muscle paralysis and can cause death from respiratory failure.
Chlamydia	*Chlamydia trachomatis*	One of the most frequently reported sexually transmitted diseases in the U.S. About 75% of infected women and 50% of infected men have no symptoms. If untreated, the infection spreads and damages reproductive organs; can lead to infertility. This pathogen can also infect eyes and causes millions of cases of blindness worldwide each year.
Cholera	*Vibrio cholerae*	Contracted by eating food or drinking water contaminated with the bacterium. Common in areas with inadequate sewage treatment and impure water. Infects intestine and can cause severe diarrhea. Rapid fluid loss can lead to dehydration and death.
Diphtheria	*Corynebacterium diphtheriae*	Transmitted from person to person by intimate respiratory and physical contact. Endemic in developing countries. Not common in U.S. since vaccine became available in 1920s. Infects the heart muscle and respiratory passageways.
Epidemic typhus	*Rickettsia prowazekii*	Transmitted by infected body lice. After an 8- to 12-day incubation period, symptoms include fever, severe headache, muscle aches, and chills. Several days later a rash appears. About 40% of untreated patients die.
Gonorrhea	*Neisseria gonorrhoeae*	Common sexually transmitted disease.
Hansen disease (leprosy)	*Mycobacterium leprae*	Thought to be spread from person to person in nasal secretions. Worldwide, this disease has disabled up to 2 million people. Typically affects the skin, nerves, and mucous membranes.
Lyme disease	*Borrelia burgdorferi*	Transmitted to humans by bite of infected blacklegged ticks. Symptoms include skin rash, headache, fever, and fatigue. If untreated, infection can spread to joints, heart, and nervous system.
Peptic ulcer disease	*Helicobacter pylori*	Causes peptic ulcer, a lesion in the lining of the stomach or duodenum (upper part of small intestine).
Pertussis (whooping cough)	*Bordetella pertussis*	Highly communicable from person to person. Causes spasms of severe coughing. Vaccination available.
Plague	*Yersinia pestis*	Transmitted from wild rodents, squirrels, and cats to people by infected fleas. If untreated, can cause death. Killed millions of people in Europe during the Middle Ages.
Pneumonia	*Streptococcus pneumoniae*	Transmitted from person to person. Strains of *S. pneumoniae* are resistant to one or more antibiotics commonly used to treat this infection. Incidence has decreased since introduction of a vaccine.
Salmonella (salmonellosis)	*Salmonella* sp.	Transmitted to people in contaminated chicken, eggs, or other food. Also transmitted from feces of infected animals, e.g., lizards, turtles, chicks, birds, even dogs and cats. Symptoms include fever, diarrhea, and stomach pain.
Tetanus	*Clostridium tetani*	Bacteria enter the body through a wound in the skin. Affects the nervous system; causes lockjaw, stiffness in neck, difficulty swallowing, fever, and muscle spasms. Vaccination available.
Travelers' diarrhea	*Escherichia coli* is most common cause	Ingested in contaminated food and water. From 30% to 50% of travelers to high-risk areas (Central and South America, Africa, Middle East, and most of Asia) develop travelers' diarrhea. The infecting bacteria produce toxins in GI tract.
Syphilis	*Treponema pallidum*	Sexually transmitted disease passed through direct contact with a syphilis sore. If untreated, eventually damages brain, liver, bone, and spleen and can cause death.
Tuberculosis	*Mycobacterium tuberculosis*	Transmitted from person to person through inhalation of air containing the pathogen. Symptoms include fatigue, cough, fever, weight loss. Not common in U.S. However, multidrug-resistant form is a growing threat.
Typhoid fever	*Salmonella typhi*	Transmitted from person to person in food or water contaminated with feces. Risk greatest for travelers in developing countries, but vaccine available. Symptoms include high fever, headache, and loss of appetite. Can cause death if not treated.

to its success are several powerful flagella used to propel the pathogen through the thick mucus lining the stomach.

Pathogens produce a variety of substances that increase their success. Some bacteria produce **exotoxins,** strong poisons that are either secreted from the cell or leak out when the bacterial cell is destroyed. The toxin, not the presence of the bacteria themselves, is responsible for the disease. Diphtheria is caused by a gram-positive bacillus (*Corynebacterium diphtheriae*) that produces a toxin only when lysogenized by a phage. The diphtheria toxin kills cells and causes inflammation.

Botulism, a type of food poisoning that can lead to paralysis and sometimes death, results from eating improperly canned food. Botulism is caused by an exotoxin released by the gram-positive, endospore-forming *Clostridium botulinum*. During the canning process, food must be heated sufficiently to kill any highly heat-resistant endospores that may be present. If not, the endospores can germinate. The resulting bacterial population grows and releases an exotoxin so powerful that 1 g could kill a million humans! Like many exotoxins, the one that causes botulism is inactivated by heating. (Food must be heated to 80°C for 10 minutes, or boiled for 3 to 4 minutes.)

The botulism exotoxin, marketed under the trade name Botox, is used in extremely tiny amounts to treat several medical conditions involving spasms (involuntary muscle contractions). Because Botox is a neurotoxin that works by paralyzing muscles, it can also relax facial wrinkles caused by contraction of the underlying muscles. However, its effects last for only three to eight months.

Endotoxins are not secreted by pathogens but are components of the cell walls of most gram-negative bacteria. These compounds affect the host only when they are released from dead bacteria. Endotoxins bind to the host's macrophages (large phagocytic cells of the immune system) and stimulate them to release substances that cause fever and other symptoms of infection. Unlike exotoxins, which cause specific symptoms, endotoxins appear to affect the entire body. Endotoxins are not destroyed by heating.

Antibiotic resistance is a major public health problem

Bacteria mutate frequently and reproduce rapidly. Many antibiotics target protein synthesis in bacteria. For example, streptomycin and related antibiotics block the initiation of protein synthesis. The tetracyclines block aminoacyl tRNA from binding to the A site on the ribosome.

Drug resistance may result from an accumulation of mutations in plasmid or chromosomal DNA. Plasmids that have genes for antibiotic resistance are called **R factors.** They have genes for resistance to a specific drug and for transferring the resistance to other bacteria. Some R factors have several genes for drug resistance, each encoding resistance to a different drug.

Methicillin-resistant *Staphylococcus aureus* (SA), referred to as **MRSA,** and vancomycin-resistant *Staphylococcus aureus,* or **VRSA,** have been directly linked to the horizontal transfer of antibiotic resistance genes by plasmids during conjugation. An estimated 1 in every 100 healthy people in the United States now carries MRSA (**FIG. 25-14**). This "superbug" can cause infection in individuals with compromised immune systems. The Centers for Disease Control estimates that MRSA causes more than 90,000 serious infections each year, resulting in more than 17,000 deaths annually.

Overuse of antibiotics is the principal contributing factor to drug resistance. In any bacterial population, there are likely at least

Janice Haney Carr/CDC

1 μm

FIGURE 25-14 Colorized SEM of methicillin resistant *Staphylococcus aureus* (MRSA). These bacteria also show increased resistance to vancomycin.

a few bacteria that are genetically resistant to a particular antibiotic. The bacteria that are *not* resistant are killed by the antibiotic, leaving the resistant bacteria to multiply and produce a resistant population. Note that this is a common, present-day example of natural selection.

Another type of drug resistance explains why some infections, for example, urinary tract infections, are difficult to cure. When *E. coli* infect the bladder, the immune system launches a powerful defense. The bacteria subvert the attack by forming *biofilms* (discussed earlier in this chapter). Each biofilm is surrounded by a matrix rich in polysaccharides and by a protective shell. The bacteria in the biofilm are resistant to antibiotics, as well as to host defenses. By one estimate, bacteria growing in a biofilm are up to 1000 times as resistant to antibiotics as are the same type of bacteria that have not formed a biofilm. Within biofilms, differential gene expression and mutation lead to diverse bacterial colonies. The biofilm strategy also explains some other types of chronic or recurrent infections. A high percentage of infections acquired in hospitals involve biofilms.

Review

- What important roles do prokaryotes play in ecosystems?
- Why is each of Koch's postulates essential?

■ SUMMARY: FOCUS ON LEARNING OBJECTIVES

25.1 *(page 518)*

1 Describe the structure and common shapes of prokaryotic cells.

- Prokaryotic cells are very small and do not have membrane-enclosed organelles such as nuclei and mitochondria.
- Prokaryotic cells have several common shapes: spherical (**cocci**), rod-shaped (**bacilli**), and spiral. Spiral bacteria include the **spirillum,** which is a rigid helix, and **spirochete,** which is a flexible helix.

2 Contrast the bacterial cell wall in gram-positive and gram-negative bacteria.

- Most bacteria have **cell walls** composed of **peptidoglycan.** The walls of **gram-positive** bacteria are very thick and consist mainly of peptidoglycan. The cell walls of **gram-negative** bacteria consist of a thin peptidoglycan layer and an outer membrane resembling the plasma membrane. Some species of bacteria produce a **capsule** or **slime layer** that surrounds the cell wall.

- Some prokaryotes have hairlike appendages called **fimbriae. Pili** also extend from the surface of some prokaryotes. Both fimbriae and pili help cells adhere to one another or to certain other surfaces, including cells they infect.

3 Describe movement in prokaryotes, and describe the structure of the bacterial flagellum.

- Bacterial **flagella** are structurally different from eukaryotic flagella; each flagellum consists of a basal body, hook, and filament. They produce a rotary motion.

CENGAGENOW™ Learn more about the structure of prokaryotes and their cell walls by clicking on the figures in CengageNOW.

25.2 (page 521)

4 Describe asexual reproduction in prokaryotes and summarize three mechanisms (transformation, transduction, and conjugation) that may lead to genetic recombination.

- The genetic material of a bacterium typically consists of a circular DNA molecule and one or more **plasmids,** smaller circular fragments of DNA.

- Prokaryotes reproduce asexually by **binary fission** (the cell divides, forming two cells), **budding** (a bud forms and separates from the mother cell), or **fragmentation** (walls form inside the cell, which then separates into several cells).

- In bacteria, genetic material can be exchanged by transformation, transduction, or conjugation. In **transformation,** a bacterial cell takes in DNA fragments released by another cell. In **transduction,** a phage carries bacterial DNA from one bacterial cell into another. In **conjugation,** a donor bacterium transfers plasmid DNA to a recipient bacterium.

CENGAGENOW™ Watch conjugation by clicking on the figure in CengageNOW.

5 State specific factors that contribute to the rapid evolution of bacteria.

- Rapid reproduction ensures that mutations are rapidly passed to new generations. Horizontal gene transfer—by transformation, transduction, and conjugation—contributes to rapid evolution in bacteria.

25.3 (page 524)

6 Describe the principal modes by which prokaryotes carry on nutrition and energy capture, and compare their requirements for oxygen.

- Most prokaryotes are **heterotrophs** that obtain carbon from other organisms; some are **autotrophs** that make their own organic molecules from simple raw materials.

- **Chemotrophs** obtain energy from chemical compounds; **phototrophs** capture energy from light.

- Autotrophs may be **photoautotrophs,** which obtain energy from sunlight, or **chemoautotrophs,** which obtain energy by oxidizing inorganic chemicals such as ammonia.

- **Photoheterotrophs** obtain carbon from other organisms but use chlorophyll and other photosynthetic pigments to trap energy from sunlight. The majority of bacteria are **chemoheterotrophs.** They are mainly free-living **decomposers** that obtain both carbon and energy from dead organic matter.

- Most bacteria are **aerobic,** that is, they require oxygen for cellular respiration. Some prokaryotes are **facultative anaerobes** that metabolize anaerobically when necessary; others are **obligate anaerobes** that can carry on metabolism *only* anaerobically.

- Some bacteria carry on **nitrogen fixation**—that is, they reduce nitrogen in the atmosphere to ammonia. Other bacteria convert ammonia to nitrite or nitrate, a process called **nitrification.**

25.4 (page 525)

7 Compare characteristics of the three domains: Archaea, Bacteria, and Eukarya.

- Prokaryotes are assigned to domain **Archaea** and domain **Bacteria.**

- Unlike those of bacteria, the cell walls of archaea do not have peptidoglycan. The translational mechanisms of eukaryotes more closely resemble those of archaea than those of bacteria.

8 Distinguish between the two main groups of archaea and identify specific types of archaea belonging to each group.

- The **Crenarchaeota** consist mainly of **extreme thermophiles,** archaea that can inhabit very hot, sometimes acidic, environments. **Euryarchaeota** include methanogens, extreme halophiles, and some extreme thermophiles. **Methanogens** are obligate anaerobes that produce methane gas from simple carbon compounds. **Extreme halophiles** inhabit saturated salt solutions.

9 Describe the main groups of bacteria discussed in this chapter.

- Major groups of bacteria include proteobacteria (gram-negative), cyanobacteria (gram-negative), gram-positive bacteria, chlamydias (gram-negative), and spirochetes (gram-negative) (see Table 25-4).

25.5 (page 530)

10 Identify the critical ecological roles played by prokaryotes.

- Many bacteria are symbiotic with other organisms. **Mutualism** is a symbiotic relationship in which both partners benefit. In **commensalism,** one partner benefits and the other is neither harmed nor helped. In **parasitism,** the **parasite** benefits and the **host** is harmed. Bacterial **pathogens** cause disease, but are usually not considered obligate parasites. Many bacteria form **biofilms,** dense communities of bacteria and other microorganisms.

- Prokaryotes play essential ecological roles as decomposers and are important in recycling nitrogen and other nutrients. Some prokaryotes carry out photosynthesis.

11 Describe some of the important roles played by prokaryotes in commerce and technology.

- Some bacteria produce antibiotics. We have developed the technology for using certain bacteria to produce vaccines, insulin, and other important compounds. We use bacteria in the production of many foods, including cheese, yogurt, vinegar, and chocolate. We also use microbes in sewage treatment and in bioremediation.

25.6 (page 532)

12 Describe the roles played by Louis Pasteur and Robert Koch in understanding infectious disease; list Koch's postulates.

- Louis Pasteur demonstrated that sterilization prevented bacterial growth. **Koch's postulates** are a set of guidelines developed by Robert Koch to demonstrate that a specific pathogen causes specific disease symptoms: (1) the pathogen must be present in every individual with the disease, (2) a sample of the microorganism taken from the diseased host can be grown in pure culture, (3) a sample of the pure culture causes the same disease when injected into a healthy host, and (4) the microorganism can be recovered from the experimentally infected host.

13 Identify adaptations that have contributed to pathogen success.

- Some pathogenic bacteria release strong poisons called **exotoxins;** others produce **endotoxins,** poisonous components of their cell walls that are released when bacteria die. Many bacteria have become resistant to antibiotics. Plasmids that have genes for antibiotic resistance are called **R factors.** See Table 25-5 for a description of some pathogenic bacteria.

1. Peptidoglycan is a chemical compound found in the cell walls of (a) most viroids (b) most archaea (c) all prokaryotes (d) most bacteria (e) most eukarya

2. Bacterial flagella (a) are homologous with eukaryotic flagella (b) exhibit a rotary motion (c) consist of a basal body and nine pairs of microtubules (d) are important in transduction (e) are characteristic of gram-positive bacteria

3. Endospores (a) are formed by some viruses (b) are extremely durable cells (c) are comparable to the reproductive spores of fungi and plants (d) cause fever and other symptoms in the host (e) are extremely vulnerable to infection by phages

4. In conjugation (a) two bacterial cells of different mating types come together, and genetic material is transferred from one to another (b) a bacterial cell develops a bulge that enlarges and eventually separates from the mother cell (c) fragments of DNA released by a broken cell are taken in by another bacterial cell (d) a phage carries bacterial genes from one bacterial cell into another (e) walls develop in the cell, which then divides into several new cells

5. The majority of heterotrophic bacteria are (a) free-living chemoheterotrophs (b) photoautotrophs (c) chemoautotrophs (d) facultative anaerobes (e) obligate anaerobes

6. Bacteria that are autotrophs (a) do not require atmospheric oxygen for cellular respiration (b) must obtain organic compounds from other organisms (c) manufacture their own organic molecules from simple raw materials (d) get their nourishment from dead organisms (e) produce endospores when oxygen levels are too low for active growth

7. Bacteria that thrive in puncture wounds are likely to be (a) chemoheterotrophs (b) photoautotrophs (c) chemoautotrophs (d) endospores (e) obligate anaerobes

8. Which of the following do *not* belong to domain Archaea? (a) prokaryotes that produce methane from carbon dioxide and hydrogen (b) thermophiles (c) halophiles (d) bacteriophages (e) prokaryotes with cell walls that lack peptidoglycan

9. Rhizobial bacteria (a) are used in the production of yogurt (b) produce antibiotics (c) cause peptic ulcers (d) are the pathogens that cause syphilis (e) form mutualistic relationships with the roots of legumes and fix nitrogen

10. Robert Koch (a) proposed a set of guidelines to demonstrate that a specific pathogen causes specific disease symptoms (b) discovered *Helicobacter* (c) discovered microorganisms in the late 1600s (d) disproved spontaneous generation (e) demonstrated that people can be stimulated to develop immunity to disease

11. Which group of bacteria contains the gram-positive, anaerobic bacterium that causes botulism? (a) clostridia (b) actinomycetes (c) enterobacteria (d) spirochetes (e) streptococci

12. Label the diagram using Figure 25-2 to check your answers.

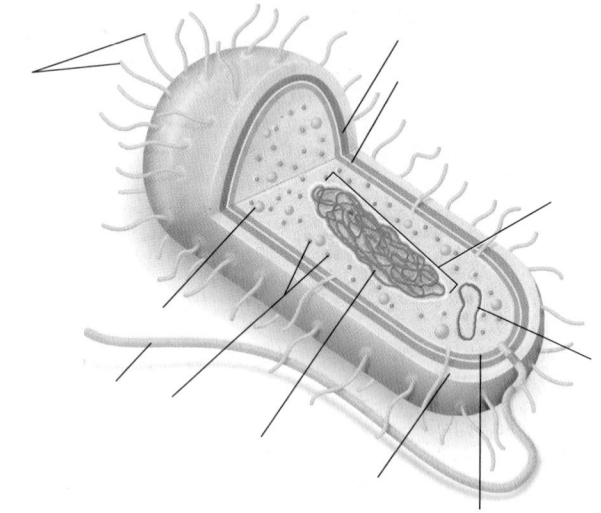

1. Imagine that you discover a new microorganism. After careful study you determine that it should be classified in domain Archaea. What characteristics might lead you to this decision?

2. In what ways would life on Earth be affected if all prokaryotes suddenly became extinct?

3. **SCIENCE, TECHNOLOGY, AND SOCIETY.** The Centers for Disease Control (CDC) considers antibiotic resistance to be one of the world's most pressing health problems. What factors are contributing to this problem?

4. **EVOLUTION LINK.** In what way does the use of antibiotics impose selective pressure on bacteria?

 Additional questions are available in CengageNOW at www.cengage.com/login.

26 Protists

Light micrograph (LM) of a marine diatom. The widely distributed diatom *Guinardia striata* forms colonies composed of spiraling chains of cells.

Wim van Egmond/Visuals Unlimited, Inc.

Protists are an informal group of primarily aquatic eukaryotic organisms with diverse body forms, types of reproduction, modes of nutrition, and lifestyles. Protists, which include algae, water molds, slime molds, and protozoa, are unicellular, colonial, or simple multicellular organisms that have a eukaryotic cell organization (see photograph). The word *protist,* from the Greek for "the very first," reflects the idea that protists were the first eukaryotes to evolve.

Protists are members of domain Eukarya, the third domain on the tree of life. (Recall the three domains depicted in Figure 23-2.) Eukaryotic cells are characteristic of protists as well as of complex multicellular organisms belonging to the kingdoms Fungi, Animalia, and Plantae. However, having a eukaryotic cell structure clearly differentiates protists from members of the prokaryotic domains Bacteria and Archaea. Recall from Chapter 4 that unlike prokaryotic cells, eukaryotic cells have nuclei and other membrane-enclosed organelles such as mitochondria and plastids, 9 + 2 flagella, and multiple chromosomes in which DNA and proteins form a complex called chromatin. Sexual reproduction, meiosis, and mitosis are also characteristic of eukaryotes.

Until recently, all protists were classified as the kingdom Protista, but this classification was by default: protists included any eukaryotes that were not land plants, fungi, or animals. Based largely on recent molecular data that have clarified many evolutionary relationships among eukaryotes, kingdom Protista is no longer a recognized clade. Although we have made great progress in understanding the evolutionary relationships among protists, many relationships remain uncertain.

Biologists currently recognize dozens of protist taxa, which, along with other eukaryotes, are classified into five "supergroups." Consideration of all protist taxa is beyond the scope of this text, but we discuss several representative examples of each supergroup and provide insights into how such diverse eukaryotes may have evolved.

26.1 DIVERSITY IN THE PROTISTS

■ LEARNING OBJECTIVE

1 Discuss in general terms the diversity inherent in protists, including means of locomotion, modes of nutrition, interactions with other organisms, habitats, and modes of reproduction.

Because of their huge numbers, protists are crucial to the natural balance of the living world. Protists are an important source of food for other organisms, and photosynthetic protists supply oxygen to aquatic and terrestrial ecosystems. Certain protists are economically important, and others cause devastating diseases such as malaria.

Body plan varies considerably among protists. Most protists are **unicellular,** with each cell forming a complete organism capable of performing all the functions characteristic of life. Some protists form **colonies,** loosely connected groups of cells; some are **coenocytic,** consisting of a multinucleate mass of cytoplasm; and some are **multicellular,** composed of many cells. Unlike the eukaryotic animals, plants, and many fungi, most multicellular protists have relatively simple body forms without specialized tissues.

Size and structural complexity are not the only variable features of protists. During the course of their long evolutionary history, protists have evolved diversity in their means of locomotion, ways of obtaining nutrients, interactions with other organisms, habitats, and modes of reproduction.

Protists, most of which are motile at some point in their life cycle, have various means of locomotion. Some move by pushing out cytoplasmic extensions (*pseudopodia*) along the leading edge and retracting the cytoplasm that trails behind, as an amoeba does. Other protists move by flexing individual cells; by gliding over surfaces; by waving *cilia,* short, hairlike organelles; or by lashing *flagella,* long, whiplike organelles. Some protists have two or more means of locomotion—for example, both flagella and pseudopodia.

Methods of obtaining nutrients differ widely among protists. Most algae are autotrophic and photosynthesize as plants do (**FIG. 26-1a**). Some heterotrophic protists obtain their nutrients by absorption, as fungi do, whereas others resemble animals in that they ingest food. Some protists switch their modes of nutrition and are autotrophic at certain times and heterotrophic at others.

Although many protists are free-living, others form stable symbiotic associations with unrelated organisms. These intimate associations range from **mutualism,** a more or less equal partnership where both partners benefit; to **commensalism,** where one partner benefits and the other is unaffected; to **parasitism,** where one partner (the parasite) lives on or in another (the host) and metabolically depends on it (see Chapter 54). Some parasitic protists are important *pathogens* (disease-causing agents) of plants or animals. Throughout this chapter, we describe specific examples of symbiotic associations involving protists.

Most protists are aquatic and live in the ocean or in freshwater streams, lakes, and ponds (**FIG. 26-1b**). They make up most of the **plankton,** the floating, often microscopic organisms that inhabit

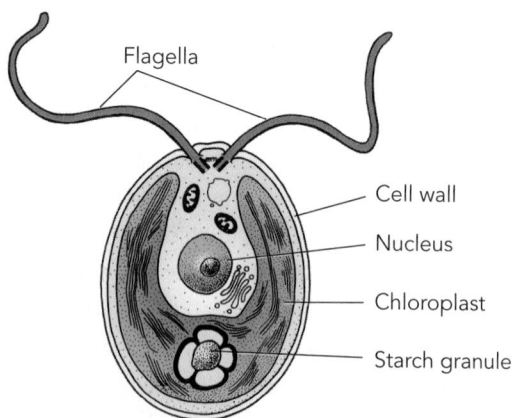

(a) *Chlamydomonas* is a photosynthetic organism with two flagella and a cup-shaped chloroplast.

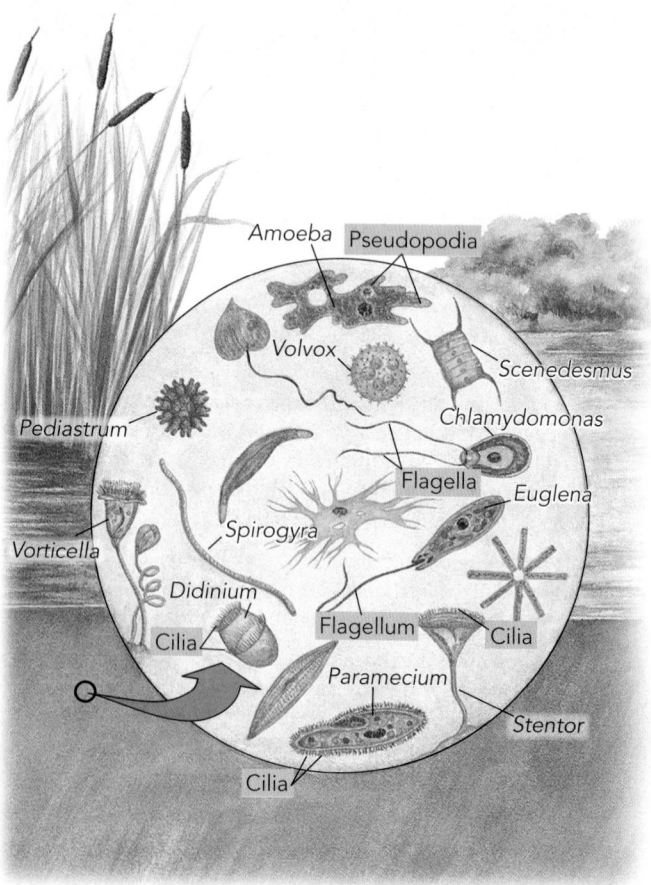

(b) Protists in a drop of pond water. Several modes of locomotion are shown.

FIGURE 26-1 Protists

surface waters and are the base of the food web in aquatic ecosystems. Other aquatic protists attach to rocks or other surfaces in the water. Even parasitic protists are aquatic because they live in the watery environments of other organisms' body fluids. Terrestrial protists are restricted to damp places such as soil, cracks in bark, and leaf litter.

Reproduction is varied among protists. Almost all protists reproduce asexually, and many also reproduce sexually. However, most protists do not develop multicellular reproductive organs, nor do they form embryos the way more complex organisms do.

Review

- How do protists vary in their means of obtaining nutrients?
- What are some of the ways protists interact with other organisms?

26.2 HOW DID EUKARYOTES EVOLVE?

▪ LEARNING OBJECTIVES

2 Discuss the hypothesis of serial endosymbiosis and briefly explain some of the evidence that supports it.

3 Describe the kinds of data biologists use to classify eukaryotes.

For many years biologists have hypothesized that protists were the first eukaryotic cells and that they evolved from ancestral prokaryotes. However, the more we study eukaryote origins, the more uncertain we are. One thing we can say with absolute certainty is that the evolution of eukaryotes was a complex process.

Eukaryotes may have appeared in the fossil record as early as 2.2 billion years ago. Other than a few protists with hard shells, such as diatoms and forams, most ancient protists did not leave many fossils because their bodies were too soft to leave permanent traces. Evolutionary studies of protists focus primarily on molecular and structural comparisons of present-day organisms, which contain many clues about their evolutionary history.

Mitochondria and chloroplasts probably originated from endosymbionts

Throughout evolutionary history, one organism has engulfed another to the mutual benefit of both. According to the hypothesis of **serial endosymbiosis,** certain eukaryotic organelles, particularly mitochondria and chloroplasts, arose from symbiotic relationships between larger cells and smaller bacteria that were incorporated and lived within them. (You might want to review serial endosymbiosis in Figure 21-8.) Cell biologists hypothesize that mitochondria originated from aerobic bacteria. Studies of mitochondrial DNA suggest it is a remnant from the mitochondrion's past, when it was an independent organism. Ribosomal RNA (rRNA) sequences from mitochondria closely match rRNAs found in purple bacteria, suggesting that ancient purple bacteria were the ancestors of mitochondria.

Chloroplast evolution is more complex, given that there were probably several endosymbiotic events (**FIG. 26-2**). Molecular evidence supports the view that incorporation of an ancient cyanobacterium within a host cell, known as *primary endosymbiosis,* resulted in the chloroplasts in today's red algae, green algae, and land plants. (The host cell was eukaryotic because mitochondria almost certainly evolved before chloroplasts.) Biologists hypothesize that these chloroplasts, which are enclosed by two external membranes, later provided other eukaryotes with their chloroplasts during *secondary endosymbiosis.*

Secondary endosymbiosis occurred frequently in eukaryote evolution, as evidenced by the presence of additional chloroplast membranes. For example, *three* membranes envelop the chloroplasts of euglenoids and dinoflagellates, and *four* membranes surround the chloroplasts of diatoms, golden algae, and brown algae. Understanding how these membranes originated is an essential aspect of serial endosymbiosis, and many researchers are studying the origin of chloroplasts in different organisms.

Even nonphotosynthetic protists may contain chloroplast relics from secondary endosymbiotic events. Apicomplexans—protists such as *Plasmodium*, which causes malaria—have a nonfunctional chloroplast surrounded by four membranes. Some researchers hypothesize that drugs that inhibit chloroplasts may also kill *Plasmodium*. This nonfunctional chloroplast, which is probably derived from a dinoflagellate, may have some medical potential in treating malaria.

A consensus in eukaryote classification is beginning to emerge

Scientists re-evaluate evolutionary relationships among the eukaryotes as additional evidence becomes available. Two types of modern research, molecular analysis and ultrastructural studies, have contributed substantially to scientific understanding of the phylogenetic relationships among protists. Molecular data were initially obtained for the gene that codes for small subunit ribosomal RNA in different eukaryotes (SSU rRNA; see Chapter 25). More recently, biologists have compared other nuclear genes, many of which code for proteins, in different protist taxa.

Ultrastructure is the fine details of cell structure revealed by electron microscopy. In many cases, ultrastructure data complement molecular data. Electron microscopy reveals similar structural patterns among those protist taxa that comparative molecular evidence suggests are **monophyletic**—that is, evolved from a common ancestor (see Chapter 23). For example, molecular and ultrastructure data suggest that water molds, diatoms, golden algae, and brown algae—protist taxa that at first glance seem to share few characteristics—are a monophyletic group.

Given the diversity in protist ultrastructure and molecular data, biologists regard the protists as a **paraphyletic group**—that is, protists contain some, but not all, of the descendants of a common eukaryote ancestor. Molecular and ultrastructural analyses continue to help biologists clarify relationships among the various protist phyla and among protists and the other eukaryotic kingdoms.

Biologists use these data to develop various classification schemes. A current scheme, which we have adopted in this edition, splits the protists and other eukaryotes (land plants, fungi, and animal) into five informal supergroups (**FIG. 26-3** and **TABLE 26-1**). This

Scientists hypothesize that plastids have evolved through both primary and secondary endosymbiosis.

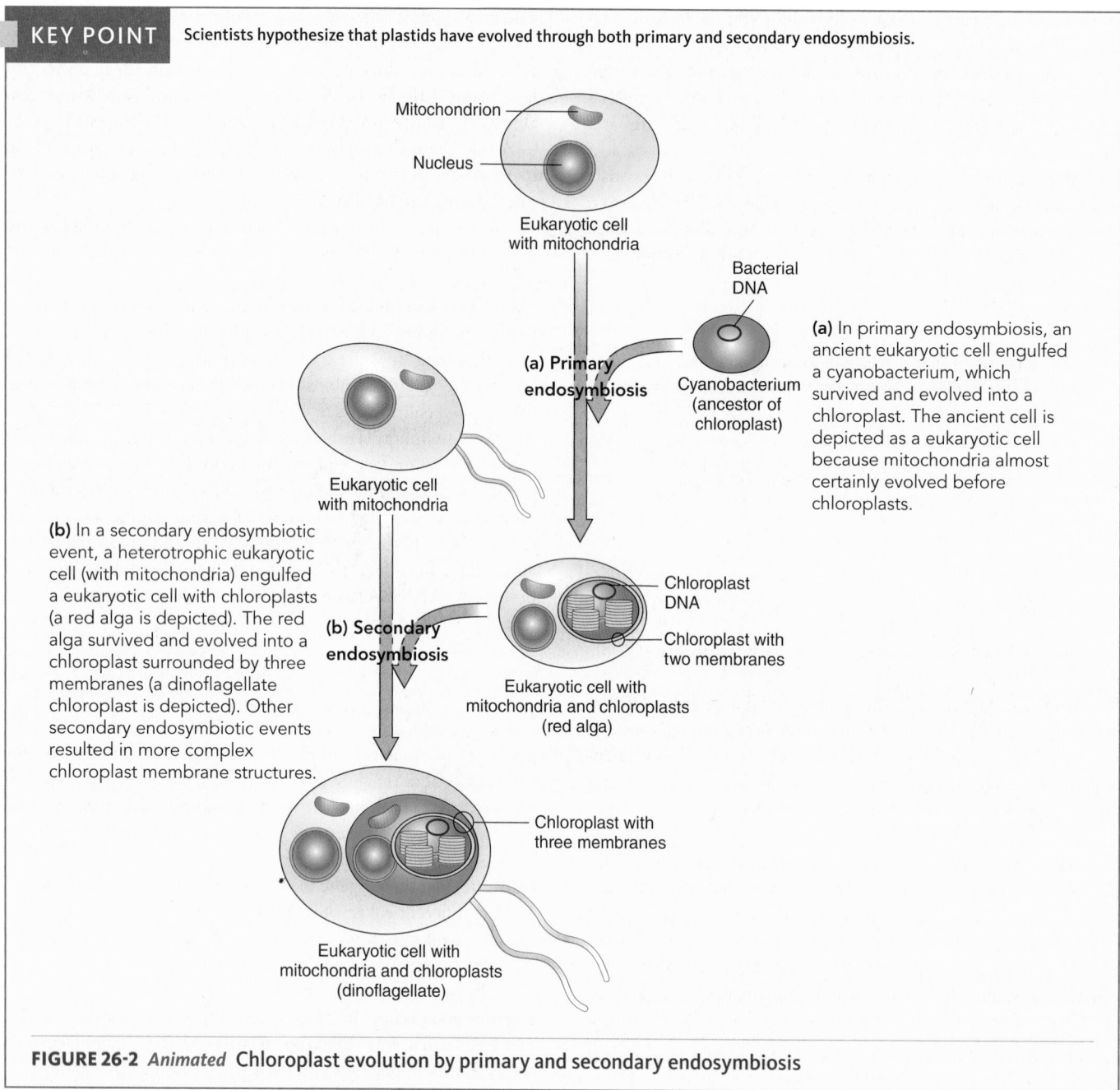

(a) In primary endosymbiosis, an ancient eukaryotic cell engulfed a cyanobacterium, which survived and evolved into a chloroplast. The ancient cell is depicted as a eukaryotic cell because mitochondria almost certainly evolved before chloroplasts.

(b) In a secondary endosymbiotic event, a heterotrophic eukaryotic cell (with mitochondria) engulfed a eukaryotic cell with chloroplasts (a red alga is depicted). The red alga survived and evolved into a chloroplast surrounded by three membranes (a dinoflagellate chloroplast is depicted). Other secondary endosymbiotic events resulted in more complex chloroplast membrane structures.

FIGURE 26-2 *Animated* **Chloroplast evolution by primary and secondary endosymbiosis**

classification scheme is different from the eukaryote classification we used in our last edition, and more changes will almost certainly be reported in future editions. Science is an ongoing enterprise, and current knowledge must always be re-evaluated in light of new discoveries.

Now that we have a basic understanding of evolution of the protists and other eukaryotes, let's examine representative protists within the five supergroups.

Review

- How does serial endosymbiosis explain the origin of chloroplasts?
- What kinds of scientific evidence support the hypothesis that protists are a paraphyletic group?

26.3 EXCAVATES

LEARNING OBJECTIVE

4 Summarize the basic features of excavates and distinguish among diplomonads, parabasilids, and euglenoids.

Excavates are a diverse group of unicellular protists with flagella. These protists are so named because many have a deep, or *excavated,* oral groove. Unlike other protists, excavates have atypical, greatly modified mitochondria. Many excavates are endosymbionts and live in anoxic (without oxygen) environments. These excavates do not carry out aerobic respiration; they obtain energy by the anaerobic pathway of glycolysis (presumably by fermentation).

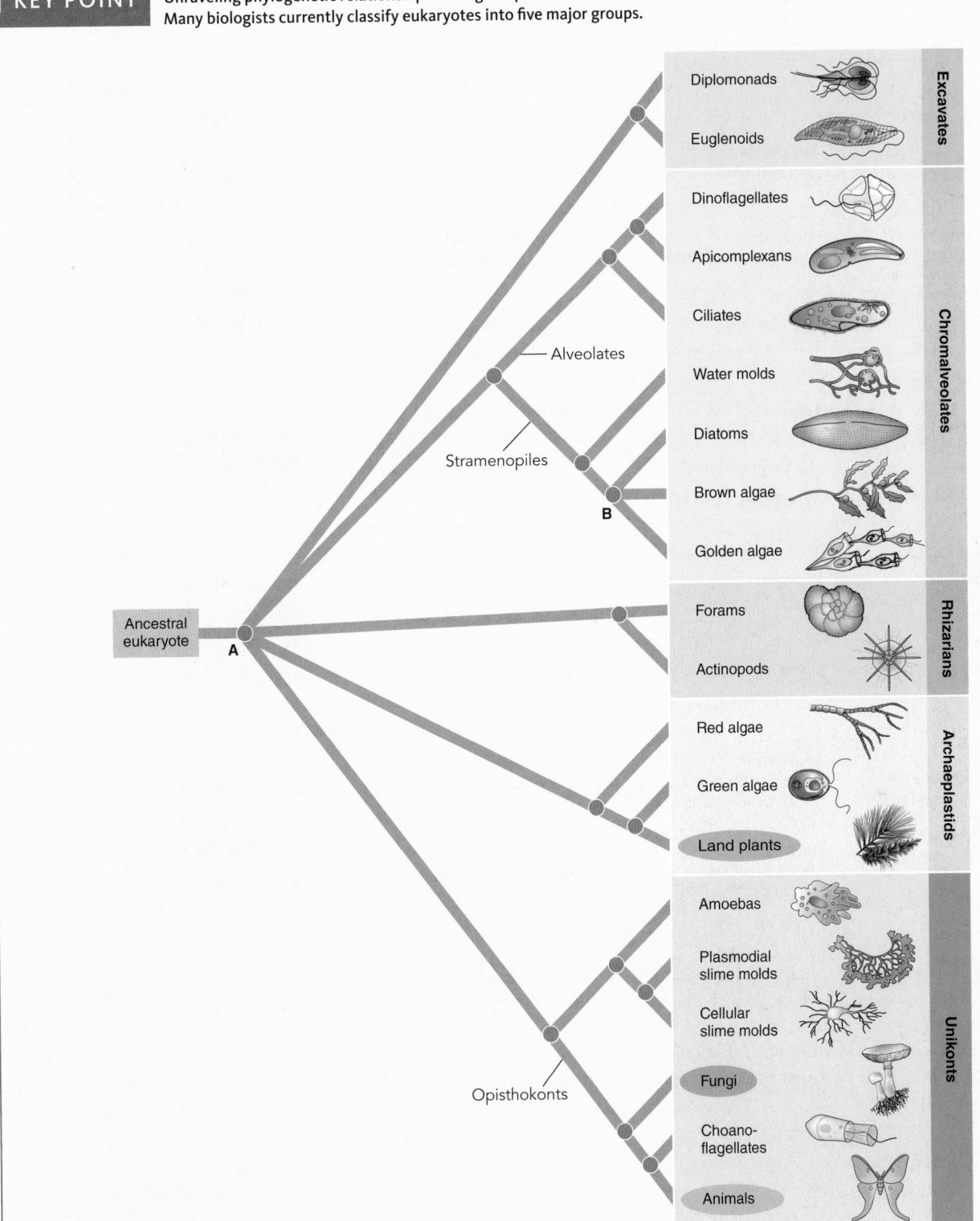

FIGURE 26-3 Evolutionary relationships among eukaryotes

This evolutionary tree presents one interpretation of relationships among eukaryotes in which the eukaryotes are placed in five "super-groups." Organisms within ovals represent separate eukaryotic kingdoms discussed in later chapters. All other eukaryotes are informally known as protists, a paraphyletic group. At node A, all five supergroups branch from the same point, indicating that the branching order is unresolved at this time. The same is true at node B for the diatoms, brown algae, and golden algae. (Based on Keeling, P. J., "Deep Questions in the Tree of Life," *Science*, Vol. 317, Sept. 28, 2007.)

TABLE 26-1   "Protist" Clades

Eukaryote "Supergroup"	Representative "Protist" Clades	Key Characters	Specific Example
Excavates Unicellular protists with atypical, greatly modified mitochondria; bikonts	**Diplomonads and parabasalids**	Two or more flagella; ventral oral (feeding) groove	SEM of *Trichomonas vaginalis*, a parabasalid
	Euglenoids and trypanosomes	Some with plastids; crystalline rod in flagella	
Chromalveolates Diverse protists that may have originated as a result of secondary endosymbiosis in which an ancestral cell engulfed a red alga; bikonts	**Alveolates** Dinoflagellates, ciliates, apicomplexans	Alveoli (flattened vesicles) just inside the plasma membrane	Darkfield LM of *Ceratium hirundinella*, a dinoflagellate
	Stramenopiles Water molds, diatoms, brown algae, golden algae	Most have two flagella, one with hairs; no flagella in some	
Rhizarians Amoeboid cells that often have tests (shells); bikonts	**Forams**	Porous tests (hard shells) through which cytoplasmic projections (pseudopods) extend	Darkfield LM of *Cibicides lobatula*, a foram
	Actinopods	Endoskeletons (internal shells) through which axopods (filamentous pseudopods) extend	
Archaeplastids Plastids bounded by outer and inner membranes; include land plants; bikonts	**Red algae**	Chloroplast pigments include phycoerythrin (red pigment) and phycocyanin (blue pigment)	Darkfield LM of *Micrasterias thomasiana*, a green alga
	Green algae	Chloroplast pigments identical to those in land plants	
Unikonts Cells that have a single flagellum or are amoebas with no flagella; have a triple-gene fusion that is lacking in other eukaryotes; include animals and fungi	**Amoebozoa** Amoebas, plasmodial slime molds, cellular slime molds	Naked amoebas (no tests) with lobelike pseudopods	Darkfield LM of *Amoeba proteus*, an amoeba
	Opisthokonts Choanoflagellates	No flagella or single posterior flagellum on motile cells	

Currently, excavates include diplomonads, parabasalids, euglenoids, and trypanosomes. The inclusion of these organisms into a single superfamily is somewhat controversial because their relationships to one another are uncertain. Additional studies will be needed to determine if the excavates as currently presented are a monophyletic group.

Diplomonads are small, mostly parasitic flagellates

Diplomonads are excavates that have one or two nuclei, no functional mitochondria, no Golgi complex, and up to eight flagella. *Giardia* is a parasitic diplomonad (**FIG. 26-4a**). Interestingly, *Giardia* has two haploid nuclei, each of which contains a complete copy of Giardia's genome. *Giardia* lacks functional mitochondria, although it contains certain genes that code for proteins associated with mitochondria in other organisms. *Giardia* also has reduced

structures that somewhat resemble mitochondria. This information suggests to some biologists that an early eukaryotic ancestor of *Giardia* may have possessed mitochondria, which were somehow lost or reduced at a later time during its evolutionary history.

Giardia intestinalis is a major cause of water-borne diarrhea throughout the world. *Giardia* is eliminated as a resistant cyst in the feces of many vertebrate animals. These cysts are a common contaminant in untreated drinking water. In a heavy infection, much of the wall of the small intestine is coated with these flagellates, which interfere with the absorption of digested nutrients and cause weight loss, abdominal cramps, and diarrhea.

Parabasilids are anaerobic endosymbionts that live in animals

Parabasilids are anaerobic, flagellated excavates that often live in animals. Trichonymphs and trichomonads are examples of para-

(a) Diplomonad. This colorized TEM of *Giardia intestinalis*, a parasitic diplomonad, reveals two nuclei.

Nuclei

2 μm

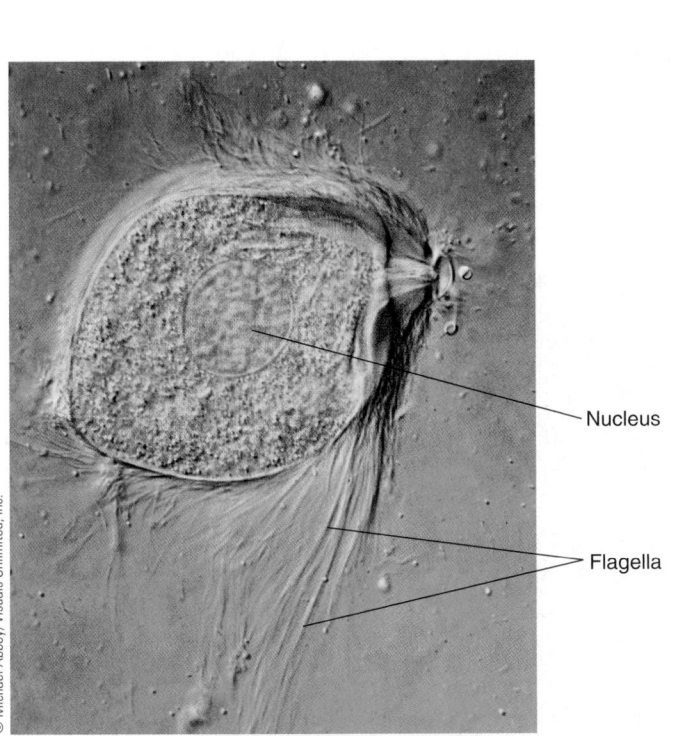

Nucleus

Flagella

50 μm

(b) Parabasalid. LM of *Trichonympha*, a parabasalid that lives in the gut of wood-eating termites and cockroaches. *Trichonympha* has hundreds of flagella.

FIGURE 26-4 Diplomonads and parabasalids

basilids. **Trichonymphs,** which have hundreds of flagella, live in the guts of termites and wood-eating cockroaches (**FIG. 26-4b**). Trichonymphs ingest wood chips from the wood that termites or roaches eat. The trichonymphs rely on endosymbiotic bacteria to digest cellulose in the wood. The insects, trichonymphs, and bacteria all obtain their nutrients from this source. This is an excellent example of mutualism.

The most well-known **trichomonad** is probably *Trichomonas vaginalis*, which causes trichomoniasis, a curable sexually transmitted disease (STD) in humans (see SEM in Table 26-1). Trichomoniasis affects both men and women, although the symptoms are more obvious in women. According to the Centers for Disease Control and Prevention, about 7.4 million new cases occur in the United States each year.

Euglenoids and trypanosomes have both free-living species and parasites

Euglenoids and *trypanosomes* are characterized by an unusual flagellum: in addition to the 9 + 2 arrangement of microtubules characteristic of all eukaryotic flagella, these excavates have a crystalline rod in their flagella; the function of this rod is unknown. Like other excavates, euglenoids and trypanosomes also have atypical mitochondria.

Most **euglenoids** are unicellular flagellates, and about one-third of them are photosynthetic (**FIGS. 26-5a** and **b**). They generally have two flagella: one long and whiplike and one that is often so short that it does not extend outside the cell. Some euglenoids, such as *Euglena*, change shape continually as they move through the water because their **pellicle,** or outer covering, is flexible.

Autotrophic euglenoids have the same photosynthetic pigments that green algae and plants have, but euglenoids are not closely related to either group, as shown in Figure 26-3. Some photosynthetic euglenoids lose their chlorophyll when grown in the dark, and they obtain their nutrients heterotrophically, by ingesting organic matter. Other euglenoids are always colorless and heterotrophic. Some heterotrophic species absorb organic compounds from the surrounding water, whereas others engulf bacteria and protists by **phagocytosis;** they digest the prey within food vacuoles.

Trypanosomes are excavates with a single mitochondrion that has an organized deposit of DNA called a **kinetoplastid.** Trypanosomes are colorless, and many are parasitic and cause disease. In

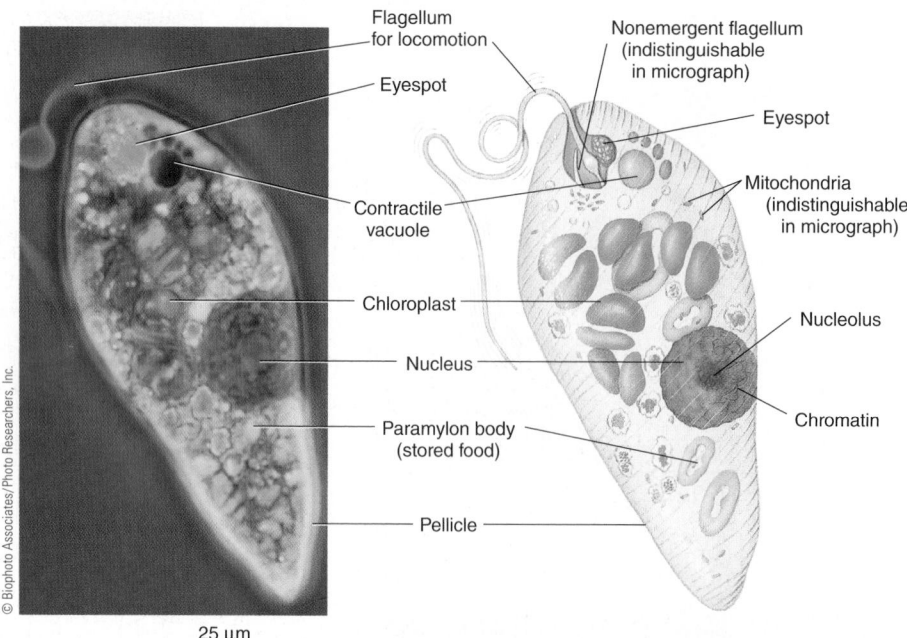

FIGURE 26-5 Euglenoids and trypanosomes ▶

vertebrates, including humans, trypanosomes live in the blood. For example, *Trypanosoma brucei* is a human parasite that causes African sleeping sickness (**FIG. 26-5c**). It is transmitted by the bite of infected tsetse flies. Early symptoms include recurring attacks of fever. Later, when the trypanosomes have invaded the central nervous system, infected people are lethargic and have difficulty speaking or walking. At least 50,000 new cases occur each year; if untreated, African sleeping sickness can cause death.

Review

- What cell organelle is atypical in excavates?
- Give an example of a human disease caused by each of the following: diplomonads, parabasilids, and trypanosomes.

(a) LM of *Euglena gracilis*, a unicellular, flagellate euglenoid.

(b) *Euglena*'s pellicle is flexible and changes shape easily. The eyespot may shield a light detector at the base of the long flagellum, thereby helping *Euglena* move to light of an appropriate intensity.

26.4 CHROMALVEOLATES

◼ LEARNING OBJECTIVES

5 Contrast the two main groups of chromalveolates: alveolates and stramenopiles.
6 Distinguish among the alveolates: dinoflagellates, apicomplexans, and ciliates.
7 Distinguish among the stramenopiles: water molds, diatoms, golden algae, and brown algae.

The **chromalveolates** are a supergroup composed of extremely diverse protists with few shared characters. Chromalveolates probably originated as a result of secondary endosymbiosis in which an ancestral cell engulfed a red alga (which itself was the result of primary endosymbiosis). Most chromalveolates are photosynthetic, and evidence suggests that heterotrophic chromalveolates, such as the water molds and ciliates, descended from autotrophic ancestors. Classification of the chromalveolates as a monophyletic supergroup is controversial because some DNA sequence data have indicated that they are not monophyletic. The chromalveolates are divided into two main groups, alveolates and stramenopiles

The unifying features of protists classified as **alveolates** include similar ribosomal DNA sequences and **alveoli** (sing., *alveolus*), flattened vesicles located just inside the plasma membrane. In some alveolates, the vesicles contain plates of cellulose. Alveolates include the dinoflagellates, apicomplexans, and ciliates.

The **stramenopiles** include water molds, diatoms, golden algae, and brown algae. At first glance, stramenopiles appear too diverse to classify together. However, most stramenopiles have motile cells with two flagella, one of which has tiny hairlike projections extending from the shaft.

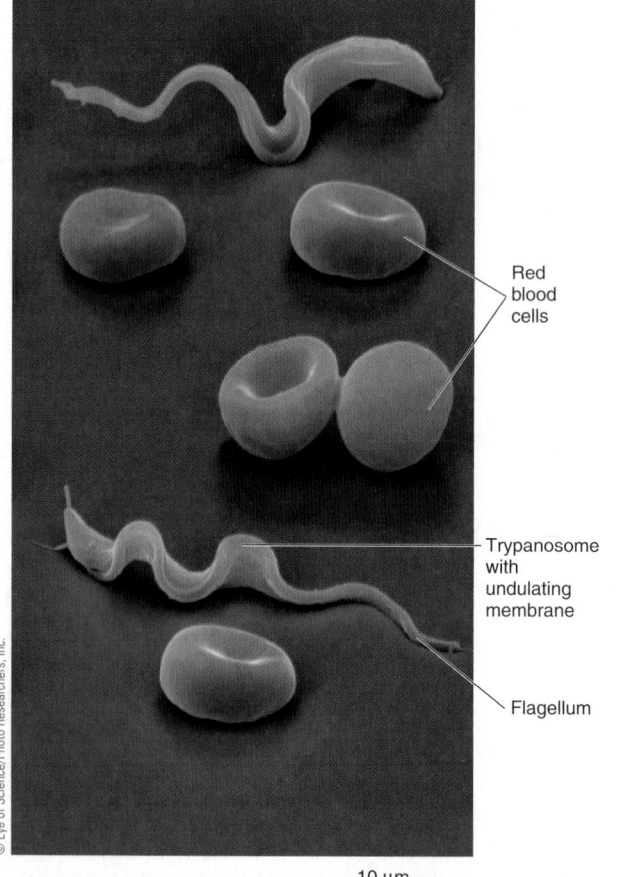

(c) SEM of the flagellate *Trypanosoma brucei* among human red blood cells. *Trypanosoma brucei* causes African sleeping sickness in humans.

Most dinoflagellates are a part of marine plankton

Dinoflagellates are generally unicellular, although a few are colonial. Their alveoli contain interlocking cellulose plates impregnated with silicates. The typical dinoflagellate has two flagella. One flagellum wraps around a transverse groove in the center of the cell like a belt, and the other lies in a longitudinal groove (perpendicular to the transverse groove), projecting behind the cell (**FIG. 26-6a**). The undulation of these flagella propels the dinoflagellate through the water like a spinning top. Indeed, the name is derived from the Greek *dinos,* meaning "whirling." Many marine dinoflagellates are bioluminescent.

Many dinoflagellates are photosynthetic (see LM in Table 26-1), but others are heterotrophic and ingest other microorganisms for food. Some dinoflagellates are endosymbionts that live in the bodies of marine invertebrates such as mollusks, jellyfish, and corals (see Fig. 54-12). These symbiotic dinoflagellates, called **zooxanthellae,** photosynthesize and provide carbohydrates for their invertebrate partners. Zooxanthellae contribute substantially to the productivity of coral reefs. Other dinoflagellates that are endosymbionts lack pigments and are parasites that live off their hosts.

Ecologically, dinoflagellates are important producers in marine ecosystems. A few dinoflagellates are known to have occasional population explosions, or blooms. These blooms, known as **red tides,** frequently color coastal waters orange, red, or brown (**FIG. 26-6b**). Dinoflagellate blooms are particularly common in warm, nutrient-enriched water. Some dinoflagellate species that form red tides produce a toxin that attacks the nervous systems of fishes, leading to fish kills. Birds sometimes die after eating contaminated fish. Research has also linked red tides to manatee and dolphin deaths in Florida.

Apicomplexans are spore-forming parasites of animals

Apicomplexans are a large group of parasitic, spore-forming alveolates, some of which cause serious diseases in humans. They contain the unpigmented remnant of a chloroplast and may have evolved from parasitic dinoflagellates living in the intestines of marine invertebrates. Apicomplexans lack specific structures for locomotion (cilia, flagella, or pseudopodia) and move by flexing.

Excavates · Chromalveolates · Rhizarians · Archaeplastids · Unikonts

Ancestral eukaryote

Dr. David Phillips/Visuals Unlimited, Inc.

Flagella

20 μm

(a) SEM of *Gymnodinium.* Note the two flagella, which are located in grooves.

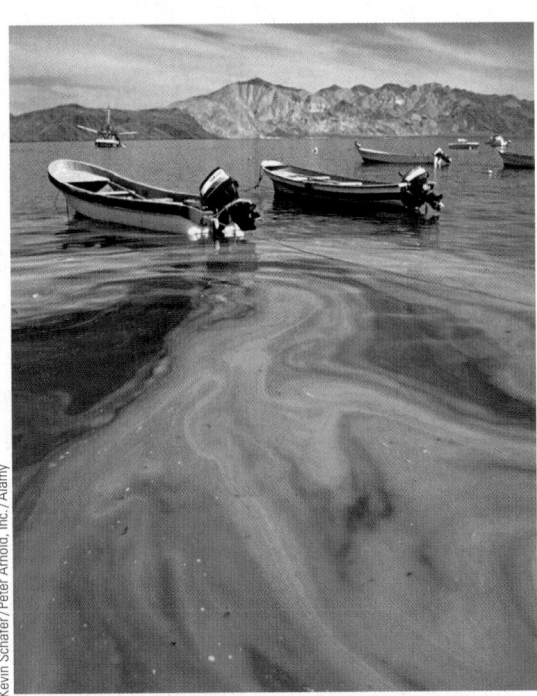

Kevin Schafer/Peter Arnold, Inc./Alamy

(b) Red tide in Mexico. Billions of dinoflagellates produce the orange cloudiness in the water.

FIGURE 26-6 Dinoflagellates

Apicomplexans have an *apical complex* of microtubules that attaches the parasite to its host cell; the apical complex is visible only by using electron microscopy. At some stage in their life cycle, apicomplexans produce **sporozoites,** small infective agents transmitted to the next host. Many apicomplexans spend part of their complex life cycle in one host species and part in a different host species.

Malaria is caused by an apicomplexan (**FIG. 26-7**). According to the World Health Organization, approximately 250 million people currently have malaria, and about 800,000 people, mostly children in developing countries, die from the disease each year. Although for centuries Chinese, Greek, Arabic, and Roman writings described the disease, its causative agent and mode of transmission were not identified until the end of the 19th century. British sci-

entist Ronald Ross received the Nobel Prize in 1902 for his role in elucidating the life cycle of *Plasmodium,* the apicomplexan that causes malaria.

Today malaria is recurring in many countries where it was under control for decades. Formerly effective control methods—antimalarial drugs and pesticides—have lost much of their effectiveness. Chloroquine and several other antimalarial drugs are taken prophylactically to prevent malaria, but *Plasmodium* has evolved resistance to several of these. Moreover, mosquitoes have evolved resistance to many pesticides. Researchers are currently testing new antimalarial drugs and several possible vaccines against malaria. The sequencing of the genomes of *P. falciparum* and the *Anopheles* mosquito may lead to new diagnostics, drugs, and vaccines.

KEY POINT *Plasmodium*, an apicomplexan that is the causative agent of malaria, lives in two hosts, mosquitoes and humans.

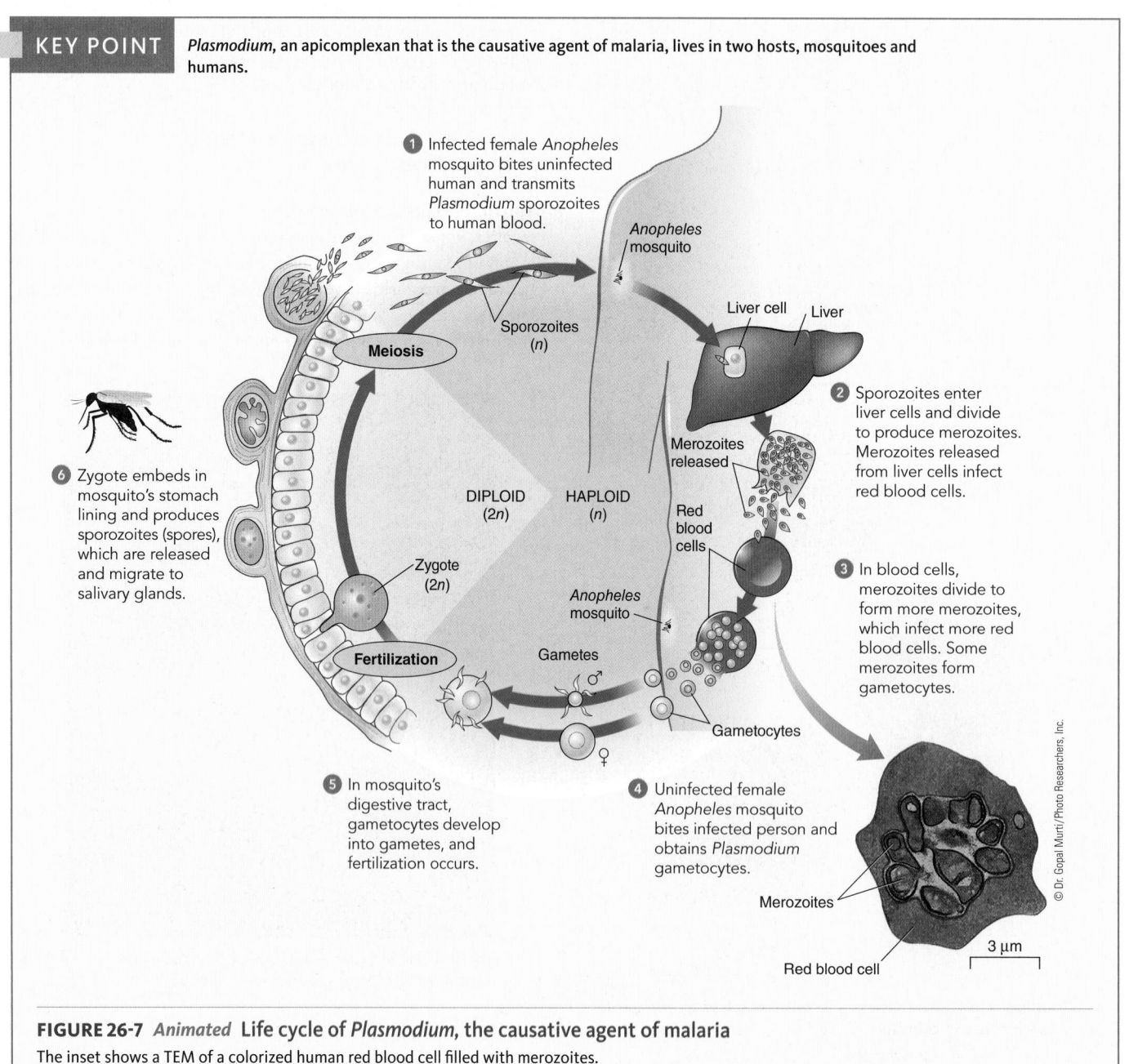

FIGURE 26-7 *Animated* **Life cycle of *Plasmodium*, the causative agent of malaria**
The inset shows a TEM of a colorized human red blood cell filled with merozoites.

Ciliates use cilia for locomotion

Ciliates are among the most complex of eukaryotic cells. These unicellular alveolates have a pellicle that gives them a definite but changeable shape. In *Paramecium*, the surface of the cell is covered with several thousand fine, short, hairlike **cilia** that extend through pores in the pellicle to facilitate movement (**FIGS. 26-8a** and **b**; also see Fig. 4-4c). The cilia beat with such precise coordination that the organism can back up and turn around as well as move forward.

Not all ciliates are motile. Some sessile forms have stalks, and others, although capable of some swimming, are more likely to remain attached to a rock or other surface at one spot. Their cilia set up water currents that draw food toward them.

Ciliates differ from other protists in having two kinds of nuclei: one or more small, diploid **micronuclei** that function in reproduction; and a larger, polyploid **macronucleus** that controls cell metabolism and growth. Most ciliates are capable of a sexual process called **conjugation**, in which two individuals come together and

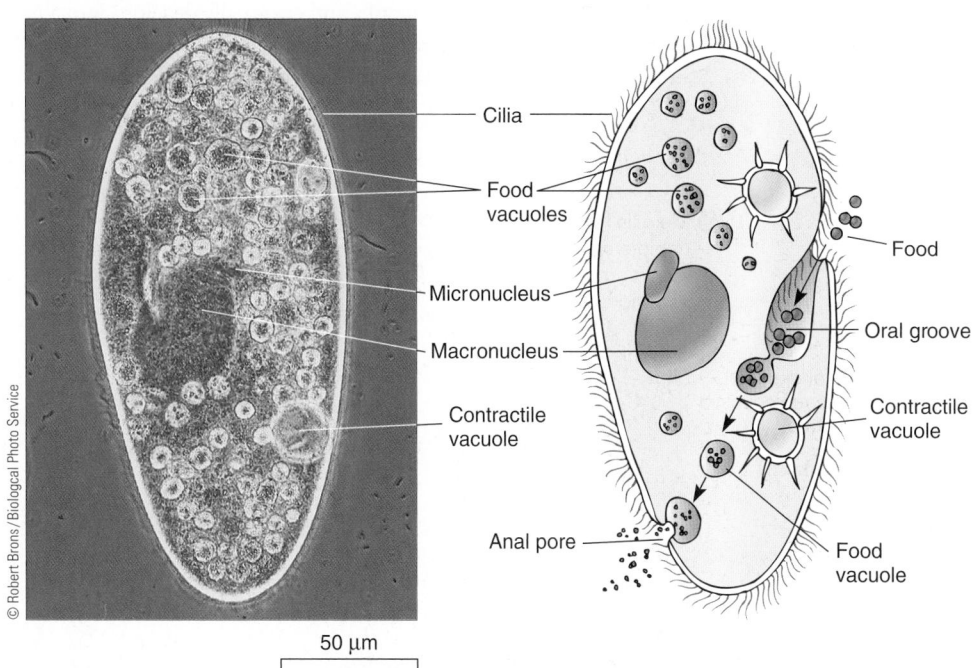

(a) Note the complex cell structure in this phase contrast LM of *Paramecium*, a freshwater ciliate. Like many ciliates, *Paramecium* has multiple nuclei: a macronucleus and one or more smaller micronuclei.

(b) Food particles are swept into *Paramecium*'s ciliated oral groove and incorporated into food vacuoles. Lysosomes fuse with the food vacuoles, and the food is digested and absorbed; undigested wastes are eliminated through the anal pore.

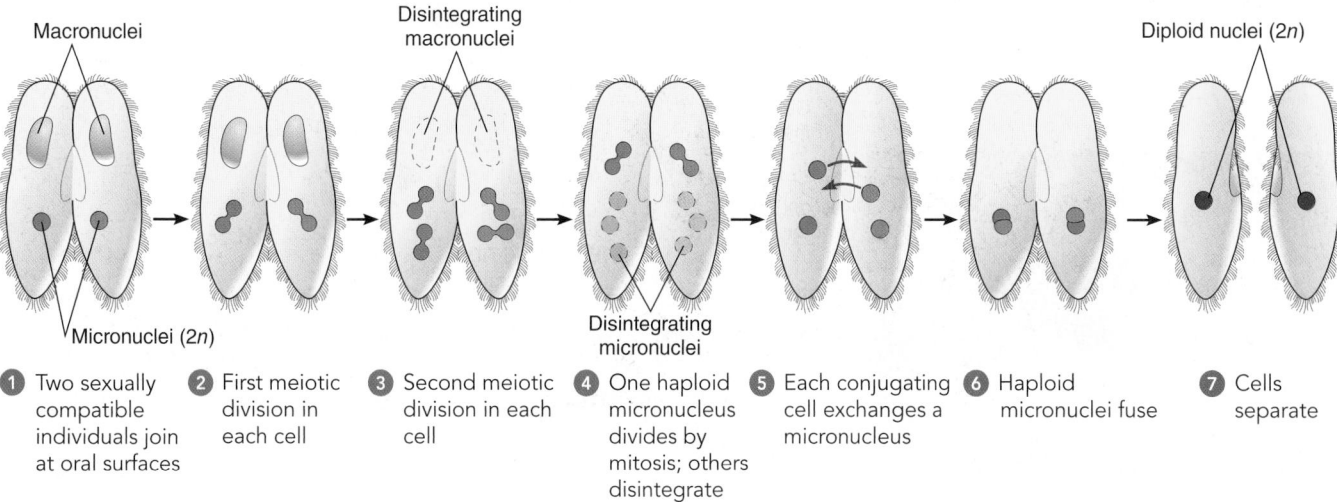

1. Two sexually compatible individuals join at oral surfaces
2. First meiotic division in each cell
3. Second meiotic division in each cell
4. One haploid micronucleus divides by mitosis; others disintegrate
5. Each conjugating cell exchanges a micronucleus
6. Haploid micronuclei fuse
7. Cells separate

(c) Conjugation in *Paramecium caudatum*.

FIGURE 26-8 Ciliates

exchange genetic material (**FIG. 26-8c**). Conjugation results in two "new" cells that are genetically identical to each other but different from what they were before conjugation. Mitosis and cell division need not follow immediately after conjugation. Ciliates usually divide perpendicularly to their longitudinal axis.

Water molds produce biflagellate reproductive cells

Water molds were once classified as fungi because of their superficial resemblance. Both water molds and fungi have a body, called a **mycelium,** that grows over organic material, digesting it and then absorbing the predigested nutrients (**FIG. 26-9**). The thread-like **hyphae** that make up the mycelium in water molds are coenocytic, meaning that there are no cross walls, and the body of these stramenopiles consists of a single multinucleate cell. The cell walls of water molds are composed of cellulose (as in plants), chitin (as in fungi), or both.

When food is plentiful and environmental conditions are favorable, water molds reproduce asexually. A hyphal tip swells and a cross wall is formed, separating the hyphal tip from the rest of the mycelium. Within this structure, called a **zoosporangium,** tiny biflagellate zoospores form, each of which swims about, lands and encysts, and eventually develops into a new mycelium. When environmental conditions worsen, water molds initiate sexual reproduction. After fusion of male and female nuclei, thick-walled

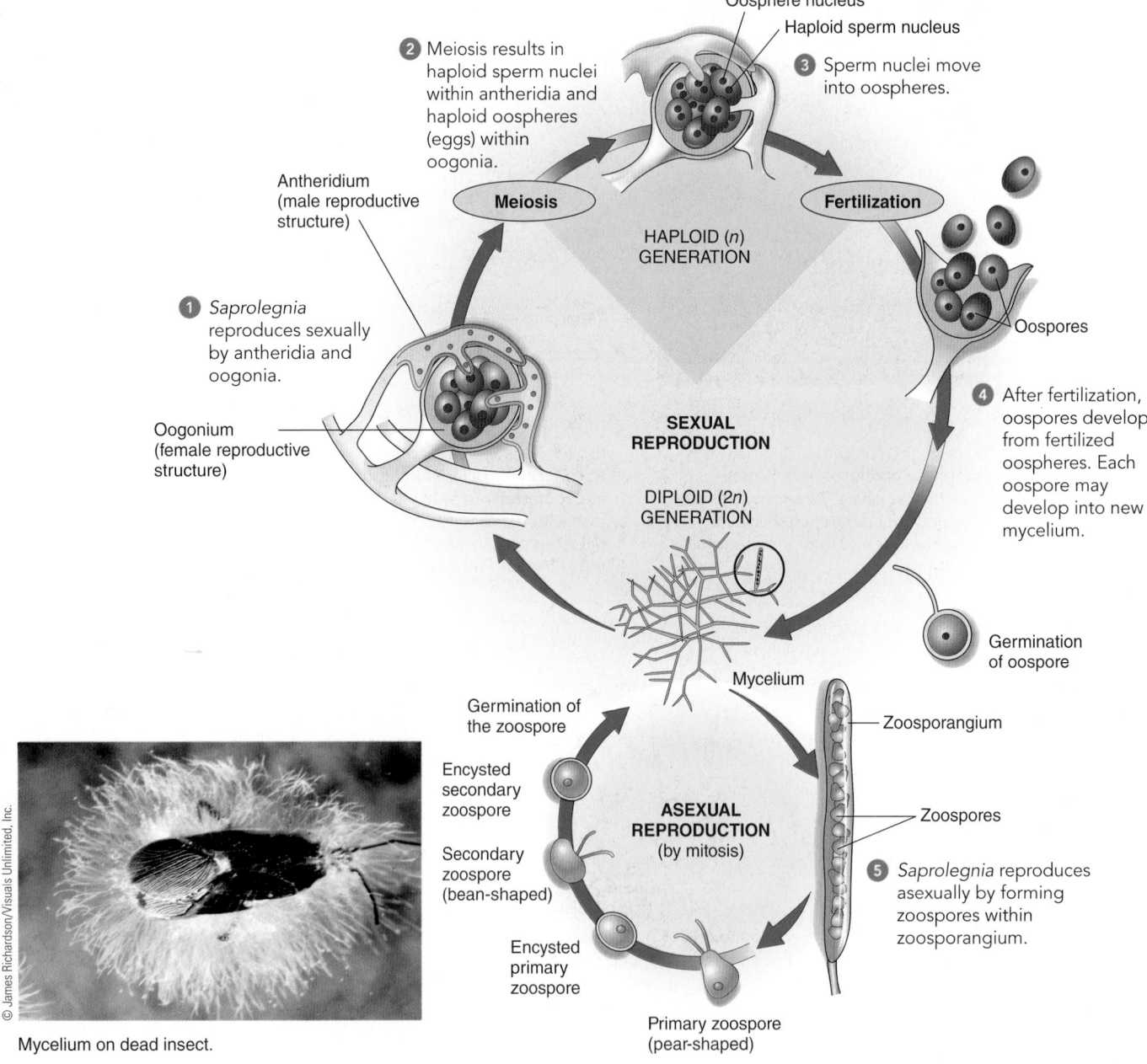

Mycelium on dead insect.

FIGURE 26-9 Water molds

The life cycle of *Saprolegnia*, a water mold. *Inset:* A mycelium of *Saprolegnia* radiates from a dead insect.

oospores develop from the oospheres (female gametes). Water molds often spend the winter as oospores.

Some water molds have played a profound role in human history. For example, the Irish potato famine of the 19th century was precipitated by the water mold *Phytophthora infestans,* which causes late blight of potatoes. (The genus *Phytophthora* is named from Greek words meaning "plant destruction.") During several rainy, cool summers in Ireland in the 1840s, the water mold multiplied unchecked, causing potato tubers to rot in the fields. Because potatoes were the staple of the Irish peasants' diet, as many as one million people starved. The famine prompted a mass migration out of Ireland to the United States and other countries.

A close relative of the late blight water mold, *P. ramorum,* causes sudden oak death, which is killing oak forests in several western states. Plant pathologists are concerned that the disease may spread to Midwestern and Eastern forests. This particular water mold also attacks redwoods, Douglas firs, bay trees, maples, and several other plant species, but most have only twig and leaf infections, not the rapid death observed in oaks.

Diatoms have shells composed of two parts

Most **diatoms** are unicellular stramenopiles, although a few exist as colonies (see chapter opener figure). The cell wall of each diatom consists of two shells that overlap where they fit together, much like a petri dish. Silica is deposited in the shell, and this glasslike material is laid down in intricate patterns (**FIG. 26-10a**). There are two basic groups of diatoms: those with radial symmetry (wheel shaped) and those with bilateral symmetry (boat shaped or needle shaped). Although some diatoms are part of the floating **plankton,** others live on rocks and sediments, where they move by gliding. This gliding movement is facilitated by the secretion of a slimy material from a small groove along the shell.

Diatoms most often reproduce asexually by mitosis. When a diatom divides, the two halves of its shell separate, and each becomes the larger half of a new diatom shell (**FIG. 26-10b**). Because the glass shell cannot grow, some diatom cells get progressively smaller with each succeeding generation. When a diatom reaches a fraction of its original size, sexual reproduction occurs, with the production of shell-less gametes. Sexual reproduction restores the diatom to its original size because the resulting *zygote,* a 2*n* cell that results from the fusion of *n* gametes, grows substantially before producing a new shell.

Diatoms are common in fresh water but are especially abundant in relatively cool ocean water. They are ecologically significant as major producers in aquatic ecosystems. At least one species is toxic and linked to shellfish poisonings, marine mammal strandings, and the deaths of sea lions along the central California coast.

When diatoms die, their shells trickle to the ocean floor and accumulate in layers that eventually become sedimentary rock. After millions of years, geologic upheaval has exposed some of these deposits on land. Called *diatomaceous earth,* these deposits are mined and used as filtering, insulating, and soundproofing materials. As a

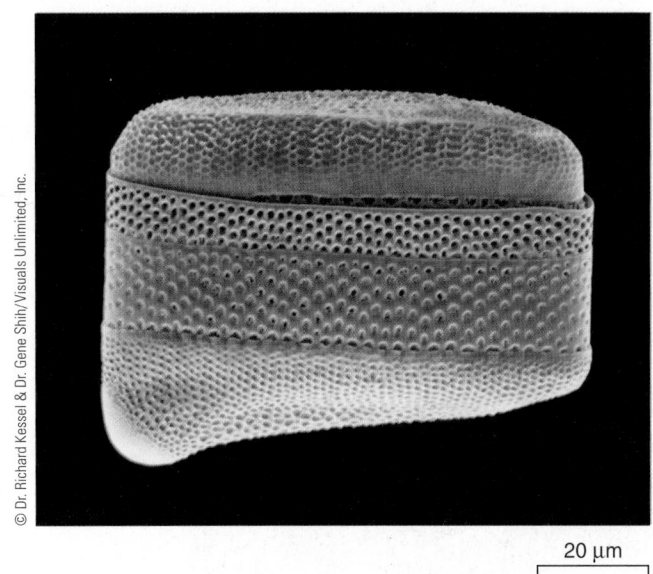

(a) SEM of a unicellular diatom. Note the striking shell that contains silica.

20 μm

(b) Asexual reproduction in diatoms. After cell division, each new cell retains half of the original shell. The newly synthesized half of the shell always fits *inside* the original half. As a result, one of the new cells is slightly smaller.

FIGURE 26-10 Diatoms

filtering agent, diatomaceous earth is used to refine raw sugar and to process vegetable oils. Because of its abrasive properties, diatomaceous earth is a common ingredient in scouring powders and metal polishes; it is no longer added to most toothpastes because it is too abrasive for tooth enamel. The intricately detailed diatom shells are often used to test microscope resolution down to 1 μm.

Brown algae are multicellular stramenopiles

Brown algae are the largest and most complex of all algae commonly called seaweeds. All brown algae are multicellular and range in size from a few centimeters (about an inch) to 75 m (about 260 ft). Their body forms are branched filaments; tufts; fleshy "ropes"; or thick, flattened branches. The largest brown algae, called *kelps,* are tough and leathery in appearance.

Many kelps have leaflike **blades** in which most photosynthesis occurs, stemlike **stipes,** and rootlike anchoring **holdfasts** (**FIG. 26-11a**). They often have gas-filled *bladders* that provide buoyancy. (The blades, stipes, and holdfasts of brown algae are not homologous to the leaves, stems, and roots of plants. Brown algae and plants arose from different unicellular ancestors, as shown in Figure 26-3.)

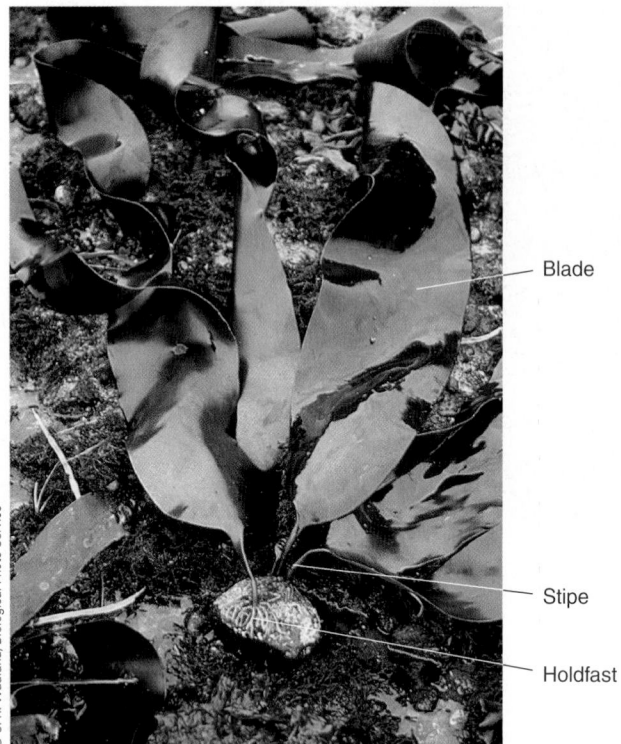

(a) *Laminaria* is widely distributed on rocky coastlines of temperate and polar seas. It grows to 2 m (6.5 ft).

FIGURE 26-11 Brown algae

(b) A kelp (*Macrocystis pyrifera*) bed is ecologically important to aquatic organisms, including the sea lion shown here. Photographed off the coast of California.

Reproduction is varied and complex in the brown algae. Their reproductive cells, both asexual zoospores and sexual gametes, are usually biflagellate. Most have a life cycle that exhibits **alternation of generations,** in which they spend part of their life as multicellular haploid organisms and part as multicellular diploid organisms (see Fig. 10-19c).

Brown algae are commercially important for several reasons. Their cell walls contain a polysaccharide called *algin* that is harvested from kelps such as *Macrocystis* and used as a thickening and stabilizing agent in ice cream, toothpaste, shaving cream, hair spray, and hand lotion. Brown algae are an important human food, particularly in eastern Asia, and they are rich sources of certain vitamins and minerals such as iodine.

Brown algae are common in cooler marine waters, especially along rocky coastlines, where they live mainly in the intertidal zone or relatively shallow offshore waters. Kelps form extensive underwater "forests," or kelp beds (**FIG. 26-11b**). They are essential in that ecosystem as important food producers, and they provide habitat for many marine invertebrates, fishes, and mammals. The diversity of life supported by kelp beds rivals that found in coral reefs.

Most golden algae are unicellular biflagellates

Golden algae are found in both freshwater and marine environments. Most species are biflagellate, unicellular organisms, although some are colonial (**FIG. 26-12a**). A few of these stramenopiles lack flagella and are similar to amoebas in appearance except that golden algae contain chloroplasts. Tiny scales of either silica

(a) LM of a colonial golden alga (*Synura*) found in freshwater lakes and ponds.

FIGURE 26-12 Golden algae

(b) SEM of a coccolithophorid (*Emiliania huxleyi*). Note the overlapping scales of calcium carbonate.

or calcium carbonate may cover the cells. Reproduction in golden algae is primarily asexual and involves the production of biflagellate, motile spores called **zoospores.**

Most golden algae are photosynthetic, and the pigment composition of golden algae gives them a golden or golden brown color. A few species ingest bacteria and other particles of food. Ecologically, golden algae are important producers in marine environments. They compose a significant portion of the ocean's **nanoplankton,** extremely minute algae (2 μm to 10 μm) that are major producers because of their great abundance.

Classification of golden algae is controversial. Some biologists lump diatoms and golden algae in a single phylum, whereas others classify both groups as brown algae. At the other extreme, some biologists divide the golden algae into two phyla by placing many of the marine species, such as **coccolithophorids** (FIG. 26-12b), in a separate phylum.

(a) SEM of a foram test. Note the pores through which cytoplasm extrudes.

FIGURE 26-13 Rhizarians

Review

- What are the two main groups of chromalveolates? What are their distinguishing characters?
- Why do some biologists think the apicomplexans descended from dinoflagellates?
- Which water mold has influenced human history? Explain your answer.
- What is the ecological significance of the diatoms? the brown algae?

26.5 RHIZARIANS

LEARNING OBJECTIVE

8   Describe the forams and actinopods, and explain why many biologists classify them in the rhizarian supergroup.

Rhizarians are a diverse supergroup of amoeboid cells that often have hard outer shells, called **tests,** through which cytoplasmic projections extend. The threadlike cytoplasmic projections suggest the name *rhizarian,* from the Greek *rhiza,* meaning "root." Forams and actinopods are rhizarians, as are certain shell-less amoebas. Not all amoebas are rhizarians, however, and many amoeba species are more closely related to other eukaryotic clades. Current molecular evidence indicates that the rhizarian supergroup is monophyletic.

Forams extend cytoplasmic projections that form a threadlike, interconnected net

Almost all **foraminiferans (forams)** are marine rhizarians that produce elaborate tests (FIG. 26-13a; also see LM in Table 26-1). The ocean contains enormous numbers of forams, which secrete chalky, many-chambered tests with pores through which cytoplasmic projections are extended. (*Foraminifera* is derived from the Latin for "bearing openings.") The cytoplasmic projections form a sticky, interconnected net that entangles prey. Many forams contain unicellular algal endosymbionts (green algae, red algae, or diatoms)

(b) LM of an unidentified living actinopod from the Red Sea. Many slender axopods project from the cell. The shell is not visible because it is an endoskeleton and cytoplasm covers it on all sides.

that provide food by photosynthesis. Many foram species live on the ocean floor, but others are part of the plankton.

Dead forams settle on the bottom of the ocean, where their tests form a gray mud that is gradually transformed into chalk. With geologic uplifting, these chalk formations become part of the land, for example, the White Cliffs of Dover in England. (The White Cliffs of Dover are the remains of a variety of carbonate organisms, not only forams.) Because foram tests often appear in rock layers covering oil deposits, geologists exploring for oil look for foram tests in rock strata. Forams are well preserved in the fossil record, and biologists use some as **index fossils,** markers to help identify ancient sedimentary rock layers (see Chapter 18).

Actinopods project slender axopods

Actinopods are mostly marine plankton rhizarians with long, filamentous cytoplasmic projections called **axopods** that protrude through pores in their shells (**FIG. 26-13b**). A cluster of microtubules strengthens each axopod. Unicellular algae and other prey become entangled in these axopods and are engulfed outside the main body of the actinopod; cytoplasmic streaming carries the prey inside the body. Many actinopods contain algal endosymbionts that provide them with the products of photosynthesis.

Some actinopods, called **radiolarians,** secrete elaborate, beautiful glassy shells made of silica. Radiolarians are an important constituent of marine plankton. When radiolarians and other actinopods die, their shells settle and become an ooze (sediment) that may be several meters thick on the ocean floor.

Review

- Why are forams and actinopods classified as rhizarians?
- What character does the term *rhizarian* indicate about the forams and actinopods?

26.6 ARCHAEPLASTIDS

■ LEARNING OBJECTIVE

9 Describe evidence supporting the hypothesis that red algae and green algae should be included in a monophyletic group with land plants.

In the classification scheme adopted in this text, the monophyletic group of **archaeplastids** includes red algae and green algae, which are discussed here, and land plants, which are in a separate kingdom (see Chapters 27 and 28). Biologists classify these groups together based on molecular data and on the presence of chloroplasts bounded by outer and inner membranes, suggesting that they developed directly from a cyanobacterial endosymbiont. All photosynthetic protists other than archaeplastids have plastids surrounded by three or four membranes.

Red algae do not produce motile cells

The vast majority of **red algae** are multicellular organisms, although there are a few unicellular species. The multicellular body form of red algae commonly consists of complex, interwoven filaments that are delicate and feathery (**FIG. 26-14a**); a few red algae

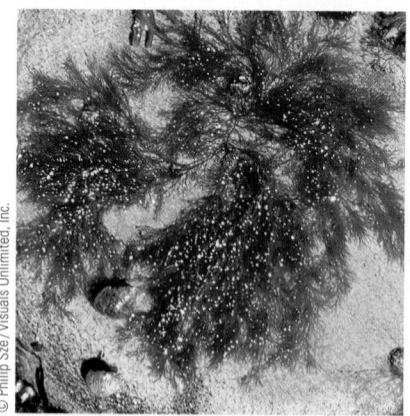

(a) *Polysiphonia*, which is widely distributed throughout the world, has a highly branched body of interwoven filaments.

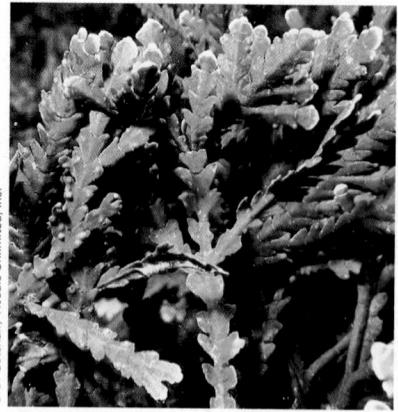

(b) *Bossiella* is a coralline red alga encrusted with calcium carbonate. It lives in the Pacific Ocean.

(c) Nori, dried and pressed sheets of the red alga *Porphyra*, surrounds sushi.

FIGURE 26-14 *Animated* Red algae

are flattened sheets of cells. Most multicellular red algae attach to rocks or other substrates by a basal holdfast. Reproduction in the red algae is remarkably complex, with an alternation of sexual and asexual stages. No flagellate cells develop during the life cycle.

Red algae primarily live in warm tropical ocean waters, although a few species occur in fresh water and in soil. Some red algae, known as *coralline algae,* incorporate calcium carbonate in their cell walls from the ocean water (**FIG. 26-14b**). The hard calcium carbonate may protect coralline algae from the rigors of wave action. These coralline red algae build "coral" reefs and are perhaps as crucial as coral animals in this process.

The cell walls of red algae often contain thick, sticky polysaccharides that have commercial value. For example, *agar* is a polysaccharide extracted from certain red algae used as a food thickener and culture medium, a substrate on which to grow microorganisms and propagate some plants, such as orchids. Another poly-

saccharide extracted from red algae, *carrageenan,* is a food additive used to stabilize chocolate milk and to provide a thick, creamy texture to ice cream and other soft processed foods. Carrageenan is also used to stabilize paints and cosmetics. Red algae are a source of vitamins (particularly A and C) and minerals, especially in Japan and other eastern Asian countries where people eat red algae fresh, dried, or toasted in such traditional foods as sushi and nori (**FIG. 26-14c**).

Green algae share many similarities with land plants

Green algae have pigments, energy reserve products, and cell walls that are chemically identical to those of land plants. Green algae are photosynthetic, with chloroplasts of a wide variety of shapes. Most green algae have cell walls with cellulose, although some lack walls. Because of these and other similarities, biologists generally accept that land plants arose from ancestral green algae (see Fig. 26-3). Based on recent molecular and ultrastructure data, some biologists classify this diverse group in the plant kingdom.

Green algae exhibit a variety of body types, from single cells to colonial forms, to coenocytic algae (multinucleate), to multicellular filaments and sheets (**FIG. 26-15**; also see LM in Table 26-1). The multicellular forms do not have cells differentiated into tissues, a characteristic that separates them from land plants. Most green algae have, or produce, flagellate cells during their life cycle, although a few are totally nonmotile.

Reproduction in the green algae is as varied as their body forms, with both sexual and asexual reproduction. Many green algae have life cycles with an alternation of haploid and diploid generations. Asexual reproduction is by mitosis and cell division in single cells or by fragmentation in multicellular forms. Many green algae produce spores asexually by mitosis; if these spores have flagella and are motile, they are called *zoospores* (**FIG. 26-16**). Sexual reproduction in the green algae involves gamete formation

50 μm

(a) LM of *Spirogyra,* a filamentous green alga with spiral chloroplasts.

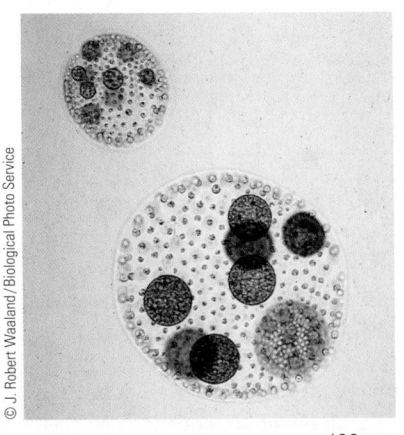

100 μm

(b) LM of two *Volvox* colonies, each composed of up to 50,000 cells. New colonies are inside the parental colonies, which eventually break apart.

(c) *Ulva's* thin, sheetlike form suggests its common name, sea lettuce.

(d) *Chara,* a green alga commonly called a stonewort, is closely related to land plants. *Chara* is widely distributed in fresh water.

FIGURE 26-15 Green algae

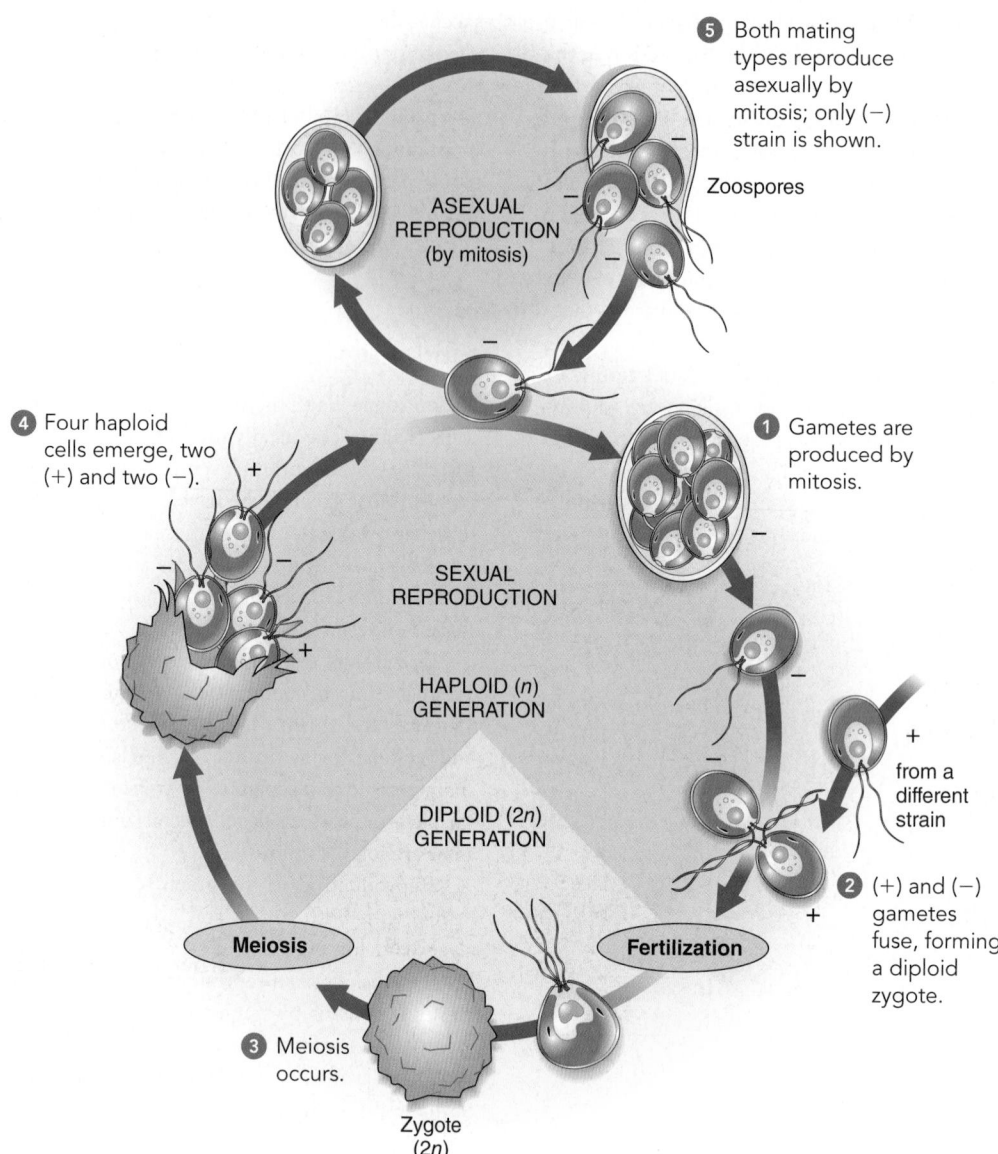

⑤ Both mating types reproduce asexually by mitosis; only (−) strain is shown.

Zoospores

ASEXUAL REPRODUCTION (by mitosis)

④ Four haploid cells emerge, two (+) and two (−).

① Gametes are produced by mitosis.

SEXUAL REPRODUCTION

HAPLOID (*n*) GENERATION

DIPLOID (2*n*) GENERATION

+ from a different strain

② (+) and (−) gametes fuse, forming a diploid zygote.

Meiosis

Fertilization

③ Meiosis occurs.

Zygote (2*n*)

FIGURE 26-16 *Animated* **The life cycle of *Chlamydomonas***

Chlamydomonas is a unicellular, haploid green alga with two mating types, (+) and (−).

in unicellular **gametangia** (sing., *gametangium*), reproductive structures in which gametes are produced. Green algae are found in both aquatic and terrestrial environments. Aquatic green algae primarily inhabit fresh water, although there are many marine species. Terrestrial green algae are restricted to damp soil, cracks in tree bark, and other moist places. Many green algae are symbionts with other organisms; some live as endosymbionts in body cells of invertebrates, and a few grow together with fungi as "dual organisms" called *lichens* (discussed in Chapter 29). Regardless of where they live, green algae are ecologically important as producers.

Review

■ Why do many biologists classify red algae and green algae with land plants?

26.7 UNIKONTS

■ LEARNING OBJECTIVE

10 Briefly describe and compare the following unikonts: amoebas, plasmodial slime molds, cellular slime molds, and choanoflagellates.

Unikonts are a supergroup composed of certain amoebas, plasmodial slime molds, cellular slime molds, choanoflagellates, fungi (discussed in Chapter 29) and animals (discussed in Chapters 30 through 32). Unikonts share a single posterior flagellum in flagellate cells such as sperm and motile spores, although some extant organisms in this supergroup have lost the flagellum. Many unikonts also have a single centriole. Examine Figure 26-3 again and note that the unikonts are divided into two clades. One of these is the **opisthokonts,** which consist of fungi, choanoflagel-lates, and animals. You will learn more about the opisthokonts in Chapters 29 and 30.

Unikonts also have a **triple-gene fusion** that has major evolutionary significance. In a triple-gene fusion, three separate genes fused into a single unit early in the course of eukaryote evolution; the fused gene codes for a multienzyme protein. You may recall that Figure 26-3 showed all five supergroups branching from the same point, indicating that the branching order is unresolved. However, triple-gene fusion provides evidence of a bifurcation, or branch of the eukaryotes into two main clades, close to the root of the common ancestor of all eukaryotes (**FIG. 26-17**). The two branches consist of (1) unikonts, which had a common ancestor with a single posterior flagellum, and (2) all other eukaryotes, collectively called **bikonts,** which had a common ancestor with two flagella.

KEY EXPERIMENT

QUESTION: How do we deduce details of eukaryote evolution near the root of the evolutionary tree?

HYPOTHESIS: Derived gene fusions, which have occurred rarely during the course of evolution, can provide insights into eukaryote evolutionary relationships.

EXPERIMENT: Alexandra Stechmann and Thomas Cavalier-Smith of Oxford University sequenced a double-gene fusion that codes for two enzymes, dihydrofolate reductase (DHFR) and thymidylate synthase (TS). In a second experiment, they sequenced a triple-fused gene involved in the enzymatic synthesis of pyrimidine nucleotides. They tested for the presence of these two gene fusions in various eukaryote groups as well as in bacteria and archaea.

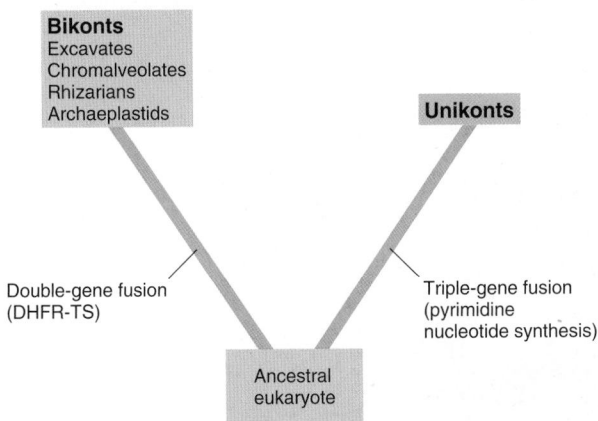

RESULTS AND CONCLUSION: The double-gene fusion is present in all eukaryotes examined except for unikonts; bacteria and archaea also lack the double-gene fusion. The unikonts have the triple-gene fusion that is lacking in all other eukaryotes, bacteria, and archaea. These gene fusions suggest a fundamental division of eukaryotes into two main clades—the unikonts and all other eukaryotes, collectively called bikonts.

Source: Stechmann, A. and T. Cavalier-Smith. "The Root of the Eukaryote Tree Pinpointed." *Current Biology,* Vol. 13, Sept. 2, 2003.

FIGURE 26-17 Stechmann and Cavalier-Smith's research on evolution of the protists

---

Amoebozoa are unikonts with lobose pseudopodia

Most **amoebozoa** produce temporary cytoplasmic projections called **pseudopodia** (sing., *pseudopodium,* meaning "false foot") at some point in their life cycle. The pseudopodia of amoebozoa are *lobose*—that is, rounded and wide—as opposed to the slender cytoplasmic projections characteristic of rhizarians. Biologists currently classify amoebas, plasmodial slime molds, and cellular slime molds as amoebozoa.

Amoebas move by forming pseudopodia

Amoebas are unicellular amoebozoa found in soil, fresh water, the ocean, and other organisms (as parasites). Because of the extreme flexibility of their outer plasma membrane, many members of this group have an asymmetrical body form and continually change shape as they move. (The word *amoeba* derives from a Greek word meaning "change.") An amoeba moves by pushing out lobose pseudopodia from the surface of the cell (see LM in Table 26-1). More cytoplasm flows into the pseudopodia, enlarging them until all the cytoplasm has entered and the organism as a whole has moved. Pseudopodia also capture and engulf food by surrounding and forming a vacuole around it (**FIG. 26-18**). Food particles are digested when the food vacuole fuses with a lysosome containing digestive enzymes. Digested materials are absorbed from the food vacuole, which gradually shrinks as it empties. Amoebas reproduce asexually, splitting into two equal parts after mitotic division of the nucleus; sexual reproduction has not been observed.

Parasitic amoebas include *Entamoeba histolytica,* which causes *amoebic dysentery,* a serious human intestinal disease characterized by severe diarrhea, bloody stools, and ulcers in the intestinal wall. In especially severe cases, the organism spreads from the large intestine and causes abscesses in the liver, lungs, or brain. *Entamoeba histolytica* is transmitted as cysts in contaminated drinking water. A **cyst** is a thick-walled, resistant, resting stage in the life cycle of some protists. Other amoebas, such as *Acanthamoeba,* are usually free-living but produce opportunistic infections such as eye infections in contact lens wearers.

Plasmodial slime molds feed as multinucleate plasmodia

The feeding stage of a **plasmodial slime mold** is a **plasmodium,** a multinucleate mass of cytoplasm that can grow up to 30 cm (1 ft) in diameter (**FIG. 26-19a**). The slimy plasmodium streams over damp, decaying logs and leaf litter, often forming a network of channels that covers a large surface area. As it creeps along, it ingests bacteria, yeasts, spores, and decaying organic matter.

When the food supply dwindles or there is insufficient moisture, the plasmodium crawls to an exposed surface and starts reproducing. Stalked structures of intricate complexity and beauty usually form from the drying plasmodium (**FIG. 26-19b**). Within these structures, called **sporangia,** meiosis produces haploid spores that are extremely resistant to adverse environmental conditions.

When conditions become favorable, the spores germinate, and a haploid reproductive cell emerges from each. This haploid cell is either a biflagellate *swarm cell* or an amoeboid *myxamoeba,*

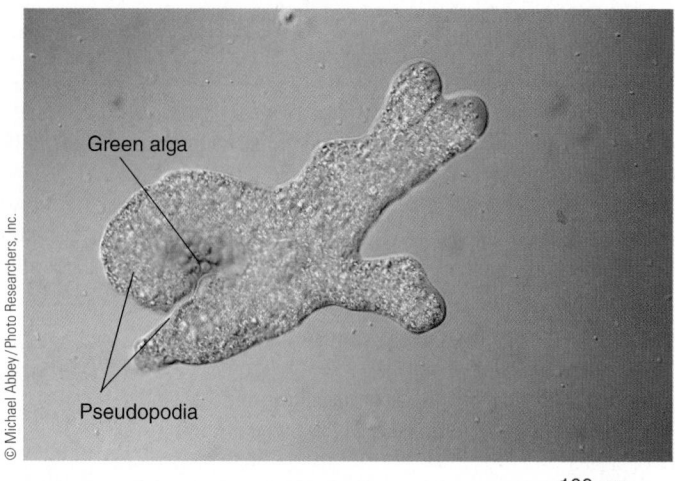

Green alga

Pseudopodia

100 μm

FIGURE 26-18 *Animated* Amoeba

LM of a giant amoeba (*Chaos carolinense*). This unicellular protist, which moves and feeds by pseudopodia, is surrounding and ingesting a colonial green alga. *Chaos* amoebas are generally scavengers that feed on debris in freshwater habitats, but they ingest living organisms when the opportunity arises.

depending on available moisture; flagellate cells form in wet conditions. Swarm cells and myxamoebas act as gametes, which fuse to form a zygote with a diploid nucleus. The resultant diploid nucleus divides many times by mitosis, but the cytoplasm does not divide, so the result is a multinucleate plasmodium.

The plasmodial slime mold *Physarum polycephalum* is a model organism that researchers use to study many fundamental biological processes, such as growth, cytoplasmic streaming, and the function of the cytoskeleton.

Cellular slime molds feed as individual amoeboid cells

The **cellular slime molds** are amoebozoa with close affinities to amoebas and plasmodial slime molds. During its feeding stage, each cellular slime mold is an individual amoeboid cell that behaves as a separate, solitary organism (**FIG. 26-20**). Each cell creeps over rotting logs and soil or swims in fresh water, ingesting bacteria and other particles of food as it goes. Each amoeboid cell has a haploid nucleus and reproduces by mitosis, as a true amoeba does.

250 μm

(a) The brightly pigmented plasmodium, shown on a dead log, feeds on bacteria and other microorganisms.

(b) The reproductive structures are sporangia on stalks.

FIGURE 26-19 The plasmodial slime mold *Physarum polycephalum*

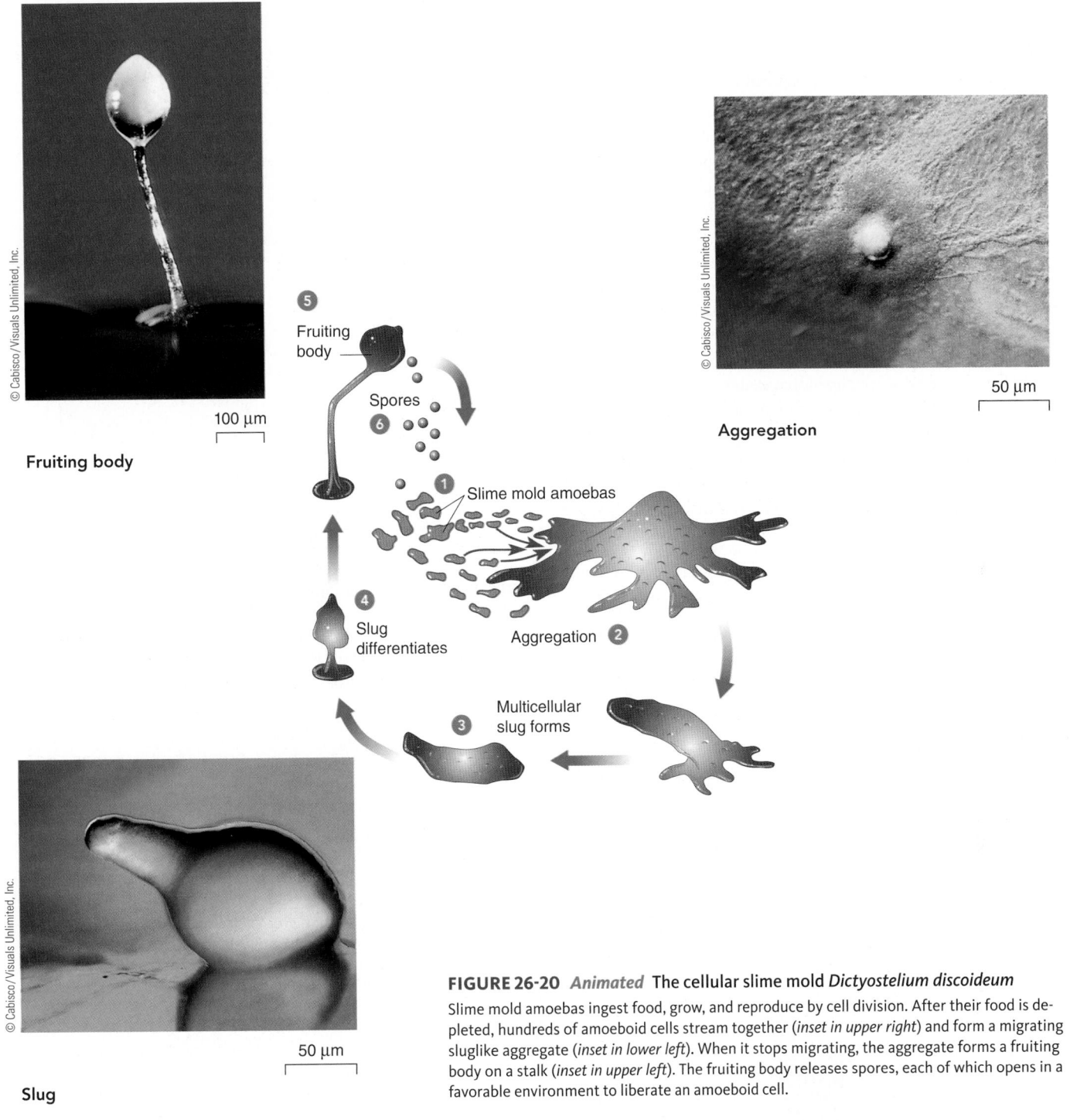

Fruiting body

© Cabisco/Visuals Unlimited, Inc.

100 µm

Aggregation

© Cabisco/Visuals Unlimited, Inc.

50 µm

⑤ Fruiting body

Spores

⑥

① Slime mold amoebas

④ Slug differentiates

Aggregation ②

Multicellular slug forms ③

Slug

© Cabisco/Visuals Unlimited, Inc.

50 µm

FIGURE 26-20 *Animated* **The cellular slime mold *Dictyostelium discoideum***

Slime mold amoebas ingest food, grow, and reproduce by cell division. After their food is depleted, hundreds of amoeboid cells stream together (*inset in upper right*) and form a migrating sluglike aggregate (*inset in lower left*). When it stops migrating, the aggregate forms a fruiting body on a stalk (*inset in upper left*). The fruiting body releases spores, each of which opens in a favorable environment to liberate an amoeboid cell.

When moisture or food becomes inadequate, certain cells send out a chemical signal, cyclic adenosine monophosphate (cAMP), that causes them to aggregate by the hundreds or thousands. During this stage the cells creep about for short distances as a single multicellular aggregate, or slug. Each cell of the slug retains its plasma membrane and individual identity. Eventually, the slug settles and reorganizes, forming a stalked fruiting body containing spores. After being released, each spore opens and a single haploid

amoeboid cell—the feeding stage—emerges. The spore-forming reproductive cycle is asexual, although sexual reproduction is observed occasionally. The life cycles of most cellular slime molds lack a flagellate stage.

The cellular slime mold *Dictyostelium discoideum* is a model organism for the study of cell differentiation, cell communication, and cell motility and adhesion. Its biology has been studied intensively, particularly as it relates to **cell signaling** molecules, such as cAMP, which are found in many organisms in addition to the cellular slime molds (see Chapter 6).

Choanoflagellates are closely related to animals

Choanoflagellates are collared flagellates. These small, inconspicuous unikonts are found globally in both freshwater and marine environments. Choanoflagellates include both free-swimming and **sessile** species that are permanently attached by a thin stalk to bacteria-rich debris. Their single flagellum is surrounded at the base by a delicate collar of microvilli that trap food (**FIG. 26-21**).

Choanoflagellates are of special interest because of their striking resemblance to collar cells in sponges (see Fig. 31-1b). Other animal phyla, such as cnidarians, flatworms, and echinoderms, also contain choanoflagellate-like cells, but no other group of protists has been observed to possess these cells. Evidence supporting the close relationship between choanoflagellates and animals includes comparative DNA sequence data of mitochondrial and nuclear genes. Given the similarities in structure and molecular genomics that has accumulated in recent years, many biologists hypothesize that choanoflagellates are the closest living non-animal relative of animals. Thus, living choanoflagellates and animals probably share a common choanoflagellate-like ancestor.

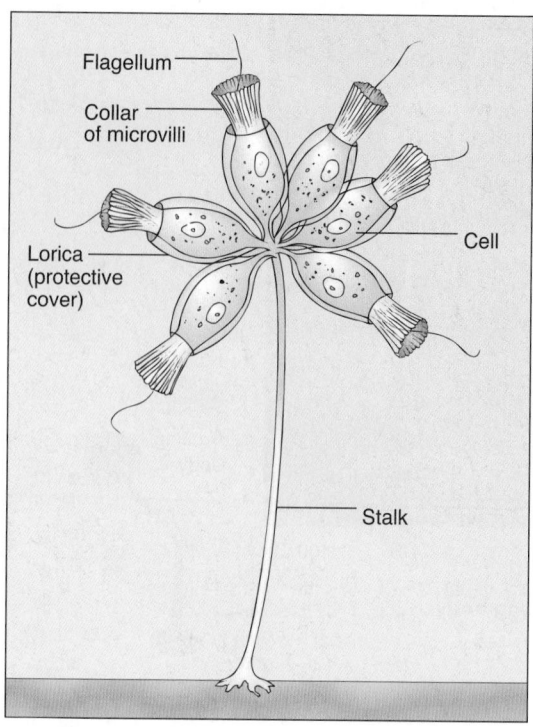

FIGURE 26-21 Choanoflagellates
Choanoflagellates are free-living flagellates that obtain food by waving their flagella, causing water currents to carry bacteria and other small particles of food into the collar of microvilli. A colonial form is shown. Each cell is 5 to 10 μm long, not including the flagellum.

Review

- Why don't we classify amoebas that have lobose pseudopodia with the rhizarians?
- Which group of unikonts is structurally and genetically most similar to animals?

■ SUMMARY: FOCUS ON LEARNING OBJECTIVES

26.1 (page 538)

1 Discuss in general terms the diversity inherent in protists, including means of locomotion, modes of nutrition, interactions with other organisms, habitats, and modes of reproduction.

- Protists have various means of locomotion, including pseudopodia, flagella, and cilia; a few are nonmotile.

- Protists obtain their nutrients autotrophically or heterotrophically. Protists are free-living or symbiotic, with symbiotic relationships ranging from **mutualism** to **parasitism.**
- Most protists live in the ocean or in freshwater ponds, lakes, and streams. Parasitic protists live in the body fluids or cells of their hosts.
- Many protists reproduce both sexually and asexually; others reproduce only asexually.

26.2 (page 539)

2 Discuss the hypothesis of serial endosymbiosis and briefly explain some of the evidence that supports it.

- According to the hypothesis of **serial endosymbiosis,** mitochondria and chloroplasts arose from symbiotic relationships between larger cells and the smaller bacteria that were incorporated and lived within them.
- Chloroplasts of red algae, green algae, and plants probably arose in a single primary endosymbiotic event in which a cyanobacterium was incorporated into a cell. Multiple secondary endosymbioses led to chloroplasts in euglenoids, dinoflagellates, diatoms, golden algae, and brown algae and to the nonfunctional chloroplasts in apicomplexans.

3 Describe the kinds of data biologists use to classify eukaryotes.

- Relationships among protists are determined largely by **ultrastructure,** which is the fine details of cell structure revealed by electron microscopy, and by comparative molecular data. Biologists have compared nuclear genes, many of which code for proteins, in different protist taxa.

26.3 (page 540)

4 Summarize the basic features of excavates and distinguish among diplomonads, parabasilids, and euglenoids.

- **Excavates** are a diverse group of unicellular protists with flagella, an excavated oral groove, and atypical, greatly modified mitochondria. The inclusion of diplomonads, parabasilids, and euglenoids in the excavate superfamily is controversial.
- **Diplomonads** are excavates, organisms with a deep, or excavated, oral groove. Diplomonads have one or two nuclei, no functional mitochondria, no Golgi complex, and up to eight flagella.

- **Parabasilids** are anaerobic, flagellated excavates that often live in animals. Trichonymphs and trichomonads are examples of parabasilids.
- **Euglenoids** are unicellular and flagellate. Some euglenoids are photosynthetic.

26.4 *(page 544)*

5 Contrast the two main groups of chromalveolates: alveolates and stramenopiles.

- **Chromalveolates** probably originated as a result of secondary endosymbiosis in which an ancestral cell engulfed a red alga. Some DNA sequence data suggest the chromalveolates are not monophyletic.
- **Alveolates** have similar ribosomal DNA sequences and alveoli, flattened vesicles located just inside the plasma membrane. Most **stramenopiles** have motile cells with two flagella, one of which has tiny hairlike projections off the shaft.

6 Distinguish among the alveolates: dinoflagellates, apicomplexans, and ciliates.

- **Dinoflagellates** are mostly unicellular, biflagellate, photosynthetic alveolates of great ecological importance as producers in marine ecosystems. Their **alveoli,** flattened vesicles under the plasma membrane, often contain cellulose plates impregnated with silicates. Some dinoflagellates produce toxic blooms known as **red tides.**
- **Apicomplexans** are parasites that produce **sporozoites** and are nonmotile. An apical complex of microtubules attaches the apicomplexan to its host cell. The apicomplexan *Plasmodium* causes malaria.

  CENGAGENOW™ Watch the life cycle of the malaria parasite by clicking on the figure in CengageNOW.

- **Ciliates** are alveolates that move by hairlike **cilia,** have **micronuclei** (for sexual reproduction) and **macronuclei** (for controlling cell metabolism and growth), and undergo a sexual process called **conjugation.**

  CENGAGENOW™ Watch conjugation by clicking on the figure in CengageNOW.

7 Distinguish among the stramenopiles: water molds, diatoms, golden algae, and brown algae.

- **Water molds** have a coenocytic **mycelium.** They reproduce asexually by forming biflagellate **zoospores** and sexually by forming **oospores.**
- **Diatoms** are mostly unicellular, with shells containing silica. Some diatoms are part of floating **plankton,** and others live on rocks and sediments where they move by gliding.
- **Golden algae** are mostly unicellular, biflagellate freshwater and marine stramenopiles that are of ecological importance as a component of the ocean's extremely minute **nanoplankton.**

- **Brown algae** are multicellular stramenopiles that are ecologically important in cooler ocean waters. The largest brown algae (kelps) possess leaflike **blades,** stemlike **stipes,** anchoring **holdfasts,** and gas-filled bladders for buoyancy.

26.5 *(page 551)*

8 Describe the forams and actinopods, and explain why many biologists classify them in the rhizarian supergroup.

- **Rhizarians** are amoeboid cells that often have hard outer shells, called **tests,** through which cytoplasmic projections extend; molecular evidence indicates this group is monophyletic.
- **Forams** secrete many-chambered tests with pores through which cytoplasmic projections extend to move and obtain food.
- **Actinopods** are mostly marine plankton that obtain food by means of **axopods,** slender cytoplasmic projections that extend through pores in their shells.

26.6 *(page 552)*

9 Describe evidence supporting the hypothesis that red algae and green algae should be included in a monophyletic group with land plants.

- Red algae, green algae, and land plants, collectively called **archaeplastids,** are considered a monophyletic group based on molecular data and on the presence of chloroplasts bounded by outer and inner membranes.
- **Red algae,** which are mostly multicellular seaweeds, are ecologically important in warm tropical ocean waters.
- **Green algae** exhibit a wide diversity in size, structural complexity, and reproduction. Botanists hypothesize that ancestral green algae gave rise to land plants.

  CENGAGENOW™ Watch the life cycles of a red alga and a green alga by clicking on the figures in CengageNOW.

26.7 *(page 554)*

10 Briefly describe and compare the following unikonts: amoebas, plasmodial slime molds, cellular slime molds, and choanoflagellates.

- **Unikonts,** which include fungi and animals, share a single posterior flagellum in flagellate cells.
- **Amoebas** move and obtain food by **phagocytosis,** using cytoplasmic extensions called **pseudopodia.**
- The feeding stage of **plasmodial slime molds** is a multinucleate **plasmodium.** Reproduction is by haploid spores produced within **sporangia.**
- **Cellular slime molds** feed as individual amoeboid cells. They reproduce by aggregating into an aggregate (slug), then forming asexual spores.

  CENGAGENOW™ Watch the life cycle of a cellular slime mold by clicking on the figures in CengageNOW.

- **Choanoflagellates** are unikonts that are probably the closest living non-animal relative of animals. A collar of microvilli surrounds their single flagellum at the base.

TEST YOUR UNDERSTANDING

1. Which of the following is *not* true of the protists? (a) they are unicellular, colonial, coenocytic, or simple multicellular organisms (b) their cilia and flagella have a 9 + 2 arrangement of microtubules (c) they are prokaryotic, as bacteria and archaea are (d) some are free-living, and some are endosymbionts (e) most are aquatic and live in the ocean or in freshwater ponds

2. Molecular evidence supports the view that all plastids evolved from an ancient (a) cyanobacterium (b) archaean (c) diplomonad (d) apicomplexan (e) unikont

3. Forams (a) are endosymbionts that live in many marine invertebrates (b) were responsible for the Irish potato famine in the 19th century (c) secrete many-chambered tests with pores through

which cytoplasmic extensions project (d) have numerous axopods that may aid in trapping and holding prey (e) have numerous cilia to direct food into the oral groove

4. *Paramecium* and other ciliates often display a sexual phenomenon called (a) oogamy (b) conjugation (c) serial endosymbiosis (d) red tide (e) alternation of generations

5. Parasitic alveolates that form spores at some stage in their life belong to which group? (a) actinopods (b) ciliates (c) cocco-lithophorids (d) apicomplexans (e) dinoflagellates

6. Malaria (a) is transmitted by the bite of a female tsetse fly (b) is caused by a parasitic flagellate, *Giardia intestinalis* (c) is a serious form of amoebic dysentery caused by *Entamoeba histolytica* (d) is caused by an apicomplexan that spends part of its life cycle in the *Anopheles* mosquito and part in humans (e) is transmitted when people drink water tainted by a red tide

7. Photosynthetic protists with shells composed of two halves that fit together like a petri dish are (a) golden algae (b) diatoms (c) euglenoids (d) brown algae (e) forams

8. The pigments, energy reserve products, and cell walls found in land plants are also characteristic of (a) green algae (b) brown algae (c) golden algae (d) diatoms (e) euglenoids and diatoms

9. Kelps are _____ with multicellular bodies differentiated into blades, stipes, holdfasts, and gas-filled floats. (a) golden algae (b) diatoms (c) euglenoids (d) brown algae (e) red algae

10. Cellular slime molds (a) include *Physarum* and *Phytophthora* (b) are more closely related to bacteria than are any other protists (c) are responsible for late blight of potatoes, which led to starva-tion in Ireland in the 1840s (d) have double-gene fusion (e) form a slug when cells aggregate in response to cyclic AMP

11. Water molds reproduce asexually by forming _____ and sexu-ally by forming _____. (a) oospores; holdfasts (b) zoospores; zooxanthellae (c) zoospores; oospores (d) holdfasts; oospores (e) oospores; zoospores

12. Label the diagrams. Use Figures 26-5b and 26-8b to check your answers.

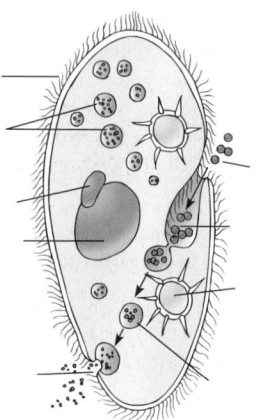

CRITICAL THINKING

1. **EVOLUTION LINK.** Why are the protists considered paraphy-letic? Use Figure 26-3 to help explain your answer.

2. **ANALYZING DATA.** Where on Figure 26-3 would you place the common ancestor of brown algae and water molds? The common ancestor of animals and fungi?

3. **ANALYZING DATA.** In the darkfield LM of unicellular choano-flagellates (at right), actin has been stained red, tubulin green, and DNA blue. Identify the cell parts that contain each of these chemi-cal materials.

4. **SCIENCE, TECHNOLOGY, AND SOCIETY.** Why has resis-tance to traditional antimalarial drugs emerged in *Plasmodium*?

Nicole King Lab, University of California, Berkeley

CENGAGENOW™ Additional questions are available in CengageNOW at www.cengage.com/login.

27 Seedless Plants

Land plants. Note the ferns in the foreground and the moss-covered dead tree. Both mosses and ferns are seedless plants.

Mark Edwards/Peter Arnold Inc.

About 445 million years ago (mya), planet Earth would have seemed an inhospitable place because, although life abounded in the ocean, it did not yet exist in abundance on land. Occasionally, perhaps, an animal would crawl out of the water onto land, but it never stayed there permanently because there was little to eat on land—not a single blade of grass, no fruit, and no seeds.

During the next 30 million years, a time corresponding roughly to the Silurian period in geologic time (see Table 21-1), plants appeared in abundance and colonized the land. Where did they come from? Although plants living today exhibit great diversity in size, form, and habitat (see photograph), biologists hypothesize that they all evolved from a common ancestor that was an ancient green alga.

Modern green algae share many biochemical and metabolic traits with modern plants. Both green algae and plants contain the same photosynthetic pigments: chlorophylls *a* and *b* and carotenoids, including xanthophylls (yellow pigments) and carotenes (orange pigments). Both store excess carbohydrates as starch and have cellulose as a major component of their cell walls. In addition, plants and some green algae share certain details of cell division, including formation of a cell plate during cytokinesis (see Chapter 10).

What exactly is a plant? A **plant** is a complex multicellular eukaryote that has cellulose cell walls, chlorophylls *a* and *b* in plastids, starch as a storage product, and may have cells with two anterior flagella. In addition, all plants develop from multicellular *embryos* that are enclosed in maternal tissues; this last character is one that distinguishes plants from green algae. Many botanists refer to land plants as *embryophytes* because of this character.

Plants range in size from minute, almost microscopic duckweeds and water-meal to massive giant sequoias, some of the largest organisms that have ever lived. Plants include hundreds of thousands of species that live in varied habitats, from frozen arctic tundra to lush tropical rain forests to harsh deserts to moist stream banks.

27.1 ADAPTATIONS OF PLANTS TO LIFE ON LAND

LEARNING OBJECTIVES

1 Discuss some environmental challenges of living on land and describe how several plant adaptations meet these challenges.
2 Name the green algal group from which plants are hypothesized to have descended and describe supporting evidence.

How were plants modified during the transition from life in the water to life on land? What are some features of plants that have let them colonize so many types of environments? One important difference between plants and algae is that a waxy **cuticle** covers the aerial portion of a plant. Essential for existence on land, the cuticle helps prevent desiccation, or drying out, of plant tissues by evaporation. Plants that are adapted to moister habitats may have a very thin layer of wax, whereas those adapted to drier environments often have a thick, crusty cuticle. (Many desert plants also have a reduced surface area, particularly of leaves, which minimizes water loss.)

Plants obtain the carbon they need for photosynthesis from the atmosphere as carbon dioxide (CO_2). To be fixed into organic molecules such as sugar, CO_2 must first diffuse into the chloroplasts that are inside green plant cells. Because a waxy cuticle covers the external surfaces of leaves and stems, however, gas exchange through the cuticle between the atmosphere and the interior of cells is negligible. Tiny pores called **stomata** (sing., *stoma*), which dot the surfaces of leaves and stems of almost all plants, facilitate gas exchange.

The sex organs, or **gametangia** (sing., *gametangium*), of most plants are multicellular, whereas the gametangia of algae are unicellular (**FIG. 27-1**). Each plant gametangium has a layer of sterile (nonreproductive) cells that surrounds and protects the delicate gametes (eggs and sperm cells). In plants, the fertilized egg develops into a multicellular **embryo** (young plant) within the female gametangium. Thus, the embryo is protected during its development. In algae, the fertilized egg develops away from its gametangium; in some algae, the gametes are released before fertilization, whereas in others the fertilized egg is released.

The plant life cycle alternates between haploid and diploid generations

Plants have a clearly defined **alternation of generations** in which they spend part of their lives in a multicellular haploid stage and part in a multicellular diploid stage (**FIG. 27-2**).[1] The haploid portion of the life cycle is called the **gametophyte generation** because it gives rise to haploid gametes by mitosis. When two gametes fuse, the diploid portion of the life cycle, called the **sporophyte generation,** begins. The sporophyte generation produces haploid spores by the process of meiosis; these spores represent the first stage in the gametophyte generation.

Let us examine alternation of generations more closely. The haploid gametophytes produce male gametangia, known as **antheridia** (sing., *antheridium*), in which sperm cells form, and/or female gametangia, known as **archegonia** (sing., *archegonium*), each bearing a single egg (**FIG. 27-3**). Sperm cells reach the female gametangium in a variety of ways, and one sperm cell fertilizes the egg to form a **zygote,** or fertilized egg.

The diploid zygote is the first stage in the sporophyte generation. The zygote divides by mitosis and develops into a multicellular embryo, the young sporophyte plant. Embryo development takes place within the archegonium; thus, the embryo is protected as it develops. Eventually, the embryo grows into a mature sporophyte plant. The mature sporophyte has special cells called *sporogenous cells* (spore-producing cells, also called *spore mother cells*) that divide by meiosis to form haploid **spores.**

fertilization of egg by sperm cell ⟶ zygote ⟶ embryo ⟶ mature sporophyte plant ⟶ sporogenous cells ⟶ meiosis ⟶ spores

---

[1]For convenience, we limit our discussion to plants that are not polyploid, although polyploidy is very common in land plants. We therefore use the terms *diploid* and *2n* (and *haploid* and *n*) interchangeably, although these terms are not actually synonymous.

FIGURE 27-1 Generalized reproductive structures of algae and plants
(a, b) In algae, gametangia are generally unicellular. When the gametes are released, only the wall of the original cell remains. **(c, d)** In plants, the gametangia are multicellular, but only the inner cells become gametes. The gametes are surrounded by a protective layer of sterile (nonreproductive) cells.

Plants have an alternation of generations, spending part of the cycle in a haploid gametophyte stage and part in a diploid sporophyte stage.

1 The gametophyte produces gametes by mitosis.

5 Each spore has the potential to undergo mitosis and develop into a gametophyte.

2 Two haploid gametes fuse to form a zygote.

4 Special cells of the sporophyte undergo meiosis to form spores.

3 The zygote (fertilized egg) develops by mitosis into the sporophyte.

Gametophyte

Spore

Sperm Egg

HAPLOID (*n*)
GAMETOPHYTE
GENERATION

Meiosis

Fertilization

DIPLOID (2*n*)
SPOROPHYTE
GENERATION

Zygote

Embryo

Sporophyte

FIGURE 27-2 The basic plant life cycle

Depending on the plant group, the haploid or the diploid stage may be greatly enlarged or reduced; as you will learn, this fact has evolutionary significance.

All plants produce spores by meiosis, in contrast with algae and fungi, which may produce spores by meiosis or mitosis. The spores represent the first stage in the gametophyte generation. Each spore divides by mitosis to produce a multicellular gametophyte, and the cycle continues. Plants therefore alternate between a haploid gametophyte generation and a diploid sporophyte generation.

spores ⟶ mature gametophyte plants

archegonia ⟶ eggs

antheridia ⟶ sperm cells

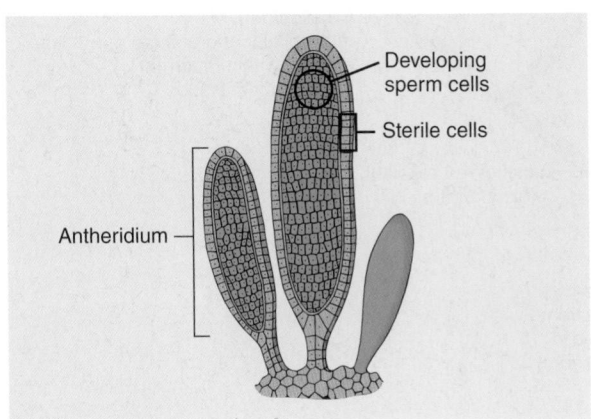

Developing sperm cells

Sterile cells

Antheridium

(a) Each antheridium, the male gametangium, produces numerous sperm cells.

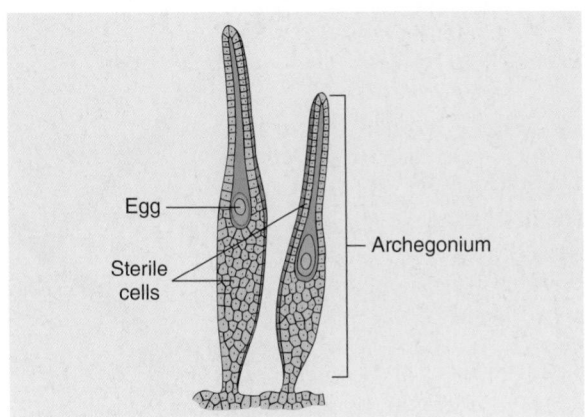

Egg

Archegonium

Sterile cells

(b) Each archegonium, the female gametangium, produces a single egg.

FIGURE 27-3 Plant gametangia

Shown are generalized moss gametangia.

Four major groups of plants exist today

Structural and molecular data indicate that land plants probably descended from a group of green algae called **charophytes** or **stoneworts** (see Fig. 26-15d, which shows a charophyte). Recall from Chapter 26 that red algae, green algae, and land plants are collectively classified as **archaeplastids.** Molecular comparisons, particularly of DNA and RNA sequences, provide compelling evidence that green algae are closely allied to plants (**FIG. 27-4**). These comparisons among plants and various green algae include sequences of chloroplast DNA, certain nuclear genes, and ribosomal RNA. In each case, the closest match occurs between charophytes and plants, indicating that modern charophytes and plants probably share a recent common ancestor.

Plants consist of four major groups: bryophytes, seedless vascular plants, and two groups of seeded vascular plants: gymnosperms and angiosperms (flowering plants) (**FIG. 27-5**; see also **TABLE 27-1**, which is an overview of the ten extant [living] plant phyla).

The mosses and other bryophytes are small nonvascular plants that lack a specialized vascular, or conducting, system to transport nutrients, water, and essential minerals (inorganic nutrients) throughout the plant body. In the absence of such a system, bryophytes rely on diffusion and osmosis to obtain needed materials. This reliance means that bryophytes are restricted in size; if they were much larger, some of their cells could not obtain enough necessary materials. Bryophytes do not form seeds, the reproductive structures discussed in Chapter 28. Bryophytes reproduce and disperse primarily via haploid spores. Recent molecular and fossil evidence, discussed later in the chapter, suggests that bryophytes may have been the earliest plants to colonize land.

The other three groups of plants—seedless vascular plants, gymnosperms, and flowering plants—have vascular tissues and are thus known as vascular plants. The two vascular tissues are **xylem,** for conducting water and dissolved minerals, and **phloem,** for conducting dissolved organic molecules such as sugar. A key step in the evolution of vascular plants was the ability to produce **lignin,** a strengthening polymer in the walls of cells that function for support and conduction (see Chapter 33 for a discussion of plant cell wall chemistry, including lignin). The stiffening property of lignin enabled plants to grow tall, which let them maximize light

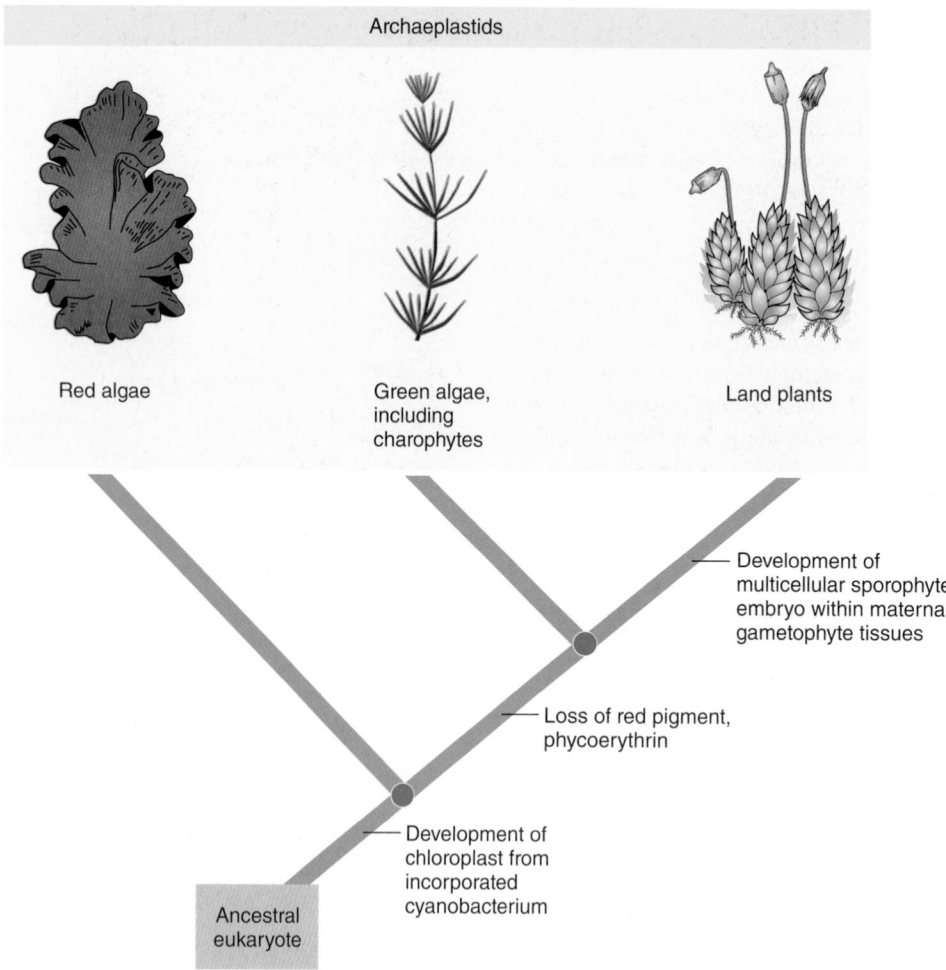

FIGURE 27-4 Evolution of land plants

Cladograms such as this one represent an emerging consensus that is open to change as new discoveries are made.

interception. The successful occupation of the land by plants, in turn, made the evolution of terrestrial animals possible by providing them with both habitat and food.

Club mosses and ferns (which include whisk ferns and horsetails) are seedless vascular plants that, like the bryophytes, reproduce and disperse primarily via spores. Seedless vascular plants arose and diversified during the Silurian and Devonian periods of the Paleozoic era, between 444 mya and 359 mya. Club mosses and ferns extend back more than 420 million years and were of considerable importance as Earth's dominant plants in past ages. Fossil evidence indicates that many species of these plants were the size of immense trees. Most living representatives of club mosses and ferns are small.

The gymnosperms are vascular plants that reproduce by forming seeds. Gymnosperms produce seeds borne exposed (unprotected) on a stem or in a cone. Plants with seeds as their primary means of reproduction and dispersal first appeared about 359 mya, at the end of the Devonian period. These early seed plants diversified into many varied species of gymnosperms.

The most recent plant group to appear is the flowering plants, or angiosperms, which arose during the early Cretaceous period of the Mesozoic era, about 130 mya. Like gymnosperms, flowering plants reproduce by forming seeds. Flowering plants, however, produce seeds enclosed within a fruit.

Review

- What are the most important environmental challenges that plants face living on land?
- What adaptations do plants have to meet these environmental challenges?
- From which group of green algae are plants hypothesized to have descended?
- Draw a simple diagram illustrating alternation of generations in plants.

27.2 BRYOPHYTES

■ LEARNING OBJECTIVES

3 Summarize the features that distinguish bryophytes from other plants.
4 Name and briefly describe the three phyla of bryophytes.
5 Describe the life cycle of mosses and compare their gametophyte and sporophyte generations.

The **bryophytes** (from the Greek words meaning "moss plant") consist of about 16,000 species of mosses, liverworts, and hornworts;

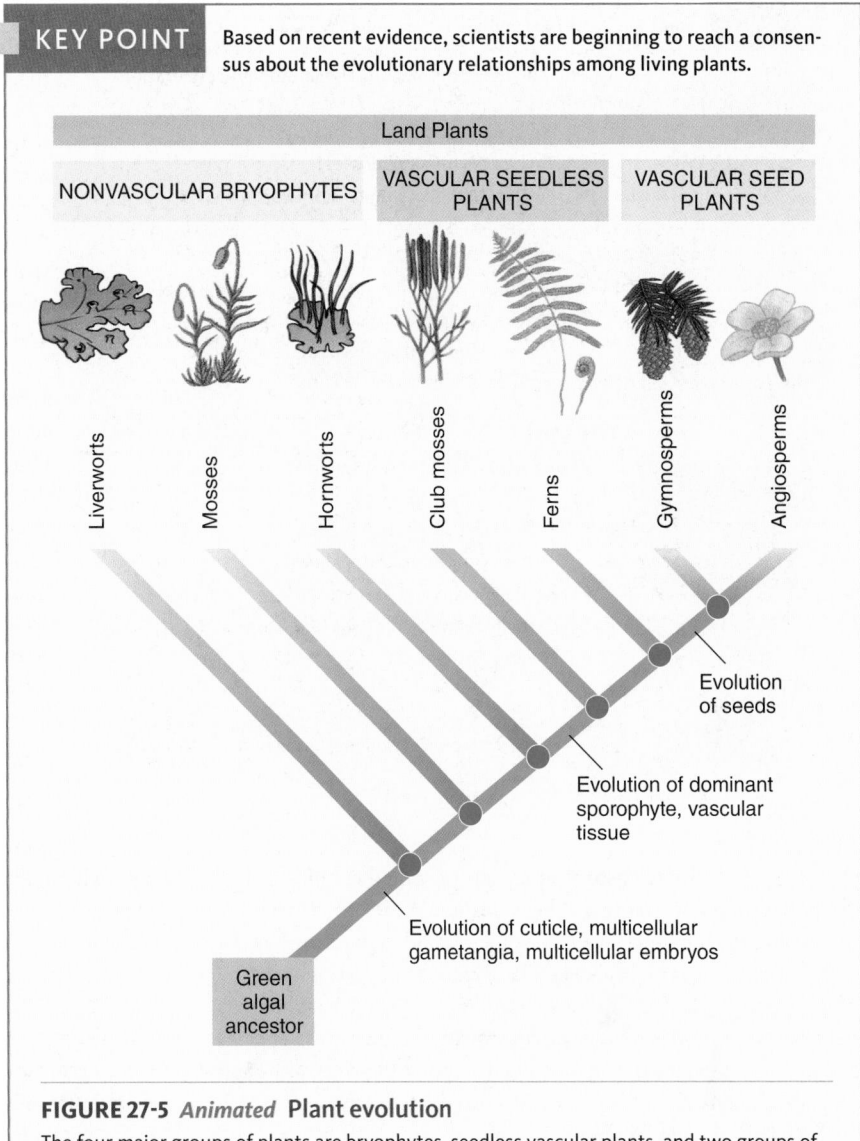

KEY POINT Based on recent evidence, scientists are beginning to reach a consensus about the evolutionary relationships among living plants.

FIGURE 27-5 *Animated* **Plant evolution**
The four major groups of plants are bryophytes, seedless vascular plants, and two groups of seed plants—gymnosperms and angiosperms. The seed plants are covered in Chapter 28.

bryophytes are the only living nonvascular plants (**TABLE 27-2**). Because they have no means for extensive internal transport of water, sugar, and essential minerals, bryophytes are typically small. They generally require a moist environment for active growth and reproduction, but some bryophytes tolerate dry areas.

The bryophytes are divided into three distinct phyla: mosses (phylum Bryophyta), liverworts (phylum Hepatophyta), and hornworts (phylum Anthocerophyta). These three groups differ in many ways and may or may not be closely related. They are usually studied together because they lack vascular tissues and have similar life cycles.

Moss gametophytes are differentiated into "leaves" and "stems"

Mosses (phylum Bryophyta), which include about 9900 species, usually live in dense colonies or beds (**FIG. 27-6a**). Each individual

TABLE 27-1   Ten Extant Plant Phyla

Nonvascular plants with a dominant gametophyte generation (bryophytes)

     Phylum Hepatophyta (liverworts)

     Phylum Bryophyta (mosses)

     Phylum Anthocerophyta (hornworts)

Vascular plants with a dominant sporophyte generation

Seedless plants

     Phylum Lycopodiophyta (club mosses)

     Phylum Pteridophyta (ferns and their allies, the whisk ferns and horsetails)

Seed plants

     Plants with naked seeds (gymnosperms)

       Phylum Coniferophyta (conifers)

       Phylum Cycadophyta (cycads)

       Phylum Ginkgophyta (ginkgoes)

       Phylum Gnetophyta (gnetophytes)

     Seeds enclosed within a fruit (angiosperms)

       Phylum Anthophyta (angiosperms or flowering plants)

         Class Eudicotyledones (eudicots)

         Class Monocotyledones (monocots)

rate sexes: male plants that bear antheridia and female plants that bear archegonia. Other mosses produce antheridia and archegonia on the same plant.

Fertilization occurs when one of the sperm cells fuses with the egg within the archegonium. Sperm cells, which have flagella, are transported from antheridium to archegonium by flowing water, such as splashing rain droplets. A raindrop lands on the top of a male gametophyte, and sperm cells are released into it from the antheridia. Another raindrop landing on the male plant may splash the sperm-laden droplet into the air and onto the top of a nearby female plant. Alternatively, arthropods such as insects and mites may touch the sperm-laden fluid and inadvertently carry it for considerable distances. Once in a film of water on the female moss, a sperm cell swims into the archegonium, which secretes chemicals to attract and guide the sperm cells, and fuses with the egg.

The diploid zygote, formed by fertilization, grows by mitosis into a multicellular embryo that develops into a mature moss sporophyte. This sporophyte grows out of the top of the female gametophyte and remains attached and nutritionally dependent on the gametophyte throughout its existence (**FIG. 27-6b**). Initially green and photosynthetic, the sporophyte becomes golden brown at maturity. It consists of three main parts: a *foot,* which anchors the sporophyte to the gametophyte and absorbs minerals and nutrients from it; a *seta,* or stalk; and a *capsule,* which contains sporogenous cells (spore mother cells). The capsule of some species is covered by a caplike structure, the *calyptra,* which is derived from the archegonium.

The sporogenous cells undergo meiosis to form haploid spores (see Fig. 27-7). When the spores are mature, the capsule opens and releases the spores, which are then transported by wind or rain. If a moss spore lands in a suitable spot, it germinates and grows into a filament of cells called a **protonema.** The protonema, which superficially resembles a filamentous green alga, forms buds, each of which grows into a green gametophyte, and the life cycle continues.

Biologists consider the haploid gametophyte generation the dominant generation in mosses because it lives independently

plant has tiny, hairlike absorptive structures called *rhizoids* and an upright, stemlike structure that bears leaflike blades, each normally consisting of a single layer of undifferentiated cells except at the midrib. Because mosses lack vascular tissues, they do not have true roots, stems, or leaves; the moss structures are not homologous to roots, stems, or leaves in vascular plants. Some moss species have water-conducting cells and sugar-conducting cells, although these cells are not lignified or as specialized or effective as the conducting cells of vascular plants.

Alternation of generations is clearly defined in the life cycle of mosses (**FIG. 27-7**). The green moss gametophyte often bears its gametangia at the top of the plant. Many moss species have sepa-

TABLE 27-2   A Comparison of Major Groups of Seedless Plants

Plant Group	Dominant Stage of Life Cycle	Representative Genera
Nonvascular; reproduce by spores (bryophytes)		
Liverworts (phylum Hepatophyta)	Gametophyte: thalloid or leafy plant	*Marchantia*
Mosses (phylum Bryophyta)	Gametophyte: leafy plant	*Polytrichum, Sphagnum, Physcomitrella*
Hornworts (phylum Anthocerophyta)	Gametophyte: thalloid plant	*Anthoceros*
Vascular; reproduce by spores		
Club mosses (phylum Lycopodiophyta)	Sporophyte: roots, rhizomes, erect stems, and leaves (microphylls)	*Lycopodium, Selaginella*
Ferns (phylum Pteridophyta)	Sporophyte: roots, rhizomes, and leaves (megaphylls)	*Pteridium, Polystichum, Azolla, Platycerium*
Whisk ferns (phylum Pteridophyta)	Sporophyte: rhizomes and erect stems; no true roots or leaves	*Psilotum*
Horsetails (phylum Pteridophyta)	Sporophyte: roots, rhizomes, erect stems, and leaves (reduced megaphylls)	*Equisetum*

Rod Planck/Dembinsky Photo Associates

(a) Moss gametophytes. Close-up of haircap moss (*Polytrichum commune*) gametophytes. The haircap moss is a popular ground cover in rock gardens, particularly in Japan.

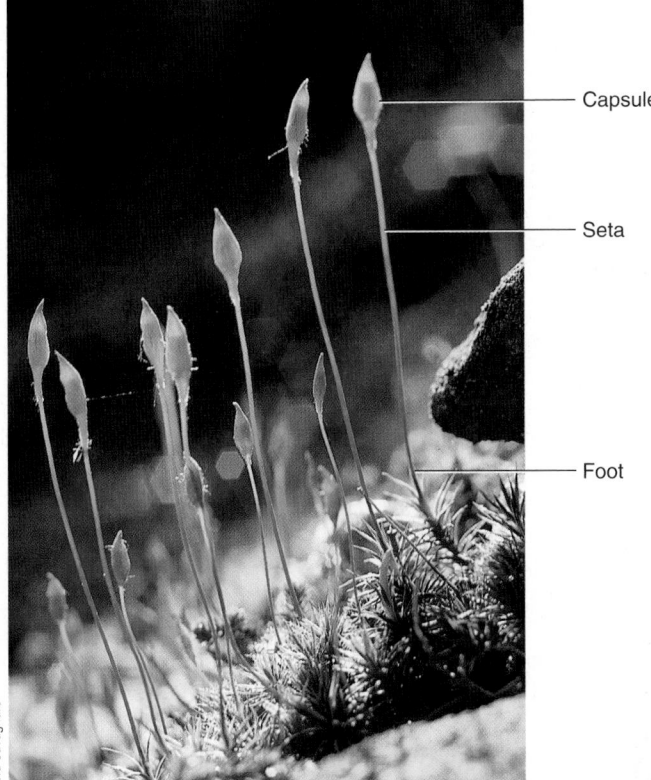

David Cavagnaro

— Capsule

— Seta

— Foot

(b) Moss sporophytes. Each consisting of a foot, seta, and capsule, the haircap moss sporophytes grow out of the top of the gametophytes. Spores are produced within the capsule.

FIGURE 27-6 Bryophytes: mosses

of the diploid sporophyte. In contrast, the moss sporophyte is attached to and nutritionally dependent on the gametophyte.

Mosses make up an inconspicuous but significant part of their environment. They play an important role in forming soil. Mosses, which form mats that cover the rock, eventually die, forming a thin layer of organic matter in which grasses and other plants can grow. Because they grow tightly packed in dense colonies, mosses hold soil in place and help prevent erosion. At the same time, they retain moisture that they and other organisms need. Waxwings and other birds use moss, along with twigs and grass, as nesting material.

Commercially, the most important mosses are the peat mosses in the genus *Sphagnum*. One of the distinctive features of *Sphagnum* "leaves" is the presence of many large, empty cells that absorb and hold water. This feature makes peat moss a useful packing material for shipping live plants as well as a good soil conditioner. Added to sandy soils, for example, peat moss helps absorb and retain moisture.

The acidic and anaerobic conditions of a peat bog retard the growth of bacterial and fungal decomposers. As a result, dead peat mosses accumulate as thick deposits—some several meters in depth—under the growing mat of living peat mosses. Over time, the organic material compresses to form *peat*. In some countries, such as Ireland and Scotland, people cut out blocks of peat that has accumulated for hundreds of years in peat bogs, dry them, and burn them for fuel. Occasionally, the remains of well-preserved humans have been uncovered during the excavations of old peat bogs in Ireland and other parts of Europe (**FIG. 27-8**).

The name *moss* is often misused to refer to plants that are not truly mosses. For example, reindeer "moss" is a lichen that is a dominant form of vegetation in the arctic tundra, Spanish "moss" is a flowering plant, and club "moss" (discussed later in the chapter) is a relative of ferns.

Liverwort gametophytes are either thalloid or leafy

Liverworts (phylum Hepatophyta) consist of about 6000 species of nonvascular plants with a dominant gametophyte generation, but the gametophytes of some liverworts are quite different from those of mosses. Their body form is often a flattened, lobed structure called a **thallus** (pl., *thalli*) that is not differentiated into leaves, stems, or roots. The common liverwort, *Marchantia polymorpha*, is thalloid (**FIGS. 27-9a** and **b**). Liverworts are so named because the lobes of their thalli superficially resemble the lobes of the human liver; *wort* is derived from the Old English word *wyrt*, meaning "plant." On the underside of the liverwort thallus are hairlike rhizoids that anchor the plant to the soil. Other liverworts, known as *leafy liverworts*, superficially resemble mosses, with leaflike blades, "stems," and rhizoids rather than a lobed thallus (**FIG. 27-9c**). As in the mosses, leafy liverwort "leaves" consist of a single layer of undifferentiated cells. Like other bryophytes, liverworts are small, generally inconspicuous plants that are largely restricted to

The dominant phase in the life cycle of mosses, like that of other bryophytes, is the gametophyte.

1 Antheridia and/or archegonia form at the tip of gametophyte shoots.

Gametophyte plants

Buds on protonema

Antheridia with sperm cells

6 When a haploid spore germinates, it forms a protonema.

Protonema

Spores released

Sperm cell

Archegonium with egg

2 Splashing raindrops transfer sperm cells from antheridia to archegonia.

HAPLOID (*n*) GAMETOPHYTE GENERATION

Meiosis

DIPLOID (*2n*) SPOROPHYTE GENERATION

Fertilization

4 The mature sporophyte is an unbranched stalk with a sporangium at its tip.

Calyptra

Capsule

Zygote

5 Sporogenous cells within each sporangium undergo meiosis to form spores.

Sporophyte

3 The fertilized egg grows by mitosis to form the embryonic sporophyte.

Gametophyte plant

Embryo

FIGURE 27-7 *Animated* The life cycle of mosses

The gametophyte generation is dominant in the moss life cycle. After sexual reproduction, the sporophyte grows out of the gametophyte.

© Robin Weaver/Alamy

damp environments. Unlike mosses, hornworts, and other plants, liverworts lack stomata, although some liverworts have surface pores thought to be analogous to stomata.

Liverworts reproduce both sexually and asexually (see Figs. 27-9a and 27-9b). Their sexual reproduction involves production of archegonia and antheridia on the haploid gametophyte. In some liverworts, these gametangia are borne on stalked structures called *archegoniophores,* which bear archegonia, and *antheridiophores,* which bear antheridia. Their life cycle is basically the same as that of mosses,

◀ **FIGURE 27-8** Preserved human remains in a peat bog in Denmark

The clothing and features of the Tollund man, estimated to be about 2000 years old, are remarkably well preserved because the bog's acidic conditions inhibited decay.

(a) Flattened, ribbon-like lobes characterize the gametophyte of the common liverwort (*Marchantia polymorpha*). This male gametophyte thallus has both asexual gemmae cups and sexual antheridiophores, which produce sperm-bearing antheridia.

Antheridiophore
Gametophyte thallus
Gemmae cup

Antheridia with sperm cells

Archegoniophore

Gametophyte thallus

Achegonia with eggs

Following fertilization, a sporophyte develops, hanging upside-down on the archegoniophore.

(b) Achegoniophores on the female gametophyte thallus of *M. polymorpha* produce egg-bearing archegonia. Liverwort sporophytes, which are always attached to and dependent on the gametophyte plant, consists of a foot, seta, and capsule. Meiosis occurs in the capsule and produces haploid spores.

Foot
Seta
Tissue derived from archegonium
Capsule
Sporogenous cells that undergo meiosis
Sporophyte

(c) *Porella* is a leafy liverwort. The leafy plant is the gametophyte. It bears antheridia and archegonia on special branches that look quite similar to the nonreproductive branches. After fertilization, a small sporophyte develops that produces spores following meiosis.

FIGURE 27-9 Bryophytes: liverworts

although some of the structures look quite different. Splashing raindrops transport sperm cells to the archegonia, where fertilization takes place. The resulting zygote develops into a multicellular embryo that becomes a mature sporophyte. The liverwort sporophyte is attached to the gametophyte, as in mosses. Sporogenous cells in the capsule of the sporophyte undergo meiosis, producing haploid spores. Each spore has the potential to develop into a green gametophyte, and the cycle continues.

Some liverworts reproduce asexually by forming tiny balls of tissue called **gemmae** (sing., *gemma*), which are borne in a saucer-shaped structure, the gemmae cup, directly on the liverwort thallus (see Fig. 27-9a). Splashing raindrops and small animals help disperse gemmae. When a gemma lands in a suitable place, it grows into a new liverwort thallus. Liverworts may also reproduce asexually by thallus branching and growth. The individual thallus lobes elongate, and each becomes a separate plant when the older part of the thallus that originally connected the individual lobes dies.

Hornwort gametophytes are inconspicuous thalloid plants

Hornworts (phylum Anthocerophyta) are a small group of about 100 species of bryophytes whose gametophytes superficially resemble those of the thalloid liverworts. Hornworts live in disturbed habitats such as fallow fields and roadsides.

Hornworts may or may not be closely related to other bryophytes. For example, their cell structure, particularly the presence of a single large chloroplast in each cell, resembles certain algal cells more than plant cells. In contrast, mosses, liverworts, and other plants have many disc-shaped chloroplasts per cell.

In the common hornwort (*Anthoceros natans*), archegonia and antheridia are embedded in the gametophyte thallus rather than on archegoniophores and antheridiophores. After fertilization and development, the needlelike sporophyte projects out of the gametophyte thallus, forming a spike or "horn"—hence the name *hornwort*. A single gametophyte often produces multiple sporophytes (**FIG. 27-10**). Meiosis occurs, forming spores within each **sporangium** (pl., *sporangia*), or spore case. The sporangium splits open from the top to release the spores; each spore can give rise to a new gametophyte thallus. A unique feature of hornworts is that the sporophytes, unlike those of mosses and liverworts, continue to grow from their bases for the remainder of the gametophyte's life, a characteristic known as **indeterminate growth.** Some botanists think that indeterminate growth may indicate that hornworts evolved from plants with larger, more complex sporophytes.

Bryophytes are used for experimental studies

Botanists use certain bryophytes as experimental models to study many fundamental aspects of plant biology, including genetics, growth and development, plant ecology, plant hormones, and *photoperiodism,* which is plant responses to varying periods of night and day length.

The moss *Physcomitrella patens* is a particularly important research organism for studying plant evolution because its features and genome can be compared to those of algae and flowering

FIGURE 27-10 Bryophytes: hornworts

The gametophyte of the common hornwort (*Anthoceros natans*) is a small thallus with unicellular rhizoids on the lower (ventral) surface. After fertilization, sporophytes project up out of the gametophyte, forming "horns."

plants (**FIG. 27-11**). In this regard, *Physcomitrella* is a plant equivalent of the fruit fly *Drosophila,* which is an important model organism for studies of animal inheritance, development, and evolution. As experimental organisms, *Physcomitrella* and other bryophytes are easy to grow on artificial media and do not require much space because they are so small.

Recap: details of bryophyte evolution are based on fossils and on structural and molecular evidence

Plants are a **monophyletic group**—that is, all plants probably evolved from a common ancestral green alga. Fossil evidence indicates that bryophytes are ancient plants, probably the first group of plants to arise from the common plant ancestor. The fossil record of ancient bryophytes is incomplete, consisting mostly of spores and small tissue fragments, and can be interpreted in different ways. As a result, it does not provide a definite answer on bryophyte evolution.

The oldest known recognizable plant fossils are dated at about 425 million years old. These fossils resemble modern liverworts in many respects, but the spores are virtually identical to those

QUESTION: Does the *Physcomitrella* genome reveal any insights in plant evolution?

HYPOTHESIS: Comparing the genome of the model organism *Physcomitrella* with genomes of other land plants as well as green algae will provide details of genes that were probably associated with the colonization of land.

EXPERIMENT: Several dozen scientists in Germany, the United States, Japan, the United Kingdom, Australia, Canada, and Belgium collaborated to produce the draft genome sequence for the model organism *Physcomitrella* (see photograph). This bryophyte was selected because researchers have used *Physcomitrella* in a wide variety of experiments and have a good understanding of its biology.

Courtesy of David J. Cove, University of Leeds

After sequencing the genome of *Physcomitrella*, it was compared with available genomes of green algae (*Ostreococcus* and *Chlamydomonas*) and land plants—the model flowering plant *Arabidopsis*, rice (*Oryza sativa*), and western balsam poplar (*Populus trichocarpa*).

RESULTS AND CONCLUSION: Researchers found that *Physcomitrella* has lost some genes needed for life in the water and gained new genes needed for life on land. Every land plant has to meet the same environmental challenges, such as obtaining enough water and preventing excessive water loss, tolerating high and low temperatures, and adapting to increased levels of solar radiation. These challenges have resulted in many modifications in plant body plans and physiological processes.

Bryophytes and vascular plants living today represent remnants of the first plants that colonized land some 450 mya. Compared to green algae, *Physcomitrella* lacks the genes needed to survive in aquatic environments but has gained genes involving plant signaling molecules (auxin, abscisic acid, and cytokinins) needed to adapt to drought, extremes of temperature, and light reception. Compared to *Physcomitrella*, other land plants have gained additional signaling molecules (gibberellins, jasmonic acid, and brassinosteroids) that enable a more complex tolerance of environmental stressors.

Because of its intermediary position in evolution (i.e., between green algae and vascular land plants), *Physcomitrella*'s genome allows biologists to reconstruct which genes may have been acquired and lost during the colonization of land by the last common ancestor of all land plants.

Source: Rensing, S. A., et al. "The *Physcomitrella* Genome Reveals Evolutionary Insights into the Conquest of Land by Plants." *Science*, Vol. 319, Jan. 4, 2008.

FIGURE 27-11 The moss *Physcomitrella*, the first bryophyte to have its genome sequenced

in 470-million-year-old rocks. In 2003, scientists reported fossil fragments of tiny liverwort-like plants associated with ancient spores that were discovered in Oman. This evidence suggests that liverwort-like plants may have been the earliest plants to colonize land.

Review

- Which of the following are parts of the gametophyte generation in mosses: antheridia, zygote, embryo, capsule, archegonia, sperm cells, egg cell, spores, and protonema?

- How are mosses, liverworts, and hornworts similar? How is each group distinctive?

27.3 SEEDLESS VASCULAR PLANTS

■ LEARNING OBJECTIVES

6 Discuss the features that distinguish seedless vascular plants from algae and bryophytes.

7 Name and briefly describe the two phyla of seedless vascular plants.

8 Describe the life cycle of ferns and compare their sporophyte and gametophyte generations.

9 Compare the generalized life cycles of homosporous and heterosporous plants.

The most important adaptation found in seedless vascular plants, though absent in algae and bryophytes, is specialized vascular tissues—xylem and phloem—for support and conduction. This system of conduction lets vascular plants grow larger than bryophytes because water, minerals, and sugar are transported to all parts of the plant. Although seedless vascular plants in temperate environments are relatively small, tree ferns in the tropics may grow to heights of 18 m (60 ft). All seedless vascular plants have true stems with vascular tissues, and most also have true roots and leaves.

Botanists have extensively studied the evolution of the leaf as the main organ of photosynthesis. The two basic types of true leaves—microphylls and megaphylls—evolved independently of each other (**FIG. 27-12**). The **microphyll,** which is usually small and has a single vascular strand, probably evolved from small, projecting extensions of stem tissue (*enations*). Only one group of living plants, the club mosses, has microphylls.

In contrast, **megaphylls** probably evolved from stem branches that gradually filled in with additional tissue (*webbing*) to form most leaves as we know them today. Megaphylls have more than one vascular strand, as we would expect if they evolved from branch systems. Ferns (with the exception of whisk ferns, discussed later in the chapter), gymnosperms, and flowering plants have megaphylls.

Recent evidence suggests megaphylls evolved over a 40-million-year period in the Late Paleozoic era in response to a gradual decline in the level of atmospheric CO_2. As CO_2 declined, plants developed a flattened blade with more stomata for gas exchange. (More stomata allowed cells inside the leaf to get enough CO_2.)

There are two main clades of seedless vascular plants: the club mosses and the ferns. Biologists originally considered horsetails

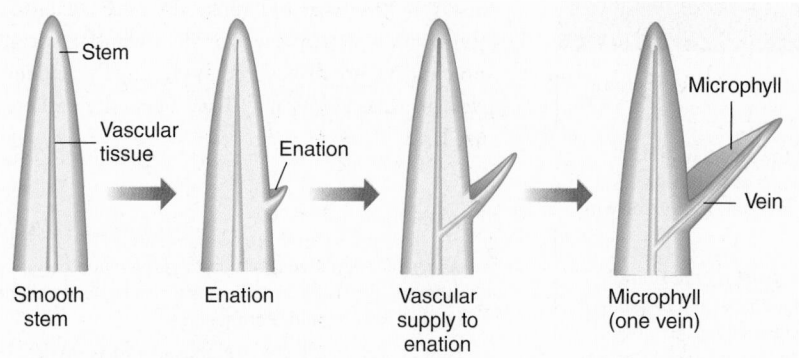

(a) Microphyll evolution. Microphylls probably originated as outgrowths (enations) of stem tissue that developed a single vascular strand later. Club mosses have microphylls.

(b) Megaphyll evolution. Megaphylls probably evolved from the evolutionary modification of side branches. Webbing is the evolutionary process in which the spaces between close branches become filled with chlorophyll-containing cells. Ferns, horsetails, gymnosperms, and flowering plants have megaphylls.

FIGURE 27-12 Evolution of microphylls and megaphylls

and whisk ferns distinct enough to be classified in separate phyla. However, many kinds of evidence, such as DNA comparisons and similarities in sperm structure, have resulted in their being reclassified as ferns. As shown in **FIGURE 27-13**, ferns, including horsetails and whisk ferns, are a monophyletic group and the closest living relatives of seed plants (also see Table 27-2).

Club mosses are small plants with rhizomes and short, erect branches

Club mosses (phylum Lycopodiophyta) were important plants millions of years ago, when species that are now extinct often reached great size (**FIG. 27-14a**). These large, treelike plants were major contributors to our present-day coal deposits (see *Inquiring About: Ancient Plants and Coal Formation*).

The 1200 or so species of club mosses living today, such as *Lycopodium* (**FIG. 27-14b**), are small (less than 25 cm, or 10 in, tall), attractive plants common in temperate woodlands. They possess true roots; both rhizomes and erect aerial stems; and small, scalelike leaves (microphylls). Sporangia are borne on reproductive leaves that are either clustered in conelike strobili at the tips

of stems or scattered in reproductive areas along the stem. Club mosses are evergreen and often fashioned into Christmas wreaths and other decorations. In some areas they are endangered by overharvesting.

That common names are sometimes misleading in biology is vividly evident in this group of plants. The most common names for the phylum Lycopodiophyta are "club mosses" and "ground pines," yet these plants are neither mosses, which are nonvascular, nor pines, which are seed plants.

Ferns are a diverse group of spore-forming vascular plants

Most of the 11,000 species of **ferns** (phylum Pteridophyta) are terrestrial, although a few have adapted to aquatic habitats. Ferns range from the tropics to the Arctic Circle, with most species living in tropical rain forests, where they perch high in the branches of trees. In temperate regions, ferns commonly inhabit swamps, marshes, stream banks, and moist woodlands (**FIG. 27-15a**). Some species grow in fields, rocky crevices on cliffs or mountains, or even deserts.

The life cycle of ferns involves a clearly defined alternation of generations. The ferns grown as houseplants (such as Boston fern, maiden-hair fern, and staghorn fern) represent the larger, more conspicuous sporophyte generation.

The fern sporophyte consists of a horizontal underground stem, or *rhizome,* that bears leaves, called *fronds,* and true roots. As each young frond first emerges from the ground, it is tightly coiled and resembles the top of a violin, hence the name *fiddlehead* (**FIG. 27-15b**). As fiddleheads grow, they unroll and expand to form fronds. Fern fronds are usually compound (the blade is divided into leaflets), with the leaflets forming beautifully complex leaves. Fronds, roots, and rhizomes all contain vascular tissues.

Spore production usually occurs in certain areas on the fronds, which develop sporangia. Many species bear the sporangia in clusters, called **sori** (sing., *sorus*) (**FIGS. 27-15c** and **d**). Within sporan-

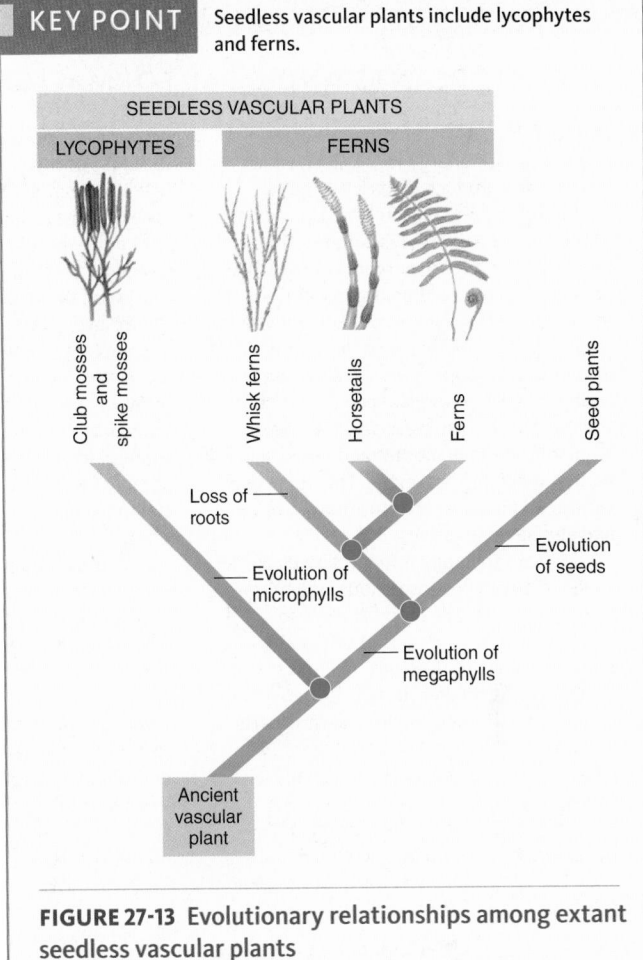

KEY POINT Seedless vascular plants include lycophytes and ferns.

SEEDLESS VASCULAR PLANTS

LYCOPHYTES | FERNS

Club mosses and spike mosses

Whisk ferns

Horsetails

Ferns

Seed plants

Loss of roots

Evolution of microphylls

Evolution of seeds

Evolution of megaphylls

Ancient vascular plant

FIGURE 27-13 Evolutionary relationships among extant seedless vascular plants
These relationships are based on structural and molecular comparisons.

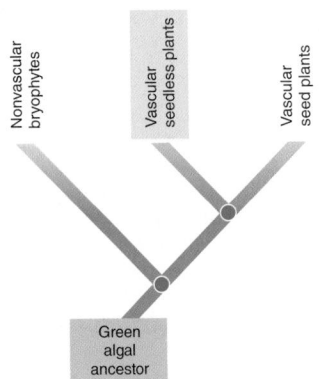

Nonvascular bryophytes

Vascular seedless plants

Vascular seed plants

Green algal ancestor

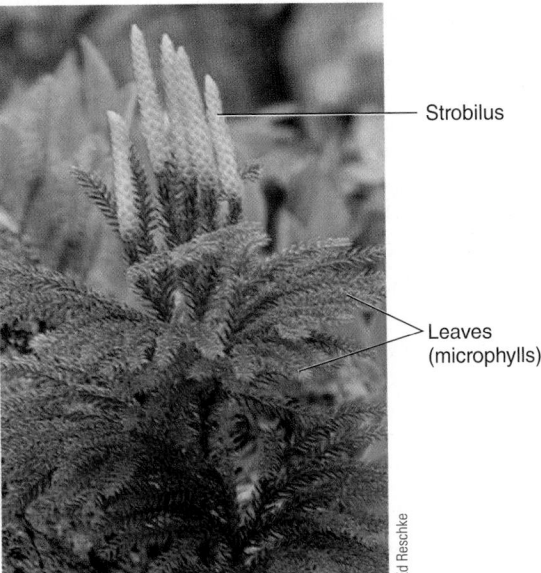

Strobilus

Leaves (microphylls)

Ed Reschke

gia, sporogenous cells (spore mother cells) undergo meiosis to form haploid spores. The sporangia burst open and discharge spores that may germinate and grow by mitosis into gametophytes.

The mature fern gametophyte, which bears no resemblance to the sporophyte, is a tiny (less than half the size of one of your fingernails), green, often heart-shaped structure that grows flat against the ground. Called a **prothallus** (pl., *prothalli*), the fern gametophyte lacks vascular tissues and has tiny, hairlike absorptive rhizoids to anchor it (**FIG. 27-15e**). The prothallus usually produces both archegonia and antheridia on its underside. Each archegonium contains

(a) Reconstruction of *Lepidodendron*, an ancient club moss the size of a large tree. Numerous fossils of *Lepidodendron* were preserved in coal deposits, particularly in Great Britain and the central United States. (Redrawn from Hirmer, M., *Handbuch der Paläobotanik,* R. Olderbourg, Munich, 1927.)

(b) The sporophyte of *Lycopodium*, a club moss, has small, scalelike, evergreen leaves (microphylls). Spores are produced in sporangia on reproductive leaves clustered in a conelike strobilus (*shown*) or, in other species, scattered along the stem.

◀ **FIGURE 27-14** Seedless vascular plants: club mosses

ANCIENT PLANTS AND COAL FORMATION

How did the coal that industrial society depends on for energy form? Coal, which is burned to produce electricity and to manufacture items of steel and iron, is one of the most important fossil fuels. Although mined, coal is not an inorganic mineral like gold or aluminum but an organic material formed from the remains of ancient vascular plants, particularly those of the Carboniferous period, approximately 320 mya. Four main groups of plants contributed to coal formation. Two were seedless vascular plants: the club mosses and ferns (see figure), including horsetails. The other two were seed plants: seed ferns (now extinct) and early gymnosperms.

It is hard to imagine that relatives of the small, relatively inconspicuous club mosses, ferns, and horsetails of today were so significant in forming vast beds of coal. However, many members of these groups that existed during the Carboniferous period were giants compared with their modern counterparts and formed immense forests. (Figure 21-12 shows a reconstruction of a Carboniferous forest.)

The climate during the Carboniferous period was warm, moist, and mild. Plants in most locations could grow year-round because of the favorable conditions. Forests of these plants often grew in low-lying, swampy areas that periodically flooded when the sea level rose. As the sea level receded, these plants would re-establish.

When these large plants died or were blown over in storms, they decomposed incompletely because they were covered by swamp water. (The anaerobic conditions of the water prevented wood-rotting fungi from decomposing the plants, and anaerobic bacteria do not decompose wood rapidly.) Thus, over time the partially decomposed plant material accumulated and consolidated.

Layers of sediment formed over the plant material each time the water level rose and flooded the low-lying swamps. With time, heat and pressure built up in these accumulated layers and converted the plant material to coal and the sediment layers to sedimentary rock. Much later, geologic upheavals raised the layers of coal and sedimentary rock. Coal is usually found in seams, underground layers that vary in thickness from 2.5 cm (1 in) to more than 30 m (100 ft).

This piece of Carboniferous coal contains a fossilized fern. The coal and fossil are about 300 million years old.

The various grades of coal (lignite, the lowest grade; sub-bituminous; bituminous; and anthracite, the highest grade) formed as a result of the different temperatures and pressures to which the layers were exposed. Coal exposed to high heat and pressure during its formation is drier, is more compact (and therefore harder), and has a higher heating value (that is, a higher energy content).

---

a single egg, whereas numerous sperm cells are produced in each antheridium.

Ferns use water as a transport medium. The flagellate sperm cells swim, usually from a nearby prothallus, to the neck of an archegonium through a thin film of water on the ground underneath the prothallus. After one of the sperm cells fertilizes the egg, a diploid zygote grows by mitosis into a multicellular embryo (an immature sporophyte). At this stage, the sporophyte embryo is attached to and dependent on the gametophyte; but as the embryo matures, the prothallus withers and dies, and the sporophyte becomes free-living.

The fern life cycle alternates between the dominant, diploid sporophyte with its rhizome, roots, and fronds, and the haploid gametophyte (prothallus) (**FIG. 27-16**). The sporophyte generation is dominant not only because it is larger than the gametophyte but also because it persists for an extended period (most fern sporophytes are perennials), whereas the gametophyte dies soon after reproducing.

Whisk ferns are classified as reduced ferns

Only about 12 species of **whisk ferns** (phylum Pteridophyta) exist today, and the fossil record contains several extinct species. Whisk ferns, which live mainly in the tropics and subtropics, are relatively simple in structure and lack true roots and leaves but have vascularized stems. *Psilotum nudum,* a representative whisk fern, has both a horizontal underground rhizome and vertical aerial stems (**FIG. 27-17a**). Whenever the stem forks, or branches, it always divides into two equal halves. Botanists call this forking **dichotomous branching.** In contrast, when most plant stems branch, one stem is more vigorous and becomes the main trunk.

The upright stems of *Psilotum* are green and are the main organs of photosynthesis. Tiny, round sporangia, borne directly on the erect, aerial stems, contain sporogenous cells that undergo meiosis to form haploid spores. After dispersal, the spores germinate to form haploid prothalli. Because they grow underground, the prothalli of whisk ferns are difficult to study (**FIG. 27-17b**). They are nonphotosynthetic as a result of their subterranean location, and they apparently have a symbiotic relationship with mycorrhizal fungi that provides them with sugar and essential minerals (see Chapter 29).

Botanists have carefully studied whisk ferns in recent years. Molecular data, including comparisons of nucleotide sequences of ribosomal RNA, chloroplast DNA, and mitochondrial DNA in living species, support the hypothesis that the whisk ferns should be classified as reduced ferns rather than as surviving representatives of extinct vascular plants (see discussion of rhyniophytes later in the chapter).

Horsetails are an evolutionary line of ferns

About 300 mya the **horsetails** (phylum Pteridophyta) were among the dominant plants and grew as large as modern trees (**FIG. 27-18a**).

(a) Fronds. The Christmas fern (*Polystichum acrostichoides*), photographed in the Great Smoky Mountains in Tennessee, has fronds that grow to 0.6 m (2 ft) in length.

(b) Fiddleheads. Some fiddleheads are edible.

(c) Sori. These round sori of rabbits foot fern (*Polypodium aureum*) are arranged in two prominent rows on the leaf's underside.

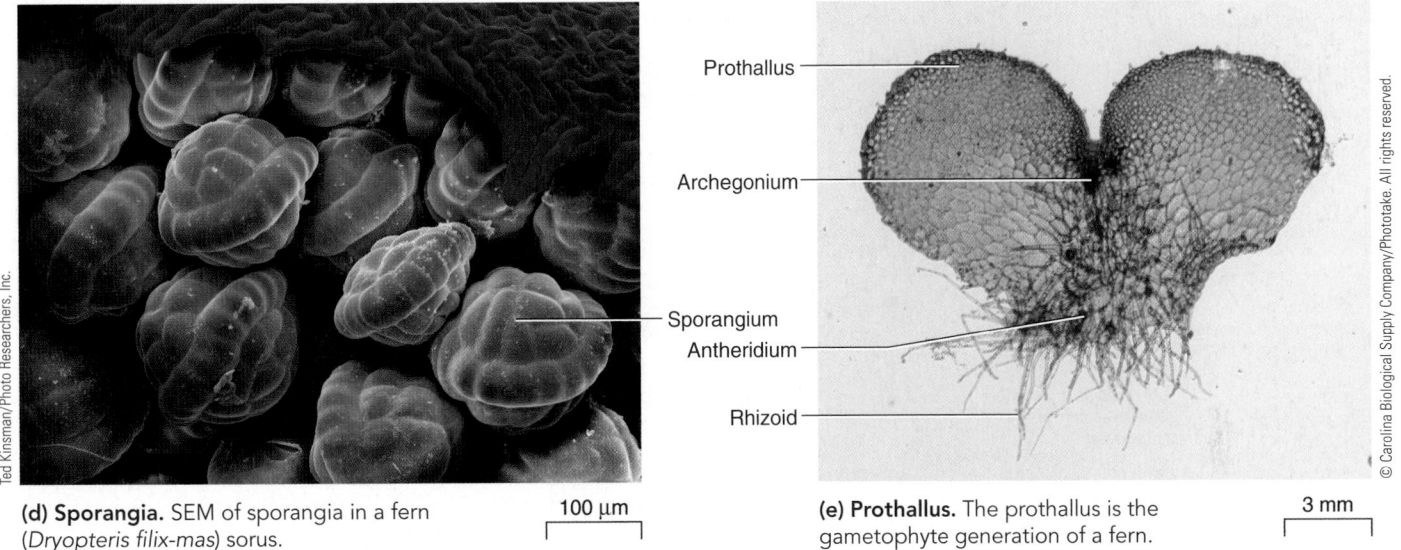

(d) Sporangia. SEM of sporangia in a fern (*Dryopteris filix-mas*) sorus.

100 μm

(e) Prothallus. The prothallus is the gametophyte generation of a fern.

Prothallus

Archegonium

Sporangium
Antheridium

Rhizoid

3 mm

FIGURE 27-15 Seedless vascular plants: ferns

Because they contributed to Earth's vast coal deposits, these ancient horsetails, like ancient club mosses, are still significant today.

The few surviving horsetails, about 15 species in the genus *Equisetum,* grow mostly in wet, marshy habitats and are less than 1.3 m (4 ft) tall, but extremely distinctive (**FIG. 27-18b**). They are widely distributed on every continent except Australia. Traditionally classified in their own phylum, horsetails are now grouped with ferns. This reclassification is based on molecular similarities between horsetails and other ferns.

Horsetails have true roots, stems (both rhizomes and erect aerial stems), and small leaves. The hollow, jointed stems are impregnated with silica, which gives them a gritty texture. Small leaves, interpreted as reduced megaphylls, are fused in whorls at each node (the area on the stem where leaves attach). The green stem is the main organ of photosynthesis. Horsetails are so named

because certain vegetative (nonreproductive) stems have whorls of branches that give the appearance of a bushy horse's tail. In the past, horsetails were called "scouring rushes" and were used to scrub pots and pans along stream banks.

Each reproductive branch of a horsetail bears a terminal cone-like **strobilus** (pl., *strobili*). The strobilus consists of several stalked, umbrella-like structures, each of which bears 5 to 10 sporangia in a circle around a common axis.

The horsetail life cycle is similar in many respects to the fern life cycle. In horsetails, as in ferns, the sporophyte is the conspicuous plant, whereas the gametophyte is a minute, lobed thallus ranging in width from the size of a pinhead to about 1 cm across. The sporophyte and gametophyte are both photosynthetic and nutritionally independent at maturity. Like ferns, horsetails require water as a medium for flagellate sperm cells to swim to the egg.

The dominant phase in the life cycle of ferns, like that of all other vascular plants, is the sporophyte.

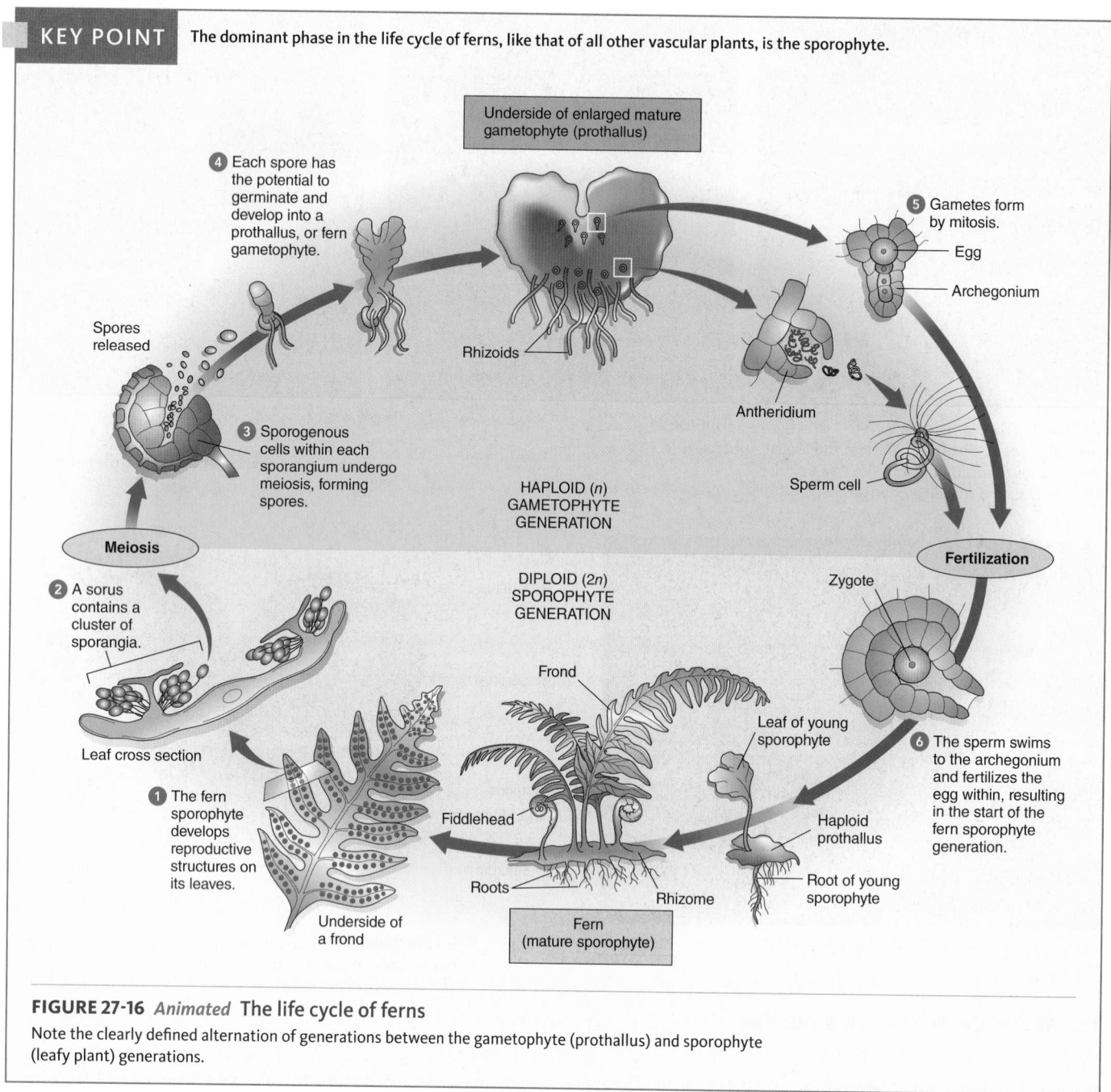

FIGURE 27-16 *Animated* **The life cycle of ferns**

Note the clearly defined alternation of generations between the gametophyte (prothallus) and sporophyte (leafy plant) generations.

Some ferns and club mosses are heterosporous

In the life cycles examined thus far, plants produce only one type of spore as a result of meiosis. This condition, known as **homospory,** is characteristic of bryophytes, horsetails, whisk ferns, and most ferns and club mosses. However, certain ferns and club mosses (known as spike mosses) exhibit **heterospory,** in which they produce two types of spores: microspores and megaspores.

FIGURE 27-19 illustrates the generalized life cycle of a heterosporous plant. The sporophyte plant produces sporangia within a conelike strobilus. Each strobilus usually bears two kinds of

sporangia: microsporangia and megasporangia. *Microsporangia* are sporangia that produce *microsporocytes* (also called *microspore mother cells*), which undergo meiosis to form microscopic, haploid **microspores.** Each microspore develops into a male gametophyte that produces sperm cells within antheridia.

Megasporangia produce *megasporocytes* (also called *megaspore mother cells*). When megasporocytes undergo meiosis, they form haploid **megaspores,** each of which develops into a female gametophyte that produces eggs in archegonia.

The development of male gametophytes from microspores and of female gametophytes from megaspores occurs within their

FIGURE 27-17 Whisk ferns ▶

Sporangia

Aerial stem with scalelike outgrowths (no leaves)

John Arnaldi

(a) The sporophyte of the whisk fern *Psilotum nudum*. The stem is the main organ of photosynthesis in this rootless, leafless, vascular plant. Sporangia, which turn yellow as they mature, are borne on short lateral branches directly on the stems.

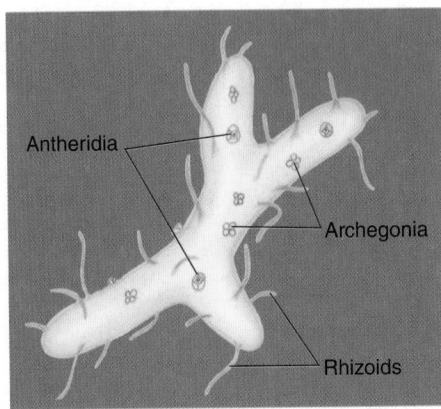

Antheridia

Archegonia

Rhizoids

(b) The gametophyte of the whisk fern *Psilotum nudum*. The gametophyte (prothallus) lives underground, nourished by mycorrhizal fungi.

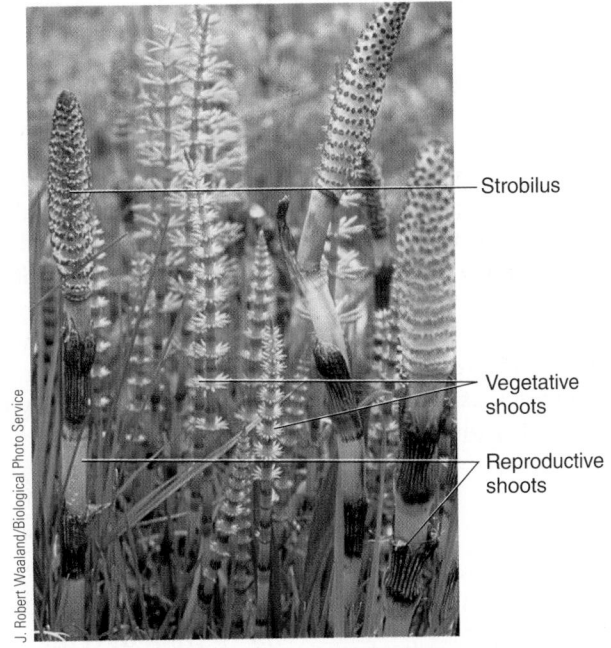

Strobilus

Vegetative shoots

Reproductive shoots

J. Robert Waaland/Biological Photo Service

(a) Reconstruction of *Calamites*, an ancient horsetail that grew as tall as many modern trees—to 20 m (about 65 ft). *Calamites* had an underground rhizome where roots and aerial shoots originated. (Redrawn from Emberger, L., *Les Plantes Fossiles*, Masson et Cie, Paris, 1968.)

(b) *Equisetum telematia*, a horsetail with a wide distribution in Eurasia, Africa, and North America, has unbranched reproductive shoots bearing conelike strobili and separate, highly branched vegetative (nonreproductive) shoots. In some horsetail species, both reproductive and vegetative shoots are unbranched.

◀ **FIGURE 27-18** Horsetails

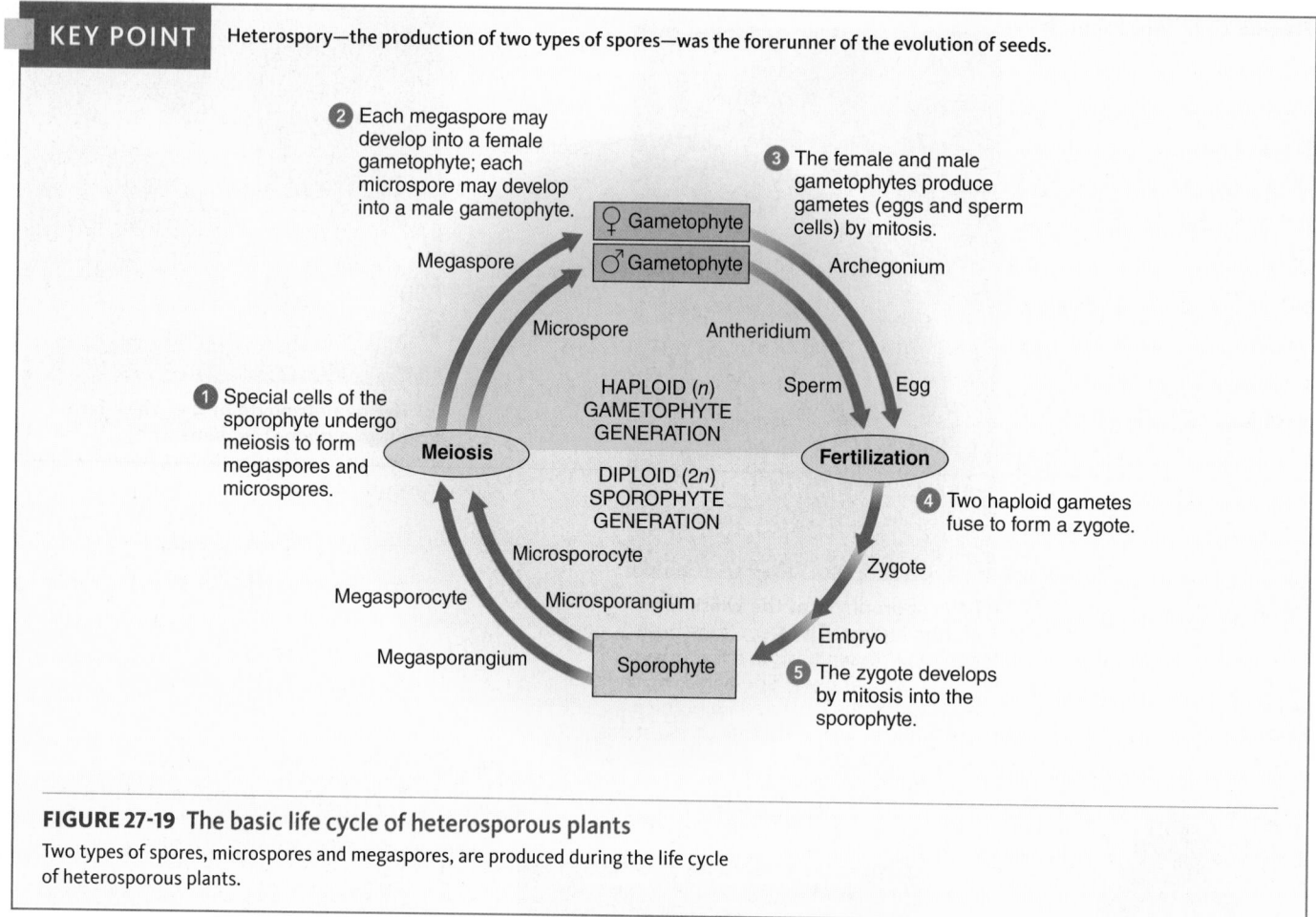

Heterospory—the production of two types of spores—was the forerunner of the evolution of seeds.

2 Each megaspore may develop into a female gametophyte; each microspore may develop into a male gametophyte.

3 The female and male gametophytes produce gametes (eggs and sperm cells) by mitosis.

Megaspore

♀ Gametophyte
♂ Gametophyte

Archegonium

Microspore

Antheridium

1 Special cells of the sporophyte undergo meiosis to form megaspores and microspores.

HAPLOID (*n*)
GAMETOPHYTE
GENERATION

Sperm   Egg

Meiosis

Fertilization

DIPLOID (*2n*)
SPOROPHYTE
GENERATION

4 Two haploid gametes fuse to form a zygote.

Microsporocyte

Zygote

Megasporocyte   Microsporangium

Megasporangium   Sporophyte

Embryo

5 The zygote develops by mitosis into the sporophyte.

FIGURE 27-19 The basic life cycle of heterosporous plants
Two types of spores, microspores and megaspores, are produced during the life cycle of heterosporous plants.

respective spore walls, using stored food provided by the sporophyte. As a result, and unlike the gametophytes of other seedless vascular plants, the male and female gametophytes are not truly free-living. Fertilization is followed by the development of a new sporophyte.

Heterospory evolved several times during the history of land plants. It was a significant development in plant evolution because it was the forerunner of the evolution of seeds. Heterospory characterizes the two most successful groups of plants existing today, the gymnosperms and the flowering plants, both of which produce seeds.

Seedless vascular plants are used for experimental studies

Botanists use many seedless vascular plants as experimental models to study certain aspects of plant biology, such as physiology, growth, and development. Ferns and other seedless vascular plants are useful in studying how apical meristems give rise to plant tissues. An **apical meristem** is the area at the tip (apex) of a root or shoot where growth—cell division, elongation, and differentiation—occurs. Ferns and other seedless vascular plants have a single large *apical cell* located at the center tip of the apical

meristem. This apical cell is the source, by mitosis, of all the cells that eventually make up the root or shoot. The apical cell divides in an orderly fashion, and the smaller daughter cells produced by the apical cell, in turn, divide and give rise to different parts of the root or shoot. It is possible to trace mature cells in the root or shoot back to their origin from the single apical cell.

Ferns are interesting research plants for studies in genetics because they are **polyploids** and have multiple sets of chromosomes. (Many ferns have hundreds of chromosomes.) However, gene expression in ferns is exactly what one would expect of a *diploid* plant. Apparently, genes in the extra sets of chromosomes are gradually silenced and therefore not expressed.

Seedless vascular plants arose more than 420 mya

Currently, the oldest known megafossils of early vascular plants are from Silurian (420 mya) deposits in Europe. (Plant *megafossils* are fossilized roots, stems, leaves, and reproductive structures.) Megafossils of several kinds of small, seedless vascular plants also occur in Silurian deposits in Bolivia, Australia, and northwestern China. Microscopic spores of early vascular plants appear in the

FIGURE 27-20 Reconstruction of *Rhynia gwynne-vaughanii*

This leafless plant, one of Earth's earliest vascular plants, is now extinct. It grew about 18 cm (7 in) tall. (Redrawn from Edwards, D., "Evidence for the Sporophytic Status of the Lower Devonian Plant *Rhynia gwynne-vaughanii*," *Review of Palaeobotany and Palynology,* Vol. 29, 1980.)

FIGURE 27-21 Reconstruction of *Aglaophyton major*

Recent evidence indicates that this plant, although superficially similar to other early vascular plants, lacked conducting tissues that are characteristic of vascular plants. For this reason, it has been reclassified into a new genus and is no longer considered a rhyniophyte. (Redrawn from Mauseth, J. D., *Botany: An Introduction to Plant Biology,* 2nd ed., Saunders College Publishing, Philadelphia, 1995.)

fossil record earlier than megafossils, suggesting that even older megafossils of simple vascular plants may be discovered.

Botanists assign the oldest vascular plants to phylum Rhyniophyta, which, according to the fossil record, arose some 420 mya and became extinct about 380 mya. The rhyniophytes are so named because many fossils of these extinct plants were found in fossil beds near Rhynie, Scotland. *Rhynia gwynne-vaughanii* is an example of an early vascular plant that superficially resembled whisk ferns in that it consisted of leafless upright stems that branched dichotomously from an underground rhizome (**FIG. 27-20**). *Rhynia* lacked roots, although it had absorptive rhizoids. Sporangia formed at the ends of short branches. The internal structure of its rhizome contained a central core of xylem cells for conducting water and minerals.

For many years, botanists considered *Rhynia major,* a plant that grew about 50 cm (20 in) tall and probably lived in marshes, a classic example of a rhyniophyte. Fossils indicate that this plant had rhizoids, dichotomously branching rhizomes, and upright stems that terminated in sporangia. However, recent microscopic studies of fossil rhizomes indicate that the central core of tissue lacked the xylem cells characteristic of vascular plants. For that reason, *R. major* was reclassified into a new genus, *Aglaophyton,* and is no longer considered a rhyniophyte (**FIG. 27-21**). Science is an ongoing enterprise, and over time, existing knowledge is re-evaluated in light of newly discovered evidence. *Aglaophyton major* is an excellent example of the self-correcting nature of science, which is in a perpetually dynamic state and changes in response to newly available techniques and data.

The oldest known megafossils of fernlike trees, discovered in New York, are dated at 380 million years old. These trees, which were about 8 m (26 feet) tall, had vascular tissues but no leaves and a minimal root system. They grew vertically and reproduced by forming spores. The trunks were discovered in the late 1800s (and named *Eospermatopteris*), but it wasn't until 2007 that a fossil of an entire tree was pieced together. The treetops had previously been found separate from the trunks and named *Wattieza*.

Review

- What adaptations do ferns have that both algae and bryophytes lack?
- How does one distinguish between megaphylls and microphylls?
- Which of the following are parts of the sporophyte generation in ferns: frond, sperm cells, egg cell, roots, sorus, sporangium, spores, prothallus, rhizome, antheridium, archegonium, and zygote?
- Why are whisk ferns and horsetails now classified as ferns?
- How does heterospory modify the plant life cycle?

27.1 *(page 562)*

1 Discuss some environmental challenges of living on land and describe how several plant adaptations meet these challenges.

- The colonization of land by plants required the evolution of many anatomical, physiological, and reproductive adaptations. Plants have a waxy **cuticle** to protect against water loss and **stomata** for gas exchange needed for photosynthesis.

- Plant life cycles have an **alternation of generations** in which they spend part of their life cycle in a haploid **gametophyte generation** and part in a diploid **sporophyte generation.** The gametophyte plant produces gametes by mitosis. During fertilization these gametes fuse to form a **zygote,** the first stage of the sporophyte generation. The zygote develops into a multicellular **embryo** that the gametophyte protects and nourishes. The mature sporophyte plant develops from the embryo and produces sporogenous cells (spore mother cells). These undergo meiosis to form **spores,** the first stage in the gametophyte generation.

- Most plants have multicellular **gametangia** with a protective jacket of sterile cells surrounding the gametes. **Antheridia** are gametangia that produce sperm cells, and **archegonia** are gametangia that produce eggs.

- Ferns and other vascular plants have **xylem** to conduct water and dissolved minerals and **phloem** to conduct dissolved sugar.

2 Name the green algal group from which plants are hypothesized to have descended and describe supporting evidence.

- Plants probably arose from a group of green algae called **charophytes.** This conclusion is based in part on molecular comparisons of DNA and RNA sequences, which show the closest match between charophytes and plants.

CENGAGENOW Explore plant evolution by clicking on the figure in CengageNOW.

27.2 *(page 565)*

3 Summarize the features that distinguish bryophytes from other plants.

- Unlike other land plants, bryophytes are nonvascular and lack xylem and phloem. Bryophytes are the only plants with a dominant gametophyte generation. Their sporophytes remain permanently attached and nutritionally dependent on the gametophytes.

4 Name and briefly describe the three phyla of bryophytes.

- Mosses (phylum Bryophyta) have gametophytes that are green plants that grow from a filamentous **protonema.**

- Many **liverworts** (phylum Hepatophyta) have gametophytes that are flattened, lobelike **thalli;** others are leafy.

- **Hornworts** (phylum Anthocerophyta) have thalloid gametophytes.

5 Describe the life cycle of mosses and compare their gametophyte and sporophyte generations.

- The green moss gametophyte bears archegonia and/or antheridia at the top of the plant. During fertilization, a sperm cell fuses with

an egg cell in the archegonium. The zygote grows into an embryo that develops into a moss sporophyte, which is attached to the gametophyte. Meiosis occurs within the capsule of the sporophyte to produce spores. When a spore germinates, it grows into a protonema that forms buds that develop into gametophytes.

CENGAGENOW Watch the life cycles of the mosses and liverworts by clicking on the figures in CengageNOW.

27.3 *(page 571)*

6 Discuss the features that distinguish seedless vascular plants from algae and bryophytes.

- Seedless vascular plants have several adaptations that algae and bryophytes lack, including vascular tissues and a dominant sporophyte generation. As in bryophytes, reproduction in seedless vascular plants depends on water as a transport medium for motile sperm cells.

7 Name and briefly describe the two phyla of seedless vascular plants.

- Sporophytes of **club mosses** (phylum Lycopodiophyta) consist of roots, rhizomes, erect branches, and leaves that are **microphylls.**

- **Ferns** (phylum Pteridophyta) are the largest and most diverse group of seedless vascular plants. The fern sporophyte consists of a rhizome that bears fronds and true roots. Phylum Pteridophyta also includes whisk ferns and horsetails. Sporophytes of **whisk ferns** have **dichotomously branching** rhizomes and erect stems; they lack true roots and leaves. **Horsetail** sporophytes have roots, rhizomes, aerial stems that are hollow and jointed, and leaves that are reduced **megaphylls.**

8 Describe the life cycle of ferns and compare their sporophyte and gametophyte generations.

- Fern sporophytes have roots, rhizomes, and leaves that are megaphylls. Their leaves, or fronds, bear sporangia in clusters called **sori.** Meiosis in sporangia produces haploid spores. The fern gametophyte, called a **prothallus,** develops from a haploid spore and bears both archegonia and antheridia.

CENGAGENOW Watch the life cycle of the ferns by clicking on the figure in CengageNOW.

9 Compare the generalized life cycles of homosporous and heterosporous plants.

- **Homospory,** the production of one kind of spore, is characteristic of bryophytes, most club mosses, and most ferns, including whisk ferns and horsetails. In homospory, spores give rise to gametophyte plants that produce both egg cells and sperm cells.

- **Heterospory,** the production of two kinds of spores (microspores and megaspores), occurs in certain club mosses, certain ferns, and all seed plants. **Microspores** give rise to male gametophytes that produce sperm cells. **Megaspores** give rise to female gametophytes that produce eggs. The evolution of heterospory was an essential step in the evolution of seeds.

1. Plants probably descended from a group of green algae called (a) rhyniophytes (b) *Calamites* (c) epiphytes (d) charophytes (e) club mosses

2. Which of the following is *not* a characteristic of plants? (a) cuticle (b) unicellular gametangia (c) stomata (d) multicellular embryo (e) alternation of generations

3. In plant life cycles (a) the first products of meiosis are gametes (b) spores are part of the diploid sporophyte generation (c) the embryo gives rise to a zygote (d) the first stage in the diploid sporophyte generation is the zygote (e) the first stage in the haploid gametophyte generation is the prothallus

4. The bryophytes (a) include mosses, liverworts, and hornworts (b) include whisk ferns, horsetails, and club mosses (c) are small plants that lack a vascular system (d) a and c (e) b and c

5. The waxy layer that covers aerial parts of plants is the (a) cuticle (b) archegonium (c) protonema (d) stoma (e) thallus

6. A strengthening compound found in cell walls of vascular plants is (a) xanthophyll (b) lignin (c) cutin (d) cellulose (e) carotenoid

7. Stomata (a) help prevent desiccation of plant tissues (b) transport water and minerals through plant tissues (c) allow gas exchange for photosynthesis (d) strengthen cell walls (e) produce male gametes

8. The green, gametangia-bearing moss plant (a) is the haploid gametophyte generation (b) is the diploid sporophyte generation (c) is called a protonema (d) contains cells with single large chloroplasts (e) b and c

9. _____ is a leaf that arose from a branch system. (a) An antheridium (b) A microphyll (c) A megaphyll (d) A sorus (e) A microspore

10. These plants have vascularized stems but lack true roots and leaves. (a) mosses (b) club mosses (c) horsetails (d) whisk ferns (e) hornworts

11. These plants have hollow, jointed stems that are impregnated with silica. (a) mosses (b) club mosses (c) horsetails (d) whisk ferns (e) hornworts

12. Which of the following statements about ferns is *not* true? (a) ferns have motile sperm cells that swim through water to the egg-containing archegonium (b) ferns are vascular plants (c) ferns are the most economically important group of bryophytes (d) the fern sporophyte consists of a rhizome, roots, and fronds (e) the diversity of ferns is greatest in the tropics

CRITICAL THINKING

1. **EVOLUTION LINK.** How may the following trends in plant evolution be adaptive to living on land?

   a. dependence on water for fertilization ⟶ no need for water as a transport medium

   b. homospory ⟶ heterospory

2. **ANALYZING DATA.** According to the cladogram in Figure 27-5, which plants evolved first: nonvascular bryophytes, seedless vascular plants, or seed plants?

3. **EVOLUTION LINK.** Where would you position the rhyniophytes on Figure 27-13? Would the line for rhyniophytes extend to the tips of the rest of the cladogram? Why or why not?

4. Label the following figures. Refer to Figs. 27-7 and 27-16 to check your answers.

28 Seed Plants

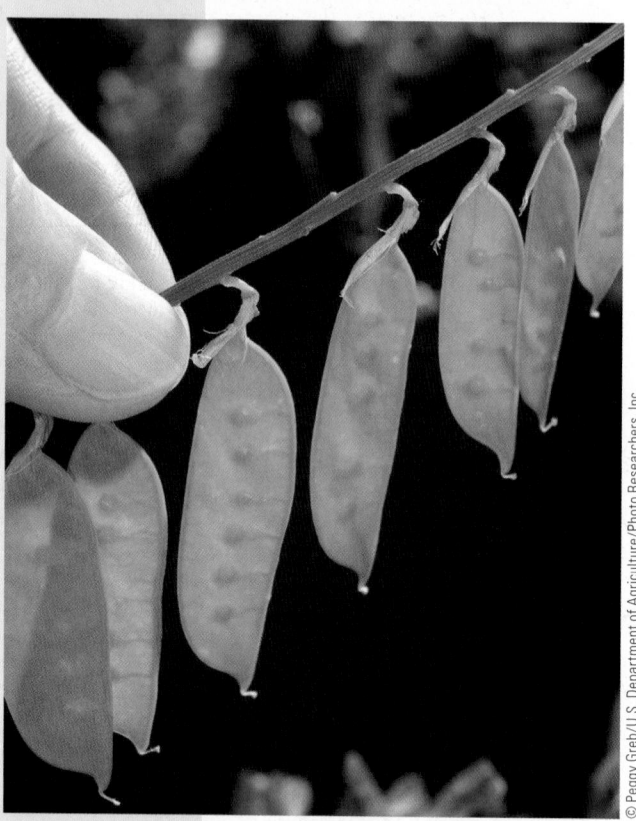

© Peggy Greb/U.S. Department of Agriculture/Photo Researchers, Inc.

Hairy vetch seed pods. The seeds are developing within each pod. Hairy vetch (*Vicia villosa*) is native to Europe and Asia but has become naturalized in the United States.

Chapter 27 focused on plants that reproduce by means of *spores,* haploid cells that disperse and germinate to produce gametophytes. Although gymnosperms and angiosperms also produce spores, their primary means of reproduction and dispersal is by **seeds,** which represent an important adaptation for life on land (see photograph). Each seed consists of an embryonic sporophyte, nutritive tissue, and a protective coat. Seeds develop from the fertilized egg cell, the female gametophyte, and its associated tissues. The two groups of seed plants, gymnosperms and angiosperms (flowering plants), exhibit the greatest evolutionary complexity of land plants and are the dominant plants in most terrestrial environments.

Seeds are reproductively superior to spores for several reasons. First, a seed is further along in its development before it is released to survive on its own: a seed contains a multicellular young plant with embryonic root, stem, and one or more leaves already formed, whereas a spore is a single cell. Second, a seed contains an abundant food supply. After germination, food stored in the seed nourishes the plant embryo until it becomes self-sufficient. Because a spore is a single cell, few food reserves exist for the plant that develops from a spore. Third, a seed is protected by a multicellular **seed coat** that is very thick and hard in some plants, as, for example, in lima beans. Like spores, seeds live for extended periods at reduced rates of metabolism and germinate when conditions become favorable.

Seeds and seed plants are intimately connected with the development of human civilization. From prehistoric times, early humans collected and used seeds for food. Seeds often contain a concentrated source of proteins, oils, carbohydrates, and vitamins, which are nourishing for humans as well as for germinating plants. Seeds are easy to store (if kept dry), so humans can collect them during times of plenty to save for times of need. Few other foods are stored as conveniently or for as long. Although flowering plants produce most seeds that humans consume, the seeds of certain gymnosperms—the piñon pine, for example—are edible.

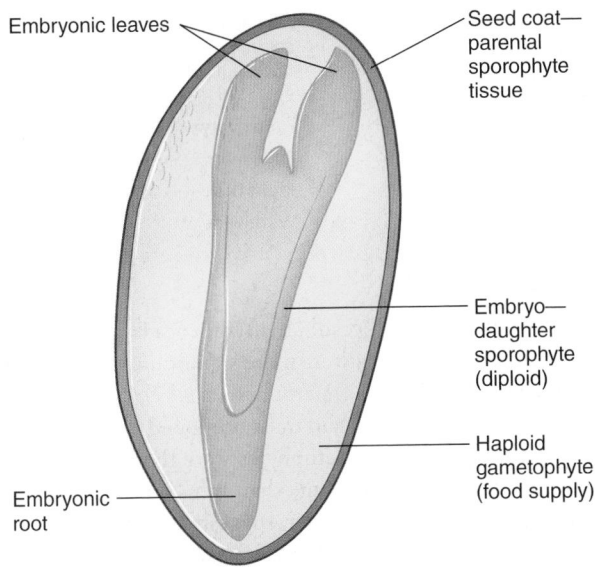

Embryonic leaves

Seed coat—
parental
sporophyte
tissue

Embryo—
daughter
sporophyte
(diploid)

Haploid
gametophyte
(food supply)

Embryonic
root

(a) Gymnosperm seed. Longitudinal section through a pine seed.

Scale

Ovule
(future seed)
surrounded by
integument
(future seed coat)

Gene Cox/Photo Researchers, Inc.

(b) Gymnosperm cone. Longitudinal section through a female pine cone, showing the ovules (which develop into seeds) borne on scales. Note the absence of an ovary wall.

FIGURE 28-1 Seeds

In this chapter we present the diversity in seed plants—both gymnosperms and angiosperms—followed by an examination of what we know about how seed plants evolved.

28.1 AN INTRODUCTION TO SEED PLANTS

■ LEARNING OBJECTIVE

1   Compare the features of gymnosperms and angiosperms.

Like the bryophytes and seedless vascular plants introduced in Chapter 27, seed plants have life cycles with an **alternation of generations;** they spend part of their lives in the multicellular diploid sporophyte stage and part in the multicellular haploid gametophyte stage. The sporophyte generation is the dominant stage in seed plants, and the gametophyte generation is significantly reduced in size and entirely dependent on the sporophyte generation. Unlike the bryophytes and ferns, seed plants do not have free-living gametophytes. Instead, the female gametophyte is attached to and nutritionally dependent on the sporophyte generation.

In Chapter 27, you learned that some seedless vascular plants are heterosporous. (Figure 27-19 shows a generalized life cycle for heterosporous plants.) However, *all* seed plants are heterosporous and produce two types of spores: microspores and megaspores. In fact, heterospory is a requirement of seed production.

Seed plants produce **ovules,** each of which is a *megasporangium* surrounded by **integuments,** layers of sporophyte tissue that enclose the megasporangium. After fertilization takes place, the ovule develops into a seed, and the integuments develop into the seed coat (**FIG. 28-1a**).

Botanists divide seed plants into two groups based on whether or not an ovary wall surrounds their ovules (an *ovary* is a structure

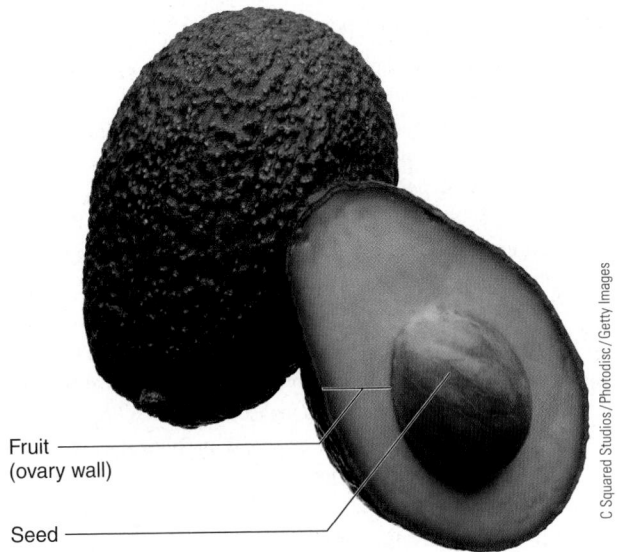

C Squared Studios/Photodisc/Getty Images

Fruit
(ovary wall)

Seed

(c) Angiosperm fruit. Longitudinal section through an avocado fruit, showing the seed surrounded by ovary tissue of the maternal sporophyte.

that contains one or more ovules). The two groups of seed plants are the **gymnosperms** and the **angiosperms** (**TABLE 28-1**). The word *gymnosperm* is derived from the Greek for "naked seed." Gymnosperms produce seeds that are totally exposed or borne on the scales of cones (**FIG. 28-1b**). In other words, an ovary wall does not surround the ovules of gymnosperms. Pine, spruce, fir, hemlock, and ginkgo are examples of gymnosperms.

The term *angiosperm* is derived from the Greek expression that means "seed enclosed in a vessel or case." Angiosperms are flowering plants that produce their seeds within a *fruit* (a mature ovary) (**FIG. 28-1c**). Thus, the ovules of angiosperms are protected. Flowering plants, which are extremely diverse, include corn, oaks, water lilies, cacti, apples, grasses, palms, and buttercups.

Both gymnosperms and flowering plants have vascular tissues: **xylem,** for conducting water and dissolved minerals (inorganic nutrients), and **phloem,** for conducting dissolved sugar.

Characteristic	Gymnosperms	Angiosperms
Growth habit	Woody trees and shrubs	Woody or herbaceous
Conducting cells in xylem	Tracheids	Vessel elements and tracheids
Reproductive structures	Cones (usually)	Flowers
Pollen grain transfer	Wind (usually)	Animals or wind
Fertilization	Egg and sperm ⟶ zygote	Double fertilization: egg and sperm ⟶ zygote; two polar nuclei and sperm ⟶ endosperm
Seeds	Exposed or borne on scales of cones	Enclosed within fruit derived from ovary
Nutritive material	Female gametophyte	Endosperm
Number of species	About 840	More than 300,000
Geographic distribution	Worldwide	Worldwide

TABLE 28-1 A Comparison of Gymnosperms and Angiosperms

Review

- What is an ovule?
- How do gymnosperm and angiosperm seeds differ?

28.2 GYMNOSPERMS

■ LEARNING OBJECTIVES

2   Trace the steps in the life cycle of a pine and compare its sporophyte and gametophyte generations.

3   Summarize the features that distinguish gymnosperms from bryophytes and ferns.

4   Name and briefly describe the four phyla of gymnosperms.

The gymnosperms include some of the most interesting plants. For example, a giant sequoia (*Sequoiadendron giganteum*) known as the General Sherman Tree, in Sequoia National Park in California, is one of the world's most massive organisms. It is 82 m (267 ft) tall and has a girth of 23.7 m (77 ft) measured 1.5 m (5 ft) above ground level. Another gymnosperm, a coast redwood (*Sequoia sempervirens*) nicknamed "Hyperion" after a giant in Greek mythology, is possibly the world's tallest tree, measuring 117 m (379 ft) in 2007. Botanists using tree-ring analysis determined that one of Earth's oldest living organisms, a bristlecone pine (*Pinus longaeva*) in the White Mountains of California, is about 5,000 years old.

Gymnosperms are usually classified into four phyla, which branch from a single evolutionary line (**FIG. 28-2**). Numbering 630 species, the largest phylum of gymnosperms is Coniferophyta, commonly called *conifers*. Two phyla of gymnosperms, Ginkgo-

phyta (the ginkgoes) and Cycadophyta (the cycads), are evolutionary remnants of groups that were more significant in the past. The fourth phylum, Gnetophyta (gnetophytes), is a collection of some unusual plants that share certain traits not found in other gymnosperms; until recently, the gnetophytes were thought to be more closely related to flowering plants than were other gymnosperm clades. Current evidence, however, suggests that gnetophytes are probably most closely related to conifers (see Fig. 28-2).

Conifers are woody plants that produce seeds in cones

The **conifers** (phylum Coniferophyta), which include pines, spruces, hemlocks, and firs, comprise the most familiar group of gymnosperms (**FIG. 28-3a**). These 630 species of woody trees or shrubs produce annual additions of secondary tissues (wood and bark); there are no herbaceous (nonwoody) conifers. The wood (*secondary xylem*) consists of **tracheids,** which are long, tapering cells with pits through which water and dissolved minerals move from one cell to another.

Many conifers produce **resin,** a viscous, clear or translucent substance consisting of several organic compounds that may protect the plant from attack by fungi or insects. The resin collects in resin ducts, tubelike cavities that extend throughout the roots, stems, and leaves. Cells lining the resin ducts produce and secrete resin.

Conifers generally have leaves called **needles** that are long, narrow, tough, and leathery (**FIG. 28-3b**). Most pines bear clusters of two to five needles, depending on the species. In a few conifers, such as American arborvitae, the leaves are scalelike and cover the stem (**FIG. 28-3c**). Most conifers are evergreen and bear their leaves throughout the year. Only a few, such as the dawn redwood, larch, and bald cypress, are deciduous and shed their needles at the end of each growing season.

Seed plants include four gymnosperm phyla and one phylum of flowering plants (angiosperms).

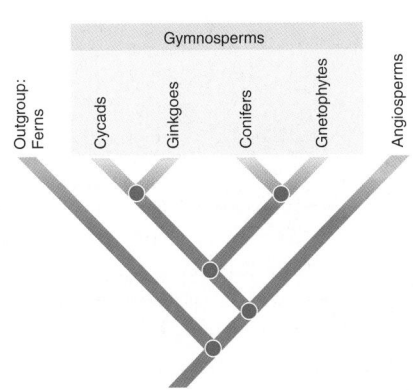

FIGURE 28-2 Gymnosperm and angiosperm evolution

This cladogram shows a current hypothesis of phylogenetic relationships among living seed plants, based on structural evidence, molecular comparisons, and fossils. Relationships among extant gymnosperm clades and angiosperms remain controversial. The arrangement of the phyla shown here may change as future analyses help clarify relationships.

Most conifers are **monoecious:** they have separate male and female reproductive parts in different locations on the same plant. These reproductive parts are generally borne in *strobili* (commonly called *cones*), hence the name *conifer*, which means "cone-bearing."

Conifers occupy extensive areas, ranging from the Arctic to the tropics, and are the dominant vegetation in the forested regions of Alaska, Canada, northern Europe, and Siberia. In addition, they are important in the Southern Hemisphere, particularly in wet, mountainous areas of temperate and tropical regions in South America, Australia, New Zealand, and Malaysia. Southwestern China, with more than 60 species of conifers, has the greatest regional diversity of conifer species in the world. California, New Caledonia (an island east of Australia), southeastern China, and Japan also have considerable diversity of conifer species. Ecologically, conifers contribute food and shelter to animals and other organisms, and their roots hold the soil in place and help prevent soil erosion.

Humans use conifers for their wood (for building materials as well as paper products), medicinal value (such as the anticancer drug Taxol from the Pacific yew), turpentine, and resins. Because of their attractive appearance, conifers such as firs, spruces, pines, and cedars are grown for landscape design and decorative holiday trees and wreaths.

Pines represent a typical conifer life cycle

The genus *Pinus,* by far the largest genus in the conifers, consists of about 100 species. A pine tree is a mature

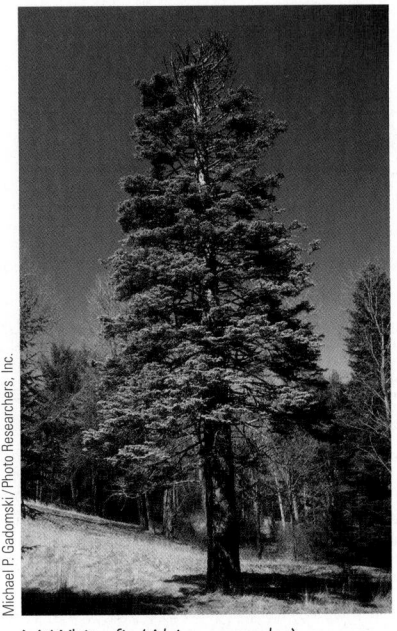

(a) White fir (*Abies concolor*). Photographed in Milford, Pennsylvania, at the historic home of Gifford Pinchot, the first Chief Forester of the U.S. Forest Service (under T. R. Roosevelt).

(b) In white pine (*Pinus strobus*), leaves are long, slender needles that occur in clusters of five.

(c) In American arborvitae (*Thuja occidentalis*), leaves are small and scalelike.

FIGURE 28-3 Conifers

sporophyte (**FIGURE 28-4**). Pine is heterosporous and therefore produces microspores and megaspores in separate cones. Male cones, usually 1 cm or less in length, are smaller than female cones and are generally produced on the lower branches each spring (**FIG. 28-5**). The more familiar, woody female cones, which are on the tree year-round, are usually found on the upper branches of the tree and bear seeds after reproduction. Female cones vary considerably in size. The sugar pine (*P. lambertiana*) that grows in California produces the world's longest female cones, which reach lengths of 60 cm (2 ft).

Each male cone, also called a *pollen cone*, consists of **sporophylls**, leaflike scales that bear sporangia on the underside. At the base of each sporophyll are two **microsporangia**, which contain numerous **microsporocytes**, also called *microspore mother cells*. In

Figure 28-4, each microsporocyte undergoes meiosis to form four haploid microspores. **Microspores** then develop into extremely reduced male gametophytes. Each immature male gametophyte, also called a **pollen grain**, consists of four cells, two of which—a *generative cell* and a *tube cell*—are involved in reproduction. The other two cells soon degenerate. Two large air sacs on each pollen grain provide buoyancy for wind dissemination. Male cones shed pollen grains in great numbers, and wind currents carry some to the immature female cones.

Many botanists think that the female cones (also called *seed cones*) are modified branch systems. Each cone scale bears two **ovules**, or **megasporangia**, on its upper surface. Within each megasporangium, meiosis of a **megasporocyte**, or *megaspore mother cell*, produces four haploid **megaspores**. One of these di-

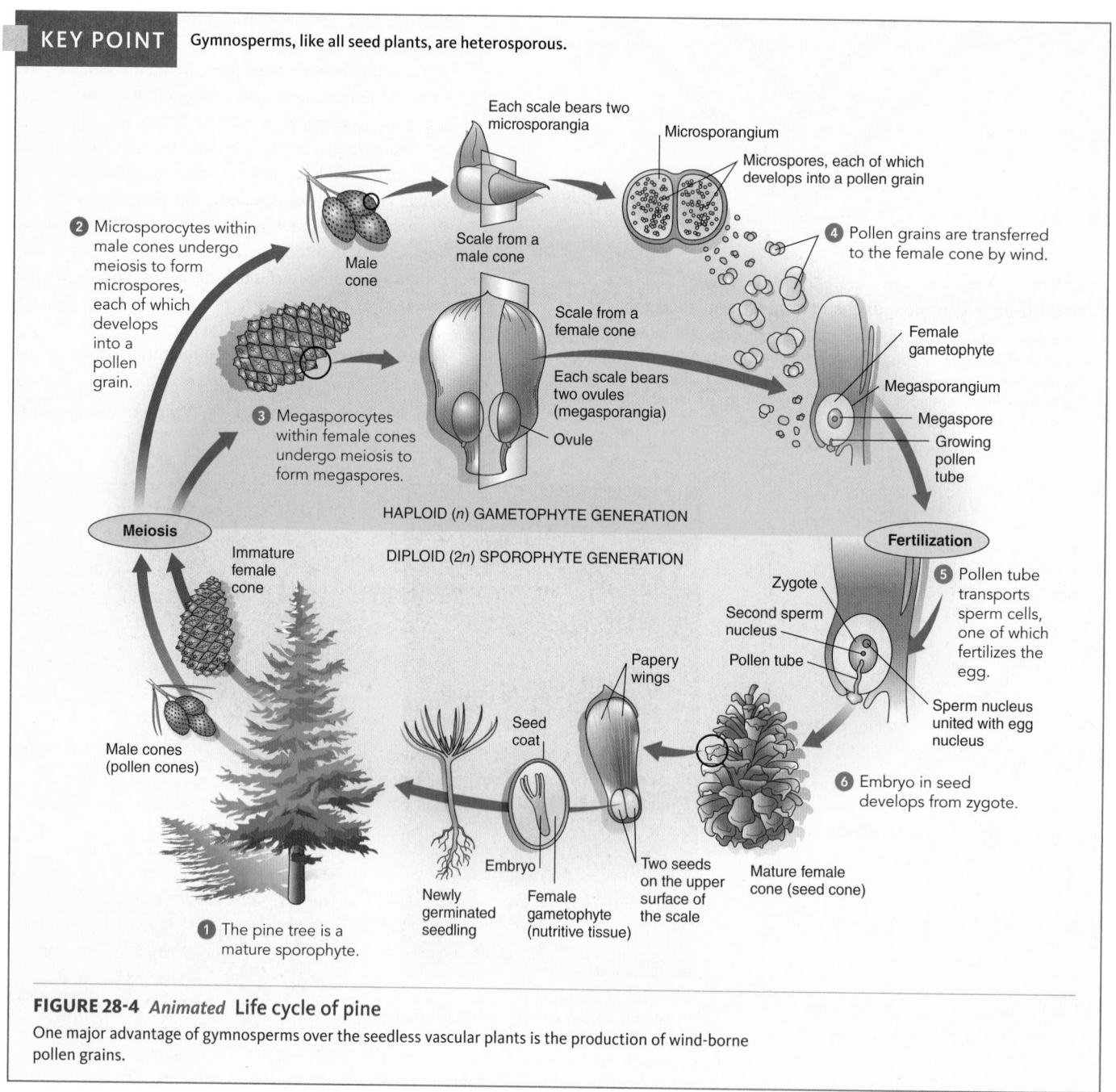

Gymnosperms, like all seed plants, are heterosporous.

FIGURE 28-4 *Animated* **Life cycle of pine**

One major advantage of gymnosperms over the seedless vascular plants is the production of wind-borne pollen grains.

Pollen grains (immature male gametophytes)

50 μm

Manfred Kage/Peter Arnold, Inc.

Walt Anderson/Visuals Unlimited

FIGURE 28-5 Male and female cones in lodgepole pine (*Pinus contorta*)

Mature woody female cones (*top*) have opened to shed their seeds. Clusters of male cones (*bottom*) produce copious amounts of pollen grains in the spring. (*Inset*) Each pollen grain develops from a microspore.

vides mitotically, developing into the female gametophyte, which produces an egg within each of several archegonia. The other three megaspores are nonfunctional and soon degenerate.

When the ovule is ready to receive pollen, it produces a sticky droplet at the opening where the pollen grains land. **Pollination,** the transfer of pollen to the female cones, occurs in the spring for a week or 10 days, after which the pollen cones wither and drop off the tree. One of the many pollen grains that adhere to the sticky female cone grows a **pollen tube,** an outgrowth that digests its way through the megasporangium to the egg within the archegonium. The germinated pollen grain with its pollen tube is the mature male gametophyte.

Ultimately, two nonmotile (nonflagellate) sperm cells form within the germinated pollen grain. When it reaches the female gametophyte, the pollen tube discharges the two sperm cells near the egg. One of these sperm cells fuses with the egg, in the process of **fertilization,** to form a zygote, or fertilized egg, which subsequently grows into a young pine embryo in the seed. The other sperm cell degenerates.

The developing embryo consists of an embryonic root and an embryonic shoot with several cotyledons (embryonic leaves). Haploid female gametophyte tissue surrounds the embryo and becomes the nutritive tissue in the mature pine seed. A tough, protective seed coat derived from the integuments encloses the embryo and nutritive tissue. The seed coat forms a thin, papery wing at one end that enables dispersal by air currents. Some seeds remain within the female cones for several years before being shed.

In the pine life cycle, the sporophyte generation is dominant, and the gametophyte generation is restricted in size to microscopic structures in the cones. Although the female gametophyte produces archegonia, the male gametophyte is so reduced that it does

not produce antheridia. The gametophyte generation in pines, as in all seed plants, depends totally on the sporophyte generation for nourishment.

A major adaptation in the pine life cycle is elimination of the need for external water as a sperm transport medium. Instead, air currents carry pine pollen grains to female cones, and nonflagellate sperm cells move through a pollen tube to the egg. Pine and other conifers are plants whose reproduction is totally adapted for life on land.

Cycads have seed cones and compound leaves

Cycads (phylum Cycadophyta) were very important during the Triassic period, which began about 251 million years ago (mya) and is sometimes referred to as the "Age of Cycads." Most species are now extinct, and the few surviving cycads, about 140 species, are tropical and subtropical plants with stout, trunklike stems and compound leaves that resemble those of palms or tree ferns (**FIG. 28-6**). Many cycads are endangered, primarily because they are popular as ornamentals and are gathered from the wild and sold to collectors. In the United States, cycads can be found in Florida, Texas, and California.

Cycad reproduction is similar to that in pines except that cycads are **dioecious** and therefore have seed cones on female plants and pollen cones on male plants. Their seed structure is most like that of the earliest seeds found in the fossil record. Cycads have also retained motile sperm cells, each of which has many hairlike flagella. Motile sperm cells are a vestige retained from the ancestors of cycads, in which sperm cells swam from antheridia to archegonia. In cycads, specialized insects (almost exclusively beetles) carry pollen grains to the female plants and their cones. Following transfer to the female cone, the pollen grain germinates and grows a pollen tube. The sperm cells are released into this tube and swim to the egg.

Ginkgo biloba is the only living species in its phylum

Ginkgo (phylum Ginkgophyta) is represented by a single **extant** (living) species, the maidenhair tree, *Ginkgo biloba* (**FIG. 28-7**). This native of eastern China grew in the wild in only two locations, although people had cultivated it for its edible seeds in China and Japan for centuries. *Ginkgo* is the oldest genus (and species) of extant trees. Fossil ginkgoes 200 million years old have been discovered that are strikingly similar to the modern ginkgo.

People often plant ginkgo in North America and Europe today, particularly in parks and along city streets, because it is hardy and somewhat resistant to air pollution. Its leaves are deciduous and turn a beautiful yellow before being shed in the fall.

Like cycads, ginkgo is dioecious, with separate male and female trees. It has flagellate sperm cells—an evolutionary vestige that is not required because ginkgo produces airborne pollen grains. Ginkgo seeds are completely exposed rather than contained within cones. Male trees are usually planted because the female trees bear seeds whose fleshy outer coverings give off a foul odor that smells like rancid butter. In China and Japan, where people eat the seeds, the female trees are more common.

Ginkgo has been an important medicinal plant for centuries and is still a common herbal remedy today. Extracts from the leaves may enhance neurological functioning by increasing blood flow to the brain, although several recent studies have concluded that ginkgo does not improve memory in elderly people.

Gnetophytes include three unusual genera

The **gnetophytes** (nee' toe phites) (phylum Gnetophyta) consist of about 70 species in three diverse and obscure genera (*Gnetum, Ephedra,* and *Welwitschia*). Gnetophytes share certain features that make them unique among the gymnosperms. For example, gnetophytes have more efficient water-conducting cells, called *vessel elements,* in their xylem (see Chapter 33). Flowering plants also have vessel elements in their xylem, but of the gymnosperms, only the gnetophytes do. In addition, the cone clusters that some gnetophytes produce resemble flower clusters, and certain details in their life cycles resemble those of flowering plants. Despite these similarities, most botanists now think that

Female strobilus (seed cone)

(a) A female Florida arrowroot (*Zamia integrifolia*) produces seed cones. This plant is the only cycad native to the United States. Like *Zamia*, most cycads are short plants, less than 2 m (6.5 ft) tall.

FIGURE 28-6 Cycads

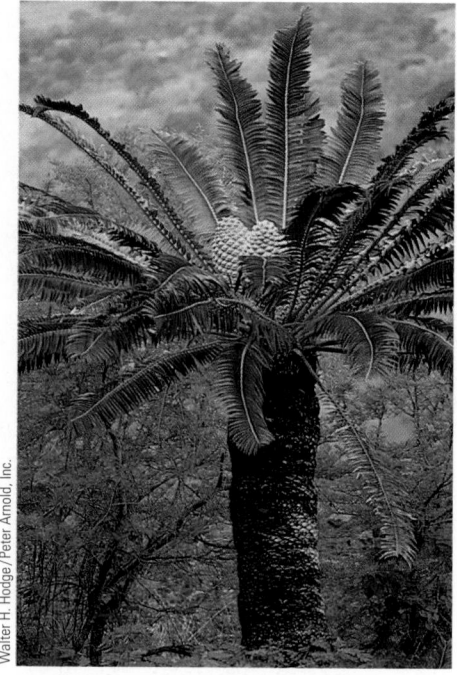

Walter H. Hodge/Peter Arnold, Inc.

(b) This female cycad (*Encephalartos transvenosus*) in South Africa has a trunk that reaches a height of about 9 m (30 ft) and resembles a palm. Note its immense seed cones that grow up to 0.8 m (30 in) in length.

Marion Lobstein

(a) Close-up of a branch from a female ginkgo, showing the exposed seeds and the distinctive, fan-shaped leaves.

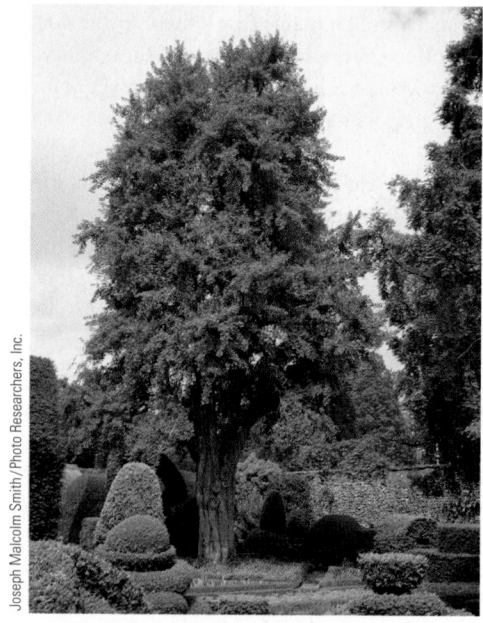

Joseph Malcolm Smith / Photo Researchers, Inc.

(b) Ginkgo (*Ginkgo biloba*) tree in a formal garden in northern England.

FIGURE 28-7 Ginkgo, or maidenhair tree

gnetophytes represent evolutionary diversity in gymnosperms and are not in a direct line to flowering plants (see Fig. 28-2).

The genus *Gnetum* contains tropical vines, shrubs, and trees with broad leaves (**FIG. 28-8a**). Species in the genus *Ephedra* include many shrubs and vines that grow in deserts and other dry temperate and tropical regions. Some *Ephedra* species resemble horsetails in that they have jointed green stems with tiny leaves (**FIG. 28-8b**). Commonly called *joint fir,* *Ephedra* has been used medicinally for centuries. An Asiatic *Ephedra* is the source of ephedrine, which stimulates the heart and raises blood pressure. At one time, ephedrine was commonly sold over the counter in weight-control medications and herbal energy boosters; several deaths were reported from chronic use or overdose of products containing ephedrine, so its use has been restricted.

The third gnetophyte genus, *Welwitschia*, contains a single species found in deserts of southwestern Africa (**FIG. 28-8c**). Most of *Welwitschia*'s body—a long taproot—grows underground. Its short, wide stem forms a shallow disc, up to 0.9 m (3 ft) in diameter, from which two ribbonlike leaves extend. These two leaves continue to grow from the stem throughout the plant's life, but their ends are usually broken and torn by the wind, giving the appearance of numerous leaves. Each leaf grows to about 2 m (6.5 ft) in length. When *Welwitschia* reproduces, cones form around the edge of its disclike stem.

(a) The leaves of *Gnetum gnemon* resemble those of flowering plants. Note the exposed seeds. The species is native to southern Asia and the Maldives.

(b) A male joint fir (*Ephedra*) has pollen cones clustered at the nodes. In the 19th century, European pioneers used species native to the American Southwest to make a beverage, Mormon tea.

(c) *Welwitschia mirabilis* is native to deserts in southwestern Africa. It survives on moisture-laden fogs that drift inland from the ocean. Photographed in the Namib Desert, Namibia.

FIGURE 28-8 Gnetophytes

Review

- What is the dominant generation in the pine life cycle? How does pollination occur in gymnosperms?
- What features distinguish gymnosperms from other plants?
- What are the four groups of gymnosperms?
- What features distinguish cycads from ginkgo? from gnetophytes?

28.3 FLOWERING PLANTS

■ LEARNING OBJECTIVES

5 Summarize the features that distinguish flowering plants from other plants.

6 Briefly explain the life cycle of a flowering plant and describe double fertilization.

7 Contrast monocots and eudicots, the two largest classes of flowering plants.

8 Discuss the evolutionary adaptations of flowering plants.

Flowering plants, or angiosperms (phylum Anthophyta), are the most successful plants today, surpassing even the gymnosperms in importance. They have adapted to almost every habitat and, with at least 300,000 species, are Earth's dominant plants. Flowering plants come in a wide variety of sizes and forms, from herbaceous violets to massive eucalyptus trees. Some flowering plants—tulips and roses, for example—have large, conspicuous flowers; others, such as grasses and oaks, produce small, inconspicuous flowers.

Flowering plants are vascular plants that reproduce sexually by forming flowers and, following a unique double fertilization process, seeds within fruits. The fruit protects the developing seeds and often aids in their dispersal (see Chapter 37). Flowering plants have efficient water-conducting cells called **vessel elements** in their xylem and efficient sugar-conducting cells called **sieve tube elements** in their phloem (see Chapter 33).

Flowering plants are extremely important to humans because our survival as a species literally depends on them. All our major food crops are flowering plants; examples include rice, wheat, corn, potatoes, tomatoes, beans, apples, and citrus fruits. Woody flowering plants such as oak, cherry, and walnut provide valuable lumber. Flowering plants give us fibers, such as cotton and linen, and medicines, such as digitalis and codeine. Products as diverse as rubber, tobacco, coffee, chocolate, wine, and aromatic oils for perfumes come from flowering plants. **Economic botany** is the subdiscipline of botany that deals with plants of economic importance.

Monocots and eudicots are the two largest classes of flowering plants

Phylum Anthophyta is divided into several classes with only a few members each and two very large classes: the monocots (class Monocotyledones) and the eudicots (class Eudicotyledones). The smaller classes will be discussed later in the chapter in the context of their evolutionary significance. For now, we restrict our discussion of flowering plants to the monocots and eudicots, which collectively represent about 97% of all flowering plant species. Eudicots are more diverse and include many more species (at least 200,000) than the monocots (at least 90,000). **TABLE 28-2** provides a comparison of some of the general features of the two classes.

Monocots include palms, grasses, orchids, irises, onions, and lilies. Monocots are mostly herbaceous plants with long, narrow leaves that have parallel veins (the main leaf veins run parallel to one another). The parts of monocot flowers usually occur in threes (**FIG. 28-9a**). For example, a flower may have three sepals, three petals, six stamens, and a compound pistil consisting of three fused

carpels (these flower parts are discussed shortly). Monocot seeds have a single **cotyledon,** or embryonic seed leaf; **endosperm,** a nutritive tissue, is usually present in the mature seed.

Eudicots include oaks, roses, mustards, cacti, blueberries, and sunflowers. Eudicots are either herbaceous (such as a tomato plant) or woody (such as a hickory tree). Their leaves vary in shape but usually are broader than monocot leaves, with netted (finely branched) veins. Flower parts usually occur in fours or fives or multiples thereof (**FIG. 28-9b**). Two cotyledons are present in eudicot seeds, and endosperm is usually absent in the mature seed, having been absorbed by the two cotyledons during seed development.

Sexual reproduction takes place in flowers

Flowers are reproductive shoots usually composed of four parts—sepals, petals, stamens, and carpels—arranged in whorls (circles)

TABLE 28-2	Distinguishing Features of Monocots and Eudicots	
Feature	**Monocots**	**Eudicots**
Flower parts	Usually in threes	Usually in fours or fives
Pollen grains	One furrow or pore	Three furrows or pores
Leaf venation	Usually parallel	Usually netted
Vascular bundles in stem cross section	Usually scattered or more complex arrangement	Arranged in a circle (ring)
Roots	Fibrous root system	Taproot system
Seeds	Embryo with one cotyledon	Embryo with two cotyledons
Secondary growth (wood and bark)	Absent	Often present

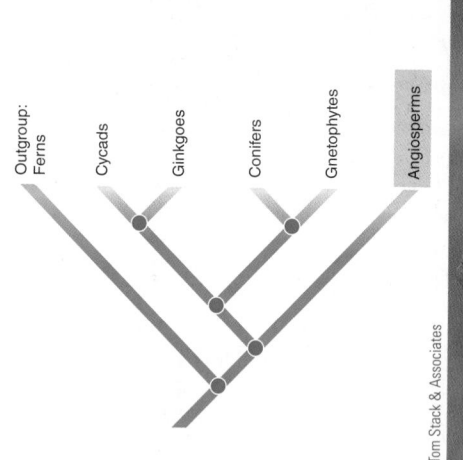

John Gerlach/Tom Stack & Associates

(a) Monocot. *Trillium erectum,* like most monocots, has floral parts in threes. Note the three green sepals, three red petals, six stamens, and three stigmas (the compound pistil consists of three fused carpels).

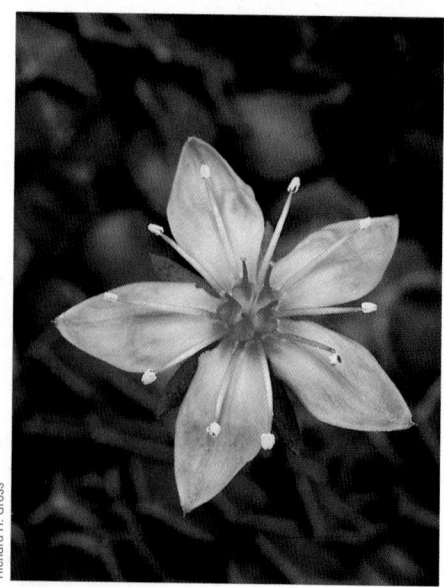

Richard H. Gross

(b) Eudicot. Most eudicots, such as this *Tacitus,* have floral parts in fours or fives. Note the five petals, 10 stamens, and five separate pistils. Five sepals are also present but barely visible against the background.

FIGURE 28-9 Flowering plants

on the end of a flower stalk, or **peduncle** (**FIG. 28-10**). The peduncle may terminate in a single flower or a cluster of flowers known as an **inflorescence.** The tip of the flower stalk that bears the flower parts is known as the **receptacle.**

All four floral parts are important in the reproductive process, but only the stamens (the "male" organs) and carpels (the "female" organs) produce gametes. A flower that has all four parts is **complete,** whereas an **incomplete** flower lacks one or more of these four parts. A flower with both stamens and carpels is **perfect,** whereas an **imperfect** flower has stamens or carpels, but not both.

Sepals, which make up the lowermost and outermost whorl on a floral shoot, are leaflike in appearance and often green (**FIG. 28-11a**). Sepals cover and protect the other flower parts when the flower is a bud. As the flower opens, the sepals fold back to reveal the more conspicuous petals. The collective term for all the sepals of a flower is the **calyx.**

The whorl just above the sepals consists of **petals,** which are broad, flat, and thin (like sepals and leaves) but vary in shape and are frequently brightly colored. Petals attract animal pollinators to the flower (see Chapter 37). Sometimes petals are fused to form a tube (as in trumpet honeysuckle flowers) or other floral shape (as in snapdragons, whose petals form two lips). The petals of a flower are referred to collectively as the **corolla.**

Just inside the petals is a whorl of **stamens** (**FIG. 28-11b**). Each stamen is composed of a thin stalk, called a **filament,** and a saclike **anther,** where meiosis occurs to form microspores that develop into pollen grains. Each pollen grain produces two cells surrounded by a tough outer wall. One cell eventually divides to form two male gametes, or sperm cells, and the other produces a pollen tube through which the sperm cells travel to reach the ovule.

In the center of most flowers are one or more closed **carpels,** the "female" reproductive organs. Carpels bear ovules, which, as

(a) An *Arabidopsis thaliana* flower.

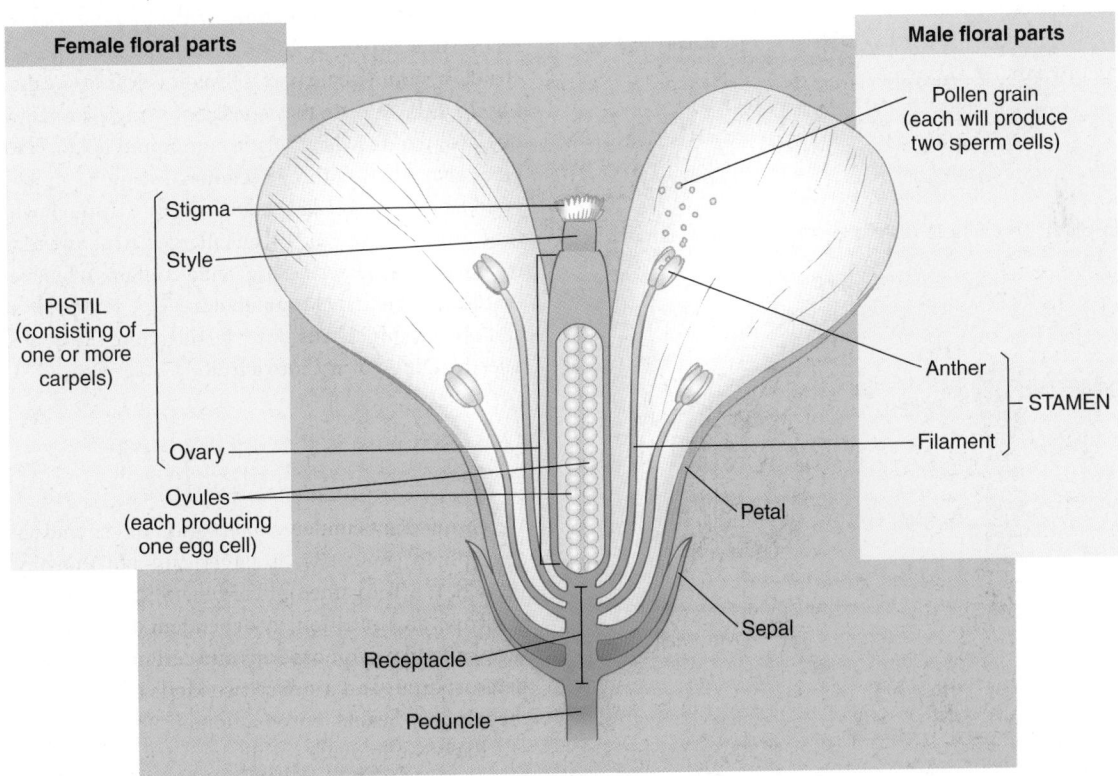

(b) This cutaway view of an *Arabidopsis* flower shows the details of basic floral structure. Each flower has four sepals (two are shown), four petals (two are shown), six stamens, and one long pistil. Four of the stamens are long, and two are short (two long and two short are shown). Pollen grains develop within sacs in the anthers. In *Arabidopsis*, the compound pistil consists of two carpels that each contain numerous ovules.

FIGURE 28-10 *Animated* Floral structure

Petals   Sepals

James Mauseth/University of Texas

(a) The leaflike sepals of a rosebud (*Rosa*) enclose and protect the inner flower parts.

FIGURE 28-11 Parts of a flower

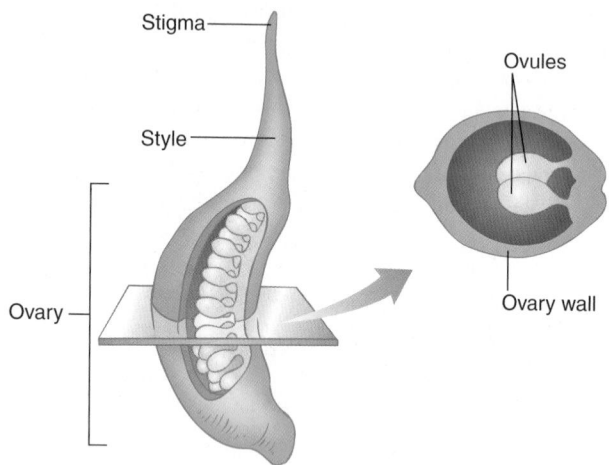

Stigma

Style

Ovary

Ovules

Ovary wall

(a) **Simple pistil.** This simple pistil consists of a single carpel.

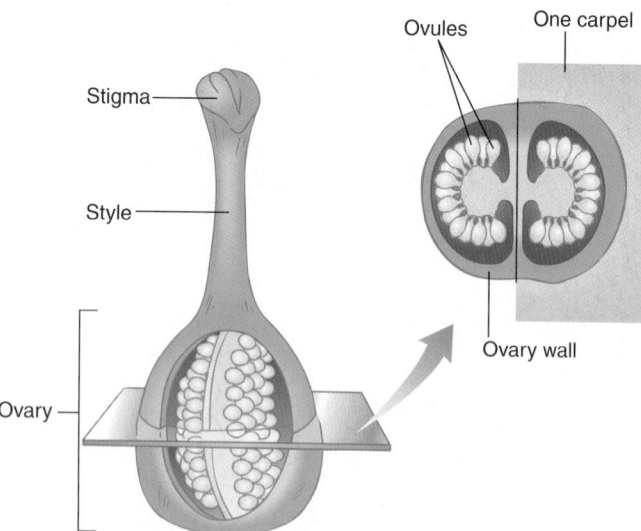

Ovules   One carpel

Stigma

Style

Ovary

Ovary wall

(b) **Compound pistil.** This compound pistil has two united carpels. In most flowers with single pistils, the pistils are compound, consisting of two or more fused carpels.

FIGURE 28-12 Simple and compound pistils

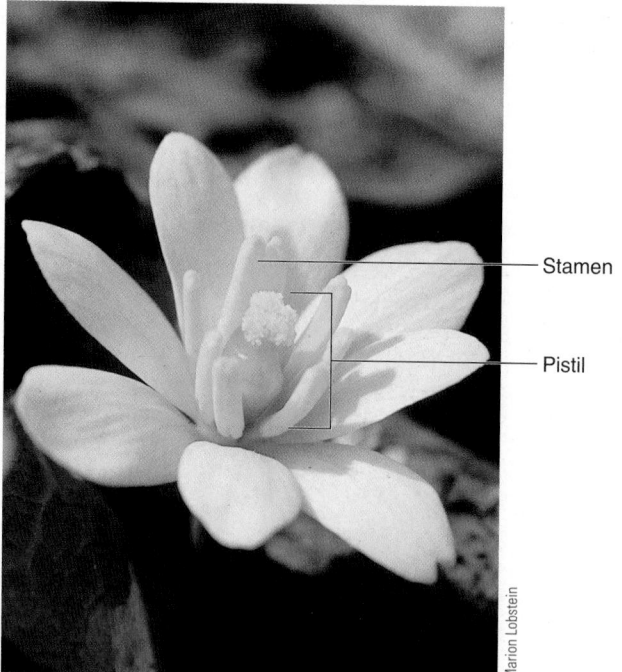

Stamen

Pistil

Marion Lobstein

(b) A twinleaf (*Jeffersonia diphylla*) flower has eight yellow stamens. Note the simple pistil with its green ovary in the center of the flower.

you may recall, are structures with the potential to develop into seeds. The carpels of a flower are separate or fused into a single structure. The female part of the flower is also called a **pistil** (see Fig. 28-11b). A pistil may consist of a single carpel (a simple pistil) or a group of fused carpels (a compound pistil) (**FIG. 28-12**). Each pistil generally has three sections: a **stigma,** on which the pollen grain lands; a **style,** a necklike structure through which the pollen tube grows; and an **ovary,** an enlarged structure that contains one or more ovules. Each young ovule contains a female gametophyte that forms one female gamete (an egg), two *polar nuclei,* and several other haploid cells. After fertilization, the ovule develops into a seed; and the ovary, into a fruit.

The life cycle of flowering plants includes double fertilization

Flowering plants undergo alternation of generations in which the sporophyte generation is larger and nutritionally independent (**FIG. 28-13**). The gametophyte generation in flowering plants is microscopic and nutritionally dependent on the sporophyte. Flowering plants, like gymnosperms and certain other vascular plants, are heterosporous and produce two kinds of spores: microspores and megaspores. Sexual reproduction occurs in the flower.

Each young ovule within an ovary contains a megasporocyte (megaspore mother cell) that undergoes meiosis to produce four haploid megaspores. Three of these usually disintegrate, and one divides mitotically and develops into a mature female gametophyte, also called an **embryo sac.**

Embryo sacs in the vast majority of angiosperms contain seven cells with eight haploid nuclei. Six of these cells, including the egg cell, contain a single nucleus each, and a central cell has two nuclei,

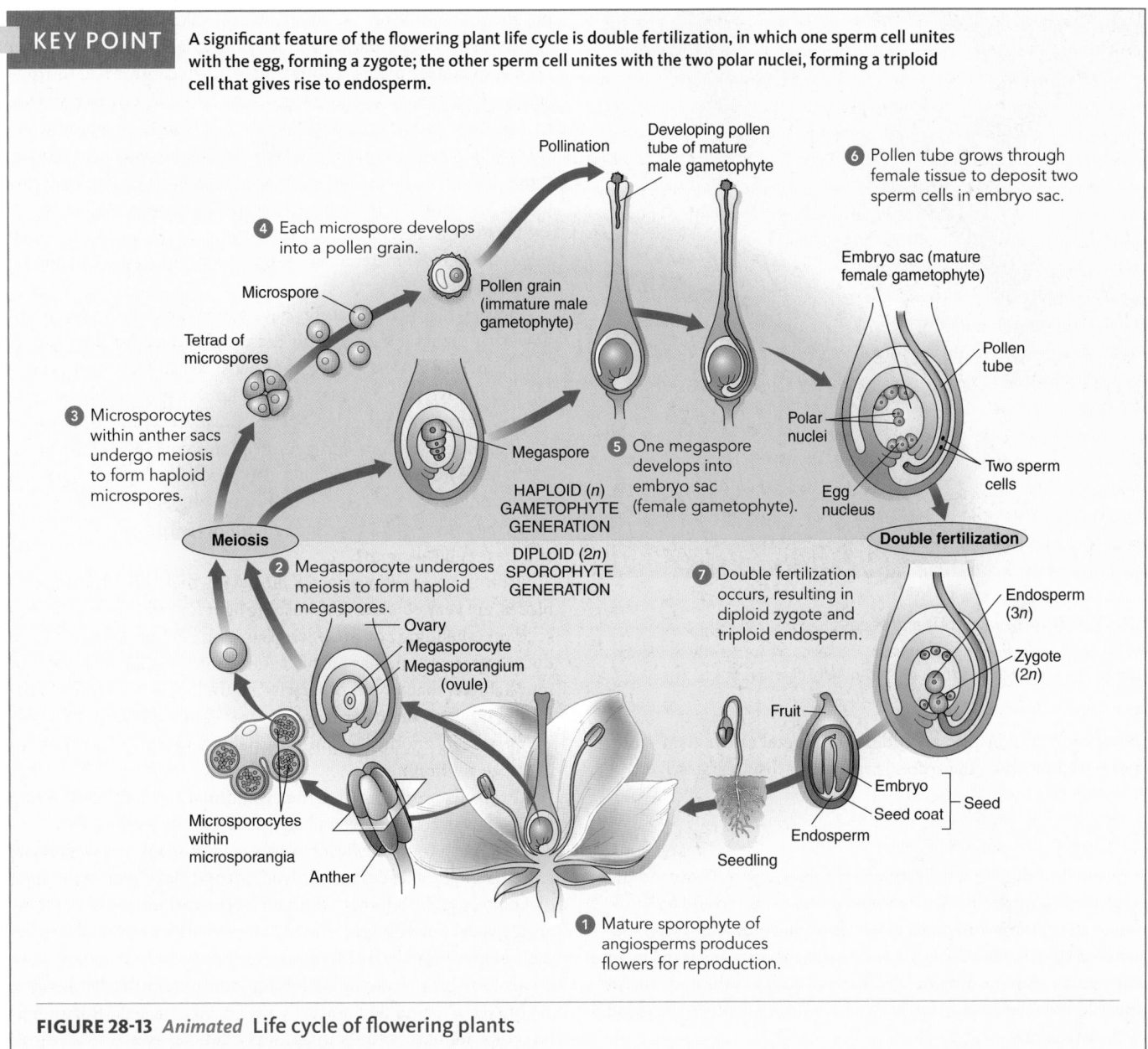

Pollination

Developing pollen tube of mature male gametophyte

6 Pollen tube grows through female tissue to deposit two sperm cells in embryo sac.

4 Each microspore develops into a pollen grain.

Microspore

Tetrad of microspores

Pollen grain (immature male gametophyte)

Embryo sac (mature female gametophyte)

Pollen tube

3 Microsporocytes within anther sacs undergo meiosis to form haploid microspores.

Megaspore

5 One megaspore develops into embryo sac (female gametophyte).

Polar nuclei

Two sperm cells

HAPLOID (n) GAMETOPHYTE GENERATION

Egg nucleus

Meiosis

Double fertilization

DIPLOID (2n) SPOROPHYTE GENERATION

2 Megasporocyte undergoes meiosis to form haploid megaspores.

7 Double fertilization occurs, resulting in diploid zygote and triploid endosperm.

Endosperm (3n)

Ovary

Zygote (2n)

Megasporocyte

Megasporangium (ovule)

Fruit

Microsporocytes within microsporangia

Embryo

Seed coat

Seed

Anther

Endosperm

Seedling

1 Mature sporophyte of angiosperms produces flowers for reproduction.

FIGURE 28-13 *Animated* Life cycle of flowering plants

called **polar nuclei.** The egg and the central cell with two polar nuclei are directly involved in fertilization; the other five cells in the embryo sac apparently have no direct role in the fertilization process and disintegrate. As the *synergids* (the two cells flanking the egg) disintegrate, however, they release chemicals that may affect the direction of pollen tube growth.

Each pollen sac, or microsporangium, of the anther contains numerous microsporocytes (microspore mother cells), each of which undergoes meiosis to form four haploid microspores. Every microspore develops into an immature male gametophyte, also called a *pollen grain*. Pollen grains are small; each consists of two cells, the *tube cell* and the *generative cell*.

The anthers split open and begin to shed pollen. A variety of agents—including wind, water, insects, and other animal pollinators—transfer pollen grains to the stigma (see Chapter 37). If compatible with the stigma, the pollen grain germinates, and a pollen tube grows down the style and into the ovary. The germi-

nated pollen grain with its pollen tube is the mature male gametophyte. Next, the generative cell divides to form two nonflagellate sperm cells. The sperm cells move down the pollen tube and are discharged into the embryo sac. Both sperm cells are involved in fertilization.

When the two sperm cells enter the embryo sac, *both* participate in fertilization. One sperm cell fuses with the egg, forming a zygote that grows by mitosis and develops into a multicellular embryo in the seed. The second sperm cell fuses with the two haploid polar nuclei of the central cell to form a triploid (3n) cell that divides by mitosis and develops into **endosperm,** a nutrient tissue rich in lipids, proteins, and carbohydrates that nourishes the growing embryo. This fertilization process, which involves two separate nuclear fusions, is called **double fertilization** and is, with two exceptions, unique to flowering plants. (Double fertilization has been reported in the gymnosperms *Ephedra nevadensis* and *Gnetum gnemon*. This process differs from double fertilization in

FIGURE 28-14 Guava fruit and seeds
Animals eat fleshy fruits such as guava. The seeds are frequently swallowed whole and pass unharmed through the animals' digestive tracts.

flowering plants in that an additional zygote, rather than endosperm, is produced. The second zygote later disintegrates.)

Seeds and fruits develop after fertilization

As a result of double fertilization and subsequent growth and development, each seed contains a young plant embryo and nutritive tissue (the endosperm), both of which are surrounded by a protective seed coat. In monocots the endosperm persists and is the main source of food in the mature seed. In most eudicots the endosperm nourishes the developing embryo, which subsequently stores food in its cotyledons.

As a seed develops from an ovule following fertilization, the ovary wall surrounding it enlarges dramatically and develops into a **fruit.** In some instances, other tissues associated with the ovary also enlarge to form the fruit (see discussion of fruits in Chapter 37). Fruits serve two purposes: to protect the developing seeds from desiccation as they grow and mature and to aid in the dispersal of seeds. For example, dandelion fruits have feathery plumes that are lifted and carried by air currents. Animals often assist in dispersing seeds found in edible fruits (**FIG. 28-14**). Once a seed lands in a suitable place, it may germinate and develop into a mature sporophyte that produces flowers, and the life cycle continues as described.

Flowering plants have many adaptations that account for their success

The evolutionary adaptations of flowering plants account for their success in terms of their ecological dominance and their great number of species. Seed production as the primary means of re-

production and dispersal, an adaptation shared with the gymnosperms, is clearly significant and provides a definite advantage over seedless vascular plants. Closed carpels, which give rise to fruits surrounding the seeds, and the process of double fertilization with its resulting endosperm, increase the likelihood of reproductive success. The evolution of a variety of interdependencies with many types of insects, birds, and bats, which disperse pollen from one flower to another of the same species, is another reason for angiosperm success. Pollen transfer results in cross-fertilization, which mixes the genetic material and promotes genetic variation among the offspring.

Several distinctive features have contributed to the success of flowering plants in addition to their highly successful reproduction involving flowers, fruits, and seeds. Recall that most flowering plants have very efficient water-conducting vessel elements in their xylem, as well as tracheids. In contrast, the xylem of almost all seedless vascular plants and gymnosperms consists exclusively of tracheids. Most flowering plants also have efficient carbohydrate-conducting sieve tube elements in their phloem. Vascular plants other than flowering plants and gnetophytes lack vessel elements and sieve tube elements.

The leaves of flowering plants, with their broad, expanded blades, are very efficient at absorbing light for photosynthesis. Abscission (shedding) of these leaves during cold or dry periods reduces water loss and has enabled some flowering plants to expand into habitats that would otherwise be too harsh for survival. The stems and roots of flowering plants are often modified for food or water storage, another feature that helps flowering plants survive in severe environments.

Probably most crucial to the evolutionary success of flowering plants, however, is the overall adaptability of the sporophyte generation. As a group, flowering plants readily adapt to new habitats and changing environments. This adaptability is evident in the great diversity of growth forms exhibited by the various species of flowering plants. For example, the cactus is remarkably well-adapted to desert environments. Its stem stores water; its leaves (spines) have a reduced surface area available for transpiration (loss of water vapor; see Chapter 34) and may also protect against thirsty herbivorous animals; and its thick, waxy cuticle reduces water loss. In contrast, the water lily is well-adapted for wet environments, in part because it has air channels that provide adequate oxygen to stems and roots living in oxygen-deficient water and mud.

Floral structure provides insights into the evolutionary process

In evolution, new structures or organs often originate by modification of previously existing structures or organs. (See Chapter 20 discussion of preadaptations.) Much evidence supports the classical interpretation that the four organs of a flower—sepals, petals, stamens, and carpels—arose from highly modified leaves. This evidence includes comparisons of the arrangement of vascular tissues in both flowers and leafy stems and of the developmental stages of floral parts and leaves.

Sepals are the most leaflike of the four floral organs, and botanists generally agree that sepals are specialized leaves. Although petals of many flowering plant species are leaflike in appearance, botanists generally view petals as modified stamens that later became sterile and leaflike. Cultivated roses and camellias provide evidence supporting this hypothesis; in some varieties the stamens have been transformed into petals, forming showy flowers with large numbers of petals.

The remarkably leaflike stamens and carpels of certain tropical trees and other species support the origin of stamens and carpels from leaves or leaflike organs. Consider, for example, the carpel of *Drimys*, a genus of flowering trees and shrubs native to Southeast Asia, Australia, and South America. This carpel resembles a leaf that is folded inward along the midrib, thereby enclosing the ovules, and joined along the entire length of the leaf's margin (**FIG. 28-15**).

The fundamental question is whether these leaflike stamens and carpels are shared ancestral characters that were conserved (retained) during the course of evolution or are highly specialized organs (that is, shared derived characters) that do not resemble early stamens and carpels. Many botanists who have studied this question have concluded that stamens and carpels are probably derived from leaves. Not all botanists accept the origin of stamens and carpels from highly modified leaves, however. As we noted in Chapter 1, uncertainty and debate are part of the scientific process, and scientists can never claim to know a final answer.

During the course of more than 130 million years of angiosperm evolution, floral structure diversified as floral organs fused or became reduced in size or number. These changes led to greater complexity in floral structure in some species and to greater simplicity in other species. Interpreting the floral structures of so many different angiosperm species is sometimes difficult, but it is important because correct interpretations are essential to devising a phylogenetic classification scheme.

Review

- How do nonreproductive adaptations of flowering plants differ from those of gymnosperms?
- How does the flowering plant life cycle differ from that of the gymnosperms?
- What are the two major classes of flowering plants, and how can one distinguish between them?
- How does fertilization differ in gymnosperms and flowering plants?

28.4 THE EVOLUTION OF SEED PLANTS

■ LEARNING OBJECTIVE

9 Summarize the evolution of gymnosperms from seedless vascular plants and trace the evolution of flowering plants from gymnosperms.

One group that descended from ancestral seedless vascular plants was the **progymnosperms,** all of which are now extinct. Progymnosperms had two derived features: leaves with branching veins (*megaphylls*) and woody tissue (*secondary xylem*) similar to that of modern gymnosperms. Progymnosperms, however, reproduced by spores, not seeds. *Archaeopteris,* a progymnosperm that lived

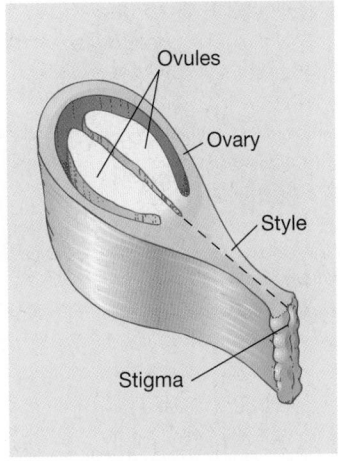

(a) The carpel resembles a folded leaf in which the ovules borne on its upper surface are enclosed.

(b) A cross section of the carpel, cut along the dashed line in **(a)**.

FIGURE 28-15 Carpel of *Drimys piperita*

about 370 mya, is one of the earliest known trees with "modern" woody tissue (**FIG. 28-16a**).

Fossils of several progymnosperms with reproductive structures intermediate between those of spore plants and seed plants have been discovered. For example, the evolution of microspores into pollen grains and of megasporangia into ovules (seed-producing structures) can be traced in fossil progymnosperms. Plants producing seeds appeared during the late Devonian period, more than 359 mya. The fossil record indicates that different groups of seed plants apparently arose independently several times.

As mentioned previously, fossilized remains of ginkgo are found in 200-million-year-old rocks, and other groups of gymnosperms were well established by 160 mya to 100 mya. Although the gymnosperms are an ancient group, some questions persist about the exact pathways of gymnosperm evolution. The fossil record indicates that progymnosperms probably gave rise to conifers and to another group of extinct plants called **seed ferns,** which were seed-bearing woody plants with fernlike leaves (**FIG. 28-16b**). The seed ferns, in turn, probably gave rise to cycads and ginkgo, as well as to several gymnosperm groups now extinct. The origin of gnetophytes remains unclear, although molecular data indicate that they are closely related to conifers.

Our understanding of the evolution of flowering plants has made great progress in recent years

Flowering plants are the most recent clade of plants to evolve. The fossil record, although incomplete, suggests that flowering plants descended from gymnosperms. By the middle of the Jurassic period, about 180 mya, several gymnosperm lines existed with some features resembling those of flowering plants. Among other traits, these derived gymnosperms possessed leaves with broad, expanded blades and the first modified seed-bearing leaves, which nearly enclose the ovules. Beetles were evidently visiting these plants, and biologists have suggested that perhaps this relationship

(a) **Progymnosperm.** *Archaeopteris*, which existed about 370 mya, had some features in common with modern seed plants but did not produce seeds.

(b) **Seed fern.** *Emplectopteris* produced seeds on fernlike leaves. Seed ferns existed from about 360 mya to 250 mya.

FIGURE 28-16 Evolution of seed plants

(**a,** Redrawn from Beck, C. B., "Reconstructions of *Archaeopteris* and Further Consideration of Its Phylogenetic Position," *American Journal of Botany*, Vol. 49, 1962. **b,** Redrawn from Andrews, H. N., *Ancient Plants and the World They Lived In*, Comstock, New York, 1947.)

was the beginning of **coevolution,** a mutual adaptation between plants and their animal pollinators (see Chapter 37).

One important task facing paleobotanists (biologists who study fossil plants) is determining which of the ancient gymnosperms are in the direct line of evolution leading to the flowering plants. Given the structural data, most botanists hypothesize that flowering plants arose only once—that is, there is only one line of evolution from the gymnosperms to the flowering plants.

Based largely on structural data, many evolutionary botanists previously thought that the gnetophytes were the gymnosperm clade most closely related to flowering plants. However, new hypotheses of angiosperm origin have been proposed in recent years with advances in molecular comparisons, genetic studies (particularly as gene function relates to reproductive development), and additional fossil discoveries. Currently, many botanists think the closest extant gymnosperms related to flowering plants are probably conifers. But this hypothesis is far from certain, and the origin and early evolution of flowering plants continue to challenge botanists.

The oldest definitive trace of flowering plants in the fossil record consists of ovules enclosed in tiny podlike fruits interpreted as carpels in Jurassic and Lower Cretaceous rocks some 125 million to 145 million years

5 mm

(a) **The oldest known fossil angiosperm.** This fossil of *Archaefructus* shows a carpel-bearing stem. Discovered in northeastern China, it is about 125 million years old.

FIGURE 28-17 Fossil angiosperms

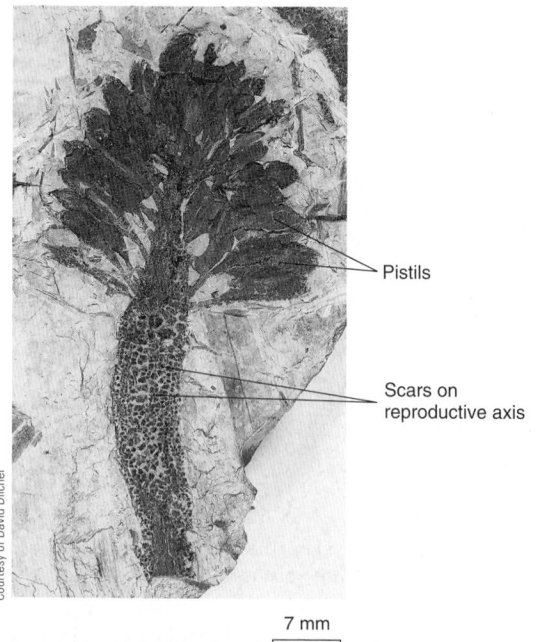

Pistils

Scars on reproductive axis

7 mm

(b) **Fossil flower.** The fossilized flower of the extinct plant *Archaeanthus linnenbergeri*, which lived about 100 mya. The scars on the reproductive axis (receptacle) may show where stamens, petals, and sepals were originally attached but abscised (fell off). Many spirally arranged pistils were still attached at the time this flower was fossilized.

old (**FIG. 28-17a**). The oldest fossilized flowers are about 118 million to 120 million years old.

By 90 mya, during the Cretaceous period, flowering plants had diversified and had begun to replace gymnosperms as Earth's dominant plants. Fossils of flowering plant leaves, stems, flowers, fruits, and seeds are numerous and diverse. They outnumber fossils of gymnosperms and ferns in Late Cretaceous deposits, indicating the rapid success of flowering plants once they appeared (**FIG. 28-17b**). Many angiosperm species apparently arose from changes in chromosome number. (See discussion of allopolyploidy and sympatric evolution in Chapter 20.)

The basal angiosperms comprise three clades

Beginning in 1999, a series of cladistic analyses of structural features and molecular comparisons have helped clarify relationships among the angiosperm classes. In the process, many long-held assumptions about early angiosperm lineages have been discarded. The evidence indicates that several clades of basal (early-diverging) angiosperms evolved before the divergence of core angiosperms (**FIG. 28-18a**). The 170 species of **basal angiosperms** represent groups thought to be ancestral to all other flowering plants.

The oldest surviving clade of basal angiosperms is represented by a single extant species, *Amborella trichopoda* (**FIG. 28-18b**). A

KEY POINT   Flowering plants evolved from ancient gymnosperms. Basal angiosperms are early diverging clades that still survive today.

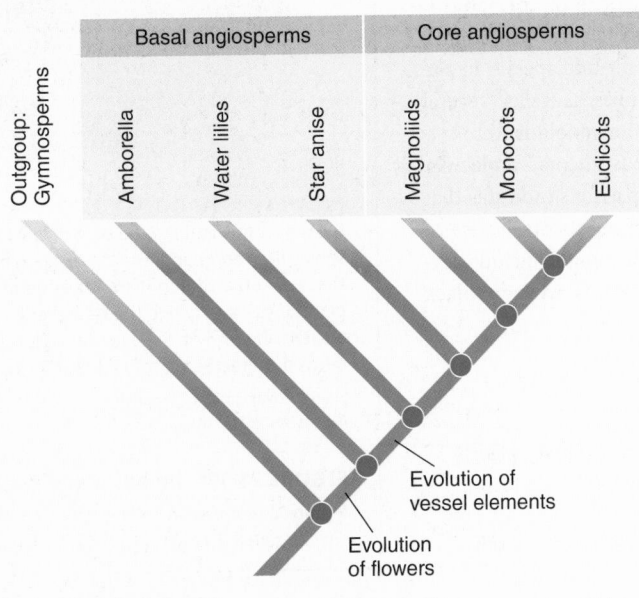

(a) One hypothesis of relationships among the flowering plants, based on fossil and molecular evidence. *Amborella*, water lilies, and star anise are living plants whose ancestors apparently branched off of the angiosperm family tree early. These early clades were followed by the magnoliids, the monocots, and the eudicots.

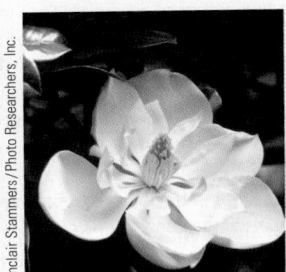

(b) *Amborella trichopoda*, a basal angiosperm.

(c) Water lily (*Nymphaea*), a basal angiosperm.

(d) Star anise (*Illicium verum*), a basal angiosperm.

(e) *Magnolia grandiflora*, a core angiosperm.

FIGURE 28-18 Evolution of flowering plants

shrub native to New Caledonia, an island in the South Pacific, *Amborella* may be the nearest living relative to the ancestor of all flowering plants. The water lilies and related families compose the second clade of basal angiosperms (**FIG. 28-18c** and **FIG. 28-19**). This clade, which contains about 70 species of aquatic or wetland herbs, may be the second-oldest surviving lineage. Star anise and relatives—the third clade of basal angiosperms—consist of about 100 species of vines, trees, and shrubs found mostly in warmer climates. Star anise is important economically because it is a source of spice used by confectioners and anise oil (**FIG. 28-18d**). Star anise is also used to make Tamiflu, one of the treatments for influenza.

The core angiosperms comprise magnoliids, monocots, and eudicots

Most angiosperm species belong to a clade of **core angiosperms,** which is divided into three subclades: magnoliids, monocots, and eudicots. **Magnoliids** include species in the magnolia, laurel, and black pepper families, as well as several related families (**FIG. 28-18e**). Although magnoliids were traditionally classified with the eudicots as "dicots," molecular evidence such as DNA sequence comparisons indicates that the magnoliids are neither eudicots nor monocots. Native to tropical or warm temperate regions, magnoliids include several economically important plants, such as avocado, black pepper, nutmeg, and bay laurel.

Review

- What features distinguish progymnosperms from seed ferns?
- Describe the significant features of the oldest known fossil angiosperm.
- Are monocots considered basal or core angiosperms? Explain your answer.

KEY EXPERIMENT

QUESTION: Hydatella sp. was incorrectly classified as a grass until recent molecular evidence indicated that it is a basal angiosperm closely related to water lilies. Does *Hydatella* have any reproductive features that may indicate it is one of the most ancient surviving lineages of angiosperms?

EXPERIMENT: *Hydatella inconspicua*, a small aquatic plant, was collected at a lake in Northland, New Zealand, and its embryo sacs were carefully analyzed.

© Justin Goh, School of Biological Sciences, University of Auckland, Auckland, New Zealand

RESULTS AND CONCLUSION: As in gymnosperms, the mother plant turns over nutrients to the seed *before* fertilization has occurred. This gymnosperm-like reproductive feature may represent a shared ancestral character that was retained during the transition from gymnosperms to flowering plants, thus supporting the view that *Hydatella* is a representative of an ancient angiosperm lineage. Alternatively, this feature may represent a shared derived character not found in earlier *Hydatella* ancestors.

Source: Friedman, W. E. "Hydatellaceae are Water Lilies with Gymnospermous Tendencies." *Nature,* Vol. 453, May 1, 2008.

FIGURE 28-19 The basal angiosperm *Hydatella*

Hydatella inconspicua belongs to an ancient clade that consists of about 10 species native to Australia, New Zealand, and India.

■ SUMMARY: FOCUS ON LEARNING OBJECTIVES

28.1 *(page 583)*

1 Compare the features of gymnosperms and angiosperms.

- The two groups of seed plants are the **gymnosperms** and the **angiosperms.** Gymnosperms produce seeds that are totally exposed or borne on the scales of cones; an ovary wall does not surround the ovules of gymnosperms. Angiosperms are flowering plants that produce their seeds within a fruit (a mature ovary).

28.2 *(page 584)*

2 Trace the steps in the life cycle of a pine and compare its sporophyte and gametophyte generations.

- A pine tree is a mature sporophyte; pine gametophytes are extremely small and nutritionally dependent on the sporophyte generation. Pine is heterosporous and produces microspores and megaspores in separate cones.
- Male cones produce **microspores** that develop into **pollen grains** (immature male gametophytes) that are carried by air currents to female cones.

- Female cones produce **megaspores.** One of each four megaspores produced by meiosis develops into a female gametophyte within an **ovule (megasporangium).**
- After **pollination,** the transfer of pollen to the female cones, a **pollen tube** grows through the megasporangium to the egg within the archegonium. After **fertilization,** the zygote develops into an embryo encased inside a seed adapted for wind dispersal.

3 Summarize the features that distinguish gymnosperms from bryophytes and ferns.

- Unlike bryophytes, gymnosperms are vascular plants. Unlike bryophytes and ferns, gymnosperms produce seeds. Gymnosperms also produce wind-borne pollen grains, a feature absent in ferns and other seedless vascular plants.

4 Name and briefly describe the four phyla of gymnosperms.

- **Conifers** (phylum Coniferophyta), the largest phylum of gymnosperms, are woody plants that bear **needles** (leaves that are usually evergreen) and produce seeds in cones. Most conifers are **monoecious** and have male and female reproductive parts in separate cones on the same plant.
- **Cycads** (phylum Cycadophyta) are palmlike or fernlike in appearance. They are **dioecious**—they have male and female reproductive structures on separate plants—but reproduce with pollen and seeds in conelike structures.
- *Ginkgo biloba,* the only surviving species in phylum Ginkgophyta, is a deciduous, dioecious tree. The female **ginkgo** produces fleshy seeds directly on branches.
- **Gnetophytes** (phylum Gnetophyta) are an obscure clade of gymnosperms that has a few traits associated with angiosperms.

28.3 (page 589)

5 Summarize the features that distinguish flowering plants from other plants.

- **Flowering plants,** or angiosperms (phylum Anthophyta), constitute the phylum of vascular plants that produce flowers and seeds enclosed within a **fruit.** They are the most diverse and most successful group of plants.
- The flower, which may contain **sepals, petals, stamens,** and **carpels,** functions in sexual reproduction. Unlike those of gymnosperms, the ovules of flowering plants are enclosed within an **ovary.** After fertilization, the ovules become seeds, and the ovary develops into a fruit.

6 Briefly explain the life cycle of a flowering plant and describe double fertilization.

- The sporophyte generation is dominant in flowering plants; gametophytes are extremely reduced in size and nutritionally dependent on the sporophyte generation. Flowering plants are heterosporous and produce microspores and megaspores within the flower.
- Each microspore develops into a pollen grain (immature male gametophyte). One of each four megaspores produced by meiosis

develops into an **embryo sac** (female gametophyte). Within the embryo sac, the egg cell and the central cell with two **polar nuclei** participate in fertilization.

- **Double fertilization,** which results in the formation of a diploid zygote and triploid **endosperm,** is characteristic of flowering plants.

CENGAGENOW˙ Explore plant life cycles by clicking on the figures in CengageNOW.

7 Contrast monocots and eudicots, the two largest classes of flowering plants.

- Most **monocots** (class Monocotyledones) have floral parts in threes, and their seeds each contain one **cotyledon.** The nutritive tissue in their mature seeds is endosperm.
- **Eudicots** (class Eudicotyledones) usually have floral parts in fours or fives or multiples thereof, and their seeds each contain two cotyledons. The nutritive organs in their mature seeds are usually the cotyledons, which have absorbed the nutrients in the endosperm.

8 Discuss the evolutionary adaptations of flowering plants.

- Flowering plants reproduce sexually by forming flowers. After double fertilization, seeds form within fruits. Flowering plants have efficient water-conducting **vessel elements** in their xylem and efficient carbohydrate-conducting **sieve tube elements** in their phloem. Wind, water, insects, or other animals transfer pollen grains in various flowering plants.

CENGAGENOW˙ Learn more about floral structure by clicking on the figure in CengageNOW.

28.4 (page 595)

9 Summarize the evolution of gymnosperms from seedless vascular plants and trace the evolution of flowering plants from gymnosperms.

- Seed plants arose from seedless vascular plants. **Progymnosperms** were seedless vascular plants that had megaphylls and "modern" woody tissue. Progymnosperms probably gave rise to conifers as well as to **seed ferns,** which in turn likely gave rise to cycads and ginkgo.
- The evolution of the gnetophytes is unclear, although molecular data indicate that they are closely related to conifers.
- Flowering plants probably descended from ancient gymnosperms that had specialized features, such as leaves with broad, expanded blades and closed carpels. Flowering plants likely arose only once—that is, there is only one line of evolution from the gymnosperms to the flowering plants.

TEST YOUR UNDERSTANDING

1. Seed plants *lack* which of the following structure(s)? (a) ovules surrounded by integuments (b) microspores and megaspores (c) vascular tissues (d) a large, nutritionally independent sporophyte (e) a large, nutritionally independent gametophyte

2. Conifers, cycads, ginkgo, and gnetophytes are collectively called (a) club mosses (b) gymnosperms (c) angiosperms (d) eudicots (e) seedless vascular plants

3. The immature male gametophytes of pine are called (a) ovules (b) stamens (c) seed cones (d) pollen grains (e) polar nuclei

4. The transfer of pollen grains from the male to the female reproductive structure is known as (a) pollination (b) fertilization

(c) embryo sac development (d) seed development (e) fruit development

5. Motile sperm cells are found as vestiges in these two gymnosperm groups: (a) monocots, eudicots (b) gnetophytes, conifers (c) gnetophytes, flowering plants (d) cycads, conifers (e) cycads, ginkgo

6. There are at least _____ species of flowering plants worldwide. (a) 235 (b) 3000 (c) 30,000 (d) 300,000 (e) 3,000,000

7. A simple pistil consists of a single (a) calyx (b) carpel (c) ovule (d) filament (e) petal

8. A flower that lacks stamens is both _____ and _____.
   (a) complete; imperfect (b) incomplete; perfect (c) complete; perfect (d) incomplete; imperfect

9. After fertilization, the _____ develop(s) into a fruit and the _____ develop(s) into a seed. (a) ovary; ovule (b) polar nuclei; ovule (c) ovary; endosperm (d) ovule; ovary (e) ovule; polar nuclei

10. The female gametophyte in flowering plants is also called the (a) polar nuclei (b) anther (c) embryo sac (d) endosperm (e) sporophyll

11. This flowering plant may be the nearest living relative to the ancestor of all flowering plants. (a) *Amborella* (b) *Archaeopteris* (c) *Gnetum* (d) water lily (e) *Archaeanthus*

12. This cross section through an ovary reveals that the pistil is (a) simple, with one carpel (b) compound, with two fused carpels (c) compound, with three fused carpels (d) compound, with six separate carpels (e) compound, with six fused carpels

CRITICAL THINKING

1. How are cones and flowers alike? How are they different? (*Hint:* Your answer should consider microspores/megaspores and seeds.)

2. How do the life cycles of seedless plants (see Chapter 27) and seed plants differ? In what fundamental way are they alike?

3. **EVOLUTION LINK.** Most flowers contain both male and female reproductive structures, in contrast to the cones of gymnosperms, which are either male or female. Explain how bisexual flowers might be an advantageous evolutionary adaptation to the flowering plants that possess them.

4. **EVOLUTION LINK.** Contrast the algae, mosses, ferns, gymnosperms, and angiosperms with respect to their dependence on water as a transport medium for reproductive cells. Suggest a hypothesis to explain how the differences might be adaptive to living on land.

5. **EVOLUTION LINK.** Where would you place the progymnosperms on Figure 28-2? Explain your reasoning.

6. You are given a plant that you have never seen before (see figure). Is it a gymnosperm or angiosperm? A monocot or eudicot? What are the features that helped you make these determinations?

Carlyn Iverson

CENGAGENOW™ Additional questions are available in CengageNOW at www.cengage.com/login.

29 The Fungi

Fungal spores. The rounded earthstar (*Geastrum saccatum*) releases a puff of microscopic spores after the sac, which is about 1.3 cm (0.5 in) wide, is hit by a raindrop. This fungus is common in leaf litter under trees throughout North America.

Jeff Lepore/Photo Researchers, Inc.

Mushrooms, morels, and truffles, delights of the gourmet, share a recent common ancestry with baker's yeast, the black mold that forms on stale bread, and the mildew that collects on damp shower curtains. All of these life-forms are classified as fungi, a diverse group of about 100,000 described species, most of which are terrestrial. Some **mycologists,** biologists who study fungi, estimate that there may be as many as 1.5 million species of fungi. Biologists who use the kingdom as a taxon group these organisms in kingdom Fungi, one of the eukaryotic kingdoms.

Fungi grow best in moist habitats, but they are found universally wherever organic material is available. They require moisture to grow, and they can obtain water from a humid atmosphere as well as from the medium on which they live. When the environment becomes dry, fungi survive by going into a resting stage or by producing spores (see photograph) that resist desiccation (drying out).

Some fungi grow to enormous size. In Washington State, a fungal clone (*Armillaria ostoyae*) has been identified that covers more than 1500 acres. This giant fungus, which is mainly underground, developed from a single spore that germinated more than a thousand years ago. The fungus has fragmented and is no longer one continuous body.

Like prokaryotes, most fungi are decomposers that obtain nutrients and energy from dead organic matter. They are vital members of ecosystems because they break down the organic compounds found in dead organisms, leaves, garbage, sewage, and other waste. When they decompose organic compounds, carbon and other elements are released into the environment, where they are recycled.

Many fungi form vital symbiotic associations. For example, most terrestrial plants have fungal partners that live in close association with their roots. The fungi help the plants obtain phosphate ions and other needed minerals from the soil. In exchange, the plants provide the fungi with organic nutrients. Some fungi live symbiotically with algae and cyanobacteria as lichens. Others are parasites and pathogens that cause disease in animals or plants.

29.1 CHARACTERISTICS OF FUNGI

◼ LEARNING OBJECTIVES

1   Describe the distinguishing characteristics of fungi.
2   Describe the body plan of a fungus.

All fungi (sing., *fungus*) are eukaryotes; their cells contain membrane-enclosed nuclei, mitochondria, and other membranous organelles. Although they vary strikingly in size and shape, fungi share certain key characters, including their way of obtaining nutrition.

The optimum pH for most fungal species is about 5.6, but various fungi can tolerate and grow in environments where the pH ranges from 2 to 9. Many fungi are less sensitive to high osmotic pressures than are bacteria. As a result, they can grow in concentrated salt solutions or in sugar solutions such as jelly, which discourage or prevent bacterial growth. Fungi also thrive over a wide temperature range. Even refrigerated food may be invaded by fungi.

Fungi absorb food from the environment

Like animals, fungi are heterotrophs. For their nutritional and energy needs, they depend on preformed carbon molecules produced by other organisms. However, fungi do not ingest food and then digest it in the body as animals do. Instead, they infiltrate a food source and secrete digestive enzymes onto it. Digestion takes place outside the body. When complex molecules are broken down into smaller compounds, the fungus absorbs the predigested food into its body.

The fungus is very efficient at absorbing nutrients and growing. It rapidly converts nutrients into new cell material. If excessive amounts of nutrients are available, fungi store them, usually as lipid droplets or glycogen.

Fungi have cell walls that contain chitin

Like the cells of bacteria, certain protists, and plants, fungal cells are enclosed by cell walls during at least some stage in their life cycle. Fungal cell walls, however, have a different chemical composition from cell walls of other organisms. In most fungi, the cell wall consists of complex carbohydrates, including **chitin,** a polymer that consists of subunits of a nitrogen-containing sugar (see Fig. 3-11). Chitin is also a component of the external skeletons of insects and other arthropods. Chitin is resistant to breakdown by most microorganisms.

Most fungi consist of a network of filaments

The simplest fungi are the **yeasts,** which are unicellular, with a round or oval shape. Yeasts are widely distributed in the soil; on leaves, fruits, and cured meats; and on and in our bodies. The importance of some yeasts in medicine, biological research, and in the food industry is discussed later in this chapter.

Most fungi are multicellular. The body consists of long, branched, threadlike filaments called **hyphae** (sing., *hypha*) (**FIGS. 29-1a** and **b**).

Hyphae

(a) A mycelium. A mass of hyphae has formed a mycelium (white area). Fruiting bodies, called sporangia, are visible as gray areas.

(b) SEM of a mycelium. The fungus *Blumeria graminis* growing on a leaf (darker area underneath the mycelium).

25 μm

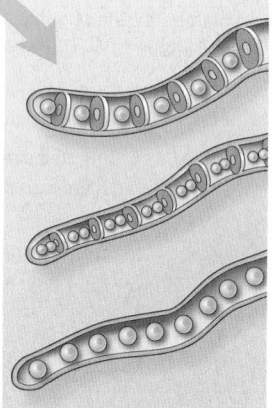

(c) A hypha divided into cells by septa. Each cell is monokaryotic (has one nucleus). In some taxa the septa are perforated, as shown.

(d) A septate hypha. In this hypha, each cell is dikaryotic (has two nuclei).

(e) A coenocytic hypha.

FIGURE 29-1 Fungus body plan
Spores carried by the air settle on food. They germinate and produce a mass of threadlike filaments called hyphae. The hyphae penetrate the food to obtain nourishment, and produce a mass of hyphae called the mycelium. Eventually, specialized hyphae grow from the mycelium giving rise to erect stalks with fruiting bodies (sporangia) at their tops. When the walls of the sporangia rupture, new spores are released into the air.

Hyphae consist of tubular cell walls surrounding the plasma membranes of the fungal cells. Hyphae are an adaptation to the fungal mode of nutrition. Growth occurs at the tips of the hyphae; as the hyphae elongate, the fungus grows into and infiltrates food sources. The fungus absorbs nutrients through its very large surface area.

As hyphae grow, they form a tangled mass or tissuelike network, called a **mycelium** (pl., *mycelia*). Fungi that form mycelia are called **molds.** The cobweb-like mold sometimes seen on bread is the mycelium of a fungus. What is not seen is the extensive mycelium that grows into the bread. Depending on environmental conditions, some fungi can alternate between a yeast phase and a phase in which they produce hyphae.

In most fungi, hyphae are divided by cross walls, called **septa** (sing., *septum*), into individual cells containing one or more nuclei (**FIGS. 29-1c** and **d**). As we will discuss, the presence of septa is an important character in the two largest fungal phyla (which include the most complex fungi). The septa of many fungi are perforated by a pore that may be large enough to permit organelles to flow from cell to cell. Some fungi, called **coenocytic** fungi, lack septa. In these species, nuclear division is not followed by cytoplasmic division. As a result, a coenocytic fungus is one elongated, multinucleated, giant cell (**FIG. 29-1e**).

Review

- What characters distinguish fungi from other organisms?
- How does the body of a yeast differ from that of a mold?

29.2 FUNGAL REPRODUCTION

■ LEARNING OBJECTIVE

3 Describe the life cycle of a typical fungus, including sexual and asexual reproduction.

Most fungi reproduce by means of microscopic **spores,** reproductive cells that can develop into new organisms. In most groups, spores are nonmotile. They are dispersed by wind, water, or animals. The air we breathe is filled with hundreds of thousands of fungal spores. When a spore germinates, it gives rise to a hypha, which then develops into a mycelium (**FIG. 29-2**).

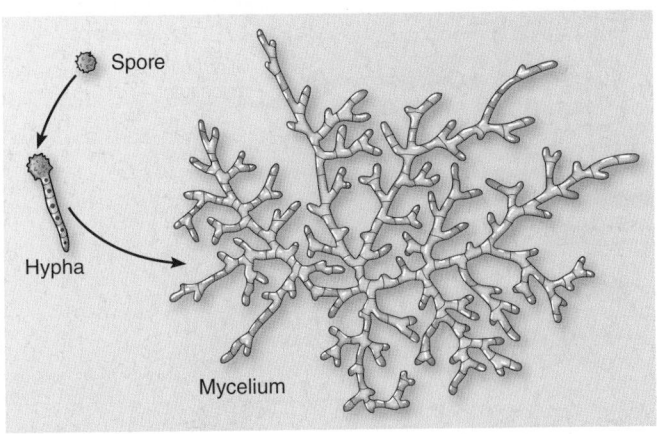

FIGURE 29-2 Germination of a spore to form a mycelium

Fungi produce spores either sexually or asexually. With asexual reproduction, new individuals are produced quickly, but there is little genetic variability. Sexual reproduction involves meiosis and generates new genotypes.

Spores are usually produced on specialized aerial hyphae or in fruiting structures. When positioned up above the ground, spores can be easily dispersed. Structures in which spores are produced are called **sporangia** (sing., *sporangium*). The aerial hyphae of some fungi produce spores in large, complex reproductive structures, referred to as **fruiting bodies.** The familiar part of a mushroom is a large fruiting body. We do not normally see the bulk of the fungus, a nearly invisible mycelium buried out of sight in the rotting material or soil on which it grows.

Many fungi reproduce asexually

Yeasts reproduce asexually, primarily by forming buds that pinch off from the parent cell (**FIG. 29-3**). Many species of multicellular fungi also reproduce asexually. Spores are produced by

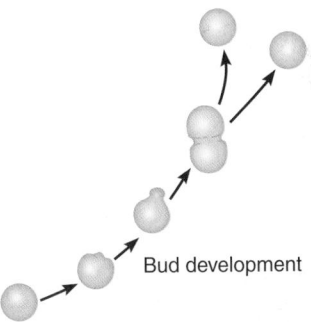

(a) Yeasts can reproduce asexually by budding.

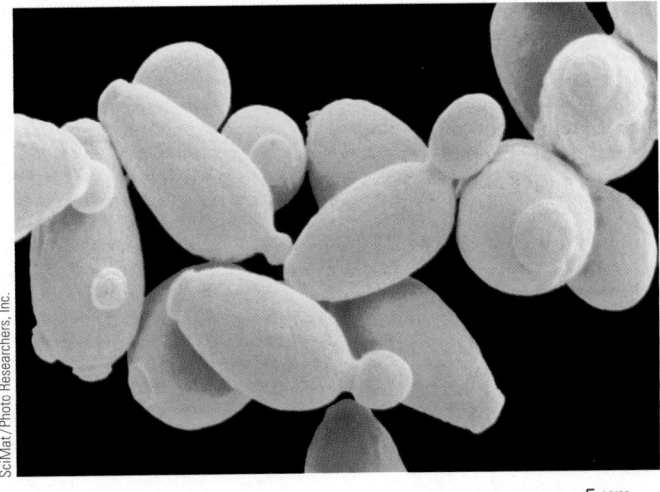

5 μm

(b) SEM (color enhanced) of *Saccharomyces cerevisiae*. Also known as baker's or brewer's yeast, this fungus can ferment sugar, producing carbon dioxide and alcohol in the process. It is used in brewing beer, in wine production, and in baking bread. Note that several yeast cells are budding, a form of asexual reproduction.

FIGURE 29-3 Yeasts are unicellular fungi

mitosis and then released into the air or water. **Conidiophores** (from the Greek, meaning "dust-bearers") are specialized hyphae that produce asexual spores called **conidia** (sing., *conidium*). The arrangement of conidia on conidiophores varies from species to species.

Most fungi reproduce sexually

Fungi are a diverse group with many variations in their life cycles. Most fungi (but not all) reproduce both asexually and sexually. **FIGURE 29-4** illustrates a generalized life cycle. Many fungal species reproduce sexually when they come into contact with other mating

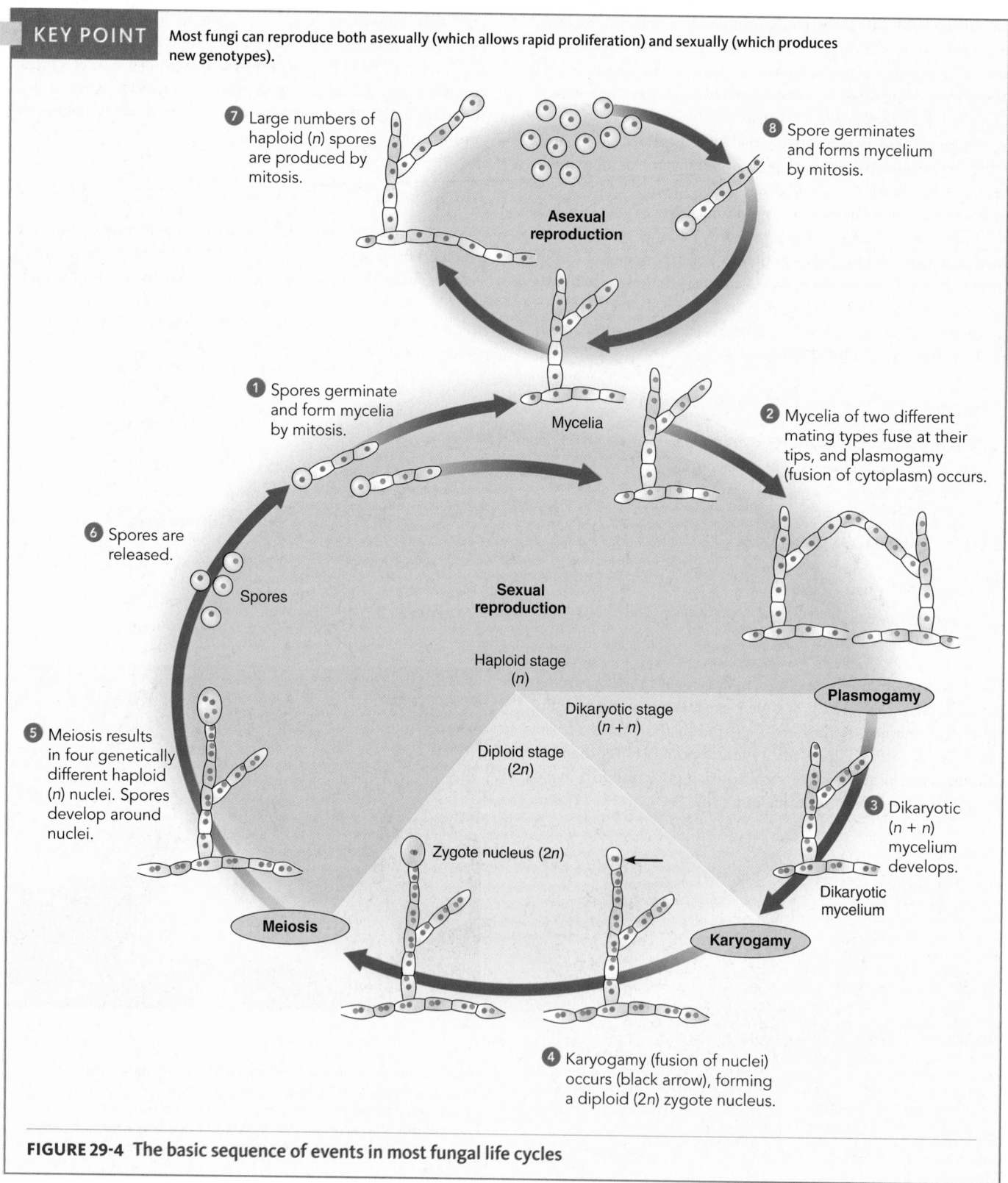

KEY POINT Most fungi can reproduce both asexually (which allows rapid proliferation) and sexually (which produces new genotypes).

7 Large numbers of haploid (*n*) spores are produced by mitosis.

8 Spore germinates and forms mycelium by mitosis.

Asexual reproduction

1 Spores germinate and form mycelia by mitosis.

Mycelia

2 Mycelia of two different mating types fuse at their tips, and plasmogamy (fusion of cytoplasm) occurs.

6 Spores are released.

Spores

Sexual reproduction

Haploid stage (*n*)

Dikaryotic stage (*n* + *n*)

Diploid stage (2*n*)

Plasmogamy

5 Meiosis results in four genetically different haploid (*n*) nuclei. Spores develop around nuclei.

3 Dikaryotic (*n* + *n*) mycelium develops.

Dikaryotic mycelium

Zygote nucleus (2*n*)

Meiosis

Karyogamy

4 Karyogamy (fusion of nuclei) occurs (black arrow), forming a diploid (2*n*) zygote nucleus.

FIGURE 29-4 The basic sequence of events in most fungal life cycles

types. In contrast to the majority of animal and plant cells, most fungal cells contain haploid nuclei. In sexual reproduction, the hyphae of two genetically compatible mating types come together, and their cytoplasm fuses, a process called **plasmogamy.** The resulting cell has two haploid nuclei, one from each fungus. This cell gives rise by mitosis to other cells with two nuclei. At some point the two haploid nuclei fuse. This process, called **karyogamy,** results in a cell containing a diploid nucleus known as a **zygote nucleus.** In some groups, the zygote nucleus is the only diploid nucleus.

In the two largest fungal phyla, the ascomycetes and basidiomycetes (discussed later in this chapter), plasmogamy occurs (hyphae fuse), but karyogamy (fusion of the two different nuclei) does not follow immediately. For a time, the nuclei remain separate within the fungal cytoplasm. Hyphae that contain two genetically distinct, sexually compatible nuclei within each cell are described as **dikaryotic** (see Fig. 29-1d). This condition is referred to as $n + n$ rather than $2n$ because there are two separate haploid nuclei. Hyphae that contain only one nucleus per cell are described as **monokaryotic.** The presence of a dikaryotic stage is an important defining character of the ascomycetes and basidiomycetes.

Fungi communicate chemically by secreting signaling molecules called **pheromones.** At least one pheromone has been identified in each major fungal group. The pheromone binds with a compatible receptor on a different mating type. For example, in the zygomycetes, a pheromone induces the formation of specialized aerial hyphae. Another pheromone causes the tips of aerial hyphae of opposite mating types to grow toward each other and fuse prior to sexual reproduction.

Review

- How is a monokaryotic nucleus different from a dikaryotic nucleus?
- Draw a generalized life cycle of a fungus.

29.3 FUNGAL DIVERSITY

■ LEARNING OBJECTIVES

4 Give arguments to support the hypothesis that fungi are opisthokonts, more closely related to animals than to plants.

5 Give arguments to support the hypothesis that chytrids may have been the earliest fungal group to evolve from the most recent common ancestor of fungi.

6 List distinguishing characteristics, describe a typical life cycle, and give examples of each of the following fungal groups: chytridiomycetes, zygomycetes, glomeromycetes, ascomycetes, and basidiomycetes.

For centuries, biologists classified fungi in the plant kingdom. Like plants, fungi have cell walls and vacuoles and are sessile, that is they cannot move around from place to place. Also, like plants, many types of fungi inhabit the soil. However, systematists began to question this classification, and in 1969, R. H. Whittaker proposed that fungi be assigned to a separate kingdom—Fungi.

Unlike plants, fungal cell walls do not contain cellulose. Rather, they contain chitin, a polysaccharide found in insect skeletons. The fungal mode of nutrition is also very different from that of plants. Unlike plants, fungi cannot produce their own organic materials from a simple carbon source (carbon dioxide). Like animals, fungi are heterotrophs.

As with systematics for other kingdoms, fungal systematics is a challenging and continuously changing process. For example, slime molds and water molds were formerly classified as fungi but are now assigned to the protist kingdom (see Chapter 26).

Fungi are assigned to the opisthokont clade

Systematists hypothesize that the common ancestor of all plants, fungi, and animals was a flagellated ancient protist. As discussed in Chapter 26, amoebozoa (a group of amoebas), fungi, animals, and a few protists, including the choanoflagellates (a group of flagellate protists), form a monophyletic "supergroup," the **unikonts.** Within this supergroup, the clade **opisthokonts** includes the choanoflagellates, the animals, and the fungi. Both genetic and structural similarities support this grouping. Like animals, fungi have plate-like cristae in their mitochondria. Another key character shared by members of this clade is that flagellate cells propel themselves with a single posterior flagellum. In other eukaryote groups, flagellate cells move by means of one or more anterior flagella. Based on structural characters and on molecular data, systematists now view fungi as more closely related to animals than to plants.

Diverse groups of fungi have evolved

Fossil evidence has not been very helpful to systematists studying evolutionary relationships among fungal groups. Most fossilized fungi recovered to date have been microscopic. For example, fossilized fungal spores have been found in amber more than 225 million years old, and fossils of hyphae associated with cyanobacteria or algae have been dated as more than 550 million years old. Few large fungal fossils, such as mushrooms, have been found.

Historically, fungi have been classified mainly on the characteristics of their sexual spores and fruiting bodies. More recently, molecular data, such as comparative DNA and RNA sequences, have helped clarify relationships among fungal groups. Currently, many mycologists assign fungi to five main groups: Chytridiomycota, Zygomycota, Glomeromycota, Ascomycota, and Basidiomycota (**FIG. 29-5** and **TABLE 29-1**). Some biologists consider each of these groups to be a phylum. However, some of these groups are not monophyletic (see Chapter 23), and mycologists are in the process of assigning fungi to additional clades.

In this edition of *Biology*, we will discuss fungi in the five phyla shown in Figure 29-5 and listed in Table 29-1. Microsporidia, a group of intracellular parasites, are classified in this text with the zygomycetes, although in the future they may be assigned to their own taxon. About 95% of all named fungi have been assigned to phyla Ascomycota and Basidiomycota. These phyla are considered *sister taxa* because they share a more recent common ancestor with each other than either does with any other group. Fungi of phyla Ascomycota and Basidiomycota have septate hyphae and a dikaryotic stage during the sexual part of their life cycle.

Until recently, mycologists had assigned about 25,000 species of fungi that did not fit into the major groups to a group called deuteromycetes (phylum Deuteromycota). This was a polyphyletic group (members did not share a recent common ancestor) lumped

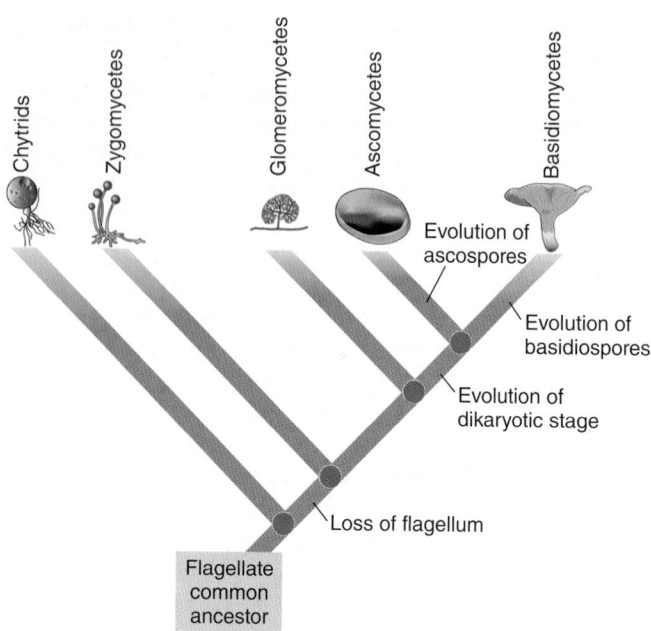

FIGURE 29-5 Cladogram of currently recognized groups of fungi
This cladogram shows phylogenetic relationships among living fungi, based on comparisons of ribosomal and nuclear gene sequence data for many species. The chytrids were the lineage that branched off first during fungal evolution. Note that ascomycetes and basidiomycetes are sister clades. Remember that the phylogeny of fungi is a work in process.

together simply as a matter of convenience. Mycologists classified fungi as deuteromycetes if no sexual stage had been observed for them at any point during their life cycle. Some of these fungi have lost the ability to reproduce sexually, whereas others reproduce sexually only rarely. Most fungi classified as deuteromycetes reproduce only by means of conidia, as ascomycetes do. Mycolo-

gists have identified relationships between deuteromycetes and their sexually reproducing relatives, based on DNA comparisons among various species. Most of the deuteromycetes have been reassigned to phylum Ascomycota, and a few reassigned to phylum Basidiomycota. (By convention, the asexual stage is still identified as a deuteromycete.)

Chytrids have flagellate spores

At one time, biologists considered the **chytrids,** also known as **chytridiomycetes** (phylum Chytridiomycota), to be funguslike protists, similar in many respects to the water molds. However, both structural and molecular characters indicate that the approximately 1000 species of chytridiomycetes are members of kingdom Fungi. Like fungi, their cell walls contain chitin, and molecular comparisons, particularly of DNA and RNA sequences, have provided compelling evidence that chytrids are indeed fungi. However, recent comparisons of rRNA sequences suggest that chytrids are not a monophyletic group and they may be divided into four clades.

Chytrids are small, relatively simple fungi that inhabit ponds and damp soil. A few species have been found in salt water. Most chytrids are decomposers that degrade organic matter. However, a few species cause disease in plants and animals. A parasitic chytrid has been partly responsible for declining amphibian populations. Infected frogs have been identified in many parts of the world (see *Inquiring About: Declining Amphibian Populations,* in Chapter 57).

Most chytrids are unicellular or composed of a few cells that form a simple body, called a **thallus.** The term *thallus* describes the simple body plan of certain algae, fungi, and plants. The thallus may have slender extensions, called **rhizoids,** that anchor it to a food source and absorb food (**FIG. 29-6**). Chytrids are the only fungi that have flagellate cells. Their spores bear a single, posterior flagellum. Sexual reproduction has not been identified in most chytrids. Species that do reproduce sexually have flagellate gametes.

	Phylum and Common Types	Asexual Reproduction	Sexual Reproduction	Other Key Characters
	Chytridiomycota (chytrids or chytridiomycetes) *Allomyces*	Flagellate, diploid zoospores produced by mitosis in zoosporangia	Flagellate, haploid gametes in some species	Haploid zoospores produced in resting sporangia; form haploid thallus
	Zygomycota (zygomycetes) Black bread mold. Microsporidia are classified with the zygomycetes	Haploid spores produced in sporangia	Zygospores develop in zygosporangia	Important decomposers; some are insect parasites. Microsporidia are opportunistic pathogens that infect animals.
	Glomeromycota (glomeromycetes)	Large, multinucleate blastospores	Has not been observed	Form arbuscular mycorrhizae with plant roots
	Ascomycota (ascomycetes) Yeasts, powdery mildews, molds, morels, truffles	Conidia pinch off from conidiophores	Ascospores develop in asci	Have a dikaryotic stage; form important symbiotic relationships as lichens and mycorrhizae
	Basidiomycota (basidiomycetes or club fungi) Mushrooms, bracket fungi, puffballs, rusts, smuts	Uncommon	Basidiospores develop on club-shaped basidia	Have a dikaryotic stage; many form mycorrhizae with tree roots

TABLE 29-1 Characteristics of Currently Recognized Phyla of Fungi

John Taylor/Visuals Unlimited, Inc.

5 μm

FIGURE 29-6 Chytrid

Nomarski differential interference micrograph of a common chytrid (*Chytridium convervae*). Many chytrids have a microscopic body form consisting of a rounded, coenocytic thallus and branched rhizoids that superficially resemble roots. The rhizoids may anchor the chytrid thallus and absorb predigested food.

Some chytrids produce branched, coenocytic mycelia. *Allomyces*, a large, common chytrid, has an unusual life cycle compared to that of most fungi. It undergoes an **alternation of generations** (common in plants, but rare in fungi), spending part of its life as a multicellular haploid (*n*) thallus and part as a multicellular diploid (*2n*) thallus (**FIG. 29-7**). The haploid and diploid thalli are similar in appearance. At the tips of its branches, the haploid thallus bears two types of sporangia, structures in which gametes form by mitosis. Each sporangium produces a different type of flagellate gamete.

Each type of gamete secretes a pheromone that attracts the other type. The two gametes fuse, and plasmogamy and karyogamy occur, resulting in a motile zygote. Each zygote can develop into a diploid thallus. The thallus bears two kinds of spore cases, zoosporangia and resting sporangia. Zoosporangia produce flagellate diploid **zoospores** that develop into new diploid thalli. Meiosis occurs within resting sporangia, producing haploid zoospores. Each zoospore has the potential to develop into a haploid thallus.

Molecular evidence suggests that chytrids were probably the earliest fungal group to evolve. Chytrids produce flagellate cells at some stage in their life history, a character that systematists trace to the protist that was the common ancestor of all opisthokonts. No other fungal group has flagellate cells. At some point in their evo-

lutionary history, other fungal groups apparently lost the ability to produce motile cells, perhaps during the transition from aquatic to terrestrial habitats.

Zygomycetes reproduce sexually by forming zygospores

Mycologists have named more than 1100 species of **zygomycetes** (phylum Zygomycota). Of all the fungi, members of this taxon appear most closely related to the chytrids. However, zygomycetes are not a monophyletic group, and as mycologists learn more about fungal relationships, they may divide this phylum into several taxa or reassign its members to other existing phyla.

Most zygomycetes are decomposers that live in the soil on decaying plant or animal matter (**FIG. 29-8**). Some zygomycetes form a type of symbiotic association (mycorrhizal relationship) with plant roots. (Recall that a symbiotic association is an intimate relationship between organisms of different species.) A few species cause disease in plants and animals, including humans.

During sexual reproduction, zygomycetes produce sexual spores, called **zygospores.** The zygospores are typically produced in spore sacs called **zygosporangia.** The hyphae in zygomycetes are coenocytic; that is, they lack regularly spaced septa. However, septa do form to separate the hyphae from reproductive structures.

Perhaps the most familiar zygomycete is the black bread mold, *Rhizopus stolonifer,* a decomposer that breaks down bread and other foods. If preservatives are not added, bread left at room temperature for a few days often becomes covered with a black, fuzzy growth. Bread becomes moldy when a spore falls on it and then germinates and grows into a mycelium (**FIG. 29-9** on page 610). Hyphae penetrate the bread and absorb nutrients. Eventually, certain hyphae grow upward and develop sporangia at their tips. Clusters of more than 50,000 black asexual spores can develop within each sporangium. The spores are released when the delicate sporangium ruptures. The spores give the black bread mold its characteristic color.

Sexual reproduction in the black bread mold occurs when the hyphae of two different mating types, designated plus (+) and minus (−), grow into contact with one another. The bread mold is **heterothallic,** meaning that an individual fungal hypha mates only with a hypha of a different mating type. That is, sexual reproduction occurs only between a member of a (+) strain and one of a (−) strain, not between members of two (+) strains or members of two (−) strains. Because there are no physical differences between the two mating types, it is not appropriate to refer to them as "male" and "female."

When hyphae of opposite mating types grow in close proximity, they signal one another with pheromones. In response to these chemical signals, the tips of the hyphae come together and form **gametangia,** which serve as gametes. Plasmogamy occurs as the gametangia fuse. Then karyogamy occurs as the (+) and (−) nuclei fuse to form the diploid zygote nucleus. The zygote develops into a zygospore. Zygospores are encased in a thick protective zygosporangium. The zygospore may lie dormant for several months. It can survive desiccation and extreme temperatures. Meiosis probably occurs at or just before germination of the zygospore.

FIGURE 29-7 Life cycle of the chytrid *Allomyces arbuscula*

Allomyces alternates between haploid and diploid stages, which are similar in appearance.

FIGURE 29-8 *Pilobolus*, a zygomycete that grows in animal dung
Stalked sporangia of *Pilobolus* protruding from a pile of dung, which contains an extensive mycelium of the fungus. The stalked sporangia, which are 5 to 10 mm tall, act like shotguns and forcefully discharge sporangia (the black tips) away from the dung onto nearby grass. When animals such as cattle or horses eat the grass, the spores pass unharmed through the animal's digestive tract and are deposited in a fresh pile of dung.

When the zygospore germinates, an aerial hypha develops with a sporangium at the tip. Mitosis within the sporangium produces haploid spores. These spores may be all (+) spores, all (−) spores, or a mixture of (+) and (−) spores. When released, the spores germinate to form new hyphae. Only the zygote and zygospore of a black bread mold are diploid; all the hyphae and the asexual spores are haploid.

Microsporidia have been a taxonomic mystery

Microsporidia are small, unicellular parasites that infect eukaryotic cells. They are opportunistic pathogens that infect animals. For example, microsporidia infect people with compromised immune systems, such as those with AIDS. Microsporidia cause a variety of diseases involving many organ systems, and some species cause lethal infections. Some species of microsporidia appear to be host-specific.

Microsporidia have two developmental stages inside their host: a feeding stage and a reproductive stage. Some microsporidian species divide into two cells by binary fission, and others divide into several cells. Some species undergo nuclear fusion and meiosis before producing spores. The spores, which have thick protective walls, can pass from cell to cell inside the host or can be excreted in urine or through the skin. The spores, the only stage with distinct characters, are used to identify groups.

Each spore is equipped with a unique structure, a long, thread-like **polar tube.** When the spore enters the gut of a new host, it discharges its polar tube and penetrates the lining of the gut. Acting as a hypodermic needle, the polar tube injects the contents of the spore into the host cell (**FIG. 29-10**).

Microbiologists estimate that there may be more than a million species of microsporidia, but only about 1500 species have been named. Microsporidia were originally classified with yeasts and bacteria. In 1976, they were assigned to the protozoa. In the 1980s, biologists viewed microsporidia as the most primitive example of a eukaryote. They were the smallest and simplest known eukaryotes, and the genomes of some species are smaller than most bacterial genomes. Microsporidia lack mitochondria, flagella, and Golgi complexes. Their ribosomes resemble those of prokaryotes.

In 1998, British biologist Thomas Cavalier-Smith reassigned microsporidia to kingdom Fungi. Molecular studies show that microsporidia have gene sequences that indicate they originally had mitochondria. Microbiologists now generally agree that these organisms have become simpler as they adapted to their parasitic way of life. Other molecular studies have provided additional evidence for their taxonomic relationship with fungi. Establishing that they are closely related to fungi is important in developing medications that will be effective in treating microsporidian infections. Recent genome studies suggest that microsporidia descended from a zygomycete ancestor. For now, we classify the microsporidia with the zygomycetes, but in the future they may be assigned to a separate taxon.

Glomeromycetes are symbionts with plant roots

Glomeromycetes (phylum Glomeromycota) have coenocytic (no septa) hyphae. They reproduce asexually with large, multinucleate spores called *blastospores*. Sexual reproduction has not been documented. Only about 200 species of glomeromycetes have been described. Glomeromycetes were previously considered zygomycetes, but in 2002 taxonomists determined that they form a separate monophyletic group. This phylogeny is based on molecular data.

Glomeromycetes are symbionts that form intracellular associations with the roots of most trees and herbaceous plants. These symbiotic associations between the hyphae of certain fungi and the roots of plants are called **mycorrhizae** (from Greek words meaning "fungus roots") (**FIG. 29-11**). Glomeromycetes extend their hyphae through the cell walls of root cells but often may not penetrate the plasma membrane. As each hypha pushes forward, the plasma membrane of the root cell surrounds it. Thus, the hyphae can be thought of as fingers pushing into a glove formed by the plasma membrane. Because they penetrate the cell wall, these fungi are referred to as **endomycorrhizal fungi.**

The most widespread endomycorrhizae are called **arbuscular mycorrhizae** because the hyphae inside the root cells form branched, tree-shaped structures known as **arbuscules** (see Fig. 29-11 and Fig. 36-11b). The arbuscules are the sites of nutrient exchange between the plant and the fungus. Arbuscular mycorrhizae live entirely underground.

In mycorrhizal relationships, the roots supply the fungus with sugars, amino acids, and other organic substances. The mycorrhizal fungus decomposes organic material in the soil and also benefits the plant by extending the reach of its roots. The slender mycelia are far thinner than roots and can extend into narrow spaces, absorbing nutrients that the plant could not capture on its own. Thus, with the help of the mycorrhizal fungus, the plant can also take in more nutrient minerals such as phosphorus and nitrogen.

What we have just described is a mutualistic symbiotic association: both partners benefit. Studies show that if a plant grows

Like most fungi, most zygomycetes reproduce both asexually and sexually.

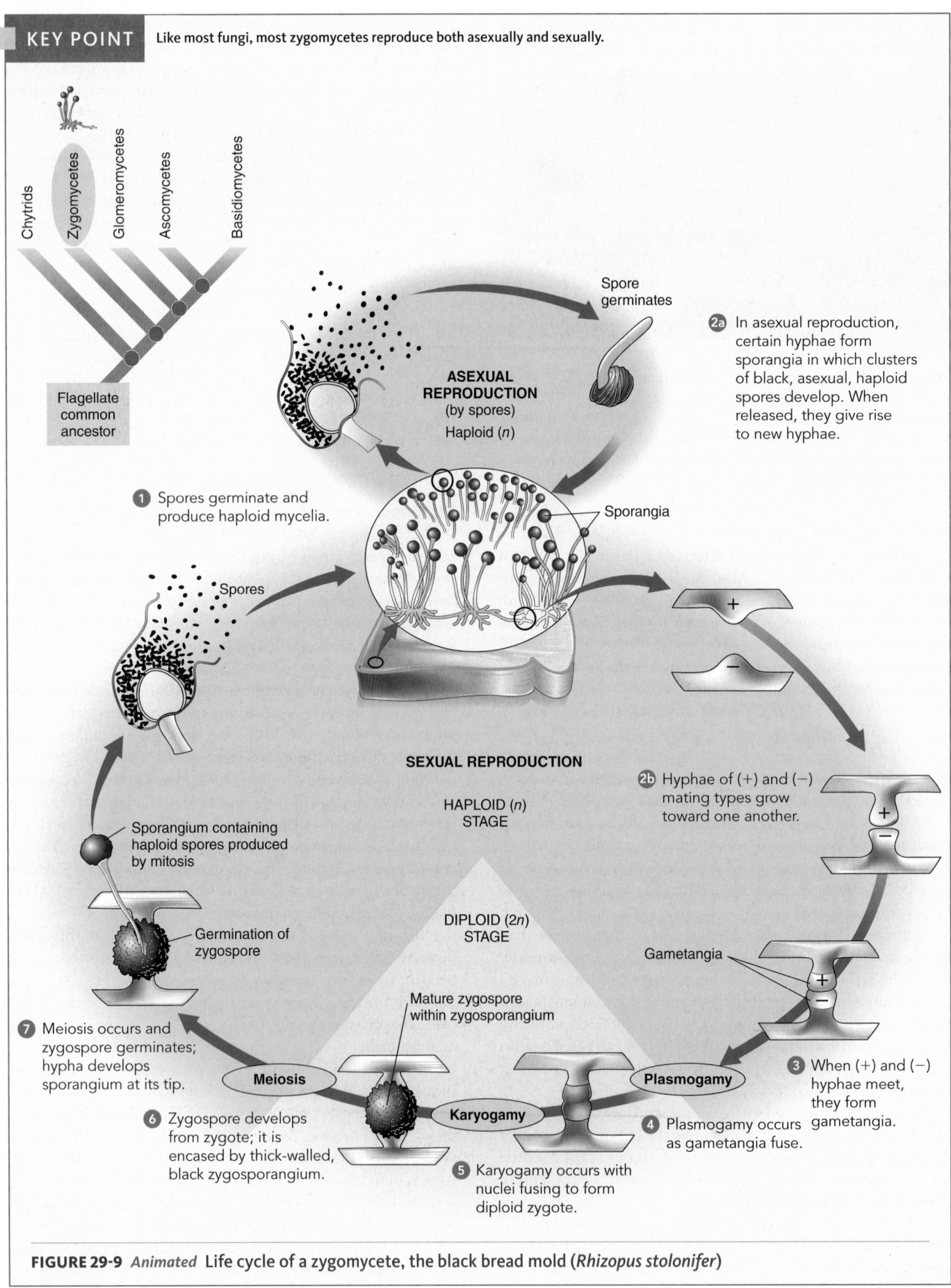

ASEXUAL REPRODUCTION (by spores) Haploid (*n*)

Spore germinates

2a In asexual reproduction, certain hyphae form sporangia in which clusters of black, asexual, haploid spores develop. When released, they give rise to new hyphae.

1 Spores germinate and produce haploid mycelia.

Sporangia

Spores

SEXUAL REPRODUCTION

HAPLOID (*n*) STAGE

DIPLOID (2*n*) STAGE

2b Hyphae of (+) and (−) mating types grow toward one another.

Gametangia

Sporangium containing haploid spores produced by mitosis

Germination of zygospore

Meiosis

Mature zygospore within zygosporangium

Karyogamy

Plasmogamy

3 When (+) and (−) hyphae meet, they form gametangia.

7 Meiosis occurs and zygospore germinates; hypha develops sporangium at its tip.

6 Zygospore develops from zygote; it is encased by thick-walled, black zygosporangium.

4 Plasmogamy occurs as gametangia fuse.

5 Karyogamy occurs with nuclei fusing to form diploid zygote.

Chytrids

Zygomycetes

Glomeromycetes

Ascomycetes

Basidiomycetes

Flagellate common ancestor

FIGURE 29-9 *Animated* Life cycle of a zygomycete, the black bread mold (*Rhizopus stolonifer*)

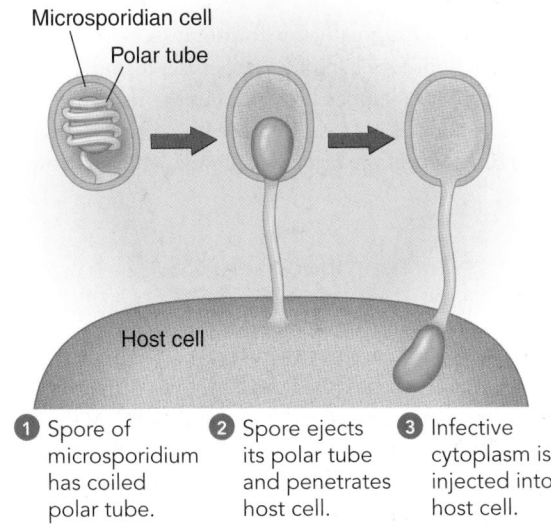

1. Spore of microsporidium has coiled polar tube.

2. Spore ejects its polar tube and penetrates host cell.

3. Infective cytoplasm is injected into host cell.

FIGURE 29-10 Infection by a microsporidium

FIGURE 29-11 Arbuscular mycorrhizae
This mycelium has grown into a plant root. Its hyphae branch between the cells of the root. Hyphae have penetrated through the cell walls of two root cells and have branched extensively to form arbuscules. The tip of one hypha between root cells has enlarged and serves as a vesicle that stores food. The tip of a hypha in the soil has enlarged, forming a spore. The spaces between the root cells have been magnified for clarity.

in phosphate-deficient soil or if it has a limited root system, its growth is enhanced by having a fungal partner. However, a plant in a phosphate-rich soil with a well-developed root system may not need fungal partners. For these plants, the fungus may be a parasite.

Much remains to be learned about mycorrhizal associations. Other, yet unknown, benefits of the symbiosis may further define the association as mutualistic. For example, some fungi release alkaloids that protect the plants from herbivores and pathogens. Plants also exchange nutrients with one another through fungi that connect them.

Scientists have discovered mycorrhizal fungi within ancient plant fossils in rocks that are about 400 million years old. These findings suggest that when plants moved onto the land, their fungal partners moved with them. In fact, the fungal partners may have been critical for early vascular plants to colonize the land because the fungal hyphae may have provided plants with water and minerals before their own root systems evolved.

Ascomycetes reproduce sexually by forming ascospores

Ascomycetes (phylum Ascomycota) comprise a large group of fungi consisting of more than 32,000 described species. The diverse ascomycetes include most yeasts; the powdery mildews; most of the blue-green, pink, and brown molds that cause food to spoil; decomposer cup fungi; and the edible morels and truffles.

The ascomycetes, more than any other group of fungi, impact humans. As we will discuss in a later section, ascomycetes are used to flavor cheeses, to bake bread (yeast), and to ferment alcohol. Some are enjoyed as foods (morels and truffles). Ascomycetes are used to produce antibiotics. They have also served as valuable model organisms for biologists studying cellular processes, including protein synthesis. Many fungi in this group form mycorrhizae with tree roots, and about 40% join with green algae or cyanobacteria to form lichens. On the negative side, ascomycetes cause

most fungal diseases of plants and animals, including humans. For example, ascomycetes cause serious plant diseases such as Dutch elm disease, ergot disease on rye, powdery mildew on fruits and ornamental plants, and chestnut blight.

Ascomycetes are sometimes referred to as *sac fungi* because their sexual spores are produced in microscopic sacs called **asci** (sing., *ascus*). Their hyphae usually have septa, but these cross walls have pores so that cytoplasm is continuous from one cell compartment to another.

In most ascomycetes, asexual reproduction involves production of spores called **conidia,** which form at the tips of certain specialized hyphae known as *conidiophores* (**FIG. 29-12**). Production of these spores is a means of rapidly propagating new mycelia when environmental conditions are favorable. Conidia occur in various shapes, sizes, and colors in different species. The color of the conidia produces the characteristic blue-green, pink, brown, or other tints of many of these molds.

Some species of ascomycetes are heterothallic. (Recall that heterothallic means that an individual fungal hypha mates only with a hypha of a different mating type.) Others are **homothallic,** which means they are self-fertile and have the ability to mate with themselves. In both heterothallic and homothallic ascomycetes, sexual reproduction takes place after two gametangia come together and their cytoplasm mingles.

Let us examine the life cycle of a typical ascomycete (**FIG. 29-13**). In our example, plasmogamy takes place as hyphae of two different mating types come together and fuse. Within this fused structure, pairs of haploid nuclei, one from each parent hypha, associate but

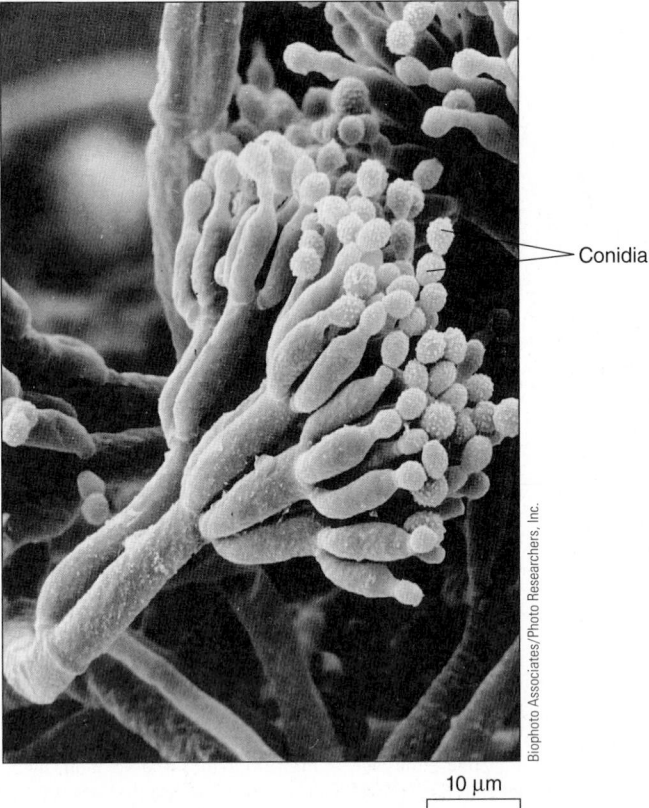

Conidia

10 μm

Biophoto Associates/Photo Researchers, Inc.

FIGURE 29-12 Conidia

SEM of *Penicillium* conidiophores, which resemble paintbrushes. Note the conidia pinching off from the tips of the "brushes." Conidia are asexual reproductive cells produced by ascomycetes and some basidiomycetes. Biologists use the arrangement of conidia on conidiophores to identify species of these fungi.

do not fuse. New hyphae, with dikaryotic cells, develop from the fused structure. The hyphae branch repeatedly until the hyphal tips reach the site where asci will be produced. As the many sac-shaped asci develop, each containing two dissimilar nuclei (one from each parent), they are surrounded by intertwining haploid (monokaryotic) hyphae. These hyphae help make a fruiting body known as an **ascocarp** (**FIG. 29-14a**).

Karyogamy occurs in each ascus. The two nuclei fuse and form a diploid zygote nucleus. The zygote nucleus then undergoes meiosis to form four haploid nuclei with different genotypes. One mitotic division of each of the four nuclei usually follows, resulting in eight haploid nuclei. Each haploid nucleus becomes incorporated into a thick-walled **ascospore;** thus, there are typically eight haploid ascospores within the ascus (**FIG. 29-14b**). The ascospores are usually released through a pore, slit, or hinged lid at the tip of the ascus. Air currents carry individual ascospores, often for long distances. If one lands in a suitable location, it germinates and forms a new mycelium. The fungus can reproduce asexually by producing conidia that can develop into new mycelia.

Phylum Ascomycota includes more than 300 species of unicellular yeasts. Asexual reproduction of yeasts is mainly by **budding;** in this process a small protuberance (bud) grows and eventually

separates from the parent cell (see Fig. 29-3). Each bud can grow into a new yeast cell.

Yeasts reproduce sexually by forming ascospores. During sexual reproduction, two haploid yeasts fuse, forming a diploid zygote. The zygote undergoes meiosis, and the resulting haploid nuclei are incorporated into ascospores. These spores remain enclosed for a time within the original cell wall, which corresponds to an ascus.

Basidiomycetes reproduce sexually by forming basidiospores

The more than 30,000 species of **basidiomycetes** (phylum Basidiomycota) include the largest and most familiar of the fungi: the mushrooms, bracket fungi, and puffballs (**FIG. 29-15**). Many basidiomycetes are decomposers that obtain nutrients by breaking down organic matter. Some species cause great economic loss because they cause dry rot in buildings. Certain basidiomycetes form mycorrhizae. Others, such as wheat rust and corn smut, infect important crops. A few basidiomycetes cause human disease.

Sometimes called *club fungi*, basidiomycetes derive their name from their microscopic club-shaped **basidia** (sing., *basidium*). Basidia are comparable in function to the asci of ascomycetes. Each basidium is an enlarged hyphal cell that undergoes meiosis to form four **basidiospores** (**FIG. 29-16**). Note that basidiospores develop on the *outside* of a basidium, whereas ascospores develop *within* an ascus.

Each individual fungus produces millions of basidiospores, and each basidiospore has the potential to give rise to a new **primary mycelium.** Hyphae of a primary mycelium consist of monokaryotic cells. The mycelium of a basidiomycete, such as the commonly cultivated mushroom *Agaricus brunnescens,* consists of a mass of white, branching, threadlike hyphae that live mostly underground. Septa divide the hyphae into cells, but as in ascomycetes, the septa are perforated and allow cytoplasmic streaming between cells.

Let us examine the life cycle of a typical basidiomycete. Asexual reproduction is less common in basidiomycetes than in other groups, so we will focus here on sexual reproduction. We begin with two compatible primary mycelia (**FIG. 29-17** on page 616). When in the course of its growth a hypha of a primary mycelium encounters a compatible monokaryotic hypha, typically of a different mating type, the two hyphae fuse (plasmogamy). As in the ascomycetes, the two haploid nuclei remain separate within each cell. In this way a **secondary mycelium** with dikaryotic hyphae is produced, in which each cell contains two haploid nuclei. The $n + n$ hyphae of the secondary mycelium grow rapidly and extensively.

When environmental conditions are favorable, the hyphae form compact masses, called *buttons,* along the mycelium. Each button grows into a fruiting body that we know as a mushroom. A mushroom is more formally referred to as a **basidiocarp.** Each basidiocarp consists of intertwined, matted hyphae, and has a stalk and a cap. The lower surface of the cap usually consists of many thin, perpendicular plates called **gills** that radiate from the stalk to the edge of the cap.

Karyogamy takes place within the young basidia on the gills of the mushroom. The haploid nuclei fuse in the dikaryotic cells,

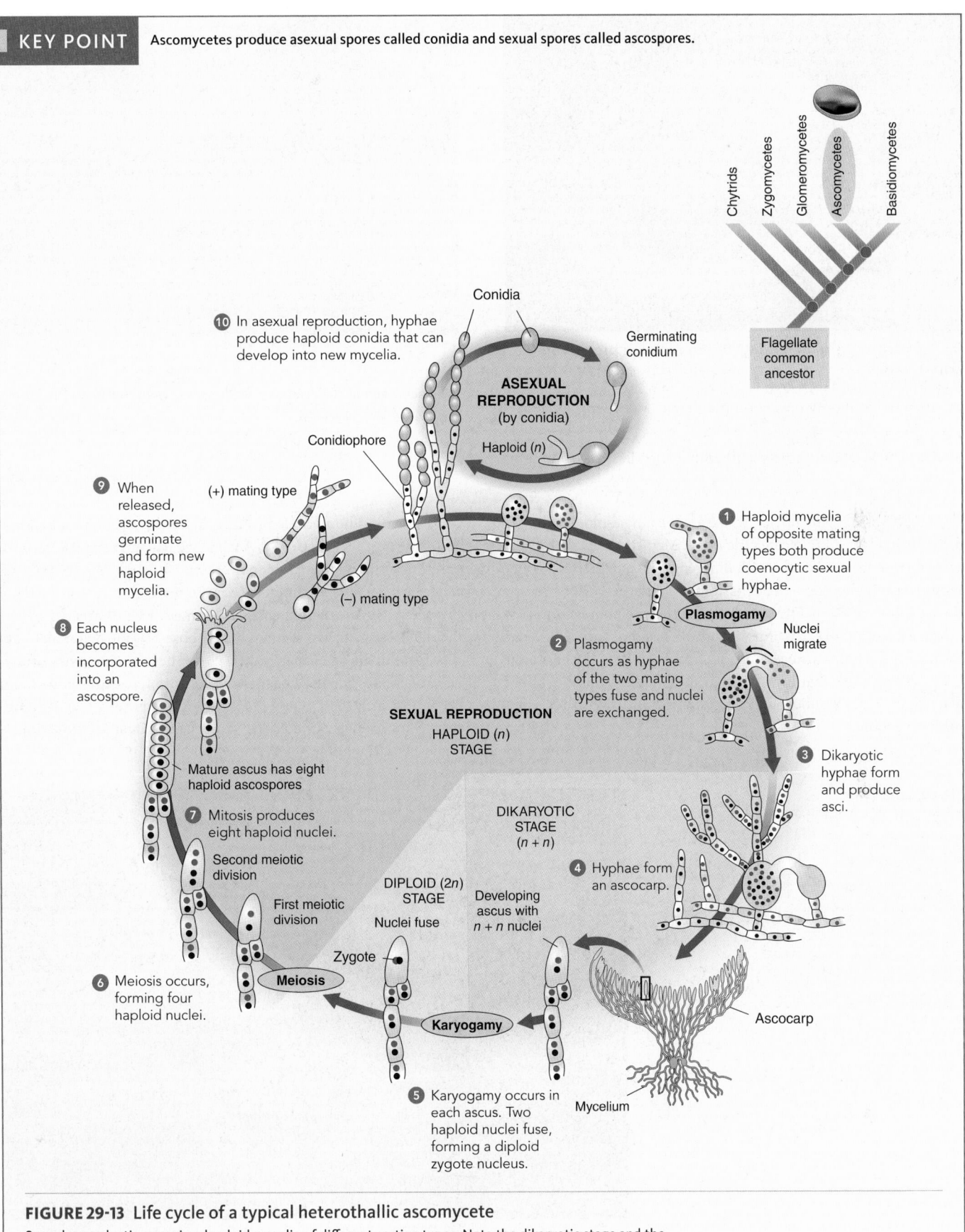

FIGURE 29-13 Life cycle of a typical heterothallic ascomycete

Sexual reproduction requires haploid mycelia of different mating types. Note the dikaryotic stage and the separation of plasmogamy and karyogamy. Steps 5 through 8 take place within an ascus in the ascocarp.

© Ed Reschke

(a) The ascocarp (fruiting body) of the common brown cup (*Peziza badio-confusa*). This ascocarp is shaped like a saucer or bowl and is 3 to 10 cm (1 to 4 in) wide. It is found on damp soil in woods throughout North America. Photographed in Muskegon, Michigan.

© Robert and Linda Mitchell

100 μm

(b) Asci. Each ascus contains eight ascospores. Asci line the inner portion of the ascocarp.

FIGURE 29-14 *Animated* Sexual reproduction in the ascomycetes

forming diploid zygote nuclei. These are the only diploid cells that form during a basidiomycete's life cycle. Meiosis then takes place, forming four haploid nuclei with different genotypes. These nuclei move to the outer edge of the basidium. Fingerlike extensions of the basidium develop, into which the nuclei and some cytoplasm move; each of these extensions becomes a basidiospore. A septum forms that separates the basidiospore from the rest of the basidium by a delicate stalk that breaks when the basidiospore is forcibly discharged. Each basidiospore can germinate and give rise to a primary mycelium.

Many basidiomycetes produce "fairy rings" in lawns and forests (**FIG. 29-18** on page 617). A fairy ring may first appear as a dark green ring surrounding an inner brown circle. The size of the ring ranges from a few centimeters to more than 15 m (about 51 ft) in diameter. The green ring consists of grass, well nourished by the nutrients released as the fungi decompose organic material. Grass dies, producing the inner brown circle, because the mass of mycelia decreases the movement of water into the area. As the fungi grow outward, the circle widens. The rings grow a few centimeters to more than a meter per year. After rainfall or irrigation, a

FIGURE 29-15 ▶
Basidiomycete fruiting bodies

Cengage

(a) Basidia line the gills of the Jack-o'-lantern mushroom (*Omphalotus olearius*). The gills of this poisonous species produce a greenish glow in the dark. Each cap is about 15 cm (6 in) wide. Photographed at the base of an oak tree in Maryland, the Jack-o'-lantern occurs throughout eastern North America and California.

ring of mushrooms may appear just outside the green circle. The name "fairy ring" comes from a legend that a ring of mushrooms appeared where fairies had danced in a circle the night before.

Review

- What evidence supports the hypothesis that chytrids were the earliest fungal group to evolve from the common ancestor of fungi?
- What are the distinguishing characteristics of each of the following fungal groups: (1) zygomycetes, (2) glomeromycetes, (3) ascomycetes, and (4) basidiomycetes?
- How does the life cycle of a typical basidiomycete differ from that of a typical ascomycete? (Draw diagrams to support your answer.)
- Distinguish among (1) ascocarp, ascus, and ascospore and among (2) basidiocarp, basidium, and basidiospore.

29.4 ECOLOGICAL IMPORTANCE OF FUNGI

■ LEARNING OBJECTIVES

7 Summarize the ecological significance of fungi as decomposers.
8 Describe the important ecological role of mycorrhizae.
9 Characterize the unique nature of a lichen.

Fungi make vital contributions to the ecological balance of our planet. Like bacteria, most fungi are free-living decomposers, chemoheterotrophs that absorb nutrients from organic wastes and dead organisms. For example, many fungal decomposers degrade cellulose and lignin, the main components of plant cell walls. When

Biophoto Associates/Photo Researchers, Inc.

5 μm

FIGURE 29-16 SEM of a basidium
Each basidium produces four basidiospores.

Basidiospore

Basidium

fungi degrade wastes and dead organisms, they release water, carbon (as CO_2), and mineral components of organic compounds, and these elements are recycled (see biogeochemical cycles in Chapter 55). Without this continuous decomposition, essential nutrients would remain locked up in huge mounds of animal carcasses, feces, branches, logs, and leaves. These nutrients would be unavailable for use by new generations of organisms, and life would eventually cease.

Fungi form important symbiotic relationships with animals, plants, bacteria, and protists. A three-way symbiotic relationship involving a fungus, a grass, and a virus has recently been reported. In the geothermal hot spots of Yellowstone National Park, a fungus infects the roots of the host grass. When infected with a specific virus, the fungus is heat tolerant and confers heat tolerance to the grass. When not infected by the virus, the fungus does not confer heat tolerance. The symbiotic relationships of fungi with other organisms have major effects on ecosystems.

Fungi form symbiotic relationships with some animals

Because animals do not have the enzymes necessary to digest cellulose and lignin, cattle and other grazing animals cannot, by themselves, obtain needed nutrients from the plant material they eat. Their survival depends on fungi that

Richard D. Poe/Visuals Unlimited

(b) The elegant stinkhorn (Phallus ravenelii) has a foul smell that attracts flies. The flies help disperse the slimy mass of basidiospores. Fruiting bodies of elegant stinkhorns grow to 18 cm (7 in) tall. Photographed in Pennsylvania.

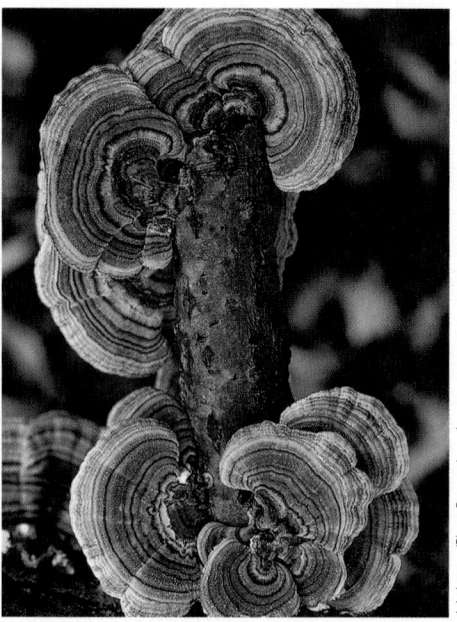

J. L. Lepore/Photo Researchers, Inc.

(c) Turkey-tail (Trametes versicolor) is a common bracket fungus. Bracket fungi grow on both dead and living trees and produce shelflike fruiting bodies. Basidiospores are produced in pores located underneath each shelf.

Basidiomycetes produce sexual basidiospores on the gills of basidiocarps (fruiting bodies).

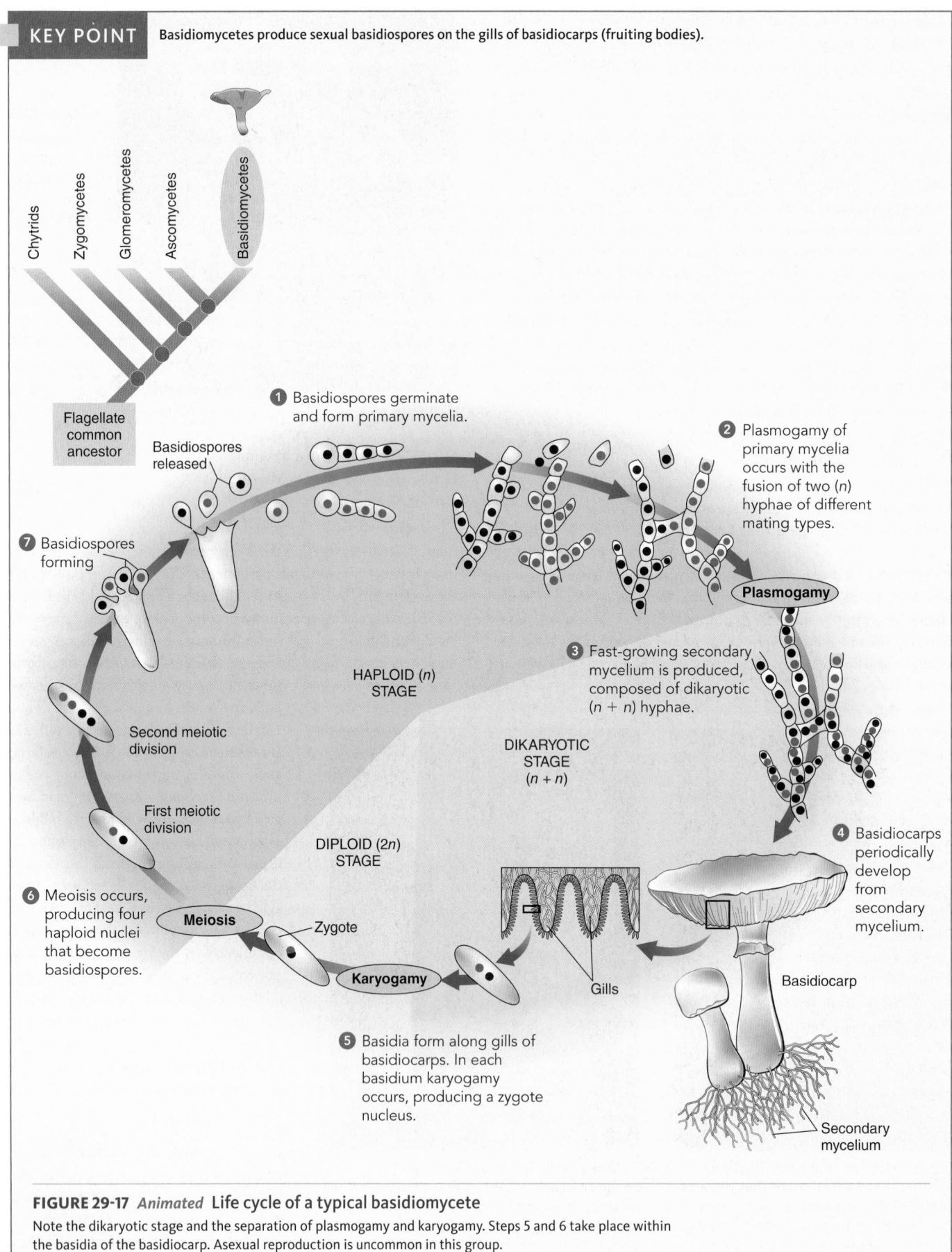

1 Basidiospores germinate and form primary mycelia.

2 Plasmogamy of primary mycelia occurs with the fusion of two (*n*) hyphae of different mating types.

Plasmogamy

3 Fast-growing secondary mycelium is produced, composed of dikaryotic (*n* + *n*) hyphae.

Basidiospores released

7 Basidiospores forming

HAPLOID (*n*) STAGE

DIKARYOTIC STAGE (*n* + *n*)

Second meiotic division

4 Basidiocarps periodically develop from secondary mycelium.

First meiotic division

DIPLOID (2*n*) STAGE

Basidiocarp

6 Meoisis occurs, producing four haploid nuclei that become basidiospores.

Meiosis

Zygote

Karyogamy

Gills

Secondary mycelium

5 Basidia form along gills of basidiocarps. In each basidium karyogamy occurs, producing a zygote nucleus.

Chytrids

Zygomycetes

Glomeromycetes

Ascomycetes

Basidiomycetes

Flagellate common ancestor

FIGURE 29-17 *Animated* **Life cycle of a typical basidiomycete**

Note the dikaryotic stage and the separation of plasmogamy and karyogamy. Steps 5 and 6 take place within the basidia of the basidiocarp. Asexual reproduction is uncommon in this group.

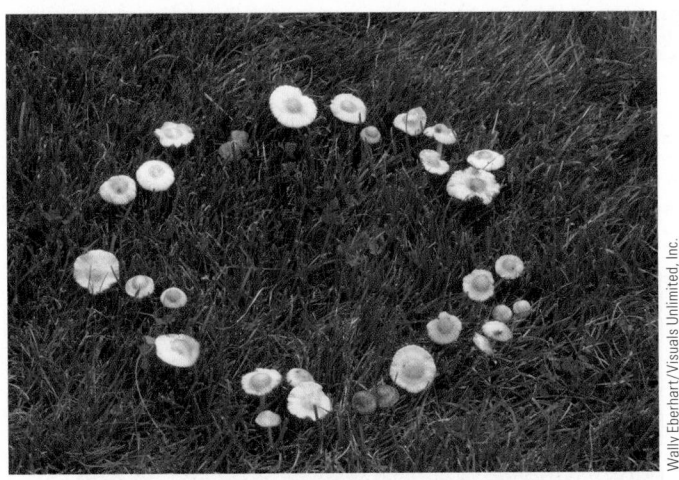

FIGURE 29-18 A fairy ring

inhabit their guts because fungi, like many other microorganisms, do have the enzymes that break down these organic compounds. The fungi benefit by living in a nutrient-rich environment.

Fungi also form symbiotic associations with ants and termites. More than 200 species of ants farm fungi. Leaf-cutting ants bring leaves to their fungi and protect them from competitors and predators. The ants also disperse the fungi to new locations. In exchange, the fungi digest the leaves, providing nutrients for the ants. This symbiosis can involve other organisms. The farmed fungi can be infested by fungal parasites. In response, the ants culture bacteria (actinomycetes) that produce antibiotics to control these parasites. These symbiotic relationships, the most complex known, are the product of 50 million years of coevolution.

Mycorrhizae are symbiotic associations between fungi and plant roots

Mycorrhizae occur in about 80% of plants (and more than 90% of all plant families). As discussed in the section on glomeromycetes, mycorrhizal fungi decompose organic material in the soil and increase the surface area of a plant's roots so that the plant can absorb more water and mineral nutrients. In exchange, the roots supply the fungus with organic nutrients.

In order to establish and maintain a symbiotic relationship, cells of the fungi and cells of the plant roots must communicate. For example, signaling molecules from the plant root cells stimulate fungal cells to shift to a presymbiotic growth phase in which their energy metabolism increases and their hyphae branch. The fungal cells then signal the root cells, activating a signaling pathway that activates gene expression in the root cells.

The importance of mycorrhizae first became evident when horticulturalists observed that orchids do not grow unless an appropriate fungus lives with them. Similarly, many forest trees, such as pines, decline and eventually die from mineral deficiencies when transplanted to mineral-rich grassland soils that lack the appropriate mycorrhizal fungi. When forest soil containing the appropriate fungi or their spores is added to the soil around these trees, they quickly resume normal growth. Studies performed with various

types of plants, including cedar, have confirmed the role of mycorrhizae in plant growth (**FIG. 29-19**).

As we have discussed, glomeromycetes form *endomycorrhizal* connections; they infiltrate the cells of plant roots. At least 5000 species of ascomycetes and basidiomycetes also form mycorrhizal connections, but their hyphae coat the plant root rather than penetrate its cells. They are referred to as **ectomycorrhizae.** Interestingly, researchers have shown that some mycorrhizal fungi harbor bacteria in their cytoplasm. Although the role of the bacteria is not yet clear, their presence suggests that they may be members of a three-way partnership: fungus, plant, and bacteria.

Mycorrhizal fungi connect plants, allowing nutrient transfer among them. Scientists have measured the movement of organic materials from one tree species to another through shared mycorrhizal connections. Mycorrhizal fungi also release chemicals that protect the plant against herbivores and pathogens.

Mycorrhizae improve the soil by decreasing water loss and erosion. Ecologists are studying the role of mycorrhizal fungi in reclaiming soils damaged by pollution. For example, mycorrhizae can modify toxic heavy metals, such as cadmium, so that plants cannot absorb them.

A lichen consists of two components: a fungus and a photoautotroph

Although a **lichen** looks like a single organism, it is actually a dual organism, a combination of a fungus and a *photoautotroph* (**FIG. 29-20a**). Almost one-fifth of all known fungal species form these symbiotic relationships. About 14,000 kinds of lichens have been described. Fossils suggest that fungi developed symbiotic partnerships with photoautotrophs before the evolution of vascular plants.

The photoautotrophic component of a lichen is either a green alga, a cyanobacterium, or both. The fungus is most often an ascomycete, although a basidiomycete is the fungal partner in some tropical lichens. Most photoautotrophic organisms found in lichens also occur as free-living species in nature, but the fungal components are generally found only as a part of the lichen. Typically, the fungus forms most of the lichen thallus (body). The fungus surrounds hundreds of photosynthetic partners and holds them in place. Lichens are named for the fungal component.

In the laboratory, researchers can isolate the fungal and photoautotrophic components of some lichens and grow them separately in appropriate culture media. The photoautotroph grows more rapidly when separated, whereas the fungus grows more slowly and requires many complex carbohydrates. Neither organism resembles a lichen in appearance when grown separately. The photoautotroph and fungus can be reassembled as a lichen thallus, but only if they are placed in a culture medium under conditions that cannot support either of them independently.

What is the nature of this partnership? The lichen was originally considered a definitive example of mutualism. The photoautotroph carries on photosynthesis, producing energy-rich carbon compounds for both members of the lichen. It is unclear how the photoautotroph benefits from the relationship. Some biologists have suggested that the photoautotroph obtains water and nutrient minerals from the fungus as well as protection against desiccation.

QUESTION: Is plant growth affected by fungi in the soil?

HYPOTHESIS: In low phosphorus soils, plants that form mycorrhizal associations with fungi exhibit enhanced growth.

EXPERIMENT: Western red cedar seedlings (*Thuja plicata*) were selected for this study. Control seedlings were grown in low phosphorus soil in the absence of the fungus. Experimental seedlings of the same age as the control plants were grown under the same conditions as the controls, except that their roots formed mycorrhizal associations.

(a) No mycorrhizal associations. Control seedlings were grown in low phosphorus soil in the absence of the fungus.

(b) Mycorrhizal associations. Experimental seedlings were grown under the same conditions as the controls, except that the fungus was present. The seedlings formed mycorrhizal associations with the fungus.

RESULTS AND CONCLUSIONS: Growth of the plants that formed mycorrhizal associations was significantly enhanced. Mycorrhizal associations enhance the growth of western red cedar plants. Many similar studies using other types of plants and other types of soil have confirmed the importance of mycorrhizal association to plant growth.

FIGURE 29-19 The effect of mycorrhizae on western red cedar (*Thuja plicata*) seedlings

More recently, researchers have suggested that the lichen partnership is not really a case of mutualism but one of controlled parasitism of the photoautotroph by the fungus.

Lichens typically exhibit one of three different growth forms (**FIG. 29-20b**). *Crustose lichens* are flat and grow tightly against their substrate (the surface they are growing on). *Foliose lichens* are also flat, but they have leaflike lobes and are not so tightly pressed to the substrate. *Fruticose lichens* grow erect and have many branches.

Able to tolerate extremes of temperature and moisture, lichens grow in almost all terrestrial environments except polluted cities. They exist farther north than any plants of the arctic region and are equally at home in the steaming equatorial rain forest. They grow on tree bark, leaves, and exposed rock surfaces, from solidified lava to tombstones. In fact, lichens are often the first organisms to inhabit rocky areas, and their growth in these areas is important in forming soil from rock. They secrete acid that gradually etches tiny cracks in the rock, releasing minerals. This process sets the stage for further disintegration of the rock by wind and rain. When the lichens themselves die and are decomposed, they become part of the soil.

Reindeer mosses of the arctic region, which serve as the main source of food for migrating herds of caribou, are actually lichens, not mosses. Some lichens produce colored pigments. One of them, orchil, is used to dye wool, and another, litmus, is widely used in chemistry laboratories as an acid–base (pH) indicator.

Lichens vary greatly in size. Some are almost invisible, whereas others, such as the reindeer mosses, may cover many square kilometers of land with an ankle-deep growth. Growth proceeds slowly; the radius of a lichen may increase by less than 1 mm each year. Some mature lichens are thought to be thousands of years old.

Lichens absorb minerals from the air, rainwater, and the surface on which they grow. They cannot excrete the elements they absorb, and perhaps for this reason they are extremely sensitive to toxic compounds. This sensitivity was first reported in 1866 by a Finnish biologist who observed that lichens growing on tree trunks in Paris were poorly developed or sterile. He deduced that lichens could be used to measure air purity. Today, reduction in lichen growth is used as a sensitive indicator of air pollution, particularly from sulfur dioxide. In one study, investigators demonstrated a relationship between lung cancer and air pollution by comparing the locations of low lichen biodiversity (and therefore of air pollution) with the locations of lung cancer deaths in young males. The return of lichens to an area indicates an improvement in air quality.

Lichens reproduce mainly by asexual means, usually by fragmentation, a process in which special dispersal units of the lichen, called **soredia,** break off and, if they land on a suitable surface, establish themselves as new lichens. Soredia contain cells of both partners. In some lichens, the fungus produces ascospores, which may be dispersed by wind and find an appropriate algal partner only by chance.

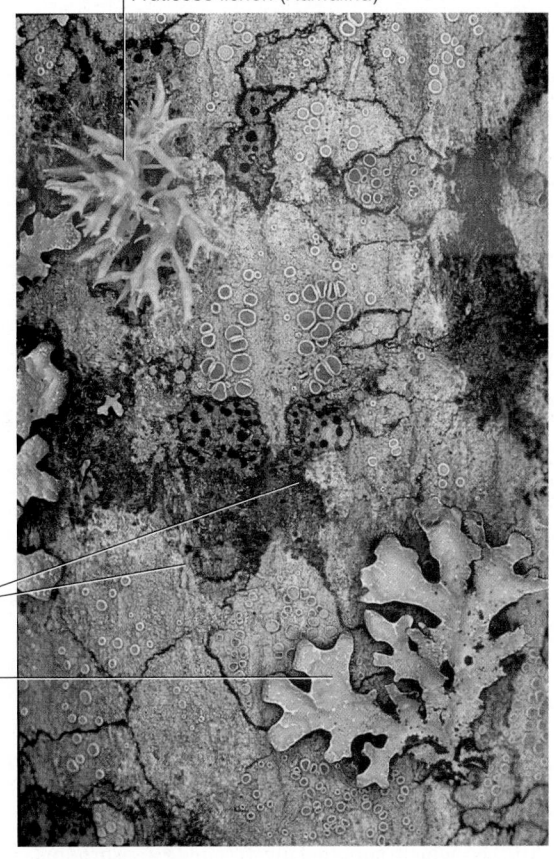
Fruticose lichen (*Ramalina*)

Crustose lichens
(*Bacidia, Lecanora*)

Foliose lichen
(*Parmelia*)

Fred M. Rhoades

(b) Lichens vary in color, shape, and overall appearance. Three growth forms—crustose, foliose, and fruticose—are shown on a maple branch in Washington State.

Soredia

Surface layer (fungal hyphae)

Fungal hyphae interwoven with photoautotroph

Loosely woven hyphae

Bottom layer (fungal hyphae)

Rock or other surface to which lichen is attached

(a) This cross section of a typical lichen shows distinct layers. The soredium (pl., *soredia*), an asexual reproductive structure, consists of clusters of algal or cyanobacterial cells enclosed by fungal hyphae.

FIGURE 29-20 *Animated* Lichens
These organisms are a combination of a fungus and an alga or cyanobacterium.

Review

- What is the ecological importance of fungal decomposers?
- What is the importance of mycorrhizae?
- What is a lichen?

29.5 ECONOMIC, BIOLOGICAL, AND MEDICAL IMPACT OF FUNGI

■ LEARNING OBJECTIVES

10 Summarize some specific ways that fungi impact humans economically.

11 Summarize the importance of fungi to biology and medicine; describe how fungi infect plants and humans, describing at least one fungal animal disease and one fungal plant disease.

The same powerful digestive enzymes that fungi use to decompose wastes and dead organisms can also be used with great efficiency to reduce wood, fiber, and food to their basic components. Many species of basidiomycetes have enzymes that break down the lignin in wood. (Lignin is the second most abundant organic compound on Earth, second only to cellulose.) From the human perspective,

various fungi cause incalculable damage to stored goods and building materials each year. Bracket fungi, for example, cause enormous losses by decaying wood, both in living trees and in stored lumber.

Some fungi cause serious diseases in animals and plants. Yet fungi also contribute to our quality of life. They are responsible for economic gains as well as losses. People eat them and grow them to make various medications, such as penicillin. We use them to make certain industrial chemicals and for bioremediation. Renewable fuel companies are actively searching for fungi and other microbes that can produce fuel. Recently, a fungus was discovered that synthesizes 55 hydrocarbons, perhaps to inhibit the growth of other organisms. Researchers may be able to use the genes of this fungus to engineer other microorganisms to more efficiently produce fuel.

Fungi provide beverages and food

Humans exploit the ability of yeasts to produce bread and alcoholic beverages. Yeasts produce ethyl alcohol and carbon dioxide from glucose and other sugars by fermentation (see Chapter 8).

Yeast species of the genus *Saccharomyces* (ascomycetes) are used to produce wine, beer, and other fermented beverages. Wine is produced when yeasts ferment fruit sugar, and beer results when yeasts ferment sugar derived from starch in grains (usually barley).

Saccharomyces cerevisiae, referred to as baker's yeast, is used to bake bread, pizza, and other wheat products. During the process of making bread, carbon dioxide produced by yeast becomes trapped in dough as bubbles, causing the dough to rise; this gives leavened bread its light quality. Both the carbon dioxide and the alcohol produced by the yeast escape during baking.

The unique flavor of cheeses such as Roquefort, Brie, Gorgonzola, and Camembert is produced by species of *Penicillium.* For example, *P. roquefortii,* found in caves near the French village of Roquefort, is used to make Roquefort cheese. By French law, only cheeses produced in this area can be called Roquefort cheese. (The blue spots in Roquefort and certain other cheeses are masses of conidia.)

Aspergillus tamarii and certain other fungi are used to produce soy sauce by fermenting soybeans with the fungi for at least three months. (In the United States, soy sauce is often made by adding flavoring to salt water rather than by soaking fermented soybeans.) Soy sauce enriches other foods with more than just its special flavor. It also adds vital amino acids from both the soybeans and the fungi themselves, which, in some parts of the world, supplement a low-protein rice diet.

Among the basidiomycetes, there are some 200 kinds of edible mushrooms and about 70 species of poisonous ones. Many edible mushrooms are cultivated commercially. The mushroom *Agaricus brunnescens* is the principal fungal species grown extensively for food. About 30 other mushroom species, such as oyster, shiitake, portobello, and straw mushrooms, are available in supermarkets. Morels, which superficially resemble mushrooms, and truffles, which produce underground fruiting bodies, are ascomycetes (**FIG. 29-21**). Truffles are now cultivated as mycorrhizal fungi on the roots of tree seedlings.

Edible and poisonous mushrooms can look very much alike and may even belong to the same genus. There is no simple way to tell them apart; an expert must identify them. Some of the most poisonous mushrooms belong to the genus *Amanita* (**FIG. 29-22**). Toxic species of this genus have been appropriately called such

names as "destroying angel" (*A. virosa*) and "death cap" (*A. phalloides*). Eating a single mushroom of either species can be fatal.

Certain species of mushrooms cause intoxication and hallucinations. The sacred mushrooms of the Aztecs—*Conocybe* and *Psilocybe*—are still used in religious ceremonies by native peoples of Central America for their hallucinogenic properties. The chemical ingredient *psilocybin* is responsible for the trances and visions experienced by those who eat these mushrooms. Ingestion of psychoactive mushrooms is dangerous because negative reactions vary considerably, from mild indigestion, sweating, and heart palpitations, to death. In addition, the possession and use of such mushrooms are illegal in the United States and some other countries.

Fungi are important to modern biology and medicine

The yeast *Saccharomyces cerevisiae* has served as a model eukaryotic cell (see Fig. 17-6a). It was the first eukaryote whose genome was sequenced, and with its 6000 genes, it has the smallest genome of any eukaryotic model organism. Molecular biologists are in the process of determining the functions of the proteins encoded by its genes. Biologists have used *S. cerevisiae* to study molecular genetics, including how genes regulate cell division. Researchers continue to use this yeast to study such problems as genetic recombination, and the correlation between cell age and cancer. *Saccharomyces cerevisiae* is also being used to study the mechanism of action of antifungal drugs and resistance to these drugs.

Biologists have used the ascomycete *Aspergillus nidulans,* an opportunistic pathogen of humans, to study mitosis and other cell processes. This fungus has provided valuable knowledge about the genetics of microtubules. Biologists are using recombinant DNA techniques to manipulate yeasts and certain filamentous fungi to produce important biological molecules, such as hormones. Among the many genes that have been cloned in yeast are those for insulin, human growth hormone, and molecules important in

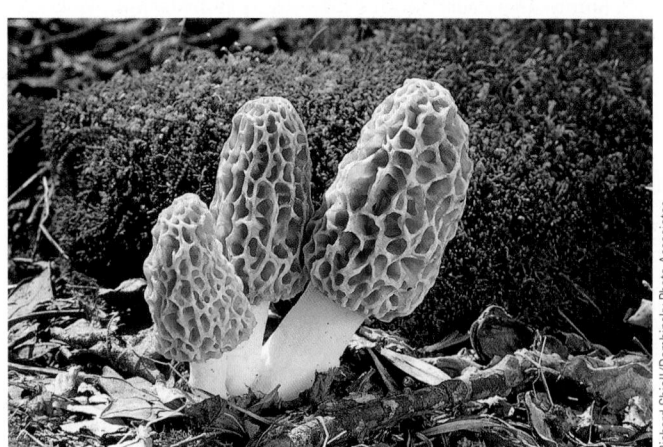

Richard Shiell/Dembinsky Photo Associates

John D. Cunningham/Visuals Unlimited

(a) The yellow morel (Morchella esculenta). This morel grows 6 to 10 cm (2.5 to 4 in) tall. It is found throughout North America. Photographed in Michigan.

FIGURE 29-21 Edible ascomycetes

(b) The Oregon white truffle (*Tuber gibbosum*). The truffle, which is found underground near Douglas firs and possibly oak trees in British Columbia and northern California, is 1 to 5 cm (0.4 to 2 in) wide. People find these subterranean ascocarps with the help of trained dogs or pigs. Here, truffles are shown whole and sectioned to show the conspicuous white, marbled tissue.

FIGURE 29-22 Poisonous mushrooms

The destroying angel (*Amanita virosa*) is an extremely poisonous mushroom that is distinguished, as are other amanitas, by the ring of tissue around its stalk and by the underground cup from which the stalk protrudes. About 50 g (2 oz) of this mushroom can kill an adult man. The destroying angel, which is 7.5 to 20 cm (3 to 8 in) tall, is found in grass or near trees throughout North America.

immune function. These procedures allow researchers to produce unlimited amounts of these compounds for study and eventual medical use.

Fungi produce useful drugs and chemicals. Discovered in 1928 by the British bacteriologist Alexander Fleming, penicillin, produced by the mold *Penicillium notatum*, is still among the most widely used and effective antibiotics (see Chapter 1). Other drugs derived from fungi include the cephalosporin antibiotics (produced by *Cephalosporium*), statins (used to lower blood cholesterol levels), and cyclosporine (used to suppress immune responses in patients who receive organ transplants). Fumagillin, a chemical produced by the ascomycete *Aspergillus fumigatus*, inhibits the formation of new blood vessels. Because solid tumors need a rich blood supply, fumagillin shows promise as an anticancer agent. Fumagillin is also used to treat diseases caused by microsporidia. Researchers have identified several other promising compounds produced by fungi that are antiviral or that destroy cancer cells.

The ascomycete *Claviceps purpurea* infects the flowers of rye plants and other cereals. It produces a structure called an *ergot* where a seed would normally form in the grain head. When livestock eat this grain or when humans eat bread made from ergot-contaminated rye flour, they may be poisoned by the extremely toxic substances in the ergot. However, some ergot compounds are now used clinically in small quantities as drugs to induce labor, to stop uterine bleeding, to treat high blood pressure, and to relieve one type of migraine headache.

Fungi are used in bioremediation and to biologically control pests

Some fungi can biodegrade pesticides, herbicides, coal tars, and petroleum. Fungi convert these products into carbon dioxide and the basic elements of which they are composed. These fungi can be used along with certain bacteria to decontaminate farm land and to clean up oil spills.

Researchers are investigating fungi—for example, certain species of microsporidia—for the biological control of pathogens and insect pests. Some of these species are already being used to parasitize insect pests. In some cases, they interfere with reproduction in their insect host. Other microsporidia completely control the metabolism and reproduction of the host. Researchers are studying the use of microsporidia in controlling the spread of malaria. A recent study showed that when female *Anopheles* mosquitoes are infected with microsporidia, their blood feeding is decreased. Fungal infection of the mosquito also interferes with development of *Plasmodium*, the protist that causes malaria.

Some fungi cause diseases in humans and other animals

Certain ascomycetes cause superficial infections in which only the skin, hair, or nails are infected. Ringworm, athlete's foot, and jock itch are examples of superficial fungal infections. Because these fungi infect dead layers of skin that are not fed by capillaries, the immune system cannot launch an effective response.

Many pathogenic fungi are opportunists that cause infections only when the body's immune system is compromised, for example, in patients with HIV. Cancer patients and organ transplant recipients who are given medication to suppress their immune systems are also at risk. *Candida* is an ascomycete that inhabits the human mouth and vagina. The immune system and the normal bacteria of these regions normally prevent this yeast from causing infection. However, when the immune system is compromised, *Candida* multiplies, causing thrush, a painful yeast infection of the mouth, throat, and vagina.

The ascomycete *Aspergillus fumigatus* is usually harmless but causes aspergillosis in people with lowered immune function. During the course of aspergillosis, the fungus can invade the lungs, heart, brain, kidneys, and other vital organs and cause death.

Other fungi infect internal tissues and organs and may spread through many regions of the body. Histoplasmosis, for example, is a lung infection caused by inhaling spores of a fungus common in soil contaminated with bird feces. Most people in the eastern and midwestern parts of the United States have been exposed to this fungus at some time, and an estimated 40 million Americans have had mild infections. Fortunately, the infection is usually confined to the lungs and is of short duration, but if the infection spreads through the blood to the heart, brain, or other parts of the body, it can be serious and sometimes fatal.

Some fungi produce poisonous compounds collectively called **mycotoxins.** A few species of *Aspergillus*, for example, produce potent mycotoxins called **aflatoxins** that harm the liver and are known carcinogens. Foods on which aflatoxin-producing fungi commonly grow include peanuts, pecans, corn, and other grains. Other foods that may contain traces of aflatoxins include animal products such as milk, eggs, and meat (from animals that consumed feed contaminated by aflatoxin). Avoiding aflatoxin in the diet is impossible, but exposure should be minimized as much as possible. Any human food or animal forage product that has become moldy should be suspected of aflatoxin contamination and should be discarded.

Fungi contribute to sick-building syndrome, a situation in which occupants of a building experience acute adverse health effects linked to the time they spend in a given building. Mold-related insurance claims amount to hundreds of millions of dollars each year. When conditions are moist, molds can grow on carpets, leather, cloth, wood, insulation, and food. Mold spores, fragments, and mold products make their way into the air, and people are exposed through inhalation as well as by skin contact.

Exposure to molds and their toxins has been linked to depressed immune function, irritation of the throat and respiratory passageways, infection, and toxicity. The most common responses to mold exposure are allergic reactions that range from mild to severe illnesses, including hay fever, sinusitis, asthma, and dermatitis.

Fungi cause many important plant diseases

Fungi are more destructive to plants than any other disease-causing organism. They are responsible for about 70% of all major crop diseases. Fungi cause serious epidemic diseases that spread rapidly and often result in complete crop failure. Fungal plant diseases costs billions of dollars in agricultural damage yearly.

All plants are apparently susceptible to some fungal infection. Damage may be localized in certain tissues or structures of the plant, or the disease may be systemic and spread throughout the entire plant. Fungal infections may cause stunting of plant parts or of the plant; they may cause wartlike growths or kill the plant.

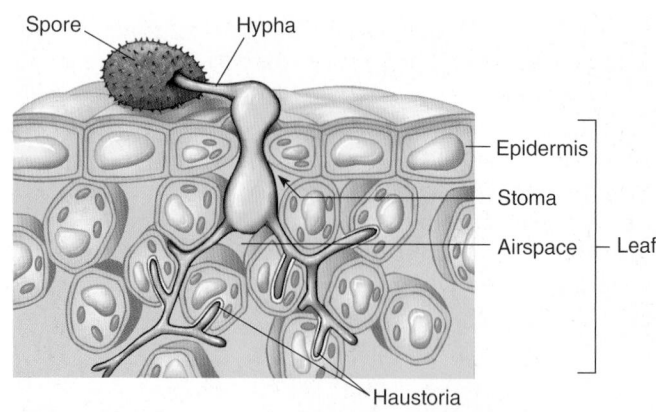

FIGURE 29-23 How a fungus parasitizes a plant
In this example, the hypha enters the leaf through a stoma. The hypha grows, branching extensively through the internal air spaces, and penetrates plant cells with specialized hyphal extensions called haustoria.

A plant often becomes infected after hyphae enter through stomata (pores) in the leaf or stem or through wounds in the plant body (**FIG. 29-23**). Alternatively, the fungus may produce *cutinase*, an enzyme that dissolves the waxy cuticle that covers the surface of leaves and stems. After dissolving the cuticle, the fungus easily invades the plant tissues. As the mycelium grows, it may stay mainly between the plant cells or it may penetrate the cells. Parasitic fungi often produce special hyphal branches called **haustoria** (sing., *haustorium*) that penetrate the host cells and obtain nourishment from the cytoplasm.

Ascomycetes cause serious plant diseases, including powdery mildew, chestnut blight, Dutch elm disease, apple scab, wilt on potatoes, and brown rot, which attacks cherries, peaches, plums, and

(a) Brown rot of peaches. This disease is caused by *Monilinia fruticola*, an ascomycete. Photographed in Oregon.

(b) Corn smut on an ear of sweet corn. This fungal disease is caused by *Ustilago maydis*, a basidiomycete.

(c) Black stem rust infection on wheat (*Triticum* sp.) stem. This plant disease is caused by *Puccinia graminis*, a basidiomycete.

FIGURE 29-24 Fungi that cause plant diseases

apricots (**FIG. 29-24a**). Basidiomycetes cause smuts and rusts that attack corn, wheat, oats, and other grains (**FIG. 29-24b** and **c**).

Some fungal parasites, such as the basidiomycete (*Puccinia graminis*) that causes black stem rust of wheat, have complex life cycles that involve two or more different host plants and the production of several kinds of spores. Before the late 1950s, black stem rust outbreaks occurred every few years somewhere in the world, destroying entire wheat crops. By the early 1960s, Nobel prize winner Norman Borlaug and other researchers had developed rust-resistant varieties of wheat, heralding in the green revolution. However, new mutations have put *Puccinia* and wheat rust back in the news. The new strain has spread through parts of Africa and into the Middle East. Each fungus releases billions of spores, which the wind can blow for hundreds of miles, spreading the fun-

gus to new regions of the world. Its spread may lead to widespread food shortages. The *Puccinia* genome has recently been sequenced, and researchers are developing methods to quickly diagnose the disease. They are also working to develop new varieties of disease-resistant wheat.

Review

- Some dictionaries erroneously define a morel as a type of mushroom. Why is this definition incorrect?
- How are fungi important in modern biology and medicine?
- What are three important fungal diseases of humans?
- Why is the mutated strain of the fungus that causes wheat rust of serious concern?

■ SUMMARY: FOCUS ON LEARNING OBJECTIVES

29.1 *(page 602)*

1 Describe the distinguishing characteristics of fungi.

- **Fungi** are eukaryotic heterotrophs that secrete digestive enzymes onto their food source and then absorb the predigested food. Fungi are characterized by cell walls that contain **chitin.**

2 Describe the body plan of a fungus.

- A fungus may be a unicellular **yeast** or a filamentous, multicellular **mold.** The body of most multicellular fungi consists of long, thread-like filaments called **hyphae** that branch and form a tangled mass called a **mycelium.**

    CENGAGENOW™   Learn more about mycelia by clicking on the figure in CengageNOW.

- In most fungi, perforated **septa,** or cross walls, divide the hyphae into individual cells. In some fungi, the hyphae are **coenocytic,** that is, they form an elongated, multinuclear cell.

29.2 *(page 603)*

3 Describe the life cycle of a typical fungus, including sexual and asexual reproduction.

- Most fungi reproduce both sexually and asexually by means of **spores.** Spores are produced on aerial hyphae. When fungal spores land in a suitable spot, they germinate.
- When fungi of two different mating types meet, their hyphae fuse, a process called **plasmogamy.** The cytoplasm fuses, but the nuclei remain separate. The fungi enter a **dikaryotic** ($n + n$) stage in which each new cell formed has one nucleus of each type.
- **Karyogamy,** fusion of the nuclei, takes place in the hyphal tip and results in a diploid ($2n$) **zygote nucleus.**
- Meiosis produces four genetically different haploid (n) nuclei. Each nucleus becomes part of a spore. When the spores germinate, they form new mycelia by mitosis.
- Genetically similar asexual spores are produced by mitosis. When these spores germinate, they also develop into mycelia.

29.3 *(page 605)*

4 Give arguments to support the hypothesis that fungi are opisthokonts, more closely related to animals than to plants.

- Like animals, some fungi have flagellate cells—for example, chytrid gametes and spores; the flagellate cells propel themselves with a single posterior flagellum. Also like animal cells, fungal mitochondria have platelike cristae.

- Based on chemical and structural characters, fungi are classified, along with animals and choanoflagellates, as **opisthokonts.**

5 Give arguments to support the hypothesis that chytrids may have been the earliest fungal group to evolve from the most recent common ancestor of fungi.

- **Chytrids,** or **chytridiomycetes,** produce flagellate spores at some stage in their life cycle. No other fungi have flagella. Thus, chytrids probably were the earliest fungi to evolve; the most recent common ancestor of all fungi was a flagellate protist.

6 List distinguishing characteristics, describe a typical life cycle, and give examples of each of the following fungal groups: chytridiomycetes, zygomycetes, glomeromycetes, ascomycetes, and basidiomycetes.

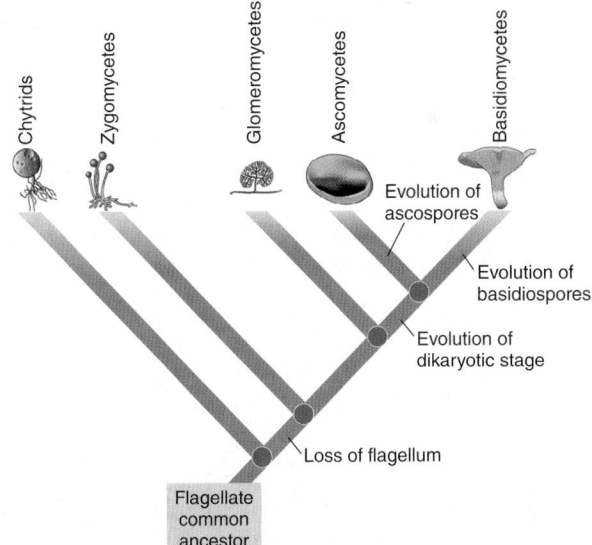

- Chytrids reproduce both asexually and sexually. Their gametes and zoospores are flagellate. *Allomyces,* a common chytrid, spends part of its life as a multicellular haploid **thallus** and part as a multicellular diploid thallus. The haploid thallus produces two types of flagellate gametes that fuse. Both plasmogamy and karyogamy occur, producing a flagellate zygote. The diploid thallus bears zoosporangia that produce diploid **zoospores** and resting sporangia in which haploid zoospores form by meiosis. The haploid zoospores form new haploid thalli.

- **Zygomycetes,** such as the black bread mold, *Rhizopus,* form a haploid thallus that produces both asexual spores and sexual spores. Asexual spores germinate and form new thalli. In sexual reproduction, hyphae of two different haploid mating types form gametangia. Plasmogamy occurs as the gametangia fuse. Karyogamy occurs, and a diploid zygote is formed; the zygote develops into a **zygospore.** Meiosis produces recombinant haploid zygospores. When zygospores germinate, each hypha develops a sporangium at its tip. Spores are released and develop into new hyphae.

- **Microsporidia,** currently classified as zygomycetes, are opportunistic pathogens that penetrate and infect animal cells with their long, threadlike **polar tubes.**

- **Glomeromycetes** have coenocytic hyphae. They reproduce asexually with large, multinucleate spores called blastospores. Glomeromycetes are symbionts that form intracellular associations called **mycorrhizae** with the roots of plants. Because they extend their hyphae into root cells, glomeromycetes are **endomycorrhizal fungi.** The most common endomycorrhizae are called **arbuscular mycorrhizae** because the hyphae inside the root cells form branched, tree-shaped structures known as **arbuscules.**

- **Ascomycetes** include yeasts, cup fungi, morels, truffles, and blue-green, pink and brown molds. Some ascomycetes form mycorrhizae; others form lichens. Ascomycetes produce asexual spores called **conidia;** they produce sexual spores called **ascospores** in saclike **asci.** The asci line a fruiting body called an **ascocarp.**

- In ascomycetes, haploid mycelia of opposite mating types produce septate hyphae. Plasmogamy occurs, and nuclei are exchanged. A dikaryotic *n* + *n* stage occurs in which hyphae form and produce asci and an ascocarp. Karyogamy occurs, followed by meiosis. The recombinant nuclei divide by mitosis, producing eight haploid nuclei that develop into ascospores. When the ascospores germinate, they can form new mycelia.

- **Basidiomycetes** include mushrooms, puffballs, bracket fungi, rusts, and smuts.

- These fungi produce sexual spores called **basidiospores** on the outside of a **basidium.** Basidia develop on the surface of **gills** in mushrooms; mushrooms are a type of **basidiocarp** (a fruiting body).

- Hyphae in the basidiomycetes have septa. Plasmogamy occurs with the fusion of two hyphae of different mating types. A dikaryotic secondary mycelium forms. Then a basidiocarp develops, and basidia form. Karyogamy occurs, producing a diploid zygote nucleus. Meiosis produces four haploid nuclei that become basidiospores. When basidiospores germinate, they form haploid primary mycelia.

CENGAGENOW™ Explore fungus life cycles by clicking on the figures in CengageNOW.

29.4 *(page 615)*

7 Summarize the ecological significance of fungi as decomposers.

- Most fungi are decomposers that break down organic compounds in dead organisms, leaves, garbage, and wastes into simpler nutrients that can be recycled.

8 Describe the important ecological role of mycorrhizae.

- Mycorrhizae are mutualistic associations between fungi and the roots of plants. The fungus supplies water and nutrient minerals to the plant; the fungus obtains organic compounds from the plant. Glomeromycetes form endomycorrhizae with roots. Ascomycetes and basidiomycetes form **ectomycorrhizae** with tree roots; they do not penetrate the root cells.

9 Characterize the unique nature of a lichen.

- A **lichen** is a combination of a fungus and a photoautotroph (an alga or cyanobacterium). In this symbiotic relationship, the photoautotroph provides the fungus with organic compounds. The fungus may provide the photoautotroph with shelter, water, and minerals. Lichens have three main forms: crustose, foliose, and fruticose.

CENGAGENOW™ Learn more about lichens by clicking on the figure in CengageNOW.

29.5 *(page 619)*

10 Summarize some specific ways that fungi impact humans economically.

- Fungi cause huge economic losses by damaging food and crops. On the other hand, some fungi, like mushrooms, are foods; others, like yeasts, are used to produce beer, wine, and bread, and still others are used to produce cheeses or industrial chemicals.

11 Summarize the importance of fungi to biology and medicine; describe how fungi infect plants and humans, describing at least one fungal animal disease and one fungal plant disease.

- Biologists use the yeast *Saccharomyces cerevisiae* and other fungi as model organisms for research in molecular biology and genetics. Fungi are also being investigated for the biological control of insects, such as the mosquitoes that transmit malaria.

- Fungi are used to make many medications, including penicillin and other antibiotics; they are used in bioremediation and to biologically control pests.

- Fungi are opportunistic pathogens in humans. They cause human diseases, such as histoplasmosis; some fungi produce **mycotoxins,** such as **aflatoxins,** which can cause liver damage and cancer.

- Fungal hyphae infect plants through stomata. Hyphal branches called **haustoria** penetrate plant cells and obtain nourishment from the cytoplasm. Fungi cause many important plant diseases, including brown rot, corn smut, and wheat rust.

TEST YOUR UNDERSTANDING

1. Fungi are (a) eukaryotes and opisthokonts (b) prokaryotes and opisthokonts (c) flagellate and dikaryotic (d) autotrophic eukaryotes (e) heterotrophs with cellulose cell walls

2. Which of the following fungi does not have a mycelium? (a) black bread mold (b) yeast (c) decomposer cup fungus (d) cultivated mushroom (e) *Penicillium*

3. A cell described as *n* + *n* is (a) monokaryotic (b) diploid (c) haploid (d) coenocytic (e) dikaryotic

4. With the exception of chytridiomycetes, fungi are generally disseminated by (a) water currents (b) fragmentation of hyphae (c) soredia (d) airborne spores (e) flagellate zoospores

5. Which statement is *not* true of the chytrids? (a) they are simple aquatic fungi (b) they produce motile cells with single, posterior flagella (c) they undergo both sexual and asexual reproduction (d) their cells are dikaryotic (e) they were the earliest fungi to evolve

6. Which statement is *not* true of the zygomycetes? (a) many members of this group form endomycorrhizae with tree roots (b) their sexual spores are called zygospores (c) they undergo both sexual and asexual reproduction (d) plasmogamy and karyogamy occur (e) they have coenocytic hyphae

7. Glomeromycetes (a) reproduce mainly by sexual spores called glomerospores (b) are characterized by unique structures called polar tubes (c) associate with cyanobacteria to form lichens (d) include many opportunistic pathogens that cause human disease (e) form arbuscular endomycorrhizae with tree roots

8. The ascomycete life cycle typically includes (a) mainly diploid thalli (b) the formation of a thick zygosporangium (c) the production of eight haploid ascospores within an ascus (d) the production of microsporidia (e) the production of ascospores, zoospores, and conidia at different stages

9. Which statement is *not* true of the basidiomycetes? (a) they produce a secondary mycelium with $n + n$ hyphae (b) their sexual spores are called basidiospores (c) they have a diploid thallus that produces zoospores (d) reproduction is mainly sexual (e) they have microscopic basidia

10. A combination organism consisting of a photoautotroph and a fungus is called _____ (a) an arbuscular endomycorrhiza (b) an ectomycorrhiza (c) a lichen (d) a pathogenic agent (e) an aflatoxin

11. Mutualistic associations between fungi and the roots of plants are called (a) lichens (b) mycorrhizae (c) pathogenic associations (d) parasitic haustoria (e) mycotoxic symbioses

12. When a fungus infects a plant, it (a) infiltrates leaves with lichens (b) forms relationships by attaching mycorrhizae to stems (c) secretes powerful digestive juices onto the leaves (d) uses haustoria to dissolve roots (e) enters leaves or stems through stomata

CRITICAL THINKING

1. Explain the statement "Mushrooms are like the tips of icebergs." If you do not see mushrooms in your lawn, can you conclude that no fungi live there? Why or why not?

2. **EVOLUTION LINK.** Justify (a) classifying fungi as opisthokonts; (b) classifying microsporidia as fungi; (c) grouping ascomycetes and basidiomycetes as sister clades.

3. **SCIENCE, TECHNOLOGY, AND SOCIETY.** Biologists have discovered that many mycorrhizal fungi are sensitive to a low pH. What human-caused environmental problem may prove catastrophic for these fungi? How may this problem affect their plant partners? What measure could we take to decrease the problem?

4. The secondary mycelium of a basidiomycete is shown here. (a) How would you describe its cells? (b) What stage of its life cycle is it in? (c) Draw the next steps in this stage of its life cycle.

Additional questions are available in CengageNOW at www.cengage.com/login.

30 An Introduction to Animal Diversity

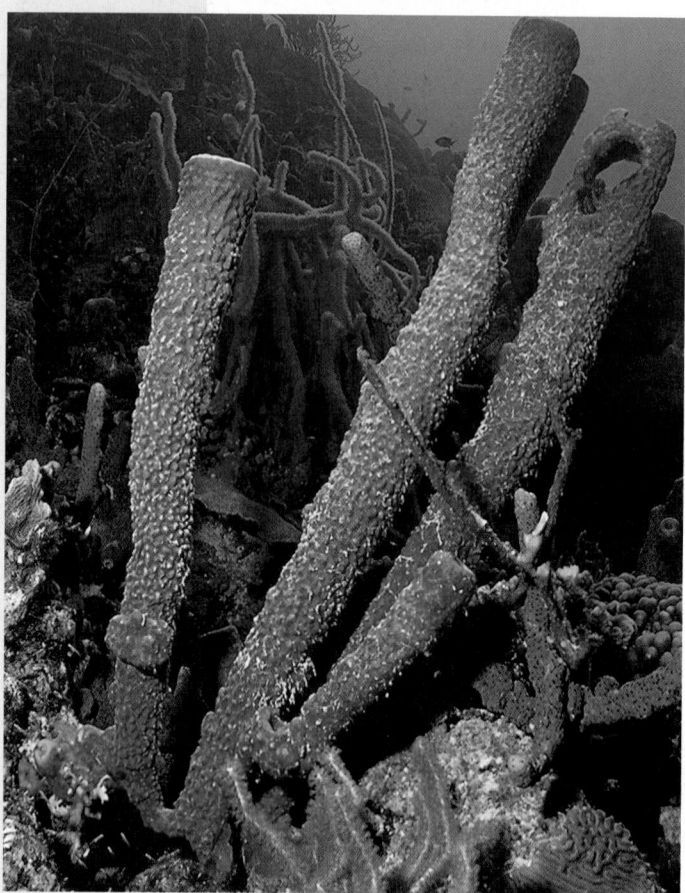

The tube sponge (*Callyspongia vaginalis*). This animal, sometimes mistaken for a plant, ranges in color from purple to blue to gray. It is common on coral reefs in the Caribbean, from Florida to Mexico.

Charles V. Angelo/Photo Researchers, Inc.

KEY CONCEPTS

30.1 Although they are a diverse group, animals share many characters. They are multicellular, eukaryotic heterotrophs composed of cells specialized to perform specific functions. Most animals are diploid organisms that reproduce sexually, and most have a nervous and muscular system.

30.2 Animals evolved in marine environments, and members of most animal phyla still inhabit marine environments. However, many animals are adapted to life in fresh water and others to terrestrial habitats.

30.3 The common ancestors of animals are choanoflagellates; choanoflagellates, fungi, and animals are a monophyletic group known as opisthokonts.

30.4 Biologists classify animals based on many characteristics, including their morphology, features of their early development, and on molecular data; they generally agree that bilateral animals split into at least three major clades.

Although members of most animal species are readily recognizable as animals, the identity of some others is less obvious. Early naturalists thought sponges were plants because they did not move from place to place. Some people still mistake certain marine animals, such as sponges and corals, for plants (see photograph). Locomotion is not a requirement for being classified as an animal.

Animal phylogeny is an exciting and rapidly changing field of study. Biologists have described and named more than 1.5 million species of animals, and 15,000 to 20,000 new species are named each year. Millions more probably remain to be discovered and classified. Interestingly, an estimated 99% of all animal species that ever inhabited our planet are extinct. Taxonomists have assigned the extant (living) animals to about 35 phyla. Molecular studies have confirmed that many of these groups are **monophyletic,** that is they consist of *all* of the descendants and *only* the descendants of a common ancestor. (Recall from Chapter 23 that a monophyletic group is called a **clade.**)

Animal groups that are not monophyletic have been split or reorganized, with some members of the groups being reassigned to other taxa. It is important to remember that the classification of animals and the relative positions of animal groups are a work in progress. As they consider new data, systematists redraw the tree of animal life.

In this chapter we discuss the characters of animals and their habitats. We then explore animal origins and some of the criteria biologists use to determine evolutionary relationships and to classify animals. In Chapter 31 we describe three phyla traditionally viewed as diverging early in the evolutionary history of animals. Then we discuss one of the major clades of animals: the protostomes. (In Chapter 32 we focus on the deuterostomes, which include the echinoderms and chordates—the clade to which we belong.) Many hypotheses are presented in these chapters, and we will discuss many examples of how systematists revise the relationships of the branches of the animal phylogenetic tree in response to new data.

30.1 ANIMAL CHARACTERS

◼ LEARNING OBJECTIVE

1   Describe several characteristics common to most animals.

Animals are so diverse that for almost any definition we can find exceptions. We can best describe animals by the characteristics they share:

1. Animals are multicellular eukaryotes. In contrast to plants, algae, and fungi, their cells lack cell walls. Instead, structural support depends on collagen and other structural proteins. Collagen is an important *shared derived character* in animals (see Chapter 23).

2. Animals are **heterotrophs.** As consumers, they depend on producers for their raw materials and energy. In contrast to the fungi, most animals ingest their food first and then digest it inside the body, usually within a digestive system.

3. Cells that make up the animal body are specialized to perform specific functions. In all but the simplest animals, cells are organized to form tissues, and tissues are organized to form organs. In small animals with simple body plans, life processes such as gas exchange, circulation of materials, and waste disposal can take place by diffusion of gases and other substances directly to and from the environment. Specialized organ systems perform these functions in large animals.

4. Animals have diverse body plans. The term **body plan** refers to the basic structure and functional design of the body. An animal's body plan and lifestyle are adapted to its methods of obtaining food and reproducing.

5. Most animals are capable of locomotion at some time during their life cycle. Some animals (such as sponges and corals) move about as larvae (immature forms) but are **sessile** (firmly attached to the ground or some other surface) as adults (see chapter opening photograph).

6. Most animals have nervous systems and muscle systems that enable them to respond rapidly to stimuli in their environment.

7. Most animals are diploid organisms that reproduce sexually, with large, nonmotile eggs and small, flagellate sperm. A haploid sperm unites with a haploid egg, forming a diploid **zygote** (fertilized egg).

8. Animals go through a period of embryonic development. The zygote undergoes **cleavage,** a series of mitotic cell divisions. During cleavage the zygote develops into a hollow ball of cells called a **blastula.** Although some animals develop directly into adults, the majority first develop into a **larva,** a sexually immature form that may look very different from the adult (**FIG. 30-1**). The larva differs from the adult in many ways, including where it lives (its habitat), how it moves, and what it eats. Larvae typically go through **metamorphosis,** a developmental process that converts the immature animal into a juvenile form that can then grow into an adult.

Review

-   For centuries, scientists classified sponges as plants, but now they are classified as animals. What criteria do biologists use to classify them as animals?

30.2 ADAPTATIONS TO OCEAN, FRESHWATER, AND TERRESTRIAL HABITATS

◼ LEARNING OBJECTIVE

2   Compare the advantages and disadvantages of life in the ocean, in fresh water, and on land.

Fossil evidence suggests that animals evolved in shallow, marine environments during the Proterozoic eon, at least 600 million years ago (mya; see Chapter 21). Although animals are now distributed in virtually every environment, at least some members of most animal phyla still inhabit marine environments.

Marine habitats offer many advantages

The buoyancy of sea water provides support, and its large volume keeps the water temperature relatively stable. The body fluids of most invertebrates have about the same osmotic concentration as sea water, so fluid and salt balance are more easily maintained than in fresh water. **Plankton,** which consists of the mainly microscopic animals and protists that are suspended in water and float with its movement, provides a ready source of food for many aquatic animals.

Life in the ocean also presents some challenges. Although the continuous motion of water brings nutrients to animals and washes their wastes away, animals must be able to cope with the water's movements and the currents that could sweep them away. Squids, fishes, and marine mammals have evolved as strong swimmers, usually able to direct their movements and maintain their location. However, most invertebrates and young

(a) Spiny lobster larva. This larva is hitching a ride on a jellyfish. Over a period of months, the larva passes through several stages before becoming an adult. Photographed in open ocean at night, Hawaii.

(b) Adult spiny lobster. The adult has two long antennae used to sense movement. Spiny lobsters lack large claws. The spines on their back help protect them. In this image you can see the two large spines above the animal's eyes. Spiny lobsters leave their hiding places at night to hunt.

FIGURE 30-1 Larva and adult spiny lobster (*Panulirus* sp.)

Most animals go through a larva stage before developing into an adult. The larva usually differs from the adult in size, appearance, and in lifestyle.

vertebrates cannot swim strongly, and they have adapted in various ways to the tides and currents.

Some sessile animals attach permanently to a stable structure such as a rock. Others burrow in the sand and silt that cover the sea bottom. Many invertebrates have adapted by maintaining a small body size and becoming part of the plankton. As they are tossed about, their food supply continues to surround them.

Some animals are adapted to freshwater habitats

Far fewer kinds of animals make their homes in fresh water than in the ocean because living in this habitat is more difficult. Fresh water is hypotonic to the tissue fluids of animals, so water tends to move into the animal by osmosis. To survive in this habitat, freshwater species must have mechanisms for removing excess water while retaining salts. This *osmoregulation* requires an expenditure of energy.

Fresh water offers a much less constant environment than sea water. Animals that inhabit fresh water must have adaptations for surviving variations in oxygen content, temperature, turbidity (because of sediments suspended in the water), and even water volume. In addition, fresh water generally contains less food than the sea.

Terrestrial living requires major adaptations

Living on land is even more difficult than living in fresh water, and the evolution of terrestrial animals involved major adaptations. Analyzing the fossil record, many biologists hypothesize that the first air-breathing terrestrial animals were scorpion-like arthropods that came ashore in the Silurian period about 444 mya. The first vertebrates to inhabit terrestrial environments, the amphibians, did not appear until the Devonian period, about 30 million years later.

The chief problem facing all terrestrial organisms is desiccation (drying out). Water is constantly lost by evaporation and is often difficult to replace. A body covering adapted to minimize fluid loss helps solve this problem in many terrestrial animals (**FIG. 30-2**). Location of the respiratory surface deep within the animal also helps prevent fluid loss. Thus, the gills of aquatic animals are typically located externally, but lungs and tracheal tubes of terrestrial animals are typically found deep within the body.

Reproduction on land also poses challenges to protect gametes and the developing offspring from desiccation. Aquatic animals typically shed their gametes in the water, where fertilization occurs. The surrounding water also serves as an effective shock absorber that protects the delicate embryos as they develop. Some land animals, including most amphibians, return to the water for reproduction, and their larval forms develop in the water.

The evolution of internal fertilization has permitted many terrestrial animals, including earthworms, land snails, insects, reptiles, birds, and mammals, to meet the desiccation challenge. Because these terrestrial animals transfer sperm from the body of the male directly into the body of the female by copulation, a watery medium continuously surrounds the sperm. Another important adaptation to reproduction on land is the tough, protective shell that surrounds the eggs of many species (see Fig. 30-2). Secreted by the female, this shell protects the developing embryo from drying out.

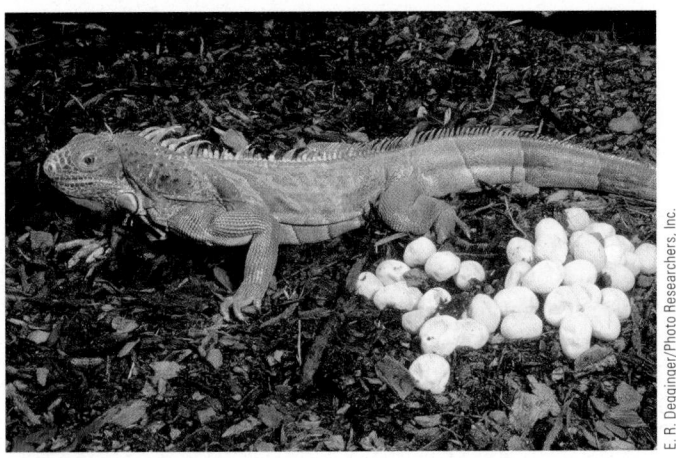

FIGURE 30-2 Adaptations to terrestrial life
The tough, horny skin of the green iguana (*Iguana iguana*) has scales and is water resistant. Leathery eggs protect the embryos from drying out.

An alternative adaptation for terrestrial reproduction is development of the embryo within the moist body of the mother.

Water has buoyancy that helps support animals that inhabit this environment. Air is less dense than water, and to inhabit the land, animals must have structures, such as a skeletal system and muscles, that support the body. The temperature extremes of terrestrial habitats also present challenges. In later chapters we discuss behavioral and physiological adaptations for maintaining body temperature.

Review

- What are some advantages of marine environments over freshwater and terrestrial habitats?
- What are some animal adaptations to the terrestrial environment?

30.3 ANIMAL EVOLUTION

■ LEARNING OBJECTIVE

3   Use current hypotheses to trace the early evolution of animals.

Biologists generally agree that animals share a common ancestor with a group of protists known as *choanoflagellates* (see Fig. 26-21). The cells of these colonial flagellates became specialized to perform specific functions, such as movement, feeding, or reproduction. As this division of labor evolved, a colony of flagellates reached the level of cooperation and coordination that qualified it to be considered a single organism—the first animal. The choanoflagellates, fungi, and animals are a monophyletic group known as **opisthokonts.** Recall from Chapter 26 that opisthokonts are characterized by a posterior flagellum on motile cells.

Historically, biologists depended on fossils, on similarities in body plan, and on patterns of development to determine evolutionary relationships among various groups of animals. **Molecu-**lar systematics, the science that focuses on molecular structure to clarify evolutionary relationships, has provided additional data that are critical in answering questions about phylogeny. In many cases, molecular data have confirmed hypotheses that were based on morphology.

Complex genomes were apparently present early during animal evolution. Molecular studies suggest that the ancestor of animals had more than 1500 genes not found in other eukaryotes. Some of these genes may be traced to horizontal gene transfer from other domains, followed by modification of the genes. Complex genomes have been described in the sea anemone and in other animals that are relatively simple morphologically.

Molecular analyses indicate that the structure of genes that control development, RNA molecules, and many other molecules are very similar among all animal groups that have been studied. According to the *principle of parsimony,* such complex molecules are unlikely to have evolved multiple times (see Chapter 23). Thus, these data support the hypothesis that animals evolved only once. Animals are a monophyletic group.

Molecular systematics helps biologists interpret the fossil record

The evolutionary history of animals has been vigorously debated, because early animals were soft-bodied forms that left few fossils. The scarcity of fossils has made it difficult to determine the age, rate of divergence, and number of branches of animal groups. In 2009, a research team found fossil traces in an oil field on the Arabian Peninsula that are thought to date back more than 635 million years. The fossil traces are steroids found only in the skeletal structures of certain sponges (demosponges). Before this discovery, the earliest known animal fossils were the **Ediacaran biota** from the Ediacaran period (600 mya to 542 mya). These fossils of small, simple animals suggest that sponges, jellyfish, and comb jellies were present during this period (see Fig. 21-9).

Paleontologists have discovered many large, complex animal fossils in Chengjiang, an Early Cambrian (542 mya to 520 mya) fossil site in China, and in the Burgess Shale in British Columbia, a Middle Cambrian fossil site (520 mya to 515 mya). Fossils of most extant phyla (and also many extinct animals) have been found at these sites. The rapid appearance of an amazing variety of body plans during this time is known as the **Cambrian radiation,** or less formally as the **Cambrian explosion** (see Fig. 21-10). According to the Cambrian radiation hypothesis, which is based on the fossil record, major modifications in body plan that occurred during this time account for many branches of the animal tree.

Studies of large molecular data sets suggest that most animal clades actually diverged over a very long period during the Proterozoic eon (2.5 bya to 542 mya). Thus, the animal phyla that first left fossils during the Cambrian radiation may have evolved several hundred million years *before* they appear in the fossil record. Biologists estimate that certain groups are about twice as old as the oldest fossils found to date. According to this view, the Cambrian radiation was a rapid evolution of new animal body plans among clades that already existed. Perhaps fossils of these early animals remain to be discovered in Proterozoic rocks. Another hypothesis holds that a change in environmental conditions that occurred prior to the Cambrian radiation allowed fossils to form.

Biologists develop hypotheses about the evolution of development

Changes in animal body plans are linked to changes in patterns of embryonic development. Biologists have long used similarities and differences in embryonic development to hypothesize how animal groups are related. Traditionally, biologists depended mainly on structural changes to compare the process of development in various groups.

During the past 20 years, researchers have begun to study the molecular basis of developmental processes. They have identified the genes that direct the early development of the body plan and have discovered that many of these genes have been conserved during animal evolution. The same basic set of genes controls early development in all animal groups. Furthermore, the same genes are used in similar fashion to regulate development.

Evolutionary developmental biology, sometimes referred to as **Evo Devo,** has become an important approach to studying animal relationships. Biologists compare molecular events, such as gene regulation during development, in various animal groups.

Recall from Chapter 17 that *Hox* **genes** are a group of regulatory genes that specify the anterior-posterior axis during development (see Figure 17-13). The presence and number of *Hox* genes provide insights about evolutionary relationships. These genes have been identified in all of the bilateral animal groups that have been studied, suggesting that the last common ancestor of all bilateral animals had similar *Hox* genes. Recently, *Hox* genes were identified in a sea anemone (*Nematostella vectensis*), which is a cnidarian. Cnidarians are marine animals with radial symmetry, such as jellyfish. This finding suggests that the cnidarians share a common ancestor with the bilateral animals.

Investigators think that all the *Hox* gene groups had evolved by the beginning of the Cambrian period. Mutations in *Hox* genes could have resulted in rapid changes in animal body plans. For example, regulation by *Hox* gene groups has been linked with the development of wings or legs. Similarities in molecular development among different animal groups suggest that they had a common ancestor.

Review

- What was the Cambrian radiation?
- According to the current hypothesis, when did most major groups of animals evolve?
- How has the discovery of *Hox* genes helped biologists understand animal evolution?

30.4 RECONSTRUCTING ANIMAL PHYLOGENY

■ LEARNING OBJECTIVES

4 Describe how biologists use morphology (including variations in body symmetry, number of tissue layers, and type of body cavity) and patterns of early development to infer relationships among animal phyla.

5 Cite specific examples of how data from molecular systematics have confirmed or modified traditional animal phylogeny. (Include identification of three major clades of bilateral animals.)

The basic animal body plan has been highly conserved throughout our evolutionary history. Biologists use similarities and differences in morphology (structure) and in early development to infer evolutionary relationships among animal groups. Variations in major characters of the body plan provide clues to animal relationships. Biologists compare variations in body symmetry, number of tissue layers, type of body cavity, and pattern of development. In addition to these traditional methods, biologists now have molecular tools to enhance our understanding of animal phylogeny.

Animals exhibit two main types of body symmetry

Symmetry refers to the arrangement of body structures in relation to the body axis. Most sponges are not symmetrical, so when a sponge is cut in half, the two halves are not similar to each other. Most other animals exhibit either radial or bilateral body symmetry.

Cnidarians (jellyfish, sea anemones, and their relatives) and adult echinoderms (sea stars and their relatives) have **radial symmetry.** In radial symmetry, the body has the general form of a wheel or cylinder, and similar structures are regularly arranged as spokes from a central axis (**FIG. 30-3a**). Multiple planes can be drawn through the central axis, each dividing the organism into two mirror images. An animal with radial symmetry receives stimuli equally from all directions in the environment. Some animals have modified radial symmetry. For example, sea anemones and ctenophores (comb jellies) have **biradial symmetry,** in which parts of the body have become specialized so that only two planes can divide the body into similar halves.

Most animals exhibit **bilateral symmetry,** at least in their larval stages. A bilaterally symmetrical animal can be divided through only one plane (which passes through the midline of the body) to produce roughly equivalent right and left halves that are mirror images (**FIG. 30-3b**).

As bilateral symmetry evolved, a corresponding evolutionary trend led toward **cephalization,** the development of a head where sensory structures are concentrated. In many animal groups, concentrations of nerve cells in the head form a brain, and a nerve cord extends from the brain toward the rear end of the animal. Bilateral symmetry and cephalization are adaptations for locomotion. The head end of the animal meets its environment first and is best equipped to capture food or respond to danger.

Some definitions of basic terms and directions will help in locating body structures in bilaterally symmetrical animals. The back surface of an animal is its **dorsal** surface; the underside (belly) is its **ventral** surface. **Anterior** (or **cephalic**) means toward the head end of the animal; **posterior,** or **caudal,** means toward the tail end. A structure is said to be **medial** if it is located toward the midline of the body and **lateral** if it is toward one side of the body; for example, the human ear is lateral to the nose. In human anatomy, the term **superior** refers to a structure located above some point of reference, or toward the head end of the body. The term **inferior**

Top view   Side view

(a) Radial symmetry. Multiple planes can be drawn through the central axis; each divides the animal into two mirror images.

Lateral view   Front view

(b) Bilateral symmetry. The head of the animal is its anterior end, and the opposite end is its posterior end. The back of the animal is its dorsal surface, and the belly is its ventral surface. The diagrams illustrate various ways the body can be sectioned (cut) to study its internal structure. A sagittal section (lengthwise vertical cut) divides the animal into right and left parts. A frontal, or longitudinal, cut (lengthwise horizontal) divides the body into dorsal and ventral parts.

FIGURE 30-3 *Animated* Radial and bilateral symmetry

Sections of animals are used in illustrations throughout this book to show the structure and arrangement of tissues and organs.

is used in human anatomy to mean located below some point of reference, or toward the feet.

A bilaterally symmetrical animal has three axes, each at right angles to the other two: an anterior-posterior axis extending from head to tail, a dorsal-ventral axis extending from back to belly, and a left-right axis extending from side to side. We can distinguish three planes or sections that divide the body into specific parts. A **sagittal plane** divides the body into right and left parts. A sagittal plane passes from anterior to posterior and from dorsal to ventral. A **frontal plane** divides a bilateral body into dorsal and ventral parts. A **transverse section,** or **cross**

section, cuts at right angles to the body axis and separates anterior and posterior parts.

Animal body plans are linked to the level of tissue development

Sponges have several types of cells, but they are not organized into **tissues,** groups of closely associated, similar cells that work together to carry out specific functions. In the early development of all animals except sponges, cells form layers, called **germ layers.** The outer germ layer, or **ectoderm,** gives rise to the tissues that form the outer covering of the body and to nervous tissue. The inner layer, or **endoderm,** forms the lining of the digestive tube and other digestive structures. These layers develop into specific types of tissues.

Biologists describe cnidarians and ctenophores as **diploblastic** because they have two tissue layers. Other animals are **triploblastic.** They have a third germ layer, the **mesoderm,** which gives rise to most other body structures, including muscles, skeletal structures, and circulatory system (when present).

Most bilateral animals have a body cavity lined with mesoderm

The vast majority of bilateral animals have a fluid-filled body cavity, or **coelom** (pronounced "see'-lum"), between the outer wall of the body and the digestive tube (**FIG. 30-4**). The flatworms and ribbon worms are exceptions. They are bilateral and triploblastic but have a solid body; that is, they have no body cavity. They are referred to as **acoelomates** (*a-,* "without"; and *coelom,* "cavity").

Most animals have a body cavity that is completely lined with mesoderm. Such a body cavity is a *true* coelom. An animal with a true coelom is referred to as a **true coelomate** animal. The coelom was one of the most important early animal adaptations. During the Proterozoic eon, animals were small, simple forms. Evolution of the coelom was an important step in the evolution of larger, more complex animals.

With the evolution of the coelom came a new body design, the **tube-within-a-tube** body plan. The coelom is a space that separates the body wall, the outer tube, from the digestive tube (gut), which is the inner tube. The digestive tube is attached to the body wall at its ends. Typically, the digestive tube has a mouth at one end for taking in food and an anus at the other end for eliminating wastes. Because the coelom separates the muscles of the body wall from those in the wall of the digestive tract, the digestive tube can move food along independently of body movements.

Because it is an enclosed compartment (or series of compartments) of fluid under pressure, the coelom can serve as a **hydrostatic skeleton** in which contracting muscles push against a tube of fluid. The hydrostatic skeleton also shapes the body of soft animals. The evolution of various shapes and divisions of the coelom

(a) Acoelomate—flatworm (liver fluke). An acoelomate animal has no body cavity.

(b) Pseudocoelomate—nematode. A pseudocoelomate animal has a body cavity that is not completely lined with mesoderm.

(c) True coelomate—vertebrate. A true coelomate animal has a true coelom, a body cavity completely lined with tissue that develops from mesoderm.

FIGURE 30-4 *Animated* Three basic body plans in triploblastic animals
The germ layer from which each tissue was derived is indicated in parentheses. Ectoderm is shown in blue, mesoderm in red, and endoderm in yellow.

provided the opportunity for animals to become specialized in swimming, crawling, or walking. Animals that can move quickly to capture food or avoid predators are more likely to survive.

Evolution of the coelom provided a space where internal organs could develop and function. For example, the pumping action of the heart is possible because of the surrounding space the coelom provides. The fluid-filled coelom also protects internal organs by cushioning them.

Some (typically, small) animals have a body cavity that is not completely lined with mesoderm. This type of body cavity is called a **pseudocoelom** ("false coelom"). Animals with a pseudocoelom, such as nematodes (roundworms) and rotifers, are called **pseudocoelomates.** Animals with a pseudocoelom are not a monophyletic group. They probably evolved through a process of simplification from more than one group of animals with a true coelom.

Bilateral animals form two main clades based on differences in development

Embryonic development begins as the zygote undergoes cleavage, the first several cell divisions of the embryo. During cleavage, the embryo develops into a hollow ball of cells, the blastula. Cells of the blastula undergo **gastrulation,** a process that forms and segregates the three germ layers.

Basic differences in the pattern of early development distinguish two main evolutionary lines of bilateral animals: protostomes (pro′-tuh-stomes), assigned to the clade **Protostomia,** and deuterostomes (doo′-ter-uh-stomes), assigned to the clade **Deuterostomia.** The **protostomes** include mollusks (for example, snails, clams, squids), annelids (for example, earthworms), arthropods (for example, crabs, insects), and several other groups. **Deuterostomes** include the echinoderms (such as sea stars and sea urchins) and chordates (which include the vertebrates).

One important difference in the development of protostomes and deuterostomes is the pattern of cleavage. In many protostomes, the early cell divisions are diagonal to the polar axis (the long axis of the egg), resulting in a somewhat spiral arrangement of cells; any one cell lies between the two cells above or below it (**FIG. 30-5a**). This pattern of division is known as **spiral cleavage. In radial cleavage,** characteristic of the deuterostomes, the early divisions are either parallel or at right angles to the polar axis. The resulting cells lie directly above or below one another (**FIG. 30-5b**).

In the protostomes, the developmental fate of each embryonic cell is typically fixed very early. For example, if the first four cells of an annelid embryo are separated, each cell develops into only a fixed quarter of the larva; this pattern of cleavage is called **determinate cleavage.** In contrast, deuterostomes typically undergo **indeterminate cleavage.** For example, if the first four cells of a sea star embryo are separated, each cell can form a complete, though small, larva. If a few cells are removed from a blastula undergoing indeterminate cleavage, other cells compensate, and the embryo develops normally. In contrast, if a few cells are removed from the blastula of an embryo undergoing determinate cleavage, some structure, such as a limb, does not develop.

During gastrulation, a group of cells moves inward, forming a sac that becomes the embryonic gut. The opening to the outside is called the **blastopore.** In most protostomes, the blastopore develops into the mouth. The word *protostome* comes from Greek words meaning "first" and "the mouth." In deuterostomes the blastopore does not give rise to the mouth but generally develops into the anus. A second opening that forms later in development gives rise to the mouth. The word *deuterostome* derives from words meaning "second" and "the mouth."

Another, though less reliable, difference between protostome and deuterostome development is the manner in which the coelom forms. In most protostomes, the mesoderm splits, and the split widens into a cavity that becomes the coelom (**FIG. 30-6**). This method

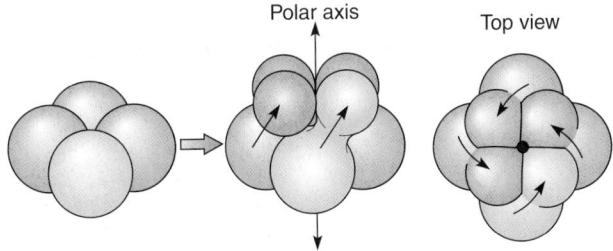

(a) Spiral cleavage is characteristic of protostomes. Note the spiral arrangement, with the upper cells centered between the lower cells.

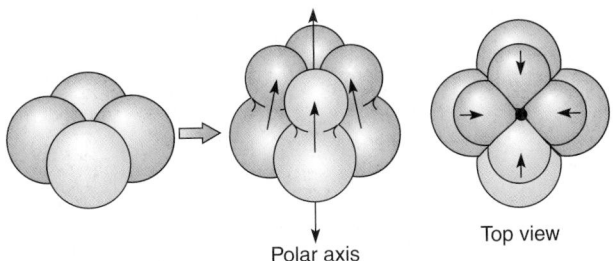

(b) Radial cleavage is characteristic of deuterostomes. The early divisions are either parallel to the polar axis or at right angles to it. The cells are stacked, with the upper cells centered directly above the lower cells.

FIGURE 30-5 Spiral and radial cleavage

The pattern of cleavage can be appreciated by comparing the positions of the purple cells in **(a)** and **(b).**

of coelom formation is known as **schizocoely.** In deuterostomes, the mesoderm forms as "outpocketings" of the developing gut, a process called **enterocoely.** These outpocketings eventually pinch off and form pouches; the cavity within the pouches becomes the coelom.

Biologists have identified major animal clades based on structure, development, and molecular data

Biologists have long inferred evolutionary relationships among animals, based on the structural variations and patterns of development we have just discussed. During the past few decades, the development of sophisticated new technology, such as new types of microscopy and cell-labeling, has helped systematists in their work. Techniques for determining the sequence of nucleotides in DNA and RNA and other molecular tools have helped systematists clarify the evolutionary relationships among animal groups. Molecular data have also challenged some traditional conclusions, for example, *when* various animal groups diverged in relation to other groups. Such questions continue to be the topic of much debate.

Animals are referred to as **metazoa.** Animals with two or three germ layers (diploblastic or triploblastic) make up the **eumetazoa.** As we have described, some animals exhibit asymmetry (sponges), radial symmetry (cnidarians), or biradial symmetry (ctenophores). The **Bilateria,** the lineage of animals with bilateral symmetry, are

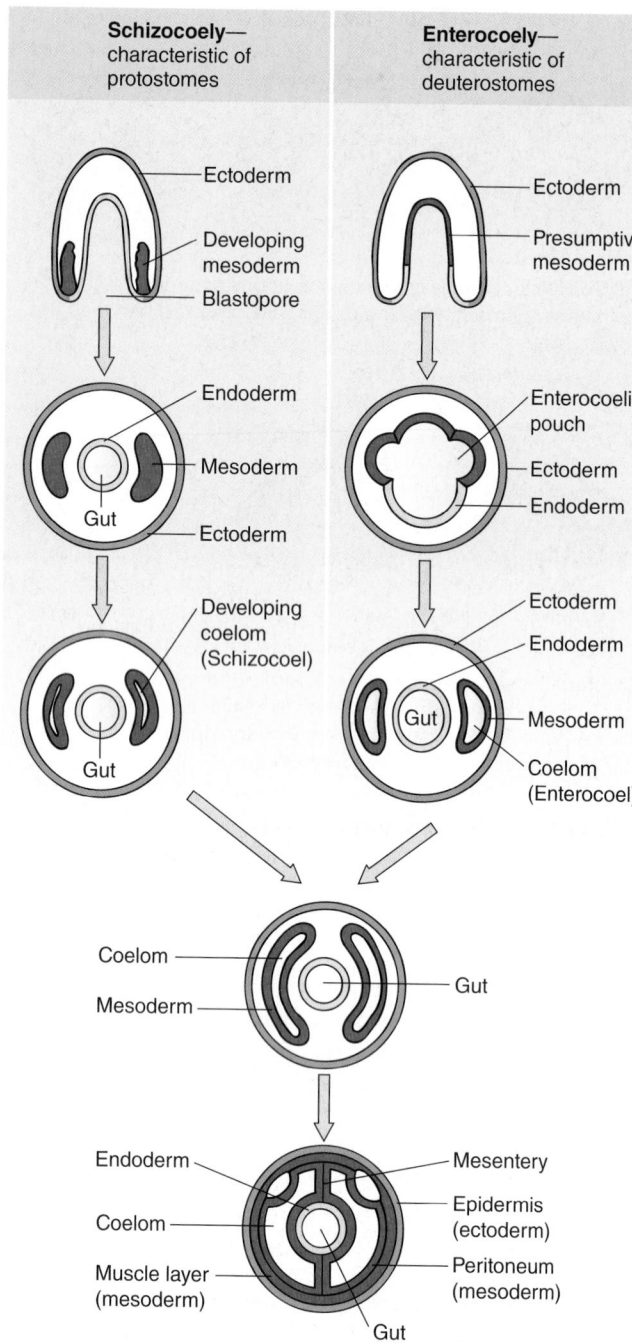

Schizocoely—
characteristic of protostomes

- Ectoderm
- Developing mesoderm
- Blastopore

- Endoderm
- Mesoderm
- Gut
- Ectoderm

- Developing coelom (Schizocoel)
- Gut

Enterocoely—
characteristic of deuterostomes

- Ectoderm
- Presumptive mesoderm

- Enterocoelic pouch
- Ectoderm
- Endoderm

- Ectoderm
- Endoderm
- Gut
- Mesoderm
- Coelom (Enterocoel)

- Coelom
- Mesoderm
- Gut

- Endoderm
- Coelom
- Muscle layer (mesoderm)
- Gut
- Mesentery
- Epidermis (ectoderm)
- Peritoneum (mesoderm)

◀ FIGURE 30-6 Two types of coelom formation

The coelem originates in the embryo from blocks of mesoderm that split off from each side of the embryonic gut. In protostomes, the coelom typically forms by the process of schizocoely. Solid blocks of mesoderm form around the gut. Programmed cell death occurs, causing the mesoderm (*red*) to split. The split widens, forming a cavity that becomes the coelom. In enterocoely, characteristic of deuterostomes, the mesoderm outpockets from the gut, forming pouches. The cavity within these pouches becomes the coelom. Ectoderm is shown in blue, endoderm in yellow. The diagrams in the top row are longitudinal sections of developing embryos; other diagrams are cross sections.

The name *Ecdysozoa* is derived from the fact that animals in this group molt, a process called *ecdysis*. The Ecdysozoa include the nematodes and arthropods. Note that the phylogeny we have described assigns bilateral animals to three major clades: Lophotrochozoa, Ecdysozoa, and Deuterostomia.

Segmentation apparently evolved three times

Over millions of years, evolutionary forces acting on the basic animal body plan have produced changes resulting in a remarkable diversity of body forms. One very important innovation has been **segmentation,** a body plan in which certain structures are repeated, producing a series of body compartments. Each compartment can be regulated somewhat independently of the others, which means that various parts of the body can become specialized to perform various functions.

Perhaps the most obvious example of segmentation can be found in the earthworm. However, as will be discussed in the following chapters, arthropods and vertebrates also have segmented body plans. Thus, segmented animals are found within each of the three major clades of bilateral animals. Molecular data suggest that segmentation evolved independently three times. This view is reflected in the cladogram in Figure 30-7. In each independent origin of segmentation, natural selection apparently acted on many of the same genes (for example, *Hox* genes).

In this chapter, we have briefly discussed characteristics common to animals and the early evolution of animals. We described animal body plans and examined some of the criteria that biologists use to reconstruct phylogenetic relationships. The cladogram shown in Figure 30-7 depicts some of the current hypotheses regarding the relationships among major animals groups, and Table 30-1 summarizes these relationships. In the next two chapters, we survey these animal groups. In Chapter 31, we describe the sponges, cnidarians, ctenophores, and the protostomes. Then, in Chapter 32, we discuss the deuterostomes, which include the echinoderms and chordates.

Review

- How are animals classified based on type of symmetry?
- What are some differences between protostomes and deuterostomes?
- What are the three main clades of bilateral animals, and how do they differ from one another?

triploblastic. (They have three germ layers: ectoderm, endoderm, and mesoderm.) As explained in the last section, biologists classify bilateral animals into protostome and deuterostome clades.

Molecular data show that the protostomes split into two major clades: **Lophotrochozoa** (pronounced "lo-fah-tro-kah-zo′-ah") and **Ecdysozoa** (pronounced "ek-dah-so-zo′-ah") (**FIG. 30-7** and **TABLE 30-1**). Animals assigned to the *Lophotrochozoa* are characterized by (1) a *lophophore,* a ciliated ring of tentacles surrounding the mouth that serves as a feeding organ, or (2) a type of larva called a *trochophore larva.* The Lophotrochozoa include the flatworms, ribbon worms, mollusks, annelids, and three groups sometimes referred to as the lophophorate phyla.

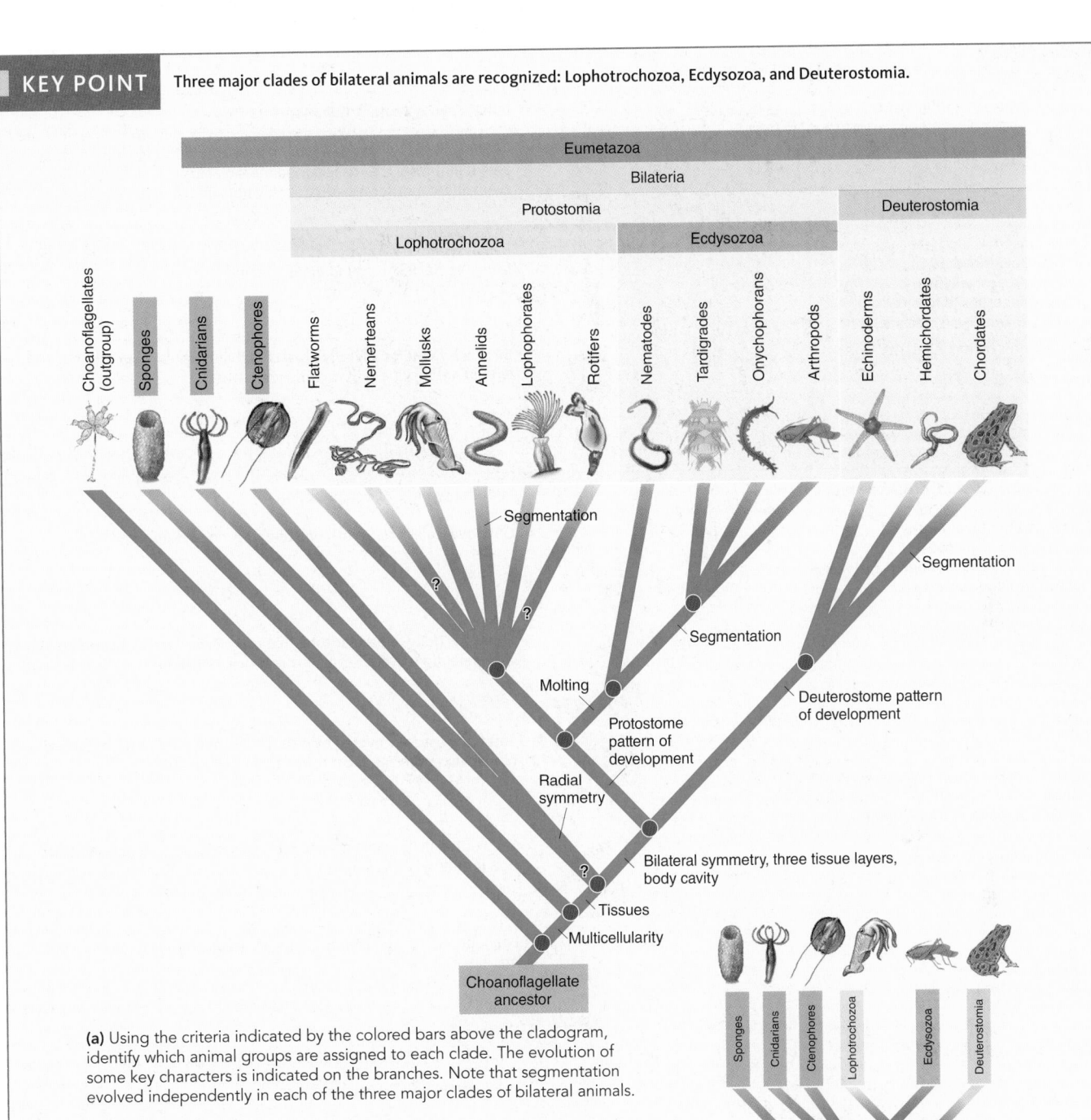

(a) Using the criteria indicated by the colored bars above the cladogram, identify which animal groups are assigned to each clade. The evolution of some key characters is indicated on the branches. Note that segmentation evolved independently in each of the three major clades of bilateral animals.

(b) Six major groups of animals.

FIGURE 30-7 Evolutionary relationships of animal clades

This cladogram is based on many forms of data, including comparisons of DNA sequences of several genes. Remember that any cladogram of animal relationships is a work in progress. As new data are considered, our understanding of relationships among animal groups changes.

Labels indicate when certain key traits originated. Note that the simplified cladogram shown in (b) is modified and used as an icon for many figures in Chapters 31 and 32.

TABLE 30-1   Overview of the Animal Kingdom

Major Groups and Subgroups		Some Key Characters/Comments
Poriferans (sponges)		Collar cells, flagellated cells that trap food; cells loosely associated and do not form true tissues; sponge larvae have flagella and can swim about; poriferans are probably not a monophyletic group

Cnidarians
  Hydrozoans: hydras
  Scyphozoans: jellyfish
  Cubozoans: box jellyfish
  Anthozoans: corals, sea anemones
		Radial symmetry; cnidocytes (stinging cells); polyp and medusa body forms; tentacles surround mouth; mainly marine

Ctenophores (comb jellies)		Biradial symmetry; eight rows of cilia that resemble combs; tentacles with adhesive glue cells; marine predators
Protostomes: Lophotrochozoan Branch		Bilateral symmetry; triploblastic

Flatworms (platyhelminths)
  Turbellarians: planarians
  Trematodes and monogeneans: flukes
  Cestodes: tapeworms
		Gastrovascular cavity with one opening; no coelom; cephalization

Nemerteans (ribbon worms)		Proboscis (long, muscular tube that can be everted to capture prey); complete digestive tube; mainly marine carnivores

Mollusks
  Chitons
  Gastropods: snails, slugs, nudibranchs
  Bivalves: clams, oysters
  Cephalopods: squids, octopods
		Soft body usually covered by dorsal shell; muscular foot; foot; mantle covers visceral mass; most have radula (belt of teeth)

Annelids
  Polychaetes: sandworms, tubeworms
  Oligochaetes: earthworms, freshwater worms
  Hirudinids: leeches
		Segmented body; most have bristles called setae, that provide traction during crawling

Lophophorates
  Brachiopods
  Phoronids
  Bryozoans (ectoprocts)
		Lophophore (ring of ciliated tentacles around mouth); mainly sessile marine organisms

Rotifera (wheel animals)		Crown of cilia at anterior end; microscopic aquatic animals
Protostomes: Ecdysozoan Branch		Protostomes with cuticle that is molted and replaced as animal grows
Nematodes (roundworms)		Fluid-filled pseudocoelom serves as hydrostatic skeleton; important decomposers; many are predators
Onycophorans (velvet worms)		Sister group of arthropods? Unjointed, paired appendages
Tardigrades ("water bears")		Sister group of arthropods? Unjointed, clawed legs

Arthropods
  Myriapods (centipedes, millipedes)
  Chelicerates (horseshoe crabs, arachnids)
  Crustaceans (lobsters, crabs, barnacles, copepods)
  Hexapods (insects)
		Segmented; exoskeleton of chitin; paired, jointed appendages; insects and many crustaceans have compound eyes

(continued)

TABLE 30-1   Overview of the Animal Kingdom (continued)

Major Groups and Subgroups	Some Key Characters/Comments
Deuterostomes	Radial, indeterminate cleavage; pharyngeal slits

Echinoderms
    Crinoids (sea lilies, feather stars)
    Asteroids (sea stars)
    Ophiuroids (basket stars, brittle stars)
    Echinoids (sea urchins, sand dollars)
    Holothuroids (sea cucumbers)
	Water vascular system; tube feet; endoskeleton with spines; larvae bilateral, ciliated; adult, pentaradial symmetry; marine

Hemichordates (acorn worms)	Proboscis, collar and trunk
Chordates	Notochord; dorsal, tubular nerve cord; postanal tail; endostyle; segmented body
Urochordates (tunicates)	Larvae have chordate characters
Cephalochordates (lancelets)	Notochord extends from anterior to posterior tip
Vertebrates (hagfishes, lampreys, cartilaginous fishes, ray-finned fishes, coelacanths, lungfishes, amphibians, reptiles [including birds], mammals)	Vertebral column, cranium, neural crest cells; endoskeleton

■ SUMMARY: FOCUS ON LEARNING OBJECTIVES

30.1 (page 627)

1 Describe several characteristics common to most animals.

- Members of **kingdom Animalia** are eukaryotic, multicellular, heterotrophic organisms with cells specialized to perform specific functions. Animals have diverse body plans. The **body plan** is the basic structure and functional design of the body.

- Most animals are capable of locomotion at some time during their life cycle, can respond adaptively to external stimuli, and can reproduce sexually.

- In sexual reproduction, sperm and egg unite to form a **zygote.** The zygote undergoes **cleavage,** a series of cell divisions that produce a hollow ball of cells called a **blastula.** Most animals develop into a **larva,** a sexually immature form that may appear and behave differently from the adult. Larvae typically go through **metamorphosis,** a developmental process that converts the immature animal into a juvenile form that grows into an adult.

   CENGAGENOW™ Explore the characteristics of animals by clicking on the figures in CengageNOW.

30.2 (page 627)

2 Compare the advantages and disadvantages of life in the ocean, in fresh water, and on land.

- Marine environments have relatively stable temperatures, provide buoyancy, and provide readily available food. Fluid and salt balance are more easily maintained than in fresh water. Currents and other water movements are a disadvantage.

- Fresh water offers a less constant environment and less food. Because fresh water is hypotonic to tissue fluid, animals must osmoregulate.

- Terrestrial animals must have adaptations that protect them from drying out and from temperature changes, and that protect their gametes and embryos.

30.3 (page 629)

3 Use current hypotheses to trace the early evolution of animals.

- Based on molecular data, biologists hypothesize that most animal clades actually diverged over a long period during the Proterozoic eon. During the **Cambrian radiation,** new animal body plans rapidly evolved among clades that already existed.

- *Hox* **genes** control early development in animal groups. These genes had evolved by the beginning of the Cambrian period, and mutations in these genes could have resulted in rapid changes in animal body plans.

30.4 (page 630)

4 Describe how biologists use morphology (including variations in body symmetry, number of tissue layers, and type of body cavity) and patterns of early development to infer relationships among animal phyla.

- Biologists hypothesize that cnidarians (which have radial symmetry) and ctenophores (which have biradial symmetry) are more closely related to each other than to animals that exhibit **bilateral symmetry. Cephalization,** the development of a head, evolved along with bilateral symmetry.

- Biologists have also inferred relationships based on level of tissue development and type of body cavity. Embryonic tissues, called **germ layers,** include the outer layer, **ectoderm,** which gives rise to the body covering and the nervous system; the inner layer, **endoderm,** which lines the gut and other digestive organs; and a middle layer, **mesoderm,** which gives rise to muscle, skeletal structures, and most other body structures.

- In bilateral animals, the type of body cavity has been used to classify animals. **Acoelomate** animals have no body cavity; **coelomate** animals have a **true coelom,** a body cavity completely lined with mesoderm. Some animals have a **pseudocoelom** (literally, a "false cavity"), a body cavity that is not completely lined with mesoderm.

Pseudocoelom

True coelom

- Two major evolutionary branches of bilateral animals are **Protostomia** (mollusks, annelids, and arthropods) and **Deuterostomia** (echinoderms and chordates).

- Protostomes undergo **spiral cleavage,** in which early cell divisions are diagonal to the polar axis. Deuterostomes undergo **radial cleavage,** in which the early cell divisions are either parallel or at right angles to the polar axis, so the cells lie directly above or below one another.

- Protostomes undergo **determinate cleavage,** in which the fate of each embryonic cell is fixed very early. Deuterostomes undergo **indeterminate cleavage,** in which the fate of each cell in early development is more flexible.

- In protostomes the **blastopore,** the opening from the embryonic gut to the outside, develops into the mouth; in **deuterostomes** the blastopore typically becomes the anus.

5 Cite specific examples of how data from molecular systematics have confirmed or modified traditional animal phylogeny. (Include identification of three major clades of bilateral animals.)

- Molecular systematics has confirmed much of animal phylogeny based on structural characters, including the axiom that animal body plans usually evolved from simple to complex. However, molecular systematics has also provided evidence for exceptions.

- Based on molecular data, biologists now subdivide the protostomes into two clades: **Lophotrochozoa** and **Ecdysozoa.** The Lophotrochozoa include the flatworms, ribbon worms, mollusks, annelids, rotifers, and animals that have a lophophore, a ciliated ring of tentacles surrounding the mouth. The Ecdysozoa, animals that molt, include the nematodes and arthropods. Thus, the three major clades of bilateral animals are Lophotrochozoa, Ecdysozoa, and Deuterostomia.

Eumetazoa			
Bilateria			
Protostomia			Deuterostomia
Lophotrochozoa		Ecdysozoa	

TEST YOUR UNDERSTANDING

1. Which of the following is *not* a defining character of animals? (a) heterotrophic (b) multicellular (c) eukaryotic (d) presence of a coelom (e) formation of a zygote that undergoes cleavage

2. Which of the following is *not* an adaptation to terrestrial living? (a) internal fertilization (b) shell surrounding egg (c) adaptations for maintaining body temperature (d) surface for gas exchange deep in body (e) ability to maintain location

3. The Cambrian radiation (a) occurred during the late Cambrian period (b) was a rapid evolution of new animal body plans during the middle Cambrian (c) was a result of prokaryotic and eukaryotic migration to many new regions (d) is supported by the great variety of Ediacaran fossils (e) b and c

4. Cephalization (a) evolved along with bilateral symmetry (b) is the development of a digestive system (c) is characteristic of protostomes but not deuterostomes (d) involves a concentration of endocrine organs (e) first evolved in deuterostomes

5. The germ layer that gives rise to the outer covering of the body and the nervous system is the (a) gastrodermis (b) ectoderm (c) mesenchyme (d) endoderm (e) mesoderm

6. Radial symmetry is characteristic of (a) protostomes (b) chordates (c) deuterostomes (d) cnidarians (e) poriferans

7. A true coelom is completely lined with (a) mesenchyme (b) ectoderm (c) mesoderm (d) endoderm (e) epidermis

8. Protostomes are characterized by (a) spiral cleavage (b) indeterminate cleavage (c) enterocoely (d) radial symmetry (e) a and c

9. The evolution of animals (a) followed an orderly progression from simple to complex (b) will be better understood as biologists continue to collect molecular and other types of data (c) has been determined by studying classification (d) began with the cnidarians (e) began with their common ancestor, a protostome

10. Which of the following would be most helpful in deciding whether an animals is a lophotrochozoan? (a) undergoes metamorphosis (b) molts (c) its zygote undergoes a series of mitotic divisions and becomes a blastula (d) has a trochophore larva (e) forms three germ layers

11. Which of the following is an example of a deuterostome? (a) lophotrochozoan (b) coral (c) chordate (d) planarian flatworm (e) insect

12. Label the branches of the diagram. Use Figure 30-7b to check your answers.

CRITICAL THINKING

1. Imagine that you discover a new organism in a lake. How would you decide whether it is an animal? What are some characteristics that might contribute to your decision?

2. **EVOLUTION LINK.** Examine the cladogram in Figure 30-7. Based on the discussion in this chapter, what were some of the types of data that biologists used to determine these phylogenetic relationships?

3. **EVOLUTION LINK.** Suggest and support a hypothesis for the view that segmentation evolved in three different animal clades.

4. **ANALYZING DATA.** Imagine that a biologist discovers evidence that a type of sponge evolved from an early protostome. Where would you place the branch for that sponge on Figure 30-7a?

 Additional questions are available in CengageNOW at www.cengage.com/login.

31 Sponges, Cnidarians, Ctenophores, and Protostomes

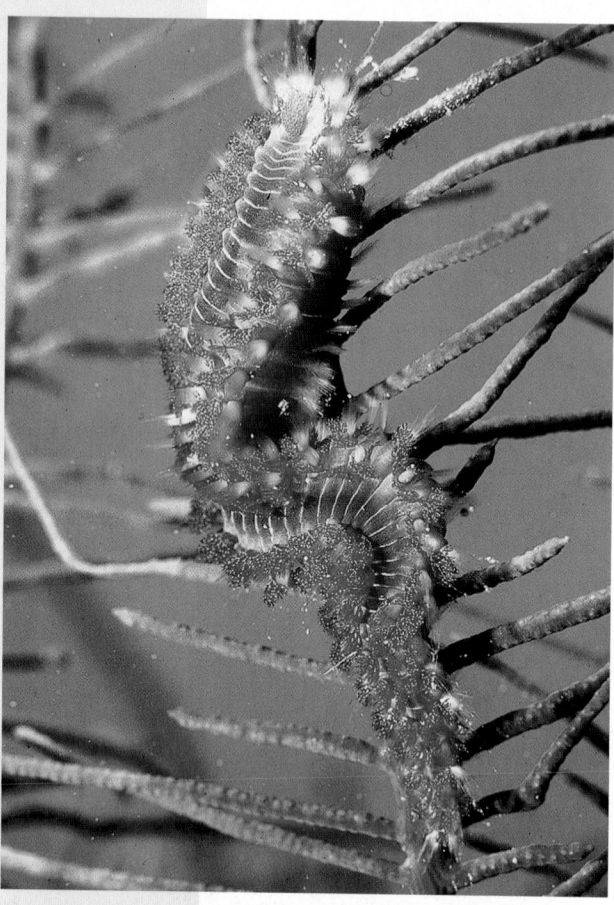

A bearded fireworm (*Hermodice carunculata*). The fireworm is a segmented worm (an annelid) that can grow up to 31 cm (11.8 in) long. It lives in shallow marine waters—in coral reefs, in beds of turtle grass, or under rocks. Fireworm bristles, which are filled with venom, can break off in the skin and cause irritation.

Marty Snyderman/Visuals Unlimited

KEY CONCEPTS

31.1 Animals with asymmetry, radial, or biradial symmetry include sponges, cnidarians (hydras, jellyfish, sea anemones), and ctenophores (comb jellies). Sponges are characterized by collar cells and by loosely associated cells that do not form true tissues; cnidarians are characterized by radial symmetry, two tissue layers, and cells that contain stinging organelles; and ctenophores have biradial symmetry, two tissue layers, eight rows of cilia, and tentacles with adhesive glue cells.

31.2 Protostomes are a monophyletic group that gave rise to two major clades: Lophotrochozoa and Ecdysozoa. The lophotrochozoans include the annelids (earthworms), mollusks, and several smaller groups.

31.3 The ecdysozoans include the nematodes (roundworms) and arthropods (horseshoe crabs, spiders, insects). The remarkable biological success of the insects can be attributed to the evolution of complex body plans and life cycles including their exoskeleton, segmentation, specialized jointed appendages, ability to fly, and metamorphosis.

In Chapter 30 we introduced the animal kingdom and explored animal phylogeny. We examined how systematists use fossils, morphology, developmental patterns, and molecular data to determine animal relationships. In this chapter we begin with an introduction to the sponges, cnidarians, and ctenophores, groups characterized by asymmetry, radial symmetry, and biradial symmetry, respectively. The phylogeny of these animals is the focus of much current research. Although sponges, cnidarians, and ctenophores are mainly small animals with simple body structures, they are of great ecological importance. They are important members of marine food chains, many provide shelter for other organisms, and some form symbiotic relationships with other animals. Corals that produce reefs are among the most ecologically important animals in the world.

Following our discussion of the sponges, cnidarians, and ctenophores, we begin our survey of the bilateral animals, the most familiar and by far the most numerous animals on Earth. More than 99% of animal species belong to the Bilateria. These diverse forms have adapted to life in almost every imaginable habitat in the ocean and in freshwater and terrestrial environments. The bearded fireworm shown in the photograph is an example of the diverse animals found among the Bilateria.

The remarkable success of the bilateral animals can be attributed to the evolution of adaptations that facilitated food capture, escape from predators, and reproduction. Among their key adaptations are cephalization (formation of a head), a central nervous system, muscles, a coelom, and compartmentalization of the body. Large animals developed body systems for gas exchange, waste disposal, and internal transport of nutrients, respiratory gases, wastes, and other materials.

Recall that based on pattern of early development, bilateral animals are classified as protostomes or deuterostomes. The protostomes form two clades: Lophotrochozoa and Ecdysozoa. In this chapter, we focus on the innovations in body plans, phylogenetic relationships, and life histories of several phyla of these two clades.

For reasons discussed in Chapter 23, some systematists now avoid using fixed ranks of the Linnaean classification hierarchy (kingdom, phylum, class, order, family). In classifying animals, we describe clades when these are known. We continue to use some Linnaean ranks, noting groups that may not be monophyletic and pointing out the controversies.

31.1 SPONGES, CNIDARIANS, AND CTENOPHORES: ANIMALS WITH ASYMMETRY, RADIAL, OR BIRADIAL SYMMETRY

■ LEARNING OBJECTIVES

1 Identify distinguishing characteristics of poriferans.
2 Identify distinguishing characteristics of cnidarians, describe four groups, and give examples of animals that belong to each group.
3 Identify distinguishing characteristics of ctenophores.

Until recently, biologists hypothesized that sponges diverged early from other animal groups and they assigned sponges to a basal group, **Parazoa** (*para*, "alongside"; and *zoa*, "animals"). They based their hypothesis on the asymmetry and simple body plan of sponges. The cells of sponges are loosely associated and do not form true tissues. Other animals have true tissues and were classified as **Eumetazoa** (*eu*, "true"; *meta*, "later"; and *zoa*, "animals"). Thus, biologists divided the animal kingdom into two major animal clades: Parazoa and Eumetazoa. Parazoa was considered a sister group of the Eumetazoa; however, this view has been challenged.

At least one group of sponges (calcareous sponges) may have become simplified as they evolved from animals with more complex body plans. Some systematists have proposed that comb jellies, rather than sponges, may be the oldest group of animals. Systematists continue to search for new clues that will settle the controversies over which branch of animals is the oldest, as well as which groups are more closely related to one another.

Sponges have collar cells and other specialized cells

Molecular data suggest that the **poriferans** (paw-rif´-er-ans; phylum **Porifera**) are not a monophyletic group. The name *Porifera*, meaning "to have pores," aptly describes the sponges, whose bodies are perforated by tiny holes. Sponges are aquatic, mainly marine animals that are most abundant in warm waters. Biologists have identified about 15,000 species of sponges. They range in size from a few millimeters to more than a meter in height and diameter (loggerhead sponges). Many sponges are asymmetrical, but they vary in shape from flat, encrusting growths to balls, cups, fans, or vases. Living sponges may be brightly colored—green, orange, red, yellow, blue, or purple—or they may be white or drab (**FIG. 31-1**). Some species are inhabited by symbiotic bacteria or algae that give them color.

Although they are multicellular and can be large, sponges function much like choanoflagellates—a group of unicellular and colonial protists. Recall that evidence suggests that animals (including sponges) and choanoflagellates share a common choanoflagellate ancestor. Choanoflagellates are characterized by a single flagellum surrounded by a collar of microvilli (see Fig. 26-21). Sponges have flagellate cells called **collar cells,** or **choanocytes,** which are strikingly similar to choanoflagellates.

Sponge larvae have flagella and can swim about. Adult sponges attach to some solid object and have long been described as sessile. However, biologists have observed adults of several species moving slowly (about 4 mm per day), perhaps by the cumulative movement of cells along the sponge's lower surface.

Although sponges are multicellular, their cells are loosely associated and do not form true tissues. However, a division of labor exists among the several types of cells that make up the sponge, with certain cells specializing in nutrition, support, contraction, or reproduction. Many sponge cells are extremely versatile and can change form and function.

Collar cells make up the inner layer of certain sponges. Each cell is equipped with a tiny collar surrounding the base of the flagellum. The collar is an extension of the plasma membrane and consists of microvilli. Collar cells create the water current that brings food and oxygen to the cells and carries away carbon dioxide and other wastes. Collar cells also trap and phagocytize food particles. Together, the collar cells of some sponges can pump a volume of water equal to the volume of the sponge each minute!

Sponges have three types of canal systems through which water circulates. In the simple *asconoid* canal system, the beating flagella of collar cells create a current that pulls water through hundreds of tiny pores, called **ostia.** Specialized tubelike cells, called **porocytes,** form the pores. These cells regulate the diameter of the pores by contracting. Water passes into the central cavity, or **spongocoel** (not a digestive cavity), and then flows out through the sponge's open end, the **osculum.** The asconoid system is illustrated in Figure 31-1.

In the *syconoid* system, water enters through canals lined by collar cells. Most types of sponges have a *leuconoid* system. The body wall is extensively folded, and complex systems of canals provide increased surface area for food capture. **Epidermal cells** form the outer layer of the sponge and line the canals. The canals lead into small chambers that are lined with collar cells.

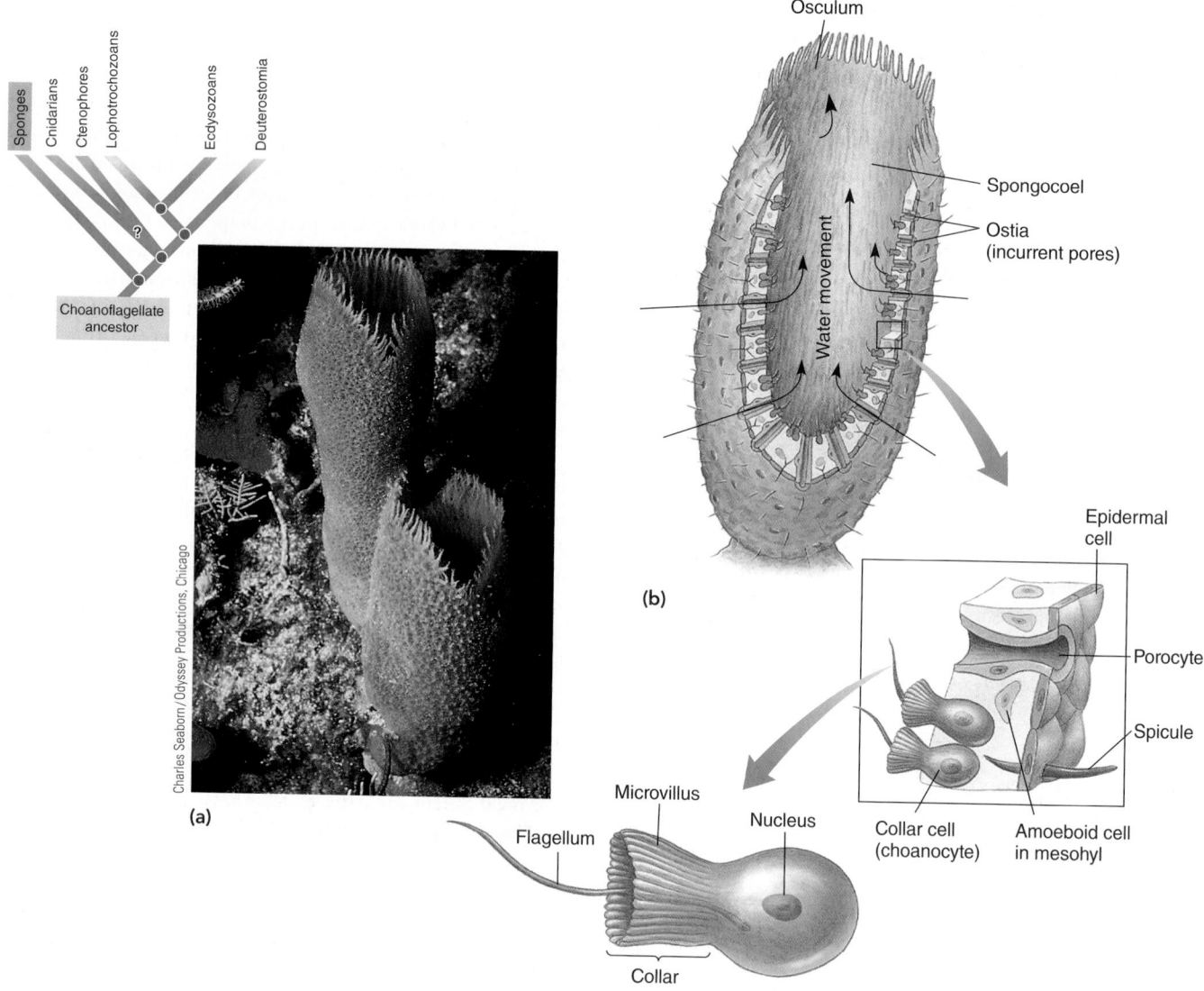

FIGURE 31-1 *Animated* **Sponge structure**

(a) Tube sponges (*Spinosella plicifera*) from the Caribbean, attached to the coral reef substrate. **(b)** Sponge cut to expose its organization. This sponge has an asconoid type of canal system.

The skeletal framework of a sponge can be both rigid and fibrous. Between the outer and inner cell layers, the sponge body has a gelatin-like layer, the **mesohyl,** which is supported by slender skeletal spikes, or **spicules. Amoeboid cells,** which wander about in the mesohyl, secrete the spicules. The spicules are made of calcium carbonate or of silica. The fibrous part of the sponge skeleton consists of **spongin,** a form of collagen.

Sponges are *suspension feeders,* adapted for trapping and eating whatever food is suspended in the water. As water circulates through the body, food is trapped along the sticky collars of the collar cells. Thus, the collars *filter* the suspended food particles out of the water. Suspension feeders that filter the suspended food are known as *filter feeders.* Food particles are either digested within the collar cell or transferred to an amoeboid cell for digestion. The amoeboid cell transports nutrients to epidermal cells. Undigested food passes out through the osculum and is simply eliminated into the water.

Gas exchange and excretion of wastes depend on diffusion into and out of individual cells. Although cells of the sponge can

react to stimuli, sponges do not have specialized nerve cells and so cannot react as a whole. However, electrical signals have been identified in certain glass sponges. Behavior appears limited to basic metabolic necessities such as capturing food and regulating the flow of water through the body.

Sponges reproduce both asexually and sexually. In asexual reproduction, a small fragment or bud may break free from the parent sponge and give rise to a new sponge. Such fragments may attach to the parent sponge, forming, or becoming part of, a colony. Most sponges are **hermaphrodites,** meaning the same individual can produce both eggs and sperm. Some of the amoeboid cells develop into sperm cells; others, into egg cells. However, hermaphroditic sponges usually produce eggs and sperm at different times, and they cross-fertilize with other sponges. They release mature sperm into the water, which are taken in by other sponges of the same species.

Fertilization and early development take place within the jelly-like mesohyl. Zygotes develop into flagellate larvae that leave the parent along with the stream of outflowing water. After swimming for a while, a larva finds a solid object, attaches to it, and settles down to a sessile life.

Sponges have a remarkable ability to repair themselves when injured and to regenerate lost parts. When the cells of a sponge are separated experimentally, they recognize one another and their place in the whole and aggregate to re-form a complete sponge.

There are three main groups of sponges: the *calcareous sponges* have spicules composed of calcium carbonate, whereas the *glass sponges* and the *demosponges* have spicules of silicon. About 95% of living sponges are demosponges. In some of the demosponges, spicules are bound together by spongin. Some demosponges do not have spicules. These soft sponges have been used for thousands of years as bath sponges and for cleaning. Unfortunately, as a result of overfishing, bath sponges are now in short supply.

Molecular data indicate that the calcareous sponges are a separate clade from the glass sponges and demosponges. The calcareous sponges may be the sister taxon to the other sponges, or they may be more closely related to lophotrochozoans than to the glass sponges and demosponges.

Cnidarians have unique stinging cells

About 10,000 species of **cnidarians** (ni-dah'-ree-ans; phylum **Cnidaria**) have been described. Most are marine. The radially symmetrical cnidarian body is organized as a hollow sac with the mouth and surrounding tentacles located at one end. Some cnidarians live a solitary existence, whereas many others, such as corals, form colonies. Based on molecular data, some systematists have proposed that cnidarians share a common ancestor with the clade of bilateral animals.

Cnidarians have two body shapes: polyp and medusa (**FIG. 31-2**). The **polyp** form, represented by *Hydra,* typically has a dorsal mouth surrounded by tentacles. In the **medusa** (pl., *medusae*), or jellyfish form, the mouth is located in the lower concave, or *oral,* surface; the

(a) Class Hydrozoa (polyp).
This hydrozoan (*Gonothyraea loveni*) forms a colony of polyps. The drawing illustrates a single polyp.

(b) Class Scyphozoa (medusa).
The sea nettle (*Chrysaora fuscescens*) uses its tentacles equipped with cnidocytes to capture small animals (zooplankton) suspended in the water.

(c) Class Anthozoa (polyp).
Coral polyps (*Montastrea cavernosa*) extended for feeding.

FIGURE 31-2 *Animated* Polyp and medusa body forms of cnidarians convex upper surface is the *aboral* surface. Some cnidarians have the polyp shape during one stage of their life cycle and the medusa form during another stage. The Portuguese man-of-war and some other cnidarians consist of colonies of many individuals, some of which are polyps and others medusae.

Cnidarians get their name from specialized cells, called **cnidocytes** (from a Greek word meaning "nettle cells"), that contain stinging organelles. Cnidocytes are located mainly in the epidermis, especially on the tentacles. The cnidocytes contain stinging "thread capsules," called **nematocysts** (**FIG. 31-3**). Each cnidocyte has a small, projecting trigger (*cnidocil*) on its outer surface and a coiled, hollow thread inside. We can compare the cnidocyte to a loaded gun, ready to fire. When stimulated by touch or certain chemicals dissolved in the water, the nematocyst fires its thread. Some types of nematocyst threads are sticky. Others are long and coil around prey. A third type bears barbs or spines that can inject a protein toxin that paralyzes prey animals, such as small crustaceans.

Cnidarians use their tentacles to capture prey and push it into the mouth. The mouth leads into the **gastrovascular cavity,** where digestion takes place. The mouth is the only opening into the gastrovascular cavity and so must serve for both ingestion of food and expulsion of undigested material. Gas exchange and excretion occur by diffusion. The body wall is thin enough that no cell is far from the surface.

More highly organized than sponges, cnidarians are diploblastic; that is, they have two definite tissue layers. The ectoderm gives rise to the outer epidermis, a protective layer covering the body. The endoderm gives rise to the inner **gastrodermis,** which lines the gastrovascular cavity and functions in digestion. These thin layers are separated by a thick, jellylike **mesoglea,** which is mainly acellular.

Cnidarians have nerve cells that form **nerve nets** connecting sensory cells in the body wall to contractile cells and gland cells. An impulse set up by one sensory cell passes in all directions more or less equally. Nerve cells are not organized to form a brain or nerve cord. In some types of medusae, sense organs are positioned around the edge of the body. The sense organs include simple "eyes," called eyespots, organs of balance (statocysts), and chemoreceptors (cells that sense certain chemicals).

Both the epidermis and gastrodermis have cells specialized to contract (however, they are not true muscle cells). Contractile fibers in the epidermal cells are arranged lengthwise, and those in the gastrodermis are arranged in a circular pattern. These two sets of contractile cells act on the water-filled gastrovascular cavity, forming a **hydrostatic skeleton.** This skeleton supports the body and allows movement. By contracting one set of contractile cells or the other, the hydra can shorten, lengthen, or bend its body (see Fig. 40-2). We consider four groups of cnidarians: hydrozoans, scyphozoans, cubozoans, and anthozoans (**TABLE 31-1**).

250 μm

(a) LM of discharged nematocysts of a Portuguese man-of-war (*Physalia physalis*). Photographed in the Gulf of Mexico.

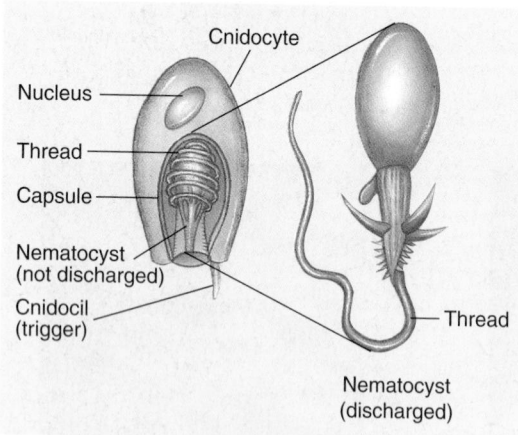

(b) Undischarged and discharged nematocyst. The cnidocil, or trigger, is a mechanoreceptor that discharges the nematocyst when it senses contact with an object.

FIGURE 31-3 *Animated* **Nematocysts**

When cnidarian stinging cells (cnidocytes) are stimulated, the nematocyst discharges, ejecting a thread that may entangle or penetrate the prey. Some nematocysts secrete a toxic substance that immobilizes the prey.

TABLE 31-1	Major Classes of Phylum Cnidaria
Class and Representative Animals	**Characteristics**
Hydrozoa *Hydra, Obelia,* Portuguese man-of-war	Mainly marine, but some freshwater species; alternation of polyp and medusa stages in most species (polyp form only in *Hydra*); some form colonies
Scyphozoa Jellyfish	Mainly marine; typically inhabit coastal water, free-swimming medusa most prominent form; polyp stage often reduced
Cubozoa "Box jellyfish"	Inhabit tropical and subtropical waters; have polyp stage, but medusa form most prominent; square shape when viewed from above; actively hunt prey; complex eyes that form blurred images
Anthozoa Sea anemones, corals, sea fans	Marine; solitary or colonial polyps; no medusa stage in most; gastrovascular cavity divided by partitions into chambers, increasing area for digestion

Most hydrozoans form colonies

Hydrozoans include hydras and *hydroids,* such as *Obelia* and the Portuguese man-of-war Although not really typical, the solitary *Hydra* is the cnidarian that beginning biology students most often study (**FIG. 31-4**). To the naked eye, *Hydra* looks like a bit of frayed string. This tiny hydrozoan is found in freshwater ponds. Because it has a remarkable ability to regenerate, biologists named *Hydra* after the multiheaded monster of Greek mythology that could grow two new heads for each head cut off. When *Hydra* is cut into several pieces, each piece can regenerate all the missing parts and become a whole animal.

Hydra lives in fresh water and typically attaches to a rock, aquatic plant, or detritus by a disc of cells at its base. Hydras reproduce asexually by budding during periods when environmental conditions are optimal. However, they differentiate as males and females and reproduce sexually in the fall or when pond water becomes stagnant. The zygote may become covered with a shell that protects it through the winter or until conditions become more favorable.

Many hydrozoans form colonies consisting of hundreds or thousands of individuals. A colony begins with a single polyp that reproduces asexually by budding. However, instead of separating from the parent, the bud remains attached and eventually forms additional buds. Several types of individuals may arise in the same colony, some specialized for feeding, some for reproduction, and others for defense.

Some marine hydrozoans are remarkable for their alternation of sessile polyp and motile medusa stages. The life cycle of the colonial marine hydrozoan *Obelia* illustrates alternation of polyp and medusa stages (**FIG. 31-5**). In *Obelia,* polyps reproduce asexually by budding, whereas the medusae reproduce sexually. Both polyp and medusa are diploid; only sperm and eggs are haploid.

Scyphozoans are the "true" jellyfish

In **scyphozoans,** the medusa is the dominant body form. Jellyfish medusae are generally larger than hydrozoan medusae, and they

(a) *Hydra viridis* with large bud. When the bud separates from its parent, it becomes an independent individual.

17 mm

Biophoto Associates/Photo Researchers, Inc.

(c) Cross section through body of *Hydra.*

Tentacles
Cnidocytes (stinging cells)
Mouth
Egg (ovum)
Bud
Ovary
Gastrovascular cavity
Epidermis
Mesoglea
Gastrodermis

(b) *Hydra* cut longitudinally to show internal structure. Asexual reproduction by budding is represented on left; sexual reproduction is represented by ovary on right. Male hydras develop testes that produce sperm.

FIGURE 31-4 Hydra, a freshwater hydrozoan

have a thick, viscous mesoglea that gives firmness to the body. In scyphozoans, the polyp stage is small and inconspicuous or may even be absent. The largest jellyfish, *Cyanea,* may be more than 2 m (6.5 ft) in diameter and have tentacles 30 m (98 ft) long. These orange and blue "monsters," among the largest invertebrates, can cause painful stings to swimmers in the North Atlantic and Pacific Oceans.

Cubozoans include the "box jellyfish"

When viewed from above, **cubozoans** have a square shape. They have four tentacles, or groups of tentacles. These fast-swimming jellyfish have complex eyes that form blurred images, and they actively hunt for prey. Found in waters off the northern Australian coast, the sea wasp (*Chironex fleckeri*) has long tentacles that can

Reproductive polyp

Feeding polyp

David M. Phillips/Visuals Unlimited

250 µm

(a) **LM of *Obelia*.** Some polyps have tentacles and are specialized for feeding, whereas others are specialized for reproduction.

extend more than 3 m (10 ft). The sea wasp produces one of the deadliest venoms in the animal kingdom. Its venom contains toxins that can stun or kill fish and other prey. These toxins can also cause respiratory failure and cardiac arrest in humans. Fatalities are mainly associated with severe stings caused by contact with tentacles over a large area of the body. Interestingly, sea turtles feed on box jellyfish, apparently unaffected by its venom.

Anthozoans are polyps

Anthozoans, which include the sea anemones and corals, are either individual or colonial polyps. There is no free-swimming medusa stage. The polyp produces eggs and sperm, and the fertilized egg develops into a small, ciliated larva called a **planula.** This larval form may swim to a new location before attaching to develop into a polyp.

Anthozoans differ from hydrozoans in that a series of vertical partitions partially divides the gastrovascular cavity into connected chambers. The partitions increase the surface area for digestion, enabling an anemone to digest an animal as large as a crab. Although corals can capture prey, many tropical species depend for nutrition on photosynthetic algae (*zooxanthellae*) that live within cells lining the coral's digestive cavity (see Chapter 26 and Fig. 54-12). The relationship between coral and zooxanthellae is symbiotic and mutually beneficial. The algae provide the coral with oxygen and with carbon and nitrogen compounds. In exchange, the coral supplies the algae with waste products such as ammonia, from which the algae make nitrogenous compounds for both partners.

In warm, shallow seas, much of the bottom is covered with coral or anemones, most of them brightly colored. Coral reefs con-

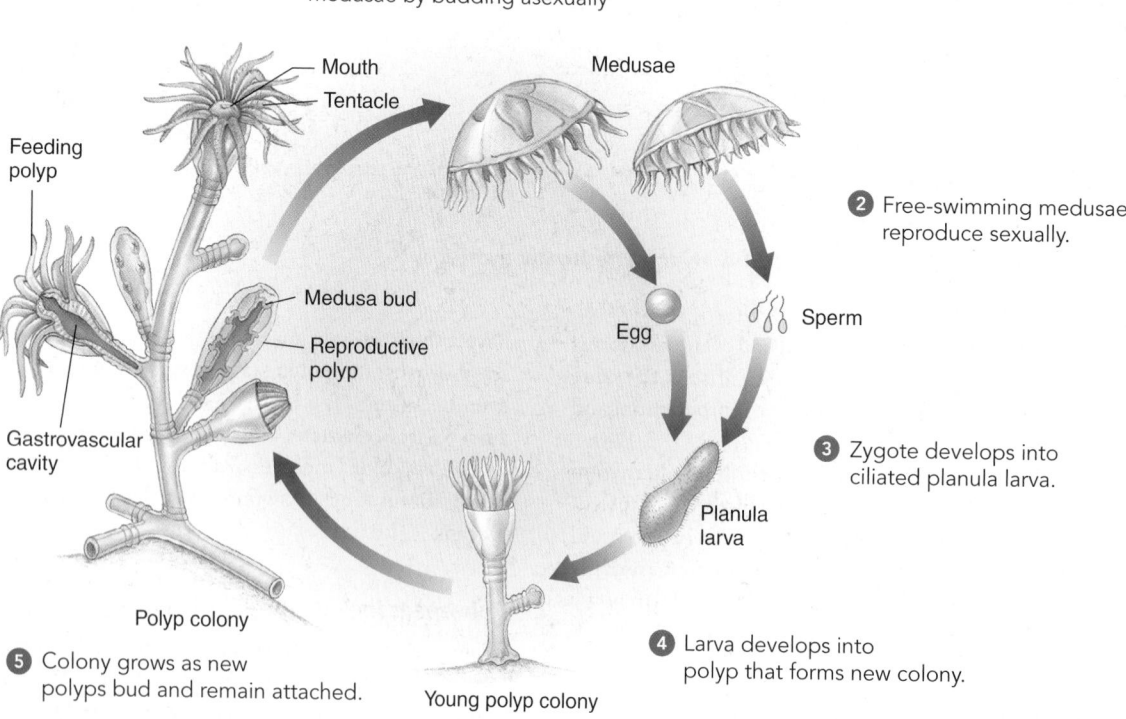

❶ Reproductive polyps produce medusae by budding asexually

Mouth
Tentacle

Medusae

Feeding polyp

Medusa bud

Reproductive polyp

Gastrovascular cavity

Egg

Sperm

❷ Free-swimming medusae reproduce sexually.

❸ Zygote develops into ciliated planula larva.

Planula larva

Polyp colony

❺ Colony grows as new polyps bud and remain attached.

Young polyp colony

❹ Larva develops into polyp that forms new colony.

(b) **Life cycle of *Obelia*.**

FIGURE 31-5 *Animated* *Obelia*, a marine colonial hydrozoan sist of colonies of millions of corals and of certain algae (mainly coralline red algae). Living colonies occur only in the uppermost regions of such reefs, adding their own skeletons to the forming rock. Coral reefs are among the most productive of all ecosystems, rivaling tropical rain forests in species diversity (see Fig. 56-21). A single reef can serve as home for more than 3000 species of fishes and other marine organisms, and an estimated one-fourth of all marine species depend on coral reefs.

A 2008 study of 704 species of reef-building corals reported that about one-third were found to be threatened or near-threatened, and may be at increased risk for extinction. Human activities are responsible for much of this damage. Contributing factors include overfishing, mining reefs for building materials, polluting coastal waters with industrial chemicals, and smothering coral with the silt washed downstream from clear-cut forests. Acidification of the ocean caused by the increase in carbon dioxide in the atmosphere is another important factor.

Coral bleaching is the stress-induced loss of the colorful symbiotic algae that inhabit coral cells (**FIG. 31-6**). When under environmental stress, coral actually expel the algae. Without their algae, coral become malnourished and die. Environmental factors suspected of contributing to coral bleaching include unusually low or high (associated with global warming) temperatures, pollution, changes in salinity, acidification, and disease.

Comb jellies have adhesive glue cells that trap prey

The fragile, luminescent **comb jellies** are marine animals known as **ctenophores.** They are assigned to phylum **Ctenophora** (teh-nof´-er-uh). Approximately 150 species of ctenophores have been described. Some are as small as a pea; others are larger than a tomato. The outer surface of a ctenophore bears eight rows of cilia that resemble combs (**FIG. 31-7**). Ctenophores are biradially symmetrical, meaning you could obtain equal halves by cutting through the body axis in two different ways. The ctenophore body plan is somewhat similar to that of a cnidarian medusa in that ctenophores have a type of radial symmetry, feeding tentacles, and two cell layers separated by a thick, jellylike mesoglea.

Some ctenophores have two tentacles. Their tentacles are equipped with adhesive glue cells. When prey comes in contact with the tentacle, the glue cells burst open, releasing sticky threads that trap the prey. Ctenophores do not have the stinging nematocysts characteristic of the cnidarians. Also unlike cnidarians, the ctenophore digestive system has a mouth for food intake at one end and two anal pores for the egestion of water and wastes at the other end.

Ctenophores have a nervous system that includes a network of nerve cells and a sensory organ called a "statocyst," which coordinates beating of the cilia in the combs. The coordinated beating of the cilia moves the animal through the water. The statocyst also functions in balance and helps the animal orient itself.

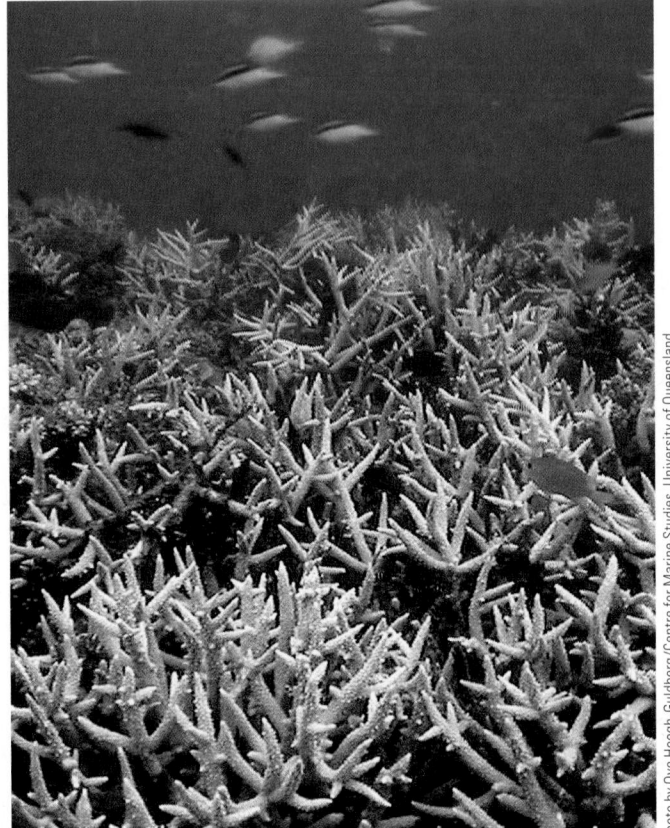

FIGURE 31-6 Bleached staghorn coral
This staghorn coral (*Acropora*) was photographed off Heron Island on the Great Barrier Reef off the coast of Australia.

Because of their similarities, biologists classify ctenophores near the cnidarians. However, their development is different, and their digestive cavity has openings at both ends. The similarities between ctenophores and cnidarians may be a result of convergent evolution from living in a similar environment, the ocean. Where, then, do the ctenophores belong on our cladogram? As systematists gather new data, their position on the animal tree will become clearer.

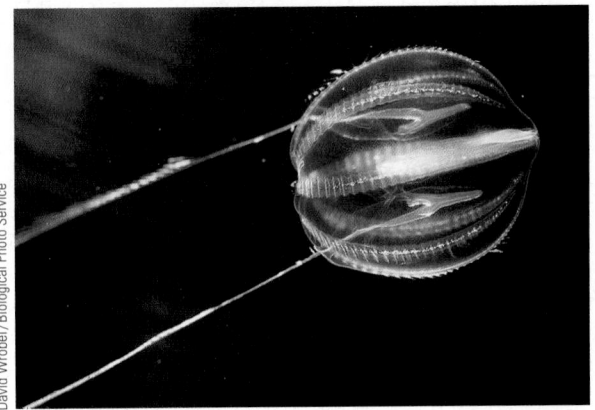

FIGURE 31-7 Ctenophore (comb jelly)
Ctenophores are free-swimming, bioluminescent hermaphrodites capable of self-fertilization. The sea gooseberry (*Pleurobrachia*) has two long tentacles with adhesive cells used to capture prey.

Review

- Why are choanocytes significant? What is their function in sponges?
- In what ways do the cells of sponges specialize?
- In what ways do cnidarians differ from sponges?
- Sketch the major events of the life cycle of *Obelia*.
- How is a ctenophore like a cnidarian? In what ways is it different?

31.2 THE LOPHOTROCHOZOA

■ LEARNING OBJECTIVES

4 Summarize what is known about the phylogeny of the lophotrochozoans and cite the adaptive advantages of having a coelom and of cephalization.

5 Identify distinguishing characteristics of flatworms and nemerteans; describe the main groups of flatworms, giving examples of animals that belong to each class.

6 Describe the distinguishing characteristics of mollusks and of the four main groups of mollusks discussed, giving examples of each group.

7 Describe the distinguishing characteristics of annelids and of the three main groups of annelids discussed, giving examples of each group.

8 Describe the distinguishing characteristics of the lophophorates and of the rotifers.

We begin our discussion of the bilateral animals with the **Lophotrochozoa,** a clade that includes the flatworms (platyhelminths), rotifers (wheel animals), nemerteans (ribbon worms), mollusks, annelids (earthworms), and the lophophorate phyla (see Fig. 30-7). Recall from Chapter 30 that the name *Lophotrochozoa* comes from two important characters of some animals in this clade: (1) the *lophophore,* a ciliated ring of tentacles surrounding the mouth in three small groups of animals; and (2) the *trochophore larva,* a type of larva that characterizes two major groups—the mollusks and annelids. Some systematists argue that flatworms and rotifers should be assigned to a separate group, the **platyzoa.** Here, we include them with the lophotrochozoa.

Most lophotrochozoans have **bilateral symmetry,** at least in their larval stages. They are **triploblastic;** that is, they have three definite tissue layers. In addition to the outer epidermis derived from ectoderm, and an inner endodermis derived from endoderm, lophotrochozoans have a middle tissue layer that develops from mesoderm.

Most lophotrochozoans have a **true coelom** and a **tube-within-a-tube body plan** (see Chapter 30). Most coelomate animals have well-developed circulatory, excretory, and nervous systems. Many internal organs are suspended within folds of the tissue lining the coelom and can move independently of the outer body wall. In addition, the coelom provides space for the gonads to develop. During the breeding season of many animals, such as birds, the gonads enlarge within the coelom as they fill with ripe gametes.

In some animals, fluid within the coelom helps transport materials such as food, oxygen, and wastes. Cells bathed by the coelomic fluid can exchange materials with it. The cells receive nutrients and oxygen from the coelomic fluid and excrete wastes into it. Some coelomates have excretory structures that remove wastes directly from the coelomic fluid.

Animals that move about typically have an elongated body with definite anterior and posterior ends. They exhibit **cephalization,** the evolution of a head with a concentration of sense organs at the anterior end. A simple brain and paired sense organs are concentrated in the "head" region. An animal with a front end generally moves forward. With a concentration of sense organs in the part of the body that first meets its environment, the animal can actively search for food, shelter, and mates or detect enemies quickly.

Flatworms are bilateral acoelomates

The **flatworms** (phylum **Platyhelminthes** [plat-ee-hel-min′-theez]) are soft-bodied animals that left few fossils to provide clues to their evolutionary history. Their flat, elongated bodies are solid; that is, they are **acoelomate** (they have no body cavity). Historically, biologists considered flatworms to be the simplest bilaterally symmetrical, triploblastic animals. However, molecular data, specifically 18S ribosomal RNA sequences, indicate that phylum Platyhelminthes, as traditionally classified, is not a monophyletic group. Based on molecular data, systematists have reclassified two orders (from class Turbellaria) that differ significantly from other flatworms. These two orders have been assigned to their own phylum (Acoelomorpha). This new group may be closely related to the common ancestor that linked radially symmetrical animals with bilateral animals.

The remaining flatworms appear more closely related to coelomates. If so, flatworms evolved from more complex animals. They originally had a body cavity, but their body plan became simplified later in their evolutionary history. Many biologists currently classify these flatworms as lophotrochozoans. The phylogeny of flatworms remains controversial. As biologists consider new data, their assessment of the phylogenetic relationships of flatworms will likely change.

Some biologists assign the 20,000 Platyhelminthes species to four classes. Class **Turbellaria** consists of the free-living flatworms, including planarians and their relatives. Classes **Trematoda** and **Monogenea** include the flukes, which are either internal or external parasites. Class **Cestoda** includes the tapeworms, which as adults are intestinal parasites of vertebrates (**TABLE 31-2**).

Flatworms typically have a simple **nervous system.** The brain consists of two masses of nervous tissue, called **ganglia,** in the

TABLE 31-2	Classes of Phylum Platyhelminthes
Class and Representative Animals	Characteristics
Turbellaria* Planarians	Mainly free-living; mainly marine; body covered by ciliated epidermis; typically carnivorous; prey on tiny invertebrates
Trematoda and Monogenea Flukes	Parasites with a wide range of vertebrate and invertebrate hosts; may require intermediate hosts; adults have suckers for attachment to host
Cestoda Tapeworms	Parasites of vertebrates; complex life cycle usually with one or two intermediate hosts; larval host may be invertebrate; typically have suckers and sometimes hooks for attachment to host; eggs produced within proglottids, which are shed; no digestive or nervous systems

*Systematists view Turbellaria as a paraphyletic group, and it will amost certainly be divided into at least three groups.

head region. In many species, the ganglia connect to two nerve cords that extend the length of the body. This nervous system is sometimes referred to as a "ladder-type nervous system" because a series of nerves connects the cords like the rungs of a ladder (see Fig. 42-2). Sense organs include simple "eyes," called eyespots, and organs of balance (statocysts).

Flatworms have no organs for circulation or gas exchange. These functions depend largely on diffusion through the body wall. The activities of some organs are coordinated and form simple organ systems, for example, the digestive and nervous systems. As in the cnidarians, the digestive system is a gastrovascular cavity with only one opening, a mouth. The gastrovascular cavity is often extensively branched.

Parasitic flatworms—flukes and tapeworms—are highly adapted to and modified for their parasitic lifestyle. They have suckers or hooks for holding on to their hosts. The bodies of those that live in digestive tracts resist the digestive enzymes secreted by their hosts. Many have complicated life cycles and produce large numbers of eggs. Other adaptations include the loss of certain structures such as sense organs. Tapeworms have also lost the digestive system.

Turbellarians are free-living flatworms

Most members of class Turbellaria are free-living, marine flatworms. However, many inhabit freshwater habitats, and some are terrestrial. Turbellarian flatworms typically have a muscular pharynx that takes in food; a simple brain, eyespots, and other sensory organs in the head; **protonephridia,** structures that function in osmoregulation (fluid balance) and metabolic waste disposal (excretion); and reproductive organs.

Planarians are turbellarian flatworms found in ponds and quiet streams throughout the world. The common American planarian *Dugesia* is about 15 mm (0.6 in) long, with what appear to be crossed "eyes" and flapping "ears" called **auricles** (**FIG. 31-8**). The auricles actually serve as organs of chemoreception, important in locating food. Planarians are capable of learning. Memory is not localized within the ganglia but appears to be retained throughout the nervous system.

Planarians are carnivorous; they trap small animals in a mucous secretion. The digestive system consists of a single opening (the mouth); a tubelike, muscular **pharynx** (the first portion of the digestive tube); and a branched gastrovascular cavity. A planarian projects its pharynx outward through its mouth, using it to suck in prey. The long, highly branched gastrovascular cavity distributes food to all parts of the body so each cell can receive nutrients by diffusion.

Although excretion takes place mainly by diffusion, some metabolic wastes are excreted by the protonephridia. Protonephridia

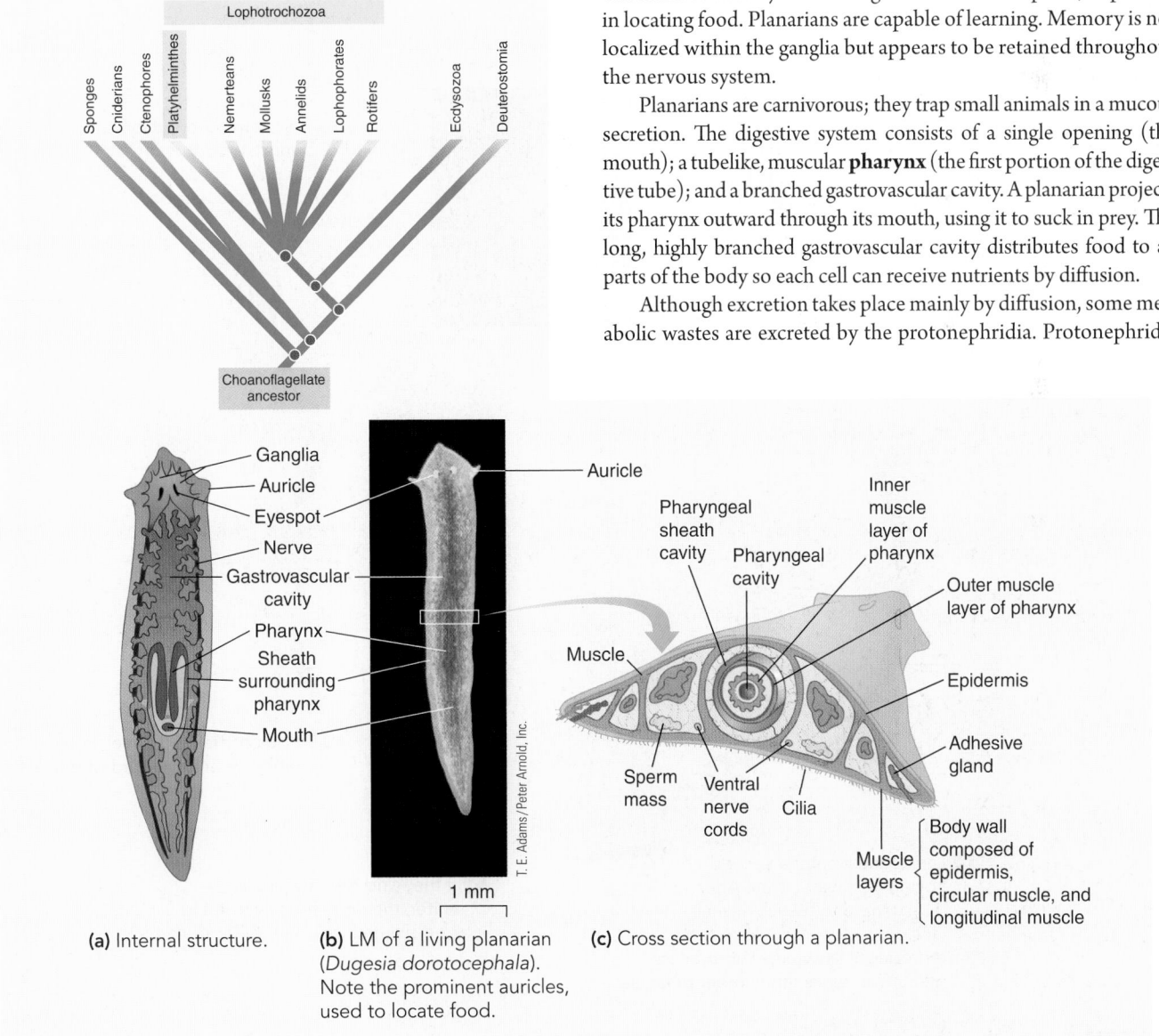

(a) Internal structure.

(b) LM of a living planarian (*Dugesia dorotocephala*). Note the prominent auricles, used to locate food.

(c) Cross section through a planarian.

T. E. Adams/Peter Arnold, Inc.

FIGURE 31-8 *Animated* The common planarian, *Dugesia*

are blind tubules that end in **flame bulbs,** collecting cells equipped with cilia. The beating of the cilia channels waste through the system of tubules and eventually out of the body through excretory pores. Osmoregulation and protonephridia are discussed further in Chapter 48 (see Fig. 48-2).

Planarians reproduce either asexually or sexually. In asexual reproduction, an individual constricts in the middle and divides into two planarians. Each regenerates its missing parts. Sexually, these animals are **hermaphrodites.** During the warm months of the year, each is equipped with a complete set of male and female organs. Two planarians come together in copulation and exchange sperm cells so that their eggs are cross-fertilized.

Flukes parasitize other animals

Although their body plan resembles that of the free-living flatworms, the **flukes,** members of classes Trematoda and Monogenea, have structures, such as hooks and suckers, for attachment to their host. Flukes also have extremely prolific reproductive organs.

Flukes that are parasitic in humans include blood flukes, widespread in tropical areas of the world, and liver flukes, common in Asia, particularly in areas where humans use their own feces for fertilizing crops. Blood flukes of the genus *Schistosoma* infect about 200 million people who live in tropical areas. Both blood flukes and liver flukes go through complicated life cycles involving several different forms. There is an alternation of sexual and asexual stages, and parasitism on one or more intermediate hosts, such as snails and fishes (**FIG. 31-9**). The aquatic snails that serve as intermediate hosts thrive in ponds, rice paddies, and the marshy areas that develop when dams are built.

Tapeworms inhabit the intestine of vertebrates

Adult members of the more than 5000 species of class Cestoda live as parasites in the intestine of probably every kind of vertebrate, including humans. Tapeworms are long, flat, ribbonlike animals strikingly specialized for their parasitic mode of life. Among their many adaptations are suckers and sometimes hooks on the "head," or **scolex,**

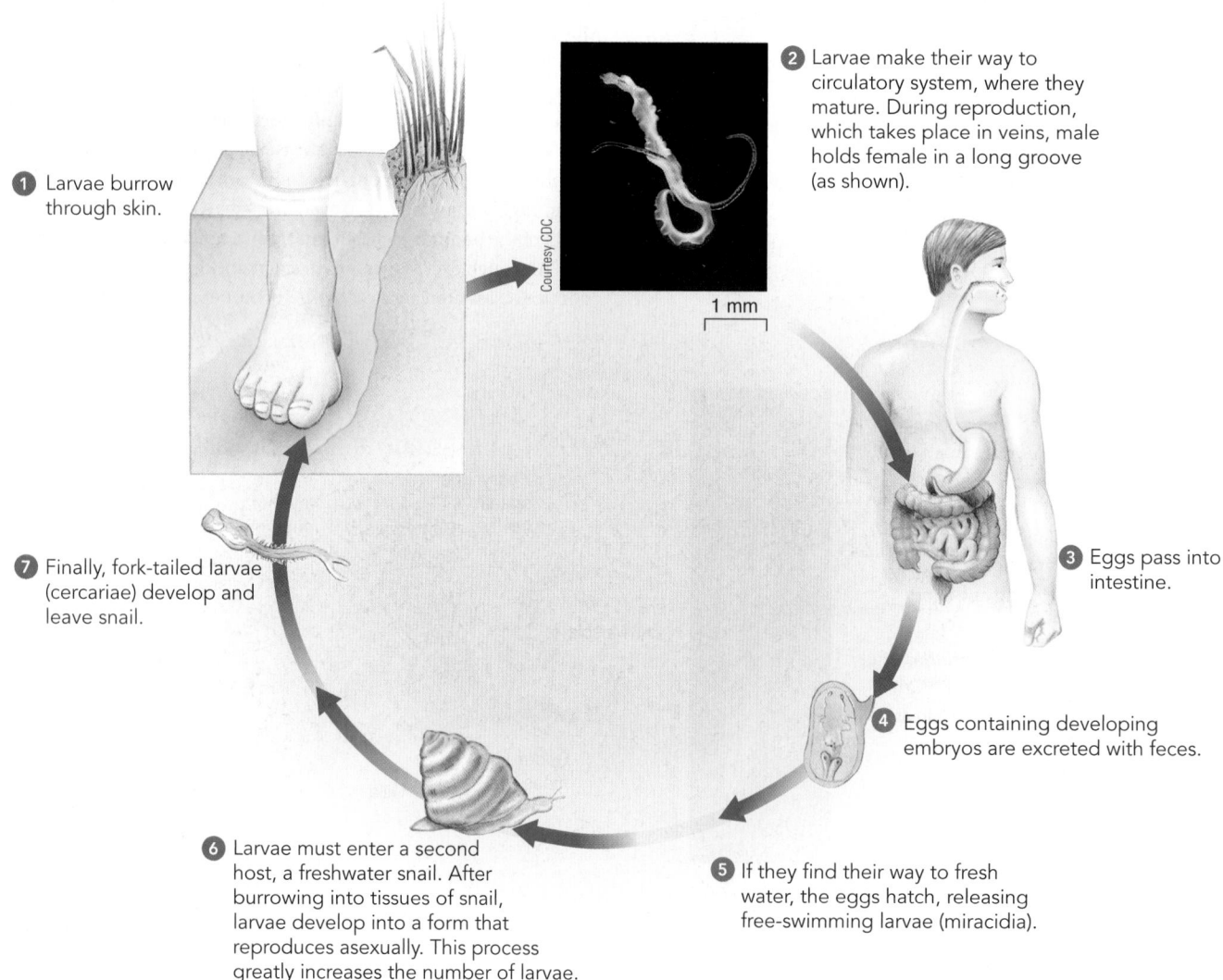

1 Larvae burrow through skin.

2 Larvae make their way to circulatory system, where they mature. During reproduction, which takes place in veins, male holds female in a long groove (as shown).

Courtesy CDC

1 mm

3 Eggs pass into intestine.

4 Eggs containing developing embryos are excreted with feces.

5 If they find their way to fresh water, the eggs hatch, releasing free-swimming larvae (miracidia).

6 Larvae must enter a second host, a freshwater snail. After burrowing into tissues of snail, larvae develop into a form that reproduces asexually. This process greatly increases the number of larvae.

7 Finally, fork-tailed larvae (cercariae) develop and leave snail.

FIGURE 31-9 *Animated* Life cycle of the blood fluke (*Schistosoma*)
The LM shows an adult male enfolding a smaller female.

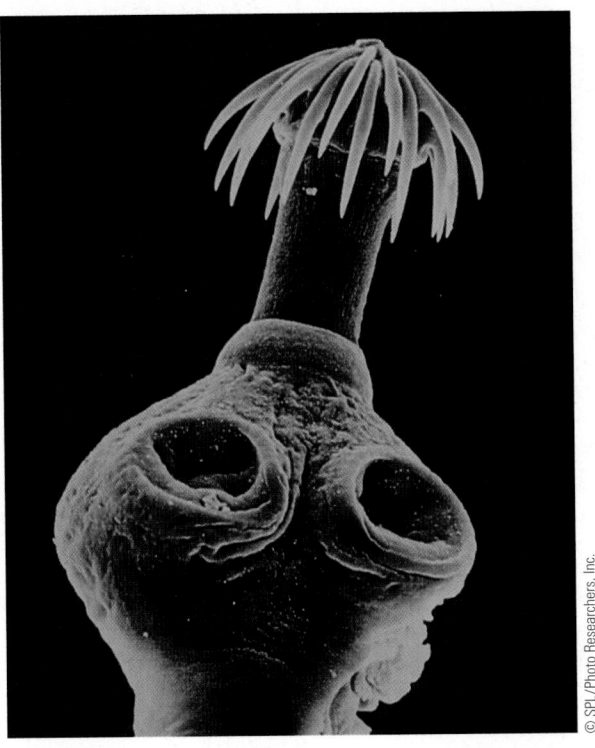

FIGURE 31-10 Scolex of a tapeworm

The small tapeworm (*Acanthrocirrus retrisrostris*) reaches maturity in the intestine of wading birds that eat barnacles. The color-enhanced SEM shows the pistonlike cluster of hooks that can be withdrawn into the head or thrust out and buried in the host's tissue. You can see two of the four powerful suckers beneath the hooks.

250 μm

© SPL/Photo Researchers, Inc.

that enable the parasite to attach to the host's intestine (**FIG. 31-10**).

The reproductive adaptations and abilities of tapeworms are extraordinary. The body of the tapeworm consists of a long chain of segments called **proglottids.** Each proglottid is an entire reproductive machine equipped with both male and female reproductive organs. A single proglottid contains up to 100,000 eggs. Because an adult tapeworm may have as many as 2000 segments, its reproductive potential is staggering. A single tapeworm can produce 600 million eggs per year! Proglottids farthest from the tapeworm's head contain the ripest eggs; these segments are shed from the host's body along with the feces.

The tapeworm has no mouth or digestive system. Digested food from the host is absorbed across the worm's body wall. The tapeworm also lacks well-developed sense organs. Some

tapeworms have complex life cycles, spending their larval stage within the body of an intermediate host and their adult life within the body of a different, final host. **FIGURE 31-11** illustrates the life cycle of the beef tapeworm, which can infect humans when they eat undercooked beef containing the larvae.

Nemerteans are characterized by their proboscis

The **nemerteans** (neh-mur'-tee-uns; phylum **Nemertea**) include the ribbon worms, a relatively small group of about 1200 species of free-living animals (**FIG. 31-12**). Most burrow in marine sediments, but a few species inhabit deep sea water, fresh water, or damp soil. Many nemerteans are carnivorous, feeding on crustaceans and annelids. Nemerteans have long, narrow bodies, either cylindrical or flattened, ranging in length from 1 mm to more than 30 m (100 ft). Some are a vivid orange, red, or green, with black or colored stripes.

Their most remarkable organ, the **proboscis,** is a long, hollow, muscular tube that can be rapidly everted (turned inside out) from the anterior end of the body. Used to capture prey, the sticky proboscis can be wrapped around a small animal. In some species the proboscis is sharp, and in various species it secretes toxic fluid that immobilizes prey. The proboscis is a *derived character* that distinguishes nemerteans from all other invertebrate groups. Because of this character, these animals are sometimes called *proboscis worms.*

Historically, the nemerteans were of special evolutionary interest because biologists thought they were the earliest animals to have a circulatory system and a complete digestive tract. Nemerteans have no heart; blood is circulated by contractions of muscular blood vessels and by movements of the body.

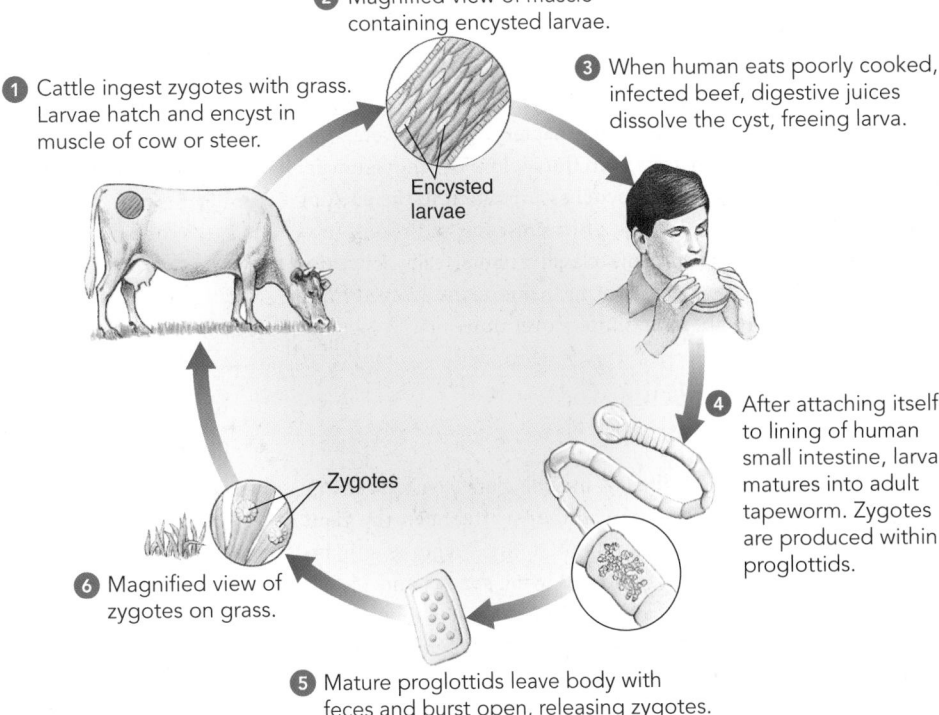

2 Magnified view of muscle containing encysted larvae.

1 Cattle ingest zygotes with grass. Larvae hatch and encyst in muscle of cow or steer.

Encysted larvae

3 When human eats poorly cooked, infected beef, digestive juices dissolve the cyst, freeing larva.

4 After attaching itself to lining of human small intestine, larva matures into adult tapeworm. Zygotes are produced within proglottids.

Zygotes

6 Magnified view of zygotes on grass.

5 Mature proglottids leave body with feces and burst open, releasing zygotes.

FIGURE 31-11 *Animated* Life cycle of the beef tapeworm, *Taenia saginata*

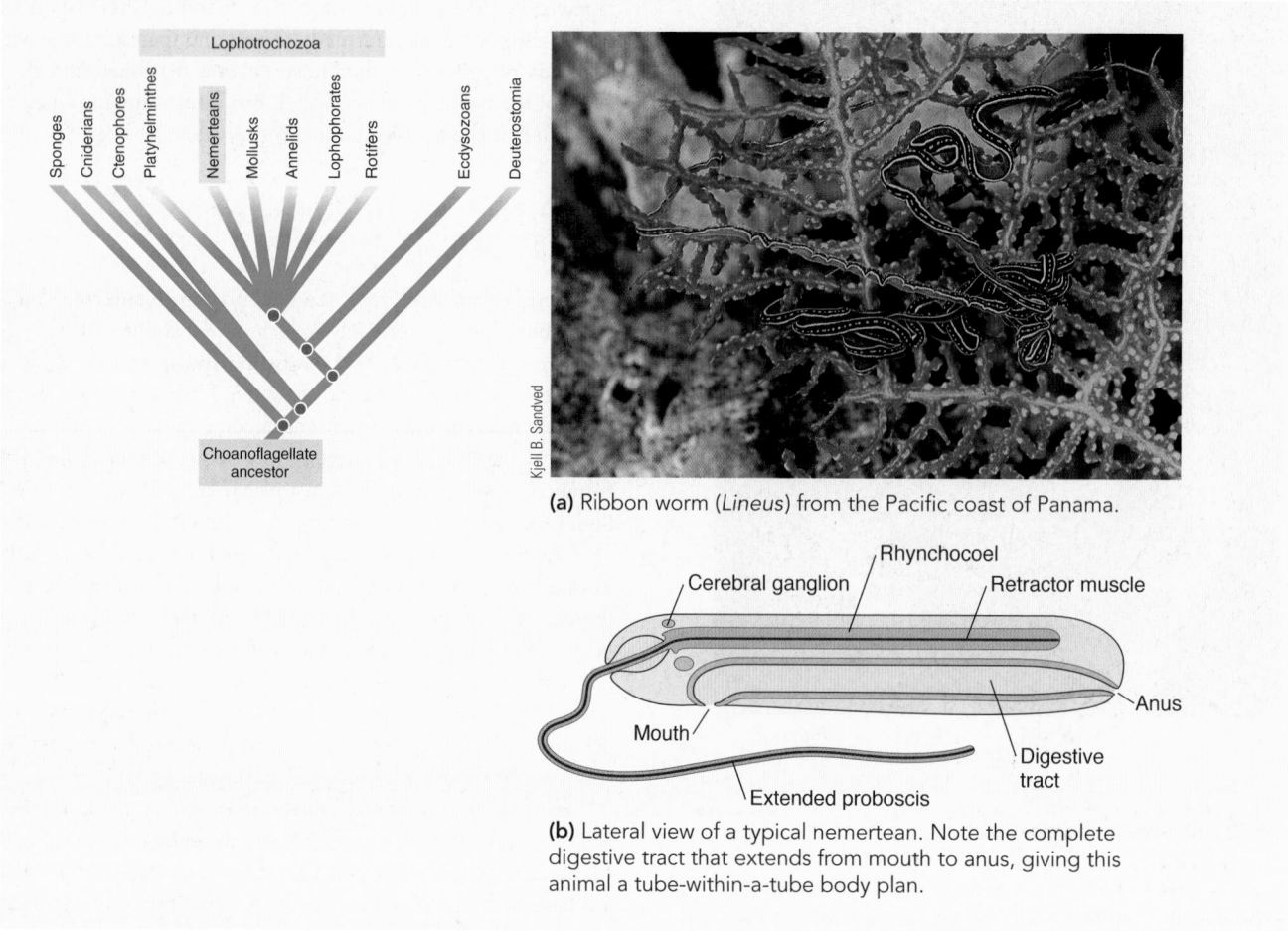

(a) Ribbon worm (*Lineus*) from the Pacific coast of Panama.

(b) Lateral view of a typical nemertean. Note the complete digestive tract that extends from mouth to anus, giving this animal a tube-within-a-tube body plan.

FIGURE 31-12 Nemerteans (ribbon worms)

The chamber surrounding the proboscis is a coelomic space, known as a **rhynchocoel.** It develops in the embryo as the coelom does in coelomate protostomes (see Chapter 30). However, it differs in position and in function from the coelom of other animals. Biologists now view the rhynchocoel as a remnant of the coelom of a coelomate ancestor. Because of its presence and recent molecular evidence, biologists now classify nemerteans with the lophotrochozoans. Like the flatworms, nemerteans evolved from coelomate animals and became simpler over time.

Mollusks have a muscular foot, visceral mass, and mantle

The **mollusks** (phylum **Mollusca**) include clams, oysters, snails, slugs, octopods, and the largest of all the invertebrates, the giant squid, which averages 9 to 16 m (about 30 to 53 ft) in length, including its tentacles. More than 80,000 living species and 35,000 fossil species (second only to the arthropods in number) have been described. Here we discuss four of eight recognized classes. We illustrate representatives of these classes in **FIGURE 31-13** and describe them in **TABLE 31-3.**

Although most mollusks are marine, many snails and clams live in fresh water, and some species of snails and slugs inhabit the land. Mollusks probably evolved early in the history of the proto-

stome clade—soon after the evolution of the coelom, but before the origin of the segmented body that is characteristic of annelids. Although mollusks vary widely in outward appearance, most share six basic characteristics:

1. A soft body, usually covered by a dorsal shell composed mainly of calcium carbonate.
2. A broad, flat, muscular **foot,** located ventrally, which is used for locomotion.
3. The body organs (viscera) concentrated as a **visceral mass** located above the foot.
4. The dorsal body wall forms a pair of folds called the **mantle.** The mantle is a thin sheet of tissue that generally overhangs the visceral mass, forming a mantle cavity. The mantle may contain glands that secrete a shell. The mantle cavity contains gills or a lung.
5. A rasplike structure called a **radula,** which is a belt of teeth in the mouth region. (The radula is not present in clams or their relatives, which are filter feeders.)
6. A coelom, generally reduced to small compartments around certain organs, including the heart and excretory organs (*metanephridia*). The main body cavity is typically a **hemocoel,** a space containing blood (see following discussion of open circulatory systems). The hemocoel is not a coelom.

TABLE 31-3	Major Classes of Phylum Mollusca

Class and Representative Animals	Characteristics
Polyplacophora Chitons	Marine; dorsal shell consisting of eight separate transverse plates; head reduced; broad foot used for locomotion
Gastropoda Snails, slugs, nudibranchs	Marine, freshwater, or terrestrial; coiled shell in many species; torsion of visceral mass; well-developed head with tentacles and eyes
Bivalvia Clams, oysters, mussels	Marine or freshwater; body laterally compressed; two-part shell hinged dorsally; hatchet-shaped foot; filter feeders
Cephalopoda Squids, octopods	Marine; predatory; foot modified into tentacles, usually bearing suckers; well-developed eyes; closed circulatory system

(a) Class Polyplacophora

Chitons are sluggish marine animals with shells composed of eight overlapping plates. This sea cradle chiton (*Tonicella lineata*), which reaches about 5 cm (2 in) in length, inhabits rocks covered with coralline algae in coastal waters off the U.S. Pacific Northwest.

(b) Class Gastropoda

The broad, flat foot of the gastropod is an adaptation to its mobile lifestyle. The mystery snail (*Pomacea bridgesi*) inhabits fresh water and can be found burrowing in the mud.

(c) Class Bivalvia

The compressed body of the horse-neck clam (*Tresus capax*) is adapted for burrowing in the North Pacific mud. Its shell grows to about 20 cm (8 in) in length.

(d) Class Cephalopoda

The squid body is streamlined for swimming. To avoid being seen by potential predators, the squid can change color to blend with its background. This northern short-fin squid (*Illex illecebrosus*), which grows to a mantle length of up to about 31 cm (about 1 ft), inhabits the North Atlantic Ocean.

FIGURE 31-13 *Animated* The mollusk body plan

Mollusks have all of the organ systems typical of complex animals. The digestive system is a tube, often coiled, consisting of a mouth, buccal cavity (mouth cavity), esophagus, stomach, intestine, and anus. The mollusk radula, located within the buccal cavity, projects out of the mouth and is used to scrape particles of food from the surface of rocks or the ocean floor. Sometimes the radula is used to drill a hole in the shell of a prey animal or to tear off pieces of a plant.

Most mollusks have an **open circulatory system** in which the blood, called **hemolymph,** bathes the tissues directly. The heart pumps blood into a single blood vessel, the aorta, which may branch into other vessels. Eventually, blood flows into a network of large spaces called *sinuses,* bringing the blood into direct contact with the tissues. This network makes up the hemocoel, or blood cavity. From the sinuses, blood drains into vessels that conduct it to the gills, where it is recharged with oxygen. After passing through the gills, the blood returns to the heart. Thus, blood flow in a mollusk follows this pattern:

heart ⟶ aorta ⟶ smaller blood vessels ⟶ blood sinuses
(hemocoel) ⟶ blood vessels to gills ⟶ heart

In open circulatory systems, blood pressure tends to be low, and tissues are not very efficiently oxygenated. Because most mollusks are slow-moving animals with low metabolic rates, this type of circulatory system is adequate. The active cephalopods (the class that includes the squids and octopods) have a **closed circulatory system** in which blood flows through a complete circuit of blood vessels.

Most marine mollusks pass through one or more larval stages. The first stage is typically a **trochophore larva,** a free-swimming, top-shaped larva with two bands of cilia around its middle (**FIG. 31-14**). In many mollusks (gastropods such as snails and bivalves such as clams), the trochophore larva develops into a **veliger larva,** which has a shell, foot, and mantle. The veliger larva is unique to the mollusks.

Chitons may be similar to ancestral mollusks

Polyplacophorans (pol-ee-plah-kof'-o-rans; meaning "many plates") are chitons, marine animals with flattened bodies (see Fig. 31-13a). Their most distinctive feature is a shell composed of eight separate but overlapping dorsal plates. The head is reduced, and there are no eyes or tentacles.

The chiton inhabits rocky intertidal zones, using its broad, flat foot to move and to hold on firmly to rocks. By pressing its mantle against the substratum and lifting the inner edge of the mantle, the chiton can produce a partial vacuum. The resulting suction lets the animal adhere powerfully to its perch. Using its radula for grazing, the chiton scrapes algae and other small organisms off rocks and shells.

Gastropods are the largest group of mollusks

The **gastropods,** the snails, slugs, conchs, sea slugs, and their relatives, are the largest and most diverse group of mollusks (see Fig. 31-13b). In fact, with more than 70,000 extant species, gastropods constitute the second-largest class in the animal kingdom, second only to insects. Most gastropods inhabit marine waters, but others make their homes in brackish or fresh water or on land. We think of snails as having a single, spirally coiled shell into which they can withdraw the body, and many do. However, other gastropods, such as limpets, have shells like flattened dunce caps. Still others, such as garden slugs and the beautiful marine slugs known as **nudibranchs,** have no shell at all (**FIG. 31-15**).

Many gastropods have a well-developed head with tentacles. Two simple eyes may be located on stalks that extend from the head. The gastropod uses its broad, flat foot for creeping. Most land snails do not have gills. Instead, the mantle is highly vascularized and functions as a lung. Biologists describe these garden snails and slugs as **pulmonate** ("having a lung").

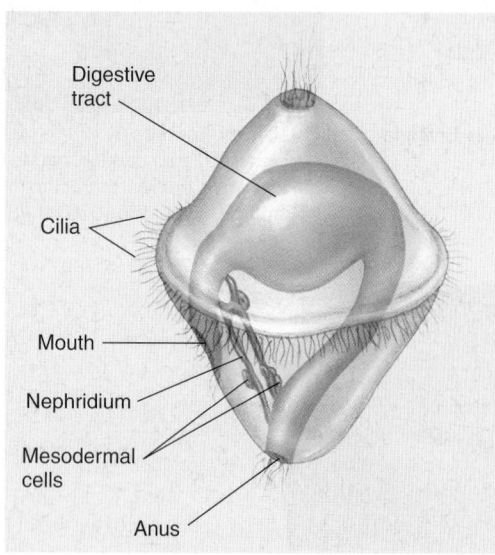

FIGURE 31-14 A trochophore larva

The first larval stage of a marine mollusk, the trochophore larva, is also characteristic of annelids. Just above the mouth a band of ciliated cells functions as a swimming organ and, in some species, collects suspended food particles.

© Bruce Watkins/Animals Animals

FIGURE 31-15 Nudibranch

A nudibranch (*Chromodoris porterae*) feeds on a lightbulb tunicate (*Clavelina huntsmani*).

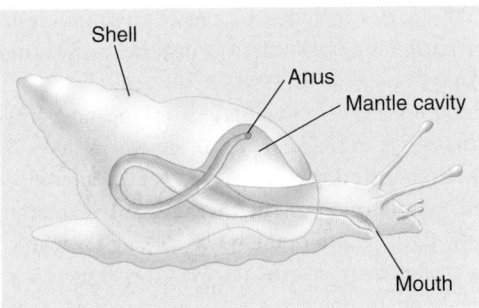

FIGURE 31-16 *Animated* Torsion in a gastropod
As the bilateral larva develops, the visceral mass twists 180 degrees relative to the head. The digestive tube coils, and the anus becomes relocated near the mouth.

Torsion, a twisting of the visceral mass, is a unique feature of gastropods. This twisting is unrelated to the coiling of the shell. As the bilateral larva develops, one side of the visceral mass grows more rapidly than the other side. This uneven growth rotates the visceral mass. The visceral mass and mantle twist permanently up to 180 degrees relative to the head. As a result, the digestive tract becomes somewhat U shaped, and the anus comes to lie above the head and gill (**FIG. 31-16**). Subsequent growth is dorsal and usually in a spiral coil. Torsion limits space in the body, and typically the gill, excretory organ (metanephridium), and gonad are absent on one side. Some biologists hypothesize that torsion is an adaptation that protects the head by allowing it to enter the shell first during withdrawal from potential predators. Without torsion, the foot would be withdrawn first.

Most bivalves are filter feeders

The **bivalves** include clams, oysters, mussels, scallops, and their relatives (see Fig. 31-13c). Typically, the soft body is laterally compressed and completely enclosed by a two-part shell that hinges dorsally and opens ventrally (**FIG. 31-17**). This arrangement allows the hatchet-shaped foot to protrude ventrally for locomotion and for burrowing in mud. The two parts, or **valves,** of the shell are connected by an elastic ligament. Stretching of the ligament opens the shell. Large, strong adductor muscles attached to the shell permit the animal to close its shell.

The inner, pearly layer of the bivalve shell is made of calcium carbonate secreted in thin sheets by the epithelial cells of the mantle. Known as *mother-of-pearl*, this material is valued for making jewelry and buttons. Should a bit of foreign matter lodge between the shell and the mantle, the epithelial cells covering the mantle secrete concentric layers of calcium carbonate around the intruding particle. Many species of oysters and clams form pearls in this way.

Some bivalves, such as oysters, attach permanently to the substrate. Others burrow

slowly through rock or wood, seeking protected dwellings. The shipworm, *Teredo,* a clam that damages dock pilings and other marine installations, is just looking for a home. A few bivalves, such as scallops, swim rapidly by clapping their two shells together with the contraction of a large adductor muscle (the part of the scallop that humans eat).

Clams and oysters are filter feeders that trap food particles suspended in sea water. They take water in through an extension of the mantle called the **incurrent siphon.** Water leaves by way of an **excurrent siphon.** As the water passes over the gills, mucus secreted by the gills traps food particles in the stream of water. Cilia move the food to the mouth. An oyster can filter more than 30 L (about 32 qt) of water per hour! As filter feeders, bivalves have no need for a radula, and indeed they are the only group of mollusks that lack this structure.

Cephalopods are active predators

In contrast with most other mollusks, members of class **Cephalopoda** (meaning "head-foot") are fast-swimming predators (see Fig. 31-13d). The cephalopod mouth is surrounded by tentacles, or arms: 8 in octopods, 10 in squids, and as many as 90 in the chambered nautilus. The large head has well-developed eyes that form images. Although they develop differently, their complex eyes are structurally similar to vertebrate eyes and function in much the same way. The octopus has no shell; and the shell of the squid, located inside the body, is greatly reduced.

Nautilus has a coiled shell consisting of many chambers built up over time. Each year the animal lives in the newest and largest chamber of the series. *Nautilus* secretes a mixture of gases similar to air into the other chambers. By regulating the amount of gas in the chambers, the animal controls its depth in the ocean.

The tentacles of squids, octopods, and cuttlefish are covered with suckers for seizing and holding prey. In addition to a radula,

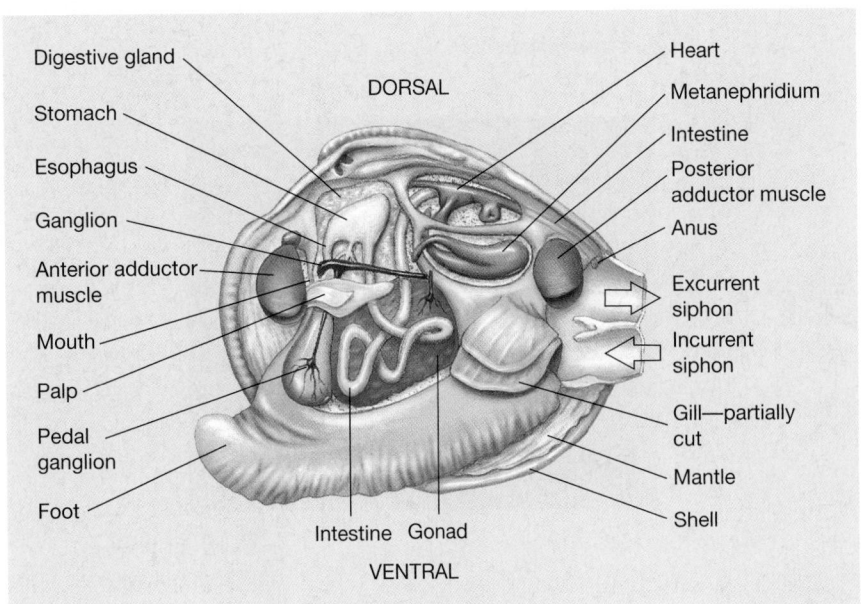

FIGURE 31-17 *Animated* Internal anatomy of a clam
The two shells of a bivalve hinge dorsally and open ventrally.

the mouth has two strong, horny beaks used to kill prey and tear it to bits. The thick, muscular mantle is fitted with a funnel-like **siphon.** By filling the cavity with water and ejecting it through the siphon, the cephalopod achieves forceful jet propulsion. Squids and cuttlefish have streamlined bodies adapted for efficient swimming.

In addition to speed, the cephalopod has two other adaptations that facilitate escape from its predators, which include certain whales and moray eels. It can confuse the enemy by rapidly changing colors. By expanding and contracting *chromatophores,* cells in the skin that contain pigment granules, the cephalopod can display an impressive variety of mottled colors. Another defense mechanism is its **ink sac,** which produces a thick, black liquid the animal releases in a dark cloud when alarmed. While its enemy pauses, temporarily blinded and confused, the cephalopod escapes. The ink inactivates the chemical receptors of some predators, making them incapable of detecting their prey.

The octopus feeds on crabs and other arthropods, catching and killing them with a poisonous secretion of its salivary glands. During the day the octopus usually hides among the rocks; in the evening it emerges to hunt for food. Its motion is incredibly fluid, giving little hint of the considerable strength in its eight arms.

Small octopods survive well in aquariums and have been studied extensively. Because octopods are relatively intelligent and can make associations among stimuli, researchers have used them as models for studying learning and memory. Their highly adaptable behavior more closely resembles that of the vertebrates than the more stereotypic patterns of behavior observed in other invertebrates (see Chapter 52).

Annelids are segmented worms

Annelids (an'-eh-lids; phylum **Annelida**) are segmented worms with bilateral symmetry and a tubular body that may be partitioned into more than 100 ringlike segments. This phylum, composed of about 15,000 species, includes three main groups: the polychaetes, a group of marine and freshwater worms; the earthworms; and the leeches (**TABLE 31-4** and **FIG. 31-18**).

The term *Annelida* (from a Latin word meaning "little rings") refers to the series of rings, or segments, which make up the annelid body. Both the body wall and many of the internal organs are segmented. Some structures, such as the digestive tract and certain nerves, extend the length of the body, passing through successive segments. Other structures, such as excretory organs, are repeated in each segment. In polychaetes and earthworms, segments are separated from one another internally by transverse partitions called **septa.**

An important advantage of **segmentation** is that it facilitates locomotion. The coelom is divided into segments, and each segment has its own muscles. This arrangement allows the animal to elongate one part of its body while shortening another part. The annelid's hydrostatic skeleton is important in movement. Polychaetes and earthworms have bristlelike structures called **setae** (sing., *seta*), located on each segment. Setae provide traction as the worm moves

TABLE 31-4	Major Classes of Phylum Annelida
Class and Representative Animals	**Characteristics**
Polychaeta Sandworms, tubeworms	Mainly marine; each segment bears a pair of parapodia with many setae; well-developed head; separate sexes; trochophore larva
Oligochaeta Earthworms	Terrestrial and freshwater worms; few setae per segment; lack well-developed head; hermaphroditic
Hirudinida Leeches	Most are blood-sucking parasites that inhabit fresh water; appendages and setae absent; prominent muscular suckers

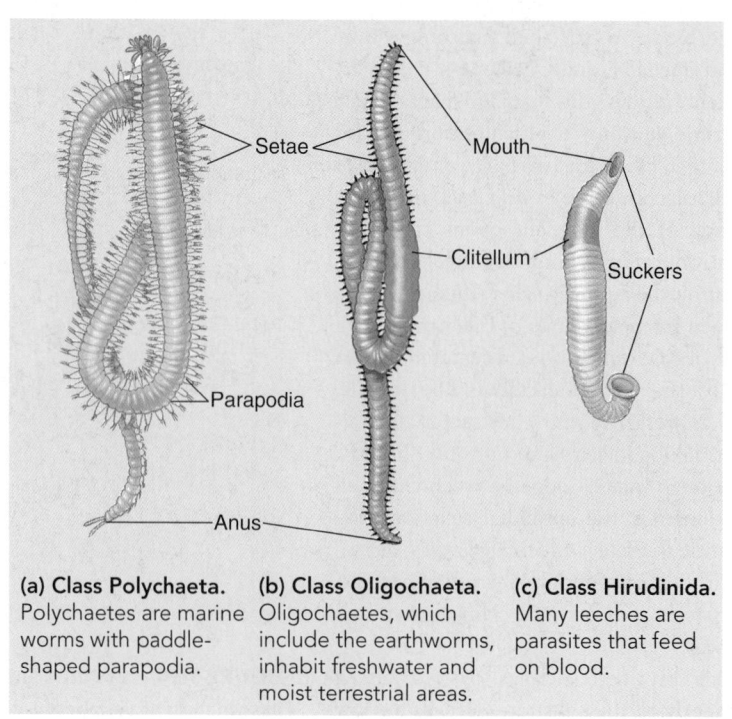

(a) Class Polychaeta. Polychaetes are marine worms with paddle-shaped parapodia.

(b) Class Oligochaeta. Oligochaetes, which include the earthworms, inhabit freshwater and moist terrestrial areas.

(c) Class Hirudinida. Many leeches are parasites that feed on blood.

FIGURE 31-18 Three major groups of annelids

along by alternating contraction of its longitudinal and circular muscles. In earthworms, setae consist mainly of chitin.

The annelid nervous system typically consists of a ventral nerve cord and a simple brain consisting of a pair of ganglia. Each segment has a pair of ganglia and lateral nerves. Annelids have a large, well-developed coelom, a closed circulatory system, and a complete digestive tract extending from mouth to anus. Respiration is *cutaneous,* that is, through the skin, or by gills. Typically, a pair of excretory tubules called **metanephridia** is located in each segment (described in Chapter 48).

Most polychaetes are marine worms with parapodia

Most **polychaetes** are marine worms, and many swim freely in the sea. Some polychaetes are part of the plankton and are important in marine food chains. Others burrow in the mud near the shore or in crevices of rocks or coral reefs. Still others live in tubes they secrete or make by cementing bits of shell and sand together with mucus. Giant tube worms have been found in deep vents in the floor of the Pacific Ocean (see *Inquiring About: Life Without the Sun* in Chapter 55).

Each body segment typically bears a pair of paddle-shaped appendages called **parapodia** (sing., *parapodium*) that function in locomotion and in gas exchange. These fleshy structures bear many stiff setae (the term *polychaete* means "many bristles"; see the fireworm in the chapter opening photograph). Most polychaetes have a well-developed head with eyes and antennae. The head may

also be equipped with tentacles and palps (feelers). Polychaetes develop from free-swimming trochophore larvae similar to those of mollusks.

Behavioral patterns that ensure fertilization have evolved in many polychaete species. By responding to certain rhythmic variations, or cycles, in the environment, nearly all the females and males of a given species release their gametes into the water at the same time. For example, more than 90% of reef-dwelling *Palolo* worms of the South Pacific shed their eggs and sperm within a 2-hour period on one night of the year. The posterior portion of the *Palolo* worm, loaded with eggs or sperm, breaks off from the rest of the body. It comes to the surface and bursts, releasing its gametes. This mass reproductive event occurs in October or November at the beginning of the last lunar quarter. Local islanders gather great numbers of the swarming polychaetes, which they bake or eat raw.

Earthworms help maintain fertile soil

The approximately 3100 species of **oligochaetes** live almost exclusively in fresh water and in moist terrestrial habitats. These worms lack parapodia, have few bristles per segment (the term *oligochaete* means "few bristles"), and lack a well-developed head. All oligochaetes are hermaphroditic.

Lumbricus terrestris, the common earthworm, is about 20 cm (8 in) long. Its body has more than 100 segments, separated externally by grooves that indicate the internal position of the septa (**FIG. 31-19**). The earthworm's body is somewhat protected from

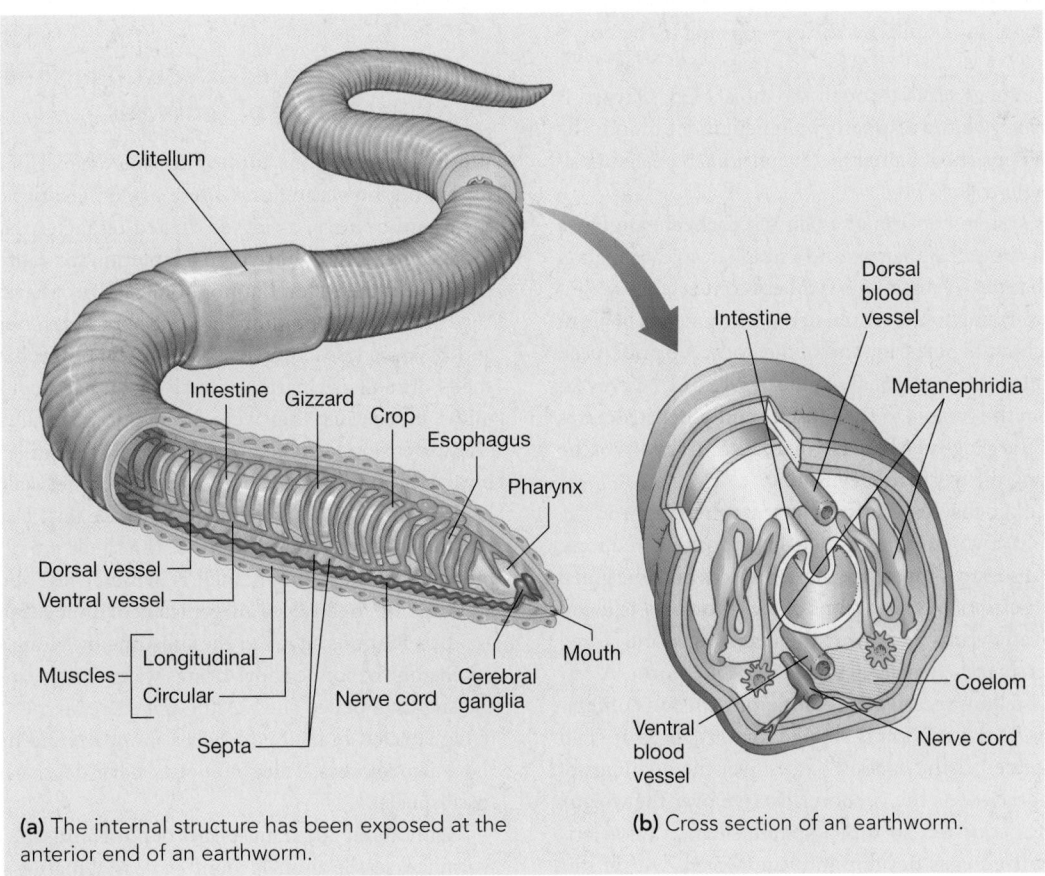

(a) The internal structure has been exposed at the anterior end of an earthworm.

(b) Cross section of an earthworm.

FIGURE 31-19 *Animated* Body plan of an earthworm

drying by a thin, transparent **cuticle** secreted by the cells of the epidermis. Mucus secreted by gland cells of the epidermis forms an additional protective layer over the body surface. The body wall has an outer layer of circular muscles and an inner layer of longitudinal muscles.

An earthworm literally eats its way through the soil. It ingests its own weight in soil and nutritious decaying vegetation every 24 hours! Earthworms enhance the formation and maintenance of fertile soil. As they move about, they turn and aerate the soil and enrich it with nitrogenous wastes.

The earthworm processes its meal of soil in a complex digestive system. Food is swallowed through the muscular **pharynx** and passes through the **esophagus,** which is modified to form a thin-walled **crop** where food is stored, and a thick-walled, muscular **gizzard.** In the gizzard, food is ground to bits by sand grains consumed along with the meal. The rest of the digestive system is a long, straight **intestine** that chemically digests food and absorbs nutrients. Wastes pass out of the intestine to the exterior through the **anus.**

The efficient closed circulatory system consists of two main blood vessels that extend longitudinally. The dorsal blood vessel, just above the digestive tract, collects blood from vessels in the segments, then contracts to pump the blood anteriorly. In the region of the esophagus, five pairs of blood vessels propel blood from the dorsal to the ventral blood vessel. Located just below the digestive tract, the ventral blood vessel carries blood posteriorly. Small vessels branch from it and deliver blood to the various structures in each segment, as well as to the body wall. Within these structures, blood flows through tiny capillaries before returning to the dorsal blood vessel.

Gas exchange takes place through the moist skin. Oxygen is transported by *hemoglobin*, a respiratory pigment in the blood. The excretory system consists of paired metanephridia, repeated in almost every segment of the body.

The nervous system consists of a pair of **cerebral ganglia** (a simple brain) just above the pharynx and a subpharyngeal ganglion just below the pharynx. A ring of nerve fibers connects these ganglia. From the lower ganglion, a ventral nerve cord extends beneath the digestive tract to the posterior end of the body. A pair of fused ganglia is present in each segment along the nerve cord. Nerves extend laterally from the ganglia to the muscles and other structures of that segment. The ganglia coordinate muscle contractions of the body wall, allowing the worm to creep along.

Like other oligochaetes, earthworms are hermaphroditic. During copulation, two worms, headed in opposite directions, press their ventral surfaces together. These surfaces become glued together by the thick mucous secretions of each worm's *clitellum,* a thickened ring of epidermis. Sperm are then exchanged and stored in the *seminal receptacles* (small sacs) of the other worm. A few days later, each clitellum secretes a membranous cocoon containing a sticky fluid. As the cocoon is slipped forward, eggs are laid in it. Sperm are added as the cocoon passes over the openings of the seminal receptacles. As the cocoon slips free over the worm's head, its openings constrict so that a spindle-shaped capsule is formed. The fertilized eggs develop into tiny worms within this capsule. This reproductive pattern is an adaptation to terrestrial

life; the cocoon protects the delicate gametes and young worms from drying out.

Many leeches are blood-sucking parasites

Leeches are members of a group called **Hirudinida.** Most leeches inhabit fresh water, but some live in the sea or in moist areas on land. Some leeches are nonparasitic predators that capture small invertebrates such as earthworms and snails. However, about 75% of the known species of leeches are blood-sucking parasites. Leeches differ from other annelids in having neither setae nor parapodia.

Leeches have muscular suckers at both the anterior and posterior ends of their body. Most parasitic leeches attach themselves to a vertebrate host, bite through the skin, and suck out a quantity of blood, which is stored in pouches in the digestive tract. *Hirudin,* an anticoagulant secreted by glands in the crop, ensures leeches a full meal of blood. In 31 minutes, a leech can suck out as much as 10 times its own weight in blood! Some leeches feed only about twice each year because they digest their food slowly over several months.

Leeches have been used since ancient times for drawing blood from areas swollen by poisonous stings and bites. During the 19th century, they were widely used to remove "bad blood," thought to be the cause of many diseases. Leeches are used in modern medicine to remove excess fluid and blood that accumulate within body tissues as a result of injury, disease, or surgery (**FIG. 31-20**). The leech attaches its sucker near the site of injury, makes an incision, and secretes hirudin. The hirudin prevents the blood from clotting and dissolves clots that already exist.

The lophophorates are distinguished by a ciliated ring of tentacles

With a few exceptions, **lophophorates** are marine animals adapted for life on the ocean floor. These coelomates are distinguished by their **lophophore,** a ring of ciliated tentacles that surrounds the mouth. The lophophore is an adaptation for capturing suspended particles in the water. Lophophorates do not have a distinct head.

The three lophophorate groups are Brachiopoda, Phoronida, and Bryozoa (also known as Ectoprocta). **Brachiopods,** or lampshells, are solitary marine animals that inhabit cold water. Until the mid-19th century, they were thought to be mollusks because they are suspension feeders that superficially resemble clams and other bivalve mollusks. Their body is enclosed between two shells and has a mantle and mantle cavity (**FIG. 31-21a**). However, they differ from bivalve mollusks in that the shells are dorsal and ventral rather than lateral; each shell is symmetrical about the midline, and the two shell valves are typically of unequal size.

Brachiopods attach to the substrate by a long stalk. The action of cilia on the lophophore brings water with suspended food into the slightly opened shell. Although there are now only about 325 living species, brachiopods were abundant and diversified during the Paleozoic era. Paleobiologists have described about 12,000 fossil species.

Only about 20 extant species of **phoronids** are known. They are wormlike, sessile animals found in coastal marine sediments. Adult phoronids secrete chitinous tubes in which they live (**FIG. 31-21b**).

(a) LM of a blood-sucking leech (*Helobdella stagnalis*) that feeds on mammals. The digestive tract (*dark area*) of its swollen body is filled with ingested blood.

(b) Medicinal leeches (*Hirudo medicinalis*) are used here to treat hematoma, an accumulation of blood within tissues that results from injury or disease.

500 μm

FIGURE 31-20 Leeches

They extend their lophophores from their tubes for feeding. Phoronids vary in length from 2 cm to more than 20 cm (less than 1 in to about 8 in), but they are only 1 to 3 mm in diameter.

Bryozoans, also known as *ectoprocts* or "moss animals," are microscopic aquatic animals. They form sessile colonies by asexual budding (**FIG. 31-21c**). Each colony can consist of millions of individuals and can extend in length up to about 31 cm (about 1 ft). The colonies typically appear plantlike, but some have the appearance of coral. Approximately 4500 living species are known.

Biologists are still debating the evolutionary position of the lophophorates. They were traditionally considered a monophyletic group and a sister group to the deuterostomes, based on certain structural similarities. However, these lophophorate groups also have several morphological characters that suggest a relationship with the lophotrochozoans. Although their phylogeny is still

(a) Brachiopods. Like other brachiopods, these northern lampshells (*Terebratulina septentrionalis*) superficially resemble clams.

(b) Phoronids. A single lophophore of a phoronid (*Phoronopsis viridis*). This animal is about 20 cm (8 in) long, but only 1–3 mm in diameter.

(c) Bryozoans. Like many bryozoans, this freshwater species (*Cristatella mucedo*) forms colonies by asexual budding.

FIGURE 31-21 Representative lophophorates

being debated, based on molecular data (18S rDNA nucleotide sequences), the lophophorate phyla are currently classified as Lophotrochozoa.

Rotifers have a crown of cilia

Rotifers (phylum **Rotifera**), or "wheel animals," are among the less familiar invertebrates. Although no larger than many protozoa, these aquatic, microscopic animals are multicellular. Most of the 2000 described species inhabit fresh water, but some live in marine environments or damp soil. Rotifers are important in cycling nutrients in aquatic ecosystems. Rotifers do not have a true coelom and were formerly classified as pseudocoelomates. Current evidence suggests that rotifers evolved from animals with a true coelom and we classify them as lophotrochozoans.

Rotifers have a characteristic crown of cilia on their anterior end. The cilia beat rapidly during swimming and feeding, giving the appearance of a spinning wheel (**FIG. 31-22**). Rotifers feed on tiny organisms suspended in the stream of water drawn into the mouth by the cilia. A muscular organ posterior to the mouth grinds the food. The complete digestive tract ends in an anus through which wastes are eliminated.

Rotifers have a nervous system with a "brain" and sense organs, including eyespots. Protonephridia with flame cells remove excess water from the body and may also excrete metabolic wastes.

Biologists have discovered that rotifers, like some other animals with a pseudocoelom, are "cell constant." Each member of a given species has exactly the same number of cells. Indeed, each part of the body has a precisely fixed number of cells arranged in a characteristic pattern. Cell division does not take place after embryonic development, and mitosis cannot be induced. Growth results from an increase in cell size. Do you think rotifers could develop cancer? One of the challenging research problems of our time is to discover the difference between such nondividing cells and the dividing cells of other animals.

Another interesting characteristic of rotifers is their ability to survive very dry conditions and temperature extremes. These interesting animals can remain in a dormant state for months or years. When conditions become favorable, they recover and become active once again.

Review

- What are some advantages of (a) bilateral symmetry, (b) cephalization, and (c) a coelom?
- On what basis have biologists classified nemerteans as lophotrochozoans?
- How does the lifestyle of a gastropod differ from that of a cephalopod? Identify adaptations that have evolved in each for its particular lifestyle.
- What are two distinguishing characteristics for each of the following: (1) flatworms, (2) mollusks, and (3) annelids?

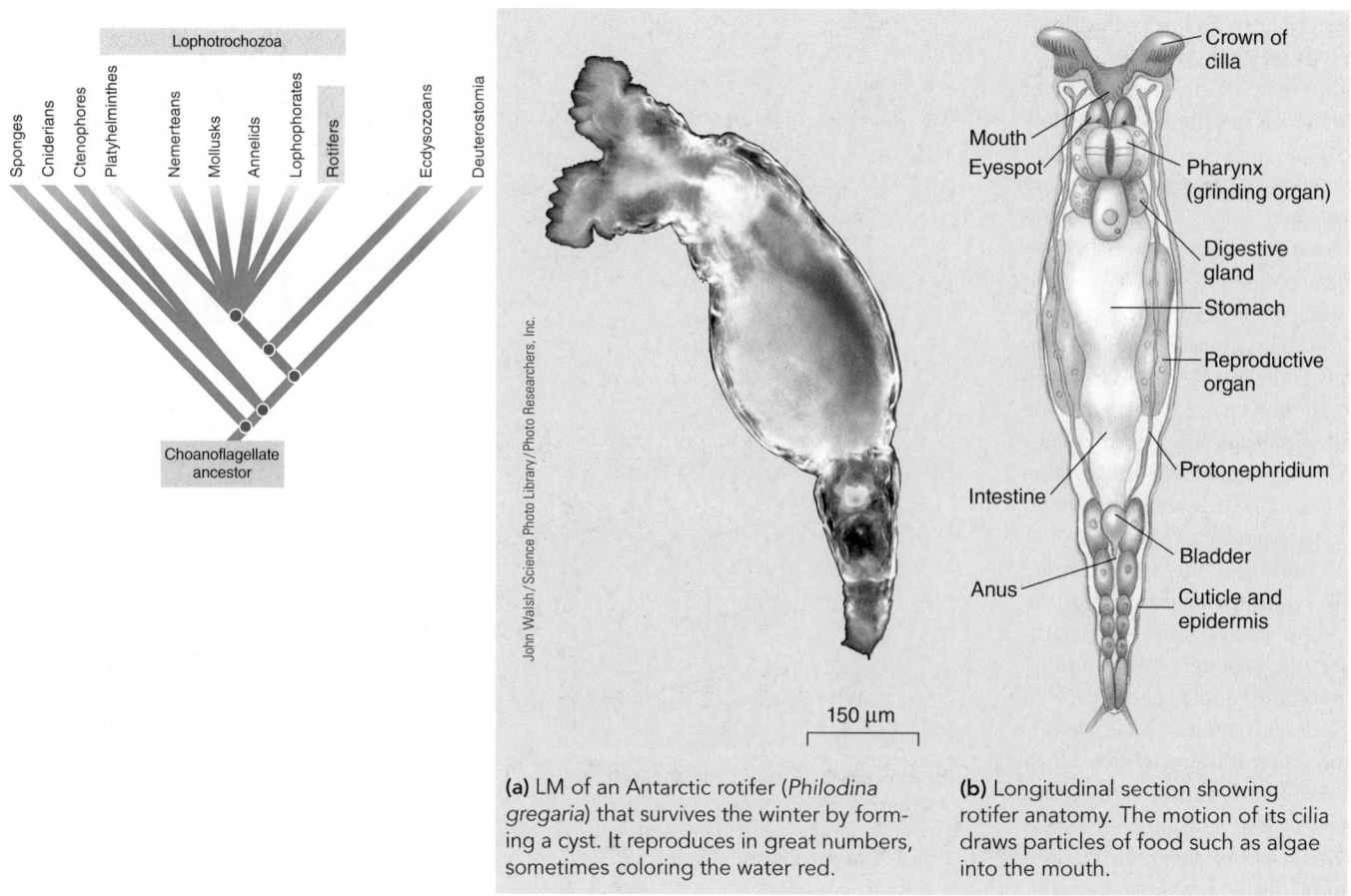

(a) LM of an Antarctic rotifer (*Philodina gregaria*) that survives the winter by forming a cyst. It reproduces in great numbers, sometimes coloring the water red.

(b) Longitudinal section showing rotifer anatomy. The motion of its cilia draws particles of food such as algae into the mouth.

FIGURE 31-22 Rotifers (wheel animals)

31.3 THE ECDYSOZOA

■ LEARNING OBJECTIVES

9 Summarize what is known about the phylogeny of the ecdysozoans.

10 Describe distinguishing characteristics of nematodes, and identify four parasitic nematodes.

11 Describe six key characteristics of arthropods, summarize proposed phylogeny of arthropods, and distinguish among arthropod subphyla and classes; give examples of animals that belong to each group.

12 Identify adaptations that have contributed to the biological success of insects.

The **Ecdysozoa** include the nematodes (roundworms) and arthropods, animals characterized by a cuticle, a noncellular body covering secreted by the epidermis. The name *Ecdysozoa* refers to the process of **ecdysis,** or **molting,** characteristic of animals in this group. During ecdysis, an animal sheds its outer covering (for example, cuticle, exoskeleton, skin), which is then replaced by the growth of a new one. The taxonomic validity of the Ecdysozoa has been supported by many types of data, including molecular data.

Roundworms are of great ecological importance

Nematodes (nem'-uh-todes; phylum **Nematoda**), or **roundworms,** play key ecological roles as decomposers and predators of smaller organisms. Many soil nematodes eat bacteria. Nematodes are numerous and widely distributed in soil and in marine and freshwater sediments. About 80,000 species have been described, and many more remain to be discovered. The nematodes rival the insects in number of individuals. A spadeful of soil may contain thousands of these mainly microscopic worms, which thrash around, coiling and uncoiling. Greater understanding of soil nematode diversity and ecology will contribute to solving some important agricultural problems. *Caenorhabditis elegans,* a free-living soil nematode, is an important model research organism for biologists studying the genetic control of development (see Chapter 17).

The elongated, cylindrical, threadlike nematode body is pointed at both ends and covered with a tough, flexible cuticle (**FIG. 31-23**). Secreted by the underlying epidermis, the thick cuticle gives the nematode body shape and offers some protection. The epidermis is unusual in that it does not consist of distinct cells.

Nematodes have a fluid-filled pseudocoelom that serves as a hydrostatic skeleton. It transmits the force of muscle contraction to the enclosed fluid. Movement of fluid in the pseudocoelom is also important in nutrient transport and distribution. Like ribbon worms, nematodes exhibit bilateral symmetry, a complete digestive tract, three definite tissue layers, and definite organ sys-

tems; however, they lack specific circulatory structures. The sexes are usually separate, and the male is generally smaller than the female.

Traditionally, biologists classified nematodes as a single phylum based on the pseudocoelom, wormlike body structure, and other characters such as absence of a well-defined head. However, molecular evidence suggests that nematodes are not a monophyletic group and that they evolved from more complex animals by a simplification in body plan. Like arthropods and other ecdysozoans, the nematode sheds its cuticle periodically. Systematists currently classify nematodes with the Ecdysozoa (see Fig. 30-7).

Although most nematodes are free-living, others are important parasites in plants and animals. More than 50 species of roundworms are human parasites, including *Ascaris,* hookworms, pinworms, and the trichina worm. The common intestinal parasite ***Ascaris*** spends its adult life in the human intestine, where it ingests partly digested food (**FIG. 31-24**). *Ascaris* is a white worm about 25 cm (10 in) long. Like most parasites, it has remarkable reproductive adaptations that ensure survival of its species. A mature female may produce as many as 200,000 eggs per day!

Hookworms attach to the lining of the intestine and suck blood, potentially causing serious tissue damage and blood loss. **Pinworms** are the most common worms found in children. The tiny pinworm eggs are often ingested by eating with hands contaminated with them. The **trichina worm** lives inside a variety of animals, including pigs, rats, and bears. Humans typically become infected by eating undercooked, infected meat. Larvae encyst in skeletal muscle.

Arthropods are characterized by jointed appendages and an exoskeleton of chitin

Arthropods (ar'-thro-pods; phylum **Arthropoda**) are the most biologically successful group of animals. More than 80% of all known animals are arthropods! They are more diverse and live in a

FIGURE 31-23 LM of a free-living nematode

This unidentified aquatic nematode is shown among the cyanobacterium *Oscillatoria,* which it eats.

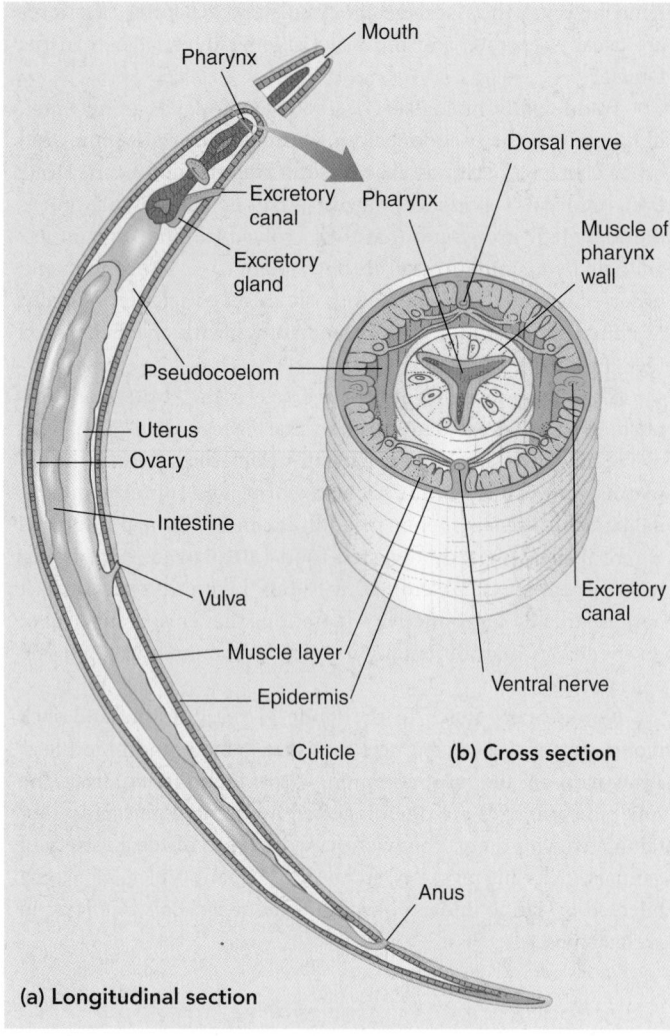

(a) Longitudinal section

Mouth
Pharynx
Pharynx
Dorsal nerve
Excretory canal
Muscle of pharynx wall
Excretory gland
Pseudocoelom
Uterus
Ovary
Intestine
Vulva
Excretory canal
Muscle layer
Epidermis
Ventral nerve
Cuticle
(b) Cross section
Anus

FIGURE 31-24 *Animated* **The roundworm** *Ascaris*
(a) Note the complete digestive tract that extends from mouth to anus.
(b) This cross section through *Ascaris* shows the tube-within-a-tube body plan. The protective cuticle that covers the body helps the animal resist drying.

A disadvantage of the exoskeleton is that it is nonliving, and the arthropod periodically outgrows it. Recall that *molting* is the process of shedding an old exoskeleton, which is then replaced by a larger one. The shed exoskeleton represents a net metabolic loss, and molting also leaves the arthropod temporarily vulnerable to predators.

3. **Paired, jointed appendages,** from which this group gets its name (*arthropod* means "jointed foot"), are modified for many functions. They serve as swimming paddles, walking legs, mouthparts for capturing and manipulating food, sensory structures, or organs for transferring sperm.

4. The nervous system, which resembles that of the annelids, consists of a "brain" (cerebral ganglia) and ventral nerve cord with ganglia. In some arthropods, successive ganglia may fuse. Arthropods have a variety of very effective sense organs. Many have organs of hearing and **antennae** that sense taste and touch. Most insects and many crustaceans have **compound eyes** composed of many light-sensitive units called **ommatidia** (see Fig. 43-17). The compound eye can form an image and is especially adapted for detecting movement.

Arthropods have an *open circulatory system*. A dorsal, tubular heart pumps **hemolymph** into a dorsal artery, which may branch into smaller arteries. From the arteries, hemolymph flows into large spaces that collectively make up the hemocoel. Eventually, hemolymph re-enters the heart through openings, called *ostia*, in its walls.

The exoskeleton presents a barrier to diffusion of oxygen and carbon dioxide through the body wall, necessitating the evolution of specialized respiratory systems for gas exchange. Most aquatic arthropods have gills that function in gas exchange, whereas many terrestrial forms have a system of internal branching air tubes called **tracheae,** or **tracheal tubes** (see Fig. 46-1b). Other terrestrial arthropods have platelike **book lungs** (see Fig. 46-1d).

The arthropod digestive system is a tube similar to that of the earthworm. Excretory structures vary somewhat among groups. The coelom is small and filled chiefly by the organs of the reproductive system.

Arthropod evolution and classification are controversial

Two groups of animals thought to be closely related to arthropods are the onychophorans and the tardigrades (**FIG. 31-25**). These three groups make up clade **Panarthropoda.** Like arthropods, onychophorans and tardigrades have a thick cuticle and must molt in order to grow. The body is segmented in all three groups, and all have legs and claws, and a ventral nervous system. Panarthropods have an open circulatory system, and the coelom is reduced to a hemocoel.

The caterpillar-like **onychophorans,** known as velvet worms, probably branched early from the arthropod line. They have paired appendages, but they are not jointed. As in arthropods, their jaws are derived from appendages. Some biologists place the **tardigrades,** known as "water bears," as the sister taxon of the arthropods. These tiny animals (typically less than 1 mm in length) have short, unjointed, clawed legs (see Fig. 2-12).

Arthropod fossils have been identified dating back to the Proterozoic eon. Early in their evolutionary history, more than 540

greater range of habitats than do the members of any other animal phylum. More than one million species have been described, and biologists predict millions more will be identified. The following adaptations have greatly contributed to their success:

1. The arthropod body, like that of the annelid, is segmented. *Segmentation* is important from an evolutionary perspective because it provides the opportunity for specialization of body regions. In arthropods, groups of segments are specialized to perform particular functions. Segments differ in shape, muscles, or the appendages they bear.

2. A hard **exoskeleton,** composed of chitin and protein, covers the entire body and appendages. The exoskeleton serves as a coat of armor that protects against predators and helps prevent excessive loss of moisture. It also supports the underlying soft tissues. Arthropods move effectively because distinct muscles attach to the inner surface of the exoskeleton and operate the joints of the body and appendages.

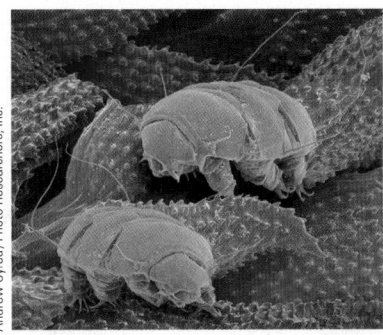

(a) Onychophoran. Note the soft segmented body and series of non-jointed legs. Extant onychophorans live in humid forests but many extinct species inhabited the ocean.

(b) Tardigrades. Commonly known as water bears, tardigrades normally live in moist habitats, such as thin films of water on mosses. Most are less than 1 mm long.

FIGURE 31-25 Onychophorans and tardigrades
These animals are thought to be close relatives of arthropods.

million years ago (mya), arthropods diverged into several groups. Arthropods evolved rapidly during the Cambrian radiation, as evidenced by many diverse fossils in the Burgess Shale and other ancient sites.

We discuss five main arthropod groups, based on emerging molecular and other data: the extinct trilobites, and the extant Myriapoda, Chelicerata, Crustacea, and Hexapoda (**TABLE 31-5**). Some systematists consider each of these groups a phylum; others

view them as subphyla or classes. In this edition, we classify these groups as subphyla of phylum Arthropoda. However, as you study the following sections, bear in mind that arthropod systematics is a work in progress. Both the relationship of arthropods to other protostomes and the relationships among arthropods continue to be topics of lively debate.

Trilobites were early arthropods

Among the earliest arthropods to evolve, **trilobites** inhabited shallow Paleozoic seas more than 500 mya. These arthropods, which have been extinct for about 250 million years, lived on the sea bottom and filtered mud to obtain food. Most ranged from 3 to 10 cm (about 1 to 4 in), but a few reached almost 1 m (39 in) in length.

Covered by a hard, segmented exoskeleton, the trilobite body was a flattened oval divided into three parts: an anterior head bearing a pair of antennae and a pair of compound eyes; a thorax; and a posterior abdomen (**FIG. 31-26**). At right angles to these divisions, two dorsal grooves extended the length of the animal, dividing the body into a median lobe and two lateral lobes. (The name *trilobite* derives from this division of the body into three longitudinal parts.) Each segment had a pair of segmented **biramous appendages**, appendages with two jointed branches extending from their base. In trilobites, each appendage consisted of an inner walking leg and an outer branch with gills.

TABLE 31-5	Extant Arthropod Subphyla					
Subphylum and Selected Classes	Body Divisions	Appendages: Antennae, Mouthparts	Appendages: Legs	Gas Exchange	Development	Main Habitat
Myriapoda Class Chilopoda (centipedes) Class Diplopoda (millipedes)	Head with segmented body	Uniramous. Antennae: one pair Mouthparts: mandibles, maxillae	Chilopods: one pair/segment Diplopods: usually two pairs/segment	Tracheae	Direct	Terrestrial
Chelicerata Class Merostoma (horseshoe crabs) Class Arachnida (spiders, scorpions, ticks, mites)	Cephalothorax and abdomen	Uniramous. Antennae: none Mouthparts: chelicerae, pedipalps	Merostomes: four pairs of walking legs Arachnids: four pairs on cephalothorax	Merostomes: gills Arachnids: book lungs or tracheae	Direct, except mites and ticks	Merostomes: marine Arachnids: mainly terrestrial
Crustacea Class Malacostraca (lobsters, crabs, shrimp, isopods) Class Cirripedia* (barnacles) Class Copepoda* (copepods)	Head, thorax, and abdomen	Biramous. Antennae: two pairs Mouthparts: mandibles, two pairs of maxillae (for handling food)	Typically one pair/segment	Gills	Usually larval stages (nauplius larva)	Marine or freshwater; a few are terrestrial
Hexapoda Class Insecta (bees, ants, grasshoppers, roaches, flies, beetles)	Head, thorax, and abdomen	Uniramous. Antennae: one pair Mouthparts: mandibles, maxillae	Three pairs on thorax	Tracheae	Typically, larval stages; most with complete metamorphosis	Mainly terrestrial

*Some systematists now include Cirripedia and Copepoda as orders under Class Maxillopoda.

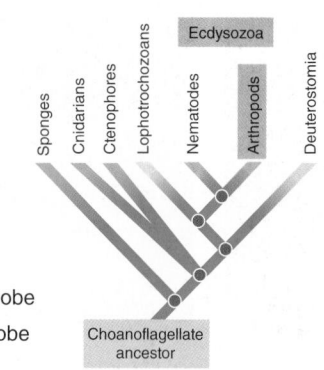

— Median lobe
— Lateral lobe

(a) Fossil trilobites. These extinct arthropods (*Phacops rana*) were about 3 cm (1.2 in) long. Note the large, well-developed eyes visible on either side of the head region.

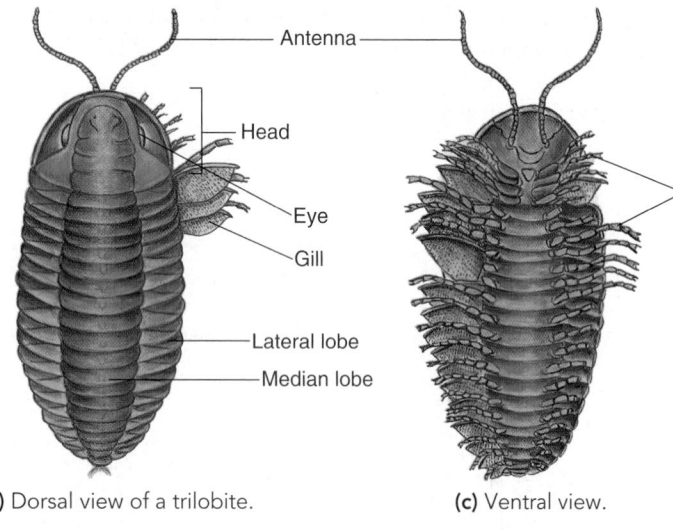

— Antenna —
— Head
— Eye
— Gill
— Lateral lobe
— Median lobe

Biramous appendages

(b) Dorsal view of a trilobite.

(c) Ventral view.

FIGURE 31-26 Trilobites

Biologists consider these extinct marine arthropods the most primitive members of phylum Arthropoda. Trilobites flourished in the ocean during the Paleozoic era.

Subphylum Myriapoda includes centipedes and millipedes

Members of subphylum **Myriapoda** are characterized by un-branched appendages called **uniramous appendages,** jawlike mandibles, and a single pair of antennae. Centipedes (class **Chilopoda**) and millipedes (class **Diplopoda**) are terrestrial and are typically found beneath stones or wood in the soil in both temperate and tropical regions. Both centipedes and millipedes have a head and an elongated trunk with many segments, each bearing uniramous legs (**FIG. 31-27**).

Centipedes ("hundred-legged") have one pair of legs on each segment behind the head. Most centipedes do not have enough legs to merit their name; typically, they have approximately 30, although a few species have 100 or more. Because centipedes have long legs, they are able to run rapidly. Centipedes are carnivorous and feed on other animals, mostly insects. Larger centipedes eat snakes, mice, and frogs. Using their poison claws located just behind the head on the first trunk segment, centipedes capture and kill their prey.

Millipedes ("thousand-legged") have two pairs of legs on most body segments. Diplopods are not as agile as chilopods, and most species can crawl only slowly over the ground. However, they can powerfully force their way through earth and rotting wood. Millipedes are generally herbivorous and feed on both living and dead vegetation.

Chelicerates have no antennae

Subphylum **Chelicerata** includes the merostomes (horseshoe crabs) and the arachnids. The chelicerate body consists of a *cephalothorax* (fused head and thorax) and an abdomen. Chelicerates are the only arthropods without antennae. They have no chewing mandibles. Instead, the first appendages, located immediately anterior to the mouth, are a pair of **chelicerae** (sing., *chelicera*), fanglike feeding appendages. Most chelicerates suck fluid food from their prey. The second appendages are the **pedipalps.** The chelicerae and pedipalps are modified to perform different functions in various groups, including manipulation of food, locomotion, defense, and copulation. The four pairs of legs on the cephalothorax are specialized for walking.

Almost all the **merostomes** are extinct. Only the horseshoe crabs have survived, essentially unchanged for more than 350 million years. *Limulus polyphemus,* the species common along the Atlantic shore of North America, is horseshoe-shaped (**FIG. 31-28a**). Its long, spikelike tail is used in locomotion, not for defense or offense. Horseshoe crabs feed at night, capturing mollusks, worms, and other invertebrates that they find on the sandy ocean floor.

Arachnids include spiders, scorpions, ticks, harvestmen (daddy longlegs), and mites (**FIGS. 31-28b** and **c**). Most of the approximately 80,000 named species are carnivorous and prey on insects and other small arthropods. Arachnids have six pairs of jointed appendages. In spiders, the first appendages, the chelicerae, are used to penetrate prey; some species use the chelicerae to inject poison into their prey. Spiders use the second pair of appendages, the pedipalps, to hold and chew food. Many arachnid species have pedipalps modified as sense organs for tasting food or for repro-

(a) Centipede (*Lithobius*), a member of class Chilopoda. Centipedes have one pair of uniramous appendages per segment.

(b) Millipede (*Diplopoda pachydesmus*), a member of class Diplopoda. Millipedes have two pairs of uniramous appendages per segment.

FIGURE 31-27 Myriapods

(a) Horseshoe crabs. The only living merostomes are a few closely related species of horseshoe crabs. Seasonally, horseshoe crabs return to beaches for mating. In this photograph *Limulus polyphemus* males are competing for a female.

(b) A female black widow spider (Latrodectus mactans) rests on her web. The venom of the black widow spider is a neurotoxin.

100 μm

(c) The house dust mite *Dermatophagoides*. This mite, a common inhabitant of homes, is associated with house dust allergies (color enhanced SEM).

duction (for sperm transfer and courtship displays). Scorpions use their very large pedipalps as pincers for capturing prey. Chelicerates use the remaining four pairs of appendages for walking.

Typically, spiders have eight eyes arranged in two rows of four each along the anterior dorsal edge of the cephalothorax. The eyes detect movement, locate objects, and in some species form a relatively sharp image.

Gas exchange in arachnids takes place by either tracheal tubes, book lungs, or both. A *book lung* consists of 15 to 20 parallel plates (like pages of a book) that contain tiny blood vessels. Air enters the body through abdominal slits and circulates between the plates. As air passes over the blood vessels in the plates, oxygen diffuses into the blood and carbon dioxide diffuses out of the blood into the air. As many as four pairs of book lungs provide an extensive surface area for gas exchange.

The spider has unique glands in its abdomen that secrete silk, an elastic protein that is spun into fibers by organs called *spinnerets*.

FIGURE 31-28 Chelicerates ▶

The silk is liquid as it emerges from the spinnerets but hardens after it leaves the body. Spiders use silk to build nests, to encase their eggs in a cocoon, and in some species, to trap prey in a web. Many spiders lay down a silken dragline that serves both as a safety line and a means of communication between members of a species. From the type of dragline, another spider can determine the sex and maturity level of the spinner.

Although all spiders (and scorpions) have poison glands useful in capturing prey, only a few produce poison toxic to humans. The most widely distributed poisonous spider in the United States is the black widow (see Fig. 31-28b). Its venom is a neurotoxin that interferes with transmission of messages from nerves to muscles. The shiny black female is about 3.8 cm (1.5 in) long with a red or orange hourglass-shaped marking on the underside of its abdomen. Adult male black widow spiders are smaller and are harmless. After mating, the female sometimes kills and eats the male.

The brown recluse spider (*Loxosceles reclusa*) is more slender than the black widow and has a violin-shaped stripe on its dorsal cephalothorax. Its venom destroys the tissues surrounding the bite. Although painful, spider bites cause fewer than three fatalities per year in the United States.

Although some mites contribute to soil fertility by breaking down organic matter, many are serious nuisances. They eat crops, infest livestock and pets, and inhabit our own bodies. Certain mites cause mange in dogs and other domestic animals. Chiggers (red bugs), the larval form of red mites, attach themselves to the skin and secrete an irritating digestive fluid that may cause itchy red welts.

Larger than mites, ticks are parasites on dogs, deer, and many other animals. They transmit the bacteria that cause diseases such as Rocky Mountain spotted fever and Lyme disease (see Fig. 54-2).

Crustaceans are vital members of marine food webs

Subphylum **Crustacea** includes lobsters, crabs, shrimp, barnacles, and their relatives (**FIG. 31-29**). Many crustaceans are primary consumers of algae and detritus. Countless billions of microscopic crustaceans are part of marine zooplankton, the free-floating, mainly microscopic organisms in the upper layers of the ocean. These crustaceans are food for many fishes and other marine animals, such as certain baleen whales. Paleobiologists have dated crustacean fossils back to the Cambrian period (more than 505 mya).

A distinctive feature of crustaceans is the *nauplius larva,* which is often the first stage after hatching. This larva has only the most anterior three pairs of appendages. Crustaceans are also characterized by mandibles, biramous appendages, and two pairs of **antennae.** Their antennae, which are the first and second pairs of appendages, serve as sensory organs for touch and taste. Most adult crustaceans have compound eyes, and many crustaceans have **statocysts,** sense organs that detect gravity (see Fig. 43-6).

The hard **mandibles,** used for biting and grinding food, are the third pair of appendages; they lie on each side of the ventral mouth. Posterior to the mandibles are two pairs of appendages, the first and second **maxillae,** used for manipulating and holding food. Several other pairs of appendages are present. Some are modified for walking. Others may be specialized for swimming, sperm transmission, carrying eggs and young, or sensation.

(a) **Goose barnacles (*Lepas* sp.) filter feeding.** These stalked barnacles are found in large numbers on intertidal rocks. The ones in this image are attached to a fisherman's float, North Pacific.

(b) **Sponge crab (*Criptodromia octodenta*) wearing a sponge on its back.** The sponge provides camouflage and shelter. The sponge crab uses its claws to cut out a fragment from a sponge and then trims the sponge to conform to its own shape. The last two pairs of the crab's legs bend upward over the crab's carapace and hold the sponge in place. The sponge grows along with the crab.

FIGURE 31-29 Crustaceans

Crustaceans are the only group of arthropods that are primarily aquatic; not surprisingly, they typically have gills for gas exchange. Two large glands located in the head excrete metabolic wastes and regulate salt balance. Most crustaceans have separate sexes. During copulation, the male uses specialized appendages to transfer sperm into the female. Newly hatched animals may resemble adults, or they may undergo successive molts as they pass through a series of larval stages before developing an adult body.

Barnacles, the only sessile crustaceans, differ markedly in external anatomy from other members of the subphylum. They are marine suspension feeders that secrete limestone cups within which they live (see Fig. 31-29a). The larvae of barnacles are free-swimming forms that go through several molts. They eventually become sessile and develop into the adult form. The 19th-century naturalist Louis Agassiz described the barnacle as "nothing more than a little shrimplike animal standing on its head in a limestone house and kicking food into its mouth." The bane of marine boaters, barnacles can proliferate on ship bottoms in great numbers. Barnacles can reduce the speed of a ship by more than 10% and increase fuel consumption by as much as 40%. The United States Office of Naval Research has been testing an underwater robot that cleans barnacles and other marine life from the hulls of ships when they are in port.

Isopods are mainly tiny (5 to 15 mm in length) marine crustaceans that inhabit the ocean floor. However, this group also includes some terrestrial animals: pill bugs and sow bugs. The most abundant crustaceans are the *copepods,* which are typically microscopic. Marine copepods are the most numerous component of zooplankton.

The largest and most familiar order of crustaceans, Decapoda, contains more than 10,000 species of lobsters, crayfish, crabs, and shrimp. Most decapods are marine, but a few, such as the crayfish, certain shrimp, and a few crabs, live in fresh water. The crustaceans in general and the decapods in particular show striking specialization and differentiation of parts in the various regions of the animal. In the lobster, the appendages in the different parts of the body differ markedly in form and function (**FIG. 31-30**).

The five segments of the lobster's head and the eight segments of its thorax are fused into a cephalothorax, which is covered on the top and sides by a shield, the **carapace,** composed of chitin impregnated with calcium salts. The two pairs of antennae serve as chemoreceptors and tactile sense organs. The mandibles are short and heavy, with opposing surfaces used in grinding and biting food. Behind the mandibles are two pairs of accessory feeding appendages: the first and second maxillae.

The appendages of the first three segments of the thorax are the maxillipeds, which aid in chopping up food and passing it to the mouth. The fourth segment of the thorax has a pair of large **chelipeds,** or pinching claws. The last four thoracic segments bear walking legs.

The appendages of the first abdominal segment are part of the reproductive system and are used by the male to transfer sperm. The following four abdominal segments bear paired **swimmerets,** small paddlelike structures used by some decapods for swimming and by the females of all species for holding eggs. Each branch of the sixth abdominal appendages consists of a large flattened structure. Together with the flattened posterior end of the abdomen, they form a tail fan used for swimming backward.

Insects are articulated, tracheated hexapods

With more than one million described species (and perhaps millions more not yet identified), class **Insecta** of subphylum

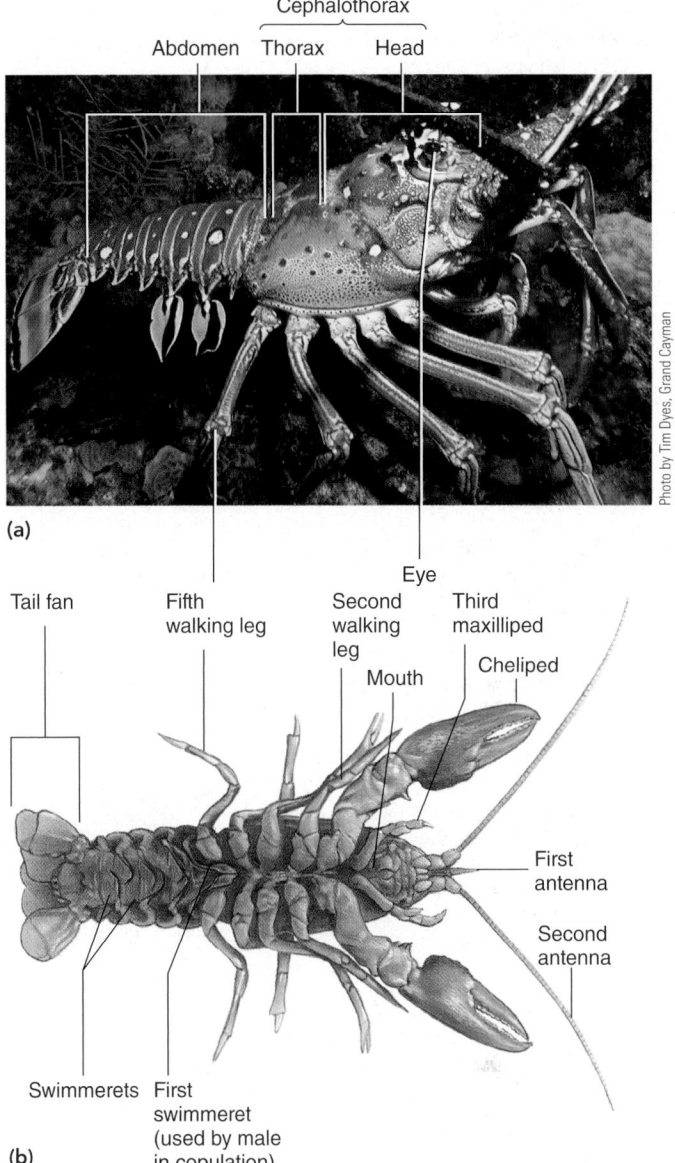

FIGURE 31-30 Anatomy of the lobster

(a) Like other decapods, the spiny lobster (*Panulirus argus*) has five pairs of walking legs. The first pair of walking legs is modified as chelipeds (*large claws*). Photographed in Grand Cayman. **(b)** Ventral view of a lobster. Note the variety of specialized appendages.

Hexapoda is the most successful group of animals on our planet in terms of number of individuals, number of species, diversity, and geographic distribution (**TABLE 31-6**). What they lack in size, insects make up in sheer numbers. If we could weigh all the insects in the world, their weight would exceed that of all the remaining terrestrial animals. Although primarily terrestrial, some insect species live in fresh water, a few are truly marine, and others inhabit the shore between the tides.

The earliest fossil insects—primitive, wingless species—date to the Devonian period more than 360 mya. Insect fossils from the Carboniferous period more than 310 mya include both wingless

TABLE 31-6   Some Orders of Insects

Order, Number of Species, Some Characteristics	Representative Adult	Order, Number of Species, Some Characteristics	Representative Adult
Homoptera (43,000)* Leafhoppers, scale insects Two pairs of membranous wings; piercing–sucking mouthparts form beak; parasites of plants; vectors of plant diseases; incomplete metamorphosis	Buffalo treehopper *Stictocephala bubalus*	**Lepidoptera (160,000)** Moths, butterflies Usually two pairs of membranous, colorful, scaled wings; larvae are wormlike caterpillars with chewing mouthparts for eating plants; adult mouthparts adapted for sucking nectar	Luna moth *Aetias luna*
Odonata (6000) Dragonflies, damselflies Two pairs of long membranous wings; chewing mouthparts; large, compound eyes; active predators; larvae very different from adult; incomplete metamorphosis	Damselfly *Ischnura*	**Diptera (150,000)** Houseflies, mosquitoes, fruit flies Only forewings functional in flying; hindwings reduced to small, knob-like balancing organs (halteres); mouthparts usually adapted for sucking (and piercing in some); larvae are maggots that damage domestic animals or food; adults transmit diseases such as sleeping sickness, yellow fever, and malaria	Deerfly *Chrysops vittatus*
Orthoptera (20,000) Grasshoppers, crickets Forewings leathery, hindwings membranous; chewing mouthparts; most herbivorous, some cause crop damage; some predatory; incomplete metamorphosis	Fork-tailed bush katydid *Scudderia furcata*	**Siphonaptera (2000)** Fleas No wings; piercing–sucking mouthparts; legs adapted for clinging and jumping; parasites on birds and mammals; vectors of bubonic plague and typhus	Dog flea *Ctenocephalides canis*
Blattodea (4000) Cockroaches When wings present, forewings leathery, hindwings membranous; chewing mouthparts; legs adapted for running; incomplete metamorphosis	American cockroach *Periplaneta americana*	**Coleoptera (360,000)** Beetles, weevils Forewings modified as protective coverings for membranous hindwings (which are sometimes absent); chewing mouthparts; largest order of insects; most herbivorous; some aquatic	Colorado potato beetle *Leptinotarsa decemlineata*
Isoptera (2100) Termites Two pairs of wings, or none; wings shed by sexual forms after mating; chewing mouthparts; social insects, form large colonies; eat wood; incomplete metamorphosis	Eastern subterranean termite *Reticulitermes flavipes*	**Hymenoptera (190,000)** Ants, bees, wasps Usually two pairs of membranous wings; mouthparts may be modified for sucking or lapping nectar; many are social insects; some sting; important pollinators	Bald-faced hornet *Vespula maculata*
Phthiraptera (3000) Lice, sucking lice No wings; piercing–sucking mouthparts; ectoparasites of mammals; head and body louse and crab louse are human parasites; vectors of typhus fever; incomplete metamorphosis	Human head and body louse *Pediculus humanus*	**Thysanura (320)** Silverfish No wings; biting–chewing mouthparts; two to three "tails" extend from posterior tip of abdomen; inhabit dead leaves; eat starch in books; direct development	Silverfish *Lepisma saccharina*
Hemiptera (80,000) Chinch bugs, bedbugs, water striders; cicadas and aphids are now assigned to this order Hindwings membranous; forewings smaller; piercing–sucking mouthparts form beak; most herbivorous; some parasitic; incomplete metamorphosis	Chinch bug *Blissus leucopterus*		

*The number of species listed for each order is approximate. Estimates vary widely.

and primitive winged species. Cockroaches, mayflies, and cicadas are among the insects that have survived relatively unchanged from the Carboniferous period to the present day.

Molecular and developmental studies suggest that hexapods are not a monophyletic group and that they are closely related to the crustaceans. At the time of this writing, many biologists classify crustaceans along with hexapods in clade **Pancrustacea.** Some systematists hypothesize that crustaceans and hexapods are *sister taxa,* closely related taxa that occupy adjacent branches in a cladogram (see Chapter 23). Others argue that hexapods evolved *within* the crustacean clade.

We describe an insect as an **articulated** (jointed), **tracheated** (having tracheal tubes for gas exchange) **hexapod** (having six feet). The insect body consists of three distinct parts: head, thorax, and abdomen (**FIG. 31-31**). An insect's uniramous (unbranched) appendages include three pairs of legs that extend from the adult thorax and, in many orders, one or two pairs of wings. One pair of antennae protrudes from the head, and the sense organs include both simple and compound eyes. The complex mouthparts, which include mandibles and maxillae, are adapted for piercing, chewing, sucking, or lapping.

The tracheal system of insects has made an important contribution to their diversity. Air enters the tracheal tubes, or tracheae, through **spiracles,** tiny openings in the body wall. Oxygen passes directly to the internal organs. This effective oxygen delivery system permits insects to have the high metabolic rate necessary for activities such as flight, even though they have an open circulatory system.

Excretion is accomplished by two or more **Malpighian tubules,** which receive metabolic wastes from the blood, concentrate the wastes, and discharge them into the intestine. Unique to terrestrial arthropods, Malpighian tubules also perform the extremely important function of conserving water (see Fig. 48-4).

The sexes are separate, and fertilization takes place internally. Several molts occur during development. The immature stages between molts are called **instars.** Primitive insects with no wings, such as silverfish, have direct, or simple, development: the young hatch as juveniles that resemble the adult form. Other insects, such as grasshoppers and cockroaches, undergo **incomplete metamorphosis** in which the egg gives rise to a larva that resembles the adult in many ways but lacks functional wings and reproductive structures. The larva goes through a series of molts during which it becomes more and more like the adult.

Most insects, including bees, butterflies, and fleas, undergo **complete metamorphosis** with four distinct stages in the life cycle: **egg, larva, pupa,** and **adult** (**FIG. 31-32**). The wormlike larva does not look at all like the adult. For example, caterpillars have a body form entirely different from that of butterflies. Typically, an insect spends most of its life as a larva, which has chewing mouthparts. Eventually, the larva stops feeding, molts, and enters a pupal stage, usually within a protective cocoon or underground burrow. The pupa does not feed and typically cannot defend itself. Energy reserves stored during the larval stage are spent remodeling its body. When it emerges as an adult, it is equipped with functional wings and reproductive organs.

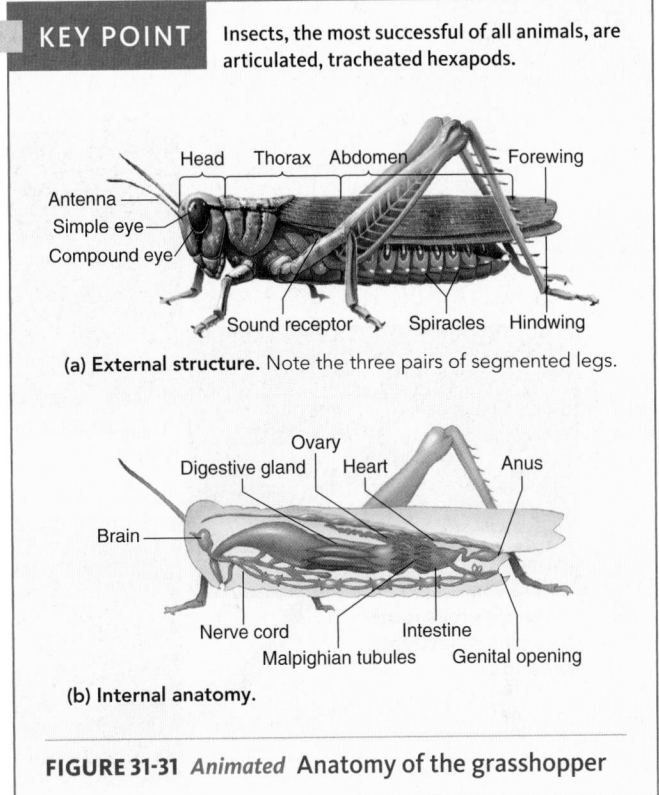

KEY POINT Insects, the most successful of all animals, are articulated, tracheated hexapods.

(a) **External structure.** Note the three pairs of segmented legs.

(b) **Internal anatomy.**

FIGURE 31-31 *Animated* Anatomy of the grasshopper

Certain species of bees, ants, and termites exist as colonies or societies made up of several different types of individuals, each adapted for some particular function. The members of some insect societies communicate with one another by "dances" and by means of **pheromones,** substances secreted to the external environment. Social insects and their communication are discussed in Chapter 52.

Adaptations that contribute to the biological success of insects
What are the secrets of insect success? The tough exoskeleton protects insects from predators and helps reduce water loss. Segmentation allows mobility and flexibility and permits regional specialization of the body. For example, cephalization and highly developed sense organs are important in both offense and defense.

The insect body plan has been modified and specialized in so many ways that insects are adapted to a remarkable number of lifestyles. The jointed appendages are specialized for various types of feeding, sensory functions, and different types of locomotion (walking, jumping, swimming). For example, grasshopper mouthparts are adapted for biting and chewing leaves. Moth and butterfly mouthparts are adapted for sucking nectar from flowers, and mosquito mouthparts are adapted for sucking blood. Aphids and leafhoppers have mouthparts specialized to pierce plants and feed on plant juices.

Another adaptation that contributes to insect success is the ability to fly. Unlike other terrestrial invertebrates, which creep slowly along on or under the ground, many insects fly rapidly through the air. Their wings and small size facilitate their wide distribution and,

Metamorphosis reduces competition among insects within the same species; larval forms do not compete with adults for food or habitats.

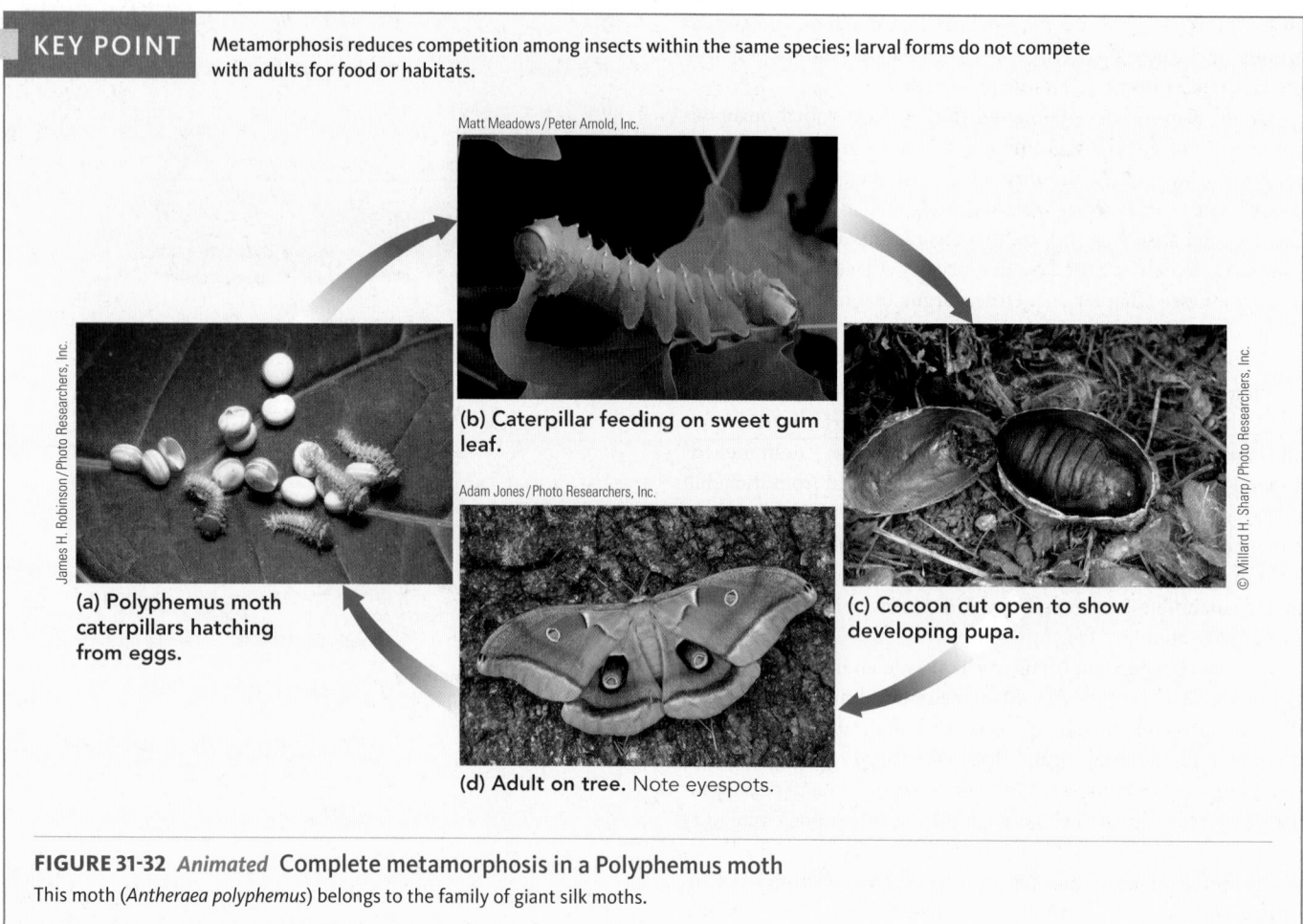

Matt Meadows / Peter Arnold, Inc.

(b) Caterpillar feeding on sweet gum leaf.

Adam Jones / Photo Researchers, Inc.

James H. Robinson / Photo Researchers, Inc.

© Millard H. Sharp / Photo Researchers, Inc.

(a) Polyphemus moth caterpillars hatching from eggs.

(c) Cocoon cut open to show developing pupa.

(d) Adult on tree. Note eyespots.

FIGURE 31-32 *Animated* **Complete metamorphosis in a Polyphemus moth**
This moth (*Antheraea polyphemus*) belongs to the family of giant silk moths.

in many instances, their immediate survival. For example, when a pond dries up, adult aquatic insects can fly to another habitat.

The reproductive capacity of insects is remarkable. Under ideal conditions, the fruit fly *Drosophila* can produce 25 generations in a single year! Insect eggs are protected by a thick membrane, and several eggs may, in addition, be enclosed in a protective egg case. By dividing the insect life cycle into different stages, metamorphosis reduces competition among members of the same species (intraspecific competition). For example, larval forms have different lifestyles, so they do not compete with adults for food or habitats.

Insects have many interesting adaptations for offense and defense (see Fig. 7-8). We all are familiar with the stingers of bees and wasps, which are specialized egg-laying structures (ovipositors). Many insects have **cryptic coloration,** which allows them to blend into the background of their habitat; some look like dead twigs or leaves. Others mimic poisonous insects, deriving protection from this resemblance. Still others "play dead" by remaining motionless.

Insects communicate by tactile, auditory, visual, or chemical signals. For example, certain ant species use pheromones to mark trails and to warn of danger. Other insects use pheromones to attract a mate.

Impact of insects on humans Not all insects compete with humans for food or cause us to scratch, swell up, or recoil from their presence. Bees, wasps, beetles, and many other insects pollinate the flowers of crops and fruit trees. Some insects destroy other insects that are harmful to humans. For example, dragonflies eat mosquitoes. And many organic farmers and home gardeners buy ladybird beetles, which are adept at ridding plants of aphids and other insect pests. Insects are important members of many food webs. Many birds, mammals, amphibians, reptiles, and some fishes depend on insects for food. Some beetles and the larvae (maggots) of flies are detritus feeders—they break down dead plants and animals and their wastes, permitting nutrients to be recycled.

Various insect products are useful to humans. Bees produce honey as well as beeswax, which we use to make candles, lubricants, and other products. Shellac is made from lac, a substance given off by certain scale insects that feed on the sap of trees. And the labor of silkworms provides us with beautiful fabric.

On the negative side, insects destroy crops worth billions of dollars each year. Termites destroy buildings, and moths damage clothing. Fire ants not only inflict painful stings but cause farmers serious economic loss because of their large mounds, which damage mowers and other farm equipment. Blood-sucking flies, screwworms, lice, fleas, and other insects annoy and transmit disease to humans and domestic animals. Mosquitoes are vectors of yellow fever and malaria (see Fig. 26-7). Fleas and lice transmit the rickettsia that cause typhus, and houseflies sometimes transmit typhoid fever and dysentery. Tsetse flies transmit African sleeping sickness, and fleas may be vectors of bubonic plague.

In this chapter, we have surveyed the major groups of protostomes. **TABLE 31-7** summarizes these groups. Chapter 32 focuses on the deuterostomes, which include the echinoderms and chordates.

Review

- What characters distinguish nematodes from flatworms?
- What are four key arthropod characters, and how does each contribute to arthropod success?
- How do myriapods differ from chelicerates?
- What are the functions of each of these appendages in a lobster: maxillae, chelipeds, and swimmerets?
- Define an insect. What are four adaptations that have contributed to insect success?

TABLE 31-7	Overview of Sponges, Cnidarians, Ctenophores, and Protostomes		
Major Groups		**Body Plan**	**Some Key Characteristics**
Poriferans (sponges)		Asymmetrical; cells loosely arranged and do not form true tissues; body is sac with pores, central cavity, and osculum	Collar cells (choanocytes); aquatic, mainly marine
Cnidarians (hydras, jellyfish, corals)		Radial symmetry; diploblastic; gastrovascular cavity with one opening	Tentacles with cnidocytes (stinging cells) that discharge nematocysts; two body forms: polyp and medusa; some form colonies; mainly marine
Ctenophores (comb jellies)		Biradial symmetry; diploblastic; gastrovascular cavity with mouth and anal pores	Eight rows of cilia that resemble combs; tentacles with adhesive glue cells; marine predators

Protostomes: Lophotrochozoan Branch

Flatworms (planarians, tapeworms, flukes)		Bilateral symmetry; triploblastic; simple organ systems; gastrovascular cavity with one opening	No body cavity; some cephalization; some are free-living carnivores; many are parasites
Nemerteans (ribbon worms)		Bilateral symmetry; triploblastic; organ systems; complete digestive tube*	Proboscis (long, muscular tube that can be everted to capture prey); true coelom reduced; mainly marine carnivores
Mollusks (clams, snails, squids)		Bilateral symmetry; triploblastic; organ systems; complete digestive tube; true coelom	Soft body usually covered by dorsal shell; flat, muscular foot; mantle covers visceral mass; most have a radula (belt of teeth)
Annelids (some marine worms, earthworms, leeches)		Bilateral symmetry; triploblastic; organ systems; complete digestive tube; true coelom	Segmented body; most have setae, bristles that provide traction during crawling
Lophophorates (brachiopods, phoronids, bryozoans)		Bilateral symmetry; triploblastic; organ systems; complete digestive tube; true coelom	Lophophore (ciliated ring of tentacles) surrounds mouth, captures suspended particles in water; mainly sessile, marine animals
Rotifers (wheel animals)		Bilateral symmetry; triploblastic; organ systems; complete digestive tube; pseudocoelom	Crown of cilia at anterior end; cell number constant; microscopic, aquatic animals

Protostomes: Ecdysozoan Branch

Nematodes (roundworms, e.g., *Ascaris*, hookworms, trichina worms)		Bilateral symmetry; triploblastic; organ systems; complete digestive tube; pseudocoelom	Cylindrical, threadlike body; widely distributed in soil and aquatic sediments; important as decomposers; many are predators; some are parasites
Arthropods (centipedes, spiders, crabs, lobsters, insects)		Bilateral symmetry; triploblastic; organ systems; complete digestive tube; true coelom	Segmented body; exoskeleton; paired, jointed appendages; insects and many crustaceans have compound eyes; insects have tracheal tubes for gas exchange

*A complete digestive tube has a mouth for food intake and an opening (anus) for elimination of wastes.

31.1 *(page 641)*

1 Identify distinguishing characteristics of poriferans.

- The **poriferans,** or sponges, are characterized by flagellate **collar cells (choanocytes)** that generate a water current that brings food and oxygen to the cells. Collar cells also trap and phagocytize food particles. The sponge body is a sac with tiny openings through which water enters; a central cavity, or **spongocoel;** and an open end, or **osculum,** through which water exits. The cells of sponges are loosely associated; they do not form true tissues.

  CENGAGENOW™ Learn more about sponge structure by clicking on the figure in CengageNOW.

2 Identify distinguishing characteristics of cnidarians, describe four groups, and give examples of animals that belong to each group.

- **Cnidarians** are characterized by radial symmetry, two tissue layers, and **cnidocytes,** cells containing stinging organelles called **nemato-cysts.** The **gastrovascular cavity** has a single opening that serves as both mouth and anus. Nerve cells form irregular, nondirectional **nerve nets** that connect sensory cells with contractile and gland cells.

- The life cycle of many cnidarians includes a sessile **polyp** stage (a form with a dorsal mouth surrounded by tentacles) and a free-swimming **medusa** (jellyfish) stage.

- Phylum Cnidaria includes four groups. **Hydrozoa** (hydras, hydroids, and the Portuguese man-of-war) are typically polyps and may be solitary or colonial. **Scyphozoa** (jellyfish) are generally medusae. **Cubozoa,** the "box jellyfish," have complex eyes that form blurred images. **Anthozoa** (sea anemones and corals) are polyps and may be solitary or colonial; anthozoans differ from hydrozoans in the organization of the gastrovascular cavity.

CENGAGENOW™ Learn more about cnidarian body forms, nemato-cysts, and life cycles by clicking on the figures in CengageNOW.

3 Identify distinguishing characteristics of ctenophores.

- **Ctenophores,** or comb jellies, are fragile, luminescent marine predators with biradial symmetry. Ctenophores have eight rows of cilia that resemble combs. They are diploblastic and have tentacles with adhesive glue cells.

31.2 *(page 648)*

4 Summarize what is known about the phylogeny of the lophotrocho-zoans and cite the adaptive advantages of having a coelom and of cephalization.

- The **Lophotrochozoa** make up a clade that includes some of the flatworms, nemerteans, mollusks, annelids, the lophophorate phyla, and rotifers.

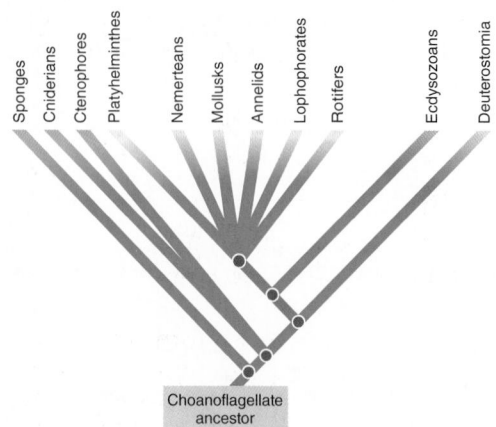

- The **true coelom** is a fluid-filled body cavity completely lined by mesoderm that lies between the digestive tube and the outer body wall. The coelom brings about the **tube-within-a-tube body plan.** The body wall is the outer tube. The inner tube is the digestive tube. The coelom can serve as a **hydrostatic skeleton** in which con-tracting muscles push against a tube of fluid. The coelom is a space in which internal organs, including gonads, can develop; it helps transport materials; and protects internal organs.

- **Cephalization,** the evolution of a head with the concentration of sense organs and nerve cells at the anterior end, increases the effectiveness of a bilateral animal to actively find food, shelter, and mates and to detect enemies.

5 Identify distinguishing characteristics of flatworms and nemerteans; describe the main groups of flatworms, giving examples of animals that belong to each class.

- The **flatworms** are **acoelomate** (have no coelom) animals with bilateral symmetry, cephalization, three definite tissue layers, and well-developed organs. Many flatworms are **hermaphrodites;** a single animal produces both sperm and eggs. Flatworms have a ladder-type nervous system, typically consisting of sense organs and a simple brain composed of two **ganglia.** The ganglia are con-nected to two nerve cords that extend the length of the body. **Protonephridia** function in osmoregulation and disposal of meta-bolic wastes.

- Four groups of flatworms are recognized: class **Turbellaria** com-prises free-living flatworms, including planarians; classes **Trema-toda** and **Monogenea** include the parasitic **flukes;** class **Cestoda** includes the parasitic tapeworms. The parasitic flukes and tape-worms typically have suckers or hooks for holding on to their hosts; they have complicated life cycles with intermediate hosts and produce large numbers of eggs.

  CENGAGENOW™ Watch the fluke and tapeworm life cycles by clicking on the figures in CengageNOW.

- **Nemerteans** (ribbon worms) are characterized by the **proboscis,** a muscular tube used in capturing food and in defense. Nemerteans have a tube-within-a-tube body plan, a complete digestive tract with mouth and anus, and a circulatory system. The coelom is reduced.

6 Describe the distinguishing characteristics of mollusks and of the four main groups of mollusks discussed, giving examples of each group.

- **Mollusks** are soft-bodied animals usually covered by a shell. They have a ventral **foot** for locomotion and a pair of folds called the **mantle** that covers the **visceral mass,** a concentration of body organs.

- Mollusks have an **open circulatory system** except for cephalopods, which have a **closed circulatory system.** A rasplike **radula** functions as a scraper in feeding in all groups except the bivalves, which are filter feeders. Typically, marine mollusks have a free-swimming, ciliated **trochophore larva.**

- **Polyplacophorans** are **chitons,** mollusks with shells consisting of eight overlapping dorsal plates. The **gastropods,** which include the snails, slugs, and their relatives, have a well-developed head with tentacles. The body undergoes **torsion,** a twisting of the visceral mass. **Bivalves** are aquatic clams, scallops, and oysters. A two-part shell, hinged dorsally, encloses the bodies of these filter feeders. **Cephalopods** include the squids, octopods, and *Nautilus.* These active, predatory swimmers have tentacles surrounding the mouth, which is located in the large head.

7 Describe the distinguishing characteristics of annelids and of the three main groups of annelids discussed, giving examples of each group.

- The **annelids,** the segmented worms, include many aquatic worms, earthworms, and leeches. Annelids have long bodies with **segmentation** both internally and externally; their large, compartmentalized coelom serves as a hydrostatic skeleton.

- **Polychaetes** are marine annelids characterized by **parapodia,** appendages used for locomotion and gas exchange. The parapodia bear many bristlelike structures called **setae.** Polychaetes also differ from other annelids in having a well-defined head with sense organs. **Oligochaetes,** the group that includes the earthworms, are characterized by a few short setae per segment. The body is divided into more than 100 segments separated internally by **septa.** Leeches belong to the group **Hirudinida.** Setae and appendages are absent. Parasitic leeches are equipped with suckers for holding on to their host.

8 Describe the distinguishing characteristics of the lophophorates and of the rotifers.

- The **lophophorates,** marine animals that have a lophophore, include the **brachiopods, phoronids,** and **bryozoans.** The **lophophore,** a ciliated ring of tentacles surrounding the mouth, is specialized for capturing suspended particles in the water.

- **Rotifers** are pseudocoelomates that are thought to have evolved from animals with a true coelom. They have a crown of cilia at their anterior end.

31.3 (page 661)

9 Summarize what is known about the phylogeny of the ecdysozoans.

- **Ecdysozoa** is one of the three major animal clades; its validity is based on many types of evidence, including molecular data. Members of this group go through the process of **ecdysis,** or **molting,** during which an animal sheds its outer covering, which is then replaced by the growth of a new one.

10 Describe distinguishing characteristics of nematodes and identify four parasitic nematodes.

- **Nematodes,** or **roundworms,** have a pseudocoelom. The body is covered by a tough **cuticle** that helps prevent desiccation. Parasitic nematodes that infect humans include *Ascaris,* hookworms, **trichina worms,** and **pinworms.**

11 Describe six key characteristics of arthropods, summarize proposed phylogeny of arthropods, and distinguish among arthropod subphyla and classes; give examples of animals that belong to each group.

- Phylum **Arthropoda** is composed of segmented animals with **paired, jointed appendages** and an armorlike **exoskeleton** of chitin. Molting is necessary for the arthropod to grow. Arthropods have an open circulatory system with a dorsal heart that pumps **hemolymph.** Aquatic forms have gills for gas exchange; terrestrial forms have either **tracheae** or **book lungs.**

- The arthropods along with the **onychophorans** (velvet worms) and **tardigrades** (water bears) make up the clade **Panarthropoda.** Based on molecular and other data, arthropods are currently assigned to five main groups: extinct trilobites and extant Myriapoda, Chelicerata, Crustacea, and Hexapoda.

- The **trilobites** are extinct marine arthropods covered by a hard, segmented shell. Each segment had a pair of **biramous appendages,** appendages with two jointed branches, an inner walking leg and an outer gill branch.

- Subphylum **Myriapoda** includes class **Chilopoda,** the centipedes, and class **Diplopoda,** the millipedes. Members of this subphylum have **uniramous** (unbranched) **appendages** and a single pair of antennae.

- Subphylum **Chelicerata** includes the **merostomes** (horseshoe crabs) and the **arachnids** (spiders, mites, and their relatives). The chelicerate body consists of a cephalothorax and abdomen; there are six pairs of uniramous, jointed appendages, of which four pairs serve as legs. The first appendages are **chelicerae;** the second are **pedipalps.** These appendages are adapted for manipulation of food, locomotion, defense, or copulation. Chelicerates have no antennae and no mandibles.

- Subphylum **Crustacea** includes lobsters, crabs, shrimp, pill bugs, and barnacles. The body consists of a cephalothorax and abdomen. Crustaceans typically have five pairs of walking legs. Appendages are biramous. Crustaceans have two pairs of **antennae** that sense taste and touch. The third appendages are **mandibles** used for chewing. Two pairs of **maxillae,** posterior to the mandibles, manipulate and hold food.

- Subphylum **Hexapoda** includes class **Insecta.** An insect is an **articulated, tracheated hexapod;** its body consists of head, thorax, and abdomen. Insects have uniramous appendages, a single pair of antennae, tracheae for gas exchange, and **Malpighian tubules** for excretion.

12 Identify adaptations that have contributed to the biological success of insects.

- The biological success of the insects can be attributed to their many adaptations, including a versatile exoskeleton, segmentation, specialized jointed appendages, highly developed sense organs, and ability to fly. **Metamorphosis,** transition from one developmental form to another, reduces competition within the same species. Insects have developed effective reproductive strategies, effective mechanisms for defense and offense, and the ability to communicate.

CENGAGENOW™ Explore the body plans of the protostomes by clicking on the figures in CengageNOW.

1. Collar cells (choanocytes) are characteristic of (a) poriferans (b) cnidarians (c) most coelomates (d) lophotrochozoans (e) ecdysozoans

2. Cnidocytes (a) are characteristic of sponges (b) are found among cells lining the gastrovascular cavity (c) contain stinging organelles (d) are lined with mesoderm (e) have two main shapes

3. Which of the following is associated with the evolution of the coelom? (a) radial symmetry (b) tube-within-a-tube body plan (c) incomplete metamorphosis (d) bilateral symmetry (e) development of ganglia

4. Trochophore larvae are characteristic of (a) arthropods (b) cnidarians (c) flatworms (d) mollusks (e) crustaceans

5. Which of the following is *not* an adaptation to parasitic life? (a) production of a few well-protected eggs (b) hooks (c) suckers (d) reduced digestive system (e) intermediate host

6. An open circulatory system (a) is characteristic of squids and other active mollusks (b) permits contracting muscles to recover quickly (c) has no blood vessels (d) is a unique characteristic of annelids (e) has hemolymph, which bathes tissues directly

7. Which of the following characteristics is associated with mollusks? (a) mandibles (b) mantle (c) pedipalps (d) chelipeds (e) setae

8. Trilobites (a) were early mollusks (b) are onychophorans (c) are characterized by parapodia and setae (d) were early

arthropods (e) are an evolutionary link between annelids and arthropods

9. Which of the following is *not* characteristic of arthropods? (a) exoskeleton (b) pseudocoelom (c) paired, jointed appendages (d) chitin (e) segmentation

10. Which of the following is characteristic of insects? (a) biramous appendages (b) two pairs of antennae (c) chelicerae (d) eight legs (e) mandibles

11. The correct sequence of complete metamorphosis of an insect is
    (a) egg ⟶ immature form ⟶ adult
    (b) egg ⟶ trochophore larva ⟶ adult
    (c) egg ⟶ pupa ⟶ larva ⟶ adult
    (d) egg ⟶ larva ⟶ pupa ⟶ adult
    (e) adult ⟶ larva ⟶ egg ⟶ pupa

12. Label the diagram. Refer to Figure 31-31 b to confirm your answers.

1. **ANALYZING DATA.** Imagine that you discover a new animal in a rain forest. It has an elongated, segmented body. Where would you place this animal in the cladogram below? Support your decision. Look at the more detailed cladogram in Figure 30-7a (in Chapter 30). What additional characteristics would help you place your animal in this cladogram? Explain your decision-making process.

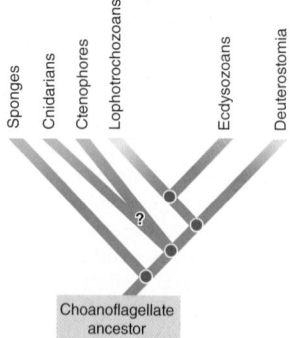

2. **EVOLUTION LINK.** Acoelomates, pseudocoelomates, and coelomates were historically classified as distinct groups of animals. In what way has this classification changed? Why have biologists stopped using type of body cavity as a major criterion for inferring relationships among animal groups?

3. **EVOLUTION LINK.** Animal body plans have generally evolved from simple to more complex. How can we explain the exceptions?

4. **EVOLUTION LINK.** Discuss important adaptations made possible by the development of the coelom.

5. **EVOLUTION LINK.** Discuss the idea that every evolutionary adaptation has both advantages and disadvantages, using each of the following as an example: (a) cephalization, (b) the arthropod exoskeleton, and (c) segmentation with specialization.

6. **EVOLUTION LINK.** Insects that undergo complete metamorphosis outnumber those that do not by more than 10 to 1. Hypothesize an explanation.

7. **SCIENCE, TECHNOLOGY, AND SOCIETY.** Several international monitoring projects are gathering data to help us understand coral reef destruction. In your opinion, why is it important to take action to protect coral reefs?

 Additional questions are available in CengageNOW at www.cengage.com/login.

32 The Deuterostomes

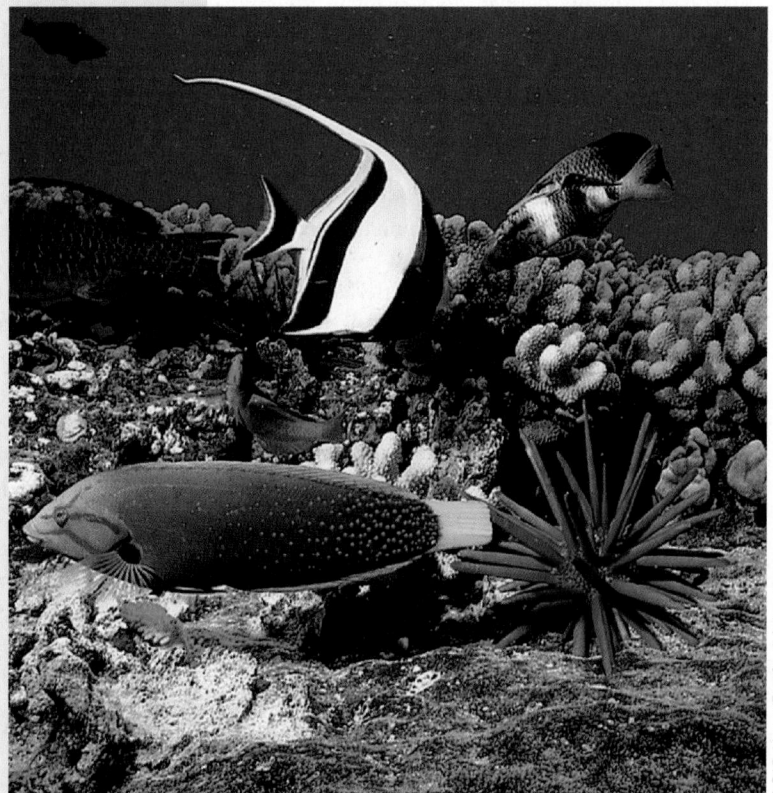

© Ed Robinson/Tom Stack & Associates

Representative deuterostomes. This marine habitat photographed in Hawaii includes an echinoderm known as a pencil urchin (*Heterocentrotrus mammilatus*); and chordates, represented by fishes, the clown wrasse (*Coris gaimard*) with its yellow tail and the Moorish idol (*Zanchus cornutus*).

KEY CONCEPTS

32.1 Echinoderms and chordates are the two most successful deuterostome lineages in terms of diversity, number of species, and number of individuals.

32.2 Echinoderms are characterized by radial symmetry in adults, a water vascular system, tube feet, and spiny skin.

32.3 At some time in its life, a chordate has a notochord; a dorsal, tubular nerve cord; a muscular postanal tail; and an endostyle (or thyroid gland).

32.4 Invertebrate chordates include tunicates and lancelets.

32.5 Shared derived characters of vertebrates include a vertebral column, cranium, neural crest cells, and an endoskeleton of cartilage or bone.

32.6 Among the earliest vertebrates, ostracoderms were armored, jawless fishes. The extant hagfishes and lampreys have neither jaws nor paired fins.

32.7 Jaws and fins were key adaptations that contributed to the success of jawed fishes, and the development of limbs was important in the transition to terrestrial life.

32.8 The evolution of the amniotic egg allowed animals to become fully terrestrial; the amniotic egg was the key adaptation leading to the evolution of reptiles, and later, to birds and mammals.

What does a sea star have in common with a fish, frog, hawk, or human? You may think it strange to group the echinoderms—the sea stars, sea urchins, and sand dollars—with the chordates, the phylum to which we humans and other animals with a backbone belong. However, even though these animals look and behave very differently, fossil evidence and morphological, developmental, and molecular data suggest that chordates and echinoderms share a common ancestor and are closely related.

In Chapter 31 we discussed the two major protostome branches of the animal kingdom, the lophotrochozoans and the ecdysozoans. In this chapter we focus on the third major branch of the animal kingdom, the deuterostomes. Some biologists speculate that the last common ancestor of the deuterostomes was an animal that obtained food by filtering ocean water. The two major groups (phyla) of living animals assigned to the deuterostomes are the echinoderms and chordates. The largest chordate subphylum is Vertebrata, which includes the animals with which we are most familiar—fishes, amphibians, reptiles (including birds), and mammals. Echinoderms are represented in the photograph by the pencil urchin, and chordates are represented by the fishes.

We begin this chapter with an introduction to the deuterostomes, and a survey of the echinoderms. With their unusual symmetry, spiny skins, water vascular system, and tube feet, echinoderms are one of the most unique animal groups. We then turn our attention to the chordates. We describe the key chordate characteristics and discuss the invertebrate chordates. After an introduction to the vertebrates, we discuss jawless fishes and the evolution of jaws and limbs. We discuss evolution of the adaptations that made the transition to life on land possible. We then describe the evolution of reptiles (including birds) and mammals.

32.1 WHAT ARE DEUTEROSTOMES?

■ LEARNING OBJECTIVE

1 Identify shared derived characters of deuterostomes and briefly describe the hemichordates.

Deuterostomia, the third major branch of the animal kingdom, includes the *echinoderms*—the sea stars, sea urchins, and sand dollars—and the *chordates,* the phylum to which we humans and other *vertebrates* (animals with a backbone) belong. Biologists also classify the **hemichordates,** a small group of wormlike marine animals, as deuterostomes. Hemichordates have a three-part body including a proboscis, collar, and trunk. These animals also have a characteristic ring of cilia surrounding the mouth. The most familiar of the hemichordates are the **acorn worms,** animals that live buried in mud or sand.

Deuterostomes evolved from a common ancestor during the Proterozoic eon more than 550 million years ago (mya). The major groups were present during the Lower Cambrian. Deuterostomes are characterized by several **shared derived characters (synapomorphies),** evolutionary novelties absent in their most recent common ancestor (see Chapter 23). Their defining characters are similarities in their patterns of development. For example, deuterostomes are characterized by radial, rather than spiral, cleavage (see Chapter 30). Their cleavage is indeterminate, which means the fate of their cells is fixed later in development than is the case in protostomes. In deuterostomes, the mouth does not develop from the blastopore as in protostomes. The blastopore of deuterostomes becomes the anus (or is located near the future site of the anus), and the mouth develops from a second opening at the anterior end of the embryo—thus the name *deuterostome,* which is derived from the Greek words for "second mouth."

Another characteristic of deuterostomes is the presence of *pharyngeal slits* (openings in the pharynx) at some time in their life cycle. Hemichordates and chordates have pharyngeal slits. Although there is evidence that some early echinoderms had pharyngeal slits, the extant (living) echinoderms have lost this character. *Basal deuterostomes* (members of the earliest deuterostome group to evolve) have a type of larva with a loop-shaped band of cilia used for locomotion. Deuterostomes have a true coelom.

Review

■ What are three shared derived characters of deuterostomes?

32.2 ECHINODERMS

■ LEARNING OBJECTIVE

2 Identify three shared derived characters of echinoderms and describe the main classes of echinoderms.

The **echinoderms** (phylum **Echinodermata**) have one of the most highly derived body plans in the animal kingdom. Echinoderm larvae are bilaterally symmetrical, ciliated, and free-swimming. However, during development the body reorganizes, and the adult exhibits **pentaradial symmetry,** in which the body is arranged in five parts around a central axis. Biologists have hypothesized that early echinoderms were sessile and that radial symmetry evolved as an adaptation to that lifestyle. Their radial symmetry allows these animals to respond effectively in every direction of their surrounding environment.

The most unique derived character of echinoderms is the **water vascular system,** a network of fluid-filled canals and chambers. In the sea star, for example, sea water enters through small pores in the *madreporite,* a sievelike structure on the body surface. Cilia lining the canals of the system move the water along. Branches of the water vascular system lead to numerous tiny **tube feet** that extend when filled with fluid. Each tube foot receives fluid from the main system of canals. A rounded muscular sac, or **ampulla,** at the base of the foot, stores fluid and is used to operate the tube foot. A valve separates each tube foot from other parts of the system. When the valve shuts, the ampulla contracts, forcing fluid into the tube foot. The fluid causes the tube foot to extend. At the bottom of the foot, a suction-type structure presses against and adheres to whatever surface the tube foot is on. The water vascular system functions in feeding and gas exchange, and serves as a hydrostatic skeleton important in locomotion.

Another unique echinoderm character is the **endoskeleton,** an internal skeleton, covered by a thin, ciliated epidermis. The endoskeleton consists of calcium carbonate ($CaCO_3$) plates and spines. The name *Echinodermata,* derived from words meaning "spiny skinned," was inspired by the spines that project outward from the endoskeleton. Some groups have pincerlike, modified spines called **pedicellariae** on the body surface. These structures, found only among the echinoderms, keep the surface of the animal free of debris.

Echinoderms have a well-developed coelom, containing coelomic fluid that transports materials. Although its structure varies in different groups, the complete digestive system is the most prominent body system. A variety of respiratory structures are found in the various classes. No excretory organs are present. The nervous system is simple, generally consisting of a nerve ring with nerves that extend out from it. Echinoderms have no brain. The sexes are usually separate, and eggs and sperm are generally released into the water, where fertilization takes place.

The echinoderms evolved from bilaterally symmetrical ancestors, probably during the Early Cambrian period. They achieved maximum diversity by the middle of the Paleozoic era, about 400 mya. By the beginning of the Mesozoic era 251 mya, they had declined, leaving five main groups that have survived to the present day. Biologists have identified about 7000 living and more than

13,000 extinct species. All echinoderms inhabit marine environments. They are found in the ocean at all depths. We consider the five extant groups: class Crinoidea, sea lilies and feather stars; class Asteroidea, sea stars; class Ophiuroidea, basket stars and brittle stars; class Echinoidea, sea urchins and sand dollars; and class Holothuroidea, sea cucumbers (**FIG. 32-1** and **TABLE 32-1**).

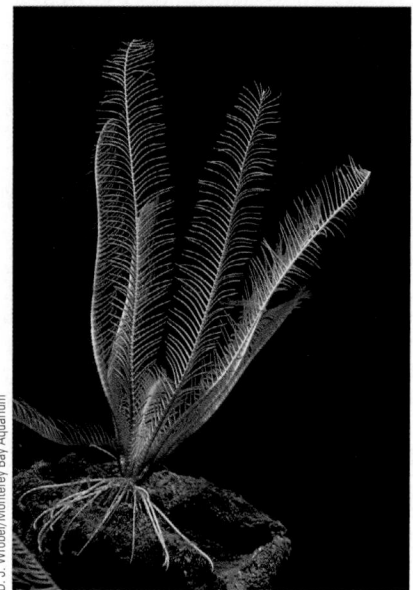

(a) **Class Crinoidea.** Feather stars use their slender, jointed appendages to cling to the surface of a rock or coral reef. They can creep and often move away to escape predators.

(b) **Class Asteroidea.** Orange and red sea star (*Fromia monilis*) on bubble coral.

(c) **Class Ophiuroidea.** Daisy brittle star (*Ophiopholis aculeata*), photographed in Muscongus Bay, Maine.

(d) **Class Echinoidea.** With its flattened, circular body, the sand dollar (*Dendraster excentricus*) is adapted for burrowing on the ocean floor.

(e) **Class Holothuroidea.** A sea cucumber (*Thelonota*) raises its body to spawn.

FIGURE 32-1 Representative echinoderms

TABLE 32-1   Classes of Echinoderms

Class and Representative Animals		Characteristics
Crinoidea Feather stars, sea lilies		Feather stars motile; sea lilies, sessile, attach to ocean floor by stalk; oral surface on upper side of disc; tube feet along feathery arms trap microscopic organisms
Asteroidea Sea stars		Arms (rays) extend from central disc; tube feet on undersurface of each arm; mouth in center of underside of disc; carnivorous predators and scavengers
Ophiuroidea Basket stars, brittle stars		Resemble sea stars, but arms long, slender, and more set off from central disc; tube feet used to collect and handle food
Echinoidea Sea urchins, sand dollars		Skeletal plates flattened and fused to form a test; sand dollars burrow in sand and feed on organic particles; sea urchins graze on algae
Holothuroidea Sea cucumbers		Body is elongated, muscular sac; mouth surrounded by tentacles that are modified tube feet; sluggish animals that live on sea bottom; many species eject organs when conditions poor; for defense, can eject tubules out of anus

Feather stars and sea lilies are suspension feeders

Feather stars and sea lilies (class **Crinoidea**) are the oldest living echinoderms (see Fig. 32-1a). Although many extinct crinoids are known, relatively few living species have been identified. The feather stars are motile, although they often remain in the same location for long periods. Sea lilies are sessile and remain attached to the ocean floor by a stalk.

Crinoids remove suspended food from the water. Several branched, feathery arms extend upward. Numerous tube feet shaped like small tentacles are located along the feathery arms. These tube feet are coated with mucus that traps microscopic organisms. The **oral surface** (location of the mouth) is on the upper side of the disc. In all other echinoderms, the mouth is located on the underside of the disc toward the substratum.

Many sea stars capture prey

Sea stars (commonly called starfish) are asteroids (class **Asteroidea**; see Fig. 32-1b). Their bodies consist of a central disc from which extend 5 to more than 20 arms, or rays (**FIG. 32-2**). The undersurface of each arm has hundreds of pairs of tube feet. The endoskeleton consists of a series of calcareous plates that permit some movement of the arms. Delicate dermal gills, small extensions of the body wall, carry on gas exchange. The mouth lies in the center of the underside of the disc.

Most sea stars are carnivorous predators and scavengers that feed on crustaceans, mollusks, annelids, and even other echinoderms. Occasionally, they catch small fish. The sea star's water vascular system does not permit rapid movement, so its prey usually consists of stationary or slow-moving animals, such as clams.

To attack a clam or other bivalve mollusk, the sea star mounts it and assumes a humped position as it straddles the edge opposite the hinge. Then, holding itself in position with its tube feet, the sea star slides its thin, flexible stomach out through its mouth and between the closed, or slightly gaping, valves (shell parts) of the clam. While the clam is still in its own shell, the sea star secretes enzymes that digest the soft parts of the clam to the consistency of a thick soup. When the partly digested meal is taken into the sea star body, it is further digested by enzymes secreted by digestive glands located in each arm.

The circulatory system in sea stars is poorly developed and probably of little help in transporting materials. Instead, the coelomic fluid, which fills the large coelom and bathes the internal tissues, assumes this function. Metabolic wastes pass to the outside by diffusion across the tube feet and dermal gills. The nervous system consists of a ring of nervous tissue encircling the mouth and a nerve extending from this ring into each arm.

Sea daisies are a curious group of asteroids characterized by small, disc-shaped, flat bodies (less than 1 cm in diameter) with no arms or mouth. They inhabit bacteria-rich wood sunk in deep water and apparently absorb bacteria through their body surface.

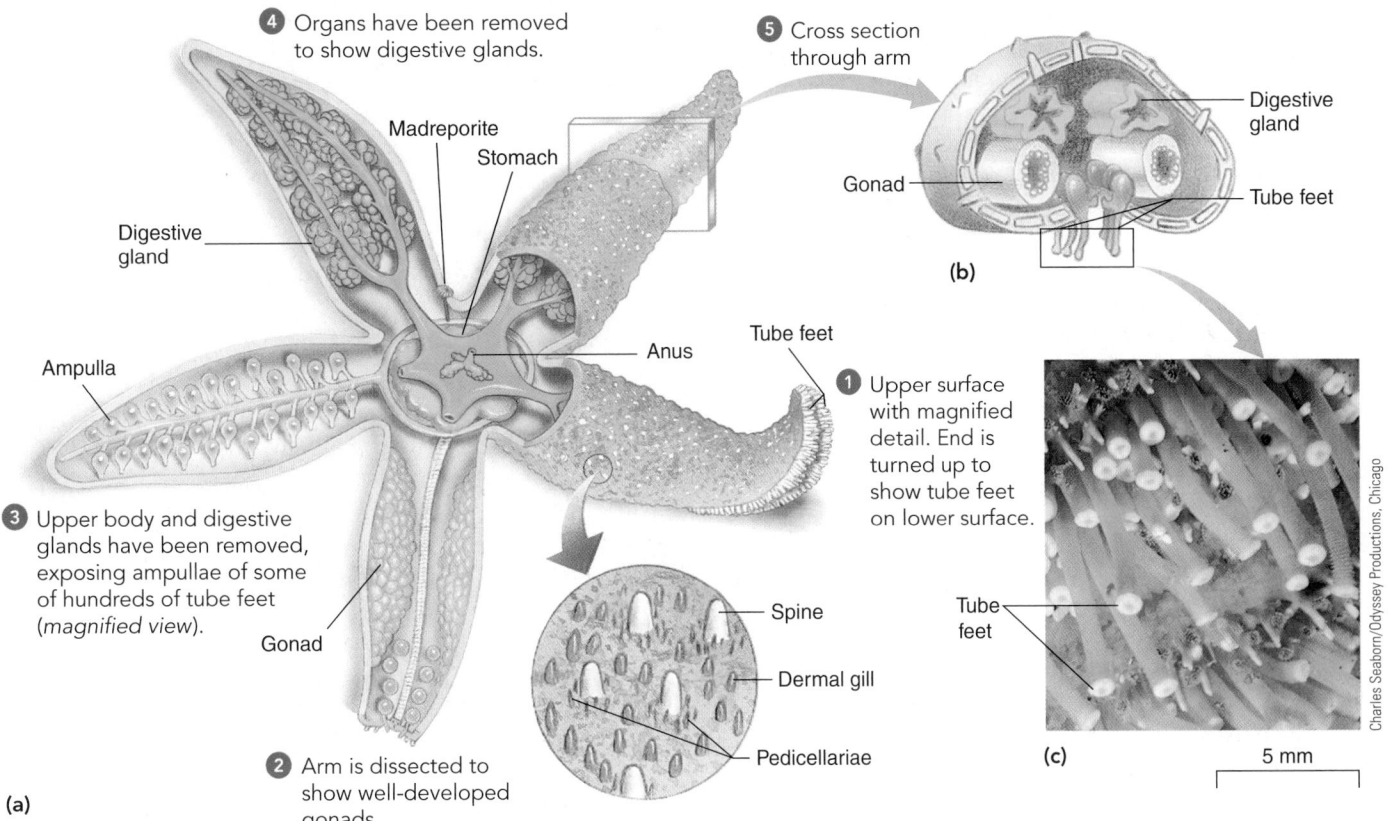

FIGURE 32-2 Body plan of a sea star

(a) A sea star viewed from above, with its arms in various stages of dissection. Similar structures are present in each arm, but some organs are not shown in order to highlight certain structures. The two-part stomach is in the central disc with the anus on the aboral (*upper*) surface and the mouth beneath on the oral surface. **(b)** Cross section through arm and tube feet. **(c)** LM of tube feet of a sea star.

In figure (a):
④ Organs have been removed to show digestive glands.

Madreporite
Stomach
Digestive gland
Ampulla

③ Upper body and digestive glands have been removed, exposing ampullae of some of hundreds of tube feet (*magnified view*).

Gonad

② Arm is dissected to show well-developed gonads.

Anus
Tube feet

① Upper surface with magnified detail. End is turned up to show tube feet on lower surface.

Spine
Dermal gill
Pedicellariae

⑤ Cross section through arm
Digestive gland
Gonad
Tube feet

(b)

Tube feet

(c)   5 mm

Charles Seaborn/Odyssey Productions, Chicago

Basket stars and brittle stars make up the largest group of echinoderms

Basket stars and brittle stars (serpent stars) make up the largest group of echinoderms (class **Ophiuroidea**) both in number of species and individuals (see Fig. 32-1c). These animals resemble sea stars in that their bodies consist of a central disc with arms. However, the arms are long and slender and more sharply set off from the central disc. Some brittle stars use their arms for locomotion, making rowing movements. Their tube feet lack suckers; they may be used to collect and handle food and may also serve a sensory function, perhaps that of taste.

Sea urchins and sand dollars have movable spines

Sea urchins and sand dollars (class **Echinoidea**) have no arms (see Fig. 32-1d and chapter opening photograph). Their skeletal plates are flattened and fused to form a solid shell called a test. The flattened body of the sand dollar is adapted for burrowing in the sand, where it feeds on tiny organic particles. Sand dollars have smaller spines than sea urchins.

Many sea urchins graze on algae, scraping the sea floor with their calcareous teeth. Sea urchins use their tube feet for locomotion. They also push themselves along with their movable spines. In some species, the spines covering the body can penetrate flesh and are difficult to remove. So threatening are these spines that swimmers on tropical beaches are often cautioned to wear shoes when venturing offshore, where these living pincushions may dwell in abundance.

Sea cucumbers are elongated, sluggish animals

Sea cucumbers (class **Holothuroidea**) are appropriately named, for some species are about the size and shape of a cucumber. The elongated body is a flexible, muscular sac (see Fig. 32-1e). The mouth is usually surrounded by a circle of tentacles that are modified tube feet. The endoskeleton consists of microscopic plates embedded in the body wall. The circulatory system, which is more highly developed than in other echinoderms, functions to transport oxygen and perhaps nutrients.

Sea cucumbers are sluggish animals that usually live on the bottom of the sea, sometimes burrowing in the mud. Some graze with their tentacles, whereas others stretch their branched tentacles out in the water and wait for dinner to float by. Algae and other morsels are trapped in mucus along the tentacles.

An interesting habit of some sea cucumbers is evisceration, in which the digestive tract, respiratory structures, and gonads are ejected from the body, usually when environmental conditions are unfavorable. When conditions improve, the lost parts are regenerated. Even more curious, when certain sea cucumbers are irritated or attacked, they direct their rear end toward the enemy and shoot red tubules out of their anus! These unusual weapons become sticky in sea water, and the attacking animal may become hopelessly entangled in the spaghetti-like tangle of tubules. Some of the tubules release a toxic substance.

Review

- What are three derived characters of echinoderms? Describe each.
- How do sea stars differ from crinoids? from sea urchins?

32.3 THE CHORDATES: DEFINING CHARACTERISTICS

■ LEARNING OBJECTIVE

3   Describe characteristics of chordates, including four shared derived characters.

Biologists currently assign the chordates (phylum **Chordata**) to three groups, or subphyla: urochordates, marine animals called *tunicates*; cephalochordates, marine animals called *lancelets*; and vertebrates, animals with backbones. Systematists are currently debating whether the urochordates or cephalochordates are the sister group of the chordates (**FIG. 32-3**).

Chordates are deuterostomes. They are coelomates with bilateral symmetry, a tube-within-a-tube body plan, and three well-developed germ layers. Four shared derived characters distinguish the chordates from all other groups of animals. These characters, which evolved in connection with their evolving methods of locomotion and obtaining food, include the notochord; the dorsal, tubular nerve cord; a postanal tail; and an endostyle or thyroid gland.

1. All chordates have a **notochord** during some time in their life cycle. The notochord is a dorsal, longitudinal rod composed of cartilage. The notochord is firm but flexible, and it supports the body.

2. At some time in their life cycle, chordates have a **dorsal, tubular nerve cord.** The chordate nerve cord differs from the nerve cord of most other animals in that it is located dorsally rather than ventrally, is hollow rather than solid, and is single rather than double.

3. Chordates have a larva or embryo with a muscular **postanal tail,** an appendage that extends posterior to the anus.

4. The **endostyle** is a groove in the floor of the pharynx that secretes mucus and traps food particles in the sea water passing through the pharynx. The endostyle is present in the urochordates, cephalochordates, and lamprey larvae. The thyroid gland evolved from the endostyle and is present in all other chordates.

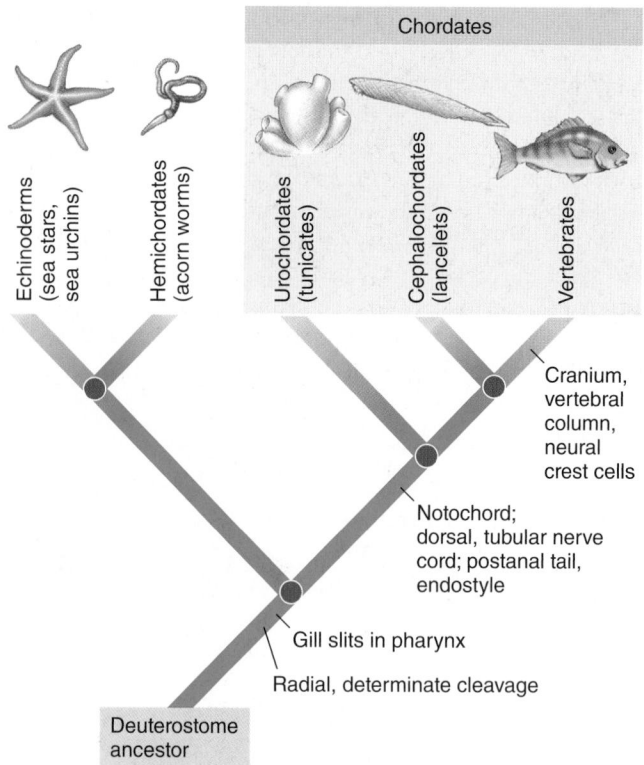

FIGURE 32-3 Evolutionary relationships of the chordates
This cladogram shows hypothesized phylogenetic relationships among deuterostomes, including chordates (*tan region*), based on structural and DNA data. The relative positions of the urochordates and cephalochordates may change as new data are considered.

Chordates have **pharyngeal slits** (also called *pharyngeal gill slits*) or pharyngeal pouches during some time in their life cycle (**FIG. 32-4**). In the embryo, a series of alternating branchial (gill) arches and grooves develop in the body wall in the pharyngeal (throat) region. Pharyngeal pouches extend laterally from the anterior portion of the digestive tract toward the grooves. In aquatic chordates, the tissue breaks through where the pouches meet the grooves, forming slits.

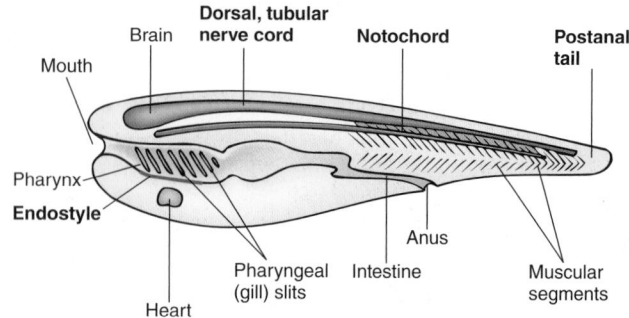

FIGURE 32-4 Generalized chordate body plan
Note the shared derived characters: notochord; dorsal, tubular nerve cord; postanal tail; and endostyle. Other key characteristics include pharyngeal (gill) slits and segmented muscles.

The perforated pharynx first evolved as an adaptation for filtering food. As water flowed through the mouth and passed out of the pharynx through the gill slits, suspended food particles were trapped in mucus. Later, modifications evolved, adapting the gill slits for gas exchange in fishes and some other aquatic vertebrates. Early in vertebrate evolution, anterior pharyngeal arches evolved into jaws. Pharyngeal slits are not a derived character of chordates because they are also present in hemichordates.

Typically, chordates have an endoskeleton and a closed circulatory system with a ventral heart. Chordates have segmented bodies, but specialization is so pronounced that the basic segmentation of the body plan may not be apparent. For example, in vertebrates, although segmentation of the body is not obvious, muscles and nerves are segmentally organized.

Review

- What are four shared derived characters of chordates?
- How is the chordate nerve cord different from the nerve cord of most other animals?

32.4 INVERTEBRATE CHORDATES

■ LEARNING OBJECTIVE

4   Compare tunicates and lancelets, and summarize the phylogeny of chordates.

Some chordates are not vertebrates. The invertebrate chordates include tunicates (urochordates) and lancelets (cephalochordates).

Tunicates are common marine animals

The **tunicates,** or **urochordates** (subphylum **Urochordata**), include the sea squirts and their relatives (**FIG. 32-5**). Larval tunicates have typical chordate characteristics and superficially resemble tadpoles. The expanded body has a pharynx with slits, and the long muscular tail contains a notochord and a dorsal, tubular nerve cord. Some tunicates (*appendicularians*) retain their chordate features and ability to swim. These animals are common members of the zooplankton.

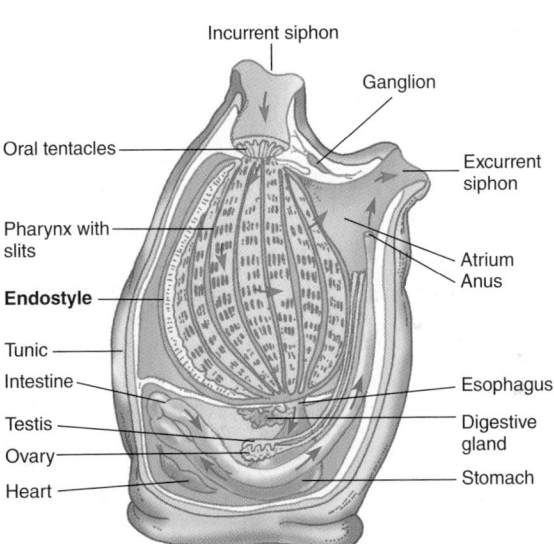

(b) Lateral view of an adult tunicate. The blue arrows represent the flow of water, and the red arrows represent the path of food.

(a) Incurrent (*top*) and excurrent (*side*) siphons of a sea peach (*Halocynthia aurantium*), a solitary tunicate.

0.5 mm

(c) Swimming larval stage of a colonial species, *Distaplia occidentalis*.

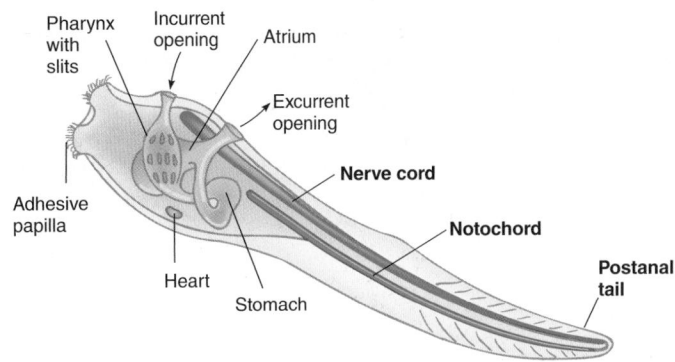

(d) Internal structure of a larval tunicate (*lateral view*).

FIGURE 32-5 *Animated* **Tunicate body plan**

Most tunicates are **ascidians,** commonly known as sea squirts (class Ascidiacea). A sea squirt larva swims for a time, then attaches itself to a rock, piling, or to the sea bottom. It loses its tail, notochord, and much of its nervous system. Adult sea squirts are barrel-shaped, sessile marine animals unlike other chordates. Indeed, they are often mistaken for sponges or cnidarians. Only the pharyngeal slits, endostyle, and the structure of its larva indicate that the sea squirt is a chordate.

Adult tunicates develop a protective covering, or **tunic,** that may be soft and transparent or quite leathery. Curiously, the tunic consists of a carbohydrate much like cellulose. The tunic has two openings: the incurrent siphon, through which water and food enter; and the excurrent siphon, through which water, waste products, and gametes pass to the outside. Sea squirts get their name from their practice of forcefully expelling a stream of water from the excurrent siphon when irritated.

Tunicates are filter feeders that remove plankton suspended in the stream of water passing through the pharynx. Food particles are trapped in mucus secreted by cells of the *endostyle,* a groove that extends the length of the pharynx. Ciliated cells of the pharynx move the stream of food-laden mucus into the esophagus. Much of the water entering the pharynx passes out through the pharyngeal slits into an **atrium** (chamber) and is discharged through the excurrent siphon.

Some species of tunicates form large colonies in which members share a common tunic and excurrent siphon. Colonial forms often reproduce asexually by budding. Sexual forms are usually hermaphroditic.

Lancelets clearly exhibit chordate characteristics

Most **cephalochordates** (subphylum **Cephalochordata**) belong to the genus *Branchiostoma,* which consists of animals commonly known as **lancelets,** or **amphioxus.** Lancelets are translucent, fish-shaped animals, 3 to 8 cm (1.3 to 3.2 in) long and pointed at both ends. They are widely distributed in shallow seas. Larvae can swim freely, but adults typically burrow in the sand in shallow water near the shore. In some parts of the world, lancelets are an important source of food. One Chinese fishery reports an annual catch of 35 tons (about one billion lancelets).

Chordate characteristics are highly developed in lancelets. The notochord extends from the anterior tip ("head"; hence the name *Cephalochordata*) to the posterior tip. A dorsal, tubular nerve cord also extends the entire length of the animal, and many pairs of pharyngeal slits are evident in the large pharyngeal region (**FIG. 32-6**). Although superficially similar to fishes, lancelets have a far simpler body plan. They do not have paired fins, jaws, sense organs, a heart, or a well-defined head or brain.

Like tunicates, lancelets are filter feeders. Cilia in the mouth and pharynx draw a current of water into the mouth. Microscopic organisms in the water are trapped in mucus secreted by the endostyle, and are then moved back to the intestine by beating cilia.

Water passes through the pharyngeal slits into the atrium, a chamber with a ventral opening (the *atriopore*) located anterior to the anus. Metabolic wastes are excreted by segmentally arranged, ciliated *protonephridia* that open into the atrium. Unlike circulation in other invertebrates, the blood flows anteriorly in the ventral vessel and posteriorly in the dorsal vessel in lancelets. This circulatory pattern is similar to that of fishes.

Systematists debate chordate phylogeny

Fossils of early chordates contribute to our understanding of chordate phylogeny. Invertebrate chordates are soft-bodied and did not leave many fossils. However, some well-preserved, key fossils that date back to the Middle Cambrian have been found in the Burgess Shale of British Columbia, Canada. Early Cambrian fossil sites have been discovered in Chengjiang and Haikou, China. At

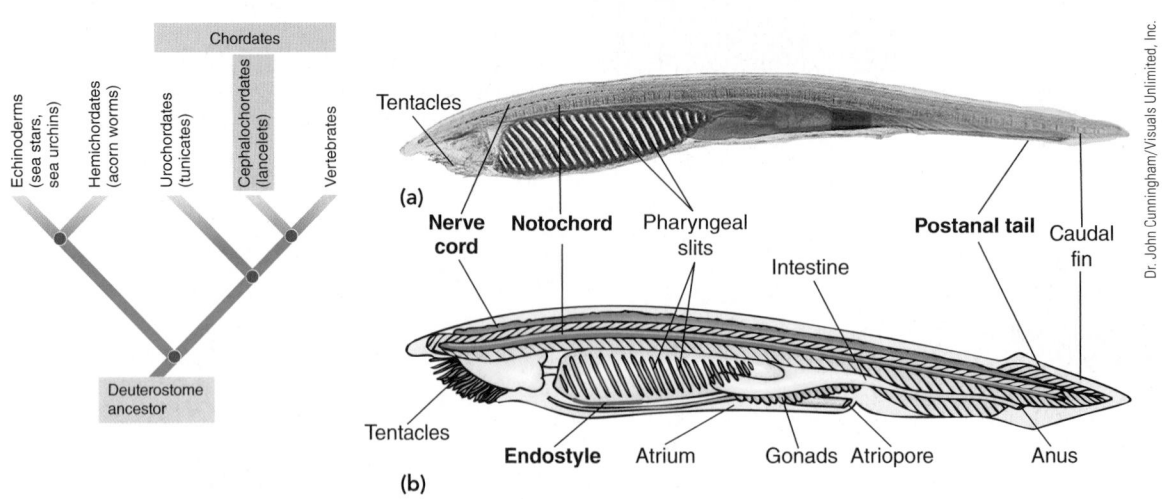

FIGURE 32-6 *Animated* Cephalochordate body plan
(a) Photograph of a lancelet, *Branchiostoma* (amphioxus). Note the prominent pharyngeal gill slits.
(b) Longitudinal section showing derived characters and other internal structures.

Chengjiang, fine-grained rocks about 530 million years old have preserved soft-bodied animals, including *Haikouella,* in some detail. *Haikouella* was about 2 to 3 cm (approximately 1 in) long and had a nerve cord, notochord, gills, muscle segments, and a brain. Many biologists view *Haikouella* as an early chordate. Some investigators hypothesize that this fossil represents a transitional form between cephalochordates and vertebrates.

Pikaia, a lancelet-like fossil discovered in the Burgess Shale, had a primitive notochord with muscles attached to it that allowed for locomotion. About 4 cm (1.5 in) in length, *Pikaia* had a tail fin and probably filtered food from the water. *Pikaia* is considered an early chordate, most likely a cephalochordate.

Are cephalochordates or urochordates the sister group of the vertebrates? Both structural and molecular data suggest that the cephalochordates are the sister group of the vertebrates. The most recent common ancestor of cephalochordates and vertebrates may have resembled a tunicate larva. Important shared derived characters include the presence of the notochord, nerve cord, and post-anal tail in the adults. Another is the presence of **somites,** a series of paired blocks of mesoderm that develop on each side of the notochord. Somites are temporary structures that define the segmentation of the embryo. In vertebrates, they give rise to the vertebrae, ribs, and certain skeletal muscles. Another similarity between cephalochordates and vertebrates is the lancelet nerve cord, which has specialized regions, corresponding to the vertebrate forebrain and midbrain. Molecular data support the cephalochordates as the vertebrate sister group based on similarities in ribosomal and mitochondrial gene sequences.

However, based on genome sequencing of tunicates (including the tunicate *Ciona intestinalis),* some biologists argue that the urochordate genome corresponds more closely to that of the chordate ancestor and that urochordates are the sister group of the vertebrates. The tunicate *Ciona intestinalis* is an excellent model organism for studying chordate development because its genome consists of only about 16,000 protein-coding genes, the basic set of genes found in chordates. Interestingly, about 80% of *Ciona's* genes are found in vertebrates. In fact, *Ciona* has most vertebrate gene families, but in simplified form. For example, *Ciona* has only a single copy of each gene family involved in cell signaling and regulation of development, whereas vertebrates have two or more copies of these gene families. (A gene family is a group of genes that evolved over time from a single ancestral gene through duplication and divergence.) Some of the "extra" copies probably evolved to code for new structures or functions. *Ciona* also has genes for some vertebrate structures and processes, even though it does not express these genes.

Although the debate about chordate phylogeny and the sister group of the vertebrates continues, in this edition of *Biology,* we consider the cephalochordates to be the sister group of the vertebrates.

Review

- How are the main derived chordate characters evident in a tunicate larva and in an adult tunicate?
- If you found a small fishlike animal along the shoreline, how would you identify it as a lancelet?

32.5 INTRODUCING THE VERTEBRATES

■ LEARNING OBJECTIVES

5   Describe four shared derived characters of vertebrates.
6   Describe the major taxa of extant vertebrates.

Numbering about 50,000 described species, the **vertebrates** (subphylum **Vertebrata**) are less diverse and much less numerous than the insects. However, vertebrates rival the insects in their adaptations to an enormous variety of lifestyles (**FIG. 32-7**). In addition to the basic chordate characteristics, vertebrates have a number of shared derived characters not found in other groups.

The vertebral column is a derived vertebrate character

The vertebrates are distinguished from other chordates in having a backbone, or **vertebral column,** that forms the skeletal axis of the body. This flexible support develops around the notochord, and in most species it largely replaces the notochord during embryonic development. The vertebral column consists of cartilaginous or bony segments called **vertebrae.** Dorsal projections of the vertebrae enclose the nerve cord along its length. Anterior to the vertebral column, a cartilaginous or bony **cranium,** or braincase, encloses and protects the brain, the enlarged anterior end of the nerve cord.

The cranium and vertebral column are part of the *endoskeleton.* In contrast with the nonliving exoskeleton of many invertebrates, the vertebrate endoskeleton is a living tissue that grows with the animal. Some vertebrates (jawless and cartilaginous fishes) have skeletons made of cartilage. However, in most vertebrates, the skeleton is mainly bone, a tissue that contains fibers made of the protein collagen. The hard matrix of bone consists of the compound hydroxyapatite, composed mainly of calcium phosphate.

Many characters common to vertebrates have been derived from a group of cells called **neural crest cells.** These cells, found only in vertebrates, appear early in development and migrate to various parts of the embryo. Neural crest cells give rise to or influence the development of many structures, including nerves, head muscles, cranium, and jaws.

Recall that *Hox* genes are important in determining pattern development in embryos (see Chapter 17). Specifically, *Hox* genes determine the fate of cells in the anterior-posterior axis. These genes occur in clusters on specific chromosomes. All invertebrates and early chordates that have been studied have one *Hox* gene cluster, but vertebrates have four duplicated clusters. Other gene clusters, including some encoding transcription factors, were also duplicated during the evolution of the early vertebrates. The significance of these genetic changes is the focus of current investigation, but it is reasonable to hypothesize that the increase in genetic complexity contributed to the development of more complex and varied bodies.

Recall that invertebrates show an evolutionary trend toward **cephalization,** the concentration of nerve cells and sense organs

This cladogram provides a framework for understanding the evolution of vertebrate diversity and adaptations to aquatic and terrestrial environments.

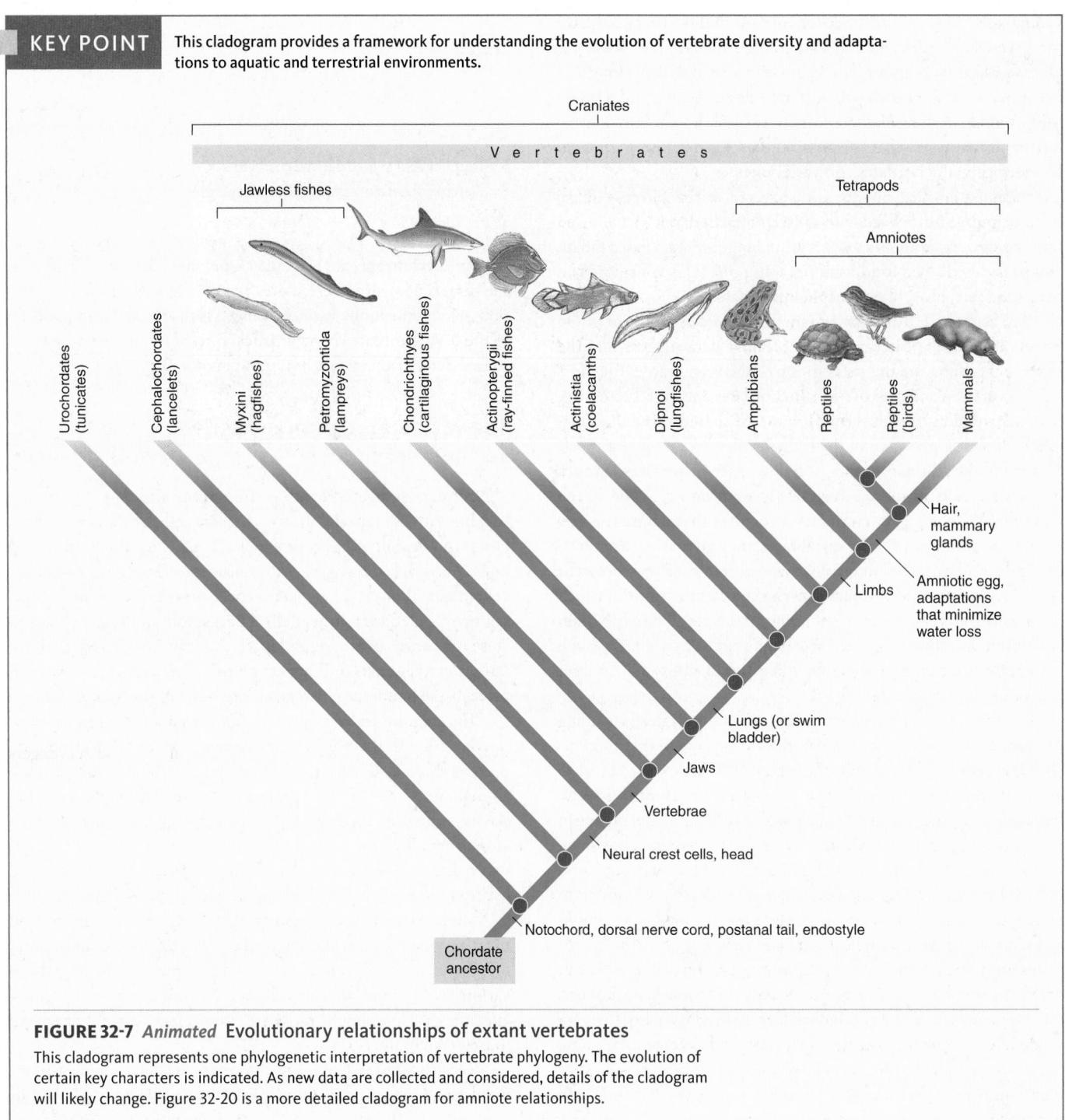

FIGURE 32-7 *Animated* Evolutionary relationships of extant vertebrates

This cladogram represents one phylogenetic interpretation of vertebrate phylogeny. The evolution of certain key characters is indicated. As new data are collected and considered, details of the cladogram will likely change. Figure 32-20 is a more detailed cladogram for amniote relationships.

in a definite head. Vertebrate evolution is characterized by *pronounced* cephalization. The brain has become larger and more elaborate, and its various regions have specialized to perform different functions. Either 10 or 12 pairs of **cranial nerves** emerge from the brain and extend to various organs of the body. Vertebrates have well-developed sense organs concentrated in the head: eyes; ears that serve as organs of balance and, in some vertebrates, for hearing as well; and organs of smell and taste.

Most vertebrates have two pairs of appendages. The fins of fishes are appendages that stabilize the fish in the water. Paired pectoral and pelvic fins are also used in steering. Biologists hypothesize that jointed appendages that facilitated locomotion on land evolved from the lobed (divided) fins of lungfishes.

Vertebrates have a closed circulatory system with a ventral heart and blood containing hemoglobin. The complete digestive tract has specialized regions and large digestive glands (the liver and pancreas). Several *endocrine glands,* which are ductless glands, secrete hormones. Paired kidneys regulate fluid balance. The sexes are typically separate.

Early vertebrates were probably marine animals. In contrast to the tunicates and lancelets, which use cilia to beat a stream of water into the mouth and filter particles of food from the water, vertebrates use muscles for feeding. Some vertebrates use muscles to draw in a current of water from which both food and oxygen can be extracted. Muscles in the wall of the digestive tube are more powerful than cilia and probably contributed to an increase in both size and activity of early vertebrates. A muscular pharynx may have permitted animals to crush small prey after capture. The evolution of more effective sensory systems, a more complex brain, and organs that could support increased activity was important in the shift from filter-feeding to a more active lifestyle.

Vertebrate taxonomy is a work in progress

The study of evolutionary relationships of vertebrates is an important focus of research. The earliest vertebrate fossils include *Haikouichthys,* conodonts, and a group known as *ostracoderms* (discussed in the next section). *Haikouichthys* was a fishlike animal about 2.5 cm (1 in) long. It had several characters found in vertebrates, and some researchers think it was an early jawless fish.

Conodonts were simple fishlike chordates with gill arches, muscular segments, and fins. They had large eyes, and complex toothlike hooks that were probably used in capturing prey. Conodonts were abundant from the Precambrian to the Late Triassic period; they have been identified in several fossil beds around the world. Cladistic analyses suggest that conodonts were early vertebrates.

The earliest extant vertebrates to evolve were *agnathans* (*a,* "without"; and *gnathos,* "jaw"): the hagfishes, followed by the lampreys. Biologists assign hagfishes to class *Myxini* (mik-sin′-y) and lampreys to class *Petromyzontida* (pet-tro-my-zon′-tih-da) (from the Greek *petros,* "stone"; and *myzon,* "sucking"; lampreys hold onto stones by their mouths to prevent being washed away by the currents).

Some systematists have argued that the hagfishes do not quite qualify as vertebrates. Although they have many vertebrate characters, including a cranium, hagfishes have no trace of vertebrae. The notochord is their only axial support. Some biologists use the term **Craniata,** based on the presence of a cranium, to designate a clade that includes the vertebrates plus the hagfishes. They view the Myxini as the sister group of all other craniates. Recent molecular analyses, however, support classifying hagfishes as vertebrates. Hagfishes may have evolved from vertebrates that had vertebrae but lost them during the course of their evolution.

If we include the Myxini, the extant vertebrates are currently assigned to nine classes: six classes of fishes and three of tetrapods (four-limbed vertebrates) (**TABLE 32-2** and see Fig. 32-7). Some biologists give fishes and tetrapods superclass status: superclass **Pisces** (fishes) and superclass **Tetrapoda.** In this classification scheme, the fishes include the hagfishes, lampreys, and four classes of jawed fishes: *Chondrichthyes, Actinopterygii, Actinistia,* and *Dipnoi.*

The four-limbed land vertebrates, or **tetrapods,** include class *Amphibia* (frogs, toads, and salamanders); class *Reptilia* (lizards, snakes, turtles, alligators and birds); and class *Mammalia,* the mammals. The reptiles and mammals form a clade known as *amniotes,* animals fully adapted to life on land.

Review

- What shared derived characters distinguish the vertebrates from the rest of the chordates?
- What are the six classes of fishes? the three classes of tetrapods?

32.6 JAWLESS FISHES

■ LEARNING OBJECTIVE

7 Distinguish among the major groups of jawless fishes.

Some of the earliest known vertebrates, collectively referred to as **ostracoderms,** consisted of several groups of small, armored, jawless fishes that lived on the bottom and strained their food from the water (see Fig. 21-11). Thick bony plates protected their heads from predators, and thick scales covered their trunks and tails. Most ostracoderms lacked fins. Fragments of ostracoderm scales have been found in rocks from the Cambrian period, but most ostracoderm fossils are from the Ordovician and Silurian periods. They became extinct by the end of the Devonian period.

Like ostracoderms, present-day hagfishes and lampreys have neither jaws nor paired fins. They are eel-shaped animals, up to 1 m (about 3 ft) long. Their smooth skin lacks scales, and they are supported by a cartilaginous skeleton and well-developed notochord.

Hagfishes, assigned to class **Myxini,** are marine scavengers (**FIG. 32-8**). They burrow for worms and other invertebrates or prey on dead and disabled fishes. Hagfishes use toothlike projections from their tongue to pull off flesh from prey. For leverage, a hagfish

FIGURE 32-8 *Animated* **Pacific hagfish (*Eptatretus stoutii*)**
The hagfish has a flexible body and can tie it into knots. It knots its tail and then slides the knot toward its head. Being knotted gives it leverage when tearing flesh from its prey. Knotting itself also helps the hagfish remove excess slime from its body.

TABLE 32-2   Extant Vertebrate Classes

Class	Examples	Characteristics
Myxini	Hagfishes	Jawless, marine fishes that lack paired appendages; the notochord is their only axial support; lack vertebrae, so some biologists classify as craniates, but not as vertebrates
Petromyzontida	Lampreys	Jawless, freshwater and marine fishes with skeleton of cartilage; complete cranium and rudimentary vertebrae; hatch as small larvae
Chondrichthyes	Sharks, rays, skates, chimaeras	Jawed marine and freshwater fishes with skeleton of cartilage; notochord replaced by vertebrae in adult; gills; placoid scales; two pairs of fins; oviparous, ovoviparous, or viviparous (a few species); well-developed sense organs (including lateral line system)
Actinopterygii (ray-finned fishes)	Perch, salmon, tuna, trout	Bony, marine and freshwater fishes; gills; swim bladder; generally oviparous
Actinistia (lobe-finned fishes)	Coelacanths	Bony fishes; marine, nocturnal predators on fish; lobed fins
Dipnoi	Lungfishes	Bony freshwater fishes; four similarly sized limbs, which are similar in structure and position to those of tetrapods
Amphibia	Salamanders, frogs and toads, caecilians	Tetrapods; aquatic larva typically undergoes metamorphosis into terrestrial adult; gas exchange through lungs and/or moist skin; heart consists of two atria and single ventricle; systemic and pulmonary circulation
Reptilia	Turtles, lizards, snakes, alligators	Amniotes* with horny scales; adapted for reproduction on land (internal fertilization, leathery shell, amnion); lungs; ventricles of heart partly divided
	Robins, pelicans, eagles, ducks, penguins, ostriches	Amniotes with feathers; anterior limbs modified as wings; compact, streamlined body; four-chambered heart; endothermic; vocal calls and complex songs
Mammalia	Monotremes (Protheria), marsupials (Metatheria), Eutheria (mammals with well-developed placentas)	Amniotes with hair; females nourish young with mammary glands; differentiation of teeth; three middle-ear bones; diaphragm; four-chambered heart; endothermic; highly developed nervous system

*A cladogram classification of amniotes is shown in Figure 32-20.

can tie itself into a knot. As a defense mechanism, hagfishes secrete large amounts of fluid that forms sticky slime in sea water. The hagfish becomes so slippery that predators cannot grasp it.

Lampreys are jawless vertebrates assigned to class **Petromyzontida.** Some spend their adult lives in the ocean and return to fresh water to reproduce. Many species of adult lampreys are parasites on other fishes (**FIG. 32-9**). Adult parasitic lampreys have a circular sucking disc around the mouth, which lies on the ventral side of the anterior end of the body. Using this disc to attach to a fish, the lamprey bores through the skin of its host with horny (made of keratin) teeth on the disc and tongue. Then the lamprey injects an anticoagulant into its host and sucks out blood and soft tissues.

As in hagfish, the notochord persists throughout life and is not replaced by a vertebral column. However, lampreys have rudiments of vertebrae, cartilaginous segments called *neural arches* that extend dorsally around the spinal cord.

(a) Three lampreys attached to a carp by their suction-cup mouths. Note the absence of jaws and paired fins.

(b) Suction-cup mouth of adult lamprey (*Entosphenus japonicus*). Note the rasplike teeth.

FIGURE 32-9 *Animated* **Lampreys**
Parasitic lampreys attach to fish and suck out body fluids. The wounds they leave in the fish may be fatal.

Review

- How do lampreys and hagfishes resemble ostracoderms?
- How do hagfishes differ from other fishes?

32.7 EVOLUTION OF JAWS AND LIMBS: JAWED FISHES AND AMPHIBIANS

■ LEARNING OBJECTIVE

8   Trace the evolution of jawed fishes and early tetrapods; describe modern amphibians.

Imagine trying to hunt for food and then eat without jaws or limbs. This was the challenge for early vertebrates and helps explain why the jawless fishes are mainly scavengers and parasites. The evolution of jaws from a portion of the gill arch skeleton and the development of fins allowed fishes to become active predators. With jaws an animal can grasp and hold on to live prey while eating it. The evolution of fins allowed fishes to swim faster and with more control. Fishes with jaws and fins had many new opportunities for capturing food.

Fossil evidence suggests that jaws and paired fins evolved during the Late Silurian and Devonian periods. Two early groups of jawed fishes, now extinct, were the **acanthodians,** armored fishes with paired spines and pectoral and pelvic fins, and **placoderms,** armored fishes with paired fins (**FIG. 32-10**). The success of the jawed vertebrates probably contributed to the extinction of the ostracoderms.

When the fins of certain fishes evolved into limbs about 370 mya, a different type of locomotion was possible. These fishes

(a) An acanthodian. *Climatius* was a spiny-skinned acanthodian with large fin spines and five pairs of accessory fins between the pectoral and pelvic pairs. *Climatius* was a small fish that reached a length of 8 cm (3 in).

(b) A placoderm. *Dinichthys* was a giant placoderm that grew to a length of 8 m (26 ft). (Most placoderms were only about 20 cm, or 8 in, long.) Its head and thorax were covered by bony armor, but the rest of the body and tail were naked.

FIGURE 32-10 **Early jawed fishes**
Acanthodians and placoderms flourished in the Devonian period.

were able to move about in shallow waters and wetlands in search of food. When the first tetrapods—the amphibians—moved onto the land, new opportunities for habitats and food became available.

Most cartilaginous fishes inhabit marine environments

The cartilaginous fishes, members of class **Chondrichthyes** (kon-drik'-thee-eez), appeared as successful marine forms in the Devonian period. Class Chondrichthyes , which is considered monophyletic, includes the sharks, rays, and skates (**FIG. 32-11**). Most species are ocean dwellers, but a few have invaded fresh water. With the exception of whales, the sharks are the largest living vertebrates. Some whale sharks (*Rhincodon*) exceed 15 m (49 ft) in length.

Most rays and skates are flattened creatures that live partly buried in the sand. Their enormous pectoral fins propel them along the bottom, where they feed on mussels and clams. The stingray has a whiplike tail with a barbed spine at its base that can inflict a painful wound. The electric ray has electric organs on either side of the head. These modified muscles can discharge enough electric current (up to 200 volts) to stun fairly large fishes as well as human swimmers.

The chondrichthyes retain their cartilaginous embryonic skeleton. Although this skeleton is not replaced by bone, a deposit of calcium salts may strengthen it. All chondrichthyes have paired jaws and two pairs of fins. The skin contains **placoid scales,** which are toothlike structures (**FIG. 32-12**). The lining of the mouth contains larger, but essentially similar, scales that serve as teeth. The teeth of other vertebrates are homologous with these scales. Shark teeth are embedded in the flesh and not attached to the jawbones; new teeth develop continuously in rows behind the functional teeth and migrate forward to replace any that are lost.

(a) Blue-spotted stingray (*Taeniura lymma*). Stingrays typically feed on shellfish and bottom-dwelling fishes.

(b) The great white shark (*Carcharodon carcharias*). Photographed in Australia, this shark is considered the most dangerous shark to humans. It is actually white only on its ventral aspect; the rest of the body is brownish gray or bluish gray.

FIGURE 32-11 *Animated* Cartilaginous fishes

The streamlined shark body is adapted for rapid swimming. Lift is provided by body shape and fins and by the action of swimming swiftly. The shark stores a great deal of oil in its large liver (which may account for up to 30% of the body weight). Fats and oils decrease the overall density of fishes and contribute to buoyancy. Even so, the shark body is denser than water, so sharks tend to sink unless they are actively swimming.

Most sharks are predators that swim actively and catch and eat other fishes as well as crustaceans and mollusks. The largest sharks and rays, like the largest whales, are filter feeders that strain plankton from the water. They gulp water through the mouth. As the water passes through the pharynx and out the gill slits, food particles are trapped in a sievelike structure.

Predatory sharks are attracted to blood, so a wounded swimmer or a skin diver towing speared fish is a target. However, despite the common portrayal of sharks in books and films as monstrous enemies, most do not go out of their way to attack humans. In fact, of the approximately 350 known shark species, fewer than 30 are known to attack humans.

The shark has a complex brain and a spinal cord that is protected by vertebrae. The well-developed sense organs effectively locate prey in the water. Sharks may detect other animals electrically before sensing them by sight or smell. **Electroreceptors** on the shark's head sense weak electric currents generated by the muscular activity of animals. The **lateral line organ,** found in all fishes, is a groove along each side of the body with many tiny openings to the outside. Sensory cells in the lateral line organ detect vibrations caused by waves and other movement in the water, including movements by predators or prey (see Fig. 43-7).

Cartilaginous fishes have no lungs. Gas exchange takes place through their five to seven pairs of gills. A current of water enters the mouth and passes over the gills and out the gill slits, constantly providing the fish with a fresh supply of dissolved oxygen. Sharks that actively swim depend on their motion to enhance gas exchange. Rays, skates, and sharks that spend time on the ocean floor use muscles of the jaw and pharynx to pump water over their gills.

The digestive tract of sharks consists of the mouth cavity; a long pharynx leading to the stomach; a short, straight intestine; and a **cloaca,** which opens on the underside of the body and is characteristic of many vertebrates (see Fig. 32-12). The liver and pancreas discharge digestive juices into the intestine. The cloaca receives digestive wastes as well as metabolic wastes from the urinary system. In females, the cloaca also serves as a reproductive organ.

The sexes are separate, and fertilization is internal. In the mature male, each pelvic fin has a slender, grooved section, known as a **clasper,** used to transfer sperm into the female's cloaca. The eggs are fertilized in the upper part of the female's oviducts. Part of the oviduct is modified as a shell gland, which secretes a protective coat around the egg.

Skates and some species of sharks are **oviparous;** that is, they lay eggs. Many species of sharks, however, are **ovoviviparous,** meaning their young are enclosed in eggs and incubated within the mother's body. During development, the young depend on stored yolk for their nourishment rather than on transfer of materials from the mother. The young are born after hatching from the eggs.

A few species of sharks are **viviparous.** Not only do the embryos develop within the uterus, but much of their nourishment is

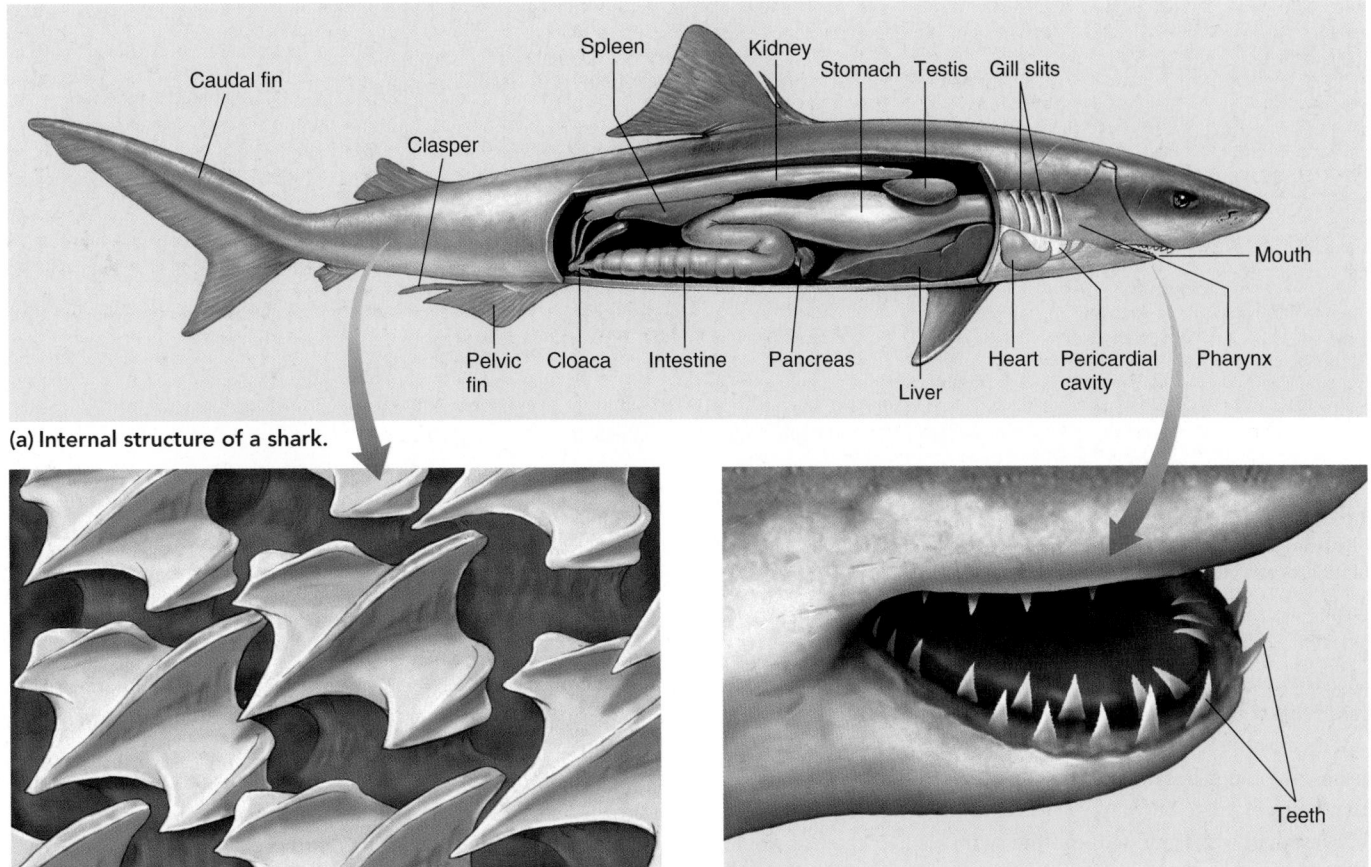

(a) Internal structure of a shark.

(b) Placoid scales. These tough scales protect the shark against predators. The base of each placoid scale is embedded in the skin. Placoid scales are modified teeth. They are covered with hard enamel.

(c) Teeth. Placoid scales are embedded in the flesh along the inner surface of the jaw cartilage where they function as teeth. Sharks have several rows of teeth. Old teeth are shed and quickly replaced.

FIGURE 32-12 Anatomy of a shark

delivered to them by the mother's blood. Nutrients are transferred between the blood vessels in the lining of the uterus and the yolk sac surrounding each embryo.

The ray-finned fishes gave rise to modern bony fishes

Although bony fishes appear earlier in the fossil record than cartilaginous fishes, both groups may have evolved about the same time, during the Devonian period. The two groups share many characteristics (such as continuous tooth replacement), but they also differ in important ways.

Most bony fishes are characterized by a bony skeleton with many vertebrae. Bone has advantages over cartilage because it provides excellent support and effectively stores calcium. Most species have flexible median and paired fins, supported by long rays made of cartilage or bone. Overlapping, bony dermal scales cover the body. A lateral bony flap, the **operculum,** extends posteriorly from the head and protects the gills.

Unlike most sharks, bony fishes are oviparous. They lay an impressive number of eggs and fertilize them externally. The ocean sunfish, for example, lays more than 300 million eggs! Of course, most of the eggs and young become food for other animals. The probability of survival is increased by certain behavioral adaptations. For example, many species of fishes build nests for their eggs and protect them.

During the Devonian period, the bony fishes diverged into two major groups: the **Sarcopterygii** and the **ray-finned fishes,** class **Actinopterygii.** Fossils of the earliest sarcopterygians date back to the Devonian period, about 400 mya. Lungs and fleshy, **lobed fins** characterized these fishes. The flexible fins were not supported by rays of bone except at their tips. Instead, the fins were supported by a group of bones with joints between them. These fins had muscles that could move them. Lobed fins may have evolved as an adaptation to life on the bottom of the sea. Fish could use the fins to push against the bottom.

Early sarcopterygians evolved along two separate lines: the **lungfishes** (class **Dipnoi**) and **lobe-finned fishes** (class **Actinistia**). Both lineages have lobed fins. Three genera of lungfishes survive today in the rivers of tropical Africa, Australia, and South America.

The ray-finned fishes underwent two important adaptive radiations. The first gave rise during the Late Paleozoic era to a group of fishes that are now mostly extinct. The second radiation began during the Early Mesozoic era and gave rise to the modern bony fishes.

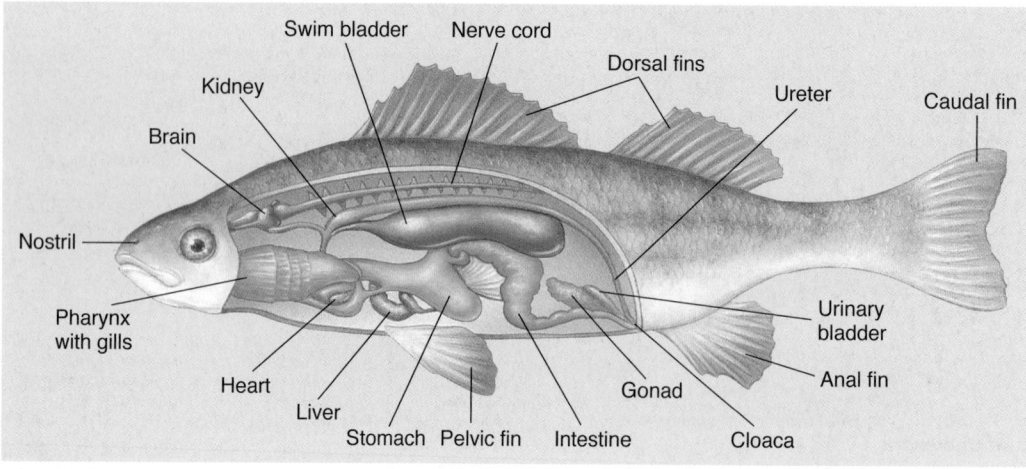

FIGURE 32-13 *Animated* Perch, a representative bony fish

The swim bladder is a hydrostatic organ that enables the fish to change the density of its body and remain stationary at a given depth. Pectoral fins (*not shown*) and pelvic fins are paired.

The common ancestor of the modern bony fishes had primitive lungs that could exchange gases in air. Lungs for gas exchange were retained by the lobe-finned fishes and lungfishes. In the ray-finned fishes, the lungs became modified as a **swim bladder,** an air sac that helps regulate buoyancy (**FIG. 32-13**). Bones and muscles are heavier than water, and without the swim bladder the fish would sink. By regulating gas exchange between its blood and swim bladder, a fish can control the amount of gas in the swim bladder and thus change the overall density of its body. This ability allows a bony fish, in contrast to a shark, to hover at a given depth of water without much muscular effort.

There are more species of bony fishes than of any other vertebrate group. Biologists have identified about 49,000 living species of freshwater and saltwater bony fishes, of many shapes and colors (**FIG. 32-14**). Bony fishes range in size from that of *Paedocypris progenetica,* which has been measured at less than 8 mm (about 0.3 in) long, to that of the ocean sunfish (or *Mola;* see Fig. 20-16c), which may reach 4 m (13 ft) and weigh about 1500 kg (about 3300 lb). *Paedocypris progenetica,* native to Indonesia, is the smallest known vertebrate.

The diversity of bony fishes may have resulted from the action of *Hox* genes. During the radiation of ray-finned fishes, entire chromosomes duplicated, resulting in one or more additional clusters of *Hox* genes. The zebrafish (see Fig.17-6d) has seven *Hox* clusters. These additional genes could have provided the genetic material for the evolution of the diverse species of ray-finned fishes.

Descendants of the lungfishes moved onto the land

Biologists thought the lobe-finned fishes were extinct by the end of the Paleozoic era, so in 1938 the scientific community was very excited when a commercial fisherman caught one off the coast of South Africa. Since that time more than 200 specimens of these giant "living fossils" have been found in the deep waters off the southeastern coast of Africa, the Comores Islands, Madagascar,

and Indonesia (**FIG. 32-15**). These fishes, known as **coelacanths,** measure nearly 2 m (about 6 ft) in length. They are nocturnal predators on other fishes.

Until the 1980s, the prevailing hypothesis was that coelacanths were the living fossil representatives of the group that gave rise to the land vertebrates. Then, a few investigators challenged this hypothesis with morphological data. The external nasal openings of fossil and living lungfishes suggested that they, rather than the coelacanths, are the ancestors of the land vertebrates. Other similarities between lungfishes and land vertebrates are tooth enamel and four limbs that have the same structure and position (**FIG. 32-16**). (Recall that the fins of lungfishes are also lobed.)

During the 1990s, the lungfish hypothesis gained support from comparisons of mitochondrial DNA. More recently, underwater studies of coelacanths have shown that these fish use their muscular fins to slowly swim rather than to "walk" on the ocean bottom. In contrast, living lungfishes do use their fins to "walk" on the river bottom. Biologists now generally agree that ancestors of lungfishes, rather than coelacanths, gave rise to the **tetrapods.**

Molecular data support the structural evidence that the limbs of tetrapods evolved from the lobed fins of fishes. Proteins encoded by certain regulatory genes, including *Hox* genes, have been found at the same developmental times and in the same locations in both limbs and fins. These findings indicate that limb and fin development are governed by the same genes.

What drove the evolution of tetrapod limbs? One hypothesis suggests that during the frequent seasonal droughts of the Devonian period, swamps became stagnant or dried up completely. Fishes with lobed fins had a tremendous advantage for survival under those conditions. They were strikingly pre-adapted for moving onto the land. They had lungs for breathing air, and their sturdy, fleshy fins allowed them to "walk" along in shallow water. These fins could support the fish's weight, so it could emerge onto dry land and make its way to another pond or stream.

A more recent hypothesis holds that limbs evolved in a fully aquatic environment. Animals with more developed limbs could

(a) The porcupinefish (*Diodon hystrix*). This fish swallows air or water to inflate its body, a strategy that discourages potential predators. Photographed in the Virgin Islands.

(b) The parrotfish (*Scarus gibbus*). The parrotfish feeds on coral, grinds it in its digestive tract, and extracts the coralline algae. The fish eliminates a fine white sand. These fishes contribute to white sand beaches in many parts of the world. Parrotfish begin life as females and later become males.

(c) Anglerfishes. In some clades of anglerfishes, the much smaller male attaches himself to a female with his sharp teeth and becomes a lifelong parasitic mate. Most species have at least one long spine projecting from the middle of the head. This "lure" is used as bait to attract prey. The more than 200 species of anglerfish are assigned to order Lophiliformes.

FIGURE 32-14 Modern bony fishes

move along in shallow water or creep through dense aquatic vegetation more efficiently than their lobe-finned ancestors. *Tiktaalik* was a transitional form between fishes and tetrapods (**FIG. 32-17**). Biologists consider *Tiktaalik,* which lived about 375 mya (during the Devonian period), a fish because it had scales and fins. However, *Tiktaalik* also had tetrapod features such as a movable neck and ribs that supported lungs.

Acanthostega was one of the earliest known tetrapods. Fossils from the Devonian period show that this animal had four legs with well-formed digits. However, its limbs were not sufficiently strong for walking effectively on land. *Acanthostega* was an aquatic animal, not an amphibian. *Ichthyostega* is the earliest amphibian fossil found to date. This animal had strong legs supported by well-developed shoulder and hip bones and muscles.

Natural selection favored animals such as *Ichthyostega* that could explore shallow wetlands and make their way onto dry land. The ability to move about on land, however awkwardly, provided

FIGURE 32-15 Diver swimming with coelacanth
For many years, biologists thought that ancestors of this lobe-finned fish (*Latimeria chalumnae*) gave rise to the amphibians.

FIGURE 32-16 South American lungfish (*Lepidosiren paradoxus*)
Lungfishes were common in Devonian and Carboniferous times (400 mya to 300 mya). South American lungfish have paired lungs on either side of the throat and can survive for long periods if the river they inhabit dries up.

FIGURE 32-17 *Animated* Tiktaalik
This extinct fish, which grew to 2.75 m (9 ft), had limblike fins and other tetrapod features.

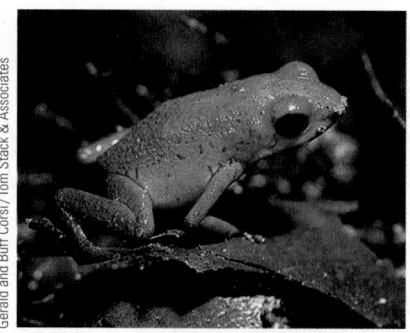

(a) Red dart frog (*Dendrobates histrionicus*). Poison dart frogs, native to Central and South America, are active during the day. Most are brightly colored. Many secrete toxins through their skin as a chemical defense against predators.

(b) Spotted salamander (*Ambystoma maculatum*). This salamander spends most of its time underground. In early spring spotted salamanders gather in woodland ponds to reproduce.

FIGURE 32-18 Modern amphibians

access to new food sources. Terrestrial plants were already established, and terrestrial insects and arachnids were rapidly evolving. A vertebrate that could survive on land had less competition for food. However, success on land required the evolution of several major adaptations in addition to legs.

As already discussed, the lungfishes had lungs for gas exchange. This was important because gills cannot function in air. Life on land also required the evolution of vertebrae and muscles strong enough to support the weight of the body in air. Body coverings and other mechanisms were needed to protect animals against the drying effect of air.

Evolution of ears that could hear sound transmitted through air and olfactory mechanisms for detecting airborne odors contributed to the ability to find food and mates, and to avoid predators. At first, animals returned to the water to reproduce, but eventually adaptations evolved that allowed animals to reproduce in terrestrial environments. The early vertebrate experience on land was so successful that this lineage gave rise to the amphibians and, later, the reptiles, including birds, and the mammals.

Amphibians were the first successful land vertebrates

Biologists classify modern amphibians (class **Amphibia**) in three orders. Order **Urodela** ("visible tail") includes salamanders, mud puppies, and newts, all animals with long tails; order **Anura** ("no tail") is made up of frogs and toads, with legs adapted for hopping; and order **Apoda** ("no feet") contains the wormlike caecilians (**FIG. 32-18**). Although some adult amphibians are quite successful as land animals and live in dry environments, most return to the water to reproduce. Eggs and sperm are typically released in the water.

Amphibians undergo **metamorphosis,** a transition from larva to adult. The embryos of most frogs and toads develop into larvae called **tadpoles.** These larvae have tails and gills, and most feed on aquatic plants. After a time, the tadpole undergoes metamorphosis, which is regulated by hormones secreted by the *thyroid gland.* During metamorphosis, gills and gill slits disappear, the tail

is resorbed, and limbs emerge. The digestive tract shortens, and food preference shifts from plant material to a carnivorous diet; the mouth widens; a tongue develops; the tympanic membrane (eardrum) and eyelids appear; and the eye lens changes shape. Many biochemical changes accompany the transformation from a completely aquatic life to an amphibious one.

Several salamanders, such as the mud puppy *Necturus,* do not undergo complete metamorphosis; they retain many larval characteristics even when sexually mature adults. Recall from Chapter 20 that this is an example of **paedomorphosis** (see Fig. 20-17). This type of development permits these salamanders to remain aquatic rather than having to compete on land.

The coloration of amphibians may conceal them in their habitat or may be very bright and striking. Many of the brightly colored species are poisonous (see Fig. 32-18a). Their distinctive colors warn predators that they are not encountering an ordinary amphibian. Some frogs camouflage themselves by changing color.

Adult amphibians do not depend solely on their primitive lungs for the exchange of respiratory gases. Their moist, glandular skin, which lacks scales and is plentifully supplied with blood vessels, also serves as a respiratory surface. The numerous mucous glands within the skin help keep the body surface moist, which is important in gas exchange. The mucus also makes the animal slippery, facilitating its escape from predators. Some amphibians have glands in their skin that secrete poisonous substances harmful to predators.

The amphibian heart is divided into three chambers: two **atria** receive blood, and a single **ventricle** pumps it into the arteries. A double circuit of blood vessels keeps oxygen-rich and oxygen-poor blood partially separate. Blood passes through the **systemic circulation** to the various tissues and organs of the body. Then, after returning to the heart, it is directed through the **pulmonary circulation** to the lungs and skin, where it is recharged with oxygen. The oxygen-rich blood returns to the heart to be pumped out into the systemic circulation again. We discuss the comparative anatomy of the heart and circulation of various vertebrate classes in Chapter 44.

Review

- From an evolutionary perspective, what is the significance of each of the following: (1) placoderms, (2) lungfishes, (3) ray-finned fishes, (4) *Ichthyostega*, and (5) *Tiktaalik*?
- What changes allow amphibians to move from aquatic life as a tadpole to terrestrial life as an adult?

32.8 AMNIOTES

■ LEARNING OBJECTIVES

9 Describe three vertebrate adaptations to terrestrial life.

10 Describe the reptiles (including the birds) and give an argument for including the birds in the reptile clade.

11 Describe five key characters of mammals; contrast protherian (monotremes), metatherian (marsupials), and eutherian mammals, giving examples of animals that belong to each group.

The evolution of reptiles from ancestral amphibians required many adaptations that allowed them to become completely terrestrial. Evolution of the **amniotic egg** was an extremely important event because it allowed terrestrial vertebrates to complete their life cycles on land. The amniotic egg contains an **amnion,** a membrane that forms a fluid-filled sac around the embryo. The amnion provides the embryo with its own private "pond," permitting independence from a watery external environment. In addition to keeping the embryo moist, the amniotic fluid serves as a shock absorber that cushions the developing embryo.

The evolution of the amniotic egg is so important to the success of terrestrial vertebrates—reptiles (including birds) and mammals—that biologists refer to these animals as **amniotes.** Amniotes are a monophyletic group because they have a recent common ancestor that was itself an amniote.

In addition to the amnion, the amniotic egg has three other extraembryonic (not part of the developing body itself) membranes: yolk sac, chorion, and allantois (**FIG. 32-19**). These membranes protect the developing embryo, store nutrients (*yolk sac*), carry on gas exchange (*chorion* and *allantois*), and store wastes (*allantois*). We discuss development of the extraembryonic membranes in Chapter 51. Although most extant mammals do not lay

FIGURE 32-19 *Animated* An amniotic egg

The amnion is a protective membrane surrounding the embryo. Other extraembryonic membranes are the yolk sac, allantois, and chorion.

eggs, their embryos have an amnion and other extraembryonic membranes.

Another important adaptation to terrestrial life is a body covering that minimizes water loss. Such a covering presents another challenge because it severely decreases gas exchange across the body surface. This challenge has been met by the evolution of efficient lungs and circulatory systems for exchange of oxygen and carbon dioxide. Amniotes also have physiological mechanisms for conserving water. For example, much of the water filtered from the blood by the kidneys is reabsorbed in the kidney tubules to decrease fluid loss during excretion of metabolic wastes.

Our understanding of amniote phylogeny is changing

Biology instructors once taught that the three classes of amniotes were Reptilia, Aves (birds), and Mammalia. However, cladistic analysis determined that class Reptilia was not a monophyletic group without the birds. Because it included some, but not all, of its descendants, it was paraphyletic (see Fig. 23-7). For this reason, most biologists now classify the birds as a group of reptiles.

Biologists hypothesize that the earliest amniotes resembled lizards. By the Late Carboniferous period, about 290 mya, amniotes had undergone an impressive adaptive radiation and diverged into two main branches: **diapsids** and **synapsids** (**FIG. 32-20** and **TABLE 32-3**). The term *diapsid* refers to the two pairs of openings in the temporal bones that characterize the skulls of these animals. Synapsid skulls have one pair of temporal openings. The diapsids comprise all extant reptilian groups, including the birds and most extinct reptiles. The synapsids include the extinct **therapsid** reptiles and the mammals.

A second great adaptive radiation of amniotes occurred during the Mesozoic era, which ended about 66 mya. During that time reptiles were the dominant terrestrial animals (see Chapter 21). In fact, the Mesozoic era is known as the "Age of Reptiles." These animals had radiated into an impressive variety of ecological lifestyles (see Figs. 21-13, 21-14, and 21-15). Some could fly, others became marine, and many filled terrestrial habitats. Among the

The diapsid reptiles gave rise to the birds, and the synapsids gave rise to the mammals. Note the five (including the birds) main branches of extant diapsids.

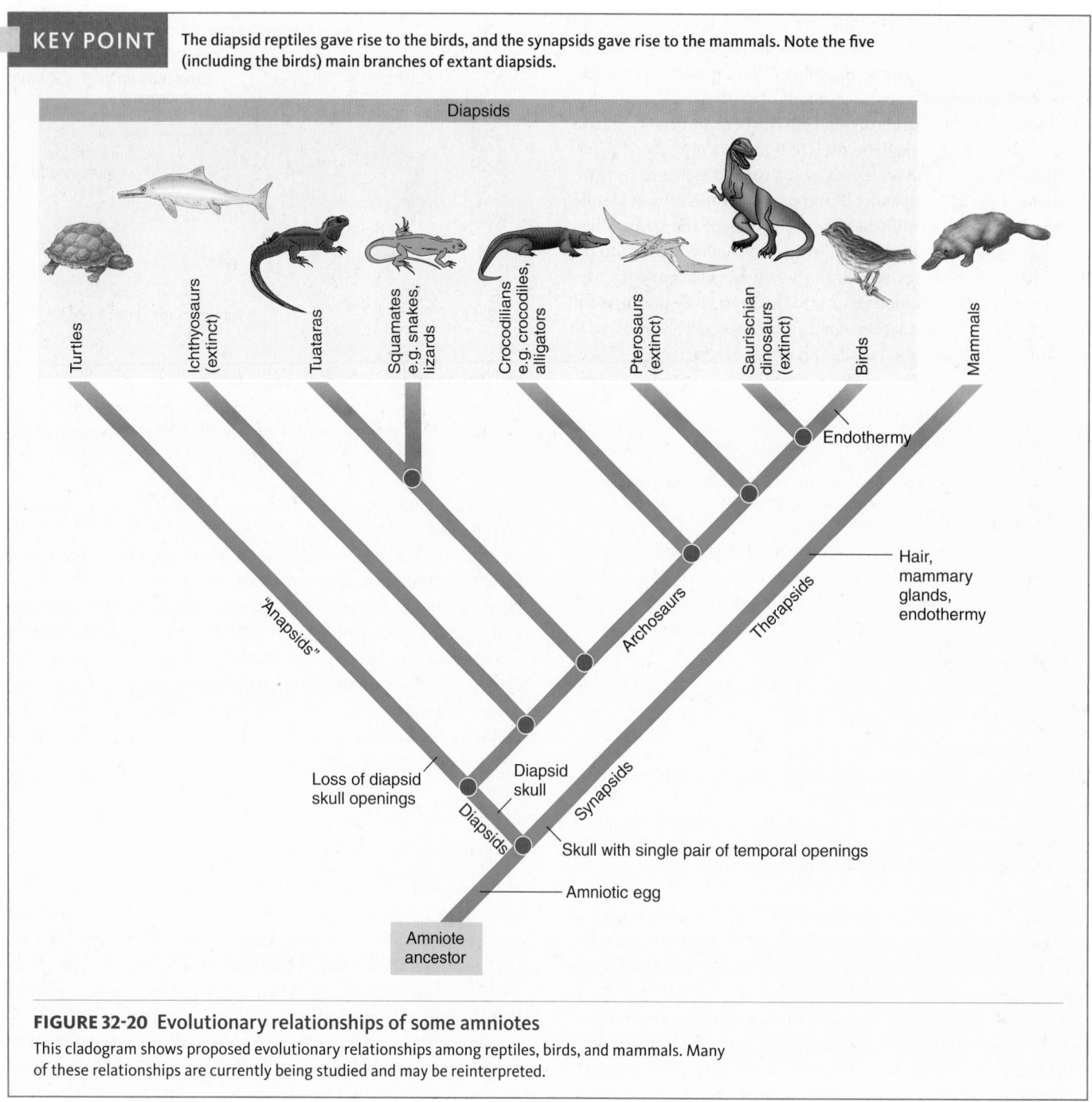

FIGURE 32-20 Evolutionary relationships of some amniotes
This cladogram shows proposed evolutionary relationships among reptiles, birds, and mammals. Many of these relationships are currently being studied and may be reinterpreted.

major groups were the **pterosaurs** (ter′-uh-sawr), the flying reptiles; the **saurischian** (saw-ris′-kee-un) **dinosaurs,** a group that included *Tyrannosaurus* and *Diplodocus*; and the **ornithischian** (awr-nuh-this′-kee-un) **dinosaurs,** including *Triceratops*.

Some of the dinosaurs were among the largest land animals to ever walk on Earth. Some dinosaurs apparently traveled in social groups and took care of their young. Fossil evidence supports the hypothesis that at least some dinosaurs were **endotherms,** meaning they used metabolic energy to maintain a constant body temperature despite changes in the temperature of the environment. An advantage of endothermy is that it allows animals to be more active. The natural history and evolution of dinosaurs and other early reptiles are discussed in more detail in Chapter 21.

The reptiles were the dominant land animals for almost 200 million years. Then, toward the end of the Mesozoic era, many, including all the dinosaurs and pterosaurs, disappeared from the fossil record. In fact, more than half of all animal species became extinct at that time (see Chapter 21). As a result of this mass extinction, there are many more extinct reptiles than living species.

Reptiles have many terrestrial adaptations

Many reptilian characters are adaptations to terrestrial life. The female reptile secretes a protective leathery shell around the egg, which helps prevent the developing embryo from drying out. The shell presents a challenge for reproduction because sperm can-

TABLE 32-3   Some Major Groups of Nonavian Reptiles

Subclass (Superorder/Order)		Important Characters
Subclass Diapsida		Skull with two pairs of temporal openings
Order Testudines (Chelonia) Turtles, terrapins, tortoises		Enclosed in bony shell; beak of keratin instead of teeth; some can withdraw head and legs into shell; temporal openings lost ("anapsids")
Superorder Lepidosauria		Overlapping scales; most successful of modern reptiles

Order Squamata
   Snakes, lizards, iguanas,
   amphisbaenians (worm lizards)
		Flexible armor of overlapping, horny scales, which are shed
		
		Lizards: Slender body, typically with four limbs; movable eyelids
		
		Snakes: Elongated body with no limbs; flexible, loosely jointed jaw; forked tongue protrusible

Order Sphenodonta Tuataras		Third eye under skin of forehead; only two extant species
Superorder Ichthyosauria (Extinct) Marine reptiles of Mesozoic		Body shaped like that of modern dolphins; large eyes; vertical tails
Superorder Archosauria		Mainly terrestrial; some specialized for flight; ventricle completely divided
Order Crocodilia Crocodiles, alligators, caimans, gavials		Four-chambered heart; closest extant relative to birds
Pterosauria (Extinct) Flying reptiles of Mesozoic		Membranous wings

Saurischia (Extinct)
   Mesozoic dinosaurs
   (*Tyrannosaurus, Diplodocus*)
   Birds descended from this lineage
		Some were two-legged carnivores; others were four-legged herbivores

Ornithischia (Extinct) Mesozoic dinosaurs (*Triceratops*)		Bipedal and quadrupedal herbivores
Subclass Synapsida		Skull with one pair of temporal openings
Therapsida (Extinct) **Mammals descended from this lineage**		Many mammal-like characters; became dominant land animals during Middle Permian

not penetrate it. Fertilization must take place within the body of the female before the shell is added. In this process, the male uses a copulatory organ (penis) to transfer sperm into the female reproductive tract. An amnion surrounds the embryo as it develops within the protective shell.

The hard, dry, horny scales that are part of the reptile's skin retard drying—another adaptation to life on land. This scaly protective armor, which also protects the reptile from predators, is shed periodically. The dry reptilian skin does not allow effective gas exchange. Reptilian lungs are better developed than the saclike lungs of amphibians. Divided into many chambers, the reptilian lung provides an increased surface area for gas exchange.

Most reptiles have a three-chambered heart that is more efficient than the amphibian heart. The single ventricle has a partition, though incomplete, that separates oxygen-rich and oxygen-poor blood, facilitating oxygenation of body tissues. In crocodiles the partition is complete, and the heart has four chambers.

Like fishes and amphibians, extant reptiles generally lack metabolic mechanisms for regulating body temperature. They are

ectothermic, meaning that their body temperature fluctuates with the temperature of the surrounding environment. Some reptiles have behavioral adaptations that help them maintain a body temperature higher than that of their environment. For example, you may have observed a lizard basking in the sun, which raises its body temperature and so increases its metabolic rate. This permits the lizard to hunt actively for food. When the body of a reptile is cold, its metabolic rate is low and the animal tends to be sluggish. Ectothermy helps explain why reptiles are more successful in warm than in cold climates.

Many reptiles are carnivorous (meat-eating). Their paired limbs, usually with five toes, are well adapted for running and climbing in search of prey. In addition, their well-developed sense organs enable them to locate prey.

We can assign extant reptiles to five groups

Biologists assign the extant reptiles to five orders, or clades. Order Testudines includes the turtles, terrapins, and tortoises. Order

Squamata includes lizards, snakes, and amphisbaenians (worm lizards). Order Sphenodonta includes the **tuataras,** lizardlike animals that live in burrows. The Archosaurs are a clade (sometimes designated a superorder) that includes the extinct flying reptiles and dinosaurs, as well as the extant order Crocodilia, and the birds. Order Crocodilia includes crocodiles, alligators, caimans, and gavials (**FIG. 32-21**).

Turtles have protective shells

Members of order **Testudines** (te-stood′-n-eez) are enclosed in a protective shell made of bony plates overlaid by horny scales. Some terrestrial species can withdraw their heads and legs completely into their shells. Their horny beak covers the jaws. Turtles do not have teeth.

(a) **Green turtle (*Chelonia mydas*).** The paddlelike appendages of this turtle are adapted for swimming.

(b) **The emerald tree boa (*Corallus canina*).** The boa inhabits tropical South American forests. It rarely leaves the trees it inhabits to go to the ground. Emerald boas use their heat-sensitive pit organs to locate prey.

(c) **Tuatara (*Sphenodon punctatus*).** These nocturnal predators reach a length of 60 cm (more than 2 ft) or longer. There are two species of tuataras. Both are classified as endangered.

(d) **Nile crocodile (*Crocodilus niloticus*).** Both parents guard the leathery eggs. When the hatchlings emerge, the mother leads them to the water. She may carry them in her mouth.

(e) **Two fledgling wood storks (*Mycteria americana*).** About 8 to 9 weeks old, these storks preen their feathers atop their nest in South Carolina's White Hall rookery.

FIGURE 32-21 *Animated* Representative extant reptiles

The size of adult turtles ranges in length from about 8 cm (3 in) to more than 2 m (6.5 ft) in leatherback turtles, which are the largest marine species. The weight of a leatherback turtle can exceed 500 kg (more than 1000 lb). The forelimbs of marine turtles are modified into flippers. Sea turtles migrate hundreds of miles from the beaches where they hatch to feeding grounds. Females return to the same beaches where they hatched to mate and nest. Most species of sea turtles are endangered as a result of human activities. Biologists sometimes refer to the aquatic forms as *turtles* and to the land species as *tortoises*. Freshwater types are sometimes called *terrapins*.

Lizards and snakes are the most common modern reptiles

Lizards and snakes are assigned to order **Squamata** (squa-ma´-tah). These animals have rows of scales that overlap like shingles on a roof, forming a continuous, flexible armor that is shed periodically. Lizards range in size from certain geckos, which weigh as little as 1 g (less than 0.1 oz), to the Komodo dragon of Indonesia, which may weigh 100 kg (220 lb). Their body sizes and shapes vary greatly. Some lizards are legless, for example, the "worm lizards" and the glass snake (which is really a lizard).

Snakes are characterized by a flexible, loosely jointed jaw structure that lets them swallow animals larger than the diameter of their own jaws. These reptiles have elongated bodies with no legs, although pythons have vestigial hind-limb bones (see Fig. 18-17). Remember that although not all the tetrapods have four limbs, all evolved from four-limbed ancestors. Snake eyes are covered by a transparent scale. They do not have movable eyelids. Also absent are an external ear opening, a tympanic membrane (eardrum), and a middle-ear cavity.

The snake uses its forked tongue as an accessory sensory organ for touch and smell. Chemicals from the ground or air adhere to the tongue. The snake rubs the tip of its tongue across the opening of a sense organ in the roof of the mouth that detects odors. Pit vipers and some boas also have a prominent **pit organ** on each side of the head that detects heat from endothermic prey (see Fig. 43-3). These snakes use their pit organs to locate and capture birds and small nocturnal mammals.

Some snakes, such as king snakes, pythons, and boa constrictors, kill their prey by rapidly wrapping themselves around the animal and squeezing so it cannot breathe. Others have fangs, which are hollow teeth connected to venom glands. When the snake bites, it pumps venom through the fangs into the prey. Some snake venoms cause the breakdown of red blood cells; others, such as that of the coral snake, are neurotoxins, which interfere with nerve function. Venomous snakes of the United States include rattlesnakes, copperheads, cottonmouths, and coral snakes. All of these except the coral snakes are pit vipers.

Amphisbaenians (am-fus-bee´-nee-uns), or worm lizards, are now considered modified lizards. They are well adapted for their burrowing lifestyle. They have elongated, legless bodies, and their eyes are hidden under their skin. Most are less than 15 cm (6 in) long. Most species inhabit South America and southern Africa. Only one species (known as the "graveyard snake") is known in the United States; it is found in Florida.

Tuataras superficially resemble lizards

Tuataras look somewhat like iguanas but have certain distinct characters. For example, they are the only amniotes with vertebrae that are concave at both ends; such vertebrae are characteristic of fish and some amphibians. The two extant species of tuataras inhabit New Zealand and several small islands off the coast of New Zealand. Tuataras have long been considered endangered species. When humans brought rats, cats, and dogs to New Zealand, these non-native animals decimated the population of tuataras by eating their eggs. Tuataras became extinct on the New Zealand mainland. In 2005, these animals were reintroduced into a sanctuary in New Zealand and are now protected.

Crocodilians have an elongated skull

The extant members of order **Crocodilia** (crok-uh-dil´-ee-uh) along with the birds, are the surviving reptiles of the archosaur lineage. This is the lineage that gave rise to the pterosaurs (flying reptiles) and most of the dinosaurs that dominated the Mesozoic era. Modern crocodilians include three groups: (1) the crocodiles of Africa, Asia, and America; (2) the alligators of the southern United States and China, plus the caimans of Central America; and (3) the gavials of South Asia. Most species live in swamps, in rivers, or along seacoasts, feeding on various kinds of animals.

Crocodiles are the largest living reptiles; some exceed 7 m (23 ft) in length. The cranial skeleton is adapted for aquatic life. The crocodile can be distinguished from the alligator or caiman by its long, slender snout and by the large fourth tooth on the bottom jaw that is visible when the mouth is closed.

How do we know that birds are really dinosaurs?

Cladistic analyses indicate that birds evolved from the lineage of saurischian dinosaurs, specifically from the **theropods** (theer´-uh-pods), a group of bipedal, saurischian dinosaurs that included *Tyrannosaurus* and *Deinonychus* (see Fig. 21-15). This view is supported by the remarkable array of fossils discovered in the Yixian Formation in China. These fossils date back to the Early Cretaceous period (128 mya to 124 mya).

Some dinosaurs had feathers

Paleontologists have identified many theropod dinosaur fossils that demonstrate the evolution of feathers from very simple, tubular structures to complex modern forms. *Caudipteryx*, one feathered dinosaur discovered in the Yixian Formation, was about the size of a turkey. It had only a few teeth in the front of its upper jaw, and its bones show many birdlike characteristics (**FIG. 32-22a**). *Caudipteryx* has well-preserved imprints of complex feathers on its tail and forelimbs. Analyzing fossil evidence and molecular data, some investigators have hypothesized that feather evolution took place in terrestrial, bipedal dinosaurs *before* the evolution of birds or flight.

Modern birds use asymmetrical feathers for flight. In 2003, paleontologists reported finding a new species of feathered dinosaur, *Microraptor gui. Microraptor* had asymmetrical feathers on both its forelimbs and hind limbs, and also on its tail (See figure in *Inquiring About: The Origin of Flight in Birds,* in Chapter 21.) However, their small size and body structure support the hypothesis that flying evolved from gliding; that is, *Microraptor* climbed trees and used the feathered limbs for gliding. These small dinosaurs, which lived about 126 mya, coexisted with early birds.

Biologists have debated why feathers may have evolved in dinosaurs. Were feathers important in courtship rituals? in camouflage? Were feathers an adaptation that conserved body heat? Insulating feathers could have contributed to the evolution of endothermy (the ability to maintain a constant body temperature), permitting animals to be more active.

In 2010, paleontologists at George Washington University and their colleagues described a nearly complete skeleton of a basal theropod discovered in northwestern China's Junggar Basin. This new fossil, named *Haplocheirus sollers,* was a feathered dinosaur that preceded the earliest known bird (*Archaeopteryx*) by about 15 million years. This finding supports the hypothesis that feather evolution took place in terrestrial, bipedal dinosaurs *before* the evolution of birds. *Haplocheirus* had organelles containing pigment that colored its feathers, suggesting that feathers first evolved for color displays in courtship rituals. The presence of feathers and the bone structure of *Haplocheirus* indicate that striking evolutionary convergence occurred between feathered dinosaurs and birds.

Early birds were transitional forms

Many extinct theropods were long-tailed animals that moved about on two feet and had forelimbs with three clawed fingers. Although the bones of birds are fragile and disintegrate quickly, paleobiologists have found a few fossils of early birds. The first birds looked very much like dinosaurs. They had teeth (which modern birds lack), a long tail, and bones with thick walls. Certain extinct theropods and modern birds have feet with three digits and thin-walled, hollow bones. Both have a **furcula,** or wishbone, which is formed by the two clavicles (collarbones) fusing in the midline. Some biologists classify modern birds as theropods.

The earliest known bird, *Archaeopteryx* (meaning "ancient wing"), was about the size of a pigeon. Ten specimens of this genus have been found in Bavaria in Jurassic limestone, which was laid down about 150 mya. Unlike those of extant birds, the jawbones of *Archaeopteryx* were armed with teeth, and its long reptilian tail was covered with feathers (**FIG. 32-22b**). Each of its short, broad wings had three claw-bearing, functional digits. Like modern birds, *Archaeopteryx* had wings, feathers, and a furcula. Its feathers were very similar to those of modern birds. Biologists do not know whether *Archaeopteryx* shared a common ancestor with other birds or whether *Archaeopteryx* itself gave rise to modern birds.

Using computer tomography and computerized three-dimensional reconstruction, researchers examined the inside of the *Archaeopteryx* skull. They found that *Archaeopteryx* had a birdlike brain with comparatively larger cerebral lobes than those of other reptiles. It had enlarged visual centers and highly developed inner ear canals similar to those of modern birds. These structures would support the coordination and agility needed for flight.

Chinese Academy of Geological Sciences

Pelvis

Leg

Feathers

(a) *Caudipteryx* exhibits both dinosaur and bird characteristics. This fossil lacks a head, but the rest of its skeleton is well preserved. The bones in the foot and the shape and orientation of the pelvis are similar to those of dinosaurs, but the fossil also has birdlike characters, including impressions of feathers.

From a painting by Rudolph Freund, courtesy of Carnegie Museum of Natural History

(b) This reconstruction represents the view that *Archaeopteryx* was a climbing animal that had at least some ability to use its wings and feathers for gliding.

FIGURE 32-22 Fossil of *Caudipteryx,* a feathered dinosaur, and reconstruction of *Archaeopteryx,* the earliest known bird

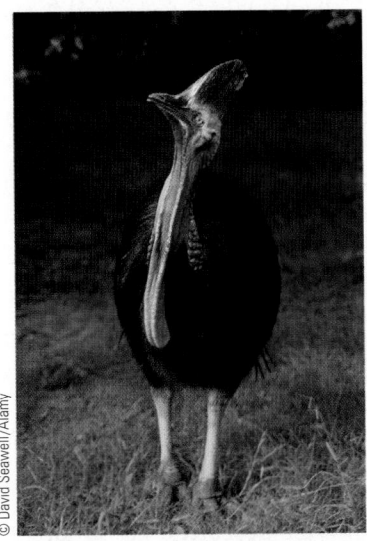

(a) **Southern cassowary (*Casuarius casuarius*), a ratite.** The flightless southern cassowary, native to Australia, is the third largest bird in the world, after the ostrich and emu. This is the only bird known to have protective armor, including a hard crest that serves as a helmet atop its head.

(b) **Male peacock (*Pavo cristatus*).** The male peacock flares out its colorful feathers to get a female's attention. Peafowl (peacocks and peahens) belong to the pheasant family.

(c) **Atlantic puffin (*Fratercula arctica*).** This puffin has caught several fish. The puffin's beak becomes brightly colored during the breeding season.

FIGURE 32-23 Modern birds
Although they are diverse, most birds are highly adapted for flight, and their basic structure is similar.

Cretaceous rocks have yielded fossils of other early birds. *Hesperornis,* which lived in North America, was a toothed, aquatic diving bird with small wings and broad, lobed feet for swimming. *Ichthyornis* was a toothed, flying bird about the size of a small tern. Based on fossils, structural similarities, and molecular data, most biologists now view birds as living dinosaurs.

Modern birds are adapted for flight

By the end of the Cretaceous period, the major clades of present-day birds had evolved: palaeognaths and neognaths. (Some biologists assign birds to class Aves and consider palaeognathae and neognathae as superorders.) **Palaeognaths** (from Greek *palaios,* "ancient," and *gnathos,* "jaw") include flightless birds such as the ostriches, kiwis, cassowaries, and emus. These birds are called **ratites.** Their sternum (breastbone) is flat and does not have a ridge for attachment of wing muscles. They have only vestigial wings, but they have well-developed legs used for running.

Most modern birds are **neognaths** (from Greek *neos,* "new," and *gnathos,* "jaw"). These birds have powerful flight muscles attached to their keeled (ridged) sternum, and most neognaths fly. The penguins are an exception. They use their strong pectoral muscles and small, flipperlike wings to swim.

Biologists have described about 9000 species of extant birds and classified them into about 23 monophyletic taxa. Birds are a diverse group (**FIG. 32-23**). They have become adapted to a variety of environments, and various species have different types of beaks, feet, wings, tails, and behavioral patterns. They can be found on all continents, most islands, and even the open sea. The largest living birds are the ostriches of Africa, which may be up to 2 m (6.5 ft) tall and weigh 136 kg (300 lb). The great condors of the Americas have wingspans of up to 3 m (10 ft). The smallest known bird is the bee hummingbird of Cuba, with a length of less than 6 cm (about 2 in) and a weight of less than 2 g (about 0.06 oz).

Like their reptilian ancestors, modern birds lay eggs and have reptilian-type scales on their legs. Birds have evolved remarkable specializations for flight. They are the only extant animals with feathers. Their feathers are an amazing example of biological engineering. They are very light, yet flexible and strong, and present a flat surface to the air. Feathers also protect the body and decrease water and heat loss. The anterior limbs of birds are wings, usually adapted for flight. The posterior limbs are modified for walking, swimming, or perching.

Other adaptations for flight include the compact, streamlined body and the fusion of many bones, which provides the rigidity needed for flying. The bones are strong but very light. Many are hollow, containing large air spaces. The avian jaw is light, and instead of teeth, birds have a light, horny beak. The breastbone is broad and keeled for the attachment of the large flight muscles.

Birds have lungs with **air sacs,** thin-walled extensions that occupy spaces between the internal organs and within certain bones. The unique "one-way" flow of air through their respiratory system is metabolically efficient because they do not need to pump air in and out of the lungs. (This respiratory system is described in more detail in Chapter 46.) Birds have a four-chambered heart and a double circuit of blood flow. After blood delivers oxygen to the tissues, it is recharged with oxygen in the lungs; then the heart pumps the blood back into the systemic circulation. The very effective respiratory and circulatory systems provide the cells with enough oxygen to permit a high metabolic rate, which is necessary for the strenuous muscular activity that flying requires. Some of the heat a bird generates by metabolic activities helps it maintain a constant body temperature. Because they are endotherms, birds can remain active in cold climates.

Birds excrete nitrogenous wastes mainly as semisolid uric acid. Because birds typically do not have a urinary bladder, these solid wastes are delivered into the cloaca. They leave the body with the feces, which are dropped frequently. This adaptive mechanism helps maintain a light body weight.

Bills are specifically adapted for the type of food the bird eats (see Fig. 1-13). Birds must eat frequently because they have a high metabolic rate and typically do not store much fat. Although the choice of food varies widely among species, most birds eat energy-rich foods such as seeds, fruits, worms, mollusks, or arthropods. Warblers and some other species eat mainly insects. Owls and hawks eat rodents, rabbits, and other small mammals. Some hawks catch snakes and lizards. Vultures feed on dead animals. Pelicans, gulls, terns, and kingfishers catch fish.

An interesting feature of the bird digestive system is the **crop,** an expanded, saclike portion of the digestive tract below the esophagus, in which food is temporarily stored. The stomach is divided into a **proventriculus,** which secretes gastric juices; and a thick, muscular **gizzard,** which grinds food. The bird swallows small bits of gravel that act as "teeth" in the gizzard to mechanically break down food.

Birds have a well-developed nervous system, with a brain that is proportionately larger than that of reptiles. Birds rely heavily on vision, and their eyes are relatively larger than those of other vertebrates. Hearing is also well developed.

In striking contrast with the relatively silent reptiles, birds are very vocal. Most have short, simple *calls* that signal danger or influence feeding, flocking, or interaction between parent and young. *Songs* are usually more complex than calls and are performed mainly by males. Birds sing songs to attract and keep a mate and to claim and defend a territory.

One of the most fascinating aspects of bird behavior is the annual migration made by many species. Some birds, such as the golden plover and Arctic tern, fly from Alaska to Patagonia, South America, and back each year, covering perhaps 40,250 km (25,000 mi) en route. Migration and navigation are discussed in Chapter 52.

Many birds have beautiful, striking colors. The color is due partly to pigments deposited during the development of the feathers and partly to reflection and refraction of light of certain wavelengths. Many birds, especially females, are protectively colored by their plumage. During the breeding season, the male often assumes brighter colors to help him attract a mate.

Mammals have hair and mammary glands

Hair is a key derived character of **mammals** (class Mammalia). All mammals have at least a few hairs at some time in their life, and no other organism has true hair. Hair insulates the body, helping to maintain the high constant body temperature required for endothermy. The benefit of endothermy is a high metabolic rate, which allows a high level of activity even in low winter temperatures.

Other derived characters of mammals are **mammary glands,** which produce milk for the young; one pair of temporal openings in the skull; **differentiation of teeth** into incisors, canines, premolars, and molars; and three **middle-ear bones** (malleus, incus, and stapes) that transmit vibrations from the tympanic membrane (eardrum) to the inner ear. The evolution of the **cochlea,** the organ of hearing in the inner ear, gives mammals an excellent sense of hearing.

Contributing significantly to the success of the mammals, the nervous system is more highly developed than in any other group of animals. The cerebrum is especially large and complex, with an outer gray region, the **cerebral cortex.** In mammals, the highly specialized cerebral cortex, called the **neocortex,** has six layers of neurons. Specific regions in the neocortex are specialized for functions such as vision, hearing, touch, movement, emotional response, and higher cognitive functions.

Fertilization in mammals is internal, and with the exception of the monotremes that lay eggs, mammals are viviparous. Most mammals develop a **placenta,** an organ of exchange between developing embryo and mother. As the mother's blood passes through blood vessels in the placenta, it delivers nourishment and oxygen to the embryo and carries off wastes. By carrying their developing young internally, mammals avoid the hazards of having their eggs consumed by predators. By nourishing the young and caring for them, the parents offer both protection and an "education" on how to obtain food and avoid being eaten.

A muscular **diaphragm** helps move air into and out of the lungs. Like birds, mammals are endotherms, but mammals may have evolved endothermy independently of birds. Some of the adaptations that allow mammals to maintain a constant body temperature include the covering of insulating hair, the four-chambered heart, and separation of pulmonary and systemic circulations. Red blood cells without nuclei serve as efficient oxygen transporters.

The limbs of mammals are variously adapted for walking, running, climbing, swimming, burrowing, or flying. In four-legged mammals, the limbs are more directly under the body than they are in extant reptiles; this contributes to speed and agility.

New fossil discoveries are changing our understanding of the early evolution of mammals

Mammals descended from **therapsids,** a group of synapsid reptiles, during the Triassic period more than 200 mya. The therapsids were doglike carnivores with differentiated teeth and legs adapted for running (**FIG. 32-24**). Until recently, early mammals were thought to be small, about the size of a mouse or shrew. However, fossil evidence indicates that mammals diversified earlier than previously thought. Some early mammals were fairly large, with limbs adapted for swimming or burrowing. Some had fur, and some were probably endothermic.

How did mammals manage to coexist with reptiles during the approximately 160 million years that reptiles ruled Earth?

FIGURE 32-24 Therapsid (*Lycaenops*)
The therapsids were synapsid reptiles. *Lycaenops*, a carnivore about the size of a coyote, lived in South Africa during the Late Permian period.

Many adaptations permitted early mammals to compete for a place on this planet. Perhaps one of the most important was their skill at being inconspicuous. Many were **arboreal** (tree dwelling) and **nocturnal** (active at night), searching for food (mainly insects and plant material, and perhaps reptile eggs) at night while the reptiles were inactive. Although their eyes may have been

small, early mammals had well-developed sense organs for hearing and smell.

As many reptiles became extinct, mammals adapted to the niches (lifestyles) that reptiles abandoned. During this time, the flowering plants, including many trees, underwent an adaptive radiation, providing new habitats, sources of food, and protection from predators. Numerous new varieties of mammals evolved. During the Early Cenozoic era (more than 55 mya), the mammals underwent an adaptive radiation; they became widely distributed and adapted to an impressive variety of ecological lifestyles.

Modern mammals are assigned to three subclasses

By the end of the Cretaceous period, three main groups of mammals had evolved (**FIG. 32-25**). Today, mammals inhabit virtually every corner of Earth; they live on land, in fresh and salt water, and in the air. They range in size from the tiny pygmy shrew, weighing about 2.5 g (less than 0.1 oz), to the blue whale, which may weigh up to 136,000 kg (150 tons) and which is probably one of the largest animals that has ever lived.

Modern mammals are classified in two main clades: **Protheria**, which includes the egg-laying mammals, or **monotremes**, and **Theria**, which includes the mammals that bear their young alive. The therian clade is further divided into two groups: **Metatheria**, the **marsupials** (pouched mammals), and **Eutheria**, mammals that are more developed at birth than the marsupials. (The eutherians are often referred to as placental mammals because they have well-developed placentas. However, some marsupials do have simple placentas.)

One group of protherians includes the duck-billed platypus and a second, the spiny anteaters or echidnas (**FIG. 32-26**; see also Figs. 1-16 and 23-5). These animals live in Australia and Tasmania; two species of spiny anteaters inhabit New Guinea. Female protherians lay eggs that they carry in a pouch on the abdomen or keep warm in a nest. When the young hatch, they lap up milk secreted by their mother's mammary glands. Unlike other mammals, monotremes do not have nipples. With their long beaks and long, sticky tongues, spiny anteaters capture ants and termites. The duck-billed platypus,

FIGURE 32-25 Evolution of mammals
This cladogram shows the current interpretation of the evolution of mammals.

FIGURE 32-26 Spiny anteater
The spiny anteater (*Tachyglossus aculeatus*) is an egg-laying monotreme.

(a) Eastern gray kangaroo (Macropus giganteus) with young, known as a joey. The kangaroo is native to Australia.

(b) A kangaroo soon after birth. Marsupials are born in the embryonic state and continue to develop in the safety of the mother's marsupium (pouch).

FIGURE 32-27 Marsupials

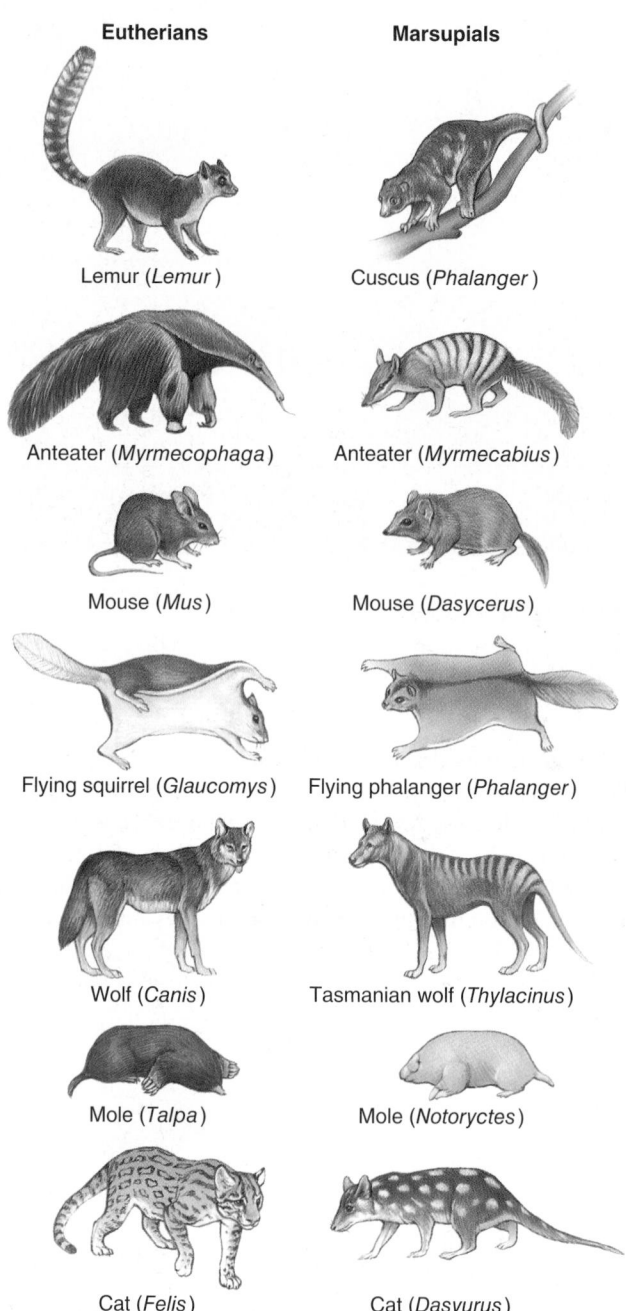

Eutherians	Marsupials
Lemur (*Lemur*)	Cuscus (*Phalanger*)
Anteater (*Myrmecophaga*)	Anteater (*Myrmecabius*)
Mouse (*Mus*)	Mouse (*Dasycerus*)
Flying squirrel (*Glaucomys*)	Flying phalanger (*Phalanger*)
Wolf (*Canis*)	Tasmanian wolf (*Thylacinus*)
Mole (*Talpa*)	Mole (*Notoryctes*)
Cat (*Felis*)	Cat (*Dasyurus*)

FIGURE 32-28 Convergent evolution in eutherian and marsupial mammals

For each mammal in one group, there is a counterpart in the other group. Their similarities include both lifestyles and structural features.

which lives in burrows along river banks, preys on freshwater invertebrates. It has webbed feet and a flat, beaverlike tail, which help it swim.

Marsupials include pouched mammals such as kangaroos and opossums (**FIG. 32-27a**). Embryos begin their development in the mother's uterus, where they are nourished by fluid and yolk. After a brief gestation, the young are born in an undeveloped stage. The young make their way to the **marsupium** (pouch), where they attach to a nipple. Nourished by the mother's milk, they complete their development (**FIG. 32-27b**).

At one time, marsupials probably inhabited much of the world, but placental mammals largely out-competed them. Now marsupials live mainly in Australia and in Central and South America. The only marsupial species that ranges into the United States is the Virginia opossum. Australia became geographically isolated from the rest of the world before placental mammals migrated there, and the marsupials remained the dominant mammals (see discussion of continental drift in Chapter 18). Australian marsupials underwent adaptive radiation, paralleling the evolution of placental mammals

(a) Wildebeest (*Connochaetes taurinus*), photographed in Tanzania. The dominant plains antelope in many areas of eastern and southern Africa, wildebeest migrate long distances during the dry season in search of food and water.

(c) Polar bears (*Ursus maritimus*), the largest living land carnivores, feed mainly on seals.

(b) Humpback whales (*Megaptera novaeangliae*) exhibiting a rare double breach.

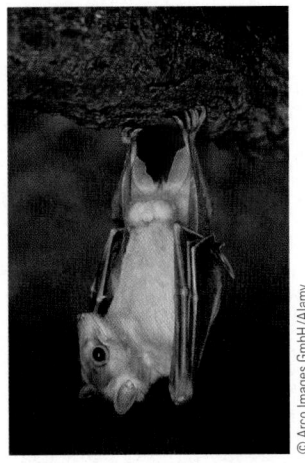

(d) Egyptian fruit bat (*Rousettus aegyptiacus*). Often called "flying foxes," these small bats cluster in large colonies. They often hang by one foot from the cave ceiling.

FIGURE 32-29 Eutherian mammals

elsewhere. Thus, marsupials that live in Australia and adjacent islands correspond to North American placental wolves, bears, rats, moles, flying squirrels, and even cats (**FIG. 32-28** on facing page).

Most familiar to us are the eutherian mammals, which are born at a more mature stage than marsupials. Indeed, among some species the young can walk and begin to interact with other members of the group within a few minutes after birth. **Eutherians** have a well-developed **placenta** (**FIG. 32-29**). The placenta develops from both embryonic membranes and the maternal uterine wall. In the placenta, blood vessels of the embryo come very close to the blood vessels of the mother, so materials can be exchanged by diffusion. (The two circulations do not normally mix.) The placenta allows the young to remain within the mother's body until embryonic development is complete. Biologists assign extant placental

mammals to about 19 orders. **TABLE 32-4** gives a brief summary of some of these orders. Remember that aquatic mammals, such as dolphins, whales, and seals, evolved from terrestrial ancestors (see Fig. 18-9). Also refer to **TABLE 32-5**, which reviews the three main deuterostome groups.

Review

- What vertebrate adaptations are important for terrestrial life?
- Which amniotes are endothermic? What are some advantages of endothermy?
- What are some arguments for classifying birds and reptiles in a single clade?
- What are the three main clades of mammals? How do they differ?

TABLE 32-4   Some Orders of Extant Eutherian Mammals

Order, Representative Members, and Some Characteristics

Insectivora (moles, hedgehogs, shrews)

Nocturnal; eat insects. Shrew is smallest living mammal; some weigh less than 5 g.

African hedgehog
Atelerix albiventris

Chiroptera (bats)

Adapted for flying; fold of skin extends from elongated fingers to body and legs, forming wing. Guided in flight by type of biological sonar; emit high-frequency squeaks and are guided by echoes from obstructions. Eat insects and fruit or suck blood of other animals.

Bat
Eptesicus fuscus

Carnivora (cats, dogs, wolves, foxes, bears, otters, mink, weasels, skunks, seals, sea lions, walruses)

Carnivores with sharp, pointed canine teeth and molars for shearing; keen sense of smell; complex social interactions; among fastest, strongest, and smartest animals. Seals, sea lions, and walruses are large marine carnivores with limbs adapted as flippers for swimming.

Wolf
Canis lupus

Perissodactyla (horses, zebras, tapirs, rhinoceroses)

Herbivores; hoofed with odd number of digits per foot; one or three toes; teeth adapted for chewing; usually large animals with long legs.

Tapir
Tapirus sp.

Lagomorpha (rabbits, hares, pikas)

Like rodents, have chisel-like incisors; typically have long hind legs adapted for jumping; many have long ears.

Pika
Ochontona sp.

Primates (lemurs, monkeys, apes, humans)

Highly developed brain and eyes; nails instead of claws; opposable thumb; eyes directed forward; omnivores; most species arboreal. (Primate evolution discussed in Chapter 22.)

Ring-tailed lemur
Lemur catta

Artiodactyla (cattle, sheep, pigs, deer, giraffes)

Hoofed with even numbers of digits per foot; most have two toes, some have four. Most have antlers or horns. Herbivores; most are ruminants, chew a cud and have series of stomachs inhabited by bacteria that digest cellulose.

American elk
Cervus elaphus

Xenarthra (sloths, anteaters, armadillos)

Teeth reduced or no teeth. Sloths are sluggish animals that hang upside down from branches; often protectively colored by green algae that grow on their hair. Armadillos are protected by bony plates; eat insects and small invertebrates.

Nine-banded armadillo
Dasypus bellus

Rodentia (squirrels, beavers, rats, mice, hamsters, porcupines, guinea pigs)

Gnawing animals with chisel-like incisors. As they gnaw, teeth are worn down, and so must grow continually. Most numerous mammals both in numbers and species.

Flying squirrel
Glaucomys volans

Proboscidea (elephants)

Largest land animals; weigh up to 7 tons; large head; broad ears; long, muscular, flexible trunk (proboscis); thick loose skin is characteristic; two upper incisors are elongated as tusks. Includes extinct mastodons and woolly mammoths.

African elephant
Loxodonta africana

Sirenia (sea cows, manatees)

Herbivorous, aquatic mammals with fin-like forelimbs and no hind limbs. They are probably the basis for most tales about mermaids.

Manatee
Trichechus manatus

Cetacea (whales, dolphins, porpoises)

Adapted for aquatic life with fish-shaped body and broad, paddlelike forelimbs (flippers); posterior limbs absent; many have thick layer of blubber under skin; some are filter feeders; mate and bear young in the water; very intelligent.

Humpback whale
Megaptera noveangliae

TABLE 32-5 Overview of the Deuterostomes

Major Groups and Phyla	Body Plan	Key Characteristics
Deuterostomes		
Echinoderms (sea stars, sea urchins; sand dollars)	Larva bilateral, ciliated; adult pentaradial; triploblastic; organ systems; complete digestive tube	Endoskeleton with spines; water vascular system functions in locomotion, feeding, and gas exchange; tube feet; marine
Hemichordates (acorn worms)	Bilateral symmetry; triploblastic; organ systems; complete digestive tube	Ring of cilia surrounds mouth; three-part body: proboscis, collar, and trunk; pharyngeal slits; wormlike marine animals
Chordates (tunicates, lancelets, vertebrates)	Bilateral symmetry; triploblastic; organ systems; complete digestive tube	Notochord; dorsal, tubular nerve cord; endostyle; pharyngeal slits during some time in life cycle; postanal tail; segmented body

■ SUMMARY: FOCUS ON LEARNING OBJECTIVES

32.1 (page 676)

1 Identify shared derived characters of deuterostomes and briefly describe the hemichordates.

- **Deuterostomia** includes echinoderms, hemichordates, and chordates. Shared derived characters include radial, indeterminate cleavage; the blastopore becomes (or is near the future site of) the anus; pharyngeal slits at some time in the life cycle. Basal deuterostomes have a larva with a loop-shaped ciliated band used for locomotion.
- **Hemichordates** (acorn worms) are marine deuterostomes with a three-part body, including proboscis, collar, and trunk.

32.2 (page 676)

2 Identify three shared derived characters of echinoderms and describe the main classes of echinoderms.

- **Echinoderms** (phylum **Echinodermata**) are marine animals with a spiny "skin," **water vascular system, tube feet,** and **endoskeleton.** The larvae exhibit bilateral symmetry; most of the adults exhibit **pentaradial symmetry.**
- Class **Crinoidea** includes sea lilies and feather stars. The **oral surface** of crinoids is turned upward; some crinoids are sessile.
- Class **Asteroidea** consists of the sea stars. They have a central disc with five or more arms, and use tube feet for locomotion.
- Class **Ophiuroidea** includes the brittle stars, which resemble sea stars but have longer, more slender arms that are set off more distinctly from the central disc. They use their arms for locomotion. Their tube feet lack suckers and are not used in locomotion.
- Class **Echinoidea** includes the sea urchins and sand dollars. Echinoids lack arms; they have a solid shell and are covered with spines. Class **Holothuroidea** consists of sea cucumbers, animals with elongated flexible bodies. The mouth is surrounded by a circle of modified tube feet that serve as tentacles.

32.3 (page 680)

3 Describe characteristics of chordates, including four shared derived characters.

- Phylum **Chordata** includes three subphyla: Urochordata, Cephalochordata, and Vertebrata. At some time in its life cycle, a chordate has a flexible, supporting **notochord;** a dorsal, tubular nerve cord; a muscular **postanal tail;** and an **endostyle,** or thyroid gland; they

are also characterized by **pharyngeal (gill) slits,** but this is a derived character of deuterostomes.

32.4 (page 681)

4 Compare tunicates and lancelets, and summarize the phylogeny of chordates.

- The **tunicates,** which belong to subphylum **Urochordata,** are suspension-feeding marine animals with **tunics.** Larvae have typical chordate characteristics and are free-swimming. Adults of most groups are sessile suspension feeders.
- Subphylum **Cephalochordata** consists of the **lancelets,** small, segmented, fishlike animals; chordate characteristics are highly developed.
- Biologists are still seeking evidence that will help determine whether the cephalochordates or the urochordates are the sister group of the vertebrates.

CENGAGENOW™ Learn more about the body plans of the deuterostomes by clicking on the figures in CengageNOW.

32.5 (page 683)

5 Describe four shared derived characters of vertebrates.

- The vertebrates have a **vertebral column** composed of **vertebrae** that forms the chief skeletal axis of the body and a braincase, or **cranium. Neural crest cells** are important in the development of many structures, including the cranium and jaws. Vertebrates have pronounced cephalization, a complex brain, and muscles attached to the endoskeleton for movement.

CENGAGENOW™ Explore the evolutionary relationships of vertebrates by clicking on the figure in CengageNOW.

6 Describe the major taxa of extant vertebrates.

- Vertebrates can be assigned to nine clades. The hagfishes, which make up the **Myxini,** and the lampreys, the **Petromyzontida,** have neither jaws nor paired fins. The **Chondrichthyes** comprise the sharks, rays, and skates; they are jawed fishes with skeletons of cartilage. The bony fishes are assigned to three groups: **Actinopterygii,** ray-finned fishes; **Actinistia,** coelacanths; and **Dipnoi,** lungfishes, which have limbs similar in size and position to the tetrapods.

- The tetrapods include the **Amphibia** (salamanders, frogs, and toads), which have aquatic larvae that undergo metamorphosis; **Reptilia** (turtles, lizards, snakes, alligators, and birds), amniotes with horny scales or feathers and reproduction adapted for terrestrial life; and **Mammalia** (monotremes, marsupials, placental mammals), amniotes with hair and mammary glands. (See Table 32-2 for a more detailed review.)

32.6 (page 685)

7 Distinguish among the major groups of jawless fishes.

- The extant jawless fishes, or **agnathans,** are the hagfishes (Myxini) and the lampreys (Petromyzontida). Jaws and paired fins are absent in both hagfishes and lampreys. Hagfishes are marine scavengers that secrete slime as a defense mechanism. Many lampreys are parasites on other fishes.

32.7 (page 687)

8 Trace the evolution of jawed fishes and early tetrapods; describe modern amphibians.

- Chondrichthyes, the cartilaginous fishes (sharks, rays, and skates), evolved during the Devonian period. They have jaws, two pairs of fins, and **placoid scales.**

- During the Devonian period, bony fishes gave rise to two evolutionary lines: the Actinopterygii, or **ray-finned fishes,** and the **Sarcopterygii,** or **lobe-finned fishes.** The ray-finned fishes gave rise to the modern bony fishes. Their lungs have been modified as a **swim bladder,** an air sac for regulating buoyancy.

- The Sarcopterygii probably gave rise to the **lungfishes** (Dipnoi) and the **coelacanths** (Actinistia). Evidence suggests that the lungfishes gave rise to the **tetrapods,** the land vertebrates. *Tiktaalik* was a transitional form between fishes and tetrapods.

- Early **amphibians** (Amphibia) were mainly aquatic animals that ventured onto the land to find food or escape predators. These early tetrapods had limbs strong enough to support the weight of their bodies on land.

- Modern amphibians include salamanders, frogs and toads, and caecilians. Most amphibians return to the water to reproduce. Frog embryos develop into **tadpoles,** which undergo **metamorphosis** to become adults. Amphibians use their moist skin as well as lungs for gas exchange. They have a three-chambered heart and systemic and pulmonary circulations.

CENGAGENOW™ Learn more about jawless, early jawed, cartilaginous, and bony fishes by clicking on the figures in CengageNOW.

32.8 (page 693)

9 Describe three vertebrate adaptations to terrestrial life.

- Terrestrial vertebrates, or **amniotes,** include reptiles (including birds) and mammals. The evolution of the **amniotic egg** with its shell and amnion was an important adaptation for life on land. The **amnion** is a membrane that forms a fluid-filled sac around the embryo.

Fertilization is internal. Amniotes have a body covering that retards water loss and physiological mechanisms that conserve water.

CENGAGENOW™ Learn more about the amniotic egg by clicking on the figure in CengageNOW.

10 Describe the reptiles (including the birds) and give an argument for including the birds in the reptile clade.

- Biologists classify amniotes in two main groups: diapsids and synapsids. **Diapsids** include the turtles, ichthyosaurs, tuataras, squamates (snakes and lizards), crocodiles, pterosaurs, saurischian dinosaurs, and birds. The **synapsids** gave rise to the **therapsids,** which gave rise to the mammals.

- Extant reptiles (including birds) are classified in five groups: turtles, terrapins, and tortoises; lizards, snakes, and amphisbaenians; tuataras; crocodiles, alligators, caimans, and gavials; and birds.

- Reptiles have dry skin with horny scales, lungs with many chambers, and a three-chambered heart with some separation of oxygen-rich and oxygen-poor blood.

- Birds have many adaptations for powered flight, including feathers; wings; and light, hollow bones containing airspaces. They have a four-chambered heart and very efficient lungs, and they excrete solid metabolic wastes (uric acid). They are **endotherms;** that is, they maintain a constant body temperature. Birds have a well-developed nervous system with excellent vision and hearing.

- Based on fossil evidence and molecular data, feather evolution took place in terrestrial, bipedal dinosaurs before the evolution of birds or flight. Birds are considered feathered reptiles that evolved from the lineage of saurischian dinosaurs, specifically from the **theropods,** a group of bipedal, saurischian dinosaurs. Like theropods, modern birds have feet with three digits; thin-walled, hollow bones; and a **furcula,** or wishbone.

11 Describe five key characters of mammals; contrast protherians (monotremes), metatherians (marsupials), and eutherian mammals, giving examples of animals that belong to each group.

- **Mammals** have **hair, mammary glands, differentiated teeth,** and three **middle-ear bones.** They are endotherms and have a highly developed nervous system and a muscular **diaphragm.**

- **Protherians,** the **monotremes,** include the duck-billed platypus and spiny anteaters. Monotremes lay eggs.

- **Metatherians,** the **marsupials,** include pouched mammals, such as kangaroos and opossums. The young, born at an immature stage, complete their development in their mother's **marsupium,** where they are nourished with milk from mammary glands.

- **Eutherians** are more developed at birth than marsupials; they are characterized by a well-developed **placenta,** an organ of exchange that develops between the embryo and the mother.

1. Which of the following is *not* a shared derived character of echinoderms? (a) water vascular system (b) notochord (c) tube feet (d) pentaradial symmetry in adult (e) endoskeleton of calcium carbonate plates and spines

2. Which of the following organisms belongs to subphylum Vertebrata? (a) lophophorate (b) lamprey (c) lancelet (d) tunicate (e) crinoid

3. Which of the following is/are found in tunicates? (a) dorsal, tubular nerve cord (b) tube feet (c) anal gill slits (d) two pairs of appendages (e) vertebral column

4. Arrange the following animals to reflect an accepted sequence of evolution.
   1. lungfish 2. dinosaur 3. amphibian 4. bird
   (a) 3, 1, 2, 4 (b) 1, 3, 2, 4 (c) 2, 1, 3, 4 (d) 1, 2, 3, 4 (e) 2, 4, 1, 3

5. A shark is characterized by (a) amnion (b) bony skeleton (c) water vascular system (d) placoid scales (e) placoid scales *and* amnion

6. Which of the following characteristics is associated with amphibians? (a) amnion (b) placoid scales (c) four-chambered heart (d) swim bladder (e) metamorphosis

7. Reptiles (a) are endothermic (b) are amniotes (c) gave rise to the birds and mammals (d) have external fertilization (e) b and c are correct

8. Which of the following is *not* characteristic of birds? (a) hollow bones (b) amnion (c) ectothermy (d) high metabolic rate (e) reptilian-like scales on legs

9. Which of the following is *not* true of the duck-billed platypus? (a) classified as a marsupial (b) lays eggs (c) has a notochord at embryo stage (d) has vertebral column (e) is a predator

10. Which of the following is a shared derived character of mammals? (a) placenta (b) amnion (c) three middle-ear bones (d) endostyle (e) notochord

11. Which of the following is *not* true? (a) feathers evolved in dinosaurs (b) birds are endothermic (c) birds excrete uric acid (d) birds have an amniotic egg (e) *Archaeopteryx* was the ancestor of feathered dinosaurs

12. Label the cladogram. See Figure 32-25 to check your answers.

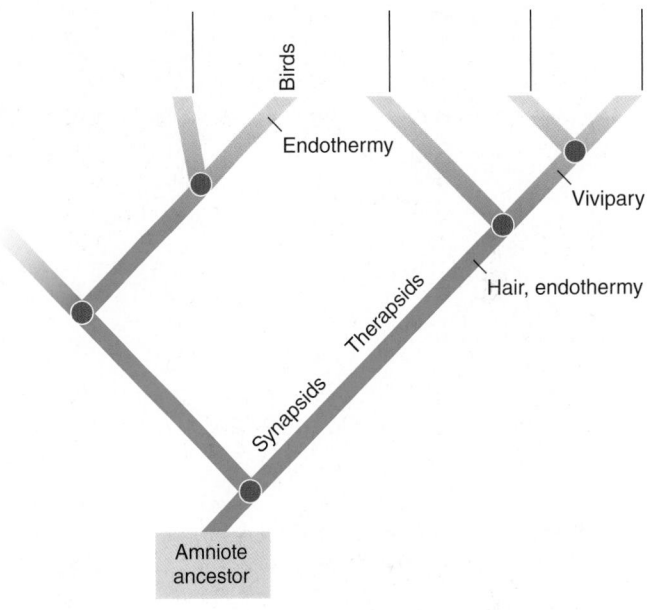

1. Sea urchins have radial symmetry. Explain why they are not classified as cnidarians.

2. **ANALYZING DATA.** Imagine that you discover an interesting new animal. You find it has a dorsal, tubular nerve cord; a cranium; skin with scales; and a heart with two atria and two ventricles. How would you classify the animal? Explain each step in your decision. Where would you place this animal on the cladogram shown in Figure 32-20?

3. **EVOLUTION LINK.** Discuss the relationships among the echinoderms and chordates, describing shared derived characters that support grouping these animals as deuterostomes.

4. **EVOLUTION LINK.** Support the hypothesis that lungfishes gave rise to tetrapods.

5. **EVOLUTION LINK.** Most biologists now consider birds as living dinosaurs. Justify this position.

6. **EVOLUTION LINK.** Some biologists consider protherians (monotremes) to be therapsid reptiles rather than mammals. Give arguments for and against this position.

7. **SCIENCE, TECHNOLOGY, AND SOCIETY.** Every year hundreds of sea turtles are injured and killed as a result of human activities. All seven species of marine turtles are listed under the Endangered Species Act. What measures would you propose to protect sea turtles?

 Additional questions are available in CengageNOW at www.cengage.com/login.

33 Plant Structure, Growth, and Development

© Organica/Alamy

Foxglove, a herbaceous biennial. Purple and white foxgloves (*Digitalis purpurea*) are popular garden plants. Foxglove is also the source for digitalis, which is used to treat heart disease.

The more than 300,000 species of flowering plants that live in and are adapted to the many environments on Earth represent remarkable variety. Yet all of these—from desert cacti with enormously swollen stems, to cattails partly submerged in marshes, to orchids growing in the uppermost tree branches of lush tropical rain forests—are recognizable as plants. Almost all plants have the same basic body plan, which consists of roots, stems, and leaves.

Plants are either herbaceous or woody. *Herbaceous* plants are non-woody. In temperate climates, the aerial parts (stems and leaves) of herbaceous plants die back to the ground at the end of the growing season. In contrast, the aerial parts of *woody* plants (trees and shrubs) persist. Botanically speaking, woody plants produce hard, lignified secondary tissues (the cell walls of secondary tissues contain *lignin*), and herbaceous plants do not. Lignin and the production of secondary tissues are discussed later in this chapter and in Chapters 35 and 36.

Annuals are herbaceous plants (such as corn, geranium, and marigold) that grow, reproduce, and die in one year or less. Other herbaceous plants (such as carrot, Queen Anne's lace, cabbage, and foxglove) are **biennials;** they take two years to complete their life cycles before dying (see photograph). During their first season, biennials produce extra carbohydrates, which they store and use during their second year, when they typically form flowers and reproduce.

Perennials are herbaceous and woody plants that have the potential to live for more than two years. In temperate climates, the aerial (aboveground) stems of herbaceous perennials such as iris, rhubarb, onion, and asparagus die back each winter. Their underground parts (roots and underground stems) become dormant during the winter and send out new growth each spring. (In **dormancy,** an organism reduces its metabolic state to a minimum level to survive unfavorable conditions.) Similarly, in certain tropical climates with pronounced wet and dry seasons, the aerial parts of herbaceous perennials die back, and the underground parts become dormant during the unfavorable dry season. Other tropical plants, such as orchids, are herbaceous perennials that grow year-round.

All woody plants are perennials, and some of them live for hundreds or even thousands of years. In temperate climates, the aerial stems of woody plants become dormant during the winter. Many temperate woody perennials are **deciduous;** that is, they shed their leaves before winter and produce new stems with new leaves the following spring. Other woody perennials are **evergreen** and shed their leaves over a long period, so some leaves are always present. Because they have permanent woody stems that are the starting points for new growth the following season, many trees attain massive sizes.

In this chapter we focus on the structure, growth, and development of flowering plants, which are vascular plants characterized by flowers, double fertilization, endosperm, and seeds enclosed within fruits (see Chapter 28). We then examine other aspects of flowering plants in Chapters 34 to 38.

33.1 THE PLANT BODY

■ LEARNING OBJECTIVES

1. Discuss the functions of various parts of the vascular plant body, including the nutrient- and water-absorbing root system and the photosynthesizing shoot system.
2. Describe the structure and functions of the ground tissue system (parenchyma tissue, collenchyma tissue, and sclerenchyma tissue).
3. Describe the structure and functions of the vascular tissue system (xylem and phloem).
4. Describe the structure and functions of the dermal tissue system (epidermis and periderm).

The plant body of flowering plants (and other vascular plants) is usually organized into a root system and a shoot system (**FIG. 33-1**). The **root system** is generally underground. The aerial portion, the **shoot system,** usually consists of a vertical stem that bears leaves and, in flowering plants, flowers and fruits that contain seeds.

Each plant typically grows in two different environments: the dark, moist soil and the illuminated, relatively dry air. Plants usually have both roots and shoots because they require resources from both environments. Thus, roots branch extensively through the soil, forming a network that anchors the plant firmly in place and absorbs water and dissolved minerals (inorganic nutrients). Leaves, the flattened organs of photosynthesis, are attached more or less regularly on the stem, where they absorb the sun's light and atmospheric carbon dioxide (CO_2) used in photosynthesis.

The plant body consists of cells and tissues

As in other organisms, the basic structural and functional unit of plants is the cell. Plants have evolved a variety of cell types, each specialized for particular functions. Plant cells are organized into tissues. A **tissue** is a group of cells that forms a structural and functional unit. *Simple tissues* are composed of only one kind of cell, whereas *complex tissues* have two or more kinds of cells.

In vascular plants, tissues are organized into three tissue systems, each of which extends throughout the plant body (**FIG. 33-2**). Each tissue system contains two or more kinds of tissues (**TABLE 33-1**). Most of the plant body is composed of the **ground tissue system,** which has a variety of functions, including photosynthesis, storage, and support. The **vascular tissue system,** an intricate conducting system that extends throughout the plant body, is responsible for conduction of various substances, including water, dissolved minerals, and food (dissolved sugar). The vascular tissue system also functions in strengthening and supporting the plant. The **dermal tissue system** provides a covering for the plant body.

Roots, stems, leaves, flower parts, and fruits are **organs** because each is composed of all three tissue systems. The tissue systems of different plant organs form an interconnected network throughout the plant. For example, the vascular tissue system of a leaf is continuous with the vascular tissue system of the stem to which it is attached, and the vascular tissue system of the stem is continuous with the vascular tissue system of the root.

The ground tissue system is composed of three simple tissues

The bulk of a herbaceous plant is its ground tissue system, which is composed of three tissues: parenchyma, collenchyma, and sclerenchyma (**TABLE 33-2** on pages 712 and 713). These tissues can be distinguished by their cell wall structures. Recall that plant cells are surrounded by a cell wall that provides structural support (see Chapter 4). A growing plant cell secretes a thin **primary cell wall,** which stretches and expands as the cell increases in size. After the cell stops growing, it sometimes secretes a thick, strong **secondary cell wall,** which is deposited *inside* the primary cell wall—that is, between the primary cell wall and the plasma membrane (see Fig. 4-31).

Plant cell walls have several important roles. As discussed later in the chapter, cell walls are involved in growth; the ability of

During the evolution of plants, the root and shoot systems specialized to obtain resources from the soil and air, respectively.

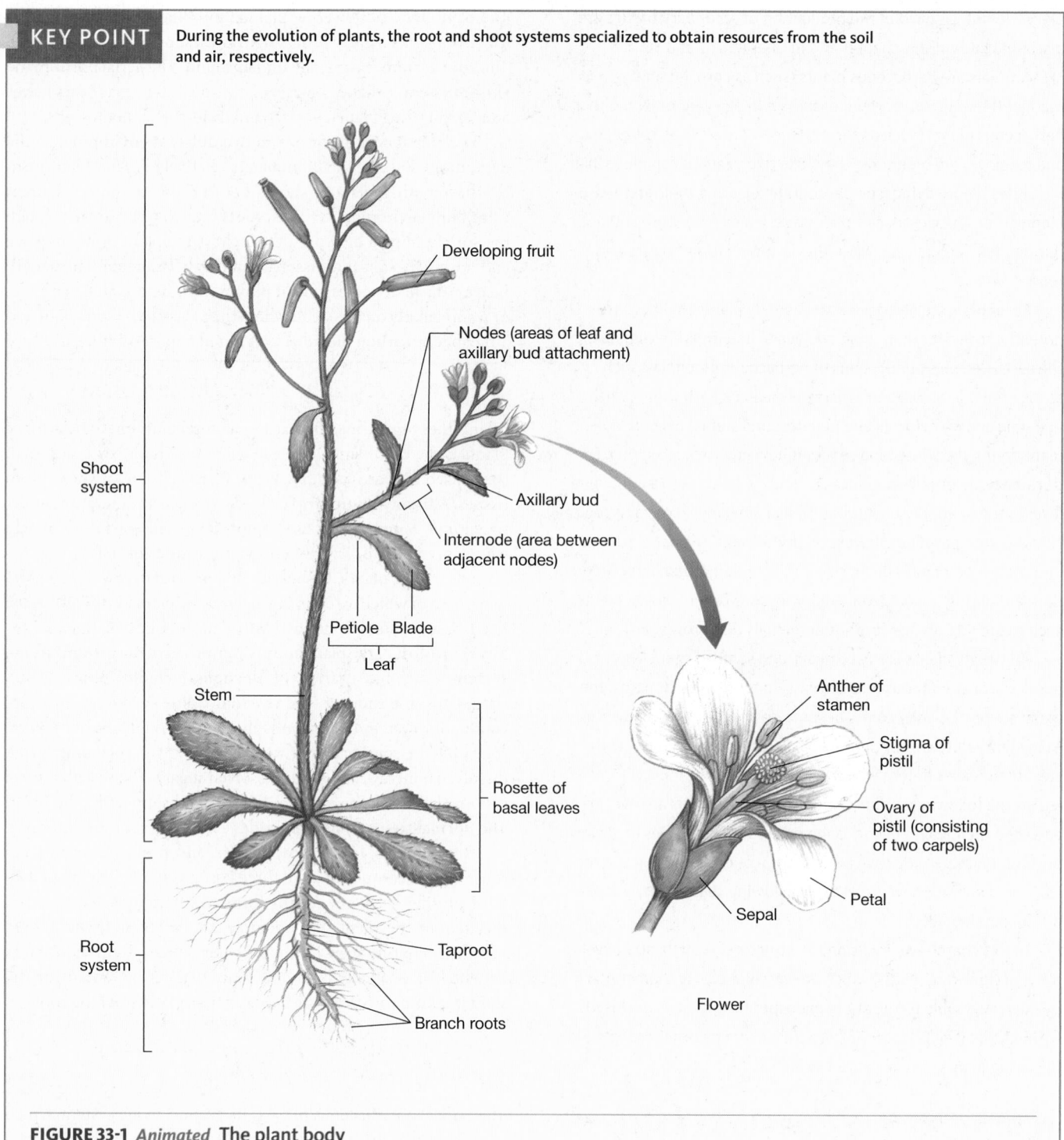

FIGURE 33-1 *Animated* **The plant body**

A plant body consists of a root system, usually underground, and a shoot system, usually aerial. Shown is mouse-ear cress (*Arabidopsis thaliana*), a small plant in the mustard family that is a model plant for biological research. *Arabidopsis* is native to North Africa and Eurasia and has been naturalized (was introduced and is now growing in the wild) in California and the eastern half of the United States.

primary cell walls to expand allows cells to increase in size. Scientists are increasingly aware that **signal transduction** takes place in plant cell walls because many carbohydrate and protein molecules in plant cell walls communicate with other molecules both inside and outside the cell. The cell wall is also the first line of defense against disease-causing organisms.

Parenchyma cells have thin primary walls

Parenchyma tissue, a simple tissue composed of parenchyma cells, is found throughout the plant body and is the most common type of cell and tissue (**FIG. 33-3a** on page 714). The soft parts of a plant, such as the edible part of an apple or a potato, consist largely of parenchyma.

The tissue systems are continuous throughout the plant. For example, the vascular tissue system in a leaf is continuous with the vascular tissue system in the stem to which it is attached.

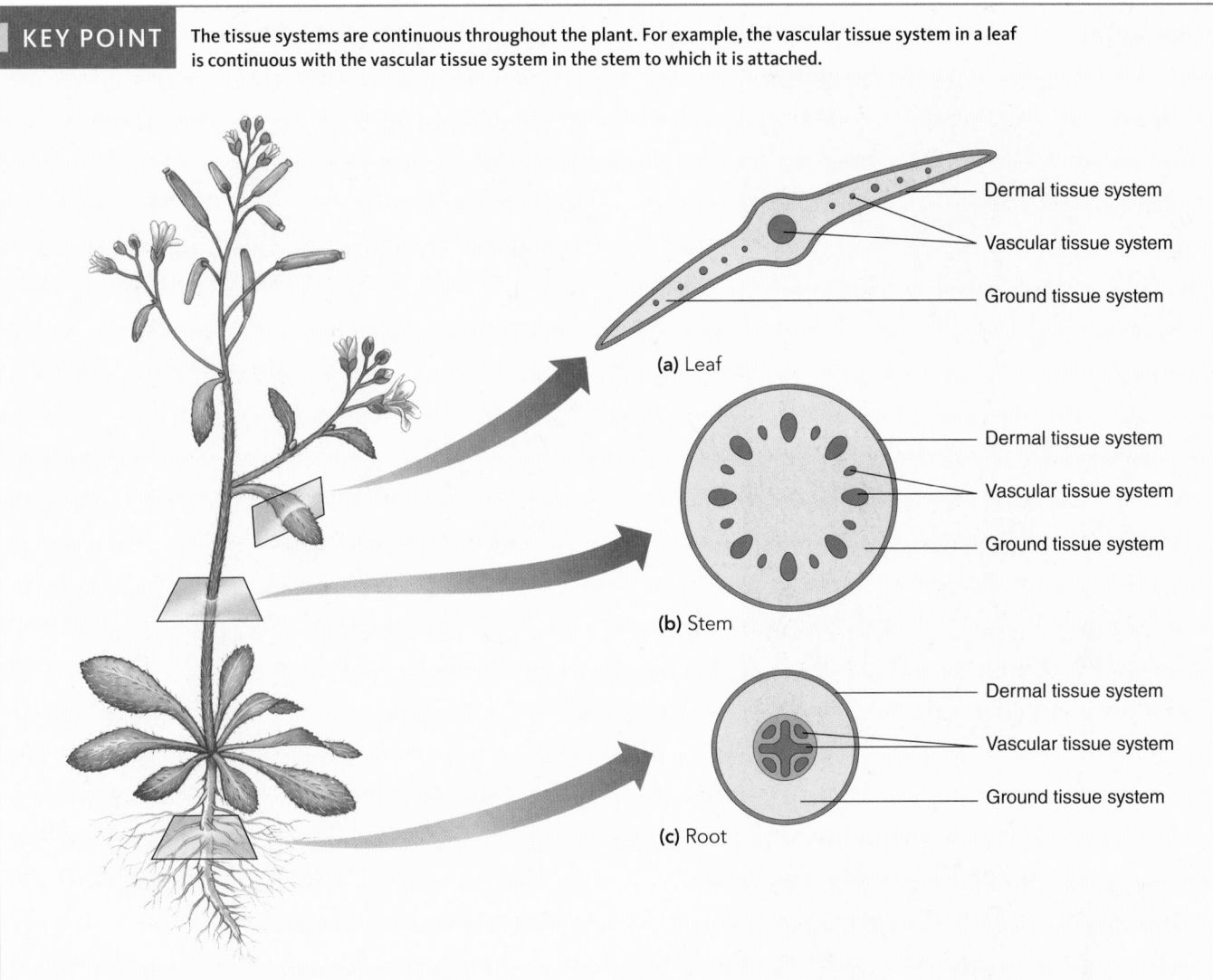

(a) Leaf
- Dermal tissue system
- Vascular tissue system
- Ground tissue system

(b) Stem
- Dermal tissue system
- Vascular tissue system
- Ground tissue system

(c) Root
- Dermal tissue system
- Vascular tissue system
- Ground tissue system

FIGURE 33-2 *Animated* **The three tissue systems in the plant body**

This figure shows the distribution of the ground tissue system, vascular tissue system, and dermal tissue system in a herbaceous eudicot such as *Arabidopsis*.

TABLE 33-1 Tissue Systems, Tissues, and Cell Types of Flowering Plants

Tissue System	Tissue	Cell Types	Main Functions of Tissue
Ground tissue system	Parenchyma tissue Collenchyma tissue Sclerenchyma tissue	Parenchyma cells Collenchyma cells Sclerenchyma cells (sclereids or fibers)	Storage, secretion, photosynthesis Support Support, strength
Vascular tissue system	Xylem	Tracheids Vessel elements Xylem parenchyma cells Fibers (sclerenchyma cells)	Conduction of water and nutrient minerals, support Conduction of water and nutrient minerals, support Storage Support, strength
	Phloem	Sieve tube elements Companion cells Phloem parenchyma cells Fibers (sclerenchyma cells)	Conduction of sugar in solution, support May control functioning of sieve tube elements, loading sugar into sieve tube elements Storage Support, strength
Dermal tissue system	Epidermis	Epidermal cells Guard cells Trichomes	Protective covering over surface of plant body Regulate stomata Variable functions
	Periderm	Cork cells Cork cambium cells Cork parenchyma cells	Protective covering over surface of plant body Meristematic (form new cells) Storage

TABLE 33-2   Cell Types in the Ground Tissue System

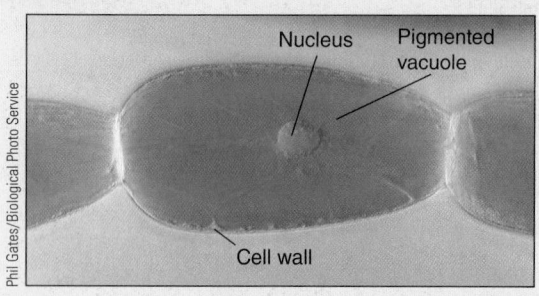

Nucleus
Pigmented vacuole
Cell wall
100 μm

Phil Gates/Biological Photo Service

Parenchyma cell

Description
Living, actively metabolizing; thin primary cell walls

Functions
Storage; secretion, and/or photosynthesis

Location and comments
Throughout the plant body; shown is an LM of a stamen hair of a spiderwort (*Tradescantia virginiana*) flower; note the large pigmented vacuole; the nucleus is not inside the vacuole but is lying on *top* of the vacuole

Chloroplasts
Cell wall
Vacuole
100 μm

Cengage

Parenchyma cell

Description
Living, actively metabolizing; thin primary cell walls

Functions
Storage; secretion; photosynthesis

Location and comments
Throughout the plant body; shown is an LM of leaf cells from an aquatic plant (*Elodea*); note the many chloroplasts in the thin layer of cytoplasm surrounding the large, transparent vacuole

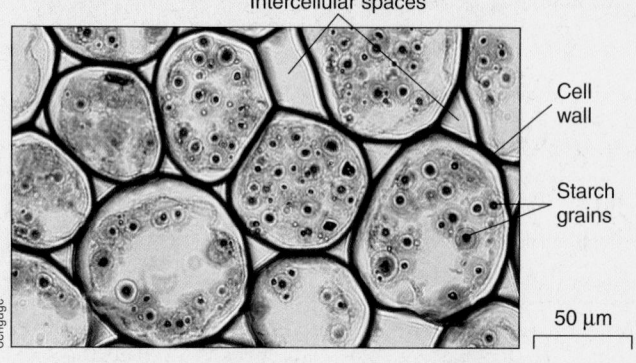

Intercellular spaces
Cell wall
Starch grains
50 μm

Cengage

Parenchyma cell

Description
Living, actively metabolizing; thin primary cell walls

Functions
Storage; secretion; photosynthesis

Location and comments
Throughout the plant body; shown is an LM of a cross section of part of a buttercup (*Ranunculus*) root; note the starch grains filling the cells

Primary cell walls are thickened in corners
50 μm

Ed Reschke/Peter Arnold, Inc.

Collenchyma cell

Description
Living; unevenly thickened primary cell walls

Function
Elastic support

Location and comments
Just under stem epidermis; shown is an LM of a cross section of an elderberry (*Sambucus*) stem; note the unevenly thickened cell walls that are especially thick in the corners, making the cell contents assume a rounded shape in cross section

(continued)

TABLE 33-2   Cell Types in the Ground Tissue System (continued)

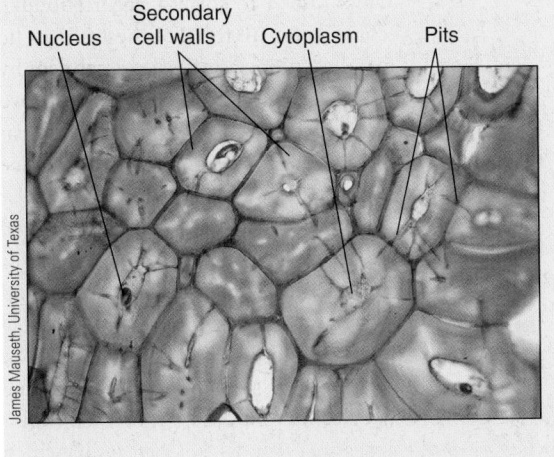

Nucleus · Secondary cell walls · Cytoplasm · Pits

James Mauseth, University of Texas

50 µm

Sclereid (sclerenchyma cell)

Description
May be living or dead at maturity; thick secondary cell walls; lacks secondary wall at pits

Functions
Strength; sclereid-rich tissue is hard and inflexible

Location and comments
Shells of walnuts and coconuts; pits of cherries and peaches; shown is an LM of living sclereids in a section through a cherry (*Prunus avium*) pit

Thick secondary cell walls · Lumen where protoplast was when these cells were alive

James Mauseth, University of Texas

50 µm

Fiber (sclerenchyma cell)

Description
Often dead at maturity; thick secondary cell walls; fewer pits than in sclereids

Functions
Support; provides strength

Location and comments
Throughout the plant body; common in stems and certain leaves; shown is an LM of a cross section through a clump of fibers from a century plant (*Agave*) leaf

Parenchyma cells perform several important functions, such as photosynthesis, storage, and secretion. Parenchyma cells that function in photosynthesis contain green chloroplasts, whereas nonphotosynthetic parenchyma cells lack chloroplasts and are often colorless. Materials stored in parenchyma cells include starch grains, oil droplets, water, and salts, which are sometimes visible as crystals. Resins, tannins, hormones, enzymes, and sugary nectar are examples of substances that may be secreted by parenchyma cells. The various functions of parenchyma require that parenchyma cells be alive and metabolically active.

Parenchyma cells have the ability to **differentiate** into other kinds of cells, particularly when a plant has been injured. If xylem (water-conducting) cells are severed, for example, adjacent parenchyma cells may divide and differentiate into new xylem cells within a few days. (Recall from Chapter 17 that it is possible to induce certain plant cells to become the equivalent of embryonic stem cells that can then differentiate into specialized cells.)

Collenchyma cells have unevenly thickened primary walls

Collenchyma tissue, a simple plant tissue composed of collenchyma cells, is an extremely flexible structural tissue that provides much of the support in soft, nonwoody plant organs (**FIG. 33-3b**).

Support is crucial for plants, in part because it lets them grow upward to compete with other plants for available sunlight in a plant-crowded area. Plants lack the bony skeletal system typical of many animals; instead, individual cells, including collenchyma cells, support the plant body.

Collenchyma cells, which are usually elongated, are alive at maturity. Their primary cell walls are unevenly thickened and are especially thick in the corners. Collenchyma is not found uniformly throughout the plant and often occurs as long strands near stem surfaces and along leaf veins. The "strings" in a celery stalk, for example, consist of collenchyma tissue.

Sclerenchyma cells have both primary walls and thick secondary walls

Another simple plant tissue specialized for structural support is **sclerenchyma** tissue, whose cells have both primary and secondary cell walls. The root of the word *sclerenchyma* is derived from the Greek word *sclero*, meaning "hard." The secondary cell walls of sclerenchyma cells become strong and hard because of extreme thickening. *Pits*, which are thin areas where secondary walls did not develop, allow an exchange of substances between adjacent living sclerenchyma cells. Mature sclerenchyma cells are unable to stretch

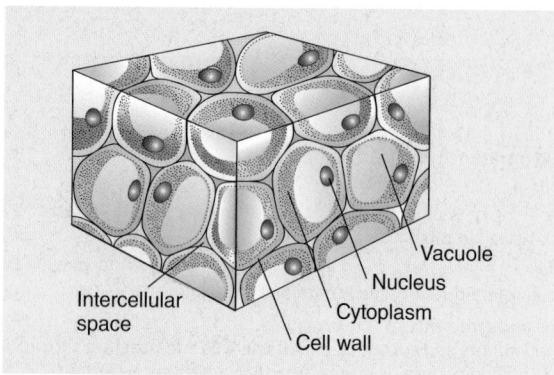

Intercellular space — Vacuole — Nucleus — Cytoplasm — Cell wall

(a) Parenchyma cells. Parenchyma cells vary in size and structure, depending on their various functions within the plant body.

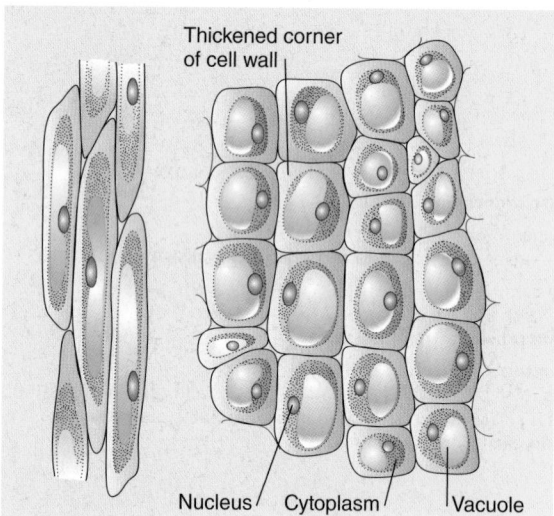

Thickened corner of cell wall

Nucleus / Cytoplasm / Vacuole

(b) Collenchyma cells in longitudinal section (*left*) and cross section. Note the elongated cells, evident in longitudinal section, and the unevenly thickened cell walls, evident in cross section.

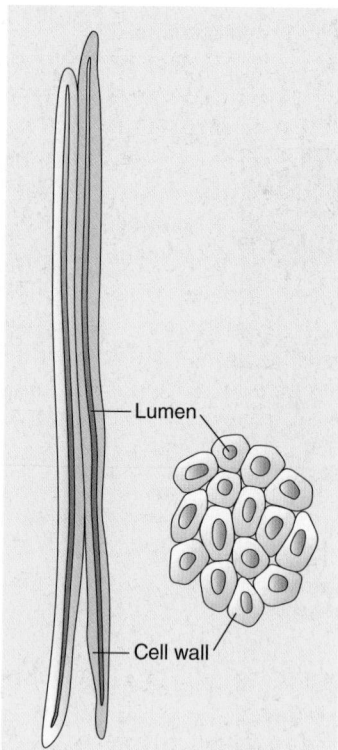

Lumen

Cell wall

(c) Sclerenchyma cells (fibers) in longitudinal section (*left*) and cross section. Mature fibers are often dead at functional maturity and therefore lack nuclei and cytoplasm; the lumen is the space formerly occupied by the living cell.

FIGURE 33-3 Cell types: parenchyma, collenchyma, and sclerenchyma

or elongate. At functional maturity, when sclerenchyma tissue is providing support for the plant body, its cells are often dead.

Sclerenchyma tissue may be located in several areas of the plant body. Two types of sclerenchyma cells are sclereids and fibers. **Sclereids** are cells of variable shape common in the shells of nuts and in the stones of fruits such as cherries and peaches. The slightly gritty texture of pears results from the presence of clusters of sclereids. **Fibers,** which are long, tapered cells that often occur in patches or clumps, are particularly abundant in the wood, inner bark, and leaf ribs (veins) of flowering plants (**FIG. 33-3c**).

Cells of the three simple tissues vary in their cell wall chemistry

Parenchyma, collenchyma, and sclerenchyma cells can be distinguished by the chemistry of their cell walls. Cell walls may contain cellulose, hemicelluloses, pectin, and lignin. **Cellulose,** the most abundant polymer in the world, accounts for about 40% to 60% of the dry weight of plant cell walls. As discussed in Chapter 3, cellulose is a **polysaccharide** composed of glucose units joined by

β-1,4 bonds. Each cellulose molecule consists of thousands of glucose subunits joined to form a flat, ribbonlike chain. From 40 to 70 of these chains lie parallel to one another and connect by hydrogen bonding to form a **cellulose microfibril,** a strong, tiny strand visible under the electron microscope (see Fig. 3-10a).

Cellulose microfibrils are cemented together by a matrix of hemicelluloses and pectins. **Hemicelluloses** are a group of polysaccharides that are more soluble than cellulose. Hemicelluloses vary in their chemical composition from one species to another. Some hemicelluloses are composed of *xyloglucan,* which consists of a backbone of β-1,4-glucose molecules to which side chains of *xylose,* a five-carbon sugar, are attached. Despite their name, the chemical structure of the hemicelluloses is significantly different from that of cellulose. **Pectin,** another cementing polysaccharide, is less variable in its monomer composition than are the hemicelluloses. Pectin monomer units are *α-galacturonic acid,* a six-carbon molecule that is a derivative of glucose.

An important component of secondary plant cell walls, particularly those of wood, is **lignin.** Composing as much as 35% of the dry weight of the secondary cell wall, lignin is a strengthening polymer made up of monomers derived from certain amino acids. Scientists have not yet determined the exact chemical structure of lignin because it is hard to remove from cellulose and other cell wall materials to which it is covalently bound.

Having discussed the four main components in plant cell walls, we can now generalize about the cell chemistry of parenchyma, collenchyma, and sclerenchyma cells. The thin primary cell walls of parenchyma cells contain predominantly cellulose, although they also contain hemicelluloses and pectin. Both parenchyma and collenchyma cells have primary cell walls, but their walls are chemically distinct because the thickened areas of collenchyma walls contain large quantities of pectin in addition to cellulose and hemicelluloses. The thick secondary walls of sclerenchyma cells are chemically different because they are rich in lignin, in addition to cellulose, hemicelluloses, and pectin.

The vascular tissue system consists of two complex tissues

The **vascular tissue system,** which is embedded in the ground tissue, transports needed materials throughout the plant via two complex tissues: xylem and phloem (**TABLE 33-3**). Both xylem and

TABLE 33-3 | Selected Cell Types in the Vascular Tissue System

John D. Cunningham/Visuals Unlimited

Tracheids

Pits

100 µm

Tracheid

Description
Dead at maturity; lacks secondary wall at pits

Functions
Conduction of water and nutrient minerals; support

Location and comments
Occurs in clumps in xylem throughout plant body; shown is an LM of a longitudinal section of tracheids from white pine (*Pinus strobus*) wood

James Mauseth, University of Texas

Fibers

Vessel element dotted with numerous pits

Perforation

Vessel element dotted with numerous pits

100 µm

Vessel element

Description
Dead at maturity; end walls have perforations; lacks secondary wall at pits

Functions
Conduction of water and nutrient minerals; support

Location and comments
Xylem throughout plant body; vessel elements are more efficient than tracheids in conduction; shown is an LM of a longitudinal section of two vessel elements from an unidentified woody eudicot

James Mauseth, University of Texas

Sieve tube element

Sieve plate

Sieve tube element

50 µm

Sieve tube element

Description
Living but lacks nucleus and other organelles at maturity; end walls are sieve plates

Function
Conduction of sugar in solution

Location and comments
Phloem throughout plant body; shown is an LM of a longitudinal section through a clump of sieve tube elements in a squash (*Cucurbita*) petiole (leaf stalk)

J. Robert Waaland/Biological Photo Service

Sieve tube elements

Companion cells

Sieve plate

Companion cell

Description
Living; has cytoplasmic connections with sieve tube element

Function
Assists in moving sugars into and out of sieve tube element

Location and comments
Phloem throughout plant body; shown is an LM of phloem from a squash (*Cucurbita*) petiole (leaf stalk) in cross section

50 µm

phloem are continuous throughout the plant body. (Chapter 35 discusses the mechanisms of transport in xylem and phloem.)

The conducting cells in xylem are tracheids and vessel elements

Xylem conducts water and dissolved minerals from the roots to the stems and leaves and provides structural support. In flowering plants, xylem is a complex tissue composed of four cell types: tracheids, vessel elements, parenchyma cells, and fibers. Two of the four cell types found in xylem, the **tracheids** and **vessel elements,** conduct water and dissolved minerals. Xylem also contains fibers that provide support, and parenchyma cells, known as *xylem parenchyma,* that perform storage functions.

Tracheids and vessel elements are highly specialized for conduction. As they develop, both types of cells undergo **apoptosis,** or programmed cell death. As a result, mature tracheids and vessel elements are dead and therefore hollow; only their cell walls remain. Tracheids, the chief water-conducting cells in gymnosperms (such as pine) and seedless vascular plants (such as ferns), are long, tapering cells located in patches or clumps (**FIG. 33-4a**). Water is conducted upward, from roots to shoots, passing from one tracheid into another through wide pits.

In addition to tracheids, flowering plants possess extremely efficient vessel elements (**FIG. 33-4b**). The cell diameters of vessel elements are usually greater than those of tracheids. Vessel elements are hollow, but unlike tracheids, the end walls have holes, known as *perforations,* or are absent. Vessel elements are stacked one on top of the other, and water is conducted readily from one vessel element into the next. A stack of vessel elements, called a **vessel,** resembles a miniature water pipe. Vessel elements also have pits in their side walls that permit the lateral transport (sideways movement) of water from one vessel to another.

Sieve tube elements are the conducting cells of phloem

Phloem conducts food materials, that is, carbohydrates formed in photosynthesis, throughout the plant and provides structural support. In flowering plants, phloem is a complex tissue composed of four cell types: sieve tube elements, companion cells, fibers, and phloem parenchyma cells (**FIGS. 33-4c** and **33-4d**). Fibers, which are usually extensive in the phloem of herbaceous plants, provide additional structural support for the plant body.

Food materials are conducted in solution—that is, dissolved in water—through the **sieve tube elements,** which are among the most specialized plant cells. Sieve tube elements are joined end to end to form long **sieve tubes.** The cells' end walls, called *sieve plates,* have a series of holes through which cytoplasm extends from one sieve tube element into the next. Sieve tube elements are living at maturity, but many of their organelles, including the nucleus, vacuole, mitochondria, and ribosomes, disintegrate or shrink as they mature.

Sieve tube elements are among the few eukaryotic cells that can function without nuclei. These cells typically live for less than a year. There are, however, notable exceptions. Certain palms have sieve tube elements that remain alive for approximately 100 years.

Adjacent to each sieve tube element is a **companion cell** that assists in the functioning of the sieve tube element. The compan-

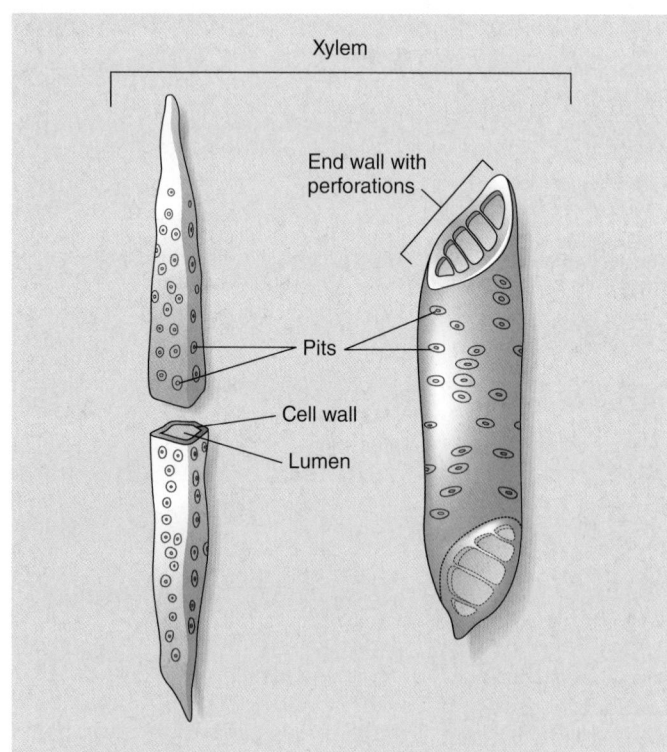

(a) Tracheid (xylem cell). The tracheid is opened to reveal the cell's appearance in cross section. At maturity, tracheids are usually dead.

(b) Vessel element (xylem cell). The end walls of vessel elements are perforated. Vessel elements are joined end to end, from roots to leaves and other shoot parts.

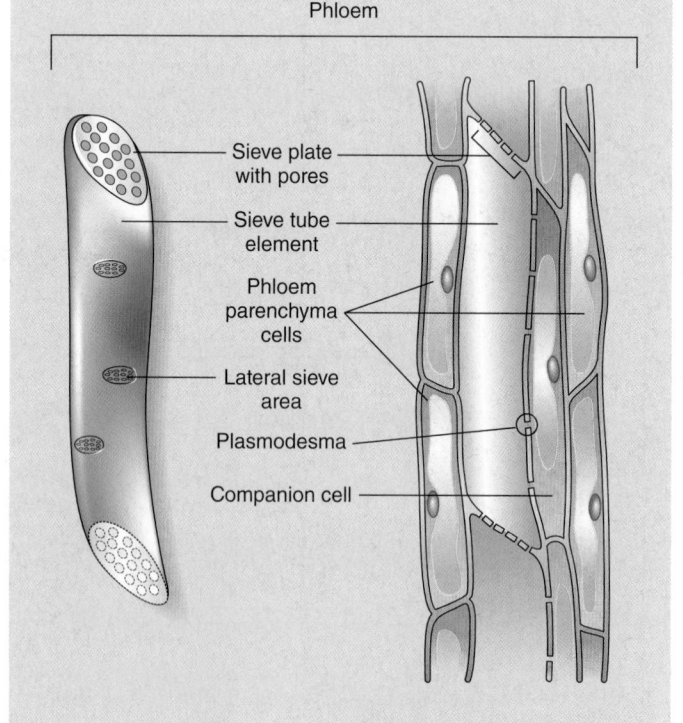

(c) Sieve tube element, showing the sieve plate. Sieve tube elements are joined end to end to form sieve tubes.

(d) Longitudinal section of phloem tissue. Sieve tube elements, companion cells, and phloem parenchyma cells. Fiber cells are not shown.

FIGURE 33-4 *Animated* Longitudinal views of cell types in xylem and phloem tissues ion cell is a living cell, complete with a nucleus. This nucleus is thought to direct the activities of both the companion cell and sieve tube element. Numerous **plasmodesmata**—cytoplasmic connections through which cytoplasm extends from one cell to another (see Chapter 5)—link a companion cell with its adjoining sieve tube element. The companion cells play an essential role in moving sugar into the sieve tube elements for transport to other parts of the plant.

The dermal tissue system consists of two complex tissues

The **dermal tissue system**—the epidermis and periderm—provides a protective covering over plant parts (**TABLE 33-4**). In herbaceous plants, the dermal tissue system is a single layer of cells called the epidermis. Woody plants initially produce an epidermis, but it splits apart as a result of the production of additional woody

TABLE 33-4	Selected Cell Types in the Dermal Tissue System

Epidermal cell

Description
Relatively unspecialized cell with thin primary wall; outer wall often thicker and covered by a noncellular waxy layer (cuticle)

Functions
Protective covering over surface of plant body; helps reduce water loss

Location and comments
Epidermis is usually one cell thick; shown is an LM of a cross section through epidermis of an ivy (*Hedera helix*) stem

Guard cell

Description
Chloroplast-containing cell that occurs in pairs; pair changes shape to open and close stomatal pore

Function
Opens and closes stomatal pore

Location and comments
Epidermis of stems and leaves; shown is an LM of the epidermis of a spiderwort (*Tradescantia virginiana*) leaf

Trichome

Description
Hair or other epidermal outgrowth; may be unicellular or multicellular; occurs in variety of sizes and shapes

Functions
Varied; absorption; secretion; excretion; protection; reduction of water loss

Location and comments
Epidermis; shown is an SEM of a nettle (*Solanum carolinense*) leaf, which has trichomes that break off inside the skin of animals and inject irritating substances that cause a stinging sensation

Cork cell

Description
Dead at maturity; cell walls impregnated with waterproof material (suberin)

Functions
Reduces water loss and prevents disease-causing organisms from penetrating

Location and comments
Produced in large numbers; cork often forms just under the epidermis; replaces epidermis in older stems and roots; shown is an LM of a cross section through periderm of a geranium (*Pelargonium*) stem

tissues inside the epidermis as the plant increases in girth. Periderm, which replaces the epidermis in the stems and roots of older woody plants, composes the outer bark.

Epidermis is the outermost layer of a herbaceous plant

The **epidermis** is a complex tissue composed primarily of relatively unspecialized living cells. Dispersed among these cells are more specialized guard cells and outgrowths called trichomes (discussed later). In most plants, the epidermis consists of a single layer of flattened cells (**FIG. 33-5**). Epidermal cells generally contain no chloroplasts and are therefore transparent, so light can penetrate the interior tissues of stems and leaves. In both stems and leaves, photosynthetic tissues lie *beneath* the epidermis.

An important requirement of the aerial parts (stems, leaves, flowers, and fruits) of a plant is the ability to control water loss. Epidermal cells of aerial parts secrete a waxy **cuticle** over the surface of their exterior walls; this waxy layer greatly restricts water loss from plant surfaces.

Although the cuticle is extremely efficient at preventing most water loss through epidermal cells, it also slows the diffusion of CO_2, needed for photosynthesis, from the atmosphere into the leaf or stem. The diffusion of CO_2 is facilitated by **stomata** (sing.,

stoma). Stomata are minute pores in the epidermis that are surrounded by two cells called **guard cells** (see Fig. 34-5). Many gases, including CO_2, oxygen, and water vapor, pass through the stomata by diffusion. Stomata are generally open during the day when photosynthesis is occurring, and the water loss that also takes place when stomata are open provides some evaporative cooling. At night, stomata usually close. In drought conditions, the need to conserve water overrides the need to cool the leaves and exchange gases. Thus, during a drought, the stomata close in the daytime. Stomata are discussed in greater detail in Chapter 34.

The epidermis also contains special outgrowths, or hairs, called **trichomes,** which occur in many sizes and shapes and have a variety of functions. Plants that tolerate salty environments such as the seashore often have specialized trichomes on their leaves to remove excess salt that accumulates in the plant. The presence of trichomes on the aerial parts of desert plants may increase the reflection of light off the plants, thereby cooling the internal tissues and decreasing water loss. Other trichomes have a protective function. For example, the trichomes on stinging nettle leaves and stems contain irritating substances that may discourage herbivorous animals from eating the plant. **Root hairs** are simple, unbranched trichomes that increase the surface area of the root epidermis (which comes into contact with the soil) for more effective water and mineral absorption.

Periderm replaces epidermis in woody plants

Periderm, a tissue that can be anywhere from several to many cell layers thick, forms under the epidermis to provide a new protective covering as the epidermis is destroyed. As a woody plant continues to increase in girth, its epidermis is sloughed off, exposing the periderm. Periderm forms the outer bark of older stems and roots. It is a complex tissue composed mainly of cork cells and cork parenchyma cells. **Cork cells** are dead at maturity, and their walls are heavily coated with a waterproof substance called *suberin,* which helps reduce water loss. **Cork parenchyma** cells function primarily in storage. Periderm is discussed further in Chapters 35 and 36.

Review

- What are some of the functions of roots? of shoots?
- What are the three tissue systems in plants? Describe the functions of each.
- How do parenchyma, collenchyma, and sclerenchyma tissues differ in cell structure and function?
- What are the functions of xylem and phloem? Describe the conducting cells that occur in each of these complex tissues.
- How are epidermis and periderm alike? How are they different?

FIGURE 33-5 Cell types: epidermal cells
Epidermal cells from three different plants. Note that regardless of the cell shape, epidermal cells fit tightly together.

Labels on figure: Cell wall, Cytoplasm, Vacuole, Nucleus

33.2 PLANT MERISTEMS

■ LEARNING OBJECTIVES

5   State how growth in plants differs from growth in animals.
6   Distinguish between primary and secondary growth.
7   Distinguish between apical meristems and lateral meristems.

One difference between plants and animals is the *location* of growth. When plants grow, their cells divide only in specific areas, called **meristems,** which are composed of cells whose primary function is to form new cells by mitotic division. (In contrast, when a young animal is growing, all parts of its body grow, although not necessarily at the same rate.) Meristematic cells, also known as *stem cells,* do not differentiate. Instead, they retain the ability to divide by mitosis, a trait that many differentiated cells lose. The persistence of mitotically active meristems means that plants, unlike most animals, can grow throughout their entire lifespan.

This ability of roots and stems to grow throughout a plant's life is known as **indeterminate growth.** In contrast, many leaves and flowers have **determinate growth;** that is, they stop growing after reaching a certain size. The size of leaves and flowers with determinate growth varies from species to species and from individual to individual, depending on the plant's genetic programming and on environmental conditions such as availability of sunlight, water, and essential minerals.

Two kinds of meristematic growth may occur in plants. **Primary growth** is an increase in stem and root length. All plants have primary growth, which produces the entire plant body in herbaceous plants and the young, soft shoots and roots in woody trees and shrubs. **Secondary growth** is an increase in the girth of a plant. For the most part, only gymnosperms and woody eudicots have secondary growth. (Woody eudicots include trees and shrubs such as oak, sycamore, ash, cherry, apple, beech, and maple.)

Tissues produced by secondary growth comprise the wood and bark, which make up most of the bulk of trees and shrubs. A few annuals—geranium and sunflower, for example—undergo limited secondary growth despite the fact that they lack obvious wood and bark tissues.

Primary growth takes place at apical meristems

Primary growth occurs as a result of the activity of **apical meristems,** areas located at the tips of roots and shoots, including within the buds of stems. **Buds** are dormant embryonic shoots that eventually develop into branches.

Primary growth is evident when a root tip is examined (**FIG. 33-6**). A protective layer of cells called a **root cap** covers the root tip. Directly behind the root cap is the root apical meristem, which consists of meristematic cells. Meristematic cells, which are cube shaped, remain small because they are continually dividing. (In meristems, as daughter cells begin to enlarge, one or both will divide again.)

Farther from the root tip, just behind the area of cell division, is an area of cell elongation where the cells have been displaced from the meristem. Here the cells are no longer dividing but instead are growing longer, pushing the root tip ahead of them, deeper into the soil. Some differentiation also begins to occur in the area of cell elongation, and immature tissues such as differentiating xylem and phloem become evident. The tissue systems continue to develop and differentiate into primary tissues (epidermis, xylem, phloem, and ground tissues) of the adult plant. Farther from the tip, behind the area of cell elongation, most cells have completely differentiated and are fully mature. Root hairs are evident in this area.

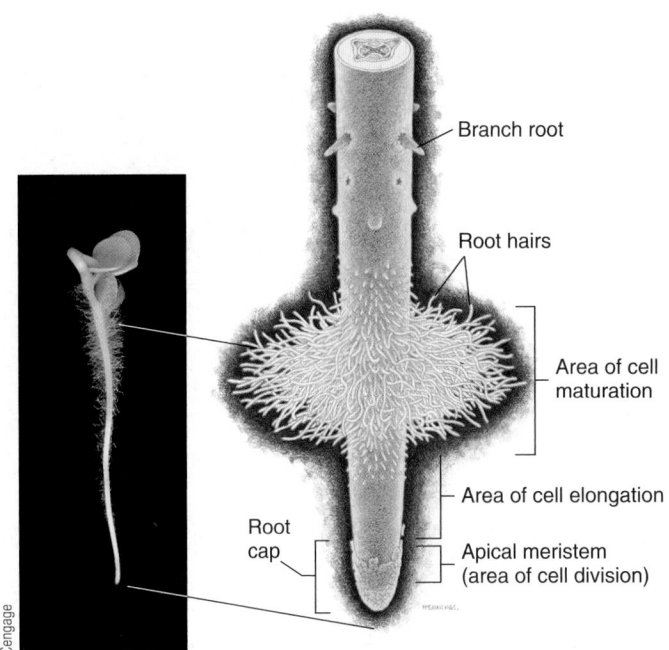

FIGURE 33-6 *Animated* A root tip

The root apical meristem (where cells divide and thus increase in number) is protected by a root cap. Farther from the tip is an area of cell elongation where cells enlarge and begin to differentiate. The area of cell maturation has fully mature, differentiated cells. Note the young root hairs in this area and on the root of a young radish (*Raphanus sativus*) seedling, which is approximately 5 cm (2 in) long (*left*).

A shoot apex (such as the terminal bud) is quite different in appearance from a root tip (**FIG. 33-7**). A dome of minute, regularly arranged meristematic cells—the shoot apical meristem—is located in each shoot apex. **Leaf primordia** (developing leaves) and **bud primordia** (developing buds) arise from the shoot apical meristem. The tiny leaf primordia cover and protect the shoot apical meristem. As the cells formed by the shoot apical meristem elongate, the shoot apical meristem is pushed upward. Subsequent cell divisions produce additional stem tissue and cause new leaf and bud primordia to appear. Farther from the stem tip, the immature cells differentiate into the three tissue systems of the mature plant body.

Secondary growth takes place at lateral meristems

Trees and shrubs undergo both primary and secondary growth. These plants increase in length by primary growth and increase in girth by secondary growth. The increase in girth, which occurs in areas that are no longer elongating, is due to cell divisions that take place in **lateral meristems,** areas extending along the entire length of the stems and roots except at the tips. Two lateral meristems, the vascular cambium and the cork cambium, are responsible for secondary growth, which is the formation of secondary tissues: secondary xylem, secondary phloem, and periderm (**FIG. 33-8**).

The **vascular cambium** is a layer of meristematic cells that forms a long, thin, continuous cylinder within the stem and root.

FIGURE 33-7 A shoot apex

LM of a longitudinal section through a shoot apex of *Coleus*, showing the shoot apical meristem, leaf primordia, and bud primordia.

It is located between the wood and bark of a woody plant. Division of cells of the vascular cambium adds more cells to the wood (secondary xylem) and inner bark (secondary phloem).

The **cork cambium,** located in the outer bark, is composed of a thin cylinder or irregular arrangement of meristematic cells. Cells of the cork cambium divide and form **cork cells** toward the outside and one or more underlying layers of **cork parenchyma** cells that function in storage. Collectively, cork cells, cork cambium, and cork parenchyma make up the periderm.

We are now ready to give a more precise definition of *bark.* **Bark,** the outermost covering over woody stems and roots, consists of all plant tissues located outside the vascular cambium.

Bark has two regions, a living inner bark composed of secondary phloem and a mostly dead outer bark composed of periderm. Chapters 35 and 36 present a more comprehensive discussion of secondary growth.

Review

- What is the role of plant meristems? Does animal growth involve meristems?
- What is primary growth? secondary growth?
- What are apical meristems? lateral meristems?

33.3 DEVELOPMENT OF FORM

◼ LEARNING OBJECTIVES

8 Distinguish between cell division and cell expansion, and describe the roles of the preprophase band and cellulose microfibrils.

9 Describe the relationship between cell determination and cell differentiation, and between pattern formation and morphogenesis.

10 Explain why the model organism *Arabidopsis* is so useful in the study of plant development.

Plants are growing, dynamic organisms. **Development** in plants encompasses all the changes that take place during the entire life of an individual. Of particular interest in developmental biology is the process by which cells specialize and organize into a complex organism. For example, how does a microscopic, unicellular zygote give rise to a multicellular embryo in a seed? (See the stages of embryonic development in a typical eudicot in Figure 37-8.) How does the embryo in the seed give rise to the leaves, stems, and roots of a *juvenile* plant, and what mechanisms underlie the transition from a nonreproductive juvenile plant to an *adult plant* capable of flowering (**FIG. 33-9**)?

We now examine several aspects of plant development that affect form in plants. Flowering is discussed elsewhere in this book (see the ABC model in Chapter 17).

FIGURE 33-8 Secondary growth

The vascular cambium, a thin layer of cells sandwiched between the wood and bark, produces the secondary vascular tissues: the wood, which is secondary xylem, and the inner bark, which is secondary phloem. The cork cambium produces the periderm, the outer bark tissue that replaces the epidermis in a plant with secondary growth.

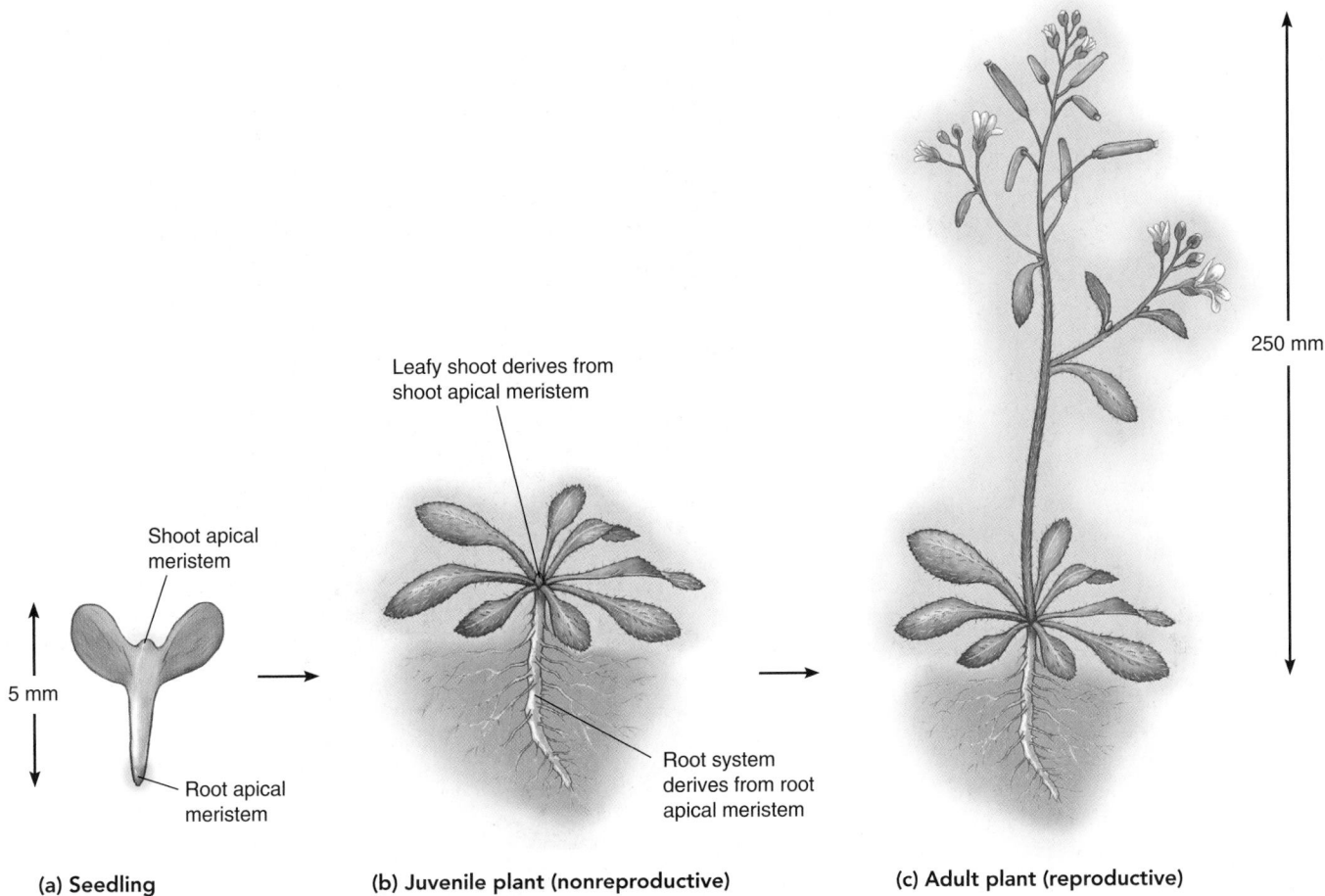

FIGURE 33-9 Growth of an *Arabidopsis* seedling into an adult plant

Almost all of the differentiated tissues formed after a seed is germinated (often referred to as postembryonic growth) come from a small number of stem cells in the root and shoot apical meristems.

The plane and symmetry of cell division affect plant form

You have seen that plant growth is localized into meristems for cell division. At these sites, the cells undergo cell division in an orderly manner. In the onion root apical meristem, for example, files of cells can be traced back to the meristem region (**FIG. 33-10**). These cells divided in the same plane to produce each file of cells. Cell divisions in one plane, two planes, or more help to establish the tissue patterns that will be produced during development.

How is the plane of cell division for a particular meristematic cell determined? In plant cells, a dense array of microtubules forms a **preprophase band** just inside of the plasma membrane, encircling the nucleus much like a belt. (Chapter 4 contains a discussion of the dynamic nature of microtubules.) The preprophase band appears just prior to mitosis and determines the plane in which the cell will divide (**FIG. 33-11**). The preprophase band, which is located where the cell plate will form following mitosis and cytokinesis, also helps to orient the mitotic spindle. The preprophase band is a plant characteristic; in animal cells, the orientation of the spindle determines the plane in which cells divide, and there is no preprophase band.

The orientation of cellulose microfibrils affects the direction of cell expansion

In plants, growth occurs by both an increase in the number of cells and an increase in cell size. Cell division and cell expansion (also called *elongation*) are governed by a genetic program that interacts with environmental signals from both the external and internal environments.

In growth, a newly formed plant cell absorbs water into its vacuole by osmosis. The water increases the cell's **turgor pressure,** hydrostatic pressure that develops within a walled cell and presses outward against the plasma membrane. Turgor pressure provides a force that exerts pressure on the cell wall and causes it to expand. In an onion root cell, the vacuole increases in size by some 30 to 150 times during elongation.

In growing tissue, the arrangement of cellulose microfibrils in the wall prevents the cell from expanding equally in all directions

3 Cells form a single file

2 Two cells become three

Cell division
in the same
plane as before

1 One cell becomes two

Plane of
cell division

Maximum rate
of cell division

Meristematic
zone

Root cap

© Visuals Unlimited/Corbis

200 μm

(a) Cells that divide in the same plane form a row, or file, of cells.

(b) A single file of cells in the onion root tip is labeled. If you look closely, you can see many other files.

FIGURE 33-10 The plane of cell division and the onion root tip
The root apical meristem maintains postembryonic root growth.

due to turgor pressure. When the microfibrils in the cell wall are oriented in the same direction, the wall expands perpendicularly to them (**FIG. 33-12**).

Cell differentiation depends in part on a cell's location

By themselves cell division and cell expansion would produce only a formless heap of similar cells. The development of plant form is the result of a balanced combination of several fundamental processes that go beyond cell division and cell expansion: cell differentiation and cell determination, and pattern formation and morphogenesis.

As growth proceeds, cell division gives rise to increasing numbers of cells, which serve as the building blocks of development. At various times certain cells become biochemically and structurally specialized to carry out specific functions through a process known as **cell differentiation.** Generally, a differentiated animal cell is irreversibly committed to its fate, but that is not the case with plants. As discussed earlier in the chapter, parenchyma cells can differentiate into other kinds of cells, for example, when the plant body is injured.

Cell differentiation occurs through **cell determination,** a series of molecular events in which the activities of certain genes are altered in ways that cause a cell to progressively commit to a particular differentiation pathway. As cell determination proceeds, a

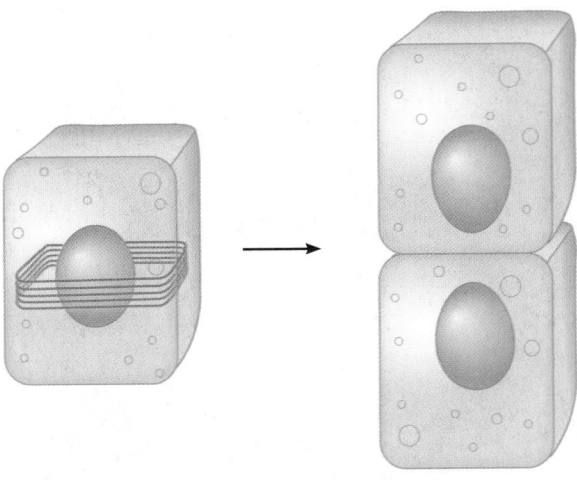

The preprophase band encircles the nucleus and indicates the plane of an upcoming cell division.

FIGURE 33-11 Preprophase band

FIGURE 33-12 *Animated* Direction of cell expansion

Following cell division, cellulose microtubules are deposited into new cell walls in an orderly fashion that permits cell expansion. The orientation of the cellulose microfibrils determines the direction of cell expansion. Note that most of the cellulose microfilbrils are oriented transversely in this figure, which results in longitudinal cell expansion.

young cell's fate becomes more and more limited, restricting its development to a limited set of tissue types.

During cell differentiation, a cell's physical appearance may or may not change significantly. Nevertheless, when cell determination is complete, a cell becomes structurally and functionally recognizable—as an epidermal cell, for example—and its pattern of gene activity differs from that of other cell types. Thus, differentiated cells of the plant body have **differential gene expression**—that is, different genes are active in different cells at the same time. Differential gene expression is responsible for variations in chemistry, behavior, and structure among cells.

Tissue cultures involve differential gene expression

Cells can be isolated from certain plants and grown in a chemically defined, sterile nutrient medium. In initial experiments with such cultures, plant cells could be kept alive, but they did not divide. Researchers later discovered that adding certain natural materials, such as the liquid endosperm of coconut, also known as coconut milk, induced cells to divide in culture. By the late 1950s, plant cells from a variety of sources could be cultured successfully, dividing to produce a mass of disorganized, relatively undifferentiated cells, or **callus.**

In 1958, F. C. Steward, a plant physiologist at Cornell University, succeeded in generating an entire carrot plant from a single callus cell derived from a carrot root (see Fig. 17-2). This demonstrated that each plant cell contains a genetic blueprint for all features of an entire organism. His work also showed that an entire plant can be grown from a single cell, provided differential gene expression occurs so that the proper genes are expressed at the appropriate times.

Since Steward's pioneering work, biologists have successfully cultured many plants by using a variety of cell sources. Plants have been regenerated from different tissues, organ explants (excised organs or parts such as root apical meristems), and single cells.

Cell and tissue culture techniques help answer many fundamental questions involving growth and development in plants. These techniques also have great practical potential. Using tissue culture, researchers can regenerate many genetically identical plants from the cells of a single, genetically superior plant. Many kinds of plants—from orchids and African violets to coastal redwoods—have been cultured in this way.

Morphogenesis occurs through pattern formation

Cell differentiation by itself does not explain overall plant form. The differentiated cells must become progressively organized, shaping the intricate pattern of tissues and organs that characterizes a multicellular plant. This development of form, in which differentiated cells in specific locations become spatially organized into recognizable structures, is known as **morphogenesis.**

Morphogenesis proceeds through the process of **pattern formation,** a series of steps requiring signaling between cells, changes in the shapes and metabolism of certain cells, and precise cell interactions. Pattern formation organizes cells into three-dimensional structures (**FIG. 33-13**). Depending on their location, cells are exposed to different concentrations of signaling molecules that specify **positional information**—that is, where the cell is located relative to the body's axes. This information affects cell differentiation and tissue formation. Thus, *where* a given cell is located often determines *what* it will become when it matures.

Arabidopsis mutants provide crucial insights into plant development

Until the late 1970s, biologists knew little about how genes interact to control development. However, rapid progress in molecular biology led scientists to search for developmental mutants and to

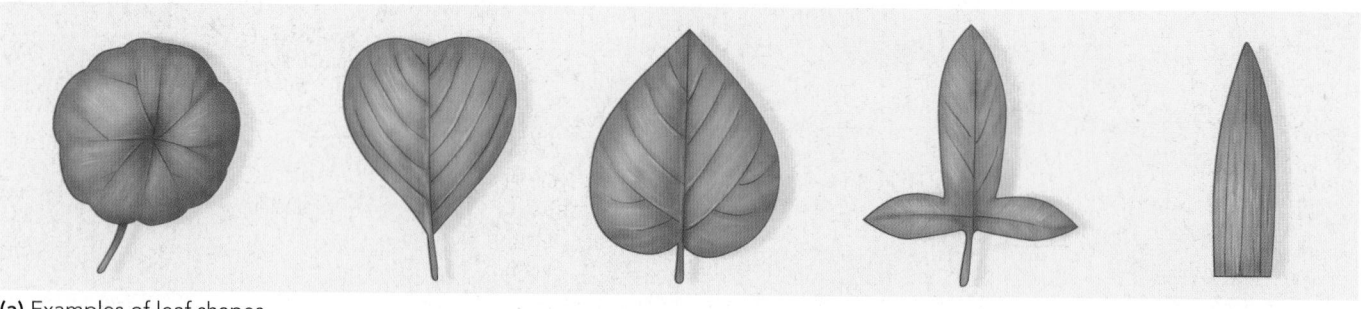

(a) Examples of leaf shapes.

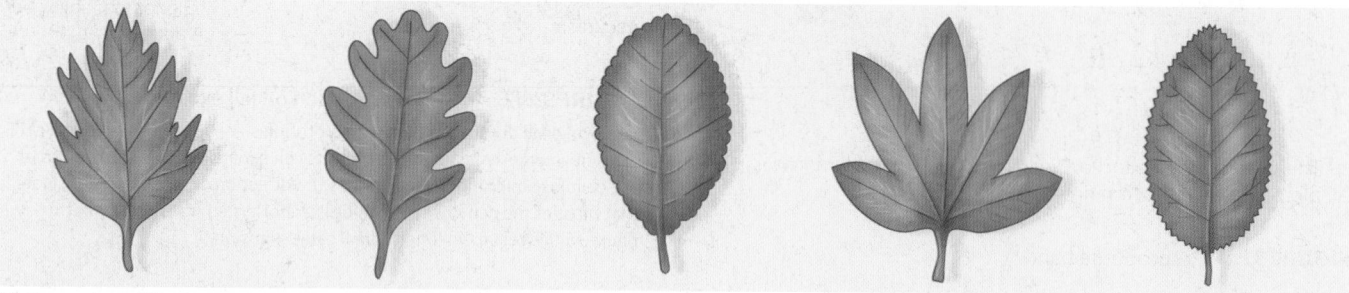

(b) Examples of leaf margins.

FIGURE 33-13 Leaf variation and pattern formation

Leaves are quite variable in form—there are dozens of different leaf shapes and margins. Leaves on juvenile plants are often shaped differently than those on adult plants, and some adult plants have several leaf shapes on the same individual. Pattern formation, which is under genetic control, is largely responsible for leaf variation. (Also see Figure 34-2 for more examples of variation in leaves.)

apply sophisticated techniques to study them. (A *mutant* is an individual with an abnormal phenotype caused by a gene mutation.) Biologists are now studying how genes are activated, inactivated, and modified to control development. Eventually, scientists expect to reach a major goal of systems biology—understanding how a single cell (a fertilized egg) develops into a multicellular plant.

You may recall from Chapter 17 that mouse-ear cress (*Arabidopsis thaliana*) is the organism most widely used to study the genetic control of development in plants. When biologists insert cloned foreign genes into *Arabidopsis* cells, the genes integrate into the chromosomes and are expressed. The researchers then induce these transformed cells to differentiate into transgenic plants.

Botanists use chemical mutagens to produce mutant strains and have isolated many developmental mutants of *Arabidopsis*. Consider the *monopteros* (*mp*) gene, which codes for a transcription factor affecting apical-basal pattern formation and the development of vascular tissues. Mutant *mp* seedlings lack basal structures, including a primary root (**FIG. 33-14**). Such mutant phenotypes have helped scientists identify the genes essential for normal development.

Arabidopsis has also had its relatively small genome—about 26,700 genes—sequenced. The success of the *Arabidopsis* sequencing project led to an international initiative by plant biologists to understand the functions of all the genes in the *Arabidopsis* genome (**TABLE 33-5**). This functional genomic information will lead to a far deeper understanding of plant development and evolutionary history.

T. Berleth / G. Jürgens

FIGURE 33-14 *Monopteros* mutation in *Arabidopsis* seedling

The *monopteros* gene affects development of the root system. The wild type seedling (*left*) has a normal *monopteros* gene, whereas the mutant (*right*) lacks basal structures.

Review

- Which process typically occurs first, cell differentiation or cell expansion?
- What are some kinds of events that contribute to pattern formation?
- How does pattern formation lead to morphogenesis?
- Why is *Arabidopsis* such a useful model organism for plant development?

TABLE 33-5	Known Gene Functions in the *Arabidopsis* Genome

Function	Percent of Genome
DNA/RNA metabolism	1
Signal transduction	2
Development	2
Energy metabolism	3
Cell division	3
Transport	4
Transcription	4
Response to environment	4
Protein metabolism	7
Other biological processes	11
Other cellular processes	17
Other metabolic functions	18
Unknown functions	24

Source: The Arabidopsis Information Resource, 2007.

© Nigel Cattlin/Alamy

■ SUMMARY: FOCUS ON LEARNING OBJECTIVES

33.1 *(page 709)*

1 Discuss the functions of various parts of the vascular plant body, including the nutrient- and water-absorbing root system and the photosynthesizing shoot system.

- The vascular plant body typically consists of a root system and a shoot system. The **root system** is generally underground and obtains water and dissolved minerals for the plant. Roots also anchor the plant firmly in place.

- The **shoot system** is generally aerial and obtains sunlight and exchanges gases such as CO_2, oxygen, and water vapor. The shoot system consists of a vertical stem that bears leaves and reproductive structures. **Buds,** undeveloped embryonic shoots, develop on stems.

CENGAGENOW™ Learn more about the plant body by clicking on the figure in CengageNOW.

2 Describe the structure and functions of the ground tissue system (parenchyma tissue, collenchyma tissue, and sclerenchyma tissue).

- The **ground tissue system** consists of three tissues with a variety of functions. **Parenchyma** tissue is composed of living parenchyma cells that have thin **primary cell walls.** Functions of parenchyma tissue include photosynthesis, storage, and secretion.

- **Collenchyma** tissue consists of collenchyma cells with unevenly thickened primary cell walls. This tissue provides flexible structural support.

- **Sclerenchyma** tissue is composed of sclerenchyma cells—**sclereids** or **fibers**—that have both primary cell walls and **secondary cell walls.** Sclerenchyma cells are often dead at maturity but provide structural support.

  CENGAGENOW™ Learn more about parenchyma, collenchyma, and sclerenchyma cells by clicking on the figure in CengageNOW.

3 Describe the structure and functions of the vascular tissue system (xylem and phloem).

- The **vascular tissue system** conducts materials throughout the plant body and provides strength and support.

- **Xylem** is a complex tissue that conducts water and dissolved minerals. The actual conducting cells of xylem are **tracheids** and **vessel elements.**

- **Phloem** is a complex tissue that conducts sugar in solution. **Sieve tube elements** are the conducting cells of phloem; they are assisted by **companion cells.**

  CENGAGENOW™ Learn more about xylem and phloem by clicking on the figure in CengageNOW.

4 Describe the structure and functions of the dermal tissue system (epidermis and periderm).

- The **dermal tissue system** is the outer protective covering of the plant body.

- The **epidermis** is a complex tissue that covers the herbaceous plant body. The epidermis that covers aerial parts secretes a waxy **cuticle** that reduces water loss. **Stomata** permit gas exchange between the interior of the shoot system and the surrounding atmosphere. **Trichomes** are outgrowths, or hairs, that occur in many sizes and shapes and have a variety of functions.
- The **periderm** is a complex tissue that covers the plant body in woody plants.

33.2 *(page 718)*

5 State how growth in plants differs from growth in animals.
- Growth in plants, unlike that in animals, is localized in specific regions called **meristems.** Meristems are composed of cells whose primary function is to form new cells by mitotic division.

6 Distinguish between primary and secondary growth.
- **Primary growth** is an increase in stem or root length. Primary growth occurs in all plants.

  CENGAGENOW™   See root and shoot development by clicking on the figures in CengageNOW.

- **Secondary growth** is an increase in stem or root girth (thickness). Secondary growth typically occurs in long cylinders of meristematic cells throughout the length of older stems and roots.

  CENGAGENOW™   Learn more about secondary growth by clicking on the figures in CengageNOW.

7 Distinguish between apical meristems and lateral meristems.
- Primary growth results from the activity of **apical meristems** that are localized at the tips of roots and shoots and within the buds of stems.
- The two **lateral meristems** responsible for secondary growth are the **vascular cambium** and the **cork cambium.**

33.3 *(page 720)*

8 Distinguish between cell division and cell expansion, and describe the roles of the preprophase band and cellulose microfibrils.

- Growth occurs by both cell division (an increase in the number of cells) and cell expansion (an increase in cell size).
- In plant cells, a dense array of microtubules forms a **preprophase band** just inside of the plasma membrane. The preprophase band appears just prior to mitosis and determines the plane in which the cell will divide.
- Absorption of water into a cell's vacuole increases the **turgor pressure,** which exerts pressure on the cell wall. The arrangement of cellulose microfibrils in the wall prevents the wall from expanding equally in all directions. When microfibrils are oriented the same way, the wall expands perpendicular to the microfibrillar orientation.

9 Describe the relationship between cell determination and cell differentiation, and between pattern formation and morphogenesis.
- In **cell differentiation,** cells become biochemically and structurally specialized to carry out specific functions. Cell differentiation occurs through **cell determination,** a series of molecular events in which the activities of certain genes are altered in ways that cause a cell to progressively commit to a particular differentiation pathway.
- The development of form, in which differentiated cells in specific locations become spatially organized into recognizable structures, is known as **morphogenesis.** Morphogenesis proceeds through the process of **pattern formation,** a series of steps requiring signaling between cells, changes in the shapes and metabolism of certain cells, and precise cell interactions.

10 Explain why the model organism *Arabidopsis* is so useful in the study of plant development.
- Botanists have isolated many developmental mutants of *Arabidopsis.* Such mutant phenotypes have helped scientists identify genes essential for normal development. The genome of *Arabidopsis* has been sequenced, and plant biologists are currently determining the functions of all of this plant's genes.

TEST YOUR UNDERSTANDING

1. Most of the plant body consists of the _____ tissue system. (a) ground (b) vascular (c) periderm (d) dermal (e) cortex

2. The cell walls of parenchyma cells (a) contain large quantities of pectin in the thickened corners (b) are rich in lignin but do not contain hemicelluloses and pectin (c) are predominantly cellulose, although they also contain hemicelluloses and pectin (d) contain cellulose, hemicelluloses, and lignin in approximately equal amounts (e) contain hemicelluloses, pectin, and lignin but no cellulose

3. Which tissue system provides a covering for the plant body? (a) ground (b) vascular (c) periderm (d) dermal (e) cortex

4. The two simple tissues that are specialized for support are (a) parenchyma and collenchyma (b) collenchyma and sclerenchyma (c) sclerenchyma and parenchyma (d) parenchyma and xylem (e) xylem and phloem

5. Sclereids and fibers are examples of which plant tissue? (a) parenchyma (b) collenchyma (c) sclerenchyma (d) xylem (e) epidermis

6. Which of the following statements about the vascular tissue system is *not* true? (a) xylem and phloem are continuous throughout the plant body (b) xylem not only conducts water and dissolved minerals but also provides support (c) four cell types occur in phloem: sieve tube elements, companion cells, tracheids, and vessel elements (d) sieve tube elements lack nuclei (e) vessel elements are hollow, and their end walls have perforations or are entirely dissolved away

7. Minute pores known as _____ dot the surface of the epidermis of leaves and stems; each pore is bordered by two _____. (a) stomata; guard cells (b) stomata; fibers (c) sieve tube elements; companion cells (d) sclereids; guard cells (e) cuticle; guard cells

8. Primary growth, an increase in the length of a plant, occurs at the (a) cork cambium (b) apical meristem (c) vascular cambium (d) lateral meristem (e) periderm

9. The preprophase band (a) appears just prior to mitosis in both plant and animal cells (b) determines the plane in which the cell will divide (c) attaches to cellulose microfibrils in the cell wall (d) is an essential part of pattern formation in plants (e) increases a cell's turgor pressure

10. Cell differentiation occurs through _____, whereas morphogenesis involves _____. (a) pattern formation; cell determination (b) cell division; cell expansion (c) cell expansion; pattern formation (d) cell determination; cell division (e) cell determination; pattern formation

11. The *monopteros* mutant (a) lacks a primary root (b) develops normally until the plant becomes reproductive (c) has abnormal leaf morphogenesis (d) was discovered in rice after its genome was sequenced (e) is one of only two developmental mutants known in *Arabidopsis*.

12. Label the three tissue systems in the plant body.

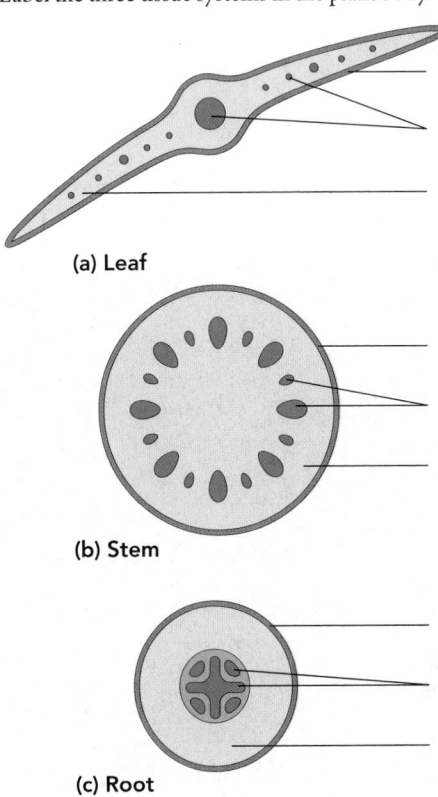

(a) Leaf

(b) Stem

(c) Root

CRITICAL THINKING

1. Grasses have a special meristem situated at the base of the leaves. Relate this information to what you know about the growth of grass after you mow the lawn.

2. A couple carved a heart with their initials into a tree trunk 4 ft above ground level; the tree was 25 ft tall at the time. Twenty years later the tree was 50 ft tall. How far above the ground were the initials? Explain your answer.

3. Sclerenchyma in plants is the functional equivalent of bone in humans (both sclerenchyma and bone provide support). However, sclerenchyma is dead, whereas bone is living tissue. What are some of the advantages of a plant having dead support cells? Can you think of any disadvantages? Explain your answer.

4. **EVOLUTION LINK.** Flowering plants have both tracheids and vessel elements in their xylem. Conifers, which evolved earlier than flowering plants, have tracheids only. Do these differences in xylem structure help explain the difference in the success of these two plant groups? Explain your answer.

5. Plant biologists are currently working to identify those *Arabidopsis* genes with unknown functions (see Table 33-5). If you were assigned to determine the function of a particular gene, how might you approach this task?

6. **SCIENCE, TECHNOLOGY, AND SOCIETY.** Why is knowledge gained from sequencing the *Arabidopsis* genome important even though *Arabidopsis* has no commercial value?

 Additional questions are available in CengageNOW at www.cengage.com/login.

34 Leaf Structure and Function

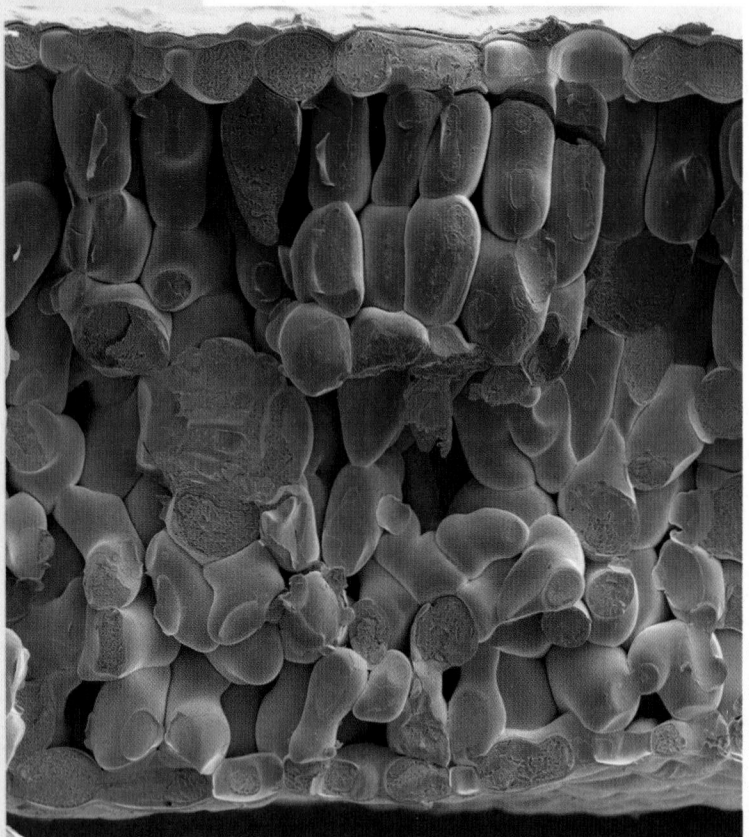

Colorized SEM of the interior of a spinach leaf. The loose arrangement of internal cells in spinach (*Spinacia oleracea*) optimizes the diffusion of necessary raw materials such as carbon dioxide and water into photosynthetic cells.

Andrew Syred/Science Photo Library

KEY CONCEPTS

34.1 Leaf structure reflects its primary function of photosynthesis.

34.2 Opening and closing of stomata affect carbon dioxide availability in the daily cycle of photosynthesis.

34.3 Transpiration, the loss of water vapor from leaf surfaces, keeps leaves from getting overheated and promotes water transport in the plant. Guttation is the exudation of liquid water from leaf margins.

34.4 Leaf abscission is the seasonal removal of deciduous leaves.

34.5 Some leaves are modified for special functions in addition to photosynthesis and transpiration.

Plants allocate many resources into the production of leaves that are often short-lived. Each year, a large maple tree, for example, may produce 47 m² (500 ft²) of leaves, which may weigh more than 113 kg (250 lb). The metabolic cost of producing so many leaves is high, but necessary. Simply put, leaves are essential to the tree's survival, so plants must invest in their production.

In most vascular plants, leaves are the primary organs to effectively collect solar energy and convert it into chemical energy. That is, leaves gather the sunlight necessary for **photosynthesis,** the biological process that converts radiant energy into the chemical energy of carbohydrate molecules. Plants use these molecules as starting materials to synthesize all other organic compounds and as fuel to provide energy for metabolism. During a single summer, the leaves of a maple tree will fix about 454 kg (1000 lb) of carbon dioxide (CO_2) into organic compounds.

The structure of a leaf is superbly adapted for its primary function of photosynthesis. Most leaves are thin and flat, a shape that allows optimal absorption of light energy and the efficient internal diffusion of gases such as CO_2 and O_2. As a result of their ordered arrangement on the stem, leaves efficiently catch the sun's rays with a minimum of "interference" from neighboring leaves. The leaves form an intricate green mosaic, bathed in sunlight and atmospheric gases.

To control water loss, a thin, transparent layer of wax covers the leaf surface. Such structural adaptations are compromises between competing needs, and some features that optimize photosynthesis promote water loss. For example, plants have minute pores that allow gas exchange for photosynthesis, but these openings also let water vapor escape into the atmosphere. Thus, leaf structure represents a trade-off between photosynthesis and water conservation.

In this chapter we examine leaf form and function. Leaf form is highly variable, and thousands of different leaf shapes have evolved over millions of years. Despite this diversity, most leaves "work" in the same way, and their internal structures (see photograph) support this similarity in function.

34.1 LEAF FORM AND STRUCTURE

◼ LEARNING OBJECTIVES

1. Discuss variation in leaf form, including simple versus compound leaves, leaf arrangement on the stem, and venation patterns.
2. Describe the major tissues of the leaf (epidermis, photosynthetic ground tissue, xylem, and phloem) and label them on a diagram of a leaf cross section.
3. Compare leaf anatomy in eudicots and monocots.
4. Relate leaf structure to its function of photosynthesis.

Foliage leaves are the most variable of plant organs, so much so that plant biologists have developed specific terminology to describe their shapes, margins (edges), vein patterns, and the way they attach to stems. Because each leaf is characteristic of the species on which it grows, many plants can be identified by their leaves alone. Leaves may be round, needlelike, scalelike, cylindrical, heart-shaped, fan-shaped, or thin and narrow. They vary in size from those of the raffia palm (*Raphia ruffia*), whose leaves often grow more than 20 m (65 ft) long, to those of water-meal (*Wolffia*), whose leaves are so small that 16 of them laid end to end measure only 2.5 cm (1 in).

The broad, flat portion of a leaf is the **blade;** the stalk that attaches the blade to the stem is the **petiole.** Some leaves also have **stipules,** which are leaflike outgrowths usually present in pairs at the base of the petiole (**FIG. 34-1**). Some leaves do not have petioles (that is, the blades are attached directly to the stem) or stipules; leaves without a petiole are said to be **sessile.**

Leaves may be *simple* (having a single blade) or *compound* (having a blade divided into two or more leaflets) (**FIG. 34-2a**). Sometimes it is difficult to tell whether a plant has formed one compound leaf or a small stem bearing several simple leaves. One easy way to determine if a plant has simple or compound leaves is to look for axillary buds, so-called because each develops in a leaf *axil* (the angle between the stem and petiole). Axillary buds form at the base of a leaf, whether it is simple or compound. However, axillary buds never develop at the base of leaflets. Also, the leaflets

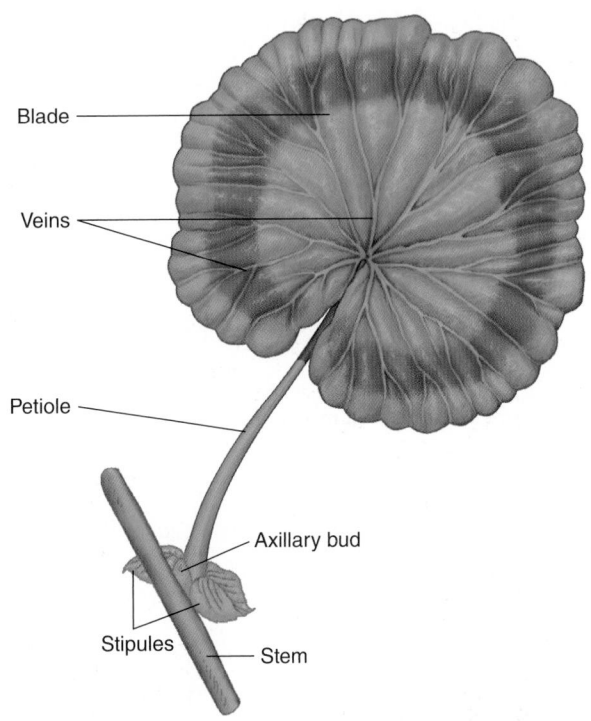

FIGURE 34-1 Parts of a leaf

A geranium leaf consists of a blade, a petiole, and two stipules at the base of the leaf. Note the axillary bud in the leaf axil.

of a compound leaf lie in a single plane (you can lay a compound leaf flat on a table), whereas simple leaves usually are not arranged in one plane on a stem.

Leaves are arranged on a stem in one of three possible ways (**FIG. 34-2b**). Plants such as beeches and walnuts have an *alternate leaf arrangement,* with one leaf at each **node,** the area of the stem where one or more leaves are attached. In an *opposite leaf arrangement,* as occurs in maples and ashes, two leaves grow at each node. In a *whorled leaf arrangement,* as in catalpa trees, three or more leaves grow at each node.

Leaf blades may possess *parallel venation,* in which the primary **veins**—strands of vascular tissue—run approximately parallel to one another (generally characteristic of monocots), or *netted venation,* in which veins are branched in such a way that they resemble a net (generally characteristic of eudicots; **FIG. 34-2c**).[1] Netted veins can be *pinnately netted,* with major veins branching off in succession along the entire length of the **midvein** (main or central vein of a leaf), or *palmately netted,* with several major veins radiating out from one point.

Plant scientists use sophisticated molecular techniques to study the genetic basis of various aspects of plant growth and development, including leaf form. Many of the genes under study code for transcription factors. As discussed in Chapter 14, *transcription factors* are DNA-binding proteins that regulate the synthesis of

---

[1]Recall that flowering plants, the focus of this chapter, are divided into two main groups, informally called *eudicots* and *monocots* (see Chapter 28). Examples of eudicots include beans, petunias, oaks, cherry trees, roses, and snapdragons; monocots include corn, lilies, grasses, palms, tulips, orchids, and bananas.

(a) Leaf form: simple and compound.

Simple — California white oak (*Quercus lobata*)

Pinnately compound — White ash (*Fraxinus americana*)

Palmately compound — Ohio buckeye (*Aesculus glabra*)

(b) Leaf arrangement on a stem.

Alternate — American beech (*Fagus grandifolia*)

Opposite — Sugar maple (*Acer saccharum*)

Whorled — Southern catalpa (*Catalpa bignonioides*)

(c) Venation patterns.

Parallel — Bermuda grass (*Cynodon dactylon*)

Pinnately netted — Black willow (*Salix nigra*)

Palmately netted — Sweetgum (*Liquidambar styraciflua*)

FIGURE 34-2 Leaf morphology

All leaves shown are woody eudicot trees from North America, except Bermuda grass, which is a herbaceous monocot native to Europe and Asia.

RNA from a DNA template. An exciting example of this type of research was recently published in the journal *Science* (**FIG. 34-3**). Eventually, research like this will help plant biologists to understand the roles of all genes involved in plant development—an important goal of systems biology.

Leaf structure is adapted for maximum light absorption

The leaf is a complex organ composed of several tissues organized to optimize photosynthesis (**FIG. 34-4**). The leaf blade has upper and lower surfaces, each consisting of a layer of epidermis. The **upper epidermis** covers the upper surface, and the **lower epidermis** covers the lower surface. Most cells in these layers lack chloroplasts and are relatively transparent. One interesting feature of leaf epidermal cells is that the cell wall facing toward the outside environment is somewhat thicker than the cell wall facing inward. This extra thickness may provide the plant with additional protection against injury or water loss.

Because leaves have such a large surface area exposed to the atmosphere, water loss by evaporation from the leaf's surface is unavoidable. However, epidermal cells secrete a waxy layer, the **cuticle,**

QUESTION: What molecular controls determine if a developing leaf will become simple or compound?

EXPERIMENT: *NAM/CUC* (NO APICAL MERISTEM/CUP-SHAPED COTYLEDON) genes were cloned and genetically manipulated in four distantly related flowering plants that normally produce compound leaves: *Aquilegia caerulea* (columbine), *Solanum lycopersicum* (tomato), *Cardamine hirsuta* (hairy bittercress), and *Pisum sativum* (garden pea). *NAM/CUC* genes were already known to code for plant transcription factors involved in the establishment and function of the shoot apical meristem.

RESULTS AND CONCLUSION: European scientists Thomas Blein, Patrick Laufs, and colleagues reported in the journal *Science* in 2008 that the *timing* of gene silencing of *NAM/CUC* genes had the potential to produce less elaborate, simpler leaf structures. If a young leaf at the shoot apical meristem of a columbine plant had already developed deeply lobed leaflets, silencing the *NAM/CUC* genes would not affect its further development (leaf 1). The leaf margins of leaves 2 and 3 developed with fewer lobes because the *NAM/CUC* genes had been silenced before much leaf development had taken place. In leaf 4, very early silencing resulted in a simple leaf with an entire margin. Similar leaf simplifications occurred due to the timing of silencing of the *NAM/CUC* genes in the developing leaves of tomato, hairy bittercress, and garden pea.

Source: Blein, T. et al. "A conserved molecular framework for compound leaf development." *Science*, Vol. 322, Dec. 19, 2008. (Photo is taken from Figure 2 on page 1837.)

FIGURE 34-3 Molecular controls and the development of leaf form

---

Leaves contain all three tissue systems found in plants: the dermal tissue system, represented by the upper and lower epidermis; the ground tissue system, represented by the mesophyll; and the vascular tissue system, represented by the xylem and phloem in the veins.

Palisade mesophyll

Vein (vascular bundle)

Spongy mesophyll

Cuticle

Upper epidermis

Bundle sheath

Xylem

Phloem

Stoma

Air space

Lower epidermis

Stoma

Guard cells

FIGURE 34-4 *Animated* **Tissues in a typical leaf blade**

An upper epidermis and lower epidermis cover the blade. The photosynthetic ground tissue, called *mesophyll*, is often arranged into palisade and spongy layers. Veins branch throughout the mesophyll.

that reduces water loss from their exterior walls (see Table 33-4). The cuticle, which consists primarily of the waxy substance **cutin,** varies in thickness in different plants, in part as a result of environmental conditions. As one might expect, the leaves of plants adapted to hot, dry climates have extremely thick cuticles. Furthermore, a leaf's exposed (and warmer) upper epidermis generally has a thicker cuticle than its shaded (and cooler) lower epidermis.

The epidermis of many leaves is covered with various hairlike structures called **trichomes,** which have several functions (see Table 33-4). Trichomes of some plants help reduce water loss from the leaf surface by retaining a layer of moist air next to the leaf and by reflecting sunlight, thereby protecting the plant from overheating. Some trichomes secrete stinging irritants for deterring *herbivores,* animals that feed on plants. In addition, a leaf covered with trichomes is difficult for an insect to walk over or eat. Other trichomes excrete excess salts absorbed from a salty soil.

The leaf epidermis contains minute openings, or **stomata** (sing., *stoma*), for gas exchange between leaf cells and the environment; the stomata are evenly spaced to optimize this gas exchange. Each stoma is flanked by two specialized epidermal **guard cells,** which are responsible for opening and closing the stoma (**FIG. 34-5**). Guard cells are usually the only epidermal cells with chloroplasts.

Stomata are especially numerous on the lower epidermis of horizontally oriented leaves (an average of about 100 stomata per square millimeter) and in many species are located *only* on the lower surface. The lower epidermis of apple (*Malus sylvestris*) leaves, for example, has almost 400 stomata per square millimeter, whereas the upper epidermis has none. This adaptation reduces water loss because stomata on the lower epidermis are shielded from direct sunlight and are therefore cooler than those on the upper epidermis. In contrast, floating leaves of aquatic plants, such as water lilies, have stomata only on the upper epidermis.

Guard cells are associated with special epidermal cells called **subsidiary cells** that are often structurally different from other epi-

FIGURE 34-5 Stoma

LM of an open stoma from the leaf epidermis of an inch plant (*Zebrina pendula*). Note the chloroplasts present in the guard cells and the thicker inner wall of each guard cell.

dermal cells. Subsidiary cells provide a reservoir of water and ions that move into and out of the guard cells as they change shape during stomatal opening and closing (discussed later in the chapter).

The photosynthetic ground tissue of the leaf, called the **mesophyll** (from the Greek *meso,* "the middle of"; and *phyll,* "leaf"), is sandwiched between the upper epidermis and the lower epidermis. Mesophyll cells, which are parenchyma cells (see Chapter 33) packed with chloroplasts, are loosely arranged, with many air spaces between them that facilitate gas exchange. These intercellular air spaces account for as much as 70% of the leaf's volume.

In many plants, the mesophyll is divided into two sublayers. Toward the upper epidermis, the columnar cells are stacked closely together in a layer called **palisade mesophyll.** In the lower portion, the cells are more loosely and irregularly arranged in a layer called **spongy mesophyll.** The two layers have different functions. Palisade mesophyll is specialized for light capture and is the main site of photosynthesis in the leaf. Photosynthesis also occurs in the spongy mesophyll, but the primary function of the spongy mesophyll is to allow diffusion of gases, particularly CO_2, within the leaf.

Palisade mesophyll may be organized into one, two, three, or even more layers of cells. The presence of additional layers is at least partly an adaptation to environmental conditions. Leaves exposed to direct sunlight contain more layers of palisade mesophyll than do shaded leaves on the same plant. In direct sunlight, the light is strong enough to effectively penetrate multiple layers of palisade mesophyll, allowing all layers to photosynthesize efficiently.

The veins, or **vascular bundles,** of a leaf extend through the mesophyll. Branching is extensive, and no mesophyll cell is more than two or three cells away from a vein. Therefore, the slow process of diffusion does not limit the movement of needed resources between mesophyll cells and veins. Each vein contains two types of vascular tissue: xylem and phloem. **Xylem,** which conducts water and dissolved minerals (inorganic nutrients), is usually located in the upper part of a vein, toward the upper epidermis. **Phloem,** which conducts dissolved sugars, is usually confined to the lower part of a vein.

One or more layers of nonvascular cells surround the larger veins and make up the **bundle sheath.** Bundle sheaths are composed of parenchyma or sclerenchyma cells (see Chapter 33). Frequently, the bundle sheath has support columns, called **bundle sheath extensions,** that extend through the mesophyll from the upper epidermis to the lower epidermis (**FIG. 34-6**). Bundle sheath extensions may be composed of parenchyma, collenchyma, or sclerenchyma cells.

Leaf structure differs in eudicots and monocots

Each eudicot leaf is usually composed of a broad, flattened blade and a petiole. As mentioned previously, eudicot leaves typically have netted venation. In contrast, many monocot leaves lack a petiole; they are narrow, and the base of the leaf often wraps around the stem to form a sheath. Parallel venation is characteristic of monocot leaves.

Eudicots and certain monocots also differ in internal leaf anatomy (**FIG. 34-7**). Although most eudicots and monocots have both palisade and spongy layers, some monocots (corn and other grasses) do not have mesophyll differentiated into distinct palisade and spongy layers. Because eudicots have netted veins, a cross sec-

FIGURE 34-6 Bundle sheath extension ▶

LM of a wheat (*Triticum aestivum*) midvein in cross section. Note the bundle sheath extensions to both the upper epidermis and lower epidermis. Photographed using fluorescence microscopy.

Phil Gates/Biological Photo Service

Upper epidermis
Bundle sheath extension
Midvein
Bundle sheath
Bundle sheath extension
Lower epidermis

250 μm

Ed Reschke/Peter Arnold, Inc.

Midvein
Upper epidermis
Palisade mesophyll
Lengthwise view of vein
Spongy mesophyll
Air space
Lower epidermis
Xylem
Phloem

250 μm

(a) Eudicot leaf. LM of part of a leaf cross section of privet (*Ligustrum vulgare*). The mesophyll has distinct palisade and spongy sections.

Dwight R. Kuhn

Midvein
Upper epidermis
Mesophyll
Bundle sheath cell
Air space
Lower epidermis
Stoma
Xylem
Phloem

25 μm

(b) Monocot leaf. LM of part of a leaf cross section of corn (*Zea mays*). Corn leaves lack distinct regions of palisade and spongy mesophyll.

tion of a eudicot blade often shows veins in both cross-sectional and lengthwise views. In a cross section of a monocot leaf, in contrast, the parallel venation pattern produces evenly spaced veins, all of which appear in cross section.

Differences between the guard cells in eudicot and certain monocot leaves also occur (**FIG. 34-8**). The guard cells of eudicots and many monocots are shaped like kidney beans. Other monocot leaves (those of grasses, reeds, and sedges) have guard cells shaped like dumbbells. These structural differences affect how the cells swell or shrink to open or close the stoma.

Leaf structure is related to function

How is leaf structure related to its primary function of photosynthesis? The epidermis of a leaf is relatively transparent and allows light to penetrate to the interior of the leaf where the photosynthetic ground tissue, the mesophyll, is located. Stomata, which dot the leaf surfaces, permit the exchange of gases between the atmosphere and the leaf's internal tissues. CO_2, a raw material of photosynthesis, diffuses into the leaf through stomata, and the oxygen produced during photosynthesis diffuses rapidly out of the leaf through stomata. Other gases, including air pollutants, also enter the leaf's interior via stomata.

Water required for photosynthesis is obtained from the soil and transported in the xylem to the leaf, where it diffuses into the mesophyll and moistens the surfaces of mesophyll cells. The loose arrangement of the mesophyll cells, with air spaces

◀ **FIGURE 34-7** Eudicot and monocot leaf cross sections

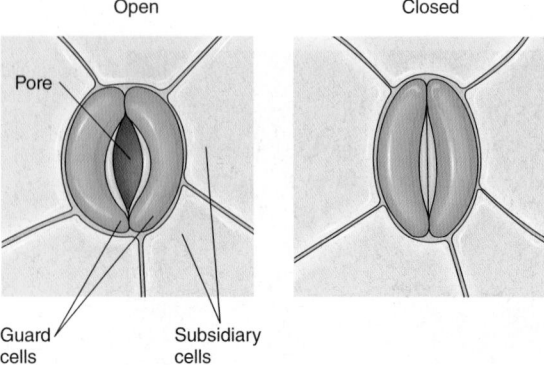

(a) Guard cells of eudicots and many monocots are bean-shaped.

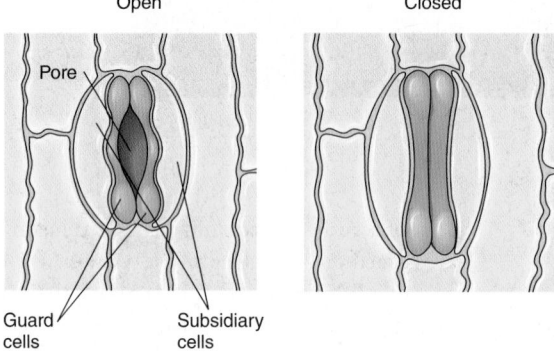

(b) Some monocot guard cells are narrow in the center and thicker at each end.

FIGURE 34-8 Variation in guard cells
Guard cells are associated with epidermal cells called subsidiary cells.

between cells, allows for rapid diffusion of CO_2 to the mesophyll cell surfaces; there it dissolves in a film of water before diffusing into the cells.

The veins not only supply the photosynthetic ground tissue with water and minerals (from the roots, by way of the xylem) but also carry (in the phloem) dissolved sugar produced during photosynthesis to all parts of the plant. Bundle sheaths and bundle sheath extensions associated with the veins provide additional support to prevent the leaf, which is structurally weak because of the large amount of air space in the mesophyll, from collapsing under its own weight.

Leaves are adapted to help a plant survive in its environment

Leaf structure reflects the environment to which a particular plant is adapted. Although both aquatic plants and those adapted to dry conditions perform photosynthesis and have the same basic leaf anatomy, their leaves are modified to enable them to survive different environmental conditions. The leaves of water lilies have petioles long enough to allow the blade to float on the water's surface. Large air spaces in the mesophyll make the floating blade buoyant. The petioles and other submerged parts have an internal system of air ducts; oxygen moves through these ducts from the floating leaves to the underwater roots and stems, which live in a poorly aerated environment.

Conifers are an important group of woody trees and shrubs that includes pine, spruce, fir, redwood, and cedar.[2] Most conifers are evergreen, which means they lose leaves throughout the year rather than during certain seasons. Conifers dominate a large portion of Earth's land area, particularly in northern forests and mountains. The leaves of most conifers are waxy needles. Their needles have structural adaptations that help them survive winter, the driest part of the year. (Winter is arid even in areas of heavy snows because roots cannot absorb water from soil when the soil temperature is very low.) Indeed, many of the structural features of needles are also found in many desert plants.

FIGURE 34-9 shows a cross section of a pine needle. Note that the needle is somewhat thickened rather than thin and bladelike. The needle's relative thickness, which results in less surface area exposed to the air, reduces water loss. Other features that help conserve water include the thick, waxy cuticle and sunken stomata; these permit gas exchange while minimizing water loss. Thus, needles help conifers tolerate the dry winds that occur during winter (*dry* refers here to low relative humidity). With the warming of spring, soil water again becomes available, and the needles quickly resume photosynthesis.

Review

- How are leaves adapted to conserve water?
- What is the photosynthetic ground tissue of a leaf called? What are its two sublayers?
- What are the two types of vascular tissue in a vascular bundle? Which vascular tissue is usually located in the upper part of the vascular bundle?
- How is the leaf organized to deliver the raw materials and remove the products of photosynthesis?

34.2 STOMATAL OPENING AND CLOSING

LEARNING OBJECTIVES

5 Explain the role of blue light in the opening of stomata.
6 Outline the physiological changes that accompany stomatal opening and closing.

Stomata are adjustable pores that are usually open during the day when CO_2 is required for photosynthesis and closed at night when photosynthesis is shut down (see the section on CAM photosynthesis in Chapter 9 for an interesting exception). The opening and closing of stomata are controlled by changes in the shape of the two guard cells that surround each pore. The guard cells' shape is determined by their rigidity. When water moves into guard cells from surrounding nonguard cells, the guard cells become turgid (swollen) and bend, producing a pore. When water leaves the guard cells, they become flaccid (limp) and collapse against one

---

[2]As discussed in Chapter 28, conifers are gymnosperms, one of the two groups of seed plants (the other group is the flowering plants, or angiosperms). Unlike flowering plants, whose seeds are enclosed in fruits, conifers bear "naked" seeds on the scales of female cones.

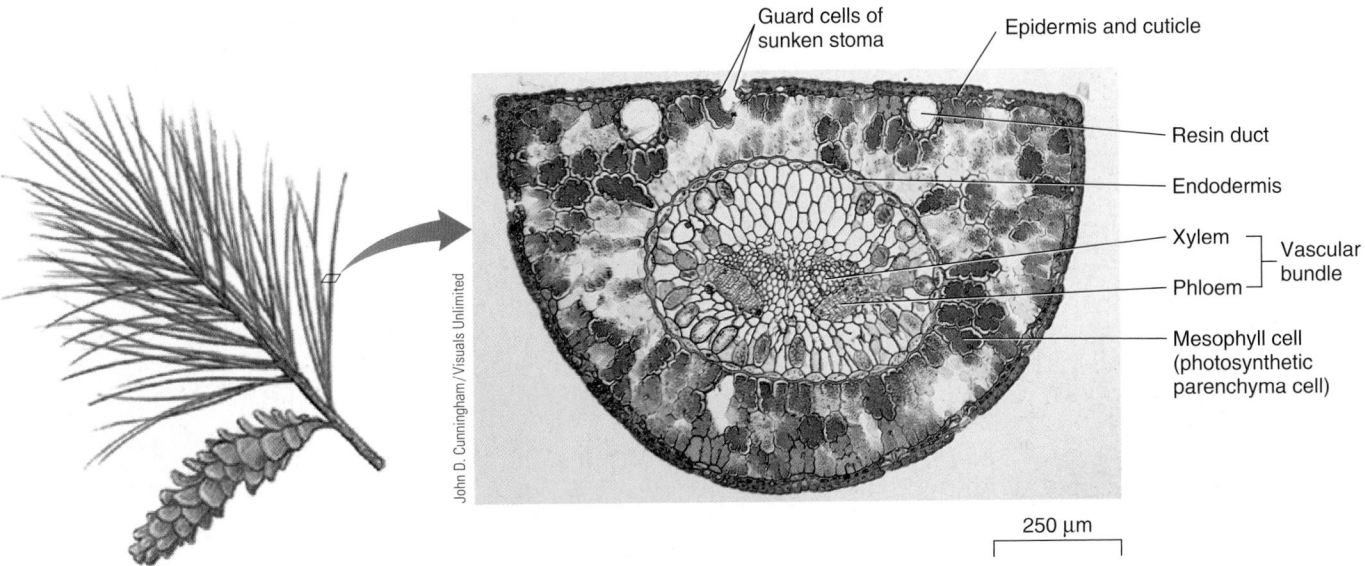

Guard cells of
sunken stoma

Epidermis and cuticle

Resin duct

Endodermis

Xylem ⎱ Vascular
Phloem ⎰ bundle

Mesophyll cell
(photosynthetic
parenchyma cell)

John D. Cunningham/Visuals Unlimited

250 μm

FIGURE 34-9 LM of a pine needle in cross section
The thick, waxy cuticle and sunken stomata are two structural adaptations that enable pine (*Pinus*) to retain its needles throughout the winter.

another, closing the pore. What causes water to move into and out of guard cells?

Blue light triggers stomatal opening

Data from numerous experiments and observations are beginning to explain the complexities of stomatal movements. Let us begin with stomatal opening, which occurs when the plant detects light from the rising sun. You already know that light is a form of energy; plants absorb light and convert it to chemical energy in the process of photosynthesis. However, light is also an important *environmental signal* for plants—that is, light provides plants with information about their environment that they use to modify various activities at the molecular and cellular levels.

In stomatal opening and several other plant responses, **blue light,** which has wavelengths from 400 to 500 nm, is an environmental signal. Any plant response to light must involve a **pigment,** a molecule that absorbs the light, before the induction of a particular biological response. Data such as the responses of stomata to different colors of light suggest that the pigment involved in stomatal opening and closing is yellow (yellow pigments strongly absorb blue light). The yellow pigment is thought to be located in the guard cells, probably in their plasma membranes.

In **FIGURE 34-10,** blue light, which is a component of sunlight, triggers the activation of proton pumps, located in the guard cell plasma membrane. Blue light also triggers the synthesis of malic acid and the **hydrolysis** (splitting) of starch (discussed later).

The proton pumps use ATP energy to actively transport protons (H^+) out of the guard cells. The H^+ that are pumped are formed when malic acid produced in the guard cells ionizes to form H^+ and negatively charged malate ions. As the proton pumps in the plasma membranes of guard cells transport protons out of the guard cells, an **electrochemical gradient**—that is, a charge

and concentration difference—forms on the two sides of the guard cell plasma membrane.

The resulting electrochemical gradient of H^+ drives the facilitated diffusion of large numbers of potassium ions *into* guard cells. This movement occurs through **voltage-activated potassium channels,** which open when a certain voltage (difference in charge between the two sides of the guard cell plasma membrane) is attained. This movement of potassium ions has been experimentally measured by the **patch clamp technique,** in which researchers seal the tip of a micropipette to a tiny patch of membrane that contains a single ion channel. They measure the flow of ions through that channel between the cytoplasm and the solution in the micropipette. (Interestingly, in animals, voltage-activated ion channels are found in the plasma membranes of nerve cells and are involved in transmitting neural impulses.)

Chloride ions are also taken into the guard cells through ion channels in the guard cell plasma membrane. The negatively charged chloride and malate ions help to electrically balance the positively charged potassium ions.

The potassium, chloride, and malate ions accumulate in the vacuoles of the guard cells, thus increasing the solute concentration in the vacuoles. You may recall from the discussion of osmosis in Chapter 5 that when a cell has a solute concentration greater than that of surrounding cells, water flows *into* the cell. Thus, water enters the guard cells from surrounding epidermal cells by osmosis. The increased turgidity of the guard cells changes their shape, because the thickened inner cell walls do not expand as much as the outer walls, so the stoma opens.

blue light activates proton pumps ⟶ proton pump moves H^+ out of guard cells ⟶ K^+ and Cl^- diffuse into guard cells through voltage-activated ion channels ⟶ water diffuses by osmosis into guard cells ⟶ guard cells change shape and stoma opens

The accumulation of osmotically active ions (K^+ and Cl^-) in the guard cells is driven by a proton (H^+) gradient.

1 Blue light activates proton pumps.

2 Protons are pumped out of guard cells, forming electro-chemical gradient.

3 Potassium ions enter guard cells through voltage-activated ion channels.

4 Chloride ions also enter guard cells through ion channels.

5 Water enters guard cells by osmosis, and stoma opens.

FIGURE 34-10 Mechanism of stomatal opening

Stomata close in the late afternoon or early evening, but not by an exact reversal of the opening process. Recent studies have demonstrated that the concentration of potassium ions in guard cells slowly decreases during the day. However, the concentration of sucrose, another osmotically active substance, increases during the day—maintaining the open pore—and then slowly decreases as evening approaches. This sucrose comes from the hydrolysis of the polysaccharide starch, which is stored in the guard cell chloroplasts. As evening approaches, the sucrose concentration in the guard cells declines as sucrose is converted back to starch (which is osmotically inactive), water leaves by osmosis, the guard cells lose their turgidity, and the pore closes.

To summarize, different mechanisms appear to regulate the opening and closing of stomata. The uptake of potassium and chloride ions is mainly associated with stomatal opening, and the declining concentration of sucrose is mainly associated with stomatal closing. In Chapter 38, we discuss other blue-light responses in plants.

Additional factors affect stomatal opening and closing

Although light and darkness trigger the opening and closing of stomata, other environmental factors are also involved, including CO_2 concentration. A low concentration of CO_2 in the leaf induces stomata to open, even in the dark. The effects of light and CO_2 concentration on stomatal opening are interrelated. Photosynthesis, which occurs in the presence of light, reduces the internal concentration of CO_2 in the leaf, triggering stomatal opening. Another

environmental factor that affects stomatal opening and closing is water stress. During a prolonged drought, stomata remain closed, even during the day. Stomatal opening and closing are under hormonal control, particularly by the plant hormone *abscisic acid* (see Table 38-1).

The opening and closing of stomata are also regulated by an internal biological clock that in some way measures time. For example, after plants are placed in continual darkness, their stomata continue to open and close at more or less the same time each day. Such biological rhythms that follow an approximate 24-hour cycle are known as **circadian rhythms.** Other examples of circadian rhythms are provided in Chapter 38.

Review

- How does blue light trigger stomatal opening?
- What physiological changes occur in guard cells during stomatal opening? during stomatal closing?

34.3 TRANSPIRATION AND GUTTATION

LEARNING OBJECTIVES

7 Discuss transpiration and its effects on plants.

8 Distinguish between transpiration and guttation.

Despite leaf adaptations such as the cuticle, approximately 99% of the water that a plant absorbs from the soil is lost by evaporation from the leaves and, to a lesser extent, the stems. Loss of water vapor by evaporation from aerial plant parts is called **transpiration.**

The cuticle is extremely effective in reducing water loss by transpiration. It is estimated that only 1% to 3% of the water lost from a plant passes directly through the cuticle. Most transpiration occurs through open stomata. The numerous stomatal pores that are so effective in gas exchange for photosynthesis also provide openings through which water vapor escapes. In addition, the loose arrangement of the spongy mesophyll cells provides a large surface area within the leaf from which water can evaporate.

Several environmental factors influence the rate of transpiration. More water is lost from plant surfaces at higher temperatures. Light increases the transpiration rate, in part because it triggers stomatal opening and in part because it increases the leaf's temperature. Wind and dry air increase transpiration, but humid air *decreases* transpiration because the air is already saturated, or nearly so, with water vapor.

Although transpiration may seem wasteful, particularly to farmers in arid lands, it is an essential process that has adaptive value. Transpiration is responsible for water movement in plants, and without it water would not reach the leaves from the soil (see discussion of the tension–cohesion model in Chapter 35). The large amount of water that plants lose by transpiration may provide some additional benefits. Transpiration, like sweating in humans, cools the leaves and stems. When water passes from a liquid state to a vapor, it absorbs a great deal of heat. When the water molecules leave the plant as water vapor, they carry this heat with them. Thus, the cooling effect of transpiration may prevent leaves from overheating, particularly in direct sunlight.

Another benefit of transpiration is that it distributes essential minerals throughout the plant. The water that a plant transpires is initially absorbed from the soil, where it is present not as pure water but as a dilute solution of dissolved mineral salts. The water and dissolved minerals are then transported in the xylem throughout the plant, including its leaves. Water moves from the plant to the atmosphere during transpiration, but minerals remain in plant tissues. Many of these minerals are required for the plant's growth. It has been suggested that transpiration enables a plant to take in sufficient water to provide enough essential minerals; it has also been suggested that plants cannot satisfy their mineral requirements if the transpiration rate is not high enough.

There is no doubt, however, that under certain circumstances excessive transpiration can be harmful to a plant. On hot summer days, plants frequently lose more water by transpiration than they can take in from the soil. Their cells experience a loss of turgor, and the plants wilt (**FIG. 34-11**). If a plant is able to recover overnight, because of the combination of negligible transpiration (recall that stomata are closed) and absorption of water from the soil, the plant is said to have experienced *temporary wilting.* Most plants recover from temporary wilting with no ill effects. In cases of prolonged drought, however,

the soil may not contain sufficient moisture to permit recovery from wilting. A plant that cannot recover is said to be *permanently wilted* and will die.

Transpiration is an important part of the **hydrologic cycle,** in which water cycles from the ocean and land to the atmosphere and then back to the ocean and land (see Fig. 55-11). As a result of transpiration, water evaporates from leaves and stems to form clouds in the atmosphere. Thus, transpiration eventually results in precipitation. As you may expect, forest trees release substantial amounts of moisture into the air by transpiration. Researchers have determined that at least half the rain that falls in the Amazon rainforest basin is recycled again and again by transpiration and precipitation.

Some plants exude liquid water

Many leaves have special structures at vein endings through which liquid water is literally forced out. This loss of liquid water, known as **guttation,** occurs when transpiration is negligible and available soil moisture is high. Guttation typically occurs in low-growing plants at night because the stomata are closed, but water continues to move into the roots by osmosis. People sometimes mistake the early morning water droplets formed on leaf margins by guttation for dew (**FIG. 34-12**). Unlike dew, which condenses from cool night air, guttation droplets come from within the plant. (The mechanism for guttation is discussed in Chapter 35.)

Review

- What is transpiration? How is leaf structure related to transpiration?
- How do environmental factors (sunlight, temperature, humidity, and wind) influence the rate of transpiration?
- How does guttation differ from transpiration?

 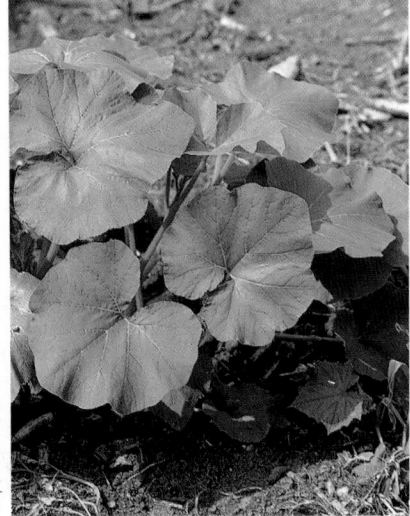

(a) In the late afternoon of a hot day, the leaves have wilted because of water loss. Note that wilting helps reduce the surface area from which transpiration occurs.

(b) The next morning, water in the leaves has been replenished. Transpiration is negligible during the night, and the plants recover by absorbing water from the soil.

FIGURE 34-11 Temporary wilting in squash (*Cucurbita pepo*) leaves

FIGURE 34-12 Guttation

Shown is a compound leaf of strawberry (*Fragaria*) with water droplets formed by guttation.

34.4 LEAF ABSCISSION

◼ LEARNING OBJECTIVE

9   Define leaf *abscission*, explain why it occurs, and describe the physiological and anatomical changes that precede it.

All trees shed leaves, a process known as **abscission.** Many conifers shed their needles in small numbers year-round. The leaves of deciduous plants turn color and abscise, or fall off, once a year—as winter approaches in temperate climates or at the beginning of the dry period in tropical climates with pronounced wet and dry seasons. In temperate forests, most woody plants with broad leaves shed their leaves to survive the low temperatures of winter. During winter, the plant's metabolism, including its photosynthetic machinery, slows down or halts temporarily.

Another reason for abscission is related to a plant's water requirements, which become critical during the physiological drought of winter. As mentioned previously, as the ground chills, absorption of water by the roots is inhibited. When the ground freezes, *no* absorption occurs. If the broad leaves were to stay on the plant during the winter, the plant would continue to lose water by transpiration but would be unable to replace it with water absorbed from the soil.

Leaf abscission is a complex process that involves many physiological changes, all initiated and orchestrated by changing levels of plant hormones, particularly *ethylene*. Briefly, the process is this: As autumn approaches, sugars, amino acids, and many essential minerals (such as nitrogen, phosphorus, and possibly potassium) are mobilized and transported from the leaves to other plant parts; these minerals will be reused during the following spring. Chlorophyll breaks down, allowing the **carotenoids** (orange carotenes and yellow xanthophylls), some of the accessory pigments in the chloroplasts of leaf cells, to become evident (see Fig. 3-14b). Accessory pigments are always present in the chloroplasts but are masked by the green of the chlorophyll. In addition, red water-soluble pigments called **anthocyanins** may accumulate in the vacuoles of epidermal leaf cells in some species; anthocyanins may protect leaves against damage by ultraviolet radiation. The various combinations of carotenoids and anthocyanins are responsible for the brilliant colors found in autumn landscapes in temperate climates.

In many leaves, abscission occurs at an abscission zone near the base of the petiole

The area where a petiole detaches from the stem is a structurally distinct area called the **abscission zone.** Composed primarily of thin-walled parenchyma cells, it is anatomically weak because it contains few fibers (**FIG. 34-13**). A protective layer of cork cells develops on the stem side of the abscission zone. These cells have a waxy, waterproof material impregnated in their walls. Enzymes then dissolve the **middle lamella** (the "cement" that holds the primary cell walls of adjacent cells together) in the abscission zone (see Fig. 4-29). Once this process is completed, nothing holds the leaf to the stem but a few xylem cells. A sudden breeze is enough to make the final break, and the leaf detaches. The protective layer of cork remains, sealing off the area and forming a leaf scar.

Although the structure of abscission zones and the physiological changes associated with abscission have been well known for many years, only recently have botanists investigated the genes responsible for the development of an abscission zone and the physiological changes of leaf abscission. Using **DNA microarrays,** for example, botanists have identified about 35 genes that are expressed in leaves only as winter approaches. As shown in Figure 15-12, a DNA microarray contains hundreds of different DNA molecules placed on a glass slide or chip. Some of these genes code for degradative enzymes involved in breaking down proteins and other molecules; others have functions not yet identified.

Review

- Why do many woody plants living in temperate zones lose their leaves in autumn?
- What physiological changes occur during leaf abscission?
- What is the abscission zone?

34.5 MODIFIED LEAVES

◼ LEARNING OBJECTIVE

10   List at least four examples of modified leaves and give the function of each.

Although photosynthesis is the main function of leaves, certain leaves have special modifications for other functions. Some plants have leaves specialized for deterring herbivores. **Spines,** modified

Axillary bud

Bud scales

Petiole

Abscission zone

Stem

James Mauseth, University of Texas

0.5 mm

FIGURE 34-13 Abscission zone

This LM of a longitudinal section through a silver maple (*Acer saccharinum*) branch shows the abscission zone at the base of a petiole. An axillary bud with its protective bud scales is also evident above the petiole.

leaves that are hard and pointed, are found on many desert plants, such as cacti (**FIG. 34-14a**). In the cactus, the main organ of photosynthesis is the stem rather than the leaf. Spines discourage animals from eating the succulent stem tissue.

Vines are climbing plants whose stems cannot support their own weight, so they often possess **tendrils** that help keep the vine attached to the structure on which it is growing. The tendrils of many vines, such as peas, cucumbers, squash, and sweet peas, are specialized leaves (**FIG. 34-14b**). However, some tendrils, such as those of ivy, Virginia creeper, and grape, are specialized stems.

The winter buds of a dormant woody plant are covered by **bud scales,** modified leaves that protect the delicate meristematic tissue of the bud from injury, freezing, or drying out (**FIG. 34-14c**).

Some leaves associated with flower clusters (inflorescences) are modified as **bracts.** In flowering dogwood, the inconspicuous flowers are clustered in the center of each inflorescence, and what appears to be four white or pink petals are actually bracts. Similarly, the red "petals" of poinsettia are not petals at all but bracts (**FIG. 34-14d**).

Leaves may also be modified for storage of water or food. For example, a **bulb** is a short, underground stem to which large, fleshy leaves are attached (**FIG. 34-14e**). Onions and tulips form bulbs. Many plants adapted to arid conditions, such as jade plant, medicinal aloe, and string-of-beads, have succulent leaves for water storage (**FIG. 34-14f**). These leaves are usually green and function in photosynthesis.

Some leaves are modified for either sexual reproduction (see discussion of flower evolution in Chapter 28, including Fig. 28-15) or asexual reproduction (see Fig. 37-17).

Modified leaves of carnivorous plants capture insects

Carnivorous plants are plants that capture insects. Most carnivorous plants grow in poor soil that is deficient in certain essential minerals, particularly nitrogen. These plants meet some of their mineral requirements by digesting insects and other small animals. The leaves of carnivorous plants are adapted to attract, capture, and digest their animal prey.

Some carnivorous plants have passive traps. The leaves of a pitcher plant, for example, are shaped so that rainwater collects and forms a reservoir that also contains acid secreted by the plant (**FIG. 34-15**). Some pitchers are quite large; in the tropics, pitcher plants may be large enough to hold 1 L (approximately 1 qt) or more of liquid. An insect attracted by the odor or nectar of the pitcher may lean over the edge and fall in. Although it may make repeated attempts to escape, the insect is prevented from crawling out by the slippery sides and the rows of stiff hairs that point downward around the lip of the pitcher. The insect eventually drowns, and part of its body disintegrates and is absorbed.

Most insects are killed in pitcher plants. However, the larvae of several insects (certain flies, midges, and mosquitoes) and a large community of microorganisms live inside the pitchers. These insect species obtain their food from the insect carcasses, and the pitcher plant digests what remains. It is not known how these insects survive the acidic environment inside the pitcher.

The Venus flytrap is a carnivorous plant with active traps. Its leaf blades resemble tiny bear traps (see Fig. 1-3). Each side of the leaf blade contains three small, stiff hairs. If an insect alights and

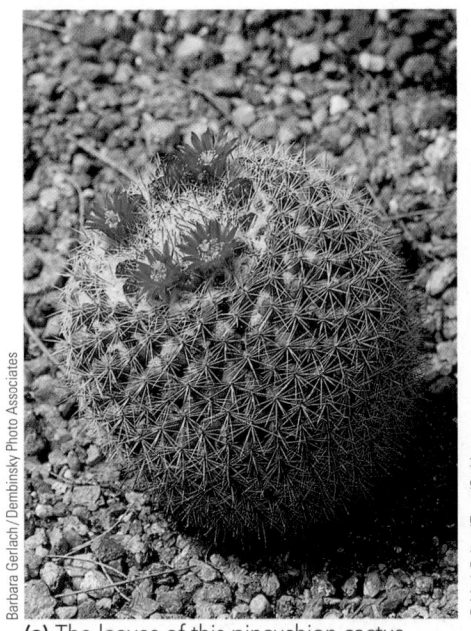

(a) The leaves of this pincushion cactus (*Mammilaria*) are spines for deterring herbivores.

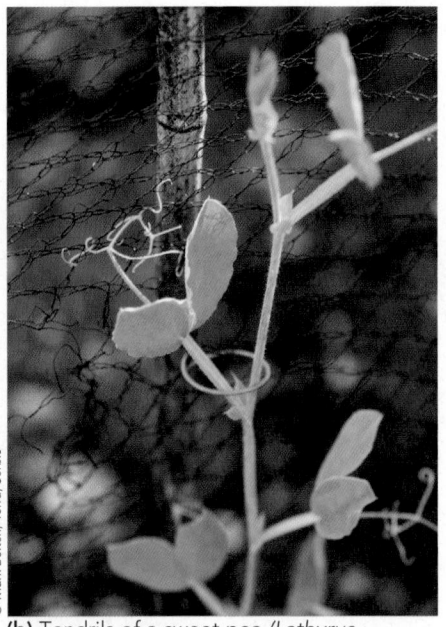

(b) Tendrils of a sweet pea (*Lathyrus odoratus*) are modified leaves that wind around objects and aid in climbing.

(c) A terminal bud and two axillary buds of a maple (*Acer*) twig have overlapping bud scales to protect the buds.

(d) Showy red bracts surround each poinsettia (*Euphorbia pulcherrima*) inflorescence; the inconspicuous flowers are in the center.

(e) The leaves of bulbs such as the onion (*Allium cepa*) are fleshy for storage of food materials and water.

(f) The succulent leaves of the string-of-beads plant (*Senecio rowleyanus*) are spherical to minimize surface area, thereby conserving water.

FIGURE 34-14 Leaf modifications

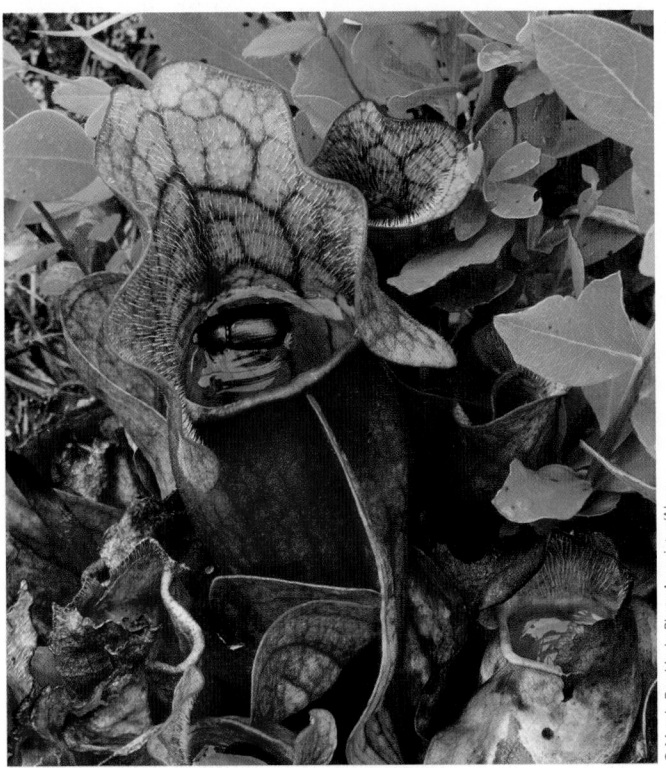

◀ **FIGURE 34-15 A common pitcher plant**
This species (*Sarracenia purpurea*), whose pitchers grow to 30.5 cm (12 in), is widely distributed in acidic bogs and marshes in eastern North America. Young pitchers are green but turn red as they age. Note the dead beetle in the pitcher.

brushes against two of the hairs, or against the same hair twice in quick succession, the trap springs shut with amazing rapidity—about 100 milliseconds. The spines along the margins of the blades fit closely together to prevent the insect from escaping. After the leaf initially traps the insect, the leaf continues to slowly close for the next several hours. Digestive glands on the surface of the trap secrete enzymes in response to the insect pressing against them. Days later, after the insect has died and been digested, the trap re-opens and the indigestible remains fall out.

Review

- What are the primary functions of each of the following modified leaves: spines, tendrils, and bud scales?
- What are the functions of bulbs? of succulent leaves?
- What are some of the specialized features of the leaves of carnivorous plants?

■ SUMMARY: FOCUS ON LEARNING OBJECTIVES

34.1 *(page 729)*

1 Discuss variation in leaf form, including simple versus compound leaves, leaf arrangement on the stem, and venation patterns.

- Leaves may be simple (having a single **blade**) or compound (having a blade divided into two or more leaflets).
- Leaf arrangement on a stem may be alternate (one leaf at each **node**), opposite (two leaves at each node), or whorled (three or more leaves at each node).
- Leaves may have parallel or netted venation. Netted venation may be palmately netted, with several major **veins** radiating from one point, or pinnately netted, with veins branching along the entire length of the midvein.

2 Describe the major tissues of the leaf (epidermis, photosynthetic ground tissue, xylem, and phloem) and label them on a diagram of a leaf cross section.

- Upper and lower surfaces of the leaf blade are covered by an **epidermis.** A waxy **cuticle** coats the epidermis, enabling the plant to survive the dry conditions of a terrestrial existence.
- **Stomata** are small pores in the epidermis that permit gas exchange needed for photosynthesis. Each pore is surrounded by two **guard cells** that are often associated with special epidermal cells called **subsidiary cells.** Subsidiary cells provide a reservoir of water and ions that move into and out of the guard cells as they change shape during stomatal opening and closing.
- **Mesophyll** consists of photosynthetic parenchyma cells. Mesophyll is divided into **palisade mesophyll,** which functions primarily for photosynthesis, and **spongy mesophyll,** which functions primarily for gas exchange.

- Leaf veins have **xylem** to conduct water and essential minerals to the leaf and **phloem** to conduct sugar produced by photosynthesis to the rest of the plant.

  CENGAGENOW™ Learn more about leaf tissues by clicking on the figure in CengageNOW.

3 Compare leaf anatomy in eudicots and monocots.

- Monocot leaves have parallel venation, whereas eudicot leaves have netted venation. Some monocots (corn and other grasses) do not have mesophyll differentiated into distinct palisade and spongy layers. Some monocots (grasses, reeds, and sedges) have guard cells shaped like dumbbells, unlike the more common bean-shaped guard cells.

4 Relate leaf structure to its function of photosynthesis.

- Leaf structure is adapted for its primary function of **photosynthesis.** Most leaves have a broad, flattened blade that efficiently collects the sun's radiant energy. The transparent epidermis allows light to penetrate into the middle of the leaf, where photosynthesis occurs.
- Stomata generally open during the day for gas exchange needed during photosynthesis and close at night to conserve water when photosynthesis is not occurring.
- Air spaces in mesophyll tissue permit the rapid diffusion of CO_2 and water into, and oxygen out of, mesophyll cells.

34.2 *(page 734)*

5 Explain the role of blue light in the opening of stomata.

- **Blue light,** which is a component of sunlight, triggers the activation of proton pumps located in the guard cell plasma membrane. Blue light also triggers the synthesis of malic acid and the **hydrolysis** of starch.

6 Outline the physiological changes that accompany stomatal opening and closing.

- Protons (H^+), produced when malic acid ionizes, are pumped out of the guard cells. As protons leave the guard cells, an **electrochemical gradient** (a charge and concentration difference) forms on the two sides of the guard cell plasma membrane.
- The electrochemical gradient drives the uptake of potassium ions (K^+) through **voltage-activated potassium channels** into the guard cells. Chloride ions (C^-) are also taken into the guard cells through ion channels. These osmotically active ions increase the solute concentration in the guard cell vacuoles. The resulting osmotic movement of water into the guard cells causes them to become turgid, forming a pore.
- As the day progresses, potassium ions slowly leave the guard cells and starch is hydrolyzed to sucrose, an osmotically active solute, which increases in concentration in the guard cells. Stomata close when water leaves the guard cells as a result of a decline in the concentration of sucrose, which occurs as evening approaches. The sucrose is converted to starch, which is osmotically inactive.

CENGAGENOW™ Watch stomata in action by clicking on the figure in CengageNOW.

34.3 (page 736)

7 Discuss transpiration and its effects on plants.

- **Transpiration** is the loss of water vapor from aerial parts of plants. Transpiration, which occurs primarily through the stomata, is affected by environmental factors such as temperature, wind, and relative humidity.
- Transpiration appears to be both beneficial and harmful to the plant—that is, transpiration represents a trade-off between the CO_2 requirement for photosynthesis and the need for water conservation.

8 Distinguish between transpiration and guttation.

- **Guttation,** the release of liquid water from leaf margins of some plants, occurs through special structures when transpiration is negligible and available soil moisture is high. In contrast, transpiration is the loss of water vapor and occurs primarily through the stomata.

34.4 (page 738)

9 Define leaf *abscission*, explain why it occurs, and describe the physiological and anatomical changes that precede it.

- Leaf **abscission** is the loss of leaves that often occurs as winter approaches in temperate climates or at the beginning of the dry period in tropical climates with wet and dry seasons.
- Abscission involves physiological and anatomical changes that occur prior to leaf fall. An **abscission zone** develops where the petiole detaches from the stem. Sugars, amino acids, and many essential minerals are transported from the leaves to other plant parts. Chlorophyll breaks down, and **carotenoids** and **anthocyanins** become evident.

34.5 (page 738)

10 List at least four examples of modified leaves and give the function of each.

- **Spines** are leaves adapted to deter herbivores. Some **tendrils** are leaves modified for grasping and holding on to other structures (to support weak stems). **Bud scales** are leaves modified to protect delicate meristematic tissue or dormant buds. **Bracts** are modified leaves associated with some inflorescences. **Bulbs** are short, underground stems with fleshy leaves specialized for storage. Many plants adapted to arid conditions have succulent leaves for water storage. Carnivorous plants have leaves modified to trap insects.

TEST YOUR UNDERSTANDING

1. Plants with an alternate leaf arrangement have (a) blades divided into two or more leaflets (b) major veins that radiate out from one point (c) one leaf at each node (d) major veins branching off along the entire length of the midvein (e) two leaves at each node

2. The primary function of the spongy mesophyll is (a) reducing water loss from the leaf surface (b) changing the shape of the guard cells (c) supporting the leaf to prevent it from collapsing under its own weight (d) diffusing gases within the leaf (e) deterring herbivores

3. Gas exchange occurs through microscopic pores formed by two (a) subsidiary cells (b) abscission cells (c) mesophyll cells (d) guard cells (e) stipules

4. The thin, noncellular layer of wax secreted by the epidermis of leaves is the (a) stoma (b) subsidiary cell (c) trichome (d) bundle sheath (e) cuticle

5. Which of the following is *not* an adaptation of pine needles to conserve water? (a) less surface area exposed to the air than thin-bladed leaves (b) a relatively thick cuticle (c) sunken stomata (d) netted veins instead of parallel veins (e) both c and d are not adaptations of pine needles

6. When transpiration is negligible, plants such as grasses exude excess water by (a) guttation (b) circadian rhythm (c) abscission (d) pumping H^+ out of and K^+ into guard cells (e) photosynthesis

7. At sunrise, the accumulation in the guard cells of the osmotically active substance _____ causes an inflow of water and the opening of the pore. (a) protons (b) starch (c) ATP synthase (d) sucrose (e) potassium ions

8. Stomatal opening is most pronounced in response to _____ light. (a) green (b) yellow (c) blue (d) ultraviolet (e) infrared

9. Anatomically, the abscission zone where a petiole detaches from a stem consists of (a) thin-walled parenchyma cells with few fibers (b) thick-walled cork parenchyma cells (c) clusters of fibers and collenchyma strands (d) hard, pointed stipules (e) epidermal cells with sunken stomata

10. Modified leaves that enable a stem to climb are called _____, whereas modified leaves that cover the winter buds of a dormant woody plant are called _____. (a) spines; bud scales (b) bud scales; tendrils (c) tendrils; bud scales (d) tendrils; spines (e) carnivorous leaves; spines

11. There is a trade-off between photosynthesis and transpiration in leaves because (a) numerous stomatal pores provide both gas exchange for photosynthesis and openings through which water vapor escapes (b) a waxy layer, the cuticle, reduces water loss (c) blue light triggers an influx of potassium ions (K^+) into the guard cells (d) leaves of deciduous plants abscise as winter approaches in temperate climates (e) stomata are closed at night, although water continues to move into the roots by osmosis

12. Label the following diagram. (Refer to Figure 34-4 to check your answers.)

CRITICAL THINKING

1. Suppose that you are asked to observe a micrograph of a leaf cross section and distinguish between the upper and lower epidermis. How would you make this decision?

2. Given that (a) xylem is located toward the upper epidermis in leaf veins and phloem is toward the lower epidermis and (b) the vascular tissue of a leaf is continuous with that of the stem, suggest one possible arrangement of vascular tissues in the stem that might account for the arrangement of vascular tissue in the leaf.

3. What might be some of the advantages of a plant having a few large leaves? What might be some disadvantages? What might be some advantages of having many small leaves? What disadvantages might this entail? How would your answers differ for plants growing in a humid environment compared to those in a desert?

4. **EVOLUTION LINK.** Why did natural selection favor the evolution of seasonal leaf abscission in woody flowering plants living in colder climates? What adaptations enable conifers to survive these climates without leaf abscission?

5. **SCIENCE, TECHNOLOGY, AND SOCIETY.** Briefly explain why research on the molecular mechanism of stomatal closure might be of future use in agriculture.

 Additional questions are available in CengageNOW at www.cengage.com/login.

35 Stem Structure and Transport

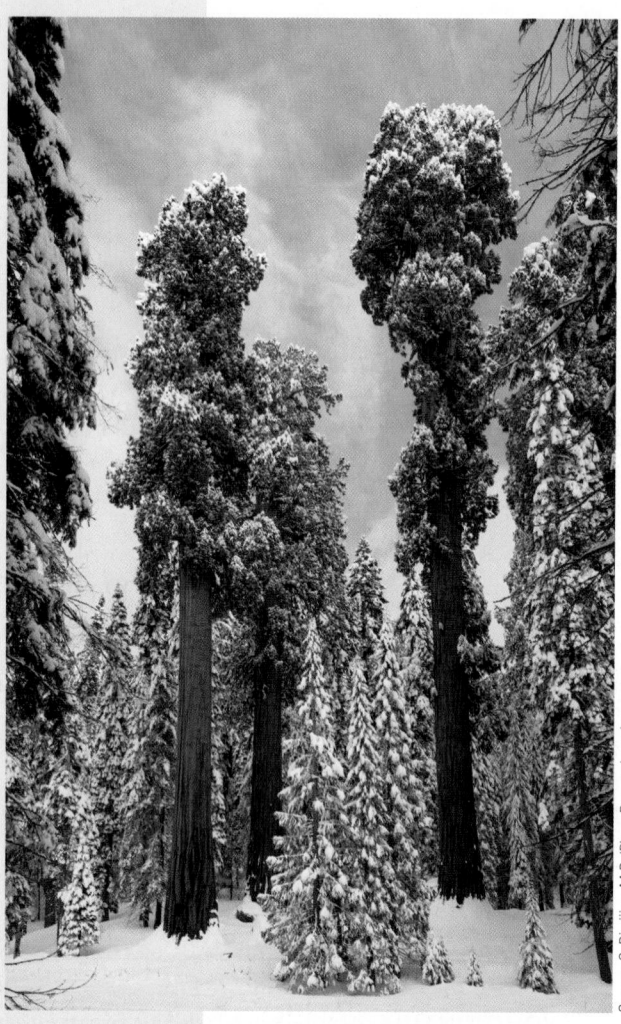

Gregory G. Dimijian, M.D./Photo Researchers, Inc.

Giant sequoias in winter. Giant sequoias (*Sequoiadendron giganteum*) are the most massive trees on Earth. Their huge stems grow to 75 m (250 ft) or more. Photographed in Sequoia National Park, California.

KEY CONCEPTS

35.1 Primary tissues (epidermis, cortex, pith, xylem, and phloem) of stems develop from shoot apical meristems. Secondary tissues (wood and bark) of stems develop from two lateral meristems, vascular cambium and cork cambium.

35.2 The concept of water potential explains the direction of water transport into, through, and out of a plant. According to the tension–cohesion model, transpiration pulls water up through the stem as water evaporates from leaves by transpiration.

35.3 According to the pressure–flow model, sucrose is translocated in phloem sap from the source, where the sugar is loaded into phloem, to the sink, where the sugar is removed from phloem.

A vegetative (not sexually reproductive) vascular plant has three parts: roots, leaves, and stems. As discussed in Chapter 33, roots serve to anchor the plant and absorb materials from the soil, whereas leaves are primarily for photosynthesis, converting radiant energy into the chemical energy of carbohydrate molecules. Stems, the focus of this chapter, link a plant's roots to its leaves and are usually located aboveground, although many plants have underground stems. Stems exhibit varied forms, ranging from ropelike vines to massive tree trunks (see photograph). They can be either herbaceous, with soft, nonwoody tissues, or they can be woody, with extensive hard tissues of wood and bark.

Stems perform three main functions in plants. First, stems of most species support leaves and reproductive structures. The upright position of most stems and the arrangement of the leaves on them allow each leaf to absorb light for use in photosynthesis. Reproductive structures (such as flowers and fruits) are located on stems in areas accessible to insects, birds, and air currents, which transfer pollen from flower to flower and help disperse seeds and fruits.

Second, stems provide internal transport. They conduct water and dissolved minerals (inorganic nutrients) from the roots, where these materials are absorbed from the soil, to leaves and other plant parts. Stems also conduct the sugar produced in leaves by photosynthesis to roots and other parts of the plant. Remember, however, that stems are not the only plant organs that conduct materials. The vascular system is continuous throughout all parts of a plant, and conduction occurs in roots, stems, leaves, and reproductive structures.

Third, stems produce new living tissue. They continue to grow throughout a plant's life, producing *buds* that develop into stems with new leaves and/or reproductive structures. In addition to the main functions of support, conduction, and production of new stem tissues, stems of some species are modified for asexual reproduction (see Chapter 37) or, if green, to manufacture sugar by photosynthesis.

35.1 STEM GROWTH AND STRUCTURE

■ LEARNING OBJECTIVES

1   Label cross sections of herbaceous eudicot and monocot stems, and describe the functions of each tissue.
2   Name the two lateral meristems and describe the tissues that arise from each.
3   Outline the transition from primary growth to secondary growth in a woody stem.

You may recall from Chapter 33 that plants have two different types of growth. **Primary growth** is an increase in the length of a plant and occurs at **apical meristems** located at the tips of roots and shoots and also within the buds of stems. **Secondary growth** is an increase in the girth (thickness) of a plant as a result of the activity of **lateral meristems** located within stems and roots. The new tissues formed by the lateral meristems are called *secondary tissues* to distinguish them from *primary tissues* produced by apical meristems.

All plants have primary growth; some plants have both primary and secondary growth. Stems with only primary growth are herbaceous, whereas those with both primary and secondary growth are generally woody. (Certain herbaceous stems, such as geranium and sunflower, also have a limited amount of secondary growth.) A woody plant increases in length by primary growth at the tips of its stems and roots, whereas its older stems and roots farther back from the tips increase in girth by secondary growth. In other words, at the same time that primary growth is increasing the length of the stem, secondary growth is adding wood and bark, thereby causing the stem to thicken.

Herbaceous eudicot and monocot stems differ in internal structure

Although considerable structural variation exists in stems, they all possess an outer protective covering (epidermis or periderm), one or more types of ground tissue, and vascular tissues (xylem and phloem). Let us first consider the structure of herbaceous eudicot stems and then of monocot stems.

Vascular bundles of herbaceous eudicot stems are arranged in a circle in cross section

A young sunflower stem is a representative herbaceous eudicot stem that exhibits primary growth (**FIG. 35-1**). Its outer covering, the **epidermis,** provides protection in herbaceous stems, as it does in leaves and herbaceous roots (see Table 33-4 and Fig. 33-5). The **cuticle,** a waxy layer of *cutin,* covers the stem epidermis and reduces water loss from the stem surface. **Stomata** permit gas exchange. (Recall from Chapter 34 that a cuticle and stomata are also associated with the leaf epidermis.)

Inside the epidermis is the **cortex,** a cylinder of ground tissue that may contain parenchyma, collenchyma, and sclerenchyma cells (see Table 33-2 and Fig. 33-3). As might be expected from the various types of cells that it contains, the cortex in herbaceous eudicot stems can have several functions, such as photosynthesis, storage, and support. If a stem is green, photosynthesis occurs in chloroplasts of cortical parenchyma cells. Parenchyma in the cortex also stores starch (in amyloplasts) and crystals (in vacuoles). Collenchyma and sclerenchyma in the cortex confer strength and structural support for the stem.

The vascular tissues provide conduction and support. In herbaceous eudicot stems, the vascular tissues are located in bundles that, when viewed in cross section, are arranged in a circle. However, viewed lengthwise, these bundles extend as long strands throughout the length of a stem and are continuous with vascular tissues of both roots and leaves.

Each vascular bundle contains both **xylem,** which transports water and dissolved minerals from roots to leaves, and **phloem,** which transports dissolved sugar (see Table 33-3 and Fig. 33-4). Xylem is located on the inner side of the vascular bundle, and phloem is found toward the outside. Sandwiched between xylem and phloem in some herbaceous stems is a single layer of cells called the *vascular cambium,* a lateral meristem responsible for secondary growth (discussed later).

Because most stems support the aerial plant body, they are much stronger than roots. The thick walls of tracheids and vessel elements in xylem help support the plant. Fibers also occur in both xylem and phloem, although they are usually more extensive in phloem. These fibers add considerable strength to the herbaceous stem. In sunflowers and certain other herbaceous eudicot stems, phloem contains a cluster of fibers toward the outside of the vascular bundle, called a **phloem fiber cap,** that helps strengthen the stem. The phloem fiber cap is not present in all herbaceous eudicot stems.

The **pith** is a ground tissue at the center of the herbaceous eudicot stem that consists of large, thin-walled parenchyma cells that function primarily in storage. Because of the arrangement of the vascular tissues in bundles, there is no distinct separation of cortex

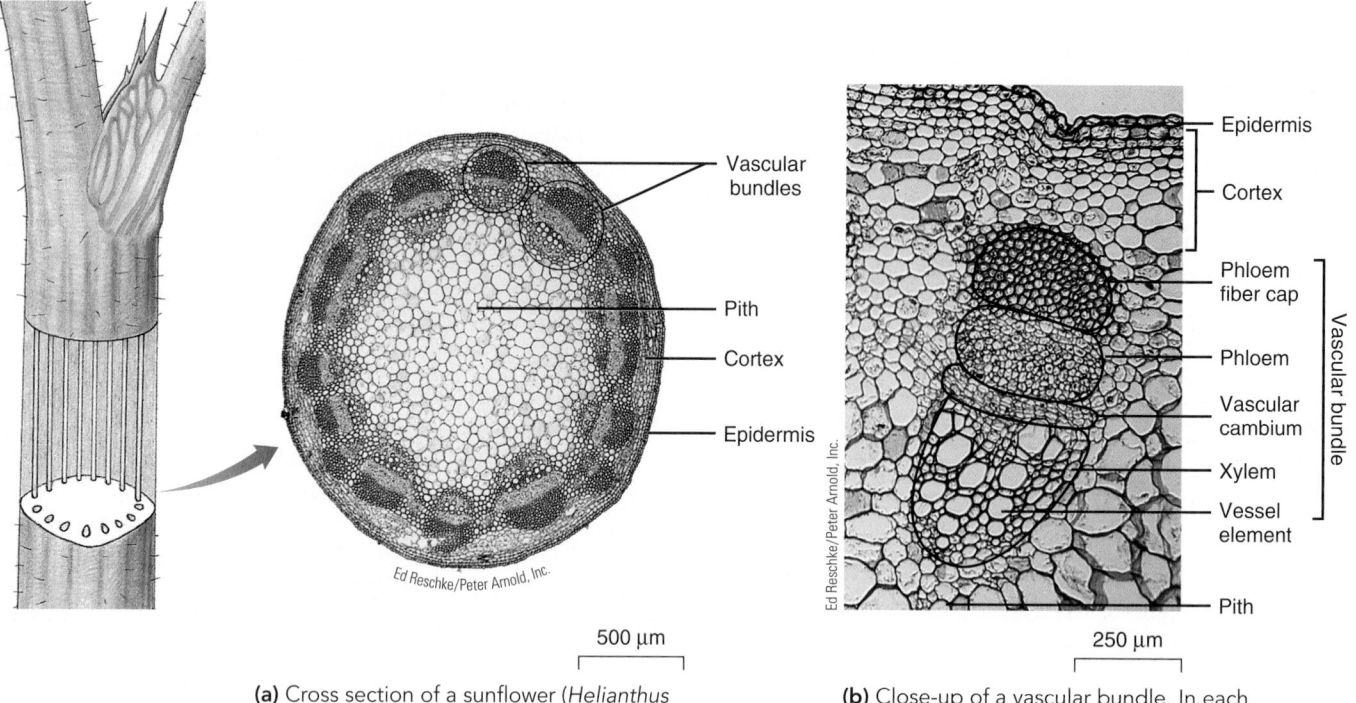

(a) Cross section of a sunflower (*Helianthus annuus*) stem. Note the vascular bundles arranged in a circle around a central core of pith.

(b) Close-up of a vascular bundle. In each bundle, xylem is located toward the stem's interior, and phloem toward the exterior. Each vascular bundle is "capped" by a batch of fibers for additional support.

FIGURE 35-1 *Animated* LMs of a herbaceous eudicot stem

and pith between the vascular bundles. The areas of parenchyma between the vascular bundles are often referred to as **pith rays.**

Vascular bundles are scattered throughout monocot stems

An epidermis with its waxy cuticle covers monocot stems, such as the herbaceous stem of corn. As in herbaceous eudicot stems, the vascular tissues run in strands throughout the length of a stem. In cross section the vascular bundles contain xylem toward the inside and phloem toward the outside. In contrast with herbaceous eudicots, however, vascular bundles of monocots are not arranged in a circle but are scattered throughout the stem (**FIG. 35-2**). Each vascular bundle is enclosed in a bundle sheath of supporting sclerenchyma cells. The monocot stem does not have distinct areas of cortex and pith. The ground tissue in which the vascular tissues are embedded performs the same functions as cortex and pith in herbaceous eudicot stems.

Monocot stems do not possess lateral meristems (vascular cambium and cork cambium) that give rise to secondary growth. Monocots have primary growth only and do not produce wood and bark. Although some treelike monocots (such as palms) attain considerable size, they do so by a modified form of primary growth in which parenchyma cells divide and enlarge. Stems of some monocots (such as bamboo and palm) contain a great deal of sclerenchyma tissue, which makes them hard and woodlike in appearance.

Woody plants have stems with secondary growth

Woody plants undergo secondary growth, an increase in the girth of stems and roots. Secondary growth occurs as a result of the activity of two lateral meristems: vascular cambium and cork cambium. Among flowering plants, only woody eudicots (such as apple, hickory, and maple) have secondary growth. Cone-bearing gymnosperms (such as pine, juniper, and spruce) also have secondary growth.

Cells in the **vascular cambium** divide and produce two conducting and supporting tissues: secondary xylem (wood) to replace primary xylem and secondary phloem (inner bark) to replace primary phloem. Primary xylem and primary phloem are not able to transport materials indefinitely and so are replaced in plants that have extended lifespans.

Cells of the outer lateral meristem, called cork cambium, divide and produce cork cells and cork parenchyma. **Cork cambium** and the tissues it produces are collectively referred to as **periderm** (outer bark), which functions as a replacement for the epidermis (see the last LM in Table 33-4).

Vascular cambium gives rise to secondary xylem and secondary phloem

Primary tissues in woody eudicot stems are organized like those in herbaceous eudicot stems, with the vascular cambium a thin layer of cells sandwiched between xylem and phloem in the vascular

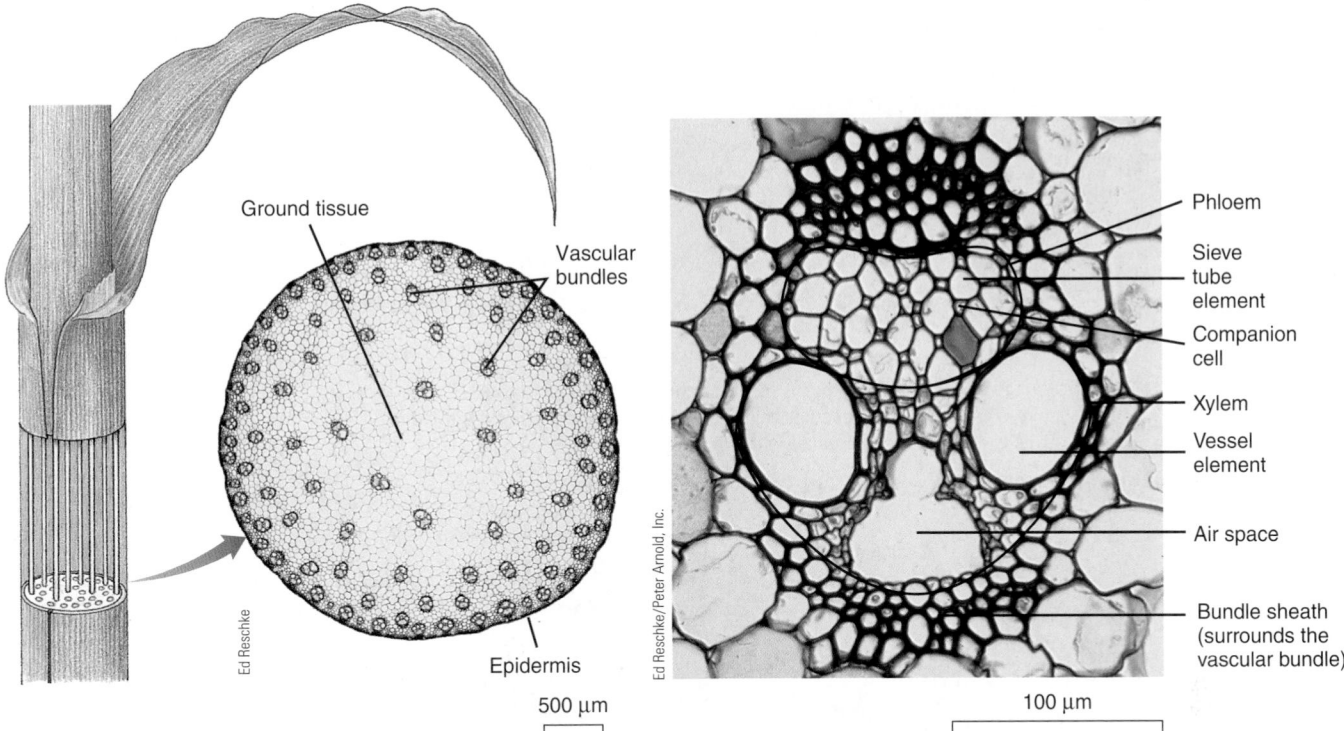

Ground tissue

Vascular bundles

Epidermis

Ed Reschke

500 μm

Phloem

Sieve tube element

Companion cell

Xylem

Vessel element

Air space

Bundle sheath (surrounds the vascular bundle)

Ed Reschke/Peter Arnold, Inc.

100 μm

(a) Cross section of a corn (*Zea mays*) stem shows vascular bundles scattered throughout ground tissue.

(b) Close-up of a vascular bundle. The air space is the site where the first xylem elements were formed and later disintegrated. The entire bundle is enclosed in a bundle sheath of sclerenchyma for additional support.

FIGURE 35-2 *Animated* LMs of a monocot stem

bundles. Once secondary growth begins, the internal structure of a stem changes considerably (**FIG. 35-3**). Although vascular cambium is not initially a continuous cylinder of cells (because the vascular bundles are separated by pith rays), it becomes continuous when production of secondary tissues begins. This continuity develops because certain parenchyma cells in each pith ray retain the ability to divide. These cells connect to vascular cambium cells in each vascular bundle, forming a complete ring of vascular cambium.

Cells in the vascular cambium divide and produce daughter cells in two directions. The cells formed from the dividing vascular cambium are located either *inside* the ring of vascular cambium (to become secondary xylem, or wood) or *outside* it (to become secondary phloem, or inner bark) (**FIG. 35-4**). When a cell in the vascular cambium divides tangentially (inward or outward), one daughter cell remains meristematic; that is, it remains part of the vascular cambium. The other cell may divide again several times, but eventually it stops dividing and develops into mature secondary tissue. Thus, vascular cambium is a thin layer of cells sandwiched between the wood and inner bark, the two tissues it produces (**FIG. 35-5**).

As the stem increases in circumference, the number of cells in the vascular cambium also increases. This increase in cells occurs by an occasional radial division of a vascular cambium cell, at right angles to its normal direction of division. In this case, both daughter cells remain meristematic.

What happens to the original primary tissues of a stem once secondary growth develops? As a stem increases in thickness, the orientation of the original primary tissues changes. For example, secondary xylem and secondary phloem are laid down between the primary xylem and primary phloem within each vascular bundle. Therefore, as vascular cambium forms secondary tissues, the primary xylem and primary phloem in each vascular bundle become separated from one another. The primary tissues located outside the cylinder of secondary growth (that is, primary phloem, cortex, and epidermis) are subjected to the mechanical pressures produced by secondary growth and are gradually crushed or torn apart and sloughed off.

Secondary tissues replace the primary tissues in function. Secondary xylem conducts water and dissolved minerals from roots to leaves in the woody plant. It contains the same types of cells found in primary xylem: water-conducting tracheids and vessel elements, in addition to xylem parenchyma cells and fibers. The arrangement of the different cell types in secondary xylem produces the distinctive wood characteristics of each species.

Secondary phloem conducts dissolved sugar from its place of manufacture or of breakdown of starch to a place of use and storage. The same types of cells found in primary phloem (sieve tube elements, companion cells, phloem parenchyma cells, and fibers) are also found in secondary phloem, although secondary phloem usually has more fibers than primary phloem.

1   At the onset of secondary growth, vascular cambium arises in the parenchyma between the vascular bundles (that is, in the pith rays), forming a cylinder of meristematic tissue (*blue circle in cross section*).

2   Vascular cambium begins to divide, forming secondary xylem on the inside and secondary phloem on the outside.

3   A young woody stem. Vascular cambium produces significantly more secondary xylem than secondary phloem.

FIGURE 35-3 Development of secondary growth

Vascular cambium and the tissues it produces are shown in cross section; cork cambium is not depicted. (The figures change in scale because of space limitations; pith and primary xylem are actually the same size in all three diagrams, but the change in scale makes those tissues appear to shrink in each succeeding diagram.)

Secondary xylem and secondary phloem transport water, minerals, and sugar vertically throughout the woody plant body. However, materials must also move horizontally (laterally). Lateral movement occurs through **rays,** which are chains of parenchyma cells that radiate from the center of the woody stem or root (see Fig. 35-5). The vascular cambium forms rays, which are often continuous from the secondary xylem to the secondary phloem. Water and dissolved minerals are transported laterally through rays, from the secondary xylem to the secondary phloem. Likewise, rays form pathways for the lateral transport of dissolved sugar, from the

To study the figure, start at the bottom and move up. Note that vascular cambium (*the blue cell*) divides in two directions, forming secondary xylem (X) to the inside and secondary phloem (P) to the outside. These cells, which are numbered in the order in which they are produced, differentiate into the mature cell types associated with xylem and phloem. As secondary xylem accumulates, vascular cambium "moves" outward, and the woody stem increases in diameter.

X_1 X_2 X_3 X_4 P_2 P_1

X_1 X_2 X_3 P_2 P_1

X_1 X_2 P_2 P_1

◄──── Secondary xylem ──── Secondary phloem ────►

X_1 X_2 P_1

X_1 P_1 — Second division of vascular cambium forms a phloem cell.

X_1 — Division of vascular cambium forms two cells, one xylem cell and one vascular cambium cell.

— Vascular cambium cell when secondary growth begins.

Vascular cambium cell

Time

FIGURE 35-5 LM of portion of a three-year-old basswood (*Tilia americana*) stem in cross section ►

Garry DeLong/Photo Researchers, Inc.

Periderm and remnants of primary tissues

Secondary phloem

Vascular cambium

Ray

Secondary xylem (3 years' growth)

Summerwood

Springwood

Remnants of primary tissues

100 μm

secondary phloem to the secondary xylem, and of waste products to the center, or heart, of the tree (discussed later).

Cork cambium produces periderm

Cork cambium, which usually arises from parenchyma cells in the outer cortex, produces **periderm,** the functional replacement for the epidermis. Cork cambium is either a continuous cylinder of dividing cells (similar to vascular cambium) or a series of overlapping arcs of meristematic cells that form from parenchyma cells in successively deeper layers of the cortex and, eventually, secondary phloem. Variation in cork cambia and their rates of division explain why the outer bark of some tree species is fissured (as in bur oak), rough and shaggy (shagbark hickory), scaly (Norway pine), or smooth and peeling (paper birch).

As is true of vascular cambium, cork cambium divides to form new tissues in two directions—to its inside and its outside. Cork cells, formed to the outside of cork cambium, are dead at maturity and have walls that contain layers of *suberin* and waxes, making them waterproof. These cork cells protect the woody stem against mechanical injury, mild fires, attacks by insects and fungi, temperature extremes, and water loss. To its inside, cork cambium sometimes forms cork parenchyma cells that store water and starch granules. Cork parenchyma is only one to several cells thick, much thinner than the cork cell layer.

Cork cells are impermeable to water and gases, yet the living internal cells of the woody stem require oxygen and must be able to exchange gases with the surrounding atmosphere. As a stem thickens from secondary growth, the epidermis, including stomata that exchange gases for the herbaceous stem, dies. Stomata are replaced by **lenticels,** which permit gas exchange through the periderm (**FIG. 35-6**).

Woody twigs of deciduous trees bear characteristic features in winter

A woody *twig* is that part of a branch produced during the current growing season. Twigs have **buds,** which are embryonic shoots. A **terminal bud** is the embryonic shoot located at the tip of a stem. The dormant (not actively growing) apical meristem of a terminal bud is covered and protected by an outer layer of **bud scales,** which are modified leaves (see Fig. 34-14c). **Axillary buds,** also called **lateral buds,** are located in the axils of a plant's leaves (see Fig. 34-1). An *axil* is the upper angle between a leaf and the stem to which it is attached. When terminal and axillary buds grow, they form branches that bear leaves and/or flowers. The area on a stem where each leaf is attached is called a **node,** and the region between two successive nodes is an **internode.**

To demonstrate certain structural features of the stem, we can use a woody branch of a deciduous tree that has shed its leaves,

FIGURE 35-6 LM of stem periderm, showing a lenticel
The epidermis has ruptured because of the proliferation of loosely arranged cork cells in the lenticel. From the bark of a calico flower (*Aristolochia elegans*) stem.

as shown in **FIGURE 35-7.** Bud scales cover the terminal bud and protect its delicate apical meristem during dormancy. When the bud resumes growth, the bud scales covering the terminal bud fall off, leaving **bud scale scars** on the stem where they were attached. Because temperate-zone woody plants form terminal buds at the end of each year's growing season, the number of sets of bud scale scars on a twig indicates its age. A **leaf scar** shows where each leaf was attached on the stem; the pattern of leaf scars can be used to determine leaf arrangement on a stem—alternate, opposite, or whorled (see Fig. 34-2b). The vascular (conducting) tissue that extends from the stem out into the leaf forms **bundle scars** within a leaf scar. Axillary buds may be found above the leaf scars. Also, the bark of a woody twig has lenticels, which look like tiny specks on the bark of a twig.

Common terms associated with wood are based on plant structure

If you have ever examined different types of lumber, you may have noticed that some trees have wood with two different colors (**FIG. 35-8**). The functional secondary xylem—the part that conducts water and dissolved minerals—is the *sapwood,* a thin layer of younger, lighter-colored wood that is closest to the bark. *Heartwood,* the older wood in the center of the tree, is typically a brownish red. A microscopic examination of heartwood reveals that its vessels and tracheids are plugged with pigments, tannins, gums, resins, and other materials. Therefore, heartwood no longer functions in conduction but instead functions as a storage site for waste products. Because it is denser than sapwood, heartwood provides structural support for trees. Some evidence suggests that heartwood is also more resistant to decay.

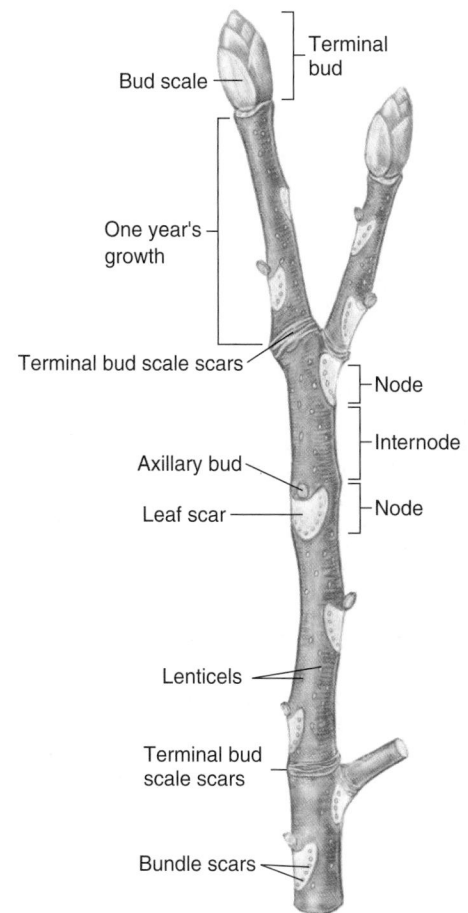

FIGURE 35-7 *Animated* **External structure of a woody branch in its winter condition**

The age of a woody branch can be determined by the number of sets of bud scale scars (do not count side branches). How old is this branch? Can you point out any twigs?

FIGURE 35-8 **Heartwood and sapwood**

The wood of older trees consists of a dense central heartwood and an outer layer of sapwood. The sapwood is the functioning xylem that conducts water and dissolved minerals. The annual rings in the heartwood are very conspicuous.

Almost everyone has heard of hardwood and softwood. Botanically speaking, *hardwood* is the wood of flowering plants and *softwood* is the wood of conifers (cone-bearing gymnosperms). The wood of pine and other conifers typically lacks fibers (with their thick secondary cell walls) and vessel elements; the conducting cells in gymnosperms are tracheids. These cell differences generally make conifer wood softer than the wood of flowering plants, although there is a substantial variation from one species to another. The balsa tree, for example, is a flowering plant whose extremely light, soft wood is used to fashion airplane models.

Woody plants that grow in temperate climates where there is a growing period (during spring and summer) and a dormant period (during winter) exhibit *annual rings,* concentric circles found in cross sections of wood. To determine the age of a woody stem in the temperate zone, simply count the annual rings. In the tropics, environmental conditions, particularly seasonal or year-round precipitation patterns, determine the presence or absence of rings, so rings are not a reliable method of determining the ages of most tropical trees.

Examination of annual rings with a magnifying lens reveals no actual "ring," or line, separating one year's growth from the next. The appearance of a ring in cross section is due to differences in cell size and cell wall thickness between secondary xylem formed at the end of the preceding year's growth and that formed at the beginning of the following year's growth. In the spring, when water is plentiful, wood formed by vascular cambium has large-diameter conducting cells (tracheids and vessel elements) and few fibers and is appropriately called *springwood* or *early wood* (see Fig. 35-5). As summer progresses and water becomes less plentiful, the wood formed, known as *summerwood* or *late wood,* has narrower conducting cells and many fibers. It is this difference in cell size between the summerwood of one year and the springwood of the following year that gives the appearance of rings.

Tree-ring analysis provides useful scientific information

In temperate climates, the number of annual rings indicates the age of a tree. The size of each ring varies depending on local weather conditions. Sometimes the variation can be attributed to a single environmental factor, and similar patterns appear in the rings of different species over a large geographic area. For example, years with adequate precipitation produce wider growth rings, and years of drought produce narrower rings. It is possible to study ring sequences that are several thousand years old by constructing a *master chronology,* a complete sample of rings dating back as far as possible (**FIG. 35-9**).

Dendrochronology, the study of both visible and microscopic details of tree rings, has been used extensively in several fields. Tree-ring analysis has helped date Native American prehistoric sites in the Southwest. For example, using tree-ring analysis, scientists determined that the Cliff Palace in Mesa Verde National Park dates back to the year 1073. Tree-ring analysis is also useful in ecology (to study changes in a forest community over time),

Why Is It Used? By matching the rings of a wood sample of unknown age to the master chronology, investigators can accurately determine the age of the sample. Tree-ring analysis provides useful information in a variety of fields, such as to date prehistoric sites, study past climate patterns, and date major prehistoric earthquakes.

Annual rings

Bark

Tilia
(basswood)

Long, slender core of wood
extracted by a boring tool

Outer bark
Vascular cambium
Annual rings
Pith

1 Sample from a living tree

1950
Outermost ring is
the year when the
tree was cut.

1940

1932

2 Sample from a dead tree
in the same forest

1940

1932   1931

1926

Matching and overlapping older and older
wood sections extends dates back in time.

3 Sample from an old building
in the same area as the forest

1931   1926

1920   1918

How Is It Done? A master chronology is developed using progressively older pieces of wood from the same geographic area. A small core of wood is bored out of the trunk of a living tree. The oldest rings (toward the center of the tree) are matched with the youngest rings (toward the outside) of an older tree, perhaps a dead one in the forest. The master chronology is extended back in time by overlapping matching ring sequences of successively older and older sections of wood, even those found in prehistoric dwellings. Currently, the longest master chronology—of bristlecone pines in the western United States—goes back almost 9000 years. Ring matching, once a tedious, painstaking job, is performed by computers today.

FIGURE 35-9 How tree rings are analyzed

environmental science (to study the effects of air pollution on tree growth), and geology (to date earthquakes and volcanic eruptions).

Climatologists are increasingly using tree-ring data to study past climate patterns. Annual rings of certain tree species that grow at high elevations are sensitive to yearly temperature variations; the rings of these trees are wider in warm years and narrower in

cool years. Studying tree rings over long periods helps researchers determine the natural pattern of global temperature fluctuations. This information is particularly important because of concerns about the human influence on global climate.

Although scientists generally agree that Earth has warmed in recent decades, they are not sure how much of the recent warming is the result of human influence rather than natural climate variability. To help answer this vital question, European scientists are currently developing a 10,000-year master chronology that will help reconstruct annual temperatures across northern Europe and Asia since the end of the last Ice Age.

Review

- How does the arrangement of vascular tissue differ in primary eudicot stems and monocot stems in cross section?
- What is the difference between vascular cambium and cork cambium? What tissues arise from vascular cambium? from cork cambium?
- What happens to the primary tissues of a stem when secondary growth occurs?
- How do growth rings form in woody stems?
- What is the difference between terminal and axillary buds?

35.2 WATER TRANSPORT

◼ LEARNING OBJECTIVES

4   Describe the pathway of water movement in plants.
5   Define *water potential*.
6   Explain the roles of tension–cohesion and root pressure as mechanisms responsible for the rise of water and dissolved minerals in xylem.

Now that we have discussed stem structure and primary and secondary growth, we examine internal transport in the vascular system of the plant (**FIG. 35-10**). Roots obtain water and dissolved minerals from the soil. Once inside roots, these materials are transported upward to stems, leaves, flowers, fruits, and seeds. Furthermore, sugar molecules are transported from their place of manufacture or of breakdown of starch throughout the plant body, including into the subterranean roots. Water and dissolved minerals are transported from roots to other parts of the plant in xylem, whereas dissolved sugar is **translocated** in phloem.

Xylem transport and phloem translocation do not resemble the movement of materials in animals because in plants nothing *circulates* in a system of vessels. Water and minerals, transported in xylem, travel in one direction only (upward), whereas translocation of dissolved sugar may occur upward or downward in separate phloem cells. In addition, xylem transport and phloem translocation differ from internal circulation in animals because movement in both xylem and phloem is driven largely by natural physical processes rather than by a pumping organ, or heart.

How do materials travel in the continuous system of the plant's vascular tissues? We first examine water and its movement through the plant, and later we discuss the translocation of dissolved sugar.

Water and minerals are transported in xylem

Water initially moves horizontally into roots from the soil, passing through several tissues until it reaches xylem. Once the water moves into the tracheids and vessel elements of root xylem, it trav-

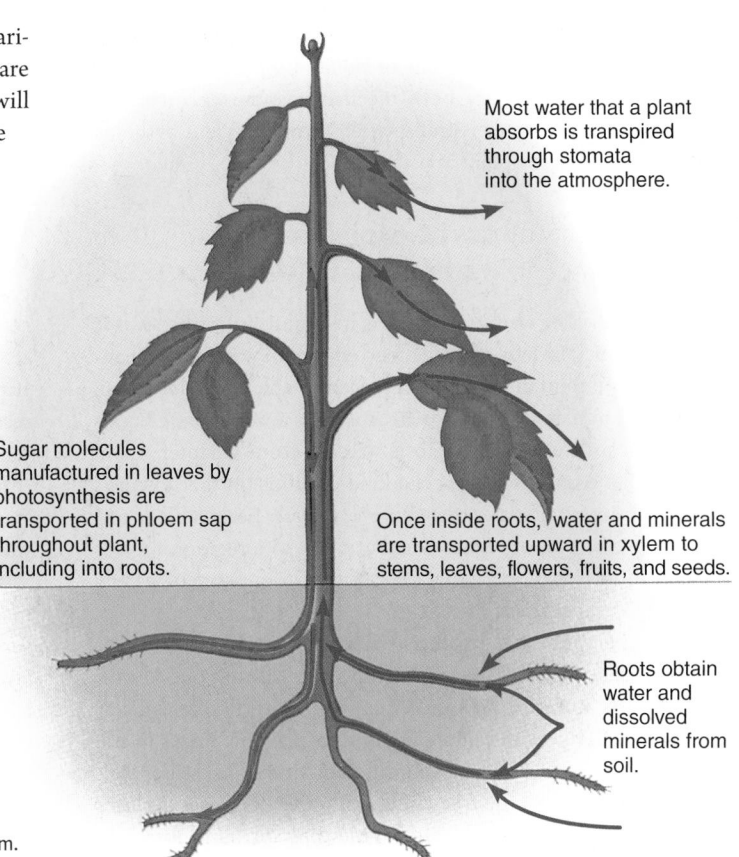

Most water that a plant absorbs is transpired through stomata into the atmosphere.

Sugar molecules manufactured in leaves by photosynthesis are transported in phloem sap throughout plant, including into roots.

Once inside roots, water and minerals are transported upward in xylem to stems, leaves, flowers, fruits, and seeds.

Roots obtain water and dissolved minerals from soil.

FIGURE 35-10 *Animated* **Overview of transport in vascular plants**
Xylem transport is explained on the right side of the figure (start at the bottom and work upward), whereas phloem transport is on the left side.

els upward through a continuous network of these hollow, dead cells from root to stem to leaf. Dissolved minerals are carried along passively in the water. The plant does not expend any energy of its own to transport water, which moves as a result of natural physical processes. The transport of xylem sap is the most rapid of any movement of materials in plants (**TABLE 35-1**).

TABLE 35-1	Xylem and Phloem Transport Rates in Selected Plants	
Plant	Maximum Rate in Xylem (cm/min)	Maximum Rate in Phloem (cm/min)
Conifer	2	0.8
Woody eudicot	73	2
Herbaceous eudicot or monocot	100	2.8–11
Herbaceous vine	250	1.2

Source: Adapted from Mauseth, J. D., *Botany: An Introduction to Plant Biology*, 2nd ed. Saunders College Publishing, Philadelphia, 1995.

Note: Xylem and phloem rates are from different plants within each general group and should be used for comparative purposes only.

How does water move to the tops of plants? It is either pushed up from the bottom of the plant or pulled up by the top of the plant. Although plants use both mechanisms, current evidence indicates that most water is transported through xylem by being *pulled* to the top of the plant.

Water movement can be explained by a difference in water potential

To understand how water moves, it is helpful to introduce **water potential,** which is defined as the **free energy** of water (see Chapter 7). Water potential (Ψ_w), represented by the Greek letter psi, is important in plant physiology because it is a measure of a cell's ability to absorb water by osmosis. (Recall from Chapter 5 and Fig. 5-12 that **osmosis** is a special kind of diffusion that involves the net movement of water through a selectively permeable membrane from a region of higher concentration to a region of lower concentration.) Water potential also provides a measure of water's tendency to evaporate from cells.

The water potential of pure water is conventionally set at 0 megapascals (MPa) because it cannot be measured directly. (A megapascal is a unit of pressure equal to about 10.2 kg/cm^2, or 145.1 lb/in^2.) However, botanists can measure differences in the free energy of water molecules in different situations. When solutes dissolve in water, the free energy of water decreases. Solutes induce **hydration,** in which water molecules surround ions and polar molecules, keeping them in solution by preventing them from coming together (see Fig. 2-10). The association of water molecules with hydrated molecules and ions reduces the motion of water molecules, decreasing their free energy. Thus, dissolved solutes lower the water potential to a negative number. Water moves from a region of higher (less negative) water potential to a region of lower (more negative) water potential.

The water potential of the soil varies, depending on how much water it contains. When a soil is extremely dry, its water potential is very low (very negative). When a soil is moister, its water potential is higher, although it still has a negative value because dissolved minerals are present in dilute concentrations (**TABLE 35-2**).

The water potential in root cells is also negative because of the presence of dissolved solutes. Roots contain more dissolved materials than soil water does, unless the soil is extremely dry. This means that under normal conditions the water potential of the root

TABLE 35-2	Representative Water Potential (Ψ_w) Values*	
Plant Parts and the Nearby Environment	Water Potentials in Megapascals (MPa)
Atmosphere near leaves	−80.0
Leaf interior	−1.5
Stem xylem	−0.7
Root interior	−0.4
Soil water	−0.1

*Actual values vary widely, depending on environmental factors such as solute concentration, hydrostatic pressure, and gravity.

is more negative than the water potential of the soil. Thus, water moves by osmosis from the soil into the root.

According to the tension–cohesion model, water is pulled up a stem

In 1896, Irish botanist Henry Dixon proposed the tension–cohesion model to explain the ascent of water against the force of gravity. Although initially met with widespread skepticism in the scientific community, this model has withstood the test of time. According to the **tension–cohesion model,** also known as the **transpiration–cohesion model,** water is pulled up the plant as a result of a *tension* produced at the top of the plant (**FIG. 35-11**). This tension, which resembles that produced when drinking a liquid through a straw, is caused by the evaporative pull of transpiration. Recall from Chapter 34 that **transpiration** is the evaporation of water vapor from plants.

Most water loss from transpiration takes place through stomata, the numerous microscopic pores present on leaf and stem surfaces. Water vapor diffuses through the stomata into a *boundary layer* of quiet air adjacent to the leaf surface. The boundary layer is thicker when the wind is calm than when it is gusty; a thicker boundary layer results in a slower rate of transpiration.

The tension extends from leaves, where most transpiration occurs, down the stems and into the roots. It draws water up stem xylem to leaf cells that have lost water as a result of transpiration and pulls water from root xylem into stem xylem. As water is pulled upward, additional water from the soil is drawn into the roots. Thus, the pathway of water movement is as follows:

> soil ⟶ root tissues (epidermis, cortex, and so forth) ⟶ root xylem ⟶ stem xylem ⟶ leaf xylem ⟶ leaf mesophyll ⟶ atmosphere

This upward pulling of water is possible only as long as there is an unbroken column of water in xylem throughout the plant. Water forms an unbroken column in xylem because of the *cohesiveness* of water molecules. Recall from Chapter 2 that water molecules are **cohesive,** that is, strongly attracted to one another, because of **hydrogen bonding.** In addition, the **adhesion** of water to the walls of xylem cells, also the result of hydrogen bonding, is an important factor in maintaining an unbroken column of water. Thus, the cohesive and adhesive properties of water enable it to form a continuous column that can be pulled up through the xylem.

The movement of water in xylem by the tension–cohesion mechanism can be explained in terms of water potential. The atmosphere has an extremely negative water potential. For example, air with a relative humidity of 50% has a water potential of −100 MPa; even moist air at a relative humidity of 90% has a negative water potential of −13 MPa. Thus, there is a water potential gradient from the least negative (the soil) up through the plant to the most negative (the atmosphere). This gradient literally pulls the water from the soil up through the plant.

Although the tension–cohesion model was first proposed toward the end of the 19th century, conclusive experimental evidence to support this mechanism was not obtained until the late

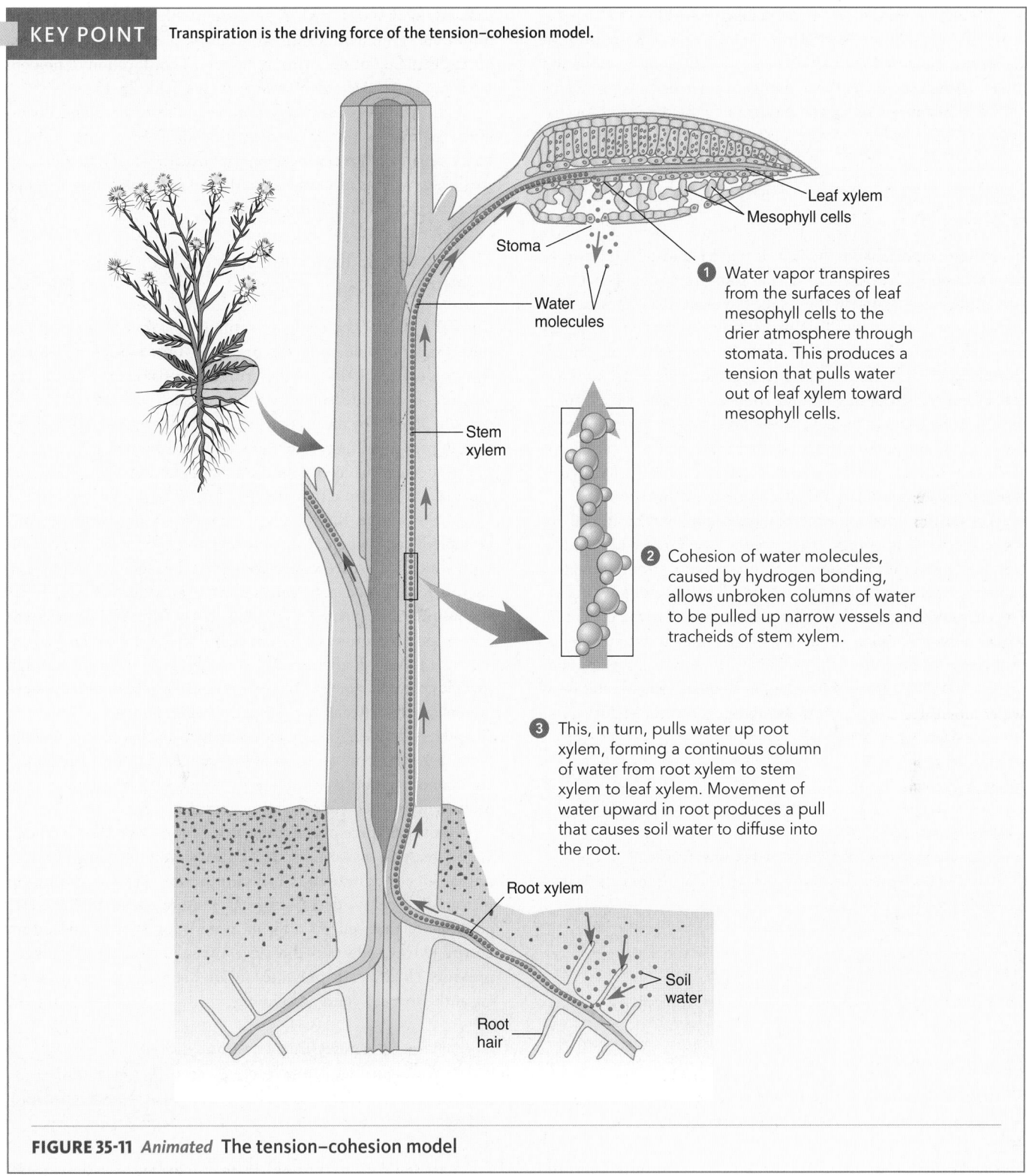

1. Water vapor transpires from the surfaces of leaf mesophyll cells to the drier atmosphere through stomata. This produces a tension that pulls water out of leaf xylem toward mesophyll cells.

2. Cohesion of water molecules, caused by hydrogen bonding, allows unbroken columns of water to be pulled up narrow vessels and tracheids of stem xylem.

3. This, in turn, pulls water up root xylem, forming a continuous column of water from root xylem to stem xylem to leaf xylem. Movement of water upward in root produces a pull that causes soil water to diffuse into the root.

Leaf xylem
Mesophyll cells
Stoma
Water molecules
Stem xylem
Root xylem
Soil water
Root hair

FIGURE 35-11 *Animated* **The tension–cohesion model**

1990s and early 2000s. At that time, several research groups made direct measurements of the large negative pressure that exists in xylem, indicating that the water potential gradients in root, stem, and leaf xylem are adequate to explain the observed movement of water.

Is the tension–cohesion model powerful enough to explain the rise of water in the tallest plants? Plant biologists have studied this question for years. For example, a 2004 study of five of the eight tallest trees in the world (all redwoods, or *Sequoia sempervirens*) concluded that the tension produced by transpiration is strong enough to pull water upward to a maximum height of 130 m (422 ft). Because the height of the tallest known living tree, a coast redwood in California, measured 117 m (379 ft) in 2007, the tension–cohesion model easily accounts for the transport of water. Botanists generally consider the tension–cohesion model to be the dominant mechanism of xylem transport in most plants.

Root pressure pushes water from the root up a stem

In the less important mechanism for water transport, known as **root pressure,** water that moves into roots from the soil is *pushed* up through xylem toward the top of the plant. Root pressure occurs because mineral ions that are actively absorbed from the soil are pumped into the xylem, decreasing its water potential. This accumulation of ions has an osmotic effect, causing water to move into xylem cells from surrounding root cells. In turn, water moves into roots by osmosis because of the difference in water potential between the soil and root cells. The accumulation of water in root tissues produces a positive pressure (as high as +0.2 MPa) that forces the water up through the root xylem into the shoot.

Guttation, a phenomenon in which liquid water is forced out through special openings in the leaves (see Fig. 34-12), results from root pressure. However, root pressure is not strong enough to explain the rise of water to the tops of tall trees. Root pressure exerts an influence in much smaller plants, particularly in the spring when the soil is moist, but it clearly does not cause water to rise to the tops of the tallest plants. Furthermore, root pressure does not occur to any appreciable extent in summer (when water is often not plentiful in soil), yet water transport is greatest during hot summer days.

Review

- What is water potential?
- How is the movement of water related to water potential?
- How does the tension–cohesion model explain the rise of water in the tallest trees?

35.3 TRANSLOCATION OF SUGAR IN SOLUTION

■ LEARNING OBJECTIVES

7 Describe the pathway of sugar translocation in plants.

8 Discuss the pressure–flow model of sugar translocation in phloem.

The sugar produced during photosynthesis is converted into sucrose (common table sugar), a disaccharide composed of one molecule of glucose and one of fructose (see Fig. 3-8b), before being loaded into phloem and translocated to the rest of the plant. Sucrose is the predominant photosynthetic product carried in phloem. Phloem sap also contains much smaller amounts of other materials, such as amino acids, organic acids, proteins, hormones,

and certain minerals (such as potassium, chloride, phosphate, and magnesium). Sometimes disease-causing plant viruses are transported throughout the plant in phloem. Translocation of phloem sap is not as rapid as xylem transport (see Table 35-1).

Fluid within phloem tissue moves both upward and downward. Sucrose is translocated in individual sieve tubes from a *source*, an area of excess sugar supply (usually a leaf), to a *sink*, an area of storage (as insoluble starch) or of sugar use, such as roots, apical meristems, fruits, and seeds.

The pressure–flow model explains translocation in phloem

Current experimental evidence supports the translocation of dissolved sugar in phloem by the **pressure–flow model,** which was first proposed in 1926 by the German scientist Ernst Münch. The pressure–flow model states that solutes (such as dissolved sugars) move in phloem by means of a pressure gradient—that is, a difference in pressure. The pressure gradient exists between the source, where the sugar is loaded into phloem, and the sink, where the sugar is removed from phloem.

At the source, the dissolved sucrose is moved from a leaf's mesophyll cells, where it was manufactured, into the companion cells, which load sucrose into the sieve tube elements of phloem. Sucrose loading occurs by active transport, a process that requires adenosine triphosphate (ATP) (**FIG. 35-12**). The ATP supplies energy to pump protons (H^+) out of the sieve tube elements, producing a proton gradient that drives the uptake of sugar through specific channels by the **cotransport** of protons back into the sieve tube elements. (Recall the discussion of a cotransport system in Chapter 5.) In the cotransport system involved in phloem loading, sugar is moved from a region of low concentration to a region of high concentration by coupling its transport to the transport of protons down their concentration gradient.

The sugar therefore accumulates in the sieve tube element. The increase in dissolved sugars in the sieve tube element at the source—a concentration that is two to three times as great as in surrounding cells—decreases (makes more negative) the water potential of that cell. As a result, water moves by osmosis from nearby xylem cells into the sieve tubes, increasing the **turgor pressure** (hydrostatic pressure) inside them. Thus, phloem loading at the source occurs as follows:

proton pump moves H^+ out of sieve tube element ⟶ sugar is actively transported into sieve tube element ⟶ water diffuses from xylem into sieve tube element ⟶ turgor pressure increases within sieve tube

At its destination (the sink), sugar is unloaded by various mechanisms, both active and passive, from the sieve tube elements. With the loss of sugar, the water potential in the sieve tube elements at the sink increases (becomes less negative). Therefore, water moves out of the sieve tubes by osmosis and into surrounding cells where the water potential is more negative. Most of this water diffuses back to the xylem to be transported upward. This water movement de-

In phloem, solutes move from sources to sinks. The pressure gradient within the sieve tube causes translocation from the area of higher turgor pressure (the source) to the area of lower turgor pressure (the sink).

1 Sucrose is actively loaded into sieve tube elements (requires ATP).

2 Water diffuses from xylem as a result of decreased (more negative) water potential in sieve tube.

3 The increase in pressure forces the fluid through the sieve tube to the root.

4 Sucrose is actively and passively unloaded into sink cell, such as parenchyma cell in the root cortex. (Active unloading requires ATP.)

5 Water diffuses from phloem to xylem as a result of increased (less negative) water potential in sieve tube.

6 Once water is in the xylem, transpiration pulls water to leaves again.

XYLEM   PHLOEM

SOURCE   Leaf cell

Companion cells

Sieve tube element

Direction of water movement

Direction of sucrose movement

SINK   Root cell

Vessel running through length of plant

Sieve tube running through length of plant

FIGURE 35-12 *Animated* The pressure–flow model

The pressure–flow model explains the movement of dissolved sugar in phloem by means of a pressure gradient. The difference in sugar concentrations between the source and the sink causes translocation in phloem as water and dissolved sugar flow along the pressure gradient. This pressure gradient pushes the sugar solution through phloem much as water is forced through a hose.

The actual translocation of dissolved sugar in phloem does not require metabolic energy. However, the loading of sugar at the source and the active unloading of sugar at the sink require energy derived from ATP to move the sugar across cell membranes by active transport.

Although the pressure–flow model adequately explains current data on phloem translocation, much remains to be learned about this complex process. Phloem translocation is difficult to study in plants. Because phloem cells are under pressure, cutting into phloem to observe it releases the pressure and causes the contents of the sieve tube elements (the phloem sap) to exude and mix with the contents of other severed cells that are also unavoidably cut. In the 1950s, scientists developed a unique research tool to avoid contaminating the phloem sap: aphids, which are small insects that insert their mouthparts into phloem sieve tubes for feeding (**FIG. 35-13**). The pressure in the punctured phloem drives the sugar solution through the aphid's mouthpart into its digestive system. When the aphid's mouthpart is severed from its body by a laser beam, the sugar solution continues to flow through the mouthpart at a rate proportional to the pressure in phloem. This rate can be measured, and the effects on phloem transport of different environmental conditions—varying light intensities, darkness, and mineral deficiencies, for example—can be ascertained.

The identity and proportions of translocated substances can also be determined using severed aphid mouthparts. This technique has verified that in most plant species the sugar sucrose is the primary carbohydrate transported in phloem; however, some species transport other sugars, such as raffinose, or sugar alcohols, such as sorbitol.

creases the turgor pressure inside the sieve tubes at the sink. Thus, phloem unloading at the sink proceeds as follows:

sugar is transported out of sieve tube element ⟶ water diffuses out of sieve tube element and into xylem ⟶ turgor pressure decreases within sieve tube

Review

- How does the direction of transport differ in xylem and phloem?
- How does the pressure–flow model explain sugar movement in phloem? Include in your answer the activities at source and sink.

QUESTION: How can phloem sap be studied without cutting nonphloem cells that would contaminate the sap?

HYPOTHESIS: An aphid mouthpart can be used to penetrate a single sieve tube.

EXPERIMENT: After allowing aphids to insert their mouthparts into phloem of a stem, researchers anesthetized the feeding aphids with CO_2 and used a laser to cut their bodies away from their mouthparts. The mouthparts remained in the phloem and functioned like miniature pipes.

25 µm

M. H. Zimmermann, SCIENCE, Vol. 133, pp. 73–79 (Fig. 4), 13 Jan. 1961. © 1961 by the American Association for the Advancement of Science

Dwight Kuhn

(a) Aphid feeding on a stem.

(b) LM of phloem cells, showing an aphid mouthpart penetrating a sieve tube element.

RESULTS AND CONCLUSION: About 1 mm³ of phloem sap exuded from each severed mouthpart per hour for several days, so researchers were able to collect and analyze the composition of the sap.

FIGURE 35-13 Collecting and analyzing phloem sap

This method, first used in the 1950s by insect physiologists studying aphids, was quickly adopted by plant physiologists studying phloem translocation.

■ SUMMARY: FOCUS ON LEARNING OBJECTIVES

35.1 *(page 745)*

1 Label cross sections of herbaceous eudicot and monocot stems, and describe the functions of each tissue.

- Herbaceous stems possess an epidermis, vascular tissue, and either ground tissue or cortex and pith. The **epidermis** is a protective layer covered by a water-conserving **cuticle. Stomata** permit gas exchange. **Xylem** conducts water and dissolved minerals, and **phloem** conducts dissolved sugar. The **cortex, pith,** and ground tissue function primarily for storage.

- All herbaceous stems have the same basic tissues, but their arrangement varies. Herbaceous eudicot stems have the vascular bundles arranged in a circle (in cross section) and have a distinct cortex and pith. Monocot stems have vascular bundles scattered in ground tissue.

    CENGAGENOW™ Learn more about eudicot and monocot stems by clicking on the figures in CengageNOW.

2 Name the two lateral meristems and describe the tissues that arise from each.

- **Vascular cambium** is the lateral meristem that produces secondary xylem (wood) and secondary phloem (inner bark).

- **Cork cambium** produces **periderm,** which consists of cork parenchyma and cork cells. Cork cells are the functional replacement for epidermis in a woody stem. Cork parenchyma functions primarily for storage in a woody stem.

3 Outline the transition from primary growth to secondary growth in a woody stem.

- **Secondary growth** (the production of the secondary tissues, wood and bark) occurs in some flowering plants (woody eudicots) and in all cone-bearing gymnosperms. During secondary growth, the vascular cambium divides in two directions to form secondary xylem (to the inside) and secondary phloem (to the outside). The primary xylem and primary phloem in the original vascular bundles become separated as secondary growth proceeds.

CENGAGENOW™ Learn more about secondary growth by clicking on the figures in CengageNOW.

35.2 *(page 753)*

4 Describe the pathway of water movement in plants.

- Water and dissolved minerals move from the soil into root tissues (epidermis, cortex, and so forth). Once in root xylem, water and minerals move upward, from root xylem to stem xylem to leaf xylem. Much of the water entering the leaf exits leaf veins and passes into the atmosphere.

5 Define *water potential*.

- **Water potential (Ψ_w)** is a measure of the **free energy** of water. Pure water has a water potential of 0 megapascals (MPa), whereas water with dissolved solutes has a negative water potential. Water moves from an area of higher (less negative) water potential to an area of lower (more negative) water potential.

6 Explain the roles of tension–cohesion and root pressure as mechanisms responsible for the rise of water and dissolved minerals in xylem.

- The **tension–cohesion model** explains the rise of water in even the tallest plants. The evaporative pull of **transpiration** causes tension at the top of the plant. This tension is the result of a water potential gradient that ranges from the slightly negative water potentials in the soil and roots to the very negative water potentials in the atmosphere. As a result of the **cohesive** and **adhesive** properties of water, the column of water pulled up through the plant remains unbroken.

CENGAGENOW™ Learn more about the tension–cohesion model by clicking on the figure in CengageNOW.

- **Root pressure,** caused by the movement of water into roots from the soil as a result of the active absorption of mineral ions from the soil, helps explain the rise of water in smaller plants, particularly when the soil is wet. Root pressure pushes water up through xylem.

35.3 *(page 756)*

7 Describe the pathway of sugar translocation in plants.

- Dissolved sugar is **translocated** upward or downward in phloem, from a source (an area of excess sugar, usually a leaf) to a sink (an area of storage or of sugar use, such as roots, apical meristems, fruits, and seeds). Sucrose is the predominant sugar translocated in phloem.

8 Discuss the pressure–flow model of sugar translocation in phloem.

- Movement of materials in phloem is explained by the **pressure–flow model.** Companion cells actively load sugar into the sieve tubes at the source; ATP is required for this process. The ATP supplies energy to pump protons out of the sieve tube elements. The proton gradient drives the uptake of sugar by the cotransport of protons back into the sieve tube elements. Sugar therefore accumulates in the sieve tube element, causing the movement of water into the sieve tubes by **osmosis.**

- Companion cells actively (requiring ATP) and passively (not requiring ATP) unload sugar from the sieve tubes at the sink. As a result, water leaves the sieve tubes by osmosis, decreasing the **turgor pressure** (hydrostatic pressure) inside the sieve tubes.

- The flow of materials between source and sink is driven by the turgor pressure gradient produced by water entering phloem at the source and water leaving phloem at the sink.

CENGAGENOW™ Learn more about how sugar travels by clicking on the figure in CengageNOW.

TEST YOUR UNDERSTANDING

1. Axillary buds are located (a) at the tips of stems (b) in unusual places, such as on roots (c) in the region between two successive nodes (d) in the upper angle between a leaf and the stem to which it is attached (e) within the loosely arranged cells of lenticels

2. Ground tissue in monocot stems performs the same functions as _____ and _____ in herbaceous eudicot stems. (a) phloem; xylem (b) cork cambium; vascular cambium (c) epidermis; periderm (d) primary xylem; secondary xylem (e) cortex; pith

3. Which of the following statements is *false*? (a) primary growth is an increase in the length of a plant (b) primary growth occurs at both apical and lateral meristems (c) all plants have primary growth (d) herbaceous stems have primary growth, whereas woody stems have both primary and secondary growth (e) buds are embryonic shoots that contain apical meristems

4. The two lateral meristems responsible for secondary growth are (a) phloem and xylem (b) cork cambium and vascular cambium (c) epidermis and periderm (d) primary xylem and secondary xylem (e) cortex and pith

5. Cork cambium and the tissues it produces are collectively called (a) periderm (b) lenticels (c) cortex (d) epidermis (e) wood

6. Each annual ring in a section of wood represents one year's growth of (a) primary xylem (b) secondary xylem (c) primary xylem or secondary xylem in alternate years (d) primary phloem (e) secondary phloem

7. Water potential is (a) the formation of a proton gradient across a cell membrane (b) the transport of a watery solution of sugar in phloem (c) the transport of water in both xylem and phloem (d) the removal of sucrose at the sink, causing water to move out of the sieve tubes (e) the free energy of water in a particular situation

8. Which of the following is a mechanism of water movement in xylem that is responsible for guttation? (a) pressure–flow (b) tension–cohesion (c) root pressure (d) active transport of potassium ions into guard cells (e) transpiration

9. Which of the following is a mechanism of water movement in xylem that combines the evaporative pull of transpiration with

the cohesive and adhesive properties of water? (a) pressure–flow (b) tension–cohesion (c) root pressure (d) active transport of potassium ions into guard cells (e) guttation

10. Which of the following is a mechanism of phloem transport in which dissolved sugar is moved by means of a pressure gradient that exists between the source and the sink? (a) pressure–flow (b) tension–cohesion (c) root pressure (d) active transport of potassium ions into guard cells (e) guttation

11. How does increasing solute concentration affect water potential? (a) water potential becomes more positive (b) water potential becomes more negative (c) water potential becomes more positive under certain conditions and more negative under other conditions (d) water potential is not affected by solute concentration (e) water potential is always zero when solutes are dissolved in water

12. Label the various tissues, give at least one function for each tissue, and identify the stem as a herbaceous eudicot, monocot, or woody plant. Use Figure 35-1 to check your answers.

(a)

(b)

CRITICAL THINKING

1. When secondary growth is initiated, certain cells become meristematic and begin to divide. Could a mature tracheid ever do this? a sieve tube element? Why or why not?

2. Why does the wood of many tropical trees lack annual rings? Why does the wood of other tropical trees possess annual rings?

3. Why is hardwood more desirable than softwood for making furniture? Explain your answer, based on the structural differences between hardwood and softwood.

4. Why should you cut off a few inches from the stem ends of cut flowers before placing them in water? Base your answer on what you have learned about the tension–cohesion model.

5. When a strip of bark is peeled off a tree branch, what tissues are usually removed?

6. Could a tree grow to a height of 150 m (488 ft)? Why or why not?

7. **EVOLUTION LINK.** Like stems in general, some vines are herbaceous and others are woody. Tropical rain forests have a greater diversity of vines than in any other environment on Earth, and most of these vines are woody. Develop a hypothesis to explain why natural selection has favored the evolution of more species of woody vines (as opposed to herbaceous vines) in tropical rain forests.

8. **ANALYZING DATA.** A plant cell with a water potential $\Psi_w = -1.5$ MPa is adjacent to a second cell with $\Psi_w = -1.8$ MPa. Will water flow by osmosis from one cell to the other? If so, in which direction?

 Additional questions are available in CengageNOW at www.cengage.com/ login.

36 Roots and Mineral Nutrition

Storage roots. Cassava (*Manihot esculenta*) plants have been dug up to show the growth habit of the storage roots. Cassava roots are an important staple crop in the tropics. Some cassava roots contain a poison (prussic acid), which is destroyed during cooking.

© Inga Spence/Alamy

KEY CONCEPTS

36.1 Root structure is related to function. Primary tissues (epidermis, cortex, endodermis, pericycle, xylem, and phloem) of roots develop from root apical meristems. Secondary tissues (wood and bark) of woody roots develop from lateral meristems.

36.2 Roots associate and interact with many organisms, including soil bacteria and fungi.

36.3 Soil, the layer of Earth's crust that has been modified by contact with weather, wind, water, and organisms, contains most of the essential elements required by plants.

Branching underground root systems are often more extensive than a plant's aerial parts. The roots of a corn plant, for example, may grow to a depth of 2.5 m (about 8 ft) and spread outward 1.2 m (4 ft) from the stem. Desert-dwelling tamarisk (*Tamarix*) trees reportedly have roots that grow to a depth of 50 m (163 ft) to tap underground water. The extent of a plant's root depth and spread varies considerably among different species and even among different individuals in the same species.

Because roots are usually underground and out of sight, people do not always appreciate the important functions they perform. First, as anyone who has ever pulled weeds can attest, roots anchor a plant securely in the soil. A plant needs a solid foundation from which to grow. Firm anchorage is essential to a plant's survival so that the stem remains upright, enabling leaves to absorb sunlight effectively. Second, roots absorb water and dissolved minerals (inorganic nutrients) such as nitrates, phosphates, and sulfates, which are necessary for synthesizing important organic molecules. These dissolved minerals are then transported throughout the plant in the xylem.

Many roots perform the function of storage. Carrots, sweet potatoes, cassava, and other root crops are important sources of human food (see photograph). Surplus sugars produced in the leaves by photosynthesis are transported in the phloem to the roots for food storage (usually as starch or sucrose) until needed. Other plants, particularly those living in arid regions, possess storage roots adapted to store water.

In certain species, roots are modified for functions other than anchorage, absorption, conduction, and storage. Roots specialized to perform uncommon functions are discussed later in the chapter.

36.1 ROOT STRUCTURE AND FUNCTION

LEARNING OBJECTIVES

1 Distinguish between taproot and fibrous root systems.
2 Compare cross sections of a primary eudicot root and a monocot root, and describe the functions of each tissue.
3 Trace the pathway of water and mineral ions from the soil through the various root tissues, and distinguish between the symplast and apoplast.
4 Discuss the structure of roots with secondary growth.
5 Describe at least three roots that are modified to perform uncommon functions.

Two types of root systems, a taproot system and a fibrous root system, occur in plants (**FIG. 36-1**). A **taproot** system consists of one main root that formed from the seedling's enlarging **radicle,** or

FIGURE 36-1 *Animated* **Root systems**
(a) A taproot system develops from the embryonic root in the seed.
(b) The roots of a fibrous root system are adventitious and develop from stem tissue.

embryonic root. Many lateral roots of various sizes branch out of a taproot. Taproots are characteristic of many eudicots and gymnosperms. A dandelion is a good example of a common herbaceous plant with a taproot system. A few trees, such as hickory, retain their taproots, which become quite massive as the plants age. Most trees, however, have taproots when young and later develop large, shallow, lateral roots from which other roots branch off and grow downward.

A **fibrous root** system has several to many roots of similar size developing from the end of the stem, with lateral roots branching off these roots. Fibrous root systems form in plants that have a short-lived embryonic root. The roots originate first from the base of the embryonic root and later from stem tissue. The main roots of a fibrous root system do not arise from pre-existing roots but from the stem; such roots are called **adventitious roots.** Adventitious organs occur in an unusual location, such as roots that develop on a stem, or buds that develop on roots. Onions, crabgrass, and other monocots have fibrous root systems.

Taproot and fibrous root systems are adapted to obtain water in different sections of the soil. Taproot systems often extend down into the soil to obtain water located deep underground, whereas fibrous root systems, which are located relatively close to the soil surface, are adapted to obtain rainwater from a larger area as it drains into the soil.

Roots have root caps and root hairs

Because of the need to adapt to the soil environment instead of the atmospheric environment, roots have several structures, such as root caps and root hairs, that shoots lack. Although stems and leaves have various types of hairs, they are distinct from root hairs in structure and function.

Each root tip is covered by a **root cap,** a protective, thimblelike layer many cells thick that covers the delicate root **apical meristem** (**FIG. 36-2a**; also see Fig. 33-6). As the root grows, pushing its way through the soil, cells of the root cap are sloughed off by the frictional resistance of the soil particles and replaced by new cells formed by the root apical meristem. The root cap cells secrete lubricating polysaccharides that reduce friction as the root passes through the soil. The root cap also appears to be involved in orienting the root so that it grows downward (see discussion of gravitropism in Chapter 38). When a root cap is removed, the root apical meristem grows a new cap. However, until the root cap has regenerated, the root grows randomly rather than in the direction of gravity.

Root hairs are short-lived tubular extensions of epidermal cells located just behind the growing root tip. Root hairs continually form in the area of cell maturation closest to the root tip to replace those that are dying off at the more mature end of the root-hair zone (**FIG. 36-2b**; also see Fig. 33-6). Each root hair is short (typically less than 1 cm, or 0.4 in, in length), but they are quite numerous. Root hairs greatly increase the absorptive capacity of roots by increasing their surface area in contact with moist soil. Soil particles are coated with a microscopically thin layer of water in which minerals are dissolved. The root hairs establish an intimate contact with soil particles, which allows efficient absorption of water and minerals.

Runk/Rannels/Grant Heilman Photography

250 μm

Cengage

Root apical
meristem
(area of
cell division)

Root cap

Root hairs

Soil air

Soil water

Soil particles

Epidermis

(a) Root cap. LM of an oak (*Quercus* sp.) root tip showing its root cap. The root apical meristem is protected by the root cap.

(b) Root hairs. Each delicate hair is an extension of a single cell of the root epidermis. Root hairs increase the surface area of the root in contact with the soil. This radish (*Raphanus sativus*) seedling is approximately 5 cm (2 in) long.

FIGURE 36-2 *Animated* Structures unique to roots

The development of root hairs is under the control of two regulatory genes that code for **transcription factors.** (You may recall from Chapter 14 that transcription factors are DNA-binding proteins that regulate the synthesis of RNA from a DNA template.) In 2007, researchers from the United Kingdom and France reported in the journal *Science* that these two genes have an ancient origin with evolutionary significance. The biologists compared two genes that control rhizoid formation in the gametophyte stage of the moss *Physcomitrella patens* to those that control root hair formation in the sporophyte stage of the angiosperm *Arabidopsis thaliana*. They found that the genes code for transcription factors that are essentially the same in both plants. Mosses such as *Physcomitrella* represent an ancient lineage of land plants (see Chapter 27). It therefore appears that these genes were conserved during the evolution from a dominant gametophyte in mosses to a dominant sporophyte in flowering plants.

The arrangement of vascular tissues distinguishes the roots of herbaceous eudicots and monocots

Although considerable variation exists in herbaceous eudicot and monocot roots, they all have an outer protective covering (epidermis), a cortex for storage of starch and other organic molecules, and vascular tissues for conduction. Let us first consider the structure of herbaceous eudicot roots.

In most herbaceous eudicot roots, the central core of vascular tissue lacks pith

The buttercup root is a representative eudicot root with primary growth (**FIG. 36-3**). Like other parts of this herbaceous eudicot, a single layer of protective tissue, the **epidermis,** covers its roots.

The root hairs are a modification of the root epidermis that enables it to absorb more water from the soil. The root epidermis does not secrete a thick, waxy cuticle in the region of root hairs because this layer would impede the absorption of water from the soil. Both the lack of a cuticle and the presence of root hairs increase absorption.

Beginning with the root hairs, most of the water that enters the root moves along the cell walls rather than enters the cells. One of the major components of cell walls is cellulose, which absorbs water as a sponge does. An example of the absorptive properties of cellulose is found in cotton balls, which are almost pure cellulose.

The **cortex,** which is composed primarily of loosely packed **parenchyma** cells, composes the bulk of a herbaceous eudicot root. Roots usually lack supporting **collenchyma** cells, probably because the soil supports the root, although roots as they age may develop some **sclerenchyma** (another supporting tissue; see Chapter 33). The primary function of the root cortex is storage. A microscopic examination of the parenchyma cells that form the cortex often reveals numerous amyloplasts (see Figs. 36-3b and 3-9a), which store starch. Starch, an insoluble carbohydrate composed of glucose subunits, is the most common form of stored energy in plants. When used at a later time, these reserves provide energy for such activities as growth and cell replacement following an injury.

The large intercellular (between-cell) spaces, a common feature of the root cortex, provide a pathway for water uptake and allow for aeration of the root. The oxygen that root cells need for aerobic respiration diffuses from air spaces in the soil into the intercellular spaces of the cortex and from there into the cells of the root.

The water and dissolved minerals that enter the root cortex from the epidermis move in solution along two pathways: the symplast and apoplast (**FIG. 36-4**). The **symplast** is the continuum of

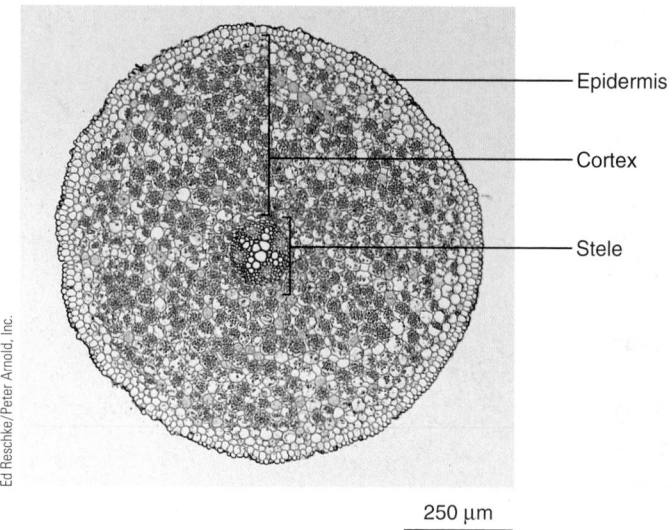

Ed Reschke/Peter Arnold, Inc.

Epidermis

Cortex

Stele

250 μm

(a) Eudicot root. Cortex composes the bulk of herbaceous eudicot roots. Note the X-shaped xylem in the center of the root.

Ed Reschke/Peter Arnold, Inc.

Cortex cells filled with amyloplasts

Endodermis cell

Pericycle cell

Phloem cell

Xylem vessel elements

Intercellular space in cortex

25 μm

(b) Stele of eudicot root. Surrounding the solid core of vascular tissues is a single layer of pericycle, which is meristematic in growing roots.

FIGURE 36-3 LMs of cross sections of a herbaceous eudicot root

Shown is a buttercup (*Ranunculus*) root.

KEY POINT The symplast pathway (*blue*) consists of living cells interconnected by plasmodesmata. The apoplast pathway (*red*) uses cell walls and intercellular spaces.

Movement upward by tension–cohesion

Xylem vessels

Endodermis

Casparian strip

Cortex

Epidermis

Symplast: interconnected cytoplasm of living cells

Phloem cells

Pericycle

Water and dissolved nutrient minerals

Plasma membrane

Plasmodesma

Cell wall

Apoplast: interconnected cell wall spaces

Root hair

FIGURE 36-4 Pathways of water and dissolved minerals in the root

Water and dissolved minerals travel from cell to cell along the interconnected porous cell walls (the apoplast) or from one cell's cytoplasm to another through plasmodesmata (the symplast). On reaching the endodermis, water and minerals can move into the root's center only if they pass through a plasma membrane and enter the cytoplasm of an endodermal cell.

living cytoplasm, which is connected from one cell to the next by cytoplasmic bridges called **plasmodesmata** (see Fig. 5-27). Some dissolved mineral ions move from the epidermis through the cortex via the symplast. The **apoplast** consists of the interconnected porous cell walls of a plant, along which water and mineral ions move freely. The water and mineral ions can diffuse across the cortex without ever crossing a plasma membrane to enter a living cell. Together the symplast and apoplast make up the entire plant body.

The inner layer of the cortex, the **endodermis,** regulates the movement of water and minerals that enter the xylem in the root's center. Structurally, the endodermis differs from the rest of the cortex. Endodermal cells fit snugly against one another, and each has a special bandlike region, called a **Casparian strip** (**FIG. 36-5**), on its radial (side) and transverse (upper and lower) walls. Casparian strips contain *suberin,* a fatty material that is waterproof. (Recall from Chapter 33 that suberin is also the waterproof material in cork cell walls.)

Until the endodermis is reached, most of the water and dissolved minerals have traveled along the apoplast and therefore have not passed through a plasma membrane or entered the cytoplasm of a root cell. However, the waterproof Casparian strip on the radial and transverse walls of the endodermal cells prevents water and minerals from continuing to move passively along the cell walls. For substances to pass farther into the root interior, they must move from the cell walls into the cytoplasm of the endodermal cells. Water enters by osmosis, both directly across the lipid bilayer of the endodermal plasma membrane and through

aquaporins, integral membrane proteins that facilitate the rapid transport of water across the membrane (**FIG. 36-6a**). As in water movement across the lipid bilayer, water moves through aquaporins only along the osmotic gradient, from a region of higher water concentration to a region of lower water concentration. The key role of aquaporins in the uptake of water by root cells is currently under active study.

Minerals enter endodermal cells by passing through carrier proteins in their plasma membranes. In **carrier-mediated active transport,** the mineral ions are pumped *against* their concentration gradient—that is, from an area of *low* concentration of that mineral in the soil solution to an area of *high* concentration in the plant's cells (**FIG. 36-6b**). One of many reasons why root cells require sugar and oxygen for aerobic respiration is that this active transport requires the expenditure of energy, usually in the form of ATP. From the endodermis, water and mineral ions enter the root xylem (botanists do not yet know precisely how this is done) and are conducted to the rest of the plant.

At the center of a eudicot primary root is the **stele,** or **vascular cylinder,** a central cylinder of vascular tissues. The outermost layer of the stele is the **pericycle,** which is just inside the endodermis. The pericycle consists of a single layer of parenchyma cells that give rise to multicellular *lateral roots,* also called branch roots (**FIG. 36-7**). Lateral roots originate when cells in a portion of the pericycle start dividing. As it grows, the lateral root pushes through several layers of root tissue (endodermis, cortex, and epidermis) before entering the soil. Each lateral root has all the structures

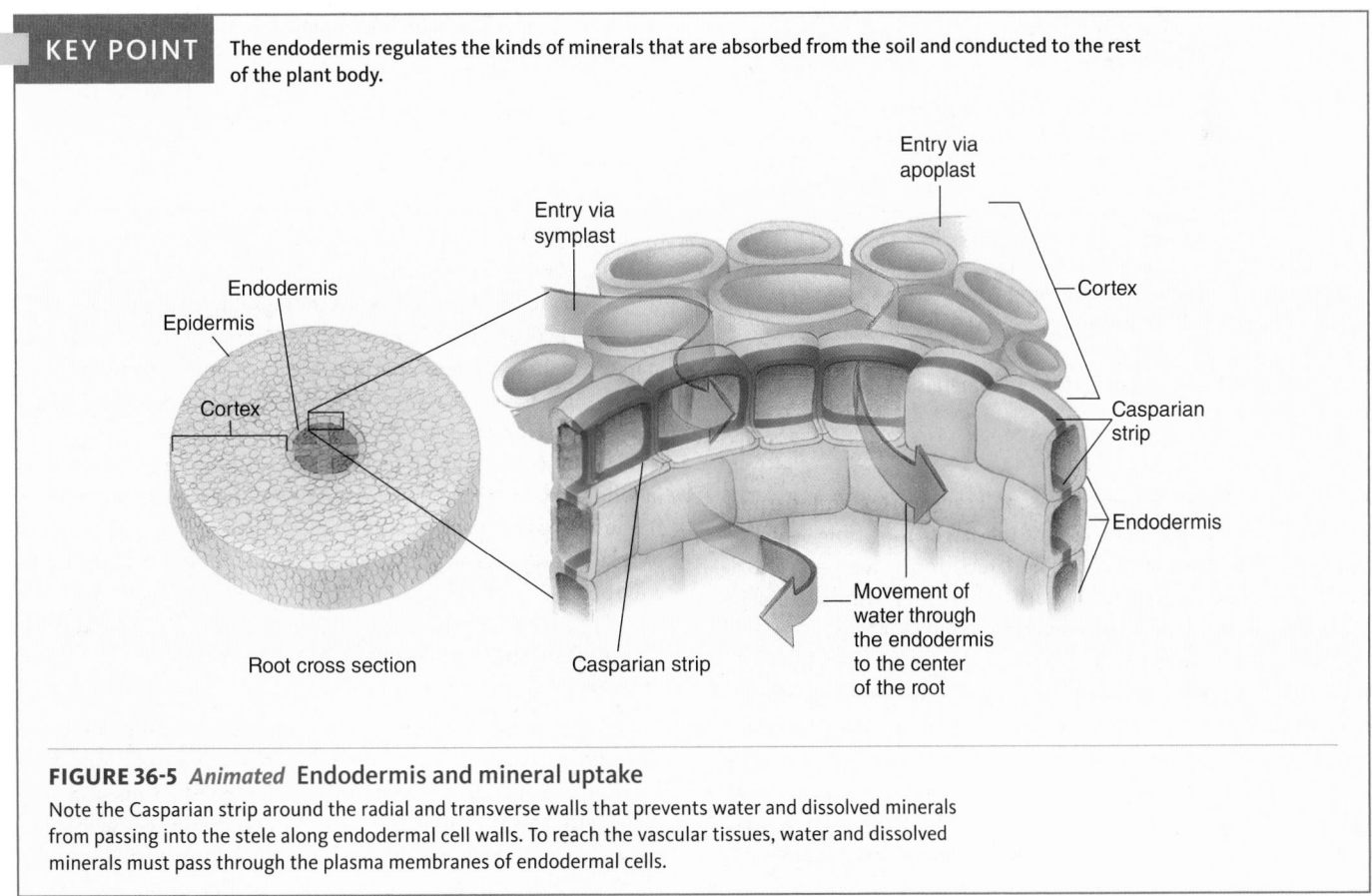

KEY POINT The endodermis regulates the kinds of minerals that are absorbed from the soil and conducted to the rest of the plant body.

Entry via symplast

Entry via apoplast

Endodermis

Epidermis

Cortex

Cortex

Casparian strip

Endodermis

Root cross section

Casparian strip

Movement of water through the endodermis to the center of the root

FIGURE 36-5 *Animated* **Endodermis and mineral uptake**

Note the Casparian strip around the radial and transverse walls that prevents water and dissolved minerals from passing into the stele along endodermal cell walls. To reach the vascular tissues, water and dissolved minerals must pass through the plasma membranes of endodermal cells.

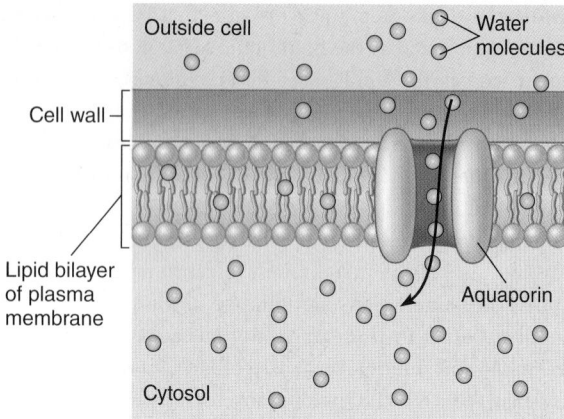

(a) Movement of water. Water crosses membranes by diffusion through the lipid layer (*left*) and, more rapidlly, through aquaporins (*right*).

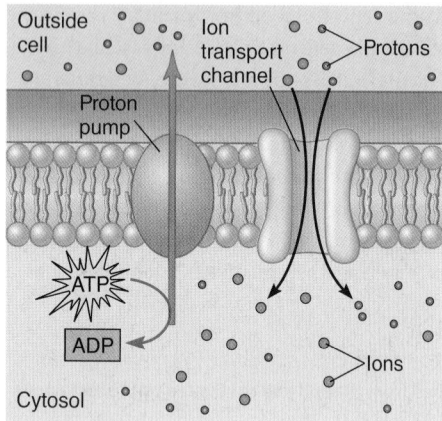

(b) Movement of mineral ions by carrier-mediated active transport. The lipid bilayer of plant membranes is impermeable to mineral ions, which can only pass through ion transport channels. The hydrolysis of ATP pumps protons outside the cell, forming an energy-charged proton gradient. Ion transport channels allow mineral ions to enter the cell with protons.

FIGURE 36-6 Transport of water and minerals across plant membranes

and features—root cap, root hairs, epidermis, cortex, endodermis, pericycle, xylem, and phloem—of the larger root from which it emerges. In addition to producing lateral roots, the pericycle is involved in forming the lateral meristems that produce secondary growth in woody roots (discussed later in the chapter).

Xylem, the centermost tissue of the stele, often has two, three, four, or more extensions, or "xylem arms" (see Fig. 36-3b). **Phloem** is located in patches between the xylem arms. The xylem and phloem of the root have the same functions and kinds of cells as in the rest of the plant: water and dissolved minerals are conducted in **tracheids** and **vessel elements** of xylem, and dissolved sugar (sucrose) is conducted in **sieve tube elements** of phloem.

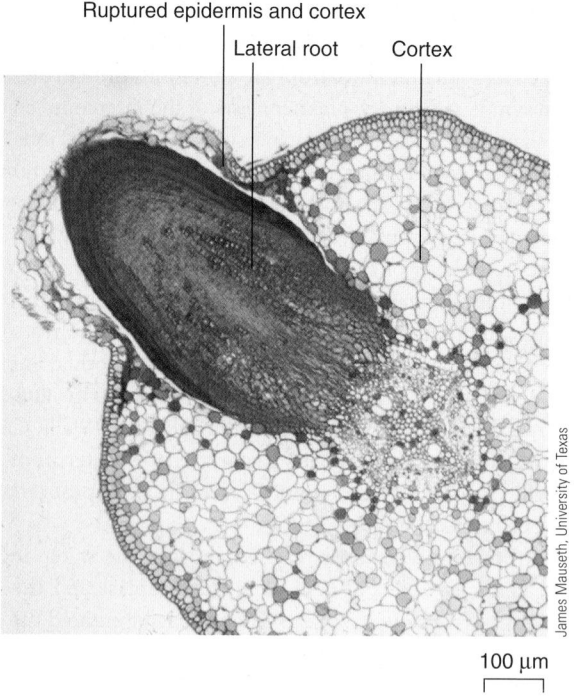

FIGURE 36-7 LM of a lateral root
Lateral roots originate at the pericycle.

After passing through the endodermal cells, water enters the root xylem, often at one of the xylem arms. Up to this point, the pathway of water has been horizontal from the soil into the center of the root:

root hair/epidermis ⟶ cortex ⟶ endodermis ⟶ pericycle ⟶ root xylem

Once water enters the xylem, it is transported upward through root xylem into stem xylem and from there to the rest of the plant.

One direction of phloem conduction is from the leaves, where sugar is made by photosynthesis, to the root, where sugar is used for the growth and maintenance of root tissues or stored, usually as starch. Another direction of phloem conduction is from the root, where sugar is stored as starch, to other parts of the plant, where sugar is used for growth and maintenance of tissues.

The *vascular cambium*, which gives rise to secondary tissues in woody plants, is sandwiched between the xylem and phloem. Because it has an inner core of vascular tissue, the primary eudicot root lacks **pith,** a ground tissue found in the centers of many stems and roots.

Xylem does not form the central tissue in some monocot roots

Monocot roots vary considerably in internal structure compared with eudicot roots. The layers found in some monocot roots, starting from the outside, are epidermis, cortex, endodermis, and pericycle (**FIG. 36-8**). Unlike the xylem in herbaceous eudicot roots, the xylem in many monocot roots does not form a solid cylinder

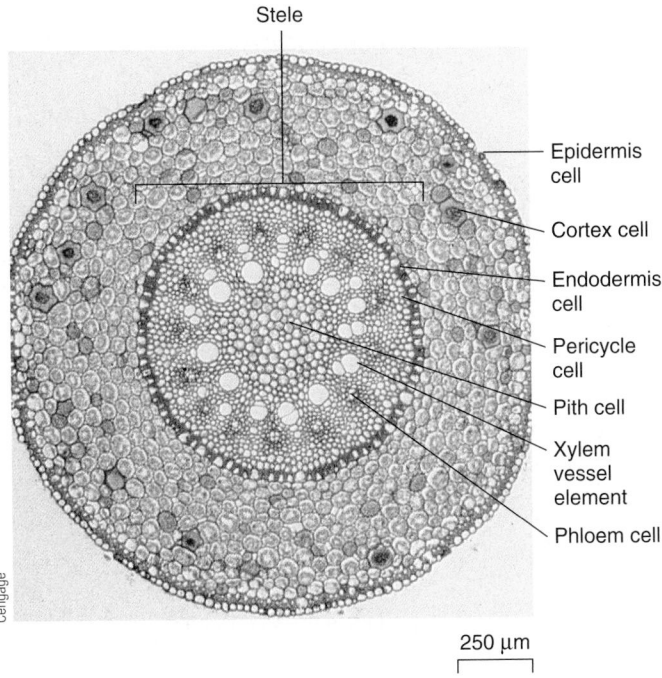

Stele

Epidermis cell

Cortex cell

Endodermis cell

Pericycle cell

Pith cell

Xylem vessel element

Phloem cell

250 μm

Cengage

FIGURE 36-8 LM of a cross section of a monocot root
Shown is a greenbrier (*Smilax*) root. As in herbaceous eudicot roots, the cortex of a monocot root is extensive.

in the center. Instead, the phloem and xylem are in separate, alternating bundles arranged around the central pith, which consists of parenchyma cells.

Because virtually no monocots have secondary growth, no vascular cambium exists in monocot roots. Despite their lack of secondary growth, long-lived monocots, such as palms, may have thickened roots produced by a modified form of primary growth in which parenchyma cells in the cortex divide and enlarge.

Woody plants have roots with secondary growth

Plants that produce stems with secondary growth also produce roots with secondary growth. These plants—gymnosperms and woody eudicots—have primary growth at apical meristems and secondary growth at lateral meristems. The production of secondary tissues occurs some distance back from the root tips and results from the activity of the same two lateral meristems found in woody stems: the vascular cambium and the cork cambium. Major roots of trees are often massive and have both wood and bark. In temperate climates, the wood of both roots and stems exhibits annual rings in cross section.

Before secondary growth starts in a root, the **vascular cambium** is sandwiched between the primary xylem and the primary phloem (**FIG. 36-9**). At the onset of secondary growth, the vascular cambium extends out to the pericycle, which develops into vascular cambium opposite the xylem arms. As a result, the pericycle links the separate sections of vascular cambium so that the vascular cambium becomes a continuous, noncircular loop of cells in cross

section. As the vascular cambium divides to produce secondary tissues, it eventually forms a cylinder of vascular cambium that continues to divide, producing secondary xylem (wood) to the inside and secondary phloem (inner bark) to the outside. The root increases in girth (thickness), and the vascular cambium continues to move outward.

The epidermis, cortex, endodermis, and primary phloem are gradually torn apart as the root increases in girth. The root epidermis is replaced by **periderm,** composed of cork cells and cork parenchyma, both produced by the **cork cambium** (the last figure in Table 33-4 shows an LM of periderm). The cork cambium in the root initially arises from regions in the pericycle.

Some roots are specialized for unusual functions

Adventitious roots often arise from the nodes of stems. Many aerial adventitious roots are adapted for functions other than anchorage, absorption, conduction, or storage. **Prop roots** are adventitious roots that develop from branches or a vertical stem and grow downward into the soil to help support the plant in an upright position (**FIG. 36-10a**). Prop roots are more common in monocots than in eudicots. Corn and sorghum, both monocots, are herbaceous plants that produce prop roots. Many tropical and subtropical eudicot trees, such as red mangrove, also produce prop roots.

The roots of many tropical rainforest trees are shallow and concentrated near the surface in a mat only a few centimeters (an inch or so) thick. The root mat catches and absorbs almost all minerals released from leaves by decomposition. Swollen bases or braces called **buttress roots** hold the trees upright and aid in the extensive distribution of the shallow roots (**FIG. 36-10b**).

In swampy or tidal environments where the soil is flooded or waterlogged, some roots grow upward until they are above the high-tide level. Even though roots live in the soil, they still require oxygen for aerobic respiration. Flooded soils are depleted of oxygen, so these aerial "breathing" roots, known as **pneumatophores,** may assist in getting oxygen to the submerged roots (**FIG. 36-10c**). Pneumatophores, which also help anchor the plant, have a well-developed system of internal air spaces that is continuous with the submerged parts of the root, presumably allowing gas exchange. Black and white mangroves are examples of plants with pneumatophores.

Climbing plants and **epiphytes,** which are plants that grow attached to other plants, have aerial roots that anchor the plant to the bark, branch, or other surface on which they grow. Some epiphytes have aerial roots specialized for functions other than anchorage. Certain epiphytic orchids, for example, have photosynthetic roots (**FIG. 36-10d**). Epiphytic roots may absorb moisture as well.

Some parasitic epiphytes, such as mistletoe, have modified roots that penetrate the host-plant tissues and absorb water. Another plant that starts its life as an epiphyte is the strangler fig, which produces long roots that eventually reach the ground and anchor the plant (now a tree rather than an epiphyte) in the soil. The tree on which the strangler fig originally grew is often killed as the strangler fig grows around it, competing with it for light and other resources and crushing its secondary phloem.

The production of secondary tissues in roots, like that in stems, is the result of the activity of two lateral meristems—the vascular cambium and the cork cambium.

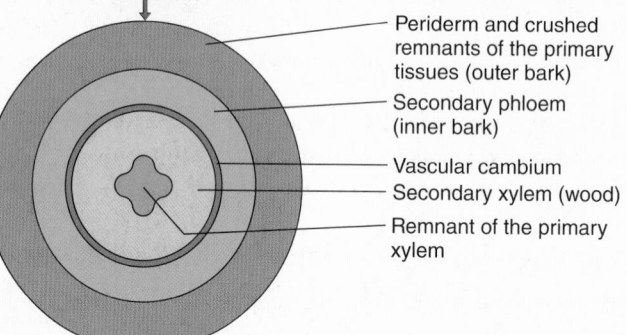

1 Tissues in primary root.

Epidermis
Cortex
Endodermis
Pericycle
Primary phloem
Vascular cambium
Primary xylem

2 At onset of secondary growth, vascular cambium extends out to pericycle, forming continuous, noncircular loop.

Pericycle
Primary phloem
Vascular cambium
Primary xylem

3 Vascular cambium produces secondary xylem to its inside and secondary phloem to its outside.

Periderm and remnants of the epidermis, cortex, endodermis, and pericycle
Remnant of the primary phloem
Secondary phloem
Vascular cambium
Secondary xylem
Primary xylem

4 Ring of vascular cambium gradually becomes circular. As vascular cambium continues to divide, epidermis, cortex, and primary phloem located in outer bark are torn apart.

Periderm and crushed remnants of the primary tissues (outer bark)
Secondary phloem (inner bark)
Vascular cambium
Secondary xylem (wood)
Remnant of the primary xylem

FIGURE 36-9 Development of secondary vascular tissues in a primary root

The figures are not drawn to scale because of space limitations; the primary xylem is actually the same size in all four diagrams, but differences in scale make the xylem appear different sizes.

Review

- What are the advantages of a taproot system? of a fibrous root system?
- If you were examining a cross section of a primary root of a flowering plant, how would you determine whether it was a eudicot or a monocot?
- What is the symplast? the apoplast?
- How does a herbaceous eudicot root develop secondary tissues?
- What are the functions of each of the following: prop roots, buttress roots, and pneumatophores?

36.2 ROOT ASSOCIATIONS AND INTERACTIONS

LEARNING OBJECTIVE

6 List and describe two mutualistic relationships between roots and other organisms.

As roots of an individual plant extend through the soil, they often encounter the roots of related or unrelated plants. The nature of

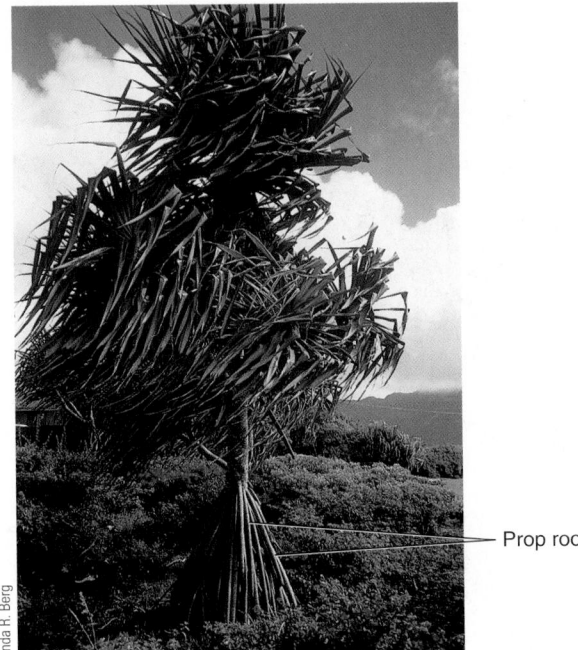

Linda R. Berg

(a) Prop roots are adventitious roots that arise near the base of the stem and provide additional support. Screw pine (*Pandanus*) has an elaborate set of aerial prop roots. Photographed in Kauai, Hawaii.

Prop roots

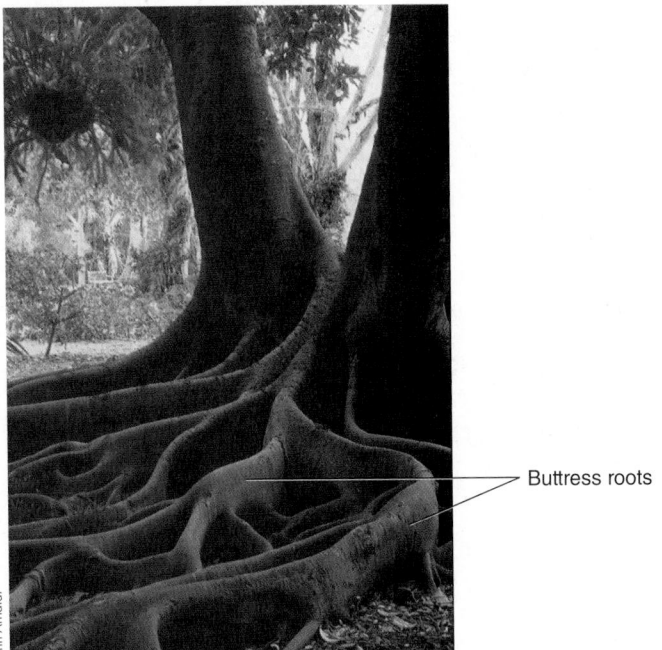

John Arnaldi

Buttress roots

(b) Tropical rainforest trees typically possess buttress roots that support them in the shallow, often wet soil. Shown are buttress roots on Australian banyan (*Ficus macrophylla*). Photographed at Selby Gardens in Sarasota, Florida.

Robert and Linda Mitchell

Pneumatophores

(c) White mangrove (*Laguncularia racemosa*) produces pneumatophores, shown protruding from the wet mud in the foreground. Pneumatophores may provide oxygen for roots buried in anaerobic (oxygen-deficient) soil. Photographed in Isla del Carmen, Mexico.

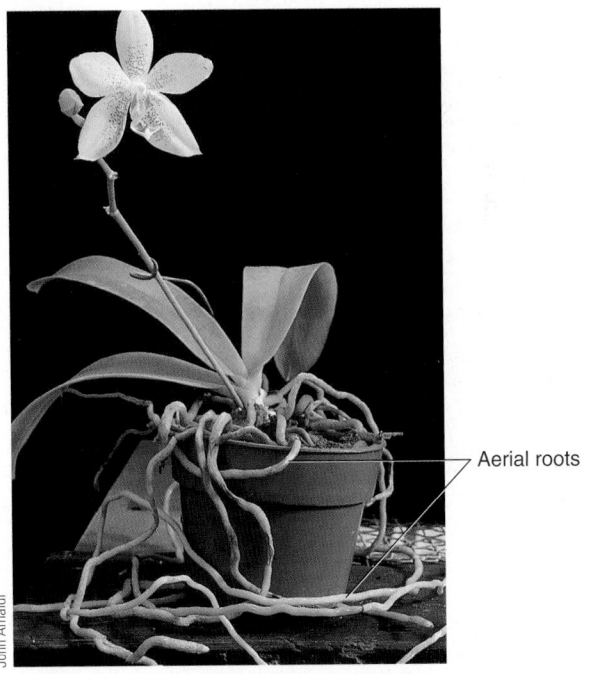

John Arnaldi

Aerial roots

(d) The moth orchid (*Phalaenopsis* hybrid) has photosynthetic aerial roots.

FIGURE 36-10 Specialized roots

Sheath of fungal hyphae encircles root

Fungal hypha between plant cells

Robert Knauft / Biology Media / Photo Researchers, Inc.

(a) LM of ectomycorrhizae, fungal associations that form a sheath around the root. The fungal hyphae penetrate the root between cortical cells but do not enter the cells.

Fungal hyphae within plant cortical cells

Cabisco / Visuals Unlimited

100 μm

(b) LM of endomycorrhizae, fungal associations in which the fungal hyphae penetrate root cells. The hyphae aid in delivering and receiving nutrients. Roots of most vascular plant species are colonized by endomycorrhizae.

U.S. Department of Energy

(c) Fruiting body of the mycorrhizal fungus *Laccaria bicolor*, which is colonizing the roots of nearby Douglas fir seedlings.

FIGURE 36-11 Mycorrhizae

Mycorrhizae enhance plant growth by providing essential minerals to the roots.

250 μm

The roots of terrestrial plant species may form **mutualistic**—that is, mutually beneficial—relationships with certain soil microorganisms: *mycorrhizal fungi* and *rhizobial bacteria*. These mutualistic relationships provide plants with access to essential minerals that are in limited supply in the soil.

Mycorrhizae facilitate the uptake of essential minerals by roots

Subterranean associations between roots and certain fungi, known as **mycorrhizae,** are found in virtually all terrestrial ecosystems. Mycorrhizae permit the transfer of materials (such as carbon compounds produced by photosynthesis) from roots to the fungus. At the same time, essential minerals, such as phosphorus, move from the fungus to the roots of the host plant. The threadlike body of the fungal partner extends into the soil, extracting minerals well beyond the reach of the plant's roots. In some mycorrhizae, the fungal mycelium encircles the root like a sheath; in others, the fungus penetrates cell walls of the root cortex and forms branching **arbuscules** (**FIG. 36-11**; also see Fig. 29-11).

The mycorrhizal relationship is an ancient one: some of the earliest known plant fossils (about 400 million years old) contain mycorrhizal fungi in the roots. The mycorrhizal relationship is mutually beneficial because when mycorrhizae are not present neither the fungus nor the plant grows as well (see Fig. 29-19). The hyphal network of mycorrhizae appears to interconnect the roots of different plant species in the community so that carbon compounds may flow from one plant to another through their mutual fungal partner.

these interactions is largely unknown, but several studies suggest that roots are involved in complex ways, sometimes recognizing the identity of neighboring roots and modifying their growth accordingly. For example, wild strawberry roots have been demonstrated to grow more vigorously when they encounter ground ivy roots; in contrast, root growth of ground ivy is inhibited by strawberry roots. Such root associations affect community dynamics in natural ecosystems and may affect the productivity of agricultural ecosystems.

In 2008, an international team of several dozen scientists reported in the journal *Nature* that the genome of an ectomycorrhizal fungus, *Laccaria bicolor,* had been sequenced. The scientists identified many genes that code for *small secreted proteins* that may be involved in establishing the mutualistic relationship between the fungus and its plant partner (see Fig. 36-11c). The functions of these proteins are not known at present, but several are expressed only when the fungus and plant root are in contact to form a mycorrhiza.

Rhizobial bacteria fix nitrogen in the roots of leguminous plants

Certain nitrogen-fixing bacteria, collectively called **rhizobia,** form associations with the roots of leguminous plants—clover, peas, and soybeans, for example. **Nodules** (swellings) that house millions of the rhizobia develop on the roots (see Fig. 55-9). Evidence indi-

cates that the rhizobial relationship evolved much later than the mycorrhizal relationship; unlike mycorrhizae, which infect most plant species, rhizobia almost exclusively infect plants of the legume family, which evolved about 70 million years ago. (A few other plant–bacteria associations that fix nitrogen have also evolved.)

As with mycorrhizae, the association between nitrogen-fixing bacteria and the roots of legumes is mutually beneficial. Bacteria receive photosynthetic products from plants while helping plants meet their nitrogen requirements by producing ammonia (NH_3) from atmospheric nitrogen.

For several decades, biologists have been studying the molecular basis of associations between plants and nitrogen-fixing bacteria. The two partners in this association use **cell signaling,** that is, a molecular dialogue back and forth between them, to establish contact and develop nodules. When soil contains a low level of nitrogen, legume roots secrete chemical attractants (flavonoids) toward which the rhizobial bacteria swim (**FIG. 36-12**).

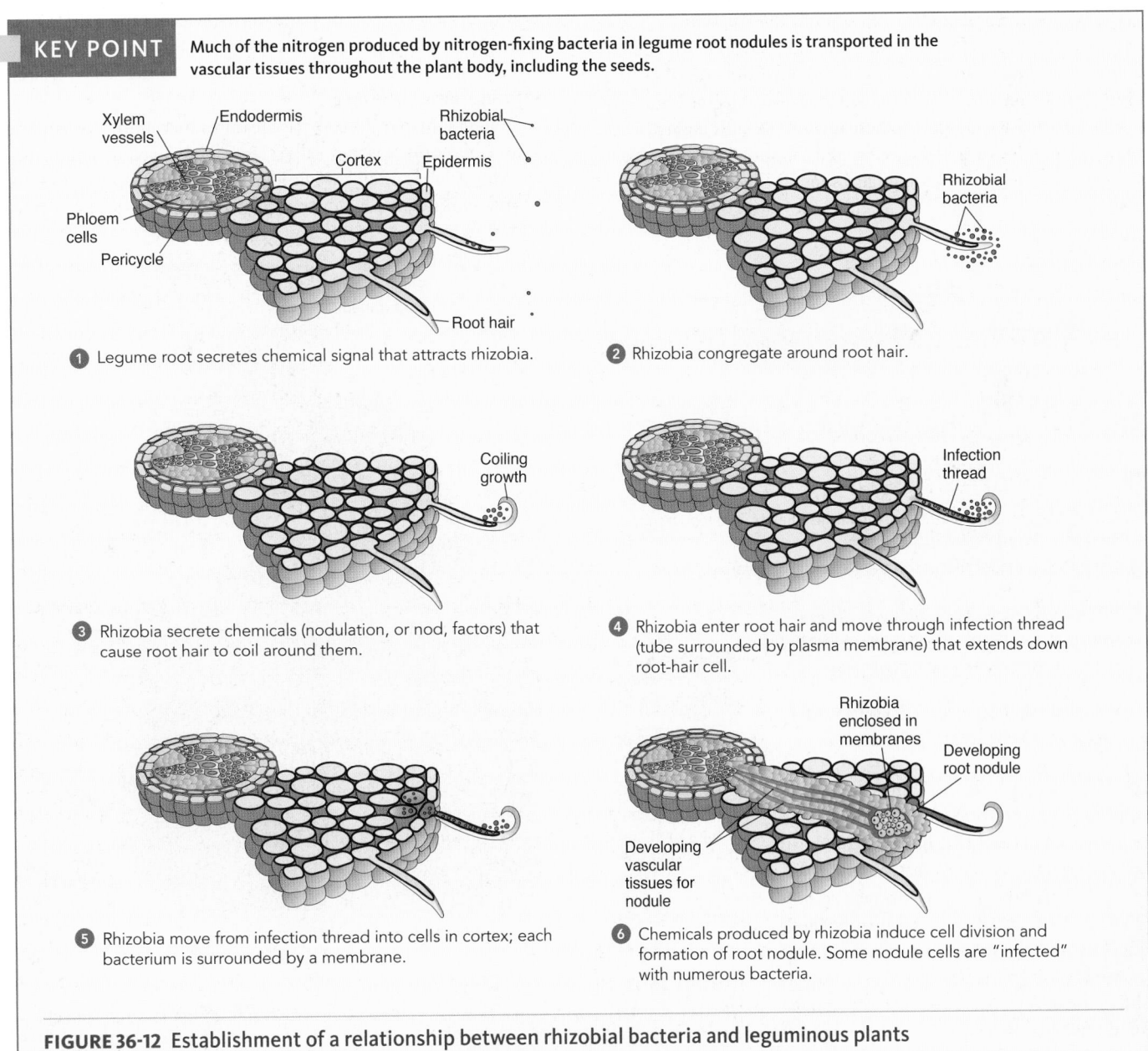

KEY POINT Much of the nitrogen produced by nitrogen-fixing bacteria in legume root nodules is transported in the vascular tissues throughout the plant body, including the seeds.

1 Legume root secretes chemical signal that attracts rhizobia.

2 Rhizobia congregate around root hair.

3 Rhizobia secrete chemicals (nodulation, or nod, factors) that cause root hair to coil around them.

4 Rhizobia enter root hair and move through infection thread (tube surrounded by plasma membrane) that extends down root-hair cell.

5 Rhizobia move from infection thread into cells in cortex; each bacterium is surrounded by a membrane.

6 Chemicals produced by rhizobia induce cell division and formation of root nodule. Some nodule cells are "infected" with numerous bacteria.

FIGURE 36-12 Establishment of a relationship between rhizobial bacteria and leguminous plants

The initial signal molecules produced by rhizobial bacteria are called *nodulation factors,* or *nod factors.* These nod factors help root-hair cells in the roots of leguminous plants recognize the presence of the bacteria; recognition is the first step in the infection by rhizobia and the development of root nodules. The nod factor apparently attaches to a plant receptor on the root-hair plasma membrane. This attachment triggers a calcium-dependent **signal transduction** cascade within root cells that alters gene expression and metabolism, resulting in nodule formation. The plant hormone **cytokinin,** which triggers cell division (see Chapter 38), is involved in root nodule formation.

Some genes are involved in the initiation of both mycorrhizal and rhizobial associations

Because both mycorrhizae and rhizobia infect plant roots, some biologists have hypothesized that the genes and signal transduction components involved in mycorrhizal relationships may have been recruited for the rhizobial relationships that evolved much later. There is experimental evidence to support this hypothesis. Some of the same genes that trigger infection and changes in root development to form rhizobial nodules are also involved in establishing mycorrhizal infections. Evidence includes several legume mutants that biologists have identified; these mutants lack the ability to develop nodules for rhizobial bacteria and cannot form mycorrhizal associations. Molecular findings also support the hypothesis.

Review

- What are mycorrhizal fungi?
- What are rhizobial bacteria?
- How are mycorrhizae and root nodules similar? How are they different?

36.3 THE SOIL ENVIRONMENT

◾ LEARNING OBJECTIVES

7 Describe the roles of weathering, organisms, climate, and topography in soil formation.
8 List the four components of soil and give the ecological significance of each.
9 Describe how roots absorb positively charged mineral ions by the process of cation exchange.
10 Distinguish between macronutrients and micronutrients.
11 Explain the impacts of mineral depletion and soil erosion on plant growth.

We now examine the soil environment in which most roots live. **Soil** is a relatively thin layer of Earth's crust that has been modified by the natural actions of weather, wind, water, and organisms. It is easy to take soil for granted. We walk on and over it throughout our lives but rarely stop to think about how important it is to our survival. Vast numbers and kinds of organisms colonize soil and depend on it for shelter and food. Most plants

anchor themselves in soil, and from it they receive water and minerals. Almost all of the elements essential for plant growth are obtained directly from the soil. With few exceptions, plants cannot survive on their own without soil, and because we depend on plants for our food, neither could humans exist without soil.

Soils are generally formed from rock (called "parent material") that is gradually broken down, or fragmented, into smaller and smaller particles by biological, chemical, and physical **weathering processes** (**FIG. 36-13**). Two important factors that work together in the weathering of rock are climate and organisms. When plant roots and other organisms living in the soil respire, they produce carbon dioxide (CO_2), which diffuses into the soil and reacts with soil water to form carbonic acid (H_2CO_3). Soil organisms such as lichens produce other kinds of acids. Recall from Chapter 29 that a lichen is a dual organism composed of a fungus and a phototroph (photosynthetic organism). These acids etch tiny cracks, or fissures, in the rock surface; water then seeps into these cracks. If the parent material is located in a temperate climate, the alternate freezing and thawing of the water during winter causes the cracks to enlarge, breaking off small pieces of rock. Small plants can then become established and send their roots into the larger cracks, fracturing the rock further.

Topography, a region's surface features such as the presence or absence of mountains and valleys, is also involved in soil formation. Steep slopes often have little or no soil on them because the soil and rock are continually transported down the slopes by grav-

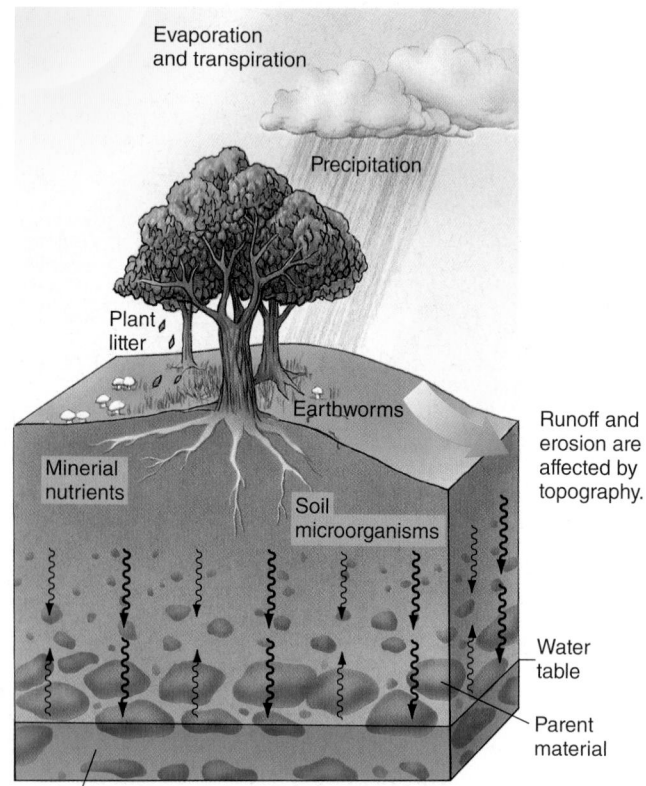

Soil organisms add organic additions underground.

Fine particles and solubles are washed downward.

Capillary action and evaporation cause some materials to rise.

FIGURE 36-13 The dynamics of soil formation
Weather, climate, topography, and organisms interact with Earth's crust to form soil, the material that supports plants and many other organisms on land.

ity. Runoff from precipitation tends to amplify erosion on steep slopes. Moderate slopes, in contrast, may encourage the formation of deep soils.

The disintegration of solid rock into finer and finer mineral particles in the soil takes an extremely long time, sometimes thousands of years. Soil forms constantly as the weathering of parent material beneath soil that is already formed continues to add new soil.

Soil is composed of inorganic minerals, organic matter, air, and water

Soil comprises four distinct components—inorganic mineral particles (which make up about 45% of a typical soil), organic matter (about 5%), water (about 25%), and air (about 25%). The plants, animals, fungi, and microorganisms that inhabit soil interact with it, and minerals are continually cycled from the soil to organisms, which use them in their biological processes. When the organisms die, bacteria and other soil organisms decompose the remains, returning the minerals to the soil.

The inorganic mineral particles, which come from weathered rock, provide anchorage and essential minerals for plants, as well as pore space for water and air. Because different rocks consist of different minerals, soils vary in mineral composition and chemical properties. Rocks rich in aluminum form acidic soils, for example, whereas rocks that contain silicates of magnesium and iron form soils that may be deficient in calcium, nitrogen, and phosphorus. Also, soils formed from the same kind of parent material may not develop in the same way because other factors, such as weather, topography, and organisms, differ.

The *texture,* or structural characteristic, of a soil is determined by the percentages (by weight) of the different-sized inorganic mineral particles—sand, silt, and clay—in it. The size assignments for sand, silt, and clay give soil scientists a way to classify soil texture. Particles larger than 2 mm in diameter, called gravel or stones, are not considered soil particles because they do not have any direct value to plants. The largest soil particles are called "sand" (0.02 to 2 mm in diameter); the medium-sized particles, "silt" (0.002 to 0.02 mm in diameter); and the smallest particles, "clay" (less than 0.002 mm in diameter). Sand particles are large enough to be seen easily with the eye, and silt particles (about the size of flour particles) can be seen with an ordinary light microscope. Most individual clay particles can be seen only under an electron microscope.

A soil's texture affects many of that soil's properties, in turn influencing plant growth. The clay component of a soil is particularly important in determining many of its characteristics because clay particles have the greatest surface area of all soil particles. If the surface areas of about 450 g (1 lb) of clay particles were laid out side by side, they would occupy 1 hectare (2.5 acres).

Each clay particle has predominantly negative electric charges on its outer surface that attract and reversibly bind **cations,** which are positively charged mineral ions such as potassium (K^+) and magnesium (Mg^{2+}). Because many cations are essential for plant growth, cation adhesion to soil particles is an important aspect of soil fertility. Roots secrete protons (H^+), which are exchanged for other positively charged mineral ions adhering to the surface of soil particles, in a process known as **cation exchange.** These "freed"

FIGURE 36-14 Cation exchange

Negatively charged clay particles bind to positively charged mineral cations, holding them in the soil. Roots pump out protons (H^+), which are exchanged for the cations, facilitating their absorption.

ions and the water that forms a film around the soil particles are absorbed by the plant's roots (**FIG. 36-14**).

In contrast, **anions,** which are negatively charged mineral ions, are repelled by the negative surface charges of clay particles and tend to remain in solution. Anions such as nitrate (NO_3^-) are often washed out of the root zone by water moving through the soil.

Soil always contains a mixture of different-sized particles, but the proportions vary from one soil to another. A *loam,* which is an ideal agricultural soil, has an optimum combination of different soil particle sizes: it contains approximately 40% each of sand and silt and about 20% of clay. Generally, the larger particles provide structural support, aeration, and permeability to the soil, whereas the smaller particles bind into aggregates, or clumps, and hold minerals and water. Soils with larger proportions of sand are not as desirable for most plants because they do not hold water and mineral ions well. Plants grown in such soils are more susceptible to drought and mineral deficiencies. Soils with larger proportions of clay are also not desirable for most plants because they provide poor drainage and often do not provide enough oxygen. Clay soils used in agriculture tend to compact, which reduces the number of soil spaces that can be filled by water and air.

A soil's organic matter consists of the wastes and remains of soil organisms

The organic matter in soil is composed of litter (dead leaves and branches on the soil's surface); droppings (animal dung); and the dead remains of plants, animals, and microorganisms in various stages of decomposition. Organic matter is decomposed by microorganisms, particularly bacteria and fungi, that inhabit the soil. During decomposition, essential mineral ions are released into the soil, where they may be bound by soil particles or absorbed by plant roots. Organic matter increases the soil's water-holding capacity by acting much like a sponge. For this reason gardeners often add organic matter to soils, especially sandy soils, which are naturally low in organic matter.

The partly decayed organic portion of the soil is referred to as **humus.** Humus, which is not a single chemical compound but a mix of many organic compounds, binds mineral ions and holds water. On average, humus persists in agricultural soil for about 20 years. Certain components of humus may persist in the soil for hundreds of years. Although humus is somewhat resistant to decay, a succession of microorganisms gradually reduces it to carbon dioxide, water, and minerals.

About 50% of soil volume is composed of pore spaces

Soil has numerous pore spaces of different sizes around and among the soil particles. Pore spaces occupy roughly 50% of a soil's volume and are filled with varying proportions of air and water. Both soil air and soil water are necessary to produce a moist but aerated soil that sustains plants and other soil-dwelling organisms. Water is usually held in the smaller pores, whereas air is found in the larger pores. After a prolonged rain, almost all the pore spaces may be filled with water, but water drains rapidly from the larger pore spaces, drawing air from the atmosphere into those spaces.

Soil air contains the same gases as atmospheric air, although they are usually present in different proportions. As a result of respiration by soil organisms, there is less oxygen and more carbon dioxide in soil air than in atmospheric air. (Aerobic respiration uses oxygen and produces carbon dioxide.) Among the important gases in soil are oxygen (O_2), required by soil organisms for aerobic respiration; nitrogen (N_2), used by nitrogen-fixing bacteria; and carbon dioxide (CO_2), involved in soil weathering.

Soil water originates as precipitation, which drains downward, or as groundwater (water stored in porous underground rock), which rises upward from the water table (the uppermost level of groundwater). Soil water contains low concentrations of dissolved minerals that enter the roots of plants when they absorb water. Water not bound to soil particles or absorbed by roots percolates (moves down) through soil, carrying dissolved minerals with it. The removal of dissolved materials from soil by percolating water is called **leaching.** The deposition of leached material in the lower layers of soil is known as **illuviation.** Iron and aluminum compounds, humus, and clay are some illuvial materials that can gather in the subsurface por-

tion of the soil. Some substances completely leach out of the soil because they are so soluble that they migrate down into the groundwater. It is also possible for water that is moving *upward* through the soil to carry dissolved materials with it.

Soil organisms form a complex ecosystem

A single teaspoon of fertile agricultural soil may contain millions of microorganisms, such as bacteria, fungi, algae, protozoa, as well as microscopic nematodes and other worms. Other organisms also colonize the soil ecosystem, including plant roots, earthworms, insects, moles, snakes, and groundhogs (**FIG. 36-15**). Most numerous in soil are bacteria, which number in the hundreds of millions per gram of soil. Scientists have identified about 170,000 species of soil organisms, but thousands remain to be identified. Little is known about the roles and interactions of soil organisms, in part because it is hard to study their activities under natural conditions.

Worms are some of the most important organisms living in soil. Earthworms, probably one of the most familiar soil inhabitants, ingest soil and obtain energy and raw materials by digesting humus. *Castings,* bits of soil that have passed through the gut of an earthworm, are deposited on or near the soil surface. In this way,

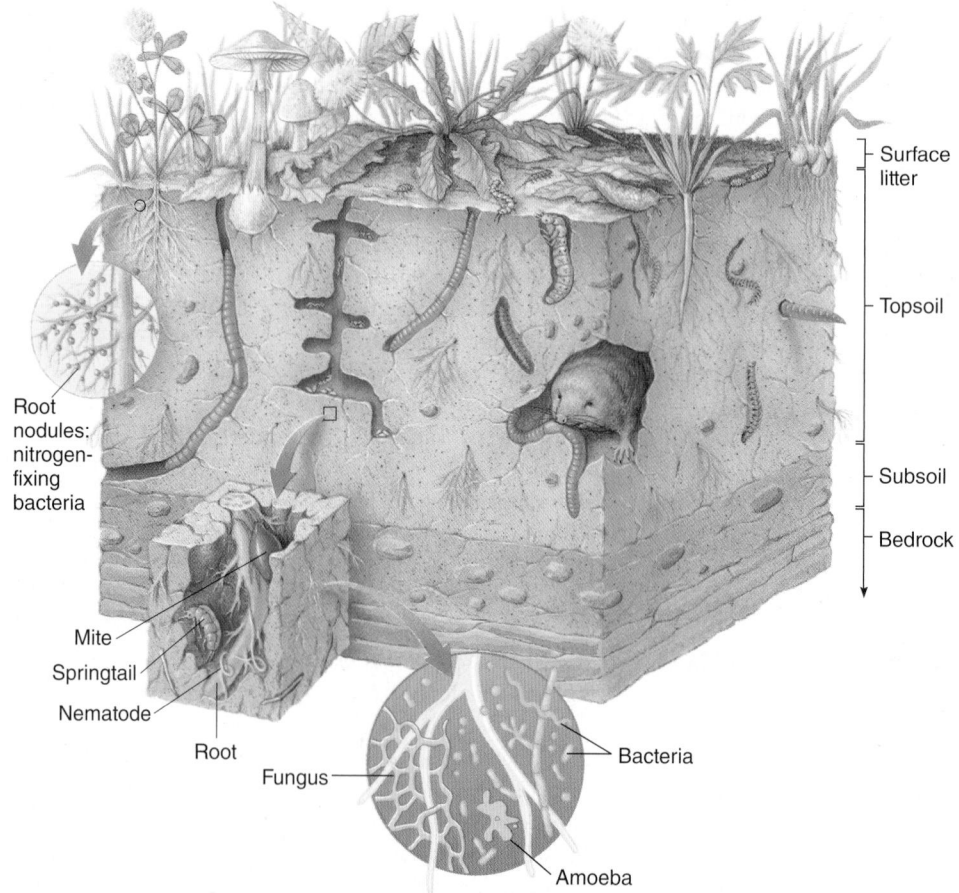

FIGURE 36-15 Diversity of life in fertile soil
Plants, algae, protozoa, fungi, bacteria, earthworms, flatworms, roundworms, insects, spiders and mites, and burrowing animals such as moles and groundhogs live in soil.

minerals from deeper layers are brought to upper layers. Earthworm tunnels serve to aerate the soil, and the worms' waste products and corpses add organic material to the soil.

Ants live in the soil in enormous numbers, constructing tunnels and chambers that help aerate it. Members of soil-dwelling ant colonies forage on the surface for bits of food, which they carry back to their nests. Not all this food is eaten, however, and its eventual decomposition helps increase the organic matter in the soil. Many ants are also indispensable in plant reproduction because they bury seeds in the soil (discussed in Chapter 37).

Soil pH affects soil characteristics and plant growth

Acidity is measured using the pH scale, which extends from 0 (extremely acidic) through 7.0 (neutral) to 14.0 (extremely alkaline). The pH of most soils ranges from 4.0 to 8.0, but some soils are outside this range. The soil of the Pygmy Forest in Mendocino County, California, is extremely acidic (pH 2.8 to 3.9). At the other extreme, certain soils in Death Valley, California, have a pH of 10.5.

Plants are affected by soil pH, partly because the solubility of certain minerals varies with differences in pH. Soluble minerals can be absorbed by the plant, whereas insoluble forms cannot. At a low pH, for example, aluminum and manganese in soil water are more soluble and are sometimes absorbed by the roots in toxic concentrations. At a higher pH, certain mineral salts essential for plant growth, such as calcium phosphate, become less soluble and thus less available to plants.

Soil pH also affects the leaching of minerals. An acidic soil has less ability to bind positively charged ions to it because the soil particles also bind the abundant protons (**FIG. 36-16**). As a result, certain mineral ions essential for plant growth, such as potassium (K^+), are leached more readily from acidic soil. The optimum soil pH for most plant growth is 6.0 to 7.0 because most essential minerals are available to plants in that pH range.

Acid precipitation, a type of air pollution in which sulfuric and nitric acids produced by human activities fall to the ground as acid rain, sleet, snow, or fog, can seriously decrease soil pH. Acid precipitation is one of several factors implicated in **forest decline,** the gradual deterioration, and often death, of trees that has been observed in many European and North American forests in recent decades. Forest decline may be partly the result of soil changes, such as leaching of essential cations, caused by acid precipitation. In central European forests that have experienced forest decline, for example, a strong correlation has been demonstrated between forest damage and soil chemistry altered by acid precipitation.

Soil provides most of the minerals found in plants

More than 90 naturally occurring elements exist on Earth, and more than 60 of these, including elements as common as carbon and as rare as gold, have been found in plant tissues. Not all of these elements are essential for plant growth, however.

Nineteen elements have been found essential for most, if not all, plants (**TABLE 36-1**). Ten of these are required in fairly large quantities (greater than 0.05% dry weight) and are therefore known as **macronutrients.** Macronutrients include carbon, hydrogen, oxygen, nitrogen, potassium, calcium, magnesium, phosphorus, sulfur, and silicon. The remaining nine **micronutrients** are needed in trace amounts (less than 0.05% dry weight) for normal plant growth and development. Micronutrients include chlorine, iron, boron, manganese, sodium, zinc, copper, nickel, and molybdenum.

Four of the 19 elements—carbon, oxygen, hydrogen, and nitrogen—come directly or indirectly from soil water or from gases in the atmosphere. Carbon is obtained from carbon dioxide in the atmosphere during photosynthesis. Oxygen is obtained from atmospheric oxygen (O_2) and water (H_2O). Water also supplies hydrogen to the plant. Plants absorb their nitrogen from the soil as ions of nitrogen salts, but the nitrogen in nitrogen salts ultimately comes from atmospheric nitrogen (N_2). The remaining 15 essential elements are obtained from the soil as dissolved mineral ions. Their ultimate source is the parent material from which the soil was formed.

Let us examine the main functions of essential elements. Carbon, hydrogen, and oxygen are found as part of the structure of all biologically important molecules, including lipids, carbohydrates, nucleic acids, and proteins. Nitrogen is part of proteins, nucleic acids, and chlorophyll.

Potassium, which plants use in fairly substantial amounts, is not found in a specific organic compound in plant cells. Instead, it

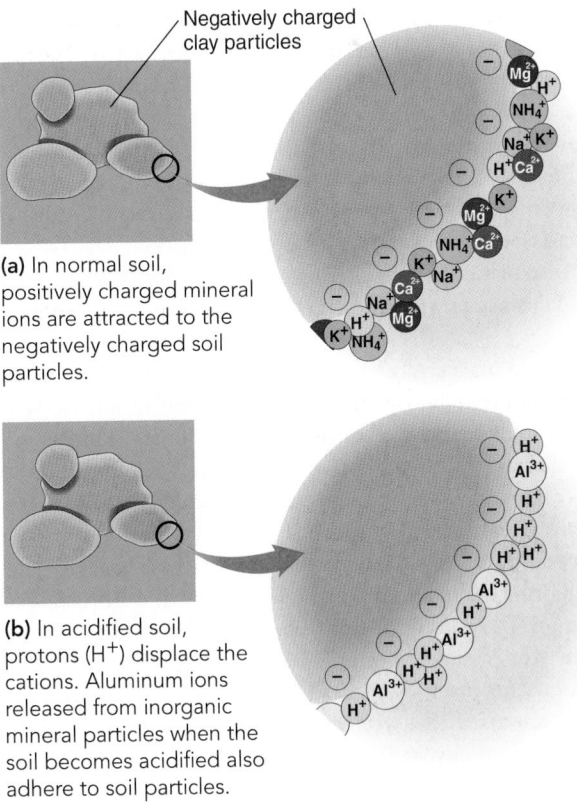

(a) In normal soil, positively charged mineral ions are attracted to the negatively charged soil particles.

(b) In acidified soil, protons (H^+) displace the cations. Aluminum ions released from inorganic mineral particles when the soil becomes acidified also adhere to soil particles.

FIGURE 36-16 How acid alters soil chemistry

TABLE 36-1   Functions of Elements Required by Most Plants

Element	Taken Up As	Major Functions
Macronutrients		
Carbon	CO_2	Component of carbohydrate, lipid, protein, and nucleic acid molecules
Hydrogen	H_2O	Component of carbohydrate, lipid, protein, and nucleic acid molecules
Oxygen	O_2, H_2O	Component of carbohydrate, lipid, protein, and nucleic acid molecules
Nitrogen	NO_3^-, NH_4^+	Component of proteins, nucleic acids, chlorophyll, certain coenzymes
Potassium	K^+	Osmotic and ionic balance; opening of stomata; enzyme activator (for 40+ enzymes)
Calcium	Ca^{2+}	In cell walls; involved in membrane permeability; enzyme activator; second messenger in metabolism
Magnesium	Mg^{2+}	In chlorophyll; enzyme activator in carbohydrate metabolism (phosphate transfer)
Phosphorus	$HPO_4^{2-}, H_2PO_4^-$	In nucleic acids, phospholipids, ATP (energy transfer compound), and coenzymes
Sulfur	SO_4^{2-}	In certain amino acids and vitamins
Silicon	SiO_3^{2-}	In cell walls; increased resistance to pests and diseases; important primarily in grasses and sedges
Micronutrients		
Chlorine	Cl^-	Ionic balance; involved in photosynthesis (production of oxygen)
Iron	Fe^{2+}, Fe^{3+}	In enzymes and electron transport molecules involved in photosynthesis, respiration, and nitrogen fixation
Boron	$H_2BO_3^-$	In cell walls; involved in nucleic acid metabolism and in cell elongation
Manganese	Mn^{2+}	In enzymes involved in respiration and nitrogen metabolism; required for photosynthesis (production of oxygen)
Sodium	Na^+	Involved in photosynthesis (in C_4 and CAM plants); substitutes for potassium in osmotic and ionic balance
Zinc	Zn^{2+}	In enzymes involved in respiration and nitrogen metabolism
Copper	Cu^+, Cu^{2+}	In enzymes involved in photosynthesis
Nickel	Ni^{2+}	In enzymes (urease) involved in nitrogen metabolism; required by nitrogen-fixing bacteria
Molybdenum	MoO_4^{2-}	In enzymes involved in nitrogen metabolism

remains as free K^+ and plays a key physiological role in maintaining the turgidity of cells because it is osmotically active. The presence of K^+ in cytoplasm causes water to pass through the plasma membrane into the cell by osmosis. Potassium is also involved in the opening of stomata.

Calcium plays a key structural role as a component of the middle lamella (the cementing layer between cell walls of adjacent plant cells). Calcium ions (Ca^{2+}) are also important in physiological roles in plants, such as altering membrane permeability and as **second messengers** in various cell signaling responses (see Chapter 6).

Magnesium is critical for plants because it is part of the chlorophyll molecule. Phosphorus is a component of nucleic acids, phospholipids (part of cell membranes), and energy transfer molecules such as ATP. Sulfur is essential because it is found in certain amino acids and vitamins. Many plants accumulate silicon in their cell walls and intercellular spaces. Silicon enhances the growth and fertility of some species and may help reinforce cell walls.

Chlorine and sodium are micronutrients that help maintain cell turgor. In addition to this osmotic role, chloride (Cl^-) and sodium (Na^+) ions are essential for photosynthesis. Six of the micronutrients (iron, manganese, zinc, copper, nickel, and molybdenum) are associated with various plant enzymes, often as **cofactors**, and are involved in certain enzymatic reactions. Boron, present in cell walls, is also involved in nucleic acid metabolism and in cell growth.

How do biologists determine whether an element is essential?

It is impossible to conduct mineral nutrition experiments by growing plants in soil because soil is too complex and contains too many elements. Therefore, nutritional studies require special methods. One of the most useful techniques to test whether an element is essential is **hydroponics,** which is the growing of plants in aerated water to which mineral salts have been added (**FIG. 36-17**). Hydroponics has commercial applications in addition to its scientific use. Lettuce is one of several crops that is grown hydroponically.

If biologists suspect that a particular element is essential for plant growth, they grow plants in a nutrient solution that contains all known essential elements *except* the one in question. If plants grown in the absence of that element cannot develop normally or complete their life cycle, the element may be essential. Additional criteria are used to confirm whether an element is essential. For example, it must be demonstrated that the element has a direct effect on the plant's metabolism and that the element is essential for a wide variety of plants.

Soil can be damaged by human mismanagement

Soil is a valuable natural resource on which humans depend for food. Many human activities generate or aggravate soil problems, including mineral depletion, soil erosion, and accumulation of salt.

Why Is It Used? Using hydroponics, it is possible to grow plants in which only the mineral under investigation is absent from a nutrient solution. (It would be impossible to design such an experiment using soil.) Growing plants hydroponically in the absence of an essential mineral produces recognizable deficiency symptoms.

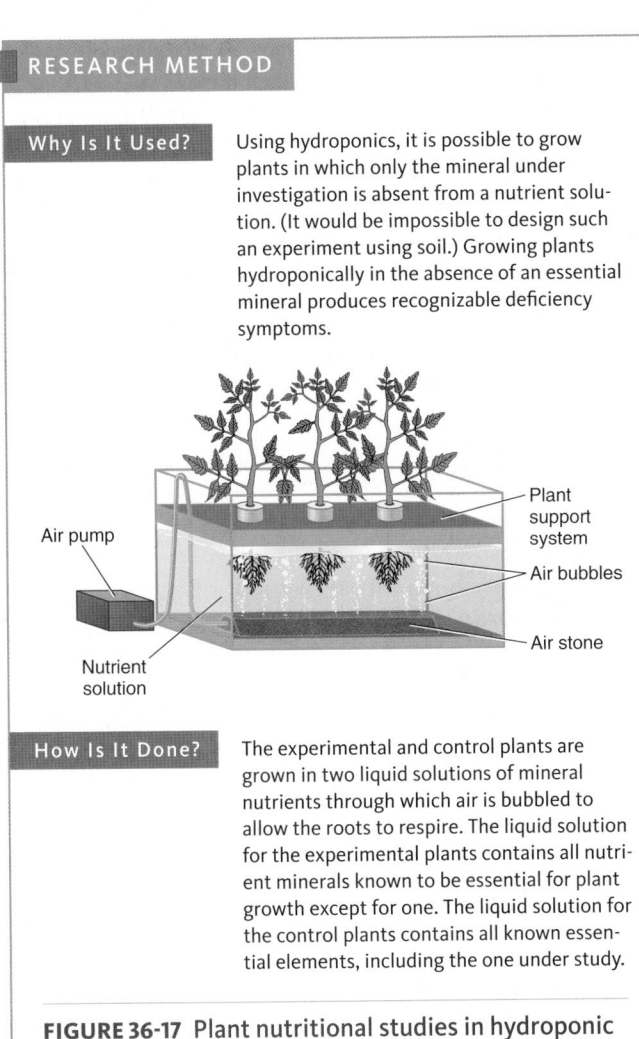

How Is It Done? The experimental and control plants are grown in two liquid solutions of mineral nutrients through which air is bubbled to allow the roots to respire. The liquid solution for the experimental plants contains all nutrient minerals known to be essential for plant growth except for one. The liquid solution for the control plants contains all known essential elements, including the one under study.

FIGURE 36-17 Plant nutritional studies in hydroponic growth systems

FIGURE 36-18 Soil erosion in an open field

Removal of plant cover exposes bare soil to erosion in heavy rains. Precipitation can cause gullies to enlarge rapidly because they provide channels for the runoff of water.

Mineral depletion may occur in agricultural soils

In a natural ecosystem, the essential minerals removed from the soil by plants are returned when the plants or the animals that eat them die and are decomposed. An agricultural system disrupts this pattern of nutrient cycling when the crops are harvested. Plant material containing minerals is removed from the nutrient cycle, and the harvested crops fail to decay and release their nutrients back to the soil. Over time, farmed soil inevitably loses its fertility, that is, its ability to produce abundant crops. Homeowners often mow their lawns and remove the clippings, similarly preventing decomposition and cycling of minerals that were in the grass blades.

The essential material (water, sunlight, or some essential element) that is in shortest supply usually limits plant growth. This phenomenon is sometimes called the concept of **limiting resources.** The three elements that are most often limiting resources for plants are nitrogen, phosphorus, and potassium. To sustain the productivity of agricultural soils, farmers periodically add fertilizers to depleted soils to replace the minerals that limit plant growth.

Soil erosion is the loss of soil from the land

Water, wind, ice, and other agents cause **soil erosion,** the wearing away or removal of soil from the land. Water and wind are particularly effective in moving soil from one place to another. Rainfall loosens soil particles that can then be transported by moving water (**FIG. 36-18**). Wind loosens soil and blows it away, particularly if the soil is barren and dry. Soil erosion is a natural process that can be greatly accelerated by human activities.

Soil erosion is a national and international problem that does not make the headlines very often. The U.S. Department of Agriculture estimates that approximately 4.2 billion metric tons (4.6 billion tons) of topsoil are eroded each year from U.S. croplands and rangelands. Erosion causes a loss in soil fertility because essential minerals and organic matter that are a part of the soil are removed. As a result of these losses, the productivity of eroded agricultural soils declines, and more fertilizer must be used to replace the nutrients lost to erosion.

Humans often accelerate soil erosion through poor soil management practices. Agriculture is not the only culprit, because the removal of natural plant communities during surface mining, unsound logging practices (such as clear-cutting large areas of forest), and the construction of roads and buildings also accelerate erosion.

Soil erosion has an impact on other natural resources. Sediment that enters streams, rivers, and lakes degrades water quality and fish habitats. Pesticides and fertilizer residues in sediment may add pollutants to the water. Also, when forests are removed within the watershed of a hydroelectric power facility, accelerated soil erosion fills the reservoir behind the dam with sediment much faster than usual. This process reduces electricity production at that facility.

Sufficient plant cover reduces the amount of soil erosion: leaves and stems cushion the impact of rainfall, and roots help hold the soil in place. Although soil erosion is a natural process, abundant plant cover makes it negligible in many natural ecosystems.

Salt accumulates in soil that is improperly irrigated

Although irrigation improves the agricultural productivity of arid and semiarid lands, it sometimes causes salt to accumulate in the soil, a process called **salinization.** In a natural scenario, as a result of precipitation runoff, rivers carry dissolved salts away. Irrigation water, however, normally soaks into the soil and does not run off the land into rivers, so when water evaporates, the salt remains behind and accumulates in the soil. Salty soil results in a decline in productivity and, in extreme cases, renders the soil completely unfit for crop production.

Most plants cannot obtain all the water they need from salty soil because a water balance problem exists: water moves by osmosis *out* of plant roots and into the salty soil. Obviously, most plants cannot survive under these conditions (see Fig. 5-14). Plant species that thrive in saline soils have special adaptations that en-

able them to tolerate the high amount of salt. Black mangroves, for example, excrete excess salt through their leaves.

Most crops, unless they have been genetically selected to tolerate high salt, are not productive in saline soil. Research on the molecular aspects of salt tolerance suggests that mutations in membrane transport proteins confer salt tolerance. Biologists genetically engineered a salt-tolerant variety of *Arabidopsis* to overexpress a single gene that codes for a sodium transport protein in the vacuolar membrane. These plants can store large quantities of sodium in their vacuoles, thereby tolerating saline soils.

Review

- What are the four components of soil, and how is each important to plants?
- What is cation exchange?
- How do weathering processes convert rock into soil?
- What are macronutrients and micronutrients?
- How are minerals lost from the soil?

■ SUMMARY: FOCUS ON LEARNING OBJECTIVES

36.1 *(page 762)*

1 Distinguish between taproot and fibrous root systems.

- A **taproot** system has one main root (formed from the **radicle**), from which many lateral roots extend. A **fibrous root** system has several to many **adventitious roots** of the same size developing from the end of the stem. Lateral roots branch from these adventitious roots.

  CENGAGENOW™ Learn more about root systems by clicking on the figure in CengageNOW.

2 Compare cross sections of a primary eudicot root and a monocot root, and describe the functions of each tissue.

- Primary roots have an epidermis, ground tissues (cortex and, in certain roots, pith), and vascular tissues (xylem and phloem). Each root tip is covered by a **root cap,** a protective layer that covers the delicate root **apical meristem** and may orient the root so that it grows downward.
- **Epidermis** protects the root. **Root hairs,** short-lived extensions of epidermal cells, aid in absorption of water and dissolved minerals.
- **Cortex** consists of parenchyma cells that often store starch. **Endodermis,** the innermost layer of the cortex, regulates the movement of water and minerals into the root xylem. Cells of the endodermis have a **Casparian strip** around their radial and transverse walls that is impermeable to water and dissolved minerals.

- Pericycle, xylem, and phloem collectively make up the root's **stele,** or **vascular cylinder. Pericycle** gives rise to lateral roots and lateral meristems. **Xylem** conducts water and dissolved minerals; **phloem** conducts dissolved sugar.
- Xylem of a herbaceous eudicot root forms a solid core in the center of the root. The center of a monocot root often consists of **pith** surrounded by a ring of alternating bundles of xylem and phloem.

3 Trace the pathway of water and mineral ions from the soil through the various root tissues, and distinguish between the symplast and apoplast.

- As water and dissolved mineral ions move from the soil into the root, they pass through the following tissues: root hair/epidermis ⟶ cortex ⟶ endodermis ⟶ pericycle ⟶ root xylem.
- Water and dissolved minerals move through the epidermis and cortex along one of two pathways, the **apoplast** (along the interconnected porous cell walls) or the **symplast** (from one cell's cytoplasm to the next through **plasmodesmata**).

  CENGAGENOW™ Explore the pathways of water and dissolved minerals in the root by clicking on the figures in CengageNOW.

4 Discuss the structure of roots with secondary growth.

- Roots of gymnosperms and woody eudicots develop secondary tissues (wood and bark). The production of secondary tissues is the result of the activity of two lateral meristems, the vascular cambium and cork cambium. The **vascular cambium** produces secondary xylem (wood) and secondary phloem (inner bark). The **cork cambium** produces **periderm** (outer bark).

5 Describe at least three roots that are modified to perform uncommon functions.

- **Prop roots** develop from branches or from a vertical stem and grow downward into the soil to help support certain plants in an upright position. **Buttress roots** are swollen bases or braces that support certain tropical rainforest trees that have shallow root systems. **Pneumatophores** are aerial "breathing" roots that may assist in getting oxygen to submerged roots.

36.2 *(page 768)*

6 List and describe two mutualistic relationships between roots and other organisms.

- **Mycorrhizae,** which are mutually beneficial associations between roots and soil fungi, enhance plant growth by providing essential minerals such as phosphorus to the roots.

- Root **nodules** are swellings that develop on roots of leguminous plants and house millions of **rhizobia** (nitrogen-fixing bacteria).

36.3 *(page 772)*

7 Describe the roles of weathering, organisms, climate, and topography in soil formation.

- Factors influencing soil formation include parent material (type of rock), climate, organisms, the passage of time, and topography. Most soils are formed from parent material that is broken into smaller and smaller particles by **weathering processes.** Climate and organisms work together in weathering rock.

- Soil organisms such as plants, algae, fungi, worms, insects, spiders, and bacteria are important not only in forming soil but also in cycling minerals.

- Topography, a region's surface features, affects soil formation. Steep slopes have little or no soil on them, whereas moderate slopes often have deep soils.

8 List the four components of soil and give the ecological significance of each.

- Soil is composed of inorganic minerals, organic matter, air, and water. Inorganic minerals provide anchorage and essential minerals for plants. Organic matter increases the soil's water-holding capacity and, as it decomposes, releases essential minerals into the soil. Soil air provides oxygen for soil organisms to use during aerobic respiration. Soil water provides water and dissolved minerals to plants and other organisms.

9 Describe how roots absorb positively charged mineral ions by the process of cation exchange.

- **Cations,** positively charged mineral ions, are attracted and reversibly bound to clay particles, which have predominantly negative charges on their outer surfaces. In **cation exchange,** roots secrete protons (H^+), which are exchanged for other positively charged mineral ions, freeing them into the soil water to be absorbed by roots.

10 Distinguish between macronutrients and micronutrients.

- Plants require 19 essential elements for normal growth. Ten elements are **macronutrients:** carbon, hydrogen, oxygen, nitrogen, potassium, calcium, magnesium, phosphorus, sulfur, and silicon. Macronutrients are required in fairly large quantities.

- Nine elements are **micronutrients:** chlorine, iron, boron, manganese, sodium, zinc, copper, nickel, and molybdenum. Micronutrients are needed in trace amounts.

11 Explain the impacts of mineral depletion and soil erosion on plant growth.

- Mineral depletion may occur in soils that are farmed because the natural pattern of nutrient cycling is disrupted when crops are harvested (and not allowed to decompose into the soil).

- **Soil erosion** is the removal of soil from the land by agents such as water and wind. Erosion causes a loss in soil fertility because essential minerals and organic matter that are a part of the soil are removed.

TEST YOUR UNDERSTANDING

1. One main root, formed from the enlarging embryonic root, with many smaller lateral roots branching off it is (a) a fibrous root system (b) an adventitious root system (c) a taproot system (d) a storage root system (e) a prop root system

2. Root hairs (a) cover and protect the delicate root apical meristem (b) increase the absorptive capacity of roots (c) secrete a waxy cuticle (d) orient the root so it grows downward (e) store excess sugars produced in the leaves

3. Certain plants adapted to flooded soil produce aerial "breathing" roots known as (a) fibrous roots (b) pneumatophores (c) mycorrhizae (d) nodules (e) prop roots

4. The waterproof region around the radial and transverse walls of endodermal cells is the (a) Casparian strip (b) pericycle (c) apoplast (d) symplast (e) pneumatophore

5. The apoplast is (a) a layer of cells that surround the vascular region in roots (b) the layer of cells just inside the endodermis (c) a system of interconnected plant cell walls through which water moves (d) the central cylinder of the root that comprises the vascular tissues (e) a continuum of cytoplasm of many cells, all connected by plasmodesmata

6. Plants obtain positively charged mineral ions from clay particles in the soil by cation exchange, in which (a) roots passively absorb the positively charged mineral ions (b) mineral ions flow freely along porous cell walls (c) roots secrete protons, which free other positively charged mineral ions to be absorbed by roots (d) the Casparian strip effectively blocks the passage of water and mineral ions along the endodermal cell wall (e) a well-developed system of internal air spaces in the root allows both gas exchange and cation exchange

7. The cell layer from which lateral roots originate is the (a) epidermis (b) cortex (c) endodermis (d) pericycle (e) vascular cambium

8. Mutually beneficial associations between certain soil fungi and the roots of most plant species are called (a) mycorrhizae (b) pneumatophores (c) nodules (d) rhizobia (e) humus

9. Which of the following statements about soil is *true*? (a) pore spaces are always filled with about 50% air and 50% water (b) a single teaspoon of fertile agricultural soil may contain up to several hundred living microorganisms (c) the texture of a soil is determined by the soil's pH (d) a soil's organic matter includes litter, droppings, and the dead remains of plants, animals,

and microorganisms (e) soil formation is unaffected by a region's climate or topography

10. Carbon, hydrogen, oxygen, nitrogen, potassium, calcium, magnesium, phosphorus, sulfur, and silicon are collectively known as (a) micronutrients (b) microvilli (c) micronuclei (d) macronuclei (e) macronutrients

11. Corn, sorghum, and red mangrove are plants that have (a) prop roots (b) buttress roots (c) pneumatophores (d) storage roots (e) root nodules

12. Label the various tissues of this herbaceous eudicot root. Use Figure 36-3 to check your answers.

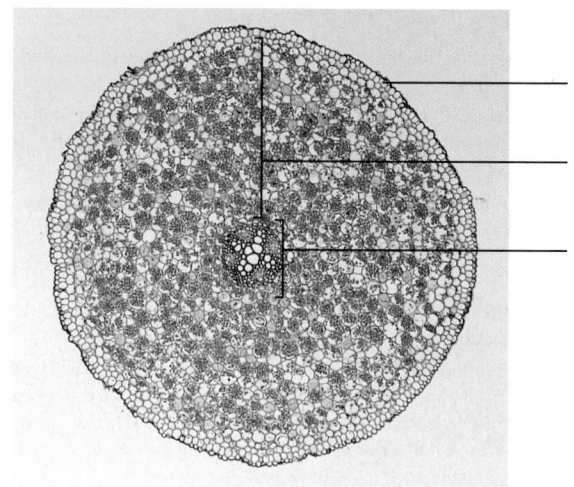

CRITICAL THINKING

1. A mesquite root is found penetrating a mine shaft about 46 m (150 ft) below the surface of the soil. How could you determine *when* the root first grew into the shaft? (*Hint:* Mesquite is a woody plant.)

2. How would you distinguish between a root hair and a small lateral root?

3. You are given a plant part that was found growing in the soil and are asked to determine whether it is a root or an underground stem. How would you identify the structure without a microscope? with a microscope?

4. How would you design an experiment to determine whether gold is essential for plant growth? What would you use for an experimental control?

5. Why does overwatering a plant often kill it?

6. Explain why, once secondary growth has occurred, that portion of the root is no longer involved in absorption. Where does absorption of water and dissolved minerals occur in plants that have roots with secondary growth?

7. **EVOLUTION LINK.** A barrel cactus that is 60 cm tall and 30 cm in diameter has roots more than 3 m long. However, all the plant's roots are found in the soil at a depth of 5 to 15 cm. What possible adaptive value does such a shallow root system confer on a desert plant?

8. **ANALYZING DATA.** When soil has become polluted with hazardous materials such as heavy metals, it is sometimes cost-effective to construct an artificial marsh around the site. Water is pumped through the contaminated soil, picking up the hazard-

ous material, and then the water is passed through the artificial wetland. In one experiment, scientists compared the effectiveness of the roots of two different marsh plants (cattails and common reeds) in absorbing the heavy metal selenium. Which plant's roots removed the most selenium? What should be done to the plants after they have absorbed selenium?

 Additional questions are available in CengageNOW at www.cengage.com/login.

37 Reproduction in Flowering Plants

Flower of the common chickweed. This plant (*Stellaria media*) is a weedy annual native to Europe but widespread in North America. Each flower has five green sepals, five deeply notched yellow petals, three to five pollen-bearing stamens (this flower has three), and a single pistil.

Dr. Jeremy Burgess/Science Photo Library/Photo Researchers, Inc.

KEY CONCEPTS

37.1 The flower is the site of sexual reproduction in angiosperms. A typical flower consists of four whorls: sepals, petals, stamens, and carpels.

37.2 Pollen grains are transported to stigmas by a variety of agents, such as animals and wind.

37.3 Double fertilization results in a plant embryo and endosperm. The seed is a mature ovule, and the fruit is a mature ovary.

37.4 Following a period of dormancy, a seed germinates, or sprouts. The young seedling becomes anchored in the ground and begins to photosynthesize.

37.5 Many vegetative organs (roots, stems, and leaves) are modified for asexual reproduction.

37.6 Sexual reproduction in flowers results in genetic variability in the offspring, whereas asexual reproduction in vegetative structures generally results in individuals that are genetically identical.

Flowering plants, or **angiosperms,** include about 300,000 species and are the largest, most successful group of plants. You may have admired flowers for their fragrances as well as their appealing colors and varied shapes (see photograph). The biological function of flowers is sexual reproduction. Their colors, shapes, and fragrances increase the likelihood that pollen grains, which produce sperm cells, will be carried from one plant to another. Sexual reproduction in plants includes *meiosis* and the fusion of reproductive cells—egg and sperm cells, collectively called **gametes.** The union of gametes, called fertilization, occurs within the flower's ovary.

Sexual reproduction offers the advantage of new gene combinations, not found in either parent, that may make an individual plant better suited to its environment. These new combinations result from the crossing-over and independent assortment of chromosomes that occur during meiosis, before the production of egg and sperm cells (see Chapter 11).

Many flowering plants also reproduce asexually. Asexual reproduction often does not involve the formation of flowers, seeds, and fruits. Instead, offspring generally form when a vegetative organ (such as a stem, root, or leaf) expands, grows, and then becomes separated from the rest of the plant, often by the death of tissues. Because asexual reproduction requires only one parent and no meiosis or fusion of gametes occurs, the offspring of asexual reproduction are virtually genetically identical to one another and to the parent plant.[1]

This chapter examines both sexual and asexual reproduction in flowering plants, including floral adaptations that are important in pollination; seed and fruit structure and dispersal; germination and early growth; and several kinds of asexual reproduction. We conclude with a discussion of the evolutionary advantages and disadvantages of sexual and asexual reproduction.

37.1 THE FLOWERING PLANT LIFE CYCLE

◼ LEARNING OBJECTIVES

1   Describe the functions of each part of a flower.
2   Identify where eggs and pollen grains are formed within the flower.

In Chapters 27 and 28 you learned that angiosperms and other plants undergo a cyclic **alternation of generations** in which they spend a portion of their life cycle in a multicellular haploid stage and a portion in a multicellular diploid stage. The haploid portion, called the **gametophyte generation,** gives rise to gametes by mitosis. When two gametes fuse during **fertilization,** the diploid portion of the life cycle, called the **sporophyte generation,** begins. The sporophyte generation produces haploid spores by meiosis. Each spore has the potential to give rise to a gametophyte plant, and the cycle continues.

In flowering plants the diploid sporophyte generation is larger and nutritionally independent. The haploid gametophyte generation, which is located in the flower, is microscopic and nutritionally dependent on the sporophyte. We say more about alternation of generations in flowering plants after our discussion of the role of flowers as reproductive structures. (It may be helpful for you to review Figure 28-13, which shows the main stages in the flowering plant life cycle.)

Flowers develop at apical meristems

How does a plant "know" it is time to start forming flowers? Correct timing in the switch from vegetative to reproductive development is crucial to ensure reproductive success. A variety of environmental cues, such as temperature and day length, ensure proper timing, and different species are adapted to respond to distinct environmental cues. These environmental signals interact with a variety of plant hormones and developmental pathways.

In recent years some biologists have focused on the molecular aspects of developmental pathways that initiate flowering in plants such as the model organism *Arabidopsis.* When environ-

mental conditions induce flowering, many genes are activated or inactivated. One gene, the *Flowering Locus C (FLC)* gene, codes for a **transcription factor** that represses flowering. Another gene, called *Flowering Locus D (FLD)* gene, codes for a protein that removes acetyl groups from histones in the chromatin where the *FLC* gene is located. When deacetylation occurs, the *FLC* gene is not transcribed (that is, the repressive transcription factor is not produced), and the shoot apical meristem undergoes a transition from vegetative growth to reproductive growth. It is intriguing that the plant FLD protein is homologous to a mammalian protein that also removes acetyl groups from chromatin.

Other genes are also involved in the initiation of flowering, and this area remains a focus of active research interest. In Chapter 38 we discuss the initiation of flowering further.

Each part of a flower has a specific function

Flowers are reproductive shoots, usually consisting of four kinds of organs—sepals, petals, stamens, and carpels—arranged in whorls (circles) on the end of a flower stalk (**FIG. 37-1**; also see Fig. 28-11). In flowers with all four organs, the normal order of whorls from the flower's periphery to the center (or from the flower's base upward) is as follows:

sepals $\longrightarrow$ petals $\longrightarrow$ stamens $\longrightarrow$ carpels

The tip of the stalk enlarges to form a **receptacle** on which some or all of the flower parts are borne. All four floral parts are important in the reproductive process, but only the stamens (the "male" organs) and carpels (the "female" organs) participate directly in sexual reproduction—sepals and petals are sterile.

Sepals, which constitute the outermost and lowest whorl on a floral shoot, cover and protect the flower parts when the flower is a bud. Sepals are leaflike in shape and form and are often green. Some sepals, such as those in lily flowers, are colored and resemble petals (**FIG. 37-2**). The collective term for all the sepals of a flower is **calyx.**

The whorl just inside and above the sepals consists of **petals,** which are broad, flat, and thin (like sepals and leaves) but widely varied in shape and frequently brightly colored, which attracts pollinators. Petals play an important role in ensuring that sexual reproduction will occur. Sometimes petals fuse to form a tube or other floral shape. The collective term for all the petals of a flower is **corolla.**

Just inside and above the petals are the **stamens,** the male reproductive organs. Each stamen has a thin stalk, called a **filament,** at the top of which is an **anther,** a saclike structure in which **pollen grains** form. For sexual reproduction to occur, pollen grains must be transferred from the anther to the female reproductive structure (the carpel), usually of another flower of the same species. At first, each pollen grain consists of two cells surrounded by a tough outer wall. One cell, the **generative cell,** divides mitotically to form two nonflagellate male gametes, known as *sperm cells.* The other cell, the **tube cell,** produces a **pollen tube,** through which the sperm cells travel to reach the ovule.

One or more **carpels,** the female reproductive organs, are located in the center or top of most flowers. Carpels bear **ovules,**

---

[1]Somatic mutations can result in some variability among asexually derived offspring.

which are structures with the potential to develop into seeds. The carpels of a flower may be separate or fused into a single structure. The female part of the flower, often called a **pistil,** may be a single carpel (a *simple pistil*) or a group of fused carpels (a *compound pistil*) (see Fig. 28-12). Each pistil has three sections: a **stigma,** on which the pollen grains land; a **style,** a necklike structure through which the pollen tube grows; and an **ovary,** a juglike structure that contains one or more ovules and can develop into a fruit.

Considerable variation in flower structure occurs from one species to another, but flower structure is virtually constant within a given species. For that reason, flower structure is important in plant identification and, if flowers are present, flowering plant species are easy to evaluate in the field.

Female gametophytes are produced in the ovary, male gametophytes in the anther

Before we proceed, it may be helpful to relate the stages in alternation of generations to floral structure. As discussed in Chapters 27 and 28, angiosperms and certain other plants are heterosporous and produce two kinds of spores: megaspores and microspores (**FIG. 37-3**).

Each young ovule within an ovary contains a diploid cell, the *megasporocyte,* which undergoes meiosis to produce four haploid **megaspores.** Three of these usually disintegrate, and the fourth, the functional megaspore, divides mitotically to produce a multicellular **female gametophyte,** also called an *embryo sac.* The female gametophyte, which is embedded in the ovule, typically contains seven cells with eight haploid nuclei. Six of these cells, including the egg cell (the female gamete), contain a single nucleus each; a large central cell has two nuclei, called **polar nuclei.** The egg and both polar nuclei participate directly in fertilization.

Darwin Dale / Photo Researchers, Inc.

(a) An *Arabidopsis thaliana* flower.

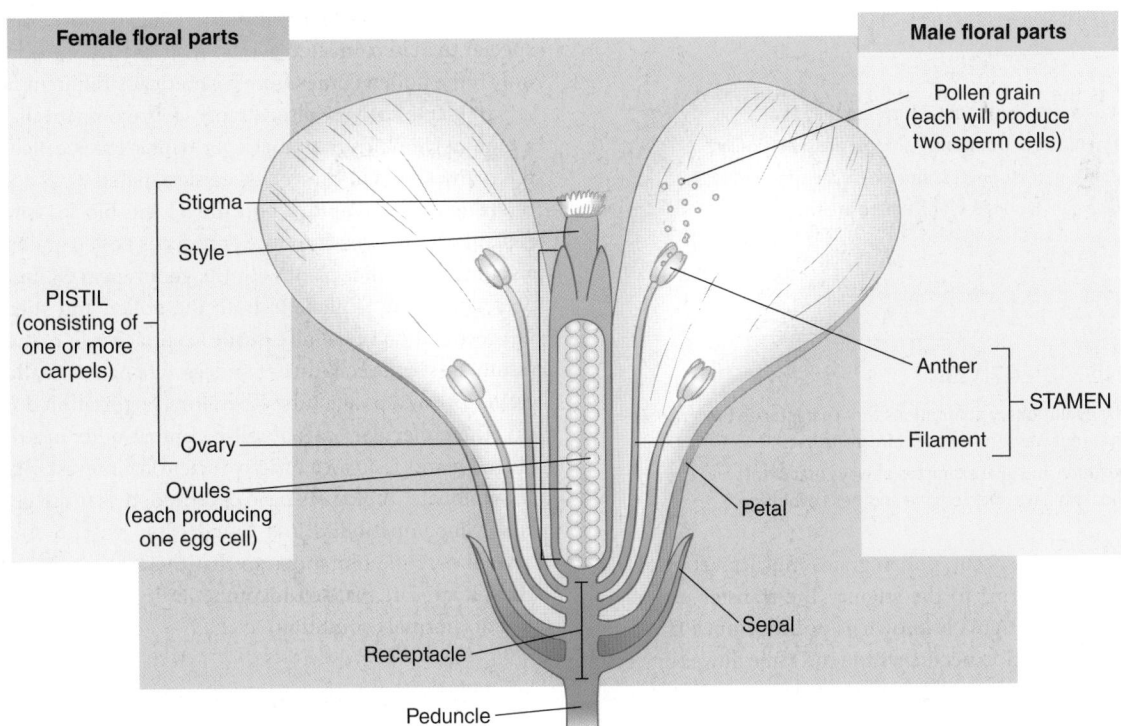

(b) Cutaway view of an *Arabidopsis* flower. Each flower has four sepals (*two are shown*), four petals (*two are shown*), six stamens, and one long pistil. Four of the stamens are long, and two are short (*two long and two short are shown*). Pollen grains develop within sacs in the anthers. In *Arabidopsis*, the compound pistil consists of two carpels that each contain numerous ovules.

FIGURE 37-1 *Animated* Floral structure

FIGURE 37-2 Lily flowers
In lily (*Lilium*) the three sepals and three petals are similar in size and color.

Pollen sacs within the anther contain numerous diploid cells called *microsporocytes,* each of which undergoes meiosis to produce four haploid cells called **microspores.** Each microspore divides mitotically to produce an immature male gametophyte, also called a pollen grain, that consists of two cells, the tube cell and the generative cell. The pollen grain becomes mature when its generative cell divides to form two nonmotile sperm cells.

Review

- How do petals differ from sepals? How are they similar?
- How do stamens differ from carpels? How are they similar?
- What are female gametophytes, and where are they formed?
- What are male gametophytes, and where are they formed?

37.2 POLLINATION

LEARNING OBJECTIVES

3   Compare the evolutionary adaptations that characterize flowers pollinated in different ways (by insects, birds, and bats).

4   Define *coevolution* and give examples of ways that plants and their animal pollinators have affected one another's evolution.

Before fertilization can occur, pollen grains must travel from the anther (where they form) to the stigma. The transfer of pollen grains from anther to stigma is known as **pollination.** Plants are *self-pollinated* if pollination occurs within the same flower or a different flower on the same individual plant. When pollen grains are transferred to a flower on another individual of the same species, the plant is *cross-pollinated.* Flowering plants accomplish pollination in a variety of ways. Beetles, bees, flies, butterflies, moths, wasps, and other insects pollinate many flowers. Animals such as birds, bats, snails, and small nonflying mammals (rodents, primates, and marsupials) also pollinate plants. Wind is an agent of pollination for certain flowers; and water, for a few aquatic flowers.

Many plants have mechanisms that prevent self-pollination

In plant sexual reproduction, the two gametes that unite to form a zygote may be from the same parent or from two different parents. The combination of gametes from two different parents increases the variation in offspring, and this variation may confer a selective advantage. Some offspring, for example, may be able to survive environmental changes better than either parent can.

Evolution has resulted in a variety of mechanisms that prevent self-pollination and thus prevent **inbreeding,** which is the mating of genetically similar individuals. Inbreeding can increase the concentration of harmful genes in the offspring. Some plants, such as asparagus and willow, have separate male and female individuals; the male plants have staminate flowers that lack carpels, and the female plants have pistillate flowers that lack stamens. Other species have flowers with both stamens and pistils, but the pollen is shed from a given flower either before or after the time when the stigma of that flower is receptive to pollen. These characteristics promote **outcrossing** (also called outbreeding), which is the mating of dissimilar individuals.

Many species have genes for **self-incompatibility,** a genetic condition in which the pollen is ineffective in fertilizing the same flower or other flowers on the same plant. In other words, an individual plant can identify and reject its own pollen. Genes for self-incompatibility usually inhibit the growth of the pollen tube in the stigma and style, thereby preventing delivery of sperm cells to the ovules. Self-incompatibility, which is more common in wild species than in cultivated plants, ensures that reproduction occurs only if the pollen comes from a genetically different individual.

In plants such as oilseed rape, self-incompatibility is based on a high degree of variation at a particular locus called the S locus; the many alleles at this locus are designated S_1, S_2, S_3, S_4, and so on. Here is an example of how the S locus blocks self-fertilization: A plant with the genotype S_1S_2 produces pollen grains that land on a stigma of another plant with the genotype S_1S_3. In this case, the presence of the S_1 allele in both the pollen and stigma triggers a self-recognition signaling cascade in surface cells of the stigma. As a result, the stigma cells do not undergo changes that allow the pollen grain to grow a pollen tube. Therefore, fertilization does not occur.

The molecular basis of self-incompatibility in *Arabidopsis* and related plants is an area of active scientific interest. *Arabidopsis* can self-pollinate. Biologists have determined that the genes involved in self-incompatibility and outcrossing exist in *Arabidopsis* but have undergone mutations so that they are no longer functional. Thus, it appears that self-incompatibility in these plants is the ancestral (normal) condition.

Flowering plants and their animal pollinators have coevolved

Animal pollinators and the plants they pollinate have had such close, interdependent relationships over time that they have affected the evolution of certain physical and behavioral features in one another. The term **coevolution** describes such reciprocal adaptation, in which two species interact so closely that they become increasingly adapted to each other as they each undergo evo-

In alternation of generations in flowering plants, the female and male gametophytes are microscopic and nutritionally dependent on the sporophyte plant.

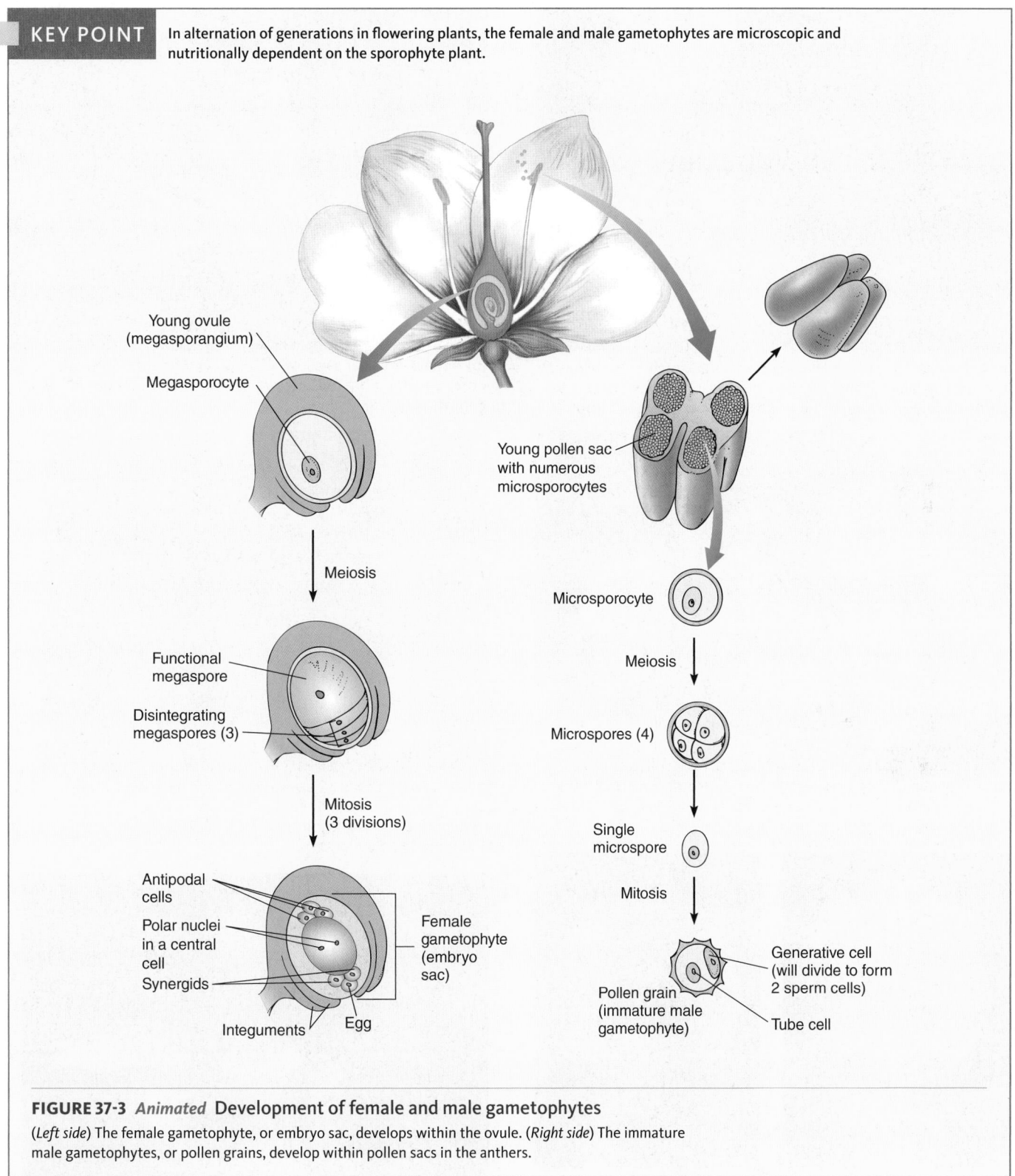

FIGURE 37-3 *Animated* **Development of female and male gametophytes**

(*Left side*) The female gametophyte, or embryo sac, develops within the ovule. (*Right side*) The immature male gametophytes, or pollen grains, develop within pollen sacs in the anthers.

lutionary change by *natural selection.* We now examine some of the features of flowers and their pollinators that may be the products of coevolution.

Flowers pollinated by animals have various features to attract their pollinators, including showy petals (a visual attractant) and scent (an olfactory attractant) (**FIG. 37-4** and **TABLE 37-1**). One reward for the animal pollinator is food. Pollen grains are a protein-rich food for many animals. As they move from flower to flower searching for food, pollinators inadvertently carry along pollen grains on their body parts, helping the plants reproduce sexually.

(a) A honeybee (*Apis mellifera*) pollinates a Scotch broom flower (*Cytisus scoparius*). When the bee presses in to obtain nectar, the stamens spring out, dropping pollen grains on the bee's body.

(b) An eastern tiger swallowtail butterfly (*Pterourus glaucas*) obtains nectar from butterfly weed (*Asclepias tuberosa*) flowers. Photographed in Michigan.

(c) An Australian long-nosed lycid beetle (*Metriorrhynchus rhipidus*) obtains nectar from an Australian tea-tree (*Leptospermum laevigatum*).

(d) The carrion flower (*Stapelia* sp.), which has petals that resemble dried blood, emits a putrid scent. This desert plant is pollinated by flies. Photographed in the Fairchild Tropical Garden in Miami, Florida.

 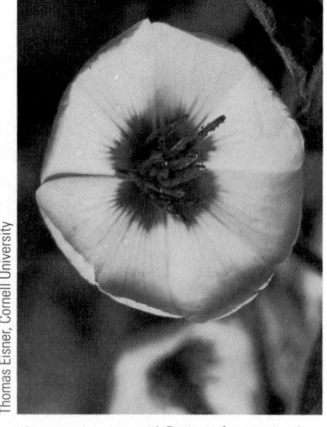

(e) Ultraviolet markings on the evening primrose (*Oenothera* sp.) draw attention to the center of the flower, where insects find nectar and pollen grains. The human eye perceives the flower as solid yellow (*left*). The same flower viewed under ultraviolet radiation (*right*) provides clues about how the insect eye perceives it. The light blue portions of the petals may appear purple to a bee, whereas the dark blue inner parts may appear yellow.

(f) A lesser longnosed bat (*Leptonycteris curasoae*) obtains nectar from a cardon cactus flower (*Pachycereus*) and transfers pollen as it moves from flower to flower. Bats pollinate several hundred species of plants.

FIGURE 37-4 Flowers and their animal pollinators

(g) A broad-billed hummingbird obtains nectar from a desert flower, ocotillo (*Fouquieria splendens*), in Arizona. The pollen grains on the bird's feathers are carried to the next plant.

FIGURE 37-4 (*continued*)

(h) An orchid flower (*Ophrys scolopax*) that mimics female bees attracts male bees, thereby accomplishing pollination.

TABLE 37-1	Floral Characteristics Associated with Various Animal Pollinators			
Animal Pollinator	**Common Flower Color**	**Scent**	**Pollinator Reward**	**Time of Flowering**
Bee	Yellow, blue, purple	Strong, floral	Nectar, pollen	Day
Butterfly	Red, pink	Weak, floral	Nectar	Day
Moth	White	Strong, sweet	Nectar	Dusk, night
Carrion fly	Reddish-brown, purple	Strong, rotten	No reward	Day, night
Beetle	Green, white	Strong, various scents	Nectar, pollen	Day, night
Bird	Red, pink	No scent	Nectar	Day
Bat	White	Strong, musklike or sweet	Nectar, pollen	Night

Some flowers produce nectar, a sugary solution, in special floral glands called *nectaries*. Pollinators use nectar, which is also rich in amino acids, alkaloids, and other floral chemicals, as an energy-rich food. Some nectars contain alkaloids such as nicotine to prevent animal pollinators from drinking all the nectar in a single visit. (Nicotine is poisonous.) Thus, pollinators are encouraged to visit multiple flowers, and each flower has multiple pollinator visitors.

Biologists estimate that insects pollinate about 70% of all flowering plant species. Bees are particularly important as pollinators of crop plants. Crops pollinated by bees provide about 30% of human food. Plants pollinated by insects often have blue or yellow petals. The insect eye does not see color the same way the human eye does. Most insects see well in the violet, blue, and yellow range of visible light but do not perceive red as a distinct color. So flowers pollinated by insects are not usually red. Insects also see in the ultraviolet range, wavelengths that are invisible to the human eye. Insects see ultraviolet radiation as a color called *bee's purple*. Many flowers have dramatic UV markings that may or may not be visible to humans but that direct insects to the center of the flower where the pollen grains and nectar are.

Insects have a well-developed sense of smell, and many insect-pollinated flowers have a strong scent that may be pleasant or foul to humans. The carrion plant, for example, is pollinated by flies and smells like the rotting flesh in which flies lay their eggs. As flies move from one reeking flower to another looking for a place to lay their eggs, they transfer pollen grains.

Birds such as hummingbirds are important pollinators. Flowers pollinated by birds are usually red, orange, or yellow because birds see well in this range of visible light. Because most birds do not have a strong sense of smell, bird-pollinated flowers usually lack a scent.

Bats, which feed at night and do not see well, are important pollinators, particularly in the tropics. Bat-pollinated flowers bloom at night and have dull white petals and a strong nighttime output of scent that usually smells like fermented fruit. Nectar-feeding bats are attracted to the flowers by the scent; they lap up the nectar with their long, extendible tongues. As they move from flower to flower, they transfer pollen grains. An unusual adaptation that encourages pollination by bats has evolved in the tropical vine *Mucana holtonii.* When the pollen in a given flower is mature, a concave petal lifts up. The petal bounces the echo from the bat's echo-locating calls back to the bat, helping it find the flower.

Specialized features such as petals, scent, and nectar to attract pollinators have coevolved with adaptations of animal pollinators. Specialized body parts and behaviors adapted animals to aid pollination as they obtain nectar and pollen grains as a reward. For example, coevolution has selected for bumblebees' hairy bodies, which catch and hold the sticky pollen grains for transport from one flower to another.

Coevolution may have led to the long, curved beaks of the ʻiʻiwi, one of the Hawaiian honeycreepers, that inserts its beak into tubular flowers to obtain nectar (see Figs. 1-13b and 20-18). The long, tubular corolla of the flowers that ʻiʻiwis visit probably also came about through coevolution. During the 20th century, some of the tubular flower species (such as lobelias) became rare, largely as a result of grazing by nonnative cows and feral goats, and about 25% of lobelia species have become extinct. The ʻiʻiwi now feeds largely on the flowers of the ʻohiʻa tree, which lacks petals, and the ʻiʻiwi bill appears to be adapting to this change in feeding preference. Comparison of the bills of ʻiʻiwi museum specimens collected in 1902 with the bills of live birds captured in the 1990s showed that ʻiʻiwi bills were about 3% shorter in the 1990s than in 1902.

Plants and the behavior of their animal pollinators have co-evolved, sometimes in bizarre and complex ways. The flowers of certain orchids (*Ophrys*) resemble female bees in coloring and shape. The unpollinated flowers secrete a scent similar to that produced by female bees, and the males are irresistibly attracted to it. The resemblance between *Ophrys* flowers and female bees is so strong that male bees mount the flowers and try to copulate with them. During this *pseudocopulation,* a pollen sac usually attaches to the back of the bee. When the frustrated bee departs and tries to copulate with another orchid flower, pollen grains are transferred to that flower. Interestingly, once a flower has been pollinated, it emits a scent like that released by female bees that have already mated. Male bees have no interest in visiting flowers that have been pollinated (just as they lose interest in female bees that have already been inseminated).

KEY EXPERIMENT

QUESTION: Can a single-gene mutation in flower color affect animal pollinators?

HYPOTHESIS: If flower color is changed by a mutation, pollinator preferences for the resulting flower may change.

EXPERIMENT: *Mimulus lewisii* has violet-pink flowers and is pollinated by bumblebees; the closely related *M. cardinalis* has orange-red flowers and is pollinated by hummingbirds. Alleles at the same locus in both species affect flower color.

Researchers transferred the allele for orange-red flowers from *M. cardinalis* to *M. lewisii*, which then produced yellow-orange petals. They also transferred the allele for pink flowers from *M. lewisii* to *M. cardinalis*, which then produced dark pink petals.

Wild-type *M. lewisii*

Wild-type *M. cardinalis*

Altered *M. lewisii*

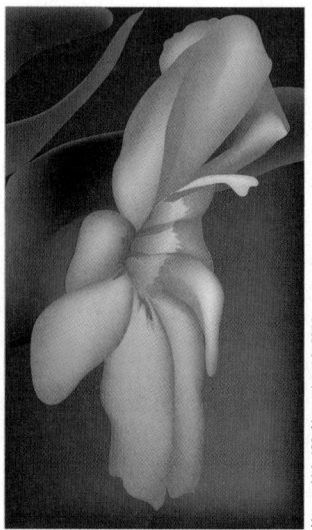
Altered *M. cardinalis*

Nature, Vol. 426, November 13, 2003

RESULTS AND CONCLUSION: The modified *M. lewisii* flowers were yellow-orange in color and had 68 times as many hummingbird visits as the unaltered *M. lewisii* flowers. The modified *M. cardinalis* flowers had dark pink petals and were visited by 74 times as many bumblebees as the unaltered *M. cardinalis* flowers. Thus, a single mutation in a gene for flower color resulted in a shift in animal pollinators.

FIGURE 37-5 Studying how pollinator preferences may have evolved
Biologists from the University of Washington and Michigan State University used monkey flowers to determine if a single gene mutation would have any effect on animal pollinators.

A single mutation in a gene for flower color can result in a shift in animal pollinators

Biologists used two species of monkey flowers, both native to western North America, to determine if a single gene mutation would have any effect on animal pollinators. The wild-type *Mimulus lewisii* has violet-pink flowers and is pollinated by bumblebees, whereas the closely related *M. cardinalis* has orange-red flowers and is pollinated by hummingbirds. Alleles at the same locus in both species affect flower color.

When the researchers transferred the allele for orange-red flowers from *M. cardinalis* to *M. lewisii,* the resulting *M. lewisii* flowers were yellow-orange instead of pink. These flowers were visited by 68 times as many hummingbirds as the wild-type *M. lewisii* flowers (**FIG. 37-5**). A shift in pollinators also occurred when *M. cardinalis* plants received the allele for pink flowers from *M. lewisii.* These *M. cardinalis* flowers were a dark pink in color and had 74 times as many bumblebee visits as the wild-type *M. cardinalis* flowers.

Biologists think that hummingbird-pollinated flowers arose from insect-pollinated flowers many times during the course of flowering plant evolution. These data suggest that a single gene mutation affecting petal color could have been partly responsible for the pollinator shift that resulted in the evolution of two species, *M. lewisii* and *M. cardinalis,* from their insect-pollinated common ancestor.

Some flowering plants depend on wind to disperse pollen

Some flowering plants, such as grasses, ragweed, maples, and oaks, are pollinated by wind. Wind-pollinated plants produce many small, inconspicuous flowers (**FIG. 37-6**). They do not produce large, colorful petals, scent, or nectar. Some have large, feathery

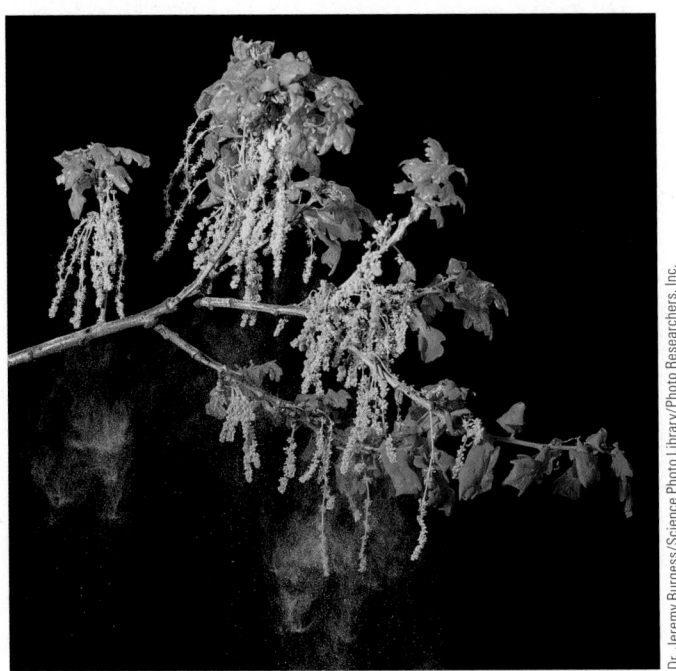

FIGURE 37-6 Wind pollination
Each cluster of male oak flowers (*Quercus*) dangles from a tree branch and sheds a shower of pollen when the wind blows. These flowers lack petals.

Dr. Jeremy Burgess/Science Photo Library/Photo Researchers, Inc.

stigmas, presumably to trap wind-borne pollen grains. Because wind pollination is a hit-or-miss affair, the likelihood of a particular pollen grain landing on a stigma of the same species of flower is slim. Wind-pollinated plants produce large quantities of pollen grains, which increase the likelihood that some pollen grains will land on the appropriate stigma.

Review

- A flower has yellow petals, a pleasant scent, and sugary nectar. How is it probably pollinated?
- A flower has small, inconspicuous flowers without petals, a scent, or nectar. How is it probably pollinated?
- What is coevolution?

37.3 FERTILIZATION AND SEED/ FRUIT DEVELOPMENT

■ LEARNING OBJECTIVES

5 Distinguish between pollination and fertilization.

6 Trace the stages of embryo development in flowering plants, and list and define the main parts of seeds.

7 Explain the relationships among the following: ovules, ovaries, seeds, and fruits.

8 Distinguish among simple, aggregate, multiple, and accessory fruits.

After pollen grains have been transferred from anther to stigma, the tube cell, one of the two cells in the pollen grain, grows a thin pollen tube down through the style and into an ovule in the ovary. How does the pollen tube "know" where to grow? Scientists have found that molecular signals from the female gametophyte guide the growing pollen tube toward the ovule. In 2001 the synergid cells located adjacent to the egg were identified as the source of these molecular signals. The chemical nature of these pollen tube attractants was not known until 2009, when two attracting signals (called LUREs), both small polypeptides, were identified in wishbone flowers (*Torenia fournieri*) and reported in the journal *Science.*

Once a pollen tube penetrates the ovule, the attracting signals are no longer produced. As a result, only one pollen tube enters each female gametophyte. The second cell within the pollen grain divides to form two male gametes (the sperm cells), which move down the pollen tube and enter the ovule (**FIG. 37-7**).

A unique double fertilization process occurs in flowering plants

The egg within the ovule unites with one of the sperm cells, forming a zygote (fertilized egg) that develops into an embryonic plant contained in the future seed. The two polar nuclei in the central cell of the ovule fuse with the second sperm cell to form the first cell of the triploid ($3n$) **endosperm,** the tissue with nutritive and hormonal functions that surrounds the developing embryonic plant in the seed. This process, in which two separate cell fusions occur, is called **double fertilization.** It is, with few exceptions, unique to flowering plants. (A type of double fertilization has been reported in two gymnosperm species, *Ephedra nevadensis* and *Gnetum gnemon.*)

After double fertilization, the ovule develops into a *seed* and the surrounding ovary develops into a *fruit* (see discussion in Chapter 28).

Embryonic development in seeds is orderly and predictable

Flowering plants package a young plant embryo, complete with stored nutrients, in a compact **seed,** which develops from the ovule after fertilization. The nutrients in seeds are not only used by germinating plant embryos but also eaten by animals, including humans. Development of the embryo and endosperm following fertilization is possible because of the constant flow of nutrients into the developing seed from the parent plant.

Cell divisions of the fertilized egg to form a multicellular embryo proceed in several ways in flowering plants. We describe eudicot embryonic development; monocot embryonic development is similar in the early stages.

The two cells (basal cell and apical cell) that are formed as a result of the first division of the fertilized egg establish *polarity,* or direction, in the embryo. The large **basal cell** (located toward the outside of the ovule) typically develops into a **suspensor,** an embryonic tissue that anchors the developing embryo and aids in nutrient uptake from the endosperm. The **apical cell** (toward the inside of the ovule) develops into the plant embryo. Scientists are currently studying molecular differences between the apical cell and basal cell to determine the initial molecular signals that are involved in establishing polarity.

Initially, the apical cell divides to form a small cluster of cells, called a *proembryo* (**FIG. 37-8**). As cell division continues, a sphere of cells, often called a *globular embryo,* develops. Cells begin to develop into specialized tissues during this stage. When the eudicot embryo starts to develop its two cotyledons (seed leaves), it has two lobes and resembles a heart; this is often called the *heart stage.* During the *torpedo stage,* the embryo continues to grow as the cotyledons elongate. As the embryo enlarges, it often curves back on itself and crushes the suspensor.

The mature seed contains an embryonic plant and storage materials

A mature seed contains an embryonic plant and food (stored in the cotyledons or endosperm), surrounded by a tough, protective **seed coat** derived from the **integuments,** which are the outermost layers of an ovule. The seed, in turn, is enclosed within a fruit.

FIGURE 37-7 *Animated* Pollination, pollen tube growth, and double fertilization

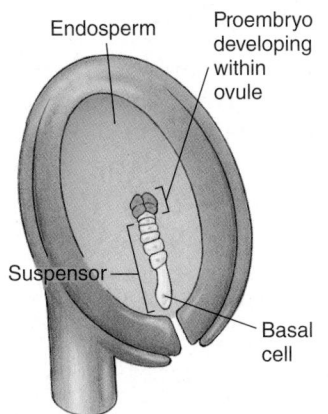

1 Proembryo. This is the earliest multicellular stage of the embryo.

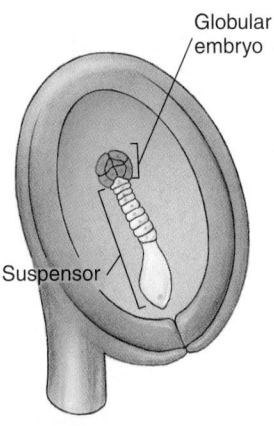

2 Globular stage embryo. As cell division continues, the embryo becomes a ball of cells.

3 Heart stage embryo. As two cotyledons begin to emerge, the embryo is shaped like a heart.

4 Torpedo stage embryo. Cotyledons continue to elongate, forming the torpedo stage.

5 Maturing embryo within seed. Food originally stored in endosperm has been almost completely depleted during embryonic growth and development, and most of the food for the embryonic plant is now stored in the cotyledons.

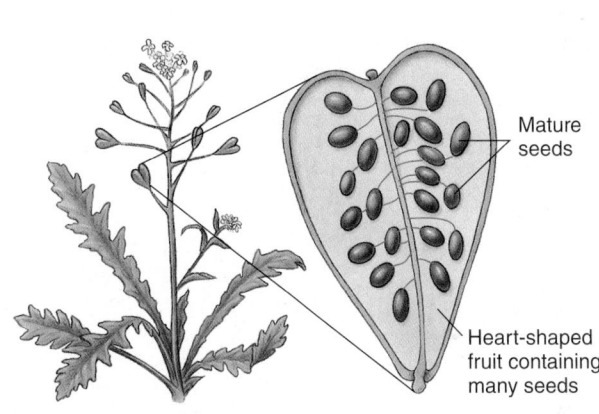

6 Fruit. Longitudinal section through a fruit of shepherd's purse reveals numerous tiny seeds, each containing a mature embryo. Each seed developed from an ovule.

FIGURE 37-8 Embryonic development in shepherd's purse (*Capsella bursa-pastoris*)
The ovule is shown apart from the ovary in parts 1 through 5.

The mature embryo within the seed consists of a short embryonic root, or **radicle;** an embryonic shoot; and one or two seed leaves, or **cotyledons** (**FIG. 37-9**). Monocots have a single cotyledon, whereas eudicots have two. The short portion of the embryonic shoot connecting the radicle to one or two cotyledons is the **hypocotyl.** The shoot apex, or terminal bud, located above the point of attachment of the cotyledon(s) is the **plumule.** After the radicle, hypocotyl, cotyledon(s), and plumule have formed, the young plant's development is arrested, usually by desiccation (drying out) or **dormancy** (a temporary state of arrested physiological activity). When conditions are right for continuing the developmental program, the seed **germinates,** and the embryo resumes growth.

Many seeds are known to remain dormant for decade or so, but only a few instances of germination after hundreds of years of dormancy have been scientifically documented. In 2008 a team

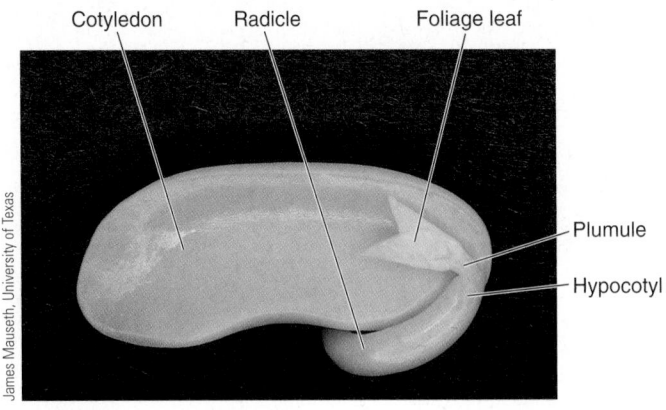

FIGURE 37-9 Seed structure
A bean seed has been dissected—its seed coat and one of its two cotyledons were removed—to show the radicle, hypocotyl, remaining cotyledon, and plumule with its foliage leaf at the shoot apex. This particular seed had begun germinating, so its radicle is larger than in an ungerminated seed.

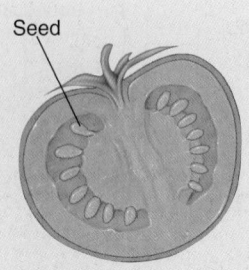

Berry (simple fruit)
A simple, fleshy fruit in which the fruit wall is soft throughout.

Tomato (*Lycopersicon lycopersicum*)

Seed

Caryopsis (simple fruit)
A simple, dry fruit in which the fruit wall is fused to the seed coat.

Wheat (*Triticum*)

Fused fruit wall and seed coat

Single seed

Drupe (simple fruit)
A simple, fleshy fruit in which the inner wall of the fruit is a hard stone.

Peach (*Prunus persica*)

Single seed inside stone

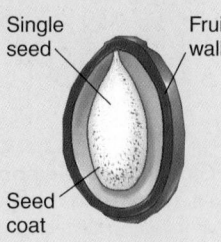

Achene (simple fruit)
A simple, dry fruit in which the fruit wall is separate from the seed coat.

Sunflower (*Helianthus annuus*)

Single seed   Fruit wall

Seed coat

Follicle (simple fruit)
A simple, dry fruit that splits open along one suture to release its seeds; fruit is formed from ovary that consists of a single carpel.

Milkweed (*Asclepias syriaca*)

Seed

Nut (simple fruit)
A simple, dry fruit that has a stony wall, is usually large, and does not split open at maturity.

Oak (*Quercus*)

Scale-covered cup

Woody fruit wall

Single seed

Legume (simple fruit)
A simple, dry fruit that splits open along two sutures to release its seeds; fruit is formed from ovary that consists of a single carpel.

Green bean (*Phaseolus vulgaris*)

Seed

Seed

Aggregate fruit
A fruit that develops from a single flower with several to many pistils (i.e., carpels are not fused into a single pistil).

Blackberry (*Rubus*)

Seed

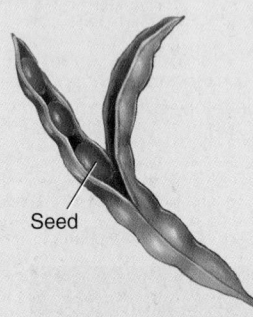

Capsule (simple fruit)
A simple, dry fruit that splits open along two or more sutures or pores to release its seeds; fruit is formed from ovary that consists of two or more carpels.

Iris (*Iris*)

Split-open suture

Seed

Multiple fruit
A fruit that develops from the ovaries of a group of flowers.

Mulberry (*Morus*)

Seed

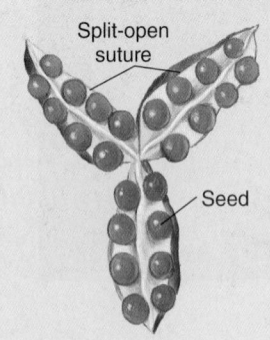

Accessory fruit
A fruit composed primarily of nonovarian tissue (such as the receptacle or floral tube).

Apple (*Malus sylvestris*)

Enlarged floral tube

Ovary wall   Seed

FIGURE 37-10 Fruit types

Fruits are botanically classified into four groups—simple, aggregate, multiple, and accessory—based on their structure and mechanism of seed dispersal.

of biologists from Israel and Switzerland successfully germinated a date seed (*Phoenix dactylifera*) that was radiocarbon dated at about 2000 years old. Before this report, the oldest documented instance of germination was a 1200-year-old lotus seed (*Nelumbo nucifera*).

Because the embryonic plant is nonphotosynthetic, it must be nourished during germination until it becomes photosynthetic and therefore self-sufficient. The cotyledons of many plants function as storage organs and become large, thick, and fleshy as they absorb the food reserves (starches, oils, and proteins) initially produced as endosperm. Seeds that store nutrients in cotyledons have little or no endosperm at maturity. Examples of such seeds are peas, beans, squashes, sunflowers, and peanuts. Other plants—wheat and corn, for example—have thin cotyledons that function primarily to help the young plant digest and absorb food stored in the endosperm.

Fruits are mature, ripened ovaries

After double fertilization takes place within the ovule, the ovule develops into a seed, and the ovary surrounding it develops into a **fruit.** For example, a pea pod is a fruit, and the peas within it are seeds. A fruit may contain one or more seeds; some orchid fruits contain several thousand to a few million seeds! Fruits provide protection for the enclosed seeds and sometimes aid in their dispersal.

There are several types of fruits; their differences result from variations in the structure or arrangement of the flowers from which they were formed. The four basic types of fruits—simple fruits, aggregate fruits, multiple fruits, and accessory fruits—are summarized in **FIGURE 37-10**.

Most fruits are simple fruits. A **simple fruit** develops from a single ovary, which may consist of a single carpel or several fused carpels. At maturity, simple fruits may be fleshy or dry. Two examples of simple, fleshy fruits are berries and drupes. A **berry** is a fleshy fruit that has soft tissues throughout and contains few to many seeds; a blueberry is a berry, as are grapes, cranberries, bananas, and tomatoes. Many so-called "berries" do not fit the botanical definition. Strawberries, raspberries, and mulberries, for example, are not berries; these three fruits are discussed shortly.

A **drupe** is a simple, fleshy or fibrous fruit that contains a hard stone (pit) surrounding a single seed. Examples of drupes include peaches, plums, olives, and almonds. The almond shell is actually the stone, which remains after the rest of the fruit has been removed.

Many simple fruits are dry at maturity; some of these split open, usually along seams, called *sutures,* to release their seeds. A milkweed pod is an example of a **follicle,** a simple, dry fruit that develops from a single carpel and splits open along one suture to release its seeds. A **legume** is a simple, dry fruit that develops from a single carpel and splits open along two sutures. Pea pods are legumes, as are green beans, although both are generally harvested before the fruit has dried out and split open. Pea seeds are usually removed from the fruit and consumed, whereas in green beans the entire fruit and seeds are eaten. A **capsule** is a simple, dry fruit that develops from two or more fused carpels and splits open along two or more sutures or pores. Iris, poppy, and cotton fruits are capsules.

Other simple, dry fruits, such as **caryopses** (sing., *caryopsis*), or **grains,** do not split open at maturity. Each caryopsis contains a single seed. Because the seed coat is fused to the fruit wall, a caryopsis looks like a seed rather than a fruit. Kernels of corn and wheat are fruits of this type.

An **achene** is similar to a caryopsis in that it is simple and dry, does not split open at maturity, and contains a single seed. However, the seed coat of an achene is not fused to the fruit wall. Instead, the single seed is attached to the fruit wall at one point only, permitting an achene to be separated from its seed. The sunflower fruit is an example of an achene. One can peel off the fruit wall (the shell) to reveal the sunflower seed within.

Nuts are simple, dry fruits that have a stony wall and do not split open at maturity. Unlike achenes, nuts are usually large, single seeded, and often derived from a compound ovary. Examples of nuts include chestnuts, acorns, and hazelnuts. Many so-called "nuts" do not fit the botanical definition. Peanuts and Brazil nuts, for example, are seeds, not nuts.

Aggregate fruits are a second main type of fruit. An **aggregate fruit** is formed from a single flower that contains several to many separate (free) carpels (**FIG. 37-11**). After fertilization, each ovary from each individual carpel enlarges. As they enlarge, the ovaries

(a)   (b)   (c)

FIGURE 37-11 An aggregate fruit
(a) Cutaway view of a blackberry flower (*Rubus*), showing the many separate carpels in the center of the flower. **(b)** A developing blackberry fruit is an aggregate of tiny drupes. The little "hairs" on the blackberry are remnants of stigmas and styles. **(c)** Developing blackberry fruits at various stages of maturity.

may fuse to form a single fruit. Raspberries, blackberries, and magnolia fruits are examples of aggregate fruits.

A third type is the **multiple fruit,** formed from the ovaries of many flowers that grow in proximity on a common floral stalk. The ovary from each flower fuses with nearby ovaries as it develops and enlarges after fertilization. Pineapples, figs, and mulberries are multiple fruits.

Accessory fruits are the fourth type. They differ from other fruits in that plant tissues in addition to ovary tissue make up the fruit. For example, the edible portion of a strawberry is the red, fleshy receptacle. Apples and pears are also accessory fruits; the outer part of each of these fruits is an enlarged *floral tube,* consisting of receptacle tissue along with portions of the calyx, that surrounds the ovary (**FIG. 37-12**).

Seed dispersal is highly varied

Wind, animals, water, and explosive dehiscence disperse the various seeds and fruits of flowering plants (**FIG. 37-13**). Effective methods of seed dispersal have made it possible for certain plants to expand their geographic range. In some cases the seed is the actual agent of dispersal, whereas in others the fruit performs this role. In tumbleweeds, such as Russian thistle, the entire plant is the agent of dispersal because it detaches and blows across the ground, scattering seeds as it bumps along. Tumbleweeds are lightweight and are sometimes blown many kilometers by the wind.

Wind is responsible for seed dispersal in many plants. Plants such as maple trees have winged fruits adapted for wind dispersal. Light, feathery plumes enable other seeds or fruits to be transported by wind, often for considerable distances. Both dandelion fruits and milkweed seeds have this type of adaptation.

Some plants have special structures that aid in dispersal of their seeds and fruits by animals. The spines and barbs of burdock burs and similar fruits catch in animal fur and fall off as the animal moves about.

Fleshy, edible fruits are also adapted for animal dispersal. Birds, bats, primates, grazing ruminants, and ants are common dispersal agents. These animals are attracted to the fruit by its color, location, odor, and taste. As the animal eats these fruits, it either discards or swallows the seeds. Many seeds that are swallowed have thick seed coats and are not digested; instead, they pass through the digestive tract and are deposited in the animal's feces some distance from the parent plant. In fact, some seeds do not germinate unless they have passed through an animal's digestive tract; the animal's digestive juices probably aid germination by helping to break down the seed coat. Some edible fruits apparently contain chemicals that function as laxatives to speed seeds through an animal's digestive tract; the less time these seeds spend in the gut, the more likely they will germinate.

Animals such as squirrels and many bird species also help disperse acorns and other fruits and seeds by burying them for winter use. Many buried seeds are never used by the animal and germinate the following spring. Ants collect the seeds of many plants and take them underground to their nests. Ants disperse and bury seeds for hundreds of plant species in almost every terrestrial environment, from northern coniferous forests to tropical rain forests to deserts.

Both ants and flowering plants benefit from their association. The ants ensure the reproductive success of the plants whose seeds they bury, and the plants supply food to the ants. A seed that is collected and taken underground by ants often contains a special structure called an *elaiosome,* or *oil body,* that protrudes from the

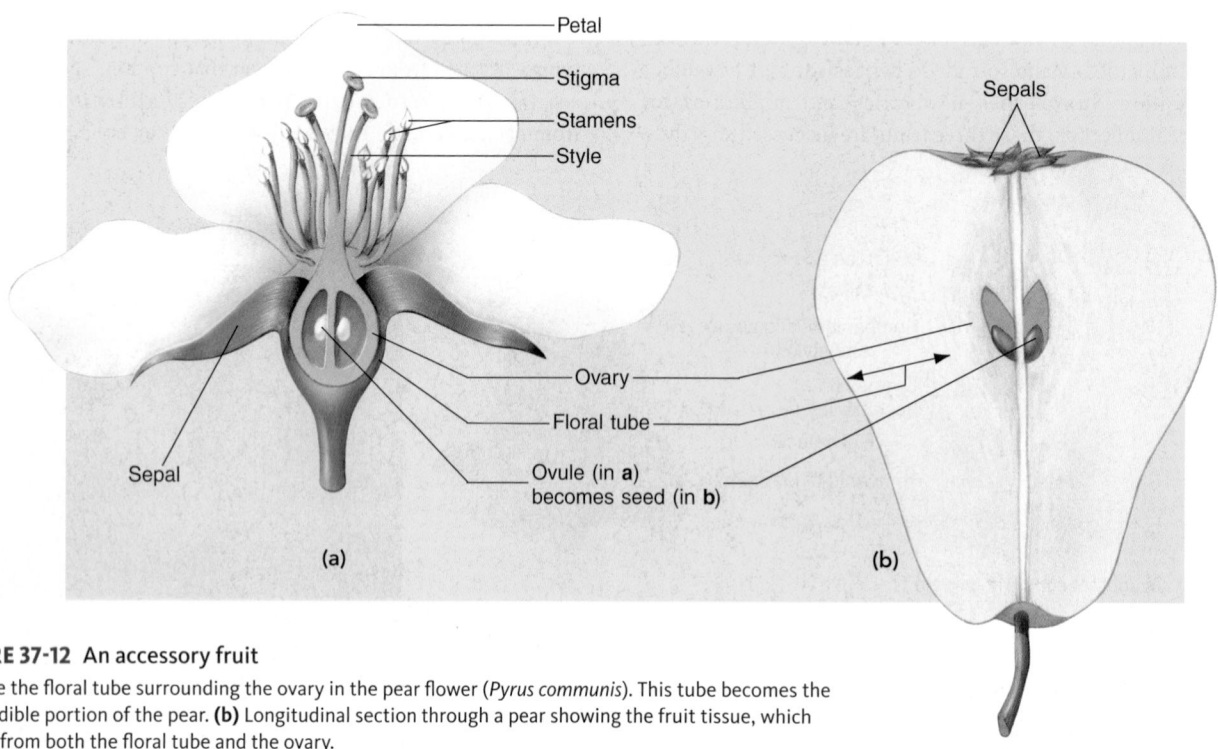

FIGURE 37-12 An accessory fruit
(a) Note the floral tube surrounding the ovary in the pear flower (*Pyrus communis*). This tube becomes the major edible portion of the pear. **(b)** Longitudinal section through a pear showing the fruit tissue, which derives from both the floral tube and the ovary.

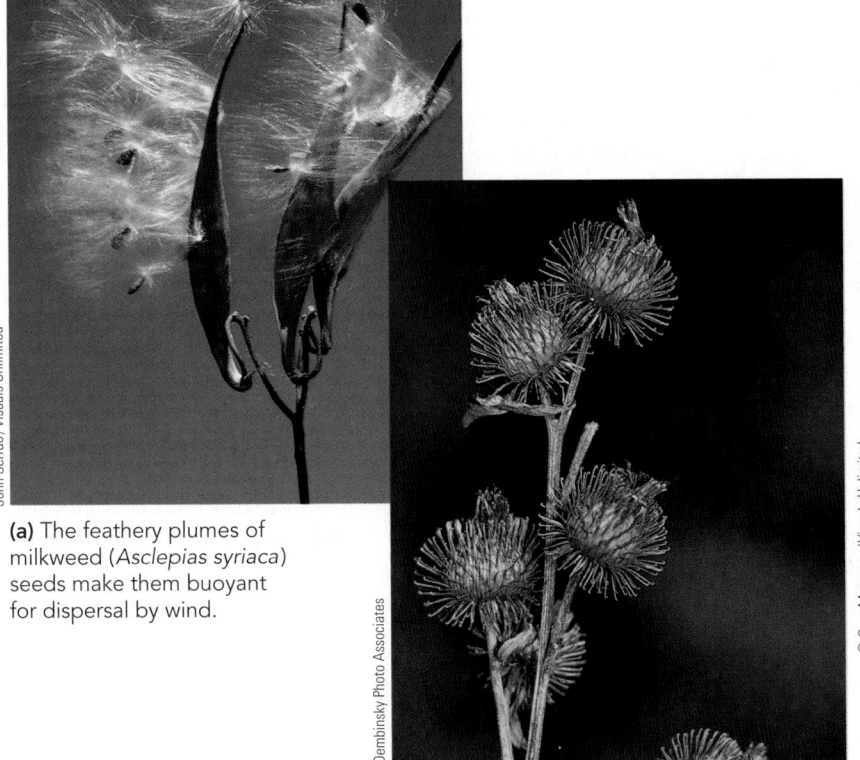

John Serrao/Visuals Unlimited

(a) The feathery plumes of milkweed (*Asclepias syriaca*) seeds make them buoyant for dispersal by wind.

DPA/Dembinsky Photo Associates

(b) Burdock (*Arctium minus*) burs (the hooked fruits) are carried away from the parent plant after sticking to bird feathers, mammal fur, or human clothing.

© Gary Meszaros/Visuals Unlimited

(c) Fleshy fruits such as blackberries (*Rubus*) are eaten by animals such as this white-footed mouse. The seeds are frequently swallowed whole and pass unharmed through the animal's digestive tract.

Marion Lobstein

(d) Dispersal of seeds by ants. The brown part of each bloodroot (*Sanguinaria canadensis*) seed is the seed proper, and the white part is the elaiosome, or oil body. The seeds have been placed along the midvein of an oak leaf to indicate scale.

(e) (*Left*) An intact fruit of bitter cress (*Cardamine pratensis*), before it has opened. (*Right*) The fruit splits open with explosive force, flinging the seeds some distance from the plant.

FIGURE 37-13 Seed (and fruit) dispersal

seed. Elaiosomes are a nutritious food for ants, which carry seeds underground before removing the elaiosome. Once an elaiosome is removed from a seed, the ants discard the undamaged seed in an underground refuse pile, which happens to be rich in organic material (such as ant droppings and dead ants) and minerals (inorganic nutrients) required by young seedlings. Thus, ants not only bury the seeds away from animals that might eat them but also place the seeds in rich soil that is ideal for germination and seedling growth.

The coconut is an example of a fruit adapted for dispersal by water. The coconut has air spaces that make it buoyant and capable of being carried by ocean currents for thousands of kilometers. When it washes ashore, the seed may germinate and grow into a coconut palm tree.

Some seeds are not dispersed by wind, animals, or water. Such seeds are found in fruits that use *explosive dehiscence,* in which the fruit bursts open suddenly and quite often violently, forcibly discharging its seeds. These fruits burst open due to pressure caused by differences in *turgor* (hydrostatic pressure) as the cells in the fruit dry out. The fruits of plants such as touch-me-not and bitter cress split open so explosively that seeds are scattered a meter or more.

Review

- What is the difference between pollination and fertilization? Which process occurs first?
- What are the main stages of eudicot embryonic development?
- What is a fruit?
- How are the following fruits distinguished: simple, aggregate, multiple, and accessory?
- What are some characteristics of animal-dispersed seeds and fruits?

37.4 GERMINATION AND EARLY GROWTH

◼ LEARNING OBJECTIVE

9 Summarize the influence of internal and environmental factors on the germination of seeds.

Pollination and fertilization are followed by seed and fruit development in flowering plants. Each seed develops from an ovule and contains an embryonic plant and food to provide nourishment for the embryo during germination. **Germination**—the process of a seed sprouting—and the growth of young seedlings into mature plants are aspects of growth and development. Within a given species, the precise requirements for seed germination represent evolutionary adaptations that protect the young seedlings from adverse environmental conditions. Environmental cues, such as the presence of water and oxygen, proper temperature, and sometimes the presence of light penetrating the soil surface, influence whether or not a seed germinates.

No seed germinates unless it has absorbed water. The embryo in a mature seed is dehydrated, and a watery environment is necessary for active metabolism. When a seed germinates, its metabolic machinery is turned on, and numerous materials are synthesized

and others degraded. Therefore, water is an absolute requirement for germination. The absorption of water by a dry seed is **imbibition.** As a seed imbibes water, it often swells to several times its original, dry size (**FIG. 37-14**). Cells imbibe water by adhesion of water onto and into materials such as cellulose, pectin, and starches within the seed.

Germination and subsequent growth require a great deal of energy. Because young plants obtain this energy by converting the energy of food molecules stored in the seed's endosperm or cotyledons to ATP during aerobic respiration, much oxygen is usually needed during germination. (Some plants, such as rice, grow in flooded soil where oxygen is absent and carry out *alcohol fermentation* during the early stages of germination and seedling growth.)

Temperature is another environmental factor that affects germination. Each species has an optimal, or ideal, temperature at which the germination percentage is highest. For most plants, the optimal germination temperature is between 25°C and 30°C (77°F and 86°F). Some seeds, such as those of apples, require prolonged exposure to low temperatures before their seeds break dormancy and germinate. Some of the environmental factors needed for germination help ensure the survival of the young plant. The requirement of a prolonged low-temperature period ensures that seeds adapted to temperate climates germinate in the spring rather than the fall.

Some plants, especially those with tiny seeds, such as lettuce, require light for germination. A light requirement ensures that a tiny seed germinates only if it is close to the soil surface. If such a seed were to germinate several centimeters below the soil surface, it might not have enough food reserves to grow to the surface. But if this light-dependent seed remains dormant until the soil is disturbed and it is brought to the surface, it has a much greater likelihood of survival.

Some seeds do not germinate immediately

A mature seed is often dormant and may not germinate immediately even if growing conditions are ideal. In certain seeds, internal factors, which are under genetic control, prevent germination even

FIGURE 37-14 Imbibition
Pinto bean seeds (*Phaseolus vulgaris*) before imbibition (*left*) and after (*right*). Dry seeds imbibe water before they germinate.

when all external conditions are favorable. Many seeds are dormant because certain chemicals are present or absent or because the seed coat restricts germination. For example, the seeds of many desert plants contain high concentrations of *abscisic acid* (discussed in Chapter 38), which inhibits germination under unfavorable conditions. Abscisic acid is washed out only when rainfall is sufficient to support the plant's growth after the seed germinates.

Some seeds, such as certain legumes, have extremely hard, thick seed coats that prevent water and oxygen from entering, thereby inducing dormancy. *Scarification,* the process of scratching or scarring the seed coat (physically with a knife or chemically with an acid) before sowing it, induces germination in these plants. Scarification in nature occurs, for example, when these seeds pass through the digestive tracts of animals or when the seed coats are partially digested by soil bacteria.

Eudicots and monocots exhibit characteristic patterns of early growth

Once conditions are right for germination, the first part of the plant to emerge from the seed is the radicle, or embryonic root. As the root grows and forces its way through the soil, it encounters considerable friction from soil particles. A root cap protects the delicate apical meristem of the root tip.

The shoot (the stem with its leaves and reproductive structures) is next to emerge from the seed. Stem tips are not protected by a structure comparable to a root cap, but plants have ways to protect the delicate stem tip as it grows through the soil to the surface. The stem of a bean seedling (a eudicot), for instance, curves over to form a hook so that the stem tip and cotyledons are actually *pulled up* through the soil (**FIG. 37-15a**). Corn and other grasses (monocots) have a special sheath of cells called a **coleoptile** that surrounds and protects the young shoot (**FIG. 37-15b**). First, the coleoptile pushes up through the soil, and then the leaves and stem grow through the tip of the coleoptile.

Review

- What factors influence the germination of seeds?
- Why are plant growth and development so sensitive to environmental cues?

37.5 ASEXUAL REPRODUCTION IN FLOWERING PLANTS

◼ LEARNING OBJECTIVES

10 Explain how the following structures may be used to propagate plants asexually: rhizomes, tubers, bulbs, corms, stolons, plantlets, and suckers.

11 Define *apomixis.*

Flowering plants have many kinds of asexual reproduction, several of which involve modified stems: rhizomes, tubers, bulbs, corms, and stolons. A **rhizome** is a horizontal underground stem that may or may not be fleshy. Fleshiness indicates that the rhizome is used for storing food materials, such as starch (**FIG. 37-16a**). Although rhizomes resemble roots, they are really stems, as indicated by the

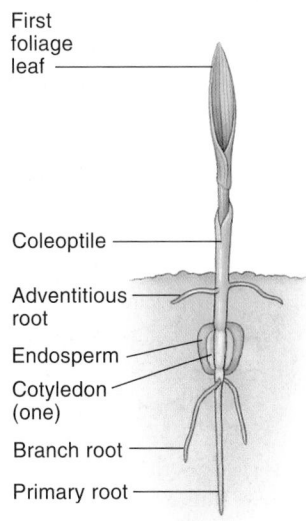

(a) Common bean, a eudicot. The hook in the stem protects the delicate stem tip as it grows through the soil. Once the shoot emerges from the soil, the hook straightens.

(b) Corn, a monocot. The coleoptile, a sheath of cells, emerges first from the soil. The shoot and leaves grow through the middle of the coleoptile.

FIGURE 37-15 *Animated* Germination and seedling growth

presence of scalelike leaves, buds, nodes, and internodes. (Roots have none of these features.) Rhizomes frequently branch in different directions. Over time, the old portion of the rhizome dies, and the two branches eventually separate to become distinct plants. Irises, bamboos, ginger, and many grasses are examples of plants that reproduce asexually by forming rhizomes.

Some rhizomes produce greatly thickened ends called **tubers,** which are fleshy underground stems enlarged for food storage. When the attachment between a tuber and its parent plant breaks, often as a result of the death of the parent plant, the tuber grows into a separate plant. Potatoes and elephant's ear (*Caladium*) are examples of plants that produce tubers (**FIG. 37-16b**). The "eyes" of a potato are axillary buds, evidence that the tuber is an underground stem rather than a storage root such as a sweet potato or carrot.

A **bulb** is a modified underground bud in which fleshy storage leaves are attached to a short stem (**FIG. 37-16c**). A bulb is globose (round) and covered by paperlike bulb scales, which are modified leaves. It frequently forms axillary buds that develop into small daughter bulbs (bulblets). These new bulbs are initially attached to the parent bulb, but when the parent bulb dies and rots away, each daughter bulb can become established as a separate plant. Lilies, tulips, onions, and daffodils are some plants that form bulbs.

A **corm** is a short, erect underground stem that superficially resembles a bulb (**FIG. 37-16d**). Unlike the bulb, whose food is stored in underground leaves, the corm's storage organ is a thickened underground stem covered by papery scales (modified leaves). Axillary buds frequently give rise to new corms; the death of the parent corm separates these daughter corms, which then become established as separate plants. Familiar garden plants that produce corms include crocus, gladiolus, and cyclamen.

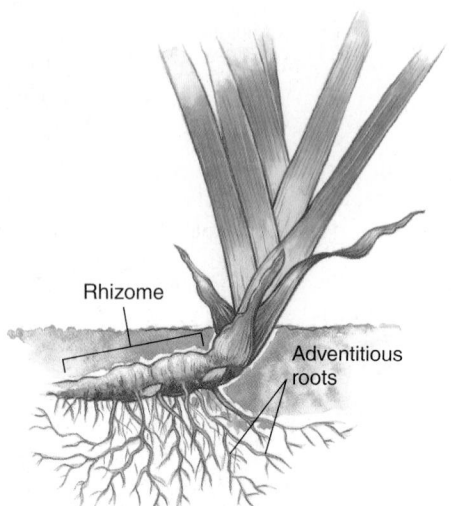

(a) Rhizome. Irises have horizontal underground stems called rhizomes. New aerial shoots arise from buds that develop on the rhizome.

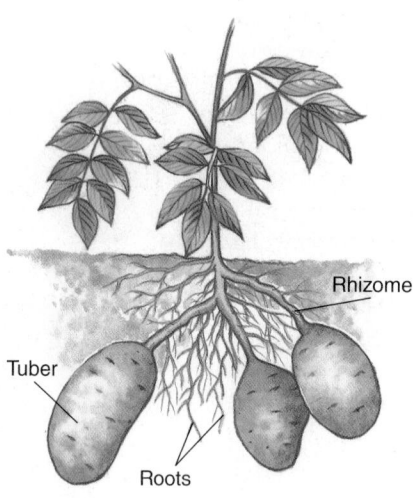

(b) Tuber. Potato plants form rhizomes, which enlarge into tubers (the potatoes) at the ends.

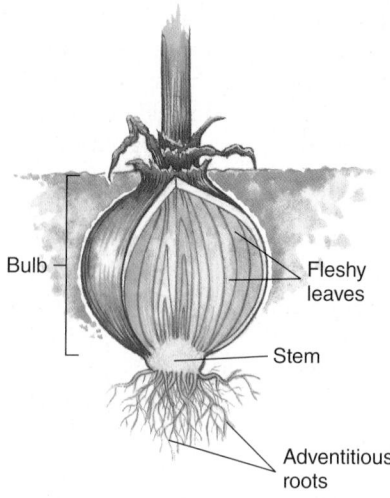

(c) Bulb. A bulb is a short underground stem to which overlapping, fleshy leaves are attached; most of the bulb consists of leaves.

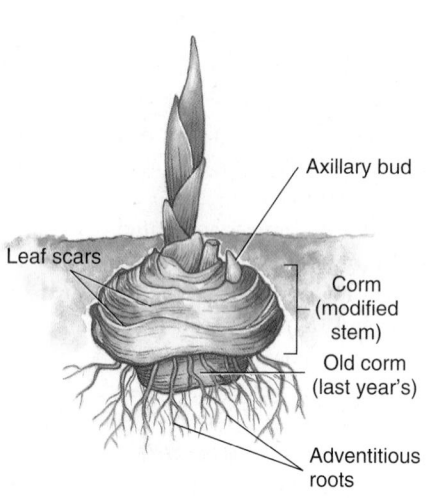

(d) Corm. A corm is an underground stem that is almost entirely stem tissue surrounded by a few papery scales.

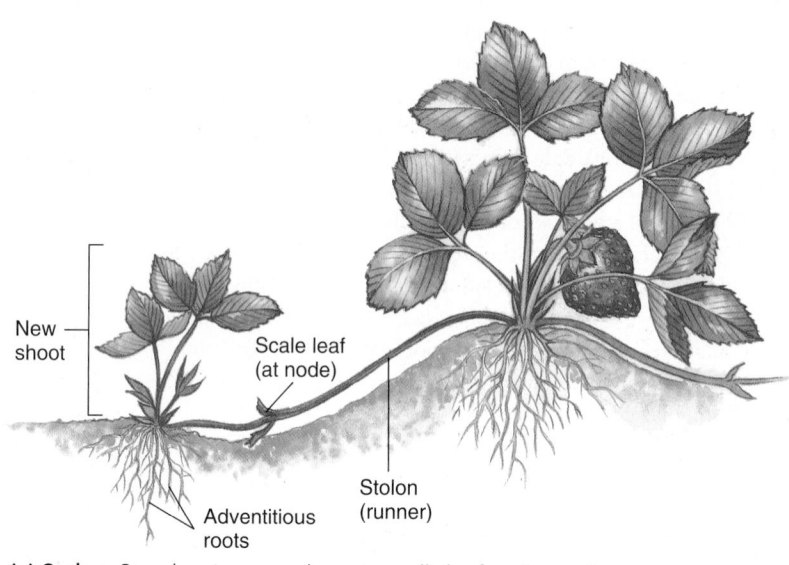

(e) Stolon. Strawberries reproduce asexually by forming stolons, or runners. New plants (shoots and roots) are produced at every other node.

FIGURE 37-16 Modified stems

Stolons, or **runners,** are horizontal, aboveground stems that grow along the surface and have long internodes (**FIG. 37-16e**). Buds develop along the stolon, and each bud gives rise to a new shoot that roots in the ground. When the stolon dies, the daughter plants live separately. The strawberry plant produces stolons.

Some plants form detachable **plantlets** (small plants) in notches along their leaf margins. *Kalanchoe,* whose common name is "mother of thousands," has meristematic tissue that gives rise to an individual plantlet at each notch in the leaf (**FIG. 37-17**). When these plantlets reach a certain size, they drop to the ground, root, and grow.

Some plants reproduce asexually by producing **suckers,** aboveground shoots that develop from adventitious buds on roots (**FIG. 37-18**). Each sucker grows additional roots and becomes an independent plant when the parent plant dies. Examples of plants that form suckers include black locust, pear, apple, cherry, blackberry, and aspen. A quaking aspen (*Populus tremuloides*) colony in the Wasatch Mountains of Utah contains at least 47,000 tree trunks formed from suckers that can be traced back to a single individual; this massive "organism" occupies almost 43 hectares (106 acres). Some weeds, such as field bindweed, produce many suckers. These plants are difficult to control because pulling the plant out of the

FIGURE 37-17 Plantlets

The "mother of thousands" (*Kalanchoe*) produces detachable plantlets along the margins of its leaves. The young plantlets drop off and root in the ground.

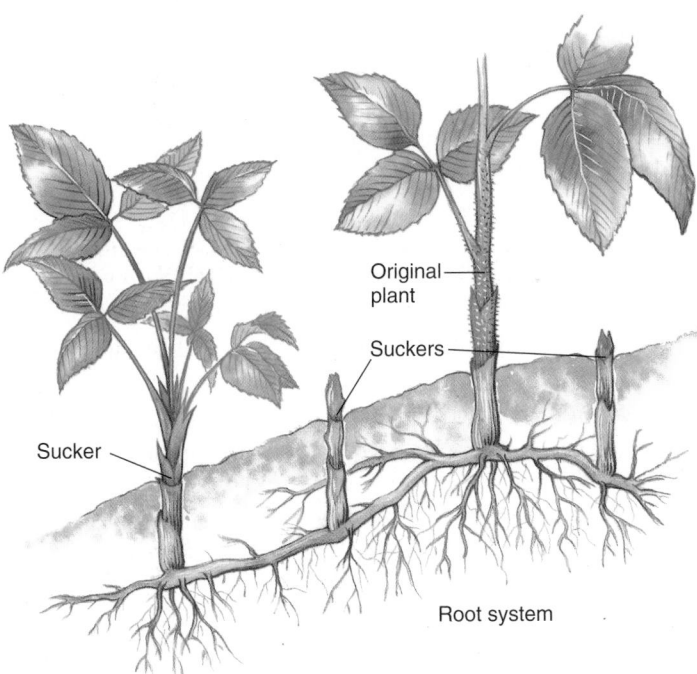

FIGURE 37-18 Suckers in various stages of development

All the suckers are connected to one another through the root system.

soil seldom removes all the roots, which can grow as deep as 3 m (10 ft). In fact, in response to wounding, the roots produce additional suckers, which can be a considerable nuisance to humans.

Apomixis is the production of seeds without the sexual process

Some flowering plants produce embryos in seeds without meiosis and the fusion of gametes. Seed production by **apomixis** is a form of asexual reproduction in which the offspring are maternal clones. For example, an embryo may develop from a diploid cell in the ovule rather than from a diploid zygote that forms from the union of two haploid gametes. Because there is no fusion of gametes, the embryo is virtually genetically identical to the maternal genotype. However, the advantage of apomixis over other methods of asexual reproduction is that the seeds and fruits produced by apomixis can be dispersed by methods associated with sexual reproduction.

Apomixis, which occurs in various species of more than 40 angiosperm families, is often found in plants that are polyploid with varying degrees of sterility. Apomixis allows these sterile plants to reproduce and therefore survive. Examples of plants that can reproduce by apomixis include dandelions, citrus trees, mango, blackberries, garlic, and certain grasses.

Plant biologists are actively engaged in identifying the genes involved in asexual reproduction by apomixis. In 2008, scientists in India reported in the journal *Nature* that they had identified a mutation of a single gene in *Arabidopsis* that results in diploid female gametes, a first step toward apomixis. If researchers can transfer this or similar genes to crop plants that possess superior traits such as high yield, they may be able to develop apomictic crop plants whose traits do not get lost or diluted during the genetic shuffling of sexual reproduction.

Review

- How are rhizomes and tubers involved in asexual reproduction?
- How are corms and bulbs similar? How are they different?
- What is apomixis? How is the ability to reproduce by apomixis advantageous?

37.6 A COMPARISON OF SEXUAL AND ASEXUAL REPRODUCTION

■ LEARNING OBJECTIVE

12 State the differences between sexual reproduction and asexual reproduction, and discuss the evolutionary advantages and disadvantages of each.

Sexual reproduction and asexual reproduction are suited for different environmental circumstances. As you know, sexual reproduction results in offspring that are genetically different from the parents; that is, the parental genotypes are not preserved in the offspring. This genetic diversity of offspring may be selectively advantageous, particularly in an unstable, or changing, environment. (We define *environment* broadly to include all external conditions, both living and nonliving, that affect an organism.) If a plant species that reproduces sexually (and is therefore genetically diverse) is exposed to increasing annual temperatures as a result of global warming, for example, some of the individuals may be more fit than the parents or other offspring. The genetic diversity from sexual reproduction may also let the individuals of a species exploit new environments, thereby expanding their range.

You have seen that asexual reproduction results in offspring that are virtually genetically identical to the parent; that is, the parental genotype is preserved. Assuming the parent is well adapted to its environment (that is, the parent has a favorable combination of alleles), this genetic similarity may be selectively advantageous if the environment remains stable (unchanging) for several generations. None of the offspring of asexual reproduction is more fit than the parent, but neither is any less fit.

Despite the apparent advantages of asexual reproduction, most plant species whose reproduction is primarily asexual occasionally reproduce sexually. Even in what appears to be a stable environment, plants are exposed to changing selective pressures, such as changes in the number and kinds of herbivores and parasites, the availability of food, competition from other species, and climate. Sexual reproduction permits species whose reproduction is primarily asexual to increase their genetic variability so at least some individuals are adapted to the changing selective pressures in a stable environment.

Sexual reproduction has some disadvantages

Although the genetic diversity produced by sexual reproduction is advantageous to a species' long-term survival, sexual reproduction is a costly form of reproduction. Sexual reproduction requires both male and female gametes, which must meet for reproduction to occur. The many adaptations of flowers for different modes of pollination represent one cost of sexual reproduction.

Sexual reproduction produces some individuals with genotypes that are well-adapted to the environment, but it also produces some individuals that are less well-adapted. Therefore, sexual reproduction is usually accompanied by high death rates among offspring, particularly when selective pressures are strong. (As discussed in Chapter 18, however, this aspect of sexual reproduction is an important part of evolution by natural selection.)

Every biological process involves trade-offs, and sexual reproduction is no exception. Although sexual reproduction has its costs, it also has adaptive advantages over asexual reproduction.

Review

- How does sexual reproduction in plants differ from asexual reproduction?
- What is an adaptive advantage of sexual reproduction? Why is sexual reproduction considered costly?

■ SUMMARY: FOCUS ON LEARNING OBJECTIVES

37.1 *(page 782)*

1 Describe the functions of each part of a flower.

- **Sepals** cover and protect the flower parts when the flower is a bud. **Petals** play an important role in attracting animal pollinators to the flower.
- **Stamens** produce pollen grains. Each stamen consists of a thin stalk (the **filament**) attached to a saclike structure (the **anther**).
- The **carpel** is the female reproductive unit. A **pistil** may consist of a single carpel or a group of fused carpels. Each pistil has three sections: a **stigma**, on which the pollen grains land; a **style**, through which the pollen tube grows; and an **ovary** that contains one or more **ovules.**

CENGAGENOW™ **Learn more about flower structure by clicking on the figure in CengageNOW.**

2 Identify where eggs and pollen grains are formed within the flower.

- **Pollen grains** form within pollen sacs in the anther.

- An egg and two **polar nuclei,** along with several other nuclei, are formed in the ovule. Both egg and polar nuclei participate directly in fertilization.

  CENGAGENOW™ **Watch plant reproduction unfold by clicking on the figure in CengageNOW.**

37.2 *(page 784)*

3 Compare the evolutionary adaptations that characterize flowers pollinated in different ways (by insects, birds, and bats).

- Flowers pollinated by insects are often yellow or blue and have a scent. Bird-pollinated flowers are often yellow, orange, or red and do not have a strong scent. Bat-pollinated flowers often have white petals and are scented.

4 Define *coevolution* and give examples of ways that plants and their animal pollinators have affected one another's evolution.

- **Coevolution** is reciprocal adaptation caused by two different species (such as flowering plants and their animal pollinators) forming an interdependent relationship and affecting the course of each other's evolution. For example, flowers with large, showy petals and scent have evolved in some plants, whereas hairy bodies that catch and hold sticky pollen grains have evolved in bees.

37.3 *(page 789)*

5 Distinguish between pollination and fertilization.

- **Pollination** is the transfer of pollen grains from anther to stigma. After pollination, **fertilization,** the fusion of gametes, occurs.
- Flowering plants undergo **double fertilization.** The egg fuses with one sperm cell, forming a zygote (fertilized egg) that eventually develops into a multicellular embryo in the **seed.** The two polar nuclei fuse with the second sperm cell, forming a triploid nutritive tissue called **endosperm.**

CENGAGENOW™ Learn more about double fertilization by clicking on the figures in CengageNOW.

6 Trace the stages of embryo development in flowering plants, and list and define the main parts of seeds.

- A eudicot embryo develops in the seed in an orderly fashion, from proembryo to globular embryo to the heart stage to the torpedo stage.

- A mature seed contains both a young plant embryo and nutritive tissue—stored in the endosperm or in the **cotyledons** (seed leaves)—for use during germination. A tough, protective **seed coat** surrounds the seed.

CENGAGENOW™ Watch embryonic development in flowering plants by clicking on the figure in CengageNOW.

7 Explain the relationships among the following: ovules, ovaries, seeds, and fruits.

- Ovules are structures with the potential to develop into seeds, whereas ovaries are structures with the potential to develop into fruits. Seeds are enclosed within **fruits,** which are mature, ripened ovaries.

8 Distinguish among simple, aggregate, multiple, and accessory fruits.

- **Simple fruits** develop from a single ovary that consists of one carpel or several fused carpels. **Aggregate fruits** develop from a single flower with many separate ovaries. **Multiple fruits** develop from the ovaries of many flowers growing in close proximity on a common axis. In **accessory fruits,** the major part of the fruit consists of tissue other than ovary tissue.

37.4 *(page 796)*

9 Summarize the influence of internal and environmental factors on the germination of seeds.

- **Germination** is the process of seed sprouting. Internal factors affecting whether a seed germinates include the maturity of the embryo; the presence or absence of chemical inhibitors; and the presence or absence of hard, thick seed coats.

- External environmental factors that may affect germination include requirements for oxygen, water, temperature, and light.

CENGAGENOW™ Learn more about germination and seedling growth by clicking on the figure in CengageNOW.

37.5 *(page 797)*

10 Explain how the following structures may be used to propagate plants asexually: rhizomes, tubers, bulbs, corms, stolons, plantlets, and suckers.

- A **rhizome** is a horizontal underground stem. A **tuber** is a fleshy underground stem enlarged for food storage. A **bulb** is a modified underground bud with fleshy storage leaves attached to a short stem. A **corm** is a short, erect underground stem covered by papery scales. A **stolon** is a horizontal aboveground stem with long internodes.

- Some leaves have meristematic tissue along their margins and give rise to detachable **plantlets.**

- Roots may develop adventitious buds that develop into **suckers.** Suckers produce additional roots and may give rise to new plants.

11 Define *apomixis.*

- **Apomixis** is the production of seeds and fruits without sexual reproduction.

37.6 *(page 799)*

12 State the differences between sexual reproduction and asexual reproduction, and discuss the evolutionary advantages and disadvantages of each.

- Sexual reproduction involves the union of two gametes; the offspring produced by sexual reproduction are genetically variable. Asexual reproduction involves the formation of offspring without the fusion of gametes; the offspring are virtually genetically identical to the single parent.

- Genetic diversity among offspring produced by sexual reproduction may let certain individuals survive in a changing environment or exploit new environments. Sexual reproduction is costly because both male and female gametes must be produced and must meet.

- Genetic similarity among offspring produced by asexual reproduction may be advantageous if the environment is stable. Most plant species whose reproduction is primarily asexual occasionally reproduce sexually, thereby increasing their genetic variability.

TEST YOUR UNDERSTANDING

1. The normal order of whorls from the flower's periphery to the center is (a) sepals, petals, carpels, stamens (b) stamens, carpels, sepals, petals (c) sepals, petals, stamens, carpels (d) petals, carpels, stamens, sepals (e) carpels, stamens, petals, sepals

2. A pistil consists of (a) stigma, style, and stamen (b) anther and filament (c) sepal and petal (d) stigma, style, and ovary (e) radicle, hypocotyl, and plumule

3. The transfer of pollen grains from anther to stigma is (a) fertilization (b) double fertilization (c) pollination (d) germination (e) apomixis

4. The observation that insects with long mouthparts pollinate long, tubular flowers and insects with short mouthparts pollinate flowers with short corollas is explained by (a) coevolution (b) germination (c) double fertilization (d) apomixis (e) explosive dehiscence

5. The process of _____ in flowering plants involves one sperm cell fusing with an egg cell and one sperm cell fusing with two polar nuclei. (a) coevolution (b) germination (c) double fertilization (d) apomixis (e) pollination

6. The nutritive tissue in the seeds of flowering plants that is formed from the union of a sperm cell and two polar nuclei is called the (a) plumule (b) endosperm (c) cotyledon (d) hypocotyl (e) radicle

7. After fertilization, the ovule develops into a _____ and the ovary develops into a _____. (a) fruit; seed (b) seed; fruit (c) calyx; corolla (d) corolla; calyx (e) follicle; legume

8. In plants that lack endosperm in their mature seeds, the cotyledons function to (a) enclose and protect the seed (b) aid in seed dispersal (c) serve as an absorptive embryonic root (d) store food reserves (e) attach the embryo within the ovule

9. _____ fruits develop from many ovaries of a single flower, whereas _____ fruits develop from the ovaries of many separate flowers. (a) multiple; accessory (b) simple; accessory (c) aggregate; multiple (d) accessory; aggregate (e) simple; multiple

10. A horizontal underground stem that may or may not be fleshy and that is often specialized for asexual reproduction is called a (a) stolon (b) bulb (c) corm (d) rhizome (e) tuber

11. Place the following events in the correct order.

    1. pollen tube grows into ovule   2. insect lands on flower to drink nectar   3. embryo develops within the seed   4. fertilization occurs   5. pollen carried by insect contacts stigma

    (a) 2, 5, 1, 4, 3   (b) 1, 4, 2, 5, 3   (c) 3, 2, 5, 1, 4   (d) 5, 1, 3, 4, 2   (e) 2, 5, 4, 3, 1

12. Label the following diagram and give the function of each part. (Refer to Figure 37-1b to check your answers.)

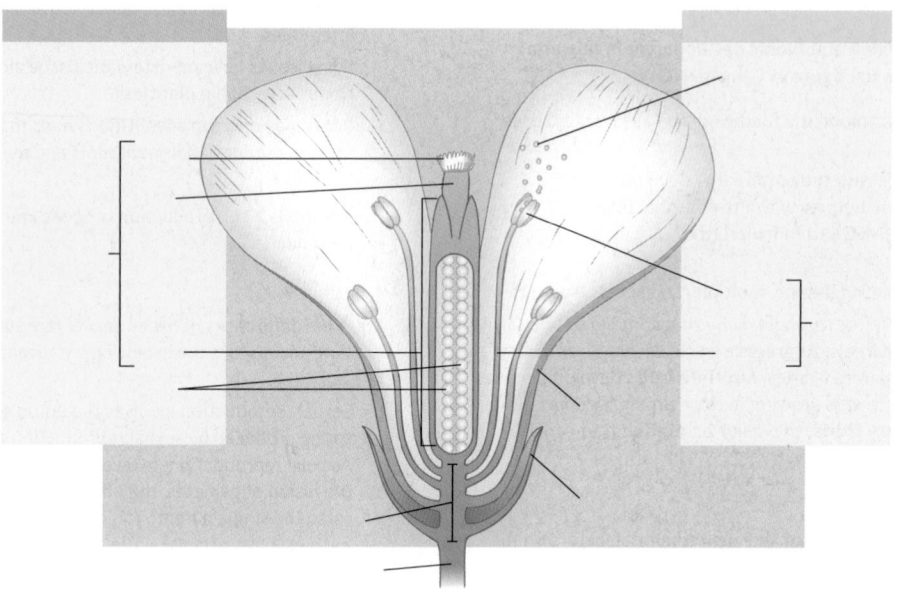

CRITICAL THINKING

1. Sketch the kinds of flowers that form simple, aggregate, multiple, and accessory fruits.

2. Using what you have learned in this chapter, speculate whether it is more likely that offspring of asexual reproduction develop in close proximity to or widely dispersed from the parent plant. Explain your reasoning. How could you design an experiment to test your hypothesis?

3. Which type of reproduction, sexual or asexual, might be more beneficial in the following circumstances, and why: (a) a perennial (plant that lives more than two years) in a stable environment; (b) an annual (plant that lives one year) in a rapidly changing environment; and (c) a plant adapted to an extremely narrow climate range?

4. Using what you have learned in this chapter, offer an explanation of why telephone poles and wires strung across grassy fields or plains often have tree seedlings growing under them.

5. **EVOLUTION LINK.** Is seed dispersal by ants an example of coevolution? Why or why not?

6. **SCIENCE, TECHNOLOGY, AND SOCIETY.** What is the value to society of research on genes that control flowering?

 Additional questions are available in CengageNOW at www.cengage.com/login.

38 Plant Developmental Responses to External and Internal Signals

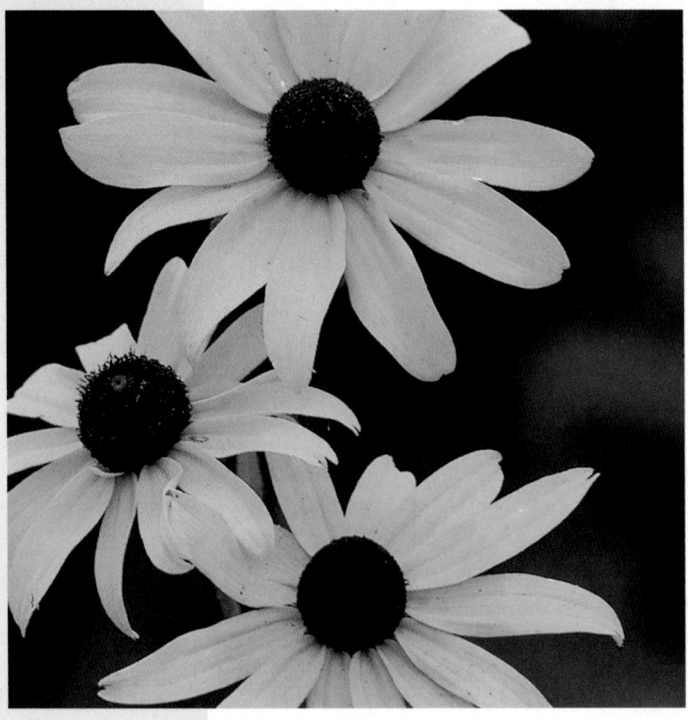

Black-eyed Susan. This plant (*Rudbeckia hirta*) produces flowers in response to the shortening nights of spring and early summer.

Dwight R. Kuhn

KEY CONCEPTS

38.1 A plant may respond to an external stimulus, such as light, gravity, or touch, by a directional growth response, or tropism. Study of tropisms has helped biologists elucidate links between the external environment and internal signals such as hormones.

38.2 Hormones are chemical signals responsible for coordinating and regulating many aspects of plant development. Although there are many plant hormones, six have been well-characterized: auxins, gibberellins, cytokinins, ethylene, abscisic acid, and brassinosteroids.

38.3 Plants have different receptors that detect various colors of light. Phytochrome detects red and far-red light, which affect several aspects of development, including the timing of flowering.

38.4 The exposure of a plant to a herbivore or pathogen causes a localized hypersensitive response that seals off the affected area. The plant also sends signals from the site of localized infection, leading to systemic acquired resistance—long-lasting, enhanced defenses throughout the plant.

The ultimate control of plant growth and development, which includes all the changes that take place during the entire life of an individual, is genetic. If the genes required for development of a particular trait, such as the shape of a leaf, the color of a flower, or the type of root system, are not present, that characteristic does not develop. When a particular gene is present, its expression—that is, how it exhibits itself as an observable feature of an organism—is determined by several factors, including signals from other genes and from the environment. The location of a cell in the young plant body also has a profound effect on gene expression during development. Chemical signals from adjacent cells help a cell "perceive" its location within the plant body. Each cell's spatial environment helps determine what that cell ultimately becomes.

Growth and development, including a plant's responses to various changes in its environment, are controlled by plant *hormones,* organic molecules that are present in very low concentrations in plant tissues and that act as chemical signals between cells. Environmental cues, such as changing day length and variations in precipitation and temperature, exert an important influence on gene expression and hormone production, as they do on all aspects of plant growth and development.

For example, the initiation of sexual reproduction is often under environmental control, particularly in temperate latitudes, and plants switch from vegetative to reproductive growth after receiving appropriate signals from the environment. Many flowering plants are sensitive to changes in the relative amounts of daylight and darkness that accompany the changing seasons, and these plants flower in response to those changes (see photograph). In this chapter we will see that plants use light as an external signal to help regulate many aspects of growth and development, such as tropisms (directional growth), time of flowering, shade avoidance, and circadian rhythms.

Other plants have temperature requirements that induce sexual reproduction. Thus, plants continually perceive information from the environment and use this information to help regulate normal growth and development. We consider these various aspects of growth and development in this chapter.

FIGURE 38-1 Phototropism

A bean seedling (*Phaseolus vulgaris*) grows in the direction of light and therefore exhibits positive phototropism. The bending is caused by greater elongation on the shaded side of the stem than on the lighted side.

38.1 TROPISMS

■ LEARNING OBJECTIVE

1   Describe phototropism, gravitropism, and thigmotropism.

Plants exhibit movements in response to environmental stimuli such as light, gravity, and touch. A plant may respond to such an external stimulus by directional growth—that is, the direction of growth depends on the direction of the stimulus. Such a directional growth response, called a **tropism,** results in a change in the position of a plant part. Tropisms are irreversible and may be positive or negative, depending on whether the plant grows toward the stimulus (a positive tropism) or away from it (a negative tropism). Tropisms are under hormonal control, which is discussed later in the chapter.

Phototropism is the directional growth of a plant caused by light (**FIG. 38-1**). Most growing shoot tips exhibit positive phototropism by bending (growing) toward light, something you may have observed if you place houseplants near a sunny window. This growth response

increases the likelihood that stems and leaves receive adequate light for photosynthesis. The bending response of phototropism is triggered by blue light with wavelengths less than 500 nm. (You may recall from Chapter 34 that blue light also induces stomata to open.)

For a plant or any organism to have a biological response to light, it must contain a light-sensitive substance, called a *photoreceptor,* to absorb the light. The photoreceptor that absorbs blue light and triggers the phototropic response and other blue-light responses (such as stomatal opening) is a family of yellow pigments called **phototropins.** Phototropins are light-activated **kinases,** enzymes that transfer phosphate groups. There is evidence that phototropins become phosphorylated—that is, a phosphate group is added—in response to blue light. Thus, phosphorylation is an early step in the blue-light-signaling pathway.

Growth in response to the direction of gravity is called **gravitropism.** Most stem tips exhibit negative gravitropism by growing away from Earth's center, whereas most root tips exhibit positive gravitropism (**FIG. 38-2**). The root cap is the site of gravity perception in

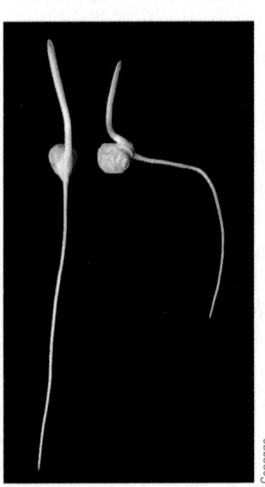

On day 3, turned on its side

One hour later

(a)

(b)

FIGURE 38-2 *Animated* Gravitropism

(a) A corn (*Zea mays*) seedling was turned on its side three days after germinating. In 1 hour the root and shoot tips had curved. **(b)** In 24 hours (*seedling on the right*), the new root growth was downward (positive gravitropism) and the new shoot growth was upward (negative gravitropism). A control seedling germinated at the same time is on the left.

roots; when the root cap is removed, the root continues to grow, but it loses any ability to perceive gravity. Special cells in the root cap possess starch-containing **amyloplasts** that collect toward the bottom of the cells in response to gravity, and these amyloplasts may initiate at least some of the gravitropic response. If the root is put in a different position, as when a potted plant is laid on its side, the amyloplasts tumble to a new position, always settling in the direction of gravity. The gravitropic response (bending) occurs shortly thereafter and involves the hormone *auxin* (discussed later in the chapter).

Despite the movement of amyloplasts in response to gravity, researchers question their role in gravitropism. A mutant *Arabidopsis thaliana* plant that lacks amyloplasts in its root cap cells still responds gravitropically when placed on its side, indicating that roots do not necessarily need amyloplasts to respond to gravity. Ongoing research may clarify how roots perceive gravity.

Thigmotropism is growth in response to a mechanical stimulus, such as contact with a solid object. The twining or curling growth of tendrils or stems, which helps attach a climbing plant such as a vine to some type of support, is an example of thigmotropism (see Fig. 34-14b).

Review

- What is phototropism? How does blue light trigger the phototropic response?
- How do phototropism and gravitropism differ?

38.2 PLANT HORMONES AND DEVELOPMENT

■ LEARNING OBJECTIVES

2 Describe a general mechanism of action for plant hormones, using auxin as your example.

3 Describe early auxin experiments involving phototropism.

4 List several ways that each of these hormones affects plant growth and development: auxins, gibberellins, cytokinins, ethylene, abscisic acid, and brassinosteroids.

A plant **hormone** is an organic compound that acts as a chemical signal eliciting a variety of responses that regulate growth and development. The study of plant hormones is challenging because hormones are effective in extremely small concentrations (less than 10^{-6} mol/L). In addition, the effects of different plant hormones overlap, and it is difficult to determine which hormone, if any, is the primary cause of a particular response. Plant hormones may also stimulate a response at one concentration and inhibit that same response at a different concentration.

For many years, biologists studied five major classes of plant hormones: auxins, gibberellins, cytokinins, ethylene, and abscisic acid. More recently, researchers have uncovered compelling evidence for brassinosteroids as a sixth plant hormone. Additional plant hormones will probably be characterized in the future. (**TABLE 38-1** summarizes the six plant hormones.)

Plant hormones act by signal transduction

Researchers have used molecular genetic techniques to better understand the biology of plant hormones. *Arabidopsis* mutants are particularly useful. For example, different mutants have defects in hormone synthesis, hormone transport, signal reception, or signal transduction (**FIG. 38-3**). In **signal transduction,** a receptor converts an extracellular signal into an intracellular signal that causes one or more cellular responses.

Such mutants enable plant biologists to identify and clone genes involved in these aspects of hormone biology. Studying the mutant phenotypes helps plant biologists establish connections between the mutant genes and specific physiological activities involved in growth and development. Using this research, biologists are elucidating the general mechanisms of plant hormone action, an important goal of systems biology.

It appears that many plant hormones bind to **enzyme-linked receptors;** the hormone binds to the receptor, where it triggers an enzymatic reaction of some sort. Let us consider a specific example that involves the plant hormone *auxin,* which is known to cause rapid changes in gene expression. One receptor for auxin is located in either the cytosol or the nucleus and has a three-dimensional shape that binds to the auxin molecule. The binding of auxin to its receptor (designated the *TIR1 receptor*) catalyzes the attachment of the molecule *ubiquitin* to repressor proteins that inhibit the transcription of certain genes, designated *auxin response genes* (**FIG. 38-4**).

TABLE 38-1	Plant Hormones	
Hormone	Site of Production	Principal Actions
Auxins (e.g., IAA)	Shoot apical meristem, young leaves, seeds	Stem elongation, apical dominance, root initiation, fruit development
Gibberellins (e.g., GA₃)	Young leaves and shoot apical meristems, embryo in seed	Seed germination, stem elongation, flowering, fruit development
Cytokinins (e.g., zeatin)	Various sites in plants	Cell division, delay of leaf senescence, inhibition of apical dominance, flower development, embryo development, seed germination
Ethylene	Stem nodes, ripening fruit, damaged or senescing tissue	Fruit ripening, responses to environmental stressors, seed germination, maintenance of apical hook on seedlings, root initiation, senescence and abscission in leaves and flowers
Abscisic acid	Almost all cells that contain plastids (leaves, stems, roots)	Seed dormancy, responses to water stress
Brassinosteroids (e.g., brassinolide)	Shoots (leaves and flower buds), seeds, fruits	Light-mediated gene expression, cell division, cell elongation, seed germination, vascular development

FIGURE 38-3 General mechanism of action for the hormone auxin

Various external and/or internal signals trigger the synthesis of auxin. Once synthesized, auxin is transported directionally, causing local auxin gradients to form in the plant. In turn, these gradients trigger specific developmental responses in certain cells by reception, signal transduction, and response (discussed shortly). *Arabidopsis* mutants have been identified with defects involving auxin synthesis, auxin transport, or other steps in the process.

(a) Auxin absent. A repressor protein binds to a transcription activator, inhibiting transcription of the auxin response gene.

(b) Auxin present. Auxin binds to the TIR1 receptor, which is part of an enzyme complex that attaches ubiquitin to the repressor protein. The ubiquitinylated rerpressor protein is then degraded into peptide fragments in a proteasome. With the repressor protein no longer bound to the transcription activator, transcription of the auxin response gene occurs.

FIGURE 38-4 Model of a signal transduction pathway for auxin

The ubiquitinylated protein is therefore targeted for degradation into peptide fragments in a **proteasome.** (See Figure 14-15, which shows the ubiquitin-proteasome degradation of proteins.) As a result, transcription of the auxin response gene occurs, resulting in changes in cell growth and development.

The identification of the *TIR1* receptor for auxin was reported in 2005 by two groups working independently. This receptor is an **F-box protein.** The *F-box* is a short sequence of amino acids found in molecules that catalyze the addition of ubiquitin tags to proteins targeted for destruction. Interestingly, all animals, plants, and fungi examined to date use ubiquitin to target proteins for destruction, but bacteria do not. This suggests that the use of ubiquitin tags evolved early in eukaryote evolution and was conserved as the various groups of eukaryotes diversified. Plants have about 700 different F-box proteins. Although not much is known about most of them, it is significant that researchers have identified other plant hormones and signaling molecules that use F-box proteins as receptors. These include gibberellin, ethylene, and abscisic acid.

Auxins promote cell elongation

Charles Darwin, the British naturalist best known for developing the theory of natural selection to explain evolution, also provided the first evidence for the existence of auxins. The experiments that Darwin and his son Francis performed in the 1870s involved positive phototropism, the directional growth of plants toward light. The plants they used were newly germinated canary grass seedlings. As in all grasses, the first part of a canary grass seedling to emerge from the soil is the coleoptile, a protective sheath that encircles the stem. When coleoptiles are exposed to light from only one direction, they bend toward the light. The bending occurs below the tip of the coleoptile.

The Darwins tried to influence this bending in several ways (**FIG. 38-5**). For example, they covered the tip of the coleoptile as soon as it emerged from the soil. When they covered that part of the coleoptile above where the bend would be expected to occur, the plants did not bend. On other plants, they removed the coleoptile tip and found bending did not occur. When the bottom of the coleoptile where the curvature would occur was shielded from the

light, the coleoptile bent toward light. From these experiments, the Darwins concluded that "some influence is transmitted from the upper to the lower part, causing it to bend."

In the 1920s, Frits Went, a young Dutch scientist, isolated the phototropic hormone from oat coleoptiles. He removed the coleoptile tips and placed them on tiny blocks of agar for a period of time. When he put one of these agar blocks squarely on a decapitated coleoptile, normal growth resumed. When he placed one of these agar blocks to one side of the tip of a decapitated coleoptile in the dark, bending occurred (**FIG. 38-6**). The results indicated that the substance had diffused from the coleoptile tip into the agar and, later, from the agar into the decapitated coleoptile. Went named this substance **auxin** (from the Greek *aux*, "enlarge" or "increase").

Auxin is a group of several natural (and artificial) plant hormones; the most common and physiologically important auxin is **indoleacetic acid (IAA).** The purification and elucidation of the primary auxin's chemical structure were accomplished in the mid-1930s by a research team led by Kenneth Thimann at the California Institute of Technology.

The movement of auxin in the plant is said to be *polar,* or unidirectional. Auxin moves downward along the shoot–root axis from its site of production, usually the shoot apical meristem. (Young leaves and seeds are also sites of auxin production.) This directional cell to cell transport results in an *auxin gradient* (a spatial difference in auxin concentration) that triggers specific responses. Special auxin transport proteins in the plasma membranes of plant cells control the movement of auxin out of cells; this process is responsible for the directional movement of auxin. Mutations in

---

KEY EXPERIMENT

QUESTION: What part of the grass coleoptile depends on light for phototropic growth?

HYPOTHESIS: The coleoptile tip is required for the growth (bending) of the coleoptile shaft that accompanies exposure to light coming from one direction.

EXPERIMENT: Some canary grass coleoptiles were uncovered, some were covered only at the tip, some had the tip removed, and some were covered everywhere but at the tip (*left*). The covers were impervious to light.

RESULTS AND CONCLUSION: After exposure to light coming from one direction, the uncovered plants and the plants with uncovered tips grew toward the light (*right*). The plants with tips covered or removed did not bend toward light. The Darwins concluded that some substance was produced in the tip and transmitted to the lower part, causing it to bend.

Sources: Darwin, C. R. *The Power of Movement in Plants.* John Murray, London, 1880; Boysen-Jensen, P. "Concerning the performance of phototropic stimuli on the *Avena* coleoptile." *Berichte der Deutschen Botanischen Gesellschaft* (Reports of the German Botanical Society), Vol. 31, pp. 559–566, 1913.

FIGURE 38-5 The Darwins' phototropism experiments

QUESTION: Is there a chemical substance responsible for elongation of coleoptiles, and can it be isolated?

HYPOTHESIS: The factor responsible for coleoptile growth is a diffusible chemical that can be isolated from coleoptile tips.

EXPERIMENT: Coleoptile tips were placed on agar blocks for a period of time **(a)**. The agar block was transferred to a decapitated coleoptile. It was placed off-center, and the coleoptile was left in darkness **(b)**.

RESULTS AND CONCLUSION: The coleoptile bent **(c),** indicating that a chemical moved from the original coleoptile tip to the agar block and from there to the same side of the decapitated coleoptile, causing that side to elongate.

Source: Went, F. "A growth substance and growth." *Recueils Travaux Botaniques Néerlandais* (Collections of Dutch Botanical Works), Vol. 25, pp. 1–116, 1928.

FIGURE 38-6 *Animated* Isolating auxin from coleoptiles

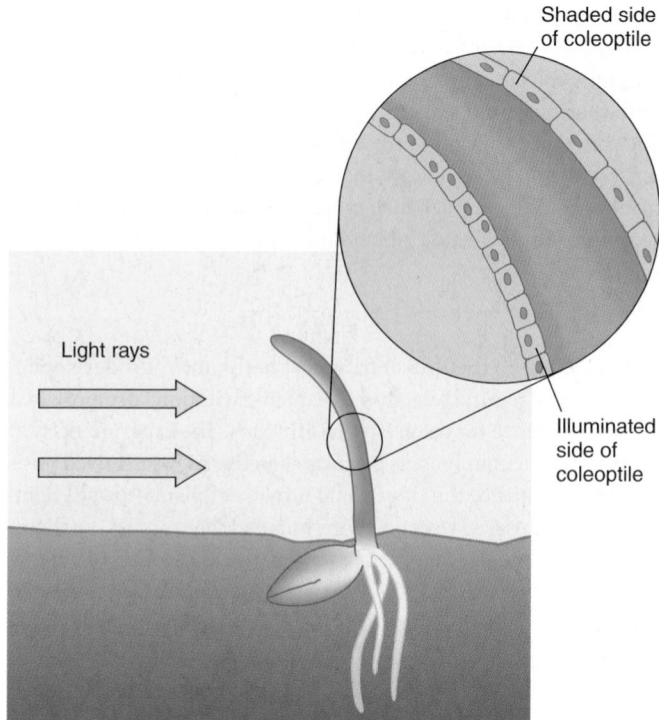

FIGURE 38-7 *Animated* Phototropism and the unequal distribution of auxin

Auxin travels down the side of the stem or coleoptile *away* from the light, causing cells on the shaded side to elongate. Therefore, the stem or coleoptile bends toward light.

auxin transport proteins inhibit the transmission of auxin, which normally moves about 1 cm per hour.

Auxin's most characteristic action is promotion of cell elongation in stems and coleoptiles. This effect, apparently exerted by acidification of cell walls, increases their plasticity and thus enables them to expand under the force of the cell's internal turgor pressure. Auxin's effect on cell elongation also provides an explanation for phototropism. When a plant is exposed to a light from only one direction, some of the auxin migrates laterally to the shaded side of the stem before moving down the stem by polar transport. Because of the greater auxin concentration on the shaded side of the stem, the cells there elongate more than the cells on the light side, and the stem bends toward the light (**FIG. 38-7**). Auxin is also involved in gravitropism and thigmotropism.

Auxin exerts other effects on plants. For example, some plants tend to branch out very little when they grow. Growth in these plants occurs almost exclusively from the apical meristem rather than from axillary buds, which do not develop as long as the terminal bud is present. Such plants are said to exhibit **apical dominance,** the inhibition of axillary bud growth by the apical meristem. In plants with strong apical dominance, auxin produced

in the apical meristem inhibits axillary buds near the apical meristem from developing into actively growing shoots. When the apical meristem is pinched off, the auxin source is removed and axillary buds grow to form branches. Apical dominance is often quickly re-established, however, as one branch begins to inhibit the growth of others. Other hormones (ethylene and cytokinin, both discussed later) are also involved in apical dominance. As with many physiological activities, the changing ratios of these hormones may be the factor responsible for apical dominance.

Auxin produced by developing seeds stimulates the development of the fruit. When auxin is applied to certain flowers in which fertilization has not occurred (and, therefore, in which seeds are not developing), the ovary enlarges and develops into a seedless fruit. Seedless tomatoes are produced in this manner.[1] Auxin is not the only hormone involved in fruit development, however.

Some manufactured, or synthetic, auxins have structures similar to that of IAA. The synthetic auxin naphthalene acetic acid stimulates root development on stem cuttings and is used for asexual propagation, particularly of woody plants with horticultural importance (**FIG. 38-8**). The synthetic auxins 2,4-D and 2,4,5-T have been used as selective herbicides (weed killers). These compounds kill plants with broad leaves but, for reasons not completely under-

---

[1]Not all seedless fruits are produced by treatment with auxin. In Thompson seedless grapes, fertilizations occurs but the embryos abort, and therefore the seeds fail to develop. Thompson seedless grapes are sprayed with the hormone gibberellin to increase berry size.

FIGURE 38-8 Auxin and root development on stem cuttings

Many adventitious roots developed on a honeysuckle (*Lonicera fragrantissima*) cutting placed in a solution with a high concentration of synthetic auxin (*left*). Fewer roots developed in a lower auxin concentration (*middle*). The cutting placed in water (no auxin) served as a control and did not form roots in the same period (*right*).

Joe Eakes, Color Advantage/Visuals Unlimited

stood, do not kill grasses. Both herbicides are similar in structure to IAA and disrupt the plants' normal growth processes. Because many of the world's most important crops are grasses (such as wheat, corn, and rice), 2,4-D and 2,4,5-T can kill broadleaf weeds that compete with these crops. The use of 2,4,5-T is no longer allowed in the United States, however, because of its association with dioxins, a group of mildly to very toxic compounds formed as byproducts when 2,4,5-T is manufactured.

Gibberellins promote stem elongation

In the 1920s and 1930s, a Japanese biologist was studying a disease of rice in which the young rice seedlings grew extremely tall and spindly, fell over, and died. The cause of the disease was a fungus (*Gibberella fujikuroi*) that produces a chemical substance named **gibberellin (GA).** Not until after World War II did scientists in Europe and North America learn of the work done by the Japanese scientists. During the 1950s and 1960s, studies in the United States and Great Britain showed that gibberellins are produced by healthy plants as well as by the fungus.

Gibberellins are hormones involved in many normal plant functions. The symptoms of the seedling disease are caused by an abnormally high GA concentration in the plant tissue (because both plant and fungus produce gibberellin). Currently, dozens of naturally occurring GAs are known, although only about four function as plant hormones; the rest are inactive precursors. There are no synthetic gibberellins.

Gibberellins promote stem elongation in many plants. When GA is applied to a plant, particularly certain dwarf varieties, this elongation may be spectacular. Some corn and pea plants that are dwarfs as a result of one or more mutations grow to a normal height when treated with GA. Short-stemmed, high-yielding varieties of wheat have short stems because they have a reduced response to GA. These varieties put less of their resources into stem height and more resources into grain production. Gibberellins are also involved in **bolting,** the rapid elongation of a floral stalk that occurs naturally in many plants when they initiate flowering (**FIG. 38-9**).

Robert Lyons/Visuals Unlimited

FIGURE 38-9 Gibberellin and stem elongation

Like many biennials, Indian blanket (*Gaillardia pulchella*) grows as a rosette, which is a circular cluster of leaves close to the ground, during its first year (*left*). It then bolts when it initiates flowering in the second year (*right*). The plant in bloom grows to 0.6 m (2 ft).

Gibberellins cause stem elongation by stimulating cells to divide as well as to elongate. The actual mechanism of cell elongation differs from that caused by auxin, however. Recall that IAA-induced cell elongation involves the acidification of the cell wall. In GA-induced cell elongation, cell wall acidification does not occur; biologists do not yet know how gibberellins modify cell wall properties to cause cell elongation.

Gibberellins affect several reproductive processes in plants. They stimulate flowering, particularly in long-day plants (discussed later in the chapter). In addition, GAs substitute for the low temperature that biennials require before they begin flowering. If GAs are applied to biennials during their first year of growth, flowering occurs without exposure to a period of low temperature. Gibberellins, like auxin, affect fruit development. Agriculturalists apply GAs to several varieties of grapes to produce larger fruits.

Gibberellins are also involved in seed germination in certain plants. In a classic experiment involving barley seed germination, researchers showed that the release of GA from the embryo triggers the synthesis of α-amylase, an enzyme that digests starch in the endosperm. As a result, glucose becomes available for absorption by the embryo. Although enzymes mobilize starch reserves in many types of seeds, GA control of seed enzymes appears restricted to cereals and other grasses. In addition to mobilizing food reserves in newly germinated grass seeds, application of gibberellins substitutes for low-temperature or light requirements for germination in seeds of plants such as lettuce, oats, and tobacco.

Scientists are actively conducting research in gibberellin signaling and have identified several GA receptors in the nucleus, repressor proteins designated *DELLA proteins,* as well as an F-box protein. When GA is not bound to the receptor, a DELLA protein inhibits transcription of *GA response genes*. When GA is present, it binds to the receptor, which triggers an enzyme that attaches ubiquitin to the DELLA protein. This protein is targeted for degradation into peptide fragments in a proteasome. With the DELLA protein no longer present, transcription of the GA response gene occurs. This signaling process may sound familiar: the GA signal transduction process shares similarities with the auxin signal transduction pathway described earlier in the chapter.

Cytokinins promote cell division

During the 1940s and 1950s, researchers were trying to find substances that might induce plant cells to divide in **tissue culture,** a technique in which cells are isolated from plants and grown in a nutrient medium. (Plant tissue culture is discussed in Chapter 33.) They discovered that cells would not divide without a substance found in coconut milk. Because coconut milk has a complex chemical composition, investigators did not chemically identify the division-inducing substance for some time. Finally, researchers isolated an active substance from a different source, aged DNA from herring sperm. They called it **cytokinin** because it induces cytokinesis, or cytoplasmic division. In 1963, researchers identified the first plant cytokinin, zeatin, in corn. Since then, similar molecules have been identified in other plants. Biologists have also synthesized several cytokinins.

Cytokinins are structurally similar to adenine, a purine base that is part of DNA and RNA molecules. Biologists are beginning to elucidate the cytokinin signal transduction pathway, which is more complex than those of auxin and gibberellin. The cytokinin pathway has multiple steps, each under the control of a number of genes. The presence of feedback loops and links to other signaling pathways adds another level of complexity to the regulation of cytokinin activity.

Cytokinins promote cell division and differentiation of young, relatively unspecialized cells into mature, more specialized cells in intact plants. They are a required ingredient in any plant tissue culture medium and must be present for cells to divide. In tissue culture, cytokinins interact with auxin during the formation of plant organs such as roots and stems (**FIG. 38-10**). For example, in tobacco tissue culture a high ratio of auxin to cytokinin induces root formation, whereas a low ratio of auxin to cytokinin induces shoot formation.

Cytokinins and auxin also interact in the control of apical dominance. Here their relationship is antagonistic: auxin inhibits the growth of axillary buds, and cytokinin promotes their growth.

One effect of cytokinins on plant cells is to delay the aging process. Plant cells, like all living cells, go through a natural aging process known as **senescence.** Senescence is accelerated in cells of plant parts that are cut, such as flower stems. Botanists think that plants must have a continual supply of cytokinins from the roots. Cut stems, of course, lose their source of cytokinins and therefore age rapidly. When cytokinins are sprayed on leaves of a cut stem of many species, they remain green, whereas unsprayed leaves turn yellow and die.

Despite their involvement in regulating many aspects of plant growth and development, cytokinins currently have few commercial applications other than plant tissue culture. However, in 1995,

FIGURE 38-10 Auxin–cytokinin interactions in tissue culture
Varying amounts of auxin and cytokinin in the culture media produce different growth responses. **(a)** The initial explant is a small piece of sterile tissue from the pith of a tobacco stem, which is placed on nutrient agar. **(b)** Nutrient agar containing 2.0 mg/L of auxin and 0.2 mg/L of cytokinin causes cells to divide and form a clump of undifferentiated tissue called a callus. **(c)** Agar with 2.0 mg/L of auxin and 0.02 mg/L of cytokinin (high ratio of auxin to cytokinin) stimulates root growth. **(d)** Agar with 2.0 mg/L of auxin and 0.5 mg/L of cytokinin (low ratio of auxin to cytokinin) stimulates shoot growth.

molecular biologists at the University of Wisconsin combined a promoter from a gene activated during normal senescence with a gene that encodes an enzyme involved in cytokinin synthesis. (Recall from Chapter 13 that the **promoter** is the nucleotide sequence in DNA to which RNA polymerase attaches to begin transcription.) The leaves of transgenic tobacco plants that contained this recombinant DNA produced more cytokinin and therefore lived longer and continued to photosynthesize (**FIG. 38-11**). This molecular technology may have the potential to increase the longevity and productivity of certain crops.

Ethylene promotes abscission and fruit ripening

During the early 20th century, scientists observed that the gas **ethylene** (C_2H_4) has several effects on plant growth, but not until 1934 did they demonstrate that plants produce ethylene. This natural hormone influences many plant processes. Ethylene inhibits cell elongation, promotes seed germination, promotes apical dominance, and is involved in plant responses to wounding or invasion by disease-causing microorganisms.

Ethylene also has a major role in many aspects of senescence, including fruit ripening. As a fruit ripens, it produces ethylene, which triggers an acceleration of the ripening process. This induces

FIGURE 38-11 Cytokinin synthesis and delay of senescence

The tobacco (*Nicotiana tabacum*) plant on the left was genetically engineered to produce additional cytokinin as it aged, whereas the tobacco plant of the same age on the right served as a control. Note the extensive senescence and death of older leaves on the control plant. Depending on the variety, tobacco grows 0.9 to 3 m (3 to 10 ft) tall.

Ethylene is involved in leaf abscission, which is actually influenced by two antagonistic hormones, ethylene and auxin. As a leaf ages (as autumn approaches, for deciduous trees in temperate climates), the level of auxin in the leaf decreases. Concurrently, cells in the abscission layer at the base of the petiole (where the leaf will break away from the stem) begin producing ethylene.

Researchers studying ethylene-signaling have identified a similar mechanism to that already described for auxin and gibberellin. When ethylene is present, it binds to a receptor. This binding triggers an enzyme that attaches ubiquitin to a protein targeted for degradation into peptide fragments in a proteasome. At least two F-box proteins are involved in the protein degradation that occurs in ethylene signal transduction.

Abscisic acid promotes seed dormancy

In 1963, two different research teams discovered **abscisic acid (ABA).** Despite its name, abscisic acid does not induce abscission in most plants. Instead, ABA is involved in a plant's response to stress and in seed **dormancy,** a temporary state of arrested physiological activity. As an environmental stress hormone, ABA particularly promotes changes in plant tissues that are water-stressed. (Recall that ethylene also affects plant responses to certain stressors, such as mechanical stressors and wounding.)

Botanists best understand the effect of abscisic acid on plants suffering from water stress. The level of ABA increases dramatically in the leaves of plants exposed to severe drought conditions. The high level of ABA in the leaves activates a signal transduction process that leads to the closing of stomata. The closing of stomata saves the water that the plant would normally lose by transpiration, thereby increasing the plant's likelihood of survival. As knowledge of ABA signaling in guard cells increases, botanists hope to use this information to engineer crops and horticultural plants that are resistant to drought.

the fruit to produce more ethylene, which further accelerates ripening. The expression "one rotten apple spoils the barrel" is true. A rotten apple is one that is overripe and produces large amounts of ethylene, which diffuses and triggers the ripening process in nearby apples. Humans use ethylene commercially to uniformly ripen bananas and tomatoes. These fruits are picked while green and shipped to their destination, where they are exposed to ethylene before they are delivered to grocery stores (**FIG. 38-12**).

Plants growing in a natural environment encounter rain, hail, wind, and contact with passing animals. All these mechanical stressors alter their growth and development, making them shorter and stockier than plants grown in a greenhouse. Ethylene regulates such developmental responses to mechanical stimuli, known as **thigmomorphogenesis.** Plants that are mechanically disturbed produce additional ethylene, which in turn inhibits stem elongation and enhances cell wall thickening in supporting cells (collenchyma and sclerenchyma). These changes are adaptive because shorter, thicker stems are less likely to be damaged by mechanical stressors.

FIGURE 38-12 Ethylene and fruit ripening

Both boxes of tomatoes were picked at the same time, while green. The tomatoes in the box on the right were exposed to an atmosphere containing 100 ppm of ethylene for three days.

Courtesy of M. G. Neuffer

FIGURE 38-13 The absence of abscisic acid causes precocious germination

In a corn (*Zea mays*) mutant that does not produce abscisic acid, some of the kernels have germinated while still on the ear, producing roots (*arrows*).

The onset of winter is also a type of stress on plants. A winter adaptation that involves abscisic acid is dormancy in seeds. Many seeds have high levels of ABA in their tissues and do not germinate until the ABA washes out. In a corn mutant unable to synthesize ABA, the seeds germinate as soon as the embryos are mature, even while attached to the ear (**FIG. 38-13**).

Abscisic acid is not the only hormone involved in seed dormancy. For example, addition of gibberellin reverses the effects of dormancy. In seeds, the level of ABA decreases during the winter, and the level of GA increases. Cytokinins are also implicated in breaking dormancy. Once again, you see that a single physiological activity such as seed dormancy may be controlled in plants by the interaction of several hormones. The plant's actual response may result from changing ratios of hormones rather than the effect of each individual hormone.

Brassinosteroids are plant steroid hormones

Although steroid hormones have long been known to have crucial roles in animals, the roles of steroid hormones in plants were not well characterized until the mid-1990s. The **brassinosteroids (BRs)** are a group of steroids that function as plant hormones. BRs are involved in several aspects of growth and development. *Arabidopsis* mutants that cannot synthesize BRs are dwarf plants with small curly leaves and reduced fertility; researchers can re-

verse this defect by applying BR exogenously to the plant. Studies of these mutants suggest that brassinosteroids are involved in multiple developmental processes, such as cell division, cell elongation, light-induced differentiation, vascular development, and seed germination (**FIG. 38-14**).

Many steps of the BR signaling pathway have been characterized. BRs bind to a receptor kinase in the plant plasma membrane (unlike steroid hormones in animals, which enter the cell and bind to receptors in the cytoplasm or nucleus). When BR binds to its receptor, the receptor phosphorylates molecules in the cytosol, which in turn triggers a signaling cascade that ultimately alters gene expression in the cell. Part of the signal transduction process involves attaching ubiquitin to nuclear proteins targeted for degradation in a proteasome. As a result, the expression of BR target genes is adjusted.

Identification of a universal flower-promoting signal remains elusive

Experiments in which different tobacco species are grafted together indicate that unidentified flower-promoting and flower-inhibiting

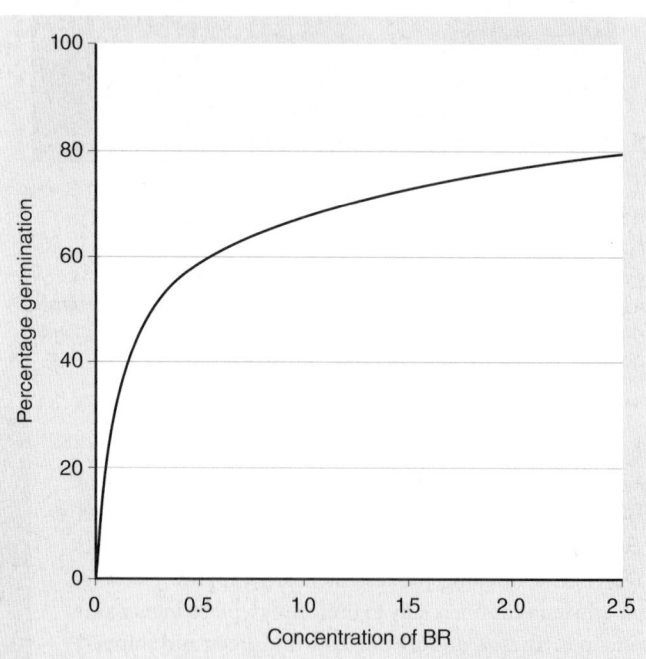

FIGURE 38-14 Brassinosteroids and seed germination in *Arabidopsis*

Researchers used a GA-insensitive *Arabidopsis* mutant that produced seeds that did not germinate. (Recall that GA promotes seed germination, so a plant that does not respond to endogenous GA is required.) The scientists overcame the inability of the mutant seeds to germinate by treating them with a brassinosteroid (BR). Note how the percentage of germination increases as the concentration of BR to which the seeds were exposed increases.

Original source: Steber, C. M. and P. McCourt. "A role for brassinosteroids in germination in *Arabidopsis*." *Plant Physiology*, Vol. 125, pp. 287–297, 2001.

Long-day
induction
(short
night)

Graft

Day-neutral plant grafted
to long-day plant

Both plants flower

FIGURE 38-15 Evidence for the existence of a flower-promoting substance

When a long-day tobacco plant (*Nicotiana silvestris*) is grafted to a day-neutral tobacco plant (*N. tabacum*) and both plants are exposed to a long-day/short-night regimen, they both flower. The day-neutral plant flowers sooner than it normally would, presumably because a flower-promoting substance passes from the long-day plant to the day-neutral one through the graft.

substances may exist. *Nicotiana silvestris* is a *long-day* tobacco plant (it requires a short night to flower); a variety of *N. tabacum* is a *day-neutral* tobacco plant (seasonal changes do not affect when it flowers). When a long-day tobacco is grafted to a day-neutral tobacco and exposed to short nights, both plants flower (**FIG. 38-15**). The day-neutral tobacco plant flowers sooner than it normally would.

Biologists hypothesize that a flower-promoting substance, **florigen,** may be induced in the long-day plant and transported to the day-neutral plant through the graft union, causing the day-neutral tobacco plant to flower sooner than expected. An intact plant may produce florigen in the leaves and transport it in the phloem to the shoot apical meristem. There, it induces a transition from vegetative to reproductive development—that is, to a meristem that produces flowers.

When a botanist grafts a long-day tobacco to a day-neutral tobacco and exposes them to long nights, neither plant flowers. As long as these conditions continue, the day-neutral plants do not flower even when they would normally do so. In this case, the long-day tobacco may produce a flower-inhibiting substance that is transported to the day-neutral tobacco through the graft union. This substance prevents the day-neutral tobacco from flowering.

Review

- How are signal reception, signal transduction, and altered cell activity part of the general mechanism of action for auxin?
- How is auxin involved in phototropism?
- Which hormones are involved in each of the following physiological processes: (1) seed germination, (2) stem elongation, (3) fruit ripening, (4) leaf abscission, and (5) seed dormancy?

38.3 LIGHT SIGNALS AND PLANT DEVELOPMENT

LEARNING OBJECTIVES

5 Explain how varying amounts of light and darkness induce flowering.

6 Describe the role of phytochrome in flowering, including a brief discussion of phytochrome signal transduction.

7 Define *circadian rhythm* and give an example.

8 Distinguish between phytochrome and cryptochrome.

Photoperiodism is any response of a plant to the relative lengths of daylight and darkness. Initiation of flowering at the shoot apical meristem is one of several physiological activities that are photoperiodic in many plants. Plants are classified into four main groups—short-day, long-day, intermediate-day, and day-neutral—on the basis of how photoperiodism affects their transition from vegetative growth to flowering.

Short-day plants (also called **long-night plants**) flower when the night length is equal to or greater than some critical period (**FIG. 38-16a**). Thus, short-day plants detect the lengthening nights of late summer or fall. There are two kinds of short-day plants: qualitative and quantitative. In *qualitative short-day plants,* flowering occurs only in short days; in *quantitative short-day plants,* flowering is accelerated by short days. The initiation of flowering in short-day plants is not due to the shorter period of daylight but to the long, uninterrupted period of darkness. The minimum critical night length varies considerably from one plant species to another but falls between 12 and 14 hours for many. Examples of short-day plants are florist's chrysanthemum, cocklebur, and poinsettia, which typically flower in late summer or fall. Poinsettias, for example, typically initiate flower buds in early October in the Northern Hemisphere and flower about 8 to 10 weeks later; hence, their traditional association with Christmas.

Long-day plants (also called **short-night plants**) flower when the night length is equal to or less than some critical period (**FIG. 38-16b**). In *qualitative long-day plants,* flowering occurs only in long days; in *quantitative long-day plants,* long days accelerate flowering. Long-day plants, such as spinach, black-eyed Susan (see photograph in chapter introduction), and the model research plant *Arabidopsis,* flower when they detect the shortening nights of spring and early summer.

Intermediate-day plants do not flower when night length is either too long or too short (**FIG. 38-16c**). Sugarcane and coleus are intermediate-day plants. These plants flower when exposed to days and nights of intermediate length.

Some plants, called **day-neutral plants,** do not initiate flowering in response to seasonal changes in the period of daylight and darkness but instead respond to some other type of stimulus, external or internal. Cucumber, sunflower, corn, and onion are examples of day-neutral plants. Many of these plants originated in the tropics, where day length does not vary appreciably during the year. In contrast, short-day, long-day, and intermediate-day plants are temperate or subtropical (midlatitude species).

(a) **Short-day plants** flower when the night length is equal to or exceeds a certain critical length in a 24-hour period.

(b) **Long-day plants** flower when the night length is equal to or less than a certain critical length in a 24-hour period. The critical length varies among different species; short-day plants may require a shorter night length than long-day plants, as shown.

(c) **Intermediate-day plants** have a narrow night-length requirement.

FIGURE 38-16 Generalized photoperiodic responses in short-day, long-day, and intermediate-day plants

Plant biologists have experimented with the effects of various light regimens on flowering. **FIGURE 38-17** shows how flowering in long-day and short-day plants is affected by different light treatments, including a short-day/long-night regimen with a *night break,* a short burst of light in the middle of the night.

Phytochrome detects day length

The main photoreceptor for photoperiodism and many other light-initiated plant responses (such as germination and seedling establishment) is **phytochrome,** a family of about five blue-green pigment proteins, each of which is coded for by a different gene. A mixture of phytochrome proteins is present in cells of all vascular plants examined so far. For example, five members of the phytochrome family, designated phyA, phyB, phyC, phyD, and phyE, oc-

FIGURE 38-17 *Animated* **Photoperiodic responses of short-day and long-day plants**

A short-day plant flowers when it is grown under long-night conditions (*top middle*), but it does not flower when exposed to a long night interrupted with a brief flash of red light (*top right*). A long-day plant does not flower when grown under long-night conditions (*bottom middle*) unless the long night is interrupted with a brief flash of red light (*bottom right*).

cur in *Arabidopsis.* Phytochrome is also a photoreceptor in certain bacteria, fungi, and slime molds.

Much of the current knowledge of phytochrome in *Arabidopsis* is based on various mutant plants that do not express a specific phytochrome gene, such as the gene that codes for phyA. By studying the physiological response of plants that do not produce an individual phytochrome, biologists have concluded that the individual forms of phytochrome have both unique and overlapping functions. PhyB appears to exert its influence at all stages of the plant life cycle, whereas the other forms of phytochrome have narrower functions at specific stages in the life cycle.

PhyA and phyB may have antagonistic (opposite) effects on flowering. In long-day plants, phyB may inhibit flowering and phyA may induce flowering. Flowering occurs more rapidly in long-day plants with mutations in the gene that codes for phyB; such mutations reduce or eliminate the production of phyB. In contrast, flowering is delayed or prevented in long-day plants with mutations in the gene that codes for phyA.

Each member of the phytochrome family exists in two forms and readily converts from one form to the other after absorption of light of specific wavelengths. One form, designated **Pr** (for *red*-absorbing *p*hytochrome), strongly absorbs light with a relatively short red wavelength (660 nm). In the process, the shape of the molecule changes to the second form of phytochrome, **Pfr,** so

FIGURE 38-18 *Animated* **Phytochrome**

Each member of the phytochrome family occurs in two forms, designated Pr and Pfr, and readily converts from one form to the other. Red light (660 nm) converts Pr to Pfr, and far-red light (730 nm) converts Pfr to Pr.

designated because it absorbs *far-r*ed light, which is light with a relatively long red wavelength (730 nm; **FIG. 38-18**). When it absorbs far-red light, Pfr reverts to the original form, Pr. Pfr is the active form of phytochrome, triggering or inhibiting physiological responses such as flowering.

What does a pigment that absorbs red light and far-red light have to do with daylight and darkness? Sunlight consists of various amounts of the entire spectrum of visible light, in addition to ultraviolet and infrared radiation. Because sunlight contains more red than far-red light, however, when a plant is exposed to sunlight, the level of Pfr increases. During the night, the level of Pfr slowly decreases as Pfr, which is less stable than Pr, is degraded.

The importance of phytochrome to plants cannot be overemphasized. Timing of day length and darkness is the most reliable way for plants to measure the change from one season to the next. This measurement, which synchronizes the stages of plant development, is crucial for survival, particularly in environments where the climate has an annual pattern of favorable and unfavorable seasons.

Competition for sunlight among shade-avoiding plants involves phytochrome

Plants sense the proximity of nearby plants, which are potential competitors, and react by changing the way they grow and develop. Many plants, from small herbs to large trees, compete for light, a response known as **shade avoidance,** in which plants tend to grow taller when closely surrounded by other plants. If successful, the shade-avoiding plant projects its new growth into direct sunlight and thereby increases its chances of survival.

Since the 1970s, botanists have recognized the environmental factor that triggers shade avoidance: plants perceive changes in the ratio of red to far-red light that result from the presence of nearby plants. The leaves of neighboring plants absorb much more red light than far-red light. (The green pigment chlorophyll strongly absorbs red light during photosynthesis.) In a densely plant-populated area, the ratio of red light to far-red light (r/fr) decreases, affect-

ing the equilibrium between the Pr and Pfr forms, particularly of phyB. This signal triggers a series of responses that cause the shade-avoiding plant, which is adapted to full-light environments, to grow taller or flower earlier. **FIGURE 38-19** shows an interesting application of additional (reflected) far-red light without the reduction in incoming sunlight that occurs in shade avoidance.

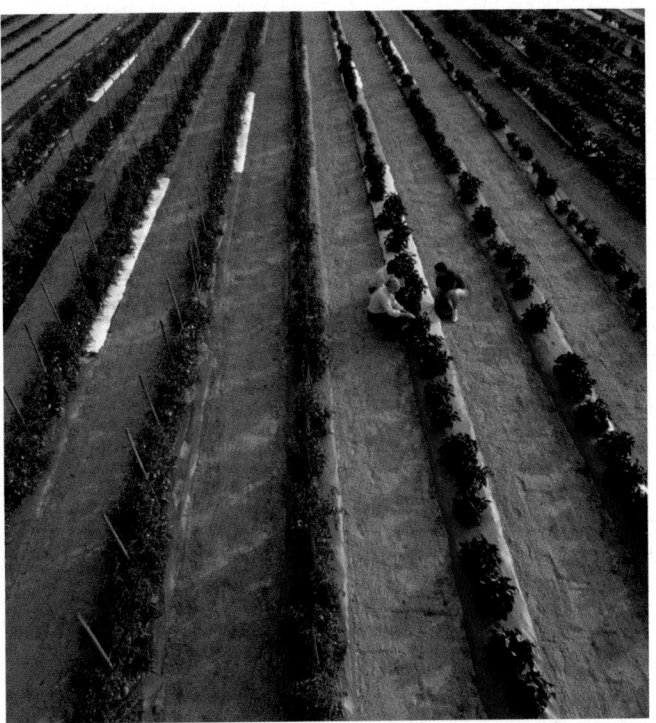

Cary Wolinsky

FIGURE 38-19 Colored mulches and plant growth processes

The red mulch reflects far-red light from the ground to the tomato plants. The plants, absorbing the extra far-red light, react as if nearby plants are present. Their aboveground growth is greater, and their fruits ripen earlier. Manipulating mulch colors also modifies yield, flavor, and nutrient content.

When a plant is using many of its resources for stem elongation, it has fewer resources for new leaves and branches, storage tissues, and reproductive tissues. However, for a shade-avoiding plant that is shaded by its neighbors, a rapid increase in stem length is advantageous, because once this plant is taller than its neighbors, it obtains a larger share of unfiltered sunlight.

Phytochrome is involved in other responses to light, including germination

Phytochrome is involved in the light requirement that some seeds have for germination. Seeds with a light requirement must be exposed to light containing red wavelengths. Exposure to red light converts Pr to Pfr, and germination occurs. Many temperate forest species with small seeds require light for germination. (Larger seeds generally do not have a light requirement.) This adaptation enables the seeds to germinate at the optimal time. During early spring, sunlight, including red light, penetrates the bare branches of overlying deciduous trees and reaches the soil between the trees. As spring temperatures warm, the seeds on the soil absorb red light and germinate. During their early growth, the newly germinated seedlings do not have to compete with the taller trees for sunlight.

Other physiological functions under the influence of phytochrome include sleep movements in leaves (discussed later); shoot dormancy; leaf abscission; and pigment formation in flowers, fruits, and leaves.

Phytochrome acts by signal transduction

Some phytochrome-induced responses are very rapid and short-term, whereas others are slower and long-term. The rapid responses probably involve reversible changes in the properties of membranes, altering cell ionic balances. Red light, for example, causes potassium ion (K^+) channels to open in cell membranes involved in plant movements caused by changes in turgor. Exposure to far-red light causes the K^+ channels to close. Slower phytochrome-induced responses involve the selective regulation of transcription of numerous genes. For example, phytochrome activates transcription of the gene for the small subunit of *rubisco*, an enzyme involved in photosynthesis (see Chapter 9).

Each phytochrome molecule consists of a protein attached to a light-absorbing photoreceptor. Biologists hypothesize that the absorption of light by the photoreceptor portion of phytochrome elicits a change in the shape of the protein portion of the phytochrome molecule. This change, in turn, triggers one or more signal transduction pathways.

One important research tool in studying phytochrome signal transduction is mutant plants that respond as if they were exposed to a particular light stimulus even if they were not. Research indicates that the active form of phytochrome moves from the cytoplasm into the nucleus, where it affects gene expression by activating a **transcription factor.** When activated, the transcription factor, which binds to the promoter of a gene, either turns on or represses transcription that leads to protein synthesis.

In one such pathway, inactive phytochrome (Pr) in the cytoplasm absorbs red light and is converted into the active form, Pfr, which moves into the nucleus. There, phytochrome binds to PIF3 (phytochrome-interacting factor 3), a transcription factor that is already bound to the promoters of light-responsive genes, thereby activating (or repressing) their transcription.

The signal transduction pathway is shut down by far-red light, which is absorbed by the Pfr in the Pfr–PIF3 complex in the nucleus. When Pfr is converted to Pr, it dissociates from PIF3.

The signal transduction pathway just described is not the end of the story. Phytochrome does not regulate just one but numerous light-responsive signaling pathways that affect gene expression. Also, we do not understand the specifics of how the transition from Pr to Pfr participates in so many signaling cascades.

Light influences circadian rhythms

Almost all organisms, including plants, animals, fungi, eukaryotic microorganisms, and many bacteria, appear to have an internal timer, or biological clock, that approximates a 24-hour cycle, the time it takes for Earth to rotate around its own axis. These internal molecular cycles are known as **circadian rhythms** (from the Latin *circum,* "around," and *diurn,* "daily"). Circadian rhythms help an organism detect the time of day, whereas photoperiodism enables a plant to detect the time of year.

Why do plants and other organisms exhibit daily circadian rhythms? Predictable environmental changes, such as sunrise and sunset, occur during the course of each 24-hour period. These predictable changes may be important to an individual organism, causing it to change its physiological activities or its behavior (in the case of animals). Researchers think that circadian rhythms help an organism synchronize repeated daily activities so that they occur at the appropriate time each day. If, for example, an insect-pollinated flower does not open at the time of day that pollinating insects are foraging for food, reproduction will be unsuccessful.

Circadian rhythms in plants affect such biological events as gene expression, the timing of photoperiodism (that is, of seasonal reproduction), the rate of photosynthesis, and the opening and closing of stomata. **Sleep movements** observed in the common bean and other plants are another example of a circadian rhythm (**FIG. 38-20**). During the day, bean leaves are horizontal, possibly for optimal light absorption, but at night the leaves fold down or up, a movement that orients them perpendicular to their daytime position. The biological significance of sleep movements is unknown at this time.

When constant environmental conditions are maintained, circadian rhythms such as sleep movements repeat every 20 to 30 hours, at least for several days. In nature, the rising and setting of the sun reset the biological clock so that the cycle repeats every 24 hours.

What happens if a plant's circadian clock is mutated so that it is not resynchronized by the day–night cycle? In 2005, biologists at the University of Cambridge in England identified mutants of the model plant *Arabidopsis* in which the circadian clock is not synchronized to match the external day–night cycle. The mutant plants contained less chlorophyll, fixed less carbon by photosynthesis, grew more slowly, and had less of a competitive advantage than *Arabidopsis* plants with a normal circadian clock.

For *Arabidopsis* and many other plants, two photoreceptors—the red light–absorbing phytochrome and the blue/ultraviolet-A light–absorbing **cryptochrome**—are implicated in resetting the biological clock. Certain amino acid sequences of the protein portion of phytochrome are homologous with amino acid sequences

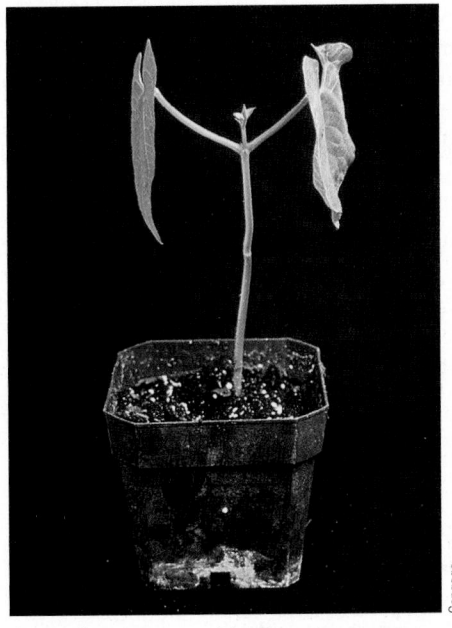

(a) Leaf position at noon in a bean (*Phaseolus vulgaris*) seedling.

(b) Leaf position at midnight.

FIGURE 38-20 *Animated* **Sleep movements**

of clock proteins in fruit flies, fungi, mammals, and bacteria; this molecular evidence strongly supports the circadian-clock role of phytochrome. The evidence for cryptochrome as a clock protein is also convincing. First discovered in plants, cryptochrome counterparts are found in the fruit fly and mouse biological-clock proteins. Possibly both photoreceptors are involved in resetting the biological clock in plants; researchers have evidence that phytochrome and cryptochrome sometimes interact to regulate similar responses.

Review

- What is phytochrome? What are two roles of phytochrome?
- What are the steps in phytochrome signal transduction?
- In what process is cryptochrome involved?

38.4 RESPONSES TO HERBIVORES AND PATHOGENS

■ LEARNING OBJECTIVE

9 Distinguish between the hypersensitive response and systemic acquired resistance.

Plants lack an immune system such as is found in humans and other mammals, but plants can defend themselves from attack by pathogenic and herbivorous enemies. Each plant cell has an innate immune system to fight against local infections. When a molecule produced by a pathogen or herbivore binds to a receptor in a plant cell, it triggers a signal transduction pathway. As a result, a **hypersensitive response** occurs that seals off the infected area, causing it to die. These *necrotic lesions,* or dead areas, prevent or slow the spread of the initial infection (**FIG. 38-21**).

The plant also sends signals from the site of localized infection, leading to **systemic acquired resistance (SAR),** a buildup of long-lasting, enhanced resistance throughout the plant. The signal travels in the phloem. Systemic acquired resistance is broad spectrum—that is, SAR is a heightened defense against many types of pathogens, not just the one that caused the initial infection.

Plant biologists continue to discover new hormonelike signaling molecules. Many of these signaling molecules are involved in the defensive responses of plants to disease organisms and insects. Here we briefly consider two groups—jasmonic acid and methyl salicylate.

Jasmonic acid activates several plant defenses

Jasmonic acid affects several plant processes, such as pollen development, root growth, fruit ripening, and senescence. This lipid-derived plant hormone, which is structurally similar to *prostaglandins* in animals, is also produced in response to the presence of insect pests and disease-causing organisms.

Jasmonic acid triggers the production of enzymes that confer an increased resistance against herbivorous (plant-eating) insects. For example, caterpillar-infested tomato plants release volatile jasmonic acid into the air that attracts natural caterpillar enemies, such as parasitic wasps; the wasps lay their eggs on the caterpillars'

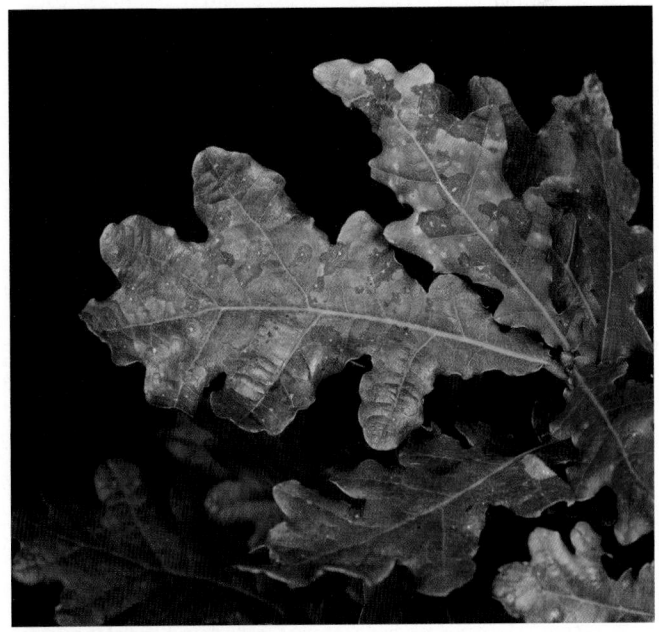

FIGURE 38-21 Hypersensitive response
The necrotic lesions on these oak leaves were produced in response to invasion by a fungal pathogen.

bodies. When the eggs hatch, the wasp larvae consume, and ultimately kill, the host insects. In one study, treating plants with jasmonic acid increased parasitism on caterpillar pests twofold over control fields in which the plants did not have jasmonic acid applications. Jasmonic acid may be of practical value in controlling certain insect pests without the use of chemical pesticides.

Biologists have made progress in identifying key aspects of the jasmonic acid signaling pathway. Interestingly, the jasmonic acid signaling pathway includes ubiquitin, which was discussed earlier in the chapter in relation to auxin (see Fig. 38-4). As in the auxin signaling pathway, the ubiquitin tags in the jasmonic acid signaling pathway cause degradation of transcription repressors, thereby altering gene expression.

Methyl salicylate may induce systemic acquired resistance

For centuries people chewed willow (*Salix*) bark to treat headaches and other types of pain. **Salicylic acid** was first extracted from willow bark and is chemically related to aspirin (acetylsali-

cylic acid). More recently, biologists have shown that salicylic acid helps plants defend against insect pests and pathogens such as viruses. When a plant is under attack, the concentration of salicylic acid increases, and it spreads systemically throughout the plant.

Based on current research, biologists think that *methyl salicylate,* a derivative of salicylic acid also known as *oil of wintergreen*, binds to a cell receptor, triggering a signal transduction pathway that switches on genes. These genes code for proteins that establish systemic acquired resistance to fight infection and promote wound healing.

Plants also use methyl salicylate, which is volatile, to signal nearby plants. Tobacco plants infected with tobacco mosaic virus release methyl salicylate into the air. When nearby healthy plants receive the airborne chemical signal, they begin synthesizing antiviral proteins that enhance their resistance to the virus.

Review

- What is the hypersensitive response?
- What is systemic acquired resistance?

■ SUMMARY: FOCUS ON LEARNING OBJECTIVES

38.1 *(page 804)*

1 Describe phototropism, gravitropism, and thigmotropism.

- **Tropisms** are directional growth responses. **Phototropism** is growth in response to the direction of light. **Gravitropism** is growth in response to the influence of gravity. **Thigmotropism** is growth in response to contact with a solid object.

  CENGAGENOW™ Learn more about phototropism and gravitropism by clicking on the figures in CengageNOW.

38.2 *(page 805)*

2 Describe a general mechanism of action for plant hormones, using auxin as your example.

- Plants produce and respond to **hormones,** organic molecules that act as highly specific chemical signals to elicit a variety of responses that regulate growth and development.
- Many plant hormones bind to **enzyme-linked receptors** located in the plasma membrane; the hormone binds to the receptor, triggering an enzymatic reaction of some sort. The receptor for auxin, which is located in the cytosol or nucleus, binds to auxin. This catalyzes the attachment of ubiquitin to a repressor protein, targeting it for destruction. When genes repressed by those proteins are then expressed, changes in cell growth and development result.

3 Describe early auxin experiments involving phototropism.

- Darwin and his son performed phototropism experiments in the 1870s on grass seedlings. When they covered the coleoptile tip, the plant did not bend. When they removed the coleoptile tip, bending did not occur. When the bottom of the coleoptile was shielded from the light, the coleoptile bent. The Darwins concluded that some substance is transmitted from the upper to the lower part that causes the plant to bend.
- In the 1920s, Frits Went isolated the phototropic hormone from oat coleoptiles by removing the coleoptile tips and placing them on agar blocks. Normal growth resumed when he put one of these agar blocks squarely on a decapitated coleoptile; the substance had dif-

fused from the coleoptile tip into the agar and, later, from the agar into the decapitated coleoptile. Went named this substance auxin.

CENGAGENOW™ See the auxin experiments in action by clicking on the figure in CengageNOW.

4 List several ways that each of these hormones affects plant growth and development: auxins, gibberellins, cytokinins, ethylene, abscisic acid, and brassinosteroids.

- **Auxin** is involved in cell elongation; tropisms; **apical dominance,** the inhibition of axillary buds by the apical meristem; and fruit development. Auxin also stimulates root development on stem cuttings.
- **Gibberellins** are involved in stem elongation, flowering, and germination.
- **Cytokinins** promote cell division and differentiation; delay **senescence,** the natural aging process; and interact with auxin and ethylene in apical dominance. Cytokinins induce cell division in **tissue culture,** a technique in which cells are isolated from plants and grown in a nutrient medium.
- **Ethylene** plays a role in ripening fruits; apical dominance; leaf abscission; wound response; **thigmomorphogenesis,** a developmental response to mechanical stressors such as wind; and senescence.

- **Abscisic acid** is an environmental stress hormone involved in stomatal closure caused by water stress and in seed **dormancy,** a temporary state of reduced physiological activity.

- Plant steroids known as **brassinosteroids** are involved in several aspects of plant growth and development, such as cell division, cell elongation, light-induced differentiation, seed germination, and vascular development.

38.3 *(page 813)*

5 Explain how varying amounts of light and darkness induce flowering.

- **Photoperiodism** is any response of plants to the duration and timing of light and dark. Flowering is a photoperiodic response in many plants. **Short-day plants** detect the lengthening nights of late summer or fall and flower at that time. **Long-day plants** detect the shortening nights of spring and early summer and flower at that time. **Intermediate-day plants** flower when exposed to days and nights of intermediate length.

CENGAGENOW™ Learn more about photoperiodism by clicking on the figure in CengageNOW.

6 Describe the role of phytochrome in flowering, including a brief discussion of phytochrome signal transduction.

- The photoreceptor in photoperiodism is **phytochrome,** a family of about five blue-green pigments. Each type of phytochrome has two forms, **Pr** and **Pfr,** named by the wavelength of light they absorb. Pfr is the active form, triggering or inhibiting physiological responses such as flowering, **shade avoidance,** and a light requirement for germination.
- The pathway in phytochrome **signal transduction** begins when inactive phytochrome in the cytoplasm absorbs red light and is converted into the active form, Pfr, which moves into the nu-

cleus. There, phytochrome binds to the transcription factor PIF3 (phytochrome-interacting factor) and activates or represses the transcription of light-responsive genes.

CENGAGENOW™ Learn more about phytochrome by clicking on the figure in CengageNOW.

7 Define *circadian rhythm* and give an example.

- A **circadian rhythm** is a regular period in an organism's growth or activities that approximates the 24-hour day and is reset by the rising and setting of the sun. Two examples of circadian rhythms are the opening and closing of stomata and **sleep movements.**

8 Distinguish between phytochrome and cryptochrome.

- Both phytochrome and **cryptochrome** are photoreceptors that sometimes interact to regulate similar responses, such as resetting the biological clock. Phytochrome strongly absorbs red light, whereas cryptochrome absorbs blue and ultraviolet-A light.

38.4 *(page 817)*

9 Distinguish between the hypersensitive response and systemic acquired resistance.

- Each plant cell has an innate immune system to fight against local infections. A **hypersensitive response** seals off the infected area, causing it to die. These dead areas prevent or slow the spread of the initial infection.
- **Systemic acquired resistance (SAR)** is a buildup of long-lasting, enhanced resistance throughout the plant. Systemic acquired resistance is broad spectrum (against many types of pathogens).

TEST YOUR UNDERSTANDING

1. In the signal transduction process for the hormone auxin, the molecule ubiquitin (a) absorbs blue light (b) becomes phosphorylated (c) tags certain proteins for destruction (d) interacts antagonistically with gibberellins (e) binds to a receptor in the plant cell's plasma membrane

2. When you prune shrubs to make them "bushier"—that is, to prevent apical dominance—you are affecting the distribution and action of which plant hormone? (a) auxin (b) jasmonic acid (c) salicylic acid (d) ethylene (e) abscisic acid

3. Research on a fungal disease of rice provided the first clues about the plant hormone (a) auxin (b) gibberellin (c) cytokinin (d) ethylene (e) abscisic acid

4. This plant hormone interacts with auxin during the formation of plant organs in tissue culture. (a) florigen (b) gibberellin (c) cytokinin (d) ethylene (e) abscisic acid

5. The stress hormone that helps plants respond to drought is (a) auxin (b) gibberellin (c) cytokinin (d) ethylene (e) abscisic acid

6. This hormone promotes seed dormancy. (a) auxin (b) gibberellin (c) cytokinin (d) ethylene (e) abscisic acid

7. The three classes of photoreceptors that enable plants to sense the presence and duration of light are (a) phytochrome, cryptochrome, and circadian rhythms (b) chlorophyll, photosynthesis, and photoperiodism (c) phytochrome, photoperiodism, and chlorophyll (d) phytochrome, cryptochrome, and phototropin (e) phototropin, photosynthesis, and photoperiodism

8. A plant's response to the relative amounts of daylight and darkness is (a) apical dominance (b) bolting (c) gravitropism (d) photoperiodism (e) phototropism

9. Pfr, the active state of _____, forms when red light is absorbed. (a) photosystem I (b) phytochrome (c) far-red light (d) phototropin (e) cryptochrome

10. Which of the following represents the correct order in the phytochrome signal transduction pathway?
    1. red light
    2. light-responsive gene is switched on (or off)
    3. movement of Pfr to nucleus
    4. conversion of Pr to Pfr
    5. formation of PFr–PIF3 complex that is bound to promoter region
       (a) 1, 3, 5, 4, 2 (b) 1, 5, 3, 2, 4 (c) 1, 2, 3, 4, 5 (d) 1, 4, 3, 2, 5 (e) 1, 4, 3, 5, 2

11. Which photoreceptor(s) is/are implicated in resetting the biological clock? (a) phytochrome only (b) cryptochrome only (c) phototropin only (d) cryptochrome and gibberellin (e) phytochrome and cryptochrome

12. Which signaling molecule triggers the release of volatile substances that attract parasitic wasps to plant-eating caterpillars? (a) phytochrome (b) jasmonic acid (c) auxin (d) methyl salicylate (e) gibberellin

CRITICAL THINKING

1. Predict whether flowering in a short-day plant with a minimum critical night length of 14 hours would be expected to occur in the following situations. Explain each answer.

   (a) The plant is exposed to 15 hours of daylight and 9 hours of uninterrupted darkness.

   (b) The plant is exposed to 9 hours of daylight and 15 hours of darkness.

   (c) The plant is exposed to 9 hours of daylight and 15 hours of darkness, with a 10-minute exposure to red light in the middle of the night.

2. If you transplanted the short-day plant discussed in question 1 to the tropics, would it flower? Explain your answer.

3. **EVOLUTION LINK.** What adaptive advantages are conferred on a plant whose stems are positively phototropic and whose roots are positively gravitropic?

4. **EVOLUTION LINK.** Explain why a plant with a mutation in one of its phytochrome genes that affects flowering time would be at an evolutionary disadvantage.

5. **ANALYZING DATA.** Examine the figure (right). When the day length is 10 hours and the night length is 14 hours, what percent of the plants flower? When the day length is 16 hours and the night

length is 8 hours, what percent of the plants flower? What is the critical night length for this plant?

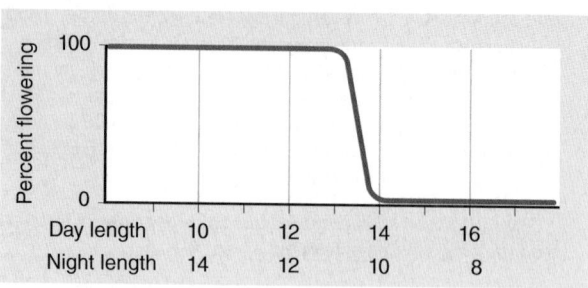

6. **SCIENCE, TECHNOLOGY, AND SOCIETY.** Do you think our expanding knowledge of the molecular basis of plant signaling molecules could improve agricultural productivity in the future? Explain your answer.

 Additional questions are available in CengageNOW at www.cengage.com/login.

39 Animal Structure and Function: An Introduction

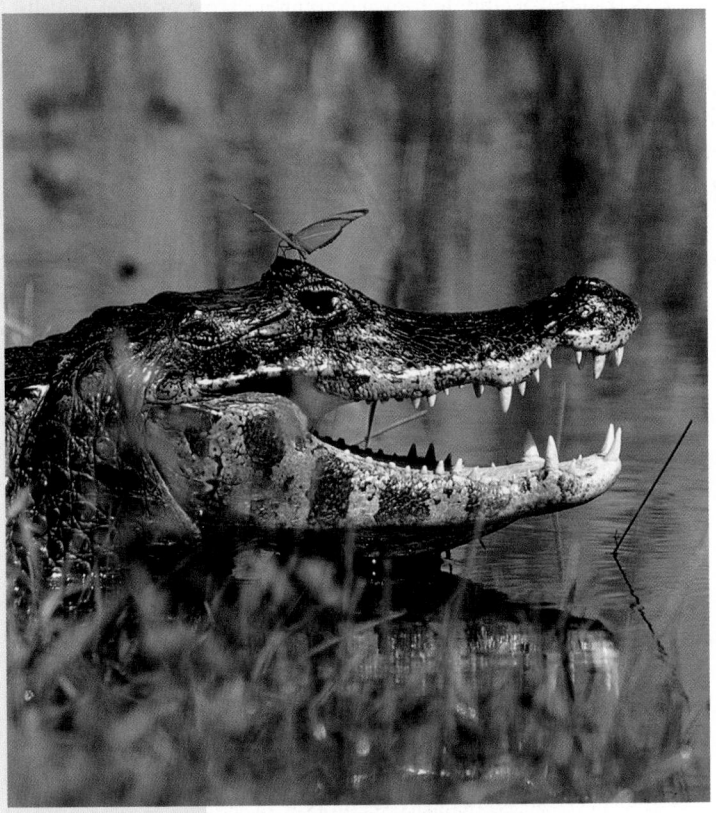

Larger body size does not mean bigger cells. The cells of the Yacare caiman (*Caiman yacare*) and the flambeau butterfly (*Dryas julia*) on its head are all about the same size. The caiman is larger because its genes specify that its body consists of a larger number of cells.

Fritz Polking/Dembinsky Photo Associates

KEY CONCEPTS

39.1 Cells make up tissues, various types of tissues make up organs, and tissues and organs working together make up organ systems. The main types of tissues found in animals are epithelial, connective, muscle, and nervous tissues.

39.2 Homeostatic mechanisms are mainly negative feedback systems that maintain a relatively stable internal environment.

39.3 Thermoregulation is the process of maintaining homeostasis of body temperature, despite changes in surrounding (or internal) temperature.

Animal groups are dramatically diverse, with radically different body structures. For example, consider how different the caiman and the butterfly are, not only in size but also in body form and lifestyle (see photograph). Despite their differences, animal groups share many characteristics, including their relatively large size.

Why are most animals larger than bacteria, protists, and fungi? The answer may be related to *ecological niches,* which are the functional roles of a species within a community. By the time animals evolved, bacteria, protists, and fungi already occupied most available ecological niches. For new species to succeed, they had to displace others from a niche or adapt to a new one. Success in a new niche required a new body plan, and new body plans often required and accommodated larger size. Increased size also provided more opportunity for capturing food. Predators are typically larger than their prey.

To grow larger than their bacterial and protist competitors, animals had to be multicellular. Recall that the size of a single cell is limited by the ratio of its surface area (plasma membrane) to its volume (see Chapter 4). The plasma membrane needs to be large enough relative to the cell's volume to permit passage of materials into and out of the cell so that the

821

conditions necessary for life can be maintained. In a multicellular animal, each cell has a large enough surface-area-to-volume ratio to effectively regulate its internal environment. Individual cells live and die and are replaced while the organism continues to maintain itself and thrive. The number of cells, not their individual sizes, is mainly responsible for the size of an animal.

In unicellular organisms, such as bacteria and many protists, the single cell carries on all the activities necessary for life. Recall that unicellular and small, flat organisms depend on diffusion for many life processes, including gas exchange and disposal of metabolic wastes. One reason they can be small is that they do not require complex organ systems.

In this chapter we focus on the basic form and function of the animal body. **Anatomy** is the study of an organism's structure. **Physiology** is the study of how the body functions. Structure and function are closely linked at every level of organization. We describe the types and functions of tissues and the principal organ systems of animals. We also discuss the important concept of *homeostasis*, using regulation of body temperature as an example. In the following chapters, we discuss how organ systems work together to maintain homeostasis, as the animal carries out its many life processes.

39.1 TISSUES, ORGANS, AND ORGAN SYSTEMS

◼ LEARNING OBJECTIVES

1 Compare the structure and function of the four main kinds of animal tissues: epithelial, connective, muscle, and nervous tissues.

2 Compare the main types of epithelial tissue and describe their functions.

3 Compare the main types of connective tissue and describe their functions.

4 Contrast the three types of muscle tissue and describe their functions.

5 Relate the structure of the neuron to its function.

6 Briefly describe the organ systems of a mammal and summarize the functions of each organ system.

In a multicellular organism, cells specialize to perform specific tasks. Recall from Chapter 1 that cells organize to form *tissues,* and tissues associate to form *organs* such as the heart or stomach. Groups of tissues and organs make up the *organ systems* of a complex *organism.* Billions of cells may be organized to form the tissues, organs, and organ systems of a complex animal.

A **tissue** consists of a group of closely associated, similar cells that carry out specific functions. Biologists classify animal tissues as epithelial, connective, muscle, or nervous tissue. Classification of tissues depends on their structure and origin. Each kind of tissue is composed of cells with characteristic sizes, shapes, and arrangements; and each type of tissue is specialized to perform a specific function or group of functions. For example, some tissues are specialized to transport materials, whereas others contract, enabling the animal to move. Still others secrete hormones that regulate

metabolic processes. Structure and function are closely linked at every level of organization. As we discuss each tissue type, notice the relationship between its form and its function.

Epithelial tissues cover the body and line its cavities

Epithelial tissue (also called **epithelium**) consists of cells fitted tightly together to form a continuous layer, or sheet, of cells. One surface of the sheet is typically exposed because it covers the body (outer layer of the skin) or lines a cavity, such as the *lumen* (the cavity in a hollow organ) of the intestine. The other surface of an epithelial layer attaches to the underlying tissue by a noncellular **basement membrane** consisting of tiny fibers and nonliving polysaccharide material that the epithelial cells produce.

Epithelial tissue forms the outer layer of the skin and the linings of the digestive, respiratory, excretory, and reproductive tracts. As a result, everything that enters or leaves the body must cross at least one layer of epithelium. Food taken into the mouth and swallowed is not really "inside" the body until it is absorbed through the epithelium of the gut and enters the blood. To a large extent, the permeabilities of the various epithelial tissues regulate the exchange of substances between the different parts of the body, as well as between the animal and the external environment.

Epithelial tissues perform many functions, including protection, absorption, secretion, and sensation. The epithelial layer of the skin, the **epidermis,** covers the entire body and protects it from mechanical injury, chemicals, bacteria, and fluid loss. The epithelial tissue lining the digestive tract absorbs nutrients and water into the body. Some epithelial cells form **glands** that secrete cell products such as hormones, enzymes, or sweat. Other epithelial cells are sensory receptors that receive information from the environment. For example, epithelial cells in taste buds and in the nose specialize as chemical receptors.

TABLE 39-1 illustrates the main types of epithelial tissue, indicates their locations in the body, and describes their functions (pages 824–825). We can distinguish three types of epithelial cells on the basis of shape. **Squamous** epithelial cells are thin, flat cells shaped like flagstones. **Cuboidal** epithelial cells are short cylinders that from the side appear cube-shaped, like dice. Actually, each cuboidal cell is typically hexagonal in cross section, making it an eight-sided polyhedron.

Columnar epithelial cells look like columns or cylinders when viewed from the side. The nucleus is usually located near the base of the cell. Viewed from above or in cross section, these cells often appear hexagonal. On its free surface, a columnar epithelial cell may have cilia that beat in a coordinated way, moving materials over the tissue surface. Most of the upper respiratory tract is lined with ciliated columnar epithelium that moves particles of dust and other foreign material away from the lungs.

Epithelial tissue is also classified by number of layers. **Simple epithelium** is composed of one layer of cells. It is usually located where substances are secreted, excreted, or absorbed, or where materials diffuse between compartments. For example, simple squamous epithelium lines the air sacs in the lungs. The structure of this thin tissue allows diffusion of gases in and out of air sacs.

Stratified epithelium, which has two or more layers, protects underlying tissues. For example, stratified squamous epithelium, which makes up the outer layer of your skin, is continuously sloughed off during normal wear and tear. It must also continuously regenerate. The cells of **pseudostratified epithelium** falsely appear layered. Although all its cells rest on a basement membrane, not every cell extends to the exposed surface of the tissue. This arrangement gives the impression of two or more cell layers. Some of the respiratory passageways are lined with pseudostratified epithelium equipped with cilia.

The lining of blood and lymph vessels is called endothelium. Endothelial cells have a different embryonic origin from "true" epithelium. However, these cells are structurally similar to squamous epithelial cells and can be included in that category.

Glands are made of epithelial cells

A **gland** consists of one or more epithelial cells specialized to produce and secrete a product such as sweat, milk, mucus, wax, saliva, hormones, or enzymes (**FIG. 39-1**). Epithelial tissue lining the cavities and passageways of the body typically has some specialized mucus-secreting cells called **goblet cells.** The mucus lubricates these surfaces, offers protection, and facilitates the movement of materials.

Glands are classified as exocrine or endocrine. **Exocrine glands,** like goblet cells and sweat glands, secrete their products onto a free epithelial surface, typically through a duct (tube). **Endocrine glands** lack ducts. These glands release their products, called **hormones,** into the **interstitial fluid** (tissue fluid) or blood; hormones are typically transported by the cardiovascular system. (Endocrine glands are discussed in Chapter 50.)

Epithelial cells form membranes

An **epithelial membrane** consists of a sheet of epithelial tissue and a layer of underlying connective tissue. Types of epithelial membranes include mucous membranes and serous membranes. A **mucous membrane,** or mucosa, lines a body cavity that opens to the outside of the body, such as the digestive or respiratory tract. Goblet cells in the epithelial layer secrete mucus that lubricates the tissue and protects it from drying.

A **serous membrane** lines a body cavity that does not open to the outside of the body. It consists of simple squamous epithelium over a thin layer of loose connective tissue. This type of membrane secretes fluid into the cavity it lines. Examples of serous membranes are the pleural membranes lining the pleural cavities around the lungs and the pericardial membranes lining the pericardial cavity around the heart.

Connective tissues support other body structures

Almost every organ in the body has a framework of **connective tissue** that supports and cushions it. Compared to epithelial tissues, connective tissues contain relatively few cells. Its cells are embedded in an extensive **intercellular substance** consisting of threadlike, microscopic **fibers** scattered throughout a **matrix,** a thin gel of polysaccharides that the cells secrete. The nature and

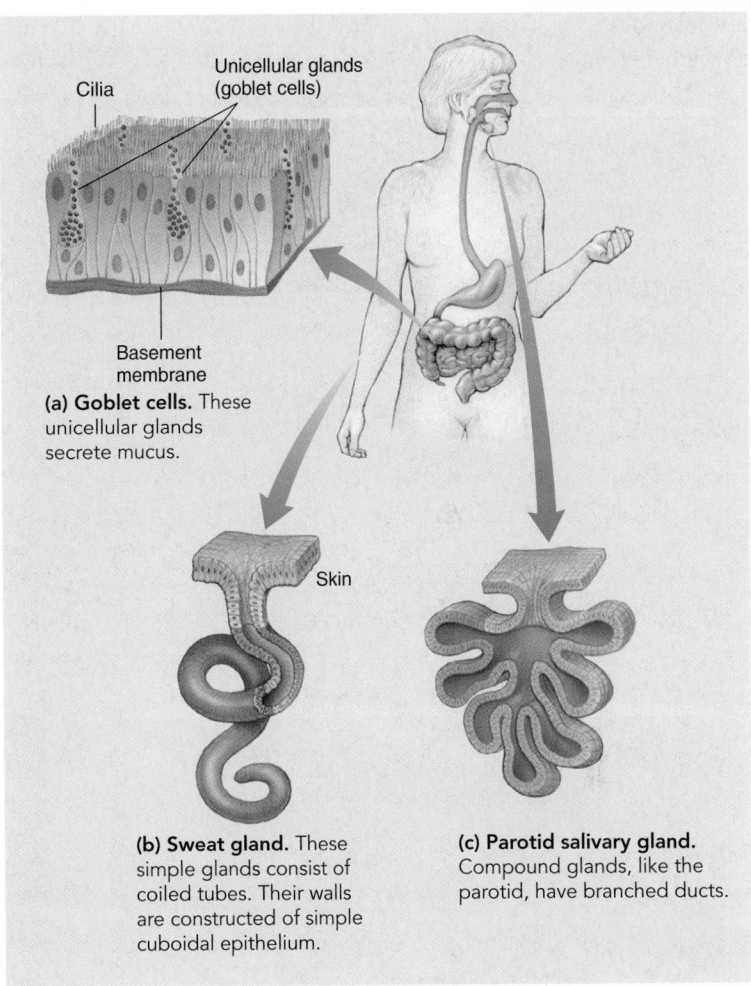

(a) **Goblet cells.** These unicellular glands secrete mucus.

(b) **Sweat gland.** These simple glands consist of coiled tubes. Their walls are constructed of simple cuboidal epithelium.

(c) **Parotid salivary gland.** Compound glands, like the parotid, have branched ducts.

FIGURE 39-1 Glands

A gland consists of one or more epithelial cells.

function of each kind of connective tissue are determined in part by the structure and properties of the intercellular substance.

Connective tissue typically contains three types of fibers: collagen, elastic, and reticular. **Collagen fibers,** the most numerous type, are made of **collagens,** a group of fibrous proteins found in all animals (see Fig. 3-22b). Collagens are the most abundant proteins in mammals, accounting for about 25% of their total protein mass. Collagen is very tough (meat is tough because of its collagen content). The tensile strength (ability to stretch without tearing) of collagen fibers is comparable to that of steel. Collagen fibers are wavy and flexible, allowing them to remain intact when tissue is stretched.

Elastic fibers branch and fuse to form networks. They can be stretched by a force and then (like a stretched rubber band) return to their original size and shape when the force is removed. Elastic fibers, composed of the protein elastin, are an important component of structures that must stretch.

Reticular fibers are very thin, branched fibers that form delicate networks joining connective tissues to neighboring tissues. Reticular fibers consist of collagen and some glycoprotein.

The cells of various kinds of connective tissues differ in their shapes and structures and in the kinds of fibers and matrices they secrete. **Fibroblasts** are connective tissue cells that produce the

TABLE 39-1   Epithelial Tissues

Nuclei of squamous epithelial cells

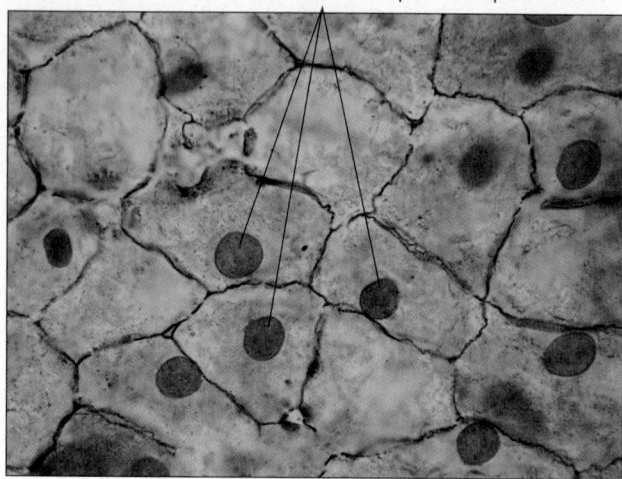

Ed Reschke

LM of simple squamous epithelium.

Simple Squamous Epithelium

Main Locations
Air sacs of lungs; lining of blood vessels

Functions
Passage of materials where little or no protection is needed and where diffusion is major form of transport

Description and Comments
Cells are flat and arranged as single layer

25 μm

Nuclei of cuboidal epithelial cells   Lumen of tubule

Ed Reschke

LM of simple cuboidal epithelium.

Simple Cuboidal Epithelium

Main Locations
Linings of kidney tubules; gland ducts

Functions
Secretion and absorption

Description and Comments
Single layer of cells; LM shows cross section through tubules; from the side each cell looks like a short cylinder; some have microvilli for absorption

25 μm

Goblet cell   Nuclei of columnar cells

Ed Reschke

LM of simple columnar epithelium.

Simple Columnar Epithelium

Main Locations
Linings of much of digestive tract and upper part of respiratory tract

Functions
Secretion, especially of mucus; absorption; protection; moves layer of mucus

Description and Comments
Single layer of columnar cells; sometimes with enclosed secretory vesicles (in goblet cells); highly developed Golgi complex; often ciliated

25 μm

(continued)

TABLE 39-1   Ephithelial Tissues (continued)

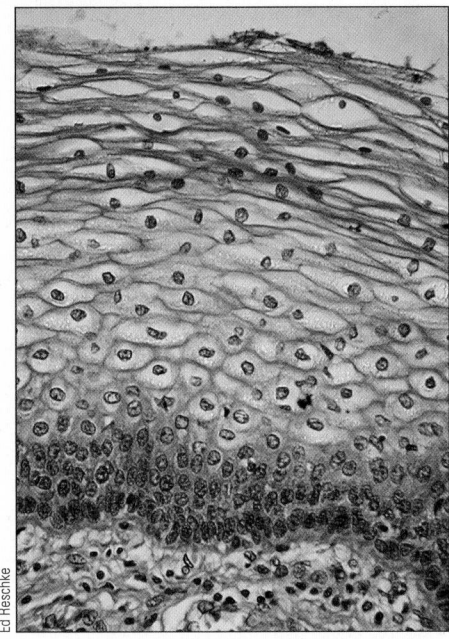

LM of stratified squamous epithelium.

Stratified Squamous Epithelium

Main Locations
Skin; mouth lining; vaginal lining

Functions
Protection only; little or no absorption or transit of materials; outer layer continuously sloughed off and replaced from below

Description and Comments
Several layers of cells, with only the lower ones columnar and metabolically active; division of lower cells causes older ones to be pushed upward toward surface, becoming flatter as they move

50 μm

— Cilia

— Epithelial cells

— Nuclei

— Basement membrane

25 μm

LM of pseudostratified columnar epithelium, ciliated.

Pseudostratified Epithelium

Main Locations
Some respiratory passages; ducts of many glands

Functions
Secretion; protection; moves layer of mucus

Description and Comments
Ciliated, mucus-secreting, or with microvilli; comparable in many ways to columnar epithelium except that not all cells are the same height; so, though all cells contact the same basement membrane, the tissue appears stratified

fibers, as well as the protein and carbohydrate complexes, of the matrix. Fibroblasts release protein components that become arranged to form the characteristic fibers. These cells are especially active in developing tissues and are important in healing wounds. As tissues mature, the number of fibroblasts decreases and they become less active. **Macrophages,** the body's scavenger cells, commonly wander through connective tissues, cleaning up cell debris and phagocytosing foreign matter, including bacteria.

Some of the main types of connective tissue are (1) loose and dense connective tissues; (2) elastic connective tissue; (3) reticular connective tissue; (4) adipose tissue; (5) cartilage; (6) bone; and (7) blood, lymph, and tissues that produce blood cells. These tissues vary widely in their structural details and in the functions they perform (**TABLE 39-2**).

Loose connective tissue is the most widely distributed connective tissue in the vertebrate body. Together with adipose tissue,

TABLE 39-2 Connective Tissues

Collagen fibers   Nuclei of fibroblasts

Elastic fibers

50 μm

LM of loose connective tissue.

Loose Connective Tissue

Main Locations
Everywhere that support must be combined with elasticity, such as sub-cutaneous tissue (the layer of tissue beneath the dermis of the skin)

Functions
Support; reservoir for fluid and salts

Description and Comments
Fibers produced by fibroblast cells embedded in semifluid matrix and mixed with miscellaneous other cells

Nucleus of fibroblast

Collagen fibers

25 μm

LM of dense connective tissue.

Dense Connective Tissue

Main Locations
Tendons; many ligaments; dermis of skin

Functions
Support; transmits mechanical forces

Description and Comments
Collagen fibers may be regularly or irregularly arranged

Elastic fibers

LM of elastic connective tissue.

50 μm

Elastic Connective Tissue

Main Locations
Structures that must both expand and return to their original size, such as lung tissue and large arteries

Function
Confers elasticity

Description and Comments
Branching elastic fibers interspersed with fibroblasts

Reticular fibers

50 μm

LM of reticular connective tissue.

Reticular Connective Tissue

Main Locations
Framework of liver; lymph nodes; spleen

Function
Support

Description and Comments
Consists of interlacing reticular fibers

(continued)

TABLE 39-2   Connective Tissues (continued)

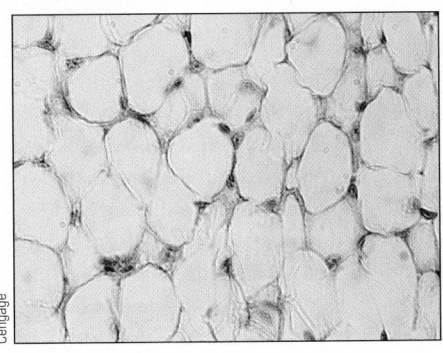

LM of adipose tissue.

Adipose Tissue

Main Locations
Subcutaneous layer; pads around certain internal organs

Functions
Food storage; insulation; supports organs such as mammary glands, kidneys

Description and Comments
Fat cells are star shaped at first; fat droplets accumulate until typical ring-shaped cells are produced

Chondrocytes   Lacuna   Intercellular substance

LM of cartilage.

Cartilage

Main Locations
Supporting skeletons in sharks and rays; ends of bones in mammals and some other vertebrates; supporting rings in walls of some respiratory tubes; tip of nose; external ear

Function
Flexible support

Description and Comments
Cells (chondrocytes) separated from one another by intercellular substance; cells occupy lacunae

Lacunae   Haversian canal   Matrix

LM of bone.

Bone

Main Locations
Forms skeletal structure in most vertebrates

Functions
Supports and protects internal organs; calcium reservoir; skeletal muscles attach to bones

Description and Comments
Osteocytes in lacunae; in compact bone, lacunae embedded in lamellae, concentric circles of matrix surrounding Haversian canals

Red blood cells   White blood cells

LM of blood.

Blood

Main Locations
Within heart and blood vessels of circulatory system

Functions
Transports oxygen, nutrients, wastes, and other materials

Description and Comments
Consists of cells dispersed in fluid intercellular substance (plasma)

loose connective tissue forms the subcutaneous (below the skin) layer that attaches skin to the muscles and other structures beneath. Nerves, blood vessels, and muscles are wrapped in loose connective tissue. This tissue also forms a thin filling between body parts and serves as a reservoir for fluid and salts. Loose connective tissue consists of fibers running in all directions through a semifluid matrix. Its flexibility permits the parts it connects to move.

Dense connective tissue, found in the dermis (lower layer) of the skin, is very strong, but is somewhat less flexible than loose connective tissue. Collagen fibers predominate. **Tendons,** the cords that connect muscles to bones, and **ligaments,** the cables that connect bones to one another, consist of dense connective tissue in which collagen bundles are arranged in a definite pattern.

Elastic connective tissue consists mainly of bundles of parallel elastic fibers. This tissue is found in structures that must expand and then return to their original size, such as lung tissue and the walls of large arteries.

Reticular connective tissue is composed mainly of interlacing reticular fibers. It forms a supporting internal framework in many organs, including the liver, spleen, and lymph nodes.

The cells of **adipose tissue** store fat and release it when fuel is needed for cellular respiration. Adipose tissue is found in the subcutaneous layer and in tissue that cushions internal organs.

The supporting skeleton of a vertebrate is made of cartilage, or of both cartilage and bone. **Cartilage** is the supporting skeleton in the embryonic stages of all vertebrates. In most vertebrates, bone replaces cartilage during development. However, cartilage remains in some supporting structures. For example, in humans, cartilage is found in the external ear, the supporting rings in the walls of the respiratory passageways, the tip of the nose, the ends of some bones, and the discs that serve as cushions between the vertebrae.

Cartilage is firm yet elastic. Its cells, called **chondrocytes,** secrete a hard, rubbery matrix that surrounds them. They also secrete collagen fibers, which become embedded in the matrix and strengthen it. Chondrocytes eventually come to lie, singly or in groups of two or four, in small cavities in the matrix called **lacunae.** These cells remain alive and are nourished by nutrients and oxygen that diffuse through the matrix. Cartilage tissue lacks nerves, lymph vessels, and blood vessels.

Bone, the main vertebrate skeletal tissue, is like cartilage in that it consists mostly of matrix material. The bone cells, called **osteocytes,** are contained within lacunae. Osteocytes secrete and maintain the matrix (**FIG. 39-2**). Unlike cartilage, however, bone is a highly vascular tissue, with a substantial blood supply. Osteocytes communicate with one another and with capillaries by tiny channels (*canaliculi*) that contain long cytoplasmic extensions of the osteocytes.

A typical bone has an outer layer of *compact bone* surrounding a filling of *spongy bone.* Compact bone consists of spindle-shaped units called **osteons.** Within each osteon, osteocytes are arranged in concentric layers of matrix called *lamellae.* In turn, the lamellae surround central microscopic channels known as **Haversian canals,** through which capillaries and nerves pass.

Bones are amazingly light and strong. Calcium salts of bone render the matrix very hard, and collagen prevents the bony matrix from being overly brittle. Most bones have a large, central **marrow cavity** that contains a spongy tissue called *marrow.* Yellow mar-

row consists mainly of fat. Red marrow is the connective tissue in which blood cells are produced. We discuss bone in more detail in Chapter 40.

Blood and **lymph** are circulating tissues that help other parts of the body communicate and interact. Like other connective tissues, they consist of specialized cells dispersed in an intercellular substance. In mammals, blood consists of **red blood cells, white blood cells,** and **platelets,** all suspended within **plasma,** the liquid, noncellular part of the blood. In humans and other vertebrates, red blood cells contain the respiratory pigment that transports oxygen. White blood cells defend the body against disease-causing microorganisms (see Chapter 45). Platelets, small fragments broken off from large cells in the bone marrow, play a key role in blood clotting. Plasma consists of water, proteins, salts, and a variety of soluble chemical messengers such as hormones that it transports from one part of the body to another. We discuss blood in Chapter 44.

Muscle tissue is specialized to contract

Most animals move by contracting the long, cylindrical or spindle-shaped cells of **muscle tissue.** Muscle cells are called muscle fibers because of their length. Each **muscle fiber** contains many thin, longitudinal, parallel contractile units called **myofibrils.** Two proteins, **myosin** and **actin,** are the chief components of myofibrils. Myosin and actin play a key role in contraction of muscle fibers.

Many invertebrates have skeletal and smooth muscle. Vertebrates have three types of muscle tissue: skeletal, cardiac, and smooth (**TABLE 39-3** on page 830). **Skeletal muscle** makes up the large muscle masses attached to the bones of the body. Skeletal muscle fibers are very long, and each fiber has many nuclei. The nuclei of skeletal muscle fibers are also unusual in their position. They lie just under the plasma membrane, which frees the entire central part of the skeletal muscle fiber for the myofibrils. This adaptation appears to increase the efficiency of contraction. When skeletal muscles contract, they move parts of the body. Whereas skeletal muscle fibers are generally under voluntary control, you do not normally contract your cardiac and smooth muscle fibers at will.

Light microscopy shows that both skeletal and cardiac fibers have alternating light and dark transverse stripes, or **striations,** that change their relative sizes during contraction. Striated muscle fibers contract rapidly but cannot remain contracted for a long period. They must relax and rest momentarily before contracting again. (Muscle contraction is discussed in Chapter 40.)

Cardiac muscle is the main tissue of the heart. When cardiac muscle contracts, the heart pumps the blood. The fibers of cardiac muscle join end to end, and they branch and rejoin to form complex networks. One or two nuclei lie within each fiber. A characteristic feature of cardiac muscle tissue is the presence of *intercalated discs,* specialized junctions where the fibers join.

Smooth muscle occurs in the walls of the digestive tract, uterus, blood vessels, and many other internal organs. Contraction of smooth muscle is necessary for these organs to perform certain functions. For example, smooth muscle contraction in the wall of the digestive tract moves food through the digestive tract. When smooth muscle in the walls of arterioles (small arteries) contracts,

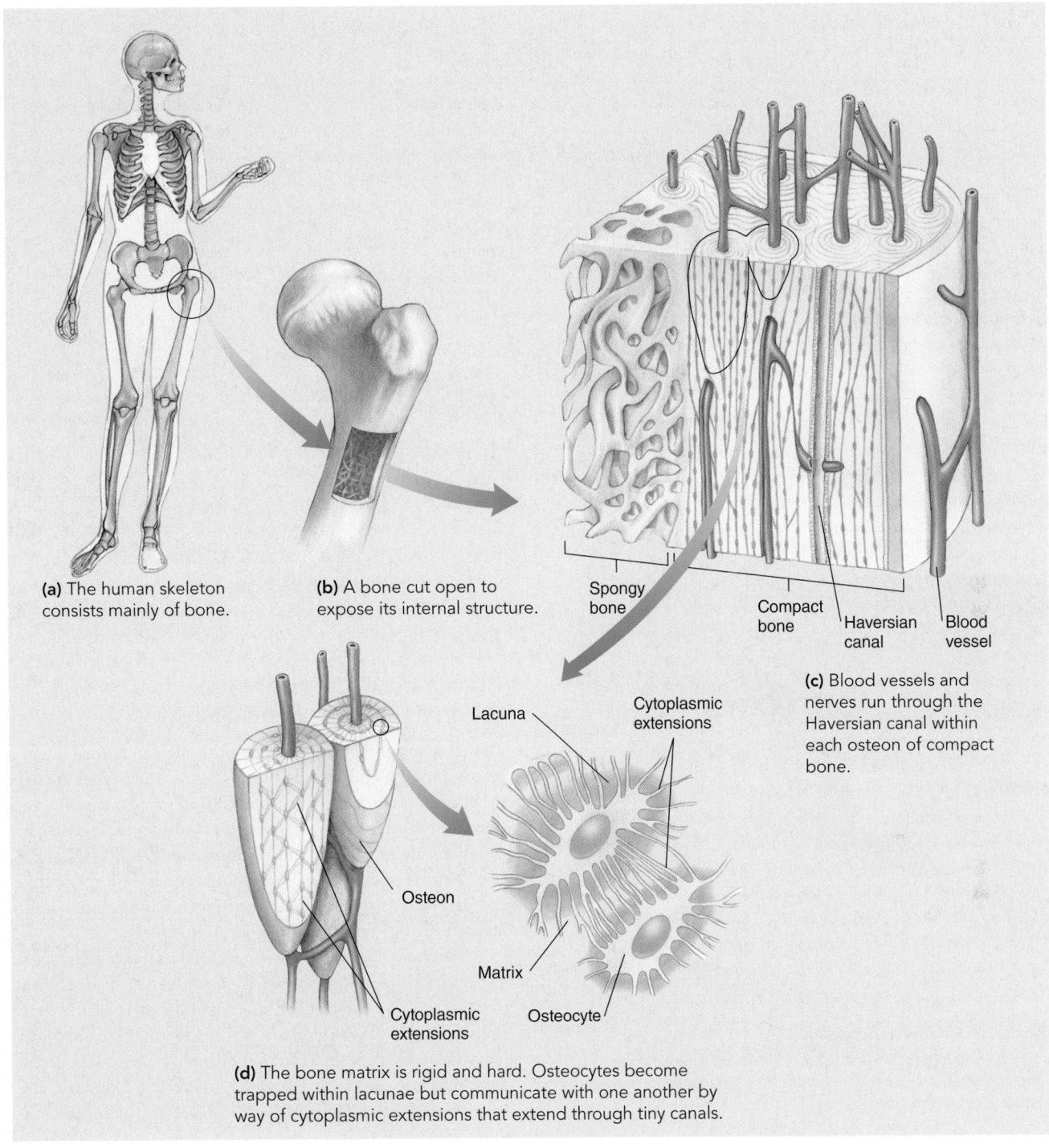

(a) The human skeleton consists mainly of bone.

(b) A bone cut open to expose its internal structure.

Spongy bone

Compact bone

Haversian canal

Blood vessel

(c) Blood vessels and nerves run through the Haversian canal within each osteon of compact bone.

Lacuna

Cytoplasmic extensions

Osteon

Matrix

Cytoplasmic extensions

Osteocyte

(d) The bone matrix is rigid and hard. Osteocytes become trapped within lacunae but communicate with one another by way of cytoplasmic extensions that extend through tiny canals.

FIGURE 39-2 *Animated* Bone

the blood vessels constrict, raising blood pressure. Each spindle-shaped smooth muscle fiber contains a single, central nucleus.

Nervous tissue controls muscles and glands

Nervous tissue consists of neurons and glial cells. **Neurons** are specialized for receiving and transmitting signals. **Glial cells** sup-port and nourish the neurons, destroy pathogens, and modulate transmission of impulses (**FIG. 39-3**).

A typical neuron has a **cell body** containing the nucleus as well as two types of cytoplasmic extensions (discussed in Chapter 41). **Dendrites** are cytoplasmic extensions specialized for receiving signals and transmitting them to the cell body. The single **axon** transmits signals, called *nerve impulses,* away from the cell body.

TABLE 39-3   Muscle Tissues

	Skeletal	Cardiac	Smooth
Location	Attached to skeleton	Walls of heart	Walls of stomach, intestines, etc.
Type of control	Voluntary	Involuntary	Involuntary
Shape of fibers	Elongated, cylindrical, blunt ends	Elongated, cylindrical, fibers that branch and fuse	Elongated, spindle shaped, pointed ends
Striations	Present	Present	Absent
Number of nuclei per fiber	Many	One or two	One
Position of nuclei	Peripheral	Central	Central
Speed of contraction	Most rapid	Intermediate (varies)	Slowest
Resistance to fatigue (with repetitive contraction)	Least	Intermediate	Greatest

Skeletal muscle fibers — Nuclei, Striations

Cardiac muscle fibers — Nuclei, Intercalated discs

Smooth muscle fibers — Nuclei

Ed Reschke

100 μm

FIGURE 39-3 LM of nervous tissue

Neurons transmit information in the form of electrochemical signals. Glial cells support, protect, and nourish neurons. They also communicate and help regulate neural function.

Neurons — Dendrite — Nuclei of glial cells — Axon

Axons range in length from 1 or 2 mm to more than a meter. Those extending from the spinal cord down the arm or leg in a human, for example, may be a meter or more in length.

Certain neurons receive signals from the external or internal environment and transmit them to the spinal cord and brain. Other neurons relay, process, or store information. Still others transmit signals from the brain and spinal cord to the muscles and glands. Neurons communicate at junctions called **synapses.** A **nerve** consists of a great many neurons bound together by connective tissue.

In this chapter, we have focused on normal tissues. For a discussion of some abnormal tissues, see *Inquiring About: Unwelcome Tissues: Cancers.*

Tissues and organs make up the organ systems of the body

Tissues associate to form **organs.** Although an animal organ may be composed mainly of one type of tissue, other types are needed to support, protect, provide a blood supply, and transmit information. For example, the heart is mainly cardiac muscle tissue, but its chambers are lined with endothelium and its walls contain blood vessels made of endothelium, smooth muscle, and connective tissue. The heart also has nerves that transmit information and help regulate the rate and strength of its contractions.

An organized group of tissues and organs that together perform a specialized set of functions make up an **organ system.** Working together in a very coordinated way, organ systems perform the functions required by the **organism.** We can identify 11 major organ systems that work together to carry out the physiological processes of a mammal: **integumentary, skeletal, muscular, digestive, cardiovascular, immune (lymphatic), respiratory, urinary, nervous, endocrine,** and **reproductive systems. FIGURE 39-4** summarizes the principal organs and functions of each organ system.

Review

- What are the main differences in structure and function between epithelial tissue and connective tissue?
- What type of tissue lines the air sacs of the lungs? How is its structure adapted to its function?
- What are some differences between the three types of muscle tissue? How is the structure of each type adapted for its function?
- What are the main functions of each of the following organ systems? (1) respiratory, (2) urinary, and (3) endocrine? (Consult Fig. 39-4 for help.)

UNWELCOME TISSUES: CANCERS

A **neoplasm** ("new growth") is an abnormal mass of cells. A **tumor** is a neoplasm that has formed a lump. A neoplasm may be benign or malignant (cancerous). A benign ("kind") neoplasm tends to grow slowly, and its cells stay together. Because benign tumors form masses with distinct borders, they can usually be removed surgically. A **malignant** ("wicked") **neoplasm,** or **cancer,** usually grows much more rapidly and invasively than a benign tumor.

In Chapter 17 you learned that cancer results from abnormal expression of specific genes critical for cell division (see Fig. 17-20). Most cancer cells divide in an uncontrolled way. Unlike normal cells, which respect one another's boundaries and form tissues in an orderly, organized manner, cancer cells grow helter-skelter and infiltrate normal tissues. They apparently no longer receive or respond appropriately to signals from surrounding cells; communication is lacking (see figure).

When a cancer cell multiplies, all the cells derived from it are also abnormal. Unlike the cells of benign neoplasms, cancer cells do not retain normal structural features. Cancers that develop from connective tissues or muscle are referred to as **sarcomas.** Most human cancers originate in epithelial tissue and are called **carcinomas.** This group includes breast, prostate, colon, lung cancer, and most ovarian cancers.

Death from cancer results from the effects of **metastasis,** migration of cancer cells through blood or lymph channels to other parts of the body. Once there, cancer cells multiply, forming new malignant neoplasms that interfere with the normal functions of the tissues being invaded. Cancer often spreads so rapidly and extensively that surgeons cannot locate or remove all the malignant masses.

Solid tumors, which account for more than 85% of cancer deaths, require blood vessels to ensure delivery of nourishment and oxygen. Some neoplasms grow to several millimeters in diameter and then enter a dormant stage, which may last for months or even years. Eventually, cancer cells release a chemical substance that stimulates nearby blood vessels to develop new capillaries. These blood vessels grow into the abnormal mass of cells. Nourished by its new blood supply, the neoplasm begins to grow rapidly. Newly formed blood vessels have leaky walls that provide a route for metastasis. Malignant cells enter the blood

through these walls and are transported to new sites.

Worldwide, cancer causes more than seven million deaths each year. In the United States, cancer is the second leading cause of death. One in three people in the United States develops cancer at some time in his or her life. Currently, the key to survival is early diagnosis and treatment with some combination of surgery, hormonal treatment, radiation therapy, chemotherapy, inhibitors that suppress development of new blood vessels, immunotherapy, and targeted therapies. Many new treatments are under investigation, including agents that inhibit the development of new blood vessels. Immunotherapy for cancer will be discussed in Chapter 45. Cancer is a large family of closely related diseases (there are hundreds of distinct varieties), and treatment must be tailored to the particular type of cancer.

Alleles of some genes appear to affect an individual's level of tolerance to *carcinogens.* Most cancers are thought to be triggered by **carcinogens,** cancer-producing agents, in the environment and by diet and lifestyle. You can decrease risk of developing cancer by following these recommendations:

1. Do not smoke or use tobacco. Smoking is responsible for more than 80% of lung

50 µm

Moredum Animal Health LTD / Photo Researchers, Inc.

When cancer cells multiply, they invade normal tissues and interfere with their functions. This SEM shows a mass of malignant cells (*pink*) in the air sac in the center. Cancer cells that have separated from the main tumor can be seen in other air sacs. Microvilli on the surface of the cancer cells give them a fuzzy appearance.

cancer cases, and it increases the risk for many other cancers.

2. Avoid prolonged exposure to the sun. When in the sun, use sunscreen or sunblock. Exposure to the sun is responsible for almost all the 400,000 cases of skin cancer reported each year in the United States alone.

3. Eat a healthy diet, including fresh, unprocessed fruits, vegetables, and grains. Limit intake of red meat. Avoid smoked, salt-cured, and nitrite-cured foods. Limit intake of alcoholic beverages. Reduce intake of foods and drinks that contribute to weight gain. Obesity increases the risk of cancer.

4. Exercise. Physical inactivity has been linked with increased risk of colon, breast, and other cancers.

5. Avoid unnecessary exposure to X-rays.

6. Self-examination/screening can lead to early diagnosis. Women should examine their breasts each month, have regular mammograms, and obtain annual Papanicolaou (Pap) and human papilloma virus (HPV) tests. Certain HPV strains can cause cervical cancer; vaccines are now available.

7. Self-examination/screening. Men should regularly examine their testes and have prostate examinations yearly after age 50. They should also have the prostate-specific antigen (PSA) blood test. These routine tests detect cancer at an early, more treatable stage.

8. Self-examination/screening. Beginning at age 50, both men and women should be screened for colorectal cancer. Detection and removal of polyps (benign growths that can become malignant) can prevent cancer.

9. Genetic testing. If you have a family history of certain cancers, you may be at higher risk genetically for cancer. Genetic tests are now available to determine if you have mutations in the BRCA1 or BRCA2 genes, which increase risk for breast, ovarian, and pancreatic cancers. Mutations in several other genes indicate increased risk for colon, uterine, stomach, and urinary tract cancer. If you are at increased risk for cancer, a genetic counselor can advise you of measures you can take to reduce that risk.

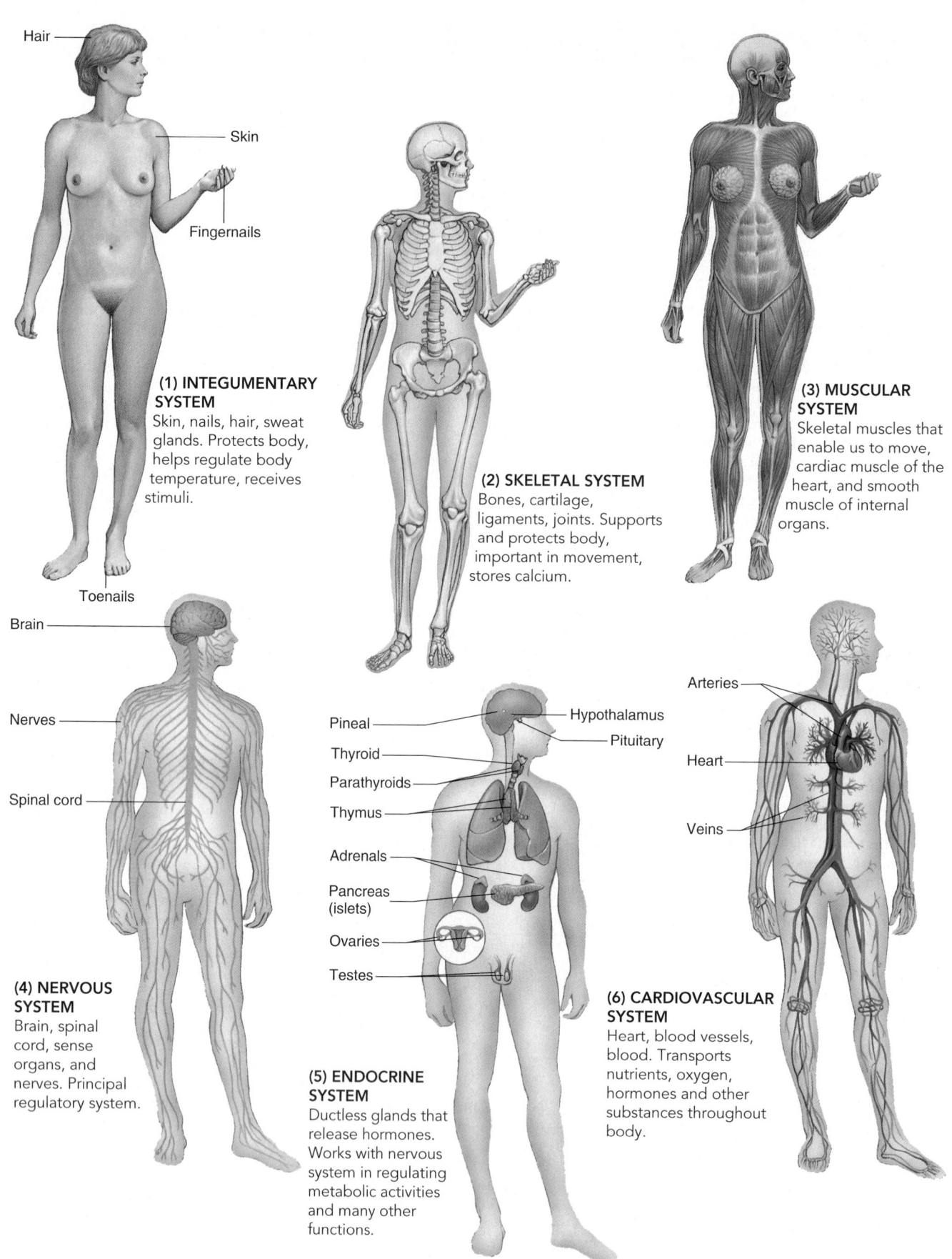

(1) INTEGUMENTARY SYSTEM
Skin, nails, hair, sweat glands. Protects body, helps regulate body temperature, receives stimuli.

Hair

Skin

Fingernails

Toenails

(2) SKELETAL SYSTEM
Bones, cartilage, ligaments, joints. Supports and protects body, important in movement, stores calcium.

(3) MUSCULAR SYSTEM
Skeletal muscles that enable us to move, cardiac muscle of the heart, and smooth muscle of internal organs.

(4) NERVOUS SYSTEM
Brain, spinal cord, sense organs, and nerves. Principal regulatory system.

Brain

Nerves

Spinal cord

(5) ENDOCRINE SYSTEM
Ductless glands that release hormones. Works with nervous system in regulating metabolic activities and many other functions.

Pineal

Hypothalamus

Thyroid

Pituitary

Parathyroids

Thymus

Adrenals

Pancreas (islets)

Ovaries

Testes

(6) CARDIOVASCULAR SYSTEM
Heart, blood vessels, blood. Transports nutrients, oxygen, hormones and other substances throughout body.

Arteries

Heart

Veins

FIGURE 39-4 *Animated* The principal organ systems of the human body

(7) IMMUNE/LYMPHATIC SYSTEM
Lymphatic vessels, lymph, lymph nodes, spleen, thymus, tonsils. Returns excess tissue fluid to blood, absorbs lipids, defends against disease.

Thymus
Thoracic duct
Lymph node
Spleen
Lymph vessels

(8) RESPIRATORY SYSTEM
Lungs and air passageways. Supplies oxygen to blood and excretes carbon dioxide.

Nasal cavity
Pharynx (throat)
Lungs
Oral cavity (mouth)
Larynx (voice box)
Bronchus
Diaphragm

(9) DIGESTIVE SYSTEM
Digestive tract and glands that secrete digestive juices. Processes food, eliminates wastes.

Pharynx
Oral cavity
Salivary glands
Esophagus
Liver
Stomach
Gallbladder
Pancreas
Small intestine
Large intestine
Rectum
Anus

(10) URINARY SYSTEM
Kidneys, urinary bladder, and associated ducts. Kidneys remove metabolic wastes and excess materials from blood; produce urine. Helps regulate blood chemistry.

Kidney
Ureter
Urinary bladder
Urethra

(11) MALE AND FEMALE REPRODUCTIVE SYSTEMS
Both consist of gonads and associated structures. Sexual reproduction; maintains sexual characteristics.

Oviduct
Ovary
Uterus
Vagina

Prostate gland
Vas deferens
Penis
Testis

39.2 REGULATING THE INTERNAL ENVIRONMENT

To survive and function, animals must regulate the composition of the fluids that bathe their cells. They must maintain pH and internal temperature within relatively narrow limits. The body must also maintain the appropriate concentration of nutrients, oxygen, and other gases, ions, and compounds needed for metabolism at all times.

Cells, tissues, organs, and organ systems work together to maintain appropriate conditions in the body. The balanced internal environment is referred to as **homeostasis.** Homeostasis is a basic concept in physiology. First coined by U.S. physiologist Walter Cannon, the word *homeostasis* is derived from the Greek *homoios,* meaning "same," and *stasis,* "standing." Although, the internal environment never really stays the same, it is a dynamic equilibrium in which conditions are maintained within narrow limits, which we call a **steady state.** The control processes that maintain these conditions are **homeostatic mechanisms.**

Stressors, changes in the internal or external environment that affect normal conditions within the body, continuously challenge homeostasis. An internal condition that moves out of its homeostatic range (either too high or too low) causes **stress.** An organism functions effectively because homeostatic mechanisms continuously operate to manage stress.

Many animals are **conformers** for certain environmental conditions. Some of their internal states vary with changes in their surroundings. For example, most marine invertebrates conform to the salinity of the surrounding sea water. Mammals are superb **regulators.** They have complex homeostatic mechanisms that maintain relatively constant internal conditions despite changes in the outside environment. How do homeostatic mechanisms work? Many are **feedback systems,** sometimes called "biofeedback systems."

Negative feedback systems restore homeostasis

In a **negative feedback system,** a change in some steady state (for example, normal body temperature) triggers a response that counteracts, or reverses, the change. A **sensor** detects a change, a deviation from the normal condition, or **set point.** The sensor signals an **integrator,** or control center. Based on the input of the sensor, the integrator activates homeostatic mechanisms that restore the steady state (**FIG. 39-5**). The response counteracts the inappropriate change, thereby restoring the steady state.

Note that in a negative feedback system, the response of the integrator is *opposite* (negative) to the output of the sensor. When some condition varies too far from the steady state (either too high or too low), a control system using negative feedback brings the condition back to the steady state. For example, when the glucose concentration in the blood *decreases* below its homeostatic level, negative feedback systems *increase* its concentration. Most homeostatic mechanisms in the body are negative feedback systems.

Let us discuss a specific example of negative feedback systems: heat regulation. The temperature-regulating system in the human body is somewhat similar to how you regulate temperature in your home. You might set a particular room temperature on your ther-

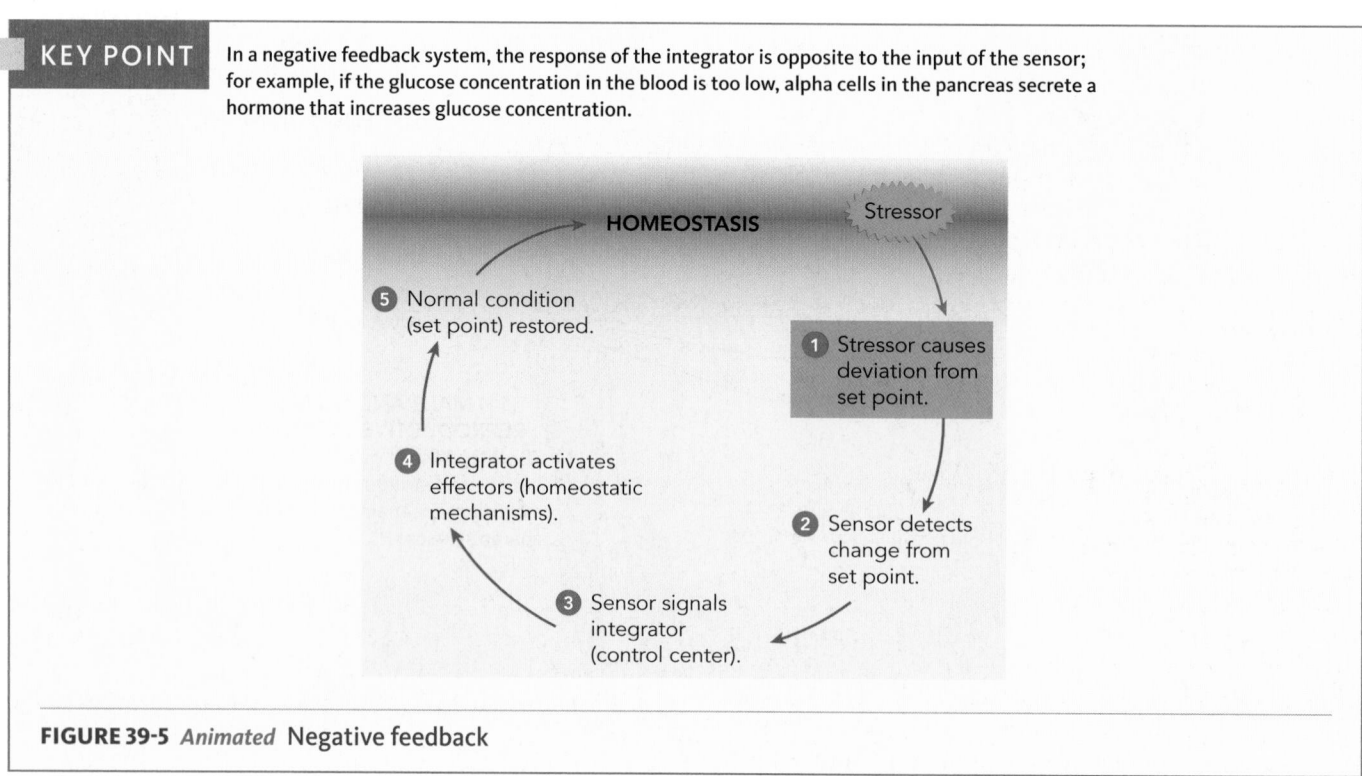

KEY POINT In a negative feedback system, the response of the integrator is opposite to the input of the sensor; for example, if the glucose concentration in the blood is too low, alpha cells in the pancreas secrete a hormone that increases glucose concentration.

HOMEOSTASIS

Stressor

⑤ Normal condition (set point) restored.

① Stressor causes deviation from set point.

④ Integrator activates effectors (homeostatic mechanisms).

② Sensor detects change from set point.

③ Sensor signals integrator (control center).

FIGURE 39-5 *Animated* Negative feedback

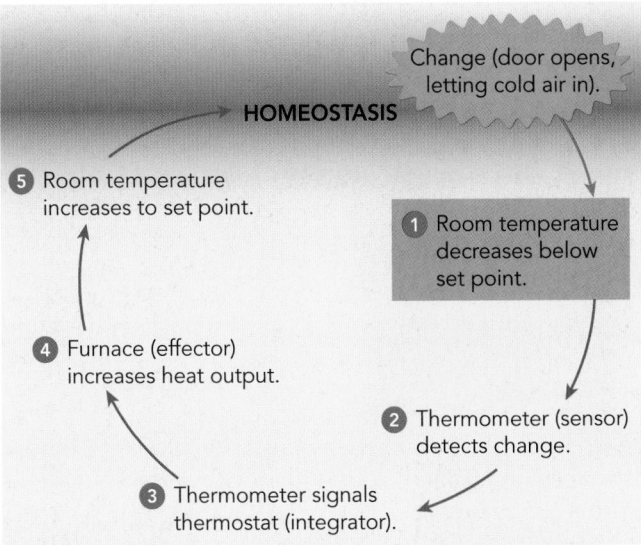

(a) **Regulation of room temperature.**

(b) **Regulation of body temperature.**

FIGURE 39-6 Negative feedback in temperature regulation
Note that the diagram in **(b)** is highly simplified. Figure 39-9 shows greater detail.

mostat. If the temperature in the room falls, the thermometer in the thermostat acts as a sensor that detects a change, or deviation, from the set point (**FIG. 39-6a**). The thermometer sends a signal to the thermostat, which then acts as an integrator, or control center. The thermostat compares the sensor's input with the set point. The thermostat then signals the furnace, which is the **effector** in this system. An effector is the device, organ, or process that helps restore the steady state. The furnace increases its heat output, a corrective response that brings the room temperature back to the set point. The thermometer no longer detects a change from the set point, so the thermostat and furnace are switched off.

Basically, the negative feedback system that regulates body temperature is similar, as shown in **FIGURE 39-6b**. When body temperature decreases below normal limits, specialized nerve cells (sensors) signal the temperature-regulating center in the hypothalamus of the brain (the integrator). The integrator activates effectors that bring the temperature back to the set point. The return to normal temperature signals the sensors, and the temperature-regulating center switches off the effectors.

A few positive feedback systems operate in the body

In a **positive feedback system,** a change in some steady state sets off a response that intensifies (rather than reverses) the changing condition. Although some positive feedback mechanisms are beneficial, they do not maintain homeostasis. For example, a positive feedback cycle operates during the birth of a baby. As the baby's head pushes against the cervix (lower part of uterus), a reflex action causes the uterus to contract. The contraction forces the head against the cervix again, stimulating another contraction, and the positive feedback cycle repeats again and again until the baby is born. Some positive feedback sequences, such as those that deepen circulatory shock

following severe hemorrhage, can disrupt steady states and lead to death. A simplified example is shown in **FIGURE 39-7**.

Homeostatic mechanisms maintain the internal environment within the physiological limits that support life. As you continue your study of animal processes, you will learn many ways in which organ systems interact to maintain the steady state of the organism. Although the nervous and endocrine systems play major roles, all organ systems participate in these regulatory processes. In the next section, we discuss some specific homeostatic mechanisms that help regulate body temperature.

Review

- What is the basic difference between negative and positive feedback systems?

39.3 THERMOREGULATION

◼ LEARNING OBJECTIVES

8   Compare the costs and benefits of ectothermy.
9   Compare the costs and benefits of endothermy, and describe strategies animals use to adjust to challenging temperature changes.

Many animals have elaborate homeostatic mechanisms for regulating body temperature. Some are physiological, and others are structural or behavioral. **Thermoregulation** is the process of maintaining body temperature within certain limits despite changes in the surrounding temperature. Animals produce heat as a byproduct of metabolic activities. Body temperature is determined by the rate at which heat is produced and the rate at which heat is lost to, or gained from, the outside environment.

KEY POINT   Positive feedback intensifies the change taking place, moving conditions further away from homeostasis; in some situations, such as hemorrhage, the results can be fatal.

FIGURE 39-7 Positive feedback

In positive feedback, the changes that occur increase the deviation from the set point. Conditions move further from the normal range. Loss of blood decreases blood pressure. Less blood reaches the heart, so heart function decreases. The resulting decrease in cardiac output further decreases blood pressure, bringing about conditions farther from homeostasis.

The strategies for maintaining body temperature that are available to an animal may restrict the type of environment it can inhabit. Each species has an optimal environmental temperature range. Some animals, such as snowshoe hares, snowy owls, and weasels, can survive in cold arctic regions. Others, such as the Cape ground squirrel, which inhabits South Africa, are adapted to hot tropical climates. Although some animals can survive at temperature extremes, most survive only within moderate temperature ranges.

Ectotherms absorb heat from their surroundings

Ectotherms are animals that depend on the environment for their body heat. Their body temperature is determined mainly by the changing temperature of their surroundings. Most of the heat for their thermoregulation comes from the sun. You may be surprised to learn that most animals are ectotherms.

A benefit of ectothermy is that very little energy is used to maintain a high metabolic rate. In fact, an ectotherm's metabolic rate tends to change with the weather. As a result, ectotherms have a much lower daily energy expenditure than do endotherms. They survive on less food and convert more of the energy in their food to growth and reproduction. Ectothermy also has costs. One disadvantage is that daily and seasonal temperature conditions may limit activity.

Many ectotherms use behavioral strategies to adjust body temperature. For example, lizards may keep warm by burrowing in the soil at night. During the day, lizards take in heat by basking in the sun, orienting their bodies to expose the maximum surface area to the sun's rays (**FIG. 39-8a**). Many animals migrate to warmer climates during the winter. Another behavioral strategy for regulating temperature is *hibernation.*

Some insects use a combination of structural, behavioral, and physiological mechanisms to regulate body temperature. The "furry" body of the moth helps conserve body heat. When a moth prepares for flight, it contracts its flight muscles with little movement of its wings. The metabolic heat generated enables the moth to sustain the intense metabolic activity needed for flight.

Endotherms derive heat from metabolic processes

Birds and mammals, as well as some species of fish (e.g., tuna and some sharks) and some insects, are **endotherms:** they have homeostatic mechanisms that maintain body temperature despite changes in the external temperature. The most important benefit of endothermy is the high metabolic rate, which can be as much as six times higher than that of ectotherms. Their constant body temperature allows a higher rate of enzyme activity than is possible for ectotherms living in the same habitat. Endotherms respond more rapidly to internal and external stimuli and can be active even in low winter temperatures. However, these animals must pay the high energy cost of thermoregulation during times when they are inactive. You must maintain your body temperature even when you are asleep.

Endotherms have structural adaptations for maintaining body temperature. For example, the insulating feathers of birds, hair of mammals, and insulating layers of fat in birds and mammals reduce heat loss from the body. Birds and mammals also have behavioral adaptations for maintaining body temperature. The Cape ground squirrel positions its tail to shade its body from the direct rays of the sun. Elephants spray themselves with cool water.

Endotherms have a variety of physiological mechanisms for maintaining temperature homeostasis. They regulate heat production and regulate heat exchange with the environment. Most of their body heat comes from their own metabolic processes (see *Inquiring About: Electron Transport and Heat,* in Chapter 8).

In mammals, receptors located in the hypothalamus of the brain and in the spinal cord regulate temperature. Heat from metabolic activities can be increased directly or can be increased indirectly by the action of hormones (such as thyroid hormones) that increase metabolic rate. Heat production is increased by contracting muscles, and in cold weather many animals shiver.

When body temperature rises, birds and many mammals pant and some mammals sweat (**FIG. 39-8b**). These processes provide fluid for evaporation, the conversion of a liquid, such as sweat, to water vapor. (Recall from Chapter 2 that when molecules enter the vapor phase, they take their heat energy with them.) Heat transfers from the body to the surroundings, resulting in evaporative cooling.

In the human body, about 2.5 million sweat glands secrete sweat. As sweat evaporates from the skin surface, body temperature decreases. Constriction and dilation of capillaries in the skin are also homeostatic mechanisms for regulating body temperature.

In humans, when body temperature increases above normal, specialized nerve cells signal the temperature-regulating center in the hypothalamus (**FIG. 39-9**). This center sends messages, by way of nerves to the sweat glands, which increase sweat secretion. At the same time, the hypothalamus sends messages to smooth muscle in the walls of blood vessels in the skin that cause them to dilate. More blood circulates through the skin, bringing heat to the body surface. The skin acts as a heat radiator that allows heat to radiate from the body surface into the environment. These homeostatic mechanisms help return body temperature to normal.

When body temperature decreases below normal, the hypothalamus signals the anterior pituitary gland to release a hormone that signals the thyroid gland. Secretion of thyroid hormones increases, which raises metabolic rate. Body tissues increase heat production. The hypothalamus also sends neural signals that cause blood vessels in the skin to constrict. As a result, less heat is brought to the body surface. In addition, nerves signal muscles to shiver or let you move muscles voluntarily to increase body temperature.

Many animals adjust to challenging temperature changes

Animals adjust to seasonal changes, a process called **acclimatization**. A familiar example is the thickening of a dog's coat in the winter. As water temperature decreases during fall and winter, a trout's enzyme systems decrease their level of activity, allowing the trout to remain active at the lowest metabolic cost.

When stressed by cold, many small endotherms sink into **torpor**, a short-term state in which metabolic rate decreases, sometimes dramatically. Torpor saves the energy that the animal would use to maintain a high body temperature. Instead, body temperature decreases below normal levels. The decrease in body temperature is brought about by a decrease in the temperature set point in the hypothalamus. Heart and respiratory rates decrease, and animals are less responsive to external stimulation. Daily torpor occurs in some small endotherms, for example, hummingbirds and shrews. We can think of torpor as an adaptive hypothermia that helps animals survive during times of cold temperatures.

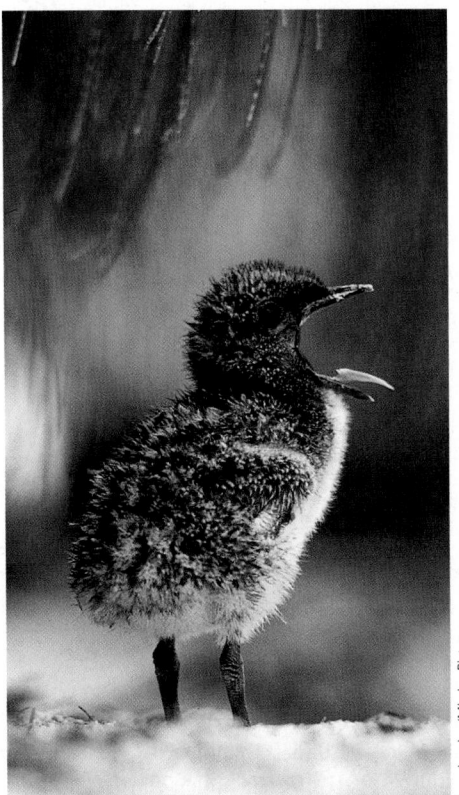

(a) **Ectotherm.** The rainbow agama (*Agama agama*) increases its body temperature by sunning itself. This insect-eating lizard was photographed in Serengeti National Park, Tanzania.

FIGURE 39-8 Behavioral adaptations for thermoregulation

(b) **Endotherm.** The body temperature of this baby sooty tern (*Sterna fuscata*) is reduced as heat leaves the body through its open mouth. Photographed in Hawaii.

Richard J. Green/Photo Researchers, Inc.

Frans Lanting/Minden Pictures

The hypothalamus maintains homeostasis of body temperature by activating mechanisms that cool (*upper arrows*) or warm (*lower arrows*) the body.

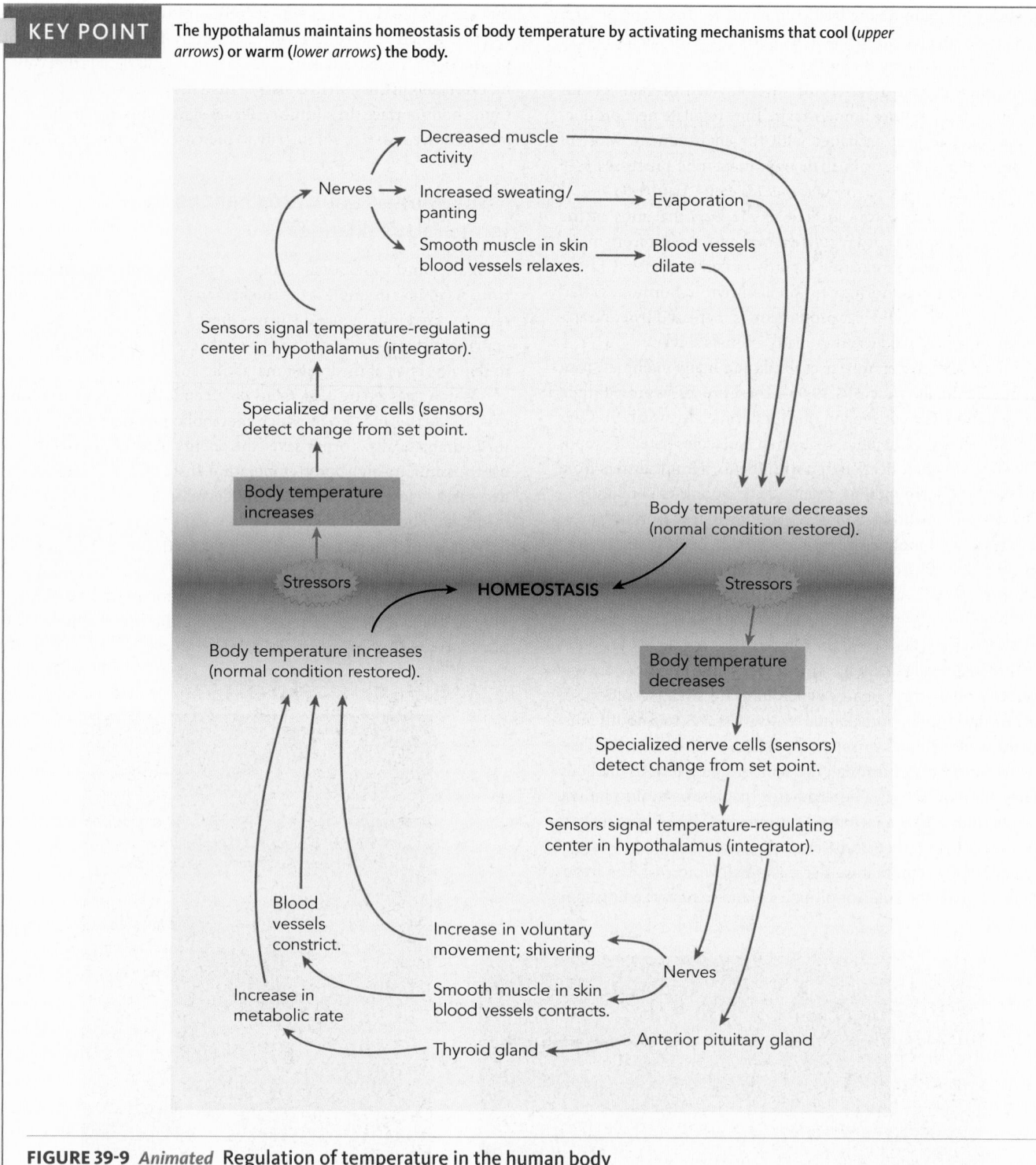

FIGURE 39-9 *Animated* Regulation of temperature in the human body

Hibernation is long-term torpor in response to winter cold and scarcity of food. Animals that hibernate store unsaturated fats as energy sources. **Estivation** is a state of torpor caused by lack of food or water during periods of high temperature. During estivation some mammals retreat to their burrows. The cactus mouse enters a state of hibernation during the winter in response to cold and scarcity of food. In summer, it estivates in response to lack of either food or water.

Review

- How do ectotherms adjust body temperature? What are some costs and benefits of ectothermy?

- What are some costs and benefits of endothermy? How is body temperature regulated in humans? Draw a diagram to illustrate your answer.

- How do hibernation and estivation differ?

39.1 *(page 822)*

1 Compare the structure and function of the four main kinds of animal tissues: epithelial, connective, muscle, and nervous tissues.

- A **tissue** consists of a group of similarly specialized cells that associate to perform specific functions. **Epithelial tissue (epithelium)** forms a continuous layer, or sheet, of cells covering a body surface or lining a body cavity. Epithelial tissue functions in protection, absorption, secretion, and sensation.

- **Connective tissue** consists of relatively few cells separated by an **intercellular substance,** composed of **fibers** scattered throughout a **matrix.** The intercellular substance contains three types of fibers.

- Connective tissue contains specialized cells such as **fibroblasts and macrophages.** Connective tissue joins other tissues of the body, supports the body and its organs, and protects underlying organs.

- **Muscle tissue** consists of cells specialized to contract. Each cell is an elongated muscle fiber containing many contractile units called **myofibrils. Nervous tissue** consists of elongated cells called neurons, specialized for transmitting impulses, and **glial cells,** which support and nourish the neurons.

2 Compare the main types of epithelial tissue and describe their functions.

- Epithelial cells may be **squamous, cuboidal,** or **columnar** in shape. Epithelial tissue may be **simple, stratified,** or **pseudostratified** (summarized in Table 39-1).

- Simple squamous epithelium lines blood vessels and the air sacs in the lungs; it permits exchange of materials by diffusion. Simple cuboidal and columnar epithelia line passageways and are specialized for secretion and absorption. Stratified squamous epithelium forms the outer layer of the skin and lines passageways into the body; it provides protection. Pseudostratified epithelium also lines passageways and protects underlying tissues.

- Some epithelial tissue is specialized to form **glands. Goblet cells** are unicellular glands that secrete mucus. Goblet cells are **exocrine glands** that secrete their product through a duct onto an exposed epithelial surface. In contrast, **endocrine glands** release hormones into the **interstitial fluid** or blood.

- An **epithelial membrane** consists of a sheet of epithelial tissue and a layer of underlying connective tissue. A **mucous membrane** lines a cavity that opens to the outside of the body. A **serous membrane** lines a body cavity that does not open to the outside.

3 Compare the main types of connective tissue and describe their functions.

- The cells of connective tissue are embedded in an intercellular substance that consists of microscopic **collagen fibers, elastic fibers,** and **reticular fibers** (thin branched fibers) scattered through a **matrix,** a thin gel of polysaccharides. **Loose connective tissue** consists of fibers running in various directions through a semifluid matrix; it forms a covering for nerves, blood vessels, and muscles.

- **Dense connective tissue** is strong but less flexible than loose connective tissue. It forms **tendons,** cords that connect muscles to bones, and **ligaments,** cables that connect bones to one another.

- **Elastic connective tissue** consists of bundles of parallel elastic fibers; it is found in lung tissue and in walls of large arteries. **Reticular connective tissue,** which consists of interlacing reticular fibers, forms a supporting framework for many organs.

- **Adipose tissue** is made up of fat cells; it is found along with loose connective tissue in subcutaneous tissue.

- **Cartilage** consists of **chondrocytes** that lie in **lacunae,** small cavities in a hard matrix. **Osteocytes** secrete and maintain the matrix of **bone.** Unlike cartilage, bone is quite vascular. Cartilage and bone form the skeleton of vertebrates.

- **Blood** and **lymph** are circulating tissues that help various parts of an animal communicate with one another. The intercellular substances of blood and lymph are more fluid than those of other tissues.

4 Contrast the three types of muscle tissue and describe their functions.

- **Skeletal muscle** is **striated** and under voluntary control. Each elongated, cylindrical **muscle fiber** has several nuclei. When skeletal muscles contract, they move parts of the body.

- **Cardiac muscle** is also striated, but its contractions are involuntary. Its elongated, cylindrical fibers branch and fuse; each fiber has one or two central nuclei. When this muscle contracts, the heart pumps the blood.

- **Smooth muscle** contracts involuntarily; its elongated, spindle-shaped fibers lack striations. Each fiber has a single central nucleus. Smooth muscle is responsible for movement of body organs; for example, it pushes food through the digestive tract.

5 Relate the structure of the neuron to its function.

- The elongated neuron is adapted for receiving and transmitting information. **Dendrites** receive signals and transmit them to the **cell body.** The **axon** transmits signals away from the cell body to other neurons or to a muscle or gland. A **synapse** is a junction between neurons.

6 Briefly describe the organ systems of a mammal and summarize the functions of each organ system.

- Tissues and **organs** work together, forming **organ systems.** In mammals, 11 organ systems work together to carry out the functions required by the **organism.** These include the **integumentary, skeletal, muscular, nervous, endocrine, cardiovascular, immune (lymphatic), respiratory, digestive, urinary,** and **reproductive systems** (summarized in Figure 39-4). Each organ system functions to maintain homeostasis.

CENGAGENOW™ Watch body systems work together by clicking on the figure in CengageNOW.

39.2 *(page 834)*

7 Define *homeostasis,* and contrast negative and positive feedback systems.

- **Homeostasis** is the balanced internal environment, or steady state. The control processes that maintain these conditions are **homeostatic mechanisms,** mainly **negative feedback systems.** When a stressor causes a change in some steady state, a response is triggered that counteracts the change. A **sensor** detects a change, a deviation from the desired condition, or **set point.** The sensor signals an **integrator,** or control center. Based on the output of the sensor, the integrator activates one or more **effectors,** organs or processes that restore the steady state.

- In a **positive feedback system,** a deviation from the steady state sets off a series of changes that intensify (rather than reverse) the changes.

39.3 *(page 835)*

8 Compare the costs and benefits of ectothermy.

- Animals have structural, behavioral, and physiological strategies for **thermoregulation,** the process of maintaining body temperature within certain limits despite changes in the surrounding temperature.
- In **ectotherms,** body temperature depends to a large extent on the temperature of the environment. Many ectotherms use behavioral strategies to adjust body temperatures. A benefit of ectothermy is that very little energy is used to maintain the metabolic rate. A disadvantage is that activity may be limited by daily and seasonal temperature conditions.

9 Compare the costs and benefits of endothermy, and describe strategies animals use to adjust to challenging temperature changes.

- **Endotherms** have homeostatic mechanisms for regulating body temperature within a narrow range. The most important benefit of endothermy is a high metabolic rate. Another advantage is that constant body temperature allows a higher rate of enzyme activity. Many endotherms are active even in low winter temperatures. A disadvantage of endothermy is its high energy cost.
- **Acclimatization** is the process of adjustment to seasonal changes.
- When challenged by a drop in surrounding temperature, many small endotherms enter a state of torpor. **Torpor** is an adaptive hypothermia; body temperature is maintained below normal levels. **Hibernation** is long-term torpor in response to winter cold. **Estivation** is torpor caused by lack of food or water during summer heat.

CENGAGENOW™ Explore negative feedback and temperature regulation in humans and other animals by clicking on the figures in CengageNOW.

TEST YOUR UNDERSTANDING

1. A group of closely associated cells that carry out specific functions is (a) a colony (b) a tissue (c) an organ system (d) an effector (e) a homeostatic mechanism

2. Epithelial cells that produce and secrete a product into a duct form (a) an endocrine gland (b) an exocrine gland (c) a pseudostratified membrane (d) an endocrine or exocrine gland (e) a serous membrane

3. A serous membrane (a) lines a body cavity that does not open to the outside of the body (b) consists of loose connective tissue (c) has a framework of reticular connective tissue (d) covers the body (e) lines the digestive and respiratory systems

4. Tissue that contains fibroblasts and a great deal of intercellular substance is (a) connective tissue (b) muscle tissue (c) nervous tissue (d) pseudostratified epithelium (e) simple squamous epithelium

5. Dense connective tissue is likely to be found in (a) the outer layer of skin (b) the framework of the lymph nodes (c) bone (d) the air sacs of lungs (e) tendons

6. Tissue that contracts and is striated and involuntary is (a) connective tissue (b) smooth muscle (c) skeletal muscle (d) pseudostratified (e) cardiac muscle

7. Glial cells are characteristic of (a) muscle that is striated and voluntary (b) cardiac muscle tissue (c) nervous tissue (d) stratified epithelium (e) loose connective tissue

8. The contractile elements in muscle tissue are (a) myofibrils (b) elastic fibers (c) collagen fibers (d) lacunae (e) dendrites

9. Which system has the homeostatic function of helping regulate volume and composition of blood and body fluids? (a) integumentary (b) muscular (c) reproductive (d) urinary (e) exocrine

10. Many homeostatic functions are maintained by (a) negative feedback systems (b) positive feedback systems (c) set points (d) stressors (e) exocrine glands

11. Which of the following is *not* true of torpor? (a) it is an adaptive state of low body temperature (b) the temperature set point in the hypothalamus decreases (c) metabolic rate increases (d) it is a strategy used by some endotherms (e) respiratory rate decreases

12. An ectotherm (a) has a higher rate of enzyme activity than a typical endotherm (b) has a variety of homeostatic mechanisms for regulating body temperature (c) depends on sensors in the hypothalamus to regulate temperature (d) may use behavioral strategies to help adjust body temperature (e) must expend more energy on thermoregulation than an endotherm

13. Identify and label the tissues. See Tables 39-1 and 39-2 to check your answers.

Ed Reschke/Peter Arnold, Inc.

CRITICAL THINKING

1. Imagine that all the epithelium in an animal, such as a human, suddenly disappeared. What effects might this have on the body and its ability to function?

2. What would connective tissue be like if it had no intercellular substance? What effect would the absence of intercellular substance have on the body?

3. A high concentration of carbon dioxide in the blood and interstitial fluid results in more rapid breathing. Explain this observation in terms of homeostasis.

4. **EVOLUTION LINK.** From an evolutionary perspective, why do you think most animals are ectotherms? (*Hint:* What are some benefits of ectothermy?)

5. **SCIENCE, TECHNOLOGY, AND SOCIETY.** Imagine that you are a healthcare professional. If a patient told you she had a family history of breast cancer, would you advise her to be genetically tested? Why or why not? What if you had a family history of cancer. Would you want to be tested?

 Additional questions are available in CengageNOW at www.cengage.com/login.

40 Protection, Support, and Movement

Stephen Dalton/NHPA

Grasshopper in midjump. The grasshopper (*Tropidacris dux*) uses powerful muscles in its hind legs to catapult itself into the air. Insect muscles attach to the exoskeleton.

KEY CONCEPTS

40.1 Many structures and processes have evolved in animals for protection, support, and movement. Epithelial coverings are adapted for protecting underlying tissues and may be specialized for gas exchange, sensory reception, secretion, or other functions.

40.2 Skeletal systems, whether they are hydrostatic skeletons, exoskeletons, or endoskeletons, are adapted for supporting and protecting the body and for transmitting mechanical forces important in movement.

40.3 Muscles are adapted for contracting; during contraction, energy from ATP is used to slide muscle filaments so that the muscle shortens. Body parts move when muscles pull on them.

In Chapter 39 we described animal tissues, organs, and organ systems, laying the foundation for the more detailed discussions in this and later chapters. Here we focus on epithelial coverings, skeletons, and muscles—structures that are closely interrelated in the functions of protection, support, and movement. In our survey of the animal kingdom (Chapters 30 to 32), we described many adaptations involving these structures. For example, we discussed how the arthropod *exoskeleton* contributes to the great biological success of insects. In this chapter we compare these systems in several animal groups and then focus on their structure and function in mammals.

The *epithelial coverings* of animals protect underlying tissues and have several other functions as well. One of the most interesting is secretion of peptides and other substances that kill harmful bacteria and certain other pathogens. Frogs and toads, in particular, secrete a variety of potent peptides that protect them against harmful bacteria, fungi, and protozoa. Secretions of the frog *Rana ridibanda* have been shown to kill "superbugs," such as MRSA (methicillin-resistant *Staphylococcus aureus;* see Chapter 25). The skin of amphibians is a promising potential source of new antibiotics and other drugs.

Most animals are also protected by a *skeletal system.* Whether it is a fluid-filled compartment, a shell, or a system of bones, the skeletal system protects internal organs and provides support for the body. The skeletal system and *muscular system* work together to produce movement. Muscle tissue is specialized to contract. Although a few animals remain rooted to one spot, sweeping their surroundings with tentacles, **locomotion**—movement from place to place in the environment—is characteristic of most animals. Muscles responsible for locomotion anchor to the skeleton, which gives them something firm on which to act. In most vertebrates, bones serve as levers that transmit the force necessary to move various parts of the body.

During the course of evolution, most animals have developed adaptations for dependable, rapid, and responsive movement. Animals creep, walk, run, jump, swim, or fly (see photograph). These adaptations enable them to find food and escape from predators. In complex animals, effective movement depends on the cooperation and interactions of several body systems, including the muscular, skeletal, nervous, circulatory, respiratory, and endocrine systems. The precisely regulated interactions among tissues, organs, and organ systems that make complex function and maintenance of homeostasis possible are a dynamic example of systems biology in action.

40.1 EPITHELIAL COVERINGS

◼ LEARNING OBJECTIVES

1 Compare the functions of the epithelial coverings of invertebrates and vertebrates.
2 Relate the structure of vertebrate skin to its functions.

Epithelial tissue covers all external and internal surfaces of the animal body. The structure and functions of the external epithelial covering are adapted to the animal's environment and lifestyle. In both invertebrates and vertebrates, epithelial coverings protect the body. Epithelial coverings may also be specialized for secretion, gas exchange, or temperature regulation, and typically contain receptors that receive sensory signals from the environment.

Invertebrate epithelium may secrete a cuticle

In many invertebrates, the outer epithelium is specialized to secrete protective or supportive layers of nonliving material. In insects and many other animals, the secreted material forms an outer covering called a **cuticle.** Some animals, including corals and mollusks, secrete a shell made mainly of calcium carbonate.

In many species, the epithelium contains cells that secrete lubricants or adhesives. Such cells may release odorous secretions used for communication or for marking trails. In other species, secretory cells produce toxins used for offense or defense. The earthworm epithelium secretes a lubricating mucus that promotes efficient diffusion of gases across the body wall and reduces friction during movement through the soil. Epithelial cells may be modified as sensory cells that are selectively sensitive to light; chemical stimuli; or mechanical stimuli, such as contact with an object, or pressure.

Vertebrate skin functions in protection and temperature regulation

The **integumentary system** of vertebrates includes the skin and structures that develop from it. In many fishes, in some reptiles, and in the anteating pangolin (a mammal; see Fig. 18-15c), skin has developed into a set of scales formidable enough to be considered armor. Even human skin has considerable strength. The thin, moist skin of many amphibians is adapted for gas exchange, as well as for defense.

Derivatives of skin differ considerably among vertebrates. Fishes have bony or toothlike scales. Amphibians have naked skin covered with mucus, and some species are equipped with poison glands. Reptiles have epidermal scales, mammals have hair, and birds have feathers that provide even more effective insulation than fur. The feathers of birds and the fur of mammals are insulating structures that help maintain body temperature by trapping heat in the body. Skin and its derivatives are often brilliantly colored in connection with courtship rituals, territorial displays, and other kinds of communication.

In mammals, structures derived from skin include claws (modified as fingernails and toenails in primates), hair, sweat glands, oil (sebaceous) glands, and several types of sensory receptors that give mammals the ability to feel pressure, temperature, and pain. The skin of mammals also contains mammary glands, specialized in females for secretion of milk.

In humans and other mammals, oil glands empty via short ducts into hair follicles. A **hair follicle** is the part of a hair below the skin surface, together with the surrounding epithelial tissue. Oil glands secrete **sebum,** a mixture of fats and waxes that inhibits the growth of harmful bacteria.

Although the skin of fishes, frogs, snakes, pelicans, and elephants appears very different, the basic structure of skin is the same in all vertebrates. The outer layer of skin, the **epidermis,** is a waterproof protective barrier. The epidermis consists of several strata, or sublayers. The deepest is **stratum basale,** and the most superficial is **stratum corneum (FIG. 40-1).** Pigment cells in stratum basale and in the dermis below produce **melanin,** a pigment that contributes to the color of the skin. In stratum basale, cells divide and are pushed outward as other cells are produced below them. Epidermal cells mature as they move toward the skin surface.

As they move toward the body surface, epidermal cells manufacture **keratin,** an elaborately coiled protein that gives the skin considerable mechanical strength and flexibility. Keratin is insoluble and serves as a diffusion barrier for the body surface. As epidermal cells move through stratum corneum, they die. When they reach the outer surface of the skin, they wear off and must be continuously replaced.

Beneath the epidermis lies the **dermis,** a dense, fibrous connective tissue made up mainly of collagen fibers (see Fig. 40-1). Collagen imparts strength and flexibility to the skin. The dermis also contains blood vessels that nourish the skin and sensory receptors for touch, pain, and temperature. Hair follicles and, in most mammals, sweat glands are embedded in the dermis. In birds and mammals, the dermis rests on a layer of **subcutaneous tissue** composed mainly of adipose tissue that insulates the body from outside temperature extremes.

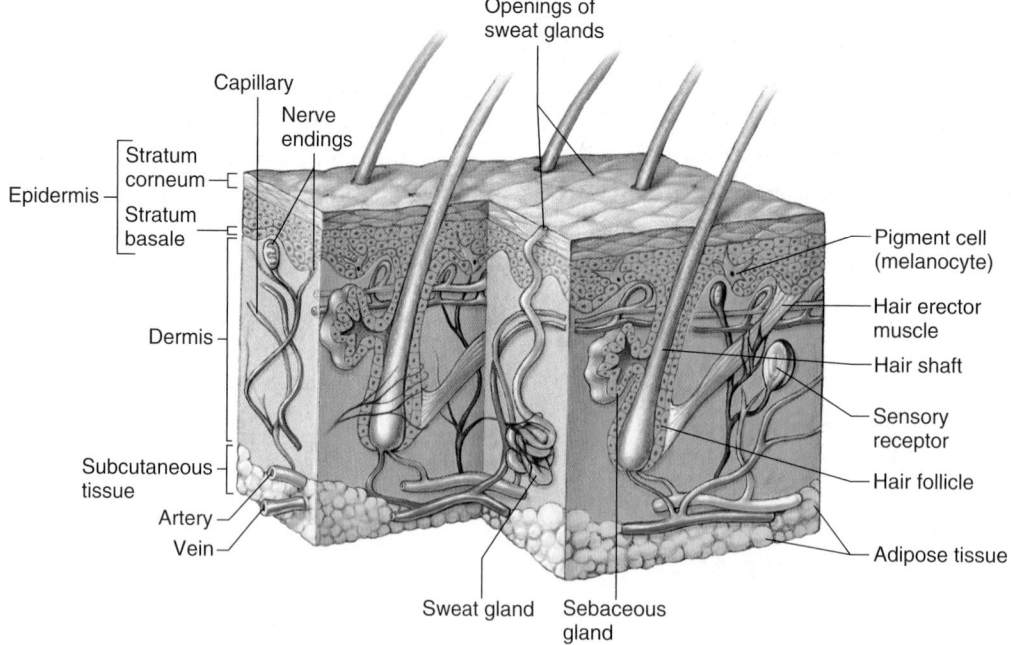

FIGURE 40-1 *Animated* **Human integumentary system**

The integumentary system of humans and other mammals is a complex organ system consisting of skin and structures such as hair and nails that are derived from the skin. Stratum basale consists of a single layer of dividing epithelial cells.

In humans, exposure to ultraviolet (UV) radiation, the short, invisible rays from the sun, causes the epidermis to thicken and stimulates pigment cells in the skin to produce melanin at an increased rate. Melanin is an important protective screen against the sun because it absorbs some of the harmful UV rays. An increase in melanin causes the skin to darken. The suntan so prized by sun worshippers is actually a sign that the skin has been exposed to too much UV radiation. When the melanin cannot absorb all the UV rays, the skin becomes inflamed, or sunburned. Dark-skinned people have more melanin and so suffer less sunburn, wrinkling, and skin cancer but still require protection from UV rays.

UV radiation damages DNA, causing mutations that lead to malignant transformation of cells (see Chapter 17). Skin cancer is the most common type of cancer in humans, and most cases of skin cancer are caused by excessive, chronic exposure to UV radiation. The incidence of *malignant melanoma,* the most lethal type of skin cancer, is increasing faster than any other type of cancer. Worldwide the number of cases has doubled during the past 20 years. Greater understanding of the Ras/ERK cell signaling pathway has led to research aimed at developing targeted drugs for treating melanoma. (Recall from Chapter 6 that this pathway is the main signaling cascade for cell division and differentiation.)

Review

- How are the body coverings of invertebrates and vertebrates alike?
- How is the structure of vertebrate skin related to its specific functions?
- What properties does keratin give human skin?
- What is the function of melanin?

40.2 SKELETAL SYSTEMS

■ LEARNING OBJECTIVES

3   Compare the structure and functions of different types of skeletal systems, including the hydrostatic skeleton, exoskeleton, and endoskeleton.

4   Describe the main divisions of the vertebrate skeleton and the bones that make up each division.

5   Describe the structure of a typical long bone and differentiate between endochondral and intramembranous bone development.

6   Compare the main types of vertebrate joints.

In addition to having an epithelial covering, many animals are protected by a **skeletal system** that forms the framework of the body. The skeleton also functions in locomotion. Muscles typically act on hard structures such as chitin or bone. These skeletal structures transmit and transform mechanical forces generated by muscle contraction into the variety of motions that animals make. Most invertebrates have *hydrostatic skeletons* or *exoskeletons.* (You may recall from Chapter 32 that echinoderms are an exception.) Vertebrates have *endoskeletons* of cartilage or bone.

In hydrostatic skeletons, body fluids transmit force

Many soft-bodied invertebrates have **hydrostatic skeletons** made of fluid-filled body compartments. Imagine an elongated balloon full of water. If you pull on the balloon, it lengthens and becomes thinner. It does the same if you squeeze it. Conversely, if you push the ends toward the center, the balloon shortens and thickens. Many invertebrates, including most cnidarians, flatworms, annelids, and roundworms, have hydrostatic skeletons that work something like a balloon filled with water. Fluid in a closed compartment of the body is held under pressure. When muscles in the compartment wall contract, they push against the tube of fluid. Because fluids cannot be compressed, the force is transmitted through the fluid, changing the shape and movement of the body.

In *Hydra* and other cnidarians, cells of the two body layers can contract. The contractile cells in the outer epidermal layer lie longitudinally, whereas the contractile cells of the inner layer (the gastrodermis) are arranged circularly around the central body axis (**FIG. 40-2**). The two groups of cells work in **antagonistic** fashion: what one can do, the other can undo. When the epidermal (longitudinal) layer contracts, the hydra shortens. Due to the fluid in the gastrovascular cavity, force is transmitted so that the hydra thickens as well. In contrast, when the inner (circular) layer contracts, the hydra thins and its fluid contents force it to lengthen.

Mechanically, the hydra is a bag of fluid. The fluid acts as a hydrostatic skeleton because it transmits force when the contractile cells contract against it. (Although technically not a closed compartment, the gastrovascular cavity functions as a hydrostatic skeleton because its opening is small.) Hydrostatic skeletons permit only crude mass movements of the body or its appendages. Delicate movements are difficult because force tends to be transmitted equally in all directions throughout the entire fluid-filled body of the animal. For example, it is not easy for the hydra to thicken one part of its body while thinning another.

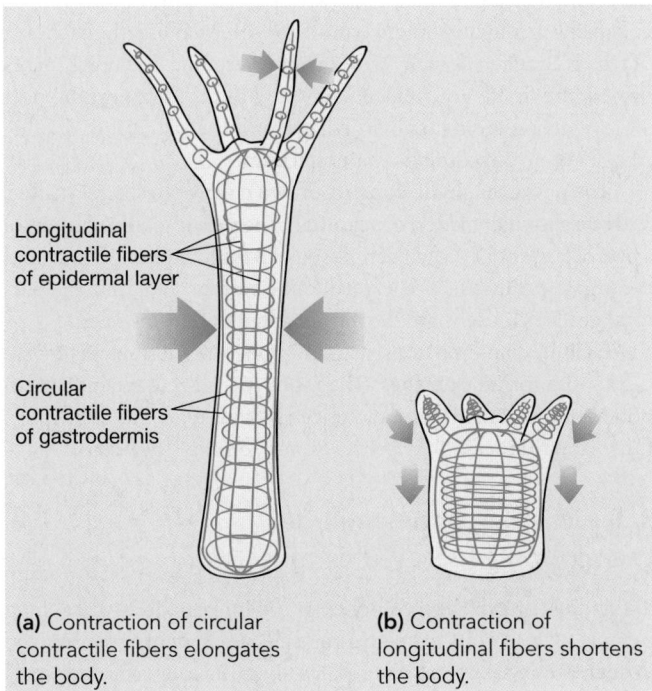

(a) Contraction of circular contractile fibers elongates the body.

(b) Contraction of longitudinal fibers shortens the body.

FIGURE 40-2 Hydrostatic skeleton

In *Hydra*, fluid in the gastrovascular cavity transmits force when contractile cells in the body wall contract against it. The longitudinally arranged contractile cells of *Hydra* are antagonistic to the cells arranged circularly around the body axis.

The more sophisticated hydrostatic skeleton of the annelid worm lets it move with more flexibility. An earthworm's body consists of a series of segments divided by transverse partitions, or septa (see Fig. 31-19). The septa isolate portions of the body cavity and the coelomic fluid they contain. This arrangement allows the hydrostatic skeletons of each segment to be largely independent of one another. Thus, contraction of the circular muscle in the elongating anterior end does not interfere with the action of the longitudinal muscle in the segments at the posterior end.

You can find some examples of hydrostatic skeletons in invertebrates equipped with shells or endoskeletons, and even in vertebrates with endoskeletons of cartilage or bone. For example, sea stars and sea urchins have an endoskeleton, but they move their tube feet by an ingenious adaptation of a hydrostatic skeleton (see Chapter 32). And the human penis becomes erect and stiff because of the turgidity of pressurized blood in its internal spaces.

Mollusks and arthropods have nonliving exoskeletons

In most animals, the skeleton is a lifeless shell, or **exoskeleton,** deposited atop the outer epithelial covering. In mollusks, the exoskeleton is a calcium carbonate shell secreted by the mantle, a thin sheet of epithelial tissue that extends from the body wall. The exoskeleton provides protection, a retreat used in emergencies, with the bulk of the naked, tasty body exposed at other times.

Exoskeletons of arthropods serve not only to protect but also to transmit forces. In this respect they are comparable to the skeletons of vertebrates. The arthropod exoskeleton is a nonliving *cuticle* that contains the polysaccharide **chitin.** Although it is a continuous, one-piece sheath covering the entire body, the arthropod exoskeleton varies greatly in thickness and flexibility. Large, thick, inflexible plates are separated from one another by thin, flexible joints arranged segmentally. Enough joints are provided to make the arthropod's body as flexible as those of many vertebrates. The arthropod exoskeleton is adapted to a vast variety of lifestyles, and parts of it are modified to function as specialized tools or weapons.

A disadvantage of the rigid arthropod exoskeleton is that to accommodate growth, an arthropod must **molt,** that is, shed its exoskeleton and replace it with a new, larger one (**FIG. 40-3**). Recall from Chapter 31 that this process, also called **ecdysis,** is characteristic of the **Ecdysozoa,** a major branch of invertebrates. During ecdysis the animal is weak and vulnerable to predators.

Internal skeletons are capable of growth

Echinoderms and chordates have **endoskeletons.** This internal skeleton consists of plates or shafts of calcium-impregnated tissue (such as cartilage or bone). Composed of living tissue, the endoskeleton grows along with the animal as a whole. The echinoderm endoskeleton consists of spines and plates of calcium salts embedded in the body wall, beneath an epidermis that covers the body. This endoskeleton forms what amounts to an internal shell that provides support and protection (**FIG. 40-4**). Many echinoderm endoskeletons bear spines that project to the outer surface.

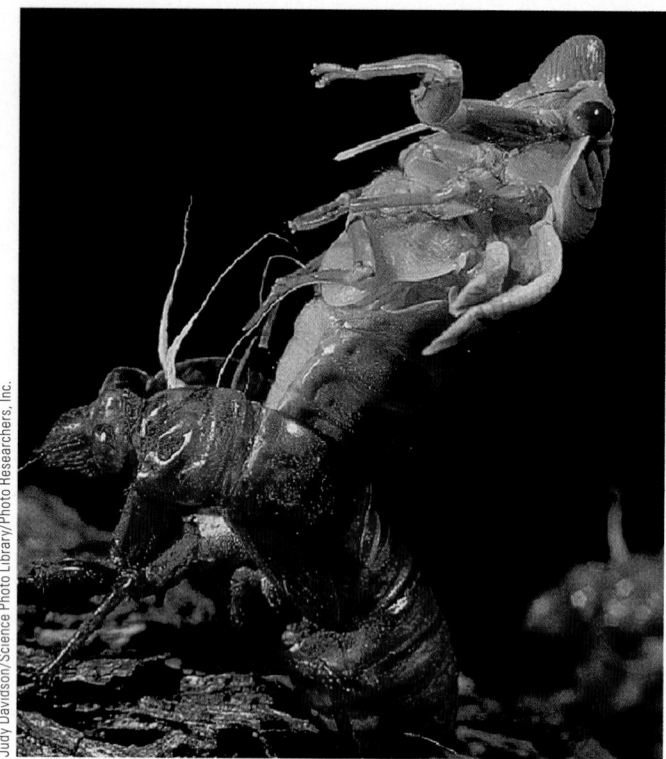

FIGURE 40-3 Ecdysis

A greengrocer cicada (*Magicicada*) requires 13 years to mature. It then emerges from the soil, climbs a tree, and sheds its exoskeleton, prior to reproducing.

You are probably most familiar with the endoskeleton of vertebrates. The internal vertebrate skeleton provides support and protection and transmits muscle forces. Members of class Chondrichthyes (sharks and rays) have skeletons of cartilage, but in most vertebrates the skeleton consists mainly of bone. Many bones form systems of levers that transmit muscle forces. Bones store calcium and are important in maintaining homeostatic levels of calcium in the blood.

The vertebrate skeleton has two main divisions

The two main divisions of the vertebrate skeleton are the axial and appendicular skeletons (**FIG. 40-5**). The **axial skeleton,** located along the central axis of the body, consists of the skull, vertebral column, ribs, and sternum (breastbone). The **appendicular skeleton** consists of the bones of the limbs (arms and legs) plus the bones making up the pectoral (shoulder) girdle and most of the pelvic (hip) girdle; these girdles connect the limbs to the axial skeleton.

The **skull,** the bony framework of the head, consists of the cranial and facial bones. In the human, 8 cranial bones enclose the brain, and 14 bones make up the facial portion of the skull. Several cranial bones that are single in the adult human result from the fusion of 2 or more bones that are separate in the fetus or newborn.

The vertebrate spine, or **vertebral column,** supports the body and bears its weight. In humans, it consists of 24 **vertebrae** and 2 bones composed of fused vertebrae, the **sacrum** and **coccyx.** The

FIGURE 40-4 The echinoderm endoskeleton

As in other echinoderms, the endoskeleton of the red sea star (*Formia milleporella*) is composed of spines and plates of nonliving calcium salts embedded in the body wall. The endoskeleton provides support and protection.

vertebral column consists of the **cervical** (neck) region, with 7 vertebrae; the **thoracic** (chest) region, with 12 vertebrae; the **lumbar** (back) region, with 5 vertebrae; the **sacral** (pelvic) region, with 5 fused vertebrae; and the **coccygeal** region, also composed of fused vertebrae.

The **rib cage** is a bony "basket" formed by the **sternum** (breastbone), thoracic vertebrae, and, in mammals, 12 pairs of ribs. The rib cage protects the internal organs of the chest, including the heart and lungs. It also supports the chest wall, preventing it from collapsing as the diaphragm contracts with each breath. Each pair of ribs is attached dorsally to a separate vertebra. Of your 12 pairs of ribs, the first 7 are attached ventrally to the sternum; the next 3 are attached indirectly by cartilage; and the last 2, the "floating ribs," have no attachments to the sternum.

The **pectoral girdle** consists of two collarbones, or **clavicles,** and two shoulder blades, or **scapulas.** The **pelvic girdle** consists of a pair of large bones, each composed of 3 fused hipbones. Whereas the pelvic girdle is securely fused to the vertebral column, the pectoral girdle is loosely and flexibly attached to it by muscles.

Each human limb consists of 30 bones and terminates in five **digits,** the fingers and toes. The more specialized appendages of other tetrapods may be characterized by four digits (as in the pig), three (the rhinoceros), two (the camel), or one (the horse).

A typical long bone amplifies the motion generated by muscles

The radius, one of the two bones of the forearm, is a typical long bone (**FIG. 40-6**). Its numerous muscle attachments are arranged in such a way that the bone rotates about its long axis and operates as a lever, amplifying the motion generated by the muscles. By themselves, muscles cannot shorten enough to produce large movements of the body parts to which they are attached.

Like other bones, the radius is covered by a connective tissue membrane, the **periosteum,** to which muscle tendons and ligaments attach. The periosteum can produce new layers of bone, thus

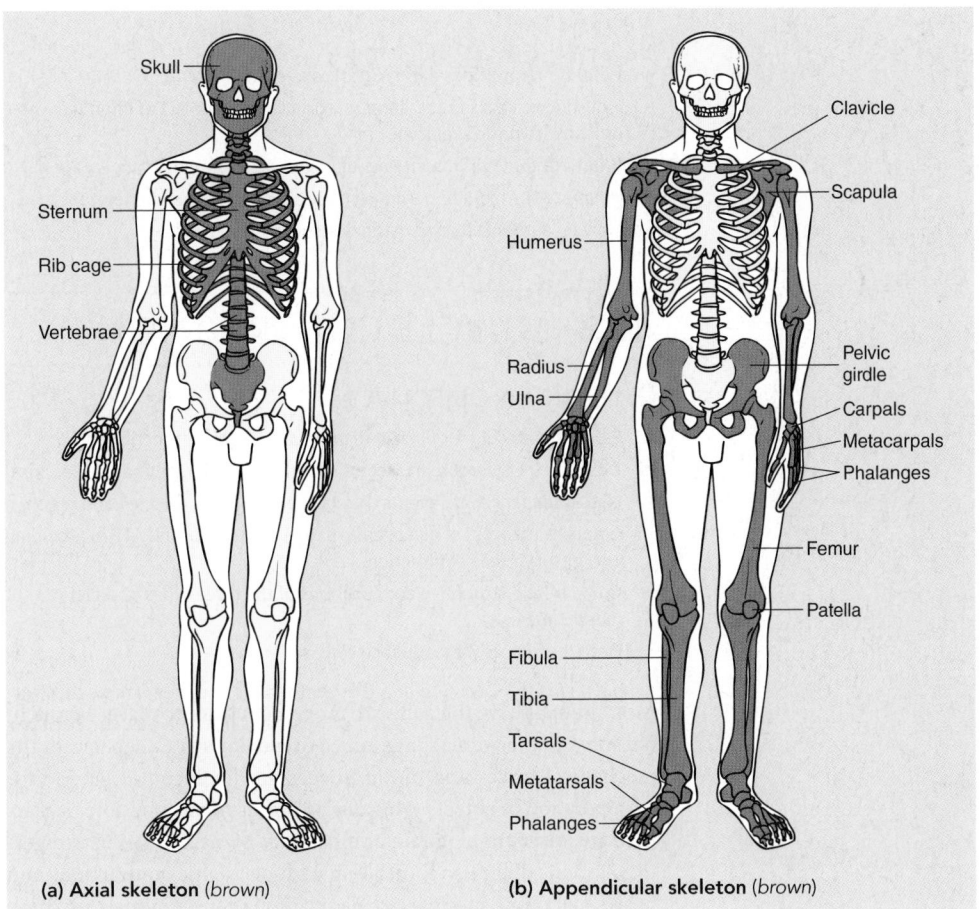

FIGURE 40-5 *Animated* **The human skeletal system**
Only a few of the 206 named bones are labeled here.

increasing the bone's diameter. The main shaft of a long bone is its **diaphysis;** each expanded end is an **epiphysis.** In children, a disc of cartilage, the **metaphysis,** lies between the epiphyses and the diaphysis. Metaphyses are growth centers that disappear at maturity, becoming vague **epiphyseal lines.** Long bones have a central cavity that contains **bone marrow.** Yellow marrow consists mainly of a fatty connective tissue; the red marrow in certain bones produces blood cells.

The radius has a thin outer shell of **compact bone,** which is very dense and hard. Compact bone lies primarily near the surfaces of a bone, where it provides great strength. Recall from Chapter 39 that compact bone consists of interlocking spindle-shaped units called **osteons** (see Fig. 39-2). Within an osteon, **osteocytes** (bone cells) lie in small cavities called **lacunae** (sing., *lacuna*). The lacunae are arranged in concentric circles around central **Haversian canals.** Blood vessels that nourish the bone tissue pass through the Haversian canals. Osteocytes are connected by threadlike extensions of their cytoplasm that extend through narrow channels called *canaliculi.*

Interior to the thin shell of compact bone is a filling of **spongy bone,** which provides mechanical strength. Spongy bone consists of a network of thin strands of bone. Its spaces are filled with bone marrow.

Bones are remodeled throughout life

During fetal development, bones form in two ways. Long bones, such as the radius, develop from cartilage templates in a process called **endochondral bone development.** A bone begins to ossify (become bony) in its diaphysis, and secondary sites of bone production develop in the epiphyses. The part of the bone between the ossified regions can grow. Eventually, the ossified regions fuse. In contrast, other bones, including the flat outer bones of the skull, develop from a noncartilage, connective tissue scaffold. This process is known as **intramembranous bone development.**

Osteoblasts are bone-building cells. They secrete the protein collagen, which forms the strong fibers of bone. The compound hydroxyapatite, composed mainly of calcium phosphate, is present in the interstitial fluid (tissue fluid). It automatically crystallizes around the collagen fibers to form the hard matrix of bone. As the matrix forms around the osteoblasts, they become isolated within the lacunae. The trapped osteoblasts are then called **osteocytes.**

Bones are modeled during growth and remodeled continuously throughout life in response to physical stresses and other changing demands. As muscles develop in response to physical activity, the bones to which they are attached thicken and become stronger. As a bone grows, tissue is removed from its interior, especially from the walls of the marrow cavity.

Osteoclasts are large, multinucleated cells that break down (resorb) bone. The osteoclasts move about, secreting hydrogen ions that dissolve the crystals, and enzymes that digest the collagen. Osteoclasts and osteoblasts are synergistic; together they shape bones. The remodeling process is extensive—the adult human skeleton is completely replaced every 10 years!

In *osteoporosis,* the most common progressive, degenerative bone disease, bone resorption takes place more rapidly than bone formation. Patients lose so much bone mass that their bones become fragile, which greatly increases their risk for fracture. Most drugs used to treat osteoporosis inhibit osteoclast-mediated bone resorption. A recent addition to the treatment arsenal stimulates osteoblasts to promote bone formation.

Joints are junctions between bones

Joints, or articulations, are junctions between two or more bones. Joints facilitate flexibility and movement. At the joint, the outer

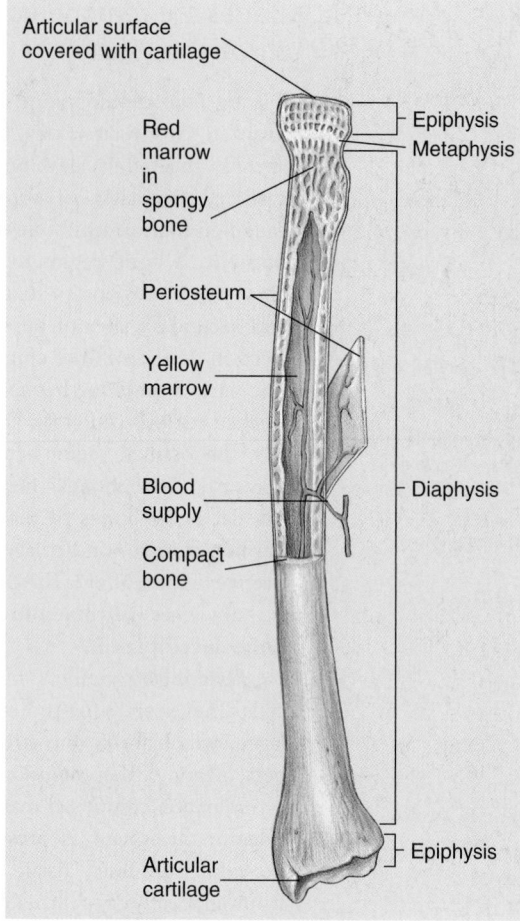

Articular surface covered with cartilage

Red marrow in spongy bone

Epiphysis

Metaphysis

Periosteum

Yellow marrow

Blood supply

Diaphysis

Compact bone

Epiphysis

Articular cartilage

FIGURE 40-6 *Animated* **A typical long bone**
A long bone has a thin shell of compact bone and a filling of spongy bone that contains marrow.

surface of each bone consists of articular cartilage. One way to classify joints is according to the degree of movement they allow. The *sutures* between bones of the human skull are **immovable joints.** In a suture, bones are held together by a thin layer of dense fibrous connective tissue, which may be replaced by bone in the adult. **Slightly movable** joints, found between vertebrae, are made of cartilage and help absorb shock.

Most joints are **freely movable joints.** Each is enclosed by a joint capsule of connective tissue and lined with a membrane that secretes a lubricant called **synovial fluid.** This viscous fluid reduces friction during movement and absorbs shock. The joint capsule is typically reinforced by **ligaments,** bands of fibrous connective tissue that connect bones and limit movement at the joint.

With time and use, joints wear down. In *osteoarthritis,* a group of common joint disorders, cartilage repair does not keep up with degeneration, and the articular cartilage wears out. Inflammation of the joint capsule may occur, and bone outgrowths, or spurs, may develop. In *rheumatoid arthritis,* an autoimmune disease, the synovial membrane thickens and becomes inflamed. Synovial fluid accumulates, causing pressure, pain, stiffness, and progressive deformity, leading to loss of function.

Review

- What functions does a hydrostatic skeleton perform?
- How do the septa in the annelid worm contribute to the effectiveness of its hydrostatic skeleton?
- What are some disadvantages of an exoskeleton? some advantages?
- What are the main bones in each division of the human skeleton?
- How do osteoblasts and osteoclasts remodel bone?

40.3 MUSCLE CONTRACTION

◼ LEARNING OBJECTIVES

7 Relate the structure of insect flight muscles to their function.
8 Describe the structure of skeletal muscles and their antagonistic actions.
9 List, in sequence, the events that take place during muscle contraction.
10 Compare the roles of glycogen, creatine phosphate, and ATP in providing energy for muscle contraction.
11 Compare the structures and functions of the three types of skeletal muscle fibers.
12 Describe factors that influence contraction.

Most animals have the ability to move from place to place. Throughout most of the animal kingdom, a **muscular system** generates the mechanical forces and motion necessary for locomotion and for manipulation of objects. Muscle also powers many physiological actions necessary to maintain homeostasis. Many animals have digestive systems that push food along with peristaltic contractions and hearts that pump internal circulating fluids. Some animals also have blood vessels that maintain their pressure with gentle squeezing.

Animals with very simple body plans do not have muscle tissue, but all eukaryotic cells do contain the contractile protein **actin.** The major component of microfilaments (see Fig. 4-28), actin is important in many cell processes, including amoeboid movement and attachment of cells to surfaces. In most cells, actin is functionally associated with the contractile protein **myosin.** Actin and myosin are most highly organized in muscle fibers.

Invertebrate muscle varies among groups

Earlier in the chapter, we discussed the contractile cells of the hydrostatic skeleton of *Hydra* and other cnidarians. In most other animal groups, muscle is a specialized tissue organized into definite layers, or straplike bands. Some invertebrate phyla have skeletal and smooth muscle. Bivalve mollusks, such as clams, have two sets of muscles for opening and closing the shell. Their specialized smooth muscle, which is capable of slow, sustained contraction at low energy cost, keeps the two shells tightly closed for long periods, even weeks at a time. Striated muscle, which contracts rapidly, is used to swim and to shut the shell quickly when the mollusk is threatened. Arthropod muscles are striated, even in the walls of the digestive tract.

Insect flight muscles are adapted for rapid contraction

Insects were the first animals in which flight evolved, an adaptation that has contributed to their impressive biological success (see Chapter 31). Just how insects fly has been an aerodynamic mystery, and scientists are working to understand their remarkable ability to maneuver. Insect flight muscles contract more rapidly than any other known muscle, up to 1000 contractions per second! Not surprisingly, insect flight muscles in action have the highest known metabolic rate of any muscle tissue.

As you might imagine, insect flight muscles are structurally well adapted to their function. They contain more mitochondria than any other known variety of muscle. Their mitochondria also have more cristae (folds of their inner membranes) and can consume oxygen twice as fast as mammalian mitochondria. Insect muscles are also elaborately infiltrated with *tracheae,* tiny air-filled tubes that carry oxygen directly to each fiber.

Many insects must warm up before they fly because an increase in body temperature increases the rate of ATP synthesis. Butterflies and some other insects bask in the sun before they fly. Honeybees "shiver" their muscles to increase body temperature.

In the common blowfly, the wings may beat at 120 cycles *per second.* Yet in the same blowfly, the neurons that innervate those furiously contracting flight muscles are delivering impulses to them at the astonishingly low frequency of three per second. In fact, about 75% of flying insect species beat their wings too rapidly for each contraction to be controlled by a signal from a motor neuron. Instead, they have **asynchronous,** or indirect, muscle contractions in which muscle contraction is not synchronized with signals from motor neurons.

In insects with asynchronous muscle contractions, the striated flight muscles do not attach directly to the wings. They attach to the flexible portions of the exoskeleton that articulate with the wings. The mechanical properties of this musculoskeletal arrangement provide the stimuli for contraction by stretching the muscle fibers at a high frequency. Each contraction of the muscles "dimples" the exoskeleton in association with a downstroke, and sometimes, depending on the exact arrangement of the muscles, on the upstroke as well. When the dimple springs back into resting position, the muscles attached to it stretch. The stretching immediately initiates another contraction, and the cycle repeats. Thus, the deformation of the exoskeleton is transmitted as a force to the wings, which beat so fast that we may perceive the sounds as a musical tone. However, nerve impulses are needed to maintain contraction.

Somehow insects create lift that is 20 times or more their body weight. A central question has been how their flapping wings generate enough force to keep them airborne. Insect flight involves much more than just flapping the wings up and down. The flapping motion of the insect wing changes direction and speed, and upstrokes alternate with downstrokes at very high rates. At each shift of stroke, the wing rotates about its long axis and tilts to just the right angle for the new direction of motion.

Vertebrate skeletal muscles act antagonistically to one another

Skeletal muscles produce movements by pulling on **tendons,** tough cords of connective tissue that anchor muscles to bone. Tendons then pull on bones. Skeletal muscles, or their tendons, pass across a joint and are attached to the bones on each side of the joint. When the muscle contracts, it pulls one bone toward or away from the bone with which it articulates.

Because muscles can only contract, they can only pull; they cannot push. Muscles act **antagonistically** to one another, which means that the movement produced by one can be reversed by another. The biceps muscle, for example, flexes (bends) your arm, whereas contraction of the triceps muscle extends it (**FIG. 40-7**). Thus, the biceps and triceps work antagonistically.

The muscle that contracts to produce a particular action is known as the **agonist.** The muscle that produces the opposite movement is the **antagonist.** When the agonist is contracting, the antagonist is relaxed. Generally, movements are accomplished by groups of muscles working together, so several agonists and several antagonists may take part in any action. Note that muscles that are agonists in one movement may serve as antagonists in another. Some of the superficial skeletal muscles of the human body are shown in **FIGURE 40-8.**

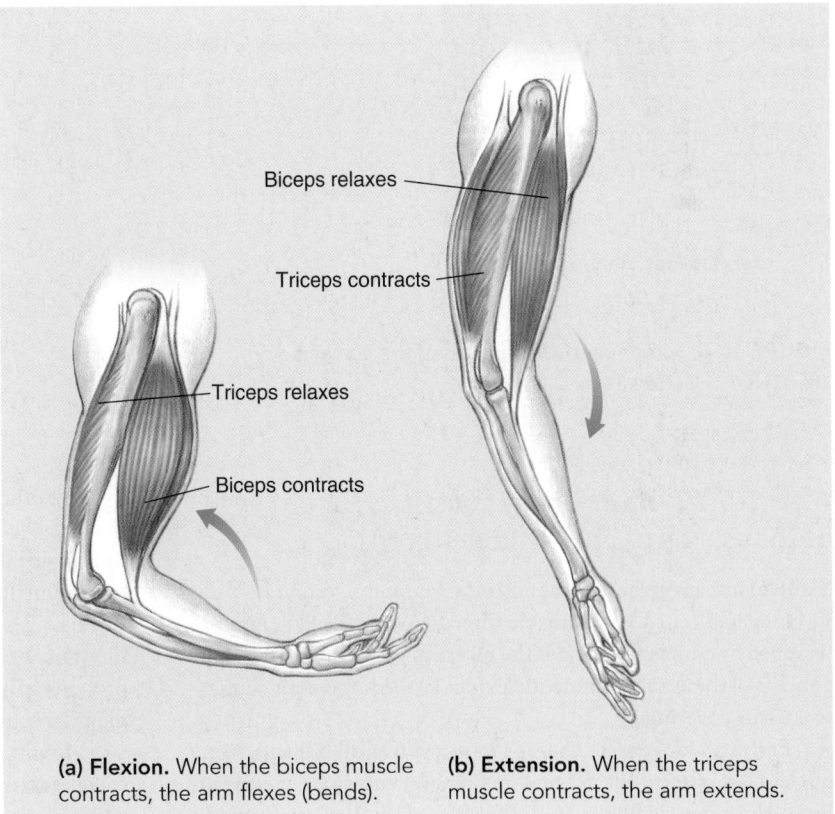

Biceps relaxes

Triceps contracts

Triceps relaxes

Biceps contracts

(a) Flexion. When the biceps muscle contracts, the arm flexes (bends).

(b) Extension. When the triceps muscle contracts, the arm extends.

FIGURE 40-7 *Animated* Muscle action

The biceps and triceps muscles function antagonistically.

Muscles that flex fingers
Platysma
Latissimus dorsi
Rectus abdominis
Linea alba
External oblique
Gluteus medius
Gracilis
Sartorius
Quadriceps femoris
Patella
Soleus

Facial muscles
Sternocleido-mastoid
Trapezius
Clavicle
Deltoid
Pectoralis major
Biceps brachii
Brachialis
Wrist and finger flexors
Triceps brachii
Gastrocnemius
Tibialis anterior
Tibia

(a) Anterior view

Sternocleidomastoid
Trapezius
Deltoid
Triceps brachii
Brachio-radialis
Muscles that flex fingers

Biceps brachii
Brachialis
Latissimus dorsi
External oblique
Gluteus maximus
Hamstring muscles
Gracilis
Semitendinosus
Biceps femoris
Semi-membranosus
Gastrocnemius
Soleus
Achilles tendon
Calcaneus

(b) Posterior view

FIGURE 40-8 Some superficial muscles of the human body
The labels in boldface are bones.

A vertebrate muscle may consist of thousands of muscle fibers

Skeletal muscle is the most abundant tissue in the vertebrate body. Its elongated cells, called **muscle fibers,** are organized in bundles wrapped by connective tissue. The biceps in your arm, for example, consists of thousands of individual muscle fibers and their connective tissue coverings.

Each striated muscle fiber is a long, cylindrical cell with many nuclei (**FIG. 40-9**). The plasma membrane, known as the **sarcolemma** in a muscle fiber, has multiple inward extensions that form a set of **T tubules** (transverse tubules). The cytoplasm of a muscle fiber is called **sarcoplasm,** and the endoplasmic reticulum is called the **sarcoplasmic reticulum.**

Myofibrils, which are threadlike structures, run lengthwise through the muscle fiber. They consist of even smaller structures, the **myofilaments,** or simply **filaments.** There are two types of myofilaments: myosin and actin filaments. **Myosin filaments** are thick, consisting mainly of the protein myosin. The thin **actin filaments** consist mostly of the protein actin; they also contain the proteins **tropomyosin** and **troponin,** which regulate the actin filament's interaction with myosin filaments.

Myosin and actin filaments are organized into repeating units called **sarcomeres,** the basic units of muscle contraction. Hundreds of sarcomeres connected end to end make up a myofibril. Sarcomeres are joined at their ends by an interweaving of filaments called the **Z line.** Each sarcomere consists of overlapping myosin and actin filaments. The filaments overlap lengthwise in the muscle

A skeletal muscle fiber contains threadlike myofibrils that consist of actin and myosin filaments; the filaments are organized into repeating units called sarcomeres.

(a) A muscle such as the biceps in the arm consists of many fascicles (bundles) of muscle fibers.

Biceps muscle

(b) A fascicle wrapped in a connective tissue covering.

Muscle fibers

Sarcolemma

Sarcoplasmic reticulum

Myofibril

T tubule   Mitochondria   Nucleus

(c) Part of a muscle fiber showing the structure of myofibrils. The Z lines mark the ends of the sarcomeres.

Z line

Myofilaments

Sarcomere

Bloom and Fawcett Textbook of Histology

(d) TEM of striated muscle.

1 µm

Ed Reschke/Peter Arnold

(e) LM showing striations.

25 µm

FIGURE 40-9 *Animated* **Muscle structure**

The regular pattern of overlapping filaments gives skeletal and cardiac muscle their striated appearance.

fibers, producing the pattern of transverse bands or striations characteristic of striated muscle (**FIG. 40-10**; also see Fig. 40-9). The bands are designated by the letters *A*, *H*, and *I*.

The **I band** consists of parts of actin filaments of two adjacent sarcomeres. The **A band** is the wide, dark region that includes overlapping myosin and actin filaments. Within the A band is a narrow, light area, the **H zone,** made up exclusively of myosin filaments; the actin filaments do not extend into this region.

Contraction occurs when actin and myosin filaments slide past one another

Muscle contraction occurs when the sarcomeres, and thus the muscle fibers, shorten. This explanation of muscle contraction, known as the **sliding filament model,** was developed in the 1950s by two British biologists, Hugh Huxley and Andrew Huxley. (The Huxleys are not related. They worked separately, and independently came to the same general conclusions at about the same time.) Thanks to the Huxleys, we now understand that the muscle shortens as the actin and myosin filaments slide past one another, increasing their overlap. You might think of an extension ladder. The overall ladder length changes as the ends get closer or farther apart, but the length of each ladder section stays the same. The I band and H zone decrease in length, but neither the actin nor myosin filaments themselves shorten.

Motor neurons transmit messages from the brain or spinal cord to muscle fibers. When a motor neuron transmits a message, it releases the neurotransmitter **acetylcholine** into the **synaptic cleft,** a small space between the motor neuron and each muscle fiber. Acetylcholine binds with receptors on each muscle fiber, causing **depolarization,** a change in the distribution of electric charge across its sarcolemma. Depolarization can cause an electrical signal, or **action potential,** to be generated in the muscle fiber.

In a muscle fiber, an action potential is a wave of depolarization that travels along the sarcolemma and into the system of T-tubule membranes. Depolarization of the T tubules opens calcium channels in the sarcoplasmic reticulum, and stored calcium ions are released into the myofibrils. Calcium ions bind to the protein troponin on the actin filaments, which changes the shape of the troponin. This change results in the troponin pushing the tropomyosin away from the **active sites** on the actin filament (**FIG. 40-11**). These active sites, also called **myosin-binding sites,** are now exposed.

One end of each myosin molecule is folded into two globular structures called *heads.* The rounded heads of the myosin molecules extend away from the body of the myosin filament. Each myosin molecule also has a long tail that joins other myosin tails to form the body of the thick filament. ATP is bound to the myosin when the muscle fiber is at rest (not contracting). Myosin is an adenosine triphosphatase (ATPase), an enzyme that splits ATP to form ADP and inorganic phosphate (P_i). Myosin converts the chemical energy of ATP into the mechanical energy of sliding filaments.

According to the current model of muscle contraction, when ATP is split, the ADP and P_i initially remain attached to the myosin head. The myosin head (with ADP and P_i still bound to it) is in an energized state; it is "cocked." The myosin head binds to an exposed active site on the actin filament, forming a **cross bridge**

linking the myosin and actin filaments. The inorganic phosphate is then released, which triggers a conformational change in the myosin head. The myosin head bends about 45 degrees, in a flexing motion. This movement, the *power stroke,* pulls the actin filament closer to the center of the sarcomere. During the power stroke, the ADP is released.

A new ATP must bind to the myosin head before the myosin can detach from the actin. If sufficient calcium ions are present, the cycle begins anew. Energized once again, myosin heads contact a second set of active sites on the actin filament; this next set is farther down the filament, closer to the end of the sarcomere. The process repeats with a third set of active sites, and so on. This series of stepping motions pulls the actin filaments toward the center of the sarcomere.

Each time the myosin heads attach, move 45 degrees, detach, and then re-attach farther along the actin filament, the muscle shortens. One way to visualize this process is to imagine the myosin heads engaging "hand over hand" with the actin filaments. When many sarcomeres contract simultaneously, they contract the muscle as a whole. The sequence of events in muscle contraction can be summarized as follows:

1. A motor neuron releases acetylcholine, which binds with receptors on the muscle fiber; binding causes depolarization and generation of an action potential.
2. The action potential spreads through T tubules, triggering Ca^{2+} release from the sarcoplasmic reticulum.
3. Ca^{2+} binds to troponin, which then undergoes a conformational change; active sites on actin filaments are exposed.
4. ATP (attached to myosin) is split, and the energized myosin head is cocked; it binds to the active site on the actin filament, forming a cross bridge.
5. The release of P_i from the myosin head triggers the power stroke.
6. During the power stroke, myosin heads pull actin filament toward the center of the sarcomere, shortening the muscle; ADP is released.
7. The myosin head binds ATP and detaches from actin. If the concentration of Ca^{2+} is high enough, the sequence repeats from step 3.

When impulses from the motor neuron cease, the enzyme acetylcholinesterase in the synaptic cleft inactivates acetylcholine. Muscle fibers return to their resting state. Calcium ions are pumped back into the sarcoplasmic reticulum by active transport, a process that requires ATP. Calcium removal is the key step in muscle relaxation. Without Ca^{2+}, tropomyosin once again covers active sites on the actin filaments. The actin filaments slide back to their original position, and the muscle relaxes. This entire series of events happens in milliseconds.

ATP powers muscle contraction

Muscle cells often perform strenuously and need large amounts of energy. As noted, the immediate source of energy for muscle contraction is ATP. Energy stored in ATP molecules powers cocking, attachment of the myosin heads to the actin filaments, flexion, and release of the myosin heads. Note that energy is needed not only

A muscle contracts when actin and myosin filaments slide past one another. The length of each filament remains the same.

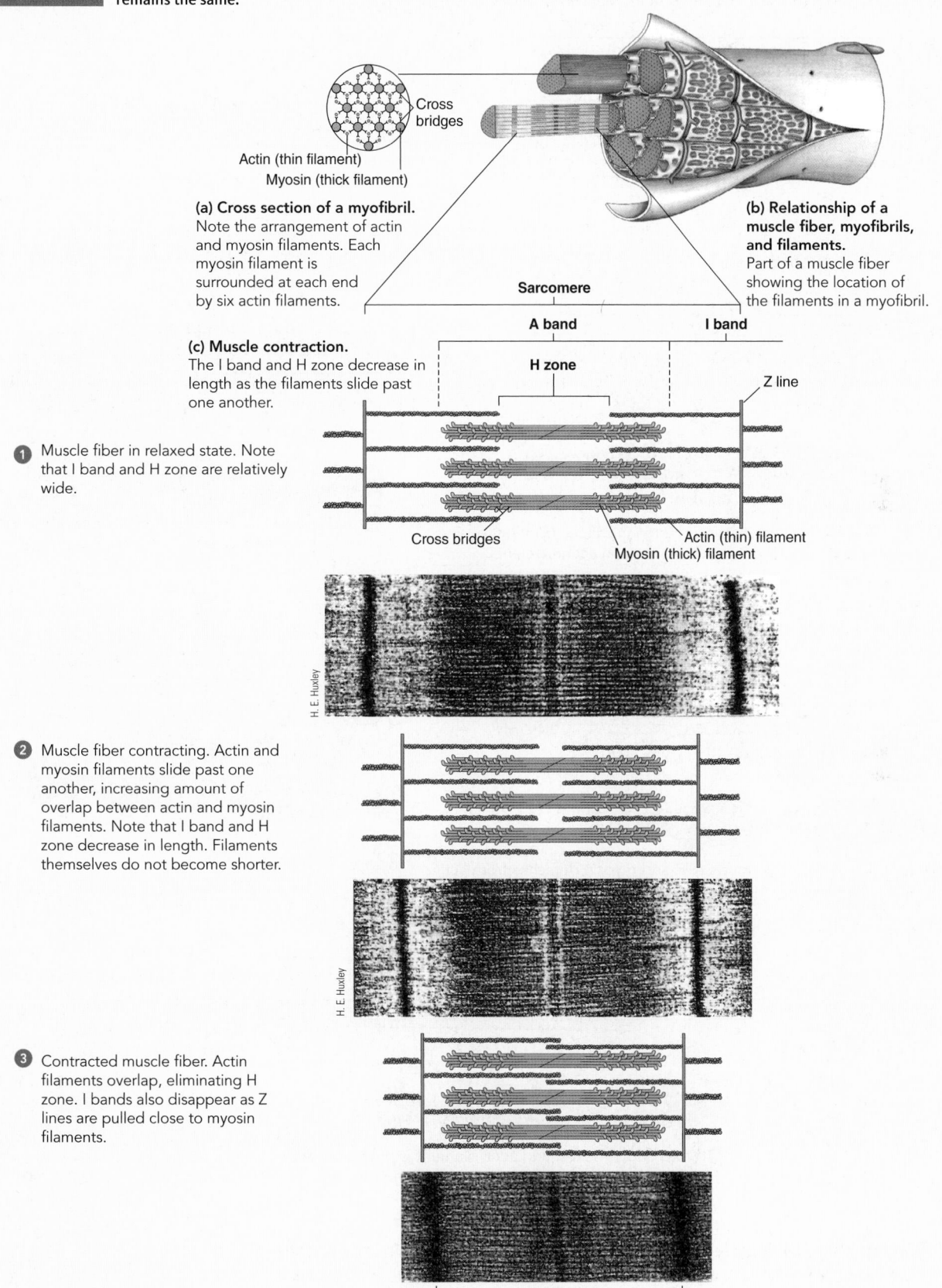

Cross bridges

Actin (thin filament)
Myosin (thick filament)

(a) Cross section of a myofibril.
Note the arrangement of actin and myosin filaments. Each myosin filament is surrounded at each end by six actin filaments.

(b) Relationship of a muscle fiber, myofibrils, and filaments.
Part of a muscle fiber showing the location of the filaments in a myofibril.

(c) Muscle contraction.
The I band and H zone decrease in length as the filaments slide past one another.

Sarcomere

A band   I band

H zone

Z line

1 Muscle fiber in relaxed state. Note that I band and H zone are relatively wide.

Cross bridges

Actin (thin) filament

Myosin (thick) filament

2 Muscle fiber contracting. Actin and myosin filaments slide past one another, increasing amount of overlap between actin and myosin filaments. Note that I band and H zone decrease in length. Filaments themselves do not become shorter.

3 Contracted muscle fiber. Actin filaments overlap, eliminating H zone. I bands also disappear as Z lines are pulled close to myosin filaments.

Sarcomere

FIGURE 40-10 *Animated* **The sliding filament model of muscle contraction**

Myosin and actin filaments are organized into repeating units called sarcomeres. As the sarcomeres become shorter, the muscle fiber short-ens, but the size of the filaments does not change. (The I band consists of actin filaments of two adjacent sarcomeres.)

The energy of ATP powers muscle contraction. During the power stroke, myosin heads move actin filaments toward the center of the sarcomere, which shortens the muscle.

1 Acetylcholine (released by motor neuron) combines with receptors on muscle fiber, causing depolarization and an action potential.

2 Neural impulse spreads through T tubules, stimulating Ca^{2+} release from sarcoplasmic reticulum.

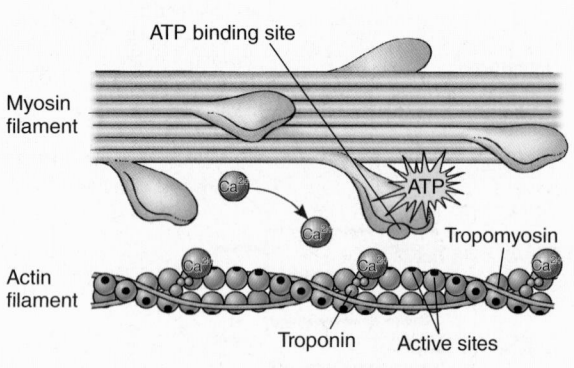

ATP binding site

Myosin filament

Actin filament

Tropomyosin

Troponin   Active sites

3 Ca^{2+} bind to troponin, causing change in shape. Troponin pushes tropomyosin away, exposing active sites on actin filaments.

4 ATP is split. Myosin head, now cocked, binds to exposed active site, forming cross bridge.

If Ca^{2+} available

7 Actin-myosin complex binds ATP, and myosin detaches from actin.

5 P_i is released.

6 Cross bridge flexes, and actin filament is pulled toward center of sarcomere. This movement is the power stroke. ADP is released.

FIGURE 40-11 *Animated* Muscle contraction: model of actin and myosin interactions

Contraction results when actin filaments slide toward the center of individual sarcomeres of a myofibril. After step 7, the cycle repeats from step 3 if calcium ions are available. In the absence of calcium ions, the muscle relaxes.

for the pull exerted by the cross bridges but also for their release from each active site.

Rigor mortis, the temporary but very marked muscle stiffening that occurs after death, results from ATP depletion. When death occurs, cellular respiration ceases and ATP is used up. However, at the time of death, many muscle fibers are in the process of contraction, and cross bridges have formed. Because ATP is essential for release of the myosin heads, cross bridges remain intact. Rigor mortis does not persist indefinitely because the entire contractile apparatus of the muscles eventually decomposes, restoring pliability. The phenomenon is temperature dependent, so given the prevailing temperature, a medical examiner can estimate the time of death of a cadaver from its degree of rigor mortis.

ATP molecules can provide energy for only a few seconds of strenuous activity. Fortunately, muscle fibers have a backup energy storage compound, **creatine phosphate,** that can be stockpiled. The energy stored in creatine phosphate is transferred to ATP as needed. But during vigorous exercise the supply of creatine phosphate is quickly depleted. Muscle cells must replenish their supplies of these energy-rich compounds.

Muscle fibers store chemical energy in **glycogen,** a large polysaccharide formed from hundreds of glucose molecules. Glycogen can be degraded, yielding glucose, which is then degraded in cellular respiration. When sufficient oxygen is available, enough energy is captured from glucose to produce needed quantities of ATP and creatine phosphate.

During a burst of strenuous exercise, the circulatory system cannot deliver enough oxygen to keep up with the demand of the rapidly metabolizing muscle fibers. This results in an **oxygen debt.** Under these conditions, muscle fibers break down fuel molecules anaerobically (without oxygen) for short periods. Lactic acid fermentation is a method of generating ATP anaerobically, but not in great quantity (see Fig. 8-14). ATP depletion results in weaker contractions and muscle fatigue. Accumulation of the waste product **lactic acid** also contributes to muscle fatigue. Well-conditioned athletes develop the ability to tolerate the high levels of lactic acid generated during high-performance activity. The period of rapid breathing that generally follows strenuous exercise pays back the oxygen debt by consuming lactic acid.

The type of muscle fibers determines strength and endurance

Three major types of skeletal muscle fibers have been identified in vertebrates: slow-oxidative, fast-glycolytic, and fast-oxidative (**TABLE 40-1**). **Slow-oxidative fibers** are well-adapted for endurance activities such as swimming and running long distances, and for maintaining posture. They contract slowly and fatigue slowly. These fibers require a steady supply of oxygen. They derive most of their energy from aerobic respiration and are rich in mitochondria and capillaries. Slow-oxidative fibers are rich in **myoglobin,** a red pigment similar to hemoglobin, which stores oxygen in red blood cells. Myoglobin enhances rapid diffusion of oxygen from blood into muscles during strenuous muscle exertion. Because of their myoglobin, slow-oxidative fibers are red and are sometimes called red fibers.

TABLE 40-1	Characteristics of Skeletal Muscle Fibers		
Characteristics	Slow-Oxidative Fibers	Fast-Glycolytic Fibers	Fast-Oxidative Fibers
Contraction speed	Slow	Fast	Fast
Rate of fatigue	Slow	Fast	Intermediate
Major pathway for ATP synthesis	Aerobic respiration	Glycolysis	Aerobic respiration
Mitochondria	Many	Few	Many
Intensity of contraction	Low	High	Intermediate
Myoglobin content	High	Low	High
Color of fiber	Red	White	Red

Fast-glycolytic fibers generate a great deal of power and carry out rapid movements but can sustain that activity for only a short time. They are important in activities such as sprinting and weight lifting. Fast-glycolytic fibers contract rapidly, have few mitochondria, and obtain most of their energy from glycolysis. When their glycogen supply is depleted, they fatigue rapidly. These fibers have a low myoglobin content and are white. (They are sometimes referred to as white fibers.) People who are sedentary have more fast-glycolytic fibers than do physically fit individuals. With physical training, these fibers change to fast-oxidative fibers.

Fast-oxidative fibers, also known as *intermediate fibers,* contract rapidly and have an intermediate rate of fatigue. Like slow-oxidative fibers, they are rich in mitochondria and obtain most of their ATP from aerobic respiration. They have a high myoglobin content and a red color.

Entire muscles may be specialized for quick or slow responses. In chickens, for instance, the white breast muscles are efficient for quick responses, perhaps because a short flight is an escape mechanism for chickens. However, they walk about on the ground all day; the dark (red) meat of the leg and thigh is muscle specialized for more sustained activity. Birds that fly have red breast muscles specialized to support sustained activity.

In humans, most muscles have a mixture of different types of fibers. The proportions of the types of fibers vary among individuals and from muscle to muscle in the same person. Aerobic exercise, such as jogging or bicycling, increases endurance. *Aerobic training* increases capillary density, the number of mitochondria, and the myoglobin content of muscle fibers. In *strength training,* for example, weight lifting, specific muscles are repeatedly contracted under heavy loads. This action increases the number of filaments in the muscle fibers, which increases the size of the muscle.

Several factors influence the strength of muscle contraction

In addition to the types of muscle fibers making up the muscle, contraction of a whole muscle depends on the number of muscle fibers contracting; the tension developed by each fiber; frequency of stimulation; the condition of the muscle, for example, whether or not it is fatigued; and the load on the muscle. The more muscle fibers that contract, the greater the tension in the muscle. In a **motor unit,** a motor neuron is functionally connected with an average of about 150 muscle fibers (**FIG. 40-12**). However, some motor units have less than a dozen motor neurons, and others have several hundred. Each junction of a motor neuron with a muscle fiber is called a **neuromuscular junction.** Messages from the brain or

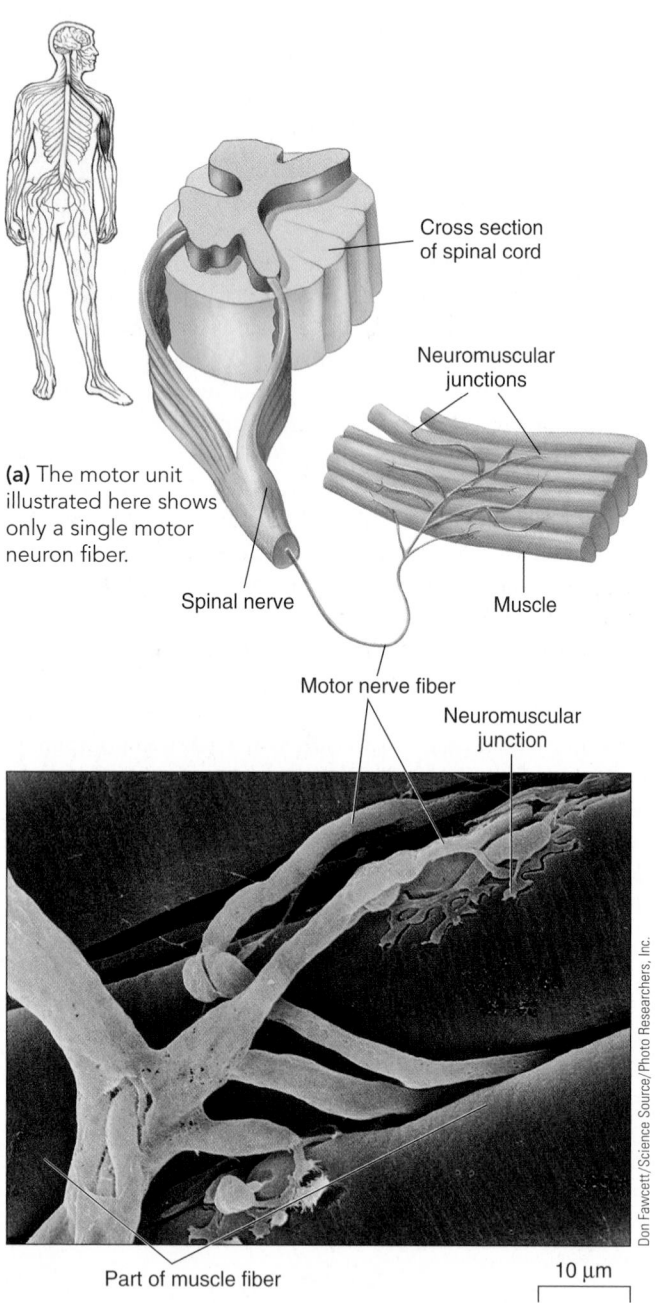

(a) The motor unit illustrated here shows only a single motor neuron fiber.

Cross section of spinal cord

Neuromuscular junctions

Spinal nerve

Muscle

Motor nerve fiber

Neuromuscular junction

Don Fawcett/Science Source/Photo Researchers, Inc.

Part of muscle fiber

10 μm

(b) SEM of some of the fibers in a motor unit. Note how neurons branch to innervate all muscle fibers in the motor unit.

FIGURE 40-12 *Animated* A motor unit

A motor unit consists of a motor neuron and the muscle fibers that it innervates.

spinal cord activate motor units. The more motor units that are *recruited,* the stronger are the contractions.

An important factor affecting the tension of contracting muscle fibers is the frequency of stimulation. In response to a single, brief electrical stimulus, skeletal muscle contracts with a single, quick contraction called a **simple twitch.** When a second stimulus is received before the first contraction is complete, the two twitches may add together, a process called **summation** (**FIG. 40-13**). Typically, skeletal muscle receives a series of separate stimuli timed very closely together. Summation results in a smooth, sustained contraction called **tetanus.** Depending on the identity and number of our muscle fibers tetanically contracting, we might thread a needle, rock a baby, or run a mile.

When you lift a heavy object, you place a load on the muscles affected. As the weight of the load increases, the muscles contract more strongly (within limits).

Even when you are not moving, your muscles are in a state of partial contraction known as **muscle tone.** At any given moment, some muscle fibers are contracted, stimulated by messages from motor neurons. Muscle tone is an unconscious process that keeps muscles prepared for action. When the motor nerve to a muscle is cut, the muscle becomes limp (completely relaxed, or flaccid) and eventually atrophies (decreases in size).

Smooth muscle and cardiac muscle are involuntary

The three types of vertebrate muscle—skeletal, smooth, and cardiac—are compared in Table 39-3. All three types of muscle have thin actin filaments that slide along thick myosin filaments in response to an increase in calcium ion concentration. All three muscle types use ATP to power contraction. However, each type of muscle is specialized for particular types of responses. Neither smooth muscle nor cardiac muscle is under voluntary control.

Smooth muscle is not attached to bones but instead forms tubes that squeeze like the muscle tissue in the body wall of the earthworm. Smooth muscle often contracts in response to simple stretching, and its contraction tends to be sustained. It is well adapted to performing such tasks as regulating blood pressure by sustained contraction of the walls of the arterioles. Although smooth muscle contracts slowly, it shortens much more than striated muscle does; it squeezes impressively.

Smooth muscle is not striated because its actin and myosin filaments are not organized into myofibrils or into sarcomeres. The fibers of smooth muscle tissue function as a unit because they are connected by *gap junctions* (see Chapter 5). Gap junctions permit electrical signals to pass rapidly from fiber to fiber. Although smooth muscle contraction is basically similar to skeletal muscle contraction (occurring by a sliding filament mechanism), the cross bridges in smooth muscle remain in the attached state longer. For this reason, less ATP is required to maintain a high level of force.

Cardiac muscle contracts and relaxes in alternating rhythm, propelling blood with each contraction. Sustained contraction of cardiac muscle would be disastrous! Like smooth muscle fibers, cardiac muscle fibers are electrically coupled by gap junctions

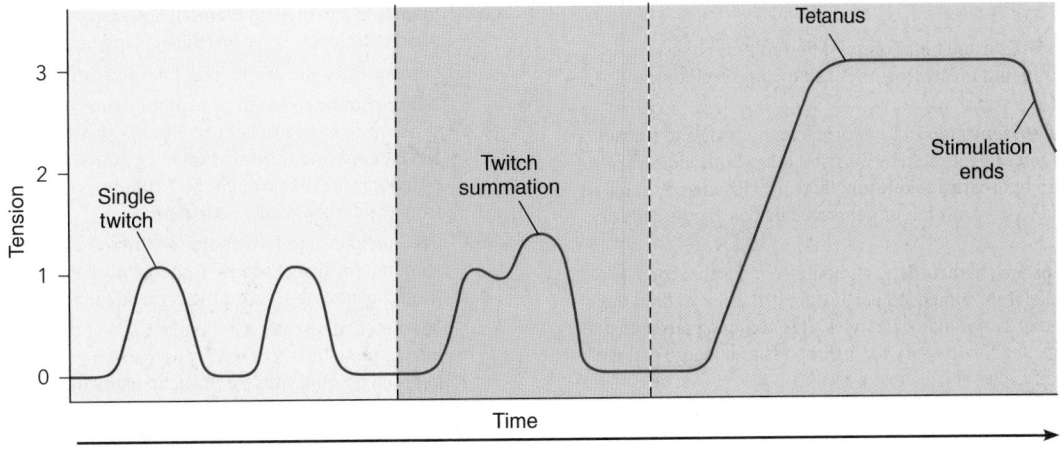

(a) When a muscle fiber is allowed to completely relax and is then stimulated a second time, the second twitch is the same magnitude as the first twitch.

(b) When a muscle fiber is stimulated a second time before it has completely relaxed, the second twitch is added on to the first twitch. The result is summation.

(c) A volley of rapid stimuli does not allow the muscle fiber to relax between stimuli. A sustained contraction, called tetanus, occurs.

FIGURE 40-13 *Animated* **Summation and tetanus**

(called intercalated discs). Each heartbeat is initiated by a *pacemaker,* a mass of specialized cardiac muscle. A conduction system transmits the signal throughout the cardiac muscle, and the heart beats in a regular rhythm independent of a nerve supply. However, the heart rate is regulated, according to the needs of the body, by neurons in the cardiac centers in the medulla of the brain (discussed in Chapter 44).

Review

- Describe a skeletal muscle fiber. What are its two types of filaments?
- What events occur when a muscle fiber contracts (begin with release of acetylcholine and include cross-bridge action)?
- What is the role of ATP in muscle contraction? What are the functions of creatine phosphate and glycogen?
- What is summation?

■ SUMMARY: FOCUS ON LEARNING OBJECTIVES

40.1 *(page 843)*

1 Compare the functions of the epithelial coverings of invertebrates and vertebrates.

- **Epithelial tissue** protects underlying tissues and may be specialized for sensory or respiratory functions. The outer epithelium may be specialized to secrete antibacterial or poisonous substances.
- In many invertebrates, the outer epithelium is specialized to secrete a protective **cuticle,** or shell.
- The **integumentary system** of vertebrates includes the skin and structures that develop from it. Mammalian skin includes hair, claws or nails, sweat glands, oil glands, and sensory receptors.

2 Relate the structure of vertebrate skin to its functions.

- The feathers of birds and the hair of mammals form an insulating layer that helps maintain a constant body temperature. Mammalian skin protects the body from the wear and tear that occurs as it interacts with the outer environment. **Stratum corneum,** the most superficial layer of the **epidermis,** consists of dead cells, filled with **keratin,** a protein that gives mechanical strength to the skin and reduces water loss. Cells in **stratum basale** of the epidermis divide and are pushed upward

toward the skin surface. These cells mature, produce keratin, and eventually die and slough off.

- The **dermis** consists of dense, fibrous connective tissue. In birds and mammals, the dermis rests on a layer of **subcutaneous tissue** composed largely of insulating fat.

3 Compare the structure and functions of different types of skeletal systems, including the hydrostatic skeleton, exoskeleton, and endoskeleton.

- The **skeletal system** supports and protects the body and transmits mechanical forces generated by muscles. Many soft-bodied invertebrates have a **hydrostatic skeleton;** fluid in a closed body compartment is used to transmit forces generated by contractile cells or muscle.

- **Exoskeletons** are characteristic of mollusks and arthropods. The arthropod skeleton, composed partly of **chitin,** is jointed for flexibility and adapted for many lifestyles. This nonliving skeleton does not grow, making it necessary for arthropods to undergo **ecdysis (molt)** periodically.

- The **endoskeletons** of echinoderms and chordates consist of living tissue and therefore can grow.

4 Describe the main divisions of the vertebrate skeleton and the bones that make up each division.

- The vertebrate skeleton consists of an **axial skeleton** and an **appendicular skeleton.** The axial skeleton consists of **skull, vertebral column, rib cage,** and **sternum.** The appendicular skeleton consists of bones of the limbs, **pectoral girdle,** and **pelvic girdle.**

5 Describe the structure of a typical long bone and differentiate between endochondral and intramembranous bone development.

- A typical long bone consists of a thin outer shell of **compact bone** surrounding the inner **spongy bone** and a central cavity that contains **bone marrow.**

- Long bones develop from cartilage templates during **endochondral bone development.** Other bones, such as the flat bones of the skull, develop from a noncartilage connective tissue model by **intramembranous bone development.**

- **Osteoblasts,** cells that produce bone, and **osteoclasts,** cells that break down bone, work together to shape and remodel bone.

  CENGAGENOW™ Learn more about the human skeletal system and a typical long bone by clicking on the figures in CengageNOW.

6 Compare the main types of vertebrate joints.

- **Joints** are junctions of two or more bones. **Ligaments** are connective tissue bands that connect bones and limit movement at the joint. The sutures of the skull are **immovable joints.** Joints between vertebrae are **slightly movable joints.** A **freely movable joint** is enclosed by a joint capsule lined with a membrane that secretes **synovial fluid.**

7 Relate the structure of insect flight muscles to their function.

- Large numbers of mitochondria and tracheae (air tubes) present in insect flight muscles support the high metabolic rate required for flight.

8 Describe the structure of skeletal muscles and their antagonistic actions.

- A **muscular system** is found in most invertebrate phyla and in vertebrates. As muscle tissue contracts (shortens), it moves body parts by pulling on them.

- Vertebrate skeletal muscles pull on **tendons,** connective tissue cords that attach muscles to bones. When a muscle contracts, it pulls a bone toward or away from the bone with which it articulates.

- Skeletal muscles act **antagonistically** to one another. The muscle that produces a particular action is the **agonist;** the **antagonist** produces the opposite movement.

- A skeletal muscle such as the biceps is an organ made up of hundreds of **muscle fibers.** Each fiber consists of threadlike **myofibrils** composed of smaller **myofilaments,** or simply **filaments.** The striations of skeletal muscle fibers reflect the overlapping of their **actin**

filaments and **myosin filaments.** A **sarcomere** is a contractile unit of actin (thin) and myosin (thick) filaments.

9 List, in sequence, the events that take place during muscle contraction.

- **Acetylcholine** released by a motor neuron binds with receptors on the surface of a muscle fiber. This may cause **depolarization** of the sarcolemma and transmission of an **action potential.** The action potential spreads through the **T tubules,** releasing calcium ions from the **sarcoplasmic reticulum.**

- Calcium ions bind to **troponin** in the actin filaments, causing the troponin to change shape. Troponin pushes **tropomyosin** away from the binding sites on the actin filaments.

- ATP binds to myosin; ATP is split, putting the myosin head in a high-energy state (it is "cocked"). Energized myosin heads attach to the exposed binding sites on the actin filaments, forming **cross bridges** that link the myosin and actin filaments.

- After myosin attaches to the actin filament, the cross bridge flexes as phosphate is released. This is the power stroke, which pulls the actin filament toward the center of the sarcomere. ADP is released during the power stroke.

- The myosin head binds a new ATP, which lets the myosin head detach from the actin. As long as the calcium ion concentration remains elevated, the new ATP is split and the sequence repeats. The myosin reattaches to new active sites so that the filaments are pulled past one another, and the muscle continues to shorten.

10 Compare the roles of glycogen, creatine phosphate, and ATP in providing energy for muscle contraction.

- ATP is the immediate source of energy for muscle contraction. ATP hydrolysis provides the energy to "cock" the myosin. Muscle tissue has an intermediate energy storage compound, **creatine phosphate. Glycogen** is the fuel stored in muscle fibers.

11 Compare the structures and functions of the three types of skeletal muscle fibers.

- **Slow-oxidative fibers** are specialized for endurance activities. They contract slowly, fatigue slowly, are rich in mitochondria, and obtain most of their ATP from aerobic respiration. These fibers have a red color because they have a high content of **myoglobin,** a red pigment that stores oxygen.

- **Fast-glycolytic fibers** generate a great deal of power for a brief period. These white fibers contract rapidly, fatigue quickly, have few mitochondria, and use glycolysis as a major pathway for ATP synthesis.

- **Fast-oxidative fibers** are specialized for rapid response. They contract fast, have an intermediate rate of fatigue, are rich in mitochondria, and obtain most of their ATP from aerobic respiration. They have a high myoglobin content and a red color.

12 Describe factors that influence contraction.

- Contraction of a whole muscle depends on several factors, including the number of muscle fibers contracting, tension developed by each fiber, frequency of stimulation, condition of the muscle, and load on the muscle.

- A **motor unit** consists of all of the skeletal muscle fibers stimulated by a single motor neuron. Messages from the brain or spinal cord activate motor units. The more motor units that are *recruited,* the stronger are the contractions.

- When activated by a brief electrical stimulus, skeletal muscle responds with a **simple twitch.** When a second stimulus is received before the first contraction is complete, the two twitches can add together, a process called **summation.** Typically, skeletal muscle is stimulated by a series of separate stimuli timed close together and responds with a smooth, sustained contraction called **tetanus.**

- **Muscle tone** is the state of partial contraction characteristic of muscles.

  CENGAGENOW™ Explore muscle action, structure, and contraction as well as summation and tetanus by clicking on the figures in CengageNOW.

1. In vertebrate skin, cells actively divide in (a) stratum basale (b) stratum corneum (c) the dermis (d) the layer with cells that contain keratin (e) stratum basale and stratum corneum

2. An endoskeleton (a) is typically composed of dead tissue (b) is characterized by fluid in a closed compartment (c) is found mainly in echinoderms and vertebrates (d) is typical of echinoderms and arthropods (e) requires the animal to molt

3. Which of the following is *not* part of the vertebrate axial skeleton? (a) skull (b) vertebral column (c) pelvic girdle (d) rib cage (e) sternum

4. The thin outer shell of a long bone is made of (a) compact bone (b) spongy bone (c) epiphyses (d) cartilage (e) mainly chondrocytes

5. In endochondral bone development, (a) osteoclasts produce bone (b) joints connect fibers (c) the skeleton consists of cartilage (d) bones develop from cartilage templates (e) bones form in noncartilage connective tissue

6. All animals have (a) muscles (b) actin (c) bones (d) endoskeleton or exoskeleton (e) dermis

7. An energy storage compound that can be stockpiled in muscle cells for short-term use is (a) myoglobin (b) ADP (c) troponin (d) myosin (e) creatine phosphate

8. Myosin binds to actin, forming a cross bridge. What happens next? (a) acetylcholine is released (b) calcium ions stimulate exposure of active sites (c) filaments slide past one another, and the muscle fiber shortens (d) myosin is activated (e) P_i is released, and the cross bridge flexes

9. Calcium ions are released from the sarcoplasmic reticulum. What happens next? (a) acetylcholine is released (b) active sites on the actin filaments are exposed (c) filaments slide past one another, and the muscle fiber shortens (d) myosin is activated (e) P_i is released, and the cross bridge flexes

10. When skeletal muscle is stimulated by a series of closely timed separate stimuli, (a) white fibers respond (b) a simple twitch occurs (c) it responds with a smooth, sustained contraction called tetanus (d) red fibers respond (e) summation is inhibited

11. Insect flight muscles (a) work best at low temperature (b) evolved after bird wings (c) do not create much lift (d) have a very high metabolic rate (e) are typically attached directly to the wing and make up the bulk of the wing

12. Label the diagram. (Refer to Fig.40-9c to check your answers.)

CRITICAL THINKING

1. What are some examples of hydrostatic support in plants?

2. Why is it important that a muscle be able to shift functions, sometimes acting as an agonist and at other times acting as an antagonist?

3. What is the functional relationship between skeletal and muscle tissues?

4. **EVOLUTION LINK.** Very different skeletal systems have evolved in arthropods and vertebrates. What are some benefits and some disadvantages of each type of skeleton? In what way is the insect skeleton an adaptation to the insect lifestyle?

5. **ANALYZING DATA.** Examine Figure 40-13. Based on the summation of two stimuli shown in this graph, draw a curve showing summation when the muscle fiber is stimulated three times.

 Additional questions are available in CengageNOW at www.cengage.com/login.

41 Neural Signaling

Nancy Kedersha/UCLA/Science Photo Library/
Photo Researchers, Inc.

Specialized cells in the nervous system. This immunofluorescent LM of mammalian spinal cord tissue includes several astrocytes (*green*). The blue dots are the nuclei of other glial cells. The smaller cells (*dark pink*) are neurons; their cell bodies appear light pink.

KEY CONCEPTS

41.1 Neural signaling involves reception, transmission, integration, and action by effectors.

41.2 Neurons are specialized to receive stimuli and transmit signals; glial cells support, protect, and nourish neurons and can modify neural signals.

41.3 The resting potential of a neuron is maintained by differences in concentrations of specific ions inside the cell relative to the extracellular fluid and by selective permeability of the plasma membrane to these ions. Depolarization of the neuron plasma membrane to threshold level generates an action potential, an electrical signal that travels as a wave of depolarization along the axon.

41.4 Most neurons signal other cells by releasing neurotransmitters at chemical synapses.

41.5 During integration, incoming neural signals are summed; temporal and spatial summation can bring a neuron to threshold level.

41.6 Neurons are organized in specific pathways called neural circuits, which, in turn, are organized to form neural networks.

An animal's ability to survive and to maintain homeostasis depends largely on how effectively it detects and responds to *stimuli*—changes in its environment. Most animals have a *nervous system* that takes in information, transmits it to the spinal cord and brain where it is integrated, and then responds. The nervous system is composed mainly of two specialized types of cells—*neurons* and *glial cells* (see photograph). Just how animals respond to stimuli depends on how their neurons are organized and connected to one another. A single neuron in the vertebrate brain may be functionally connected to thousands of other neurons.

The nervous system is the principal regulatory system in animals. Regulation requires communication, and the nervous system transmits information to and from all parts of the body. As you will learn, the endocrine system works with the nervous system to regulate many behaviors and physiological processes. In general, the endocrine system provides relatively slow and long-lasting regulation, whereas the nervous system responds rapidly, but briefly.

Neurobiology is one of the most exciting areas of biological research. Active areas of research include *neurotransmitters,* the chemical messengers used by neurons to signal other neurons, and the *receptors* that bind with the neurotransmitters. Some neurobiologists are focused on how neural networks in the brain function in cognitive and emotional experience. For example, researchers have recently identified an area of the prefrontal cortex important in self-control and decision-making. They have also identified neural circuits that appear to be responsible for our experiences of physical pain and pleasure.

A very active area of research focuses on neurogenesis, the production of new neurons. One of the most time-honored views about nervous system function was that the brain of mammals cannot generate new neurons after birth. Nobel laureate Santiago Ramon y Cajal promoted this concept at the beginning of the 20th century, and the idea that we are born with all the brain cells we will ever have was widely held for almost a century. Another enduring idea was that glial cells, the most common cells in the brain, simply provide support services for neurons. As we will discuss in this chapter, both of these concepts have been shown to be incorrect.

In this chapter we focus on how information is communicated by neurons and glial cells. In Chapter 42 we discuss nervous systems, and in Chapter 43 we explore sensory reception.

41.1 NEURAL SIGNALING: AN OVERVIEW

◼ LEARNING OBJECTIVE

1   Describe the processes involved in neural signaling: reception, transmission, integration, and action by effectors.

Thousands of stimuli constantly bombard an animal. Survival depends on identifying these stimuli and responding effectively. Information about each stimulus must be transmitted *to* the nervous system and then information *from* the nervous system must be transmitted to the muscles (and glands). Animals respond to changes in temperature, sound, light, odors, and movement that may indicate the presence of a predator or of prey. Internal signals, such as hunger, pain, fluctuations in blood pressure, or changes in blood sugar concentration, also demand responses. In most animals, responses to stimuli depend on **neural signaling,** information transfer by networks of nerve cells, called **neurons.** In most animals, neural signaling involves four processes: reception, transmission, integration, and action by effectors (muscles or glands).

Reception, the process of detecting a stimulus, is the job of neurons and of specialized *sensory receptors* such as those in the skin, eyes, and ears (**FIG. 41-1**). **Transmission** is the process of sending messages along a neuron, from one neuron to another or from a neuron to a muscle or gland. In vertebrates, a neural message is transmitted from a receptor to the **central nervous system (CNS),** which consists of the brain and spinal cord. Neurons that transmit information to the CNS are called **afferent** (meaning "to carry toward") **neurons,** or **sensory neurons.**

Afferent neurons generally transmit information to **interneurons,** or association neurons, in the CNS. Most neurons, perhaps 99%, are interneurons. Their function is to integrate input and out-

FIGURE 41-1 *Animated* **Response to a stimulus**

Whether a stimulus originates in the outside world or inside the body, information must be received; transmitted to the central nervous system; integrated; and then transmitted to effectors, muscles or glands that carry out some action, the actual response.

put. **Integration** involves sorting and interpreting incoming sensory information and determining the appropriate response.

Neural messages are transmitted from the CNS by **efferent** (meaning "to carry away") **neurons** to **effectors**—muscles and glands. Efferent neurons that signal skeletal muscle are called **motor**

neurons. The **action by effectors** is the actual response to the stimulus. Sensory receptors and afferent and efferent neurons are part of the **peripheral nervous system (PNS).** In summary, information flows through the nervous system in the following sequence:

reception by sensory receptor ⟶ transmission by afferent neuron ⟶ integration by interneurons in CNS ⟶ transmission by efferent neuron ⟶ action by effectors

Review

- Imagine you are swimming and you suddenly spot a shark fin moving in your direction. What processes must take place within your nervous system before you can make your escape?
- What happens after neural signals are integrated in the CNS?

41.2 NEURONS AND GLIAL CELLS

◼ LEARNING OBJECTIVES

2   Describe the structure of a typical neuron and give the function of each of its parts.
3   Name the main types of glial cells and describe the functions of each.

Neurons and glial cells are unique to the nervous system. Neurons are specialized to receive and send information. Glial cells support and protect neurons and carry out many regulatory functions.

Neurons receive stimuli and transmit neural signals

The neuron is highly specialized to receive and transmit information. Neurons produce and transmit electrical signals called **nerve impulses,** or *action potentials.* The neuron is distinguished from all other cells by its long **processes** (cytoplasmic extensions). Ex-

amine the structure of a common type of neuron, the multipolar neuron shown in **FIGURE 41-2.**

The largest portion of the neuron, the **cell body,** contains the nucleus, the bulk of the cytoplasm, and most of the organelles. Typically, two types of processes project from the cell body of a multipolar neuron. Numerous dendrites extend from one end, and a long, single axon projects from the opposite end. **Dendrites** are typically short, highly branched processes specialized to receive stimuli and send signals to the cell body. The cell body integrates incoming signals.

Although microscopic in diameter, an **axon** may be 1 m (more than 1 yard) or more in length and may divide, forming branches called **axon collaterals.** The axon conducts nerve impulses away from the cell body to another neuron or to a muscle or gland. At its end the axon divides, forming many **terminal branches** that end in **synaptic terminals.** The synaptic terminals release **neurotransmitters,** chemicals that transmit signals from one neuron to another or from a neuron to an effector. The junction between a synaptic terminal and another neuron (or effector) is called a **synapse.** Typically, a small space exists between these two cells.

In vertebrates, the axons of many neurons outside the CNS are surrounded by a series of **Schwann cells.** The plasma membranes of these glial cells contain **myelin,** a white, fatty material. Schwann cells wrap their plasma membranes around the axon, forming an insulating covering called the **myelin sheath.** Gaps in the myelin sheath, called **nodes of Ranvier,** occur between successive Schwann cells. At these points the axon is not insulated with myelin. Axons more than 2 μm in diameter have myelin sheaths and are described as *myelinated.* Those of smaller diameter are generally unmyelinated.

Certain regions of the CNS produce new neurons

At the beginning of the chapter, we described Cajal's idea that **neurogenesis,** the production of new neurons, does not occur in the CNS. The paradigm shift that has occurred with regard to

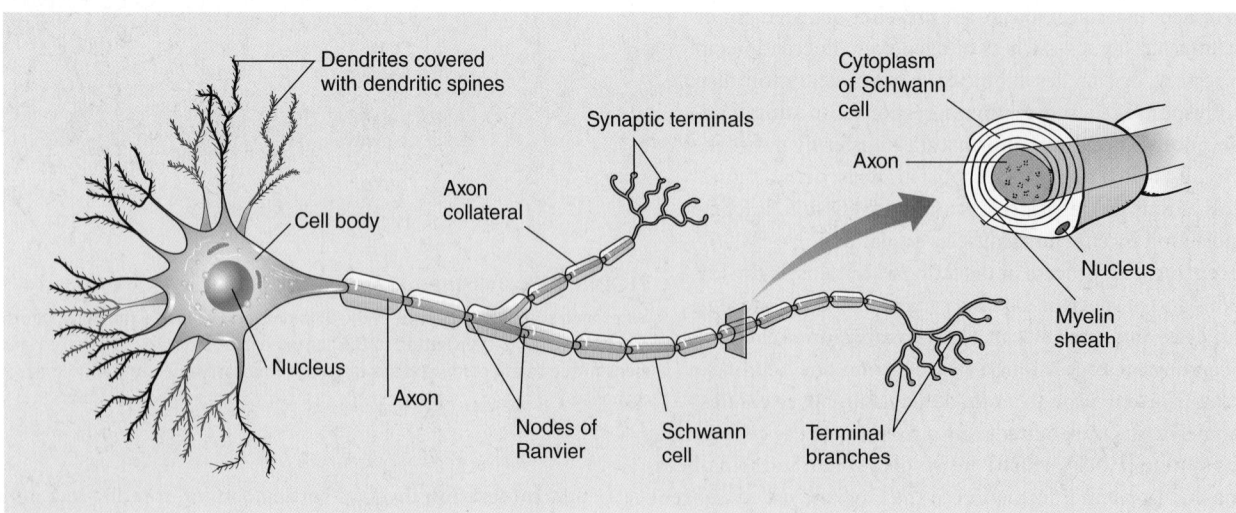

FIGURE 41-2 *Animated* **Structure of a multipolar neuron**
The cell body contains most of the organelles. Many dendrites and a single axon extend from the cell body. Schwann cells form a myelin sheath around the axon by wrapping their own plasma membranes around the neuron in jelly-roll fashion.

this view demonstrates the power and importance of the process of science. Cajal's idea was so entrenched that for many years the researchers who attempted to study the issue were discouraged and discounted. Even images produced by an electron microscope showing neurons dividing were ridiculed and rejected.

During the 1980s, studies on rhesus monkey brains appeared to support Cajal's idea. No new neurons were found in the monkeys' brains. The matter appeared settled. However, matters are almost never settled in science. Researchers investigating a variety of seemingly unrelated problems made observations that shed new light on the neurogenesis issue. For more than 25 years, Fernando Nottebohm at Rockefeller University has studied birdsong, including its neural basis. Nottebohm found that birds produce new neurons daily in the brain center that regulates their songs. His work was at first dismissed as a phenomenon peculiar to birds and not relevant to mammals.

However, other investigators, most notably psychologist Elizabeth Gould at Princeton University, have provided additional data that together have falsified Cajal's concept. Gould demonstrated neuron proliferation in primates. She and her research team also discovered that stress damages the brain and inhibits mitosis in neurons. They stressed newborn rats by separating them from their mothers for up to 3 hours a day. These rats did not learn how to cope with stress, and as adults, they had fewer new neurons in certain areas of their brains than control rats. Earlier investigations may have failed to show new neurons in the brain because the animals being studied were in a state of stress and neurogenesis was inhibited. Neurobiologists now agree that neurogenesis does occur regularly in the adult mammalian brain, at least in the olfactory bulb and hippocampus. The paradigm has shifted.

Axons aggregate to form nerves and tracts

A **nerve** consists of hundreds or even thousands of axons wrapped together in connective tissue (**FIG. 41-3**). We can compare a nerve to a telephone cable. The individual axons correspond to the wires that run through the cable, and the sheaths and connective tissue coverings correspond to the insulation. Within the CNS, bundles of axons are called **tracts** or **pathways** rather than nerves.

Outside the CNS, the cell bodies of neurons are usually grouped in masses called **ganglia** (sing., *ganglion*). Inside the CNS, collections of cell bodies are generally called *nuclei* rather than *ganglia*.

Glial cells play critical roles in neural function

Glial cells collectively make up the **neuroglia** (literally, "nerve glue"). Until recently, glial cells were thought to be passive cells that simply support and protect the neurons. Armed with more sophisticated technology, researchers are discovering that glial cells communicate and carry out major regulatory functions.

More than 75% of the cells in the human CNS are glial cells. They account for about 50% of the brain volume because they do not branch as extensively as neurons. Four types of glial cells are found in the vertebrate CNS: astrocytes, oligodendrocytes, ependymal cells, and microglia (**TABLE 41-1**).

Astrocytes are star-shaped glial cells that provide physical support for neurons and provide neurons with nutrients. Astrocytes help regulate the composition of the extracellular fluid in the CNS by removing excess potassium ions. This action helps maintain normal neuron excitability. Some astrocytes position the ends of their long processes on blood vessels in the brain. In response,

(a) A nerve consists of bundles of axons held together by connective tissue. The cell bodies belonging to the axons of a nerve are grouped in a ganglion.

(b) SEM showing a cross section through a myelinated afferent nerve of a bullfrog.

FIGURE 41-3 *Animated* Structure of a myelinated nerve

TABLE 41-1	Functions of Glial Cells
Type of Glial Cell	**Functions**
Astrocytes 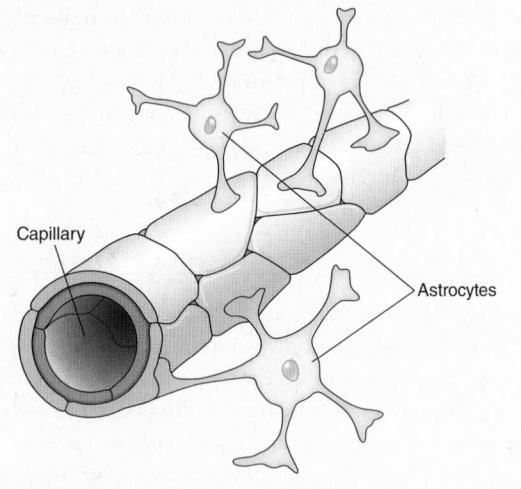 Capillary Astrocytes	Physically support neurons Provide neurons with nutrients Remove excess K^+, which helps regulate composition of extracellular fluid in CNS Induce blood vessels to form blood–brain barrier Communicate with one another and with neurons Induce synapse formation and strengthen activity of synapses Respond to neurotransmitters and help regulate neurotransmitter reuptake May be important in memory and learning Guide neurons during embryonic development
Oligodendrocytes 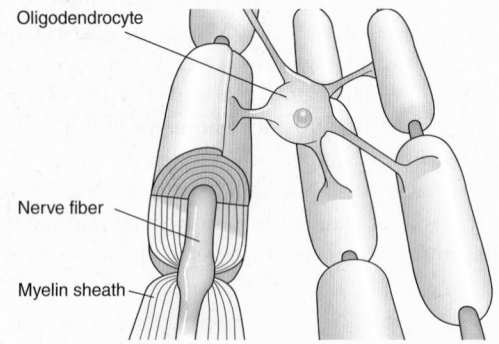 Oligodendrocyte Nerve fiber Myelin sheath	Form myelin sheaths around neurons in CNS
Ependymal cells Cilia Ependymal cells	Line cavities of CNS Help produce and circulate cerebrospinal fluid May function as neural stem cells
Microglia 	Phagocytosis of bacteria and debris Release signaling molecules that mediate inflammation

endothelial cells lining the blood vessels form *tight junctions* (see Chapter 5) that prevent many substances in the blood from entering the brain tissue. This protective wall is the *blood–brain barrier*.

Neurobiologists have shown that astrocytes are functionally connected throughout the brain. These interesting glial cells may participate in information signaling in the brain by coordinating activity among neurons. They communicate through *gap junctions* and with signaling molecules. Although astrocytes can generate only weak electrical signals, they communicate with one another and with neurons by means of chemical signals. Astrocytes appear to respond to neurotransmitters released by neurons. They also help regulate the reuptake of excess neurotransmitters from synapses. Neurobiologists have demonstrated that astrocytes induce synapse formation and can strengthen activity of synapses in the brain. Their actions appear to be important in learning and memory.

Astrocytes play a role in development by guiding neurons to appropriate locations in the body. Neurobiologists have shown that certain astrocytes function as stem cells in the brain and spinal cord. These cells can give rise to new neurons, additional astrocytes, and certain other glial cells. Taken out of their normal environment in the adult mouse brain, astrocytes can give rise to cells of all germ layers (the embryonic tissue layers: ectoderm, mesoderm, and endoderm). Human astrocytes may someday be used to produce specific types of cells needed for treating various medical conditions.

Oligodendrocytes are glial cells that envelop neurons in the CNS, forming insulating myelin sheaths around them. Because myelin is an excellent electrical insulator, its presence speeds transmission of neural impulses. In the neurological disease **multiple sclerosis,** which affects about 400,000 people in North America alone, patches of myelin deteriorate at irregular intervals along axons in the CNS and are replaced by scar tissue. This damage interferes with conduction of neural impulses, and the victim suffers loss of coordination, tremor, and partial or complete paralysis of parts of the body.

Do not confuse oligodendrocytes with Schwann cells. Although sometimes considered glial cells, Schwann cells are located outside the CNS. Schwann cells form myelin sheaths around axons of many neurons that are part of the PNS.

Ependymal cells are ciliated glial cells that line the internal cavities of the CNS. Ependymal cells help produce and circulate the *cerebrospinal fluid* that bathes the brain and spinal cord of vertebrates (discussed in Chapter 42). Investigators have recently suggested that ependymal cells might function as neural stem cells.

Microglia are actually specialized macrophages (phagocytic cells that ingest and digest cell debris and bacteria). Microglia respond to signals from neurons and are important in mediating responses to injury or disease. These cells are found near blood vessels. When the brain is injured or infected, microglia multiply and move to the affected area. There they remove bacteria and cell debris by phagocytosis. They also release signaling molecules (also produced by macrophages and certain other cells in the immune system) that mediate inflammation.

Review

- What are the functions of (1) dendrites, (2) synaptic terminals, and (3) the myelin sheath?
- How is a neuron different from a nerve?
- What are the functions of astrocytes? of microglia?

41.3 TRANSMITTING INFORMATION ALONG THE NEURON

■ LEARNING OBJECTIVES

4 Explain how the neuron develops and maintains a resting potential.

5 Compare a graded potential with an action potential, describing the production and transmission of each.

6 Contrast continuous conduction with saltatory conduction.

Most animal cells have a difference in electric charge across the plasma membrane—the electric charge inside the cell is more negative than the electric charge of the extracellular fluid. The plasma membrane is said to be electrically **polarized,** meaning that one side, or pole, has a different charge than the other side. When electric charges are separated in this way, a potential energy difference exists across the membrane.

The difference in electric charge across the plasma membrane gives rise to an *electrical gradient*. Voltage is the force that causes charged particles to flow between two points. The voltage measured across the plasma membrane is called the **membrane potential.** If the charges are permitted to come together, they have the ability to do work. Thus, the cell can be thought of as a biological battery. In excitable cells, such as neurons and muscle cells, the membrane potential can change rapidly. Such changes can transmit signals to other cells.

Ion channels and pumps maintain the resting potential of the neuron

The membrane potential in a resting (not excited) neuron or muscle cell is its **resting potential.** The resting potential is generally expressed in units called *millivolts* (mV). (A millivolt equals one thousandth of a volt.) Like other cells that can produce electrical signals, the neuron has a resting potential of about 70 mV. By convention this is expressed as −70 mV because the cytosol close to the plasma membrane is negatively charged relative to the extracellular fluid (**FIG. 41-4a**).

Biologists can measure the potential across the membrane by placing one electrode inside the cell and a second electrode outside the cell and connecting them through a very sensitive voltmeter or oscilloscope. If you place both electrodes on the outside surface of the neuron, no potential difference between them is registered. (All points on the same side of the membrane have the same charge.) However, once one of the electrodes penetrates the cell, the voltage changes from zero to approximately −70 mV.

Two main factors determine the magnitude of the membrane potential: (1) differences in the concentrations between specific ions inside the cell and those in the extracellular fluid and (2) selective permeability of the plasma membrane to these ions. The distribution of ions inside neurons and in the extracellular fluid surrounding them is like that of most other cells in the body. The potassium ion (K^+) concentration is about 10 times greater inside the cell than outside the cell. In contrast, the sodium ion (Na^+) concentration is about 10 times greater outside than inside. This asymmetric distribution of ions across the plasma membrane at

(a) Measuring the resting potential of a neuron. The axon is negatively charged compared with the surrounding extracellular fluid. The difference in electric charge across the plasma membrane is measured by placing an electrode just inside the neuron and a second electrode in the extracellular fluid just outside the plasma membrane.

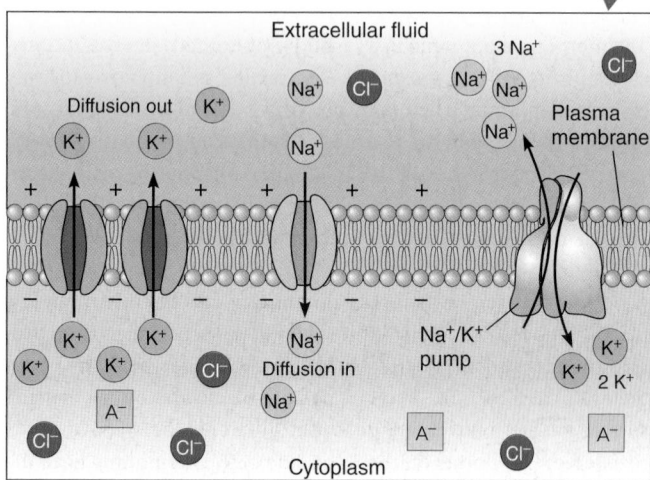

(b) Permeability of the neuron membrane. The membrane is less permeable to Na^+ than to K^+. Passive ion channels allow K^+ to diffuse out along their concentration gradient. Potassium ions are mainly responsible for the voltage across the membrane. Sodium–potassium pumps in the plasma membrane actively pump Na^+ out of the cell and pump K^+ in. The plasma membrane is permeable to negatively charged Cl^-, and they contribute slightly to the negative charge. Large anions (A^-) such as proteins also contribute to the negative charge.

FIGURE 41-4 *Animated* Resting potential

rest is brought about by the action of selective ion channels and ion pumps. In vertebrate neurons (and skeletal muscle fibers), the resting membrane potential depends mainly on the diffusion of ions down their *concentration gradients* (see discussion of diffusion in Chapter 5).

Ions cross the plasma membrane by diffusion through ion channels

Recall that net movement of ions occurs from an area of higher concentration of that type of ion to one of lower concentration. Membrane proteins form ion channels that typically allow only specific types of ions to pass. Neurons have three types of ion channels: *passive ion channels, voltage-activated channels,* and *chemically activated ion channels.* **Passive ion channels** permit the passage of specific ions such as Na^+, K^+, Cl^-, and Ca^{2+} (**FIG. 41-4b**). Unlike voltage-activated and chemically activated ion channels, passive ion channels are not controlled by gates.

Potassium channels are the most common type of passive ion channel in the plasma membrane, and cells are more permeable to potassium than to other ions. In fact, in the resting neuron, the plasma membrane is up to 100 times more permeable to K^+ than to Na^+. When pumped out of the neuron, Na^+ cannot easily pass back into the cell. However, K^+ pumped into the neuron easily diffuses out.

Potassium ions leak out through passive ion channels following their concentration gradient. As K^+ diffuse out of the neuron, they increase the positive charge in the extracellular fluid relative to the charge inside the cell. The resulting change in the electrical gradient across the membrane influences the flow of ions. This electrical gradient forces some of the positively charged potassium ions back into the cell.

The membrane potential at which the flux (flow) of K^+ inward (due to the electrical gradient) equals the flux of K^+ outward (because of the concentration gradient) is the **equilibrium potential** for K^+. The equilibrium potential for any particular ion is a steady state in which opposing chemical and electrical fluxes are equal and there is no net movement of the ion. The equilibrium potential for K^+ in the typical neuron is -80 mV. The equilibrium potential for Na^+ is -40 mV; it differs from the equilibrium potential of K^+ because of the difference in concentration of Na^+ across the membrane (concentration is high outside and low inside the cell). Because the membrane is much more permeable to K^+ than to Na^+, the resting potential of the neuron is closer to the potassium equilibrium potential than to the sodium equilibrium potential. (Remember that the resting potential of the neuron is about -70 mV.)

The resting potential is primarily established by the net flow of K^+ into the neuron. However, the net flow of Na^+ outward contributes to the resting potential. Because the plasma membrane is permeable to negatively charged chloride ions, Cl^- also contribute slightly. These ions accumulate in the cytosol close to the plasma membrane. Negative charges on large molecules such as proteins add to the negative charge in the cytosol. These large anions cannot cross the plasma membrane.

Ion pumping maintains the gradients that determine the resting potential

The neuron plasma membrane has very efficient **sodium–potassium pumps** that actively transport Na^+ out of the cell and

K^+ into the cell (see Fig. 41-4b; also see Fig. 5-17). These pumps require ATP to pump Na^+ and K^+ against their concentration and electrical gradients. For every three Na^+ pumped out of the cell, two K^+ are pumped in. Thus, more positive ions are pumped out than in. The sodium–potassium pumps maintain a higher concentration of K^+ inside the cell than outside, and a higher concentration of Na^+ outside than inside.

In summary, the development of the resting potential depends mainly on the diffusion of K^+ out of the cell. However, once the neuron reaches a steady state, net Na^+ diffusion into the cell is greater than net K^+ diffusion out of the cell. This situation is offset by the sodium–potassium pumps that pump three Na^+ out of the cell for every two K^+ pumped in.

Graded local signals vary in magnitude

Neurons are excitable cells. They respond to stimuli and can convert stimuli into nerve impulses. An electrical, chemical, or mechanical stimulus may alter the resting potential by increasing the membrane's permeability to sodium ions.

When a stimulus causes the membrane potential to become less negative (closer to zero) than the resting potential, that region of the membrane is **depolarized.** Because depolarization brings a neuron closer to transmitting a neural impulse, it is described as *excitatory*. In contrast, when the membrane potential becomes more negative than the resting potential, the membrane is **hyperpolarized.** Hyperpolarization is *inhibitory*; it decreases the ability of the neuron to generate a neural impulse.

A stimulus may change the potential in a relatively small region of the plasma membrane. Such a **graded potential** is a local response. It functions as a signal only over a very short distance because it fades out within a few millimeters of its point of origin. A graded potential varies in magnitude; that is, the potential charge varies depending on the strength of the stimulus applied. The larger the stimulus is, the larger the change in permeability and the greater the change in membrane potential.

Axons transmit signals called action potentials

When a stimulus is strong enough, a rapid, large change in membrane potential occurs, depolarizing the membrane to a critical point known as the **threshold level.** At that point, the neuron fires a nerve impulse, or **action potential,** an electrical signal that travels rapidly down the axon into the synaptic terminals. All cells can generate graded potentials, but only neurons, muscle cells, and a few cells of the endocrine and immune systems can generate action potentials.

In a series of experiments in the 1940s, pioneering English researchers Alan Hodgkin and Andrew Huxley inserted electrodes into large axons found in squids. By measuring voltage changes as they varied ion concentrations, these investigators showed that passage of Na^+ ions *into* the neuron and K^+ ions *out* of the neuron resulted in an action potential. The process of Na^+ rushing into the cell can be compared to the gas pedal of the action, whereas the process of K^+ leaving the cell brakes the action. In 1963, Hodgkin and Huxley received the Nobel Prize in Physiology or Medicine for this research.

We now know that changes in voltage regulate specific **voltage-activated ion channels** (also called **voltage-gated ion channels**) in the plasma membrane of the axon and cell body. Biologists can study these channels by using the **patch clamp technique** to measure currents across a very small segment of the plasma membrane rather than across the entire membrane (**FIG. 41-5**). The patch of membrane measured is so small that it may contain a single channel.

Biologists have used certain toxins that affect the nervous system to investigate how membrane channels function. For example, the poison tetrodotoxin (TTX) binds to voltage-activated Na^+ channels, blocking the passage of Na^+. Using TTX and other toxins, researchers were able to identify the channel protein. TTX was first isolated from the Japanese puffer fish, which is eaten as a delicacy (**FIG. 41-6**). In small amounts TTX tingles the taste buds, but in a larger dose it can prevent breathing. (The Japanese government operates a certification program for puffer fish chefs!)

Investigators have established that voltage-activated ion channels have charged regions that act as gates. Voltage-activated Na^+ channels have two gates—an *activation gate* and an *inactivation gate* (**FIG. 41-7a**). Voltage-activated K^+ channels have a single gate (**FIG. 41-7b**).

Local anesthetics such as procaine (novocaine) and lidocaine (Xylocaine), as well as cocaine, bind to voltage-activated Na^+ channels and block them. The channels cannot open in response to depolarization, and the neuron cannot transmit an impulse through the anesthetized region. Signals do not reach the brain, so pain is not experienced.

An action potential is generated when the voltage reaches threshold level

The membrane of most neurons can depolarize by about 15 mV, that is, to a potential of about -55 mV, without initiating an action potential. However, when depolarization is greater than -55 mV, the threshold level is reached and an action potential is generated. The neuron membrane quickly reaches zero potential and even **overshoots** to $+35$ mV or more as a momentary reversal in polarity takes place. The sharp rise and fall of the action potential is called a *spike*. **FIGURE 41-8a** on page 870 illustrates an action potential recorded by placing one electrode inside an axon and one just outside.

At resting potentials, activation gates of the voltage-activated Na^+ channels are closed and Na^+ cannot pass into the neuron (**FIG. 41-8b**; follow the steps illustrated in this figure as you read about transmission of action potentials, repolarization, and return to the resting state). When the voltage reaches threshold level, the channel proteins change shape, opening the activation gates. Sodium ions can then flow through the voltage-activated Na^+ channels. As a result, the inside of the neuron becomes positively charged relative to the fluid outside the plasma membrane, generating an action potential. Inactivation gates that are open in the resting neuron close slowly in response to depolarization. Sodium ions can pass through the channel only during the brief period when both activation and inactivation gates are open.

The generation of an action potential depends on a **positive feedback system.** (Recall from Chapter 39 that in a positive feedback system, a change in some condition triggers a response that *intensifies* the change.) As just discussed, when a neuron is

Why Is It Used? The patch clamp technique allows researchers to study the action of a single ion channel over time, even in very small cells. This research method was developed in the mid-1970s by Erwin Neher and Bert Sakmann, both of the Max Planck Institute in Germany. They were awarded a Nobel Prize in 1991 for this work.

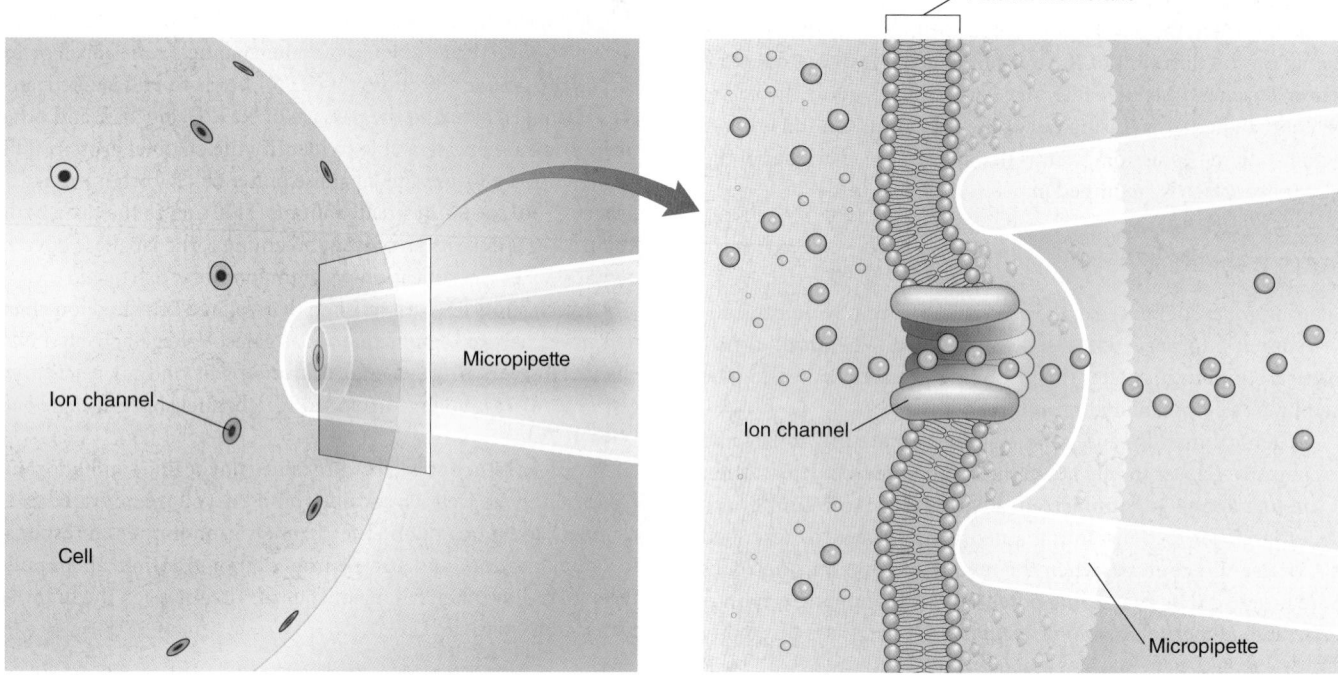

How Is It Done? The tip of a micropipette is tightly sealed to a patch of membrane so small that it generally contains only a single ion channel. The flow of ions through the channel can be measured using an extremely sensitive recording device. Cell biologists have found that the current flow is intermittent and corresponds to the opening and closing of the ion channel. The permeability of the channel affects the magnitude of the current.

FIGURE 41-5 The patch clamp technique

The patch clamp technique has been modified in many ways and has been applied to studies of the roles of ion channels in a wide range of cellular processes in both plants and animals. For example, until recently neuroscientists thought that transmitting action potentials was a very inefficient process. They thought that there was a high degree of overlap between the time that Na^+ rush into the cell and K^+ move out of the cell. This would be a waste of energy because it would be like stepping on the gas and the brake at the same time. Henrik Alle, a neuroscientist at the Max Planck Institute for Brain Research in Frankfurt, Germany, and his colleagues recently used the patch clamp technique to record currents in neurons of the learning and memory areas of rat brains. They found that the flow of Na^+ and of K^+ were almost completely separated in time. Na^+ have almost finished entering the neuron before K^+ ions begin to exit. In contrast to earlier estimates of 30% efficiency for transmission of signals along the neuron, neurons may transmit action potentials with more than 70% efficiency.

depolarized, voltage-activated Na^+ channels open, increasing the membrane permeability to Na^+. Sodium ions diffuse into the cell, moving from an area of higher concentration to an area of lower concentration. As Na^+ flow into the cell, the cytosol becomes positively charged relative to the extracellular fluid. This charge further depolarizes the neuron so that more voltage-activated Na^+ channels open, which increases membrane permeability to Na^+.

The neuron repolarizes and returns to a resting state

After a certain period, inactivation gates close in the Na^+ channels, and the membrane again becomes impermeable to Na^+. This

inactivation begins the process of **repolarization,** during which the membrane potential returns to its resting level. Voltage-activated K^+ channels slowly open in response to depolarization. When Na^+ have almost stopped rushing into the neuron, K^+ channels open and K^+ leak out of the neuron. This decrease in intracellular K^+ returns the interior of the membrane to its relatively negative state, repolarizing the membrane. Voltage-activated K^+ channels remain open until the resting potential has been restored.

As a wave of depolarization moves down the membrane of the neuron, the normal polarized state is quickly re-established behind

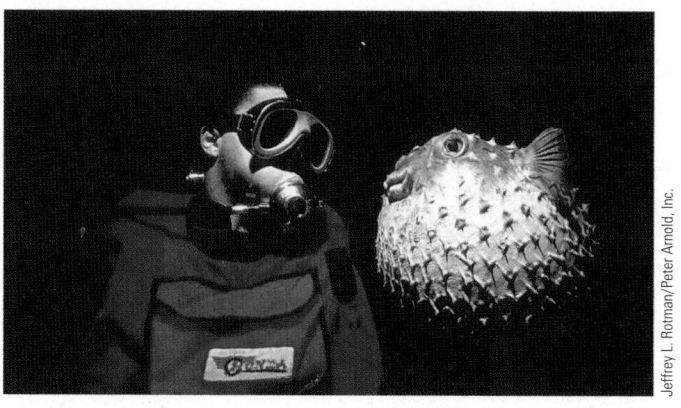

FIGURE 41-6 Japanese puffer fish

A poison, tetrodotoxin, isolated from this fish (*Fugu rubripes*) binds to voltage-activated sodium ion channels, allowing neurobiologists to study them.

it. The entire process—depolarization and then repolarization—can take place in less than 1 millisecond.

During the millisecond or so in which it is depolarized, the axon membrane is in an **absolute refractory period:** it cannot transmit another action potential no matter how great a stimulus is applied because the voltage-activated Na^+ channels are inactivated. Until their gates are reset, they cannot open again. When enough Na^+ channel gates have been reset, the neuron enters a **relative refractory period** that lasts for a few more milliseconds. During this period, the axon can transmit impulses, but the threshold is higher (less negative). Even with the limits imposed by their

refractory periods, most neurons can transmit several hundred impulses per second.

In summary, neural action proceeds as follows:

neuron in resting state ⟶ stimulus causes depolarization ⟶ threshold reached ⟶ action potential transmits signal ⟶ repolarization and return to resting state

The action potential is an all-or-none response

Any stimulus too weak to depolarize the plasma membrane to threshold level cannot fire the neuron. It merely sets up a local signal that fades and dies within a few millimeters from the point of stimulus. Only a stimulus strong enough to depolarize the membrane to its critical threshold level results in transmission of an impulse along the axon. An action potential is an **all-or-none response** because either it occurs or it does not. No variation exists in the strength of a single impulse.

If the all-or-none law is valid, how can we explain differences in the levels of intensity of sensations? After all, we have no difficulty distinguishing between the pain of a severe toothache and that of a minor cut on the arm. We can explain this apparent inconsistency by understanding that the intensity of sensation depends on several factors, including the *number of neurons stimulated* and on their *frequency of discharge.* For example, suppose you burn your hand. If a large area is burned, more pain receptors are stimulated and more neurons become depolarized. Also, each neuron transmits more action potentials per unit of time.

(a) Sodium channels. In the resting state, voltage-activated Na^+ channels are closed (*left*). When the voltage reaches threshold level, activation gates open quickly, allowing Na^+ to pass into the cell (*right*). After a certain time, inactivation gates close, blocking the channels (not shown). Inactivation gates are open when a neuron is in the resting state; they close slowly in response to depolarization. The ion channel is open only during the brief period when both activation and inactivation gates are open.

(b) Potassium channels. Voltage-activated K^+ channels have activation gates that open slowly in response to depolarization. The activation gates close after the resting potential has been restored. Potassium channels have no inactivation gates.

FIGURE 41-7 Voltage-activated ion channels

When the neuron plasma membrane is depolarized to threshold level, voltage-activated Na^+ channels open and Na^+ rush in, causing greater depolarization; an action potential is generated.

(a) Action potential. When the axon depolarizes to about −55 mV, an action potential is generated. (The numerical values vary for different nerve cells.)

1 Resting state. Voltage-activated Na^+ and K^+ channels are closed.

2 Depolarization. At threshold, voltage-activated Na^+ channels open. Na^+ rush into the neuron, causing further depolarization. Action potential is generated.

3 Repolarization. Voltage-activated Na^+ channels become inactivated. Voltage-activated K^+ channels are open; K^+ diffuse out of cell, restoring negative charge to inside of cell.

4 Return to resting state. Voltage-activated Na^+ and K^+ channels close. Na^+/K^+ pumps (not shown) move Na^+ out of the cell and K^+ into the cell, restoring the original ion distribution.

(b) The action of ion channels in the plasma membrane determines the state of the neuron.

FIGURE 41-8 *Animated* **Neural signaling along a neuron**

Generation of an action potential depends on the action of ion channels in the plasma membrane.

An action potential is self-propagating

Once initiated, an action potential continues along the neuron. During depolarization, the affected area of the membrane is more positive relative to adjacent regions where the membrane is still at resting potential. The difference in potentials between active and resting membrane regions causes ions to flow between them (an electric current). The flow of Na^+ into the adjacent region induces the opening of voltage-activated Na^+ channels in that area of the

membrane (**FIG. 41-9**). The process is repeated like a chain reaction until the end of the axon is reached. Thus, an action potential is a **wave of depolarization** that travels down the length of the axon.

Transmission of an action potential is sometimes compared with a flame moving along a trail of gunpowder. Once the gunpowder is ignited at one end of the trail, the flame moves steadily to the other end by igniting the powder particles ahead of it. An amazing difference is that, after a brief refractory period, the neuron recovers and is able to transmit another action potential.

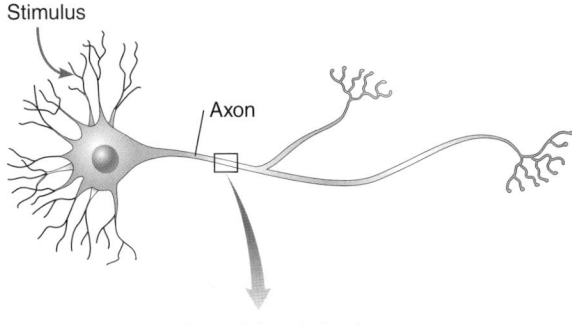

Stimulus

Axon

Area of depolarization

Potassium channel

Sodium channel

Action potential

1 Action potential is transmitted as wave of depolarization that travels down axon. At region of depolarization, Na⁺ diffuse into cell.

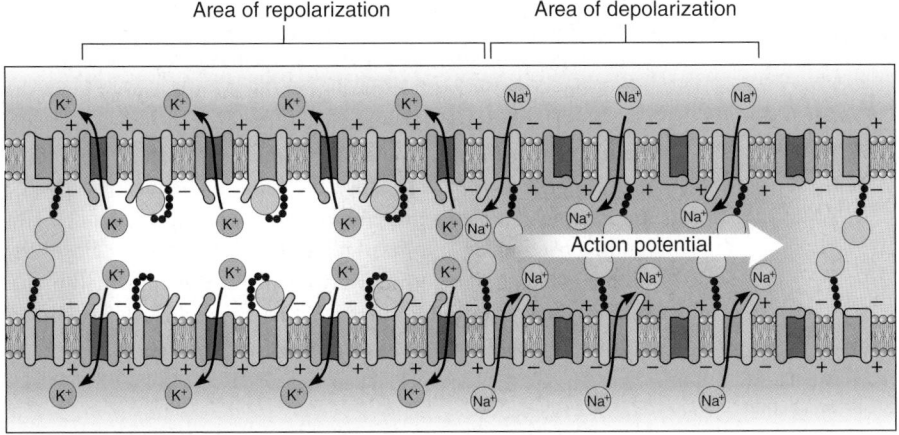

Area of repolarization

Area of depolarization

Action potential

2 As action potential progresses along axon, repolarization occurs quickly behind it.

FIGURE 41-9 Transmission of an action potential along the axon

When the dendrites (or cell body) of a neuron are stimulated sufficiently to depolarize the membrane to its threshold level, a strong pulse of voltage change travels down the axon. This pulse is an action potential.

Several factors determine the velocity of an action potential

Compared with the flow of electrons in electrical wiring or the speed of light, a nerve impulse travels rather slowly. Most axons transmit impulses at about 1 to 10 m per second. The smooth, progressive impulse transmission just described, called **continuous conduction,** occurs in unmyelinated neurons. In these axons, the speed of transmission is proportional to the diameter of the axon.

Axons with larger diameters transmit faster than do those with smaller diameters because an axon with a large diameter presents less internal resistance to the ions flowing along its length. Squids and certain other invertebrates have giant axons, up to 1 mm in diameter, which allow them to respond rapidly when escaping from predators.

In vertebrates, another strategy has evolved that speeds transmission—myelinated neurons. Myelin acts as an effective electrical insulator around the axon. However, the axon is not myelinated at the nodes of Ranvier. At these nodes, the plasma membrane of the axon makes direct contact with the surrounding extracellular fluid. Voltage-activated Na⁺ and K⁺ channels are concentrated at the nodes. In fact, in myelinated neurons, ion movement across the membrane occurs only at the nodes.

The ion activity at an active node results in diffusion of ions along the axon that depolarize the next node. The action potential appears to jump from one node of Ranvier to the next (**FIG. 41-10**). This type of impulse transmission is known as **saltatory conduction** (from the Latin word *saltus,* which means "to leap").

In myelinated neurons, the distance between successive nodes of Ranvier affects speed of transmission. When nodes are farther apart, less of the axon must depolarize and the axon conducts the impulse faster. Using saltatory conduction, a myelinated axon can conduct an impulse up to 50 times faster than the fastest unmyelinated axon.

Saltatory conduction has another advantage over continuous conduction: it requires less energy. Ions move across the plasma membrane only at the nodes, so fewer Na⁺ and K⁺ are displaced. As a result, the sodium–potassium pumps do not expend as much ATP to re-establish resting conditions each time an impulse is conducted.

Review

- How do ion channels and sodium–potassium pumps contribute to the resting potential?
- What sequence of events occurs when threshold level is reached in a neuron?
- How do voltage-activated ion channels work?
- How does an action potential differ from a graded potential?
- What are the benefits of saltatory conduction compared with continuous conduction?

In saltatory conduction, Na⁺ rapidly diffuse from one node of Ranvier to the next in a myelinated neuron. Action potentials appear to leap from node to node.

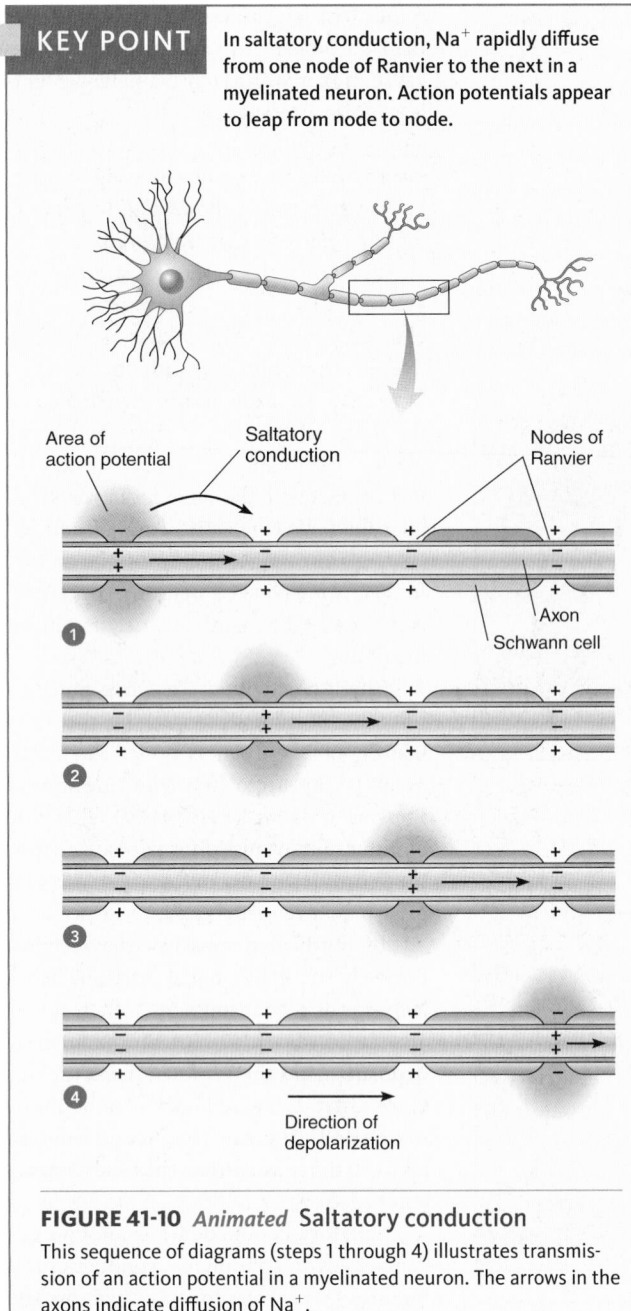

FIGURE 41-10 *Animated* **Saltatory conduction**

This sequence of diagrams (steps 1 through 4) illustrates transmission of an action potential in a myelinated neuron. The arrows in the axons indicate diffusion of Na^+.

41.4 TRANSMITTING INFORMATION ACROSS SYNAPSES

■ LEARNING OBJECTIVES

7   Describe the actions of the neurotransmitters identified in the chapter.

8   Trace the events that take place in synaptic transmission and draw diagrams to support your description.

9   Compare excitatory and inhibitory signals and their effects.

A **synapse** is a junction between two neurons or between a neuron and an effector, such as between a neuron and a muscle cell. A

neuron that *terminates* at a specific synapse is called a **presynaptic neuron,** whereas a neuron that *begins* at that synapse is a **postsynaptic neuron.** Note that these terms are relative to a specific synapse. A neuron that is postsynaptic with respect to one synapse may be presynaptic to the next synapse in the sequence.

Signals across synapses can be electrical or chemical

Based on how presynaptic and postsynaptic neurons communicate, two types of synapses have been identified: electrical synapses and chemical synapses. In **electrical synapses,** the presynaptic and postsynaptic neurons occur very close together (within 2 nm of one another) and form *gap junctions* (see Chapter 5). The interiors of the two cells are physically connected by a protein channel. Electrical synapses let ions pass from one cell to another, permitting an impulse to be directly and rapidly transmitted from a presynaptic to a postsynaptic neuron. The escape responses of many animals involve electrical synapses. For example, the "tail-flick" escape response of the crayfish involves giant neurons in the nerve cord that form electrical synapses with large motor neurons. The motor neurons signal muscles in the abdomen to contract. Electrical synapses are important in the mammalian nervous system as well. For example, many interneurons communicate by way of electrical synapses.

The majority of synapses are **chemical synapses.** Presynaptic and postsynaptic neurons are separated by a space, the **synaptic cleft,** about 20 nm wide (less than one-millionth of an inch). Because depolarization is a property of the plasma membrane, when an action potential reaches the end of the axon, it cannot jump the gap. The electrical signal must be converted into a chemical one. **Neurotransmitters** are the chemical messengers that conduct the neural signal across the synapse and bind to chemically activated ion channels in the membrane of the postsynaptic neuron. This binding triggers specific gated ion channels to open (or close), resulting in changes in permeability of the postsynaptic membrane. When a postsynaptic neuron reaches its threshold level of depolarization, it transmits an action potential.

Neurons use neurotransmitters to signal other cells

Many chemical compounds are now known or suspected to function as neurotransmitters, chemical messengers used by neurons to signal other neurons or to signal muscle or gland cells. We can categorize neurotransmitters into several chemical groups, including acetylcholine, biogenic amines, amino acids, neuropeptides, and gaseous neurotransmitters (**TABLE 41-2**).

Acetylcholine is a low-molecular-weight neurotransmitter that is released from motor neurons and triggers muscle contraction. Acetylcholine is also released by some neurons in the brain and in the autonomic nervous system (see *Inquiring About: Alzheimer's Disease;* also see Chapter 42). Cells that release acetylcholine are called **cholinergic neurons.**

Neurons that release norepinephrine are called **adrenergic neurons. Norepinephrine, epinephrine,** and the neurotrans-

TABLE 41-2   Selected Neurotransmitters

Neurotransmitter	Structure	Site of Action	Action
Acetylcholine	$H_2C-\overset{\displaystyle O}{\overset{\|}{C}}-O-CH_2-CH_2-N^+-[CH_3]_3$	CNS, neuromuscular junctions	Excitatory effect on skeletal muscle; inhibitory effect on cardiac muscle; excitatory or inhibitory at other sites; acetylcholine concentration in the brain decreases during the progression of Alzheimer's disease
Biogenic Amines Norepinephrine	(structure: catechol ring with HO, HO groups and side chain $-CH-CH_2-NH_2$ with OH)	CNS, PNS	Excitatory or inhibitory; concentration in brain affects mood, sleep, wakefulness, attention
Dopamine	(structure: catechol ring with HO, HO groups and side chain $-CH_2-CH_2-NH_2$)	CNS	Helps maintain balance between excitation and inhibition of neurons; important in motor functions; concentration in brain affects mood; also involved in motivation and reward
Serotonin (5-hydroxytryptamine, 5-HT)	(structure: indole ring with HO group and side chain $C-CH_2-CH_2-NH_2$)	CNS	Excitatory effect on pathways that control muscle action; inhibitory effect on sensory pathways; helps regulate food intake, sleep, and wakefulness; affects mood
Amino Acids Glutamate	$H_2N-\overset{\displaystyle}{\underset{\displaystyle COOH}{CH}}-CH_2-CH_2-COOH$	CNS, invertebrate neuromuscular junctions	Principal excitatory neurotransmitter in vertebrate brain; functions in learning and memory; excitatory effect at invertebrate neuromuscular junctions
Aspartate	$H_2N-\overset{\displaystyle}{\underset{\displaystyle COOH}{CH}}-CH_2-COOH$	CNS	Excitatory; functions in learning and memory
Glycine	H_2N-CH_2-COOH	CNS	Inhibitory (mainly in spinal cord)
Gamma-aminobutyric acid (GABA)	$H_2N-CH_2-CH_2-CH_2-COOH$	CNS, invertebrate neuromuscular junctions	Major inhibitory neurotransmitter in mammalian brain
Neuropeptides Endorphins and enkephalins	Y—G—G—F—M* (Methionine enkephalin)	CNS, PNS	Endogenous opiates; bind with opiate receptors on afferent fibers that transmit pain signals; inhibit release of substance P
Substance P	R—P—K—P—Q—Q—F—F—G—L—M	CNS, PNS	Activates ascending pathways that transmit pain signals
Gaseous Neurotransmitters Nitric oxide	NO	Most neurons?	Retrograde messenger; transmits signals from postsynaptic to presynaptic neuron
Carbon monoxide	CO	Most neurons?	May be neuromodulator

*Letters represent amino acids; refer to Figure 3-17.

mitter **dopamine** are **catecholamines.** The catecholamines and the neurotransmitters **serotonin** and **histamine** belong to a class of compounds called **biogenic amines.** Biogenic amines affect mood, and their imbalance has been linked to several disorders, including major depression, anxiety disorders, attention deficit hyperactivity disorder (ADHD), and schizophrenia.

ALZHEIMER'S DISEASE

What is Alzheimer's disease and what causes it? **Alzheimer's disease (AD)** is a progressive, degenerative brain disorder in which neural signaling is disrupted and neurons become damaged and die prematurely. Alzheimer's disease is the leading cause of senile dementia, the loss of memory, judgment, and ability to reason that is sometimes associated with aging. AD can affect the ability to recognize family members and to carry on routine daily activities, such as dressing, bathing, and eating. More than five million people in the United States have AD, and it is one of the top ten leading causes of death.

The development of AD may be a lifelong process. One startling study demonstrated that a person's writing early in life can predict the disease. Young adults whose writings had a lower density of ideas were more likely to develop the disease. One approach to detecting development of AD is the use of positron emission tomography (PET) scans to study glucose uptake in the brain. Low glucose uptake in certain areas of the brain suggests that neurons in these areas may be damaged. More recently, new genetic markers for AD have been identified.

In AD, neurons are damaged in certain parts of the brain, including the cerebral cortex and hippocampus, areas that are important in thinking and remembering. Neurons that secrete the neurotransmitter acetylcholine are especially affected. Investigators have demonstrated that two of the abnormalities that develop in brain tissue as we age, *amyloid plaques* and *neurofibrillary tangles,* are especially characteristic of AD. Understanding the biochemistry and genetic basis of both plaques and tangles may provide clues to the causes and cures of AD.

Amyloid plaques were first identified in autopsied brains in 1906 by the German physician Alois Alzheimer. These plaques are extracellular deposits of a peptide called amyloid-beta (amyloid-β). Neurons near these plaques appear swollen and misshapen. Microglia are typically present, suggesting an attempt to remove the damaged cells or the plaques themselves.

Researchers have found that amyloid-β is cut from a precursor protein called β-APP, a large transmembrane protein coded by a gene on chromosome 21. Normal amyloid-β molecules have 40 amino acids. However, about 10% of the peptides produced have two additional amino acids. This longer peptide appears to form the plaques. Investigators have identified mutations in specific genes that result in the production of abnormal amyloid-β.

Just how the longer amyloid-β leads to AD is not known. The abnormal peptide appears to disrupt calcium regulation, killing neurons in the brain. The peptide may also damage mitochondria, releasing harmful free radicals. AD appears to begin with subtle changes in synaptic function in the hippocampus, a region of the brain important in memory. An early symptom is decreased ability to encode new memories. The loss of synaptic function may be caused by abnormal amyloid-β. Mutations in two other proteins, presenillin 1 and presenillin 2, have been linked to AD. These proteins also reduce the ability to regulate calcium concentration. (They affect Ca^+ release from the ER.)

Recent studies have linked amyloid-β with sleep deprivation. Short-term sleep deprivation (three weeks) apparently increases deposition of amyloid plaque in mouse models. Another group of investigators have demonstrated that amyloid-β can destroy certain types of bacteria, and therefore may have an immune function.

Neurofibrillary tangles, which form in the neuron cytoplasm, are another piece of the AD puzzle. The cytoskeletal protein tau normally associates with the protein tubulin, which forms microtubules. Mutations in the *tau* gene may interfere with the way the tau protein binds to microtubules, resulting in abnormal microtubules that cannot effectively transport materials through axons.

Abnormal tau proteins accumulate in the cytoplasm, forming fibrous deposits that make up the neurofibrillary tangles (see figure). These tangles interfere with neural signaling.

Mechanisms that cause amyloid plaques and neurofibrillary tangles are connected. Using transgenic mice, researchers have demonstrated that amyloid-β deposits in the brain are responsible for the formation of neurofibrillary tangles in areas of the brain known to be affected in Alzheimer's disease.

The drug memantine (Namenda), one of the few drugs approved for treating AD, slows cognitive decline but does not prevent the eventual damage that occurs in the brain. Memantine blocks one type of glutamate receptor (NMDA receptor), which appears to help restore calcium balance. Donepezil (Aricept) inhibits acetylcholinesterase so that it does not break down acetylcholine as rapidly. Acetylcholine is a neurotransmitter in the brain important for memory and thought.

Several other drugs designed to slow the progress of Alzheimer's disease are in clinical trials. One of the challenges of developing a drug has been getting the medication through the blood–brain barrier. Some drugs block formation of β-amyloid, whereas others dissolve the abnormal β-amyloid deposits that are already present. Immune mechanisms that target β-amyloid are being investigated. Anti-inflammatory drugs are also being tested as strategies that may prevent or slow the development of AD.

Amyloid plaques

Neurofibrillary tangles

Thomas Deerinck, NCMIR/Photo Researchers, Inc.

Brain tissue from the cerebral cortex of a patient with Alzheimer's disease, showing characteristic amyloid plaques (rounded brown areas) and neurofibrillary tangles (dark teardrop shapes).

Several amino acids function as neurotransmitters. **Glutamate** is the major excitatory neurotransmitter in the brain. One type of glutamate receptor is the target of several mind-altering drugs, including phencyclidine ("angel dust").

The amino acid **glycine** and a modified amino acid, **gamma-aminobutyric acid (GABA),** are neurotransmitters that inhibit neurons in the spinal cord and brain. Glycine is the main inhibitory neurotransmitter in the spinal cord. GABA is the neurotransmitter used at most rapid inhibitory synapses throughout the brain. Many drugs that reduce anxiety enhance the actions of GABA by permitting lower concentrations of GABA to open Cl^- channels. These drugs include benzodiazepines, such as diazepam (Valium) and alprazolam (Xanax), and barbiturates, such as phenobarbital.

Neuropeptides, such as endorphins and enkephalins, appear to function mainly as **neuromodulators,** messenger molecules that stimulate long-term changes that enhance or inhibit synaptic function. Some neurobiologists consider them a group of neurotransmitters, but others classify them as a separate group. **Endorphins,** such as **beta-endorphin,** and **enkephalins** are the body's own endogenous opioids. Opiate drugs, for example, morphine and codeine, are powerful analgesics, drugs that relieve pain without causing loss of consciousness. Endorphins and enkephalins bind to opioid receptors (the same receptors to which opiate drugs bind) and block pain signals. Opioids modulate the effect of other neurotransmitters, including **substance P,** which activates pathways that transmit pain signals from certain sensory neurons to the CNS. (We discuss pain perception in Chapter 43.)

The signaling molecule **nitric oxide (NO)** is a gas that acts as a *retrograde messenger* at some synapses. It transmits information from the postsynaptic neuron to the presynaptic neuron, the opposite direction of transmission from other neurotransmitters. Carbon monoxide has also been identified as a gaseous neurotransmitter that may function as a neuromodulator. Some neurobiologists consider nitric oxide and carbon monoxide to be second messengers rather than neurotransmitters.

Neurotransmitters bind with receptors on postsynaptic cells

Neurotransmitters are stored in synaptic terminals within hundreds of small membrane-enclosed sacs called **synaptic vesicles** (**FIG. 41-11a**). Each time an action potential reaches a synaptic terminal, voltage-gated Ca^{2+} channels open. Calcium ions from the extracellular fluid then flow into the synaptic terminal. The Ca^{2+} induce synaptic vesicles to fuse with the presynaptic membrane and release neurotransmitter molecules into the synaptic cleft by exocytosis (**FIG. 41-11b**).

Neurotransmitter molecules diffuse across the synaptic cleft and bind with specific receptors on the dendrites or cell bodies of postsynaptic neurons (or on the plasma membranes of effector cells). Many neurotransmitter receptors are chemically activated ion channels known as **ligand-gated ion channels.** (See Chapter 6.) When the neurotransmitter, the *ligand,* binds with the receptor, the ion channel opens (**FIG. 41-11c**). (Recall that a ligand is a molecule that binds to a specific site in a receptor.) The acetyl-choline receptor, for example, is a ligand-gated ion channel that permits the passage of Na^+ and K^+.

Some neurotransmitters, such as serotonin, operate by a different mechanism. They work indirectly through a **second messenger.** Binding of the neurotransmitter with a receptor activates a **G protein.** The G protein then activates an enzyme, such as adenylyl cyclase, in the postsynaptic membrane. Adenylyl cyclase converts ATP to **cyclic AMP (cAMP),** which acts as a second messenger (see Chapters 6 and 49). Cyclic AMP activates a kinase that phosphorylates a protein, which then closes K^+ channels.

For a postsynaptic neuron to repolarize quickly, any excess neurotransmitter in the synaptic cleft must be removed. Some neurotransmitters are inactivated by enzymes. For example, excess acetylcholine is degraded into its chemical components, choline and acetate, by the enzyme acetylcholinesterase. Other neurotransmitters, such as the biogenic amines, are actively transported back into the synaptic terminals, a process known as **reuptake.** These neurotransmitters are repackaged in vesicles and recycled.

Many drugs inhibit the reuptake of neurotransmitters. For example, some antidepressants are selective serotonin reuptake inhibitors (SSRIs). SSRIs such as fluoxetine (Prozac) and escitalopram (Lexapro) selectively inhibit the reuptake of serotonin in the brain. This action concentrates serotonin in the synaptic cleft, elevating mood. Some antidepressants (and cocaine) also inhibit the reuptake of dopamine.

Activated receptors can send excitatory or inhibitory signals

A postsynaptic neuron may have receptors for several types of neurotransmitters. Some of its receptors may be excitatory, and others may be inhibitory. Depending on the type of postsynaptic receptor with which it combines, the same neurotransmitter can have different effects. For example, acetylcholine has an excitatory effect on skeletal muscle and an inhibitory effect on cardiac muscle.

When neurotransmitter molecules bind to receptors, the activated receptor can directly or indirectly open or close ion channels; this action changes the permeability of the postsynaptic membrane to certain ions. The resulting redistribution of ions changes the electrical potential of the membrane, and the membrane may depolarize. For example, when neurotransmitter molecules combine with receptors that open Na^+ channels, the resulting influx of Na^+ partially depolarizes the membrane. If sufficiently intense, a local depolarization can set off an action potential.

A change in membrane potential that brings the neuron closer to firing is called an **excitatory postsynaptic potential (EPSP).** Imagine that sufficient sodium ions enter to change the membrane potential from -70 mV to -60 mV. The membrane would be only -5 mV away from threshold. Under such conditions, an additional relatively weak stimulus, causing a small influx of Na^+, can cause the neuron to fire. *Note that unlike action potentials, postsynaptic potentials are graded responses.*

Some neurotransmitter–receptor combinations hyperpolarize the postsynaptic membrane. The membrane potential becomes more negative. Because such an action takes the neuron farther

At most synapses the action potential cannot jump across the synaptic cleft between the two neurons. This problem is solved by chemical signaling across synapses.

(a) The TEM shows synaptic terminals filled with synaptic vesicles.

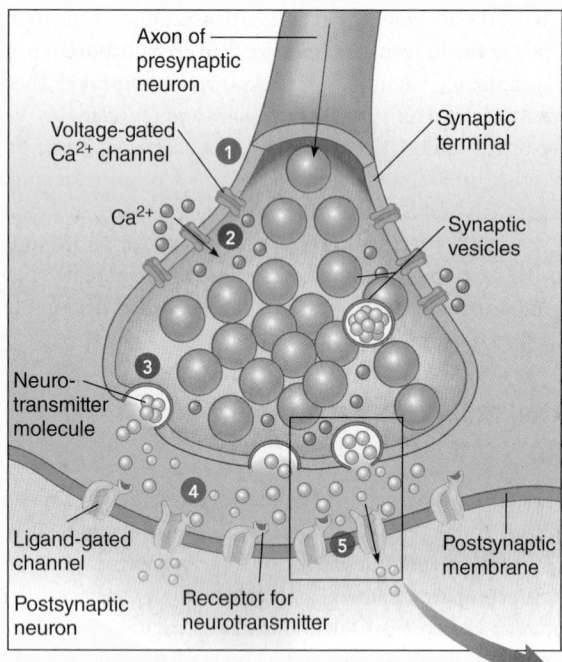

Axon of presynaptic neuron

Voltage-gated Ca²⁺ channel

Ca^{2+}

Synaptic terminal

Synaptic vesicles

Neurotransmitter molecule

Ligand-gated channel

Postsynaptic neuron

Receptor for neurotransmitter

Postsynaptic membrane

(b) How a neural impulse is transmitted across a synapse.

1 Action potential reaches synaptic terminals at end of presynaptic neuron.

2 Calcium channels open in membrane, letting Ca^{2+} from extracellular fluid enter the synaptic terminal.

3 Ca^{2+} cause synaptic vesicles to fuse with plasma membrane and release neurotransmitter into synaptic cleft.

4 Neurotransmitter binds with receptors on membrane of postsynaptic neuron.

5 In response, specific ion channels open or close, resulting in either depolarization or hyperpolarization. When depolarization reaches threshold level, an action potential is generated in postsynaptic neuron.

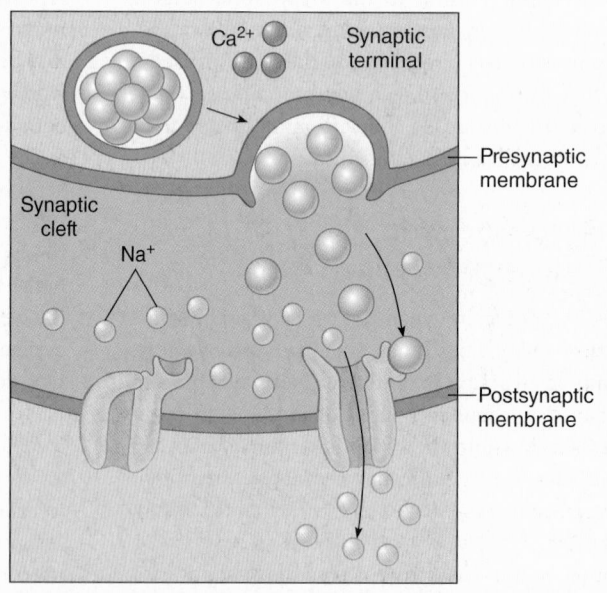

(c) Neurotransmitter binds with receptor. Ligand-gated channel opens, resulting in depolarization.

FIGURE 41-11 *Animated* Neural signaling across a synapse away from the firing level, a potential change in this direction is called an **inhibitory postsynaptic potential (IPSP).** For example, if the membrane potential changes from -70 mV to -80 mV, the membrane is farther away from threshold and a stronger stimulus is required to fire the neuron.

Like an EPSP, an IPSP can be produced in several ways. Two types of GABA receptors are known to produce IPSPs. When GABA binds to a $GABA_B$ receptor, K^+ channels open. As K^+ diffuse out, the neuron becomes more negative, hyperpolarizing the membrane. Activated $GABA_A$ receptors produce IPSPs by opening Cl^- channels. In this case, the influx of negative ions hyperpolarizes the membrane. Although the mechanisms are different, the inhibiting effect of GABA is the same in both cases.

In summary, neural signaling across synapses involves the following sequence of events:

> action potential reaches synaptic terminals $\longrightarrow$ calcium ions enter synaptic terminal $\longrightarrow$ synaptic vesicles release neurotransmitter into the synaptic cleft $\longrightarrow$ neurotransmitter diffuses across synaptic cleft $\longrightarrow$ neurotransmitter binds with receptors in membrane of postsynaptic neuron $\longrightarrow$ ion channels open or close, resulting in depolarization or hyperpolarization of postsynaptic membrane

Review

- What are some functions of biogenic amines? of GABA?
- What events take place at a chemical synapse?
- How are EPSPs produced? IPSPs?

41.5 NEURAL INTEGRATION

■ LEARNING OBJECTIVE

10 Define *neural integration* and describe how a postsynaptic neuron integrates incoming stimuli and "decides" whether to fire.

Each neuron may synapse with hundreds of other neurons. Indeed, thousands of synaptic terminals of presynaptic neurons may cover as much as 40% of a postsynaptic neuron's dendritic surface and cell body. It is the job of the dendrites and the cell body of every neuron to integrate the messages that continually bombard them.

Neural integration is the process of summing, or integrating, incoming signals. EPSPs and IPSPs are produced continually in postsynaptic neurons, and IPSPs cancel the effects of some EPSPs. It is important to remember that each EPSP and IPSP is not an all-or-none response. Rather, each is a graded response that does not travel like an action potential but may be added to or subtracted from other EPSPs and IPSPs.

As the postsynaptic neuron membrane continuously updates its molecular tabulations, the neuron may be inhibited or brought to threshold level. This mechanism integrates hundreds of signals (EPSPs and IPSPs) before an action potential is actually transmitted along the axon of a postsynaptic neuron. Local responses permit the neuron and the entire nervous system a far greater range of response than would be possible if every EPSP generated an action potential.

Postsynaptic potentials are summed over time and space

Each EPSP or IPSP is a graded potential that varies in magnitude depending on the strength of the stimulus applied. One EPSP is usually too weak to trigger an action potential by itself. Its effect is below threshold level. However, even though subthreshold EPSPs do not produce an action potential, they do affect the membrane potential. EPSPs can be added together in a process called **summation** (**FIG. 41-12**).

Temporal summation occurs when repeated stimuli cause new EPSPs to develop before previous EPSPs have decayed. The summation of several EPSPs may bring the neuron to the critical firing level.

(a) Subthreshold (no summation). Each stimulus is at a subthreshold level, so no action potential is generated.

(b) Temporal summation. The second EPSP occurs before the first dies off, so the two EPSPs are summed. An action potential is generated.

(c) Spatial summation. EPSPs generated by input from two different presynaptic neurons are summed.

(d) Spatial summation of EPSPs and IPSPs. EPSPs and IPSPs are also summed and can cancel each other out.

FIGURE 41-12 Neural integration

E_1 and E_2 are excitatory stimuli. I represents an inhibitory stimulus.

Spatial summation can also bring the postsynaptic neuron to threshold level. **Spatial summation** occurs when several closely spaced synaptic terminals release neurotransmitter simultaneously. The postsynaptic neuron is stimulated at several places at once.

Neurons also sum IPSPs. As IPSPs are added together as a result of temporal and spatial summation, they move the membrane potential farther away from threshold.

Where does neural integration take place?

On a molecular level, every neuron sorts through the thousands of bits of information simultaneously bombarding it. In vertebrates more than 90% of the neurons in the body are located in the CNS, so most neural integration takes place there, within the brain and spinal cord. These neurons are responsible for making most of the "decisions." In the next chapter, the brain and spinal cord are examined in some detail.

Review

- What is neural integration?
- How do temporal and spatial summation differ?
- Where does most neural integration take place in vertebrates?

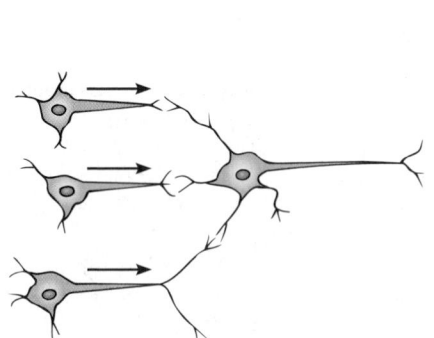

(a) Convergence of neural input.
Several presynaptic neurons synapse with one postsynaptic neuron.

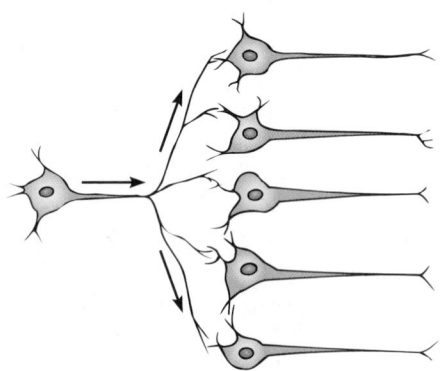

(b) Divergence of neural output.
A single presynaptic neuron synapses with many postsynaptic neurons.

FIGURE 41-13 Neural circuits

41.6 NEURAL CIRCUITS: COMPLEX INFORMATION SIGNALING

■ LEARNING OBJECTIVE

11 Distinguish between convergence and divergence, and explain why each is important.

The CNS contains millions of neurons, but it is not just a tangled mass of nerve cells. Its neurons are organized into **neural networks,** and within each network the neurons are arranged in specific pathways, or **neural circuits.** Although each network has some special characteristics, the neural circuits in all the networks share many organizational features. For example, convergence and divergence are probably characteristic of them all.

In **convergence,** a single neuron is controlled by converging signals from two or more presynaptic neurons (**FIG. 41-13a**). An interneuron in the spinal cord, for instance, may receive converging information from sensory neurons entering the cord, from neurons bringing information from various parts of the brain, and from neurons coming from different levels of the spinal cord. Information from all these sources must be integrated before an action potential is transmitted and an appropriate motor neuron is stimulated. Convergence is an important mechanism by which the CNS integrates the information that impinges on it from various sources.

In **divergence,** a single presynaptic neuron stimulates many postsynaptic neurons (**FIG. 41-13b**). Each presynaptic neuron may branch and synapse with thousands of different postsynaptic neurons. For example, a single neuron transmitting an impulse from the motor area of the brain may synapse with hundreds of interneurons in the spinal cord, and each of these may diverge, in turn, so that hundreds of muscle fibers are stimulated.

Review

- How does convergence differ from divergence?

■ SUMMARY: FOCUS ON LEARNING OBJECTIVES

41.1 *(page 861)*

1 Describe the processes involved in neural signaling: reception, transmission, integration, and action by effectors.

- Neural signaling involves (1) **reception** of information by a sensory receptor; (2) **transmission** by an **afferent neuron** to the **central nervous system (CNS),** which consists of the brain and spinal cord; (3) **integration** by **interneurons** in the central nervous system; (4) transmission by an **efferent neuron** to other neurons or to an effector; and (5) **action by effectors,** the muscles and glands.

Sensory receptors and neurons outside the CNS make up the **peripheral nervous system (PNS).**

41.2 *(page 862)*

2 Describe the structure of a typical neuron and give the function of each of its parts.

- **Neurons** are specialized to receive stimuli and transmit electrical and chemical signals. In a typical neuron, a **cell body** contains the nucleus and most of the organelles. Many branched **dendrites** extend from the cell body; they are specialized to receive stimuli and send signals to the cell body.

- The single long **axon** extends from the cell body and forms branches called **axon collaterals.** The axon transmits signals into its **terminal branches,** which end in **synaptic terminals.** Many axons are surrounded by an insulating **myelin sheath.** In the PNS the myelin sheath is formed by **Schwann cells.** In the CNS the sheath is formed by other glial cells. **Nodes of Ranvier** are gaps in the sheath between successive Schwann cells. A **nerve** consists of several hundred axons wrapped in connective tissue; a **ganglion** is a mass of neuron cell bodies in the PNS.

CENGAGENOW˙ Learn more about the structure of neurons and nerves by clicking on the figures in CengageNOW.

3 Name the main types of glial cells and describe the functions of each.

- **Glial cells** support and nourish neurons and are important in neural communication. **Astrocytes** are glial cells that physically support neurons. They help regulate the composition of the extracellular fluid in the CNS by taking up excess potassium ions. Astrocytes communicate with one another and with neurons; they also induce and stabilize synapses.

- **Oligodendrocytes** are glial cells that form myelin sheaths around axons in the CNS; Schwann cells form sheaths around axons in the PNS.

- **Ependymal cells** line cavities in the CNS and help produce and circulate cerebrospinal fluid. They may also serve as neural stem cells.

- **Microglia** are phagocytic cells.

41.3 *(page 865)*

4 Explain how the neuron develops and maintains a resting potential.

- Neurons use electrical signals to transmit information along axons. The plasma membrane of a resting neuron, one that is not transmitting an impulse, is **polarized.** The inner surface of the plasma membrane is negatively charged relative to the extracellular fluid just outside the membrane.

- The **resting potential** is the potential difference of about -70 mV that exists across the membrane. The magnitude of the resting potential is determined by (1) differences in concentrations of specific ions (mainly Na^+ and K^+) inside the cell relative to the extracellular fluid and (2) selective permeability of the plasma membrane to these ions.

- Ions pass through specific **passive ion channels.** K^+ leak out more readily than Na^+ can leak in. The resting potential is mainly due to the net flow of K^+ into the neuron. Cl^- and large anions inside the neuron contribute negative charges.

- The gradients that determine the resting potential are maintained by ATP-requiring **sodium–potassium pumps** that continuously transport three Na^+ out of the neuron for every two K^+ transported in.

5 Compare a graded potential with an action potential, describing the production and transmission of each.

- If a stimulus causes the membrane potential to become less negative, the membrane becomes **depolarized.** If the membrane

potential becomes more negative than the resting potential, the membrane is **hyperpolarized.**

- A **graded potential** is a local response that varies in magnitude depending on the strength of the applied stimulus. A graded potential fades out within a few millimeters of its point of origin.

- If voltage across the membrane declines to a critical **threshold level, voltage-activated ion channels** open, allowing Na^+ to flow into the neuron, and an **action potential** is generated. The action potential is a **wave of depolarization** that moves down the axon.

- As the action potential moves down the axon, **repolarization** occurs behind it. During depolarization, the axon enters an **absolute refractory period,** a time when it cannot transmit another action potential. When enough gates controlling Na^+ channels have been reset, the neuron enters a **relative refractory period,** a time when the threshold to fire the neuron is higher.

CENGAGENOW˙ Learn more about ion channels and action potentials by clicking on the figures in CengageNOW.

- The action potential conforms to an **all-or-none response;** no variation exists in the strength of a single impulse. Either the membrane potential exceeds threshold level, leading to transmission of an action potential, or it does not. Once begun, an action potential is self-propagating.

6 Contrast continuous conduction with saltatory conduction.

- **Continuous conduction,** which involves the entire axon plasma membrane, takes place in unmyelinated neurons.

- **Saltatory conduction,** which is more rapid than continuous conduction, takes place in myelinated neurons. Depolarization appears to skip along the axon from one node of Ranvier to the next; these are sites where the axon is not covered by myelin and where Na^+ channels are concentrated.

41.4 *(page 872)*

7 Describe the actions of the neurotransmitters identified in the chapter.

- The junction between two neurons or between a neuron and effector is a **synapse.** Although there are electrical synapses, most synapses are chemical. In synaptic transmission, a **presynaptic neuron** releases **neurotransmitter,** a chemical messenger, from its **synaptic vesicles.**

- **Acetylcholine** triggers contraction of skeletal muscle.

- The **biogenic amines** include **norepinephrine, epinephrine, serotonin, dopamine,** and **histamine.** These neurotransmitters play important roles in regulating mood. Dopamine is also important in motor function.

- Several amino acids function as neurotransmitters, including **glutamate,** the main excitatory neurotransmitter in the brain, and **GABA,** a widespread inhibitory neurotransmitter.

- The neuropeptides, which are opioids, include the **endorphins** (for example, **beta-endorphin)** and the **enkephalins.**

- **Nitric oxide (NO),** a gaseous neurotransmitter, transmits signals from a postsynaptic neuron to a presynaptic neuron, the opposite direction from most neurotransmitters.

8 Trace the events that take place in synaptic transmission and draw diagrams to support your description.

- Calcium ions induce synaptic vesicles to fuse with the presynaptic membrane and release neurotransmitter into the **synaptic cleft.** The neurotransmitter diffuses across the synaptic cleft and combines with specific receptors on a postsynaptic neuron.

- Many neurotransmitter receptors are proteins that form **ligand-gated ion channels.** Others activate a G protein and work through a **second messenger** such as **cAMP.**

CENGAGENOW˙ Learn more about synaptic transmission by clicking on the figure in CengageNOW.

9 Compare excitatory and inhibitory signals and their effects.

- Binding of a neurotransmitter to a receptor can cause either an **excitatory postsynaptic potential (EPSP)** or an **inhibitory postsynaptic potential (IPSP),** depending on the type of receptor. EPSPs bring the neuron closer to firing. IPSPs move the neuron farther away from its firing level.

41.5 *(page 877)*

10 Define *neural integration* and describe how a postsynaptic neuron integrates incoming stimuli and "decides" whether to fire.

- **Neural integration** is the process of summing, or integrating, incoming signals.
- Each EPSP or IPSP is a graded potential that varies in magnitude depending on the strength of the stimulus applied. **Summation** is the process of adding and subtracting incoming signals. By summation of several EPSPs, the neuron may be brought to critical firing level.

- **Temporal summation** occurs when repeated stimuli cause new EPSPs to develop before previous EPSPs have decayed. **Spatial summation** occurs when several closely spaced synaptic terminals release neurotransmitter simultaneously, stimulating the postsynaptic neuron at several different places.

41.6 *(page 878)*

11 Distinguish between convergence and divergence, and explain why each is important.

- Complex **neural circuits** are possible because of associations such as convergence and divergence. In **convergence,** a single neuron is affected by converging signals from two or more presynaptic neurons. Convergence allows the CNS to integrate incoming information from various sources. In **divergence,** a single presynaptic neuron stimulates many postsynaptic neurons, allowing widespread effect.

TEST YOUR UNDERSTANDING

1. Summing incoming neural signals is part of (a) reception (b) transmission (c) integration (d) action by effectors (e) afferent neuron transmission

2. Action potentials are transmitted to synaptic terminals by the (a) ganglia (b) axon (c) dendrites (d) cell body (e) nodes

3. The myelin sheath is produced around axons in the PNS by (a) axons (b) neuron cell bodies (c) dendrites (d) Schwann cells (e) oligodendrocytes

4. Which of the following does *not* contribute to the resting potential of a neuron? (a) sodium–potassium pumps (b) ion channels (c) differences in concentration of ions across the membrane (d) differences in permeability to certain ions (e) graded potentials

5. Which of the following occurs first when voltage reaches the threshold level? (a) gates of certain voltage-activated ion channels open (b) K^+ channels close (c) the membrane hyperpolarizes (d) neurotransmitter is released (e) neurotransmitter reuptake takes place at the synapse

6. Saltatory conduction (a) requires more energy than continuous conduction (b) occurs in unmyelinated neurons (c) occurs when the action potential jumps from one node of Ranvier to the next (d) slows transmission of an impulse (e) depends on the action of GABA

7. Acetylcholine (a) is a biogenic amine (b) is recycled (c) is released by motor neurons and by some neurons in the brain (d) is deactivated by G proteins (e) binds to opioid receptors

8. Receptors for serotonin and some other neurotransmitters (a) are voltage-activated ion channels (b) permit influx of chloride ions, leading to depolarization of the membrane (c) work through a second messenger (d) inhibit reuptake of the neurotransmitter (e) are passive ion channels

9. IPSPs (a) excite presynaptic neurons (b) excite postsynaptic neurons (c) can cancel the effects of some EPSPs (d) release large amounts of neurotransmitters (e) are released by postsynaptic cell bodies

10. A presynaptic neuron in the cerebrum transmits information to hundreds of other neurons. This is an example of (a) convergence (b) divergence (c) temporal summation (d) spatial summation (e) a graded potential

11. In spatial summation (a) repeated stimuli cause new EPSPs to develop before previous ones decay (b) divergence occurs at two or more synapses (c) EPSPs and IPSPs cancel each other in the space of the axon (d) two or more EPSPs transmit a summed chemical signal (e) several closely spaced synaptic terminals release neurotransmitter simultaneously

12. Describe the action taking place at each of the numbered steps. Use Figure 41-11c to check your answers.

CRITICAL THINKING

1. Discuss several specific ways in which the nervous system helps maintain homeostasis.

2. Stimulant drugs such as amphetamines increase the activity of the nervous system. Describe two mechanisms involving synaptic transmission that could explain the action of such drugs.

3. Develop a hypothesis to explain the fact that acetylcholine has an excitatory effect on skeletal muscle but an inhibitory effect on cardiac muscle.

4. **EVOLUTION LINK.** From the perspective of adaptation, hypothesize the advantages of neural circuits characterized by a great deal of convergence and divergence.

5. **ANALYZING DATA.** State whether each of the following would result in an EPSP or IPSP (explain your answer): (a) Na^+ enter postsynaptic neuron; (b) K^+ diffuse out of postsynaptic neuron; (c) Cl^- enter postsynaptic neuron.

6. **SCIENCE, TECHNOLOGY, AND SOCIETY.** A test for AD risk is now on the market. Based on gene markers that can be identified in a saliva sample, a healthy person can learn his or her approximate risk for AD. Do you think that this information will be useful to people? Would you worry about the psychological consequences of a person knowing that he or she had a high risk? Would you want to know?

7. **SCIENCE, TECHNOLOGY, AND SOCIETY.** Investigators have genetically engineered cells to produce acetylcholine, dopamine, GABA, and other neurotransmitters. In what ways might these cells be useful in neurobiological research? How might they be useful in clinical medicine?

 Additional questions are available in CengageNOW at www.cengage.com/login.

42 Neural Regulation

The brain during speech. In this functional magnetic resonance image (fMRI) of the brain, red indicates areas of greatest activation during speech; yellow indicates medium activation.

Volker Steger/Peter Arnold, Inc.

KEY CONCEPTS

42.1 Trends in invertebrate nervous system evolution include increased number and concentration of neurons and interneurons, more complex synaptic contacts, specialization of function, and cephalization.

42.2 The vertebrate nervous system consists of a central nervous system (CNS), which includes the brain and spinal cord and a peripheral nervous system (PNS), which includes sensory receptors and nerves.

42.3 Although different regions of the brain are specialized in various vertebrate classes, the brain develops in the same way and has the same basic structure; during the evolution of the vertebrate brain, the cerebrum and cerebellum have become larger and more complex.

42.4 As in other vertebrates, the human CNS receives sensory information from both the internal and external environment, integrates it, and determines appropriate responses. The association areas of the brain are responsible for learning, memory, language, thought, and judgment.

42.5 The peripheral nervous system has two divisions: the somatic division transmits information between the external environment and the CNS, whereas the autonomic division transmits information between the internal environment and the CNS.

42.6 Many prescribed and illicit drugs affect mood by affecting neurotransmitter concentrations in the brain.

A frog flicks out its tongue with lightning speed to capture a fly, a rabbit escapes from a predator, and you learn biology—perhaps not that quickly. In a complex nervous system, millions of neurons work together to transmit information from the external environment to the central nervous system (CNS). After the information is integrated, neural signals are transmitted to the effectors that can produce effective responses.

The nervous system also regulates heart rate, breathing, and hundreds of other internal activities. Nerves must transmit information from all of the organs in the body to the CNS. Then, other nerves transmit back the information that will allow organs to make the adjustments necessary to maintain homeostasis. Researchers have focused extensively on just how neurons interact, and we are only beginning to understand the mechanisms that permit the many vital functions of the nervous system.

Neurobiologists use a variety of methods to study the mechanisms of neural function. For example, improved imaging methods have revolutionized the study of the brain. Functional magnetic resonance imaging (fMRI) has provided investigators with a window through which to observe brain function. Functional MRI allows neurobiologists to study the responses of neural networks in the brain while an individual is actually performing a task, such as speaking (see photograph). During the performance of the task, an area of the brain becomes active and flow of oxygenated blood to that area increases. Functional MRI detects changes that take place in response to a very brief stimulus. For example, a visual stimulus lasting only 30 milliseconds stimulates brain activation that can be detected by fMRI.

In this chapter we compare several types of nervous systems. We then examine the structure and function of the vertebrate nervous system, with emphasis on the function of the human brain. We explore some of the frontiers of neurobiology, such as mechanisms involved in information processing and drug addiction.

42.1 INVERTEBRATE NERVOUS SYSTEMS: TRENDS IN EVOLUTION

▪ LEARNING OBJECTIVES

1 Contrast nerve nets and radial nervous systems with bilateral nervous systems.
2 Identify trends in the evolution of the invertebrate nervous system.

An animal's lifestyle is closely related to the organization and complexity of its nervous system. *Hydra* and other cnidarians have a **nerve net** consisting of interconnected neurons with no central control organ. Sensory cells are located in the epidermis, and the cnidarian can respond to stimuli from any direction (see Chapter 31). When a neuron is stimulated, electrical signals are sent from neuron to neuron in all directions (**FIG. 42-1**). Responses may involve large parts of the body.

An advantage of the nerve net is that the cnidarian responds effectively to predator or prey approaching from any direction. *Hydra* responds by discharging nematocysts (stinging structures) and coordinating the movements of its tentacles to capture food. Some cnidarians have two or more nerve nets. In some jellyfish, a slow-transmission nerve net coordinates movement of the tentacles, and a second nerve net, which is faster, coordinates swimming.

The **radial nervous system** of the sea star and other echinoderms (see Chapter 32) is a modified nerve net. This system shows some degree of selective organization of neurons into more than a diffuse network. It consists of a nerve ring around the mouth, from which a large radial nerve extends into each arm. Branches of these nerves, which form a network somewhat similar to the nerve net of *Hydra*, coordinate the animal's movement.

Bilaterally symmetrical animals have a **bilateral nervous system.** In planarian flatworms, the head region contains concentrations of nerve cells called **cerebral ganglia** (**FIG. 42-2**). These serve as a primitive brain and have some control over the rest of the nervous system. Typically, two solid, ventral, longitudinal nerve cords extend from the ganglia to the posterior end of the body. Transverse nerves connect the two nerve cords and connect the brain with the eyespots. This arrangement is called a "ladder-type" nervous system.

Annelids and arthropods typically have a solid ventral nerve cord (**FIG. 42-3**). The cell bodies of many of the neurons are massed into ganglia. Afferent and efferent neurons lie in lateral nerves that link the ganglia with muscles and other body structures. If an earthworm's brain is removed, the animal can move almost as well as before. However, when it bumps into an obstacle, it persists in a futile effort to move forward rather than turn aside. The earthworm needs its brain in order to respond adaptively to environmental change.

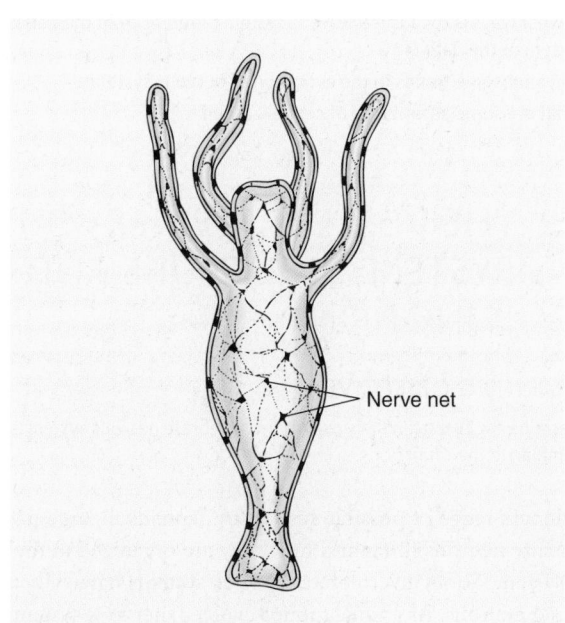

FIGURE 42-1 *Animated* **Hydra's nerve net**

Hydra and other cnidarians have a network of neurons with no central control organ.

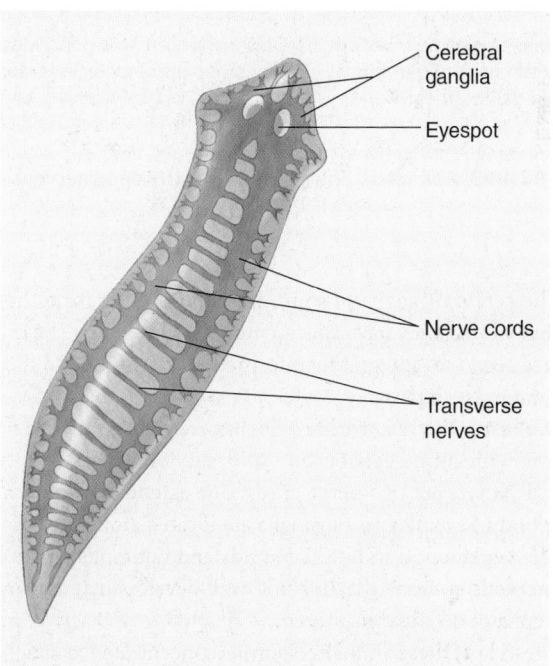

FIGURE 42-2 *Animated* Ladder-type nervous system of flatworms

Cerebral ganglia in the head region serve as a simple brain. The longitudinal nerve cords are connected by transverse nerves.

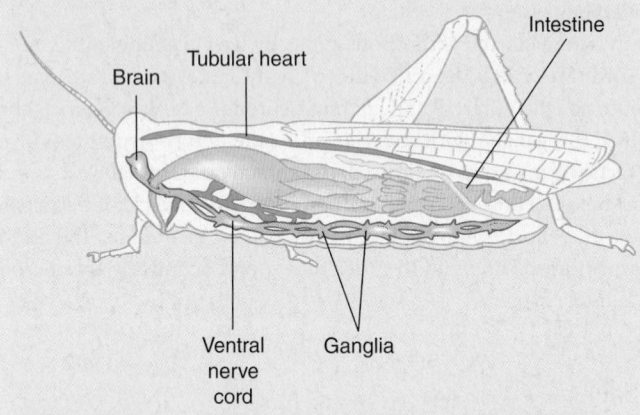

(a) **Earthworm nervous system.** Annelids have a dorsal anterior brain and one or more ventral nerve cords. Cell bodies of the neurons are located in ganglia that are connected by the ventral nerve cord.

(b) **Insect nervous system.** The arthropod brain is continuous with the ventral nerve cord. The brain is more specialized than in annelids.

FIGURE 42-3 *Animated* The annelid and arthropod nervous systems

The cerebral ganglia of some arthropods differ from those of annelids in that they have specific functional regions. These areas are specialized for integrating information transmitted to the ganglia from sense organs.

Mollusks with inactive lifestyles have relatively simple nervous systems with little cephalization and very simple sense organs. Typically, there are two nerve cords; one extends down each side of the body. Several pairs of ganglia are located along the cords.

The cephalopod mollusks (squids and octopods) have complex nervous systems that include well-developed sense organs. The cephalopod nervous system is adapted to the active, predatory lifestyle of these animals. Neurons concentrated in ganglia are massed in a ring surrounding the esophagus; they make up a brain that contains about 168 million nerve cells. Like the vertebrate brain, the cephalopod brain has lobes and intricate folds, and particular areas are specialized as centers for specific functions. The

octopus is capable of considerable learning and can be taught difficult tasks. In fact, cephalopods are considered the most intelligent invertebrates.

We can identify the following trends in the evolution of nervous systems:

1. *Increased number of nerve cells.*
2. *Concentration of nerve cells.* The nerve cells form masses of tissue that become **ganglia** (concentrations of cell bodies) and **brain,** and form thick cords of tissue that become **nerve cords** and **nerves.**
3. *Specialization of function.* For example, transmission of nerve impulses in one direction requires both **afferent nerves,** which conduct impulses toward a central nervous system (CNS), and **efferent nerves,** which transmit impulses away from the CNS to the **effectors** (muscles and glands). Certain parts of the CNS become specialized to perform specific functions, and distinct structural and functional regions can be identified.
4. *Increased number of interneurons and more complex synaptic contacts.* These contacts permit greater integration of incoming messages, provide a greater range of responses, and allow more precise responses.
5. **Cephalization,** *or formation of a head.* A bilaterally symmetrical animal generally moves in a forward direction. Concentration of sense organs at the front end of the body lets the animal detect an enemy quickly enough to escape, or to see or smell food in time to capture it. Response can be rapid if short pathways link sense organs to decision-making nerve cells nearby. Therefore, nerve cells are typically concentrated in the head region and organized to form ganglia or a brain.

Review

- In what ways is the insect nervous system different from the nervous system of the flatworm?
- What are some trends in the evolution of nervous systems?
- What are some advantages of cephalization?

42.2 THE VERTEBRATE NERVOUS SYSTEM: STRUCTURE AND FUNCTION

◼ LEARNING OBJECTIVE

3 Describe the two main divisions of the vertebrate nervous system and summarize their functions.

An animal's range of possible responses depends in large part on how many neurons it has and how they are organized in the nervous system. Some invertebrate nervous systems have only a few hundred neurons. As animal groups evolved, nervous systems became increasingly complex. The human brain has an estimated 100 billion neurons. How neurons are organized is critical in determining learning ability and flexibility of behavior.

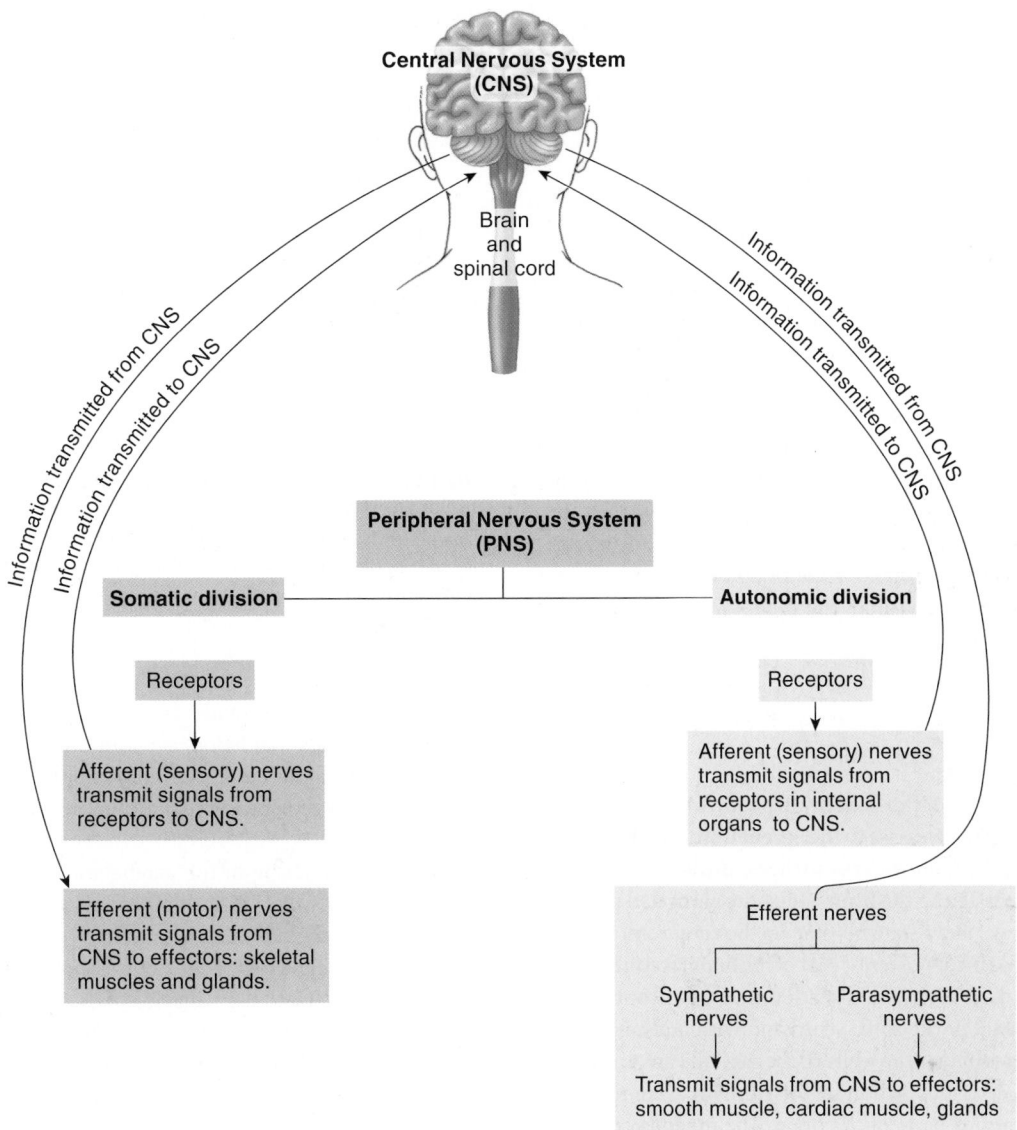

FIGURE 42-4 *Animated* Organization of the vertebrate nervous system

The vertebrate nervous system has two main divisions: the **central nervous system (CNS)** and the **peripheral nervous system (PNS)** (**FIG. 42-4**). The CNS consists of a highly developed brain that is continuous with the dorsal, tubular **spinal cord.** Serving as central control, these organs integrate incoming information and determine appropriate responses.

The PNS is made up of the sensory receptors (for example, tactile, auditory, and visual receptors) and the nerves, which are the communication lines. Various parts of the body are linked to the brain by cranial nerves and to the spinal cord by spinal nerves. Afferent (sensory) neurons in these nerves continuously inform the CNS of changing conditions. Then efferent neurons transmit the "decisions" of the CNS to appropriate muscles and glands, which make the adjustments needed to maintain homeostasis.

For convenience the PNS is subdivided into somatic and autonomic divisions. Most of the receptors and nerves concerned with changes in the external environment are somatic. Those that regulate the internal environment are autonomic. Both divisions have afferent nerves, which transmit messages from receptors to the CNS, and efferent nerves, which transmit information back from the CNS to the structures that respond. The autonomic division has two kinds of efferent pathways: sympathetic and parasympathetic nerves (discussed later in the chapter).

Review

- What are the main components of the CNS?
- What are the main components and functions of the PNS?

42.3 EVOLUTION OF THE VERTEBRATE BRAIN

■ LEARNING OBJECTIVE

4　Trace the development of the principal vertebrate brain regions from the hindbrain, midbrain, and forebrain, and compare the brains of fishes, amphibians, reptiles, birds, and mammals.

All vertebrates, from fishes to mammals, have the same basic brain structure, although different parts of the brain are specialized in the various vertebrate classes. The evolutionary trend is toward increasing complexity, especially of the cerebrum and cerebellum.

In the early vertebrate embryo, the brain and spinal cord differentiate from a single tube of tissue, the **neural tube.** Anteriorly, the tube expands and develops into the brain. Posteriorly, the tube becomes the spinal cord. Brain and spinal cord remain continuous, and their cavities communicate. As the brain begins to differentiate, three bulges become visible: the hindbrain, midbrain, and forebrain (**FIG. 42-5**).

The hindbrain develops into the medulla, pons, and cerebellum

As indicated in **TABLE 42-1**, the **hindbrain** subdivides to form the **metencephalon,** which gives rise to the **cerebellum** and **pons,** and the **myelencephalon,** which gives rise to the **medulla.** The medulla, pons, and midbrain make up the **brain stem,** the elongated portion of the brain that looks like a stalk holding up the cerebrum.

The medulla, the most posterior part of the brain, is continuous with the spinal cord. Its cavity, the **fourth ventricle,** is continuous with the central canal of the spinal cord and with a channel that runs through the midbrain. The walls of the medulla are thick and made up largely of *nerve tracts* (bundles of axons) that connect the spinal cord with various parts of the brain. The medulla contains centers that regulate life-sustaining functions such as respiration, heartbeat, and blood pressure. Other reflex centers in the medulla regulate activities such as swallowing, coughing, and vomiting.

The cerebellum is responsible for muscle tone, posture, and equilibrium. It also refines and coordinates muscle activity. In hu-

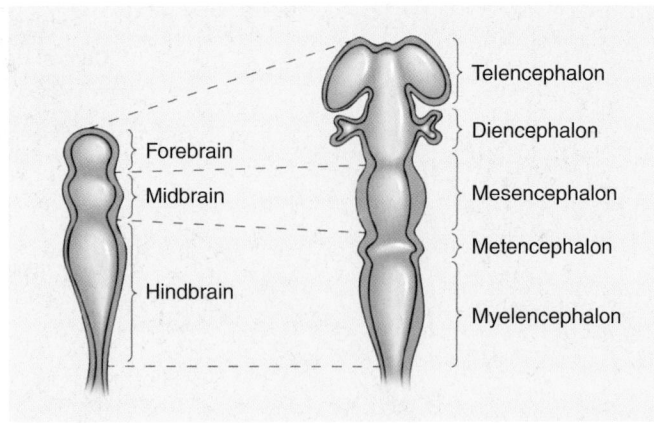

FIGURE 42-5 *Animated* **Early development of the vertebrate nervous system**

Early in the development of the vertebrate embryo, the anterior end of the neural tube differentiates into the hindbrain, midbrain, and forebrain. These primary divisions subdivide and eventually give rise to specific structures of the adult brain.

mans, the cerebellum provides input to motor areas in the cerebral cortex, and in this way helps plan and initiate voluntary activity. Certain regions of the cerebellum store implicit memories (unconscious memories for perceptual and motor skills, such as swimming or skating).

The size and shape of the cerebellum vary among the vertebrate classes (**FIG. 42-6**). Development of the cerebellum is roughly correlated with the extent and complexity of muscular activity, reflecting the principle that the relative size of a brain part correlates with its importance to the behavior of the species. In some fishes, birds, and mammals, the cerebellum is highly developed, whereas it tends to be small in jawless fishes, amphibians, and reptiles. In birds and mammals, the cerebellum is large with many folds.

Injury or removal of the cerebellum results in impaired muscle coordination. A bird without a cerebellum cannot fly, and its wings thrash about jerkily. When the human cerebellum is injured by a blow or by disease, muscular movements are uncoordinated. Any activity requiring delicate coordination, such as threading a needle, becomes very difficult, if not impossible.

TABLE 42-1	Differentiation of CNS Structures		
Early Embryonic Divisions	Subdivisions	Derivatives in Adult	Cavity
Brain			
Forebrain	Telencephalon	Cerebrum	Lateral ventricles (first and second ventricles)
	Diencephalon	Thalamus, hypothalamus, epiphysis (pineal body)	Third ventricle
Midbrain	Mesencephalon	Optic lobes in fish and amphibians; superior and inferior colliculi in mammals	Cerebral aqueduct
Hindbrain	Metencephalon	Cerebellum, pons	
	Myelencephalon	Medulla	Fourth ventricle
Spinal cord	Spinal cord	Spinal cord	Central canal

Although different parts of the brain are specialized in various vertebrate groups, there is an evolutionary trend toward larger size and greater complexity of the cerebrum and cerebellum.

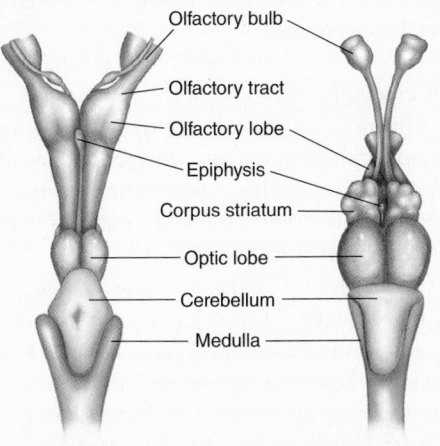

Olfactory bulb
Olfactory tract
Olfactory lobe
Epiphysis
Corpus striatum
Optic lobe
Cerebellum
Medulla

(a) Shark

(b) Codfish

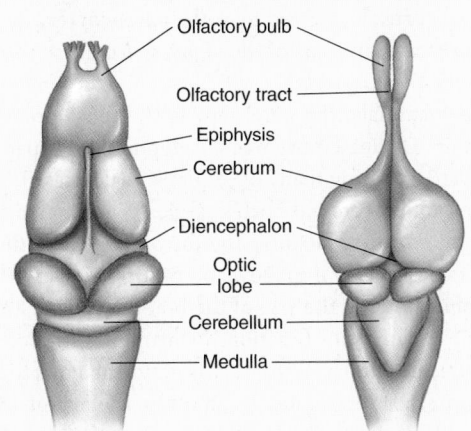

Olfactory bulb
Olfactory tract
Epiphysis
Cerebrum
Diencephalon
Optic lobe
Cerebellum
Medulla

(c) Amphibian (frog)

(d) Reptile (alligator)

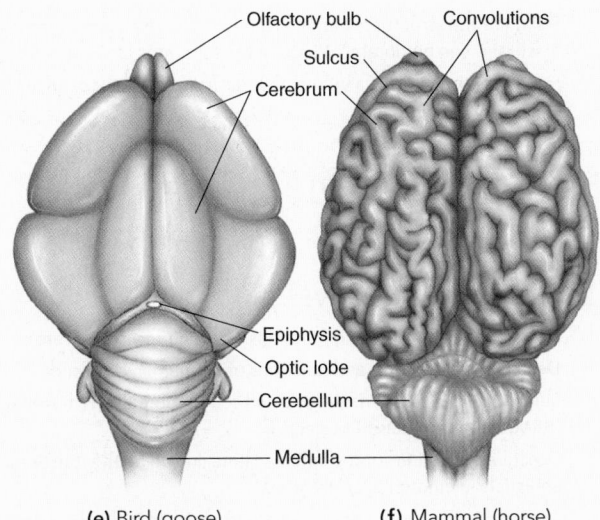

Olfactory bulb
Sulcus
Cerebrum
Convolutions
Epiphysis
Optic lobe
Cerebellum
Medulla

(e) Bird (goose)

(f) Mammal (horse)

FIGURE 42-6 *Animated* Evolution of the vertebrate brain

Comparison of the brains of members of six vertebrate classes reveals basic similarities and evolutionary trends. (Brains are not drawn to scale.) Note that different parts of the brain are specialized in the various groups. The large olfactory lobes in the shark brain **(a)** are essential to this predator's highly developed sense of smell. **(b–f)** During the course of evolution, the cerebrum and cerebellum have become larger and more complex. In mammals **(f)**, the cerebrum is the most prominent part of the brain; the cerebral cortex, the thin outer layer of the cerebrum, is highly convoluted (folded), which greatly increases its surface area. In **(f)**, the diencephalon and part of the brain stem are covered by the large cerebrum.

In mammals, the pons contains a thick bundle of fibers that transmits information between the two sides of the cerebellum. The pons also serves as a bridge that connects the medulla and cerebellum with other regions of the brain. The pons contains centers that help regulate respiration and nuclei that relay impulses from the cerebrum to the cerebellum. Recall from Chapter 41 that a **nucleus** is a group of cell bodies within the CNS.

The midbrain is prominent in fishes and amphibians

In fishes and amphibians, the **midbrain, or mesencephalon,** is the most prominent part of the brain and serves as the main association area. It receives incoming sensory information, integrates it, and sends decisions to appropriate motor nerves. The dorsal portion of the midbrain is differentiated to some extent. For example, the optic lobes are specialized for visual interpretations.

In reptiles, birds, and mammals, many functions of the optic lobes are assumed by the cerebrum, which develops from the forebrain. In mammals, the midbrain consists of the **superior colliculi,** centers for visual reflexes such as pupil constriction, and the **inferior colliculi,** centers for certain auditory reflexes. The inferior colliculi are major integration centers for incoming auditory information. The mammalian midbrain also contains a center (the *red nucleus*) that helps maintain muscle tone and posture.

The forebrain gives rise to the thalamus, hypothalamus, and cerebrum

The **forebrain** subdivides to form the *telencephalon* and *diencephalon.* The **diencephalon** gives rise to the thalamus and hypothalamus.

In all vertebrate classes, the **thalamus** is a relay center for motor and sensory messages. In mammals, all sensory messages except those from the olfactory receptors are delivered to the thalamus, where they are integrated before they are relayed to the sensory areas of the cerebrum.

The **hypothalamus,** which lies below the thalamus, forms the floor of the third ventricle. The hypothalamus is a major coordinating center for regulating autonomic and somatic responses. It integrates incoming information and provides input to centers in the medulla and spinal cord that regulate activities such as heart rate, respiration, and digestive system function. In birds and mammals, the hypothalamus controls body temperature. It also contains olfactory centers, regulates appetite and water balance, and is important in emotional and sexual responses. As discussed in Chapter 49, the hypothalamus links the nervous and endocrine systems and produces certain hormones.

The **telencephalon** gives rise to the **cerebrum.** The *lateral ventricles* (also called the first and second ventricles) lie within the cerebrum. Each lateral ventricle connects with the third ventricle (within the diencephalon) by way of a channel. In most vertebrate groups, the telencephalon also gives rise to the **olfactory bulbs.** These structures are important in the chemical sense of smell—the dominant sense in most aquatic and terrestrial vertebrates. In fact, much of brain development in vertebrates appears to focus on integrating olfactory information. In fishes and amphibians, a large part of the cerebrum is devoted to this function. Birds are an exception among the vertebrates in that their sense of smell is generally poor. A part of their cerebrum, the *corpus striatum,* however, is highly developed. This structure controls eating, flying, singing, and other action patterns.

In most vertebrates, the cerebrum is divided into right and left **cerebral hemispheres.** Most of the cerebrum is made of **white matter,** which consists mainly of myelinated axons that connect various parts of the brain. In mammals and in the majority of reptiles, a layer of **gray matter,** the **cerebral cortex,** makes up the outer portion of the cerebrum. Gray matter is unmyelinated and contains cell bodies and dendrites.

Certain reptiles and all mammals have a type of cerebral cortex called the **neocortex.** Most of the neocortex consists of *association areas*—regions that link sensory and motor functions and are responsible for higher functions, such as learning and reasoning. The neocortex is very extensive in mammals, making up the bulk of the cerebrum. In humans, most of the cerebral cortex is neocortex, which consists of six distinct cell layers. The remaining part of the cerebral cortex is referred to as the **paleocortex.** In mammals the paleocortex forms part of the *limbic system* (discussed later in this chapter).

In mammals, the cerebrum is the most prominent part of the brain. During embryonic development, it expands and grows backward, covering many other brain structures. The surface area of the human cerebral cortex is greatly expanded by numerous folds called **convolutions.** The furrows between them are called **sulci** (sing., *sulcus*) if shallow and **fissures** if deep. The number of convolutions (not the size of the brain) has been associated with complexity of brain function. In mammals, the cerebrum is responsible for numerous functions performed by other parts of the brain in other vertebrates. In addition, the mammalian cerebrum has highly developed association functions.

Review

- What are the structures derived from the vertebrate embryonic forebrain? the hindbrain? What are the functions of these structures?
- How does the brain of a mammal differ from the brain of an amphibian?

42.4 THE HUMAN CENTRAL NERVOUS SYSTEM

LEARNING OBJECTIVES

5 Describe the structure and functions of the human spinal cord.
6 Describe the structure and functions of the human cerebrum.
7 Summarize the sleep–wake cycle and contrast rapid-eye-movement (REM) sleep with non-REM sleep.
8 Describe the actions of the limbic system, including the role of the amygdala in emotional expression.
9 Summarize how the brain processes information, including a description of synaptic plasticity and the neurobiological changes that take place during learning.

The soft, fragile human brain and spinal cord are well-protected. Encased within bone, they are covered by three layers of connective tissue, the **meninges.** The three meningeal layers are the tough, outer **dura mater;** the middle **arachnoid;** and the thin, vascular **pia mater,** which adheres closely to the tissue of the brain and spinal cord (**FIG. 42-7**). *Meningitis* is a disease in which these coverings become infected and inflamed.

The space between the arachnoid and the pia mater is the sub-arachnoid space, which contains **cerebrospinal fluid (CSF).** This shock-absorbing fluid cushions the brain and spinal cord against mechanical injury. It also serves as a medium for exchange of nutrients and waste products between the blood and brain. CSF is produced by special networks of capillaries, collectively called the **choroid plexus,** which extend from the pia mater into the ventricles. After circulating through the ventricles, CSF passes into the subarachnoid space. It is then reabsorbed into large blood sinuses within the dura mater.

(a) **Frontal section through the superior part of the brain.** Note the dural sinus, a blood sinus, between two layers of the dura mater. Blood leaving the brain flows into such sinuses and then circulates to the large jugular veins in the neck.

Dural sinus (superior sagittal sinus)

Skin of scalp
Skull
Dura mater
Arachnoid
Subarachnoid space
Pia mater
Cortex of brain

Cerebral aqueduct
Fourth ventricle
Dura mater
Choroid plexus

Skin
Skull
Subarachnoid space
Pia mater
Choroid plexus
Third ventricle

(b) **Sagittal section through brain.** The CSF, which cushions the brain and spinal cord, is produced by the choroid plexi in the walls of the ventricles. This fluid circulates through the ventricles and subarachnoid space. It is continuously produced and then reabsorbed into the blood of the dural sinuses.

FIGURE 42-7 Protection of the brain and spinal cord
The CNS is well-protected by the skull and meninges, and by cerebrospinal fluid (CSF).

The spinal cord transmits impulses to and from the brain

The tubular **spinal cord** extends from the base of the brain to the level of the second lumbar vertebra. A cross-section view through the spinal cord reveals a small **central canal** surrounded by an area of gray matter shaped a bit like the letter H (**FIG. 42-8**). The gray matter consists of large masses of cell bodies, dendrites, un-myelinated axons, and glial cells.

The white matter, found outside the gray matter, consists of myelinated axons arranged in bundles called **tracts** or **pathways. Ascending tracts** conduct impulses up the cord to the brain. For example, the spinothalamic tracts in the anterior and lateral columns of the white matter conduct pain and temperature information from sensory neurons in the skin. The pyramidal tracts are **descending tracts** that convey impulses from the cerebrum to motor nerves at various levels in the cord. We describe the spinal nerves later in this chapter.

In addition to transmitting impulses to and from the brain, the spinal cord controls many reflex activities. A **reflex action** is a relatively simple, involuntary motor response to a stimulus. Although most reflex actions are more complex, let us consider a **withdrawal reflex,** in which a neural circuit consisting of three types of neurons carries out a response to a stimulus (**FIG. 42-9**). Suppose that your hand accidentally touches a flame. Almost instantly, and even before you become consciously aware of what has happened, you jerk your hand away.

The instant your skin contacts the flame, a sensory neuron transmits a message from pain receptors in the skin to the spinal cord. Within the spinal cord, a sensory neuron transmits the signal to an interneuron. The interneuron integrates the information and signals an appropriate efferent (motor) neuron, which conducts the information to groups of muscles. The muscles respond by contracting,

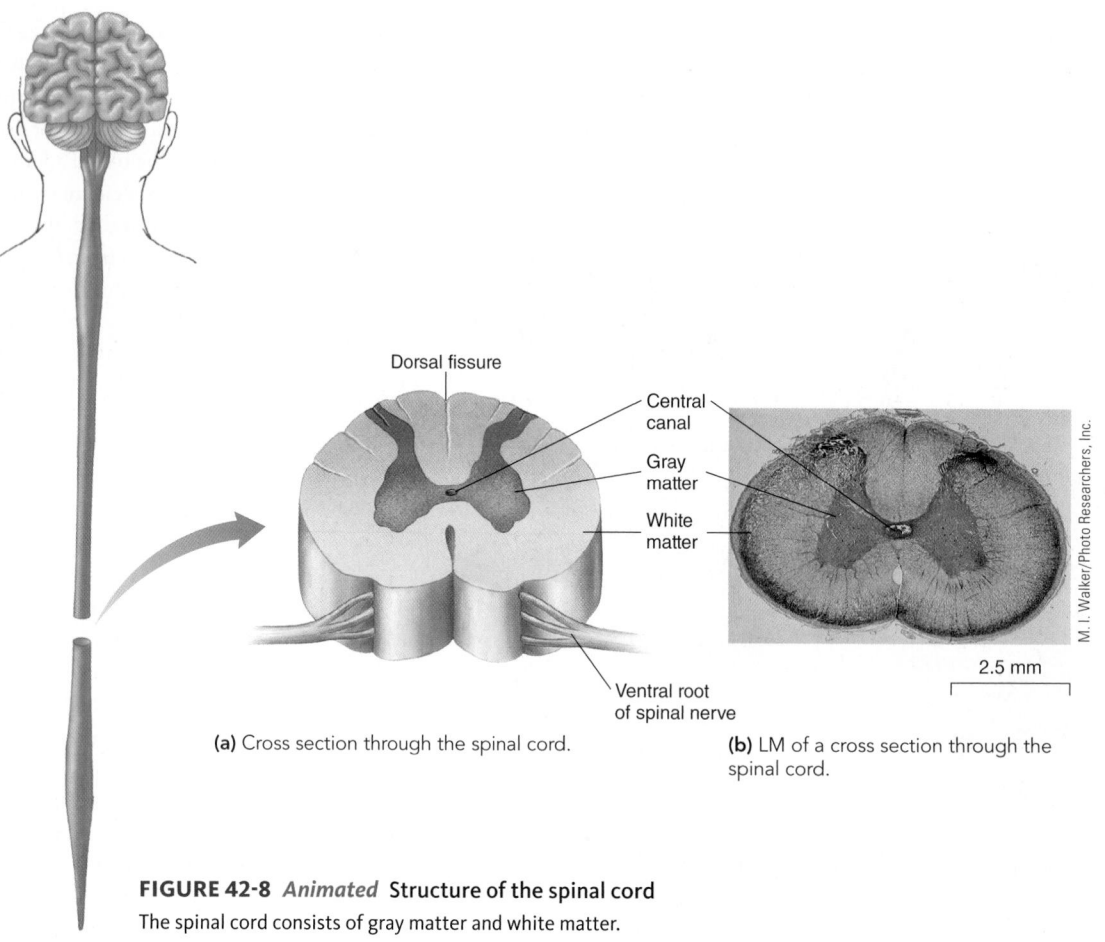

Dorsal fissure

Central
canal

Gray
matter

White
matter

Ventral root
of spinal nerve

(a) Cross section through the spinal cord.

M. I. Walker/Photo Researchers, Inc.

2.5 mm

(b) LM of a cross section through the
spinal cord.

FIGURE 42-8 *Animated* Structure of the spinal cord
The spinal cord consists of gray matter and white matter.

KEY POINT   A reflex action is a coordinated, involuntary motor response to a stimulus.

Synapse between sensory
neuron and interneuron

Nerve cell body
of sensory neuron

Interneuron

Receptor

Muscle

Sensory neuron

Nerve cell body
of motor neuron

❶ Reception.
Sensory receptor
signals sensory
neuron.

❷ Transmission.
Sensory neuron
transmits signal
to CNS.

❸ Integration.
Interneuron
integrates
information.

❹ Transmission.
Appropriate
motor neuron
(*shown in red*)
transmits impulses
to muscle.

❺ Action by effector.
Muscle contracts,
moving hand away
from flame (actual
response).

FIGURE 42-9 Withdrawal reflex

jerking the hand away from the flame. Actually, many neurons in sensory, association, and motor nerves participate in such a reflex action. Generally, we are not even consciously aware that all these responding muscles exist. In summary, signals are transmitted through a withdrawal reflex in the following sequence:

> reception by sensory receptor in skin ⟶ sensory neuron transmits signal to CNS ⟶ interneuron in CNS integrates information ⟶ efferent (motor) neuron transmits signal to muscle ⟶ muscle contracts

At the same time that the reflex pathway is activated, a message is sent up the spinal cord to the conscious areas of the brain. As you pull your hand away from the flame, you become aware of what has happened and feel the pain. This awareness, however, is not part of the reflex response.

The spinal cord has some plasticity and is capable of training. For example, sensory feedback from exercise increases the strength of neural connections in the spinal cord. When descending connec-

tions with the brain are intact, some victims of spinal cord injury (more than 1.2 million people in the United States alone) can develop at least some limited ability to walk again.

The most prominent part of the human brain is the cerebrum

The structure and functions of the main parts of the human brain are summarized in **TABLE 42-2**, and major regions of the brain are illustrated in **FIGURES 42-10** and **42-11**. As in other mammals, the human cerebral cortex consists of right and left *cerebral hemispheres*.

Specific areas of the cerebrum are specialized for performing specific functions

The cerebral cortex is functionally divided into three areas: (1) **sensory areas** receive incoming signals from the sense organs; (2) **motor areas** control voluntary movement; and (3) **association areas** link the sensory and motor areas and are responsible for thought, learning, language, memory, judgment, decision

TABLE 42-2	The Human Brain	
Structure	Description	Function
Brain stem		
Medulla	Continuous with spinal cord; primarily made up of nerves passing from spinal cord to rest of brain	Contains vital centers (clusters of neuron cell bodies) that control heartbeat, respiration, and blood pressure; contains centers that control swallowing, coughing, vomiting
Pons	Forms bulge on anterior surface of brain stem	Connects various parts of brain with one another; contains respiratory and sleep centers
Midbrain	Just above pons	Center for visual and auditory reflexes (e.g., pupil reflex, blinking, adjusting ear to volume of sound)
Thalamus	At top of brain stem	Main sensory relay center for conducting information between spinal cord and cerebrum; neurons in thalamus sort and interpret all incoming sensory information (except olfaction) before relaying messages to appropriate neurons in cerebrum
Hypothalamus	Just below thalamus; pituitary gland is connected to hypothalamus by stalk of neural tissue	Contains centers for control of body temperature, appetite, and fat metabolism; regulates pituitary gland; important in emotional and sexual responses, and in sleep–wake cycle
Cerebellum	Second-largest division of brain	Muscle coordination and refinement of movements; muscle tone, posture, equilibrium; helps plan and initiate voluntary activity; stores implicit memories
Cerebrum	Largest, most prominent part of human brain; longitudinal fissure divides cerebrum into right and left hemispheres, each divided into lobes: frontal, parietal, temporal, and occipital lobes	Center of intellect, memory, consciousness, and language; also controls sensation and motor functions
Cerebral cortex (outer gray matter)	Arranged into convolutions (folds) that increase surface area; functionally, cerebral cortex is divided into:	
	1. Motor areas	1. Control movement of voluntary muscles
	2. Sensory areas	2. Receive incoming information from eyes, ears, pressure and touch receptors, etc.
	3. Association areas	3. Sites of intellect, memory, language, and emotion; interpret incoming sensory information
White matter	Consists of myelinated axons of neurons that connect various regions of brain; axons are arranged into bundles (tracts)	Connects the following:
		1. Neurons within same hemisphere
		2. Right and left hemispheres
		3. Cerebrum with other parts of brain and spinal cord

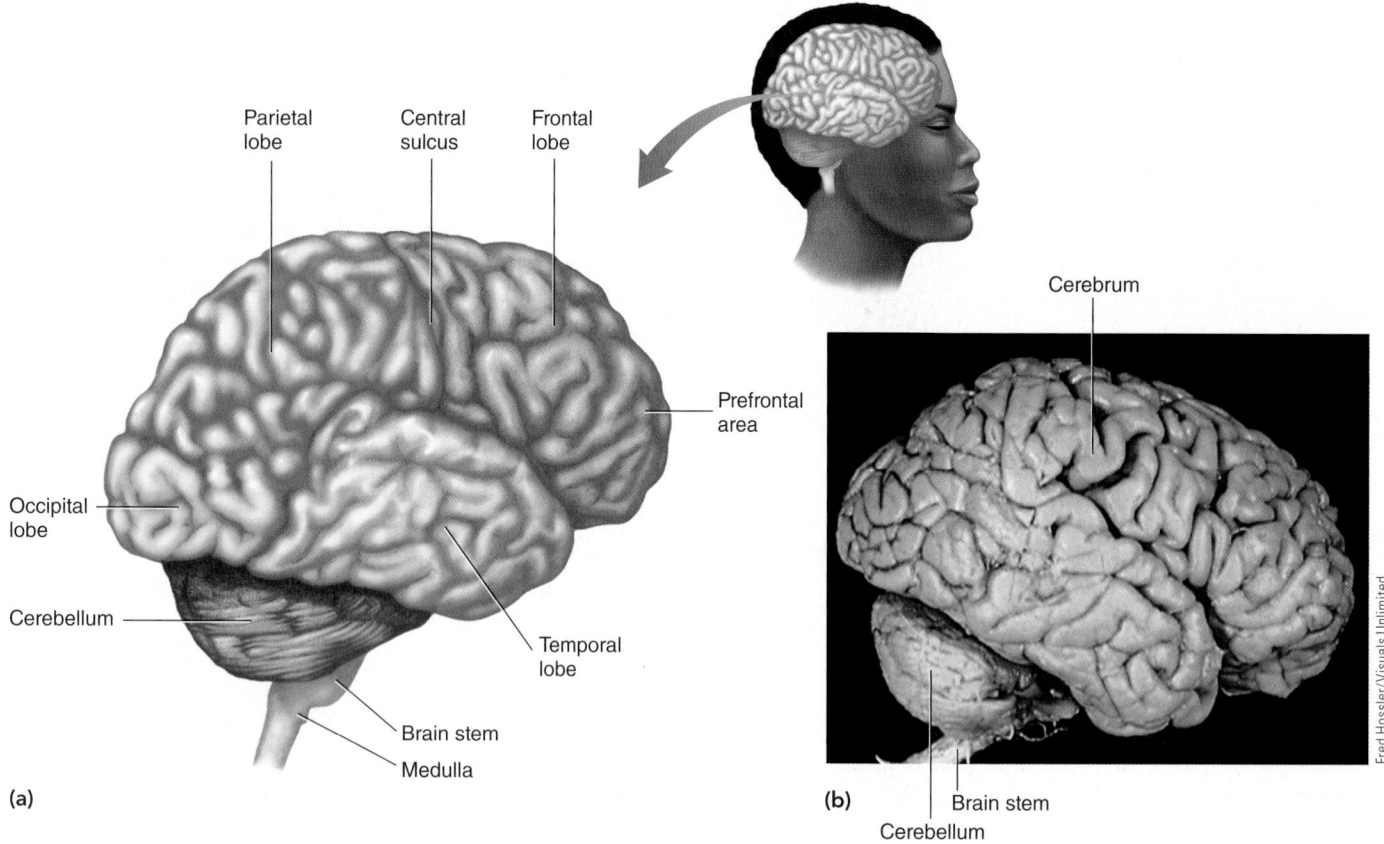

Parietal lobe

Central sulcus

Frontal lobe

Prefrontal area

Occipital lobe

Cerebellum

Temporal lobe

Brain stem

Medulla

(a)

Cerebrum

Brain stem

Cerebellum

(b)

Fred Hossler/Visuals Unlimited

FIGURE 42-10 *Animated* **The human brain**

Human brain, lateral view. Each cerebral hemisphere is divided into four major lobes. The diencephalon and part of the brain stem are covered by the cerebrum. Compare the diagram **(a)** with the photograph of the human brain **(b).**

making, and personality. You can see positron-emission tomography (PET) scans showing some functional areas of the cerebrum in **FIGURE 42-12**.

Investigators have mapped the cerebral cortex, locating the areas responsible for different functions. The **occipital lobes** contain the visual centers. Stimulation of these areas, even by a blow on the back of the head, causes the sensation of light; their removal causes blindness. The centers for hearing are located in the **temporal lobes** of the brain above the ear; stimulation by a blow causes a sensation of noise. Removal of both auditory areas causes deafness. Removal of one does not cause deafness in one ear; instead, it produces a decrease in the auditory acuity of both ears. Association areas in the temporal lobes help us identify incoming stimuli.

A groove called the **central sulcus** crosses the top of each hemisphere from medial to lateral edge. This groove partially separates the **frontal lobes** from the **parietal lobes.** The frontal lobes have important motor and association areas. The **prefrontal cortex** is an association area in each frontal lobe that is crucial in evaluating information, making judgments and decisions, planning, and organizing responses. The **motor areas** in the frontal lobes control the skeletal muscles. The **somatosensory area** in the anterior region of the parietal lobes receives information regarding touch, pressure, heat, cold, and pain from sense organs in the skin. This

region also receives information regarding position of the body. Association areas in the parietal lobes are important in helping us pay attention to such incoming information.

The size of the motor area in the brain for any given part of the body is proportional to the complexity of movement involved, not to the amount of muscle. Predictably, areas that control the hands and face are relatively large (**FIG. 42-13** on page 895). A similar relationship exists between the sensory area and the sensitivity of the region of the skin from which it receives impulses. These relationships are visually represented as the sensory homunculus ("little person") and the motor homunculus in Figure 42-13.

Neural fibers in the brain cross so that one side of the brain controls the opposite side of the body. As a result of another "reversal," the uppermost part of the cortex controls the lower limbs of the body.

When all the areas of known function are plotted, they cover almost all of the rat's cortex, a large part of the dog's, a moderate amount of the monkey's, and only a small part of the total surface of the human cortex. The remaining cortical areas are association areas. Somehow the association regions integrate the diverse impulses reaching the brain so that an appropriate response is made. When disease or accident destroys the functioning of one or more association areas, the ability to recognize certain kinds of symbols

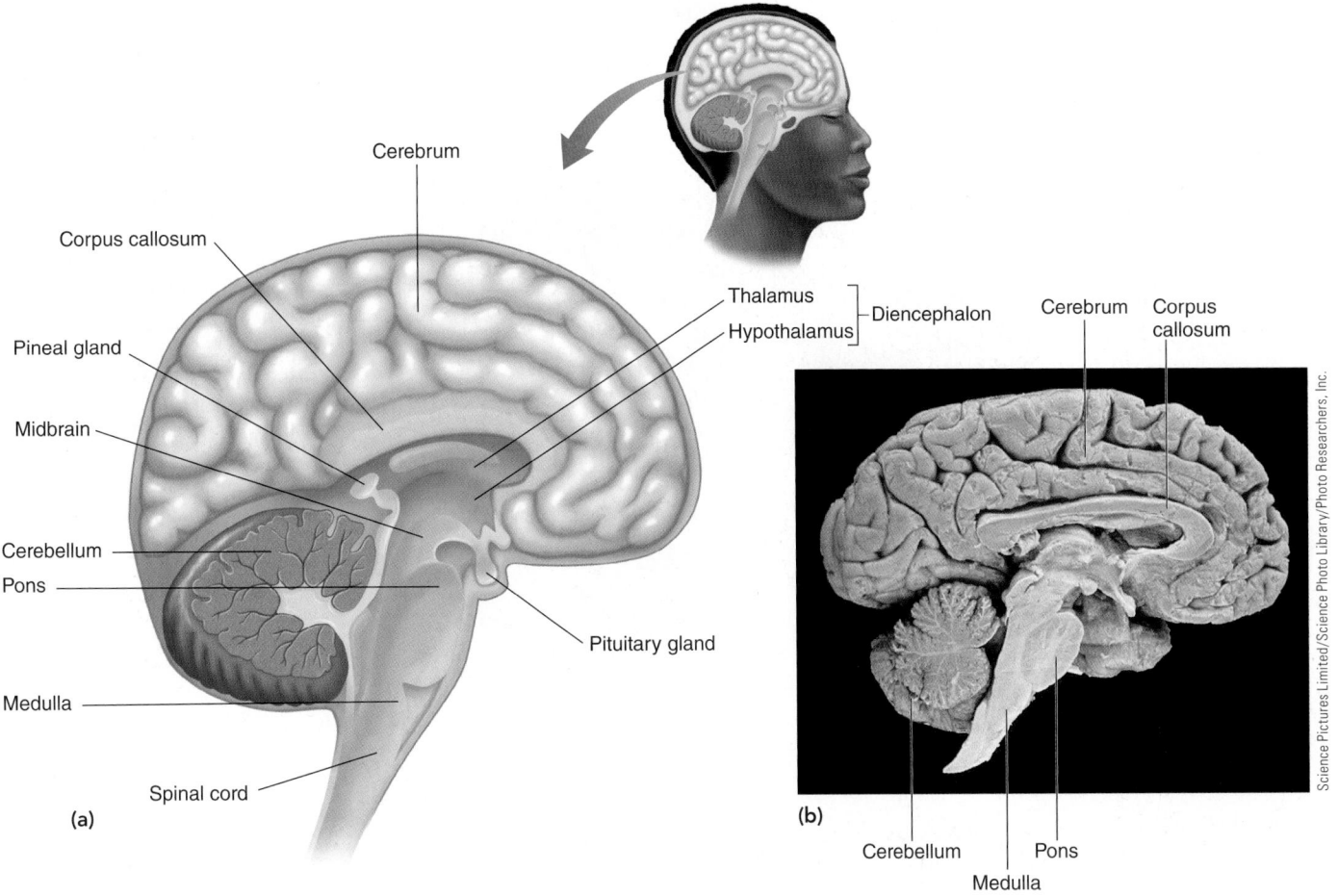

Cerebrum

Corpus callosum

Pineal gland

Midbrain

Cerebellum

Pons

Medulla

Spinal cord

(a)

Thalamus
Hypothalamus
} Diencephalon

Pituitary gland

Cerebrum   Corpus callosum

Cerebellum   Pons

Medulla

(b)

Science Pictures Limited/Science Photo Library/Photo Researchers, Inc.

FIGURE 42-11 Midsagittal section through the human brain

Half of the brain has been cut away, exposing structures normally covered by the cerebrum. Compare the diagram **(a)** with the photograph of the human brain **(b)**.

may be lost. For example, the names of objects may be forgotten, although their functions are remembered and understood.

The two cerebral hemispheres are specialized for certain functions. As will be discussed later in this chapter, the left hemisphere is specialized for language functions. This part of the brain is also specialized for logical decision making and retrieval of facts. The right hemisphere is specialized for emotional processing and for visual-spatial tasks such as recognizing faces.

Axons in the white matter of the cerebrum connect parts of the brain

The white matter of the cerebrum lies beneath the cerebral cortex. Nerve fibers of the white matter connect the cortical areas with one another and with other parts of the nervous system (see Table 42-2). A large band of white matter, the **corpus callosum,** connects the right and left hemispheres (see Fig. 42-11).

Deep within the white matter of the cerebrum lie the **basal ganglia,** paired groups of nuclei (gray matter). These nuclei play an important role in coordinating movement. The basal ganglia send signals to and receive signals from the **substantia nigra** in

the midbrain. Neurons from the substantia nigra that project (extend) to the basal ganglia produce **dopamine,** a neurotransmitter that helps balance inhibition and excitation of neurons involved in motor function. (See discussion of neurotransmitters in Chapter 41.) Other neurons from the substantia nigra signal nuclei in the thalamus, which in turn relay information to the motor cortex. Neurons from the substantia nigra that signal the thalamus release the neurotransmitter **gamma-aminobutyric acid (GABA).** Just how these areas work together to coordinate motor function is not yet fully understood.

More than one-half million people in the United States alone are affected by Parkinson's disease, a progressive neurological disorder that affects movement. In this disease, dopamine-producing neurons die over time, decreasing the available dopamine. As a result there is a progressive decrease in effective neural messages regarding motor responses. This results in tremors in the limbs and face, a slowing of movement, poor muscle coordination, and impaired walking and balance. Several medications, including a dopamine precursor (L-DOPA) are used to treat symptoms of the disorder.

Supplementary motor area (on inner surface—not visible; programming of complex movements)

Primary motor area (voluntary movement)

Somatosensory area (sensations from body surface and awareness of body position)

CENTRAL SULCUS

Premotor area (coordination of complex movements)

Posterior parietal area (integration of somato-sensory and visual input; important for complex movements)

Prefrontal association area (planning for voluntary activity; decision making; personality traits)

Wernicke's area (speech understanding)

FRONTAL LOBE

PARIETAL LOBE

Broca's area (controls ability to speak)

Parietal-temporal-occipital association area (integration of all sensory input; important in language)

Primary auditory area (receives and interprets auditory information)

OCCIPITAL LOBE

Primary visual area (receives and interprets visual information)

Limbic association cortex (mostly on inner and bottom surface of temporal lobe; motivation and emotion; memory)

TEMPORAL LOBE

CEREBELLUM

BRAIN STEM

SPINAL CORD

(a) Various areas of the cerebral cortex are responsible for specific types of neural processing. (Lateral view of the brain).

FIGURE 42-12 Functional areas of the cerebrum

The body follows a circadian cycle of sleep and wakefulness

Researchers have determined that many animals sleep, including nematodes and fruit flies. Predators typically sleep for longer periods than animals that are preyed upon. For example, rabbits sleep for a few minutes at a time. In some birds and aquatic mammals, one cerebral hemisphere sleeps at a time, allowing the animal to remain aware of its environment. Sleeping with one hemisphere permits eared seals and whales to move to the surface to breathe without awakening.

Humans and many other animals follow a 24-hour **circadian** (daily) **cycle** of sleeping and then being awake. When we are awake, we are typically aware of the external world and of ourselves, including our thoughts, perceptions, and emotions. In contrast, when we are asleep, the body receives messages from the environment, but we are not aware of them.

The **suprachiasmatic nucleus,** the most important of the body's biological clocks, is located in the hypothalamus. The suprachiasmatic nucleus receives information about the duration of light and dark from the retina of the eye and transmits information to other nuclei and neurons. The suprachiasmatic nucleus signals

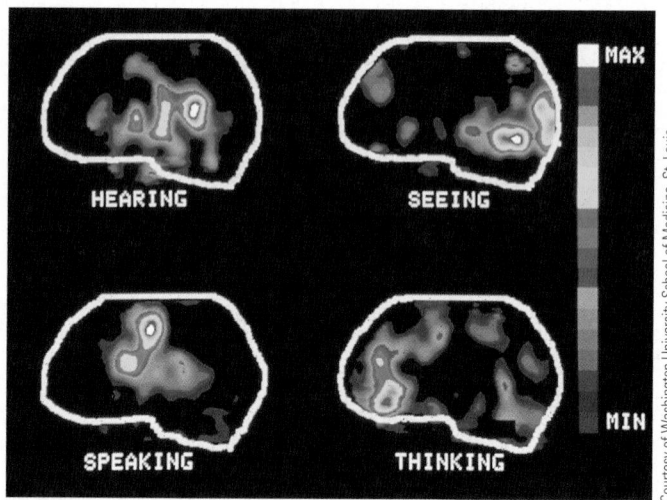

(b) Specific areas of the brain "light up" on positron-emission tomography (PET) scans as an individual performs various tasks. When a specific region of the brain is more active, more blood flows to the area. PET scans detect the magnitude of blood flow. Thus, PET scans are pictures of the brain at work at specific tasks. The color scale at the right indicates progressively more activity from the purple color at the bottom to the white at the top, which indicates maximum activity.

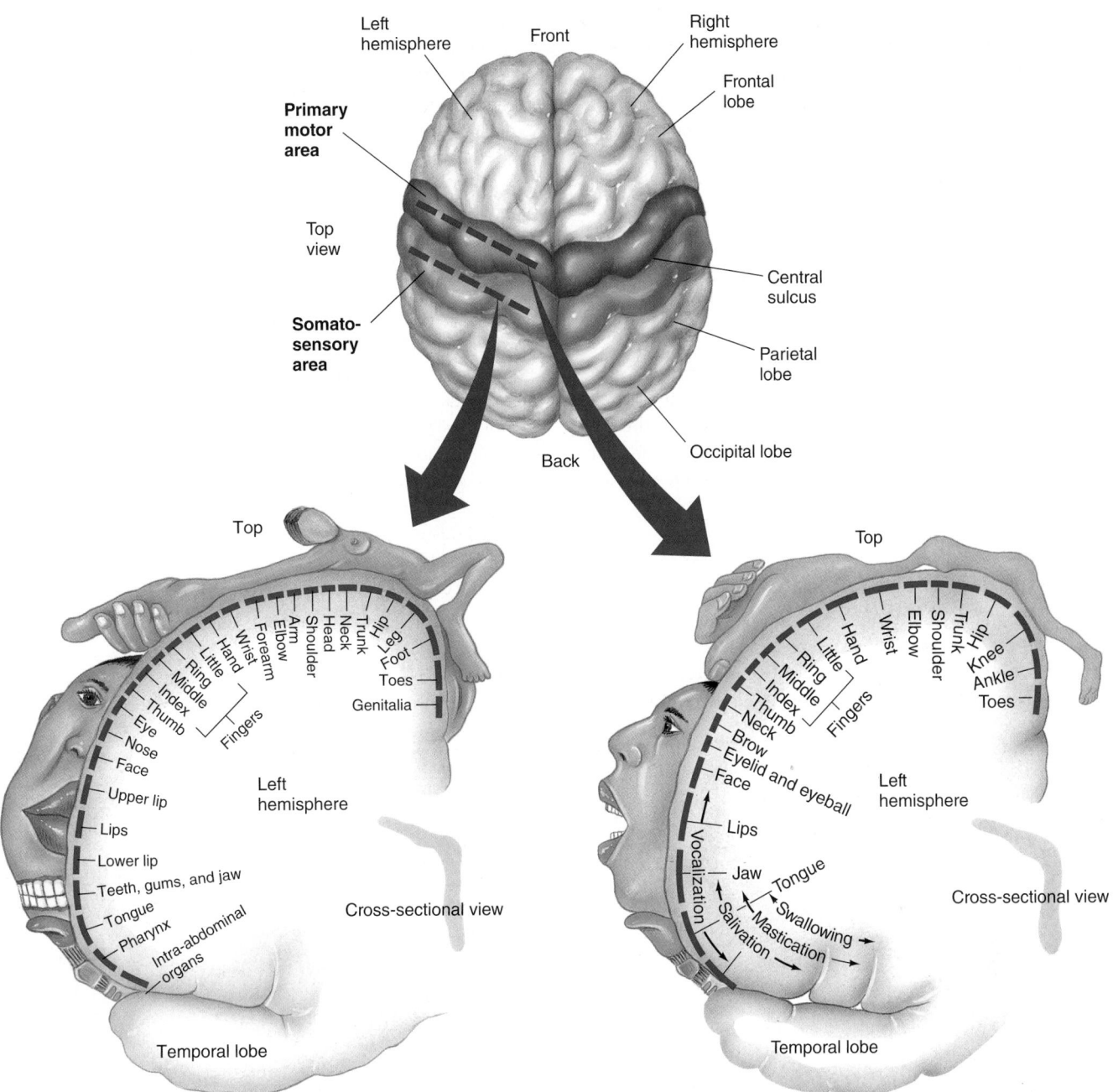

(a) Sensory homunculus. This cross section through the anterior region of the parietal lobe shows the distribution of sensory input to the somatosensory area from various parts of the body. The homunculus is proportioned to reflect the relative amount of cerebral cortex that receives sensory information from each body part.

(b) Motor homunculus. This cross section through the posterior part of the frontal lobe shows which area of the cerebral cortex controls each body part. Note that more of the cerebral cortex is devoted to controlling those body structures capable of skilled, complex movement. The primary motor area is involved in coordinated movement of many muscle groups.

FIGURE 42-13 Maps of the primary sensory and motor areas

the **pineal gland** about light and dark. This endocrine gland is located in the midline of the diencephalon.

The pineal gland produces **melatonin,** a hormone that plays a role in regulating the sleep–wake cycle. The pineal gland secretes up to ten times as much melatonin during darkness as during day-light. *Jet lag,* the state of fatigue and decreased physical and mental performance we experience when we fly to a different time zone, occurs because the body is no longer synchronized with its light–dark cycle. Some individuals take melatonin supplements to promote sleep, but their effectiveness has not been proven.

The hypothalamus, thalamus, and brain stem are all involved in regulating the sleep–wake cycle. Neurons in these regions secrete several neurotransmitters important in regulating sleep, including acetylcholine, norepinephrine, and serotonin. The **reticular activating system (RAS)** is a neural pathway within the brain stem and thalamus. The RAS receives messages from neurons in the spinal cord and from many other parts of the nervous system, and communicates with the cerebral cortex by complex neural circuits. When certain neurons of the RAS bombard the cerebral cortex with stimuli, an individual feels alert and can focus on specific thoughts. If the RAS is severely damaged, the person may pass into a deep, permanent coma.

After many hours of activity, the sleep–wake cycle may be affected by fatigue of the RAS. Sleep centers are then activated, and their neurons release serotonin. During *REM sleep,* a stage of sleep characterized by rapid eye movement, neurons in the RAS stimulate heightened activity in certain regions of the brain. After sufficient rest, the inhibitory neurons of the sleep centers become less excitable, and the excitatory neurons of the RAS become more excitable.

Specific types of activity are associated with certain brain wave patterns

Brain activity can be studied by measuring and recording the electrical potentials, or "brain waves," generated by thousands of active neurons in various parts of the brain. This electrical activity can be recorded by a device known as an *electroencephalograph.* A recording of this electrical activity, called an **electroencephalogram (EEG),** can be obtained by taping a set of electrodes to standard regions of the scalp and measuring the activity of the cerebral cortex (**FIG. 42-14**). The EEG shows that the brain is continuously active.

Certain patterns of brain waves are elicited by specific types of activity. For example, when you are resting quietly with eyes closed, your brain emits **alpha rhythm patterns.** In contrast, as you are reading this biology text, your brain is emitting **beta rhythm patterns,** which have a fast-frequency rhythm. Beta rhythm patterns are characteristic of heightened mental activity, such as information processing. During certain stages of sleep, the brain emits slow, high-amplitude **theta waves** and **delta waves.**

Certain brain conditions and diseases change the pattern of brain waves. Individuals with epilepsy, for example, exhibit a recognizable, abnormal wave pattern. The location of a brain tumor or the site of brain damage caused by a blow to the head can sometimes be determined by noting the part of the brain that emits abnormal waves.

Sleep progresses through several stages

Sleep is an alteration of consciousness during which there is decreased electrical activity in the cerebral cortex and from which a person can be aroused. Based on changes in electrical activity, we can identify four stages of **non-REM** (nonrapid eye move-

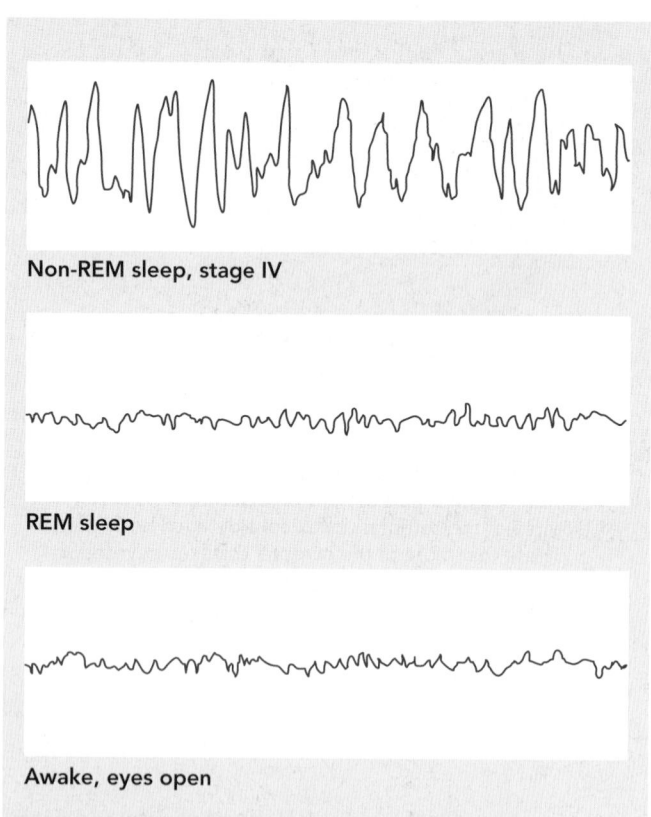

(a) EEG rhythms during different stages of sleep. During non-REM, stage IV sleep, the brain emits delta waves, slow-frequency, high-amplitude waves. During REM sleep, the brain emits high-frequency activity similar to that of a person who is awake.

(b) A typical cyclical sleep pattern in a young adult.

FIGURE 42-14 EEG rhythms and cyclical pattern of sleep

ment; *REM* is an acronym for *rapid eye movement*) sleep during the first hour of sleep. The deepest sleep is thought to occur during the fourth stage, when it is difficult to awaken the sleeping person. Slower-frequency, higher-amplitude waves (theta and delta waves) are characteristic of non-REM sleep. This electrical activity is thought to be generated spontaneously by the cerebral cortex when it is not driven by impulses from other parts of the brain. During non-REM sleep, body movement, heart rate, breathing, blood pressure, metabolic rate, and body temperature all decrease.

Every 90 minutes or so, a sleeping person enters the **REM sleep** stage for a time. During this stage (about 20% of total sleep time), the eyes move about rapidly beneath the closed but fluttering lids. Brain waves change to a desynchronized pattern. Everyone dreams, especially during REM sleep. PET scans of sleeping subjects indicate that during REM sleep, blood flow in the frontal lobes is reduced. In contrast, blood flow increases in limbic system areas that produce visual scenes and emotion. During REM sleep, body movement, heart rate, breathing, blood pressure, metabolic rate, and body temperature all increase. Increased secretion of the neurotransmitter GABA by certain neurons in the brain and spinal cord inhibits muscle contraction in some large groups of muscles. This results in a type of temporary paralysis.

Sleep may have several functions

Although birds, mammals, and many other animals have a sleep–wake cycle, neurophysiologists are not certain why sleep is necessary. One hypothesis holds that memories are consolidated during REM sleep. Another hypothesis suggests that sleep allows less important synaptic connections set during the day to reset. Non-REM sleep may provide time for the brain to restore itself. When a person stays awake for unusually long periods, fatigue and irritability result, and even routine tasks are not performed well. For example, fatigue is a leading cause of automobile accidents. Sleep also provides the body with the opportunity to conserve energy and to replace glycogen stores.

The limbic system affects emotional aspects of behavior

The **limbic system,** present in all mammals, influences the emotional aspects of behavior, evaluates rewards, and is important in motivation. It plays a role in sexual behavior, biological rhythms, and autonomic responses. The limbic system includes regions of the cerebrum (parts of the prefrontal cortex, cingulate cortex, temporal lobe, basal ganglia, the hippocampus, amygdala, and olfactory bulb), regions of the thalamus, hypothalamus, several nuclei in the midbrain, and the neural pathways that connect these structures (**FIG. 42-15**). The limbic system influences the endocrine system and the autonomic division of the nervous system.

Emotions are feeling states that we experience both physiologically and cognitively. Humans are born with the capacity to experience and express emotions, including fear, anger, sadness, and happiness. The **amygdala** filters incoming sensory information and interprets it in the context of emotional needs and survival. When it perceives danger, the amygdala sends information to other parts of the brain so that appropriate responses can be made. This part of the limbic system is important in the experience of fear and aggression. The amygdala becomes hypersensitive to possible danger following a traumatic experience (see *Inquiring About: The Neurobiology of Traumatic Experience*).

Structures of the limbic system are essential in an infant's bonding with a caregiver during the first year of life. The development of a secure attachment bond between infant and caregiver is the foundation for all future emotional and social connections between the child and other human beings. The quality of early attachment between child and caregiver affects brain development and future behavior. Healthy attachment allows the baby to express emotions and provides the basis for learning how to regulate emotions. Attachment also determines how vulnerable (or resilient) the individual will be to traumatic experiences later in life.

Researchers first discovered in the 1950s that the limbic system is part of an important motivational system when they implanted electrodes in certain areas of the brains of laboratory animals. They found that a rat quickly learns to press a lever that stimulates **reward centers** in the brain. In fact, the rat will press the lever as

FIGURE 42-15 The limbic system

The limbic system consists of a ring of forebrain structures that surround the brain stem and are interconnected by complex neural pathways. This system includes the amygdala, hippocampus, parts of the prefrontal cortex, the cingulate cortex, and areas in the thalamus, and hypothalamus. The limbic system is important in evaluating threat, in emotional expression, sexual behavior, motivation, and learning.

THE NEUROBIOLOGY OF TRAUMATIC EXPERIENCE

Have you been involved in a serious automobile accident or have you been the victim of a violent crime? Are you a combat veteran of Iraq or Afghanistan? Perhaps you are a survivor of a natural disaster, such as a hurricane or earthquake. Or you may have endured childhood neglect or abuse. Whether you are a survivor of any of these experiences, or of other terrifying events, you may have experienced the effects of trauma. A *traumatic experience* is an event that causes intense fear, helplessness, or horror and that overwhelms normal coping and defense mechanisms.

Most of us have strategies for processing *moderately* disturbing experiences. For example, if you were involved in a minor car accident, or if you were one of the millions of people who watched by television as people were wounded in Iraq or pulled from the rubble of buildings after earthquakes in Chile or Haiti, you may have been disturbed by the events you experienced or witnessed. You probably processed what you saw and heard by thinking about it and talking to your friends and family about what happened. You may have dreamed about your experience. As the brain actively reviews and sorts out a disturbing experience, we make sense of what happened. The emotional intensity decreases, and we store the memory along with other memories of more ordinary past events. The memory of the uncomfortable experience fades in importance and intensity.

Traumatic events are more difficult to process. If you survived an experience in which you thought you were going to die or be seriously hurt or if you witnessed someone else being wounded or killed, your body's response to real or perceived danger may be very intense. Years later, your brain may still be secreting abnormally high amounts of stress hormones and certain neurotransmitters, and you may remain on red alert, your body ready to deal with any new threat.

How does the brain respond in a traumatic experience, and how does the experience affect the brain? When danger threatens, the amygdala sends messages to both the hypothalamus (which signals the autonomic division of the nervous system and the endocrine system) and the neocortex (which allows us to be aware of our experience). The amygdala is programmed to remember the smells, sounds, and sensations that are part of the experience. Until the memories of the experience are fully processed, similar smells, sounds, and sensations remind us of the traumatic event and trigger the body to prepare for danger. The traumatized individual experiences fear and anxiety.

Because they are so overwhelming, traumatic memories are very difficult to process. They cause us so much discomfort and anxiety that we tend to avoid them rather than intentionally focus on them and sort them out. As a result, traumatic memories seem to stay "stuck" in the limbic system. When triggered, the experience may be replayed with its original emotional intensity (a flashback). Some trauma survivors develop Post-traumatic Stress Disorder (PTSD), a condition in which they experience (1) intrusive thoughts, images, sensory experiences, memories, and dreams; (2) an urge to avoid reminders of the traumatic event; and (3) physiological hyperarousal, a condition in which the body remains on high-alert status, continuously scanning the environment for potential danger.

Several studies have shown an association between prolonged trauma (for example, severe child abuse) and long-term changes in the brain. These changes include EEG abnormalities, smaller size of certain areas of the brain, compromised right brain development (the right brain is specialized for processing information related to emotion, social interaction, and physiological states); differences in neural circuits connecting cortical and subcortical areas (can decrease the individual's sense of self and lead to poor connections with other people); abnormal concentrations of certain neurotransmitters (affect mood, ability to inhibit inappropriate behavior); inappropriate modulation of the limbic system (its responses are exaggerated); and long-term changes in the sympathetic nervous system and endocrine response to stress (faster, more intense response to stress).

Neuroimaging studies have demonstrated changes in brain function, including over-response by the amygdala and decreased response by the medial prefrontal cortex (which normally inhibits the amygdala). When the amygdala over-responds, the individual experiences anxiety, distress, and physiological hyperarousal. These physiological states can lead to intense emotional responses that are rooted in the traumatic experience.

Broca's area, a region in the posterior part of the left frontal cortex, is also affected by trauma. Broca's area is critically important in generating words and thus in expressing language (see Fig. 42-12). Researchers have shown that when subjects are exposed to accounts of their traumatic experiences, activity in Broca's area decreases. This deactivation appears to be the physiological basis for the difficulty that trauma survivors have describing their experience in words. Trauma survivors have described a state of "speechless terror" that they experience during flashbacks of traumatic experiences. Without words, it is difficult to process and resolve a traumatic experience.

Based on many studies, it is clear that traumatic experiences can cause both structural and functional changes in the brain. The exaggerated responses of the amygdala to harmless stimuli perceived as threatening are dissociated from cortical (medial prefrontal) activation. Responses generated by the limbic system are rooted in emotion rather than in rationality and judgment (see figure below). PTSD can severely affect and limit one's life. However, this disorder can be resolved with appropriate treatment.

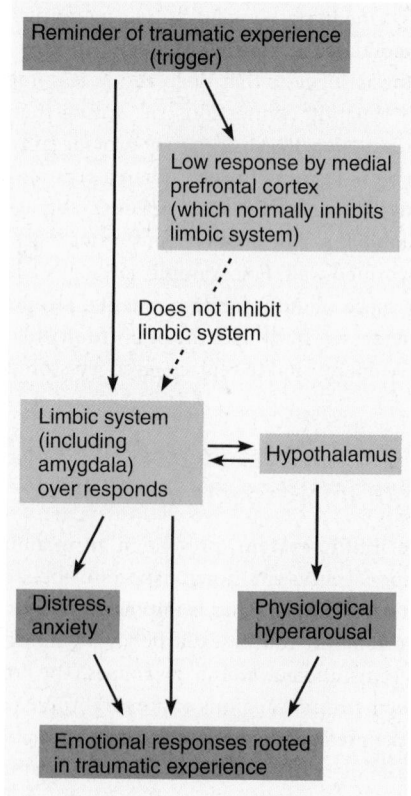

Some limbic system responses to reminders of traumatic experiences many as 5000 times per hour, choosing this self-stimulation over food and water, until it drops from exhaustion.

We now know that the brain has reward centers that give us pleasure when we carry out vital activities such as eating, drinking, and sexual activity. These centers are important in experiencing emotion and in motivation. When stimulated, they activate reward circuits that allow us to feel pleasure in response to certain experiences.

The **mesolimbic dopamine pathway,** a major reward circuit, includes two important midbrain areas, the substantia nigra and the adjacent ventral tegmental area. These areas, which extend into behavioral control centers in the limbic system, contain the largest group of neurons in the brain that release dopamine. Novel stimuli associated with reward or pleasure activate these dopamine neurons. The neurons signal information about surprising events or stimuli that predict rewards. Such signals may motivate us to act when something important is happening. Dopamine pathways are also important in the neurobiology of drug addiction (discussed later in this chapter).

As researchers continue to unravel the mechanisms of dopamine pathways, we may better understand such disorders as attention deficit hyperactivity disorder (ADHD) and schizophrenia, conditions associated with excessive amounts of dopamine and other neurotransmitters in the brain. People with these disorders have difficulty filtering out sensory stimuli. The presence of excess dopamine may drive them to divert their attention to so many sensory stimuli that they have difficulty focusing on the most important stimuli.

Learning and memory involve long-term changes at synapses

Neurobiologists are beginning to understand how the nervous system functions, including how we learn and remember. **Learning** is the process by which we acquire knowledge or skills as a result of experience. For learning to occur, we must be able to remember what we experience. **Memory** is the process of encoding, storing, and retrieving information or learned skills.

An interesting question has been: To what extent are the brain's functions **hard-wired,** that is, preset? Many areas of the brain once thought to be hard-wired are now known to be flexible and capable of change. Even animals with very simple nervous systems can learn to repeat behaviors associated with reward and to avoid behaviors that cause pain. Such changes in behavior are possible because of **synaptic plasticity,** the ability of synaptic connections to change in response to experience. Such change involves structure and function.

Familiar examples of plasticity in human motor skills include learning to walk, ride a bicycle, or catch a baseball. At first, you were probably clumsy, but with practice your performance became smoother and more precise. For that to happen, changes must occur at synapses in neural circuits. Similarly, the ability to learn languages, solve problems, and perform scientific experiments depends on synaptic plasticity.

What are the mechanisms by which we learn diverse activities, such as skilled movement and the study of biology? Canadian psychologist Donald O. Hebb proposed in 1949 that when two neurons connected by a synapse (that is, presynaptic and postsynaptic neurons) are active simultaneously, the synapse is strengthened. In 1973, British researchers T.V.P. Bliss and T. J. Lomo found experimental evidence for Hebb's hypothesis. Investigating rabbit brains, these researchers applied a series of high-frequency electrical stimuli to neurons in the hippocampus, a region that helps convert information into memories. The result was a long-term increase in synaptic strength. We can also credit Hebb for the axiom "Neurons that fire together, wire together." Experience influences how neural circuits in our brains organize themselves.

Learning involves the storage of information and its retrieval

Implicit memory, also called *procedural memory,* is unconscious memory for perceptual and motor skills, such as riding a bicycle. Implicit memory is about "how" to do something and involves repeating the behavior until it becomes routine. **Declarative memory,** also called *explicit memory,* involves factual knowledge of people, places, or objects and requires conscious recall of the information. The hippocampus is critical in forming and retrieving declarative memories.

How long do you remember? You are constantly bombarded with thousands of bits of sensory information. At this very moment, your eyes are receiving information about the words on this page, the objects around you, and the intensity of the light in the room. At the same time, you may be hearing a variety of sounds—music, your friends talking in the next room, the hum of an air conditioner. Your olfactory epithelium may sense cologne or the smell of coffee. Maybe you are eating as you read. Sensory receptors in your hands may be receiving information regarding the weight and position of your book. We may hold such sensory information in **immediate memory** for fractions of a second. Most sensory stimuli are not important to remember any longer and are filtered out.

Short-term memory lasts only for seconds or for a few minutes. Typically, we can hold only about seven chunks of information (for example, seven words or numbers) at a time in short-term memory. Short-term memory lets us recall information for a few minutes. When we look up a phone number, for example, we usually remember it only long enough to call it. If we need the same number an hour later, most of us have to look it up again.

When we select information for **long-term memory,** we must process it. The brain rehearses the material and *encodes* it. We recognize patterns and meaningfully *associate* the stimuli to past experience or knowledge. The **hippocampus** functions in the formation and retrieval of memories. The hippocampus temporarily holds new information and may integrate various aspects of an experience, including odors, sounds, and other information. It helps place our experiences in categories so that they can be stored along with similar memories. We integrate new information with other knowledge already stored in the brain.

Memory consolidation allows memories to be transferred to the cerebral cortex and *stored* for long periods. Consolidation involves expression of genes and protein synthesis and depends on new neural connections at synapses. Time (several minutes, hours, or even longer) is required for the brain to *consolidate* a new memory.

If a person suffers a brain concussion, memory of what happened immediately before the incident may be completely lost. This is known as *retrograde amnesia*. When the hippocampus is damaged, long-term memory may not be impaired, and the patient may be able to recall information stored in the past. However, new short-term memories can no longer be converted to long-term memories.

Where are memories stored? When large areas of the mammalian cerebral cortex are destroyed, information is lost somewhat in proportion to the extent of lost tissue. No specific area can be labeled the "memory bank." Rather, memories seem to be stored within many areas of the brain. For example, visual memories may be stored in the visual centers of the occipital lobes, and auditory memories may be stored in the temporal lobes. Researchers think that memories are integrated in many areas of the brain, including association areas of the cerebral cortex, the amygdala, hippocampus, thalamus, and hypothalamus. *Wernicke's area* in the temporal lobe has been identified as an important association area for complex thought processes. Neurons within the association areas form interconnected pathways that permit complicated information transfer.

Retrieval of information stored in long-term memory is of considerable interest—especially to students! The challenge is to find information when you need it. When you seem to forget something, the problem may be that you have not searched effectively for the memory. Information retrieval can be improved by careful encoding, for example, by forming strong associations between items. On the other hand, unimportant, unused memories are typically forgotten over time. Forgetting can be useful when it clears the brain of unnecessary information.

Neurobiological changes occur during learning

Short-term memory involves changes in the neurotransmitter receptors of postsynaptic neurons. These changes strengthen synaptic connections. The receptors are linked by second messengers (for example, cyclic AMP) to ion channels in the plasma membrane.

In some types of learning, changes take place in presynaptic terminals or postsynaptic neurons that permanently enhance or inhibit the transmission of impulses. In some cases, specific neurons may become more sensitive to a particular neurotransmitter. Neurons typically transmit action potentials in bursts, and the amount of a neurotransmitter released by each action potential may increase or decrease.

Repeated electrical stimulation of neurons causes a functional change at synapses. When a presynaptic neuron continues to transmit action potentials at a high rate for a minute or longer, there is a long-lasting strengthening of the connection between the presynaptic and postsynaptic neurons. This increased strength of the synaptic connection is known as **long-term potentiation (LTP).** *Potentiation* means "to strengthen or make more potent."

In contrast, low-frequency stimulation of neurons results in a long-lasting *decrease* in the strength of their synaptic connections. This decrease is called **long-term depression (LTD;** not related to the mood disorder). Information storage and forgetting depend on the strengthening and weakening of synaptic connections brought about by LTP and LTD.

Induction of LTP and LTD requires activation of two types of glutamate receptors: **NMDA receptors** and **AMPA receptors.**

(Each of these receptors is named for the compound that artificially activates it. NMDA is the acronym for N-methyl-D-aspartate and AMPA stands for α-amino-3-hydroxyl-5-methyl-4-isoxazole-propionate.) NMDA and AMPA receptors are present on the plasma membranes of postsynaptic neurons. They control the passage of calcium ions into neurons. NMDA receptors respond to the neurotransmitter *glutamate* by opening Ca^{2+} channels. However, when the postsynaptic neuron is at its resting potential, NMDA ion channels are blocked by Mg^{2+}.

A model for the mechanism of LTP is illustrated in **FIGURE 42-16.** A presynaptic neuron releases glutamate, which binds with AMPA receptors. The postsynaptic neuron becomes depolarized. If depolarization of the postsynaptic neuron is sufficiently strong, Mg^{2+} move away from the NMDA receptors, unblocking them. Glutamate can then bind with these receptors, opening Ca^{2+} channels and letting Ca^{2+} move into the cell. Calcium ions appear to be an important trigger for LTP.

Calcium ions act as second messengers that initiate long-term changes ultimately responsible for LTP. For example, calcium ions activate a Ca^{2+}-dependent second-messenger pathway that results in the insertion of more AMPA receptors in the postsynaptic membrane. This is important because additional AMPA receptors increase sensitivity to glutamate. More EPSPs (excitatory postsynaptic potentials) are produced, which strengthens the synapse (that is, helps maintain the LTP). Recall from Chapter 41 that an EPSP is a change in membrane potential that brings the neuron closer to its threshold level.

Calcium ions also activate a pathway that leads to release of a retrograde signal, a signal that moves backward, from the postsynaptic neuron to the presynaptic neuron. The soluble gas *nitric oxide (NO)* has been identified as the retrograde signal. This signal enhances neurotransmitter release by the presynaptic neuron. Note that this is a positive feedback loop that strengthens the connection between the two neurons.

Long-term memory involves gene expression

Gene expression and protein synthesis take place during the process of establishing long-term memory. This process involves slower, but longer-lasting, changes in synaptic connections. Long-term memory depends on activated receptors linked to G proteins (see Chapter 6). Cyclic AMP acts as a second messenger.

A high level of cyclic AMP activates a protein kinase that enters the nucleus, leading to gene activation and protein synthesis. In this process, protein kinase phosphorylates a transcription factor known as **CREB** (for "cyclic AMP response element binding protein"). CREB then turns on the transcription process of certain genes. CREB has been shown to be a signaling molecule in the memory pathway in many animals, including fruit flies and mice. The molecules and processes involved in learning and memory have been highly conserved during evolution.

Experience affects development and learning

Many studies have demonstrated synaptic plasticity in rats, mice, and other laboratory animals exposed to enriched environments. In contrast with rats housed in standard cages and provided with the basic necessities, those exposed to enriched environments are

When glutamate binds to NMDA receptors, Ca^{2+} enter the postsynaptic neuron and activate intracellular signaling systems that lead to changes responsible for LTP.

1 Stimulated presynaptic neuron releases glutamate.

Presynaptic neuron

Glutamate

AMPA receptor

2 Glutamate binds with AMPA receptors on postsynaptic neuron.

Postsynaptic neuron

Mg^{2+}

NMDA receptor blocked by Mg^{2+}

3 Ion channels open, allowing Na^+ to pass into postsynaptic neuron. Na^+ depolarize membrane.

Presynaptic neuron

Glutamate

Na^+

Mg^{2+}

Ca^{2+}

4 If postsynaptic neuron is strongly depolarized, Mg^{2+} move away from NMDA receptors, allowing glutamate to bind with them.

5 Ca^{2+} channels open.

Presynaptic neuron

6 Ca^{2+} cause more AMPA receptors to be inserted into membrane.

Ca^{2+}

Signaling pathway

NO

Retrograde signal

7 Ca^{2+} stimulate release of NO, which diffuses into presynaptic neuron and stimulates release of more glutamate.

(a) Activation of AMPA receptors. Glutamate released by a presynaptic neuron binds with AMPA receptors on the postsynaptic neuron. Note that NMDA receptors are blocked by Mg^{2+}.

(b) Activation of NMDA receptors. The combination of strong stimulation and glutamate binding activates NMDA receptors.

(c) Long-term potentiation. Calcium ions activate pathways, leading to changes that are ultimately responsible for LTP.

FIGURE 42-16 A proposed model for the mechanism of long-term potentiation (LTP)

given toys and other stimulating objects, as well as the opportunity to socially interact with other rats. Animals reared in an enriched environment exhibit increased synaptic contacts and process and remember information more quickly than animals lacking such advantages. Mice exposed to enriched environments develop significantly greater numbers of neurons in the hippocampus and learn mazes faster than control animals.

Early environmental stimulation can also enhance the development of motor areas in the brain. For example, the brains of rats encouraged to exercise become slightly heavier than those of control animals. Characteristic changes occur within the cerebellum, including the development of larger dendrites.

Apparently, during early life certain critical or sensitive periods of nervous system development occur that are influenced by environmental stimuli. For example, when the eyes of young mice first open, neurons in the visual cortex develop large numbers of dendritic spines (structures on which synaptic contact takes place). If the animals are kept in the dark and deprived of visual stimuli, fewer dendritic spines form. If the mice are exposed to light later in life, some new dendritic spines form but never as many as develop in a mouse reared in a normal environment.

Studies linking the development of the human brain with environmental experience have demonstrated that early stimulation is important for the sensory, motor, intellectual, and social development of children. Such studies argue for the importance of informed parenting, as well as for early education programs. Inves-

tigators have also shown that environmental stimulation is needed to maintain the status of the cerebral cortex in later life.

Language involves comprehension and expression

Language is a form of communication in which we use words to symbolize objects and convey ideas. In about 97% of humans, including most who are left-handed, the areas of the brain responsible for language are located in the left hemisphere (see Fig. 42-12). **Wernicke's area,** located in the temporal lobe, is an important center for language comprehension. This area helps us recognize and interpret both spoken and written words. Wernicke's area also helps us formulate the choice and sequence of words and transfers information to **Broca's area.** Located near motor areas in the left frontal lobe, Broca's area controls our ability to speak. Broca's area is also important in language processing and speech comprehension.

Review

- How is the human CNS protected? What is the function of the cerebrospinal fluid?
- What are two main functions of the vertebrate spinal cord?
- What are the functions of each of the major lobes of the cerebrum?
- What role does the limbic system play in the emotional aspects of behavior?
- What role does synaptic plasticity play in information processing?

42.5 THE PERIPHERAL NERVOUS SYSTEM

■ LEARNING OBJECTIVES

10 Describe the organization of the peripheral nervous system and compare its somatic and autonomic divisions.

11 Contrast the sympathetic and parasympathetic divisions of the autonomic system and give examples of the effects of these systems on specific organs such as the heart and intestine.

The peripheral nervous system consists of the sensory receptors, the nerves that link these receptors with the central nervous system, and the nerves that link the CNS with effectors (muscles and glands). The somatic division of the PNS helps the body respond to changes in the external environment. The nerves and receptors that maintain homeostasis despite internal changes make up the autonomic division.

The somatic division helps the body adjust to the external environment

The **somatic division** of the PNS includes the receptors that react to changes in the external environment, the sensory neurons that inform the CNS of those changes, and the motor neurons that adjust the positions of the skeletal muscles that help maintain the body's posture and balance. In mammals, 12 pairs of **cranial nerves** emerge from the brain. They transmit information to the brain from the sensory receptors for smell, sight, hearing, and taste. For example, cranial nerve II, the optic nerve, transmits signals from the retina of the eye to the brain. The cranial nerves also transmit information to the brain from general sensory receptors, especially in the head region.

Cranial nerves also bring orders from the CNS to the voluntary muscles that control movements of the eyes, face, mouth, tongue, pharynx, and larynx. Cranial nerve VII, the facial nerve, transmits signals to the muscles used in facial expression and to the salivary glands.

In humans, 31 pairs of **spinal nerves** emerge from the spinal cord. Named for the general region of the vertebral column from which they originate, they comprise 8 pairs of cervical, 12 pairs of thoracic, 5 pairs of lumbar, 5 pairs of sacral, and 1 pair of coccygeal spinal nerves. The ventral branches of several spinal nerves form tangled networks called *plexi* (sing., *plexus*). Within a plexus, the fibers of a spinal nerve may separate and then regroup with fibers that originated in other spinal nerves. Thus, nerves emerging from a plexus consist of neurons from several different spinal nerves.

The autonomic division regulates the internal environment

The **autonomic division** helps maintain homeostasis in the internal environment. For example, it regulates the heart rate and helps maintain a constant body temperature. The autonomic system works automatically and without voluntary input. Its effectors are smooth muscle, cardiac muscle, and glands. Like the somatic system, it is functionally organized into reflex pathways. Receptors within the viscera relay information via afferent nerves

to the CNS. The information is integrated at various levels. Then the "decisions" are transmitted along efferent nerves to the appropriate muscles or glands.

Afferent and efferent neurons of the autonomic division lie within cranial and spinal nerves. For example, afferent fibers of cranial nerve X, the **vagus nerve**, transmit signals from many organs of the chest and upper abdomen to the CNS. Its efferent fibers transmit signals from the brain to the heart, stomach, small intestine, and several other organs.

The efferent portion of the autonomic division is subdivided into **sympathetic** and **parasympathetic systems** (TABLE 42-3). Many organs are innervated by both types of nerves. In general, sympathetic and parasympathetic systems have *opposite* effects (FIGS. 42-17 and 42-18). For example, the heart rate is speeded up by messages from sympathetic nerve fibers and slowed by impulses from its parasympathetic nerve fibers. In many cases sympathetic nerves operate to stimulate organs and to mobilize energy, especially in response to stress; whereas the parasympathetic nerves influence organs to conserve and restore energy, particularly during quiet, calm activities.

Instead of using a single efferent neuron, as in the somatic system, the autonomic system uses a relay of two neurons between the CNS and the effector. The first neuron, called the **preganglionic neuron,** has a cell body and dendrites within the CNS. Its axon, part of a peripheral nerve, ends by synapsing with a **postganglionic neuron.** The dendrites and cell body of the postganglionic

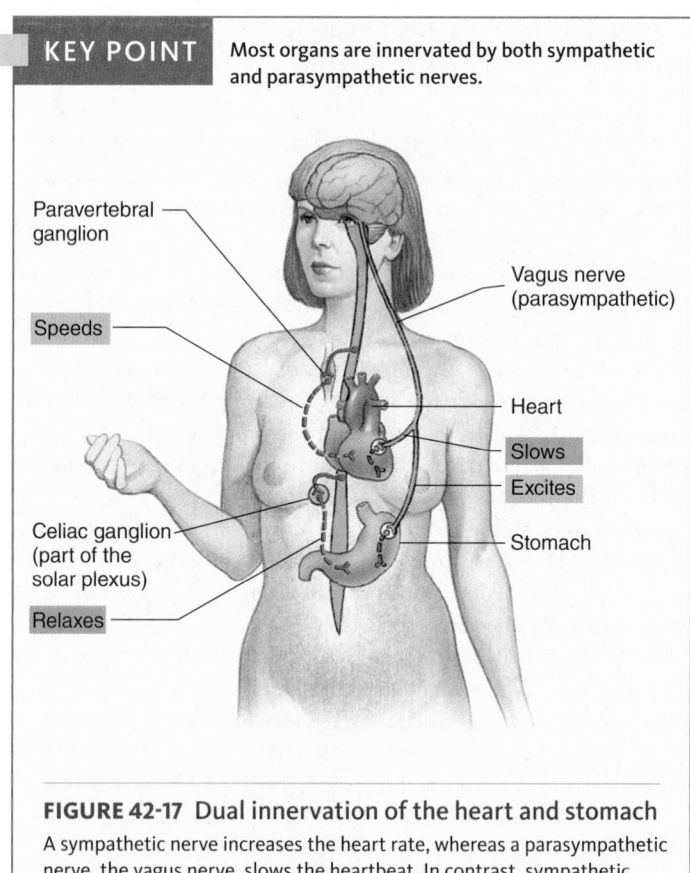

KEY POINT Most organs are innervated by both sympathetic and parasympathetic nerves.

Paravertebral ganglion

Speeds

Celiac ganglion (part of the solar plexus)

Relaxes

Vagus nerve (parasympathetic)

Heart

Slows

Excites

Stomach

FIGURE 42-17 Dual innervation of the heart and stomach
A sympathetic nerve increases the heart rate, whereas a parasympathetic nerve, the vagus nerve, slows the heartbeat. In contrast, sympathetic nerves slow contractions of the stomach and intestine, whereas the vagus nerve stimulates contractions of the digestive organs. Sympathetic nerves are shown in red; postganglionic fibers are shown as dotted lines.

TABLE 42-3 Comparison of Sympathetic and Parasympathetic Systems

	Sympathetic System	Parasympathetic System
General effect	Prepares body to cope with stressful situations	Restores body to resting state after stressful situation; actively maintains normal body functions
Extent of effect	Widespread throughout body	Localized
Duration of effect	Lasting	Brief
Outflow from CNS	Thoracic and lumbar nerves from spinal cord	Cranial nerves and sacral nerves from spinal cord
Location of ganglia	Chain and collateral ganglia	Terminal ganglia
Neurotransmitters released	Preganglionic: acetylcholine	Acetylcholine
	Postganglionic: norepinephrine (usually)	Acetylcholine

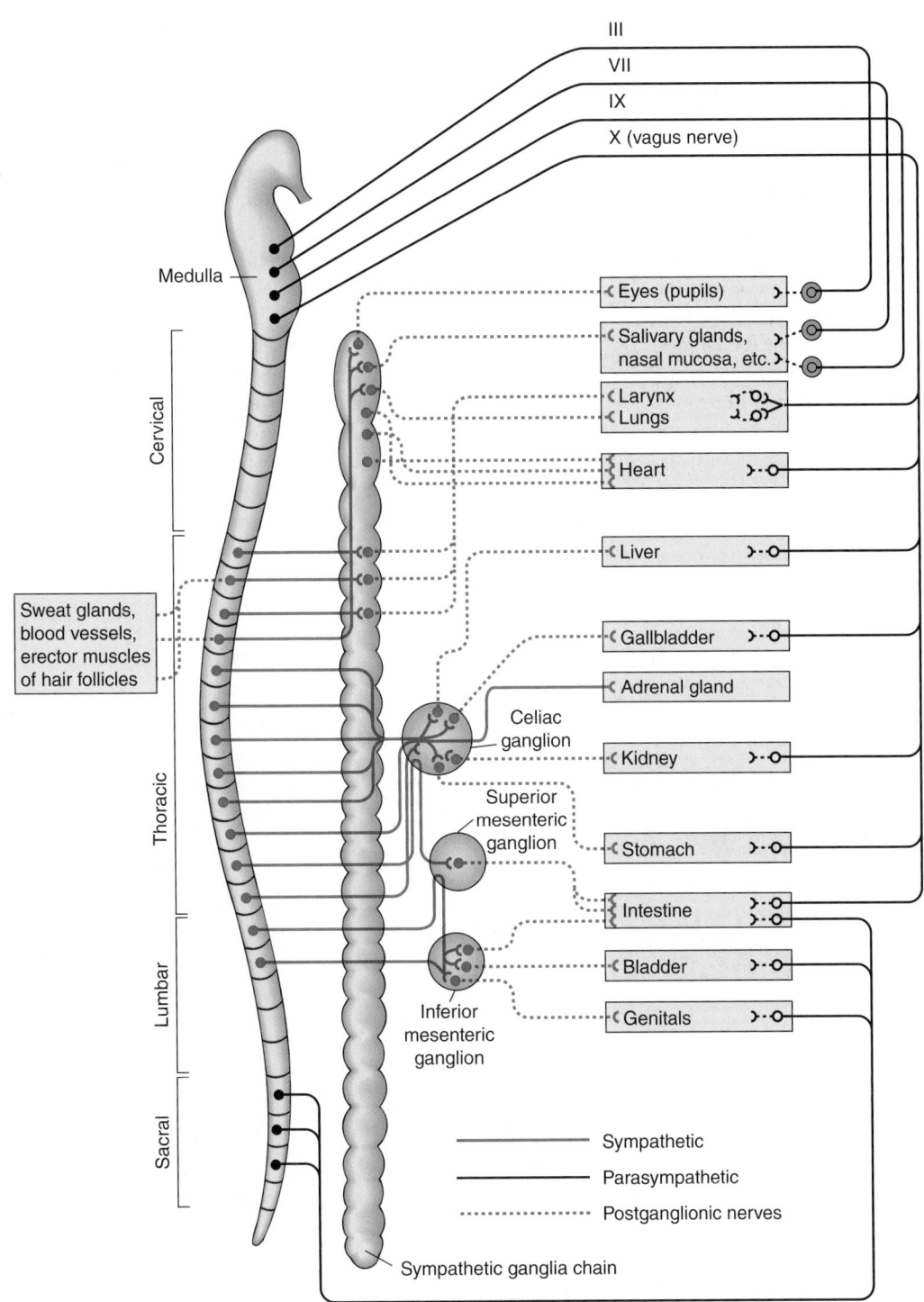

FIGURE 42-18
The sympathetic and parasympathetic systems

Complex as it appears, this diagram has been greatly simplified. Red lines represent sympathetic nerves, black lines represent parasympathetic nerves, and dotted lines represent postganglionic nerves.

neuron are in a ganglion outside the CNS. Its axon terminates near or on the effector.

The sympathetic ganglia are paired, and a chain of them, the **paravertebral sympathetic ganglion chain,** runs on each side of the spinal cord from the neck to the abdomen. Some sympathetic preganglionic neurons do not end in these ganglia but pass on to **collateral ganglia** in the abdomen, close to the aorta and its major branches. Parasympathetic preganglionic neurons synapse with postganglionic neurons in **terminal ganglia** near or within the walls of the organs they innervate.

The sympathetic and parasympathetic systems also differ in the neurotransmitters they release at the synapse with the effector. Both preganglionic and postganglionic parasympathetic neurons secrete acetylcholine. Sympathetic postganglionic neurons release norepinephrine (although preganglionic sympathetic neurons secrete acetylcholine).

The autonomic division got its name from the original idea that it was independent of the CNS, that is, autonomous. Neurobiologists have disproved this and shown that the hypothalamus and many other parts of the CNS help regulate the autonomic system. Although the autonomic system usually functions automatically, its activities can be consciously influenced. Biofeedback provides a person with visual or auditory evidence concerning the status of an autonomic body function. For example, a tone may be sounded when blood pressure reaches a desirable level. Using such techniques, individuals have learned to control autonomic activities such as blood pressure, brain wave pattern, heart rate, and blood sugar level. Even certain abnormal heart rhythms can be consciously modified.

Review

- What are some differences between the somatic division and the autonomic division?
- What are some differences in structure and function of the sympathetic system and the parasympathetic system?

42.6 EFFECTS OF DRUGS ON THE NERVOUS SYSTEM

◼ LEARNING OBJECTIVE

12 Distinguish among psychological dependence, tolerance, and drug addiction, and describe the biological actions and effects on mood of alcohol, antidepressants, barbiturates, antianxiety drugs, antipsychotic drugs, opiates, stimulants, hallucinogens, and marijuana.

About 25% of all prescribed drugs are taken to alter psychological conditions, and almost all the commonly abused drugs affect mood. Many act by changing the levels of neurotransmitters within the brain. In particular, changing levels of norepinephrine, serotonin, and dopamine influence mood. According to the Substance Abuse and Men-

tal Health Services Administration, an estimated 20.1 million individuals (8% of the population) ages 12 or older in the United States use drugs that are not legal (based on individuals who acknowledged using an illicit drug at least once during the 30 days prior to the interview). Abuse of prescription drugs, particularly pain killers, has become a serious problem, especially among teens and young adults.

Although legal, alcohol is the most commonly used and abused drug. (See *Inquiring About: Alcohol: The Most Abused Drug.*) More than 9 million children live with a parent who is dependent on alcohol and/or illicit drugs. **TABLE 42-4** lists several commonly used and abused drugs and gives their effects.

Habitual use of almost any mood-altering drug can result in **psychological dependence,** in which the user becomes emotionally dependent on the drug. When deprived of it, the user craves the feeling of euphoria (well-being) the drug induces. Some drugs induce **tolerance** after several days or weeks. Response to the drug decreases, and greater amounts are required to obtain the desired effect. Tolerance often occurs because the liver cells are stimulated to produce more of the enzymes that metabolize and inactivate the drug. It can also occur when the number of postsynaptic receptors that bind with the drug decrease (*down-regulation*).

Drug addiction is a serious societal problem that involves compulsive use of a drug despite negative health consequences and negative effects on the ability to function socially and occupationally. Use of some drugs, such as heroin, tobacco, alcohol, and barbiturates, may also result in physical dependence, in which physiological changes occur that make the user dependent on the drug. For example, when heroin or alcohol is withheld, the addict suffers characteristic withdrawal symptoms. Physical addiction can occur when a drug, for example, morphine, has components similar to substances that body cells normally manufacture on their own. Some highly addictive drugs, such as crack cocaine and methamphetamine, do not cause serious withdrawal symptoms.

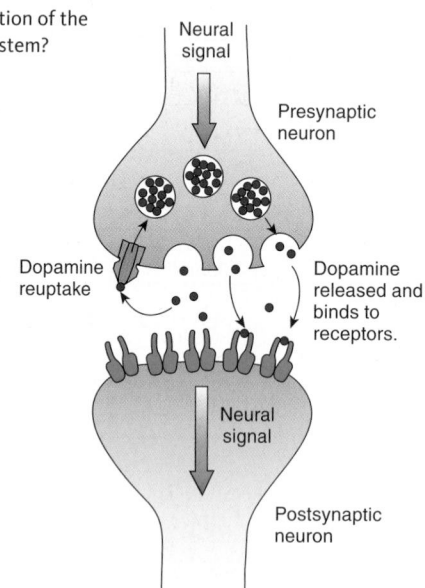

(a) Reuptake of the neurotransmitter dopamine. Dopamine binds with a transporter (*green*) that shuttles it back into the presynaptic terminal.

(b) Cocaine blocks the reuptake of dopamine by binding competitively with the dopamine reuptake transporter. As a result, more dopamine is available to bind with postsynaptic receptors.

FIGURE 42-19 Mechanism of cocaine action

ALCOHOL: THE MOST ABUSED DRUG

What makes alcohol one of the leading preventable risk factors for premature death in the United States? An estimated 90,000 individuals in the United States alone die each year as a result of alcohol-related cancers and other diseases, alcohol-related violence, traffic accidents, and other injuries. Alcohol abuse costs our society more than $100 billion annually.

An estimated 18 million adults in the United States have problems with alcohol abuse or dependence. More than half of the adults in the United States report that one or more of their close relatives has a drinking problem. According to the most recent U.S. Department of Health and Human Services study, the 2008 National Survey on Drug Use and Health: National Findings, 23% of Americans had binged (five or more drinks within two hours) at least once during the 30 days prior to being surveyed. More than 23% had drunk heavily (five or more drinks on five or more occasions). The highest prevalence of binge and heavy drinking was among young adults ages 18 to 25 years. More than seven million binge drinkers in the United States are under age 21.

According to the U.S. Department of Health and Human Services, alcohol use by individuals under age 21 is a major public health problem. Adolescents ages 12 to 20 consume 11% of all alcohol consumed in the United States, and more than 90% of this alcohol was consumed during bingeing. Based on many studies, the Centers for Disease Control and Prevention (CDC) reports that youth who drink alcohol are likely to experience serious problems, including disruption of normal growth and sexual development, abnormal brain development that may have life-long effects, memory problems, as well as school, social, and legal problems and higher risk for suicide, homicide, and death from alcohol poisoning.

Investigators have reported that adults who first used alcohol when they were 14 years old or younger were more than five times as likely to have a problem with alcohol dependence or abuse than adults who had their first drink at age 21 or older. Alcohol abuse results in physiological, psychological, and social impairment and has serious negative consequences for family, friends, and society. Alcohol abuse has been linked to the following:

- More than 30% of all traffic fatalities
- Almost 50% of violent crime
- More than 60% of child-abuse and spouse-abuse cases
- More than 50% of college sexual assaults
- About 25% of suicides
- The birth each year of thousands of babies with serious birth defects because their mother drank alcohol during pregnancy. Fetal alcohol spectrum disorders are the leading cause of preventable mental retardation in the United States.
- Increased risk of mouth, larynx, and throat cancers. Alcohol is also a risk factor for primary liver cancer, breast cancer, and colon cancer. These cancers have been linked to regular alcohol consumption.

A single drink, that is, 12 oz of beer, 5 oz of wine, or 1.5 oz of 80-proof liquor, results in a blood alcohol concentration of approximately 20 mg/dL (milligrams per deciliter). This represents about 0.5 oz of pure alcohol in the blood. Alcohol accumulates in the blood because absorption occurs more rapidly than oxidation and excretion. Every cell in the body can take in alcohol from the blood.

At first the drinker may feel stimulated, but alcohol actually depresses the CNS. As blood alcohol concentration rises, information processing, judgment, memory, sensory perception, and motor coordination all become progressively impaired. Depression and drowsiness generally occur. Contrary to popular belief, alcohol decreases sexual performance. Some individuals become loud, angry, or violent.

A blood alcohol concentration of 80 mg/dL (or 0.08 gm/100 mL) legally defines driving under the influence (DUI). A 170-pound man typically reaches this level by drinking four drinks in an hour on an empty stomach. Alcohol metabolism occurs at a fixed rate in the liver so only time, not coffee, decreases its effects. Because alcohol inhibits water reabsorption in the kidneys, more fluid is excreted as urine than is consumed in the alcohol. This results in dehydration that, together with low blood sugar level, may cause the stupor produced by excessive drinking.

In chronic drinkers, cells of the CNS adapt to the presence of the drug. This causes *tolerance* (more and more alcohol is needed to experience the same effect) and physical dependence. Abrupt withdrawal can result in sleep disturbances, severe anxiety, tremors, seizures, hallucinations, and psychoses.

The *A1* allele of the D2 dopamine receptor gene increases the risk for alcoholism. Individuals with this allele have fewer D2 dopamine receptors in their brain. Alcohol, like cocaine, heroin, amphetamines, and nicotine, enhances dopamine activity in the *mesolimbic dopamine pathway* of the brain. Individuals with the *A1* allele may compensate for their low dopamine levels by using alcohol and other drugs. However, the mechanisms underlying alcohol addiction are far more complex. Evidence suggests that many neurotransmitters are involved, including glutamate, serotonin, GABA, and opioid peptides. Recently, researchers identified a cluster of genes on chromosome 11 that appear to be associated with alcohol dependence.

Treatment for alcohol problems includes various forms of psychotherapy and use of drugs such as naltrexone and acamprosate. The group support offered by Alcoholics Anonymous (AA) has proved effective for many struggling with alcohol dependence. Participation in AA includes attending frequent meetings, having a sponsor within the program, and working on the 12 steps.

The neurobiological mechanisms for drug addiction involve the *mesolimbic dopamine pathway,* a major reward circuit (described earlier in this chapter in connection with the limbic system). Many of the neurons in this pathway project from the *ventral tegmental area* in the midbrain and signal neurons in the limbic system, including the amygdala and an area called the *nucleus accumbens.* Projections of this nucleus are thought to be involved in the reinforcement people experience from taking drugs.

Effects on neurons in the mesolimbic dopamine pathway have been demonstrated in nicotine, heroin, amphetamine, and cocaine addiction. For example, amphetamines stimulate dopamine release. Cocaine blocks the reuptake of dopamine into presynaptic neurons, thus prolonging the stimulation (**FIG. 42-19**). Amphetamines or cocaine can increase dopamine concentration in the limbic system by up to 1000 times normal amounts! Prolonged drug use alters gene expression and changes neuron structure.

Review

- How does each of the following drugs affect the CNS: (1) alcohol, (2) antipsychotic drugs, (3) antidepressants, (4) amphetamines, and (5) MDMA ("Ecstasy")?

TABLE 42-4   Effects of Some Commonly Used Drugs

Name of Drug	Effect on Mood	Actions on Body	Side Effects/Dangers Associated with Abuse
Antidepressants			
Tricyclic antidepressants (e.g., Elavil, Anafranil)	Elevate mood; relieve depression; used to treat obsessive-compulsive behavior	Most block reuptake of biogenic amines (especially norepinephrine), increasing their concentration in synapses	Sedation, weight gain, sexual dysfunction
Selective serotonin reuptake inhibitors (SSRIs) (e.g., Prozac, Zoloft, Lexapro, Celexa)	Relieve depression; used to treat obsessive-compulsive behavior	Block serotonin reuptake	Nausea, headache, insomnia, anxiety
MAO (monoamine oxidase) inhibitors (e.g., Parnate, Nardil)	Relieve depression	Block enzymatic breakdown of biogenic amines, increasing their concentration in synapses	Liver toxicity, excessive CNS stimulation; overdose may affect blood pressure, cause hallucinations
Anti-anxiety Medications			
Benzodiazepines (e.g., Xanax, Valium, Librium)	Sedation; induce sleep	Bind to GABA receptors on post-synaptic neuron; increase effectiveness of GABA in opening chloride channels, causing hyperpolarization; cause relaxation of skeletal muscles	Drowsiness, confusion; psychological dependence, addiction; effects additive with alcohol
Barbiturates ("downers") (e.g., phenobarbital)	Sedation; induce sleep	Bind to receptor adjacent to GABA receptor on chloride channels; chloride channels open so more chloride ions move in, causing hyperpolarization	Drowsiness, confusion; psychological dependence, tolerance, addiction; severe CNS depression, resulting in coma and death (especially lethal in combination with alcohol)
Antipsychotic Medications			
Phenothiazines (e.g., Thorazine, Mellaril, Stelazine)	Relieve symptoms of schizophrenia; reduce impulsive and aggressive behavior	Block dopamine receptors	Muscle spasms, shuffling gait, and other symptoms of Parkinson's disease
Atypical antipsychotic medications (e.g., Abilify, Risperdal)	Similar to phenothiazines, but also increase motivation	Block dopamine receptors and other neurotransmitter receptors	Fewer side effects than with the phenothiazines
Narcotic Analgesics			
Opiates (e.g., morphine, codeine, Demerol, heroin)	Euphoria; sedation; relieve pain	Mimic actions of endorphins; bind to opiate receptors	Depress respiration; constrict pupils; impair coordination; tolerance, psychological dependence, addiction; convulsions, death from overdose
Cocaine	Brief, intense high with euphoria, followed by fatigue and depression	Stimulates release and inhibits reuptake of norepinephrine and dopamine, leading to CNS stimulation followed by depression; autonomic stimulation; dilation of pupils; local anesthesia	Mental impairment, convulsions, hallucinations, unconsciousness; death from overdose
Marijuana	Euphoria	Impairs coordination; impairs depth perception and alters sense of timing; impairs short-term memory (probably by decreasing acetylcholine levels in the hippocampus); inflames eyes; causes peripheral vasodilation	In large doses, sensory distortions, hallucinations, evidence of lowered sperm counts and testosterone levels
Amphetamines			
"Uppers," "pep pills," "crystal meth" (e.g., Dexedrine); methamphetamine is a popular club drug	Euphoria, stimulation, hyperactivity	Stimulate release and block reuptake of dopamine and norepinephrine; enhance flow of impulses in RAS, leading to increased heart rate, blood pressure; pupil dilation	Tolerance, physical dependence; hallucinations; increased blood pressure; psychotic episodes; death from overdose

TABLE 42-4 (Continued)

Name of Drug	Effect on Mood	Actions on Body	Side Effects/Dangers Associated with Abuse
Amphetamines *(continued)*			
Amphetamine-type prescription stimulants commonly used to treat attention deficit hyper-activity disorder (ADHD) (e.g., methylphenidate: Ritalin, Concerta)	CNS stimulation, but has calming effect on many children and adults who have ADHD; increases focus	Increases heart rate, blood pressure, and body temperature; like cocaine, amphetamines block dopamine transporter which increases dopamine concentration in synapses	Not addictive at prescribed doses; used illegally and abused by some high school and college students who use them in higher doses than would be prescribed; can cause irregular heartbeat and respiration, hallucinations, delusions, and convulsions; abuse can lead to tolerance and physical addiction
MDMA (3,4-methylene-dioxymethamphetamine) "Ecstasy" (most popular of club drugs)	Stimulation, sense of pleasure, self-confidence, feelings of closeness to others; mild hallucinogenic	CNS stimulant; damages serotonin pathways in rat and monkey brains	Hyperthermia (excessive body heat); overdose causes rapid heartbeat, high blood pressure, panic attacks, and seizures; long-term neurological changes; cognitive impairment
Rohypnol (flunitrazepam) "Date rape" drug, "roofies," "roach"	Sedative-hypnotic	Muscle relaxation; amnesia	Physical and psychological dependence; withdrawal may cause seizures; may be lethal when mixed with alcohol and/or other depressants
PCP (phencyclidine) "Angel dust," "ozone"	Feelings of strength, power, invulnerability, and a numbing effect on the mind	Increase in blood pressure and heart rate; shallow respiration; flushing, profuse sweating; numbness of extremities; muscular incoordination; changes in body awareness, similar to those associated with alcohol intoxication	Psychological dependence, craving; in adolescents, interferes with hormones related to growth and development; may interfere with learning; causes hallucinations, delusions, disordered thinking; high doses cause drop in blood pressure and heart rate, seizures, coma, and death; chronic use causes memory loss, difficulties with speech and thinking, and depression
LSD (lysergic acid diethylamide)	Overexcitation; sensory distortions, hallucinations	Alters levels of neurotransmitters in brain; potent CNS stimulator; dilates pupils, sometimes unequally; increases heart rate; raises blood pressure	Impaired judgment leading to irrational behavior; panic attacks; psychosis; flashbacks
Methaqualone (e.g., Quaalude, Sopor)	Hypnotic	Depresses CNS; depresses certain spinal reflexes	Tolerance, physical dependence; convulsions, death
Caffeine	Increases mental alertness; decreases fatigue and drowsiness	Acts on cerebral cortex; relaxes smooth muscle; stimulates cardiac and skeletal muscle; increases urine volume	Very large doses stimulate centers in the medulla (may slow the heart); toxic doses may cause convulsions
Nicotine	Decreases psychological tension	Stimulates sympathetic nervous system; increases dopamine in mesolimbic pathway	Tolerance, physical dependence; stimulates development of atherosclerosis by stimulating synthesis of lipid in arterial wall
Alcohol	Euphoria, relaxation, release of inhibitions	Depresses CNS; impairs vision, coordination, judgment; lengthens reaction time	Physical dependence; damage to pancreas and liver (e.g., cirrhosis); brain damage; increased risk of depression

42.1 (page 883)

1 Contrast nerve nets and radial nervous systems with bilateral nervous systems.

- **Nerve nets** and **radial nervous systems** are typical of radially symmetrical invertebrates, such as cnidarians. An animal with a radial nervous system can respond effectively to predator or prey approaching from any direction.

- In planarian flatworms the **bilateral nervous system** includes **cerebral ganglia** and, usually, two solid ventral nerve cords connected by transverse nerves. Annelids and arthropods typically have a ventral nerve cord and numerous ganglia. The cerebral ganglia of arthropods have specialized regions. Octopods and other cephalopod mollusks have highly developed nervous systems with neurons concentrated in a central region.

- The bilateral nervous system is adaptive for bilaterally symmetrical animals that typically move in a forward direction. Nerve cells concentrate to form **nerves, nerve cords, ganglia,** and **brain;** typically, sense organs are concentrated in the head region.

    CENGAGENOW™ Learn more about various nervous systems by clicking on the figures in CengageNOW.

2 Identify trends in the evolution of the invertebrate nervous system.

- Trends in nervous system evolution include increased numbers and concentration of nerve cells; specialization of function; increased number of association neurons; more complex synaptic contacts; and **cephalization,** formation of a head.

42.2 (page 884)

3 Describe the two main divisions of the vertebrate nervous system and summarize their functions.

- The **central nervous system (CNS),** which consists of the brain and spinal cord, is specialized to integrate incoming information. The **peripheral nervous system (PNS),** which consists of sensory receptors and nerves, transmits signals between sensory receptors and the CNS, and between the CNS and effectors.

    CENGAGENOW™ Learn more about the vertebrate nervous system by clicking on the figure in CengageNOW.

42.3 (page 886)

4 Trace the development of the principal vertebrate brain regions from the hindbrain, midbrain, and forebrain, and compare the brains of fishes, amphibians, reptiles, birds, and mammals.

- In the vertebrate embryo, the brain and spinal cord arise from the **neural tube.** The anterior end of the tube differentiates into **hindbrain, midbrain,** and **forebrain.**

- The hindbrain subdivides into the **metencephalon** and **myelencephalon.** The myelencephalon develops into the **medulla,** which contains vital centers and other reflex centers. The **fourth ventricle,** the cavity of the medulla, communicates with the central canal of the spinal cord. The metencephalon gives rise to the **cerebellum,** which is responsible for muscle tone, posture, and equilibrium, and to the **pons,** which connects various parts of the brain.

- The midbrain is the largest part of the brain in fishes and amphibians. It is their main association area, linking sensory input and motor output. In reptiles, birds, and mammals, the midbrain serves as a center for visual and auditory reflexes. The medulla, pons, and midbrain make up the **brain stem.**

- The forebrain differentiates to form the **diencephalon** and **telencephalon.** The diencephalon develops into the thalamus and hypothalamus. The **thalamus** is a relay center for motor and sensory information. The **hypothalamus** controls autonomic functions; links nervous and endocrine systems; controls temperature, appetite, and fluid balance; and is involved in some emotional and sexual responses.

- The telencephalon develops into the cerebrum and **olfactory bulbs.** In most vertebrates, the **cerebrum** is divided into right and left **cerebral hemispheres.** In fishes and amphibians, the cerebrum mainly integrates incoming sensory information. In birds, the corpus striatum controls complex behavior patterns, such as flying and singing.

- In mammals, the **neocortex** accounts for a large part of the **cerebral cortex,** the **gray matter** of the brain. The cerebrum has complex association functions.

    CENGAGENOW™ Explore the early development of the vertebrate nervous system and the evolution of the vertebrate brain by clicking on the figures in CengageNOW.

42.4 (page 888)

5 Describe the structure and functions of the human spinal cord.

- The human brain and spinal cord are protected by bone and three **meninges**—the **dura mater, arachnoid,** and **pia mater;** the brain and spinal cord are cushioned by **cerebrospinal fluid (CSF).**

- The spinal cord transmits impulses to and from the brain and controls many **reflex actions.** The spinal cord consists of **ascending tracts,** which transmit information to the brain, and **descending tracts,** which transmit information from the brain. Its gray matter contains nuclei that serve as reflex centers.

    CENGAGENOW™ Learn more about the spinal cord by clicking on the figure in CengageNOW.

- A **withdrawal reflex** involves sensory receptors; sensory neurons, interneurons, and motor neurons; and effectors, such as muscles.

6 Describe the structure and functions of the human cerebrum.

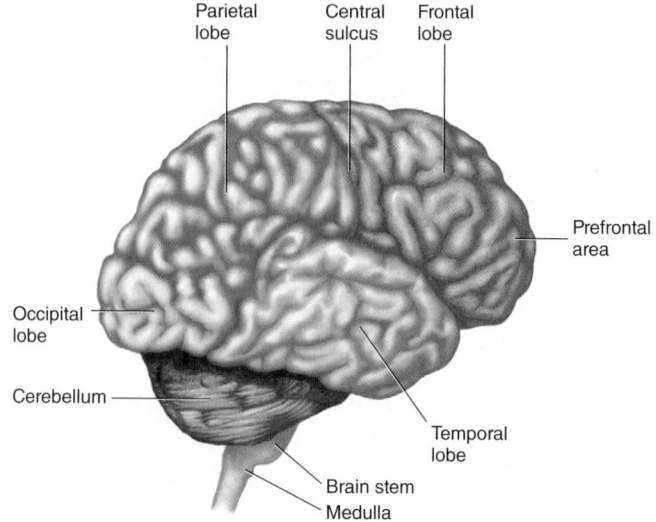

- The human cerebral cortex consists of gray matter, which forms folds or **convolutions.** Deep furrows between the folds are called **fissures.**
- The cerebrum is functionally divided into **sensory areas** that receive incoming sensory information; **motor areas** that control voluntary movement; and **association areas** that link sensory and motor areas and are responsible for learning, language, thought, and judgment. The cerebrum consists of lobes, including the **frontal lobes, parietal lobes, temporal lobes,** and **occipital lobes.**
- The **white matter** of the cerebrum lies beneath the cerebral cortex. The **corpus callosum,** a large band of white matter, connects right and left hemispheres. The **basal ganglia,** a cluster of nuclei within the white matter, are important centers for motor function.

CENGAGENOW™ Learn more about the human brain by clicking on the figures in CengageNOW.

7 Summarize the sleep–wake cycle and contrast rapid-eye-movement (REM) sleep with non-REM sleep.
- The body's main biological clock—the **suprachiasmatic nucleus**—receives information about light and dark and transmits it to other nuclei that regulate sleep.
- The **reticular activating system (RAS)** is an arousal system; its neurons filter sensory input, selecting which information is transmitted to the cerebrum.
- The hypothalamus, thalamus, and brain stem regulate the sleep–wake cycle. **Sleep** is an alteration of consciousness with decreased electrical activity in the cerebral cortex.
- Electrical activity of the cerebral cortex and metabolic rate slow during **non-REM sleep,** whereas dreaming characterizes **REM sleep.**

8 Describe the actions of the limbic system, including the role of the amygdala in emotional expression.
- The **limbic system** affects the emotional aspects of behavior, motivation, sexual activity, autonomic responses, and biological rhythms. The **amygdala** evaluates incoming information and signals danger; it is especially important in the experience of fear and aggression.

9 Summarize how the brain processes information, including a description of synaptic plasticity and the neurobiological changes that take place during learning.
- **Synaptic plasticity** is the ability of the nervous system to modify synapses, which allows learning and remembering.
- **Learning** is the process by which we acquire knowledge or skills as a result of experience. **Memory** is the process by which information is encoded, stored, and retrieved. **Implicit memory** is unconscious ("how-to") memory for perceptual and motor skills. **Declarative memory** is factual memory of people, places, or objects.
- **Immediate memory** holds sensory information for fractions of a second. **Short-term memory** holds a small amount of information, for a few minutes. Information can be transferred from short-term memory to **long-term memory.** The **hippocampus** is important in categorizing information and consolidating memories.
- Learning and memory involve long-term functional changes at synapses. Known as **long-term potentiation (LTP),** such changes involve increased sensitivity to an action potential by a postsynaptic neuron. **Long-term depression (LTD)** is a long-lasting decrease in the strength of synaptic connections. Long-term memory storage involves gene expression. The transcription factor **CREB** is an important signaling molecule in the memory pathway.

42.5 (page 902)

10 Describe the organization of the peripheral nervous system and compare its somatic and autonomic divisions.
- The PNS consists of sensory receptors and nerves, including the **cranial nerves** and **spinal nerves** and their branches. The **somatic division** of the PNS responds to changes in the external environment. The **autonomic division** regulates the internal activities of the body.

11 Contrast the sympathetic and parasympathetic divisions of the autonomic system and give examples of the effects of these systems on specific organs such as the heart and intestine.
- The **sympathetic system** permits the body to respond to stressful situations. The **parasympathetic system** influences organs to conserve and restore energy. Many organs are innervated by sympathetic and parasympathetic nerves, which function in opposite ways. For example, the sympathetic system increases heart rate, whereas the parasympathetic system decreases heart rate.

42.6 (page 904)

12 Distinguish among psychological dependence, tolerance, and drug addiction, and describe the biological actions and effects on mood of alcohol, antidepressants, barbiturates, anti-anxiety drugs, antipsychotic drugs, opiates, stimulants, hallucinogens, and marijuana.
- Many drugs alter mood by increasing or decreasing the concentrations of specific neurotransmitters within the brain. See Table 42-4 for a summary of these drugs.
- Habitual use of mood-altering drugs can result in **psychological dependence** or **drug addiction.** Many drugs induce **tolerance,** in which the body's response to the drug decreases so that greater amounts are needed to obtain the desired effect.

TEST YOUR UNDERSTANDING

1. A radially symmetrical animal such as *Hydra* is likely to have (a) a forebrain (b) a nerve net (c) cerebral ganglia (d) a ventral nerve cord (e) cerebral ganglia and a nerve net

2. In vertebrate embryos the brain develops from the (a) spinal cord (b) sympathetic nervous system (c) parasympathetic nervous system (d) neural tube (e) forebrain

3. Which part of the brain maintains posture, muscle tone, and equilibrium? (a) cerebrum (b) medulla (c) cerebellum (d) neocortex (e) thalamus

4. The most prominent part of the amphibian brain is the (a) midbrain (b) medulla (c) cerebellum (d) neocortex (e) cerebrum

5. Which part of the brain controls autonomic functions and regulates body temperature? (a) cerebrum (b) hypothalamus (c) cerebellum (d) pons (e) thalamus

6. Which sequence best describes transmission of information in a withdrawal reflex? 1. afferent neuron transmits signal to CNS 2. muscle contracts 3. reception by sensory neuron 4. interneuron in CNS integrates information 5. efferent neuron transmits signal (a) 3, 1, 4, 5, 2 (b) 2, 1, 4, 5, 3 (c) 3, 5, 1, 4, 2 (d) 3, 1, 5, 4, 2 (e) 5, 3, 1, 4, 2

7. The human brain is protected by (a) arachnoid, pia mater, cerebrospinal fluid, and ganglia (b) meninges and skull bones only

(c) dura mater and fourth ventricle (d) pia mater and skull bones (e) meninges, cerebrospinal fluid, and skull bones

8. The suprachiasmatic nucleus (a) secretes melatonin (b) stimulates beta waves (c) filters incoming sensory information and determines whether it is threatening (d) is critical in memory consolidation (e) is important in regulating the sleep–wake cycle

9. Long-term potentiation (LTP) (a) is mainly the responsibility of cranial nerve II (b) is a long-lasting increase in synaptic strength (c) is associated with short-term memory (d) is a long-lasting decrease in synaptic strength (e) is a long-lasting decrease in synaptic strength that occurs mainly during REM sleep

10. The heart rate is slowed by (a) sympathetic nerves (b) parasympathetic nerves (c) rapid firing in the corpus callosum (d) both sympathetic and parasympathetic nerves (e) the hippocampus working together with sympathetic nerves

11. Amphetamines (a) affect neurons in the mesolimbic dopamine pathway (b) decrease the amount of dopamine secreted (c) have the same types of effects as alcohol (d) are often prescribed to reduce anxiety (e) are CNS depressants

12. Label the diagram. Use Figure 42-11a to check your answers.

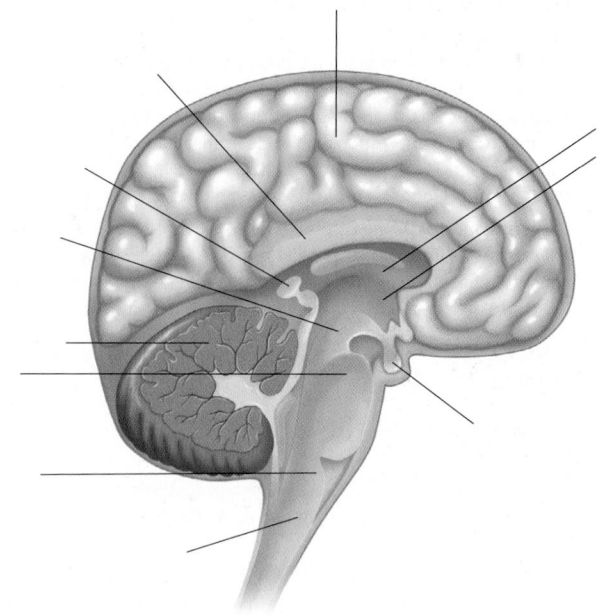

CRITICAL THINKING

1. What is the adaptive function of the limbic system when you are in danger?

2. Hypothesize a possible relationship between inheritance and intelligence based on gene activation during information processing.

3. **EVOLUTION LINK.** What general trends can you identify in the evolution of the vertebrate brain?

4. **EVOLUTION LINK.** CREB has been shown to be a signaling molecule in the memory pathway in many animals, including fruit flies and mice. What does this suggest about the evolution of learning and memory?

5. **SCIENCE, TECHNOLOGY, AND SOCIETY.** Imagine that you have just become a parent. What kinds of things can you do to enhance the development of your child's intellectual abilities?

 Additional questions are available in CengageNOW at www.cengage.com/login.

43 Sensory Systems

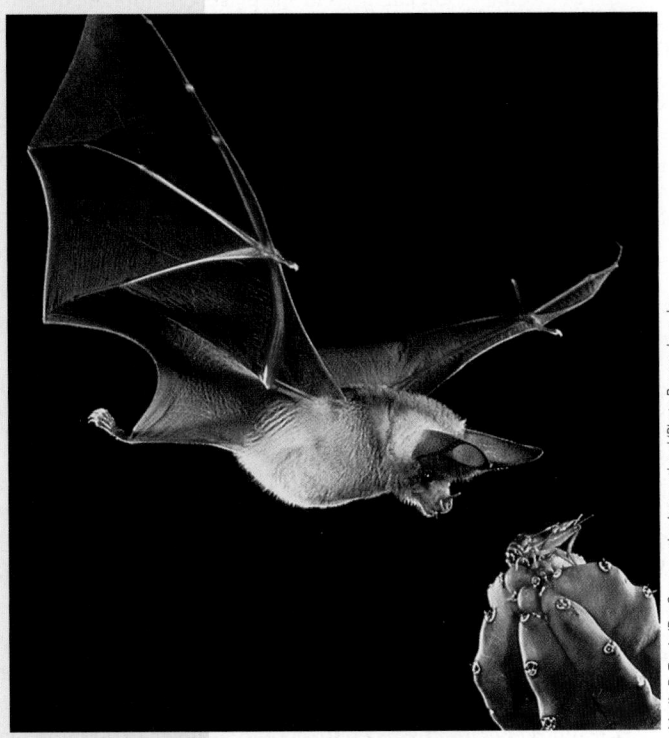

Bats are guided by echoes. This California leaf-nosed bat (*Macrotus californicus*) has located an insect.

Merlin D. Tuttle/Bat Conservation International/Photo Researchers, Inc.

Have you heard dolphins make clicking sounds? Humans can hear only a limited number of the wide range of sound frequencies that dolphins emit. Dolphins, bats, and a few other vertebrates detect distant objects by *echolocation,* sometimes called biosonar. Echolocation works something like radar but uses sound rather than radio waves. For example, a bat emits high-pitched sounds that bounce off objects in its path and echo back. By rapidly responding to the echo, the bat skillfully avoids obstacles and captures prey (see photograph). Using echolocation, bats and dolphins determine the size, shape, texture, and density of an object, as well as its location.

The ability to detect sounds emitted by some foraging bats has evolved in certain moths and other insect prey. Through the course of evolution, some species of bats have adapted to this ability of their prey; they now emit even higher-frequency sounds that their prey cannot detect. Researchers have recently reported another interesting adaptation. There is evidence that some moths emit ultrasonic clicks that jam the bats' echolocation.

Sensory systems transfer information from the outside world to the animal. They inform the animal about predators, food, water, possible mates, temperature, and other changes in the environment. The kinds of sensory receptors an animal has and the way in which the brain *perceives* incoming sensory information determine what the animal's world is like.

911

We humans live in a world of rich colors, numerous shapes, and varied sounds. But we cannot hear the high-pitched whistles that are audible to dogs and cats or the ultrasonic echoes by which bats navigate. Nor do we ordinarily recognize our friends by their distinctive odors! And although vision is our dominant and most refined sense, we are blind to the ultraviolet (UV) hues that light up the world for insects. Unlike birds and some other animals, we cannot detect changes in magnetic fields. Nor can we detect electric fields like sharks and several other species of fishes.

We humans are most familiar with the senses of sight, hearing, smell, taste, and touch, but there are other senses. In fact, touch is a compound sense that allows us to detect pressure, pain, and temperature. Some sensory receptors allow us to sense balance, muscle tension, and joint position, providing us with an awareness of our bodies.

In this chapter we will first examine how sensory systems function. Next we will introduce the major types of sensory receptors. We then discuss several types of sensory receptors with emphasis on auditory and visual receptors.

43.1 HOW SENSORY SYSTEMS WORK

■ LEARNING OBJECTIVES

1 Describe how sensory systems function; include descriptions of sensory receptors, energy transduction, receptor potential, sensory adaptation, and perception.

2 Classify sensory receptors according to the location of stimuli to which they respond and according to the types of energy they transduce.

Sensory receptors detect information about changes in the external and internal environment. These receptors consist of specialized neuron endings or specialized cells in close contact with neurons. Sensory receptors, along with other types of cells, make up complex **sense organs,** such as eyes, ears, nose, and taste buds. A human taste bud, for example, consists of modified epithelial cells that detect chemicals dissolved in saliva.

Several steps take place in sensory processing, including sensory reception, energy transduction, transmission of the signal, and interpretation in the brain. With minor variations, this is how all sensory systems operate.

Sensory receptors receive information

Sensory receptors receive stimuli from the external or internal environment. In the process of reception, they absorb a small amount of energy from some stimulus. Each kind of sensory receptor is especially sensitive to one particular form of energy. The photoreceptors of the human eye are stimulated by an extremely faint beam of light, and taste receptors are stimulated by a minute amount of a chemical compound.

Sensory receptors transduce energy

Sensory receptors *transduce,* or convert, the energy of the stimulus into electrical signals, the information currency of the nervous system. This process is known as **energy transduction.** When unstimulated, a sensory receptor maintains a *resting potential,* that is, a difference in charge between the inside and outside of the cell (see Chapter 41). Transduction couples a stimulus with the opening or closing of ion channels in the plasma membrane of sensory receptors. The permeability of the plasma membrane to various ions is altered.

A change in ion distribution causes a change in voltage across the membrane. If the difference in charge increases, the receptor becomes hyperpolarized. If the potential decreases, the receptor becomes depolarized. A change in membrane potential is a **receptor potential.** A receptor potential does not directly trigger an action potential. Like an excitatory postsynaptic potential, or EPSP (see Chapter 41), the receptor potential is a **graded response** in which the magnitude of change depends on the energy of the stimulus.

If the receptor is a separate cell, receptor potentials stimulate the release of a neurotransmitter, which flows across the synapse and binds to receptors on a **sensory neuron,** also known as an *afferent neuron* (**FIG. 43-1**). When a sensory neuron becomes sufficiently depolarized to reach its threshold level, an action potential is generated. Thus, receptor potentials can generate action potentials that transmit information to the central nervous system (CNS).

Many receptors are specialized neurons rather than separate cells. In these neurons, the specialized region of the plasma membrane that transduces energy does not generate action potentials. Current generated by receptor potentials flows to a region along the axon where an action potential can be generated.

We can summarize the process of sensory reception as follows:

stimulus (such as light energy) ⟶ sensory receptor absorbs energy from stimulus ⟶ transduces energy of stimulus into electrical energy ⟶ receptor potential ⟶ action potential in sensory neuron ⟶ signal transmitted to CNS

Sensory input is integrated at many levels

Sensory integration begins in the receptor itself. For example, receptor potentials produced by various stimuli are integrated by summation (see Chapter 41). However, integration occurs mainly in the spinal cord and at various locations in the brain.

Sensory receptors adapt to stimuli

Many sensory receptors do not continue to respond at the initial rate, even if the stimulus continues at the same intensity. This change in response rate, called **sensory adaptation,** occurs for two reasons. First, during a sustained stimulus, the receptor sensitivity decreases and produces a smaller receptor potential (resulting in a lower frequency of action potentials in the sensory neurons). Second, changes take place at synapses in the neural pathway activated by the receptor. For example, the release of neurotransmitter from

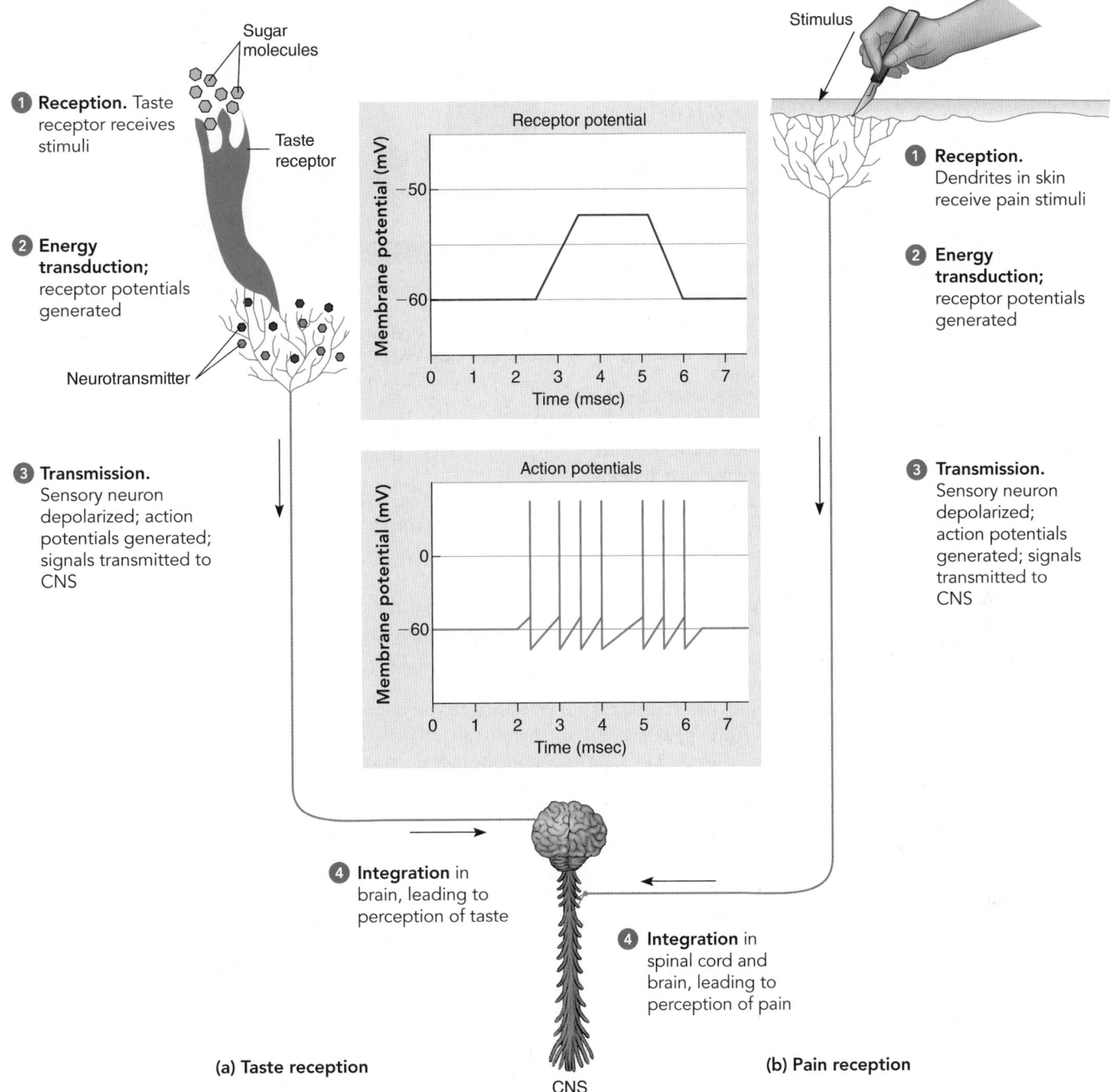

① Reception. Taste receptor receives stimuli

Sugar molecules

Taste receptor

② Energy transduction; receptor potentials generated

Neurotransmitter

③ Transmission. Sensory neuron depolarized; action potentials generated; signals transmitted to CNS

④ Integration in brain, leading to perception of taste

(a) Taste reception

Receptor potential

Membrane potential (mV)

−50

−60

0 1 2 3 4 5 6 7
Time (msec)

Action potentials

Membrane potential (mV)

0

−60

0 1 2 3 4 5 6 7
Time (msec)

CNS

Stimulus

① Reception. Dendrites in skin receive pain stimuli

② Energy transduction; receptor potentials generated

③ Transmission. Sensory neuron depolarized; action potentials generated; signals transmitted to CNS

④ Integration in spinal cord and brain, leading to perception of pain

(b) Pain reception

FIGURE 43-1 How sensory systems work

Sensory receptors receive stimuli from the environment. They transduce the energy of the stimulus into electrical signals, and thus generate receptor potentials. Action potentials are generated in sensory neurons that transmit signals to the CNS, where they are integrated.

a presynaptic terminal may decrease in response to a series of action potentials.

Some receptors, such as those for pain or cold, adapt so slowly that they continue to trigger action potentials as long as the stimulus persists. Other receptors adapt rapidly, permitting us to ignore persistent unpleasant or unimportant stimuli. For example, when you first pull on a pair of tight jeans, your pressure receptors let you

know that you are being squished, and you may feel uncomfortable. Soon, though, these receptors adapt, and you hardly notice the sensation of the tight fit. In the same way, people quickly adapt to odors that at first seem to assault their senses. Sensory adaptation enables an animal to discriminate between unimportant background stimuli that can be ignored and new or important stimuli that require attention.

Sensation depends on transmission of a coded message

How do you know whether you are seeing a blue sky, tasting a doughnut, or hearing a note played on a piano? All action potentials are qualitatively the same. Light of the wavelength 450 nm (blue), sugar molecules (sweet), and sound waves of 440 hertz (Hz) (A above middle C) all cause transmission of similar action potentials. Our ability to differentiate stimuli depends on both the sensory receptor itself and on the brain. We can distinguish the color of a blue sky from the scent of cologne; a sweet taste from a light breeze; or the sound of a piano from the heat of the sun because cells of each sensory receptor are connected to specific neurons in particular parts of the brain. Because a receptor normally responds to only one type of stimulus (for example, light), the brain interprets a message arriving from a particular receptor as meaning that a certain type of stimulus occurred (such as a flash of color).

When stimulated, a sensory receptor initiates what might be considered a coded message, composed of action potentials transmitted by sensory neurons. This coded message is later decoded in the brain. Impulses from the sensory receptor may differ in the (1) total number of sensory neurons transmitting the signal, (2) specific neurons transmitting action potentials and their targets, (3) total number of action potentials transmitted by a given neuron, and (4) frequency of the action potentials transmitted by a given fiber. The intensity of a stimulus is coded by the frequency of action potentials fired by sensory neurons during the stimulus. A strong stimulus results in a greater depolarization of the receptor membrane, so the sensory neuron fires action potentials with greater frequency than would a weak stimulus. This variation is possible because, as a graded response, the receptor potential can vary in magnitude.

The difference in sound intensity between the gentle rustling of leaves and a clap of thunder depends on the number of neurons transmitting action potentials as well as the frequency of the action potentials transmitted by each neuron. Just how the sensory receptor initiates different codes and how the brain analyzes and interprets them to produce various sensations are not yet completely understood.

Sensation takes place in the brain. Interpretation of the message and the type of sensation depends on which interneurons receive the message. The rods and cones of the eye do not see. When stimulated, they send a message to the brain that interprets the signals and translates them into a rainbow, an elephant, or a child. Artificial (for example, electrical) stimulation of brain centers can also result in sensation. In contrast, many sensory messages never give rise to sensations at all. For example, certain chemoreceptors sense internal changes in the body but never stir our consciousness.

Sensory perceptions are constructed by the mind

The brain interprets sensations by converting them to perceptions of stimuli. Sensory **perception** is the process of selecting, interpreting, and organizing sensory information. Sensory perceptions are constructed by the mind by comparing present sensory experience with our memories of past experiences. You may perceive the incoming visual and auditory input of a hissing snake very differently than does your friend who is terrified of snakes, or a herpetologist who studies them. Perceptions are influenced by our state of mind at the time we receive sensory information. Optical illu-

(a) Your perception of the same visual input can vary. Do you see a wineglass or the profiles of two faces?

(b) Do you "see" a white square? If so, your brain is completing a familiar pattern suggested by the right-angle wedges taken out of each of the four red circles.

FIGURE 43-2 Visual perception

sions demonstrate that the brain can interpret sensory stimuli in various ways (**FIG. 43-2a**). The brain also modifies stimuli to make them more complete, familiar, or logical (**FIG. 43-2b**).

We can classify sensory receptors based on location of stimuli or on the type of energy they transduce

Sensory receptors can be classified according to the location of the stimuli to which they respond. **Exteroceptors** receive stimuli from the outside environment, enabling an animal to know and explore the world, search for food, find and attract a mate, recognize friends, and detect enemies. **Interoceptors** are sensory receptors within body organs that detect changes in pH, osmotic pressure, body temperature, and the chemical composition of the blood. You are not usually aware of messages sent to the CNS by these receptors as they work continuously to maintain homeostasis. You become aware of their activity when they signal certain internal conditions such as thirst, hunger, nausea, pain, and orgasm.

We can also classify sensory receptors based on the type of energy they transduce (**TABLE 43-1**). *Thermoreceptors* respond to heat and cold. *Electroreceptors* sense differences in electrical potential. *Electromagnetic receptors* are electroreceptors that are sensitive enough to detect Earth's magnetic field. *Nociceptors* (pain receptors) respond to mechanical, temperature, and other stimuli that could be damaging. *Mechanoreceptors* transduce mechanical energy—touch, pressure, gravity, stretching, and movement. These receptors convert mechanical forces directly into electrical signals. *Chemoreceptors* transduce the energy of certain chemical compounds, and *photoreceptors* transduce light energy.

Review

- What is a receptor potential?
- What is the function of sensory adaptation?
- How is sensory information integrated?
- Name five kinds of sensory receptors based on the type of energy they transduce. What is the specific function of each?

TABLE 43-1 Classification of Receptors by Type of Energy They Transduce

Type of Receptor	Type of Energy Transduced	Examples
Thermoreceptors	Heat	Temperature receptors in blood-sucking insects and ticks; pit organs in pit vipers; nerve endings and receptors in skin and tongues of many animals
Electroreceptors and electromagnetic receptors	Electrical; receptors sense differences in electrical potential; electromagnetic receptors detect magnetic fields	Electrical currents in water used to navigate by many fish and some amphibian species; magnetic fields used for orientation and migration
Nociceptors (pain receptors)	Mechanical; physical force such as strong touch, pressure; heat, temperature extremes; damaging chemicals	Neuron endings in skin and other tissues
Mechanoreceptors	Mechanical; change shape as a result of being pushed or pulled	Tactile receptors (free nerve endings, Merkel cells, Meissner corpuscles, Ruffini endings, Pacinian corpuscles); respond to touch and pressure
		Proprioceptors; respond to movement and body position Muscle spindles; respond to muscle contraction Golgi tendon organs; respond to stretch of a tendon Joint receptors; respond to movement in ligaments
		Statocysts in invertebrates; have hair cells that respond to gravity
		Lateral line organs in fish; detect vibrations in the water; respond to waves and currents
		Vestibular apparatus Hair cells in saccule and utricle; respond to gravity, linear acceleration Hair cells in semicircular canals; respond to angular acceleration Hair cells in organ of Corti in cochlea; respond to pressure waves (sound)
Chemoreceptors	Specific chemical compounds	Taste buds; olfactory epithelium
Photoreceptors	Light	Eyespots; ommatidia in compound eye of arthropods; rods and cones in retina of vertebrates

43.2 THERMORECEPTORS

■ LEARNING OBJECTIVE

3   Identify three functions of thermoreceptors.

Thermoreceptors respond to heat and cold. Mosquitoes, ticks, and other blood-sucking arthropods use thermoreception in their search for an endothermic host. Some have temperature receptors on their antennae that are sensitive to changes of less than 0.5°C. At least two types of snakes—pit vipers and boas—use thermoreceptors to locate their prey (**FIG. 43-3**).

In mammals, which are endothermic, free nerve endings (and perhaps, specialized receptors) in the skin and tongue detect temperature changes in the outside environment. In addition, pain receptors sense extreme temperatures that pose a threat to the body. Thermoreceptors in the hypothalamus detect internal changes in temperature. They also receive and integrate information from receptors on the body surface. The hypothalamus then initiates homeostatic mechanisms that ensure a constant body temperature.

Review

■   What are the functions of thermoreceptors in mosquitoes, snakes, and mammals?

Zig Lesczynski/Animals Animals

FIGURE 43-3 Thermoreception

The pit organ of the bamboo viper (*Trimeresurus stejnegeri*) is a sense organ located between each eye and nostril. Thermoreceptors in the pit organ can detect the heat emitted by an endothermic animal up to a distance of 1 to 2 m.

43.3 ELECTRORECEPTORS AND ELECTROMAGNETIC RECEPTORS

LEARNING OBJECTIVE

4 Describe the functions of electroreceptors and electromagnetic receptors.

Electroreceptors sense differences in electrical potential. Some predatory species of sharks, rays, and bony fishes detect electric fields generated in the water by the muscle activity of their prey. Several groups of fishes have electric organs, specialized muscle or nerve cells that emit electrical signals and receive a feedback signal. In species that produce a weak electric current, electroreceptors may help in navigation. This mechanism is particularly useful in murky water, where visibility and olfaction are poor.

Electroreception also appears important in communication, for example, in recognizing a potential mate. Males and females have different frequencies of electric discharge. A few fishes, such as electric eels or electric rays, have electric organs in their heads capable of delivering powerful shocks (up to several hundred volts) that stun prey or predators. Weaker electrical signals are emitted continuously to help in assessing the environment, orienting themselves, and communicating.

Some electroreceptors, called **electromagnetic receptors,** are sensitive enough to detect Earth's magnetic field. When a shark, ray, or skate swims across one of Earth's magnetic field lines, its electromagnetic receptors detect changes that occur in electric currents. This information, which is integrated in the brain, helps the animal orient itself. Many other animals, including some insects, bony fishes, amphibians, reptiles, birds, and a few mammals, can also detect magnetic fields and use this information to orient themselves. Migratory birds and sea turtles are well-known examples of animals that use magnetic fields to navigate (discussed further in Chapter 52).

Review

- What are two functions of electroreceptors?
- What is the function of electromagnetic receptors?

43.4 NOCICEPTORS

LEARNING OBJECTIVE

5 Describe the functions of nociceptors and identify the roles of glutamate and substance P.

Pain receptors, called **nociceptors** (from the Latin *nocere,* meaning "to injure"), are free nerve endings (dendrites) of certain sensory neurons found in almost every tissue. Three main types of nociceptors have been identified. Mechanical nociceptors respond to strong tactile stimuli such as cutting, crushing, or pinching. Thermal nociceptors respond to temperature extremes (temperatures

above 45°C or below 5°C). Other nociceptors respond to a variety of damaging stimuli, including certain chemicals.

When stimulated, nociceptors transmit signals through sensory neurons to interneurons in the spinal cord. The sensory neurons release the neurotransmitter **glutamate,** as well as several neuropeptides, including **substance P,** that enhance and prolong the actions of glutamate. The interneuron transmits the message to the opposite side of the spinal cord and then upward to the thalamus, where pain perception begins. From the thalamus, impulses are sent into the parietal lobes and several other cortical regions, including areas of the limbic system where the emotional aspects of the pain are processed. When pain signals reach the cerebrum, we become fully aware of our pain and can evaluate the situation.

Review

- What is the function of each main type of nociceptor?
- What is the function of substance P?

43.5 MECHANORECEPTORS

LEARNING OBJECTIVES

6 Compare the functions and mechanisms of action of the following mechanoreceptors: tactile receptors, proprioceptors, statocysts, hair cells, and lateral line organs.

7 Compare the structure and function of the saccule and utricle with that of the semicircular canals in maintaining equilibrium.

8 Trace the path taken by sound waves through the structures of the ear and explain how the organ of Corti functions as an auditory receptor.

Mechanoreceptors are activated when they change shape as a result of being mechanically pushed or pulled. They transduce mechanical energy, permitting animals to feel, hear, and maintain balance. These receptors provide information about the shape, texture, weight, and topographic relations of objects in the external environment. Some mechanoreceptors are extremely sensitive. For example, alligators have pressure receptors on their faces that can detect the movement in the surrounding water caused by a single drop of falling water.

Certain mechanoreceptors enable an organism to maintain its body position with respect to gravity (for us, head up and feet down; for a dog, dorsal side up and ventral side down; for a tree sloth, ventral side up and dorsal side down). When displaced from its normal position, the animal quickly adjusts its body to reassume its normal orientation. Mechanoreceptors continuously send information to the CNS regarding the position and movements of the body. These receptors also provide information about the operation of internal organs. For example, they inform us about the presence of food in the stomach, feces in the rectum, urine in the bladder, and a fetus in the uterus.

Tactile receptors are located in the skin

The simplest mechanoreceptors are free nerve endings in the skin. They detect touch, pressure, vibration, and pain when stimulated by objects that contact the body surface. In many invertebrates and vertebrates, **tactile** (touch) **receptors** lie at the base of a hair or bristle. These receptors may sense the body's orientation in space with respect to gravity. They may also detect air and water vibrations and contact with other objects. The tactile receptor is stimulated indirectly when the hair is bent or displaced. A receptor potential develops, and a few action potentials may be generated. This type of receptor responds only when the hair is moving. Even though the hair may be maintained in a displaced position, the receptor is not stimulated unless there is motion.

Thousands of specialized tactile receptors are located in mammalian skin (**FIG. 43-4**). **Merkel cells** form discs in the deep regions of the epidermis that extend down into the dermis. Merkel cells are important in sensing light touch and enable us to distinguish among the softness of a baby's skin, the fuzziness of a peach, or the hardness of a book cover. They adapt slowly, permitting us to know that an object continues to touch the skin.

Three types of mechanoreceptors in the skin have encapsulated endings: Meissner corpuscles, Ruffini endings, and Pacinian corpuscles. **Meissner corpuscles,** located in the upper dermis, are sensitive to light touch and vibration. They adapt quickly to a sustained stimulus. **Ruffini endings,** which are located in the dermis, inform us of heavy, continuous pressure and stretch of the skin. They adapt very slowly and are thought to provide information about the position of our fingers and hand.

Pacinian corpuscles, which are located deep in the dermis, are sensitive to deep pressure that causes rapid movement of the tissues. They are especially sensitive to stimuli that vibrate. The Pacinian corpuscle consists of a neuron ending surrounded by concentric connective tissue layers interspersed with fluid. Compression causes displacement of the layers, which stimulates the axon. Even though the displacement is maintained under steady compression, the receptor potential rapidly falls to zero, and action potentials cease—an excellent example of sensory adaptation.

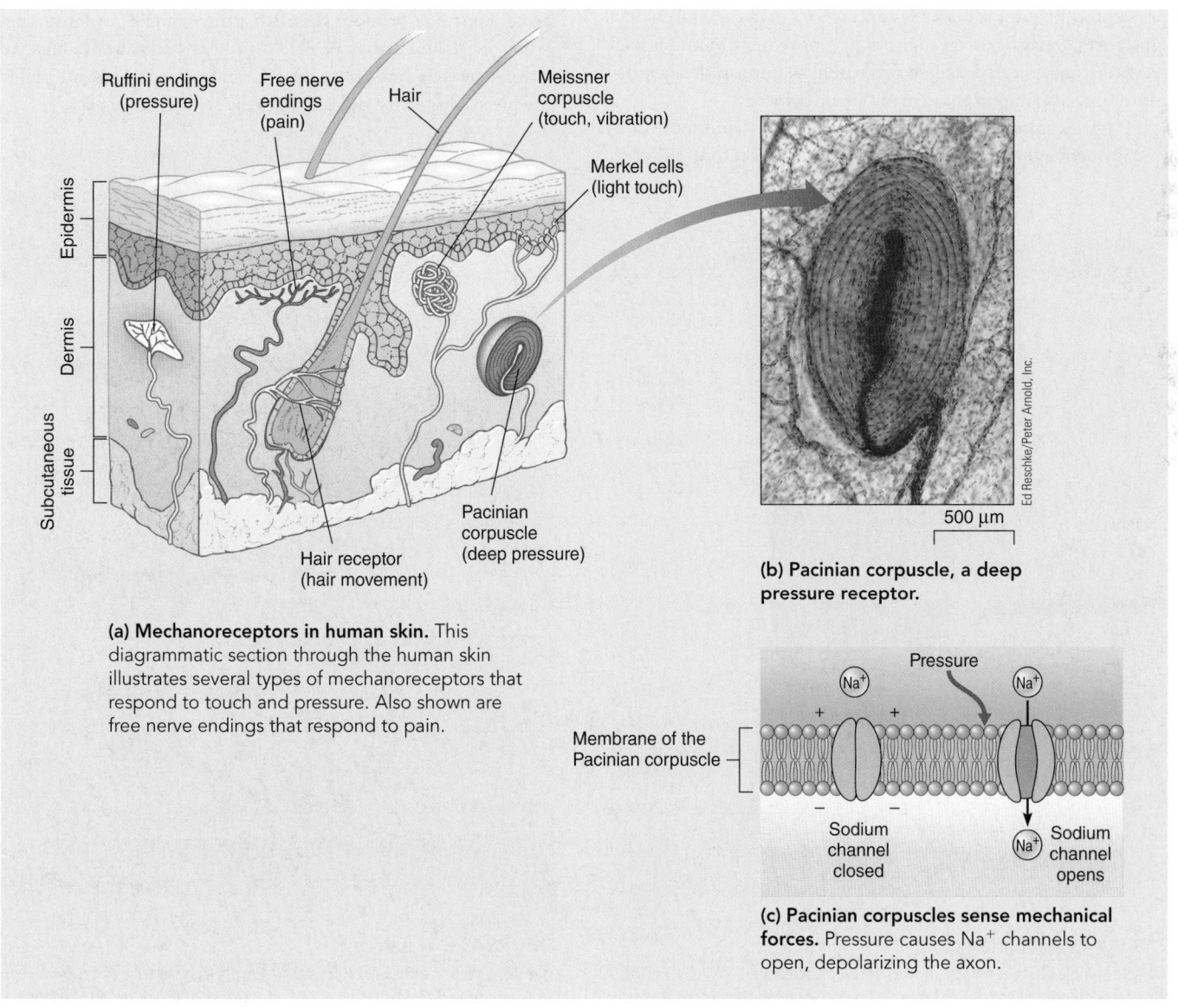

(a) **Mechanoreceptors in human skin.** This diagrammatic section through the human skin illustrates several types of mechanoreceptors that respond to touch and pressure. Also shown are free nerve endings that respond to pain.

(b) **Pacinian corpuscle, a deep pressure receptor.**

(c) **Pacinian corpuscles sense mechanical forces.** Pressure causes Na⁺ channels to open, depolarizing the axon.

FIGURE 43-4 *Animated* Sensory receptors in human skin

Proprioceptors help coordinate muscle movement

Proprioceptors help animals maintain postural relations—the position of one part of the body with respect to another. Located within muscles, tendons, and joints, proprioceptors continuously respond to tension and movement. With their continuous input, an animal can perceive the positions of its arms, legs, head, and other body parts, along with the orientation of its body as a whole. This information is essential for all forms of locomotion and for all coordinated and skilled movements, from spinning a cocoon to completing a reverse one-and-a-half dive with a twist. With the help of proprioceptors, we carry out activities such as dressing or playing the piano even in the dark.

Vertebrates have three main types of proprioceptors: **muscle spindles,** which detect muscle movement (**FIG. 43-5**); **Golgi tendon organs,** which respond to tension in contracting muscles and in the tendons that attach muscle to bone; and **joint receptors,** which detect movement in ligaments. Impulses from proprioceptors help coordinate the contractions of the several distinct muscles that may be involved in a single movement. Without such receptors, complicated, skilled acts would be impossible. Proprioceptors are also important in maintaining balance.

Proprioceptors are probably more numerous and more continually active than any of the other sensory receptors, although we are less aware of them than of most of the others. As long as the stimulus is present, receptor potentials are maintained (although not at constant magnitude) and action potentials continue to be generated. Proprioceptors continuously send signals to inform the brain about position.

The mammalian muscle spindle, one of the more versatile stretch receptors, helps maintain muscle tone. It is a bundle of specialized muscle fibers, with a central region encircled by sensory neuron endings. These neurons continue to transmit signals for a prolonged period, in proportion to the degree of stretch.

Many invertebrates have gravity receptors called statocysts

Many invertebrates—from jellyfish to crayfish—have gravity receptors called **statocysts** (**FIG. 43-6**). Statocysts are the simplest organs of equilibrium. A statocyst is basically an infolding of the epidermis lined with receptor cells, called *sensory hair cells.* These hair cells are equipped with sensory hairs (not true hairs). The cavity contains one or more **statoliths,** tiny granules of loose sand grains or calcium carbonate held together by an adhesive material secreted by cells of the statocyst. Normally, the particles are pulled downward by gravity and stimulate the sensory hair cells.

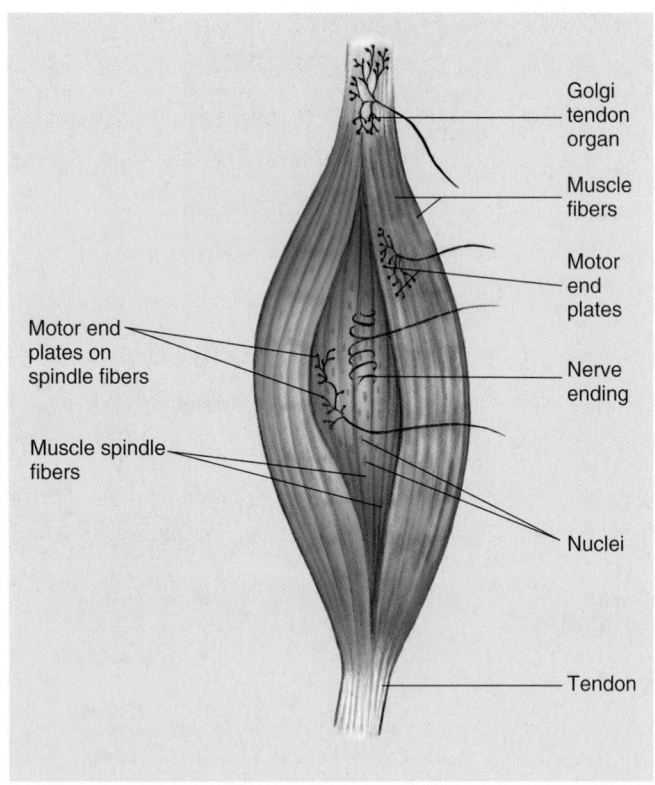

FIGURE 43-5 Proprioceptors
Muscle spindles detect muscle movement. A muscle spindle consists of an elongated bundle of specialized muscle fibers. Golgi tendon organs respond to tension in muscles and their associated tendons.

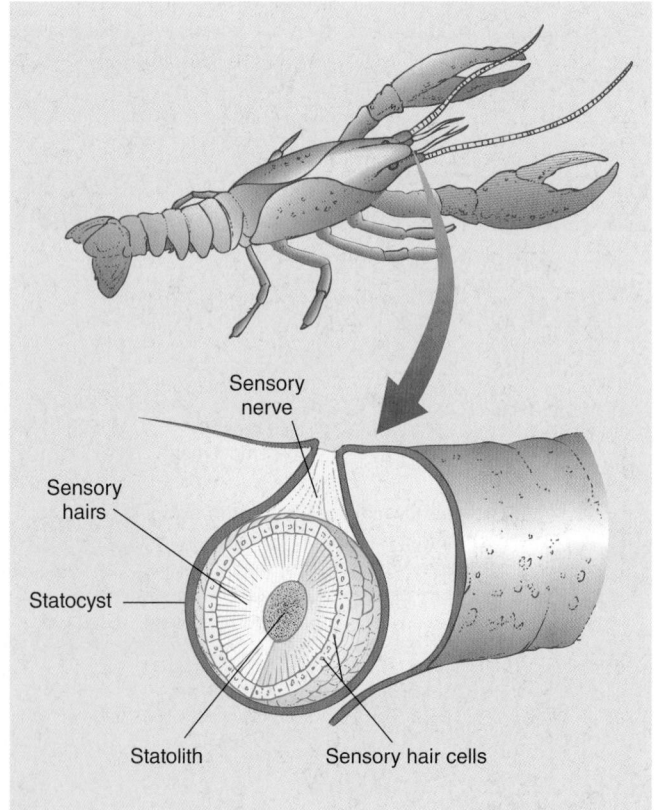

FIGURE 43-6 A statocyst
Many invertebrates have statocysts, receptors that sense gravitational force and provide information about orientation of the body with respect to gravity.

When the animal changes position, the statocyst tilts and the statolith moves in the same direction. This movement bends the sensory hairs. Each sensory hair cell responds maximally when the animal is at a particular position with respect to gravity. The mechanical displacement results in receptor potentials and action potentials that inform the CNS of the change in position. By "knowing" which sensory cells are firing, the animal knows where "down" is and can correct any abnormal orientation.

In a classic experiment, the function of the statocyst was demonstrated by substituting iron filings for sand grains in the statocysts of crayfish. The force of gravity was overcome by holding magnets above the animals. The iron filings were attracted upward toward the magnets, and the crayfish began to swim upside down in response to the new information provided by their gravity receptors.

Hair cells are characterized by stereocilia

Vertebrate **hair cells** are mechanoreceptors that detect movement. They are the sensory receptors, located in the lateral line of fishes, that detect water movements (**FIG. 43-7**). Hair cells also help maintain position and equilibrium and are important in hearing.

The surface of a vertebrate hair cell typically has a single long **kinocilium** and many shorter **stereocilia,** hairlike projections that increase in length from one side of the hair cell to the other (see Fig. 43-7c). A kinocilium is a true cilium with a 9 + 2 arrangement of microtubules (see Chapter 4). In contrast, stereocilia are not really cilia. They are microvilli that contain actin filaments.

Mechanical stimulation of the stereocilia causes voltage changes. Mechanical stimulation in one direction causes depolarization and release of neurotransmitter, whereas mechanical stimulation in the opposite direction results in hyperpolarization. However, hair cells have no axons and do not produce their own action potentials. Rather, they release neurotransmitter that depolarizes associated neurons.

Lateral line organs supplement vision in fishes

Lateral line organs of fishes and aquatic amphibians detect vibrations in the water. They inform the animal of obstacles in its way and of moving objects such as prey, enemies, and others in its school. Typically, the lateral line organ is a long canal running the length of the body and continuing into the head. The canal is lined with sensory hair cells. The tips of the stereocilia are enclosed by a **cupula,** a mass of gelatinous material secreted by the hair cells.

Pressure waves, currents, and even slight movement in the water cause vibrations in the lateral line organ. As the water moves the cupula, the stereocilia bend. This changes the membrane potential of the hair cell, which may then release neurotransmitter. If an associated sensory neuron is sufficiently stimulated, an action potential may be dispatched to the CNS.

The vestibular apparatus maintains equilibrium

When you think of the ear, you probably think of hearing. However, in vertebrates its main function is to help maintain equilibrium. Many vertebrates do not have outer or middle ears, but all have inner ears (**FIG. 43-8**). The mammalian **inner ear** includes organs of equilibrium equipped with hair cells that sense the position of the body with respect to gravity.

The inner ear is a group of interconnected canals and sacs, called the **labyrinth,** which includes a membranous labyrinth that fits inside a bony labyrinth. In mammals the membranous labyrinth has two saclike chambers—the **saccule** and the **utricle**—and three **semicircular canals.** Collectively, the saccule, utricle, and semicircular canals are called the **vestibular apparatus** (see Fig. 43-8b). Destruction of these organs leads to a considerable loss of the sense of equilibrium. A pigeon whose vestibular apparatus has been destroyed cannot fly but in time can relearn how to maintain equilibrium by using visual stimuli.

(a) The lateral line organ is a canal that extends the length of the body.

(b) The canal has numerous groupings of hair cells and openings to the outside environment.

(c) The receptor cells are hair cells. Each hair cell has stereocilia and a kinocilium that are covered with a gelatinous cupula. The hair cells respond to waves, currents, and other disturbances in the water.

FIGURE 43-7 Lateral line organs of fishes
These mechanoreceptors detect vibrations in the water, informing the fish of obstacles or moving objects.

(a) Structure of the human ear, anterior view.

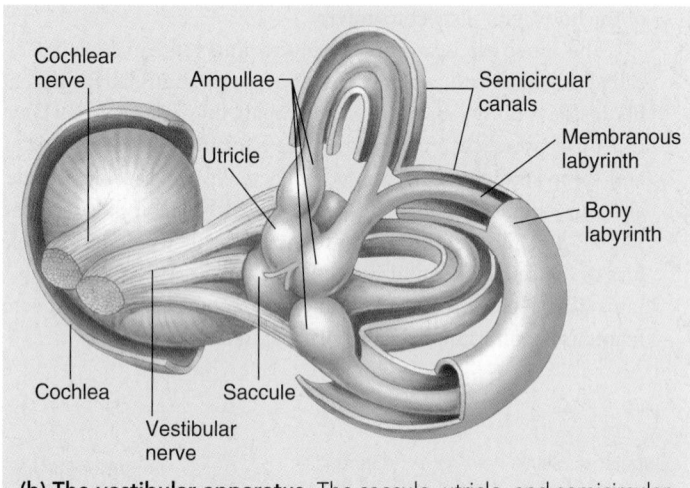

(b) The vestibular apparatus. The saccule, utricle, and semicircular canals together make up the vestibular apparatus. The utricle and saccule are best seen in the posterior view shown here.

FIGURE 43-8 *Animated* The human ear: hearing and equilibrium

The sensory cells of the saccule and utricle are hair cells similar to those of the lateral line organ (**FIG. 43-9**). The stereocilia projecting from the hair cells are covered by a gelatinous cupula in which calcium carbonate ear stones, called **otoliths,** are embedded. The hair cells in the saccule and utricle lie in different planes.

Normally, the pull of gravity causes the otoliths to press against the stereocilia, stimulating them to initiate impulses. Sensory neurons at the bases of the hair cells transmit these signals to the brain. When the head is tilted or in linear acceleration (increasing speed when the body is moving in a straight line), otoliths press on the stereocilia of different cells, deflecting them. Deflection of the stereocilia toward the kinocilium depolarizes the hair cell. Deflection in the opposite direction hyperpolarizes the hair cell. Thus, depending on the direction of movement, the hair cells release more or less neurotransmitter. The brain interprets the neural messages so the animal is aware of its full body position relative to the ground regardless of how its head is positioned.

Information about turning movements, referred to as angular acceleration, is provided by the three semicircular canals. Each canal, a hollow ring connected with the utricle, lies at right angles to the other two and is filled with fluid called **endolymph.** At one of the openings of each canal into the utricle, there is a small, bulb-like enlargement, the **ampulla.** Within each ampulla lies a clump of hair cells called a **crista** (pl., *cristae*), similar to the groups of hair cells in the utricle and saccule. No otoliths are present. The stereocilia of the hair cells of the cristae are stimulated by movements of the endolymph in the canals (**FIG. 43-10** on page 922).

When the head is turned, there is a lag in the movement of the fluid within the canals. The stereocilia move in relation to the fluid and are stimulated by its flow. This stimulation produces not only the consciousness of rotation but also certain reflex movements in response to it. These reflexes cause the eyes and head to move in a direction opposite that of the original rotation. Because the three canals are in three different planes, head movement in any direction stimulates fluid movement in at least one of the canals.

We humans are used to movements in the horizontal plane but not to vertical movements (parallel to the long axis of the upright body). The motion of an elevator or of a ship pitching in a rough sea stimulates the semicircular canals in an unusual way and may cause seasickness or motion sickness, with resultant nausea or vomiting. When a seasick person lies down, the movement stimulates the semicircular canals in a more familiar way and nausea is less likely to occur.

Auditory receptors are located in the cochlea

Many arthropods and most vertebrates have sound receptors, but for many of them hearing does not seem to be a sensory priority. It is important in tetrapods, however, and both birds and mammals have a highly developed sense of hearing. Their auditory receptors, located in the **cochlea** of the inner ear, contain mechanoreceptor hair cells that detect pressure waves.

The utricle and saccule sense changes in the position of the head relative to gravity, as well as changes in the rate of motion when moving in a straight line.

(a) A group of sensory cells in the utricle.

Stereocilium

Otoliths

Kinocilium

Cupula

Hair cell

Supporting cell

Nerve fiber

(b) Bending the head activates the sensory cells.

FIGURE 43-9 *Animated* **The saccule and utricle: maintaining equilibrium**

The saccule and utricle sense linear acceleration, allowing us to know our position relative to the ground. Compare the positions of the oto-liths and hair cells in **(a)** with those in **(b).** Changes in head position cause the force of gravity to distort the cupula, which in turn distorts the stereocilia of the hair cells. The hair cells respond by releasing neu-rotransmitters. Impulses are transmitted along the vestibulocochlear nerve to the brain.

The cochlea is a spiral tube that resembles a snail's shell (**FIG. 43-11**). If the cochlea were uncoiled, you would see that it consists of three canals separated from one another by thin membranes. The canals come almost to a point at the apex. Two of these canals, the **vestibular canal** and the **tympanic canal,** connect at the apex of the cochlea and are filled with a fluid called **perilymph.** The middle canal, the **cochlear duct,** is filled with endolymph and contains the auditory organ, the **organ of Corti.**

Each organ of Corti contains about 18,000 hair cells, in rows that extend the length of the coiled cochlea. The stereocilia of each hair cell extend into the cochlear duct. The hair cells rest on the **basilar membrane,** which separates the cochlear duct from the tympanic canal. Another membrane, the **tectorial membrane,** overhangs and is in contact with the hair cells.

Sound waves are amplified in the middle ear

In terrestrial vertebrates, sound waves in the air are transformed into pressure waves in the cochlear fluid. In the human ear, for example, sound waves pass through the **external auditory canal** and vibrate the **tympanic membrane,** or eardrum, which separates the outer ear and the middle ear. The vibrations are transmitted across the middle ear by three tiny bones—the **malleus, incus,** and **stapes** (or hammer, anvil, and stirrup, so called because of their shapes). The malleus is in contact with the eardrum, and the stapes is in contact with a thin, membranous region of the cochlea called the **oval window.** The **eustachian tube,** which connects the middle ear with the pharynx (throat region), helps equalize pressure between the middle ear and the atmosphere.

The malleus, incus, and stapes act as three interconnected levers that amplify vibrations. A small movement in the malleus causes a larger movement in the incus and a very large movement in the stapes. The vibrations pass through the oval window to the perilymph in the vestibular canal. If sound waves were conducted directly from air to the oval window, much energy would be lost. The middle ear functions to couple sound waves in the air with the pressure waves conducted through the fluid in the cochlea.

Because liquids cannot be compressed, the oval window could not cause movement of the fluid in the vestibular canal if there were no escape valve for the pressure. This valve is provided by the membranous **round window** at the end of the tympanic canal. The pressure wave presses on the membranes separating the three ducts, and is transmitted to the tympanic canal. The pressure wave makes the round window bulge. The movements of the basilar membrane produced by these pulsations cause the stereocilia of the organ of Corti to rub against the overlying tectorial membrane.

Stereocilia are bent by their contact with the tectorial membrane. As a result, ion channels in the plasma membrane of the hair cells open. Calcium ions move into the hair cell, causing the release of *glutamate*. This neurotransmitter binds to receptors on sensory neurons that synapse with each hair cell, leading to depolarization of these sensory neurons. Axons of the sensory neurons join to form the **cochlear nerve,** a component of the vestibulocochlear nerve (cranial nerve VIII; also referred to as the *auditory nerve*). We can summarize the sequence of events involved in hearing as follows:

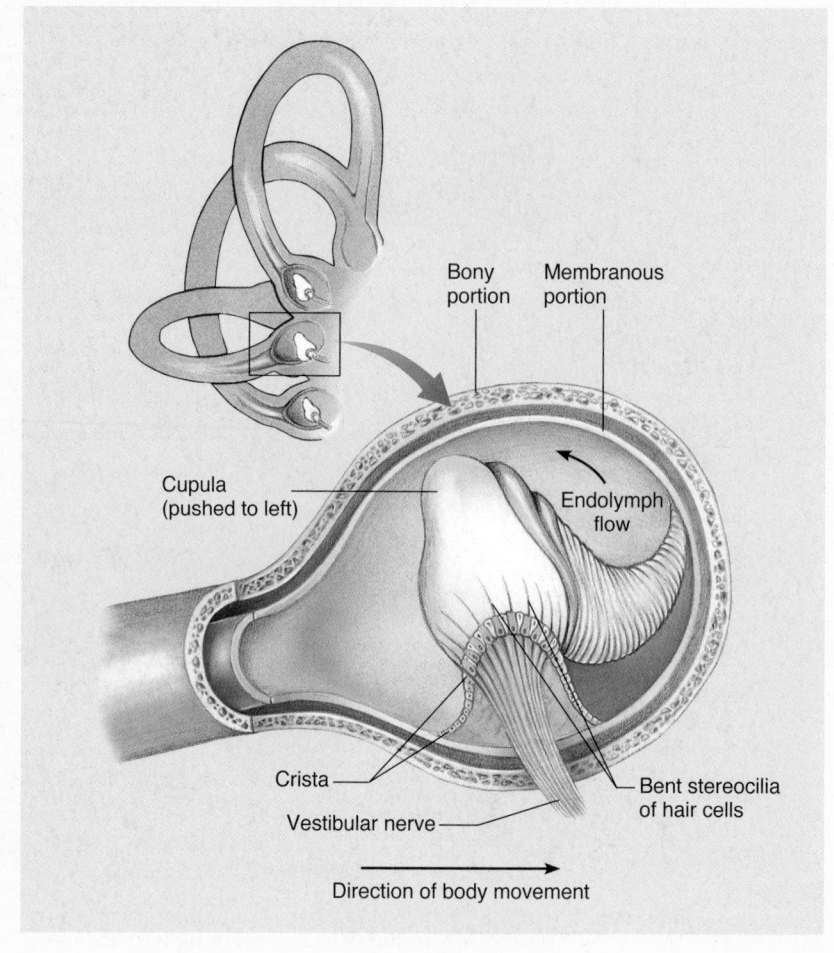

KEY POINT The semicircular canals detect angular acceleration or deceleration of the head (changes in the position of the head when you are turning it).

Bony portion   Membranous portion

Cupula (pushed to left)   Endolymph flow

Crista   Bent stereocilia of hair cells

Vestibular nerve

Direction of body movement

FIGURE 43-10 Semicircular canals and equilibrium
When the head changes its rate of rotation, endolymph within the ampulla of the semicircular canal distorts the cupula. The stereocilia of the hair cells bend, increasing the frequency of action potentials in sensory neurons. Information is transmitted to the brain via the vestibular nerve.

sound waves enter external auditory canal ⟶ tympanic membrane vibrates ⟶ malleus, incus, and stapes amplify vibrations ⟶ oval window vibrates ⟶ vibrations are conducted through fluid ⟶ basilar membrane vibrates ⟶ hair cells in organ of Corti are stimulated ⟶ cochlear nerve transmits impulses to brain

Sounds differ in pitch, loudness, and tone quality

Pitch depends on frequency of sound waves, or number of vibrations per second, and is expressed as hertz (Hz). Low-frequency vibrations result in the sensation of low pitch, whereas high-frequency vibrations result in the sensation of high pitch. Sounds of a given frequency set up resonance waves in the cochlear fluid that cause a particular section of the basilar membrane to vibrate. High frequencies are detected by hair cells located near the base of the cochlea, whereas low frequencies are sensed by hair cells near the apex of the cochlea. The brain infers the pitch of a sound from the particular hair cells that are stimulated.

The human ear typically registers sound frequencies between about 20 and 20,000 Hz (also expressed as 20 kilohertz), and is most sensitive to sounds between 1000 and 4000 Hz (**FIG. 43-12** on page 924). Comparing the energy of audible sound waves with the energy of visible light waves, your ear is ten times more sensitive than your eye. Dogs can hear sounds up to 40,000 Hz, and bats can detect frequencies as high as 100,000 Hz.

Loud sounds cause resonance waves of greater amplitude (height). The hair cells are more intensely stimulated, and the cochlear nerve transmits a greater number of impulses per second. Variations in tone quality, or timbre, such as when an oboe, a cornet, and a violin play the same note, depend on the number and

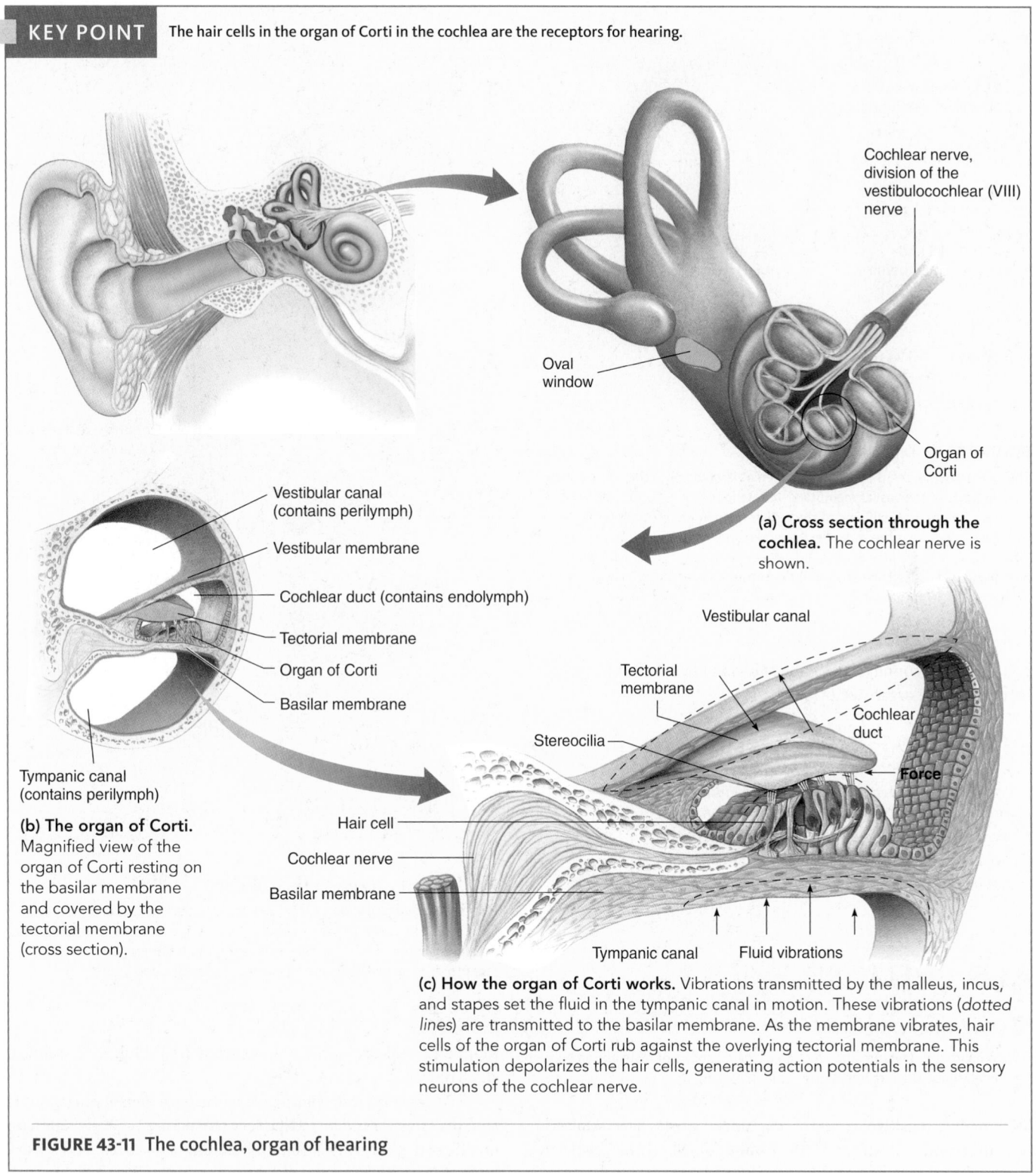

Cochlear nerve, division of the vestibulocochlear (VIII) nerve

Oval window

Organ of Corti

(a) Cross section through the cochlea. The cochlear nerve is shown.

Vestibular canal (contains perilymph)

Vestibular membrane

Cochlear duct (contains endolymph)

Tectorial membrane

Organ of Corti

Basilar membrane

Tympanic canal (contains perilymph)

(b) The organ of Corti. Magnified view of the organ of Corti resting on the basilar membrane and covered by the tectorial membrane (cross section).

Vestibular canal

Tectorial membrane

Cochlear duct

Stereocilia

Force

Hair cell

Cochlear nerve

Basilar membrane

Tympanic canal   Fluid vibrations

(c) How the organ of Corti works. Vibrations transmitted by the malleus, incus, and stapes set the fluid in the tympanic canal in motion. These vibrations (*dotted lines*) are transmitted to the basilar membrane. As the membrane vibrates, hair cells of the organ of Corti rub against the overlying tectorial membrane. This stimulation depolarizes the hair cells, generating action potentials in the sensory neurons of the cochlear nerve.

FIGURE 43-11 The cochlea, organ of hearing

kinds of overtones, or harmonics, produced. Many hair cells along the basilar membrane are stimulated and vibrate simultaneously, in addition to the main vibration common to all three instruments. Thus, differences in tone quality are recognized in the pattern of the hair cells stimulated.

Deafness may be caused by injury to, or malformation of, either the sound-transmitting mechanism of the outer, middle, or inner ear or the sound-perceiving mechanism of the inner ear. Efferent neurons from the brain stem protect the hair cells of the organ of Corti by dampening their response. Even so, exposure to

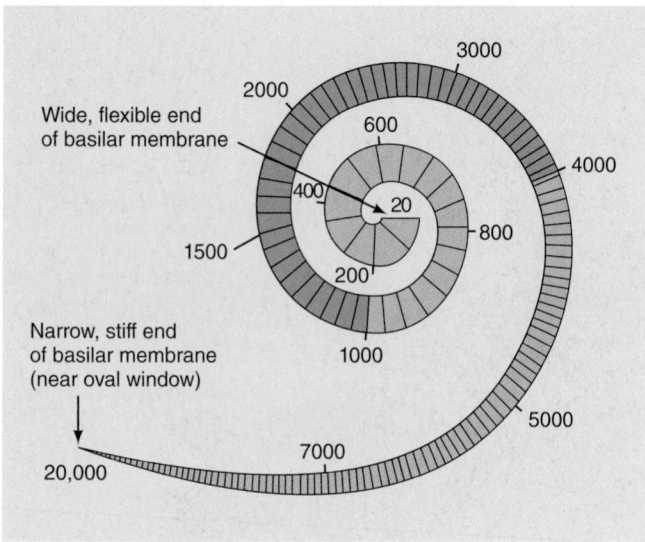

FIGURE 43-12 Distinguishing pitch

The basilar membrane is shown here coiled as it would be within the cochlea. Various parts of the basilar membrane vibrate in response to specific frequencies. The narrow, stiff end of the basilar membrane responds to higher frequencies, whereas the wide, flexible end responds to lower frequencies. Pitch depends on frequency of sound waves expressed as hertz (Hz). The human ear is most sensitive to sounds between 1000 and 4000 Hz (*darker color*).

high-intensity sound, such as heavily amplified music, damages hair cells in the organ of Corti.

Review

- Which sensory receptors permit you to perform actions such as getting dressed or finding your way into bed in the dark?
- How do hair cells work?
- What are otoliths, and what is their role in maintaining equilibrium?
- What is the sequence of events involved in hearing?

43.6 CHEMORECEPTORS

■ LEARNING OBJECTIVE

9   Compare the structure and function of the receptors of taste and smell, and describe the function of the vomeronasal organ.

Two highly sensitive types of **chemoreceptors** have evolved for **gustation,** or taste, and **olfaction,** or smell. These chemical senses, found throughout the animal kingdom, allow animals to detect chemical substances in food, water, and air. Evaluating such chemical cues allows animals to find food and mates and to avoid predators. Members of the same species use chemoreception to communicate about these critical issues.

For terrestrial vertebrates, the sense of smell involves gaseous substances that reach olfactory receptors through the air. The sense of taste depends on materials dissolved in water (or saliva) in the

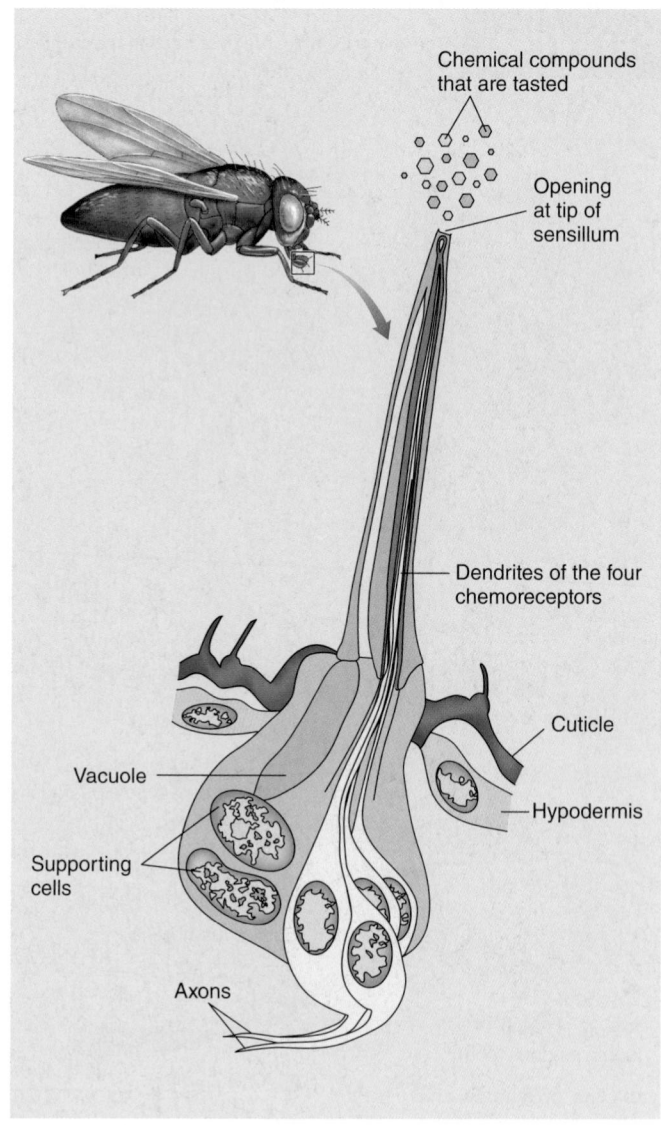

FIGURE 43-13 An insect taste receptor

Insects respond to a wide variety of chemical substances found in foods. Each sensillum in the blowfly contains four chemoreceptors. Dendrites that extend to an opening at the tip sense taste. The other end of each chemoreceptor is an axon that transmits sensory signals to the brain.

mouth. For aquatic animals, these distinctions blur. Does a catfish smell or taste the water?

The organs of taste and smell in insects are sensory hairs called **sensilla** (sing., *sensillum*). Olfactory sensilla are typically found on the antennae. In some insects, including ants, bees, and wasps, taste sensilla are also located on the antennae. Taste sensilla typically project from the mouthparts. In butterflies and flies, they may also project from the end of the leg.

In the blowfly, each sensillum contains four chemoreceptors (**FIG. 43-13**). Dendrites from each cell extend to an opening at the tip, and axons transmit sensory signals to the brain. Recent findings suggest that insects can distinguish among various bitter tastes more precisely than mammals can. This ability is important in dis-

(a) **Location of taste buds.** Taste buds are concentrated in the papillae that cover the surface of the tongue.

(b) **LM of a taste bud.** Each taste bud is an epithelial capsule containing several taste receptor cells. A single taste receptor cell may respond to more than one category of taste.

① Sugar molecule binds with receptor in plasma membrane of taste receptor cell.

② G protein is activated, and activates adenylyl cyclase.

③ ATP is converted to cyclic AMP (cAMP).

④ Cyclic AMP activates a protein kinase that closes K⁺ channels.

(c) **Tasting sweet foods.** A sugar molecule activates a signal transduction process that leads to an increase in K⁺ in the cell. The membrane becomes depolarized, resulting in action potentials in sensory neurons.

FIGURE 43-14 *Animated* Chemoreception: taste

criminating tastes associated with spoiled, bacteria-laden foods or toxins.

Taste receptors detect dissolved food molecules

As just described for insects, the ability to discriminate among tastes has survival value. Poisons are generally bitter. In contrast, foods with a high caloric value often taste sweet. Mammals sense taste with **taste buds** located in the mouth. In humans, taste buds lie mainly in tiny elevations, or papillae, on the tongue. Each of the 10,000 or so taste buds is an oval epithelial capsule containing about 50 taste receptor cells interspersed with supporting cells (**FIG. 43-14**). Taste receptor cells are replaced about every ten days. One sensory neuron can innervate several taste buds.

The plasma membrane at the tip of each taste receptor cell has microvilli that extend into a taste pore on the surface of the tongue, where they are bathed in saliva. The taste receptors detect chemical substances dissolved in saliva. Certain molecules, such as those perceived as sweet, activate a signal transduction process involving a G protein (see Fig. 43-14c). According to one model, adenylyl cyclase activity increases, elevating cyclic AMP levels. A protein kinase is activated that phosphorylates and closes K^+ channels. This decrease in K^+ permeability sets up a depolarizing receptor potential. Action potentials are then generated in sensory neurons that synapse with the taste receptor cell. A second model proposes a pathway involving IP_3, which leads to opening of Ca^{2+} channels (see Chapter 6). When Ca^{2+} rush into the cell, they also depolarize the taste cell.

Traditionally, four basic tastes have been recognized: sweet, sour, salty, and bitter. Recently, a fifth taste, umami, was added. Umami, which is a savory, or meaty taste, is stimulated by glutamate. Umami was first suggested as a basic taste in 1908 by the Japanese physiologist Kikunae Ikeda. In 1908, Ikeda identified glutamate as the compound that triggers the taste. Umami is responsible for the savoriness of certain aged cheeses, soy sauce, anchovy, and some types of seafood. Additional basic tastes have been proposed, including *fatty*, which is stimulated by fatty acids.

Flavor depends on the four or five basic tastes in combination with smell, texture, and temperature. Smell affects flavor because odors pass from the nasal chamber to the mouth. No doubt you have observed that when your nose is congested, food seems to have little "taste." The taste buds are not affected, but the blockage of nasal passages severely reduces the participation of olfactory reception in the composite sensation of flavor.

Awareness of the genetic component of taste can be traced to 1931 when Arthur L. Fox, a chemist at the DuPont Company, synthesized a compound called *phenylthiocarbamide (PTC)*. Some PTC blew into the air and was inhaled by a colleague, who experienced it as very bitter. Because Fox himself could not taste it, he became intrigued and asked other people to taste it. Fox found that about 25% of people were nontasters. Everyone else experienced PTC as bitter. Further research showed that the ability to taste PTC is inherited as a dominant trait.

Since that time, taste researchers have found that some tasters are especially sensitive to bitter tastes. In fact, about 25% of the U.S. population are supertasters, 50% are regular tasters, and 25% are nontasters. Supertasters tend to avoid vegetables and fruits that taste bitter, such as broccoli, brussels sprouts, and cabbage. This can be a problem because these foods contain flavonoids and other compounds that may protect against cancer. Continuing investigation of taste preferences and their nutritional consequences may lead to more effective approaches to improving nutrition and to a better understanding of the relative importance of genetics and learning in food selection.

The olfactory epithelium is responsible for the sense of smell

Most invertebrates depend on olfaction, the detection of odors, as their main sensory modality. Recent findings indicate that the mechanisms for chemoreception have been highly conserved throughout the animal kingdom.

In terrestrial vertebrates, olfaction occurs in the nasal epithelium. In humans, the **olfactory epithelium** is found in the roof of the nasal cavity (**FIG. 43-15**). It contains about 100 million olfactory receptor cells with ciliated tips. The long, nonmotile cilia extend into a layer of mucus on the epithelial surface of the nasal passageway. Receptor molecules on the cilia bind with compounds dissolved in the mucus. The other end of each olfactory receptor cell is an axon that projects directly to the brain. These axons make up the **olfactory nerve** (cranial nerve I), which extends to the olfactory bulb in the brain. From there, information is transmitted to the **olfactory cortex,** which is in the limbic system. (Recall that the limbic system is also associated with emotional behavior. Odors are often associated with feelings and memories.)

When an *odorant,* a molecule that can be smelled, binds with a receptor on a cilium of an olfactory receptor cell, a signal transduction process is initiated (see Fig. 43-15c). A G protein is activated, leading to the synthesis of cyclic AMP, which opens nonspecific gated channels in the plasma membrane. These channels permit Na^+ and other cations to enter the cell, causing depolarization; this is the receptor potential. The number of odorous molecules determines the intensity, which in turn determines the magnitude of the receptor potential.

Genome projects indicate that mammals have about 1000 genes that code for 1000 types of olfactory receptors. However, humans have only about 350 functional olfactory genes. Humans can detect at least seven groups of odors: camphor, musky, floral, peppermint, ether, pungent, and putrid. Each odor consists of several component chemical groups, and each type of receptor may bind with a particular component. The combination of receptors activated determines what odor you perceive. You are capable of perceiving about 10,000 scents.

The olfactory receptors respond to remarkably small amounts of a substance. For example, most people can detect ionone, the synthetic substitute for the odor of violets, when it is present in a concentration of only 1 part to more than 30 billion parts of air. Smell is perhaps the sense that adapts most quickly. The olfactory receptors adapt about 50% in the first second or so after stimulation, so even offensively odorous air may seem odorless after only a few minutes.

Many animals communicate with pheromones

Animals within many species communicate with one another by releasing **pheromones,** small, volatile molecules that are secreted into the environment. For example, female moths release pheromones that attract males. Dogs and wolves use pheromones to mark territory.

Mammals have specialized chemoreceptor cells that detect pheromones. These cells make up the **vomeronasal organ** located in the epithelium of the nose (separate from the main olfactory epithelium). The vomeronasal sensory neurons send signals to areas of the hypothalamus, which serves as a link with the endocrine system. (We discuss pheromones further in Chapter 52.)

Review

- How is signal transduction similar in taste buds and olfactory receptor cells? How is it different?

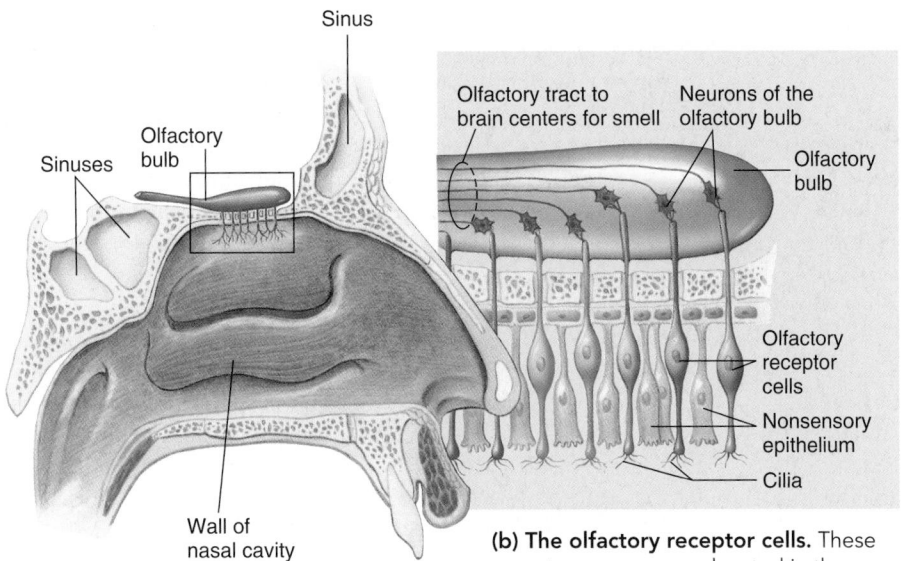

(a) **Location of olfactory receptor cells.** Smell depends on thousands of chemoreceptor cells in the roof of the nasal cavity.

(b) **The olfactory receptor cells.** These receptors are neurons located in the olfactory epithelium.

1. Odorant binds to receptor in plasma membrane of olfactory cell.

2. G protein is activated and activates adenylyl cyclase.

3. ATP is converted to cyclic AMP.

4. Gated Na⁺ channels open, leading to depolarization.

(c) **The chemistry of smelling.** An odorant activates a signal transduction process that leads to an increase in Na⁺ permeability. The membrane becomes depolarized, resulting in transmission of action potentials that transmit information to the brain.

FIGURE 43-15 *Animated* Chemoreception: olfaction

43.7 PHOTORECEPTORS

■ LEARNING OBJECTIVES

10 Contrast simple eyes, compound eyes, and vertebrate eyes.

11 Describe the function of each structure of the vertebrate eye.

12 Compare the two types of photoreceptors, describe the signal transduction pathway that is activated when rhodopsin responds to light, and summarize the visual pathway.

Most animals have **photoreceptors** that use pigments to absorb light energy. **Rhodopsins** are the photopigments in the eyes of cephalopod mollusks (squids and octopods), arthropods, and vertebrates. Light energy striking a light-sensitive receptor cell containing these pigments triggers chemical changes in the pigment molecules that result in receptor potentials.

Invertebrate photoreceptors include eyespots, simple eyes, and compound eyes

The simplest light-sensitive structures in animals are found in certain cnidarians and flatworms (**FIG. 43-16**). They are **eyespots,** called **ocelli,** that detect light but do not form images. Eyespots are often bowl-shaped clusters of light-sensitive cells within the epidermis. They may detect the direction of the light source and distinguish light intensity.

Effective image formation requires a more complex **eye,** usually with a lens. A **lens** is a structure that concentrates light on a group of photoreceptors. Vision also requires a brain that can interpret the action potentials generated by the photoreceptors. The brain integrates information about movement, brightness, location, position, and shape of the visual stimulus. Two fundamentally different types of eyes evolved: the compound eye of arthropods and the camera eye of vertebrates and cephalopod mollusks.

The **compound eyes** of crustaceans and insects differ structurally and functionally from vertebrate eyes. The surface of a compound eye appears faceted, which means "having many faces," like a diamond (**FIG. 43-17**). Each **facet** is the convex *cornea* of one of the eye's visual units, called **ommatidia** (sing., *ommatidium*). The number of ommatidia varies with the species. For example, each eye of certain crustaceans has only 20 ommatidia, whereas the dragonfly eye has as many as 28,000.

The optical part of each ommatidium includes a biconvex lens and a **crystalline cone.** The lens and crystalline cone focus light onto photoreceptor cells called **retinular cells.** These cells have a light-sensitive membrane made up of microvilli that contain rhodopsin. The membranes of several retinular cells may fuse to form a central rod-shaped **rhabdome** that is sensitive to light.

Compound eyes do not perceive form well. Although the lens system of each ommatidium is adequate to focus a small inverted image, there is little evidence that the animal actually perceives them as images. However, all the ommatidia together produce a composite image, or **mosaic** picture. Each ommatidium, in gathering a point of light from a narrow sector of the visual field, is in fact

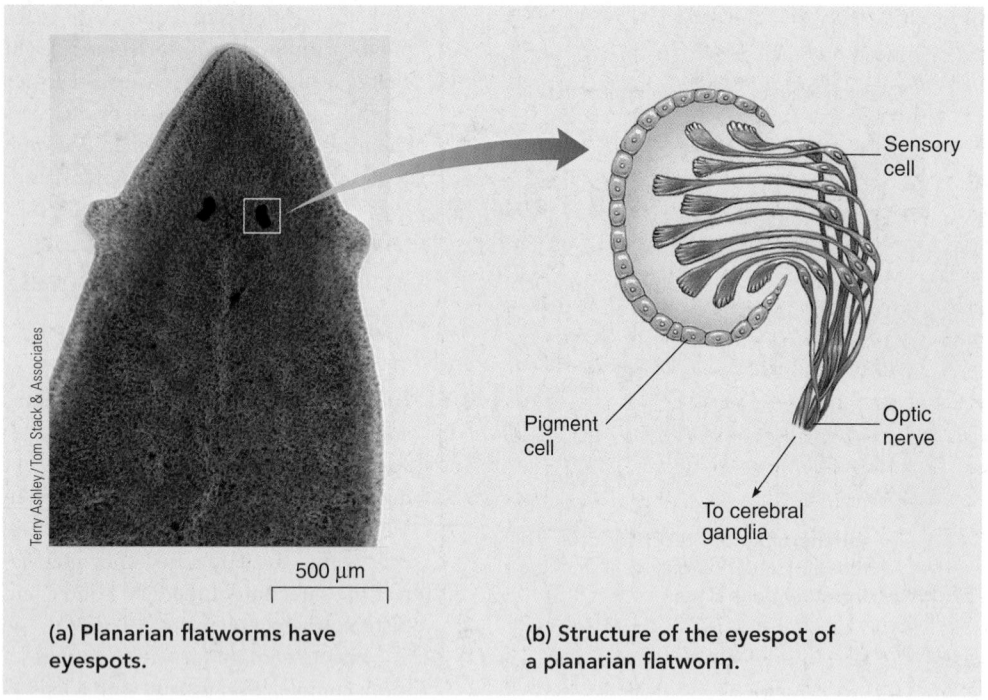

(a) Planarian flatworms have eyespots.

Sensory cell

Pigment cell

Optic nerve

To cerebral ganglia

500 μm

Terry Ashley/Tom Stack & Associates

(b) Structure of the eyespot of a planarian flatworm.

FIGURE 43-16 Photoreception: eyespots

The simplest light-sensitive structures are the ocelli, or eyespots, found in certain invertebrates.

violet (UV). Accordingly, an insect can see UV light well, and its world of color is very different from ours. Because they reflect UV light to various degrees, flowers that appear identically colored to humans may appear strikingly dissimilar to insects (see Fig. 37-4e).

Vertebrate eyes form sharp images

The position of the eyes in the front of the head of primates and certain birds allows both eyes to focus on the same object. The overlap in information they receive results in the same visual information striking the two retinas (light-sensitive areas) at the same time. This **binocular vision** is important in judging distance and in depth perception.

The vertebrate eye can be compared to an old-fashioned camera. An adjustable lens can be focused for different distances, and a diaphragm, called the **iris,** regulates the size of the light opening, called the **pupil** (**FIG. 43-18**). The **retina** corresponds to the light-sensitive film used in a camera. Outside the retina is the **choroid** layer, a sheet of cells filled with black pigment that absorbs extra light. This mechanism prevents light from being reflected back into the photoreceptors, which would cause blurring of images. (Cameras are also black on the inside.) The choroid is rich in blood vessels that supply the retina.

The outer coat of the eyeball, called the **sclera,** is a tough, opaque, curved sheet of connective tissue that protects the inner structures and helps maintain the rigidity of the eyeball. On the front surface of the eye, this sheet becomes the thinner, transparent **cornea,** through which light enters. The cornea serves as a fixed *lens* that focuses light.

The **lens** of the eye is a transparent, elastic ball just behind the iris. It bends the light rays coming in and brings them to a focus on the retina. The lens is aided by the curved surface of the cornea and by the refractive properties (ability to bend light rays) of the liquids inside the eyeball. The **anterior cavity** between the cornea and the lens is filled with a watery substance, the aqueous fluid. The larger **posterior cavity** between the lens and the retina is filled with a more viscous fluid, the **vitreous body.** Both fluids are important in maintaining the shape of the eyeball by providing an internal fluid pressure.

At its anterior margin, the choroid is thick and projects medially into the eyeball, forming the **ciliary body,** which consists of ciliary processes and the ciliary muscle. The ciliary processes are glandlike folds that project toward the lens and secrete the aqueous fluid.

sampling a mean intensity from that sector. All these points of light taken together form a mosaic picture (see Fig. 43-17d).

Arthropod eyes usually adapt to different intensities of light. A sheath of pigmented cells envelops each ommatidium, and screening pigments are present in *iris cells* and in retinular cells. In nocturnal and crepuscular (active at dusk) insects and many crustaceans, pigment migrates proximally and distally within each pigmented cell. When the pigment is in the proximal position, each ommatidium is shielded from its neighbor, and only light entering directly along its axis can stimulate the receptors. When the pigment is in the distal position, light striking at any angle can pass through several ommatidia and stimulate many retinal units. As a result, sensitivity is increased in dim light and the eye is protected from excessive stimulation in bright light. Pigment migration is under neural control in insects and under hormonal control in crustaceans. In some species it follows a daily rhythm.

Although the compound eye can form only coarse images, it compensates by following flickers to higher frequencies. Flies can detect up to about 265 flickers per second. In contrast, the human eye can detect only 45 to 53 flickers per second; for us, flickering lights fuse above these values, so we see light provided by an ordinary bulb as steady and the movement in motion pictures as smooth. To an insect, both room lighting and motion pictures must flicker horribly. The insect's high critical flicker fusion threshold permits immediate detection of even slight movement by prey or enemy. The compound eye is an important adaptation to the arthropod's way of life.

Compound eyes differ from our eyes in another respect. They are sensitive to wavelengths of light in the range from red to ultra-

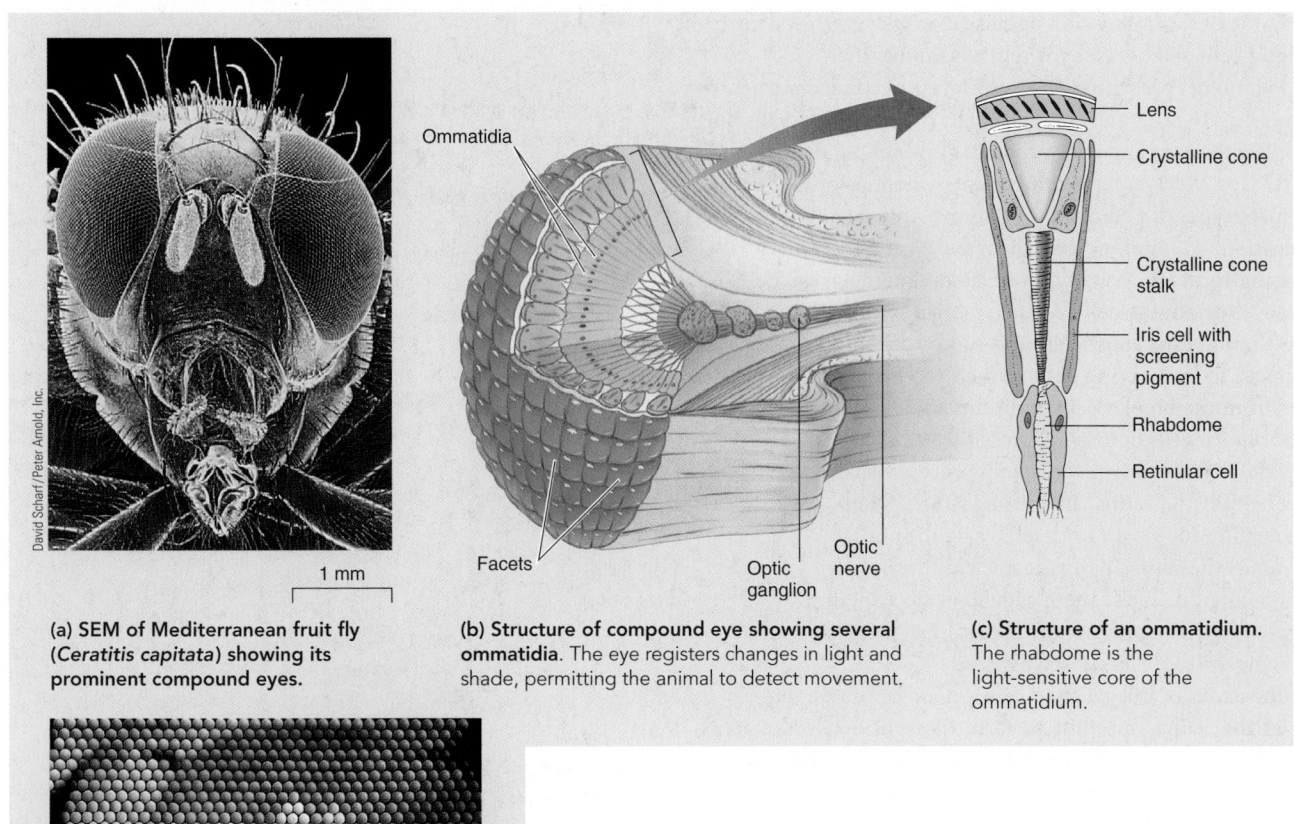

(a) SEM of Mediterranean fruit fly (*Ceratitis capitata*) showing its prominent compound eyes.

(b) Structure of compound eye showing several **ommatidia**. The eye registers changes in light and shade, permitting the animal to detect movement.

(c) Structure of an ommatidium. The rhabdome is the light-sensitive core of the ommatidium.

(d) A bee's-eye view of a flower. This photograph was taken using an optical device to achieve an approximate simulation of how the bee might see this flower. However, the bee would see UV light rather than red, and circles would be vertically elongated ellipses.

FIGURE 43-17 Photoreception: compound eyes

We focus a camera by changing the distance between the lens and the film. The eye has the **power of accommodation,** the ability to change focus for near or far vision by changing the shape of the lens (**FIG. 43-19**). This accommodation is accomplished by the **ciliary muscle,** a part of the ciliary body. To focus on close objects, the ciliary muscle contracts, making the elastic lens rounder. To focus on more distant objects, the ciliary muscle relaxes and the lens assumes a flattened (ovoid) shape.

The amount of light entering the eye is regulated by the iris, a ring of smooth muscle that appears as blue, green, gray, or brown depending on the amount and nature of pigment present. The iris consists of two mutually antagonistic sets of muscle fibers. One set is arranged circularly and contracts to *decrease* the size of the pupil. The other is arranged radially and contracts to *increase* the size of the pupil.

Each eye also has six muscles that extend from the surface of the eyeball to various points in the bony socket. These muscles enable the eye as a whole to move and be oriented in a given direction. Cranial nerves innervate the muscles in such a way that the eyes normally move together and focus on the same area.

The retina contains light-sensitive rods and cones

The light-sensitive structure in the vertebrate eye is the retina, which lines the posterior two-thirds of the eyeball and covers the choroid. The retina, which is composed of ten layers, contains the photoreceptor cells called, according to shape, **rods** and **cones.** In both rod and cone cells, infoldings of the plasma membrane form stacks of membranous discs that contain the photopigments. The discs greatly increase the light-absorbing surface.

The human eye has about 125 million rods and 6.5 million cones. Rods function in dim light allowing us to detect shape and movement. They are not sensitive to colors. Because the rods are more numerous in the periphery of the retina, you can see an object better in dim light if you look slightly to one side of it (allowing the image to fall on the rods).

Cones respond to light at higher levels of intensity, such as daylight, and they allow us to perceive fine detail. Cones are responsible for color vision; they are differentially sensitive to different wavelengths (colors) of light. In primates and certain hunting birds (such as eagles), the cones are most concentrated in the fovea, a small, depressed area in the center of the retina. The **fovea** is the region of sharpest vision because it has the greatest density of receptor cells and because the retina is thinner there.

Light must pass through several layers of connecting neurons in the retina to reach the rods and cones (**FIG. 43-20**). This arrangement lets the rods and cones contact a layer of pigmented epithelium that provides *retinal,* a component of rhodopsin. The retina has five main types of neurons: (1) Photoreceptors (rods and cones) synapse on (2) **bipolar cells,** which make synaptic contact with (3) **ganglion cells.** Two types of lateral interneurons are the (4) **horizontal cells,** which receive information from the photoreceptor cells and send it to bipolar cells, and (5) **amacrine cells,** which receive messages from the bipolar cells and send signals back to the bipolar cells or to ganglion cells (**FIG. 43-21**). Horizontal and amacrine cells help process visual input within the retina. Interestingly, one group of ganglion cells *project* to (that is, have axons that extend to) the suprachiasmatic nucleus, the body's main biological clock. These ganglion cells contain a light-sensitive pigment (melanopsin) that is important in nonvisual responses to light.

The axons of the ganglion cells extend across the surface of the retina and unite to form the *optic nerve.* The area where the optic nerve passes out of the eyeball, the **optic disk,** is known as the *blind spot;* because it lacks rods and cones, images falling on it cannot be perceived.

Here is a simplified summary of the visual pathway:

light passes through cornea ⟶ through aqueous fluid ⟶ through lens ⟶ through vitreous body ⟶ image forms on photoreceptor cells in retina ⟶ signal bipolar cells ⟶ signal ganglion cells ⟶ optic nerve transmits signals to thalamus ⟶ integration by visual areas of cerebral cortex

Light activates rhodopsin

How is light converted into the neural signals that transmit information about environmental stimuli into pictures in the brain? Rod cells are so sensitive to light that they can respond to a single

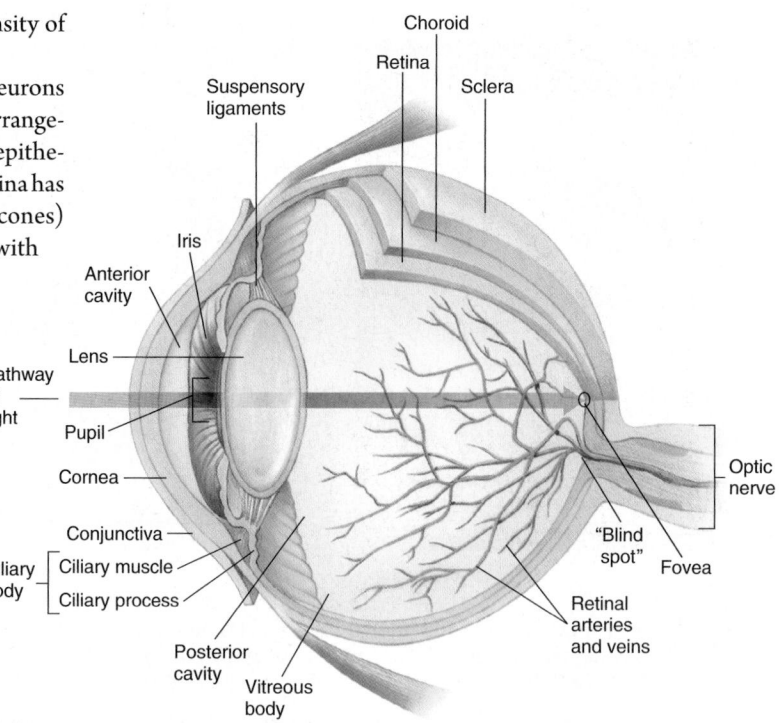

FIGURE 43-18 *Animated* Photoreception: structure of the human eye

Light passes through the human eye to photoreceptor cells in the retina. In this lateral view, the eye is shown partly sectioned along the sagittal plane to expose its internal structures.

photon. Rhodopsin in the rod cells and some very closely related photopigments in the cone cells are responsible for the ability to see. **Rhodopsin** consists of *opsin,* a large protein that is chemically joined with *retinal,* an aldehyde of vitamin A (see Fig. 3-14). Two isomers of retinal exist: the *cis* form, which is folded, and the *trans* form, which is straight.

In the dark, opsin binds to retinal in the *cis* form. Cyclic GMP (cyclic guanosine monophosphate, a molecule similar to cyclic AMP) opens nonspecific channels that permit passage of Na^+ and other cations into the rod cell (**FIG. 43-22**). This process depolar-

(a) Near vision

(b) Distant vision

FIGURE 43-19 *Animated* Accommodation

How the eye changes focus for **(a)** near and **(b)** distant vision.

The rods and cones in the retina are the photoreceptors in vertebrates.

Retina

Optic nerve

Ganglion cell

Bipolar cell

Vitreous body

Retina

Choroid layer & sclera

Front of retina

Optic nerve fibers

Cone cell

Rod cell

Pigmented epithelium

(a) Neurons in the retina. The elaborate interconnections among the various layers of neurons in the retina allow them to interact and influence one another.

© Lennart Nilsson/from *The Incredible Machine*, p. 279

10 μm

(b) SEM of rods and cones. The red, elongated structures are rods. The two shorter, thicker, yellow structures are cones. The rods function in dim light and allow you to see shapes and movement. The cones allow you to view the world in color.

FIGURE 43-20 *Animated* **Organization of the retina**

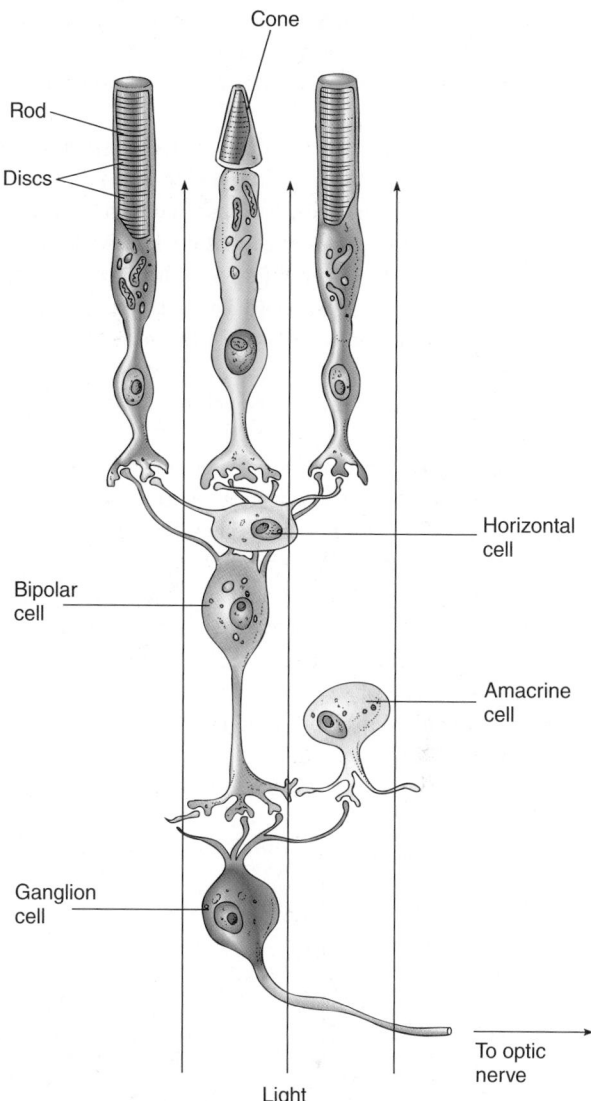

Cone

Rod

Discs

Horizontal cell

Bipolar cell

Amacrine cell

Ganglion cell

To optic nerve

Light

FIGURE 43-21 Neural pathway in the retina

The photoreceptor cells (rods and cones) are located in the back of the retina. They transmit information to bipolar cells. The bipolar cells synapse with ganglion cells. The horizontal and amacrine cells are important in local processing of visual input within the retina. Axons of ganglion cells make up the optic nerve.

izes the rod cell, which then releases the neurotransmitter glutamate. The glutamate hyperpolarizes the membrane of the bipolar cell so it does not transmit messages.

Note that the photoreceptor differs from other neurons in that the ion channels in its membrane are normally open; it is depolarized and continuously releases neurotransmitter. The steady flow of ions into the cell when the environment is dark is called the *dark current.* Another unusual characteristic of photoreceptors, and of bipolar cells, is that they do not produce action potentials. Their release of neurotransmitter is graded, regulated by the extent of depolarization.

When light strikes rhodopsin, light energy is transduced. This process can be considered in three stages:

1. Light activates rhodopsin. Light transforms *cis*-retinal to *trans*-retinal. Rhodopsin changes shape and breaks down into its components, opsin and retinal. This is the light-dependent process in vision.

2. Rhodopsin is part of a signal transduction pathway. When it changes shape, it binds with **transducin,** a G protein. Transducin activates an esterase that hydrolyzes cyclic GMP (cGMP) to GMP, reducing the concentration of cGMP.

3. The decrease in concentration of cGMP in the rod causes the Na^+ channels to close. Fewer cations pass into the rod cell, and it becomes more negative (hyperpolarized). The rod cell then releases less glutamate. Thus, light decreases the number of neural signals from the rod cells.

The release of glutamate normally hyperpolarizes the membrane of the bipolar cell, so a decrease in glutamate release results in its depolarization. The depolarized bipolar cell increases its release of a neurotransmitter, which typically stimulates the ganglion cell.

When you move from bright daylight to a dark room, you experience "blindness" for a few moments while your eyes adapt. During exposure to bright light, rhodopsin breaks down, decreasing the sensitivity of your eyes. **Dark adaptation** occurs as enzymes restore rhodopsin to a form in which it can respond to light. In dim light, vision depends on the rods. Conversely, when you move from the dark to bright light, your eyes are very sensitive and you may feel "blinded" by the light. **Light adaptation** occurs as some of the photopigments break down and the sensitivity of your eyes decreases.

Color vision depends on three types of cones

Many invertebrates and at least some animals in each vertebrate class have color vision. Color perception depends on cones. Most mammals have two types of cones, but humans and other primates have three types: blue, green, and red. Each contains a slightly different photopigment. Although the retinal portion of the pigment molecule is the same as in rhodopsin, the opsin protein differs slightly in each type of photoreceptor.

Each type of cone responds to light within a considerable range of wavelengths but is named for the ability of its pigment to absorb a particular wavelength more strongly than other cones do. For example, red light can be absorbed by all three types of cones, but those cones most sensitive to red act as red receptors. By comparing the relative responses of the three types of cones, the brain can detect colors of intermediate wavelengths. Color blindness occurs when there is a deficiency of one or more of the three types of cones. This is usually an inherited X-linked condition (see Fig. 11-15).

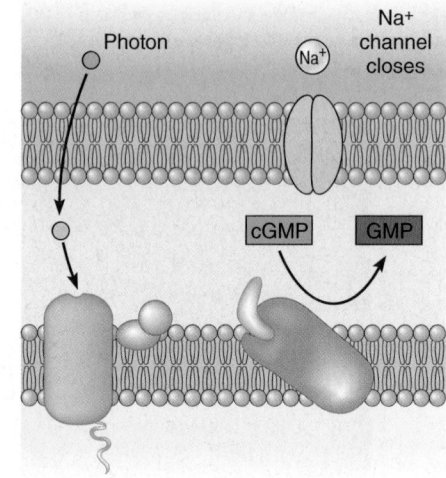

(a) In the dark. Sodium channels are open. The rod cell membrane is depolarized and releases the inhibitory neurotransmitter glutamate (not shown).

(b) In the light. When rhodopsin absorbs light, it changes shape, activating a signal transduction pathway. The concentration of cGMP is reduced. As a result cGMP-gated sodium channels close, hyperpolarizing the membrane. Hyperpolarization results in a decrease in inhibitory signals from the rod cell.

FIGURE 43-22 The biochemistry of vision
Inward foldings of the plasma membrane produce a series of discs in each rod cell. In the dark, the rod cell is depolarized; in the light it becomes hyperpolarized.

Integration of visual information begins in the retina

The size, intensity, and location of light stimuli determine initial processing in the retina. Rods and cones send signals directly to bipolar cells, and bipolar cells send signals directly to ganglion cells. However, as illustrated in Figure 43-21, photoreceptor cells can also transmit signals to horizontal cells, and bipolar cells can transmit signals to amacrine cells. Ganglion cells are inhibited by amacrine cells and can be inhibited indirectly by horizontal cells as a result of their action on bipolar cells. Thus, the horizontal and amacrine cells integrate signals laterally.

Bipolar, horizontal, and amacrine cells combine signals from several photoreceptors. Each ganglion cell has a **receptive field,** a specific group of photoreceptors that light must strike for the ganglion cell to be stimulated. Ganglion cells are activated or inhibited depending on which photoreceptor cells have been stimulated.

The pattern of neuron firing in the retina is very important. The signals sent to ganglion cells depend on spatial patterns and timing of the light striking the retina. Ganglion cells receive signals about specific types of visual stimuli, such as color, brightness, and motion, and transmit this information about the characteristics of a visual image. Ganglion cells produce action potentials, in contrast with rods and cones and most other neurons of the retina, which produce only graded potentials.

The retina begins the construction of visual images, but those images are interpreted in the brain. Axons of more than one million ganglion cells form the optic nerves that transmit information to the brain by complex, encoded signals. The optic nerves cross in the floor of the hypothalamus, forming an X-shaped structure, the **optic chiasm** (**FIG. 43-23**). Some of the axons of the optic nerves cross over and then extend to the opposite side of the brain.

Axons of the **optic nerves** end in the **lateral geniculate nuclei** of the thalamus. From there, neurons send signals to the **primary visual cortex** in the occipital lobe of the cerebrum. The lateral geniculate nucleus controls which information is sent to the visual cortex. Neurons in the reticular activating system are involved in this integration. Information is transmitted from the primary visual cortex to other cortical areas for further processing.

Different types of ganglion cells receive information about different aspects of a visual stimulus. As a result, information from each point in the retina is transmitted in parallel by several types of ganglion cells. These cells project to different kinds of neurons in the lateral geniculate nucleus and primary visual cortex.

Neurobiologists have not yet discovered all the mechanisms by which the brain makes sense out of the visual information it receives. We know that a large part of the association areas of the

FIGURE 43-23 *Animated* **Neural pathway for transmission of visual information**

Axons of ganglion cells form the optic nerves. The optic nerves cross, forming the optic chiasm. Many optic nerve fibers end in the lateral geniculate nuclei of the thalamus. From there, signals are sent to the visual area in the occipital lobe. (Brain is viewed from above with overlying structures removed.)

cerebrum are involved in integrating visual input. The neurons of the visual cortex are organized as a map of the external visual field. They are also organized into columns. Each column of neurons receives signals originating from light entering either the right or left eye. Columns are also organized by orientation of light. Neurons in a column receive signals originally triggered by light with the same orientation. However, these signals originate from different locations in the retina.

Review

- How does the insect's compound eye compare with the vertebrate eye?
- What happens when light strikes rhodopsin? (Include a description of the signal transduction pathway in your answer.)
- What is the sequence of neural signaling in the retina?
- What is meant by the statement "Vision happens mainly in the brain"?

■ SUMMARY: FOCUS ON LEARNING OBJECTIVES

43.1 *(page 912)*

1 Describe how sensory systems function; include descriptions of sensory receptors, energy transduction, receptor potential, sensory adaptation, and perception.

- **Sensory receptors** are neuron endings or specialized receptor cells in close contact with neurons. **Sense organs** consist of sensory receptors and accessory cells.
- Sensory receptors absorb energy from a stimulus and transduce that energy—**energy transduction**—into electrical energy. Sensory receptors produce **receptor potentials,** which are depolarizations

or hyperpolarizations of the membrane. Receptor potentials are **graded responses.** Receptor potentials can generate action potentials in **sensory neurons,** which transmit coded signals to the CNS.

- **Sensory adaptation,** the decrease in frequency of action potentials in a sensory neuron even when the stimulus is maintained, decreases response to that stimulus.

- The brain interprets sensations by converting them to perceptions of stimuli. Sensory **perception** is the process of selecting, interpreting, and organizing sensory information.

CENGAGENOW™ Learn more about sensory reception in human skin by clicking on the figure in CengageNOW.

2 Classify sensory receptors according to the location of stimuli to which they respond and according to the types of energy they transduce.

- **Exteroceptors** receive stimuli from the outside environment. **Interoceptors** detect changes within the body, such as changes in pH, osmotic pressure, body temperature, and the chemical composition of the blood.

- Sensory receptors can be classified according to the types of energy they transduce. Thermoreceptors respond to heat and cold. Electroreceptors sense differences in electrical potential. Some electromagnetic receptors can detect Earth's magnetic field. Nociceptors (pain receptors) respond to mechanical, temperature, and other stimuli that could be damaging. Mechanoreceptors transduce mechanical energy—touch, pressure, gravity, stretching, and movement. Chemoreceptors transduce certain chemical compounds, and photoreceptors transduce light energy.

43.2 *(page 915)*

3 Identify three functions of thermoreceptors.

- **Thermoreceptors** transduce thermal energy; they respond to heat and cold. Some parasites use thermoreceptors to find an endothermic host. Some predators use thermoreceptors to locate endothermic prey. In endothermic animals, thermoreceptors provide cues about body temperature.

43.3 *(page 916)*

4 Describe the functions of electroreceptors and electromagnetic receptors.

- **Electroreceptors,** used by predatory fishes to detect prey, respond to electrical stimuli.

- Some electroreceptors, called **electromagnetic receptors,** are sensitive enough to detect Earth's magnetic field. Some animals use information about magnetic fields to orient themselves. Many migratory animals use magnetic fields to navigate.

43.4 *(page 916)*

5 Describe the functions of nociceptors and identify the roles of glutamate and substance P.

- **Nociceptors** are pain receptors; they are free nerve endings of certain sensory neurons that respond to strong tactile stimuli, temperature extremes, and certain chemicals. Sensory neurons that transmit pain signals release the neurotransmitters **glutamate** and **substance P.** Substance P enhances and prolongs the actions of glutamate.

43.5 *(page 916)*

6 Compare the functions and mechanisms of action of the following mechanoreceptors: tactile receptors, proprioceptors, statocysts, hair cells, and lateral line organs.

- **Mechanoreceptors** transduce mechanical energy, permitting animals to feel, hear, and maintain balance. Mechanoreceptors respond to touch, pressure, gravity, stretch, or movement. They are activated when they change shape as a result of being mechanically pushed or pulled.

- **Tactile receptors** in the skin respond to mechanical displacement of hairs or to displacement of the receptor cells themselves. The **Pacinian corpuscle** is a tactile receptor that responds to touch and pressure.

- **Proprioceptors** allow an animal to perceive orientation of its body and the positions of its parts. **Muscle spindles, Golgi tendon organs,** and **joint receptors** are proprioceptors that continuously respond to tension and movement.

- **Statocysts,** gravity receptors found in many invertebrates, are simple organs of equilibrium. A statocyst consists of a chamber lined with ciliated mechanoreceptors; the chamber contains **statoliths,** granules of sand grains or calcium carbonate that change position as the animal moves. As statoliths move, sensory hairs bend and different sensory cells are stimulated. This mechanical displacement results in receptor potentials and action potentials that inform the CNS of the change in position.

- Vertebrate **hair cells** detect movement; they are found in the lateral line of fishes, the vestibular apparatus, semicircular canals, and cochlea. Each hair cell has a single **kinocilium,** which is a true cilium, and **stereocilia,** which are microvilli that contain actin filaments.

- **Lateral line organs** supplement vision in fishes and some amphibians by informing the animal of moving objects or objects in its path.

7 Compare the structure and function of the saccule and utricle with that of the semicircular canals in maintaining equilibrium.

- The vertebrate **inner ear** consists of a **labyrinth** of fluid-filled chambers and canals that help maintain equilibrium. The **vestibular apparatus** in the upper part of the labyrinth consists of the **saccule, utricle,** and **semicircular canals.**

- The saccule and utricle contain **otoliths** that change position when the head is tilted or when the body is moving in a straight line. The otoliths stimulate hair cells that send signals to the brain, enabling the animal to perceive the direction of gravity.

- The semicircular canals inform the brain about turning movements. Clumps of hair cells, called **cristae,** are located within each bulblike enlargement, called an **ampulla.** Cristae are stimulated by movements of the **endolymph,** a fluid that fills each canal.

8 Trace the path taken by sound waves through the structures of the ear and explain how the organ of Corti functions as an auditory receptor.

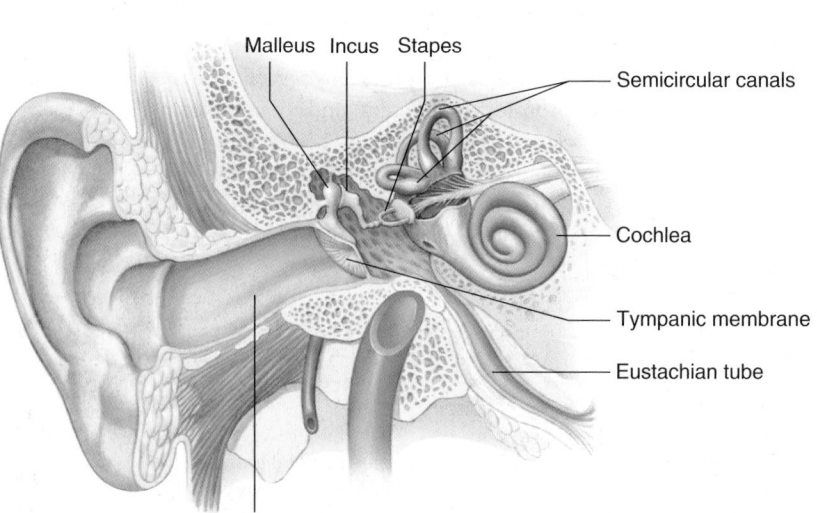

Malleus Incus Stapes

Semicircular canals

Cochlea

Tympanic membrane

Eustachian tube

External ear canal

- In terrestrial vertebrates, the **organ of Corti** within the **cochlea** contains auditory receptors.

- Sound waves pass through the **external auditory canal** and cause the **tympanic membrane** (eardrum) to vibrate. The ear bones—**malleus, incus,** and **stapes**—transmit and amplify the vibrations through the middle ear. Vibrations pass through the **oval window** to fluid within the vestibular canal. Pressure waves press on the membranes that separate the three ducts of the cochlea.

- The bulging of the **round window** serves as an escape valve for the pressure. The pressure waves cause movements of the **basilar membrane.** These movements stimulate the hair cells of the organ of Corti by rubbing them against the overlying **tectorial membrane.**

- Neural impulses are initiated in the dendrites of neurons that lie at the base of each hair cell and are transmitted by the **cochlear nerve** to the brain.

CENGAGENOW Watch the human ear in action by clicking on the figures in CengageNOW.

43.6 (page 924)

9 Compare the structure and function of the receptors of taste and smell, and describe the function of the vomeronasal organ.

- **Chemoreceptors** transduce certain kinds of chemical compounds, allowing **gustation,** or taste, and **olfaction,** or smell.

- In vertebrates, taste receptor cells are specialized epithelial cells in **taste buds.** The **olfactory epithelium** contains specialized olfactory cells with axons that extend to the brain as fibers of the **olfactory nerves.**

- When a molecule binds with a receptor on a taste receptor cell or an olfactory receptor cell, a signal transduction process involving a G protein is initiated.

- Receptors that make up the **vomeronasal organ,** located in the nasal epithelium of mammals, detect **pheromones,** small, volatile signaling molecules released by animals.

CENGAGENOW Learn more about taste buds and olfactory epithelium by clicking on the figures in CengageNOW.

43.7 (page 927)

10 Contrast simple eyes, compound eyes, and vertebrate eyes.

- **Photoreceptors** transduce light energy and serve as the sensory receptors in eyespots and eyes. **Eyespots,** or **ocelli,** found in cnidarians and flatworms, detect light but do not form images.

- The **compound eye** of insects and crustaceans consists of visual units called **ommatidia,** which collectively produce a **mosaic** image.

- Each ommatidium has a transparent lens and a **crystalline cone** that focus light onto receptor cells called **retinular cells.**

- Vertebrate eyes form sharp images.

11 Describe the function of each structure of the vertebrate eye.

- In the human eye, light enters through the **cornea,** is focused by the **lens,** and produces an image on the **retina.** The **iris** regulates the amount of light that can enter. The internal surface of the eye is covered by the **choroid,** a black coat that prevents light rays from scattering.

- The eye has the power of **accommodation,** the ability to change focus for near or far vision by changing the shape of the lens. The lens is attached to the **ciliary muscles.** When the ciliary muscles contract, the lens becomes rounder. When they relax, the lens flattens.

CENGAGENOW Learn more about the human eye and the organization of the retina by clicking on the figures in CengageNOW.

12 Compare the two types of photoreceptors, describe the signal transduction pathway that is activated when rhodopsin responds to light, and summarize the visual pathway.

- The retina contains the photoreceptor cells: **rods,** which function in dim light and form images in black and white; and **cones,** which function in bright light and permit color vision.

- The retina also contains **bipolar cells** that send signals to **ganglion cells.** Two types of lateral interneurons integrate information: **horizontal cells** receive signals from the rods and cones and send signals to bipolar cells, and **amacrine cells** receive signals from bipolar cells and send signals back to bipolar cells and to ganglion cells.

- When the environment is dark, ion channels in the plasma membranes of rod cells are open and the cells are depolarized; they release glutamate, which hyperpolarizes the membranes of bipolar cells so they do not send signals.

- When light strikes the photopigment **rhodopsin** in the rod cells, its retinal portion changes shape and initiates a signal transduction process that involves **transducin.** This G protein activates an esterase that hydrolyzes cGMP, reducing its concentration. As a result, ion channels close and the membrane becomes hyperpolarized. The rod cells release less glutamate, and fewer signals are transmitted. As a result, bipolar cells become depolarized and release neurotransmitter that stimulates ganglion cells.

- Axons of the ganglion cells make up the **optic nerves.** The optic nerves transmit information to the **lateral geniculate nuclei** in the thalamus. From there, neurons project to the **primary visual cortex** and then to integration centers in the cerebral cortex.

CENGAGENOW See how vision disorders change the eye by clicking on the figure in CengageNOW.

TEST YOUR UNDERSTANDING

1. Which of the following is *not* true of a sensory receptor? (a) detects a stimulus in the environment (b) converts energy of the stimulus into electrical energy (c) produces a receptor potential (d) produces a graded response (e) interprets sensory stimuli

2. A sensory receptor absorbs energy from some stimulus. The next step is (a) release of neurotransmitter (b) transmission of an action potential (c) energy transduction (d) transmission of a receptor potential (e) sensory adaptation

3. Interoceptors (a) help maintain homeostasis (b) are located in the skin (c) are photoreceptors (d) adapt rapidly (e) convert absorbed energy directly into action potentials

4. Which of the following are *not* correctly matched? (a) mechanoreceptors—touch, pressure (b) electroreceptors—voltage (c) photoreceptors—light (d) chemoreceptors—gravity (e) nociceptors—extreme temperature

5. Which of the following is/are associated with informing the brain about turning movements? (a) semicircular canals (b) saccule (c) lymph (d) otoliths (e) utricle

6. The auditory receptors are located in the (a) utricle (b) organ of Corti (c) vestibular apparatus (d) saccule (e) semicircular canals

7. Which of the following receptors do *not* have hair cells? (a) lateral line organ (b) saccule (c) utricle (d) semicircular canals (e) rods

8. In the process of hearing, the basilar membrane vibrates. Which event occurs next? (a) tympanic membrane vibrates (b) bones in middle ear amplify and conduct vibrations (c) cochlear nerve transmits impulses to organ of Corti (d) hair cells in organ of Corti are stimulated (e) vibrations conducted to chemoreceptors

9. In olfaction, (a) pheromones stimulate the taste buds (b) the number of odorous molecules determines the magnitude of the receptor potential (c) chemical signals are converted directly into electrical signals (d) a G protein is activated and leads to the closing of gated channels (e) the concentration of cyclic AMP increases, leading to hyperpolarization of the receptor

10. In the human visual pathway, after light passes through the cornea, it next (a) stimulates ganglion cells (b) passes through the lens (c) sends signals through the optic nerve (d) depolarizes horizontal cells (e) hyperpolarizes rod cells

11. When rhodopsin is activated, it (a) concentrates in bipolar cells (b) transmits more action potentials (c) binds with a G protein (d) sends signals to the lateral geniculate nuclei (e) activates substance P

12. Label the diagram. Refer to Figure 43-18 to check your answers.

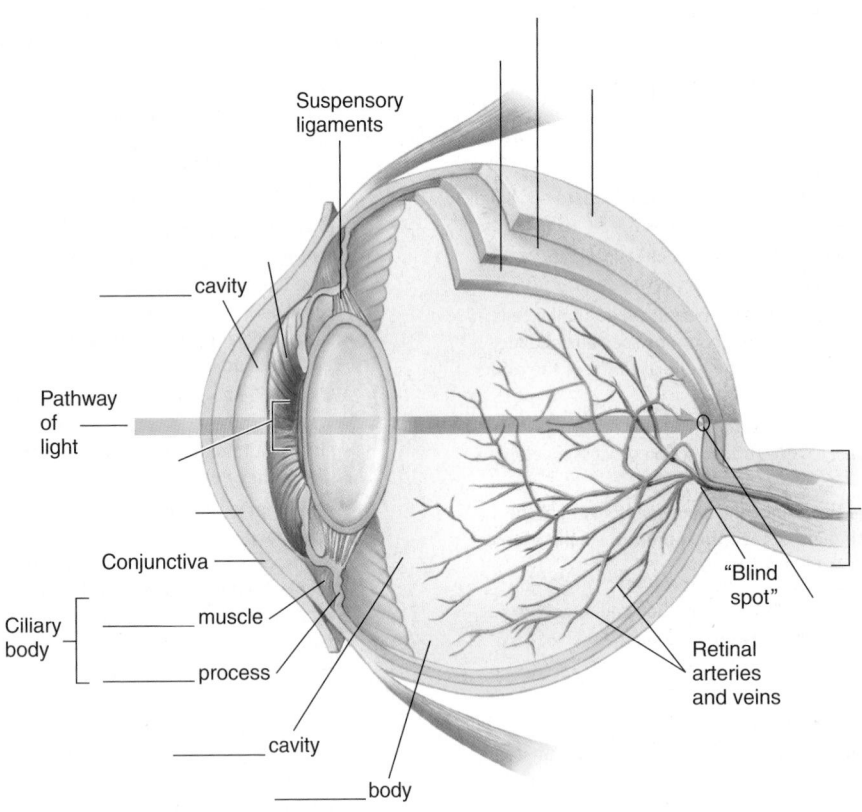

Suspensory ligaments

_____ cavity

Pathway of light

Conjunctiva _____

Ciliary body

_____ muscle

_____ process

_____ cavity

_____ body

"Blind spot"

Retinal arteries and veins

CRITICAL THINKING

1. If all neurons transmit the same type of message, how do you know the difference between sound and light? How are you able to distinguish between an intense pain and a mild one? How are these discriminations adaptive?

2. Connoisseurs can recognize many varieties of cheese or wine by "tasting." How can this be, when there are only a few types of taste receptors? Organisms have only a few basic tastes. How might that be adaptive?

3. Design a synaptic mechanism by which the same neurotransmitter has an excitatory effect on one bipolar cell in the retina and an inhibitory effect on another.

4. **EVOLUTION LINK.** Proteins known as opsins are present in the photoreceptors of all light-sensitive receptors that have been studied. What does this suggest about the relationships of organisms as diverse as amoebas, flatworms, crayfish, and elephants?

5. **EVOLUTION LINK.** Once the ability to produce images evolved, eyes evolved relatively rapidly. Hypothesize why image-forming eyes evolved quickly and are now present in the majority of animal groups.

 Additional questions are available in CengageNOW at www.cengage.com/login.

44 Internal Transport

Colored 3D computed tomography (CT) scan of the human heart and some of its blood vessels. The large cream structures at upper center above the heart are blood vessels that carry blood to and from the heart. The fine blood vessels on the surface of the chambers are coronary arteries, which supply the heart muscle itself with oxygenated blood and nutrients.

James D. Mauseth, University of Texas

Most cells require a continuous supply of nutrients and oxygen and removal of waste products. In very small animals, these metabolic needs are met by simple **diffusion,** the net movement of particles from a region of higher concentration to a region of lower concentration as a result of random motion. A molecule can diffuse 1 micrometer (μm) in less than 1 millisecond (msec), so diffusion is adequate over microscopic distances. In invertebrates that are only a few cells thick, diffusion is an effective mechanism for distributing materials to and from their cells. Consequently, many small, aquatic invertebrates have no circulatory system. Fluid between the cells, called **interstitial fluid,** or tissue fluid, bathes the cells and provides a medium for diffusion of oxygen, nutrients, and wastes.

How much time diffusion requires increases with the square of the distance over which diffusion occurs. A cell that is 10 μm away from its oxygen (or nutrient) supply can receive oxygen by diffusion in about 50 msec, but a cell that is 1000 μm (1 mm) away from its oxygen supply would have to wait several minutes! At this distance, a cell could not survive if it had to depend on diffusion alone. The evolution of specialized **circulatory systems** allowed animals to increase in size and become many cells thick. A circulatory system reduces the diffusion distance that needed materials must travel. It transports oxygen, nutrients, hormones, and other materials to the interstitial fluid surrounding all the cells and removes metabolic wastes. In most animals, a circulatory system interacts with every organ system in the body.

The computed tomography (CT) scan shown on the previous page visualizes the human heart and several blood vessels. The human circulatory system, known as the **cardiovascular system,** is the focus of extensive research because cardiovascular disease is the leading cause of death in the United States and throughout the world. A major risk factor for cardiovascular disease is elevated levels of cholesterol and low-density lipoprotein (LDL) in the blood. In contrast, high-density lipoprotein (HDL) seems to play a protective role, removing excess cholesterol from the blood and tissues. Cells in the liver and certain other organs bind with the HDL, remove the cholesterol, and use it in synthesizing needed compounds.

Researchers have identified a gene in mice that codes for an HDL receptor. When investigators knock out this gene, cholesterol levels more than double. As new receptors and mechanisms involved in lipid transport and metabolism are discovered, they serve as targets for new drugs and other treatments for cardiovascular disease.

44.1 TYPES OF CIRCULATORY SYSTEMS

■ LEARNING OBJECTIVE

1   Compare and contrast internal transport in animals with no circulatory system, those with an open circulatory system, and those with a closed circulatory system.

No specialized circulatory structures are present in sponges, cnidarians (hydras, jellyfish), ctenophores (comb jellies), flatworms, or nematodes (roundworms). In cnidarians, the central gastrovascular cavity serves as a circulatory organ as well as a digestive organ (**FIG. 44-1a**). As the animal stretches and contracts, body movements stir up the contents of the gastrovascular cavity and help distribute nutrients.

The flattened body of the flatworm permits effective gas exchange by diffusion (**FIG. 44-1b**). Its branched gastrovascular cavity brings nutrients close to all the cells. As in cnidarians, circulation is aided by contractions of the body wall muscles, which move the fluid throughout the gastrovascular cavity. The branching excretory system of planarians provides for internal transport of metabolic wastes that are then expelled from the body.

Fluid in the body cavity of nematodes and other pseudocoelomate animals helps circulate materials. Nutrients, oxygen, and wastes dissolve in this fluid and diffuse through it to and from the

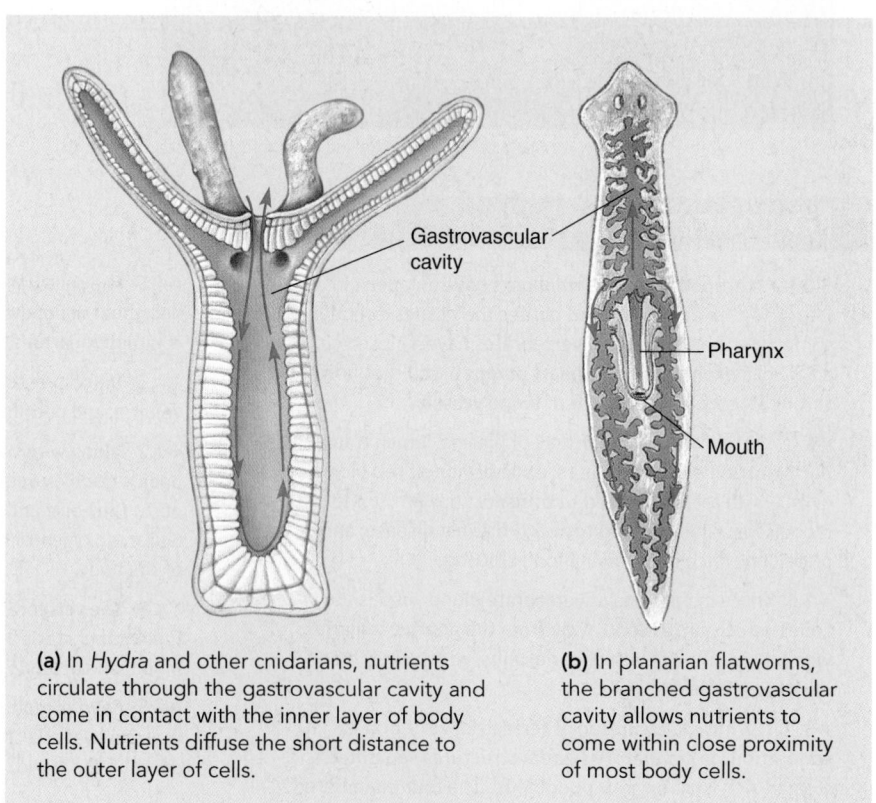

(a) In *Hydra* and other cnidarians, nutrients circulate through the gastrovascular cavity and come in contact with the inner layer of body cells. Nutrients diffuse the short distance to the outer layer of cells.

(b) In planarian flatworms, the branched gastrovascular cavity allows nutrients to come within close proximity of most body cells.

FIGURE 44-1 Invertebrates with no circulatory system
Red arrows indicate the path of nutrient circulation through the gastrovascular cavity.

cells. Body movements of the animal move the fluid and thus distribute these materials.

Larger animals require a circulatory system to efficiently distribute materials. A circulatory system typically has the following components: (1) **blood,** a connective tissue consisting of cells and cell fragments dispersed in fluid, usually called *plasma;* (2) a pumping organ, generally a **heart;** and (3) a system of **blood vessels** or spaces through which blood circulates. Two main types of circulatory systems are open and closed systems.

Many invertebrates have an open circulatory system

Arthropods and most mollusks have an **open circulatory system,** in which the heart pumps blood into vessels that have open ends. Their blood and interstitial fluid are collectively referred to as **hemolymph.** This fluid spills out of the open ends of the blood vessels, filling large spaces, called *sinuses.* The sinuses make up the **hemocoel** (blood cavity), which is not part of the coelom. (In arthropods and mollusks, the coelom is reduced.) The hemolymph bathes the cells of the body directly. Hemolymph re-enters the circulatory system through openings in the heart (in arthropods) or through open-ended vessels that lead to the gills (in mollusks).

In the open circulatory system of most mollusks, the heart has three chambers (**FIG. 44-2a**). The two *atria* receive hemolymph from the gills. Then the single *ventricle* pumps the oxygen-rich hemolymph into blood vessels that conduct it into the large sinuses of the hemocoel. After bathing the body cells, the hemolymph passes into vessels that lead to the gills, where it is recharged with oxygen. The hemolymph then returns to the heart.

Some mollusks, as well as arthropods, have a hemolymph pigment, **hemocyanin,** containing copper that transports oxygen. When oxygenated, hemocyanin is blue and imparts a bluish color to the hemolymph of these animals (the original blue bloods!).

In arthropods, a tubular heart pumps hemolymph into arteries, blood vessels that deliver it to the sinuses of the hemocoel (**FIG. 44-2b**). Hemolymph then circulates through the hemocoel, eventually returning to the pericardial cavity surrounding the heart. Hemolymph enters the heart through ostia, tiny openings equipped with valves that prevent backflow. The rate of hemolymph circulation increases when the animal moves. Thus, when an animal is active and most needs nutrients for fuel, its own movement ensures effective circulation.

In crayfish and other crustaceans, gas exchange takes place as hemolymph circulates through the gills. However, an open circulatory system cannot provide enough oxygen to maintain the active lifestyle of insects. Hemolymph mainly distributes nutrients and hormones in insects. Oxygen diffuses directly to the cells through a system of air tubes (tracheae) that make up the respiratory system (see Figure 46-2).

Some invertebrates have a closed circulatory system

Annelids, some mollusks (cephalopods), and echinoderms have a **closed circulatory system.** In them, blood flows through a continuous circuit of blood vessels. The walls of the smallest blood

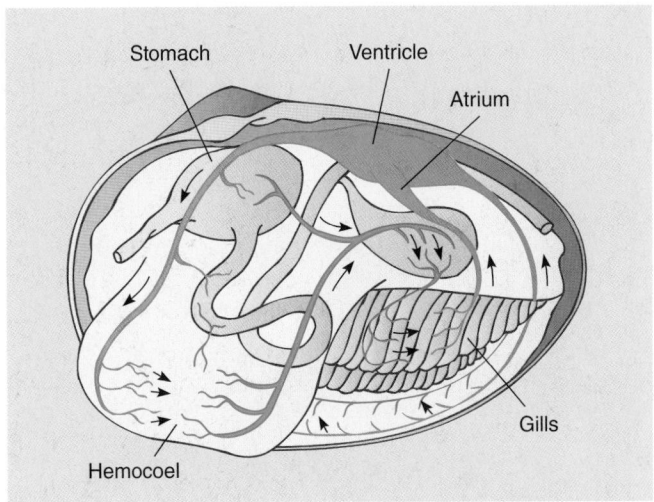

(a) In most mollusks, the heart pumps hemolymph into blood vessels that conduct it to the hemocoel. After bathing the cells, the hemolymph enters vessels that conduct it to the gills. The hemolymph is recharged with oxygen and then returned to the heart.

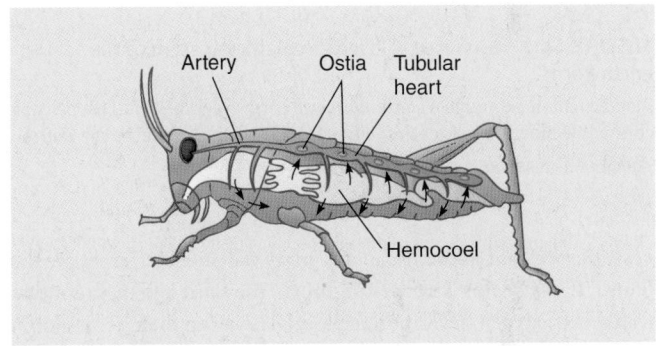

(b) In arthropods, a tubular heart pumps hemolymph into arteries that deliver it to the sinuses of the hemocoel. After circulating, hemolymph re-enters the heart through ostia in the heart wall.

FIGURE 44-2 *Animated* **Open circulatory systems**
In mollusks and arthropods, a heart pumps the blood into arteries that end in sinuses of the hemocoel. Hemolymph circulates through the hemocoel.

vessels, the *capillaries,* are thin enough to permit diffusion of gases, nutrients, and wastes between blood in the vessels and the interstitial fluid that bathes the cells.

Proboscis worms (phylum Nemertea) have a rudimentary closed circulatory system. Their system consists of a complete network of blood vessels but no heart. Blood flow depends on movements of the animal and on contractions in the walls of large blood vessels.

Earthworms and other annelids have a closed circulatory system in which two main blood vessels extend lengthwise in the body (**FIG. 44-3**). The ventral vessel conducts blood posteriorly, and the dorsal vessel conducts blood anteriorly. Dorsal and ventral vessels are connected by lateral vessels in every segment. Branches of the lateral vessels deliver blood to the surface, where it is oxygenated. In the anterior part of the worm, five pairs of contractile blood vessels (sometimes called "hearts") connect dorsal and ventral vessels. Contractions of these paired vessels and of the dorsal

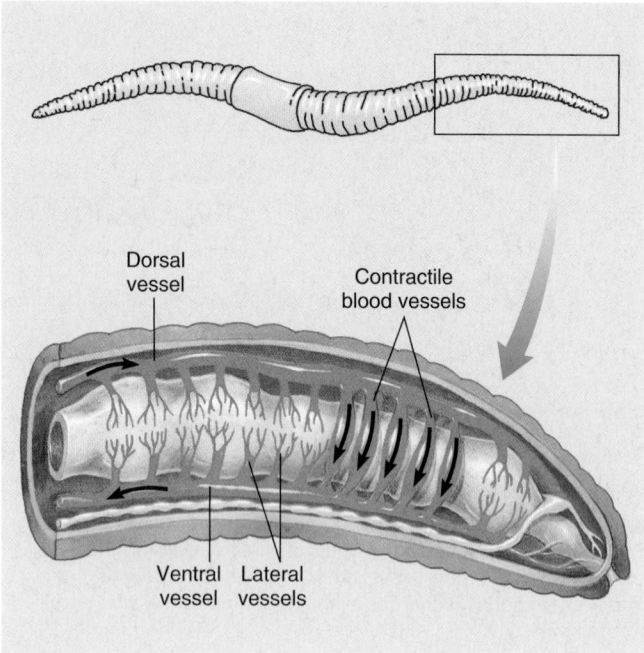

FIGURE 44-3 *Animated* **Closed circulatory system of the earthworm**

Blood circulates through a continuous system of blood vessels. Five pairs of contractile blood vessels deliver blood from the dorsal vessel to the ventral vessel.

Labels in figure: Dorsal vessel; Contractile blood vessels; Ventral vessel; Lateral vessels

vessel, as well as contraction of the body wall muscles, circulate the blood. Earthworms have **hemoglobin,** the same red pigment that transports oxygen in vertebrate blood. However, their hemoglobin is not contained within red blood cells but is dissolved in the blood plasma.

Although other mollusks have an open circulatory system, the fast-moving cephalopods, such as the squid and octopus, require a more efficient means of internal transport. They have a closed system made even more effective by accessory "hearts" at the base of the gills, which speed passage of blood through the gills.

Vertebrates have a closed circulatory system

All vertebrates have a ventral, muscular heart that pumps blood into a closed system of blood vessels. **Capillaries,** the tiniest blood vessels, have very thin walls that permit exchange of materials between blood and interstitial fluid. The vertebrate circulatory system consists of heart, blood vessels, blood, lymph, lymph vessels, and associated organs such as the thymus, spleen, and liver. This system performs several functions:

1. Transports nutrients from the digestive system and from storage depots to each cell
2. Transports oxygen from respiratory structures (gills or lungs) to the cells
3. Transports metabolic wastes from each cell to organs that excrete them
4. Transports hormones from endocrine glands to target tissues
5. Helps maintain fluid balance

6. Helps distribute metabolic heat within the body, which helps maintain a constant body temperature in endothermic animals
7. Helps maintain appropriate pH
8. Defends the body against invading microorganisms

Review

- How are nutrients and oxygen transported to the body cells in a hydra, flatworm, earthworm, insect, and frog?
- How does an open circulatory system differ from a closed circulatory system?
- What are five functions of the vertebrate circulatory system?

44.2 VERTEBRATE BLOOD

■ **LEARNING OBJECTIVES**

2   Compare the structure and function of plasma, red blood cells, white blood cells, and platelets.

3   Summarize the sequence of events involved in blood clotting.

In vertebrates, blood consists of a pale yellowish fluid called **plasma,** in which red blood cells, white blood cells, and platelets are suspended (**FIG. 44-4** and **TABLE 44-1**). In humans the total circulating blood volume is approximately 5 L (5.3 qt) in an adult female and about 5.5 L (5.8 qt) in an adult male. About 55% of the blood volume is plasma. The remaining 45% is made up of blood cells and platelets. Because cells and platelets are heavier than plasma, they can be separated from it by centrifugation. Plasma does not separate from blood cells in the body because the blood is constantly mixed as it circulates in the blood vessels.

Plasma is the fluid component of blood

Plasma consists of water (about 92%), proteins (about 7%), salts, and a variety of materials being transported, such as dissolved gases, nutrients, wastes, and hormones. Plasma is in dynamic equilibrium with the interstitial fluid bathing the cells and with the intracellular fluid. As blood passes through the capillaries, substances continuously move into and out of the plasma. Any deviation from its normal composition signals one or more organs to restore homeostasis.

Plasma contains several kinds of **plasma proteins,** each with specific properties and functions: **fibrinogen;** alpha, beta, and gamma **globulins;** and **albumin.** Fibrinogen is one of the proteins involved in the clotting process. When the proteins involved in blood clotting have been removed from the plasma, the remaining liquid is called **serum.** Alpha globulins include certain hormones and proteins that transport hormones; prothrombin, a protein involved in blood clotting; and high-density lipoproteins (HDL), which transport fats and cholesterol. Beta globulins include other lipoproteins that transport fats and cholesterol, as well as proteins that transport certain vitamins and minerals. The **gamma globulin** fraction of plasma contains many types of antibodies that provide immunity to diseases such as measles and infectious hepatitis. Purified human gamma globulin is sometimes used to treat certain diseases or to reduce the possibility of contracting a disease.

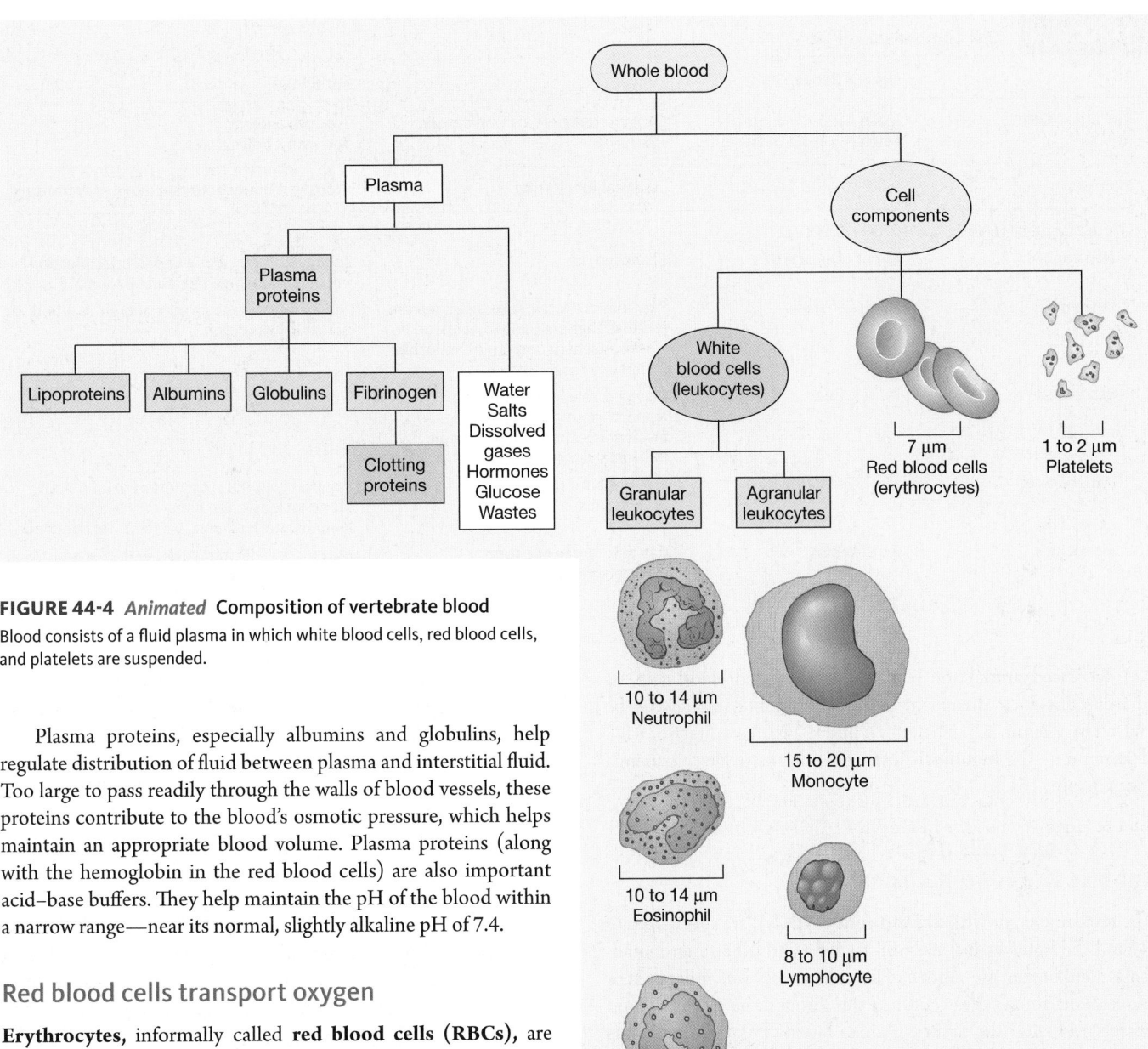

FIGURE 44-4 *Animated* **Composition of vertebrate blood**
Blood consists of a fluid plasma in which white blood cells, red blood cells, and platelets are suspended.

Plasma proteins, especially albumins and globulins, help regulate distribution of fluid between plasma and interstitial fluid. Too large to pass readily through the walls of blood vessels, these proteins contribute to the blood's osmotic pressure, which helps maintain an appropriate blood volume. Plasma proteins (along with the hemoglobin in the red blood cells) are also important acid–base buffers. They help maintain the pH of the blood within a narrow range—near its normal, slightly alkaline pH of 7.4.

Red blood cells transport oxygen

Erythrocytes, informally called **red blood cells (RBCs),** are highly specialized for transporting oxygen. In most vertebrates except mammals, circulating RBCs have nuclei. For example, birds have large, oval, nucleated RBCs. In mammals, the nucleus is ejected from the RBC as the cell develops. Each mammalian RBC is a flexible, biconcave disc 7 to 8 μm in diameter and 1 to 2 μm thick. An internal elastic framework maintains the disc shape and permits the cell to bend and twist as it passes through blood vessels even smaller than its own diameter. Its biconcave shape provides a high ratio of surface area to volume, allowing efficient diffusion of oxygen and carbon dioxide into and out of the cell. In an adult human, about 30 trillion RBCs circulate in the blood, approximately 5 million per μL.

Erythrocytes are produced within the red bone marrow of certain bones: vertebrae, ribs, breastbone, skull bones, and long bones. As an RBC develops, it produces large quantities of **hemoglobin,** the oxygen-transporting pigment that gives vertebrate blood its red color. (Oxygen transport is discussed in Chapter 46.) The lifespan of a human RBC is about 120 days. As blood circulates through the liver and spleen, phagocytic cells remove worn-out RBCs from the circulation. These RBCs are then disassembled, and some of their components are recycled. In the human body, more than 2.4 million RBCs are destroyed every second, so an equal number must be produced in the bone marrow to replace them. Red blood cell production is regulated by the hormone **erythropoietin,** which the kidneys release in response to a decrease in oxygen.

Anemia is a deficiency in hemoglobin (often accompanied by a decrease in the number of RBCs). When hemoglobin is insufficient, the amount of oxygen transported is inadequate to supply the body's needs. An anemic person may complain of feeling weak and may become easily fatigued. Three general causes of anemia are (1) loss of blood from hemorrhage or internal bleeding;

TABLE 44-1   Cell Components of Blood

	Normal Range	Function	Pathology
Red Blood Cells (RBCs)	Male: 4.2–5.4 million/μL Female: 3.6–5.0 million/μL	Oxygen transport; carbon dioxide transport	Too few: anemia Too many: polycythemia
Platelets	150,000–400,000/μL	Essential for clotting	Clotting malfunctions; bleeding; easy bruising
White Blood Cells (WBCs)	5000–10,000/μL		
Neutrophils	About 60% of WBCs	Phagocytosis	Too many: may be due to bacterial infection, inflammation, myelogenous leukemia
Eosinophils	1%–3% of WBCs	Play role in allergic responses; release proteins that are toxic to parasitic worms; release compounds important in immune responses	Too many: may result from allergic reaction, parasitic infestation
Basophils	1% of WBCs	May play role in prevention of inappropriate clotting; release histamine, which is important in inflammatory responses	
Lymphocytes	25%–35% of WBCs	Produce antibodies; destroy foreign cells	Atypical lymphocytes present in infectious mononucleosis; too many may be due to lymphocytic leukemia, certain viral infections
Monocytes	6% of WBCs	Can differentiate to form macrophages and dendritic cells	May increase in monocytic leukemia and fungal infections

(2) decreased production of hemoglobin or red blood cells, as in iron-deficiency anemia or pernicious anemia (which can be caused by vitamin B_{12} deficiency); and (3) increased rate of RBC destruction—the **hemolytic anemias,** such as sickle cell anemia (see Chapter 16).

White blood cells defend the body against disease organisms

The **leukocytes,** or **white blood cells (WBCs),** are specialized to defend the body against harmful bacteria and other microorganisms. Leukocytes are amoeba-like cells capable of independent movement. Some types routinely slip through the walls of blood vessels and enter the tissues. Human blood contains three kinds of granular leukocytes and two types of agranular leukocytes (see Fig. 44-4). Both types are manufactured in the red bone marrow.

The **granular leukocytes** are characterized by large, lobed nuclei and distinctive granules in their cytoplasm. The three varieties of granular leukocytes are the neutrophils, eosinophils, and basophils. **Neutrophils,** the principal phagocytic cells in the blood, are especially adept at seeking out and ingesting bacteria. They also phagocytose dead cells, a cleanup task that is especially demanding after injury or infection. Most granules in neutrophils contain enzymes that digest ingested material.

Eosinophils have large granules that stain bright red with eosin, an acidic dye. Eosinophils increase in number during allergic reactions and during parasitic (for example, tapeworm) infestations. The lysosomes of these WBCs contain enzymes such as peroxidases that degrade the cell membranes of parasitic worms and protozoa. These substances may also injure normal tissue. Eosiniphils also produce substances that promote inflammation.

Basophils exhibit deep blue granules when stained with basic dyes. Like eosinophils, these cells play a role in allergic reactions.

Basophils do not contain lysosomes. Granules in their cytoplasm contain **histamine,** a substance that dilates blood vessels and makes capillaries more permeable. Basophils release histamine in injured tissues and in allergic responses. Other basophil granules contain **heparin,** which speeds up fat removal from the blood after you eat a meal high in fat. Heparin is an anticoagulant that may help prevent blood from clotting inappropriately within the blood vessels.

Agranular leukocytes lack large, distinctive granules, and their nuclei are rounded or kidney-shaped. Two types of agranular leukocytes are lymphocytes and monocytes. Some **lymphocytes** are specialized to produce antibodies, whereas others directly attack foreign invaders such as bacteria or viruses (discussed in Chapter 45).

Monocytes are the largest WBCs, reaching 20 μm in diameter. During infection, monocytes migrate from the blood into the tissues. They can phagocytose cells and remove toxic molecules. Monocytes can also differentiate into macrophages or dendritic cells. **Macrophages** are giant scavenger cells that voraciously engulf bacteria, dead cells, and debris. **Dendritic cells** are also important cells of the immune system. For example, some dendritic cells produce compounds that help the body fight viral infection. We will discuss macrophages and dendritic cells further in Chapter 45.

Human blood normally has about 7000 WBCs per μL of blood (only 1 for every 700 RBCs). During bacterial infections the number may rise sharply, so a WBC count is useful in diagnosis. The proportion of each kind of WBC is determined by a differential WBC count. The normal distribution of WBCs is indicated in Table 44-1.

Leukemia is a form of cancer in which any one of the various kinds of WBCs multiplies rapidly within the bone marrow. Many of these cells do not mature, and their large numbers crowd out developing RBCs and platelets, leading to anemia and impaired clotting. A common cause of death from leukemia is internal hemorrhaging, especially in the brain. Another frequent cause of death is infection; although the WBC count may rise dramatically, the cells are immature and abnormal and cannot defend the body against disease organisms.

Leukemia is treated with chemotherapy, and sometimes with radiation therapy or bone marrow transplant. Thanks to new treatments, survival rates for individuals with leukemia have increased sharply during the past few years, particularly for children. For example, the survival rate for children younger than five years old with acute lymphocytic leukemia is more than 90%.

Platelets function in blood clotting

In most vertebrates other than mammals, the blood contains small, oval, nucleated cells called **thrombocytes** that function in blood clotting. Mammals have **platelets,** tiny spherical or disc-shaped bits of cytoplasm that lack nuclei. About 300,000 platelets per μL are present in human blood. Platelets are pinched off from very large cells in the bone marrow. Thus, a platelet is not a whole cell but a fragment of cytoplasm enclosed by a membrane.

Platelets function in blood clotting and may also stimulate the immune system. When a blood vessel is cut, it constricts to reduce blood loss. Platelets physically patch the break by sticking to the rough, cut edges of the vessel. As platelets begin to gather, they release substances that attract other platelets. The platelets become sticky and adhere to collagen fibers in the blood vessel wall. Within about 5 minutes after injury, they form a platelet plug, or temporary clot.

At the same time that the temporary clot forms, a stronger, more permanent clot begins to develop. More than 30 chemical substances interact in this complex process. The series of reactions that leads to clotting is triggered when one of the clotting factors in the blood is activated by contact with the injured tissue. In **hemophilia,** one clotting factor is absent, as a result of an inherited genetic mutation (see Chapter 16).

Prothrombin, a plasma protein manufactured in the liver, requires vitamin K for its production. In the presence of clotting factors, calcium ions, and compounds released from platelets, prothrombin is converted to **thrombin.** Then thrombin catalyzes the conversion of the soluble plasma protein **fibrinogen** to an insoluble protein, **fibrin.** Once formed, fibrin polymerizes, producing long threads that stick to the damaged surface of the blood vessel and form the webbing of the clot. These threads trap blood cells and platelets, which help strengthen the clot. The clotting process is summarized in **FIGURE 44-5.**

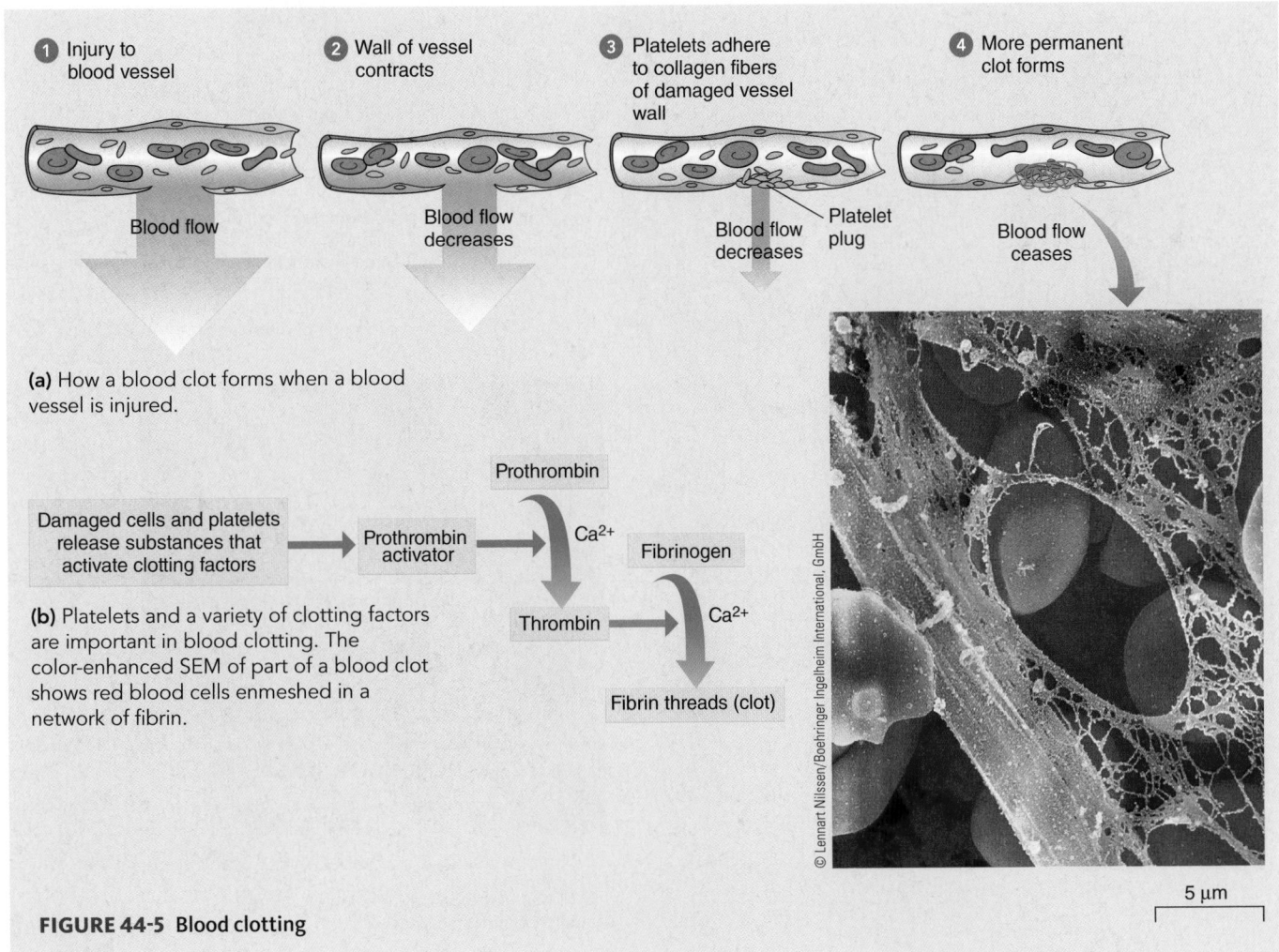

① Injury to blood vessel

② Wall of vessel contracts

③ Platelets adhere to collagen fibers of damaged vessel wall

④ More permanent clot forms

Blood flow

Blood flow decreases

Blood flow decreases

Platelet plug

Blood flow ceases

(a) How a blood clot forms when a blood vessel is injured.

Damaged cells and platelets release substances that activate clotting factors → Prothrombin activator → Prothrombin + Ca^{2+} → Thrombin + Fibrinogen + Ca^{2+} → Fibrin threads (clot)

(b) Platelets and a variety of clotting factors are important in blood clotting. The color-enhanced SEM of part of a blood clot shows red blood cells enmeshed in a network of fibrin.

© Lennart Nilsson/Boehringer Ingelheim International, GmbH

5 µm

FIGURE 44-5 Blood clotting

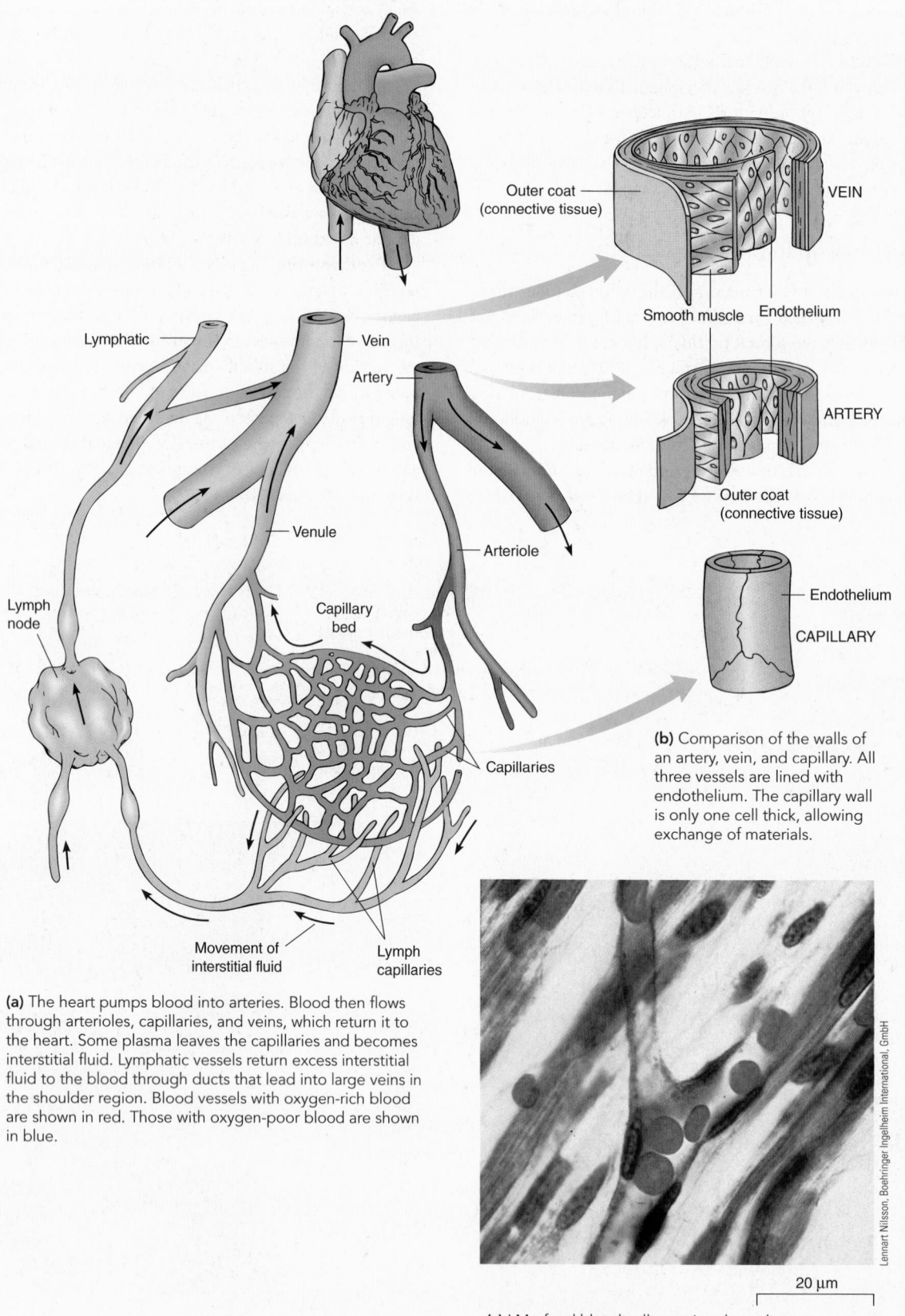

Outer coat (connective tissue)

VEIN

Smooth muscle   Endothelium

Lymphatic

Vein

Artery

ARTERY

Venule

Arteriole

Outer coat (connective tissue)

Lymph node

Capillary bed

Endothelium

CAPILLARY

Capillaries

(b) Comparison of the walls of an artery, vein, and capillary. All three vessels are lined with endothelium. The capillary wall is only one cell thick, allowing exchange of materials.

Movement of interstitial fluid

Lymph capillaries

(a) The heart pumps blood into arteries. Blood then flows through arterioles, capillaries, and veins, which return it to the heart. Some plasma leaves the capillaries and becomes interstitial fluid. Lymphatic vessels return excess interstitial fluid to the blood through ducts that lead into large veins in the shoulder region. Blood vessels with oxygen-rich blood are shown in red. Those with oxygen-poor blood are shown in blue.

20 μm

Lennart Nilsson, Boehringer Ingelheim International, GmbH

(c) LM of red blood cells passing through capillaries almost in single file.

FIGURE 44-6 *Animated* **Blood and lymphatic vessels**

Review

- What are the functions of the main groups of plasma proteins?
- What is the function of red blood cells? of neutrophils?
- What are the major steps in blood clotting?

44.3 VERTEBRATE BLOOD VESSELS

◼ LEARNING OBJECTIVE

4   Compare the structure and function of different types of blood vessels, including arteries, arterioles, capillaries, and veins.

The vertebrate circulatory system includes three main types of blood vessels: arteries, capillaries, and veins (**FIG. 44-6**). An **artery** carries blood away from a heart chamber toward other tissues. When an artery enters an organ, it divides into many smaller branches called **arterioles.** The arterioles deliver blood into the microscopic **capillaries.** After blood circulates through capillary networks within an organ or tissues, capillaries merge to form **veins** that channel the blood back toward the heart.

The wall of an artery or vein has three layers (see Fig. 44-6b). The innermost layer, which lines the blood vessel, consists mainly of **endothelium,** a tissue that resembles squamous epithelium (see Chapter 39). The middle layer is connective tissue and smooth muscle cells, and the outer coat is connective tissue rich in elastic and collagen fibers.

Gases and nutrients cannot pass through the thick walls of arteries and veins. Materials are exchanged between the blood and interstitial fluid bathing the cells through the capillary walls, which are only one cell thick. Capillary networks in the body are so extensive that at least one of these tiny vessels is located close to every cell in the body. The total length of all capillaries in the body has been estimated to be more than 96,000 km!

Smooth muscle in the arteriole wall can constrict (**vasoconstriction**) or relax (**vasodilation**), changing the radius of the arteriole. Such changes help maintain appropriate blood pressure and help control the volume of blood passing to a particular tissue. Changes in blood flow are regulated by the nervous system in response to the metabolic needs of the tissue, as well as by the demands of the body as a whole. For example, when a tissue is metabolizing rapidly, it needs more nutrients and oxygen. During exercise, arterioles within skeletal muscles dilate, increasing by more than tenfold the amount of blood flowing to these muscle tissues.

If all your blood vessels dilated at the same time, you would not have enough blood to fill them completely. Normally, your liver, kidneys, and brain receive the lion's share of blood. However, if an emergency suddenly occurred requiring rapid action, your blood would be rerouted quickly in favor of the heart and muscles. At such a time, the digestive system and kidneys can do with less blood because they are not crucial in responding to the crisis.

The small vessels that directly link arterioles with venules (small veins) are **metarterioles.** The true capillaries branch off from the metarterioles and then rejoin them (**FIG. 44-7**). True capillaries also interconnect with one another. Wherever a capillary branches from a metarteriole, a smooth muscle cell serves as a *precapillary sphincter* that opens and closes continuously, directing blood first to one and then to another section of tissue. These precapillary sphincters (along with the smooth muscle in the walls of arteries and arterioles) regulate the blood supply to each organ and its subdivisions.

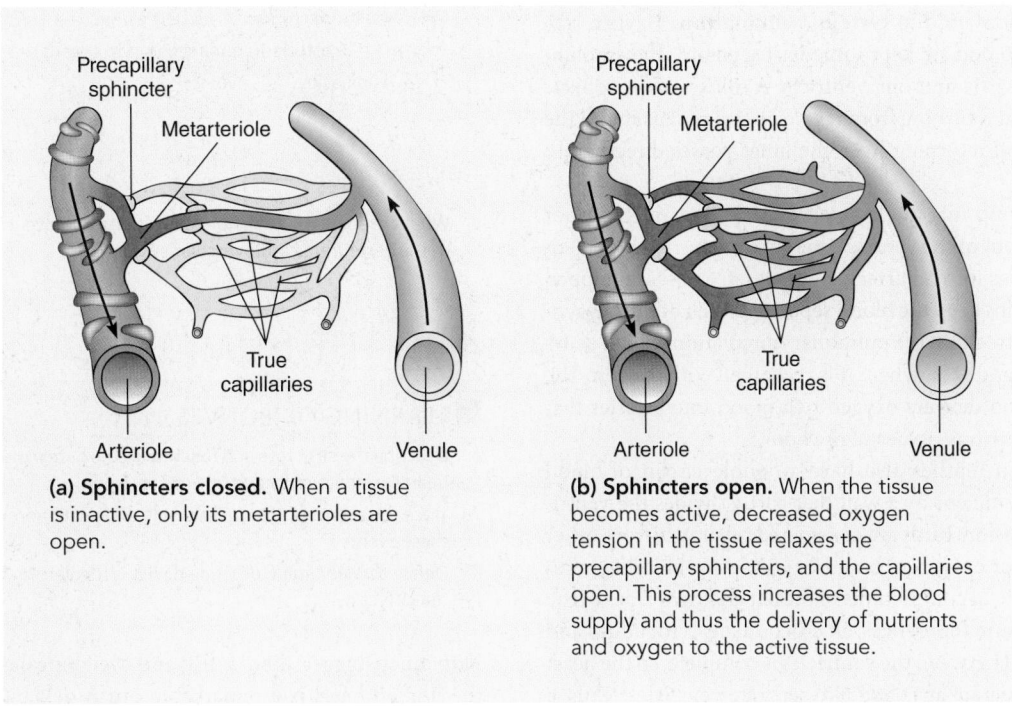

(a) Sphincters closed. When a tissue is inactive, only its metarterioles are open.

(b) Sphincters open. When the tissue becomes active, decreased oxygen tension in the tissue relaxes the precapillary sphincters, and the capillaries open. This process increases the blood supply and thus the delivery of nutrients and oxygen to the active tissue.

FIGURE 44-7 Blood flow through a capillary network
As a tissue becomes active, the pattern of blood flow through its capillary networks changes.

44.4 EVOLUTION OF THE VERTEBRATE CARDIOVASCULAR SYSTEM

■ LEARNING OBJECTIVE

5 Trace the evolution of the vertebrate cardiovascular system from fish to mammal.

The vertebrate cardiovascular system became modified in the course of evolution, as the site of gas exchange shifted from gills to lungs and as certain vertebrates became active, endothermic animals with higher metabolic rates. The vertebrate heart has one or two **atria** (sing., *atrium*), chambers that receive blood returning from the tissues, and one or two **ventricles** that pump blood into the arteries (**FIG. 44-8**). Vertebrates in some groups have additional chambers.

The fish heart has one atrium and one ventricle. The atrium pumps blood into the ventricle, which pumps blood into a single circuit of blood vessels. Blood is oxygenated as it passes through capillaries in the gills. After blood circulates through the gill capillaries, its pressure is low, so blood passes very slowly to the other organs. The fish's swimming movements facilitate circulation. Blood returning to the heart has a low oxygen content. A thin-walled sinus venosus receives blood returning from the tissues and pumps it into the atrium.

In amphibians, blood flows through a double circuit: the **pulmonary circulation** and the **systemic circulation.** Oxygen-rich and oxygen-poor blood are kept somewhat separate. The amphibian heart has two atria and one ventricle. A *sinus venosus* collects oxygen-poor blood returning from the veins and pumps it into the right atrium. Blood returning from the lungs passes directly into the left atrium.

Both atria pump into the single ventricle, but oxygen-poor blood is pumped out of the ventricle before oxygen-rich blood enters it. Blood passes into an artery, the *conus arteriosus,* equipped with a fold that helps keep the blood separate. Much of the oxygen-poor blood is directed into the pulmonary circulation, which delivers it to the lungs and skin, where it is recharged with oxygen. The systemic circulation delivers oxygen-rich blood into arteries that conduct it to the various tissues of the body.

Most nonavian reptiles also have a double circuit of blood flow, made more efficient by a wall that partly divides the ventricles. (In this discussion, birds are considered separately from other reptiles.) Mixing of oxygen-rich and oxygen-poor blood is minimized by the timing of contractions of the left and right sides of the heart and by pressure differences. In crocodilians (crocodiles and alligators), the wall between the ventricles is complete, so the heart consists of two separate atria and two separate ventricles. Thus, a four-chambered heart first evolved among the nonavian reptiles. In contrast to birds and mammals, amphibians and nonavian rep-

tiles do not ventilate their lungs continuously. Therefore, it would be inefficient to pump blood through the pulmonary circulation continuously. The shunts between the two sides of the heart allow blood to be distributed to the lungs as needed.

In all birds and mammals (and in crocodilians), the *septum* (wall) between the ventricles is complete. Biologists hypothesize that the completely divided heart evolved twice during the course of vertebrate evolution; first in the crocodilian–bird clade and then independently in mammals. The septum between the ventricles prevents oxygen-rich blood in the left chamber from mixing with oxygen-poor blood in the right chamber. The conus arteriosus has split and become the base of the **aorta** (the largest artery) and the pulmonary artery. No sinus venosus is present as a separate chamber, but a vestige remains as the *sinoatrial node* (the pacemaker).

Complete separation of the right and left sides of the heart requires blood to pass through the heart twice each time it tours the body. The complete double circuit allows birds and mammals to maintain relatively high blood pressures in the systemic circulation and modest pressures in the pulmonary circulation. The higher pressure is necessary for efficient circulation of blood through the body. However, the delicate air sacs and capillaries of the lungs would be damaged by this pressure.

The double circulatory circuit delivers materials to the tissues rapidly and efficiently. Because their blood contains more oxygen per unit volume and circulates more rapidly than in other vertebrates, the tissues of birds and mammals receive more oxygen. As a result, these animals can maintain a higher metabolic rate and a constant high body temperature even in cold surroundings.

The pattern of blood circulation in birds and mammals can be summarized as follows:

veins (conduct blood from organs) ⟶ right atrium ⟶ right ventricle ⟶ pulmonary arteries ⟶ capillaries in the lungs ⟶ pulmonary veins ⟶ left atrium ⟶ left ventricle ⟶ aorta ⟶ arteries (conduct blood to organs) ⟶ arterioles ⟶ capillaries ⟶ veins

Review

- What are some of the major adaptations that occurred in the evolution of the vertebrate cardiovascular system?

44.5 THE HUMAN HEART

■ LEARNING OBJECTIVES

6 Describe the structure and function of the human heart. (Include the heart's conduction system in your answer.)
7 Trace the events of the cardiac cycle and relate normal heart sounds to these events.
8 Define *cardiac output*, describe how it is regulated, and identify factors that affect it.

Not much bigger than a fist and weighing less than a pound, the human heart is a remarkable organ that beats about 2.5 billion times in an average lifetime, pumping about 300 million L (80 million gallons) of blood. To meet the body's changing needs,

The four-chambered heart and double circuit that separates oxygen-rich from oxygen-poor blood are important adaptations that evolved as vertebrates diversified and some became active, terrestrial, endothermic animals.

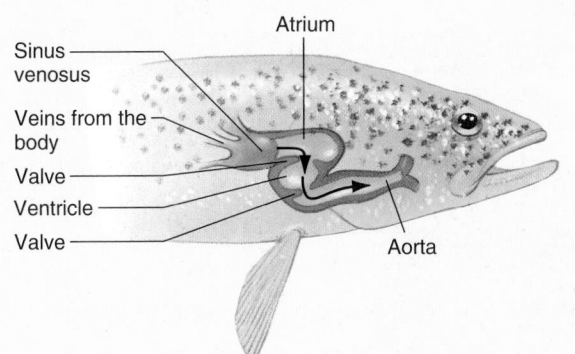

(a) Fishes. The single atrium and ventricle of the fish heart are part of a single circuit of blood flow.

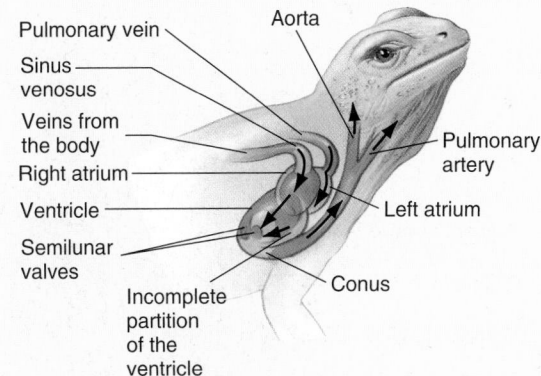

(c) Reptiles (except birds). The reptilian heart has two atria and two ventricles. In most nonavian reptiles, the wall separating the ventricles is incomplete, so blood from the right and left chambers mixes to some extent. In crocodiles and alligators, the septum is complete and the heart consists of four separate chambers.

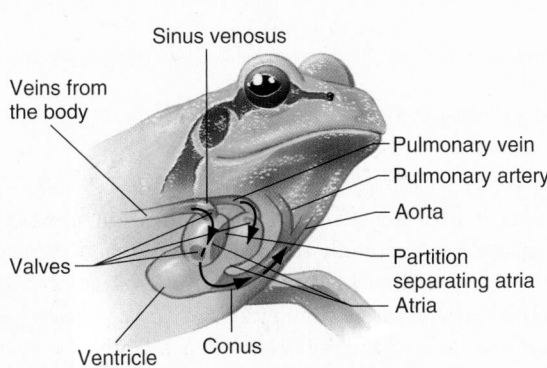

(b) Amphibians. In amphibians, the heart consists of two atria and one ventricle; blood flows through a double circuit.

(d) Birds and mammals. In birds and mammals, the two atria and two ventricles separate oxygen-rich blood from oxygen-poor blood.

FIGURE 44-8 Evolution of the vertebrate cardiovascular system

the heart can vary its output from 5 L to more than 20 L of blood per minute.

Your heart is a hollow, muscular organ located in the chest cavity directly under the breastbone. Its wall consists mainly of cardiac muscle attached to a framework of collagen fibers. The **pericardium,** a tough connective tissue sac, encloses the heart. A smooth layer of endothelium covers the inner surface of the pericardium and the outer surface of the heart. Between these two surfaces is a small **pericardial cavity** filled with fluid, which reduces friction to a minimum as the heart beats.

A wall, or **septum,** separates the right atrium and ventricle from the left atrium and ventricle. Between the atria, the wall is

known as the **interatrial septum;** between the ventricles, the **interventricular septum.** A shallow depression, the **fossa ovalis,** on the interatrial septum marks the place where an opening, the **foramen ovale,** was located in the fetal heart. In the fetus, the foramen ovale lets the blood flow directly from right to left atrium, so very little passes to the nonfunctional lungs. A small muscular pouch, called an **auricle,** lies at the upper surface of each atrium.

To keep blood from flowing backward, the heart has valves that close automatically (**FIG. 44-9**). The valve between the right atrium and right ventricle is called the **right atrioventricular (AV) valve,** or **tricuspid valve.** The **left AV valve** (between the left atrium and left ventricle) is the **mitral valve,** or **bicuspid valve.** The AV valves

Superior vena cava

Right pulmonary arteries

Pulmonary valve

Right atrium

Pulmonary veins

Tricuspid valve

Right ventricle

Inferior vena cava

Aorta

Left pulmonary arteries

Pulmonary artery

Pulmonary veins

Left atrium

Mitral valve

Aortic valve

Chordae tendineae ("heartstrings")

Papillary muscles

Left ventricle

Interventricular septum

Aorta

FIGURE 44-9 *Animated* Section through the human heart showing the valves
Note the right and left atria, which receive blood, and the right and left ventricles, which pump blood into the arteries. Arrows indicate the direction of blood flow.

are held in place by stout cords, or "heartstrings," the **chordae tendineae.** These cords attach the valves to the papillary muscles that project from the walls of the ventricles.

When blood returning from the tissues fills the atria, blood pressure on the AV valves forces them to open into the ventricles, filling the ventricles with blood. As the ventricles contract, blood is forced back against the AV valves, pushing them closed. Contraction of the papillary muscles and tensing of the chordae tendineae prevent the valves from opening backward into the atria. These valves are like swinging doors that open in only one direction.

Semilunar valves (named for their flaps, which are shaped like half-moons) guard the exits from the heart. The semilunar valve between the left ventricle and the aorta is the **aortic valve,** and the one between the right ventricle and the pulmonary artery is the **pulmonary valve.** When blood passes out of the ventricles, the flaps of the semilunar valves are pushed aside and offer no resistance to blood flow. But when the ventricles are relaxing and filling with blood from the atria, blood pressure in the arteries is higher than in the ventricles. Blood then fills the pouches of the valves, stretching them across the artery so blood cannot flow back into the ventricle.

Each heartbeat is initiated by a pacemaker

Horror films sometimes feature a scene in which a heart cut out of a human body continues to beat. Scriptwriters of these tales

actually have some factual basis for their gruesome fantasies because a heart carefully removed from the body can continue to beat for many hours if kept in a nutritive, oxygenated fluid. This is possible because the contractions of cardiac muscle begin within the muscle itself and can occur independently of any nerve supply (**FIG. 44-10a**).

At their ends cardiac muscle cells are joined by dense bands called **intercalated discs** (**FIGS. 44-10b** and **c**). These complex junctions contain *gap junctions.* Recall from Chapter 5 that in a gap junction, two cells connect through pores. Gap junctions are of great physiological importance because they offer very little resistance to the passage of an action potential. Ions move easily through the gap junctions, allowing the entire atrial (or ventricular) muscle mass to contract as one giant cell.

Compared with skeletal muscle that has action potentials typically lasting 1 to 2 milliseconds, the action potentials of cardiac muscle are much longer, several hundred milliseconds. Voltage-activated Ca^{2+} channels open during depolarization of cardiac muscle fibers. Entry of Ca^{2+} contributes to the longer depolarization time. Another factor is a type of K^+ channel that stays open when the cell is at its resting potential but closes during depolarization, lengthening depolarization time by decreasing the permeability of the membrane to K^+. From experiments on isolated cardiac muscle fibers, investigators determined that spontaneous contraction results from the combination of a slow decrease in K^+ permeability and a slow increase in Na^+ and Ca^{2+} permeability.

SA node or pacemaker
Right atrium
AV node
Purkinje fibers
Right ventricle

Left atrium
AV bundle
Left ventricle
Right and left branches of AV bundle

(a) The sinoatrial (SA) node initiates each heartbeat. The action potential spreads through the muscle fibers of the atria, producing atrial contraction. Transmission is briefly delayed at the atrioventricular (AV) node before the action potential spreads through specialized muscle fibers into the ventricles.

Ed Reschke

Nucleus

(b) LM of cardiac muscle.

25 μm

Intercalated discs

Don Fawcett/Visuals Unlimited

Z-line

Mitochondria

(c) TEM of cardiac muscle.

1 μm

FIGURE 44-10 *Animated* **Conduction system of the heart**
When action potentials are initiated by the pacemaker cells in the SA node, the gap junctions within the intercalated discs allow the impulses to spread easily from one cardiac muscle fiber to the next within the atria (and within the ventricles). The atria (and then the ventricles) contract as a functional unit.

A specialized conduction system ensures that the heart beats in a regular and effective rhythm. Each beat is initiated by the **pacemaker,** a small mass of specialized cardiac muscle fibers in the **sinoatrial (SA) node.** The SA node is located in the posterior wall of the right atrium near the opening of a large vein, the superior vena cava. The action potential in the SA node is triggered mainly by the opening of Ca^{2+} channels. Ends of the SA node fibers fuse with ordinary atrial muscle fibers, so each action potential spreads through the cardiac muscle fibers of both atria, producing atrial contraction.

One group of atrial muscle fibers conducts the action potential directly to the **atrioventricular (AV) node,** located in the right atrium along the lower part of the septum. Here transmission is delayed briefly so that the atria finish contracting before the ventricles begin to contract. From the AV node, the action potential spreads into specialized muscle fibers that make up the **AV bundle.** The AV bundle divides, sending branches into each ventricle. Fibers of the bundle branches divide further, eventually forming small *Purkinje fibers.* These fibers conduct impulses to the muscle fibers of both ventricles.

SA node ⟶ atrial muscle fibers (atria contract) ⟶ AV node ⟶ AV bundle ⟶ right and left bundle branches ⟶ Purkinje fibers ⟶ conduct impulses to muscle fibers of both ventricles ⟶ ventricles contract

As each wave of contraction spreads through the heart, electric currents flow into the tissues surrounding the heart and onto the body surface. By placing electrodes on the body surface on opposite sides of the heart, a physician can amplify and record the electrical activity. The graph produced is called an **electrocardiogram (EKG** or **ECG).** Abnormalities in the EKG indicate disorders in the heart or its rhythm. For example, in **heart block,** impulse transmission is delayed or blocked at some point in the conduction system. **Artificial pacemakers** can help patients with severe heart block. The pacemaker is implanted beneath the skin and its electrodes connected to the heart. This device provides continuous rhythmic impulses that avoid the block and drive the heartbeat.

The cardiac cycle consists of alternating periods of contraction and relaxation

Each minute the heart beats about 70 times. One complete heartbeat takes about 0.8 second and is referred to as a **cardiac cycle.** That portion of the cycle in which contraction occurs is known as **systole;** the period of relaxation is **diastole. FIGURE 44-11** shows the sequence of events that occur during one cardiac cycle.

When you listen to the heartbeat with a stethoscope, you can hear two main heart sounds, "lub-dup," which repeat rhythmically. These sounds result from the heart valves closing. When the valves close, they cause turbulence in blood flow that sets up vibrations in the walls of the heart chambers. The first heart sound, "lub," is low-pitched, not very loud, and fairly long-lasting. It is caused mainly by the closing of the AV (mitral and tricuspid) valves and marks the beginning of ventricular systole. The "lub" sound is quickly followed by the higher-pitched, louder, sharper, and shorter "dup" sound. Heard almost as a quick snap, the "dup" marks the closing of the semilunar valves and the beginning of ventricular diastole.

The rhythmic changes in electrical activity of the heart are responsible for the cardiac cycle, the pattern of contraction and relaxation that takes place during each heartbeat.

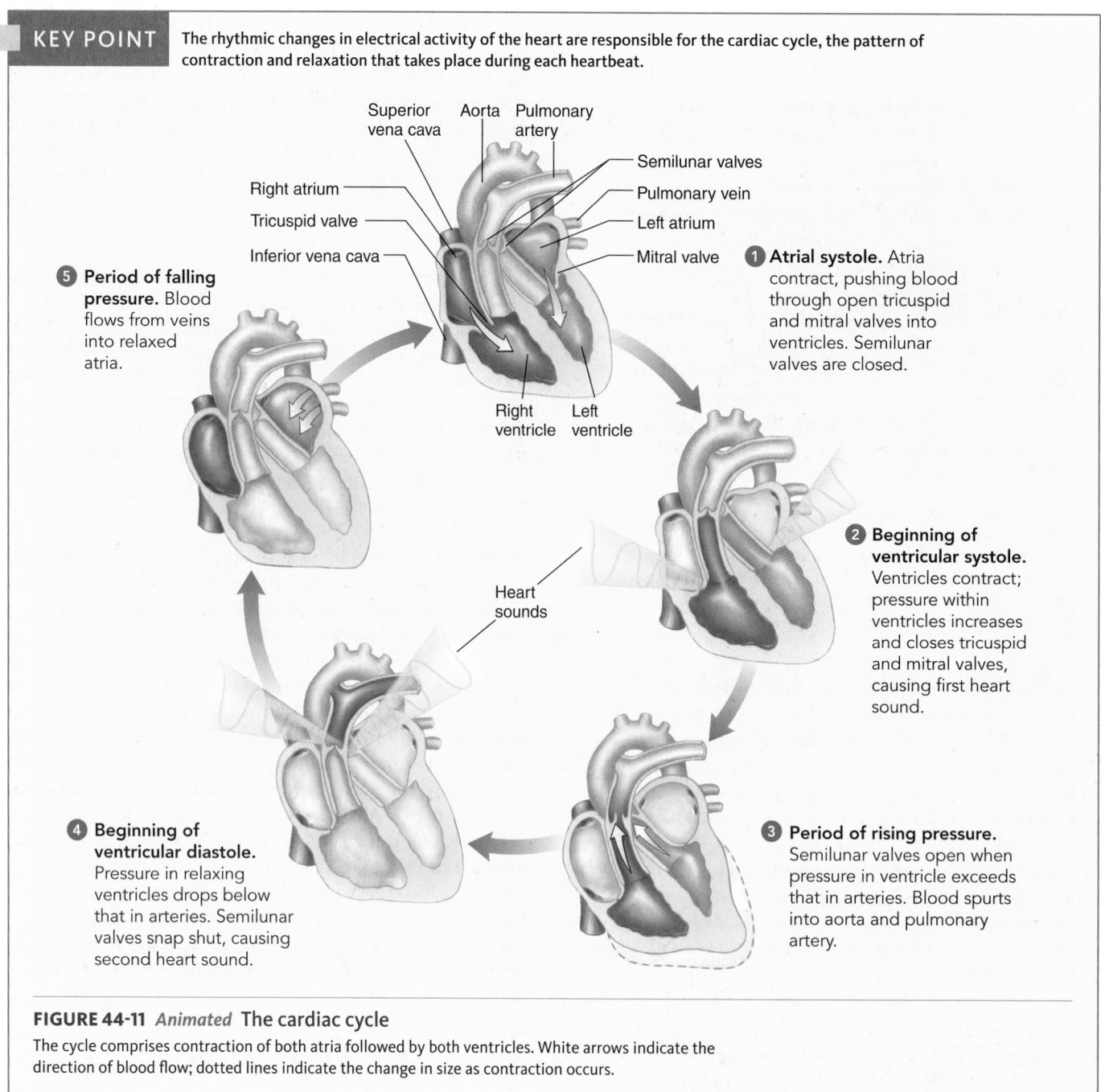

FIGURE 44-11 *Animated* **The cardiac cycle**

The cycle comprises contraction of both atria followed by both ventricles. White arrows indicate the direction of blood flow; dotted lines indicate the change in size as contraction occurs.

The quality of these sounds tells a discerning physician much about the state of the valves. For example, when a valve does not close tightly, blood may flow backward. When the semilunar valves are injured, a soft, hissing noise ("lub-shhh") known as a **heart murmur** is heard in place of the normal sound. Valve deformities are sometimes present at birth, or they may result from certain diseases, such as rheumatic fever or syphilis. Diseased or deformed valves can be surgically repaired or replaced with artificial valves.

You can measure your heart rate by placing a finger over the radial artery in your wrist or the carotid artery in your neck and counting the pulsations for 1 minute. **Arterial pulse** is the alternate expansion and recoil of an artery. Each time the left ventricle pumps blood into the aorta, the elastic wall of the aorta expands to accommodate the blood. This expansion moves in a wave down the aorta and the arteries that branch from it. When this pressure wave passes, the elastic arterial wall snaps back to its normal size.

The nervous system regulates heart rate

Although the heart can beat independently, its rate is, in fact, carefully regulated by the nervous and endocrine systems (**FIG. 44-12**). Sensory receptors in the walls of certain blood vessels and heart chambers are sensitive to changes in blood pressure. When stimulated, the receptors send messages to **cardiac centers** in the medulla of the brain. These cardiac centers govern two sets of autonomic nerves that pass to the SA node: parasympathetic and sympathetic

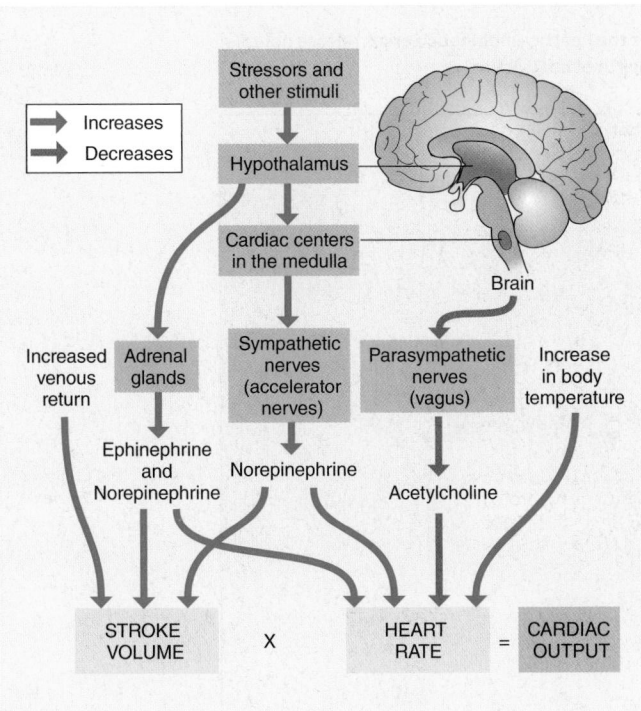

FIGURE 44-12 Some factors that influence cardiac output

nerves. Parasympathetic and sympathetic nerves have opposite effects on heart rate (see Fig. 42-17).

Parasympathetic nerves release the neurotransmitter *acetylcholine,* which slows the heart. Acetylcholine slows the rate of depolarization by increasing the membrane's permeability to K^+ (**FIG. 44-13a**). Sympathetic nerves release norepinephrine, which speeds the heart rate and increases the strength of contraction. Norepinephrine stimulates Ca^{2+} channel opening during depolarization (**FIG. 44-13b**).

Both norepinephrine and acetylcholine act indirectly on ion channels. They activate a *signal transduction* process involving a G protein (see Chapter 6).

Norepinephrine binds to *beta-adrenergic receptors,* one of the two main types of adrenergic receptors. These receptors are targeted by *beta blockers,* drugs that block the actions of norepinephrine on the heart and are used clinically in treating hypertension (high blood pressure) and other types of heart disease.

In response to physical and emotional stressors, the adrenal glands release epinephrine and norepinephrine, which speed the heart. An elevated body temperature also increases heart rate. During fever, the heart may beat more than 100 times per minute. As you might expect, heart rate decreases when body temperature is lowered. This is the reason that physicians may deliberately lower a patient's temperature during heart surgery.

Stroke volume depends on venous return

The volume of blood one ventricle pumps during one beat is the **stroke volume.** Stroke volume depends mainly on **venous return,** the amount of blood the veins deliver to the heart. According to **Starling's law of the heart,** if the veins deliver more blood

to the heart, the heart pumps more blood into the arteries (within physiological limits). Increased venous return stretches the cardiac muscle fibers more and they contract with greater force, increasing stroke volume. Norepinephrine released by sympathetic nerves and epinephrine released by the adrenal glands during stress also increase the force of contraction of cardiac muscle fibers.

Cardiac output varies with the body's need

By multiplying the stroke volume by the number of times the left ventricle beats per minute, we can compute the **cardiac output (CO).** The CO is the volume of blood pumped by the left ventricle into the aorta in 1 minute. For example, in a resting adult the heart may beat about 72 times per minute and pump about 70 mL of blood with each contraction.

$$CO = \text{stroke volume} \times \text{heart rate (number of ventricular contractions per minute)}$$
$$= 70 \text{ mL/stroke} \times 72 \text{ strokes/min}$$
$$= 5040 \text{ mL/min (about 5 L/min)}$$

Cardiac output varies with changes in either stroke volume or heart rate (see Fig. 44-12). When stroke volume increases, CO increases. The CO varies dramatically with the changing needs of the body. During stress or heavy exercise, the normal heart can increase its CO fivefold so that it pumps 20 to 30 L of blood per minute.

Review

- What sequence of events occurs during cardiac conduction?
- How is the heart regulated? (Include a description of the actions of acetylcholine and norepinephrine.)
- What factors influence cardiac output?

44.6 BLOOD PRESSURE

LEARNING OBJECTIVE

9 Identify factors that determine and regulate blood pressure, and compare blood pressure in different types of blood vessels.

Blood pressure is the force exerted by the blood against the inner walls of the blood vessels. It is determined by CO, blood volume, and resistance to blood flow (**FIG. 44-14a**). When CO increases, the increased blood flow causes a rise in blood pressure. When CO decreases, the decreased blood flow causes a fall in blood pressure. If the volume of blood is reduced by hemorrhage or by chronic bleeding, the blood pressure drops. In contrast, an increase in blood volume results in an increase in blood pressure. For example, a high dietary intake of salt causes water retention. This increases blood volume and raises blood pressure.

Blood flow is impeded by resistance; when the resistance to flow increases, blood pressure rises. **Peripheral resistance** is the resistance to blood flow caused by blood viscosity and by friction between blood and the blood vessel wall. In the blood of a healthy person, viscosity remains fairly constant and is only a minor influence on changes in blood pressure. More important is the friction

1 Parasympathetic neuron releases acetylcholine.

2 Acetylcholine binds with receptors on plasma membrane of cardiac muscle.

3 Receptor activates G protein.

4 G protein binds with K^+ channel, opening it.

5 K^+ leaves the cell, hyperpolarizing the membrane. Action potentials occur more slowly.

(a) Parasympathetic action on cardiac muscle

1 Sympathetic neuron releases norepinephrine.

2 Norepinephrine binds with receptors on the plasma membrane of cardiac muscle.

3 Receptor activates G protein.

4 G protein activates adenylyl cyclase, which converts ATP to cyclic AMP (cAMP).

5 Cyclic AMP activates protein kinase.

6 Protein kinase phosphorylates Ca^{2+} channels so that they open more easily when neuron is depolarized. Action potentials occur more rapidly.

(b) Sympathetic action on cardiac muscle

FIGURE 44-13 Actions of sympathetic and parasympathetic neurons on cardiac muscle cells
Sympathetic and parasympathetic neurons release neurotransmitters that initiate a signal transduction process.

between blood and the blood vessel wall. The length and diameter of a blood vessel determine the amount of surface area in contact with the blood. Blood vessel length does not change, but the diameter, especially of an arteriole, does. A small change in blood ves-

sel diameter causes a big change in blood pressure. Constriction of blood vessels raises blood pressure; dilation lowers blood pressure.

Blood pressure in arteries rises during systole and falls during diastole. The National Institutes of Health defines *normal blood*

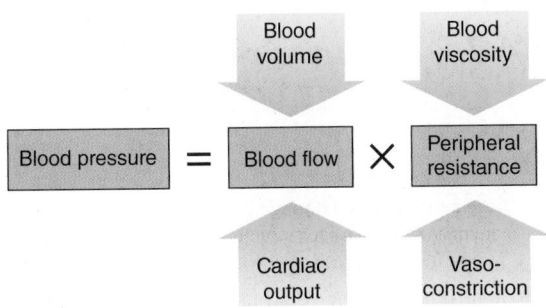

(a) **Blood pressure depends on blood flow and resistance to that flow.** A variety of factors affect blood flow and resistance.

FIGURE 44-14 Blood pressure

Area in graph refers to the surface area of blood vessels in contact with blood.

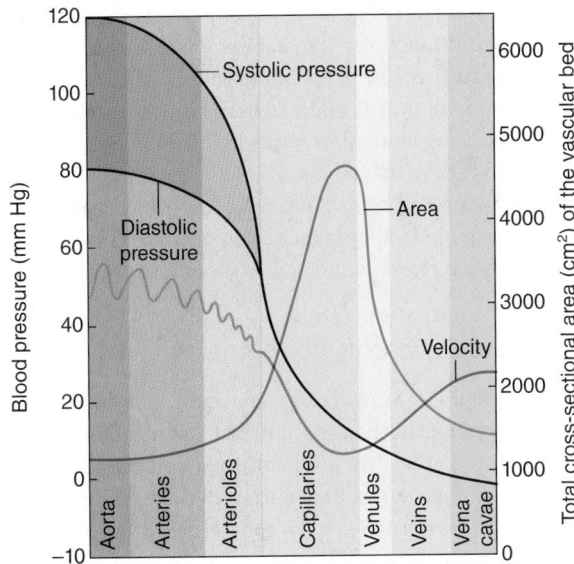

(b) **Blood pressure varies in different types of blood vessels.** Systolic and diastolic variations in arterial blood pressures are shown. Note that the venous pressure drops below zero (below atmospheric pressure) near the heart.

pressure as a systolic pressure of less than 120 and a diastolic pressure of less than 80. An example of a normal blood pressure, measured in the upper arm with a sphygmomanometer, is 110/73 mm of mercury, abbreviated mm Hg. Systolic pressure is indicated by the first number, diastolic by the second.

If you have a blood pressure of 120 to 139 systolic over 80 to 89 diastolic, you are considered *prehypertensive,* and you need to modify your lifestyle to prevent cardiovascular disease and stroke. Lifestyle changes that will reduce your risk include exercising, losing excess weight, following a heart-healthy diet, reducing salt intake, limiting alcohol, and not smoking.

If your systolic pressure consistently measures 140 mm Hg or higher or your diastolic pressure measures 90 mm Hg or higher, you have **hypertension,** or high blood pressure. Hypertension is a risk factor for atherosclerosis and other cardiovascular disease (discussed later in this chapter).

In hypertension, there is usually increased vascular resistance, especially in the arterioles and small arteries. The heart's workload increases because it must pump against this greater resistance. If this condition persists, the left ventricle enlarges and may deteriorate in function. Heredity, aging, and ethnicity contribute to the development of hypertension.

Blood pressure varies in different blood vessels

As you might guess, blood pressure is greatest in the large arteries, decreasing as blood flows away from the heart and through the smaller arteries and capillaries (**FIG. 44-14b**). By the time blood enters the veins, its pressure is very low, even approaching zero. Flow rate can be maintained in veins at low pressure because they are low-resistance vessels. Their diameter is larger than that of corresponding arteries, and their walls have little

smooth muscle. Flow of blood through veins depends on several factors, including skeletal muscle movement, which compresses veins. Most veins larger than 2 mm (0.08 in) in diameter that conduct blood against the force of gravity are equipped with *valves* to prevent backflow. Such valves usually consist of two cusps formed by inward extensions of the vein wall (**FIG. 44-15**).

When a person stands perfectly still for a long time, as when a soldier stands at attention or a store clerk stands at a cash register, blood tends to pool in the veins. When fully distended, veins can accept no more blood from the capillaries. Pressure in the

(a) **Resting condition.**

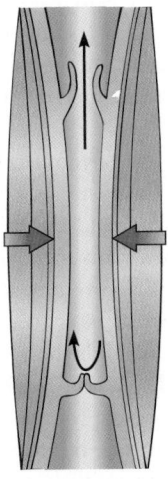

(b) **Muscles contract.** Muscles bulge, compressing veins and forcing blood toward the heart. The lower valve prevents backflow.

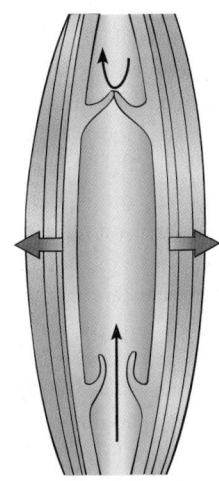

(c) **Muscles relax.** The vein expands and fills with blood from below. The upper valve prevents backflow.

FIGURE 44-15 Venous blood flow

Contraction of skeletal muscles helps move blood through the veins.

capillaries increases, and large amounts of plasma are forced out of the circulation through the thin capillary walls. Within just a few minutes, as much as 20% of the blood volume can be lost from the circulation—with drastic effect. Arterial blood pressure falls dramatically, reducing blood flow to the brain. Sometimes the resulting lack of oxygen in the brain causes fainting. This is a protective response because lying in a prone position increases blood supply to the brain. In fact, lifting a person who has fainted to an upright position can result in circulatory shock and even death.

Blood pressure is carefully regulated

Each time you get up from a horizontal position, your blood pressure changes. Several mechanisms interact to maintain normal blood pressure so that you do not faint when you get out of bed each morning or change position during the day. When blood pressure decreases, sympathetic nerves to the blood vessels stimulate vasoconstriction, causing the pressure to rise again.

Baroreceptors, specialized receptors in the walls of certain arteries and in the heart wall, are sensitive to changes in blood pressure. When an increase in blood pressure stretches the baroreceptors, messages are sent to the cardiac and vasomotor centers in the medulla of the brain. The cardiac center stimulates parasympathetic nerves that slow the heart, lowering blood pressure. The vasomotor center inhibits sympathetic nerves that constrict arterioles; this action causes vasodilation, which also lowers blood pressure. These neural reflexes continuously work in a complementary way to maintain blood pressure within normal limits.

Several hormones are also involved in regulating blood pressure (discussed in more detail in Chapters 48 and 49). In response to low blood pressure, the kidneys release **renin,** which activates the **renin–angiotensin–aldosterone pathway.** Renin acts on a plasma protein (angiotensinogen), triggering a cascade of reactions that produces the hormone **angiotensin II,** a powerful vasoconstrictor. Vasoconstriction *increases* blood pressure, restoring homeostasis. Angiotensin II also acts indirectly to maintain blood pressure by increasing the synthesis and release of the hormone **aldosterone** by the adrenal glands. Aldosterone increases retention of Na$^+$ by the kidneys, resulting in greater fluid retention and increased blood volume.

When the body becomes dehydrated, the osmotic concentration of the blood increases. In response, the posterior lobe of the pituitary gland releases **antidiuretic hormone (ADH).** ADH increases reabsorption of water in the kidneys (and only a small volume of concentrated urine is produced). Blood volume increases, raising blood pressure and restoring homeostasis.

When blood volume increases, the atria of the heart release a hormone called **atrial natriuretic peptide (ANP).** This hormone increases sodium excretion. As a result, a large volume of dilute urine is produced and blood pressure *decreases.* Nitric oxide also helps regulate blood pressure by causing vasodilation, thus decreasing blood pressure.

Review

- What is peripheral resistance? How does it affect blood pressure?
- Blood pressure is low in capillaries. How does this help retain fluid in the circulation?

44.7 THE PATTERN OF CIRCULATION

◼ LEARNING OBJECTIVE

10 Trace a drop of blood through the pulmonary and systemic circulations, naming in sequence each structure through which it passes.

Most vertebrates other than fishes have a double circuit of blood vessels: (1) the **pulmonary circulation** connects the heart and lungs; and (2) the **systemic circulation** connects the heart with all the body tissues. You can trace this general pattern of circulation in **FIGURE 44-16.**

KEY POINT

The right side of the heart receives oxygen-poor blood and pumps it into the pulmonary circulation. The left side of the heart receives oxygen-rich blood from the lungs and pumps it into the systemic circulation.

FIGURE 44-16 Systemic and pulmonary circulation
In this highly simplified diagram, red represents oxygen-rich blood and blue represents oxygen-poor blood. Blue screen highlights systemic circulation. Red screen highlights pulmonary circulation.

The pulmonary circulation oxygenates the blood

Blood from the tissues returns to the right atrium of the heart. This oxygen-poor blood, loaded with carbon dioxide, is pumped by the right ventricle into the pulmonary circulation. As it emerges from the heart, the large pulmonary trunk branches to form the **pulmonary arteries** that deliver blood to the lungs. *The pulmonary arteries are the only arteries in the body that carry oxygen-poor blood.*

In the lungs the pulmonary arteries branch into smaller and smaller vessels. These blood vessels give rise to extensive networks of pulmonary capillaries that surround the air sacs of the lungs. As blood circulates through the pulmonary capillaries, carbon dioxide diffuses out of the blood and into the air sacs. Oxygen from the air sacs diffuses into the blood so that by the time it enters the **pulmonary veins** leading back to the left atrium of the heart, the blood is charged with oxygen. *Pulmonary veins are the only veins in the body that carry blood rich in oxygen.* In summary, blood flows through the pulmonary circulation in the following sequence:

right atrium ⟶ right ventricle ⟶ pulmonary arteries ⟶ pulmonary capillaries (in lungs) ⟶ pulmonary veins ⟶ left atrium

The systemic circulation delivers blood to the tissues

Blood entering the systemic circulation is pumped by the left ventricle into the **aorta,** the largest artery. Arteries that branch off from the aorta conduct blood to all regions of the body. Some of the principal branches include the **coronary arteries** to the heart wall itself, the **carotid arteries** to the brain, the **subclavian arteries** to the shoulder region, the **mesenteric artery** to the intestine, the **renal arteries** to the kidneys, and the **iliac arteries** to the legs (**FIG. 44-17**). Each of these arteries gives rise to smaller and smaller vessels, somewhat like branches of a tree that divide until they form tiny twigs. Eventually, blood flows into capillary networks within each tissue or organ.

Blood returning from the capillary networks within the brain passes through the **jugular veins.** Blood from the shoulders and arms drains into the **subclavian veins.** These veins and others returning blood from the upper portion of the body merge to form a very large vein that empties blood into the right atrium. In humans this vein is called the **superior vena cava.** The **renal veins** from the kidneys, **iliac veins** from the lower limbs, **hepatic veins** from the liver, and other veins from the lower portion of the body return

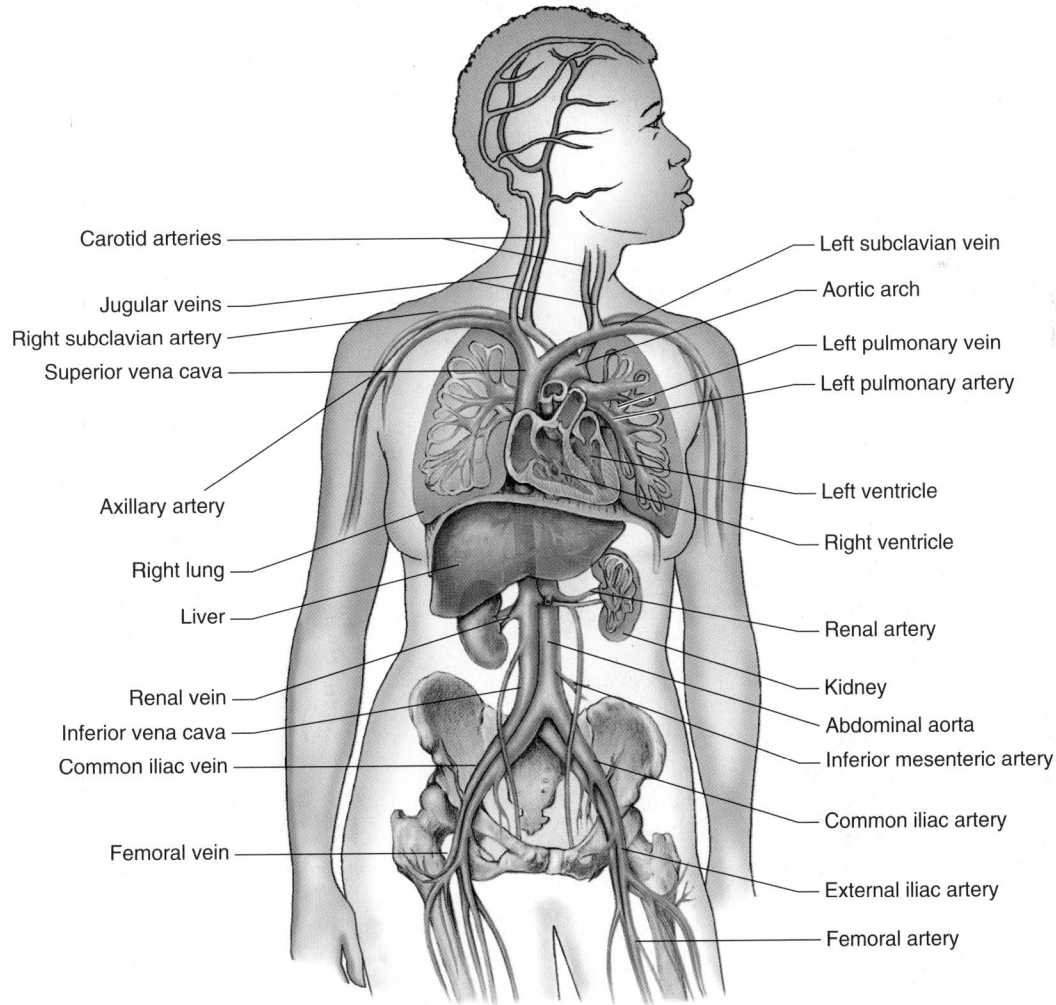

FIGURE 44-17 Blood circulation through some of the principal arteries and veins of the human body
Blood vessels carrying oxygen-rich blood are red; blood vessels carrying oxygen-poor blood are blue.

blood to the large **inferior vena cava,** which delivers blood to the right atrium.

As an example of blood circulation through the systemic circuit, let us trace a drop of blood from the heart to the right leg and back to the heart:

left atrium ⟶ left ventricle ⟶ aorta ⟶ right common iliac artery ⟶ smaller arteries in leg ⟶ capillaries in leg ⟶ small veins in leg ⟶ common iliac vein ⟶ inferior vena cava ⟶ right atrium

In most fishes, amphibians, and nonavian reptiles, the heart muscle is spongy and receives oxygen directly from the blood as it passes through the heart chambers. However, in birds and mammals the walls of the heart are too thick for nutrients and oxygen to reach all the muscle fibers by diffusion. Instead, the cardiac muscle has its own system of blood vessels. In humans, **coronary arteries** give rise to a network of capillaries within the heart wall. The **coronary veins** join to form a large vein, the **coronary sinus,** which empties directly into the right atrium.

Blood almost always travels from artery to capillary to vein to the heart. An exception occurs in the **hepatic portal system.** Instead of leading directly back to the heart (as most veins do), the hepatic portal vein delivers nutrients from the intestine to the liver. Within the liver, the hepatic portal vein gives rise to an extensive network of tiny blood sinuses. As blood courses through the hepatic sinuses, liver cells remove nutrients and store them. Eventually, liver sinuses merge to form hepatic veins, which deliver blood to the inferior vena cava.

Review

- What sequence of blood vessels and heart chambers would a red blood cell pass through on its way (1) from the inferior vena cava to the aorta and (2) from the renal vein to the renal artery?

- What is the function of the hepatic portal system? How does its sequence of blood vessels differ from that in most other circulatory routes?

44.8 THE LYMPHATIC SYSTEM

■ LEARNING OBJECTIVE

11 Describe the structure and functions of the lymphatic system.

In addition to the blood circulatory system, vertebrates have an accessory circulatory system, the **lymphatic system** (**FIG. 44-18**). The lymphatic system (1) collects and returns interstitial fluid to the blood, (2) launches immune responses that defend the body against disease organisms, and (3) absorbs lipids from the digestive tract. In this section we focus on the first function. We discuss immunity in Chapter 45 and lipid absorption in Chapter 47.

The lymphatic system consists of lymphatic vessels and lymph tissue

The lymphatic system consists of (1) an extensive network of **lymphatic vessels,** or simply **lymphatics,** that conduct **lymph,** the

clear, watery fluid formed from interstitial fluid and (2) **lymph tissue,** a type of connective tissue with large numbers of lymphocytes. Lymph tissue is organized into small masses of tissue called **lymph nodes** and **lymph nodules.** The tonsils, thymus gland, and spleen, which consist mainly of lymph tissue, are also part of the lymphatic system.

Tiny "dead-end" capillaries of the lymphatic system extend into almost all body tissues (**FIG. 44-19**). Interstitial fluid enters lymph capillaries, where it becomes lymph. Lymph capillaries join to form larger lymphatics (which you can think of as lymph veins). There are no lymph arteries.

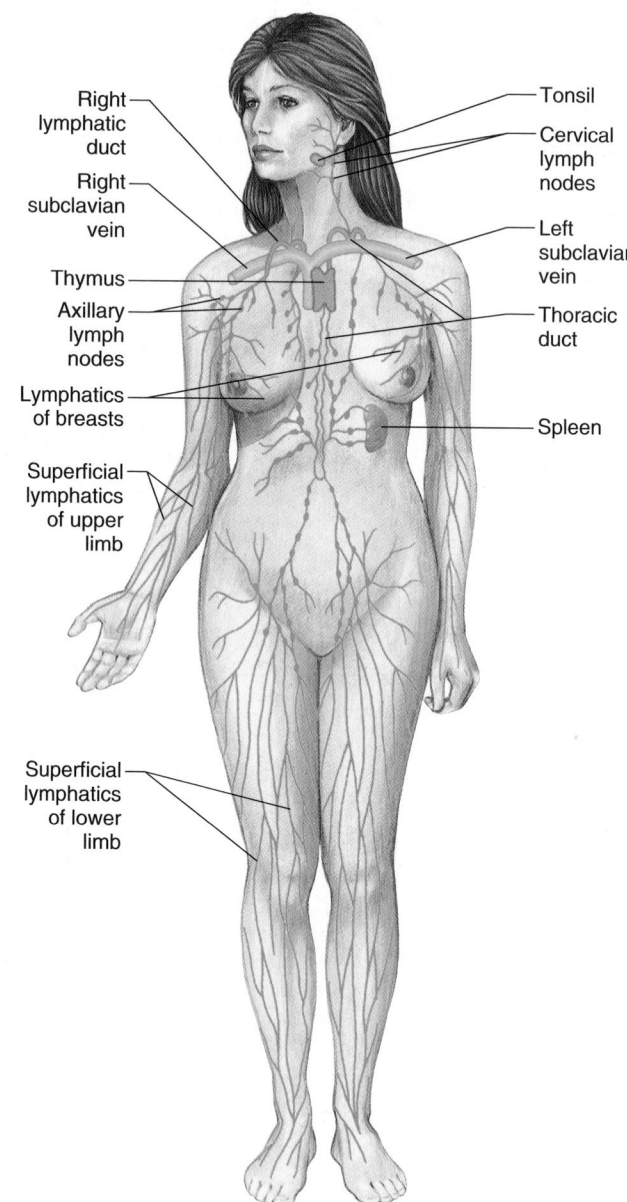

FIGURE 44-18 *Animated* **Human lymphatic system**
Note that the lymphatic vessels extend into most tissues of the body, but the lymph nodes are clustered in certain regions. The right lymphatic duct drains lymph from the upper right quadrant of the body. The thoracic duct drains lymph from other regions of the body. Both ducts return fluid to the blood.

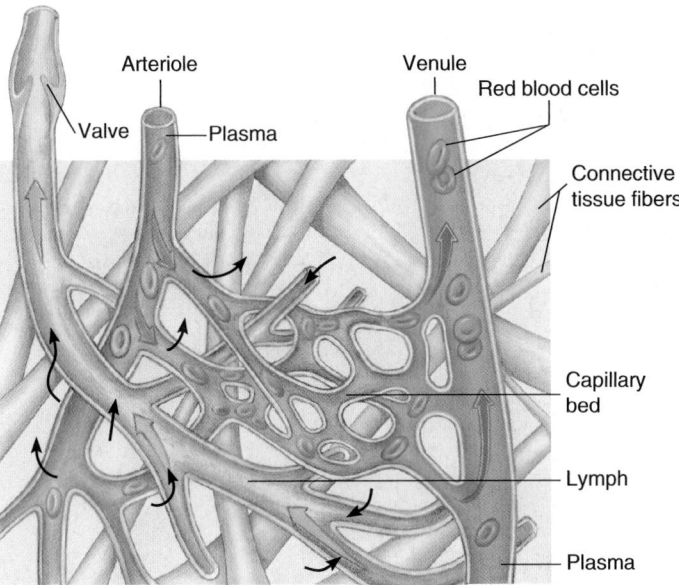

FIGURE 44-19 *Animated* **Lymph capillaries**
Lymph capillaries drain excess interstitial fluid from the tissues. Note that blood capillaries are connected to vessels at both ends, whereas lymph capillaries (*shown in green*) are "dead-end streets." The arrows indicate direction of flow.

Arteriole
Venule
Red blood cells
Valve
Plasma
Connective tissue fibers
Capillary bed
Lymph
Plasma

Lymph passes from lymph capillaries into lymphatics, which at certain locations empty into lymph nodes. As lymph circulates through the lymph nodes, phagocytes filter out bacteria and other harmful materials. The lymph then flows into lymphatics that conduct it away from the lymph node. Lymphatics from all over the body conduct lymph toward the shoulder region. These vessels join the circulatory system at the base of the subclavian veins by way of ducts: the **thoracic duct** on the left side and the **right lymphatic duct** on the right.

Tonsils are masses of lymph tissue under the lining of the oral cavity and throat. (When enlarged, the pharyngeal tonsils in back of the nose are called **adenoids.**) Tonsils help protect the respiratory system from infection by destroying bacteria and other foreign matter that enter the body through the mouth or nose. Unfortunately, tonsils are sometimes overcome by invading bacteria and become the site of frequent infection themselves.

Some vertebrates, such as frogs, have lymph "hearts," which pulsate and squeeze lymph along. However, in mammals the walls of lymphatic vessels themselves pulsate. Valves within the lymphatics prevent lymph from flowing backward. When muscles contract or when arteries pulsate, pressure on the lymphatic vessels increases lymph flow. The rate at which lymph flows is slow and variable. The total lymph flow is about 100 mL per hour—far slower than the 5 L per minute of blood flowing in the cardiovascular system.

The lymphatic system plays an important role in fluid homeostasis

When blood enters a capillary network, it is under rather high pressure, so some plasma is forced out of the capillaries into the tissues. Once it leaves the blood vessels, this fluid is called *inter-*

stitial fluid, or tissue fluid. It contains no red blood cells or platelets and only a few white blood cells. Its protein content is about one-fourth that found in plasma because proteins are too large to pass easily through capillary walls. However, smaller molecules dissolved in the plasma do pass out with the fluid leaving the blood vessels. Thus, interstitial fluid contains glucose, amino acids, other nutrients, and oxygen, as well as a variety of salts. This nourishing fluid bathes all the cells.

Three factors are responsible for **net filtration pressure,** which is the tendency for plasma to leave the blood at the arterial end of a capillary and enter the interstitial fluid (**FIG. 44- 20**). The main force is *hydrostatic pressure,* the blood pressure against the capillary wall. This effect is augmented by the osmotic pressure of the interstitial fluid. The principal opposing force is the osmotic pressure of the blood, which is greater than the osmotic pressure of the interstitial fluid and restrains fluid loss from the capillary.

At the venous ends of the capillaries, the blood hydrostatic pressure is much lower, and the osmotic pressure of the blood draws fluid back into the capillary. However, not as much fluid is absorbed back into the circulation at the venous ends of capillaries as is filtered out at the arterial ends. Furthermore, protein does not return effectively into the venous capillaries and instead tends to accumulate in the interstitial fluid. These potential problems are so serious that without the lymphatic system, fluid balance in the body would be significantly disturbed within a few hours, and death would occur within about 24 hours. The lymphatic system preserves fluid balance by collecting interstitial fluid, including the protein that accumulates in it, and returning it to the circulation.

The walls of the lymph capillaries consist of endothelial cells that overlap slightly. When interstitial fluid accumulates, it presses against these cells, pushing them inward like tiny swinging doors that swing in only one direction. As fluid accumulates within the lymph capillary, these cell doors are pushed closed.

Obstruction of lymphatic vessels causes *lymphedema,* swelling from excessive accumulation of interstitial fluid. Lymphatic vessels can be blocked as a result of injury, inflammation, surgery, or parasitic infection. For example, when a breast is removed (mastectomy) because of cancer, lymph nodes in the armpit are often removed to prevent the spread of cancer cells. The disrupted lymph circulation may cause the patient's arm to swell. Treatment focuses on minimizing the swelling and controlling discomfort and pain.

Review

- What are the relationships among plasma, interstitial fluid, and lymph?
- How does the lymphatic system help maintain fluid balance?

44.9 CARDIOVASCULAR DISEASE

◼ LEARNING OBJECTIVE

12 Trace the progression of atherosclerosis and describe at least five risk factors for cardiovascular disease.

Cardiovascular disease is the leading cause of death in the world, accounting for about 30% of deaths each year. In the United States, cardiovascular disease is responsible for about 40% of all deaths,

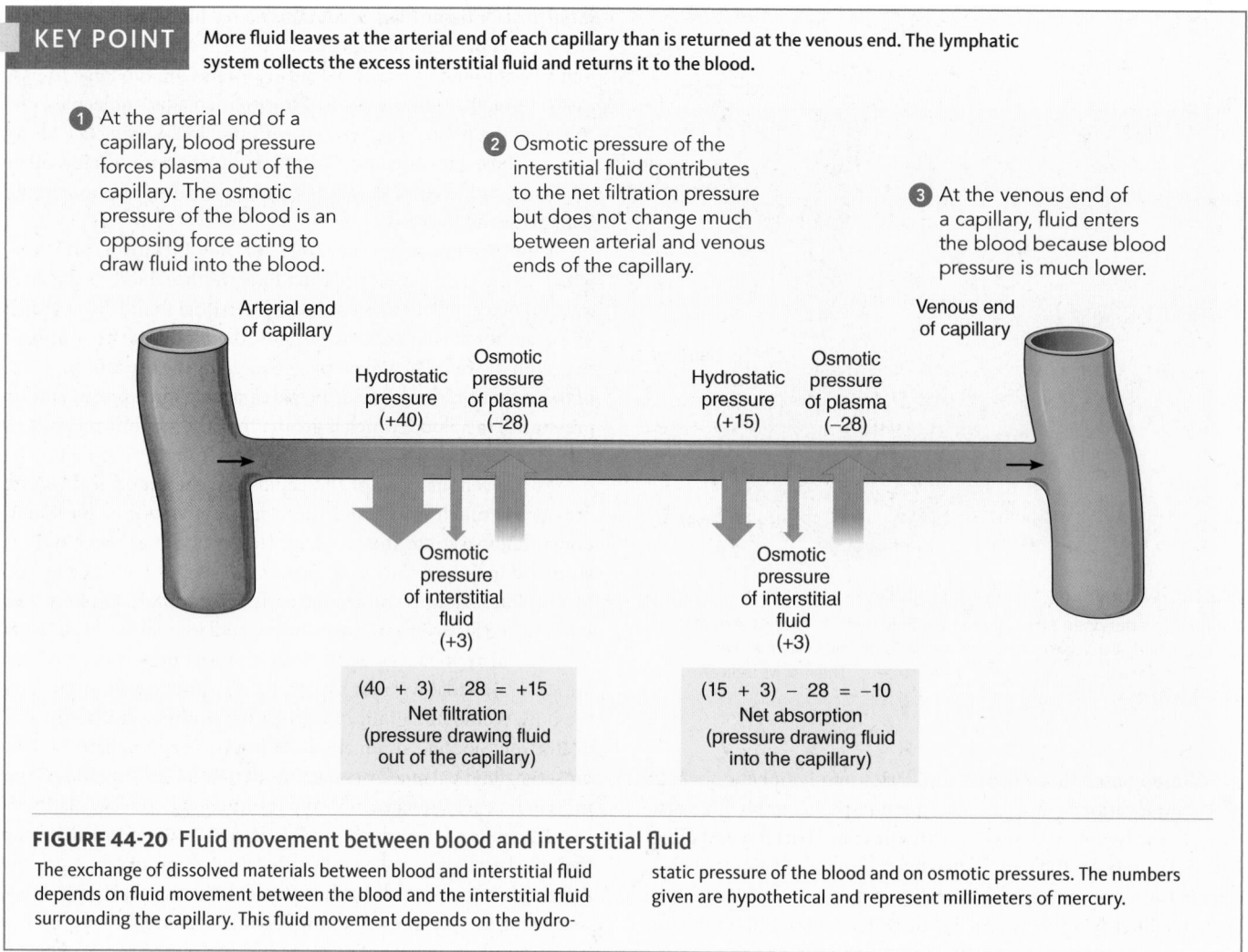

More fluid leaves at the arterial end of each capillary than is returned at the venous end. The lymphatic system collects the excess interstitial fluid and returns it to the blood.

1 At the arterial end of a capillary, blood pressure forces plasma out of the capillary. The osmotic pressure of the blood is an opposing force acting to draw fluid into the blood.

2 Osmotic pressure of the interstitial fluid contributes to the net filtration pressure but does not change much between arterial and venous ends of the capillary.

3 At the venous end of a capillary, fluid enters the blood because blood pressure is much lower.

Arterial end of capillary

Hydrostatic pressure (+40)

Osmotic pressure of plasma (−28)

Venous end of capillary

Hydrostatic pressure (+15)

Osmotic pressure of plasma (−28)

Osmotic pressure of interstitial fluid (+3)

Osmotic pressure of interstitial fluid (+3)

(40 + 3) − 28 = +15
Net filtration
(pressure drawing fluid out of the capillary)

(15 + 3) − 28 = −10
Net absorption
(pressure drawing fluid into the capillary)

FIGURE 44-20 Fluid movement between blood and interstitial fluid

The exchange of dissolved materials between blood and interstitial fluid depends on fluid movement between the blood and the interstitial fluid surrounding the capillary. This fluid movement depends on the hydro-static pressure of the blood and on osmotic pressures. The numbers given are hypothetical and represent millimeters of mercury.

more than all types of cancer combined. According to the Centers for Disease Control and Prevention, heart disease costs the United States more than three billion dollars annually (based on figures for 2010). This cost includes health-care services, medications, and lost productivity. Death often results from some complication of *atherosclerosis, thrombosis* (clotting), or *hypertension* (high blood pressure). All three of these conditions are typically involved.

Atherosclerosis is a progressive disease in which the walls of certain arteries are damaged, inflamed, and narrowed as a result of lipid deposits in their walls. Although it can affect almost any artery, the disease most often develops in the aorta and in the coronary and cerebral arteries. The earliest events in atherosclerosis begin when excess low-density lipoprotein (LDL), known as "bad" cholesterol, in the blood enters the inner layer of blood vessels. (LDLs will be discussed further in Chapter 47; uptake of LDL by cells was described in Chapter 5.)

Recall that the inner layer of a blood vessel is made up of endothelial cells. Excess LDLs in the blood vessel wall become oxidized by free radicals and accumulate between and beneath the endothelial cells. Macrophages phagocytose them and become filled with LDLs. These macrophages are called *foam cells*. Large numbers of foam cells lead to the development of fatty streaks, thought to be the initial lesion in the progression of atherosclerosis. Interestingly, fatty streaks have been identified in the arteries of some children and adolescents.

Underlying smooth muscle fibers migrate to the inner lining of the artery and multiply there. Connective tissue fibers also proliferate and produce collagen. White blood cells including monocytes and T cells (a type of lymphocyte important in immune responses) move into the region. These cells produce substances that maintain chronic inflammation in the inner layer of the arterial wall. Inflammation, discussed in Chapter 45, is one of the body's most important responses to infection or injury.

The buildup of fatty substances, smooth muscle fibers, macrophages and other cells, collagen, and sometimes, calcium form the **atherosclerotic plaque.** As the plaque increases in size, remodeling of the artery takes place, so that for a time the size of the lumen (opening) of the blood vessel is maintained. Smooth muscle fibers form a protective *fibrous cap,* which walls off the plaque from the inner lining of the artery and the blood. Macrophages and other cells eventually die within the plaque, recruiting more macrophages to the area to clean up the debris.

The progression of atherosclerosis can continue for decades without causing symptoms. However, as atherosclerotic plaque builds, arteries eventually lose their ability to stretch when filled with blood. As the walls thicken, the diameter of the artery decreases, and it gradually becomes occluded (blocked), as shown in **FIGURE 44-21.** The occluded vessels deliver less blood to the tissues, which then become **ischemic,** or lacking in blood. Now the tissue is deprived of an adequate oxygen and nutrient supply.

In **ischemic heart disease,** the increased need for oxygen during exercise or emotional stress results in the pain characteristic of **angina pectoris.** Nitroglycerin, in the form of pills or a patch, dilates veins, decreasing venous return. Cardiac output is lowered so the heart is not working as hard and requires less oxygen. Nitroglycerin also dilates the coronary arteries slightly, allowing more blood to reach the heart muscle. *Calcium ion channel blockers* are drugs that slow the heart by inhibiting the passage of Ca^{2+} into cardiac muscle fibers. They also dilate the coronary arteries.

Myocardial infarction (MI), or heart attack, is a very serious, often fatal, consequence of cardiovascular disease. MI is the first symptom of atherosclerotic cardiovascular disease for about 65% of men and almost 50% of women. MI is the leading cause of death and disability in the United States. MI often results from a sudden decrease in coronary blood supply. If only a small region of cardiac muscle is affected, the heart may continue to function. Cells in the region deprived of oxygen die and are replaced by scar tissue.

The sudden decrease in blood supply associated with MI often occurs when inflammation causes the fibrous cap over the atherosclerotic plaque to break open. Platelets adhere to the roughened arterial wall and initiate clotting. A **thrombus** is a clot that forms within a blood vessel or within the heart; a thrombus that forms within a coronary artery can block a sizable branch of the artery. Blood flow to a portion of heart muscle may be impeded or completely halted. When a critical region of cardiac muscle is deprived of its blood supply, the heart may stop beating. This condition, called **cardiac arrest,** can result in death within a few minutes.

An episode of ischemia may trigger a fatal arrhythmia such as **ventricular fibrillation,** a condition in which the ventricles contract very rapidly without actually pumping blood. The pulse may stop, and blood pressure may fall precipitously. Ventricular fibrillation has been linked with about 65% of cardiac arrests. The only effective treatment for fibrillation is **defibrillation** with electric shock. The shock appears to depolarize all of the muscle fibers in the heart so that its timing mechanism can reset.

When atherosclerosis develops in the cerebral arteries, less blood is delivered to the brain. This condition can lead to a **cerebrovascular accident (CVA),** commonly referred to as a *stroke.* Most CVAs are caused by ischemia, typically as a result of thrombosis.

Current treatment for patients with progressive cardiovascular disease includes certain drugs; surgical procedures aimed at restoring and improving blood flow; and most importantly, education regarding lifestyle changes that reduce risk factors. Among the

500 μm

500 μm

(a) Normal coronary artery.

(b) This artery is severely occluded by the atherosclerotic plaque that has built up within its wall.

FIGURE 44-21 Progression of atherosclerosis
LMs of cross sections through two arteries showing changes that take place in atherosclerosis.

types of medications used are statins, medications that lower cholesterol level; aspirin, which reduces the tendency for blood clotting; and ACE (angiotensin-converting enzyme) inhibitors, drugs that decrease blood pressure. By inhibiting ACE, a key enzyme responsible for the synthesis of angiotensin II, these drugs decrease blood pressure. (Angiotensin II is a powerful vasoconstrictor and also promotes production of the hormone aldosterone, which increases sodium reabsorption in the kidneys and thus, retention of water. Angiotensin II and aldosterone are discussed further in Chapter 48.)

Surgical procedures include angioplasty and stent placement, and coronary bypass surgery. *Angioplasty* involves inserting a small balloon into an occluded coronary artery. Inflating the balloon breaks up the plaque in the arterial wall and thus widens the vessel. A stent (a mesh tube) left in the artery helps keep the artery open. In *coronary bypass surgery,* veins from another location in the patient's body are grafted around occluded coronary arteries. The newly positioned blood vessels allow blood to flow around the blocked arteries, restoring adequate blood flow to the affected area. Future treatment for damaged hearts may include stem cell therapies. Researchers have demonstrated that cardiac stem cells can differentiate into cardiac muscle cells and other types of heart cells.

Several major *modifiable* risk factors for cardiovascular disease have been identified:

1. *Elevated LDL-cholesterol levels in the blood.* These levels are associated with diets rich in total calories, total fats, saturated fats, and cholesterol.
2. *Hypertension.* The higher the blood pressure is, the greater the risk. The hormone angiotensin II, which at abnormally high levels is thought to contribute to hypertension, also stimulates inflammation.
3. *Cigarette smoking.* The risk of developing atherosclerosis is three to six times as great in smokers as in nonsmokers and is directly proportional to the number of cigarettes smoked daily. Nicotine constricts blood vessels, and carbon monoxide in the

smoke damages the inner lining of blood vessels. Components of cigarette smoke cause oxidants to form, which may contribute to the inflammation by increasing oxidation of the altered LDL in the arterial wall.

4. *Diabetes mellitus.* In this endocrine disorder, glucose is not metabolized normally. The body shifts to fat metabolism, and there is a marked increase in circulating lipids, leading to atherosclerosis. Impaired glucose tolerance is also a risk factor.

5. *Physical inactivity.* Physical inactivity contributes to more than one-third of the approximately 500,000 deaths related to heart disease in the United States each year. Exercise reduces the concentrations of triacylglycerols (triglycerides) and cholesterol in the blood. (These lipids have been associated with heart disease.) At the same time, exercise increases the concentration of high-density lipoproteins (HDLs), which protect against heart disease.

6. *Overweight and obesity.* Being overweight can affect cholesterol levels and increase the risk of hypertension and diabetes.

The risk of developing cardiovascular disease also increases with age. Other probable risk factors currently being studied are hereditary predisposition, hormone levels, stress and behavior patterns, and dietary factors.

Review

- What happens when excess LDL enters the inner layer of arteries?
- What is ventricular fibrillation?
- In what way does cigarette smoking contribute to atherosclerosis?

■ SUMMARY: FOCUS ON LEARNING OBJECTIVES

44.1 *(page 938)*

1 Compare and contrast internal transport in animals with no circulatory system, those with an open circulatory system, and those with a closed circulatory system.

- Small, simple invertebrates, such as sponges, cnidarians, and flatworms, depend on **diffusion** for internal transport. Larger animals require a specialized **circulatory system,** which typically consists of **blood,** a **heart,** and a system of **blood vessels** or spaces through which blood circulates. In all animals, **interstitial fluid,** the tissue fluid between cells, brings oxygen and nutrients into contact with cells.

- Arthropods and most mollusks have an **open circulatory system** in which blood flows into a **hemocoel,** bathing the tissues directly.

- Some invertebrates and all vertebrates have a **closed circulatory system** in which blood flows through a continuous circuit of blood vessels.

- The vertebrate circulatory system consists of a muscular heart that pumps blood into a system of blood vessels. The circulatory system transports nutrients, oxygen, wastes, and hormones; helps maintain fluid balance, appropriate pH, and body temperature; and defends the body against disease.

  CENGAGENOW™ Learn more about open and closed circulatory systems by clicking on the figures in CengageNOW.

44.2 *(page 940)*

2 Compare the structure and function of plasma, red blood cells, white blood cells, and platelets.

- **Plasma** consists of water, salts, substances in transport, and **plasma proteins,** including albumins, globulins, and fibrinogen.

- **Red blood cells (RBCs),** also called **erythrocytes,** transport oxygen and carbon dioxide. Red blood cells produce large quantities of **hemoglobin,** a red pigment that transports oxygen.

- **White blood cells (WBCs),** also called **leukocytes,** defend the body against disease organisms. **Lymphocytes** and **monocytes** are agranular white blood cells; **neutrophils, eosinophils,** and **basophils** are granular white blood cells. Monocytes can develop into **macrophages** and **dendritic cells.**

- **Platelets** patch damaged blood vessels and release substances essential for blood clotting.

  CENGAGENOW™ Learn more about the composition of vertebrate blood by clicking on the figures in CengageNOW.

3 Summarize the sequence of events involved in blood clotting.

- Damaged cells and platelets release substances that activate clotting factors. Prothrombin is converted to **thrombin,** which catalyzes the conversion of **fibrinogen** to an insoluble protein, **fibrin.** Fibrin forms long threads that make up the webbing of the clot.

44.3 *(page 945)*

4 Compare the structure and function of different types of blood vessels, including arteries, arterioles, capillaries, and veins.

- **Arteries** carry blood away from the heart. **Arterioles** are small arteries that regulate blood pressure by constricting (**vasoconstriction**) and dilating (**vasodilation**). **Capillaries** are the thin-walled exchange vessels through which blood and tissues transfer materials. **Veins** return blood to the heart.

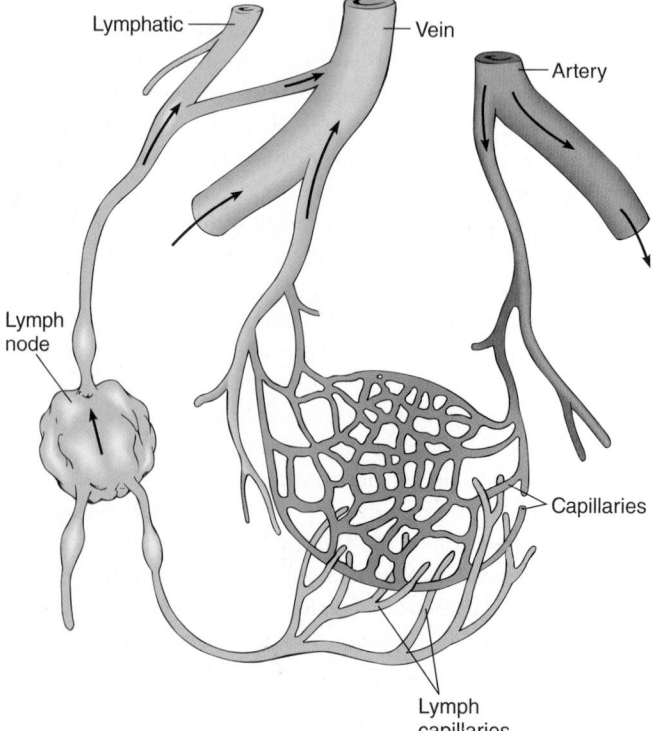

Lymphatic

Vein

Artery

Lymph node

Capillaries

Lymph capillaries

44.4 (page 946)

5 Trace the evolution of the vertebrate cardiovascular system from fish to mammal.

  ▪ The vertebrate heart has one or two **atria,** which receive blood, and one or two **ventricles,** which pump blood into the arteries. The fish heart consists of a single atrium and ventricle that are part of a single circuit of blood flow.

  ▪ In terrestrial vertebrates, circulatory systems separate oxygen-rich from oxygen-poor blood; this allows the higher metabolic rate needed to support an active terrestrial lifestyle. Amphibians have two atria and a single ventricle. Blood flows through a double circuit so that oxygen-rich blood is partly separated from oxygen-poor blood. Most nonavian reptiles have a wall that partly divides the ventricles, minimizing the mixing of oxygen-rich and oxygen-poor blood.

  ▪ The four-chambered hearts of birds and mammals separate oxygen-rich blood from oxygen-poor blood.

44.5 (page 946)

6 Describe the structure and function of the human heart. (Include the heart's conduction system in your answer.)

  ▪ The heart is enclosed by a **pericardium** and has valves that prevent backflow of blood. The valve between the right atrium and ventricle is the **right atrioventricular (AV) valve,** or **tricuspid valve.** The valve between the left atrium and ventricle is the **mitral valve. Semilunar valves** guard the exits from the heart. Cardiac muscle fibers are joined by **intercalated discs.**

  ▪ The **pacemaker** in the sinoatrial **(SA) node** initiates each heartbeat. A specialized electrical conduction system coordinates heartbeats.

  CENGAGENOW˜ Learn more about heart anatomy by clicking on the figure in CengageNOW.

  CENGAGENOW˜ See cardiac conduction by clicking on the figure in CengageNOW.

7 Trace the events of the cardiac cycle and relate normal heart sounds to these events.

  ▪ One complete heartbeat makes up a **cardiac cycle.** Contraction occurs during **systole.** The period of relaxation is **diastole.** At the beginning of ventricular systole, the closing of the AV valves makes a low-pitched "lub" sound. The closing of the semilunar valves, the beginning of ventricular diastole, makes a short, loud "dup" sound.

  CENGAGENOW˜ Watch the cardiac cycle by clicking on the figure in CengageNOW.

8 Define *cardiac output,* describe how it is regulated, and identify factors that affect it.

  ▪ **Cardiac output (CO)** equals **stroke volume** times heart rate. Stroke volume depends on **venous return** and on neural messages and hormones, especially epinephrine and norepinephrine. According to **Starling's law of the heart,** the more blood delivered to the heart by the veins, the more blood the heart pumps.

  ▪ Heart rate is regulated mainly by the nervous system and is influenced by hormones and body temperature.

44.6 (page 951)

9 Identify factors that determine and regulate blood pressure, and compare blood pressure in different types of blood vessels.

  ▪ **Blood pressure** is the force blood exerts against the inner walls of the blood vessel. Blood pressure is greatest in the arteries and decreases as blood flows through the capillaries.

  ▪ Blood pressure depends on cardiac output, blood volume, and resistance to blood flow. **Peripheral resistance** is the resistance to blood flow caused by blood viscosity and by friction between blood and the blood vessel wall.

  ▪ **Baroreceptors** sensitive to blood pressure changes send messages to the cardiac and vasomotor centers in the medulla of the brain. When informed of an increase in blood pressure, the cardiac center stimulates parasympathetic nerves that slow the heart rate. The vasomotor center inhibits sympathetic nerves that constrict blood vessels. These actions reduce blood pressure.

  ▪ **Angiotensin II** is a hormone that raises blood pressure. **Aldosterone** helps regulate salt excretion, which affects blood volume and blood pressure.

  CENGAGENOW˜ Learn more about determining blood pressure by clicking on the figure in CengageNOW.

44.7 (page 954)

10 Trace a drop of blood through the pulmonary and systemic circulations, naming in sequence each structure through which it passes.

  ▪ The **pulmonary circulation** connects the heart and the lungs; the **systemic circulation** connects the heart and the tissues. In the pulmonary circulation, the right ventricle pumps blood into the **pulmonary arteries,** which go to the lungs. Blood circulates through pulmonary capillaries in the lung and then is conducted to the left atrium by a **pulmonary vein.**

  ▪ In the systemic circulation, the left ventricle pumps blood into the **aorta,** which branches into arteries leading to the body organs. After flowing through capillary networks within various organs, blood flows into veins that conduct it to the **superior vena cava** or **inferior vena cava.** These large veins return blood to the right atrium.

  ▪ The **coronary arteries** supply the heart muscle with blood. The **hepatic portal system** circulates nutrient-rich blood through the liver.

  CENGAGENOW˜ Learn more about systemic and pulmonary circulation by clicking on the figures in CengageNOW.

44.8 (page 956)

11 Describe the structure and functions of the lymphatic system.

  ▪ The **lymphatic system** helps maintain homeostasis of fluids by collecting interstitial fluid and returning it to the blood. The lymphatic system also defends the body against disease and absorbs lipids from the digestive tract.

  ▪ **Lymphatic vessels** conduct **lymph,** a clear fluid formed from interstitial fluid, to the **thoracic duct** and **right lymphatic duct** in the shoulder region. These ducts return lymph to the blood. **Lymph nodes** are small masses of tissue that filter bacteria and harmful materials out of lymph.

  CENGAGENOW˜ Learn more about the human lymphatic system by clicking on the figure in CengageNOW.

44.9 (page 957)

12 Trace the progression of atherosclerosis and describe at least five risk factors for cardiovascular disease.

  ▪ Atherosclerosis progresses as the inner walls of certain arteries become inflamed and blocked by the accumulation of fatty deposits and cells that mediate inflammation. The blood supply of tissues served by these vessels becomes increasingly compromised.

  ▪ Risk factors include elevated LDL-cholesterol levels in the blood, hypertension, cigarette smoking, diabetes mellitus, physical inactivity, and being overweight or obese.

1. An open circulatory system (a) is found in flatworms (b) typically includes a hemocoel (c) has a continuous circuit of vessels with openings in the capillaries (d) is characteristic of vertebrates (e) is typically found in animals with a two-chambered heart

2. Which of the following is *not* a function of the vertebrate circulatory system? (a) helps maintain appropriate pH (b) transports nutrients, oxygen, and metabolic wastes (c) helps maintain fluid balance (d) produces hemocyanin (e) provides internal defense

3. Which of the following are most closely associated with oxygen transport? (a) red blood cells (b) platelets (c) neutrophils (d) basophils (e) lymphocytes

4. Which of the following are most closely associated with blood clotting? (a) red blood cells (b) platelets (c) neutrophils (d) basophils (e) lymphocytes

5. Which choice most accurately describes one sequence of blood flow?
   1. right atrium 2. right ventricle 3. left ventricle 4. left atrium
   5. pulmonary artery 6. aorta
   (a) 1, 2, 5 (b) 1, 4, 3 (c) 4, 3, 5 (d) 3, 4, 6 (e) 4, 3, 1

6. Which choice most accurately describes one sequence of blood flow?
   1. pulmonary artery 2. pulmonary vein 3. left atrium 4. right atrium 5. pulmonary capillaries
   (a) 2, 1, 4, 3 (b) 3, 4, 2, 5 (c) 1, 5, 2, 3 (d) 4, 1, 5, 2 (e) 1, 5, 2, 4

7. A cardiac cycle (a) consists of one ventricular heartbeat (b) includes a systole (c) equals stroke volume times heart rate (d) includes a diastole (e) includes a systole and a diastole

8. Blood pressure is determined by (a) cardiac output (b) peripheral resistance (c) blood volume (d) a, b, and c (e) b and c

9. Lymph forms from (a) fluid in the lymph nodes (b) blood serum (c) plasma combined with protein (d) fluid released by lymph nodes (e) interstitial fluid

10. Norepinephrine (a) slows heart rate (b) is released in cardiac muscle by parasympathetic nerves (c) causes K^+ channels in cardiac muscle to open (d) decreases stroke volume (e) causes Ca^{2+} channels in cardiac muscle to open

11. Baroreceptors (a) stimulate renin release (b) activate the renin–angiotensin–aldosterone pathway (c) stimulate sympathetic nerves (d) are stimulated by increased blood pressure (e) send messages to cardiac centers that increase blood pressure

12. Label the diagram. See Figure 44-9 to check your answers.

1. When the nerves to the heart are cut, the heart rate increases to about 100 contractions per minute. What does this indicate about the regulation of the heart rate?

2. **EVOLUTION LINK.** A heart divided into four chambers independently evolved in birds and mammals. What are the advantages of this adaptation?

3. **EVOLUTION LINK.** How is the heart of a fish specifically adapted to its lifestyle?

4. **SCIENCE, TECHNOLOGY, AND SOCIETY.** Explain the association between atherosclerosis and ischemic heart disease. Imagine that you were the Surgeon General. What types of programs would you advocate in order to decrease heart disease? As a society, do you think we should invest resources into the development of stem cell therapies for more effectively treating myocardial infarction?

 Additional questions are available in CengageNOW at www.cengage.com/login.

45 The Immune System: Internal Defense

Immune response to infection. This SEM shows a macrophage (large, deep blue cell) engulfing bacteria (small green cells). The SEM has been color-enhanced.

Dr. David M. Phillips/Visuals Unlimited/Getty Images

KEY CONCEPTS

45.1 During animal evolution, defenses that depend on protein receptors to recognize dangerous pathogens became part of the genome of every animal.

45.2 Nonspecific immune responses provide general and immediate protection against pathogens, some toxins, and cancer cells.

45.3 Specific immune responses include cell-mediated immunity and antibody-mediated immunity.

45.4 In cell-mediated immunity, specific lymphocytes known as T cells are activated; they release proteins that destroy cells infected with viruses or other intracellular pathogens.

45.5 In antibody-mediated immunity, specific lymphocytes known as B cells are activated; they multiply and differentiate into plasma cells, which produce antibodies.

45.6 Some diseases, such as cancer, and disease-causing organisms, for example HIV, the virus that causes AIDS, compromise or overcome the immune system. Some immune responses have negative effects on health: for example, immediate hypersensitivity reactions can result in allergic responses that can cause discomfort, rashes, and even death; and immune responses directed at self can cause autoimmune disease.

The **immune system,** our internal defense system, is made up of the cells and molecules that protect the body against disease-causing organisms and certain toxins. Derived from the Latin for "safe," the word *immune* refers to the early observation that when people recovered from smallpox and other serious infections, they were safe from contracting the same illnesses again.

Disease-causing organisms, or **pathogens,** include certain viruses, bacteria, fungi, protozoa, and worms. Pathogens enter the body with air, food, and water; during copulation; and through wounds in the skin. The immune system recognizes pathogens and many types of toxins and rapidly responds to eliminate them. For example, macrophages act quickly to destroy invading bacteria (see photograph).

The immune system normally functions very effectively. However some pathogens, and also cancer cells, sometimes evade or overcome the body's internal defenses, resulting in disease. Certain genetic mutations and some pathogens can prevent or compromise immune function. For example, HIV, the retrovirus that causes AIDS, destroys T cells, an important component of the immune system. At times, the immune system overreacts, as in allergic reactions. Immune responses are sometimes directed against our own tissues, resulting in *autoimmune disease* such as rheumatoid arthritis or multiple sclerosis. At times, the immune system attacks when we would prefer it did not. For example immune responses can destroy the cells of heart or kidney transplants.

Immunology, the study of internal defense systems of humans and other animals, is one of the most rapidly changing and exciting fields of biomedical research. The immune system is a collection of many types of cells and tissues scattered throughout the body. Effective **cell signaling** among these cells is critical. Cells of the immune system communicate directly by means of their surface molecules and indirectly by releasing messenger molecules. Understanding the complex signaling systems of the immune system is a major focus of research. Investigators are also working to better understand the evolution of the immune system.

One of the greatest accomplishments of immunologists has been the development of vaccines that prevent disease. Another has been developing techniques for successful tissue and organ transplantation. Sophisticated research strategies, such as gene transfer, have enabled immunologists to expand their knowledge of the cells and molecules that interact to generate immune responses. These techniques have led to the development of new approaches to the prevention and treatment of disease. Much has been learned, and many challenges lie ahead.

45.1 EVOLUTION OF IMMUNE RESPONSES

◼ LEARNING OBJECTIVES

1   Distinguish between nonspecific and specific immune responses.
2   Compare, in general terms, the immune responses that have evolved in invertebrates and vertebrates.

An **immune response** is the process of recognizing foreign or dangerous macromolecules and responding to eliminate them. The immune system distinguishes between *self* and *nonself.* Such recognition is possible because each individual is biochemically unique. Cells have surface proteins different from those on the cells of other species or even other individuals of the same species. An animal's immune system recognizes its own cells and can identify those of other organisms as foreign. Thus, the distinctive macromolecules of a pathogen that invades an animal stimulate the animal's defensive responses. A single bacterium may have from 10 to more than 1000 distinctive macromolecules on its surface. The immune system also responds to danger signals from injured tissues, such as proteins released when cell membranes are damaged.

Two main types of immune responses protect the body: nonspecific and specific (**FIG. 45-1**). **Nonspecific immune responses** provide immediate, general protection against pathogens, parasites, some toxins and drugs, and cancer cells. Nonspecific immune responses are referred to as *innate immunity.* Nonspecific immune responses prevent most pathogens from entering the body and rapidly destroy those that do penetrate the outer defenses. For example, the cuticle or skin provides a physical barrier to pathogens that come in contact with an animal's body. The *inflammatory response* and phagocytosis are nonspecific defenses that destroy bacteria that manage to penetrate the outer defenses.

Specific immune responses are highly specific for distinct macromolecules. Specific immune responses are also referred to as *acquired immunity.* Any molecule that cells of the immune system specifically recognize as foreign is called an **antigen.** Proteins are the most powerful antigens, but some polysaccharides and lipids are also antigenic. Specific immune responses are directed toward particular antigens and typically include the production of **antibodies,** highly specific proteins that recognize and bind to specific antigens. An important characteristic of specific immune responses is **immunological memory,** which means that the system "remembers" foreign or dangerous molecules and responds more effectively to repeated encounters with the same molecules.

Immunologists do not yet understand what signals the immune system *not* to respond to foreign molecules that are harmless. Some researchers have suggested that the evolution of the immune system allowed animals to *manage* bacteria and other microbes that are beneficial, as well as to defend against harmful ones.

Invertebrates launch nonspecific immune responses

Many invertebrates (cnidarians, annelids, and mollusks) are covered by mucus that traps and kills pathogens. Tough external skeletons, such as cuticles, shells, or chitinous exoskeletons, shield the bodies of nematodes, most mollusks, arthropods, and many other invertebrates (see Chapter 31). All animal species studied have **phagocytes** that move through the body, engulfing and destroying bacteria and other foreign matter. In mollusks, substances in the hemolymph (blood) enhance phagocytosis. Annelids are the only invertebrates known to have *natural killer cells,* a type of lymphocyte that destroys tumor cells and cells infected by viruses.

Researchers have described more than 800 **antimicrobial peptides,** chemicals that inactivate or kill pathogens. Investigators have identified antimicrobial peptides in all eukaryotes (including plants) that have been studied, suggesting an early common origin of these molecules. When researchers inject an antigen into an insect, as many as 15 different antimicrobial peptides are produced within a few hours. These chemicals are very effective in part because of their small size (a dozen or fewer amino acids), which facilitates their rapid production and diffusion.

What stimulates an animal to produce antimicrobial peptides and other immune defenses? Animal cells have receptors that recognize common types of pathogen molecules and then activate one or more signal transduction pathways, resulting in the production of antimicrobial peptides. All animals studied produce molecules and cells that rush to the location of an infection and produce an inflammatory response.

Invertebrates distinguish between their own cells and those of other species. For example, sponge cells have specific glycoproteins on their surfaces that enable them to recognize their own species. When cells of two different species are mixed, they sort themselves out according to species. When two different species

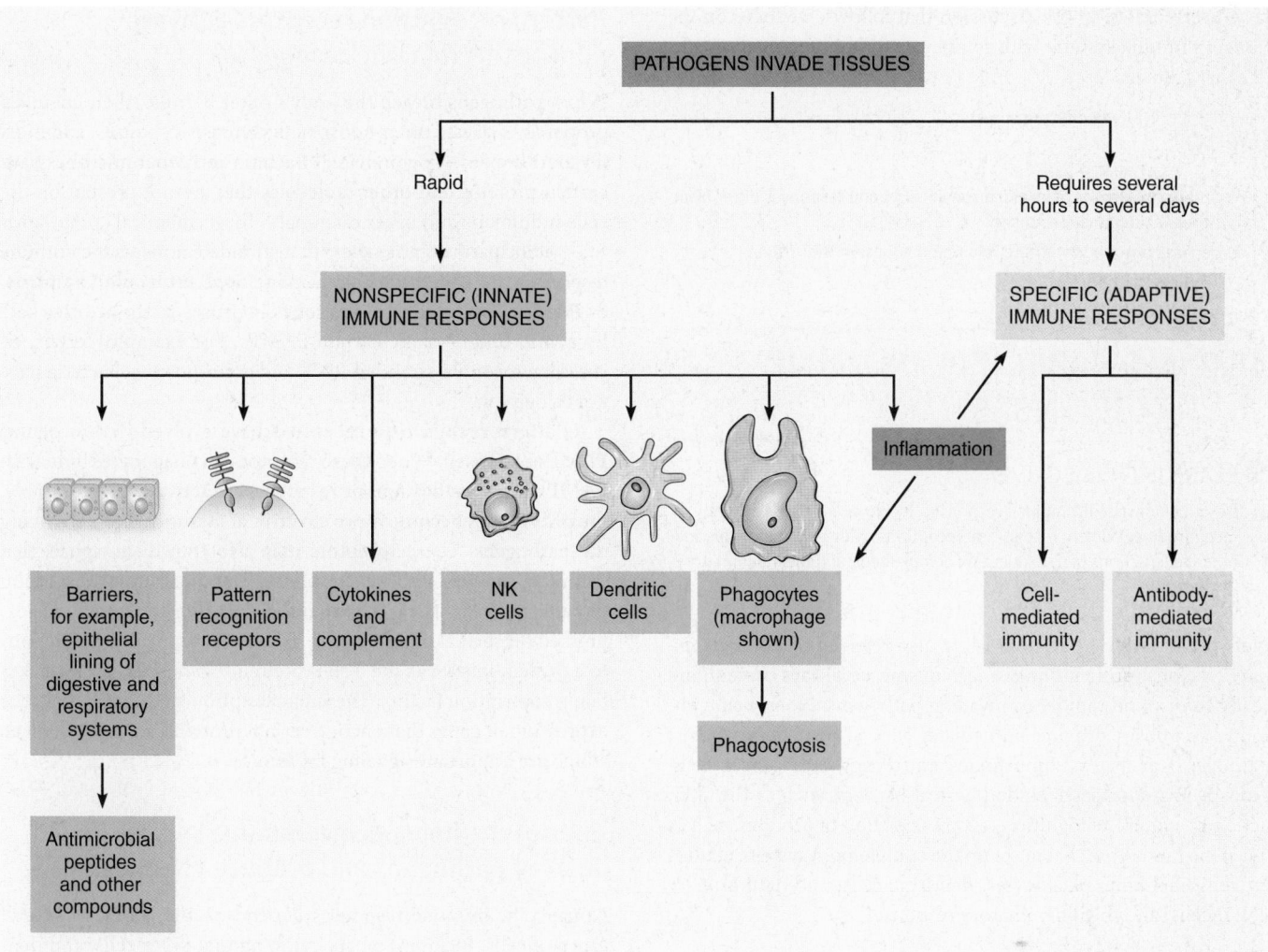

FIGURE 45-1 *Animated* Overview of human immune responses

Nonspecific immune responses include barriers that prevent the entrance of pathogens; pattern recognition receptors; cytokines and complement; natural killer (NK) cells, dendritic cells, and phagocytes; and inflammation. During inflammation, certain cells release cytokines that activate specific immune responses: cell-mediated immunity and antibody-mediated immunity.

of sponges are forced to grow in contact with each other, tissue is destroyed along the region of contact. Cnidarians (such as corals), annelids (such as earthworms), arthropods (such as insects), and echinoderms (such as sea stars) reject tissue grafted from other animals, even from the same species.

Certain cnidarians, arthropods, some echinoderms, and simple chordates (such as tunicates) appear to remember antigens for a short period. As mentioned earlier, immunological memory enables the body to respond more effectively when it encounters the same pathogens again. Although certain invertebrates demonstrate some specificity and memory, their immune responses are primarily nonspecific.

Echinoderms and tunicates are the most ancient groups of animals known to have differentiated white blood cells that perform limited immune functions. Investigators have identified two genes in the purple sea urchin that are very similar to vertebrate genes

important in producing antibodies. This discovery suggests that some invertebrates may have some capacity to launch specific immune responses.

Vertebrates launch nonspecific and specific immune responses

Like invertebrates, vertebrates depend on nonspecific immune responses for their initial assault on invading pathogens. However, their specific immune responses rapidly fine-tune the more general nonspecific responses.

The specialized lymphatic system that has evolved in vertebrates includes cells such as **lymphocytes,** white blood cells specialized to carry out immune responses, and organs such as lymph nodes (see Chapter 44). Specific immune responses, including action by lymphocytes and antibodies, may have first evolved in jawed vertebrates. In the discussion that follows, we focus on the human immune system, with references to immune mechanisms of other animals.

Review

- What are two key ways in which specific immune responses differ from nonspecific immune responses?
- In general, how do vertebrate immune responses differ from invertebrate responses?

45.2 NONSPECIFIC IMMUNE RESPONSES

■ LEARNING OBJECTIVE

3 Describe nonspecific immune responses, including physical barriers; recognition by pattern recognition receptors; actions of phagocytes and other cells; actions of cytokines and complement; and the inflammatory response.

Nonspecific immune responses are also referred to as *innate immunity*. Nonspecific immune mechanisms are always present and ready to respond rapidly to invading pathogens. Nonspecific immune responses provide immediate, general protection against pathogens, parasites, some toxins and drugs, and cancer cells. Nonspecific defenses include physical barriers, such as the skin; action by pattern recognition receptors; action of proteins such as cytokines and those that make up the complement system; actions by cells, including phagocytes, dendritic cells, and natural killer (NK) cells; and the inflammatory response.

Physical barriers prevent most pathogens from entering the body

An animal's first line of defense is its outer covering—cuticle, shell, chitin, or skin—which blocks the entry of pathogens. The digestive (gastrointestinal) tract, respiratory passageways, urinary tract, and vagina all open to the outside of the body. The epithelial linings of these passageways are barriers between the outside environment and the inside of the body. Various mechanisms within epithelial barriers expel, trap, or destroy pathogens. For example, pathogens that enter the body with inhaled air may be filtered out by hairs in the nose or trapped in the sticky mucous lining of the respiratory tract. Once trapped, they are destroyed by phagocytes.

Physical barriers are also equipped with chemical weapons. For example, antimicrobial peptides called **defensins** are produced by the epithelium of the skin of many animals, including mammals. Defensins, which are also found in saliva, are toxic to bacteria and fungi. Mucus contains a substance called *mucin,* which chemically destroys invaders. **Lysozyme,** an enzyme found in tears and other body fluids, attacks the cell walls of many gram-positive bacteria.

Mucus, tears, urine, and other body fluids flush pathogens out of the body. Invading bacteria must also compete with the populations of microbes that inhabit our skin and other surface tissues. These resident microbes are normally not harmful.

Pattern recognition receptors activate nonspecific immune responses

When pathogens breach the body's outer barriers, their chemical properties activate other nonspecific defense responses, and most invaders are quickly eliminated. Bacteria and other microbes have certain proteins and other molecules that are not present on the cells of humans and other mammals. These chemical compounds (or specific parts of molecules) that stimulate nonspecific immune responses are called **pathogen-associated molecular patterns,** or **PAMPs.** Each group of microbes—viruses, gram-positive bacteria, and fungi—share certain PAMPs. For example, certain viruses have double-stranded RNA and gram-positive bacteria have peptidoglycan.

Pattern recognition receptors have evolved that recognize PAMPs as nonself. When these receptors on phagocytes bind with PAMPs, nonspecific immune responses are activated. For example, the phagocytes become more effective at taking in and destroying the pathogens. These receptors may also transduce signals that stimulate the inflammatory response. The most important group of pattern recognition receptors, the **Toll-like receptors,** are expressed on several types of cells. Toll-like receptors (homologous to a protein known as the Toll protein in *Drosophila*) activate certain transcription factors. These transcription factors stimulate the expression of genes that encode certain proteins, such as *cytokines,* which are important signaling molecules.

Cells of the nonspecific immune system destroy pathogens and produce chemicals

Nonspecific immune responses depend on the action of several types of cells, including phagocytes, natural killer cells, and dendritic cells. **Neutrophils,** the most common type of white blood cell (see Chapter 44), and macrophages are the main phagocytes in the body. Recall that **phagocytosis** is the process by which cells engulf microorganisms, foreign matter, or other cells (see Fig. 5-21). A neutrophil can phagocytose about 20 bacteria before it becomes inactivated (perhaps by leaking lysosomal enzymes) and dies.

Macrophages are large phagocytes that develop from *monocytes,* a type of nongranular white blood cell. A macrophage can phagocytose about 100 bacteria during its lifespan (**FIG. 45-2**). Macrophages also release antiviral agents. Some macrophages patrol the body's tissues, engulfing damaged cells or foreign matter (including bacteria). Other macrophages stay in one place and destroy bacteria that pass by. For example, air sacs in the lungs contain large numbers of macrophages that destroy foreign matter entering with inhaled air.

Vertebrate macrophages have Toll-like receptors that recognize certain PAMPs and respond by producing cytokines. For example, a lipopolysaccharide found on gram-negative bacteria stimulates macrophages. In response, macrophages release *cytokines* that enhance the inflammatory response.

Can bacteria counteract the phagocyte's attack? Many strategies have evolved in bacteria that protect them from their hosts. *Streptococcus pneumoniae,* for example, has cell walls or capsules that resist the action of the phagocyte's lysosomal enzymes. Other

(a) A macrophage extends a pseudopod toward an invading *Escherichia coli* bacterium that is already multiplying.

(b) A bacterium is trapped within the engulfing pseudopod.

FIGURE 45-2 Phagocytosis

Macrophages are efficient warriors. These colorized SEMs show macrophages phagocytosing bacteria.

bacteria release enzymes that destroy lysosomal membranes. The powerful lysosomal enzymes then spill out into the cytoplasm and may destroy the phagocyte.

Natural killer (NK) cells are large, granular lymphocytes that originate in the bone marrow. They account for about 10% of circulating lymphocytes. NK cells are active against tumor cells and cells infected with some types of viruses. They destroy target cells by both nonspecific and specific (antibody-mediated) processes.

(c) A macrophage takes in trapped bacteria along with its own plasma membrane. The macrophage plasma membrane will seal over the bacteria, and powerful lysosomal enzymes will destroy them.

NK cells release cytokines, as well as enzymes that destroy target cells. **Perforins** are enzymes that cause pores to form in the plasma membrane of the target cell, allowing **granzymes,** another type of enzyme, to enter the cell. Granzymes then activate a cascade of reactions that cause the cell to self-destruct by **apoptosis,** programmed cell death. Several cytokines stimulate NK cell activity. When NK cell levels are high, resistance to certain cancers may be strengthened. Psychological stressors may decrease NK cell activity and thus enhance tumor growth.

Biologists first identified **dendritic cells** in 1868 and then rediscovered them in 1973, but the small numbers of these cells made them hard to study until sophisticated techniques became available in the 1990s. Their name derives from their long cytoplasmic extensions called *dendrites* (not to be confused with the dendrites of neurons). Dendritic cells develop from precursor cells in the bone marrow and from monocytes.

Dendritic cells are strategically stationed in all tissues of the body that come into contact with the environment—the skin and the epithelial linings of the digestive, respiratory, urinary, and vaginal passageways. When pathogens infect a tissue, PAMPs activate dendritic cells. One type of dendritic cell responds to viral infection. Dendritic cells produce *interferons,* cytokines that are antiviral. Certain types of activated dendritic cells capture microbial antigens by phagocytosis or by receptor-mediated endocytosis (see Chapter 5).

Cytokines and complement mediate immune responses

Cells of the immune system secrete a remarkable number of regulatory and antimicrobial peptides and proteins. Two major groups of molecules that are critical in nonspecific defense responses are cytokines and complement.

Cytokines are important signaling molecules

Cytokines are a large, diverse group of peptides and proteins (most are glycoproteins) that serve as important signaling molecules and perform regulatory functions. The same kinds of cytokines can be produced by many different types of cells. Also, a cytokine may affect many different kinds of cells. Just as the functions of nonspecific and specific immune responses overlap, the actions of cytokines of these subsystems also overlap. For example, cytokines produced by nonspecific cells such as macrophages can activate lymphocytes involved in specific immune responses.

Cytokines help regulate the intensity and duration of immune responses. They are also important in regulating many other biological processes, such as cell growth, repair, and cell activation. Cytokines bind to specific membrane receptors on target cells. These signaling molecules can act as *autocrine agents,* which affect the very cells that produce them, or as *paracrine agents,* which regulate the activity of nearby cells (see Chapter 49). When produced in large amounts, some cytokines act as hormones that circulate in the blood and affect distant tissues. Biologists name the types of cytokines for their function or origin. We discuss several examples, including *interferons, tumor necrosis factors, interleukins,* and *chemokines.*

When infected by viruses or other intracellular parasites (some types of bacteria, fungi, and protozoa), certain cells respond by secreting cytokines called **interferons.** *Type I interferons* are produced by either macrophages or *fibroblasts,* cells that produce the fibers of connective tissues. Type I interferons inhibit viral replication and activate NK cells that have antiviral actions. Viruses produced in cells exposed to Type I interferons are not very effective at infecting other cells. Interestingly, even though Type I interferons are produced as part of the nonspecific immune response, once released they can regulate the action of certain cells of the specific immune response. This interaction of nonspecific and specific immune mechanisms is an example of the power and complexity of the immune system.

Type II interferon (also called IFN-gamma) is critical in both nonspecific and specific immunity. In nonspecific immunity, Type II interferon stimulates macrophages to destroy tumor cells and host cells that have been infected by viruses. (The interferon activates transcription of genes that encode enzymes needed to produce antimicrobial compounds in lysosomes.)

Since their discovery in 1957, interferons have been the focus of a great deal of research. Pharmaceutical companies now use recombinant DNA techniques to produce large quantities of some interferons. The U.S. Food and Drug Administration (FDA) has approved interferons for treating several diseases, including hepatitis B and hepatitis C, genital warts, several types of cancer (for example, leukemia), a type of multiple sclerosis, and AIDS-related Kaposi's sarcoma.

In response to gram-negative bacteria, certain other pathogens, or some tumors, **tumor necrosis factor (TNF)** stimulates immune cells to initiate an inflammatory response. In fact, TNF was so-named because it was first identified as a compound that destroyed tumor cells. TNF is secreted mainly by macrophages and by *T cells,* a type of lymphocyte. In severe infections, large amounts of TNF are produced. TNF is then circulated in the blood and can have widespread effects. For example, it acts on the hypothalamus, inducing fever.

Sometimes infection by gram-negative bacteria, such as *Salmonella typhi,* results in the release of large amounts of TNF and other cytokines. This results in a cascade of reactions leading to *septic shock,* a potentially fatal condition that may involve high fever and malfunction of the circulatory system. Thus, cytokines can sometimes have harmful effects.

Interleukins are a diverse group of cytokines secreted mainly by macrophages and lymphocytes. Interleukins are numbered according to their order of discovery. They regulate interactions between white blood cells, such as lymphocytes and macrophages, and other cells. *Interleukin-1 (IL-1)* functions with TNF in mediating inflammation. *Interleukin-12 (IL-12)* stimulates NK cells, as well as T cells, to produce IFN-gamma. Some interleukins have widespread effects. During infection IL-1 can reset the body's thermostat in the hypothalamus, resulting in fever and its symptoms. The overproduction of certain interleukins has been associated with clinical disease, including atherosclerosis.

Chemokines, a large group of cytokines, are signaling molecules that attract, activate, and direct the movement of various cells of the immune system. For example, they regulate the migration of white blood cells from the blood to the tissues. Some chemokines are produced in response to infection and are mediators of the inflammatory response.

Complement promotes destruction of pathogens and enhances inflammation

Phagocytes secrete cytokines that activate the *complement system.* **Complement,** so named because it "complements" the action of other defensive responses, consists of more than 20 proteins present in plasma and other body fluids. Similarities in complement proteins in many species, including horseshoe crabs, sea urchins, tunicates, and mammals, suggest that these molecules evolved millions of years ago and have been highly conserved.

Normally, complement proteins are inactive until the body is exposed to an antigen. Certain pathogens activate the complement system directly. In other cases, the binding of an antigen and antibody stimulates activation. Complement activation involves a cascade of reactions; each component acts on the next in the series. Proteins of the complement system then work to destroy pathogens.

Complement proteins are active against many antigens, and their actions are nonspecific: they (1) lyse viruses, bacteria, and other cells; (2) coat pathogens, making them less "slippery" so that macrophages and neutrophils phagocytose them more easily; (3) attract white blood cells to the site of infection, a process called *chemotaxis;* and (4) bind to specific receptors on cells of the immune system, stimulating specific actions, such as secreting regulatory molecules and enhancing the inflammatory response.

Inflammation is a protective response

The **inflammatory response,** or *inflammation,* is one of the body's key responses to infection or injury. Tissue injury caused by pathogen invasion or physical injury activates a clotting factor in the blood plasma that turns on three different interconnecting molecular cascades in the plasma, including the clotting cascade. Many of these reactions generate molecules—for example, the peptide *bradykinin*—that mediate the inflammatory process. These plasma mediators dilate blood vessels and increase capillary permeability (**FIG. 45-3** and **45-4**). Many cytokines signal white blood cells to launch the inflammatory response, and some cytokines help regulate the process. Inflammation also activates the complement system. The clinical characteristics of inflammation are heat, redness, edema (swelling), and pain.

The inflammatory response includes three main processes.

1. *Vasodilation.* Macrophages and **mast cells** stationed in the tissues respond rapidly to damaged tissue or infection. Mast cells, which are found in most tissues close to blood vessels, release **histamine,** cytokines, and other compounds that dilate blood vessels in the affected area. Expanded blood vessel diameter brings more blood to the area. The increased blood flow warms the skin and reddens skin that contains little pigment.

2. *Increased capillary permeability.* Histamine and other compounds released by mast cells increase capillary permeability.

Fluid and antibodies leave the circulation and enter the tissues. As the volume of interstitial fluid increases, *edema* occurs. The edema, along with the action of certain enzymes in the plasma, causes the pain that characterizes inflammation.

3. *Increased phagocytosis.* Increased blood flow brings large numbers of neutrophils and other phagocytic cells to the inflamed region within a few hours of tissue injury or infection. The phagocytes migrate out of the capillaries and into the infected tissues. Macrophages secrete chemokines and other cytokines that recruit and activate additional neutrophils. One of the main functions of inflammation is increased phagocytosis.

Although the inflammatory response begins as a local response, sometimes the entire body may become involved. **Fever,** a common clinical symptom of widespread inflammation, helps the body fight infection. Elevated body temperature increases phagocytosis and interferes with the growth and replication of microorganisms. Fever breaks down lysosomes, destroying cells infected by viruses. Fever also promotes the activity of certain lymphocytes. A short-term, low fever speeds recovery.

The inflammatory response is vital in overcoming infection, but *chronic inflammation* contributes to many chronic diseases.

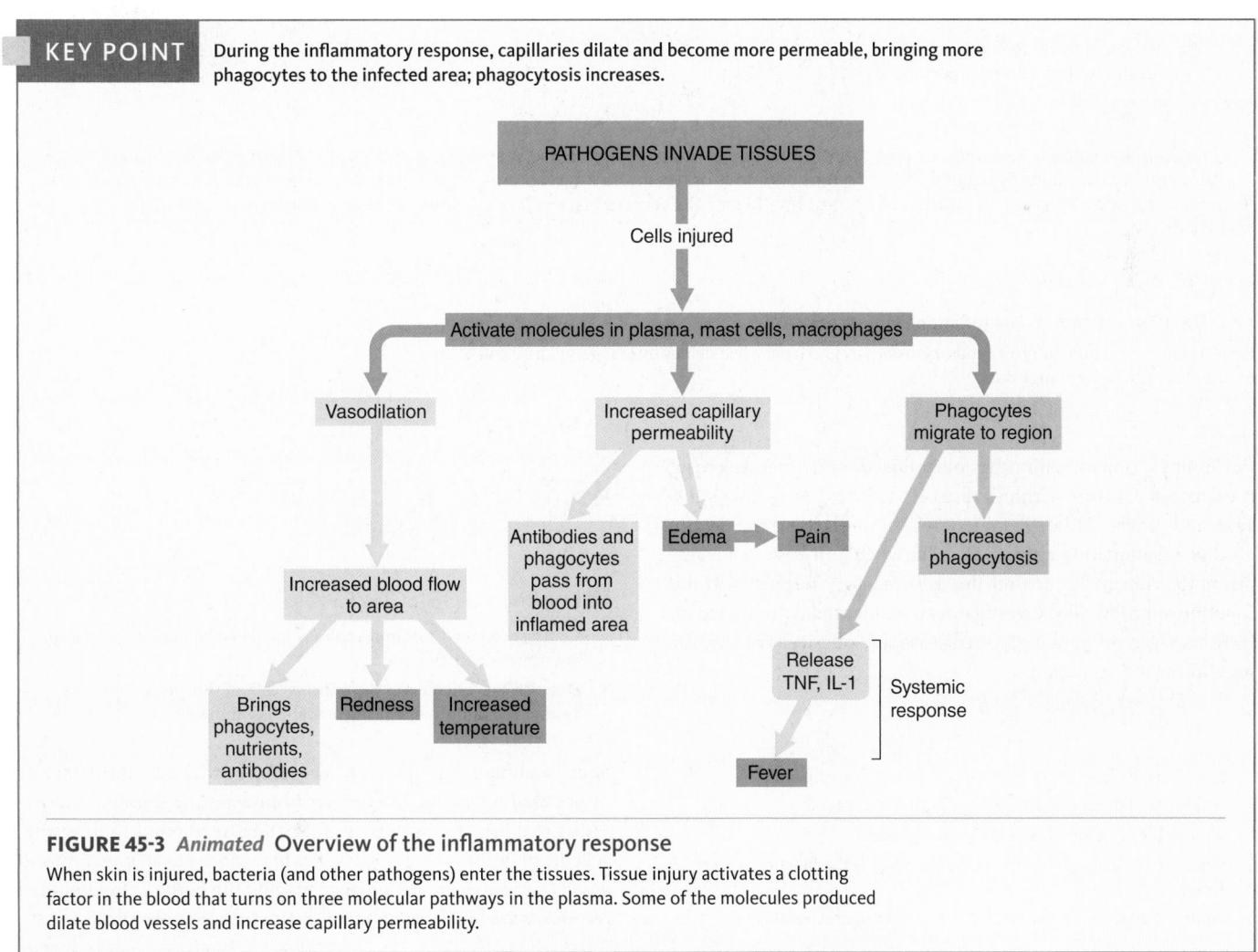

KEY POINT During the inflammatory response, capillaries dilate and become more permeable, bringing more phagocytes to the infected area; phagocytosis increases.

FIGURE 45-3 *Animated* Overview of the inflammatory response

When skin is injured, bacteria (and other pathogens) enter the tissues. Tissue injury activates a clotting factor in the blood that turns on three molecular pathways in the plasma. Some of the molecules produced dilate blood vessels and increase capillary permeability.

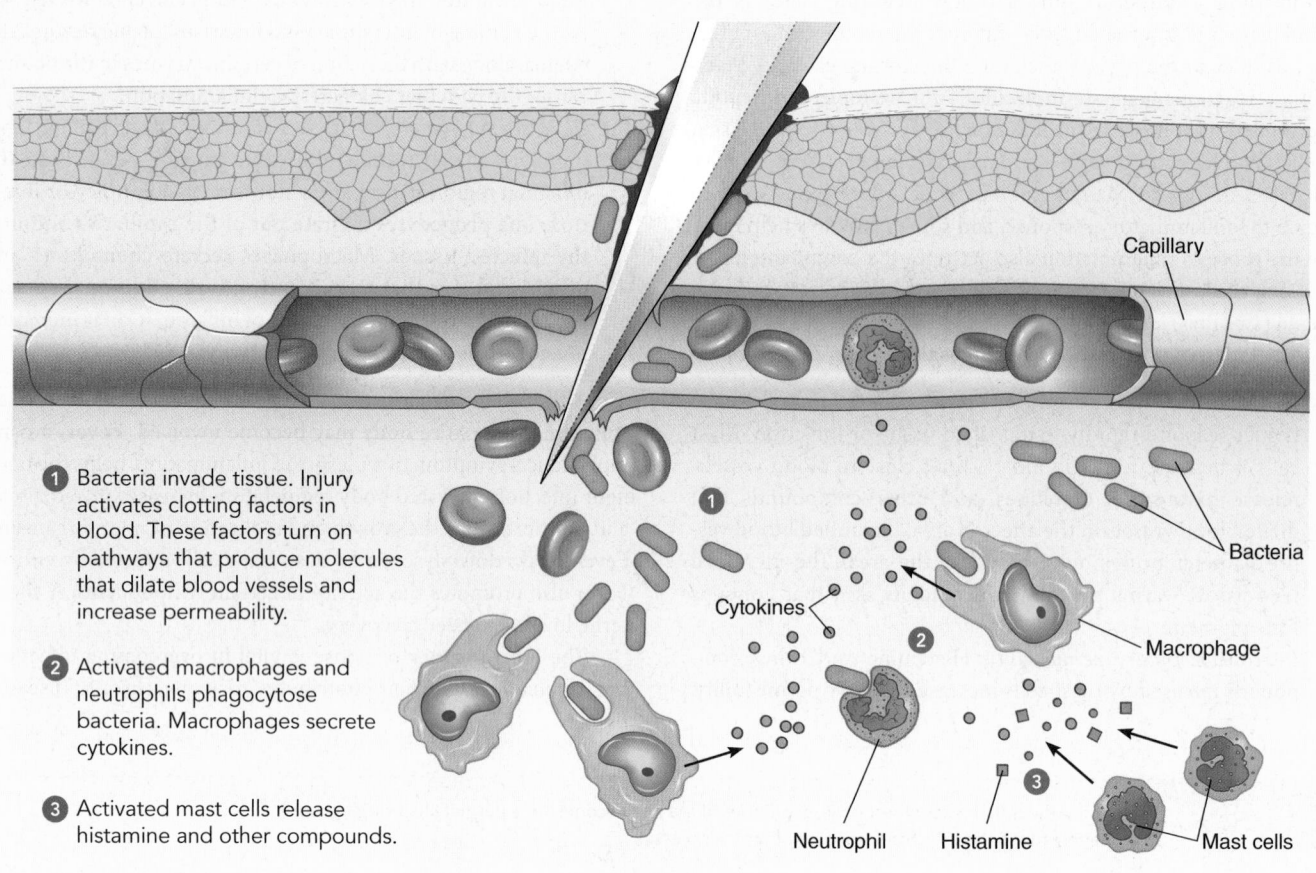

① Bacteria invade tissue. Injury activates clotting factors in blood. These factors turn on pathways that produce molecules that dilate blood vessels and increase permeability.

② Activated macrophages and neutrophils phagocytose bacteria. Macrophages secrete cytokines.

③ Activated mast cells release histamine and other compounds.

(a) Histamine, cytokines, and other compounds released by mast cells increase vasodilation and capillary permeability. Certain cytokines attract phagocytic cells. Macrophages and neutrophils in the infected area engulf and destroy bacteria. Macrophages secrete cytokines that recruit additional neutrophils. Mast cells secrete histamine, cytokines, and other substances that dilate blood vessels.

FIGURE 45-4 *Animated* **The inflammatory response**
Bacteria are represented by brown rods; cytokines by green dots; histamines by orange squares; and other mast cell secretions by orange dots.

For example, inflammation has been linked with atherosclerosis, rheumatoid arthritis, Crohn's disease, diabetes, Alzheimer's disease, and cancer. Although we do not yet understand the details, chronic inflammation appears to occur when homeostatic mechanisms that normally turn off the inflammatory response do not function appropriately. Investigators have identified prolonged infections, cigarette smoking, gum disease, and obesity as risk factors for chronic inflammation.

Review

- What barriers keep most pathogens from invading the body?
- What is the function of pattern recognition receptors?
- What is the function of NK cells? macrophages?
- What are the main groups of cytokines? What is the function of each group?
- What processes are involved in the inflammatory response?

45.3 SPECIFIC IMMUNE RESPONSES

◼ LEARNING OBJECTIVES

4 Contrast cell-mediated and antibody-mediated immunity, and give an overview of each process.
5 Describe the functions of the principal cells of the specific immune system and of the major histocompatibility complex.

Specific immune responses are also referred to as *adaptive immunity* or *acquired immunity*. In contrast to nonspecific immune mechanisms that are always present and ready to respond to infection, specific immune responses develop in response to an infection and *adapt* to the specific pathogens invading the body. These immune responses are highly specific for distinct macromolecules.

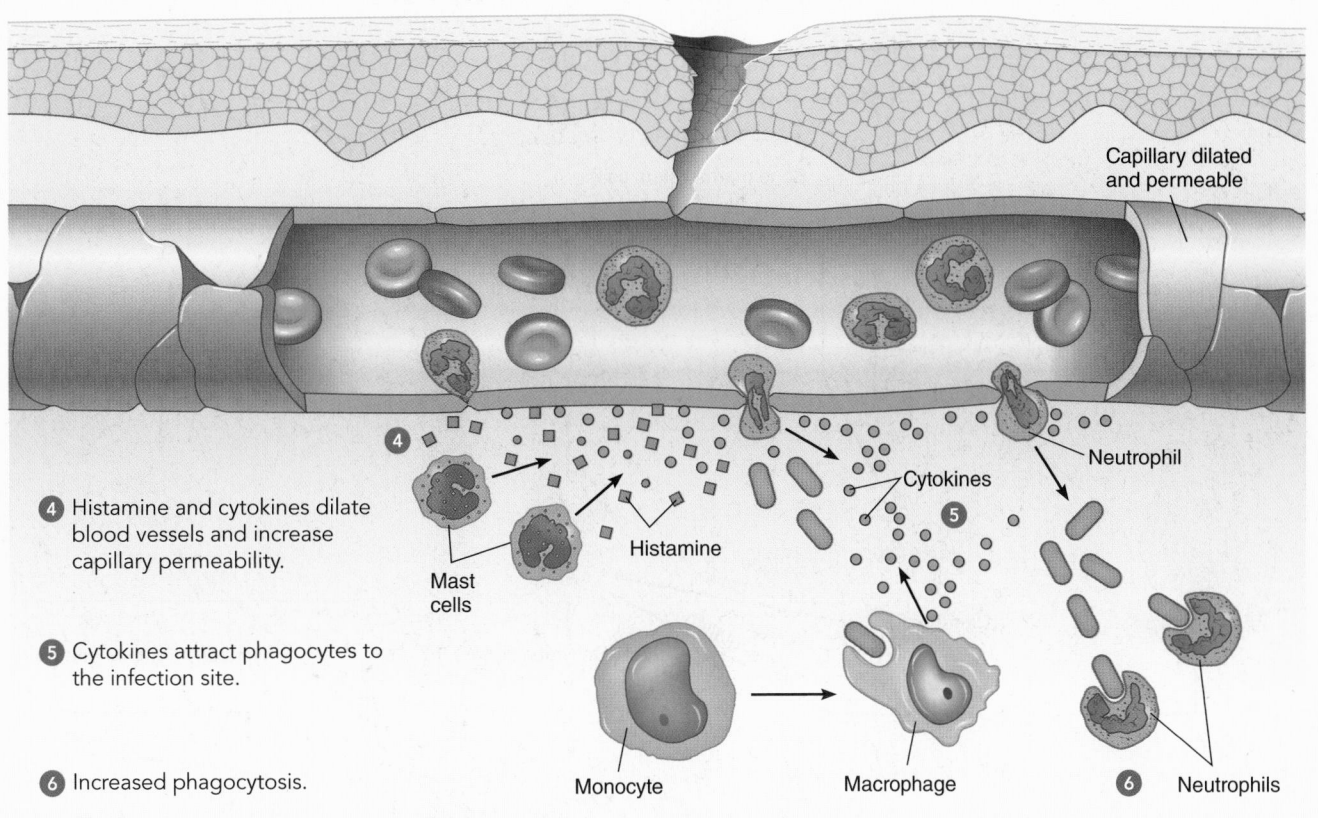

④ Histamine and cytokines dilate blood vessels and increase capillary permeability.

⑤ Cytokines attract phagocytes to the infection site.

⑥ Increased phagocytosis.

(b) Large numbers of monocytes and phagocytic cells pass through the now dilated, permeable capillaries into the infected area. Monocytes develop into macrophages. Phagocytosis increases.

While nonspecific immune responses destroy pathogens and prevent the spread of infection, the body mobilizes its specific immune responses. It takes several days to activate specific immune responses, but once in gear, these mechanisms are extremely effective. As discussed earlier, specific immune responses are precisely targeted to destroy specific antigens, and they have immunological memory. Two types of specific immune responses are *cell-mediated immunity* and *antibody-mediated immunity*.

Many types of cells are involved in specific immune responses

The main types of cells of the specific immune system are shown in **FIGURE 45-5**. Two key cell types that participate in specific immune responses are lymphocytes and *antigen-presenting cells*. Phagocytes and many other cells important in nonspecific immune responses also participate in specific responses. **Eosinophils,** for example, are white blood cells that release proteins, including cytokines, from their granules. Some of these cytokines are important in spe-

cific immune responses. Eosinophils also release proteins that are toxic to parasitic worms.

Lymphocytes are the principal warriors in specific immune responses

Lymphocytes are important in both specific and nonspecific immunity. Natural killer cells (NK cells) were discussed in the previous discussion of nonspecific immunity. Recall that NK cells are lymphocytes that kill virally infected cells and tumor cells. **T lymphocytes,** or **T cells,** and **B lymphocytes,** or **B cells,** function in specific immunity.

T cells are responsible for **cell-mediated immunity.** They are the body's cellular soldiers. T cells travel to the site of infection and attack body cells infected by invading pathogens, as well as foreign cells (such as those introduced in tissue grafts or organ transplants). T cells also destroy cells altered by mutation (cancer cells).

B cells are responsible for **antibody-mediated immunity.** B cells mature into **plasma cells,** which produce specific antibodies. Antibodies bind to specific antigens, neutralizing them or marking

Cells important in specific immune responses include antigen-presenting cells (macrophages and dendritic cells) and lymphocytes (T cells and B cells). These cells interact through complex signaling.

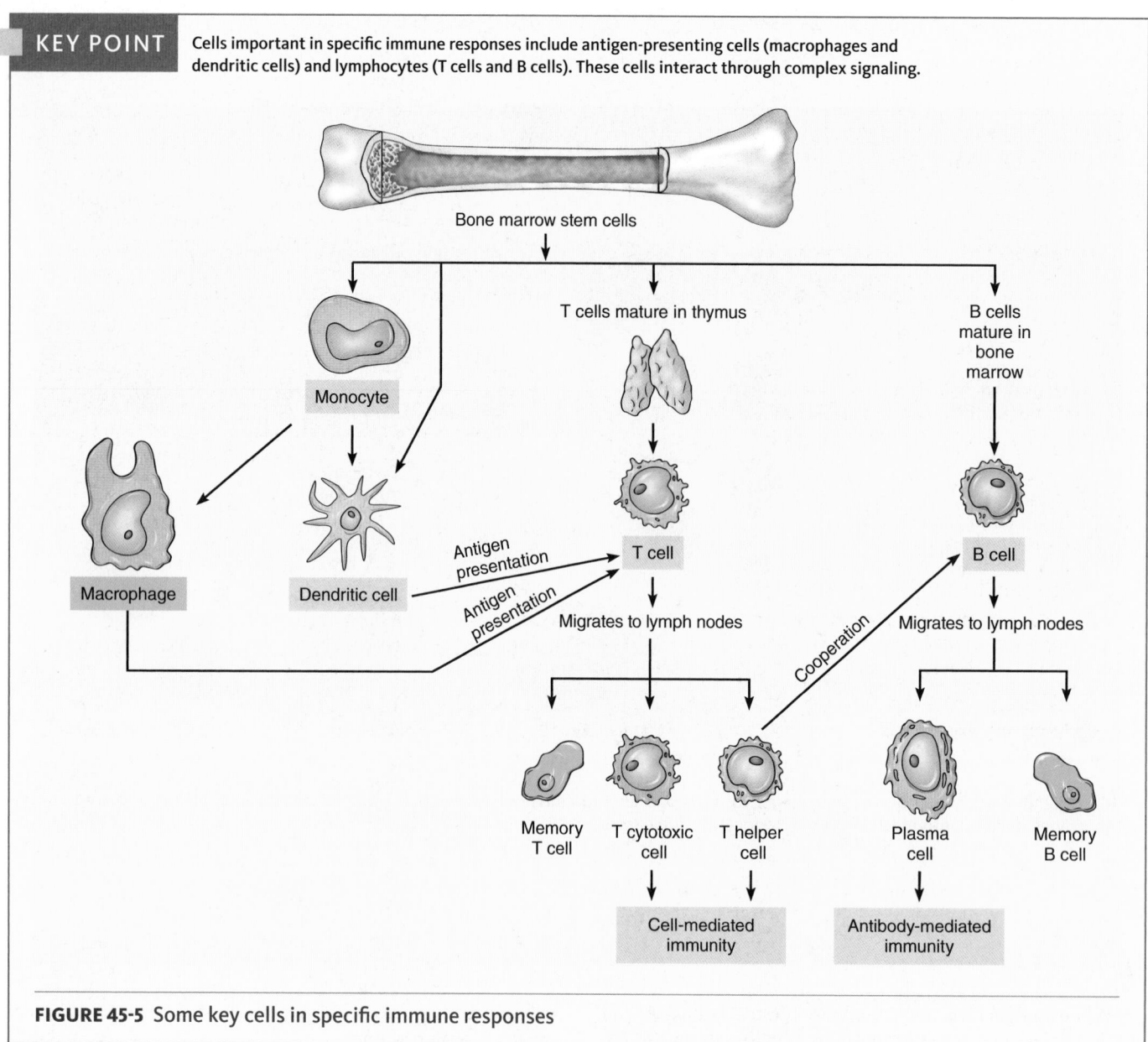

FIGURE 45-5 Some key cells in specific immune responses

them for destruction. Antibody-mediated immunity is one of the body's chief chemical defense strategies.

All lymphocytes develop from stem cells in the bone marrow. B cells complete their development in the adult bone marrow. T cells mature in the **thymus gland** (from which the *T* in their name derives). Large numbers of mature lymphocytes reside in lymph organs, including the spleen, lymph nodes, tonsils, and other lymph tissues strategically positioned throughout the body.

Although T cells and B cells are similar in appearance when viewed with a light microscope, sophisticated techniques such as fluorescence microscopy demonstrate that these cells can be differentiated by their unique cell-surface macromolecules. T cells and B cells have different functions and life histories and tend to locate in (or "home" to) separate regions of the spleen, lymph nodes, and other lymph tissues.

Millions of B cells are produced in the bone marrow daily. Each B cell is genetically programmed to encode a glycoprotein receptor that can bind with a specific type of antigen. When a B cell comes into contact with an antigen that binds to its receptors, the B cell becomes activated. B-cell activation is a complex process that typically requires the participation of a particular type of T cell.

Once activated, a B cell divides rapidly to form a clone of identical cells. The cloned B cells differentiate into *plasma cells,* which produce antibodies. A plasma cell can produce more than ten million molecules of antibody per hour! The antibody binds to the antigen that originally activated the B cells. Some activated B cells do not become plasma cells but instead become long-living **memory B cells** that continue to produce small amounts of antibody after the body overcomes an infection.

On their way from the bone marrow to the lymph tissues, T cells are processed in the thymus gland. The thymus makes T cells *immunocompetent,* capable of immunological response. As T cells move through the thymus, they divide many times and develop specific surface proteins with distinctive receptor sites.

The T-cell population undergoes positive and negative selection. In *negative selection,* T cells in the thymus that react to self-antigens undergo apoptosis. Immunologists estimate that more than 90% of developing T cells are negatively selected.

In *positive selection,* T cells are allowed to mature if they recognize self-antigens and bind with foreign antigens. These T cells differentiate and leave the thymus to take up residence in other lymph tissues or to launch immune responses in infected tissues. By selecting only appropriate T cells, the thymus gland ensures that T cells can distinguish between the body's own molecules and foreign antigens.

Most T cells in the thymus differentiate just before birth and during the first few months of postnatal life. If the thymus is removed before this processing takes place, an animal does not develop cell-mediated immunity. If the thymus is removed after that time, cell-mediated immunity is less seriously impaired.

T cells are distinguished by the **T-cell receptor (TCR),** which recognizes specific antigens. Two main populations of T cells are T cytotoxic cells and T helper cells. **T cytotoxic (T_C) cells** are also known as *CD8 cells* because they have a glycoprotein designated CD8 on their plasma membrane surface. Known less formally as *killer T cells,* T_C cells recognize and destroy cells with foreign antigens on their surfaces. Their target cells include virus-infected cells, cancer cells, and foreign tissue grafts.

T helper (T_H) cells, also known as *CD4 cells,* have a surface glycoprotein designated CD4. T_H cells secrete cytokines that activate B cells, T cells, and macrophages. **Regulatory T cells,** known as **Tregs,** are a subpopulation of T_H cells. Tregs help regulate immune responses by suppressing the function of certain T cells. After an infection, **memory T cells** (both memory T_C cells and memory T_H cells) remain in the body.

Antigen-presenting cells activate T helper cells

Macrophages, dendritic cells, and B cells function as "professional" **antigen-presenting cells (APCs)** that display foreign antigens as well as their own surface proteins. APCs are inactive until their pattern recognition receptors recognize PAMPs on pathogens. Once activated, an APC ingests the pathogen. Lysosomal enzymes inside the APC degrade most, but not all, of the bacterial antigens. The APC displays fragments of the foreign antigens on its cell surface in association with a type of self-molecule (class II MHC, discussed later). The activated APC expresses additional signaling molecules, called **costimulatory molecules,** along with the displayed antigen. These fully functional APCs present displayed antigens to T cells.

In addition to their function as APCs, macrophages secrete more than 100 different compounds, including cytokines and enzymes that destroy bacteria. When stimulated by bacteria, macrophages secrete interleukins that activate B cells and certain T cells. We have seen that interleukins also promote nonspecific immune responses, such as fever.

Receptors on dendritic cells bind antigens of microbes. Dendritic cells take these antigens, process them, and display antigen fragments on their cell surface. Now APCs, the dendritic cells leave the epithelial lining and, guided by chemokines, migrate to the lymph nodes. Costimulatory molecules, along with the displayed antigen, attract and activate specific T cells capable of responding to the antigen. Thus, dendritic cells are specialized to bind, process, transport, and present antigens to T cells.

The major histocompatibility complex is responsible for recognition of self

The ability of the vertebrate immune system to distinguish self from nonself depends largely on a cluster of closely linked genes known as the **major histocompatibility complex (MHC).** In humans, the MHC is also called the **human leukocyte antigen complex (HLA).** The MHC genes are polymorphic (variable). Within the population there are multiple alleles, more than 40 for each locus. As a result, the cell-surface proteins for which they code are generally different in each individual. With so many possible combinations, no two people, except identical twins, are likely to have all the same MHC proteins on their cells. The more closely related two individuals are, the more MHC genes they have in common. You can think of your MHC proteins as a biochemical "fingerprint."

The MHC genes encode **MHC antigens,** referred to as self-antigens, which differ in chemical structure, function, and tissue distribution. Class I MHC genes encode glycoproteins expressed on the surface of most nucleated cells. These antigens bind with foreign antigens from viruses or other pathogens within the cell to form a foreign antigen–class I MHC glycoprotein complex. The cell displays this complex on its surface and presents it to T_C cells. Thus, any infected cell can function as an antigen-presenting cell and can activate certain T_C cells.

Class II MHC genes encode glycoproteins expressed primarily on "professional" APCs—dendritic cells, macrophages, and B cells. These class II MHC antigens combine with foreign antigen from bacteria, and the cell presents the complex to T_H cells. Class III MHC genes encode many secreted proteins involved in the immune response, including components of the complement system and TNFs.

Review

- How are cell-mediated immunity and antibody-mediated immunity different?
- What are two main types of T cells? What is the function of B cells?
- What is the function of antigen-presenting cells? Describe two types.

45.4 CELL-MEDIATED IMMUNITY

■ LEARNING OBJECTIVE

6 Describe the sequence of events in cell-mediated immunity.

T cells and APCs (mainly dendritic cells and macrophages) are responsible for cell-mediated immunity. T cells destroy cells infected with viruses and macrophages that have ingested "smart" bacteria. These bacteria escape from the vesicles in which they are enclosed during phagocytosis. They escape destruction by lysosomal

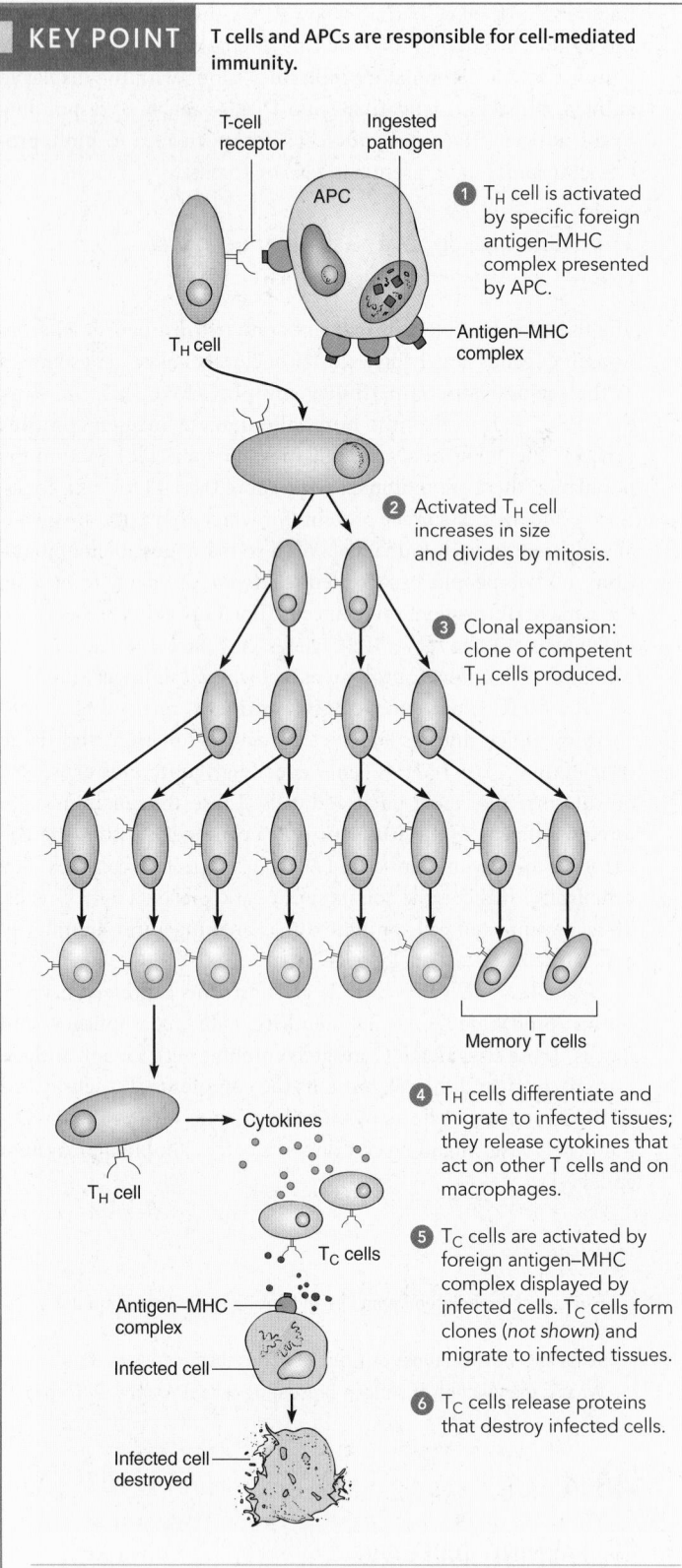

T-cell receptor

Ingested pathogen

APC

Antigen–MHC complex

T$_H$ cell

1 T$_H$ cell is activated by specific foreign antigen–MHC complex presented by APC.

2 Activated T$_H$ cell increases in size and divides by mitosis.

3 Clonal expansion: clone of competent T$_H$ cells produced.

Memory T cells

Cytokines

T$_H$ cell

T$_C$ cells

Antigen–MHC complex

Infected cell

Infected cell destroyed

4 T$_H$ cells differentiate and migrate to infected tissues; they release cytokines that act on other T cells and on macrophages.

5 T$_C$ cells are activated by foreign antigen–MHC complex displayed by infected cells. T$_C$ cells form clones (*not shown*) and migrate to infected tissues.

6 T$_C$ cells release proteins that destroy infected cells.

FIGURE 45-6 *Animated* **Cell-mediated immunity**

When activated by a foreign antigen–MHC complex presented by an APC and by cytokines, a T$_H$ cell divides and gives rise to a clone of T$_H$ cells. T$_C$ cells are also activated by antigens presented on the surfaces of infected cells, and they also form a clone. Both types of T cells migrate to the site of infection. T$_H$ cells release cytokines that stimulate T$_C$ cells and activate macrophages so that they phagocytose pathogens. T$_C$ cells release proteins that destroy infected cells.

enzymes by "hiding" in the cytoplasm of macrophages. T cells destroy cells that have been altered in some way, such as cancer cells. They also destroy the cells of foreign grafts such as a transplanted kidney or liver.

How do T cells know which cells to target? T cells do not recognize antigens unless they are presented properly. Recall that when a virus (or other pathogen) infects a cell, some of the viral protein is broken down to peptides and displayed with class I MHC molecules on the cell surface. Only T cells with receptors that bind to the specific antigen–MHC complex become activated.

There are two general populations of T cells: T$_H$ cells and T$_C$ cells. Each T$_H$ cell expresses the glycoprotein called CD4 and each T$_C$ cell expresses CD8. Within each general population of T cell, there are thousands of different antigen specificities that the T-cell receptors (TCRs) can recognize. Activation of T$_H$ cells, for example, occurs when phagocytic cells digest antigen and parts of the antigen are placed within their surface MHC complexes. They then present these antigens to the TCR on T$_H$ cells as part of a foreign antigen–class II MHC glycoprotein complex.

Once activated by the foreign antigen–MHC class II antigen complex displayed on the surface of APCs, the activated T$_H$ cells secrete interleukin 2. This cytokine is a growth factor that stimulates the activated cells to proliferate. The T$_H$ cells divide several times, giving rise to a clone of T$_H$ cells (**FIG. 45-6**). This process is called **clonal expansion.**

Some of the T$_H$ cells produced migrate to the site of infection. These cells can produce many different types of cytokines. Some attract macrophages to the site of infection and promote the destruction of intracellular pathogens. Others function mainly in promoting antibody-mediated immunity.

Each T$_C$ cell expresses the CD8 molecule on its surface, as well as more than 50,000 identical TCRs that bind to one specific type of antigen. T$_C$ cells recognize antigens presented to them as part of a foreign antigen–class I MHC glycoprotein complex. Generally, fewer than 1 in 100,000 T cells have the same antigen specificity and can respond. After clonal expansion, as many as 1 in 10 T$_C$ cells may be specific for the targeted antigen. T$_C$ cell activation requires at least two signals in addition to the presented antigen: a co-stimulatory signal and an interleukin signal. Once activated, a T$_C$ cell increases in size and gives rise to a clone of many effector T$_C$ cells.

Effector T$_C$ cells make up the cell infantry. They leave the lymph nodes and make their way to the infected area, where they destroy target cells within seconds after contact. When a T$_C$ cell combines with antigen on the surface of the target cell, it destroys the cell in much the same way that NK cells destroy their target cells. The T$_C$ secretes perforins that perforate the plasma membrane of the target cell. Granzymes then induce the cell to self-destruct by apoptosis. After releasing cytotoxic substances, the T cell disengages itself from its victim cell and seeks out a new target.

The sequence of events for production and function of T$_C$ cells in cell-mediated immunity can be summarized as follows:

virus invades body cell ⟶ infected cell displays foreign antigen–MHC class I antigen complex ⟶ specific T$_C$ cell activated by this complex ⟶ clone of T$_C$ cells produced ⟶ effector T$_C$ cells migrate to area of infection ⟶ T$_C$ cells stimulated by cytokines released by T$_H$ cells ⟶ T$_C$ cells release enzymes that destroy target cells

Review

- How do T$_H$ cells function in cell-mediated immunity?
- How do APCs function in cell-mediated immunity?
- How do T$_C$ cells function in cell-mediated immunity?

45.5 ANTIBODY-MEDIATED IMMUNITY

◼ LEARNING OBJECTIVES

7 Summarize the sequence of events in antibody-mediated immunity, including the effects of antigen–antibody complexes on pathogens.

8 Describe the basic structure and function of an antibody, and explain the basis of antibody diversity.

9 Describe the basis of immunological memory, and contrast secondary and primary immune responses.

10 Compare active and passive immunity, and give examples of each.

We have discussed two types of molecules that recognize specific antigens: T-cell receptors and MHC molecules. Here we turn our attention to the third type, antibodies. B cells are responsible for antibody-mediated immunity. A given B cell can produce many copies of one specific antibody. Antibody molecules serve as cell-surface receptors that combine with antigens. Only a B cell with a receptor complementary in shape to a particular antigen can bind that antigen. The antigen enters the B cell by receptor-mediated endocytosis (see Chapter 5). The antigen is then degraded into peptide fragments, and the B cell displays peptide fragments together with MHC protein class II on its surface.

In most cases, the activation of B cells involves APCs and T$_H$ cells (**FIG. 45-7**). T$_H$ cells stimulate B cells to divide and produce antibodies. However, the T$_H$ cell itself must first be activated. T$_H$ cells do not recognize an antigen that is presented alone. The antigen must be presented as part of a foreign antigen–class II MHC complex on the surface of an APC. When an APC displaying a foreign antigen–MHC complex contacts a T$_H$ cell with complementary T-cell receptors, a complicated interaction occurs. Multiple chemical signals are sent back and forth between cells. For example, the APC secretes interleukins, such as IL-1, that activate T$_H$ cells.

B cells serve as APCs to T cells. An activated T$_H$ cell binds with the foreign antigen–MHC complex on the B cell. The T$_H$ cell then releases interleukins, which together with antigen activate the B cell.

Once activated, a B cell divides by mitosis, giving rise to a clone of identical cells (**FIG. 45-8**). This clonal expansion in response to a specific antigen is known as *clonal selection* (discussed later). The cloned B cells mature into plasma cells that secrete antibod-

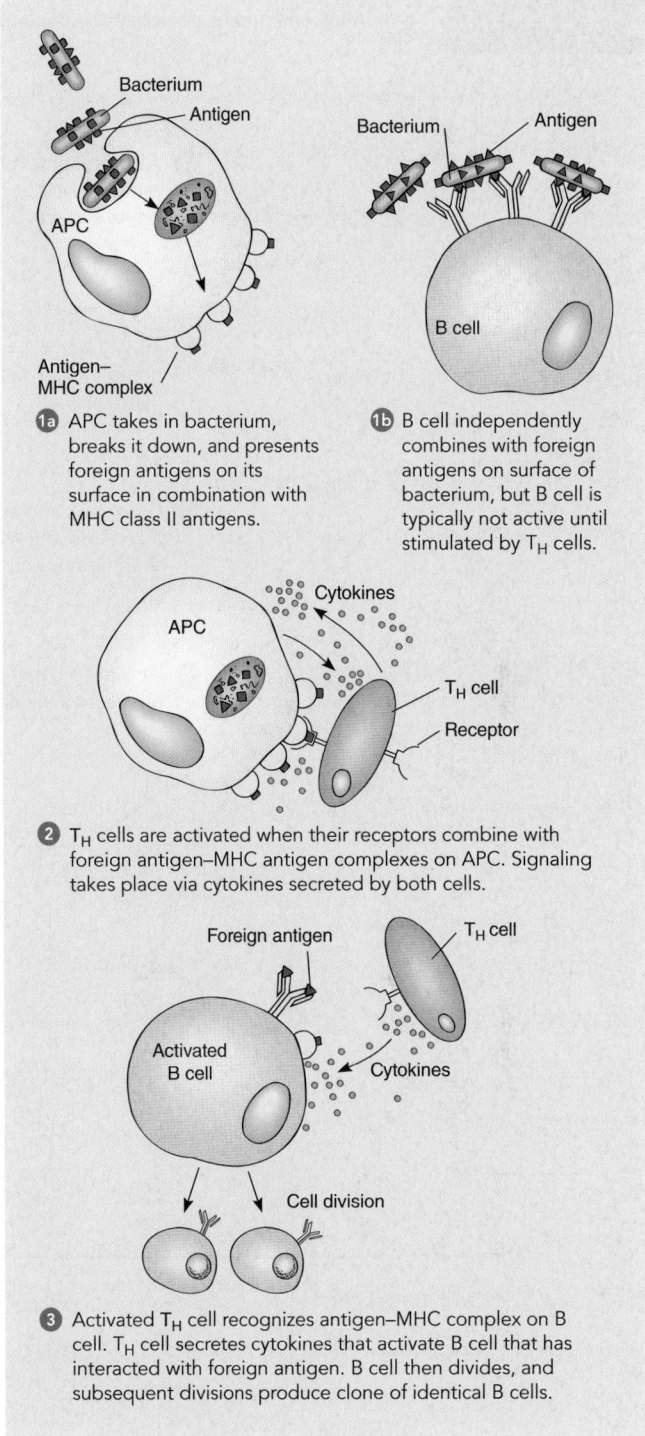

1a APC takes in bacterium, breaks it down, and presents foreign antigens on its surface in combination with MHC class II antigens.

1b B cell independently combines with foreign antigens on surface of bacterium, but B cell is typically not active until stimulated by T$_H$ cells.

2 T$_H$ cells are activated when their receptors combine with foreign antigen–MHC antigen complexes on APC. Signaling takes place via cytokines secreted by both cells.

3 Activated T$_H$ cell recognizes antigen–MHC complex on B cell. T$_H$ cell secretes cytokines that activate B cell that has interacted with foreign antigen. B cell then divides, and subsequent divisions produce clone of identical B cells.

FIGURE 45-7 *Animated* **B-cell activation**
This figure is a detailed illustration of the first four steps in Figure 45-8.

ies. These antibodies are specific to the antigen that activated the original B cell. It is important to remember that the specificity of the clone is determined *before* the B cell encounters the antigen.

Unlike T cells, most plasma cells do not leave the lymph nodes. Only the antibodies they secrete pass out of the lymph tissues and make their way via the lymph and blood to the infected area. The

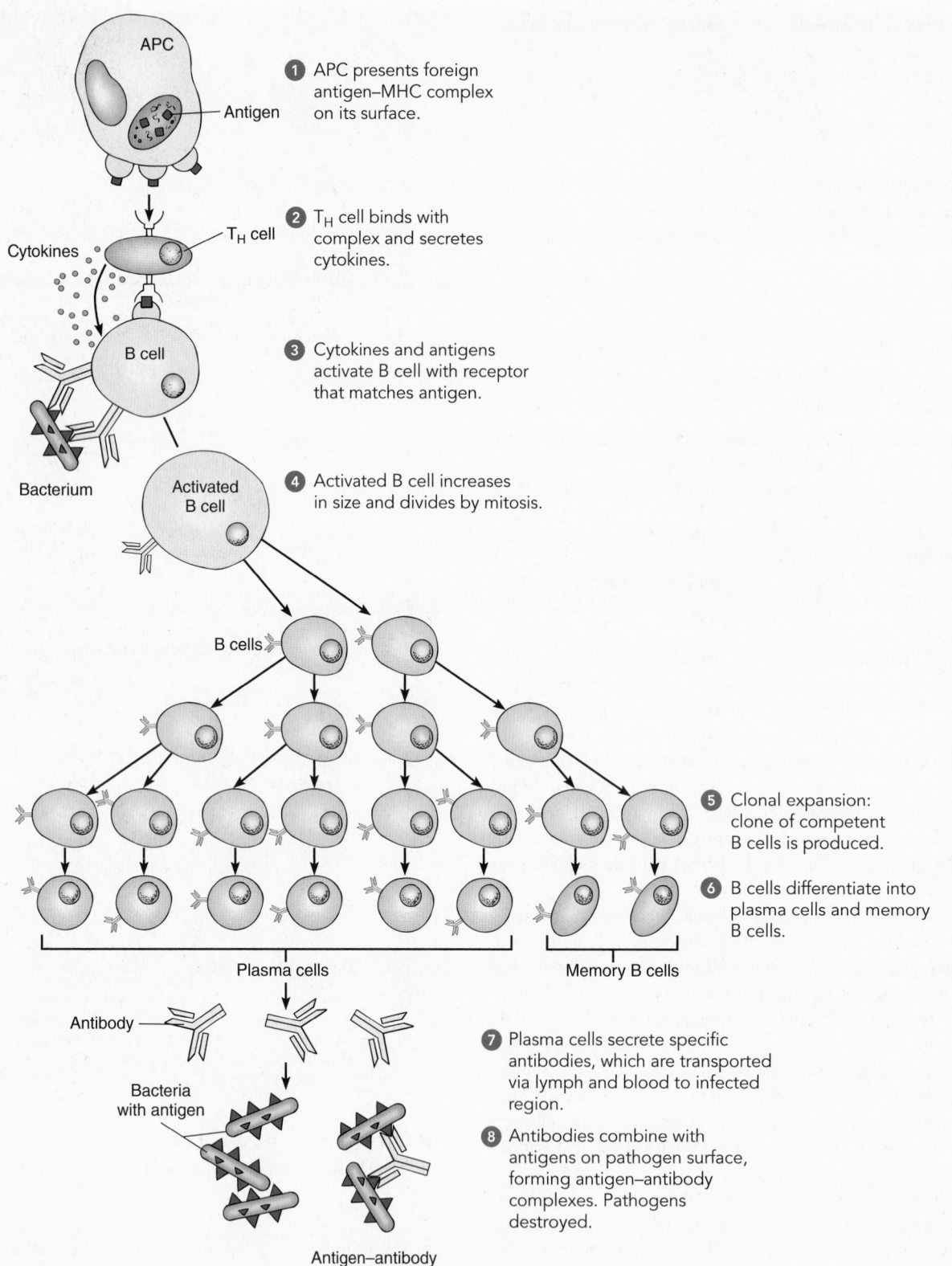

APC

Antigen

① APC presents foreign antigen–MHC complex on its surface.

Cytokines

T_H cell

② T_H cell binds with complex and secretes cytokines.

B cell

③ Cytokines and antigens activate B cell with receptor that matches antigen.

Bacterium

Activated B cell

④ Activated B cell increases in size and divides by mitosis.

B cells

⑤ Clonal expansion: clone of competent B cells is produced.

⑥ B cells differentiate into plasma cells and memory B cells.

Plasma cells

Memory B cells

Antibody

Bacteria with antigen

⑦ Plasma cells secrete specific antibodies, which are transported via lymph and blood to infected region.

⑧ Antibodies combine with antigens on pathogen surface, forming antigen–antibody complexes. Pathogens destroyed.

Antigen–antibody complex

FIGURE 45-8 *Animated* **Antibody-mediated immunity**

A specific B cell may be activated when a specific antigen binds to im-munoglobulin receptors on the B-cell surface. Typically, the B cell also requires cytokine stimulation from an activated T_H cell (see Fig. 45-7). Once activated, the B cell divides and produces a clone of B cells. These cells differentiate and become plasma cells that secrete antibodies. The plasma cells remain in the lymph tissues, but the antibodies are trans-ported to the site of infection by the blood or lymph. After the infection has been overcome, memory B cells remain in the tissues.

secreted antibody is a soluble form of the glycoprotein receptor of the activated B cell.

The sequence of events in antibody-mediated immunity can be summarized as follows:

pathogen invades body ⟶ APC phagocytoses pathogen ⟶ foreign antigen–MHC complex displayed on APC surface ⟶ T$_H$ cell binds with foreign antigen–MHC complex ⟶ activated T$_H$ cell interacts with a B cell that displays the same antigen ⟶ B cell activated ⟶ clone of B cells produced ⟶ B cells differentiate, becoming plasma cells ⟶ plasma cells secrete antibodies ⟶ antibodies form complexes with pathogen ⟶ pathogen is destroyed

Some activated B cells do not differentiate into plasma cells but instead become memory B cells (discussed in a later section).

A typical antibody consists of four polypeptide chains

An antibody molecule, also called **immunoglobulin (Ig),** has several functions. It combines with antigen, and it activates processes that destroy the antigen that binds to it. For example, an antibody may stimulate phagocytosis. Note that an antibody does not destroy an antigen directly; rather, it *labels* the antigen for destruction. The antibody molecule also serves as the B-cell receptor for antigen when it is attached to the B-cell surface.

Rodney Porter, of the University of Oxford in England, and Gerald Edelman, of Rockefeller University in New York, clarified the basic structure of the immunoglobulin molecule during the 1960s. Porter used the plant enzyme papain, a protease, to split Ig molecules into fragments. Based on his findings, Porter developed a working model of the structure of the Ig molecule and was the first to suggest that it is Y shaped. These researchers then constructed an accurate model of the antibody molecule. Porter and Edelman were awarded the 1972 Nobel Prize in Medicine for their contributions.

In a Y-shaped antibody molecule, the tail of the Y is called the *Fc fragment* (*c* indicates that this fragment crystallizes during cold storage). The Fc fragment binds with receptors on phagocytes and other cells of the immune system. This region of the antibody molecule also binds with molecules of the complement system. The two arms of the Y are referred to as *Fab fragments* (*Fab* stands for *fragment, antigen-binding*). The tips of the Fab fragments bind with antigen (**FIG. 45-9**). The Y shape permits the antibody molecule to combine with two antigen molecules, which allows the formation of **antigen–antibody complexes.**

Each antibody molecule consists of four polypeptide chains: two long chains, called *heavy chains,* and two short chains, called *light chains.* Each chain has a constant region and a variable region. In the **constant (C) region** of the heavy chains, the amino acid sequence is constant within a particular immunoglobulin class. The C region of the heavy chains is the tail of the Y part of the antibody molecule. You can think of this C region as the handle portion of a door key.

The **variable (V) region** has a unique amino acid sequence, like the pattern of bumps and notches on the part of a key that fits into a lock. At its variable regions, the antibody folds three-

(a) The antibody molecule is composed of two light chains and two heavy chains joined by disulfide bonds. The constant (C) and variable (V) regions of the chains are labeled.

(b) The Fab portion of the antibody binds to antigen. The Fc portion of the molecule binds to a cell of the immune system (*not shown*). Antigen–antibody complexes directly inactivate pathogens and increase phagocytosis. They also activate the complement system.

FIGURE 45-9 *Animated* **Antibody structure and function**

Antibodies combine with antigens to form antigen–antibody complexes. These complexes destroy or promote the destruction of pathogens in a variety of ways.

dimensionally, assuming a shape that enables it to combine with a specific antigen. When they meet, antigen and antibody fit together somewhat like a lock and key. They must fit in just the right way for the antibody to be effective (**FIG. 45-10**).

(a) A portion of the antigenic determinant (*red*) fits into a groove in the antibody molecule.

(b) The antigen–antibody complex has been pulled apart to show its structure.

FIGURE 45-10 An antigen–antibody complex

The components of an antigen–antibody complex fit together as shown in this computer simulation of their molecular structure. Antigen lysozyme, *green;* heavy chain of the antibody, *blue;* light chain, *yellow.*

The specific part of the antigen molecule that is recognized by an antibody or T-cell receptor is called an **antigenic determinant,** or *epitope.* An antigen may have many antigenic determinants on its surface; some have hundreds. Antigenic determinants often differ from one another, so several different kinds of antibodies can combine with a single antigen. A given antibody can bind with different strengths, or *affinities,* to different antigens. In the course of an immune response, higher affinity antibodies are generated. This occurs because as activated B cells are replicated, mutations occur in genes that encode the antibodies. Cells with antibodies that bind more tightly are selected during the ongoing immune response—a striking example of microevolution in action.

Antibodies are grouped in five classes

Antibodies are grouped in five classes, defined by unique amino acid sequences in the C regions of the heavy chains. The classes are named using the abbreviation *Ig* for *immunoglobulin* and are designated IgG, IgM, IgA, IgD, and IgE. In humans, about 75% of the circulating antibodies belong to the **IgG** class; these are part of the gamma globulin fraction of the plasma. **IgM** is the first antibody that humans make in an immune response. IgG and IgM share some functional properties. Both interact with macrophages and activate the complement system. They defend against many pathogens carried in the blood, including bacteria, viruses, and some fungi. IgG is the antibody that crosses the *placenta* (the organ of exchange between mother and developing fetus) and protects the fetus and, later, the newborn baby.

IgA, present in mucus, tears, saliva, and breast milk, prevents viruses and bacteria from attaching to epithelial surfaces. This immunoglobulin, which defends against inhaled or ingested pathogens, is strategically secreted into the respiratory, digestive, urinary, and reproductive tracts. Like IgM, **IgD** is an important immunoglobulin on the B-cell surface. It has a critical role in maturation of B cells and helps activate B cells following antigen binding. IgD has a low concentration in plasma (less than 1% of circulating antibodies).

IgE, which has an even lower plasma concentration than IgD, binds to mast cells, which contain histamine and other potent signaling molecules. These chemicals are released when an antigen binds to IgE on a mast cell. Histamine triggers many allergy symptoms, including inflammation. IgE is also responsible for an immune response to invading parasitic worms.

Antigen–antibody binding activates other defenses

Antibodies mark a pathogen as foreign by combining with an antigen on its surface. Generally, several antibodies bind with several antigens, creating a mass of clumped antigen–antibody complexes. The combination of antigen and antibody activates several defensive responses (see Fig. 45-9).

1. The antigen–antibody complex may inactivate the pathogen or its toxin. For example, when an antibody attaches to its surface, a virus may lose the ability to attach to a host cell.
2. The antigen–antibody complex stimulates phagocytic cells to ingest the pathogen.
3. Antibodies of the IgG and IgM groups work mainly through the complement system.

When antibodies combine with a specific antigen on a pathogen, complement proteins destroy the pathogen. IgG molecules have an Fc fragment that binds Fc receptors; these receptors are expressed on many cells, including macrophages and neutrophils. When an antibody molecule is bound to a pathogen and the Fc portion of the antibody binds with an Fc receptor on a phagocyte, the pathogen is more easily destroyed.

The immune system responds to millions of different antigens

How can the immune system recognize every possible antigen, even those produced by newly mutated viruses never before encountered during the evolution of our species? In the 1950s, the Danish researcher Niels Jerne, of the Basel Institute for Immunology in Basel, Switzerland; David Talmage, of the University of Chicago; and Frank Macfarlane Burnet, of the Walter and Eliza Hall

Institute for Medical Research in Melbourne, Australia, developed the **clonal selection** hypothesis. This hypothesis proposes that before a lymphocyte ever encounters an antigen, the lymphocyte has specific receptors for that antigen on its surface. (Jerne and Burnet later were awarded Nobel Prizes in Physiology or Medicine for their work in immunology.)

When an antigen binds to a matching receptor on a lymphocyte, it activates the lymphocyte, which then gives rise to a clone of cells with identical receptors. A problem with this hypothesis when it was initially proposed was its suggestion that our cells must contain millions of separate antibody genes, each coding for an antibody with a different specificity. Although each human cell has a large amount of DNA, it is not enough to provide a different gene to encode each of the millions of possible specific antibody molecules.

An explanation for how the immune system could have so many different specificities came later. In 1965, W. J. Dreyer of the Institute of Biochemistry at the University of Zurich, Switzerland, and Joe Claude Bennett of the University of Alabama at Birmingham suggested that the C region and the V region of an immunoglobulin are encoded by two separate genes. Their hypothesis was at first rejected by many biologists because it contradicted the prevailing hypothesis that one gene codes for one polypeptide.

The technology needed to test Dreyer and Bennett's hypothesis was not immediately available, and it was not until 1976 that Susumu Tonegawa of the Massachusetts Institute of Technology and his colleagues demonstrated that separate genes encode the V and C regions of immunoglobulins. Tonegawa further showed that three separate families of genes code for immunoglobulins and that each gene family contains a large number of DNA segments that code for V regions. Recombination of these DNA segments during the differentiation of B cells is responsible for antibody diversity. Tonegawa was awarded the 1987 Nobel Prize in Physiology or Medicine for his work, which transformed the emerging science of immunology.

We now understand that in undifferentiated B cells, gene segments are present for a number of different V regions, for one or more junction (J) regions, and for one or more different C regions (**FIG. 45-11**). Rearrangement of these DNA segments produces an enormous number of potential combinations. Millions of different types of B (and T) cells are produced. By chance, one of those B cells may produce just the right antibody to destroy a pathogen that invades the body. To appreciate the capacity for antibody diversity, consider the diverse combinations of things you create in your everyday life. A familiar example is making an ice cream sundae. Imagine the varied combinations that are possible using 10 flavors of ice cream, 6 types of sauce, and 15 kinds of toppings.

Researchers have identified additional sources of antibody diversity. For example, the DNA of the mature B cells that codes for the regions of immunoglobulins mutates very readily. These somatic mutations produce genes that code for slightly different antibodies.

We have used antibody diversity here as an example, but similar genetic mechanisms account for the diversity of T-cell receptors. Although we may actually use only a relatively few types of antibodies or T cells in a lifetime, the remarkable diversity of the immune system prepares it to attack most potentially harmful antigens that may invade the body.

Monoclonal antibodies are highly specific

Before 1975, the only method for obtaining antibodies for medicine or research was immunizing animals and collecting their blood. Then Cesar Milstein and Georges Kohler at the Laboratory of Molecular Biology in Cambridge, England, developed **monoclonal antibodies,** identical antibodies produced by cells cloned from a single cell.

One way to produce monoclonal antibodies in the laboratory is to inject mice with the antigen of interest, for example, an antigen from a particular bacterium. After the mice have produced antibodies to the antigen, their plasma cells are collected. However, these normal plasma cells survive in culture for only a few generations, limiting the amount of antibody that can be produced. In contrast, cancer cells live and divide in tissue culture indefinitely.

B cells can be suspended in a culture medium together with lymphoma cells from other mice. (Lymphoma is a cancer of lymphocytes.) Then the B cells and lymphoma cells are induced to fuse. They form hybrid cells, known as **hybridomas,** which have properties of the two "parent" cells. Hybridomas can be cultured indefinitely (a cancer cell property) and continue to secrete antibodies (a B-cell property). Researchers select hybrid cells that are manufacturing the specific antibody needed and then clone them in a separate cell culture. Cells of this clone secrete large amounts of the particular antibody—thus the name *monoclonal antibodies.* Each type of monoclonal antibody is specific for a single antigenic determinant.

Immunologists also use recombinant DNA technology to produce monoclonal antibodies. Because of their purity and specificity, monoclonal antibodies have proved to be invaluable tools in modern biology. For example, a researcher may want to detect a specific molecule present in very small amounts in a mixture. The reaction of that molecule (the antigen) with a specific monoclonal antibody makes its presence known. Monoclonal antibodies are used in similar ways in various diagnostic tests. Home pregnancy tests make use of a monoclonal antibody that is specific for human chorionic gonadotropin (hCG), a hormone produced by a developing human embryo (see Chapters 50 and 51). Several monoclonal antibodies are being used clinically to treat cancer. The drug Herceptin is a monoclonal antibody used in treating a form of breast cancer.

Immunological memory is responsible for long-term immunity

Immunological memory depends on memory B cells and memory T cells. Following an immune response, memory T cells group strategically in many nonlymphatic tissues, including the lung, liver, kidney, and intestine. Many infections occur at such sites, and T cells stationed in those locations can respond quickly. In response to antigen, memory T cells rapidly become T_C cells and produce substances that kill invading cells.

Memory B cells have a "survival gene" that prevents apoptosis, the programmed cell death that is the eventual fate of plasma cells. Memory B cells continue to live and produce small amounts of antibody long after the body has overcome an infection. This circulating antibody is part of the body's arsenal of chemical weapons.

FIGURE 45-11 *Animated* Antibody diversity

In undifferentiated cells, gene segments are present for several different variable (V) regions, for one or more junction (J) regions, and for one or more different constant (C) regions. During differentiation, these DNA segments become rearranged. A gene segment extending from the end of one V segment to the beginning of one J segment may be deleted, thus producing a gene that can be transcribed. The RNA transcript is processed to remove introns, and the mRNA is translated. Each of the polypeptide chains of an antibody molecule is produced in this way.

If the same pathogen enters the body again, the antibody immediately targets it for destruction. At the same time, specific memory cells are stimulated to divide, producing new clones of plasma cells that produce the same antibody. The presence of circulating antibodies is used clinically to detect previous exposure to specific pathogens. For example, some HIV screening tests measure antibody to the virus that causes AIDS.

A secondary immune response is more effective than a primary response

The first exposure to an antigen stimulates a **primary immune response.** An infection, or an antigen injected into an animal, causes specific antibodies to appear in the blood plasma in 3 to 14 days. After antigen injection, there is a brief *latent period* during which

the antigen is recognized and appropriate lymphocytes begin to form clones. A *logarithmic phase* follows, during which the antibody concentration rises rapidly for several days until it reaches a peak (**FIG. 45-12**). IgM is the principal antibody synthesized during the primary immune response. Finally, there is a *decline phase*, during which the antibody concentration decreases to a very low level.

A second exposure to the same antigen, even years later, results in a **secondary immune response.** Because memory B cells bearing antibodies to that antigen (and also memory T cells with their specific T-cell receptors) persist for many years, the secondary immune response is much more rapid than the primary immune response and has a shorter latent period. Much less antigen is necessary to stimulate a secondary immune response than a primary response, and more antibodies are produced. In addition, the

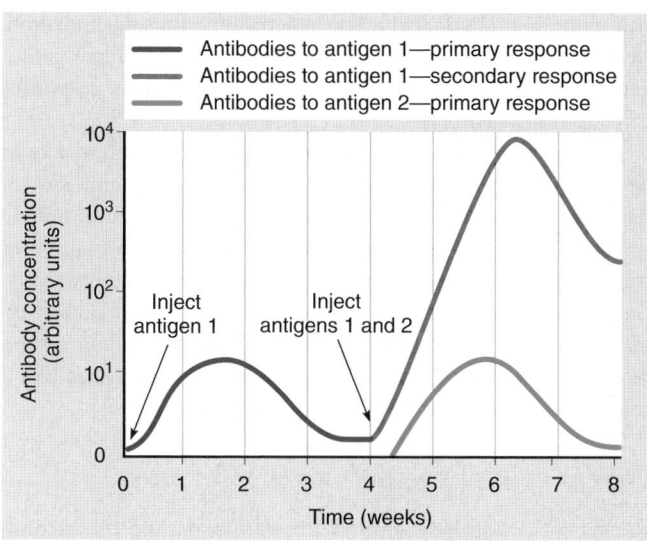

FIGURE 45-12 *Animated* **Immunological memory**

Antigen 1 was injected at day 0, and the immune response was assessed by measuring levels of antibody specific for antigen 1. At week 4, the primary immune response had subsided. Antigen 1 was injected again, together with a new protein, antigen 2. The secondary immune response was greater and more rapid than the primary response. It was also specific to antigen 1. A primary immune response was made to the newly encountered antigen 2.

affinity of antibodies is generally much higher. The predominant antibody in a secondary immune response is IgG.

The body's ability to launch a rapid, effective response during a second encounter with an antigen explains why we do not usually suffer from the same infectious disease several times. For example, a person who contracts measles or chickenpox is unlikely to become re-infected in the future. When someone is exposed a second time, the immune system responds quickly, destroying the pathogens before they have time to multiply and cause symptoms of the disease. Booster shots of vaccine are given to elicit a secondary immune response, thus reinforcing immunological memory.

You may wonder how a person can get influenza (the flu) or a cold more than once. The reason is that there are many varieties of these viral diseases, each caused by a virus with slightly different antigens. For example, more than 100 different viruses cause the common cold, and new varieties of cold and flu viruses evolve continuously by mutation (a survival mechanism for them). As viruses evolve, changes may occur in their surface antigens. Even a slight change may prevent recognition by memory cells. Because the immune system is so specific, each different antigen is treated by the body as a new immunological challenge.

Immunization induces active immunity

We have been considering **active immunity,** which develops following exposure to antigens. Active immunity can be naturally or artificially induced (**TABLE 45-1**). If someone with measles sneezes near you and you contract the disease, you develop active immunity naturally. Active immunity can also be artificially induced by **immunization,** that is, by exposure to antigens in a *vaccine.* When an effective vaccine is introduced into the body, the immune system actively develops clones of cells, produces antibodies, and develops memory cells.

The first vaccine was prepared in 1796 by British physician Edward Jenner against vaccinia, the cowpox virus. (The term *vaccination* was derived from the name of the cowpox virus.) Jenner's vaccine provided humans with immunity against the deadly disease smallpox, which closely resembles cowpox. Jenner had no knowledge of microorganisms or of immunology, and 100 years passed before French chemist Louis Pasteur began to develop scientific methods for preparing vaccines.

Pasteur showed that inoculations with preparations of attenuated (weakened) pathogens could be used to develop immunity against the virulent (infectious) form of the pathogen. However, not until 20th-century advances in immunology—for example, Burnet's clonal selection theory in 1957 and the discovery of T cells and B cells in 1965—did scientists gain a modern understanding of vaccines. Effective vaccination stimulates the body to launch an immune response against the antigens contained in the vaccine. Memory cells develop, and future encounters with the same pathogen are dealt with rapidly.

Microbiologists prepare effective vaccines in various ways. They can attenuate a pathogen so it loses its ability to cause disease. When pathogens are cultured for long periods in nonhuman cells, mutations adapt the pathogens to the nonhuman host so that they no longer cause disease in humans. This method is used to produce the Sabin polio, measles, mumps, and rubella vaccines. Tetanus and diphtheria vaccines are made from toxins secreted by the respective pathogens. The toxin is altered so that it can no longer destroy tissues, but its antigenic determinants are still intact.

Researchers are developing **DNA vaccines** (or RNA vaccines) made from a part of the pathogen's genetic material. The DNA of

TABLE 45-1	Active and Passive Immunity		
Type of Immunity	When Developed	Development of Memory Cells	Duration of Immunity
Active			
Naturally induced	After pathogens enter the body through natural encounters (e.g., a person with measles sneezes on you)	Yes	Many years
Artificially induced	After immunization with a vaccine	Yes	Many years
Passive			
Naturally induced	After transfer of antibodies from mother to developing baby	No	Few months
Artificially induced	After injection with gamma globulin	No	Few months

the pathogen is altered so that it transfers genes that specify antigens. When injected into a patient, the altered DNA is taken up by cells and makes its way to the nucleus. The encoded antigens are manufactured and stimulate both cell-mediated and antibody-mediated immunity. Several DNA vaccines, including vaccines to prevent and treat HIV infection, are in clinical trials.

Passive immunity is borrowed immunity

To provide **passive immunity,** physicians inject people with antibodies actively produced by another organism. The serum or gamma globulin that contains these antibodies is obtained from humans or other animals. Nonhuman serums are less desirable because nonhuman proteins can act as antigens, stimulating an immune response that may result in serum sickness.

Passive immunity is borrowed immunity. Its effects are temporary whether the immunity is artificially or naturally induced (see Table 45-1). Physicians use artificially induced passive immunity to boost the body's defenses temporarily against a particular disease. For example, when exposed to hepatitis A, a form of viral hepatitis spread through contaminated food or water, people at risk of infection may be injected with gamma globulin containing antibodies to the hepatitis pathogen. However, gamma globulin injections offer protection for only a few weeks. Because the body has not actively launched an immune response, it has no memory cells and cannot produce antibodies to the pathogen. Once the injected antibodies are broken down, the immunity disappears.

Pregnant women confer naturally induced passive immunity on their developing babies by manufacturing antibodies for them. These maternal antibodies, of the IgG class, pass through the placenta and provide the fetus and newborn infant with a defense system until its own immune system matures. Babies who are breast-fed continue to receive immunoglobulins, particularly IgA, in their milk, during the critical months when their own immune system is developing.

Review

- How do antibodies recognize antigens?
- What are three ways that antigen–antibody complexes affect pathogens?
- What is the basis of immunological memory?
- How is passive immunity different from active immunity?

45.6 RESPONSE TO DISEASE, IMMUNE FAILURES, AND HARMFUL REACTIONS

◼ LEARNING OBJECTIVES

11 Describe the body's response to cancer cells and HIV.
12 Describe examples of hypersensitivity, including autoimmune diseases, Rh incompatibility, and allergic reactions, and summarize the immunological basis of graft rejection.

The immune system is generally very effective in defending the body against invading pathogens. However, many factors can impair immune function, including genetic mutations, malnutrition, sleep deprivation, pre-existing disease, stress, and virulent pathogens. Ineffective or inappropriately directed immune responses can also result in disease states.

Exaggerated, damaging immune responses are referred to as **hypersensitivity.** For example, sometimes the immune system malfunctions, and attacks its own tissues, causing autoimmune disease. In allergic reactions, individuals are overresponsive to mild environmental antigens. The immune system's ability to distinguish self from nonself sometimes interferes with clinical interventions. Physicians must carefully consider immune system responses when employing such life-saving procedures as blood transfusions or organ transplants.

Cancer cells evade the immune system

Cancer is a leading cause of death worldwide and the second-leading cause of death in Western countries. An estimated one person in three in the United States will develop cancer, and one in five will die of cancer. Worldwide, lung cancer in men and breast cancer in women are the main types of cancer resulting in death. (In our earlier discussions of cancer in Chapters 17 and 39, we explained that cancer is actually a complex group of diseases characterized by dysregulation of normal control mechanisms for cellular growth.) Here we focus on the interaction between cancer cells and cells of the immune system and on new treatment strategies based on immune mechanisms.

Cancer cells are body cells that have been transformed in a way that alters their normal growth-regulating mechanisms. Every day, a few normal cells may be transformed into precancer cells in each of us in response to the sun's UV rays, X-rays, certain viruses, tobacco smoke, asbestos, and other chemical carcinogens in the environment, as well as other unknown factors. How does the immune system respond? And why is immune response sometimes ineffective?

Cancer cell antigens are classified according to their molecular structure and their source. Some cancer cell antigens are produced by mutant genes that are associated with cancer cells. T cells may respond to them because these antigens are not found in normal cells. Other cancer cell antigens are normal proteins that may stimulate immune responses because they are expressed in abnormally large quantities.

The human papillomavirus (HPV), which has been linked to cervical cancer, produces antigens that stimulate T cells to respond. Specific immune responses sometimes prevent the development of such DNA virus-induced cancers.

Cancer cell antigens induce both cell-mediated and antibody-mediated immunity

NK cells and macrophages destroy cancer cells. Macrophages produce cytokines, including TNFs that inhibit tumor growth. Dendritic cells present antigens to T cells, stimulating them to produce interferons, which have an antitumor effect. T_C cells attack cancer cells directly and also produce interleukins, which attract and activate macrophages and NK cells (**FIG. 45-13**). Although the immune system recognizes many cancer cell antigens, these antigens often stimulate only weak immune responses that are not effective.

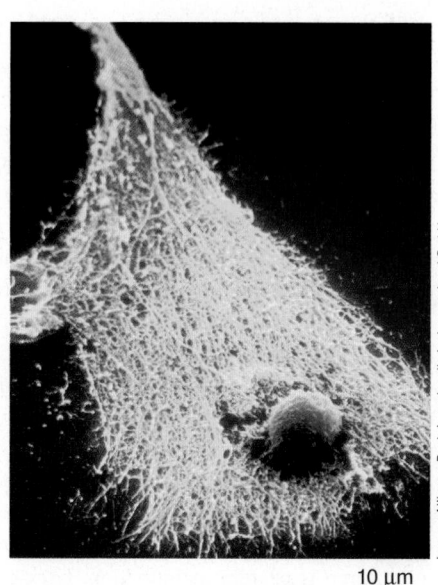

(a) An army of T$_C$ cells surrounds a large cancer cell. The T$_C$ cells recognize the cancer cell as nonself because it displays altered or unique antigens on its surface.

(b) Some T$_C$ cells elongate as they chemically attack the cancer cell and break down its plasma membrane.

(c) The cancer cell has been destroyed. Only a collapsed fibrous cytoskeleton remains.

FIGURE 45-13 Destroying cancer cells
This series of colorized SEMs shows T$_C$ cells (*green*) attacking and destroying a cancer cell (*yellow*).

Sometimes cancer cells evade the immune system and multiply unchecked. Some types of cancer cells can block T$_C$ cells. Others dramatically decrease their expression of class I MHC molecules. Recall that T$_C$ cells recognize only antigens associated with class I MHC, so a low level of these molecules prevents tumor destruction. Some cancer cells do not produce co-stimulatory molecules needed to activate T$_C$ cells.

Future cancer treatment will be more targeted

Conventional cancer treatments, such as chemotherapy and radiation, are designed to kill cells that are rapidly dividing. However, these treatments destroy normal cells as well as cancer cells. To treat cancer effectively, treatment strategies must be more specific, or even customized to the particular cancer. For example, cancer researchers are genetically engineering cancer cells to secrete cytokines that would stimulate the patient's immune response.

A few cancer drugs, such as Herceptin, are monoclonal antibodies. Herceptin binds with a growth-factor receptor that is present in excessive numbers on the cells of about 30% of metastatic breast cancers. Herceptin blocks the growth factors that would stimulate proliferation of the cells.

The spread of cancer typically depends on the development of blood vessels that bring nutrients and oxygen to the tumor. *Angiogenesis inhibitors* slow the development of blood vessels, and thereby slow the spread of cancer. Many studies underway are attempting to optimize the clinical benefits of these drugs.

Researchers are developing cancer vaccines that contain cancer cells or tumor antigens; they stimulate the patient's immune system to launch cell-mediated responses to tumor-associated antigens. These vaccines differ from traditional vaccines that are used to destroy pathogens *before* they cause disease. DNA vaccines are made from bits of DNA from a patient's cancer cells. When injected into the patient, the vaccine stimulates increased antigen production. In response, the patient's immune system produces more T cells.

Investigators are making dendritic cell vaccines by taking dendritic cells from a cancer patient and exposing them to antigens from the patient's cancer cells. The combination of dendritic cells and antigens is then injected into the patient. The dendritic cells display the antigens to T$_C$ cells, which then attack the cancer cells. Another approach that has recently shown promise is the development of drugs that deactivate proteins that activate key signaling pathways.

Effective treatment protocols for cancer will almost certainly utilize a systems approach and combinations of medications. Cellular mechanisms are complex, and when a drug blocks one signaling pathway, cancer cells can work around the blocked reaction or take advantage of a redundant pathway. When combinations of drugs are used, more than one signaling pathway, or different parts of the same pathway, can be targeted.

Immunodeficiency disease can be inherited or acquired

The absence or failure of some component of the immune system can result in **immunodeficiency disease,** a condition that increases susceptibility to infection. Inherited immunodeficiencies have an estimated incidence of 1 per 10,000 births. *Severe combined immunodeficiency syndromes (SCIDs)* are X-linked and autosomal recessive disorders that profoundly affect both cell-mediated immunity and antibody-mediated immunity, resulting in multiple infections. Babies born with SCID typically die by two years of age unless they are maintained in a protective bubble until they can be effectively treated, typically with bone marrow transplants.

In *DiGeorge syndrome,* the thymus is reduced or absent and the patient is deficient in T cells. Children born with this disorder are prone to serious viral infections. Treatment involves transplanting bone marrow or fetal thymus tissue. Other tissues may take over T-cell production, and function typically improves by age five years.

Researchers use several animal models to study immunodeficiency. For example, the nude mouse (a hairless mutant mouse) does not develop a functional thymus. Because nude mice are deficient in mature T cells, they are used to study the effects of compromised cell-mediated immunity, as well as possible treatments. *Stem cell research* and advances in genetic engineering suggest new approaches to treating immunodeficiency (see Chapters 16 and 17).

Worldwide, the leading cause of *acquired* immunodeficiency in children is protein malnutrition. Lack of protein decreases T-cell numbers and decreases the ability to manufacture antibodies, which impairs the immune system. This condition increases the risk of contracting *opportunistic infections,* infections by microbes that do not typically cause disease. Another important cause of acquired immunodeficiency is chemotherapy administered to cancer patients because chemotherapy is most damaging to cells that divide rapidly, including blood stem cells and activated lymphocytes.

HIV is the major cause of acquired immunodeficiency in adults

The **human immunodeficiency virus (HIV)** was first isolated in 1983 and was shown to be the cause of **acquired immunodeficiency syndrome (AIDS)** in 1984. HIV, which is a retrovirus, has been studied more than any other virus. (Recall from Chapter 24 that a retrovirus is an RNA virus that uses its RNA as a template to make DNA with the help of reverse transcriptase.) Several different strains of the virus are known; HIV-1 is the most virulent form in humans.

The AIDS pandemic has claimed more than 30 million lives. HIV kills more than 2 million people every year, making it the sixth-highest cause of death globally. Epidemiologists estimate that more than 33 million people, including more than 2 million children, worldwide are now infected with HIV. More than 2.7 million people are newly infected with HIV each year. The General Assembly of the United Nations has called AIDS a "global emergency" and has outlined measures for mobilizing world resources to combat this disease. HIV/AIDS is more than a medical issue; it is a political, economic, and human rights threat.

HIV is transmitted mainly during sexual intercourse with an infected person or by direct exposure to infected blood or blood products. Sharing needles and/or syringes (usually for drug injection) with an infected person is a major risk factor. The virus is not spread by casual contact. People do not contract HIV by hugging, casual kissing, or using the same bathroom facilities. Friends and family members who have contact with AIDS patients are not more likely to become infected.

In the United States, more than 50,000 new HIV infections are occurring each year. Of these new infections, about 75% occur in men. Sexual contact with persons who have HIV infection is a risk factor that can be modified. Use of a latex condom during sexual intercourse provides some protection against HIV transmission, and use of a spermicide containing nonoxynol-9 may provide additional protection.

As many as one-third of untreated pregnant women infected with HIV will transmit the virus to their babies during pregnancy, childbirth, or breast-feeding. Recent drug treatment protocols have reduced the rate of HIV transmission between mother and fetus. In highly developed countries, effective blood-screening procedures now safeguard blood bank supplies, markedly reducing the risk of infection by blood transfusion.

HIV destroys the host immune system

HIV typically enters the body through the mucosa that lines passageways. A protein on the outer envelope of the virus attaches to CD4 on the surface of T_H cells, which are the main target (**FIG. 45-14**; also see Chapter 23 opening photograph). The virus also binds to a coreceptor that normally binds a chemokine. HIV enters the T_H cell and is reverse-transcribed to form DNA. Its DNA is then incorporated into the host genome. The virus reproduces itself, causing death of the host cell. The first phase of HIV infection is the *acute* phase of the infection. Within two weeks of infection, large numbers of T_H and memory T cells are destroyed. HIV also infects dendritic cells and macrophages. Dendritic cells in the mucous membranes transport HIV from their point of entry to the lymph nodes. The virus further spreads through the blood.

The body launches an immune response following HIV infection. Nonspecific responses include production of antimicrobial peptides and action by NK cells, dendritic cells, and the complement system. Specific immune responses include activation and mobilization of T_C cells.

An estimated 25% of HIV-infected individuals in the United States do not know they are infected. Many individuals experience mild flulike symptoms (fever, headache, sore throat, swollen lymph glands, aching muscles) about two weeks after contracting the virus. However, some individuals have no symptoms.

The acute phase transitions into the latent period, a *chronic* phase, as the immune system decreases HIV in the blood. Some cells infected by HIV are not destroyed, and the virus may continue to replicate slowly for many years. T_C cells appear to be the main cells that attack HIV, limiting viral replication and delaying the progress of the disease. However, over time HIV continues to destroy T_H cells, resulting in a dramatic decrease in the T_H cell population. This decrease severely impairs the body's ability to resist infection because there are no longer T_H cells to release the cytokines necessary to activate T_C cells and B cells. After a time, a progression of symptoms occurs, including swollen lymph glands, night sweats, fever, and weight loss (**FIG. 45-15**). Too often, the virus eventually wins the battle.

In most HIV-infected individuals, the disease eventually progresses to AIDS, the final, and often lethal, stage. This process can take more than ten years, and antiretroviral drugs slow the process. By the time the disease progresses to AIDS, lymph tissue has been destroyed and the blood T_H cell count has dropped below a critical level of 200 cells/μL. As a consequence of this immunosuppression, many AIDS patients develop serious opportunis-

300 nm

(a) HIV (*blue particles*) attacking T$_H$ cells (*light green*).

100 nm

(b) HIV (*purple/blue*) budding from the ends of the branched microvilli of a T$_H$ cell.

FIGURE 45-14 Colorized SEMS of HIV infecting T helper cells
HIV infection depletes T$_H$ lymphocytes. This is the main reason for the failure of the immune system in AIDS.

tic infections, such as tuberculosis, or rare forms of cancer, such as Kaposi's sarcoma (a tumor of the endothelial cells lining blood vessels that causes purplish spots on the skin). In about one-third of AIDS patients, the virus infects the nervous system and causes

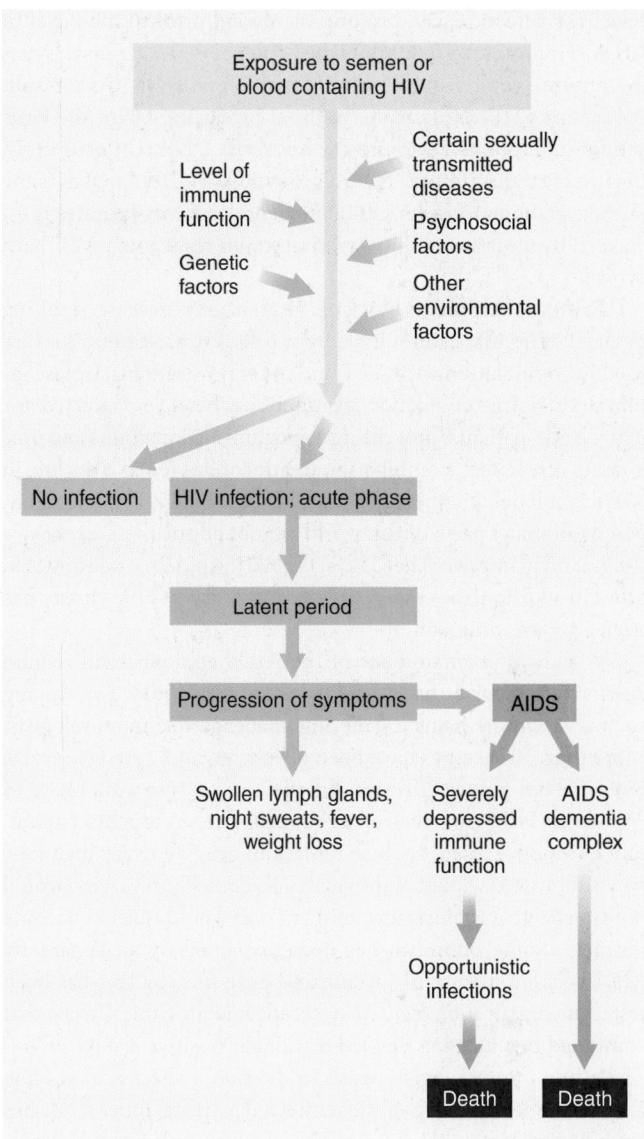

FIGURE 45-15 *Animated* **The course of HIV infection**
Exposure to semen or blood that contains HIV can lead to HIV infection. The acute (early) infection begins in lymph nodes and other lymph tissues associated with epithelial linings. Most T$_H$ cells may be destroyed within two weeks of infection. During the latent period, chronic infection develops and the virus replicates at a low level. Eventually, viral replication may increase and lead to a progression of symptoms and to AIDS, the final, often lethal, stage. Although some exposed individuals apparently do not become infected, the risk increases with multiple exposures. Many factors determine whether a person exposed to HIV will develop AIDS.

AIDS dementia complex. These patients exhibit progressive cognitive, motor, and behavioral dysfunction that typically ends in coma and death.

Researchers are searching for effective treatments

Researchers throughout the world are searching for drugs that will successfully combat the AIDS virus. Because HIV often infects the central nervous system, an effective drug must cross the blood–brain barrier. **AZT (azidothymidine),** the first drug developed to treat HIV infection, can prolong the period prior to the onset of AIDS symptoms. AZT inhibits the action of reverse transcriptase, the enzyme the retrovirus uses to synthesize DNA. As a result, AZT blocks HIV replication. Without producing DNA, the virus cannot incorporate itself into the host cell's DNA. Unfortunately, the reverse transcriptase HIV uses to synthesize DNA makes many mistakes: about 1 in every 2000 nucleotides it incorporates is incorrect. By mutating in this way, viral strains resistant to AZT have evolved.

Protease inhibitors block the viral enzyme protease, resulting in viral copies that cannot infect new cells. Protease inhibitors are used in combination with AZT and other reverse transcriptase inhibitors. Triple-combination treatment has been very effective for many AIDS patients, preventing opportunistic infections and prolonging life. In fact, combination treatment has led to a decline in AIDS incidence and mortality in the United States. Unfortunately, people in many parts of the world cannot afford these expensive drugs, and in impoverished areas, the AIDS epidemic continues to grow. In addition, the emergence of drug-resistant HIV viruses has been a serious problem.

Worldwide containment of the AIDS epidemic will require an effective vaccine that prevents the spread of HIV. Developing such a vaccine remains a daunting challenge for immunologists. More than 50 vaccines have been developed and tested clinically, but none has proved effective. An effective vaccine would have to counteract HIV's destruction of key cells needed to mount an immune response. Also, because mutations arise at a very high rate, new viral strains with new antigens evolve quickly. A vaccine would not be effective against new antigens and would quickly become obsolete. Some optimism has been generated by an apparently effective combination of vaccine and gene therapy that has been tested in simian monkeys. Also, recent human clinical trials that combined two vaccines yielded marginally positive results.

While immunologists work to develop a successful vaccine and more effective drugs to treat infected patients, other strategies are being utilized with some success. For example, we now know that male circumcision reduces the risk of HIV infection through sexual contact.

Massive educational programs have been launched to slow the spread of HIV. Educating the public that having multiple sexual partners increases the risk of AIDS and teaching sexually active individuals the importance of "safe sex" may help contain the pandemic. Some have suggested that public health facilities should provide free condoms to those who are sexually active and free sterile hypodermic needles to those addicted to intravenous drugs. The cost of these measures would be far less than the cost of medical care for increasing numbers of AIDS patients and the toll in human suffering.

In an autoimmune disease, the body attacks its own tissues

Self-tolerance, the ability to recognize self, is established during lymphocyte development. Lymphocytes do not normally attack cells and tissues of their own body. However, some lymphocytes have the potential to be *autoreactive,* that is, to launch an immune response against self-tissues. In about 5% of adults in highly developed countries, such autoreactivity can lead to a form of hypersensitivity known as *autoimmunity,* or **autoimmune disease,** in which immune cells react against the body's own cells. Some of the diseases that result from such failure in self-tolerance are rheumatoid arthritis, systemic lupus erythematosus (SLE), insulin-dependent diabetes, scleroderma, and multiple sclerosis.

In autoimmune diseases, antibodies and T cells attack the body's own tissues. In **rheumatoid arthritis,** T cells in the area of inflammation produce a cytokine that promotes inflammation. In addition, antibodies to a joint protein may generate antigen–antibody complexes that are deposited in the small joints. In **multiple sclerosis,** an autoimmune disease of the central nervous system, T_H cells attack self-myelin antigens. MRI scans show the loss of myelin sheaths in multiple areas around axons in the brain and spinal cord that are normally myelinated. Scar tissue forms and compromises the ability of these damaged neurons to transmit signals.

Multiple genes, including MHC genes, contribute to the development of autoimmune disease. Mutations that cause abnormal apoptosis or inadequate clearing of dead cells may result in danger signals that activate the immune system. Another important factor is that viral or bacterial infection often precedes the onset of an autoimmune disease. Some pathogens have evolved a tactic known as *molecular mimicry.* They trick the body by producing molecules that look like self-molecules. For example, an adenovirus that causes respiratory and intestinal illness produces a peptide that mimics myelin protein. When the body launches responses to the adenovirus peptide, it may also begin to attack the similar self-molecule, myelin.

To maintain homeostasis and health, the numerous types of cells, regulatory and signaling molecules, and the complex actions of the immune system must be carefully regulated. Specific T cells and B cells proliferate and respond to challenges by pathogens, but after an effective immune response the expanded populations of T cells and B cells must be decreased to normal numbers. Cells that are no longer needed die by apoptosis. Overactivation of critical components can result in inflammation and autoimmune disease. Underactivation allows pathogens to cause serious disease. Either situation can lead to death.

Rh incompatibility can result in hypersensitivity

Named for the rhesus monkeys in whose blood it was first found, the Rh system consists of more than 40 kinds of Rh antigens, each referred to as an **Rh factor.** By far the most important of these factors is *antigen D.* About 85% of U.S. residents who are of Western European descent are Rh positive—they have antigen D on the surfaces of their red blood cells (in addition to the antigens of the ABO system and other blood group antigens). The 15% or so of this population who are Rh negative have no antigen D.

Unlike the situation discussed in Chapter 11 for the ABO blood group, Rh-negative individuals do not naturally produce antibodies against antigen D (anti-D). However, they do produce anti-D antibodies if they are exposed to Rh-positive blood. The allele coding for antigen D is dominant to the allele for the absence of antigen D. For this reason, Rh-negative people are homozygous recessive, and Rh-positive people are heterozygous or homozygous dominant.

Although several kinds of maternal-fetal blood type incompatibilities are known, **Rh incompatibility** is the most serious (**FIG. 45-16**). If a woman is Rh negative and the father of the fetus she is carrying is Rh positive, the fetus may also be Rh positive, having inherited the D allele from the father. Ordinarily, the maternal and fetal blood do not mix; nutrients, oxygen, and other substances are exchanged between these two circulatory systems across the placenta. However, late in pregnancy or during the birth process, a small quantity of blood from the fetus may pass through a defect in the placenta.

If any maternal blood mixes with fetal blood, fetal red blood cells, which bear antigen D, activate the mother's immune system. The mother's B cells then produce antibodies to antigen D. If the woman becomes pregnant again, anti-D antibodies cross the placenta and enter the fetal blood. They combine with antigen D molecules on the surface of the fetal red blood cells, causing hemolysis (cells rupture and release hemoglobin into the circulation). The ability to transport oxygen is reduced, and breakdown products of the released hemoglobin damage organs, including the brain. In extreme cases of this disease, known as *erythroblastosis fetalis,* so many fetal red blood cells are destroyed that the fetus may die.

When Rh-incompatibility problems are suspected, fetal blood can be exchanged by transfusion before birth, but this is a risky procedure. More commonly, Rh-negative women are treated just after childbirth (or at termination of pregnancy by miscarriage or abortion) with a preparation of anti-D antibodies known as RhoGAM. These antibodies clear the Rh-positive fetal red blood cells from the mother's blood very quickly, minimizing the chance for her own white blood cells to become sensitized and develop memory cells. The antibodies are also soon eliminated from her body. As a result, if she becomes pregnant again, her blood does not contain the anti-D that could harm the developing fetus.

Allergic reactions are directed against ordinary environmental antigens

About 20% of the U.S. population is plagued by an allergic disorder, such as allergic asthma or hay fever. A predisposition toward these disorders appears to be inherited. In **allergic reactions,** hypersensitivity results in the manufacture of antibodies against mild antigens, called **allergens,** which normally do not stimulate an immune response. Common environmental agents, such as pollen, house-dust mites, roach feces, and pet dander, can trigger allergic reactions in some individuals. In many kinds of allergic reactions, distinctive IgE immunoglobulins are produced.

Let us examine a common allergic reaction, **allergic rhinitis,** commonly known as hay fever. This allergic response is triggered in some individuals by breathing pollen (**FIG. 45-17**). Exposure to pollen causes *sensitization.* Macrophages degrade the allergen and present fragments of it to T cells. The activated T cells then stimulate B cells to become plasma cells and produce pollen-specific IgE. These antibodies attach to receptors on mast cells. The Fc end of each IgE molecule attaches to a mast cell receptor; its V region is free to combine with the pollen allergen.

When a sensitized, allergic person inhales the microscopic pollen, allergen molecules rapidly attach to the IgE on sensitized mast cells. In response to IgE antibody binding with the allergen, mast cells release granules filled with histamine and other molecules that stimulate inflammation. Blood vessels dilate, and capillaries become more permeable, leading to edema and redness. Such responses cause the nasal passages to become swollen and irritated. A runny nose, sneezing, watery eyes, and a general feeling of discomfort are common.

A prolonged allergic response occurs when neutrophils are attracted by chemical compounds released by the mast cells. Neutrophils migrate to the inflamed area and release compounds that lengthen the allergic reaction.

In **allergic asthma,** an allergen–IgE response occurs in the bronchioles of the lungs. Mast cells release substances that cause smooth muscle

FIGURE 45-16 *Animated* **Rh incompatibility**
When an Rh-negative woman produces Rh-positive offspring, her immune system may become sensitized. In subsequent pregnancies she may produce anti-D antibodies that cross the placenta and destroy fetal red blood cells.

FIGURE 45-17 An allergic reaction
Many people respond to breathing pollen with allergic rhinitis (hay fever), a common type of allergic reaction.

① Previous exposure to pollen causes plasma cells to make pollen-specific IgE.

② IgE combines with mast cell receptors in lining of nasal passages.

③ Pollen is inhaled.

④ Allergen combines with region of IgE on surface of sensitized mast cell.

⑤ Mast cell releases histamine and other chemicals.

⑥ This release causes increased vasodilation and increased capillary permeability. Symptoms result: edema, redness, constriction of respiratory passageways, mucus.

to contract, and the airways in the lungs sometimes constrict for several hours, making breathing difficult. Allergic asthma is treated with steroids, which block cytokine production, and with drugs, such as leukotriene inhibitors, that block inflammatory mediators from binding to smooth muscle in the airway. Leukotrienes are inflammatory compounds released by mast cells. Leukotriene inhibitors reduce inflammation and decrease the incidence of asthma and hay fever episodes in individuals with hypersensitive immune systems. Monoclonal antibodies to IgE are also useful in treating these disorders because they reduce IgE levels in the blood.

Certain foods or drugs act as allergens in some people, causing a reaction in the walls of the digestive tract that leads to discomfort and diarrhea. The allergen may be absorbed and cause mast cells to release granules elsewhere in the body. When the allergen–IgE reaction takes place in the skin, the histamine released by mast cells causes the swollen red welts known as urticaria, or hives.

Systemic anaphylaxis is a dangerous allergic reaction that can occur when a person develops an allergy to a specific drug, such as penicillin; to compounds in the venom injected by a stinging insect; or even to certain foods. Within minutes after the substance enters the body, a widespread allergic reaction takes place. Mast cells release large amounts of histamine and other compounds into the circulation that cause extreme vasodilation and capillary permeability. So much plasma may be lost from the blood that circulatory shock and death can occur within a few minutes.

The symptoms of allergic reactions are often treated with **antihistamines,** drugs that block the effects of histamine. These drugs compete for the same receptors on cells targeted by histamine. When the antihistamine combines with the receptor, it prevents the histamine from binding and thus prevents its harmful effects. Antihistamines are useful clinically in relieving the symptoms of hives and hay fever. They are not completely effective because mast cells release molecules other than histamine that also cause allergic symptoms.

Graft rejection is an immune response against transplanted tissue

Skin can be successfully transplanted from one part of the same body to another or from one identical twin to another. However, when skin is taken from one person and grafted onto the body of a nontwin, it is rejected and sloughs off. Why? Recall that tissues from the same individual or from identical twins have identical MHC alleles and thus the same MHC antigens. Such tissues are compatible. Because there are many alleles for each of the MHC genes, it is difficult to find identical matches among nonidentical twins.

When a tissue or organ is taken from a donor and transplanted to the body of a nontwin host, several of the MHC antigens are likely to be different. The host's immune system regards the graft as foreign and launches an immune response known as **graft rejection.** In the first stage of rejection, the *sensitization stage,* T_H cells and T_C cells recognize the foreign antigens. In the second stage, the *effector stage,* T_C cells, the complement system, and cytokines secreted by T_H cells attack the transplanted tissue and can destroy it within a week. The sequence of events in graft rejection can be summarized as follows:

tissue from donor transplanted into body of recipient $\longrightarrow$ T_H cells and T_C cells recognize MHC antigens on transplant cells as foreign $\longrightarrow$ T_H cells secrete cytokines, complement system is activated, and T_C cells destroy transplant cells

To avoid graft rejection, tissues from the patient and from potential donors must be typed and matched as closely as possible. Cell typing is somewhat similar to blood typing but is more complex. If all the MHC antigens are matched, the graft has about a 95% chance of surviving the first year. Unfortunately, not many people are lucky enough to have an identical twin to supply spare parts, so perfect matches are difficult to find. Furthermore, some organs, such as the heart, cannot be spared. Most transplanted organs, therefore, come from unrelated donors, often from patients who have just died.

To prevent graft rejection in less compatible matches, physicians use antirejection drugs such as cyclosporine to suppress the immune system. Cyclosporine prevents T cells from producing cytokines. Unfortunately, immunosuppression makes the transplant patient more vulnerable to pneumonia or other infections and increases the risk of certain types of cancer. After the first few months, immunosuppressant drug dosages may be reduced. Researchers are working to develop more effective immunosuppression techniques.

In the United States, thousands of patients are in need of organ transplants. Because the number of human donors does not meet this need, investigators are developing techniques for culturing stem cells as replacement tissues. Some researchers are working on more effective methods for transplanting animal tissues and organs to humans. Challenges include risks of transmitting animal diseases to humans and graft rejection. Pigs have been used as donors, but destructive immune responses are launched against these transplanted organs. Because they are closely related, chimpanzees and other primates can be used as donors with lower risk of graft rejection. However, ethical concerns have limited such transplants.

Researchers are developing methods for genetically engineering pigs and other animals so that they do not produce antigens that stimulate immune responses in human recipients. These animals could then be cloned and used as donors of hearts, kidneys, and other organs. Effective artificial organs are also being developed.

The body has a few immunologically privileged locations where foreign tissue is accepted. For example, corneal transplants are highly successful because the cornea has almost no associated blood or lymphatic vessels and is thus out of reach of most lymphocytes. Furthermore, antigens in the corneal graft probably would not find their way into the circulatory system and therefore could not stimulate an immune response.

Review

- How does the body defend itself against cancer?
- How does HIV infect the body? How does it affect the body?
- What is an autoimmune disease? Give two examples.
- What is the sequence of immunological events that take place in a common type of allergic reaction, such as hay fever?
- What is the immunological basis for graft rejection?

■ SUMMARY: FOCUS ON LEARNING OBJECTIVES

45.1 *(page 964)*

1 Distinguish between nonspecific and specific immune responses.

- **Immune responses** are the body's defensive responses against **pathogens** (disease-causing organisms), toxins, and other harmful agents. In immune responses, the body recognizes foreign or dangerous macromolecules and responds to eliminate them. **Nonspecific immune responses** provide general and immediate protection against pathogens, some toxins and drugs, and cancer cells.
- **Specific immune responses** target distinct **antigens,** molecules recognized as foreign or dangerous by cells of the immune system. The immune system produces **antibodies,** highly specific proteins that recognize and bind to specific antigens. Another defining feature of specific immunity is **immunological memory,** that is, the system "remembers" foreign or dangerous molecules and responds more strongly to repeated encounters with the same molecules.

2 Compare, in general terms, the immune responses that have evolved in invertebrates and vertebrates.

- Invertebrates depend mainly on nonspecific immune responses, such as physical barriers; **phagocytosis** (engulfing and destroying pathogens); receptors that recognize molecular patterns associated

with pathogens; and **antimicrobial peptides** (soluble molecules that destroy pathogens).
- Vertebrates use both nonspecific and specific immune responses.

45.2 *(page 966)*

3 Describe nonspecific immune responses, including physical barriers; recognition by pattern recognition receptors; actions of phagocytes and other cells; actions of cytokines and complement; and the inflammatory response.

- Nonspecific immune responses include physical barriers, such as the skin and the epithelial linings of the respiratory and digestive tracts. Antimicrobial peptides are produced by epithelial membranes.
- When pathogens break through the first-line defenses, **pathogen-associated molecular patterns,** or **PAMPs,** bind with **pattern recognition receptors** and activate other nonspecific defenses. PAMPs are sets of common molecular features that are characteristic of each class of pathogens. The best known pattern recognition receptors are **Toll-like receptors,** receptors on phagocytes and certain other types of cells.

- **Phagocytes,** including **neutrophils** and **macrophages,** destroy bacteria. **Natural killer (NK) cells** destroy cells infected with viruses and foreign or altered cells such as tumor cells. **Dendritic cells** release antiviral proteins called **interferons.**

- **Cytokines** are signaling proteins that regulate interactions between cells. Important groups are interferons, tumor necrosis factors, interleukins, and chemokines. Interferons inhibit viral replication and activate natural killer cells. **Tumor necrosis factor (TNF)** stimulates immune cells to initiate an inflammatory response. **Interleukins** help regulate interactions between lymphocytes and other cells of the body, help mediate inflammation, and can mediate fever. **Chemokines** attract, activate, and direct the movement of certain cells of the immune system.

- **Complement** proteins lyse the cell wall of pathogens; coat pathogens, thereby enhancing phagocytosis; and attract white blood cells to the site of infection. These actions enhance the inflammatory response.

- When pathogens invade tissues, they trigger an **inflammatory response,** which includes three main processes: vasodilation, which brings more blood to the area of infection; increased capillary permeability, which allows fluid and antibodies to leave the circulation and enter the tissues; and increased phagocytosis. In response to infection, **mast cells** release **histamine** and other compounds that cause vasodilation and increased capillary permeability.

  CENGAGENOW™ Watch immune responses, including the inflammatory response, by clicking on the figures in CengageNOW.

45.3 *(page 970)*

4 Contrast cell-mediated and antibody-mediated immunity, and give an overview of each process.

- In **cell-mediated immunity,** specific T cells are activated; T cells release proteins that destroy cells infected with viruses or other intracellular pathogens.

- In **antibody-mediated immunity,** specific B cells are activated; B cells multiply and differentiate into plasma cells, which produce antibodies.

5 Describe the functions of the principal cells of the specific immune system and of the major histocompatibility complex.

- Two main types of cells important in specific immune responses are lymphocytes and antigen-presenting cells. Lymphocytes develop from stem cells in the bone marrow. **T cells** are lymphocytes responsible for cell-mediated immunity. The **thymus gland** confers immunocompetence on T cells by making them capable of distinguishing between self and nonself. There are several types of T cells, including **T cytotoxic cells (T_C cells), T helper cells (T_H),** memory T_C cells, memory T_H cells, and **regulatory T cells (Tregs).** T cells are distinguished by their **T-cell receptors (TCRs).**

- **B cells** are lymphocytes responsible for antibody-mediated immunity. B cells differentiate into **plasma cells,** which produce antibodies. Some activated B cells become **memory B cells,** which continue to produce antibodies after the body overcomes the infection.

- **Antigen-presenting cells (APCs),** including dendritic cells, macrophages, and B cells, display foreign antigens as well as their own surface proteins. Dendritic cells are specialized to process, transport, and present antigens.

- Immune responses depend on the **major histocompatibility complex (MHC),** a group of genes that encode MHC proteins. Class I MHC genes encode self-antigens, glycoproteins expressed on the surface of most nucleated cells. Class II MHC genes encode glycoproteins expressed on APCs of the immune system. Class III MHC genes encode components of the complement system and TNFs.

6 Describe the sequence of events in cell-mediated immunity.

- In cell-mediated immunity, specific T cells are activated by a foreign antigen–MHC complex on the surface of an infected cell. A **costimulatory molecule** and interleukins are also required. Activated T_C cells multiply and give rise to a clone, a process called **clonal expansion.** These differentiated cells migrate to the site of infection and destroy pathogen-infected cells. Activated T_H cells give rise to a clone of T_H cells, which secrete cytokines that activate B cells and macrophages.

45.5 *(page 975)*

7 Summarize the sequence of events in antibody-mediated immunity, including the effects of antigen–antibody complexes on pathogens.

- In antibody-mediated immunity, B cells are activated when they combine with antigen. Activation requires both an APC (such as a dendritic cell or macrophage) that has a foreign antigen–MHC complex displayed on its surface and a T_H cell that secretes interleukins.

- When activated B cells multiply, they give rise to clones of cells. The cloned cells differentiate and form plasma cells. Plasma cells produce specific antibodies, called **immunoglobulins (Ig),** in response to the specific antigens that activated them. An antibody combines with a specific antigen to form an **antigen–antibody complex,** which may inactivate the pathogen, stimulate phagocytosis, or activate the complement system.

  CENGAGENOW™ See cell-mediated and antibody-mediated immunity by clicking on the figures in CengageNOW.

8 Describe the basic structure and function of an antibody, and explain the basis of antibody diversity.

- An antibody molecule consists of four polypeptide chains: two identical heavy chains and two shorter light chains. Each chain has a **constant (C) region** and a **variable (V) region.** In a Y-shaped antibody, the two arms combine with antigen.

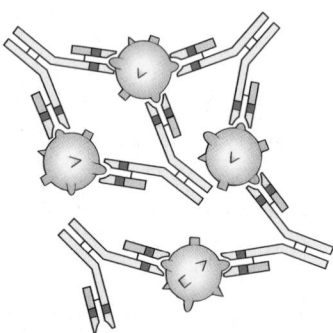

- Rearrangement of DNA segments during the differentiation of B cells is the main factor responsible for antibody diversity; millions of different types of B (and T) cells are produced.

  CENGAGENOW™ Learn more about antibody structure, function, and diversity by clicking on the figures in CengageNOW.

9 Describe the basis of immunological memory, and contrast secondary and primary immune responses.

- After an infection, memory B cells and memory T cells remain in the body. These cells are responsible for long-term immunity.

- The first exposure to an antigen stimulates a **primary immune response.** A second exposure to the same antigen evokes a **secondary immune response,** which is more rapid and more intense than the primary response.

10 Compare active and passive immunity, and give examples of each.

- **Active immunity** develops as a result of exposure to antigens; it may occur naturally after recovery from a disease or can be artificially induced by immunization with a vaccine.

- **Passive immunity** is a temporary condition that develops when an individual receives antibodies produced by another person or animal.

45.6 (page 982)

11 Describe the body's response to cancer cells and HIV.

- NK cells, macrophages, T cells, and other cells of the immune system recognize antigens on cancer cells and launch an immune response against them. Cancer cells evade the immune system by blocking T_C directly or by decreasing the class I MHC molecules on T_C cells.

- **Acquired immunodeficiency syndrome (AIDS)** is caused by the **human immunodeficiency virus (HIV)**, a retrovirus. HIV destroys T helper cells, severely impairing immunity and placing the patient at risk for opportunistic infections.

12 Describe examples of hypersensitivity, including autoimmune diseases, Rh incompatibility, and allergic reactions, and summarize the immunological basis of graft rejection.

- In **autoimmune diseases,** the body reacts immunologically against its own tissues.

- When an Rh-negative woman gives birth to an Rh-positive baby, she may develop anti-D antibodies. **Rh incompatibility** can then occur in future pregnancies.

- In an **allergic reaction,** an **allergen** stimulates the production of IgE, which combines with receptors on mast cells. The mast cells release histamine and other molecules that cause inflammation and other symptoms of allergy. **Systemic anaphylaxis** is a rapid, widespread allergic reaction that can lead to death.

- Transplanted tissues have MHC antigens that stimulate **graft rejection,** an immune response in which T cells destroy the transplant.

TEST YOUR UNDERSTANDING

1. Nonspecific (innate) immune responses include all but (a) inflammation (b) antigen–antibody complexes (c) binding of PAMPs with pattern recognition receptors (d) complement (e) phagocytosis

2. Cytokines (a) are regulatory Toll-like receptors (b) prevent the inflammatory response (c) include interferons and interleukins (d) are immunoglobulins (e) b and c are correct

3. Which of the following is *not* an action of complement? (a) enhances phagocytosis (b) enhances inflammatory response (c) coats pathogens (d) lyses viruses (e) stimulates production of memory T cells

4. Which of the following cells are antigen-presenting cells? (a) NK cells and monocytes (b) macrophages and plasma cells (c) dendritic cells and macrophages (d) mast cells and B cells (e) memory T cells and plasma cells

5. Which of the following cells are especially adept at destroying tumor cells? (a) NK cells (b) plasma cells (c) neutrophils (d) B cytotoxic cells (e) mast cells

6. Which of the following cells become immunologically competent after processing in the thymus gland? (a) NK cells (b) T cells (c) macrophages (d) B cells (e) plasma cells

7. The major histocompatibility complex (MHC) (a) consists of Y-shaped molecules (b) encodes certain antibodies (c) encodes Toll-like receptors (d) inhibits complement release from macrophages (e) encodes a group of cell-surface proteins

8. Which sequence most accurately describes antibody-mediated immunity?
   1. B cell divides and gives rise to clone 2. antibodies produced
   3. cells differentiate and form plasma cells 4. activated T helper cell interacts with B cell displaying same antigen complex
   5. B cell activated
   (a) 1, 2, 3, 4, 5 (b) 3, 2, 1, 4, 5 (c) 4, 5, 3, 2, 1 (d) 4, 5, 1, 3, 2
   (e) 4, 3, 1, 2, 5

9. Immunoglobulin A (a) recognizes pathogen-associated molecular patterns (b) binds with NK cells (c) prevents pathogens from attaching to epithelial surfaces (d) is found mainly on dendritic cell surfaces (e) is found mainly on T-cell surfaces

10. When a person is exposed to the same antigen a second time, the response is (a) less specific (b) more rapid (c) mediated by dendritic cells (d) likely to lead to development of an autoimmune disease (e) a hypersensitivity reaction

11. In an allergic reaction, (a) an allergen binds with IgE (b) the body is immunodeficient (c) T helper cells release histamine (d) allergens are produced by plasma cells (e) mast cells are deactivated

12. Label the diagram and explain what this diagram illustrates. (Consult Figure 45-7, step 3 to check your answers.)

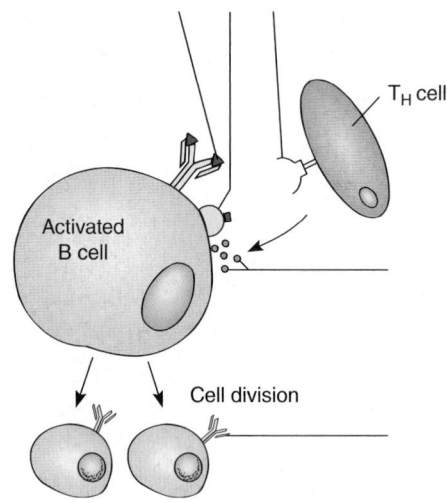

CRITICAL THINKING

1. Specificity, diversity, and memory are key features of the immune system. Giving specific examples, explain how each of these features is important.

2. What would be the effects of total loss of macrophages in the body? Which do you think would have a greater effect on the immune system, loss of macrophages or loss of B cells?

3. What are the advantages of having MHC antigens? disadvantages? What do you think would be the consequences of not having them?

4. A playmate in kindergarten exposes John and Jack to measles. John has been immunized against measles, but Jack has not received the measles vaccine. How are their immune responses different? Five years later, John and Jack are playing together when Judy, who is coming down with measles, sneezes on both of them. Compare their immune responses.

5. **EVOLUTION LINK.** The enzymes Rag1 and Rag2 cut and rearrange DNA, producing millions of specific antibodies and T-cell receptors. Until recently, immunologists thought that the genes (*Rag1* and *Rag2*) that encode these enzymes were found only in jawed vertebrates. However, investigators recently found similar genes in the purple sea urchin. What does this finding suggest about the evolution of the specific immune system?

6. **EVOLUTION LINK.** Fishes have only one class of antibodies, IgM. Amphibians have two classes, and the number increases to five main classes in mammals. Hypothesize an adaptive advantage of having a greater variety of antibody groups.

7. **SCIENCE, TECHNOLOGY, AND SOCIETY.** Imagine that you are a researcher developing new HIV treatments. What approaches might you take? What public policy decisions would you recommend that might help slow the spread of AIDS while new treatments or vaccines are being developed?

 Additional questions are available in CengageNOW at www.cengage.com/login.

46 Gas Exchange

Ventilation. Terrestrial vertebrates, like the white-tailed deer (*Odocoileus virginanus*), ventilate their lungs by breathing air.

Skip Moody/Dembinsky Photo Associates

KEY CONCEPTS

46.1 Air has a higher concentration of molecular oxygen than water does, and animals require less energy to move air than to move water over a gas exchange surface; however, animals that respire in air must have adaptations that reduce water loss so that their respiratory surfaces do not dry out.

46.2 Adaptations for gas exchange include a thin, moist body surface; gills in aquatic animals; and tracheal tubes and lungs in terrestrial animals.

46.3 In mammals, oxygen and carbon dioxide are exchanged between alveoli and blood by diffusion; the pressure of a particular gas determines its direction and rate of diffusion. Respiratory pigments combine with oxygen and transport it; carbon dioxide is transported mainly as bicarbonate ions.

46.4 Several defense mechanisms protect the lungs from harmful substances that are inhaled; tobacco smoke and other air pollutants are major causes of disease, disability, and death.

Most animal cells require a continuous supply of oxygen for cellular respiration. Mammalian brain cells, and some other cells, may be damaged beyond repair if their oxygen supply is cut off for only a few minutes. To stay alive, animals must take in oxygen and release excess carbon dioxide. The exchange of gases between an organism and its environment is called **respiration.**

There are two phases of respiration. During **organismic respiration,** oxygen from the environment is taken up by the animal and delivered to its individual cells. At the same time, carbon dioxide generated during *cellular respiration* is excreted into the environment. **Aerobic cellular respiration** takes place in mitochondria. Oxygen is essential because it serves as the final electron acceptor in the mitochondrial electron transport chain (see Chapter 8). Carbon dioxide is a metabolic waste product of cellular respiration.

Sponges, hydras, flatworms, and many other small, aquatic organisms exchange gases entirely by simple **diffusion,** the passive movement of particles (atoms, ions, or molecules) from a region of higher concentration to a region of lower concentration, that is, down a concentration gradient (see Chapter 5). In these animals, most cells are in direct contact with the environment. Dissolved oxygen from the surrounding water diffuses into the cells, while carbon dioxide diffuses out of the cells and into the water. No specialized respiratory structures are needed.

In an animal more than about 1 mm thick, oxygen cannot diffuse quickly enough through layers of cells to support life. Specialized respiratory structures, such as gills or lungs, deliver oxygen to the cells or to a transport system. These structures also facilitate excretion of carbon dioxide. Animals with lungs carry on *ventilation* by breathing air (see photograph).

In many animal groups, including vertebrates, respiratory systems and circulatory systems are functionally connected. They work together to provide efficient intake and transport of oxygen. Such systems provide sufficient oxygen to support high metabolic rates. As we will discuss, different strategies for gas exchange have evolved in the arthropods.

In this chapter, we will examine adaptations for gas exchange in air and water and describe various types of respiratory surfaces. We will then focus on the structure and function of the mammalian respiratory system. We end the chapter with a discussion of the effects of breathing polluted air, including cigarette smoke.

46.1 ADAPTATIONS FOR GAS EXCHANGE IN AIR OR WATER

◼ LEARNING OBJECTIVE

1   Compare the advantages and disadvantages of air and water as mediums for gas exchange, and describe adaptations for gas exchange in air.

Gas exchange in air has certain advantages over gas exchange in water. Air contains a much higher concentration of molecular oxygen (at least 20 times more) than water does. In addition, oxygen diffuses about 10,000 times faster through air than through water. Another advantage is that less energy is needed to move air than to move water over a gas exchange surface because air is less dense and less viscous. A mammal uses less than 2% of its energy budget to breathe compared to a fish, which must spend as much as 20% of its energy to obtain its oxygen from water.

Gas exchange in air presents a major challenge: the threat of desiccation. Animals that respire in air struggle continuously with water loss. Respiratory surfaces must be kept moist because oxygen and carbon dioxide are dissolved in the fluid that bathes the cells of these surfaces. Whether an animal makes its home on land or water, gas exchange takes place across a moist surface.

Adaptations have evolved that keep respiratory surfaces moist and minimize desiccation. For example, the lungs of air-breathing vertebrates are located deep within the body, not exposed as gills are. Air is humidified and brought to body temperature as it passes through the moist upper respiratory passageways. Expired air must

again pass through these airways (providing opportunity for retaining water) before leaving the body. These adaptations protect the lungs from the drying and cooling effects of air.

Review

■   What are some advantages of gas exchange in air over gas exchange in water?

46.2 TYPES OF RESPIRATORY SURFACES

◼ LEARNING OBJECTIVE

2   Describe the following adaptations for gas exchange: body surface, tracheal tubes, gills, and lungs.

Respiratory structures must be moist, and must also have thin walls through which diffusion can easily occur. Four main types of respiratory surfaces have evolved in animals: the animal's own body surface, tracheal tubes, gills, and lungs (**FIG. 46-1**). Some animals use a combination of these adaptations. Gills are adapted for gas exchange in water, and the tracheal tubes of insects and lungs of vertebrates are respiratory structures adapted for gas exchange in air. With the important exception of insect tracheal tubes, respiratory structures are richly supplied with blood vessels that facilitate exchange and transport of respiratory gases.

Most animals carry on **ventilation,** that is, they actively move air or water over their respiratory surfaces. If the air or water supplying oxygen to the cells can be continuously renewed, more oxygen will be available. Sponges use their flagella to set up a current of water through the channels of their bodies. Most fishes gulp water, which then passes over their gills. Terrestrial vertebrates have lungs and breathe air. When mammals breathe, the diaphragm and other muscles move air in and out of the lungs.

The body surface may be adapted for gas exchange

Gas exchange occurs through the entire body surface in many animals, including nudibranch mollusks, most annelids, and some amphibians. These animals are small, with a high surface area to volume ratio. They also have a low metabolic rate that requires smaller quantities of oxygen per cell. In aquatic animals, the body surface is kept moist by the surrounding water. In terrestrial animals, the body secretes fluids that keep its surface moist. Many animals that exchange gases across the body surface also have gills or lungs.

Tracheal tube systems deliver air directly to the cells

In insects and some other arthropods (such as chilopods, diplopods, some mites, and some spiders), the respiratory system is a network of **tracheal tubes,** also called **tracheae** (**FIG. 46-2**). This very efficient respiratory system delivers air directly to the cells.

Earthworm

(a) Body surface. Some small, multicellular animals exchange gases through the body surface.

Grasshopper

(b) Tracheal tubes. Insects and some other arthropods exchange gases through a system of tracheal tubes, or tracheae.

Internal gills

External gills

Fish

Mud puppy

Gills

(c) Gills. Most aquatic animals exchange gases through gills, thin structures that extend from the body surface. Gills can be internal or external.

Book lung

Spider

Lungfish

Mammal

(d) Lungs. Lungs are adaptations for terrestrial gas exchange.

FIGURE 46-1 Adaptations for gas exchange

The efficient tracheal tube system of insects delivers air directly to the cells.

Spiracle

Tracheal tube

(a) Location of spiracles and tracheal tubes. Air enters the system of tracheal tubes through openings called spiracles.

Epithelial cell

Tracheal tube

Tracheole

O_2

Spiracle

CO_2

Muscle

(b) Structure and function of tracheal tubes. Air passes through a system of branching tracheal tubes that conduct oxygen to all cells of the insect.

Courtesy of Dr. James L. Nation and Stain Technology, Vol. 58, 1983

100 μm

(c) SEM of a mole cricket trachea. The wrinkles are a part of a long spiral that wraps around the tube, strengthening the tracheal wall somewhat as a spring strengthens the plastic hoses of many vacuum cleaners. The tracheal wall is composed of chitin.

FIGURE 46-2 Gas exchange in insects: tracheal tubes

Air enters the tracheal tubes through a series of as many as 20 tiny openings called **spiracles** along the body surface. In some insects, especially large, active ones, muscles help ventilate the tracheae by pumping air in and out of the spiracles. For example, the grasshopper draws air in through the first four pairs of spiracles when the abdomen expands. Then the abdomen contracts, forcing air out through the last six pairs of spiracles.

Once inside the body, the air passes through a system of branching tracheal tubes, which extend to all parts of the animal. The tracheal tubes terminate in microscopic, fluid-filled tracheoles. Gases are exchanged between this fluid and the body cells. The tracheal system supplies enough oxygen to support the high metabolic rates required by many insects.

Gills are the respiratory surfaces in many aquatic animals

Found mainly in aquatic animals, **gills** are moist, thin structures that extend from the body surface. They are supported by the buoyancy of water but tend to collapse in air. In many animals, the outer surface of the gills is exposed to water, whereas the inner side is in close contact with networks of blood vessels.

Sea stars and sea urchins have **dermal gills** that project from the body wall. Their ciliated epidermal cells ventilate the gills by beating a stream of water over them. Gases are exchanged between the water and the coelomic fluid inside the body by diffusion through the gills.

Various types of gills are found in some annelids, aquatic mollusks, crustaceans, fishes, and amphibians. Mollusk gills are folded, providing a large surface for respiration. In clams and other bivalve mollusks and in simple chordates, gills may also be adapted for trapping and sorting food. The rhythmic beating of cilia draws water over the gill area, and food is filtered out of the water while gases are exchanged. In mollusks, gas exchange also takes place through the mantle.

In chordates, gills are usually internal. A series of slits perforates the pharynx, and the gills lie along the edges of these gill slits (see Fig. 32-4). In bony fishes, the fragile gills are protected by an external bony plate, the **operculum.** In some fishes, movements of the jaw and operculum help pump water rich in oxygen through the mouth and across the gills. The water leaves through the gill slits.

Each gill in the bony fish consists of many **gill filaments,** which provide an extensive surface for gas exchange (**FIGS. 46-3a** and **b**). The filaments extend out into the water, which continuously flows over them. A capillary network delivers blood to the gill filaments, facilitating diffusion of oxygen and carbon dioxide between blood and water. This system is extremely efficient because blood flows in a direction opposite to the movement of the water. This arrangement, called a **countercurrent exchange system,** maximizes the difference in oxygen concentration between blood and water throughout the area where the two remain in contact (**FIG. 46-3c**).

If blood and water flowed in the *same* direction, that is, *concurrent exchange,* the difference between the oxygen concentrations in blood (low) and water (high) would be very large initially and very small at the end (**FIG. 46-3d**). The oxygen concentration in the water would decrease as the concentration in the blood increased. When the concentrations in the two fluids became equal, equilibrium would be reached, and the net diffusion of oxygen would stop. Only about 50% of the oxygen dissolved in the water could diffuse into the blood.

In the countercurrent exchange system, however, blood low in oxygen comes in contact with water that is partly depleted of oxygen. Then, as the blood flowing through the capillaries becomes progressively richer in oxygen, the blood comes in contact with water with an increasingly higher concentration of oxygen. Thus, all along the capillaries, the diffusion gradient favors passage of oxygen from the water into the gill. A high rate of diffusion is maintained, ensuring that a very high percentage (more than 80%) of the available oxygen in the water diffuses into the blood.

Oxygen and carbon dioxide do not interfere with each other's diffusion, and they simultaneously diffuse in opposite directions. The reason is that oxygen is more concentrated outside the gills than inside but carbon dioxide is more concentrated inside the gills than outside. Thus, the same countercurrent exchange mechanism that ensures efficient inflow of oxygen also results in equally efficient outflow of carbon dioxide.

Terrestrial vertebrates exchange gases through lungs

Lungs are respiratory structures that develop as ingrowths of the body surface or from the wall of a body cavity such as the pharynx (throat region). For example, the **book lungs** of spiders are enclosed in an inpocketing of the abdominal wall. These lungs consist of a series of thin, parallel plates of tissue (like the pages of a book) filled with hemolymph (see Fig. 46-1d). The plates of tissue are separated by air spaces that receive oxygen from the outside environment through a spiracle. A different type of lung evolved in land snails and slugs. (These terrestrial mollusks lack gills.) Gas exchange takes place through a lung, which is a vascular region of the mantle.

Fossil evidence suggests that early lobe-finned fishes had lungs somewhat similar to those of modern lungfishes. The Australian lungfish can use either its gills or its lungs, depending on the conditions in its environment. The gills of African and South American lungfishes degenerate with age, so adults must rise to the surface and exchange gases entirely through their lungs. Some paleontologists hypothesize that all early bony fishes had lungs or lunglike structures. Most modern bony fishes have no lungs, but nearly all have homologous **swim bladders** (see Chapter 32). By adjusting the amount of gas in its swim bladder, the fish can control its buoyancy.

Most amphibians have lungs (**FIG. 46-4**). However, most of their gas exchange takes place across the body surface. The lungs of salamanders are two long, simple sacs richly supplied with capillaries. Frogs and toads have ridges containing connective tissue on the inside of the lungs, which increases the respiratory surface. Some amphibians do not have lungs. Among plethodontid (lungless) salamanders, for example, gas exchange takes place across the thin, wet skin and through the moist, vascular walls of the mouth and pharynx.

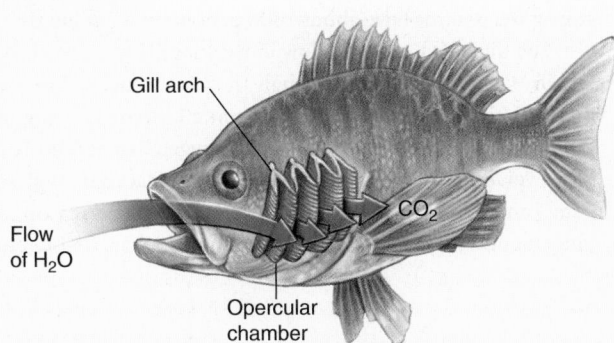

Gill arch

Flow of H_2O

CO_2

Opercular chamber

(a) Location of gills. The gills form the lateral wall of the pharyngeal cavity. They lie under a bony plate, the operculum, which has been removed in this side view.

Gill arch

Blood vessels

Gill filaments

(b) Structure of a gill. Each gill consists of a cartilaginous gill arch to which two rows of leaflike gill filaments attach. Each gill filament has many smaller extensions rich in capillaries. As water flows past the gill filament, oxygen passes from the water into blood circulating through the capillaries.

Afferent blood vessel (low O_2 concentration)

Efferent blood vessel (rich in O_2)

(c) Countercurrent flow. Blood entering the capillaries of the gill filament is deficient in oxygen. The blood flows through the capillaries in a direction opposite to that taken by the water. This countercurrent exchange system efficiently charges the blood with oxygen.

(d) Concurrent flow (hypothetical). If the system were concurrent, that is, if blood flowed through the capillaries in the same direction as the flow of the water, much less of the oxygen dissolved in the water could diffuse into the blood.

Bernard Photo Production/Animals Animals

(e) Gills of the salmon.

FIGURE 46-3 *Animated* Gas exchange in bony fishes: gills

Reptiles have better developed lungs than amphibians. The respiratory surface of each lung is divided into large sacs that increase the surface for gas exchange. In some turtles, lizards, and crocodiles, the lungs have many subdivisions that give them a spongy texture. Reptiles ventilate their lungs by drawing air into the lungs, but the muscles involved differ in the various reptile groups. Gas exchange is not very efficient and does not supply enough oxygen to sustain long periods of activity.

Birds have the most efficient respiratory system of any living vertebrate. Very active, endothermic animals with high metabolic

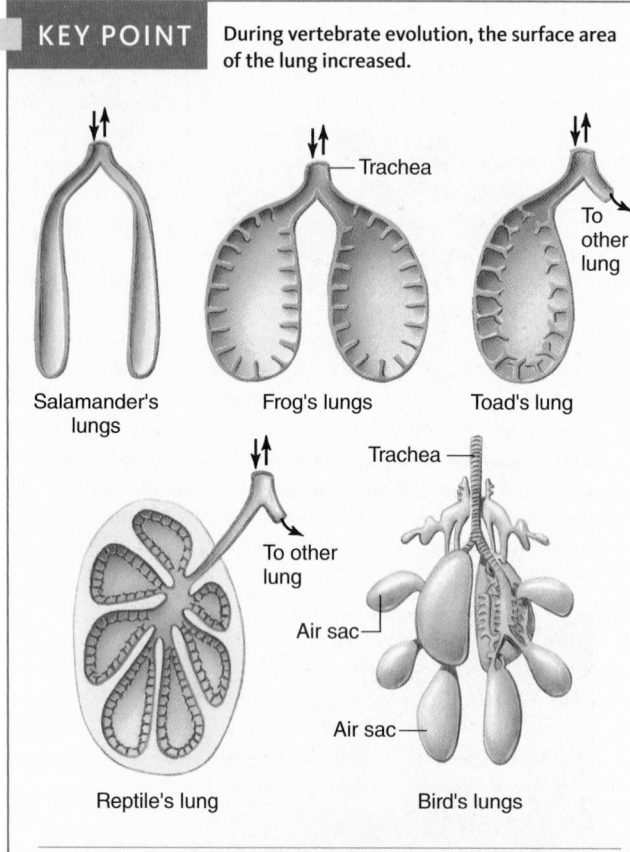

During vertebrate evolution, the surface area of the lung increased.

Salamander's lungs

Frog's lungs

Toad's lung

Trachea

To other lung

Reptile's lung

Trachea

To other lung

Air sac

Air sac

Bird's lungs

FIGURE 46-4 *Animated* **Evolution of vertebrate lungs**
Salamander lungs are simple sacs. Other amphibians and reptiles have lungs with small ridges or folds that increase surface area. Birds have an elaborate system of lungs and air sacs. Mammalian lungs have millions of air sacs (alveoli) that increase the surface available for gas exchange (see Fig. 46-7).

flows through them. Gas exchange takes place across the walls of these tubes, which are rich in capillaries. Chickens and other weak-flying birds have about 400 parabronchi per lung; pigeons and other strong-flying birds have about 1800 parabronchi per lung.

The direction of blood flow in the lungs is in a different direction from that of airflow through the parabronchi. This arrangement, similar in principle to the countercurrent exchange in the gills of fishes, increases the amount of oxygen that enters the blood. However, in birds the capillaries are oriented at right angles to the parabronchi rather than along their length. For this reason, this arrangement is referred to as *crosscurrent* rather than countercurrent.

Review

- Why are specialized respiratory structures necessary in a tadpole but not in a flatworm?
- How does gas exchange differ among the following animals: (1) earthworm, (2) grasshopper, (3) fish, and (4) bird?
- How does the countercurrent exchange system increase the efficiency of gas exchange between a fish's gills and blood?

46.3 THE MAMMALIAN RESPIRATORY SYSTEM

LEARNING OBJECTIVES

3 Trace the passage of oxygen through the human respiratory system from nostrils to alveoli.

4 Summarize the mechanics of breathing in humans, and describe gas exchange in the lungs and tissues.

5 Summarize the mechanisms by which oxygen and carbon dioxide are transported in the blood and identify factors that determine the oxygen–hemoglobin dissociation curve.

6 Describe the regulation of breathing in humans and summarize the physiological effects of hyperventilation and of sudden decompression when a diver surfaces too quickly from deep water.

The respiratory system of mammals consists of the lungs and a series of tubes through which air passes on its journey from the nostrils to the lungs and back (**FIG. 46-6**). The complex lungs have an enormous surface area. As in all vertebrates, the respiratory and circulatory systems are functionally connected. The circulatory system delivers oxygen-rich blood to all of the cells in the body. In the following sections, we focus mainly on the human respiratory system.

The airway conducts air into the lungs

A breath of air enters the body through the **nostrils** and flows through the **nasal cavities.** Air passing through the nose is filtered, moistened, and brought to body temperature. The nasal cavities are lined with a moist, ciliated epithelium rich in blood vessels. Inhaled dirt, bacteria, and other foreign particles are trapped in the stream of mucus produced by cells within the epithelium and pushed along toward the throat by the cilia. In this way, foreign particles are de-

rates, birds require large amounts of oxygen to sustain flight and other activities. Their small, bright red lungs have extensions (usually nine) called **air sacs,** which reach into all parts of the body and even connect with air spaces in some of the bones. The air sacs act as bellows, drawing air into the system. Collapse of the air sacs during exhalation forces air out. Gas exchange does not take place across the walls of the air sacs.

The high-performance bird respiratory system is arranged so that air flows in one direction through the lungs and is renewed during a two-cycle process (**FIG. 46-5**). Air entering the body passes into the posterior air sacs and the part of the lungs closest to these air sacs. The posterior air sacs are reservoirs for fresh air. When the bird exhales, that air flows into the lungs. At the second breath, the air flows from the lungs to the anterior air sacs. Finally, at the second exhalation, the air leaves the body as another breath of air enters the lungs. Thus, a bird gets fresh air across its lungs through both inhalation and exhalation.

In birds the narrowest branches of the airway end in tiny, thin-walled tubes called **parabronchi.** In contrast to the saclike alveoli of mammals, parabronchi are open at both ends and air continuously

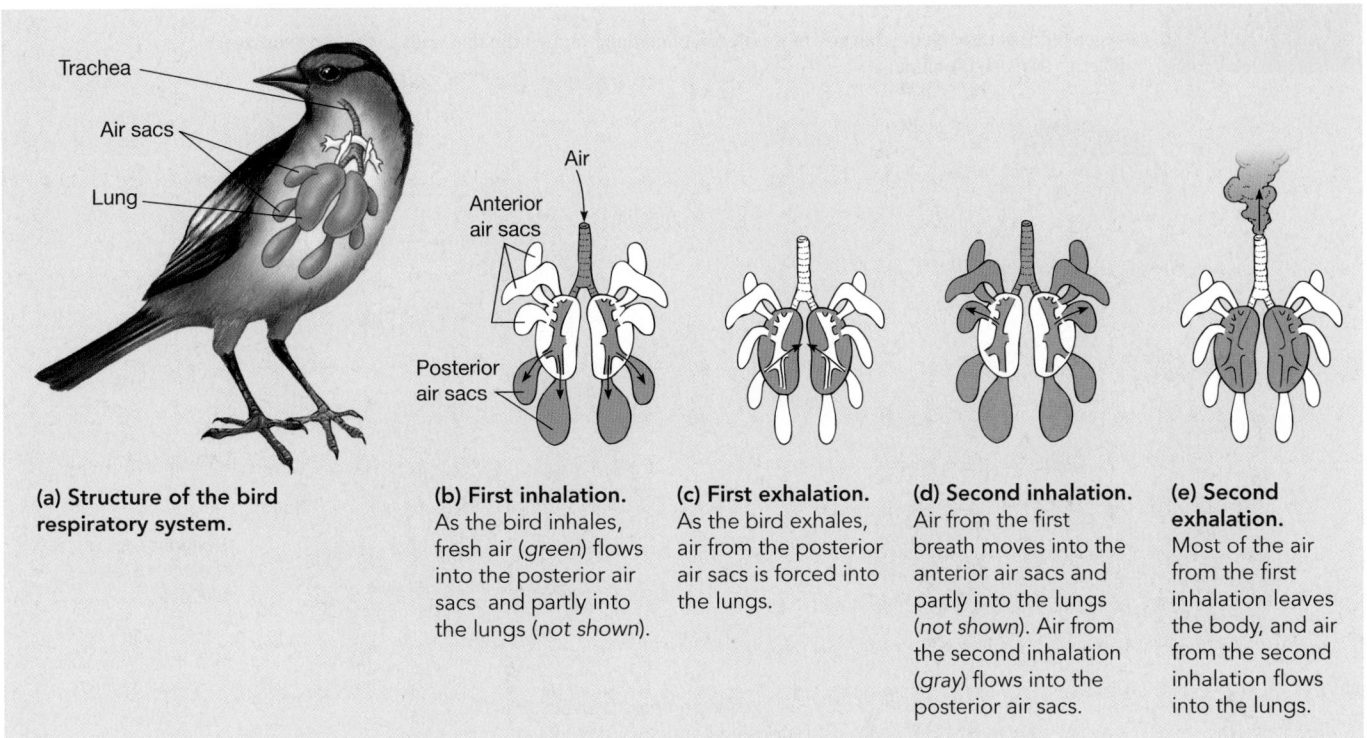

(a) Structure of the bird respiratory system.

(b) First inhalation. As the bird inhales, fresh air (*green*) flows into the posterior air sacs and partly into the lungs (*not shown*).

(c) First exhalation. As the bird exhales, air from the posterior air sacs is forced into the lungs.

(d) Second inhalation. Air from the first breath moves into the anterior air sacs and partly into the lungs (*not shown*). Air from the second inhalation (*gray*) flows into the posterior air sacs.

(e) Second exhalation. Most of the air from the first inhalation leaves the body, and air from the second inhalation flows into the lungs.

FIGURE 46-5 *Animated* Gas exchange in birds

The bird respiratory system includes lungs and air sacs. The bird's breathing process requires two cycles of inhalation and exhalation to support a one-way flow of air through the lungs.

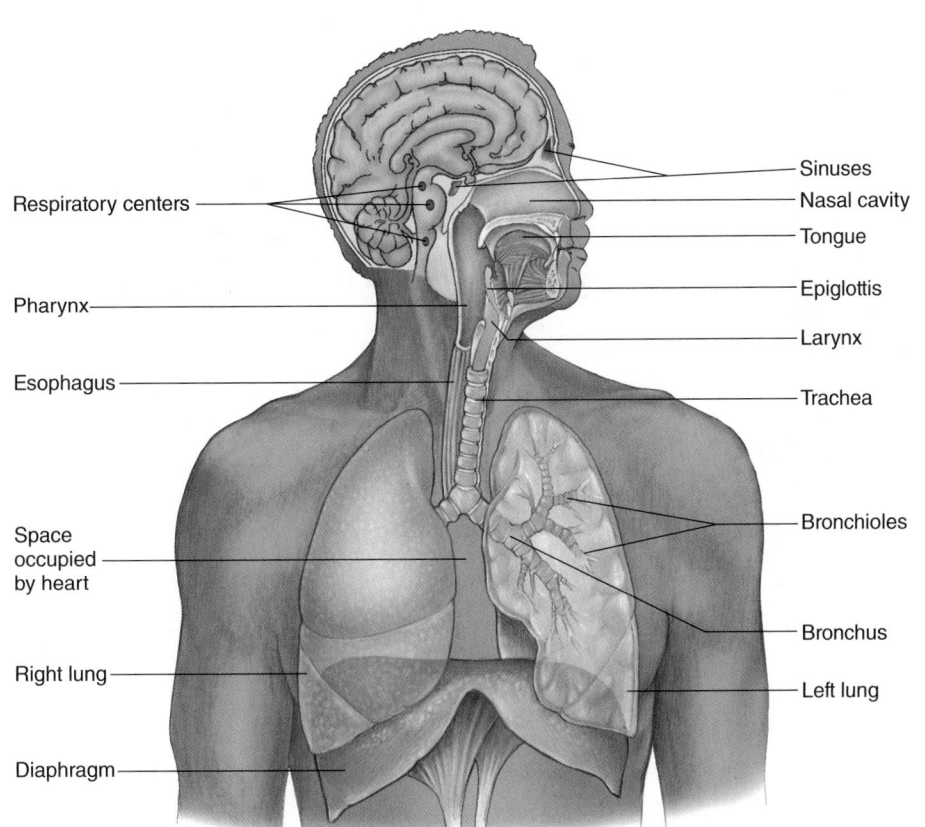

livered to the digestive system, which can more effectively dispose of such materials than can the delicate lungs. A person normally swallows more than a pint of nasal mucus each day, and even more during an infection or allergic reaction.

The back of the nasal cavities is continuous with the throat region, or **pharynx.** Air finds its way into the pharynx whether one breathes through the nose or mouth. An opening in the floor of the pharynx leads into the **larynx.** Because the larynx contains the vocal cords, it is also referred to as the "voice box." Cartilage embedded in its wall prevents the larynx from collapsing and makes it hard to the touch when felt through the neck.

◀**FIGURE 46-6** *Animated* **The human respiratory system**

The internal view of one lung illustrates a portion of its extensive system of air passageways. The muscular diaphragm forms the floor of the thoracic cavity. The respiratory centers in the brain regulate the rate of respiration.

KEY POINT Oxygen diffuses through the thin wall of the alveolus and then through the thin walls of the surrounding capillaries to reach the blood.

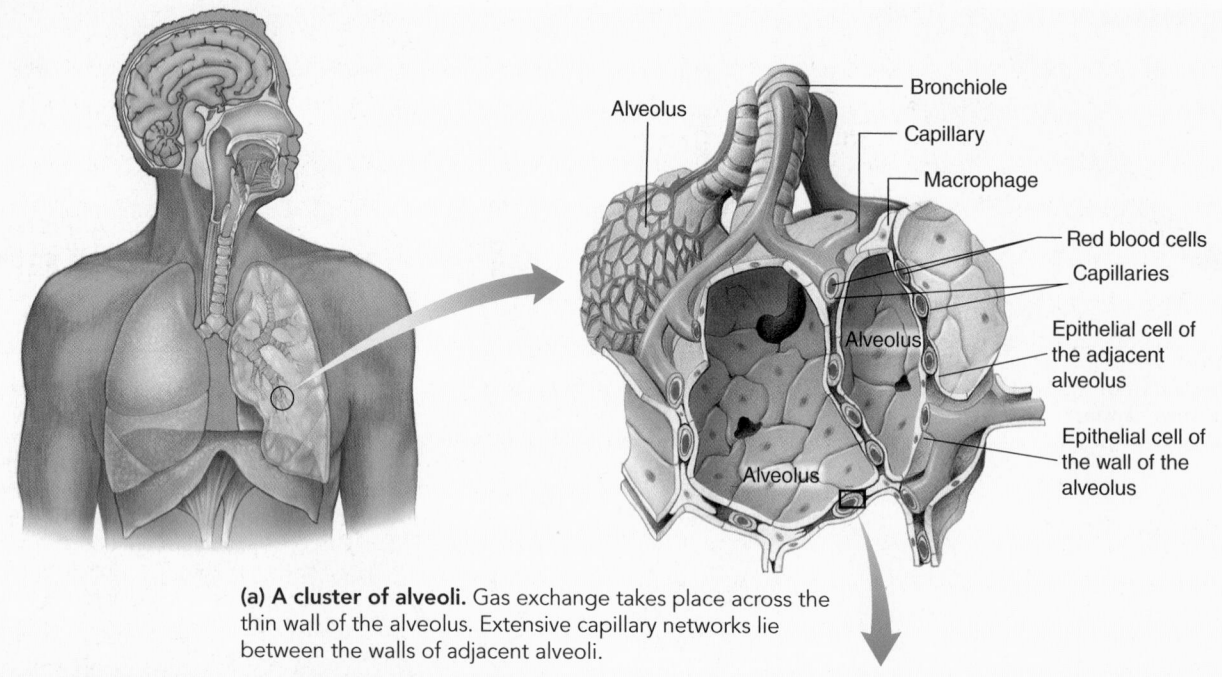

(a) A cluster of alveoli. Gas exchange takes place across the thin wall of the alveolus. Extensive capillary networks lie between the walls of adjacent alveoli.

Dr. Richard Kessel & Dr. Randy K./Visuals Unlimited/Corbis

30 µm

(b) Capillaries in lung. Capillaries surround the individual alveoli (air sacs), allowing for the exchange of oxygen and carbon dioxide between the blood and the alveoli.

Courtesy of Drs. Peter Gehr, Marianne Bachofen, and Ewald R. Wiebel

Wall of alveolus   Wall of capillary   Red blood cell

1 µm

(c) Color-enhanced TEM of a portion of a capillary and the wall of an alveolus. The dark structure extending through the capillary is part of a red blood cell. Notice the very short distance oxygen must diffuse to get from the air within the alveolus to the red blood cells that transport it to the body tissues.

FIGURE 46-7 *Animated* **Structure and function of alveoli**

· The alveoli are the air sacs through which gases are exchanged between the air in the lung and the blood in the capillaries.

During swallowing, a flap of tissue called the **epiglottis** automatically closes off the larynx so that food and liquid enter the esophagus rather than the lower airway. If this mechanism fails and foreign matter enters the sensitive larynx, a cough reflex expels the material. Despite these mechanisms, choking sometimes occurs.

From the larynx, air passes into the **trachea,** or windpipe, which is kept from collapsing by rings of cartilage in its wall. The trachea divides into two branches, the **bronchi** (sing., *bronchus*); one bronchus connects to each lung. Both trachea and bronchi are lined by a mucous membrane containing ciliated cells. These cells trap medium-sized particles that escape the cleansing mechanisms of the nose and larynx. Mucus containing these particles is constantly beaten upward by the cilia to the pharynx, where it is periodically swallowed. This mechanism, functioning as a cilia-propelled elevator of mucus, helps keep foreign material out of the lungs.

Gas exchange occurs in the alveoli of the lungs

The lungs are large, paired, spongy organs occupying the *thoracic* (chest) *cavity*. The right lung is divided into three lobes, the left lung into two lobes. Each lung is covered with a **pleural membrane,** which forms a continuous sac that encloses the lung and extends outward to become the lining of the thoracic cavity. The *pleural cavity* is the space between the pleural membranes. A film of fluid in the pleural cavity provides lubrication between the lungs and the chest wall.

Because the lung consists largely of air tubes and elastic connective tissue, it is a spongy, elastic organ with a very large internal surface area for gas exchange. Within each lung the bronchi branch, becoming progressively shorter, narrower, and more numerous, similar to the branching of a tree. Small branches give rise to the even smaller **bronchioles** in each lung. Each bronchiole ends in a cluster of tiny air sacs, the **alveoli** (sing., *alveolus*) (**FIG. 46-7**). Each human lung contains more than 200 million alveoli, which provide an internal surface area the approximate size of a tennis court!

Each alveolus is lined by an extremely thin, single layer of epithelial cells. Gases diffuse freely through the wall of the alveolus and into the capillaries that surround it. Only two thin cell layers—the epithelium of the alveolar wall and the epithelium of the capillary wall—separate the air in the alveolus from the blood.

In summary, air passes through the following sequence of structures after it enters the body:

nostrils ⟶ nasal cavities ⟶ pharynx ⟶ larynx ⟶
trachea ⟶ bronchi ⟶ bronchioles ⟶ alveoli

Ventilation is accomplished by breathing

Breathing is the mechanical process of moving air from the environment into the lungs and of expelling air from the lungs. Inhaling air is called **inhalation** or *inspiration*; exhaling air is **exhalation** or *expiration*. The thoracic cavity is closed so no air can enter except through the trachea. (When the chest wall is punctured, for example, by a fractured rib or gunshot wound, air enters the pleural space and the lung collapses.)

During inhalation, the volume of the thoracic cavity is increased by the contraction of the **diaphragm,** the dome-shaped muscle that forms its floor. When the diaphragm contracts, it moves downward, increasing the volume of the thoracic cavity (**FIG. 46-8**). During forced inhalation, when a large volume of air is inhaled, the *external intercostal muscles* contract as well. This action moves the ribs upward, which also increases the volume of the thoracic cavity.

Because the lungs adhere to the walls of the thoracic cavity, when the volume of the thoracic cavity increases, the space within each lung also increases. The air in the lungs now has more space in which to move about. As a result, air pressure in the lungs falls by 2 or 3 millimeters of mercury (mm Hg) below the air pressure outside the body. Because of this pressure difference, air from the

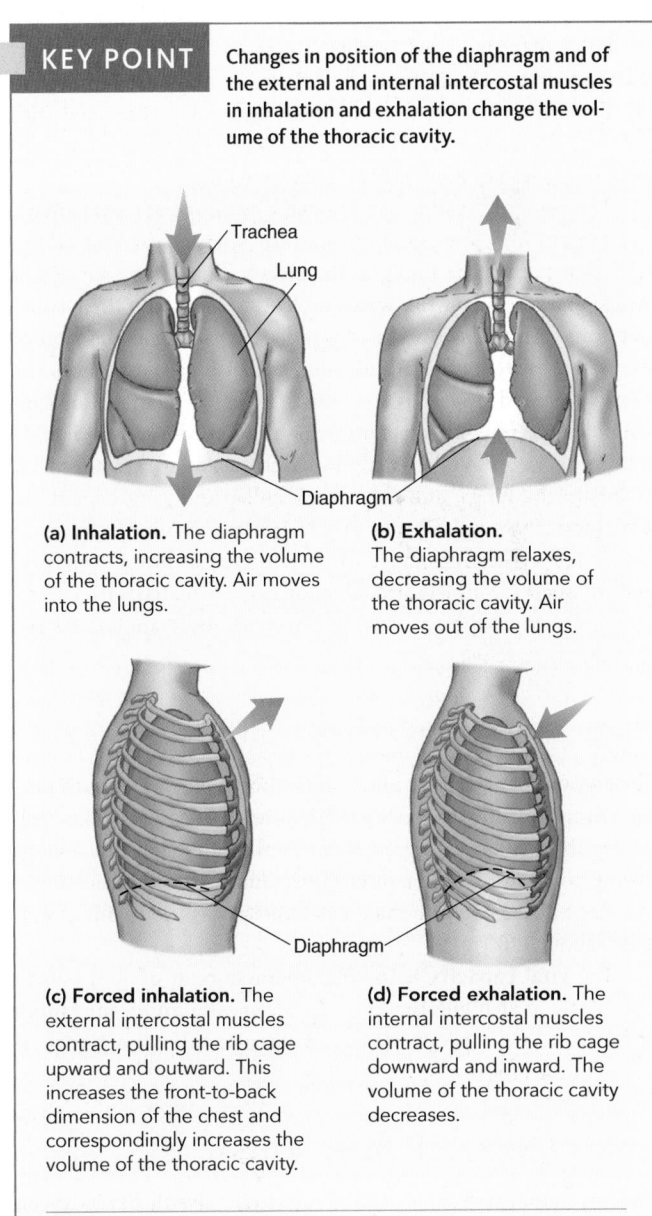

KEY POINT Changes in position of the diaphragm and of the external and internal intercostal muscles in inhalation and exhalation change the volume of the thoracic cavity.

Trachea
Lung
Diaphragm

(a) Inhalation. The diaphragm contracts, increasing the volume of the thoracic cavity. Air moves into the lungs.

(b) Exhalation. The diaphragm relaxes, decreasing the volume of the thoracic cavity. Air moves out of the lungs.

Diaphragm

(c) Forced inhalation. The external intercostal muscles contract, pulling the rib cage upward and outward. This increases the front-to-back dimension of the chest and correspondingly increases the volume of the thoracic cavity.

(d) Forced exhalation. The internal intercostal muscles contract, pulling the rib cage downward and inward. The volume of the thoracic cavity decreases.

FIGURE 46-8 *Animated* Mechanics of breathing

outside rushes in through the respiratory passageways and fills the lungs until the two pressures are equal once again.

Exhalation occurs when the diaphragm relaxes. The volume of the thoracic cavity decreases, raising the pressure in the lungs to 2 to 3 mm Hg above atmospheric pressure. The millions of distended air sacs partially deflate and expel the inhaled air. The pressure then returns to normal, and the lung is ready for another inhalation. To summarize: during inhalation the millions of alveoli fill with air like so many tiny balloons. Then, during exhalation, the air rushes out of the alveoli, partially deflating them.

During deep or forced inhalation, the *external intercostal muscles* also contract, pulling the rib cage upward and outward. This action further increases the volume of the thoracic cavity and more air moves into the lungs. During forced exhalation, muscles of the abdominal wall and the *internal intercostal muscles* contract, pushing the diaphragm up and the ribs down. This action decreases the volume of the thoracic cavity, pushing air out of the lungs.

Some of the work in stretching the thorax and the lungs is necessary to stretch elastic connective tissue. Work is also required to overcome the cohesive force of water molecules associated with the pleural membranes. The forces between the water molecules produce a surface tension that resists stretching.

The work of breathing is reduced by **pulmonary surfactant,** a detergent-like phospholipid mixture secreted by specialized epithelial cells in the lining of the alveoli. Pulmonary surfactant intersperses between the water molecules, reducing their cohesive force. This action markedly reduces the surface tension of the water, prevents the alveoli from collapsing, and reduces the energy required to stretch the lungs. Premature infants often cannot produce enough surfactant, which causes respiratory distress syndrome. In these infants, high surface tension makes it difficult to inflate the lungs, and the alveoli collapse during expiration. Breathing is labored. Respiratory failure as a result of surfactant deficiency is a leading cause of morbidity and mortality in premature infants. Surfactant deficiency can be treated with surfactant replacement therapy in which artificial surfactant is delivered through the trachea.

The quantity of respired air can be measured

The amount of air moved into and out of the lungs with each normal resting breath is called the **tidal volume.** The normal tidal volume is about 500 mL. A great deal of stale air remains in the lungs during normal resting breathing. The volume of air that remains in the lungs at the end of a maximal expiration is the **residual volume** (about 1200 mL).

The **vital capacity** is the maximum amount of air a person can exhale after filling the lungs to the maximum extent (about 4500 mL). Vital capacity is a useful measure of the functional capacity of the lungs.

Gas exchange takes place in the alveoli

The respiratory system delivers oxygen to the alveoli, but if oxygen remained in the lungs, all the other body cells would soon die. The vital link between alveolus and body cell is the circulatory system. Pulmonary capillaries bring blood very close to the alveolar air.

Each alveolus serves as a tiny depot from which oxygen diffuses into the blood (**FIG. 46-9**).

Oxygen molecules efficiently pass by simple diffusion from the alveoli, where they are more concentrated, into the blood in the pulmonary capillaries, where they are less concentrated. At the same time, carbon dioxide moves from the blood, where it is more concentrated, to the alveoli, where it is less concentrated. Each gas diffuses through the single layer of cells lining the alveoli and the single layer of cells lining the capillaries.

Recall that in aerobic respiration, oxygen is the final electron acceptor; it accepts two electrons, which are added to two protons to produce water (see Chapter 8). Inhaled (atmospheric) air contains about 20.9% oxygen, but because oxygen is used during cellular respiration, exhaled (alveolar) air contains only 14% oxygen. Carbon dioxide is produced during aerobic respiration. For this reason, exhaled air contains more than 100 times as much (5.6%) carbon dioxide as inhaled air (almost .04% carbon dioxide).

The concentration of oxygen in the cells is lower than in the capillaries entering the tissues, and the concentration of carbon dioxide is higher in the cells than in the capillaries. As blood circulates through capillaries of a tissue such as brain or muscle, oxygen moves by simple diffusion from the blood to the cells, and carbon dioxide moves from the cells into the blood.

The factor that determines the direction and rate of diffusion is the pressure or tension of the particular gas. According to **Dalton's**

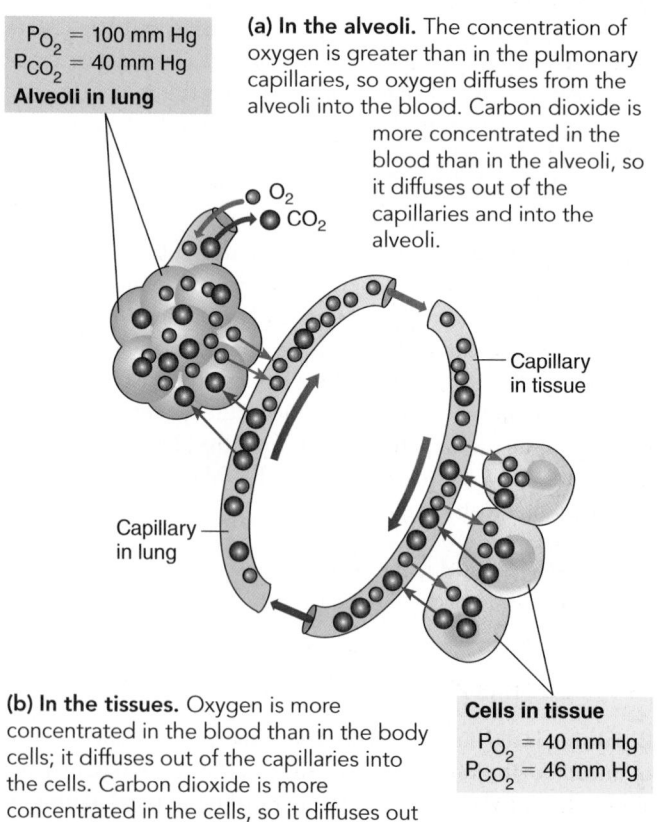

P_{O_2} = 100 mm Hg
P_{CO_2} = 40 mm Hg
Alveoli in lung

O_2
CO_2

(a) In the alveoli. The concentration of oxygen is greater than in the pulmonary capillaries, so oxygen diffuses from the alveoli into the blood. Carbon dioxide is more concentrated in the blood than in the alveoli, so it diffuses out of the capillaries and into the alveoli.

Capillary in tissue

Capillary in lung

(b) In the tissues. Oxygen is more concentrated in the blood than in the body cells; it diffuses out of the capillaries into the cells. Carbon dioxide is more concentrated in the cells, so it diffuses out of the cells and moves into the blood.

Cells in tissue
P_{O_2} = 40 mm Hg
P_{CO_2} = 46 mm Hg

FIGURE 46-9 Gas exchange in the lungs and tissues
Note the differences in partial pressures of oxygen and carbon dioxide before and after gases are exchanged in the tissues.

law of partial pressures, in a mixture of gases the total pressure of the mixture is the sum of the pressures of the individual gases. Each gas exerts, independently of the others, a **partial pressure**—the same pressure it would exert if it were present alone. At sea level, the barometric pressure (the pressure of Earth's atmosphere) typically supports a column of mercury 760 mm high. Because oxygen makes up about 21% of the atmosphere, oxygen's share of that pressure is $0.21 \times 760 = 160$ mm Hg. Thus, 160 mm Hg is the partial pressure of atmospheric O_2, abbreviated P_{O_2}. In contrast, the partial pressure of atmospheric CO_2 is 0.3 mm Hg, abbreviated P_{CO_2}.

Fick's law of diffusion explains that the amount of oxygen or carbon dioxide that diffuses across the membrane of an alveolus depends on the differences in partial pressure on the two sides of the membrane, and on the surface area of the membrane. The gas diffuses faster if the difference in pressure or the surface area increases.

Gas exchange takes place in the tissues

The partial pressure of oxygen in arterial blood is about 100 mm Hg. The P_{O_2} in the tissues is still lower, averaging about 40 mm Hg. Consequently, oxygen diffuses out of the capillaries and into the tissues. Not all the oxygen leaves the blood, however. The blood passes through the tissue capillaries too rapidly for equilibrium to be reached. As a result, the partial pressure of oxygen in venous blood returning to the lungs is about 40 mm Hg. Thus, exhaled air has had only part of its oxygen removed—a good thing for those in need of mouth-to-mouth resuscitation!

Respiratory pigments increase capacity for oxygen transport

Respiratory pigments combine reversibly with oxygen and greatly increase the capacity of blood to transport it. **Hemocyanins** are copper-containing proteins dispersed in the hemolymph of many species of mollusks and arthropods. Without oxygen, these pigments are colorless. When oxygen combines with the copper, hemocyanins are blue.

Hemoglobin and **myoglobin** are the most common respiratory pigments in animals. Hemoglobin is the pigment found in the blood of vertebrates. It is also present in many invertebrate species, including annelids, nematodes, mollusks, and arthropods. In some of these animals, the hemoglobin is dispersed in the plasma rather than confined to blood cells. Recall that myoglobin is a form of hemoglobin found in muscle fibers (see Chapter 40).

In humans and other mammals, inhaled oxygen diffuses out of the alveoli and enters the pulmonary capillaries. Plasma in equilibrium with alveolar air can take up only 0.25 mL of oxygen per 100 mL. However, oxygen diffuses into red blood cells (RBCs) and combines with hemoglobin. The properties of hemoglobin permit whole blood to carry some 20 mL of oxygen per 100 mL. Hemoglobin transports almost 99% of the oxygen. The rest is dissolved in the plasma.

The term *hemoglobin* is actually a general name for a group of related compounds, all of which consist of an iron–porphyrin, or heme, group bound to a protein known as a *globin*. The protein portion of the molecule varies in size, amino acid composition, and physical properties among various species.

The protein portion of hemoglobin is composed of four peptide chains, typically two α and two β chains, each attached to a heme (iron–porphyrin) ring (see Fig. 3-22a). An iron atom is bound in the center of each heme ring. Hemoglobin has the remarkable property of forming a weak chemical bond with oxygen. An oxygen molecule can attach to the iron atom in each heme. In the lung (or gill), oxygen diffuses into the RBCs and combines with hemoglobin (Hb) to form **oxyhemoglobin (HbO_2).** When combined with oxygen, hemoglobin is bright red; without oxygen, it appears dark red, imparting a purplish color to venous blood.

Because the chemical bond formed between the oxygen and the hemoglobin is weak, the reaction is readily reversible. As blood circulates through tissues where the oxygen concentration is low, the reaction proceeds to the left. Hemoglobin releases oxygen, which diffuses out of the blood and into the cells of the tissues.

$$Hb + O_2 \rightleftharpoons HbO_2$$

The maximum amount of oxygen that hemoglobin can transport is its **oxygen-carrying capacity.** The *actual* amount of oxygen bound to hemoglobin is the **oxygen content.** The ratio of O_2 content to oxygen-carrying capacity is the **percent O_2 saturation** of the hemoglobin. The percent O_2 saturation is highest in the pulmonary capillaries, where the concentration of oxygen is greatest. In the capillaries of the tissues, where there is less oxygen, oxyhemoglobin dissociates, releasing oxygen. There, the percent saturation of hemoglobin is correspondingly lower.

The **oxygen–hemoglobin dissociation curve** shown in **FIGURE 46-10a** illustrates the relationship between partial pressure of oxygen and percent saturation of hemoglobin. As oxygen concentration increases, there is a progressive increase in the percentage of hemoglobin that is combined with oxygen. The ability of oxygen to combine with hemoglobin and be released from oxyhemoglobin is influenced by several factors in addition to percent O_2 saturation. These factors include pH, carbon dioxide concentration, and temperature.

Carbon dioxide produced in respiring tissue reacts with water in the plasma to form carbonic acid, H_2CO_3. For this reason, any increase in carbon dioxide concentration also increases the acidity (lowers the pH) of the blood. Oxyhemoglobin unloads oxygen more readily in an acidic environment than in an environment with normal pH. Displacement of the oxygen–hemoglobin dissociation curve by a change in pH is known as the **Bohr effect** (**FIG. 46-10b**). Lactic acid released from active muscles also lowers blood pH and has a similar effect on the oxygen–hemoglobin dissociation curve—more oxygen is unloaded and available for muscle contraction.

Some carbon dioxide is transported by the hemoglobin molecule. Although carbon dioxide attaches to the hemoglobin molecule in a different way and at a different site than oxygen does, the attachment of a carbon dioxide molecule releases an oxygen molecule from the hemoglobin. This effect of carbon dioxide concentration on the oxygen–hemoglobin dissociation curve is important. In the capillaries of the lungs (or gills in fishes), carbon dioxide concentration is relatively low and oxygen concentration is high, so oxygen combines with a very high percentage of hemoglobin. In the capillaries of the tissues, carbon dioxide concentration is high and oxygen concentration is low, so hemoglobin readily unloads oxygen.

The oxygen and carbon dioxide bound to hemoglobin in RBCs do not contribute to the partial pressures that govern diffusion. Loading and unloading of gases onto hemoglobin depend on partial pressures of the plasma and interstitial fluid (which is determined by the gases dissolved in these fluids).

Carbon dioxide is transported mainly as bicarbonate ions

Blood transports carbon dioxide in three forms. About 10% of carbon dioxide dissolves in plasma. Another 30% enters the RBCs and combines with hemoglobin. Because the bond between the hemoglobin and carbon dioxide is very weak, the reaction is readily reversible. Most carbon dioxide (about 60%) moves through plasma as **bicarbonate ions** (HCO_3^-).

In plasma, carbon dioxide slowly combines with water to form carbonic acid. This reaction proceeds much more rapidly inside RBCs as a result of the action of the enzyme **carbonic anhydrase** (**FIG. 46-11**). Carbonic acid dissociates, forming hydrogen ions and bicarbonate ions.

$$\underset{\substack{\text{Carbon}\\\text{dioxide}}}{CO_2} + \underset{\text{Water}}{H_2O} \xrightarrow{\text{Carbonic anhydrase}} \underset{\substack{\text{Carbonic}\\\text{acid}}}{H_2CO_3} \longrightarrow \underset{\substack{\text{Hydrogen}\\\text{ion}}}{H^+} + \underset{\substack{\text{Bicarbonate}\\\text{ion}}}{HCO_3^-}$$

Most hydrogen ions released from carbonic acid combine with hemoglobin, which is a very effective buffer. Many of the bicarbonate ions diffuse into the plasma. The action of carbonic anhydrase in the RBCs maintains a diffusion gradient for carbon dioxide to move into and then out of RBCs. As the negatively charged bicarbonate ions move out of RBCs, chloride ions (Cl^-) in the plasma diffuse into the RBCs to replace them, a process known as the **chloride shift.** In the alveolar capillaries, CO_2 diffuses out of the plasma and into the alveoli. As the CO_2 concentration decreases, the reaction sequence just described reverses.

Any condition (such as emphysema) that interferes with the removal of carbon dioxide by the lungs can lead to *respiratory acidosis*. In this situation, carbon dioxide is produced more rapidly than it is excreted by the lungs. As a result, the concentration of

carbonic acid in the blood increases. When blood pH falls below 7, the central nervous system becomes depressed and the individual becomes disoriented. Untreated respiratory acidosis can cause coma and death.

Breathing is regulated by respiratory centers in the brain

Breathing is a rhythmic, involuntary process regulated by **respiratory centers** in the brain stem (see Fig. 46-6). Groups of neurons in the medulla regulate the basic rhythm of breathing. These neurons send a burst of impulses to the diaphragm and external intercostal muscles, which causes them to contract. After several seconds, these neurons become inactive, the muscles relax, and exhalation occurs. Respiratory centers in the pons help control the transition from inspiration to exhalation. These centers can stimulate or inhibit the respiratory centers in the medulla. The cycle of activity and inactivity repeats itself so that at rest you breathe about 14 times per minute. Overdose of certain medications, such as barbiturates, depresses the respiratory centers and may lead to respiratory failure.

The basic rhythm of respiration changes in response to the body's needs. When you are playing a fast game of tennis, you need

---

As oxygen concentration increases, the percentage of hemoglobin that combines with oxygen increases.

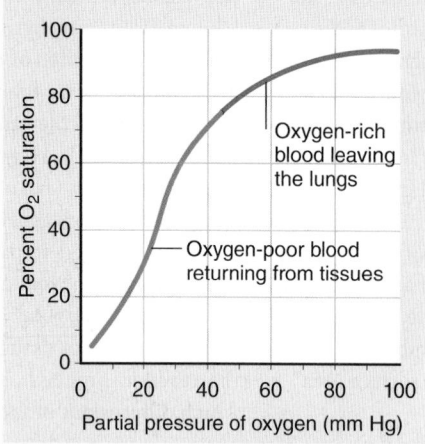

(a) Normal oxygen–hemoglobin dissociation curve. Look at the relationship between the partial pressure of oxygen and the percent O_2 saturation of hemoglobin. Oxygen binds to hemoglobin in the lungs and unloads from hemoglobin in the tissues.

(b) Effect of pH on the oxygen–hemoglobin curve (Bohr effect). The normal pH of human blood is 7.4. Find the location on the horizontal axis where the partial pressure of oxygen is 40, and follow the line up through the curves. Notice that the saturation of hemoglobin with oxygen differs among the three curves, even though the partial pressure of oxygen is the same. Oxygen loading increases at higher pH (7.6). At lower pH (7.2), hemoglobin unloads more oxygen.

FIGURE 46-10 *Animated* Oxygen–hemoglobin dissociation curves

---

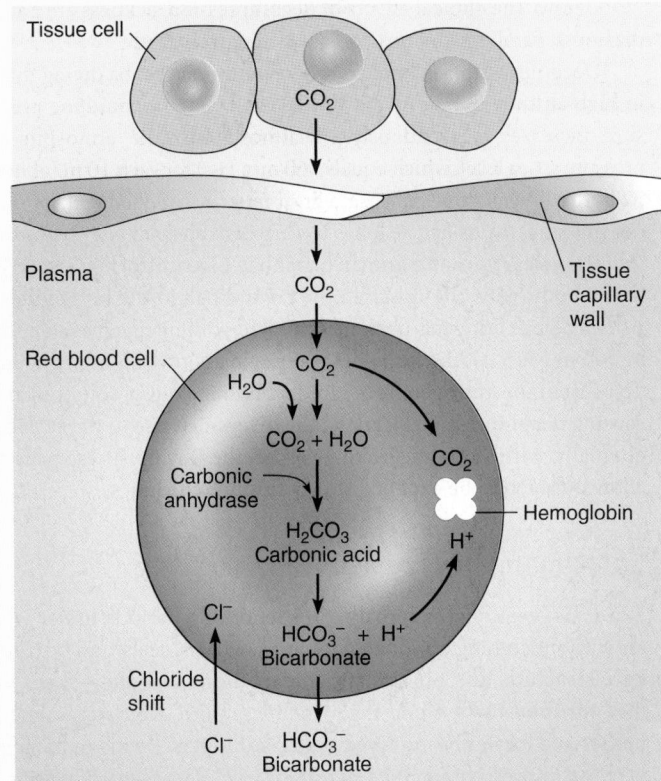

(a) In the tissues, carbon dioxide diffuses from cells into the plasma. Most of the carbon dioxide enters red blood cells, where the enzyme carbonic anhydrase rapidly converts it to carbonic acid. Carbonic acid dissociates, producing bicarbonate ions (HCO_3^-) and H^+. As bicarbonate ions move out into the plasma, chloride ions replace them. Hemoglobin combines with H^+, preventing a decrease in pH.

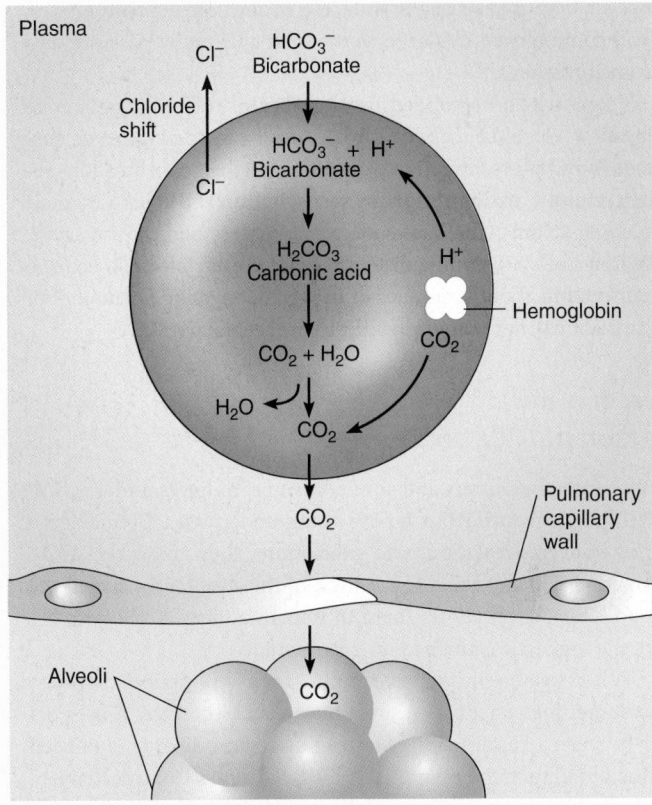

(b) In the lungs, carbon dioxide diffuses out of the plasma and into the alveoli. The reactions described in (a) are reversed. Bicarbonate ions diffuse from the plasma into the red blood cells. H^+ released from hemoglobin combines with bicarbonate ions, producing carbonic acid. Carbon dioxide produced from the carbonic acid diffuses out of the blood and into the alveoli.

FIGURE 46-11 Carbon dioxide transport

more oxygen than when you are studying biology. During exercise the rate of aerobic cellular respiration increases, producing more carbon dioxide. Your body must dispose of this carbon dioxide through increased ventilation.

Carbon dioxide concentration is the most important chemical stimulus for regulating the rate of respiration. Specialized **chemoreceptors** in the medulla and in the walls of the aorta and carotid arteries are sensitive to changes in arterial carbon dioxide concentration. When stimulated, they send impulses to the respiratory centers, which increase breathing rate.

The chemoreceptors in the walls of the aorta, called *aortic bodies,* and those in the walls of the carotid arteries, the *carotid bodies,* are sensitive to changes in hydrogen ion concentration and oxygen concentration, as well as to carbon dioxide levels. Recall that an increase in carbon dioxide concentration increases hydrogen ions (from carbonic acid) and lowers blood pH. Even a slight decrease

in pH stimulates these chemoreceptors, leading to faster breathing. As the lungs remove carbon dioxide, the hydrogen ion concentration in the blood and other body fluids decreases, and homeostasis is re-established.

Interestingly, oxygen concentration generally does not play an important role in regulating respiration. Only if the partial pressure of oxygen falls markedly do the chemoreceptors in the aorta and carotid arteries become stimulated to send messages to the respiratory centers.

Shallow breathing, which occurs in anxiety and in many respiratory diseases, causes **hypoxia,** a deficiency of oxygen. Even *rapid, shallow* breathing results in hypoxia because we do not clear out the stale air in the airway and ventilate the lungs. Hypoxia causes drowsiness, mental fatigue, headache, and sometimes euphoria. The ability to think and make judgments is impaired, as is the ability to perform tasks requiring coordination.

Although breathing is involuntary, the action of the respiratory centers can be consciously influenced for a short time by stimulating or inhibiting them. For example, you can inhibit respiration by holding your breath. You cannot hold your breath indefinitely, however, because eventually you feel a strong urge to breathe. Even if you could ignore this urge, you would eventually pass out and resume breathing.

People who have stopped breathing because of drowning, smoke inhalation, electric shock, or cardiac arrest can sometimes be sustained by mouth-to-mouth resuscitation until their own breathing reflexes return. **Cardiopulmonary resuscitation (CPR)** is a method for aiding victims who have suffered respiratory and cardiac arrest. CPR must be started immediately because irreversible brain damage occurs within about 4 minutes of oxygen deprivation. A number of organizations offer training in CPR to the general public.

Hyperventilation reduces carbon dioxide concentration

Underwater swimmers and some Asian pearl divers undergo voluntary **hyperventilation** before going underwater. By making a series of deep inhalations and exhalations, they "blow off" CO_2, markedly reducing the CO_2 content of the alveolar air and of the blood. This action allows them to remain underwater longer before the urge to breathe becomes irresistible.

When hyperventilation continues for a long period, dizziness and sometimes unconsciousness may result. These responses occur because a certain concentration of carbon dioxide is needed in the blood to maintain normal blood pressure. (This mechanism operates by way of the vasoconstrictor center in the brain, which maintains the muscle tone of blood vessel walls.) Furthermore, if divers hold their breath too long, the low concentration of oxygen may result in unconsciousness and drowning.

High flying or deep diving can disrupt homeostasis

The barometric pressure decreases at progressively higher altitudes. Because the concentration of oxygen in the air remains at 21%, the partial pressure of oxygen decreases along with the barometric pressure. When a person moves to a high altitude, his or her body adjusts over time by producing a greater number of RBCs.

Getting sufficient oxygen from the air becomes an ever-increasing problem as we ascend to progressively higher altitudes. All high-flying jets have airtight cabins pressurized to the equivalent of the barometric pressure at an altitude of about 2000 m (6600 ft). If a jet flying at 11,700 m (more than 38,000 ft) suddenly decompressed, the pilot would lose consciousness in about 30 seconds and become comatose in about 1 minute.

In addition to the problems of hypoxia, a rapid decrease in barometric pressure causes **decompression sickness** (commonly known as the "bends" because those suffering from it bend over in pain). When the barometric pressure drops below the total pressure of all gases dissolved in the blood and other body fluids, the dissolved gases tend to come out of solution and form gas bubbles. A familiar example occurs each time you uncap a bottle of soda, reducing pressure in the bottle. Carbon dioxide is released from solution and bubbles out into the air. In the body, nitrogen has a low solubility in blood and tissues. When it comes out of solution, the bubbles produced may damage tissues and block capillaries, interfering with blood flow. The clinical effects of decompression sickness are pain, dizziness, paralysis, unconsciousness, and even death.

Decompression sickness is more common in scuba diving than in high-altitude flying. As a diver descends, the surrounding pressure increases tremendously—1 atmosphere (the atmospheric pressure at sea level, which equals 760 mm Hg) for each 10 m (about 32 ft). To prevent lung collapse, a diver must be supplied with air under pressure, exposing the lungs to very high alveolar gas pressures.

At sea level an adult human has about 1 L of nitrogen dissolved in the body, with about half in the fat and half in the body fluids. After a diver's body has become saturated with nitrogen at a depth of 100 m (325 ft), the body fluids contain about 10 L of nitrogen. To prevent this nitrogen from rapidly bubbling out of solution and causing decompression sickness, the diver must rise to the surface gradually, with stops at certain levels on the way up. These pauses allow nitrogen to be expelled slowly through the lungs.

Some mammals are adapted for diving

Some air-breathing mammals can spend long periods under water without coming up for air. Dolphins, whales, seals, and beavers have structural and physiological adaptations that allow them to dive for food or to elude their enemies. With their streamlined bodies and forelimbs modified as fins or flippers, diving mammals perform impressive aquatic feats. The Weddell seal can swim under the ice at a depth of 596 m (1955 ft) for more than an hour without coming up for air. The enormous elephant seal, which measures about 5 m (16 to 18 ft) in length and weighs 2 to 4 tons, can plunge even deeper (**FIG. 46-12**). A female elephant seal can dive to depths of more than 1500 m (almost 5000 ft) in less than 20 minutes and stay beneath the surface for more than an hour.

Physiological adaptations, including ways to distribute and store oxygen, permit some mammals to dive deeply and remain underwater for long periods. Turtles and birds that dive depend on oxygen stored in their lungs. However, diving mammals do not take in and store extra air before a dive. In fact, seals exhale before they dive. With less air in their lungs, they are less buoyant. Their lungs collapse at about 50 to 70 m into their dive and then reinflate as they ascend, so their lungs do not function for most of the dive. These adaptations are thought to reduce the chance of decompression sickness because with less air in the lungs there is less nitrogen in the blood to dissolve during the dive.

Seals have about twice the volume of blood, relative to their body weight, as nondiving mammals. Diving mammals also have high concentrations of myoglobin, which stores oxygen in muscles. These animals have up to ten times as much myoglobin as do terrestrial mammals. The very large spleen typical of many diving mammals stores oxygen-rich red blood cells. During a dive, the increased pressure squeezes the spleen, releasing the stored red blood cells into the circulation.

Diving mammals markedly reduce the energy expended in deep diving (more than 200 m) by gliding. Filmed video sequences of diving seals and whales show that they glide most of the way down. Gliding is possible because the animal's buoyancy decreases as the lungs gradually collapse and the amount of air in the lungs is reduced. Gravity then pulls the animal downward.

When a mammal dives to its limit, physiological mechanisms known collectively as the **diving reflex** are activated. Metabolic rate decreases by about 20%, which conserves oxygen. Breathing stops, and bradycardia (slowing of the heart rate) occurs. The heart rate may decrease to one-tenth the normal rate, reducing the body's consumption of oxygen and energy. Blood is redistributed so that the heart and brain receive the greatest share; skin, muscles, digestive organs, and other internal organs can survive with less oxygen, and less blood is directed to these organs while an animal is submerged.

The diving reflex is present to some extent in humans, where it may act as a protective mechanism during birth, when an infant may be deprived of oxygen for several minutes. Cases of near drownings, especially of young children, have been documented in which the victim was submerged for as long as 45 minutes in very cold water before being rescued and resuscitated. Many of these survivors showed no brain damage. The shock of icy water slows heart rate, increases blood pressure, and shunts blood to internal organs of the body that most need oxygen (blood flow in arms and legs decreases). Metabolic rate decreases, so less oxygen is required.

Review

- What is the sequence of inhaled airflow through the respiratory structures in a mammal? What happens in the alveoli?
- Why does alveolar air differ in composition from atmospheric air? Explain.
- How does carbon dioxide concentration affect the oxygen–hemoglobin dissociation curve?
- What physiological mechanisms bring about an increase in rate and depth of breathing during exercise? Why is such an increase necessary?

46.4 BREATHING POLLUTED AIR

■ LEARNING OBJECTIVE

7   Describe the defense mechanisms that protect the lungs and describe the effects of polluted air and cigarette smoking on the respiratory system.

Several defense mechanisms protect the delicate lungs from the harmful substances we breathe (**FIG. 46-13**). Hairs in the nostrils, the ciliated mucous lining in the nose and pharynx, and the cilia–mucus elevator of the trachea and bronchi trap foreign particles in inspired air. Researchers recently reported that cilia of epithelial cells lining the human airway function as chemoreceptors that sense bitter taste. Bitter compounds increase the concentration of Ca^{2+}, which, in turn, increase the rate of ciliary beating. As a result the harmful compound is more rapidly removed.

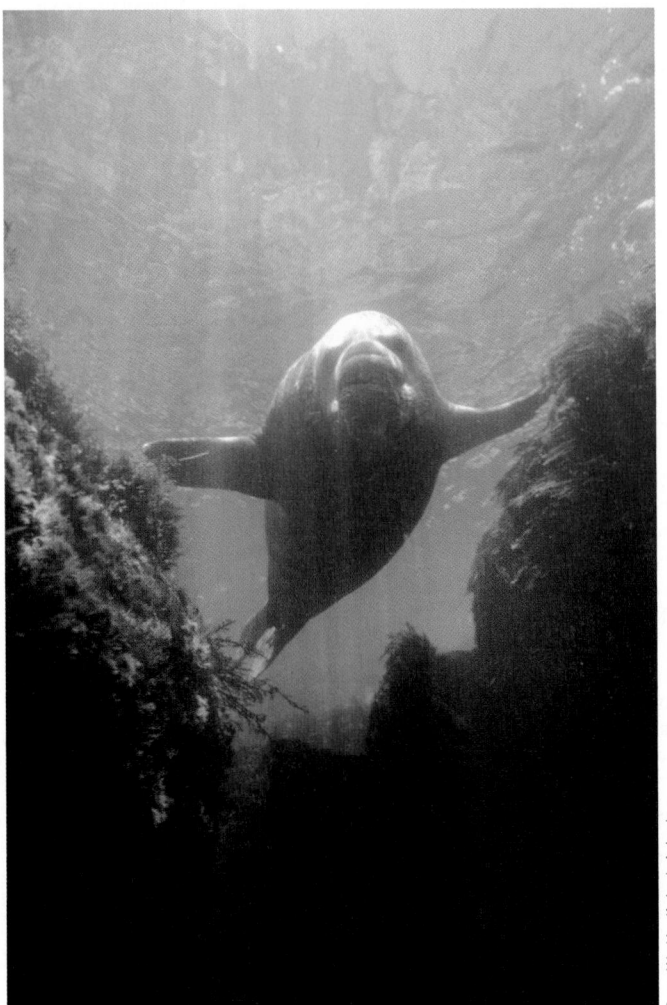

FIGURE 46-12 Deep diver
Elephant seals, like this northern elephant seal (*Mirounga angustirostris*), may be the deepest divers on Earth. Researchers have recorded their dives at depths of more than 1500 m (almost 5000 ft).

FIGURE 46-13 Urban air pollution
Industry continues to spew tons of pollutants into the atmosphere. Despite modern technology, air pollution still poses a significant health risk.

THE EFFECTS OF SMOKING

What is the single most preventable cause of disease, disability, and death in the United States? According to the Centers for Disease Control, it is tobacco use. Cigarette smoking kills more people than alcohol, car accidents, suicide, AIDS, homicide, and illegal drugs combined. More than 443,000 people die prematurely each year from smoking or exposure to secondhand smoke. An additional 8.6 million have a serious illness caused by smoking.[1]

Tobacco smoke is by far the most important risk factor for lung cancer, the most common lethal cancer worldwide. It is also associated with many other types of cancer and accounts for at least 30% of all cancer deaths. Tobacco smoke is also an important risk factor for cardiovascular disease, chronic obstructive pulmonary disease, and many other diseases. Despite these grim facts, approximately 20% of both high school students and adults in the United States continue to smoke cigarettes. (This amounts to more than 43 million U.S. adults and 71 million teens.)

Secondhand tobacco smoke is a known human carcinogen. It causes the deaths of an estimated 49,000 individuals each year in the United States alone. Millions of children and adults are exposed to secondhand smoke in their homes and workplaces. This exposure causes disease and premature death in children and adults who do not smoke. Babies and children exposed to secondhand smoke are at increased risk for sudden infant death syndrome (SIDS), acute respiratory infections, pneumonia, bronchitis, ear infections, and asthma. In adults, secondhand smoke causes cardiovascular disease and lung cancer. About 60% of nonsmokers in the United States exhibit biological evidence of exposure to secondhand smoke.

[1]Statistics quoted are from the Centers for Disease Control and the American Cancer Society.

Nicotine is highly addictive. Like morphine, amphetamines, and cocaine, nicotine increases dopamine concentration in the limbic system. This area helps integrate emotion, and dopamine may facilitate learning an association between the pleasurable effects of the drug and other stimuli, such as the smell of smoke. Nicotine, like cocaine and other abused drugs, causes long-lasting changes in the brain. Cell signaling and other mechanisms underlying drug addiction are very similar to those of learning and memory.

An estimated 70% of smokers (more than 33 million) want to quit, but only 2.5% per year succeed in quitting permanently. Nicotine replacement with gum, patches, nasal spray, inhalers, or lozenges has been shown to be effective as an aid to smoking cessation, especially when used with behavioral therapy. Certain antidepressants are used to reduce the craving for nicotine. A newer prescription medication (Chantix) works by blocking nicotine receptors in the brain. It reduces symptoms of nicotine withdrawal and also decreases the pleasurable effects of smoking.

Here are some facts about smoking:

- Smoking shortens the life of an adult male smoker by an average of 13.2 years and shortens the life of an adult female smoker by an average of 14.5 years.
- If you smoke more than one pack per day, you are about 20 times as likely as a nonsmoker to develop lung cancer. According to the American Cancer Society, cigarette smoking causes almost nine out of ten lung cancer deaths.
- If you smoke, you double your chances of dying from cardiovascular disease.
- If you smoke, you are 20 times as likely as a nonsmoker to develop chronic bronchitis and emphysema. About 90% of all deaths from COPD are caused by cigarette smoking.

- If you smoke, you have about 5% less oxygen circulating in your blood (because carbon monoxide binds to hemoglobin) than does a nonsmoker.
- If you smoke when you are pregnant, your baby will weigh about 6 ounces less at birth, and there is a higher risk of miscarriage, premature birth (early delivery), stillbirth, and sudden infant death syndrome.
- Infants whose parents smoke have double the risk of contracting pneumonia or bronchitis in their first year of life.
- There is no risk-free level of exposure to secondhand smoke. Nonsmokers who are exposed to secondhand smoke increase their risk of developing heart disease by 25% to 30% and lung cancer by 20% to 30%.
- When smokers quit smoking, their risk of dying from chronic obstructive pulmonary disease, cardiovascular disease, or cancer gradually decreases. (Precise changes in risk depend on the number of years the person smoked, the number of cigarettes smoked per day, the age of starting to smoke, and the number of years since quitting.)
- Almost every American who takes up smoking is a teenager—more than 3500 teens smoke their first cigarette every day. About one-third of these teens will die prematurely from a smoking-related disease.
- The younger you are when you begin to smoke, the more likely you are to be an adult smoker.
- The direct medical costs of tobacco use amount to more than $96 billion annually.
- Smokeless tobacco products (snuff, chewing tobacco) are not a safe alternative to tobacco smoking. All forms of these products have chemicals that cause cancer.

One of the body's most rapid defense responses to breathing dirty air is **bronchial constriction.** In this process, the bronchial tubes narrow, increasing the chance that inhaled particles will land on the sticky mucous lining. Unfortunately, bronchial constriction narrows the airway. Less air can reach the lungs, decreasing the amount of oxygen available to body cells. Fifteen puffs on a cigarette during a 5-minute period increases airway resistance as much as threefold, and this added resistance to breathing lasts more than 30 minutes. Chain-smokers and those who breathe heavily polluted air are in a state of chronic bronchial constriction.

Neither the smallest bronchioles nor the alveoli are equipped with mucus or ciliated cells. Foreign particles that get through other respiratory defenses and find their way into the alveoli may be engulfed by macrophages. The macrophages may then accumulate in the lymph tissue of the lungs. Lung tissues of cigarette smokers and those who work in dirty industries burning fossil fuel contain large blackened areas where carbon particles have been deposited (**FIG. 46-14**).

Continued insult to the respiratory system results in disease. Chronic bronchitis, pulmonary emphysema, and lung cancer have

(a) Lungs and major bronchi of a nonsmoker.

(b) Lungs and heart of a cigarette smoker. The dark spots visible in the lung tissue are particles of carbon, tar, and other substances that passed through the respiratory defenses and lodged in the lungs.

FIGURE 46-14 Effects of cigarette smoking

been linked to cigarette smoking and breathing polluted air. More than 75% of patients with **chronic bronchitis** have a history of heavy cigarette smoking (see *Inquiring About: The Effects of Smoking*). People with chronic bronchitis often develop **pulmonary em-**physema, a disease also most common in cigarette smokers. In this disorder, alveoli lose their elasticity, and walls between adjacent alveoli are destroyed. The surface area of the lung is so reduced that gas exchange is seriously impaired. Air is not expelled effectively, and stale air accumulates in the lungs.

The emphysema victim struggles for every breath, and still the body does not get enough oxygen. To compensate, the right ventricle of the heart pumps harder and becomes enlarged. Emphysema patients frequently die of heart failure.

Most patients with **chronic obstructive pulmonary disease (COPD),** a condition characterized by obstructed airflow, have both chronic bronchitis and emphysema. Asthma also contributes to COPD. People with asthma respond to inhaled stimuli with exaggerated bronchial constriction, and the airway is typically inflamed.

Cigarette smoking is also the main cause of **lung cancer.** More than 69 of the 4800 chemical compounds in tobacco smoke cause cancer in animals, including humans. These carcinogenic substances irritate the cells lining the respiratory passages and alter their metabolic balance. Normal cells are transformed into cancer cells, which may multiply rapidly and invade surrounding tissues.

Review

- What mechanisms does the human respiratory system have for getting rid of inhaled particles?
- What happens when so much dirty air is inhaled that these mechanisms cannot function effectively?

■ SUMMARY: FOCUS ON LEARNING OBJECTIVES

46.1 *(page 994)*

1 Compare the advantages and disadvantages of air and water as mediums for gas exchange, and describe adaptations for gas exchange in air.

- Air contains a higher concentration of molecular oxygen than does water, and oxygen diffuses more rapidly through air than through water. Air is less dense and less viscous than water, so less energy is needed to move air over a gas exchange surface.
- Terrestrial animals have adaptations that protect their respiratory surfaces from drying.

46.2 *(page 994)*

2 Describe the following adaptations for gas exchange: body surface, tracheal tubes, gills, and lungs.

- Small aquatic animals exchange gases by diffusion; they require no specialized respiratory structures. Some invertebrates, including most annelids, and a few vertebrates (many amphibians) exchange gases across the body surface.
- In insects and some other arthropods, air enters a network of **tracheal tubes,** or **tracheae,** through openings, called **spiracles,** along the body surface. Tracheal tubes branch and extend to all regions of the body.
- **Gills** are moist, thin projections of the body surface found mainly in aquatic animals. In chordates, gills are usually internal, located along the edges of the gill slits. In bony fishes an **operculum** pro-tects the gills. A **countercurrent exchange system** maximizes diffusion of oxygen into the blood and diffusion of carbon dioxide out of blood.

- Animals carry on **ventilation,** the process of actively moving air or water over respiratory surfaces. Terrestrial vertebrates have **lungs** and some means of ventilating them.
- In birds, the lungs have extensions, called **air sacs,** that act as bellows, drawing air into the system. Two cycles of inhalation and exhalation support a one-way flow of air through the lungs. Air from the outside flows into the posterior air sacs, to the lung, through the anterior air sacs, and then out of the body. Gas exchange takes place through the walls of the **parabronchi,** small, open tubes in the lungs. A crosscurrent arrangement, in which blood flow is at right angles to the parabronchi, increases the amount of oxygen that enters the blood.

CENGAGENOW™ Learn more about adaptations for gas exchange, including gills in bony fishes, vertebrate lungs, and the bird respiratory system, by clicking on the figures in CengageNOW.

46.3 *(page 998)*

3 Trace the passage of oxygen through the human respiratory system from nostrils to alveoli.

- The human respiratory system includes the lungs and a system of airways. Each breath of air passes in sequence through the **nostrils, nasal cavities, pharynx, larynx, trachea, bronchi, bronchioles,** and **alveoli.** Each lung occupies a pleural cavity and is covered with a **pleural membrane.**

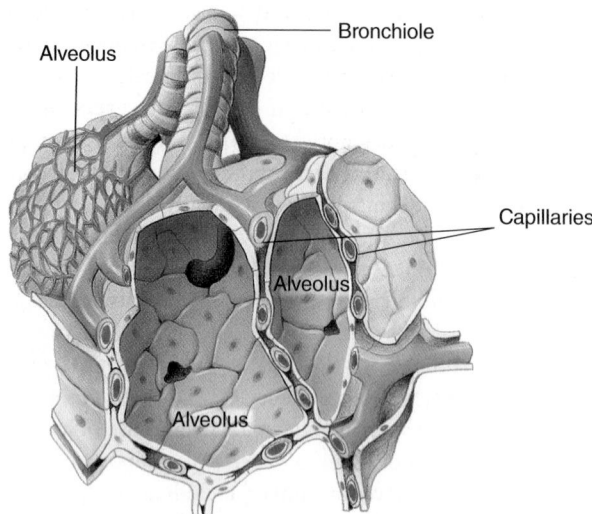

Alveolus

Bronchiole

Capillaries

Alveolus

Alveolus

CENGAGENOW™ Learn more about the human respiratory system by clicking on the figures in CengageNOW.

4 Summarize the mechanics of breathing in humans, and describe gas exchange in the lungs and tissues.

  ▪ During breathing, the **diaphragm** contracts, expanding the chest cavity. The membranous walls of the lungs move outward along with the chest walls, lowering pressure within the lungs. Air from outside the body rushes in through the air passageways and fills the lungs until the pressure equals atmospheric pressure.

  ▪ **Tidal volume** is the amount of air moved into and out of the lungs with each normal breath. The volume of air that remains in the lungs at the end of a maximal expiration is the **residual volume. Vital capacity** is the maximum volume of air that can be exhaled after the lungs fill to the maximum extent.

  ▪ Oxygen and carbon dioxide are exchanged between alveoli and blood by diffusion. The pressure of a particular gas determines its direction and rate of diffusion.

  ▪ **Dalton's law of partial pressures** explains that in a mixture of gases, the total pressure of the mixture is the sum of the pressures of the individual gases. Thus, each gas in a mixture of gases exerts a **partial pressure,** the same pressure it would exert if it were present alone. The partial pressure of atmospheric oxygen, P_{O_2}, is 160 mm Hg at sea level.

  ▪ According to **Fick's law of diffusion,** the greater the difference in pressure on the two sides of a membrane and the larger the surface area, the faster the gas diffuses across the membrane.

CENGAGENOW™ See the breathing mechanisms in action by clicking on the figures in CengageNOW.

5 Summarize the mechanisms by which oxygen and carbon dioxide are transported in the blood and identify factors that determine the oxygen–hemoglobin dissociation curve.

  ▪ **Hemoglobin** is the respiratory pigment in the blood of vertebrates. Almost 99% of the oxygen in human blood is transported as **oxyhemoglobin (HbO_2).**

  ▪ The maximum amount of oxygen that hemoglobin can transport is the **oxygen-carrying capacity.** The actual amount of oxygen bound to hemoglobin is the **oxygen content.** The **percent O_2 saturation,** the ratio of oxygen content to oxygen-carrying capacity, is highest in pulmonary capillaries, where oxygen concentration is greatest.

  ▪ The **oxygen–hemoglobin dissociation curve** shows that as oxygen concentration increases, there is a progressive increase in the amount of hemoglobin that combines with oxygen. The curve is affected by pH, temperature, and CO_2 concentration.

  ▪ Oxyhemoglobin dissociates more readily as carbon dioxide concentration increases because carbon dioxide combines with water and produces carbonic acid, which lowers the pH. Displacement of the oxygen–hemoglobin dissociation curve by a change in pH is called the **Bohr effect.**

  ▪ About 60% of the carbon dioxide in the blood is transported as bicarbonate ions. About 30% combines with hemoglobin, and another 10% is dissolved in plasma.

  ▪ **Carbonic anhydrase** catalyzes the production of carbonic acid from carbon dioxide and water. Carbonic acid dissociates, producing bicarbonate ions (HCO_3^-) and hydrogen ions (H^+).

  ▪ Hemoglobin combines with H^+, which buffers the blood. Many bicarbonate ions diffuse from red blood cells into the plasma; they are replaced by Cl^-. This exchange is known as the **chloride shift.**

6 Describe the regulation of breathing in humans and summarize the physiological effects of hyperventilation and of sudden decompression when a diver surfaces too quickly from deep water.

  ▪ **Respiratory centers** in the medulla and pons regulate respiration. These centers are stimulated by **chemoreceptors** sensitive to an increase in carbon dioxide concentration. They also respond to an increase in hydrogen ions and to very low oxygen concentration.

  ▪ **Hyperventilation** reduces the concentration of carbon dioxide in the alveolar air and in the blood.

  ▪ As altitude increases, barometric pressure falls, and less oxygen enters the blood. This situation can lead to **hypoxia,** or oxygen deficiency, which in turn can lead to loss of consciousness and death. Rapid decrease in barometric pressure can also cause **decompression sickness,** especially common among divers who ascend too rapidly from a dive.

  ▪ Diving mammals have high concentrations of **myoglobin,** a pigment that stores oxygen, in their muscles. The **diving reflex,** a group of physiological mechanisms, including a decrease in metabolic rate, is activated when a mammal dives to its limit.

46.4 *(page 1007)*

7 Describe the defense mechanisms that protect the lungs and describe the effects of polluted air and cigarette smoking on the respiratory system.

  ▪ The ciliated mucous lining of the airway traps inhaled particles. Inhaling polluted air results in **bronchial constriction,** increased mucus secretion, damage to ciliated cells, and coughing. Breathing polluted air or inhaling cigarette smoke can cause many diseases, including **chronic bronchitis, pulmonary emphysema,** and **lung cancer.**

TEST YOUR UNDERSTANDING

1. Which of the following is a benefit of gas exchange in air compared with gas exchange in water? (a) air has a higher concentration of molecular oxygen (b) oxygen diffuses more slowly in air (c) no energy is required for ventilation (d) moist respiratory surface is not needed (e) air is denser than water

2. Which of the following are accurately matched? (a) bony fish—operculum (b) insect—alveoli (c) bird—spiracles (d) aquatic mammal—gill filaments (e) shark—dermal gills

3. Tracheal tubes (tracheae) (a) are linked to the circulatory system (b) are highly vascular (c) branch and extend to all the cells (d) are characteristic of many vertebrates (e) a, b, and c

4. The most efficient vertebrate respiratory system is that of (a) amphibians (b) birds (c) reptiles (d) mammals (e) humans

5. In a bird, the correct sequence for a breath of air is
   1. anterior air sacs 2. posterior air sacs 3. parabronchi 4. alveoli
   (a) 1, 2, 4 (b) 2, 1, 3 (c) 2, 3, 1 (d) 2, 4, 1 (e) 1, 3, 2

6. Which sequence most accurately describes the sequence of airflow in the human respiratory system?
   1. pharynx 2. bronchus 3. trachea 4. larynx 5. alveolus
   6. bronchiole
   (a) 4, 1, 3, 2, 5, 6 (b) 1, 4, 3, 2, 5, 6 (c) 4, 1, 3, 2, 6, 5
   (d) 1, 4, 3, 2, 6, 5 (e) 1, 3, 4, 2, 6, 5

7. The amount of air moved in and out of the lungs with each normal resting breath is the (a) vital capacity (b) residual volume (c) vital volume (d) partial pressure (e) tidal volume

8. According to Fick's law of diffusion, a gas will diffuse faster if the (a) surface is reduced (b) difference in pressure is decreased (c) difference in pressure is increased (d) pH is lowered (e) a and c

9. The concentration of which substance is most important in regulating the rate of respiration? (a) chloride ions (b) oxygen (c) bicarbonate ions (d) nitrogen (e) carbon dioxide

10. When a diver ascends too rapidly, (a) bronchial constriction occurs (b) a diving reflex is activated (c) nitrogen rapidly bubbles out of solution in the body fluids (d) nitrogen hypoxia occurs (e) carbon dioxide bubbles damage the alveoli

11. Which of the following is *not* true of the diving reflex? (a) breathing stops (b) the heart slows (c) less blood is distributed to the muscles (d) metabolic rate increases by about 20% (e) energy consumption decreases

12. Label the figure. Use Figure 46-6 to check your answers.

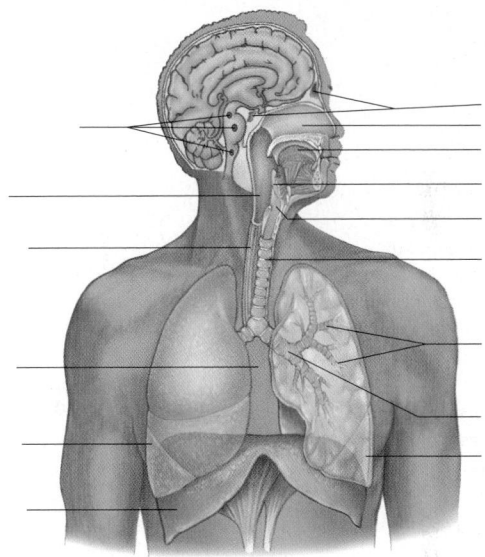

CRITICAL THINKING

1. What problems would be faced by a terrestrial animal having gills instead of lungs?

2. **EVOLUTION LINK.** Under what conditions might it be advantageous for a fish to have lungs as well as gills? What function do the "lungs" of modern fishes serve?

3. **EVOLUTION LINK.** Aquatic mammals such as whales and dolphins use lungs rather than gills for gas exchange. Propose a hypothesis to explain this.

4. **EVOLUTION LINK.** What are the advantages of having millions of alveoli rather than a pair of simple, balloonlike lungs?

5. **ANALYZING DATA.** Look at Figure 46-10b. How would strenuous muscle activity affect the oxygen–hemoglobin disso-

ciation curve? (*Hint:* How does muscular activity affect pH? See Chapter 40 if you need to review this concept.) What would be the advantage of the shift in the curve?

6. **SCIENCE, TECHNOLOGY, AND SOCIETY.** How would you solve the tobacco smoking problem, which is extremely expensive to our society in economic and health costs, as well as in human suffering?

 Additional questions are available in CengageNOW at www.cengage.com/login.

47 Processing Food and Nutrition

Atlantic wolffish (*Anarhichas lupus*) eating a sea urchin. Also known as the seawolf and as the Atlantic catfish, this fish lives on the ocean floor where it hunts and eats hard-shelled prey. The Atlantic wolffish can weigh up to 40 pounds. Its population has decreased drastically as a result of overfishing, unintentional harm by fishermen (bycatch), and habitat damage. Photographed in Maine.

Jonathan Bird/Peter Arnold, Inc.

KEY CONCEPTS

47.1 Many animal adaptations are associated with mode of nutrition; food processing includes ingestion, digestion, absorption, and elimination.

47.2 Various parts of the vertebrate digestive system are specialized to perform specific functions; accessory glands (liver, pancreas, and salivary glands) secrete fluids and enzymes that are important in digestion.

47.3 Most animals require the same basic nutrients: carbohydrates, lipids, proteins, vitamins, and minerals.

47.4 Basal metabolic rate is the body's cost of metabolic living; energy metabolism is regulated by complex signaling pathways. Both overnutrition and undernutrition can result in malnutrition.

Sponges and baleen whales feed on food particles suspended in the water. Giraffes eat leaves, and antelope graze on grasses. Frogs, lions, and some insects capture other animals. Although their choices of food and feeding mechanisms are diverse, all animals are **heterotrophs,** organisms that must obtain their energy and nourishment from the organic molecules manufactured by other organisms. What they eat, how they obtain food, and how they process and use food are the focus of this chapter.

Nutrients are substances in food that are used as energy sources to power the systems of the body, as ingredients to make compounds needed for metabolic processes, and as building blocks in the growth and repair of tissues. Obtaining nutrients is of such vital importance that both individual organisms and ecosystems are structured around the central theme of **nutrition,** the process of taking in and using food.

An animal's body plan and its lifestyle are adapted to its particular mode of obtaining food. For example, the seawolf lives on the ocean floor at depths of up to 120 m (400 ft). It hunts clams, crabs, sea stars, and sea urchins (see photograph). Both its upper and lower jaw have four to six fanglike teeth that stab and tear its prey. Behind these fangs, there are three rows of teeth that crush the hard shells of its prey. It also has serrated teeth in its throat.

Nutrition has been an important force in human evolution. Through natural selection, the human diet became more varied than the diets of other primates. Humans also became very efficient at obtaining food. Their higher-quality diet supported the evolution of a larger, more complex brain.

With only slight variations, all animals require the same basic nutrients: carbohydrates, lipids, proteins, vitamins, and minerals. Carbohydrates, lipids, and proteins are used as energy sources. Eating too much of any of these nutrients can result in weight gain, whereas eating too few nutrients or an unbalanced diet can result in malnutrition and death. **Malnutrition,** or poor nutritional status, results from dietary intake that is either below or above required needs. In human populations, both undernutrition (particularly protein deficiency) and obesity (which results from overnutrition) are serious health problems. Food processing and nutrition are active areas of research.

47.1 NUTRITIONAL STYLES AND ADAPTATIONS

◼ LEARNING OBJECTIVE

1   Describe food processing, including ingestion, digestion, absorption, and egestion or elimination, and compare the digestive system of a cnidarian (such as *Hydra*) with that of an earthworm and vertebrate.

Feeding is the selection, acquisition, and ingestion of food. Most animals have a specialized digestive system that processes the food they eat. **Ingestion** is the process of taking food into the digestive cavity. In many animals, including vertebrates, ingestion includes taking food into the mouth and swallowing it.

The process of breaking down food is called **digestion.** Because animals eat the macromolecules made by and for other organisms, they must break down these molecules and synthesize new macromolecules for their own needs. For example, we humans cannot incorporate the proteins and other organic compounds from a hamburger directly into our own cells. We must *mechanically digest* the meat and then *chemically digest* it by enzymatic hydrolysis (see Chapter 3). During digestion, complex organic compounds are degraded into smaller molecular components. For example, proteins are broken down into their component amino acids. These amino acids will later be used to synthesize proteins tailored for the needs of that individual at that particular time.

Amino acids and other nutrients pass through the lining of the digestive tract and into the blood by **absorption.** Then the circulatory system transports the nutrients to all the cells of the body. Cells use nutrients to synthesize proteins and other organic compounds, or as fuel for cellular respiration. Food that is not digested and absorbed is discharged from the body, a process called **egestion** or **elimination.**

Animals are adapted to their mode of nutrition

We classify animals as herbivores, carnivores, or omnivores on the basis of the type of food they typically eat (**FIG. 47-1**). Many adaptations have evolved for each type of feeding. For example, the beaks of birds and the teeth of many vertebrates are specialized for cutting, tearing, crushing, or chewing food.

Animals that feed directly on producers are **herbivores,** or primary consumers. Most of what an herbivore eats is not efficiently digested and is eliminated from the body, almost unchanged, as waste. For this reason herbivores must eat large quantities of food to obtain the nourishment they need. Many herbivores—grasshoppers, locusts, elephants, and cattle, for example—spend a major part of their lives eating.

Animals cannot digest the cellulose of plant cell walls, and many adaptations have evolved for extracting nutrients from the plant material they eat. Many herbivores, including termites, cows, and horses, have a symbiotic relationship with bacteria, fungi, and other microorganisms that inhabit their digestive tracts. **Ruminants** (cattle, sheep, deer, giraffes) are hooved animals with a stomach divided into four chambers. Symbiotic bacteria and protists living in the first two chambers digest cellulose, splitting some of the molecule into sugars, which are then used by the host and the bacteria themselves. The bacteria produce fatty acids during their metabolism, some of which are absorbed by the animal and serve as an important energy source.

Solid bits of food clump together to form a cud. The cud is regurgitated into the animal's mouth, where it is mixed with saliva and chewed again. When the cud is reswallowed, the partly digested food is further broken down. Partially digested food passes into the third chamber, where water and minerals are absorbed into the blood. Digestion is completed in the fourth chamber, which corresponds to the stomach of humans and other animals with a single stomach.

Herbivores are sometimes eaten by flesh-eating **carnivores,** which may also eat one another. Many carnivores (secondary and higher-level consumers in ecosystems) are predators, adapted for capturing and killing prey. Some carnivores seize their victims and swallow them alive and whole (see Fig. 47-1d). Others paralyze, crush, or shred their prey before ingesting it. Adaptations for this type of feeding include tentacles, claws, fangs, poison glands, and teeth.

Carnivorous mammals have well-developed canine teeth for stabbing their prey during combat. Spotted hyenas, which are formidable predators as well as scavengers, have massive jaws that allow them to consume an entire elephant carcass, including bones and hide. Few nutrients are wasted. Meat is more easily digested than plant food, and carnivore digestive tracts are shorter than those of herbivores.

Omnivores, such as pigs, humans, most bears, and some fishes, consume both plants and animals. Earthworms ingest large amounts of soil containing both animal and plant material. The blue whale, the largest animal, filters out tiny algae and animals from the water as it swims. Omnivores often have adaptations that help them distinguish among a wide range of smells and tastes and thereby select a variety of foods.

(a) **Unusual adaptation of an acorn-eating insect.** The impressively long "snout" of the herbivorous acorn weevil (*Curculio*) is adapted both for feeding and for making a hole in the acorn through which it deposits an egg. When it has hatched, the larva feeds on the contents of the acorn seed.

(b) **An herbivorous bear.** The giant panda's (*Ailuropoda melanoleuca*) large, flat teeth and well-developed jaws and jaw muscles are adaptations for grinding high-fiber plant food. Most bears are omnivores.

(c) **A carnivorous fish.** The mouth (*on left*) of the long-nose butterfly fish (*Forcipiger longirostris*) is adapted for extracting small worms and crustaceans from tight spots in coral reefs.

(d) **Snakes are carnivorous.** This snake (*Dromicus*) is strangling a lava lizard (*Tropidurus*). A snake can swallow very large prey whole because of the structure of the jaws. The very flexible lower jaw expands during swallowing.

FIGURE 47-1 Adaptations for obtaining and processing food

Animals can also be classified according to the mechanisms they use to feed. Many omnivores are **filter feeders** that remove suspended food particles from the water they inhabit. For example, clams and oysters trap suspended food particles in mucus secreted by their gills. Some echinoderms trap food particles along their tentacles, which are coated with mucus. Baleen whales use rows of hard plates (baleen) suspended from the roof of the mouth to filter small crustaceans.

Some animals feed on fluids by piercing and sucking. Mosquitoes have highly adapted structures for piercing skin and sucking blood. Bats that feed on nectar have a long tongue and reduced dentition (number of teeth). Birds that feed on pollen and nectar have long bills

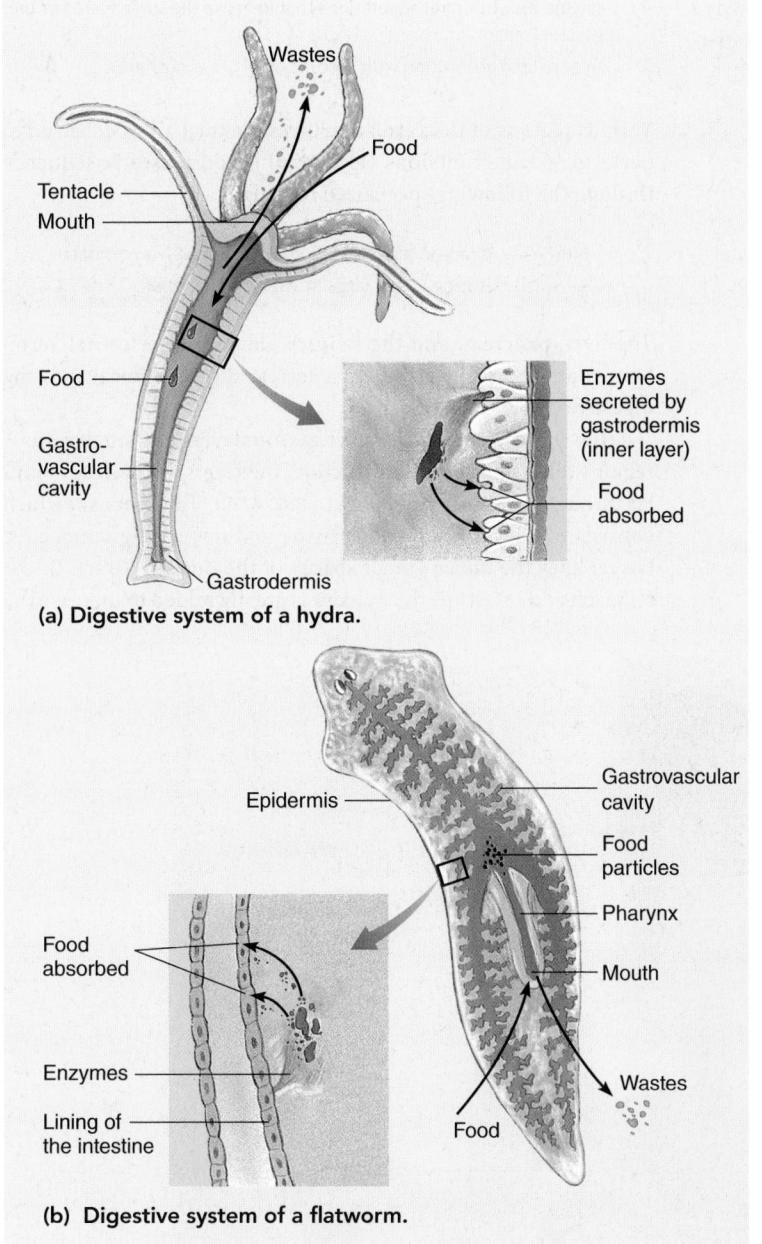

(a) Digestive system of a hydra.

(b) Digestive system of a flatworm.

(a) Hydras and **(b)** flatworms (planarians) have a gastrovascular cavity, a digestive tract with a single opening that serves as both mouth and anus.

have a **gastrovascular cavity,** a central digestive cavity with a single opening. Cnidarians capture small aquatic animals with the help of their stinging cells and tentacles (**FIG. 47-2a**). The mouth opens into the gastrovascular cavity. Cells lining this digestive cavity secrete enzymes that break down proteins. Digestion continues intracellularly within food vacuoles, and digested nutrients diffuse into other cells. Body contractions promote egestion of undigested food particles through the mouth.

Free-living flatworms begin to digest their prey even before ingesting it. They extend the pharynx out through their mouth and secrete digestive enzymes onto their prey (**FIG. 47-2b**). After it is ingested, the food enters the branched gastrovascular cavity, where enzymes continue to digest it. Cells lining the gastrovascular cavity phagocytose partly digested food fragments, and digestion is completed within food vacuoles. As in cnidarians, the flatworm digestive cavity has only one opening, so undigested wastes are egested through the mouth.

Most animal digestive systems have two openings

Most invertebrates, and all vertebrates, have a tube-within-a-tube body plan. The body wall forms the outer tube. The inner tube is a digestive tract with two openings, sometimes referred to as a complete digestive system (**FIG. 47-3**). Food enters through the mouth, and undigested food is eliminated through the anus. The mixing and propulsive movements of the digestive tract are referred to as **motility.** The propulsive activity characteristic of most regions of the digestive tract is **peristalsis,** waves of muscular contraction that push the food in one direction. More food can be taken in while

and tongues. The shape, size, and curve of the beak may be specialized for feeding on or capturing a particular type of food (see Fig. 1-11).

Some invertebrates have a digestive cavity with a single opening

Sponges, very simple invertebrates, obtain food by filtering microscopic organisms from the surrounding water. Individual cells phagocytose the food particles, and digestion is *intracellular* within food vacuoles. Wastes are egested into the water that continuously circulates through the sponge body.

Most animals have a digestive cavity. Digestion within a cavity is more efficient than intracellular digestion because digestive enzymes can be released into one confined space. Less surface area is required. Cnidarians (such as hydras and jellyfish) and flatworms

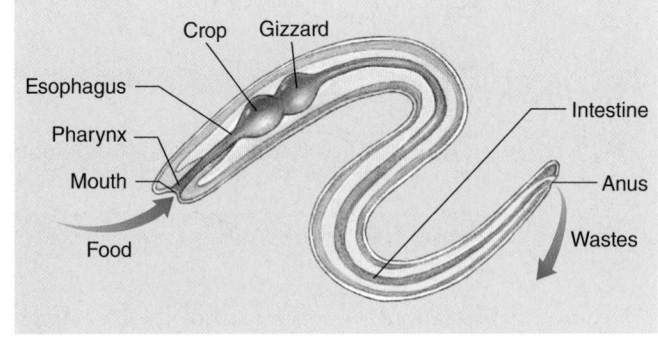

FIGURE 47-3 Digestive tract with two openings
The earthworm, like most animals, has a complete digestive tract extending from mouth to anus. Various regions of the digestive tract are specialized to perform different food-processing functions.

previously eaten food is being digested and absorbed farther down the digestive tract. In a digestive tract with two openings, various regions of the tube are adapted to perform specific functions.

Review

- How have carnivores adapted to their mode of nutrition?
- How does food processing differ in earthworms and flatworms?
- What are the advantages of a digestive tract with two openings?

47.2 THE VERTEBRATE DIGESTIVE SYSTEM

■ LEARNING OBJECTIVES

2 Trace the pathway traveled by an ingested meal through the human digestive system and describe the structure and function of each organ involved.

3 Trace the step-by-step digestion of carbohydrate, protein, and lipid.

4 Describe the structural adaptations that increase the surface area of the digestive tract.

5 Compare lipid absorption with absorption of other nutrients.

Various regions of the vertebrate digestive tract are specialized to perform specific functions (**FIG. 47-4**). Food passes in sequence through the following specialized regions:

mouth ⟶ pharynx (throat) ⟶ esophagus ⟶ stomach ⟶ small intestine ⟶ large intestine ⟶ anus

The liver, pancreas, and the salivary glands (in terrestrial vertebrates) are accessory glands that secrete digestive juices into the digestive tract.

The wall of the digestive tract has four layers. Although various regions differ somewhat in structure, the layers are basically similar throughout the digestive tract (**FIG. 47-5**). The **mucosa,** which consists of a layer of epithelial tissue and underlying connective tissue, lines the *lumen* (inner space) of the digestive tract. In the stomach and intestine, the mucosa is greatly folded to increase the

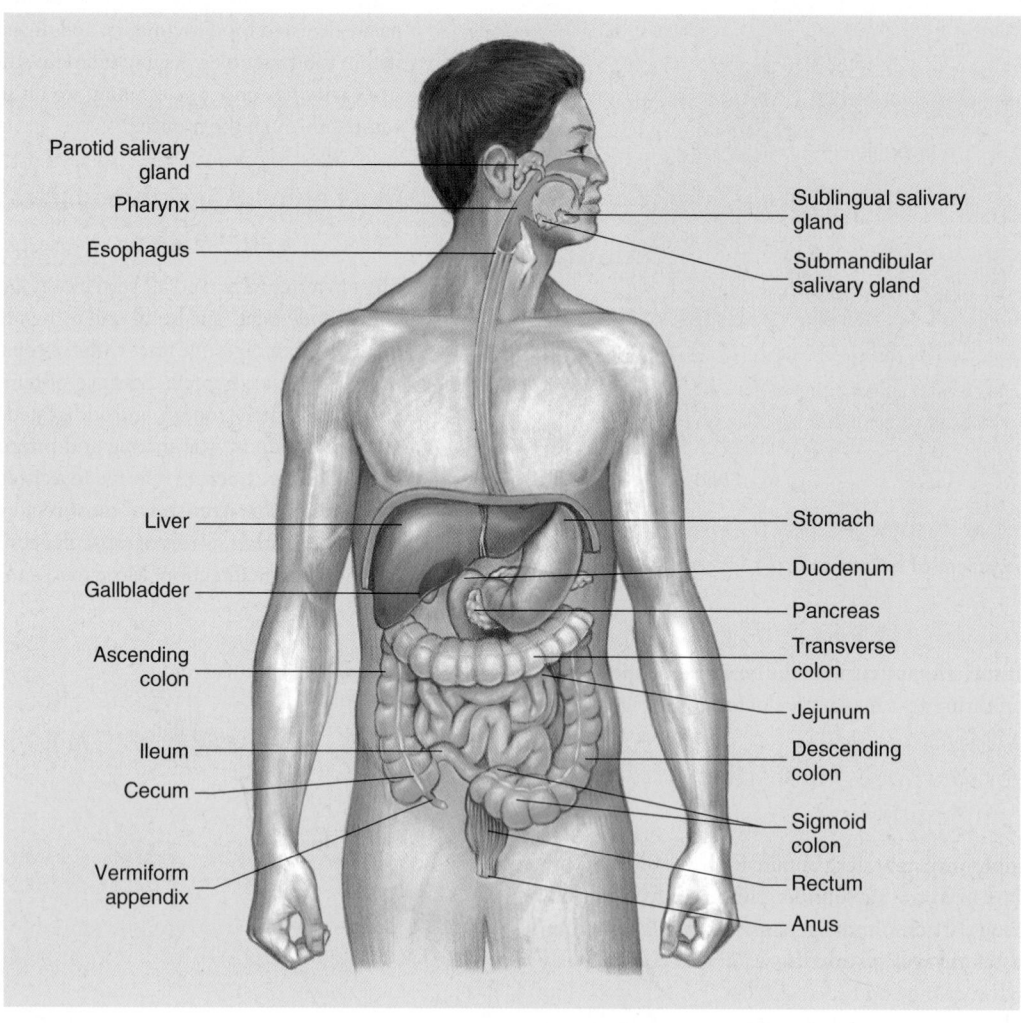

FIGURE 47-4 *Animated* Human digestive system

The human digestive tract is a long, coiled tube extending from mouth to anus. The small intestine consists of the duodenum, jejunum, and ileum. The large intestine includes the cecum, colon, rectum, and anus. Locate the three types of accessory glands: the liver, pancreas, and salivary glands.

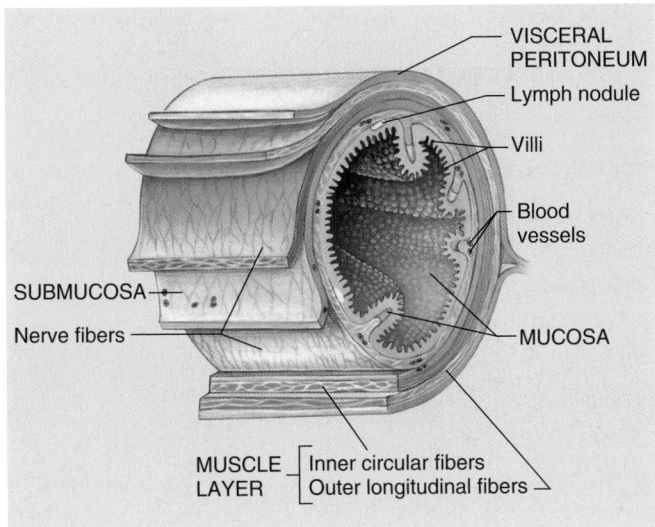

FIGURE 47-5 Wall of the digestive tract
From inside out, the layers of the wall are the mucosa, submucosa, muscle layer, and visceral peritoneum.

secreting and absorbing surface. Surrounding the mucosa is the **submucosa,** a connective tissue layer rich in blood vessels, lymphatic vessels, and nerves.

A **muscle layer,** consisting of two sublayers of smooth muscle, surrounds the submucosa. In the inner sublayer, the muscle fibers are arranged circularly around the digestive tube. In the outer sublayer, the muscle fibers are arranged longitudinally. Below the level of the diaphragm, the outer connective tissue coat of the digestive tract is called the **visceral peritoneum.** By various folds it is connected to the **parietal peritoneum,** a sheet of connective tissue that lines the walls of the abdominal and pelvic cavities. The visceral and parietal peritonea enclose part of the coelom, the **peritoneal cavity.** Inflammation of the peritoneum, called **peritonitis,** can be very serious because infection can spread along the peritoneum to most of the abdominal organs.

Food processing begins in the mouth

Imagine that you have just taken a big bite of a hamburger in a bun. The mouth is specialized for ingestion and for beginning the digestive process. Mechanical digestion begins as you bite, grind, and chew the meat and bun with your teeth. Unlike the simple, pointed teeth of fish, amphibians, and reptiles, the teeth of mammals vary in size and shape and are specialized to perform specific functions. The chisel-shaped **incisors** are used for biting and cutting food, whereas the long, pointed **canines** are adapted for piercing prey and tearing food (**FIG. 47-6**). The flattened surfaces of the **premolars** and **molars** are specialized for crushing and grinding.

Each tooth is covered by **enamel,** the hardest substance in the body (**FIG. 47-7**). Most of the tooth consists of **dentin,** which resembles bone in composition and hardness. The **pulp cavity,** which lies beneath the dentin, is a soft connective tissue containing blood vessels, lymph vessels, and nerves.

While food is being mechanically disassembled by the teeth, it is moistened by saliva. As some of the food molecules dissolve,

(a) Carnivore. The skull of a coyote shows the pointed incisors and canines, adaptations for ripping flesh.

(b) Herbivore. Horses and other herbivores have incisors (and sometimes canines) adapted for cutting off bits of vegetation. Canines are absent in some herbivores. The broad, ridged surfaces of the molars are adapted for grinding plant material.

(c) Omnivore. The teeth of humans and other omnivores are adapted for chewing a variety of foods.

FIGURE 47-6 Teeth and diet

you can taste the food. (Recall from Chapter 43 that taste buds are located on the tongue and other surfaces of the mouth.) Three pairs of **salivary glands** secrete about a liter of saliva into the mouth cavity each day. Saliva contains an enzyme, **salivary amylase,** which begins the chemical digestion of starch into sugar.

The pharynx and esophagus conduct food to the stomach

After being chewed and fashioned into a lump called a **bolus,** the bite of food is swallowed—moved through the **pharynx** into the

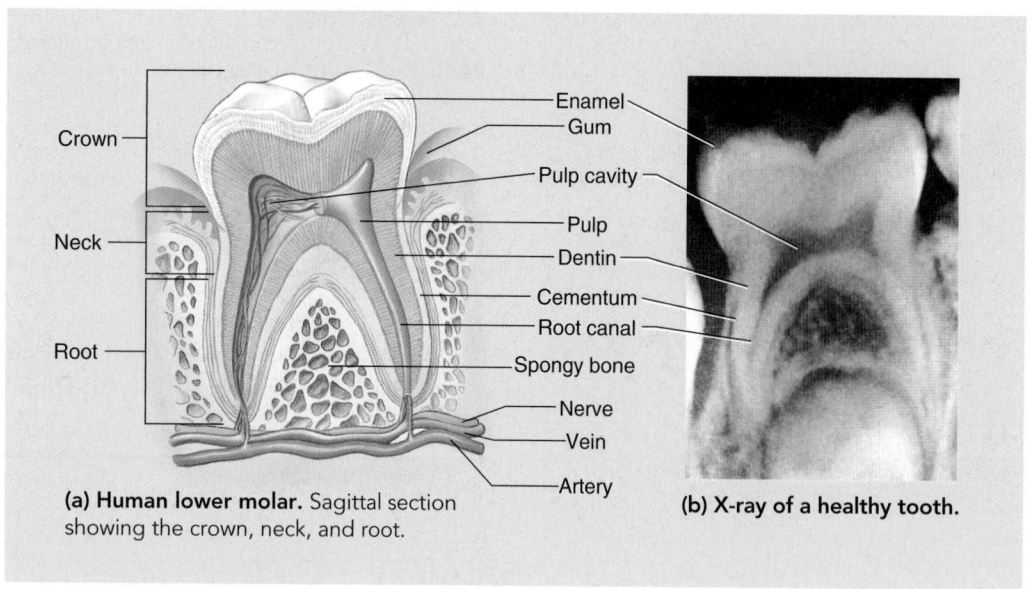

(a) **Human lower molar.** Sagittal section showing the crown, neck, and root.

(b) **X-ray of a healthy tooth.**

FIGURE 47-7 Tooth structure

esophagus. The pharynx, or throat, is a muscular tube that serves as the hallway of both the respiratory system and the digestive system. During swallowing, a small flap of tissue, the **epiglottis,** closes the opening to the airway.

Waves of peristalsis sweep the bolus through the pharynx and esophagus toward the stomach (**FIG. 47-8**). Circular muscle fibers in the wall of the esophagus contract around the top of the bolus and push it downward. Almost at the same time, longitudinal muscles around the bottom of the bolus and below it contract, which shortens the tube.

When the body is in an upright position, gravity helps move the food through the esophagus, but gravity is not essential. Astronauts eat in its absence, and even if you are standing on your head, food will reach your stomach.

Food is mechanically and enzymatically digested in the stomach

The entrance to the large, muscular **stomach** is normally closed by a ring of muscle at the lower end of the esophagus. When a peristaltic wave passes down the esophagus, the muscle relaxes and the bolus enters the stomach (**FIG. 47-9**). When empty, the stomach is collapsed and shaped almost like a hot dog. Folds of the stomach wall, called **rugae,** give the inner lining a wrinkled appearance. As food enters, the rugae gradually smooth out, which expands the capacity of the stomach to more than a liter.

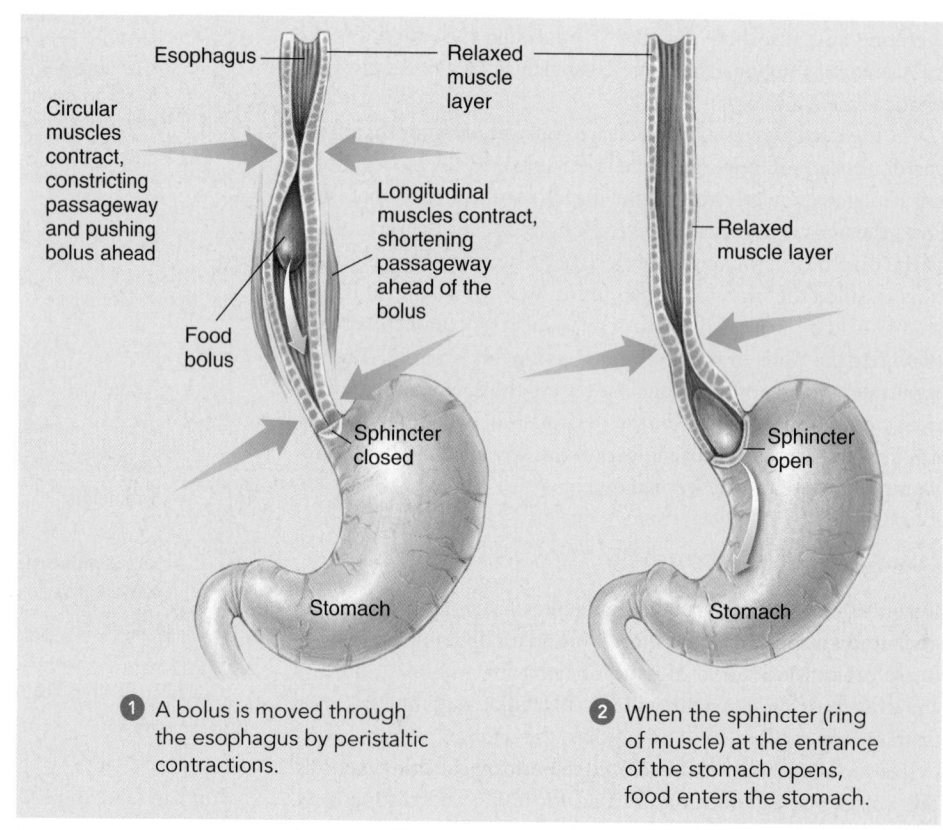

① A bolus is moved through the esophagus by peristaltic contractions.

② When the sphincter (ring of muscle) at the entrance of the stomach opens, food enters the stomach.

FIGURE 47-8 *Animated* **Peristalsis**

The stomach is lined with a simple, columnar epithelium that secretes large amounts of mucus. Tiny pits mark the entrances to the millions of **gastric glands,** which extend deep into the stomach wall. **Parietal cells** in the gastric glands secrete hydrochloric acid and *intrinsic factor,* a substance needed for adequate absorption of vitamin B_{12}. **Chief cells** in the gastric glands secrete **pepsinogen,**

The structure of the stomach is adapted for its function of digesting food; gastric glands in its mucosa secrete digestive juices, and three layers of muscle in the stomach wall are important in mechanically digesting food.

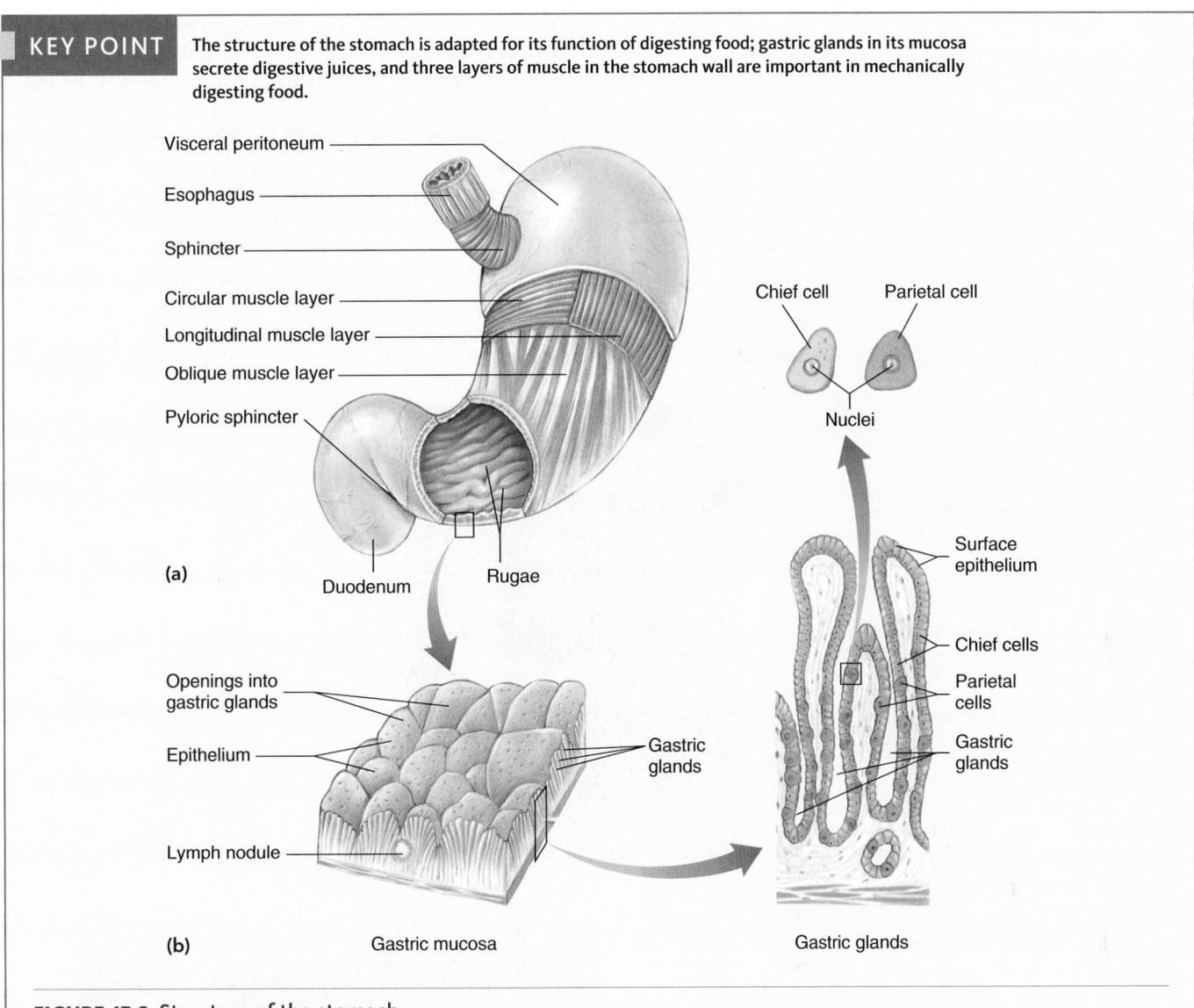

FIGURE 47-9 Structure of the stomach

The stomach is adapted for mechanically and enzymatically digesting food. **(a)** The wall of the stomach has been progressively removed to show muscle layers and rugae. **(b)** Stomach lining and gastric glands.

an inactive enzyme precursor. When it comes in contact with the acidic gastric juice in the stomach, pepsinogen is converted to pepsin, the main digestive enzyme of the stomach. **Pepsin** hydrolyzes proteins, converting them to short polypeptides.

Several protective mechanisms prevent the gastric juice from digesting the wall of the stomach. Cells of the gastric mucosa secrete alkaline mucus that coats the stomach wall and neutralizes the acidity of the gastric juice along the lining. In addition, the epithelial cells of the lining fit tightly together, preventing gastric juice from leaking between them and into the tissue beneath. If some of the epithelial cells become damaged, they are quickly replaced. In fact, about a half million of these cells are shed and replaced every minute!

Sometimes, these protective mechanisms malfunction and part of the stomach lining is digested, leaving an open sore, or **peptic ulcer.** Such ulcers also occur in the duodenum and sometimes in the lower part of the esophagus. The bacterium *Helicobacter pylori* has been implicated as a causative factor in ulcers (see Fig. 25-13). *Helicobacter pylori* infects the mucus-secreting cells of the stomach lining, decreasing the protective mucus, which can lead to peptic ulcers or cancer. This type of infection responds to antibiotic therapy.

What changes occur in a bite of hamburger during its 3- to 4-hour stay in the stomach? The stomach churns and chemically degrades the food so that it assumes the consistency of a thick soup; this partially digested food is called **chyme.** Protein digestion then degrades much of the hamburger protein to polypeptides. Digestion of the starch in the bun to small polysaccharides and maltose continues until salivary amylase is inactivated by the acidic pH of the stomach. Over a period of several hours, peristaltic waves release the chyme in spurts through the stomach exit, the **pylorus,** and into the small intestine.

Most enzymatic digestion takes place in the small intestine

Digestion of food is completed in the **small intestine,** and nutrients are absorbed through its wall. The small intestine, which is 5 to 6 m (about 17 ft) in length, has three regions: the **duodenum, jejunum,** and **ileum.** Most chemical digestion takes place in the duodenum, the first portion of the small intestine, not in the stomach. Bile from the liver and enzymes from the pancreas are released into the duodenum and act on the chyme. Then enzymes produced by the epithelial cells lining the duodenum catalyze the final steps in the digestion of the major types of nutrients.

The lining of the small intestine appears velvety because of its millions of tiny fingerlike projections, the intestinal **villi** (sing., *villus*) (**FIG. 47-10**). The villi increase the surface area of the small intestine for digestion and absorption of nutrients. The intestinal surface is further expanded by **microvilli,** projections of the

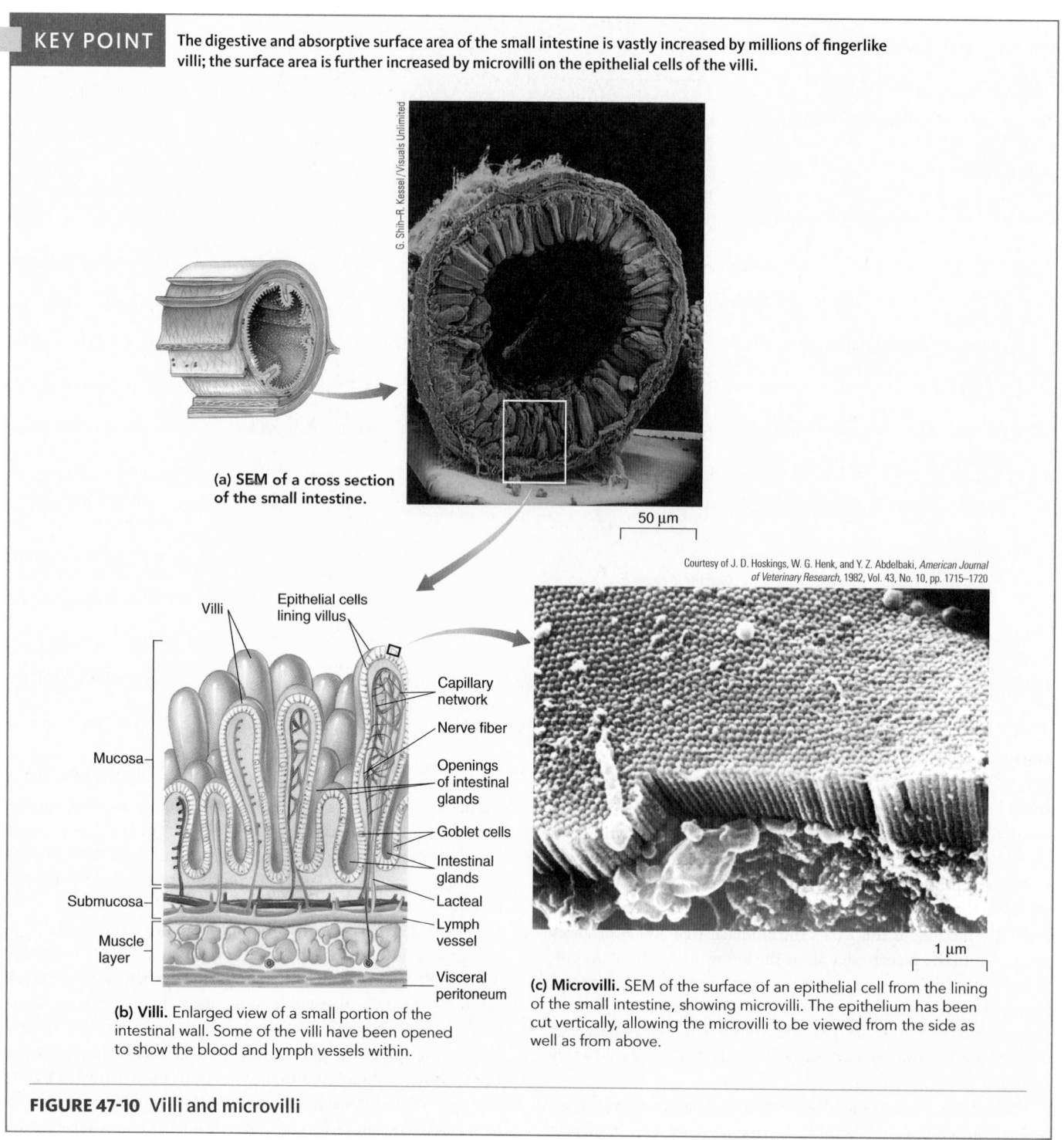

KEY POINT
The digestive and absorptive surface area of the small intestine is vastly increased by millions of fingerlike villi; the surface area is further increased by microvilli on the epithelial cells of the villi.

G. Shih–R. Kessel/Visuals Unlimited

(a) SEM of a cross section of the small intestine.

50 μm

Courtesy of J. D. Hoskings, W. G. Henk, and Y. Z. Abdelbaki, *American Journal of Veterinary Research*, 1982, Vol. 43, No. 10, pp. 1715–1720

Villi

Epithelial cells lining villus

Capillary network

Nerve fiber

Openings of intestinal glands

Goblet cells

Intestinal glands

Lacteal

Lymph vessel

Visceral peritoneum

Mucosa

Submucosa

Muscle layer

(b) Villi. Enlarged view of a small portion of the intestinal wall. Some of the villi have been opened to show the blood and lymph vessels within.

1 μm

(c) Microvilli. SEM of the surface of an epithelial cell from the lining of the small intestine, showing microvilli. The epithelium has been cut vertically, allowing the microvilli to be viewed from the side as well as from above.

FIGURE 47-10 Villi and microvilli

plasma membrane of the simple columnar epithelial cells of the villi. About 600 microvilli protrude from the exposed surface of each cell, giving the epithelial lining a fuzzy appearance when viewed with the light microscope.

If the intestinal lining were smooth, like the inside of a water pipe, food would zip right through the intestine, and many valuable nutrients would not be digested or absorbed. Folds in the wall of the intestine, the villi, and microvilli together increase the surface area of the small intestine by about 600 times. If we could unfold and spread out the lining of the small intestine of an adult human, its surface would approximate the size of a tennis court.

The liver secretes bile

The **liver,** the largest internal organ and also one of the most complex organs in the body, lies in the upper-right part of the abdomen just under the diaphragm (**FIG. 47-11**). The liver secretes **bile,** which mechanically digests fats by a detergent-like action (discussed in a later section). Bile consists of water, bile salts, bile pigments, cholesterol, salts, and lecithin (a phospholipid). Because it contains no digestive enzymes, bile does not enzymatically digest food. The pear-shaped **gallbladder** stores and concentrates bile and releases it into the duodenum as needed.

A single liver cell can carry on more than 500 separate, specialized metabolic activities! The liver performs these vital functions:

1. Secretes bile that mechanically digests fats
2. Helps maintain homeostasis by removing or adding nutrients to the blood
3. Converts excess glucose to glycogen and stores it
4. Converts excess amino acids to fatty acids and urea
5. Stores iron and certain vitamins
6. Detoxifies alcohol and other drugs and poisons

The pancreas secretes digestive enzymes

The **pancreas** is an elongated gland that secretes both digestive enzymes and hormones that help regulate the level of glucose in the blood. The cells that line the pancreatic ducts secrete an alkaline solution rich in bicarbonate ions. This pancreatic juice neutralizes the stomach acid in the duodenum and provides the optimal pH for action of the pancreatic enzymes. Pancreatic enzymes include **trypsin** and **chymotrypsin,** which digest polypeptides to dipeptides; **pancreatic lipase,** which degrades fats; **pancreatic amylase,** which breaks down almost all types of complex carbohydrates, except cellulose, to disaccharides; and **ribonuclease** and **deoxyribonuclease,** which split the nucleic acids ribonucleic acid (RNA) and deoxyribonucleic acid (DNA) to free nucleotides.

Nutrients are digested as they move through the digestive tract

Chyme moves through the digestive tract by peristalsis, mixing contractions, and motions of the villi. As nutrients in the chyme move through the small intestine, they come into contact with enzymes that digest them (**TABLE 47-1**).

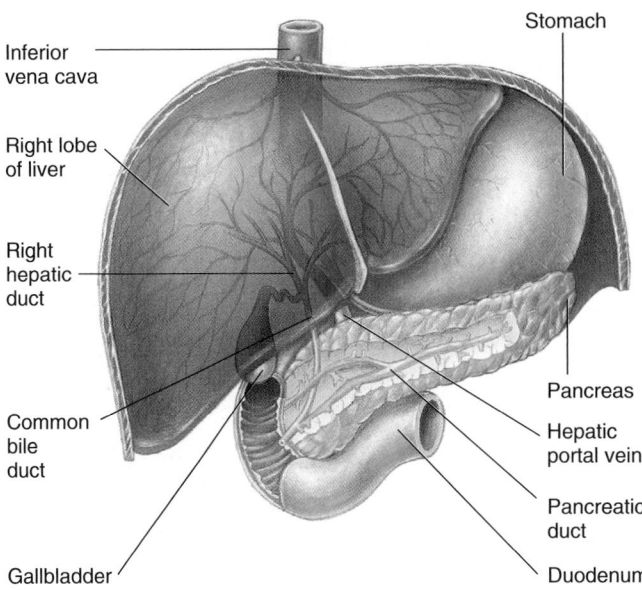

FIGURE 47-11 The liver and pancreas
The gallbladder stores bile from the liver. Note the ducts that conduct bile to the gallbladder and the duodenum. The stomach has been displaced to expose the pancreas, which secretes several digestive enzymes into the duodenum.

Carbohydrates are digested to monosaccharides

Polysaccharides, such as starch and glycogen, are important components of the food ingested by most animals. The glucose units of these large molecules are connected by glycosidic bonds linking carbon 4 (or 6) of one glucose molecule with carbon 1 of the adjacent glucose molecule. These bonds are hydrolyzed by **amylases** that digest polysaccharides to the disaccharide maltose. Although amylase can split the α-glycosidic linkages present in starch and glycogen, it cannot split the β-glycosidic linkages present in cellulose (see Figs. 3-9 and 3-10).

Amylase cannot split the bond between the two glucose units of maltose. Enzymes produced by the cells lining the small intestine break down disaccharides such as maltose to monosaccharides. **Maltase,** for example, splits maltose into two glucose molecules (see Fig. 3-8a). Hydrolysis occurs while the disaccharides are being absorbed through the epithelium of the small intestine.

Proteins are digested to amino acids

Several proteolytic enzymes are secreted into the digestive tract. Each breaks peptide bonds at one or more specific locations in a polypeptide chain. Trypsin, secreted in an inactive form by the pancreas, is activated by an enzyme called *enterokinase.* The trypsin then activates chymotrypsin and carboxypeptidase, as well as additional trypsin.

Pepsin, trypsin, and chymotrypsin break certain internal peptide bonds of proteins and polypeptides. Carboxypeptidase removes amino acids with free terminal carboxyl groups from the end of polypeptide chains. **Dipeptidases** released by the duodenum then split the small peptides to amino acids.

TABLE 47-1   Summary of Digestion

	Carbohydrates	Proteins	Lipids
Mouth	Polysaccharides ↓ Salivary amylase Maltose and small polysaccharides		
Stomach	Action continues until acidic pH inactivates salivary amylase	Protein ↓ Pepsin Short polypeptides	
Small intestine	Undigested polysaccharides ↓ Pancreatic amylase Maltose and other disaccharides ↓ Maltase, sucrase, lactase Monosaccharides	Polypeptides ↓ Trypsin, chymotrypsin Short polypeptides and peptides ↓ Carboxypeptidase, peptidases, dipeptidases Amino acids	Glob of fat ↓ Bile salts Emulsified fat droplets ↓ Pancreatic lipase Fatty acids and glycerol

Fats are digested to fatty acids and monoacylglycerols

Lipids are usually ingested as large masses of triacylglycerols (also called triglycerides). They are digested mainly within the duodenum by pancreatic lipase. Like many other proteins, lipase is water soluble, but its substrates are not. Thus, the enzyme can attack only the fat molecules at the surface of a mass of fat. Bile salts act like detergents, reducing the surface tension of fats. Their action, called **emulsification,** breaks large masses of fat into smaller droplets. Emulsification greatly increases the surface area of fat exposed to the action of pancreatic lipase and so increases the rate of lipid digestion.

Conditions in the intestine are usually not optimal for the complete hydrolysis of lipids to glycerol and fatty acids. Consequently, the products of lipid digestion include monoacylglycerols (monoglycerides) and diacylglycerols (diglycerides) as well as glycerol and fatty acids. Undigested triacylglycerols also remain, some of which are absorbed without digestion.

Nerves and hormones regulate digestion

Most digestive enzymes are produced only when food is present in the digestive tract. Salivary gland secretion is controlled entirely by the nervous system, but secretion of other digestive juices is regulated by both nerves and hormones. The wall of the digestive tract contains dense networks of neurons. This so-called *enteric nervous system* continues to regulate many motor and secretory activities of the digestive system even if sympathetic and parasympathetic nerves to these organs are cut. Many neuropeptides present in the brain are also released by neurons in the digestive tract and help regulate digestion. For example, *substance P* stimulates smooth muscle contraction of the digestive tract, and *enkephalin* inhibits it (see Table 41-2).

Several hormones, including **gastrin, secretin, cholecystokinin (CCK),** and **glucose-dependent insulinotropic peptide (GIP),** help regulate the digestive system (**TABLE 47-2**). These hormones are polypeptides secreted by endocrine cells in the mucosa

TABLE 47-2   Some Hormones That Regulate Digestion

Hormone	Source	Target Tissue	Actions	Factors That Stimulate Release
Gastrin	Stomach (mucosa)	Stomach (gastric glands)	Stimulates gastric glands to secrete pepsinogen and HCl; stimulates gastric motility	Distention of the stomach by food; certain substances such as partially digested proteins and caffeine
Secretin	Duodenum (mucosa)	Pancreas	Signals secretion of sodium bicarbonate	Acidic chyme acting on mucosa of duodenum
		Liver	Stimulates bile secretion	
		Stomach	Inhibits gastric secretion	
Cholecystokinin (CCK)	Duodenum (mucosa)	Pancreas	Stimulates release of digestive enzymes	Presence of fatty acids and partially digested proteins in duodenum
		Gallbladder	Stimulates emptying of bile	
		Brain	Signals satiety	
Glucose-dependent insulinotropic peptide (GIP)	Duodenum (mucosa)	Pancreas	Stimulates insulin secretion	Presence of glucose in duodenum

of certain regions of the digestive tract. Investigators are studying several other messenger peptides that are important in regulating digestive activity.

As an example of the regulation of the digestive system, consider the secretion of gastric juice. Seeing, smelling, tasting, or even thinking about food causes the brain to send neural signals to the gastric glands in the stomach. These signals stimulate these glands to secrete gastric juice. In addition, when food distends the stomach, stretch receptors send neural messages to the medulla. The medulla then sends messages to endocrine cells in the stomach wall that secrete gastrin. This hormone is absorbed into the blood; it stimulates the stomach to release gastric juice and also stimulates gastric emptying and intestinal motility.

Absorption takes place mainly through the villi of the small intestine

Only a few substances—water, simple sugars, salts, alcohol, and certain drugs—are small enough to be absorbed through the stomach wall. Absorption of nutrients is primarily the job of the intestinal villi. As illustrated in Figure 47-10, the wall of a villus is a single layer of epithelial cells. Inside each villus is a network of capillaries and a central lymph vessel, called a **lacteal.**

To reach the blood (or lymph), a nutrient molecule must pass through an epithelial cell lining the intestine and through a cell lining a blood or lymph vessel. Absorption occurs by a combination of simple diffusion, facilitated diffusion, and active transport. Because glucose and amino acids cannot diffuse through the intestinal lining, they must be absorbed by active transport. Absorption of these nutrients is coupled with the active transport of sodium (see Chapter 5). Fructose is absorbed by facilitated diffusion.

Amino acids and glucose are transported directly to the liver by the **hepatic portal vein.** In the liver this vein divides into a vast network of tiny blood sinuses, vessels similar to capillaries. As the nutrient-rich blood moves slowly through the liver, nutrients and certain toxic substances are removed from the circulation.

The products of lipid digestion are absorbed by a different process and different route. After free fatty acids and monoacylglycerols enter an epithelial cell in the intestinal lining, they are reassembled as triacylglycerols in the smooth endoplasmic reticulum. The triacylglycerols, along with absorbed cholesterol and phospholipids, are packaged into protein-covered fat droplets, called **chylomicrons.**

After they are released into the interstitial fluid, chylomicrons enter the lacteal (lymph vessel) of the villus. Chylomicrons are transported in the lymph to the subclavian veins, where the lymph and its contents enter the blood. About 90% of absorbed fat enters the blood circulation in this indirect way. The rest, mainly short-chain fatty acids such as those in butter, are absorbed directly into the blood. After a meal rich in fats, the great number of chylomicrons in the blood may give the plasma a turbid, milky appearance for a few hours. Chylomicrons transport fats to the liver and other tissues.

Most of the nutrients in the chyme are absorbed by the time it reaches the end of the small intestine. What is left (mainly waste) passes through a sphincter, the **ileocecal valve,** into the large intestine.

The large intestine eliminates waste

Undigested material, such as the cellulose of plant foods, along with unabsorbed chyme, passes into the **large intestine** (see Fig. 47-4). Although only about 1.3 m (about 4 ft) long, this part of the digestive tract is referred to as "large" because its diameter is greater than that of the small intestine. The small intestine joins the large intestine about 7 cm (2.8 in) from the end of the large intestine, forming a blind pouch, the **cecum.** The **vermiform appendix** projects from the end of the cecum. (Appendicitis is an inflammation of the appendix.) Herbivores such as rabbits have a large, functional cecum that holds food while bacteria digest its cellulose. In humans, the functions of the cecum and appendix are not known, and these structures are generally considered vestigial organs.

From the cecum to the **rectum** (the last portion of the large intestine), the large intestine is known as the **colon.** The regions of the large intestine are the cecum; ascending colon; transverse colon; descending colon; sigmoid colon; rectum; and **anus,** the opening for the elimination of wastes.

As chyme passes slowly through the large intestine, water and sodium are absorbed from it, and it gradually assumes the consistency of normal feces. Bacteria inhabiting the large intestine are nourished by the last remnants of the meal; in exchange, they benefit their host by producing vitamin K and certain B vitamins that can be absorbed and used.

A distinction should be made between elimination and excretion. *Elimination* is the process of getting rid of digestive wastes—materials that have not been absorbed from the digestive tract and did not participate in metabolic activities. In contrast, *excretion* is the process of getting rid of metabolic wastes, which in mammals is mainly the function of the kidneys and lungs. The large intestine, however, does *excrete* bile pigments.

When chyme passes through the intestine too rapidly, **defecation** (expulsion of feces) becomes more frequent, and the feces are watery. This condition, called *diarrhea,* may be caused by anxiety, certain foods, or pathogens that irritate the intestinal lining. Prolonged diarrhea results in loss of water and salts and leads to dehydration—a serious condition, especially in infants. *Constipation* results when chyme passes through the intestine too slowly. Because more water than usual is removed from the chyme, the feces may be hard and dry. Constipation is often caused by a diet deficient in fiber.

Colorectal cancer occurs in the colon or rectum (**FIG. 47-12**). In Western countries, colorectal cancer is the third most common cancer, and in the United States, it is the second leading cancer killer. Several factors contribute to the risk of developing colon cancer, including family history, certain genetic factors, smoking, physical inactivity, heavy use of alcohol, and obesity. A diet high in red meat and processed meat and low in fresh fruit, vegetables, poultry, and fish appears to increase the risk.

Review

- Imagine that you have just taken a bite of a chicken sandwich. List in sequence the structures through which it passes in its journey through the digestive system. What happens in each structure?
- What is the function of villi? How do they function?
- What is the function of the pancreas?
- What are chylomicrons?

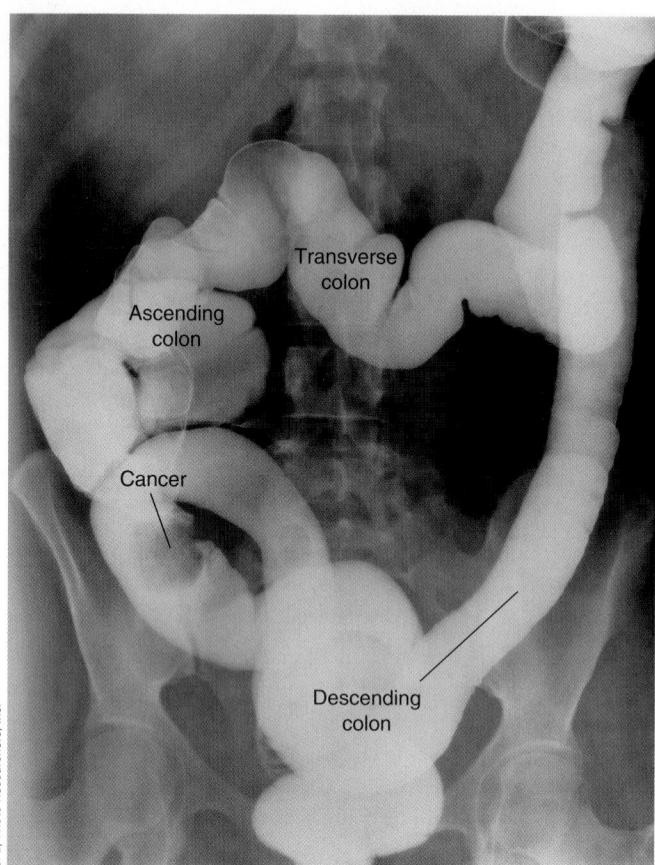

FIGURE 47-12 Colon cancer

In this radiographic view of the large intestine, cancer is evident as a mass that projects into the lumen of the colon. The large intestine has been filled with a suspension of barium sulfate, which makes irregularities in the wall visible.

47.3 REQUIRED NUTRIENTS

◼ LEARNING OBJECTIVES

6 Summarize the nutritional requirements for dietary carbohydrates, lipids, and proteins, and trace the fate of glucose, lipids, and amino acids after their absorption.

7 Describe the nutritional functions of vitamins, minerals, and phytochemicals.

Adequate amounts of essential nutrients are necessary for metabolic processes. Animals require carbohydrates, lipids, proteins, vitamins, and minerals. Nutritionists are also investigating plant compounds called *phytochemicals* that are important in nutrition. Although not considered a nutrient in a strict sense, water is a necessary dietary component. Enough fluid must be ingested to replace fluid lost in urine, sweat, feces, and breath.

Nutritionists consider new data and continually re-examine the *relative* amounts of various types of nutrients recommended for a healthy diet. According to the U.S. Department of Agriculture's *Dietary Guidelines for Americans,* 45% to 65% of our calories should come from carbohydrates, 20% to 35% from fat, and 10% to 35% from protein.

Recall from Chapter 1 that **metabolism** includes all the chemical processes that take place in the body. Metabolism includes anabolic and catabolic processes. **Anabolism** includes the synthetic aspects of metabolism, such as the production of proteins and nucleic acids. **Catabolism** includes breakdown processes, such as hydrolysis. Nutritionists measure the energy value of food in kilocalories, or simply Calories. A Calorie, spelled with a capital C, denotes a **kilocalorie (kcal),** defined as the amount of heat required to raise the temperature of a kilogram of water 1 degree Celsius.

Carbohydrates provide energy

Sugars and starches are important sources of energy in the human diet. Most carbohydrates are ingested in the form of starch and cellulose, both polysaccharides composed of long chains of glucose subunits. (You may want to review the discussion of carbohydrates in Chapter 3.) Nutritionists refer to *polysaccharides* as **"complex carbohydrates."** Foods rich in complex carbohydrates include rice, potatoes, corn, and other cereal grains.

When we eat an excess of carbohydrate-rich food, the liver cells become fully packed with glycogen and convert excess glucose to fatty acids and glycerol. Liver cells convert these compounds to triacylglycerols and send them to the fat depots of the body for storage.

Refined carbohydrates, such as white bread and white rice, are unhealthy because the refining process removes fiber and many vitamins and minerals. The refining process also produces a form of starch that the digestive system rapidly breaks down to glucose. The resulting rapid increase in glucose concentration in the blood stimulates the pancreas to release a large amount of insulin. This hormone lowers blood glucose level by signaling the liver and muscles to remove glucose from the blood. When glucose and insulin levels are high, triacylglycerol levels increase and high-density lipoprotein (HDL; the good cholesterol) concentration decreases. These metabolic events can lead to cardiovascular disease and increase the risk of type 2 diabetes (discussed in Chapter 49).

Dietary *fiber* decreases cholesterol concentration in the blood and is associated with a lower risk for cardiovascular disease and diabetes. **Fiber** is mainly a mixture of cellulose and other indigestible carbohydrates. We obtain dietary fiber by eating fruits, vegetables, and whole grains. The U.S. diet is low in fiber because of low intake of fruits and vegetables and use of refined flour. Increasing fiber in the diet has a variety of health benefits. Fiber stimulates the feeling of being satisfied (satiety) after food intake and thus is useful in treating obesity.

Lipids provide energy and are used to make biological molecules

Cells use ingested lipids to provide energy and to make a variety of lipid compounds, such as components of cell membranes, steroid hormones, and bile salts. We ingest about 98% of our dietary lipids in the form of triacylglycerols (triglycerides). (Recall from Chapter 3 that a triacylglycerol is a glycerol molecule chemically combined with three fatty acids; see Fig. 3-12b.) Triacylglycerols may be saturated, that is, fully loaded with hydrogen atoms, or their fatty acids may be monounsaturated (containing one double bond) or polyunsaturated (containing two or more double bonds).

Three polyunsaturated fatty acids (linoleic, linolenic, and arachidonic acids) are essential fatty acids that humans must obtain from food. Given these and sufficient nonlipid nutrients, the body can make all the lipid compounds (including fats, cholesterol, phospholipids, and prostaglandins) that it needs. The average U.S. diet provides far more cholesterol than the recommended daily maximum of 300 mg. High-cholesterol sources include egg yolks, butter, and meat.

How are lipids transported? Recall that chylomicrons transport lipids from the intestine to the liver and to other tissues. As chylomicrons circulate in the blood, the enzyme **lipoprotein lipase** breaks down triacylglycerols. The fatty acids and glycerol can then be taken up by the cells. What is left of the chylomicron, a remnant made up mainly of cholesterol and protein, is taken up by the liver.

Liver cells repackage cholesterol and triacylglycerols. These lipids are bound to proteins and transported as large molecular complexes, called **lipoproteins.** Some plasma cholesterol is transported by **high-density lipoproteins,** or **HDLs** ("good" cholesterol), but most is transported by **low-density lipoproteins,** or **LDLs** ("bad" cholesterol). LDLs deliver cholesterol to the cells. For cells to take in LDLs, a protein (apolipoprotein B) on the LDL surface must bind with a protein **LDL receptor** on the plasma membrane (see Fig. 5-23). After binding, the LDL enters the cell, and its cholesterol and other components are used. When cholesterol levels are high, HDLs collect the excess cholesterol and transport it to the liver. HDLs decrease risk for cardiovascular disease.

When needed, stored fats are hydrolyzed to fatty acids and released into the blood. Before cells can use these fatty acids as fuel, they are broken down into smaller compounds and combined with coenzyme A to form molecules of acetyl coenzyme A (acetyl CoA; **FIG. 47-13**). Acetyl CoA enters the citric acid cycle (see Chapter 8). The conversion of fatty acids to acetyl CoA is accomplished in the liver by a process known as β-oxidation.

For transport to the cells, acetyl coenzyme A is converted into one of three types of *ketone bodies* (four-carbon ketones). Normally, the level of ketone bodies in the blood is low, but in certain abnormal conditions, such as starvation and diabetes mellitus, fat metabolism is tremendously increased. Ketone bodies are then produced so rapidly that their level in the blood becomes excessive, which may make the blood too acidic. Such disrupted pH balance can lead to death.

What is the relationship between fat and cholesterol intake and cardiovascular disease? Lipids play a key role in the development of atherosclerosis, a progressive disease in which the arteries become clogged with fatty material (see Chapter 44). LDLs are the main source of the cholesterol that builds up in the walls of arteries. The type of fat consumed, as well as other dietary and lifestyle factors, is important. You can promote a healthy proportion of HDL to LDL by exercising regularly, following a healthy diet, maintaining appropriate body weight (obesity raises LDL and triacylglycerol levels), and not smoking cigarettes.

In general, animal foods are rich in both saturated fats and cholesterol, whereas most plant foods contain unsaturated fats and no cholesterol. Butter contains mainly saturated fats. Commonly used polyunsaturated vegetable oils are corn, soybean, and safflower oils. Monounsaturated fats raise HDL level, as does stearic acid, the saturated fat in chocolate. Olive, canola, and peanut oils contain large amounts of monounsaturated fats. A few plant oils, including palm oil and coconut oil, are high in saturated fats. **Omega-3 fatty acids** (found in fish and some plant oils) decrease LDL levels and play other protective roles in decreasing the risk for coronary heart disease.

A diet high in saturated fats and cholesterol raises the blood cholesterol level by as much as 25%. Because polyunsaturated fats decrease the blood cholesterol level, many people now cook with vegetable oils rather than with butter and lard, drink skim milk rather than whole milk, and eat low-fat ice cream. Some use margarine instead of butter. However, during production of many margarines, vegetable oils are partially hydrogenated (some of the carbons accept hydrogen to become fully saturated). During hydrogenation, some double bonds are transformed from a *cis* arrangement to a *trans* arrangement (see Fig. 3-3b), forming ***trans* fatty acids;** the harder the margarine, the higher the *trans* fatty acid content. Health

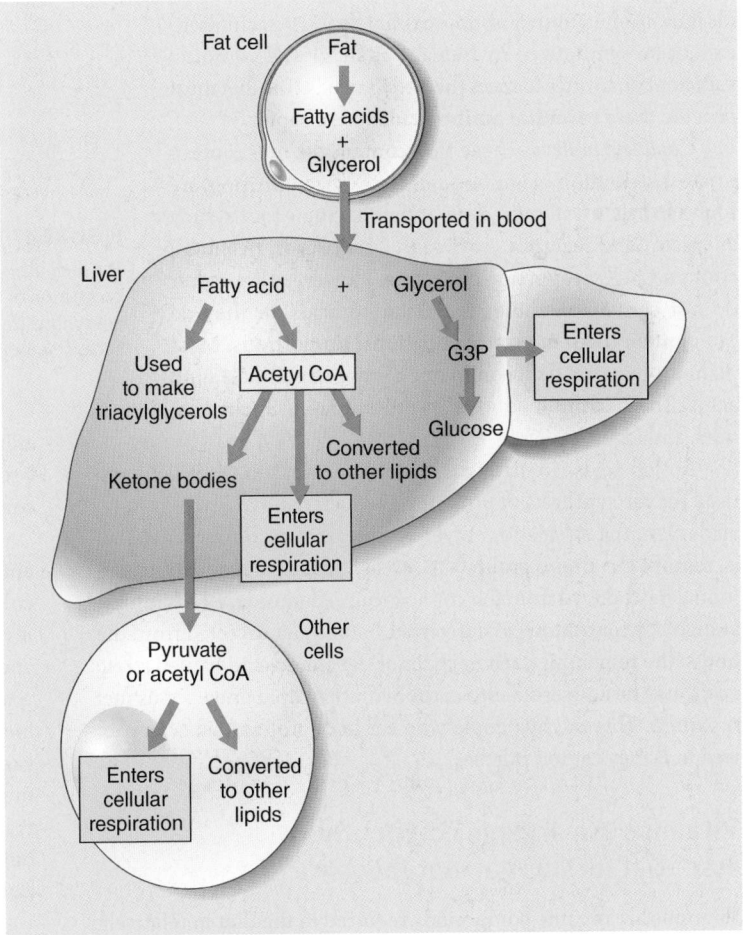

FIGURE 47-13 How the body uses fat

The liver converts glycerol and fatty acids to compounds that are used as fuel in cellular respiration. Recall from Chapter 8 that G3P is glyceraldehyde-3-phosphate.

concerns have been raised because *trans* fatty acids increase LDL cholesterol in the blood and lower HDL. Many processed foods, including cakes, doughnuts, cookies, crackers, and potato chips, contain *trans* fatty acids.

Although some fats, such as *trans* fatty acids and saturated fats, are unhealthy, others, such as omega-3 fatty acids and monounsaturated fat, promote health. The Inuits in Greenland eat diets extremely high in fat. However, because their dietary fat is rich in omega-3 fatty acids, they have a low incidence of heart disease.

Proteins serve as enzymes and as structural components of cells

Proteins are essential building blocks of cells, serve as enzymes, and are used to make essential compounds such as receptors, hemoglobin and myosin. Protein consumption is an index of a country's (or an individual's) economic status because high-quality protein tends to be the most expensive and least available of the nutrients. In many parts of the world, protein poverty is one of the most pressing health problems.

Ingested proteins are degraded in the digestive tract to small peptides and amino acids. Of the 20 or so amino acids important in nutrition, approximately 9 (10 in children) cannot be synthesized by humans at all, or at least not in sufficient quantities to meet the body's needs. The diet must provide these **essential amino acids** (see Chapter 3).

Complete proteins, those that contain the most appropriate distribution of amino acids for human nutrition, are found in fish, meat, nuts, eggs, and milk. Some foods, such as gelatin and legumes (soybeans, beans, peas, peanuts), contain a high proportion of protein. However, they either do not contain all the essential amino acids, or they do not contain them in proper nutritional proportions. Most plant proteins are deficient in one or more essential amino acids. The healthiest sources of protein are fish, chicken, nuts, and legumes.

Amino acids circulating in the blood are taken up by cells and used for the synthesis of proteins. The liver removes excess amino acids from the circulation. Liver cells deaminate amino acids, that is, remove the amino group (**FIG. 47-14**). During deamination, ammonia is produced from the amino group. Ammonia, which is toxic at high concentrations, is converted to urea and excreted from the body. The remaining carbon chain of the amino acid (called a *keto acid*) may be converted into carbohydrate or lipid and used as fuel or stored. This is why people who eat high-protein diets can gain weight if they eat too much.

Vitamins are organic compounds essential for normal metabolism

Vitamins are organic compounds required in the diet in relatively small amounts for normal biochemical functioning. Many are components of coenzymes (see Chapter 7). Nutritionists divide vitamins into two main groups. **Fat-soluble vitamins** include vitamins A, D, E, and K. **Water-soluble vitamins** are the B and C vita-

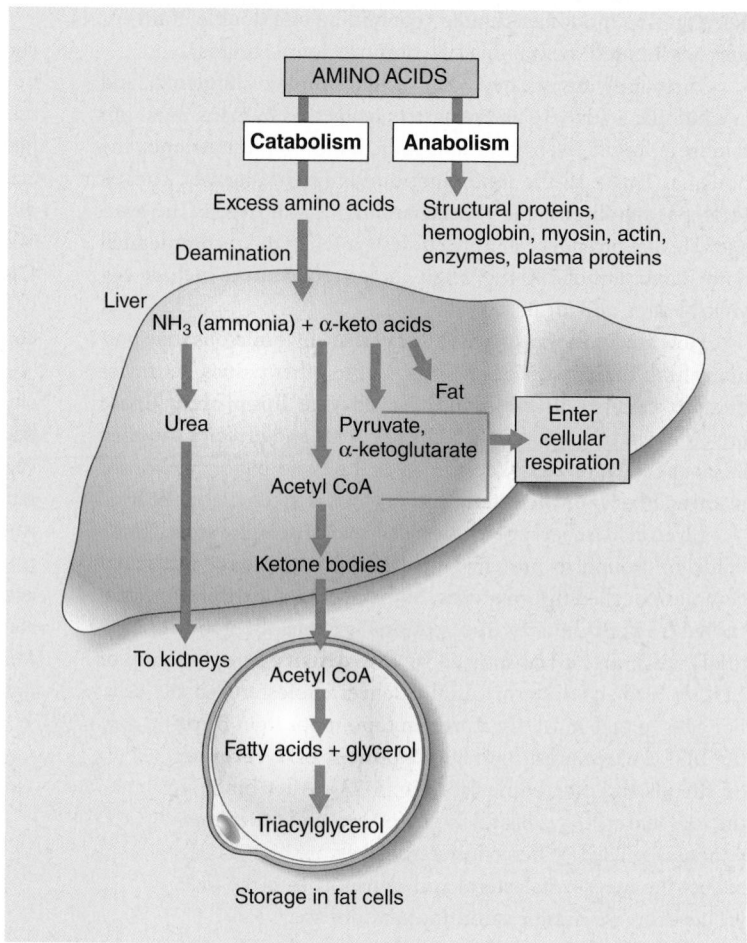

FIGURE 47-14 How the body uses protein

The liver plays a central role in protein metabolism. Deamination of amino acids and conversion of the amino groups to urea take place there. In addition, many proteins are synthesized in the liver. Note that you can gain weight on a high-protein diet because excess amino acids can be converted to fat.

mins. Fruit and vegetables are rich sources of vitamins. **TABLE 47-3** provides the sources, functions, and consequences of deficiency for most of the vitamins.

Health professionals debate the advisability of taking large amounts of certain specific vitamins, such as vitamin C to prevent colds or vitamin E to protect against vascular disease. Some studies suggest that vitamin A (found in yellow and green vegetables) and vitamin C (found in citrus fruit and tomatoes) help protect against certain forms of cancer. We do not yet understand all the biochemical roles played by vitamins or the interactions among various vitamins and other nutrients. We do know that, like vitamin deficiency, large overdoses of vitamins can be harmful. Moderate overdoses of the B and C vitamins are excreted in the urine, but surpluses of the fat-soluble vitamins are not easily excreted and can accumulate to harmful levels.

Minerals are inorganic nutrients

Minerals are inorganic nutrients ingested in the form of salts dissolved in food and water (**TABLE 47-4**). We need certain miner-

TABLE 47-3 The Vitamins

Vitamins and U.S. RDA*	Actions	Effect of Deficiency	Sources
Fat soluble			
Vitamin A, retinol 5000 IU†	Converted to retinal; essential for normal vision; essential for normal growth and differentiation of cells; reproduction; immunity	Growth retardation; night blindness; world-wide millions of children are at risk of blindness from vitamin A deficiency	Liver, fortified milk, orange and green vegetables such as carrots and broccoli; orange fruits such as cantaloupe
Vitamin D, calciferol 400 IU	Promotes calcium and phosphorus absorption from digestive tract; essential to normal growth and maintenance of bone	Weak bones; bone deformities; rickets in children, osteomalacia in adults	Fish oils, egg yolk, fortified milk, butter, margarine, salmon
Vitamin E, tocopherols 30 IU	Antioxidant; protects unsaturated fatty acids and cell membranes	Increased catabolism of unsaturated fatty acids so that not enough are available for maintenance of cell membranes; prevention of normal growth; nerve damage	Polyunsaturated plant oils, nuts, leafy greens, whole-grain products
Vitamin K, about 80 mcg‡	Synthesis of blood-clotting proteins and proteins important in bone production	Prolonged blood-clotting time	Normally supplied by intestinal bacteria; leafy greens, legumes
Water soluble			
Vitamin C, ascorbic acid 60 mg	Collagen synthesis; antioxidant; needed for synthesis of some hormones and neurotransmitters; important in immune function	Scurvy (wounds heal very slowly, and scars become weak and split open; capillaries become fragile; bone does not grow or heal properly); immune system suppressed	Citrus fruit, strawberries, tomatoes, leafy vegetables, cabbage
B-complex vitamins **Vitamin B₁,** thiamine 1.5 mg	Active form is a coenzyme in many enzyme systems; important in carbohydrate and amino acid metabolism	Beriberi (weakened heart muscle, enlarged right side of heart, nervous sytem and digestive tract disorders); common in alcoholics	Liver, yeast, whole and enriched grains, meat, green leafy vegetables
Vitamin B₂, riboflavin 1.7 mg	Used to make coenzymes (e.g., FAD) essential in cellular respiration	Dermatitis, inflammation and cracking at corners of mouth; confusion	Liver, milk, eggs, green leafy vegetables, enriched grains
Niacin, 20 mg	Component of important coenzymes (NAD^+ and $NADP^+$); essential to cellular respiration	Pellagra (dermatitis, diarrhea, mental symptoms, muscular weakness, fatigue)	Liver, chicken, tuna, milk, green leafy vegetables, enriched grains
Vitamin B₆, pyridoxine 2 mg	Derivative is coenzyme in many reactions in amino acid metabolism	Dermatitis, digestive tract disturbances; convulsions	Meat, whole grains, legumes, green leafy vegetables
Pantothenic acid, 10 mg	Constituent of coenzyme A (important in cellular metabolism)	Deficiency extremely rare	Meat, whole grains, legumes
Folate, 400 mcg	Coenzyme needed for nucleic acid synthesis and for maturation of red blood cells	A type of anemia; certain birth defects; increased risk of cardiovascular disease; deficiency in alcoholics, smokers, and pregnant women	Liver, legumes, dark green leafy vegetables, orange juice, grains
Biotin, 30 mcg	Coenzyme important in metabolism	Deficiency uncommon; depression, skin irritation, seizures	Produced by intestinal bacteria; liver, chocolate, egg yolk
Vitamin B₁₂, 2.4 mcg	Coenzyme important in metabolism; contains cobalt	A type of anemia	Liver, meat, fish, eggs, cheese

*RDA is the recommended dietary allowance, established by the Food and Nutrition Board of the National Research Council, to maintain good nutrition for healthy adults.

†International Unit: the amount that produces a specific biological effect and is internationally accepted as a measure of the activity of the substance.

‡mcg = micrograms.

als, including sodium, chloride, potassium, calcium, phosphorus, magnesium, manganese, and sulfur, in amounts of 100 mg or more daily. These are referred to as *major minerals.* Several others, such as iron, copper, iodide, fluoride, and selenium, are **trace elements,** minerals that we require in amounts less than 100 mg per day.

Minerals are necessary components of body tissues and fluids. Salt content (about 0.9% in plasma) is vital in maintaining the fluid balance of the body, and because salts are lost from the body daily in sweat, urine, and feces, they must be replaced by dietary intake. Sodium chloride (common table salt) is the salt needed in largest quantity in blood and other body fluids. Deficiency results

in dehydration. Iron is the mineral most often deficient in the diet. In fact, iron deficiency is one of the most widespread nutritional problems in the world.

Antioxidants protect against oxidants

Normal cell processes that require oxygen produce **oxidants,** highly reactive molecules such as free radicals, peroxides, and superoxides. **Free radicals,** molecules or ions with one or more unpaired electrons, are also generated by ionizing radiation, tobacco smoke, and other forms of air pollution. Oxidants damage DNA,

TABLE 47-4 Some Important Minerals and Their Functions

Mineral	Functions	Sources; Comments
Calcium	Main mineral of bones and teeth; essential for normal blood clotting, muscle function, nerve function, and regulation of cell activities	Milk and other dairy products, fish, green leafy vegetables; bones serve as calcium reservoir
Phosphorus	Performs more functions than any other mineral; structural component of bone; component of ATP, DNA, RNA, and phospholipids	Meat, dairy products, cereals
Sulfur	Component of many proteins and vitamins	High-protein foods such as meat, fish, legumes, nuts
Potassium	Principal positive ion within cells; important in muscle contraction and nerve function	Meat, milk, fruit, vegetables, grains
Sodium	Principal positive ion in interstitial fluid; important in fluid balance; neural transmission	Many foods, table salt; too much ingested in average American diet; excessive amounts may contribute to high blood pressure
Chloride	Principal negative ion of interstitial fluid; important in fluid balance and in acid–base balance	Many foods, table salt
Magnesium	Needed for normal muscle and nerve function	Nuts, whole grains, green leafy vegetables, seafood, chocolate
Copper	Component of several enzymes; essential for hemoglobin synthesis	Liver, eggs, fish, whole wheat flour, beans
Iodide	Component of thyroid hormones (hormones that increase metabolic rate); deficiency results in goiter (abnormal enlargement of thyroid gland)	Seafood, iodized salt, vegetables grown in iodine-rich soils
Manganese	Activates many enzymes	Whole-grain cereals, nuts, leafy green vegetables; poorly absorbed from intestine
Iron	Component of hemoglobin, myoglobin, important respiratory enzymes (cytochromes), and other enzymes essential to oxygen transport and cellular respiration; deficiency results in anemia and may impair cognitive function	Mineral most likely to be deficient in diet. Good sources: meat (especially liver), fish, nuts, egg yolk, legumes, dried fruit
Fluoride	Component of bones and teeth; makes teeth resistant to decay; excess causes tooth mottling	Fish; in areas where it does not occur naturally, fluoride may be added to municipal water supplies (fluoridation)
Zinc	Cofactor for at least 70 enzymes; helps regulate synthesis of certain proteins; needed for growth and repair of tissues; deficiency associated with loss of appetite, depressed immune function, retarded growth in children	Meat, fish, milk, yogurt, grains, vegetables
Selenium	Antioxidant (cofactor for a peroxidase that breaks down peroxides); appears to protect against prostate cancer in men	Seafood, eggs, meat, whole grains

proteins, and unsaturated fatty acids by snatching electrons. Damage to DNA causes mutations that may lead to cancer, and injury to unsaturated fatty acids can damage cell membranes. Free radicals are thought to contribute to atherosclerosis by causing oxidation of LDL cholesterol. Oxidative damage to the body over many years contributes to the aging process.

Cells have **antioxidants** that destroy free radicals and other reactive molecules. Antioxidants in tissues include certain enzymes, for example, catalase and peroxidase. Their action requires minerals such as selenium, zinc, manganese, and copper. Certain vitamins—vitamin C, vitamin E, and vitamin A—have strong antioxidant activity. Vitamins A and E protect cell membranes from free radicals. In addition, a variety of *phytochemicals* are potent antioxidants (discussed in next section).

Nutritionists recommend that we increase the antioxidants in our diet by eating fruits, vegetables, and other foods high in antioxidants. We do not yet know whether antioxidant supplements are useful.

Phytochemicals play important roles in maintaining health

A diet that includes all the essential nutrients does not provide the same health benefits as one also rich in fruit and vegetables. The missing ingredients are **phytochemicals,** plant compounds that promote health. Many phytochemicals are antioxidants. For example, *lycopenes,* responsible for the red color of tomatoes, are powerful antioxidants. *Flavonoids,* found in cocoa, especially in dark chocolate, are antioxidants that also appear to lower blood pressure, lower cholesterol, and improve cardiovascular health in other ways.

Nutritionists have begun to intensively investigate phytochemicals. Some important classes of phytochemicals are carotenoids (which include vitamin A and lycopene) in deeply pigmented fruits and vegetables such as carrots and tomatoes; flavonoids in berries, herbs, vegetables, barley, soy, black and green tea, and cocoa; isothiocyanates and indoles in broccoli and other cruciferous vegetables; and organosulfur compounds in garlic and onions. In Asian countries where diets are low in fat and high in soy and green tea, the incidence of breast, prostate, and colorectal cancer is low.

Diets rich in fruits and vegetables lower the incidence of heart disease and of certain types of cancer. Studies comparing diets in various countries suggest that intake of fruits and vegetables may be more important than differences in dietary fat. Yet nutritionists estimate that in the United States only about 1 in 11 people eats the daily recommended 2 to 6.5 cups of fruits and vegetables a day (the equivalent of 4 to 13 servings). In the United States, the National Fruit and Vegetable Program (a public private partnership that includes government agencies, industry, and not-for-profit groups) promotes a public health initiative known as Fruit & Veggies–More Matters. This group is committed to increasing the number of daily servings of fruits and vegetables based on current dietary guidelines.

Review

- How do complex carbohydrates affect the body?
- What is the function of glucose? of essential amino acids?
- What is the function of high-density lipoproteins (HDLs)?
- What measures can you take to lower your risk for heart disease?

47.4 ENERGY METABOLISM

■ LEARNING OBJECTIVES

8 Contrast basal metabolic rate with total metabolic rate; write the basic energy equation for maintaining body weight and describe the consequences of altering it in either direction.

9 Identify components of the regulatory pathways that regulate food intake and energy homeostasis.

10 In general terms, describe the effects of malnutrition, including both overnutrition and undernutrition.

The amount of energy liberated by the body per unit time is a measure of its **metabolic rate.** Much of the energy expended by the body is ultimately converted to heat. Metabolic rate may be expressed either in kilocalories of heat energy expended per day or as a percentage above or below a standard normal level.

The **basal metabolic rate (BMR)** is the rate at which the body releases heat as a result of breaking down fuel molecules. BMR is the body's basic cost of living, that is, the rate of energy use during resting conditions. This energy is required to maintain body functions such as heart contraction, breathing, and kidney function. A person's **total metabolic rate** is the sum of his or her BMR and the energy used to carry on daily activities. A laborer has a greater total

metabolic rate than an account executive who is inactive most of the day and who does not exercise regularly.

An average-sized man who does not exercise and who sits at a desk all day expends about 2100 kcal daily (women expend less energy). If the food the individual eats each day also contains about the same number of kilocalories, the body will be in a state of energy balance; that is, energy input will equal energy output. This is an extremely important concept because body weight remains constant when:

$$\text{energy input} = \text{energy output}$$

When energy output is greater than energy input, stored fat is burned and body weight decreases. People gain weight when they take in more energy in food than they expend in daily activity, in other words, when:

$$\text{energy input} > \text{energy output}$$

Energy metabolism is regulated by complex signaling

The hypothalamus regulates energy metabolism and food intake. Biologists have identified several signaling molecules that form complex signaling pathways involving the hypothalamus and digestive system. For example, several appetite regulators signal us to eat or to stop eating. When the stomach is empty, it secretes the peptide hormone **ghrelin** (grell'-in), which stimulates appetite. Ghrelin activates neurons in the hypothalamus that produce the appetite-stimulating neurotransmitter **neuropeptide Y (NPY).**

The gastrointestinal tract releases several peptides that signal satiety and suppress food intake. **Peptide YY,** secreted by the intestine, signals the hypothalamus to stop secreting NPY. The decrease in NPY slows gastric emptying. Other compounds that signal satiety include the gastrointestinal hormone *cholecystokinin* (CCK) and *melanocortins* released by the hypothalamus.

Leptin and **insulin** are also critical in regulating energy metabolism. Leptin, a hormone released by adipose tissue, is important in regulating normal body weight. Leptin signals centers in the brain about the status of energy stores in adipose tissue. The brain then adjusts feeding behavior and energy metabolism. The pancreatic hormone insulin is secreted when the concentration of glucose and other nutrients increases after we eat. Insulin stimulates cells, especially liver, muscle, and fat cells, to take in glucose from the blood and use or store it. The actions of insulin inhibit the hypothalamus from secreting NPY. Thus, insulin inhibits further food intake.

The hypothalamus integrates input from these signaling molecules with other information, such as the concentration of nutrients circulating in the blood. The brain then sends signals that adjust feeding behavior and metabolism so that homeostasis of stored fat and fuel metabolism is maintained. When food is available and energy stores are adequate, energy use increases and fat stores are mobilized. Energy intake and glucose production in the liver are inhibited. In contrast, when food intake is low, as during dieting or starvation, the hypothalamus increases secretion of neuropeptide Y. Appetite increases and metabolism slows, actions that help restore energy homeostasis.

Obesity is a serious nutritional problem

Overnutrition can cause malnutrition. **Obesity,** the excess accumulation of body fat, is a serious form of malnutrition that has become a problem of epidemic proportions in affluent societies. The World Health Organization considers obesity among the most important global health problems. Obesity contributes to about 300,000 deaths annually in the United States and is the second leading preventable cause of death (second only to smoking). It is a major risk factor for heart disease, diabetes mellitus, certain types of cancer (including breast and colon cancers), hypertension, osteoarthritis, and liver and gallbladder disease. In the well-known Framingham study of more than 2000 men, those who were 20% overweight had a significantly higher mortality rate from all causes.

Body mass index (BMI), now used worldwide as a measure of body size, is an index of weight in relation to height. It is calculated by dividing the square of the weight (kg^2) by height (m). The equivalent in the United States is 4.89 times the weight (lb) divided by the square of the height (ft^2). An adult who has a BMI between 25 and 29.9 is considered overweight. An adult who has a BMI of 30 or more is considered obese. Approximately 33% of U.S. adults are overweight and another 34% of U.S. adults are obese. An estimated 17% of U.S. children and adolescents are overweight.

Each of us appears to have a **set point,** or steady state, around which body weight is regulated. Dieting can be difficult because when BMI decreases below an individual's set point, energy-conserving mechanisms are activated and energy expenditure decreases.

Many factors affect weight

In addition to an array of signaling molecules that affect energy metabolism and body weight, researchers have identified several gene mutations that affect food intake and energy homeostasis. For example, mice with a mutated allele at the *ob* locus become grossly obese. The normal *ob* gene product is leptin. When researchers inject leptin into grossly obese mice, the appetites of the mice decrease and their energy use increases. They lose weight, mainly from loss of body fat (**FIG. 47-15**). Unfortunately, most obese humans are resistant to the actions of leptin.

The number of fat cells in the adult is apparently determined mainly by the amount of fat stored during infancy and childhood. When we are overfed early in life, abnormally large numbers of fat cells are formed. Later in life, these fat cells may be fully stocked with excess lipids or may shrink in size, but they are always there. People with such increased numbers of fat cells are thought to be at greater risk for obesity than are those with normal numbers.

Eating activates the dopamine reward circuit in the brain. (Recall that this circuit is also activated in drug addiction.) The amount of dopamine released corresponds to the intensity of pleasure experienced by eating the food. One hypothesis holds that obese individuals may have an underactive dopamine reward system. They overeat to compensate and may develop a food addiction.

Although many factors involved in obesity are inherited, behavior is critically important. High-calorie diets, overeating, and underexercising lead to obesity, and psychosocial factors influence these behaviors. A sedentary lifestyle combined with the ready availability of high-energy foods contributes to the problem. One researcher cleverly described the roots of the obesity problem as the combination of "computer chips and potato chips." For every 9.3 kcal of excess food taken into the body, about 1 g of fat is stored. (An excess of about 140 kcal, less than a typical candy bar, per day for a month results in a 1-pound weight gain.)

Researchers have identified targets for obesity treatment

As researchers discover the genetic and biochemical mechanisms that regulate energy metabolism, they provide potential targets for the development of pharmacological treatments for obesity. The following are among the many targets for drug action that are the focus of research: (1) reduce appetite so that food intake is decreased; (2) block absorption of fat; (3) uncouple metabolism from energy production so that food energy is dissipated as heat (see *Inquiring About: Electron Transport and Heat,* in Chapter 8); and (4) block receptors for molecules that send signals leading to increased energy storage.

Undernutrition can cause serious health problems

Millions of people do not have enough to eat or do not eat a balanced diet. Individuals suffering from *undernutrition* are malnourished. They may feel weak, are easily fatigued, and are highly susceptible to infection as a result of depressed immune function. Iron, calcium, and vitamin A are commonly deficient, but essential amino acids are the nutrients most often deficient in the diet. Millions of people suffer from poor health and lowered resistance to disease because of protein deficiency. Children's physical and mental development are retarded when these essential building blocks of cells are not provided in the diet. Because these children's bodies cannot manufacture antibodies (which are proteins) and cells needed to fight infection, common childhood diseases, such as measles, whooping cough, and chickenpox, are often fatal in children suffering from protein malnutrition.

FIGURE 47-15 Effect of leptin
Mutant *ob* mice before (*left*) and after (*right*) treatment with leptin.

FIGURE 47-16 Protein deficiency
Millions of children suffer from kwashiorkor, a disease caused by severe protein deficiency. Note the characteristic swollen belly, which results from fluid imbalance.

In young children, severe protein malnutrition results in the condition known as **kwashiorkor.** This Ashanti (West African) word means "first-second." It refers to the situation in which a first child is displaced from its mother's breast when a younger sibling is born. The older child is then given a diet of starchy cereal or cassava that is deficient in protein. Growth becomes stunted, muscles are wasted, and edema develops (as displayed by a swollen belly); the child becomes apathetic and anemic, with an impaired metabolism (**FIG. 47-16**). Without essential amino acids, digestive enzymes cannot be manufactured, so what little protein is ingested cannot be digested. Deficiencies in trace elements and antioxidants have also been associated with the development of kwashiorkor.

Review

- Write an equation to describe energy balance and explain what happens when the equation is altered in either direction.
- What is body mass index (BMI)?
- What is the function of ghrelin? of leptin?

◼ SUMMARY: FOCUS ON LEARNING OBJECTIVES

47.1 (page 1013)

1 Describe food processing, including ingestion, digestion, absorption, and egestion or elimination, and compare the digestive system of a cnidarian (such as *Hydra*) with that of an earthworm and vertebrate.

- **Nutrition** is the process of taking in and using food. **Feeding** is the selection, acquisition, and **ingestion** of food, that is, taking food into the body. **Digestion** is the process of breaking down food mechanically and chemically. Nutrients pass through the lining of the digestive tract and into the blood by **absorption.** Food that is not digested and absorbed is discharged from the body by **egestion** or **elimination.**

- In cnidarians and flatworms, food is digested in the **gastrovascular cavity.** This cavity has only one opening that serves as both mouth and anus. In more complex invertebrates and in all vertebrates, the digestive tract is a complete tube with an opening at each end. Digestion takes place as food passes through the tube. Various parts of the digestive tract are specialized to perform specific functions.

CENGAGENOW™ Explore various digestive systems by clicking on the figure in CengageNOW.

47.2 (page 1016)

2 Trace the pathway traveled by an ingested meal through the human digestive system and describe the structure and function of each organ involved.

- Mechanical and enzymatic digestion of carbohydrates begins in the mouth. Mammalian teeth include **incisors,** which are adapted for biting and cutting food; **canines** adapted for tearing food; and

premolars and **molars** adapted for crushing and grinding. Three pairs of **salivary glands** secrete saliva, which contains the enzyme **salivary amylase** that digests starch.

- As food is swallowed, it is propelled through the **pharynx** and **esophagus.** A **bolus** of food is moved along through the digestive tract by **peristalsis,** waves of muscular contraction that push food along.

- In the **stomach,** food is mechanically digested by vigorous churning, and proteins are enzymatically digested by the action of **pepsin** in the gastric juice. **Rugae** are folds in the stomach wall that expand as the stomach fills with food. **Gastric glands** secrete hydrochloric acid and **pepsinogen,** the precursor of pepsin.

- After several hours, a soup of partly digested food, called **chyme,** leaves the stomach through the **pylorus** and enters the **small intestine** in spurts. Most enzymatic digestion takes place in the **duodenum,** which produces several digestive enzymes and receives secretions from the liver and pancreas.

- The **liver** produces **bile,** which emulsifies fats. The **pancreas** releases enzymes that digest carbohydrate, lipid, and protein as well as RNA and DNA. **Pancreatic amylase** digests complex carbohydrates. **Pancreatic lipase** degrades fats, and **trypsin** and **chymotrypsin** digest polypeptides to dipeptides.

- The **large intestine,** which consists of the **cecum, colon, rectum,** and **anus,** is responsible for eliminating undigested wastes. It also incubates bacteria that produce vitamin K and certain B vitamins.

CENGAGENOW™ Learn more about human digestion by clicking on the figures in Cengage NOW.

3 Trace the step-by-step digestion of carbohydrate, protein, and lipid.

- Nutrients in chyme are enzymatically digested as they move through the digestive tract. Polysaccharides are digested to the disaccharide maltose by salivary and pancreatic amylases. **Maltase** in the small intestine splits maltose into glucose, the main product of carbohydrate digestion.

- Proteins are split by pepsin in the stomach and by proteolytic enzymes in the pancreatic juice. **Dipeptidases** split small peptides to amino acids.

- Lipids are emulsified by bile salts and then hydrolyzed by pancreatic lipase.

4 Describe the structural adaptations that increase the surface area of the digestive tract.

- The surface area of the small intestine is greatly expanded by folds in its wall; by the intestinal **villi,** elongated projections of the mucosa; and by **microvilli,** projections of the plasma membrane of the epithelial cells of the villi.

Villi

5 Compare lipid absorption with absorption of other nutrients.

- Nutrients are absorbed through the thin walls of intestinal villi. The **hepatic portal vein** transports amino acids and glucose to the liver.

- Fatty acids and monoacylglycerols enter epithelial cells in the intestinal lining, where they are reassembled into triacylglycerols. They are packaged into **chylomicrons,** droplets that also contain cholesterol and phospholipids and are covered with a protein coat. The lymphatic system transports chylomicrons to the blood circulation.

47.3 (page 1024)

6 Summarize the nutritional requirements for dietary carbohydrates, lipids, and proteins, and trace the fate of glucose, lipids, and amino acids after their absorption.

- Most carbohydrates are ingested in the form of polysaccharides—starch and cellulose. Polysaccharides are referred to as **complex carbohydrates. Fiber** is mainly a mixture of cellulose and other indigestible carbohydrates. Carbohydrates are used mainly as an energy source. Glucose concentration in the blood is carefully regulated. Excess glucose is stored as glycogen and can also be converted to fat.

- Lipids are used to provide energy, to form components of cell membranes, and to synthesize steroid hormones and other lipid substances. Most lipids are ingested in the form of triacylglycer-

ols. Fatty acids are converted to molecules of acetyl coenzyme A, which enter the citric acid cycle. Excess fatty acids are converted to triacylglycerol and stored as fat.

- Lipids are transported as large molecular complexes called **lipoproteins. Low-density lipoproteins (LDLs)** deliver cholesterol to the cells. **High-density lipoproteins (HDLs)** collect excess cholesterol and transport it to the liver.

- Proteins serve as enzymes and are essential structural components of cells. The best distribution of **essential amino acids** is found in the complete proteins of animal foods. Excess amino acids are deaminated by liver cells. Amino groups are converted to urea and excreted in urine; the remaining keto acids are converted to carbohydrate and used as fuel or converted to lipid and stored in fat cells.

7 Describe the nutritional functions of vitamins, minerals, and phytochemicals.

- **Vitamins** are organic compounds required in small amounts for many biochemical processes. Many serve as components of coenzymes. **Fat-soluble vitamins** include vitamins A, D, E, and K. **Water-soluble vitamins** are the B and C vitamins.

- **Minerals** are inorganic nutrients ingested as salts dissolved in food and water. **Trace elements** are minerals required in amounts less than 100 mg per day.

- **Phytochemicals** are plant compounds that promote health. Many phytochemicals are **antioxidants** that destroy **oxidants.** which are reactive molecules, such as **free radicals.** These molecules damage DNA, proteins, and unsaturated fatty acids by snatching electrons.

47.4 (page 1029)

8 Contrast basal metabolic rate with total metabolic rate; write the basic energy equation for maintaining body weight and describe the consequences of altering it in either direction.

- **Basal metabolic rate (BMR)** is the body's cost of metabolic living. **Total metabolic rate** is the BMR plus the energy used to carry on daily activities.

- When energy (kilocalories) input equals energy output, body weight remains constant. When energy output is greater than energy input, body weight decreases. When energy input exceeds energy output, body weight increases.

9 Identify components of the regulatory pathways that regulate food intake and energy homeostasis.

- Complex pathways of signaling molecules regulate food intake and energy metabolism.

- **Ghrelin** and **neuropeptide Y (NPY)** stimulate appetite. Peptide YY, cholecystokinin (CCK), and melanocortins signal satiety.

- The hormone **leptin** signals the brain about the status of energy stores in adipose tissue. Leptin and **insulin** inhibit food intake.

   CENGAGENOW˜ Learn more about leptins and body weight by clicking on the figure in CengageNOW.

10 In general terms, describe the effects of malnutrition, including both overnutrition and undernutrition.

- In **obesity** an excess amount of fat accumulates in adipose tissues. Obesity is a major risk factor for several major disorders, including heart disease and diabetes mellitus. A person gains weight by taking in more energy, in the form of kilocalories, than is expended in activity. Genes, signaling molecules that affect energy metabolism, and certain behaviors contribute to obesity.

- Millions of people suffer from undernutrition, a form of malnutrition that causes fatigue and depressed immune function. Essential amino acids are the nutrients most often deficient in the diet.

TEST YOUR UNDERSTANDING

1. Teeth adapted for crushing and grinding are (a) incisors (b) canines (c) premolars and molars (d) incisors and premolars (e) canines and molars

2. The layer of tissue that lines the lumen of the digestive tract is the (a) muscle layer (b) visceral peritoneum (c) parietal peritoneum (d) mucosa (e) submucosa

3. Which of the following are accessory digestive glands? (a) salivary glands (b) pancreas (c) liver (d) a, b, and c (e) a and b

4. Arrange the following into the correct sequence.
   1. stomach 2. esophagus 3. pharynx 4. small intestine 5. colon
   (a) 2, 3, 1, 4, 5 (b) 3, 2, 1, 5, 4 (c) 3, 2, 5, 1, 4 (d) 2, 3, 1, 5, 4 (e) 3, 2, 1, 4, 5

5. Amylase is produced by the (a) pancreas and salivary glands (b) stomach and pancreas (c) colon and salivary glands (d) liver and pancreas (e) duodenum and pancreas

6. Which sequence most accurately describes the digestion of protein?
   1. dipeptide 2. amino acid 3. protein 4. polypeptide 5. glycerol
   (a) 4, 3, 1, 2 (b) 3, 4, 1, 2 (c) 3, 4, 1, 5 (d) 4, 3, 5, 1, 2 (e) 2, 1, 4, 5

7. The surface area of the small intestine is increased by (a) folds in its wall (b) villi (c) microvilli (d) a, b, and c (e) a and b

8. Lipids are transported from the intestine to the liver by (a) chylomicrons (b) HDLs (c) LDLs (d) glycerol transporters (e) leptin

9. Most vitamins are (a) inorganic compounds (b) components of coenzymes (c) used as fuel (d) electrolytes (e) required by herbivores and carnivores but not omnivores

10. When energy input is greater than energy output, (a) weight loss occurs (b) weight remains stable (c) weight gain occurs (d) leptin secretion is inhibited (e) the *ob* gene is deactivated

11. A hormone that stimulates gastric glands to secrete pepsinogen is (a) secretin (b) GIP (c) gastrin (d) cholecystokinin (CCK) (e) substance P

12. Label the diagram. Use Figure 47-4 to check your answers.

CRITICAL THINKING

1. Design an experiment to test the hypothesis that the B vitamin pyridoxine is an essential nutrient in mice.

2. Proteolytic enzymes are produced in an inactive form. What, if any, benefit might this have?

3. **EVOLUTION LINK.** If you were presented with an unfamiliar animal and asked to determine its nutritional lifestyle, how would you do so? (*Hint:* Consider adaptations.)

4. **SCIENCE, TECHNOLOGY, AND SOCIETY.** Investigators are unraveling the biochemical pathways that help regulate body weight. How might their work lead to a cure for obesity? How might a cure for obesity affect our society?

 Additional questions are available in CengageNOW at www.cengage.com/login.

48 Osmoregulation and Disposal of Metabolic Wastes

Most terrestrial animals inhabit areas near water sources. Zebra, wildebeest, and a variety of birds drink at a lake in Ngorongoro Crater in Tanzania.

McMurray Photography

Water, the most abundant molecule both in the cell and on Earth's surface, shapes life and is a critical factor in the distribution of organisms on our planet. Like the animals in the photograph, most animals need a dependable source of water with which to replenish their body fluids. For this reason, animals often inhabit areas near water sources.

Ions are dissolved in water, the medium in which most metabolic reactions take place. The volume and ionic composition of an animal's body fluids must be maintained within homeostatic limits. Through natural selection a variety of homeostatic mechanisms have evolved that regulate the volume and composition of fluids in the internal environment.

Many small animals live in the ocean and get their food and oxygen directly from the sea water that surrounds them; they release waste products into the sea water. In larger animals and in most terrestrial animals, the cells are bathed by fluid that serves as an internal sea. Terrestrial animals have a continuous need to conserve water. Water loss from the body must be carefully regulated, and water lost must be replaced. Water is taken in with food and drink and is also produced in metabolic reactions.

Two processes that help maintain fluid and electrolyte (salt) homeostasis in animals are *osmoregulation* and *excretion*, the disposal of metabolic wastes. In this chapter we discuss these processes in both invertebrates and vertebrates inhabiting various environments. Then we focus on the structure and functions of the mammalian kidney. We end the chapter with a description of the hormones that regulate kidney function.

48.1 MAINTAINING FLUID AND ELECTROLYTE BALANCE

■ LEARNING OBJECTIVE

1   Describe how the processes of *osmoregulation* and *excretion* contribute to fluid and electrolyte homeostasis.

Intracellular fluid, the fluid within cells, accounts for most of the body fluid. **Extracellular fluid,** the fluid outside the cells, includes interstitial fluid (the fluid between cells), lymph, and blood plasma (or hemolymph). In vertebrates, blood plasma, which is mainly water, transports nutrients, gases, waste products, and other materials throughout the body. **Interstitial fluid** forms from the blood plasma and bathes all the cells. Excess water evaporates from the body surface or is excreted by specialized structures.

Electrolytes are compounds such as inorganic salts, acids, and bases that form ions in solution. Electrolytes are very important solutes in body fluids. Many homeostatic mechanisms regulate fluid and electrolyte balance.

Recall from Chapter 5 that *osmosis* is the diffusion of water through a selectively permeable membrane. The net flow of water is from a more dilute solution (one with a lower solute concentration) to a less dilute solution (one with a higher solute concentration). If the solute concentrations of two solutions are equal, they are *isotonic* to each other. If solution A has a greater solute concentration than solution B, solution A is *hypertonic* to solution B. Solution B, with a lower solute concentration relative to solution A, is *hypotonic* to solution A. Remember that the total solute concentration of a solution is responsible for the direction of water movement. The *osmotic pressure* of a solution is the pressure that must be exerted on the hypertonic side of a selectively permeable membrane to prevent net movement of water from the hypotonic side.

An **osmole** is related to a mole (see Chapter 2), but takes into account the number of particles produced when a solute dissolves. For example, glucose dissolves to give only one kind of particle, so a mole of glucose in solution is one osmole. A mole of NaCl in solution produces two kinds of particles (Na^+ and Cl^-), so a mole of NaCl is two osmoles. Both types of ions affect the osmotic pressure of the solution. A *milliosmole* is 1/1000 of an osmole.

Osmolarity is a measure of the number of osmoles of solute per liter of solution. Solutions with the same osmolarity are described as *isoosmotic*. If solution X has a higher osmolarity than solution Y, it is described as *hyperosmotic*. Solution Y would be described as *hypoosmotic* relative to solution X.

Osmoregulation is the process by which organisms control the concentration of water and salt so that their body fluids do not become too dilute or too concentrated. **Excretion** is the process of ridding the body of metabolic wastes. **Excretory systems** have evolved that function in both osmoregulation and in disposal of metabolic wastes. Excretory systems rid the body of excess water and ions, metabolic wastes, and harmful substances. As we will discuss, hormones are important signaling molecules in these regulatory processes.

Review

- What is osmoregulation?
- What is excretion?

48.2 METABOLIC WASTE PRODUCTS

■ LEARNING OBJECTIVE

2   Contrast the benefits and costs of excreting ammonia, uric acid, or urea.

Metabolic wastes must be excreted so that they do not accumulate and reach concentrations that would disrupt homeostasis. The principal metabolic waste products produced by most animals are water, carbon dioxide, and **nitrogenous wastes,** those that contain nitrogen. Carbon dioxide is excreted mainly by respiratory structures (see Chapter 46). In terrestrial animals, some water is also lost from respiratory surfaces. However, specialized excretory organs, such as kidneys, remove and excrete most of the water and nitrogenous wastes.

Nitrogenous wastes include ammonia, uric acid, and urea. Recall that amino acids and nucleic acids contain nitrogen. During the metabolism of amino acids, the nitrogen-containing amino group is removed (in a process known as deamination) and converted to **ammonia** (**FIG. 48-1**). However, ammonia is highly toxic. Some aquatic animals excrete it into the surrounding water before it can build up to toxic concentrations in their tissues. A few terrestrial animals, including some snails and wood lice, vent it directly into the air. But many animals, humans included, convert ammonia to some less toxic nitrogenous waste such as uric acid or urea.

Uric acid is produced both from ammonia and by the breakdown of nucleotides from nucleic acids. Uric acid is insoluble in water and forms crystals that are excreted as a crystalline paste, so little fluid loss results. This is an important water-conserving adaptation in many terrestrial animals, including insects, certain reptiles, and birds. Also, because uric acid is not toxic and can be safely stored, its excretion is an adaptive advantage for species whose young begin their development enclosed in eggs.

Urea, the principal nitrogenous waste product of amphibians and mammals, is synthesized in the liver from ammonia and carbon dioxide by a sequence of reactions known as the urea cycle. Like the formation of uric acid, these reactions require specific enzymes and the input of energy by the cells. Compared with the

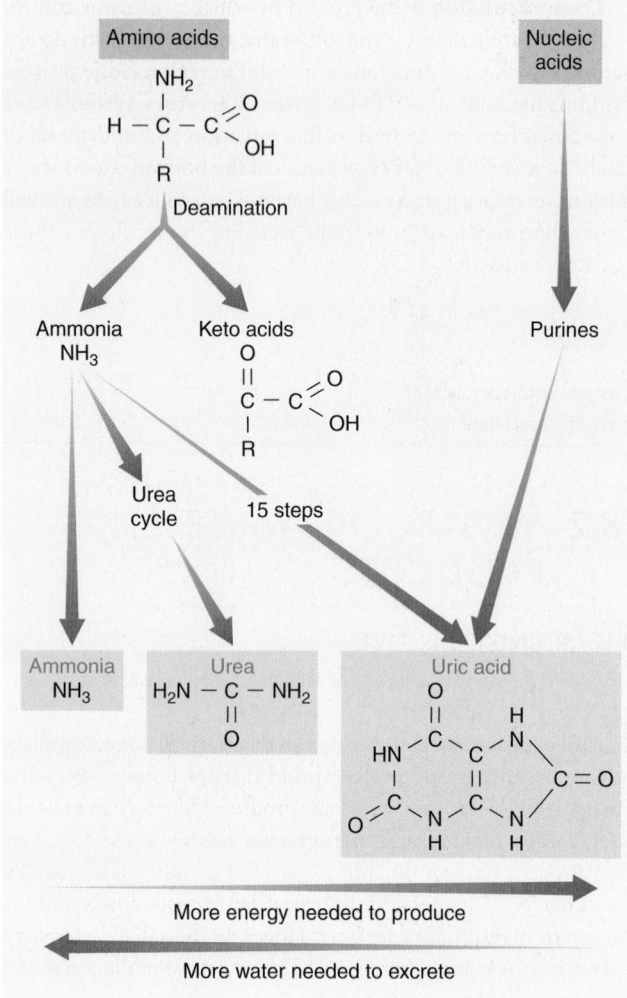

FIGURE 48-1 Formation of nitrogenous wastes

Deamination of amino acids and metabolism of nucleic acids produce nitrogenous wastes. Ammonia is the first metabolic product of deamination. Many aquatic animals excrete ammonia, but terrestrial animals convert it to urea and uric acid, which are less toxic. Most amphibians and mammals convert ammonia to urea via the urea cycle. Insects, many reptiles, and birds convert ammonia to uric acid. Energy is required to convert ammonia to urea and uric acid, but less water is required to excrete these wastes.

energy cost of producing ammonia, that of producing urea and uric acid is high.

Urea has the advantage of being far less toxic than ammonia and can accumulate in higher concentrations without causing tissue damage; thus, it can be excreted in more concentrated form. Because urea is highly soluble, however, it is dissolved in water, and more water is needed to excrete urea than to excrete uric acid.

Review

- What are the principal types of nitrogenous wastes? Give examples of animals that excrete each type.
- What are the benefits of excreting nitrogenous wastes in the form of uric acid? in the form of urea?

48.3 OSMOREGULATION AND EXCRETION IN INVERTEBRATES

LEARNING OBJECTIVES

3   Compare osmoconformers and osmoregulators.
4   Describe protonephridia, metanephridia, and Malpighian tubules, and compare their functions.

The ocean is a stable environment, and its salt concentration does not vary much. The electrolyte concentration in the cells and body fluids of marine sponges and cnidarians is very similar to sea water, so these animals do not require specialized excretory structures. They expend little or no energy in excreting wastes because wastes simply diffuse from their cells to the external environment and are washed away by water currents. When water stagnates and currents do not wash away wastes, aquatic environments, such as coral reefs, are damaged by the waste accumulation.

The body fluids of most marine invertebrates are in osmotic equilibrium with the surrounding sea water. These animals are known as **osmoconformers** because the concentration of their body fluids varies along with changes in the sea water. However, many osmoconforming marine animals still regulate some ions in their body fluids.

Coastal habitats, such as estuaries that contain brackish water, are much less stable environments than is the open ocean. Salt concentrations change frequently with shifting tides. Many invertebrates and vertebrates that inhabit these environments are **osmoregulators.** These animals have homeostatic mechanisms that maintain an optimal salt concentration in their tissues regardless of changes in the salt concentration of their surroundings.

In a coastal environment where fresh water enters the ocean, the water may have a lower salt concentration than an animal's body fluids. Water osmotically moves into the animal's body, and salt diffuses out. An animal adapted to this environment has excretory structures that remove the excess water. Certain polychaete worms and the blue crab are among the animals that can be osmoconformers or osmoregulators depending on environmental conditions.

Dehydration is a constant threat to terrestrial animals. Because their fluid concentration is higher than that of the air around them, they tend to lose water by evaporation from both the body surface and respiratory surfaces. Terrestrial animals may also lose water as wastes are excreted. As animals moved onto the land, natural selection favored the evolution of structures and processes that conserve water.

Excretory systems help maintain fluid and electrolyte homeostasis by selectively adjusting the concentrations of salts and other substances in blood and other body fluids. Typically, an excretory system collects fluid, generally from the blood or interstitial fluid. It then adjusts the composition of this fluid by selectively returning needed substances to the body fluid. Finally, the body releases the adjusted excretory product containing excess or potentially toxic substances.

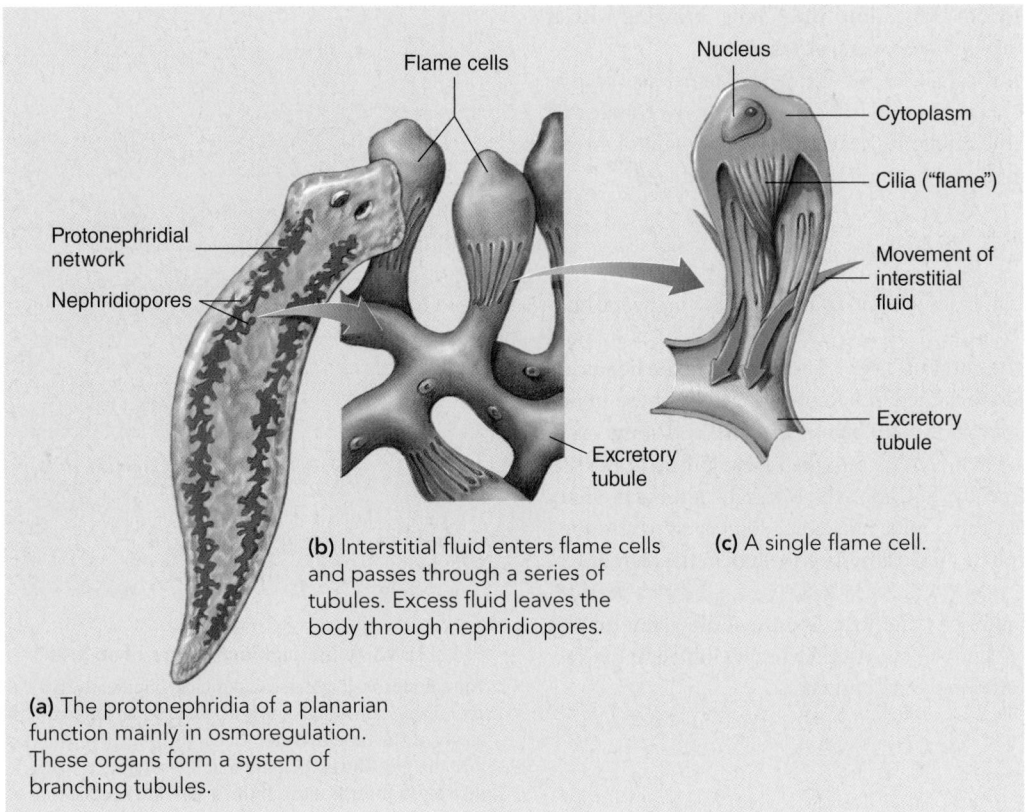

(b) Interstitial fluid enters flame cells and passes through a series of tubules. Excess fluid leaves the body through nephridiopores.

(c) A single flame cell.

(a) The protonephridia of a planarian function mainly in osmoregulation. These organs form a system of branching tubules.

FIGURE 48-2 Protonephridia of a flatworm

Nephridial organs are specialized for osmoregulation and/or excretion

Nephridial organs, or nephridia, are structures that function in osmoregulation and excretion in many invertebrates, including flatworms, nemerteans, rotifers, annelids, mollusks, and lancelets. Each nephridial organ consists of simple or branching tubes that typically open to the outside of the body through pores, called *nephridiopores.* Two types of nephridial organs are protonephridia and metanephridia.

In flatworms and nemerteans, metabolic wastes pass through the body surface by diffusion, but these animals also have **protonephridia** (FIG. 48-2). The protonephridia are composed of tubules with no internal openings. Their enlarged blind ends consist of **flame cells** with brushes of cilia, so named because their constant motion reminded early biologists of flickering flames. The flame cells lie in the interstitial fluid that bathes the body cells. Fluid enters the flame cells, and the beating of the cilia propels the fluid through the tubules. Excess fluid leaves the body through nephridiopores.

Most annelids and mollusks have more complex nephridial organs called **metanephridia** (FIG. 48-3). Each segment of an earthworm has a pair of metanephridia. A metanephridium is a tubule open at both ends. The inner end opens into the coelom as a ciliated funnel, and the outer end opens to the outside through a nephridiopore. A network of capillaries surrounds each tubule.

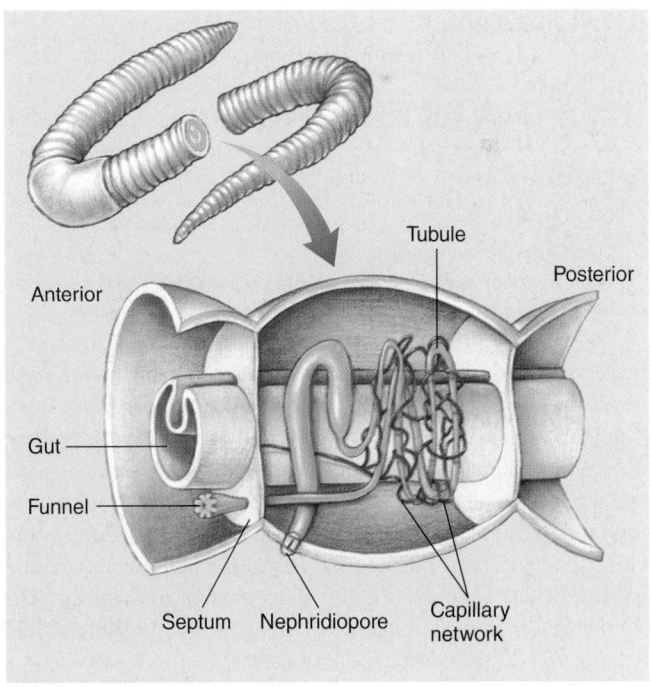

FIGURE 48-3 Metanephridium of an earthworm

Each metanephridium consists of a ciliated funnel opening into the coelom, a coiled tubule, and a nephridiopore opening to the outside. This 3-D internal view shows parts of three segments of the earthworm body.

Fluid from the coelom passes into the tubule, bringing with it whatever it contains—glucose, salts, or wastes.

As fluid moves through the tubule, needed materials (such as water and glucose) are removed from the fluid by the tubule and are reabsorbed by the capillaries, leaving the wastes behind. In this way, urine that contains concentrated wastes is produced.

Malpighian tubules conserve water

The excretory system of insects and spiders consists of several hundred **Malpighian tubules** (**FIG. 48-4**). Malpighian tubules are slender extensions of the gut wall. Their blind ends lie in the hemocoel (blood cavity) and are bathed in hemolymph. Cells of the tubule wall actively transport uric acid, potassium ions, and some other substances from the hemolymph into the tubule lumen. Other solutes and water follow by diffusion. The Malpighian tubules empty into the gut. Water, some salts, and other solutes are reabsorbed into the hemolymph by a specialized epithelium in the rectum.

Uric acid, the major waste product, is excreted as a semidry paste with a minimum of water loss. Because Malpighian tubules effectively conserve body fluids, they have contributed to the success of insects in terrestrial environments.

Review

- How are nephridial organs and Malpighian tubules alike? How are they different?

48.4 OSMOREGULATION AND EXCRETION IN VERTEBRATES

■ LEARNING OBJECTIVES

5   Relate the function of the vertebrate kidney to the success of vertebrates in a wide variety of habitats.

6   Compare adaptations for osmoregulation in freshwater fishes, marine bony fishes, sharks, marine mammals, and terrestrial vertebrates.

Vertebrates live successfully in a wide range of habitats—in fresh water, the ocean, tidal regions, and on land, even in extreme environments such as deserts. In response to the requirements of these diverse environments, adaptations have evolved for regulating salt and water content and for excreting wastes. The main osmoregulatory and excretory organ in most vertebrates is the **kidney.** The kidney excretes most nitrogenous wastes and helps maintain fluid balance by adjusting the salt and water content of the urine. The skin, lungs or gills, and digestive system also help maintain fluid balance and dispose of metabolic wastes.

Freshwater vertebrates must rid themselves of excess water

As fishes began to move into freshwater habitats about 470 million years ago (mya), there must have been strong selection for ad-

FIGURE 48-4 Malpighian tubules of an insect
The slender Malpighian tubules have blind ends that extend into the hemocoel. Their cells transfer uric acid and some ions from the hemolymph to the cavity of the tubule. Water follows by diffusion. The wastes are discharged into the gut. The epithelium that lines the rectum (part of the hindgut) actively reabsorbs most of the water and needed ions.

aptations that promoted effective osmoregulation. The evolution of body fluids more dilute than sea water was a major adaptation. However, the salt concentration of the body fluids of these fishes is still higher than that of the fresh water that surrounds them. They are hypertonic to their watery environment. As a result, water moves into the body, and they are in constant danger of becoming waterlogged.

Freshwater fishes are covered by scales and a mucous secretion that retard the passage of water into the body. However, water constantly enters through the gills and through the mouth (with food). How do these animals meet this challenge? Some water leaves the body through the gills. Furthermore, the kidneys of freshwater fishes are adapted to excrete large amounts of dilute urine (**FIG. 48-5a**). The kidneys have large *glomeruli,* capillary clusters that filter the blood and produce urine.

Water entry is only part of the challenge of osmoregulation in freshwater fishes. These animals also tend to lose salts by diffusion through the gills into the surrounding water. To compensate, special gill cells have evolved that actively transport salts (mainly sodium chloride) from the water into the body.

The gills excrete most of the nitrogenous wastes of freshwater fishes, but the kidneys are also important excretory organs. Ammonia is the main nitrogenous waste; about 10% of nitrogenous wastes are excreted as urea.

Most amphibians are at least semi-aquatic, and their mechanisms of osmoregulation are similar to those of freshwater fishes. They, too, produce large amounts of dilute urine. In its urine and through its skin, a frog can lose an amount of water equivalent to one-third of its body weight in one day. Active transport of salt into the body by special cells in the skin compensates for loss of salt through skin and in urine.

Marine vertebrates must replace lost fluid

Freshwater fishes adapted very successfully to their aquatic habitats. Thus, when some freshwater fishes returned to the sea about 200 mya, their blood and body fluids were less salty than their surroundings; that is, they were hypotonic to their environment. These fishes lose water osmotically and take in salt. To compensate for fluid loss, many marine bony fishes drink sea water (**FIG. 48-5b**). They retain the water and excrete salt by the action of specialized cells in their gills. The gills are also responsible for ammonia excretion. Very little urine is excreted by the kidneys, which have only small (or no) glomeruli.

Marine cartilaginous fishes (sharks and rays) have different osmoregulatory adaptations that allow them to tolerate the salt concentrations of their environment. These animals accumulate and tolerate urea (**FIG. 48-5c**). Their tissues are adapted to function at concentrations of urea that would be toxic to most other animals. The high urea concentration makes the body fluids slightly hypertonic to sea water, resulting in a net inflow of water. Marine cartilaginous fishes have well-developed kidneys that excrete a large volume of urine. Excess salt is excreted by the kidneys and, in many species, by a rectal gland.

Certain reptiles and marine birds ingest sea water and take in a lot of salt in their food. Glands in their heads excrete salt. These salt glands are usually inactive; they function only in response to osmotic stress.

Whales, dolphins, and other marine mammals ingest sea water along with their food. Their kidneys produce concentrated urine, much saltier than sea water. This is an important physiological adaptation, especially for marine carnivores. The high-protein diet of these animals results in the production of large amounts of urea, which must be excreted in urine without losing much water.

Terrestrial vertebrates must conserve water

Adult amphibians generally inhabit moist environments. They excrete urea and reabsorb some water from the urinary bladder. Amniotes (reptiles, birds, and mammals) have more effective adaptations for life on land. Their skin minimizes water loss by evaporation, and many amniotes excrete uric acid, which requires very little water.

Because birds and mammals are endothermic (maintain a constant body temperature) and have a high rate of metabolism, they produce a relatively large volume of nitrogenous wastes. They have numerous adaptations, including very efficient kidneys, for conserving water. An extreme example is the desert-dwelling kangaroo rat, which obtains most of its water from its own metabolism. (Recall from Chapter 8 that aerobic respiration produces water. The kangaroo rat's kidneys are so efficient that it loses little fluid as urine.)

Birds conserve water by excreting nitrogen as uric acid and by efficiently reabsorbing water from the cloaca and intestine. Mammals excrete urea. Their kidneys produce very concentrated (hypertonic) urine.

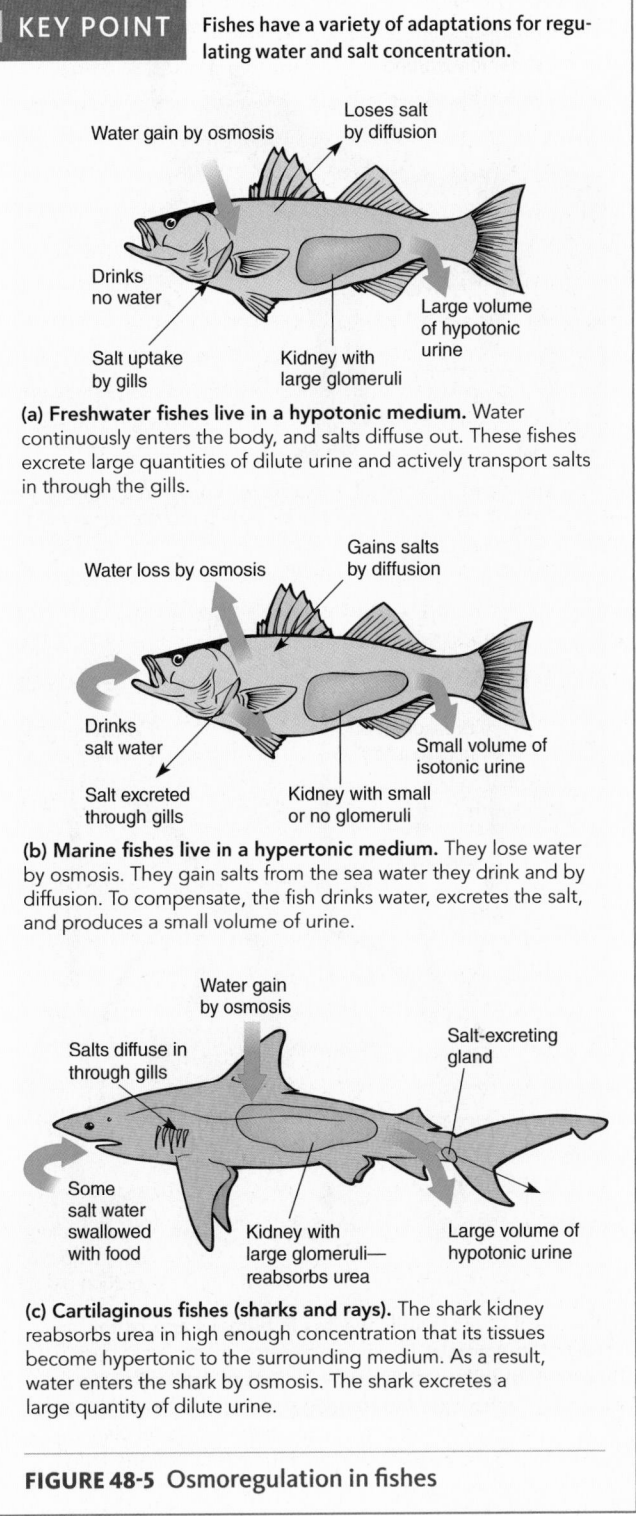

KEY POINT Fishes have a variety of adaptations for regulating water and salt concentration.

(a) Freshwater fishes live in a hypotonic medium. Water continuously enters the body, and salts diffuse out. These fishes excrete large quantities of dilute urine and actively transport salts in through the gills.

(b) Marine fishes live in a hypertonic medium. They lose water by osmosis. They gain salts from the sea water they drink and by diffusion. To compensate, the fish drinks water, excretes the salt, and produces a small volume of urine.

(c) Cartilaginous fishes (sharks and rays). The shark kidney reabsorbs urea in high enough concentration that its tissues become hypertonic to the surrounding medium. As a result, water enters the shark by osmosis. The shark excretes a large quantity of dilute urine.

FIGURE 48-5 Osmoregulation in fishes

In terrestrial vertebrates, the lungs, skin, and digestive system are important in osmoregulation and waste disposal (**FIG. 48-6**). Most carbon dioxide is excreted by the lungs. In birds and mammals, some water is lost from the body as water vapor in exhaled air. Although primarily concerned with the regulation of body

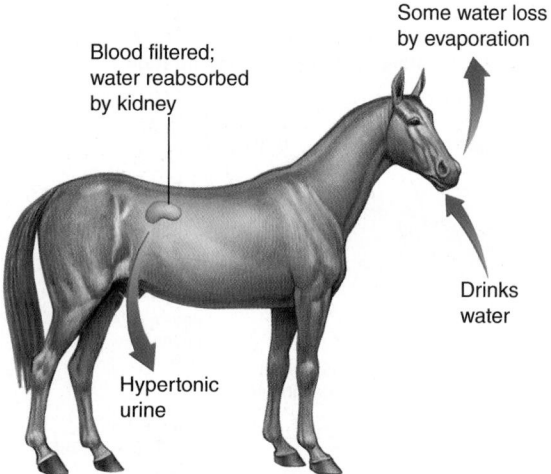

(a) **The kidney of terrestrial vertebrates conserves water by reabsorbing it.** Birds and mammals can produce concentrated urine.

Blood filtered; water reabsorbed by kidney

Some water loss by evaporation

Drinks water

Hypertonic urine

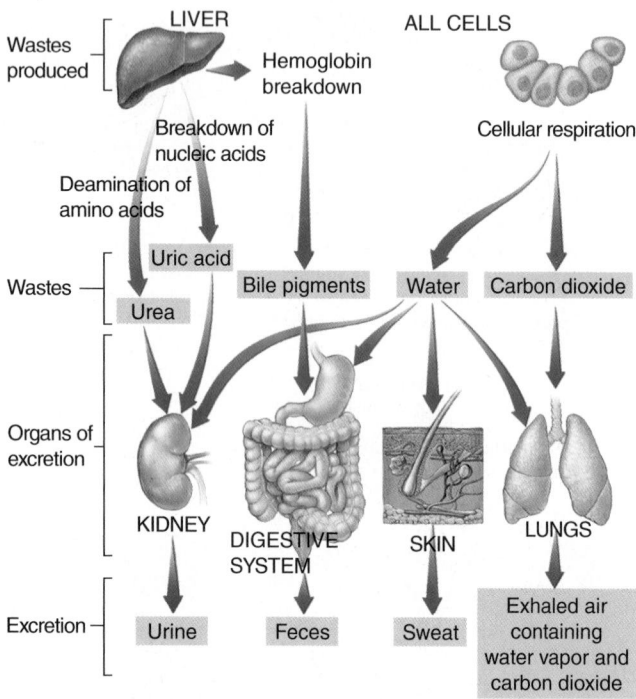

(b) **Disposal of metabolic wastes in humans and other terrestrial mammals.** To conserve water, mammals produce a small amount of hypertonic urine. Nitrogenous wastes are produced by the liver and transported to the kidneys. All cells produce carbon dioxide and some water during cellular respiration. These waste products are excreted by the lungs.

FIGURE 48-6 Excretory organs in terrestrial vertebrates

temperature, the sweat glands of humans and some other mammals excrete 5% to 10% of all metabolic wastes.

The liver produces both urea and uric acid, which are transported by the blood to the kidneys. Most of the bile pigments produced by the breakdown of red blood cells are excreted by the liver into the intestine. From the intestine they pass out of the body with the feces.

Review

- What type of osmoregulatory challenge is faced by marine fishes? by freshwater fishes? What mechanisms have evolved to meet these challenges?
- What adaptations in aquatic birds and mammals help meet the challenges of osmoregulation and metabolic waste disposal? in terrestrial birds and mammals?

48.5 THE URINARY SYSTEM

■ LEARNING OBJECTIVES

7 Describe (or label on a diagram) the organs of the mammalian urinary system and give the functions of each.

8 Describe (or label on a diagram) the structures of a nephron (including associated blood vessels) and give the functions of each structure.

9 Trace a drop of filtrate from Bowman's capsule to its release from the body as urine.

10 Describe the hormonal regulation of fluid and electrolyte balance by antidiuretic hormone (ADH), the renin–angiotensin–aldosterone system, and atrial natriuretic peptide (ANP).

The mammalian **urinary system** consists of the kidneys, the urinary bladder, and associated ducts. The overall structure of the human urinary system is shown in **FIGURE 48-7**. Located just below the diaphragm in the "small of the back," the kidneys look like a pair of giant, dark red lima beans, each about the size of a fist. Each kidney is covered by a connective tissue capsule (**FIG. 48-8**). The outer portion of the kidney is the **renal cortex;** the inner portion is the **renal medulla.** The renal medulla contains eight to ten cone-shaped structures called **renal pyramids.** The tip of each pyramid is a **renal papilla.** Each papilla has several pores, the openings of **collecting ducts.**

As urine is produced, it flows from collecting ducts through a renal papilla and into the **renal pelvis,** a funnel-shaped chamber. Urine then flows into one of the paired **ureters,** ducts that connect each kidney with the **urinary bladder.** The urinary bladder is a remarkable organ capable of holding (with practice) up to 800 mL (about a pint and a half) of urine. Emptying the bladder changes it from the size of a small melon to that of a pecan. This feat is made possible by the smooth muscle and specialized epithelium of the bladder wall, which is capable of great shrinkage and stretching.

During **urination,** urine is released from the bladder and flows through the **urethra,** a duct leading to the outside of the body. In the male, the urethra is lengthy and passes through the penis. Semen, as well as urine, passes through the male urethra. In the female, the urethra is short and transports only urine. Its opening to the outside is just above the opening of the vagina. The length of the male urethra discourages bacterial invasions of the bladder. This length difference helps explain why bladder infections are more common in females than in males. In summary, urine flows through the following structures:

kidney (through renal pelvis) ⟶ ureter ⟶ urinary bladder ⟶ urethra

FIGURE 48-7 *Animated*
The human urinary system ▶
The kidneys produce urine, which passes through the ureters to the urinary bladder for temporary storage. During urination, the urethra conducts urine from the bladder to the outside of the body through an opening, the external urethral orifice.

Adrenal gland

Left renal artery

Right kidney

Right renal vein

Left kidney

Inferior vena cava

Abdominal aorta

Ureteral orifices

Right and left ureters

Urinary bladder

Urethra

External urethral orifice

Renal pyramids (medulla)

Capsule
Renal cortex
Renal medulla

Renal artery

Renal vein

Renal pelvis

Ureter

(a) Internal structure of the kidney. The outer region of the kidney is the cortex; the inner region is the medulla. As urine is produced, it flows into the renal pelvis and leaves the kidney through the ureter.

FIGURE 48-8 *Animated* **Structure of the kidney**

Juxtamedullary nephron   Distal convoluted tubule   **Cortical nephron**

Capsule

Proximal convoluted tubule

Renal cortex

Glomerulus

Bowman's capsule

Artery and vein

Loop of Henle

Renal medulla

Collecting duct

Papilla

(b) Juxtamedullary and cortical nephrons. Longitudinal section showing the location and structure of the two main types of nephrons.

The nephron is the functional unit of the kidney

The principal function of the kidneys is to help maintain homeostasis by regulating fluid balance and excreting metabolic wastes. However, the kidneys have other functions as well. They produce the enzyme *renin*, which helps regulate fluid balance and blood pressure (discussed later in the chapter). They also produce at least two hormones: *erythropoietin*, which stimulates red blood cell production, and *1,25-dihydroxy-vitamin D_3*, which stimulates calcium absorption by the intestine.

Each kidney has up to one million functional units called **nephrons.** A nephron consists of a cuplike **Bowman's capsule** connected to a long, partially coiled **renal tubule** (**FIG. 48-9**). Positioned within Bowman's capsule is a cluster of capillaries called a **glomerulus.** Three main regions of the renal tubule are (1) the **proximal convoluted tubule** (or simply, *proximal tubule*), which conducts the *filtrate* (the fluid filtered from the blood) from Bowman's capsule; (2) the **loop of Henle,** an elongated, hairpin-shaped portion; and (3) the **distal convoluted tubule** (or *distal tubule*), which conducts the filtrate to a collecting duct. Thus, filtrate passes through the following structures:

Bowman's capsule ⟶ proximal convoluted tubule ⟶ loop of Henle ⟶ distal convoluted tubule ⟶ collecting duct

The human kidney has two types of nephrons: the more numerous (85%) cortical nephrons and the more internal juxtamedullary nephrons (see Fig. 48-8b). **Cortical nephrons** have

(a) Location and the basic structure of a nephron. Urine forms by filtration of the blood in the glomerulus and by adjustment of the filtrate as it passes through the series of tubules that drain Bowman's capsule.

(b) Cutaway view of Bowman's capsule. Note that the distal tubule is adjacent to the afferent and efferent arterioles. The juxtaglomerular apparatus (discussed later in the chapter) is a small group of cells located in the walls of the tubule and arterioles.

Steve Gschmeissner/Photo Researchers, Inc.

100 μm

(c) Low-power SEM of a portion of the kidney cortex. The tissue was treated to remove some structures and to show glomeruli and associated blood vessels.

FIGURE 48-9 Nephron structure

relatively small glomeruli and are located almost entirely within the cortex or outer medulla. **Juxtamedullary nephrons** have large glomeruli, and their very long loops of Henle extend deep into the medulla. The loop of Henle consists of a *descending limb* that receives filtrate from the proximal convoluted tubule and an *ascending limb,* through which the filtrate passes on its way to the distal convoluted tubule. The juxtamedullary nephrons contribute to the ability of the mammalian kidney to concentrate urine. Excretion of urine that is hypertonic to body fluids is an important mechanism for conserving water.

Blood is delivered to the kidney by the **renal artery.** Small branches of the renal artery give rise to **afferent arterioles** (*afferent* means "to carry toward"). An afferent arteriole conducts blood into the capillaries that make up each glomerulus. As blood flows through the glomerulus, some of the plasma is forced into Bowman's capsule.

You may recall that in a typical circulatory route, capillaries deliver blood into veins. Circulation in the kidneys is an exception because blood flowing from the glomerular capillaries next passes into an **efferent arteriole.** Each efferent arteriole conducts blood *away* from a glomerulus. The efferent arteriole delivers blood to a second capillary network, the **peritubular capillaries** surrounding the renal tubule.

Blood is filtered as it flows through the first set of capillaries, those of the glomerulus. The peritubular capillaries receive materials returned to the blood by the renal tubule. Blood from the peritubular capillaries enters small veins that eventually lead to the **renal vein.** In summary, blood circulates through the kidney in the following sequence:

renal artery ⟶ an afferent arteriole ⟶ capillaries of a
glomerulus ⟶ an efferent arteriole ⟶ peritubular capillaries
⟶ small veins ⟶ renal vein

Urine is produced by filtration, reabsorption, and secretion

Urine, the watery discharge of the urinary system, is produced by a combination of three processes: filtration, reabsorption, and tubular secretion (**FIG. 48-10**).

Filtration is not selective with regard to ions and small molecules

Blood flows through the glomerular capillaries under high pressure, forcing more than 10% of the plasma out of the capillaries and into Bowman's capsule. **Filtration** is similar to the mechanism whereby interstitial fluid is formed as blood flows through other capillary networks in the body. However, blood flow through

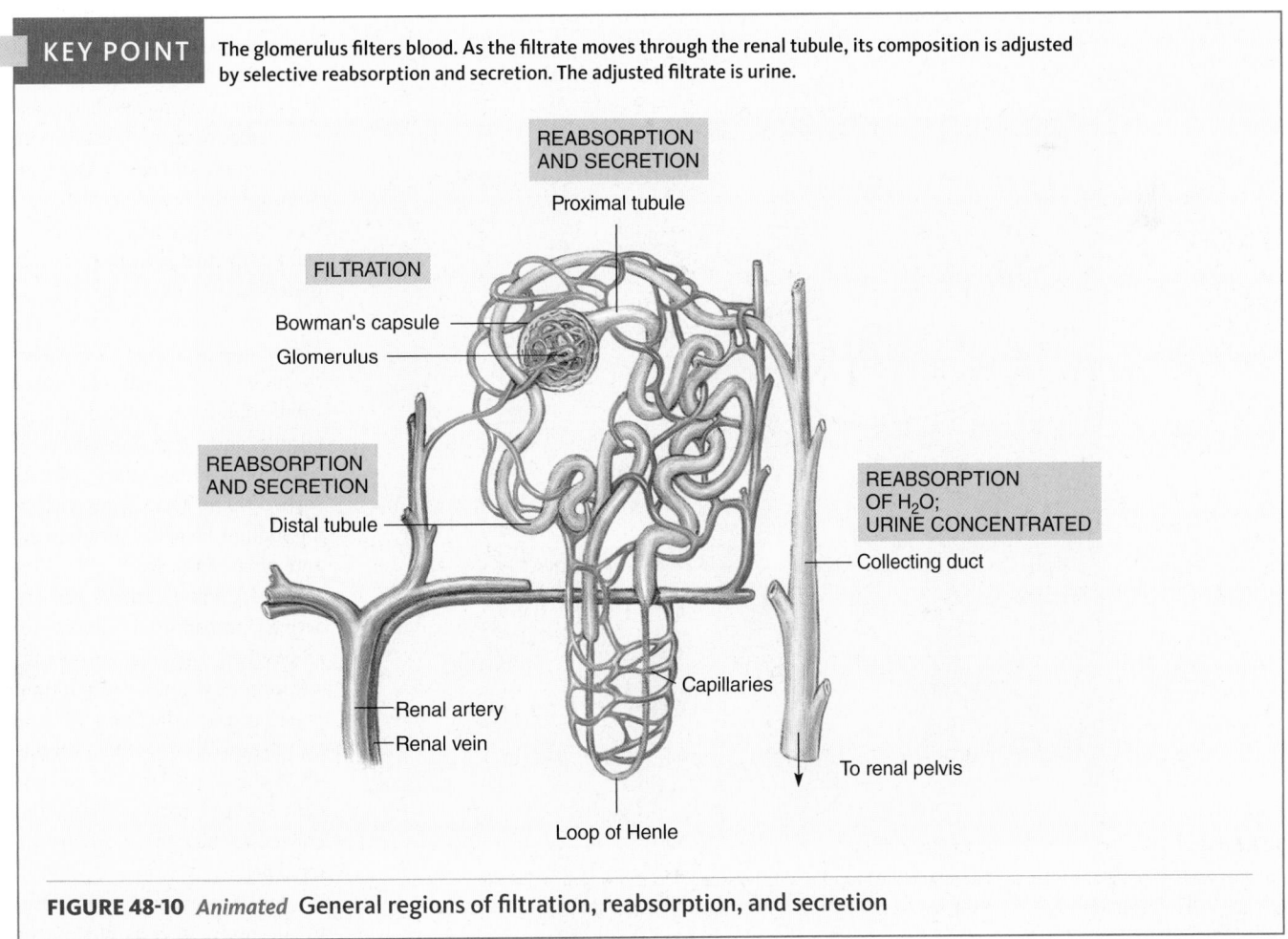

KEY POINT The glomerulus filters blood. As the filtrate moves through the renal tubule, its composition is adjusted by selective reabsorption and secretion. The adjusted filtrate is urine.

REABSORPTION AND SECRETION
Proximal tubule

FILTRATION
Bowman's capsule
Glomerulus

REABSORPTION AND SECRETION
Distal tubule

REABSORPTION OF H_2O; URINE CONCENTRATED
Collecting duct

Capillaries

Renal artery
Renal vein

To renal pelvis

Loop of Henle

FIGURE 48-10 *Animated* General regions of filtration, reabsorption, and secretion glomerular capillaries is at much higher pressure, so more plasma is filtered in the kidney.

Several factors contribute to filtration. First, the hydrostatic blood pressure in the glomerular capillaries is higher than in other capillaries. This high pressure is mainly due to the high resistance to outflow presented by the efferent arteriole, which is smaller in diameter than the afferent arteriole (see Fig. 48-9b). A second factor contributing to the large amount of **glomerular filtrate** is the large surface area for filtration provided by the highly coiled glomerular capillaries. A third factor is the great permeability of the glomerular capillaries. Numerous small pores between the endothelial cells that form their walls make the glomerular capillaries more porous than typical capillaries.

The wall of Bowman's capsule in contact with the capillaries consists of specialized epithelial cells called **podocytes.** These cells have numerous cytoplasmic extensions called *foot processes* that cover most of the surfaces of the glomerular capillaries (**FIG. 48-11**). Foot processes of adjacent podocytes are separated by narrow gaps called **filtration slits.** The porous walls of the glomerular capillaries and the filtration slits of the podocytes form a **filtration membrane** that permits fluid and small solutes dissolved in the plasma (including glucose, amino acids, sodium, potassium, chloride, bicarbonate, other salts, and urea) to pass through and become part of the

filtrate. This filtration membrane holds back blood cells, platelets, and most of the plasma proteins.

The total volume of blood passing through the kidneys is about 1200 mL per minute, or about one-fourth of the entire cardiac output. As plasma passes through the glomerulus, it loses more than 10% of its volume to the glomerular filtrate. The normal glomerular filtration rate amounts to about 180 L (about 45 gallons) each 24 hours. This is 4.5 times the amount of fluid in the entire body! Common sense tells us that urine could not be excreted at that rate. Within a few moments, dehydration would become life-threatening.

Reabsorption is highly selective

The threat to homeostasis posed by the vast amounts of fluid filtered by the kidneys is avoided by **reabsorption.** The renal tubules reabsorb about 99% of the filtrate into the blood, leaving only about 1.5 L to be excreted as urine during a 24-hour period. Reabsorption permits precise regulation of blood chemistry by the kidneys. Wastes, excess salts, and other materials remain in the filtrate and are excreted in the urine, while needed substances such as glucose and amino acids are returned to the blood. Each day the tubules reabsorb more than 178 L of water, 1200 g (2.6 lb) of salt, and about 250 g (0.5 lb) of glucose. Most of this, of course, is reabsorbed many times over.

The simple epithelial cells lining the renal tubule are well adapted for reabsorbing materials. Their abundant microvilli increase the surface area for reabsorption. These epithelial cells contain numerous mitochondria that provide the energy for running the cell pumps that actively transport materials.

Most (about 65%) of the filtrate is reabsorbed as it passes through the proximal convoluted tubule. Glucose, amino acids, vitamins, and other substances of nutritional value are entirely reabsorbed there. Many ions, including sodium, chloride, bicarbonate, and potassium, are partially reabsorbed. Some of these ions are actively transported; others are reabsorbed by diffusion. Reabsorption continues as the filtrate passes through the loop of Henle and the distal convoluted tubule. Then the filtrate is further concentrated as it passes through the collecting duct that leads to the renal pelvis.

Substances that are useful to the body, such as glucose or

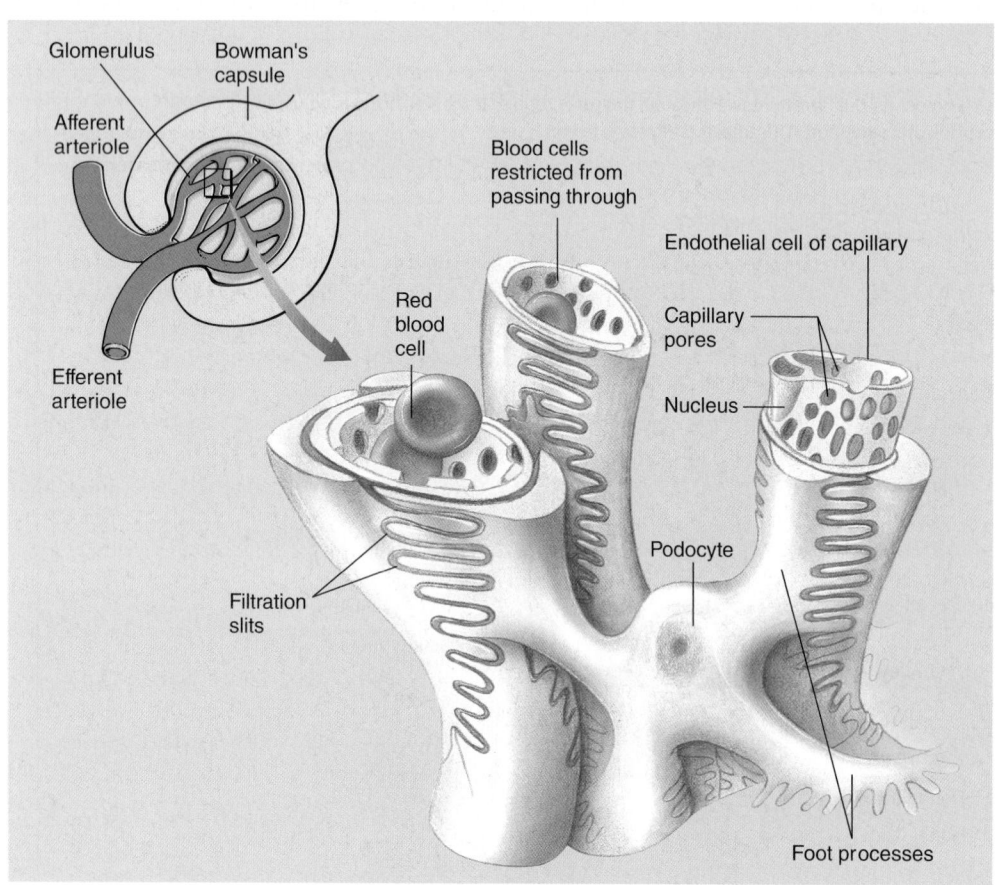

FIGURE 48-11 Filtration membrane of the kidney
The porous walls of the glomerular capillaries and the filtration slits between podocytes form a filtration membrane that is highly permeable to water and small molecules but restricts the passage of blood cells and large molecules.

amino acids, are normally reabsorbed from the renal tubules. If the concentration of a particular substance in the blood is high, however, the tubules may not be able to reabsorb it all. The maximum rate at which a substance can be reabsorbed is its **tubular transport maximum (Tm).** When that rate is reached, the binding sites are saturated on the membrane proteins that transport the substance. For example, the tubular load of glucose is about 125 mg per minute, and almost all of it is normally reabsorbed. However, in a person with uncontrolled diabetes mellitus, the concentration of glucose in the blood exceeds its Tm (glucose concentration in excess of 320 mg per minute). The excess glucose cannot be reabsorbed and is excreted in the urine (glucosuria), a symptom of diabetes (discussed in Chapter 49).

Some substances are actively secreted from the blood into the filtrate

Tubular **secretion** is the selective transfer of substances from the blood in the peritubular capillaries into the renal tubule. Note that in tubular secretion ions and other substances are moved across the tubule epithelium in the opposite direction of reabsorption. Potassium, hydrogen ions, and ammonium ions, as well as some organic ions such as creatinine (a metabolic waste), are secreted into the filtrate. Certain drugs, such as penicillin, are also removed from the blood by secretion. Secretion occurs mainly in the region of the distal convoluted tubule.

Secretion of hydrogen ions by the collecting ducts is an important homeostatic mechanism for regulating the pH of the blood. Carbon dioxide, which diffuses from the blood into the cells of the distal tubules and collecting ducts, combines with water, which produces carbonic acid. This acid then dissociates to form hydrogen ions and bicarbonate ions. When the blood becomes too acidic, the collecting ducts secrete more hydrogen ions into the urine:

$$CO_2 + H_2O \rightleftharpoons H_2CO_3 \rightleftharpoons H^+ + HCO_3^-$$

Potassium ion secretion is another important homeostatic mechanism. When K^+ concentration is too high, nerve impulses are not effectively transmitted, and the strength of muscle contraction decreases. The heart rhythm becomes irregular, and cardiac arrest can occur. When K^+ concentration exceeds its homeostatic level, K^+ are secreted from the blood into the renal tubules and then excreted in the urine. Secretion results partly from a direct effect of the K^+ on the tubules. In addition, the adrenal cortex (a region of the adrenal gland) increases its output of the hormone aldosterone, which further stimulates secretion of K^+.

Urine becomes concentrated as it passes through the renal tubule

We can survive with limited fluid intake because the kidneys can produce highly concentrated urine—more than four times as concentrated as blood. The osmolarity of human blood is about 300 milliosmoles per liter (mOsm/L). The kidneys can produce urine with an osmolarity of about 1200 mOsm/L.

As the filtrate passes through various regions of the renal tubule, salt (NaCl) is reabsorbed into the interstitial fluid, and a salt concentration gradient is established (**FIGS. 48-12** and **48-13**). The gradient is used to produce concentrated urine.

When filtrate flows from Bowman's capsule to the proximal tubule, its osmolarity is the same as that of blood (about 300 mOsm/L). Water and salt are reabsorbed from the proximal tubule. Sodium ions are actively transported out of the proximal tubule, and chloride follows passively. As salt passes into the interstitial fluid, water follows osmotically.

The walls of the descending limb of the loop of Henle are relatively permeable to water but relatively impermeable to sodium and urea. The interstitial fluid has a high concentration of Na^+, so as the filtrate passes down the loop of Henle, water moves out by osmosis. This process concentrates the filtrate inside the loop of Henle.

The loop of Henle is specialized to highly concentrate sodium chloride in the interstitial fluid of the medulla. It maintains a highly hypertonic interstitial fluid in the medulla near the bottom of the loop, which in turn lets the kidneys produce concentrated urine. At the turn of the loop of Henle, the walls become more permeable to salt and less permeable to water. As the concentrated filtrate begins to move up the ascending limb (the thin region), salt diffuses out into the interstitial fluid. This contributes to the high salt concentration of the interstitial fluid in the medulla surrounding the loop of Henle. Farther along the ascending limb (the thick region), sodium is actively transported out of the tubule.

Because water passes out of the descending limb of the loop of Henle, the filtrate at the bottom of the loop has a high salt concentration. However, because salt (but not water) is removed in the ascending limb, by the time the filtrate moves into the distal tubule, its osmolarity may be the same as or even lower than that of blood.

As it passes through the distal tubule, the filtrate may become even more dilute. The distal tubule is relatively impermeable to water but actively transports salt out into the interstitial fluid. The filtrate passes from the renal tubule into a larger collecting duct that eventually empties into the renal pelvis.

Note the *counterflow* of fluid through the two limbs of the loop of Henle. Filtrate passing down through the descending limb is flowing in a direction opposite that of the filtrate moving upward through the ascending limb. The filtrate becomes concentrated as it moves down the descending limb and diluted as it moves up the ascending limb. This countercurrent mechanism helps maintain a high salt concentration in the interstitial fluid of the medulla. The hypertonic interstitial fluid draws water osmotically from the filtrate in the collecting ducts.

The inner medullary collecting ducts are permeable to urea, so some of the concentrated urea in the filtrate can diffuse out into the interstitial fluid. The urea contributes to the high solute concentration of the inner medulla. This process helps concentrate urine.

The collecting ducts pass through the zone of very salty interstitial fluid. As the filtrate moves through the collecting duct, water passes osmotically into the interstitial fluid. Excess interstitial fluid continuously enters capillaries and becomes part of the blood. Sufficient water can leave the collecting ducts to produce a highly concentrated urine. A hypertonic urine conserves water.

Some of the water that diffuses from the filtrate into the interstitial fluid is removed by the **vasa recta,** which are long,

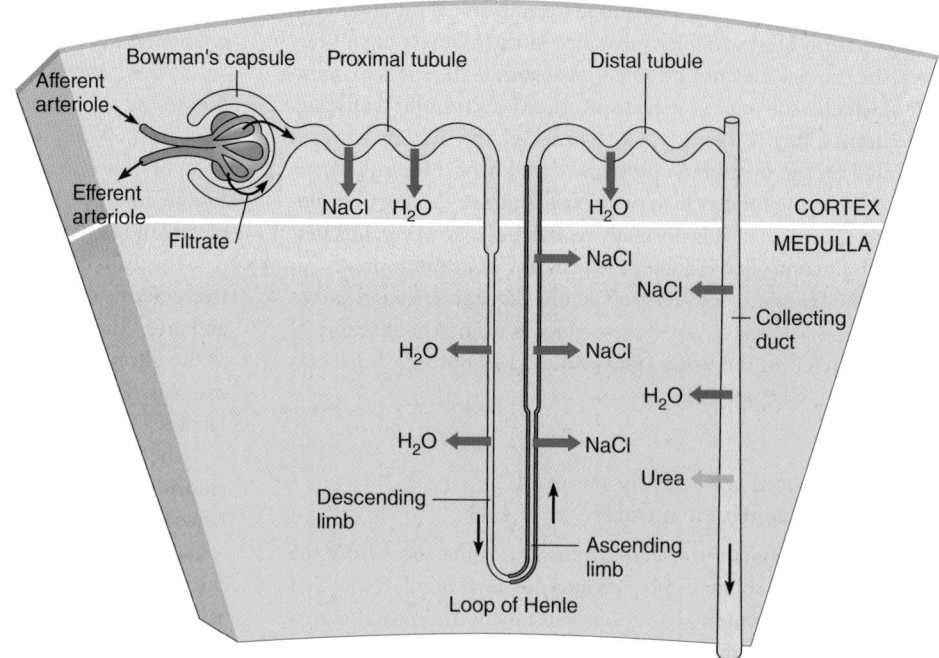

FIGURE 48-12 *Animated* Movement of water, ions, and urea through the renal tubule and collecting duct ▶

Water passes out of the descending limb of the loop of Henle, leaving a more concentrated filtrate inside. The heavy outline along the ascending limb indicates that this region is relatively impermeable to water. NaCl diffuses out from the lower (*thin*) part of the ascending limb. In the upper (*thick*) part of the ascending limb, NaCl is actively transported into the interstitial fluid. The saltier the interstitial fluid becomes, the more water moves out of the descending limb. This process leaves a concentrated filtrate inside, so more salt passes out. Note that this is a positive feedback system. Some urea also moves out into the interstitial fluid through the collecting ducts. Water from the collecting ducts moves out osmotically into this hypertonic interstitial fluid and is carried away by capillaries.

straight capillaries that extend from the efferent arterioles of the juxtamedullary nephrons. The vasa recta extend deep into the medulla, only to negotiate a hairpin curve and return to the cortical venous drainage of the kidney. These capillaries parallel the renal tubules.

Blood flows in opposite directions in the ascending and descending regions of the vasa recta, just as filtrate flows in opposite directions in the ascending and descending limbs of the loop of Henle. As a consequence of this countercurrent flow, much of the salt and urea that enter the blood through the descending region of the vasa recta leave again from the ascending region. As a result, the solute concentration of the blood leaving the vasa recta is only slightly higher than that of the blood entering. This mechanism helps maintain the high solute concentration of the interstitial fluid in the renal medulla.

Urine consists of water, nitrogenous wastes, and salts

By the time the filtrate reaches the renal pelvis, its composition has been precisely adjusted. The adjusted filtrate, called *urine,* consists of approximately 96% water, 2.5% nitrogenous wastes (mainly urea), 1.5% salts, and traces of other substances, such as bile pigments, that may contribute to the characteristic color and odor. Healthy urine is sterile and has been used to wash battlefield wounds when clean water was not available. However, when exposed to bacterial action, urine swiftly decomposes and forms ammonia and other products. Ammonia produces the diaper rash of infants.

The composition of urine yields many clues to body function and malfunction. **Urinalysis,** the physical, chemical, and microscopic examination of urine, is a very important diagnostic tool that has been used to monitor diabetes mellitus and many other disorders. Urinalysis is also extensively used in drug testing be-

cause breakdown products of some drugs can be identified in the urine for several days or weeks after the drugs are taken.

Hormones regulate kidney function

The kidneys maintain the body's fluid volume and electrolyte concentration. They help maintain the concentration of Na^+ and K^+ in the blood within narrow limits and also regulate blood pH. The endocrine system regulates these homeostatic functions of the kidneys. Hormones involved include antidiuretic hormone (ADH), aldosterone, angiotensin II, and atrial natriuretic peptide (ANP) (**TABLE 48-1**).

ADH increases water reabsorption

The amount of urine produced depends on the body's need to retain or rid itself of water. When fluid intake is low, the body begins to dehydrate, and the blood volume decreases. As blood volume decreases, the concentration of salts dissolved in the blood becomes greater, causing an increase in osmotic pressure. Certain receptors in the hypothalamus are sensitive to this osmotic change. They signal the posterior lobe of the pituitary gland to release **antidiuretic hormone (ADH).** This hormone is actually produced in the hypothalamus but is stored in the posterior pituitary and released as needed. A thirst center in the hypothalamus also responds to dehydration, stimulating an increase in fluid intake.

ADH makes the collecting ducts more permeable to water so that more water is reabsorbed. As a result, a small volume of concentrated urine is produced (**FIG. 48-14**). ADH acts on aquaporin-2, a membrane protein that forms gated water channels in the wall of the collecting ducts (see Chapter 5). These channels allow water to pass rapidly through the plasma membrane.

When you drink a large volume of water, your blood becomes diluted and its osmotic pressure falls. Release of ADH by the pi-

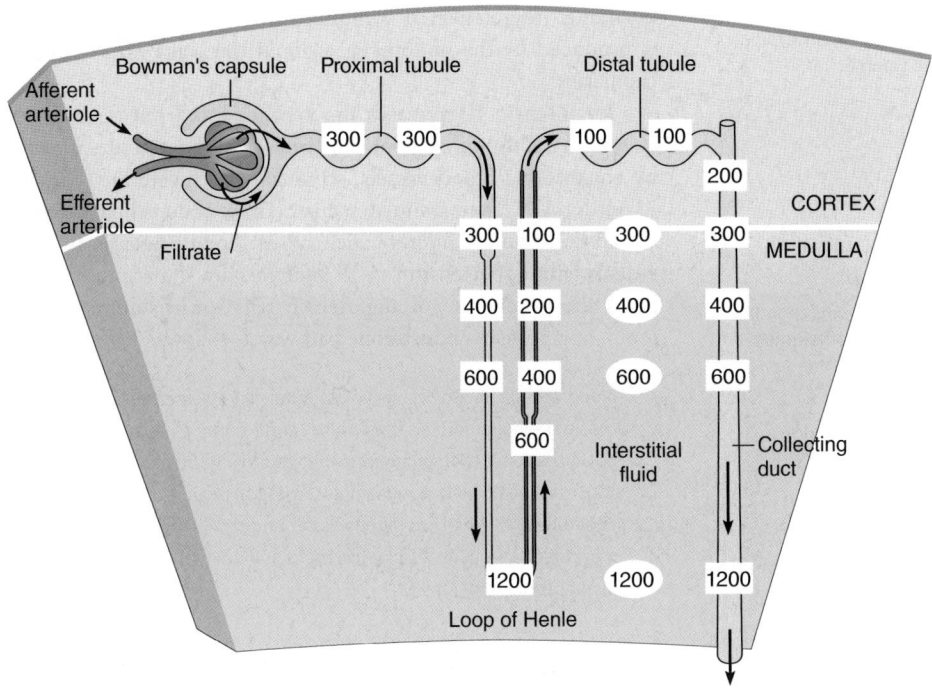

Bowman's capsule Proximal tubule   Distal tubule

Afferent arteriole

Efferent arteriole

Filtrate

300 300   100 100
                    200
                         CORTEX
300 100   300   300   MEDULLA

400 200   400   400

600 400   600   600

600   Interstitial fluid   Collecting duct

1200   1200   1200

Loop of Henle

◀ **FIGURE 48-13 Concentration of the filtrate as it moves through the nephron**

This figure shows the relative concentration of ions, mainly Na^+ and Cl^-, during formation of a very concentrated urine. Numbers indicate the concentration of salt in the filtrate and interstitial fluid expressed in milliosmoles per liter. The more hypertonic a solution is, the higher its osmotic pressure. The very hypertonic interstitial fluid near the renal pelvis draws water osmotically from the filtrate in the collecting ducts. The heavy outline along the ascending loop indicates that this region is relatively impermeable to water.

tuitary gland decreases, lessening the amount of water reabsorbed from the collecting ducts. The kidneys produce a large volume of dilute urine.

In the disorder *diabetes insipidus* (not to be confused with the more common disorder, diabetes mellitus) the pituitary gland malfunctions and does not release enough ADH. Diabetes insipidus can also develop from an acquired insensitivity of the kidney to ADH. In diabetes insipidus, water is not efficiently reabsorbed from the ducts, so the body produces a large volume of urine. A person with severe diabetes insipidus may excrete up to 25 quarts of urine each day, a serious water loss. The affected individual becomes dehydrated and must drink almost continually to offset fluid loss. A synthetic hormone (desmopressin) is used to treat diabetes insipidus.

The renin–angiotensin–aldosterone pathway increases sodium reabsorption

Sodium is the most abundant extracellular ion, accounting for about 90% of all positive ions in the extracellular fluid. Several hormones work together to regulate sodium concentration. **Aldosterone,** which is secreted by the cortex of the adrenal glands, stimulates the distal tubules and collecting ducts to increase sodium reabsorption. When researchers remove the adrenal glands

TABLE 48-1 Endocrine Regulation of Kidney Function

Hormone	Source	Target Tissue	Actions	Factors That Stimulate Release
Antidiuretic hormone (ADH)	Produced in hypothalamus; released by posterior pituitary gland	Collecting ducts	Increases permeability of collecting ducts to water, which increases reabsorption and decreases water excretion	Low fluid intake decreases blood volume and increases osmotic pressure of blood; receptors in hypothalamus stimulate posterior pituitary
Aldosterone	Adrenal glands (cortex)	Distal tubules and collecting ducts	Increases sodium reabsorption, which raises blood pressure	Angiotensin II; decrease in blood pressure
Angiotensin II	Produced from angiotensin I	Blood vessels and adrenal glands	Constricts blood vessels, which raises blood pressure; stimulates aldosterone secretion; stimulates thirst	Decrease in blood pressure causes renin secretion; renin catalyzes conversion of angiotensinogen to angiotensin I, which is then converted to angiotensin II by ACE
Atrial natriuretic peptide (ANP)	Atrium of heart	Afferent arterioles; collecting ducts	Dilates afferent arterioles; inhibits sodium reabsorption by collecting ducts; inhibits aldosterone secretion; decreases blood pressure	Stretching of atria due to increased blood volume

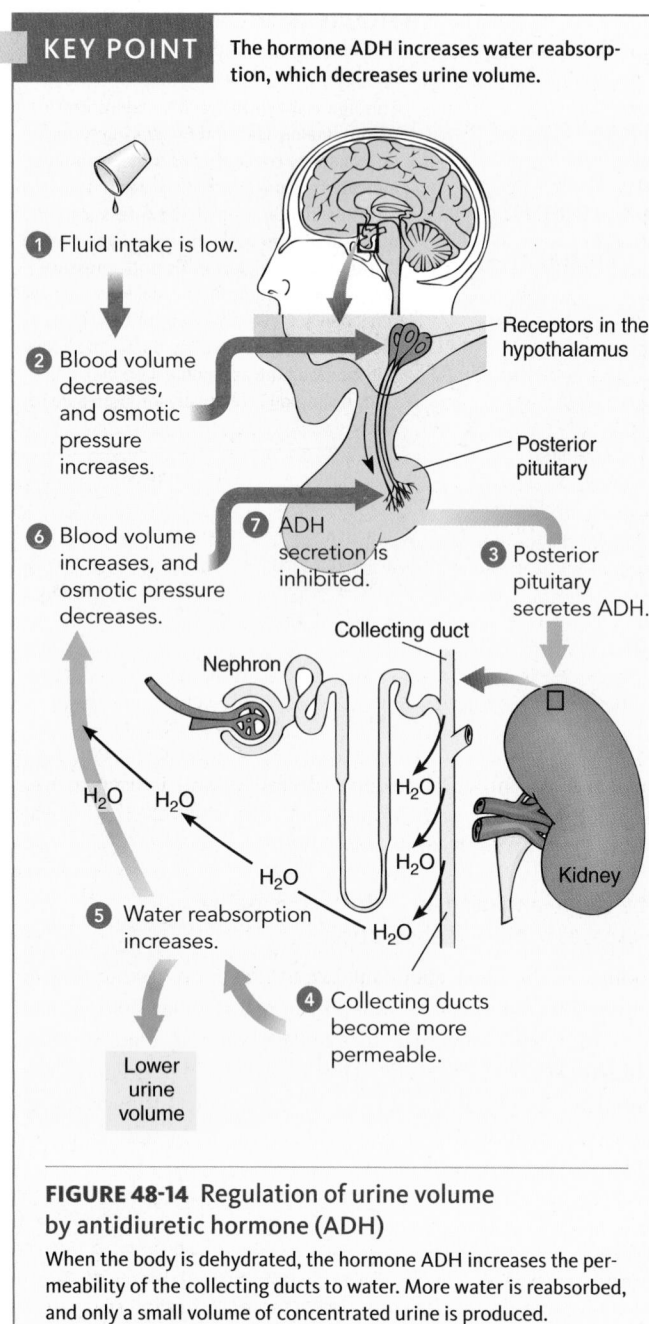

1 Fluid intake is low.

2 Blood volume decreases, and osmotic pressure increases.

Receptors in the hypothalamus

Posterior pituitary

6 Blood volume increases, and osmotic pressure decreases.

7 ADH secretion is inhibited.

3 Posterior pituitary secretes ADH.

Collecting duct

Nephron

H_2O H_2O H_2O

H_2O

H_2O

H_2O

Kidney

5 Water reabsorption increases.

4 Collecting ducts become more permeable.

Lower urine volume

FIGURE 48-14 Regulation of urine volume by antidiuretic hormone (ADH)

When the body is dehydrated, the hormone ADH increases the permeability of the collecting ducts to water. More water is reabsorbed, and only a small volume of concentrated urine is produced.

hormone. Angiotensin II stimulates aldosterone secretion. ACE is produced by the endothelial cells in the walls of pulmonary capillaries.

Angiotensin II increases the synthesis and release of aldosterone. In addition, angiotensin II raises blood pressure directly by constricting blood vessels, stimulates the posterior pituitary to release ADH, and stimulates thirst. These actions help increase extracellular fluid volume, which raises blood pressure. In individuals with hypertension, *ACE inhibitors* are sometimes used to block the production of angiotensin II. We can summarize the renin–angiotensin–aldosterone pathway as follows:

blood volume decreases ⟶ blood pressure decreases ⟶ cells of juxtaglomerular apparatus secrete renin ⟶ renin catalyzes conversion of angiotensinogen to angiotensin I ⟶ ACE catalyzes conversion of angiotensin I to angiotensin II ⟶ angiotensin II constricts blood vessels and stimulates aldosterone secretion ⟶ aldosterone increases sodium reabsorption ⟶ blood pressure increases

Atrial natriuretic peptide inhibits sodium reabsorption

Atrial natriuretic peptide (ANP), a hormone produced by the heart, increases sodium excretion and decreases blood pressure. ANP is stored in granules in atrial muscle cells. When Na^+ concentration increases, fluid is retained, and blood volume increases. Atrial muscle cells are stretched and respond by releasing ANP into the circulation.

ANP dilates afferent arterioles, thereby increasing the glomerular filtration rate. This hormone inhibits sodium reabsorption by the collecting ducts directly and also indirectly by inhibiting aldosterone secretion. ANP also reduces plasma aldosterone concentration by inhibiting renin release. These actions of ANP increase sodium excretion and urine output, which lowers blood volume and blood pressure. Note that the renin–angiotensin–aldosterone pathway and ANP work antagonistically in regulating fluid balance, electrolyte balance, and blood pressure.

blood volume increases ⟶ blood pressure increases ⟶ atria of heart stretched ⟶ atria release ANP ⟶ directly inhibits sodium reabsorption and inhibits aldosterone secretion (which also inhibits sodium reabsorption) ⟶ larger urine volume ⟶ blood volume decreases ⟶ blood pressure decreases

of experimental animals, too much sodium is excreted, leading to serious depletion of the extracellular fluid.

Aldosterone secretion is stimulated both by hormones and by a decrease in blood pressure (caused by a decrease in volume of blood and interstitial fluid). When blood pressure falls, cells of the **juxtaglomerular apparatus** secrete the enzyme **renin,** which activates the **renin–angiotensin–aldosterone pathway.** The juxtaglomerular apparatus is a small group of cells in the region where the renal tubule contacts the afferent and efferent arterioles (see Fig. 48-9b). Renin converts the plasma protein angiotensinogen to angiotensin I. *Angiotensin-converting enzyme (ACE)* converts angiotensin I into its active form, **angiotensin II,** which is a peptide

Review

- Which structure(s) is/are associated with each of the following processes: (1) urea formation; (2) urine formation; (3) temporary storage of urine; (4) conduction of urine out of the body?
- Which part(s) of the nephron is/are associated with the following processes: (1) filtration; (2) reabsorption; (3) secretion?
- Through what sequence of structures does a drop of filtrate pass as it moves from Bowman's capsule to the urinary bladder?
- Through what sequence of blood vessels does a drop of blood pass as it is conducted to and from a nephron?
- How does the kidney regulate the composition of the blood?
- What are the actions of the renin–angiotensin–aldosterone pathway?

48.1 *(page 1035)*

1 Describe how the processes of *osmoregulation* and *excretion* contribute to fluid and electrolyte homeostasis.

  ▪ **Osmoregulation** is the active regulation of osmotic pressure of body fluids so that fluid and electrolyte homeostasis is maintained. **Excretion** is the process of ridding the body of metabolic wastes.

48.2 *(page 1035)*

2 Contrast the benefits and costs of excreting ammonia, uric acid, or urea.

  ▪ The principal waste products of animal metabolism are water; carbon dioxide; and **nitrogenous wastes,** including ammonia, uric acid, and urea. **Ammonia** is toxic and is excreted mainly by aquatic animals.

  ▪ **Uric acid** and **urea** are far less toxic than ammonia, but their synthesis requires energy. Uric acid can be excreted as a semisolid paste, a water-conserving adaptation. Urea excretion requires water.

48.3 *(page 1036)*

3 Compare osmoconformers and osmoregulators.

  ▪ Most marine invertebrates are **osmoconformers**—the salt concentration of their body fluids varies with changes in the sea water. Some marine invertebrates, especially those inhabiting coastal habitats, are **osmoregulators** that maintain an optimal salt concentration despite changes in salinity of their surroundings.

4 Describe protonephridia, metanephridia, and Malpighian tubules, and compare their functions.

  ▪ **Nephridial organs** help maintain homeostasis by regulating the concentration of body fluids through osmoregulation and excretion of metabolic wastes. **Protonephridia,** nephridial organs found in flatworms and nemerteans, are tubules with no internal openings. Interstitial fluid enters their blind ends, which consist of **flame cells,** cells with brushes of cilia. The cilia propel fluid through the tubules; excess fluid exits through nephridiopores.

  ▪ Most annelids and mollusks have nephridial organs called **metanephridia,** which are tubules open at both ends. As fluid from the coelom moves through the tubule, needed materials are reabsorbed by capillaries. Urine, containing wastes, exits the body through nephridiopores.

  ▪ **Malpighian tubules,** extensions of the insect gut wall, have blind ends that lie in the hemocoel. Cells of the tubule actively transport uric acid and some other substances from the hemolymph into the tubule, and water follows by diffusion. The contents of the tubule pass into the gut. Water and some solutes are reabsorbed in the rectum. Malpighian tubules effectively conserve water and have contributed to the success of insects as terrestrial animals.

48.4 *(page 1038)*

5 Relate the function of the vertebrate kidney to the success of vertebrates in a wide variety of habitats.

  ▪ The vertebrate **kidney** excretes nitrogenous wastes and helps maintain fluid balance by adjusting the salt and water content of the urine. Freshwater, marine, and terrestrial habitats present different problems for maintaining internal fluid balance and for the excretion of nitrogenous wastes. The structure and function of the vertebrate kidney have adapted to meet the various osmotic challenges presented by these different habitats.

6 Compare adaptations for osmoregulation in freshwater fishes, marine bony fishes, sharks, marine mammals, and terrestrial vertebrates.

  ▪ Freshwater fishes take in water osmotically; they excrete a large volume of hypotonic urine.

  ▪ Marine bony fishes lose water osmotically. They compensate by drinking sea water and excreting salt through their gills; they produce only a small volume of isotonic urine. Sharks and other marine cartilaginous fishes retain large amounts of urea, allowing them to take in water osmotically through the gills. They excrete a large volume of hypotonic urine. Marine mammals ingest sea water with their food. They produce concentrated urine.

  ▪ Terrestrial vertebrates must conserve water. Endotherms have a high metabolic rate and produce a large volume of nitrogenous wastes. They have numerous adaptations for conserving water, including efficient kidneys.

48.5 *(page 1040)*

7 Describe (or label on a diagram) the organs of the mammalian urinary system and give the functions of each.

  ▪ The **urinary system** is the principal excretory system in humans and other mammals. In mammals, the kidneys produce urine, which passes through the **ureters** to the **urinary bladder** for storage. During urination, the urine is released from the body through the **urethra.**

  ▪ The outer portion of each kidney is the **renal cortex;** the inner portion is the **renal medulla.** The renal medulla contains eight to ten **renal pyramids.** The tip of each pyramid is a **renal papilla.** As urine is produced, it flows into **collecting ducts,** which empty through a renal papilla into a funnel-shaped chamber, the **renal pelvis.** Each kidney has more than one million functional units called **nephrons.**

CENGAGENOW™ Explore the human urinary system and kidney structure by clicking on the figures in CengageNOW.

8 Describe (or label on a diagram) the structures of a nephron (including associated blood vessels) and give the functions of each structure.

  ▪ Each nephron consists of a cluster of capillaries called a **glomerulus,** which is surrounded by a **Bowman's capsule** that opens into a long, coiled **renal tubule.** The renal tubule consists of a **proximal convoluted tubule, loop of Henle,** and **distal convoluted tubule.**

  ▪ **Cortical nephrons,** located almost entirely within the cortex or outer medulla, have small glomeruli. **Juxtamedullary nephrons** have large glomeruli and long loops of Henle that extend deep into the medulla. These nephrons are important in concentrating urine.

  ▪ Blood flows from small branches of the **renal artery** to **afferent arterioles** and then to glomerular capillaries. Blood then flows into an **efferent arteriole** that delivers blood into a second set of capillaries, the **peritubular capillaries** that surround the renal tubule. Blood leaves the kidney through the **renal vein.**

9 Trace a drop of filtrate from Bowman's capsule to its release from the body as urine.

  ▪ Urine is produced by **filtration** of plasma, **reabsorption** of needed materials, and **secretion** of a few substances, such as potassium and hydrogen ions, into the renal tubule.

- Plasma filters through the glomerular capillaries and into Bowman's capsule. The permeable walls of the capillaries and **filtration slits** between **podocytes,** specialized epithelial cells that make up the inner wall of Bowman's capsule, serve as a **filtration membrane.** Filtration is nonselective with regard to small molecules; glucose and other needed materials, as well as metabolic wastes, become part of the filtrate.

- About 99% of the filtrate is reabsorbed from the renal tubules into the blood. Reabsorption is a highly selective process that returns usable materials to the blood but leaves wastes and excesses of other substances to be excreted in the urine. The maximum rate at which a substance can be reabsorbed is its **tubular transport maximum (Tm).**

- In secretion, hydrogen ions, certain other ions, and some drugs are actively transported into the renal tubule to become part of the urine.

- Production of concentrated urine depends on a high salt and urea concentration in the interstitial fluid of the kidney medulla. The interstitial fluid in the medulla has a concentration gradient in which the salt is most concentrated around the bottom of the loop of Henle. This gradient is maintained, in part, by salt reabsorption from various parts of the renal tubule. A counterflow of fluid through the two limbs of the loop of Henle concentrates filtrate as it moves down the descending loop and dilutes it as it moves up the ascending loop.

- Water is drawn by osmosis from the filtrate as it passes through the collecting ducts. This process concentrates urine in the collecting ducts.

- Some of the water that diffuses from the filtrate into the interstitial fluid is removed by the **vasa recta,** a system of capillaries that extend from the efferent arterioles.

- **Urine** is a watery solution of nitrogenous wastes, excess salts, and other substances not needed by the body.

CENGAGENOW™ Watch renal processes in action by clicking on the figures in CengageNOW.

10 Describe the hormonal regulation of fluid and electrolyte balance by antidiuretic hormone (ADH), the renin–angiotensin–aldosterone system, and atrial natriuretic peptide (ANP).

- When the body needs to conserve water, the posterior pituitary gland increases its release of **antidiuretic hormone (ADH).** The pituitary gland responds to an increase in osmotic concentration of the blood (caused by dehydration). ADH increases the permeability of the collecting ducts to water. As a result, more water is reabsorbed and only a small volume of urine is produced.

- The renin–angiotensin–aldosterone pathway and atrial natriuretic peptide work antagonistically. When blood pressure decreases, cells of the **juxtaglomerular apparatus** secrete the enzyme **renin,** which activates a pathway leading to production of **angiotensin II.** This hormone stimulates aldosterone release. **Aldosterone** increases sodium reabsorption, and angiotensin II constricts arterioles; both actions raise blood pressure.

- When blood pressure increases, **atrial natriuretic peptide (ANP)** increases sodium excretion and inhibits aldosterone secretion. These actions increase urine output and lower blood pressure.

TEST YOUR UNDERSTANDING

1. The process that maintains homeostasis of body fluids by keeping them from becoming too dilute or too concentrated is (a) excretion (b) elimination (c) osmoregulation (d) glomerular filtration (e) tubular secretion

2. Which of the following is *not* a correct pair? (a) protonephridia; flatworm (b) metanephridia; annelid (c) flame cell; flatworm (d) Malpighian tubule; mollusk (e) kidney; vertebrate

3. To compensate for fluid loss, many marine bony fishes (a) accumulate urea (b) have glands that excrete glucose (c) eat a low-protein diet (d) excrete a large volume of hypertonic urine (e) drink sea water

4. Arrange the following structures into an accurate sequence through which urine passes.
   1. urethra 2. urinary bladder 3. kidney 4. ureter
   (a) 4, 3, 2, 1 (b) 3, 4, 2, 1 (c) 1, 2, 3, 4 (d) 4, 2, 1, 3 (e) 3, 1, 2, 4

5. Arrange the following structures into an accurate sequence through which filtrate passes.
   1. proximal convoluted tubule 2. loop of Henle 3. collecting duct
   4. distal convoluted tubule 5. Bowman's capsule
   (a) 5, 4, 3, 2, 1 (b) 3, 4, 2, 5, 1 (c) 1, 5, 2, 3, 4 (d) 5, 4, 2, 3, 1
   (e) 5, 1, 2, 4, 3

6. The afferent arteriole delivers blood to the (a) renal artery (b) efferent arteriole (c) renal vein (d) capillaries of the glomerulus (e) peritubular capillaries

7. Which of the following does *not* contribute to the process of filtration? (a) active transport by epithelial cells lining renal tubules (b) large surface area for filtration (c) permeability of glomerular capillaries (d) high hydrostatic blood pressure in glomerular capillaries (e) podocytes

8. Tubular transport maximum (Tm) is (a) the maximum concentration of a substance in the plasma that can be reabsorbed by the kidney (b) the most rapid rate at which urine can be transported through the ureter (c) the maximum rate at which a substance can be reabsorbed from the filtrate in the renal tubules (d) the maximum rate at which a substance can pass through the loop of Henle (e) the maximum rate at which a substance can be secreted into the filtrate

9. Which of the following does *not* contribute to the high salt concentration in the interstitial fluid in the medulla of the kidney? (a) active transport of sodium from the upper part of the ascending limb (b) diffusion of salt from the ascending limb of the loop

of Henle (c) reabsorption of salt from various regions of Bowman's capsule (d) counterflow of fluid through the two limbs of the loop of Henle (e) diffusion of urea out of the collecting duct

10. Which is *not* true of ADH? (a) released by posterior lobe of the pituitary gland (b) increases water reabsorption (c) secretion increases when osmotic pressure in body increases (d) increases urine volume (e) secretion decreases when you drink a lot of water

11. Aldosterone (a) is released by the posterior pituitary gland (b) decreases sodium reabsorption (c) secretion is stimulated by an increase in blood pressure (d) is an enzyme that converts angiotensin into angiotensin II (e) secretion increases in response to angiotensin II

12. Label the diagram. Use Figure 48-9a to check your answers.

CRITICAL THINKING

1. Why is glucose normally not present in urine? Why is it present in the urine of individuals with diabetes mellitus? Why do you suppose that people with diabetes mellitus experience an increased output of urine?

2. What types of osmoregulatory challenges do humans experience? Explain. What mechanisms do we have to meet these challenges?

3. **EVOLUTION LINK.** The number of protonephridia in a planarian is related to the salinity of its environment. Planaria inhabiting slightly salty water develop fewer protonephridia, but the number quickly increases when the concentration of salt in the environment is lower. How is this adaptive? Explain.

4. **EVOLUTION LINK.** The kangaroo rat's diet consists of dry seeds, and it drinks no water. What types of osmoregulatory adaptations might help this animal survive?

5. **EVOLUTION LINK.** Although the kidney is basically similar in all vertebrates, its structure and function vary somewhat among

vertebrate taxa. What are some of the adaptations that have occurred during the evolution of the vertebrate kidney?

6. **SCIENCE, TECHNOLOGY, AND SOCIETY.** A person with kidney disease lives 10 to 15 years longer with a kidney transplant than on continued dialysis. However, in the United States many individuals have difficulty being accepted by a transplant program because they do not have adequate insurance. The immunosuppressive drugs required after the surgery are very expensive, costing about $1500 per month. Should economic status be a deciding factor about whether a person lives or dies? or about quality of life?

 Additional questions are available in CengageNOW at www.cengage.com/login.

49 Endocrine Regulation

Endocrine regulation of color changes in a crustacean. Hormones regulate the distribution of pigment in the cells, resulting in color changes. This juvenile Puget Sound king crab (*Lopholithodes mandtii*) blends with its background by changing color.

Shark Song/M. Kazmers/Dembinsky Photo Associates

KEY CONCEPTS

49.1 Endocrine glands and tissues secrete hormones, chemical messengers that bind to specific receptors on (or in) target cells and regulate physiological processes. Endocrine regulation depends mainly on negative feedback systems, often involving concentrations of specific ions or chemical compounds.

49.2 Several types of endocrine signaling are known: in classical endocrine signaling, endocrine glands secrete hormones that are transported to target cells by the blood; in neuroendocrine signaling, neuroendocrine cells produce hormones that are transported down axons and released into interstitial fluid; in autocrine signaling, a hormone acts on the very cells that produce it; and in paracrine signaling, a hormone acts on nearby cells.

49.3 Receptors are responsible for the specificity of the endocrine system. Small, lipid-soluble hormones enter target cells, bind to receptors inside the cell, and then activate or repress specific genes; hydrophilic hormones bind to cell-surface receptors and initiate signal transduction, leading to changes in cell processes.

49.4 Many invertebrate hormones are neurohormones secreted by neuroendocrine cells. Invertebrate hormones regulate metabolism, growth, and development, including molting and metamorphosis.

49.5 In vertebrates, many organs and tissues secrete hormones that interact to regulate growth and development, metabolism, fluid balance, reproduction, response to stress, and many other processes.

A caterpillar becomes a butterfly. A crustacean changes color to blend with its background (see photograph). A young girl develops into a woman. An adult copes with chronic stress. The **endocrine system** regulates these physiological processes and many more, including growth and development; metabolism; fluid balance and concentrations of specific ions and chemical compounds in the blood, urine, and other body fluids; reproduction; and response to stress. The tissues and organs of the endocrine system secrete *hormones,* chemical messengers that signal other cells.

Endocrinology, the study of endocrine activity, is an active, exciting field of biomedical research. This branch of biology has its roots in experiments performed by German physiologist A. A. Berthold in the 1840s. Berthold removed the testes from young roosters and observed that the roosters' combs (a male secondary sex characteristic) did not grow as large as those in normal roosters. He then transplanted testes into some of the birds and observed that the combs grew to normal size. Berthold's methods became a model for subsequent studies in endocrinology and are still used by researchers today.

Investigators are actively studying mechanisms of hormone action, including characterizing receptors and identifying the molecules involved in *signal transduction.* Some endocrinologists use a reverse strategy for discovering new hormones and signaling pathways within the cell. They focus on "orphan" nuclear receptors, those for which ligands (the molecules that bind with them) are not yet known. Some of these "orphan" receptors are receptors for hormones that have not yet been identified. Using this strategy, researchers have identified intracellular signaling pathways for steroids, fatty acids, and several other compounds. Interestingly, many signaling pathways share the same molecules even though they respond to different stimuli and activate different responses. Much remains to be learned about how similar pathways lead to many different, and very specific, cell actions.

In this chapter we discuss how the endocrine system regulates life processes. We focus on how hormones maintain homeostasis, and we examine how overproduction or deficiency of various hormones interferes with normal functioning.

49.1 AN OVERVIEW OF ENDOCRINE REGULATION

■ LEARNING OBJECTIVES

1 Compare endocrine with nervous system function and describe how these systems work together to regulate body processes.
2 Summarize the regulation of endocrine action by negative feedback systems.
3 Identify four main chemical groups to which hormones are assigned and give two examples for each group.

The endocrine system is a diverse collection of cells, tissues, and organs including specialized **endocrine glands** that produce and secrete **hormones,** chemical messengers that regulate many physiological processes. The term *hormone* is derived from a Greek word meaning "to excite." Hormones excite, or stimulate, changes in specific tissues. Endocrine glands differ from **exocrine glands** (such as sweat glands and gastric glands) that release their secretions into ducts. Endocrine glands have no ducts and secrete their hormones into the surrounding interstitial fluid or blood.

Endocrinologists have identified about ten discrete endocrine glands. They have also discovered specialized cells in the digestive tract, heart, kidneys, and many other parts of the body that release hormones or hormone-like substances. As a result of these discoveries, the scope of endocrinology now includes the production and actions of chemical messengers produced by a wide variety of organs, tissues, and cells.[1]

Hormones are typically transported by the blood. They produce a characteristic response only after they bind with specific receptors on **target cells,** the cells influenced by a particular hormone. Target cells may be in another endocrine gland or in an entirely different type of organ, such as a bone or kidney. Target cells may be located far from the endocrine gland. For example,

---

[1]Pheromones are chemical messengers that animals release to communicate with other animals of the same species. Because pheromones are generally produced by exocrine glands and do not regulate metabolic activities within the animal that produces them, most biologists do not classify them as hormones. Their role in regulating behavior is discussed in Chapter 52.

the vertebrate thyroid gland secretes hormones that stimulate metabolism in tissues throughout the body.

Several types of hormones may be involved in regulating the metabolic activities of a particular type of cell. In fact, many hormones produce a synergistic effect in which the presence of one hormone enhances the effects of another.

The endocrine system and nervous system interact to regulate the body

The endocrine system works closely with the nervous system to maintain **homeostasis,** the balanced internal environment of the body. Recall from Chapters 41 and 42 that the nervous system responds rapidly to stimuli by transmitting electrical and chemical signals. Neurons signal muscle and gland cells, including endocrine cells. The endocrine system signals a much wider range of target cell types than the nervous system does.

In general, the endocrine system responds more slowly than the nervous system, but its responses may be longer-lasting. As we will learn, the nervous system helps regulate many endocrine responses. For example, when the body is threatened, the hypothalamus signals the adrenal glands to secrete the hormone epinephrine. The hypothalamus, which is the link between the nervous and endocrine systems, also produces several hormones (neurohormones), including hormones that regulate the pituitary gland.

Nervous system and endocrine function further blur when we consider that the same signal molecule can function as either a neurotransmitter or a hormone, depending on its source. (You may recall from Chapters 41 and 42 that norepinephrine is secreted at synapses by neurons in the brain and by the sympathetic system.) Norepinephrine is also secreted as a hormone by the adrenal medulla, an endocrine organ.

Negative feedback systems regulate endocrine activity

Although present in minute amounts, more than 50 different hormones may be circulating in the blood of a vertebrate at any given time. Hormone molecules continuously move out of the circulation and bind with target cells. They are removed from the blood by the liver, which inactivates some hormones, and by the kidneys, which excrete them.

Most endocrine action is regulated by **negative feedback systems,** discussed in Chapter 39. The parathyroid glands, located in the neck of tetrapod vertebrates, provide a good example of how negative feedback works in endocrine regulation (**FIG. 49-1**). The parathyroid glands regulate the calcium concentration of the blood. When the calcium concentration is not within homeostatic limits, nerves and muscles cannot function properly. For instance, when too few calcium ions are present, neurons fire spontaneously, causing muscle spasms. When calcium concentration varies too far from the steady state (either too high or too low), negative feedback systems restore homeostasis.

A decrease in calcium concentration in the plasma signals the parathyroid glands to release more parathyroid hormone. This hormone increases the concentration of calcium in the blood.

FIGURE 49-1 Regulation by negative feedback ▶

Whether the calcium concentration in the blood is too high or too low, negative feedback mechanisms restore homeostasis. Parathyroid hormone increases calcium concentration by stimulating calcium release from bone and calcium reabsorption from the kidney tubules.

(See Figure 49-11 for more detailed diagrams of parathyroid hormone regulation.)

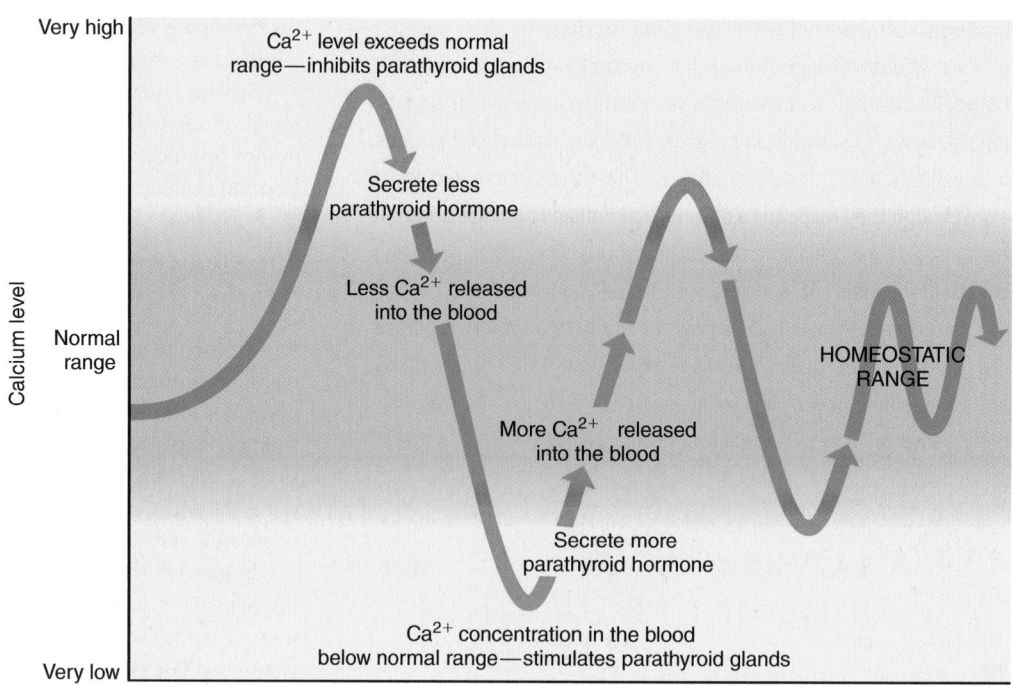

Ca^{2+} level exceeds normal range—inhibits parathyroid glands

Secrete less parathyroid hormone

Less Ca^{2+} released into the blood

Normal range

HOMEOSTATIC RANGE

More Ca^{2+} released into the blood

Secrete more parathyroid hormone

Ca^{2+} concentration in the blood below normal range—stimulates parathyroid glands

Very high

Calcium level

Very low

Time

When the calcium concentration rises above normal limits, the parathyroid glands slow their output of hormone. Both responses are negative feedback systems. An increase in calcium concentration results in decreased release of parathyroid hormone, whereas a decrease in calcium leads to increased hormone secretion. In each case, the response counteracts the inappropriate change, restoring the steady state. (Parathyroid action is discussed in greater detail later in the chapter.)

Hormones are assigned to four chemical groups

Although hormones are chemically diverse, they generally belong to one of four chemical groups: (1) fatty acid derivatives, (2) steroids, (3) amino acid derivatives, or (4) peptides or proteins. *Prostaglandins* and the juvenile hormones of insects are **fatty acid derivatives** (**FIG. 49-2a**). Prostaglandins are synthesized from arachidonic acid, a 20-carbon fatty acid. A prostaglandin has a five-carbon ring in its structure.

The molting hormone of insects is a **steroid hormone** (**FIG. 49-2b**). In vertebrates, the adrenal cortex, testis, ovary, and placenta secrete steroid hormones synthesized from cholesterol. Examples of steroid hormones are cortisol, secreted by the adrenal cortex; the male reproductive hormone testosterone secreted by the testis; and the female reproductive hormones progesterone and estrogen produced by the ovary. Athletes (and others) sometimes abuse synthetic hormones known as anabolic steroids (see *Inquiring About: Anabolic Steroids and Other Abused Hormones*).

Chemically, the simplest hormones are **amino acid derivatives** (**FIG. 49-2c**). The thyroid hormones (T_3 and T_4) are synthesized from the amino acid tyrosine and iodide. Epinephrine (also

known as adrenaline) and norepinephrine (also known as noradrenaline), produced by the medulla of the adrenal gland, are also derived from tyrosine. Melatonin is synthesized from the amino acid tryptophan.

The water-soluble **peptide hormones** are the largest hormone group. (Many endocrinologists include protein hormones in this group.) **Neuropeptides** are a large group of signaling molecules produced by neurons. Oxytocin and antidiuretic hormone (ADH), produced in the hypothalamus, are short neuropeptides, each composed of nine amino acids (**FIG. 49-2d**). Seven of the amino acids are identical in the two hormones, but the actions of these hormones are quite different. The hormones glucagon (see Fig. 3-19), secretin, adrenocorticotropic hormone (ACTH), and calcitonin are somewhat longer peptides that each consist of about 30 amino acids.

Insulin is a small protein that consists of two peptide chains joined by disulfide bonds. Growth hormone, thyroid-stimulating hormone, and the gonadotropic hormones, all secreted by the anterior lobe of the pituitary gland, are large proteins with molecular weights of 25,000 or more.

Review

- What are target cells?
- How do the nervous and endocrine systems work together?
- How does negative feedback work?
- How does the body respond when the concentration of calcium in the blood is below the homeostatic level?
- What are four major chemical groups of hormones? Give an example of each.

(a) Hormones derived from fatty acids

(b) Steroid hormones

Molting hormone (ecdysone)

Cortisol

Estradiol (principal estrogen)

(c) Amino acid derivatives

Norepinephrine

Epinephrine

Thyroid hormones

Thyroxine (T$_4$)

Triiodothyronine (T$_3$)

(d) Peptide hormones

Oxytocin

ADH

FIGURE 49-2 Major chemical groups of hormones

49.2 TYPES OF ENDOCRINE SIGNALING

■ LEARNING OBJECTIVE

4 Compare four types of endocrine signaling.

Hormones signal their target cells by classical endocrine signaling, neuroendocrine signaling, autocrine signaling, and paracrine signaling. In **classical endocrine signaling,** hormones are secreted by endocrine glands and are transported by the blood to target cells (**FIG. 49-3a**). Steroid hormones and thyroid hormones are transported bound to plasma proteins. The water-soluble peptide hormones are dissolved in the plasma. Hormones move out of the blood with plasma and are present in interstitial fluid.

Neurohormones are transported in the blood

Certain neurons, known as **neuroendocrine cells,** are an important link between the nervous and endocrine systems. In **neuroendocrine signaling,** neuroendocrine cells produce **neurohormones** that are transported down axons and released into the interstitial fluid. They typically diffuse into capillaries and are transported by the blood (**FIG. 49-3b**). Invertebrate endocrine systems are largely neuroendocrine. In vertebrates, the hypothalamus produces neurohormones that link the nervous system with the pituitary gland, an endocrine gland that secretes several hormones.

Some local regulators are considered hormones

A **local regulator** is a signaling molecule that diffuses through the interstitial fluid and acts on nearby cells. Most endocrinologists include at least certain local regulators as hormones. Also, some chemical compounds that act as classical hormones (transported by the blood) function as local regulators under some conditions.

ANABOLIC STEROIDS AND OTHER ABUSED HORMONES

Why are anabolic steroids and some other hormones abused? An estimated one million people in the United States, half of them adolescents, abuse certain hormones in order to enhance their physical performance. Anabolic steroids, a group of synthetic hormones, are officially called anabolic-androgenic steroids (AAS). Anabolic steroids are synthetic androgens (male reproductive hormones) that were developed in the 1930s to prevent muscle atrophy in patients with diseases that prevented them from moving.

In the 1950s, anabolic steroids became popular with professional athletes, who used them to increase muscle mass, physical strength, endurance, and aggressiveness. In truth, their athletic performance was probably enhanced, at least in part, by drug-induced euphoria and increased enthusiasm for training. The term *doping* refers to the use of substances such as anabolic steroids, which may enhance performance but are potentially harmful.

As with other hormones, the concentration of steroids circulating in the body is precisely regulated, so use of anabolic steroids interferes with normal physiological processes. These drugs remain in the body for a long time. Their metabolites (breakdown products) can be detected in the urine for up to six months.

Even during short-term use and at relatively low doses, anabolic steroids have a significant effect on mood and behavior. At higher doses, users experience disturbed thought processes, forgetfulness, and confusion and often find themselves easily distracted. The term *roid rage* refers to

the mood swings, unpredictable anger, increased aggressiveness, and irrational behavior exhibited by many users.

Misuse of anabolic steroids poses many health hazards. These drugs increase the risk of cardiovascular disease by elevating blood pressure and decreasing the concentration of high-density lipoproteins (HDL; "good" cholesterol). Anabolic steroids cause kidney and liver damage and increase the risk of liver cancer. Abuse of these hormones also reduces sexual function. In males, testosterone secretion decreases and the testes shrink, leading to sterility. In females, abuse of anabolic steroids can cause infertility as well as masculine features such as facial hair and decreased breast size. In adolescents, these steroids cause severe acne and stunt growth by prematurely closing the growth plates in bones.

Anabolic steroids are both injected and taken in pill form. Steroid abusers who share needles or use nonsterile techniques when they inject steroids are at risk for contracting hepatitis, HIV, and other serious infections.

When their serious side effects became known in the 1960s, anabolic steroid use became controversial, and in 1973 the Olympic Committee banned their use. They are now prohibited worldwide by amateur and professional sports organizations. In the United States, possession of anabolic steroids without a prescription is a federal offense. However, despite the risks, the black market for these synthetic hormones is estimated at more than $1 billion per year.

A recent analysis determined that almost one-third of anabolic steroids purchased illegally did not contain the drugs listed on

their labels. Almost 50% of anabolic steroids that did contain the promised drug were delivered in much lower or much higher dosage. In addition, illegally purchased drugs are often contaminated with toxic heavy metals (for example, lead and arsenic).

The typical anabolic steroid user is a male (95%) athlete (65%), most often a football player, weight lifter, or wrestler. Surprisingly, though, about 10% of male high school students have used anabolic steroids, and about one-third of these students are not even on a high school team. These adolescents use the hormone only to change their physical appearance—to pump up their muscles ("bulk up")—and increase endurance. Many anabolic steroid users have difficulty realistically perceiving their body images. They remain unhappy even after dramatic increases in muscle mass.

Some people also abuse other hormones, including human growth hormone (HGH) and erythropoietin. Human growth hormone, like anabolic steroids, helps build muscle mass but also causes acromegaly, a condition in which certain bones thicken abnormally. Human growth hormone can also cause diabetes and increase heart size, which can lead to heart failure.

Erythropoietin, a hormone produced by the kidney, increases the concentration of red blood cells, which increases oxygen transport. This hormone can enhance the performance of an endurance athlete by as much as 10% for short periods. However, abnormally high concentrations of red blood cells can cause serious cardiovascular problems. Erythropoietin abuse has caused the deaths of several athletes.

Local regulators use *autocrine* or *paracrine* signaling. In **autocrine signaling,** a hormone or other regulator acts on the very cells that produce it (**FIG. 49-3c**). For example, the female hormone estrogen, which functions as a classical hormone, can also exert an autocrine effect that stimulates additional estrogen secretion. At times, estrogen acts on nearby cells, a type of local regulation known as **paracrine signaling** (**FIG. 49-3d**).

Local regulators include chemical mediators such as growth factors, histamine, nitric oxide, and prostaglandins. More than 50 **growth factors,** typically peptides, stimulate cell division and normal development in specific types of cells. (Recall from Chapter 45 that **histamine** is stored in mast cells and is released in response to allergic reactions, injury, or infection.) Histamine causes blood vessels to dilate and capillaries to become more permeable. **Nitric oxide (NO),** another local regulator, is a gas produced by many types of cells, including those lining blood vessels. NO relaxes

smooth muscle fibers in the blood vessel wall, causing the blood vessel to dilate. (See discussion of nitric oxide in Chapter 6.)

Prostaglandins are modified fatty acids released continuously by the cells of most tissues. These local hormones use paracrine signaling. Although present in very small quantities, prostaglandins affect a wide range of physiological processes. They modify cyclic AMP levels and interact with other hormones to regulate various metabolic activities.

The major prostaglandin target is smooth muscle. Some prostaglandins stimulate smooth muscle to contract, whereas others cause relaxation. Thus, some reduce blood pressure, whereas others raise it. Prostaglandins synthesized in the temperature-regulating center of the hypothalamus cause fever. In fact, nonsteroidal anti-inflammatory drugs (NSAIDs), such as aspirin and ibuprofen, reduce fever and decrease inflammation and pain by inhibiting prostaglandin synthesis.

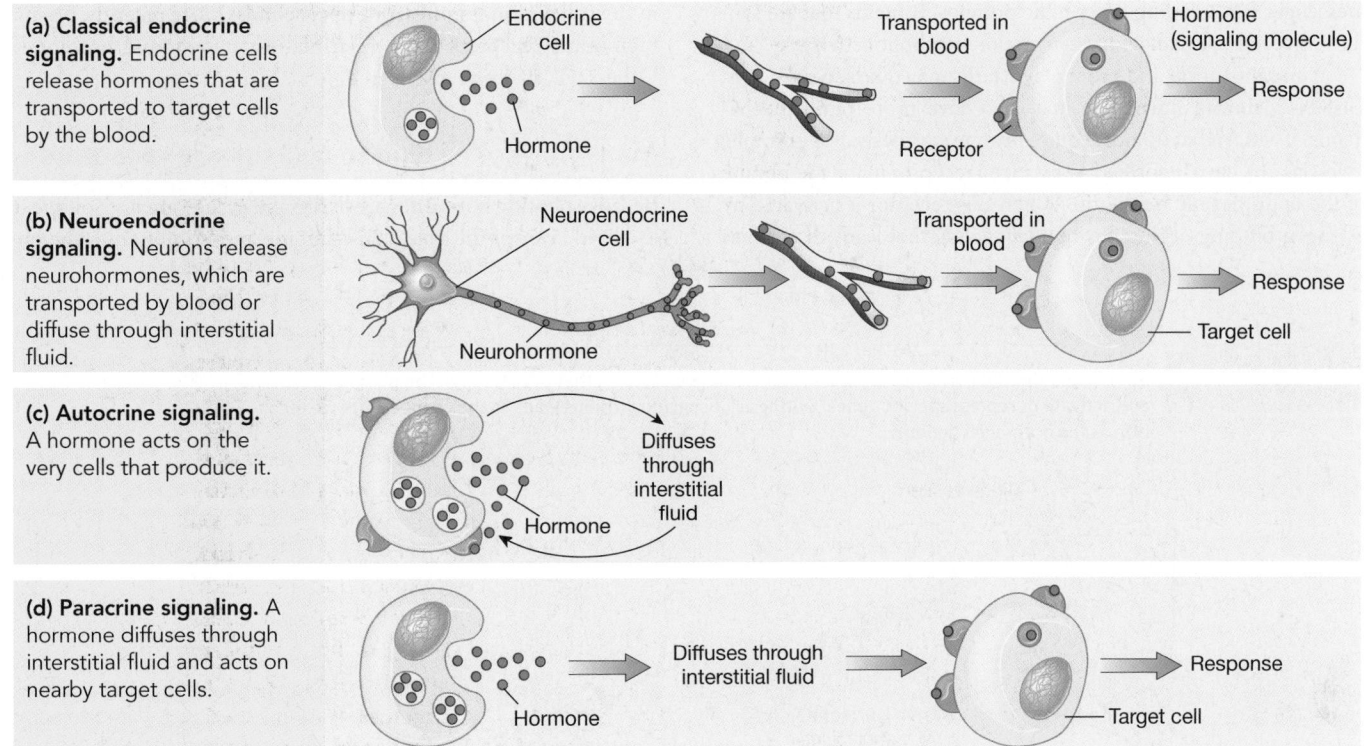

FIGURE 49-3 Some types of endocrine signaling
Endocrine cells secrete hormones that signal target cells, leading to a change in one or more cell processes.

Because prostaglandins are involved in the regulation of so many metabolic processes, they have great potential for a variety of clinical uses. Physicians use them to induce labor in pregnant women, to induce abortion, and to promote the healing of ulcers in the stomach and duodenum. Prostaglandins may someday be used to treat a variety of illnesses, including asthma, arthritis, kidney disease, certain cardiovascular disorders, and some forms of cancer.

Review

- What is neuroendocrine signaling?
- What are local regulators?
- How are autocrine and paracrine signaling different?
- What are two functions of prostaglandins?

49.3 MECHANISMS OF HORMONE ACTION

■ LEARNING OBJECTIVE

5 Compare the mechanism of action of small, lipid-soluble hormones with that of hydrophilic hormones; include the role of second messengers, such as cyclic AMP.

A hormone present in the interstitial fluid remains "unnoticed" until it reaches its target cells, which have receptors that recognize and bind it. Hormone receptors are large proteins or glycoproteins. Recall that the receptor site is somewhat similar to a lock, and the hormones are like different keys. Only the hormone that fits the specific receptor can influence the metabolic machinery of the cell (see Chapter 6). Receptors are responsible for the specificity of the endocrine system.

Receptors are continuously synthesized and degraded. Their numbers are increased or decreased by **receptor down-regulation** and **receptor up-regulation.** For example, when the concentration of a hormone is too high for an extended period, cells decrease the number of receptors for that hormone. Down-regulation decreases the sensitivity of target cells to the hormone, so it dampens the hormone's ability to carry out its function. Up-regulation occurs when the concentration of a particular hormone is too low. Increasing the number of receptors on the plasma membrane increases the hormone's effect on the cell.

Some hormones enter target cells and activate genes

Steroid hormones and thyroid hormones are relatively small, lipid-soluble (hydrophobic) molecules that easily pass through the plasma membrane of the target cell. Specific protein receptors in the cytoplasm or in the nucleus bind with the hormone to form a hormone–receptor complex (**FIG. 49-4**). For example, thyroid hormones bind with receptors in the nucleus that are transcription factors. When activated by the hormone, they activate or repress transcription of messenger RNA coding for specific proteins. Proteins that are synthesized produce changes in structure or metabolic activity.

Gene activation and protein synthesis may take several hours. However, steroid hormones may also have more rapid mechanisms of action that do not require protein synthesis. For example, investigators have identified an estrogen receptor in the membrane of the endoplasmic reticulum. When this receptor is activated by estrogen binding, it initiates rapid signaling that leads to changes in the cell within minutes, or even seconds. More recently, plasma membrane receptors were described for two steroid hormones. Others will likely be discovered.

Many hormones bind to cell-surface receptors

Because peptide hormones are hydrophilic, they are not soluble in the lipid layer of the plasma membrane and do not enter the tar-

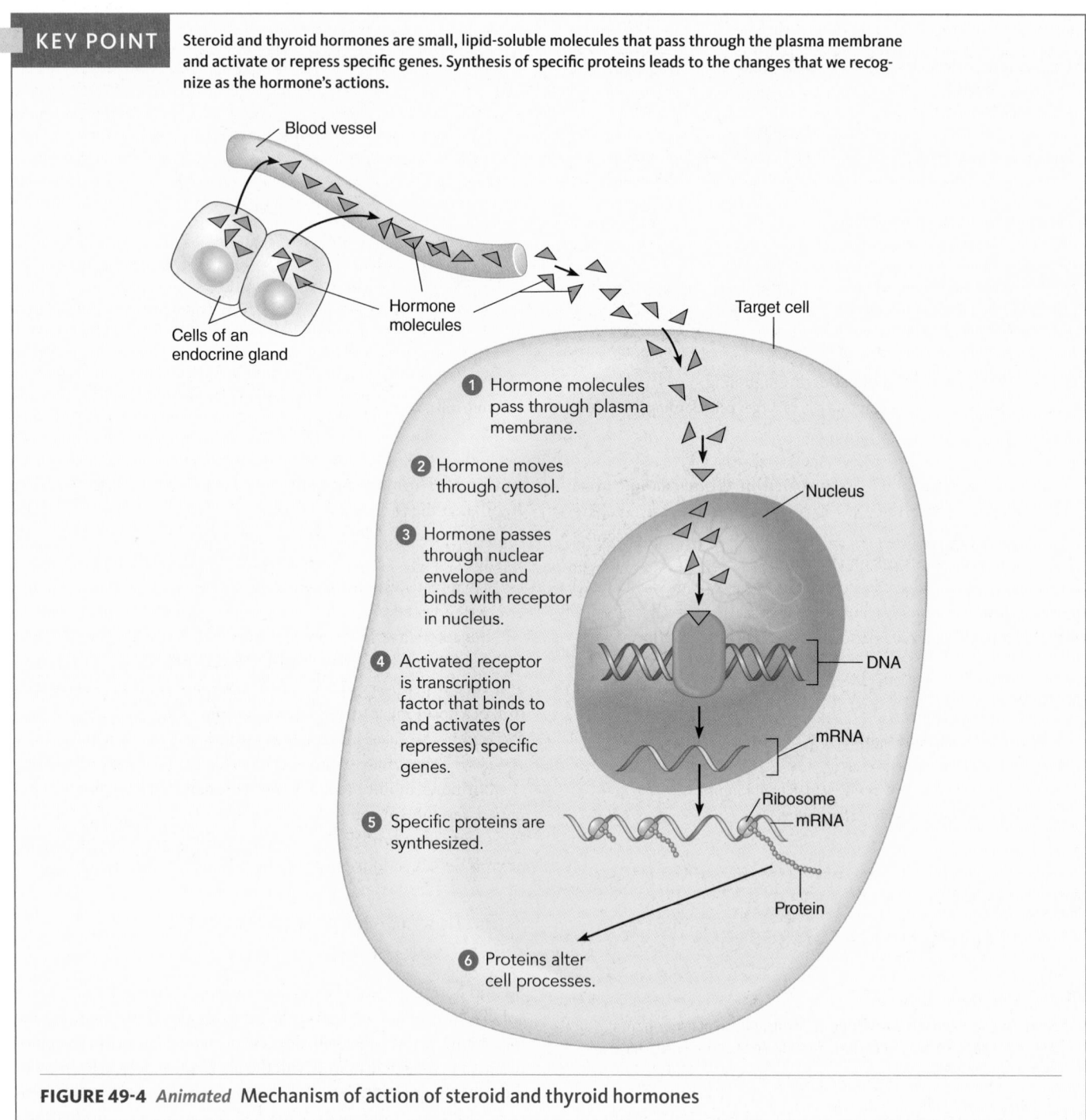

KEY POINT Steroid and thyroid hormones are small, lipid-soluble molecules that pass through the plasma membrane and activate or repress specific genes. Synthesis of specific proteins leads to the changes that we recognize as the hormone's actions.

Blood vessel

Hormone molecules

Cells of an endocrine gland

Target cell

1 Hormone molecules pass through plasma membrane.

2 Hormone moves through cytosol.

3 Hormone passes through nuclear envelope and binds with receptor in nucleus.

4 Activated receptor is transcription factor that binds to and activates (or represses) specific genes.

5 Specific proteins are synthesized.

6 Proteins alter cell processes.

Nucleus

DNA

mRNA

Ribosome
mRNA

Protein

FIGURE 49-4 *Animated* Mechanism of action of steroid and thyroid hormones get cell. Instead, they bind to a specific cell-surface receptor in the plasma membrane. Two main types of cell-surface receptors that bind hormones are G protein–linked receptors and enzyme-linked receptors. These receptors were discussed in detail in Chapter 6. Here we will review some basic concepts.

G protein–linked receptors initiate signal transduction

G protein–linked receptors are transmembrane proteins that initiate **signal transduction;** they convert an extracellular hormone signal into an intracellular signal that affects some cell process. The hormone does not enter the cell. It serves as the **first messenger** and relays information to a **second messenger,** or intracellular signal. The second messenger then signals effector molecules that carry out the action.

G protein–linked receptors activate **G proteins,** a group of integral regulatory proteins (**FIG. 49-5**). The G indicates that they bind **guanosine triphosphate (GTP),** which, like ATP, is an important molecule in energy reactions. When the system is inactive, G protein binds to **guanosine diphosphate (GDP),** which is similar to ADP, the hydrolyzed form of ATP. G proteins shuttle a signal between the receptor and a second messenger.

When a hormone-bound receptor binds to it, a stimulatory G protein releases GDP and replaces it with GTP. The G protein undergoes a change in shape that allows it to bind with and activate the enzyme **adenylyl cyclase** on the cytoplasmic side of the plasma membrane. Once activated, adenylyl cyclase catalyzes the conversion of ATP to **cyclic AMP (cAMP).** By coupling the hormone–receptor complex to an enzyme that generates a signal, G proteins amplify hormone effects, and many second-messenger molecules are rapidly produced. One type of G protein, G_s, stimulates adenylyl cyclase, and another, G_i, inhibits it.

Cyclic AMP activates **protein kinases,** enzymes that phosphorylate (add a phosphate group to) specific proteins. When phosphorylated, protein kinase is activated and may phosphorylate the next protein in the pathway. A chain of reactions leads to some metabolic change. The substrates for protein kinases are

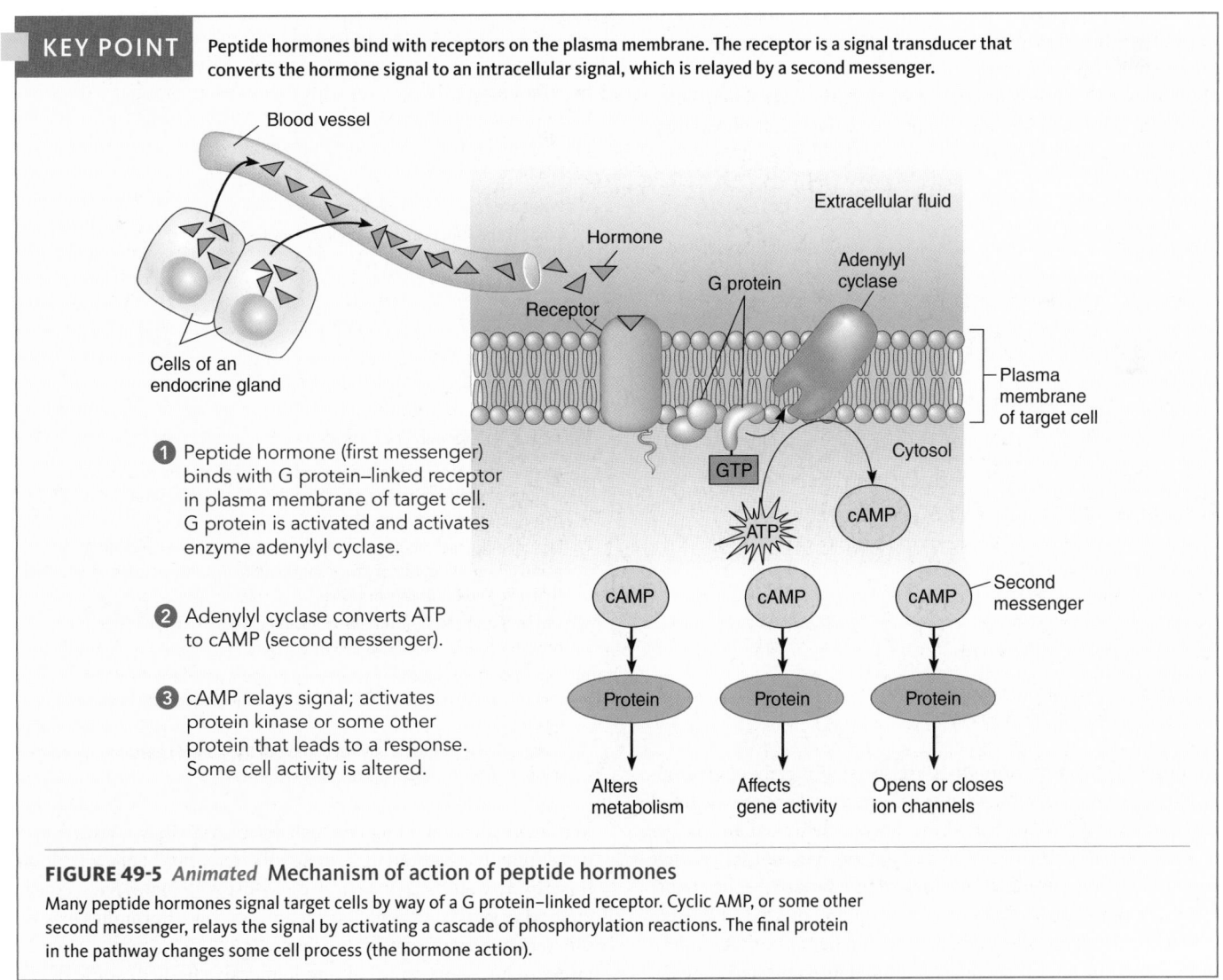

KEY POINT Peptide hormones bind with receptors on the plasma membrane. The receptor is a signal transducer that converts the hormone signal to an intracellular signal, which is relayed by a second messenger.

1 Peptide hormone (first messenger) binds with G protein–linked receptor in plasma membrane of target cell. G protein is activated and activates enzyme adenylyl cyclase.

2 Adenylyl cyclase converts ATP to cAMP (second messenger).

3 cAMP relays signal; activates protein kinase or some other protein that leads to a response. Some cell activity is altered.

FIGURE 49-5 *Animated* **Mechanism of action of peptide hormones**
Many peptide hormones signal target cells by way of a G protein–linked receptor. Cyclic AMP, or some other second messenger, relays the signal by activating a cascade of phosphorylation reactions. The final protein in the pathway changes some cell process (the hormone action).

different in various cell types, so the effect of cAMP varies. In skeletal muscle cells, a protein kinase triggers the breakdown of glycogen to glucose, whereas in cells of the hypothalamus, a protein kinase activates the gene that encodes a growth-inhibiting hormone.

Recall from Chapter 6 that some G proteins use phospholipids as second messengers. Certain hormone–receptor complexes activate a G protein that then activates phospholipase C, a membrane-bound enzyme (see Fig. 6-9). This enzyme splits a membrane phospholipid into two products, **inositol trisphosphate (IP$_3$)** and **diacylglycerol (DAG).** Both act as second messengers. DAG (in combination with calcium ions) activates a protein kinase that phosphorylates a variety of proteins. IP$_3$ opens calcium channels in the endoplasmic reticulum, releasing calcium ions into the cytosol. Calcium ions bind to certain proteins, such as **calmodulin.** The activated calmodulin then activates other proteins.

Enzyme-linked receptors function directly

Enzyme-linked receptors are transmembrane proteins with a hormone-binding site outside the cell and an enzyme site inside the cell (see Fig. 6-5c). These receptors are not linked to G proteins. They function directly as enzymes or are directly linked to enzymes. Most enzyme-linked receptors are **receptor tyrosine kinases** that bind growth factors and other signal molecules, including insulin. When the receptor is activated, it phosphorylates the amino acid tyrosine in specific signaling proteins inside the cell.

Review

- What are the roles of receptors and second messengers in hormone action?
- How do steroid and peptide hormones differ in their mechanisms of action?
- What is the mechanism of action of a hormone that uses cyclic AMP as a second messenger?

49.4 NEUROENDOCRINE REGULATION IN INVERTEBRATES

■ LEARNING OBJECTIVE

6 Identify four functions of invertebrate neurohormones and describe the regulation of insect development.

Among invertebrates, hormones are secreted mainly by neurons rather than by endocrine glands. These *neurohormones* regulate regeneration in hydras, flatworms, and annelids; color changes in crustaceans; and growth, development, metabolism, gamete production, and reproduction (including reproductive behavior) in many other groups. Trends in the evolution of invertebrate endocrine systems include an increasing number of both neurohormones and hormones secreted by endocrine glands and a greater role of hormones in physiological processes.

Insects have endocrine glands and neuroendocrine cells. Their various hormones and neurohormones interact with one another to regulate metabolism, growth, and development, including molting and metamorphosis. Hormonal control of development in insects varies among species. Generally, some environmental factor (such as temperature change) activates neuroendocrine cells in the brain. These cells then produce a neurohormone referred to as **brain hormone (BH),** which is transported down axons and stored in the paired **corpora cardiaca** (sing., *corpus cardiacum;* **FIG. 49-6**). When released from the corpora cardiaca, BH stimulates the **prothoracic glands,** endocrine glands in the prothorax, to produce **molting hormone (MH),** also called **ecdysone** (see Fig. 49-2b). Molting hormone, a steroid hormone, stimulates growth and molting.

In the immature insect, paired endocrine glands called **corpora allata** (sing., *corpus allatum*) secrete **juvenile hormone (JH).** This hormone suppresses metamorphosis at each larval molt so that the insect increases in size while remaining in its immature state; after the molt, the insect is still in a larval stage. When the concentration of JH decreases below some critical level, metamorphosis occurs, and the insect is transformed into a pupa (see Chapter 31). In the absence of JH, the pupa molts and becomes an adult. The nervous system regulates the secretory activity of the corpora allata, and the amount of JH decreases with successive molts.

Review

- What are four actions of hormones in invertebrates?
- What is the function of juvenile hormone in insects?

49.5 ENDOCRINE REGULATION IN VERTEBRATES

■ LEARNING OBJECTIVES

7 Identify the classical vertebrate endocrine glands and describe the actions of their hormones. Describe the effects of hypersecretion and hyposecretion on homeostasis.

8 Describe the mechanisms by which the hypothalamus and pituitary gland integrate regulatory functions; summarize the actions of the hypothalamic and pituitary hormones.

9 Describe the actions of the thyroid and parathyroid hormones, their regulation, and the effects of malfunction.

10 Contrast the actions of insulin and glucagon, and describe diabetes mellitus and hypoglycemia, including the metabolic effects of these disorders.

11 Summarize the actions and regulation of the adrenal hormones, including their role in the body's response to stress.

Vertebrate hormones regulate such diverse activities as growth and development, reproduction, metabolic rate, fluid balance, blood homeostasis, and response to stress. Most vertebrates have similar endocrine glands, although the actions of some hormones may be different in various vertebrate groups. **TABLE 49-1** gives the sources, target tissues, and principal physiological actions of some of the major vertebrate hormones. The hypothalamus and pituitary gland

FIGURE 49-6 Regulation of growth and molting in insects

Hormones regulate insect development. Most insects go through a series of larval stages and then undergo metamorphosis to the adult form. This dissection of an insect head shows the brain, paired corpora allata, and paired corpora cardiaca.

The figure labels include:

Brain · Antenna · Neuroendocrine cells · Compound eye · Corpus cardiacum · Tracheal tube · Esophagus · Corpus allatum · Thorax · BH · JH absent · JH low · Prothoracic gland · JH · MH · MH · MH · Larva · Pupa · Adult

1. Neuroendocrine cells secrete brain hormone (BH), which is stored in corpora cardiaca.

2. When released, BH stimulates prothoracic glands to secrete molting hormone (MH), which stimulates growth and molting.

3. In immature insect, corpora allata secrete juvenile hormone (JH), which suppresses metamorphosis at each larval molt.

4. Metamorphosis to adult form occurs when MH acts in absence of JH.

regulate many of these hormones. The principal human endocrine glands are illustrated in **FIGURE 49-7**.

Homeostasis depends on normal concentrations of hormones

When a disorder or disease process affects an endocrine gland, the rate of secretion may become abnormal. If **hyposecretion** (abnormally reduced output) occurs, target cells are deprived of needed stimulation. If **hypersecretion** (abnormally increased output) occurs, the target cells may be overstimulated. In some endocrine disorders, an appropriate amount of hormone is secreted, but the target cell receptors do not function properly. As a result, the target cells cannot respond to the hormone. Any of these abnormalities leads to loss of homeostasis, resulting in predictable metabolic malfunctions and clinical symptoms (**TABLE 49-2**).

The hypothalamus regulates the pituitary gland

Most endocrine activity is controlled directly or indirectly by the **hypothalamus,** which links the nervous and endocrine systems both anatomically and physiologically. The **pituitary gland** is connected to the hypothalamus by the pituitary stalk. In response to input from other areas of the brain and from hormones in the blood, neurons of the hypothalamus secrete neurohormones that regulate specific physiological processes.

Because secretions of the pituitary gland control the activities of several other endocrine glands, biologists refer to it as the master gland of the body. Although it is the size of a large pea and weighs only about 0.5 g (0.02 oz), the pituitary gland produces six peptide hormones that exert far-reaching influence over growth, metabolism, reproduction, and many other body activities. The human pituitary gland consists of two main parts: the *anterior lobe* and the *posterior lobe*. In some vertebrates, an intermediate lobe is present.

The posterior lobe of the pituitary gland releases hormones produced by the hypothalamus

The **posterior lobe** of the pituitary gland develops from brain tissue. This neuroendocrine organ *secretes* two peptide hormones, **oxytocin** and **antidiuretic hormone,** or **ADH,** also known as

TABLE 49-1 Some Vertebrate Endocrine Glands and Their Hormones

Gland	Hormone	Target Tissue	Principal Actions
Hypothalamus	Releasing and inhibiting hormones	Anterior lobe of pituitary	Regulate secretion of hormones by the anterior pituitary
Posterior pituitary (storage and release of hormones produced by hypothalamus)	Oxytocin	Uterus	Stimulates contraction
		Mammary glands	Stimulates ejection of milk into ducts
	Antidiuretic hormone (ADH)	Kidneys (collecting ducts)	Stimulates reabsorption of water
Anterior pituitary	Growth hormone (GH)	General	Stimulates growth of skeleton and muscle
	Prolactin	Mammary glands	Stimulates milk production
	Melanocyte-stimulating hormones (MSH)	Pigment cells in skin	Stimulate melanin production in some animals; in humans, help regulate food intake
	Thyroid-stimulating hormone (TSH)	Thyroid gland	Stimulates secretion of thyroid hormones; helps regulate bone remodeling
	Adrenocorticotropic hormone (ACTH)	Adrenal cortex	Stimulates secretion of adrenal cortical hormones
	Gonadotropic hormones* (follicle-stimulating hormone [FSH]; luteinizing hormone [LH])	Gonads	Stimulate gonad function and growth
Thyroid gland	Thyroxine (T_4) and triiodothyronine (T_3)	General	Stimulate metabolic rate; regulate energy metabolism
	Calcitonin	Bone	Lowers blood calcium level
Parathyroid glands	Parathyroid hormone	Bone, kidneys, digestive tract	Regulates blood calcium level
Pancreas	Insulin	General	Lowers blood glucose concentration
	Glucagon	Liver, adipose tissue	Raises blood glucose concentration
Adrenal medulla	Epinephrine and norepinephrine	Muscle; blood vessels; liver; adipose tissue	Help body cope with stress; increase metabolic rate; raise blood glucose level; increase heart rate and blood pressure
Adrenal cortex	Mineralocorticoids	Kidney tubules	Maintain sodium and potassium balance
	Glucocorticoids	General	Help body cope with long-term stress; raise blood glucose level
Pineal gland	Melatonin	Hypothalamus	Regulates biological rhythms
Ovary*	Estrogens	General; uterus	Develop and maintain sex characteristics in female; stimulate growth of uterine lining
	Progesterone	Uterus; breast	Stimulates development of uterine lining
Testis	Testosterone	General; reproductive structures	Develops and maintains sex characteristics in males; promotes spermatogenesis

*Reproductive hormones are discussed in Chapter 50; see Tables 50-1 and 50-2.

vasopressin. Oxytocin and ADH are actually *produced* by neuroendocrine cells in two distinct areas of the hypothalamus. These hormones are enclosed within vesicles and transported down the axons of the neuroendocrine cells into the posterior lobe of the pituitary gland (**FIG. 49-8**). The vesicles are stored in the axon terminals until the neuron is stimulated. Then the hormones are released and diffuse into surrounding capillaries.

We discussed the function of ADH in Chapter 48. Recall that ADH stimulates reabsorption of water in the kidneys. Oxytocin concentration in the blood rises toward the end of pregnancy, stimulating the strong contractions of the uterus needed to expel a baby. Oxytocin is sometimes administered clinically to initiate or speed labor.

After birth, when an infant sucks at its mother's breast, sensory neurons signal the pituitary to release oxytocin. The hormone stimulates contraction of smooth muscle cells surrounding the milk glands so that milk is let down into the ducts, making it available to the nursing infant. Because oxytocin also stimulates the uterus to contract, breastfeeding promotes recovery of the uterus to nonpregnant size.

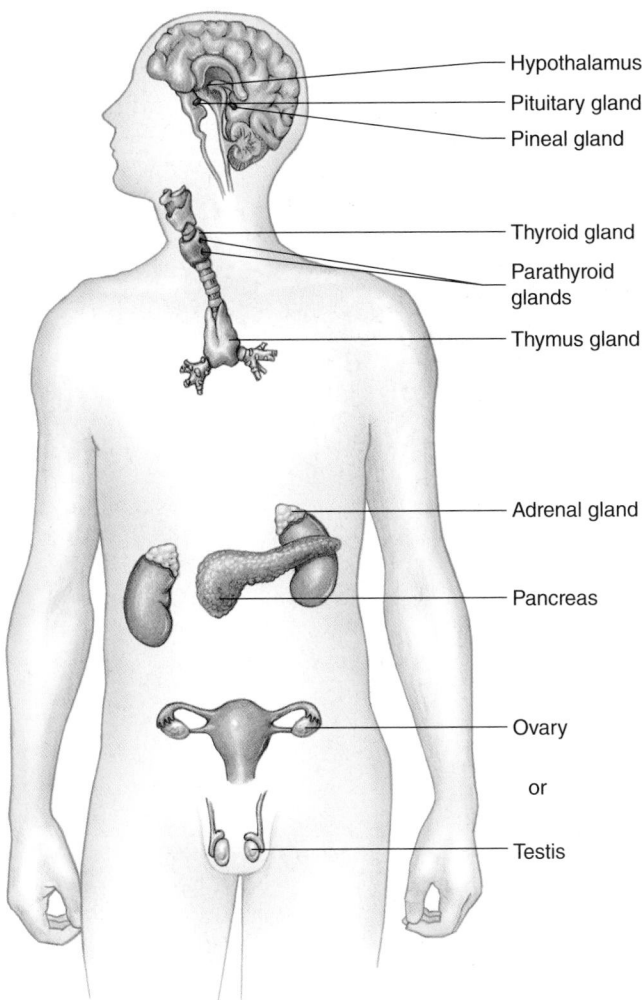

FIGURE 49-7 *Animated* **The principal human endocrine glands**
Many of the hormones produced by these glands and their actions are discussed in this chapter.

Labels in figure:
- Hypothalamus
- Pituitary gland
- Pineal gland
- Thyroid gland
- Parathyroid glands
- Thymus gland
- Adrenal gland
- Pancreas
- Ovary
- or
- Testis

Recent studies suggest that oxytocin also plays a role in social behavior. For example, in voles, males with higher concentrations of oxytocin are more likely to be monogamous (have a single sexual partner). In humans, oxytocin affects maternal behavior. Of critical importance, this hormone facilitates attachment between mother and infant. Oxytocin also appears to help us recognize familiar faces and trust other people.

The anterior lobe of the pituitary gland regulates growth and other endocrine glands

The **anterior lobe** of the pituitary develops from epithelial cells rather than neural cells. The anterior lobe functions like a classical endocrine gland: it receives signals by way of the blood and releases its hormones into the blood. The *hypothalamus* produces several **releasing hormones** and **inhibiting hormones** that regulate the production and secretion of specific hormones by the anterior pituitary gland.

Releasing and inhibiting hormones are produced by specific endocrine cells in the hypothalamus and are stored in vesicles in the axon terminals. When signaled to do so, the cell secretes a particular releasing (or inhibiting) hormone, which then enters a capillary. The hormone is transported in the blood through special portal veins that connect the hypothalamus with the anterior lobe of the pituitary. (These portal veins, like the hepatic portal vein, do not deliver blood to a larger vein directly; they connect two sets of capillaries.) Within the anterior lobe of the pituitary, the portal veins divide into a second set of capillaries.

Releasing and inhibiting hormones pass through the capillary walls into the tissue of the anterior lobe of the pituitary. These hormones control the secretion of anterior pituitary hormones. For example, when the body is stressed, the hypothalamus secretes *corticotropin-releasing factor*. This releasing factor stimulates the anterior pituitary to secrete *adrenocorticotropic hormone (ACTH)*.

The anterior lobe secretes prolactin, melanocyte-stimulating hormones, growth hormone, and several **tropic hormones** that stimulate other endocrine glands (**FIG. 49-9**). **Prolactin** stimulates the cells of the mammary glands to produce milk in a nursing mother. Recently, investigators have discovered that this hormone has diverse roles in various vertebrate groups. For example, in fishes and amphibians it helps maintain water and electrolyte balance by decreasing Na^+ and K^+ loss in the urine. Prolactin also inhibits metamorphosis in amphibians and stimulates molting in reptiles. There is some evidence that this versatile hormone has a role in immune function and in formation of new blood vessels.

Melanocyte-stimulating hormones (MSH) (also called *melanocortins*) are a group of peptide hormones secreted by the anterior pituitary gland and also by certain neurons in the hypothalamus.

TABLE 49-2	Consequences of Endocrine Malfunction	
Hormone	Hyposecretion	Hypersecretion
Growth hormone	Pituitary dwarfism	Gigantism if malfunction occurs in childhood; acromegaly in adult
Thyroid hormones	Cretinism (in children); myxedema, a condition of prounounced adult hypothyroidism; dietary iodine deficiency leads to hyposecretion and goiter	Hyperthyroidism; increased metabolic rate, nervousness, irritability; goiter; Graves' disease
Parathyroid hormone	Spontaneous discharge of nerves; spasms; tetany; death	Weak, brittle bones; kidney stones
Insulin	Diabetes mellitus	Hypoglycemia
Hormones of adrenal cortex	Addison's disease	Cushing's syndrome

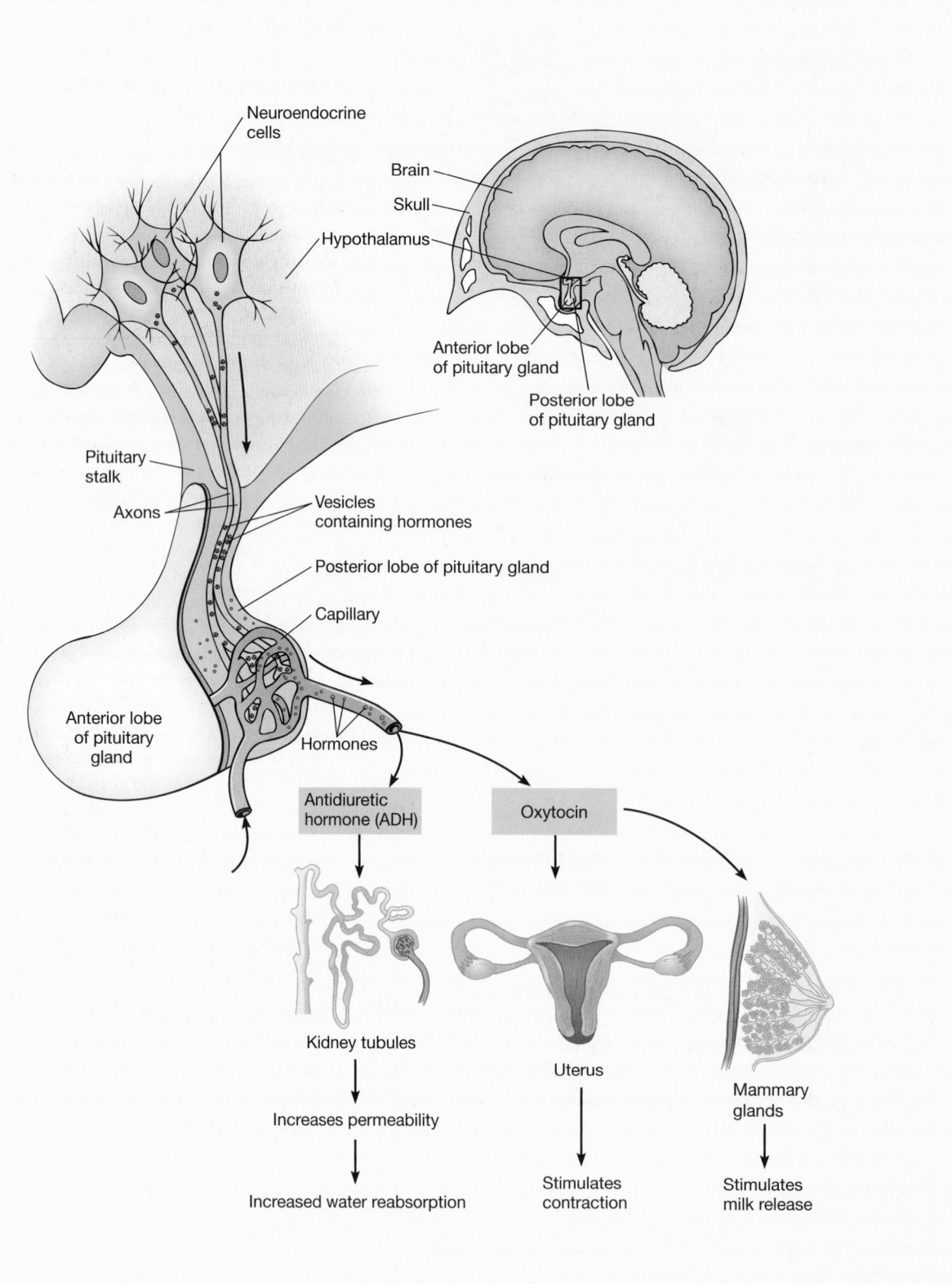

FIGURE 49-8 Synthesis and secretion of posterior pituitary hormones

Neuroendocrine cells in the hypothalamus manufacture hormones that are later secreted by the posterior lobe of the pituitary gland. The axons of these neurons extend into the posterior lobe. The hormones are packaged in vesicles that are transported through the axons and stored in the axon ends. When needed, the hormones are secreted, enter the blood, and are transported by the circulatory system.

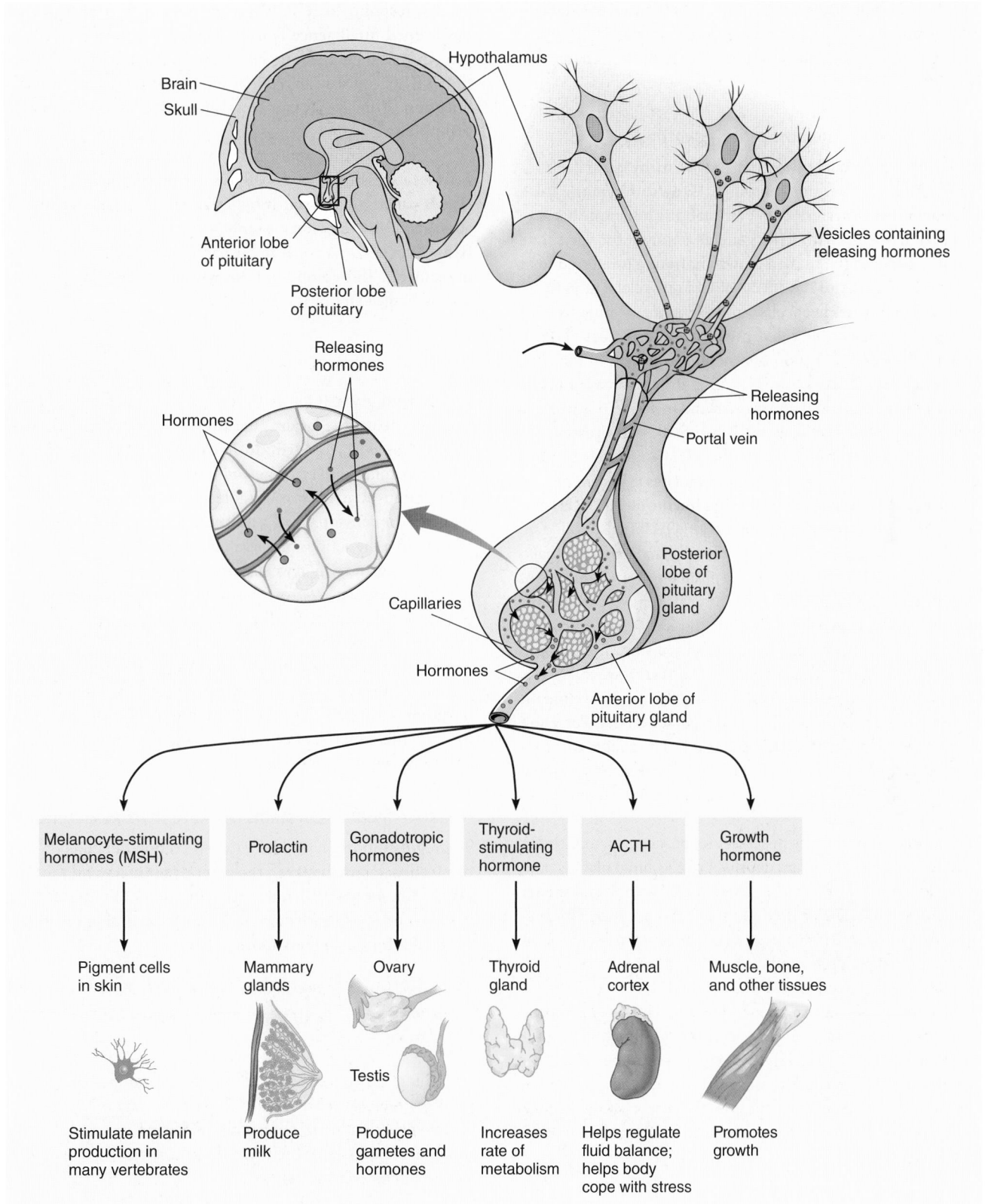

FIGURE 49-9 Synthesis and secretion of anterior pituitary hormones

The hypothalamus secretes several specific releasing and inhibiting hormones that are transported to the anterior lobe of the pituitary gland by way of portal veins. These regulatory hormones stimulate or inhibit the release of specific hormones by cells of the anterior lobe. The anterior lobe secretes hormones that act on a wide variety of target tissues. (ACTH, adrenocorticotropic hormone)

In some fishes, amphibians, and reptiles, MSH causes skin darkening; this is important in camouflage in some animals. In humans, MSH suppresses appetite and is important in regulating energy and body weight.

Growth hormone stimulates protein synthesis

Whether someone is tall or short depends on many factors, including genes, diet, and hormonal balance. **Growth hormone** (also called *somatotropin*) is referred to as an **anabolic hormone** because it promotes tissue growth. (The general acronym for vertebrate growth hormone is GH; human growth hormone is referred to as HGH or hGH.) Many of the effects of GH on skeletal growth are indirect. GH stimulates liver cells (and cells of many other tissues) to produce peptides called **insulin-like growth factors (IGFs).** These growth factors (1) promote the linear growth of the skeleton by stimulating cartilage formation in growth areas of bones and (2) stimulate general tissue growth and increase in organ size by promoting protein synthesis and other anabolic processes.

In adults as well as in growing children, GH is secreted in pulses throughout the day. The hypothalamus regulates GH secretion by secreting a **growth hormone–releasing hormone (GHRH)** and a **growth hormone–inhibiting hormone** (**GHIH;** also called *somatostatin*). A high level of GH in the blood signals the hypothalamus to secrete GHIH; in response, the pituitary slows its release of GH. A low level of GH in the blood stimulates the hypothalamus to secrete GHRH, which stimulates the pituitary gland to release more GH. Many other factors, including blood sugar level, amino acid concentration, and stress, influence GH secretion.

Research supports the age-old notions that to grow children need plenty of sleep, a proper diet, and regular exercise. Secretion of GH increases during exercise, probably because rapid metabolism by muscle cells lowers the blood glucose level. GH is secreted about 1 hour after the onset of deep sleep and in a series of pulses 2 to 4 hours after a meal.

Emotional support is also necessary for proper growth. Growth is retarded in children who are deprived of cuddling, playing, and other forms of nurture, even when their needs for food and shelter are met. In extreme cases, childhood stress can produce a form of retarded development known as *psychosocial dwarfism*. Some emotionally deprived children exhibit abnormal sleep patterns, which may be the basis for decreased secretion of GH.

Other hormones also influence growth. Thyroid hormones appear necessary for normal GH secretion and function and for normal tissue response to IGFs. Sex hormones must be present for the adolescent growth spurt to occur. However, the presence of sex hormones eventually causes the growth centers within the long bones to ossify so that no further increase in height can occur even when GH is present.

Inappropriate amounts of growth hormone secretion result in abnormal growth

Have you ever wondered why some people fail to grow normally? Extreme deficiency in GH during childhood causes pituitary dwarfism. This condition is usually caused by insufficient production of GH by the pituitary gland. However, dwarfism also occurs when the liver produces insufficient IGF or when target tissues do not respond to IGF. Although miniature, a pituitary dwarf has normal intelligence and is usually well-proportioned. If the growth centers in the long bones are still active when this condition is diagnosed, it can often be effectively treated by human GH injection. Human GH can be synthesized by recombinant DNA technology.

A person grows abnormally tall when the anterior pituitary secretes excessive amounts of GH during childhood. This condition is called **gigantism.** If hypersecretion of GH occurs during adulthood, the individual cannot grow taller. Instead, connective tissue thickens, and bones in the hands, feet, and face may increase in diameter. This condition is known as **acromegaly** (*acromegaly* means "large extremities").

Thyroid hormones increase metabolic rate

The **thyroid gland** is located in the neck region, in front of the trachea and below the larynx. The **thyroid hormones—thyroxine,** also known as T_4, and **triiodothyronine,** or T_3—are synthesized from the amino acid tyrosine and from iodine. Thyroxine has four iodine atoms attached to each molecule; T_3 has three. In most target tissues, T_4 is converted to T_3, the more active form (see Fig. 49-2c). We describe the actions of calcitonin, another hormone secreted by the thyroid gland, when we discuss the parathyroid glands.

In vertebrates, thyroid hormones are essential for normal growth and development. These hormones increase the rate of metabolism in most body tissues. After T_3 binds with its receptor in the nucleus of a target cell, the T_3 receptor complex induces or suppresses synthesis of specific enzymes and other proteins. Thyroid hormones also help regulate the synthesis of proteins necessary for cell differentiation. For example, tadpoles cannot develop into adult frogs without thyroxine.

Negative feedback systems regulate thyroid secretion

The regulation of thyroid hormone secretion depends on a negative feedback loop between the anterior pituitary and the thyroid gland (**FIG. 49-10**). When the concentration of thyroid hormones in the blood rises above normal, the anterior pituitary secretes less **thyroid-stimulating hormone (TSH):**

thyroid hormone concentration high $\longrightarrow$ inhibits anterior pituitary $\longrightarrow$ secretes less TSH $\longrightarrow$ thyroid gland secretes less hormone $\longrightarrow$ homeostasis

When the concentration of thyroid hormones decreases, the pituitary secretes more TSH. TSH acts by way of cAMP to promote synthesis and secretion of thyroid hormones and also to promote increased size of the thyroid gland itself. The effect of TSH can be summarized as follows:

thyroid hormone concentration low $\longrightarrow$ anterior pituitary secretes more TSH $\longrightarrow$ thyroid gland secretes more hormone $\longrightarrow$ homeostasis

In some mammals, changes in weather affect the hypothalamus. Exposure to very cold temperature stimulates the hypothalamus to increase secretion of **TSH-releasing hormone (TRH).**

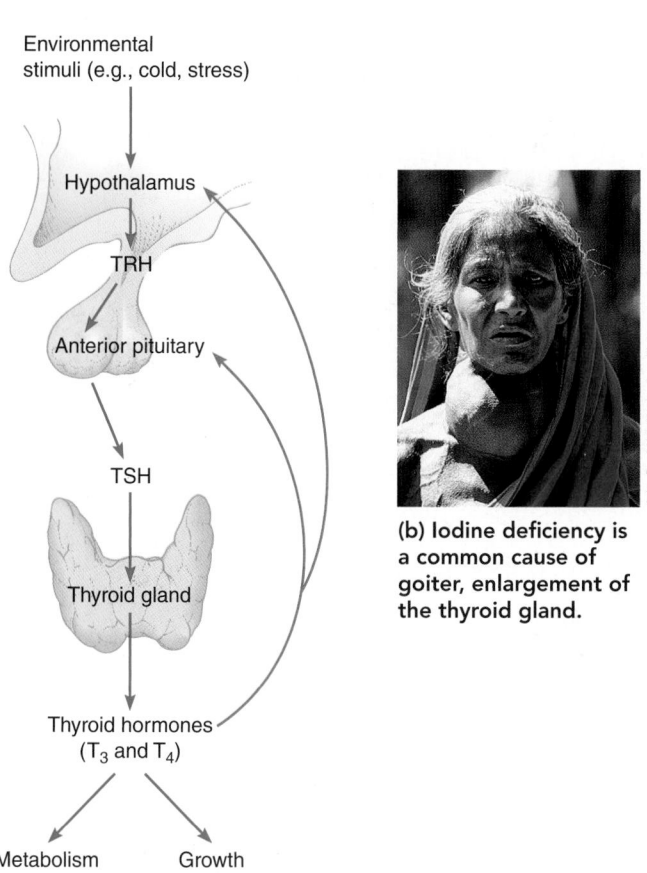

Environmental
stimuli (e.g., cold, stress)

Hypothalamus

TRH

Anterior pituitary

TSH

Thyroid gland

Thyroid hormones
(T$_3$ and T$_4$)

Metabolism   Growth

(a) Regulation of thyroid hormone secretion by negative feedback. An increase in concentration of thyroid hormones above normal levels signals the anterior pituitary to slow thyroid-stimulating hormone (TSH) production. Thus, thyroid hormones limit their own production by negative feedback. Green arrows indicate stimulation; red arrows indicate inhibition. (TRH, TSH-releasing hormone)

John Paul Kay/Peter Arnold, Inc.

(b) Iodine deficiency is a common cause of goiter, enlargement of the thyroid gland.

FIGURE 49-10 *Animated* Regulation of thyroid hormone secretion

This action causes a dramatic increase in thyroid hormone secretion. Metabolic rate increases, which also increases heat production, so the body temperature rises. Increased body temperature has a negative feedback effect, limiting further secretion of thyroid hormones.

Malfunction of the thyroid gland leads to specific disorders

Extreme hypothyroidism during infancy and childhood results in low metabolic rate and can lead to **cretinism,** a condition characterized by retarded mental and physical development. When diagnosed early enough, hypothyroidism can be treated with thyroid hormones, and cretinism can be prevented.

An adult who feels like sleeping all the time, has little energy, and is mentally slow or confused may be suffering from hypothyroidism. When there is almost no thyroid function, the basal metabolic rate is reduced by about 40% and the patient develops **myxedema,** characterized by a slowing down of physical and mental activity. Hypothyroidism is treated by oral administration of the missing hormone.

Hyperthyroidism does not cause abnormal growth but does increase metabolic rate by 60% or even more. This increase in metabolism results in the rapid use of nutrients, causing the individual to be hungry and to eat more. But this is not sufficient to meet the demands of the rapidly metabolizing cells, so people with this condition often lose weight. They also tend to be nervous, irritable, and emotionally unstable. The most common form of hyperthyroidism is **Graves' disease,** an autoimmune disease. Abnormal antibodies bind to TSH receptors and activate them. This leads to increased production of thyroid hormones.

An abnormal enlargement of the thyroid gland, or **goiter,** may be associated with either hypersecretion or hyposecretion (see Fig. 49-10b). In Graves' disease, the abnormal antibodies that activate TSH receptors can cause the development of a goiter. Hyposecretion can be caused by dietary iodine deficiency. Without iodine the gland cannot make thyroid hormones, so their concentration in the blood decreases. The anterior pituitary compensates by secreting large amounts of TSH, which stimulates growth of the thyroid gland, sometimes to gigantic proportions. However, enlargement of the gland does not increase production of the hormones because the needed ingredient is still missing.

Seafood is a rich source of iodine, and iodine is also added to table salt as a nutritional supplement. In fact, thanks to iodized salt, goiter is no longer common in the United States and other highly developed countries. In other parts of the world, however, hundreds of thousands still suffer from this easily preventable disorder. Because it results in hypothyroidism, iodine deficiency also causes retarded mental and physical development. *Lancet,* a well-respected British medical journal, has referred to iodine deficiency as "the single greatest preventable cause of mental retardation."

The parathyroid glands regulate calcium concentration

The **parathyroid glands** are typically embedded in the connective tissue surrounding the thyroid gland. These glands secrete **parathyroid hormone (PTH),** a polypeptide that helps regulate the calcium level of the blood and interstitial fluid (**FIG. 49-11a**). Parathyroid hormone acts by way of a G protein–linked receptor and cAMP to stimulate calcium release from bones and to increase calcium reabsorption from the kidney tubules. It also activates vitamin D, which then increases the amount of calcium absorbed from the intestine.

Calcitonin, a peptide hormone secreted by the thyroid gland, works antagonistically to parathyroid hormone (**FIG. 49-11b**). When the concentration of calcium rises above homeostatic levels, calcitonin is released and rapidly inhibits removal of calcium from bone.

The islets of the pancreas regulate glucose concentration

In addition to secreting digestive enzymes (see Chapter 47), the pancreas is an important endocrine gland. Its hormones, insulin and glucagon, are secreted by cells that occur in little clusters, the **islets of Langerhans,** throughout the pancreas (**FIG. 49-12**). About one million islets are present in the human pancreas. They consist

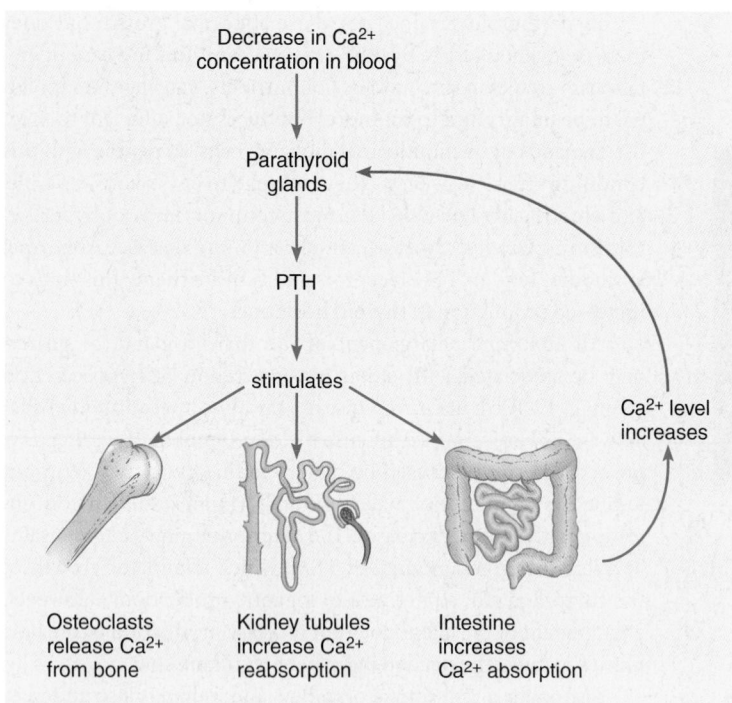

(a) Calcium concentration too low. When calcium concentration decreases below the normal range, the parathyroid glands secrete parathyroid hormone (PTH). PTH stimulates homeostatic mechanisms that restore appropriate calcium concentration.

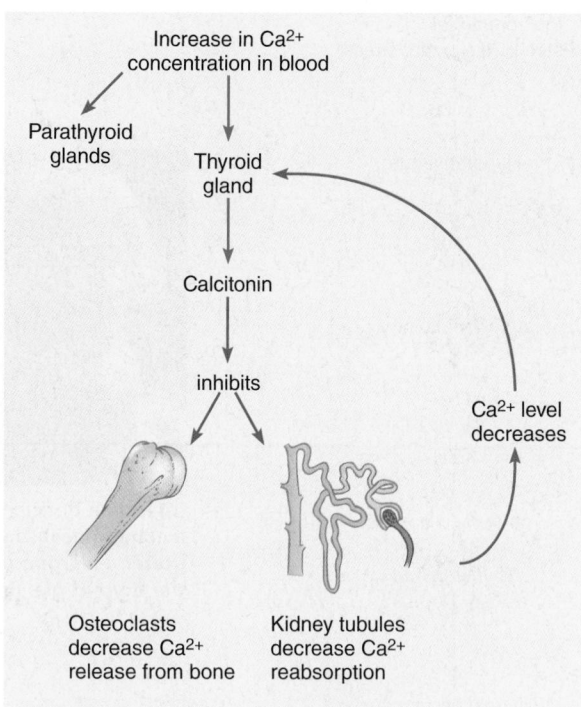

(b) Calcium concentration too high. When calcium concentration increases above its set point, the parathyroid glands are inhibited. The thyroid gland secretes calcitonin, which inhibits Ca^{2+} release from bone and decreases Ca^{2+} reabsorption in the kidneys.

FIGURE 49-11 Regulation of calcium homeostasis
Green arrows indicate stimulation; red arrows indicate inhibition.

mainly of **beta cells,** which secrete insulin, and **alpha cells,** which secrete glucagon.

Insulin lowers the concentration of glucose in the blood

Insulin is an anabolic hormone that regulates the use and storage of nutrients. Insulin stimulates cells of many tissues, including liver, muscle, and fat cells, to take up glucose from the blood by facilitated diffusion (see Chapter 5). Once glucose enters muscle cells, it is either used immediately as fuel or stored as glycogen. Insulin also inhibits liver cells from releasing glucose. Thus, insulin activity *lowers* the glucose level in the blood.

Insulin also helps regulate fat and protein metabolism. It reduces the use of fatty acids as fuel and instead stimulates their storage in adipose tissue. Insulin has an anabolic effect on protein metabolism, resulting in a net increase in protein in cells. It promotes protein synthesis by increasing the number of amino acid transporters in the plasma membrane, thus stimulating the transport of certain amino acids into cells. Insulin also promotes transcription and translation.

Glucagon raises the concentration of glucose in the blood

The effects of **glucagon** are opposite to those of insulin. Glucagon's main action is to raise blood glucose level. It does this by stimulating liver cells to convert glycogen to glucose, a process known as *glycogenolysis*. Glucagon also stimulates *gluconeogenesis*, the production of glucose from other metabolites. Glucagon mobilizes fatty acids by promoting breakdown of fat and inhibiting triacylglycerol synthesis. This hormone also stimulates the liver to degrade proteins and inhibits protein synthesis.

Glucose concentration regulates insulin and glucagon secretion

The concentration of glucose in the blood directly controls insulin and glucagon secretion (**FIG. 49-13**). After a meal, when the blood glucose level rises as a result of intestinal absorption, beta cells are stimulated to increase insulin secretion. Then, as cells remove glucose from the blood, decreasing its concentration, insulin secretion decreases.

high blood glucose concentration ⟶ beta cells secrete insulin ⟶ blood glucose concentration decreases ⟶ homeostasis

When you have not eaten for several hours, the concentration of glucose in your blood begins to fall. When it decreases from its normal fasting level of about 90 mg of glucose per 100 mL of blood to about 70 mg of glucose, the alpha cells of the islets increase their

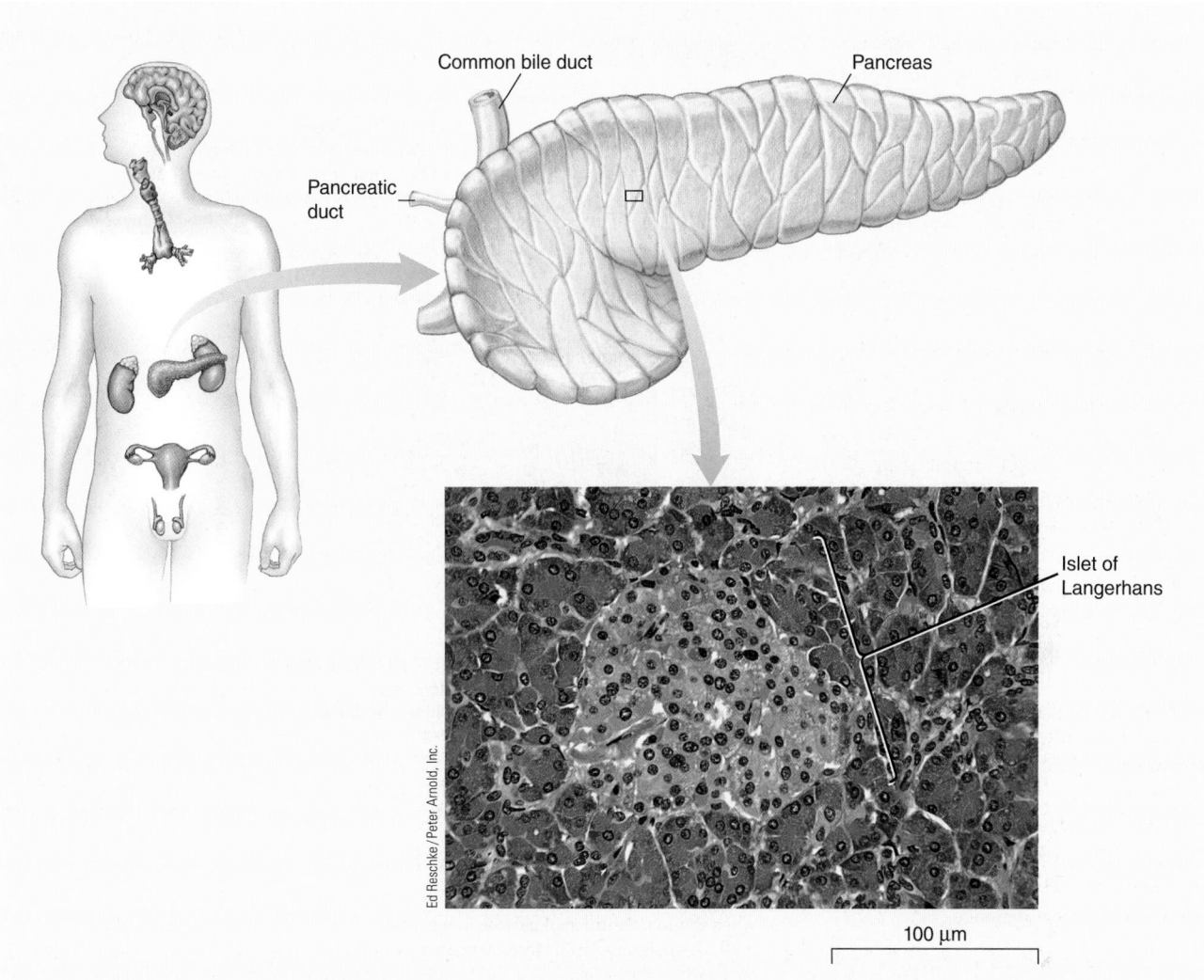

FIGURE 49-12 An islet of Langerhans in the pancreas

Scattered throughout the pancreas, clusters of endocrine cells (such as the one shown in this LM) secrete insulin and glucagon.

secretion of glucagon. Glucose is mobilized from storage in the liver cells, and blood glucose concentration returns to normal:

low blood glucose concentration ⟶ alpha cells secrete glucagon ⟶ blood glucose concentration increases ⟶ homeostasis

Alpha cells respond to the glucose concentration within their own cytoplasm, which reflects the blood glucose level. When blood glucose level is high, there is generally a high level of glucose within the alpha cells, and glucagon secretion is inhibited.

Note that these are negative feedback systems and that insulin and glucagon work antagonistically to keep blood glucose concentration within normal limits. When the glucose level rises, insulin release brings it back to normal; when the glucose concentration falls, glucagon acts to raise it again. The insulin–glucagon system is a powerful, fast-acting mechanism for keeping blood glucose level

within normal limits. Why is it important to maintain a constant blood glucose level? Recall that brain cells ordinarily are unable to use other nutrients as fuel, so they depend on a continuous supply of glucose. As we will discuss, several other hormones also affect blood glucose concentration.

Diabetes mellitus is a serious disorder of carbohydrate metabolism

Diabetes mellitus, the most common endocrine disorder, is a serious health problem, and according to the World Health Organization, its global prevalence is increasing. More than 150 million people worldwide have this disorder. Diabetes is a leading cause of premature death. It is a major risk factor for cardiovascular disease, blindness, neurological disease, kidney disorders, and gangrene of the limbs. (Note that diabetes mellitus is an entirely different disorder from diabetes insipidus, which was discussed in Chapter 48.) Approximately one-half of the people suffering from diabetes are unaware that they have this disorder; consequently, they do not receive treatment and are at high risk for its serious effects.

Diabetes mellitus is actually a group of related disorders characterized by high blood glucose concentrations. Two main types of diabetes are type 1 and type 2. *Type 1 diabetes* is an autoimmune disease in which antibodies mark the beta cells for destruction. T cells destroy the beta cells, resulting in insulin deficiency. Insulin injections are needed to correct the carbohydrate imbalance that results. This disorder usually develops before age 30, often during childhood. Type 1 diabetes is caused by a combination of genetic predisposition and environmental factors, possibly including infection by a virus.

More than 90% of diabetics have *type 2 diabetes*. This disorder develops gradually, typically in overweight people. Type 2 diabetes usually begins as **insulin resistance,** a condition in which cells cannot use insulin effectively. In type 2 diabetes, normal (or greater than normal) concentrations of insulin are present in the blood, but target cells cannot use it.

Similar metabolic disturbances occur in both types of diabetes mellitus: disruption of carbohydrate, fat, and protein metabolism and electrolyte imbalance.

1. *Glucose use decreases.* In a diabetic, the cells have difficulty taking up glucose from the blood, and its accumulation causes hyperglycemia. Instead of the normal fasting concentration of about 90 mg of glucose per 100 mL of blood, the level may exceed 140 mg per 100 mL and may reach concentrations of more than 500 mg per 100 mL. Recall from Chapter 48 that when glucose concentration exceeds its **tubular transport maximum (Tm),** the maximum rate at which it can be reabsorbed, glucose is excreted in the urine. Despite the large quantities of glucose in the blood, insulin-dependent cells in a diabetic can take in only about 25% of the glucose they require for fuel.

2. *Fat mobilization increases.* Cells turn to fat and protein for energy. The absence of insulin promotes the mobilization of fat stores to provide nutrients for cellular respiration. But unfortunately, the blood lipid level may reach five times the normal level, leading to the development of atherosclerosis (see Chapter 44). Increased fat metabolism also increases the formation of ketone bodies, which build up in the blood. This accumulation can cause *ketoacidosis,* a condition in which the body fluids and blood become too acidic. When the ketone level in the blood rises, ketones appear in the urine, another clinical indication of diabetes mellitus. If severe, ketoacidosis can lead to coma and death.

KEY POINT Insulin and glucagon work antagonistically to regulate the concentration of glucose in the blood.

INSULIN RELEASE:
(a) Stimulates cells to take in glucose
(b) Stimulates muscles and liver to store glucose as glycogen
(c) Stimulates storage of amino acids and fat

High

Stimulates beta cells

Stressor: Eating carbohydrates

Glucose level

Normal range

Stressor: Fasting

HOMEOSTATIC RANGE

Stimulates alpha cells

GLUCAGON RELEASE:
(a) Stimulates mobilization of amino acids and fat
(b) Stimulates gluconeogenesis
(c) Stimulates liver to release stored glucose (glycogenolysis)

Low

Time

FIGURE 49-13 *Animated* Regulation of glucose concentration
When the concentration of glucose in the blood increases above normal, beta cells secrete insulin. This hormone lowers blood glucose concentration, thus restoring homeostasis. When the concentration of glucose in the blood decreases below normal, alpha cells secrete glucagon. This hormone increases blood glucose concentration, restoring homeostasis.

3. *Protein use increases.* Lack of insulin also results in increased protein breakdown relative to protein synthesis, so the untreated diabetic becomes thin and emaciated.

4. *Electrolyte imbalance.* When ketone bodies and glucose are excreted in the urine, water follows by osmosis; as a result, urine volume increases. The resulting dehydration causes thirst and challenges electrolyte homeostasis. When ketones are excreted, they also take sodium, potassium, and some other cations with them, contributing to electrolyte imbalance.

Many type 2 diabetics can keep their blood glucose levels within normal range by diet management, weight loss, and regular exercise. When this treatment approach is not effective, the disorder is treated with oral drugs that stimulate insulin secretion and promote its actions. Approximately one-third of type 2 diabetics eventually need insulin injections.

The dramatic increase in type 2 diabetes is a public health problem resulting from a sedentary lifestyle and increased prevalence of obesity. Because type 2 diabetes is associated with insulin resistance, researchers are looking for causes and cures of diabetes by studying this metabolic problem. Researchers have found a strong association between increased fat tissue and insulin resistance. When insulin-resistant individuals lose weight, they become more sensitive to insulin.

Investigators are testing two main hypotheses: the inflammation hypothesis and the lipid-overload hypothesis. The *inflammation hypothesis* holds that macrophages are attracted to enlarged fat cells, which are abundant in obese individuals. The macrophages release cytokines and other inflammatory signals that shut down the insulin-signaling pathway in muscle fibers.

According to the *lipid-overload hypothesis,* when fat cells are fully enlarged and cannot store additional fat, they leak fatty acids. Fat accumulates in muscle fibers and in liver cells. Accumulated diacylglycerols (DAGs) inhibit the insulin-signaling pathway. Both of these hypotheses may be valid.

Adipose tissue produces several hormones and other signaling molecules that play a role in insulin resistance and diabetes. These include resistin and adiponectin. *Resistin* antagonizes the action of insulin, thus contributing to insulin resistance. *Adiponectin* promotes insulin's effects, but obese people produce low amounts. Insulin resistance has a strong genetic component, and some investigators are searching for specific genes that may be involved. Others are focusing on education and lifestyle changes.

More than 20% of obese children have impaired glucose tolerance, an early warning sign of diabetes. Impaired glucose tolerance, which affects more than 200 million people worldwide, is defined as *hyperglycemia* (a blood glucose concentration that is abnormally high) following ingestion of a large amount of glucose (a glucose load).

In hypoglycemia the blood glucose concentration is too low

Low blood glucose concentration, or *hypoglycemia,* sometimes occurs in people who later develop diabetes. These individuals may have impaired glucose tolerance in which the islets overreact to glucose challenge. When carbohydrates are ingested, there is a delayed insulin response, followed after about 3 hours by too much insulin secretion. This hypersecretion causes glucose levels to fall, and the individual feels drowsy. If this reaction is severe, the person may become uncoordinated or even unconscious.

Serious hypoglycemia can develop if diabetics receive injections of too much insulin or if the islets, because of a tumor, secrete too much insulin. The blood glucose concentration may then fall drastically, depriving brain cells of their needed fuel supply. These events can lead to **insulin shock,** a condition in which the patient may appear drunk or may become unconscious, suffer convulsions, and even die.

The adrenal glands help the body respond to stress

The paired **adrenal glands** are small, yellow masses of tissue that lie in contact with the upper ends of the kidneys (**FIG. 49-14**). Each gland consists of a central portion, the **adrenal medulla,** and a larger outer section, the **adrenal cortex.** Although joined anatomically, the adrenal medulla and cortex develop from different types of tissue in the embryo and function as distinctly different glands. However, both secrete hormones that help regulate metabolism and help the body respond to stress.

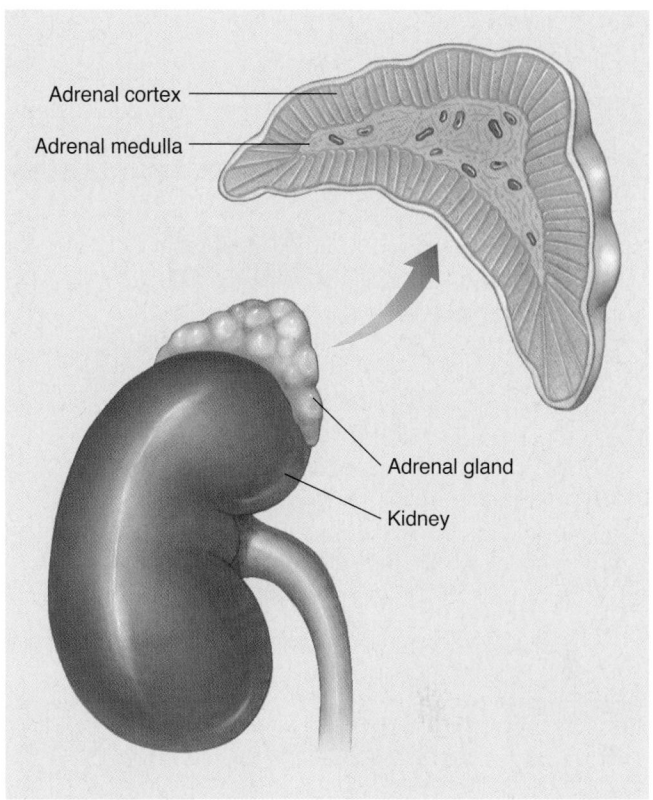

FIGURE 49-14 Adrenal gland

The adrenal glands are located above the kidneys. Each gland consists of a central adrenal medulla surrounded by an adrenal cortex.

The adrenal medulla initiates an alarm reaction

The adrenal medulla is a neuroendocrine gland that is coupled to the sympathetic nervous system. It develops from neural tissue, and its secretion is controlled by sympathetic nerves. The adrenal medulla secretes **epinephrine** and **norepinephrine.** Chemically, these hormones are very similar; they are amino acid derivatives that belong to the chemical group known as **catecholamines** (see Fig. 49-2c). Most of the hormone output of the adrenal medulla is epinephrine. Recall that norepinephrine also serves as a neurotransmitter released by sympathetic neurons and by some neurons in the central nervous system (see Chapter 41).

Under normal conditions, the adrenal medulla continuously secretes small amounts of both epinephrine and norepinephrine. Their secretion is under neural control. When anxiety is aroused, the hypothalamus sends signals via sympathetic nerves to the adrenal medulla. Sympathetic neurons release acetylcholine, which triggers the adrenal medulla to release larger amounts of epinephrine and norepinephrine.

During a stressful situation, adrenal medullary hormones initiate an *alarm reaction* that enables you to think more quickly, fight harder, or run faster than usual. Metabolic rate increases by as much as 100%. Blood is rerouted to those organs essential for emergency action (**FIG. 49-15**). Blood vessels going to the brain, muscles, and heart are dilated, whereas those to the skin and kidneys are constricted. Constriction of blood vessels serving the skin has the added advantage of decreasing blood loss in case of hemorrhage

FIGURE 49-15 Response to stress

The adrenal glands help the body respond to stressful experiences. (RAS, reticular activating system; CRF, corticotropin-releasing factor; ACTH, adrenocorticotropic hormone)

(and explains the sudden paling that comes with fear). At the same time, the heart beats faster. Strength of muscle contraction increases. Thresholds in the reticular activating system of the brain are lowered, so you become more alert (see Chapter 42). The adrenal medullary hormones also raise fatty acid and glucose levels in the blood, ensuring needed fuel for extra energy.

The adrenal cortex helps the body deal with chronic stress

The adrenal cortex synthesizes steroid hormones from cholesterol (which in turn is made in the liver from acetyl coenzyme A). Al-

though the adrenal cortex produces more than 30 types of steroids, it secretes only three types of hormones in significant amounts: sex hormone precursors, mineralocorticoids, and glucocorticoids.

In both sexes, the adrenal cortex secretes sex hormone precursors, such as androgens (masculinizing hormones). Certain tissues convert sex hormone precursors to **testosterone,** the principal male sex hormone, and **estradiol,** the principal female sex hormone. In males, androgen production by the adrenal cortex is not significant because the testes produce testosterone. However, in females, the adrenal cortex secretes the androgen used to produce most of the testosterone circulating in the blood.

The principal **mineralocorticoid** is **aldosterone.** (Recall from Chapter 48 that aldosterone helps regulate fluid balance by regulating salt balance.) In response to aldosterone, the kidneys reabsorb more sodium and excrete more potassium. As a result of increased sodium, extracellular fluid volume increases, which results in greater blood volume and elevated blood pressure.

When the adrenal glands do not produce enough aldosterone, large amounts of sodium are excreted in the urine. Water leaves the body with the sodium (because of osmotic pressure), and the blood volume may be so markedly reduced that the patient dies of low blood pressure.

Cortisol, also called *hydrocortisone,* accounts for about 95% of the **glucocorticoid** activity of the human adrenal cortex (see Fig. 49-2b). Cortisol helps ensure adequate fuel supplies for the cells when the body is under stress. Its principal action is to stimulate production of glucose from other nutrients in liver cells.

Cortisol helps provide nutrients for glucose production by stimulating amino acid transport into liver cells (see Fig. 49-15). It also promotes mobilization of fats so that glycerol from triacylglycerol molecules is available for conversion to glucose. These actions ensure that glucose and glycogen are produced in the liver, and the concentration of glucose in the blood rises. Thus, the adrenal cortex provides an important backup system for the adrenal medulla, ensuring adequate glucose supplies when the body is under stress and in need of extra energy.

During stress, the brain and the adrenal glands work together to help the body respond effectively (see Fig. 49-15; also see *Inquiring About: The Neurobiology of Traumatic Experience,* in Chapter 42). Almost any type of stress stimulates the hypothalamus to secrete **corticotropin-releasing factor (CRF),** which stimulates the anterior pituitary to secrete **adrenocorticotropic hormone (ACTH).** ACTH regulates both glucocorticoid and aldosterone secretion. ACTH is so potent that it can result in a 20-fold increase in cortisol secretion within minutes. When the body is not under stress, high levels of cortisol in the blood inhibit both CRF secretion by the hypothalamus and ACTH secretion by the pituitary.

Addison's disease results when the adrenal cortex produces insufficient amounts of aldosterone and cortisol. This disorder is most commonly caused by autoimmune destruction of the adrenal cortex. Reduction in cortisol prevents the body from regulating the blood glucose concentration because the liver cannot synthesize enough glucose. The cortisol-deficient patient also loses the ability to respond to stress. If cortisol levels are significantly depressed, even the stress of mild infections can cause death.

Glucocorticoids are used clinically to reduce inflammation in allergic reactions, infections, arthritis, and certain types of cancer. These hormones inhibit production of prostaglandins (which are mediators of inflammation). Glucocorticoids also reduce inflammation by decreasing capillary permeability, which reduces swelling. In addition, they reduce the effects of histamine and so are used to treat allergic symptoms.

When used in large amounts over long periods, glucocorticoids can cause serious side effects. Although they help stabilize lysosome membranes so that they do not destroy tissues with their potent enzymes, the ability of lysosomes to degrade foreign molecules is also decreased. Glucocorticoids decrease interleukin-1 production, blocking cell-mediated immunity and reducing the patient's ability to fight infections. Other side effects include ulcers, hypertension, diabetes mellitus, and atherosclerosis.

Abnormally large amounts of glucocorticoids, whether due to disease or steroid medication, can result in **Cushing's syndrome.** In this condition, excess glucose is converted to fat and deposited about the trunk. Edema gives the patient's face a full-moon appearance. Blood glucose level may increase by as much as 50% above normal, causing *adrenal diabetes.* If this condition persists for several months, the beta cells in the pancreas may "burn out" from secreting excessive amounts of insulin, leading to permanent diabetes mellitus. Reduction in protein synthesis causes weakness and decreased immune responses.

Many other hormones are known

Many other tissues of the body secrete hormones. The **pineal gland,** located in the brain, produces **melatonin,** which is derived from the amino acid tryptophan and influences biological rhythms and the onset of sexual maturity. In humans, melatonin facilitates the onset of sleep. Exposure to light suppresses melatonin secretion.

Several hormones secreted by the digestive tract and by adipose tissue regulate digestive processes (see Chapter 47). The **thymus gland** produces **thymosin,** a hormone that plays a role in immune responses. **Atrial natriuretic factor (ANF),** secreted by the atrium of the heart, promotes sodium excretion and lowers blood pressure (see Chapter 48). We discuss reproductive hormones in Chapter 50.

Review

- Why is the hypothalamus considered the link between the nervous and endocrine systems? What is the role of the anterior lobe of the pituitary? of the posterior lobe?
- How are thyroid hormone secretion and parathyroid hormone secretion regulated?
- What are the antagonistic actions of insulin and glucagon in regulating blood glucose level? What is insulin resistance?
- What are the actions of epinephrine and norepinephrine? of cortisol?
- How is regulation of the adrenal medulla different from regulation of the adrenal cortex?

49.1 (page 1053)

1 Compare endocrine with nervous system function and describe how these systems work together to regulate body processes.

- The **endocrine system** consists of endocrine glands, cells, and tissues that secrete **hormones,** chemical signals that regulate physiological processes. Most endocrine responses are slow, but long-lasting. The endocrine system signals a wide range of **target cells.**

- The nervous system responds rapidly to stimuli by transmitting electrical and chemical signals. Neurons signal other neurons, muscle cells, and gland cells, including endocrine cells. The nervous system helps regulate many endocrine responses.

2 Summarize the regulation of endocrine action by negative feedback systems.

- Hormone secretion is typically regulated by **negative feedback systems.** A hormone is released in response to some change in a steady state and triggers a response that counteracts the changed condition; this process restores homeostasis.

3 Identify four main chemical groups to which hormones are assigned, and give two examples for each group.

- Prostaglandins and the juvenile hormone of insects are **fatty acid derivatives.** Hormones secreted by the adrenal cortex, ovary, and testis, as well as the molting hormone of insects, are **steroid hormones.**

- Thyroid hormones and epinephrine are **amino acid derivatives.** Antidiuretic hormone (ADH) and glucagon are examples of **peptide hormones.** Insulin is a small protein.

CENGAGENOW™ Watch the mechanisms of action of steroid and peptide hormones by clicking on the figures in CengageNOW.

49.2 (page 1055)

4 Compare four types of endocrine signaling.

- In **classical endocrine signaling,** discrete **endocrine glands,** glands without ducts, secrete hormones into the interstitial fluid. Hormones are transported by the blood. They bind with receptors on or in specific **target cells.**

- In **neuroendocrine signaling,** neurons secrete **neurohormones.** These hormones are transported down axons and then secreted; they are typically transported by the blood.

- In **autocrine signaling,** a hormone (or other signal molecule) is secreted into the interstitial fluid and then acts on the very cell that produced it. In **paracrine signaling,** a hormone (or other signal molecule) diffuses through interstitial fluid and acts on nearby target cells.

- Some **local regulators** are considered hormones; they use autocrine or paracrine signaling. Local regulators include **growth factors,** peptides that stimulate cell division and development, and **prostaglandins,** a group of local hormones that help regulate many metabolic processes.

49.3 (page 1057)

5 Compare the mechanism of action of small, lipid-soluble hormones with that of hydrophilic hormones; include the role of second messengers, such as cyclic AMP.

- Steroid hormones and thyroid hormones are small, lipid-soluble molecules that pass through the plasma membrane and combine with receptors within the target cell; the hormone–receptor complex may activate or repress transcription of messenger RNA coding for specific proteins.

- Peptide hormones are hydrophilic and do not enter target cells. They combine with receptors on the plasma membrane of target cells. Many hormones bind to **G protein–linked receptors** that act via **signal transduction.** An extracellular hormone signal is transduced into an intracellular signal by the receptor.

- Most peptide hormones are first messengers that carry out their actions by way of **second messengers,** such as **cyclic AMP (cAMP).** The G protein–linked receptor activates a **G protein.** The G protein either stimulates or inhibits an enzyme that affects the second messenger. For example, G proteins stimulate or inhibit **adenylyl cyclase,** the enzyme that catalyzes the conversion of ATP to cAMP.

- Many second messengers stimulate the activity of **protein kinases,** enzymes that phosphorylate specific proteins that affect some cell process.

- Some G proteins use phospholipid derivatives as second messengers. **Inositol trisphosphate (IP₃)** and **diacylglycerol (DAG)** are second messengers that increase calcium concentration and activate enzymes. Calcium ions bind with **calmodulin,** which activates certain enzymes.

- **Receptor tyrosine kinases** are **enzyme-linked receptors** that bind growth factors, including insulin and nerve growth factor.

49.4 (page 1060)

6 Identify four functions of invertebrate neurohormones and describe the regulation of insect development.

- Invertebrate hormones and neurohormones help regulate metabolism, growth and development, regeneration, color changes, molting, metamorphosis, reproduction, and behavior.

- Hormones control development in insects. When stimulated by some environmental factor, neuroendocrine cells in the insect brain secrete **brain hormone (BH).** BH stimulates the prothoracic glands to produce **molting hormone (MH),** which stimulates growth and molting.

- In the immature insect, the **corpora allata** secrete **juvenile hormone (JH),** which suppresses metamorphosis at each larval molt. The amount of JH decreases with successive molts.

49.5 (page 1060)

7 Identify the classical vertebrate endocrine glands and describe the actions of their hormones. Describe the effects of hypersecretion and hyposecretion on homeostasis.

- Consult Table 49-1 for a description of the main endocrine glands and their actions. Vertebrate hormones regulate growth and development, reproduction, salt and fluid balance, and many aspects of metabolism and behavior.

- **Hyposecretion** (abnormally reduced output) or **hypersecretion** (abnormally increased output) of hormones leads to disruption of homeostasis and specific endocrine disorders.

8 Describe the mechanisms by which the hypothalamus and pituitary gland integrate regulatory functions; summarize the actions of the hypothalamic and pituitary hormones.

- Nervous and endocrine regulation is integrated in the **hypothalamus,** which regulates the activity of the **pituitary gland.**

- The neurohormones **oxytocin** and **antidiuretic hormone (ADH)** are produced by the hypothalamus and released by the **posterior lobe** of the pituitary. Oxytocin stimulates contraction of the uterus and stimulates ejection of milk by the mammary glands. ADH stimulates reabsorption of water by the kidney tubules.

- The hypothalamus secretes **releasing hormones** and **inhibiting hormones** that regulate the hormone output of the **anterior lobe** of the pituitary gland.

- The anterior lobe of the pituitary secretes prolactin, melanocyte-stimulating hormones, growth hormone, and several **tropic hormones** that stimulate other endocrine glands. **Melanocyte-stimulating hormones (MSH)** suppress appetite and are important in regulating energy and body weight. **Prolactin** stimulates the mammary glands to produce milk.

- **Growth hormone (GH)** is an **anabolic hormone** that stimulates body growth by promoting protein synthesis. GH stimulates the liver to produce **insulin-like growth factors (IGFs),** which promote skeletal growth and general tissue growth.

  CENGAGENOW™ Explore the human endocrine glands and hormones by clicking on the figures in CengageNOW.

9 Describe the actions of the thyroid and parathyroid hormones, their regulation, and the effects of malfunction.

- The **thyroid gland** secretes thyroid hormones: **thyroxine,** or T_4, and **triiodothyronine,** or T_3. Thyroid hormones stimulate the rate of metabolism.

- Regulation of thyroid secretion depends mainly on a negative feedback system between the anterior pituitary gland and the thyroid gland.

- Hyposecretion of thyroxine during childhood may lead to **cretinism;** during adulthood it may result in **myxedema. Goiter,** an abnormal enlargement of the thyroid gland, is associated with both hyposecretion and hypersecretion. The most common cause of hyperthyroidism is **Graves' disease,** an autoimmune disease.

- The **parathyroid glands** secrete **parathyroid hormone (PTH),** which regulates the calcium level in the blood. Parathyroid hormone increases calcium concentration by stimulating calcium release from bones, increasing calcium reabsorption by kidney tubules, and increasing calcium reabsorption from the intestine.

- **Calcitonin,** secreted by the thyroid gland, acts antagonistically to parathyroid hormone.

10 Contrast the actions of insulin and glucagon, and describe diabetes mellitus and hypoglycemia, including the metabolic effects of these disorders.

- The **islets of Langerhans** in the pancreas secrete **insulin** and **glucagon.** Insulin and glucagon secretion is regulated directly by glucose concentration. Insulin stimulates cells to take up glucose from the blood, so it lowers blood glucose concentration. Glucagon raises blood glucose concentration by stimulating conversion of glycogen to glucose and by stimulating production of glucose from other nutrients.

- In **diabetes mellitus,** either insulin deficiency or **insulin resistance** results in decreased use of glucose, increased fat mobilization, increased protein use, and electrolyte imbalance. In hypoglycemia, impaired glucose tolerance results in a delayed insulin response, followed by hypersecretion of insulin. The glucose concentration falls, causing drowsiness.

11 Summarize the actions and regulation of the adrenal hormones, including their role in the body's response to stress.

- The **adrenal glands** secrete hormones that help the body respond to stress and are important in regulating fluid balance.

- The **adrenal medulla** secretes **epinephrine** and **norepinephrine,** hormones that increase heart rate, metabolic rate, and strength of muscle contraction. These hormones reroute blood to organs needed for fight or flight. The adrenal medulla is regulated by the nervous system.

- The **adrenal cortex** secretes sex hormones; **mineralocorticoids,** such as **aldosterone;** and **glucocorticoids,** such as **cortisol.** Aldosterone increases the rate of sodium reabsorption and potassium excretion by the kidneys.

- During stress, the adrenal cortex ensures adequate fuel supplies for the rapidly metabolizing cells. Cortisol promotes glucose synthesis from other nutrients. During stress, the hypothalamus secretes **corticotropin-releasing factor (CRF),** which stimulates the anterior pituitary gland to secrete **adrenocorticotropic hormone (ACTH).** ACTH regulates both aldosterone and cortisol secretion.

  CENGAGENOW™ Learn more about the hormonal response to stress by clicking on the figure in CengageNOW.

TEST YOUR UNDERSTANDING

1. Which of the following is *not* true of endocrine glands? (a) they secrete hormones (b) they have ducts (c) their product is typically transported by the blood (d) they are typically regulated by negative feedback (e) an experimental animal exhibits symptoms of deficiency when they are removed

2. A cell secretes a product that diffuses through the interstitial fluid and acts on nearby cells. This is an example of (a) neuroendocrine secretion (b) autocrine signaling (c) paracrine signaling (d) classical endocrine regulation (e) peptide hormone function

3. Which of the following is/are *true* of steroid hormones? (a) hydrophilic (b) secreted by the posterior pituitary (c) typically work through G proteins and cyclic AMP (d) typically bind with receptor in nucleus and affect transcription (e) a and c

4. Which of the following activates a second messenger? (a) hormone–receptor complex (b) calcium ions (c) inositol trisphosphate (IP_3) (d) cyclic AMP (e) diacylglycerol (DAG)

5. Which of the following is *not* a correct pair? (a) neurohormone; insect brain hormone (b) calcium; calmodulin (c) posterior lobe of pituitary; releasing hormone (d) anterior lobe of pituitary; growth hormone (e) thyroid hyposecretion; cretinism

6. Growth hormone (a) signals the hypothalamus to produce a releasing hormone (b) is regulated mainly by calcium level (c) is a catabolic hormone (d) stimulates metabolic rate (e) stimulates the liver to produce insulin-like growth factors

7. Arrange the following events into an appropriate sequence. 1. high thyroid hormone concentration 2. anterior pituitary inhibited 3. homeostasis 4. lower level of thyroid-stimulating hormone 5. thyroid gland secretes less thyroid hormone (a) 1, 2, 4, 5, 3 (b) 5, 4, 3, 2, 1 (c) 1, 2, 5, 4, 3 (d) 4, 5, 2, 3, 1 (e) 1, 4, 2, 5, 3

8. Arrange the following events into an appropriate sequence. 1. blood glucose concentration increases 2. alpha cells in islets stimulated 3. homeostasis 4. low blood glucose concentration 5. glucagon secretion increases (a) 1, 2, 3, 5, 4 (b) 5, 4, 2, 1, 3 (c) 1, 2, 5, 4, 3 (d) 4, 2, 5, 1, 3 (e) 4, 5, 1, 2, 3

9. Which of the following occurs in diabetes mellitus? (a) decreased use of glucose (b) decreased fat metabolism (c) decreased protein use (d) increased concentration of TSH-releasing hormone (e) b and c

10. Which of the following is an action of epinephrine? (a) decreases glucose use (b) increases cardiac output (c) constricts blood vessels in brain (d) reduces inflammation (e) mobilizes fat

11. Aldosterone (a) is released by posterior pituitary (b) is an androgen (c) secretion is stimulated by an increase in thyroid-stimulating hormone (d) is an enzyme that converts epinephrine to norepinephrine (e) increases sodium reabsorption

12. Label the diagram. Use Figure 49-7 to check your answers.

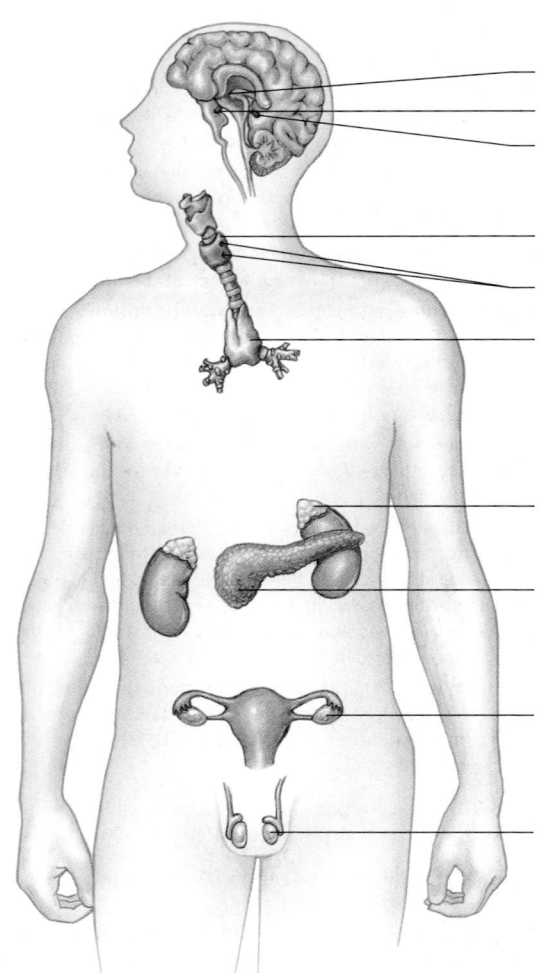

CRITICAL THINKING

1. How do receptors impart specificity within the endocrine system? What might be some advantages of having complex mechanisms for hormone action (such as second messengers)?

2. Why is it important to maintain a constant blood glucose level? Several hormones discussed in this chapter affect carbohydrate metabolism. Why is it important to have more than one? How do they interact?

3. An injection of too much insulin may cause a diabetic to go into insulin shock, in which the person may appear drunk or may become unconscious, suffer convulsions, and even die. From what you know about the actions of insulin, explain the physiological causes of insulin shock.

4. **EVOLUTION LINK.** The receptor for aldosterone appears to have evolved much earlier than aldosterone itself. Propose a hypothesis to explain how this might have occurred.

5. **SCIENCE, TECHNOLOGY, AND SOCIETY.** The "thrifty gene" hypothesis holds that the genes that increase risk for type 2 diabetes allow efficient utilization of food (and fat accumulation) when food is available to increase chances of survival in times of food scarcity. Use this hypothesis to explain the rising rate of diabetes in the United States.

 Additional questions are available in CengageNOW at www.cengage.com/ login.

50 Reproduction

Mating nudibranchs (*Chromodoris*). Photographed in Indonesia.

Bruce Watkins/Animals Animals

KEY CONCEPTS

50.1 Most animals reproduce sexually by fusion of sperm and egg, but some animals reproduce asexually and others can reproduce either way, depending on conditions.

50.2 In male vertebrates, testes produce sperm and reproductive hormones. In humans and other mammals, reproduction is regulated by hormones produced by the hypothalamus, pituitary gland, and gonads.

50.3 In female vertebrates, ovaries produce ova and reproductive hormones. In human females, hormones maintain a monthly menstrual cycle that prepares the body for possible pregnancy; ovulation typically occurs midcycle.

50.4 When a secondary oocyte is fertilized, development begins and the embryo implants in the wall of the uterus; hormones from the developing embryo, from the corpus luteum, and later from the placenta maintain the pregnancy.

50.5 In both human males and females, sexual response includes four physiological stages: excitement phase, plateau phase, orgasmic phase, and resolution phase.

50.6 A variety of highly reliable contraceptives are available; most hormone contraceptives prevent ovulation.

50.7 Sexually transmitted diseases are prevalent communicable diseases; among the most common STDs are human papillomavirus (HPV), genital herpes, and pelvic inflammatory disease caused by chlamydia.

The survival of each species requires that its members produce new individuals to replace those that die. The ability to reproduce and perpetuate its species is a basic characteristic of living things. To paraphrase American sociobiologist E. O. Wilson, animal reproduction is an animal's way of making more copies of its genes. How this is accomplished depends on the relative benefits (and costs) of the reproductive strategies available in any given situation.

The mating nudibranchs (marine slugs) in the photograph are *hermaphrodites*. Each animal has both male and female organs and produces both sperm and eggs. However, they do not self-fertilize. Two nudibranchs come together to mate and exchange sperm through a tube near the head. Each then goes its own way and lays masses containing millions of eggs.

In this chapter we summarize some major features of animal reproduction and discuss the evolutionary advantages of sexual reproduction. We then focus on the process of human reproduction and on the hormones that regulate reproduction. We conclude the chapter with discussions of contraception and sexually transmitted disease.

50.1 ASEXUAL AND SEXUAL REPRODUCTION

1 Compare the benefits of asexual and sexual reproduction, and describe each mode of reproduction, giving specific examples.

Most animals carry on *sexual reproduction,* and some carry on *asexual reproduction.* Some animals reproduce asexually under some conditions and sexually at other times. As we will discuss, many variations of both asexual and sexual reproduction have evolved.

Asexual reproduction is an efficient strategy

In **asexual reproduction,** a single parent gives rise to offspring that are genetically identical to the parent (unless there are mutations). Many invertebrates, including sponges, cnidarians, and some rotifers, flatworms, and annelids, can reproduce asexually. Some vertebrates also reproduce asexually under certain conditions. Asexual reproduction is an adaptation of some sessile animals that cannot move about to search for mates. For animals that do move about, asexual reproduction can be advantageous when the population density is low and mates are not readily available.

In asexual reproduction, a single parent may split, bud, or fragment to give rise to two or more offspring. Sponges and cnidarians are among the animals that can reproduce by **budding.** A small part of the parent's body separates from the rest and develops into a new individual (**FIG. 50-1**). Sometimes the buds remain attached and become more or less independent members of a colony.

Oyster farmers learned long ago that when they tried to kill sea stars by chopping them in half and throwing the pieces back into the sea, the number of sea stars preying on the oyster bed doubled! In some flatworms, nemerteans, and annelids, this ability to regenerate is part of a method of reproduction known as **fragmentation.** The body of the parent breaks into several pieces; each piece regenerates the missing parts and develops into a whole animal.

Parthenogenesis ("virgin development") is a form of asexual reproduction in which an unfertilized egg develops into an adult animal. The adult is typically haploid. Parthenogenesis is common among insects (especially honeybees and wasps) and crustaceans; it also occurs among some other invertebrate and vertebrate groups, including some species of nematodes, gastropods, fishes, amphibians, and reptiles.

Although a few species appear to reproduce solely by parthenogenesis, in most species episodes of parthenogenesis alternate with periods of sexual reproduction. Parthenogenesis may occur for several generations, followed at some point by sexual reproduction in which males develop, produce sperm, and mate with the females to fertilize their eggs. In some species, parthenogenesis is a means of rapidly producing individuals when conditions are favorable.

Most animals reproduce sexually

Sexual reproduction in animals involves the production and fusion of two types of **gametes**—sperm and eggs. Typically, two different individuals are required. A male parent contributes a **sperm,**

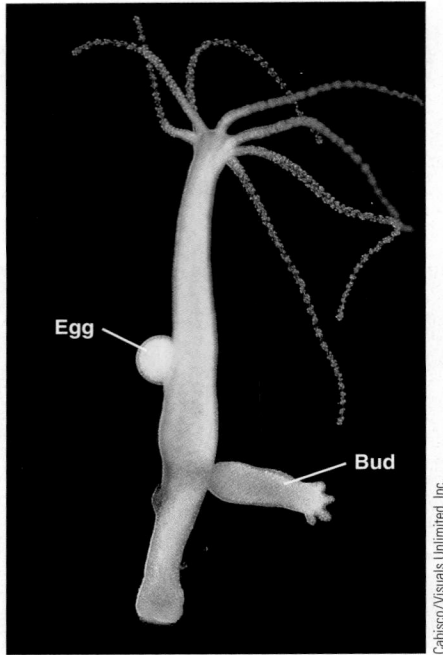

FIGURE 50-1 Asexual reproduction by budding

A part of the *Hydra*'s body grows outward, then separates and develops into a new individual. The region of the parent body that buds is not specialized exclusively for reproduction. The *Hydra* shown here is also reproducing sexually, as evidenced by the egg (*left*).

and a female parent contributes an egg, or **ovum** (pl., *ova*). The sperm provides genes coding for some of the male parent's traits, and the egg contributes genes coding for some of the female parent's traits. The egg is typically large and nonmotile, with a store of nutrients that supports the development of the embryo. The sperm is usually small and motile and adapted to propel itself by beating its long, whiplike flagellum.

When sperm and egg unite, a **zygote,** or fertilized egg, is produced. The zygote develops into a new animal, similar to both parents but not identical to either. Sexual reproduction typically involves remarkably complex structural, functional, and behavioral processes. In vertebrates, hormones secreted by the hypothalamus, pituitary gland, and gonads regulate these processes.

Many aquatic animals practice **external fertilization** in which the gametes meet outside the body (**FIG. 50-2a**). Mating partners usually release eggs and sperm into the water simultaneously. Gametes live for only a short time, and many are lost in the water; some are eaten by predators. However, so many gametes are released that sufficient numbers of sperm and egg cells meet to perpetuate the species.

In **internal fertilization,** matters are left less to chance. The male generally delivers sperm cells directly into the body of the female. Her moist tissues provide the watery medium required for the movement of sperm, and the gametes fuse inside the body. Most terrestrial animals, sharks, and aquatic reptiles, birds, and mammals practice internal fertilization (**FIG. 50-2b**).

Hermaphroditism is a form of sexual reproduction in which a single individual produces both eggs and sperm. A few hermaph-

(a) **External fertilization.** Like many aquatic animals, these spawning frogs (*Rana temporaria*) release their gametes into the water. The female lays a mass of eggs, while the male mounts her and simultaneously deposits his sperm in the water.

Carmela Leszcynski/Animals Animals

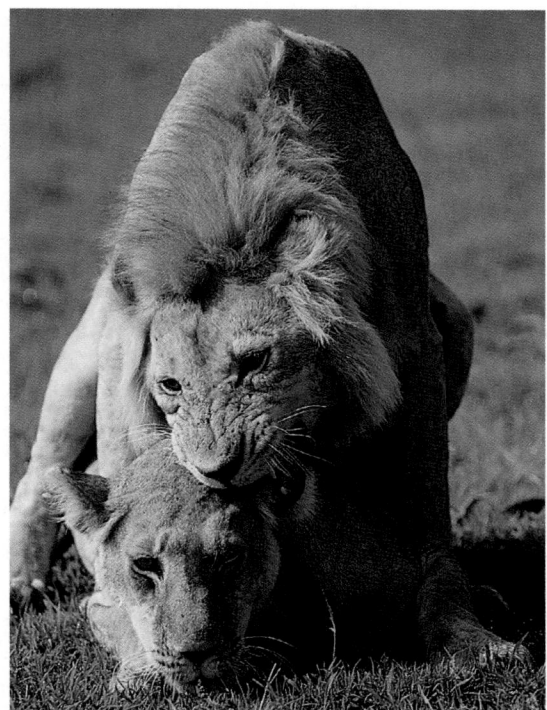

Fritz Polking/Dembinsky Photo Associates

(b) **Internal fertilization.** In most terrestrial animals, such as these lions (*Panthera leo*), the male deposits sperm inside the female body. Internal fertilization is also practiced by some fishes and some aquatic reptiles and mammals.

FIGURE 50-2 Sexual reproduction by external and internal fertilization

rodites, such as the tapeworm, are capable of self-fertilization. More typically, two animals come together and fertilize each other's eggs (see photograph of mating nudibranchs at beginning of chapter). The common earthworm is also a hermaphrodite. Two animals copulate and mutual cross-fertilization occurs. Each earthworm inseminates the other. In some hermaphroditic species, self-fertilization is prevented by the development of testes and ovaries at different times.

Sexual reproduction increases genetic variability

Asexual reproduction is the fastest and most efficient way to reproduce. Each cell can produce two new cells. Sexual reproduction is less efficient because two cells, rather than just one, are required to make a new organism. (Two parents are required.) Sexual reproduction is also more expensive in terms of energy than asexual reproduction because the animal must produce gametes and find mates. Why, then, do most animals reproduce sexually?

A major benefit of sexual reproduction is that it increases the *fitness* (reproductive success) of offspring. In contrast to asexual reproduction, in which an animal passes all of its genes to its offspring, sexual reproduction has the biological advantage of promoting genetic variety among the members of a species. Each offspring is the product of a particular combination of genes contributed by both parents, rather than a genetic copy of a single individual. By combining inherited traits of two parents, sexual reproduction gives rise to at

least some offspring that may be better able to survive than either parent. Also, because the offspring are diploid, they have a backup copy of their genes in case one copy gets damaged by mutation.

Although they agree that sexual reproduction has some selective advantage, biologists do not agree on the details. They are exploring several hypotheses. One hypothesis holds that sexual reproduction permits beneficial mutations from each parent to come together in offspring that can reproduce and spread these mutations through the population. For example, certain beneficial mutations may permit animals to protect themselves from predators or resist parasites. Sexual reproduction provides a mechanism for such mutations to spread through the population.

Another hypothesis holds that sexual reproduction is more efficient than asexual reproduction at removing harmful mutations from a population. As you have learned in earlier chapters, mutations occur constantly, and most mutations are harmful. When animals reproduce asexually, all the offspring inherit all the harmful mutations. As mutations accumulate in a population, individuals carry a bigger and bigger load of harmful genes. In contrast, when animals with different mutations mate, offspring inherit varying numbers and combinations of mutations. Offspring that inherit too many harmful mutations are selected against. They may not live to reproduce, so their harmful mutations are removed from the population.

Wayne Getz, an applied mathematician at the University of California, Berkeley, developed a mathematical model that predicts whether asexual or sexual reproduction will exist within a population. According to his model, clones of animals produced by asexual reproduction would be favored in an unchanging environment. The model further predicts that sexual reproduction will be adaptive in an unstable, changing environment and that both types of reproduction can coexist under conditions of moderate change.

Competing hypotheses are an expected part of the scientific process because scientific discovery is rarely a straightforward, linear sequence of question–answer, question–answer. In fact, as scientific knowledge expands, many creative hypotheses are discarded as dead ends. Sometimes researchers show that competing hypotheses may each explain part of the problem under scrutiny.

Review

- How would you distinguish among budding, fragmentation, and parthenogenesis?
- What are the advantages and disadvantages of asexual reproduction compared to sexual reproduction?

50.2 HUMAN REPRODUCTION: THE MALE

■ LEARNING OBJECTIVES

2　Relate the structure of each organ of the human male reproductive system to its function.

3　Trace the passage of sperm cells through the human male reproductive system from their origin in the seminiferous tubules to their expulsion from the body in the semen. (Include a description of spermatogenesis.)

4　Describe endocrine regulation of reproduction in the human male.

The human male, like other male mammals, has the reproductive role of producing sperm cells and delivering them into the female reproductive tract. When a sperm combines with an egg, the sperm contributes its genes and determines the sex of the offspring.

The testes produce gametes and hormones

In humans and other vertebrates, **spermatogenesis,** the process of sperm cell production, occurs in the paired male gonads, or **testes** (sing., *testis*) (**FIG. 50-3a**). Spermatogenesis takes place within a vast tangle of hollow tubules, the **seminiferous tubules,** within each testis (**FIG. 50-3b**). Spermatogenesis begins with undifferentiated cells, the **spermatogonia** in the walls of the tubules (**FIG. 50-4**).

The spermatogonia, which are diploid cells, divide by mitosis and produce more spermatogonia. Some enlarge and become **primary spermatocytes,** which undergo **meiosis** and produce haploid gametes. (You may want to review the discussion of meiosis in Chapter 10.) In many animals, gamete production occurs only in the spring or fall, but humans have no special breeding season. In the human adult male, spermatogenesis proceeds continuously, and millions of sperm are produced each day.

Each primary spermatocyte undergoes a first meiotic division, which produces two haploid **secondary spermatocytes** (**FIG. 50-5**). During the second meiotic division, each of the two secondary spermatocytes gives rise to two haploid **spermatids.** Four spermatids are produced from the original primary spermatocyte. Each spermatid differentiates into a mature sperm. The sequence is as follows:

spermatogonium (diploid) ⟶ primary spermatocyte (diploid) ⟶ two secondary spermatocytes (haploid) ⟶ four spermatids (haploid) ⟶ four mature sperm (haploid)

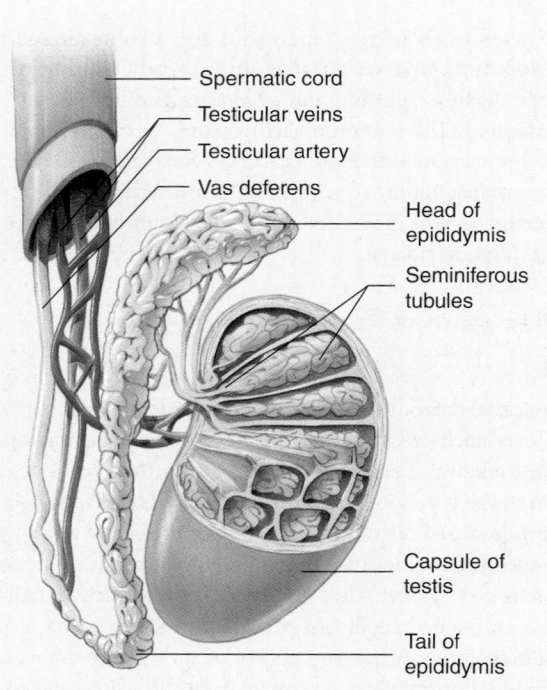

- Spermatic cord
- Testicular veins
- Testicular artery
- Vas deferens
- Head of epididymis
- Seminiferous tubules
- Capsule of testis
- Tail of epididymis

(b) The testis, epididymis, and spermatic cord are shown partly dissected and exposed. The testis is shown in sagittal section to illustrate the arrangement of the seminiferous tubules.

- Seminal vesicle
- Ejaculatory duct
- Prostate
- Rectum
- Bulbourethral gland
- Epididymis
- Scrotum
- Bladder
- Pubic bone
- Vas deferens
- Cavernous body
- Spongy body
- Urethra
- Glans penis
- Testis

(a) The scrotum, penis, and pelvic region of the human male are shown in sagittal section to illustrate their internal structure.

FIGURE 50-3 *Animated* Male reproductive system

Spermatogonium Mature sperm cells

Custom Medical Stock Photo

100 μm

Primary
spermatocyte

Spermatogonium

Sertoli
cells

(a) Color-enhanced SEM of a transverse section through a seminiferous tubule.

Mature
sperm
cells

Spermatid

Secondary
spermatocyte

Primary
spermatocyte

Spermatogonium

Sertoli
cell

Wall of
the seminiferous
tubule

(b) Sperm cells in various stages of development. Note that the developing sperm cells lie between the large, nutritive Sertoli cells.

FIGURE 50-4 *Animated* Spermatogenesis in the seminiferous tubules

Each mature sperm consists of a head, midpiece, and flagellum (**FIG. 50-6**). The head consists almost entirely of the nucleus. Part of the nucleus is covered by the **acrosome,** a large vesicle that differentiates from the Golgi complex. The acrosome contains enzymes that help the sperm penetrate the egg.

Mitochondria, located in the midpiece of the sperm, provide the energy for movement of the flagellum. The sperm flagellum has the typical eukaryotic 9 + 2 arrangement of microtubules. During its development, most of the sperm's cytoplasm is discarded and is phagocytosed by the large **Sertoli cells** that ring the fluid-filled lumen of the seminiferous tubule. These cells provide nutrients for the developing sperm cells. Sertoli cells also secrete hormones and other signaling molecules.

Each Sertoli cell extends from the outer membrane of the seminiferous tubule to its lumen. Sertoli cells are joined to one another by *tight junctions* at a place just within the outer membrane of the tubule (see Chapter 5 for discussion of tight junctions). Together, Sertoli cells form a blood–testis barrier that prevents harmful substances from entering the tubule and interfering with spermatogenesis. This barrier also prevents sperm from passing out of the tubule into the blood, where they could stimulate an immune response. The tight junctions between Sertoli cells form compartments that separate sperm cells in various stages of development.

Human sperm cells cannot develop at body temperature. Although the testes develop within the abdominal cavity of the male embryo, about two months before birth they descend into the **scrotum,** a skin-covered sac suspended from the groin. The scrotum serves as a cooling unit, maintaining sperm below body temperature. In rare cases, the testes do not descend. If this condition is not corrected by surgery or hormone treatment, the seminiferous tubules eventually degenerate and the male becomes **sterile,** unable to produce offspring.

The scrotum is an outpocketing of the pelvic cavity and is connected to it by the **inguinal canals.** As they descend, the testes pull their blood vessels, nerves, and conducting tubes after them. The inguinal region is a weak place in the abdominal wall. Straining the abdominal muscles by lifting heavy objects sometimes tears the inguinal tissue. A loop of intestine can then bulge into the scrotum through the tear, a condition known as an *inguinal hernia.*

A series of ducts store and transport sperm

Sperm cells leave the seminiferous tubules of each testis and pass into a larger coiled tube, the **epididymis.** There, sperm finish maturing and are stored. During ejaculation, sperm pass from each epididymis into a sperm duct, the **vas deferens** (pl., *vasa deferentia*). The vas deferens extends from the scrotum through the inguinal canal and into the pelvic cavity.

Each vas deferens empties into a short **ejaculatory duct,** which passes through the prostate gland and then opens into the single **urethra.** The urethra, which at different times conducts urine and semen, passes through the penis to the outside of the body. Thus, the sperm pass through the following structures:

seminiferous tubules ⟶ epididymis ⟶ vas deferens ⟶
ejaculatory duct ⟶ urethra ⟶ release from body

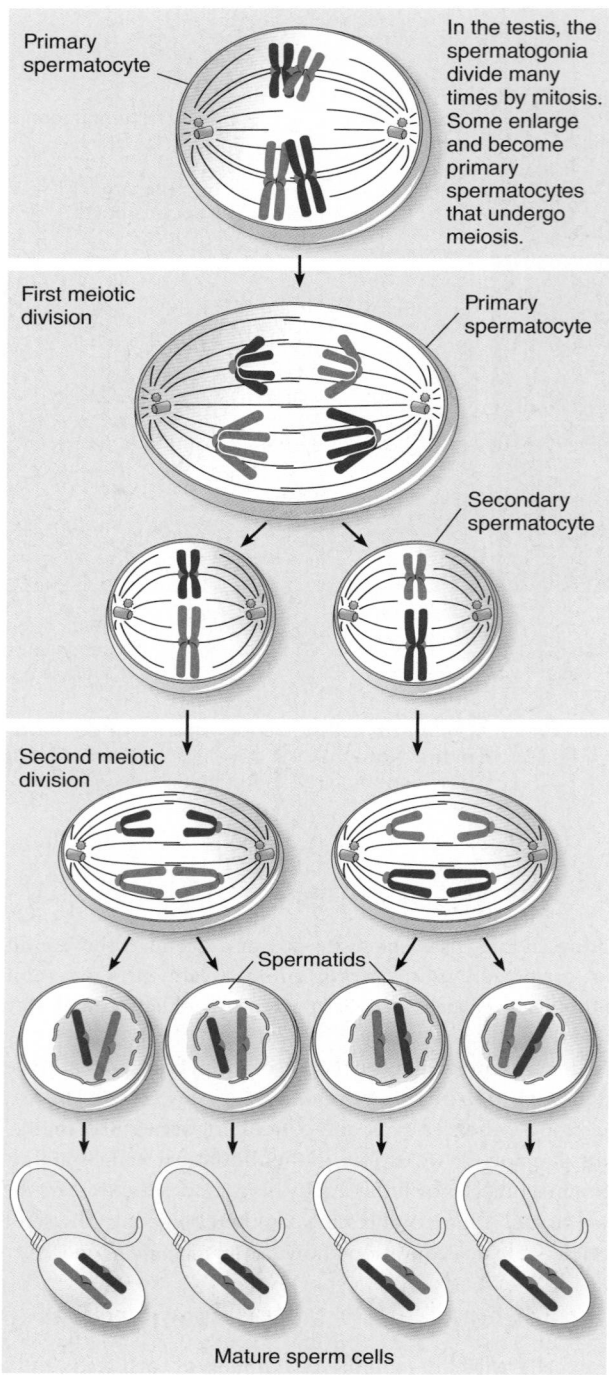

FIGURE 50-5 Spermatogenesis

Note in this example that four chromosomes are present in the primary spermatocyte (*2n*) and that meiosis produces the haploid (*n*) number (2) in the secondary spermatocytes, spermatids, and mature sperm cells.

In the testis, the spermatogonia divide many times by mitosis. Some enlarge and become primary spermatocytes that undergo meiosis.

Primary spermatocyte

First meiotic division — Primary spermatocyte

Secondary spermatocyte

Second meiotic division

Spermatids

Mature sperm cells

The accessory glands produce the fluid portion of semen

As sperm travel through the conducting tubes, they mix with secretions from three types of accessory glands. Approximately 3 mL of **semen** is ejaculated during sexual climax. Semen consists

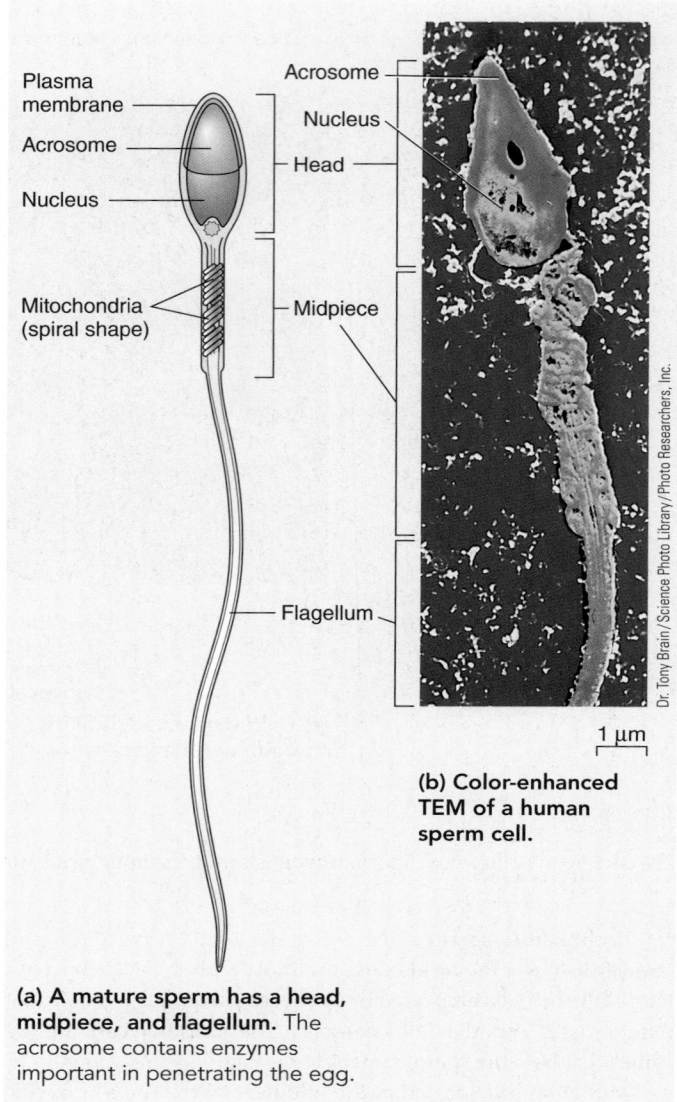

Plasma membrane
Acrosome
Nucleus
Mitochondria (spiral shape)
Flagellum

Acrosome
Nucleus — Head
Midpiece

Dr. Tony Brain/Science Photo Library/Photo Researchers, Inc.

1 μm

(b) Color-enhanced TEM of a human sperm cell.

(a) A mature sperm has a head, midpiece, and flagellum. The acrosome contains enzymes important in penetrating the egg.

FIGURE 50-6 Structure of a mature sperm

of about 200 million sperm cells suspended in the secretions of these glands.

The paired **seminal vesicles** secrete a fluid rich in fructose and prostaglandins into the vasa deferentia (see Fig. 50-3). The fructose provides energy for the sperm after they are ejaculated. Prostaglandins stimulate contractions of smooth muscle in both male and female reproductive tracts. These contractions help transport the sperm down the male reproductive tract and up the female tract to the oviduct where fertilization occurs. The seminal vesicles also secrete fibrinogen, which clots the semen. The fluid secreted by the seminal vesicles accounts for about 60% of the semen volume.

The single **prostate gland** secretes an alkaline fluid that neutralizes the acidic secretions of the vagina. This is important because sperm are more active and survive longer in a slightly alkaline environment. Prostate gland secretion also contains clotting enzymes and **prostate-specific antigen (PSA).** The clotting enzymes act on fibrinogen from the seminal vesicles, producing fibrin. You may recall from Chapter 43 that fibrin threads form blood clots. In this case, fibrin clots the semen. When semen is ejaculated, the clotted semen helps keep the sperm in the female reproductive tract while the penis is withdrawn. The clot is then broken down by PSA, and mobile sperm make their way through the female reproductive tract to the ovum.

In the United States, prostate cancer is the most common cancer in males and is also the leading cause of cancer death among males. As with all cancer, early detection is important. Screening tests for prostate cancer include the digital rectal exam (DRE) and the prostate specific antigen blood test (PSA). The PSA measures the concentration of PSA in the blood. Elevated concentrations of PSA are associated with prostate cancer, prostate infection, and certain benign changes in the prostate. An elevated PSA indicates a need for further evaluation, typically a prostate biopsy. Prostate cancer can be treated with surgery, hormone therapy, or radiation treatment.

During sexual arousal, the paired **bulbourethral glands,** located on each side of the urethra, release a mucous secretion. This fluid lubricates the penis, facilitating its penetration into the vagina.

A major cause of male infertility is insufficient sperm production. When sperm counts drop below 35 million per milliliter of semen, fertility is impaired, and males with a sperm count lower than 20 million per milliliter are usually considered sterile. When a couple's attempts to produce a child are unsuccessful, a sperm count and analysis may be performed in a clinical laboratory. Sometimes semen is found to contain large numbers of abnormal sperm or, occasionally, no sperm at all.

In the United States in the 1970s, an average healthy young man produced about 100 million sperm per milliliter of semen. Today that average has dropped to about 60 million. Although the cause of this decrease is not known, low sperm counts have been linked to a variety of environmental factors, including chronic marijuana use, alcohol abuse, and cigarette smoking. Studies also show that men who smoke tobacco are more likely than nonsmokers to produce abnormal sperm. Exposure to industrial and environmental toxins such as DDT and PCBs (polychlorinated biphenyls) may contribute to low sperm count and sterility. The use of anabolic steroids by athletes to accelerate muscle development can cause sterility in both males and females (see *Inquiring About: Anabolic Steroids and Other Abused Hormones* in Chapter 49).

The penis transfers sperm to the female

The **penis** is an erectile copulatory organ that delivers sperm into the female reproductive tract. It is a long shaft that enlarges to form an expanded tip, the **glans.** Part of the loose-fitting skin of the penis folds down and covers the proximal portion of the glans, forming a cuff called the **prepuce,** or foreskin. The foreskin is removed during circumcision, a procedure commonly performed on male babies either for hygienic or religious reasons. Studies have documented that male circumcision significantly reduces the male's risk of acquiring HIV during vaginal sexual intercourse.

(a) Longitudinal section through the prostate gland and penis. Note the three parallel columns of erectile tissue, the two cavernous bodies, and the spongy body in the penis.

(b) Cross sections through a flaccid and an erect penis. The erectile tissues become engorged with blood in the erect penis.

FIGURE 50-7 Internal structure of the penis

Under the skin, the penis consists of three parallel columns of **erectile tissue:** two **cavernous bodies** and one **spongy body** (**FIG. 50-7**). The spongy body surrounds the portion of the urethra that passes through the penis. Erectile tissue contains numerous blood vessels. When the male is sexually stimulated, parasympathetic neurons dilate the arteries in the penis. As blood fills the blood vessels of the erectile tissue, the tissue swells. This compresses veins that conduct blood away from the penis, slowing the outflow of blood. Thus, more blood enters the penis than can leave, further engorging the erectile tissue with blood. **Penile erection** occurs; the penis increases in length, diameter, and firmness. Although the human penis contains no bone, penis bones do occur in some other mammals, such as bats, rodents, and some primates.

Erectile dysfunction, the chronic inability to sustain an erection, prevents effective sexual intercourse. Associated with a variety of physical causes and psychological issues, this common disorder is now treated with sildenafil (Viagra) and related drugs (Levitra, Cialis). These drugs block the action of an enzyme that breaks down the signaling molecule that sustains erection (see Chapter 6 for a more detailed discussion).

Testosterone has multiple effects

Testosterone is the principal **androgen,** or male sex hormone. It is a steroid produced by the **interstitial cells** between the seminiferous tubules in the testes. Testosterone has many functions, beginning during early embryonic development when it stimulates development of the primary male reproductive organs (**TABLE 50-1**). Later in development, testosterone stimulates descent of the testes into the scrotum.

Puberty is the period of sexual maturation during which the secondary sex characteristics begin to develop and the individual becomes capable of reproducing. In males, puberty typically begins between ages 10 and 12 and continues until ages 16 to 18. Testosterone directly affects muscle and bone and stimulates the adolescent growth spurt in males at puberty. It produces the male's **primary sex characteristics:** growth of the reproductive organs and spermatogenesis. Testosterone also stimulates the development of the **secondary sex characteristics** at puberty, including growth of facial and body hair, muscle development, and the increase in vocal cord length and thickness that causes the voice to deepen. Testosterone is necessary for normal sex drive.

In some of its target tissues, testosterone is converted to other steroids. Interestingly, in brain cells testosterone is converted to *estradiol,* the principal female sex hormone. The implications of this transformation are not yet understood.

The hypothalamus, pituitary gland, and testes regulate male reproduction

As you read the following description of male hormone action and regulation, follow the steps in **FIGURE 50-8**. When a boy is about 10 years old, the hypothalamus begins to secrete **gonadotropin-releasing hormone (GnRH).** GnRH stimulates the anterior pituitary to secrete the *gonadotropic hormones* **follicle-stimulating hormone (FSH)** and **luteinizing hormone (LH).** Both FSH and LH are glycoproteins that use cyclic AMP as a second messenger (see Chapter 49). FSH stimulates Sertoli cells to secrete **androgen-binding protein (ABP)** and other signaling molecules that are necessary for spermatogenesis. LH stimulates the interstitial cells to secrete testosterone.

FSH, LH, and testosterone all directly or indirectly stimulate testosterone secretion and spermatogenesis. A high concentration of testosterone in the testes is required for spermatogenesis. Testosterone and FSH stimulate Sertoli cells to produce ABP, which binds to testosterone and concentrates it in the tubules. Testosterone also maintains the male secondary sex characteristics.

Reproductive hormone concentrations are regulated by negative feedback mechanisms (see Fig. 50-8b). Testosterone acts on the hypothalamus, decreasing its secretion of GnRH, which decreases FSH and LH secretion by the pituitary. Testosterone also directly inhibits the anterior lobe of the pituitary by blocking the normal actions of GnRH on LH synthesis and release.

FSH secretion is inhibited mainly by **inhibin,** a peptide hormone secreted by Sertoli cells. FSH itself stimulates inhibin secretion. The endocrine regulation of reproductive function is complex, and it is likely that other hormones and signaling molecules will be identified.

Insufficient testosterone results in sterility. If a male is **castrated,** that is, the testes are removed, before puberty, he is deprived of testosterone and becomes a eunuch. He retains childlike sexual organs and does not develop secondary sexual characteristics. If castration occurs after puberty, increased secretion of male hormones by the adrenal glands helps maintain masculinity.

Review

- What are the functions of the testes?
- Through what structures must a sperm pass in its journey from a seminiferous tubule until it leaves the male body during ejaculation?
- What is the physiological basis for erection of the penis?
- What are the actions of testosterone? Give an overview of the endocrine regulation of male reproduction.

50.3 HUMAN REPRODUCTION: THE FEMALE

▄ LEARNING OBJECTIVES

5   Relate the structure of each organ of the human female reproductive system to its function.

TABLE 50-1	Principal Male Reproductive Hormones	
Endocrine Gland and Hormones	**Principal Target Tissue**	**Principal Actions**
Hypothalamus Gonadotropin-releasing hormone (GnRH)	Anterior pituitary	Stimulates release of FSH and LH
Anterior Pituitary Follicle-stimulating hormone (FSH)	Testes	Stimulates development of seminiferous tubules; stimulates spermatogenesis
Luteinizing hormone (LH)	Testes	Stimulates interstitial cells to secrete testosterone
Testes Testosterone	General	**Before birth:** stimulates development of primary sex organs and descent of testes into scrotum **At puberty:** responsible for growth spurt; stimulates development of reproductive structures and secondary sex characteristics **In adult:** maintains secondary sex characteristics; stimulates spermatogenesis
Inhibin	Anterior pituitary	Inhibits FSH secretion

① Hypothalamus secretes GnRH, which stimulates anterior pituitary.

② Pituitary secretes FSH and LH.

③ FSH stimulates Sertoli cells to secrete ABP and other signaling molecules necessary for spermatogenesis. LH stimulates interstitial cells to secrete testosterone.

④ Testosterone stimulates Sertoli cells, leading to stimulation of spermatogenesis.

⑤ Testosterone maintains secondary sex characteristics.

⑥ Testosterone inhibits GnRH secretion by hypothalamus and FSH and LH secretion by pituitary.

⑦ Inhibin inhibits FSH secretion.

(a) Overview of hormone action.

(b) Negative feedback systems regulate hormone concentrations.

FIGURE 50-8 Regulation of male reproduction

Green arrows indicate stimulation; red arrows indicate inhibition. (GnRH, gonadotropin-releasing hormone; FSH, follicle-stimulating hormone; LH, luteinizing hormone; ABP, androgen-binding protein)

6 Trace the development of a human egg and trace its passage through the female reproductive system until it is fertilized.

7 Describe the endocrine regulation of reproduction in the human female, and identify the important events of the menstrual cycle, such as ovulation and menstruation.

The female reproductive system produces oocytes (immature gametes), receives the penis and sperm released from it during sexual intercourse, houses and nourishes the embryo during prenatal development, gives birth, and produces milk for the young (lactation). Hormones secreted by the hypothalamus, pituitary gland, and ovaries interact to regulate and coordinate these processes.

The ovaries produce gametes and sex hormones

Like the male gonads, the female gonads, or **ovaries,** produce both gametes and sex hormones. About the size and shape of large almonds, the ovaries lie close to the lateral walls of the pelvic cav-

ity and are held in position by several connective tissue ligaments (**FIG. 50-9**). Internally, the ovary consists mainly of connective tissue containing scattered ova in various stages of maturation.

The process of ovum production, called **oogenesis,** begins in the ovaries. Before birth, hundreds of thousands of **oogonia** are present in the ovaries. All of a female's oogonia form during embryonic development. No new oogonia are formed after birth. During prenatal development, the oogonia increase in size and become **primary oocytes.** By the time of birth, they are in the prophase of the first meiotic division. At this stage, they enter a resting phase that lasts throughout childhood and into adult life.

A primary oocyte and the **granulosa cells** surrounding it together make up a **follicle** (**FIG. 50-10**). The granulosa cells are connected by tight junctions that form a protective barrier around the oocyte. With the onset of puberty, a few follicles begin to mature each month in response to FSH secreted by the anterior pituitary gland. As a follicle grows, the granulosa cells proliferate, forming

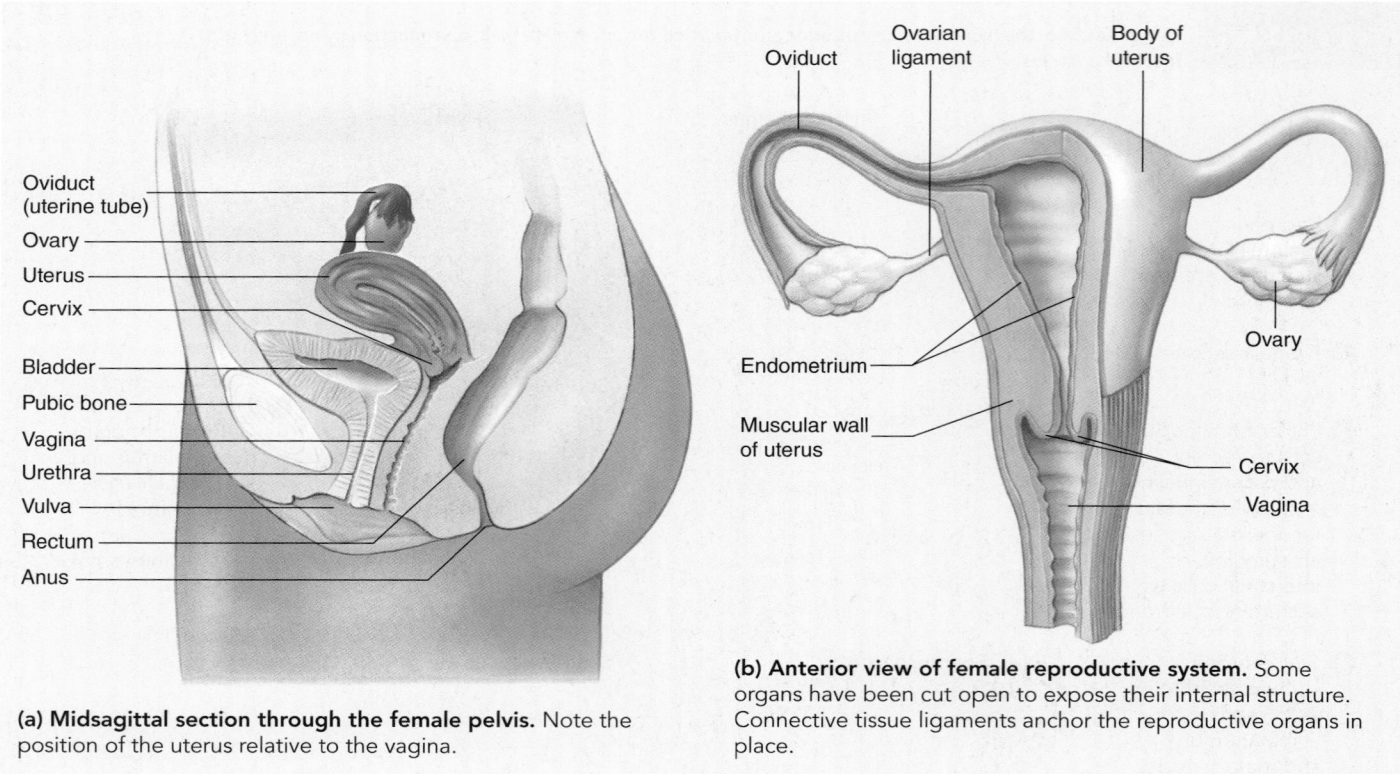

Oviduct (uterine tube)
Ovary
Uterus
Cervix
Bladder
Pubic bone
Vagina
Urethra
Vulva
Rectum
Anus

(a) Midsagittal section through the female pelvis. Note the position of the uterus relative to the vagina.

Oviduct
Ovarian ligament
Body of uterus
Endometrium
Muscular wall of uterus
Ovary
Cervix
Vagina

(b) Anterior view of female reproductive system. Some organs have been cut open to expose their internal structure. Connective tissue ligaments anchor the reproductive organs in place.

FIGURE 50-9 *Animated* Female reproductive system

several layers. Connective tissue cells surrounding the granulosa cells differentiate to form a layer of **theca cells.**

As the follicle matures, the primary oocyte completes its first meiotic division. The two haploid cells produced differ in size (**FIG. 50-11**). The smaller one, the first **polar body,** may later divide, forming two polar bodies, but these eventually disintegrate. The larger cell, the **secondary oocyte,** proceeds to the second meiotic division but remains in metaphase II until it is fertilized. When meiosis continues, the second meiotic division gives rise to a single ovum and a second polar body. The polar bodies are small and apparently dispose of unneeded chromosomes with a minimal amount of cytoplasm. The sequence is as follows:

oogonium (diploid) ⟶ primary oocyte (diploid) ⟶ secondary oocyte + first polar body (both haploid) ⟶ (after fertilization) ovum + second polar body (both haploid)

Recall that in the male, each primary spermatocyte gives rise to four functional sperm cells. In contrast, each primary oocyte generates only one ovum.

As an oocyte develops, it becomes separated from its surrounding follicle cells by a layer of glycoproteins called the **zona pellucida.** As the follicle develops, follicle cells secrete fluid, which collects in the antrum (space) between them (see Fig. 50-10). The follicle cells also secrete **estrogens,** female sex hormones. The principal estrogen is **estradiol** (see Fig. 49-2b). Typically, only one follicle fully matures each month. Several others may develop for a while and then deteriorate by apoptosis.

As a follicle matures, it moves closer to the surface of the ovary, eventually resembling a fluid-filled bulge on the ovarian surface. Follicle cells secrete proteolytic enzymes that break down a small area of the ovary wall. During **ovulation,** the secondary oocyte ejects through the ovary wall and into the pelvic cavity. The portion of the follicle that remains in the ovary develops into the **corpus luteum,** a temporary endocrine gland that secretes estrogen and **progesterone.**

The oviducts transport the secondary oocyte

Almost immediately after ovulation, the secondary oocyte is swept into the funnel-shaped opening of the **oviduct,** also called the **uterine tube** or *fallopian tube.* Ciliated epithelial cells lining the oviduct sweep the secondary oocyte into the oviduct and move it along toward the uterus. Fertilization takes place within the oviduct. If fertilization does not occur, the secondary oocyte degenerates there.

Scarring of the oviducts (for example, by *pelvic inflammatory disease,* caused by a sexually transmitted disease) can block the tubes so that the fertilized ovum cannot pass to the uterus. Women with blocked oviducts may be infertile. Sometimes partial constriction of the oviduct results in *tubal pregnancy.* The embryo cannot progress to the uterus, and it begins to develop in the wall of the oviduct. Because oviducts are not adapted to bear the burden of a developing embryo, the oviduct and the embryo it contains must be surgically removed before it ruptures and endangers the life of the mother.

The uterus incubates the embryo

The oviducts open into the upper corners of the pear-shaped **uterus** (see Fig. 50-9b). About the size of a fist, the uterus (or womb) occupies a central position in the pelvic cavity. It has thick walls of smooth muscle and an epithelial lining, the **endometrium,** which thickens each month in preparation for possible pregnancy. Up to 15% of women (more than five million women in the United States alone) are affected by **endometriosis,** a painful disorder in which fragments of the endometrium migrate to other areas, such as the oviducts or ovaries. Like pelvic inflammatory disease, endometriosis causes scarring that can lead to infertility.

If a secondary oocyte is fertilized, the tiny embryo enters the uterus and implants in the endometrium. As it grows and develops, it is sustained by nutrients and oxygen delivered by surrounding maternal blood vessels. If fertilization does not occur during the monthly cycle, the endometrium sloughs off and is discharged in the process known as **menstruation.**

The lower portion of the uterus, called the **cervix,** extends slightly into the vagina. Cervical cancer is the second most common type of cancer in the world. Almost all cases of cervical cancer are linked to infection with human papillomavirus (HPV). Detection of cervical cancer is usually possible by the routine Papanicolaou test (Pap smear), in which a few cells are scraped from the cervix during a regular gynecological examination and studied microscopically. When cervical cancer is detected at an early stage, there is a good chance that the patient can be cured.

The vagina receives sperm

The **vagina** is an elastic, muscular tube that extends from the uterus to the exterior of the body. The vaginal opening is located in the *perineal region* between the opening of the urethra (anteriorly) and the opening of the anus (posteriorly). The vagina serves as a receptacle for sperm during sexual intercourse and as part of the birth canal (see Fig. 50-9).

(a) **LM of a developing follicle.** The secondary oocyte is surrounded by the zona pellucida (a layer of glycoproteins) and by granulosa cells. Connective tissue cells surrounding the granulosa cells form a layer of theca cells.

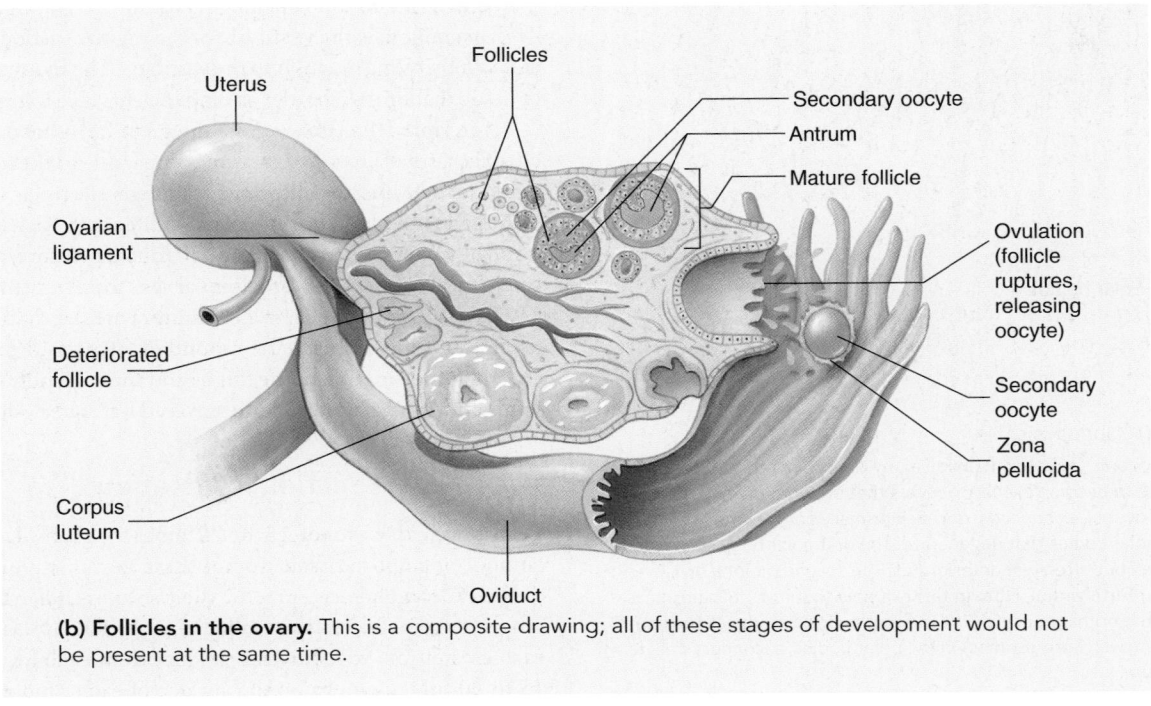

(b) **Follicles in the ovary.** This is a composite drawing; all of these stages of development would not be present at the same time.

FIGURE 50-10 *Animated* Follicle development in the ovary

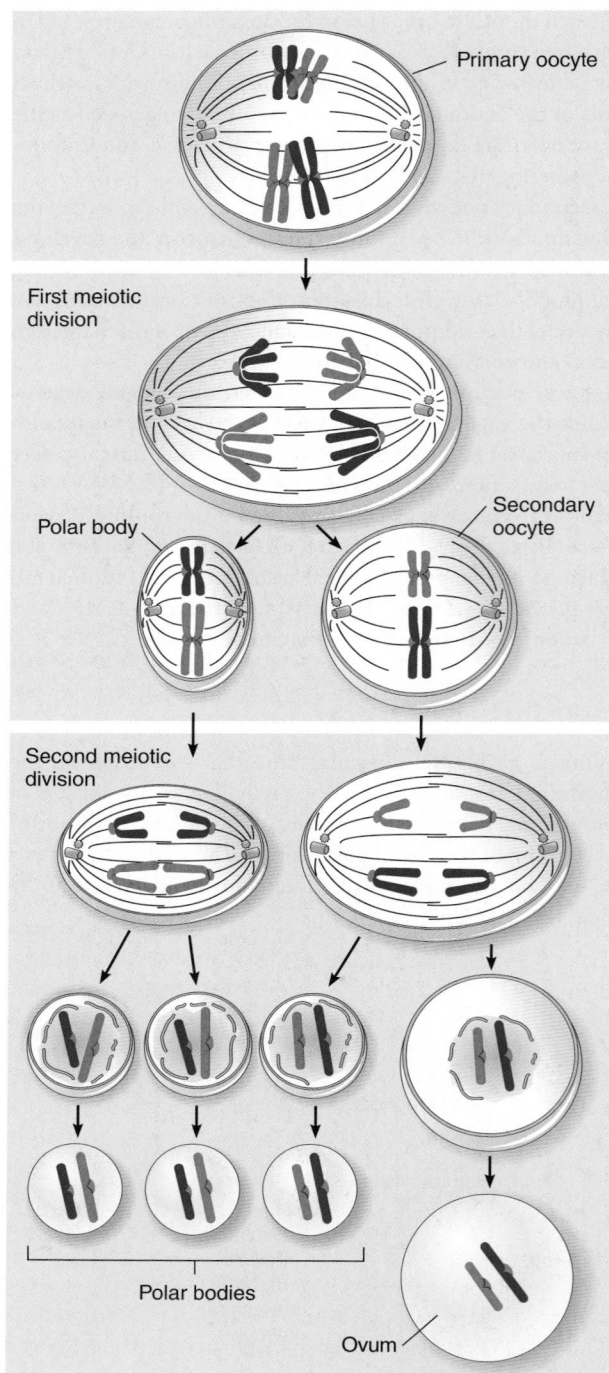

FIGURE 50-11 Oogenesis

Before birth, oogonia (*not shown*) divide many times by mitosis. Some oogonia differentiate to become primary oocytes that undergo meiosis. Only one functional ovum is produced from each primary oocyte. The other cells produced are polar bodies that degenerate. The first polar body sometimes divides as shown but often just deteriorates. The second meiotic division is completed after fertilization. Note in this example that four chromosomes are present in the primary oocyte (2*n*) and that meiosis produces the haploid (*n*) number (two chromosomes) in the polar bodies, secondary oocyte, and mature ovum.

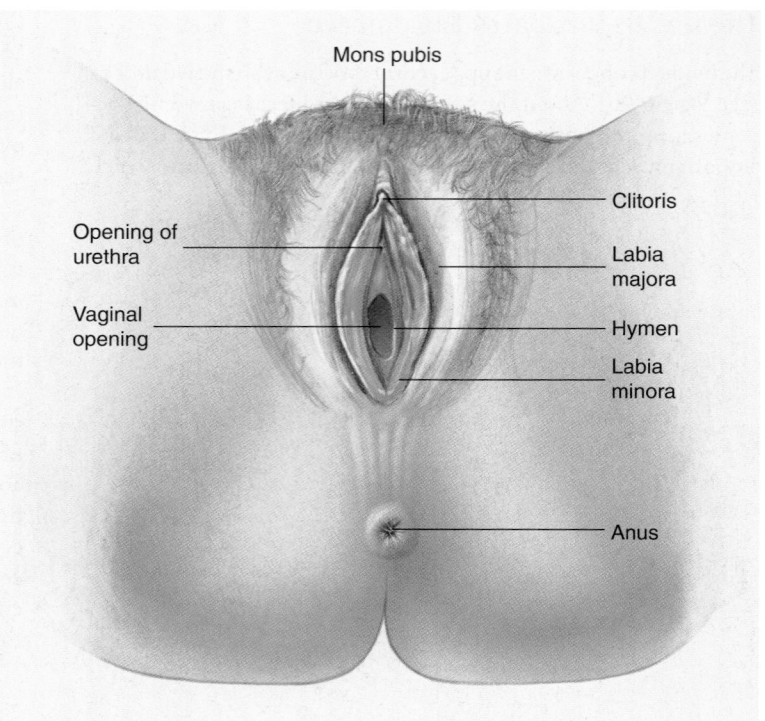

FIGURE 50-12 External female genital structures

Collectively, the structures shown (excluding the anus) are referred to as the vulva.

The vulva are external genital structures

The female external genitalia, collectively known as the **vulva,** include several structures. Liplike folds, the **labia minora,** surround the vaginal and urethral openings (**FIG. 50-12**). The area enclosed by the labia minora is the **vestibule** of the vagina. Vestibular glands secrete a lubricating mucus into the vestibule. The **hymen** is a thin ring of tissue that forms a border around the entrance to the vagina.

Anteriorly, the labia minora merge to form the prepuce of the **clitoris,** a small erectile structure comparable to the male glans penis. Like the penis, the clitoris contains erectile tissue that becomes engorged with blood during sexual excitement. Rich in nerve endings, the clitoris is highly sensitive to touch, pressure, and temperature, and serves as a center of sexual sensation in the female.

External to the delicate labia minora are the thicker **labia majora.** The **mons pubis** is the mound of fatty tissue just above the clitoris at the junction of the thighs and torso. At puberty the mons pubis and labia majora become covered by coarse pubic hair.

The breasts function in lactation

Each breast consists of 15 to 20 lobes of glandular tissue. The amount of adipose tissue around these lobes determines the size of the breasts and accounts for their softness. Gland cells are arranged in grapelike clusters called **alveoli** (**FIG. 50-13**). Ducts from each cluster join to form a single duct from each lobe, producing 15 to 20 tiny openings on the surface of each nipple. The breasts are the most common site of cancer in women, except for the skin (see *Inquiring About: Breast Cancer*).

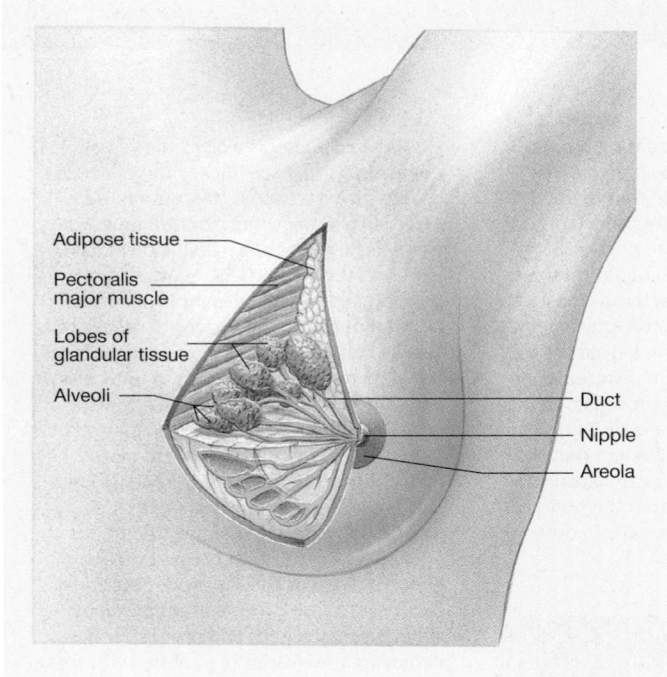

FIGURE 50-13 Structure of the mature female breast
The breast contains lobes of glandular tissue. This tissue consists of alveoli, clusters of gland cells.

Lactation is the production of milk for nourishing the young. During pregnancy, high concentrations of the female reproductive hormones, estrogen and progesterone, stimulate the breasts to increase in size. For the first few days after childbirth, the mammary glands produce a fluid called *colostrum,* which contains proteins and antibodies, but little fat. When the baby suckles, the hormone **prolactin,** secreted by the anterior pituitary, stimulates milk production. Nursing also stimulates the posterior pituitary to release **oxytocin.** This hormone stimulates ejection of milk from the alveoli into the ducts.

Breast-feeding promotes recovery of the uterus because oxytocin released during breast-feeding stimulates the uterus to contract to nonpregnant size. Breast-feeding offers advantages to the baby as well. It promotes bonding between mother and child, and provides milk tailored to the nutritional needs of the human infant. Breast milk contains a variety of immune cells (B cells, T cells, neutrophils, and macrophages) and antibodies. As a result, breast-fed infants have a lower incidence of diarrhea, ear and respiratory infections, and hospital admissions than do formula-fed babies.

The hypothalamus, pituitary gland, and ovaries regulate female reproduction

As in the male, regulation of female reproduction involves many hormones and other signal molecules. In the male, concentration of sex hormones is kept within a narrow range. In contrast, concentrations of female sex hormones change dramatically during the course of each monthly cycle. **TABLE 50-2** lists the actions of the principal female reproductive hormones.

TABLE 50-2	Principal Female Reproductive Hormones		
Endocrine Gland and Hormones	**Principal Target Tissue**	**Principal Actions**	
Hypothalamus			
Gonadotropin-releasing hormone (GnRH)	Anterior pituitary	Stimulates release of FSH and LH	
Anterior Pituitary			
Follicle-stimulating hormone (FSH)	Ovary	Stimulates development of follicles and secretion of estrogen	
Luteinizing hormone (LH)	Ovary	Stimulates ovulation and development of corpus luteum	
Prolactin	Breast	Stimulates milk production (after breast has been prepared by estrogen and progesterone)	
Posterior Pituitary			
Oxytocin	Uterus	Stimulates contraction and stimulates prostaglandin release	
	Mammary glands	Stimulates ejection of milk into ducts	
Ovaries			
Estrogen (estradiol)	General	Stimulates growth of sex organs at puberty and development of secondary sex characteristics	
	Reproductive structures	Induces maturation; stimulates monthly preparation of endometrium for pregnancy; makes cervical mucus thinner and more alkaline	
Progesterone	Uterus	Completes preparation of endometrium for pregnancy	
Inhibin	Anterior pituitary	Inhibits secretion of FSH	

Like testosterone in the male, *estrogens* are responsible for growth of the sex organs at puberty, for body growth, and for the development of secondary sexual characteristics. In the female, these include development of the breasts, broadening of the pelvis, and the characteristic development and distribution of muscle and fat responsible for the female body shape. In females, *puberty* typically begins between ages 10 and 12 and continues until ages 14 to 16.

Hormones of the hypothalamus, anterior pituitary, and ovaries regulate the **menstrual cycle,** the monthly sequence of events that prepares the body for possible pregnancy. (The term *menstrual cycle* is sometimes used more narrowly to refer to the changes that occur in the uterus; we use the term here to include both the ovarian and uterine cycles.) The menstrual cycle runs its course every month from puberty until *menopause,* which occurs at about age 50. Although wide variations exist, a typical menstrual cycle is 28 days long (**FIG. 50-14**).

BREAST CANCER

How common is breast cancer? According to the American Cancer Society, breast cancer is the most common type of cancer among women, other than skin cancer. It is a leading cause of cancer deaths in women, second only to lung cancer. Almost 200,000 new cases of invasive breast cancer are diagnosed each year, and more than 40,000 women die of breast cancer every year in the United States alone. Risk factors for breast cancer include being overweight (especially after menopause), alcohol use (more than two drinks per day), and lack of exercise. Some studies show that cigarette smoking is also a risk factor.

Women with a family history of breast cancer are at higher risk. An estimated 10% of breast cancers are familial, and about half of these patients have mutations in a tumor suppressor gene, either *BRCA1* or *BRCA2*. When the *normal* protein product of the *BRCA1* gene is phosphorylated by a specific protein kinase, it interacts with the normal protein product of the *BRCA2* gene and certain other compounds to repair DNA damage. Women with a family history of breast (or ovarian) cancer should seek genetic counseling and consider genetic testing. For those who test positive, there are now drugs available that decrease the risk of cancer. Some women choose preventive surgery.

About 50% of breast cancers begin in the upper, outer quadrant of the breast. As a malignant tumor grows, it may adhere to the deep tissue of the chest wall. Sometimes it extends to the skin, causing dimpling. Eventually, the cancer spreads to the lymphatic system. About two-thirds of breast cancers have metastasized (spread) to the lymph nodes by the time they are first diagnosed. When diagnosis and treatment begin early, 86% of patients survive for 5 years, and 65% survive for 20 years or longer. Untreated patients have a 5-year survival rate of only 20%.

Common methods of treating breast cancer include mastectomy (surgical removal of the breast), chemotherapy, and radiation treatment. Lumpectomy (surgical removal of only the affected portion of the breast) in conjunction with radiation treatment appears to be as effective as mastectomy in some cases. *Chemotherapy* (chemo) is treatment with drugs that kill cancer cells. Chemotherapy is often administered after surgery to destroy any cancer cells that may have broken away from the main tumor and escaped surgical removal. Even in the early stages of cancer, *metastasis* can occur: cancer cells may move away from the primary tumor and establish new tumors in other parts of the body.

Mammogram showing area of breast cancer. Cancer is seen as a dense mass (*blue*) in this colorized mammogram. The healthy fibrous tissue (*lavender*) supports the glandular structures.

Targeted therapy involves the use of newer drugs that specifically target certain changes in cancer cells. Targeted therapy is often used along with chemotherapy. For example, in about one in five individuals with breast cancer, HER2, a protein that promotes growth, is present in abnormally large amounts on the surface of cancer cells. Cancer cells with HER2 spread more aggressively than other cancer cells. A monoclonal antibody called Herceptin helps slow the growth of these cells. Herceptin may also stimulate the immune system to more effectively destroy the cancer. Monoclonal antibodies are also now available that target new blood vessels that supply the tumors.

About two-thirds of breast cancers have estrogen or progesterone receptors. Growth of these cancers is enhanced by circulating estrogens and progesterone. Removing the ovaries in patients with these tumors relieves the symptoms and may cause remission of the disease for months or even years. Drugs (for example, tamoxifen and aromatase inhibitors) have been developed that antagonize the action of estrogen receptors.

According to the American Cancer Society, when breast cancer is confined to the breast, the 5-year survival rate is almost 100%. Because early detection of breast cancer greatly increases the chances of cure and survival, self-examination and screening are important. The American Cancer Society recommends that women in their 20s and 30s should have a clinical breast exam by a health professional at least every 3 years. After age 40, women should have an annual breast exam by a health professional. Women age 40 and older should have a screening mammogram annually. *Mammography*, a soft-tissue radiological study of the breast, is helpful in detecting very small lesions that might not be identified by routine examination. In mammography, lesions show on an X-ray plate as areas of increased density (see figure).

The first two weeks of the menstrual cycle make up the **preovulatory phase.** Ovulation occurs on about the 14th day of the cycle. The third and fourth weeks of the menstrual cycle are the **postovulatory phase.** As you read the following description of the menstrual cycle, follow the steps illustrated in **FIGURE 50-15.**

The preovulatory phase spans the first two weeks of the cycle

The first five days or so of the preovulatory phase are known as the *menstrual phase.* In fact, the first day of the menstrual cycle is marked by the onset of *menstruation,* the monthly discharge through the vagina of blood and tissue from the endometrium. During the first part of the preovulatory phase, the hypothalamus releases *gonadotropin-releasing hormone (GnRH).* This hormone stimulates the anterior pituitary to release gonadotropic hormones: *follicle-stimulating hormone (FSH)* and *luteinizing hormone (LH).* GnRH, FSH, and LH are the same hormones that help regulate reproduction in the male.

The preovulatory phase is also called the *follicular phase,* because during this period, FSH stimulates a few follicles to begin to develop. FSH also stimulates the granulosa cells of the follicle to multiply and produce estrogen. Some estrogen diffuses into the

Gonadotropic hormones and ovarian hormones regulate the monthly sequence of events that take place within the ovary and uterus.

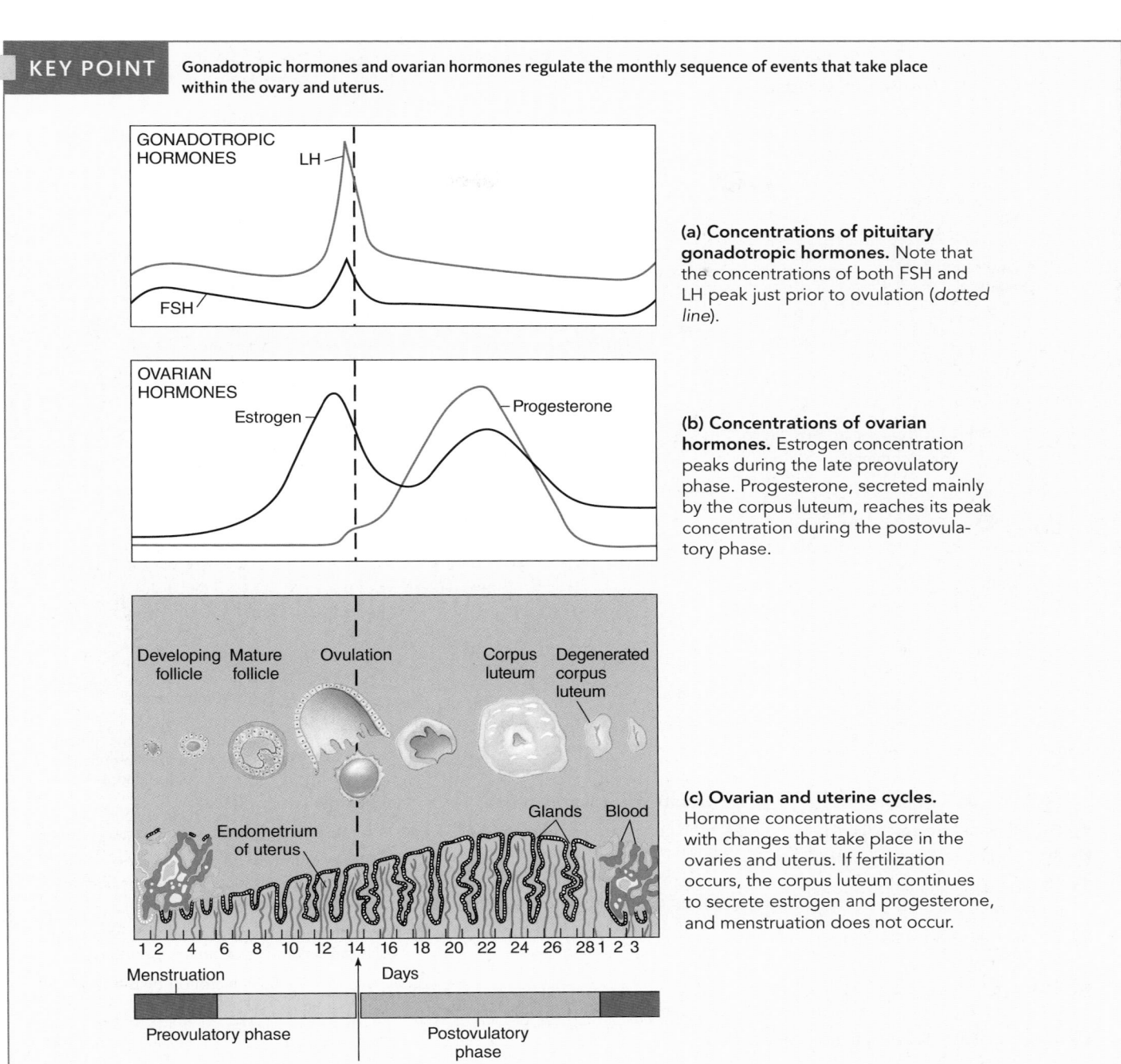

(a) Concentrations of pituitary gonadotropic hormones. Note that the concentrations of both FSH and LH peak just prior to ovulation (*dotted line*).

(b) Concentrations of ovarian hormones. Estrogen concentration peaks during the late preovulatory phase. Progesterone, secreted mainly by the corpus luteum, reaches its peak concentration during the postovulatory phase.

(c) Ovarian and uterine cycles. Hormone concentrations correlate with changes that take place in the ovaries and uterus. If fertilization occurs, the corpus luteum continues to secrete estrogen and progesterone, and menstruation does not occur.

FIGURE 50-14 *Animated* **Endocrine regulation of the menstrual cycle**

When fertilization does not occur, the menstrual cycle repeats about every 28 days. Note the changes in hormone concentrations during the menstrual cycle. (FSH, follicle-stimulating hormone; LH, luteinizing hormone)

blood, but estrogen also has an *autocrine* action on the granulosa cells that produce it and a *paracrine* effect on nearby granulosa cells (see Chapter 49 for a discussion of autocrine and paracrine regulation). The amount of estrogen secreted by the granulosa cells is enhanced by the action of LH on the theca cells. LH stimulates the theca cells to proliferate and produce androgens. The androgens diffuse into the granulosa cells, where they are converted to estrogen. Estrogen stimulates growth of the endometrium, which begins to thicken and develop new blood vessels and glands.

Typically, after the first week of the menstrual cycle, only one follicle continues to develop. Its granulosa cells become sensitive to LH as well as to FSH. This dominant follicle now secretes enough estrogen to cause a rise in the concentration of estrogen in the blood. *Although still at relatively low concentration,* estrogen

The hypothalamus, anterior pituitary, and ovary secrete hormones that regulate the menstrual cycle through feedback systems.

(a) Preovulatory phase.

1 Hypothalamus releases GnRH.

2 FSH stimulates follicle development.

3 LH indirectly stimulates estrogen production.

4 Estrogen stimulates thickening of endometrium.

5 Estrogen has a negative feedback effect on the pituitary and hypothalamus.

6 Inhibin inhibits FSH secretion by pituitary.

(b) Late preovulatory phase.

7 High concentration of estrogen has a positive feedback effect on the pituitary and hypothalamus.

8 Surge of LH stimulates ovulation.

(c) Postovulatory phase.

9 LH stimulates development of corpus luteum.

10 High concentration of progesterone strongly inhibits hypothalamus and anterior pituitary. FSH and LH secretion decreases.

11 Estrogen has a negative feedback effect on the hypothalamus and anterior pituitary.

12 Inhibin inhibits FSH secretion by pituitary.

FIGURE 50-15 Feedback mechanisms in endocrine regulation of female reproduction

Green arrows indicate stimulation; red arrows indicate inhibition. (GnRH, gonadotropin-releasing hormone; FSH, follicle-stimulating hormone; LH, luteinizing hormone)

inhibits secretion of FSH from the pituitary and may also act on the hypothalamus, decreasing secretion of GnRH. In addition, the granulosa cells secrete *inhibin,* a hormone that mainly inhibits FSH secretion. As a result of these negative feedback signals, FSH concentration decreases.

As its concentration in the blood peaks during the late preovulatory phase, estrogen signals the anterior pituitary to secrete LH. This is a positive feedback mechanism. The surge of LH secreted at the middle of the menstrual cycle stimulates the final maturation

of the follicle. The LH surge also stimulates *ovulation,* the ejection of the secondary oocyte from the ovary. The granulosa cells of the follicle decrease their estrogen output, resulting in a temporary decrease in estrogen concentration.

The corpus luteum develops during the postovulatory phase

The postovulatory phase, also called the *luteal phase,* begins after ovulation. LH stimulates development of the corpus luteum, which secretes a large amount of progesterone and estrogen, as well as inhibin. These hormones stimulate the uterus to continue its preparation for pregnancy. Progesterone stimulates tiny glands in the endometrium to secrete a fluid rich in nutrients.

During the postovulatory phase, the high concentration of progesterone in the blood, along with estrogen, inhibits secretion of GnRH, FSH, and LH. Progesterone is thought to act mainly on the hypothalamus. Inhibin acts on the pituitary to further inhibit FSH secretion. As a result of these negative feedback systems, FSH and LH concentrations are low during the postovulatory phase, and no new follicles develop.

If the secondary oocyte is not fertilized, the corpus luteum begins to degenerate after about eight days. Although the mechanism responsible for corpus luteum degeneration is not completely understood, a decrease in LH may be a factor. In addition, the corpus luteum may become less sensitive to LH.

When the corpus luteum stops secreting progesterone and estrogen, the concentrations of these hormones in the blood fall markedly. As a result, small arteries in the endometrium constrict, reducing the oxygen supply. Menstruation, which marks the beginning of a new cycle, begins as cells die and damaged blood vessels rupture and bleed. The concentrations of estrogen and progesterone are now too low to inhibit the anterior pituitary, and secretion of FSH and LH increases once again.

Menstrual cycles stop at menopause

At about age 51, a woman enters **menopause**—a period when ova are no longer produced and the woman becomes infertile. Apparently, a change in the hypothalamus triggers menopause. Although gonadotropic hormones are produced, the ovaries become less responsive to them, and the oocytes in the ovaries begin to degenerate. The ovaries secrete less estrogen and progesterone, and the menstrual cycle becomes irregular and eventually halts.

Women in menopause sometimes experience a sensation of heat ("hot flashes"), probably because of less stable regulation of blood flow through blood vessels in the skin. Periodic increases of warm blood through these blood vessels may cause the sensation of a hot flash. Other physiological changes associated with menopause include night sweats, mood swings, and weight gain. Although its use is controversial, hormone replacement therapy with estrogen and progesterone relieves many of the symptoms of menopause.

In contrast to humans, females of other species maintain their ability to reproduce throughout the lifespan. They do not experience menopause. Researchers have suggested that the infertile postmenopausal period allows older women to help their daughters with grandchildren, increasing their survival rate. This practice helps ensure that the older woman's genes will be transmitted to future generations.

Most mammals have estrous cycles

Only humans and some other primates have menstrual cycles. Most other mammals have **estrous cycles.** Although their reproductive organs and hormones are generally similar, there are some important differences. In animals with estrous cycles, the uterus reabsorbs the thickened lining of the endometrium if conception does not occur. As we have just learned, in animals with a menstrual cycle, the endometrium is expelled during menstruation.

Female animals with estrous cycles, are sexually receptive ("in heat") only during the **estrus** phase of the cycle. The frequency and length of the estrus phase vary. In dogs, the estrus phase typically occurs twice a year and lasts 4 to 13 days. Estrus occurs every 4 to 5 days in rodents. In cats, cycles can occur about every 3 weeks, and the estrus phase averages 7 days. The resting phase of the cycle is prolonged in the fall and early winter. (Why might that be advantageous?) Animals with estrous cycles typically display physiological and behavioral changes that signal sexual readiness to potential mates.

Review

- How is oogenesis different from spermatogenesis? Why are so many sperm produced in the male and so few ova produced in the female?
- What is the function of the corpus luteum? What is the fate of the corpus luteum when the ovum is not fertilized?
- What are specific actions of FSH and LH in the female? of estrogens? of progesterone?

50.4 FERTILIZATION, PREGNANCY, AND BIRTH

■ LEARNING OBJECTIVE

8 Describe the process of human fertilization and summarize the actions of hormones that regulate pregnancy and birth.

Hormones play key roles in preparing the body for fertilization and pregnancy. These signaling molecules are also critical in initiating the birth process.

Fertilization is the fusion of sperm and egg

Fertilization and the subsequent establishment of pregnancy together are referred to as **conception.** After ejaculation into the female reproductive tract, sperm typically remain alive and retain their ability to fertilize an ovum for about 48 hours. However, sperm can survive up to 5 days in the female reproductive tract. The ovum remains fertile for 12 to 24 hours after ovulation. Therefore, in a very regular 28-day menstrual cycle, sexual intercourse during the middle of the cycle is most likely to result in fertilization. However, many women do not have regular menstrual cycles, and many factors can cause an irregular cycle even in women who are generally regular.

When conditions in the vagina and cervix are favorable, sperm begin to arrive at the site of fertilization in the upper oviduct within 30 minutes after ejaculation. At the time of ovulation, when estrogen concentration is high, the cervical mucus has a thin consistency that permits passage of sperm from the vagina into the uterus. During the rest of the menstrual cycle, the cervical mucus is too thick and sticky for sperm to penetrate.

Once sperm enter the uterus, contractions of the muscular uterine wall help transport them. When they reach the oviduct,

NOVEL ORIGINS

What are some benefits of reproductive technology? About five million couples in the United States are affected by infertility, the inability to achieve conception after using no contraception for at least one year. About 30% of cases involve both male and female factors. Male infertility is often attributed to low sperm count. Among the common causes of female infertility are failure to ovulate, production of infertile eggs (common in older women), and oviduct scarring (often caused by pelvic inflammatory disease). Women with blocked oviducts can usually ovulate and incubate an embryo normally but need clinical assistance in getting the young embryo to the uterus.

In the United States, more than three million infertile couples consult health-care professionals each year. Some are helped with conventional treatment, for example with hormone therapy that regulates ovulation or with fertility drugs. But more than 40,000 couples need more sophisticated clinical help. They turn to high-tech, assisted reproductive techniques that have been developed through reproduction and human embryo research. At present these techniques are expensive, and the success rate is low, less than one-third.

The most common assisted reproductive procedure is **artificial insemination,** in which a catheter is used to inject sperm directly into the cervix or uterus. Transfer into the uterus is called **intrauterine insemination (IUI).** More than 600,000 IUI procedures are performed annually with a success rate of about 10%. If a male is infertile because of a low sperm count, his sperm can be concentrated, or alternatively, sperm from a donor can be used. Although the sperm donor usually remains anonymous to the prospective birth parents, his genetic qualifications are screened by physicians.

With **in vitro fertilization (IVF),** a woman takes a fertility drug that induces ovulation of several eggs. The eggs are retrieved by needle aspiration through the vagina. The eggs are placed in a dish with sperm and fertilization takes place in vitro (outside the patient's body). Embryos are cultured for three to five days and then screened for chromosome or gene abnormalities. Healthy ones are transferred into the uterus through the vagina. IVF was first used in England in 1978 to help a couple who

Courtesy of Betsy Dresser

Newborn bongo with its surrogate mother, an eland. As a young embryo, the bongo was transplanted into the eland's uterus, where it implanted and developed. Bongos are a rare and elusive species that inhabits dense forests in Africa. The larger and more common elands inhabit open areas.

had tried unsuccessfully for several years to have a child. Since that time, thousands of "test-tube babies" have been conceived in this way and born to previously infertile women. The success rate of in vitro fertilization is more than 30%; women less than 35 years old have the highest rate of pregnancy, and the rate declines with age.

In **gamete intrafallopian transfer (GIFT),** a laparoscope (a fiber-optic instrument) is used to guide the transfer of eggs and sperm into a woman's oviduct through a small incision in her abdomen. More than 4000 of these expensive procedures are performed each year with a success rate of about 28%. In **zygote intrafallopian transfer (ZIFT),** ova are fertilized in the laboratory. A laparoscope is used to guide the transfer of the resulting zygotes into the oviduct. In these procedures, the woman's own ova may be used. However, if she does not produce fertile eggs, they can be contributed by a donor (**oocyte donation**).

Another novel procedure is **host mothering.** An embryo is removed from its natural mother and implanted into a female

substitute. The foster mother can support the developing embryo either until birth or temporarily until it is implanted again into the original mother or another host. This technique has proved useful to animal breeders. For example, embryos from prize sheep can be temporarily implanted into rabbits for easy shipping by air and then implanted into a host ewe, perhaps one of inferior quality. Host mothering allows an animal with superior genetic traits to produce more offspring than would be naturally possible. This procedure is also used to increase the populations of certain endangered species (see figure).

Technology is available to freeze the gametes or embryos of many species, including humans, and then transplant them into their donors or into host mothers. Freezing eggs may be an effective strategy for women with cancer who undergo chemotherapy or for young women not yet ready to become parents but who want to preserve young eggs with lower risk for chromosome abnormality. These eggs can be implanted at a later time.

---

contractions of smooth muscle in the wall of the oviduct help move sperm toward the egg. The uterine and oviduct contractions are induced by the high estrogen concentration present just before ovulation. Prostaglandins in the semen contribute to this muscle

contraction. The sperm's own motility is important, especially in approaching and fertilizing the secondary oocyte. Also, the secondary oocyte is thought to release a compound that attracts the sperm.

When a sperm encounters an egg, openings develop in the sperm acrosome, exposing enzymes that digest a path through the zona pellucida surrounding the secondary oocyte. As soon as one sperm enters the secondary oocyte, changes occur that prevent the entrance of other sperm. As the fertilizing sperm enters, it usually loses its flagellum (**FIG. 50-16**). Sperm entry stimulates the secondary oocyte to complete its second meiotic division. The head of the haploid sperm then swells to form the **male pronucleus** and fuses with the **female pronucleus** to form the diploid nucleus of the zygote. The process of fertilization is described in more detail in Chapter 51 (also see *Inquiring About: Novel Origins*).

If only one sperm is needed to fertilize a secondary oocyte, why are nearly 200 million ejaculated? Many die as a result of unfavorable pH or phagocytosis by white blood cells and macrophages in the female tract. Only a few hundred succeed in making their way up the correct oviduct and reaching the vicinity of the secondary oocyte. In addition, the enzymes released by the acrosomes of many sperm are needed to break down the barriers that surround the secondary oocyte.

If the secondary oocyte is fertilized, development begins while the embryo is still in the oviduct. After three or four days, the progesterone concentration is sufficiently high to induce changes that permit the oviduct to move the embryo to the uterus. The embryo is moved along by muscle contractions and by the cilia lining the oviduct. By the time it enters the uterus, cleavage has occurred and the embryo consists of a ball of about 32 cells. After floating free in the uterus for another three to four days, the embryo (which has developed into a *blastocyst*) begins to implant in the thick endometrium. Implantation occurs on about the seventh day after fertilization (**FIG. 50-17**). (See Chapter 51 for a discussion of development.)

Hormones are necessary to maintain pregnancy

Estrogen and progesterone are necessary to maintain conditions required for pregnancy. Estrogen stimulates development of the uterine wall, including the muscle needed to expel the fetus during delivery. Progesterone inhibits uterine contractions so that the fetus is not expelled too soon. Because these hormones also inhibit FSH and LH, new follicles do not develop and the menstrual cycle stops during pregnancy.

Membranes that develop around the embryo secrete **human chorionic gonadotropin (hCG),** a peptide hormone that signals the mother's corpus luteum to continue to function. (The presence of hCG in urine or blood is used as an early pregnancy test.) Concentrations of estrogen and progesterone remain high throughout pregnancy. During the first two months, the corpus luteum secretes almost all the estrogen and progesterone necessary to maintain the pregnancy. During this time, membranes surrounding the embryo, together with uterine tissue, form the **placenta,** the organ of exchange between the mother and de-

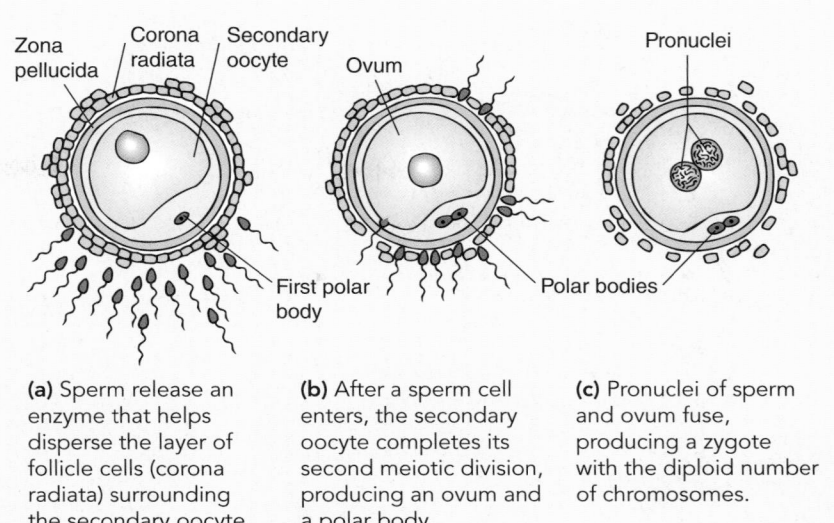

(a) Sperm release an enzyme that helps disperse the layer of follicle cells (corona radiata) surrounding the secondary oocyte.

(b) After a sperm cell enters, the secondary oocyte completes its second meiotic division, producing an ovum and a polar body.

(c) Pronuclei of sperm and ovum fuse, producing a zygote with the diploid number of chromosomes.

10 μm

(d) Color-enhanced SEM of human sperm cells surrounding a test ovum. Sperm are being tested for viability.

FIGURE 50-16 *Animated* **Fertilization**

veloping embryo. By the 10th week of pregnancy, hCG secretion decreases and the corpus luteum begins to deteriorate. The placenta takes over and secretes large amounts of estrogen and progesterone.

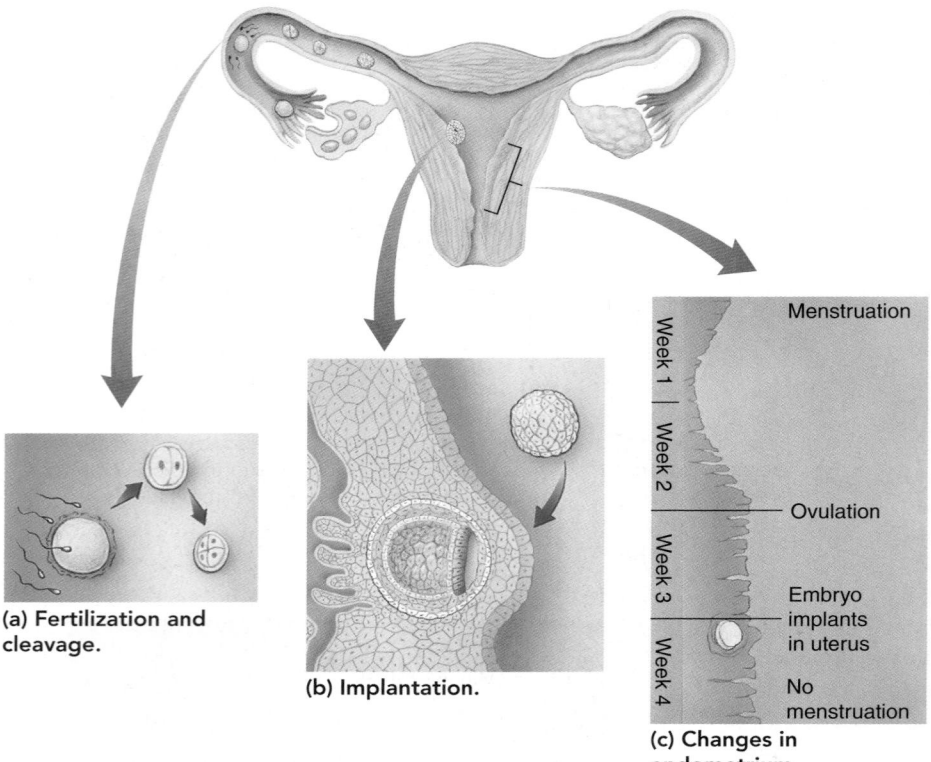

(a) Fertilization and cleavage.

(b) Implantation.

Menstruation

Week 1 | Week 2 | Week 3 | Week 4

Ovulation

Embryo implants in uterus

No menstruation

(c) Changes in endometrium.

FIGURE 50-17 Events following fertilization

The ovarian and uterine cycles are interrupted when pregnancy occurs. The corpus luteum does not degenerate, and menstruation does not take place. Instead, the wall of the uterus thickens even more, permitting the embryo to implant and develop within it. (Cleavage is the early series of mitotic divisions that converts the zygote to a multicellular embryo.)

The birth process depends on a positive feedback system

A normal human pregnancy is about 38 weeks long, counting from the day of fertilization, or about 40 weeks from the first day of the last menstrual cycle. The mechanisms that terminate pregnancy and initiate the birth process, called **parturition,** depend on several hormones. High levels of estrogen secreted by the placenta greatly increase the number of receptors for oxytocin in the uterine wall. As a result, the uterus becomes about one hundred times more responsive to oxytocin, the hormone that stimulates uterine contractions. (Other hormones are involved, but discussion of their roles is beyond the scope of this chapter.)

At the end of pregnancy, the stretching of the uterine muscle by the growing fetus combined with the effects of increased estrogen concentration and oxytocin produce strong uterine contractions. A long series of involuntary contractions of the uterus are experienced as **labor.** Real labor begins when uterine contractions occur in a frequent, regular pattern and cause the cervix to change in preparation for delivery.

Labor can be divided into three stages. During the first stage, which typically lasts 8 to 10 hours, the contractions of the uterus move the fetus toward the cervix, causing the cervix to *dilate* (open) to a maximum diameter of 10 cm (4 in). The cervix also becomes *effaced*; that is, it thins out so that the fetal head can pass through. During the first stage of labor, the amnion (the membrane that forms a fluid-filled sac around the embryo/fetus) usually ruptures and releases about a liter of amniotic fluid, which flows out through the vagina.

A positive feedback cycle operates during the birth process. As the baby's head pushes against the cervix, a reflex action causes the uterus to contract. The contraction forces the head against the cervix again, resulting in another contraction, and the positive feedback cycle repeats again and again until the baby descends through the cervix.

During the second stage, which normally lasts between 20 minutes and an hour, the fetus passes through the cervix and the vagina and is born, or "delivered" (**FIG. 50-18**). With each uterine contraction, the woman bears down so that the fetus is expelled by the combined forces of uterine contractions and contractions of abdominal wall muscles.

At birth, the baby is still connected to the placenta by the umbilical cord. Contractions of the uterus squeeze much of the fetal blood from the placenta into the infant. The cord is tied and cut, separating the child from the mother. (The stump of the cord gradually shrivels until nothing remains but the scar, the **navel.**)

During the third stage of labor, which can last 5 to 30 minutes after the birth, the placenta and the fetal membranes are loosened from the lining of the uterus by another series of contractions and expelled. At this stage they are collectively called the **afterbirth** because these tissues are expelled from the vagina after the baby has been delivered.

During labor an obstetrician may administer oxytocin to increase the contractions of the uterus or may assist delivery with special forceps or a vacuum device. In some women, the opening between the pelvic bones is too small to permit the passage of the baby vaginally. In this situation, the obstetrician performs a **cesarean section,** a surgical procedure in which the baby is delivered through an incision made in the abdominal and uterine walls. A cesarean section may also be performed if the baby's position prevents normal delivery or if the baby shows signs of distress.

Review

- If only one sperm is needed to fertilize an egg, why are so many released?
- What is the function of hCG?
- What are the actions of estrogen and progesterone in maintaining pregnancy?
- What is the role of estrogen in initiating the birth process? of oxytocin?

(a) The mother bears down hard with her abdominal muscles, helping to push the baby out. When the head fully appears, the physician or midwife gently grasps it and guides the baby's entrance into the outside world.

(b) Once the head has emerged, the rest of the body usually follows readily. The physician gently aspirates the mouth and pharynx to clear the upper airway of amniotic fluid, mucus, or blood. At this time the newborn takes its first breath.

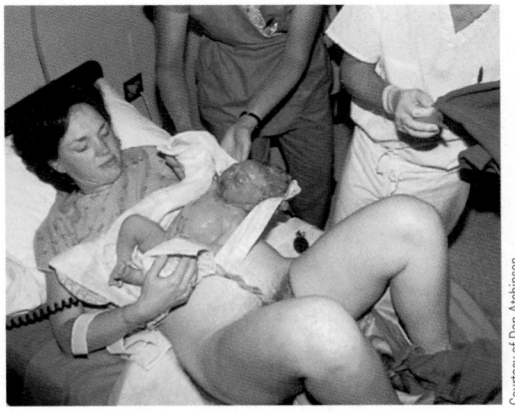

(c) The baby, still attached to the placenta by its umbilical cord, is presented to its mother.

(d) During the third stage of labor, the placenta is delivered.

FIGURE 50-18 The birth process
Uterine contractions during labor expel the fetus from the uterus. In about 95% of all human births, the baby descends through the cervix and vagina in the head-down position.

50.5 HUMAN SEXUAL RESPONSE

■ LEARNING OBJECTIVE

9   Describe the physiological changes that take place during human sexual response.

During **sexual intercourse,** also called *coitus* or *copulation,* the male deposits semen into the upper end of the vagina. The complex structures of the male and female reproductive systems, and the physiological, endocrine, and psychological processes associated with sexual activity, are adaptations that promote fertilization of the secondary oocyte and development of the resulting embryo.

Sexual stimulation results in two basic physiological responses: (1) vasocongestion, the concentration of blood in reproductive structures as well as in certain other areas of the body, and (2) increased muscle tension. Sexual response includes four phases: sexual excitement, plateau, orgasm, and resolution. The *desire* to have sexual activity may be motivated by fantasies or thoughts about sex. This anticipation can lead to (physical) sexual excitement and a sense of sexual pleasure.

Physiologically, the **sexual excitement phase** involves vasocongestion and increased muscle tension. Penile erection is the first male response to sexual excitement. The penis must be erect in order to enter the vagina and function in coitus. In the female, vasocongestion occurs in the vagina, clitoris, and breasts, and the vaginal epithelium secretes a sticky lubricant. Vaginal lubrication is the female's first response to effective sexual stimulation. During the excitement phase, the vagina lengthens and expands in preparation for receiving the penis.

If erotic stimulation continues, sexual excitement heightens to the **plateau phase.** Vasocongestion and muscle tension increase markedly. In both sexes, muscle tension, heart rate, blood pressure, and respiration rate all increase. Sexual intercourse is usually initiated during the plateau phase. The penis creates friction as it is moved inward and outward in the vagina, in actions referred to as pelvic thrusts.

Physical sensations resulting from this friction and the psychological experience of emotional intimacy lead to **orgasm,** the intense physical pleasure that is the climax of sexual excitement. In the female, stimulation of the clitoris heightens the sexual excitement that leads to orgasm.

Although it lasts only a few seconds, orgasm is the phase of maximum sexual tension and its release. In both sexes, orgasm is marked by rhythmic contractions of the muscles of the pelvic floor and reproductive structures. These muscular contractions continue at about 0.8-second intervals for several seconds. After the first few contractions, their intensity decreases, and they become less regular and less frequent.

Heart rate and respiration more than double, and blood pressure increases markedly, just before and during orgasm. Musculoskeletal contractions occur throughout the body. In the male, orgasm is marked by the *ejaculation* of semen from the penis. No fluid ejaculation accompanies orgasm in the female. Orgasm is followed by the **resolution phase,** a state of well-being during which the body is restored to its unstimulated state.

Review

- What physiological changes take place during the sexual response cycle?

50.6 BIRTH CONTROL METHODS AND ABORTION

■ LEARNING OBJECTIVE

10 Compare the modes of action, effectiveness, advantages, and disadvantages of the methods of birth control discussed, including sterilization and emergency contraception; distinguish between spontaneous and induced abortions.

Worldwide, about 180 million pregnancies occur each year, resulting in about 100 million births annually. Population experts estimate that about one-fourth of these are unplanned. An estimated 41 million induced abortions are performed annually. Although most couples worldwide might agree it is best to have babies by choice rather than by chance, most do not have contraceptives available to them. (More than 100 million married women in developing countries have an unmet need for contraception.)

In the United States, almost half of all pregnancies are unplanned. Teen pregnancy is a particularly serious problem. More than 700,000 teenagers become pregnant each year in the United States, and more than 400,000 give birth. Thousands of these girls are ages 14 or younger. The majority of teen births are unintended. Teens often lack the knowledge and means of protecting themselves from unwanted pregnancy.

Many birth control methods are available

When a fertile, heterosexually active woman uses no form of birth control, her chances of becoming pregnant during the course of a year are about 90%. Any method for deliberately separating sexual intercourse from reproduction is **contraception** (literally, "against conception").

Since ancient times, humans have searched for effective methods of preventing fertilization and pregnancy. Of course, fertilization can be avoided by abstaining from sexual intercourse. Some couples avoid having intercourse around the time of ovulation. This cyclical temporary abstinence is called the **rhythm method,** or **natural family planning.** Because the time of ovulation is difficult to determine, the rhythm method has a high failure rate (about 25%).

Scientists continue to develop a variety of contraceptives with a high percentage of reliability. Some of the more common methods of birth control are described in the following paragraphs and in **TABLE 50-3** (see also **FIG. 50-19**). Oral contraceptives, intrauterine devices (IUDs), and female sterilization account for more than two-thirds of all contraception practiced worldwide.

Most hormone contraceptives prevent ovulation

Hormone contraceptives include oral contraceptives, contraceptive patches, rings, implants, and injectable contraceptives. More than 80 million women worldwide (more than 8 million in the United States alone) use oral contraceptives. When taken correctly, oral contraceptives are about 99.7% effective in preventing pregnancy. They are also used to regulate menstrual cycles, control bleeding, and help with symptoms of menses. The most common preparations are combinations of progestin (synthetic progesterone) and synthetic estrogen. (Natural hormones are destroyed by the liver almost immediately, but synthetic ones are chemically modified during production so that they can be absorbed effectively and metabolized slowly.) In a typical regimen, a woman takes one pill each day for about three weeks. Then, for one week she takes a sugar pill that allows menstruation to occur as a result of the withdrawal of the hormones. One type of oral contraceptive works on a 91-day regimen, reducing menstruation to four times per year. Other new oral contraceptives are being marketed as methods to manipulate menstrual cycles so that menstruation is shorter.

Oral contraceptives prevent ovulation. When postovulatory levels of ovarian hormones are maintained in the blood, the body is tricked into responding as though conception has occurred. The pituitary gland is inhibited and does not produce the surge of LH that stimulates ovulation.

Studies suggest that women older than the age of 35, who smoke or have other risk factors, such as untreated hypertension, should not take oral contraceptives. Women in this category who take oral contraceptives have an increased risk of death from stroke and myocardial infarction. Low-dose oral contraceptive pills appear safe for nonsmokers up to the time of menopause. Oral contraceptives are linked to deaths in about 3 per 100,000 users. This compares favorably with the death rate of about 9 per 100,000 pregnancies.

Trends in contraception are geared toward convenience and improved compliance. The birth control patch (Ortho Evra) delivers estrogen and progestin through the skin. The patch is applied weekly for three weeks and removed for the fourth week. During the patch-free week, menstruation usually occurs because the hor-

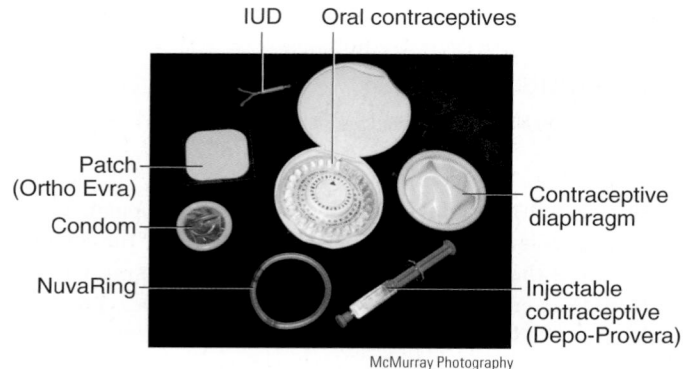

FIGURE 50-19 Some commonly used contraceptives
The only common male method of contraception is the condom, but researchers are developing other methods.

TABLE 50-3 Selected Contraceptive Methods

Method	Failure Rate*	Mode of Action	Advantages	Disadvantages
Oral contraceptives	0.3; 5	Inhibit ovulation; may affect endometrium and cervical mucus and prevent implantation	Highly effective; regulate menstrual cycle	Minor discomfort in some women; should not be used by women over age 35 who smoke or have other risk factors
Injectable contraceptives (Depo-Provera)	About 1	Inhibit ovulation	Effective; long-lasting	Irregular menstrual bleeding; fertility may not return for 6–12 months after contraceptive is discontinued
Intrauterine device (IUD)	1; 1	Prevents fertilization; some IUDs may prevent ovulation	Provides continuous protection; highly effective for several years	Cramps; increased menstrual flow; increased risk of pelvic inflammatory disease and infertility; not recommended for women who have not had a child
Spermicides: foams, jellies, creams	3; 20	Chemically kill sperm	No known side effects; can be used with a condom or diaphragm to improve efficacy	Messy; must be applied before intercourse
Contraceptive diaphragm (with jelly)†	3; 14	Diaphragm mechanically blocks entrance to cervix; jelly is spermicidal	No side effects	Must be inserted prior to intercourse and left in place for several hours afterward
Condom	2.6; 14	Mechanically prevents sperm from entering vagina	No side effects; some protection against STDs, including HIV	Slightly decreased sensation for male; could break
Rhythm‡ (natural family planning)	7; 35	Abstinence during fertile period	No known side effects	Not very reliable
Withdrawal (coitus interruptus)	9; 30	Male withdraws penis from vagina prior to ejaculation	No side effects	Not reliable; sperm in fluid secreted before ejaculation may be sufficient for conception
Sterilization Tubal sterilization	0.04	Prevents oocyte from leaving oviduct	Most reliable method	Requires surgery; considered permanent
Vasectomy	0.15	Prevents sperm from leaving vas deferens	Most reliable method	Requires surgery; considered permanent
Chance (no contraception)	About 90			

*Lower figure is the failure rate of method; higher figure is rate of method failure plus failure of the user to apply the method correctly. Based on number of failures per 100 women who use method per year in the United States.

†Failure rate is lower when diaphragm is used with spermicides.

‡There are several variations of rhythm method. For those who use the calendar method alone, the failure rate is about 35. However, if body temperature is taken daily and careful records are kept (temperature rises after ovulation), failure rate can be reduced. When women use some method to determine time of ovulation and have intercourse *only* more than 48 hours *after* ovulation, failure rate can be reduced to about 7.

mone is withdrawn. Another approach is a thin, flexible plastic ring (NuvaRing) that women can flatten like a rubber band and insert into the vagina once a month. The ring releases progestin and estrogen in the amounts present in low-dose birth control pills.

Injectable progestin (Depo-Provera) is injected intramuscularly every three months. It prevents ovulation by suppressing anterior pituitary function; it also thickens the cervical mucus (which makes it more difficult for the sperm to reach the egg). Implanon, an implant system, consists of a single plastic progestin rod (the size of a cardboard matchstick). The progestin is released over a three-year period. Implanon is considered one of the most effective birth control methods available.

Intrauterine devices are widely used

The **intrauterine device (IUD)** is the most widely used method of reversible contraception in the world, used by an estimated 90 million women. However, in the United States only a small percentage of women use them. The IUD is a small device that is inserted into the uterus by a medical professional. The safety of IUDs in current use has been demonstrated, and they are about 99% effective. Disadvantages of the IUD include uterine cramping and bleeding in a small percentage of women.

One IUD presently being used in the United States, the Copper T380 (ParaGard), can be left in place for 10 years. Another IUD (Mirena), also a small, plastic T-shaped device, releases a very small amount of progestin onto the inner wall of the uterus. This IUD can be left in place for up to five years and can improve the symptoms of a woman's menstrual periods.

The IUD apparently prevents fertilization. The hormone slowly released from certain IUDs may prevent ovulation. Some IUDs cause the cervical mucus to thicken, which impedes passage of sperm into the uterus. The copper in an IUD apparently also reduces the ability of sperm to fertilize the egg. In addition, white blood cells mobilized in response to the foreign body (IUD) in the uterus may produce substances toxic to sperm.

Barrier methods of contraception include the diaphragm and condom

The **contraceptive diaphragm** mechanically blocks the passage of sperm from the vagina into the cervix. It is covered with spermicidal jelly or cream and inserted just prior to sexual intercourse.

The **condom** is also a mechanical method of birth control. The only contraceptive device currently sold for men, the condom provides a barrier that contains the semen so that sperm cannot enter the female tract. The latex condom is the only contraceptive that provides some protection against infection with **human immunodeficiency virus (HIV)** and other sexually transmitted diseases (STDs). The female condom is a strong, soft, polyurethane pouch, or sheath, inserted in the vagina before sexual intercourse. When used correctly, it provides protection against both pregnancy and sexually transmitted infections.

Emergency contraception is available

Emergency contraception is after-the-fact contraception for rape victims and others who have had unprotected sexual intercourse. The use of emergency contraception has significantly reduced the number of abortions. If physicians actively advocated and more women used emergency contraception, many more unwanted pregnancies that occur each year (as a result of contraceptive failure, unprotected sex, or sexual assault) and thousands more abortions could be prevented in the United States alone.

The most common types of emergency contraception are progestin pills, known as Plan B, or combination progestin-and-estrogen pills. Emergency contraception pills are sometimes called morning-after pills, but they can actually be taken up to five days after unprotected intercourse. Emergency contraception pills prevent fertilization or ovulation. Progestin pills decrease the probability

of pregnancy by about 89%. Plan B is now available from health centers and pharmacies without a prescription.

A less common type of emergency contraception is insertion of a copper IUD within a week of unprotected intercourse. This method is more than 99% effective in preventing pregnancy.

Sterilization renders an individual incapable of producing offspring

Sterilization is the only method of contraception not affected by noncompliance or failure to use a contraceptive method correctly. Worldwide, female sterilization is the most common contraceptive method and accounts for one-third of all contraceptive use.

Male sterilization is performed by vasectomy

An estimated one million **vasectomies** are performed each year in the United States. After using a local anesthetic, the physician makes a small incision on each side of the scrotum. Then each vas deferens is cut and its ends sealed so that they cannot grow back together (**FIG. 50-20a**). Because testosterone secretion and transport are not affected, vasectomy does not affect masculinity. Sperm continue to be produced, though at a much slower rate, and are destroyed by macrophages in the testes. No change in amount of semen ejaculated is noticed because sperm account for very little of the semen volume.

By surgically reuniting the ends of the vasa deferentia, surgeons can successfully reverse sterilization in about 50% of males. Some sterilized men eventually develop antibodies against their own sperm and remain sterile even after their vasectomies have been surgically reversed. Therefore, fertility rates are low (about 30%) for men who undergo vasectomy reversal after 10 or more years.

An alternative to vasectomy reversal is the storage of frozen sperm in sperm banks. Such banks have been established throughout the United States. If the male should decide to father another child after he has been sterilized, he "withdraws" his sperm to artificially inseminate his mate. However, sperm do not always survive freezing, and even if it remains viable, there may be an increased risk of genetic defects.

(a) **Vasectomy.** The vas deferens (sperm duct) on each side is cut and cauterized.

(b) **Tubal sterilization.** Each oviduct is cut and cauterized so that oocyte and sperm can no longer meet.

FIGURE 50-20 Sterilization

Female sterilization is by tubal sterilization

In the United States, **tubal sterilization** is the most common means of birth control. A surgeon performs this procedure while the patient is under general anesthesia by making a small abdominal incision and using a laparoscope to locate and cut the oviducts (**FIG. 50-20b**). The tubes are then burned (cauterized), or they may be clipped or clamped. Sometimes a small section of the tube is removed. This procedure is often performed at the time of cesarean section (C-section).

Tubal sterilization can be accomplished without an incision. A physician inserts two small metal coils through the vagina, cervix, uterus, and up into the oviducts. The coils cause scar tissue to develop, which blocks the oviducts. As with the male, hormone balance and sexual performance of the female are not affected by sterilization.

Future contraceptives may control regulatory peptides

Ideal contraceptives have not yet been developed. Among the issues that must be considered in developing contraceptives are safety, effectiveness, cost, convenience, and ease of use. Risks of cancer, birth defects in case the method fails and the woman becomes pregnant, permanent infertility, and side effects such as menstrual abnormalities must be minimized.

Some researchers predict that future contraceptive methods will control regulatory peptides and the genes that code for them. For example, the genes that code for certain hormone signals could be interrupted. Another approach being studied is development of contraceptive vaccines that would stimulate the immune system to produce antibodies against hCG or some other protein essential to reproduction. Some investigators are exploring methods for interfering with sperm motility or with fertilization. It is likely that current methods of contraception will be replaced by more sophisticated molecular methods within the next several years.

Abortions can be spontaneous or induced

Abortion is the termination of pregnancy that results in the death of the embryo or fetus. **Spontaneous abortions** (commonly referred to as miscarriages) occur without intervention. Embryos that are spontaneously aborted are frequently abnormal. **Induced abortions** are performed deliberately either for therapeutic reasons or as a means of birth control. **Therapeutic abortions** are performed when the mother's life is in danger or when there is reason to suspect that the embryo is grossly abnormal.

Abortions are sometimes used as a means of birth control. Worldwide, more unplanned than planned pregnancies occur each year, and more than half of the unplanned pregnancies end in abortion. An estimated 41 million induced abortions are performed each year (more than a million in the United States).

Most first-trimester abortions (those performed during the first three months of pregnancy) are performed by a suction method or by administering drugs that interrupt the pregnancy and induce expulsion of the embryo. In the suction method of abortion, the cervix is dilated, and a suction aspirator is inserted into the uterus. The embryo and other products of conception are evacuated.

Drugs are also used to interrupt pregnancy. The drug *RU-496* (mifepristone) binds competitively with progesterone receptors in the uterus but does not activate them. Because the normal actions of progesterone are blocked, the endometrium breaks down and uterine contractions occur. These conditions prevent implantation of an embryo. The action of methotrexate, a drug used to treat cancer, is similar to that of RU-496. Both of these drugs interrupt pregnancy. Prostaglandins may then be administered to induce the uterine contractions that expel the embryo.

After the first trimester, abortions are performed mainly because of fetal abnormalities or maternal illness. The method most commonly used is dilation and evacuation. The cervix is dilated, forceps are used to remove the fetus, and suction is used to aspirate the remaining contents of the uterus. Drugs such as prostaglandins are also used to induce labor in second-trimester abortions.

When abortions are performed by skilled medical personnel, they are relatively safe. The mortality rate in the United States is less than 1 per 100,000. In countries where abortion is illegal (and unsafe), the death rate is as high as 700 per 100,000. These statistics can be contrasted with the death rate from pregnancy and childbirth of about 9 per 100,000. The World Health Organization estimates that one-third of all maternal deaths result from poorly performed illegal abortions.

Review

- How do hormone contraceptives work?
- What is emergency contraception?
- What is a spontaneous abortion? a therapeutic abortion?

50.7 SEXUALLY TRANSMITTED DISEASES

◼ LEARNING OBJECTIVE

11 Identify common sexually transmitted diseases and describe their symptoms, effects, and treatments.

Sexually transmitted diseases (STDs), also called *venereal diseases (VDs)* or *sexually transmitted infections (STIs),* are, next to the common cold, the most prevalent communicable diseases in the world. The World Health Organization has estimated that more than 62 million people are infected each year with **gonorrhea,** and more than 12 million are infected with **syphilis.** Globally, more than 33 million people are living with HIV and more than 30 million have died of AIDS since 1981 (discussed in Chapter 45).

In the United States, more than 65 million people are currently living with an STD, and more than 12 million people (including 3 million teens) are diagnosed with new STD infections each year. One in three sexually active young people will acquire an STD by age 24.

Human papillomavirus (HPV) is now the most common STD in the United States. An estimated 20 million people in the United States are currently infected with HPV. At least 50% of sexually active men and women will become infected with this virus at sometime during their lives. In most infected individuals, the

TABLE 50-4 Some Common Sexually Transmitted Diseases

Disease and Causative Organism	Course of Disease	Treatment
Human papillomavirus (HPV; about 30 strains of HPV can infect reproductive organs)	Causes abnormal Pap smears and cervical cancer; some strains cause genital warts	Immune modifiers; interferon; vaccines now available
Chlamydia (*Chlamydia trachomatis*, a bacterium)	Discharge and burning with urination, or asymptomatic; men 15–30 years old with multiple sex partners are most at risk; in women can cause pelvic inflammatory disease (PID), infection of reproductive organs and pelvic cavity that may lead to sterility (> 15% of cases)	Antibiotics
Gonorrhea (*Neisseria gonorrhoeae*, a gonococcus bacterium)	Bacterial toxin may produce redness and swelling at infection site; symptoms in males are painful urination and discharge of pus from penis; in about 60% of infected women no symptoms initially; can spread to epididymis (in males) or oviducts and ovaries (in females), causing sterility; can cause widespread infection; damage to heart valves, meninges (outer coverings of brain and spinal cord), and joints	Antibiotics
Syphilis (*Treponema pallidum*, a spirochete bacterium)	Bacteria enter body through defect in skin; primary chancre (small, painless ulcer) at site of initial infection; highly infectious at this stage; secondary stage, widespread rash and influenza-like symptoms; scaly lesions may occur that are highly infectious; latent stage that follows can last 20 years; eventually, lesions called gummae may form that damage liver, brain, bone, or spleen; death results in 5%–10% of untreated cases	Penicillin
Genital herpes (herpes simplex type 2 virus)	Symptoms may be absent or minimal. When they occur, symptoms include painful blisters in genital area that develop into ulcers; symptoms recur periodically; threat to fetus or newborn infant	No effective cure; some drugs may shorten outbreaks or reduce severity; medication can be taken to prevent outbreak
Trichomoniasis (a protozoon)	Itching, discharge, soreness; can be contracted from dirty toilet seats and towels; may be asymptomatic in males	Metronidazole (an antibiotic)
"Yeast" infections (genital candidiasis; *Candida albicans*)	Irritation, soreness, discharge; especially common in females; rare in males; can be acquired nonsexually	Antifungal drugs
Acquired immunodeficiency syndrome (AIDS)* (caused by human immunodeficiency virus, HIV)	Influenza-like symptoms: swollen lymph glands, fever, night sweats, weight loss; decreased immunity, leading to pneumonia, rare forms of cancer	No effective cure; a variety of drugs reduce symptoms and prolong life

*AIDS was discussed in Chapter 45.

immune system destroys the virus before it causes serious health problems. However, HPV can cause abnormal Pap smears and cervical cancer. Some strains of HPV cause genital warts. Two vaccines (Gardasil and Cervarix) prevent infection by several harmful HPV strains. Health professionals anticipate that such vaccines will lead to the decline of genital warts and cervical cancer. For the vaccine to be most effective, individuals must be vaccinated before they become sexually active. These vaccines are recommended for 11- and 12-year-old girls and are available for women through age 26. The vaccine Gardasil protects boys and men against genital warts and is available for males 9 to 26 years old.

Chlamydia, another common STD, causes no symptoms in about 50% of infected men and 75% of infected women. Infected men may notice a discharge from the penis and infected women may have a vaginal discharge. In women, the infection can spread and cause **pelvic inflammatory disease (PID).** This serious infection leads to infertility in about 20% of infected women.

One out of four women and one out of five men are infected with **genital herpes,** which is caused by a virus. Most infected individuals have minimal symptoms, or no symptoms. When outbreaks occur, symptoms include blisters around the genital area.

Some common STDs are described in **TABLE 50-4.** (See Chapter 45 for a discussion of HIV.)

Review

- What is now the most common STD in the United States?
- What is PID? What causes it?

■ SUMMARY: FOCUS ON LEARNING OBJECTIVES

50.1 *(page 1078)*

1 Compare the benefits of asexual and sexual reproduction, and describe each mode of reproduction, giving specific examples.

- In **asexual reproduction,** a single parent endows its offspring with a set of genes identical to its own. Asexual reproduction is energy efficient, and is most successful in stable environments.

- In **budding,** a part of the parent's body grows and separates from the rest of the body. In **fragmentation,** the parent's body may break into several pieces; each piece can develop into a new animal. In **parthenogenesis,** an unfertilized egg develops into an adult.

- In **sexual reproduction,** offspring are produced by the fusion of two types of gametes—**ovum** and **sperm.** When a sperm and egg fuse, a fertilized egg, or **zygote,** is produced. Sexual reproduction promotes genetic variety and is especially adaptive in unstable, changing environments.

- In **external fertilization,** mating partners typically release eggs and sperm into the water simultaneously. In **internal fertilization,** the male delivers sperm into the female's body.

- In **hermaphroditism,** a single individual produces both eggs and sperm.

50.2 *(page 1080)*

2 Relate the structure of each organ of the human male reproductive system to its function.

- The human male reproductive system includes the testes, which produce sperm and testosterone; a series of conducting ducts; accessory glands; and the **penis.**

- The **testes,** housed in the **scrotum,** contain the **seminiferous tubules,** where **spermatogenesis** (sperm production) takes place. The **interstitial cells** in the testes secrete testosterone. **Sertoli cells** produce signaling molecules and a fluid that nourishes sperm cells.

- Sperm complete their maturation and are stored in the **epididymis** and **vas deferens.** During ejaculation, sperm pass from the vas deferens to the **ejaculatory duct** and then into the **urethra,** which passes through the penis.

- The penis consists of three columns of **erectile tissue,** two **cavernous bodies** and one **spongy body,** which surrounds the urethra. When its erectile tissue becomes engorged with blood, the penis becomes erect and functions as the copulatory organ.

CENGAGENOW™ Learn more about the male reproductive system by clicking on the figure in CengageNOW.

3 Trace the passage of sperm cells through the human male reproductive system from their origin in the seminiferous tubules to their expulsion from the body in the semen. (Include a description of spermatogenesis.)

- Spermatogenesis takes place in the seminiferous tubules of the testes. **Spermatogonia** divide by mitosis; some differentiate and become **primary spermatocytes,** which undergo **meiosis.** The first meiotic division produces two **secondary spermatocytes.** In the second meiotic division, each secondary spermatocyte produces two **spermatids.** Each spermatid differentiates to form a mature sperm. The head of a sperm consists of the nucleus and a cap, or **acrosome,** containing enzymes that help the sperm penetrate the egg.

- Sperm pass in sequence through the seminiferous tubules of the testis, epididymis, vas deferens, ejaculatory duct, and urethra.

- Each ejaculate of semen contains about 200 million sperm suspended in the secretions of the **seminal vesicles** and **prostate gland.** The **bulbourethral glands** release a mucous secretion.

CENGAGENOW™ Learn more about spermatogenesis by clicking on the figure in CengageNOW.

4 Describe endocrine regulation of reproduction in the human male.

- **Testosterone** establishes and maintains male **primary sex characteristics,** growth of reproductive organs, and spermatogenesis. Testosterone also stimulates development of **secondary sex characteristics** at puberty: growth of facial and body hair, muscle development, and deepened voice.

- Endocrine regulation of male reproduction involves the hypothalamus, pituitary gland, and testes. The hypothalamus secretes **gonadotropin-releasing hormone (GnRH),** which stimulates the anterior pituitary gland to secrete the gonadotropic hormones: **follicle-stimulating hormone (FSH)** and **luteinizing hormone (LH).**

- FSH, LH, and testosterone directly or indirectly stimulate sperm production. LH stimulates the interstitial cells of the testes to produce testosterone. FSH stimulates the Sertoli cells to produce (1) **androgen-binding protein (ABP),** which binds to testosterone and concentrates it, and (2) **inhibin,** a hormone that inhibits FSH secretion.

CENGAGENOW™ Learn more about the hormonal control of sperm production by clicking on the figure in CengageNOW.

50.3 *(page 1084)*

5 Relate the structure of each organ of the human female reproductive system to its function.

- The **ovaries** produce gametes and the steroid hormones **estrogen** and **progesterone.** Fertilization takes place in the **oviducts** (uterine tubes).

- The **uterus** serves as an incubator for the developing embryo. The epithelial lining of the uterus, the **endometrium,** thickens each month in preparation for possible pregnancy. The lower part of the uterus, the **cervix,** extends into the vagina.

- The **vagina** receives the penis during sexual intercourse and is the lower part of the birth canal. The **vulva** includes the **labia majora, labia minora, vestibule** of the vagina, **clitoris,** and **mons pubis.**

- The breasts function in **lactation,** production of milk for the young. Each breast consists of 15 to 20 lobes of glandular tissue. The hormone **prolactin** stimulates milk production; **oxytocin** stimulates ejection of milk from the alveoli into the ducts, making it available to the nursing infant.

CENGAGENOW™ Learn more about the female reproductive system by clicking on the figure in CengageNOW.

6 Trace the development of a human egg and trace its passage through the female reproductive system until it is fertilized.

- **Oogenesis** takes place in the ovaries. **Oogonia** differentiate into **primary oocytes.** A primary oocyte and the **granulosa cells** surrounding it make up a **follicle.**

- As the follicle grows, connective tissue cells surrounding the granulosa cells form a layer of **theca cells.** As the follicle matures, the primary oocyte undergoes the first meiotic division, giving rise to a **secondary oocyte** and a **polar body.**

- During **ovulation,** the secondary oocyte is ejected from the ovary and enters one of the paired oviducts, where it may be fertilized. The part of the follicle remaining in the ovary develops into a **corpus luteum,** a temporary endocrine gland.

CENGAGENOW™ Learn more about oogenesis by clicking on the figure in CengageNOW.

7 Describe the endocrine regulation of reproduction in the human female, and identify the important events of the menstrual cycle, such as ovulation and menstruation.

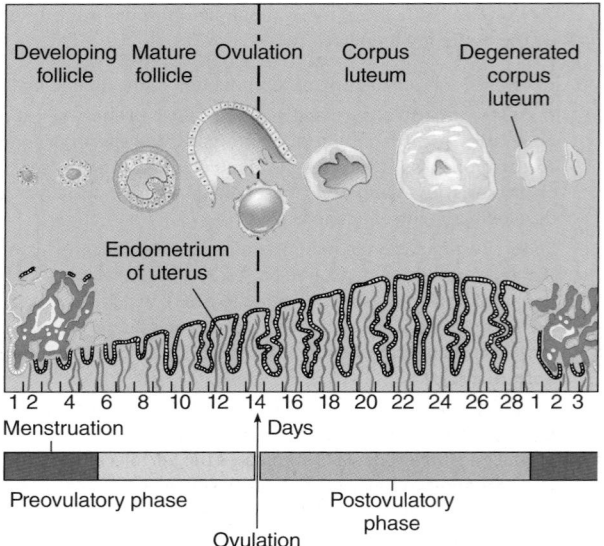

- Endocrine regulation of female reproduction involves the hypothalamus, pituitary gland, and ovaries. The first day of the **menstrual cycle** is marked by the beginning of menstrual bleeding. Ovulation occurs at about day 14 in a typical 28-day menstrual cycle.

- During the **preovulatory phase,** gonadotropin-releasing hormone (GnRH) from the hypothalamus stimulates the anterior lobe of the pituitary to secrete follicle-stimulating hormone (FSH) and luteinizing hormone (LH). FSH stimulates follicle development and stimulates the granulosa cells to produce estrogen. LH stimulates theca cells to multiply and produce androgens, which are converted to estrogen.

- Estrogen is responsible for primary and secondary female sex characteristics and stimulates development of the endometrium.

- After the first week, only one follicle continues to develop. Although at relatively low concentration, estrogen inhibits FSH secretion by negative feedback. Granulosa cells produce inhibin, which also inhibits FSH secretion.

- During the late preovulatory phase, estrogen concentration peaks. Through a positive feedback mechanism, estrogen signals the anterior pituitary to secrete LH. This hormone stimulates final maturation of the follicle and stimulates ovulation.

- During the **postovulatory phase,** LH promotes development of the corpus luteum. The corpus luteum secretes progesterone and estrogen, which stimulate final preparation of the uterus for pregnancy. During the postovulatory phase, progesterone, along with estrogen, inhibits secretion of GnRH, FSH, and LH.

- If fertilization does not occur, the corpus luteum degenerates, concentrations of estrogen and progesterone in the blood fall, and menstruation occurs.

CENGAGENOW™ Explore hormonal control of the menstrual cycle by clicking on the figures in CengageNOW.

50.4 (page 1093)

8 Describe the process of human fertilization and summarize the actions of hormones that regulate pregnancy and birth.

- Human **fertilization** is the fusion of secondary oocyte and sperm to form a zygote. The processes of fertilization and establishing pregnancy together are called **conception.**

- If the secondary oocyte is fertilized, development begins and the embryo implants in the uterus. Membranes that develop around the embryo secrete **human chorionic gonadotropin (hCG),** a hormone that maintains the corpus luteum. During the first two to three months of pregnancy, the corpus luteum secretes the large amounts of estrogen and progesterone needed to maintain pregnancy. After three months, the **placenta,** the organ of exchange between mother and embryo, assumes this function.

CENGAGENOW™ Learn more about fertilization by clicking on the figure in CengageNOW.

- Several hormones, including estrogen, oxytocin, and prostaglandins, regulate **parturition,** the birth process. Labor can be divided into three stages; the baby is delivered during the second stage.

50.5 (page 1097)

9 Describe the physiological changes that take place during human sexual response.

- Vasocongestion and increased muscle tension are physiological responses to sexual stimulation. The phases of sexual response include **sexual excitement, plateau, orgasm,** and **resolution.**

50.6 (page 1098)

10 Compare the modes of action, effectiveness, advantages, and disadvantages of the methods of birth control discussed, including sterilization and emergency contraception; distinguish between spontaneous and induced abortions.

- Effective methods of **contraception** include **hormone contraceptives,** such as oral contraceptives and injectable progestin; **intrauterine devices (IUDs); condoms; contraceptive diaphragms;** and **sterilization (vasectomy** in the male and **tubal sterilization** in the female); see Table 50-3. Emergency contraception can be used to prevent unwanted pregnancy after rape or unprotected intercourse.

- **Spontaneous abortions** (miscarriages) occur without intervention. **Induced abortions** include **therapeutic abortions,** performed when the mother's health is in danger or when the embryo is thought to be grossly abnormal. Abortions are also induced as a means of birth control.

50.7 (page 1101)

11 Identify common sexually transmitted diseases and describe their symptoms, effects, and treatments.

- Among the common types of **sexually transmitted diseases (STDs)** are **human papillomavirus (HPV), chlamydia** (the most common cause of **pelvic inflammatory disease**), genital herpes, gonorrhea, syphilis, and **human immunodeficiency virus, HIV** (see Table 50-4).

TEST YOUR UNDERSTANDING

1. Hermaphroditism (a) is a form of asexual reproduction (b) occurs when an unfertilized egg develops into an adult animal (c) is a form of sexual reproduction in which an animal produces both eggs and sperm (d) typically involves self-fertilization (e) typically requires only a male animal

2. In contrast to asexual reproduction, sexual reproduction (a) is a faster way to produce offspring (b) is more efficient (c) is more effective at increasing fitness (d) is less efficient at removing harmful mutations from a population (e) limits genetic variety among members of a population

3. The seminiferous tubules (a) are the site of spermatogenesis (b) produce most of the seminal fluid (c) empty directly into the vas deferens (d) are located within the cavernous body (e) receive fluid from the bulbourethral glands

4. Arrange the following stages into the correct sequence.
   1. spermatogonium 2. spermatid 3. primary spermatocyte
   4. secondary spermatocyte 5. sperm
   (a) 2, 1, 3, 4, 5 (b) 5, 1, 3, 4, 2 (c) 4, 3, 1, 2, 5 (d) 1, 4, 3, 2, 5
   (e) 1, 3, 4, 2, 5

5. Which sequence best describes the passage of sperm?
   1. seminiferous tubules 2. vas deferens 3. epididymis
   4. ejaculatory duct 5. urethra
   (a) 3, 1, 2, 4, 5 (b) 1, 3, 2, 4, 5 (c) 5, 4, 2, 3, 1 (d) 1, 3, 4, 2, 5
   (e) 3, 1, 4, 2, 5

6. Which of the following cells is haploid? (a) primary oocyte (b) oogonium (c) secondary oocyte (d) cells of the corpus luteum (e) follicle cell

7. The corpus luteum (a) is surrounded by ova (b) degenerates if fertilization occurs (c) develops in the preovulatory phase (d) is maintained by prostaglandins (e) serves as a temporary endocrine gland

8. After ovulation, the secondary oocyte enters the (a) oviduct (b) corpus luteum (c) cervix (d) ovary (e) vagina

9. Uterine contraction is strongly stimulated by (a) progesterone (b) FSH (c) LH (d) oxytocin (e) inhibin

10. Hormone contraceptives (a) prevent ovulation (b) decrease estrogen concentration in the blood (c) are not as effective as barrier methods of contraception (d) decrease risk of STDs (e) a and b

11. Pelvic inflammatory disease is commonly caused by (a) syphilis (b) gonorrhea (c) genital herpes (d) HIV (e) chlamydia

12. Label the diagram. Use Figure 50-9b to check your answers.

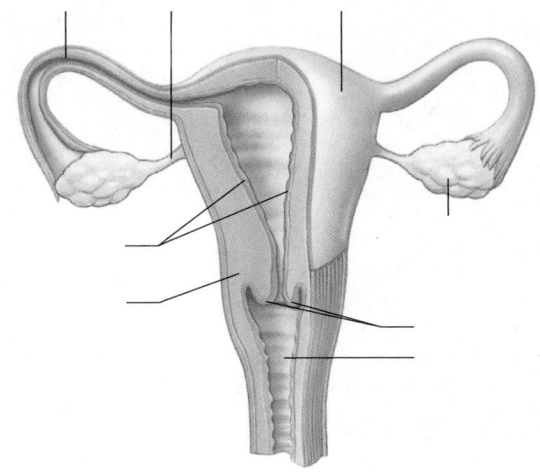

CRITICAL THINKING

1. How would a woman be affected if ovulation occurred but no corpus luteum developed?

2. **EVOLUTION LINK.** Contrast the biological advantages of hermaphroditism that involves cross-fertilization with hermaphroditism that involves self-fertilization.

3. **EVOLUTION LINK.** Asexual reproduction is more common in habitats with few parasites. Sexual reproduction is more common in habitats with larger numbers of parasites. Develop a hypothesis to explain why.

4. **ANALYZING DATA.** Examine Figure 50-14. Which hormones are present in largest concentration just before ovulation? During which part of the menstrual cycle is the endometrium most prepared to receive an embryo? Which hormones stimulate thickening of the endometrium?

5. **SCIENCE, TECHNOLOGY, AND SOCIETY.** Why do you think a variety of effective methods of male contraception have not yet been developed? If you were a researcher, what are some approaches you might take to development of a method of male contraception?

6. **SCIENCE, TECHNOLOGY, AND SOCIETY.** The incidence of abortion has declined more in countries where abortions are legal (and safe) than in countries in which they are illegal (and unsafe). Can you suggest an explanation?

 Additional questions are available in CengageNOW at www.cengage.com/login.

51 Animal Development

Human embryo in its seventh week of development. The embryo is 2 cm (0.8 in) long.

Lennart Nilsson, from *A Child Is Born*, Dell Publishing, 1989

Development includes all the changes that take place during the entire life of an individual. In this chapter, however, we focus mainly on the fertilization of the egg to form a zygote and the subsequent development of the young animal before birth or hatching.

Just how does a microscopic, unicellular zygote give rise to the bones, muscles, brain, and other structures of a complex animal? The zygote divides by mitosis, forming an **embryo** that subsequently undergoes an orderly sequence of cell divisions. In animals, growth (that is, increase in mass) occurs primarily by an increase in the number of cells; but it also occurs by an increase in cell size, as in fat cells. Although the very early embryo usually does not grow, later cell divisions typically contribute to growth. However, by itself cell division, which is governed by a genetic program that interacts with environmental signals (see Chapter 10), would produce only a formless heap of similar cells. We therefore begin this chapter with a discussion of the fundamental processes introduced in Chapter 17 that contribute to the development of form: cell determination and cell differentiation; and pattern formation and morphogenesis.

The photograph shows a human embryo, as well as part of the placenta (large, fluffy mass in the lower right-hand corner). In this chapter you have an opportunity to compare and contrast the sequences of developmental events in several different animals in addition to humans. Researchers have chosen these model organisms because they have certain desirable characteristics. For example, the embryos of certain types of animals, such as echinoderms and amphibians, can be obtained in large quantities, which facilitates studies in which biochemical changes are correlated with developmental landmarks. The embryos of echinoderms are particularly easy to observe because they are transparent. The embryos of echinoderms, amphibians, and birds are easily grown in the laboratory. As you read, note the intimate interrelationships among the sequential developmental processes, as well as the fundamental similarities among the early developmental events in the different animal groups featured. Many decades of painstaking investigations on these similarities became the foundations of the science of evolutionary developmental biology, popularly known as **Evo Devo,** introduced in Chapters 17 and 30.

51.1 DEVELOPMENT OF FORM

■ LEARNING OBJECTIVES

1   Analyze the relationship between cell determination and cell differentiation, and between pattern formation and morphogenesis.
2   Relate differential gene expression to nuclear equivalence.

The development of the form of an animal is a consequence of a balanced combination of several fundamental processes that go beyond cell division and growth: cell determination and cell differentiation, and pattern formation and morphogenesis.

As embryonic development proceeds, cell division gives rise to increasing numbers of cells, which serve as the building blocks of development. At various times certain cells become biochemically and structurally specialized to carry out specific functions through a process known as **cell differentiation.** In our discussion of the genetic control of development in Chapter 17, you learned how cell differentiation occurs through **cell determination,** a series of molecular events in which the activities of certain genes are altered in ways that cause a cell to progressively commit to a particular differentiation pathway. This process proceeds even though there may not be any immediate changes in the cell's morphology. You also evaluated evidence supporting the principle of **nuclear equivalence,** which states that in most cases neither cell determination nor cell differentiation entails a loss of genetic information from the cell nucleus. That is, the nuclei of virtually all differentiated cells of an animal contain the same genetic information present in the zygote, but each cell type *expresses* a different subset of that information. In fact, nuclear equivalence is the principle that underlies the cloning of organisms.

Cell differentiation is therefore an expression of changes in the activity of specific genes, which in turn is influenced by a variety of factors inside and outside the cell. This **differential gene expression** is responsible for variations in chemistry, behavior, and structure among cells. Through this process, an embryo can develop into an organism of more than 200 types of cells, each specialized to perform specific functions. However, not all cells differentiate. Some, known as **stem cells,** remain in a relatively undifferentiated state and retain the ability to give rise to various cell types.

Cell differentiation by itself does not explain development. The differentiated cells must become progressively organized, shaping the intricate pattern of tissues and organs that characterizes a multicellular animal. This development of form, known as **morphogenesis,** proceeds through the process of pattern formation. **Pattern formation** is a series of steps requiring signaling between cells, changes in the shapes of certain cells, precise cell migrations, interactions with the extracellular matrix, and even **apoptosis** (programmed cell death; see Chapter 4) of some cells.

Review

■   Which typically comes first, cell differentiation or cell determination?
■   What are some kinds of events that contribute to pattern formation? How does pattern formation lead to morphogenesis?

51.2 FERTILIZATION

■ LEARNING OBJECTIVES

3   Describe the four processes involved in fertilization.
4   Describe fertilization in echinoderms and point out some ways in which mammalian fertilization differs.

In Chapter 50 you studied **spermatogenesis** and **oogenesis,** the processes by which meiosis leads to the formation of haploid cells, which differentiate as sperm and eggs, respectively. In **fertilization** a usually flagellated, motile sperm fuses with a much larger, immotile **ovum** to produce a **zygote,** or fertilized egg.

Fertilization has two important genetic consequences: restoration of the diploid chromosome number and, in mammals and many other animals, determination of the sex of the offspring (see Chapter 11). Fertilization also has profound physiological effects because it activates the egg, thus initiating reactions that permit development.

Fertilization involves four events, some of which may occur simultaneously: (1) the sperm contacts the egg and recognition occurs; (2) the sperm or sperm nucleus enters the egg; (3) the egg becomes activated, and certain developmental changes begin; and (4) the sperm and egg nuclei fuse. These events do not necessarily follow the same temporal sequence in all animals. Unless otherwise stated, our discussion applies to sea urchins and other echinoderms such as sea stars, which have been studied intensively because they produce large numbers of gametes and because fertilization is external.

The first step in fertilization involves contact and recognition

Although eggs are immotile, they are active participants in fertilization. An egg is surrounded by a plasma membrane and by one or more external coverings that are important in fertilization. For example, a mammalian egg is enclosed by a thick, noncellular **zona** pellucida, which is surrounded by a layer of granulosa cells derived from the follicle in which the egg developed.

The egg coverings not only facilitate fertilization by sperm of the same species but also bar interspecific fertilization, a particularly important function in species that practice external fertilization. External to the plasma membrane of a sea urchin egg are two acellular layers that interact with sperm: a very thin **vitelline envelope** and, outside this, a thick glycoprotein layer called the **jelly coat.** Sea urchin sperm become motile when released into sea water, and their motility increases when they reach the vicinity of a sea urchin egg. Motility improves the probability that sperm will encounter the egg, but motility alone may not be sufficient to ensure actual contact with the egg. In sea urchins, as well as certain fishes and some cnidarians, the egg or one of its coverings secretes a chemotactic substance that attracts sperm from the same species. However, for many species, researchers have not found a specific chemical that attracts the sperm to the egg.

When a sea urchin sperm contacts the jelly coat, the sperm undergoes an **acrosome reaction,** in which the membranes surrounding the acrosome (the cap at the head of the sperm; see Fig. 50-6) fuse, and pores in the membrane enlarge. Calcium ions from the sea water move into the acrosome, which swells and begins to disorganize. The acrosome then releases proteolytic enzymes that digest a path through the jelly coat to the vitelline envelope of the egg. If the sperm and egg are of the same species, **bindin,** a species-specific binding protein located on the acrosome, adheres to species-specific bindin receptors located on the egg's vitelline envelope.

Before a mammalian sperm participates in fertilization, it first undergoes **capacitation,** a maturation process in the female reproductive tract. During capacitation, which in humans can take several hours, sperm become increasingly motile and capable of undergoing an acrosome reaction when they encounter an egg. Evidence indicates that mammalian fertilization requires interaction between sperm and species-specific glycoproteins in the egg's zona pellucida.

Sperm entry is regulated

In sea urchins, once contact occurs between acrosome and vitelline envelope, enzymes dissolve a bit of the vitelline envelope in the area of the sperm head. The plasma membrane of the egg is covered with microvilli, several of which elongate to surround the head of the sperm. As they do so, the plasma membranes of sperm and egg fuse and a **fertilization cone** is formed that contracts to draw the sperm into the egg (**FIG. 51-1**).

Fertilization of the egg by more than one sperm, a condition known as polyspermy, results in an offspring with extra sets of chromosomes, which is usually lethal. Two reactions, known as the *fast* and *slow blocks* to **polyspermy,** prevent this occurrence. In the fast block to polyspermy, the egg plasma membrane depolarizes, which prevents its fusion with additional sperm. An unfertilized egg is polarized, that is, the cytoplasm is negatively charged relative to the outside. However, within a few seconds after sperm fusion, ion channels in the plasma membrane open, permitting positively charged calcium ions to diffuse across the membrane and depolarize the egg.

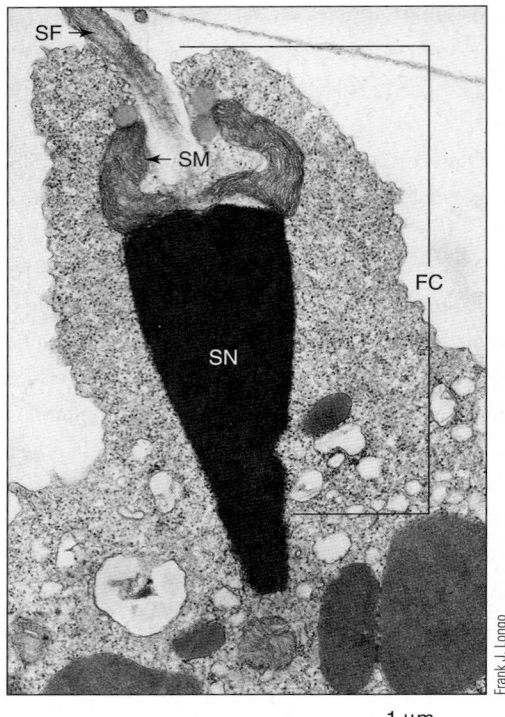

Frank J. Longo

1 μm

FIGURE 51-1 Fertilization
In this TEM, a fertilization cone (FC) forms as a sperm enters a sea urchin egg. (SN, sperm nucleus; SM, sperm mitochondrion; SF, sperm flagellum)

The slow block to polyspermy, the **cortical reaction,** requires up to several minutes to complete, but it is a complete block. Binding of the sperm to receptors on the vitelline envelope activates one or more *signal transduction* pathways (see Chapter 6) in the egg. These events cause calcium ions stored in the egg endoplasmic reticulum to be released into the cytosol. This rise in the level of intracellular calcium causes thousands of cortical granules, membrane-enclosed vesicles in the egg cortex (region close to the plasma membrane), to release enzymes, various proteins, and other substances by exocytosis into the space between the plasma membrane and the vitelline envelope (**FIG. 51-2**). Some of the enzymes dissolve the protein linking the two membranes; thus, the space enlarges as additional substances released by the cortical granules raise the osmotic pressure, which causes an influx of water from the surroundings. Thus, the vitelline envelope becomes elevated away from the plasma membrane and forms the fertilization envelope, a hardened covering that prevents entry of additional sperm.

In mammals, a fertilization envelope does not form, but the enzymes released during exocytosis of the cortical granules alter the sperm receptors on the egg's zona pellucida so that no additional sperm bind to them.

Not all species have these types of blocks to polyspermy. In some, such as salamanders, several sperm usually enter the egg, but only one sperm nucleus fuses with the egg nucleus, and the rest degenerate.

Reprinted from E. Anderson, *The Journal of Cell Biology*, 1968, Vol. 37, pp. 514–539, by copyright permission of the Rockefeller University Press

1 µm

FIGURE 51-2 The cortical reaction

Three cortical granules are undergoing exocytosis in this TEM of the plasma membrane of a sea urchin egg shortly after fertilization. This release of the contents of the cortical granules initiates the slow block to polyspermy.

Fertilization activates the egg

Release of calcium ions into the egg cytoplasm does more than stimulate the cortical reaction; it also triggers the *activation program,* a series of metabolic changes within the egg. Aerobic respiration increases; certain maternal enzymes and other proteins become active; and within a few minutes after sperm entry, a burst of protein synthesis occurs. In addition, the egg nucleus is stimulated to complete meiosis. (Recall from Chapter 50 that in most animal species, including mammals, at the time of fertilization an egg is actually a secondary oocyte, arrested early in the second meiotic division.)

In some species, an egg can be artificially activated without sperm penetration by swabbing it with blood and pricking the plasma membrane with a needle, by calcium injection, or by certain other treatments. These haploid eggs go through some developmental stages *parthenogenetically,* that is, without fertilization (see Chapter 50), but they cannot complete development. Special mechanisms of egg activation have evolved in species that are naturally parthenogenetic.

Sperm and egg pronuclei fuse, restoring the diploid state

After the sperm nucleus enters the egg, researchers think it is guided toward the egg nucleus by a system of microtubules that forms within the egg. The sperm nucleus swells and forms the **male pronucleus.** The nucleus formed during completion of meiosis in the egg becomes the **female pronucleus.** (Recall from Figure 50-11 that the other nucleus formed during meiosis II in the egg becomes the second polar body.) The haploid male and female pronuclei then fuse to form the diploid nucleus of the zygote, and DNA synthesis occurs in preparation for the first cell division.

Review

- How do the mechanisms of fertilization ensure control of both quality (fertilization by a sperm of the same species) and quantity (fertilization by only one sperm)?
- What happens as a result of the cortical reaction in echinoderms? in mammals?

51.3 CLEAVAGE

■ LEARNING OBJECTIVES

5 Trace the generalized pattern of early development of the embryo from zygote through early cleavage and formation of the morula and blastula.

6 Contrast early development, including cleavage, in the echinoderm (or in amphioxus), the amphibian, and the bird, paying particular attention to the importance of the amount and distribution of yolk.

Despite its simple appearance, the zygote is **totipotent,** that is, it gives rise to all the cell types of the new individual. Because the ovum is very large compared with the sperm, the bulk of the zygote cytoplasm and organelles comes from the ovum. However, the sperm and ovum usually contribute equal numbers of chromosomes.

Shortly after fertilization, the zygote undergoes **cleavage,** a series of rapid mitotic divisions with no period of growth during each cell cycle. For this reason, although the cell number increases, the embryo does not increase in size. The zygote initially divides to form a 2-celled embryo. Then each of these cells undergoes mitosis and divides, bringing the number of cells to 4. Repeated divisions increase the number of cells, called **blastomeres,** that make up the embryo. At about the 32-cell stage, the embryo is a solid ball of blastomeres called a **morula.** Eventually, anywhere from 64 to several hundred blastomeres form the **blastula,** which is usually a hollow ball with a fluid-filled cavity, the **blastocoel.**

The pattern of cleavage is affected by yolk

Many animal eggs contain **yolk,** a mixture of proteins, phospholipids, and fats that serves as food for the developing embryo. The amount and distribution of yolk vary among different animal groups, depending on the needs of the embryo. Mammalian eggs have very little yolk because the embryo obtains maternal nutritional support throughout most of its development, whereas the eggs of birds and reptiles must contain sufficient yolk to sustain the embryo until hatching. Echinoderm eggs typically need only enough yolk to nourish the embryo until it becomes a tiny larva capable of obtaining its own food.

Most invertebrates and simple chordates have **isolecithal eggs** with relatively small amounts of yolk uniformly distributed through the cytoplasm. Isolecithal eggs divide completely; this is called **holoblastic cleavage.** Cleavage of these eggs is radial or spiral. Radial cleavage is characteristic of *deuterostomes,* such as chordates and echinoderms; spiral cleavage is common in the embryos of *protostomes,* such as annelids and mollusks (see Fig. 30-5).

In **radial cleavage,** the first division is vertical and splits the egg into two equal cells. The second cleavage division, also vertical, is at right angles to the first division and separates the two

Cleavage in sea stars is radial and holoblastic.

(a) Unfertilized egg   100 μm

Nucleus

a–i: Carolina Biological Company of Phototake, NYC

(b) 2-cell stage   50 μm

(c) 4-cell stage   50 μm

(d) 16-cell stage   50 μm

(e) Blastula   50 μm

Blastocoel

Archenteron   Blastopore

(f) Early gastrula   50 μm

Archenteron

Blastopore

(g) Middle gastrula   50 μm

Mouth

Anus

Stomach

(h) Sea star larva   50 μm

(i) Young sea star   1 mm

FIGURE 51-3 LMs showing sea star development

(a) The isolecithal egg has a small amount of uniformly distributed yolk. **(b–e)** The cleavage pattern is radial and holoblastic (the entire egg becomes partitioned into cells). **(f, g)** The three germ layers form during gastrulation. The blastopore is the opening into the developing gut cavity, the archenteron. The rudiments of organs are evident in the sea star larva **(h)** and the young sea star **(i)**. All views are side views with the animal pole at the top, except **(c)** and **(i)**, which are top views. Note that the sea star larva is bilaterally symmetrical, but differential growth produces a radially symmetrical young sea star.

cells into four equal cells. The third division is horizontal, at right angles to the other two, and separates the four cells into eight cells: four above and four below the third line of cleavage. This pattern of radial cleavage occurs in echinoderms and in the cephalochordate amphioxus (**FIGS. 51-3** and **51-4**).

In **spiral cleavage,** after the first two divisions, the plane of cytokinesis is diagonal to the polar axis (**FIG. 51-5**). This results in a spiral arrangement of cells, with each cell located above and between the two underlying cells. This pattern is typical of annelids and mollusks.

Many vertebrate eggs are **telolecithal,** meaning they have large amounts of yolk concentrated at one end of the cell, known as the **vegetal pole.** The opposite, more metabolically active, pole is the **animal pole.** The eggs of amphibians are moderately telolecithal (mesolecithal). Although cleavage is radial and holoblastic, the divisions in the vegetal hemisphere are slowed by the presence of the inert yolk. As a result, the blastula consists of many small cells in the animal hemisphere and fewer but larger cells in the vegetal hemisphere (**FIG. 51-6**). The blastocoel is displaced toward the animal pole.

The telolecithal eggs of reptiles and birds have very large amounts of yolk at the vegetal pole and only a small amount of cytoplasm concentrated at the animal pole. The yolk of such eggs never cleaves. Cell division is restricted to the **blastodisc,** the small disc of cytoplasm at the animal pole (**FIG. 51-7**); this type of cleavage is termed **meroblastic cleavage.** In birds and some reptiles, the blastomeres form two layers separated by the blastocoel cavity: an upper *epiblast* and a lower, thin layer of flat cells, the *hypoblast*.

Cleavage may distribute developmental determinants

The pattern of cleavage in a particular species depends on both yolk and other factors. Recall from Chapter 17 that some animals have relatively rigid developmental patterns, known as **mosaic**

KEY POINT Cleavage in amphioxus is radial and holoblastic.

FIGURE 51-4 Cleavage and gastrulation in amphioxus

As in the sea star, cleavage is holoblastic and radial. The embryos are shown from the side. **(a)** Mature egg with polar body. **(b–e)** The 2-, 4-, 8-, and 16-cell stages. **(f)** Embryo cut open to show the blastocoel. **(g)** Blastula. **(h)** Blastula cut open. **(i)** Early gastrula showing beginning of invagination at vegetal pole. **(j)** Late gastrula. Invagination is completed, and the blastopore has formed.

KEY POINT Cleavage in annelids is spiral and holoblastic.

FIGURE 51-5 Spiral cleavage in an annelid embryo

(a–f) Top views of the animal pole. The successive cleavage divisions occur in a spiral pattern as illustrated. **(g)** A typical trochophore larva. The upper half of the trochophore develops into the extreme anterior end of the adult worm; all the rest of the adult body develops from the lower half.

KEY POINT Cleavage in the moderately telolecithal frog egg is radial and holoblastic but is retarded by yolk in the vegetal hemisphere.

Animal pole

Vegetal pole

(a)　　(b)　　(c)　　(d)

FIGURE 51-6 *Animated* **Cleavage pattern in a frog egg**
(a–d) Although cleavage is holoblastic, the large amount of yolk concentrated in the vegetal hemisphere slows cleavage. As a result, fewer cells develop at the vegetal hemisphere than at the animal hemisphere. These embryos are shown from the side.

development. This type of development is largely a consequence of the unequal distribution of important materials in the cytoplasm of the zygote. Because the zygote cytoplasm is not homogeneous, cytoplasmic developmental determinants portioned out to each new cell during cleavage may be different. Such differences help determine the course of development. At the other extreme are mammals, which have zygotes with very homogeneous cytoplasm. They exhibit highly **regulative development,** in which individual

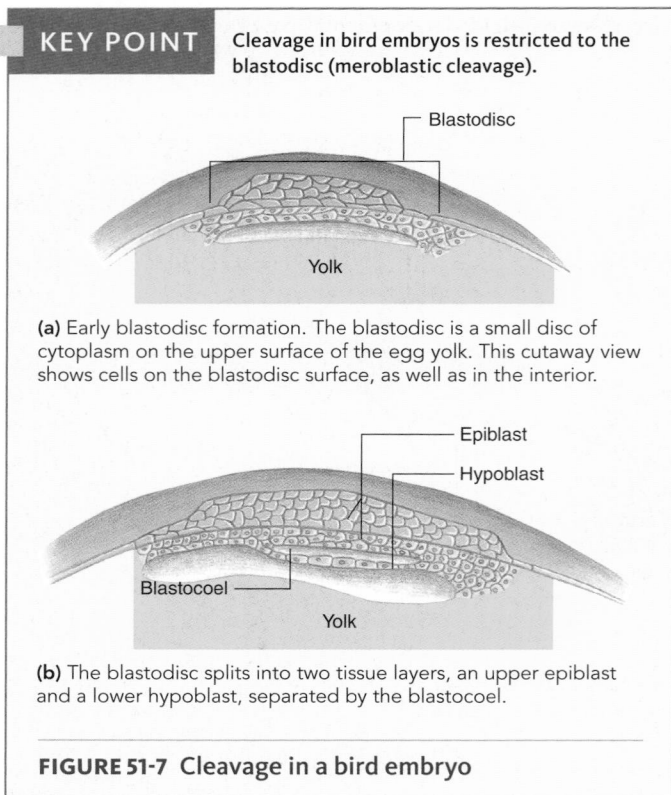

KEY POINT Cleavage in bird embryos is restricted to the blastodisc (meroblastic cleavage).

Blastodisc

Yolk

(a) Early blastodisc formation. The blastodisc is a small disc of cytoplasm on the upper surface of the egg yolk. This cutaway view shows cells on the blastodisc surface, as well as in the interior.

Epiblast

Hypoblast

Blastocoel

Yolk

(b) The blastodisc splits into two tissue layers, an upper epiblast and a lower hypoblast, separated by the blastocoel.

FIGURE 51-7 **Cleavage in a bird embryo**

cells produced by the cleavage divisions are equivalent, thus allowing the embryo to develop as a self-regulating whole. Developmental patterns of most animals fall somewhere on a continuum between these two extremes.

In some species the distribution of developmental determinants in the unfertilized egg is maintained in the zygote. In others sperm penetration initiates rearrangement of the cytoplasm. For example, fertilization in the amphibian egg causes a shift of some of the cortical cytoplasm. These cytoplasmic movements can be easily followed because the egg cortex contains dark pigment granules. As a result of this rearrangement, a crescent-shaped region of underlying lighter colored (gray) cytoplasm becomes evident directly opposite the point on the cell where the sperm penetrated the egg. This **gray crescent** region is thought to contain growth factors and other developmental determinants. The first cleavage bisects the gray crescent, distributing half to each of the first two blastomeres; in this way the position of the gray crescent establishes the future right and left halves of the embryo. As cleavage continues, the gray crescent material becomes partitioned into certain blastomeres. Those that contain parts of the gray crescent eventually develop into the dorsal region of the embryo.

Experiments have confirmed the importance of determinants in the gray crescent to development. If the first two frog blastomeres are separated experimentally, each develops into a complete tadpole (**FIG. 51-8a**). When the plane of the first division is altered so that the gray crescent is completely absent from one of the cells, that cell does not develop normally (**FIG. 51-8b**).

Cleavage provides building blocks for development

Cleavage partitions the zygote into many small cells that serve as the basic building blocks for subsequent development. At the end of cleavage, the small cells that make up the blastula begin to move about with relative ease, arranging themselves into the patterns necessary for further development. Surface proteins are important in helping cells "recognize" one another and therefore in determining which ones adhere to form tissues.

Review

- What is radial cleavage? spiral cleavage?
- What type of cleavage is characteristic of telolecithal eggs of reptiles and birds?
- How does the cytoplasm influence early development?

51.4 GASTRULATION

◼ LEARNING OBJECTIVE

7 Identify the significance of gastrulation in the developmental process and compare gastrulation in the echinoderm (or in amphioxus), the amphibian, and the bird.

The process by which the blastula becomes a three-layered embryo, or **gastrula,** is called **gastrulation.** Thus, early development proceeds through the following stages:

zygote ⟶ early cleavage stages ⟶ morula ⟶ blastula ⟶ gastrula

During gastrulation, the embryo begins to approximate its body plan as cells arrange themselves into three distinct **germ layers,** or embryonic tissue layers: the outermost layer, the **ectoderm;** the innermost, the **endoderm;** and the **mesoderm,** which develops between them. Additional cell divisions take place during gastrulation, and the germ layers become established through a combi-

nation of processes. Many cells lose their old cell-to-cell contacts and establish new ones through cell recognition and adhesion processes involving interactions among the integrins and other plasma membrane proteins and the extracellular matrix (see Chapters 4 and 5). Many cells undergo cytoskeletal changes, particularly alterations in the distribution of actin microfilaments; these changes in the internal architecture of the cells allow them to change shape and/or undergo specific, directional, amoeboid movements. As a result of these movements, many cells ultimately take up new positions in the interior of the embryo.

Each of the germ layers develops into specific parts of the embryo. As you study the illustrations, keep in mind that a conventional color code accepted by developmental biologists is used to depict the germ layers: endoderm, yellow; mesoderm, red or pink; and ectoderm, blue.

The amount of yolk affects the pattern of gastrulation

The simple type of gastrulation that occurs in echinoderms and in amphioxus is illustrated in Figures 51-3f and g and 51-4i and j, respectively. Gastrulation begins when a group of cells at the vegetal pole undergoes a series of changes in shape that cause that part of the blastula wall to first flatten and then bend inward (invaginate). The invaginated wall eventually meets the opposite wall, obliterating the blastocoel.

You can roughly demonstrate this type of gastrulation by pushing inward on the wall of a partly deflated rubber ball until it rests against the opposite wall. In a similar way, the embryo is converted into a double-walled, cup-shaped structure. The new internal wall lines the **archenteron,** the newly formed cavity of the developing gut. The opening of the archenteron to the exterior, the **blastopore,** is the site of the future anus in deuterostomes.

This simple type of gastrulation cannot occur in the amphibian embryo because the large yolk-laden cells in the vegetal half of the blastula obstruct any inward movement at the vegetal pole. Instead, cells from the animal pole move down the embryo surface; when they reach the region derived from the gray crescent, they move into the interior. This inward movement is accomplished as the cells change shape, first becoming flask- or bottle-shaped (so that most of their mass is actually below the surface) and then sinking into the interior as they lose their remaining connections with other cells on the surface. This spot on the embryo's surface, referred to as the **dorsal lip of the blastopore,** is marked by a dimple, shaped like a C lying on its side (**FIG. 51-9**). As the process continues, the blastopore becomes ring-shaped as cells lateral, and then ventral, to its dorsal lip become involved in similar movements. The yolk-filled cells fill the space enclosed by the lips of the blastopore, forming the yolk plug.

The archenteron forms and is lined on all sides by cells that have moved in from the surface. At first, the archenteron is a narrow slit, but it gradually expands at the anterior end of the embryo. As a result, the blastocoel progressively shrinks and eventually disappears.

Although the details differ somewhat, gastrulation in birds is basically similar to amphibian gastrulation. Cells that make up the upper layer (the epiblast) migrate toward the midline to form a

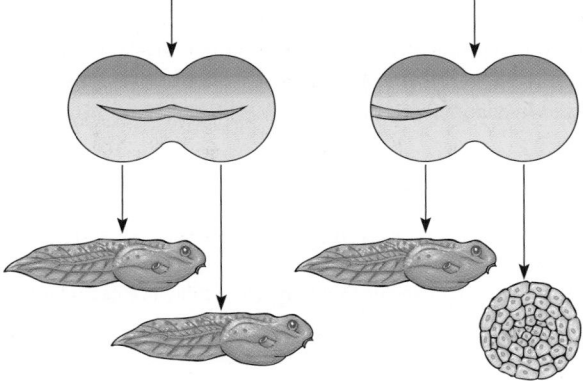

Blastocoel

(a) Late blastula

Blastocoel

Dorsal lip of
the blastopore

(b) Early gastrula

Archenteron

Endoderm

Mesoderm

Dorsal lip of
the blastopore

Blastocoel

(c) Middle gastrula

Neural plate

Archenteron

Mesoderm

(d) Late gastrula

Neural fold

Archenteron

(e) Early development
of the nervous system

FIGURE 51-9 *Animated* Gastrulation in a frog embryo

The embryos in the diagrams are cut in half longitudinally to show the formation of the germ layers.

---

thickened region known as the **primitive streak,** which elongates and narrows as it develops. At its center is a narrow furrow, the **primitive groove.** The primitive streak is a dynamic structure. Its cells constantly change as they migrate in from the epiblast, sink inward at the primitive groove, then move out laterally and anteriorly in the interior (**FIG. 51-10**). The primitive groove is the functional equivalent of the blastopore of the echinoderm, amphioxus, and amphibian embryos. However, a bird embryo contains no cavity homologous to the archenteron.

At the anterior end of the primitive streak, cells destined to form the **notochord** (supporting rod of mesodermal cartilage-like cells that serves as the flexible skeletal axis in all chordate embryos) concentrate in a thickened knot known as **Hensen's node.** These cells sink into the interior and then move anteriorly just beneath the epiblast, forming a narrow extension from the node. Cells that will form other types of mesoderm move laterally and anteriorly from the primitive streak, between the epiblast (which becomes

FIGURE 51-10 Gastrulation in birds ▶

A three-layered embryo forms as cells move toward the primitive streak, move inward at the primitive groove, and migrate laterally and anteriorly in the interior. The red cells will develop as mesoderm. Cells shown just above the double-headed arrow have migrated into the hypoblast; they are moving laterally and will eventually become endoderm.

ectoderm) and the hypoblast. Other cells that form the endoderm displace the hypoblast cells and cause them to move laterally. These displaced cells will form part of the extraembryonic membranes, discussed in a later section.

Review

- What is the archenteron? Is an archenteron formed in sea stars? in amphibians? in birds?
- How do the amount and distribution of yolk influence gastrulation?

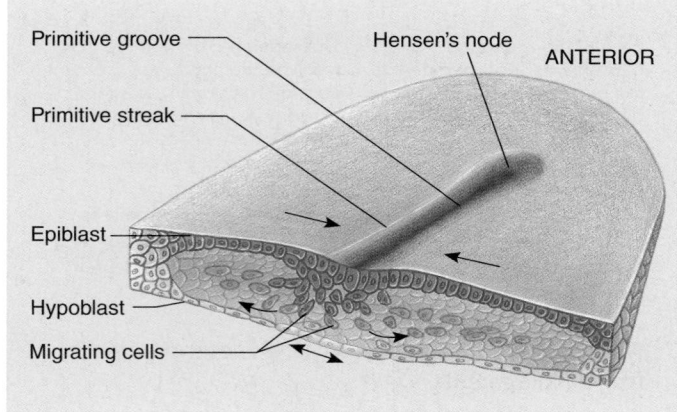

Primitive groove

Hensen's node

ANTERIOR

Primitive streak

Epiblast

Hypoblast

Migrating cells

51.5 ORGANOGENESIS

▪ LEARNING OBJECTIVES

8 Define *organogenesis* and summarize the fate of each of the germ layers.
9 Trace the early development of the vertebrate nervous system.

Gastrulation leads to **organogenesis,** or organ formation, in which the cells of the three germ layers continue the processes of pattern formation that lead to the formation of specific structures. The ectoderm eventually forms the outer layer of the skin and gives rise to the nervous system and sense organs. Tissues that eventually line the digestive tract, and organs that develop as outgrowths of the digestive tract (including the liver, pancreas, and lungs), are all of endodermal origin. Skeletal tissue, muscle, and the circulatory, excretory, and reproductive systems all are derived from mesoderm (**TABLE 51-1**; see Fig. 17-1).

The notochord, brain, and spinal cord are among the first organs to develop in the early vertebrate embryo (**FIG. 51-11**; see also Fig. 51-9d and e). First, the notochord, which is mesodermal tissue, grows forward along the length of the embryo as a cylindrical rod of cells. The notochord eventually is replaced by the vertebral column, although notochord remnants will remain in the cartilage discs between the vertebrae.

The developing notochord has yet another crucial function. Numerous experiments in which researchers have transplanted portions of the notochord mesoderm to other locations in the embryo show that the notochord causes the overlying ectoderm to thicken and differentiate to form the precursor of the central nervous system, the **neural plate.** Such phenomena, in which certain cells stimulate or otherwise influence the differentiation of their neighbors, are examples of **induction** (see Chapter 17).

Repeated testing supports the hypothesis that induction of the neural plate cells does not require direct cell-to-cell contact with the developing notochord cells. Researchers therefore think that this induction involves the diffusion of some type of signal molecule, although they have not yet identified the chemical signal itself. The induction of the neural plate by the notochord is a good example of the importance of a cell's position in relation to other cells. That position is often critical in determining the fate of a cell because it determines the cell's exposure to substances released from other cells.

The cells of the neural plate undergo changes in shape that cause the central cells of the neural plate to move downward and form a depression called the **neural groove;** the cells flanking the groove

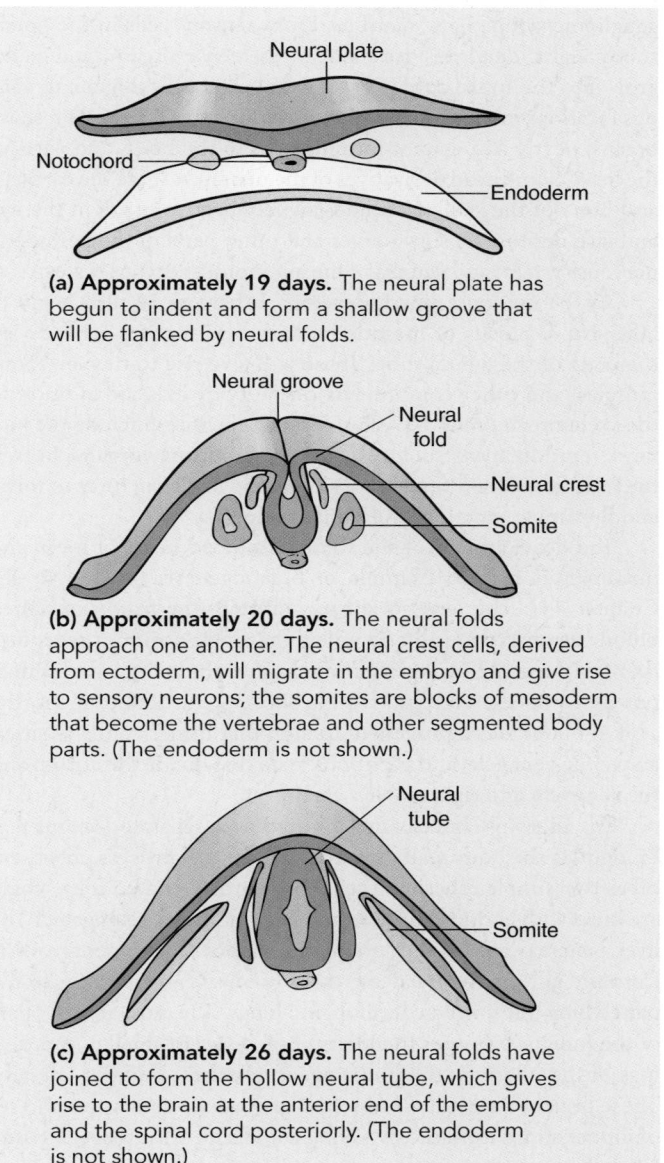

(a) **Approximately 19 days.** The neural plate has begun to indent and form a shallow groove that will be flanked by neural folds.

(b) **Approximately 20 days.** The neural folds approach one another. The neural crest cells, derived from ectoderm, will migrate in the embryo and give rise to sensory neurons; the somites are blocks of mesoderm that become the vertebrae and other segmented body parts. (The endoderm is not shown.)

(c) **Approximately 26 days.** The neural folds have joined to form the hollow neural tube, which gives rise to the brain at the anterior end of the embryo and the spinal cord posteriorly. (The endoderm is not shown.)

FIGURE 51-11 *Animated* **Development of the human nervous system**

TABLE 51-1	Fate of the Germ Layers Formed at Gastrulation

Ectoderm
  Nervous system and sense organs
  Outer layer of skin (epidermis) and its associated structures (nails, hair, etc.)
  Pituitary gland

Mesoderm
  Notochord
  Skeleton (bone and cartilage)
  Muscles
  Circulatory system
  Excretory system
  Reproductive system
  Inner layer of skin (dermis)
  Outer layers of digestive tube and of structures that develop from it, such as part of respiratory system

Endoderm
  Lining of digestive tube and of structures that develop from it, such as lining of the respiratory system

on each side form **neural folds.** Continued changes in cell shape bring the folds closer together until they meet and fuse to form the **neural tube.** In this process, the hollow neural tube comes to lie beneath the surface. The ectoderm overlying it will form the outer layer of skin. The anterior portion of the neural tube grows and differentiates into the brain; the rest of the tube develops into the spinal cord. The brain and the spinal cord remain hollow, even in the adult; the ventricles of the brain and central canal of the spinal cord are persistent reminders of their embryonic origins.

Various motor nerves grow out of the developing brain and spinal cord, but sensory nerves have a separate origin. When the neural folds fuse to form the neural tube, bits of nervous tissue known as the **neural crest** arise from ectoderm on each side of the tube. Neural crest cells migrate downward from their original position and form the dorsal root ganglia of the spinal nerves and the postganglionic sympathetic neurons. From sensory cells in the dorsal root ganglia, dendrites grow out to the sense organs, and axons grow into the spinal cord. Other neural crest cells migrate to various locations in the embryo. They give rise to parts of certain sense organs, nearly all pigment-forming cells in the body, and parts of the head. Some head derivatives of the neural crest are the cartilage and bone of the skull, face, and jaw; connective tissue in the eye and face dermis; sensory nerves and other parts of the peripheral nervous system; and ganglia of the autonomic nervous system.

As the nervous system develops, other organs also begin to take shape. Blocks of mesoderm known as somites form on either side of the neural tube. These will give rise to the vertebrae, muscles, and other components of the body axis. In addition to the skeleton and muscles, mesodermal structures include the kidneys, reproductive structures, and the circulatory organs. In fact, the heart and blood vessels are among the first structures to form, and they must function while still developing.

The development of the four-chambered heart of birds and mammals is a good example of organogenesis (**FIG. 51-12**; see Chapter 44). The heart originates through the fusion of paired blood vessels. Venous blood enters the single atrium; passes into the single ventricle, which is located above the atrium; and is then pumped into the embryo. During subsequent development, the atrium undergoes a process of torsion that brings it to a position above the ventricle, and partitions form that divide the atrium and the ventricle into right and left chambers.

The digestive tract is first formed as a separate foregut and hindgut as the body wall grows and folds; this process cuts them off as two simple tubes. As the embryo grows, these tubes, which are lined with endoderm, grow and become greatly elongated. The liver, pancreas, and trachea originate as hollow, tubular outgrowths from the gut. As the trachea grows downward, it gives rise to the paired lung buds, which develop into lungs. The most anterior part of the foregut becomes the pharynx. A series of small outpocketings of the pharynx, the **pharyngeal pouches,** bud out laterally. These pouches meet the **branchial grooves,** a corresponding set of inpocketings from the overlying ectoderm. The arches of tissue formed between the grooves are called **branchial arches.** They contain the rudimentary skeletal, neural, and vascular elements of the face, jaws, and neck.

In fishes and some amphibians, the pharyngeal pouches and branchial grooves meet and form a continuous passage from the

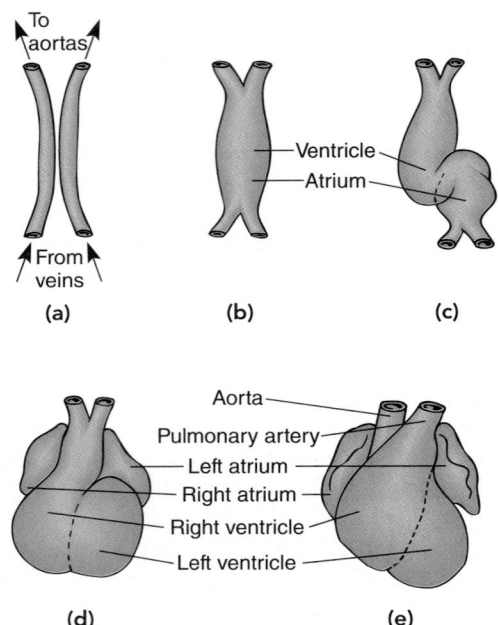

FIGURE 51-12 Formation of the heart in birds and mammals
These ventral views of successive stages show that the heart forms from the fusion of two blood vessels and that at first the end that receives blood from the veins is at the bottom. The developing heart twists to carry the atrium to a position above the ventricle, and the chambers then divide to form the four-chambered heart.

pharynx to the outside; these gill slits function as respiratory organs. In terrestrial vertebrates, each branchial groove remains separated from the corresponding pharyngeal pouch by a thin membrane of tissue, and these structures give rise to organs more appropriate for life on land. For example, the middle-ear cavity and its connection to the pharynx, the eustachian tube, derive from a pharyngeal pouch.

Review

- What adult structures develop from each germ layer?
- How do cell division, growth, cell differentiation, and morphogenesis interact in the formation of the neural tube?
- What is the developmental significance of the neural crest cells?

51.6 EXTRAEMBRYONIC MEMBRANES

LEARNING OBJECTIVE

10 Give the origins and functions of the chorion, amnion, allantois, and yolk sac.

In terrestrial vertebrates, the three germ layers also give rise to four **extraembryonic membranes:** the chorion, amnion, allantois, and yolk sac (**FIG. 51-13**). Although they develop from the germ layers, these membranes are not part of the embryo itself and are discarded at hatching or birth. The extraembryonic membranes are adaptations to the challenges of embryonic development on land. They protect the embryo, prevent it from drying out, and help in obtaining food and oxygen and eliminating wastes.

The outermost membrane, the **chorion,** encloses the entire embryo as well as the other membranes. Lying underneath the eggshell in birds and reptiles, it functions as the major organ of gas exchange. As you will see in the next section, its functions have been extended in humans and most other mammals.

Like the chorion, the **amnion** encloses the entire embryo. The amniotic cavity, the space between the embryo and the amnion, becomes filled with amniotic fluid secreted by the membrane. (Recall from Chapter 32 that terrestrial vertebrates are known as *amniotes* because their embryos develop within this pool of fluid.) The amniotic fluid prevents the embryo from drying out and permits it a certain freedom of motion. The fluid also serves as a protective cushion that absorbs shocks and prevents the amniotic membrane from sticking to the embryo. In current medical practice, a sample of amniotic fluid can be obtained through a procedure known as *amniocentesis* and analyzed for biochemical or chromosomal abnormalities that indicate a possible birth defect (see Fig. 16-12).

The **allantois** is an outgrowth of the developing digestive tract. In reptiles and birds, it stores nitrogenous wastes. In humans, the allantois is small and nonfunctional, except that its blood vessels contribute to the formation of umbilical vessels joining the embryo to the placenta. In vertebrates with yolk-rich eggs, the **yolk**

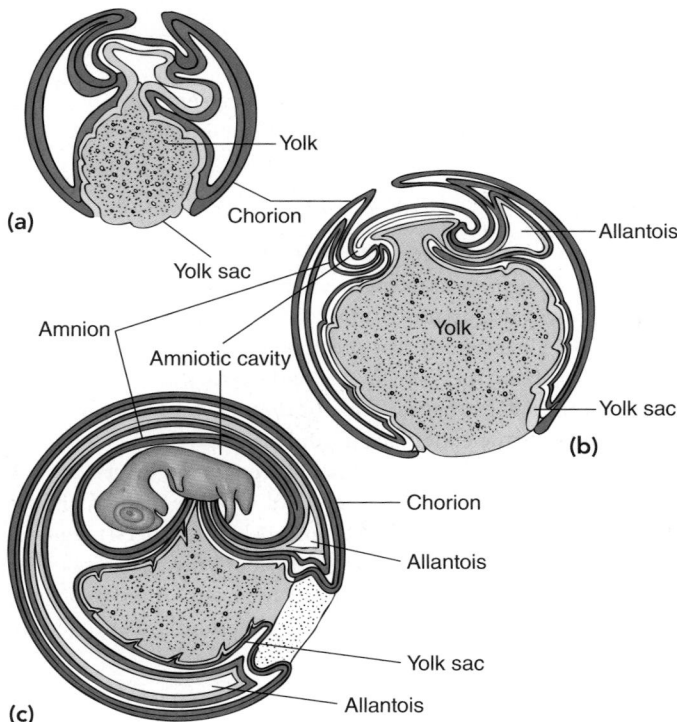

(a)

Yolk
Chorion
Yolk sac
Amnion
Amniotic cavity
Yolk
Allantois
Yolk sac
(b)
Chorion
Allantois
Yolk sac
Allantois
(c)

FIGURE 51-13 Extraembryonic membranes
The formation of the extraembryonic membranes of the chick is illustrated at **(a)** four days, **(b)** five days, and **(c)** nine days of development. Each of the membranes develops from a combination of two germ layers. The chorion and amnion form from lateral folds of the ectoderm and mesoderm that extend over the embryo and fuse. The allantois and the yolk sac develop from endoderm and mesoderm.

sac encloses the yolk, slowly digests it, and makes it available to the embryo. A yolk sac, connected to the embryo by a yolk stalk, develops even in mammalian embryos that have little or no yolk. Its walls serve as temporary centers for the formation of blood cells.

Review

- What are the roles of the chorion and amnion in terrestrial vertebrate embryos?
- How do the functions of the allantois and yolk sac differ between birds and mammals?

51.7 HUMAN DEVELOPMENT

◼ LEARNING OBJECTIVES

11 Describe the general course of early human development, including fertilization, the fates of the trophoblast and inner cell mass, implantation, and the role of the placenta.

12 Contrast postnatal with prenatal life, describing several changes that occur at or shortly after birth that allow the neonate to live independently.

13 Describe some anatomical and physiological changes that occur with aging.

The human **gestation period,** the duration of pregnancy, averages 266 days (38 weeks, or about 9 months) from the time of fertilization to the birth of the baby (**TABLE 51-2**). We will use this system of timing when discussing the events of early development.

TABLE 51-2	Some Important Developmental Events in the Human Embryo
Time from Fertilization	**Event**
24 hours	Embryo reaches two-cell stage
3 days	Morula reaches uterus
7 days	Blastocyst begins to implant
2.5 weeks	Notochord and neural plate are formed; tissue that will give rise to heart is differentiating; blood cells are forming in yolk sac and chorion
3.5 weeks	Neural tube forming; primordial eye and ear visible; pharyngeal pouches forming; liver bud differentiating; respiratory system and thyroid gland just beginning to develop; heart tubes fuse, bend, and begin to beat; blood vessels are laid down
4 weeks	Limb buds appear; three primary divisions of brain forming
2 months	Muscles differentiating; embryo capable of movement; gonad distinguishable as testis or ovary; bones begin to ossify; cerebral cortex differentiating; principal blood vessels assume final positions
3 months	Sex can be determined by external inspection; notochord degenerates; lymph glands develop
4 months	Face begins to look human; lobes of cerebrum differentiate; eyes, ears, and nose look more "normal"
Third trimester	Downy hair covers the fetus, then later is shed; neuron myelination begins; tremendous growth of body
266 days	Birth

Because the time of fertilization is not easily marked, obstetricians usually time the pregnancy by counting from the date of onset of the woman's last menstrual period; by this calculation, an average pregnancy is 280 days (40 weeks).

Fertilization occurs in the oviduct, and within 24 hours the human zygote has divided to become a two-celled embryo (**FIG. 51-14**). Cleavage continues as the embryo is propelled along the oviduct by ciliary action.

When the embryo enters the uterus on about the fifth day of development, the *zona pellucida* (its surrounding coat) is dissolved. During the next few days, the embryo floats free in the uterine cavity and is nourished by a nutritive fluid secreted by the glands of the uterus. Its cells arrange themselves, forming a blastula, which in mammals is called a **blastocyst.** The outer layer of cells, the **trophoblast,** eventually forms the chorion and amnion that surround the embryo. A little cluster of cells, the **inner cell mass,** projects into the cavity of the blastocyst. The inner cell mass gives rise to the embryo proper.

On about the seventh day of development, the embryo begins the process of **implantation,** in which it embeds in the endometrium of the uterus (**FIG. 51-15**). The trophoblast cells in contact with the endometrium secrete enzymes that erode an area just large enough to accommodate the tiny embryo. As the embryo slowly works its way into the underlying connective and vascular tissues, the opening in the endometrium repairs itself. All further development of the embryo takes place *within* the endometrium.

The placenta is an organ of exchange

In placental mammals, the **placenta** is the organ of exchange between mother and embryo (see Fig. 51-15). The placenta provides nutrients and oxygen for the fetus and removes wastes, which the mother then excretes. In addition, the placenta is an endocrine organ that secretes estrogens and progesterone to maintain pregnancy. The placenta develops from both the chorion of the embryo and the uterine tissue of the mother. In early development, the chorion grows rapidly, invading the endometrium and forming fingerlike projections known as *chorionic villi.* The chorionic villus sampling technique allows prenatal detection of certain genetic disorders (see Fig. 16-13). The villi become vascularized (infiltrated with blood vessels) as the embryonic circulation develops.

As the human embryo grows, the **umbilical cord** develops and connects the embryo to the placenta (see Fig. 51-15e). The umbilical cord contains the two umbilical arteries and the umbilical vein. The umbilical arteries connect the embryo to a vast network of capillaries developing within the chorionic villi. Blood from the villi returns to the embryo through the umbilical vein.

The placenta consists of the portion of the chorion that develops villi, together with the underlying uterine tissue that contains maternal capillaries and small pools of maternal blood. The fetal blood in the capillaries of the chorionic villi comes in close contact with the mother's blood in the tissues between the villi. The two circulations are always separated by a membrane through which substances may diffuse or be actively transported. Maternal and fetal blood do not normally mix in the placenta or any other place.

(a) Male and female pronuclei prior to fusion

50 μm

(b) 2-cell stage

50 μm

(c) 8-cell stage

50 μm

(d) Cleavage continues, giving rise to a morula

50 μm

FIGURE 51-14 *Animated* Cleavage in a human embryo
(From Nilsson, Lennart. *Being Born*, pp. 14, 15, 17. Putnam Publishing Group, 1992.)

The placenta produces several hormones. From the time the embryo first begins to implant itself, its trophoblastic cells release **human chorionic gonadotropin (hCG),** which signals the corpus luteum (see Chapter 50) that pregnancy has begun. In response, the corpus luteum increases in size and releases large amounts of progesterone and estrogens. These hormones stimulate continued development of the endometrium and placenta.

Without hCG, the corpus luteum would degenerate and the embryo would abort and be flushed out with the menstrual flow. The woman would probably not even know she had been pregnant. If the corpus luteum is removed before about the 11th week after fertilization, the embryo spontaneously aborts. After that time, the placenta itself produces enough progesterone and estrogens to maintain pregnancy.

Organ development begins during the first trimester

Gastrulation occurs during the second and third weeks of development. Then the notochord begins to form and induces formation of the neural plate. The neural tube develops, and the forebrain, midbrain, and hindbrain are evident by the fifth week

(a) 7 days. About 7 days after fertilization, the blastocyst drifts to an appropriate site along the uterine wall and begins to implant. The cells of the trophoblast proliferate and invade the endometrium.

(b) 10 days. About 10 days after fertilization, the chorion has formed from the trophoblast.

Courtesy of Carnegie Institute of Washington

(c) 12 days. This LM shows an implanted blastocyst at about 12 days after fertilization.

(d) 25 days. After 25 days, the maternal blood vessels provide the embryo with oxygen and nutrients. Note the specialized region of the chorion that will become the placenta.

(e) 45 days. At about 45 days, the embryo and its membranes together are about the size of a Ping-Pong ball, and the mother still may be unaware of her pregnancy. The amnion filled with amniotic fluid surrounds and cushions the embryo. The yolk sac has been incorporated into the umbilical cord. Blood circulation has been established through the umbilical cord to the placenta.

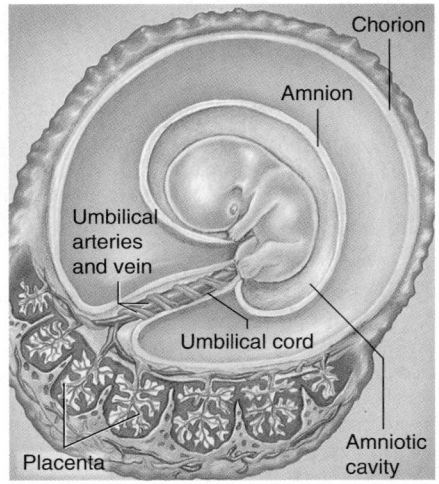

FIGURE 51-15 Implantation and early development in the uterus

of development. A week or so later the forebrain begins to grow outward, forming the rudiments of the cerebral hemispheres.

The heart begins to develop and after 3.5 weeks begins to beat spontaneously. Pharyngeal pouches, branchial grooves, and branchial arches form in the region of the developing pharynx. In the floor of the pharynx, a tube of cells grows downward to form the primordial trachea, which gives rise to the lung buds. The digestive system also gives rise to outgrowths that develop into the liver, gallbladder, and pancreas. A thin tail becomes evident but does not grow as rapidly as the rest of the body, and so becomes inconspicuous by the end of the second month. Near the end of the fourth week, the limb buds begin to differentiate; these eventually give rise to arms and legs.

All the organs continue to develop during the second month (**FIG. 51-16**). Muscles develop, and the embryo becomes capable of movement. The brain begins to send impulses that regulate the functions of some organs, and a few simple reflexes are evident. After the first two months of development, the embryo is referred to as a **fetus** (**FIG. 51-17**).

By the end of the **first trimester** (the first three months of development), the fetus is about 56 mm (2.2 in) long and weighs about 14 g (0.5 oz). Although small, it looks human. The external genital structures have differentiated, indicating the sex of the fetus. Ears and eyes approach their final positions. Some of the skeleton becomes distinct, and the developing vertebral column has replaced the notochord. The fetus performs breathing movements, pumping amniotic fluid into and out of its lungs, and even makes sucking motions.

Development continues during the second and third trimesters

During the second trimester (months four through six), the fetal heart can be heard with a stethoscope. The fetus moves freely within the amniotic cavity, and during the fifth month the mother usually becomes aware of relatively weak fetal movements ("quickening"). The fetus grows rapidly during the final trimester (months seven through nine), and final differentiation of tissues and organs occurs. If born at 24 weeks (out of 40 weeks), the fetus has only about a 50% chance of surviving, even with the best of medical care. Its brain is not yet sufficiently developed to sustain vital functions such as rhythmic breathing, and the kidneys and lungs are immature.

During the seventh month, the cerebrum grows rapidly and develops convolutions. The grasping and sucking reflexes are evident, and the fetus may suck its thumb. Any infant born before 37 weeks (out of 40) is considered premature. According to statistics made available by the March of Dimes, premature birth is an increasing problem in the United States, its incidence having risen from 9.6% in 1983 to 12.8% in 2006 (a 33% increase). Well over half a million premature babies are born each year. Babies born at 28 weeks or less are at greatest risk of death and severe defects. Babies born closer to 37 weeks have a greater chance of survival with competent medical care but may still face multiple long-term health problems.

At birth the average full-term baby weighs about 3000 g (6.6 lb) and measures about 52 cm (20 in) in total length. A baby

FIGURE 51-16 The second month of development
The amnion is prominent as a transparent fluid-filled sac surrounding this 5.5-week-old human embryo, which is 1 cm (0.4 in) long. Note the limb buds and the eyes. The balloonlike object at the left, connected to the embryo by a stalk, is the yolk sac. This embryo is in a period of very rapid development, as you can see by a comparison with the chapter opening photograph of a human embryo in its seventh week.

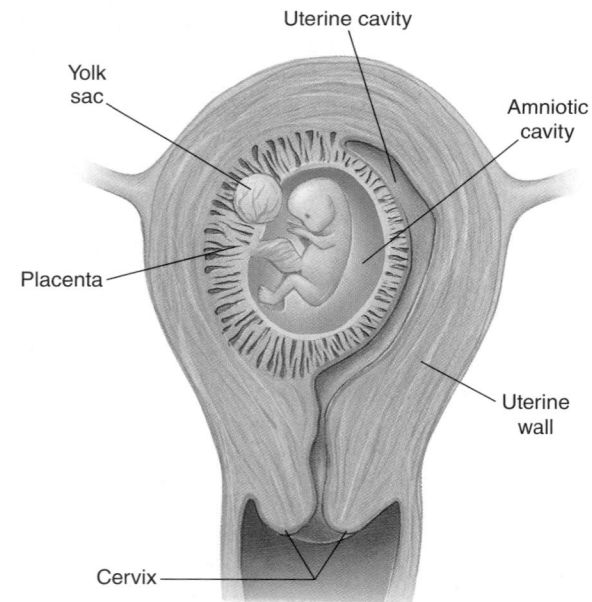

FIGURE 51-17 Human fetus at 10 weeks
Note the position of the fetus within the uterine wall.

that weighs less than 2500 g (5.5 lb) is considered low birth weight and is at risk even if not premature.

More than one mechanism can lead to a multiple birth

Occasionally, the cells of the two-cell embryo separate, and each cell develops into a complete organism. Or sometimes the inner cell mass subdivides, forming two groups of cells, each of which develops independently. Because these cells have identical sets of genes, the individuals formed are exactly alike—**monozygotic,** or identical, twins. Very rarely, the two inner cell masses do not completely separate and so give rise to **conjoined twins,** who are physically attached and usually share one or more body parts.

Dizygotic twins, also called fraternal twins, develop when two eggs are ovulated and each is fertilized by a different sperm. Each zygote has its own distinctive genetic endowment, so the individuals produced are not identical. They may not even be of the same sex. Similarly, triplets (and other multiple births) may be either identical or fraternal.

Before fertility-inducing agents became available in the United States, twins were born once in about 80 births (about 30% of twins are monozygotic), triplets once in 80^2 (or 1 in 6400), and quadruplets once in 80^3 (or 1 in 512,000). However, widespread use of drugs to improve fertility has been linked to an increase in multiple births. The March of Dimes reports that between 1980 and 2000 the rate of twin births increased by about 74% and the rate of triplet births increased fivefold. These rates may be stabilizing; the rate of twin births does not appear to be increasing, and the rate of triplet births has declined slightly.

A family history of twinning increases the probability of having dizygotic twins. However, giving birth to monozygotic twins is probably not influenced by heredity, age of the mother, or other known factors. An estimated two-thirds of multiple pregnancies end in the birth of a single baby; the other embryo(s) may be absorbed within the first ten weeks of pregnancy, or spontaneously aborted. Ultrasound imaging techniques are used to produce a type of image known as a **sonogram,** which can provide valuable data regarding the presence of multiple embryos. This is medically important because multiple births are associated with higher infant mortality, which is largely a consequence of an increased risk of prematurity and low birth weight.

Environmental factors affect the embryo

We all know that the growth and development of babies are influenced by the food they eat, the air they breathe, the disease organisms that infect them, and the chemicals or drugs to which they are exposed. **Prenatal development** is also affected by these environmental influences. Life before birth is even more sensitive to environmental changes than it is for the fully formed baby. Although there is no direct mixing of maternal and fetal blood, diffusion and various other mechanisms allow many substances—nutrients, drugs, pathogens, and gases—to travel across the placenta.

TABLE 51-3 describes some environmental influences on development. Some of these are **teratogens,** drugs or other substances that interfere with morphogenesis and so cause malformations. Many factors, such as smoking, alcohol use, and poor nutrition, contribute to low birth weight, a condition responsible for many infant deaths.

About one out of every 33 newborns (more than 120,000 babies per year) in the United States has a defect of clinical significance. Such birth defects account for more than 20% of deaths among newborns. Birth defects may be caused by genetic or environmental factors, or a combination of the two. Genetic factors were discussed in Chapter 17. In this section we examine some environmental conditions that affect the well-being of the embryo.

Timing is important. Each developing structure has a critical period during which it is most susceptible to unfavorable conditions. Generally, this critical period occurs early in the structure's development, when interference with cell movements or divisions may prevent formation of normal shape or size, resulting in permanent malformation. Because most structures form during the first three months of embryonic life, the embryo is most susceptible to environmental factors during this early period. During part of this time, the woman may not even realize she is pregnant and so may not take special precautions to minimize potential dangers.

Physicians diagnose some defects while the embryo is in the uterus. In some cases, treatment is possible before birth. Amniocentesis and chorionic villus sampling, discussed in Chapter 16, are techniques used to detect certain defects. Ultrasound imaging techniques mentioned previously help diagnose defects and determine the position of the fetus. Ultrasound has been used for more than 30 years, and unlike imaging techniques that use radiation, no risk of harm to the fetus has been traced to its use. New methods currently under development or refinement include special types of MRI and high-resolution, three-dimensional ultrasound imaging (**FIG. 51-18**).

The neonate must adapt to its new environment

Important changes take place after birth. During prenatal life, the fetus received both food and oxygen from the mother through the placenta. Now the newborn's own digestive and respiratory systems must function. Correlated with these changes are several major changes in the circulatory system.

Normally, the **neonate** (newborn infant) begins to breathe within a few seconds of birth and cries within half a minute. If anesthetics have been given to the mother, however, the fetus may also be anesthetized, and its breathing and other activities may be depressed. Some infants may not begin breathing until several minutes have passed. This is one reason why many women request childbirth methods that minimize the use of medication.

Researchers think that the neonate's first breath is initiated by the accumulation of carbon dioxide in the blood after the umbilical cord is cut. Carbon dioxide stimulates the respiratory centers in the medulla. The resulting expansion of the lungs enlarges its blood vessels (which in the uterus were partially collapsed). Blood from the right ventricle flows in increasing amounts through these larger pulmonary vessels. (During fetal life, blood bypasses the lungs in two ways: by flowing through an opening, the *foramen ovale,* which

TABLE 51-3   Environmental Influences on the Embryo

Factor	Example and Effect	Comment
Nutrition	Severe protein malnutrition doubles number of defects, fewer brain cells are produced, and learning ability may be permanently affected; deficiency of folic acid (a vitamin) linked to CNS defects such as spina bifida (open spine), low birth weight.	Growth rate mainly determined by rate of net protein synthesis by embryo's cells.
Medications	Many medications, even aspirin, affect development of the fetus.	Herbal drugs and dietary supplements are unregulated.
Excessive vitamins	Vitamin D essential, but excessive amounts may result in a form of mental retardation; an excess of vitamins A and K may also be harmful.	Vitamin supplements are normally prescribed for pregnant women, but only the recommended dosage should be taken.
Thalidomide	Thalidomide, marketed in Europe as a mild sedative, was responsible for serious malformations in about 10,000 babies born in the late 1950s in 20 countries; principal defect was phocomelia, a condition in which babies are born with extremely short limbs, often with no fingers or toes.	This teratogenic drug interferes with the development of blood vessels and nerves; most hazardous when taken during fourth to fifth weeks, when limbs are developing; thalidomide has been approved for the treatment of leprosy and certain cancers (e.g., myeloma), and clinical trials are being conducted to test its usefulness in the treatment of other cancers and some of the complications of AIDS.*
Accutane (isotretinoin)	Accutane, a synthetic derivitive of vitamin A, is used for the treatment of cystic acne. A woman who takes Accutane during pregnancy has a 1 in 5 chance of having a child with serious malformations of the brain (causing mental retardation), head and face, thymus gland (interfering with immune function), or heart.	Although Accutane is marketed with severe restrictions to prevent pregnant women from taking this teratogenic drug, several children are born each year with birth defects attributable to Accutane exposure.
Pathogens		
Rubella	Rubella (German measles) virus crosses placenta and infects embryo; interferes with normal metabolism and cell movements; causes syndrome that involves blinding cataracts, deafness, heart malformations, and mental retardation; risk is greatest (about 50%) when rubella is contracted during the first month of pregnancy; risk declines with each succeeding month.	Rubella epidemic in the United States in 1963–1965 resulted in about 20,000 fetal deaths and 30,000 infants born with serious defects; immunization is available but must be administered several months before conception.
HIV*	HIV can be transmitted from mother to baby before birth, during birth, or by breastfeeding.	See discussion of AIDS in Chapter 45.
Syphilis	Syphilis is transmitted to fetus in about 40% of infected women; fetus may die or be born with defects and congenital syphilis.	Pregnant women are routinely tested for syphilis during prenatal examinations; most cases can be safely treated with antibiotics.
Ionizing radiation	When a pregnant woman is subjected to X-rays or other forms of radiation, infant has a higher risk of birth defects and leukemia.	Radiation was one of the earliest causes of birth defects to be recognized.
Recreational and/or abused substances		
Alcohol	When a woman drinks heavily during pregnancy, the baby may be born with fetal alcohol syndrome (FAS), which includes certain physical deformities and mental and physical retardation; low birth weight and structural abnormalities have been associated with as little as two drinks a day; some cases of hyperactivity and learning disabilities have occurred.	Fetal alcohol syndrome is the leading cause of preventable mental retardation in the United States.
Cigarette smoking	Cigarette smoking reduces the amount of oxygen available to the fetus because some of the maternal hemoglobin is combined with carbon monoxide; may slow growth and can cause subtle forms of damage.	Mothers who smoke deliver babies with lower-than-average birth weights and have a higher incidence of spontaneous abortions, stillbirths, and neonatal deaths, especially from SIDS;* studies also indicate a possible relationship between maternal smoking and slower intellectual development in offspring.
Cocaine	Constricts fetal arteries, resulting in retarded development and low birth weight; in severe cases, there may be learning and behavioral problems, heart defects, and other medical problems.	Cocaine users frequently abuse alcohol as well, so it is difficult to separate the effects.
Heroin	High rates of mortality and prematurity; low birth weight.	Infants that survive are born addicted and must be treated for weeks or months; risk of SIDS is increased 10-fold.

*AIDS, acquired immunodeficiency syndrome; HIV, human immunodeficiency virus; SIDS, sudden infant death syndrome

FIGURE 51-18 Three-dimensional ultrasound image of a human fetus at about 16 weeks gestation
Note the enhanced soft tissue detail.

shunts blood from the right atrium to the left atrium, and by flowing through an arterial duct connecting the pulmonary artery and aorta. Both of these routes close off after birth.)

Aging is not a uniform process

We have examined briefly the development of the embryo and fetus, the birth process, and the adjustments required of the neonate. The human life cycle then proceeds through the stages of infant, child, adolescent, young adult, middle-aged adult, and elderly adult.

Development encompasses any biological change within an organism over time, including the changes commonly called **aging.** Changes during the aging process decrease function in the older individual. The declining capacities of the various systems in the human body, although most apparent in the elderly, may begin much earlier in life.

The aging process is far from uniform among different individuals or in various parts of the body. The body systems generally decline at different times and rates. On average, between the ages of 30 and 75 a man loses 64% of his taste buds, 44% of the glomeruli in his kidneys, and 37% of the axons in his spinal nerves. His nerve impulses are propagated at a 10% slower rate, the blood supply to his brain is 20% less, his glomerular filtration rate has decreased 31%, and the vital capacity of his lungs has declined 44%. However, the human body has considerable functional capacity in reserve, so bodily functions are usually adequate. Furthermore, there is evidence that some of these declines can be significantly lessened by modifying lifestyle (such as diet and exercise). Women also undergo body system declines in function, although, on average, they live about five years longer than men.

Although marked improvements in medicine and public health have led to longer life expectancies, there has been no corresponding increase in the *maximum* life expectancy. Relatively little is known about the aging process itself; this is now an active field of investigation, and researchers are gaining considerable insight through genetic studies on model organisms such as the nematode worm, *Caenorhabditis elegans*; the fruit fly, *Drosophila melanogaster*; and the laboratory mouse, *Mus musculus* (see Chapter 17).

Homeostatic response to stress decreases during aging

Research findings support the idea that most aging occurs because a combination of inheritance and environmental stress makes the individual less able to respond to additional stressors. One major question is whether a genetic program has evolved to cause aging or whether genetic involvement in the process is more circumstantial. Most available evidence favors the latter view.

However, some genetically programmed developmental events do seem related to the aging process. Cells that normally stop dividing when they differentiate appear more subject to the changes of aging than cells that continue to divide throughout life. Furthermore, researchers have hypothesized that certain parts of the body begin to malfunction because a genetic program stops key cells from dividing and replenishing themselves. In one model known as **cell aging,** when grown in culture, normal human cells eventually lose their ability to divide. Furthermore, cells taken from an older person divide fewer times than those from a younger person. Cell aging appears related to the fact that most normal human somatic cells are genetically programmed to lose the ability to produce active telomerase, an enzyme that replicates the DNA of the end caps (telomeres) of the chromosomes (see Fig. 12-18).

Genetically programmed cell death, *apoptosis,* is an essential developmental mechanism that may play a role in aging. However, researchers think that most aging is not a direct consequence of the genetic program leading to apoptosis; instead, mistakes in the *control* of apoptosis may lead to certain degenerative conditions, such as Alzheimer's disease, or to some of the cell deaths that occur following a heart attack or stroke.

Researchers are investigating genes that affect how the body is maintained and repaired in the face of various stressors. Like other life processes, aging may be accelerated by certain environmental influences and may vary because of inherited differences among individuals. Evidence also indicates that premature aging can be precipitated by hormonal changes; by various malfunctions of the immune system, including autoimmune responses; by accumulation of specific waste products within the cells; by changes in the molecular structure of macromolecules such as collagen; and by damage to DNA from continued exposure to cosmic radiation and X-rays.

Of course, researchers tend to be less interested in mechanisms that accelerate aging and more interested in those that might increase the maximum lifespan. In nematode worms, fruit flies, and mice, decreasing the activity of a gene encoding IGF-1 (insulin-like growth factor 1), a cell signaling molecule, can increase the lifespan by 100%. Severe caloric restriction in rats, mice, and some other mammals can also delay aging. Some researchers have obtained experimental evidence that calorie restriction is a stressor that activates genes responsible for regulating an organism's adaptive response to stress. They are in the process of identifying those genes and investigating interactions among them, with the goal of developing treatments capable of activating these adaptive pathways.

Review

- How does a human blastocyst form and implant?
- How does the placenta form, and what is its function?
- During which trimester does each of the following occur: cerebrum develops convolutions; limb buds develop; mother feels fetal movements?
- What adaptations must the neonate make immediately after birth?
- What changes take place during the aging process?
- How are model organisms contributing to the study of aging?

■ SUMMARY: FOCUS ON LEARNING OBJECTIVES

51.1 *(page 1107)*

1 Analyze the relationship between cell determination and cell differentiation, and between pattern formation and morphogenesis.

- **Cell determination** is a series of molecular events that lead to **cell differentiation,** in which a cell becomes specialized and carries out specific functions. Relatively undifferentiated cells are known as **stem cells.**
- **Morphogenesis,** the development of form, occurs through **pattern formation,** a series of events in which cells may communicate by signaling, migrate, undergo changes in shape, and even undergo **apoptosis** (programmed cell death).

2 Relate differential gene expression to nuclear equivalence.

- Usually no genetic changes occur in cell determination and cell differentiation (the principle of **nuclear equivalence**). Instead, various types of differentiated cells express different subsets of their genes (**differential gene expression**).

51.2 *(page 1107)*

3 Describe the four processes involved in fertilization.

- Contact and recognition occur between noncellular egg coverings and sperm.
- Sperm entry is regulated to prevent interspecific fertilization and **polyspermy,** which is fertilization of the egg by more than one sperm.
- Fertilization activates the egg, triggering the events of early development.
- Sperm and egg pronuclei fuse and initiate DNA synthesis.

4 Describe fertilization in echinoderms and point out some ways in which mammalian fertilization differs.

- The coverings of echinoderm eggs are the **vitelline envelope** and the **jelly coat;** a **zona pellucida** encloses the mammalian egg.
- On contact, a sperm undergoes an **acrosome reaction,** which facilitates penetration of the egg coverings; in mammals the acrosome reaction is preceded by **capacitation,** a maturation process that results in the ability of a sperm to fertilize an egg.
- Sea urchin fertilization is followed by a fast block to polyspermy (depolarization of the plasma membrane) and a slow block to polyspermy (the **cortical reaction**); changes in the zona pellucida prevent polyspermy in mammals.

51.3 *(page 1109)*

5 Trace the generalized pattern of early development of the embryo from zygote through early cleavage and formation of the morula and blastula.

- The zygote undergoes **cleavage,** a series of rapid cell divisions without a growth phase. The main effect of cleavage is to partition the zygote into many small **blastomeres.**
- Cleavage forms a solid ball of cells called the **morula** and then usually a hollow ball of cells called the **blastula.**

6 Contrast early development, including cleavage, in the echinoderm (or in amphioxus), the amphibian, and the bird, paying particular attention to the importance of the amount and distribution of yolk.

- The **isolecithal eggs** of most invertebrates and simple chordates have evenly distributed yolk. They undergo **holoblastic cleavage,** which involves division of the entire egg.
- In the moderately **telolecithal eggs** of amphibians, a concentration of yolk at the **vegetal pole** slows cleavage so that only a few large cells form there, compared to a large number of smaller cells at the **animal pole.**
- The highly telolecithal eggs of reptiles and birds, with a large concentration of yolk at one end, undergo **meroblastic cleavage,** which is restricted to the **blastodisc.**
- Animals whose zygotes have relatively homogeneous cytoplasm exhibit **regulative development,** in which the embryo develops as a self-regulating whole. The relatively rigid developmental patterns of some animals (**mosaic development**) is a consequence of the unequal distribution of cytoplasmic components.
- The **gray crescent** of an amphibian zygote determines the body axis of the embryo.

51.4 *(page 1112)*

7 Identify the significance of gastrulation in the developmental process and compare gastrulation in the echinoderm (or in amphioxus), the amphibian, and the bird.

- In **gastrulation,** the basic body plan is laid down as three germ layers form: the outer **ectoderm,** the inner **endoderm,** and the **mesoderm** between them.
- The **archenteron,** the forerunner of the digestive tube, forms in some groups; its opening to the exterior is the **blastopore.**
- In gastrulation in the sea star and in amphioxus, cells from the blastula wall invaginate and eventually meet the opposite wall, forming the archenteron.

- In the amphibian, invagination at the vegetal pole is obstructed by large, yolk-laden cells; instead, cells from the animal pole move down over the yolk-rich cells and invaginate, forming the **dorsal lip of the blastopore.**
- In the bird, invagination occurs at the primitive streak, and no archenteron forms.

CENGAGENOW™   Explore the frog life cycle by clicking on the figures in CengageNOW.

51.5 *(page 1115)*

8 Define *organogenesis* and summarize the fate of each of the germ layers.
- **Organogenesis** is the process of organ formation.
- Ectoderm becomes the nervous system, sense organs, and outer layer of skin (epidermis).
- Mesoderm becomes the notochord, skeleton, muscles, circulatory system, and inner layer of skin (dermis).
- Endoderm becomes the lining of the digestive tube.

9 Trace the early development of the vertebrate nervous system.

- The developing **notochord** is responsible for **induction,** which causes the overlying ectoderm to differentiate as the **neural plate,** the precursor of the central nervous system.
- The cells of the neural plate undergo changes in shape to form the hollow **neural tube,** from which the brain and spinal cord develop.

CENGAGENOW™   Explore nervous system development by clicking on the figure in CengageNOW.

51.6 *(page 1116)*

10 Give the origins and functions of the chorion, amnion, allantois, and yolk sac.

- The **chorion** and **amnion** derive from ectoderm and mesoderm; the **allantois** and **yolk sac,** from endoderm and mesoderm.
- The chorion is used in gas exchange. The amnion is a fluid-filled sac that surrounds the embryo and keeps it moist; it also acts as a shock absorber. The allantois stores nitrogenous wastes. The yolk sac makes food available to the embryo.

51.7 *(page 1117)*

11 Describe the general course of early human development, including fertilization, the fates of the trophoblast and inner cell mass, implantation, and the role of the placenta.
- Fertilization occurs in the oviduct.
- Cleavage takes place as the embryo is moved down the oviduct.
- In the uterus, the embryo develops into a **blastocyst** consisting of an outer **trophoblast,** which gives rise to the chorion and amnion, and an **inner cell mass,** which becomes the embryo proper. The blastocyst undergoes implantation in the endometrium.
- The **umbilical cord** connects the embryo to the **placenta,** the organ of exchange between the maternal and fetal circulation. The placenta derives from the embryonic chorion and maternal tissue.

CENGAGENOW™   Learn more about cleavage, implantation, and the development of the human embryo by clicking on the figures in CengageNOW.

12 Contrast postnatal with prenatal life, describing several changes that occur at or shortly after birth that allow the neonate to live independently.
- Human **prenatal development** requires 266 days from the time of fertilization; organogenesis begins during the **first trimester.** After the first two months of development, the embryo is referred to as a **fetus.** Growth and refinement of the organs continue in the second and third trimesters.
- The **neonate** (newborn) must undergo rapid adaptations, especially changes in the respiratory and digestive systems.

13 Describe some anatomical and physiological changes that occur with aging.
- The **aging** process is marked by a decrease in homeostatic response to stress.
- All body systems decline with age, but not at the same rate.

TEST YOUR UNDERSTANDING

1. The mechanism that leads directly to morphogenesis is (a) differential gene expression (b) pattern formation (c) nuclear equivalence (d) cell differentiation (e) cell determination

2. The main function of the acrosome reaction is to (a) activate the egg (b) improve sperm motility (c) prevent interspecific fertilization (d) facilitate penetration of the egg coverings by the sperm (e) cause fusion of the sperm and egg pronuclei

3. The fast block to polyspermy in sea urchins (a) is a depolarization of the egg plasma membrane (b) requires exocytosis of the cortical granules (c) includes the elevation of the fertilization envelope (d) involves the hardening of the jelly coat (e) is a complete block

4. Place the following events of sea urchin fertilization in the proper sequence.
   1. fusion of egg and sperm pronuclei 2. DNA synthesis 3. increased protein synthesis 4. release of calcium ions into the egg cytoplasm
   (a) 4, 3, 1, 2 (b) 3, 2, 4, 1 (c) 2, 3, 1, 4 (d) 1, 2, 3, 4 (e) 4, 1, 2, 3

5. The cleavage divisions of a sea urchin embryo (a) occur in a spiral pattern (b) do not include DNA synthesis (c) do not include cytokinesis (d) are holoblastic (e) do not occur at the vegetal pole

6. Meroblastic cleavage is typical of embryos formed from _____ eggs. (a) moderately telolecithal (b) highly telolecithal (c) isolecithal (d) b and c (e) a, b, and c

7. The primitive groove of the bird embryo is the functional equivalent of the _____ in the amphibian embryo. (a) yolk plug (b) archenteron (c) blastocoel (d) gray crescent (e) blastopore

8. Which of the following are mismatched? (a) endoderm; lining of the digestive tube (b) ectoderm; circulatory system (c) mesoderm; notochord (d) mesoderm; reproductive system (e) ectoderm; sense organs

9. Which of the following has three germ layers? (a) morula (b) gastrula (c) blastula (d) blastocyst (e) trophoblast

10. An unidentified substance (or substances) released from the developing notochord causes the overlying ectoderm to form the neural plate. This phenomenon is known as (a) activation (b) determination (c) induction (d) implantation (e) mosaic development

11. Which of the following consists of both fetal and maternal tissues? (a) umbilical cord (b) placenta (c) amnion (d) allantois (e) yolk sac

12. The embryo proper of a mammal develops from the (a) trophoblast (b) umbilical cord (c) inner cell mass (d) entire blastocyst (e) yolk sac

CRITICAL THINKING

1. For almost 200 years, scientists debated whether an egg or sperm cell contains a completely formed, miniature human (preformation) or whether structures develop gradually from a formless zygote (epigenesis). Relate these views to current concepts of development.

2. Not all teratogenic medications are banned by the U.S. Food and Drug Administration. Why?

3. **EVOLUTION LINK.** Consider the chordate characteristics described in Chapter 32 (notochord, dorsal hollow nerve cord, postanal tail, and pharynx with slits, a deuterostome characteristic). How are they evident in a human embryo? Do they have the same functions in humans as they do in a less specialized chordate, such as amphioxus? Why have they persisted in humans?

4. **EVOLUTION LINK.** What is the adaptive value of developing a placenta?

5. **EVOLUTION LINK.** Can you think of a rationale for natural selection for increased lifespan in humans, even though most individuals live past reproductive age?

6. **SCIENCE, TECHNOLOGY, AND SOCIETY.** As a public health official, what policies might you promote to reduce the incidence of prematurity and/or low birth weight? of malformations at birth?

 Additional questions are available in CengageNOW at www.cengage.com/login.

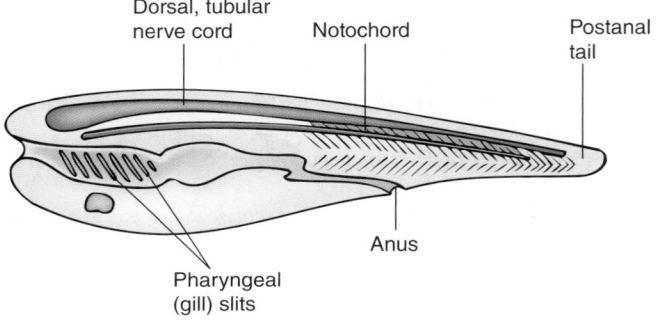

Dorsal, tubular nerve cord   Notochord   Postanal tail

Anus

Pharyngeal (gill) slits

52 Animal Behavior

The sand wasp (*Philanthus triangulum*) digging a burrow. How does the wasp know how to carry out the complex set of behaviors that ensure her reproductive success?

E. S. Ross

KEY CONCEPTS

52.1 Proximate causes of behavior are the immediate causes, such as the genetic, developmental, and physiological processes, that explain *how* an animal carries out a specific behavior. Ultimate causes of behavior are the evolutionary explanations for *why* a certain behavior occurs. If its benefits are greater than its costs, a behavior is adaptive.

52.2 The capacity for behavior is inherited, but behavior is modified in response to environmental experience; this is learned behavior. Types of learned behavior include habituation, imprinting, classical conditioning, operant conditioning, and cognition.

52.3 Biologically successful animals are physiologically and behaviorally adapted to the continuous changes that take place in the environment. Biological clocks regulate biological rhythms. Migration is an example of a behavior that involves interactions among biological rhythms, physiology, and the environment.

52.4 Optimal foraging is the most efficient way for an animal to obtain food.

52.5 Social behavior requires communication among animals in the group. Dominance hierarchies and defense of a territory benefit many social groups.

52.6 Sexual selection is a type of natural selection in which individuals with reproductive advantages are selected over others of the same sex and species. In many animal species, sexual selection favors polygynous mating systems in which males fertilize the eggs of as many females as they can during each breeding season.

52.7 Altruism is a type of cooperative behavior in which one animal behaves in a way that appears to benefit others rather than itself. Kin selection is a form of natural selection that increases inclusive fitness (the number of genes an animal perpetuates in offspring plus the number of genes its close relatives perpetuate) through the successful reproduction of close relatives.

52.8 Some bird and mammal species transmit culture, which is defined as learned behavior common to a population that one generation can teach to the next.

Suppose your professor gave you a hypodermic syringe full of poison and told you to find a particular type of insect, one that you had never seen before and that was armed with active defenses. You then had to inject the ganglia of your prey's nervous system (about which you had been taught nothing) with just enough poison to paralyze but not kill it. You would have difficulty accomplishing these tasks—but a solitary wasp no larger than the first joint of your thumb does it all with elegance and surgical precision, without instruction.

Philanthus, the sand wasp, captures a bee (or beetle), stings it, and places the paralyzed insect in a burrow excavated in the sand (see photograph on previous page). She then lays an egg on her prey, which is devoured alive by the larva that hatches from that egg. From time to time, *Philanthus* brings provisions to her hidden burrow, until autumn, when the larva becomes a hibernating pupa. Her offspring will repeat this behavior, precisely executing each step without ever having seen it done.

An animal's **behavior** is what it *does* and how it does it, usually in response to stimuli in its environment. A dog may wag its tail, a bird may sing, a butterfly may release a volatile sex attractant. Behavior is just as diverse as biological structure and just as characteristic of a given species as its anatomy or physiology. Like its morphology and physiology, an animal's behavior is the product of natural selection on phenotypes and indirectly on the genotypes that code for those phenotypes. Thus, an animal's repertoire of behavior is a set of adaptations that equip it for survival in a particular environment.

Whether biologists study behavior in an animal's natural environment or in the laboratory, they must consider that what an animal does cannot be isolated from the way in which it lives. **Behavioral ecology** is the study of behavior in natural environments from an evolutionary perspective. For more than two decades, behavioral ecology has been the main approach of biologists who study animal behavior. Before this approach emerged, the study of animal behavior was called *ethology*, and this term is sometimes still used to refer to the overall study of animal behavior.

In this chapter, we consider how an animal's behavior contributes to its reproductive success and to the survival of its species. We discuss types of learning and then focus on the *hows* and *whys* of some key types of behavior, including migration, foraging, and social behavior. We also explore sexual selection and helping behavior.

52.1 BEHAVIOR AND ADAPTATION

■ LEARNING OBJECTIVES

1 Distinguish between proximate and ultimate causes of behavior, and apply the concepts of ultimate cause and cost–benefit analysis to decide whether a particular behavior is adaptive.
2 Describe the interactions of heredity, environment, and maturation in animal behavior.

In considering the reproductive behavior of *Philanthus*, we might wonder *how* she accomplishes her task, and *why* she behaves as she does. Early investigators of animal behavior focused on *how* questions. These questions address **proximate causes**, immediate causes such as the genetic, developmental, and physiological processes that permit the animal to carry out the particular behavior.

Today, biologists also ask *why* questions that address the **ultimate causes** of behavior. These questions, which have evolutionary explanations, ask *why* a particular behavior has evolved. Ultimate considerations address costs and benefits of behavior patterns. When studying ultimate causes, we may ask what the adaptive value of a particular behavior might be. An understanding of behavior requires consideration of both proximate and ultimate causes.

Behaviors have benefits and costs

Behavioral ecologists use **cost–benefit analysis** to understand specific behaviors. A behavior may help an animal obtain food or water, protect itself, reproduce, or acquire and maintain territory in which to live. The benefits typically contribute to **direct fitness**, which is an individual's reproductive success, measured by the number of viable offspring it produces. Reproduction is, of course, the key to evolutionary success.

Behaviors also involve costs. A particular behavior may have risks. For example, while a parent is off hunting for food for its offspring, the youngsters may be killed by predators. Behaviors also have energy costs and costs of missed opportunities to carry out other behaviors. When an animal is out foraging for food, it may be missing opportunities to mate. If the benefits are greater than the costs, a behavior is adaptive.

The ultimate cause of a behavior is therefore to increase the probability that the genes of the individual animal will be passed to future generations. Certain responses may lead to the death of the individual while increasing the chance that copies of its genes will survive through the enhanced production or survival of its offspring or other relatives.

Genes interact with environment

Early biologists debated nature versus nurture, that is, the relative importance of genes compared with environmental experience. They defined **innate behavior** (inborn behavior, popularly referred to as *instinct*) as genetically programmed and **learned behavior** as behavior that has been modified in response to environmental experience. More recently, behavioral ecologists have recognized that no true dichotomy exists. All behavior has a genetic basis. Even the *capacity* for learned behavior is inherited. However, behavior is modified by the environment in which an animal lives; behavior is a product of the interaction between genetic capacity and environmental influences. Thus, behavior begins with an inherited framework that experience can modify.

We can think of a range of behaviors from the more rigidly genetically programmed types through those that, although they have a genetic component, are extensively developed through experience. The sand wasp *Philanthus*, discussed in the chapter introduction, efficiently carries out a sequence of behaviors that depends mainly on genetic programming. How to dig the burrow, how to cover it, how to kill the bees—these behaviors are genetically determined. Yet some of her behavior is learned. There is no way her ability to locate the burrow could be genetically programmed. Because a burrow can be dug only in a suitable spot, its location must be learned *after* it is dug. When *Philanthus* covers her burrow with sand, she takes precise bearings of its location by circling the area a few times before flying off again to hunt.

The Dutch ethologist Niko Tinbergen studied this behavior of *Philanthus*. He surrounded the wasp's burrow with a circle of pine cones as potential landmarks (**FIG. 52-1**). Before the wasp returned with another bee, Tinbergen rearranged or removed the pine cones. Without them, the wasp could not find her burrow. When Tinbergen moved the pine cones to an area where there was no burrow, the female wasp responded as though the burrow were there. When the investigator completely removed them, the female seemed very confused. Only when Tinbergen restored the cones to their original location could the wasp find her burrow.

When Tinbergen substituted a ring of stones for the cones, the wasp responded as though the burrow were in the center of the stones. Thus, *Philanthus* responded to the *arrangement* of the cones rather than to the cones themselves. Tinbergen's findings demonstrated that for *Philanthus*, learning the landmarks surrounding the burrow was critical for burrow locating.

Studies of fruit fly courtship and mating have provided interesting examples of interaction between genes and behavior. A ritual consisting of a complex sequence of steps, almost like a dance, must occur before mat-

ing takes place. This courtship ritual involves an exchange of visual, auditory, tactile, and chemical signals between the male and female. J. B. Hall, of Brandeis University, and his colleagues identified more than a dozen genes controlling these actions, suggesting that courtship behavior is largely inherited and preprogrammed. Nevertheless, the fruit fly has the capacity to learn from experience, a capacity that, of course, is also inherited.

KEY EXPERIMENT

QUESTION: How does *Philanthus* locate her burrow when she returns to provision it with food?

HYPOTHESIS: *Philanthus* uses visual cues to locate her burrow.

EXPERIMENT:
1. While *Philanthus* was in the burrow, Tinbergen placed a circle of pine cones around its entrance.
2. While the wasp was out foraging, Tinbergen moved the cones to a new position.
3. In a second experiment, Tinbergen left the pine cones around the burrow but rearranged them in a triangle shape in the wasp's absence. Nearby, he made a circle of stones.

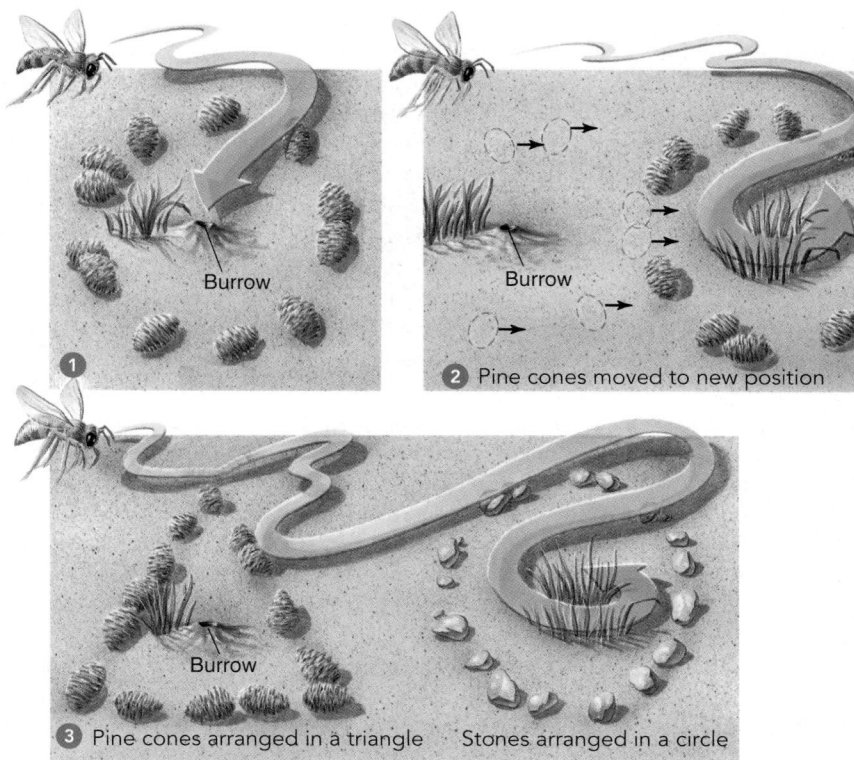

RESULTS:
1. When *Philanthus* emerged from her burrow, she responded to the circle of pine cones by circling the site, an orientation flight. When she returned with prey, she flew to the middle of the circle of pine cones.
2. When Tinbergen relocated the circle of pine cones, *Philanthus* flew to the middle of the new circle because she had learned the position of the burrow in relation to the cones.
3. When Tinbergen rearranged the cones in the shape of a triangle, and made a circle of stones nearby, *Philanthus* flew to the middle of the circle of stones.

CONCLUSION: *Philanthus* used visual cues to locate her burrow. She responded to the *arrangement* of cones rather than to the cones themselves. Landmark learning is critical for locating the burrow.

Source: Tinbergen, N. *The Animal in Its World*, Vol. 1. Harvard University Press, Cambridge, MA, 1972.

FIGURE 52-1 Niko Tinbergen's experiments determining how the wasp *Philanthus* locates her burrow

The interaction between genes and environment has been studied in many vertebrates. Several species of the love-bird (*Agapornis*) differ not only in appearance but in behavior. One species uses its bill to transport small pieces of bark for building a nest. Another species tucks nest-building materials under its rump feathers. Hybrid birds attempt to tuck material under their feathers, then try to carry it in their bills, repeating the pattern several times.

Eventually, most of the birds carry the material in their bills, but it takes them up to three years to perfect this behavior, and most continue to make futile attempts to tuck material into their feathers. Thus, the method of transporting materials is inherited but somewhat flexible. (In nature, hybrids would likely experience dramatically reduced fitness because of the long delay in breeding onset.)

Behavior depends on physiological readiness

Although behavior involves all body systems, it is influenced mainly by the nervous and endocrine systems. The capacity for behavior depends on the genetic characteristics that govern the development and functions of these systems. Before an animal can exhibit any pattern of behavior, it must be physiologically ready to produce the behavior. For example, breeding behavior does not ordinarily occur among birds or most mammals unless sufficient concentrations of sex hormones are present in their blood. A human baby cannot walk until its muscles and neurons are sufficiently developed. These states of physiological readiness are themselves produced by a continuous interaction with the environment. The level of sex hormones in a bird's blood may be determined by seasonal variations in day length. The baby's muscles develop with experience, as well as age.

Several factors influence the development of song in male white-crowned sparrows (generally only male songbirds sing a complex song). These birds show considerable regional variation in their song. During early development, young sparrows normally hear adult males sing the distinctive song of their population. Days 10 to 52 after hatching are a critical period for learning the song. When he is several months old, a young male sparrow "practices" the song over several weeks until he eventually sings in the local "dialect."

In laboratory experiments, birds kept in isolation and deprived of the acoustic experience of hearing the song of mature males eventually sing a poorly developed but recognizable white-crowned sparrow song. When a young white-crowned sparrow is permitted to interact socially with a strawberry finch (which belongs to a different genus of birds), it learns the song of the finch rather than its own species-specific song. This occurs even if the

white-crowned sparrow can hear the song of other sparrows but does not interact with them socially. From these experiments, investigators have concluded that the white-crowned sparrow is hatched equipped with a rough genetic pattern of its song, but social and acoustic stimuli are important in developing its ability to sing its specific song.

Many behavior patterns depend on motor programs

Many behaviors that we think of as automatic depend on coordinated sequences of muscle actions called **motor programs.** Some motor programs—for example, walking in newborn gazelles—seem mainly innate. Others, such as walking in human infants, have a greater learned component.

A classic example of a motor program in vertebrates is egg rolling in the European graylag goose (**FIG. 52-2**). Once activated by a simple sensory stimulus, egg-rolling behavior continues to completion regardless of sensory feedback. There is little flexibility. Behavioral ecologists call this behavior a **behavioral pattern.** Certain behavioral patterns can be elicited by a **sign stimulus,** or **releaser,** a simple signal that triggers a specific behavioral response. A wooden egg is a sign stimulus that elicits egg-rolling behavior in the graylag goose.

In a set of classic experiments performed in 1951, Tinbergen showed that the red stripe on the ventral surface (belly) of a male stickleback fish is a sign stimulus. The ventral surface of the male stickleback is normally silver but turns red at the beginning of the breeding season. The male stickleback selects a territory, builds a nest, and defends his territory against rival males. After a female lays her eggs, she leaves and the male guards the eggs and, later, the newly hatched fish.

Tinbergen showed that the red stripe triggers aggressive behavior by a male whose territory is being invaded. Tinbergen found that crude models painted with a red belly were more likely to be attacked than more realistic models lacking the red belly (**FIG. 52-3**). Aggressive behavior is triggered by the red belly rather than by recognition based on a combination of features.

FIGURE 52-2 Egg-rolling behavior in the European graylag goose
In this rather rigid behavioral pattern, the goose reaches out by extending her neck and uses her bill to pull the egg back into the nest. If the investigator quickly removes the egg while the goose is in the process of reaching for it or pulling it back, she continues the behavior to completion, as though pulling the now absent egg back to the nest.

QUESTION: What triggers aggressive behavior in the male stickleback?

HYPOTHESIS: The red ventral surface (belly) of a male stickleback is a sign stimulus that triggers aggressive behavior in other male sticklebacks.

EXPERIMENT: Niko Tinbergen presented male sticklebacks with two series of models.
1 The models in the neutral series were the neutral color of the male in the nonbreeding season.
2 The models in the red series were red on the ventral surface.

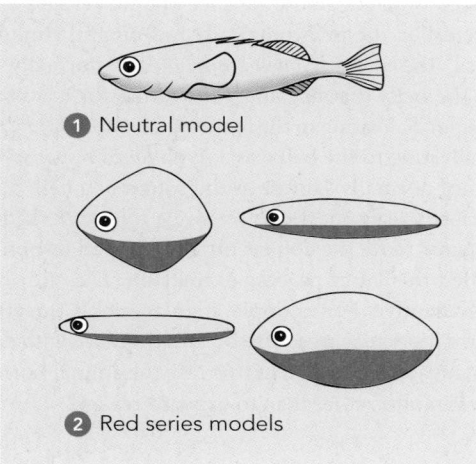

1 Neutral model

2 Red series models

RESULTS: The male fish did not attack realistic models of another male stickleback when they lacked a red belly. The male fish did attack other models, however unrealistic, that had red ventral surfaces.

CONCLUSION: Aggressive behavior in the male stickleback is triggered by the red belly of another male fish. The red belly is a sign stimulus, or releaser, for aggressive behavior.

FIGURE 52-3 Niko Tinbergen's experiments on aggressive behavior in the male stickleback fish

Review

- In what ways are the behaviors of *Philanthus*, the sand wasp, adaptive?
- Give an example showing that behavior capacity is inherited and is modified by learning.
- How does physiological readiness affect innate behavior? How does it affect learned behavior?

52.2 LEARNING: CHANGING BEHAVIOR AS A RESULT OF EXPERIENCE

■ LEARNING OBJECTIVE

3 Discuss the adaptive significance of habituation, imprinting, classical conditioning, operant conditioning, and cognition.

Based on our discussion thus far, it should be clear that much inherited behavior can be modified by experience. **Learning** involves persistent changes in behavior that result from experience. The capacity to learn new responses to new situations is adaptive, enabling animals to survive as their environment changes.

Learning abilities are biased; information most important to survival appears most easily learned. A rat may have taken a dozen trials to learn the artificial task of pushing a lever to get a reward. However, the same rat learns from *one* experience to avoid a food that has made it ill. People who poison rats to get rid of them can readily appreciate the adaptive value of this learning ability. Such quick learning in response to an unpleasant experience forms the basis of **warning coloration,** or **aposematic coloration,** which is found in many poisonous insects and brilliantly colored, but distasteful, bird eggs. Once made ill by such a meal, predators quickly learn to avoid them. In the following sections, we consider several types of learning, including habituation, imprinting, classical conditioning, operant conditioning, and cognition.

An animal habituates to irrelevant stimuli

Habituation is a type of learning in which an animal learns to ignore a repeated, irrelevant stimulus, that is, one that neither rewards nor punishes. Pigeons gathered in a city park learn by repeated harmless encounters that humans are not dangerous to them and behave accordingly. This behavior benefits them. A pigeon intolerant of people might waste energy by flying away each time a human approached and might not get enough to eat. Many African animals habituate to humans on photo safari and to the vans that transport them (**FIG. 52-4**). Urban humans habituate to the noise of traffic. In fact, many urban dwellers report that they do not sleep well when they visit a quiet rural area.

Imprinting occurs during an early critical period

Anyone who has watched a mother goose with her goslings must have wondered how she can "keep track" of such a horde of almost identical little creatures tumbling about in the grass, let alone distinguish them from those of another goose (**FIG. 52-5**). Although she can recognize her offspring to some extent, basically *they* have the responsibility of keeping track of *her*. The survival of a gosling requires that it quickly learn to discriminate its mother (care provider) from other geese.

Imprinting, a type of social learning based on early experience, has been studied in some mammals as well as birds. It occurs during a **critical period,** usually within a few hours or days after

FIGURE 52-4 Habituation

After repeated safe encounters with vans transporting humans on photo safari, many animals, including giraffes, zebras, and lions in the Serengeti, learn to ignore them. Elephants typically ignore the vans unless the driver provokes them by moving too close. In that event an elephant may challenge and even charge the van.

birth (or hatching). Konrad Lorenz, an Austrian physician and early ethologist, discovered that a newly hatched bird imprints on the first moving object it sees—even a human or an inanimate object such as a colored sphere or light. Although the process of imprinting is genetically determined, the bird *learns* to respond to a particular animal or object.

Among many types of birds, especially ducks and geese, older embryos can exchange calls with their nest mates and parents through the porous eggshell. When they hatch, at least one parent is normally on hand, emitting the characteristic sounds with which the hatchlings are already familiar. If the parent moves, the chicks follow. This movement and the sounds produce imprinting.

FIGURE 52-5 Imprinting

Parent–offspring bonds generally form during an early critical period. These goslings have imprinted on their mother, an upland goose (*Chloephaga picta*).

During a brief critical period after hatching, the chicks learn the appearance of the parent.

Imprinting in some mammals depends on scent. Baby shrews, for example, become imprinted on the odor of their mother (or any female nursing them). In many species, the mother also learns to distinguish her offspring during a critical period. The mother in some species of hooved mammals, such as sheep, will accept her offspring for only a few hours after its birth. If they are kept apart past that time, the young are rejected. Normally, the mother learns to distinguish her own offspring from those of others by olfactory cues.

In classical conditioning, a reflex becomes associated with a new stimulus

In **classical conditioning,** an association forms between some normal body function and a new stimulus. If you have observed dog or cat behavior, you know that the sound of a can opener at dinner time can captivate a pet's attention! Early in the 20th century, Ivan Pavlov, a Russian physiologist, discovered that if he rang a bell just before he fed a dog, the dog learned to associate the sound of the bell with food. Eventually, the dog salivated even when the bell was rung in the absence of food (**FIG. 52-6**).

Pavlov called the physiologically meaningful stimulus (food, in this case) the *unconditioned stimulus.* The normally irrelevant stimulus (the bell) that became a substitute for it was the *conditioned stimulus.* Salivating to the food was an *unconditioned response,* whereas salivating to the bell was a *conditioned response.* Because a dog does not normally salivate at the sound of a bell, the association was clearly learned. It could also be forgotten. If the bell no longer signaled food, the dog eventually stopped responding to it. Pavlov called this latter process **extinction.** Classical conditioning can be adaptive. For example, if an animal is threatened by a predator in a particular area, it associates the place with danger and avoids that area in the future. In this case the animal learns to *avoid* a negative stimulus rather than to expect a reward.

In operant conditioning, spontaneous behavior is reinforced

In **operant conditioning,** the animal must do something to gain a reward (positive reinforcement) or avoid punishment. Operant conditioning has been studied in many animals, including flatworms, insects, spiders, birds, and mammals. In a typical laboratory experiment, a rat is placed in a cage containing a movable bar. When random actions of the rat result in pressing the bar, a pellet of food rolls down a chute to the rat. Thus, the rat is positively reinforced for pressing the bar. Eventually, the rat learns the association and presses the bar to obtain food.

In negative reinforcement, removal of a stimulus increases the probability that a behavior will occur. For example, a rat may be subjected to an unpleasant stimulus, such as a low-level electric shock. When the animal presses a bar, this negative reinforcer is removed.

Many variations of these techniques have been developed. A pigeon may be trained to peck at a lighted circle to obtain food, a chimpanzee may learn to perform some task to get tokens that can

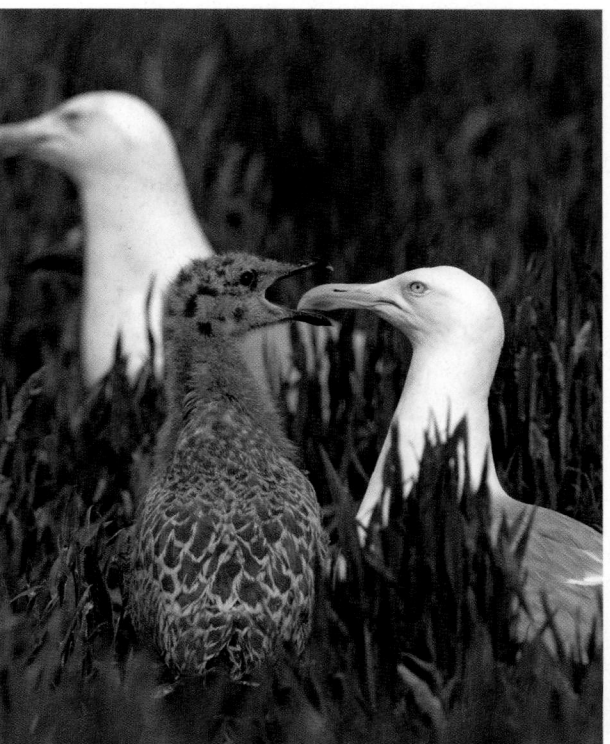

ARCO/J. De Cuveland

FIGURE 52-7 Operant conditioning
When the pelican chick pecks its parent's beak, the chick is positively reinforced with food. After many tries, the chick learns to be more accurate in begging for food from a parent.

ever, pecking behavior becomes more efficient with practice. Thus, a behavior that might appear to be entirely genetic is improved by learning (**FIG. 52-7**).

Animal cognition is controversial

Cognition is the process of gaining knowledge; it includes thinking, processing information, learning, reasoning, and awareness of thoughts, perceptions, and self. Cognition allows humans to carry out high-level mental functions. For example, we can make difficult decisions; solve problems, including mathematical problems; plan; and develop and comprehend languages. How closely animal cognition approximates human thought processes has been hotly debated and is the focus of a great deal of research. One controversial issue is whether any animals have a sense of self-awareness.

Some animals have a form of cognition called **insight learning,** the ability to adapt past experiences that may involve different stimuli to solve a new problem. A dog can be placed in a blind alley that it must circumvent to reach a reward. The difficulty lies in the fact that the animal must move *away* from the reward to get to it. Typically, the dog flings itself at the barrier nearest the food. Eventually, by trial and error, the frustrated dog may find its way around the barrier and reach the reward.

In contrast to the dog, a chimpanzee placed in a new situation is likely to make new associations between tasks it has learned previously to solve the problem (**FIG. 52-8**). Primates are especially

be exchanged for food, or children may learn to sit quietly in their seats at school to obtain the teacher's praise.

Operant conditioning plays a role in the development of some behaviors that appear genetically programmed. An example is the feeding behavior of gull chicks. Herring gull chicks peck the beaks of the parents, which stimulates the parents to regurgitate partially digested food for them. The chicks are attracted by two stimuli: the general appearance of the parent's beak with its elongated shape and distinctive red spot, and its downward movement as the parent lowers its head. Like the rat's chance pressing of the bar, the chicks' initial exploratory pecking behavior is sufficiently functional for them to get their first meal, but they waste a lot of energy in pecking. Some pecks are off target and are therefore not rewarded. How-

FIGURE 52-8 Cognition

Confronted with the problem of reaching food hanging from the ceiling, a chimpanzee may draw on past experience to solve the problem. When provided with boxes, many chimps stack them until they can climb and reach the food. What former experience might the chimp be applying to this new situation?

skilled at insight learning, but some other mammals and a few birds, notably crows, also seem to have this ability to some degree.

Play may be practice behavior

Perhaps you have watched a kitten pouncing on a dead leaf or practicing a carnivore neck bite or a hind-claw disemboweling stroke on a littermate without causing injury. Many animals, especially young birds and mammals, appear to practice adult patterns of behavior

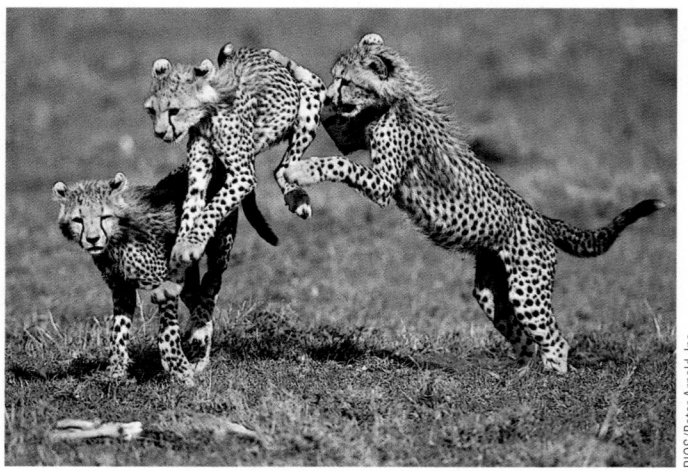

BIOS/Peter Arnold, Inc.

FIGURE 52-9 Cheetah cubs playing

Play may serve as a means of practicing behavior that will be useful later in life, possibly in hunting, fighting for territory, or competing for mates.

while they play (**FIG. 52-9**). They may improve their ability to escape, hunt, kill prey, or perform sexual behavior. Play may be an example of operant conditioning in action. Hypotheses for the ultimate causes of play behavior include exercising, learning to coordinate movements, and learning social skills. Of course, there could be other unknown explanations.

Review

- How is imprinting adaptive?
- How is operant conditioning adaptive?

52.3 BEHAVIORAL RESPONSES TO ENVIRONMENTAL STIMULI

■ LEARNING OBJECTIVES

4 Give examples of biological rhythms and describe some of the physiological mechanisms responsible for them.
5 Analyze costs and benefits of migrations, and distinguish between directional orientation and navigation.

Biologically successful animals are physiologically and behaviorally adapted to the continuous changes that take place in the environment. Think of the many variations that take place in our natural surroundings: cycles of day and night, changes in length of day with changing seasons, lunar cycles, high and low tide, changes in weather, and variations in amount and distribution of food. The biochemical, physiological, and behavioral responses animals make to the periodic changes in the environment are referred to as **biological rhythms.**

Biological rhythms regulate many behaviors

Biologists have identified many types of biological rhythms, including daily, monthly, and annual rhythms. Among many animals, physiological cycles such as body-temperature fluctuations and hormone secretion are rhythmic. Human body temperature, for example, follows a typical daily curve with the lowest temperature early in the morning and the highest in the late afternoon. (Women also have a monthly temperature rhythm with the highest body temperature during the last half of the menstrual cycle.) Biological rhythms control various behaviors, including activity, sleep, feeding, drinking, reproduction, and migration.

The behavior of many animals, like the activities of many plants, is organized around **circadian** (meaning "approximately 1 day") **rhythms,** which are daily, 24-hour cycles of activity. **Diurnal** animals, such as honeybees and pigeons, are most active during the day. Most bats, moths, and cats are **nocturnal** animals, most active during the hours of darkness. **Crepuscular** animals, like many mosquitoes and fiddler crabs, are busiest at dawn or dusk, or both. Generally, there are ecological reasons for these patterns. If an animal's food is most plentiful in the early morning, for example, its cycle of activity must be regulated so that it becomes active shortly before dawn.

Some biological rhythms of animals reflect the **lunar** (moon) **cycle.** The most striking rhythms are those in marine organisms that are attuned to changes in tides and phases of the moon. For instance, a combination of tidal, lunar, and annual rhythms governs the reproductive behavior of the grunion, a small fish that lives off the Pacific coast of North America. Grunions swarm from April through June on those three or four nights when the highest tides of the year occur. At precisely the high point of the tide, the fish squirm onto the beach and deposit eggs and sperm in the sand. They return to the sea in the next wave. By the time the next tide reaches that portion of the beach 15 days later, the young fish have hatched in the damp sand and are ready to enter the sea. This synchronization may help protect fish eggs from aquatic predators.

An animal's metabolic processes and behavior are typically synchronized with the cyclic changes in its external environment. Its behavior anticipates these regular changes. The little fiddler crabs of marine beaches often emerge from their burrows at low tide to engage in social activities such as territorial disputes. To avoid being washed away, they must return to their burrows before the tide returns. How do the crabs "know" that high tide is about to occur? One might guess that the crabs recognize clues present in the seashore. However, when the crabs are isolated in the laboratory away from any known stimulus that could relate to time and tide, their characteristic behavioral rhythms persist.

Many biological rhythms are regulated by *internal* timing mechanisms that serve as **biological clocks.** As illustrated by the fiddler crabs, these timing mechanisms do not simply respond to environmental cues but are capable of sustaining biological rhythms independently. Such internal clocks have been identified in almost every eukaryote, as well as some bacteria. Molecular biologists have demonstrated that genes control biological clocks. In *Drosophila,* seven genes produce clock proteins that seem to interact in feedback loops in many cell types both inside and outside the nervous system. Researchers have identified similar genes and proteins in many animal groups, including mammals. The principal clock is located in specific areas of the central nervous system.

In mammals, the master clock is located in the **suprachiasmatic nucleus (SCN)** in the hypothalamus (see Chapter 42). This SCN clock generates approximately 24-hour cycles even without input from the environment. However, the SCN-generated cycles are normally adjusted every day based on visual input received from the retina. Signals from the retina reflecting changes in light intensity adjust internal circadian rhythms to light–dark cycles in the environment. The SCN sends rhythmic signals, in the form of neuropeptides, to the **pineal gland,** an endocrine gland located in the brain. In response, the pineal gland secretes *melatonin,* a hormone that promotes sleep in humans. Clock genes in the SCN are turned on and off by the very proteins they encode, setting up feedback loops that have a 24-hour cycle.

In addition to the master clock, most cells have timing mechanisms that use many of the same clock proteins. These peripheral clocks may function independently of the SCN.

Environmental signals trigger physiological responses that lead to migration

Ruby-throated hummingbirds cross the vast distance of the Gulf of Mexico twice each year, and the sooty tern travels across the entire South Atlantic from Africa to reach its tiny island breed-

ing grounds south of Florida. Birds, butterflies, fishes, sea turtles, wildebeest, zebras, and whales are among the many animals that travel long distances. Behavioral ecologists define **migration** as a periodic long-distance travel from one location to another. Many migrations involve astonishing feats of endurance and navigation.

Why do animals migrate? Ultimate causes of migration apparently involve the advantages of moving from an area that seasonally becomes less hospitable to a region more likely to support reproduction or survival. Seasonal changes include shifts in climate, availability of food resources, and safe nesting sites. For example, as winter approaches, many birds migrate to a warmer region.

Proximate causes of migration include signals from the environment that trigger physiological responses leading to migration. In migratory birds, for example, the pineal gland senses changes in day length and then releases hormones that cause restless behavior. The birds show an increased readiness to fly and to fly for longer periods.

Migration has costs and benefits

An interesting example of migration is the annual journey of millions of monarch butterflies (*Danaus plexippus*) from Canada and the continental United States to Mexico, a journey of 2520 km (about 1520 mi) for some. Their dramatic annual migration appears related to the availability of milkweed plants on which females lay their eggs. On hatching, the larvae (caterpillars) feed on the leaves of the milkweed plant. In cold regions these plants die in late autumn and grow again with the warmer weather of spring.

The wintering destinations of monarchs also may be determined by temperature and humidity. Possible benefits include the opportunity to winter in an area that offers an abundant food supply, nonfreezing temperatures, and moist air. Thus, the investment made by migrating monarch butterflies in their long journey increases their chances of surviving the winter.

The benefits of migration are not without costs in time, energy, and even survival. Many weeks may be spent each year on energy-demanding journeys. Some animals may become lost or die along the way from fatigue or predation. When in unfamiliar areas, migrating individuals are often at greater risk from predators.

In recent years, human activities have interfered with migrations of many kinds of animals. For example, after millions of years of biological success, survival of sea turtles is threatened by fishing and shrimping nets in which they become entangled. As a result, thousands of migrating turtles drown each year. Sea turtles also die as a result of oil from oil spills and from ingesting floating plastic bags they mistake for jellyfish.

Animals find their way using directional orientation and navigation

How do migrating animals find their way? The term **directional orientation** refers to travel in a specific direction. To travel in a straight line toward a destination requires a sense of direction, or **compass sense.** Many animals use the sun to orient themselves. Because the sun appears to move across the sky each day, an animal must have a sense of time. Biological clocks seem to sense time and regulate circadian rhythms.

Navigation is more complex, requiring both compass sense and **map sense,** which is an "awareness" of location. Navigation

FIGURE 52-10 Navigation by light and magnetic field
To study turtle navigation, researcher Kenneth Lohmann harnessed leatherback turtles (*Dermochelys coriacea*), such as this hatchling, and wired them to a computer that recorded their swimming direction.

involves the use of cues to change direction when necessary to reach a specific destination. When navigating, an animal must integrate information about distance and time, as well as direction.

DNA tests confirm that loggerhead sea turtles that hatch on Florida beaches along the Atlantic swim hundreds of miles across the ocean to the Mediterranean Sea, an area rich in food. Several years later, those that survive to become adults mate, and the females navigate back, often to the same beach, to lay their eggs. Their journey requires both compass sense and map sense.

Marine biologist Kenneth Lohmann, of the University of North Carolina, fitted hatchling turtles with harnesses connected to a swivel arm in the center of a large tank (**FIG. 52-10**). A computer connected to the swivel arm recorded the turtles' swimming movements. Manipulating light and magnetic fields, Lohmann demonstrated that both these environmental cues are important in turtle migration. The turtles swam toward the east until Lohmann reversed the magnetic field. The turtles reversed their direction to swim toward the new "magnetic east," which was now actually west. Recent work suggests that young turtles use wave direction to help set magnetic direction preference.

Some biologists suspect that turtles also use their sense of smell to guide them, particularly to guide the females to the very same beach to lay their eggs. Similarly, adult salmon use the unique odors of different streams to help find their way back to the same stream from which they hatched.

Birds and some other animals that navigate by day rely on the position of the sun (our local star); those that travel at night use the stars to guide them. When birds see the star patterns of the night sky, they seek to fly in the appropriate migration direction for their species, even when they have had no opportunity to learn this feat from other birds.

Studies by Stephen Emlen, of Cornell University, showed that young indigo buntings learn the constellations, using the position of the North Star as their reference point. (Other stars in the Northern Hemisphere appear to rotate about the North Star.) When Emlen rearranged the constellations in a planetarium sky, birds learned the altered patterns of stars and later attempted to fly in a direction consistent with the artificial pattern. These and other

studies suggested that birds have a genetic ability to learn constellation patterns and use them to orient during migration.

Investigators have long observed that some species of birds navigate even when the sky is overcast and they cannot see the stars. They hypothesized that these birds use Earth's magnetic field to navigate. Studies of garden warblers indicate that as these birds make their way from central Europe to Africa each winter, they navigate both by the stars and by Earth's magnetic field. The warblers use stars to determine the general direction of travel, then use magnetic information to refine and correct their course. In addition to birds and sea turtles, honeybees, some fishes, and some other animals are sensitive to Earth's magnetic field and use it as a guide.

Review

- Why is it adaptive for some species to be diurnal but for others to be nocturnal or crepuscular?
- What is the difference between directional orientation and navigation?

52.4 FORAGING BEHAVIOR

■ LEARNING OBJECTIVE

6 Define *optimal foraging behavior* and explain how it is adaptive.

Feeding behavior, or **foraging,** involves locating and selecting food, as well as gathering and capturing food. Some behavioral ecologists study the costs and benefits of searching for and selecting certain types of food, as well as the mechanisms used to locate prey. For example, many camouflage strategies have evolved that make potential prey difficult to detect. As predators experience repeated success in locating a particular prey species, they are thought to develop a *search image*, a constellation of cues that help them identify hidden prey.

Why do grizzly bears spend hours digging arctic ground squirrels out of burrows while ignoring larger prey such as caribou? It is more energy efficient to dig for squirrels because the bears' efforts most probably will be rewarded, whereas caribou are more likely to escape, leaving the bears hungry. This is an example of **optimal foraging,** the most efficient way for an animal to obtain food. According to *optimal foraging theory,* when animals forage, they maximize their energy intake per unit of foraging time. When animals maximize energy obtained per unit of foraging time, they may maximize their reproductive success. Many factors, such as avoiding predators while foraging, must be considered in determining efficient or optimal strategies.

In habitats where the most preferred food items are abundant and an animal does not have to travel far to obtain them, animals can afford to be selective. In contrast, the optimal strategy in poor habitats, where it takes longer to find the best food items, is to select less preferred items. Animals may learn to forage efficiently through operant conditioning, that is, by randomly trying various strategies and selecting the one associated with the most rewards (and the fewest hunger pangs at the end of the day).

Foraging is also affected by the forager's risk of predation. British biologist Guy Cowlishaw studied foraging behavior in a population of baboons in Namibia. He found that the baboons spent more time foraging in a habitat in which food was relatively scarce than in an area with more abundant food that had a high risk of predation by lions and leopards.

Lions live, and often forage, in social units called *prides*. A pride typically consists of a group of related adult females, their cubs, and unrelated males. Biologist Craig Packer, of the University of Minnesota, and his research team studied lion behavior in Serengeti National Park, Tanzania. Packer radio-collared at least one female in each of 21 prides and tracked them for several years. During the season when prey was abundant, lions hunted wildebeest, gazelle, and zebra that migrated into the area. When these herds migrated out of the area during the dry season, these prey become scarce, and lions fed mainly on warthog and Cape buffalo.

Packer reported that when prey was abundant, the size of the foraging group had little effect on daily food intake. Whether a lion hunted individually or in small (two to four females) or large (five to seven) groups, food was captured by individuals or groups of any size. During the season when prey was scarce, however, lions were more successful if they hunted alone or in large groups (**FIG. 52-11**). Nevertheless, Packer's data from radio-collared lions indicated that females typically foraged in as large a group as they could, even if the group consisted of three or four females, an approach that decreased foraging efficiency. Thus, selection pressure seems to be stronger to protect cubs and defend territory against larger prides than to forage maximally (alone).

Review

- What is optimal foraging?
- How is optimal foraging adaptive?

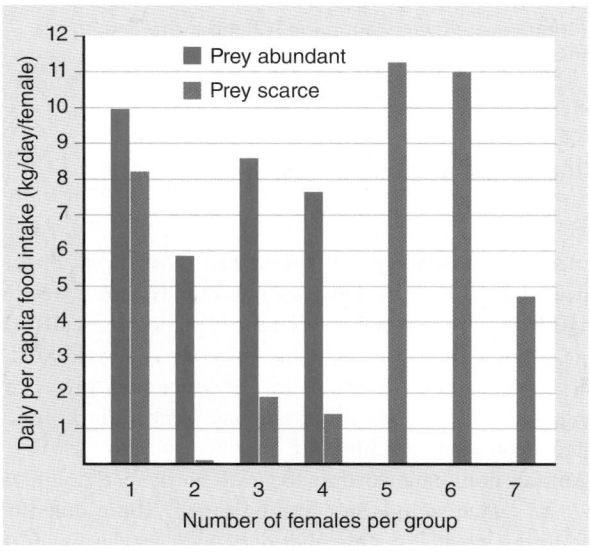

FIGURE 52-11 Optimal foraging and group size in lions
During times of prey scarcity, optimal foraging is related to group size: lions hunt most successfully alone or in large groups of five to seven. Observations of group size suggest that the benefits of optimal defense often outweigh the benefits of optimal foraging. (Based on data from Packer, C., D. Scheel, and A. E. Pusey. "Why Lions Form Groups: Food Is Not Enough." *American Naturalist*, Vol. 136, July 1990.)

52.5 COSTS AND BENEFITS OF SOCIAL BEHAVIOR

LEARNING OBJECTIVES

7 Analyze social behavior in terms of costs and benefits, and compare different types of social groups, including societies of social insects.

8 Describe common modes of animal communication, including signaling by pheromones.

9 Describe costs and benefits of dominance hierarchies and of territoriality.

The mere presence of more than one individual does not mean a behavior is social. Many factors of the physical environment bring animals together in **aggregations,** but whatever interaction they experience may be circumstantial. A light shining in the dark is a stimulus that draws large numbers of moths, and the high humidity under a log attracts wood lice. Although these aggregations may have adaptive value, they are not truly social because the animals are not communicating with one another.

We can define **social behavior** as the interaction of two or more animals, usually of the same species. In the same way that natural selection led to the evolution of behaviors in response to environmental factors, natural selection has resulted in the evolution of social behavior. We will examine several familiar types of social behavior, including communication, living together, dominance behaviors, territoriality, mating rituals, parenting, and helping behavior.

An organized **society** is an actively cooperating group of individuals belonging to the same species and often closely related. Many insects, such as tent caterpillars, which spin communal nests, cooperate socially. A school of fish, a flock of birds, a pack of wolves, and a hive of bees are other examples of societies. Some societies are loosely organized, whereas others are elaborately structured.

Many animals benefit from living in groups. Schools of fishes tend to confuse predators, so individuals within the school may be less vulnerable to predators than a solitary fish would be (see Fig. 53-1b). Zebra stripes appear to be a visual antipredator adaptation. When viewed from a distance, the stripes tend to visually break up the form of the animal so that individuals cannot be distinguished. A herd of zebras confuses predators, whereas a solitary animal is easy prey for lions, cheetahs, or spotted hyenas (**FIG. 52-12**).

Social foraging is an adaptive strategy used routinely by many animal species. A pack of wolves has greater success in hunting than an individual wolf would have. Among some birds of prey, such as certain hawks, group hunting locates prey more quickly.

Social behavior has benefits in addition to defense against predators and, in some cases more successful foraging. Living together provides opportunities for interfering with reproduction of competitors, for example, destroying their eggs. Social living also provides the opportunity to receive help from others in the group. Thus, for many types of animals, social behavior increases direct fitness. However, social behavior also has certain costs. Living together means increased competition for food and habitats, increased risk of attracting predators, and increased risk of transmitting disease. In addition, time and energy must often be invested in gaining and maintaining social status.

FIGURE 52-12 Social behavior in zebras
The social unit consists of a fairly stable group of females with young and a dominant stallion. The stripes of a group of zebras confuse predators.

Communication is necessary for social behavior

One animal can influence the behavior of another only if the two of them can exchange mutually recognizable signals (**FIG. 52-13**). **Communication** is most evident when one animal performs an act that changes the behavior of another. Animals may communicate to hold a group together, warn of danger, signal social status, indicate willingness to accept or provide care, identify members of the same species, or indicate sexual maturity or readiness to mate. Communication may also be important in finding food, as in the elaborate dances of honeybees. Animals use electrical, tactile, visual, auditory, and chemical signals to transmit information to one another.

Certain fishes (gymnotids) emit electric pulses that generate electric fields in the water. These electric pulses can be used for navigation and communication, including territorial threat, in a fashion similar to bird vocalization. As Harvard sociobiologist Edward O. Wilson said, "The fish, in effect, sing electrical songs."

Examples of animal touch include grooming and sharing food. Social insects, such as ants, groom and stroke one another with their antennae and mouthparts. Many types of bird chicks stimulate their parents to feed them by pecking at their beaks.

Visual signals can be transmitted quickly

Visual signals are fast, communicate a great deal of information, and indicate the position of the animal sending the signal. An animal's own body, such as its coloration, may serve as the visual message. Numerous species communicate with visual displays that serve as social signals. For example, many birds present visual displays along with their songs.

Auditory signals can be conveyed in the dark

Most animals cannot communicate effectively with visual signals when it is dark. However, animals can hear at night as well as during the day. Auditory signals can also be transmitted over longer

(a) A male spring peeper frog (*Hyla crucifer*) calling to locate a mate.

(b) Communicating with language. Chimpanzee Tatu (*top*) is signing "food" to Washoe (*below*), the first chimp to learn American Sign Language from a human. Washoe then taught other chimps how to sign.

FIGURE 52-13 Animal communication

distances than visual signals. Sound can move in all directions at once, and an auditory signal can be rapidly terminated. Most animals that communicate with auditory signals use **calls,** short, simple sounds. Birds and mammals use more complex auditory signals. In many bird species, males announce their presence and willingness to interact socially by singing. Some birds respond to a particular sound by matching it.

Among nonhuman mammals, only bottlenose dolphins are known to match sounds in communicating. These dolphins respond to the whistle of a member of its own species by imitating and emitting the same sound. (Researchers suggest that vocal matching was important in the evolution of human language.)

Orcas (formerly known as killer whales) communicate by sounds and songs. Members of a given pod (social group) have an average of 12 different calls, which vary in pitch and duration and appear to reflect their "emotional" state.

Some animals communicate by scent

Dogs and wolves mark territory by frequent urination. Antelopes, deer, and cats rub facial gland secretions on conspicuous objects in their vicinity and urinate on the ground. **Pheromones** are chemical signals secreted into the environment that convey information between members of a species. These small, volatile molecules provide a simple, widespread means of communication. Animals use pheromones to communicate danger, ownership of territory, and availability for mating. For example, female moths release pheromones that attract males. Ants mark their trails with pheromones.

Most pheromones elicit a very specific, immediate, but transitory type of behavior. Others trigger hormonal activities that result in slow but long-lasting responses. Still other pheromones may elicit both transitory and more lasting responses. An advantage to pheromone communication is that relatively little energy is needed to synthesize the simple, but distinctive, organic compounds involved. Members of the same species have receptors that fit the molecular configuration of the pheromone; other species usually ignore it or do not detect it at all. Pheromones are effective in the dark, can pass around obstacles, and last for several hours or longer. A major disadvantage of pheromone communication is that pheromones are transmitted slowly. Also, their information content is limited. However, some animals secrete several pheromones with different meanings.

Pheromones are important in attracting the opposite sex and in sex recognition in many species. Many social insects use these chemical signals to regulate reproduction. Humans have taken advantage of some sex-attractant pheromones to help control pests such as gypsy moths. They lure the males to traps baited with synthetic versions of female gypsy moth pheromones.

In honeybees, certain fatty acids are mixed with hydrocarbons from wax glands, and this mixture is transferred onto worker bees when they touch the comb. This mixture serves as a pheromone that identifies all the bees that belong to a particular hive. Should a bee from another hive attempt to enter, guard bees sting and may even kill the foreigner.

In vertebrates, pheromones affect sexual cycles and reproductive behavior, including choice of a mate. Pheromones may also play a role in defending territory. Among some mammals, an ovulating female (one physiologically ready to mate) releases pheromones as part of her vaginal secretion. When males detect these chemical odors, their sexual interest increases. When the odor of a male mouse is introduced among a group of females, the reproductive cycles of the female mice synchronize. In some species of mice, the odor of a strange male, a sign of high population density, causes a newly impregnated female to abort.

The extent to which humans respond to pheromones is the focus of research. One interesting finding suggests that an unconsciously perceived body odor can synchronize the menstrual cycles of women who associate closely (for instance, college roommates or cell mates in prison). Human steroids used in commercial fragrances such as perfumes may act as subtle signals that modulate mood and behavior.

As discussed in Chapter 43, mammals detect pheromones with specialized chemoreceptor cells that make up the **vomeronasal organ** in the epithelium of the nose. The vomeronasal sensory neurons signal the amygdala and hypothalamus, brain structures that regulate emotional responses and certain endocrine processes. When neurons of the vomeronasal system are damaged in virgin mice, they do not mate. Biologists have identified about 100 genes that code for pheromone receptors in the mouse and rat. These receptors initiate **signal transduction** pathways that involve G proteins.

Dominance hierarchies establish social status

In the spring, female paper wasps awaken from hibernation and begin to build a nest together. During the early course of construction, a series of squabbles among the females takes place in which the combatants bite one another's bodies or legs. Finally, one of the wasps emerges as dominant. After that, she is rarely challenged. This queen wasp spends more and more time tending the nest and less and less time out foraging for herself. She takes the food she needs from the others as they return.

The queen then begins to take an interest in raising a family—her family. Because she is almost always in the nest, she can prevent other wasps from laying eggs in the brood cells by rushing at them, jaws agape. Because of her supreme dominance, the queen can bite any other wasp without serious risk of retaliation.

The other wasps of the nest are further organized into a **dominance hierarchy,** a ranking of social status in which each wasp has more status than the wasps that are lower in rank. Wasps lower in the hierarchy are subordinate to those above them, as follows:

queen $\longrightarrow$ wasp A $\longrightarrow$ wasp B $\longrightarrow$ . . . wasp M $\longrightarrow$ wasp N

Once a dominance hierarchy is established, little or no time is wasted in fighting. When challenged, subordinate wasps communicate with submissive poses that inhibit the queen's aggressive behavior. Consequently, few or no colony members are lost through wounds sustained in fighting one another. This social organization ensures greater reproductive success for the colony.

In many species, males and females have separate dominance systems. For example, both female and male chimpanzees establish dominance hierarchies. Some females apparently become dominant through aggressive behavior, whereas others achieve high rank by virtue of their mother's status. Dominant females are more successful reproductively than those with lower social status. In many monogamous animals, especially birds, the female acquires the dominance status of her mate by virtue of their relationship and the male's willingness to defend her.

Like many fishes and some invertebrates, certain coral reef fishes (labrids) are capable of sex reversal. The largest, most dominant individual of a group is always male, and the remaining fish within his territory are all female. If the male dies or is removed, the most dominant female becomes the new male. Should any harm come to him, the next-ranking female undergoes sex reversal, takes charge, and protects the group territory. Other fishes exhibit the reverse behavior, in which the most dominant fish is always female. In such species, size is less important for aggressive defense than for maximal egg production.

In establishing dominance, males may expend energy in posturing, roaring, leaping about, or sometimes fighting fiercely. These

FIGURE 52-14 Communicating dominance

This baboon (*Papio*) bares his teeth and screams in an unmistakable show of aggression, a signal that allows him to establish and maintain dominance. In many social groups, animals send signals that help them establish and maintain dominance.

behaviors appear to be a test of male quality. The male with the greatest endurance will likely gain dominance and will have the greatest opportunity to mate and perpetuate his genes. In many animals, social dominance is a function of aggressiveness (**FIG. 52-14**). Tremendous energy is often needed for the fights engaged in by some birds and many mammals, including baboons, rams, and elephant seals. Establishing dominance is often strenuous and dangerous.

Sex hormones, particularly the male reproductive hormone testosterone, increase aggressiveness. The female hormone estrogen sometimes reduces dominance. Among chickens, the rooster is the most dominant. If a hen receives testosterone injections, her place in the dominance hierarchy shifts upward. When male rhesus monkeys are dominant, their testosterone levels are much higher than when they have been defeated. Not only can testosterone increase dominance but dominance may even increase testosterone production. It is not always easy to determine cause and effect. (Studies suggest that the effects of testosterone on human mood and behavior may be different from those in other vertebrates.)

Social status affects many organs and systems, including brain structure. For example, dominant male rats have more new neurons in the hippocampus than subordinate rats or controls.

Many animals defend a territory

Most animals have a **home range,** a geographic area they seldom leave (**FIG. 52-15**). Because the animal has the opportunity to become familiar with everything in that range, it has an advantage over its competitors, predators, and prey in negotiating the terrain and finding food. Some, but not all, animals exhibit **territoriality.** They defend a **territory,** a portion of the home range, often against other individuals of their species and sometimes against individuals of other species. Many species are territorial for only part of the year, often during the breeding season, but others are territorial throughout the year. Territoriality has been positively correlated with the availability of needed resources that occur in small areas that can be defended.

Territoriality is easily studied in birds. Typically, the male chooses a territory at the beginning of the breeding season. This behavior results from high sex hormone concentrations in his blood.

FIGURE 52-15 Home range

The Cape buffalo (*Syncerus caffer*) lives in herds of several hundred animals. Each herd, such as this one photographed in the Serengeti, has a fairly constant home range. Buffalo protect herd members, especially calves, from potential predators.

The males of adjacent territories fight until territorial boundaries become established. Generally, the dominance of a male is directly associated with how close he is to the center of his territory. Close to home he acts like a lion, but when invading some other bird's territory, he may behave more like a lamb. Sometimes males respect a neutral line, an area between their territories in which neither is dominant.

Bird songs announce the territory and often substitute for fighting. Songs also announce to eligible females that a propertied male resides in the territory. Typically, male birds take up a conspicuous station, sing, and sometimes display striking patterns of coloration or aerial acrobatics to their neighbors, their rivals, and sometimes their mates.

The costs of territoriality include the time and energy expended in staking out and defending a territory and the risks involved in fighting for it. Benefits often include exclusive rights to food within the territory and greater reproductive success. The males of a lion pride father all the cubs born within that pride. Their ability to defend their territory from invasion by strange males ensures their reproductive success. Among many species, animals that fail to establish territories fail to reproduce. Territoriality also tends to reduce conflict among members of the same species and ensures efficient use of environmental resources by encouraging individuals to spread throughout a habitat.

Usually, territorial behavior is related to the specific lifestyle of the animal and to whatever aspect of its environment is most critical to its reproductive success. For instance, seabirds may range over hundreds of square kilometers of open water but exhibit territorial behavior only at crowded nesting sites on an island. The nesting sites are their scarcest resource and the one for which competition is keenest.

Some insect societies are highly organized

Social insects form elaborate societies. Characteristics of a highly organized society include cooperation and division of labor among animals of different sexes, age groups, or castes. An intricate system of communication reinforces the organization of the society. The members tend to remain together and to resist attempts by outsiders to enter the group.

By cooperation and division of labor, some insects construct elaborate nests and raise young by mass-production methods. Bees, ants, wasps, and termites form the most organized insect societies. (The first three of these all belong, not coincidentally, to the same order, Hymenoptera.) Insect societies are held together by a complex system of sign stimuli that are keyed to social interaction, and their behaviors tend to be quite rigid.

The social organization of honeybees has been studied more extensively than that of any other social insect. Instructions for the honeybee society are inherited and preprogrammed, and the size and structure of the bee's nervous system permit only a limited range of behavioral variation. Yet these insects are not automatons. Within those limits, the complex bee society can respond with some flexibility to food and other stimuli in the environment.

A honeybee society generally consists of a single adult queen, up to 80,000 worker bees (all female), and at certain times, a few males called drones that fertilize newly developed queens. The

FIGURE 52-16 Maintaining a complex social structure
Numerous worker honeybees surround their queen (*center*). Workers constantly lick secretions from the queen bee. These secretions, transmitted throughout the hive, suppress the activity of the workers' ovaries.

queen, the only female in the hive capable of reproduction, deposits about 1000 fertilized eggs per day in the wax cells of a comb.

The composition of a bee society is generally controlled by a pheromone secreted by the queen. It inhibits the workers from raising a new queen and prevents development of ovaries in the workers (**FIG. 52-16**). If the queen dies or if the colony becomes so large that the inhibiting effect of the pheromone dissipates, the workers begin to feed some larvae special food that promotes their development into new queens.

The queen bee stores sperm cells from previous matings in a seminal receptacle. If she releases sperm to fertilize an egg as it is laid, the resulting offspring is female; otherwise, it is male. Thus, males develop by parthenogenesis from unfertilized eggs and are haploid. Because a drone is haploid, each of his sperm cells has *all* his chromosomes; that is, meiosis does not occur during sperm production. The queen bee stores this sperm throughout her lifetime and uses it to produce worker bees.

The worker bees of a hive are more closely related to one another than would be sisters born of a diploid father. Indeed, they have up to three-fourths of their genes in common. (Assuming the queen bred with a single drone, they share half of the queen's chromosomes and all of the drone's chromosomes.) As a consequence, they are more closely related to one another than they would be to their own offspring, if they could have any. (A worker bee's female offspring would have only half of its genes in common with its worker mother.) New queens are also their sisters. Worker bees are therefore more likely to pass on copies of their genes to the next generation by raising these individuals than they would if they were to produce their own offspring.

Division of labor among worker bees is mostly determined by age. The youngest worker bees serve as nurses that nourish larval bees. After about a week as nurse bees, workers begin to produce wax and build and maintain the wax cells. Older workers are foragers, bringing home nectar and pollen. Most worker bees die at the ripe old age of 42 days.

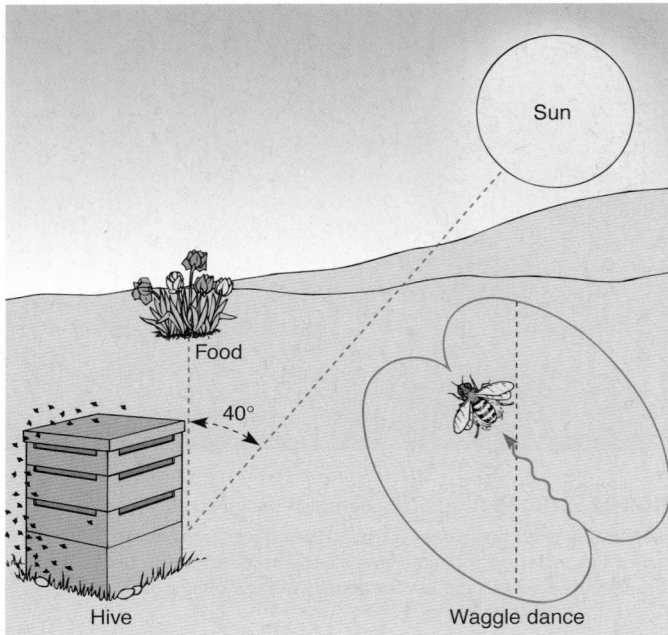

FIGURE 52-17 *Animated* **The honeybee waggle dance**
The scout is waggling upward, indicating that the food is toward the sun, and inclined 40 degrees to the left, which reveals the angle of the food source relative to the sun. The dance takes place inside the hive.

Bees have the most sophisticated mode of communication known among nonmammals. They perform a stereotyped series of body movements called a *dance.* The dance re-enacts, in miniature, the bee's flight to the food. When a honeybee scout locates a rich source of nectar, it apparently observes the angles among the food, hive, and the sun. The forager bee then communicates the direction and distance of the food source relative to the hive (**FIG. 52-17**). If the food supply is within about 52 m (about 55 yd), the scout performs a **round dance,** which generally excites the other bees and prompts them to fly short distances in all directions from the hive until they find the nectar. If the food is distant, however, the scout performs a **waggle dance,** which follows a figure-eight pattern.

In the 1940s, the German zoologist Karl von Frisch pioneered studies in bee communication. He found that the waggle dance conveys information about both distance and direction. During the straight run part of the figure eight, the number and frequency of the waggles indicate the distance. The orientation of the movements indicates the direction of the food source in reference to the position of the sun. For example, if the bee dances straight up, the nectar is located directly toward the sun. If the bee dances 40 degrees to the left of the vertical surface of the comb, the nectar is located 40 degrees to the left of a line between the hive and the sun.

The forager bee typically performs the dance in the dark hive on the vertical surface of the comb. How then does its audience "see" the dance? Investigators have shown that the bee produces sounds as it dances. The auditory signals apparently communicate the position of the dancing bee.

Review

- What are some benefits of living in groups? some costs?
- What are some advantages of pheromones? some limitations?
- How does an animal establish dominance? What costs and benefits accrue to dominant individuals in a dominance hierarchy? to subordinate individuals?
- What are some benefits of territoriality?
- How does the dance of bees compare with human language?

52.6 SEXUAL SELECTION

LEARNING OBJECTIVE

10 Define *sexual selection* and describe different types of mating systems and approaches to parental care.

Sexual selection is a type of natural selection for successful mating. Animals vary in their ability to compete for mates. Individuals with some inherited advantage, such as males with large size, have a greater chance to mate and pass on their genes to the next generation. The beneficial trait becomes more common in the population over time. Thus, sexual selection results in the reproductive advantage that some individuals have over others of the same species and sex.

For a male, reproductive success depends on how many females he can impregnate. For a female, reproductive success depends on how many eggs she can produce during her reproductive lifetime, on the quality of the sperm that fertilize them, and on the survival of her offspring to reproductive age. Recall that an animal's reproductive success is a measure of its *direct fitness.* We can distinguish between *intrasexual selection* and *intersexual selection.*

Animals of the same sex compete for mates

In **intrasexual selection,** individuals of the same sex actively compete for mates. Typically, in such populations abundant males compete for a limited number of receptive females. Competition may take the form of physical combat. Among many species, for example, baboons and elephant seals, the largest male has the advantage.

Often, males establish dominance in more subtle ways. Many males use elaborate ornamental displays to establish dominance. For example, the male deer with the largest antlers may discourage his competitors. The male bird with the most dramatic plumage and brightest colors may have a psychological advantage over competing males.

Several studies confirm that males ranking higher in a dominance hierarchy mate more frequently than males that rank lower. However, exceptions demonstrate the complexity of reproductive behavior among some species. For example, among baboons with a definite dominance hierarchy, males lower in the hierarchy copulated with females as frequently as did males of higher status. Investigators observed, though, that dominant males copulated more frequently with females who were in *estrus,* their fertile period.

Animals select quality mates

Females frequently have the opportunity to select a sexual partner from among several males. In **intersexual selection,** females select their mates on the basis of some physical trait or some resource offered by the winning suitors. The physical trait typically indicates genetic quality or good health. In many species, success of a male in dominance encounters with other males indicates his quality to the female, and she allows the victorious male to court her. Some lower-ranking males develop alternative strategies for attracting females. For instance, a male may win a female's interest by protecting her baby, even though it is not his own.

Females of some species select their mates based on ornamental displays. A female fish may select the most brightly colored male. Female birds often select males with the showiest plumage and brightest colors, and female deer prefer males that display elaborate antlers. Expression of ornamental traits may give the female important information about the male's physical condition and ability to fight. The size of the antlers of red deer, for example, may indicate combat effectiveness, as well as proper nutrition and good health. Female lions are attracted to males with thick, dark manes, an indicator of good nutrition and plenty of testosterone (which regulates growth of hair and melanin production). Thus, in some species ornaments signal good health and good genes.

Among crickets and many other insect species, a courting male offers a gift of food to a prospective mate. Studies show that the larger or higher quality the food offering is, the better the chances the male will be accepted.

Among some species of insects, birds, and bats, males gather in a small display area called a **lek,** where they compete for females. When a receptive female appears, males may excitedly display themselves and compete for her attention. Among some species, the female selects a male based on his location in the lek rather than on his appearance. The dominant male may occupy a central position and be chosen by most of the females. The female selects a male, mates with him, and then leaves the lek. The male remains to woo other females.

Courtship rituals ensure that the male is indeed a male and is a member of the same species. Rituals provide the female further opportunity to evaluate him. In some species, courtship may also be necessary as a signal to trigger nest building or ovulation. Courtship rituals can last seconds, hours, or days and often involve a series of behavioral patterns (**FIG. 52-18**). The first display by the male releases a counter-behavior by the female. This, in turn, releases additional male behavior, and so on until the pair is physiologically ready for copulation. Specific cues enable courtship rituals to function as reproductive isolating mechanisms among species (see Fig. 20-3).

An extreme courtship ritual has been described for redback spiders, which are closely related to the black widow spider. During copulation, the small male spider positions himself above his larger mate's jaws. During 65% of matings, the finale is that the female eats her suitor. The apparent explanation for this behavior is that the risk-taking male is able to copulate for a longer period and thus fertilize more eggs than males who are not cannibalized. Also, the female is more likely to reject additional mates.

Sexual selection favors polygynous mating systems

In most species, males make little parental investment in their offspring, apart from providing sperm. Males ensure reproductive success by impregnating many females, increasing the probability that their genes will be propagated in multiple offspring. Thus, sexual selection often favors **polygyny,** a mating system in which males fertilize the eggs of many females during a breeding season.

(a) The male great frigatebird (*Frigata minor*) inflates his red throat sac in display as part of a courtship ritual. Photographed on Christmas Island in the Pacific.

(b) Egrets (*Egretta rufescens*) performing a mating dance.

FIGURE 52-18 Courtship rituals

Elaborate courtship rituals help animals determine that a potential mate is of the same species and gives each animal a chance to evaluate the other as a potential mate.

In the mating system known as **polyandry,** one female mates with several males. Benefits may include receiving gifts from several males or enlisting several males' help in caring for the young. Data collected at Jane Goodall's research center at Gombe National Park in Tanzania indicate that female chimpanzees practice polyandry. Females mate with males of their own group, but when they are most fertile, many females slip off to neighboring communities and copulate with less familiar males. Perhaps these sexual rendezvous protect against inbreeding.

Investigators also hypothesize that mating with many males provides insurance against infanticide. Males do not aggress against infants of mothers with whom they have copulated. Recent studies indicate that females with multiple mates are more fertile and produce more offspring.

Polyandry and polygyny sometimes occur in the same species. After mating, a female giant water bug attaches a clutch of eggs to her mate's back (**FIG. 52-19a**). He cares for the eggs until they hatch. She then may mate with a different male and glue the new clutch of eggs to his back. However, if the male has more space for eggs, he may mate with another female.

Apparently, in most species it is not certain who fathered the offspring. However, raising some other male's offspring is a genetic disadvantage, so males of some species may compromise mate chasing in favor of **mate guarding.** The male guards his partner after copulation to ensure that she does not copulate with another male. Mate-guarding behavior is likely to occur when the female is receptive and has eggs that might be fertilized by another male. For example, dominant male African elephants guard a female only during the phase of estrus when she is most likely to be fertile. Before that time, or later in estrus after mating has already occurred, younger male elephants of lesser social status can copulate with the female. A high cost of mate guarding is the loss of opportunity for a dominant male to mate with other females.

Sexual selection favors males that inseminate many females and produce many offspring. Perhaps for this reason, **monogamy,** a mating system in which a male mates with only one female during a breeding season, is not common. Less than 10% of mammals are monogamous.

Researchers long thought monogamy was common among birds because many species form **pair bonds,** which are stable relationships that ensure cooperative behavior in mating and the rearing of the young. However, genetic evidence shows that some offspring are fathered by males other than the one caring for them. For example, DNA tests show that among eastern bluebirds, 15% to 20% of the chicks are fathered by other males. The extra-pair male contributes new genes. The female then produces offspring with greater genetic variability, increasing the chance that at least some of her offspring will survive. Some researchers distinguish between *sexual monogamy* and *social monogamy,* in which animals form a pair bond.

Monogamy does occur in some species, typically when males are needed to protect and feed the young. For example, the California mouse is sexually, as well as socially, monogamous. The offspring need their parents' body heat to survive, and the parents take turns keeping them warm.

Some animals care for their young

Parental investment is the contribution that each parent makes in producing and rearing offspring. The benefit of parental investment is the greater probability that each offspring will survive. However, most animals do not invest time and energy in caring for their offspring because the costs of parenting are high. For example, an animal busy feeding and protecting offspring might produce fewer additional offspring. There are also risks in protecting the young from predators.

Natural selection has favored parental care in species in which the female produces few young or reproduces only once during a breeding season. Parental care is an important part of successful reproduction in some invertebrates, including some cnidarians (jellyfish), rotifers, mollusks, and arthropods (crustaceans, insects, spiders, and scorpions), and is a common practice among vertebrates (**FIG. 52-19b, c, d**).

Females of many vertebrate species produce relatively few, large eggs. Because of the time and energy invested in producing eggs and carrying the developing embryo, the female has more to lose than the male if the young do not develop. Thus, females are more likely than males to brood eggs and young, and usually females invest more in parental care. Parental care is especially skewed toward the female in mammals because females provide milk to nourish their young. Investing time and effort in care of the young is usually less advantageous to a male (assuming the female can handle the job by herself) because time spent in parenting is time lost from inseminating other females.

In some situations, a male benefits by helping rear his own young or even those of a genetic relative. Receptive females may be scarce, breeding territories may be difficult to establish or guard, and gathering sufficient food may require more effort than one parent can provide. In some habitats, the young need protection against predators or cannibalistic males of the same species. Among wolves and many other carnivores, for example, males defend the young and the food supply.

Among many species of fish, the male cares for the young. Apparently, parenting costs to the males are less than they would be for the females. A male fish must have a territory to attract a female. While guarding his territory, the male guards the fertilized eggs as well. Having eggs also appears to make the male more attractive to potential mates. In contrast, when a female is caring for her eggs or young, she is not able to feed optimally. As a result, her body size is smaller and her fertility is reduced.

Behavioral ecologist Bryan D. Neff, of the University of Western Ontario, showed that male bluegill sunfish (*Lepomis macrochirus*) adjust their level of caregiving according to their degree of certainty that the offspring are indeed their own. Adult males, called parentals, defend a nest, attract females, and care for the eggs and newly hatched offspring. Some males, called *sneaker males* (or cuckolders), sneak into nests and fertilize eggs during spawning. Other sneaker males have developed in a way that gives them characteristics of females. The parental male is tricked into regarding the sneaker male as another female, allowing it access to the eggs (**FIG. 52-20**).

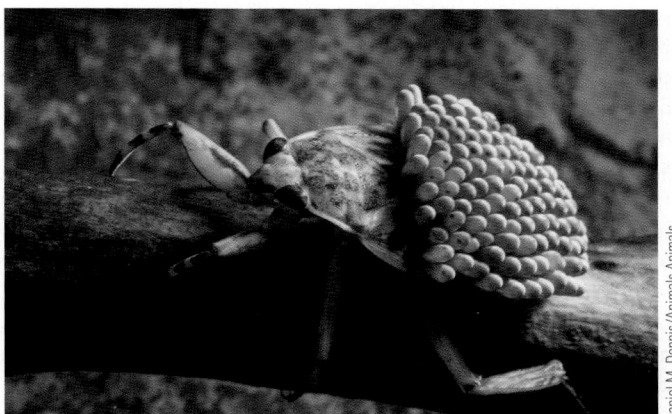

(a) Giant water bug (*Belostomatidae*) male carrying eggs on his back.

(c) Adult robins invest energy in feeding their young.

(b) A female crocodile in South Africa transports hatchlings in her mouth from their nest site to Lake St. Lucia.

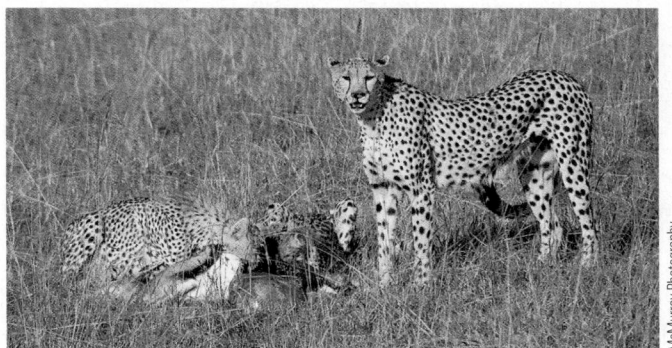

(d) Female cheetah (*Acinonyx jubatus*) stands watch as her cubs eat the Thompson's gazelle she has hunted and killed for them.

FIGURE 52-19 Caring for the young
Parental investment in offspring increases the probability that the young will survive.

Neff performed a series of experiments in which he placed sneaker males in transparent containers so they could not fertilize eggs, but the parentals could see them. In response, parentals reduced their level of protecting the eggs (**FIG. 52-21**). However, after the eggs hatched, the parentals increased their level of care. Apparently, olfactory cues indicated that these young fish were indeed the offspring of the parental caring for them. (They smelled right.)

In a second experiment, Neff exchanged about one-third of the eggs between two nests. Parentals continued to protect the eggs, but after the eggs hatched, parentals decreased their level of care. Neff showed that parentals responded to olfactory cues. At least some of their offspring did not smell right. (The odor may

be produced by the offspring's urine.) Neff suggested that an animal learns its own odor (or appearance) and forms a template of what its relatives should smell (or look) like. If they don't match up closely enough, they may be rejected.

Review

- What is sexual selection? What are some factors that influence mate choice?
- Under what conditions does sexual selection favor polygynous (or polyandrous) mating systems? Why is monogamy uncommon?
- What are some advantages of courtship rituals?
- Why do more females than males invest in caring for their offspring? Explain in terms of costs, benefits, and fitness.

FIGURE 52-20 Deception in mating

A large parental (adult male) bluegill sunfish (*Lepomis macrochirus*) courts a female (*center*). Another male, impersonating a female, swims close to the female (*right*). The parental is not aware that the sneaker is a rival male. In about 20% of spawnings, a sneaker fertilizes some of the eggs and then swims away.

Courtesy Dr. Bryan D. Neff

52.7 HELPING BEHAVIOR

■ LEARNING OBJECTIVE

11 Relate the concepts of inclusive fitness and kin selection to altruism.

Among wild turkeys and many other species, subordinate males help dominant males attract a mate, but the subordinate males do not reproduce. If an animal's principal evolutionary mandate is to perpetuate its genes, we must wonder why some animals spend time and energy in helping others.

Altruistic behavior can be explained by inclusive fitness

In a type of cooperative behavior known as **altruism,** one individual behaves in a way that seems to benefit others rather than itself,

with no potential payoff. In fact, the helper experiences a fitness cost, while the recipient of the altruistic behavior benefits. How could true altruistic behavior be adaptive if the animal's response decreases its reproductive success relative to individuals that do not exhibit the altruistic behavior? In 1964, the British evolutionary biologist William D. Hamilton offered a plausible explanation. He suggested that evolution does not distinguish between genes transmitted directly from parent to offspring and those transmitted indirectly through close relatives.

According to Hamilton, natural selection favors animals that help a relative because the relative's offspring carries some of the helper's alleles. **Inclusive fitness** is the sum of direct fitness (which can be measured by the number of alleles an animal perpetuates in its offspring) plus indirect fitness (the alleles it helps perpetuate in the offspring of its kin).

We can measure the potential genetic gain from helping relatives by the **coefficient of relatedness,** the probability that two individuals inherit the same uncommon allele from a recent common ancestor. The coefficient of relatedness for two animals that are not related is 0, whereas between a parent and its offspring this coefficient is 0.5, indicating that half of their genes are the same. The coefficient of relatedness for siblings is also 0.5; for first cousins it is 0.125. The higher the coefficient of relatedness, the more likely an animal will help a relative.

Hamilton developed a mathematical model to show how an allele that promotes altruistic behavior can increase in frequency in a population. According to **Hamilton's rule,** an altruistic act is adaptive if (1) its indirect fitness benefits are high for the animals that profit; (2) the recipients are close relatives of the altruist; and (3) the direct fitness cost to the altruistic animal is low.

Behavioral ecologists have DNA-fingerprinted lions in the Serengeti National Park and in the Ngorongoro Crater (both in Tanzania). Their findings confirm that lion brothers that cooperate in prides have a greater probability of perpetuating their genes than those that go off on their own. This is true even if the lion perpetuates his genes only by proxy, through his brother. **Kin selection,** also called *indirect selection,* is a form of natural selection that increases inclusive fitness through the breeding success of close relatives.

The bee society provides an interesting example of kin selection. Recall that worker bees do not reproduce, but they nourish larval bees. The worker bees have up to three-fourths of their genes in common with the larval bees. For this reason, worker bees are more likely to pass on copies of their genes to the next generation by raising larval bees than they would by producing their own offspring.

Among some birds (such as Florida jays), nonreproducing individuals aid in the rearing of the young. Nests tended by these additional helpers as well as parents produce more young than do nests with the same number of eggs overseen only by parents. The nonreproducing helpers are close relatives who increase their own biological success by ensuring the successful, though indirect, perpetuation of their genes. Helpers may be prevented from producing their own offspring by limiting factors such as a shortage of mates or territories.

QUESTION: Does a male bluegill sunfish adjust his level of caregiving if he perceives that he is not the genetic parent of the eggs or offspring he is guarding?

HYPOTHESIS: Behavioral ecologist Bryan D. Neff hypothesized that male bluegill sunfish adjust the level of their parental care according to their level of perceived paternity.

EXPERIMENT: Dr. Neff manipulated visual and olfactory cues.

In **Experiment 1,** Dr. Neff manipulated sneaker males. He placed two transparent containers with sneaker males near the nests of 34 parentals (adult males) and left them there during spawning. Empty containers were placed around 20 control nests. After the fish spawned, a potential egg predator (a pumpkinseed sunfish in a clear plastic container) was presented, and the parental's defensive behavior was observed and quantified for both experimental and control groups.

In **Experiment 2,** Dr. Neff removed one-third of the eggs from the nests of 20 parentals and replaced them with eggs from other nests. Sham egg swaps were carried out on eggs of 15 control parentals. Parental defensive behavior was observed before and after the eggs hatched.

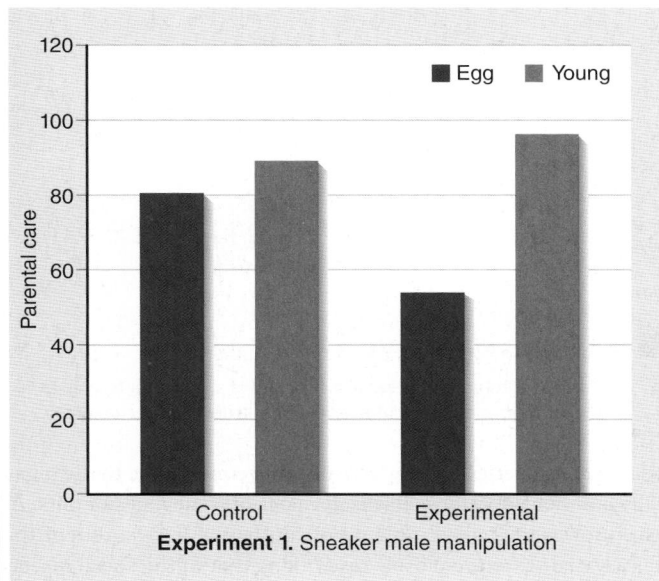

Experiment 1. Sneaker male manipulation

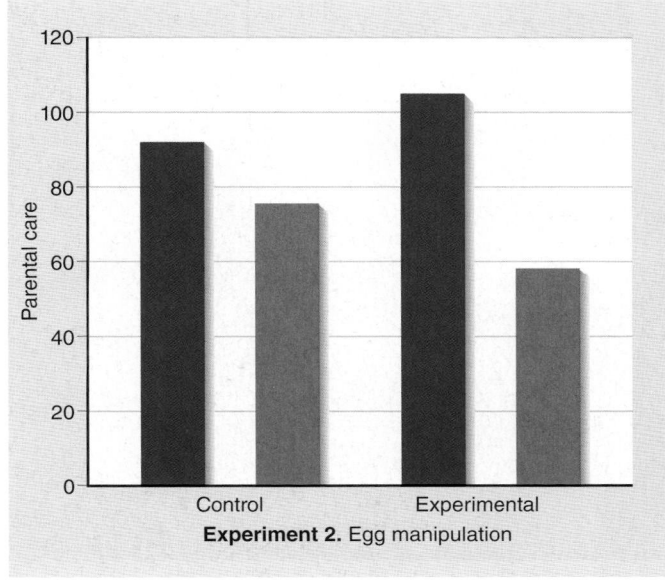

Experiment 2. Egg manipulation

RESULTS:

Experiment 1: As indicated on the y axis, which measures level of parental care, parentals reduced their level of guarding the eggs. Eight of the males in the experimental group abandoned their nests, and egg defense was significantly lower in this group compared to that in the control group. However, after eggs hatched, there was little difference in parental care between the two groups.

Experiment 2: During the egg phase, there was little difference in level of parental care between experimental and control groups. However, after eggs hatched, the experimental parentals significantly decreased their level of guarding the nest.

CONCLUSION: Male bluegill sunfish adjust their level of parental care according to their level of perceived paternity.

In **Experiment 1,** parentals provided less care when they perceived that the eggs may have been fertilized by sneaker males. After the eggs hatched, olfactory cues indicated that the offspring were indeed their own, and their level of care increased.

In **Experiment 2,** parentals cared for the eggs even though some had been swapped. However, after they hatched, olfactory cues from the offspring indicated that they were not the parental's own offspring. The level of parental care decreased significantly.

Source: Neff, B. D. *Nature,* Vol. 422, pp. 716–719, April 17, 2003.

FIGURE 52-21 Decisions about parental care

Helping behavior may have alternative explanations

Some behavioral ecologists are questioning the role of kin selection in helping behavior. One of the time-honored examples of kin selection has been sentinel behavior, keeping watch for predators and warning other members of the group when danger threatens. Until recently, biologists thought that sentinels were at greater risk

for predation, yet selflessly engaged in risky behavior that benefited their relatives. This explanation appears valid for some species, including prairie dogs and ground squirrels (**FIG. 52-22**). However, some studies suggest an opposing hypothesis for guarding behavior in other species.

U.S. biologist Peter A. Bednekoff developed a model to explain how guarding could result from selfish behavior. Bednekoff observed that for some species sentinels are not at higher risk than

FIGURE 52-22 Kin selection in prairie dogs
Low-ranking members of this social rodent group act as sentries, risking their own lives by exposing themselves outside their burrows. However, by protecting their siblings, they ensure that the genes shared in common will be perpetuated in the population.

others in their group. In fact, the opposite may be true, and sentinels may actually have an advantage. By detecting predators first, the sentinels can escape more rapidly.

Studies of sentinel behavior in the African mongoose, commonly known as the meerkat, support Bednekoff's model. During 2000 hours of researcher observation, no sentinel was killed. In fact, investigators concluded that guarding is a selfish behavior in meerkat populations because sentinels were able to escape quickly into their nearby burrows. This research is an important reminder that it is risky for biologists to generalize the meanings of complex social behavior from one species to another. Many explanations are possible. Helpers often derive direct benefits in safety and eventual reproductive success. Among some species, for example, younger animals that help are permitted to remain in the social group and derive the benefits of group protection. These helpers are also positioned to take over territories and mates when older members of the group die.

Some animals help nonrelatives

Occasionally, an animal helps a nonrelative in a fight, grooms it, or even shares food. Evolutionary biologist Robert L. Trivers, of Rutgers University, explained this behavior in 1971 with his hypothesis of **reciprocal altruism.** According to this hypothesis, one animal helps a nonrelative with no immediate benefit, but at some later time the animal that was helped repays the debt. In this way, the original helper experiences a net fitness benefit. A vampire bat that has just fed regurgitates blood for hungry bats that share the roost. If a bat does not share blood with a neighbor who has fed it in the past, the "cheater" will probably not be helped in the future.

Review

- How does kin selection explain the evolution of altruistic behavior?
- What other hypotheses may account for cooperative behavior?

52.8 CULTURE IN VERTEBRATE SOCIETIES

■ LEARNING OBJECTIVE

12 Contrast a vertebrate society with a society of social insects, give examples of transmission of culture, and briefly describe sociobiology.

Vertebrate societies usually have nothing comparable to the physically and behaviorally specialized castes of honeybees or ants. An exception is the naked mole rat of southern Africa, a rodent that has a social structure closely resembling that of the social insects. Although most vertebrate societies seem simpler than insect societies, they are also more flexible. Vertebrate societies share a great range and plasticity of potential behaviors and can effectively modify behavior to meet environmental challenges.

Some vertebrates transmit culture

The behavioral plasticity of vertebrates makes possible the transmission of culture in some bird and mammal species. **Culture** is behavior common to a population, learned from other members of the group, and transmitted from one generation to another. Culture is not inherited. It is maintained by *social learning*—for example, through imitation or teaching.

About 17 behaviors that may be considered cultural have been described among cetaceans (whales, dolphins, porpoises). For example, female orcas teach their offspring to hunt seals according to the custom of their particular group. Orcas also have local dialects that have been documented for at least six generations, suggesting that they are passed on from parent to offspring. Separate dialects are maintained even when various populations of orcas interact socially. Bottlenose dolphins are well-known for their ability to learn by imitation. Behavioral ecologists have documented foraging practices that appear to be cultural, that is, transmitted by social learning.

Teaching is an efficient form of social learning. If adult animals can teach younger ones, critical information can be rapidly transferred from one generation to the next. Researchers Alex Thornton and Katherine McAuliffe, both of the University of Cambridge, reported that helper meerkats teach pups skills for capturing prey. Meerkats feed on a variety of animals, many difficult to subdue. Some, such as scorpions, are potentially dangerous. Young pups cannot find and capture their own prey. Instead, the pups emit begging calls that induce helpers to feed them. Helpers monitor and nudge the pups to handle the prey efficiently. As they grow older, the pups' begging calls change. In response, helpers modify their teaching, giving the pups the opportunity to practice a greater range of skills. The helpers gradually introduce the pups to live prey.

Recent studies of nonhuman primates demonstrate that some groups develop local customs and teach them to their offspring. Using data provided by researchers at seven chimpanzee research sites, animal behaviorists identified 39 chimpanzee behaviors that they considered cultural variations. These behaviors included various ways of using tools, courtship rituals, and grooming techniques. Each of these local customs was learned from other chimpanzees in the population, and customs varied among different populations. For example, chimpanzees on the western side of the Sassandra-N'Zo River use stone hammers to crack coula nuts. Researchers have photographed mother chimpanzees teaching this behavior to their offspring. Just a few miles away on the eastern side of the river, chimpanzees do not crack nuts, even though they are available. When a chimp migrates and joins a new population, it can transmit knowledge learned in its previous culture. In this way, customs spread from one population to another.

As researchers continue to study cultural variation among chimpanzee populations, learning ever more about our closest relatives, it is important to remember that the capacity to learn such behaviors is the product of natural selection. The behaviors that are maintained are adaptive for these animals in their environment. Studying culture in nonhuman primates may provide insights into the evolutionary origins of human culture. Human society is based to a great extent on the symbolic transmission of culture through spoken and written language.

Sociobiology explains human social behavior in terms of adaptation

Sociobiology focuses on the evolution of social behavior through natural selection. In his landmark book, *Sociobiology: The New Synthesis,* published in 1975, Edward O. Wilson combined principles of population genetics, evolution, and animal behavior to present a comprehensive view of the evolution of social behavior. Like Darwin and many other biologists of the past, Wilson suggested that human behavior can be studied in evolutionary terms. Many of the concepts discussed in this chapter, such as paternal investment in care of the young, are based on contributions made by Wilson and other sociobiologists. Wilson's work greatly influenced the development of behavioral ecology, evolutionary psychology, and evolutionary anthropology.

Sociobiology has been controversial, at least in part because of its application to human behavior and the possible ethical implications of that. Some critics have complained that according to sociobiology human behavior may not be flexible enough to permit substantial improvements in the quality of our social lives. Yet sociobiologists agree with their critics that human behavior *is* flexible. At least some of the debate focuses on the *degree* to which human behavior is genetically determined and the extent to which it can be modified.

As sociobiologists acknowledge, people can, through culture, change their way of life far more profoundly in a few years than could a hive of bees or a troop of baboons in hundreds of generations of genetic evolution. This capacity to make changes is indeed genetically determined, and that is a great gift. How we use it and what we accomplish with it are not a gift but a responsibility on which our own well-being and the survival of other species depend.

Review

- How are vertebrate societies different from those of social insects?
- What are some examples of culture?
- What is sociobiology?

■ SUMMARY: FOCUS ON LEARNING OBJECTIVES

52.1 *(page 1128)*

1 Distinguish between proximate and ultimate causes of behavior, and apply the concepts of ultimate cause and cost–benefit analysis to decide whether a particular behavior is adaptive.

- **Behavior** is what an animal does and how it does it, usually in response to stimuli in its environment. **Proximate causes** of behavior are immediate causes, such as genetic, developmental, and physiological processes that permit the animal to carry out a specific behavior. Proximate causes answer *how* questions. **Ultimate causes** are the evolutionary explanations for *why* a certain behavior occurs.
- We can use **cost–benefit analysis** to determine whether a behavior is adaptive. Benefits contribute to **direct fitness,** the animal's reproductive success measured by the number of viable offspring. If benefits outweigh costs, the behavior is adaptive.

2 Describe the interactions of heredity, environment, and maturation in animal behavior.

- Behavior results from the interaction of genes (**innate behavior**) and environmental factors. The capacity for behavior is inherited, but behavior is modified in response to environmental experience.
- An organism must be mature—physiologically ready to produce a given behavior—before it can perform that pattern of behavior. Walking and many other behaviors that we view as automatic are **motor programs,** coordinated sequences of muscle actions.
- A **behavioral pattern** is an automatic behavior that, once activated by a simple sensory stimulus, continues to completion regardless of sensory feedback. A behavioral pattern can be triggered by a specific unlearned **sign stimulus,** or **releaser.**

3 Discuss the adaptive significance of habituation, imprinting, classical conditioning, operant conditioning, and cognition.

- **Learning** is a change of behavior that results from experience. **Habituation** is a type of learning in which an animal learns to ignore a repeated, irrelevant stimulus so it can focus on finding food and carrying out other life activities.

- **Imprinting** establishes a parent–offspring bond during a **critical period** early in development, ensuring that the offspring recognizes its mother.

- In **classical conditioning,** an association is formed between some normal body function and a new stimulus. This type of learning allows an animal to make an association between two stimuli.

- In **operant conditioning,** an animal learns a behavior in order to receive positive reinforcement or to avoid punishment. This type of learning is important in many natural situations; for example, young herring gulls perfect their pecking behavior in order to obtain food.

- **Cognition** is the process of gaining knowledge; it includes thinking, processing information, learning, reasoning, and awareness of thoughts, perceptions, and self. **Insight learning** is the ability to adapt past experiences to solve a new problem that may involve different stimuli.

52.3 *(page 1134)*

4 Give examples of biological rhythms and describe some of the physiological mechanisms responsible for them.

- It is adaptive for an organism's metabolic processes and behavior to be synchronized with cyclical changes in the environment. In many species, physiological processes and activities follow **circadian rhythms,** which are daily cycles of activity.

- **Diurnal** animals are most active during the day; **nocturnal** animals, at night; and **crepuscular** animals, at dawn or dusk. Some biological rhythms reflect the **lunar cycle,** for example, the changes in tides due to changes in the phase of the moon.

- Many biological rhythms are regulated by internal timing mechanisms that serve as **biological clocks.** In mammals the master clock is located in the **suprachiasmatic nucleus (SCN)** in the hypothalamus.

5 Analyze costs and benefits of migrations, and distinguish between directional orientation and navigation.

- **Migration** is periodic long-distance travel from one location to another. Proximate causes of migration include physiological responses that are triggered by environmental changes. Ultimate causes of migration include the benefit of moving away from an area that seasonally becomes too cold, dry, or depleted of food to a more hospitable area. Costs of migration include time, energy, and greater risk of predation.

- **Directional orientation** is travel in a specific direction and requires **compass sense,** a sense of direction. Many migrating animals use the sun to orient themselves.

- **Navigation** requires both compass sense and **map sense,** an awareness of location. Birds that navigate at night use the stars as guides. Birds and many other animals also use Earth's magnetic field to navigate.

52.4 *(page 1136)*

6 Define *optimal foraging behavior* and explain how it is adaptive.

- **Optimal foraging,** the most efficient strategy for an animal to get food, can enhance reproductive success.

52.5 *(page 1137)*

7 Analyze social behavior in terms of costs and benefits, and compare different types of social groups, including societies of social insects.

- **Social behavior** is the interaction of two or more animals, usually of the same species. An organized **society** is an actively cooperat-

ing group of individuals belonging to the same species and often closely related. In some species, social organization ensures greater reproductive success. Many animal societies are characterized by a means of communication, cooperation, division of labor, and a tendency to stay together. Benefits include cooperative foraging or hunting and defense from predators. Costs include increased competition for food and habitats and increased risks of attracting predators and transmitting disease.

8 Describe common modes of animal communication, including signaling by pheromones.

- Animal **communication** involves the exchange of mutually recognizable signals, which can be electrical, tactile, visual, auditory, or chemical. **Pheromones** are chemical signals that convey information between members of a species.

9 Describe costs and benefits of dominance hierarchies and of territoriality.

- A **dominance hierarchy** is a ranking of status within a group in which more dominant members are accorded benefits (such as food or mates) by subordinates, often without overt aggressive behavior. Social ranking reduces costly physical fights.

- Animals often inhabit a **home range,** a geographic area that they seldom leave but do not necessarily defend. A defended area within a home range is called a **territory,** and the defensive behavior is **territoriality.** Costs of territoriality include time and energy expended in staking out and defending a territory, and risks in fighting for it. Benefits include rights to food in the territory and reduction in conflict among members of a population.

52.6 *(page 1142)*

10 Define *sexual selection* and describe different types of mating systems and approaches to parental care.

- **Sexual selection,** a type of natural selection, occurs when individuals vary in their ability to compete for mates. Individuals with reproductive advantages are selected over others of the same sex and species. In **intrasexual selection,** animals of the same sex actively compete for mates.

- In **intersexual selection,** females may choose their mates based on dominance, gifts, ornaments, or courtship displays. Males of some species gather in a **lek,** a small display area where they compete for females. **Courtship rituals** ensure that the male is a member of the same species and permit the female to assess the quality of the male.

- Sexual selection often favors **polygyny,** a mating system in which a male mates with many females. In **polyandry,** a female mates with several males. **Monogamy,** mating with a single partner during a breeding season, is less common. Among many species, males engage in **mate guarding,** especially when the female is most fertile, to prevent other males from fertilizing her eggs.

- A **pair bond** is a stable relationship between a male and a female that may involve cooperative behavior in mating and in rearing the young. **Parental investment** in care of eggs and offspring increases the probability that offspring will survive. A high investment in parenting is typically less advantageous to the male than to the female.

52.7 (page 1146)

11 Relate the concepts of inclusive fitness and kin selection to altruism.

- **Altruism** is a type of cooperative behavior in which one individual appears to behave in a way that benefits others rather than itself. **Inclusive fitness** is the sum of an individual's direct fitness and indirect fitness (number of offspring of kin). This concept suggests that natural selection favors animals that help a relative because this is an indirect way to perpetuate some of the helper's own alleles.

- According to **Hamilton's rule,** an altruistic act is adaptive if its indirect fitness benefits are high for the animals that are helped, if the recipients are close relatives of the altruist, and if the direct fitness cost to the altruist is low.

- **Kin selection** is a type of natural selection that increases inclusive fitness through successful reproduction of close relatives. Some types of cooperative behavior may increase the direct fitness of the helper.

- In a type of cooperative behavior known as **reciprocal altruism,** the helper does not immediately benefit but is helped later by the animal it helped.

52.8 (page 1148)

12 Contrast a vertebrate society with a society of social insects, give examples of transmission of culture, and briefly describe sociobiology.

- Compared to insect societies, vertebrate societies are more flexible and the role of the individual is less narrowly defined. Some bird and mammal species develop **culture,** learned behavior common to a population that is transmitted from one generation to the next. For example, orcas have local dialects that are passed from parent to offspring. Symbolic transmission of culture is important in human societies.

- **Sociobiology** focuses on the evolution of social behavior through natural selection.

TEST YOUR UNDERSTANDING

1. The responses of an organism to signals from its environment are its (a) behavior (b) culture (c) ultimate behavior (d) releasers (e) motor programs

2. A behavioral pattern is elicited by (a) a motor program (b) a sign stimulus (c) an ultimate releaser (d) a, b, and c (e) b and c

3. A form of learning in which an animal forms a strong attachment to a moving object (usually its parent) within a few hours of birth is (a) classical conditioning (b) operant conditioning (c) imprinting (d) insight learning (e) parental investment

4. Both compass sense and map sense are necessary for (a) navigation (b) migration (c) directional orientation (d) both navigation and migration (e) the action of biological clocks

5. In optimal foraging, (a) animals always hunt in social groups (b) an animal obtains food in the most efficient way (c) animals can rarely afford to be selective (d) groups of five to seven animals are most successful (e) animals are typically most successful when they hunt alone

6. Chemical signals that convey information between members of a species are (a) pheromones (b) hormones (c) neurotransmitters (d) leks (e) neuropeptides

7. The benefits of territoriality include (a) right to defend a home range (b) higher potential for monogamy (c) energy investment in staking out and defending the area (d) increased reproductive success (e) pair bonding

8. Sexual selection (a) occurs mainly among animals that practice polyandry (b) occurs when animals are very similar in their ability to compete for mates (c) results in animals that have lower direct fitness (d) occurs mainly among animals that practice polygyny (e) is a form of natural selection

9. In most species, mate choice is least likely influenced by (a) ornamental displays such as antlers (b) fidelity of the male (c) gifts (d) courtship behavior (e) dominance

10. Behavior that appears to have no payoff, that is, an individual appears to act to benefit others rather than itself, is known as (a) mutualism (b) helping behavior (c) reciprocal altruism (d) inclusive fitness (e) altruism

11. Kin selection (a) increases inclusive fitness through the breeding success of close relatives (b) is a way of perpetuating genes of non-relatives (c) accounts for some forms of migration (d) typically involves mate guarding (e) involves ornamental displays and use of a lek

12. Culture (a) is common among invertebrate groups (b) does not vary within the same species (c) is behavior learned from other members of the group and shared by members of a population (d) has a strong genetic component in primates (e) is a shared derived character of humans

CRITICAL THINKING

1. Behavioral ecologists have demonstrated that young tiger salamanders can become cannibals and devour other salamanders. Investigators observed that the cannibal salamanders preferred eating unrelated salamanders over their own cousins and preferred eating cousins over their siblings. Explain this behavior based on what you have learned in this chapter.

2. How is the society of a social insect different from human society? What are some similarities between the transmission of information by heredity and by culture? What are some differences?

3. **EVOLUTION LINK.** What might be the adaptive value of sea turtle migration? Consider how this adaptive value has changed if, as a result of human activities, migration now puts sea turtles

at greater risk than if they restricted their habitat to a single location. Discuss the possible evolutionary mechanisms by which the behavior of these species may (or may not) adapt to these environmental pressures. What conservation efforts should we take to increase the probability of successful migration?

4. **ANALYZING DATA.** Look at the diagram (Fig. 52-11) and identify the groups most likely to be hungry at the end of the day's hunt during times of prey scarcity. Develop a hypothesis to explain why these groups hunt as they do.

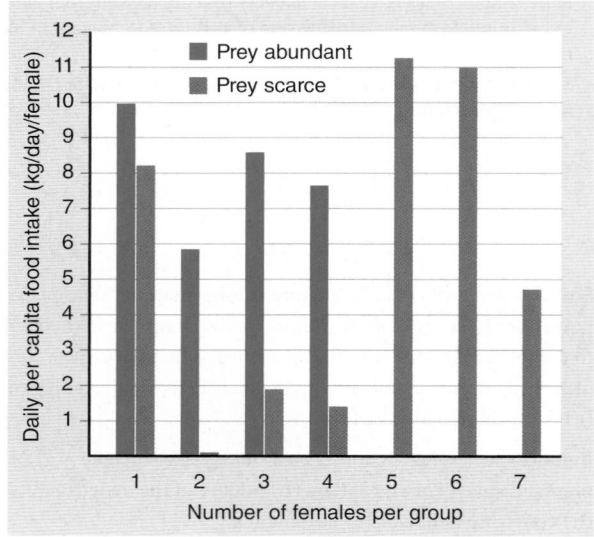

5. **ANALYZING DATA.** Look at the two graphs (at right). In which experiment did the parentals in the experimental group guard the eggs more closely? In which experiment did the experimental parentals guard the young more closely? Account for these differences.

 Additional questions are available in CengageNOW at www.cengage.com/login.

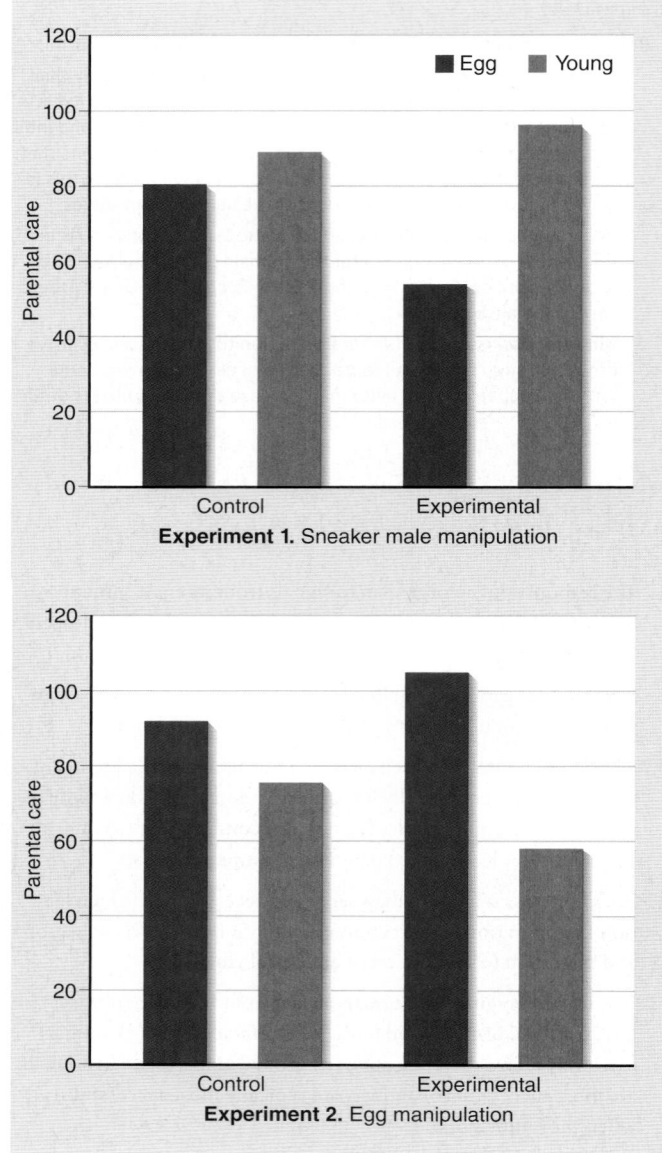

Experiment 1. Sneaker male manipulation

Experiment 2. Egg manipulation

53 Introduction to Ecology: Population Ecology

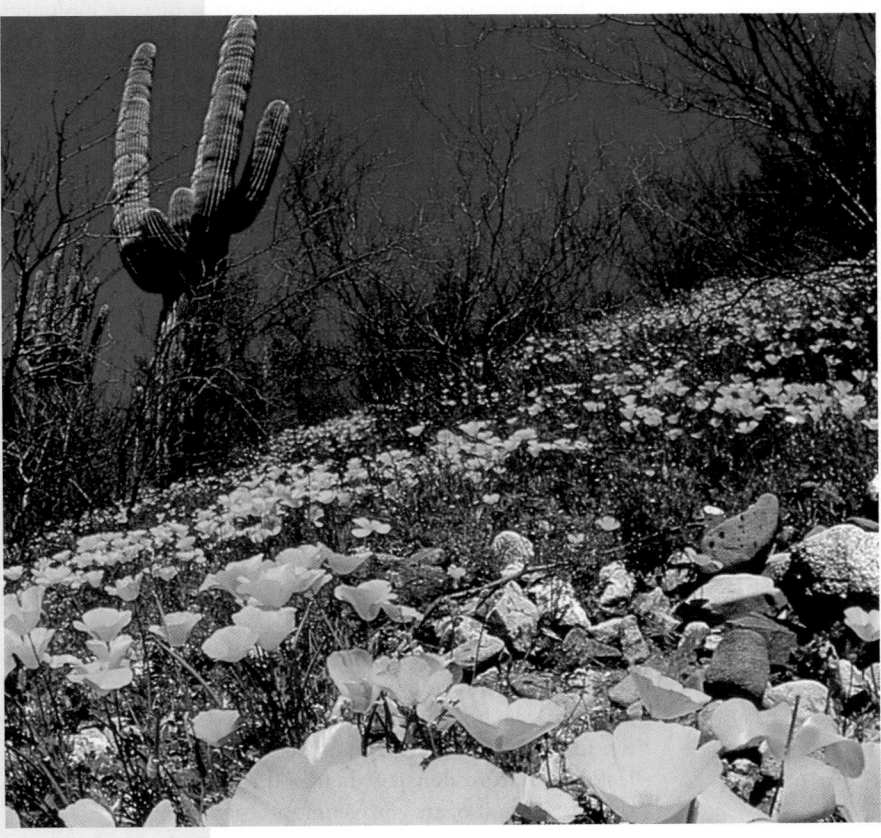

A population of Mexican poppies. Mexican poppies (*Eschsolzia mexicana*), which thrive on gravelly desert slopes, bloom in the desert after the winter rains.

Jim Brandenburg/Minden Pictures

KEY CONCEPTS

53.1 A population can be described in terms of its density, dispersion, birth and death rates, growth rate, survivorship, and age structure.

53.2 Changes in population size are caused by natality, mortality, immigration, and emigration.

53.3 Population size may be influenced by density-dependent factors and density-independent factors.

53.4 Life history traits of a population are adaptations that affect the ability of individuals to survive and reproduce.

53.5 A metapopulation consists of two or more local populations with dispersal occurring among them.

53.6 Human population structure differs among countries in ways that are primarily related to differences in level of development.

The science of **ecology** is the study of how living organisms and the physical environment interact in an immense and complicated web of relationships. Biologists call the interactions among organisms **biotic factors** and those between organisms and their nonliving, physical environment **abiotic factors.** Abiotic factors include precipitation, temperature, pH, wind, and chemical nutrients. Ecologists formulate hypotheses to explain such phenomena as the distribution and abundance of life, the ecological roles of specific species, the interactions among species in communities, and the importance of ecosystems in maintaining the health of the biosphere. They then test these hypotheses.

The focus of ecology can be local or global, specific or generalized, depending on what questions the scientist is asking and trying to answer. Ecology is the broadest field in biology, with explicit links to evolution and every other biological discipline. It includes studies on transfer of information among organisms and analyses of the transfer of energy for life. Its universality encompasses subjects that are not traditionally part of biology. Earth science, geology, chemistry, oceanography, climatology, and meteorology are extremely important to ecology, especially when ecologists examine the abiotic environment of planet Earth. Because humans are part of Earth's web of life, all our activities, including economics and politics, have profound ecological implications. **Environmental science,** a scientific discipline with ties to ecology, focuses on how humans interact with the environment.

As you learned in Chapter 1, most ecologists are interested in the levels of biological organization including and above the level of the individual organism: population, community, ecosystem, landscape, and biosphere. Each level has its own characteristic composition, structure, and functioning.

An individual belongs to a **population,** a group consisting of members of the same species that live together in a prescribed area at the same time. The boundaries of the area are defined by the ecologist performing a particular study. A population ecologist might study a population of microorganisms, animals, or plants, like the Mexican poppies in the photograph, to see how individuals within it live and interact with one another, with other species in their community, and with their physical environment.

In this chapter we begin our study of ecological principles by focusing on the study of populations as functioning systems and end with a discussion of the human population. Subsequent chapters examine the interactions among different populations within communities (Chapter 54), the dynamic exchanges between communities and their physical environments (Chapter 55), the characteristics of Earth's major biological ecosystems (Chapter 56), and biological diversity and conservation biology (Chapter 57).

53.1 FEATURES OF POPULATIONS

■ LEARNING OBJECTIVE

1   Define *population density* and *dispersion*, and describe the main types of population dispersion.

Populations exhibit characteristics distinctive from those of the individuals of which they are composed. Some features discussed in this chapter that characterize populations are population density, population dispersion, birth and death rates, growth rates, survivorship, and age structure.

Although communities consist of all the populations of all the different species that live together within an area, populations have properties that communities lack. Populations, for example, share a common gene pool (see Chapter 19). Consequently, natural selection can cause changes in allele frequencies in populations. As a result, allele frequency changes resulting from natural selection occur in populations. Natural selection, therefore, acts directly to produce adaptive changes in populations and only indirectly affects the community level.

Population ecology considers both the number of individuals of a particular species that are found in an area and the dynamics of the population. **Population dynamics** is the study of changes in populations—how and why those numbers increase or decrease over time. Population ecologists try to determine the processes common to all populations. They study how a population interacts with its environment, such as how individuals in a population compete for food or other resources, and how predation, disease, and other environmental pressures affect the population. Population growth, whether of bacteria, maples, or giraffes, cannot increase indefinitely because of such environmental pressures.

Additional aspects of populations that interest biologists are their reproductive success or failure (extinction), their evolution, their genetics, and the way they affect the normal functioning of communities and ecosystems. Biologists in applied disciplines, such as forestry, agronomy (crop science), and wildlife management, must understand population ecology to manage populations of economic importance, for example, forests, field crops, game animals, or fishes. Understanding the population dynamics of endangered and threatened species plays a key role in efforts to prevent their slide to extinction. Knowledge of population ecology helps in efforts to prevent the increase of pest populations to levels that cause significant economic or health impacts.

Density and dispersion are important features of populations

The concept of population size is meaningful only when the boundaries of that population are defined. Consider, for example, the difference between 1000 mice in 100 hectares (250 acres) and 1000 mice in 1 hectare (2.5 acres). Often a population is too large to study in its entirety. Researchers examine such a population by sampling a part of it and then expressing the population in terms of density. Examples include the number of dandelions per square meter of lawn, the number of water fleas per liter of pond water, or the number of cabbage aphids per square centimeter of cabbage leaf. **Population density,** then, is the number of individuals of a species per unit of area or volume at a given time.

Different environments vary in the population density of any species they can support. This density may also vary in a single habitat from season to season or year to year. For example, red grouse are ground-dwelling game birds whose populations are managed for hunting. Consider two red grouse populations in the treeless moors of northwestern Scotland, at locations only 2.5 km (1.5 mi) apart. At one location the population density remained stationary during a three-year period, but at the other site it almost doubled in the first two years and then declined to its initial density in the third year. The reason was likely a difference in habitat. Researchers had experimentally burned the area where the population density increased initially and then decreased. Young heather shoots (*Calluna vulgaris*) produced after the burn provided nutritious food for the red grouse. So population density may be determined in large part by biotic or abiotic factors in the environment that are external to the individuals in the population.

The individuals in a population often exhibit characteristic patterns of **dispersion,** or spacing, relative to one another. Individuals may be spaced in a random, clumped, or uniform dispersion. **Random dispersion** occurs when individuals in a population are spaced throughout an area in a manner that is unrelated to the presence of others (**FIG. 53-1a**). Of the three major types of disper-

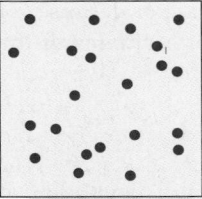

(a) Random dispersion, illustrated for comparison, rarely, if ever, occurs in nature.

(b) Clumped dispersion is evident in the schooling behavior of certain fish species. Shown are bluestripe snappers (*Lutjanus kasmira*), photographed in Hawaii. This introduced fish, which grows to 30 cm (12 in), may be displacing native fish species in Hawaiian waters.

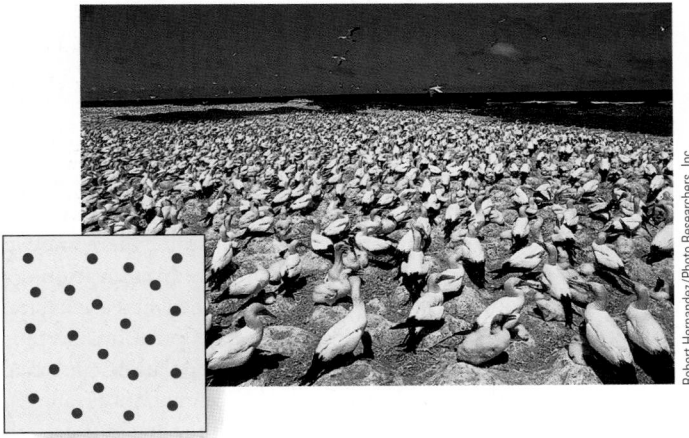

(c) Uniform dispersion is characteristic of these nesting Cape gannets (*Morus capensis*) on the coast of South Africa. The birds space their nests more or less evenly.

FIGURE 53-1 *Animated* **Dispersion of individuals within a population**

sion, random dispersion is least common and hardest to observe in nature, leading some ecologists to question its existence. Trees of the same species, for example, sometimes appear to be distributed randomly in a tropical rain forest. However, an international team of 13 ecologists studied six tropical forest plots that were 25 to 52 hectares (62 to 130 acres) in area and reported that most of the 1000 tree species observed were clumped and not randomly dispersed. (Ecologists determine both clumped and uniform dispersion by statistically testing for differences from an assumed random distribution.) Random dispersion may occur infrequently because important environmental factors affecting dispersion usually do not occur at random. Flour beetle larvae in a container of flour are randomly dispersed, but their environment (flour) is unusually homogeneous.

Perhaps the most common spacing is **clumped dispersion,** also called **aggregated distribution** or **patchiness,** which occurs when individuals are concentrated in specific parts of the habitat. Clumped dispersion often results from the patchy distribution of resources in the environment. It also occurs among animals because of the presence of family groups and pairs, and among plants because of limited seed dispersal or asexual reproduction. An entire grove of aspen trees, for example, may originate asexually from a single plant. Clumped dispersion may sometimes be advantageous because social animals derive many benefits from their association. Many fish species, for example, associate in dense schools for at least part of their life cycle, possibly because schooling may reduce the risk of predation for any particular individual (**FIG. 53-1b**). The many pairs of eyes of schooling fish tend to detect predators more effectively than a single pair of eyes of a single fish. When threatened, schooling fish clump together more closely, so it is difficult for a predator to single out an individual.

Uniform dispersion occurs when individuals are more evenly spaced than would be expected from a random occupation of a given habitat. A nesting colony of seabirds, in which the birds are nesting in a relatively homogeneous environment and place their nests at a more or less equal distance from one another, is an example of uniform dispersion (**FIG. 53-1c**). What might this spacing pattern tell us? In this case, uniform dispersion may occur as a result of nesting territoriality. Aggressive interactions among the nesting birds as they peck at one another from their nests cause each pair to place its nest just beyond the reach of nearby nesting birds. Uniform dispersion also occurs when competition among individuals is severe, when plant roots or leaves that have been shed produce toxic substances that inhibit the growth of nearby plants, or when animals establish feeding or mating territories.

Some populations have different spacing patterns at different ages. Competition for sunlight among same-aged sand pine in a Florida scrub community resulted in a change over time from either random or clumped dispersion when the plants were young to uniform dispersion when the plants were old. Sand pine is a fire-adapted plant with cones that do not release their seeds until they have been exposed to high temperatures (45°C to 50°C or higher). As a result of seed dispersal and soil conditions following a fire, the seedlings grow back in dense stands that exhibit random or slightly clumped dispersion. Over time, however, many of the more crowded trees tend to die from shading or competition, resulting in uniform dispersion of the surviving trees (**TABLE 53-1**).

Review

- What is the difference between population density and dispersion?
- What are some biological advantages of a clumped dispersion? What are some disadvantages?

TABLE 53-1	Dispersion in a Sand Pine Population in Florida	
Tree Trunks Examined	Density (per m²)	Dispersion
All (alive and dead)	0.16	Random
Alive only	0.08	Uniform

Source: Adapted from Laessle, A. M. "Spacing and Competition in Natural Stands of Sand Pine." *Ecology*, Vol. 46, pp. 65–72, 1965. Data were collected 51 years after a fire.

53.2 CHANGES IN POPULATION SIZE

▪ LEARNING OBJECTIVES

2 Explain the four factors (natality, mortality, immigration, and emigration) that produce changes in population size and solve simple problems involving these changes.

3 Define *intrinsic rate of increase* and *carrying capacity*, and explain the differences between J-shaped and S-shaped growth curves.

One goal of science is to discover common patterns among separate observations. As mentioned previously, population ecologists wish to understand general processes that are shared by many different populations, so they develop mathematical models based on equations that describe the dynamics of a single population. Population models are not perfect representations of a population, but models help illuminate complex processes. Moreover, mathematical modeling enhances the scientific process by providing a framework with which experimental population studies can be compared. We can test a model and see how it fits or does not fit with existing data. Data that are inconsistent with the model are particularly useful because they demand that we ask how the natural system differs from the mathematical model that we developed to explain it. As more knowledge accumulates from observations and experiments, the model is refined and made more precise.

Population size, whether of sunflowers, elephants, or humans, changes over time. On a global scale, this change is ultimately caused by two factors, expressed on a per capita (that is, per individual) basis: **natality,** the average per capita birth rate, and **mortality,** the average per capita death rate. In humans the birth rate is usually expressed as the number of births per 1000 people per year and the death rate as the number of deaths per 1000 people per year.

To determine the rate of change in population size, we must also take into account the time interval involved, that is, the change in time. To express change in equations, we employ the Greek letter delta (Δ). In equation (1), ΔN is the change in the number of individuals in the population, Δt the change in time, N the number of individuals in the existing population, b the natality, and d the mortality.

$$(1)\ \Delta N/\Delta t = N(b - d)$$

The growth rate (r), or rate of change (increase or decrease) of a population on a per capita basis, is the birth rate minus the death rate:

$$(2)\ r = b - d$$

As an example, consider a hypothetical human population of 10,000 in which there are 200 births per year (that is, by convention, 20 births per 1000 people) and 100 deaths per year (10 deaths per 1000 people):

$$r = 20/1000 - 10/1000 = 0.02 - 0.01 = 0.01, \text{ or 1\% per year}$$

A modification of equation (1) tells us the rate at which the population is growing at a particular instant in time, that is, its instantaneous growth rate (dN/dt). (The symbols dN and dt are the mathematical differentials of N and t, respectively; they are not products, nor should the d in dN or dt be confused with the death rate, d.) Using differential calculus, this growth rate can be expressed as follows:

$$(3)\ dN/dt = rN$$

where N is the number of individuals in the existing population, t the time, and r the per capita growth rate.

Because $r = b - d$, if individuals in the population are born faster than they die, r is a positive value and population size increases. If individuals in the population die faster than they are born, r is a negative value and population size decreases. If r is equal to zero, births and deaths match and population size is stationary despite continued reproduction and death.

Dispersal affects the growth rate in some populations

In addition to birth and death rates, **dispersal,** which is movement of individuals among populations, must be considered when examining changes in populations on a *local* scale. There are two types of dispersal: immigration and emigration. **Immigration** occurs when individuals enter a population and thus increase its size. **Emigration** occurs when individuals leave a population and thus decrease its size. The growth rate of a local population must take into account birth rate (b), death rate (d), immigration rate (i), and emigration rate (e) on a per capita basis. The per capita growth rate equals the birth rate minus the death rate, plus the immigration rate minus the emigration rate:

$$(4)\ r = (b - d) + (i - e)$$

For example, the growth rate of a human population of 10,000 that has 200 births (by convention, 20 per 1000), 100 deaths (10 per 1000), 10 immigrants (1 per 1000), and 100 emigrants (10 per 1000) in a given year would be calculated as follows:

$$r = (20/1000 - 10/1000) + (1/1000 - 10/1000)$$
$$= 0.001, \text{ or 0.1\% per year}$$

Each population has a characteristic intrinsic rate of increase

The maximum rate at which a population of a given species could increase under ideal conditions, when resources are abundant and its population density is low, is known as its **intrinsic rate of increase (r_{max})**. Different species have different intrinsic rates of increase. A particular species' intrinsic rate of increase is influenced by several factors. These include the age at which reproduction begins, the fraction of the **lifespan** (duration of the individual's life) during which the individual is capable of reproducing, the number of reproductive periods per lifetime, and the number of offspring the individual is capable of producing during each period of reproduction. These factors, which we discuss in greater detail later in the chapter, determine whether a particular species has a large or small intrinsic rate of increase.

Generally, large species such as blue whales and elephants have the smallest intrinsic rates of increase, whereas microorganisms have the greatest intrinsic rates of increase. Under ideal conditions (an environment with unlimited resources), certain bacteria can reproduce by binary fission every 20 minutes. At this rate of growth, a single bacterium would increase to a population of more than one billion in just ten hours!

If we plot the population size versus time, under optimal conditions, the graph has a J shape that is characteristic of **exponential population growth,** which is the accelerating population growth rate that occurs when optimal conditions allow a constant per capita growth rate (**FIG. 53-2**). When a population grows exponentially, the larger that population gets, the faster it grows.

Regardless of which species we are considering, whenever a population is growing at its intrinsic rate of increase, population size plotted versus time gives a curve of the same shape. The only variable is time. It may take longer for an elephant population than for a bacterial population to reach a certain size (because elephants do not reproduce as rapidly as bacteria), but both populations will always increase exponentially as long as their per capita growth rates remain constant.

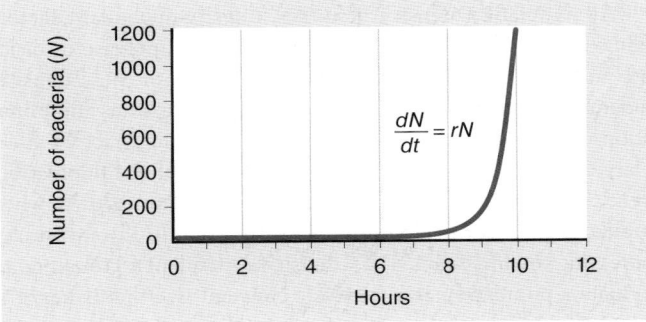

FIGURE 53-2 *Animated* **Exponential population growth**
When bacteria divide every 20 minutes, their numbers (expressed in millions) increase exponentially. The curve of exponential population growth has a characteristic J shape. The ideal conditions under which bacteria or other organisms reproduce exponentially rarely occur in nature, and when these conditions do occur, they are of short duration.

No population can increase exponentially indefinitely

Certain populations may grow exponentially for brief periods. Exponential growth has been experimentally demonstrated in certain insects and in cultures of bacteria or protists (by continually supplying nutrients and removing waste products). However, organisms cannot reproduce indefinitely at their intrinsic rate of increase because the environment sets limits. These limits include such unfavorable environmental conditions as the limited availability of food, water, shelter, and other essential resources (resulting in increased competition) as well as limits imposed by disease and predation.

In the earlier example, bacteria in nature would never be able to reproduce unchecked for an indefinite period because they would run out of food and living space, and poisonous wastes would accumulate in their vicinity. With crowding, bacteria would also become more susceptible to parasites (high population densities facilitate the spread of infectious organisms such as viruses among individuals) and predators (high population densities increase the likelihood of a predator catching an individual). As the environment deteriorated, their birth rate (b) would decline and their death rate (d) would increase. Conditions might worsen to a point where d would exceed b, and the population would decrease. The number of individuals in a population, then, is controlled by the ability of the environment to support it. As the number of individuals in a population (N) increases, environmental limits act to control population growth.

Over longer periods, the rate of population growth may decrease to nearly zero. This leveling out occurs at or near the limits of the environment to support the population. The **carrying capacity (K)** represents the largest population that can be maintained for an indefinite period by a particular environment, assuming there are no changes in that environment. In nature, the carrying capacity is dynamic and changes in response to environmental changes. An extended drought, for example, could decrease the amount of vegetation growing in an area, and this change, in turn, would lower the carrying capacity for deer and other herbivores in that environment.

When a population regulated by environmental limits is graphed over longer periods, the curve has a characteristic S shape. The curve shows the population's initial exponential increase (note the curve's J shape at the start, when environmental limits are few), followed by a leveling out as the carrying capacity of the environment is approached (**FIG. 53-3**). The S-shaped growth curve, also called **logistic population growth,** can be modeled by a modified growth equation called a *logistic equation*. The logistic model of population growth was developed to explain population growth in continually breeding populations. Similar models exist for populations that have specific breeding seasons.

The logistic model describes a population increasing from a small number of individuals to a larger number of individuals that are ultimately limited by the environment. The logistic equation takes into account the carrying capacity of the environment:

$$(5)\ dN/dt = rN[(K - N)/K]$$

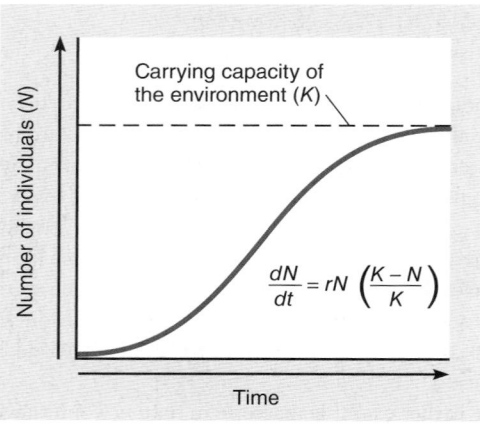

FIGURE 53-3 Carrying capacity and logistic population growth
In many laboratory studies, exponential population growth slows as the carrying capacity (*K*) of the environment is approached. The logistic model of population growth, when graphed, has a characteristic S-shaped curve.

Note that part of the equation is the same as equation (3). The added element $[(K - N)/K]$ reflects a decline in growth as a population size approaches its carrying capacity. When the number of organisms (N) is small, the rate of population growth is unchecked by the environment because the expression $[(K - N)/K]$ has a value of almost 1. But as the population (N) begins to approach the carrying capacity (K), the growth rate declines because the value of $[(K - N)/K]$ approaches zero.

Although the S curve is an oversimplification of how most populations change over time, it does appear to fit some populations that have been studied in the laboratory as well as a few that have been studied in nature. For example, Georgyi F. Gause, a Russian ecologist who conducted experiments during the 1930s, grew a population of a single species, *Paramecium caudatum,* in a test tube. He supplied a limited amount of food (bacteria) daily and replenished the growth medium occasionally to eliminate the accumulation of metabolic wastes. Under these conditions, the population of *P. caudatum* increased exponentially at first, but then its growth rate declined to zero, and the population size leveled off (see Fig. 54-5, middle graph).

A population rarely stabilizes at *K* (carrying capacity) but may temporarily rise higher than *K*. It will then drop back to, or below, the carrying capacity. Sometimes a population that overshoots *K* will experience a *population crash,* an abrupt decline from high to low population density. Such an abrupt change is commonly observed in bacterial cultures, zooplankton, and other populations whose resources have been exhausted.

The carrying capacity for reindeer, which live in cold northern habitats, is determined largely by the availability of winter forage. In 1910, humans introduced a small herd of 26 reindeer onto one of the Pribilof Islands of Alaska. The herd's population increased exponentially for about 25 years until there were approximately 2000 reindeer, many more than the island could support, particularly in winter. The reindeer overgrazed the vegetation until the plant life was almost wiped out. Then, in slightly over a decade, as reindeer died from starvation, the number of reindeer plunged

to 8, one-third the size of the original introduced population. Recovery of subarctic and arctic vegetation after overgrazing by reindeer can take 15 to 20 years, during which time the carrying capacity for reindeer is greatly reduced.

Review

- What effect does each of the following have on population size: (1) natality, (2) mortality, (3) immigration, and (4) emigration?
- How does a J-shaped population growth curve differ from an S-shaped curve in terms of intrinsic rate of increase and carrying capacity?
- What would be the main difference between graphs representing the long-term growth of two populations of bacteria cultured in test tubes, one in which the nutrient medium is replenished and the other in which it is not replenished?

53.3 FACTORS INFLUENCING POPULATION SIZE

■ LEARNING OBJECTIVE

4 Contrast the influences of density-dependent and density-independent factors on population size, and give examples of each.

Certain natural mechanisms influence population size. Factors that affect population size fall into two categories: density-dependent factors and density-independent factors. These two sets of factors vary in importance from one species to another and, in most cases, probably interact simultaneously to determine the size of a population.

Density-dependent factors regulate population size

Sometimes the influence of an environmental factor on the individuals in a population varies with the density or crowding of that population. If a change in population density alters how an environmental factor affects that population, then the environmental factor is said to be a **density-dependent factor.**

As population density increases, density-dependent factors tend to slow population growth by causing an increase in death rate and/or a decrease in birth rate. The effect of these density-dependent factors on population growth increases as the population density increases; that is, density-dependent factors affect a larger proportion, not just a larger number, of the population. Density-dependent factors can also affect population growth when population density declines by decreasing the death rate and/or increasing the birth rate. Thus, density-dependent factors tend to regulate a population at a relatively constant size that is near the carrying capacity of the environment. (Keep in mind, however, that the carrying capacity of the environment frequently changes.) Density-dependent factors are an excellent example of a **negative feedback system** (FIG. 53-4).

Predation, disease, and competition are examples of density-dependent factors. As the density of a population increases, predators are more likely to find an individual of a given prey species. When population density is high, the members of a population

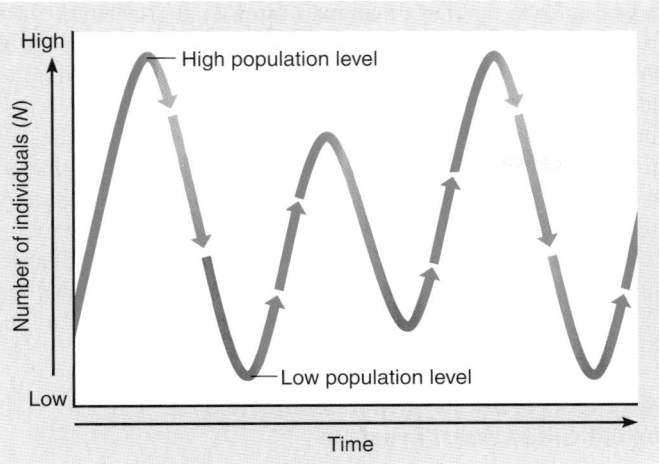

Density-dependent factors are increasingly severe: Population peaks and begins to decline.

Density-dependent factors are increasingly relaxed: Population bottoms out and begins to increase.

FIGURE 53-4 Density-dependent factors and negative feedback
When the number of individuals in a population increases, density-dependent factors cause a decline in the population. When the number of individuals in a population decreases, a relaxation of density-dependent factors allows the population to increase.

encounter one another more frequently, and the chance of their transmitting parasites and infectious disease organisms increases. As population density increases, so does competition for resources such as living space, food, cover, water, minerals, and sunlight; eventually, the point may be reached at which many members of a population fail to obtain the minimum amount of whatever resource is in shortest supply. At higher population densities, density-dependent factors raise the death rate and/or lower the birth rate, inhibiting further population growth. The opposite effect occurs when the density of a population decreases. Predators are less likely to encounter individual prey, parasites and infectious diseases are less likely to be transmitted from one host to another, and competition among members of the population for resources such as living space and food declines.

Density-dependent factors may explain what makes certain populations fluctuate cyclically over time

Lemmings are small, stumpy-tailed rodents that are found in colder regions of the Northern Hemisphere (**FIG. 53-5**). They are herbivores that feed on sedges and grasses in the arctic tundra. It has long been known that lemming populations have a three- to four-year cyclical oscillation that is often described as "boom or bust." That is, the population increases dramatically and then crashes; the population peaks may be 100 times as high as the low points in the population cycle. Many other populations, such as snowshoe hares and red grouse, also exhibit cyclic fluctuations.

What is the driving force behind these fluctuations? Several hypotheses have been proposed to explain the cyclical periodicity of lemming and other boom-or-bust populations; many hypotheses involve density-dependent factors. One possibility is that as a

FIGURE 53-5 Lemming
The brown lemming (*Lemmus trimucronatus*) lives in the arctic tundra. Although lemming populations have been studied for decades, much about the cyclic nature of lemming population oscillations and their effects on the rest of the tundra ecosystem is still not well understood. This species ranges from Alaska eastward to the Hudson Bay.

prey population becomes more dense, it overwhelms its food supply; as a result, the population declines. In the lemming example, researchers have studied the shape of several lemming population curves during their oscillations; the data suggest that lemming populations crash because they overgraze the plants, not because predators eat them.

Another explanation is that the population density of predators, such as long-tailed jaegers (birds related to gulls that eat lemmings), increases in response to the increasing density of prey. Few jaegers breed when the lemming population is low. However, when the lemming population is high, most jaegers breed, and the number of eggs per clutch is greater than usual. As more predators consume the abundant prey, the prey population declines. Later, with fewer prey in an area, the population of predators declines (some disperse out of the area, and fewer offspring are produced).

In 2003, researchers at the University of Helsinki, Finland, reported the results of a long-term study of collared lemmings in Greenland, in which they observed four-year cycles of lemming population density that were not affected by availability of food or living space. They developed a model in which the fluctuations in the lemming population are most accurately predicted by the fact that the population of the stoat, a member of the weasel family that preys almost exclusively on lemmings, peaks a year after a peak in the lemming population. On the other hand, populations of three other lemming predators—snowy owls, arctic foxes, and long-tailed skuas (birds related to gulls)—respond more immediately to changes in the lemming population, and thus tend to stabilize the population cycle established by the stoats.

Climate change may also be affecting lemming population dynamics. In 2008, researchers from the University of Oslo, Norway, and a group of international collaborators reported a correlation between climate and lemming cycles. They found that lemming populations increase in the years in which they can survive by eating moss in the space between the ground and the snow pack. Populations are reduced in warmer years, when slight melting and refreezing of the snow eliminates this space.

Parasites may also interact with their hosts to cause regular cyclic fluctuations. Detailed studies of red grouse have shown that even managed populations in wildlife preserves may have significant cyclic oscillations. Reproduction in red grouse is related to the density of parasitic nematodes (roundworms) living in adult intestines. Fewer birds breed successfully when adults are infected with worms; thus, a high density of worms leads to a population crash. Hypothesizing that red grouse populations fluctuate in response to the parasites, ecologists at the University of Stirling in Scotland successfully reduced or eliminated population fluctuations in several red grouse populations. They accomplished this by catching and orally treating the birds with a chemical that causes worms to be ejected from their bodies.

Competition is an important density-dependent factor

Competition is an interaction among two or more individuals that attempt to use the same essential resource, such as food, water, sunlight, or living space, that is in limited supply. The use of the resource by one of the individuals reduces the availability of that resource for other individuals. Competition occurs both within a given population (**intraspecific competition**) and among populations of different species (**interspecific competition**). We consider the effects of intraspecific competition here; interspecific competition is discussed in Chapter 54.

Individuals of the same species compete for a resource in limited supply by interference competition or by exploitation competition. In **interference competition,** also called **contest competition,** certain dominant individuals obtain an adequate supply of the limited resource at the expense of other individuals in the population; that is, the dominant individuals actively interfere with other individuals' access to resources. In **exploitation competition,** also called **scramble competition,** all the individuals in a population "share" the limited resource more or less equally so that at high population densities none of them obtains an adequate amount. The populations of species in which exploitation competition operates often oscillate over time, and there is always a risk that the population size will drop to zero. In contrast, those species in which interference competition operates experience a relatively small drop in population size, caused by the death of individuals that are unable to compete successfully.

Intraspecific competition among red grouse involves interference competition. When red grouse populations are small, the birds are less aggressive, and most young birds establish a feeding territory (an area defended against other members of the same species). However, when the population is large, establishing a territory is difficult because there are more birds than there are territories, and the birds are much more aggressive. Those birds without territories often die from predation or starvation. Thus, birds with territories use a larger share of the limited resource (the territory with its associated food and cover), whereas birds without territories cannot compete successfully.

The moose population on Isle Royale, Michigan, the largest island in Lake Superior, provides a vivid example of exploitation competition that is similar to that of the reindeer population on the Pribilof Islands (discussed earlier). Isle Royale differs from most islands in that large mammals can walk to it when the lake freezes over in winter. The minimum distance to be walked is 24 km (15 mi), however, so this movement has happened infrequently. Around 1900, a small herd of moose wandered across the ice of frozen Lake Superior and reached the island for the first time. By 1934, the moose population on the island had increased to about 3000 and had consumed almost all the edible vegetation. In the absence of this food resource, there was massive starvation in 1934. More than 60 years later, in 1996, a similar die-off claimed 80% of the moose after they had again increased to a high density. Thus, exploitation competition for scarce resources can result in dramatic population oscillations.

The effects of density-dependent factors are difficult to assess in nature

Most studies of density dependence have been conducted in laboratory settings where all density-dependent (and density-independent) factors except one are controlled experimentally. But populations in natural settings are exposed to a complex set of variables that continually change. As a result, in natural communities it is difficult to evaluate the relative effects of different density-dependent factors.

Ecologists from the University of California at Davis noted that few spiders occur on tropical islands inhabited by lizards, whereas more spiders and more species of spiders are found on lizard-free islands. Deciding to study these observations experimentally, David Spiller and Thomas Schoener staked out plots of vegetation (mainly seagrape shrubs) and enclosed some of them with lizard-proof screens (**FIG. 53-6**). Some of the plots were emptied of all lizards; each control enclosure had approximately nine lizards. Nine web-building spider species were observed in the enclosures. Spiders were counted approximately 30 times from 1989 to 1994. During the 4.5 years of observations reported here, spider population densities were higher in the lizard-free enclosures than in enclosures with lizards. Moreover, the enclosures without lizards had more species of spiders. Therefore, we might conclude that lizards control spider populations.

But even this relatively simple experiment may be explained by a combination of two density-dependent factors, predation (lizards eat spiders) and interspecific competition (lizards compete with spiders for insect prey—that is, both spiders and lizards eat insects). In this experiment, the effects of the two density-dependent factors in determining spider population size cannot be evaluated separately. Additional lines of evidence support the actions of both competition and predation at these sites.

Density-independent factors are generally abiotic

Any environmental factor that affects the size of a population but is not influenced by changes in population density is called a **density-independent factor.** Such factors are typically abiotic. Random weather events that reduce population size serve as density-independent factors. These often affect population density in unpredictable ways. A killing frost, severe blizzard, or hurricane, for example, may cause extreme and irregular reductions in a vulnerable population, regardless of its size, and thus may be considered largely density-independent.

KEY EXPERIMENT

QUESTION: What is the influence of density-dependent factors on population size in a natural habitat?

HYPOTHESIS: Lizards reduce the size of spider populations.

EXPERIMENT: Researchers conducted a field experiment in which they constructed enclosed plots (see photograph); spiders and insects could pass freely into and out of the enclosures, but the lizards could not. Some plots included lizards; the other plots were lizard-free. The spiders were periodically counted over a period of 4.5 years. An earlier experiment indicated that the enclosures themselves have no effect on the number of web-building spiders.

RESULTS AND CONCLUSION: The graph of the mean number of web-building spiders at each count per enclosure with lizards (*control, blue*) and per enclosure with lizards removed (*red*) demonstrates that the number of web-building spiders was consistently higher in the absence of lizards. Lizards may control spider populations by preying on them, by competing with them for insect prey, or by a combination of these factors.

Source: Graph from Spiller, D. A., and T. W. Schoener. "Lizards Reduce Spider Species Richness by Excluding Rare Species." *Ecology*, Vol. 79, No. 2, 1998. Copyright © 1998 Ecological Society of America. Reprinted with permission.

FIGURE 53-6 Interaction of density-dependent factors

Consider a density-independent factor that influences mosquito populations in arctic environments. These insects produce several generations per summer and achieve high population densities by the end of the season. A shortage of food does not seem to be a limiting factor for mosquitoes, nor is there any shortage of ponds in which to breed. What puts a stop to the skyrocketing mosquito population is winter. Not a single adult mosquito survives winter, and the entire population must grow afresh the next summer from the few eggs and hibernating larvae that survive. Thus, severe winter weather is a density-independent factor that affects arctic mosquito populations.

Density-independent and density-dependent factors are often interrelated. Social animals, for example, often resist dangerous weather conditions by collective behavior, as in the case of sheep huddling together in a snowstorm. In this case it appears that the greater the population density of the sheep, the better their ability to resist the environmental stress of a density-independent event (such as a snowstorm).

Review

- What are three examples of density-dependent factors that affect population growth?
- What are three density-independent factors?

53.4 LIFE HISTORY TRAITS

LEARNING OBJECTIVES

5 Contrast semelparous and iteroparous reproduction.

6 Distinguish among species exhibiting an *r* strategy, those with a *K* strategy, and those that do not easily fit either category.

7 Describe Type I, Type II, and Type III survivorship curves, and explain how life tables and survivorship curves indicate mortality and survival.

Each species is uniquely suited to its lifestyle. Many years pass before a young magnolia tree flowers and produces seeds, whereas

Introduction to Ecology: Population Ecology   **1161**

an annual plant grows from seed, flowers, and dies within a single season. A mating pair of black-browed albatrosses produces a single chick every year, but a mating pair of gray-headed albatrosses produces a single chick biennially (every other year).

Species that expend their energy in a single, immense reproductive effort are said to be **semelparous.** Most insects and invertebrates, many plants, and some species of fish exhibit semelparity. Pacific salmon, for example, hatch in fresh water and swim to the ocean, where they live until they mature. Adult salmon swim from the ocean back into the same rivers or streams in which they hatched to spawn (reproduce). After they spawn, the salmon die.

Agaves are semelparous plants that are common in arid tropical and semitropical areas. The thick, fleshy leaves of the agave plant are crowded into a rosette at the base of the stem. Commonly called the century plant because it was mistakenly thought to flower only once in a century, agaves can flower after they are ten years old or so, after which the entire plant dies (**FIG. 53-7**).

Many species are **iteroparous** and exhibit repeated reproductive cycles—that is, reproduction during several breeding seasons—throughout their lifetimes. Iteroparity is common in most vertebrates, as well as in perennial herbaceous plants, shrubs, and trees. The timing of reproduction, earlier or later in life, is a crucial as-

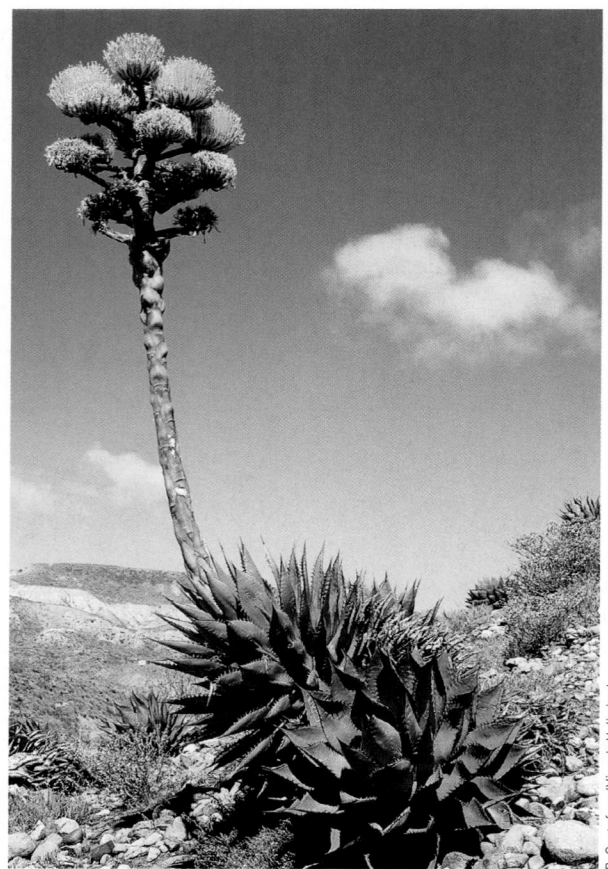

FIGURE 53-7 Semelparity

Agaves flower once and then die. The agave is a succulent with sword-shaped leaves arranged as a rosette around a short stem. Shown is *Agave shawii*, whose leaves grow to 61 cm (2 ft). Note the floral stalk, which can grow more than 3 m (10 ft) tall.

pect of iteroparity and involves trade-offs. On the one hand, reproducing earlier in life may mean a reduced likelihood of survival (because an individual is expending energy toward reproduction instead of its own growth), which reduces the potential for later reproduction. On the other hand, reproducing later in life means the individual has less time for additional reproductive events.

Ecologists try to understand the adaptive consequences of various **life history traits,** such as semelparity and iteroparity. Adaptations such as reproductive rate, age at maturity, and **fecundity** (potential capacity to produce offspring), all of which are a part of a species' life history traits, influence an organism's survival and reproduction. The ability of an individual to reproduce successfully, thereby making a genetic contribution to future generations of a population, is called its **fitness** (recall the discussion of fitness in Chapter 19).

Although many different life histories exist, some ecologists recognize two extremes: *r*-selected species and *K*-selected species. Keep in mind, as you read the following descriptions of *r* selection and *K* selection, that these concepts, although useful, oversimplify most life histories. Species tend to possess a combination of *r*-selected and *K*-selected traits, as well as traits that cannot be classified as either *r*-selected or *K*-selected. In addition, some populations within a species may exhibit the characteristics of *r* selection, whereas other populations in different environments may assume *K*-selected traits.

Populations described by the concept of *r* **selection** have traits that contribute to a high population growth rate. Recall that *r* designates the per capita growth rate. Because such organisms have a high *r*, biologists call them *r* **strategists** or *r*-**selected species.** Small body size, early maturity, short lifespan, large broods, and little or no parental care are typical of many *r* strategists, which are usually opportunists found in variable, temporary, or unpredictable environments where the probability of long-term survival is low. Some of the best examples of *r* strategists are insects, such as mosquitoes, and plants such as the poppies shown in the chapter opening photograph. Following a rainy period, these desert annuals rapidly grow from seed, flower and set seed, and then die.

In populations described by the concept of *K* **selection,** traits maximize the chance of surviving in an environment where the number of individuals is near the carrying capacity (*K*) of the environment. These organisms, called *K* **strategists** or *K*-**selected species,** do not produce large numbers of offspring. They characteristically have long lifespans with slow development, late reproduction, large body size, and a low reproductive rate. *K* strategists tend to be found in relatively constant or stable environments, where they have a high competitive ability. Redwood trees, as well as most tropical rainforest trees, are classified as *K* strategists. Animals that are *K* strategists typically invest in parental care of their young. Tawny owls (*Strix aluco*), for example, are *K* strategists that pair-bond for life, with both members of a pair living and hunting in adjacent, well-defined territories. Their reproduction is regulated in accordance with the resources, especially the food supply, present in their territories. In an average year, 30% of the birds do not breed at all. If food supplies are more limited than initially indicated, many of those that do breed fail to incubate their eggs. Rarely do the owls lay the maximum number of eggs that they are physiologically capable of laying, and breeding is often delayed until late in the season, when the rodent populations on which they depend have become large. Thus, the behavior of tawny owls ensures better reproductive success of the individual and leads to a stable population at or near the carrying capacity of the environment. Starvation, an indication that the tawny owl population has exceeded the carrying capacity, rarely occurs.

Life tables and survivorship curves indicate mortality and survival

A **life table** can be constructed to show the mortality and survival data of a population or **cohort,** a group of individuals of the same age, at different times during their lifespan. Insurance companies were the first to use life tables, to calculate the relationship between a client's age and the likelihood of the client surviving to pay enough insurance premiums to cover the cost of the policy. Ecologists construct such tables for animals and plants, based on data that rely on a variety of population sampling methods and age determination techniques.

TABLE 53-2 shows a life table for a cohort of 530 gray squirrels. The first two columns show the units of age (years) and the number of individuals in the cohort that were alive at the beginning of each age interval (the actual data collected in the field by the ecologist). The values for the third column (the proportion alive at the beginning of each age interval) are calculated by dividing each number in column 2 by 530, the number of squirrels in the original cohort. The values in the fourth column (the proportion dying during each age interval) are calculated using the values in the third column—by subtracting the number of survivors at the beginning of the next interval from those alive at the beginning of the current interval. For example, the proportion dying during interval 0–1 years is $1.000 - 0.253 = 0.747$. The last column, the death rate for each age interval, is calculated by dividing the proportion dying during the age interval (column 4) by the proportion alive at the beginning of the age interval (column 3). For example, the death rate for the age interval 1–2 years is $0.147 \div 0.253 = 0.581$.

Survivorship is the probability that a given individual in a population or cohort will survive to a particular age. Plotting the logarithm (base 10) of the number of surviving individuals against age, from birth to the maximum age reached by any individual, produces a **survivorship curve. FIGURE 53-8** shows the three main survivorship curves that ecologists recognize.

In *Type I survivorship,* as exemplified by bison and humans, the young and those at reproductive age have a high probability of surviving. The probability of survival decreases more rapidly with increasing age; mortality is concentrated later in life. **FIGURE 53-9** shows a survivorship curve for a natural population of Drummond phlox, an annual native to East Texas that became widely distributed in the southeastern United States after it escaped from cultivation. Because most Drummond phlox seedlings survive to reproduce, after germination the plant exhibits a Type I survivorship that is typical of annuals.

In *Type III survivorship,* the probability of mortality is greatest early in life, and those individuals that avoid early death subse-

TABLE 53-2	Life Table for a Cohort of 530 Gray Squirrels (*Sciurus carolinensis*)			
Age Interval (years)	Number Alive at Beginning of Age Interval	Proportion Alive at Beginning of Age Interval	Proportion Dying during Age Interval	Death Rate for Age Interval
0–1	530	1.000	0.747	0.747
1–2	134	0.253	0.147	0.581
2–3	56	0.106	0.032	0.302
3–4	39	0.074	0.031	0.418
4–5	23	0.043	0.021	0.488
5–6	12	0.022	0.013	0.591
6–7	5	0.009	0.006	0.666
7–8	2	0.003	0.003	1.000
8–9	0	0.000	0.000	—

Source: Adapted from Smith, R. L., and T. M. Smith. *Elements of Ecology*, 4th ed., table 13.1, p. 150. Benjamin/Cummings Science Publishing, San Francisco, 1998.

quently have a high probability of survival, that is, the probability of survival increases with increasing age. Type III survivorship is characteristic of oysters; young oysters have three free-swimming larval stages before settling down and secreting a shell. These larvae are vulnerable to predation, and few survive to adulthood.

In *Type II survivorship,* which is intermediate between Types I and III, the probability of survival does not change with age. The probability of death is equally likely across all age groups, resulting in a linear decline in survivorship. This constancy probably results from essentially random events that cause death with little age bias. Although this relationship between age and survivorship is rare, some lizards have Type II survivorship.

The three survivorship curves are generalizations, and few populations exactly fit one of the three. Some species have one type of survivorship curve early in life and another type as adults. Herring gulls, for example, start out with a Type III survivorship curve but develop a Type II curve as adults (**FIG. 53-10**). The survivorship curve shown in this figure is characteristic of birds in general. Note

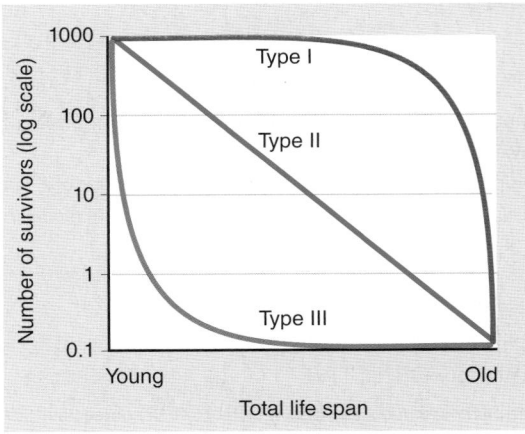

FIGURE 53-8 *Animated* **Survivorship curves**
These curves represent the ideal survivorships of species in which mortality is greatest in old age (Type I), spread evenly across all age groups (Type II), and greatest among the young (Type III). The survivorship of most organisms can be compared to these curves.

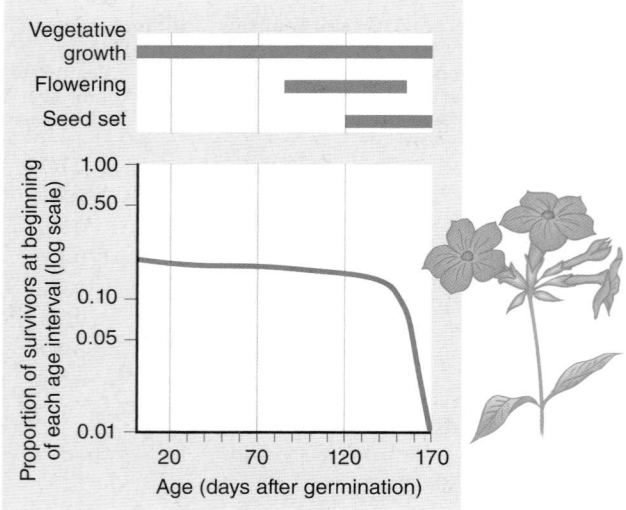

FIGURE 53-9 Survivorship curve for a Drummond phlox population

Drummond phlox has a Type I survivorship after germination of the seeds. Bars above the graph indicate the various stages in the Drummond phlox life history. Data were collected at Nixon, Texas, in 1974 and 1975. Survivorship on the *y*-axis begins at 0.296 instead of 1.00 because the study took into account death during the seed dormancy period prior to germination (*not shown*). (From Leverich, W. J., and D. A. Levin. "Age-Specific Survivorship and Reproduction in *Phlox drummondii.*" *American Naturalist*, Vol. 113, No. 6, p. 1148, 1979. Copyright © 1979 University of Chicago Press. Reprinted with permission.)

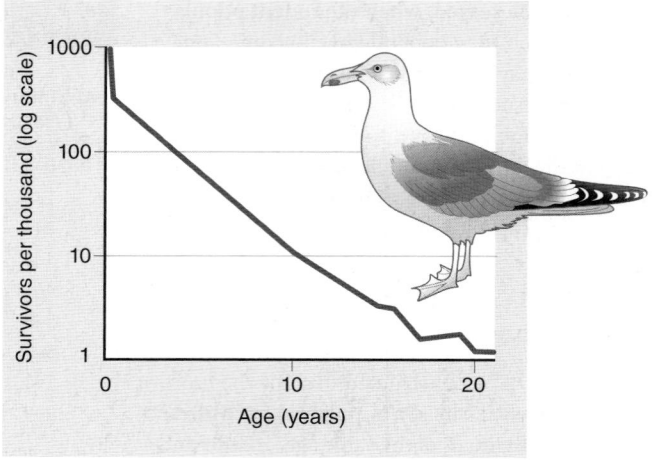

FIGURE 53-10 Survivorship curve for a herring gull population

Herring gulls (*Larus argentatus*) have Type III survivorship as chicks and Type II survivorship as adults. Data were collected from Kent Island, Maine, during a five-year period in the 1930s; baby gulls were banded to establish identity. The very slight increase just prior to 20 years of age is due to sampling error. (Paynter, R. A., Jr. "A New Attempt to Construct Lifetables for Kent Island Herring Gulls." *Bulletin of the Museum of Comparative Zoology*, Vol. 133, No. 11, pp. 489–528, 1966.)

that most death occurs almost immediately after hatching, despite the protection and care given to the chicks by the parent bird. Herring gull chicks die from predation or attack by other herring gulls, inclement weather, infectious diseases, or starvation following death of the parent. Once the chicks become independent, their survivorship increases dramatically, and death occurs at about the same rate throughout their remaining lives. Few or no herring gulls die from the degenerative diseases of "old age" that cause death in most humans.

Review

- What are the advantages of semelparity? of iteroparity? Are there disadvantages?
- Why is parental care of young a common characteristic of *K* strategists?
- Do all survivorship curves neatly fit the Type I, II, or III models? Explain.

53.5 METAPOPULATIONS

◼ LEARNING OBJECTIVE

8 Define *metapopulation*, and distinguish between source habitats and sink habitats.

The natural environment is a heterogeneous **landscape** consisting of interacting ecosystems that provide a variety of habitat patches. Landscapes, which are typically several to many square kilometers in area, cover larger land areas than individual ecosystems. Consider

a forest, for example. The forest landscape is a mosaic of different elevations, temperatures, levels of precipitation, soil moisture, soil types, and other properties. Because each species has its own habitat requirements, this heterogeneity in physical properties is reflected in the different organisms that occupy the various patches in the landscape (**FIG. 53-11**). Some species occur in very narrow habitat ranges, whereas others have wider habitat distributions.

Population ecologists have discovered that many species are not distributed as one large population across the landscape. Instead, many species exist as a series of local populations distributed in distinct habitat patches. Each local population has its own characteristic demographic features, such as birth, death, emigration, and immigration rates. A population that is divided into several local populations among which individuals occasionally disperse (emigrate and immigrate) is known as a **metapopulation.** For example, note the various local populations of red oak on the mountain slope in Figure 53-11b.

The spatial distribution of a species occurs because different habitats vary in suitability, from unacceptable to preferred. The preferred sites are more productive habitats that increase the likelihood of survival and reproductive success for the individuals living there. Good habitats, called **source habitats,** are areas where local reproductive success is greater than local mortality. **Source populations** generally have greater population densities than populations at less suitable sites, and surplus individuals in the source habitat disperse and find another habitat in which to settle and reproduce.

Individuals living in lower quality habitats may suffer death or, if they survive, poor reproductive success. Lower quality habitats, called **sink habitats,** are areas where local reproductive success is less than local mortality. Without immigration from other areas, a **sink population** declines until extinction occurs. If a local popu-

(a) This early spring view of Deep Creek Valley in the Great Smoky Mountains National Park gives some idea of the heterogeneity of the landscape. During the summer, when all the vegetation is a deep green, the landscape appears homogeneous.

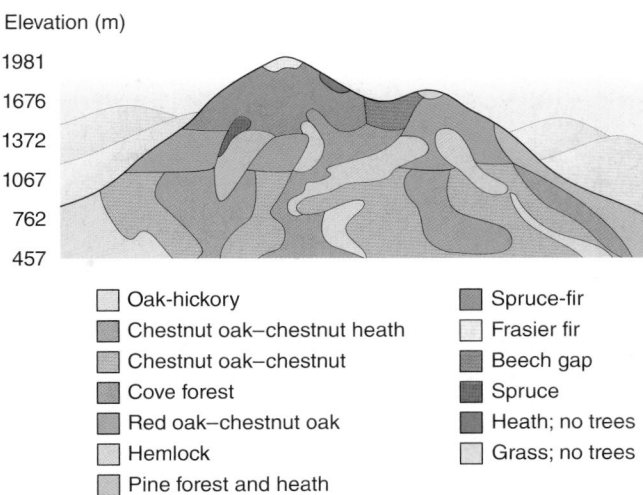

Oak-hickory
Chestnut oak–chestnut heath
Chestnut oak–chestnut
Cove forest
Red oak–chestnut oak
Hemlock
Pine forest and heath

Spruce-fir
Frasier fir
Beech gap
Spruce
Heath; no trees
Grass; no trees

(b) An evaluation of the distribution of vegetation on a typical west-facing slope in the Great Smoky Mountains National Park reveals that the landscape consists of patches. Chestnut oak is a species of oak (*Quercus prinus*); chestnut heath is an area within chestnut oak forest where the trees are widely scattered and the slopes underneath are covered by a thick growth of laurel (*Kalmia*) shrubs; cove forest is a mixed stand of deciduous trees.

FIGURE 53-11 The mosaic nature of landscapes
(Adapted from Whittaker, R. H. "Vegetation of the Great Smoky Mountains." *Ecological Monographs*, Vol. 26, 1956.)

lation becomes extinct, individuals from a source habitat may recolonize the vacant habitat at a later time. Source and sink habitats, then, are linked to one another by dispersal (**FIG. 53-12**).

Metapopulations are becoming more common as humans alter the landscape by fragmenting existing habitats to accommodate homes and factories, agricultural fields, and logging. As a result, the concept of metapopulations, particularly as it relates to endangered and threatened species, has become an important area of study in conservation biology.

Review

■ What is a metapopulation?
■ How do you distinguish between a source habitat and a sink habitat?

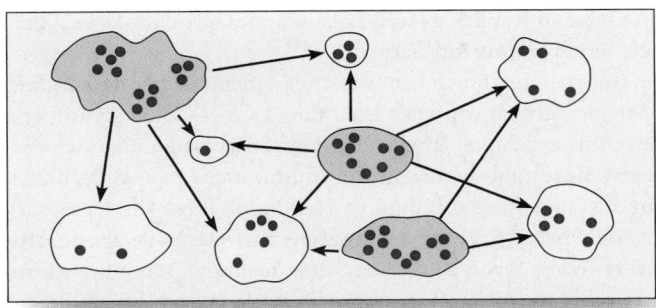

◯ Source population in a suitable habitat
◯ Sink population in a low-quality habitat
● Individual within a local population
→ Dispersal event

FIGURE 53-12 Source and sink populations in a hypothetical metapopulation
The local populations in the habitat patches shown here collectively make up the metapopulation. Source habitats provide individuals that emigrate and colonize sink habitats. Studied over time, the metapopulation is shown to exist as a shifting pattern of occupied and vacant habitat patches.

53.6 HUMAN POPULATIONS

◼ LEARNING OBJECTIVES

9 Summarize the history of human population growth.
10 Explain how highly developed and developing countries differ in population characteristics such as infant mortality rate, total fertility rate, replacement-level fertility, and age structure.
11 Distinguish between people overpopulation and consumption overpopulation.

Now that we have examined some of the basic concepts of population ecology, we can apply those concepts to the human population. Examine **FIGURE 53-13**, which shows the world increase in the human population since the development of agriculture approximately 10,000 years ago. Now look back at Figure 53-2 and compare the two curves. The characteristic J curve of exponential population growth shown in Figure 53-13 reflects the decreasing amount of time it has taken to add each additional billion people

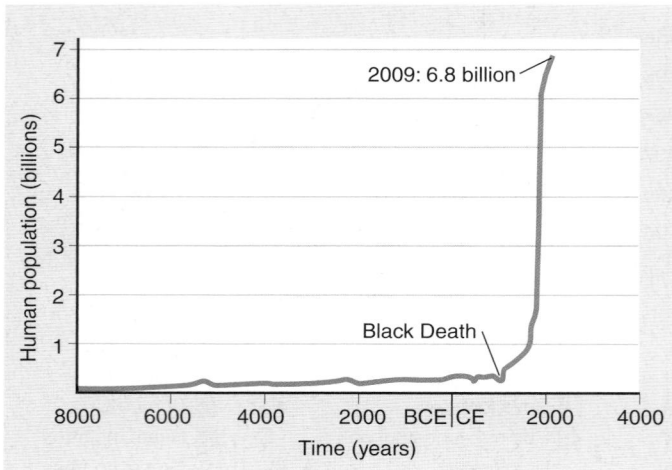

FIGURE 53-13 Human population growth

During the last 1000 years, the human population has been increasing nearly exponentially. Population experts predict that the population will level out during the 21st century, forming the S curve observed in other species. (Black Death refers to a devastating disease, probably bubonic plague, that decimated Europe and Asia in the 14th century.)

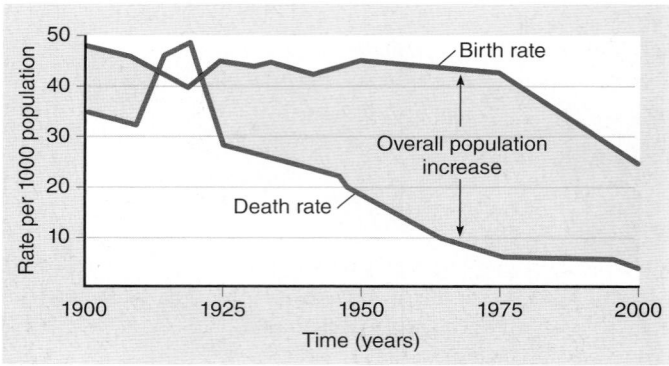

FIGURE 53-14 Birth and death rates in Mexico, 1900 to 2000

Both birth and death rates declined during the 20th century, but because the death rate declined much more than the birth rate, Mexico has experienced a high growth rate. (The high death rate prior to 1920 was caused by the Mexican Revolution; Population Reference Bureau.)

to our numbers. It took thousands of years for the human population to reach one billion, a milestone that took place around 1800. It took 130 years to reach two billion (in 1930), 30 years to reach three billion (in 1960), 15 years to reach four billion (in 1975), 12 years to reach five billion (in 1987), and 12 years to reach six billion (in 1999). The United Nations projects that the human population will reach about seven billion by 2012.

Thomas Malthus (1766–1834), a British clergyman and economist, was one of the first to recognize that the human population cannot continue to increase indefinitely (see Chapter 18). He pointed out that human population growth is not always desirable (a view contrary to the beliefs of his day and to those of many people even today) and that the human population is capable of increasing faster than the food supply. He maintained that the inevitable consequences of population growth are famine, disease, and war.

The world population is currently increasing by about 83 million people per year. It reached 6.8 billion in mid-2009. This change was not caused by an increase in the birth rate (b). In fact, the world birth rate has actually declined during the past 200 years. The increase in population is due instead to a dramatic decrease in the death rate (d). This decrease in mortality has occurred primarily because greater food production, better medical care, and improved sanitation practices have increased the life expectancies of a great majority of the global population. For example, from 1920 to 2000, the death rate in Mexico fell from approximately 40 per 1000 individuals to 4 per 1000, whereas the birth rate dropped from approximately 40 per 1000 individuals to 24 per 1000 (**FIG. 53-14**).

The human population has reached a turning point. Although our numbers continue to increase, the world per capita growth rate (r) has declined over the past several years, from a peak of 2.2% per year in the mid-1960s to 1.2% per year in 2009. Population experts at the United Nations and the World Bank have projected that the growth rate may continue to slowly decrease until zero population

growth is attained. Thus, exponential growth of the human population may end, and if it does, the S curve will replace the J curve. Demographers project that **zero population growth,** the point at which the birth rate equals the death rate ($r = 0$), will occur toward the end of the 21st century.

The latest (2009) projections available through the Population Reference Bureau, based on data from the United Nations, forecast that the human population will exceed 9.4 billion in the year 2050. This is a "medium" projection; such population projections are "what if" exercises. Given certain assumptions about future tendencies in natality, mortality, and dispersal, population experts can calculate an area's population for a given number of years into the future. Population projections indicate the changes that may occur, but they must be interpreted with care because they vary depending on what assumptions have been made. Small differences in fertility, as well as death rates, produce large differences in population forecasts.

The main unknown factor in any population growth scenario is Earth's carrying capacity. According to Joel Cohen, who has a joint professorship at Rockefeller University and Columbia University, most published estimates of how many people Earth can support range from 4 billion to 16 billion. These estimates vary so widely because of the assumptions that are made about standard of living, resource consumption, technological innovations, and waste generation. If we want all people to have a high level of material well-being equivalent to the lifestyles common in highly developed countries, then Earth will clearly be able to support far fewer humans than if everyone lives just above the subsistence level. Thus, Earth's carrying capacity for the human population is not decided simply by natural environmental constraints. Human choices and values have to be factored into the assessment.

It is also not clear what will happen to the human population if or when the carrying capacity is approached. Optimists suggest that the human population will stabilize because of a decrease in the birth rate. Some experts take a more pessimistic view and predict that the widespread degradation of our environment caused by our ever-expanding numbers will make Earth uninhabitable for humans and other species. These experts contend that a massive wave of human suffering and death will occur. Some experts think that the human population has already exceeded the carrying capacity of the environment, a potentially dangerous situation that threatens our long-term survival as a species.

Not all countries have the same growth rate

Although world population figures illustrate overall trends, they do not describe other important aspects of the human population story, such as population differences from country to country. **Human demographics,** the science that deals with human population statistics such as size, density, and distribution, provides information on the populations of various countries. As you probably know, not all parts of the world have the same rates of population increase. Countries can be classified into two groups, highly developed and developing, based on their rates of population growth, degrees of industrialization, and relative prosperity (**TABLE 53-3**).

Highly developed countries, such as the United States, Canada, France, Germany, Sweden, Australia, and Japan, have low rates of population growth and are highly industrialized relative to the rest of the world. Highly developed countries have the lowest birth rates in the world. Indeed, some highly developed countries such as Germany have birth rates just below that needed to sustain the population and are thus declining slightly in numbers. Highly developed countries also have low **infant mortality rates** (the number of infant deaths per 1000 live births). The infant mortality rate of the United States was 6.6 in 2009, for example, compared with a world infant mortality rate of 46.

Highly developed countries also have longer life expectancies (78 years at birth in the United States versus 69 years worldwide) and higher average GNI PPP per capita ($46,970 in the United States versus $10,090 worldwide). GNI PPP per capita is gross national income (GNI) in purchasing power parity (PPP) divided by midyear population. It indicates the amount of goods and services an average citizen of that particular region or country could buy in the United States.

Developing countries fall into two subcategories: moderately developed and less developed. Mexico, Turkey, Thailand, and most countries of South America are examples of *moderately developed countries.* Their birth rates and infant mortality rates are generally higher than those of highly developed countries, but the rates are declining. Moderately developed countries have a medium level of industrialization, and their average GNI PPP per capita is lower than those of highly developed countries.

Bangladesh, Niger, Ethiopia, Laos, and Cambodia are examples of *less developed countries.* These countries have the highest birth rates, the highest infant mortality rates, the lowest life expectancies, and the lowest average GNI PPP per capita in the world.

One way to represent the population growth of a country is to determine the **doubling time,** the amount of time it would take for its population to double in size, assuming its current growth rate did not change. A simplified formula for doubling time (t_d) is $t_d = 70 \div r$. (The actual formula involves calculus and is beyond the scope of this text. This simplified formula actually has many practical applications; for example, you can use it to estimate how long it will take to double your money in a savings account at a specific rate of compound interest.)

A look at a country's doubling time identifies it as a highly, moderately, or less developed country: the shorter the doubling time, the less developed the country. At rates of growth in 2009, the approximate doubling time is 26 years for Ethiopia, 33 years for Laos, 58 years for Turkey, 117 years for Thailand, 117 years for the United States, and 175 years for France.

It is also instructive to examine **replacement-level fertility,** the number of children a couple must produce to "replace" themselves. Replacement-level fertility is usually given as 2.1 children in highly developed countries and 2.7 children in developing countries. The number is always greater than 2.0 because some children die before they reach reproductive age. Higher infant mortality rates are the main reason that replacement levels in developing countries are greater than in highly developed countries. The **total fertility rate**—the average number of children born to a woman during her lifetime—is 2.6 worldwide, which is well above replacement levels. However, it has fallen below replacement levels, to 1.7, in the highly developed countries. The total fertility rate in the United States is higher than in other industrialized countries—2.1.

The population in many developing countries is beginning to approach stabilization. The fertility rate must decline for the population to stabilize (**TABLE 53-4**; note the general decline in total fertility rate from the 1960s to 2009 in selected developing countries). The total fertility rate in developing countries has decreased from

TABLE 53-3	Comparison of 2009 Population Data in Selected Developed and Developing Countries		
	Developed	Developing	
	(Highly Developed) United States	(Moderately Developed) Brazil	(Less Developed) Ethiopia
Fertility rate	2.1	2.0	5.3
Doubling time	117 years	70 years	26 years
Infant mortality rate	6.6 per 1000	24 per 1000	77 per 1000
Life expectancy at birth	78 years	73 years	53 years
GNI PPP per capita (U.S. $)	$46,970	$10,070	$870
Married women 15–49 using modern contraception	68%	70%	14%

Source: Population Reference Bureau.

TABLE 53-4	Fertility Changes in Selected Developing Countries	
	Total Fertility Rate	
Country	1960–1965	2009
Bangladesh	6.7	2.5
Brazil	6.2	2.0
China	5.9	1.6
Egypt	7.1	3.0
Guatemala	6.9	4.4
India	5.8	2.7
Kenya	8.1	4.9
Mexico	6.8	2.3
Nepal	5.9	3.1
Nigeria	6.9	5.7
Thailand	6.4	1.8

Source: Population Reference Bureau.

an average of 6.1 children per woman in 1970 to 3.1 in 2009 (excluding China), or 2.7 if China is included. Fertility is highly variable among developing countries, and although the fertility rates in most of these countries have declined, it should be remembered that most still exceed replacement-level fertility. Consequently, the populations in these countries are still increasing. Also, even when fertility rates equal replacement-level fertility, population growth will still continue for some time. To understand why this is so, we now examine the age structure of various countries.

The age structure of a country helps predict future population growth

To predict the future growth of a population, it is important to know its **age structure,** which is the number and proportion of people at each age in a population. The number of males and number of females at each age, from birth to death, are represented in **an age structure diagram.**

The overall shape of an age structure diagram indicates whether the population is increasing, stationary, or shrinking (**FIG. 53-15**). The age structure diagram for less developed countries is shaped like a pyramid. Because the largest percentage of the population is in the prereproductive age group (that is, 0 to 14 years of age), the probability of future population growth is great. A strong **population growth momentum** exists because when all these children mature they will become the parents of the next generation, and this group of parents will be larger than the previous group. Thus, even if the fertility

rates in these countries decline to replacement level (that is, couples have smaller families than their parents did), the population will continue to grow for some time. Population growth momentum can have either a positive value (that is, the population will grow) or a negative value (that is, the population will decline). However, it is usually discussed in a positive context, to explain how the future growth of a population is affected by its present age distribution.

In contrast, the more tapered bases of the age structure diagrams of highly developed countries with slowly growing, stable, or declining populations indicate that a smaller proportion of the population will become the parents of the next generation. The age structure diagram of a stable population, one that is neither growing nor shrinking, demonstrates that the number of people at prereproductive and reproductive ages are approximately the same. Also, a larger percentage of the population is older, that is, postreproductive, than in a rapidly increasing population. Many countries in Europe have stable populations. In a population that is shrinking in size, the prereproductive age group is smaller than either the reproductive or postreproductive group. Germany, Russia, and Bulgaria are examples of countries with slowly shrinking populations.

Worldwide, 27% of the human population is younger than age 15. When these people enter their reproductive years, they have the potential to cause a large increase in the growth rate. Even if the birth rate does not increase, the growth rate will increase simply because more people are reproducing.

Most of the world population increase since 1950 has taken place in developing countries as a result of the younger age struc-

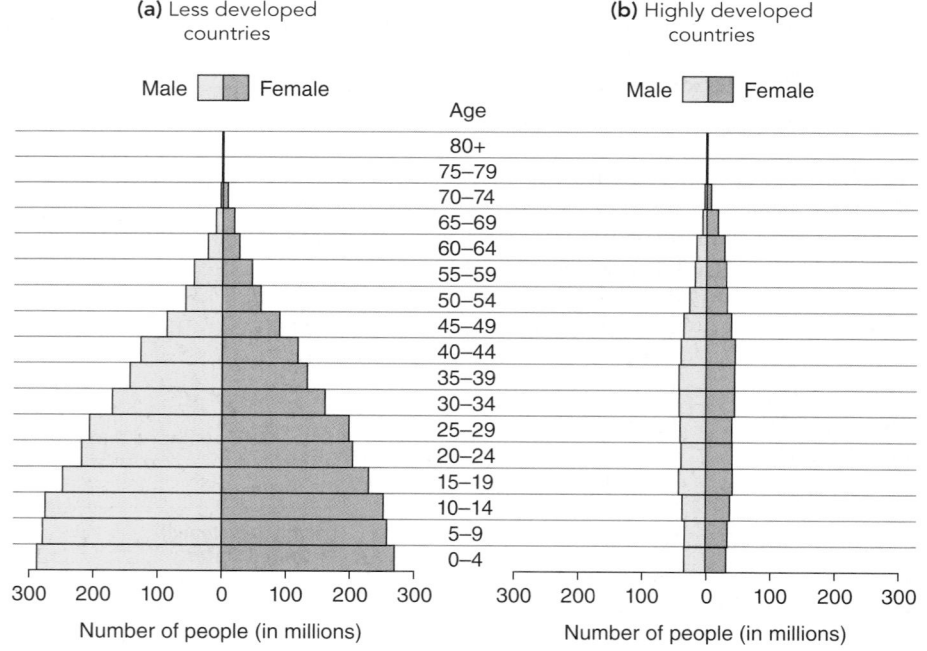

FIGURE 53-15 *Animated* Age structure diagrams

These age structure diagrams for **(a)** less developed countries and **(b)** highly developed countries indicate that less developed regions have a greater percentage of young people than do highly developed countries. As a result, less developed countries are projected to have greater population growth than are highly developed countries. (Adapted from Population Reference Bureau using data from United Nations, World Population Prospects: The 2002 Revision, 2003.)

ture and the higher-than-replacement-level fertility rates of their populations. In 1950, 66.8% of the world's population was in the developing countries in Africa, Asia (minus Japan), and Latin America. Between 1950 and 2009, the world's population more than doubled in size, but most of that growth occurred in developing countries. As a reflection of this, in 2009 the people in developing countries had increased to almost 82% of the world's population. Most of the population increase that will occur during the 21st century will also take place in developing countries, largely the result of their young age structures. These countries, most of which are poor, are least able to support such growth.

Environmental degradation is related to population growth and resource consumption

The relationships among population growth, use of natural resources, and environmental degradation are complex, but we can make two useful generalizations. First, although the amount of resources essential to an individual's survival may be small, a rapidly increasing population (as in developing countries) tends to overwhelm and deplete a country's soils, forests, and other natural resources (**FIG. 53-16a**). Second, in highly developed nations individual resource demands are large, far above requirements for survival. To satisfy their desires rather than their basic needs, people in more affluent nations exhaust resources and degrade the global environment through excessive consumption and "throwaway" lifestyles (**FIG 53-16b**).

Rapid population growth can cause natural resources to be overexploited. For example, large numbers of poor people must grow crops on land that is inappropriate for farming, such as mountain slopes or some tropical rain forests. Although this practice may provide a short-term solution to the need for food, it does not work in the long run, because when these lands are cleared for farming, their agricultural productivity declines rapidly and severe environmental deterioration occurs.

The effects of population growth on natural resources are particularly critical in developing countries. The economic growth of developing countries is often tied to the exploitation of natural resources, often for export to highly developed countries. Developing countries are faced with the difficult choice of exploiting natural resources to provide for their expanding populations in the short term (to pay for food or to cover debts) or conserving those resources for future generations. It is instructive to note that the economic growth and development of the United States and of other highly developed nations came about through the exploitation of and, in some cases, the destruction of their natural resources.

Although resource issues are clearly related to population size (more people use more resources), an equally, if not more, important factor is a population's resource consumption. People in highly developed countries are extravagant consumers—their use of resources is greatly out of proportion to their numbers. A single child born in a highly developed country such as the United States causes a greater impact on the environment and on resource depletion than a dozen or more children born in a developing country. Many natural resources are needed to provide the automobiles, air-conditioners, disposable diapers, cell phones, computers, clothes, athletic shoes, furniture, pleasure boats, and other "comforts" of

(a) The rapidly increasing number of people in developing countries overwhelms their natural resources, even though individual resource requirements may be low. Shown is a typical Indian family, from Ahraura Village, with all their possessions.

(b) People in highly developed countries consume a disproportionate share of natural resources. Shown is a typical American family from Pearland, Texas, with all their possessions.

FIGURE 53-16 People and natural resources

life in highly developed nations. Thus, the disproportionately large consumption of resources by the United States and other highly developed countries affects natural resources and the environment as much as or more than the population explosion in the developing world does.

A country is overpopulated if the level of demand on its resource base results in damage to the environment. If we compare human impact on the environment in developing and highly developed countries, we see that a country can be overpopulated in two ways. **People overpopulation** occurs when the environment is worsening from too many people, even if those people consume few resources per person. People overpopulation is the current problem in many developing nations.

In contrast, **consumption overpopulation** occurs when each individual in a population consumes too large a share of resources. The effect of consumption overpopulation on the environment is the same as that of people overpopulation—pollution and degradation of the environment. Most affluent highly developed nations, including the United States, suffer from consumption overpopulation. Highly developed nations represent about 18% of the world's population, yet they consume significantly more than half its resources. According to the Worldwatch Institute, a private research institution in Washington, D.C., highly developed nations account for the lion's share of total resources consumed, as follows: 86% of aluminum used, 76% of timber harvested, 68% of energy produced, 61% of meat eaten, and 42% of fresh water consumed. These nations also generate 75% of the world's pollution and waste.

Review

- What is replacement-level fertility? Why is it greater in developing countries than in highly developed countries?
- How can a single child born in the United States have a greater effect on the environment and natural resources than a dozen children born in Kenya?

■ SUMMARY: FOCUS ON LEARNING OBJECTIVES

53.1 *(page 1154)*

1 Define *population density* and *dispersion*, and describe the main types of population dispersion.

- **Population density** is the number of individuals of a species per unit of area or volume at a given time.

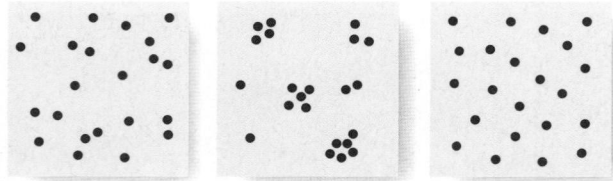

Random dispersion   **Clumped dispersion**   **Uniform dispersion**

- Population **dispersion** (spacing) may be **random dispersion** (unpredictably spaced), **clumped dispersion** (clustered in specific parts of the habitat), or **uniform dispersion** (evenly spaced).

53.2 *(page 1156)*

2 Explain the four factors (natality, mortality, immigration, and emigration) that produce changes in population size and solve simple problems involving these changes.

- Population size is affected by the average per capita birth rate (b), average per capita death rate (d), and two measures of dispersal: average per capita **immigration** rate (i) and average per capita **emigration** rate (e).
- The **growth rate (r)** is the rate of change (increase or decrease) of a population on a per capita basis. On a global scale (when dispersal is not a factor), $r = b - d$. Populations increase in size as long as the average per capita birth rate **(natality)** is greater than the average per capita death rate **(mortality).**
- For a local population (where dispersal is a factor), $r = (b - d) + (i - e)$.

3 Define *intrinsic rate of increase* and *carrying capacity*, and explain the differences between J-shaped and S-shaped growth curves.

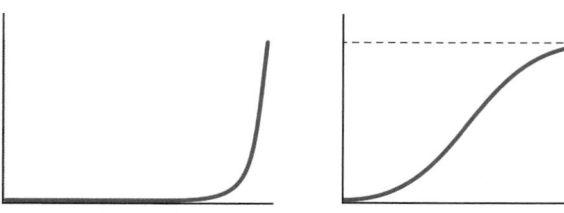

Exponential population growth   Logistic population growth

- **Intrinsic rate of increase (r_{max})** is the maximum rate at which a species or population could increase in number under ideal conditions.

- Although certain populations exhibit an accelerated pattern of growth known as **exponential population growth** for limited periods of time (the J-shaped curve), eventually the growth rate decreases to around zero or becomes negative.
- Population size is modified by limits set by the environment. The **carrying capacity (K)** of the environment is the largest population that can be maintained for an indefinite time by a particular environment. **Logistic population growth,** when graphed, shows a characteristic S-shaped curve. Seldom do natural populations follow the logistic growth curve very closely.

CENGAGENOW™   Learn more about population growth curves by clicking on the figures in CengageNOW.

53.3 *(page 1158)*

4 Contrast the influences of density-dependent and density-independent factors on population size, and give examples of each.

- **Density-dependent factors** regulate population growth by affecting a larger proportion of the population as population density rises. Predation, disease, and competition are examples.
- **Density-independent factors** limit population growth but are not influenced by changes in population density. Hurricanes and blizzards are examples.

53.4 *(page 1161)*

5 Contrast semelparous and iteroparous reproduction.

- **Semelparous** species expend their energy in a single, immense reproductive effort. **Iteroparous** species exhibit repeated reproductive cycles throughout their lifetimes.

6 Distinguish among species exhibiting an *r* strategy, those with a *K* strategy, and those that do not easily fit either category.

- Although many different combinations of life history traits exist, some ecologists recognize two extremes: *r* strategy and *K* strategy.
- An *r* strategy emphasizes a high growth rate. Organisms characterized as ***r* strategists** often have small body sizes, high reproductive rates, and short **lifespans,** and they typically inhabit variable environments.
- A *K* strategy maintains a population near the carrying capacity of the environment. Organisms characterized as ***K* strategists** often have large body sizes, low reproductive rates, and long lifespans, and they typically inhabit stable environments.
- The two strategies oversimplify most life histories. Many species combine *r*-selected and *K*-selected traits, as well as traits that cannot be classified as either *r*-selected or *K*-selected.

7 Describe Type I, Type II, and Type III survivorship curves, and explain how life tables and survivorship curves indicate mortality and survival.

- A **life table** shows the mortality and survival data of a population or **cohort**—a group of individuals of the same age—at different times during their lifespan.

- **Survivorship** is the probability that a given individual in a population or cohort will survive to a particular age. There are three general survivorship curves: *Type I survivorship*, in which mortality is greatest in old age; *Type II survivorship*, in which mortality is spread evenly across all age groups; and *Type III survivorship*, in which mortality is greatest among the young.

  CENGAGENOW™ Explore survivorship curves by clicking on the figure in CengageNOW.

53.5 *(page 1164)*

8 Define *metapopulation*, and distinguish between source habitats and sink habitats.

- Many species exist as a **metapopulation**, a set of local populations among which individuals are distributed in distinct habitat patches across a **landscape**, which is a large area of terrain (several to many square kilometers) composed of interacting ecosystems.

- Within a metapopulation, individuals occasionally disperse from one local habitat to another, by emigration and immigration. **Source habitats** are preferred sites where local reproductive success is greater than local mortality. Surplus individuals disperse from source habitats. **Sink habitats** are lower quality habitats where individuals may suffer death or, if they survive, poor reproductive success. If extinction of a local **sink population** occurs, individuals from a **source population** may recolonize the vacant habitat at a later time.

53.6 *(page 1165)*

9 Summarize the history of human population growth.

- The world population increases by about 83 million people per year and reached 6.8 billion in mid-2009.

- Although our numbers continue to increase, the per capita growth rate (*r*) has declined over the past several years, from a peak in 1965 of about 2% per year to a 2009 growth rate of 1.2% per year.

- Scientists who study **human demographics** (human population statistics) project that the world population will become stationary (*r* = 0, or **zero population growth**) by the end of the 21st century.

  CENGAGENOW™ Explore human population and the future by clicking on the figures in CengageNOW.

10 Explain how highly developed and developing countries differ in population characteristics such as infant mortality rate, total fertility rate, replacement-level fertility, and age structure.

- **Highly developed countries** have the lowest birth rates, lowest infant mortality rates, lowest total fertility rates, longest life expectancies, and highest GNI PPP per capita (a measure of the amount of goods and services the average citizen could purchase in the United States). **Developing countries** have the highest birth rates, highest infant mortality rates, highest total fertility rates, shortest life expectancies, and lowest GNI PPP per capita.

- The **age structure** of a population greatly influences population dynamics. It is possible for a country to have **replacement-level fertility** and still experience population growth if the largest percentage of the population is in the prereproductive years. A young age structure causes a positive **population growth momentum** as the very large prereproductive age group matures and becomes parents.

11 Distinguish between people overpopulation and consumption overpopulation.

- Developing countries tend to have **people overpopulation,** in which population increase degrades the environment even though each individual uses few resources.

- Highly developed countries tend to have **consumption overpopulation,** in which each individual in a slow-growing or stationary population consumes a large share of resources, which results in environmental degradation.

TEST YOUR UNDERSTANDING

1. Population _____ is the number of individuals of a species per unit of habitat area or volume at a given time. (a) dispersion (b) density (c) survivorship (d) age structure (e) demographics

2. Which of the following patterns of cars parked along a street is an example of uniform dispersion? (a) five cars parked next to one another in the middle, leaving two empty spaces at one end and three empty spaces at the other end (b) five cars parked in this pattern: car, empty space, car, empty space, and so on (c) five cars parked in no discernible pattern, sometimes having empty spaces on each side and sometimes parked next to another car

3. The per capita growth rate of a population where dispersal is not a factor is expressed as (a) $i + e$ (b) $b - d$ (c) dN/dt (d) $rN(K - N)$ (e) $(K - N) \div K$

4. The maximum rate at which a population could increase under ideal conditions is known as its (a) total fertility rate (b) survivorship (c) intrinsic rate of increase (d) doubling time (e) age structure

5. When *r* is a positive number, the population size is (a) stable (b) increasing (c) decreasing (d) either increasing or decreasing, depending on interference competition (e) either increasing or stable, depending on whether the species is semelparous

6. In a graph of population size versus time, a J-shaped curve is characteristic of (a) exponential population growth (b) logistic population growth (c) zero population growth (d) replacement-level fertility (e) population growth momentum

7. The largest population that can be maintained by a particular environment for an indefinite period is known as a (a) semelparous population (b) population undergoing exponential growth (c) metapopulation (d) population's carrying capacity (e) source population

8. Giant bamboos live many years without reproducing, then send up a huge flowering stalk and die shortly thereafter. Giant bamboo is therefore an example of (a) iteroparity (b) a source population (c) a metapopulation (d) an *r* strategist (e) semelparity

9. Predation, disease, and competition are examples of _____ factors. (a) density-dependent (b) density-independent (c) survivorship (d) dispersal (e) semelparous

10. _____ competition occurs within a population, and _____ competition occurs among populations of different species. (a) Interspecific; intraspecific (b) Intraspecific; interspecific (c) Type I survivorship; Type II survivorship (d) Interference; exploitation (e) Exploitation; interference

11. A highly developed country has a (a) long doubling time (b) low infant mortality rate (c) high GNI PPP per capita (d) a and b (e) a, b, and c

12. The continued growth of a population with a young age structure, even after its fertility rate has declined, is known as (a) population doubling (b) iteroparity (c) population growth momentum (d) *r* selection (e) density dependence

CRITICAL THINKING

1. How might pigs at a trough be an example of exploitation competition? of interference competition?

2. Explain why the population size of a species that competes by interference competition is often near the carrying capacity, whereas the population size of a species that competes by exploitation competition is often greater than or below the carrying capacity.

3. A female elephant bears a single offspring every two to four years. Based on this information, which survivorship curve do you think is representative of elephants? Explain your answer.

4. **EVOLUTION LINK.** In developing his scientific theory of evolution by natural selection, Charles Darwin considered four main observations: heritable variation among individuals in a population, overproduction of offspring, limits on population growth, and differential reproductive success. Compare how these observations may apply to populations that tend to fit the concepts of *r* selection and *K* selection.

5. **ANALYZING DATA.** In Bolivia, 39% of the population is younger than age 15, and 4% is older than 65. In Austria, 16% of the population is younger than 15, and 16% is older than 65. Which country will have the highest growth rate over the next two decades? Why?

6. **ANALYZING DATA.** The 2009 population of the Netherlands was 16.5 million, and its land area is 15,768 square miles. The 2009 population of the United States was 306.8 million, and its land area is 3,717,796 square miles. Which country has the greater population density?

7. **ANALYZING DATA.** The population of India in 2009 was 1.171 million, and its growth rate was 1.6% per year. Calculate the 2010 population of India.

8. **ANALYZING DATA.** The world population in 2009 was 6.8 billion, and its annual growth rate was 1.2%. If the birth rate was 20 per 1000 people in the year 2009, what was the death rate, expressed as number per 1000 people?

9. **ANALYZING DATA.** Consider the age structure diagrams for counties (a) and (b) following. Which diagram is consistent with negative growth momentum? Why?

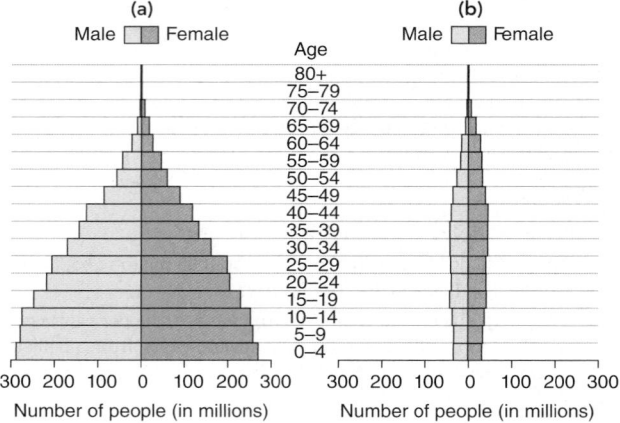

10. **SCIENCE, TECHNOLOGY, AND SOCIETY.** In what ways has technology contributed to consumption overpopulation? Can you propose some applications of technology that might help alleviate its effects?

 Additional questions are available in CengageNOW at www.cengage.com/login.

54 Community Ecology

Community in a rotting log. Fallen logs, called "nurse logs," shelter plants and other organisms and enrich the soil as they decay. Photographed in Pennsylvania.

Michael P. Gadomski/Photo Researchers, Inc.

In Chapter 53 we examined the dynamics of populations. In the natural world, most populations are part of a **community,** which consists of an association of populations of different species that live and interact in the same place at the same time. The definition for *community* is deliberately broad because it refers to ecological categories that vary greatly in size, lack precise boundaries, and are rarely completely isolated.

Smaller communities nest within larger communities. A forest is a community, but so is a rotting log in that forest (see photograph). Insects, plants, and fungi invade a fallen tree as it undergoes decay. Termites and other wood-boring insects forge tunnels through the bark and wood. Other insects, plant roots, and fungi follow and enlarge these openings. Mosses and lichens on the log's surface trap rainwater and extract minerals (inorganic nutrients), and fungi and bacteria speed decay, which provides nutrients for other inhabitants. As decay progresses, small mammals burrow into the wood and eat the fungi, insects, and plants.

Organisms exist in an abiotic (nonliving) environment that is as essential to their lives as their interactions with one another. Minerals, air, water, and sunlight are just as much a part of a honeybee's environment,

1173

for example, as the flowers it pollinates and from which it takes nectar. A biological community and its abiotic environment together compose an **ecosystem.** Like communities, ecosystems are broad entities that refer to ecological units of various sizes.

We now present some of the challenges in trying to find common patterns and processes that govern communities. The living community is emphasized in this chapter, and the abiotic components of ecosystems, including energy flow and trophic structure (feeding relationships), nutrient cycling, and climate, are considered in Chapter 55.

Jardin Lautaret/Station Alpine Joseph Fourier

(a) *Laretia acaulis* plants increase the survival rate of certain nearby plants at 2800 m (9100 ft) in the Andes Mountains of Chile. The effect is less pronounced at higher elevations.

54.1 COMMUNITY STRUCTURE AND FUNCTIONING

■ LEARNING OBJECTIVES

1   Define *ecological niche*, and distinguish between an organism's fundamental niche and its realized niche.
2   Define *competition*, and distinguish between interspecific and intraspecific competition.
3   Summarize the concepts of the competitive exclusion principle, resource partitioning, and character displacement.
4   Define *predation*, and describe the effects of natural selection on predator–prey relationships.
5   Distinguish among mutualism, commensalism, and parasitism, and give examples of each.

Communities exhibit characteristic properties that populations lack. These properties, known collectively as *community structure* and *community functioning,* include the number and types of species present, the relative abundance of each species, the interactions among different species, community resilience to disturbances, energy and nutrient flow throughout the community, and productivity. **Community ecology** is the description and analysis of patterns and processes within the community. Finding common patterns and processes in a wide variety of communities—for example, a pond community, a pine forest community, and a sagebrush desert community—helps ecologists understand community structure and functioning.

Communities are exceedingly difficult to study because a large number of individuals of many different species interact with

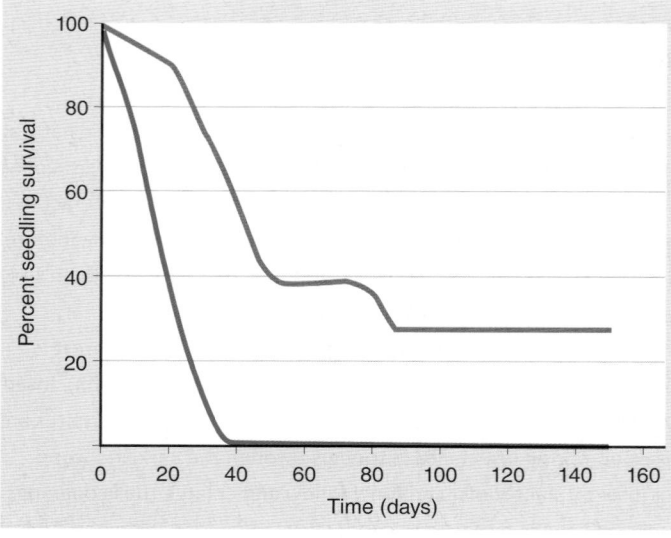

(b) Field mouse-ear chickweed (*Cerastium arvense*) plants were planted and grown within (*red*) and outside (*blue*) clumps of *Laretia acaulis.*

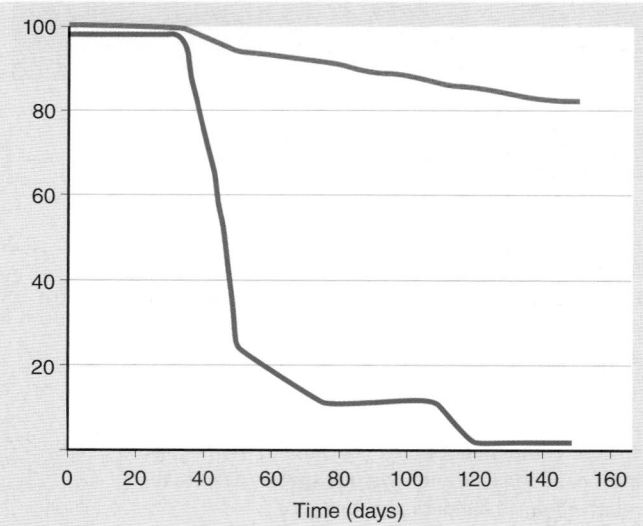

(c) Alpine barley (*Hordeum comosum*) plants were planted and grown within (*red*) and outside (*blue*) clumps of *Laretia acaulis.*

FIGURE 54-1 Facilitation in alpine communities

(**b** and **c,** Adapted from Cavieres, L. A. et al. "Positive Interactions between Alpine Plant Species and the Nurse Cushion Plants *Laretia acaulis* Do Not Increase with Elevation in the Andes of Central Chile." *New Phytologist,* 2005.)

one another and are interdependent in a variety of ways. Species compete with one another for food, water, living space, and other resources. (Used in this context, a *resource* is anything from the environment that meets needs of a particular species.) Some organisms kill and eat other organisms.

Some species form intimate associations with one another, whereas other species seem only distantly connected. Certain species interact in positive ways, in a process known as **facilitation,** which modifies and enhances the local environment for other species. For example, alpine plants in harsh mountain environments grow faster and larger and reproduce more successfully when certain other plants are growing nearby (**FIG. 54-1**).

Also, each organism plays one of three main roles in community life: producer, consumer, or decomposer. Unraveling the many positive and negative, direct and indirect interactions of organisms living together as a community is one of the goals of community ecologists.

Community interactions are complex and often not readily apparent

During the late 1990s, an intricate relationship emerged among acorn production, white-footed mice, deer, gypsy moth population growth, and the potential occurrence of Lyme disease in humans (**FIG. 54-2**). Large-scale experiments conducted in oak forests of the northeastern United States linked bumper acorn crops, which occur every three to four years, to booming mouse populations (the mice eat the acorns). Because the mice also eat gypsy moth pupae, high acorn conditions also lead to low populations of

gypsy moths. This outcome helps the oaks because gypsy moths cause serious defoliation. However, abundant acorns also attract tick-bearing deer to oak forests. The ticks' hungry offspring feed on the mice, which often carry the Lyme disease–causing bacterium. The bacterium infects the maturing ticks and, in turn, spreads to humans who are bitten by affected ticks. In 2006, scientists concluded that it is possible to predict which years pose the greatest potential threat of Lyme disease to humans based on when oaks are most productive. The risk of Lyme disease is greater two years following a bumper acorn crop.

Within a community, no species exists independently of other species. As the preceding example shows, the populations of a community interact with and affect one another in complex ways that are not always obvious. Three main types of interactions occur among species in a community: competition, predation, and symbiosis. Before we address these interactions, however, we need to examine the way of life of a given species in its community.

The niche is a species' ecological role in the community

Every species is thought to have its own ecological role within the structure and function of a community; we call this role its **ecological niche.** Although the concept of ecological niche has been in use in ecology since early in the 20th century, Yale ecologist G. E. Hutchinson first described in 1957 the multidimensional nature of the niche that is accepted today. An ecological niche takes into account all biotic and abiotic aspects of the species' existence—that is, all the physical, chemical, and biological factors that the

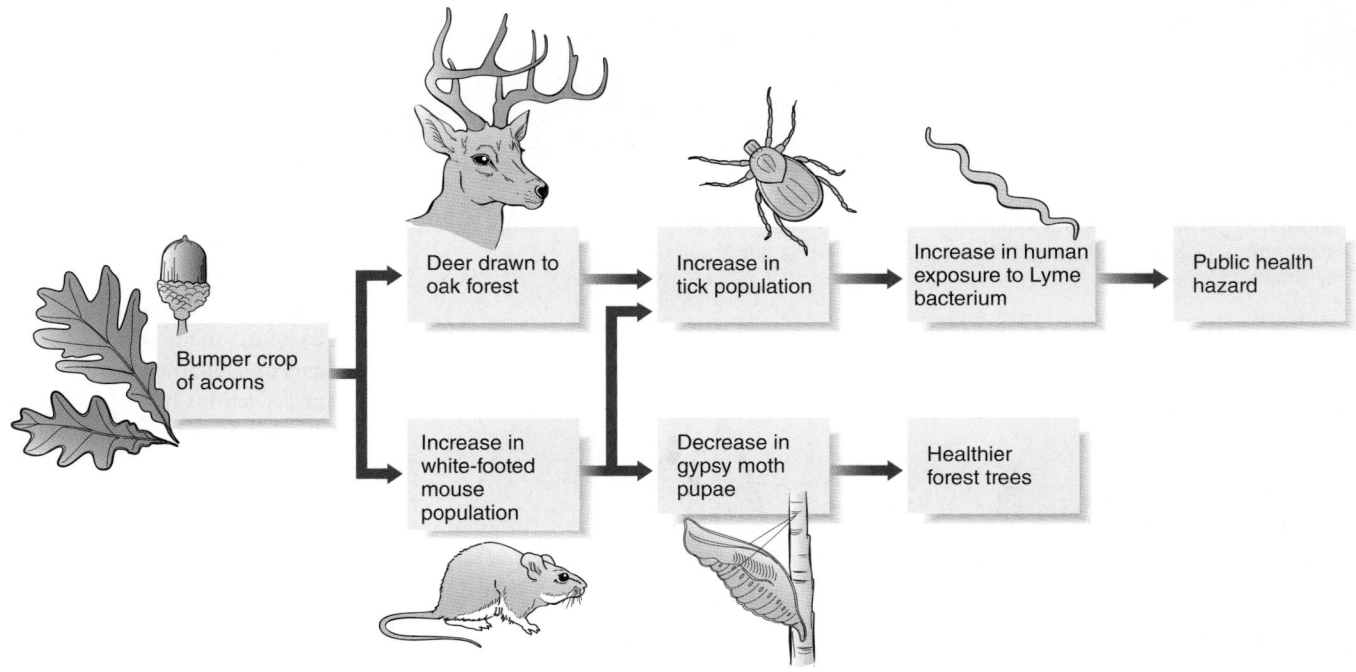

FIGURE 54-2 Connections to the size of an acorn crop

When there is a bumper crop of acorns, more mice survive and breed in winter, and more deer are attracted to oak forests. Both mice and deer are hosts of ticks that may carry the Lyme disease bacterium to humans. Abundant mice also reduce gypsy moth populations, thereby improving the health of forest trees.

species needs to survive, remain healthy, and reproduce. Among other things, the niche includes the local environment in which a species lives—its **habitat.** A niche also encompasses what a species eats, what eats it, what organisms it competes with, and how it interacts with and is influenced by the abiotic components of its environment, such as light, temperature, and moisture. The niche thus represents the totality of adaptations by a species to its environment, its use of resources, and the lifestyle to which it is suited. Although a complete description of an organism's ecological niche involves many dimensions and is difficult to define precisely, ecologists usually confine their studies to one or a few niche variables, such as feeding behaviors or ability to tolerate temperature extremes.

The ecological niche of a species is far broader hypothetically than in actuality. A species is usually capable of using much more of its environment's resources or of living in a wider assortment of habitats than it actually does. The potential ecological niche of a species is its **fundamental niche,** but various factors, such as competition with other species, may exclude it from part of this fundamental niche. Thus, the lifestyle that a species actually pursues and the resources it actually uses make up its **realized niche.**

An example may help make this distinction clear. The green anole, a lizard native to Florida and other southeastern states, perches on trees, shrubs, walls, or fences during the day, waiting for insect and spider prey (**FIG. 54-3a**). In the past these little lizards were widespread in Florida. Several years ago, however, a related species, the brown anole, was introduced from Cuba into southern Florida and quickly became common (**FIG. 54-3b**). Suddenly, the green anoles became rare, apparently driven out of their habitat by competition from the slightly larger brown anoles. Careful investigation disclosed, however, that green anoles were still around. They were now confined largely to the vegetation in wetlands and to the foliated crowns of trees, where they were less easily seen.

The habitat portion of the green anole's fundamental niche includes the trunks and crowns of trees, exterior house walls, and many other locations. Once the brown anoles became established in the green anole habitat, they drove the green anoles from all but wetlands and tree crowns; competition between the two species shrank the green anoles' realized niche (**FIGS. 54-3c** and **d**). Because communities consist of numerous species, many of which compete to some extent, the interactions among them produce each species' realized niche.

Limiting resources restrict the ecological niche of a species

A species' structural, physiological, and behavioral adaptations determine its tolerance for environmental extremes. If any feature of an environment lies outside the bounds of its tolerance, then the species cannot live there. Just as you would not expect to find a cactus living in a pond, you would not expect water lilies in a desert.

The environmental factors that actually determine a species' ecological niche are difficult to identify. For this reason, the concept of ecological niche is largely abstract, although some of its dimensions can be experimentally determined. Any environmental resource that, because it is scarce or unfavorable, tends to restrict the ecological niche of a species is called a **limiting resource.**

Most of the limiting resources that have been studied are simple variables, such as the soil's mineral content, temperature extremes, and precipitation amounts. Such investigations have disclosed that any factor exceeding the tolerance of a species, or present in quantities smaller than the required minimum, limits the presence of that species in a community. By their interaction, such factors help define the ecological niche for a species.

Limiting resources may affect only part of an organism's life cycle. For example, although adult blue crabs live in fresh or slightly brackish water, they do not be-

(a) The green anole (*Anolis carolinensis*) is the only anole species native to North America. Males are about 12.5 cm (5 in) long; females are slightly smaller.

(b) The 15.2 cm (6 in) long brown anole (*A. sagrei*) was introduced to Florida. It is native to Cuba and the Bahamas.

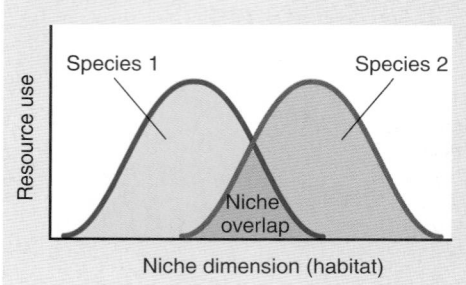

(c) Positions of the two species along a single niche dimension (in this case, habitat). Species 1 represents the green anole, and Species 2 represents the brown anole. The fundamental niches of the two lizards overlap.

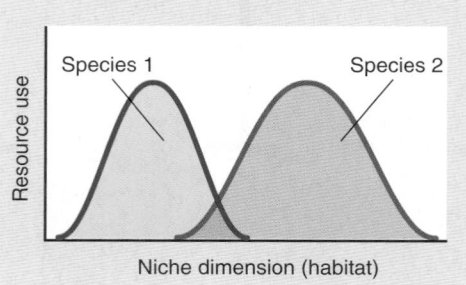

(d) The brown anole outcompetes the green anole in the area where their niches overlap, restricting the niche of the green anole.

FIGURE 54-3 Effect of competition on an organism's realized niche

come permanently established in such areas because their larvae (immature forms) require salt water. Similarly, the ring-necked pheasant, a popular game bird native to Eurasia, has been widely introduced in North America but has not become established in the southern United States. The adult birds do well there, but the eggs do not develop properly in the warmer southern temperatures.

Biotic and abiotic factors influence a species' ecological niche

In the 1960s, U.S. ecologist Joseph H. Connell investigated biotic and abiotic factors that affect the distribution of two barnacle species in the rocky *intertidal zone* along the coast of Scotland. The intertidal zone is a challenging environment, and organisms in the intertidal zone must tolerate exposure to the drying air during low tides. Barnacles are sessile crustaceans whose bodies are covered by a shell of calcium carbonate (see Fig. 31-22a). When the shell is open, feathery appendages extend to filter food from the water.

Along the coast of Scotland, more adults of one barnacle species, *Balanus balanoides,* are attached on lower rocks in the intertidal zone than are adults of the other species, *Chthamalus stellatus* (**FIG. 54-4**). The distributions of the two species do not overlap, although immature larvae of both species live together in the intertidal zone. Connell manipulated the two populations to determine what factors were affecting their distribution. When he removed *Chtha-*

malus from the upper rocks, *Balanus* barnacles did not expand into the vacant area. Connell's experiments showed that *Chthamalus* is more resistant than *Balanus* to desiccation when the tide retreats. However, when Connell removed *Balanus* from the lower rocks, *Chthamalus* expanded into the lower parts of the intertidal zone. The two species compete for space, and *Balanus,* which is larger and grows faster, outcompetes the smaller *Chthamalus* barnacles.

Competition among barnacle species for the limiting resource of living space was one of the processes that Connell's research demonstrated. We now examine other aspects of competition that various ecologists have revealed in both laboratory and field studies.

Competition is intraspecific or interspecific

Competition occurs when two or more individuals attempt to use the same essential resource, such as food, water, shelter, living space, or sunlight. Because resources are often in limited supply in the environment, their use by one individual decreases the amount available to others (**TABLE 54-1**). If a tree in a dense forest grows taller than surrounding trees, for example, it absorbs more of the incoming sunlight. Less sunlight is therefore available for nearby trees that are shaded by the taller tree. Competition occurs among individuals within a population (**intraspecific competition**) or between different species (**interspecific competition**). (Intraspecific competition was discussed in Chapter 53.)

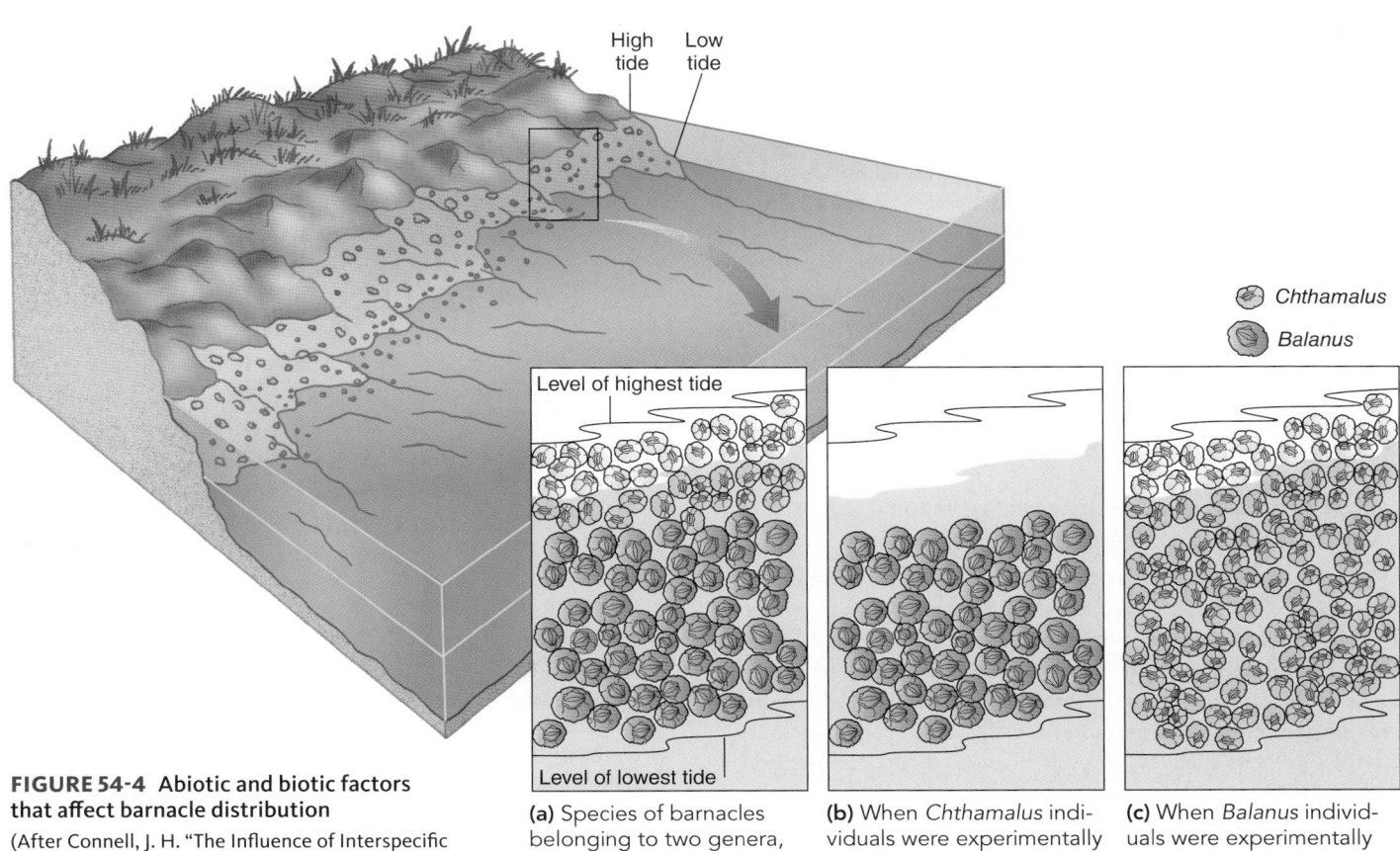

FIGURE 54-4 Abiotic and biotic factors that affect barnacle distribution
(After Connell, J. H. "The Influence of Interspecific Competition and Other Factors on the Distribution of the Barnacle *Chthamalus stellatus*." *Ecology*, Vol. 42, 1961.)

(a) Species of barnacles belonging to two genera, *Chthamalus* and *Balanus,* grow in the intertidal zone of a rocky shore in Scotland.

(b) When *Chthamalus* individuals were experimentally removed, *Balanus* individuals did not expand into their section of the rock.

(c) When *Balanus* individuals were experimentally removed, *Chthamalus* individuals spread into the empty area.

TABLE 54-1

TABLE 54-1 Ecological Interactions among Species

Interaction	Effect on Species 1	Effect on Species 2
Competition between species 1 and species 2	Harmful	Harmful
Predation of species 2 (prey) by species 1 (predator)	Beneficial	Harmful
Symbiosis		
Mutualism of species 1 and species 2	Beneficial	Beneficial
Commensalism of species 1 with species 2	Beneficial	No effect
Parasitism by species 1 (parasite) on species 2 (host)	Beneficial	Harmful

Ecologists traditionally assumed that competition is the most important determinant of both the number of species found in a community and the size of each population. Today ecologists recognize that competition is only one of many interacting biotic and abiotic factors that affect community structure. Furthermore, competition is not always a straightforward, direct interaction. Several kinds of flowering plants, for example, live in a young pine forest and presumably compete with the conifers for such resources as soil moisture and soil minerals. Their relationship, however, is more complex than simple competition. The flowers produce nectar that is consumed by some insect species that also prey on needle-eating insects, thereby reducing the number of insects feeding on pines. It is therefore difficult to assess the overall effect of flowering plants on pines. If the flowering plants were removed from the community, would the pines grow faster because they were no longer competing for necessary resources? Or would the increased presence of needle-eating insects (caused by fewer predatory insects) inhibit pine growth?

Short-term experiments in which one competing plant species is removed from a forest community often have demonstrated an improved growth for the remaining species. However, very few studies have tested the long-term effects on forest species of the removal of a single competing species. These long-term effects may be subtle, indirect, and difficult to ascertain; they may lessen or negate the short-term effects of competition for resources.

Competition between species with overlapping niches may lead to competitive exclusion

When two species are similar, as are the green and brown anoles or the two species of barnacles, their fundamental niches may overlap. However, based on experimental and modeling work, many ecologists think that no two species indefinitely occupy the same niche in the same community. According to the **competitive exclusion principle,** it is hypothesized that one species excludes another from its niche as a result of interspecific competition. Although it is possible for species to compete for some necessary resource without being total competitors, two species with absolutely identical ecological niches cannot coexist. Coexistence occurs, however, if the overlap between the two niches is reduced. In the lizard example, direct competition between the two species

was reduced as the brown anole excluded the green anole from most of its former habitat.

The initial evidence that interspecific competition contributes to a species' realized niche came from a series of laboratory experiments by the Russian biologist Georgyi F. Gause in the 1930s (see descriptions of other experiments by Gause in Chapter 53). In one study Gause grew populations of two species of protozoa, *Paramecium aurelia* and the larger *P. caudatum,* in controlled conditions (**FIG. 54-5**). When grown in separate test tubes, that is, in the absence of the second species, the population of each species quickly increased to a level imposed by the resources and remained there

KEY EXPERIMENT

QUESTION: Can competitive exclusion be demonstrated in the laboratory under controlled conditions?

HYPOTHESIS: When two species of paramecia (ciliated protozoa) are grown together in a mixed culture, one species outcompetes the other.

EXPERIMENT: Gause grew two species of paramecia, both separately and together.

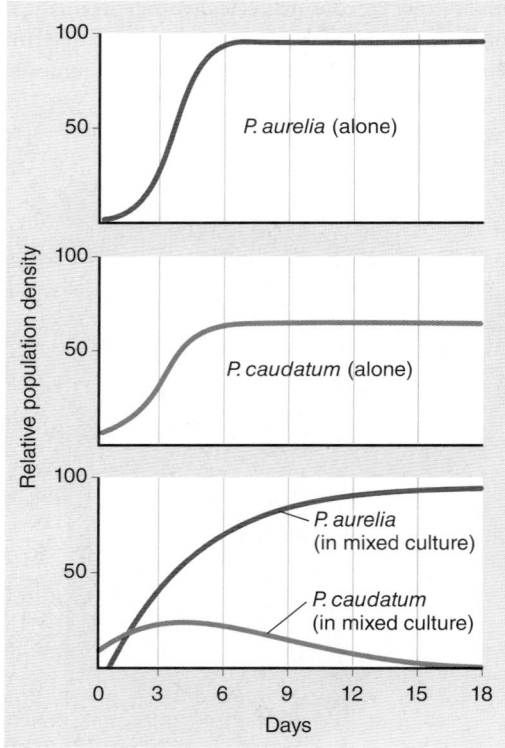

RESULTS AND CONCLUSION: The top and middle graphs show how each species of *Paramecium* flourishes when grown alone. The bottom graph shows how they grow together, in competition with each other. In a mixed culture, *P. aurelia* outcompetes *P. caudatum,* resulting in competitive exclusion.

Source: Adapted from Gause, G. F. *The Struggle for Existence.* Williams & Wilkins, Baltimore, 1934.

FIGURE 54-5 *Animated* G. F. Gause's classic experiment on interspecific competition for some time thereafter. When grown together, however, only *P. aurelia* thrived, whereas *P. caudatum* dwindled and eventually died out. Under different sets of culture conditions, *P. caudatum* prevailed over *P. aurelia*. Gause interpreted these results to mean that although one set of conditions favored one species, a different set favored the other. Nonetheless, because both species were so similar, in time one or the other would eventually triumph. Similar experiments with competing species of fruit flies, mice, beetles, and annual plants have supported Gause's results: one species thrives, and the other eventually dies out.

Thus, competition has adverse effects on species that use a limited resource and may result in competitive exclusion of one or more species. It therefore follows that over time natural selection should favor individuals of each species that avoid or reduce competition for environmental resources. Reduced competition among coexisting species as a result of each species' niche differing from the others in one or more ways is called **resource partitioning.** Resource partitioning is well-documented in animals; studies in tropical forests of Central and South America demonstrate little overlap in the diets of fruit-eating birds, primates, and bats that coexist in the same habitat. Although fruits are the primary food for several hundred bird, primate, and bat species, the wide variety of fruits available has allowed fruit eaters to specialize, which reduces competition.

Resource partitioning may also include timing of feeding, location of feeding, nest sites, and other aspects of a species' ecological niche. Princeton ecologist Robert MacArthur's study of five North American warbler species is a classic example of resource partitioning (**FIG. 54-6**). Although initially the warblers' niches seemed nearly identical, MacArthur found that individuals of each species spend most of their feeding time in different portions of the spruces and other conifer trees they frequent. They also move in different directions through the canopy, consume different combinations of insects, and nest at slightly different times.

Difference in root depth is an example of resource partitioning in plants. For example, three common annuals found in certain abandoned fields are smartweed, Indian mallow, and bristly foxtail. Smartweed roots extend deep into the soil, Indian mallow roots grow to a medium depth, and bristly foxtail roots are shallow. This difference reduces competition for the same soil resources—water and minerals—by allowing the plants to exploit different portions of the resource.

Character displacement is an adaptive consequence of interspecific competition

Sometimes populations of two similar species occur together in some locations and separately in others. Where their geographic distributions overlap, the two species tend to differ more in their structural, ecological, and behavioral characteristics than they do where each occurs in separate geographic areas. Such divergence in traits in two similar species living in the same geographic area is known as **character displacement.** Biologists think that character displacement reduces competition between two species because their differences give them somewhat different ecological niches in the same environment.

There are several well-documented examples of character displacement between two closely related species. The flowers of

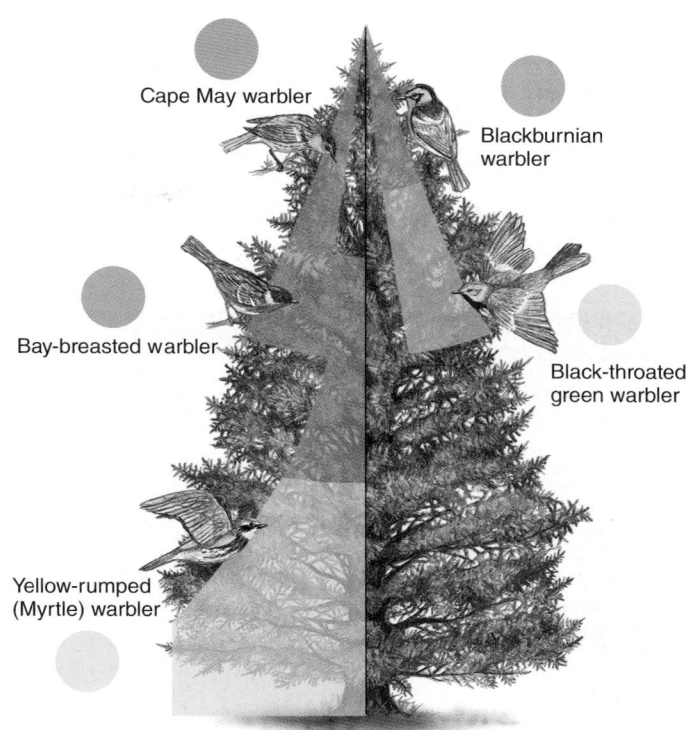

FIGURE 54-6 *Animated* **Resource partitioning**
Each warbler species spends at least half its foraging time in its designated area of a spruce tree, thereby reducing the competition among warbler species. (After MacArthur, R. H. "Population Ecology of Some Warblers of Northeastern Coniferous Forests." *Ecology*, Vol. 39, 1958.)

two *Solanum* species in Mexico are quite similar in areas where either one or the other occurs. However, where their distributions overlap, the two species differ significantly in flower size and are pollinated by different kinds of bees. In other words, character displacement reduces interspecific competition, in this case for the same animal pollinator.

The bill sizes of Darwin's finches provide another example of character displacement (**FIG. 54-7**). On large islands in the Galápagos where the medium ground finch (*Geospiza fortis*) and the small ground finch (*G. fuliginosa*) occur together, their bill depths are distinctive. *Geospiza fuliginosa* has a smaller bill depth that enables it to crack small seeds, whereas *G. fortis* has a larger bill depth that enables it to crack medium-sized seeds. However, *G. fortis* and *G. fuliginosa* also live on separate islands. Where the two species live separately, bill depths are about the same intermediate size, perhaps because there is no competition from the other species.

Although these examples of the coexistence of similar species are explained in terms of character displacement, the character displacement hypothesis has been demonstrated in nature in only a few instances. In 2006, Peter and Rosemary Grant, who have studied Darwin's finches in the Galápagos Islands for more than 30 years, reported in the journal *Science* another example of character displacement in Darwin's finches. The medium ground finch (*G. fortis*) originally lived on one of the small Galápagos islands by itself. Different *G. fortis* individuals had varying beak sizes that allowed them to eat small, medium, or large seeds. However, in recent years the large ground finch (*G. magnirostris*) colonized the island and began to compete with the medium ground finch for the larger seeds. A severe drought reduced the seed supply, putting additional pressure on the medium finch population. In response, the medium ground finch's beak quickly diverged, becoming significantly smaller in length, depth, and width on average than it had been. The altered population of medium ground finches now

---

KEY EXPERIMENT

QUESTION: Can character displacement be demonstrated in the wild?

HYPOTHESIS: Two species of finches are more different where they occur together than where they occur separately.

EXPERIMENT: Two species of Darwin's finches in the Galápagos Islands were observed on islands where they occur separately and on an island where they exist together. Bill depth **(a),** which varies considerably in the two species, was measured in the different environments.

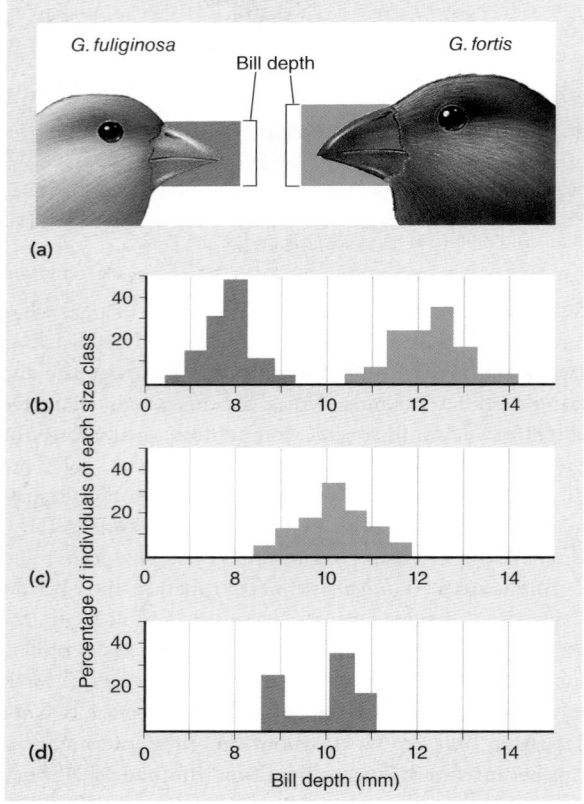

RESULTS AND CONCLUSION: (b) Where the two species are found on the same island (Santa Cruz), *G. fuliginosa* (*pink*) has a smaller average bill depth than *G. fortis* (*blue*). Where they occur on separate islands (**c,** on Daphne Major and **d,** on Los Hermanos), the average bill depths of each are similar. Thus, this is an example of character displacement.

Source: After Lack, D. *Darwin's Finches.* Cambridge University Press, Cambridge, 1947.

FIGURE 54-7 Character displacement

---

consumes small seeds almost exclusively; their small beaks cannot crack the larger seeds preferred by the large ground finch.

Natural selection shapes the bodies and behaviors of both predator and prey

Predation is the consumption of one species, the **prey,** by another, the **predator** (see Table 54-1). Predation includes animals eating other animals, as well as animals eating plants (*herbivory*). Predation has resulted in an evolutionary "arms race," with the evolution of predator strategies (more efficient ways to catch prey) and prey strategies (better ways to escape the predator). A predator that is more efficient at catching prey exerts a strong selective force on its prey. Over time, adaptations that reduce the probability of being captured may evolve in the prey species. These adaptations, in turn, exert a strong selective force on the predator. This type of interdependent evolution of two interacting species is known as **coevolution** (see discussion of coevolution in Chapter 37).

We now consider several adaptations related to predator–prey interactions. These include predator strategies (pursuit and ambush) and prey strategies (plant defenses and animal defenses). Keep in mind as you read these descriptions that such strategies are not "chosen" by the respective predators or prey. New traits arise randomly in a population as a result of genetic changes. Some new traits are beneficial, some are harmful, and others have no effect. Beneficial strategies, or traits, persist in a population because such characteristics make the individuals that have them well suited to thrive and reproduce. In contrast, characteristics that make the individuals that have them poorly suited to their environment tend to disappear in a population.

Pursuit and ambush are two predator strategies

A brown pelican sights its prey—a fish—while in flight. Less than 2 seconds after diving into the water at a speed as great as 72 km/h (45 mph), it has its catch. Orcas (formerly known as killer whales) hunt in packs and often herd salmon or tuna into a cove so they are easier to catch. Any trait that increases hunting efficiency, such as the speed of brown pelicans or the intelligence of orcas, favors predators that pursue their prey. Because these carnivores must process information quickly during the pursuit of prey, their brains are generally larger, relative to body size, than those of the prey they pursue.

Ambush is another effective way to catch prey. The yellow crab spider, for example, is the same color as the white or yellow flowers on which it hides (**FIG. 54-8**). This camouflage keeps unwary insects that visit the flower for nectar from noticing the spider until it is too late. It also fools birds that prey on the crab spider.

Predators that *attract* prey are particularly effective at ambushing. For example, a diverse group of deep-sea fishes called anglerfish possess rodlike luminescent lures close to their mouths to attract prey.

Chemical protection is an effective plant defense against herbivores

Plants cannot escape predators by fleeing, but they have several physical and chemical adaptations that protect them from be-

FIGURE 54-8 Ambush

A yellow crab spider (*Misumena vatia*) blends into its surroundings, waiting for an unwary insect to visit the flower. An effective predator strategy, ambush relies on surprising the prey.

ing eaten. The presence of spines, thorns, tough leathery leaves, or even thick wax on leaves discourages foraging herbivores from grazing. Other plants produce an array of protective chemicals that are unpalatable or even toxic to herbivores. The active ingredients in such plants as marijuana and tobacco affect hormone activity and nerve, muscle, liver, and kidney functions and may discourage foraging by herbivores. Interestingly, many of the chemical defenses in plants are useful to humans. India's neem tree, for example, contains chemicals effective against more than 100 species of herbivorous insects, mites, and nematodes. Nicotine from tobacco, pyrethrum from chrysanthemum, and rotenone from the derris plant are other examples of chemicals extracted and used as insecticides.

Milkweeds are an excellent example of the biochemical coevolution between plants and herbivores (**FIG. 54-9**). Milkweeds produce alkaloids and cardiac glycosides, chemicals that are poisonous to all animals except a small group of insects. The ability to either tolerate or metabolize the milkweed toxins has evolved in these insects. They eat milkweeds and avoid competition from other herbivorous insects because few others tolerate milkweed toxins. Predators also learn to avoid these insects, which accumulate the toxins in their tissues and therefore become toxic themselves. The black, white, and yellow coloration of the monarch caterpillar, a milkweed feeder, clearly announces its toxicity to predators that have learned to associate bright colors with illness. Conspicuous colors or patterns, which advertise a species' unpalatability to potential predators, are known as **aposematic coloration** (pronounced "ap'-uh-suh-mat'-ik"; from the Greek *apo*, "away," and *semat*, "a mark or sign"), or **warning coloration.**

Animal prey possess various defensive adaptations to avoid predators

Many animals, such as prairie voles and woodchucks, flee from predators by running to their underground burrows. Others have mechanical defenses, such as the barbed quills of a porcupine and the shell of a pond turtle. To discourage predators, the porcupine

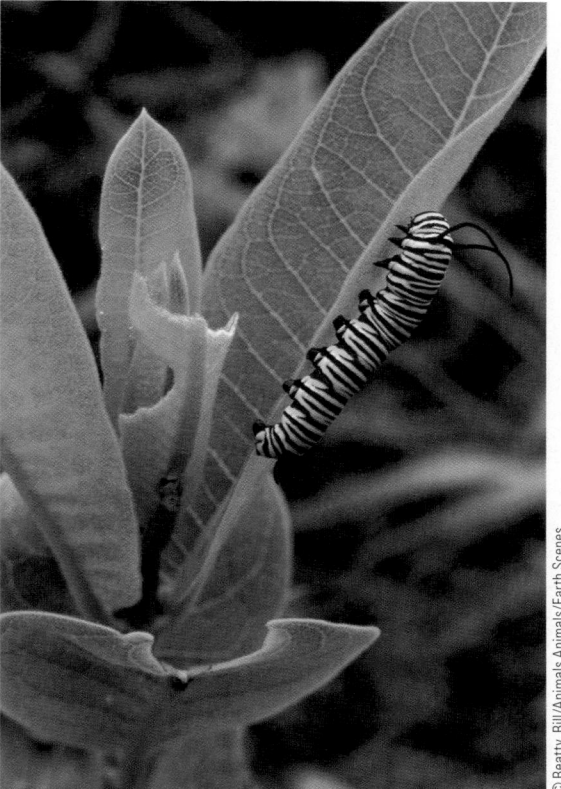

FIGURE 54-9 Plant chemical defenses

Toxic chemicals protect the common milkweed (*Asclepias syriaca*). Its leaves are poisonous to most herbivores except monarch caterpillars (*Danaus plexippus*) and a few other insects. Monarch caterpillars have bright aposematic coloration. Photographed in Michigan.

fish inflates itself to three times its normal size by pumping water into its stomach (see Fig. 32-14a). Some animals live in groups—for example, a herd of antelope, colony of honeybees, school of anchovies, or flock of pigeons. Because a group has so many eyes, ears, and noses watching, listening, and smelling for predators, this social behavior decreases the likelihood of a predator catching any one of them unaware.

Chemical defenses are also common among animal prey. The South American poison arrow frog (*Dendrobates*) stores poison in its skin. (These frogs obtain the toxins from ants and other insects in their diet.) The frog's bright aposematic coloration prompts avoidance by experienced predators (see Fig. 32-18a). Snakes and other animals that have tried once to eat a poisonous frog do not repeat their mistake! Other examples of aposematic coloration occur in the striped skunk, which sprays acrid chemicals from its anal glands, and the bombardier beetle, which spews harsh chemicals at potential predators (see Fig. 7-8).

Some animals have **cryptic coloration,** colors or markings that help them hide from predators by blending into their physical surroundings. Certain caterpillars resemble twigs so closely that you would never guess they were animals unless they moved. Pipefish are slender green fish that are almost perfectly camouflaged in green eelgrass. Leaf-tailed geckos in southern Madagascar resemble dead leaves or mossy bark, depending on the species (**FIG. 54-10**). Such

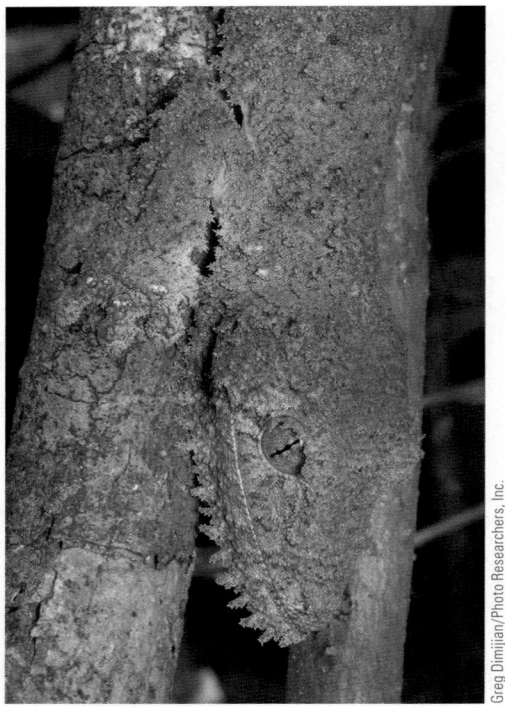

FIGURE 54-10 Cryptic coloration

The mossy leaf-tailed gecko (*Uroplatus sikorae*) hunts for insects by night and sleeps pressed against a tree branch by day. It is virtually invisible when it sleeps (look closely to see its head and front foot). Photographed in a rain forest in southern Madagascar.

cryptic coloration has been preserved and accentuated by means of natural selection. Predators are less likely to capture animals with cryptic coloration. Such animals are therefore more likely to live to maturity and produce offspring that also carry the genes for cryptic coloration.

Sometimes a defenseless species (a *mimic*) is protected from predation by its resemblance to a species that is dangerous in some way (a *model*). Such a strategy is known as **Batesian mimicry.** Many examples of this phenomenon exist. For example, a harmless scarlet king snake looks so much like a venomous coral snake that predators may avoid it (**FIG. 54-11**). Interestingly, the range of the scarlet king snake extends far beyond that of the coral snake. In an area where coral snakes do not occur, having the coloration of the model confers no special advantage to the king snake and may be harmful, triggering natural selection. This seems to be the case: in 2008 scientists reported in the journal *Nature* that scarlet king snake populations located far from coral snakes have undergone natural selection and look less like their model.

In **Müllerian mimicry,** different species (*co-models*), all of which are poisonous, harmful, or distasteful, resemble one another. Although their harmfulness protects them as individual species, their similarity in appearance works as an added advantage because potential predators more easily learn a single common aposematic coloration. Scientists hypothesize that viceroy and monarch butterflies are an example of Müllerian mimicry (see *Inquiring About: Mimicry in Butterflies*).

Symbiosis involves a close association between species

Symbiosis is any intimate relationship or association between members of two or more species. Usually, symbiosis involves one species living on or in another species. The partners of a symbiotic relationship, called **symbionts,** may benefit from, be unaffected by, or be harmed by the relationship (see Table 54-1). Examples of symbiosis occur across all of the domains and kingdoms of life. Most of the thousands, or perhaps even millions, of symbiotic associations are products of coevolution. Symbiosis takes three forms: mutualism, commensalism, and parasitism.

(a) Scarlet king snake

(b) Eastern coral snake

FIGURE 54-11 Batesian mimicry

In this example, **(a)** the scarlet king snake (*Lampropeltis triangulum elapsoides*) is the mimic and **(b)** the eastern coral snake (*Micrurus fulvius fulvius*) is the model. Note that the red and yellow warning colors touch on the coral snake but do not touch on the harmless mimic.

MIMICRY IN BUTTERFLIES

Why do some butterfly species resemble one another? The monarch butterfly (*Danaus plexippus*), for example, is an attractive insect found throughout much of North America (see figure, *left side*). As a caterpillar, it feeds exclusively on milkweed leaves. The milky white liquid produced by the milkweed plant contains poisons that the insect tolerates but that remain in its tissues for life. When a young bird encounters and tries to eat its first monarch butterfly, the bird becomes sick and vomits. Thereafter, the bird avoids eating the distinctively marked insect.

Many people confuse the viceroy butterfly (*Limenitis archippus;* see figure, *right side*) with the monarch. The viceroy, which is found throughout most of North America, is approximately the same size, and the color and markings of its wings are almost identical to those of the monarch. As caterpillars, viceroys eat cottonwood, aspen, and willow leaves, which apparently do not contain poisonous substances.

During the past century, it was thought that the viceroy butterfly was a tasty food for birds but that its close resemblance to monarchs gave it some protection against being eaten. In other words, birds that had learned to associate the distinctive markings and coloration of the monarch butterfly with its bad taste tended to avoid viceroys because they were similarly marked. The viceroy butterfly was therefore considered a classic example of Batesian mimicry.

In 1991, ecologists David Ritland and Lincoln Brower of the University of Florida reported the results of an experiment that tested the long-held notion that birds like the taste of viceroys but avoid eating them because of their resemblance to monarchs. They removed the wings of different kinds of butterflies—monarchs, viceroys, and several tasty species—and fed the seemingly identical wingless bodies to red-winged blackbirds. The results were surprising: monarchs and viceroys were equally distasteful to the birds.

As a result of this work, ecologists are re-evaluating the evolutionary significance of different types of mimicry. Rather than an example of Batesian mimicry, monarchs and viceroys may be an example of Müllerian mimicry, in which two or more different species that are distasteful or poisonous have come to resemble each other during the course of evolution. This likeness provides an adaptive advantage because predators learn quickly to avoid all butterflies with the coloration and markings of monarchs and viceroys. As a result, fewer butterflies of either species die, and more individuals survive to reproduce.

The butterfly study provides us with a useful reminder about the process of science. Expansion of knowledge in science is an ongoing enterprise, and newly acquired evidence helps scientists re-evaluate current models or ideas. Thus, scientific knowledge and understanding are continually changing.

Müllerian mimicry. Evidence suggests that monarch (*left*) and viceroy (*right*) butterflies are an example of Müllerian mimicry, in which two or more poisonous, harmful, or distasteful organisms resemble each other.

Benefits are shared in mutualism

Mutualism is a symbiotic relationship in which both partners benefit. Mutualism is either obligate (essential for the survival of both species) or facultative (either partner can live alone under certain conditions).

The association between **nitrogen-fixing bacteria** of the genus *Rhizobium* and legumes (plants such as peas, beans, and clover) is an example of mutualism (see Fig. 55-9). Nitrogen-fixing bacteria, which live inside nodules on the roots of legumes, supply the plants with most of the nitrogen they require to manufacture such nitrogen-containing compounds as chlorophylls, proteins, and nucleic acids. The legumes supply sugars and other energy-rich organic molecules to their bacterial symbionts.

Another example of mutualism is the association between reef-building animals and dinoflagellates called **zooxanthellae.** These symbiotic protists live inside cells of the coral polyp (the coral forms a vacuole around the algal cell), where they photosynthesize and provide the animal with carbon and nitrogen compounds as well as oxygen (**FIG. 54-12**). Calcium carbonate skeletons form around the coral bodies much faster when zooxanthellae are

FIGURE 54-12 Mutualism

The greenish brown specks in these polyps of stony coral (*Pocillopora*) are zooxanthellae, algae that live symbiotically within the coral's translucent cells and supply the coral with carbon and nitrogen compounds. In return, the coral provides the zooxanthellae with nitrogen in the form of ammonia.

present; their faster growth helps the corals to dominate their location on a reef. The corals, in turn, supply the zooxanthellae with waste products such as ammonia, which the algae use to make nitrogen compounds for both partners.

Mycorrhizae are mutualistic associations between fungi and the roots of plants. The association is common; biologists think that about 80% of all plant species have mycorrhizae. The fungus, which grows around and into the root as well as into the surrounding soil, absorbs essential minerals, especially phosphorus, from the soil and provides them to the plant. In return, the plant provides the fungus with organic molecules produced by photosynthesis. Plants grow more vigorously in the presence of mycorrhizal fungi (see Figs. 29-19 and 36-11), and they better tolerate environmental stressors such as drought and high soil temperatures. Indeed, some plants cannot maintain themselves under natural conditions if the fungi with which they normally form mycorrhizae are not present.

Commensalism is taking without harming

Commensalism is a type of symbiosis in which one species benefits and the other one is neither harmed nor helped. One example of commensalism is the relationship between social insects and scavengers, such as mites, beetles, or millipedes, that live in the social insects' nests. Certain types of silverfish, for example, move along in permanent association with marching columns of army ants and share the abundant food caught in the ant raids. The army ants derive no apparent benefit or harm from the silverfish.

Another example of commensalism is the relationship between a host tree and its epiphytes, which are smaller plants, such as orchids, ferns, or Spanish moss, attached to the host's branches (**FIG. 54-13**). The epiphyte anchors itself to the tree but does not obtain nutrients or water directly from it. Living on the tree enables it to obtain adequate light, water (as rainfall dripping down the branches), and required minerals (washed out of the tree's leaves by rainfall). Thus, the epiphyte benefits from the association, whereas the tree is apparently unaffected. (Epiphytes harm their host, however, if they are present in a large enough number to block sunlight from the host's leaves; in this instance, the relationship is no longer commensalism.)

Parasitism is taking at another's expense

Parasitism is a symbiotic relationship in which one member, the **parasite,** benefits, whereas the other, the **host,** is adversely affected. The parasite obtains nourishment from its host. A parasite rarely kills its host directly but may weaken it, rendering it more vulnerable to predators, competitors, or abiotic stressors. When a parasite causes disease and sometimes the death of a host, it is called a **pathogen.**

Ticks and other parasites that live outside the host's body are called **ectoparasites.** Figure 32-9 shows a lamprey, an ectoparasite on fish. Parasites such as tapeworms that live within the host are called **endoparasites.** Parasitism is a successful lifestyle; by one estimate, more than two-thirds of all species are parasites, and more than 100 species of parasites live in or on the human species alone! Examples of human parasites include *Entamoeba histolytica,*

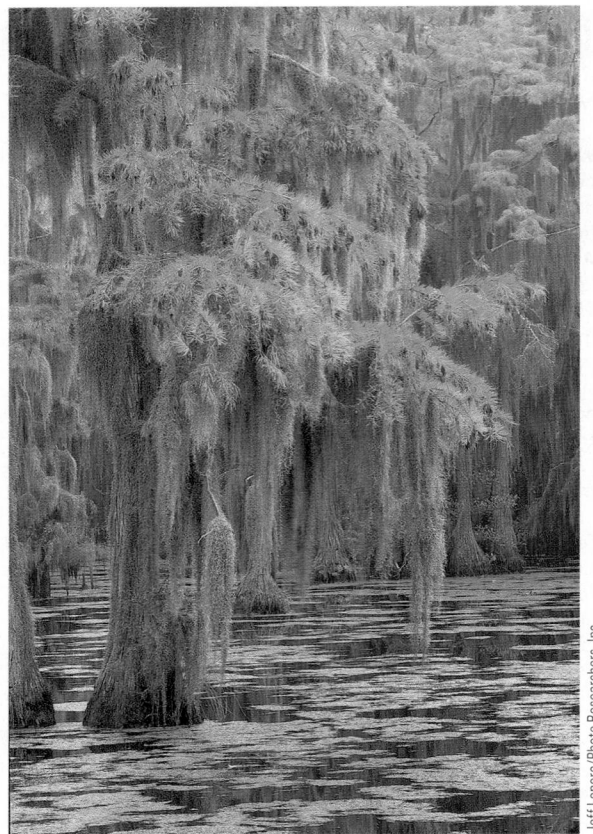

FIGURE 54-13 Commensalism

Spanish moss (*Tillandsia usneoides*) is a gray-colored epiphyte that hangs suspended from larger plants in the southeastern United States. Spanish moss is not a moss but a flowering plant in the pineapple family. Although it is often 6 m (20 ft) or longer, it is nonparasitic and does not harm the host tree. Photographed in autumn in North Carolina, hanging from a bald cypress whose foliage has turned color.

an amoeba that causes amoebic dysentery; *Plasmodium,* an apicomplexan that causes malaria; and a variety of parasitic worms, such as blood flukes, tapeworms, pinworms, and hookworms (see Figs. 31-9 and 31-11).

Since the 1980s, wild and domestic honeybees in the United States have been dying off; for example, beekeepers lost roughly half of their bees in 2005, according to the U.S. Department of Agriculture. Although habitat loss, severe weather, and pesticide use have contributed to the problem, varroa mites and smaller tracheal mites have been a major reason for the honeybee decline (**FIG. 54-14**).

Review

- How are acorns, gypsy moths, and Lyme disease related?
- Why is an organism's realized niche usually narrower, or more restricted, than its fundamental niche?
- What is the principle of competitive exclusion?
- What are the three kinds of symbiosis?

100 μm

FIGURE 54-14 Parasitism

Microscopic tracheal mites (*Acarapis woodi*) are endoparasites that live in the tracheal tubes of honeybees, clogging their airways so they cannot breathe efficiently. Tracheal mites also suck the bees' circulatory fluid, weakening and eventually killing them. Entomologists think the larger varroa mites (*not shown*), which are ectoparasites that also feed on the circulatory fluid, are more devastating to honeybee populations than tracheal mites. Mites may also transmit viruses to their honeybee hosts.

54.2 STRENGTH AND DIRECTION OF COMMUNITY INTERACTIONS

LEARNING OBJECTIVES

6   Distinguish between keystone species and dominant species.

7   Distinguish between bottom-up and top-down processes in ecosystem regulation.

There is a great deal of variation in the strength and direction of interactions among species within ecological communities. Some species, known as *keystone species,* are present in a community in low abundance and/or biomass but have strong effects on their communities. Other species, known as *dominant species,* exert strong effects on their communities because they are present in great abundance and/or biomass.

Two types of control affect ecological communities, bottom-up processes and top-down processes. In *bottom-up processes,* nutrient availability or food organisms whose population is directly affected by nutrient availability affect the abundance of other community organisms. In *top-down processes,* predators affect the abundance of other populations in the community. We now examine these aspects of interactions among species within ecological communities.

Other species of a community depend on or are greatly affected by keystone species

Certain species, called **keystone species,** are crucial in determining the nature of the entire community, that is, its species composition and ecosystem functioning. Keystone species are usually not the most abundant species in the community. Although present in relatively small numbers, the individuals of a keystone species profoundly influence the entire community because they often affect the amount of available food, water, or some other resource. Thus, the impact of keystone species is greatly disproportionate to their abundance. Identifying and protecting keystone species are crucial goals of conservation biology (see Chapter 57). If a keystone species disappears from a community, many other species in that community may become more common or rarer, or may even disappear.

The term *keystone* species was coined by ecologist Robert T. Paine in 1969, based on his experimental studies along the Pacific coast in the state of Washington (**FIG. 54-15**). Paine removed a predatory sea star, *Pisaster ochraceus,* from a rocky intertidal community that included barnacles, mussels, limpets, and chitons, all of which the sea star preyed on. He observed the changes in community structure that resulted and compared these changes to a nearby control area in which the sea stars were left intact. After the sea stars were removed, about half of the 15 species disappeared from the test area, crowded out by certain mussel and barnacle populations, which increased rapidly when freed from predation by the sea stars. Paine noted that when a keystone predator such as the sea star is removed from a community, the species diversity of that community changes dramatically.

One problem with the concept of keystone species is that it is often difficult to measure all the direct and indirect impacts of a keystone species on an ecosystem. Consequently, most evidence

FIGURE 54-15 Rocky intertidal community at low tide

Pisaster sea stars and chitons cling to the rock during low tide. *Pisaster* sea stars range in color from purple to brown to orange. Photographed in the summer in the Pacific Northwest.

for the existence of keystone species is based on indirect observations rather than on experimental manipulations. For example, consider the fig tree. Because fig trees produce a continuous crop of fruits, they may be keystone species in tropical rain forests of Central and South America. Fruit-eating monkeys, birds, bats, and other fruit-eating vertebrates of the forest do not normally consume large quantities of figs in their diets.

During that time of the year when other fruits are less plentiful, however, fig trees become important in sustaining fruit-eating vertebrates. It is therefore assumed that should the fig trees disappear, most of the fruit-eating vertebrates would also disappear. In turn, should the fruit eaters disappear, the spatial distribution of other fruit-bearing plants would become more limited because the fruit eaters help disperse their seeds. Thus, protecting fig trees in such tropical rainforest ecosystems probably increases the likelihood that monkeys, birds, bats, and many other tree species will survive. The question is whether this anecdotal evidence of fig trees as keystone species is strong enough for policymakers to grant special protection to fig trees.

Like the *Pisaster* sea stars, many keystone species are top predators; for example, consider the gray wolf. Where wolves were hunted to extinction, populations of elk, deer, and other larger herbivores increased exponentially. As these herbivores overgrazed the vegetation, many plant species that could not tolerate such grazing pressure disappeared. Smaller animals such as rodents, rabbits, and insects declined in number because the plants they depended on for food were now less abundant. The number of foxes, hawks, owls, and badgers that prey on these small animals decreased, as did the number of ravens, eagles, and other scavengers that eat wolf-kill. Thus, the disappearance of the wolf resulted in communities with considerably less biological diversity.

The reintroduction of wolves to Yellowstone National Park in 1995 has given ecologists a unique opportunity to study the impacts of a keystone species. The wolf's return has already caused substantial changes for other residents in the park. The top predator's effects have ranged from altering relationships among predator and prey species to transforming vegetation profiles. Coyotes are potential prey for wolves, and wolf packs have decimated some coyote populations. A reduction in coyotes has allowed populations of the coyotes' prey, such as ground squirrels and chipmunks, to increase. Scavengers such as ravens, bald eagles, and grizzly bears have benefited from dining on scraps from wolf-kills.

Prey populations such as elk have declined in recent years, but biologists are not sure if the pruning effect of wolves is the main reason. Climate (in this case, an extended drought) and human harvest are other possible factors.

Dominant species influence a community as a result of their greater size or abundance

In contrast to keystone species, which have a large impact out of proportion to their abundance, **dominant species** greatly affect the community because they are very common. Trees, the dominant species of forests, change the local environment. Trees provide shade, which changes both the light and moisture availability on the forest floor. Trees provide numerous habitats and *microhabitats* (such as a hole in a tree trunk) for other species. Forest trees also

provide food for many organisms and therefore play a large role in energy flow through the forest ecosystem. Similarly, cordgrass (*Spartina*) is the dominant species in salt marshes, prairie grass in grasslands, and kelp in kelp beds. Animals are also dominant species. For example, corals are dominant species in coral reefs, and cattle are dominant species in overgrazed rangelands. Typically, a community has one or a few dominant species, and most other species are relatively rare.

Ecosystem regulation occurs from the bottom up and top down

One question that ecologists have recently considered is which regulatory process—bottom-up or top-down—is more significant in the regulation of various ecosystems. Both energy flow (see Fig. 1-8) and cycles of matter are involved in bottom-up and top-down processes. **Bottom-up processes** are based on **food webs,** the interconnected series of organisms through which energy flows in an ecosystem. Food webs always have plants or other producers at the first (lowest) trophic level (**FIG. 54-16a**). (A *trophic level* is an organism's position in a food web; for example, producers are the first trophic level, and plant-eating herbivores are the second level.) In a sense, the biogeochemical cycles that regenerate nutrients such as nitrates and phosphates for producers to assimilate are located "under" the first trophic level. Thus, bottom-up processes regulate ecosystem function by nutrient cycling and by availability of other resources. If bottom-up processes dominate an ecosystem, the availability of resources such as water or soil minerals controls the number of producers, which in turn controls the number of herbivores, which controls the number of carnivores. (Recall from Chapter 53 that *limiting resources* tend to restrict the ecological niches of organisms, thereby affecting population size.)

Bottom-up processes apparently predominate in certain aquatic ecosystems in which nitrogen or phosphorus is limiting. An experiment in which phosphorus was added to a phosphorus-deficient river (the Kaparuk River in Alaska) resulted in an increase

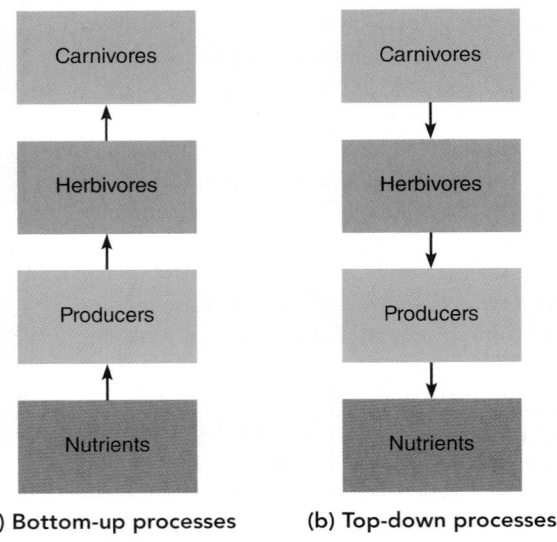

(a) Bottom-up processes   (b) Top-down processes

FIGURE 54-16 Bottom-up and top-down processes

in algae, followed over time by increased populations of aquatic insects, other invertebrates, and fishes.

In contrast, **top-down processes** regulate ecosystem function by trophic interactions, particularly from the highest trophic level (**FIG. 54-16b**). Ecosystem regulation by top-down processes occurs because carnivores eat herbivores, which in turn eat producers, which affects levels of nutrients. If top-down processes dominate an ecosystem, the effects of an increase in the population of top predators cascade down the food web through the herbivores and producers. In fact, top-down processes are also known as a *trophic cascade.*

A change in the feeding preferences of orcas, formerly known as killer whales, off the coast of Alaska provides an excellent example of a trophic cascade. A few decades ago, when orcas began preying on sea otters, the sea otter population sharply declined. As sea otters have declined, the number of sea urchins, which sea otters eat, has increased. Sea urchins eat kelp, the producers at the base of the food web; the increase in the number of sea urchins has caused a decline in kelp populations.

Top-down regulation appears to predominate in ecosystems with few trophic levels and low species richness. Such ecosystems may have only one or a few species of dominant herbivores, but those species have a strong impact on the producer populations. An excellent example of top-down regulation was discussed in Chapter 53: reindeer introduced to the Pribilof Islands of Alaska overgrazed the vegetation until the plants were almost wiped out.

It may be that top-down and bottom-up regulatory processes are not mutually exclusive. In a 13-year study of a thorn-scrub community in north-central Chile, ecologists demonstrated that top-down regulation predominates in certain small desert mammals and plant species. However, during periodic El Niño events (discussed later in the chapter), the increase in precipitation resulted in bottom-up increases in producers and consumers. In this ecosystem, it appears that both top-down and bottom-up regulatory processes are important in trophic dynamics over an extended period.

Review

- Both dominant and keystone species exert strong effects on the character of a community, but in different ways. How do dominant species and keystone species differ?
- Biologists think the reintroduction of wolves to Yellowstone National Park, which began in 1995, will ultimately result in a more varied and lush plant composition. Is this an example of a bottom-up or top-down process? Why?

54.3 COMMUNITY BIODIVERSITY

■ LEARNING OBJECTIVES

8 Summarize the main determinants of species richness in a community, and relate species richness to community stability.

9 State the results of the analysis of the distance effect in South Pacific bird species.

Species diversity, species richness, and species evenness vary greatly from one community to another and are influenced by many biotic and abiotic factors. **Species diversity** is a measure of both the number of species within a community (*species richness*) and the relative importance of each species, based on its abundance, productivity, or size (*species evenness*).

Species richness, the number of species in a community, is determined by counting the species of interest. Tropical rain forests and coral reefs are examples of communities with extremely high species richness. In contrast, geographically isolated islands and mountaintops exhibit low species richness. **Species evenness** tells us about the relative abundance of one species compared to other species (**FIG. 54-17**).

Ecologists have developed various mathematical expressions, such as the *Shannon index,* to represent species diversity quantitatively. These *diversity indices* enable ecologists to compare species diversity in different communities. Conservation biologists use

(a) Low species evenness. In this community the abundance of broomsedge is high relative to the abundance of other wildflowers (burdock, yarrow, and oxeye daisy). Therefore, the community has low species evenness.

(b) High species evenness. In this community each species has the same abundance, and the community has high species evenness.

FIGURE 54-17 Species evenness

Shown are two hypothetical communities with different species evenness but the same species richness (that is, each has four species of wildflowers).

diversity indices as part of a comprehensive approach to saving biodiversity.

Ecologists seek to explain why some communities have more species than others

What determines the number of species in a community? No single conclusive answer exists, but several explanations appear plausible. These include the structural complexity of habitats, geographic isolation, habitat stress, closeness to the margins of adjacent communities, dominance of one species over others, and geologic history. Although these and other environmental factors have positive or negative effects on species richness, there are exceptions and variations in every explanation. Some explanations vary at different spatial scales: an explanation that seems to work at a large geographic scale (such as a continent) may not work at a smaller local scale (such as a meadow).

In many habitats, species richness is related to the structural complexity of habitats. In terrestrial environments, the types of plants growing in an area typically determine structural complexity. A structurally complex community, such as a forest, offers a greater variety of potential ecological niches than does a simple community, such as an arid desert or semiarid grassland (**FIG. 54-18**). An already complex habitat, such as a coral reef, may become even more complex if species potentially capable of filling vacant ecological niches evolve or migrate into the community because these species create "opportunities" for additional species. Thus, it appears that species richness is self-perpetuating to some degree.

Species richness is inversely related to the geographic isolation of a community. Isolated island communities are generally much less diverse than are communities in similar environments found on continents. This is due partly to the *distance effect,* the difficulty encountered by many species in reaching and successfully colonizing the island (**FIG. 54-19**). Also, sometimes species become locally extinct as a result of random events. In isolated habitats, such as islands or mountaintops, locally extinct species are not readily replaced.

KEY POINT A community in which the vegetation is structurally complex generally provides animals with more kinds of food and hiding places than a community with a lower structural complexity.

FIGURE 54-18 Effect of community complexity on species richness

Data were compiled in comparable chaparral habitats (shrubby and woody areas) in Chile, South Africa, and California. The structural complexity of vegetation (*x-axis*) is a numerically assigned gradient of habitats, based on height and density of vegetation, from low complexity (very dry scrub) to high complexity (woodland). (After Cody, M. L., and J. M. Diamond, eds. *Ecology and Evolution of Communities.* Harvard University, Cambridge, MA, 1975.)

KEY EXPERIMENT

QUESTION: Does the geographic isolation of a community affect its species richness?

HYPOTHESIS: Islands close to the mainland (or to a large island) have a higher species richness than the islands that are farther from the mainland.

EXPERIMENT: The number of bird species was catalogued on South Pacific islands that are various distances from New Guinea, a source of colonizing species for these smaller islands. Each point on the graph represents a different island.

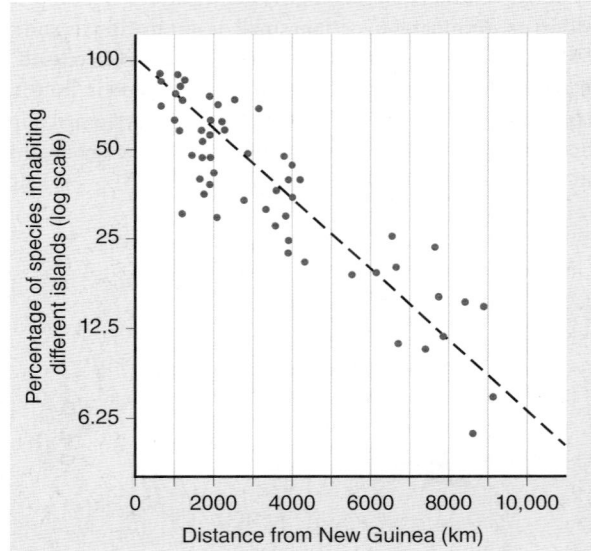

RESULTS AND CONCLUSION: The percentage of South Pacific bird species found on each island in the South Pacific is related to its distance from New Guinea. (New Guinea has 100% of the bird species living in that region.) Thus, species richness declines as the distance from New Guinea increases.

Source: After Diamond, J. M. "Biogeographic Kinetics: Estimation of Relaxation Times for Avifaunas of Southwest Pacific Islands." *Proceedings of the National Academy of Sciences,* Vol. 69, 1972.

FIGURE 54-19 The distance effect

Isolated areas are usually small and have fewer potential ecological niches.

Generally, species richness is inversely related to the environmental stress of a habitat. Only those species capable of tolerating extreme conditions live in an environmentally stressed community. Thus, the species richness of a highly polluted stream is low compared with that of a nearby pristine stream. Similarly, the species richness of high-latitude (farther from the equator) communities exposed to harsh climates is lower than that of lower latitude (closer to the equator) communities with milder climates (**FIG. 54-20**). This observation, known as the *species richness–energy hypothesis,* suggests that different latitudes affect species richness because of variations in solar energy. Greater energy may permit more species to coexist in a given region. Although the equatorial countries of Colombia, Ecuador, and Peru occupy only 2% of Earth's land, they contain a remarkable 45,000 native plant species. The continental United States and Canada, with a significantly larger land area, host a total of 19,000 native plant species. Ecuador alone contains more than 1300 native species of birds—twice as many as the United States and Canada combined.

Species richness is usually greater at the margins of distinct communities than in their centers. The reason is that an **ecotone,** a transitional zone where two or more communities meet, contains all or most of the ecological niches of the adjacent communities as well as some that are unique to the ecotone (see Fig. 56-24). This change in species composition produced at ecotones is known as the **edge effect.**

Species richness is reduced when any one species enjoys a position of dominance within a community; a dominant species may appropriate a disproportionate share of available resources, thus crowding out, or outcompeting, other species. Ecologist James H. Brown of the University of New Mexico has addressed species composition and richness in experiments conducted since 1977 in the Chihuahuan Desert of southeastern Arizona. In one experiment, the removal of three dominant species, all kangaroo rats, from several plots resulted in an increased diversity of other rodent species. This increase was ascribed both to lowered competition for food and to an altered habitat because the

abundance of grass species increased dramatically after the removal of the kangaroo rats.

Species richness is greatly affected by geologic history. Many scientists think that tropical rain forests are old, stable communities that have undergone relatively few widespread disturbances through Earth's history. (In ecology, a **disturbance** is any event in time that disrupts community or population structure.) During

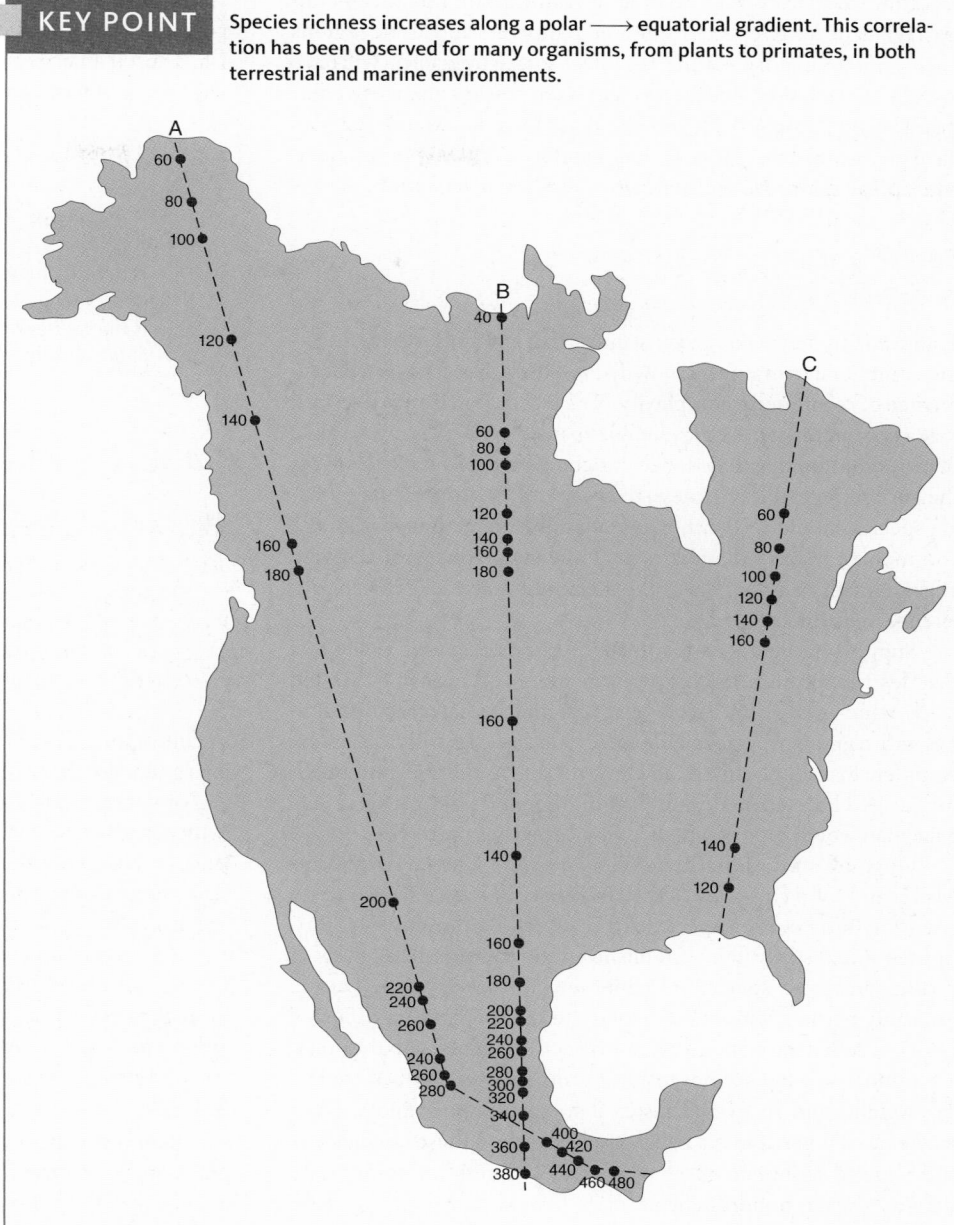

Species richness increases along a polar ⟶ equatorial gradient. This correlation has been observed for many organisms, from plants to primates, in both terrestrial and marine environments.

FIGURE 54-20 *Animated* Effect of latitude on species richness of breeding birds in North America

The species richness for three north–south transects (A, B, and C) are shown. Note that the overall number of breeding bird species is greater at lower latitudes toward the equator than at higher latitudes. However, this pattern is strongly modified by other factors, such as precipitation and surface features (such as mountains). (After Cook, R. E. "Variation in Species Density of North American Birds." *Systematic Zoology,* Vol. 18, 1969.)

this time, myriad species evolved in tropical rain forests. In contrast, glaciers have repeatedly altered temperate and arctic regions during Earth's history. An area recently vacated by glaciers will have low species richness because few species have had a chance to enter it and become established. The idea that older, more stable habitats have greater species richness than habitats subjected to frequent, widespread disturbances is known as the *time hypothesis.*

Species richness may promote community stability

Traditionally, most ecologists assumed that community stability—the ability of a community to withstand disturbances—is a consequence of community complexity. That is, ecologists hypothesized that a community with considerable species richness is more stable than a community with less species richness. According to this view, the greater the species richness, the less critically important any single species should be. With many possible interactions within the community, it appears unlikely that any single disturbance could affect enough components of the system to make a significant difference in its functioning.

Supporting evidence for this hypothesis is found in the fact that destructive outbreaks of pests are more common in cultivated fields, which have a low species richness, than in natural communities with a greater species richness. As another example, the almost complete loss of the American chestnut tree to the chestnut blight fungus had little ecological impact on the moderately diverse Appalachian woodlands of which it was formerly a part.

Ongoing studies by David Tilman of the University of Minnesota and John Downing of the University of Iowa have strengthened the link between species richness and community stability. In their initial study, they established and monitored 207 plots of various grassland species in Minnesota for seven years. During the study period, Minnesota's worst drought in 50 years occurred (1987–1988). The ecologists found that those plots with the greatest number of plant species lost less ground cover, as measured by dry weight, and recovered faster than species-poor plots. Later studies by Tilman and his colleagues supported these conclusions and showed a similar effect of species richness on community stability during nondrought years. Similar work by almost three dozen ecologists at eight grassland sites in Europe also supports the link between species richness and community stability.

Some scientists do not agree with the conclusions of Tilman and other research groups that the presence of more species confers greater community stability. These critics argue that it is difficult to separate species number from other factors that could affect productivity. They suggest it would be better to start with established ecosystems and study what happens to their productivity when plants are removed.

Another observation that adds a layer of complexity to the species richness–community stability debate is that populations of individual species within a species-rich community often vary significantly from year to year. It may seem paradoxical that variation within populations of individual species relates to the stability of the entire community. When you consider all the interactions among the organisms in a community, however, it is obvious that

some species benefit at the expense of others. If one species declines in a given year, other species that compete with it may flourish. Thus, if an ecosystem contains more species, it is likely that at least some will be resistant to any given disturbance.

Review

- How is the species richness of a community related to geographic isolation?
- How is the structural complexity of habitats relevant to species richness?
- How is the species richness of a community related to the environmental stress of a habitat?

54.4 COMMUNITY DEVELOPMENT

■ LEARNING OBJECTIVES

10 Define *succession*, and distinguish between primary and secondary succession.

11 Describe the intermediate disturbance hypothesis.

12 Discuss the two traditional views of the nature of communities: Clements's organismic model and Gleason's individualistic model.

A community does not spring into existence full-blown but develops gradually through a series of stages, each dominated by different organisms. The process of community development over time, which involves species in one stage being replaced by different species, is called **succession.** An area is initially colonized by certain early successional species that give way over time to others, which in turn give way much later to late-successional species.

Succession is usually described in terms of the changes in the species composition of an area's vegetation, although each successional stage also has its own characteristic kinds of animals and other species. The time involved in succession is on the order of tens, hundreds, or thousands of years, not the millions of years involved in the evolutionary time scale.

Ecologists distinguish between two types of succession, primary and secondary. **Primary succession** is the change in species composition over time in a habitat that was not previously inhabited by organisms. No soil exists when primary succession begins. Bare rock surfaces, such as recently formed volcanic lava and rock scraped clean by glaciers, are examples of sites where primary succession might take place (**FIG. 54-21**).

The Indonesian island of Krakatoa has provided scientists with a perfect long-term study of primary succession in a tropical rain forest. In 1883, a volcanic eruption destroyed virtually all life on the island. Ecologists have surveyed the ecosystem during the more than 100 years since the devastation to document the return of life-forms. As of the 1990s, ecologists had found that the progress of primary succession was extremely slow, in part because of Krakatoa's isolation (recall the distance effect discussed earlier in the chapter). Many species are limited in their ability to disperse over water. Krakatoa's forest, for example, may have only one-tenth the tree species richness of undisturbed tropical rain forest of nearby islands. The lack of plant diversity has, in turn, limited the

(a) After the glacier's retreat, lichens initially colonize the gravel moraine. Mosses and shallow rooted herbs such as mountain avens (*Dryas*) follow.

(b) Dense mats of low-growing *Dryas* plants dominate the landscape, stabilizing the thin layer of developing soil.

(d) As the condition of the soil improves, Sitka spruce (*Picea sichensis*) replaces the alder community. After several hundred years, the forest consists of Sitka spruce and western hemlock (*Tsuga heterophylla*).

(c) Alders replace the *Dryas* community. Both alders (*Alnus*) and *Dryas* have nitrogen-fixing bacteria in root nodules that improve the nitrogen content of the soil.

FIGURE 54-21 *Animated* **Primary succession following retreating glaciers**
Ecologists have documented primary succession as glaciers have retreated at Glacier Bay, Alaska.

number of colonizing animal species. In a forested area of Krakatoa where zoologists would expect more than 100 butterfly species, for example, there are only 2 species.

Secondary succession is the change in species composition that takes place after some disturbance removes the existing vegetation; soil is already present at these sites. Abandoned agricultural fields or open areas produced by forest fires are common examples of sites where secondary succession occurs. During the summer of 1988, wildfires burned approximately one-third of Yellowstone National Park. This natural disaster provided a valuable chance for ecologists to study secondary succession in areas that had been forests. After the conflagration, gray ash covered the forest floor, and most of the trees, although standing, were charred and dead. Secondary succession in Yellowstone has occurred rapidly since 1988. Less than a year later, in the spring of 1989, trout lily and other herbs sprouted and covered much of the ground. By 1998, a

young forest of knee-high to shoulder-high lodgepole pines dominated the area. Douglas fir seedlings also began appearing in 1998. Ecologists continue to monitor the changes in Yellowstone as secondary succession unfolds.

Disturbance influences succession and species richness

Early studies suggested that succession inevitably progressed to a stable and persistent community, known as a *climax community*, which was determined solely by climate. Periodic disturbances, such as fires or floods, were not thought to exert much influence on climax communities. If the climax community was disturbed in any way, it would return to a self-sustaining, stable equilibrium in time.

This traditional view of stability has fallen out of favor. The apparent end-point stability of species composition in a "climax" forest is probably the result of how long trees live relative to the human lifespan. It is now recognized that forest communities never reach a state of permanent equilibrium but instead exist in a state of continual disturbance. The species composition and relative abundance of each species vary in a mature community over a range of environmental gradients, although the community retains a relatively uniform appearance overall.

Because all communities are exposed to periodic disturbances, both natural and human-induced, ecologists have long tried to understand the effects of disturbance on species richness. A significant advance was the development of the **intermediate disturbance hypothesis** by Joseph H. Connell. When he examined species richness in tropical rain forests and coral reefs, he proposed that species richness is greatest at moderate levels of disturbance (**FIG. 54-22**). At a moderate level of disturbance, the community is a mosaic of habitat patches at different stages of succession; a range of sites exists, from those that were recently disturbed to those that have not been disturbed for many years. When disturbances are frequent or intense, only those species best adapted to earlier stages of succession persist, whereas low levels of disturbance allow late-successional species to dominate to such a degree that other species disappear. For example, when periodic wildfires are suppressed in forests, reducing disturbance to a low level, some of the "typical" forest herbs decline in number or even disappear.

One of the difficulties with the intermediate disturbance hypothesis is defining precisely what constitutes an "intermediate" level of disturbance. Despite this problem, the intermediate disturbance hypothesis has important ramifications for conservation biology because it tells us that we cannot maintain a particular community simply by creating a reserve around it. Both natural and human-induced disturbances will cause changes in species composition, and humans may have to intentionally intervene to maintain the species richness of the original community. What kind of and how much human intervention is necessary to maintain species richness is controversial.

Ecologists continue to study community structure

One of the major issues in community ecology, from the early 1900s to the present, is the nature of communities. Are communities highly organized systems of predictable species, or are they abstractions produced by the minds of ecologists?

U.S. botanist Frederick E. Clements (1874–1945) was struck by the worldwide uniformity of large tracts of vegetation, for example, tropical rain forests in South America, Africa, and Southeast Asia. He also noted that even though the species composition of a community in a particular habitat may be different from that of a community in a habitat with a similar climate elsewhere in the world, overall the components of the two communities are usually similar. He viewed communities as something like "superorganisms," whose member species cooperated with one another in a manner that resembled the cooperation of the parts of an individual organism's body. Clements's view was that a community went through certain stages of development, like the embryonic stages of an organism, and eventually reached

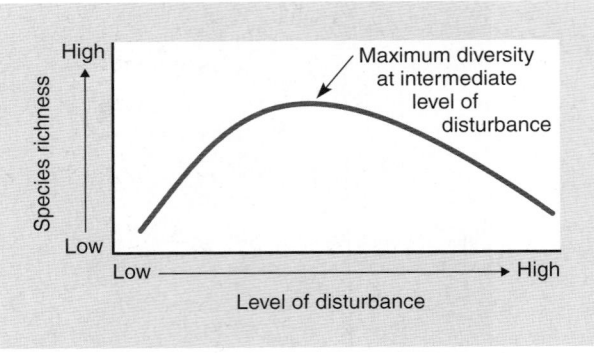

FIGURE 54-22 Intermediate disturbance hypothesis
Species richness is greatest at an intermediate level of disturbance. (After Connell, J. H. "Diversity in Tropical Rain Forests and Coral Reefs." *Science,* Vol. 199, 1978.)

an adult state; the developmental process was succession, and the adult state was the climax community. This cooperative view of the community, called the **organismic model,** stresses the interaction of the members, which tend to cluster in tightly knit groups within discrete community boundaries (**FIG. 54-23a**).

Opponents of the organismic model, particularly U.S. ecologist Henry A. Gleason (1882–1975), held that biological interactions are less important in the production of communities than are environmental gradients (such as climate and soil) or even chance. Indeed, the concept of a community is questionable. It may be a classification category with no reality, reflecting little more than the tendency of organisms with similar environmental requirements to live in similar places. This school of thought, called the **individualistic model,** emphasizes species individuality, with each species having its own particular abiotic living requirements. It holds that communities are therefore not interdependent associations of organisms. Rather, each species is independently distributed across a continuum of areas that meets its own individual requirements (**FIG. 54-23b**).

Debates such as this one over the nature of communities are an integral part of the scientific process because they fuel discussion and research that lead to a better understanding of broad scientific principles. Studies testing the organismic and individualistic hypotheses of communities do not support Clements's interactive concept of communities as discrete units. Instead, most studies favor the individualistic model. As shown in **FIGURE 54-23c**, tree species in Wisconsin forests are distributed in a gradient from wet to dry environments. Also, studies of plant and animal movements during the past 14,000 years support the individualistic model because it appears that individual species, not entire communities, became redistributed in response to changes in climate.

Review

- What is succession?
- How does primary succession differ from secondary succession?
- What is Connell's intermediate disturbance hypothesis?
- How do the organismic and individualistic models of the nature of communities differ?

(a) Organismic model. According to this hypothesis, communities are organized as distinct units. Each of the four communities shown (*numbered brackets*) consists of an assemblage of distinct species (*each colored curve represents a single species*). The arrows indicate ecotones, regions of transition along community boundaries.

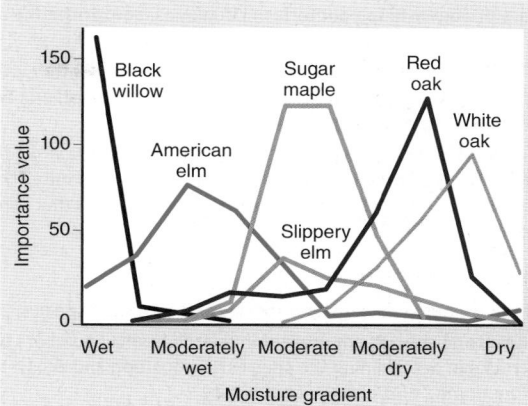

(c) Tree species in Wisconsin forests, which are distributed along a moisture gradient, more closely resemble the individualistic model. The "importance value" (*y-axis*) of each species in a given location combines three aspects (population density, frequency, and size).

(b) Individualistic model. This model predicts a more random assemblage of species along a gradient of environmental conditions.

FIGURE 54-23 Nature of communities

(**c,** Adapted from Curtis, J. T. *The Vegetation of Wisconsin.* University of Wisconsin Press, Madison, 1959.)

■ SUMMARY: FOCUS ON LEARNING OBJECTIVES

54.1 *(page 1174)*

1 Define *ecological niche,* and distinguish between an organism's fundamental niche and its realized niche.

- The distinctive lifestyle and role of an organism in a community is its **ecological niche.** An organism's ecological niche takes into account all abiotic and biotic aspects of the organism's existence. An organism's **habitat** (where it lives) is one of the parameters used to describe the niche.

- Organisms potentially exploit more resources and play a broader role in the life of their community than they actually do. The potential ecological niche for an organism is its **fundamental niche,** whereas the niche it actually occupies is its **realized niche.**

2 Define *competition,* and distinguish between interspecific and intraspecific competition.

- **Competition** occurs when two or more individuals attempt to use the same essential resource, such as food, water, shelter, living space, or sunlight.

- Competition occurs among individuals within a population (**intraspecific competition**) or between different species (**interspecific competition**).

3 Summarize the concepts of the competitive exclusion principle, resource partitioning, and character displacement.

- According to the **competitive exclusion principle,** two species cannot occupy the same niche in the same community for an indefinite

period; one species is excluded by another as a result of competition for a limiting resource.

- The evolution of differences in resource use, known as **resource partitioning,** reduces competition between similar species.

- Competition among some species is reduced by **character displacement,** in which their structural, ecological, and behavioral characteristics diverge where their ranges overlap.

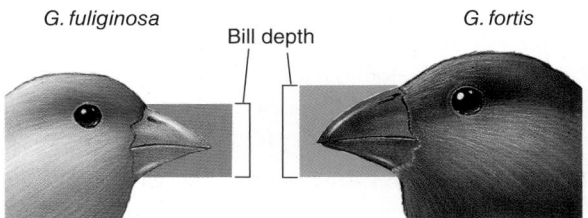

4 Define *predation,* and describe the effects of natural selection on predator–prey relationships.

- **Predation** is the consumption of one species (the **prey**) by another (the **predator**). During **coevolution** between predator and prey, more efficient ways to catch prey evolve in the predator species, and better ways to escape the predator evolve in the prey species.

5 Distinguish among mutualism, commensalism, and parasitism, and give examples of each.

- **Symbiosis** is any intimate or long-term association between two or more species. The three types of symbiosis are mutualism, commensalism, and parasitism.
- In **mutualism,** both partners benefit. Three examples of mutualism are **nitrogen-fixing bacteria** and legumes, **zooxanthellae** and corals, and **mycorrhizae** (fungi and plant roots).
- In **commensalism,** one organism benefits and the other is unaffected. Two examples of commensalism are silverfish and army ants, and epiphytes and larger plants.
- In **parasitism,** one organism (the **parasite**) benefits while the other (the **host**) is harmed. One example of parasitism is mites that grow in or on honeybees. Some parasites are **pathogens** that cause disease.

54.2 *(page 1185)*

6 Distinguish between keystone species and dominant species.
- **Keystone species** are present in relatively small numbers but are crucial in determining the species composition and ecosystem functioning of the entire community.
- In contrast to keystone species, which have an impact that is out of proportion to their abundance, **dominant species** greatly affect the community of which they are a part because they are very common.

7 Distinguish between bottom-up and top-down processes in ecosystem regulation.
- If **bottom-up processes** dominate an ecosystem, the availability of resources such as minerals controls the number of producers (that is, the lowest trophic level), which in turn controls the number of herbivores, which in turn controls the number of carnivores.
- **Top-down processes** regulate ecosystems from the highest trophic level—by consumers eating producers. If top-down processes dominate an ecosystem, an increase in the number of top predators cascades down the food web through the herbivores and producers.

54.3 *(page 1187)*

8 Summarize the main determinants of species richness in a community and relate species richness to community stability.
- Community complexity is expressed in terms of **species richness,** the number of species within a community, and **species diversity,** a measure of the relative importance of each species within a community based on abundance, productivity, or size.
- Species richness is often great in a habitat that has structural complexity; in a community that is not isolated (the distance effect)

or severely stressed; in a community where more energy is available (the species richness–energy hypothesis); in **ecotones** (transition zones between communities); and in communities with long histories without major **disturbances,** events that disrupt community or population structure.
- Several studies suggest that species richness may promote community stability.

9 State the results of the analysis of the distance effect in South Pacific bird species.
- The number of bird species found on each island in the South Pacific is inversely related to its geographic isolation—that is, to its distance from New Guinea. Species richness declines as the distance from New Guinea increases.

54.4 *(page 1190)*

10 Define *succession,* and distinguish between primary and secondary succession.
- **Succession** is the orderly replacement of one community by another. **Primary succession** occurs in an area that has not previously been inhabited (such as bare rock). **Secondary succession** begins in an area where there was a pre-existing community and well-formed soil (such as abandoned farmland).

11 Describe the intermediate disturbance hypothesis.
- Disturbance affects succession and species richness. According to the **intermediate disturbance hypothesis,** species richness is greatest at moderate levels of disturbance, which create a mosaic of habitat patches at different stages of succession.

12 Discuss the two traditional views of the nature of communities: Clements's organismic model and Gleason's individualistic model.
- The **organismic model** views a community as a "superorganism" that goes through certain stages of development (succession) toward adulthood (climax). In this view, biological interactions are primarily responsible for species composition, and organisms are highly interdependent.
- Most ecologists support the **individualistic model,** which challenges the concept of a highly interdependent community. According to this model, abiotic environmental factors are the primary determinants of species composition in a community, and organisms are somewhat independent of one another.

CENGAGENOW™ Explore interspecific competition, resource partitioning, mimicry, and the distance effect by clicking on the figures in CengageNOW.

TEST YOUR UNDERSTANDING

1. A limiting resource does all of the following *except* that it (a) tends to restrict the ecological niche of a species (b) is in short supply relative to a species' need for it (c) limits the presence of a species in a given community (d) results in an intermediate disturbance (e) may be limiting for only part of an organism's life cycle

2. Based on current evidence, monarch and viceroy butterflies are probably an example of (a) Batesian mimicry (b) character displacement (c) resource partitioning (d) Müllerian mimicry (e) cryptic coloration

3. A symbiotic association in which organisms are beneficial to one another is known as (a) predation (b) interspecific competition (c) intraspecific competition (d) commensalism (e) mutualism

4. A species' _____ is the totality of its adaptations, its use of resources, and its lifestyle. (a) habitat (b) ecotone (c) ecological niche (d) competitive exclusion (e) coevolution

5. Competition with other species helps determine an organism's (a) ecotone (b) fundamental niche (c) realized niche (d) limiting resource (e) ecosystem

6. "Complete competitors cannot coexist" is a statement of the principle of (a) primary succession (b) limiting resources (c) Müllerian mimicry (d) competitive exclusion (e) character displacement

7. The _____ signifies that species richness is greater where two communities meet than at the center of either community. (a) edge effect (b) fundamental niche (c) character displacement (d) realized niche (e) limiting resource

8. Primary succession occurs on (a) bare rock (b) newly cooled lava (c) abandoned farmland (d) a and b (e) a, b, and c

9. The tendency for two similar species to differ from each other more markedly in areas where they occur together is known as (a) Müllerian mimicry (b) Batesian mimicry (c) resource partitioning (d) competitive exclusion (e) character displacement

10. An unpalatable species demonstrates its threat to potential predators by displaying (a) character displacement (b) limiting resources (c) cryptic coloration (d) aposematic coloration (e) competitive exclusion

11. An ecologist studying several forest-dwelling, insect-eating bird species does not find any evidence of interspecific competition.

The most likely explanation is (a) lack of a keystone species (b) low species richness (c) pronounced intraspecific competition (d) coevolution of predator–prey strategies (e) resource partitioning

12. Support for the individualistic model of community structure includes (a) the decline of honeybees because of two species of parasitic mites (b) the identification of fig trees as a keystone species in tropical forests (c) the competitive exclusion of one *Paramecium* species by another (d) the distribution of trees along a moisture gradient in Wisconsin forests (e) the effects of the removal of a dominant rodent species from an Arizona desert

CRITICAL THINKING

1. In what symbiotic relationships are humans involved?

2. **SCIENCE, TECHNOLOGY, AND SOCIETY.** Describe the ecological niche of humans. Do you think our realized niche has changed during the past 1000 years? Why or why not? What role has technology played?

3. How is the vertical distribution of barnacles in Scotland an example of competitive exclusion?

4. In your opinion, are humans a dominant species or a keystone species? Explain your answer.

5. Many plants that produce nodules for nitrogen-fixing bacteria are common on disturbed sites. Explain how these plants might simultaneously compete with and facilitate other plant species.

6. **EVOLUTION LINK.** The rough-skinned newt, which lives in western North America, stores a poison in its skin and is avoided by predators. However, several populations of garter snakes have undergone one or a few mutations that enable them to tolerate the toxin, and these snakes eat the newts with no ill effects. How has natural selection affected this predator–prey relationship? Based on what you have learned about evolutionary arms races, predict what may happen to the newts and the poison-resistant garter snakes over time.

7. **EVOLUTION LINK.** Competition is an important part of Darwin's theory of evolution by natural selection, and the evolution of features that reduce competition increases a population's overall fitness. Relate this idea to character displacement and resource partitioning in Darwin's finches.

8. **EVOLUTION LINK.** Ecologist Charles Krebs said that "evolution operates through natural selection, which is ecology in action." Explain what he meant and relate his idea to one example of ecosystem regulation from the bottom up or the top down.

9. **ANALYZING DATA.** Examine the top and middle graphs in Figure 54-5. Are these examples of exponential or logistic population growth? Where is K in each graph? (You may need to refer to Chapter 53 to answer these questions.)

10. **ANALYZING DATA.** Examine Figure 54-19 (shown below). Approximately what percentage of species have colonized islands 2000 km from New Guinea? 6000 km from New Guinea? Based on your answers, explain the relationship between species richness and geographic isolation.

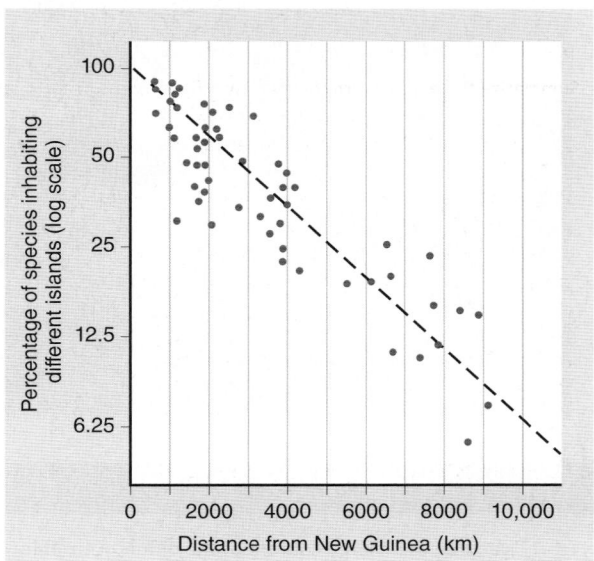

CENGAGENOW™ Additional questions are available in CengageNOW at www.cengage.com/login.

55 Ecosystems and the Biosphere

Beaver pond. Beavers constructed a dam out of branches and mud (*at far end of pond*), converting a small creek into a pond. Photographed on Shingle Creek, Utah.

Michael Stubben/Visuals Unlimited

KEY CONCEPTS

55.1 Studying the energy content of the different trophic levels provides insight into how energy flows through the biotic and abiotic components of ecosystems.

55.2 Carbon, nitrogen, water, and other materials cycle through both biotic and abiotic parts of ecosystems.

55.3 The abiotic environment—including solar radiation, the atmosphere, the ocean, climate, and fire—helps shape the biotic portion of ecosystems.

55.4 Ecosystem ecologists focus on chemical, physical, and biological processes of ecosystems to learn how ecosystems function.

Almost completely isolated from everything in the universe but sunlight, planet Earth has often been compared to a vast spaceship whose life-support system consists of the communities of organisms that inhabit it, plus energy from the sun. These organisms produce oxygen, transfer energy, and recycle water and minerals (inorganic nutrients) with great efficiency. Yet none of these ecological processes would be possible without the abiotic (nonliving) environment of spaceship Earth. As the sun warms the planet, it powers the hydrologic cycle (causes precipitation), drives ocean currents and atmospheric circulation patterns, and produces much of the climate to which organisms have adapted. The sun also supplies the energy that almost all organisms use to carry on life processes.

Individual communities and their abiotic environments are **ecosystems**, which are the basic units of ecology. An ecosystem encompasses all the interactions among organisms living together in a particular place, and among those organisms and their abiotic environment. **Ecosystem ecology** is a subfield of ecology that studies energy flow and the cycling of chemicals among the interacting biotic and abiotic parts of an ecosystem.

Ecosystem interactions are complex because each organism responds not only to other organisms but to conditions in the atmosphere, soil, and water. In turn, organisms exert an effect on the abiotic environment, as when a beaver dam creates a pond in a formerly forested area (see photograph). The pond is formed as the beaver builds an island lodge that will be safe from predators. However, the beaver dam also regulates the flow of water in the stream or river: it holds back water during rainy periods and releases a controlled amount of water throughout the year, even during periods of drought.

Like communities, ecosystems vary in size, lack precise boundaries, and are nested within larger ecosystems. Earth's largest ecosystem is the biosphere, which consists of all of Earth's communities and their interactions and connections with the planet's abiotic environment—its water, soil, rock, and atmosphere.

55.1 ENERGY FLOW THROUGH ECOSYSTEMS

LEARNING OBJECTIVES

1 Summarize the concept of energy flow through a food web.
2 Explain typical pyramids of numbers, biomass, and energy.
3 Distinguish between gross primary productivity and net primary productivity.

The passage of energy in a one-way direction through an ecosystem is known as **energy flow.** Energy enters an ecosystem as radiant energy (sunlight), a tiny portion (less than 1%) of which *producers* trap and use during photosynthesis. The energy, now in chemical form, is stored in the bonds of organic (carbon-containing) molecules such as glucose. When cellular respiration breaks these molecules apart, energy becomes available (in the form of ATP) to do work, such as repairing tissues, producing body heat, moving about, or reproducing. As the work is accomplished, energy escapes the organisms and dissipates into the environment as heat. Ultimately, this heat energy radiates into space. Thus, once an organism has used energy, the energy is unavailable for reuse (**FIG. 55-1**). (See also the discussion of the second law of thermodynamics in Chapter 7.)

In an ecosystem, energy flow occurs in **food chains,** in which energy from food passes from one organism to the next

KEY POINT Ecologists gain insights into how ecosystems function by examining energy flow and the energy content of each trophic level.

Heat   Heat   Heat   Heat   Heat

Energy from sun

First trophic level: producers

Second trophic level: primary consumers

Third trophic level: secondary consumers

Fourth trophic level: tertiary consumers

Decomposers (saprotrophs)

FIGURE 55-1 *Animated* **Energy flow through ecosystems**
Energy enters ecosystems from an external source (the sun) and exits as heat loss.

in a sequence. **Primary producers,** also called *autotrophs,* or simply, *producers,* form the beginning of the food chain by capturing the sun's energy through photosynthesis. Producers, by incorporating the chemicals they manufacture into their own *biomass* (living material), become potential food resources for other organisms. Plants are the most significant producers on land, whereas algae and cyanobacteria are important producers in aquatic environments.

All other organisms in a community are **consumers,** also called *heterotrophs,* that extract energy from organic molecules produced by other organisms. **Herbivores** are consumers that eat plants, from which they obtain the chemical energy of the producers' molecules and the building materials used to construct their own tissues. Herbivores are, in turn, consumed by **carnivores,** consumers that reap the energy stored in the herbivores' molecules. Other consumers, called **omnivores,** eat a variety of organisms, both plant and animal.

Some consumers, called **detritus feeders,** or **detritivores,** eat **detritus,** which is dead organic matter that includes animal carcasses, leaf litter, and feces. Detritus feeders and microbial decomposers destroy dead organisms and waste products. **Decomposers,** also called **saprotrophs,** include microbial heterotrophs that supply themselves with energy by breaking down organic molecules in the remains (carcasses and body wastes) of all members of the food chain. They typically release simple inorganic molecules, such as carbon dioxide and mineral salts, which may be reused by producers. Most bacteria and fungi are important decomposers.

Simple food chains such as the one just described rarely occur in nature because few organisms eat just one kind, or are eaten by just one other kind, of organism. More typically, the flow of energy and materials through ecosystems takes place in accordance with a range of food choices for each organism. In an ecosystem of average complexity, hundreds of alternative pathways are possible. Thus, a **food web,** which is a complex of interconnected food chains, is a more realistic

model of the flow of energy and materials through ecosystems (**FIG. 55-2**).

Food webs are divided into **trophic levels** (from the Greek *tropho,* which means "nourishment"). Producers (organisms that photosynthesize) occupy the first trophic level, primary consumers (herbivores) occupy the second, secondary consumers (carnivores and omnivores) the third, and so on (see Fig. 55-1).

Because food chains and food webs are descriptions of "who eats whom," they indicate the negative effects predators have on their prey. For example, consider a simple food chain: grass ⟶

> **KEY POINT** Food webs in all but the simplest ecosystems are too complex to depict all the species and links actually present. Rarely do food-web diagrams take into account that some links are strong and others weak. Moreover, food webs change over time, with additions and deletions of links.

FIGURE 55-2 *Animated* **A food web at the edge of an Eastern deciduous forest**
This diagram is greatly simplified compared with what actually happens in nature.

field mouse ⟶ owl. The owl, which kills and eats mice, obviously exerts a negative effect on the mouse population; in like manner, field mice, which eat grass seeds, reduce the grass population.

A trophic level in a food web also influences other trophic levels to which it is not directly linked. Producers and top carnivores do not exert direct effects on one another, yet each indirectly affects the other. In our example, the owls help the grasses by keeping the population of seed-eating mice under control. Likewise, the grasses benefit owls by supporting a population of mice on which the owl population feeds. These indirect interactions may be as important in food-web dynamics as direct predator–prey interactions.

The most important thing to remember about energy flow in ecosystems is that it is linear, or one-way. That is, energy moves along a food web from one trophic level to the next trophic level. Once an organism has used energy, however, it is lost as heat and is unavailable to any other organism in the ecosystem.

Ecological pyramids illustrate how ecosystems work

Ecologists sometimes compare trophic levels by determining the number of organisms, the biomass, or the relative energy found at each level. This information is presented graphically as **ecological pyramids**. The base of each ecological pyramid represents the producers, the next level is the primary consumers (herbivores), the level above that is the secondary consumers (carnivores), and so on. The relative area of each bar of the pyramid is proportional to what is being demonstrated.

A **pyramid of numbers** shows the number of organisms at each trophic level in a given ecosystem, with a larger area illustrating greater numbers for that section of the pyramid. In most pyramids of numbers, fewer organisms occupy each successive trophic level. Thus, in African grasslands the number of herbivores, such as zebras and wildebeests, is greater than the number of carnivores, such as lions. Inverted pyramids of numbers, in which higher trophic levels have more organisms than lower trophic levels, are often observed among decomposers, parasites, and herbivorous insects. One tree provides food for thousands of leaf-eating in-

sects, for example. Pyramids of numbers are of limited usefulness because they do not indicate the biomass of the organisms at each level and they do not indicate the amount of energy transferred from one level to another.

A **pyramid of biomass** illustrates the total biomass at each successive trophic level. **Biomass** is a quantitative estimate of the total mass, or amount, of living material; it indicates the amount of fixed energy at a particular time. Biomass units of measure vary: biomass may be represented as total volume, dry weight, or live weight. Typically, these pyramids illustrate a progressive reduction of biomass in succeeding trophic levels (**FIG. 55-3a**). Assuming an average biomass reduction of about 90% for each trophic level, 10,000 kg of grass should support 1000 kg of grasshoppers, which in turn support 100 kg of frogs. (The 90% reduction in biomass is an approximation; actual biomass reduction from one trophic level to the next varies widely.) If we use this logic, the biomass of frog eaters (such as snakes) could weigh, at most, only about 10 kg. From this brief exercise, you see that although carnivores do not eat producers, a large producer biomass is required to support carnivores in a food web.

Occasionally, we find an inverted pyramid of biomass in which the primary consumers outweigh the producers (**FIG. 55-3b**). In these instances, herbivores such as fishes and zooplankton (protozoa, tiny crustaceans, and immature stages of many aquatic animals) consume large numbers of producers, which are usually unicellular algae that are short-lived and reproduce quickly. Thus, although at any point in time relatively few algae are present, the rate of biomass production of the primary consumers is much less than that of the producers.

A **pyramid of energy** indicates the energy content, often expressed as kilocalories per square meter per year, of the biomass of each trophic level. A common method ecologists use to measure energy content is to burn a sample of tissue in a calorimeter; the heat released during combustion is measured to determine the energy content of the organic material in the sample. Energy pyramids always have large bases and get progressively smaller through succeeding trophic levels to show that most energy dissipates into the environment when there is a transition from one trophic level to the next. Less energy reaches each successive

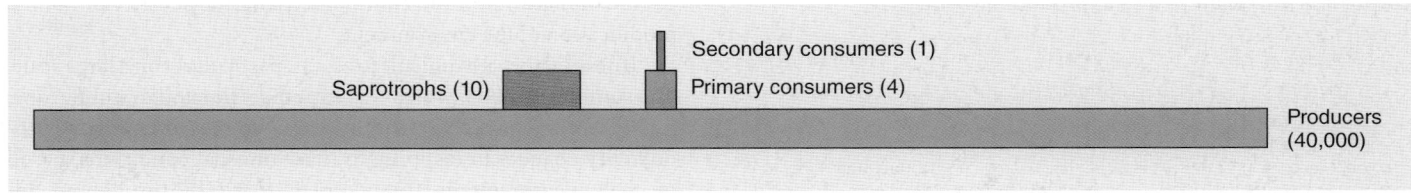

(a) A pyramid of biomass for a tropical forest in Panama.

(b) An inverted biomass pyramid, such as that for plankton in the English Channel, occurs when a highly productive lower trophic level experiences high rates of turnover. Plankton are free-floating, mainly microscopic algae and animals.

FIGURE 55-3 Pyramids of biomass

These pyramids are based on the biomass at each trophic level and generally have a pyramid shape with a large base and progressively smaller areas for each succeeding trophic level. Biomass values are in grams of dry weight per square meter. (**a, b,** Adapted from Odum, E. P. *Fundamentals of Ecology*, 3rd ed., W. B. Saunders Company, Philadelphia, 1971, and based on studies by F. B. Golley and G. I. Child **[a]** and H. W. Harvey **[b]**.)

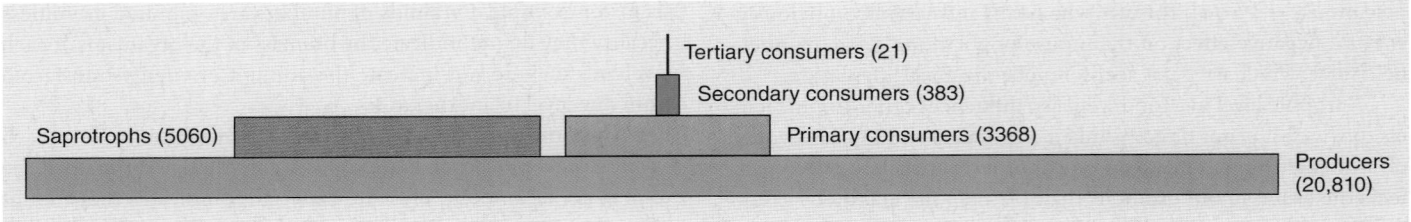

FIGURE 55-4 Pyramid of energy

A pyramid of energy for Silver Springs, Florida, represents energy flow, the functional basis of ecosystem structure. Energy values are in kilocalories per square meter per year. Note the substantial loss of usable energy from one trophic level to the next. The Silver Springs ecosystem is complex, but tape grass (producers), spiral-shelled snails (primary consumers), young river turtles (secondary consumers), gar (fish; tertiary consumers), and bacteria and fungi (saprotrophs) are representative organisms. When they are young, river turtles are carnivores and consume snails, aquatic insects, and worms; as adults, river turtles are herbivores. (Based on Odum, H. T. "Trophic Structure and Productivity of Silver Springs, Florida." *Ecological Monographs*, Vol. 27, 1957.)

trophic level from the level beneath it because those organisms at the lower level use some of the energy to perform work, and some of it is lost as heat (**FIG. 55-4**). (Remember that no biological process is 100% efficient.) The second law of thermodynamics explains why there are few trophic levels: energy pyramids are short because of the dramatic reduction in energy content that occurs at each successive trophic level.

Ecosystems vary in productivity

The **gross primary productivity (GPP)** of an ecosystem is the rate at which energy is captured during photosynthesis.[1] Thus, GPP is the total amount of photosynthetic energy captured in a given period. Of course, plants and other producers must respire to provide energy for their life processes, and cellular respiration acts as a drain on photosynthetic output. Energy that remains in plant tissues after cellular respiration has occurred is called **net primary productivity (NPP)**. That is, NPP is the amount of biomass (the energy stored in plant tissues) found in excess of that broken down by a plant's cellular respiration for normal daily activities. NPP represents the rate at which this organic matter is actually incorporated into plant tissues to produce growth.

net primary productivity	=	gross primary productivity	−	plant respiration
(plant growth per unit area per unit time)		(total photosynthesis per unit area per unit time)		(per unit area per unit time)

Only the energy represented by net primary productivity is available for consumers, and of this energy only a portion is actually used by them. Both GPP and NPP are expressed as energy per unit area per unit time (for example, kilocalories of energy fixed by photosynthesis per square meter per year) or as dry weight (that

is, grams of carbon incorporated into tissue per square meter per year).

Herbivores and other consumers eventually consume all of a plant's net primary production. What happens to this energy? Consider the transfer of net primary production from a plant to a deer that eats the plant. Much of the energy stored in the plant material that the deer consumes—about 25%—is not digested and is lost in its feces. (This energy is not lost from the ecosystem because detritivores and decomposers will make use of it; it is lost from the deer's point of view, however.) Perhaps 55% of the energy that the deer takes in as food is released during cellular respiration and used to do work such as muscle contraction and to maintain and repair the deer's body. The remaining energy—less than 20%—is available to produce new biomass, that is, new tissues. This net energy available for biomass production by consumer organisms is called **secondary productivity.** An ecosystem's secondary productivity is based on its primary productivity.

Many factors may interact to determine primary productivity. Some plants are more efficient than others in fixing carbon. Environmental factors are also important. These include the availability of solar energy, minerals, and water; other climate factors; the degree of maturity of the community; and the severity of human modification of the environment.

These factors are difficult to assess, particularly on a large scale. The summer of 2003, which was extremely hot and dry in Europe, provided ecologists there with a chance to measure primary productivity changes in response to these unusual conditions. Based on their measurements, they estimate that GPP throughout Europe was reduced by 30% as a result of the heat and drought.

Ecosystems differ strikingly in their primary productivities (**FIG. 55-5** and **TABLE 55-1**). On land, tropical rain forests have the highest productivity, probably as a result of the abundant rainfall, warm temperatures, and intense sunlight. As you might expect, tundra, because of its short, cool growing season, and deserts, because of their lack of precipitation, are the least productive terrestrial ecosystems. In ecosystems with comparable annual temperatures (such as temperate deciduous forest, temperate

---

[1]Gross and net primary productivities are referred to as primary because plants and other producers occupy the first position in food webs.

FIGURE 55-5 A measure of Earth's primary productivity

The data are from a satellite launched as part of NASA's Mission to Planet Earth in 1997. The satellite measured the amount of plant life on land as well as the concentration of phytoplankton (algae) in the ocean. On land, the most productive areas, such as tropical rain forests, are dark green, and the least productive ecosystems (deserts) are orange. In the ocean and other aquatic ecosystems, the most productive regions are red, followed by orange, yellow, green, and blue (the least productive). Data are not available for the gray area.

TABLE 55-1 Net Primary Productivities (NPP) for Selected Ecosystems

Ecosystem	Average NPP (g dry matter/m²/year)
Algal beds and reefs	2500
Tropical rain forest	2200
Swamp and marsh	2000
Estuaries	1500
Temperate evergreen forest	1300
Temperate deciduous forest	1200
Savanna	900
Boreal (northern) forest	800
Woodland and shrubland	700
Agricultural land	650
Temperate grassland	600
Upwelling zones in ocean	500
Lake and stream	250
Arctic and alpine tundra	140
Open ocean	125
Desert and semidesert scrub	90
Extreme desert (rock, sand, ice)	3

Source: Based on Whittaker, R. H. *Communities and Ecosystems*, 2nd ed. Macmillan, New York, 1975.

grassland, and temperate desert), water availability affects NPP. Availability of essential minerals such as nitrogen and phosphorus also affects NPP.

Wetlands (swamps and marshes) connect terrestrial and aquatic environments and are extremely productive. The most productive aquatic ecosystems are algal beds, coral reefs, and estuaries. The lack of available minerals in the sunlit region of the open ocean makes this area extremely unproductive, equivalent to an aquatic desert. Earth's major aquatic and terrestrial ecosystems are discussed in Chapter 56.

As primary productivity increases, species richness declines

Ecologists have observed that an ecosystem's species richness declines with increasing productivity. For example, the resource-poor depths of the Atlantic Ocean's abyssal plain have more species richness than productive shallow waters near the coasts. Ecologists are designing experiments to help explain the pattern, which has been documented with rodents in Israel, birds in South America, and large mammals in Africa. Mathematical ecosystem models suggest that a less productive environment has a *patchy distribution of resources* that reduces competition and allows a greater variety of organisms to coexist.

The bad news for global biodiversity is that humans are constantly enriching the environment, for example, with nitrogen and phosphorus inputs from fossil fuels, fertilizers, and livestock. This continual enrichment may make the Earth's ecosystems more and more productive, a shift that some ecologists think could cost the world a substantial loss of species richness. (Other factors that affect species richness were discussed in Chapter 54.)

Humans consume an increasingly greater percentage of global primary productivity

Humans consume far more of Earth's resources than do any of the other millions of animal species. Peter Vitousek and coworkers at Stanford University calculated in 1986 how much of the global NPP is appropriated for the human economy. When both direct and indirect human impacts are accounted for, Vitousek estimated that humans use 32% to 40% of land-based annual NPP. Since 1986, scientists have done additional research on global ecology, resulting in improved data sets. In 2001, Stuart Rojstaczer and coworkers at Duke University used current satellite-based data to determine a conservative estimate of land-based annual NPP appropriation by humans at 32%.

The take-home message from Vitousek's and Rojstaczer's research is simple. Essentially, human use of global productivity is competing with other species' needs for energy. Our use of so much of the world's productivity may contribute to the loss, through extinction or genetic impoverishment, of many species that have unique roles in maintaining functional ecosystems. Clearly, at these levels of consumption and exploitation of the Earth's resources, human population growth threatens the planet's ability to support all of its occupants.

Food chains and poisons in the environment

You have seen how energy flows through food chains in ecosystems. Before leaving the discussion of food chains, let us consider how certain toxins, including some pesticides, radioactive isotopes, heavy metals such as mercury, and industrial chemicals such as PCBs, enter and pass through food chains. The effects of the pesticide DDT on some bird species first drew attention to the problem. Falcons, pelicans, bald eagles, ospreys, and many other birds are sensitive to traces of DDT in their tissues. A substantial body of scientific evidence indicates that one effect of DDT on these birds is that their eggs have extremely thin, fragile shells that usually break during incubation, causing the chicks' deaths. In 1962, U.S. biologist Rachel Carson published *Silent Spring,* which heightened public awareness about the dangers of DDT and other pesticides. After 1972, the year DDT was banned in the United States, the reproductive success of many birds gradually improved.

The impact of DDT on birds is the result of three characteristics of DDT (and other toxins that cause problems in food webs):

its persistence, bioaccumulation, and biological magnification. Some toxins are extremely stable and may take many years to break down into less toxic forms. The **persistence** of synthetic pesticides and industrial chemicals is a result of their novel chemical structures. These toxins accumulate in the environment because ways to degrade them have not evolved in natural decomposers such as bacteria.

When an organism does not metabolize (break down) or excrete a persistent toxin, the toxin simply gets stored, usually in fatty tissues. Over time, the organism may accumulate high concentrations of the toxin. The buildup of such a toxin in an organism's body is known as **bioaccumulation.**

Organisms at higher trophic levels in food webs tend to store greater concentrations of bioaccumulated toxins in their bodies than do those at lower levels. The increase in concentration as the toxin passes through successive levels of the food web is known as **biological magnification.**

As an example of the concentrating characteristic of persistent toxins, consider a food chain studied in a Long Island salt marsh that was sprayed with DDT over a period of years for mosquito control (**FIG. 55-6**). Although this example involved a bird at the top of the food chain, it is important to recognize that *all* top carnivores, from fishes to humans, are at risk from biological magnification of persistent toxins. Because of this risk, currently approved pesticides have been tested to ensure they do not persist and accumulate in the environment.

KEY EXPERIMENT

QUESTION: Does DDT exhibit biological magnification as it moves through a food chain?

HYPOTHESIS: DDT, a persistent insecticide, increases in concentration at each level of a food chain.

EXPERIMENT: Biologists sampled the concentration of DDT in various organisms of a Long Island salt marsh.

TROPHIC LEVEL	AMOUNT OF DDT IN TISSUE
Tertiary consumer	Ring-billed gull (75.5 ppm)
Secondary consumer	Atlantic needlefish (2.07 ppm)
Secondary consumer	American eel (0.28 ppm)
Primary consumer	Shrimp (0.16 ppm)
Producers, primary consumers	Plankton (0.04 ppm)

RESULTS AND CONCLUSION: The level of DDT increased in the tissues of various organisms as DDT moved through the food chain from producers to consumers. Ring-billed gulls at the top of the food chain had approximately 1 million times as much DDT in their tissues as the concentration of DDT in the water (0.00005 ppm). (Plankton consisted of a mixture of phytoplankton and zooplankton.)

Source: Based on data from Woodwell, G. M., C. F. Worster Jr., and P. A. Isaacson. "DDT Residues in an East Coast Estuary: A Case of Biological Concentration of a Persistent Insecticide." *Science,* Vol. 156, May 12, 1967.

FIGURE 55-6 Biological magnification of DDT (expressed as parts per million) in a Long Island salt marsh

Review

- How does energy flow through a food web such as a deciduous forest?
- What are trophic levels, and how are they related to ecological pyramids?
- How do gross primary productivity (GPP) and net primary productivity (NPP) differ?

55.2 CYCLES OF MATTER IN ECOSYSTEMS

■ LEARNING OBJECTIVE

4 Describe the main steps in each of these biogeochemical cycles: the carbon, nitrogen, phosphorus, and hydrologic cycles.

Matter moves in numerous cycles from one part of an ecosystem to another—that is, from one organism to another (in food chains) and from living organisms to the abiotic environment and back again. We call these cycles of matter **biogeochemical cycles** because they involve biological, geologic, and chemical interactions. For all practical purposes, matter cannot escape from Earth's boundaries. The materials organisms use cannot be "lost," although this matter can end up in locations outside the reach of organisms for a long period. Usually, materials are reused and often recycled both within and among ecosystems.

We discuss four different biogeochemical cycles of matter—carbon, nitrogen, phosphorus, and water—as representative of all biogeochemical cycles. These four cycles are particularly important to organisms because they involve materials used to make the chemical components of cells.

Carbon dioxide is the pivotal molecule in the carbon cycle

Proteins, nucleic acids, lipids, carbohydrates, and other molecules essential to life contain carbon. Carbon is present in the atmosphere as the gas carbon dioxide (CO_2), which makes up approximately 0.04% of the atmosphere. It is also present in the ocean and fresh water as dissolved carbon dioxide, that is, carbonate (CO_3^{2-}) and bicarbonate (HCO_3^-); other forms of dissolved inorganic carbon; and dissolved organic carbon from decay processes. Carbon is also present in rocks such as limestone ($CaCO_3$). The global movement of carbon between the abiotic environment, including the atmosphere and ocean, and organisms is known as the **carbon cycle** (**FIG. 55-7**).

During photosynthesis, plants, algae, and cyanobacteria remove carbon dioxide from the air and *fix*, or incorporate, it into organic compounds such as glucose. Plants use much of the glucose to make cellulose, starch, amino acids, nucleic acids, and other compounds.

Many of these compounds are used as fuel for cellular respiration by the producer that made them, by a consumer that eats the

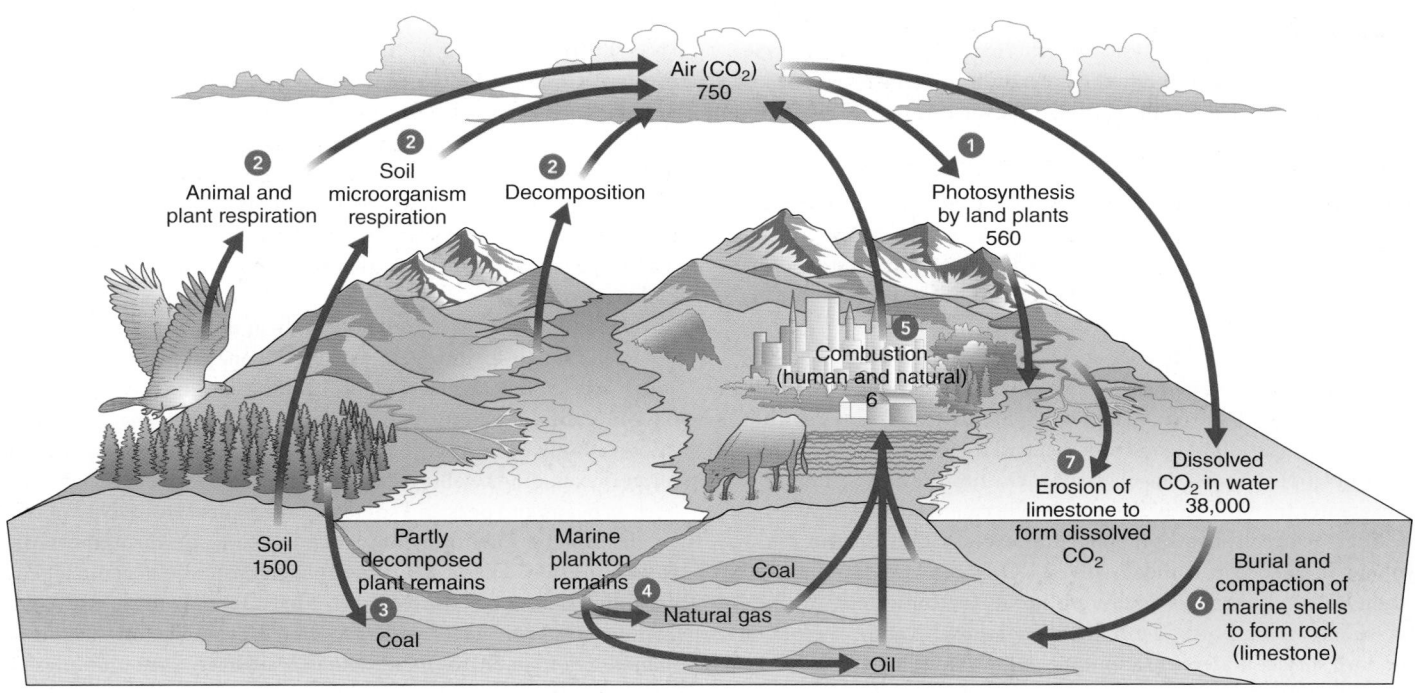

FIGURE 55-7 *Animated* A simplified diagram of the carbon cycle

All but a tiny fraction of Earth's estimated 10^{23} g of carbon is buried in sedimentary rocks and fossil fuel deposits. The values shown for some of the active pools in the global carbon budget are expressed as 10^{15} g of carbon. For example, the soil contains an estimated 1500×10^{15} g of carbon. (Values from Schlesinger, W. H. *Biogeochemistry: An Analysis of Global Change*, 2nd ed., Academic Press, San Diego, 1997, and several other sources.)

producer, or by a decomposer that breaks down the remains of the producer or consumer. The process of cellular respiration returns carbon dioxide to the atmosphere. A similar carbon cycle occurs in aquatic ecosystems between aquatic organisms and dissolved carbon dioxide in the water (not shown in Figure 55-7).

Sometimes the carbon in biological molecules is not recycled back to the abiotic environment for a long time. Carbon stored in the wood of trees may stay for several hundred years or even longer. Also, millions of years ago vast coal beds formed from the bodies of ancient trees that were buried and subjected to anaerobic conditions before they had fully decayed. Similarly, the oils of unicellular marine organisms probably gave rise to the underground deposits of oil and natural gas that accumulated in the geologic past. Coal, oil, and natural gas, called **fossil fuels** because they formed from the remains of ancient organisms, are vast deposits of carbon compounds, the end products of photosynthesis that occurred millions of years ago.

The process of burning, or combustion, may return the carbon in coal, oil, natural gas, and wood to the atmosphere. In combustion, organic molecules are rapidly oxidized (combined with oxygen) and converted to carbon dioxide and water with an accompanying release of light and heat.

An even greater amount of carbon that is stored for millions of years is incorporated into the shells of marine organisms. When these organisms die, their shells sink to the ocean floor, and sediments cover them, forming seabed deposits thousands of meters thick. The deposits are eventually cemented together to form limestone, a sedimentary rock. Earth's crust is dynamically active, and over millions of years, sedimentary rock on the bottom of the seafloor may lift to form land surfaces. When the process of geologic uplift exposes limestone, chemical and physical weathering processes slowly erode it away. This returns carbon to the water and atmosphere, where it is available to participate in the carbon cycle once again.

Human activities have disturbed the global carbon budget

Before the Industrial Revolution, around 1750, the global carbon cycle was in a steady state. Enormous amounts of carbon moved to and from the atmosphere, ocean, and terrestrial ecosystems, but these movements within the global carbon cycle just about canceled out one another.

Since 1750, our industrial society has required a lot of energy, and we have burned increasing amounts of fossil fuels—coal, oil, and natural gas—to obtain this energy. This trend, along with a greater combustion of wood as a fuel and the burning of large sections of tropical forest, has released CO_2 into the atmosphere at a rate greater than the natural carbon cycle can handle.

Earth's ocean absorbs much of this excess CO_2 from the atmosphere. In the ocean, some dissolved CO_2 is converted to carbonic acid (H_2CO_3), which is acidifying surface ocean waters. According to research reported in 2003 in the journal *Nature,* the pH of modern surface waters are about 0.1 pH unit lower than they were in preindustrial times, and models predict up to 1.4 pH units of further acidification during the next 300 years. *Ocean acidification* harms marine organisms, particularly those that produce skeletons and shells of calcium carbonate ($CaCO_3$), which dissolve in the presence of acid.

The level of atmospheric CO_2 increased dramatically beginning in the last half of the 20th century (see Fig. 57-16), and this rise of CO_2 appears to have initiated human-induced changes in global climate. Global climate change could result in a rise in sea level, changes in precipitation patterns, death of forests, extinction of organisms, and problems for agriculture. It could force the displacement of thousands or even millions of people, particularly from coastal areas. (Chapter 57 contains a more thorough discussion of increasing atmospheric CO_2 and the potential impact of global climate change.)

Bacteria are essential to the nitrogen cycle

Nitrogen is crucial for all organisms because it is an essential part of proteins, nucleic acids, and chlorophyll. Because Earth's atmosphere is about 78% nitrogen gas (N_2), it would appear there could be no possible shortage of nitrogen for organisms. However, molecular nitrogen is so stable that it does not readily combine with other elements. Therefore, the N_2 molecule must be broken apart before the nitrogen atoms combine with other elements to form proteins, nucleic acids, and chlorophyll. Chemical reactions that break up N_2 and combine nitrogen with other elements require a great deal of energy.

The **nitrogen cycle,** in which nitrogen cycles between the abiotic environment and organisms, has five steps: nitrogen fixation, nitrification, assimilation, ammonification, and denitrification (**FIG. 55-8**). Bacteria are exclusively involved in all these steps except assimilation.

The first step in the nitrogen cycle, biological **nitrogen fixation** involves conversion of gaseous nitrogen (N_2) to ammonia (NH_3). This process fixes nitrogen into a form that organisms can use. Combustion, volcanic action, lightning discharges, and industrial processes also fix nitrogen as nitrate (NO_3^-). *Nitrogen-fixing bacteria,* including cyanobacteria and certain other free-living and symbiotic bacteria, carry on biological nitrogen fixation in soil and aquatic environments. Nitrogen-fixing bacteria employ an enzyme called **nitrogenase** to break up molecular nitrogen and combine the resulting nitrogen atoms with hydrogen.

Because nitrogenase functions only in the absence of oxygen, the bacteria that fix nitrogen insulate the enzyme from oxygen in some way. Some nitrogen-fixing bacteria live beneath layers of oxygen-excluding slime on the roots of several plant species. Other important nitrogen-fixing bacteria, in the genus *Rhizobium*, live in oxygen-excluding swellings, or **nodules,** on the roots of legumes such as beans and peas and some woody plants (**FIG. 55-9**).

In aquatic environments, cyanobacteria perform most nitrogen fixation. Filamentous cyanobacteria have special oxygen-excluding cells called **heterocysts** that function to fix nitrogen. Some water ferns have cavities in which cyanobacteria live, in a manner comparable to the way *Rhizobium* lives in root nodules of legumes. Other cyanobacteria fix nitrogen in symbiotic association with cycads and other terrestrial plants or as the photosynthetic partner of certain lichens.

The second step of the nitrogen cycle is **nitrification** (see Fig. 55-8), the conversion of ammonia (NH_3) or ammonium

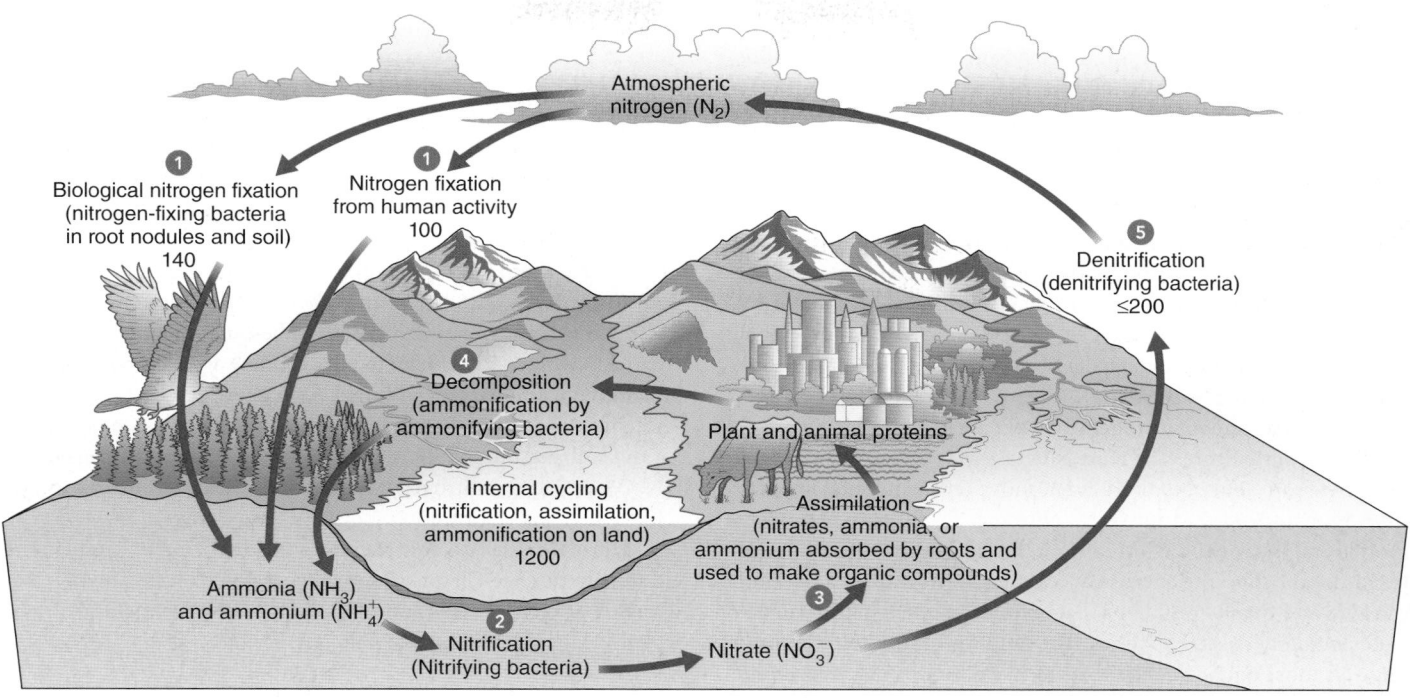

FIGURE 55-8 *Animated* **A simplified diagram of the nitrogen cycle**

The largest pool of nitrogen, estimated at 3.9×10^{21} g, is in the atmosphere. The values shown for selected nitrogen fluxes in the global nitrogen budget are expressed as 10^{12} g of nitrogen per year and represent terrestrial values. For example, each year humans fix an estimated 100×10^{12} g of nitrogen. (Values from Schlesinger, W. H. *Biogeochemistry: An Analysis of Global Change*, 2nd ed., Academic Press, San Diego, 1997, and several other sources.)

(NH_4^+), formed when water reacts with ammonia, to nitrate (NO_3^-). Soil bacteria are responsible for the two-phase process of nitrification, which furnishes these bacteria, called *nitrifying bacteria*, with energy.

In the third step, **assimilation,** roots absorb ammonia (NH_3), ammonium (NH_4^+), or nitrate (NO_3^-) formed by nitrogen fixation and nitrification, and incorporate the nitrogen into proteins, nucleic acids, and chlorophyll. When animals consume plant tissues, they assimilate nitrogen by taking in plant nitrogen compounds and converting them to animal nitrogen compounds.

The fourth step, **ammonification,** is the conversion of organic nitrogen compounds into ammonia (NH_3) and ammonium ions (NH_4^+). Ammonification begins when organisms produce nitrogen-containing wastes such as urea in urine and uric acid in the wastes of birds (see Fig. 48-1). As these substances, along with the nitrogen compounds in dead organisms, decompose, nitrogen is released into the abiotic environment as ammonia (NH_3). The bacteria that perform ammonification in both the soil and aquatic environments are called *ammonifying bacteria.* Most available nitrogen in the soil derives from the recycling of organic nitrogen by ammonification.

The fifth step of the nitrogen cycle is **denitrification,** the reduction of nitrate (NO_3^-) to gaseous nitrogen (N_2). Denitrifying bacteria reverse the action of nitrogen-fixing and nitrifying bacteria by returning nitrogen to the atmosphere as nitrogen gas.

FIGURE 55-9 **Root nodules and nitrogen fixation**

Root nodules on the roots of a pea plant provide an oxygen-free environment for nitrogen-fixing *Rhizobium* bacteria that live in them.

Denitrifying bacteria are anaerobic and therefore live and grow best where there is little or no free oxygen. For example, they are found deep in the soil near the water table, an environment that is nearly oxygen-free.

Human activities have changed the global nitrogen budget

Human activities have disturbed the balance of the global nitrogen cycle. During the 20th century, humans more than doubled the amount of fixed nitrogen (nitrogen that has been chemically combined with hydrogen, oxygen, or carbon) entering the global nitrogen cycle. The excess nitrogen is seriously altering many terrestrial and aquatic ecosystems.

Large quantities of nitrogen fertilizer are produced from nitrogen gas for agriculture. The increasing use of fertilizer has resulted in higher crop yields, but there are negative environmental impacts from human-produced nitrogen. Nitrogen fertilizer is extremely mobile and is easily transferred from the land to rivers to estuaries to the ocean. Thus, the overuse of commercial fertilizer on the land causes water-quality problems that may help explain long-term declines in many coastal fisheries. The amount of nitrate or ammonium in most aquatic ecosystems is in limited supply and limits the growth of algae. Rain washes fertilizer into rivers and lakes, where it stimulates the growth of algae, some of which are toxic. As these algae die, their decomposition by bacteria robs the water of dissolved oxygen, which in turn causes other aquatic organisms, including many fishes, to suffocate.

Nitrates from fertilizer also leach (dissolve and wash down) through the soil and contaminate groundwater. Many people who live in rural areas drink groundwater. Groundwater contaminated by nitrates is dangerous, particularly for infants and small children.

Another human activity that affects the nitrogen cycle is the combustion of fossil fuels. When fossil fuels are burned, the nitrogen locked in organic compounds in the fuel is chemically altered and transferred to the atmosphere. In addition, the high temperature of combustion converts some atmospheric nitrogen to **nitrogen oxides.** Automobile exhaust is one of the main sources of nitrogen oxides. Nitrogen oxides are a necessary ingredient in the production of **photochemical smog,** a mixture of several air pollutants that injure plant tissues, irritate eyes, and cause respiratory problems in humans.

Nitrogen oxides also react with water in the atmosphere to form nitric acid (HNO_3) and nitrous acid (HNO_2). When these and other acids leave the atmosphere as **acid deposition,** they decrease the pH of surface waters (lakes and streams) and soils. Acid deposition has been linked to declining animal populations in aquatic ecosystems. On land, acid deposition alters soil chemistry: certain essential minerals, such as calcium and potassium, wash out of the soil and are therefore unavailable for plants. Nitrous oxide (N_2O), one of the nitrogen oxides, retains heat in the atmosphere (like CO_2) and so promotes global climate change.

Nitrous oxide also contributes to the depletion of ozone in the stratosphere. (See Chapter 2 for a discussion of acids and pH, and Chapter 57 for a discussion of global climate change and stratospheric ozone depletion.)

The phosphorus cycle lacks a gaseous component

Phosphorus does not exist in a gaseous state and therefore does not enter the atmosphere. In the **phosphorus cycle,** phosphorus cycles from the land to sediments in the ocean and back to the land (**FIG. 55-10**).

As water runs over rocks containing phosphorus, it gradually erodes the surface and carries off inorganic phosphate (PO_4^{3-}). The erosion of phosphorus rocks releases phosphate into the soil, where it is taken up by roots in the form of inorganic phosphates. Once in cells, phosphates are incorporated into a variety of bio-

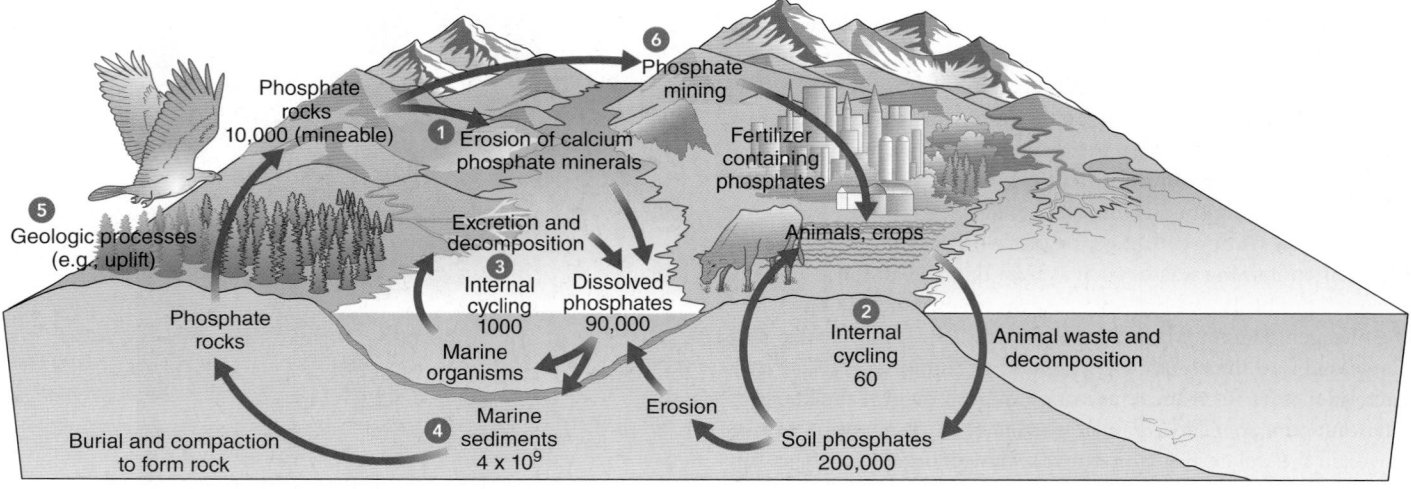

FIGURE 55-10 *Animated* A simplified diagram of the phosphorus cycle

Some values of the global phosphorus budget are given, in units of 10^{12} g phosphorus per year. For example, each year an estimated 60×10^{12} g of phosphorus cycles from the soil to terrestrial organisms and back to the soil. (Values from Schlesinger, W. H. *Biogeochemistry: An Analysis of Global Change*, 2nd ed., Academic Press, San Diego, 1997, and several other sources.)

logical molecules, including nucleic acids, ATP, and the phospholipids that make up cell membranes. Animals obtain most of their required phosphorus from the food they eat, although in some places drinking water may contain a substantial amount of inorganic phosphate. Phosphate released by decomposers becomes part of the pool of inorganic phosphate in the soil that plants reuse. Thus, like carbon and nitrogen, phosphorus moves through the food web as one organism consumes another.

Phosphorus cycles through aquatic ecosystems in much the same way as through terrestrial ecosystems. Dissolved phosphate enters aquatic ecosystems through absorption by algae and aquatic plants, which zooplankton and larger organisms consume. In turn, a variety of fishes and mollusks eat the zooplankton. Ultimately, decomposers break down wastes and dead organisms to release inorganic phosphate into the water, making it available for use again by aquatic producers.

Phosphate can be lost for varying time periods from biological cycles. Streams and rivers carry some phosphate to the ocean, where it is deposited on the seafloor and remains for millions of years. The geologic process of uplift may someday expose these seafloor sediments as new land surfaces, from which phosphate will be once again eroded. Phosphate deposits are also mined for agricultural use in phosphate fertilizers.

Humans affect the natural cycling of phosphorus

In natural terrestrial communities, very little phosphorus is lost from the cycle, but few communities today are in a natural state,

that is, unaltered in some way by humans. Land-denuding practices, such as the clear-cutting of timber, and erosion of agricultural and residential lands accelerate phosphorus loss from the soil into waterways. Excess phosphorus enriches the water, causing algal blooms that rob the water of dissolved oxygen. For practical purposes, phosphorus that washes from the land into the ocean is permanently lost from the terrestrial phosphorus cycle (and from further human use) because it remains in the ocean for millions of years.

Ecologists are also concerned that we are mining phosphorus faster than is sustainable. At its current rate of use, U.S. deposits of phosphorus will probably be depleted during the 21st century.

Water moves among the ocean, land, and atmosphere in the hydrologic cycle

Life would be impossible without water, which makes up a substantial part of the mass of most organisms. All species, from bacteria to plants and animals, use water as a medium for chemical reactions as well as for the transport of materials within and among cells. (Recall from Chapter 2 that water has many unique properties that help shape the continents, moderate climate, and allow organisms to survive.)

In the **hydrologic cycle** water continuously circulates from the ocean to the atmosphere to the land and back to the ocean (**FIG. 55-11**). Water moves from the atmosphere to the land and ocean in the form of precipitation (rain, sleet, snow, or hail). Water

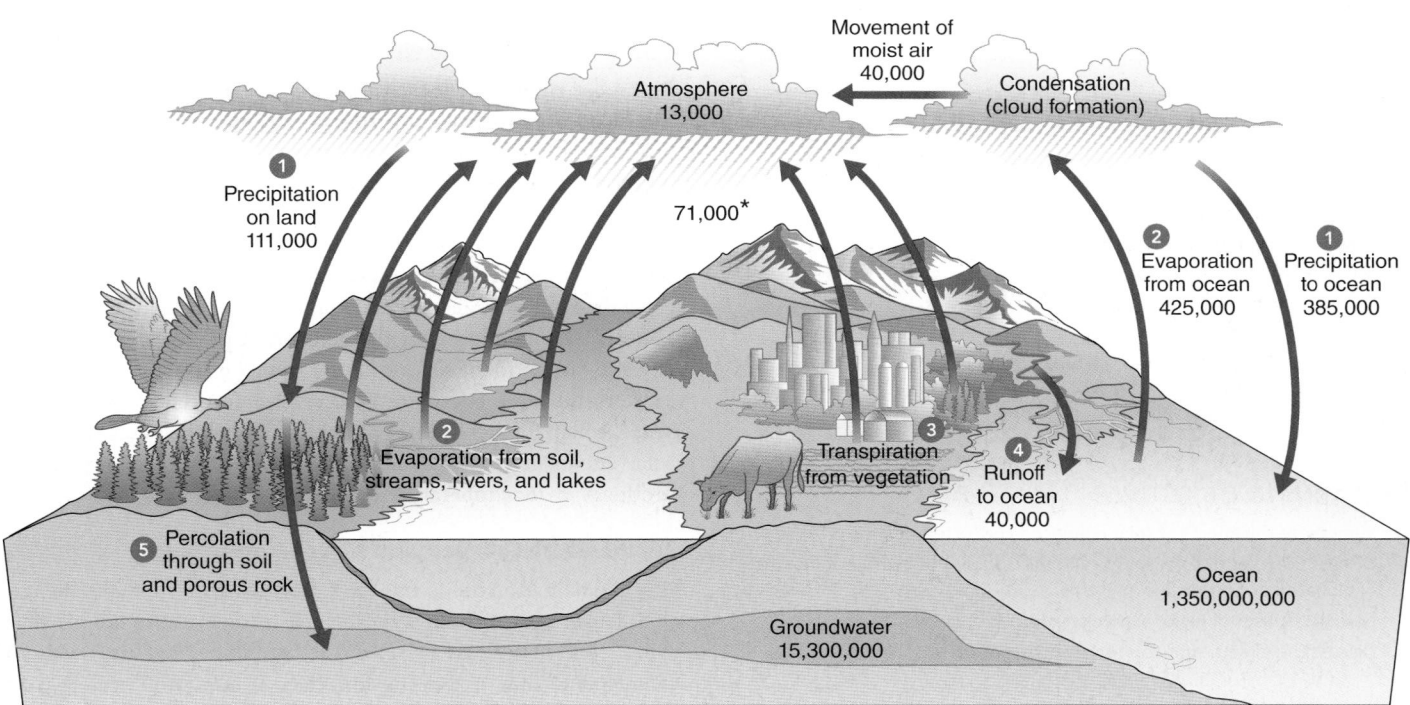

FIGURE 55-11 A simplified diagram of the hydrologic cycle
The global water budget values shown for pools are expressed as cubic kilometers; values for fluxes (movements associated with arrows) are in cubic kilometers per year. The starred value (71,000 km³/yr) is the sum of both transpiration and evaporation from soil, streams, rivers, and lakes. (Values from Schlesinger, W. H. *Biogeochemistry: An Analysis of Global Change*, 2nd ed., Academic Press, San Diego, 1997, and several other sources.)

that evaporates from the ocean surface and from soil, streams, rivers, and lakes eventually condenses and forms clouds in the atmosphere. In addition, **transpiration,** the loss of water vapor from land plants, adds a considerable amount of water vapor to the atmosphere. Roughly 97% of the water a plant absorbs from the soil is transported to the leaves, where it is lost by transpiration.

Water may evaporate from land and re-enter the atmosphere directly. Alternatively, it may flow in rivers and streams to coastal **estuaries,** where fresh water meets the ocean. The movement of surface water from land to ocean is called *runoff,* and the area of land drained by runoff is called a *watershed.* Water also percolates (seeps) downward in the soil to become *groundwater,* where it is trapped and held for a time. The underground caverns and porous layers of rock in which groundwater is stored are called *aquifers.* Groundwater may reside in the ground for hundreds to many thousands of years, but eventually it supplies water to the soil, streams and rivers, plants, and the ocean. The human removal of more groundwater than precipitation or melting snow recharges, called *aquifer depletion,* eliminates groundwater as a water resource.

Regardless of its physical form (solid, liquid, or vapor) or location, every molecule of water eventually moves through the hydrologic cycle. Tremendous amounts of water cycle annually between Earth and its atmosphere. The volume of water entering the atmosphere from the ocean each year is estimated at about 425,000 km^3. Approximately 90% of this water re-enters the ocean directly as precipitation over water; the remainder falls on land. As is true of the other cycles, water (in the form of glaciers, polar ice caps, and certain groundwater) can be lost from the cycle for thousands of years.

Review

- What are the roles of the following processes in the carbon cycle: photosynthesis, cellular respiration, combustion, and erosion?
- What is accomplished in each of the five steps in the nitrogen cycle?
- How does the phosphorus cycle proceed without a gaseous component?

55.3 ABIOTIC FACTORS IN ECOSYSTEMS

◾ LEARNING OBJECTIVES

5 Summarize the effects of solar energy on Earth's temperatures.
6 Discuss the roles of solar energy and the Coriolis effect in the generation of global air and water flow patterns.
7 Give two causes of regional precipitation differences.
8 Discuss the effects of fire on certain ecosystems.

You have seen how ecosystems depend on the abiotic environment to supply energy and essential materials (in biogeochemical cycles). Other abiotic factors such as solar radiation, the atmosphere, the ocean, climate, and fire also affect ecosystems. For a given abiotic factor, each organism living in an ecosystem has an optimal range in which it survives and reproduces. Water and temperature

are probably the two abiotic factors that most affect organisms in ecosystems.

The sun warms Earth

The sun makes life on Earth possible. Without the sun's energy, the temperature on planet Earth would approach absolute zero (0 K or $-273°C$), and all water would be frozen, even in the ocean. The sun powers the hydrologic cycle, carbon cycle, and other biogeochemical cycles and is the primary determinant of climate. Photosynthetic organisms capture the sun's energy and use it to make organic compounds that almost all forms of life require. Most of our fuels, such as wood, oil, coal, and natural gas, represent solar energy captured by photosynthetic organisms. Without the sun, almost all life on Earth would cease (see *Inquiring About: Life without the Sun* for an interesting exception).

The sun's energy, which is the product of a massive nuclear fusion reaction, is emitted into space in the form of electromagnetic radiation, especially ultraviolet, visible, and infrared radiation. About one-billionth of the total energy the sun releases strikes the atmosphere, and of this tiny trickle of energy, a minute part operates the biosphere. On average, clouds and surfaces—especially snow, ice, and the ocean—immediately reflect away 30% of the solar radiation that falls on Earth (**FIG. 55-12**). Earth's surface and atmosphere absorb the remaining 70%, which runs the water cycle, drives winds and ocean currents, powers photosynthesis, and warms the planet. Ultimately, the continual radiation of long-wave infrared (heat) energy returns all this energy to space. If heat gains did not exactly balance losses, Earth would heat up or cool down.

Temperature changes with latitude

The most significant local variations in Earth's temperature are produced because the sun's energy does not uniformly reach all places. Our planet's roughly spherical shape and the tilted angle of its axis produce significant variation in the exposure of the surface to sunlight. The sun's rays strike almost vertically near the equator, concentrating the energy and producing warmer temperatures. Near the poles the sun's rays strike more obliquely and, as a result, are spread over a larger surface area. Also, rays of light entering the atmosphere obliquely near the poles must pass through a deeper envelope of air than those entering near the equator. This causes more of the sun's energy to be scattered and reflected back into space, which further lowers temperatures near the poles. Thus, the solar energy that reaches polar regions is less concentrated and produces lower temperatures.

Temperature changes with season

Earth's inclination on its axis (23.5 degrees from a line drawn perpendicular to the orbital plane) primarily determines the seasons. During half of the year (March 21 to September 22) the Northern Hemisphere tilts toward the sun, concentrating the sunlight and making the days longer (**FIG. 55-13**). During the other half of the year (September 22 to March 21) the Northern Hemisphere tilts away from the sun, giving it a lower concentration of sunlight and shorter days. The orientation of the Southern Hemisphere is just the opposite at these times. Summer in the Northern Hemisphere corresponds to winter in the Southern Hemisphere.

LIFE WITHOUT THE SUN

Is the sun the energy source for all ecosystems? A notable exception was discovered in the late 1970s in a series of hydrothermal vents in the eastern Pacific where sea water apparently had penetrated and been heated by the radioactive rocks below. During its time within Earth, the water had become charged with inorganic mineral compounds, including hydrogen sulfide (H_2S).

No light is available for photosynthesis, but hydrothermal vents support a rich ecosystem that contrasts with the surrounding "desert" of the deep-ocean floor. Giant, blood-red tube worms almost 3 m (10 ft) in length cluster in great numbers around the vents (see figure). Other animals around the hydrothermal vents include unique species of clams, crabs, barnacles, and mussels.

Scientists initially wondered what energy source sustains the organisms in this dark environment. Most deep-sea communities depend on the organic matter that drifts down from the surface waters; in other words, they rely on energy ultimately derived from photosynthesis. Hydrothermal vent communities, however, are too densely clustered and too productive to be dependent on chance encounters with organic material from surface waters.

Instead, chemoautotrophic prokaryotes occupy the base of the food web in these aquatic oases. These prokaryotes have enzymes that catalyze the oxidation of hydrogen sulfide, yielding water plus sulfur or sulfate. Such chemical reactions are exergonic and provide the energy required to fix CO_2, which is dissolved in the water, into organic compounds. Many of the animals

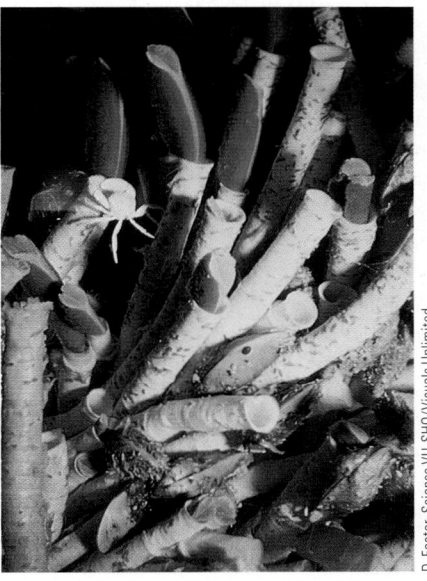

D. Foster, Science VU-SHO/Visuals Unlimited

consume the prokaryotes directly by filter-feeding, but others, such as the giant tube worms, get their energy from prokaryotes that live in their tissues.

Scientists continue to generate questions about hydrothermal vent communities. How do the organisms find and colonize vents, which are ephemeral and widely scattered on the ocean floor? How have the inhabitants of these communities adapted to survive the harsh living conditions, including high pressure, high temperatures, and toxic chemicals? As vent community research continues, scientists hope to discover answers to these and other questions.

Hydrothermal vent ecosystem. Chemoautotrophic prokaryotes living in the tissues of these tube worms (*Riftia pachyptila*) extract energy from hydrogen sulfide to manufacture organic compounds. These worms lack digestive systems and depend on the organic compounds the prokaryotes provide, along with materials filtered from the surrounding water. Also visible in the photograph are some filter-feeding clams (*yellow*) and a crab (*white*).

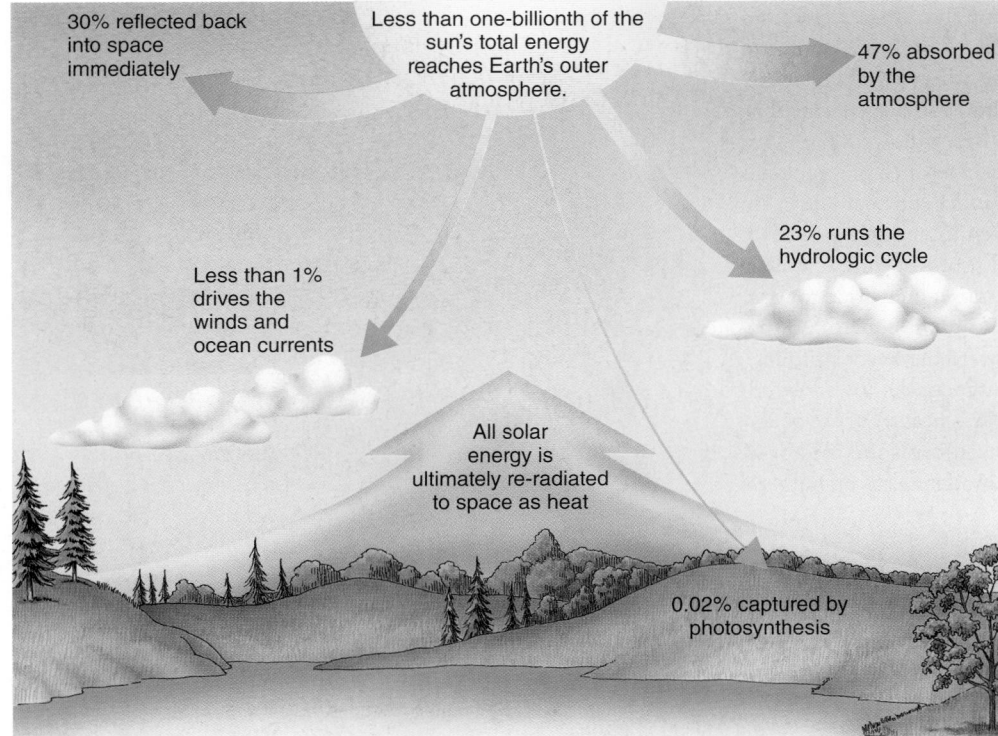

30% reflected back into space immediately

Less than one-billionth of the sun's total energy reaches Earth's outer atmosphere.

47% absorbed by the atmosphere

Less than 1% drives the winds and ocean currents

23% runs the hydrologic cycle

All solar energy is ultimately re-radiated to space as heat

0.02% captured by photosynthesis

FIGURE 55-12 The fate of solar radiation that reaches Earth

Most of the energy released by the sun never reaches Earth. The solar energy that does reach Earth warms the planet's surface, drives the hydrologic and other biogeochemical cycles, produces the climate, and powers almost all life through the process of photosynthesis.

The atmosphere contains several gases essential to organisms

The atmosphere is an invisible layer of gases that envelops Earth. Oxygen (21%) and nitrogen (78%) are the predominant gases in the atmosphere, accounting for about 99% of dry air; other gases, including argon, carbon dioxide, neon, and helium, make up the remaining 1%. In addition, water vapor and trace amounts of various air pollutants, such as methane, ozone, dust particles, pollen, microorganisms, and chlorofluorocarbons (CFCs) are present. Atmospheric oxygen is essential to plants, animals, and other organisms that respire aerobically; and plants and other photosynthetic organisms also require carbon dioxide.

The atmosphere performs several essential ecological functions. It protects Earth's surface from most of the sun's ultraviolet radiation and X-rays, and from lethal amounts of cosmic rays from space. Without this atmospheric shielding, life as we know it would cease. Although the atmosphere protects Earth from high-energy radiation, visible light and some infrared radiation can penetrate, and they warm the surface and the lower atmosphere. This interaction between the atmosphere and solar energy is responsible for weather and climate.

Organisms depend on the atmosphere, but they also help maintain and, in certain instances, modify its composition. For example, atmospheric oxygen increased to its present level as a result of billions of years of photosynthesis. Today, an approximate balance between oxygen-producing photosynthesis and oxygen-using aerobic respiration helps maintain the level of atmospheric oxygen.

The sun drives global atmospheric circulation

In large measure, differences in temperature that are due to variations in the amount of solar energy at different locations on Earth drive the circulation of the atmosphere. The warm surface near the equator heats the air with which it comes into contact, causing this air to expand and rise. As the warm air rises, it flows away from the equator, cools, and sinks again (**FIG. 55-14**). Much of it recirculates to the same areas it left, but the remainder splits and flows in two directions, toward the poles. The air chills enough to sink to the surface at about 30 degrees north and south latitudes. Similar upward movements of warm air and its subsequent flow toward the poles occur at higher latitudes, farther from the equator. At the poles, the cold polar air sinks and flows toward the lower latitudes, generally beneath the warm air that simultaneously flows toward the poles. The constant motion of air transfers heat from the equator toward the poles, and as the air returns, it cools the land over which it passes. This continuous turnover moderates temperatures over Earth's surface.

The atmosphere exhibits complex horizontal movements

In addition to global circulation patterns, the atmosphere exhibits complex horizontal movements called **winds.** The nature of wind, with its turbulent gusts, eddies, and lulls, is difficult to understand or predict. It results in part from differences in atmospheric pressure and from Earth's rotation.

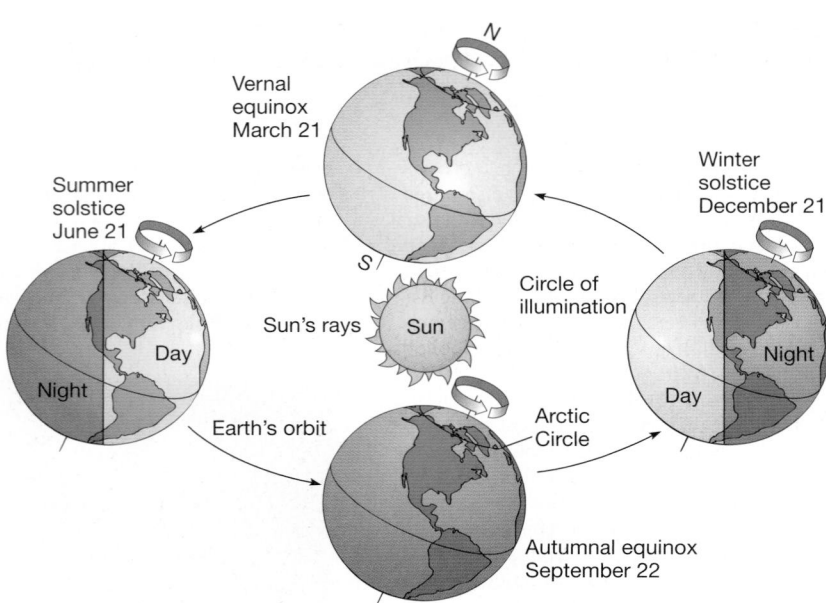

FIGURE 55-13 Seasonal changes in temperature

Earth's inclination on its axis remains the same as Earth travels around the sun. Thus, the sun's rays hit the Northern Hemisphere obliquely during winter months and more directly during summer months. In the Southern Hemisphere, the sun's rays are oblique during the winter, which corresponds to the Northern Hemisphere's summer. At the equator, the sun's rays are approximately vertical on March 21 and September 22.

FIGURE 55-14 *Animated* Atmospheric circulation

The greatest solar energy input occurs at the equator and heats air most strongly in that area. The air rises and travels poleward (*left*) but is cooled in the process so that much of it descends again around 30 degrees latitude in both hemispheres. At higher latitudes the patterns of air movement are more complex.

The gases that constitute the atmosphere have weight and exert a pressure that is, at sea level, about 1013 millibars (14.7 lb/in²). Air pressure is variable, however, and changes with altitude, temperature, and humidity. Winds tend to blow from areas of high atmospheric pressure to areas of low pressure; the greater the difference between the high and low pressure areas, the stronger the wind.

Earth's rotation influences the direction that wind blows. Because Earth rotates from west to east, wind swerves to the right in the Northern Hemisphere and to the left in the Southern Hemisphere. This tendency of moving air to be deflected from its path by Earth's rotation is known as the **Coriolis effect.**

The global ocean covers most of Earth's surface

The global ocean is a huge body of salt water that surrounds the continents and covers almost three-fourths of Earth's surface. It is a single, continuous body of water, but geographers divide it into four sections separated by the continents: the Pacific, Atlantic, Indian, and Arctic Oceans. The Pacific Ocean, which covers one-third of Earth's surface and contains more than half of Earth's water, is the largest by far.

Winds drive surface ocean currents

The persistent prevailing winds blowing over the ocean produce mass movements of surface ocean water known as **ocean currents** (**FIG. 55-15**). The prevailing winds generate circular ocean currents called *gyres.* For example, in the North Atlantic, the tropical trade winds tend to blow toward the west, whereas the westerlies in the midlatitudes blow toward the east (see Fig. 55-14). This helps establish a clockwise gyre in the North Atlantic. Thus, surface ocean currents and winds tend to move in the same direction, although there are many variations on this general rule.

The Coriolis effect is partly responsible for the paths that surface ocean currents travel. Earth's rotation from west to east causes surface ocean currents to swerve to the right in the Northern Hemisphere, producing a clockwise gyre of water currents. In the Southern Hemisphere, ocean currents swerve to the left, producing a counterclockwise gyre.

The ocean interacts with the atmosphere

The ocean and the atmosphere are strongly linked. Wind from the atmosphere affects the ocean currents, and heat from the ocean affects atmospheric circulation. One of the best examples of the interaction between ocean and atmosphere is the **El Niño–Southern**

KEY POINT The driving force of wind produces Earth's major surface ocean currents.

FIGURE 55-15 *Animated* Major surface ocean currents
Each current has characteristic temperature and flow patterns.

Oscillation (ENSO) event. ENSO is a periodic warming of surface waters of the tropical eastern Pacific that alters both oceanic and atmospheric circulation patterns and results in unusual weather in areas far from the tropical Pacific. Normally, westward-blowing trade winds restrict the warmest waters to the western Pacific (near Australia). Every three to seven years, however, the trade winds weaken and the warm water mass expands eastward to South America, raising surface temperatures in the eastern Pacific. Ocean currents, which normally flow westward in this area, slow down, stop altogether, or even reverse and go eastward. The phenomenon is called El Niño (Spanish for "the child") because the warming usually reaches the fishing grounds off Peru just before Christmas. Most ENSOs last from one to two years.

An ENSO event changes biological productivity in parts of the ocean. The warmer sea-surface temperatures and accompanying changes in ocean circulation patterns off the west coast of South America prevent colder, nutrient-laden deeper waters from **upwelling** (coming to the surface) (**FIG. 55-16**). The lack of nutrients in the water results in a severe decrease in the populations of anchovies and many other marine fishes. Other species, such as shrimp and scallops, thrive during an ENSO event. Along the Pacific coast of North America, ENSO shifts the distribution of tropical fishes northward and even affects the salmon run in Alaska.

Climate profoundly affects organisms

Climate is the average weather conditions, plus extremes (records), that occur in a given place over a period of years. The two most important factors that determine an area's climate are temperature (both average temperature and temperature extremes)

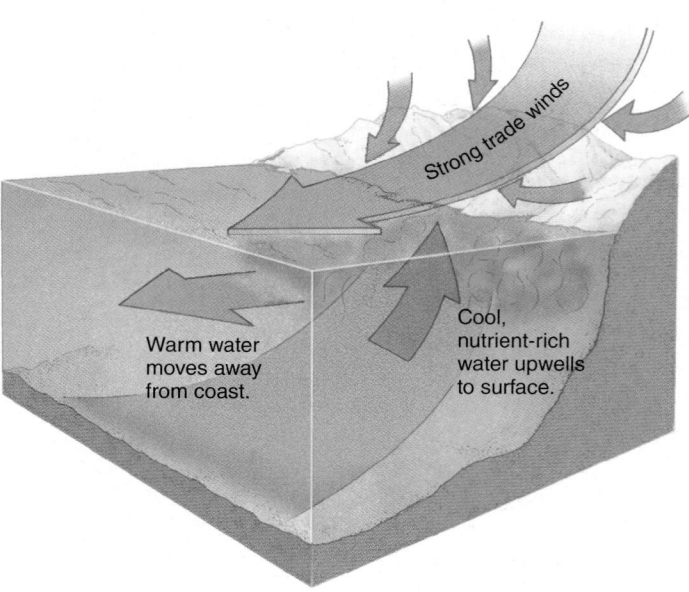

FIGURE 55-16 *Animated* **Upwelling**
Coastal upwelling, where deeper waters come to the surface, occurs in the Pacific Ocean along the South American coast. Upwelling provides nutrients for microscopic algae, which in turn support a complex food web. Coastal upwelling weakens considerably during years with ENSO events, temporarily reducing fish populations.

and precipitation (both average precipitation and seasonal distribution). Other climate factors include wind, humidity, fog, cloud cover, and lightning-caused wildfires. Unlike weather, which changes rapidly, climate generally changes slowly, over hundreds or thousands of years.

Day-to-day variations, day-to-night variations, and seasonal variations are also important dimensions of climate that affect organisms. Latitude, elevation, topography, vegetation, distance from the ocean or other large bodies of water, and location on a continent or other landmass all influence temperature, precipitation, and other aspects of climate.

Earth has many different climates, and because they are relatively constant for many years, organisms have adapted to them. The wide variety of organisms on Earth evolved in part because of the many different climates, ranging from cold, snow-covered, polar climates to hot, tropical climates where it rains almost every day.

Air and water movements and surface features affect precipitation patterns

Precipitation varies from one location to another and has a profound effect on the distribution and kinds of organisms present. One of the driest places on Earth is in the Atacama Desert in Chile, where the average annual rainfall is 0.05 cm (0.02 in). In contrast, Mount Waialeale in Hawaii, Earth's wettest spot, receives an average annual precipitation of 1200 cm (472 in).

Differences in precipitation depend on several factors. The heavy-rainfall areas of the tropics result mainly from the uplifting of moisture-laden air. High surface-water temperatures (recall the enormous amount of solar energy striking the equator) cause the evaporation of vast quantities of water from tropical parts of the ocean. Prevailing winds blow the resulting moist, warm air over landmasses. Land surfaces warmed by the sun heat the air and cause moist air to rise. As it rises, the air cools and its moisture-holding ability decreases. (Cool air holds less water vapor than warm air.) When air reaches its saturation point, it cannot hold any additional water vapor; clouds form, and water is released as precipitation. The air eventually returns to the surface on both sides of the equator near the Tropics of Cancer and Capricorn (latitudes 23.5 degrees north and south, respectively). By then, most of the moisture has precipitated so that dry air returns to the equator. This dry air makes little biological difference over the ocean, but its lack of moisture produces some of the great subtropical deserts, such as the Sahara.

Air is also dried during long journeys over landmasses. Near the windward (side from which the prevailing wind blows) coasts of continents, rainfall may be heavy. However, in the temperate zones—the areas between the tropical and polar zones—continental interiors are usually dry because they are far from the ocean that replenishes water vapor in the air passing over it.

Mountains force air to rise, removing moisture from humid air. As it gains altitude, the air cools, clouds form, and precipitation typically occurs, primarily on the windward slopes of the mountains. As the air mass moves down on the other side of the mountain, it is warmed and clouds evaporate, thereby lessening the chance of precipitation of any remaining moisture. This situation exists on the west coast of North America, where precipitation falls on the western slopes of mountains that are close to the coast. The dry lands on the sides of the mountains away from the

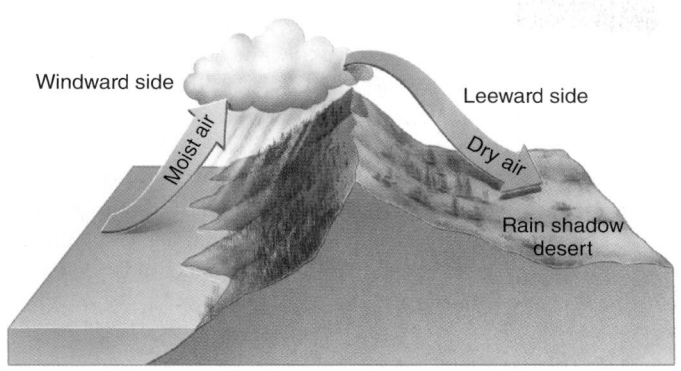

FIGURE 55-17 *Animated* **Rain shadow**

A rain shadow is the arid or semiarid land that occurs on the leeward side of a mountain. Such a rain shadow occurs east of the Cascade Range in Washington State. The western side of the range receives more than 500 cm of precipitation annually, whereas the eastern side receives 40 to 50 cm.

prevailing wind (in this case, east of the mountain range) are called **rain shadows** (**FIG. 55-17**).

Microclimates are local variations in climate

Differences in elevation, in the steepness and direction of slopes, and therefore in exposure to sunlight and prevailing winds may produce local variations in climate known as **microclimates,** which are sometimes quite different from their overall surroundings. Patches of sun and shade on a forest floor, for example, produce a variety of microclimates for plants, animals, and microorganisms living there. The microclimate of an organism's habitat is of primary importance because that is the climate an organism actually experiences and must cope with. (Keep in mind, however, that microclimates are largely affected by the regional climates in which they are located.)

Sometimes organisms modify their own microclimate. For example, trees modify the local climate within a forest so that in summer the temperature is usually lower, and the relative humidity greater, than outside the forest. The temperature and humidity beneath the litter of the forest floor differ still more; in the summer the microclimate of this area is considerably cooler and moister than the surrounding forest. As another example, many desert-dwelling animals burrow to avoid surface climate conditions that would kill them in minutes. The cooler daytime microclimate in their burrows permits them to survive until night, when the surface cools off and they come out to forage or hunt.

Fires are a common disturbance in some ecosystems

Wildfires, which are fires started by lightning, are an important ecological force in many geographic areas. Those areas most prone to wildfires have wet seasons followed by dry seasons. Vegetation that grows and accumulates during the wet season dries out enough during the dry season to burn easily. When lightning hits vegetation or ground litter, it ignites the dry organic material and a fire spreads through the area.

Fires have several effects on organisms. First, combustion frees the minerals that were locked in dry organic matter. The ashes re-

maining after a fire are rich in potassium, phosphorus, calcium, and other minerals essential for plant growth. With the arrival of precipitation, vegetation flourishes following a fire. Second, fire removes plant cover and exposes the soil. This change stimulates the germination and establishment of seeds requiring bare soil, as well as encourages the growth of shade-intolerant plants. Third, fire causes increased soil erosion because it removes plant cover, leaving the soil more vulnerable to wind and water.

African savanna, California chaparral, North American grasslands, and ponderosa pine forests of the western United States are some fire-adapted ecosystems (see Chapter 56). Fire helps maintain grasses as the dominant vegetation in grasslands by removing fire-sensitive hardwood trees.

Humans try to prevent fires, and sometimes this effort has disastrous consequences. When fire is excluded from a fire-adapted ecosystem, deadwood and other plant litter accumulate. As a result, when a fire does occur, it is much more destructive. The sometimes deadly wildfires in Colorado and other western states and provinces are blamed in part on decades of suppressing fires in the region. Prevention of fire also converts grassland to woody vegetation and facilitates the invasion of fire-sensitive trees into fire-adapted forests.

Controlled burning is a tool of ecological management in which the undergrowth and plant litter are deliberately burned under controlled conditions before they have accumulated to dangerous levels (**FIG. 55-18**). Controlled burns are also used to suppress fire-sensitive trees, thereby maintaining the natural fire-adapted ecosystem. However, little scientific evidence exists on when controlled burning is appropriate or how often it should be carried out. Moreover, there are major practical and political problems in implementing controlled burns.

FIGURE 55-18 **Fire as a tool of ecological management**

Here, a controlled burn helps maintain a ponderosa pine (*Pinus ponderosa*) stand in Oregon.

Review

- What basic forces determine the circulation of the atmosphere?
- What basic forces produce the main ocean currents?
- What are some of the factors that produce regional differences in precipitation?

55.4 STUDYING ECOSYSTEM PROCESSES

■ LEARNING OBJECTIVE

9 Briefly describe some of the long-term ecological research conducted at Hubbard Brook Experimental Forest.

Ecologists conduct detailed ecosystem studies in laboratory simulations and in the field to measure such processes as energy flow, the cycling of nutrients, and the effects of natural and human-induced disturbances (such as air pollution, tree harvesting, and land-use changes). Some ecosystem studies, such as those performed at the Hubbard Brook Experimental Forest (HBEF), a 3100-hectare (7750-acre) reserve in the White Mountain National Forest in New Hampshire, are long term. Beginning in the late 1950s and continuing to the present, HBEF has been the site of numerous studies that address the hydrology (for example, precipitation, surface runoff, and groundwater flow), biology, geology, and chemistry of forests and associated aquatic ecosystems. The National Science Foundation (NSF) has designated HBEF as one of its 24 long-term ecological research sites.

Many of the experiments at HBEF are based on field observations. For example, salamander populations were originally surveyed in forest communities in 1970 and have been resurveyed in recent years. Other studies involve manipulative experiments. In 1978, scientists added dilute sulfuric acid to a small stream in HBEF to study the chemical and biological effects of acidification. This experiment was of practical value because *acid deposition,* a form of air pollution, has acidified numerous lakes and streams in industrialized countries.

Several researchers have studied the effects on HBEF stream ecosystems of **deforestation,** the clearance of large expanses of forest for agriculture or other uses. When a forest is removed, the total amount of water and minerals that flow into streams increases drastically. **FIGURE 55-19** shows a concrete dam called a *catchment,* constructed across a stream so ecologists can measure the flow of water and chemical components out of the ecosystem. Typically, outflow is measured in two separate ecosystems: one serves as a control and one is experimentally manipulated. These studies demonstrate that deforestation causes soil erosion and leaching of essential minerals that result in decreased soil fertility. The summer temperatures in streams running through deforested areas are higher than in shady streams running through uncut forests. Many stream organisms do not fare well in deforested areas, in part because they are adapted to cooler temperatures.

Detailed studies such as those at HBEF provide ecologists with insights into how ecological processes function in individual ecosystems. Ecologists compare these data with similar information from other ecosystem studies to develop generalized insights into how ecosystems are structured and how they function. Long-term ecosystem experiments enable ecologists to evaluate and predict the effects of environmental change, including human-induced change.

Ecosystem experiments also contribute to our practical knowledge about how to maintain water quality, wildlife habitat, and productive forests. **Ecosystem management,** a conservation approach that emphasizes restoring and maintaining the quality of an entire ecosystem rather than the conservation of individual species, makes use of such knowledge.

Review

- What are some of the environmental effects observed in the deforestation study at Hubbard Brook Experimental Forest?

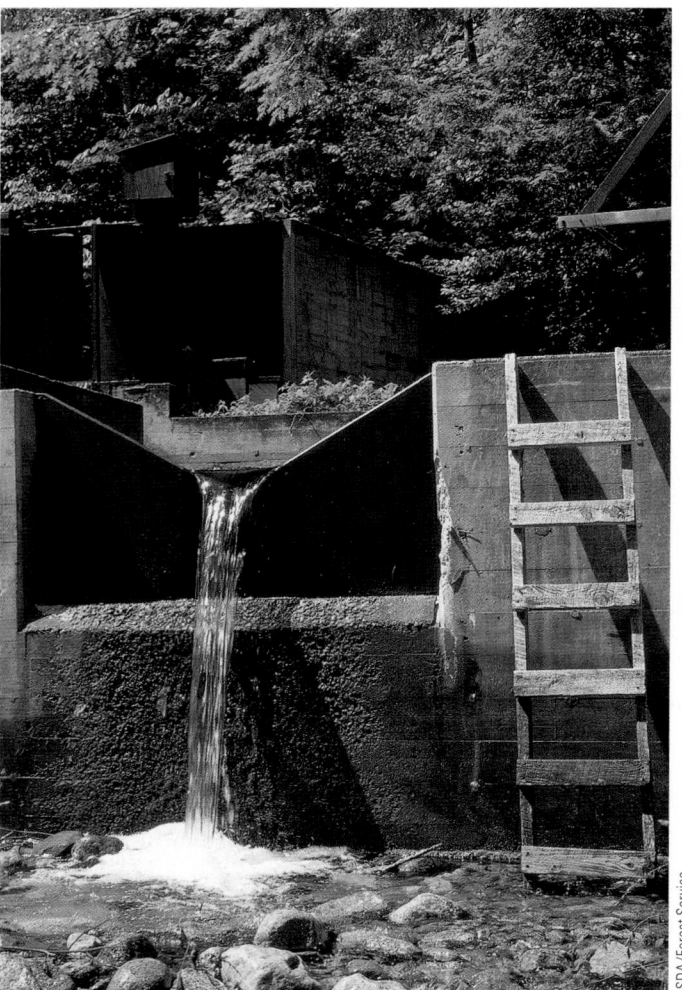

FIGURE 55-19 *Animated* Catchment at Hubbard Brook Experimental Forest

Scientists who study streams investigate processes such as how water enters and is discharged from the stream, how sediments and chemicals move, and the effects of these physical factors on stream habitats. Catchments help scientists to measure the quantity, timing, and quality of water flowing from a forested watershed.

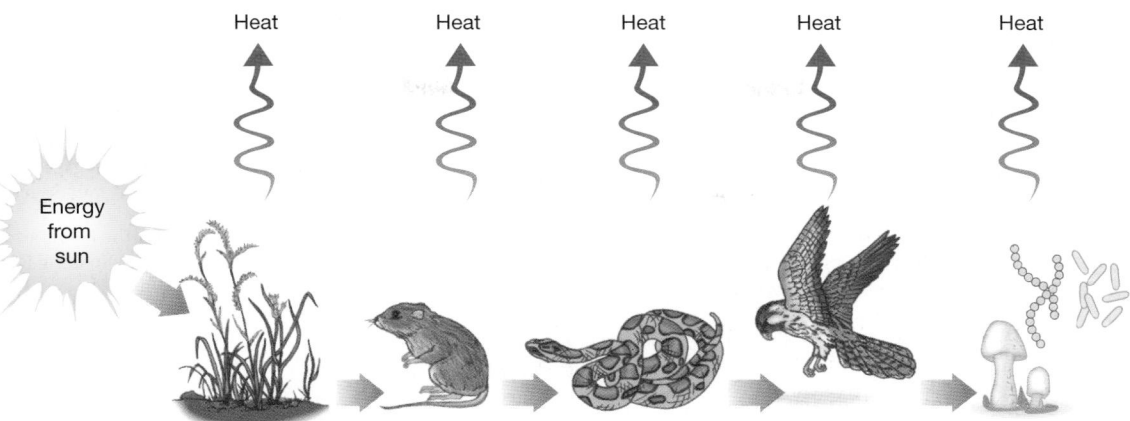

Heat   Heat   Heat   Heat   Heat

Energy from sun

55.1 *(page 1197)*

1 Summarize the concept of energy flow through a food web.

- **Energy flow** through an ecosystem is linear, from the sun to producer to consumer to decomposer. Much of this energy is converted to heat as it moves from one organism to another, so organisms occupying the next **trophic level** cannot use it.

- Trophic relationships may be expressed as **food webs,** which show the many alternative pathways that energy may take among the producers, consumers, and decomposers of an ecosystem.

CENGAGENOW™   Learn more about how trophic levels interact by clicking on the figures in CengageNOW.

2 Explain typical pyramids of numbers, biomass, and energy.

- **Ecological pyramids** typically express the progressive reduction in numbers of organisms, biomass, and energy found in successive trophic levels. A **pyramid of numbers** shows the number of organisms at each trophic level in a given ecosystem. A **pyramid of biomass** shows the total biomass at each successive trophic level. A **pyramid of energy** indicates the energy content of the biomass of each trophic level.

3 Distinguish between gross primary productivity and net primary productivity.

- **Gross primary productivity (GPP)** of an ecosystem is the rate at which photosynthesis captures energy. **Net primary productivity (NPP)** is the energy that remains (as biomass) after plants and other producers carry out cellular respiration.

55.2 *(page 1203)*

4 Describe the main steps in each of these biogeochemical cycles: the carbon, nitrogen, phosphorus, and hydrologic cycles.

- Carbon dioxide is the important gas of the **carbon cycle.** Carbon enters plants, algae, and cyanobacteria as CO_2, which photosynthesis incorporates into organic molecules. Cellular respiration, combustion, and erosion of limestone return CO_2 to the water and atmosphere, where it is again available to producers.

- The **nitrogen cycle** has five steps. **Nitrogen fixation** is the conversion of nitrogen gas to ammonia. **Nitrification** is the conversion of ammonia or ammonium to nitrate. **Assimilation** is the conversion of nitrates, ammonia, or ammonium to proteins and other nitrogen-containing compounds by plants; conversion of plant proteins into animal proteins is also assimilation. **Ammonification** is the conversion of organic nitrogen to ammonia and ammonium ions. **Denitrification** is the conversion of nitrate to nitrogen gas.

- The **phosphorus cycle** has no biologically important gaseous compounds. Phosphorus erodes from rock as inorganic phosphate, which the roots of plants absorb from the soil. Animals obtain the phosphorus they need from their diets. Decomposers release inorganic phosphate into the environment. When phosphorus washes into the ocean and is subsequently deposited in seabeds, it is lost from biological cycles for millions of years.

- The **hydrologic cycle** involves an exchange of water between the land, ocean, atmosphere, and organisms. Water enters the atmosphere by evaporation and **transpiration** and leaves the atmosphere as precipitation. On land, water filters through the ground or runs off to lakes, rivers, and the ocean. Aquifers are underground caverns and porous layers of rock in which groundwater is stored.

CENGAGENOW™   Explore the carbon, nitrogen, phosphorus, and hydrologic cycles by clicking on the figures in CengageNOW.

55.3 *(page 1208)*

5 Summarize the effects of solar energy on Earth's temperatures.

- Of the solar energy that reaches Earth, 30% is immediately reflected away; the atmosphere and surface absorb the remaining 70%. Ultimately, all absorbed solar energy is reradiated into space as infrared (heat) radiation.

- A combination of Earth's roughly spherical shape and the tilted angle of its axis concentrates solar energy at the equator and dilutes it at the poles; the tropics are hotter and less variable in climate than are temperate and polar areas.

6 Discuss the roles of solar energy and the Coriolis effect in the generation of global air and water flow patterns.

- Visible light and some infrared radiation warm the surface and the lower part of the atmosphere. Atmospheric heat transferred from the equator to the poles produces movement of warm air toward the poles and of cool air toward the equator.

- **Winds** result in part from differences in atmospheric pressure and from the **Coriolis effect,** the tendency of moving air or water, because of Earth's rotation, to be deflected to the right in the Northern Hemisphere and to the left in the Southern Hemisphere.

- Surface **ocean currents** result in part from prevailing winds and the Coriolis effect.

CENGAGENOW™   Learn more about atmospheric circulation, ocean currents, and upwelling by clicking on the figures in CengageNOW.

7 Give two causes of regional precipitation differences.

■ Latitude, elevation, topography, vegetation, distance from the ocean or other large bodies of water, and location on a continent or other landmass influence precipitation.

■ Precipitation is greatest where warm air passes over the ocean, absorbs moisture, and then cools, such as in areas where mountains force humid air upward. Deserts develop in the **rain shadows** of mountain ranges or in continental interiors.

CENGAGENOW™ Learn more about rain shadows by clicking on the figure in CengageNOW.

8 Discuss the effects of fire on certain ecosystems.

■ Fire frees the minerals locked in dry organic matter, removes plant cover and exposes the soil, and increases soil erosion. Many ecosys-tems, such as savanna, chaparral, grasslands, and certain forests, contain fire-adapted organisms.

55.4 (page 1214)

9 Briefly describe some of the long-term ecological research conducted at Hubbard Brook Experimental Forest.

■ Hubbard Brook Experimental Forest (HBEF) is the site of numer-ous studies that address the hydrology (precipitation, surface runoff, and groundwater flow), biology (effects of deforestation and changes in salamander populations), geology, and chemistry (acid precipitation) of forests and associated aquatic ecosystems.

CENGAGENOW™ Learn more about the Hubbard Brook Experi-mental Forest by clicking on the figure in CengageNOW.

TEST YOUR UNDERSTANDING

1. The movement of matter is _____ in ecosystems, and the movement of energy is _____. (a) linear; linear (b) linear; cyclic (c) cyclic; cyclic (d) cyclic; linear (e) cyclic; linear or cyclic

2. A complex of interconnected food chains in an ecosystem is called (a) an ecosystem (b) a pyramid of numbers (c) a pyramid of bio-mass (d) a biosphere (e) a food web

3. The quantitative estimate of the total amount of living material is called (a) biomass (b) energy flow (c) gross primary productivity (d) plant respiration (e) net primary productivity

4. Which of the following equations shows the relationship between gross primary productivity (GPP) and net primary productivity (NPP)? (a) GPP = NPP − photosynthesis (b) NPP = GPP − photosynthesis (c) GPP = NPP − plant respiration (d) NPP = GPP − plant respiration (e) NPP = GPP − animal respiration

5. Which of the following processes increase(s) the amount of atmo-spheric carbon in the carbon cycle? (a) photosynthesis (b) cellular respiration (c) combustion (d) a and c (e) b and c

6. In the carbon cycle, carbon is found in (a) limestone rock (b) oil, coal, and natural gas (c) living organisms (d) the atmosphere (e) all of the preceding

7. In the nitrogen cycle, gaseous nitrogen is converted to ammonia during (a) nitrogen fixation (b) nitrification (c) assimilation (d) ammonification (e) denitrification

8. The conversion of ammonia to nitrate, known as _____, is a two-step process performed by soil bacteria. (a) nitrogen fixation (b) nitrification (c) assimilation (d) ammonification (e) denitrification

9. This biogeochemical cycle does not have a gaseous component but cycles from the land to sediments in the ocean and back to the land. (a) carbon cycle (b) nitrogen cycle (c) phosphorus cycle (d) hydrologic cycle (e) neither a nor c has a gaseous component

10. Which of the following processes is *not* directly involved in the hydrologic cycle? (a) transpiration (b) evaporation (c) precipita-tion (d) nitrification (e) condensation

11. The periodic warming of surface waters of the tropical eastern Pa-cific that alters both oceanic and atmospheric circulation patterns is known as (a) upwelling (b) prevailing wind (c) ocean current (d) El Niño–Southern Oscillation (e) Coriolis effect

12. A mountain range may produce a downwind arid (a) upwelling (b) rain shadow (c) ocean current (d) microclimate (e) ecological pyramid

CRITICAL THINKING

1. Describe the simplest stable ecosystem you can imagine.

2. How might a food web change if all decomposers were eliminated from it?

3. What trophic level(s) (producer, consumer, or decomposer) is/are you eating when you eat each of the following: a. steamed broccoli b. chicken c. eggs d. mushrooms

4. Why is the cycling of matter essential to the long-term continu-ance of life?

5. What would happen to the nitrogen cycle if all bacteria were absent? Explain your answer.

6. What is the energy source that powers the wind?

7. How do ocean currents affect climate on land?

8. Would the microclimate of an ant be the same as that of an ele-phant living in the same area? Why or why not?

9. **ANALYZING DATA.** Examine Figure 55-3b (shown here). Explain why this pyramid of biomass is inverted. In other words, how can 4 g of producers support 21 g of primary consumers?

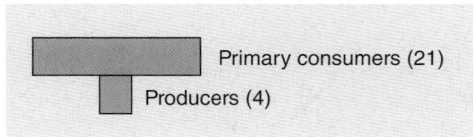

10. **ANALYZING DATA.** Scientists recently compiled databases of large forest wildfires in the western United States and compared them to climate and land-surface data. Examine the graph showing wildfire frequency compared to average spring–summer temperature. Do you see a correlation? Describe it. Based on these data, do you think climate warming is causing more wildfires? Explain your answer.

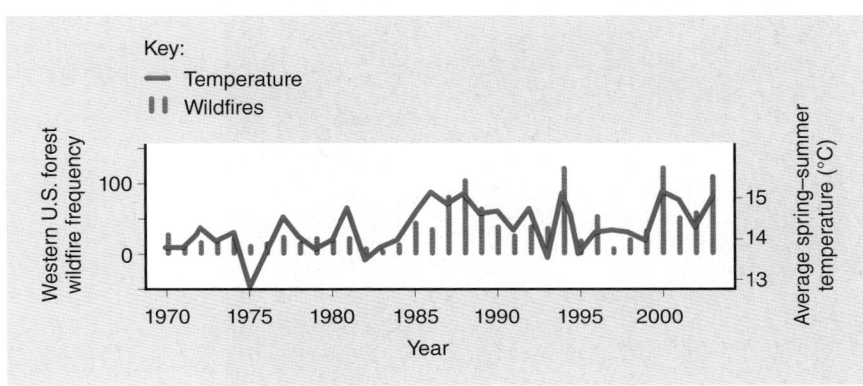

Source: Adapted from Westerling, A. L., H. G. Hidalgo, D. R. Cayan, and T. W. Swetnam. "Warming and Earlier Spring Increase Western U.S. Forest Wildfire Activity." *Science*, Vol. 313, Aug. 18, 2006.

11. **SCIENCE, TECHNOLOGY, AND SOCIETY.** How do humans alter the nitrogen cycle?

Additional questions are available in CengageNOW at www.cengage.com/login.

56 Ecology and the Geography of Life

Black-tailed prairie dog. Prairie dogs (*Cynomys ludovicianus*) never wander far from their burrows, which they use to escape from predators.

Raymond Gehman/Corbis

Earth has many different environments. *Natural selection* affects an organism's ability to survive and reproduce in a given environment. In natural selection, both **abiotic** (nonliving) and **biotic** (living) factors eliminate the least-fit individuals in a population. Over time, succeeding generations of organisms that live in each biome or major aquatic ecosystem become better adapted to local environmental conditions.

Black-tailed prairie dogs are superbly adapted to their environment. Their teeth and digestive tracts are modified to eat and easily digest the seeds and leaves of grasses that grow in great profusion on the Great Plains of western North America.

Prairie dogs live in large colonies of about 500 individuals. The eyes of every individual in the colony watch for potential danger, and when they see it, prairie dogs call out to warn the rest of the colony (see photograph). When danger approaches, each prairie dog dives into its underground home. Each burrow has at least two openings and consists of an elaborate network of long tunnels with several chambers: a nursery for the young, a sleeping chamber, a toilet chamber, and a listening chamber (close to an entrance). Piles of excavated soil surround the burrow entrances and help prevent flooding during rainstorms.

To survive winter, black-tailed prairie dogs hibernate in their burrows. Their metabolism slows, and they subsist on the stored fat in their bodies.

They do not hibernate deeply, however, and may leave their burrows to look for food when the weather warms.

Like prairie dogs, each species has structural, behavioral, and physiological adaptations for its own particular environment. As you examine Earth's major terrestrial and aquatic ecosystems, including the species characteristic of each, think about the variety of adaptations that natural selection has produced in organisms in response to their particular environments.

56.1 BIOMES

■ LEARNING OBJECTIVES

1   Define *biome* and briefly describe the nine major terrestrial biomes, giving attention to the climate, soil, and characteristic plants and animals of each.
2   Describe at least one human effect on each of the biomes discussed.

A **biome** is a large, relatively distinct terrestrial region that has similar climate, soil, plants, and animals regardless of where it occurs. Because it covers such a large geographic area, a biome encompasses many interacting landscapes. Recall from Chapter 53 that a **landscape** is a large land area (several to many square kilometers) composed of interacting ecosystems.

Biomes largely correspond to major climate zones, with temperature and precipitation being most important (**FIG. 56-1**). Near the poles, temperature is generally the overriding climate factor; whereas in tropical and temperate regions, precipitation becomes more significant than temperature. Other abiotic factors to which biomes are sensitive include temperature extremes, rapid temperature changes, floods, droughts, strong winds, and fires (see section on fires in Chapter 55).

We discuss nine major biomes in this chapter: tundra, boreal forest, temperate rain forest, temperate deciduous forest, temperate grassland, chaparral, desert, savanna, and tropical rain forest. Although we discuss each biome as a distinct entity, biomes intergrade into one another at their boundaries.

Tundra is the cold, boggy plains of the far north

Tundra (also called **arctic tundra**) occurs in extreme northern latitudes wherever snow melts seasonally (**FIG. 56-2**). The Southern Hemisphere has no equivalent of the arctic tundra because it has no land in the proper latitudes. A similar ecosystem located in the higher elevations of mountains, above the tree line, is called **alpine tundra** to distinguish it from arctic tundra (see *Inquiring About: The Distribution of Vegetation on Mountains*).

Arctic tundra has long, harsh winters and extremely short summers. Although the growing season, with its warmer temperatures, is as short as 50 days, the days are long. Above the Arctic Circle the sun does not set at all for many days in midsummer, although the amount of light at midnight is only one tenth that at noon. There is

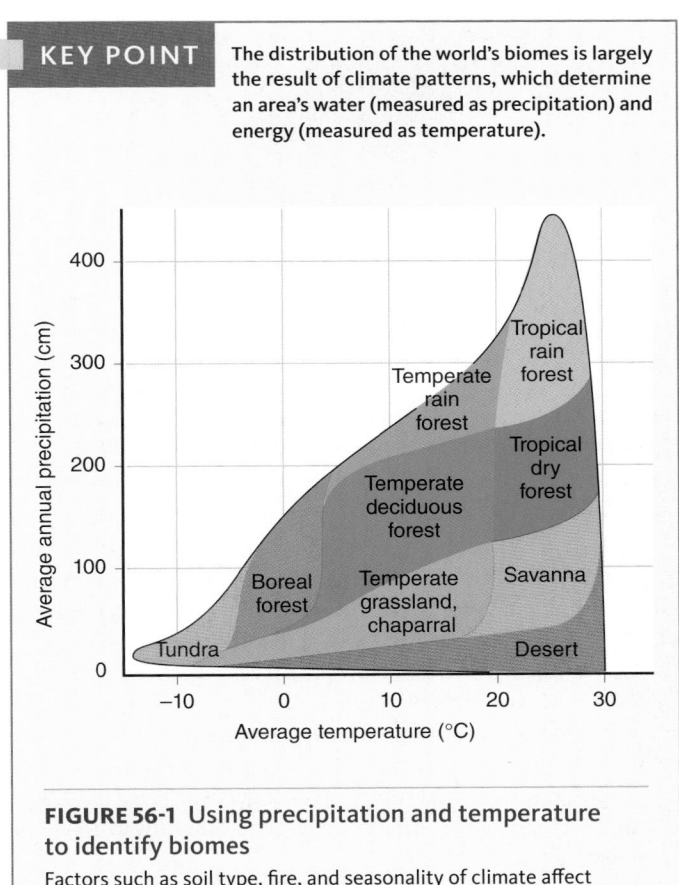

KEY POINT   The distribution of the world's biomes is largely the result of climate patterns, which determine an area's water (measured as precipitation) and energy (measured as temperature).

FIGURE 56-1 Using precipitation and temperature to identify biomes

Factors such as soil type, fire, and seasonality of climate affect whether temperate grassland or chaparral develops. (Adapted from Whittaker, R. H. *Communities and Ecosystems*, 2nd ed. Macmillan, New York, 1975.)

© Eastcott/Momatiuk/Animals Animals

FIGURE 56-2 Arctic tundra

Because of the short growing season and permafrost in arctic tundra, only small, hardy plants grow in the northernmost biome that encircles the Arctic Ocean. Photographed during autumn in Northwest Territories, Canada.

THE DISTRIBUTION OF VEGETATION ON MOUNTAINS

Does the type of vegetation change at different elevations on a mountain? Hiking up a mountain is similar to traveling toward the North Pole with respect to the major life zones encountered (see figure). This elevation–latitude similarity occurs because the temperature drops as one climbs a mountain, just as it does when one travels north; the temperature drops about 6°C (11°F) with each 1000 m increase in elevation. The types of species growing on the mountain change as the temperature changes.

Deciduous trees, which shed their leaves every autumn, may cover the base of a mountain in Colorado, for example. At higher elevations, where the climate is colder and more severe, a coniferous *subalpine forest* resembling boreal forest grows. Spruces and firs are the dominant trees here.

Higher still, the forest thins, and the trees become smaller, gnarled, and shrublike. These twisted, shrublike trees, called *krummholz* (a German word meaning "crooked wood"), are found at their elevational limit (the *tree line*). The exact elevation at which the tree line occurs depends on the latitude and distance from the ocean. In the Rocky Mountains, between 35° and 50° north latitude, the tree line drops 100 m with each 1° latitude northward.

Above the tree line, where the climate is quite cold, a kind of tundra occurs, with vegetation composed of grasses, sedges, and small tufted plants, most of which are hardy perennials. Some alpine plants (for example, buttercups) are lowland species that have adapted to the alpine environment, whereas other plants (for example, mountain douglasia) live exclusively in the mountains. This tundra is called *alpine tundra* to distinguish it from arctic tundra. At the top of the mountain, a permanent ice cap or snowcap might be found, similar to the nearly lifeless polar land areas.

Important environmental differences exist between high elevations and high latitudes that affect the types of organisms found in each place. Alpine tundra typically lacks permafrost and receives more precipitation than does arctic tundra. High elevations of temperate mountains do not have the great extremes of day length that are associated with the changing seasons in high-latitude biomes. The intensity of solar radiation is greater at high elevations than at high latitudes. At high elevations, the sun's rays pass through less atmosphere, which results in greater exposure to ultraviolet radiation (less is filtered out by the atmosphere) than occurs at high latitudes.

Comparison of elevation and latitude zones. The cooler temperatures at higher elevations of a mountain produce a series of ecosystems similar to those encountered when going toward the North Pole.

little precipitation (10 to 25 cm, or 4 to 10 in, per year) over much of the tundra, and most of it falls during summer months.

Tundra soils tend to be geologically young because most were formed only after the last Ice Age.[1] These soils are usually nutrient poor and have little organic litter (dead leaves and stems, animal droppings, and remains of organisms) in the uppermost layer of soil. Although the soil surface melts during the summer, tundra has a layer of permanently frozen ground called **permafrost** that varies in depth and thickness. Because permafrost interferes with drainage, the thawed upper zone of soil is usually waterlogged during the summer. Limited precipitation, combined with low temperatures, flat topography (surface features), and permafrost, produces a landscape of broad, shallow lakes, sluggish streams, and bogs.

Low species richness and low primary productivity characterize tundra. Mosses, lichens (such as reindeer moss), grasses, and grasslike sedges dominate tundra vegetation; most of these short plants are herbaceous perennials that live 20 to 100 years. No readily recognizable trees or shrubs grow except in sheltered locations, although dwarf willows, dwarf birches, and other dwarf trees are common.

Year-round animal life of the tundra includes voles, weasels, arctic foxes, gray wolves, snowshoe hares, ptarmigan, snowy owls, musk oxen, and lemmings (see Fig. 53-5 and the discussion of lemming population cycles in Chapter 53). In the summer, caribou

---

[1]Glacier ice, which occupied about 30% of Earth's land during the last Ice Age, began retreating about 17,000 years ago. Today, glacier ice occupies about 10% of the land surface.

migrate north to the tundra to graze on sedges, grasses, and dwarf willow. Dozens of bird species also migrate north in summer to nest and feed on abundant insects. Mosquitoes, blackflies, and deerflies survive the winter as eggs or pupae and occur in great numbers during summer weeks.

Tundra regenerates quite slowly after it has been disturbed. Even casual use by hikers causes damage. Long-lasting injury, likely to persist for hundreds of years, has been done to large portions of the arctic tundra as a result of oil exploration and military use.

Boreal forest is the evergreen forest of the north

Just south of the tundra is the **boreal forest,** or **taiga,** which stretches across both North America and Eurasia. Boreal forest is the world's largest biome, covering approximately 11% of Earth's land (**FIG. 56-3**). A biome comparable to the boreal forest is not found in the Southern Hemisphere because it has no land at the corresponding latitudes. Winters are extremely cold and severe, although not as harsh as in the tundra. Boreal forest receives little precipitation, perhaps 50 cm (20 in) per year, and its soil is typically acidic, is low in minerals (inorganic nutrients), and has a deep layer of partly decomposed conifer needles at the surface. (Conifers are cone-bearing evergreens.) Boreal forest contains numerous ponds and lakes in water-filled depressions that grinding ice sheets dug during the last Ice Age.

Black and white spruces, balsam fir, eastern larch, and other conifers dominate the boreal forest, but **deciduous** trees such as aspen or birch, which shed their leaves in autumn, form striking stands. Conifers have many drought-resistant adaptations, such as needlelike leaves with a minimal surface area to reduce water loss (see Fig. 34-9). Such an adaptation enables conifers to withstand the "drought" of the northern winter months, when roots do not absorb water because the ground is frozen. Natural selection also favors conifers in the boreal forest because, being evergreen, they resume photosynthesis as soon as warmer temperatures return.

Animal life of the boreal forest includes some larger species, such as caribou (which migrate from the tundra to the boreal forest for winter), wolves, bears, and moose. However, most animal life is medium-sized to small and includes rodents, rabbits, and fur-bearing predators such as lynx, sable, and mink. Most species of birds are seasonally abundant but migrate to warmer climates for winter. Insects are numerous, but there are few amphibians and reptiles except in the southern boreal forest.

Most of the boreal forest is not suitable for agriculture because of its short growing season and mineral-poor soil. The boreal forest, which is harvested primarily by clear-cutting, is currently the primary source of the world's industrial wood and wood fiber.

Temperate rain forest has cool weather, dense fog, and high precipitation

Coniferous **temperate rain forest** grows on the northwestern coast of North America. Similar vegetation exists in southeastern Australia and in southwestern South America. Annual precipitation in this biome is high, from 200 to 380 cm (80 to 150 in); condensation of water from dense coastal fog augments the annual precipitation. The proximity of temperate rain forest to the coastline moderates the temperature so that seasonal fluctuation is narrow; winters are mild, and summers are cool. Temperate rain forest has a relatively nutrient-poor soil, although its organic content may be high. Cool temperatures slow the activity of bacterial and fungal decomposers. Thus, needles and large fallen branches and trunks accumulate on the ground as litter that takes many years to decay and release inorganic minerals to the soil.

The dominant vegetation type in the North American temperate rain forest is large evergreen trees, such as western hemlock, Douglas fir, Sitka spruce, and western red cedar. Temperate rain forest is rich in epiphytic vegetation, which consists of smaller plants that grow nonparasitically on the trunks and branches of large trees (**FIG. 56-4**). Epiphytes in this biome are mainly mosses, lichens, and ferns, all of which also carpet the ground. Squirrels, wood rats, mule deer, elk, numerous bird species (such as jays, nuthatches, and chickadees), several species of reptiles (such as painted turtles and western terrestrial garter snakes), and amphibians (such as Pacific giant salamanders and Pacific treefrogs) are common temperate rainforest animals.

Temperate rain forest, one of the richest wood producers in the world, supplies us with lumber and pulpwood. It is also one of the most complex ecosystems in terms of species richness. Care must be taken to avoid overharvesting original old-growth forest because such an ecosystem takes hundreds of years to develop. When the logging industry harvests old-growth forest, it typically replants the area with a monoculture (a single species) of trees that it harvests in 40- to 100-year cycles. Thus, the old-growth forest ecosystem, once harvested, never has a chance to redevelop. A small fraction of the original, old-growth temperate rain forest in Washington, Oregon, and northern California remains untouched. These stable forest ecosystems provide biological habitat for many organisms, including 40 endangered and threatened species.

Beth Davidow/Visuals Unlimited

FIGURE 56-3 Boreal forest
Boreal forest is coniferous forest that occurs in cold regions of the Northern Hemisphere adjacent to the tundra. Photographed in Yukon, Canada.

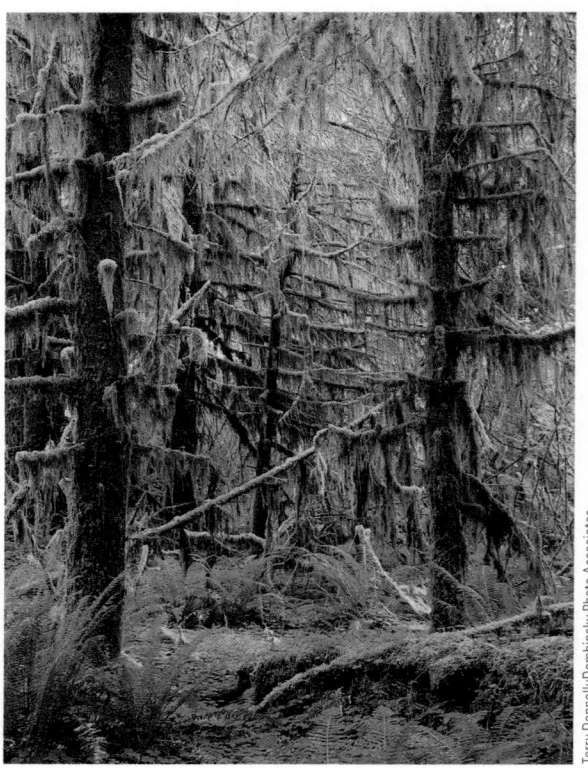

FIGURE 56-4 Temperate rain forest

Large amounts of precipitation characterize temperate rain forest. Note the epiphytes hanging from the branches of coniferous trees. Photographed in Olympic National Park in Washington State.

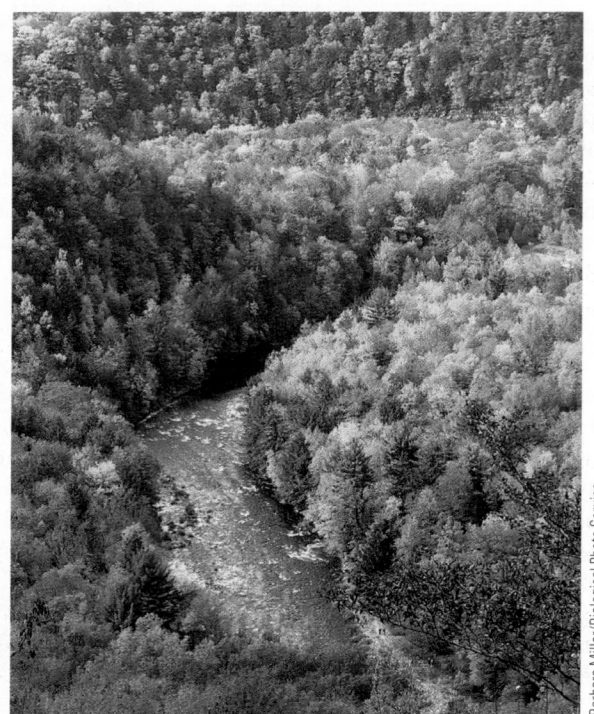

FIGURE 56-5 Temperate deciduous forest

The broad-leaf trees that dominate the temperate deciduous forest shed their leaves before winter. Photographed during autumn in Pennsylvania.

Temperate deciduous forest has a canopy of broad-leaf trees

Seasonality (hot summers and cold winters) is characteristic of **temperate deciduous forest,** which occurs in temperate areas where precipitation ranges from about 75 to 126 cm (30 to 50 in) annually. Typically, the soil of a temperate deciduous forest consists of both a topsoil rich in organic material and a deep, clay-rich lower layer. As organic materials decay, mineral ions are released. If roots of living trees do not absorb these ions, they leach into the clay, where they may be retained.

Broad-leaf hardwood trees, such as oak, hickory, maple, and beech, that lose their foliage annually dominate temperate deciduous forests of the northeastern and Mid-Atlantic United States (**FIG. 56-5**). The trees of the temperate deciduous forest form a dense canopy that overlies saplings and shrubs.

Temperate deciduous forests originally contained a variety of large mammals such as mountain lions, wolves, bison, and other species now regionally extinct, plus deer, bears, and many small mammals and birds (such as wild turkeys, blue jays, and scarlet tanagers). Both reptiles (such as box turtles and rat snakes) and amphibians (such as spotted salamanders and wood frogs) abounded, together with a denser and more varied insect life than exists today.

In Europe and North America, logging and land clearing for farms, tree plantations, and cities have removed much of the original temperate deciduous forest. Where it has regenerated, temper-

ate deciduous forest is often in a semi-natural state—that is, highly modified by humans for recreation, livestock foraging, timber harvest, and other uses. Although these returning forests do not have the biological diversity of virgin stands, many forest organisms have successfully become re-established.

Worldwide, temperate deciduous forest was among the first biomes to be converted to agricultural use. In Europe and Asia, many soils that originally supported temperate deciduous forest have been cultivated by traditional agricultural methods for thousands of years without a substantial loss in fertility. During the 20th century, however, intensive agricultural practices were adopted; these, along with overgrazing and deforestation, have contributed to the degradation of some agricultural lands.

Temperate grasslands occur in areas of moderate precipitation

Summers are hot, winters are cold, fires help shape the landscape, and rainfall is often uncertain in **temperate grasslands.** Annual precipitation averages 25 to 75 cm (10 to 30 in). In grasslands with less precipitation, minerals tend to accumulate in a marked layer just below the topsoil. These minerals tend to leach out of the soil in areas with more precipitation. Grassland soil contains considerable organic material because surface parts of many grasses die off each winter and contribute to the organic content of the soil (the roots and rhizomes survive underground). Many grasses are sod formers: their roots and rhizomes form a thick, continuous underground mat.

Moist temperate grasslands, also known as *tallgrass prairies*, occur in the United States in Iowa, western Minnesota, eastern Nebraska, and parts of other Midwestern states and across Canada's prairie provinces. Although few trees grow except near rivers and streams, grasses, some as tall as 2 m (6.5 ft), grow in great profusion in the deep, rich soil (**FIG. 56-6**). Before most of this area was converted to arable land, it was covered with herds of grazing animals, particularly bison. The principal predators were wolves, although in sparser, drier areas coyotes took their place. Smaller fauna included prairie dogs and their predators (foxes, black-footed ferrets, and birds of prey such as prairie falcons), western meadowlarks, bobolinks, reptiles (such as gopher snakes and short-horned lizards), and great numbers of insects.

Shortgrass prairies, in which the dominant grasses are less than 0.5 m (1.6 ft) tall, are temperate grasslands that receive less precipitation than the moister grasslands just described but more precipitation than deserts. In the United States, shortgrass prairies occur in the eastern half of Montana, the western half of South Dakota, and parts of other Midwestern states, as well as western Alberta in Canada. The plants grow in less abundance than in the moister grasslands, and occasionally some bare soil is exposed.

The North American grassland, particularly the tallgrass prairie, was so well suited to agriculture that little of it remains. More than 90% has vanished under the plow, and the remainder is so fragmented that almost nowhere can we see even an approximation of what European settlers saw when they settled in the Midwest. Today, the tallgrass prairie is considered North America's rarest biome.

In recent decades woody shrubs and small trees such as juniper have invaded many of the world's grasslands in North and South America, Africa, and Australia. These plants displace native grasses, reducing the amount of food available for grazing animals. Fires in such altered ecosystems are more catastrophic, and the deep roots of these invasive plants tap into water, altering the area's hydrology. Scientists are not sure why this change is occurring, but suggest that climate change, increased droughts, overgrazing, and fire suppression may all play a role.

Chaparral is a thicket of evergreen shrubs and small trees

Some hilly temperate environments have mild winters with abundant rainfall, combined with extremely dry summers. Such Mediterranean climates, as they are called, occur not only in the area around the Mediterranean Sea, but also in California, Western

FIGURE 56-6 Temperate grassland
The Nature Conservancy owns this tallgrass prairie preserve in Oklahoma. Like other moist temperate grasslands, it is mostly treeless but contains a profusion of grasses and other herbaceous flowering plants. As bison graze on the plants, they affect community structure and diversity.

Australia, portions of Chile, and South Africa. In southern California this environment is called **chaparral.** This vegetation type is also known as maquis in the Mediterranean region, mallee scrub in Australia, matorral in Chile, and Cape scrub in Africa. Chaparral soil is thin and infertile. Frequent fires occur naturally in this environment, particularly in late summer and autumn.

Chaparral vegetation looks strikingly similar in different areas of the world, even though the individual species are quite different. A dense growth of evergreen shrubs, often of drought-resistant pine or scrub oak trees, dominates chaparral (**FIG. 56-7**). During the rainy winter season the landscape may be lush and green, but during the hot, dry summer the plants lie dormant. Trees and shrubs often have hard, small, leathery leaves that resist water loss. Many plants are also fire-adapted and grow best in the months following a fire. Such growth is possible because fire releases minerals that were tied up in the plants that burned. With the new availability of essential minerals, plants sprout vigorously during winter rains. Mule deer, wood rats, brush rabbits, skinks and other lizards, and many species of birds (such as Anna's hummingbird, scrub jay, and bushtit) are common animals of the chaparral.

Fires, which occur at irregular intervals in California chaparral vegetation, are often quite costly because they consume expensive homes built on the hilly chaparral landscape. Unfortunately, efforts to control naturally occurring fires sometimes backfire. Denser, thicker vegetation tends to accumulate when periodic fires are prevented; then, when a fire does occur, it is much more severe. Removing the chaparral vegetation, whose roots hold the

FIGURE 56-7 Chaparral

Chaparral, which consists primarily of drought-resistant evergreen shrubs and small trees, develops where hot, dry summers alternate with mild, rainy winters. Photographed in the Santa Lucia Mountains, California.

neighboring states is a cold desert dominated by sagebrush. The Mojave Desert in Nevada and California is a warm desert known for its Joshua trees (a type of yucca with an erect, woody stem). The Chihuahuan Desert, home of century plants (agaves; see Fig. 53-7), is a warm desert found in Texas, New Mexico, and Mexico. The warm Sonoran Desert, with its many species of cacti, is found in Arizona, California, and Mexico (**FIG. 56-8**).

The low water-vapor content of the desert atmosphere leads to daily temperature extremes of heat and cold, so a major change in temperature occurs in each 24-hour period. Deserts vary greatly depending on the amount of precipitation they receive, which is generally less than 25 cm (10 in) per year. A few deserts are so dry that virtually no plant life occurs in them. As a result of sparse vegetation, desert soil is low in organic material but often high in mineral content, particularly the salts NaCl, $CaCO_3$, and $CaSO_4$.

soil in place, also causes problems—witness the mud slides that sometimes occur during winter rains in these areas.

Deserts are arid ecosystems

Deserts are dry areas found in temperate (*cold deserts*) and subtropical or tropical regions (*warm deserts*). North America has four distinct deserts. The Great Basin Desert in Nevada, Utah, and

Desert vegetation includes both perennials (cacti, yuccas, Joshua trees, and sagebrushes) and, after a rain, flowering annuals. Desert plants tend to have reduced leaves or no leaves, an adaptation that conserves water. In cacti such as the giant saguaro, for example, the stem carries out photosynthesis and also expands accordion-style to store water; the leaves are modified into spines, which discourage herbivores. Other desert plants shed their leaves for most of the year, growing only during the brief moist season.

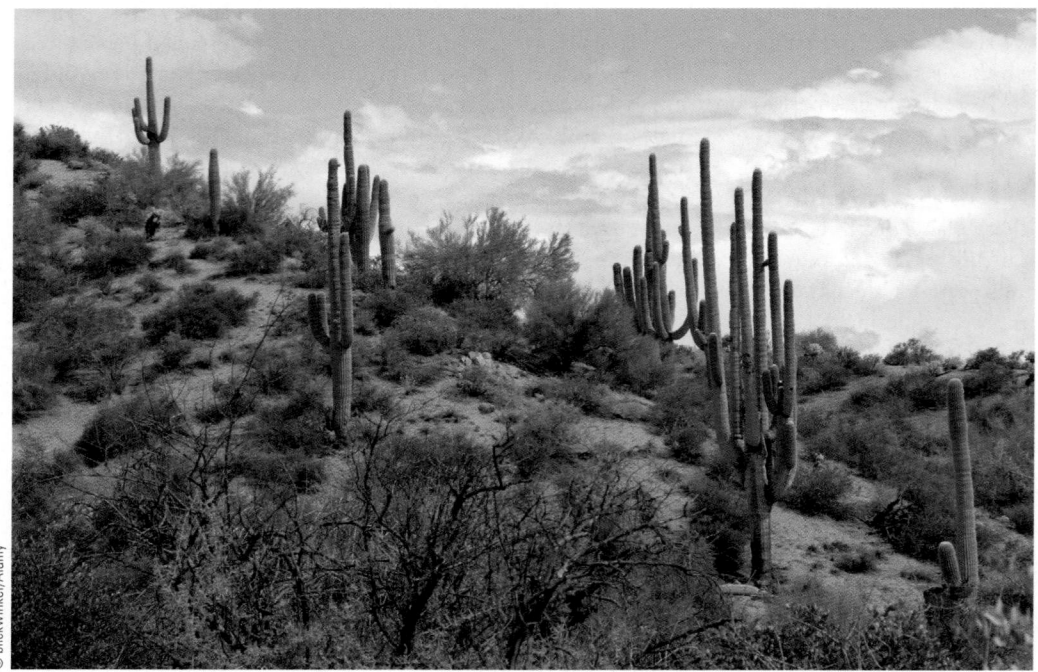

◀**FIGURE 56-8** Desert

Summer rainfall characterizes the warmer deserts of North America, such as the Sonoran Desert shown here. The Sonoran Desert contains many species of cacti, including the large, treelike saguaro (*Carnegiea gigantea*), which grows 15 to 18 m (50 to 60 ft) tall. Photographed in Arizona.

Desert animals tend to be small. During the heat of the day, they remain under cover or return to shelter periodically, whereas at night they come out to forage or hunt. In addition to desert-adapted insects, there are many specialized desert reptiles (such as desert iguanas, desert tortoises, and rattlesnakes) and a few desert-adapted amphibians (such as western spadefoot toads). Mammals include such rodents as the American kangaroo rat, which does not need to drink water but subsists solely on the water content of its food (primarily seeds and insects). American deserts are also home to jackrabbits, and kangaroos live in Australian deserts. Carnivores such as the African fennec fox and some birds of prey, especially owls, live on rodents and rabbits. During the driest months of the year, many desert insects, amphibians, reptiles, and mammals tunnel underground, where they remain inactive; this period of dormancy is known as *estivation.*

Humans have altered North American deserts in several ways. Off-road vehicles damage desert vegetation, which sometimes takes years to recover. When the top layer of desert soil is disturbed, erosion occurs more readily, and less vegetation grows to support native animals. Another problem is that certain cacti and desert tortoises have become rare as a result of poaching. Houses, factories, and farms built in desert areas require vast quantities of water, which must be imported from distant areas. Irrigation of desert soils often causes them to become salty and unfit for crops or native vegetation. Increased groundwater consumption by many desert cities has caused groundwater levels to drop. Aquifer depletion in U.S. deserts is particularly critical in southern Arizona and southwestern New Mexico.

Savanna is a tropical grassland with scattered trees

The **savanna** biome is a tropical grassland with widely scattered clumps of low trees (**FIG. 56-9**). Savanna is found in areas of relatively low or seasonal rainfall with prolonged dry periods. Temperatures in savannas vary little throughout the year, and precipitation, not temperature as in temperate grasslands, regulates seasons. Annual precipitation is 85 to 150 cm (34 to 60 in). Savanna soil is low in essential minerals, in part because it is strongly leached. Savanna soil is often rich in aluminum, which resists leaching, and in places the aluminum reaches levels that are toxic to many plants. Although the African savanna is best known, savanna also occurs in South America and northern Australia.

Wide expanses of grasses interrupted by occasional trees characterize savanna. Trees such as *Acacia* bristle with thorns that provide protection against herbivores. Both trees and grasses have fire-adapted features, such as extensive underground root systems, that enable them to survive seasonal droughts as well as periodic fires that sweep through the savanna.

The world's greatest assemblage of hooved mammals occurs in the African savanna. Here live great herds of herbivores, including wildebeests, antelopes, giraffes, zebras, and elephants. Large predators, such as lions and hyenas, kill and scavenge the herds. In areas of seasonally varying rainfall, the herds and their predators may migrate annually.

Savanna is rapidly being converted to rangeland for cattle and other domesticated animals, which are replacing the big herds of wild animals. The problem is particularly acute in Africa, which has the most rapidly growing human population of any continent. In some places severe overgrazing by domestic animals has contributed to the conversion of marginal savanna into desert, a process known as **desertification.** In desertification, the reduced grass cover caused by overgrazing allows wind and water to erode the soil; erosion removes the topsoil and decreases the soil's ability to support crops or livestock. (Desertification is not restricted to savanna. Temperate grasslands and tropical dry forests can also be degraded to desert.)

There are two basic types of tropical forests

There are many kinds of tropical forests, but ecologists generally classify them as one of two types: tropical dry forests or tropical rain forests. **Tropical dry forests** occur in regions with a wet season and a dry season (usually two to three months each year). Annual precipitation is 150 to 200 cm (60 to 80 in). During the

FIGURE 56-9 Savanna
In this photograph of African savanna in Tanzania, the smaller animals in the foreground are Thomson's gazelles (*Gazella thomsonii*), and the larger ones near the trees are wildebeests (*Connochaetes taurinus*).

Carlyn Iverson

dry season, many tropical trees shed their leaves and remain dormant, much as temperate trees do during the winter. India, Brazil, Thailand, and Mexico are some of the countries that have tropical dry forests. Tropical dry forests intergrade with savanna on their dry edges and with tropical rain forests on their wet edges. Logging and overgrazing by domestic animals have fragmented and degraded many tropical dry forests.

The annual precipitation of **tropical rain forests** is 200 to 450 cm (80 to 180 in). Much of this precipitation, which occurs almost daily, comes from locally recycled water that enters the atmosphere by transpiration from the forest's own trees. Tropical rain forests are often located in areas with ancient, highly weathered, mineral-poor soil. Little organic matter accumulates in such soils. Because temperatures are high and soil moisture is abundant year-round, decay organisms and detritus-feeding ants and termites decom-

pose organic litter quite rapidly. Vast networks of roots and mycorrhizae quickly absorb minerals from decomposing materials. Thus, minerals of tropical rain forests are tied up in the vegetation rather than in the soil.

Tropical rain forests are found in Central and South America, Africa, and Southeast Asia. Tropical rain forest is very productive despite the scarcity of minerals in the soil. Its plants, stimulated by abundant solar energy and precipitation, capture considerable energy by photosynthesis. Of all the biomes, the tropical rain forest is unrivaled in species richness.

Most trees of tropical rain forests are evergreen flowering plants. A fully developed rain forest has several distinct stories of vegetation (**FIG. 56-10**). The topmost story, called the *emergent layer,* consists of the crowns of the oldest, tallest trees, some 40 m (130 ft) or more in height; these trees are exposed to direct sun-

FIGURE 56-10 Tropical rain forest

Tropical rainforest vegetation is stratified. Except at river banks, tropical rain forest has a closed canopy that admits little light to the forest floor. The animals highlighted in this figure occupy a variety of ecological niches in the rain forest. (Adapted from Miller, G. T. *Living in the Environment*, 16th ed. Cengage/Brooks Cole, Belmont, CA, 2007, p. 156, Figure 7-17.)

light and are subject to the warmest temperatures, lowest humidities, and strongest winds. The next story, the *canopy*, reaches a height of 30 to 35 m (100 to 115 ft) and lets in little sunlight for the support of the sparse *understory*, shrub layer, and ground layer, all of which consist of smaller plants specialized for life in the shade as well as seedlings of taller trees. Vegetation of tropical rain forests is generally not dense at ground level except near stream banks or where a fallen tree has opened the canopy.

Tropical rainforest trees support extensive epiphytic communities of smaller plants such as orchids and bromeliads. Although epiphytes grow in crotches of branches, on bark, or even on the leaves of their hosts, most use their host trees only for physical support, not for nourishment.

Because little light penetrates to the understory, many plants living there are adapted to climb already-established host trees. Lianas (woody tropical vines), some as thick as a human thigh, twist up through the branches of tropical rainforest trees. Once in the canopy, lianas grow from the upper branches of one tree to another, connecting the tops of the trees and providing a walkway for many of the canopy's residents.

Not counting bacteria and other soil-dwelling organisms, about 90% of tropical rainforest organisms live in the middle and upper canopies. Rainforest animals include the most abundant and varied insect, reptile, and amphibian fauna on Earth. Birds, too, are diverse, with some specialized to consume fruits (such as parrots),

some to consume nectar (such as hummingbirds and sunbirds), and others to consume insects. Most rainforest mammals, such as sloths and monkeys, live only in the trees and never climb down to the ground. Some large ground-dwelling mammals, including elephants, are also found in tropical rain forests.

Unless strong conservation measures are initiated soon, human population growth and agricultural and industrial expansion in tropical countries may spell the end of tropical rain forests by the middle of the 22nd century. Many rainforest species may become extinct before they are even identified and scientifically described. (Tropical rainforest destruction is discussed in detail in Chapter 57.)

To review, examine **FIGURE 56-11**, which shows the geographic distribution of the world's biomes.

Review

- What climate and soil factors produce the major biomes?
- What representative organisms are found in each of these forest biomes: (1) boreal forest, (2) temperate deciduous forest, (3) temperate rain forest, (4) tropical rain forest?
- In which biome do you live? Does it match the description given in this text? If not, explain the discrepancy.
- How does tundra compare to desert? How does temperate grassland compare to savanna?

FIGURE 56-11 *Animated* **The world's major biomes**

This simplified diagram shows sharp boundaries between biomes. Biomes actually intergrade at their boundaries, sometimes over large areas. Note that mountains are keyed separately because they have variable vegetation. (Adapted from Miller, G. T. *Living in the Environment*, 16th ed. Cengage/Brooks Cole, Belmont, CA, 2007, p. 146, Figure 7-8.)

56.2 AQUATIC ECOSYSTEMS

■ LEARNING OBJECTIVES

3 Explain the important environmental factors that affect aquatic ecosystems.

4 Distinguish among plankton, nekton, and benthos.

5 Briefly describe the various freshwater, estuarine, and marine ecosystems, giving attention to the environmental characteristics and representative organisms of each.

6 Describe at least one human effect on each of the aquatic ecosystems discussed.

Aquatic "biomes" do not exist, in the sense that aquatic ecologists do not distinguish aquatic ecosystems based on the dominant form of vegetation. Aquatic ecosystems are classified primarily on abiotic factors, such as salinity, that help determine an aquatic life zone's boundaries. **Salinity,** the concentration of dissolved salts in a body of water, affects the kinds of organisms present in aquatic ecosystems, as does the amount of dissolved oxygen. Water greatly interferes with the penetration of light, so floating aquatic organisms that photosynthesize remain near the water's surface, and vegetation attached to the bottom grows only in shallow water. In addition, low levels of essential minerals often limit the number and distribution of organisms in certain aquatic environments. Other abiotic determinants of species composition in aquatic ecosystems include water depth, temperature, pH, and presence or absence of waves and currents.

Aquatic ecosystems contain three main ecological categories of organisms: free-floating plankton, strongly swimming nekton, and bottom-dwelling benthos. **Plankton** are usually small or microscopic organisms that are relatively feeble swimmers. For the most part, they are carried about at the mercy of currents and waves. They are unable to swim far horizontally, but some species are capable of large vertical migrations and are found at different depths of water at different times of the day or at different seasons. Plankton are generally subdivided into two major categories: phytoplankton and zooplankton. **Phytoplankton** (photosynthetic cyanobacteria and free-floating algae) are producers that form the base of most aquatic food webs. **Zooplankton** are nonphotosynthetic organisms that include protozoa, tiny crustaceans, and the larval stages of many animals. **Nekton** are larger, actively swimming organisms such as fishes, turtles, and whales. **Benthos** are bottom-dwelling organisms that fix themselves to one spot (sponges, oysters, and barnacles), burrow into the sand (many worms and echinoderms), or walk or swim about on the bottom (crayfish, aquatic insect larvae, and brittle stars).

Freshwater ecosystems are linked to land and marine ecosystems

Freshwater ecosystems include streams and rivers (flowing-water ecosystems), ponds and lakes (standing-water ecosystems), and marshes and swamps (freshwater wetlands). Each type of freshwater ecosystem has its own specific abiotic conditions and characteristic organisms. Although freshwater ecosystems occupy a relatively small portion—about 2%—of Earth's surface, they are important in the hydrologic cycle: they assist in recycling precipitation that flows as surface runoff to the ocean (see discussion of hydrologic cycle in Chapter 55). Freshwater habitats also provide homes for many species.

Streams and rivers are flowing-water ecosystems

Many different conditions exist along the length of a stream or river (**FIG. 56-12**). The nature of a **flowing-water ecosystem** changes greatly from its source (where it begins) to its mouth (where it empties into another body of water). Headwater streams (small streams that are the sources of a river) are usually shallow, clear,

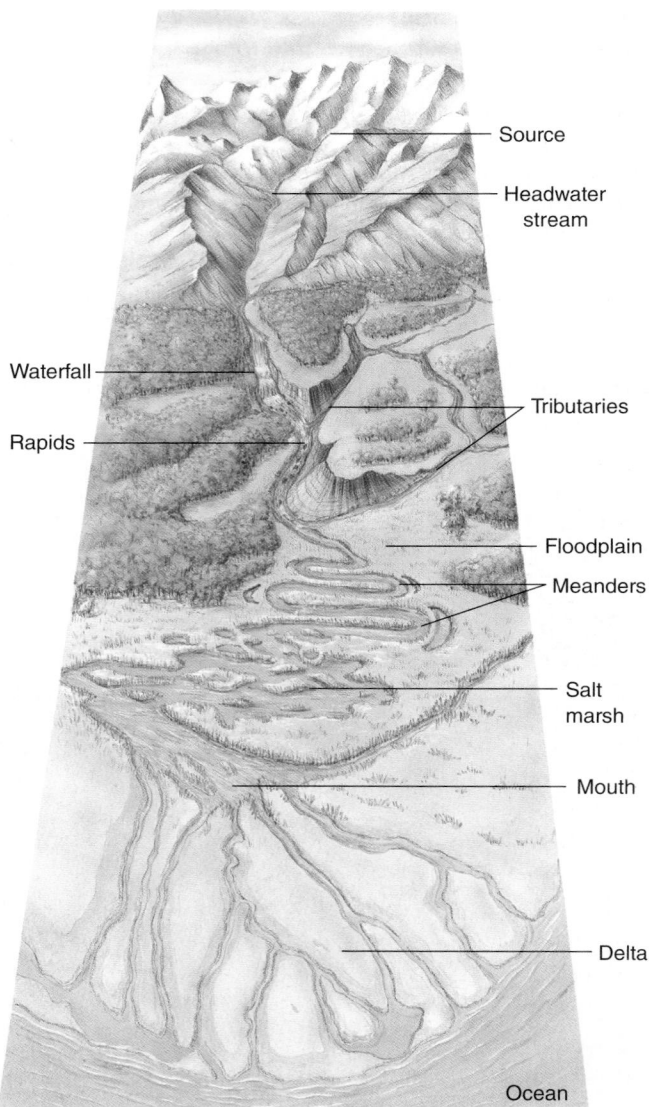

FIGURE 56-12 Features of a typical river
The river begins at a source, often high in mountains and fed by melting snows or glaciers. Headwater streams flow downstream rapidly, often over rocks (as rapids) or bluffs (as waterfalls). Along the way, tributaries feed into the river. As the river's course levels, the river flows more slowly and winds from side to side, forming meanders. The floodplain is the area on either side of the river that is subject to flooding. Near the ocean, the river may form a salt marsh where fresh water from the river and salt water from the ocean mix. Sediments deposited by the river as it empties into the ocean form the delta, a fertile, low-lying plain at the river's mouth.

cold, swiftly flowing, and highly oxygenated. In contrast, rivers downstream from the headwaters are wider and deeper, cloudy (that is, they contain suspended particulates), not as cold, slower flowing, and less oxygenated. Surrounding forest may shade certain parts of the stream or river, whereas other parts may be exposed to direct sunlight. Along parts of a stream or river, groundwater wells up through sediments on the bottom; this local input of water moderates the water temperature so that summer temperatures are cooler and winter temperatures are warmer than in adjacent parts of the flowing-water ecosystem.

The kinds of organisms in flowing-water ecosystems vary greatly from one stream to another, depending primarily on the strength of the current. In streams with fast currents, inhabitants have adaptations such as suckers to attach themselves to rocks so they are not swept away. The larvae of blackflies, for example, attach themselves with suction discs located on the ends of their abdomens. Some stream inhabitants, such as immature water-penny beetles, have flattened bodies that enable them to slip under or between rocks. The water-penny beetle larva gets its common name from its flattened, nearly circular shape. Alternatively, inhabitants such as the brown trout are streamlined and muscular enough to swim in the current.

Streams and rivers depend on land for much of their energy. In headwater streams, up to 99% of the energy input comes from detritus (dead organic material such as leaves) carried from the land into streams and rivers by wind or surface runoff. Downstream, rivers contain more producers and therefore depend slightly less on detritus as a source of energy than do the headwaters.

Human activities have several adverse impacts on rivers and streams, including water pollution and the effects of dams built to contain the water of rivers or streams. Pollution alters the physical environment of a flowing-water ecosystem and changes the biotic component downstream from the pollution source. Dams change the nature of flowing-water ecosystems, both upstream and downstream from the dam location. A dam causes water to back up, resulting in flooding of large areas of land and formation of a reservoir, which destroys terrestrial habitat. Below the dam, the once-powerful river is reduced to a relative trickle, so the flowing-water ecosystem is altered.

Ponds and lakes are standing-water ecosystems

Zonation characterizes **standing-water ecosystems.** A large lake has three basic zones: the littoral, limnetic, and profundal zones (**FIG. 56-13**). Smaller lakes and ponds typically lack a profundal zone.

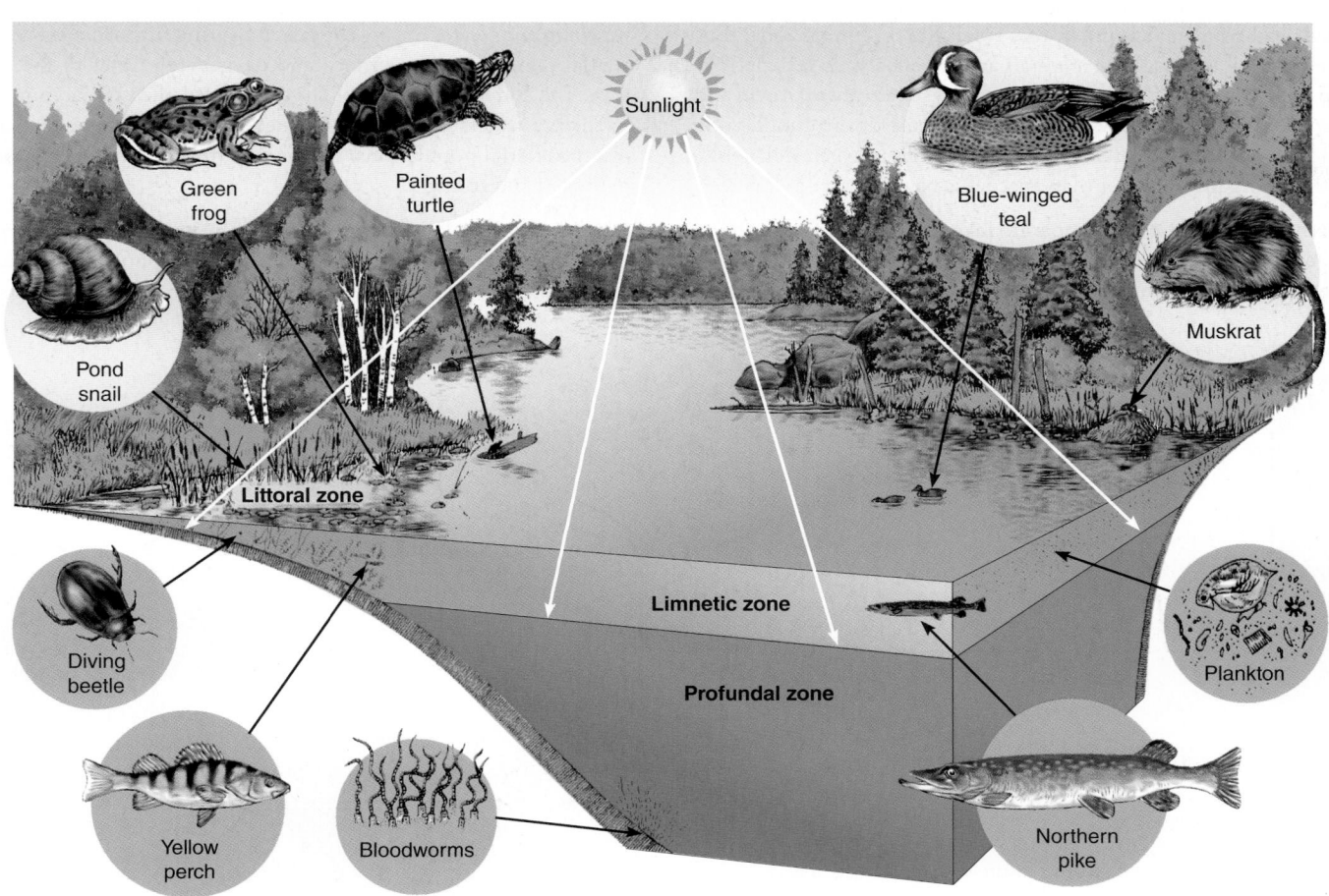

FIGURE 56-13 Zonation in a large, deep, temperate lake
A lake is a standing-water ecosystem surrounded by land. (Adapted from Miller, G. T. *Living in the Environment*, 16th ed. Cengage/Brooks Cole, Belmont, CA, 2007, p. 175, Figure 8-15.)

The **littoral zone** is a shallow-water area along the shore of a lake or pond. It includes rooted, emergent vegetation, such as cattails and burreeds, plus several deeper-dwelling aquatic plants and algae. The littoral zone is the most productive zone of the lake. Photosynthesis is greatest in the littoral zone, in part because light is abundant and because the littoral zone receives nutrient inputs from surrounding land that stimulate the growth of plants and algae. In addition, ponds and lakes—like streams and rivers—depend on detritus carried from the land for much of their energy. Animals of the littoral zone include frogs and their tadpoles, turtles, worms, crayfish and other crustaceans, insect larvae, and many fishes such as perch, carp, and bass. Surface dwellers, such as water striders and whirligig beetles, are found in the quieter areas.

The **limnetic zone** is the open water beyond the littoral zone, that is, away from the shore; it extends down as far as sunlight penetrates to permit photosynthesis. The main organisms of the limnetic zone are microscopic phytoplankton and zooplankton. Larger fishes also spend some of their time in the limnetic zone, although they may visit the littoral zone to feed and reproduce. Because of the depth of this zone, less vegetation grows in the limnetic zone than in the littoral zone.

Beneath the limnetic zone of a large lake is the **profundal zone.** Because light does not penetrate effectively to this depth, plants and algae do not live in this zone. Food drifts into the profundal zone from the littoral and limnetic zones. Bacteria decompose dead plants and animals that reach the profundal zone, thus liberating minerals. These minerals are not effectively recycled because no photosynthetic organisms are present to absorb them and incorporate them into the food web. As a result, the profundal zone tends to be both mineral rich and anaerobic (oxygen deficient), with few organisms other than anaerobic bacteria occupying it.

Thermal stratification in temperate lakes. The marked layering of large temperate lakes caused by light penetration is accentuated by **thermal stratification,** in which the temperature changes sharply with depth (**FIG. 56-14a**). Thermal stratification occurs because the summer sunlight penetrates and warms surface water, making it less dense. (Recall from Chapter 2 that the density of water is greatest at 4°C; both above and below this temperature, water is less dense.) In summer, cool (and therefore *more* dense) water remains at the lake bottom and is separated from warm (and therefore *less* dense) water above by an abrupt temperature transition called the **thermocline.** Seasonal distribution of temperature and oxygen (more oxygen dissolves in water at cooler temperatures) affects the distribution of fish in the lake.

In temperate lakes, falling temperatures in autumn cause a mixing of the lake waters called the **fall turnover** (**FIG. 56-14b**). As surface water cools, its density increases, and it sinks and displaces the less dense, warmer, mineral-rich water beneath. Warmer water then rises to the surface where it, in turn, cools and sinks. This process of cooling and sinking continues until the lake reaches a uniform temperature throughout. In winter, surface water cools to below 4°C, its temperature of greatest density. Ice, which forms at 0°C, is less dense than cold water. Thus, ice forms on the surface, and the water on the lake bottom is warmer than the ice on the surface. In the spring, a **spring turnover** occurs as ice melts and surface water reaches 4°C. Surface water again sinks to the bottom, and bottom water returns to the surface. As summer arrives, thermal stratification occurs once again.

The mixing of deeper, nutrient-rich water with surface, nutrient-poor water during the fall and spring turnovers brings essential minerals to the surface and oxygenated water to the bottom. The sudden presence of large amounts of essential minerals in surface waters encourages the development of large algal and cyanobacterial populations, which may form temporary **blooms** in the fall and spring.

Increased nutrients and algal growth. The presence of high levels of plant and algal nutrients such as nitrogen and phosphorus causes *enrichment*, the fertilization of a body of water. Excess amounts of

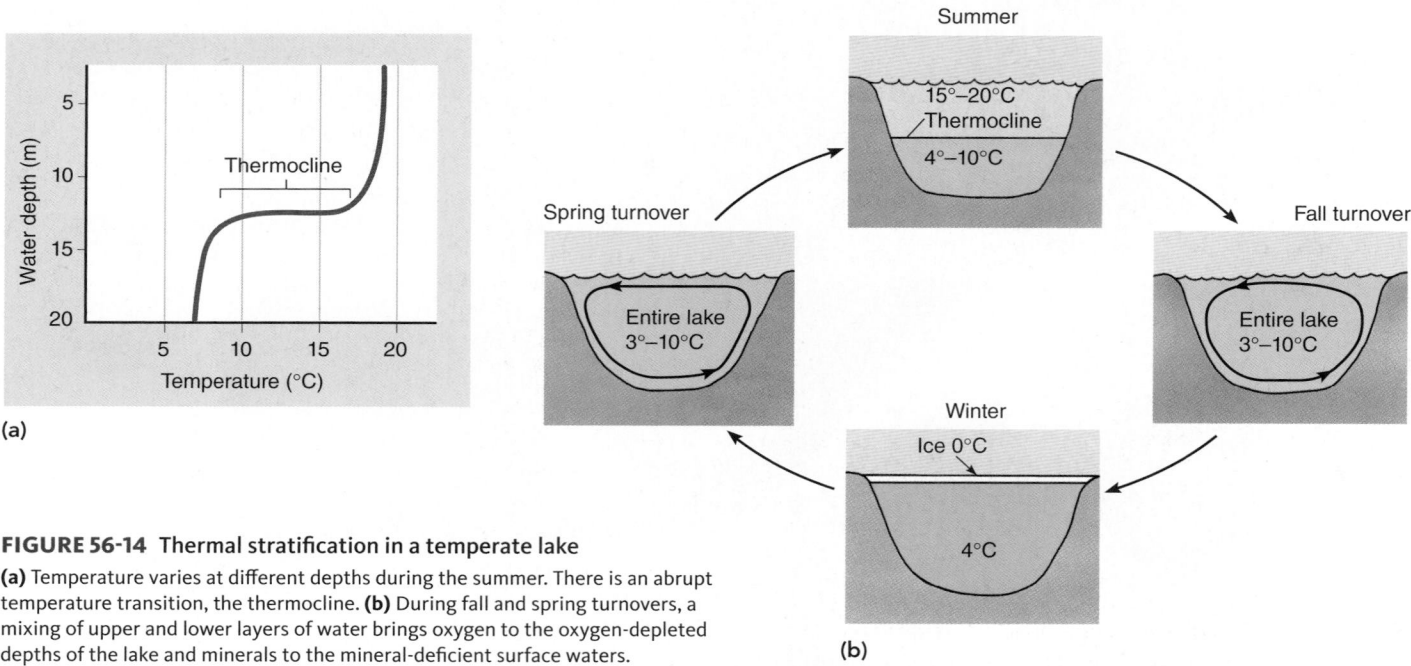

FIGURE 56-14 Thermal stratification in a temperate lake
(a) Temperature varies at different depths during the summer. There is an abrupt temperature transition, the thermocline. **(b)** During fall and spring turnovers, a mixing of upper and lower layers of water brings oxygen to the oxygen-depleted depths of the lake and minerals to the mineral-deficient surface waters.

these nutrients enter waterways from sewage and from fertilizer runoff from lawns and fields. The water in an enriched pond or lake is cloudy because of the vast numbers of algae and cyanobacteria that the nutrients support. The species composition is different in enriched and unenriched lakes. For example, an unenriched lake in the northeastern United States may contain pike, sturgeon, and whitefish in the deeper, colder part of the lake where there is a higher concentration of dissolved oxygen. In contrast, the deeper, colder levels of water in enriched lakes are depleted of dissolved oxygen because of the greater amount of decomposition on the lake floor. Fishes such as pike, sturgeon, and whitefish die out, and fishes such as catfish and carp, which tolerate lower concentrations of dissolved oxygen, replace them.

Enrichment is reversible and has declined in North America since the 1970s because the passage of legislation limits the phosphate content of detergents and because better sewage treatment plants have been constructed. Agriculture is the leading source of water-quality impairment of U.S. surface waters today. Fertilizer runoff, as well as animal wastes and plant residues in waterways, still causes enrichment problems.

Freshwater wetlands are transitional between aquatic and terrestrial ecosystems

Freshwater wetlands, which are usually covered by shallow water for at least part of the year, have characteristic soils and water-tolerant vegetation. They include marshes, dominated by grasslike plants, and swamps, in which woody trees or shrubs dominate (**FIG. 56-15**). Freshwater wetlands also include hardwood bottomland forests (lowlands along streams and rivers that are periodically flooded), prairie potholes (small, shallow ponds that formed when glacial ice melted at the end of the last Ice Age), and peat moss bogs (peat-accumulating wetlands where sphagnum moss dominates).

FIGURE 56-15 Freshwater swamp

Trees, such as bald cypress (*shown*), dominate freshwater swamps. In this wetland, photographed in northeastern Texas, a floating carpet of tiny aquatic plants covers the water's surface.

Wetlands are valued as a wildlife habitat for migratory waterfowl and many other bird species, beavers, otters, muskrats, and game fishes. Wetlands are holding areas for excess water when rivers flood their banks. The floodwater stored in wetlands then drains slowly back into the rivers, providing a steady flow of water throughout the year. Wetlands also serve as groundwater recharging areas. One of their most important roles is to trap and hold pollutants in the flooded soil, thereby cleansing and purifying the water. Such important environmental functions as these are known as **ecosystem services.**

At one time wetlands were considered wastelands, areas to be filled in or drained so that farms, housing developments, and industrial plants could be built on them. Wetlands are also breeding places for mosquitoes and therefore were viewed as a menace to public health. The crucial ecosystem services that wetlands provide are widely recognized today, and wetlands have some legal protection. Agriculture, pollution, engineering (dams), and urban and suburban development still threaten wetlands, however.

Estuaries occur where fresh water and salt water meet

Where the ocean meets the land, there may be one of several kinds of ecosystems: a rocky shore, a sandy beach, an intertidal mudflat, or a tidal estuary. An **estuary** is a coastal body of water, partly surrounded by land, with access to the open ocean and a large supply of fresh water from rivers. Water levels in an estuary rise and fall with the tides, and salinity fluctuates with tidal cycles, the time of year, and precipitation. Salinity also changes gradually within the estuary, from fresh water at the river entrance to salty ocean water at the mouth of the estuary. Because estuaries undergo marked daily, seasonal, and annual variations in temperature, salinity, and other physical properties, estuarine organisms have a wide tolerance to such changes.

Estuaries are among the most fertile ecosystems in the world, often having much greater productivities than the adjacent ocean or freshwater river (see Table 55-1). This high productivity is the result of four factors: (1) The action of tides promotes a rapid circulation of nutrients and helps remove waste products. (2) Minerals are transported from land into streams and rivers that empty into the estuary. (3) A high level of light penetrates the shallow water. (4) The presence of many plants provides an extensive photosynthetic carpet and also mechanically traps detritus, forming the basis of detritus food webs. Most commercially important fishes and shellfish spend their larval stages in estuaries among the protective tangle of decaying stems.

Temperate estuaries usually contain **salt marshes,** shallow wetlands in which salt-tolerant grasses dominate (**FIG. 56-16**). Uninformed people have often considered salt marshes as worthless, empty stretches of land. As a result, people have used them as dumps, severely polluting them, or filled them with dredged bottom material to form artificial land for residential and industrial development. A large part of the estuarine environment is lost in this way, along with many of its ecosystem services, for example, biological habitats, sediment and pollution trapping, groundwater supply, and storm buffering (salt marshes absorb much of the energy of a storm surge and therefore prevent flood damage elsewhere).

FIGURE 56-16 Salt marsh
Cordgrass (*Spartina alterniflora*) is the dominant vegetation in this salt marsh in Georgia.

Mangrove forests, the tropical equivalent of salt marshes, cover perhaps 70% of tropical and subtropical coastal mudflats where tides and waves fluctuate (**FIG. 56-17**). Like salt marshes, mangrove forests provide valuable ecosystem services. Mangrove roots stabilize the sediments, preventing coastal erosion and providing a barrier against the ocean during storms. Their interlacing roots are breeding grounds and nurseries for commercially important fish and shellfish species, such as blue crabs, shrimp, mullet, and spotted sea trout. Mangrove branches are nesting sites for many species of birds, such as pelicans, herons, egrets, and roseate spoonbills. Mangroves are under assault from coastal development, including aquaculture facilities, and unsustainable logging. Some countries, such as the Philippines, Bangladesh, and Guinea-Bissau, have cut down more than two-thirds of their mangrove forests.

Marine ecosystems dominate Earth's surface

Although lakes and the ocean are comparable in many ways, they have many differences. Depths of even the deepest lakes do not approach those of the ocean, which has areas that extend more than 6 km (3.6 miles) below the sunlit surface. Tides and currents profoundly influence the ocean. Gravitational pulls of both sun and moon produce two tides a day throughout the ocean, but the height of those tides varies with season, local topography, and phases of the moon (full moons and new moons cause the highest tides).

The immense, complex marine environment is subdivided into several zones: the intertidal zone, the benthic (ocean floor) environment, and the pelagic (ocean water) environment (**FIG. 56-18**). The pelagic environment is, in turn, divided into two provinces— the neritic province and the oceanic province.

The intertidal zone is transitional between land and ocean

The **intertidal zone** is the shoreline area between low and high tide. Although high levels of light and nutrients, together with an abundance of oxygen, make the intertidal zone a biologically productive environment, it is also a stressful one. If an intertidal beach is sandy, inhabitants must contend with a constantly shifting environment that threatens to engulf them and gives them scant protection against wave action. Consequently, most sand-dwelling organisms, such as mole crabs, are continual and active burrowers. Because they follow the tides up and down the beach, most do not have any notable adaptations to survive drying or exposure.

A rocky shore provides a fine anchorage for seaweeds and invertebrate animals. However, it is exposed to constant wave action when immersed during high tides and to drying and temperature changes when exposed to the air during low tides. A typical rocky-shore inhabitant has some way of sealing in moisture, perhaps by closing its shell, if it has one, plus a powerful means of anchoring itself to rocks. Mussels, for example, have horny, threadlike anchors, and barnacles have special cement glands. Rocky-shore intertidal algae (seaweeds) usually have thick, gummy polysaccharide coats,

FIGURE 56-17 Mangroves
Red mangroves (*Rhizophora mangle*) have stiltlike roots that support the tree. Many animals live in the complex root systems of mangrove forests. Photographed at low tide along the coast of Florida, near Miami.

FIGURE 56-18 Zonation in the ocean

*Labels in figure:*

High tide

Pelagic environment

Sun

Intertidal zone

Neritic province

Oceanic province

Depth in meters

Low tide

Sea level

Photosynthesis

Benthic environment

0

50

100

200

Continental shelf

500

1000

Twilight

Bathyal zone of benthic environment

1500

2000

3000

Darkness

4000

Abyssal zone of benthic environment

5000

Hadal zone of benthic environment

10,000

The ocean has three main life zones: the intertidal zone, the benthic environment, and the pelagic environment. The pelagic environment consists of the neritic and oceanic provinces. Note that the slopes of the ocean floor are not as steep as shown; they are exaggerated to save space. (Adapted from Miller, G. T. *Living in the Environment,* 16th ed. Cengage/Brooks Cole, Belmont, CA, 2007, p. 166, Figure 8-5.)

which dry out slowly when exposed, and flexible bodies not easily broken by wave action (**FIG. 56-19**). Some rocky-shore community inhabitants hide in burrows or crevices at low tide.

Seagrass beds, kelp forests, and coral reefs are part of the benthic environment

The **benthic environment** is the ocean floor. It is divided into zones based on distance from land, light availability, and depth.

FIGURE 56-19 Seaweeds in a rocky intertidal zone ▶

Sea palms (*Postelsia*), which are 50 to 75 cm (20 to 30 in) tall, are common on the rocky Pacific coast from Vancouver Island to California. The bases of these brown algae are firmly attached to the rocky substrate, enabling them to withstand heavy surf action. Photographed at low tide.

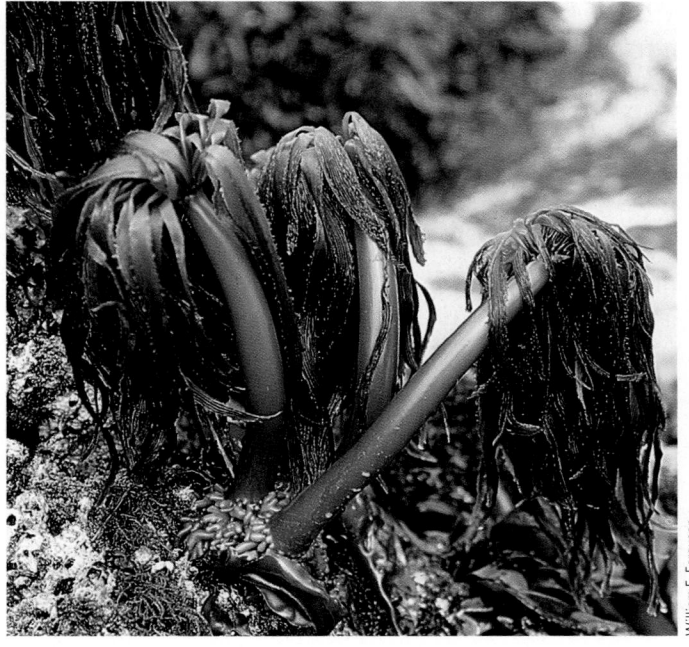

William E. Ferguson

The benthic environment consists of sediments (mostly sand and mud) in which many marine animals, such as worms and clams, burrow. Archaea and bacteria are common in marine sediments, and living archaea and bacteria have been found in deeply buried ocean sediments at least 800 m (2600 ft) below the ocean floor at several different sites in the Pacific Ocean.

The **abyssal zone** is that part of the benthic environment that extends from a depth of 4000 to 6000 m (2.5 to 3.7 miles). (In Chapter 55, *Inquiring About: Life without the Sun* describes some of the unusual organisms in hydrothermal vents in the abyssal zone.) The **hadal zone** is that part of the benthic environment deeper than 6000 m.

Here we describe benthic communities in shallow ocean waters—seagrass beds, kelp forests, and coral reefs. **Sea grasses** are flowering plants that have adapted to complete submersion in ocean water (**FIG. 56-20**). They are not true grasses. Sea grasses live in shallow water, to depths of 10 m (33 ft), where they receive enough light to photosynthesize efficiently. Extensive beds of sea grasses occur in quiet temperate, subtropical, and tropical waters; no sea grasses live in polar waters. Sea grasses have a high primary productivity and are therefore ecologically important in shallow marine areas. Their roots and rhizomes stabilize the sediments, reducing surface erosion. Sea grasses provide food and habitat for many marine organisms. In temperate waters, ducks and geese eat sea grasses; in tropical waters, manatees, green turtles, parrot fish, sturgeon fish, and sea urchins eat them. These herbivores consume only about 5% of the sea grasses. The remaining 95% eventually enter the detritus food web when the sea grasses die and bacteria decompose them. In turn, a variety of animals such as mud shrimp, lug worms, and mullet (a type of fish) consume the bacteria.

Kelps, which may reach lengths of 60 m (200 ft), are the largest brown algae (see Fig. 26-11b). Kelps are common in cooler temperate marine waters of both the Northern and Southern Hemispheres. They are especially abundant in relatively shallow waters (depths of about 25 m, or 82 ft) along rocky coastlines. Kelps are

Ron Philips

FIGURE 56-20 Seagrass bed
Turtle grasses (*Thalassia*) have numerous invertebrates and algal epiphytes attached to their leaves. These shallow underwater meadows of marine flowering plants are ecologically important for shelter and food for many organisms. Photographed off the coast of Mexico.

photosynthetic and are therefore the primary food producers for the kelp forest ecosystem. Kelp forests also provide habitats for many marine animals. Tube worms, sponges, sea cucumbers, clams, crabs, fishes (such as tuna), and mammals (such as sea otters) find refuge in the algal blades. Some animals eat the blades, but kelps are consumed mainly in the detritus food web. Bacteria that decompose dead kelp provide food for sponges, tunicates, worms, clams, and snails. Kelp beds support a diversity of life that almost rivals that found in coral reefs.

Coral reefs, which are built from accumulated layers of calcium carbonate ($CaCO_3$), are found in warm (temperature usually greater than 21°C), shallow sea water. The living portions of coral reefs grow in shallow waters where light penetrates. Many coral reefs are composed principally of red coralline algae that require light for photosynthesis. Coral animals also require light for the large number of symbiotic dinoflagellates, known as **zooxanthellae,** that live and photosynthesize in their tissues (see Fig. 54-12). Although species of coral without zooxanthellae exist, only those with zooxanthellae build reefs. In addition to obtaining food from the zooxanthellae living inside them, coral animals capture food at night; they use their stinging tentacles to paralyze small animals that drift nearby.

Coral reefs grow slowly in warm, shallow water, as coral organisms build on the calcareous remains of countless organisms before them. The waters in which coral reefs are found are often poor in nutrients. Other factors favor high productivity, however, including the presence of symbiotic zooxanthellae, warm temperatures, and plenty of sunlight.

Coral reef ecosystems are the most diverse of all marine environments and contain hundreds or even thousands of species of fishes and invertebrates, such as giant clams, sea urchins, sea stars, sponges, brittle stars, sea fans, and shrimp (**FIG. 56-21**). The Great Barrier Reef, along the northeastern coast of Australia, occupies only 0.1% of the ocean's surface, but 8% of the world's fish species live there. The multitude of relationships and interactions that occur at coral reefs is comparable only to those in tropical rain forests among terrestrial ecosystems. As in the rain forest, competition is intense, particularly for light and space to grow.

Coral reefs are ecologically important because they both provide habitat for a wide variety of marine organisms and protect coastlines from shoreline erosion. They also provide humans with seafood, pharmaceuticals, and income from tourism and recreation. Although coral formations are important ecosystems, they are being degraded and destroyed. According to the UN Environment Program, 27% of the world's coral reefs are at high risk. Coral reefs of southeastern Asia, which contain the most species of all coral reefs, are the most threatened of any region.

In some areas, silt washing downstream from clear-cut inland forests has smothered reefs under a layer of sediment. Some scientists hypothesize that high salinity resulting from the diversion of fresh water to supply the growing human population is killing Florida reefs. Overfishing, pollution from sewage discharge and agricultural runoff, oil spills, boat groundings, fishing with dynamite or cyanide, hurricane damage, disease, coral bleaching, land reclamation, tourism, and the mining of corals for building material are also taking a heavy toll. (Coral reef problems are also discussed in Chapter 31.)

FIGURE 56-21 *Animated* Coral reef organisms

A panoramic view of a coral reef in the Indian Ocean off the coast of the Maldives shows the many animals that live on and around coral reefs.

The neritic province consists of shallow waters close to shore

The **neritic province** is open ocean that overlies the continental shelves, that is, the ocean floor from the shoreline to a depth of 200 m (650 ft). Organisms that live in the neritic province are floaters or swimmers (**FIG. 56-22**). The upper reaches of the neritic province make up the **euphotic zone,** which extends from the surface to a depth of approximately 100 m (325 ft). Enough light penetrates the euphotic zone to support photosynthesis.

Large numbers of phytoplankton, particularly diatoms in cooler waters and dinoflagellates in warmer waters, produce food by photosynthesis and are thus the base of food webs. Zooplankton (including tiny crustaceans; jellyfish; comb jellies; protists such as foraminiferans; and larvae of barnacles, sea urchins, worms, and crabs) feed on phytoplankton.

Plankton-eating nekton, such as herring, sardines, squid, manta rays, and baleen whales, consume zooplankton. These, in turn, become prey for carnivorous nekton such as sharks, tuna, dolphins, and toothed whales. Nekton are thought to be mostly confined to the shallower neritic waters (less than 60 m, or 195 ft, deep) because that is where their food is. However, not much is known about the behavior and migration patterns of marine nekton. Many fishes appear to be wide-ranging. For example, an individual fish tagged on one side of an ocean may be recaptured on the other side a few months later. Whether the fish traveled alone or in a school is not known at this time.

The oceanic province makes up most of the ocean

The average depth of the world's ocean is 4000 m (2.4 mi). The **oceanic province** is that part of the open ocean that covers the deep-ocean basin, that is, the ocean floor at depths more than 200 m. It is the largest marine environment and contains about 75% of the ocean's water. Cold temperatures, high hydrostatic pressure, and an absence of sunlight characterize the oceanic province; these environmental conditions are uniform throughout the year.

Most organisms of the oceanic province depend on **marine snow,** organic debris that drifts down into the **aphotic** ("without light") **region** from the upper, lighted regions. Organisms of this little-known realm are filter-feeders, scavengers, or predators. Many are invertebrates, some of which attain great sizes. The giant squid, for example, measures up to 18 m (59 ft) in length, including its

FIGURE 56-22 *Animated* Fish in the open ocean

Rough triggerfish (*Canthidermis maculatus*) are tropical fish usually found in the open ocean to depths of 92 m (300 ft). Sometimes they spend time on deep rocky slopes. Photographed in the Pacific Ocean near Hawaii.

FIGURE 56-23 Gulper eel from the oceanic province ▶

The gulper eel (*Saccopharynx laven-bergi*) uses its "trap-door" jaws to swallow prey as large as itself. The tail, of which only a small portion is shown, makes up most of the length of a gulper eel's body. Gulper eels grow to 1.8 m (6 ft). Shown is a live specimen, photographed in an aquarium aboard ship after being captured at a depth of 1500 m (4921 ft) off southern California.

Bruce H. Robison/Monterey Bay Aquarium Research Institute

tentacles. Fishes of the oceanic province are strikingly adapted to darkness and food scarcity. For example, the gulper eel's huge jaws enable it to swallow large prey (**FIG. 56-23**). (An organism that encounters food infrequently needs to eat as much as possible when it has the chance.) Many animals of the oceanic province have illuminated organs that enable them to see one another to mate or to capture food. Adapted to drifting or slow swimming, these fishes often have reduced bone and muscle mass.

Human activities are harming the ocean

Because the ocean is so vast, it is hard to visualize that human activities could affect, much less harm, it. They do, however. Development of resorts, cities, industries, and agriculture along coasts alters or destroys many coastal ecosystems, including mangrove forests, salt marshes, seagrass beds, and coral reefs. Coastal and marine ecosystems receive pollution from land, from rivers emptying into the ocean, and from atmospheric contaminants that enter the ocean via precipitation. Disease-causing viruses and bacteria from human sewage contaminate shellfish and other seafood and sometimes threaten public health. Millions of tons of trash, including plastic, fishing nets, and packaging materials, end up in coastal and marine ecosystems; some of this trash entangles and kills marine organisms.

Less visible ocean contaminants include fertilizers, pesticides, heavy metals, and synthetic chemicals from agriculture and industry. Coastal dead zones have been reported in more than 400 locations, the consequence of enrichment caused by runoff of fertilizers and the burning of fossil fuels; these dead zones have severely depleted dissolved oxygen levels in bottom waters.

Offshore mining and oil drilling pollute the neritic province with oil and other contaminants. Millions of ships dump oily ballast and other wastes overboard in the neritic and oceanic prov-

inces. Fishing is highly mechanized, and new technologies can remove every single fish in a targeted area of the ocean. Scallop dredges and shrimp trawls are dragged across the benthic environment, destroying entire communities with a single swipe. Most countries recognize the importance of the ocean to life on this planet, but few have the resources or programs to protect and manage the ocean effectively.

Review

- What are plankton, nekton, and benthos?
- What environmental factors are most important in determining the adaptations of organisms that live in aquatic environments?
- How do you distinguish between freshwater wetlands and estuaries? between flowing-water and standing-water ecosystems?
- What are the four main marine environments?
- Which aquatic ecosystem is often compared to tropical rain forests? Why?

56.3 ECOTONES

◼ LEARNING OBJECTIVE

7   Define *ecotone* and describe some of its features.

We have discussed the various terrestrial biomes and aquatic ecosystems as if they were distinct and separate entities, but within landscapes, ecosystems intergrade with one another at their boundaries. The transition zone where two communities or biomes meet and intergrade is called an **ecotone** (see Chapter 54). Ecotones range in size from quite small, such as the area where an agricultural field meets a woodland or where a stream flows through a forest, to continental in scope. For example, at the border between tundra and boreal forest an extensive ecotone exists that consists of tundra vegetation interspersed with small, scattered conifers. Such ecotones provide habitat diversity. In fact, often a greater variety and density of organisms populate ecotones than live in either adjacent ecosystem (**FIG. 56-24**).

Ecologists who study ecotones look for adaptations that enable organisms to survive there. They also examine the relationship between species richness and ecotones and how ecotones change over time. Long-term studies of ecotones have revealed they are far from static. The ecotone boundary between desert and semiarid grassland in southern New Mexico, for example, has moved during the past 50 years as the desert ecosystem has expanded into the grassland.

KEY EXPERIMENT

QUESTION: Does species richness vary among ecotones and their adjoining communities?

HYPOTHESIS: Ecotones have greater species richness than the communities they connect.

EXPERIMENT: Plant species were sampled for two communities in southwestern Oregon and for the ecotone between them. The communities, one with nonserpentine soil and one with serpentine soil, are defined largely by soil conditions. Nonserpentine soils (samples 1 to 10) are "normal" soils. Serpentine soils (samples 18 to 28) contain high levels of elements such as chromium, nickel, and magnesium that are toxic to many plants.

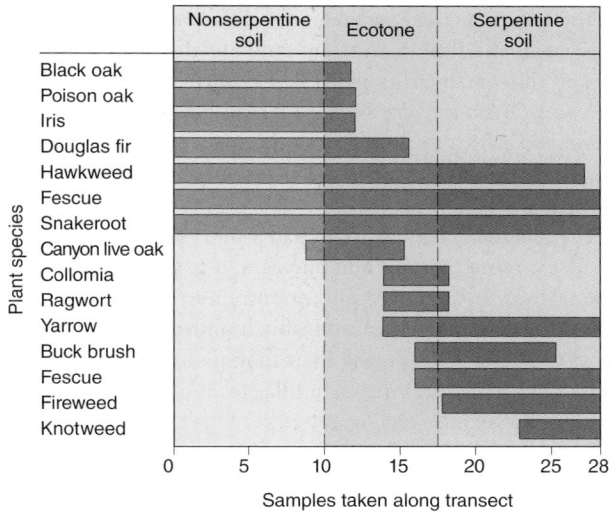

RESULTS AND CONCLUSION: Shown are the various plant species found in the two communities (*yellow and blue*) and in the ecotone between them (*green*). The ecotone had a greater richness than either adjoining community.

Source: Modified from White, C. D. "Vegetation-Soil Chemistry Correlations in Serpentine Ecosystems." Ph.D. dissertation, University of Oregon, Eugene, 1971. Reprinted with permission of Dr. Charles D. White.

FIGURE 56-24 Ecotones and species richness
Note that the two fescues in the figure are different species.

Review

- What is an ecotone?
- Where do ecotones occur?

56.4 BIOGEOGRAPHY

LEARNING OBJECTIVE

8 Define *biogeography* and briefly describe Wallace's biogeographic realms.

The study of the geographic distribution of plants and animals is called **biogeography** (see Chapter 18). Biogeographers search for patterns in geographic distribution and try to explain how such patterns arose, including where populations originated, how they spread, and when. Biogeographers recognize that geologic and climate changes such as mountain building, continental drift, and periods of extensive glaciation influence the distribution of species. Biogeography is linked to evolutionary history and provides insights into how organisms may have interacted in ancient ecosystems. Studying biogeography helps us relate ancient ecosystems to modern ones because ancient ecosystems form a continuum with modern ecosystems.

One of the basic tenets of biogeography is that each species originated only once. The particular place where this occurred is known as the species' **center of origin.** The center of origin is not a single point but the distribution of the population when the new species originated. From its center of origin, each species spreads until a barrier of some kind halts it. Examples of barriers include the ocean, a desert, or a mountain range; unfavorable climate; or the presence of organisms that compete successfully for food or shelter.

Most plant and animal species have characteristic geographic distributions. The **range** of a particular species is that portion of Earth in which it is found. The range of some species may be a relatively small area. For example, wombats, the marsupial equivalent of groundhogs, are found only in drier parts of southeastern Australia and nearby islands. Such localized, native species are said to be **endemic,** that is, they are not found anywhere else in the world. In contrast, some species have a nearly worldwide distribution and occur on more than one continent or throughout much of the ocean. Such species are said to be **cosmopolitan.**

One of the early observations of biogeographers is that the ranges of different species do not include everywhere that they *could* survive. Central Africa has elephants, gorillas, chimpanzees, lions, antelopes, umbrella trees, and guapiruvu trees, whereas areas in South America with a similar climate have none of these. These animals and plants originated in Africa after continental drift had already separated the supercontinent Pangaea into several landmasses. The organisms could not expand their range into South America because the Atlantic Ocean was an impassable barrier. Likewise, the ocean was a barrier to South American monkeys, sloths, tapirs, balsa trees, and snakewood trees, none of which are found in Africa.

FIGURE 56-25 Wallace's biogeographic realms

Certain unique species characterize each of the six biogeographic realms. The boundary between the Oriental and Australian realms, for example, is a deep-water gap. Wallace noted that hornbills, Sumatran tigers, orangutans, and tree shrews live west of the boundary, whereas tree kangaroos, cockatoos, birds of paradise, and cuscus live east of the boundary. Many of the Australian species are endemic—that is, they evolved in Australia and are found nowhere else. Wallace's studies of biogeography helped him develop his theory of evolution by natural selection.

Land areas are divided into six biogeographic realms

As the various continents were explored and their organisms studied, biologists observed that the world could be divided into major blocks of vegetation, such as forests, grasslands, and deserts, and that these vegetation types corresponded to specific climates. The relationship between animal distribution, geography, and climate was not deduced until 1876. At that time, Alfred Wallace, who independently discovered the same theory of evolution by natural selection as Charles Darwin, divided Earth's land areas into six major biogeographic realms: the Palearctic, Nearctic, Neotropical, Ethiopian, Oriental, and Australian (**FIG. 56-25**). A major barrier separates each of the six biogeographic realms from the others and helps maintain each region's biological distinctiveness.

Many biologists quickly embraced Wallace's classification system, which is still considered valid today. However, human activities, such as the intentional and unintentional introduction of foreign species, are contributing to a homogenization of the biogeographic realms (see Chapter 57).

Refer to Figure 56-25 as we briefly consider some of the characteristic animals in each realm. The *Nearctic* and *Palearctic realms* are more closely related than the other regions, especially in their northern parts, where they share many animals such as wolves, hares, and caribou. This similarity may be due to a land bridge that has periodically connected Siberia and Alaska. This bridge was present until late in the Pleistocene epoch, about 10,000 years ago. Animals adapted to cold environments may have dispersed between Asia and North America along this bridge.

The *Neotropical realm* was almost completely isolated from the Nearctic realm and other landmasses for most of the past 70 mil-

lion years. During this time, many marsupial species evolved. The isthmus of Panama, which formed a dry-land connection about 3 million years ago, linked North and South America and provided a route for dispersal. Only three species, the opossum, armadillo, and porcupine, are descendants of animals that survived the northward dispersal from South America, but many species, such as the tapir and llama, are descendants of animals that survived the southward dispersal from North America. Competition from these species caused many of South America's marsupial species to go extinct.

The Sahara Desert separates the *Ethiopian realm* from other landmasses. The Ethiopian realm contains the most varied vertebrates of all six realms. Some overlap exists between the Ethiopian realm and *Oriental realm* because a land bridge with a moist climate linked Africa to Asia during the Miocene and Pliocene epochs. The Oriental realm has the fewest endemic species of all the tropical realms.

The *Australian realm* has not had a land connection with other regions for more than 85 million years. It has no native placental mammals, and marsupials and monotremes, including the duck-billed platypus and the spiny anteater, dominate it. Adaptive radiation of the marsupials during their long period of isolation led to species with ecological niches similar to those of placental mammals of other realms (see Fig. 32-28).

Review

- What is biogeography?
- Which biogeographic realm has been separated from the other biogeographic realms for the longest period? What animals characterize this biogeographic realm?

56.1 *(page 1219)*

1 Define *biome* and briefly describe the nine major terrestrial biomes, giving attention to the climate, soil, and characteristic plants and animals of each.

- A **biome** is a large, relatively distinct terrestrial region with characteristic climate, soil, plants, and animals.

- A frozen layer of subsoil (**permafrost**) and low-growing vegetation that is adapted to extreme cold and a short growing season characterize **tundra,** the northernmost biome.

- Coniferous trees adapted to cold winters; a short growing season; and acidic, mineral-poor soil dominate the **boreal forest, or taiga.**

- Large conifers dominate **temperate rain forest,** which receives high precipitation.

- **Temperate deciduous forest** occurs where precipitation is relatively high and soils are rich in organic matter. Broad-leaf trees that lose their leaves seasonally dominate temperate deciduous forest.

- **Temperate grassland** typically has a deep, mineral-rich soil and has moderate but uncertain precipitation.

- Thickets of small-leaf evergreen shrubs and trees and a climate of wet, mild winters and dry summers characterize **chaparral.**

- **Desert,** found in both temperate (cold deserts) and subtropical or tropical regions (warm deserts) with low levels of precipitation, contains organisms with specialized water-conserving adaptations.

- Tropical grassland, called **savanna,** has widely scattered trees interspersed with grassy areas. Savanna occurs in tropical areas with low or seasonal rainfall.

- Mineral-poor soil and high rainfall that is evenly distributed throughout the year characterize **tropical rain forest.** Tropical rain forest has high species richness and high productivity.

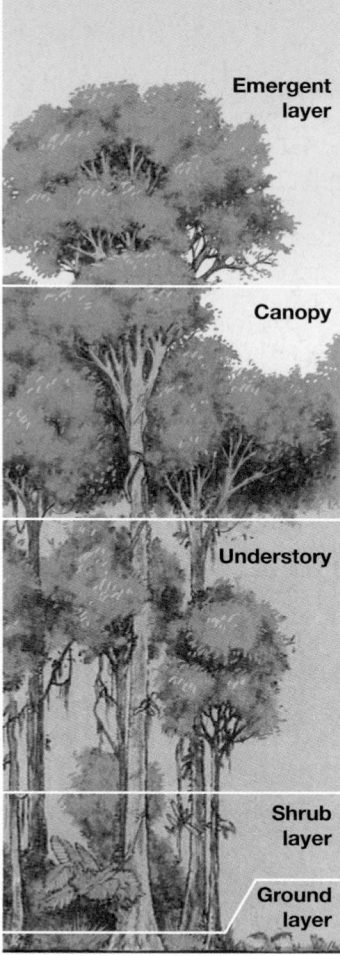

Emergent layer

Canopy

Understory

Shrub layer

Ground layer

CENGAGENOW™ Learn more about biomes by clicking on the figure in CengageNOW.

2 Describe at least one human effect on each of the biomes discussed.

- Oil exploration and military exercises result in long-lasting damage to tundra. Clear-cut logging destroys boreal and temperate rain forests. Temperate deciduous forests are removed for logging, farms and tree plantations, and land development.

- Human population growth and its accompanying agricultural and industrial expansion threaten most of the world's tropical rain forests.

- Farmland has replaced most temperate grasslands; savannas are increasingly converted to rangeland for cattle. Development of hilly chaparral results in mud slides and costly fires. Land development in deserts reduces wildlife habitat.

56.2 *(page 1228)*

3 Explain the important environmental factors that affect aquatic ecosystems.

- In aquatic ecosystems, important environmental factors include **salinity** (concentration of dissolved salts), amount of dissolved oxygen, availability of light, levels of essential minerals, water depth, temperature, pH, and presence or absence of waves and currents.

4 Distinguish among plankton, nekton, and benthos.

- Aquatic life is ecologically divided into **plankton** (free-floating organisms), **nekton** (strongly swimming organisms), and **benthos** (bottom-dwelling organisms).

- **Phytoplankton** are photosynthetic algae and cyanobacteria; **zooplankton** include protozoa, tiny crustaceans, and the larval stages of many animals.

5 Briefly describe the various freshwater, estuarine, and marine ecosystems, giving attention to the environmental characteristics and representative organisms of each.

- Freshwater ecosystems include flowing-water ecosystems, standing-water ecosystems, and freshwater wetlands. In **flowing-water ecosystems,** the water flows in a current. Flowing-water ecosystems have few phytoplankton and depend on detritus from the land for much of their energy.

- Large **standing-water ecosystems** (freshwater lakes) are divided into zones on the basis of water depth. The marginal **littoral zone** contains emergent vegetation and algae. The **limnetic zone,** open water away from the shore that extends as far down as sunlight penetrates, contains phytoplankton, zooplankton, and larger fishes. The deep, dark **profundal zone** holds little life other than bacterial decomposers.

- **Freshwater wetlands,** lands that are transitional between fresh water and terrestrial ecosystems, are usually covered at least part of the year by shallow water and have characteristic soils and vegetation. Freshwater wetlands perform many valuable **ecosystem services.**

- An **estuary** is a coastal body of water, partly surrounded by land, with access to both the ocean and a large supply of fresh water from rivers. Salinity fluctuates with tidal cycles, the time of year, and precipitation. Temperate estuaries usually contain **salt marshes,** whereas **mangrove forests** dominate tropical coastlines.

- Four important marine environments are the intertidal zone, the benthic environment, the neritic province, and the oceanic province. The **intertidal zone** is the shoreline area between low and high tides. Organisms of the intertidal zone have adaptations to resist wave action and being exposed to air (low tide).

- The **benthic environment** is the ocean floor. **Sea grasses, kelps, and coral reefs** are important benthic communities in shallow ocean waters.
- The **neritic province** is open ocean from the shoreline to a depth of 200 m. Organisms that live in the neritic province are all floaters or swimmers. Phytoplankton are the base of the food web in the **euphotic zone,** where enough light penetrates to support photosynthesis.
- The **oceanic province** is that part of the open ocean that is deeper than 200 m. The uniform environment is one of darkness, cold temperature, and high pressure. Animal inhabitants of the oceanic province are either predators or scavengers that subsist on **marine snow,** detritus that drifts down from other areas of the ocean.

    CENGAGENOW Learn more about lake and ocean zonation by clicking on the figures in CengageNOW.

6 Describe at least one human effect on each of the aquatic ecosystems discussed.
- Water pollution and dams adversely affect flowing-water ecosystems. Increased nutrients, supplied by human activities, stimulate algal growth, resulting in enriched ponds and lakes. Agriculture, pollution, and land development threaten wetlands and estuaries. Pollution, coastal development, offshore mining and oil drilling, and overfishing threaten marine ecosystems.

56.3 *(page 1236)*

7 Define *ecotone* and describe some of its features.
- An **ecotone** is the transition zone where two communities or biomes meet and intergrade. Ecotones provide habitat diversity and are often populated by a greater variety of organisms than lives in either adjacent ecosystem.

56.4 *(page 1237)*

8 Define *biogeography* and briefly describe Wallace's biogeographic realms.
- **Biogeography** is the study of the geographic distribution of plants and animals, including where populations came from, how they got there, and when. Each species originated only once, at its **center of origin.** From its center of origin, each species spreads until a physical, environmental, or biological barrier halts it. The **range** of a particular species is that portion of Earth in which it is found.
- Alfred Wallace divided Earth's land areas into six major biogeographic realms: the Palearctic, Nearctic, Neotropical, Ethiopian, Oriental, and Australian. Each realm is biologically distinctive because a mountain range, desert, deep water, or other barrier separates it from the others.

TEST YOUR UNDERSTANDING

1. The northernmost biome, known as _____, typically has little precipitation, a short growing season, and permafrost. (a) chaparral (b) boreal forest (c) tundra (d) northern deciduous forest (e) savanna

2. Forests of the northeastern and Mid-Atlantic United States, which have broad-leaf hardwood trees that lose their foliage annually, are called (a) temperate deciduous forests (b) tropical dry forests (c) boreal forests (d) temperate rain forests (e) tropical rain forests

3. The deepest, richest soil in the world occurs in (a) temperate rain forest (b) tropical rain forest (c) savanna (d) temperate grassland (e) chaparral

4. This biome, with its thicket of evergreen shrubs and small trees, is found in areas with Mediterranean climates. (a) temperate rain forest (b) tropical rain forest (c) savanna (d) temperate grassland (e) chaparral

5. This biome is a tropical grassland interspersed with widely spaced trees. (a) temperate rain forest (b) tropical rain forest (c) savanna (d) temperate grassland (e) chaparral

6. This biome has the greatest species richness. (a) temperate rain forest (b) tropical rain forest (c) savanna (d) temperate grassland (e) chaparral

7. Organisms in aquatic environments fall into three categories: free-floating _____, strongly swimming _____, and bottom-dwelling _____. (a) nekton; benthos; plankton (b) nekton; plankton; benthos (c) plankton; benthos; nekton (d) plankton; nekton; benthos (e) benthos; nekton; plankton

8. Temperate-zone lakes are thermally stratified, with warm and cold layers separated by a transitional (a) aphotic region (b) thermocline (c) barrier reef (d) ecotone (e) littoral zone

9. Emergent vegetation grows in the _____ zone of freshwater lakes. (a) littoral (b) limnetic (c) profundal (d) neritic (e) intertidal

10. The _____ is open ocean from the shoreline to a depth of 200 m. (a) benthic environment (b) intertidal zone (c) neritic province (d) oceanic province (e) aphotic region

11. The transition zone where two ecosystems or biomes meet and intergrade is called (a) a biosphere (b) an aphotic region (c) a thermocline (d) a biogeographic realm (e) an ecotone

12. Which biogeographic realm has been separated from the other landmasses for more than 85 million years? (a) Ethiopian (b) Palearctic (c) Nearctic (d) Oriental (e) Australian

CRITICAL THINKING

1. In which biomes would migration be most common? hibernation? estivation? Explain your answers.

2. Develop a hypothesis to explain why animals adapted to the desert are usually small. How would you test your hypothesis?

3. Why do most of the animals of the tropical rain forest live in trees?

4. What would happen to the organisms in a river with a fast current if a dam were built? Would there be any differences in habitat if the dam were upstream or downstream of the organisms in question? Explain your answers.

5. **EVOLUTION LINK.** When a black-tailed prairie dog or other small animal dies, other prairie dogs bury it. Develop a hypothesis to explain how this behavior may be adaptive. How would you test this hypothesis?

6. **ANALYZING DATA.** Examine Figure 56-1. What is the lowest average annual precipitation characteristic of tropical rain forests? the highest? What is the range of average temperature in tropical rain forests?

7. **ANALYZING DATA.** Examine Figure 56-24. How many of the sampled species are found in the nonserpentine soil? in the serpentine soil? in the ecotone? What generalization about ecotones do these data support?

8. **ANALYZING DATA.** The climate graphs below show the monthly temperature and precipitation averages for three different temperate biomes in North America. Identify the temperate desert, temperate deciduous forest, and temperate grassland. Explain your answers.

9. **SCIENCE, TECHNOLOGY, AND SOCIETY.** Imagine that you are a graduate student working with university scientists on the effects on sea turtles of the 2010 oil spill in the Gulf of Mexico. What data would you want to collect? Knowing that the turtles' life cycle includes laying eggs on beaches, why would it be important to involve local communities in your research?

 Additional questions are available in CengageNOW at www.cengage.com/login.

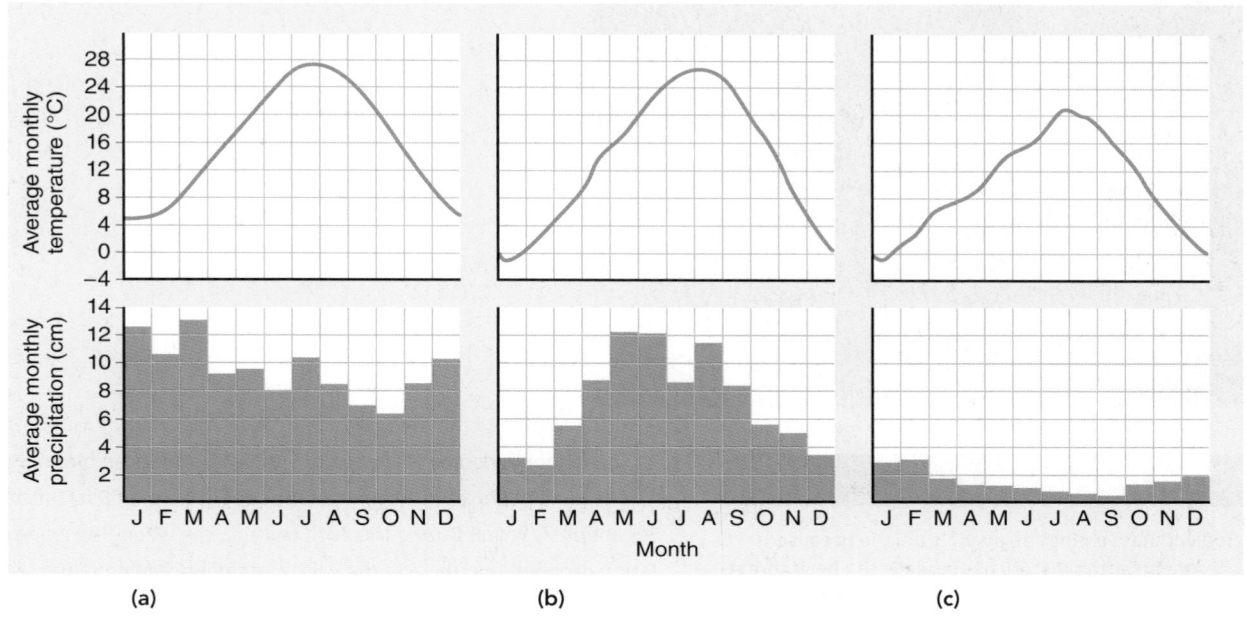

(a)　　　　　(b)　　　　　(c)

57 Biological Diversity and Conservation Biology

Lucky, the whooping crane (*Grus americana*). Photographed with one of his parents in Florida.

Steve Nesbitt/Florida Fish and Wildlife Conservation Commission

KEY CONCEPTS

57.1 Today's mass extinction event is unique because never before in Earth's history has biodiversity been threatened with extinction in such a compressed time period.

57.2 Conservation biology is a multidisciplinary science that studies human effects on biodiversity and devises practical solutions to address these effects.

57.3 Globally, removal of large expanses of forest for timber, agriculture, and other uses is contributing to the loss of biological diversity and valuable ecosystem services.

57.4 There is strong evidence of global climate change, which scientists predict will adversely affect biodiversity, human health, and agriculture.

57.5 Although the stratospheric ozone layer is slowly recovering, harmful effects on biodiversity and humans will continue for several decades.

The whooping crane is a magnificent North American bird named for its loud, penetrating voice. It stands about 1.4 m (4.5 ft) tall and lives for about 50 years. During the 20th century, the whooping crane population dropped to only 16 in the wild, and their breeding range shrank from much of central North America to one remote location in Canada. Whooping crane numbers declined primarily due to the loss of their wetland habitat, which humans filled in for farmland, housing developments, and industrial plants.

Thanks to intensive efforts by conservation organizations and government agencies in Canada and the United States, the wild flock of whooping cranes still exists and now contains about 387 birds. The wild population spends summer in Canada and migrates to the Texas coast to winter.

Concerned that bad weather, disease, or some other natural or human-caused disaster could wipe out the single wild population, in the 1990s biologists started reintroducing a second population of whooping cranes to the eastern part of North America. Captive-bred whooping cranes are released in central Florida to establish this population, where a population of related sandhill cranes with similar habitat requirements resides.

A breeding pair of whooping cranes made history in 2002 when they successfully reproduced. An eagle killed one of the offspring, but the other chick, named Lucky, survived (see photograph). Lucky is the first whooping crane to be produced by captive-reared, released parents and the first to hatch in the wild in the United States since 1939.

Whooping cranes are an excellent example of the kinds of injuries humans inflict on biological diversity. They also exemplify human efforts to maintain the world's declining biological diversity, which is a serious problem. For example, according to the International Union for the Conservation of Nature (IUCN), which monitors the status of Earth's biological diversity, as many as one-third of the world's mammals are at risk of extinction.

We conclude this text by focusing our attention on declining biological diversity and conservation biology. We also consider three environmental issues that harm biological diversity—deforestation, climate change, and ozone depletion in the stratosphere.

57.1 THE BIODIVERSITY CRISIS

◼ LEARNING OBJECTIVES

1 Identify the various levels of biodiversity: genetic diversity, species richness, and ecosystem diversity.
2 Distinguish among threatened species, endangered species, and extinct species.
3 Discuss at least four causes of declining biological diversity and identify the most important cause.

The human species (*Homo sapiens*) has been present on Earth for about 195,000 years (see Chapter 22), which is a brief span of time compared with the age of our planet, some 4.6 billion years. Despite our relatively short tenure on Earth, our biological impact on other species is unparalleled. Our numbers have increased dramatically—the human population reached 6.8 billion in mid-2009—and we have expanded our biological range, moving into almost every habitat on Earth.

Wherever we have gone, we have altered the environment and shaped it to meet our needs. In only a few generations we have transformed the face of Earth, placed a great strain on Earth's resources and resilience, and profoundly affected other species. As a result of these changes, many people are concerned with **environmental sustainability,** the ability to meet humanity's current needs without compromising the ability of future generations to meet their needs. The impact of humans on the environment merits special study in biology, not merely because we ourselves are humans but because our impact on the rest of the biosphere is so extensive.

Extinction, the death of a species, occurs when the last individual member of a species dies. (Chapter 20 introduced the important concept of extinction.) Although extinction is a natural biological process, human activities have greatly accelerated it (**FIG. 57-1**). Extinction is happening at a rate as much as 1000 times the normal background rate of extinction, according to the 2005 Millennium Ecosystem Assessment report. The burgeoning human population has forced us to spread into almost all areas of Earth. Whenever humans invade an area, the habitats of many plants and animals are disrupted or destroyed, which can contribute to their extinction.

Biological diversity, also called **biodiversity,** is the variation among organisms (**FIG. 57-2**). Biological diversity includes much more than simply **species richness,** the number of species of archaea, bacteria, protists, plants, fungi, and animals. Biological diversity occurs at all levels of ecological organization, from populations to ecosystems. It takes into account **genetic diversity,** the genetic variety within a species, both among individuals within a given population and among geographically separate populations. (An individual species may have hundreds of genetically distinct populations.) Biological diversity also includes **ecosystem diversity,** the variety of ecosystems found on Earth—the forests, prairies, deserts, lakes, coastal estuaries, coral reefs, and other ecosystems.

| Passenger pigeon | Great auk | Dodo | Golden toad | Aepyornis |

FIGURE 57-1 Selected animal extinctions
These animals became extinct largely as a result of human activities such as destruction of their habitats and hunting. (Adapted from Miller, G. T., and S. E. Spoolman. *Living in the Environment*, 16th ed. Brooks/Cole, Belmont, CA, 2009.)

Genetic diversity affects a population's ability to thrive. This in turn affects species richness within an ecosystem, which ultimately helps determine ecosystem diversity across a large spatial scale.

Genetic diversity in an American oystercatcher population

Species richness in an Eastern sandy shore ecosystem

Ecosystem diversity across an entire region (ocean and shore)

FIGURE 57-2 Levels of biodiversity

The single unduplicated chromosome below each oystercatcher represents the genetic variation among individuals within a population. Conservation at all three ecological levels must occur to protect biological diversity.

Biologists must consider all three levels of biological diversity—species richness, genetic diversity, and ecosystem diversity—as they address the human impact on biodiversity. For example, the disappearance of populations (that is, a decline in genetic diversity) indicates an increased risk that a species will become extinct (a decline in species richness). Biologists perform detailed analyses to quantify how large a population must be to ensure a given species' long-term survival. The smallest population that has a high chance of enduring into the future is known as the **minimum viable population (MVP).**

Biological diversity is currently decreasing at an unprecedented rate (see *Inquiring About: Declining Amphibian Populations*). For example, the IUCN Red List of Threatened Plants, which is based on 20 years of data collection and analysis around the world, lists about 34,000 species of plants currently threatened with extinction. Because Red Lists are not yet available for many tropical countries, it is difficult to know the true scale of the biodiversity crisis.

We may have entered the greatest period of mass extinction in Earth's history, but the current situation differs from previous periods of mass extinction in several respects. First, its cause is directly attributable to human activities. Second, it is occurring in a tremendously compressed period (just a few decades, as opposed to hundreds of thousands of years), much faster than rates of speciation (or replacement). Perhaps even more sobering, larger numbers of plant species are becoming extinct today than in previous mass extinctions. Because plants are the base of terrestrial food webs, extinction of animals that depend on plants is not far behind. It is crucial that we determine how the loss of biodiversity affects the stability and functioning of ecosystems, which make up our life-support system.

The legal definition of an **endangered species,** as stipulated by the U.S. Endangered Species Act, is a species in imminent danger of extinction throughout all or a significant part of its range. (The area in which a particular species is found is its **range.**) Unless humans intervene, an endangered species will probably become extinct.

When extinction is less imminent but the population of a particular species is quite small, the species is classified as threatened. The legal definition of a **threatened species** is a species likely to become endangered in the foreseeable future, throughout all or a significant part of its range.

Endangered and threatened species represent a decline in biological diversity, because as their numbers decrease, their genetic diversity is severely diminished. Endangered and threatened species are at greater risk of extinction than species with greater genetic variability because long-term survival and evolution depend on genetic diversity (see the section on genetic drift in Chapter 19).

Endangered species have certain characteristics in common

Many threatened and endangered species share certain characteristics that may make them more vulnerable to extinction. Some of these characteristics include having an extremely small (localized) range, requiring a large territory, living on islands, having a

DECLINING AMPHIBIAN POPULATIONS

What is happening to our amphibian populations? Since the 1970s, many of the world's frog populations have dwindled or disappeared. According to the IUCN Global Amphibian Assessment, as many as 168 amphibian species may have disappeared since 1980 and are presumed extinct. About one-third of all amphibian species are in decline, and about 500 will probably become extinct in the next 50 years if they are not taken into captivity.

The declines are not limited to areas with obvious habitat destruction (such as drainage of wetlands where frogs live), degradation from pollutants, or overharvesting. Some remote, pristine locations also show dramatic declines in amphibians. No single factor seems responsible for these declines. Factors with scientific support include pollutants, infectious diseases, and *climate change.*

Agricultural chemicals are implicated in amphibian declines in California's Sierra Nevadas. Frog populations on the eastern slopes are relatively healthy, but about eight species are declining on the western slopes, where prevailing winds carry residues of 15 different pesticides from the Central Valley's agricultural region. Agricultural chemicals are also implicated in amphibian declines on the eastern shore of Maryland and in Ontario, Canada.

Infectious diseases are strongly implicated in some of the declines. In 1998, a chytrid (fungus) was first connected to amphibian declines. Climate change may be exacerbating chytrid-induced amphibian deaths. At certain altitudes and temperatures, the chytrid has infected and killed 85% of the amphibians.

Amphibian Deformities

The discovery of amphibians with deformities adds another layer of complexity to the amphibian crisis (see photograph). Frogs with extra legs, extra toes, eyes located on the shoulder or back, deformed jaws, missing legs, missing toes, or missing eyes usually die before they reproduce. Predators easily catch frogs with extra or missing legs. Deformed amphibians have been reported on four continents and in almost all states in the United States.

Biologists have investigated many possible causes of amphibian deformities during development, and no single factor explains the deformities found in all locations. Several pesticides affect normal development in frog embryos. Also, infecting tadpoles with a trematode (a parasitic flatworm) causes the adults that develop from the tadpoles to exhibit limb deformities. Multiple environmental stressors, such as habitat loss, disease, and pollution, may interact synergistically with one another to cause deformities. For example, northern leopard frogs stressed by the presence of the herbicide atrazine in water are more likely to be infected by trematodes.

Frans Lanting/Corbis

Frog deformity. Pollution and parasites are implicated in developmental abnormalities in amphibians, such as this Pacific tree frog.

---

low reproductive success, needing specialized breeding areas, and possessing specialized feeding habits.

Many endangered species have a small natural range, which makes them particularly prone to extinction if their habitat is altered. The Tiburon mariposa lily, for example, is found nowhere in nature except on a single hilltop near San Francisco. Development of that hilltop would almost certainly cause the extinction of this species.

Species that need extremely large territories may be threatened with extinction when all or part of their territory is modified by human activity. The California condor, for example, is a scavenger bird that lives off carrion and requires hundreds of square kilometers of undisturbed territory to find adequate food. The condor is slowly recovering from the brink of extinction. From 1987 to 1992, it existed only in zoos and was not found in nature. A program to reintroduce zoo-bred California condors into the wild began in 1992. Currently, there are about 327 condors, with more than half of them living in the wild in California and adjacent areas in Mexico and Arizona. The condor story is not an unqualified success because the condors have yet to become a self-sustaining population that replaces its numbers without captive breeding.

Many **endemic** island species are endangered. (*Endemic* means they are not found anywhere else in the world.) These species often have small populations that cannot be replaced by immigration if their numbers decline. Because they evolved in isolation from competitors, predators, and disease organisms, island species have few defenses when such organisms are introduced, usually by humans. It is not surprising that of the 171 bird species that have become extinct in the past few centuries, 155 of them lived on islands.

For a species to survive, its members must be present within their range in large enough numbers for males and females to mate. The minimum viable population that ensures reproductive success varies from one type of organism to another. For all species, when the population size falls below the MVP, the population goes into a decline and becomes susceptible to extinction.

Endangered species often have low reproductive rates. The female blue whale produces a single calf every other year, whereas no more than 6% of swamp pinks, an endangered species of small flowering plant, produce flowers in a given year (**FIG. 57-3**). Some endangered species breed only in specialized areas; for example, the green sea turtle lays its eggs on just a few beaches.

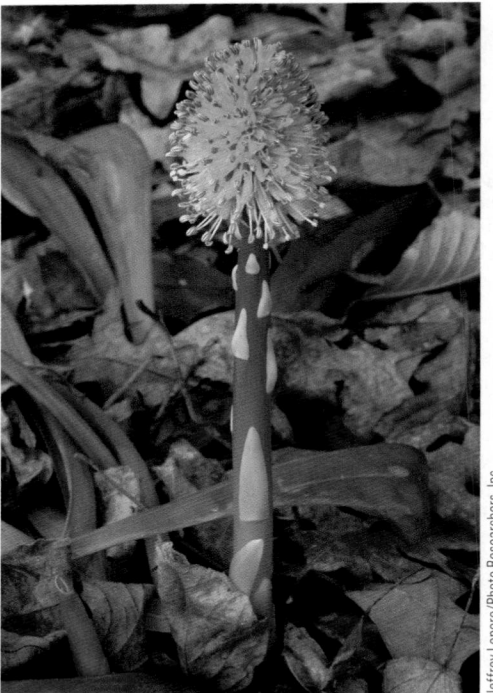

FIGURE 57-3 The swamp pink, an endangered species
The swamp pink (*Helonias bullata*) lives in boggy areas of the eastern United States. Photographed in Killens Pond State Park, Delaware.

Highly specialized feeding habits endanger a species. In nature, the giant panda eats only bamboo. Periodically, all the bamboo plants in a given area flower and die together; when this occurs, panda populations face starvation. Like many other endangered species, giant pandas are also endangered because their habitat has been fragmented, and there are few intact habitats where they can survive. China's 1600 wild giant pandas live in 24 isolated habitats that represent a small fraction of their historic range.

Human activities contribute to declining biological diversity

Species become endangered and extinct for a variety of reasons, including the destruction or modification of habitats (that is, land use change) and the production of pollution, including the greenhouse gases that cause climate change. Humans also upset the delicate balance of organisms in a given area by introducing invasive species. Overexploitation such as overfishing is also a factor. **FIGURE 57-4** shows the interactions between these direct causes of declining biological diversity and indirect human factors such as human population increase.

To save species, we must protect their habitats

Most species facing extinction today are endangered by destruction, fragmentation, or degradation of natural habitats. Building roads, parking lots, bridges, and buildings; clearing forests to grow

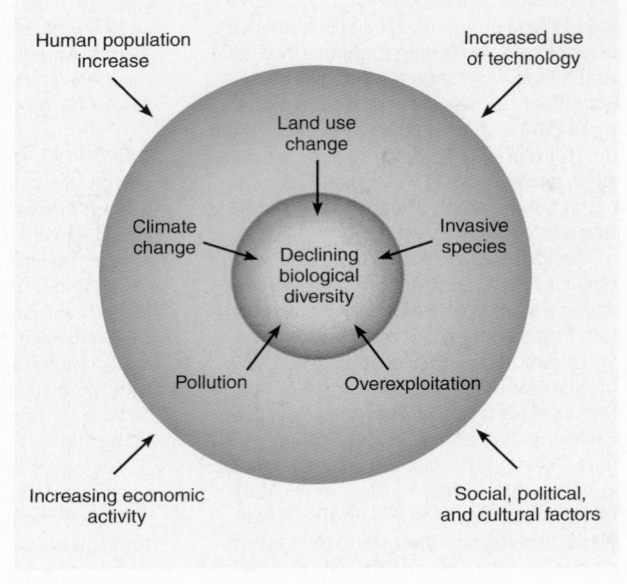

KEY POINT Because direct and indirect causes interact in complex ways, it is more effective to deal with declining biological diversity from a systems biology perspective.

FIGURE 57-4 Causes of declining biological diversity
Indirect causes (*blue*) interact with and amplify the effects of one another and of direct causes (*green*).

crops or graze domestic animals; and logging forests for timber all take their toll on natural habitats. Draining marshes converts aquatic habitats to terrestrial ones, whereas building dams and canals floods terrestrial habitats (**FIG. 57-5**). Because most organisms require a particular type of environment, habitat destruction reduces their biological range and ability to survive.

Humans often leave small, isolated patches of natural landscape that roads, fences, fields, and buildings completely surround. In ecological terms, *island* refers not only to any landmass surrounded by water but also to any isolated habitat surrounded by an expanse of unsuitable territory. Accordingly, a small patch of forest surrounded by agricultural and suburban lands is considered an island.

Habitat fragmentation, the breakup of large areas of habitat into small, isolated segments (that is, islands), is a major threat to the long-term survival of many populations and species (**FIG. 57-6**). Species from the surrounding "developed" landscape may intrude into the isolated habitat (the *edge effect,* discussed in Chapter 54), whereas rare and wide-ranging species that require a large patch of undisturbed habitat may disappear altogether. Habitat fragmentation encourages the spread of *invasive species,* disease organisms, and other "weedy" species and makes it difficult for organisms to migrate. Generally, habitat fragments support only a fraction of the species found in the original, unaltered environment. However,

FIGURE 57-5 *Animated* **Habitat destruction**
This tiny island lies in the Panama Canal. It was once a hilltop in a forest that was flooded when the canal was built.

much remains to be learned about precisely how habitat fragmentation affects specific populations, species, and ecosystems.

Human activities that produce acid precipitation and other forms of pollution indirectly modify habitats left undisturbed and in their natural state. Acid precipitation has contributed to the decline of large stands of forest trees and to the biological death of many freshwater lakes, for example, in the Adirondack Mountains and in Nova Scotia. Other types of pollutants, such as chemicals from industry and agriculture, organic pollutants from sewage, acid wastes seeping from mines, and thermal pollution from the heated wastewater of industrial plants, also adversely affect organisms.

To save native species, we must control intrusions of invasive species

Biotic pollution, the introduction of a foreign species into an area where it is not native, often upsets the balance among the organisms living in that area and interferes with the ecosystem's normal functioning. Unlike other forms of pollution, which may be cleaned up, biotic pollution is usually permanent. The foreign species may prey on native species or compete with them for food or habitat. If the foreign species causes economic or environmental harm, it is known as an **invasive species.** Generally, a foreign competitor or predator harms local organisms more than do native competitors or predators. Most invasive species lack natural agents (such as parasites, predators, and competitors) that would otherwise control them. Also, without a shared evolutionary history, most native species typically are less equipped to cope with invasive species. Although foreign species sometimes spread into new areas on their own, humans are usually responsible for such introductions, either knowingly or accidentally.

One of North America's greatest biological threats is the zebra mussel, a native of the Caspian Sea. It was probably introduced by a foreign ship that flushed ballast water into the Great Lakes

---

KEY EXPERIMENT

QUESTION: How does habitat fragmentation affect predation of juvenile bay scallops in the marine environment?

HYPOTHESIS: Predation of juvenile bay scallops is greater in patchy areas of sea grass than in undisturbed (continuous) seagrass meadows.

EXPERIMENT: Predation rates of juvenile bay scallops were measured over a 4-week period in three seagrass environments: continuous, patchy, and very patchy.

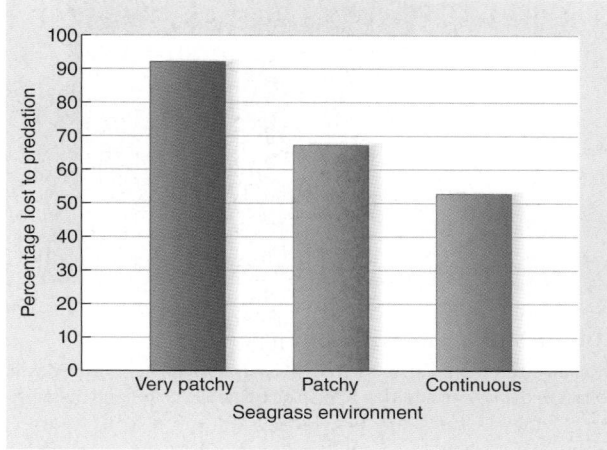

RESULTS AND CONCLUSION: The lowest rate of predation (52%) occurred in the continuous seagrass meadow, and the highest predation rate (92%) occurred in the very patchy environment. The patchy (fragmented) areas provided the predators with easier access to the young scallops. It was more difficult for the predators to intrude from surrounding areas into the continuous seagrass meadow.

Source: Irlandi, E. A., W. G. Ambrose, and B. A. Orando. "Landscape Ecology and the Marine Environment: How Spatial Configuration of Seagrass Habitat Influences Growth and Survival of the Bay Scallop." *Oikos,* Vol. 72, 1995.

FIGURE 57-6 **Effects of habitat fragmentation in a shallow marine environment**

---

in 1985 or 1986. Since then, the tiny freshwater mussel, which clusters in extraordinary densities, has massed on hulls of boats, piers, buoys, water intake systems, and, most damaging of all, on native clam and mussel shells. The zebra mussel's strong appetite for algae, phytoplankton, and zooplankton is also cutting into the food supply of native fishes, mussels, and clams, threatening their survival. The zebra mussel is currently found throughout most of the Mississippi River and its tributary rivers. According to the U.S. Coast Guard, the United States spends about $5 billion each year to control the spread of the zebra mussel and to repair damage such as clogged pipes (**FIG. 57-7**).

Islands are particularly susceptible to the introduction of invasive species. In Hawaii, the introduction of sheep has imperiled both the mamane tree (because the sheep eat it) and a species of

FIGURE 57-7 Zebra mussels clog a pipe
Thumbnail-sized zebra mussels (*Dreissena polymorpha*) have caused billions of dollars in damage in addition to displacing native clams and mussels.

FIGURE 57-8 Illegal commercial harvesting
These hyacinth macaws (*Anodorhynchus hyacinthus*) were seized in French Guiana in South America as part of the illegal animal trade there. The hyacinth macaw population is much reduced in South America.

honeycreeper, an endemic bird that relies on the tree for food. Hawaii's plants evolved in the absence of herbivorous mammals and therefore have no defenses against introduced sheep, pigs, goats, and deer.

Other human activities affect biodiversity directly or indirectly

Sometimes species become endangered or extinct as a result of deliberate efforts to eradicate or control their numbers, often because they prey on game animals or livestock. In the past, ranchers, hunters, and government agents decimated populations of large predators such as the wolf, mountain lion, and grizzly bear. Some animals are killed because their lifestyles cause problems for humans. The Carolina parakeet, a beautiful green, red, and yellow bird endemic to the southeastern United States, was extinct by 1920, exterminated by farmers because it ate fruit from their trees.

Unregulated hunting, or overhunting, has caused the extinction of certain species in the past but is now strictly controlled in most countries. The passenger pigeon was one of the most common birds in North America in the early 1800s, but a century of overhunting resulted in its extinction in the early 1900s.

Illegal commercial hunting, or *poaching*, endangers larger animals such as the tiger, cheetah, and snow leopard, whose beautiful furs are quite valuable. Rhinoceroses are slaughtered for their horns (used for ceremonial dagger handles in the Middle East and for purported medicinal purposes in Asian medicine). Bears are killed for their gallbladders (which Asian doctors use to treat ailments ranging from indigestion to hemorrhoids). Bush meat—meat from rare primates, elephants, anteaters, and such—is sold to urban restaurants. Although laws protect these animals, demand

for their products on the black market has promoted illegal hunting, particularly in impoverished countries where a sale of contraband products can support a family for months.

Commercial harvest is the collection of live organisms from nature. Most commercially harvested organisms end up in zoos, aquaria, biomedical research labs, circuses, and pet stores. For example, several million birds are commercially harvested each year for the pet trade, but many die in transit, and many more die from improper treatment in their owners' homes. At least 40 parrot species are now threatened or endangered, in part because of commercial harvest. Although it is illegal to capture endangered animals from the wild, a thriving black market exists, mainly because collectors in the United States, Europe, and Japan pay extremely large sums for rare tropical birds (**FIG. 57-8**).

Commercial harvest also threatens plants. Many unique or rare plants have been so extensively collected from the wild that they are now classified as endangered. These include certain carnivorous plants, wildflower bulbs, cacti, and orchids. In contrast, carefully monitored and regulated commercial use of animal and plant resources creates an economic incentive to ensure that these resources do not disappear.

Review

- What are the three levels of biological diversity?
- Which organism is more likely to become extinct, an endangered species or a threatened species? Explain your answer.
- How does habitat fragmentation contribute to declining biological diversity?
- How do invasive species contribute to the biodiversity crisis?

57.2 CONSERVATION BIOLOGY

■ LEARNING OBJECTIVES

4 Define *conservation biology* and compare in situ and ex situ conservation measures.

5 Describe the benefits and shortcomings of the U.S. Endangered Species Act and the Convention on International Trade in Endangered Species of Wild Flora and Fauna.

Conservation biology is the scientific study of how humans impact organisms and of the development of ways to protect biological diversity. Conservation biologists develop models, design experiments, and perform fieldwork to address a wide range of questions. For example, what are the processes that influence a decline in biological diversity? How do we protect and restore populations of endangered species? If we are to preserve entire ecosystems and landscapes, which ones are the most important to save?

Conservation biologists have determined that a single large area of habitat capable of supporting several populations is more effective at safeguarding an endangered species than several habitat fragments, each capable of supporting a single population. Also, a large area of habitat typically supports greater species richness than several habitat fragments.

Conservation is more successful when habitat areas for a given species are in close proximity rather than far apart. If an area of habitat is isolated from other areas, individuals may not effectively disperse from one habitat to another. Because the presence of humans adversely affects many species, habitat areas that lack roads or are inaccessible to humans are better than human-accessible areas.

According to conservation biologists, it is more effective and, ultimately, more economical to preserve intact ecosystems in which many species live than to try to preserve individual species. Conservation biologists generally consider it a higher priority to preserve areas with greater biological diversity.

Conservation biology includes two problem-solving approaches that save organisms from extinction: in situ and ex situ conservation. **In situ conservation,** which includes the establishment of parks and reserves, concentrates on preserving biological diversity in nature. A high priority of in situ conservation is identifying and protecting sites that harbor a great deal of diversity. With increasing demands on land, however, in situ conservation cannot preserve all types of biological diversity. Sometimes only ex situ conservation can save a species.

Ex situ conservation conserves individual species in human-controlled settings. Breeding captive species in zoos and storing seeds of genetically diverse plant crops are examples of ex situ conservation.

In situ conservation is the best way to preserve biological diversity

Protecting animal and plant habitats—that is, conserving and managing ecosystems as a whole—is the single best way to protect biological diversity. Many nations have set aside areas for wildlife habitats. Such natural ecosystems offer the best strategy for the long-term protection and preservation of biological diversity. Currently, more than 100,000 national parks, marine sanctuaries, wildlife refuges, forests, and other areas are protected throughout the world. These encompass a total area almost as large as Canada. However, many protected areas have multiple uses that sometimes conflict with the goal of preserving species. National parks provide for recreational needs, for example, whereas national forests are used for logging, grazing, and mineral extraction. The mineral rights to many wildlife refuges are privately owned, and oil, gas, and other mineral development has occurred on some wildlife refuges.

Protected areas are not always effective in preserving biological diversity, particularly in developing countries where biological diversity is greatest, because there is little money or expertise to manage them. Another shortcoming of the world's protected areas is that many are in lightly populated mountain areas, tundra, and the driest deserts, places that often have spectacular scenery but relatively few kinds of species. In reality, such remote areas are often designated reserves because they are unsuitable for commercial development.

In contrast, ecosystems in which biological diversity is greatest often receive little attention. Protected areas are urgently needed in tropical rain forests, the tropical grasslands and savannas of Brazil and Australia, and dry forests that are widely scattered around the world. Desert organisms are underprotected in northern Africa and Argentina, and the species of many islands and temperate river basins also need protection.

Many of these unprotected areas are part of what some biologists have identified as the world's 25 **biodiversity hotspots** (**FIG. 57-9**). The hotspots collectively make up 1.4% of Earth's land but contain as many as 44% of all vascular plant species, 29% of the world's endemic bird species, 27% of endemic mammal species, 38% of endemic reptile species, and 53% of endemic amphibian species. Nearly 20% of the world's human population lives in the hotspots. Fifteen of the 25 hotspots are tropical, and 9 are mostly or solely islands. The 25 hotspots are somewhat arbitrary, as additional hotspots are recognized when different criteria are used.

Not all conservation biologists support focusing limited conservation resources on protecting biodiversity hotspots because doing so ignores the many **ecosystem services** provided by entire ecosystems that are rapidly vanishing due to habitat destruction. For example, the vast boreal forests in Canada and Russia are critically important to the proper functioning of the global carbon and nitrogen cycles. These forests are being logged at unprecedented rates. Yet conservation organizations do not recognize them as hotspots. Landscape ecology takes a larger view of ecosystem conservation.

Landscape ecology considers ecosystem types on a regional scale

The subdiscipline of ecology that studies the connections in a heterogeneous **landscape** consisting of multiple interacting ecosystems is known as **landscape ecology.** Increasingly, biologists are focusing efforts on preserving biodiversity in landscapes. But what is the minimum ecosystem/landscape size needed to preserve species numbers and distributions?

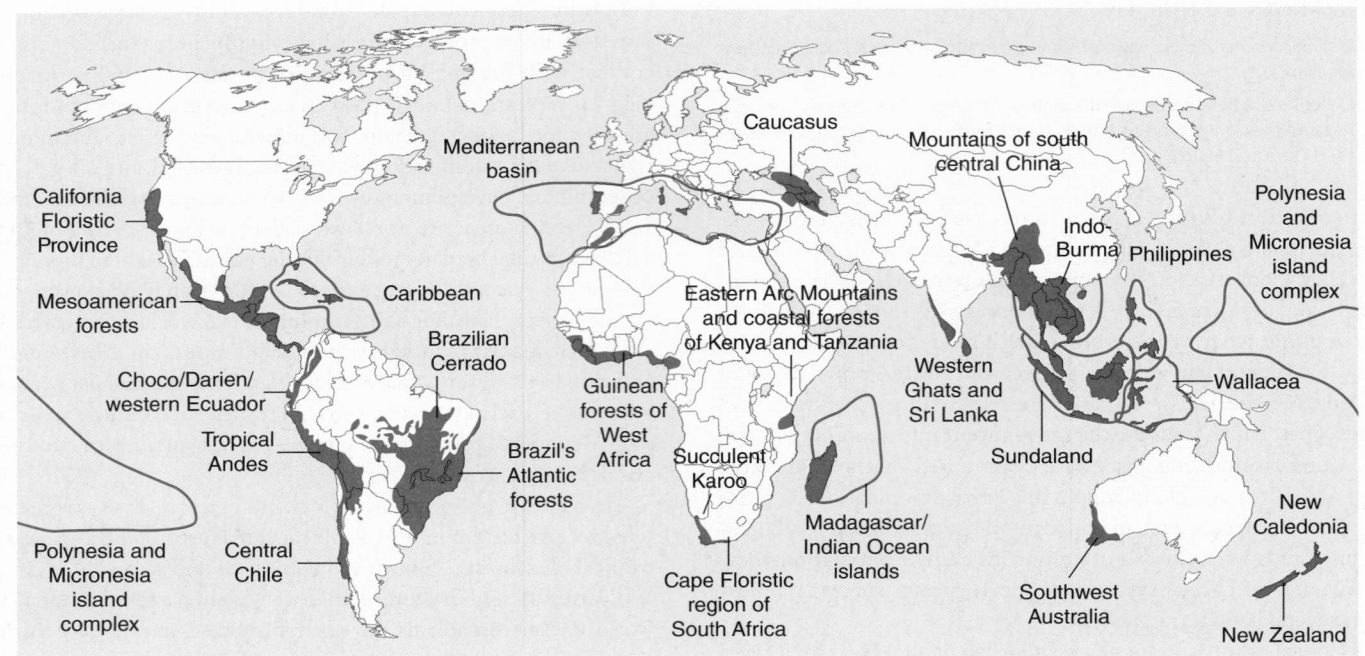

FIGURE 57-9 *Animated* **Biodiversity hotspots**

Rich in endemic species, these hotspots are under pressure from the number of humans living in them.
(Data from Conservation International.)

FIGURE 57-10 **Biological Dynamics of Forest Fragment Project**

Shown are 1-hectare and 10-hectare plots of a long-term (about three decades) study under way in Brazil on the effects of fragmentation on Amazonian rain forest. Plots with an area of 100 hectares are also under study,
along with identically sized sections of intact forest, which are controls.

One long-term study addressing this question in tropical rain
forests is the Biological Dynamics of Forest Fragment Project (formerly the Minimum Critical Size of Ecosystems Project), which
is studying a series of Amazonian rainforest fragments varying in
size from 1 to 100 hectares (**FIG. 57-10**). Preliminary data from this
study, which began in 1979, indicate that smaller forest fragments
do not maintain their ecological integrity. For example, large
trees near forest edges often die or are damaged from exposure to
wind, desiccation (from lateral exposure of the forest fragment to
sunlight), and invasion by parasitic woody vines. In addition, biologists have documented that various species adapted to forest
interiors do not prosper in the smaller fragments and eventually
die out, whereas species adapted to forest edges invade the smaller
fragments and thrive.

Unfortunately, human colonization and other activities are
beginning to threaten the Biological Dynamics of Forest Fragment
Project itself. Agriculture is expanding in the area, nearby forests
are being burned, and logging and hunting are increasing. Should
human expansion spread into the research site, the potential benefits that might be derived from understanding the effects of forest
fragmentation will be lost.

Habitat corridors. To remedy widespread habitat fragmentation
and its associated loss of biodiversity, conservation biologists have
proposed linking isolated fragments with **habitat corridors,** strips
of habitat connecting isolated habitat patches. Habitat corridors

allow wildlife to move about so they can feed, mate, and recolonize habitats after local extinctions take place. Research has also shown that habitat fragments linked by habitat corridors retain more native plant species than do isolated fragments.

Habitat corridors range from a local scale (such as an overpass that allows wildlife to cross a road safely) to a landscape scale that connects separate reserves (**FIG. 57-11**). The minimum corridor width for landscape-scale corridors varies depending on the size of home ranges for various species. For example, to link two reserves and protect wolves in Minnesota, the corridor must have a minimum width of 12 km (7.2 miles), whereas the minimum corridor width for bobcats in South Carolina must be 2.5 km (1.5 miles).

Restoring damaged or destroyed habitats is the goal of restoration ecology

Although preserving habitats is an important part of conservation biology, the realities of our world, including the fact that the land-hungry human population continues to increase, dictate a variety of other conservation measures. Sometimes scientists reclaim disturbed lands and convert them into areas with high biological diversity. **Restoration ecology,** in which the principles of ecology are used to return a degraded environment to one that is more functional and sustainable, is an important part of in situ conservation.

Since 1934, the University of Wisconsin–Madison Arboretum has carried out one of the most famous examples of ecological restoration (**FIG. 57-12**). Several distinct natural communities have been carefully developed on damaged agricultural land. These communities include a tallgrass prairie, a xeric (dry) prairie, and several types of pine and maple forests native to Wisconsin.

Restoration of disturbed lands not only creates biological habitats but also has additional benefits, such as the regeneration of soil that agriculture or mining damaged. The disadvantages of restoration ecology include the time and expense required to restore an area. Nonetheless, restoration ecology is an important aspect of conservation biology, as it is thought that restoration will reduce extinctions.

Ex situ conservation attempts to save species on the brink of extinction

Zoos, aquaria, and botanical gardens often attempt to save certain endangered species from extinction. Eggs are collected from nature, or the remaining few animals are captured and bred in zoos and other research facilities.

Special techniques, such as artificial insemination and host mothering, increase the number of offspring. In **artificial insemination,** sperm is collected from a suitable male of a rare species and used to impregnate a female, perhaps located in another zoo in a different city or even in another country. In **host mothering,**

FIGURE 57-11 Proposed habitat corridors

Five wilderness areas are already established in northern California and southern Oregon. These areas would more effectively preserve biodiversity if they were joined by habitat corridors to form a single landscape-scale conservation unit. To date, the U.S. Forest Service has not adopted this habitat corridor proposal. (*Arrows show the direction of other nearby wilderness areas.*) (From Pace, F. "The Klamath Corridors: Preserving Biodiversity in the Klamath National Forest," in *Landscape Linkages and Biodiversity*, edited by W. E. Hudson, pp. 105–116, Island Press, Washington, D.C., 1991. Reprinted by permission of Island Press.)

a female of a rare species is treated with fertility drugs, which cause her to produce multiple eggs. Some of these eggs are collected, fertilized with sperm, and surgically implanted into females of a related but less rare species, which later give birth to offspring of the rare species (see *Inquiring About: Novel Origins,* in Chapter 50). Plans are under way to clone endangered species, such as the giant panda, that do not reproduce well in captivity. Another technique involves hormone patches, which are being developed to stimulate reproduction in endangered birds; the patch is attached under the female bird's wing.

A few spectacular successes have occurred in captive-breeding programs, in which large enough numbers of a species have been produced to re-establish small populations in the wild. Conservation efforts, for example, let the bald eagle make a remarkable comeback in the lower 48 states, and in 2007, the U.S. Fish and

(a) The restoration of the prairie by the University of Wisconsin–Madison Arboretum was at an early stage in 1935. The men are digging holes to plant prairie grass sod.

(b) The prairie as it looks today. This picture was taken at about the same location as the 1935 photograph.

FIGURE 57-12 Restoring damaged lands

Wildlife Service (FWS) removed the bald eagle from the endangered list.

Attempting to save a species on the brink of extinction is usually expensive; therefore, only a small proportion of endangered species can be saved. Moreover, zoos, aquaria, and botanical gardens do not have the space to try to save all endangered species. This means that conservation biologists must set priorities on which species to attempt to save. Zoos have traditionally focused on large, charismatic animals, such as pandas, bald eagles, and whooping cranes, because the public is more interested in them. Such conservation efforts ignore millions of ecologically important species. However, zoos, aquaria, and botanical gardens serve a useful purpose because they educate the public about the value of biodiversity. Clearly, controlling unchecked human development so that species do not become endangered in the first place is a more effective way to protect and maintain natural habitat.

The Endangered Species Act provides some legal protection for species and habitats

In 1973, the *Endangered Species Act (ESA)* was passed in the United States, authorizing the FWS to protect endangered and threatened species in the United States and abroad. Many other countries now have similar legislation. The FWS conducts a detailed study of a species to determine if it should be listed as endangered or threatened (**TABLE 57-1**). The ESA provides legal protection to listed species so that their danger of extinction is reduced. For example, the act makes it illegal to sell or buy any product made from an endangered or threatened species.

The ESA requires officials of the FWS to select critical habitats and design a recovery plan for each species listed. The recovery plan includes an estimate of the current population size, an analysis of what factors contributed to its endangerment, and a list of activities that may help the species recover.

The Endangered Species Act is considered one of the strongest pieces of environmental legislation in the United States, in part because species are designated as endangered or threatened entirely on biological grounds. Currently, economic considerations cannot influence the designation of endangered or threatened species. Biologists generally agree that as a result of passage of the ESA in 1973, fewer species became extinct than would have had the law never been passed.

The ESA is also one of the most controversial pieces of environmental legislation. For example, the ESA does not provide compensation for private property owners who suffer financial losses because they cannot develop their land if a threatened or endangered species lives there. The ESA has also interfered with some federally funded development projects.

It currently takes, on average, about 17 years for a candidate species with declining numbers to be listed as threatened or endangered. This backlog is due to both the high cost of evaluating each species and the limited funds allocated to the FWS for these studies. Meanwhile, 27 species on the ESA's "candidate list" have become extinct since 1973, without ever being classified as threatened or endangered so that they could have some measure of protection.

The ESA is geared more to saving a few popular or unique endangered species than to saving the much larger number of less popular species that perform valuable ecosystem services. About one-third of the annual funding for the ESA is used to help just ten species. Yet it is the less glamorous organisms, such as plants, fungi, bacteria, and insects, that play central roles in ecosystems and contribute most to their functioning. Bacteria and fungi, for example, provide the critically important ecosystem service of breaking down dead organic materials into simple substances (CO_2, water, and minerals) that are subsequently recycled to plants and other autotrophs.

Conservationist biologists would like to see the ESA strengthened in such a way as to manage whole ecosystems and maintain complete biological diversity rather than attempt to save endangered species as isolated entities. This approach would offer collective protection to many declining species rather than to single species.

<table>
<tr><td>**TABLE 57-1**</td><td colspan="3">Organisms Listed as Endangered or Threatened in the United States, 2008</td></tr>
<tr><td>Type of Organism</td><td>Number of Endangered Species</td><td>Number of Threatened Species</td></tr>
<tr><td>Mammals</td><td>69</td><td>12</td></tr>
<tr><td>Birds</td><td>75</td><td>14</td></tr>
<tr><td>Reptiles</td><td>13</td><td>24</td></tr>
<tr><td>Amphibians</td><td>13</td><td>10</td></tr>
<tr><td>Fishes</td><td>74</td><td>65</td></tr>
<tr><td>Snails</td><td>64</td><td>11</td></tr>
<tr><td>Clams</td><td>62</td><td>8</td></tr>
<tr><td>Crustaceans</td><td>19</td><td>3</td></tr>
<tr><td>Insects</td><td>47</td><td>10</td></tr>
<tr><td>Spiders</td><td>12</td><td>0</td></tr>
<tr><td>Flowering plants</td><td>570</td><td>143</td></tr>
<tr><td>Conifers and cycads</td><td>2</td><td>1</td></tr>
<tr><td>Ferns and other plants</td><td>24</td><td>2</td></tr>
</table>

Source: U.S. Fish and Wildlife Service.

International agreements provide some protection of species and habitats

The *Convention on International Trade in Endangered Species of Wild Flora and Fauna (CITES)* is an international agreement that went into effect in 1975. Originally drawn up to protect endangered animals and plants considered valuable in the highly lucrative international wildlife trade, CITES bans hunting, capturing, and selling of endangered or threatened species and regulates trade of organisms listed as potentially threatened. Unfortunately, enforcement of this treaty varies from country to country, and even where enforcement exists, the penalties are not very severe. As a result, illegal trade in rare, commercially valuable species continues.

The goals of CITES often stir up controversy over such issues as who actually owns the world's wildlife and whether global conservation concerns take precedence over competing local interests. These conflicts often highlight socioeconomic differences between wealthy consumers of products protected by CITES and poor people who trade the endangered organisms.

Another international treaty, the *Convention on Biological Diversity,* requires that each signatory nation inventory its own biodiversity and develop a **national conservation strategy,** a detailed plan for managing and preserving the biological diversity of that specific country.

Review

- What is conservation biology?
- Are landscape biology and restoration ecology examples of in situ or ex situ conservation?
- Which type of conservation measure, in situ or ex situ, helps the greatest number of species? Why?
- Why is the U.S. Endangered Species Act so controversial?

57.3 DEFORESTATION

LEARNING OBJECTIVES

6 Discuss the ecosystem services of forests and describe the consequences of deforestation.

7 State at least three reasons why forests (tropical rain forests and boreal forests) are disappearing today.

The most serious problem facing the world's forests and their biological diversity is **deforestation,** which is the temporary or permanent clearance of large expanses of forest for agriculture or other uses (**FIG. 57-13**). According to the UN Food and Agriculture Organization (FAO), which provides world statistics on forest cover, forests are currently shrinking about 9 million hectares (22.2 million acres) each year.

When forests are destroyed, they no longer contribute valuable ecosystem services to the environment or to people who depend on them. Deforestation increases soil erosion and thus decreases soil fertility. Soil erosion causes increased sedimentation of waterways, which harms downstream aquatic ecosystems by reducing light penetration, covering aquatic organisms, and filling in waterways. Uncontrolled soil erosion, particularly on steep deforested slopes, causes mudflows that endanger human lives and property and reduces production of hydroelectric power as silt builds up behind dams. In drier areas, deforestation can lead to the formation of deserts.

Deforestation contributes to the loss of biological diversity. Many species have limited ranges within a forest, particularly in the tropics, so these species are especially vulnerable to habitat destruction or modification. Migratory species, such as birds and butterflies, also suffer from tropical deforestation.

By trapping and absorbing precipitation, forests on hillsides and mountains help protect nearby lowlands from floods. When a forest is cut down, the watershed cannot absorb and hold water

FIGURE 57-13 *Animated* **Deforestation**
Aerial view of clear-cut areas in the Gifford Pinchot National Forest in southwestern Washington State. The lines are roads built at taxpayer expense to haul away logs.

as well, and the total amount of surface runoff flowing into rivers and streams increases. This not only causes soil erosion but puts lowland areas at extreme risk of flooding.

Deforestation may affect regional and global climate changes. Transpiring trees release substantial amounts of moisture into the air. This moisture falls back to the surface in the hydrologic cycle. When a large forest is removed, rainfall may decline, and droughts may become common in that region. Studies suggest that the local climate has become drier in parts of Brazil where tracts of the rain forest have been burned. Temperatures may also rise slightly in a deforested area because there is less evaporative cooling from the trees.

Deforestation may increase global temperature by releasing carbon stored in the trees into the atmosphere as carbon dioxide, which enables the air to retain heat. The carbon in forests is released immediately if the trees are burned or more slowly when unburned parts decay. If trees are harvested and logs are removed, roughly one-half of the forest carbon remains as dead materials (branches, twigs, roots, and leaves) that decompose, releasing carbon dioxide. When an old-growth forest is harvested, it may take 200 years for the replacement forest to accumulate the amount of carbon that was stored in the original forest.

Why are tropical rain forests disappearing?

Most of the remaining undisturbed tropical rain forests, in the Amazon and Congo River basins of South America and Africa, are being cleared and burned at a rate unprecedented in human history. Tropical rain forests are also being destroyed at an extremely rapid rate in southern Asia, Indonesia, Central America, and the Philippines.

Several studies show a strong statistical correlation between population growth and deforestation. More people need more food, so they clear forests for agricultural expansion. However, tropical deforestation cannot be attributed simply to population pressures. The main causes of deforestation vary from place to place, and a variety of economic, social, and governmental factors interact to cause deforestation. Government policies sometimes provide incentives that favor the removal of forests. For example, in the late 1950s the Brazilian government constructed the Belem–Brasilia Highway, which cut through the Amazon Basin and opened the Amazonian frontier for settlement (**FIG. 57-14**). Sometimes economic conditions encourage deforestation. The

farmer who converts more forest to pasture can maintain a larger herd of cattle, which is a good hedge against inflation.

If we keep in mind that tropical deforestation is a complex problem, three agents are probably the most immediate causes of deforestation in tropical rain forests: subsistence agriculture, commercial logging, and cattle ranching. Other reasons for the destruction of tropical forests include the development of hydroelectric power, which inundates large areas of forest; mining, particularly when ore smelters burn charcoal produced from rainforest trees; and plantation-style agriculture of crops such as citrus fruits and bananas.

Subsistence agriculture, in which a family produces enough food to feed itself, accounts for perhaps 60% of tropical deforestation. In many developing countries where tropical rain forests are located, the majority of people do not own the land on which they live and work. Most subsistence farmers have no place to go except into the forest, which they clear to grow food. Land reform in Brazil, Madagascar, Mexico, the Philippines, Thailand, and many other countries would make the land owned by a few available to everyone, thereby easing the pressure of subsistence farmers on tropical

FIGURE 57-14 Human settlements in Brazil's tropical rain forest
This satellite photograph shows numerous smaller roads extending perpendicularly from the main roads. As people settle along the roads, they clear out more and more forest (*dark green*) for their croplands and pastures (*tans and pinks*).

forests. This scenario is unlikely because wealthy landowners have more economic and political clout than impoverished peasants.

Subsistence farmers often follow loggers' access roads until they find a suitable spot. They first cut down the trees and allow them to dry; then they burn the area and plant crops immediately after burning. This is known as **slash-and-burn agriculture.** Yields from the first crop are often quite high because the nutrients that were in the trees are now available in the soil. However, soil productivity declines rapidly, and subsequent crops are poor. In a few years the farmer must move to a new part of the forest and repeat the process. Cattle ranchers often claim the abandoned land for grazing because land that is not fertile enough to support crops can still support livestock.

Slash-and-burn agriculture done on a small scale, with periods of 20 to 100 years between cycles, is sustainable. The forest regrows rapidly after a few years of farming. But when millions of people try to obtain a living in this way, the land is not allowed to lie uncultivated long enough to recover. Globally, at least 200 million subsistence farmers obtain a living from slash-and-burn agriculture, and the number is growing. To compound the problem, there is only half as much forest available today as there was 50 years ago.

About 20% of tropical deforestation is the result of commercial logging, and vast tracts of tropical rain forests, particularly in Southeast Asia, are harvested for export abroad. Most tropical countries allow commercial logging to proceed much faster than is sustainable because it supplies them with much-needed revenues. In the final analysis, uncontrolled tropical deforestation does not contribute to economic development; rather, it reduces or destroys the value of an important natural resource.

Approximately 12% of tropical rainforest destruction is carried out to provide open rangeland for cattle. Cattle ranching is particularly important in Central America. Much of the beef raised on these ranches, which foreign companies often own, is exported to restaurant chains in North America and Europe. After the forests are cleared, cattle graze on the land for as long as 20 years, after which time the soil fertility is depleted. When this occurs, shrubby plants, or *scrub savanna,* take over the range.

Why are boreal forests disappearing?

Tropical rain forests are not the only forests at risk from deforestation. Extensive logging of certain boreal forests began in the late 1980s and continues to the present. Coniferous evergreen trees such as spruce, fir, cedar, and hemlock dominate these northern forests of Alaska, Canada, Scandinavia, and northern Russia.

Boreal forests, harvested primarily by clear-cut logging, are currently the primary source of the world's industrial wood and wood fiber. About 1 million hectares (2.5 million acres) of Canadian forests are logged annually, and most of Canada's forests are under logging tenures. (*Tenures* are agreements between provinces and companies that give companies the right to cut timber.) Canada is the world's biggest timber exporter, and most of its forest products are exported to the United States. On the basis of current harvest quotas, logging in Canada is unsustainable. Extensive tracts of boreal forests in Russia are also harvested, although exact estimates are unavailable. Alaska's boreal forests are also at risk be-

cause the U.S. government may increase logging on public lands there in the future.

Review

- What are three ecosystem services that forests provide?
- What are two reasons for deforestation in tropical rain forests? What is the main reason for deforestation of boreal forests?

57.4 CLIMATE CHANGE

■ LEARNING OBJECTIVES

8   Name at least three greenhouse gases and explain how greenhouse gases contribute to climate change.
9   Describe how climate change may affect sea level, precipitation patterns, organisms (including humans), and food production.

Earth's average temperature is based on daily measurements from several thousand land-based meteorological stations around the world, as well as data from weather balloons, orbiting satellites, transoceanic ships, and hundreds of sea-surface buoys with temperature sensors. *Data indicate that the 14 warmest years since the mid-1800s have occurred since 1990.* The 1990s was the warmest decade of the 20th century, and the early 2000s continued the warming trend (**FIG. 57-15**). Because the climate is changing so rapidly, it imposes stresses on many living organisms and ultimately could lower biological diversity.

Scientists around the world have studied **climate change** for several decades. As the evidence has accumulated, those most qualified to address the issue have reached a strong consensus that the 21st century will experience significant climate change and

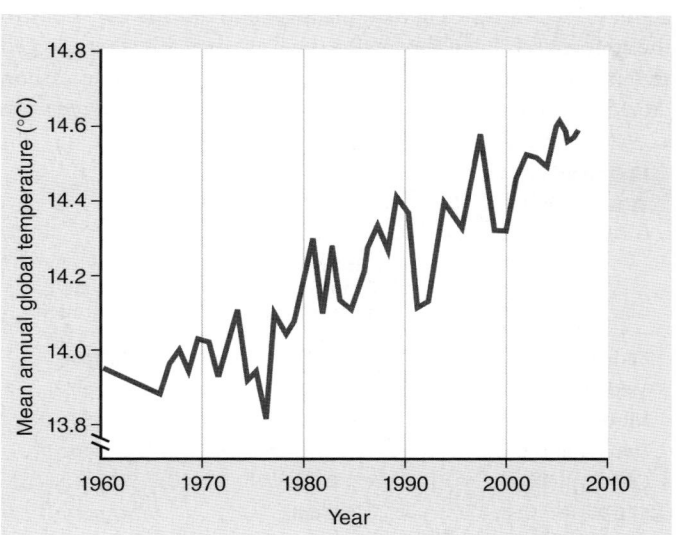

FIGURE 57-15 Mean annual global temperature, 1960 to 2007
Data are presented as surface temperatures (°C) for 1960, 1965, and every year thereafter. The measurements, which naturally fluctuate, clearly show the warming trend of the last several decades. (Surface Air Temperature Analysis, Goddard Institute for Space Studies, NASA.)

that human activities will be responsible for much of this change.

In response to the growing scientific agreement about both climate change and its human cause, governments around the world organized the UN Intergovernmental Panel on Climate Change (IPCC) in 1988. The IPCC reviews all published literature about global climate change, especially articles published over the past five years, and summarizes the current state of knowledge and uncertainty. The observed and projected impacts of climate change in each IPCC report have gotten progressively worse. The 2007 IPCC Fourth Assessment Report concluded that human-produced air pollutants have caused most of the climate change observed in the past 50 years. The IPCC report projects up to a 0.2°C (0.4°F) increase in global average temperature in each of the next two decades.

By the year 2100, depending on whether and how much we can control greenhouse gas emissions, temperatures may rise anywhere from 1.8 to 4.0°C (3.2 to 7.2°F). Thus, Earth may become warmer during the 21st century than it has been for several million years.

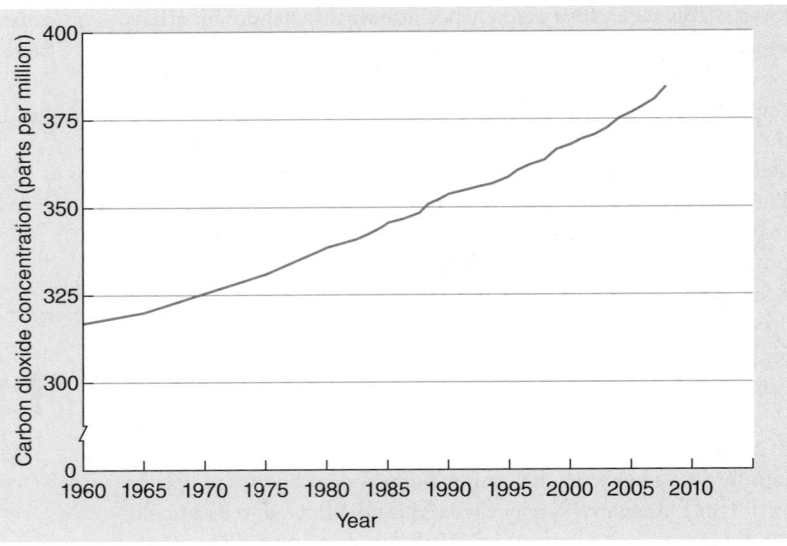

FIGURE 57-16 *Animated* Carbon dioxide in the atmosphere, 1960 to 2008

Note the steady increase in the concentration of atmospheric carbon dioxide. Measurements are taken at the Mauna Loa Observatory, Hawaii, far from urban areas where factories, power plants, and motor vehicles emit carbon dioxide. (Scripps Institution of Oceanography, University of California, La Jolla, California.)

Greenhouse gases cause climate change

Carbon dioxide (CO_2) and certain other trace gases, including methane (CH_4), surface ozone (O_3), nitrous oxide (N_2O), and chlorofluorocarbons (CFCs), are accumulating in the atmosphere as a result of human activities (**TABLE 57-2**). The concentration of atmospheric CO_2 has increased from about 288 parts per million (ppm) approximately 250 years ago (before the Industrial Revolution began) to 384 ppm in 2008 (**FIG. 57-16**). Burning carbon-containing fossil fuels—coal, oil, and natural gas—accounts for about three-fourths of human-made carbon dioxide emissions to the atmosphere. Land conversion, such as when forests are logged or burned, also releases carbon dioxide. (Burning releases carbon dioxide into the atmosphere; also, because trees normally remove

carbon dioxide from the atmosphere during photosynthesis, tree removal prevents this process.) The levels of the other trace gases associated with climate change are also rising.

Climate change occurs because these gases absorb infrared radiation, that is, heat, in the atmosphere. This absorption slows the natural heat flow into space, warming the lower atmosphere. Some of the heat from the lower atmosphere is transferred to the ocean and raises its temperature as well. This retention of heat in the atmosphere is a natural phenomenon that has made Earth habitable for its millions of species. However, as human activities increase the atmospheric concentration of these gases, the atmosphere and ocean continue to warm, and the overall global temperature rises.

Because carbon dioxide and other gases trap the sun's radiation somewhat like glass does in a greenhouse, the natural trapping of heat in the atmosphere is called the **greenhouse effect**, and the gases that absorb infrared radiation are known as **greenhouse gases.** This natural heating of the atmosphere prevents Earth from becoming a frozen planet. However, the additional warming produced when increased levels of gases produced by human activities absorb additional infrared radiation, called the **enhanced greenhouse effect,** has potentially catastrophic implications (**FIG. 57-17**).

Although current rates of fossil fuel combustion and deforestation are high, causing the carbon dioxide level in the atmosphere to increase markedly, scientists think the warming trend is slower than the increasing level of carbon dioxide might indicate. The reason is that water requires more heat to raise its temperature than gases in the atmosphere do. (Recall the high specific heat of water discussed in Chapter 2.) As a result, the ocean takes longer to warm than the atmosphere. Most climate scientists think that warming will be more pronounced in the second half of the 21st century than in the first half.

TABLE 57-2	Changes in Selected Atmospheric Greenhouse Gases, Preindustrial Times to Present	
Gas	Estimated Preindustrial Concentration	Present Concentration
Carbon dioxide	288 ppm*	384 ppm
Methane	848 ppb†	1851 ppb
Nitrous oxide	285 ppb	321 ppb
Tropospheric ozone	25 ppb	34 ppb
CFC-12	0 ppt‡	541 ppt
CFC-11	0 ppt	247 ppt

Note: The preindustrial value is for the 17th and 18th centuries.

Source: Carbon Dioxide Information Analysis Center, Environmental Sciences Division, Oak Ridge National Laboratory.

*ppm = parts per million.

†ppb = parts per billion.

‡ppt = parts per trillion.

Greenhouse gases accumulating in the atmosphere are causing an enhanced greenhouse effect.

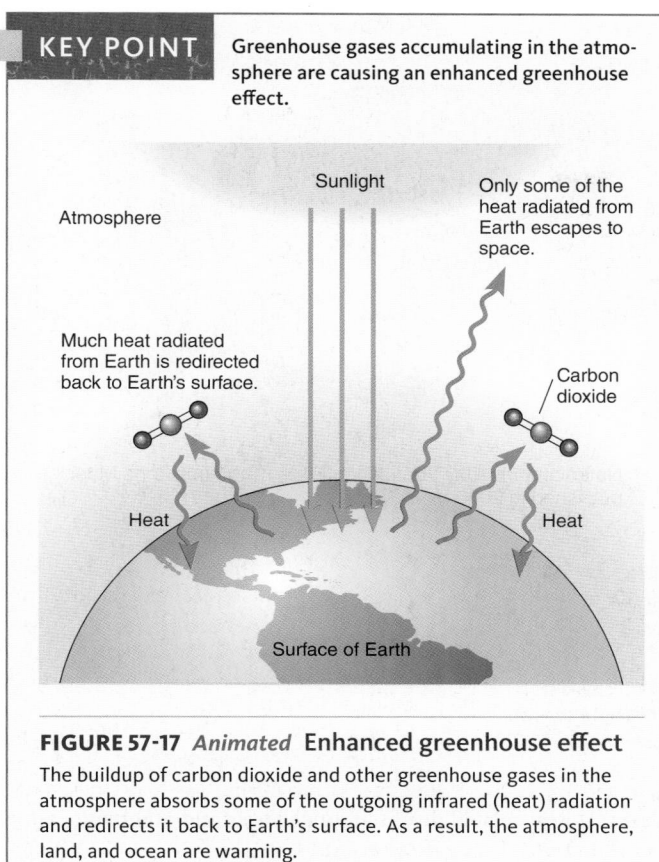

Atmosphere

Sunlight

Only some of the heat radiated from Earth escapes to space.

Much heat radiated from Earth is redirected back to Earth's surface.

Carbon dioxide

Heat

Heat

Surface of Earth

FIGURE 57-17 *Animated* **Enhanced greenhouse effect**
The buildup of carbon dioxide and other greenhouse gases in the atmosphere absorbs some of the outgoing infrared (heat) radiation and redirects it back to Earth's surface. As a result, the atmosphere, land, and ocean are warming.

What are the probable effects of climate change?

We now consider some of the probable effects of climate change, including changes in sea level; changes in precipitation patterns; effects on biological diversity, including humans; and effects on agriculture. These changes will persist for centuries because many greenhouse gases remain in the atmosphere for hundreds of years. Furthermore, even after greenhouse gas concentrations have stabilized, scientists think that Earth's mean surface temperature will continue to rise because the ocean adjusts to climate change on a delayed time scale.

With climate change, the global average sea level is rising

As Earth's overall temperature increases by just a few degrees, there could be a major thawing of glaciers and the polar ice caps. In addition to sea-level rise caused by the retreat of glaciers and thawing of polar ice, the sea level will rise because of thermal expansion of the warming ocean. Water, like other substances, expands as it warms.

The IPCC estimates that sea level will rise 18 to 59 cm (0.6 to 1.9 ft) by 2100 and notes that it could be even higher. Such an increase will flood low-lying coastal areas, such as parts of southern Louisiana and South Florida. Coastal areas that are not inundated will more likely suffer erosion and other damage from more frequent and more intense weather events such as hurricanes.

Countries particularly at risk include Bangladesh, Egypt, Vietnam, Mozambique, and many island nations such as the Maldives.

With climate change, precipitation patterns will change

Computer simulations of weather changes as climate warming occurs indicate that precipitation patterns will be altered, causing some areas such as midlatitude continental interiors to have more frequent droughts. At the same time, heavier snowstorms and rainstorms may cause more frequent flooding in other areas. Changes in precipitation patterns could affect the availability and quality of fresh water in many places. Arid or semiarid areas, such as the Sahel region just south of the Sahara Desert, may have the most serious water shortages as the climate warms. Closer to home, water experts predict water shortages in the American West because warmer winter temperatures will cause more precipitation to fall as rain rather than snow; melting snow currently provides 70% of stream flows in the West during summer months.

The frequency and intensity of storms over warm surface waters may also increase. Scientists at the National Oceanic and Atmospheric Administration developed a computer model that examines how climate change may affect hurricanes. When the model was run with a sea-surface temperature 2.2°C warmer than today, more intense hurricanes resulted. (The question of whether hurricanes will occur *more frequently* in a warmer climate remains uncertain.) Changes in storm frequency and intensity are expected because as the atmosphere warms, more water evaporates, which in turn releases more energy into the atmosphere. (Recall the discussion of water's heat of vaporization in Chapter 2.) This energy generates more powerful storms.

With climate change, the ranges of organisms are changing

Dozens of studies report on the effects of climate change on organisms, from flowering times in plants to breeding times in birds. For example, researchers determined that populations of zooplankton in the California Current have declined 80% since 1951, apparently because the current has warmed slightly. (The California Current flows from Oregon southward along the California coast.) The decline in zooplankton has affected the entire ecosystem's food web, and populations of seabirds and plankton-eating fishes have also declined.

Warmer temperatures in Antarctica—during the past 50 years the average annual temperature on the Antarctic Peninsula has increased 2.6°C (5°F)—have contributed to reproductive failure in Adélie penguins. The birds normally lay their eggs in snow-free rocky outcrops, but the warmer temperatures have caused more snowfall (recall that warmer air holds more moisture), which melts when the birds incubate the eggs. The melted snow forms cold pools of slush that kill the developing chick embryos.

Biologists generally agree that climate change will have an especially severe impact on plants, which cannot migrate as quickly as animals when environmental conditions change. (The speed of seed dispersal has definite limitations.) During past climate changes, such as during the glacial retreat that took place some 12,000 years ago, the upper limit of dispersal for tree species was probably 200 km (124 miles) per century. If Earth warms as much during the 21st century as projections indicate, the ranges

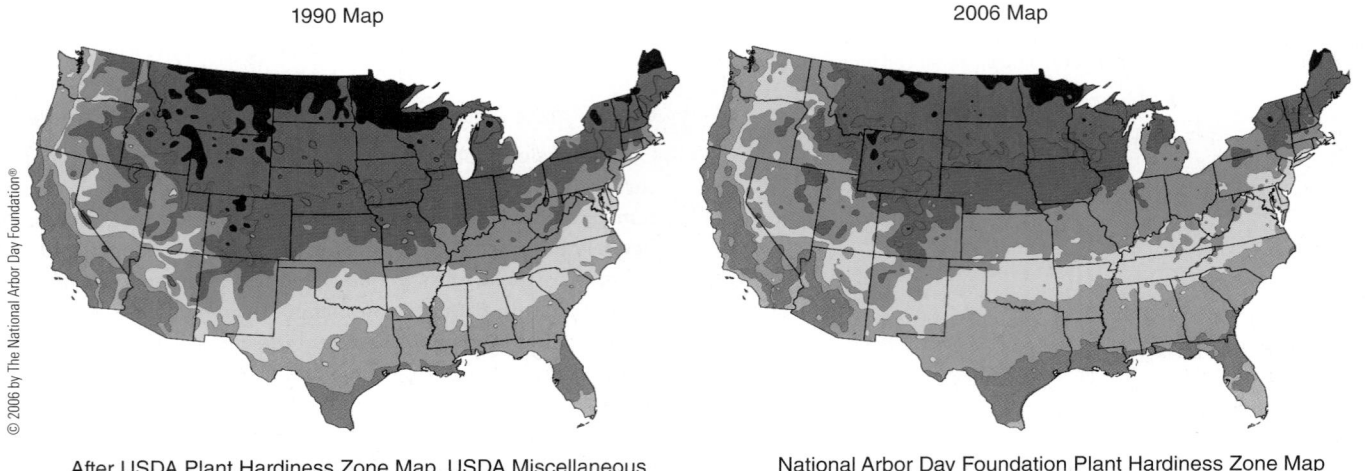

1990 Map

2006 Map

After USDA Plant Hardiness Zone Map, USDA Miscellaneous
Publication No. 1475, Issued January 1990

National Arbor Day Foundation Plant Hardiness Zone Map
published in 2006

Zone

2 3 4 5 6 7 8 9 10

© 2006 by The National Arbor Day Foundation®

FIGURE 57-18 Changes in U.S. plant hardiness zones, 1990 to 2006

Plant hardiness zones were developed for farmers and gardeners to help them identify which plants
are most suitable for their location. The zones had to be redrawn in 2006 as a result of climate change.
(Courtesy of the USDA and National Arbor Day Foundation.)

for some temperate tree species may shift northward as much as
480 km (300 miles).

The U.S. Department of Agriculture reports hardiness zones,
based on the average low temperature in an area. Hardiness zones,
which indicate which plants will do well at different locations
around the country, have shifted considerably over the past two
decades (**FIG. 57-18**).

Each species reacts to changes in temperature differently. In
response to climate change, some species will probably become
extinct, particularly those with narrow temperature requirements,
those confined to small reserves or parks, and those living in fragile
ecosystems. Other species may survive in greatly reduced numbers
and ranges. Ecosystems considered most vulnerable to species loss
in the short term are polar seas, coral reefs and atolls, prairie wetlands, coastal wetlands, tundra, boreal forests, tropical forests, and
mountains, particularly alpine tundra.

In response to climate change, some species may disperse into
new environments or adapt to the changing conditions in their present habitats. Climate change may not affect certain species, whereas
other species may emerge as winners, with greatly expanded numbers and ranges. Those considered most likely to prosper include
weeds, pests, and disease-carrying organisms, all of which are gen-
eralists that are already common in many different environments.

Climate change will have a more pronounced
effect on human health in developing countries

Data linking climate change and human health problems are accumulating. Since 1950, the United States has experienced an
increased frequency of extreme heat-stress events, which are extremely hot, humid days during summer months. Medical records
show that heat-related deaths among elderly and other vulnerable
people increase during these events.

Climate change has also affected human health indirectly.
Mosquitoes and other disease carriers could expand their range
into the newly warm areas and spread malaria, dengue fever, yellow
fever, Rift Valley fever, and viral encephalitis. As many as 50 million to 80 million additional cases of malaria could occur annually
in tropical, subtropical, and temperate areas.

Highly developed countries are less vulnerable to such disease
outbreaks because of better housing (which keeps mosquitoes outside), medical care, pest control, and public health measures such
as water treatment plants. Texas reported a few cases of dengue
fever in the late 1990s, for example, whereas nearby Mexico had
thousands of cases during that period.

Climate change may increase problems for agriculture

Several studies show that the rising sea level will inundate river
deltas, which are some of the world's best agricultural lands. The
Nile River (Egypt), Mississippi River (United States), and Yang-
tze River (China) are examples of river deltas that have been studied. Certain agricultural pests and disease-causing organisms will
probably proliferate. As mentioned earlier, climate change may
also increase the frequency and duration of droughts and, in some
areas, crop-damaging floods.

On a regional scale, current global-warming models forecast
that agricultural productivity will increase in some areas and decline in others. Models suggest that Canada and Russia will increase their agricultural productivity in a warmer climate, whereas
tropical and subtropical regions, where many of the world's poor-
est people live, will decline in agricultural productivity. Central

(a) Stratospheric ozone absorbs 99% of incoming ultraviolet radiation, effectively shielding Earth's surface.

(b) When stratospheric ozone is reduced, more high-energy ultraviolet radiation penetrates the atmosphere to the surface, where it harms organisms.

FIGURE 57-19 *Animated* **Ultraviolet radiation and the ozone layer**

America and Southeast Asia may experience some of the greatest declines in agricultural productivity.

Review

- What is the enhanced greenhouse effect?
- How do greenhouse gases cause the enhanced greenhouse effect?
- What are some of the significant problems that climate change may cause during the 21st century?

57.5 DECLINING STRATOSPHERIC OZONE

■ LEARNING OBJECTIVES

10 Distinguish between surface ozone and stratospheric ozone.
11 Cite the causes and potential effects of ozone destruction in the stratosphere.

Ozone (O_3) is a form of oxygen that is a human-made pollutant in the lower atmosphere but a naturally produced, essential part of the stratosphere (see Fig. 21-7). The **stratosphere,** which encircles the planet some 10 to 45 km (6 to 28 miles) above the surface, contains a layer of ozone that shields the surface from much of the ultraviolet radiation from the sun (**FIG. 57-19**). If ozone disappeared from the stratosphere, Earth would become unlivable for most forms of life. Ozone in the lower atmosphere is converted back to oxygen in a few days and so does not replenish the ozone depleted in the stratosphere.

A slight thinning in the ozone layer over Antarctica forms naturally for a few months each year. In 1985, however, scientists observed a greater thinning than usual. This increased thinning, which begins each September, is commonly referred to as the "ozone hole" (**FIG. 57-20**). During the 1990s, the ozone-thinned area continued to grow, and by 2000 it had reached the record size of 28.3 million km^2 (11.3 million miles^2), larger than the North American continent.

In addition, worldwide levels of stratospheric ozone decreased for several decades. According to the National Center for Atmospheric Research, since the 1970s ozone levels over Europe and North America have dropped almost 10%.

Certain chemicals destroy stratospheric ozone

Both chlorine- and bromine-containing substances catalyze ozone destruction. The primary chemicals responsible for ozone loss in the stratosphere are a group of chlorine compounds called *chlorofluorocarbons (CFCs)*. Chlorofluorocarbons have been used as propellants in aerosol cans, coolants in air conditioners and refrigerators, foam-blowing agents for insulation and packaging, and solvents and cleaners for the electronics industry. Additional compounds that also attack ozone include halons (found in many fire extinguishers), methyl bromide (a pesticide), methyl chloroform (an industrial solvent), and carbon tetrachloride (used in many industrial processes, including the manufacture of pesticides and dyes).

After release into the lower troposphere, CFCs and similar compounds slowly drift up to the stratosphere, where ultraviolet radiation breaks them down, releasing chlorine. Similarly, the breakdown of halons and methyl bromide releases bromine. The thinning in the ozone layer over Antarctica occurs annually between September and November (spring in the Southern Hemisphere).

Ozone (Dobson Units)

110   220   330   440   550

FIGURE 57-20 Ozone thinning

A computer-generated image of part of the Southern Hemisphere, taken on September 30, 2009, reveals the ozone thinning (*purple and blue areas*). The ozone-thinned area is not stationary but is moved about by air currents. (Dobson units measure stratospheric ozone. They are named after British scientist Gordon Dobson, who studied ozone levels over Antarctica during the late 1950s.)

At this time, two important conditions occur: sunlight returns to the polar region, and the *circumpolar vortex,* a mass of cold air that circulates around the southern polar region and isolates it from the warmer air in the rest of the planet, is well developed.

The cold air causes polar stratospheric clouds to form; these clouds contain ice crystals to which chlorine and bromine adhere, making them available to destroy ozone. The sunlight promotes the chemical reaction in which chlorine or bromine breaks ozone molecules apart, converting them into O_2 molecules. The chemical reaction in which ozone is destroyed does not alter the chlorine or bromine, and thus a single chlorine or bromine atom breaks down many thousands of ozone molecules. The chlorine and bromine remain in the stratosphere for many years. When the circumpolar vortex breaks up, the ozone-depleted air spreads northward, diluting ozone levels in the stratosphere over South America, New Zealand, and Australia.

Ozone depletion harms organisms

With depletion of the ozone layer, more ultraviolet radiation reaches the surface. Excessive exposure to UV radiation is linked to human health problems, such as cataracts, skin cancer, and a weakened immune system. The lens of the eye contains transparent proteins that are replaced at a very slow rate. Exposure to excessive UV radiation damages these proteins, and over time, the damage accumulates; a cataract forms as the lens becomes cloudy.

Cataracts can be surgically treated, but millions of people in developing nations cannot afford the operation and so remain partially or totally blind.

Increased levels of UV radiation disrupt certain ecosystems. For example, the productivity of Antarctic phytoplankton, the microscopic drifting algae that are the base of the Antarctic food web, has declined from increased exposure to UVB. (UVB, one of three types of UV radiation, is particularly damaging to DNA.) Research shows that surface UV radiation inhibits photosynthesis in these phytoplankton. Biologists have also documented direct damage to natural populations of Antarctic fish. Increased DNA mutations in icefish eggs and larvae (young fish) were matched to increased levels of UV radiation; researchers are currently studying if these mutations lessen the animals' ability to survive.

There is also concern that high levels of UV radiation may damage crops and forests, but the effects of UVB radiation on plants are very complex and have not been adequately studied. Plants interact with many other species in both natural ecosystems and agricultural ecosystems, and the effects of UV radiation on each of these organisms, in turn, affect plants indirectly. For example, exposure to higher levels of UVB radiation may increase wheat yields by inhibiting fungi that cause disease in wheat. In contrast, exposure to higher levels of UV radiation may decrease cucumber yields because it increases the incidence of disease.

International cooperation
is helping repair the ozone layer

In 1987, representatives from many countries met in Montreal to sign the **Montreal Protocol,** an agreement that originally stipulated a 50% reduction of CFC production by 1998. After scientists reported that decreases in stratospheric ozone occurred over the heavily populated midlatitudes of the Northern Hemisphere in all seasons, the Montreal Protocol was modified to include stricter measures to limit CFC production. Industrial companies that manufacture CFCs quickly developed substitutes.

Production of CFCs, carbon tetrachloride, and methyl chloroform was completely phased out in the United States and other highly developed countries in 1996, with the exception of a relatively small amount exported to developing countries. Existing stockpiles could be used after the deadline, however. Developing countries phased out CFC use in 2005. Methyl bromide was supposed to be phased out by 2005 in highly developed countries, which are responsible for 80% of the global use of that chemical. However, these countries have been given more time to find effective substitutes. Hydrochlorofluorocarbons (HCFCs) will be phased out in 2030.

Satellite measurements taken in 1997 provided the first evidence that the levels of ozone-depleting chemicals were starting to decline in the stratosphere. In the early 2000s, the first signs of recovery of the ozone layer were evident: the *rate* of stratospheric ozone depletion was declining.

However, atmospheric levels of two chemicals (CFC-12 and halon-1211) still produced by developing countries may have increased. CFCs are extremely stable, and those being used today probably will continue to deplete stratospheric ozone for at least 50 years. Assuming that countries continue to adhere to the Montreal Protocol, however, scientists expect that human-exacerbated ozone thinning will gradually decline over time.

What is the take-home message from this chapter? Humans share much in common with the fate of other organisms on the planet. We are not immune to the environmental damage we have produced. We differ from other organisms, however, in our capacity to reflect on the consequences of our actions and to alter our behavior accordingly. Humans, both individually and collectively, can bring about change. The widespread substitution of construc-

tive change for destructive change is the key to ensuring the biosphere's survival.

Review

- What environmental service does the stratospheric ozone layer provide?
- How does ozone depletion occur?
- What are some of the consequences of the thinning ozone layer?

■ SUMMARY: FOCUS ON LEARNING OBJECTIVES

57.1 *(page 1243)*

1 Identify the various levels of biodiversity: genetic diversity, species richness, and ecosystem diversity.

- **Genetic diversity** is the genetic variety within a species, both within a given population and among geographically separate populations. **Species richness** is the number of species of archaea, bacteria, protists, plants, fungi, and animals. **Ecosystem diversity** is the variety of Earth's ecosystems, such as forests, prairies, deserts, lakes, coastal estuaries, and coral reefs.

2 Distinguish among threatened species, endangered species, and extinct species.

- A species' **extinction** occurs when its last individual member dies. A species whose severely reduced numbers throughout all or a significant part of its **range** put it in imminent danger of extinction is classified as an **endangered species.** When extinction is less imminent but the population is quite small, a species is classified as a **threatened species.**

Dodo

3 Discuss at least four causes of declining biological diversity and identify the most important cause.

- Human activities that reduce biological diversity include habitat loss and **habitat fragmentation,** pollution, introduction of **invasive species,** pest and predator control, illegal commercial hunting, and **commercial harvest.** Of these, habitat loss and fragmentation are the most significant.

57.2 *(page 1249)*

4 Define *conservation biology* and compare in situ and ex situ conservation measures.

- **Conservation biology** is the study of how humans affect organisms and of the development of ways to protect biological diversity.
- Efforts to preserve biological diversity in the wild, known as **in situ conservation,** are urgently needed in the world's **biodiversity hotspots.** Increasingly, biologists are focusing efforts on preserving biodiversity in entire ecosystems and **landscapes,** which consist of multiple interacting ecosystems.

- **Ex situ conservation** involves conserving individual species in human-controlled settings. Breeding captive species in zoos and storing seeds of genetically diverse plant crops are examples.

5 Describe the benefits and shortcomings of the U.S. Endangered Species Act and the Convention on International Trade in Endangered Species of Wild Flora and Fauna.

- The Endangered Species Act (ESA) authorizes the U.S. Fish and Wildlife Service to protect endangered and threatened species, both in the United States and abroad. The ESA does not compensate private property owners for financial losses because they cannot develop their land if a threatened or endangered species lives there. Conservationists would like to strengthen the ESA to manage whole ecosystems rather than endangered species and individual entities.
- At the international level, the Convention on International Trade in Endangered Species of Wild Flora and Fauna (CITES) protects endangered animals and plants considered valuable in the highly lucrative international wildlife trade. Enforcement varies from country to country; where enforcement exists, penalties are not severe, so illegal trade in rare species continues.

57.3 *(page 1253)*

6 Discuss the ecosystem services of forests and describe the consequences of deforestation.

- Forests provide many **ecosystem services,** including wildlife habitat, protection of watersheds, prevention of soil erosion, moderation of climate, and protection from flooding.
- **Deforestation** is the temporary or permanent clearance of forests for agriculture or other uses. Deforestation increases soil erosion and decreases soil fertility; contributes to loss of biological diversity; adversely affects watersheds; and may affect regional and global climate changes.

  CENGAGENOW™ Learn more about deforestation by clicking on the figure in CengageNOW.

7 State at least three reasons why forests (tropical rain forests and boreal forests) are disappearing today.

- Forests are destroyed to provide subsistence farmers with agricultural land, to produce timber, to provide open rangeland for cattle, and to supply fuel wood. **Subsistence agriculture,** in which a family produces enough food to feed itself, accounts for much of tropical rainforest deforestation. Extensive logging of boreal forests in Alaska, Canada, and Russia is the world's primary source of industrial wood and wood fiber.
- In **slash-and-burn agriculture,** trees are cut down and burned so that crops can be grown on the soil. Yields from the first crop are high because the nutrients that were in the trees are now available in the soil. When soil productivity declines, the farmer moves to a new part of the forest and repeats the process.

57.4 (page 1255)

8 Name at least three greenhouse gases and explain how greenhouse gases contribute to climate change.

- **Greenhouse gases**—carbon dioxide, methane, surface ozone, nitrous oxide, and chlorofluorocarbons—cause the **greenhouse effect,** in which the atmosphere retains heat and warms Earth's surface. Increased levels of CO_2 and other human-produced greenhouse gases in the atmosphere are causing concerns about an **enhanced greenhouse effect,** which is additional warming produced by increased levels of gases that absorb infrared radiation.

   CENGAGENOW™ Watch the development of the enhanced greenhouse effect by clicking on the figure in CengageNOW.

9 Describe how climate change may affect sea level, precipitation patterns, organisms (including humans), and food production.

- During the 21st century, **climate change** is causing a rise in sea level. Precipitation patterns are changing, resulting in more frequent droughts in some areas and more frequent flooding in other areas.

- Biologists think that climate change will cause some species to go extinct, some to be unaffected, and others to expand their numbers and ranges. Data linking climate change and human health problems (particularly in developing countries) are accumulating. Problems for agriculture include increased flooding, increased droughts, and declining agricultural productivity in tropical and subtropical areas.

57.5 (page 1259)

10 Distinguish between surface ozone and stratospheric ozone.

- **Ozone (O_3)** is a form of oxygen that is a human-made pollutant in the lower atmosphere but a naturally produced, essential part of the stratosphere. The **stratosphere,** which encircles Earth some 10 to 45 km above the surface, contains a layer of ozone that shields the surface from much of the damaging ultraviolet radiation from the sun.

11 Cite the causes and potential effects of ozone destruction in the stratosphere.

- Large areas of ozone thinning develop over Antarctica each year. Chlorofluorocarbons and similar chlorine- and bromine-containing compounds attack the ozone layer.

- Excessive exposure to UV radiation is linked to human health problems, including cataracts, skin cancer, and a weakened immune system. Increased levels of UV radiation may disrupt ecosystems, such as the Antarctic food web. High levels of UV radiation may damage crops and forests.

   CENGAGENOW™ Learn more about ultraviolet radiation and the ozone layer by clicking on the figure in CengageNOW.

TEST YOUR UNDERSTANDING

1. Which of the following statements about extinction is *not* correct? (a) extinction is the permanent loss of a species (b) extinction is a natural biological process (c) once a species is extinct, it never reappears (d) human activities have little impact on extinctions (e) thousands of plant and animal species are currently threatened with extinction

2. An endangered species (a) is severely reduced in number (b) is in imminent danger of becoming extinct throughout all or a significant part of its range (c) usually does not have reduced genetic variability (d) is not in danger of extinction in the foreseeable future (e) a and b

3. The most important reason for declining biological diversity is (a) air pollution (b) introduction of foreign (invasive) species (c) habitat destruction and fragmentation (d) illegal commercial hunting (e) commercial harvesting

4. Habitat corridors (a) surround a given habitat (b) cut through a continuous habitat, producing an edge effect (c) vary in width depending on the species they are designed to protect (d) are an important strategy of ex situ conservation (e) have been widely adopted by restoration ecologists

5. In situ conservation (a) includes breeding captive species in zoos (b) includes seed storage of genetically diverse crops (c) concentrates on preserving biological diversity in the wild (d) focuses exclusively on large, charismatic animals (e) a and b

6. Restoration ecology (a) is the study of how humans impact organisms (b) returns a degraded environment as close as possible to its former state (c) is an example of ex situ conservation (d) has been used to successfully reverse the decline in amphibian populations (e) is an important provision of the Endangered Species Act

7. Which of the following is linked to the decline of amphibian populations? (a) agricultural chemicals (b) increased UV radiation (c) infectious diseases (d) global climate change (e) all of the preceding

8. About 60% of tropical rainforest deforestation is the result of (a) commercial logging (b) cattle ranching (c) hydroelectric dams (d) mining (e) subsistence agriculture

9. Which of the following gases contributes to both climate change and thinning of the ozone layer? (a) CO_2 (b) CH_4 (c) surface O_3 (d) CFCs (e) N_2O

10. Climate change occurs because (a) carbon dioxide and other greenhouse gases react chemically to produce excess heat (b) Earth has too many greenhouses and other glassed buildings (c) volcanic eruptions produce large quantities of sulfur and other greenhouse gases (d) carbon dioxide and other greenhouse gases trap infrared radiation in the atmosphere (e) carbon dioxide and other greenhouse gases allow excess heat to pass out of the atmosphere

11. What gas is a human-made pollutant in the lower (surface) atmosphere but a natural and beneficial gas in the stratosphere? (a) CO_2 (b) CH_4 (c) O_3 (d) CFCs (e) N_2O

12. Where is stratospheric ozone depletion most pronounced? (a) over Antarctica (b) over the equator (c) over South America (d) over North America and Europe (e) over Alaska and Siberia

CRITICAL THINKING

1. Why might captive-breeding programs that reintroduce species into natural environments fail?

2. Conservation biologists often say that their discipline is less about biology than it is about economics and human decision-making. What do you think they mean?

3. A more descriptive name for *Homo sapiens* is *Homo dangerous*. Explain this specific epithet, given what you have learned in this chapter.

4. **EVOLUTION LINK.** Because new species will eventually evolve to replace those that humans are driving to extinction, why is declining biological diversity such a threat?

5. **EVOLUTION LINK.** Biologists have wondered how introduced species that would probably have limited genetic variation (due to the founder effect) survive and adapt so successfully that they become invasive. Part of the answer may be that invasive species are the result of multiple introductions instead of a single one. Explain how multiple introductions from a species' native area to an introduced area could increase that species' invasion success.

6. **EVOLUTION LINK.** Conservation biologists have altered the evolution of salmon populations in captive-breeding programs. Wild female salmon tend to produce fewer large eggs because the large eggs contain more nutrients for the offspring, giving each individual a greater chance to survive. After just a few generations, however, captive-bred females now lay greater numbers of small eggs. Suggest a possible adaptive advantage for many small eggs in the captive-bred environment. What would you predict regarding the reproductive success of captive-bred females released in the wild?

7. **ANALYZING DATA.** Study the graph, which shows the combined effects of various factors on biological diversity in 12 different terrestrial and aquatic ecosystems. Which factor is most important overall? Why do you think that climate change and

increasing atmospheric CO_2 are represented as separate factors? What is nitrogen pollution? (Adapted from Sala, O. E. et al. *Science,* Vol. 287, 2000.)

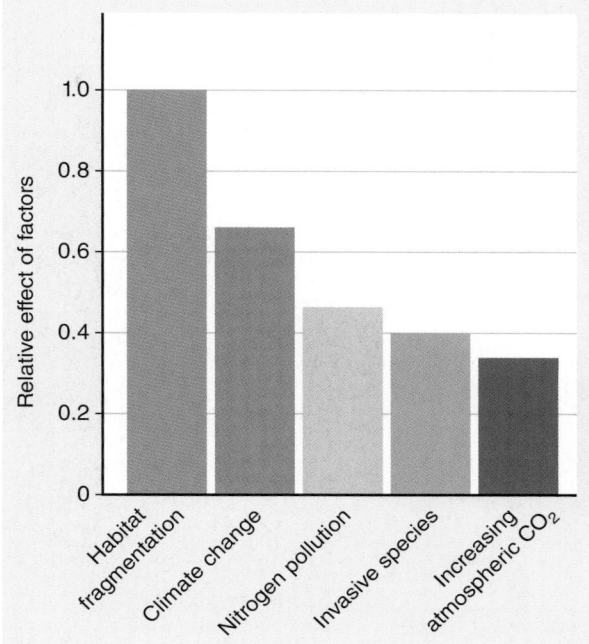

8. **SCIENCE, TECHNOLOGY, AND SOCIETY.** If you were given the task of developing a policy for the United States to deal with global climate change during the next 50 years, what would you propose? Explain your answer.

 Additional questions are available in CengageNOW at www.cengage.com/login.

Appendix A

Periodic Table of the Elements

State: S Solid, L Liquid, G Gas, X Not found in nature

Legend: Main Group metals; Transition metals, lanthanide series, actinide series; Metalloids; Nonmetals, noble gases

Atomic number 92, Symbol U, Atomic mass 238.0289

Group headers: 1A, 2A, 3B, 4B, 5B, 6B, 7B, 8B, 1B, 2B, 3A, 4A, 5A, 6A, 7A, 8A

1 H Hydrogen 1.0079
2 He Helium 4.0026
3 Li Lithium 6.941
4 Be Beryllium 9.0122
5 B Boron 10.811
6 C Carbon 12.011
7 N Nitrogen 14.0067
8 O Oxygen 15.9994
9 F Fluorine 18.9984
10 Ne Neon 20.1797
11 Na Sodium 22.9898
12 Mg Magnesium 24.3050
13 Al Aluminum 26.9815
14 Si Silicon 28.0855
15 P Phosphorus 30.9738
16 S Sulfur 32.066
17 Cl Chlorine 35.4527
18 Ar Argon 39.948
19 K Potassium 39.0983
20 Ca Calcium 40.078
21 Sc Scandium 44.9559
22 Ti Titanium 47.88
23 V Vanadium 50.9415
24 Cr Chromium 51.9961
25 Mn Manganese 54.9380
26 Fe Iron 55.847
27 Co Cobalt 58.9332
28 Ni Nickel 58.693
29 Cu Copper 63.546
30 Zn Zinc 65.39
31 Ga Gallium 69.723
32 Ge Germanium 72.61
33 As Arsenic 74.9216
34 Se Selenium 78.96
35 Br Bromine 79.904
36 Kr Krypton 83.80
37 Rb Rubidium 85.4678
38 Sr Strontium 87.62
39 Y Yttrium 88.9059
40 Zr Zirconium 91.224
41 Nb Niobium 92.9064
42 Mo Molybdenum 95.94
43 Tc Technetium (98)
44 Ru Ruthenium 101.07
45 Rh Rhodium 102.9055
46 Pd Palladium 106.42
47 Ag Silver 107.8682
48 Cd Cadmium 112.411
49 In Indium 114.82
50 Sn Tin 118.710
51 Sb Antimony 121.757
52 Te Tellurium 127.60
53 I Iodine 126.9045
54 Xe Xenon 131.29
55 Cs Cesium 132.9054
56 Ba Barium 137.327
57 La Lanthanum 138.9055
72 Hf Hafnium 178.49
73 Ta Tantalum 180.9479
74 W Tungsten 183.85
75 Re Rhenium 186.207
76 Os Osmium 190.2
77 Ir Iridium 192.22
78 Pt Platinum 195.08
79 Au Gold 196.9665
80 Hg Mercury 200.59
81 Tl Thallium 204.3833
82 Pb Lead 207.2
83 Bi Bismuth 208.9804
84 Po Polonium (209)
85 At Astatine (210)
86 Rn Radon (222)
87 Fr Francium (223)
88 Ra Radium 227.0254
89 Ac Actinium 227.0278
104 Rf Rutherfordium (261)
105 Db Dubnium (262)
106 Sg Seaborgium (263)
107 Bh Bohrium (262)
108 Hs Hassium (265)
109 Mt Meitnerium (266)
110 (269)
111 (272)
112 (277)

Lanthanide series:
58 Ce Cerium 140.115
59 Pr Praseodymium 140.9076
60 Nd Neodymium 144.24
61 Pm Promethium (145)
62 Sm Samarium 150.36
63 Eu Europium 151.965
64 Gd Gadolinium 157.25
65 Tb Terbium 158.9253
66 Dy Dysprosium 162.50
67 Ho Holmium 164.9303
68 Er Erbium 167.26
69 Tm Thulium 168.9342
70 Yb Ytterbium 173.04
71 Lu Lutetium 174.967

Actinide series:
90 Th Thorium 232.0381
91 Pa Protactinium 231.0359
92 U Uranium 238.0289
93 Np Neptunium 237.0482
94 Pu Plutonium (244)
95 Am Americium (243)
96 Cm Curium (247)
97 Bk Berkelium (247)
98 Cf Californium (251)
99 Es Einsteinium (252)
100 Fm Fermium (257)
101 Md Mendelevium (258)
102 No Nobelium (259)
103 Lr Lawrencium (260)

Appendix B
Classification of Organisms

The system of cataloguing organisms used in this book is described in Chapter 1 and in Chapters 23 through 32. In this ninth edition of *Biology,* we use the three-domain classification. The three domains are Bacteria, Archaea, and Eukarya (eukaryotes). We also discuss the five "supergroups" of eukaryotes based on molecular data. We describe the kingdoms Bacteria (which corresponds to domain Bacteria); Archaea (which corresponds to domain Archaea); and Plantae, Fungi, and Animalia (kingdoms assigned to domain Eukarya). The protists are no longer considered a kingdom. We assign them to several supergroups.

In this classification overview, we have included select groups. (We have also omitted many groups, especially extinct ones.) We have omitted viruses from this survey because they are not considered living organisms and are not assigned to any of the three domains.

PROKARYOTES

Domains Bacteria and Archaea are made up of prokaryotic organisms. They are distinguished from eukaryotic organisms by their smaller ribosomes and absence of membranous organelles, including the absence of a discrete nucleus surrounded by a nuclear envelope. Prokaryotes reproduce mainly asexually by binary fission. When present, flagella are simple and solid; they do not have the 9 + 2 microfilament structure typical of eukaryotes.

DOMAIN BACTERIA, KINGDOM BACTERIA

Very large, diverse group of prokaryotic organisms. Typically unicellular, but some form colonies or filaments. Mainly heterotrophic, but some groups are photosynthetic or chemosynthetic. Bacteria are nonmotile or move by rotating flagella. Typically have peptidoglycan in their cell walls. Estimated 100,000 to 200,000 species. Bacterial nomenclature and taxonomic practices are controversial and changing. See Table 25-4.

Proteobacteria Large, diverse group of gram-negative bacteria. Five subgroups are designated alpha, beta, gamma, delta, and epsilon. The alpha proteobacteria group includes *Rhizobium* and rickettsias. Beta proteobacteria include the bacterium that causes gonorrhea. Gamma proteobacteria include the enterobacteria, the group to which the intestinal bacterium *Escherichia coli* belongs, and the purple sulfur bacteria. The delta proteobacteria group includes the myxobacteria, and the epsilon bacteria include *Helicobacter,* which can cause peptic ulcers.

Cyanobacteria Gram-negative, photosynthetic.

Gram-positive bacteria Diverse group; includes actinomycetes, lactic acid bacteria, mycobacteria, streptococci, staphylococci, clostridia. Thick cell wall of peptidoglycan; many produce spores.

Mycoplasmas Lack cell walls. Extremely small bacteria bounded by plasma membrane.

Chlamydias Lack peptidoglycan in their cell walls. Energy parasites dependent on host for ATP.

Spirochetes Spiral-shaped bacteria with flexible cell walls.

DOMAIN ARCHAEA, KINGDOM ARCHAEA

Prokaryotes with unique cell membrane structure and cell walls lacking peptidoglycan. Also distinguished by their ribosomal RNA, lipid structure, and specific enzymes. Archaea are found in extreme environments—hot springs, sea vents, dry and salty seashores, boiling mud, and near ash-ejecting volcanoes. Fewer than 225 named species. Based on molecular data, there are two main clades: **Crenarchaeota** and **Euryarchaeota.** See Table 25-3. Three main types of archaea based on their metabolism and ecology are *methanogens, extreme halophiles,* and *extreme thermophiles.*

Methanogens Anaerobes that produce methane gas from simple carbon compounds.

Extreme halophiles Inhabit saturated salt solutions.

Extreme thermophiles Grow at 70°C or higher; some thrive above boiling point.

DOMAIN EUKARYA, PROTISTS

Primarily unicellular or simple multicellular eukaryotic organisms that do not form tissues and that exhibit relatively little division of labor. Most modes of nutrition occur in this group. Life cycles may include both sexually and asexually reproducing phases and may be extremely complex, especially in parasitic forms. Locomotion is by cilia, flagella, amoeboid movement, or by other means; flagella and cilia have 9 + 2 structure. Many biologists recognize five supergroups: Excavates, Chromalveolates, Rhizarians, Archaeplastids, and Unikonts.

Excavates Unicellular protists that have deep, or excavated, oral (feeding) groove. Have atypical, greatly modified mitochondria or lack them. Many are endosymbionts. Currently include diplomonads, parabasilids, euglenoids, and trypanosomes.

Diplomonads Excavates with one or two nuclei, no functional mitochondria, no Golgi complex, and up to eight flagella.

Parabasilids Anaerobic, flagellated excavates that often live in animals. Include trichonymphs and trichomonads.

Euglenoids and trypanosomes Unicellular flagellates with crystalline rod in flagella; some free-living and some pathogenic. Many are heterotrophic, but some (about one-third) have plastids and are photosynthetic. At least 900 species.

Chromalveolates Diverse protists that may have originated as a result of secondary endosymbiosis in which an ancestral cell engulfed a red alga. Include alveolates (dinoflagellates, ciliates, and apicomplexans) and stramenopiles (water molds, diatoms, golden algae, and brown algae).

Alveolates Chromalveolates with alveoli, flattened vesicles located inside plasma membrane.

Dinoflagellates Unicellular (some colonial), photosynthetic, biflagellate. Cell walls composed of overlapping cell plates; contain cellulose. Contain chlorophylls *a* and *c* and carotenoids, including fucoxanthin. About 2000 to 4000 species.

Ciliates Unicellular protists that move by means of cilia. Reproduction is asexual by binary fission or sexual by conjugation. About 7200 species.

Apicomplexans Parasitic unicellular protists that lack specific structures for locomotion. At some stage in life cycle, they develop spores (small infective agents). Some pathogenic. About 3900 species.

Stramenopiles Diverse group; most have motile cells with two flagella, one with tiny, hairlike projections off shaft; no flagella in some. Include water molds, diatoms, golden algae, and brown algae.

Water molds Consist of branched, coenocytic mycelia. Cellulose and/or chitin in cell walls. Produce biflagellate asexual spores. Sexual stage involves production of oospores. Some parasitic. About 700 species.

Diatoms Unicellular (some colonial), photosynthetic. Most nonmotile, but some move by gliding. Cell walls composed of silica rather than cellulose. Contain chlorophylls *a* and *c* and carotenoids, including fucoxanthin. At least 100,000 species estimated.

Golden algae Unicellular (some colonial), photosynthetic, biflagellate (some lack flagella). Cells covered by tiny scales of either silica or calcium carbonate. Contain chlorophylls *a* and *c* and carotenoids, including fucoxanthin. About 1000 species.

Brown algae Multicellular, often quite large (kelps). Photosynthetic; contain chlorophylls *a* and *c* and carotenoids, including fucoxanthin. Biflagellate reproductive cells. About 1500 species.

Rhizarians Amoeboid cells that often have tests (shells). Include forams and actinopods.

Foraminiferans (forams) Unicellular protists that produce calcareous tests (shells) with pores through which cytoplasmic projections extend, forming sticky net to entangle prey.

Actinopods Unicellular protists that produce axopods (long, filamentous cytoplasmic projections) that protrude through pores in their siliceous shells.

Archaeplastids Photosynthetic organisms with chloroplasts bounded by outer and inner membranes. This monophyletic group includes Plantae (land plants) and protists (red algae and green algae).

Red algae Most multicellular (some unicellular), mainly marine. Some (coralline algae) have bodies impregnated with calcium carbonate. No motile cells. Photosynthetic; contain chlorophyll *a*, carotenoids, phycocyanin, and phycoerythrin. About 5000 species.

Green algae Unicellular, colonial, siphonous, and multicellular forms. Some motile and flagellate. Photosynthetic; contain chlorophylls *a* and *b* and carotenoids. About 17,000 species.

Unikonts Cells that have a single flagellum or are amoebas with no flagella. Have a triple gene fusion that is lacking in other eukaryotes. Includes organisms currently classified in two kingdoms: Animalia and Fungi; and certain protists (amoebozoa and opisthokonts).

Amoebozoa Amoeboid protists that lack tests and move by means of lobose pseudopodia. Include amoebas, plasmodial slime molds, and cellular slime molds.

Amoebas Free-living and parasitic unicellular protists whose movement and capture of food are associated with pseudopodia.

Plasmodial slime molds Spend part of life cycle as thin, streaming, multinucleate plasmodium that creeps along on decaying leaves or wood. Flagellate or amoeboid reproductive cells; form spores in sporangia. About 700 species.

Cellular slime molds Vegetative (nonreproductive) form is unicellular; move by pseudopods. Amoeba-like cells aggregate to form multicellular pseudoplasmodium that eventually develops into fruiting body that bears spores. About 50 species.

Opisthokonts Opisthokonts (Greek *opistho*, "rear," and *kontos*, "pole") have a single posterior flagellum in flagellate cells. Includes animals, fungi, and choanoflagellates.

Choanoflagellates Have a single flagellum surrounded at its base by a collar of microvilli. Probably related to the common ancestor of animals.

DOMAIN EUKARYA, KINGDOM PLANTAE

Multicellular eukaryotic organisms with differentiated tissues and organs. Cell walls contain cellulose. Cells frequently contain large vacuoles; photosynthetic pigments in plastids. Photosynthetic pigments are chlorophylls *a* and *b* and carotenoids. Nonmotile. Reproduce both asexually and sexually, with alternation of gametophyte (*n*) and sporophyte (*2n*) generations. Some biologists classify plants as Archaeplastids (along with red algae and green algae).

Phylum Bryophyta *Mosses* Nonvascular plants that lack xylem and phloem. Marked alternation of generations with dominant gametophyte generation. Motile sperm. Gametophytes generally form dense green mat consisting of individual plants. At least 9900 species.

Phylum Hepatophyta *Liverworts* Nonvascular plants that lack xylem and phloem. Marked alternation of generations with dominant gametophyte generation. Motile sperm. Gametophytes of certain species have flat, liverlike thallus; other species more mosslike in appearance. About 6000 species.

Phylum Anthocerophyta *Hornworts* Nonvascular plants that lack xylem and phloem. Marked alternation of generations with dominant gametophyte generation. Motile sperm. Gametophyte is small, flat, green thallus with scalloped edges. Spores produced on erect, hornlike stalk. About 100 species.

Phylum Pteridophyta Vascular plants with dominant sporophyte generation. Reproduce by spores. Motile sperm.

Ferns Generally homosporous. Gametophyte is free-living and photosynthetic. About 11,000 species.

Whisk ferns Homosporous. Sporophyte stem branches dichotomously; lacks true roots and leaves. Gametophyte is subterranean and nonphotosynthetic and forms mycorrhizal relationship with fungus. About 12 species.

Horsetails Homosporous. Sporophyte has hollow, jointed stems and reduced, scalelike leaves. Gametophyte is tiny photosynthetic plant. About 15 species.

Phylum Lycopodiophyta *Club mosses* Sporophyte plants are vascular with branching rhizomes and upright stems that bear microphylls.

Although modern representatives are small, some extinct species were treelike. Some homosporous; others heterosporous. Motile sperm. About 1200 species.

Phylum Coniferophyta *Conifers* Heterosporous vascular plants with woody tissues (trees and shrubs) and needle-shaped or scalelike leaves. Most are evergreen. Seeds usually borne naked on surface of cone scales. Nutritive tissue in seed is haploid female gametophyte tissue. Nonmotile sperm. About 630 species.

Phylum Cycadophyta *Cycads* Heterosporous, vascular, dioecious plants that are small and shrubby or larger and palmlike. Produce naked seeds in conspicuous cones. Flagellate sperm. About 140 species.

Phylum Ginkgophyta *Ginkgo* Broadleaf deciduous trees that bear naked seeds directly on branches. Dioecious. Contain vascular tissues. Flagellate sperm. Ginkgo tree is only living representative. One species.

Phylum Gnetophyta *Gnetophytes* Woody shrubs, vines, or small trees that bear naked seeds in cones. Contain vascular tissues. Possess many features similar to flowering plants. About 70 species.

Phylum Anthophyta *Flowering plants or angiosperms* Largest, most successful group of plants. Heterosporous; dominant sporophytes with extremely reduced gametophytes. Contain vascular tissues. Bear flowers, fruits, and seeds (enclosed in fruit; seeds contain endosperm as nutritive tissue). Double fertilization. More than 300,000 species.

DOMAIN EUKARYA, KINGDOM FUNGI

Eukaryotic, mainly multicellular organisms with cell walls containing chitin. Heterotrophs that secrete digestive enzymes onto food source and then absorb predigested food. Most decomposers, but some parasites. Body form typically a mycelium. Cells usually haploid or dikaryotic, with brief diploid period following fertilization. Reproduce by means of spores, which may be produced sexually or asexually. No flagellate stages except in chytrids. Classified as opisthokonts (along with choanoflagellates and animals) because flagellate cells, where present, have a single posterior flagellum (Greek *opistho*, "rear," and *kontos*, "pole").

Phylum Chytridiomycota *Chytridiomycetes or chytrids* Parasites and decomposers found mainly in fresh water. Motile cells (gametes and zoospores) contain single, posterior flagellum. Reproduce both sexually and asexually. About 1000 species.

Phylum Zygomycota *Zygomycetes (molds)* Important decomposers; some are insect parasites. Produce sexual resting spores called *zygospores*; and nonmotile, haploid, asexual spores in sporangium. Hyphae are coenocytic. Many are heterothallic (two mating types). About 1100 species.

Phylum Glomeromycota *Glomeromycetes* Symbionts that form intracellular mycorrhizal associations within roots of most trees and herbaceous plants. Reproduce asexually with large, multinucleate spores called *blastospores*. About 200 species.

Phylum Ascomycota *Ascomycetes or sac fungi (yeasts, powdery mildews, molds, morels, truffles)* Important symbionts; 98% of lichen-forming fungi are ascomycetes; some form mycorrhizae. Sexual reproduction: form ascospores in sacs called *asci*. Asexual reproduction: produce spores called *conidia*, which pinch off from conidiophores. Hyphae usually have perforated septa. Dikaryotic stage. About 32,000 species.

Phylum Basidiomycota *Basidiomycetes or club fungi (mushrooms, bracket fungi, puffballs)* Many form mycorrhizae with tree roots. Sexual reproduction: form basidiospores on basidium. Asexual reproduction

uncommon. Heterothallic. Hyphae usually have perforated septa. Dikaryotic stage. More than 30,000 species.

DOMAIN EUKARYA, KINGDOM ANIMALIA

Eukaryotic, multicellular heterotrophs with differentiated cells. In most animals, cells are organized to form tissues, tissues form organs, and tissues and organs form specialized organ systems that carry on specific functions. Most have a well-developed nervous system and respond adaptively to changes in their environment. Most are capable of locomotion during some time in their life cycle. Most diploid and reproduce sexually; flagellate haploid sperm unites with large, nonmotile, haploid egg, forming diploid zygote that undergoes cleavage. Classified as opisthokonts (along with choanoflagellates and fungi) because flagellate cells, where present, have a single posterior flagellum (Greek *opistho*, "rear," and *kontos*, "pole").

Phylum Porifera *Sponges* Mainly marine; solitary or colonial. Body bears many pores through which water circulates. Food is filtered from water by collar cells (choanocytes). Asexual reproduction by budding; external sexual reproduction in which sperm are released and swim to internal egg. Larva is motile. About 15,000 species.

Phylum Cnidaria *Hydras, jellyfish, sea anemones, corals* Marine, with a few freshwater species; solitary or colonial; polyp and medusa forms. Radial symmetry. Tentacles surrounding mouth. Stinging cells (cnidocytes) contain stinging structures called *nematocysts*. Planula larva. About 10,000 species.

Phylum Ctenophora *Comb jellies* Marine; free-swimming. Biradial symmetry. Two tentacles and eight longitudinal rows of cilia resembling combs; animal moves by means of these bands of cilia. About 150 species.

Protostomes: Lophotrochozoa

Coelomates (characterized by true coelom, that is, body cavity completely lined with mesoderm). Spiral, determinate cleavage, and mouth typically develops from blastopore. There are two branches of protostomes: Lophotrochozoa and Ecdysozoa. The Lophotrochozoa include the platyhelminths, nemerteans (ribbon worms), mollusks, annelids, the lophophorate phyla, and the rotifers. The name *Lophotrochozoa* comes from two characteristics of some animals in this clade: the lophophore, a ciliated ring of tentacles surrounding the mouth in three small groups of animals, and the trochophore larva that characterizes its two major groups—the mollusks and annelids.

Phylum Platyhelminthes *Flatworms* Acoelomate (no body cavity); region between body wall and internal organs filled with tissue. Planarians are free-living; flukes and tapeworms are parasitic. Body dorsoventrally flattened; cephalization; three tissue layers. Simple nervous system with ganglia in head region. Excretory organs are protonephridia with flame cells. About 20,000 species.

Phylum Nemertea *Proboscis worms (also called ribbon worms)* Long, dorsoventrally flattened body with complex proboscis used for defense and for capturing prey. Functionally acoelomate but have small true coelom in proboscis. Definite organ systems. Complete digestive tract. Circulatory system with blood. About 1200 species.

Phylum Mollusca *Snails, clams, squids, octopods* Unsegmented, soft-bodied animals usually covered by dorsal shell. Have ventral, muscular foot. Most organs located above foot in visceral mass. Shell-secreting mantle covers visceral mass and forms mantle cavity, which contains gills. Trochophore and/or veliger larva. More than 80,000 species.

Phylum Annelida *Segmented worms: polychaetes, earthworms, leeches* Both body wall and internal organs are segmented. Body segments separated by septa. Some have nonjointed appendages. Setae used in locomotion. Closed circulatory system; metanephridia; specialized regions of digestive tract. Trochophore larva. About 15,000 species.

Phylum Brachiopoda *Lamp shells* One of lophophorate phyla. Marine; body enclosed between two shells. About 325 species.

Phylum Phoronida One of lophophorate phyla. Tube-dwelling marine worms. About 20 species.

Phylum Bryozoa One of lophophorate phyla. Mainly marine; sessile colonies produced by asexual budding. About 4500 species.

Phylum Rotifera *Wheel animals* Aquatic, microscopic. Anterior end has ciliated crown that looks like wheel when cilia beat. Posterior end tapers to foot. Characterized by pseudocoelom (body cavity not completely lined with mesoderm). Constant number of cells in adult. About 2000 species.

Protostomes: Ecdysozoa

Animals in this group of protostomes characterized by ecdysis (molting).

Phylum Nematoda *Roundworms: ascaris, hookworms, pinworms* Slender, elongated, cylindrical worms; covered with cuticle. Characterized by pseudocoelom (body cavity not completely lined with mesoderm). Free-living and parasitic forms. About 80,000 species.

Phylum Arthropoda *Arachnids (spiders, mites, ticks), crustaceans (lobsters, crabs, shrimp), insects, centipedes, millipedes* Segmented animals with paired, jointed appendages and hard exoskeleton made of chitin. Open circulatory system with dorsal heart. Hemocoel occupies most of body cavity, and coelom is reduced. More than 1 million species.

Deuterostomes

Coelomates with radial, indeterminate cleavage. Blastopore develops into anus, and mouth forms from second opening.

Phylum Echinodermata *Sea stars, sea urchins, sand dollars, sea cucumbers* Marine. Pentaradial symmetry as adults; bilateral symmetry as larvae. Endoskeleton of small, calcareous plates. Water vascular system; tube feet for locomotion. About 7000 species.

Phylum Hemichordata *Acorn worms* Marine with ring of cilia around mouth. Anterior muscular proboscis is connected by collar region to long, wormlike body. Larval form resembles echinoderm larva. About 100 species.

Phylum Chordata *Subphylum Urochordata (tunicates), subphylum Cephalochordata (lancelets), subphylum Vertebrata (fishes, amphibians, reptiles, birds, mammals)* Notochord; dorsal, tubular nerve cord; postanal tail; endostyle; and pharyngeal slits present at some time in life cycle. About 60,000 species.

Appendix C

Understanding Biological Terms

Your task of mastering new terms will be greatly simplified if you learn to dissect each new word. Many terms can be divided into a prefix, the part of the word that precedes the main root; the word root itself; and often a suffix, a word ending that may add to or modify the meaning of the root. As you progress in your study of biology, you will learn to recognize the more common prefixes, word roots, and suffixes. Such recognition will help you analyze new terms so that you can more readily determine their meaning and will help you remember them.

Prefixes

a-, ab- from, away, apart (*abduct,* move away from the midline of the body)

a-, an-, un- less, lack, not (*asymmetrical,* not symmetrical)

ad- (also **af-, ag-, an-, ap-**) to, toward (*adduct,* move toward the midline of the body)

allo- different (*allometric growth,* different rates of growth for different parts of the body during development)

ambi- both sides (*ambidextrous,* able to use either hand)

andro- a man (*androecium,* the male portion of a flower)

anis- unequal (*anisogamy,* sexual reproduction in which the gametes are of unequal sizes)

ante- forward, before (*anteflexion,* bending forward)

anti- against (*antibody,* proteins that have the capacity to react against foreign substances in the body)

auto- self (*autotroph,* organism that manufactures its own food)

bi- two (*biennial,* a plant that takes two years to complete its life cycle)

bio- life (*biology,* the study of life)

circum-, circ- around (*circumcision,* a cutting around)

co-, con- with, together (*congenital,* existing with or before birth)

contra- against (*contraception,* against conception)

cyt- cell (*cytology,* the study of cells)

di- two (*disaccharide,* a compound made of two sugar molecules chemically combined)

dis- apart (*dissect,* cut apart)

ecto- outside (*ectoderm,* outer layer of cells)

end-, endo- within, inner (*endoplasmic reticulum,* a network of membranes found within the cytoplasm)

epi- on, upon (*epidermis,* upon the dermis)

ex-, e-, ef- out from, out of (*extension,* a straightening out)

extra- outside, beyond (*extraembryonic membrane,* a membrane that encircles and protects the embryo)

gravi- heavy (*gravitropism,* growth of a plant in response to gravity)

hemi- half (*cerebral hemisphere,* lateral half of the cerebrum)

hetero- other, different (*heterozygous,* having unlike members of a gene pair)

homeo- unchanging, steady (*homeostasis,* reaching a steady state)

homo-, hom- same (*homologous,* corresponding in structure; *homozygous,* having identical members of a gene pair)

hyper- excessive, above normal (*hypersecretion,* excessive secretion)

hypo- under, below, deficient (*hypotonic,* a solution whose osmotic pressure is less than that of a solution with which it is compared)

in-, im- not (*incomplete flower,* a flower that does not have one or more of the four main parts)

inter- between, among (*interstitial,* situated between parts)

intra- within (*intracellular,* within the cell)

iso- equal, like (*isotonic,* equal osmotic pressure)

macro- large (*macronucleus,* a large, polyploid nucleus found in ciliates)

mal- bad, abnormal (*malnutrition,* poor nutrition)

mega- large, great (*megakaryocyte,* giant cell of bone marrow)

meso- middle (*mesoderm,* middle tissue layer of the animal embryo)

meta- after, beyond (*metaphase,* the stage of mitosis after prophase)

micro- small (*microscope,* instrument for viewing small objects)

mono- one (*monocot,* a group of flowering plants with one cotyledon, or seed leaf, in the seed)

oligo- small, few, scant (*oligotrophic lake,* a lake deficient in nutrients and organisms)

oo- egg (*oocyte,* cell that gives rise to an egg cell)

paedo- a child (*paedomorphosis,* the preservation of a juvenile characteristic in an adult)

para- near, beside, beyond (*paracentral,* near the center)

peri- around (*pericardial membrane,* membrane that surrounds the heart)

photo- light (*phototropism,* growth of a plant in response to the direction of light)

poly- many, much, multiple, complex (*polysaccharide,* a carbohydrate composed of many simple sugars)

post- after, behind (*postnatal,* after birth)

pre- before (*prenatal,* before birth)

pseudo- false (*pseudopod,* a temporary protrusion of a cell, i.e., "false foot")

retro- backward (*retroperitoneal,* located behind the peritoneum)

semi- half (*semilunar,* half-moon)

sub- under (*subcutaneous tissue,* tissue immediately under the skin)

super, supra- above (*suprarenal,* above the kidney)

sym- with, together (*sympatric speciation,* evolution of a new species within the same geographic region as the parent species)

syn- with, together (*syndrome,* a group of symptoms that occur together and characterize a disease)

trans- across, beyond (*transport,* carry across)

Suffixes

-able, -ible able (*viable,* able to live)

-ad used in anatomy to form adverbs of direction (*cephalad,* toward the head)

-asis, -asia, -esis condition or state of (*euthanasia,* state of "good death")

-cide kill, destroy (*biocide,* substance that kills living things)

-emia condition of blood (*anemia,* a blood condition in which there is a lack of red blood cells)

-gen something produced or generated or something that produces or generates (*pathogen,* an organism that produces disease)

-gram record, write (*electrocardiogram,* a record of the electrical activity of the heart)

-graph record, write (*electrocardiograph,* an instrument for recording the electrical activity of the heart)

-ic adjective-forming suffix that means *of* or *pertaining to* (*ophthalmic,* of or pertaining to the eye)

-itis inflammation of (*appendicitis,* inflammation of the appendix)

-logy study or science of (*cytology,* study of cells)

-oid like, in the form of (*thyroid,* in the form of a shield, referring to the shape of the thyroid gland)

-oma tumor (*carcinoma,* a malignant tumor)

-osis indicates disease (*psychosis,* a mental disease)

-pathy disease (*dermopathy,* disease of the skin)

-phyll leaf (*mesophyll,* the middle tissue of the leaf)

-scope instrument for viewing or observing (*microscope,* instrument for viewing small objects)

Some Common Word Roots

abscis cut off (*abscission,* the falling off of leaves or other plant parts)

angi, angio vessel (*angiosperm,* a plant that produces seeds enclosed within a fruit or "vessel")

apic tip, apex (*apical meristem,* area of cell division located at the tips of plant stems and roots)

arthr joint (*arthropods,* invertebrate animals with jointed legs and segmented bodies)

aux grow, enlarge (*auxin,* a plant hormone involved in growth and development)

blast a formative cell, germ layer (*osteoblast,* cell that gives rise to bone cells)

brachi arm (*brachial artery,* blood vessel that supplies the arm)

bry grow, swell (*embryo,* an organism in the early stages of development)

cardi heart (*cardiac,* pertaining to the heart)

carot carrot (*carotene,* a yellow, orange, or red pigment in plants)

cephal head (*cephalad,* toward the head)

cerebr brain (*cerebral,* pertaining to the brain)

cervic, cervix neck (*cervical,* pertaining to the neck)

chlor green (*chlorophyll,* a green pigment found in plants)

chondr cartilage (*chondrocyte,* a cartilage cell)

chrom color (*chromosome,* deeply staining body in nucleus)

cili small hair (*cilium,* a short, fine cytoplasmic hair projecting from the surface of a cell)

coleo a sheath (*coleoptile,* a protective sheath that encircles the stem in grass seedlings)

conjug joined (*conjugation,* a sexual phenomenon in certain protists)

cran skull (*cranial,* pertaining to the skull)

decid falling off (*deciduous,* a plant that sheds its leaves at the end of the growing season)

dehis split (*dehiscent fruit,* a fruit that splits open at maturity)

derm skin (*dermatology,* study of the skin)

ecol dwelling, house (*ecology,* the study of organisms in relation to their environment, i.e., "their house")

enter intestine (*enterobacteria,* a group of bacteria that includes species that inhabit the intestines of humans and other animals)

evol to unroll (*evolution,* descent with modification, gradual directional change)

fil a thread (*filament,* the thin stalk of the stamen in flowers)

gamet a wife or husband (*gametangium,* the part of a plant, protist, or fungus that produces reproductive cells)

gastr stomach (*gastrointestinal tract,* the digestive tract)

glyc, glyco sweet, sugar (*glycogen,* storage form of glucose)

gon seed (*gonad,* an organ that produces gametes)

gutt a drop (*guttation,* loss of water as liquid "drops" from plants)

gymn naked (*gymnosperm,* a plant that produces seeds that are not enclosed with a fruit, i.e., "naked")

hem blood (*hemoglobin,* the pigment of red blood cells)

hepat liver (*hepatic,* of or pertaining to the liver)

hist tissue (*histology,* study of tissues)

hydr water (*hydrolysis,* a breakdown reaction involving water)

leuk white (*leukocyte,* white blood cell)

menin membrane (*meninges,* the three membranes that envelop the brain and spinal cord)

morph form (*morphogenesis,* development of body form)

my, myo muscle (*myocardium,* muscle layer of the heart)

myc a fungus (*mycelium,* the vegetative body of a fungus)

nephr kidney (*nephron,* microscopic unit of the kidney)

neur, nerv nerve (*neuromuscular,* involving both the nerves and muscles)

occiput back part of the head (*occipital,* back region of the head)

ost bone (*osteology,* study of bones)

path disease (*pathologist,* one who studies disease processes)

ped, pod foot (*bipedal,* walking on two feet)

pell skin (*pellicle,* a flexible covering over the body of certain protists)

phag eat (*phagocytosis,* process by which certain cells ingest particles and foreign matter)

phil love (*hydrophilic,* a substance that attracts, i.e., "loves," water)

phloe bark of a tree (*phloem,* food-conducting tissue in plants that corresponds to bark in woody plants)

phyt plant (*xerophyte,* a plant adapted to xeric, or dry, conditions)

plankt wandering (*plankton,* microscopic aquatic protists that float or drift passively)

rhiz root (*rhizome,* a horizontal, underground stem that superficially resembles a root)

scler hard (*sclerenchyma,* cells that provide strength and support in the plant body)

sipho a tube (*siphonous,* a type of tubular body form found in certain algae)

som body (*chromosome,* deeply staining body in the nucleus)

sor heap (*sorus,* a cluster or "heap" of sporangia in a fern)

spor seed (*spore,* a reproductive cell that gives rise to individual offspring in plants, protists, and fungi)

stom a mouth (*stoma,* a small pore, i.e., "mouth," in the epidermis of plants)

thigm a touch (*thigmotropism,* plant growth in response to touch)

thromb clot (*thrombus,* a clot within a blood vessel)

troph nourishment (*heterotroph,* an organism that must depend on other organisms for its nourishment)

tropi turn (*thigmotropism,* growth of a plant in response to contact with a solid object, such as a tendril "turning" or wrapping around a wire fence)

visc pertaining to an internal organ or body cavity (*viscera,* internal organs)

xanth yellow (*xanthophyll,* a yellowish pigment found in plants)

xyl wood (*xylem,* water-conducting tissue in plant, the "wood" of woody plants)

zoo an animal (*zoology,* the science of animals)

Appendix D
Abbreviations

The biological sciences use a great many abbreviations and with good reason. Many technical terms in biology and biological chemistry are both long and difficult to pronounce. Yet it can be difficult for beginners, when confronted with something like NADPH or EPSP, to understand the reference. Here, for your ready reference, are some of the common abbreviations used in biology.

A adenine
ABA abscisic acid
ABC transporters ATP-binding cassette transporters
ACTH adrenocorticotropic hormone
AD Alzheimer's disease
ADA adenosine deaminase
ADH antidiuretic hormone
ADP adenosine diphosphate
AIDS acquired immunodeficiency syndrome
AMP adenosine monophosphate
amu atomic mass unit (dalton)
ANP atrial natriuretic peptide
APC anaphase-promoting complex *or* antigen-presenting cell
AS Angelman syndrome
ATP adenosine triphosphate
AV node or valve atrioventricular node or valve (of heart)
B lymphocyte or B cell lymphocyte responsible for antibody-mediated immunity
BAC bacterial artificial chromosome
BH brain hormone (of insects)
BMR basal metabolic rate
BR brassinosteroid
bya billion years ago
C cytosine
C$_3$ three-carbon pathway for carbon fixation (Calvin cycle)
C$_4$ four-carbon pathway for carbon fixation
CAM crassulacean acid metabolism
cAMP cyclic adenosine monophosphate
CAP catabolite activator protein
CD4 T cell T helper cell (T_H); T cell with a surface marker designated CD4
CD8 T cell T cell with a surface marker designated CD8; includes T cytotoxic cells (T_C)
Cdk cyclin-dependent protein kinase
cDNA complementary deoxyribonucleic acid
CFCs chlorofluorocarbons
CFTR cystic fibrosis transmembrane conductance regulator
CITES Convention on International Trade in Endangered Species of Wild Flora and Fauna
CNS central nervous system
CNVs copy number variations
CO cardiac output
CoA coenzyme A

COPD chronic obstructive pulmonary disease
CP creatine phosphate
CPR cardiopulmonary resuscitation
CREB cyclic AMP response element binding protein
CSF cerebrospinal fluid
CVA cardiovascular accident
CVS cardiovascular system
CVS chorionic villus sampling
DAG diacylglycerol
DNA deoxyribonucleic acid
DOC dissolved organic carbon
E$_A$ activation energy (of an enzyme)
ECG electrocardiogram
ECM extracellular matrix
EEG electroencephalogram
EKG electrocardiogram
EM electron microscope or micrograph
ENSO El Niño–Southern Oscillation
EPSP excitatory postsynaptic potential (of a neuron)
ER endoplasmic reticulum
ERK extracellular signal-regulated kinases
ES cells embryonic stem cells
EST expressed sequence tag
F$_1$ first filial generation
F$_2$ second filial generation
Fab portion the part of an antibody that binds to an antigen
Factor VIII blood-clotting factor (absent in hemophiliacs)
FAD/FADH$_2$ flavin adenine dinucleotide (oxidized and reduced forms, respectively)
FAP fixed action pattern
Fc portion the part of an antibody that interacts with cells of the immune system
FISH fluorescent in situ hybridization
FSH follicle-stimulating hormone
G guanine
G$_1$ phase first gap phase (of the cell cycle)
G$_2$ phase second gap phase (of the cell cycle)
G3P glyceraldehyde-3-phosphate
GINA Genetic Information Nondiscrimination Act
G protein cell-signaling molecule that requires GTP
GA gibberellin
GAA Global Amphibian Assessment (by World Conservation Union)
GABA gamma-aminobutyric acid
GH growth hormone (somatotropin)
GnRH gonadotropin-releasing hormone
GTP guanosine triphosphate
GWA genome-wide association
Hb hemoglobin
HBEF Hubbard Brook Experimental Forest

HBO$_2$ oxyhemoglobin
HCFCs hydrochlorofluorocarbons
hCG human chorionic gonadotropin
HD Huntington disease
HDL high-density lipoprotein
HFCs hydrofluorocarbons
hGH human growth hormone
HIV human immunodeficiency virus
HLA human leukocyte antigen
HPV human papillomavirus
HUGO Human Genome Organization
IAA indole acetic acid (natural auxin)
Ig immunoglobulin, as in IgA, IgG, etc.
IGF insulin-like growth factor
IP$_3$ inositol trisphosphate
IPCC United Nations Intergovernmental Panel on Climate Change
IPS induced pluripotent stem cells
IPSP inhibitory postsynaptic potential (of a neuron)
IUCN World Conservation Union
IUD intrauterine device
JH juvenile hormone (of insects)
kb kilobase
LDH lactate dehydrogenase enzyme
LDL low-density lipoprotein
LH luteinizing hormone
LM light microscope or micrograph
LSD lysergic acid diethylamide
LTP long-term potentiation
MAO monoamine oxidase
MAP mitogen-activated protein
MAPs microtubule-associated proteins
MHC major histocompatibility complex
MI myocardial infarction
miRNA microribonucleic acid
MPF mitosis-promoting factor
MRI magnetic resonance imaging
mRNA messenger RNA
MSAFP maternal serum α-fetoprotein
MSH melanocyte-stimulating hormone
mtDNA mitochondrial DNA
MTOC microtubule organizing center
MVP minimum viable population
mya million years ago
9 + 2 structure cilium or flagellum (of a eukaryote)
9 × 3 structure centriole or basal body (of a eukaryote)
n, $2n$ the chromosome number of a gamete and of a zygote, respectively
NAD$^+$/NADH nicotinamide adenine dinucleotide (oxidized and reduced forms, respectively)
NADP$^+$/NADPH nicotinamide adenine dinucleotide phosphate (oxidized and reduced forms, respectively)
NAG *N*-acetyl glucosamine
NK cell natural killer cell
NMDA *N*-methyl-D aspartate (an artificial ligand)
NO nitric oxide
NSF National Science Foundation
P generation parental generation
P53 a tumor suppressor gene

P680 reaction center of photosystem II
P700 reaction center of photosystem I
PABA para-aminobenzoic acid
PAMPs pathogen-associated molecular patterns
PCR polymerase chain reaction
PEP phosphoenolpyruvate
Pfr phytochrome (form that absorbs far-red light)
PGA phosphoglycerate
PGD preimplantation genetic diagnosis
PID pelvic inflammatory disease
PIF3 phytochrome-interacting factor-3
PKU phenylketonuria
PNS peripheral nervous system
pre-mRNA precursor messenger RNA (in eukaryotes)
Pr phytochrome (form that absorbs red light)
PTH parathyroid hormone
PWS Prader-Willi syndrome
RAO recent African origin
RAS reticular activating system
RBC red blood cell (erythrocyte)
REM sleep rapid-eye-movement sleep
RFLP restriction fragment length polymorphism
r_{max} intrinsic rate of increase (of a population)
RNA ribonucleic acid
RNAi ribonucleic acid interference
rRNA ribosomal RNA
rubisco ribulose bisphosphate carboxylase/oxygenase
RuBP ribulose bisphosphate
S phase DNA synthetic phase (of the cell cycle)
SA node sinoatrial node (of heart)
SCID severe combined immunodeficiency
SEM scanning electron microscope or micrograph
siRNA small interfering ribonucleic acid
snRNA small nuclear ribonucleic acid
snoRNA small nucleolar ribonucleic acid
SNPs single nucleotide polymorphisms
snRNP small nuclear ribonucleoprotein complex
SRP RNA signal recognition particle ribonucleic acid
SSB protein single-strand binding protein
ssp subspecies
STD sexually transmitted disease
STR short tandem repeat
T thymine
T lymphocyte or T cell lymphocyte responsible for cell-mediated immunity
T$_C$ lymphocyte T cytotoxic cell (CD8 T cell)
T$_H$ lymphocyte T helper cell (CD4 T cell)
TATA box base sequence in eukaryotic promoter
TCA cycle tricarboxylic acid cycle (synonym for citric acid cycle)
TCR T-cell receptor
TEM transmission electron microscope or micrograph
Tm tubular transport maximum
TNF tumor necrosis factor
tRNA transfer RNA
U uracil
UV light ultraviolet light
WBC white blood cell (leukocyte)

Appendix E
Answers to Test Your Understanding Questions

Chapter 1: 1. a 2. c 3. a 4. d 5. b 6. e 7. c 8. d 9. b
10. c 11. e 12. e

Chapter 2: 1. c 2. e 3. a 4. b 5. c 6. d 7. a 8. a 9. d
10. e 11. e 12. e

Chapter 3: 1. d 2. b 3. e 4. c 5. c 6. a 7. a 8. b 9. e
10. c 11. e 12. b

Chapter 4: 1. b 2. a 3. d 4. d 5. a 6. e 7. d 8. a 9. b
10. e 11. a

Chapter 5: 1. c 2. c 3. e 4. a 5. b 6. e 7. d 8. e 9. b
10. b 11. c 12. e

Chapter 6: 1. a 2. e 3. e 4. d 5. c 6. a 7. d 8. b 9. a
10. c 11. d 12. c

Chapter 7: 1. e 2. d 3. b 4. c 5. b 6. c 7. e 8. e 9. b
10. b 11. b 12. a

Chapter 8: 1. d 2. c 3. a 4. a 5. b 6. c 7. d 8. d 9. d
10. e 11. b

Chapter 9: 1. a 2. d 3. c 4. a 5. a 6. e 7. a 8. c 9. a
10. c 11. b

Chapter 10: 1. d 2. c 3. a 4. d 5. e 6. d 7. c 8. a 9. c
10. b 11. b 12. (1) −c, (2) −e, (3) −b, (4) −d, (5) −a

Chapter 11: 1. d 2. c 3. c 4. e 5. c 6. b
7. The short-winged condition is recessive. Both parents are heterozygous.
8. The F_1 offspring are expected to be black, short-haired. There is a 1/16 chance of brown and tan, long-haired offspring in the F_2 generation.
9. Yes.
10. The rooster is *PpRr*; hen A is *PpRR*; hen B is *Pprr*; and hen C is *PPRR*.
11. This is a two-point test cross involving linked loci. The parental classes of offspring are *Aabb* and *aaBb*; the recombinant classes are *AaBb* and *aabb*. There is a 4.6% recombination, which corresponds to 4.6 map units between the loci.
12. If genes B and C are 10 map units apart, gene A is in the middle. If genes B and C are two map units apart, gene C is in the middle.

Chapter 12: 1. c 2. d 3. d 4. e 5. b 6. d 7. b 8. e 9. d
10. b 11. a 12. b

Chapter 13: 1. e 2. a 3. b 4. d 5. b 6. a 7. e 8. c 9. a
10. d 11. b 12. e

Chapter 14: 1. a 2. c 3. a 4. c 5. c 6. c 7. b 8. c 9. e
10. a 11. c

Chapter 15: 1. a 2. b 3. e 4. e 5. a 6. b 7. a 8. c 9. a
10. c 11. b 12. a

Chapter 16: 1. e 2. a 3. c 4. e 5. a 6. d 7. c 8. e 9. d
10. e 11. a

Chapter 17: 1. c 2. d 3. b 4. a 5. c 6. d 7. b 8. e 9. c
10. b 11. d 12. c

Chapter 18: 1. d 2. b 3. c 4. c 5. b 6. b 7. d 8. e 9. b
10. b 11. c

Chapter 19: 1. b 2. b 3. b 4. d 5. b 6. b 7. c 8. a 9. e
10. b 11. c 12. d

Chapter 20: 1. a 2. a 3. c 4. d 5. b 6. c 7. b 8. e 9. c
10. d

Chapter 21: 1. a 2. b 3. d 4. c 5. e 6. c 7. a 8. a 9. b
10. b 11. c 12. c

Chapter 22: 1. c 2. a 3. a 4. b 5. e 6. a 7. b 8. b 9. d
10. c 11. c 12. e

Chapter 23: 1. b 2. a 3. e 4. c 5. a 6. a 7. e 8. c 9. b
10. e 11. d 12. a

Chapter 24: 1. e 2. a 3. b 4. c 5. a 6. c 7. e 8. a 9. c
10. d 11. b

Chapter 25: 1. d 2. b 3. b 4. a 5. a 6. c 7. e 8. d 9. e
10. a 11. a

Chapter 26: 1. c 2. a 3. c 4. b 5. d 6. d 7. b 8. a 9. d
10. e 11. c

Chapter 27: 1. d 2. b 3. d 4. d 5. a 6. b 7. c 8. a 9. c
10. d 11. c 12. c

Chapter 28: 1. e 2. b 3. d 4. a 5. e 6. d 7. b 8. d 9. a
10. c 11. a 12. c

Chapter 29: 1. a 2. b 3. e 4. d 5. d 6. a 7. e 8. c 9. c
10. c 11. b 12. e

Chapter 30: 1. d 2. e 3. b 4. a 5. b 6. d 7. c 8. a 9. b
10. d 11. c

Chapter 31: 1. a 2. c 3. b 4. d 5. a 6. e 7. b 8. d 9. b
10. e 11. d

Chapter 32: 1. b 2. b 3. a 4. b 5. d 6. e 7. e 8. c 9. a
10. c 11. e

Chapter 33: 1. a 2. c 3. d 4. b 5. c 6. c 7. a 8. b 9. b
10. e 11. a

Chapter 34: 1. c 2. d 3. d 4. e 5. d 6. a 7. e 8. c 9. a
10. c 11. a

Chapter 35: 1. d 2. e 3. b 4. b 5. a 6. b 7. e 8. c 9. b
10. a 11. b

Chapter 36: 1. c 2. b 3. b 4. a 5. c 6. c 7. d 8. a 9. d
10. e 11. a

Chapter 37: 1. c 2. d 3. c 4. a 5. c 6. b 7. b 8. d 9. c
10. d 11. a

Chapter 38: 1. c 2. a 3. b 4. c 5. e 6. e 7. d 8. d 9. b
10. e 11. e 12. b

Chapter 39: 1. b 2. b 3. a 4. a 5. e 6. e 7. c 8. a 9. d 10. a 11. c 12. d

Chapter 40: 1. a 2. c 3. c 4. a 5. d 6. b 7. e 8. e 9. b 10. c 11. d

Chapter 41: 1. c 2. b 3. d 4. e 5. a 6. c 7. c 8. c 9. c 10. b 11. e

Chapter 42: 1. b 2. d 3. c 4. a 5. b 6. a 7. e 8. e 9. b 10. b 11. a

Chapter 43: 1. e 2. c 3. a 4. d 5. a 6. b 7. e 8. d 9. b 10. b 11. c

Chapter 44: 1. b 2. d 3. a 4. b 5. a 6. c 7. e 8. d 9. e 10. e 11. d

Chapter 45: 1. b 2. c 3. e 4. c 5. a 6. b 7. e 8. d 9. c 10. b 11. a

Chapter 46: 1. a 2. a 3. c 4. b 5. c 6. d 7. e 8. c 9. e 10. c 11. d

Chapter 47: 1. c 2. d 3. d 4. e 5. a 6. b 7. d 8. a 9. b 10. c 11. c

Chapter 48: 1. c 2. d 3. e 4. b 5. e 6. d 7. a 8. a 9. c 10. d 11. e

Chapter 49: 1. b 2. c 3. d 4. a 5. c 6. e 7. a 8. d 9. a 10. b 11. e

Chapter 50: 1. c 2. c 3. a 4. e 5. b 6. c 7. e 8. a 9. d 10. a 11. e

Chapter 51: 1. b 2. d 3. a 4. a 5. d 6. b 7. e 8. b 9. b 10. c 11. b 12. c

Chapter 52: 1. a 2. b 3. c 4. a 5. b 6. a 7. d 8. e 9. b 10. e 11. a 12. c

Chapter 53: 1. b 2. b 3. b 4. c 5. b 6. a 7. d 8. e 9. a 10. b 11. e 12. c

Chapter 54: 1. d 2. d 3. e 4. c 5. c 6. d 7. a 8. d 9. e 10. d 11. e 12. d

Chapter 55: 1. d 2. e 3. a 4. d 5. e 6. e 7. a 8. b 9. c 10. d 11. d 12. b

Chapter 56: 1. c 2. a 3. d 4. e 5. c 6. b 7. d 8. b 9. a 10. c 11. e 12. e

Chapter 57: 1. d 2. e 3. c 4. c 5. c 6. b 7. e 8. e 9. d 10. d 11. c 12. a

Glossary

abiotic factors Elements of the nonliving, physical environment that affect a particular organism. Compare with *biotic factors.*

abscisic acid (ab-sis'-ik) A plant hormone involved in dormancy and responses to stress.

abscission (ab-sizh'-en) The normal (usually seasonal) fall of leaves or other plant parts, such as fruits or flowers.

abscission layer The area at the base of the petiole where the leaf will break away from the stem. Also known as *abscission zone.*

absorption (ab-sorp'-shun) (1) The movement of nutrients and other substances through the wall of the digestive tract and into the blood or lymph. (2) The process by which chlorophyll takes up light for photosynthesis.

absorption spectrum A graph of the amount of light at specific wavelengths that is absorbed as light passes through a substance. Each type of molecule has a characteristic absorption spectrum. Compare with *action spectrum.*

accessory fruit A fruit consisting primarily of tissue other than ovary tissue, e.g., apple, pear. Compare with *aggregate, simple,* and *multiple fruits.*

acclimatization Adjustment to seasonal changes.

acetyl coenzyme A (acetyl CoA) (as'-uh-teel) A key intermediate compound in metabolism; consists of a two-carbon acetyl group covalently bonded to coenzyme A.

acetyl group A two-carbon group derived from acetic acid (acetate).

acetylcholine (ah"-see-til-koh'-leen) A common neurotransmitter released by cholinergic neurons, including motor neurons.

achene (a-keen') A simple, dry fruit with one seed in which the fruit wall is separate from the seed coat, e.g., sunflower fruit.

acid A substance that is a hydrogen ion (proton) donor; acids unite with bases to form salts. Compare with *base.*

acid precipitation Precipitation that is acidic as a result of both sulfur and nitrogen oxides forming acids when they react with water in the atmosphere.

acidic solution A solution in which the concentration of hydrogen ions $[H^+]$ exceeds the concentration of hydroxide ions $[OH^-]$. An acidic solution has a pH less than 7. Compare with *basic solution* and *neutral solution.*

acoelomate (a-seel'-oh-mate) An animal lacking a body cavity (coelom). Compare with *coelomate* and *pseudocoelomate.*

acquired immune responses See *specific immune responses.*

acquired immunodeficiency syndrome (AIDS) A serious, potentially fatal disease caused by the human immunodeficiency virus (HIV).

acromegaly (ak"-roh-meg'-ah-lee) A condition characterized by overgrowth of the extremities of the skeleton, fingers, toes, jaws, and nose. It may be produced by excessive secretion of growth hormone by the anterior pituitary gland.

acrosome reaction (ak'-roh-sohm) A series of events in which the acrosome, a caplike structure covering the head of a sperm cell, releases proteolytic (protein-digesting) enzymes and undergoes other changes that permit the sperm to penetrate the outer covering of the egg.

actin (ak'-tin) The protein of which microfilaments consist. Actin, together with the protein myosin, is responsible for muscle contraction.

actin filaments Thin filaments consisting mainly of the protein actin; actin and myosin filaments make up the myofibrils of muscle fibers.

actinopods (ak-tin'-o-podz) Protists characterized by axopods that protrude through pores in their shells. See *rhizarians.*

action potential An electrical signal resulting from depolarization of the plasma membrane in a neuron or muscle cell. Compare with *resting potential.*

action spectrum A graph of the effectiveness of light at specific wavelengths in promoting a light-requiring reaction. Compare with *absorption spectrum.*

activation energy (E_A) The kinetic energy required to initiate a chemical reaction.

activator protein A positive regulatory protein that stimulates transcription when bound to DNA. Compare with *repressor protein.*

active immunity Immunity that develops as a result of exposure to antigens; it can occur naturally after recovery from a disease or can be artificially induced by immunization with a vaccine. Compare with *passive immunity.*

active site A specific region of an enzyme (generally near the surface) that accepts one or more substrates and catalyzes a chemical reaction. Compare with *allosteric site.*

active transport Transport of a substance across a membrane that does not rely on the potential energy of a concentration gradient for the substance being transported and therefore requires an additional energy source (often ATP); includes carrier-mediated active transport, endocytosis, and exocytosis. Compare with *diffusion* and *facilitated diffusion.*

adaptation (1) An evolutionary modification that improves an organism's chances of survival and reproductive success. (2) A decline in the response of a receptor subjected to repeated or prolonged stimulation.

adaptive immune responses See *specific immune responses.*

adaptive radiation The evolution of a large number of related species from an unspecialized ancestral organism.

adaptive zone A new ecological opportunity that was not exploited by an ancestral organism; used by evolutionary biologists to explain the ecological paths along which different taxa evolve.

addiction Physical dependence on a drug, generally based on physiological changes that take place in response to the drug; when the drug is withheld, the addict may suffer characteristic withdrawal symptoms.

adenine (ad'-eh-neen) A nitrogenous purine base that is a component of nucleic acids and ATP.

adenosine triphosphate (ATP) (a-den′-oh-seen) An organic compound containing adenine, ribose, and three phosphate groups; of prime importance for energy transfers in cells.

adhering junction A type of anchoring junction between cells; connects epithelial cells.

adhesion The property of sticking to some other substance. Compare with *cohesion.*

adipose tissue (ad′-i-pohs) Tissue in which fat is stored.

adrenal cortex (ah-dree′-nul kor′-teks) The outer region of each adrenal gland; secretes steroid hormones, including mineralocorticoids and glucocorticoids.

adrenal glands (ah-dree′-nul) Paired endocrine glands, one located just superior to each kidney; secrete hormones that help regulate metabolism and help the body cope with stress.

adrenal medulla (ah-dree′-nul meh-dull′-uh) The inner region of each adrenal gland; secretes epinephrine and norepinephrine.

adrenergic neuron (ad-ren-er′-jik) A neuron that releases norepinephrine or epinephrine as a neurotransmitter. Compare with *cholinergic neuron.*

adventitious (ad″-ven-tish′-us) Of plant organs, such as roots or buds, that arise in an unusual position on a plant.

aerobe Organism that grows or metabolizes only in the presence of molecular oxygen. Compare with *anaerobe.*

aerobic (air-oh′bik) Growing or metabolizing only in the presence of molecular oxygen. Compare with *anaerobic.*

aerobic respiration See *respiration.*

afferent (af′fer-ent) Leading toward some point of reference. Compare with *efferent.*

afferent neurons Neurons that transmit action potentials from sensory receptors to the brain or spinal cord. Compare with *efferent neurons.*

age structure The number and proportion of people at each age in a population. Age structure diagrams represent the number of males and females at each age, from birth to death, in the population.

aggregate fruit A fruit that develops from a single flower with many separate carpels, e.g., raspberry. Compare with *simple, accessory,* and *multiple fruits.*

aggregated distribution See *clumped dispersion.*

aging Progressive changes in development in an adult organism.

agnathans (ag-na′-thanz) Jawless fishes; historical class of vertebrates, including lampreys, hagfishes, and many extinct forms.

AIDS See *acquired immunodeficiency syndrome.*

albinism (al′-bih-niz-em) A hereditary inability to form melanin pigment, resulting in light coloration.

albumin (al-bew′-min) A class of protein found in most animal tissues; a fraction of plasma proteins.

aldehyde An organic molecule containing a carbonyl group bonded to at least one hydrogen atom. Compare with *ketone.*

aldosterone (al-dos′-tur-ohn) A steroid hormone produced by the vertebrate adrenal cortex; stimulates sodium reabsorption. See *mineralocorticoids.*

algae (al′-gee) (sing., *alga*) An informal group of unicellular, or simple multicellular, photosynthetic protists that are important producers in aquatic ecosystems.

allantois (a-lan′-toe-iss) An extraembryonic membrane of reptiles, birds, and mammals that stores the embryo's nitrogenous wastes; most of the allantois is detached at hatching or birth.

allele frequency The proportion of a specific allele in the population.

alleles (al-leelz′) Genes governing variation of the same character that occupy corresponding positions (loci) on homologous chromosomes; alternative forms of a gene.

allelopathy (uh-leel′-uh-path″-ee) An adaptation in which toxic substances secreted by roots or shed leaves inhibit the establishment of competing plants nearby.

allergen A substance that stimulates an allergic reaction.

allergy A hypersensitivity to some substance in the environment, manifested as hay fever, skin rash, asthma, food allergies, etc.

allometric growth Variation in the relative rates of growth for different parts of the body during development.

allopatric speciation (al-oh-pa′-trik) Speciation that occurs when one population becomes geographically separated from the rest of the species and subsequently evolves. Compare with *sympatric speciation.*

allopolyploid (al″-oh-pol′-ee-ployd) A polyploid whose chromosomes are derived from two species. Compare with *autopolyploid.*

all-or-none law The principle that neurons transmit an impulse in a similar way no matter how weak or strong the stimulus; the neuron either transmits an action potential (all) or does not (none).

allosteric regulators Substances that affect protein function by binding to allosteric sites.

allosteric site (al-oh-steer′-ik) A site on an enzyme other than the active site, to which a specific substance binds, thereby changing the shape and activity of the enzyme. Compare with *active site.*

alpha (α) helix A regular, coiled type of secondary structure of a polypeptide chain, maintained by hydrogen bonds. Compare with *beta (β)-pleated sheet.*

alpine tundra An ecosystem located in the higher elevations of mountains, above the tree line and below the snow line. Compare with *tundra.*

alternation of generations A type of life cycle characteristic of plants and a few algae and fungi in which they spend part of their life in a multicellular *n* gametophyte stage and part in a multicellular *2n* sporophyte stage.

alternative splicing A genetic mechanism in which exons are spliced in different ways to produce different mRNAs from a single gene.

altruistic behavior Behavior in which one individual helps another, seemingly at its own risk or expense.

alveolates Protists that have alveoli, flattened vesicles located just inside the plasma membrane; include the dinoflagellates, apicomplexans, and ciliates. See *chromalveolates.*

alveolus (al-vee′-o-lus) (pl., *alveoli*) (1) An air sac of the lung through which gas exchange with the blood takes place. (2) Saclike unit of some glands, e.g., mammary glands. (3) One of several flattened vesicles located just inside the plasma membrane in certain protists.

Alzheimer's disease (AD) A progressive, degenerative brain disorder characterized by amyloid plaques and neurofibrillary tangles.

amino acid (uh-mee′-no) An organic compound containing an amino group ($-NH_2$) and a carboxyl group ($-COOH$); may be joined by peptide bonds to form a polypeptide chain.

amino group A weakly basic functional group; abbreviated $-NH_2$.

aminoacyl-tRNA (uh-mee″-no-ace′-seel) Molecule consisting of an amino acid covalently linked to a transfer RNA.

aminoacyl-tRNA synthetase One of a family of enzymes, each responsible for covalently linking an amino acid to its specific transfer RNA.

ammonification (uh-moe″-nuh-fah-kay′-shun) The conversion of nitrogen-containing organic compounds to ammonia (NH_3) by certain soil bacteria (ammonifying bacteria); part of the nitrogen cycle.

amniocentesis (am″-nee-oh-sen-tee′-sis) Sampling of the amniotic fluid surrounding a fetus to obtain information about its development and genetic makeup. Compare with *chorionic villus sampling.*

amnion (am'-nee-on) In terrestrial vertebrates, an extraembryonic membrane that forms a fluid-filled sac for the protection of the developing embryo.

amniotes Terrestrial vertebrates: reptiles, birds, and mammals; animals whose embryos are enclosed by an amnion.

amoeba (a-mee'-ba) (pl., *amoebas*) A unicellular protist that moves by means of pseudopodia.

amphibians Members of vertebrate class that includes salamanders, frogs, and caecilians.

amphipathic molecule (am''-fih-pa'-thik) A molecule containing both hydrophobic and hydrophilic regions.

ampulla Any small, saclike extension, e.g., the expanded structure at the end of each semicircular canal of the ear.

amylase (am'-uh-laze) Starch-digesting enzyme, e.g., human salivary amylase or pancreatic amylase.

amyloplasts See *leukoplasts.*

anabolic steroids Synthetic androgens that increase muscle mass, physical strength, endurance, and aggressiveness but cause serious side effects; these drugs are often abused.

anabolism (an-ab'-oh-lizm) The aspect of metabolism in which simpler substances are combined to form more complex substances, resulting in the storage of energy, the production of new cell materials, and growth. Compare with *catabolism.*

anaerobe Organism that can grow or metabolize in the absence of molecular oxygen. See *facultative anaerobe* and *obligate anaerobe.* Compare with *aerobe.*

anaerobic (an''-air-oh'-bik) Growing or metabolizing in the absence of molecular oxygen. Compare with *aerobic.*

anaerobic respiration See *respiration.*

anaphase (an'uh-faze) Stage of mitosis in which the chromosomes move to opposite poles of the cell; anaphase occurs after metaphase and before telophase.

anaphylaxis (an''-uh-fih-lak'-sis) An acute allergic reaction following sensitization to a foreign substance or other substance.

ancestral characters See *shared ancestral characters.*

androgen (an'-dro-jen) Any substance that has masculinizing properties, such as a sex hormone. See *testosterone.*

androgen-binding protein (ABP) A protein produced by Sertoli cells in the testes; binds and concentrates testosterone.

anemia (uh-nee'-mee-uh) A deficiency of hemoglobin or red blood cells.

aneuploidy (an'-you-ploy-dee) Any chromosomal aberration in which there are either extra or missing copies of certain chromosomes.

angiosperms (an'-jee-oh-spermz'') The traditional name for flowering plants, a very large (more than 300,000 species), diverse phylum of plants that form flowers for sexual reproduction and produce seeds enclosed in fruits; include monocots and eudicots.

angiotensin I (an-jee-o-ten'-sin) A polypeptide produced by the action of renin on the plasma protein angiotensinogen.

angiotensin II A peptide hormone formed by the action of angiotensin-converting enzyme on angiotensin I; stimulates aldosterone secretion by the adrenal cortex.

animal pole The nonyolky, metabolically active pole of a vertebrate or echinoderm egg. Compare with *vegetal pole.*

anion (an'-eye-on) A particle with one or more units of negative charge, such as a chloride ion (Cl^-) or hydroxide ion (OH^-). Compare with *cation.*

anisogamy (an''-eye-sog'-uh-me) Sexual reproduction involving motile gametes of similar form but dissimilar size. Compare with *isogamy* and *oogamy.*

annelid (an'-eh-lid) A member of phylum Annelida; segmented worm such as the earthworm.

annual plant A plant that completes its entire life cycle in one year or less. Compare with *perennial* and *biennial.*

antenna complex The arrangement of chlorophyll, accessory pigments, and pigment-binding proteins into light-gathering units in the thylakoid membranes of photoautotrophic eukaryotes. See *reaction center* and *photosystem.*

antennae (sing., *antenna*) Sensory structures characteristic of some arthropod groups.

anterior Toward the head end of a bilaterally symmetrical animal. Compare with *posterior.*

anther (an'-thur) The part of the stamen in flowers that produces microspores and, ultimately, pollen grains.

antheridium (an''-thur-id'-ee-im) (pl., *antheridia*) In plants, the multicellular male gametangium (sex organ) that produces sperm cells. Compare with *archegonium.*

anthropoid (an'-thra-poid) A member of a suborder of primates that includes monkeys, apes, and humans.

antibody (an'-tee-bod''-ee) A specific protein (immunoglobulin) that recognizes and binds to specific antigens; produced by plasma cells.

antibody-mediated immunity A type of specific immune response in which B cells differentiate into plasma cells and produce antibodies that bind with foreign antigens, leading to the destruction of pathogens. Compare with *cell-mediated immunity.*

anticodon (an''-tee-koh'-don) A sequence of three nucleotides in transfer RNA that is complementary to, and combines with, the three-nucleotide codon.

antidiuretic hormone (ADH) (an''-ty-dy-uh-ret'-ik) A hormone secreted by the posterior lobe of the pituitary that controls the rate of water reabsorption by the kidney.

antigen (an'-tih-jen) Any molecule, usually a protein or large carbohydrate, that is specifically recognized as foreign by cells of the immune system.

antigen–antibody complex The combination of antigen and antibody molecules.

antigen-presenting cell (APC) A cell that displays foreign antigens as well as its own surface proteins. Dendritic cells, macrophages, and B cells are APCs.

antimicrobial peptides Soluble molecules that destroy pathogens.

anti-oncogene See *tumor suppressor gene.*

antioxidants Certain enzymes (e.g., catalase and peroxidase), vitamins, and other substances that destroy free radicals and other reactive molecules. Compare with *oxidants.*

antiparallel Said of a double-stranded nucleic acid in which the 5' to 3' direction of the sugar–phosphate backbone of one strand is reversed in the other strand.

anus (ay'nus) The distal end and outlet of the digestive tract.

aorta (ay-or'-tah) The largest and main systemic artery of the vertebrate body; arises from the left ventricle and branches to distribute blood to all parts of the body except the lungs.

aphotic region (ay-fote'-ik) The lower layer of the ocean (deeper than 100 m or so) where light does not penetrate.

apical dominance (ape'-ih-kl) The inhibition of lateral buds by a shoot tip.

apical meristem (mehr'-ih-stem) An area of dividing tissue, located at the tip of a shoot or root, that gives rise to primary tissues; apical meristems cause an increase in the length of the plant body. Compare with *lateral meristems.*

apicomplexans A group of parasitic protists that lack structures for locomotion and that produce sporozoites as infective agents; malaria is caused by an apicomplexan.

apoenzyme (ap″-oh-en′-zime) Protein portion of an enzyme; requires the presence of a specific coenzyme to become a complete functional enzyme.

apomixis (ap″-uh-mix′-us) A type of reproduction in which fruits and seeds are formed asexually.

apoplast A continuum consisting of the interconnected, porous plant cell walls, along which water moves freely. Compare with *symplast.*

apoptosis (ap-uh-toe′-sis) Programmed cell death; apoptosis is a normal part of an organism's development and maintenance. Compare with *necrosis.*

aposematic coloration The conspicuous coloring of a poisonous or distasteful organism that enables potential predators to easily see and recognize it. Also called *warning coloration.* Compare with *cryptic coloration.*

aquaporin One of a family of transport proteins located in the plasma membrane that facilitate the rapid movement of water molecules into or out of cells.

arachnids (ah-rack′-nidz) Eight-legged arthropods, such as spiders, scorpions, ticks, and mites.

arachnoid The middle of the three meningeal layers that cover and protect the brain and spinal cord; see *pia mater* and *dura mater.*

archaea (ar′-key-ah) Prokaryotic organisms with a number of features, such as the absence of peptidoglycan in their cell walls, that set them apart from the bacteria. Archaea is the name of one of the two prokaryotic domains. Compare with *bacteria.*

Archaean eon The period of Earth's history from its beginnings approximately 4.6 billion up to 2.5 billion years ago; life originated during the Archaean.

archaeplastids A monophyletic supergroup of eukaryotes with chloroplasts bounded by outer and inner membranes; include red algae, green algae, and land plants.

archegonium (ar′-ke-go′-nee-um) (pl., *archegonia*) In plants, the multicellular female gametangium (sex organ) that contains an egg. Compare with *antheridium.*

archenteron (ark-en′-ter-on) The central cavity of the gastrula stage of embryonic development that is lined with endoderm; primitive digestive system.

arctic tundra See *tundra.*

arterial pulse See *pulse, arterial.*

arteriole (ar-teer′-ee-ole) A very small artery. Vasoconstriction and vasodilation of arterioles help regulate blood pressure.

artery A thick-walled blood vessel that carries blood away from a heart chamber and toward the body organs. Compare with *vein.*

arthropod (ar′-throh-pod) An invertebrate that belongs to phylum Arthropoda; characterized by a hard exoskeleton; a segmented body; and paired, jointed appendages.

artificial insemination The impregnation of a female by artificially introducing sperm from a male.

artificial selection The selection by humans of traits that are desirable in plants or animals and breeding only those individuals that have the desired traits.

ascocarp (ass′-koh-karp) The fruiting body of an ascomycete.

ascomycete (ass″-koh-my′-seat) Member of a phylum of fungi characterized by the production of nonmotile asexual conidia and sexual ascospores.

ascospore (ass′-koh-spor) One of a set of sexual spores, usually eight, contained in a special spore case (an ascus) of an ascomycete.

ascus (ass′-kus) A saclike spore case in ascomycetes that contains sexual spores called *ascospores.*

asexual reproduction Reproduction in which there is no fusion of gametes and in which the genetic makeup of parent and of offspring is usually identical. Compare with *sexual reproduction.*

assimilation (of nitrogen) The conversion of inorganic nitrogen (nitrate, NO_3^-, or ammonia, NH_3) to the organic molecules of living things; part of the nitrogen cycle.

association areas Areas of the brain that link sensory and motor areas; responsible for thought, learning, memory, language abilities, judgment, and personality.

association neuron See *interneuron.*

assortative mating Sexual reproduction in which individuals pair nonrandomly, i.e., select mates on the basis of phenotype.

asters Clusters of microtubules radiating out from the poles in dividing cells that have centrioles.

astrocyte A type of glial cell; some are phagocytic; others regulate the composition of the extracellular fluid in the central nervous system.

atherosclerosis (ath″-ur-oh-skle-row′-sis) A progressive disease in which lipid deposits accumulate in the inner lining of arteries, leading eventually to impaired circulation and heart disease.

atom The smallest quantity of an element that retains the chemical properties of that element.

atomic mass The total number of protons and neutrons in an atom; expressed in atomic mass units or daltons.

atomic mass unit (amu) The approximate mass of a proton or neutron; also called a *dalton.*

atomic number The number of protons in the atomic nucleus of an atom, which uniquely identifies the element to which the atom corresponds.

ATP See *adenosine triphosphate.*

ATP synthase Large enzyme complex that catalyzes the formation of ATP from ADP and inorganic phosphate by chemiosmosis; located in the inner mitochondrial membrane, the thylakoid membrane of chloroplasts, and the plasma membrane of bacteria.

atrial natriuretic peptide (ANP) A hormone released by the atrium of the heart; helps regulate sodium excretion and lowers blood pressure.

atrioventricular (AV) node (ay″-tree-oh-ven-trik′-you-lur) Mass of specialized cardiac tissue that receives an impulse from the sinoatrial node (pacemaker) and conducts it to the ventricles.

atrioventricular (AV) valve (of the heart) A valve between each atrium and its ventricle that prevents backflow of blood. The right AV valve is the tricuspid valve; the left AV valve is the mitral valve.

atrium (of the heart) (ay′-tree-um) A heart chamber that receives blood from the veins.

australopithecines Early hominids that lived between about 6 mya and 1 mya, based on fossil evidence. Includes several species in three genera: *Ardipithecus, Australopithecus,* and *Paranthropus.*

autocrine regulation A type of regulation in which a signaling molecule (e.g., a hormone) is secreted into interstitial fluid and then acts on the cells that produce it. Compare with *paracrine regulation.*

autoimmune disease (aw″-toh-ih-mune′) A disease in which the body produces antibodies against its own cells or tissues. Also called *autoimmunity.*

autonomic nervous system (aw-tuh-nom′-ik) The portion of the peripheral nervous system that controls the visceral functions of the body, e.g., regulates smooth muscle, cardiac muscle, and glands. Its divisions are the sympathetic and parasympathetic nervous systems. Compare with *somatic nervous system.*

autopolyploid A polyploid whose chromosomes are derived from a single species. Compare with *allopolyploid*.

autoradiography Method for detecting radioactive decay; radiation causes the appearance of dark silver grains in special X-ray film.

autosome (aw′-toh-sohm) A chromosome other than the sex (X and Y) chromosomes.

autotroph (aw′-toh-trof) An organism that synthesizes complex organic compounds from simple inorganic raw materials; also called *producer* or *primary producer*. Compare with *heterotroph*. See *chemoautotroph* and *photoautotroph*.

auxin (awk′-sin) A plant hormone involved in various aspects of growth and development, such as stem elongation, apical dominance, and root formation on cuttings, e.g., indole acetic acid (IAA).

avirulence Properties that render an infectious agent nonlethal, i.e., unable to cause disease in its host. Compare with *virulence*.

Avogadro's number The number of units (6.02×10^{23}) present in one mole of any substance.

axillary bud A bud in the axil of a leaf. Compare with *terminal bud*.

axon (aks′-on) The long extension of the neuron that transmits nerve impulses away from the cell body. Compare with *dendrite*.

axopods (aks′-o-podz) Long, filamentous, cytoplasmic projections characteristic of actinopods.

B cell (B lymphocyte) The type of white blood cell responsible for antibody-mediated immunity. When stimulated, B cells differentiate to become plasma cells that produce antibodies. Compare with *T cell*.

bacillus (bah-sill′-us) (pl., *bacilli*) A rod-shaped bacterium. Compare with *coccus, spirillum, vibrio,* and *spirochete*.

background extinction The continuous, low-level extinction of species that has occurred throughout much of the history of life. Compare with *mass extinction*.

bacteria (bak-teer′-ee-ah) Prokaryotic organisms that have peptidoglycan in their cell walls; most are decomposers, but some are parasites and others are autotrophs. Bacteria is the name of one of the two prokaryotic domains. Compare with *archaea*.

bacterial artificial chromosome (BAC) Genetically engineered segments of chromosomal DNA with the ability to carry large segments of foreign DNA.

bacteriophage (bak-teer′-ee-oh-fayj) A virus that infects a bacterium (literally, "bacteria eater"). Also called *phage*.

balanced polymorphism (pol″-ee-mor′-fizm) The presence in a population of two or more genetic variants that are maintained in a stable frequency over several generations.

bark The outermost covering over woody stems and roots; consists of all plant tissues located outside the vascular cambium.

baroreceptors (bare″-oh-ree-sep′-torz) Receptors within certain blood vessels that are stimulated by changes in blood pressure.

Barr body A condensed and inactivated X chromosome appearing as a distinctive dense spot in the interphase nucleus of certain cells of female mammals.

basal angiosperms (bay′-sl) Three clades of angiosperms that are thought to be ancestral to all other flowering plants. Compare with *core angiosperms*.

basal body Structure involved in the organization and anchorage of a cilium or flagellum. Structurally similar to a centriole; each is in the form of a cylinder composed of nine triplets of microtubules $(9 \times 3 \text{ structure})$.

basal metabolic rate (BMR) The amount of energy expended by the body at resting conditions, when no food is being digested and no voluntary muscular work is being performed.

base (1) A substance that is a hydrogen ion (proton) acceptor; bases unite with acids to form salts. Compare with *acid*. (2) A nitrogenous base in a nucleotide or nucleic acid. See *purines* and *pyrimidines*.

basement membrane The thin, noncell layer of an epithelial membrane that attaches to the underlying tissues; consists of tiny fibers and polysaccharides produced by the epithelial cells.

base-pair substitution mutation A change in one base pair in DNA. See *missense mutation* and *nonsense mutation*.

basic solution A solution in which the concentration of hydroxide ions $[\text{OH}^-]$ exceeds the concentration of hydrogen ions $[\text{H}^+]$. A basic solution has pH greater than 7. Compare with *acidic solution* and *neutral solution*.

basidiocarp (ba-sid′-ee-o-karp) The fruiting body of a basidiomycete, e.g., a mushroom.

basidiomycete (ba-sid″-ee-o-my′-seat) Member of a phylum of fungi characterized by the production of sexual basidiospores.

basidiospore (ba-sid′-ee-o-spor) One of a set of sexual spores, usually four, borne on a basidium of a basidiomycete.

basidium (ba-sid′-ee-um) The clublike spore-producing organ of basidiomycetes that bears sexual spores called *basidiospores*.

basilar membrane The multicellular tissue in the inner ear that separates the cochlear duct from the tympanic canal; the sensory cells of the organ of Corti rest on this membrane.

Batesian mimicry (bate′-see-un mim′-ih-kree) The resemblance of a harmless or palatable species to one that is dangerous, unpalatable, or poisonous so that predators are more likely to avoid them. Compare with *Müllerian mimicry*.

behavioral ecology The scientific study of behavior in natural environments from the evolutionary perspective.

behavioral isolation A prezygotic reproductive isolating mechanism in which reproduction between similar species is prevented because each group exhibits its own characteristic courtship behavior; also called *sexual isolation*.

benthos (ben′-thos) Bottom-dwelling sea organisms that fix themselves to one spot, burrow into the sediment, or simply walk about on the ocean floor.

berry A simple, fleshy fruit in which the fruit wall is soft throughout, e.g., tomato, banana, grape.

beta (β) oxidation Process by which fatty acids are converted to acetyl CoA before entry into the citric acid cycle.

beta (β)-pleated sheet A regular, folded, sheetlike type of protein secondary structure, resulting from hydrogen bonding between two different polypeptide chains or two regions of the same polypeptide chain. Compare with *alpha (α) helix*.

biennial plant (by-en′-ee-ul) A plant that takes two years to complete its life cycle. Compare with *annual* and *perennial*.

bikonts One of two main clades of all eukaryotes that had a common ancestor with two flagella. Compare with *unikonts*.

bilateral symmetry A body shape with right and left halves that are approximately mirror images of each other. Compare with *radial symmetry*.

bile The fluid secreted by the liver; emulsifies fats.

binary fission (by′-nare-ee fish′-un) Equal division of a prokaryotic cell into two; a type of asexual reproduction.

binomial system of nomenclature (by-nome′-ee-ul) System of naming a species by the combination of the genus name and a specific epithet.

bioaccumulation The buildup of a persistent toxic substance, such as certain pesticides, in an organism's body.

biodiversity See *biological diversity*.

biofilm An irregular layer of microorganisms embedded in the slime they secrete and concentrated at a solid or liquid surface.

biogenic amines A class of neurotransmitters that includes norepinephrine, serotonin, and dopamine.

biogeochemical cycle (bye"-o-jee"-o-kem′-ee-kl) Process by which matter cycles from the living world to the nonliving, physical environment and back again, e.g., the carbon cycle, the nitrogen cycle, and the phosphorus cycle.

biogeography The study of the past and present geographic distributions of organisms.

bioinformatics The storage, retrieval, and comparison of biological information, particularly DNA or protein sequences within a given species and among different species.

biological clocks Mechanisms by which activities of organisms are adapted to regularly recurring changes in the environment. See *circadian rhythm.*

biological diversity The variety of living organisms considered at three levels: genetic diversity, species diversity, and ecosystem diversity. Also called *biodiversity.*

biological magnification The increased concentration of toxic chemicals, such as PCBs, heavy metals, and certain pesticides, in the tissues of organisms at higher trophic levels in food webs.

biological species concept See *species.*

biomass (bye′-o-mas) A quantitative estimate of the total mass, or amount, of living material in a particular ecosystem.

biome (by′-ohm) A large, relatively distinct terrestrial region characterized by a similar climate, soil, plants, and animals, regardless of where it occurs on Earth.

bioremediation A method to clean up a hazardous waste site that uses microorganisms to break down toxic pollutants, or plants to selectively accumulate toxins.

biosphere All of Earth's living organisms, collectively.

biotic factors Elements of the living world that affect a particular organism, i.e., its relationships with other organisms. Compare with *abiotic factors.*

biotic potential See *intrinsic rate of increase.*

bipedal Walking on two feet.

bipolar cell A type of neuron in the retina of the eye; receives input from the photoreceptors (rods and cones) and synapses on ganglion cells.

biramous appendages Appendages with two jointed branches at their ends; characteristic of crustaceans.

blade (1) The thin, expanded part of a leaf. (2) The flat, leaflike structure of certain multicellular algae.

blastocoel (blas′-toh-seel) The fluid-filled cavity of a blastula.

blastocyst The mammalian blastula. See *blastula.*

blastodisc A small disc of cytoplasm at the animal pole of a reptile or bird egg; cleavage is restricted to the blastodisc (meroblastic cleavage).

blastomere A cell of an early embryo.

blastopore (blas′-toh-pore) The primitive opening into the body cavity of an early embryo that may become the mouth (in protostomes) or anus (in deuterostomes) of the adult organism.

blastula (blas′-tew-lah) In animal development, a hollow ball of cells produced by cleavage of a fertilized ovum. In mammalian development, known as a *blastocyst.*

blood A fluid, circulating connective tissue that transports nutrients and other materials through the bodies of many types of animals.

blood pressure The force exerted by blood against the inner walls of the blood vessels.

bloom The sporadic occurrence of huge numbers of algae in freshwater and marine ecosystems.

body mass index (BMI) An index of weight in relation to height; calculated by dividing the square of the weight (square kilograms) by height (meters).

Bohr effect Increased oxyhemoglobin dissociation due to lowered pH; occurs as carbon dioxide concentration increases.

bolting The production of a tall flower stalk by a plant that grows vegetatively as a rosette (growth habit with a short stem and a circular cluster of leaves).

bond energy The energy required to break a particular chemical bond.

bone tissue Principal vertebrate skeletal tissue; a type of connective tissue.

boreal forest (bor′-ee-uhl) The northern coniferous forest biome found primarily in Canada, northern Europe, and Siberia; also called *taiga.*

bottleneck A sudden decrease in a population size caused by adverse environmental factors; may result in genetic drift; also called *genetic bottleneck* or *population bottleneck.*

bottom-up processes Control of ecosystem function by nutrient cycles and other parts of the abiotic environment. Compare with *top-down processes.*

Bowman's capsule A double-walled sac of cells that surrounds the glomerulus of each nephron.

brachiopods (bray′-kee-oh-podz) The phylum of solitary marine invertebrates having a pair of shells and, internally, a pair of coiled arms with ciliated tentacles; one of the lophophorate phyla.

brain A concentration of nervous tissue that controls neural function; in vertebrates, the anterior, enlarged portion of the central nervous system.

brain stem The part of the vertebrate brain that includes the medulla, pons, and midbrain.

branchial Pertaining to the gills or gill region.

brassinosteroid (BR) One of a group of steroids that function as plant hormones and are involved in several aspects of growth and development.

bronchiole (bronk′-ee-ole) Air duct in the lung that branches from a bronchus; divides to form air sacs (alveoli).

bronchus (bronk′-us) (pl., *bronchi*) One branch of the trachea and its immediate branches within the lung.

brown alga One of a group of predominantly marine algae that are multicellular and contain the pigments chlorophyll *a* and *c,* and carotenoids, including fucoxanthin.

bryophytes (bry′-oh-fites) Nonvascular plants including mosses, liverworts, and hornworts.

bryozoans Animals belonging to phylum Bryozoa, one of the three lophophorate phyla; form sessile colonies by asexual budding.

bud An undeveloped shoot that develops into flowers, stems, or leaves. Buds are enclosed in bud scales.

bud scale A modified leaf that covers and protects a dormant bud.

bud scale scar Scar on a twig left when a bud scale abscises from the terminal bud.

budding Asexual reproduction in which a small part of the parent's body separates from the rest and develops into a new individual; characteristic of yeasts and certain other organisms.

buffer A substance in a solution that tends to lessen the change in hydrogen ion concentration (pH) that otherwise would be produced by adding an acid or base.

bulb A globose, fleshy, underground bud that consists of a short stem with fleshy leaves, e.g., onion.

bundle scar Marks on a leaf scar left when vascular bundles of the petiole break during leaf abscission.

bundle sheath cells Tightly packed cells that form a sheath around the veins of a leaf.

bundle sheath extension Support cells that extend from the bundle sheath of a leaf vein toward the upper and/or lower epidermis.

buttress root A bracelike root at the base of certain trees that provides upright support.

C_3 plant Plant that carries out carbon fixation solely by the Calvin cycle. Compare with *C_4 plant* and *CAM plant*.

C_4 plant Plant that fixes carbon initially by a pathway in which the reaction of CO_2 with phosphoenolpyruvate is catalyzed by PEP carboxylase in leaf mesophyll cells; the products are transferred to the bundle sheath cells, where the Calvin cycle takes place. Compare with *C_3 plant* and *CAM plant*.

calcitonin (kal-sih-toh'-nin) A hormone secreted by the thyroid gland that rapidly lowers the calcium content in the blood.

callus (kal'-us) Undifferentiated tissue formed on an explant (excised tissue or organ) in plant tissue culture.

calmodulin A calcium-binding protein; when bound, it alters the activity of certain enzymes or transport proteins.

calorie The amount of heat energy required to raise the temperature of 1 g of water 1°C; equivalent to 4.184 joules. Compare with *kilocalorie*.

Calvin cycle Cyclic series of reactions in the chloroplast stroma in photosynthesis; fixes carbon dioxide and produces carbohydrate. See *C_3 plant*.

calyx (kay'-liks) The collective term for the sepals of a flower.

CAM plant Plant that carries out crassulacean acid metabolism; carbon is initially fixed into organic acids at night in the reaction of CO_2 and phosphoenolpyruvate, catalyzed by PEP carboxylase; during the day the acids break down to yield CO_2, which enters the Calvin cycle. Compare with *C_3 plant* and *C_4 plant*.

cambium See *lateral meristems*.

Cambrian Radiation A span of 40 million years, beginning about 542 mya, during which many new animal groups appeared in the fossil record.

cAMP See *cyclic AMP*.

cancer cells See *malignant cells*.

CAP See *catabolite activator protein*.

capillaries (kap'-i-lare-eez) Microscopic blood vessels in the tissues that permit exchange of materials between cells and blood.

capillary action The ability of water to move in small-diameter tubes as a consequence of its cohesive and adhesive properties.

capping See *mRNA cap*.

capsid Protein coat surrounding the nucleic acid of a virus.

capsule (1) The portion of the moss sporophyte that contains spores. (2) A simple, dry, dehiscent fruit that develops from two or more fused carpels and opens along many sutures or pores to release seeds. (3) A gelatinous coat that surrounds some bacteria.

carbohydrate Compound containing carbon, hydrogen, and oxygen, in the approximate ratio of C:2H:O, e.g., sugars, starch, and cellulose.

carbon cycle The worldwide circulation of carbon from the abiotic environment into living things and back into the abiotic environment.

carbon fixation reactions Reduction reactions of photosynthesis in which carbon from carbon dioxide becomes incorporated into organic molecules, leading to the production of carbohydrate. See *Calvin cycle*.

carbonyl group A polar functional group consisting of a carbon attached to an oxygen by a double bond; found in aldehydes and ketones.

carboxyl group A weakly acidic functional group; abbreviated —COOH.

carcinogen (kar-sin'-oh-jen) An agent that causes cancer or accelerates its development.

cardiac cycle One complete heartbeat.

cardiac muscle Involuntary, striated type of muscle found in the vertebrate heart. Compare with *smooth muscle* and *skeletal muscle*.

cardiac output The volume of blood pumped by the left ventricle into the aorta in 1 minute.

cardiovascular disease Disease of the heart or blood vessels; the leading cause of death in most industrial societies.

carnivore (kar'-ni-vor) An animal that feeds on other animals; flesh eater; also called *secondary* or *tertiary consumer*. Secondary consumers eat primary consumers (herbivores), whereas tertiary consumers eat secondary consumers.

carotenoids (ka-rot'-n-oidz) A group of yellow to orange plant pigments synthesized from isoprene subunits; include carotenes and xanthophylls.

carpel (kar'-pul) The female reproductive unit of a flower; carpels bear ovules. Compare with *pistil*.

carrier-mediated active transport Transport across a membrane of a substance from a region of low concentration to a region of high concentration; requires both a transport protein with a binding site for the specific substance and an energy source (often ATP).

carrier-mediated transport Any form of transport across a membrane that uses a membrane-bound transport protein with a binding site for a specific substance; includes both facilitated diffusion and carrier-mediated active transport.

carrying capacity (K) The largest population that a particular habitat can support and sustain for an indefinite period, assuming there are no changes in the environment.

cartilage A flexible skeletal tissue of vertebrates; a type of connective tissue.

caryopsis See *grain*.

Casparian strip (kas-pare'-ee-un) A band of waterproof material around the radial and transverse walls of endodermal root cells.

caspase Any of a group of proteolytic enzymes that are active in the early stages of apoptosis.

catabolism The aspect of metabolism in which complex substances are broken down to form simpler substances; catabolic reactions are particularly important in releasing chemical energy stored by the cell. Compare with *anabolism*.

catabolite activator protein (CAP) A positively acting regulator that becomes active when bound to cAMP; active CAP stimulates transcription of the *lac* operon and other operons that code for enzymes used in catabolic pathways.

catalyst (kat'-ah-list) A substance that increases the speed at which a chemical reaction occurs without being used up in the reaction. Enzymes are biological catalysts.

catecholamine (cat"-eh-kole'-ah-meen) A class of compounds including dopamine, epinephrine, and norepinephrine; these compounds serve as neurotransmitters and hormones.

cation A particle with one or more units of positive charge, such as a hydrogen ion (H^+) or calcium ion (Ca^{2+}). Compare with *anion*.

CD4 T cell See *T helper cell*.

CD8 T cell See *T cytotoxic cell*.

cDNA library A collection of recombinant plasmids that contain complementary DNA (cDNA) copies of mRNA templates. The cDNA, which lacks introns, is synthesized by reverse transcriptase. Compare with *genomic DNA library*.

cell The basic structural and functional unit of life, which consists of living material enclosed by a membrane.

cell cycle Cyclic series of events in the life of a dividing eukaryotic cell; consists of mitosis, cytokinesis, and the stages of interphase.

cell determination See *determination*.

cell differentiation See *differentiation*.

cell fractionation The technique used to separate the components of cells by subjecting them to centrifugal force. See *differential centrifugation* and *density gradient centrifugation*.

cell plate The structure that forms during cytokinesis in plants, separating the two daughter cells produced by mitosis.

cell signaling Mechanisms of communication between cells. Cells signal one another with secreted signaling molecules, or a signaling molecule on one cell combines with a receptor on another cell. See *signal transduction*.

cell theory The scientific theory that the cell is the basic unit of life, of which all living things are composed, and that all cells are derived from pre-existing cells.

cell wall The structure outside the plasma membrane of certain cells; may contain cellulose (plant cells), chitin (most fungal cells), peptidoglycan and/or lipopolysaccharide (most bacterial cells), or other material.

cell-cycle control system Regulatory molecules that control key events in the cell cycle; common to all eukaryotes.

cell-mediated immunity A type of specific immune response carried out by T cells. Compare with *antibody-mediated immunity*.

cellular respiration See *respiration*.

cellular slime mold A group of funguslike protists whose feeding stage consists of unicellular, amoeboid organisms that aggregate to form a pseudoplasmodium during reproduction.

cellulose (sel'-yoo-lohs) A structural polysaccharide consisting of beta glucose subunits; the main constituent of plant primary cell walls.

Cenozoic era A geologic era that began about 66 million years ago and extends to the present.

center of origin The geographic area where a given species originated.

central nervous system (CNS) In vertebrates, the brain and spinal cord. Compare with *peripheral nervous system*.

centrifuge A device used to separate cells or their components by subjecting them to centrifugal force.

centriole (sen'-tree-ohl) One of a pair of small, cylindrical organelles lying at right angles to each other near the nucleus in the cytoplasm of animal cells and certain protist and plant cells; each centriole is in the form of a cylinder composed of nine triplets of microtubules (9×3 structure).

centromere (sen'-tro-meer) A specialized constricted region of a chromatid; contains the kinetochore. In cells at prophase and metaphase, sister chromatids are joined in the vicinity of their centromeres.

centrosome (sen'-tro-sowm) An organelle in animal cells that is the main microtubule-organizing center; typically contains a pair of centrioles and is important in cell division.

cephalization The evolution of a head; the concentration of nervous tissue and sense organs at the front end of the animal.

cephalochordates Members of the chordate subphylum that includes the lancelets.

cerebellum (ser-eh-bel'-um) A convoluted subdivision of the vertebrate brain concerned with coordination of muscular movements, muscle tone, and balance.

cerebral cortex (ser-ee'-brul kor'-teks) The outer layer of the cerebrum composed of gray matter and consisting mainly of nerve cell bodies.

cerebrospinal fluid (CSF) The fluid that bathes the central nervous system of vertebrates.

cerebrum (ser-ee'-brum) A large, convoluted subdivision of the vertebrate brain; in humans, it functions as the center for learning, voluntary movement, and interpretation of sensation.

chaparral (shap"-uh-ral') A biome with a Mediterranean climate (mild, moist winters and hot, dry summers). Chaparral vegetation is characterized by drought-resistant, small-leaved evergreen shrubs and small trees.

chaperones See *molecular chaperones*.

character displacement The tendency for two similar species to diverge (become more different) in areas where their ranges overlap; reduces interspecific competition.

Chargaff's rules A relationship in DNA molecules based on nucleotide composition data; the number of adenines equals the number of thymines, and the number of guanines equals the number of cytosines.

chelicerae (keh-lis'-er-ee) The first pair of appendages in certain arthropods; clawlike appendages located immediately anterior to the mouth and used to manipulate food into the mouth.

chemical bond A force of attraction between atoms in a compound. See *covalent bond*, *hydrogen bond*, and *ionic bond*.

chemical compound Two or more elements combined in a fixed ratio.

chemical evolution The origin of life from nonliving matter.

chemical formula A representation of the composition of a compound; the elements are indicated by chemical symbols with subscripts to indicate their ratios. See *molecular formula*, *structural formula*, and *simplest formula*.

chemical symbol The abbreviation for an element; usually the first letter (or first and second letters) of the English or Latin name.

chemiosmosis Process by which phosphorylation of ADP to form ATP is coupled to the transfer of electrons down an electron transport chain; the electron transport chain powers proton pumps that produce a proton gradient across the membrane; ATP is formed as protons diffuse through transmembrane channels in ATP synthase.

chemoautotroph (kee"-moh-aw'-toh-trof) Organism that obtains energy from inorganic compounds and synthesizes organic compounds from inorganic raw materials; includes some bacteria and many archaea. Compare with *photoautotroph*, *photoheterotroph*, and *chemoheterotroph*.

chemoheterotroph (kee"-moh-het'-ur-oh-trof) Organism that uses organic compounds as a source of energy and carbon; includes animals, fungi, many bacteria, and a few archaea. Compare with *photoautotroph*, *photoheterotroph*, and *chemoautotroph*.

chemoreceptor (kee"-moh-ree-sep'-tor) A sensory receptor that responds to chemical stimuli.

chemotroph (kee'-moh-trof) Organism that uses organic compounds or inorganic substances, such as iron, nitrate, ammonia, or sulfur, as sources of energy. Compare with *phototroph*. See *chemoautotroph* and *chemoheterotroph*.

chiasma (ky-az'-muh) (pl., *chiasmata*) An X-shaped site in a tetrad usually marking the location where homologous (nonsister) chromatids previously crossed over.

chimera (ky-meer'-uh) An organism consisting of two or more kinds of genetically dissimilar cells.

chitin (ky'-tin) A nitrogen-containing structural polysaccharide that forms the exoskeleton of insects and the cell walls of many fungi.

chlorophyll (klor'-oh-fil) A group of light-trapping green pigments found in most photosynthetic organisms.

chlorophyll-binding proteins About 15 different proteins associated with chlorophyll molecules in the thylakoid membrane.

chloroplasts (klor'-oh-plastz) Membranous organelles that are the sites of photosynthesis in eukaryotes; occur in some plant and algal cells.

cholinergic neuron (kohl"-in-air'-jik) A neuron that releases acetylcholine as a neurotransmitter. Compare with *adrenergic neuron.*

chondrichthyes (kon-drik'-thees) The class of cartilaginous fishes that includes the sharks, rays, and skates.

chondrocytes Cartilage cells.

chordates (kor'-dates) Deuterostome animals that, at some time in their lives, have a cartilaginous, dorsal skeletal structure called a *notochord;* a dorsal, tubular, nerve cord; pharyngeal gill grooves; a postanal tail; and an endostyle (or its derivative, a thyroid gland).

chorion (kor-'ee-on) An extraembryonic membrane in reptiles, birds, and mammals that forms an outer cover around the embryo, and in mammals contributes to the formation of the placenta.

chorionic villus sampling (CVS) (kor"ee-on'ik) Study of extraembryonic cells that are genetically identical to the cells of an embryo, making it possible to assess its genetic makeup. Compare with *amniocentesis.*

choroid layer A layer of cells filled with black pigment that absorbs light and prevents reflected light from blurring the image that falls on the retina; the layer of the eyeball outside the retina.

chromalveolates A supergroup composed of diverse protists with few shared characters; most are photosynthetic, and heterotrophic chromalveolates, such as the water molds and ciliates, probably descended from autotrophic ancestors. Divided into two main groups, alveolates and stramenopiles.

chromatid (kroh'-mah-tid) One of the two identical halves of a duplicated chromosome; the two chromatids that make up a chromosome are referred to as *sister chromatids.*

chromatin (kro'-mah-tin) The complex of DNA and protein that makes up eukaryotic chromosomes.

chromoplasts Pigment-containing plastids; found mainly in flowers and fruits.

chromosome theory of inheritance A basic principle in biology that states that inheritance can be explained by assuming that genes are linearly arranged in specific locations along the chromosomes.

chromosomes Structures in the cell nucleus that consist of chromatin and contain the genes. The chromosomes become visible under the microscope as distinct structures during cell division.

chylomicrons (kie-low-my'-kronz) Protein-covered fat droplets produced in the intestinal cells; they enter the lymphatic system and are transported to the blood.

chytrid See *chytridiomycete.*

chytridiomycete (ki-trid"-ee-o-my'-seat) A member of a phylum of fungi characterized by the production of flagellate cells at some stage in their life history. Also called *chytrid.*

ciliate (sil'-e-ate) A unicellular protist covered by many short cilia.

cilium (sil'-ee-um) (pl., *cilia*) One of many short, hairlike structures that project from the surface of some eukaryotic cells and are used for locomotion or movement of materials across the cell surface.

circadian rhythm (sir-kay'-dee-un) An internal rhythm that approximates the 24-hour day. See *biological clocks.*

circulatory system The body system that functions in internal transport and protects the body from disease.

cisternae (sing., *cisterna*) Stacks of flattened membranous sacs that make up the Golgi complex.

citrate (citric acid) A six-carbon organic acid.

citric acid cycle Series of chemical reactions in aerobic respiration in which acetyl coenzyme A is completely degraded to carbon dioxide and water with the release of metabolic energy that is used to produce ATP; also known as the *Krebs cycle* and the *tricarboxylic acid (TCA) cycle.*

clade A group of organisms containing a common ancestor and all its descendants; a monophyletic group.

cladistics An approach to classification based on recency of common ancestry rather than degree of structural similarity. Also called *phylogenetic systematics.* Compare with *phenetics* and *evolutionary systematics.*

cladogram A branching diagram that illustrates taxonomic relationships based on the principles of cladistics.

class A taxonomic category made up of related orders.

classical conditioning A type of learning in which an association is formed between some normal response to a stimulus and a new stimulus, after which the new stimulus elicits the response.

cleavage furrow A constricted region of the cytoplasm that forms and progressively deepens during cytokinesis of animal cells, thereby separating the two daughter cells.

cleavage Series of mitotic cell divisions, without growth, that converts the zygote to a multicellular blastula.

cline Gradual change in phenotype and genotype frequencies among contiguous populations that is the result of an environmental gradient.

clitoris (klit'-o-ris) A small, erectile structure at the anterior part of the vulva in female mammals; homologous to the male penis.

cloaca (klow-a'-ka) An exit chamber in some animals that receives digestive wastes and urine; may also serve as an exit for gametes.

clonal expansion The increase in number of T cells or B cells specific for an antigen; occurs when specific T cells or B cells are activated by the antigen.

clonal selection Lymphocyte activation in which a specific antigen causes activation, cell division, and differentiation only in cells that express receptors with which the antigen binds.

clone (1) A population of cells descended by mitotic division from a single ancestral cell. (2) A population of genetically identical organisms asexually propagated from a single individual. Also see *DNA cloning.*

cloning The process of forming a clone.

closed circulatory system A type of circulatory system in which the blood flows through a continuous circuit of blood vessels; characteristic of annelids, cephalopods, and vertebrates. Compare with *open circulatory system.*

closed system An entity that does not exchange energy with its surroundings. Compare with *open system.*

club mosses A phylum of seedless vascular plants with a life cycle similar to that of ferns.

clumped dispersion The spatial distribution pattern of a population in which individuals are more concentrated in specific parts of the habitat. Also called *aggregated distribution* and *patchiness.* Compare with *random dispersion* and *uniform dispersion.*

cnidarians (ni-dah'-ree-anz) Phylum of animals that have stinging cells called *cnidocytes,* two tissue layers, and radial symmetry; include hydras and jellyfish.

cnidocytes Stinging cells characteristic of cnidarians.

coated pit A depression in the plasma membrane, the cytosolic side of which is coated with the protein clathrin; important in receptor-mediated endocytosis.

coccus (kok'-us) (pl., *cocci*) A bacterium with a spherical shape. Compare with *bacillus, spirillum, vibrio,* and *spirochete.*

cochlea (koke'-lee-ah) The structure of the inner ear of mammals that contains the auditory receptors (organ of Corti).

codominance (koh"-dom'-in-ants) Condition in which two alleles of a locus are expressed in a heterozygote.

codon (koh'-don) A triplet of mRNA nucleotides. The 64 possible codons collectively constitute a universal genetic code in which each codon specifies an amino acid in a polypeptide, or a signal to either start or terminate polypeptide synthesis.

coelacanths A genus of lobe-finned fishes that has survived to the present day.

coelom (see'lum) The main body cavity of most animals; a true coelom is lined with mesoderm. Compare with *pseudocoelom*.

coelomate (seel'-oh-mate) Animal that has a true coelom. Compare with *acoelomate* and *pseudocoelomate*.

coenocyte (see'-no-site) An organism consisting of a multinucleate cell, i.e., the nuclei are not separated from one another by septa.

coenzyme (koh-en'-zime) An organic cofactor for an enzyme; generally participates in the reaction by transferring some component, such as electrons or part of a substrate molecule.

coenzyme A (CoA) Organic cofactor responsible for transferring groups derived from organic acids.

coevolution The reciprocal adaptation of two or more species that occurs as a result of their close interactions over a long period.

cofactor A nonprotein substance needed by an enzyme for normal activity; some cofactors are inorganic (usually metal ions); others are organic (coenzymes).

cohesion The property of sticking together. Compare with *adhesion*.

cohort A group of individuals of the same age.

colchicine A drug that blocks the division of eukaryotic cells by binding to tubulin subunits, which make up the microtubules, the major component of the mitotic spindle.

coleoptile (kol-ee-op'-tile) A protective sheath that encloses the young stem in certain monocots.

collagens (kol'-ah-gen) Proteins found in the collagen fibers of connective tissues.

collecting duct A tube in the kidney that receives filtrate from several nephrons and conducts it to the renal pelvis.

collenchyma (kol-en'-kih-mah) Living cells with moderately but unevenly thickened primary cell walls; collenchyma cells help support the herbaceous plant body.

colony An association of loosely connected cells or individuals of the same species.

commensalism (kuh-men'-sul-izm) A type of symbiosis in which one organism benefits and the other one is neither harmed nor helped. Compare with *mutualism* and *parasitism*.

commercial harvest The collection of commercially important organisms from the wild. Examples include the commercial harvest of parrots (for the pet trade) and cacti (for houseplants).

community An association of populations of different species living together in a defined habitat with some degree of interdependence. Compare with *ecosystem*.

community ecology The description and analysis of patterns and processes within the community.

compact bone Dense, hard bone tissue found mainly near the surfaces of a bone.

companion cell A cell in the phloem of flowering plants that governs loading and unloading sugar into the sieve tube element for translocation.

compass sense The sense of direction an animal requires to travel in a straight line toward a destination.

competition The interaction among two or more individuals that attempt to use the same essential resource, such as food, water, sunlight, or living space. See *interspecific* and *intraspecific competition*. See *interference* and *exploitation competition*.

competitive exclusion principle The concept that no two species with identical living requirements can occupy the same ecological niche indefinitely.

competitive inhibitor A substance that binds to the active site of an enzyme, thus lowering the rate of the reaction catalyzed by the enzyme. Compare with *noncompetitive inhibitor*.

complement A group of proteins in blood and other body fluids that are activated by an antigen–antibody complex and then destroy pathogens.

complementary DNA (cDNA) DNA synthesized by reverse transcriptase, using RNA as a template.

complete flower A flower that has all four parts: sepals, petals, stamens, and carpels. Compare with *incomplete flower*.

compound eye An eye, such as that of an insect, consisting of many light-sensitive units called *ommatidia*.

concentration gradient A difference in the concentration of a substance from one point to another, as for example, across a cell membrane.

condensation synthesis A reaction in which two monomers are combined covalently through the removal of the equivalent of a water molecule. Compare with *hydrolysis*.

cone (1) In botany, a reproductive structure in many gymnosperms that produces either microspores or megaspores. (2) In zoology, one of the conical photoreceptive cells of the retina that is particularly sensitive to bright light and, by distinguishing light of various wavelengths, mediates color vision. Compare with *rod*.

conidiophore (kah-nid'-e-o-for") A specialized hypha that bears conidia.

conidium (kah-nid'-e-um) (pl., *conidia*) An asexual spore that is usually formed at the tip of a specialized hypha called a *conidiophore*.

conifer (kon'-ih-fur) Any of a large phylum of gymnosperms that are woody trees and shrubs with needlelike, mostly evergreen leaves and with seeds in cones.

conjugation (kon"-jew-gay'-shun) (1) A sexual process in ciliate protists that involves exchange of haploid nuclei with another cell. (2) A mechanism for DNA exchange in bacteria that involves cell-to-cell contact.

connective tissue Animal tissue consisting mostly of an intercellular substance (fibers scattered through a matrix) in which the cells are embedded, e.g., bone.

conservation biology A multidisciplinary science that focuses on the study of how humans impact organisms and on the development of ways to protect biological diversity.

constitutive gene A gene that is constantly transcribed.

consumer See *heterotroph*.

consumption overpopulation A situation in which each individual in a human population consumes too large a share of resources; results in pollution, environmental degradation, and resource depletion. Compare with *people overpopulation*.

contest competition See *interference competition*.

continental drift The scientific theory that continents were once joined and later split and drifted apart.

contraception Any method used to intentionally prevent pregnancy.

contractile root (kun-trak'-til) A specialized type of root that contracts and pulls a bulb or corm deeper into the soil.

contractile vacuole A membrane-enclosed organelle found in certain freshwater protists, such as *Paramecium*; appears to have an osmoregulatory function.

control group In a scientific experiment, a group in which the experimental variable is kept constant. The control provides a standard of comparison used to verify the results of the experiment.

controlled mating A mating in which the genotypes of the parents are known.

convergent circuit (kun-vur'-jent) A neural pathway in which a postsynaptic neuron is controlled by signals coming from two or more presynaptic neurons. Compare with *divergent circuit.*

convergent evolution (kun-vur'-jent) The independent evolution of structural or functional similarity in two or more distantly related species, usually as a result of adaptations to similar environments.

copy number variations (CNVs) Genetic variation among individuals in a population as measured by segments of DNA that have been gained or lost, compared to a reference genome.

core angiosperms The clade to which most angiosperm species belong. Core angiosperms are divided into three subclades: magnoliids, monocots, and eudicots. Compare with *basal angiosperms.*

corepressor Substance that binds to a repressor protein, converting it to its active form, which is capable of preventing transcription.

Coriolis effect (kor"-e-o'-lis) The tendency of moving air or water to be deflected from its path to the right in the Northern Hemisphere and to the left in the Southern Hemisphere. Caused by the direction of Earth's rotation.

cork cambium (kam'-bee-um) A lateral meristem that produces cork cells and cork parenchyma; cork cambium and the tissues it produces make up the outer bark of a woody plant. Compare with *vascular cambium.*

cork cell A cell in the bark that is produced outwardly by the cork cambium; cork cells are dead at maturity and function for protection and reduction of water loss.

cork parenchyma (par-en'-kih-mah) One or more layers of parenchyma cells produced inwardly by the cork cambium.

corm A short, thickened underground stem specialized for food storage and asexual reproduction, e.g., crocus, gladiolus.

cornea (kor'-nee-ah) The transparent covering of an eye.

corolla (kor-ohl'-ah) Collectively, the petals of a flower.

corpus callosum (kah-loh'-sum) In mammals, a large bundle of nerve fibers interconnecting the two cerebral hemispheres.

corpus luteum (loo'-tee"-um) The temporary endocrine tissue in the ovary that develops from the ruptured follicle after ovulation; secretes progesterone and estrogen.

cortex (kor'-teks) (1) The outer part of an organ, such as the cortex of the kidney. Compare with *medulla.* (2) The tissue between the epidermis and vascular tissue in the stems and roots of many herbaceous plants.

cortical reaction Process occurring after fertilization that prevents additional sperm from entering the egg; also known as the "slow block to polyspermy."

cortisol A steroid hormone, secreted by the adrenal cortex, that helps the body adjust to long-term stress; stimulates conversion of other nutrients to glucose in the liver, resulting in increased blood glucose concentration.

cosmid cloning vector A cloning vector with features of both bacteriophages and plasmids and with the ability to carry large segments of foreign DNA.

cosmopolitan species Species that have a nearly worldwide distribution and occur on more than one continent or throughout much of the ocean. Compare with *endemic species.*

cotransport The active transport of a substance from a region of low concentration to a region of high concentration by coupling its transport to the transport of a substance down its concentration gradient.

cotyledon (kot"-uh-lee'-dun) The seed leaf of a plant embryo, which may contain food stored for germination.

cotylosaurs The first reptiles; also known as *stem reptiles.*

countercurrent exchange system A biological mechanism that enables maximum exchange between two fluids. The two fluids must be flowing in opposite directions and have a concentration gradient between them.

coupled reactions A set of reactions in which an exergonic reaction provides the free energy required to drive an endergonic reaction; energy coupling generally occurs through a common intermediate.

covalent bond The chemical bond involving shared pairs of electrons; may be single, double, or triple (with one, two, or three shared pairs of electrons, respectively). Compare with *ionic bond* and *hydrogen bond.*

covalent compound A compound in which atoms are held together by covalent bonds; covalent compounds consist of molecules. Compare with *ionic compound.*

cranial nerves The 10 to 12 pairs of nerves in vertebrates that emerge directly from the brain.

cranium The bony framework that protects the brain in vertebrates.

crassulacean acid metabolism See *CAM plant.*

creatine phosphate An energy-storing compound in muscle cells.

cretinism (kree'-tin-izm) A chronic condition caused by lack of thyroid secretion during fetal development and early childhood; results in retarded physical and mental development if untreated.

cri du chat syndrome A human genetic disease caused by losing part of the short arm of chromosome 5 and characterized by mental retardation, a cry that sounds like a kitten mewing, and death in infancy or childhood.

cristae (kris'-tee) (sing., *crista*) Shelflike or fingerlike inward projections of the inner membrane of a mitochondrion.

Cro-Magnons Prehistoric humans (*Homo sapiens*) with modern features (tall, erect, lacking a heavy brow) who lived in Europe some 30,000 years ago.

cross bridges The connections between myosin and actin filaments in muscle fibers; formed by the binding of myosin heads to active sites on actin filaments.

crossing-over A process in which genetic material (DNA) is exchanged between paired, homologous chromosomes.

cryptic coloration Colors or markings that help some organisms hide from predators by blending into their physical surroundings. Compare with *aposematic coloration.*

cryptochrome A proteinaceous pigment that strongly absorbs blue light; implicated in resetting the biological clock in plants, fruit flies, and mice.

ctenophores (ten'-oh-forz) Phylum of marine animals (comb jellies) whose bodies consist of two layers of cells enclosing a gelatinous mass. The outer surface is covered with comblike rows of cilia, by which the animal moves.

cuticle (kew'-tih-kl) (1) A noncell, waxy covering over the epidermis of the aerial parts of plants that reduces water loss. (2) The outer covering of some animals, such as roundworms.

cyanobacteria (sy-an"-oh-bak-teer'-ee-uh) Prokaryotic photosynthetic microorganisms that possess chlorophyll and produce oxygen during photosynthesis.

cycad (sih'-kad) Any of a phylum of gymnosperms that live mainly in tropical and semitropical regions and have stout stems (to 20 m in height) and fernlike leaves.

cyclic AMP (cAMP) A form of adenosine monophosphate in which the phosphate is part of a ring-shaped structure; acts as a regulatory molecule and second messenger in organisms ranging from bacteria to humans.

cyclic electron transport In photosynthesis, the cyclic flow of electrons through photosystem I; ATP is formed by chemiosmosis, but no photolysis of water occurs, and O_2 and NADPH are not produced. Compare with *noncyclic electron transport*.

cyclin-dependent kinases (Cdks) Protein kinases involved in controlling the cell cycle.

cyclins Regulatory proteins whose levels oscillate during the cell cycle; activate cyclin-dependent kinases.

cystic fibrosis A genetic disease with an autosomal recessive inheritance pattern; characterized by secretion of abnormally thick mucus, particularly in the respiratory and digestive systems.

cytochromes (sy'-toh-krohmz) Iron-containing heme proteins of an electron transport system.

cytokines Signaling proteins that regulate interactions between cells in the immune system. Important groups include interferons, interleukins, tumor necrosis factors, and chemokines.

cytokinesis (sy"-toh-kih-nee'-sis) Stage of cell division in which the cytoplasm divides to form two daughter cells.

cytokinin (sy"-toh-ky'-nin) A plant hormone involved in various aspects of plant growth and development, such as cell division and delay of senescence.

cytoplasm The plasma membrane and cell contents with the exception of the nucleus.

cytosine A nitrogenous pyrimidine base that is a component of nucleic acids.

cytoskeleton The dynamic internal network of protein fibers that includes microfilaments, intermediate filaments, and microtubules.

cytosol The fluid component of the cytoplasm in which the organelles are suspended.

cytotoxic T cell See *T cytotoxic cell*.

dalton See *atomic mass unit (amu)*.

day-neutral plant A plant whose flowering is not controlled by variations in day length that occur with changing seasons. Compare with *long-day, short-day,* and *intermediate-day plants*.

deamination (dee-am-ih-nay'-shun) The removal of an amino group ($—NH_2$) from an amino acid or other organic compound.

decarboxylation A reaction in which a molecule of CO_2 is removed from a carboxyl group of an organic acid.

deciduous A term describing a plant that sheds leaves or other structures at regular intervals, e.g., during autumn. Compare with *evergreen*.

declarative memory Factual knowledge of people, places, or objects; requires conscious recall of the information.

decomposers Microbial heterotrophs that break down dead organic material and use the decomposition products as a source of energy. Also called *saprotrophs* or *saprobes*.

deductive reasoning The reasoning that operates from generalities to specifics and can make relationships among data more apparent. Compare with *inductive reasoning*. See *hypothetico-deductive approach*.

deforestation The temporary or permanent removal of forest for agriculture or other uses.

dehydrogenation (dee-hy"-dro-jen-ay'-shun) A form of oxidation in which hydrogen atoms are removed from a molecule.

deletion (1) A chromosome abnormality in which part of a chromosome is missing, e.g., cri du chat syndrome. (2) The loss of one or more base pairs from DNA, which can result in a frameshift mutation.

demographics The science that deals with human population statistics, such as size, density, and distribution.

denature (dee-nay'-ture) To alter the physical properties and three-dimensional structure of a protein, nucleic acid, or other macromolecule by treating it with excess heat, strong acids, or strong bases.

dendrite (den'-drite) A branch of a neuron that receives and conducts nerve impulses toward the cell body. Compare with *axon*.

dendritic cells A set of immune cells present in many tissues that capture antigens and present them to T cells.

dendrochronology (den"-dro-kruh-naal'-uh-gee) A method of dating that uses the annual rings of trees.

denitrification (dee-nie"-tra-fuh-kay'-shun) The conversion of nitrate (NO_3^-) to nitrogen gas (N_2) by certain bacteria (denitrifying bacteria) in the soil; part of the nitrogen cycle.

dense connective tissue A type of tissue that may be irregular, as in the dermis of the skin, or regular, as in tendons.

density gradient centrifugation Procedure in which cell components are placed in a layer on top of a density gradient, usually a sucrose solution and water. Cell structures migrate during centrifugation, forming a band at the position in the gradient where their own density equals that of the sucrose solution.

density-dependent factor An environmental factor whose effects on a population change as population density changes; tends to retard population growth as population density increases and enhance population growth as population density decreases. Compare with *density-independent factor*.

density-independent factor An environmental factor that affects the size of a population but is not influenced by changes in population density. Compare with *density-dependent factor*.

deoxyribonucleic acid (DNA) Double-stranded nucleic acid; contains genetic information coded in specific sequences of its constituent nucleotides.

deoxyribose Pentose sugar lacking a hydroxyl ($—OH$) group on carbon-2'; a constituent of DNA.

depolarization (dee-pol"-ar-ih-zay'-shun) A decrease in the charge difference across a plasma membrane; may result in an action potential in a neuron or muscle cell.

derived characters See *shared derived characters*.

dermal tissue system The tissue that forms the outer covering over a plant; the epidermis or periderm.

dermis (dur'-mis) The layer of dense connective tissue beneath the epidermis in the skin of vertebrates.

desert A temperate or tropical biome in which lack of precipitation limits plant growth.

desertification The degradation of once-fertile land into nonproductive desert; caused partly by soil erosion, deforestation, and overgrazing by domestic animals.

desmosomes (dez'-moh-sohmz) Buttonlike plaques, present on two opposing cell surfaces, that hold the cells together by means of protein filaments that span the intercellular space.

determinate growth Growth of limited duration, as for example, in flowers and leaves. Compare with *indeterminate growth*.

determination The developmental process by which one or more cells become progressively committed to a particular fate. Determination is a series of molecular events usually leading to differentiation. Also called *cell determination*.

detritivore (duh-try'-tuh-vore) An organism, such as an earthworm or crab, that consumes fragments of freshly dead or decomposing organisms; also called *detritus feeder*.

detritus (duh-try'-tus) Organic debris from decomposing organisms.

detritus feeder See *detritivore*.

deuteromycetes (doo"-ter-o-my'-seats) An artificial grouping of fungi characterized by the absence of sexual reproduction but usually having other traits similar to ascomycetes; also called *imperfect fungi*.

deuterostome (doo′-ter-oh-stome) Major division of the animal kingdom in which the anus develops from the blastopore; includes the echinoderms and chordates. Compare with *protostome.*

development All the progressive changes that take place throughout the life of an organism.

diabetes mellitus (mel′-i-tus) The most common endocrine disorder. In type 1 diabetes, there is a marked decrease in the number of beta cells in the pancreas, resulting in insulin deficiency. In the more common type 2 diabetes, insulin receptors on target cells do not bind with insulin (insulin resistance).

diacylglycerol (DAG) (di″-as-il-glis′-er-ol) A lipid consisting of glycerol combined chemically with two fatty acids; also called *diglyceride.* Compare with *monoacylglycerol* and *triacylglycerol.*

dialysis The diffusion of certain solutes across a selectively permeable membrane.

diaphragm In mammals, the muscular floor of the chest cavity; contracts during inhalation, expanding the chest cavity.

diastole (di-ass′-toh-lee) Phase of the cardiac cycle in which the heart is relaxed. Compare with *systole.*

diatom (die′-eh-tom″) A usually unicellular alga that is covered by an ornate, siliceous shell consisting of two overlapping halves; an important component of plankton in both marine and fresh waters.

dichotomous branching (di-kaut′-uh-mus) In botany, a type of branching in which one part always divides into two more or less equal parts.

diencephalon See *forebrain.*

differential centrifugation Separation of cell particles according to their mass, size, or density. In differential centrifugation, the supernatant is spun at successively higher revolutions per minute.

differential gene expression The expression of different subsets of genes at different times and in different cells during development.

differentiated cell A specialized cell; carries out unique activities, expresses a specific set of proteins, and usually has a recognizable appearance.

differentiation (dif″-ah-ren-she-ay′-shun) Development toward a more mature state; a process changing a young, relatively unspecialized cell to a more specialized cell. Also called *cell differentiation.*

diffusion The net movement of particles (atoms, molecules, or ions) from a region of higher concentration to a region of lower concentration (i.e., down a concentration gradient), resulting from random motion. Compare with *facilitated diffusion* and *active transport.*

digestion The breakdown of food to small molecules.

diglyceride See *diacylglycerol.*

dihybrid cross (dy-hy′-brid) A genetic cross that takes into account the behavior of alleles of two loci. Compare with *monohybrid cross.*

dikaryotic (dy-kare-ee-ot′-ik) Condition of having two nuclei per cell (i.e., *n* + *n*), characteristic of certain fungal hyphae. Compare with *monokaryotic.*

dimer An association of two monomers (e.g., a disaccharide or a dipeptide).

dinoflagellate (dy″-noh-flaj′-eh-late) A unicellular, biflagellate, typically marine protist that is an important component of plankton; usually photosynthetic.

dioecious (dy-ee′-shus) Having male and female reproductive structures on separate plants; compare with *monoecious.*

dipeptide See *peptide.*

diploid (dip′-loyd) The condition of having two sets of chromosomes per nucleus. Compare with *haploid* and *polyploid.*

diplomonads Small, mostly parasitic zooflagellates with one or two nuclei, no functional mitochondria, and one to four flagella.

direct fitness An individual's reproductive success, measured by the number of viable offspring it produces. Compare with *inclusive fitness.*

directed evolution See *in vitro evolution.*

directional selection The gradual replacement of one phenotype with another because of environmental change that favors phenotypes at one of the extremes of the normal distribution. Compare with *stabilizing selection* and *disruptive selection.*

disaccharide (dy-sak′-ah-ride) A sugar produced by covalently linking two monosaccharides (e.g., maltose or sucrose).

disomy The normal condition in which both members of a chromosome pair are present in a diploid cell or organism. Compare with *monosomy* and *trisomy.*

dispersal The movement of individuals among populations. See *immigration and emigration.*

dispersion The pattern of distribution in space of the individuals of a population relative to their neighbors; may be clumped, random, or uniform.

disruptive selection A special type of directional selection in which changes in the environment favor two or more variant phenotypes at the expense of the mean. Compare with *stabilizing selection* and *directional selection.*

distal Remote; farther from the point of reference. Compare with *proximal.*

distal convoluted tubule The part of the renal tubule that extends from the loop of Henle to the collecting duct. Compare with *proximal convoluted tubule.*

disturbance In ecology, any event that disrupts community or population structure.

divergent circuit A neural pathway in which a presynaptic neuron stimulates many postsynaptic neurons. Compare with *convergent circuit.*

diving reflex A group of physiological mechanisms, such as decrease in metabolic rate, that are activated when a mammal dives to its limit.

dizygotic twins Twins that arise from the separate fertilization of two eggs; commonly known as *fraternal twins.* Compare with *monozygotic twins.*

DNA See *deoxyribonucleic acid.*

DNA cloning The process of selectively amplifying DNA sequences so their structure and function can be studied.

DNA fingerprinting The analysis of DNA fragments extracted from an individual; the resulting pattern is unique to that individual.

DNA ligase Enzyme that catalyzes the joining of the 5′ and 3′ ends of two DNA fragments; essential in DNA replication and used in recombinant DNA technology.

DNA methylation A process in which gene inactivation is perpetuated by enzymes that add methyl groups to DNA.

DNA microarray A diagnostic test involving thousands of DNA molecules placed on a glass slide or chip.

DNA polymerases Family of enzymes that catalyze the synthesis of DNA from a DNA template by adding nucleotides to a growing 3′ end.

DNA probe A labeled single-stranded DNA fragment used to detect a gene of interest in a hybridization experiment.

DNA provirus Double-stranded DNA molecule that is an intermediate in the life cycle of an RNA tumor virus (retrovirus).

DNA replication The process by which DNA is duplicated; ordinarily a semiconservative process in which a double helix gives rise to two double helices, each with an "old" strand and a newly synthesized strand.

DNA sequencing Procedure by which the sequence of nucleotides in DNA is determined.

domain (1) A structural and functional region of a protein. (2) The broadest taxonomic category; each domain includes one or more kingdoms.

dominance hierarchy A linear "pecking order" into which animals in a population may organize according to status; regulates aggressive behavior within the population.

dominant allele (al-leel') An allele that is always expressed when it is present, regardless of whether it is homozygous or heterozygous. Compare with *recessive allele.*

dominant species In a community, a species that as a result of its large biomass or abundance exerts a major influence on the distribution of populations of other species.

dopamine A neurotransmitter of the biogenic amine group.

dormancy A temporary period of arrested growth in plants or plant parts such as spores, seeds, bulbs, and buds.

dorsal (dor'-sl) Toward the uppermost surface or back of an animal. Compare with *ventral.*

dosage compensation Genetic mechanism by which the expression of X-linked genes in mammals is made equivalent in XX females and XY males by rendering all but one X chromosome inactive.

double fertilization A process in the flowering plant life cycle in which there are two fertilizations; one fertilization results in formation of a zygote, whereas the second results in formation of endosperm.

double helix The structure of DNA, which consists of two antiparallel polynucleotide chains twisted around each other.

doubling time The amount of time it takes for a population to double in size, assuming that its current rate of increase does not change. Doubling time can be estimated by dividing 70 by the rate of increase (percent increase per unit of time).

Down syndrome An inherited condition in which individuals have abnormalities of the face, eyelids, tongue, and other parts of the body and are physically and mentally retarded; usually results from trisomy of chromosome 21.

drupe (droop) A simple, fleshy fruit in which the inner wall of the fruit is a hard stone, e.g., peach, cherry.

duodenum (doo"-o-dee'-num) The portion of the small intestine into which the contents of the stomach first enter.

duplication An abnormality in which a set of chromosomes contains more than one copy of a particular chromosomal segment; the translocation form of Down syndrome is an example.

dura mater The tough, outer meningeal layer that covers and protects the brain and spinal cord. Also see *arachnoid* and *pia mater.*

dynamic equilibrium The condition of a chemical reaction when the rate of change in one direction is exactly the same as the rate of change in the opposite direction, i.e., the concentrations of the reactants and products are not changing, and the difference in free energy between reactants and products is zero.

ecdysis Molting; shedding outer skin; common process in insects, crustaceans, snakes.

ecdysone (ek'-dih-sone) See *molting hormone.*

Ecdysozoa A branch of the protostomes that includes animals that molt, such as the rotifers, nematodes, and arthropods.

echinoderms (eh-kine'-oh-derms) Phylum of spiny-skinned marine deuterostome invertebrates characterized by a water vascular system and tube feet; include sea stars, sea urchins, and sea cucumbers.

echolocation Determination of the position of objects by detecting echoes of high-pitched sounds emitted by an animal; a type of sensory system used by bats and dolphins.

ecological niche See *niche.*

ecological pyramid A graphical representation of the relative energy value at each trophic level. See *pyramid of biomass* and *pyramid of energy.*

ecological succession See *succession.*

ecology (ee-kol'-uh-jee) A discipline of biology that studies the interrelations among living things and their environments.

ecosystem (ee'-koh-sis-tem) The interacting system that encompasses a community and its nonliving, physical environment. Compare with *community.*

ecosystem ecology A subfield of ecology that studies energy flow and the cycling of chemicals among the interacting biotic and abiotic parts of an ecosystem.

ecosystem management A conservation focus that emphasizes restoring and maintaining ecosystem quality rather than the conservation of individual species.

ecosystem services Important environmental services, such as clean air to breathe, clean water to drink, and fertile soil in which to grow crops, that ecosystems provide.

ecotone The transition zone where two communities meet and intergrade.

ectoderm (ek'-toh-derm) The outer germ layer of the early embryo; gives rise to the skin and nervous system. Compare with *mesoderm* and *endoderm.*

ectoparasite A tick or other parasite that lives outside its host's body. Compare with *endoparasite.*

ectotherm An animal whose temperature fluctuates with that of the environment; may use behavioral adaptations to regulate temperature; sometimes referred to as *cold-blooded.* Compare with *endotherm.*

edge effect The ecological phenomenon in which ecotones between adjacent communities often contain a greater number of species or greater population densities of certain species than either adjacent community.

Ediacaran period (ee-dee-ack'-uh-ran") The last (most recent) period of the Proterozoic eon, from 600 million to 542 million years ago; named for early animal fossils found in the Ediacara Hills in South Australia.

effector (1) A muscle or gland that contracts or secretes in direct response to nerve impulses. (2) In homeostasis, an organ or process that helps restore a steady state.

efferent (ef'-fur-ent) Leading away from some point of reference. Compare with *afferent.*

efferent neurons Neurons that transmit action potentials from the brain or spinal cord to muscles or glands. Compare with *afferent neurons.*

ejaculation (ee-jak"-yoo-lay'-shun) A sudden expulsion, as in the ejection of semen from the penis.

El Niño–Southern Oscillation (ENSO) (el nee'-nyo) A recurring climatic phenomenon that involves a surge of warm water in the Pacific Ocean and unusual weather patterns elsewhere in the world.

electrolyte A substance that dissociates into ions when dissolved in water; the resulting solution can conduct an electric current.

electron A particle with one unit of negative charge and negligible mass, located outside the atomic nucleus. Compare with *neutron* and *proton.*

electron configuration The arrangement of electrons around the atom. In a Bohr model, the electron configuration is depicted as a series of concentric circles.

electron microscope A microscope capable of producing high-resolution, highly magnified images through the use of an electron beam (rather than light). Transmission electron microscopes (TEMs) produce images of thin sections; scanning electron microscopes (SEMs) produce images of surfaces.

electron shell Group of orbitals of electrons with similar energies.

electron transport system A series of chemical reactions during which hydrogens or their electrons are passed along an electron transport chain from one acceptor molecule to another, with the release of energy.

electronegativity A measure of an atom's attraction for electrons.

electrophoresis, gel See *gel electrophoresis.*

electroreceptor A receptor that responds to electrical stimuli.

element A substance that cannot be changed to a simpler substance by a normal chemical reaction.

elimination Ejection of undigested food from the body. Compare with *excretion.*

elongation (in protein synthesis) Cyclic process by which amino acids are added one by one to a growing polypeptide chain. See *initiation* and *termination.*

embryo (em′-bree-oh) (1) A young organism before it emerges from the egg, seed, or body of its mother. (2) Developing human until the end of the second month, after which it is referred to as a fetus. (3) In plants, the young sporophyte produced following fertilization and subsequent development of the zygote.

embryo sac The female gametophyte generation in flowering plants.

embryo transfer See *host mothering.*

emergent properties Characteristics of an object, process, or behavior that could not be predicted from its component parts; emergent properties can be identified at each level as we move up the hierarchy of biological organization.

emigration The movement of individuals out of a population. Compare with *immigration.*

enantiomers (en-an′-tee-oh-merz) Two isomeric chemical compounds that are mirror images.

end product inhibition See *feedback inhibition.*

endangered species A species whose numbers are so severely reduced that it is in imminent danger of extinction throughout all or part of its range. Compare with *threatened species.*

endemic species Localized, native species that are not found anywhere else in the world. Compare with *cosmopolitan species.*

endergonic reaction (end′-er-gon″-ik) A nonspontaneous reaction; a reaction requiring a net input of free energy. Compare with *exergonic reaction.*

endocrine gland (en′-doh-crin) A gland that secretes hormones directly into the blood or tissue fluid instead of into ducts. Compare with *exocrine gland.*

endocrine system The body system that helps regulate metabolic activities; consists of ductless glands and tissues that secrete hormones.

endocytosis (en″-doh-sy-toh′-sis) The active transport of substances into the cell by the formation of invaginated regions of the plasma membrane that pinch off and become cytoplasmic vesicles. Compare with *exocytosis.*

endoderm (en′-doh-derm) The inner germ layer of the early embryo; becomes the lining of the digestive tract and the structures that develop from the digestive tract—liver, lungs, and pancreas. Compare with *ectoderm* and *mesoderm.*

endodermis (en″-doh-der′-mis) The innermost layer of the plant root cortex. Endodermal cells have a waterproof Casparian strip around their radial and transverse walls that ensures that water and minerals enter the xylem only by passing through the endoderm cells.

endolymph (en′-doh-limf) The fluid of the membranous labyrinth and cochlear duct of the ear.

endomembrane system See *internal membrane system.*

endometrium (en″-doh-mee′-tree-um) The uterine lining.

endoparasite A parasite such as a tapeworm that lives within the host. Compare with *ectoparasite.*

endoplasmic reticulum (ER) (en′-doh-plaz″-mik reh-tik′-yoo-lum) An interconnected network of internal membranes in eukaryotic cells enclosing a compartment, the ER lumen. Rough ER has ribosomes attached to the cytosolic surface; smooth ER, a site of lipid biosynthesis, lacks ribosomes.

endorphins (en-dor′-finz) Neuropeptides released by certain brain neurons; block pain signals.

endoskeleton (en″-doh-skel′-eh-ton) Bony and/or cartilaginous structures within the body that provide support. Compare with *exoskeleton.*

endosperm (en′-doh-sperm) The 3*n* nutritive tissue that is formed at some point in the development of all angiosperm seeds.

endospore A resting cell formed by certain bacteria; highly resistant to heat, radiation, and disinfectants.

endostyle A shared derived character of chordates; a groove in the floor of the pharynx that secretes mucus and traps food particles in sea water passing through the pharynx. In vertebrates, the thyroid gland is derived from the endostyle.

endosymbiont (en″-doe-sim′-bee-ont) An organism that lives inside the body of another kind of organism. Endosymbionts may benefit their host (mutualism) or harm their host (parasitism).

endothelium (en-doh-theel′-ee-um) The tissue that lines the cavities of the heart, blood vessels, and lymph vessels.

endotherm (en′-doh-therm) An animal that uses metabolic energy to maintain a constant body temperature despite variations in environmental temperature; e.g., birds and mammals. Compare with *ectotherm.*

endotoxin A poisonous substance in the cell walls of gram-negative bacteria. Compare with *exotoxin.*

energy The capacity to do work; expressed in kilojoules or kilocalories.

energy of activation See *activation energy.*

enhanced greenhouse effect See *greenhouse effect.*

enhancers Regulatory DNA sequences that enhance gene transcription; can be located long distances away from the actual coding regions of a gene.

enkephalins (en-kef′-ah-linz) Neuropeptides released by certain brain neurons that block pain signals.

enterocoely (en′-ter-oh-seely) The process by which the coelom forms as a cavity within mesoderm produced by outpocketings of the primitive gut (archenteron); characteristic of many deuterostomes. Compare with *schizocoely.*

enthalpy The total potential energy of a system; sometimes referred to as the "heat content of the system."

entropy (en′-trop-ee) Disorderliness; a quantitative measure of the amount of the random, disordered energy that is unavailable to do work.

environmental resistance Unfavorable environmental conditions, such as crowding, that prevent organisms from reproducing indefinitely at their intrinsic rate of increase.

environmental sustainability The ability to meet humanity's current needs without compromising the ability of future generations to meet their needs.

enzyme (en′-zime) An organic catalyst (usually a protein) that accelerates a specific chemical reaction by lowering the activation energy required for that reaction.

enzyme–substrate complex The temporary association between enzyme and substrate that forms during the course of a catalyzed reaction; also called *ES complex.*

eon The largest division of the geologic time scale; eons are divided into eras.

eosinophil (ee-oh-sin′-oh-fil) A type of white blood cell whose cytoplasmic granules absorb acidic stains; functions in parasitic infestations and allergic reactions.

epidermis (ep-ih-dur′-mis) (1) An outer layer of cells that covers the body of plants and functions primarily for protection. (2) The outer layer of vertebrate skin.

epididymis (ep-ih-did′-ih-mis) (pl., *epididymides*) A coiled tube that receives sperm from the testis and conveys it to the vas deferens.

epigenetic inheritance Inheritance that involves changes in how a gene is expressed without any change in that gene's nucleotide sequence.

epiglottis A thin, flexible structure that guards the entrance to the larynx, preventing food from entering the airway during swallowing.

epinephrine (ep-ih-nef′-rin) Hormone produced by the adrenal medulla; stimulates the sympathetic nervous system.

epistasis (ep-ih-sta′-sis) Condition in which certain alleles of one locus alter the expression of alleles of a different locus.

epithelial tissue (ep-ih-theel′-ee-al) The type of animal tissue that covers body surfaces, lines body cavities, and forms glands; also called *epithelium.*

epoch The smallest unit of geologic time; a subdivision of a period.

equilibrium See *dynamic equilibrium, genetic equilibrium,* and *punctuated equilibrium.*

era An interval of geologic time that is a subdivision of an eon; eras are divided into periods.

erythroblastosis fetalis (eh-rith″-row-blas-toe′-sis fi-tal′-is) Serious condition in which Rh$^+$ red blood cells (which bear antigen D) of a fetus are destroyed by maternal anti-D antibodies.

erythrocyte (eh-rith′-row-site) A vertebrate red blood cell; contains hemoglobin, which transports oxygen.

erythropoietin (eh-rith″-row-poy′-ih-tin) A peptide hormone secreted mainly by kidney cells; stimulates red blood cell production.

ES complex See *enzyme–substrate complex.*

esophagus (e-sof′-ah-gus) The part of the digestive tract that conducts food from the pharynx to the stomach.

essential nutrient A nutrient that must be provided in the diet because the body cannot make it or cannot make it in sufficient quantities to meet nutritional needs, e.g., essential amino acids and essential fatty acids.

ester linkage Covalent linkage formed by the reaction of a carboxyl group and a hydroxyl group, with the removal of the equivalent of a water molecule; the linkage includes an oxygen atom bonded to a carbonyl group.

estivation A state of torpor caused by lack of food or water during periods of high temperature. Compare with *hibernation.*

estrogens (es′-troh-jenz) Female sex hormones produced by the ovary; promote the development and maintenance of female reproductive structures and of secondary sex characteristics.

estuary (es′-choo-wear-ee) A coastal body of water that connects to an ocean, in which fresh water from the land mixes with salt water.

ethology (ee-thol′-oh-jee) The study of animal behavior under natural conditions from the point of view of adaptation.

ethyl alcohol A two-carbon alcohol.

ethylene (eth′-ih-leen) A gaseous plant hormone involved in various aspects of plant growth and development, such as leaf abscission and fruit ripening.

euchromatin (yoo-croh′-mah-tin) A loosely coiled chromatin that is generally capable of transcription. Compare with *heterochromatin.*

eudicot (yoo-dy′-kot) One of the two clades of flowering plants; eudicot seeds contain two cotyledons, or seed leaves. Compare with *monocot.*

euglenoids (yoo-glee′-noidz) A group of mostly freshwater, flagellate, unicellular algae that move by means of an anterior flagellum and are usually photosynthetic.

eukaryote (yoo″-kar′-ee-ote) An organism whose cells have nuclei and other membrane-enclosed organelles. Includes protists, fungi, plants, and animals. Compare with *prokaryote.*

euphotic zone The upper reaches of the ocean, in which enough light penetrates to support photosynthesis.

eustachian tube (yoo-stay′-shee-un) The auditory tube passing between the middle-ear cavity and the pharynx in vertebrates; permits the equalization of pressure on the tympanic membrane.

eutrophic lake A lake enriched with nutrients such as nitrate and phosphate and consequently overgrown with plants or algae.

evergreen A plant that sheds leaves over a long period, so some leaves are always present. Compare with *deciduous.*

Evo Devo The study of the evolution of the genetic control of development.

evolution Any cumulative genetic changes in a population from generation to generation. Evolution leads to differences in populations and explains the origin of all the organisms that exist today or have ever existed.

evolutionary species concept See *phylogenetic species concept.*

evolutionary systematics An approach to classification that considers both evolutionary relationships and the extent of divergence that has occurred since a group branched from an ancestral group. Compare with *cladistics* and *phenetics.*

ex situ conservation Conservation efforts that involve conserving individual species in human-controlled settings, such as zoos. Compare with *in situ conservation.*

excitatory postsynaptic potential (EPSP) A change in membrane potential that brings a neuron closer to the firing level. Compare with *inhibitory postsynaptic potential (IPSP).*

excretion (ek-skree′-shun) The discharge from the body of a waste product of metabolism (not to be confused with the elimination of undigested food materials). Compare with *elimination.*

excretory system The body system in animals that functions in osmoregulation and in the discharge of metabolic wastes.

exergonic reaction (ex′-er-gon″-ik) A reaction characterized by a release of free energy. Also called *spontaneous reaction.* Compare with *endergonic reaction.*

exocrine gland (ex′-oh-crin) A gland that excretes its products through a duct that opens onto a free surface, such as the skin (e.g., sweat glands). Compare with *endocrine gland.*

exocytosis (ex″-oh-sy-toh′-sis) The active transport of materials out of the cell by fusion of cytoplasmic vesicles with the plasma membrane. Compare with *endocytosis.*

exon (1) A protein-coding region of a eukaryotic gene. (2) The mRNA transcribed from such a region. Compare with *intron.*

exoskeleton (ex″-oh-skel′-eh-ton) An external skeleton, such as the shell of mollusks or outer covering of arthropods; provides protection and sites of attachment for muscles. Compare with *endoskeleton.*

exotoxin A poisonous substance released by certain bacteria. Compare with *endotoxin.*

exploitation competition Intraspecific competition in which all the individuals in a population "share" the limited resource equally, so that at high population densities, none of them obtains an adequate amount. Also called *scramble competition*. Compare with *interference competition*.

exponential population growth The accelerating population growth that occurs when optimal conditions allow a constant per capita growth rate. Compare with *logistic population growth*.

exteroceptor (ex′-tur-oh-sep″-tor) One of the sense organs that receives sensory stimuli from the outside world, such as the eyes or touch receptors. Compare with *interoceptor*.

extinction The elimination of a species; occurs when the last individual member of a species dies.

extracellular matrix (ECM) A network of proteins and carbohydrates that surrounds many animal cells.

extraembryonic membranes Multicellular membranous structures that develop from the germ layers of a terrestrial vertebrate embryo but are not part of the embryo itself. See *chorion, amnion, allantois,* and *yolk sac.*

F_1 generation (first filial generation) The first generation of hybrid offspring resulting from a cross between parents from two different true-breeding lines.

F_2 generation (second filial generation) The offspring of the F_1 generation.

facilitated diffusion The passive transport of ions or molecules by a specific carrier protein in a membrane. As in simple diffusion, net transport is down a concentration gradient, and no additional energy has to be supplied. Compare with *diffusion* and *active transport.*

facilitation In ecology, a situation in which one species has a positive effect on other species in the community, for example, by enhancing the local environment.

facultative anaerobe An organism capable of carrying out aerobic respiration but able to switch to fermentation when oxygen is unavailable, e.g., yeast. Compare with *obligate anaerobe.*

FAD/FADH$_2$ Oxidized and reduced forms, respectively, of flavin adenine dinucleotide, a coenzyme that transfers electrons (as hydrogen) in metabolism, including cellular respiration.

fallopian tube See *oviduct.*

family A taxonomic category made up of related genera.

fatty acid A lipid that is an organic acid containing a long hydrocarbon chain, with no double bonds (saturated fatty acid), one double bond (monounsaturated fatty acid), or two or more double bonds (polyunsaturated fatty acid); components of triacylglycerols and phospholipids, as well as monoacylglycerols and diacylglycerols.

fecundity The potential capacity of an individual to produce offspring.

feedback inhibition A type of enzyme regulation in which the accumulation of the product of a reaction inhibits an earlier reaction in the sequence; also known as *end product inhibition.*

fermentation An anaerobic process by which ATP is produced by a series of redox reactions in which organic compounds serve both as electron donors and terminal electron acceptors.

fern One of a phylum of seedless vascular plants that reproduce by spores produced in sporangia; ferns undergo an alternation of generations between the dominant sporophyte and the gametophyte (prothallus).

fertilization The fusion of two *n* gametes; results in the formation of a 2*n* zygote. Compare with *double fertilization.*

fetus The unborn human offspring from the third month of pregnancy to birth.

fiber (1) In plants, a type of sclerenchyma cell; fibers are long, tapered cells with thick walls. Compare with *sclereid*. (2) In animals, an elongated cell such as a muscle or nerve cell. (3) In animals, the

microscopic, threadlike protein and carbohydrate complexes scattered through the matrix of connective tissues.

fibrin An insoluble protein formed from the plasma protein fibrinogen during blood clotting.

fibroblasts Connective tissue cells that produce the fibers and the protein and carbohydrate complexes of the matrix of connective tissues.

fibronectins Glycoproteins of the extracellular matrix that bind to integrins (receptor proteins in the plasma membrane).

fibrous root system A root system consisting of several adventitious roots of approximately equal size that arise from the base of the stem. Compare with *taproot system.*

Fick's law of diffusion A physical law governing rates of gas exchange in animal respiratory systems; states that the rate of diffusion of a substance across a membrane is directly proportional to the surface area and to the difference in pressure between the two sides.

filament In flowering plants, the thin stalk of a stamen; the filament bears an anther at its tip.

fimbriae Hairlike structures that project from the cell surface of some prokaryotes; help bacteria to adhere to one another and to attach to the surfaces of cells they infect.

first law of thermodynamics The law of conservation of energy, which states that the total energy of any closed system (any object plus its surroundings, i.e., the universe) remains constant. Compare with *second law of thermodynamics.*

fitness See *direct fitness.*

fixed action pattern (FAP) An innate behavior triggered by a sign stimulus.

flagellate A unicellular nonphotosynthetic protist that has one or more long, whiplike flagella.

flagellum (flah-jel′-um) (pl., *flagella*) A long, whiplike structure extending from certain cells and used in locomotion. (1) Eukaryote flagella consist of two central, single microtubules surrounded by nine double microtubules (9 + 2 structure), all covered by a plasma membrane. (2) Prokaryote flagella are filaments rotated by special structures located in the plasma membrane and cell wall.

flame cells Collecting cells that have cilia; part of the osmoregulatory system of flatworms.

flavin adenine dinucleotide See *FAD/FADH$_2$.*

flowering plants See *angiosperms.*

flowing-water ecosystem A river or stream ecosystem.

fluid mosaic model The currently accepted model of the plasma membrane and other cell membranes, in which protein molcules "float" in a fluid phospholipid bilayer.

fluorescence The emission of light of a longer wavelength (lower energy) than the light originally absorbed.

fluorescent in situ hybridization (FISH) A technique to detect specific DNA segments by hybridization directly to chromosomes; visualized microscopically by using a fluorescent dye.

follicle (fol′-i-kl) (1) A simple, dry, dehiscent fruit that develops from a single carpel and splits open at maturity along one suture to liberate the seeds. (2) A small sac of cells in the mammalian ovary that contains a maturing egg. (3) The pocket in the skin from which a hair grows.

follicle-stimulating hormone (FSH) A gonadotropic hormone secreted by the anterior lobe of the pituitary gland; stimulates follicle development in the ovaries of females and sperm production in the testes of males.

food chain The series of organisms through which energy flows in an ecosystem. Each organism in the series eats or decomposes the preceding organism in the chain. See *food web.*

food web A complex interconnection of all the food chains in an ecosystem.

foramen magnum The opening in the vertebrate skull through which the spinal cord passes.

foraminiferan (for″-am-in-if′-er-an) A marine protist that produces a shell, or test, that encloses an amoeboid body. Also called *foram*. See *rhizarians*.

forebrain In the early embryo, one of the three divisions of the developing vertebrate brain; subdivides to form the telencephalon, which gives rise to the cerebrum, and the diencephalon, which gives rise to the thalamus and hypothalamus. Compare with *midbrain* and *hindbrain*.

forest decline A gradual deterioration (and often death) of many trees in a forest; can be caused by a combination of factors, such as acid precipitation, toxic heavy metals, and surface-level ozone.

fossil Parts or traces of an ancient organism usually preserved in rock.

fossil fuel Combustible deposits in Earth's crust that are composed of the remnants of prehistoric organisms that existed millions of years ago, e.g., oil, natural gas, and coal.

founder cell A cell from which a particular cell lineage is derived.

founder effect Genetic drift that results from a small population colonizing a new area.

fovea (foe′-vee-ah) The area of sharpest vision in the retina; cone cells are concentrated here.

fragile site A weak point at a specific location on a chromosome where part of a chromatid appears attached to the rest of the chromosome by a thin thread of DNA.

fragile X syndrome A human genetic disorder caused by a fragile site that occurs near the tip on the X chromosome; effects range from mild learning disabilities to severe mental retardation and hyperactivity.

frameshift mutation A mutation that results when one or two nucleotide pairs are inserted into or deleted from the DNA. The change causes the mRNA transcribed from the mutated DNA to have an altered reading frame such that all codons downstream from the mutation are changed.

fraternal twins See *dizygotic twins*.

free energy The maximum amount of energy available to do work under the conditions of a biochemical reaction.

free radicals Toxic, highly reactive compounds with unpaired electrons that bond with other compounds in the cell and interfere with normal function.

frequency-dependent selection Selection in which the relative fitness of different genotypes is related to how frequently they occur in the population.

freshwater wetlands Land that is transitional between freshwater and terrestrial ecosystems and is covered with water for at least part of the year, e.g., marshes and swamps.

frontal lobes In mammals, the anterior part of the cerebrum.

fruit In flowering plants, a mature, ripened ovary. Fruits contain seeds and usually provide seed protection and dispersal.

fruiting body A multicellular structure that contains the sexual spores of certain fungi; refers to the ascocarp of an ascomycete and the basidiocarp of a basidiomycete.

fucoxanthin (few″-koh-zan′-thin) The brown carotenoid pigment found in brown algae, golden algae, diatoms, and dinoflagellates.

functional genomics The study of the roles of genes in cells.

functional group A group of atoms that confers distinctive properties on an organic molecule (or region of a molecule) to which it is attached, e.g., hydroxyl, carbonyl, carboxyl, amino, phosphate, and sulfhydryl groups.

fundamental niche The potential ecological niche that an organism could occupy if there were no competition from other species. Compare with *realized niche*.

fungus (pl., *fungi*) A heterotrophic eukaryote with chitinous cell walls and a body usually in the form of a mycelium of branched, threadlike hyphae. Most fungi are decomposers; some are parasitic.

G protein One of a group of proteins that bind GTP and are involved in the transfer of signals across the plasma membrane.

G_1 phase The first gap phase within the interphase stage of the cell cycle; G_1 occurs before DNA synthesis (S phase) begins. Compare with S and G_2 *phases*.

G_2 phase Second gap phase within the interphase stage of the cell cycle; G_2 occurs after DNA synthesis (S phase) and before mitosis. Compare with S and G_1 *phases*.

gallbladder A small sac that stores bile.

gametangium (gam″-uh-tan′-gee-um) Special multicellular or unicellular structure of plants, protists, and fungi in which gametes are formed.

gamete (gam′-eet) A sex cell; in plants and animals, an egg or sperm. In sexual reproduction, the union of gametes results in the formation of a zygote. The chromosome number of a gamete is designated *n*.

gametic isolation (gam-ee′-tik) A prezygotic reproductive isolating mechanism in which sexual reproduction between two closely related species cannot occur because of chemical differences in the gametes.

gametogenesis The process of gamete formation. See *spermatogenesis* and *oogenesis*.

gametophyte generation (gam-ee′-toh-fite) The *n*, gamete-producing stage in the life cycle of a plant. Compare with *sporophyte generation*.

gamma-aminobutyric acid (GABA) A neurotransmitter that has an inhibitory effect.

ganglion (gang′-glee-on) (pl., *ganglia*) A mass of neuron cell bodies; in vertebrates, refers to aggregations of cell bodies in the peripheral nervous system. Compare with *nucleus* (definition 3).

ganglion cell A type of neuron in the retina of the eye; receives input from bipolar cells.

gap junction Structure consisting of specialized regions of the plasma membrane of two adjacent cells; contains numerous pores that allow the passage of certain small molecules and ions between them.

gastrin (gas′-trin) A hormone released by the stomach mucosa; stimulates the gastric glands to secrete pepsinogen.

gastrovascular cavity A central digestive cavity with a single opening that functions as both mouth and anus; characteristic of cnidarians and flatworms.

gastrula (gas′-troo-lah) A three-layered embryo formed by the process of gastrulation.

gastrulation (gas-troo-lay′-shun) Process in embryonic development during which the three germ layers (ectoderm, mesoderm, and endoderm) form.

gel electrophoresis Procedure by which proteins or nucleic acids are separated on the basis of size and charge as they migrate through a gel in an electric field.

gene A segment of DNA that serves as a unit of hereditary information; includes a transcribable DNA sequence (plus associated sequences regulating its transcription) that yields a protein or RNA product with a specific function.

gene amplification The developmental process in which certain cells produce multiple copies of a gene by selective replication, thus allowing for increased synthesis of the gene product. Compare with *nuclear equivalence* and *genomic rearrangement*.

gene flow The movement of alleles between local populations due to the migration of individuals; can have significant evolutionary consequences.

gene locus See *locus*.

gene pool All the alleles of all the genes present in a freely interbreeding population.

gene therapy Any of a variety of methods designed to correct a disease or alleviate its symptoms through the introduction of normal, therapeutic genes into the affected person's cells.

genetic bottleneck See *bottleneck*.

genetic code See *codon*.

genetic counseling Medical and genetic information provided to couples who are concerned about the risk of abnormality in their children.

genetic drift A random change in allele frequency in a small breeding population.

genetic engineering Manipulation of genes, often through recombinant DNA technology. Also called *molecular modification*.

genetic equilibrium The condition of a population that is not undergoing evolutionary change, i.e., in which allele and genotype frequencies do not change from one generation to the next. See *Hardy–Weinberg principle*.

genetic polymorphism (pol″-ee-mor′-fizm) The presence in a population of two or more alleles for a given gene locus.

genetic recombination See *recombination, genetic*.

genetic screening A systematic search through a population for individuals with a genotype or karyotype that might cause a serious genetic disease in them or their offspring.

genetics The science of heredity; includes genetic similarities and genetic variation between parents and offspring or among individuals of a population.

genome (jee′-nome) Originally, all the genetic material in a cell or individual organism. The term is used in more than one way depending on context, e.g., an organism's haploid genome is all the DNA contained in one haploid set of its chromosomes, and its mitochondrial genome is all the DNA in a mitochondrion. See *human genome*.

genomic DNA library A collection of recombinant plasmids in which all the DNA in the genome is represented. Compare with *cDNA library*.

genomic imprinting See *imprinting* (definition 1).

genomic rearrangement A physical change in the structure of one or more genes that occurs during the development of an organism and leads to an alteration in gene expression; compare with *nuclear equivalence* and *gene amplification*.

genomics The emerging field of biology that studies the entire DNA sequence of an organism's genome to identify all the genes, determine their RNA or protein products, and ascertain how the genes are regulated.

genotype (jeen′-oh-type) The genetic makeup of, or combination of alleles in, an individual. Compare with *phenotype*.

genotype frequency The proportion of a particular genotype in the population.

genus (jee′-nus) A taxonomic category made up of related species.

geometric isomer One of two or more chemical compounds having the same arrangement of covalent bonds but differing in the spatial arrangement of their atoms or groups of atoms.

germ layers In animals, three embryonic tissue layers: endoderm, mesoderm, and ectoderm.

germ line cell In animals, a cell that is part of the line of cells that will ultimately undergo meiosis to form gametes. Compare with *somatic cell*.

germination Resumption of growth of an embryo or spore; occurs when a seed or spore sprouts.

germplasm Any plant or animal material that may be used in breeding; includes seeds, plants, and plant tissues of traditional crop varieties and the sperm and eggs of traditional livestock breeds.

gibberellin (jib″-ur-el′-lin) A plant hormone involved in many aspects of plant growth and development, such as stem elongation, flowering, and seed germination.

gills (1) The respiratory organs characteristic of many aquatic animals, usually thin-walled projections from the body surface or from some part of the digestive tract. (2) The spore-bearing, platelike structures under the caps of mushrooms.

ginkgo (ging′-ko) A member of an ancient gymnosperm group that consists of a single living representative (*Ginkgo biloba*), a hardy, deciduous tree with broad, fan-shaped leaves and naked, fleshy seeds (on female trees).

gland See *endocrine gland* and *exocrine gland*.

glial cells (glee′-ul) In nervous tissue, cells that support and nourish neurons; they also communicate with neurons and have several other functions; also see *astrocyte, microglia,* and *oligodendrocyte*.

globulin (glob′-yoo-lin) One of a class of proteins in blood plasma, some of which (gamma globulins) function as antibodies.

glomeromycetes A group of fungal symbionts that form arbuscular mycorrhizae with the roots of many plants; belong to phylum Glomeromycota.

glomerulus (glom-air′-yoo-lus) The cluster of capillaries at the proximal end of a nephron; the glomerulus is surrounded by Bowman's capsule.

glucagon (gloo′-kah-gahn) A hormone secreted by the pancreas that stimulates glycogen breakdown, thereby increasing the concentration of glucose in the blood. Compare with *insulin*.

glucose A hexose aldehyde sugar that is central to many metabolic processes.

glutamate An amino acid that functions as the major excitatory neurotransmitter in the vertebrate brain.

glyceraldehyde-3-phosphate (G3P) Phosphorylated three-carbon compound that is an important intermediate in glycolysis and in the Calvin cycle.

glycerol A three-carbon alcohol with a hydroxyl group on each carbon; a component of triacylglycerols and phospholipids, as well as monoacylglycerols and diacylglycerols.

glycocalyx (gly″-koh-kay′-lix) A coating on the outside of an animal cell, formed by the polysaccharide portions of glycoproteins and glycolipids associated with the plasma membrane.

glycogen (gly′-koh-jen) The principal storage polysaccharide in animal cells; formed from glucose and stored primarily in the liver and, to a lesser extent, in muscle cells.

glycolipid A lipid with covalently attached carbohydrates.

glycolysis (gly-kol′-ih-sis) The first stage of cellular respiration, literally the "splitting of sugar." The metabolic conversion of glucose into pyruvate, accompanied by the production of ATP.

glycoprotein (gly′-koh-pro-teen) A protein with covalently attached carbohydrates.

glycosidic linkage Covalent linkage joining two sugars; includes an oxygen atom bonded to a carbon of each sugar.

glyoxysomes (gly-ox'-ih-sohmz) Membrane-enclosed structures in cells of certain plant seeds; contain a large array of enzymes that convert stored fat to sugar.

gnetophyte (nee'-toe-fite) One of a small phylum of unusual gymnosperms that have some features similar to those of flowering plants.

goblet cells Unicellular glands that secrete mucus.

goiter (goy'-ter) An enlargement of the thyroid gland.

golden alga A member of a group of algae, most of which are biflagellate, are unicellular, and contain pigments, including chlorophylls *a* and *c* and carotenoids, including fucoxanthin.

Golgi complex (goal'-jee) Organelle composed of stacks of flattened, membranous sacs. Mainly responsible for modifying, packaging, and sorting proteins that will be secreted or targeted to other organelles of the internal membrane system or to the plasma membrane; also called *Golgi body* or *Golgi apparatus.*

gonad (goh'-nad) A gamete-producing gland; an ovary or a testis.

gonadotropic hormones (go-nad-oh-troh'-pic) Hormones produced by the anterior pituitary gland that stimulate the testes and ovaries; include follicle-stimulating hormone (FSH) and luteinizing hormone (LH).

gonadotropin-releasing hormone (GnRH) A hormone secreted by the hypothalamus that stimulates the anterior pituitary to secrete the gonadotropic hormones: follicle-stimulating hormone (FSH) and luteinizing hormone (LH).

graded potential A local change in electrical potential that varies in magnitude depending on the strength of the applied stimulus.

gradualism The idea that evolution occurs by a slow, steady accumulation of genetic changes over time. Also called *phyletic gradualism.* Compare with *punctuated equilibrium.*

graft rejection An immune response directed against a transplanted tissue or organ.

grain A simple, dry, one-seeded fruit in which the fruit wall is fused to the seed coat, e.g., corn and wheat kernels. Also called *caryopsis.*

granulosa cells In mammals, cells that surround the developing oocyte and are part of the follicle; produce estrogens and inhibin.

granum (pl., *grana*) A stack of thylakoids within a chloroplast.

gravitropism (grav"-ih-troh'-pizm) Growth of a plant in response to gravity.

gray crescent The grayish area of cytoplasm that marks the region where gastrulation begins in an amphibian embryo.

gray matter Nervous tissue in the brain and spinal cord that contains cell bodies, dendrites, and unmyelinated axons. Compare with *white matter.*

green alga A member of a diverse group of algae that contain the same pigments as plants (chlorophylls *a* and *b* and carotenoids).

greenhouse effect The natural global warming of Earth's atmosphere caused by the presence of carbon dioxide and other gases that trap the sun's radiation. The additional warming produced when increased levels of greenhouse gases absorb infrared radiation is known as the *enhanced greenhouse effect.*

greenhouse gases Trace gases in the atmosphere that allow the sun's energy to penetrate to Earth's surface but do not allow as much of it to escape as heat.

gross primary productivity The rate at which energy accumulates (is assimilated) in an ecosystem during photosynthesis. Compare with *net primary productivity.*

ground state The lowest energy state of an atom.

ground tissue system All tissues in the plant body other than the dermal tissue system and vascular tissue system; consists of parenchyma, collenchyma, and sclerenchyma.

growth factors A group of more than 50 extracellular peptides that signal certain cells to grow and divide.

growth hormone (GH) A hormone secreted by the anterior lobe of the pituitary gland; stimulates growth of body tissues; also called *somatotropin.*

growth rate The rate of change of a population's size on a per capita basis.

guanine (gwan'-een) A nitrogenous purine base that is a component of nucleic acids and GTP.

guanosine triphosphate (GTP) An energy transfer molecule similar to ATP that releases free energy with the hydrolysis of its terminal phosphate group.

guard cell One of a pair of epidermal cells that adjust their shape to form a stomatal pore for gas exchange.

guttation (gut-tay'-shun) The appearance of water droplets on leaves, forced out through leaf pores by root pressure.

gymnosperm (jim'-noh-sperm) Any of a group of seed plants in which the seeds are not enclosed in an ovary; gymnosperms frequently bear their seeds in cones. Includes four phyla: conifers, cycads, ginkgoes, and gnetophytes.

habitat The natural environment or place where an organism, population, or species lives.

habitat fragmentation The division of habitats that formerly occupied large, unbroken areas into smaller pieces by roads, fields, cities, and other human land-transforming activities.

habitat isolation A prezygotic reproductive isolating mechanism in which reproduction between similar species is prevented because they live and breed in different habitats.

habituation (hab-it"-yoo-ay'-shun) A type of learning in which an animal becomes accustomed to a repeated, irrelevant stimulus and no longer responds to it.

hair cell A vertebrate mechanoreceptor found in the lateral line of fishes, the vestibular apparatus, semicircular canals, and cochlea.

half-life The period of time required for a radioisotope to change into a different material.

haploid (hap'-loyd) The condition of having one set of chromosomes per nucleus. Compare with *diploid* and *polyploid.*

"hard-wiring" Refers to how neurons signal one another, how they connect, and how they carry out basic functions such as regulating heart rate, blood pressure, and sleep–wake cycles.

Hardy–Weinberg principle The mathematical prediction that allele frequencies do not change from generation to generation in a large population in the absence of microevolutionary processes (mutation, genetic drift, gene flow, natural selection).

haustorium (hah-stor'-ee-um) (pl., *haustoria*) In parasitic fungi, a specialized hypha that penetrates a host cell and obtains nourishment from the cytoplasm.

Haversian canals (ha-vur'-zee-un) Channels extending through the matrix of bone; contain blood vessels and nerves.

heat The total amount of kinetic energy in a sample of a substance.

heat energy The thermal energy that flows from an object with a higher temperature to an object with a lower temperature.

heat of vaporization The amount of heat energy that must be supplied to change one gram of a substance from the liquid phase to the vapor phase.

helicases Enzymes that unwind the two strands of a DNA double helix.

helper T cell See *T helper cell.*

hemichordates A phylum of sedentary, wormlike deuterostomes.

hemizygous (hem"-ih-zy'-gus) Possessing only one allele for a particular locus; a human male is hemizygous for all X-linked genes. Compare with *homozygous* and *heterozygous.*

hemocoel Blood cavity characteristic of animals with an open circulatory system.

hemocyanin A hemolymph pigment that transports oxygen in some mollusks and arthropods.

hemoglobin (hee'-moh-gloh"-bin) The red, iron-containing protein pigment in blood that transports oxygen and carbon dioxide and aids in regulation of pH.

hemolymph (hee'-moh-limf) The fluid that bathes the tissues in animals with an open circulatory system, e.g., arthropods and most mollusks.

hemophilia (hee"-moh-feel'-ee-ah) A hereditary disease in which blood does not clot properly; the form known as *hemophilia A* has an X-linked, recessive inheritance pattern.

Hensen's node See *primitive streak*.

hepatic (heh-pat'-ik) Pertaining to the liver.

hepatic portal system The portion of the circulatory system that carries blood from the intestine through the liver.

herbivore (erb'-uh-vore) An animal that feeds on plants or algae. Also called *primary consumer*.

heredity The transmission of genetic information from parent to offspring.

hermaphrodite (her-maf'-roh-dite) An organism that has both male and female sex organs.

heterochromatin (het"-ur-oh-kroh'-mah-tin) Highly coiled and compacted chromatin in an inactive state. Compare with *euchromatin*.

heterocyst (het'-ur-oh-sist") An oxygen-excluding cell of cyanobacteria that is the site of nitrogen fixation.

heterogametic A term describing an individual that produces two classes of gametes with respect to their sex chromosome constitutions. Human males (XY) are heterogametic, producing X and Y sperm. Compare with *homogametic*.

heterospory (het"-ur-os'-pur-ee) Production of two types of *n* spores, microspores (male) and megaspores (female). Compare with *homospory*.

heterothallic (het"-ur-oh-thal'-ik) Pertaining to certain algae and fungi that have two mating types; only by combining a plus strain and a minus strain can sexual reproduction occur. Compare with *homothallic*.

heterotroph (het'-ur-oh-trof) An organism that cannot synthesize its own food from inorganic raw materials and therefore must obtain energy and body-building materials from other organisms. Also called *consumer*. Compare with *autotroph*. See *chemoheterotroph* and *photoheterotroph*.

heterozygote advantage A phenomenon in which the heterozygous condition confers some special advantage on an individual that either homozygous condition does not (i.e., *Aa* has a higher degree of fitness than does *AA* or *aa*).

heterozygous (het-ur"-oh-zye'-gus) Having a pair of unlike alleles for a particular locus. Compare with *homozygous*.

hexose A monosaccharide containing six carbon atoms.

hibernation Long-term torpor in response to winter cold and scarcity of food. Compare with *estivation*.

high-density lipoprotein (HDL) See *lipoprotein*.

hindbrain In the early embryo, one of the three divisions of the developing vertebrate brain; subdivides to form the metencephalon, which gives rise to the cerebellum and pons, and the myelencephalon, which gives rise to the medulla. Compare with *forebrain* and *midbrain*.

histamine (his'-tah-meen) Substance released from mast cells that is involved in allergic and inflammatory reactions.

histones (his'-tohnz) Small, positively charged (basic) proteins in the cell nucleus that bind to the negatively charged DNA. See *nucleosomes*.

holdfast The basal structure for attachment to solid surfaces found in multicellular algae.

holoblastic cleavage A cleavage pattern in which the entire embryo cleaves; characteristic of eggs with little or moderate yolk (isolecithal or moderately telolecithal), e.g., the eggs of echinoderms, amphioxus, and mammals. Compare with *meroblastic cleavage*.

home range A geographic area that an individual animal seldom or never leaves. Compare with *range*.

homeobox A short (180-nucleotide) DNA sequence that characterizes many homeotic genes as well as some other genes that play a role in development.

homeodomain A functional region of certain transcription factors; consists of approximately 60 amino acids specified by a homeobox DNA sequence and includes a recognition alpha helix, which binds to specific DNA sequences and affects their transcription.

homeostasis (home"-ee-oh-stay'-sis) The balanced internal environment of the body; the automatic tendency of an organism to maintain such a steady state.

homeostatic mechanisms (home"-ee-oh-stat'-ik) The regulatory mechanisms that maintain homeostasis.

homeotic gene (home"-ee-ah'-tik) A gene that controls the formation of specific structures during development. Such genes were originally identified through insect mutants in which one body part is substituted for another.

hominin (hah'-min-in) Any of a group of extinct and living humans. Also called *hominid*.

hominoid (hah'-min-oid) The apes and hominids.

homogametic Term describing an individual that produces gametes with identical sex chromosome constitutions. Human females (XX) are homogametic, producing all X eggs. Compare with *heterogametic*.

homologous chromosomes (hom-ol'-ah-gus) Chromosomes that are similar in morphology and genetic constitution. In humans there are 23 pairs of homologous chromosomes; one member of each pair is inherited from the mother, and the other from the father.

homologous features See *homology*.

homology Similarity in different species that results from their derivation from a common ancestor. The features that exhibit such similarity are called *homologous features*. Compare with *homoplasy*.

homoplastic features See *homoplasy*.

homoplasy Similarity in the characters in different species that is due to convergent evolution, not common descent. Characters that exhibit such similarity are called *homoplastic features*. Compare with *homology*.

homospory (hoh"-mos'-pur-ee) Production of one type of *n* spore that gives rise to a bisexual gametophyte. Compare with *heterospory*.

homothallic (hoh"-moh-thal'-ik) Pertaining to certain algae and fungi that are self-fertile. Compare with *heterothallic*.

homozygous (hoh"-moh-zy'-gous) Having a pair of identical alleles for a particular locus. Compare with *heterozygous*.

hormone A chemical messenger, often produced in one region of the body of a multicellular organism and transported to another region where it signals cells to alter some aspect of growth, development, or metabolism.

hornwort A phylum of spore-producing, nonvascular, thallose plants with a life cycle similar to that of mosses.

host mothering The introduction of an embryo from one species into the uterus of another species, where it implants and develops; the host mother subsequently gives birth and may raise the offspring as her own.

Hox genes Clusters of homeobox-containing genes that specify the anterior-posterior axis of various animals during development.

human chorionic gonadotropin (hCG) A hormone secreted by cells surrounding the early embryo; signals the mother's corpus luteum to continue to function.

human genetics The science of inherited variation in humans.

human genome The totality of genetic information in human cells; includes the DNA content of both the nucleus and mitochondria. See *genome.*

human immunodeficiency virus (HIV) The retrovirus that causes AIDS (acquired immunodeficiency syndrome).

human leukocyte antigen (HLA) See *major histocompatibility complex.*

humus (hew'-mus) Organic matter in various stages of decomposition in the soil; gives soil a dark brown or black color.

Huntington disease A genetic disease that has an autosomal dominant inheritance pattern and causes mental and physical deterioration.

hybrid The offspring of two genetically dissimilar parents.

hybrid breakdown A postzygotic reproductive isolating mechanism in which, although an interspecific hybrid is fertile and produces a second (F_2) generation, the F_2 has defects that prevent it from successfully reproducing.

hybrid inviability A postzygotic reproductive isolating mechanism in which the embryonic development of an interspecific hybrid is aborted.

hybrid sterility A postzygotic reproductive isolating mechanism in which an interspecific hybrid cannot reproduce successfully.

hybrid vigor The genetic superiority of an F_1 hybrid over either parent, caused by the presence of heterozygosity for a number of different loci.

hybrid zone An area of overlap between two closely related populations, subspecies, or species in which interbreeding occurs.

hybridization (1) Interbreeding between members of two different taxa. (2) Interbreeding between genetically dissimilar parents. (3) In molecular biology, complementary base pairing between nucleic acid (DNA or RNA) strands from different sources.

hydration Process of association of a substance with the partial positive and/or negative charges of water molecules.

hydrocarbon An organic compound composed solely of hydrogen and carbon atoms.

hydrogen bond A weak attractive force existing between a hydrogen atom with a partial positive charge and an electronegative atom (usually oxygen or nitrogen) with a partial negative charge. Compare with *covalent bond* and *ionic bond.*

hydrologic cycle The water cycle, which includes evaporation, precipitation, and flow to the ocean; supplies terrestrial organisms with a continual supply of fresh water.

hydrolysis Reaction in which a covalent bond between two subunits is broken through the addition of the equivalent of a water molecule; a hydrogen atom is added to one subunit and a hydroxyl group to the other. Compare with *condensation synthesis.*

hydrophilic Interacting readily with water; having a greater affinity for water molecules than they have for each other. Compare with *hydrophobic.*

hydrophobic Not readily interacting with water; having less affinity for water molecules than they have for each other. Compare with *hydrophilic.*

hydroponics (hy"-dra-paun'-iks) Growing plants in an aerated solution of dissolved inorganic minerals, i.e., without soil.

hydrostatic skeleton A type of skeleton found in some invertebrates in which contracting muscles push against a tube of fluid.

hydroxide ion An anion (negatively charged particle) consisting of oxygen and hydrogen; usually written OH^-.

hydroxyl group (hy-drok'-sil) Polar functional group; abbreviated —OH.

hyperpolarize To change the membrane potential so that the inside of the cell becomes more negative than its resting potential.

hypertonic A term referring to a solution having an osmotic pressure (or solute concentration) greater than that of the solution with which it is compared. Compare with *hypotonic* and *isotonic.*

hypha (hy'-fah) (pl., *hyphae*) One of the threadlike filaments composing the mycelium of a water mold or fungus.

hypocotyl (hy'-poh-kah"-tl) The part of the axis of a plant embryo or seedling below the point of attachment of the cotyledons.

hypothalamus (hy-poh-thal'-uh-mus) Part of the vertebrate brain; in mammals it regulates the pituitary gland, the autonomic system, emotional responses, body temperature, water balance, and appetite; located below the thalamus.

hypothesis A testable statement about the nature of an observation or relationship. Compare with *theory.*

hypothetico-deductive approach Emphasizes the use of deductive reasoning to test hypotheses. Compare with *hypothetico-inductive approach.* See *deductive reasoning.*

hypothetico-inductive approach Emphasizes the use of inductive reasoning to discover new general principles. Compare with *hypothetico-deductive approach.* See *inductive reasoning.*

hypotonic A term referring to a solution having an osmotic pressure (or solute concentration) less than that of the solution with which it is compared. Compare with *hypertonic* and *isotonic.*

hypotrichs A group of dorsoventrally flattened ciliates that exhibit an unusual creeping–darting locomotion.

identical twins See *monozygotic twins.*

illuviation The deposition of material leached from the upper layers of soil into the lower layers.

imaginal discs Paired structures in an insect larva that develop into specific adult structures during complete metamorphosis.

imago (ih-may'-go) The adult form of an insect.

imbibition (im"-bi-bish'-en) The absorption of water by a seed prior to germination.

immigration The movement of individuals into a population. Compare with *emigration.*

immune response Process of recognizing foreign macromolecules and mounting a response aimed at eliminating them. See *specific* and *nonspecific immune responses; primary* and *secondary immune responses.*

immunoglobulin (im-yoon"-oh-glob'-yoo-lin) See *antibody.*

imperfect flower A flower that lacks either stamens or carpels. Compare with *perfect flower.*

imperfect fungi See *deuteromycetes.*

implantation The embedding of a developing embryo in the inner lining (endometrium) of the uterus.

implicit memory The unconscious memory for perceptual and motor skills, e.g., riding a bicycle.

imprinting (1) The expression of a gene based on its parental origin; also called *genomic imprinting* or *parental imprinting.* (2) A type of learning by which a young bird or mammal forms a strong social attachment to an individual (usually a parent) or object within a few hours after hatching or birth.

monomer (mon'-oh-mer) A molecule that can link with other similar molecules; two monomers join to form a dimer, whereas many form a polymer. Monomers are small (e.g., sugars or amino acids) or large (e.g., tubulin or actin proteins).

monophyletic group (mon"-oh-fye-let'-ik) A group of organisms that includes a recent common ancestor and all its descendants; a clade. Compare with *polyphyletic group* and *paraphyletic group*.

monosaccharide (mon-oh-sak'-ah-ride) A sugar that cannot be degraded by hydrolysis to a simpler sugar (e.g., glucose or fructose).

monosomy A type of aneuploidy in which an individual lacks one member of a pair of chromosomes; designated $2n - 1$.

monotremes (mon'-oh-treemz) Egg-laying mammals such as the duck-billed platypus of Australia.

monounsaturated fatty acid See *fatty acid.*

monozygotic twins Genetically identical twins that arise from the division of a single fertilized egg; commonly known as *identical twins.* Compare with *dizygotic twins.*

morphogen Any chemical agent thought to govern the processes of cell differentiation and pattern formation that lead to morphogenesis.

morphogenesis (mor-foh-jen'-eh-sis) The development of the form and structures of an organism and its parts; proceeds by a series of steps known as *pattern formation.*

mortality The rate at which individuals die; the average per capita death rate.

morula (mor'-yoo-lah) An early embryo consisting of a solid ball of cells.

mosaic development A rigid developmental pattern in which the fates of cells become restricted early in development. Compare with *regulative development.*

mosses A phylum of spore-producing nonvascular plants with an alternation of generations in which the dominant *n* gametophyte alternates with a 2*n* sporophyte that remains attached to the gametophyte.

motor neuron An efferent neuron that transmits impulses away from the central nervous system to skeletal muscle.

motor program A coordinated sequences of muscle actions responsible for many behaviors we think of as automatic.

motor unit Functional unit consisting of a single motor neuron and the muscle fibers it innervates.

mRNA cap An unusual nucleotide, 7-methylguanylate, that is added to the 5′ end of a eukaryotic messenger RNA. Capping enables eukaryotic ribosomes to bind to mRNA.

mucosa (mew-koh'-suh) See *mucous membrane.*

mucous membrane A type of epithelial membrane that lines a body cavity that opens to the outside of the body, e.g., the digestive and respiratory tracts; also called *mucosa.*

mucus (mew'-cus) A sticky secretion composed of covalently linked protein and carbohydrate; serves to lubricate body parts and trap particles of dirt and other contaminants. (The adjectival form is spelled *mucous.*)

Müllerian mimicry (mul-ler'-ee-un mim'-ih-kree) The resemblance of dangerous, unpalatable, or poisonous species to one another so that potential predators recognize them more easily. Compare with *Batesian mimicry.*

multiple alleles (al-leelz') Three or more alleles of a single locus (in a population), such as the alleles governing the ABO series of blood types.

multiple fruit A fruit that develops from many ovaries of many separate flowers, e.g., pineapple. Compare with *simple, aggregate,* and *accessory fruits.*

muscle (1) A tissue specialized for contraction. (2) An organ that produces movement by contraction.

mutagen (mew'-tah-jen) Any agent capable of entering the cell and producing mutations.

mutation Any change in DNA; may include a change in the nucleotide base pairs of a gene, a rearrangement of genes within the chromosomes so that their interactions produce different effects, or a change in the chromosomes themselves.

mutualism In ecology, a symbiotic relationship in which both partners benefit from the association. Compare with *parasitism* and *commensalism.*

mycelium (my-seel'-ee-um) (pl., *mycelia*) The vegetative body of most fungi and certain protists (water molds); consists of a branched network of hyphae.

mycorrhizae (my"-kor-rye'-zee) Mutualistic associations of fungi and plant roots that aid in the plant's absorption of essential minerals from the soil.

mycotoxins Poisonous chemical compounds produced by fungi, e.g., aflatoxins that harm the liver and are known carcinogens.

myelencephalon See *hindbrain.*

myelin sheath (my'-eh-lin) The white, fatty material that forms a sheath around the axons of certain nerve cells, which are then called *myelinated fibers.*

myocardial infarction (MI) Heart attack; serious consequence occurring when the heart muscle receives insufficient oxygen.

myofibrils (my-oh-fy'-brilz) Tiny threadlike structures in the cytoplasm of striated and cardiac muscle that are composed of myosin filaments and actin filaments; these filaments are responsible for muscle contraction; see *myosin filaments* and *actin filaments.*

myoglobin (my'-oh-glo"-bin) A hemoglobin-like, oxygen-transferring protein found in muscle.

myosin (my'-oh-sin) A protein that together with actin is responsible for muscle contraction.

myosin filaments Thick filaments consisting mainly of the protein myosin; actin and myosin filaments make up the myofibrils of muscle fibers.

n The chromosome number of a gamete. The chromosome number of a zygote is 2*n*. If an organism is not polyploid, the *n* gametes are haploid and the 2*n* zygotes are diploid.

NAD^+/NADH Oxidized and reduced forms, respectively, of nicotinamide adenine dinucleotide, a coenzyme that transfers electrons (as hydrogen), particularly in catabolic pathways, including cellular respiration.

$NADP^+$/NADPH Oxidized and reduced forms, respectively, of nicotinamide adenine dinucleotide phosphate, a coenzyme that acts as an electron (hydrogen) transfer agent, particularly in anabolic pathways, including photosynthesis.

nanoplankton Extremely minute (<10 μm in length) algae that are major producers in the ocean because of their great abundance; part of phytoplankton.

natality The rate at which individuals produce offspring; the average per capita birth rate.

natural killer cell (NK cell) A large, granular lymphocyte that functions in both nonspecific and specific immune responses; releases cytokines and proteolytic enzymes that target tumor cells and cells infected with viruses and other pathogens.

natural selection The mechanism of evolution proposed by Charles Darwin; the tendency of organisms that have favorable adaptations to their environment to survive and become the parents of the next generation. Evolution occurs when natural selection results in changes in allele frequencies in a population.

necrosis Uncontrolled cell death that causes inflammation and damages other cells. Compare with *apoptosis*.

nectary (nek′-ter-ee) In plants, a gland or other structure that secretes nectar.

negative feedback system A regulatory system in which a change in some steady state triggers a response that counteracts, or reverses, the change, restoring homeostasis, e.g., how mammals maintain body temperature. Compare with *positive feedback system*.

nekton (nek′-ton) Free-swimming aquatic organisms such as fish and turtles. Compare with *plankton*.

nematocyst (nem-at′-oh-sist) A stinging structure found within cnidocytes (stinging cells) in cnidarians; used for anchorage, defense, and capturing prey.

nematodes The phylum of animals commonly known as *roundworms*.

nemerteans The phylum of animals commonly known as *ribbon worms*; each has a proboscis (tubular feeding organ) for capturing prey.

neonate Newborn individual.

neoplasm See *tumor*.

nephridial organ (neh-frid′-ee-al) The excretory organ of many invertebrates; consists of simple or branching tubes that usually open to the outside of the body through pores; also called *nephridium*.

nephron (nef′-ron) The functional, microscopic unit of the vertebrate kidney.

neritic province (ner-ih′-tik) Ocean water that extends from the shoreline to where the bottom reaches a depth of 200 m. Compare with *oceanic province*.

nerve A bundle of axons (or dendrites) wrapped in connective tissue that conveys impulses between the central nervous system and some other part of the body.

nerve net A system of interconnecting nerve cells found in cnidarians and echinoderms.

nervous tissue A type of animal tissue specialized for transmitting electrical and chemical signals.

net primary productivity The energy that remains in an ecosystem (as biomass) after cellular respiration has occurred; net primary productivity equals gross primary productivity minus respiration. Compare with *gross primary productivity*.

neural crest (noor′-ul) A group of cells along the neural tube that migrate and form various parts of the embryo, including parts of the peripheral nervous system.

neural plasticity The ability of the nervous system to change in response to experience.

neural plate See *neural tube*.

neural transmission See *transmission, neural*.

neural tube The hollow, longitudinal structure in the early vertebrate embryo that gives rise to the brain and spinal cord. The neural tube forms from the neural plate, a flattened, thickened region of the ectoderm that rolls up and sinks below the surface.

neuroendocrine cells Neurons that produce neurohormones.

neurohormones Hormones produced by neuroendocrine cells; transported down axons and released into interstitial fluid; common in invertebrates; in vertebrates, the hypothalamus produces neurohormones.

neuron (noor′-on) A nerve cell; a conducting cell of the nervous system that typically consists of a cell body, dendrites, and an axon.

neuropeptide One of a group of peptides produced in neural tissue that function as signaling molecules; many are neurotransmitters.

neuropeptide Y A signaling molecule produced by the hypothalamus that increases appetite and slows metabolism; helps restore energy homeostasis when leptin levels and food intake are low.

neurotransmitter A chemical signal used by neurons to transmit impulses across a synapse.

neutral solution A solution of pH 7; there are equal concentrations of hydrogen ions [H^+] and hydroxide ions [OH^-]. Compare with *acidic solution* and *basic solution*.

neutral variation Variation that does not appear to confer any selective advantage or disadvantage to the organism.

neutron (noo′-tron) An electrically neutral particle with a mass of 1 atomic mass unit (amu) found in the atomic nucleus. Compare with *proton* and *electron*.

neutrophil (new′-truh-fil) A type of granular leukocyte important in immune responses; a type of phagocyte that engulfs and destroys bacteria and foreign matter.

niche (nich) The totality of an organism's adaptations, its use of resources, and the lifestyle to which it is fitted in its community; how an organism uses materials in its environment as well as how it interacts with other organisms; also called *ecological niche*. See *fundamental niche* and *realized niche*.

nicotinamide adenine dinucleotide See *NAD⁺/NADH*.

nicotinamide adenine dinucleotide phosphate See *NADP⁺/NADPH*.

nitric oxide (NO) A gaseous signaling molecule; a neurotransmitter.

nitrification (nie″-tra-fuh-kay′-shun) The conversion of ammonia (NH_3) to nitrate (NO_3^-) by certain bacteria (nitrifying bacteria) in the soil; part of the nitrogen cycle.

nitrogen cycle The worldwide circulation of nitrogen from the abiotic environment into living things and back into the abiotic environment.

nitrogen fixation The conversion of atmospheric nitrogen (N_2) to ammonia (NH_3) by certain bacteria; part of the nitrogen cycle.

nitrogenase (nie-traa′-jen-ase) The enzyme responsible for nitrogen fixation under anaerobic conditions.

nociceptors (no′-sih-sep-torz) Pain receptors; free endings of certain sensory neurons whose stimulation is perceived as pain.

node The area on a stem where each leaf is attached. Compare with *internode*.

nodules Swellings on the roots of plants, such as legumes, in which symbiotic nitrogen-fixing bacteria (*Rhizobium*) live.

noncompetitive inhibitor A substance that lowers the rate at which an enzyme catalyzes a reaction but does not bind to the active site. Compare with *competitive inhibitor*.

noncyclic electron transport In photosynthesis, the linear flow of electrons, produced by photolysis of water, through photosystems II and I; results in the formation of ATP (by chemiosmosis), NADPH, and O_2. Compare with *cyclic electron transport*.

nondisjunction Abnormal separation of sister chromatids or of homologous chromosomes caused by their failure to disjoin (move apart) properly during mitosis or meiosis.

nonpolar covalent bond Chemical bond formed by the equal sharing of electrons between atoms of approximately equal electronegativity. Compare with *polar covalent bond*.

nonpolar molecule Molecule that does not have a positively charged end and a negatively charged end; nonpolar molecules are generally insoluble in water. Compare with *polar molecule*.

nonsense mutation A base-pair substitution mutation that results in an amino acid–specifying codon being changed to a termination (stop) codon; when the abnormal mRNA is translated, the resulting protein is usually truncated and nonfunctional. Compare with *missense mutation*.

nonspecific immune responses Mechanisms such as physical barriers (e.g., the skin) and phagocytosis that provide immediate and general protection against pathogens. Also called *innate immunity*. Compare with *specific immune responses*.

norepinephrine (nor-ep-ih-nef´-rin) A neurotransmitter that is also a hormone secreted by the adrenal medulla.

norm of reaction The range of phenotypic possibilities that can develop from a single genotype under different environmental conditions.

Northern blot A technique in which RNA fragments, previously separated by gel electrophoresis, are transferred to a nitrocellulose membrane and detected by autoradiography or chemical luminescence. Compare with *Southern blot* and *Western blot*.

notochord (no´-toe-kord) The flexible, longitudinal rod in the anterior-posterior axis that serves as an internal skeleton in the embryos of all chordates and in the adults of some.

nuclear area Region of a prokaryotic cell that contains DNA; not enclosed by a membrane. Also called *nucleoid*.

nuclear envelope The double membrane system that encloses the cell nucleus of eukaryotes.

nuclear equivalence The concept that the nuclei of all differentiated cells of an adult organism are genetically identical to one another and to the nucleus of the zygote from which they were derived. Compare with *genomic rearrangement* and *gene amplification*.

nuclear pores Structures in the nuclear envelope that allow passage of certain materials between the cell nucleus and the cytoplasm.

nucleoid See *nuclear area*.

nucleolus (new-klee´-oh-lus) (pl., *nucleoli*) Specialized structure in the cell nucleus formed from regions of several chromosomes; site of assembly of the ribosomal subunits.

nucleoplasm The contents of the cell nucleus.

nucleoside triphosphate Molecule consisting of a nitrogenous base, a pentose sugar, and three phosphate groups, e.g., adenosine triphosphate (ATP).

nucleosomes (new´-klee-oh-sohmz) Repeating units of chromatin structure, each consisting of a length of DNA wound around a complex of eight histone molecules. Adjacent nucleosomes are connected by a DNA linker region associated with another histone protein.

nucleotide (noo´-klee-oh-tide) A molecule consisting of one or more phosphate groups, a five-carbon sugar (ribose or deoxyribose), and a nitrogenous base (purine or pyrimidine).

nucleotide excision repair A DNA repair mechanism commonly used to repair a damaged segment of DNA caused by the sun's ultraviolet radiation or by harmful chemicals.

nucleus (new´-klee-us) (pl., *nuclei*) (1) The central region of an atom that contains the protons and neutrons. (2) A cell organelle in eukaryotes that contains the DNA and serves as the control center of the cell. (3) A mass of nerve cell bodies in the central nervous system. Compare with *ganglion*.

nut A simple, dry fruit that contains a single seed and is surrounded by a hard fruit wall.

nutrients The chemical substances in food that are used as components for synthesizing needed materials and/or as energy sources.

nutrition The process of taking in and using food (nutrients).

obesity Excess accumulation of body fat; a person is considered obese if the body mass index (BMI) is 30 or higher.

obligate anaerobe An organism that grows only in the absence of oxygen. Compare with *facultative anaerobe*.

occipital lobes Posterior areas of the mammalian cerebrum; interpret visual stimuli from the retina of the eye.

oceanic province That part of the open ocean that overlies an ocean bottom deeper than 200 m. Compare with *neritic province*.

Okazaki fragment One of many short segments of DNA, each 100 to 1000 nucleotides long, that must be joined by DNA ligase to form the lagging strand in DNA replication.

olfactory epithelium Tissue containing odor-sensing neurons.

oligodendrocyte A type of glial cell that forms myelin sheaths around neurons in the CNS.

ommatidium (om″-ah-tid´-ee-um) (pl., *ommatidia*) One of the light-detecting units of a compound eye, consisting of a lens and a crystalline cone that focus light onto photoreceptors called *retinular cells*.

omnivore (om´-nih-vore) An animal that eats a variety of plant and animal materials.

oncogene (on´-koh-jeen) An abnormally functioning gene implicated in causing cancer. Compare with *proto-oncogene* and *tumor suppressor gene*.

oocytes (oh´-oh-sites) Meiotic cells that give rise to egg cells (ova).

oogamy (oh-og´-uh-me) The fertilization of a large, nonmotile female gamete by a small, motile male gamete. Compare with *isogamy* and *anisogamy*.

oogenesis (oh″-oh-jen´-eh-sis) Production of female gametes (eggs) by meiosis. Compare with *spermatogenesis*.

oospore A thick-walled, resistant spore formed from a zygote during sexual reproduction in water molds.

open circulatory system A type of circulatory system in which the blood bathes the tissues directly; characteristic of arthropods and many mollusks. Compare with *closed circulatory system*.

open system An entity that exchanges energy with its surroundings. Compare with *closed system*.

operant conditioning A type of learning in which an animal is rewarded or punished for performing a behavior it discovers by chance.

operator site One of the control regions of an operon; the DNA segment to which a repressor binds, thereby inhibiting the transcription of the adjacent structural genes of the operon.

operculum In bony fishes, a protective flap of the body wall that covers the gills.

operon (op´-er-on) In prokaryotes, a group of structural genes that are coordinately controlled and transcribed as a single message, plus their adjacent regulatory elements.

opposable thumb The arrangement of the fingers so that they are positioned opposite the thumb, enabling the organism to grasp objects.

optimal foraging The process of obtaining food in a manner that maximizes benefits and/or minimizes costs.

orbital Region in which electrons occur in an atom or molecule.

order A taxonomic category made up of related families.

organ A specialized structure, such as the heart or liver, made up of tissues and adapted to perform a specific function or group of functions.

organ of Corti The structure within the inner ear of vertebrates that contains receptor cells that sense sound vibrations.

organ system An organized group of tissues and organs that work together to perform a specialized set of functions, e.g., the digestive system or circulatory system.

organelle One of the specialized structures within the cell, such as the mitochondria, Golgi complex, ribosomes, or contractile vacuole; many organelles are membrane-enclosed.

organic compound A compound consisting of a backbone made up of carbon atoms. Compare with *inorganic compound*.

organism Any living system consisting of one or more cells.

organismic respiration See *respiration*.

organogenesis The process of organ formation.

orgasm (or'-gazm) The climax of sexual excitement.

origin of replication A specific site on the DNA where replication begins.

orthologous genes Homologous genes found in different species because they were inherited from a common ancestor.

osmoconformer An animal in which the salt concentration of body fluids varies along with changes in the surrounding sea water so that it stays in osmotic equilibrium with its surroundings. Compare with *osmoregulator.*

osmoregulation (oz"-moh-reg-yoo-lay'-shun) The active regulation of the osmotic pressure of body fluids so that they do not become excessively dilute or excessively concentrated.

osmoregulator An animal that maintains an optimal salt concentration in its body fluids despite changes in salinity of its surroundings. Compare with *osmoconformer.*

osmosis (oz-moh'-sis) The net movement of water (the principal solvent in biological systems) by diffusion through a selectively permeable membrane from a region of higher concentration of water (a hypotonic solution) to a region of lower concentration of water (a hypertonic solution).

osmotic pressure The pressure that must be exerted on the hypertonic side of a selectively permeable membrane to prevent diffusion of water (by osmosis) from the side containing pure water.

osteichthyes (os"-tee-ick'-thees) Historically, the vertebrate class of bony fishes. Biologists now divide bony fishes into three classes: Actinopterygii, the ray-finned fishes; Actinistia, the lobe-finned fishes; and Dipnoi, the lungfishes.

osteoblast (os'-tee-oh-blast) A type of bone cell that secretes the protein matrix of bone. Also see *osteocyte.*

osteoclast (os'-tee-oh-clast) Large, multinucleate cell that helps sculpt and remodel bones by dissolving and removing part of the bony substance.

osteocyte (os'-tee-oh-site) A mature bone cell; an osteoblast that has become embedded within the bone matrix and occupies a lacuna.

osteon (os'-tee-on) The spindle-shaped unit of bone composed of concentric layers of osteocytes organized around a central Haversian canal containing blood vessels and nerves.

otoliths (oh'-toe-liths) Small calcium carbonate crystals in the saccule and utricle of the inner ear; sense gravity and are important in static equilibrium.

outbreeding The mating of individuals of unrelated strains, also called *outcrossing.* Compare with *inbreeding.*

outcrossing See *outbreeding.*

outgroup In cladistics, a taxon that represents an approximation of the ancestral condition; the outgroup is related to the *ingroup* (the members of the group under study) but separated from the ingroup lineage before they diversified.

ovary (oh'-var-ee) (1) In animals, one of the paired female gonads responsible for producing eggs and sex hormones. (2) In flowering plants, the base of the carpel that contains ovules; ovaries develop into fruits after fertilization.

oviduct (oh'-vih-dukt) The tube that carries ova from the ovary to the uterus, cloaca, or body exterior. Also called *fallopian tube* or *uterine tube.*

oviparous (oh-vip'-ur-us) Bearing young in the egg stage of development; egg laying. Compare with *viviparous* and *ovoviviparous.*

ovoviviparous (oh"-voh-vih-vip'-ur-us) A type of development in which the young hatch from eggs incubated inside the mother's body. Compare with *viviparous* and *oviparous.*

ovulation (ov-u-lay'-shun) The release of an egg from the ovary.

ovule (ov'-yool) The structure (i.e., megasporangium) in the plant ovary that develops into the seed following fertilization.

ovum (pl., *ova*) Female gamete of an animal.

oxaloacetate Four-carbon compound; important intermediate in the citric acid cycle and in the C_4 and CAM pathways of carbon fixation in photosynthesis.

oxidants Highly reactive molecules such as free radicals, peroxides, and superoxides that are produced during normal cell processes that require oxygen; can damage DNA and other molecules by snatching electrons. Compare with *antioxidants.*

oxidation The loss of one or more electrons (or hydrogen atoms) by an atom, ion, or molecule. Compare with *reduction.*

oxidative phosphorylation (fos"-for-ih-lay'-shun) The production of ATP using energy derived from the transfer of electrons in the electron transport system of mitochondria; occurs by chemiosmosis.

oxygen debt The oxygen necessary to metabolize the lactic acid produced during strenuous exercise.

oxygen-carrying capacity The maximum amount of oxygen transported by hemoglobin.

oxygen–hemoglobin dissociation curve A curve depicting the percentage saturation of hemoglobin with oxygen, as a function of certain variables such as oxygen concentration, carbon dioxide concentration, or pH.

oxyhemoglobin Hemoglobin that has combined with oxygen.

oxytocin (ok"see-tow'-sin) Hormone secreted by the hypothalamus and released by the posterior lobe of the pituitary gland; stimulates contraction of the pregnant uterus and the ducts of mammary glands.

ozone A blue gas, O_3, with a distinctive odor that is a human-made pollutant near Earth's surface (in the troposphere) but a natural and essential component of the stratosphere.

P generation (parental generation) Members of two different true-breeding lines that are crossed to produce the F_1 generation.

P680 Chlorophyll *a* molecules that serve as the reaction center of photosystem II, transferring photoexcited electrons to a primary acceptor; named by their absorption peak at 680 nm.

P700 Chlorophyll *a* molecules that serve as the reaction center of photosystem I, transferring photoexcited electrons to a primary acceptor; named by their absorption peak at 700 nm.

pacemaker (of the heart) See *sinoatrial (SA) node.*

Pacinian corpuscle (pah-sin'-ee-an kor'-pus-el) A receptor located in the dermis of the skin that responds to pressure.

paedomorphosis Retention of juvenile or larval features in a sexually mature animal.

pair bond A stable relationship between animals of opposite sex that ensures cooperative behavior in mating and rearing the young.

paleoanthropology (pay"-lee-o-an-thro-pol'-uh-gee) The study of human evolution.

Paleozoic era That part of geologic time extending from roughly 542 million to 251 million years ago.

palindromic Reading the same forward and backward; DNA sequences are palindromic when the base sequence of one strand reads the same as its complement when both are read in the 5' to 3' direction.

palisade mesophyll (mez'-oh-fil) The vertically stacked, columnar mesophyll cells near the upper epidermis in certain leaves. Compare with *spongy mesophyll.*

pancreas (pan'-kree-us) Large gland located in the vertebrate abdominal cavity. The pancreas produces pancreatic juice containing digestive enzymes; also serves as an endocrine gland, secreting the hormones insulin and glucagon.

parabasilids Anaerobic, flagellated excavates that often live in animals; examples include trichonymphs and trichomonads.

parabronchi (sing., *parabronchus*) Thin-walled ducts in the lungs of birds; gases are exchanged across their walls.

paracrine regulation A type of regulation in which a signal molecule (e.g., certain hormones) diffuses through interstitial fluid and acts on nearby target cells. Compare with *autocrine regulation*.

paraphyletic group A group of organisms made up of a common ancestor and some, but not all, of its descendants. Compare with *monophyletic group* and *polyphyletic group*.

parapodia (par″-uh-poh′-dee-ah) (sing., *parapodium*) Paired, thickly bristled paddlelike appendages extending laterally from each segment of polychaete worms.

parasite A heterotrophic organism that obtains nourishment from the living tissue of another organism (the host).

parasitism (par′-uh-si-tiz″-m) A symbiotic relationship in which one member (the parasite) benefits and the other (the host) is adversely affected. Compare with *commensalism* and *mutualism*.

parasympathetic nervous system A division of the autonomic nervous system concerned with the control of the internal organs; functions to conserve or restore energy. Compare with *sympathetic nervous system*.

parathyroid glands Small, pea-sized glands closely adjacent to the thyroid gland; they secrete parathyroid hormone, which regulates calcium and phosphate metabolism.

parathyroid hormone (PTH) A hormone secreted by the parathyroid glands; regulates calcium and phosphate metabolism.

parenchyma (par-en′-kih-mah) Highly variable living plant cells that have thin primary walls; function in photosynthesis, the storage of nutrients, and/or secretion.

parsimony The principle based on the experience that the simplest explanation is most probably the correct one.

parthenogenesis (par″-theh-noh-jen′-eh-sis) The development of an unfertilized egg into an adult organism; common among honeybees, wasps, and certain other arthropods.

partial pressure (of a gas) The pressure exerted by a gas in a mixture, which is the same pressure it would exert if alone. For example, the partial pressure of atmospheric oxygen (P_{O_2}) is 160 mm Hg at sea level.

parturition (par″-to-rish′-un) The birth process.

passive immunity Temporary immunity that depends on the presence of immunoglobulins produced by another organism. Compare with *active immunity*.

passive ion channel A channel in the plasma membrane that permits the passage of specific ions such as Na^+, K^+, or Cl^-.

patch–clamp technique A method that allows researchers to study the ion channels of a tiny patch of membrane by tightly sealing a micropipette to the patch and measuring the flow of ions through the channels.

patchiness See *clumped dispersion*.

pathogen (path′-oh-gen) An organism, usually a microorganism, capable of producing disease.

pathogen-associated molecular patterns (PAMPs) Distinctive molecules on bacteria and other pathogens that are not found in animals; pattern recognition receptors bind them.

pattern formation See *morphogenesis*.

pattern recognition receptors Receptors on certain types of animal cells that bind pathogen-associated molecular patterns (PAMPs); binding activates nonspecific immune responses.

pedigree A chart constructed to show an inheritance pattern within a family through multiple generations.

peduncle The stalk of a flower or inflorescence.

pellicle A flexible outer covering consisting of protein; characteristic of certain protists, e.g., ciliates and euglenoids.

penis The male sexual organ of copulation in reptiles, mammals, and a few birds.

pentose A sugar molecule containing five carbons.

people overpopulation A situation in which there are too many people in a given geographic area; results in pollution, environmental degradation, and resource depletion. Compare with *consumption overpopulation*.

pepsin (pep′-sin) An enzyme produced in the stomach that initiates digestion of protein.

pepsinogen The precursor of pepsin; secreted by chief cells in the gastric glands of the stomach.

peptide (pep′-tide) A compound consisting of a chain of amino acid groups linked by peptide bonds. A dipeptide consists of two amino acids, a polypeptide of many.

peptide bond A distinctive covalent carbon-to-nitrogen bond that links amino acids in peptides and proteins.

peptidoglycan (pep″-tid-oh-gly′-kan) A modified protein or peptide having an attached carbohydrate; component of the bacterial cell wall.

peptidyl transferase The ribosomal enzyme that catalyzes the formation of a peptide bond.

perennial plant (purr-en′-ee-ul) A woody or herbaceous plant that grows year after year, i.e., lives more than two years. Compare with *annual* and *biennial*.

perfect flower A flower that has both stamens and carpels. Compare with *imperfect flower*.

pericentriolar material Fibrils surrounding the centrioles in the microtubule-organizing centers in cells of animals and other organisms having centrioles.

pericycle (pehr′-eh-sy″-kl) A layer of meristematic cells typically found between the endodermis and phloem in roots.

periderm (pehr′-ih-durm) The outer bark of woody stems and roots; composed of cork cells, cork cambium, and cork parenchyma, along with traces of primary tissues.

period An interval of geologic time that is a subdivision of an era; each period is divided into epochs.

peripheral membrane protein A protein associated with one of the surfaces of a biological membrane. Compare with *integral membrane protein*.

peripheral nervous system (PNS) In vertebrates, the nerves and receptors that lie outside the central nervous system. Compare with *central nervous system (CNS)*.

peristalsis (pehr″-ih-stal′-sis) Rhythmic waves of muscular contraction and relaxation in the walls of hollow tubular organs, such as the ureter or parts of the digestive tract, that serve to move the contents through the tube.

permafrost Permanently frozen subsoil characteristic of frigid areas such as the tundra.

peroxisomes (pehr-ox′-ih-sohmz) In eukaryotic cells, membrane-enclosed organelles containing enzymes that produce or degrade hydrogen peroxide.

persistence A characteristic of certain chemicals that are extremely stable and may take many years to be broken down into simpler forms by natural processes.

petal One of the parts of the flower attached inside the whorl of sepals; petals are usually colored.

petiole (pet′-ee-ohl) The part of a leaf that attaches to a stem.

pH The negative logarithm of the hydrogen ion concentration of a solution (expressed as moles per liter). Neutral pH is 7, values less than 7 are acidic, and those greater than 7 are basic.

phage See *bacteriophage*.

phagocytosis (fag″-oh-sy-toh′-sis) Literally, "cell eating"; a type of endocytosis by which certain cells engulf food particles, microorganisms, foreign matter, or other cells.

pharmacogenetics A field of gene-based medicine in which drugs are personalized to match a patient's genetic makeup.

pharyngeal slits (fair-in′-jel) Openings that lead from the pharyngeal cavity to the outside; evolved as part of a filter-feeding system in chordates and later became modified for other functions, including gill slits in many aquatic vertebrates.

pharynx (fair′-inks) Part of the digestive tract. In complex vertebrates, it is bounded anteriorly by the mouth and nasal cavities and posteriorly by the esophagus and larynx; the throat region in humans.

phenetics (feh-neh′-tiks) An approach to classification based on measurable similarities in phenotypic characters without consideration of homology or other evolutionary relationships. Compare with *cladistics* and *evolutionary systematics*.

phenotype (fee′-noh-type) The physical or chemical expression of an organism's genes. Compare with *genotype*.

phenotype frequency The proportion of a particular phenotype in the population.

phenylketonuria (PKU) (fee″-nl-kee″-toh-noor′-ee-ah) An inherited disease in which there is a deficiency of the enzyme that normally converts phenylalanine to tyrosine; results in mental retardation if untreated.

pheromone (fer′-oh-mone) A substance secreted by an organism to the external environment that influences the development or behavior of other members of the same species.

phloem (flo′-em) The vascular tissue that conducts dissolved sugar and other organic compounds in plants.

phosphate group A weakly acidic functional group that can release one or two hydrogen ions.

phosphodiester linkage Covalent linkage between two nucleotides in a strand of DNA or RNA; includes a phosphate group bonded to the sugars of two adjacent nucleotides.

phosphoenolpyruvate (PEP) Three-carbon phosphorylated compound that is an important intermediate in glycolysis and is a reactant in the initial carbon fixation step in C_4 and CAM photosynthesis.

phosphoglycerate (PGA) Phosphorylated three-carbon compound that is an important metabolic intermediate.

phospholipids (fos″-foh-lip′-idz) Lipids in which two fatty acids and a phosphorus-containing group are attached to glycerol; major components of cell membranes.

phosphorus cycle The worldwide circulation of phosphorus from the abiotic environment into living things and back into the abiotic environment.

phosphorylation (fos″-for-ih-lay′-shun) The introduction of a phosphate group into an organic molecule. See *kinases*.

photoautotroph An organism that obtains energy from light and synthesizes organic compounds from inorganic raw materials; includes plants, algae, and some bacteria. Compare with *photoheterotroph, chemoautotroph,* and *chemoheterotroph*.

photoheterotroph An organism that can carry out photosynthesis to obtain energy but cannot fix carbon dioxide and therefore requires organic compounds as a carbon source; includes some bacteria and archaea. Compare with *photoautotroph, chemoautotroph,* and *chemoheterotroph*.

photolysis (foh-tol′-uh-sis) The photochemical splitting of water in the light-dependent reactions of photosynthesis; a specific enzyme is needed to catalyze this reaction.

photon (foh′-ton) A particle of electromagnetic radiation; one quantum of radiant energy.

photoperiodism (foh″-teh-peer′-ee-o-dizm) The physiological response (such as flowering) of plants to variations in the length of daylight and darkness.

photophosphorylation (foh″-toh-fos-for-ih-lay′-shun) The production of ATP in photosynthesis.

photoreceptor (foh″-toh-ree-sep′-tor) (1) A sense organ specialized to detect light. (2) A pigment that absorbs light before triggering a physiological response.

photorespiration (foh″-toh-res-pur-ay′-shun) The process that reduces the efficiency of photosynthesis in C_3 plants during hot spells in summer; consumes oxygen and produces carbon dioxide through the degradation of Calvin cycle intermediates.

photosynthesis The biological process that captures light energy and transforms it into the chemical energy of organic molecules (e.g., carbohydrates), which are manufactured from carbon dioxide and water.

photosystem One of two photosynthetic units responsible for capturing light energy and transferring excited electrons; photosystem I strongly absorbs light of about 700 nm, whereas photosystem II strongly absorbs light of about 680 nm. See *antenna complex* and *reaction center*.

phototroph (foh′-toh-trof) Organism that uses light as a source of energy. Compare with *chemotroph*. See *photoautotroph* and *photoheterotroph*.

phototropism (foh″-toh-troh′-pizm) The growth of a plant in response to the direction of light.

phycocyanin (fy″-koh-sy-ah′-nin) A blue pigment found in cyanobacteria and red algae.

phycoerythrin (fy″-koh-ee-rih′-thrin) A red pigment found in cyanobacteria and red algae.

phylogenetic species concept An alternative to the biological species concept in which for a population to be declared a separate species, it must have undergone evolution long enough for statistically significant differences to emerge. Also called *evolutionary species concept*. Compare with *species*.

phylogenetic systematics See *cladistics*.

phylogenetic tree A branching diagram that shows lines of descent among a group of related species.

phylogeny (fy-loj′-en-ee) The complete evolutionary history of a group of organisms.

phylum (fy′-lum) (pl., *phyla*) A taxonomic grouping of related, similar classes; a category beneath the kingdom and above the class.

phytoalexins Antimicrobial compounds produced by plants that limit the spread of pathogens such as fungi.

phytochemicals Compounds found in plants that play important roles in preventing certain diseases; some function as antioxidants.

phytochrome (fy′-toh-krome) A blue-green, proteinaceous pigment involved in a wide variety of physiological responses to light; occurs in two interchangeable forms depending on the ratio of red to far-red light.

phytoplankton (fy″-toh-plank′-tun) Microscopic floating algae and cyanobacteria that are the base of most aquatic food webs. Compare with *zooplankton*. See *plankton* and *nanoplankton*.

pia mater (pee′-a may′-ter) The inner membrane covering the brain and spinal cord; the innermost of the meninges; also see *dura mater* and *arachnoid*.

pigment A substance that selectively absorbs light of specific wavelengths.

pili (pie′-lie) (sing., *pilus*) Hairlike structures on the surface of many bacteria; function in conjugation or attachment.

pineal gland (pie-nee′-al) Endocrine gland located in the brain.

pinocytosis (pin″-oh-sy-toh′-sis) Cell drinking; a type of endocytosis by which cells engulf and absorb droplets of liquids.

pioneer The first organism to colonize an area and begin the first stage of succession.

pistil The female reproductive organ of a flower; consists of either a single carpel or two or more fused carpels. See *carpel*.

pith The innermost tissue in the stems and roots of many herbaceous plants; primarily a storage tissue.

pituitary gland (pi-too′-ih-tehr″-ee) An endocrine gland located below the hypothalamus; secretes several hormones that influence a wide range of physiological processes.

placenta (plah-sen′-tah) The partly fetal and partly maternal organ whereby materials are exchanged between fetus and mother in the uterus of placental mammals.

placoderms (plak′-oh-durmz) A group of extinct jawed fishes.

plankton Free-floating, mainly microscopic aquatic organisms found in the upper layers of the water; consisting of phytoplankton and zooplankton. Compare with *nekton*.

planula larva (plan′-yoo-lah) A ciliated larval form found in cnidarians.

plasma The fluid portion of blood in which red blood cells, white blood cells, and platelets are suspended.

plasma cell Cell that secretes antibodies; a differentiated B lymphocyte (B cell).

plasma membrane The selectively permeable surface membrane that encloses the cell contents and through which all materials entering or leaving the cell must pass.

plasma proteins Proteins such as albumins, globulins, and fibrinogen that circulate in the blood plasma.

plasmid (plaz′-mid) Small, circular, double-stranded DNA molecule that carries genes separate from those in the main DNA of a cell.

plasmodesmata (sing., *plasmodesma*) Cytoplasmic channels connecting adjacent plant cells and allowing for the movement of molecules and ions between cells.

plasmodial slime mold (plaz-moh′-dee-uhl) A funguslike protist whose feeding stage consists of a plasmodium.

plasmodium (plaz-moh′-dee-um) A multinucleate mass of living matter that moves and feeds in an amoeboid fashion.

plasmogamy (1) Fusion of the cytoplasm of two cells without fusion of nuclei. (2) A stage in the asexual reproduction of some fungi; hyphae of two compatible mating types come together, and their cytoplasm fuses.

plasmolysis (plaz-mol′-ih-sis) The shrinkage of cytoplasm and the pulling away of the plasma membrane from the cell wall when a plant cell (or other walled cell) loses water, usually in a hypertonic environment.

plastids (plas′-tidz) A family of membrane-enclosed organelles occurring in photosynthetic eukaryotic cells; include chloroplasts, chromoplasts, and amyloplasts and other leukoplasts.

platelets (playt′-lets) Cell fragments in vertebrate blood that function in clotting; also called *thrombocytes*.

platyhelminths The phylum of acoelomate animals commonly known as *flatworms*.

pleiotropy The ability of a single gene to have multiple effects.

plesiomorphic characters See *shared ancestral characters*.

pleural membrane (ploor′-ul) The membrane that lines the thoracic cavity and envelops each lung.

ploidy The number of chromosome sets in a nucleus or cell. See *haploid, diploid,* and *polyploid*.

plumule (ploom′-yool) The embryonic shoot apex, or terminal bud, located above the point of attachment of the cotyledon(s).

pluripotent (ploor-i-poh′-tent) A term describing a stem cell that can divide to give rise to many, but not all, types of cells in an organism. Compare with *totipotent*.

pneumatophore (noo-mat′-uh-for″) Roots that extend up out of the water in swampy areas and are thought to provide aeration between the atmosphere and submerged roots.

polar body A small *n* cell produced during oogenesis in female animals that does not develop into a functional ovum.

polar covalent bond Chemical bond formed by the sharing of electrons between atoms that differ in electronegativity; the end of the bond near the more electronegative atom has a partial negative charge, and the other end has a partial positive charge. Compare with *nonpolar covalent bond*.

polar molecule Molecule that has one end with a partial positive charge and the other with a partial negative charge; polar molecules are generally soluble in water. Compare with *nonpolar molecule*.

polar nucleus In flowering plants, one of two *n* cells in the embryo sac that fuse with a sperm during double fertilization to form the 3*n* endosperm.

pollen grain The immature male gametophyte of seed plants (gymnosperms and angiosperms) that produces sperm capable of fertilization.

pollen tube In gymnosperms and flowering plants, a tube or extension that forms after germination of the pollen grain and through which male gametes (sperm cells) pass into the ovule.

pollination (pol″-uh-nay′-shen) In seed plants, the transfer of pollen from the male to the female part of the plant.

poly-A tail See *polyadenylation*.

polyadenylation (pol″-ee-a-den-uh-lay′-shun) That part of eukaryotic mRNA processing in which multiple adenine-containing nucleotides (a poly-A tail) are added to the 3′ end of the molecule.

polyandry A mating system in which a female mates with several males during a breeding season. Compare with *polygyny*.

polygenic inheritance (pol″-ee-jen′-ik) Inheritance in which several independently assorting or loosely linked nonallelic genes modify the intensity of a trait or contribute to the phenotype in additive fashion.

polygyny A mating system in which a male animal mates with many females during a breeding season. Compare with *polyandry*.

polymer (pol′-ih-mer) A molecule built up from repeating subunits of the same general type (monomers); examples include proteins, nucleic acids, or polysaccharides.

polymerase chain reaction (PCR) A method by which a targeted DNA fragment is amplified in vitro to produce millions of copies.

polymorphism (pol″-ee-mor′-fizm) (1) The existence of two or more phenotypically different individuals within a population. (2) The presence of detectable variation in the genomes of different individuals in a population.

polyp (pol′-ip) A hydralike animal; the sessile stage of the life cycle of certain cnidarians. Compare with *medusa*.

polypeptide See *peptide*.

polyphyletic group (pol″-ee-fye-let′-ik) A group made up of organisms that evolved from two or more different ancestors. Compare with *monophyletic group* and *paraphyletic group*.

polyploid (pol′-ee-ployd) The condition of having more than two sets of chromosomes per nucleus. Compare with *diploid* and *haploid*.

polyribosome A complex consisting of a number of ribosomes attached to an mRNA during translation; also known as a *polysome*.

polysaccharide (pol-ee-sak'-ah-ride) A carbohydrate consisting of many monosaccharide subunits (e.g., starch, glycogen, and cellulose).

polysome See *polyribosome*.

polyspermy The fertilization of an egg by more than one sperm.

polytene A term describing a giant chromosome consisting of many parallel DNA double helices. Polytene chromosomes are typically found in cells of the salivary glands and some other tissues of certain insects, such as the fruit fly, *Drosophila*.

polyunsaturated fatty acid See *fatty acid*.

pons (ponz) The white bulge that is the part of the brain stem between the medulla and the midbrain; connects various parts of the brain.

population A group of organisms of the same species that live in a defined geographic area at the same time.

population bottleneck See *bottleneck*.

population crash An abrupt decline in the size of a population.

population density The number of individuals of a species per unit of area or volume at a given time.

population dynamics The study of changes in populations, such as how and why population numbers change over time.

population ecology That branch of biology that deals with the numbers of a particular species that are found in an area and how and why those numbers change (or remain fixed) over time.

population genetics The study of genetic variability in a population and of the forces that act on it.

population growth momentum The continued growth of a population after fertility rates have declined, as a result of a population's young age structure.

poriferans Sponges; members of phylum Porifera.

positional information In plants, the exposure of cells to different concentrations of signaling molecules that specify where the cell is located relative to the body's axes; this information affects cell differentiation and tissue formation.

positive feedback system A system in which a change in some steady state triggers a response that intensifies the changing condition. Compare with *negative feedback system*.

posterior Toward the tail end of a bilaterally symmetrical animal. Compare with *anterior*.

postsynaptic neuron A neuron that transmits an impulse away from a synapse. Compare with *presynaptic neuron*.

postzygotic barrier One of several reproductive isolating mechanisms that prevent gene flow between species after fertilization has taken place, e.g., hybrid inviability, hybrid sterility, and hybrid breakdown. Compare with *prezygotic barrier*.

potential energy Stored energy; energy that can do work as a consequence of its position or state. Compare with *kinetic energy*.

potentiation A form of synaptic enhancement (increase in neurotransmitter release) that can last for several minutes; occurs when a presynaptic neuron continues to transmit action potentials at a high rate for a minute or longer.

preadaptation A novel evolutionary change in a pre-existing biological structure that enables it to have a different function; feathers, which evolved from reptilian scales, represent a preadaptation for flight.

prebiotic soup hypothesis The hypothesis that simple organic molecules that are the precursors of life originated and accumulated at Earth's surface, in shallow seas or on rock or clay surfaces. Compare with *iron–sulfur world hypothesis*.

predation Relationship in which one organism (the predator) devours another organism (the prey).

pre-mRNA RNA precursor to mRNA in eukaryotes; contains both introns and exons.

prenatal Pertaining to the time before birth.

preprophase band In plant cells, a dense array of microtubules just inside of the plasma membrane that appears just prior to mitosis and determines the plane in which the cell will divide.

pressure-flow model The mechanism by which dissolved sugar is thought to be transported in phloem; caused by a pressure gradient between the source (where sugar is loaded into the phloem) and the sink (where sugar is removed from phloem).

presynaptic neuron A neuron that transmits an impulse to a synapse. Compare with *postsynaptic neuron*.

prezygotic barrier One of several reproductive isolating mechanisms that interfere with fertilization between male and female gametes of different species, e.g., temporal isolation, habitat isolation, behavioral isolation, mechanical isolation, and gametic isolation. Compare with *postzygotic barrier*.

primary consumer See *herbivore*.

primary growth An increase in the length of a plant that occurs at the tips of the shoots and roots due to the activity of apical meristems. Compare with *secondary growth*.

primary immune response The response of the immune system to first exposure to an antigen. Compare with *secondary immune response*.

primary mycelium A mycelium in which the cells are monokaryotic and haploid; a mycelium that grows from either an ascospore or a basidiospore. Compare with *secondary mycelium*.

primary producer See *autotroph*.

primary productivity The amount of light energy converted to organic compounds by autotrophs in an ecosystem over a given period. Compare with *secondary productivity*. See *gross primary productivity* and *net primary productivity*.

primary structure (of a protein) The complete sequence of amino acids in a polypeptide chain, beginning at the amino end and ending at the carboxyl end. Compare with *secondary, tertiary,* and *quaternary protein structure*.

primary succession An ecological succession that occurs on land that has not previously been inhabited by plants; no soil is present initially. See *succession*. Compare with *secondary succession*.

primates Mammals that share such traits as flexible hands and feet with five digits; a strong social organization; and front-facing eyes; includes lemurs, tarsiers, monkeys, apes, and humans.

primer See *RNA primer*.

primitive streak Dynamic, constantly changing structure that forms at the midline of the blastodisc in birds, mammals, and some other vertebrates and is active in gastrulation. The anterior end of the primitive streak is Hensen's node.

primosome A complex of proteins responsible for synthesizing the RNA primers required in DNA synthesis.

principle In science, a statement of a rule that explains how something works. A scientific principle has withstood repeated testing.

prion (pri'-on) An infectious agent that consists only of protein.

producer See *autotroph*.

product Substance formed by a chemical reaction. Compare with *reactant*.

product rule The rule for combining the probabilities of independent events by multiplying their individual probabilities. Compare with *sum rule*.

profundal zone (pro-fun'-dl) The deepest zone of a large lake, located below the level of penetration by sunlight. Compare with *littoral zone* and *limnetic zone*.

progesterone (pro-jes'-ter-own) A steroid hormone secreted by the ovary (mainly by the corpus luteum) and placenta; stimulates the uterus (to prepare the endometrium for implantation) and breasts (for milk secretion).

progymnosperm (pro-jim'-noh-sperm) An extinct group of plants that may have been the ancestors of gymnosperms.

prokaryote (pro-kar'-ee-ote) A cell that lacks a nucleus and other membrane-enclosed organelles; includes the bacteria and archaea (kingdoms Bacteria and Archaea). Compare with *eukaryote.*

prometaphase Stage of mitosis during which spindle microtubules attach to kinetochores of chromosomes, which begin to move toward the cell's midplane; occurs after prophase and before metaphase.

promoter The nucleotide sequence in DNA to which RNA polymerase attaches to begin transcription.

prop root An adventitious root that arises from the stem and provides additional support for a plant such as corn.

prophage (pro'-faj) Bacteriophage nucleic acid that is inserted into the bacterial DNA.

prophase The first stage of mitosis. During prophase the chromosomes become visible as distinct structures, the nuclear envelope breaks down, and a spindle forms.

proplastids Organelles that are plastid precursors; may mature into various specialized plastids, including chloroplasts, chromoplasts, or leukoplasts.

proprioceptors (pro"-pree-oh-sep'-torz) Receptors in muscles, tendons, and joints that respond to changes in movement, tension, and position; enable an animal to perceive the position of its body.

prostaglandins (pros"-tah-glan'-dinz) A group of local regulators derived from fatty acids; synthesized by most cells of the body and produce a wide variety of effects; sometimes called *local hormones.*

prostate gland A gland in male animals that produces an alkaline secretion that is part of the semen.

proteasome A large multiprotein structure that recognizes and degrades protein molecules tagged with ubiquitin into short, nonfunctional peptide fragments.

protein A large, complex organic compound composed of covalently linked amino acid subunits; contains carbon, hydrogen, oxygen, nitrogen, and sulfur.

protein kinase One of a group of enzymes that activate or inactivate other proteins by phosphorylating (adding phosphate groups to) them.

proteomics The study of all the proteins expressed by a cell at a given time.

Proterozoic eon The period of Earth's history that began approximately 2.5 billion years ago and ended 542 million years ago; marked by the accumulation of oxygen and the appearance of the first multicellular eukaryotic life-forms.

prothallus (pro-thal'-us) (pl., *prothalli*) The free-living, *n* gametophyte in ferns and other seedless vascular plants.

protist (pro'-tist) One of a vast informal group of eukaryotic organisms, primarily unicellular or simple multicellular; mostly aquatic.

protobionts (pro"-toh-by'-ontz) Assemblages of organic polymers that spontaneously form under certain conditions. Protobionts may have been involved in chemical evolution.

proton A particle present in the nuclei of all atoms that has one unit of positive charge and a mass of 1 atomic mass unit (amu). Compare with *electron* and *neutron.*

protonema (pro"-toh-nee'-mah) (pl., *protonemata*) In mosses, a filament of *n* cells that grows from a spore and develops into leafy moss gametophytes.

protonephridia (pro"-toh-nef-rid'-ee-ah) (sing., *protonephridium*) The flame-cell excretory organs of flatworms and some other simple invertebrates.

proto-oncogene A gene that normally promotes cell division in response to the presence of certain growth factors; when mutated, it may become an oncogene, possibly leading to the formation of a cancer cell. Compare with *oncogene.*

protostome (pro'-toh-stome) A major division of the animal kingdom in which the blastopore develops into the mouth, and the anus forms secondarily; includes the annelids, arthropods, and mollusks. Compare with *deuterostome.*

protozoa (proh"-toh-zoh'-a) (sing., *protozoon*) An informal group of unicellular, animal-like protists, including amoebas, foraminiferans, actinopods, ciliates, flagellates, and apicomplexans. (The adjectival form is *protozoan.*)

provirus (pro-vy'-rus) A part of a virus, consisting of nucleic acid only, that was inserted into a host genome. See *DNA provirus.*

proximal convoluted tubule The part of the renal tubule that extends from Bowman's capsule to the loop of Henle. Compare with *distal convoluted tubule.*

proximal Closer to the point of reference. Compare with *distal.*

proximate causes (of behavior) The immediate causes of behavior, such as genetic, developmental, and physiological processes that permit the animal to carry out a specific behavior. Compare with *ultimate causes of behavior.*

pseudocoelom (sue'-doh-see'-lom) A body cavity between the mesoderm and endoderm; derived from the blastocoel. Compare with *coelom.*

pseudocoelomate (sue"-doh-seel'-oh-mate) An animal having a pseudocoelom. Compare with *coelomate* and *acoelomate.*

pseudoplasmodium (sue"-doe-plaz-moh'-dee-um) In cellular slime molds, an aggregation of amoeboid cells that forms a spore-producing fruiting body during reproduction.

pseudopodium (sue"-doe-poe'-dee-um) (pl., *pseudopodia*) A temporary extension of an amoeboid cell that is used for feeding and locomotion.

puff In a polytene chromosome, a decondensed region that is a site of intense RNA synthesis.

pulmonary circulation The part of the circulatory system that delivers blood to and from the lungs for oxygenation. Compare with *systemic circulation.*

pulse, arterial The alternate expansion and recoil of an artery.

punctuated equilibrium The idea that evolution proceeds with periods of little or no genetic change, followed by very active phases, so that major adaptations or clusters of adaptations appear suddenly in the fossil record. Compare with *gradualism.*

Punnett square The grid structure, first developed by Reginald Punnett, that allows direct calculation of the probabilities of occurrence of all possible offspring of a genetic cross.

pupa (pew'-pah) (pl., *pupae*) A stage in the development of an insect, between the larva and the imago (adult); a form that neither moves nor feeds and may be in a cocoon.

purines (pure'-eenz) Nitrogenous bases with carbon and nitrogen atoms in two attached rings, e.g., adenine and guanine; components of nucleic acids, ATP, GTP, NAD^+, and certain other biologically active substances. Compare with *pyrimidines.*

pyramid of biomass An ecological pyramid that illustrates the total biomass, as, for example, the total dry weight, of all organisms at each trophic level in an ecosystem.

pyramid of energy An ecological pyramid that shows the energy flow through each trophic level of an ecosystem.

pyrimidines (pyr-im'-ih-deenz) Nitrogenous bases, each composed of a single ring of carbon and nitrogen atoms, e.g., thymine, cytosine, and uracil; components of nucleic acids. Compare with *purines.*

pyruvate (pyruvic acid) A three-carbon compound; the end product of glycolysis.

quadrupedal (kwad'-roo-ped"-ul) Walking on all fours.

quantitative trait A trait that shows continuous variation in a population (e.g., human height) and typically has a polygenic inheritance pattern.

quaternary structure (of a protein) The overall conformation of a protein produced by the interaction of two or more polypeptide chains. Compare with *primary, secondary,* and *tertiary protein structure.*

r selection A reproductive strategy recognized by some ecologists, in which a species typically has a small body size, rapid development, and short lifespan and devotes a large proportion of its metabolic energy to the production of offspring. Compare with *K selection.*

radial cleavage The pattern of blastomere production in which the cells are located directly above or below one another; characteristic of early deuterostome embryos. Compare with *spiral cleavage.*

radial symmetry A body plan in which any section through the mouth and down the length of the body divides the body into similar halves. Jellyfish and other cnidarians have radial symmetry. Compare with *bilateral symmetry.*

radicle (rad'-ih-kl) The embryonic root of a seed plant.

radioactive decay The process in which a radioactive element emits radiation, and as a result, its nucleus changes into the nucleus of a different element.

radioisotopes Unstable isotopes that spontaneously emit radiation; also called *radioactive isotopes.*

radiolarians Those actinopods that secrete elaborate shells of silica (glass).

radula (rad'-yoo-lah) A rasplike structure in the digestive tract of chitons, snails, squids, and certain other mollusks.

rain shadow An area that has very little precipitation, found on the downwind side of a mountain range. Deserts often occur in rain shadows.

random dispersion The spatial distribution pattern of a population in which the presence of one individual has no effect on the distribution of other individuals. Compare with *clumped dispersion* and *uniform dispersion.*

range The area where a particular species occurs. Compare with *home range.*

ray A chain of parenchyma cells (one to many cells thick) that functions for lateral transport in stems and roots of woody plants.

ray-finned fishes A class (Actinopterygii) of modern bony fishes; contains about 95% of living fish species.

reabsorption The selective removal of certain substances from the glomerular filtrate by the renal tubules and collecting ducts of the kidney, and their return into the blood.

reactant Substance that participates in a chemical reaction. Compare with *product.*

reaction center The portion of a photosystem that includes chlorophyll *a* molecules capable of transferring electrons to a primary electron acceptor, which is the first of several electron acceptors in a series. See *antenna complex* and *photosystem.*

realized niche The lifestyle that an organism actually pursues, including the resources that it actually uses. An organism's realized niche is narrower than its fundamental niche because of interspecific competition. Compare with *fundamental niche.*

receptacle The end of a flower stalk where the flower parts (sepals, petals, stamens, and carpels) are attached.

reception Process of detecting a stimulus.

receptor (1) In cell biology, a molecule on the surface of a cell, or inside a cell, that serves as a recognition or binding site for signaling molecules such as hormones, antibodies, or neurotransmitters. (2) A sensory receptor. See *sensory receptor.*

receptor down-regulation The process by which some hormone receptors decrease in number, thereby suppressing the sensitivity of target cells to a hormone. Compare with *receptor up-regulation.*

receptor up-regulation The process by which some hormone receptors increase in number, thereby increasing the sensitivity of the target cells to a hormone. Compare with *receptor down-regulation.*

receptor-mediated endocytosis A type of endocytosis in which extracellular molecules become bound to specific receptors on the cell surface and then enter the cytoplasm enclosed in vesicles.

recessive allele (al-leel') An allele that is not expressed in the heterozygous state. Compare with *dominant allele.*

recombinant DNA Any DNA molecule made by combining genes from different organisms.

recombination, genetic The appearance of new allele combinations. Recombination in eukaryotes generally results from meiotic events, either crossing-over or shuffling of chromosomes.

red alga A member of a diverse group of algae that contain the pigments chlorophyll *a,* carotenoids, phycocyanin, and phycoerythrin.

red blood cell (RBC) See *erythrocyte.*

red tide A red or brown coloration of ocean water caused by a population explosion, or bloom, of dinoflagellates.

redox reaction (ree'-dox) The chemical reaction in which one or more electrons are transferred from one substance (the substance that becomes oxidized) to another (the substance that becomes reduced). See *oxidation* and *reduction.*

reduction The gain of one or more electrons (or hydrogen atoms) by an atom, ion, or molecule. Compare with *oxidation.*

reflex action An automatic, involuntary response to a given stimulus that generally functions to restore homeostasis.

refractory period The brief period that elapses after the response of a neuron or muscle fiber, during which it cannot respond to another stimulus.

regulative development The very plastic developmental pattern in which each individual cell of an early embryo retains totipotency. Compare with *mosaic development.*

regulatory gene Gene that turns the transcription of other genes on or off.

reinforcement The increase in reproductive isolation that often occurs over time in a hybrid zone because natural selection strengthens and increases the number of prezygotic barriers between the two species.

releasing hormone A hormone secreted by the hypothalamus that stimulates secretion of a specific hormone by the anterior lobe of the pituitary gland.

renal (ree'-nl) Pertaining to the kidney.

renal pelvis The funnel-shaped chamber of the kidney that receives urine from the collecting ducts; urine then moves into the ureters.

renin (reh'-nin) An enzyme released by the kidney in response to a decrease in blood pressure; activates a pathway leading to production of angiotensin II, a hormone that increases aldosterone release; aldosterone increases blood pressure.

replacement-level fertility The number of children a couple must produce to "replace" themselves. The average number is greater than two, because some children die before reaching reproductive age.

replication See *DNA replication.*

replication fork Y-shaped structure produced during the semiconservative replication of DNA.

repolarization The process of returning membrane potential to its resting level.

repressible operon An operon that is normally active, but can be controlled by a repressor protein, which becomes active when it binds to a corepressor; the active repressor binds to the operator, making the operon transcriptionally inactive. Compare with *inducible operon.*

repressor protein A negative regulatory protein that inhibits transcription when bound to DNA; some repressors require a corepressor to be active; some other repressors become inactive when bound to an inducer molecule. Compare with *activator protein.*

reproduction The process by which new individuals are produced. See *asexual reproduction* and *sexual reproduction.*

reproductive isolating mechanisms The reproductive barriers that prevent a species from interbreeding with another species; as a result, each species' gene pool is isolated from those of other species. See *prezygotic barrier* and *postzygotic barrier.*

reptiles A class of vertebrates characterized by dry skin with horny scales and adaptations for terrestrial reproduction; include turtles, snakes, and alligators; reptiles are a paraphyletic group.

residual volume The volume of air that remains in the lungs at the end of a normal exhalation.

resin A viscous organic material that certain plants produce and secrete into specialized ducts; may play a role in deterring disease organisms or plant-eating insects.

resolution See *resolving power.*

resolving power The ability of a microscope to show fine detail, defined as the minimum distance between two points at which they are seen as separate images; also called *resolution.*

resource partitioning The reduction of competition for environmental resources such as food that occurs among coexisting species as a result of each species' niche differing from the others in one or more ways.

respiration (1) Cellular respiration is the process by which cells generate ATP through a series of redox reactions. In aerobic respiration the terminal electron acceptor is molecular oxygen; in anaerobic respiration the terminal acceptor is an inorganic molecule other than oxygen. (2) Organismic respiration is the process of gas exchange between a complex animal and its environment, generally through a specialized respiratory surface, such as a lung or gill.

respiratory centers Centers in the medulla and pons that regulate breathing.

resting potential The membrane potential (difference in electric charge between the two sides of the plasma membrane) of a neuron in which no action potential is occurring. The typical resting potential is about -70 millivolts. Compare with *action potential.*

restoration ecology The scientific field that uses the principles of ecology to help return a degraded environment as closely as possible to its former undisturbed state.

restriction enzyme One of a class of enzymes that cleave DNA at specific base sequences; produced by bacteria to degrade foreign DNA; used in recombinant DNA technology.

restriction map A physical map of DNA in which sites cut by specific restriction enzymes serve as landmarks.

reticular activating system (RAS) (reh-tik'-yoo-lur) A diffuse network of neurons in the brain stem; responsible for maintaining consciousness.

retina (ret'-ih-nah) The innermost of the three layers (retina, choroid layer, and sclera) of the eyeball, which is continuous with the optic nerve and contains the light-sensitive rod and cone cells.

retinular cells See *ommatidium.*

retrovirus (ret'-roh-vy"-rus) An RNA virus that uses reverse transcriptase to produce a DNA intermediate, known as a *DNA provirus,* in the host cell. See *DNA provirus.*

reverse transcriptase An enzyme produced by retroviruses that catalyzes the production of DNA using RNA as a template.

reversible inhibitor A substance that forms weak bonds with an enzyme, temporarily interfering with its function; a reversible inhibitor is either competitive or noncompetitive. Compare with *irreversible inhibitor.*

Rh factors Red blood cell antigens, known as *D antigens,* first identified in *Rhesus* monkeys. People who have these antigens are Rh^+; people lacking them are Rh^-. See *erythroblastosis fetalis.*

rhizarians A diverse supergroup of amoeboid cells that often have hard outer shells, called tests, through which cytoplasmic projections extend; include forams, actinopods, and certain shell-less amoebas.

rhizome (ry'-zome) A horizontal underground stem that bears leaves and buds and often serves as a storage organ and a means of asexual reproduction, e.g., iris.

rhodopsin (rho-dop'-sin) Visual purple; a light-sensitive pigment found in the rod cells of the vertebrate eye; a similar molecule is employed by certain bacteria in the capture of light energy to make ATP.

ribonucleic acid (RNA) A family of single-stranded nucleic acids that function mainly in protein synthesis

ribose The five-carbon sugar present in RNA and in important nucleoside triphosphates such as ATP.

ribosomal RNA (rRNA) See *ribosomes.*

ribosomes (ry'-boh-sohmz) Organelles that are part of the protein synthesis machinery of both prokaryotic and eukaryotic cells; consist of a larger and smaller subunit, each composed of ribosomal RNA (rRNA) and ribosomal proteins.

ribozyme (ry'-boh-zime) A molecule of RNA that has catalytic properties.

ribulose bisphosphate (RuBP) A five-carbon phosphorylated compound with a high energy potential that reacts with carbon dioxide in the initial step of the Calvin cycle.

ribulose bisphosphate carboxylase/oxygenase See *rubisco.*

RNA interference (RNAi) Phenomenon in which certain small RNA molecules interfere with the expression of genes or their RNA transcripts; RNA interference involves small interfering RNAs, microRNAs, and a few other kinds of short RNA molecules.

RNA polymerase An enzyme that catalyzes the synthesis of RNA from a DNA template.

RNA primer The sequence of about five RNA nucleotides that are synthesized during DNA replication to provide a 3' end to which DNA polymerase adds nucleotides. The RNA primer is later degraded and replaced with DNA.

RNA world A model that proposes that during the evolution of cells, RNA was the first informational molecule to evolve, followed at a later time by proteins and DNA.

rod One of the rod-shaped, light-sensitive cells of the retina that are particularly sensitive to dim light and mediate black-and-white vision. Compare with *cone.*

root cap A covering of cells over the root tip that protects the delicate meristematic tissue directly behind it.

root graft The process of roots from two different plants growing together and becoming permanently attached to each other.

root hair An extension, or outgrowth, of a root epidermal cell. Root hairs increase the absorptive capacity of roots.

root pressure The pressure in xylem sap that occurs as a result of the active absorption of mineral ions followed by the osmotic uptake of water into roots from the soil.

root system The underground portion of a plant that anchors it in the soil and absorbs water and dissolved minerals.

rough ER See *endoplasmic reticulum.*

rubisco The common name of ribulose bisphosphate carboxylase/ oxygenase, the enzyme that catalyzes the fixation of carbon dioxide in the Calvin cycle.

rugae (roo´-jee) Folds, such as those in the lining of the stomach.

runner See *stolon.*

S phase Stage in interphase of the cell cycle during which DNA and other chromosomal constituents are synthesized. Compare with G_1 and G_2 phases.

saccule The structure within the vestibule of the inner vertebrate ear that along with the utricle houses the receptors of static equilibrium.

salicylic acid A signaling molecule that helps plants defend against insect pests and pathogens such as viruses by helping activate systemic acquired resistance.

salinity The concentration of dissolved salts (e.g., sodium chloride) in a body of water.

salivary glands Accessory digestive glands found in vertebrates and some invertebrates; in humans there are three pairs.

salt An ionic compound consisting of an anion other than a hydroxide ion and a cation other than a hydrogen ion. A salt is formed by the reaction between an acid and a base.

salt marsh A wetland dominated by grasses in which the salinity fluctuates between that of sea water and fresh water; salt marshes are usually located in estuaries.

saltatory conduction The transmission of a neural impulse along a myelinated neuron; ion activity at one node depolarizes the next node along the axon.

saprobe See *decomposer.*

saprotroph (sap´-roh-trof) See *decomposer.*

sarcolemma (sar″-koh-lem´-mah) The muscle cell plasma membrane.

sarcomere (sar´-koh-meer) A segment of a striated muscle cell located between adjacent Z lines that serves as a unit of contraction.

sarcoplasmic reticulum The system of vesicles in a muscle cell that surrounds the myofibrils and releases calcium in muscle contraction; a modified endoplasmic reticulum.

saturated fatty acid See *fatty acid.*

savanna (suh-van´-uh) A tropical grassland containing scattered trees; found in areas of low rainfall or seasonal rainfall with prolonged dry periods.

scaffolding proteins (1) Proteins that organize groups of intracellular signaling molecules into signaling complexes. (2) Nonhistone proteins that help maintain the structure of a chromosome.

schizocoely (skiz´-oh-seely) The process of coelom formation in which the mesoderm splits into two layers, forming a cavity between them; characteristic of protostomes. Compare with *enterocoely.*

Schwann cells Supporting cells found in nervous tissue outside the central nervous system; produce the myelin sheath around peripheral neurons.

sclera (skler´-ah) The outer coat of the eyeball; a tough, opaque sheet of connective tissue that protects the inner structures and helps maintain the rigidity of the eyeball.

sclereid (skler´-id) In plants, a sclerenchyma cell that is variable in shape but typically not long and tapered. Compare with *fiber.*

sclerenchyma (skler-en´-kim-uh) Cells that provide strength and support in the plant body, are often dead at maturity, and have extremely thick walls; includes fibers and sclereids.

scramble competition See *exploitation competition.*

scrotum (skroh´-tum) The external sac of skin found in most male mammals that contains the testes and their accessory organs.

second law of thermodynamics The physical law stating that the total amount of entropy in the universe continually increases. Compare with *first law of thermodynamics.*

second messenger A substance, e.g., cyclic AMP or calcium ions, that relays a message from a hormone bound to a cell-surface receptor; leads to some change in the cell.

secondary consumer See *carnivore.*

secondary growth An increase in the girth of a plant due to the activity of the vascular cambium and cork cambium; secondary growth results in the production of secondary tissues, i.e., wood and bark. Compare with *primary growth.*

secondary immune response The rapid production of antibodies induced by a second exposure to an antigen several days, weeks, or even months after the initial exposure. Compare with *primary immune response.*

secondary mycelium A dikaryotic mycelium formed by the fusion of two primary hyphae. Compare with *primary mycelium.*

secondary productivity The amount of food molecules converted to biomass by consumers in an ecosystem over a given period. Compare with *primary productivity.*

secondary structure (of a protein) A regular geometric shape produced by hydrogen bonding between the atoms of the uniform polypeptide backbone; includes the alpha helix and the beta-pleated sheet. Compare with *primary, tertiary,* and *quaternary protein structure.*

secondary succession An ecological succession that takes place after some disturbance destroys the existing vegetation; soil is already present. See *succession.* Compare with *primary succession.*

secretory vesicles Small cytoplasmic vesicles that move substances from an internal membrane system to the plasma membrane.

seed A plant reproductive body consisting of a young, multicellular plant and nutritive tissue (food reserves), enclosed by a seed coat.

seed coat The outer protective covering of a seed.

seed fern An extinct group of seed-bearing woody plants with fern-like leaves; seed ferns probably descended from progymnosperms and gave rise to cycads and possibly ginkgoes.

segmentation genes In *Drosophila,* genes transcribed in the embryo that are responsible for generating a repeating pattern of body segments within the embryo and adult fly.

segregation, principle of The genetic principle, first noted by Gregor Mendel, that states that two alleles of a locus become separated into different gametes.

selectively permeable membrane A membrane that allows some substances to cross it more easily than others. Biological membranes are generally permeable to water but restrict the passage of many solutes.

self-incompatibility A genetic condition in which the pollen cannot fertilize the same flower or flowers on the same plant.

semelparity The condition of having a single reproductive effort in a lifetime. Compare with *iteroparity.*

semen The fluid consisting of sperm suspended in various glandular secretions that is ejaculated from the penis during orgasm.

semicircular canals The passages in the vertebrate inner ear containing structures that control the sense of equilibrium (balance).

semiconservative replication See *DNA replication.*

semilunar valves Valves between the ventricles of the heart and the arteries that carry blood away from the heart; aortic and pulmonary valves.

seminal vesicles (1) In mammals, glandular sacs that secrete a component of semen (seminal fluid). (2) In some invertebrates, structures that store sperm.

seminiferous tubules (sem-ih-nif´-er-ous) Coiled tubules in the testes in which spermatogenesis takes place in male vertebrates.

senescence (se-nes´-cents) The aging process.

sensory neuron A neuron that transmits an impulse from a receptor to the central nervous system.

sensory receptor A cell (or part of a cell) specialized to detect specific energy stimuli in the environment.

sepal (see´-pul) One of the outermost parts of a flower, usually leaflike in appearance, that protect the flower as a bud.

septum (pl., *septa*) A cross wall or partition, e.g., the walls that divide a hypha into cells.

sequencing See *DNA sequencing.*

serial endosymbiosis The hypothesis that certain organelles such as mitochondria and chloroplasts originated as symbiotic prokaryotes that lived inside other, free-living prokaryotic cells.

serotonin A neurotransmitter of the biogenic amine group.

Sertoli cells (sur-tole´-ee) Supporting cells of the tubules of the testis.

sessile (ses´-sile) Permanently attached to one location, e.g., coral animals.

set point A normal condition maintained by homeostatic mechanisms.

setae (sing., *seta*) Bristlelike structures that aid in annelid locomotion.

sex chromosome Chromosome that plays a role in sex determination.

sex-influenced trait A genetic trait that is expressed differently in males and females.

sex-linked gene A gene carried on a sex chromosome. In mammals almost all sex-linked genes are borne on the X chromosome, i.e., are X-linked.

sexual dimorphism Marked phenotypic differences between the two sexes of the same species.

sexual isolation See *behavioral isolation.*

sexual reproduction A type of reproduction in which two gametes (usually, but not necessarily, contributed by two different parents) fuse to form a zygote. Compare with *asexual reproduction.*

sexual selection A type of natural selection that occurs when individuals of a species vary in their ability to compete for mates; individuals with reproductive advantages are selected over others of the same sex.

shade avoidance The tendency of plants that are adapted to high light intensities to grow taller when they are closely surrounded by other plants.

shared ancestral characters Traits that were present in an ancestral species that have remained essentially unchanged; suggest a distant common ancestor. Also called *plesiomorphic characters.* Compare with *shared derived characters.*

shared derived characters Homologous traits found in two or more taxa that are present in their most recent common ancestor but not in earlier common ancestors. Also called *synapomorphic characters.* Compare with *shared ancestral characters.*

shoot system The aboveground portion of a plant, such as the stem and leaves.

short tandem repeats (STRs) Molecular markers that are short sequences of repetitive DNA; because STRs vary in length from

one individual to another, they are useful in identifying individuals with a high degree of certainty.

short-day plant A plant that flowers in response to lengthening nights; also called *long-night plant.* Compare with *long-day, intermediate-day,* and *day-neutral plants.*

short-night plant See *long-day plant.*

sickle cell anemia An inherited form of anemia in which there is abnormality in the hemoglobin beta chains; the inheritance pattern is autosomal recessive.

sieve tube elements Cells that conduct dissolved sugar in the phloem of flowering plants.

sign stimulus Any stimulus that elicits a fixed action pattern in an animal.

signal amplification The process by which a few signaling molecules can effect major responses in the cell; the strength of each signaling molecule is magnified.

signal transduction A process in which a cell converts and amplifies an extracellular signal into an intracellular signal that affects some function in the cell. Also see *cell signaling.*

signaling molecule A molecule such as a hormone, local regulator, or neurotransmitter that transmits information when it binds to a receptor on the cell surface or within the cell.

signal-recognition particle (SRP) A protein–RNA complex that directs the ribosome–mRNA–polypeptide complex to the surface of the endoplasmic reticulum.

silencer A regulatory element that associates with a eukaryotic gene and can decrease its transcription.

simple fruit A fruit that develops from a single ovary. Compare with *aggregate, accessory,* and *multiple fruits.*

simplest formula A type of chemical formula that gives the smallest whole-number ratio of the component atoms. Compare with *molecular formula* and *structural formula.*

single nucleotide polymorphisms (SNPs) Genetic variation among individuals in a population as measured by alleles of specific loci that differ by as little as a single nucleotide.

single-strand binding proteins (SSBs) Proteins involved in DNA replication that bind to single DNA strands and prevent the double helix from re-forming until the strands are copied.

sink habitat A lower-quality habitat in which local reproductive success is less than local mortality. Compare with *source habitat.*

sinoatrial (SA) node The mass of specialized cardiac muscle in which the impulse triggering the heartbeat originates; the pacemaker of the heart.

sister chromatids See *chromatid.*

sister taxa Groups of organisms that share a more recent common ancestor with one another than either taxon does with any other group shown on a cladogram.

skeletal muscle The voluntary striated muscle of vertebrates, so called because it usually is directly or indirectly attached to some part of the skeleton. Compare with *cardiac muscle* and *smooth muscle.*

slash-and-burn agriculture A type of agriculture in which tropical rain forest is cut down, allowed to dry, and burned. The crops that are planted immediately afterward thrive because the ashes provide nutrients; in a few years, however, the soil is depleted and the land must be abandoned.

slow block to polyspermy See *cortical reaction.*

small interfering RNAs (siRNAs) Double-stranded RNA molecules about 23 nucleotides in length that silence genes at the post-transcriptional level by selectively cleaving mRNA molecules with base sequences complementary to the siRNA.

small intestine Portion of the vertebrate digestive tract that extends from the stomach to the large intestine.

small nuclear ribonucleoprotein complexes (snRNP) Aggregations of RNA and protein responsible for binding to pre-mRNA in eukaryotes; catalyze the excision of introns and the splicing of exons.

smooth ER See *endoplasmic reticulum.*

smooth muscle Involuntary muscle tissue that lacks transverse striations; found mainly in sheets surrounding hollow organs, such as the intestine. Compare with *cardiac muscle* and *skeletal muscle.*

social behavior Interaction of two or more animals, usually of the same species.

sociobiology The branch of biology that focuses on the evolution of social behavior through natural selection.

sodium–potassium pump Active transport system that transports sodium ions out of, and potassium ions into, cells.

soil erosion The wearing away or removal of soil from the land; although soil erosion occurs naturally from precipitation and runoff, human activities (such as clearing the land) accelerate it.

solute A dissolved substance. Compare with *solvent.*

solvent Substance capable of dissolving other substances. Compare with *solute.*

somatic cell In animals, a cell of the body not involved in formation of gametes. Compare with *germ line cell.*

somatic nervous system That part of the vertebrate peripheral nervous system that keeps the body in adjustment with the external environment; includes sensory receptors on the body surface and within the muscles, and the nerves that link them with the central nervous system. Compare with *autonomic nervous system.*

somatomedins See *insulin-like growth factors.*

somatotropin See *growth hormone.*

somites A series of paired blocks of mesoderm that develop on each side of the notochord in cephalochordates and vertebrates. Somites define the segmentation of the embryo, and in vertebrates, they give rise to the vertebrae, ribs, and certain skeletal muscles.

sonogram See *ultrasound imaging.*

soredium (sor-id'e-um) (pl., *soredia*) In lichens, a type of asexual reproductive structure that consists of a cluster of algal cells surrounded by fungal hyphae.

sorus (soh'rus) (pl., *sori*) In ferns, a cluster of spore-producing sporangia.

source habitat A good habitat in which local reproductive success is greater than local mortality. Surplus individuals in a source habitat may disperse to other habitats. Compare with *sink habitat.*

Southern blot A technique in which DNA fragments, previously separated by gel electrophoresis, are transferred to a nitrocellulose or nylon membrane and detected by autoradiography or chemical luminescence. Compare with *Northern blot* and *Western blot.*

speciation Evolution of a new species.

species According to the biological species concept, one or more populations whose members are capable of interbreeding in nature to produce fertile offspring and do not interbreed with members of other species. Compare with *phylogenetic species concept.*

species diversity A measure of the relative importance of each species within a community; represents a combination of species richness and species evenness.

species richness The number of species in a community.

specific epithet The second part of the name of a species; designates a specific species belonging to that genus.

specific heat The amount of heat energy that must be supplied to raise the temperature of 1 g of a substance 1°C.

specific immune responses Defense mechanisms that target specific macromolecules associated with a pathogen. Includes cell-mediated immunity and antibody-mediated immunity. Also known as *acquired* or *adaptive immune responses.*

sperm The motile male gamete of animals and some plants and protists; also called a *spermatozoan.*

spermatid (spur'-ma-tid) An immature sperm cell.

spermatocyte (spur-mah'-toh-site) A meiotic cell that gives rise to spermatids and ultimately to mature sperm cells.

spermatogenesis (spur″-mah-toh-jen'-eh-sis) The production of male gametes (sperm) by meiosis and subsequent cell differentiation. Compare with *oogenesis.*

spermatozoan (spur-mah-toh-zoh'-un) See *sperm.*

sphincter (sfink'-tur) A group of circularly arranged muscle fibers, the contractions of which close an opening, e.g., the pyloric sphincter at the exit of the stomach.

spinal cord In vertebrates, the dorsal, tubular nerve cord.

spinal nerves In vertebrates, the nerves that emerge from the spinal cord.

spindle See *mitotic spindle.*

spine A leaf that is modified for protection, such as a cactus spine.

spiracle (speer'-ih-kl) An opening for gas exchange, such as the opening of a trachea on the body surface of an insect.

spiral cleavage A distinctive spiral pattern of blastomere production in an early protostome embryo. Compare with *radial cleavage.*

spirillum (pl., *spirilla*) A long, rigid, helical bacterium. Compare with *spirochete, vibrio, bacillus,* and *coccus.*

spirochete A long, flexible, helical bacterium. Compare with *spirillum, vibrio, bacillus,* and *coccus.*

spleen An abdominal organ located just below the diaphragm that removes worn-out blood cells and bacteria from the blood and plays a role in immunity.

spliceosome A large nucleoprotein particle that catalyzes the reactions that remove introns from pre-mRNA.

spongy mesophyll (mez'-oh-fil) The loosely arranged mesophyll cells near the lower epidermis in certain leaves. Compare with *palisade mesophyll.*

spontaneous reaction See *exergonic reaction.*

sporangium (spor-an'-jee-um) (pl., *sporangia*) A spore case, found in plants, certain protists, and fungi.

spore A reproductive cell that gives rise to individual offspring in plants, fungi, and certain algae and protozoa.

sporophyll (spor'-oh-fil) A leaflike structure that bears spores.

sporophyte generation (spor'-oh-fite) The 2*n*, spore-producing stage in the life cycle of a plant. Compare with *gametophyte generation.*

sporozoite The infective sporelike state in apicomplexans.

stabilizing selection Natural selection that acts against extreme phenotypes and favors intermediate variants; associated with a population well adapted to its environment. Compare with *directional selection* and *disruptive selection.*

stamen (stay'-men) The male part of a flower; consists of a filament and anther.

standing-water ecosystem A lake or pond ecosystem.

starch A polysaccharide composed of alpha glucose subunits; made by plants for energy storage.

start codon The codon AUG, which signals the beginning of translation of messenger RNA. Compare with *stop codon.*

stasis Long periods in the fossil record in which there is little or no evolutionary change.

statocyst (stat'-oh-sist) An invertebrate sense organ containing one or more granules (statoliths); senses gravity and motion.

statoliths (stat′-uh-liths) Granules of loose sand or calcium carbonate found in statocysts.

stele The cylinder in the center of roots and stems that contains the vascular tissue.

stem cell A relatively undifferentiated cell capable of repeated cell division. At each division at least one of the daughter cells usually remains a stem cell, whereas the other may differentiate as a specific cell type.

stereocilia Hairlike projections of hair cells; microvilli that contain actin filaments.

sterilization A procedure that renders an individual incapable of producing offspring; the most common surgical procedures are vasectomy in the male and tubal ligation in the female.

steroids (steer′-oids) Complex molecules containing carbon atoms arranged in four attached rings, three of which contain six carbon atoms each and the fourth of which contains five, e.g., cholesterol and certain hormones, including the male and female sex hormones of vertebrates.

stigma The portion of the carpel where pollen grains land during pollination (and before fertilization).

stipe A short stalk or stemlike structure that is a part of the body of certain multicellular algae.

stipule (stip′-yule) One of a pair of scalelike or leaflike structures found at the base of certain leaves.

stolon (stow′-lon) An aboveground, horizontal stem with long internodes; stolons often form buds that develop into separate plants, e.g., strawberry; also called *runner.*

stomach Muscular region of the vertebrate digestive tract, extending from the esophagus to the small intestine.

stomata (sing., *stoma*) Small pores located in the epidermis of plants that provide for gas exchange for photosynthesis; each stoma is flanked by two guard cells, which are responsible for its opening and closing.

stop codon Any of the three codons in mRNA that do not code for an amino acid (UAA, UAG, or UGA) but signal the termination of translation. Compare with *start codon.*

stramenopiles Protists that have motile cells with two flagella, one of which has tiny hairlike projections off the shaft; include water molds, diatoms, golden algae, and brown algae. See *chromalveolates.*

stratosphere The layer of the atmosphere between the troposphere and the mesosphere. It contains a thin ozone layer that protects life by filtering out much of the sun's ultraviolet radiation.

stratum basale (strat′-um bah-say′-lee) The deepest sublayer of the human epidermis, consisting of cells that continuously divide. Compare with *stratum corneum.*

stratum corneum The most superficial sublayer of the human epidermis. Compare with *stratum basale.*

strobilus (stroh′-bil-us) (pl., *strobili*) In certain plants, a conelike structure that bears spore-producing sporangia.

stroke volume The volume of blood pumped by one ventricle during one contraction.

stroma A fluid space of the chloroplast, enclosed by the chloroplast inner membrane and surrounding the thylakoids; site of the reactions of the Calvin cycle.

stromatolite (stroh-mat′-oh-lite) A columnlike rock that consists of many minute layers of prokaryotic cells, usually cyanobacteria.

structural formula A type of chemical formula that shows the spatial arrangement of the atoms in a molecule. Compare with *simplest formula* and *molecular formula.*

structural isomer One of two or more chemical compounds having the same chemical formula but differing in the covalent arrangement of their atoms, e.g., glucose and fructose.

style The neck connecting the stigma to the ovary of a carpel.

subsidiary cell In plants, a structurally distinct epidermal cell associated with a guard cell.

substance P A peptide neurotransmitter released by certain sensory neurons in pain pathways; signals the brain regarding painful stimuli; also stimulates other structures, including smooth muscle in the digestive tract.

substrate A substance on which an enzyme acts; a reactant in an enzymatically catalyzed reaction.

succession The sequence of changes in the species composition of a community over time. See *primary succession* and *secondary succession.*

sucker A shoot that develops adventitiously from a root; a type of asexual reproduction.

sulcus (sul′-kus) (pl., *sulci*) A groove, trench, or depression, especially one occurring on the surface of the brain, separating the convolutions.

sulfhydryl group Functional group abbreviated —SH; found in organic compounds called thiols.

sum rule The rule for combining the probabilities of mutually exclusive events by adding their individual probabilities. Compare with *product rule.*

summation The process of adding together excitatory postsynaptic potentials (EPSPs).

suppressor T cell T lymphocyte that suppresses the immune response.

supraorbital ridge (soop″-rah-or′-bit-ul) The prominent bony ridge above the eye socket; ape skulls have prominent supraorbital ridges.

surface tension The attraction that the molecules at the surface of a liquid may have for one another.

survivorship The probability that a given individual in a population or cohort will survive to a particular age; usually presented as a survivorship curve.

survivorship curve A graph of the number of surviving individuals of a cohort, from birth to the maximum age attained by any individual.

suspensor (suh-spen′-sur) In plant embryo development, a multicellular structure that anchors the embryo and aids in nutrient absorption from the endosperm.

sustainability See *environmental sustainability.*

swim bladder The hydrostatic organ in bony fishes that permits the fish to hover at a given depth.

symbiosis (sim-bee-oh′-sis) An intimate relationship between two or more organisms of different species. See *commensalism, mutualism,* and *parasitism.*

sympathetic nervous system A division of the autonomic nervous system; its general effect is to mobilize energy, especially during stress situations; prepares the body for fight-or-flight response. Compare with *parasympathetic nervous system.*

sympatric speciation (sim-pa′-trik) The evolution of a new species within the same geographic region as the parental species. Compare with *allopatric speciation.*

symplast A continuum consisting of the cytoplasm of many plant cells, connected from one cell to the next by plasmodesmata. Compare with *apoplast.*

synapomorphic characters See *shared derived characters.*

synapse (sin′-aps) The junction between two neurons or between a neuron and an effector (muscle or gland).

synapsis (sin-ap'-sis) The process of physical association of homologous chromosomes during prophase I of meiosis.

synaptic enhancement An increase in neurotransmitter release thought to occur as a result of calcium ion accumulation inside the presynaptic neuron.

synaptic plasticity The ability of synapses to change in response to certain types of stimuli. Synaptic changes occur during learning and memory storage.

synaptonemal complex The structure, visible with the electron microscope, produced when homologous chromosomes undergo synapsis.

systematics The scientific study of the diversity of organisms and their evolutionary relationships. Taxonomy is an aspect of systematics. See *taxonomy*.

systemic acquired resistance A defensive response in infected plants that helps fight infection and promote wound healing.

systemic anaphylaxis A rapid, widespread allergic reaction that can lead to death.

systemic circulation The part of the circulatory system that delivers blood to and from the tissues and organs of the body. Compare with *pulmonary circulation*.

systems biology A field of biology that synthesizes knowledge of many small parts to understand the whole. Also referred to as *integrative biology* or *integrative systems biology*.

systole (sis'-tuh-lee) The phase of the cardiac cycle when the heart is contracting. Compare with *diastole*.

T cell (T lymphocyte) The type of white blood cell responsible for a wide variety of immune functions, particularly cell-mediated immunity. T cells are processed in the thymus. Compare with *B cell*.

T cytotoxic cell (T_C) T lymphocyte that destroys cancer cells and other pathogenic cells on contact. Also known as *CD8 T cell* and *killer T cell*.

T helper cell (T_H) T lymphocyte that activates B cells (B lymphocytes) and stimulates T cytotoxic cell production. Also known as *CD4 T cell*.

T tubules Transverse tubules; system of inward extensions of the muscle fiber plasma membrane.

taiga (tie'-gah) See *boreal forest*.

taproot system A root system consisting of a prominent main root with smaller lateral roots branching off it; a taproot develops directly from the embryonic radicle. Compare with *fibrous root system*.

target cell or tissue A cell or tissue with receptors that bind a hormone.

TATA box A component of a eukaryotic promoter region; consists of a sequence of bases located about 30 base pairs upstream from the transcription initiation site.

taxon A formal taxonomic group at any level, e.g., phylum or genus.

taxonomy (tax-on'-ah-mee) The science of naming, describing, and classifying organisms; see *systematics*.

Tay–Sachs disease A serious genetic disease in which abnormal lipid metabolism in the brain causes mental deterioration in affected infants and young children; inheritance pattern is autosomal recessive.

tectorial membrane (tek-tor'-ee-ul) The roof membrane of the organ of Corti in the cochlea of the ear.

telencephalon See *forebrain*.

telolecithal egg An egg with a large amount of yolk, concentrated at the vegetal pole. Compare with *isolecithal egg*.

telomerase A special DNA replication enzyme that can lengthen telomeric DNA by adding repetitive nucleotide sequences to the ends of eukaryotic chromosomes; typically present in cells that divide an unlimited number of times.

telomeres The protective end caps of chromosomes that consist of short, simple, noncoding DNA sequences that repeat many times.

telophase (teel'-oh-faze or tel'-oh-faze) The last stage of mitosis and of meiosis I and II when, having reached the poles, chromosomes become decondensed, and a nuclear envelope forms around each group.

temperate deciduous forest A forest biome that occurs in temperate areas where annual precipitation ranges from about 75 cm to 125 cm.

temperate grassland A grassland characterized by hot summers, cold winters, and less rainfall than is found in a temperate deciduous forest biome.

temperate rain forest A coniferous biome characterized by cool weather, dense fog, and high precipitation, e.g., the north Pacific coast of North America.

temperate virus A virus that integrates into the host DNA as a prophage.

temperature The average kinetic energy of the particles in a sample of a substance.

temporal isolation A prezygotic reproductive isolating mechanism in which genetic exchange is prevented between similar species because they reproduce at different times of the day, season, or year.

tendon A connective tissue structure that joins a muscle to another muscle, or a muscle to a bone. Tendons transmit the force generated by a muscle.

tendril A leaf or stem that is modified for holding or attaching onto objects.

tension–cohesion model The mechanism by which water and dissolved inorganic minerals are thought to be transported in xylem; water is pulled upward under tension because of transpiration while maintaining an unbroken column in xylem because of cohesion; also called *transpiration–cohesion model*.

teratogen Any agent capable of interfering with normal morphogenesis in an embryo, thereby causing malformations; examples include radiation, certain chemicals, and certain infectious agents.

terminal bud A bud at the tip of a stem. Compare with *axillary bud*.

termination (of protein synthesis) The final stage of protein synthesis, which occurs when a termination (stop) codon is reached, causing the completed polypeptide chain to be released from the ribosome. See *initiation* and *elongation*.

termination codon See *stop codon*.

territoriality Behavior pattern in which one organism (usually a male) stakes out a territory of its own and defends it against intrusion by other members of the same species and sex.

tertiary consumer See *carnivore*.

tertiary structure (of a protein) (tur'-she-air"-ee) The overall three-dimensional shape of a polypeptide that is determined by interactions involving the amino acid side chains. Compare with *primary, secondary*, and *quaternary protein structure*.

test A shell.

testcross The genetic cross in which either an F_1 individual, or an individual of unknown genotype, is mated to a homozygous recessive individual.

testis (tes'-tis) (pl., *testes*) The male gonad that produces sperm and the male hormone testosterone; in humans and certain other mammals; the testes are located in the scrotum.

testosterone (tes-tos'-ter-own) The principal male sex hormone (androgen); a steroid hormone produced by the interstitial cells of the testes; stimulates spermatogenesis and is responsible for primary and secondary sex characteristics in the male.

tetrad The chromosome complex formed by the synapsis of a pair of homologous chromosomes (i.e., four chromatids) during meiotic prophase I.

tetrapods (tet′-rah-podz) Four-limbed vertebrates: the amphibians, reptiles, birds, and mammals.

thalamus (thal′-uh-mus) The part of the vertebrate brain that serves as a main relay center, transmitting information between the spinal cord and the cerebrum.

thallus (thal′-us) (pl., *thalli*) The simple body of an alga, fungus, or nonvascular plant that lacks root, stems, or leaves, e.g., a liverwort thallus or a lichen thallus.

theca cells The layer of connective tissue cells that surrounds the granulosa cells in an ovarian follicle; stimulated by luteinizing hormone (LH) to produce androgens, which are converted to estrogen in the granulosa cells.

theory In science, a widely accepted explanation supported by a large body of observations and experiments. A scientific theory relates facts that appear unrelated; it predicts new facts and suggests new relationships. Compare with *hypothesis.*

therapsids (ther-ap′-sidz) A group of mammal-like reptiles of the Permian period; gave rise to the mammals.

thermal stratification The marked layering (separation into warm and cold layers) of temperate lakes during the summer. See *thermocline.*

thermocline (thur′-moh-kline) A marked and abrupt temperature transition in temperate lakes between warm surface water and cold deeper water. See *thermal stratification.*

thermodynamics Principles governing energy transfer (often expressed in terms of heat transfer). See *first law of thermodynamics* and *second law of thermodynamics.*

thermoreceptor A sensory receptor that responds to heat.

thigmomorphogenesis (thig″-moh-mor-foh-jen′-uh-sis) An alteration of plant growth in response to mechanical stimuli, such as wind, rain, hail, and contact with passing animals.

thigmotropism (thig″-moh-troh′-pizm) Plant growth in response to contact with a solid object, such as the twining of plant tendrils.

threatened species A species in which the population is small enough for it to be at risk of becoming extinct throughout all or part of its range but not so small that it is in imminent danger of extinction. Compare with *endangered species.*

threshold level The potential that a neuron or other excitable cell must reach for an action potential to be initiated.

thrombocytes See *platelets.*

thylakoid lumen See *thylakoids.*

thylakoids (thy′-lah-koidz) An interconnected system of flattened, saclike, membranous structures inside the chloroplast.

thymine (thy′-meen) A nitrogenous pyrimidine base found in DNA.

thymus gland (thy′-mus) An endocrine gland that functions as part of the lymphatic system; processes T cells; important in cell-mediated immunity.

thyroid gland An endocrine gland that lies anterior to the trachea and releases hormones that regulate the rate of metabolism.

thyroid hormones Hormones, including thyroxin, secreted by the thyroid gland; stimulate rate of metabolism.

tidal volume The volume of air moved into and out of the lungs with each normal resting breath.

tight junctions Specialized structures that form between some animal cells, producing a tight seal that prevents materials from passing through the spaces between the cells.

tissue A group of closely associated, similar cells that work together to carry out specific functions.

tissue culture The growth of tissue or cells in a synthetic growth medium under sterile conditions.

tissue engineering A developing technology that is striving to grow human tissues and organs (for transplantation) in cell cultures.

tissue fluid See *interstitial fluid.*

tolerance A decreased response to a drug over time.

Toll-like receptors A type of pattern recognition receptor. Cell-surface receptors on several cell types that recognize pathogen-associated molecular patterns (certain common features of classes of pathogens). See also *pathogen-associated molecular patterns (PAMPs).*

tonoplast The membrane surrounding a vacuole.

top-down processes Control of ecosystem function by trophic interactions, particularly from the highest trophic level. Compare *bottom-up processes.*

topoisomerases (toe-poe-eye-sahm′-er-ases) Enzymes that relieve twists and kinks in a DNA molecule by breaking and rejoining the strands.

torpor An energy-conserving state of low metabolic rate and inactivity. See *estivation* and *hibernation.*

torsion The twisting of the visceral mass characteristic of gastropod mollusks.

total fertility rate The average number of children born to a woman during her lifetime.

totipotent (toh-ti-poh′-tent) A term describing a cell or nucleus that contains the complete set of genetic instructions required to direct the normal development of an entire organism. Compare with *pluripotent.*

trace element An element required by an organism in very small amounts.

trachea (tray′-kee-uh) (pl., *tracheae*) (1) Principal thoracic air duct of terrestrial vertebrates; windpipe. (2) One of the microscopic air ducts (or tracheal tubes) branching throughout the body of most terrestrial arthropods and some terrestrial mollusks.

tracheal tubes See *trachea.*

tracheid (tray′-kee-id) A type of water-conducting and supporting cell in the xylem of vascular plants.

tract A bundle of nerve fibers within the central nervous system.

transcription factors DNA-binding proteins that regulate transcription in eukaryotes; include positively acting activators and negatively acting repressors.

transcription The synthesis of RNA from a DNA template.

transduction (1) The transfer of a genetic fragment from one cell to another, e.g., from one bacterium to another, by a virus. (2) In the nervous system, the conversion of energy of a stimulus to electrical signals.

transfer RNA (tRNA) RNA molecules that bind to specific amino acids and serve as adapter molecules in protein synthesis. The tRNA anticodons bind to complementary mRNA codons.

transformation (1) The incorporation of genetic material into a cell, thereby changing its phenotype. (2) The conversion of a normal cell to a cancer cell (called a malignant transformation).

transgenic organism A plant or animal that has foreign DNA incorporated into its genome.

translation The conversion of information provided by mRNA into a specific sequence of amino acids in a polypeptide chain; process also requires transfer RNA and ribosomes.

translocation (1) The movement of organic materials (dissolved food) in the phloem of a plant. (2) Chromosome abnormality in which part of one chromosome has become attached to another. (3) Part of the elongation cycle of protein synthesis in which a transfer RNA attached to the growing polypeptide chain is transferred from the A site to the P site.

transmembrane protein An integral membrane protein that spans the lipid bilayer.

transmission, neural The conduction of a neural impulse along a neuron or from one neuron to another.

transpiration The loss of water vapor from the aerial surfaces of a plant (i.e., leaves and stems).

transpiration–cohesion model See *tension–cohesion model*.

transport vesicles Small cytoplasmic vesicles that move substances from one membrane system to another.

transposon (tranz-poze′-on) A DNA segment that is capable of moving from one chromosome to another or to different sites within the same chromosome; also called a *mobile genetic element*.

transverse tubules See *T tubules*.

triacylglycerol (try-ace″-il-glis′-er-ol) The main storage lipid of organisms, consisting of a glycerol combined chemically with three fatty acids; also called *triglyceride*. Compare with *monoacylglycerol* and *diacylglycerol*.

tricarboxylic acid (TCA) cycle See *citric acid cycle*.

trichome (try′-kohm) A hair or other appendage growing out from the epidermis of a plant.

tricuspid valve See *atrioventricular valve*.

triglyceride See *triacylglycerol*.

triose A sugar molecule containing three carbons.

triple-gene fusion The fusion of three separate genes into a single unit early in the course of eukaryote evolution; provides evidence of a bifurcation; characteristic of unikonts.

triplet code The sequences of three nucleotides that compose the codons, the units of genetic information in mRNA that specify the order of amino acids in a polypeptide chain.

triplet A sequence of three nucleotides that serves as the basic unit of genetic information.

trisomy (try′-sohm-ee) A type of aneuploidy in which an individual has two copies of each chromosome except for one, which has three copies; designated $2n + 1$. Compare with *monosomy* and *disomy*.

trochophore larva (troh′-koh-for) A larval form found in mollusks and many polychaetes.

trophic level (troh′-fik) Each sequential step of matter and energy in a food web, from producers to primary, secondary, or tertiary consumers; each organism is assigned to a trophic level based on its primary source of nourishment.

trophoblast (troh′-foh-blast) The outer cell layer of a late blastocyst, which in placental mammals gives rise to the chorion and to the fetal contribution to the placenta.

tropic hormone (trow′-pic) A hormone that regulates the secretion of another hormone.

tropical dry forest A tropical forest where enough precipitation falls to support trees but not enough to support the lush vegetation of a tropical rain forest; often occurs in areas with pronounced rainy and dry seasons.

tropical rain forest A lush, species-rich forest biome that occurs in tropical areas where the climate is very moist throughout the year. Tropical rain forests are also characterized by old, infertile soils.

tropism (troh′-pizm) In plants, a directional growth response that is elicited by an environmental stimulus.

tropomyosin (troh-poh-my′-oh-sin) A muscle protein involved in regulation of contraction.

true-breeding strain A genetic strain of an organism in which all individuals are homozygous at the loci under consideration.

tube feet Structures characteristic of echinoderms; function in locomotion and feeding.

tuber A thickened end of a rhizome that is fleshy and enlarged for food storage, e.g., white potato.

tubular transport maximum (Tm) The maximum rate at which a substance is reabsorbed from the renal tubules of the kidney.

tumor A mass of tissue that grows in an uncontrolled manner; a neoplasm.

tumor necrosis factors (TNFs) Cytokines that kill tumor cells and stimulate immune cells to initiate an inflammatory response.

tumor suppressor gene A gene (also known as an *anti-oncogene*) whose normal role is to block cell division in response to certain growth-inhibiting factors; when mutated, may contribute to the formation of a cancer cell. Compare with *oncogene*.

tundra (tun′-dra) A treeless biome between the boreal forest in the south and the polar ice cap in the north that consists of boggy plains covered by lichens and small plants. Also called *arctic tundra*. Compare with *alpine tundra*.

tunicates Chordates belonging to subphylum Urochordata; sea squirts.

turgor pressure (tur′-gor) Hydrostatic pressure that develops within a walled cell and presses outward against the plasma membrane.

Turner syndrome An inherited condition in which only one sex chromosome (an X chromosome) is present in cells; karyotype is designated XO; affected individuals are sterile females.

tyrosine kinase An enzyme that phosphorylates the tyrosine part of proteins.

tyrosine kinase receptor A plasma membrane receptor that phosphorylates the tyrosine part of proteins; when a ligand binds to the receptor, the conformation of the receptor changes and it may phosphorylate itself as well as other molecules; important in immune function and serves as a receptor for insulin.

ultimate causes (of behavior) Evolutionary explanations for why a certain behavior occurs. Compare with *proximate causes of behavior*.

ultrasound imaging A technique in which high-frequency sound waves (ultrasound) are used to provide an image (sonogram) of an internal structure.

ultrastructure The fine detail of a cell, generally only observable by use of an electron microscope.

umbilical cord In placental mammals, the organ that connects the embryo to the placenta.

uniform dispersion The spatial distribution pattern of a population in which individuals are regularly spaced. Compare with *random dispersion* and *clumped dispersion*.

unikonts One of two main clades of all eukaryotes that had a common ancestor with a single posterior flagellum. Compare with *bikonts*.

unsaturated fatty acid See *fatty acid*.

upwelling An upward movement of water that brings nutrients from the ocean depths to the surface. Where upwelling occurs, the ocean is very productive.

uracil (yur′-ah-sil) A nitrogenous pyrimidine base found in RNA.

urea (yur-ee′-ah) The principal nitrogenous excretory product of mammals; one of the water-soluble end products of protein metabolism.

ureter (yur′-ih-tur) One of the paired tubular structures that conducts urine from the kidney to the bladder.

urethra (yoo-ree′-thruh) The tube that conducts urine from the bladder to the outside of the body.

uric acid (yoor′-ik) The principal nitrogenous excretory product of insects, birds, and reptiles; a relatively insoluble end product of protein metabolism; also occurs in mammals as an end product of purine metabolism.

urinary bladder An organ that receives urine from the ureters and temporarily stores it.

urinary system The body system in vertebrates that consists of kidneys, urinary bladder, and associated ducts.

urochordates A subphylum of chordates; includes the tunicates.

uterine tube (yoo′-tur-in) See *oviduct*.

uterus (yoo′-tur-us) The hollow, muscular organ of the female reproductive tract in which the fetus undergoes development.

utricle The structure within the vestibule of the vertebrate inner ear that, along with the saccule, houses the receptors of static equilibrium.

vaccine (vak-seen′) A commercially produced, weakened or killed antigen associated with a particular disease that stimulates the body to make antibodies.

vacuole (vak′-yoo-ole) A fluid-filled, membrane-enclosed sac found within the cytoplasm; may function in storage, digestion, or water elimination.

vagina The elastic, muscular tube, extending from the cervix to its external opening, that receives the penis during sexual intercourse and serves as the birth canal.

valence electrons The electrons in the outer electron shell, known as the *valence shell,* of an atom; in the formation of a chemical bond, an atom can accept electrons into its valence shell or donate or share valence electrons.

van der Waals interactions Weak attractive forces between atoms; caused by interactions among fluctuating charges.

vas deferens (vas def′-ur-enz) (pl., *vasa deferentia*) One of the paired sperm ducts that connects the epididymis of the testis to the ejaculatory duct.

vascular cambium A lateral meristem that produces secondary xylem (wood) and secondary phloem (inner bark). Compare with *cork cambium.*

vascular tissue system The tissues specialized for translocation of materials throughout the plant body, i.e., the xylem and phloem.

vasoconstriction Narrowing of the diameter of blood vessels.

vasodilation Expansion of the diameter of blood vessels.

vector (1) Any carrier or means of transfer. (2) Agent, e.g., a plasmid or virus, that transfers genetic information. (3) Agent that transfers a parasite from one host to another.

vegetal pole The yolky pole of a vertebrate or echinoderm egg. Compare with *animal pole.*

vein (1) A blood vessel that carries blood from the tissues toward a chamber of the heart (compare with *artery*). (2) A strand of vascular tissue that is part of the network of conducting tissue in a leaf.

veliger larva The larval stage of many marine gastropods (snails) and bivalves (e.g., clams); often is a second larval stage that develops after the trochophore larva.

ventilation The process of actively moving air or water over a respiratory surface.

ventral Toward the lowermost surface or belly of an animal. Compare with *dorsal.*

ventricle (1) A cavity in an organ. (2) One of the several cavities of the brain. (3) One of the chambers of the heart that receives blood from an atrium.

vertebrates A subphylum of chordates that includes fishes, amphibians, reptiles, birds, and mammals; possess a bony vertebral column.

vesicle (ves′-ih-kl) Any small sac, especially a small, spherical, membrane-enclosed compartment, within the cytoplasm.

vessel element A type of water-conducting cell in the xylem of vascular plants.

vestibular apparatus Collectively, the saccule, utricle, and semicircular canals of the inner ear.

vestigial (ves-tij′-ee-ul) Rudimentary; an evolutionary remnant of a formerly functional structure.

vibrio A spirillum (spiral-shaped bacterium) that is shaped like a comma. Compare with *spirillum, spirochete, bacillus,* and *coccus.*

villus (pl., *villi*) A multicellular, minute, elongated projection from the surface of an epithelial membrane, e.g., villi of the mucosa of the small intestine.

virion A complete virus particle that is outside a cell.

viroid (vy′-roid) A tiny, naked, infectious particle consisting only of nucleic acid.

virulence Properties that render an infectious agent pathogenic (and often lethal) to its host. Compare with *avirulence.*

virus A tiny pathogen consisting of a core of nucleic acid usually encased in protein and capable of infecting living cells; a virus is characterized by total dependence on a living host.

viscera (vis′-ur-uh) The internal body organs, especially those located in the abdominal or thoracic cavities.

visceral mass The concentration of body organs (viscera) located above the foot in mollusks.

vital capacity The maximum volume of air a person exhales after filling the lungs to the maximum extent.

vitamin A complex organic molecule required in very small amounts for normal metabolic functioning.

vitelline envelope An acellular covering of the eggs of certain animals (e.g., echinoderms), located just outside the plasma membrane.

viviparous (vih-vip′-er-us) Bearing living young that develop within the body of the mother. Compare with *oviparous* and *ovoviviparous.*

voltage-activated ion channels Ion channels in the plasma membrane of neurons that are regulated by changes in voltage. Also called *voltage-gated channels.*

vomeronasal organ In mammals, an organ in the epithelium of the nose, made up of specialized chemoreceptor cells that detect pheromones.

vulva The external genital structures of female mammals.

warning coloration See *aposematic coloration.*

water mold A funguslike protist with a body consisting of a coenocytic mycelium that reproduces asexually by forming motile zoospores and sexually by forming oospores.

water potential Free energy of water; the water potential of pure water is zero and that of solutions is a negative value. Differences in water potential are used to predict the direction of water movement (always from a region of less negative water potential to a region of more negative water potential).

water vascular system Unique hydraulic system of echinoderms; functions in locomotion and feeding.

wavelength The distance from one wave peak to the next; the energy of electromagnetic radiation is inversely proportional to its wavelength.

weathering processes Chemical or physical processes that help form soil from rock; during weathering processes, the rock is gradually broken into smaller and smaller pieces.

Western blot A technique in which proteins, previously separated by gel electrophoresis, are transferred to paper. A specific labeled antibody is generally used to mark the location of a particular protein. Compare with *Southern blot* and *Northern blot.*

white matter Nervous tissue in the brain and spinal cord that contains myelinated axons. Compare with *gray matter*.

wild type The phenotypically normal (naturally occurring) form of a gene or organism.

wobble The ability of some tRNA anticodons to associate with more than one mRNA codon; in these cases the 5′ base of the anticodon is capable of forming hydrogen bonds with more than one kind of base in the 3′ position of the codon.

work Any change in the state or motion of matter.

X-linked gene A gene carried on an X chromosome.

X-ray diffraction A technique for determining the spatial arrangement of the components of a crystal.

xylem (zy′-lem) The vascular tissue that conducts water and dissolved minerals in plants.

XYY karyotype Chromosome constitution that causes affected individuals (who are fertile males) to be unusually tall, with severe acne.

yeast A unicellular fungus (ascomycete) that reproduces asexually by budding or fission and sexually by ascospores.

yolk sac One of the extraembryonic membranes; a pouchlike outgrowth of the digestive tract of embryos of certain vertebrates (e.g., birds) that grows around the yolk and digests it. Embryonic blood cells are formed in the mammalian yolk sac, which lacks yolk.

zero population growth Point at which the birth rate equals the death rate. A population with zero population growth does not change in size.

zona pellucida (pel-loo′-sih-duh) The thick, transparent covering that surrounds the plasma membrane of a mammalian ovum.

zooplankton (zoh″-oh-plank′-tun) The nonphotosynthetic organisms present in plankton, e.g., protozoa, tiny crustaceans, and the larval stages of many animals. See *plankton*. Compare with *phytoplankton*.

zoospore (zoh′-oh-spore) A flagellated motile spore produced asexually by chytrids, certain algae, water molds, and other protists.

zooxanthellae (zoh″-oh-zan-thel′-ee) (sing., *zooxanthella*) Endosymbiotic, photosynthetic dinoflagellates found in certain marine invertebrates; their mutualistic relationship with corals enhances the corals' reef-building ability.

zygomycetes (zy″-gah-my′-seats) Fungi characterized by the production of nonmotile asexual spores and sexual zygospores.

zygosporangium (zy″-gah-spor-an′-gee-um) A thick-walled sporangium containing a zygospore.

zygospore (zy′-gah-spor) A sexual spore produced by a zygomycete.

zygote The 2*n* cell that results from the union of *n* gametes in sexual reproduction. Species that are not polyploid have haploid gametes and diploid zygotes.

zygotic genes Genes that are transcribed after fertilization, either in the zygote or in the embryo. Compare with *maternal effect genes*.

Index

anabolic steroids: abuse of, 1054, 1056, 1083
anabolism, 156, 172, 1024
anaerobes, 452, 453, 463
    bacteria as, 453, 524
    facultative, 188, 524
    obligate, 453, 524
anaerobic respiration, 173, 187–189
    vs. aerobic respiration, 188t
    ATP synthesis in, 187–188, 855
    vs. fermentation, 188t, 190
analgesics, 875
anaphase
    in meiosis. *See* anaphase I; anaphase II
    metaphase–anaphase checkpoint (mitosis), *225*
    in mitosis, *219, 221*
anaphase I (in meiosis), *229, 231*
anaphase II (in meiosis), *228, 231*
anaphase-promoting complex (APC), 224–225
anaphylaxis, systemic, 988
Anarhichas lupus (Atlantic wolffish), 1012–1013, *1012*
anatomy, 822
    See also comparative anatomy
ancestors
    of animals. *See* choanoflagellates
    of birds, 458, 461
    of crocodiles, 458
    of dinosaurs, 458
    of humans, 462
    of land vertebrates. *See* lungfishes
    See also common ancestry
ancestral characters, shared (plesiomorphies), 489, 490, 493
anchor cell, 382
anchoring (of cells to the ECM), 114, *114*
anchoring junctions, 127–128
androgen-binding protein (ABP), 1084
anemia, 941
    causes of, 941–942
    See also sickle cell anemia
anemones, sea, 630, 646
aneuploidies, 352
    genetic disorders from, 352–355, 352t
    in sex chromosomes, 354–355
Anfinsen, Christian B., 66
"angel dust" (phencyclidine), 875, 907t
Angelman syndrome (AS): genomic imprinting and, 316, 356–358, *357*
angina pectoris, 959
angiogenesis inhibitors, 983
angioplasty, 959
angiosperms. *See* flowering plants
angiotensin I, 1048
angiotensin II, 954, 959, 1047t, 1048
angiotensin-converting enzyme. *See* ACE
angiotensinogen, 1048
anglerfishes, *691*
animal cell division, 100
animal cells, *83, 85*
    centrosome, 98. *See also* centrioles
    chemical mediators, 59–60
    components, 82–83, *83, 85*. *See also* cell membranes; cytoskeleton; nucleus/nuclei (in eukaryotic cells); organelles; *and other specific components*
    cytokinesis in, 222, *223*
    generation times, 223
    Golgi complexes in, 91
    interphase in, *218, 228*
    meiosis in, 228–229
    membranes, 223
    mitosis in, *218–219*
    pH value, 41
    size, 76
    surface compounds, 55
    See also cells; eukaryotic cells; specialized cells
animal cognition, 1133
animal development, 1106–1126
    allometric growth, 440, *440*, 444
    bone(s), 847
    crustaceans, 666–667
    differentiation and, 1107, 1124

embryo(s). *See* embryonic development (in animals)
    environmental stimulation and, 900–901
    fertilization in, 1107–1109, 1124
    gastrulation in, 1112–1114, 1115
    humans. *See* human development
    hybrid inviability/sterility/breakdown, 430, *431*
    insects, 1060, *1061*, 1074
    mammals, 384–386
    mosaic development, 382, 384, 389, 1111–1112
    novel features. *See* evolutionary novelties
    organogenesis in, 1115–1116, 1118, 1120
    regulative development, 384, 389, 1112
    the vertebrate brain, 886–888, *886*
    See also developmental genetics
animal digestion: and germination, 794
animal embryo(s), *693*, 1106–1107, 1112–1117
    anterior–posterior axis specification, 381, *381*
    cleavage of. *See* cleavage
    development of. *See* embryonic development (in animals)
    Drosophila embryo, *369*; development of, 376–379, *379*
    environmental influences on, 1121, 1122t
    extraembryonic membranes, 402, *693*
    gastrulation in, 633, 1111, 1112–1114, 1115
    of humans. *See* human embryo
    hybrid inviability, 430, *431*
    implantation of, 1118
    kangaroo embryo, 702
    mouse embryo, *307*
    segmentation of, 683
animal evolution, 455–462, 456t, 627, 629–630, 637
    adaptations to habitats, 627–629, 637
    amphibians, 443, 456t, 457, 628, 690–692
    birds, 456t, 460, 461, 490, *494*, 697–699, 706
    bony fishes, 689–690
    cartilaginous fishes, 689
    choanoflagellates and, 151, 558, 629
    coral(s), 455
    echinoderms, 676
    fast evolution among vertebrates, 436
    fins, 687
    hominins, 471–477, *473*
    humans. *See* human evolution
    insects (hexapods), 669
    invertebrates, 446–447, 456t, *635*
    jaws, 681, 684, 687
    on land, 443, 456t, 457, 628–629, 690–692
    mammals, 456t, 462, 466, 700–701, *701*; on islands, 476
    marsupials, 702–703
    mollusks, 652
    primates, 465–466, 467–470, 471–477, *473*
    reptiles, 456t
    snails, 455, 458
    sponges, 455, 641
    tetrapods, 443, 456t, 457, 690–692
    trilobites, 447, 455, 663
    vertebrates, 456t, 683–684, *684, 685*
animal fat, 57
animal hormones: mitosis stimulators, 225
animal pollinators, 670, 784–789, *786–787*
    coevolution of flowering plants and, 594, 595–596, 784–785, 788, 800
    floral attractants for, 785–788, 787t
animal reproduction, 627, 637
    in earthworms, 658
    fertilization, 1107–1109
    in flukes, 650
    in hydrozoans, 645, *646*
    on land, 628–629
    in planarians, 650
    in reptiles, 694–695
    in sharks, 688
    in sponges, 642–643
animal starch. *See* glycogen

animal steroid hormones, 139, 141, 148
Animalia (kingdom), 14, 483–485, 486t
animals
    adaptations: to marine and freshwater habitats, 627–628; to terrestrial environments, 443, 457, 628–629, 690–692, 693, 694–695, 700–701, 1035, 1036, 1039–1040. *See also under* adaptation(s)
    amino acid synthesis, 61
    ancestors. *See* choanoflagellates
    artificial selection of, 394
    behavior (of animals)
    in benthic environment, 1234
    in biogeographical realms, 1238
    biogeography, 1237–1238, *1238*
    biomass of Earth, 517
    biomes. *See* biomes
    of boreal forest, 1221
    in chaparral, 1223
    characters/characteristics, 14, 486t, 627, 637
    circadian rhythms, 894–895, 1134. *See also* sleep–wake cycle
    classification, *13*, 486t, *541, 626, 629, 635, 641*
    climate change and the range of, 1257
    coat color, 254, 255, 256, 257, *258*, 258–259, *259*
    commercial harvest, 1248, *1248*
    communication among, 1138–1139, 1150
    as consumers, 10
    decline of biodiversity, 1243–1248
    defensive adaptations, 911, 1181–1182, *1182*
    in the desert, 1225
    development of. *See* animal development
    domestication of, 478
    Ediacaran animals, 455, 456t
    embryos. *See* animal embryo(s)
    endangered. *See* endangered species
    energy storage, 9, 54
    evolution of. *See* animal evolution
    extinction of. *See* extinction
    fertilization in. *See under* fertilization
    in flowing-water ecosystems, 1229–1230
    in freshwater wetlands ecosystem, 1231
    fungal diseases, 611, 621–622
    gas exchange in, 993–1010
    genetic engineering of, 340–342
    geographic distribution of, 400–402, *402*
    growth of, 719, 1106
    habitats: adaptations to, 627–629, 637
    homologous features, 402, *403*
    homoplastic features, 403–404, *404*
    interactions among. *See* social behavior
    interdependencies with flowering plants, 594, 595–596
    in kelp forest ecosystem, 1234
    life cycle, 232, *233, 235*
    major groups, 633–634, *635*
    in mangrove forests, 1232
    in marine ecosystems, 1232
    movement of, 4. *See also* movement
    as multicellular organisms, 821–822
    navigation by, 916, 1135–1136
    nutritional mode, 10, 209; adaptations to, 1013–1015, *1014*
    in the oceanic province, 1235, *1236*
    oldest group, 641
    origins, 151, 641
    phyla, 626
    phylogeny, 626, 630–637, 637–638
    pollinators. *See* animal pollinators
    polyploidy in, 351–352
    predation strategies, 1180
    reproduction. *See* animal reproduction
    reproduction of, 1162
    in rocky intertidal zone, 1232
    in the savanna, 1225
    seed dispersal by, 794, 795
    sex determination in, 252
    size, 821
    in standing-water ecosystem, *1228*, 1230
    steroid hormones, 139, 141, 148

    sympatric speciation in, 435–437
    in temperate deciduous forests, 1222
    in temperate grasslands, 1222
    in temperate rain forests, 1221
    terrestrial. *See* terrestrial animals
    thermoregulation in, 835–838, *835, 838*, 840, 915
    transgenic animals, *323*, 340–342, *341*, 384–385, 385
    in tropical rain forests, 1227
    in tundra, 1220–1221
    viral diseases, 507–512
    See also invertebrates; vertebrates; *and specific animals*
anions, 34–35
    in organisms, 42
    in soils, 773
Ankylosaurus, 460
Annelida (phylum), 656, 656t
annelids (segmented worms), 648, 656–658, 673
    characters/characteristics, 636t, 671t
    circulatory system, 939
    classification, 633, 635, 636t, 661
    hydrostatic skeleton, 661, 845
    immune responses in, 964, 965
    metanephridia, 657, *657*, 1037–1038, *1037*
    nervous system, 657, 658, 883, *884*
    See also earthworms; leeches; polychaetes
annual plants: life history, 1161–1162
annual rings in wood. *See* tree rings
annuals (herbaceous plants), 709
Anolis carolinensis (green anole), 1176, *1176*, 1178
Anolis sagrei (brown anole), 1176, *1176*, 1178
Anopheles mosquito, 546, 621
ANP. *See* atrial natriuretic peptide
antagonist muscle, 849
Antarctica
    climate change and, 1257
    ozone layer thinning over, 1259, 1260
anteaters, 403, 704t
    giant, *404*; marsupial counterpart, 702
    spiny, 17, 701–702, *701*
antelopes, 1139
antenna complexes of chlorophyll, 200, *200*
antennae (of arthropods), 662
    crustaceans/lobsters, 666, 667, *667*
    insects, 669, 924; homeotic leg substitutes, 380, *380*
Antennapedia mutations, 380, *380*
anterior cavity of eye, 928, *930*
anterior end of body, 630, *631*
anterior pituitary gland, 837, 1063–1066
    hormones, 1054, 1062t, 1063–1066, 1075, 1084, 1084t, 1089t, 1090; synthesis and secretion of, *1065*
anterior–posterior axis (of embryo), 381, *381*
antheridia, 562, *563*
    of ferns, 573, *575, 576*
    of hornworts, 570, *570*
    of liverworts, 568, *569*
    of water molds, 548
antheridiophores (of liverworts), 568, *569*
anthers (of stamens), 591, *591*, 593, 710, 782, *783*
Anthocerophyta (phylum). *See* hornworts
Anthoceros natans, 570, *570*
anthocyanins as revealed in leaf abscission, 738
anthozoans, *643*, 644t, 646–647
    See also coral(s)
anthrax, 533t
    cause of, 520, 532, 533t
Anthropoidea (suborder), 467, *467*
anthropoids, 467–470, *467*, 479
    See also apes; humans; monkeys
anthropology
    molecular anthropology, 470, 477
    paleoanthropology, 465–466
anti-anxiety medications, 875, 906t
antibiotics, 512, 529t, 534, 621
    resistance genes against, 326, *326*, 534
    source microorganisms, 531
    See also penicillin

ozone depletion, 1259–1261, *1259, 1260,*
1262
atomic mass, 29
atomic mass unit (amu), 28–29
atomic nucleus, 27
atomic number, 27–28
atomic orbitals, 30, *30*
atomic weight, 29
atoms, 6, 27–31, 43
   electronegativity, 34
   light interactions with, 194–195, *195*
   models of. *See* Bohr models
   nucleus, 27
ATP (adenosine triphosphate), 68, 72, 94,
   159–160, 169
   and ADP, 160, *160*
   as a coenzyme, 165
   components, 159
   concentration level, 160
   depletion of, 855
   hydrolysis of, 100, *159, 160*
   in muscle contraction, 100, 852, 852–855,
   854
   in photosynthesis: carbon fixation
      reactions, 204, *205, 208*
   pumps driven by, 121–123, *122, 123*
   synthesis of. *See* ATP synthesis
ATP synthase, 184, *185,* 203
ATP synthesis, 94–95, 123
   in aerobic respiration: chemiosmosis,
      182–184, *183, 185,* 190; citric acid
      cycle, 177, *180, 181;* glycolysis, 175,
      176, 179
   in anaerobic respiration, 187–188, 855
   as coupled to the electron transport chain,
      182–184; or uncoupled, 183
   cyclic AMP from, 143, *144*
   in fermentation, 188, *188,* 189
   in photosynthesis, 198, *199,* 202–204, *203*
   yield from aerobic respiration, 184–186, *186*
atria (of heart), 946, *947*
   in humans, 948, *948*
   in mollusks, 939, *939*
atrial natriuretic factor (ANF), 1073
atrial natriuretic peptide (ANP), 954, 1047t
   and salt reabsorption, 1048
atrioventricular bundle (AV bundle), 949, *949*
atrioventricular node (AV node), 949, *949*
atrioventricular valves (AV valves), 947–948,
   948
atrium (of tunicates), 682
attachment of viruses to cells, 505, *506,*
   507–508
attention deficit hyperactivity disorder
   (ADHD): causes of, 873, 899
auditory receptors, 920–924, *923*
auditory signals: and animal communication,
   1138
Augustine, Saint, 482
auricles
   of the heart, 947
   in planarians, 649, *649*
Australia
   biogeography, 401
   fossil sites/deposits, 451–452, *452,*
      453–454, 455
   human demographics in, 1167
Australian banyan (*Ficus macrophylla*), 769
Australian long-nosed lycid beetle (*Metri-*
   orrhynchus rhipidus), 786
Australian realm, 1238, *1238*
Australian tea-tree (*Leptospermum laevigatum*),
   786
australopithecines, 472–474, 479
Australopithecus (genus), 473–474
Australopithecus afarensis, 473, *473,* 474, *474*
Australopithecus africanus, 473–474, *473*
Australopithecus anamensis, 473, *473*
autocrine agents, 968
autocrine signaling, 1056
autoimmune diseases, 848, 963–964, 986
   causes of, 141, 986
automated DNA-sequencing techniques/
   machines, 333, 335
   results printout, *335*

automobile exhaust from fossil fuel combustion, 1206
autonomic division of the PNS, 885, *885,* 897,
   902–904
   regulation of, 888, 904
autopolyploidy, 434
autoradiography, 29, *29,* 217, 329
autosomal dominant disease, 360–361, 367
autosomal monosomies/trisomies, 352
autosomal recessive diseases, 358–360, 367
autosomal trisomy. *See* trisomy 21
autosomes, 251–252
   as evidence of evolution, 477
autotrophs, 9–10, 208, 209, 452, 463, 524,
   524t, 535, 1198
   See also chemoautotrophs; photoauto-
      trophs; producers
auxin(s), 805–807, 805t, 807–809, 818
   action mechanism, 805–807, *806,* 818
   and cell elongation, 808
   isolation of, 807
   movement of, 807–808, *808*
   receptors, 805, 806, 807
   signal transduction pathway, *806*
AV bundle (atrioventricular bundle), 949, *949*
AV node (atrioventricular node), 949, *949*
AV valves (atrioventricular valves), 947–948,
   948
Avery, Oswald T., 265, 267t, 523
avirulence (of bacteria), 265
Avogadro, Amadeo, 32
Avogadro's number, 32
axial filaments, 529t
axial skeleton, 846, *847*
axil, 729, 750
axillary buds, 710, 729, *729, 739, 750, 751,*
   797
axolotl salamander (*Ambystoma mexicanum*),
   441
axon collaterals, 862, *862*
axons, 98, 829–830, *830, 862, 862, 863*
   membrane. *See* neuron membrane
   tracts (nerve tracts), 886, 889
axopods, *551,* 552
AZT (azidothymidine), 985–986

B cells, 971–972, *972, 973,* 975
   activation and clonal expansion of, 975,
      975, 976
   diversity, 979
   V, J, and C region gene segments, 979, *980*
B-complex vitamins, 1023, 1027t
baboons, 469
   Anubis baboon, *468*
   foraging behavior in, 1136–1137
   intrasexual selection, 1142
bacilli/bacilli bacteria, 518, *518,* 531
Bacillus anthracis, 13, 520, 532, 533t
backbone. *See* vertebral column
background extinction, 441
BACs (bacterial artificial chromosomes), 326
bacteria, 3, 11, 485, 486t, 525–526, 527
   as aerobes/anaerobes, 174, 453, 524, 535
   ammonifying bacteria, 1205
   vs. archaea, 485, 525–526, 535
   ATP synthesis in, 123
   in benthic environment, 1234
   biofilms. *See* biofilms
   biomolecule production, 531
   cell division, 222–223, *224,* 517, 522
   cell walls, 519, *519, 520,* 534
   cellular respiration in, 524
   cellulose digestion, 54–55, 543, 1013,
      1023
   chloroplasts as evolved from, 94, 454, *454*
   classification, *13,* 21, 427, 485, *485,* 486t,
      525–526, *525*
   commercial/technological uses, 531, 535
   conjugation in, 523, *523*
   as decomposers and recyclers, 10, *10,*
      517–518, 524, 530–531
   denitrifying bacteria, 1206
   diseases caused by, 520, 532–534, 533t
   DNA replication, 223
   dormancy, 520

ecological roles, 530–531
   enclosure of, 93
   endospores, 520, *520*
   as endosymbionts, 454, 543, 617
   enzyme inhibitors, 168–169, *168*
   evolution of, 456t, 523–524, 525, 535
   and the evolution of other species, 530
   fermentation by, 188, 189
   flagella, *4,* 521, *521,* 535
   in flowing-water ecosystems, 1230
   on food chain, 1198
   gene regulation in, 308–309, *309,* 314
   gene transfer in, 487, 522–523
   gram-negative, 519, 527, 528t, 529t
   gram-positive, 519, 527, 529t, 531
   horizontal gene transfer among, 427, 487,
      488, 522–523, 524, 525, 530
   vs. macrophages, 966–967
   major groups, 526, 527, 528–529t, 535
   mitochondria as evolved from, 94, 454,
      454
   mRNA in, 290–291, *291,* 298, 304, 319
   mutualism: with legumes, 531; with
      ruminants, 54–55, 530; with termites,
      55, 543
   neutrophil movement toward, 148
   and the nitrogen cycle, 1204–1206, *1205*
   nitrogen fixation by, 525, 531
   nitrogen-fixing, 525. *See also* rhizobial
      bacteria
   nutritional modes, 9–10, 208–209, 524,
      524t
   operons in, 309–312
   pathogens, 517, 524t, 528–529t, 532–534,
      533t
   percent identified, 481
   in phagocytosis, 125, *125*
   photosynthetic. *See* cyanobacteria
   population growth, 1157, *1157,* 1158
   posttranscriptional controls, 313–314
   quorum sensing, 134–135
   reproduction of, 521–523
   shapes, 518
   size, 76
   "smart" bacteria, 973–974
   in soil, 774
   structure (components), 81–82, *82,*
      518–521, *519. See also specific*
      components
   taxonomy, 525–526
   transcription in, 289–291, 309–313; as
      coupled with translation, 297–298, *298*
   transformation of DNA in, 264–265, 279,
      324, *325,* 327, 522–523, *522*
   translation as coupled with transcription
      in, 297–298, *298*
   translation initiation in, 294–295, *295,* 526
   viruses. *See* bacteriophages
   vitamin production, 1023
   See also prokaryotes; *and specific bacteria*
Bacteria (domain), 13, *13,* 485, *485,* 486t, 487,
   525, *525, 525,* 530
   phylogeny, 527, 528–529t
Bacteria (kingdom), 13, 486t
bacteria studies: applicability to other
   organisms, 26
bacterial artificial chromosomes (BACs), 326
bacterial diseases, 520, 532–534, 533t
bacterial plasmids. *See* plasmids
bacterial promoters, 289
bacterial viruses. *See* bacteriophages
bacteriophage vectors, 326
bacteriophages (phages), 265, 324, 502–503,
   503, 505, 515
   DNA transduction, *522,* 523
   reproduction of, 265, *266,* 505–506, *505,*
      506
   structure, 505
   See also macrophages
bacteriorhodopsin, 527
Bacteroides, 530
Badlands (South Dakota), 458
baker's yeast. *See Saccharomyces cerevisiae*
Balaenoptera. See blue whale
balance. *See* equilibrium maintenance

balanced polymorphism, 420–422
Balanus balanoides: competition for limiting
   resources, 1177, *1177*
bald cypress, 584, *1184,* 1231
bald eagles: conservation efforts, 1251–1252
bald-faced hornet (*Vespula maculata*), 668
balsa wood, 751
Baltimore, David, 300
Baltimore classification system, 504
bamboo: giant pandas and, 1245
bamboo viper (*Trimersurus stejnegeri*), 915
Bangladesh
   fertility rate in, 1168t
   human demographics in, 1167
banteng: cloning of, 373
banyan, Australian (*Ficus macrophylla*), 769
bar code, DNA, 490
barberry, Japanese (*Berberis thunbergii*), 405
Barberton rocks (South Africa), 451–452
barbiturates, 141, 875, 906t
bark, 720, *720*
   See also periderm; secondary phloem
barley, Alpine, *1174*
barnacles, 663t, *666,* 667
   competition for limiting resources, 1177,
      1177
   in hydrothermal vent ecosystems, 1209
   in rocky intertidal zone, 1232
baroreceptors, 954
Barr body, *254,* 255, 315, 316, 354
barriers: in biogeography, 1237
basal angiosperms, 597–598, *597*
basal bodies, 99, *100*
basal cell of flowering plant embryo, 790, *791*
basal deuterostomes, 676
basal ganglia (cerebrum), 893
basal metabolic rate (BMR), 1029
base composition of DNA, 267–268, 267t
base pairs/pairing
   in DNA, 269, 270–271, *270,* 273, 276, 280
   errors in, 301
   in tRNAs, 294
base sequences. *See* DNA sequences; RNA
   sequences
base-pair substitution mutations, 301, *302*
basement membrane, 822, 825
bases (compounds), 40–42, 43
   acids mixed with, 42
   dissociation of, 40
bases (nucleotide bases), 68
   in DNA, 68, 267, 269
   sequences. *See* DNA sequences; RNA
      sequences
   See also base pairs/pairing; complementary
      base pairing
basic amino acids, 63
basic solutions, 41
basidia, 612, *615, 616*
basidiocarps, 612, *615, 616*
basidiomycetes, 605, 606t, *606,* 612–615,
   624
   life cycle, 605, 612–614, *616*
   symbiosis in lichens, 617
   See also mushrooms
basidiospores, 612, *616*
Basilosaurus, 398, *400*
basket stars, 678t, *679*
basophils, *941,* 942, 942t
Batesian mimicry, 1182, *1182, 1183*
bath sponges, 643
bathyal zone (of ocean), *1233*
bats, 704t
   adaptations for feeding, 1014
   California leaf-nosed bat, *911*
   classification, 490
   echolocation system, 911
   Egyptian fruit bat, *703*
   flowers pollinated by, 787–788
   lesser long-nosed bat, *786*
   prey adaptations, 911
   wing structure, 402, *403*
battery acid: pH value, *41*
bay scallops: habitat fragmentation and
   predation of, *1247*
bay-breasted warblers, *1179*

dust mite (*Dermatophagoides*), 665
Dutch elm disease, 611, 622
dwarfism, 339, 1066
    achondroplasia, 353
        Ellis–van Creveld syndrome, 417
    pituitary dwarfism, 339, 1066
    psychosocial dwarfism, 1066
dynactin, 98
dynamic equilibrium, 32, 42, 116, 158, 169
dynein, 98, 99, *100*

E site (on ribosomes), 294, *294, 296*
E. coli. See Escherichia coli
E-face (of cell membranes), *112*
E$_A$. *See* activation energy
ear bones. *See* middle-ear bones
early growth in plants, 797
Early Proterozoic period, 456t
ears
    bones in the middle ear, 489, 490,
        491–492, 497, 700, 920, 921
    human ear, *920*
    as needed for terrestrial life, 692
    sensitivity, 922
    vestibular apparatus, 919–920, *920*
Earth
    biomass, 517
    chemical evolution on early Earth, 446,
        447–449, 463
    climate change on. *See* climate change
    climates, 1212–1213, *1212*
    conditions on early Earth, 447, *447*, 463
    continental drift, 401–402, *401*
    crust, 1204
    extraterrestrial object impacts on, 442, 458,
        460–461
    global carbon budget, 1204
    global ocean, 1211–1212, *1211*
    landmasses, 401–402, *401, 402*
    mean annual global temperature, *1255*
    plate tectonics, 402
    precipitation patterns, 1212–1213, *1213,*
        1216, 1257
    primary productivity, 1201–1202, *1201*
    rotation, 1211
    solar radiation on, 1208, *1209*
    sun and, 1208–1210, *1209, 1210*
    temperature. *See* temperature of Earth
    winds, 1210, *1210,* 1211, 1215
earthstar, rounded (*Geastrum saccatum*), 601
earthworms, 656–657, 656t, *656, 657*–658,
    1079
    characters/characteristics, 636t, 671t
    circulatory system, 658, 939, *940*
    classification, 633, 636t
    digestive system/tract, 658, *1015*
    epithelial secretions, 843
    "hearts," 939
    hemoglobin, 658, 940
    ingestion, 1013
    internal anatomy, *657*
    metanephridia in, 657, *657*
    in soils, 774–775, *774*
eastern coral snake (*Micrurus fulvius fulvius*),
    1182
eastern gray kangaroo (*Macropus giganteus*),
    702
eastern subterranean termite (*Reticulitermes
    flavipes*), 668
eastern tiger swallowtail butterfly (*Pterurus
    glaucas*), 786
ecdysis. *See* molting
ecdysone. *See* molting hormone
ecdysozoa, 634, 661–671, 673
    characters/characteristics, 636t, 661, 671t
    classification, *635*, 636t
    See also arthropods; nematodes;
        onychophorans; tardigrades
ECGs (electrocardiograms), 949
echidna. *See* spiny anteater
Echiniscus. See tardigrades
echinoderms, 630, 676–680
    characters/characteristics, 637t, 678t, 705,
        705t
    classification, 633, *635*, 637t, *680*

embryo cleavage, 1109, 1124
endoskeletons, 845, *846*
evolution of, 676
fertilization in, 1108, 1109, 1124
immune responses in, 965
main groups (classes), 676–677, 678t, 705
tube feet, 676, 678, 679, *679*, 845
    See also sand dollars; sea stars; sea urchins
echinoids (Echinoidea), 677, *677*, 678t, *679*
echolocation, 911
ECM. *See* extracellular matrix
ecological change(s)
    dating, 751–753
    and sympatric speciation, 435–437
    See also environmental change(s)
ecological communities. *See* communities
ecological importance
    of fungi, 615–619, 624
    of nematodes, 661
    of protists, sponges, cnidarians, and
        ctenophores, 538, 640
    of rotifers, 660
ecological niches, 441, 821, 1175–1177, *1176,
    1177,* 1193
    abiotic factors influencing, 1177
    and animal size, 821
    fundamental niche, 1176, 1193
    habitat and, 1176
    limiting resources, 777, 1176–1177, 1186
    for plants, 777
    realized niche, 1176, 1193
ecological organization levels, 6, 7, 23
ecological pyramids, 1198–1200, *1199, 1200,*
    1215
ecological restoration, 1251, *1252*
ecology, 6, 1153
    behavioral ecology, 1128, 1149
    community. *See* community ecology
    geography of life, 1218–1240
    population. *See* population ecology
    prokaryote roles, 530–531, 535
    See also ecosystems
economic botany, 590
EcoRI enzyme, 324
ecosystem diversity, 1243, 1244, *1244,* 1261
ecosystem ecology, 1197
ecosystem management, 1214
ecosystem services, 1231, 1239, 1249, 1261
ecosystems, 6, 1174, 1197
    abiotic factors in. *See* abiotic factors
    aquatic ecosystems, 1228–1236, 1239;
        estuaries, 1231–1232, 1239; freshwater
        ecosystems, 1228–1231, *1228–1231,*
        1239; marine ecosystems, 1232–1236,
        1233–1236, 1239
    biogeochemical cycles, 1203–1208, 1215
    biological diversity. *See* biological diversity
    biosphere and, 1196–1216
    carbon cycle, 1203–1204, *1203,* 1215
    climate and, 1212–1213, *1212*
    climate change and, 1159–1160, 1204,
        1257–1258, 1262
    conservation biology, 1249–1253, 1261
    cycle of matter, 1203–1208
    ecological pyramids, 1198–1200, *1199,*
        1200, 1215
    ecological research at Hubbard Brook
        Experimental Forest, 1214, *1214,* 1216
    ecology, 1197
    ecotones, 1189, 1194, 1236–1237, 1240
    energy flow through, 1197–1202, *1197,*
        1215
    energy transfer/flow through, 2, 9, *9,* 23
    fire and, 1213, 1216
    food chains, 1197–1198, *1197*
    interactions in, 1197
    organization levels, 6, 7
    and precipitation patterns, 1212, 1216
    productivity, 1200–1202, 1201t, *1201*
    regulation: bottom-up processes, 1185,
        1186–1187, *1186,* 1194; top-down
        processes, 1185, 1186, *1186,* 1187,
        1194
    solar radiation and, 1208, *1209;* at high
        elevations, 1220

sun and, 1208–1210, *1209*
temperature and, 1208, *1210,* 1215
    See also aquatic ecosystems; biomes;
        freshwater ecosystems; marine eco-
        systems; standing-water ecosystems
ecotones, 438, 1189, 1194, 1236–1237, 1240
    species richness in, *1237*
"ecstasy," 907t
ectoderm, 631–632
    in animal development, 1113, *1114,* 1115t,
        1116
ectomycorrhizal fungi, 617, 770, 771
ectoparasites, 1184
ectoprocts (bryozoans), 659, *659*
ectothermy, 695, 836, *837,* 840
Ecuador: species richness in, 1189
Edelman, Gerald, 977
edema, 957
    in the inflammatory response, 969, *969*
    in undernourished children's bellies, 1031,
        1031
edge effect (in communities), 1189, 1246
Ediacara Hills (South Australia), 455
Ediacaran period, 456t
    organisms in, 455, *455,* 456t, 463, 629
Edidin, Michael, 109–110, *109*
Edwards syndrome (trisomy 18), 352t
EEGs (electroencephalograms): brain waves
        during REM/non-REM sleep, 896, *896*
eels, electric, 916
effector T$_C$ cells, 974
effectors (in feedback systems), 835
effectors (in neural signaling), 861, 884
efferent arterioles, *1042,* 1043, 1044, *1044*
efferent nerves, 884, *885,* 902
efferent neurons, 861–862, 885, 902
    See also motor neurons
egestion (elimination), 1013, 1023
EGF (epidermal growth factor), 148, *149,* 225
egg polarity genes, 378
egg shell: as adapted for terrestrial life, 628,
    694–695
egg(s)/egg cells (ovum/ova), 1078
    activation of, 1109
    amniotic. *See* amniotic egg
    donor nucleus and egg cell cycle synchro-
        nization, 373
    of flowering plants, 592–593, 783
    formation of, 800
    nuclear transplantation experiments, 372,
        373
    oospheres, *548*
    in sexual reproduction, 5
    shell. *See* egg shell
    size, 76
    wood frog egg masses, *14*
    yolk and pattern of cleavage, 1109–1111,
        1124
    See also oocytes
egg-laying mammals (monotremes), 401
Egypt: fertility rate in, 1168t
Egyptian fruit bat (*Rousettus aegyptiacus*), 703
Einstein, Albert: on scientific theories, 19
EKGs (electrocardiograms), 949
El Niño–Southern Oscillation events,
    1211–1212
elaiosome(s) (oil body), 794–796
elastic connective tissue, *826,* 828
elastic fibers (in connective tissue), 823
electric eels, 916
electric fields: detection of, 916
electric organs, 916
electric ray, 688, 916
electrical gradients, 121, 865
    See also proton gradients
electrical signaling
    and fish communication, 1138
    in plants, 130
electrical synapses, 872
electrocardiograms (ECG/EKGs), 949
electrochemical gradients, 82–83, 121–123,
    122
electroencephalograms. *See* EEGs
electrolyte balance, 1035
electrolytes, 42, 1035

electromagnetic receptors, 914, 915t, 916, 934
electromagnetic spectrum, 194, *194*
electron acceptors/carriers
    in aerobic respiration, 177–182, 185, 186
    in anaerobic respiration, 187
    in photosynthesis, 194–195, *195,* 200
    in redox reactions, 161, *161,* 162
electron clouds, 30
electron configurations in elements. *See* Bohr
    models
electron microscopes (EMs), 79, *80,* 108, 502
electron sharing, 32–33, 33
electron shells, 30–31
    valence shell, 31
electron transfer/transport, 36–37, 161–162,
    169–170
    in aerobic respiration, *174,* 175, 177, 186;
        chain, 174t, 175, 177–184, *182, 185,* 186
    in anaerobic respiration, 187
    in photosynthesis, 198, 200–202, *201,* 206t
electron transport chain(s)
    in aerobic respiration, 174t, 175, 177–184,
        182, 185, 186
    in anaerobic respiration, 187
    chemiosmosis (ATP synthesis) as coupled
        to, 182–184; or uncoupled, 183
    in photosynthesis, 200–202, *201,* 206t
electron transport complexes, 180, *182,* 184,
    185
electronegativity (of atoms), 34, 37
electrons, 27
    characteristics, 29t
    configurations in elements. *See* Bohr
        models
    in covalent bonds, 32–33, 33
    energy levels, 30–31, *30*
    in ionic bonds, 35
    in ions, 34
    orbitals, 30, *30*
    sharing of, 32–33, 33
    transfer of. *See* electron transfer/transport
    valence electrons, 31
electroporation, 324
electroreceptors, 688, 914, 915t, 916, 934
elegant stinkhorn (*Phallus ravenelii*), 615
elements (chemical elements), 27–31, 42
    electron configurations. *See* Bohr models
    functions in organisms/plants, 27t,
        775–776, 776t
    isotopes, 29–30, *29*
    moles of, 32
    nutritional studies, 776, 777
    periodic table. *See* periodic table
    with similar chemical properties, 31
    trace elements, 27, 27t, 164
elephant seal (*Mirounga angustirostris*): diving
    adaptations, 1006–1007, *1007*
elephant's ear (*Caladium*), 797
elephants, 704t, 1157
    African, *704*
    mate guarding, 1144
elimination, 1013, 1023
elk, 514, *704*
Ellis–van Creveld syndrome, 417
Elodea, 199
elongation of cells. *See* cell elongation/
    expansion
elongation stage of transcription, 289, *290*
elongation stage of translation, 295–296
embryo sac (of flower), 592–593, *593,* 783
    development of, 785
embryo(s). *See* animal embryo(s); plant
    embryo(s)
embryogenesis
    in *Drosophila,* 376–379, *379*
    in mice, 384
embryoid bodies, 372
embryonic development (in animals), 627,
    1106–1126
    in *Drosophila,* 376–379, *379*
    evolutionary relationships and, *381,* 630
    in sharks, 688–689
    in vertebrates, 406, *407,* 490; brain, 886,
        886t, *886,* 888, 908
    See also cleavage; homeotic genes

exhalation (expiration), 1001, *1001,* 1002
exocrine glands, 823, *823,* 1053
exocytosis, 123–124, *124,* 131
exon shuffling: evolution by, 298
exons (expressed coding sequences), 292, 319
    locating, 329
    splicing of, 293, 319, *319*
    See also exon shuffling
exoskeleton(s), 845
    of arthropods, 55, *56,* 662, 669, 845, *846*
    in insect flight mechanics, 849
    of mollusks. *See under* shells
exotoxins, 533–534
experimental group, 18
experiments (scientific)
    on bacterial diseases, 532
    bias in, 19
    on biological diversity loss in cichlids, 436–437, *437*
    on cell totipotency, 372, *372,* 723
    chance discovery in, 17
    chemical evolution simulations, 448, *448, 449*
    on chimpanzee learning, 19, *20*
    on chlorophyll and photosynthesis, *197*
    in cloning, 373, *374*
    in comparative genomics, 491, *491,* 570, *571*
    data from, 15–16; large data set integration, 21
    on DNA replication, 271–272, *272*
    on eukaryote evolution, *555*
    experimental and control groups in, 18
    in flower color gene mutation, *788,* 789
    on flowering plant evolution, *598*
    on frequency-dependent selection, 421–422, *422*
    on gene linkage, *250*
    on genotype determination, *244*
    on human–mouse membrane fusion, 109–110, *109*
    in in vitro evolution (of RNA), 450, *451*
    on inbreeding, 415, *415*
    interpreting, 19
    Mendel's breeding experiments, 237–238, 238–241, 240t, *240,* 245
    on mycorrhizae and plant growth, 617, *618*
    on natural selection, 407–408, *408,* 421–422, *422*
    on nuclear transplantation/totipotency, 372, 373, *373, 374*
    on nucleus removal, 18–19, *18*
    observations in, 16–17
    on the one-gene, one-enzyme hypothesis, 283–284, *284*
    on oxidative phosphorylation, *183*
    in phototropism, 807–808, *807, 808,* 818
    on plant evolution, 570, *571*
    on polydnaviruses, 512, *513*
    on rapid evolution, 407–408, *408*
    on regeneration, 86–87
    on signaling molecules ERK 1 and ERK 2, *150*
    on spindle microtubules, 222
    on transformation (of DNA), *264*
    on transgenic mice, 341, *341,* 384–385, *385*
    on viral reproduction, 265, *266*
explicit memory, 899
exploitation competition, 1160
explosive dehiscence: seed dispersal by, *795,* 796
exponential population growth, 1157, *1157,* 1170, *1170*
export from cells, 92
expressed sequence tags (ESTs), 336
expression of genes. *See* gene expression
external face (of cell membranes), *112*
external fertilization, 1078, *1079*
external gills, 995
    of salamanders, 440, *441*
external intercostal muscles, 1002
exteroceptors, 914
extinction, 441–442, 444, 482, 1243, *1243,* 1244, 1261
    and adaptive radiation, 441
    of amphibians, 1245

and biological diversity, 440, 441–442, 478, 482
    biological factors, 442
    causes of, 442, 462
    in classical conditioning, 1132
    of the dinosaurs, 441–442, 456t, 460–461, 694
    and evolution, 441
    of gymnosperms, 460
    humans and, 442, 462, 478, 482
    minimum viable population (MVP), 1244, 1245
    preventing, 1154
    species extinction estimate, 626
    See also mass extinction(s)
extracellular fluid, 1035
extracellular matrix (ECM), 74, 102, *102*
    anchoring of cells to, 114, *114*
extraembryonic membranes, 693
extraordinary events. *See* chance (random events)
extraterrestrial object impacts on Earth, 442, 458, 460–461
extreme environments
    archaea in, 165, *165,* 486t, 526–527, *527, 528t*
    endospores in, 520, *520*
extreme halophiles, 486t, 527, *527*
extreme thermophiles, 165, *165,* 486t, 526–527, *527,* 528t
eyes (simple), 928–933, 935
    accommodation power, 929, *930*
    in cephalopods, 655
    human. *See* human eye
    primate adaptation, 466
    of snakes, 697
    structure, 928–929, *930*
    vestigial, 404
    See also compound eyes; retina
eyespots, *544,* 649, *649, 660,* 927, 928

F$^+$ cells, F$^-$ cells, 523
F factor, 523
F-box proteins, 806–807
F$_1$ generation, 240
F$_2$ generation, 240
Fab fragments, 977, *977*
facilitated diffusion, 119–121, *120,* 131
facilitation, *1174,* 1175
factor VIII. *See* clotting factor VIII
facts (in science), 16
facultative anaerobes, 188, 524
facultative mutualism, 1183
FAD (flavin adenine dinucleotide), 162
FADH$_2$, 162
    in aerobic respiration: citric acid cycle, 175, 177, *180, 181;* electron transport chain, 177, 180, *182,* 184
Fagus grandifolia (American beech), 730
fainting, 954
fairy rings, 614–615, *617*
fall colors, 198, 738
fall turnover (of lake temperature), 1230, *1230*
fallopian tubes. *See* oviducts
false feet. *See* pseudopodia
falsifiable hypotheses, 17
families (in taxonomy), 11, 483
family pedigrees (pedigrees), 349, *350,* 366
far-red light, 814–815, 816
farmers. *See* agriculture
fast block to polyspermy, 1108
fast-glycolytic fibers, 855, 855t
fast-oxidative fibers, 855, 855t
fat (adipose tissue), 183, *827,* 828
fat-soluble vitamins, 1026
fats, 57, 70t
    animal fat, 57
    catabolic pathway, 187
    digestion of, 1022, 1022t
    emulsification of, 1022
    metabolism of, 1025, *1025*
    See also lipids; triacylglycerols
fatty acid derivatives (hormones), 1054, *1055*
fatty acids, 57–58, *57, 58*
    breaking down of, 94

digestion of fats/lipids to, 1022, 1022t
    energy yield, 187
    essential, 1025
    ester linkages to glycerol, 57, *57,* 525–526
    hormones derived from, 1054, *1055*
    as hydrophobic, 38, 56
    reassembly of, 1023
Fc fragment, 977, *977*
FDA (Food and Drug Administration), 340, 343
feather stars, 677, 678, 678t
feathers, 699, 843
    coloration of, 698
    dinosaurs with, 461, *461,* 490, 697–698
    evolution of, 440, 461
    as a shared character, 490
fecundity, 1162
feedback inhibition (of enzymes), 167, *167,* 313–314
feedback regulation of glycolysis, 186
feedback systems, 834–835, *834, 835, 836*
    See also negative feedback systems; positive feedback systems
feeding, 1013
feeding behavior (foraging), 1136–1137
feet: primate adaptations, 466, *466*
    See also tube feet
Felis catus. See domestic cat
female dominance hierarchy, 1139–1140, 1143
female pronucleus, 1095, 1109
female reproductive system (in humans), 833, 1084–1093, *1086*
females
    care for the young, 1144–1145, *1145*
    male–female ratio in humans, 252–253
    sex determination in, 251–252
    variegation in, 255
    X-linked genes as equalized in males and, 254–255, *254*
    X-linked genetic disorders in, 253–254, 354
fermentation, 173, 188–189, *188*
    aerobic respiration vs., 188t, 453
    of alcohol, 188–189, *188*
    anaerobic respiration vs., 188t, 190
    by first cells, 452
    in food/beverage production, 531
    inefficiency, 189
    lactate fermentation, *188,* 189, 855
ferns, 216, 565, *565,* 566t, 572–575, *575,* 580
    endangered species, 1253t
    evolution of, 456t, 457
    in experimental studies, 578
    leaves (megaphylls), 571
    life cycle, 573–574, *576,* 580
    seed ferns, 457, 574
    tree ferns, 571
Ferocactus wislizenii. See fishhook cactus
ferredoxin, 200, 201
ferredoxin–NADP reductase, 200, *203*
fertility
    human population growth and, 1167–1168, 1168t, 1169
    interspecific barriers to, 430, *431,* 1121
    replacement-level fertility, 1167, 1168, 1171
    total fertility rate, 1167
fertility drugs: and multiple births, 1121
fertility rate: in developing countries, 1167–1168, 1168t, 1169
    See also birth rate
fertilization, 5, 232, 241, 243
    in animals, 1107–1109, 1124; external, 1078, *1079;* humans, 1093–1095, *1094; in vitro,* 363–364, 374, *1094;* internal, 694–695, 700, 1078, *1079;* interspecific, 1108; mammals, 700; polychaetes, 657; reptiles, 695; sponges, 642
    chromosome doubling during: in interspecific hybrids, 434; as resolved in meiosis, 226–227, 232
    interspecific barriers to, 428–430, 430, *431,* 444

in plants: conifers, *586,* 587; ferns, 574; flowering plants, 592–594, *592, 593,* 781, 789–790, *790,* 800; mosses, 566
fertilization cone, 1108
fertilizer runoff, 436, 1231
fetal alcohol spectrum disorders, 905
fetal heart, 947
α-fetoprotein, 363
fever, 969
fiber, dietary, 1024
fibers
    in cellulose, *56*
    in connective tissue, 823, *826*
    sclerenchyma cells, 711t, 714, *714*
    in stems, 745
    See also skeletal muscle cells (muscle fibers)
fibrillation, ventricular, 959
fibrin, 943, *943*
fibrinogen, 940, 943, *943,* 1082–1083
fibroblasts, *101,* 148, 823–824, 968
fibroin: structure, 64
fibronectins, 102, *102*
fibrous proteins, 64
    See also collagen
fibrous root system, 762, *762*
Fick's law of diffusion, 1003
Ficus macrophylla (Australian banyan), 769
fiddleheads (of ferns), 573, *575, 576*
fiddler crab, 440, 1134–1135
field mice: food-web dynamics, 1199
field mouse-ear chickweed (*Cerastium arvense*), 1174
fig trees, 1186
filamentous cyanobacteria, 1204
filaments
    of algae: green, 553, *553;* red, 552, *552*
    in cells. *See* intermediate filaments; microfilaments
    of fungi. *See* hyphae
    of muscles. *See* myofilaments
    of stamens, 591, *591,* 782, *783*
filial generations (F generations), 239–240
films. *See* biofilms
filoviruses, 508t
filter feeders, 1014
    bivalves, 655
    cartilaginous fishes, 688
    sponges, 642
    tunicates, 682
filtration (of the blood), 1043–1044, *1043, 1044*
filtration membrane, 1044, *1044*
filtration slits, 1044, *1044*
fimbriae (in prokaryotic cells), 82, *82,* 519–520, 535
finches
    Darwin's finches, 1179–1180, *1180*
    of Galápagos, 395, *396,* 406, 419, *419,* 420
Finland: founder effect in, 417, *417*
fins
    evolution of, 687
    limbs as evolved from, 684, *684,* 687
    lobed fins, 689
    pelvic fin, 688, *690*
fir, white (*Abies concolor*), 585
fire
    in chaparral, 1223
    and ecosystems, 1213, 1216
    in temperate grasslands, 1223
fire ants, 670
firefly gene expression in tobacco plant, *288*
first law of thermodynamics, 155–156, 169
first messengers, 143
first trimester: organ development in, 1118, 1120
FISH (fluorescent in situ hybridization), 348–349
fish–tetrapod transition, 443, 457, 690–692
Fisher, Ronald, 396
fishes, 675
    adaptation to freshwater habitats, 1038
    adaptive radiation, 457, 689
    Age of Fishes, 457
    bony. *See* bony fishes

hair cells (sensory), 915t
   sound receptors, 921, 922–924, *923*
   water movement receptors, 919, *919*
   See also gravity receptors
hair follicles, 843, *844*
hairy vetch (*Vicia villosa*), 582
Haldane, J. B. S., 396, 448
Haleakala silversword (*Argyroxyphium sandwicense*), 443
half-life of mRNAs, 291, 298, 310, 319
half-life of radioisotopes, 398–400
Hall, J. B., 1129
hallucinogenic mushrooms, 620
Halocynthia aurantium (sea peach), *681*
halogens, 31
halons: ozone destruction and, 1259, 1260
halophiles, 528t
   See also extreme halophiles
Hamilton, William D., 1146
Hamilton's rule, 1146
Hamlin Pool (Western Australia), *452*
Hämmerling, J., 86, 87
hamsters, 704t
hand(s)
   formation of, 382–383
   primate adaptations, 466, *466*
Hansen disease. *See* leprosy
Haplocheirus sollers, 698
haploid cells, 227, 229, 231, 233, 234
haploid chromosome numbers, 227
haploid generation. *See* gametophyte generation
haploid individuals/organisms, 256, 283
hardiness zones, 1258
hardwood, 750
hardwood bottomland forests: as freshwater ecosystem, 1231
Hardy, Godfrey, 413
Hardy–Weinberg principle, 412–414, *413*, 423
hares, 704t
Hartwell, Leland, 224
haustoria (of hyphae), 622, *622*
Haversian canals, 828, *829*, 847
Hawaii: invasive species in, 1247
Hawaiian goose (*Branta sandvicensis*), *433*
Hawaiian honeycreepers, 15, *15*, 441, 442
Hawaiian Islands: colonization of, 432
Hawaiian silverswords, 441, *443*
hawthorn, downy (*Crataegus mollis*), 405
hawthorn maggot flies, 435–436, *435*
hay fever, 987
   cause of, 622, 987, *988*
Hayflick, Leonard, 278
HBEF (Hubbard Brook Experimental Forest), 1214, *1214*, 1216
HCFCs (hydrochlorofluorocarbons), 1260
HD. *See* Huntington's disease
HDL receptor gene, 938
HDLs (high-density lipoproteins), 938, 1025
head louse (*Pediculus humanus*), 668
head movements: equilibrium maintenance during, 920, *921*, 922
headwater streams, 1228–1229, *1228*
health insurance: genetic discrimination and, 365
hearing: sequence of events in, 921–922, 934–935
   See also ears
hearing area (cerebral cortex), 892, *894*
heart attack (myocardial infarction), 959
heart block, 949
heart cells: electron transfer in, 186
heart disease: causes of, 141, 300
heart murmur, 950
heart rate
   measuring, 950
   regulation of, 857, *902*, 950–951, *952*
heart stage embryo (in seed), 790, *791*
heart valves, 947–948, *948*
heart(s)
   in amphibians, 693, 946, *947*
   in arthropods, 939, *939*
   in birds, 700, 946, *947*, 1116
   in cephalopods, 940
   divided heart, 946

earthworm "hearts," 939
   evolution of, 946, *947*
   fetal heart, 947
   in fishes, 946, *947*
   four-chambered heart, 946, *948*
   in humans. *See* human heart
   lymph "hearts," 957
   in mammals, 946, *947*, 1116; development of, 1116
   in mollusks, 939, *939*
   in reptiles, 695, 946, *947*
   in vertebrates, 684, 946, *947*
   See also cardiac ...
heartbeat, 948–949
   initiation of, 949, *949*
   See also heart rate
heartstrings (chordae tendineae), 948, *948*
heartwood, 750, *751*
heat, 39, 156
   body heat source, 183
   measuring energy as, 184
   plants generating, 183
   specific heat, 40
   of vaporization, 39–40
heat energy, 155, 156
heat of vaporization, 39–40
heat-shock genes, 314
heat-shock proteins, 314
heather (*Calluna vulgaris*), 1154
heavy metals: and food chains, 1202
Hebb, Donald O., 899
hedgehogs, 704t
height in humans, 259
Helianthus annuus. *See* sunflower
helical viruses, 502–503
Helicobacter pylori, 4, 532–533, *532*, 533t, 1019
helium, 31
helix: α-helix protein structures, 64, 65, 66, 111, *111*
   See also double helix of DNA
helix-turn-helix, 318, *318*
Helobdella stagnalis (blood-sucking leech), *659*
Helonias bullata (swamp pink), 1246
helping behavior, 1146–1148
hematomas: leeches in treatment of, 658, *659*
heme (in hemoglobin), 195
hemicelluloses, 714
hemichordates, 635, 676
   characters/characteristics, 637t, 705t
   classification, 637t, *680*
Hemignathus munroi ('Akiapola'au), 15, *442*
Hemiptera (order), 668
hemispheres of the brain, 893
hemizygosity in males, 253
hemocoel, 652, 662, 939, *939*
hemocyanin(s), 939
hemoglobin, 60, 66, 67, 658, 941, 1003
   in anthropoids vs. humans, 470
   in earthworms, 658, 940
   heme in, 195
   loading/unloading of gases onto, 1003–1004
   percent O_2 saturation of, 1003
   polypeptide chains, 66, 67
   production of, 941
   in sickle cell anemia, 67, 284, 358–359, 413, 421
hemolymph, 654, 662, 939
hemolysis, 987
hemolytic anemias, 942
   See also sickle cell anemia
hemophilia, 255, 943
hemophilia A, 339, 361
   probability of inheriting, 364–365
hemp nettles (*Galeopsis*), 435
Henle, loop of. *See* loop of Henle
Hensen's node, 1114
Henslow, John, 393
heparin, 942
hepatic portal system, 956
hepatic veins, 955
   portal vein, *1021*, 1023
hepatitis A
   cause of, 508t
   gamma globulin injections for, 982

hepatitis B: vaccine for, 340
hepatitis C: cause of, 508t
Hepatophyta (phylum). *See* liverworts
herbaceous eudicots
   leaf structure, *590*, 732–733, *733*
   root structure, 763–766, *764*, *765*, *766*, 778
   root system, 762, 762
   stem system, 745–746, *746*, *748*, 758
herbaceous plants, 590, 708–709
   growth process, 719, 745
   See also herbaceous eudicots; monocots (herbaceous monocots)
herbicides, 808–809
herbivores, 1013, *1014*, 1198
   plant defenses against, 817–818, 1180–1181, *1181*
   and productivity, 1200
   teeth, *1017*
herbivory, 1180
Herceptin, 979, 983
hereditary material. *See* genetic material
heredity. *See* inheritance
hermaphrodites, 1078–1079
   among *C. elegans*, 382
   earthworms as, 658
   planarians as, 650
   sponges as, 642
heroin, 906t
herpes, 508, 508t
   genital, 1102, 1102t
herpesviruses, 508t
herring gull (*Larus argentatus*), 1163–1164, *1164*
Hershey, Alfred, 265, 267t
Hershey-Chase experiments, 265, *266*
Hesperornis, 699
Heterocentrotus mammillatus (pencil urchin), *675*
heterochromatin, 315, *316*
heterocysts, 1204
heterosporous plants, 576, 586
   life cycle, 576–578, *578*
   seed plants as, 583
   See also flowering plants (angiosperms); gymnosperms
heterospory, 576, 578, 580
heterothallic fungi, 607, 611
heterotrophs, 10, 209, 452, 463, 524, 524t, 535, 1012, 1198
   first cells as, 452–453
   See also chemoheterotrophs; consumers; decomposers; photoheterotrophs
heterozygosity
   detection of, 244–245, *244*
   inbreeding and, 416
heterozygote advantage, 359, 360, 421, *421*
heterozygous individuals, 242–243, 260, 364, 413
   autosomal recessive diseases in, 358
   incomplete dominance/codominance in, 255–256, *256*
   variegation in mice and cats, 255
Hexapoda (subphylum), 663t, 667
hexapods, 663t, 667–669
   See also insects
hexokinase, *164*, *178*
hexose sugars, 52–53, *52*
HGH (human growth hormone). *See* growth hormone
hibernation, 836, 838
hierarchical classification. *See* systematics; taxonomy
hierarchy of taxonomic categories, 11, 483
high altitude: respiratory trouble at, 1006
high blood pressure, 953
high-density lipoproteins (HDLs), 938, 1025
highly developed countries
   consumption overpopulation in, 1170, 1171
   human demographics in, 1167, 1167t, 1171
highly organized societies, 1141–1142
Himalayan rabbits, 258–259, *259*
Himalayas: formation of, 402
hindbrain, 886, 886t, *886*

HindIII enzyme, 324
hippocampus, 874, 897, 899
hippos: and whales, 405–406, *407*
hirudin, 658
Hirudinida (class), 656t
   See also leeches
Hirudo medicinalis (medicinal leech), 658, *659*
histamine, 873, 942, 978, 1056
   in cell signaling, 137
   in the inflammatory response, 969, 970–971
histidine, 47, 61, *63*
histidine kinases, 139–141
histones, 214–215, *215*, *216*, 217, 315
histoplasmosis, 613
history of life. *See* evolutionary history
HIV (human immunodeficiency virus), 300, *501*, 502, *503*, 509, 984–986
   diagnostic technique, 331
   infection by, 984–985, *985*; treatments for, 985–986
   life cycle, *511*
   protection against, 984, 1100
   transmission of, 984
   vaccines for, 986
   See also AIDS
hives (urticaria), 988
HLA complex (human leukocyte antigen complex), 973
"hobbits," 476
Hodgkin, Alan, 867
holdfasts
   of *Acetabularia*, 86–87
   of brown algae/kelp, 549, *550*
Holocene epoch, 456t, 461
holothuroids (Holothuroidea), 677, *677*, 678t, 679–680
home range, 1140
homeobox genes, 381, 385
homeodomains, 381
homeostasis, 3, 75, 93, 103, 834
   aging and, 1123–1124
   communication and, 134–135
   endocrine and nervous system interactions and, 1053, 1074
   excretory systems and, 1036
   hormones and, 1061
   the lymphatic system and, 957
homeostatic mechanisms, 3, 834–835, 839–840, *839*
   blood-buffering system, 42
homeotic genes, 379t, 380–381, 389
   ABC model, 386
   Arabidopsis mutants, 386, *386*, 724, *725*
   mutations in, 380, *380*, 381, 406
   transcription factors coded for, 381, 386
   See also Hox genes
hominins/hominids, 469, 479
   and chimpanzees: common ancestry, 467, 472
   dead ends, 474, 476
   evolution of, 471–477, *473*
   fossils, 471–477
   origins of, 470, 472
   sexual dimorphism in, 473, 474
   smallest humans, 476
   tools. *See* stone tools of hominins
   See also humans
hominoids, 467, 469–470, 479
Homo (genus): origin, 462
Homo antecessor, 473, 475, 479
Homo erectus, 473, 474–475, 476, 479
Homo ergaster, 473, 474, 479
Homo floresiensis, 476
Homo habilis, 473, 474, 479
Homo heidelbergensis, 473, 475, 479
Homo neanderthalensis, 473, 475–476, 479
Homo sapiens. *See* humans
homogentisic acid, 283
homologous chromosomes, 226–227, *227*, 228–229, 230–231, 233, 234, 242
   alleles on, 242–245
   loci on. *See* gene loci
   separation of, *228*, 229, 231, 241, *241*
   sex chromosomes as/as not, 252

lysogenic conversion, 506, 515
lysogenic cycle, 506, *506*, 515
lysosomal storage diseases, 93
lysosomes (membranous sacs), *85*, 90t, 93, *93*, 103, *547*, 942
  in endocytosis, 125, *125*, 126–127, *126*
  fever and, 969
  manufacture of, 91
  in Tay–Sachs disease, 360
lysozyme, 164, 966
Lystrosaurus, 402
lytic cycle, 505–506, *505*, 515

M phase (cell cycle), 217
  See also cytokinesis; mitosis
M-Cdk, 224–225, 226
macaques, 469, 470
MacArthur, Robert, 1179
Mackenzie Mountains (Canada): fossil deposits, 455
MacKinnon, Roderick, 115
MacLeod, Colin M., 265, 267t
Macrocystis (*pyrifera*), 550, *550*
macroevolution, 392, 439–443, 444
  chance and, 397
  See also evolution; speciation
macromolecules, 7, 47, 51, 71, 135
  origin, 446
  See also nucleic acids; polymers; proteins; receptors
macronucleus in ciliates, 547, *547*
macronutrients for plants, 775–776, 776t
macrophages, 127, 825, 942, *963*, 966–967, *967*, 972, 973
  bacteria vs., 966–967
  in the inflammatory response, 969, *970–971*
  microglia, *864*, 865, 874
  secretions from, 968, 973
  and tumor necrosis factor, 968
Macropus giganteus (eastern gray kangaroo), 702
Macrotus californicus (California leaf-nosed bat), *911*
mad cow disease, 68, 514
magnesium, 1028t
  Bohr model, 28
  as a cofactor, 164
  function in organisms/plants, 27t, 776, 776t
magnetic fields
  detection of, 916
  and migration, 1136
magnification: of microscopes, 77
Magnolia grandiflora, 597
magnolia tree, 1161
magnoliids, *597*, 598
maidenhair tree. *See Ginkgo biloba*
maize: transposons in, 303
  See also corn
major histocompatibility complex (MHC), 973
Malacostraca (class), 663t
malaria, 546, 1184
  cause of (parasite), 338, 546. *See also Plasmodium*
  climate change and, 1258
  control methods, 621
  and sickle cell anemia, 359, 421; geographic distribution, *421*
malate, *181*
  decarboxylation of, 207, 208, *208*
malate ions: and stomatal opening, 735
male dominance hierarchy, 1139–1140, 1142
male pronucleus, 1095, 1109
male reproductive system (in humans), *833*, 1080–1084, *1080*
male–female ratio in humans, 252–253
males
  care for the young, 1144–1145, *1145*
  hemizygosity in, 253
  sex determination in, 251–252
  X-linked genes as equalized in females and, 254–255, *254*
  X-linked genetic disorders in, 253–254, 354–355
malignant melanoma, 844
malignant transformation of cells, 387, 388

malignant tumors/neoplasms, 831
mallee scrub, 1223
malnutrition, 1013
  and obesity, 1030
  protein deficiency, 1031, *1031*
  undernutrition, 1030–1031
Malpighian tubules, 669, 1038
maltase, 1021
maltose, 53, *54*, 209, 1021
Malthus, Thomas, 394, 1166
mamane tree, 1247
mammal-like reptiles, 457, 458, 466
Mammalia (class), 11
mammalian respiratory system, 998–1007
  air volume measurements, 1002
  airway, 998–1001, 1009–1010
  breathing mechanics, 1001–1002, *1001*, 1009
  breathing regulation, 1004–1006, 1009
  defense mechanisms against polluted air, 1007–1008, 1009
  diving adaptations, 1006–1007
  gas exchange in, 1001–1004, *1002*
  in humans, *833*, 999
mammals, 834
  adaptations to terrestrial life, 629, 700–701
  adaptive radiation, 441, 462, 701
  Age of Mammals, 461–462
  bear/give birth to live young hypothesis, 17–18
  and biological clocks, 1135
  brain, 700, 887, 888
  characters/characteristics, 489–490, 491–492, 686t, 700, 706
  circulatory system, 946, *947*
  classification, 684, 694, 701
  cloning of, 373, *374*
  communication and pheromones, 1139
  development of, 384–386
  diving mammals, 1006–1007, *1007*
  embryo cleavage, 1109
  endangered species, 1253t
  as endotherms, 700, 836–837
  equilibrium maintenance in, 919–920, *921*, *922*
  estrous cycles, 1093
  evolution of, 456t, 462, 466, 700–701, *701*; on islands, 476
  fertilization in, 1108
  groups: orders, 704t; subclasses, 701–703, 706
  hair. *See* hair
  heart, 946, *947*, 1116
  imprinting in, 1132
  inner ears, 919–920, *920*
  large mammal extinction, 456t, 462
  lungs, 995
  marsupials, 401
  middle-ear bones, 489, 490, 491–492, *497*, 700
  monotremes, 401
  mouse model of development, 384–386
  organ systems in, 830, *832–833*
  origin, 456t
  osmoregulation and excretion in, 1039–1040, *1040*
  parental care by, 1144–1145
  placental. *See* placental mammals
  reproduction in: regulation of, *150*
  and reptiles. *See* amniotes
  respiratory system. *See* mammalian respiratory system
  scaffold proteins in, 147
  sex determination in, 251–253, *252*
  shared characters, 489–490, 491–492, *497*
  skin (epithelial cells), 127
  skin derivatives, 843
  urinary system. *See* urinary system
mammary gland cell, *124*
mammary glands, 489–490, 700, *701*
manatees, 545, 704t, *704*
mandibles (of crustaceans), 666
manganese, 1028t
  function in organisms/plants, 27t, 776, 776t

mangrove forests, 1232, *1232*, 1239
mangroves: pneumatophores (breathing roots), 767, 769
Manihot esculenta (cassava), *761*
Manis crassicaudata (pangolin), 403, *404*
mantle: of mollusks, 652, 654
mantle of Earth, 402
MAO inhibitors, 906t
MAP kinase pathways, 147, 148, *149*
MAP protein kinases, 148, *149*
map sense, 1135
map units in genetics, 250
maples (*Acer*)
  communication among, 135
  leaf arrangement, *730*
  leaf cell cytokinesis, 223
  pollination of, 789
  seed dispersal, 794
  silver maple, 223, 739
  sugar maple, *730*
  water mold infections, 549
mapping
  of chromosomes, 347
  of genes, 250–251, *251*, 310
  See also DNA sequencing
MAPs (microtubule-associated proteins), 97, 98, *99*
MAPs (mitogen-activated proteins), 148
maquis, 1223
Marchantia polymorpha (common liverwort), 567, 569
marijuana, 906t, 1181
marine birds, 1039
marine ecosystems, 1232–1236, *1233–1236*, 1239
  human activities and, 1236, 1240
  zones, 1232, *1233*
marine ecosystems/environment
  animal adaptations to, 627–628
  deep-sea vents, 165
marine invertebrates, 834
marine nekton, 1235
marine organisms
  mass extinction, 442, 458
  shells of, 1204
marine plankton. *See* plankton
marine reptiles. *See* ichthyosaurs
marine sanctuaries, 1249
marine slugs. *See* nudibranch
marine snow, 1235, 1240
marine worms. *See* polychaetes
Marrella splendens fossil, 457
marriage: consanguineous matings, 365
marrow. *See* bone marrow
marshes
  productivity, 1201t
  as wetland ecosystem, 1231, *1231*
marsupials, 401, 686t, 701, *701*, 702–703, *702*, 1238
  adaptive radiation, 702–703
  eutherian counterparts, 702–703, *702*
marsupium (pouch), 702
Martin–Bell syndrome, 356
mass, 29n2, 155
  molecular mass, 31–32
mass extinction(s), 440, 441–442, 444
  causes of, 442, 462
  Cretaceous period-/Mesozoic era-ending extinction, 441–442, 456t, 460–461
  Permian period-/Paleozoic era-ending extinction, 456t, 458
  Pleistocene epoch-ending extinction, 456t, 462
mast cells: in the inflammatory response, 969, *970–971*
mastectomy, 957
mate chasing, 1143–1144
mate guarding, 1144
maternal age: and Down syndrome, 353–354
maternal antibodies
  passive immunity from, 982
  from Rh incompatibility, 987
maternal effect genes, 378, 379, 379t, 389
maternal homologue, 230

maternal imprinting (genomic imprinting), 316, 356–358, *357*
maternal PKU, 358
maternal serum α-fetoprotein (MSAFP), 363
mathematical models: of population size, 1156
mating systems, 1143–1144
mating(s)
  consanguineous, 365
  controlled matings, 347
  nonrandom mating: and genotype frequencies, 415–416, *415*, 424
  random mating: and genetic equilibrium, 414
  See also reproduction; sexual intercourse
matorral, 1223
matrix. *See* extracellular matrix; mitochondrial matrix
matter, 27, 155
  cycles of. *See* biogeochemical cycles
  See also states of matter
Matthaei, Heinrich, 287
mature embryo (in seed), 790–791, *791*
maxillae (of crustaceans/lobsters), 666, 667
maxillipeds (of lobsters), 667, 667
maximum likelihood in molecular systematics, 497
mayflies, 669
Mayr, Ernst, 396, 427
McAuliffe, Katherine, 1149
McCarty, Maclyn, 265, 267t
McClintock, Barbara, 303
MDMA, 907t
measles (*rubeola*): cause of, 508t
  See also German measles
measles virus, 507–508
mechanical energy, 155
mechanical isolation (of species), 429, *431*
mechanical nociceptors, 916
mechanoreceptors, 914, 915t, 916–924, 934
  for gravity, 916, 918–919, *918*, 919–920, *920*
  for muscle movement, 918, *918*
  for sound, 920–924, *923*
  for touch, 916–917, *917*
  for water movement, 919, *919*
Medawar, Sir Peter, 506
medial structure of body, 630, *631*
medical applications of DNA technology, 338, 339–340
medical research: evolution and, 392
medicinal leeches, 658, *659*
medicinal plants: ginkgo, 588
medicine (medical practice)
  evolution and, 392
  fungi as used in, 620–621, 624
  leeches as used in, 658, 659
  radioisotopes as used in, 29–30
medicines: genetically modified protein products, 339–340
  See also drugs
Mediterranean fruit fly (*Ceratitis capitata*), 929
Mediterranean rabbits, 433
medium ground finch (*Geospiza fortis*), 1179, 1180, *1180*
medulla (brain organ), 886, 886t, *887*, 891t, 893
  breathing regulation, 1004
medulla, adrenal. *See* adrenal medulla
medulla, renal. *See* renal medulla
medusa body form, 643–644, *643*, 645
meerkat (African mongoose), 1148, 1149
megafossils, 578–579
megaphylls, 571
  evolution of, 571, *572*
Megaptera novaeangliae (humpback whale), 703, *704*
megasporangia (of heterosporous plants), 576, 578
  See also ovules
megaspores (of heterosporous plants), 576, 578
  of conifers, 586–587, *586*
  of flowering plants, 592, 783

perfect flower, 591
perforins, 967
pericardial cavity, 947
pericardium, 947
pericentriolar material, 219–220
pericycle, 764, 765, 766, 767, 767
periderm (outer bark), 711t, 718, 720, 720, 746, 748, 749, 750
  in roots, 767
periosteum, 846–847, 848
peripheral membrane proteins, 108, 110, 111–112, 111
peripheral nervous system (PNS), 862, 885, 885, 902–904, 909
peripheral resistance to blood flow, 951–952
Periplaneta americana (American cockroach), 668t
Perissodactyla (order), 704t
Perissodus microlepis (cichlid), 421–422, 422
peristalsis, 1015–1016, 1018, 1018
peritoneal cavity, 1017
peritoneum, 1017
peritonitis, 1017
peritubular capillaries, 1042, 1043
permafrost, 1219, 1220, 1239
permeability of membranes, 115
  selectively permeable membranes, 115, 117, 117, 130–131
Permian period, 402, 456t
  mass extinction at the end, 456t, 458
  organisms appearing in, 456t, 458, 701
Peromyscus eremicus (cactus mouse), 838
Peromyscus leucopus. See white-footed mouse
peroxisomes (membranous sacs), 90t, 93–94, 94, 103
persistence (of synthetic pesticides), 1202
pertussis (whooping cough), 533t
Peru: species richness in, 1189
pest control
  biological methods, 621, 817–818
  plant signaling in, 817–818
pesticides
  and amphibian deformities, 1245
  biological magnification, 1202, 1202
  and food chains, 1202
  GM crops and, 342–343
  resistance to, 546
PET scans (positron-emission tomography), 874
petals (of flower), 386, 591, 591, 592, 710, 782, 783
  bracts as, 739, 740
  evolution of, 594–595
  pollinator attractants, 787–788, 788, 789
Peteinosaurus, 459
petioles, 710, 729, 729
petrified wood, 399
Petromyzontida (class), 685, 686, 686t
  See also lampreys
Peziza badio-confusa (brown cup), 614
Pfr phytochrome, 814–815, 815, 816
PGA (phosphoglycerate), 204, 205
PGD (preimplantation genetic diagnosis), 363–364, 367
pH value(s), 41, 43
  of amino acids, 61
  of blood, 41, 42, 941, 1003, 1004; regulation of, 1045
  calculation of, 41, 41t
  of cells, 41
  of common solutions, 41t, 41
  of enzymes, 165–166, 165
  of fungi, 602
  of soil(s): and mineral availability, 775
Phacops rana, 664
phages. See bacteriophages
phagocytes, 957, 964, 965, 966–969, 969, 971, 977, 977, 978, 990
phagocytosis, 125, 125, 543, 942, 964, 966, 967
  in the inflammatory response, 969, 969
Phalaenopsis hybrid (moth orchid), 769

Phalanger (cuscus), 702
Phalanger (flying phalanger), 702
Phallus revenelii (elegant stinkhorn), 615
Phanerozoic eon, 456t
pharmacogenetics, 338–339, 345
pharming, 341–342, 343
pharyngeal pouches, 680, 1116
pharyngeal slits/gill slits, 676, 680, 680, 681
pharynx, 1016, 1017–1018, 1018
  in earthworms, 657, 658, 1017
  jaws as evolved from, 681, 684
  muscular pharynx, 685
  in nematodes/*Ascaris*, 662
  in planarians, 649, 649
  in vertebrates, 1017–1018; humans, 999, 999, 1016
phase contrast microscopy, 78–79, 78, 80
phencyclidine, 875, 907t
phenetic approach to systematics, 493
phenobarbital, 875
phenotype frequencies, 412, 423
phenotypes, 239
  assessment of, 255
  the environment and, 258–260, 259, 1128
  epigenetic variation in, 316–317, 316
  gene expression and, 257, 258–260, 259, 261, 283
  gene interaction and, 257–258, 257, 258
  and genotypes, 243, 249, 259, 260
  mate selection by, 415–416
  monohybrid F_2 phenotypic ratios, 243
  mutagenesis screening for genes involved in, 336
  natural selection modes/processes changing, 418–420, 418, 424
  norm of reaction in, 259, 261
  novel features. See evolutionary novelties
  polygenic inheritance and, 257–258, 258, 261
phenylalanine, 61, 63, 358
phenylketonuria (PKU), 358
  newborn screening for, 358, 364
phenylthiocarbamide (PTC), 926
pheophytin, 200
pheromones, 1139
  in animal communication, 1139
  in fungi, 605, 607
  in insect communication, 669, 670, 1139
  queen bee control of hive, 1139
Philodendron selloum (splitleaf philodendron), 183
Philodina roseola (bdelloid rotifer), 427, 427
phloem, 564, 584, 711t, 716–717, 716
  conducting cells, 715, 716–717, 716
  functions, 747–750
  in leaves, 732
  primary phloem, 746, 747, 748
  in roots: of herbaceous eudicots, 766; of monocots, 766–767, 767
  secondary. See secondary phloem
  sieve tube elements in. See sieve tube elements
  in stems, 745, 746, 746, 747, 748
  sugar translocation in. See sugar translocation in plants
phloem fiber cap, 745, 746
phloem loading, 756–757, 757
phloem parenchyma, 711t, 716
phloem transport, 747–750, 753t, 753, 756–757
phlox, Drummond, 1163, 1164
Phoenix dactylifera (date palm), 791–793
phoronids, 658–659, 659
phosphatases, 141, 146, 150, 164, 320
phosphate: phosphorus cycle, 1206, 1206
phosphate group transfer, 122, 139, 141, 142, 159, 160, 175, 179, 320
  See also phosphorylation
phosphate group(s), 50–51, 50, 68, 159, 267
  See also phosphate group transfer
phosphodiester linkages, 68, 69, 267, 267
phosphodiesterase, 143, 144, 149–150
phosphoenolpyruvate (PEP), 179, 207, 208
phosphofructokinase, 178, 186
2-phosphoglycerate, 179

3-phosphoglycerate, 179
phosphoglycerate (PGA), 204, 205
phospholipase C, 145, 145, 1060
phospholipid bilayer(s). See lipid bilayer(s)
phospholipids (in cell membranes), 58–59, 70t, 71, 107
  as hydrophobic/hydrophilic, 58, 59, 107, 110
  movement, 109, 109
  as second messengers, 145–146, 145, 1060
  shape, 107, 107
  synthesis of, 89, 94
  in water. See lipid bilayer(s)
phosphorus, 1028t
  Bohr model, 28
  covalent bonding, 33t
  function in organisms/plants, 27t, 776, 776t
  radioisotope, 29
phosphorus cycle, 1206–1207, 1206, 1215
  human activity and, 1207
phosphorus-32, 29
phosphorylation, 139, 141, 160, 175
  in ATP hydrolysis, 100, 159, 160
  in cell signaling, 139, 141, 142, 146
  dephosphorylation, 141
  of glucose, 121, 160, 175, 178–179
  photophosphorylation, 202
  of proteins, 224, 320
  in the sodium–potassium pump, 122
  See also oxidative phosphorylation; substrate-level phosphorylation
photoautotrophs, 208–209, 524, 524t
photochemical smog, 1206
photoheterotrophs, 209, 524, 524t
photolysis (light splitting)
  of hydrogen sulfide, 452
  of water, 200–201, 452
photomicrographs, 74, 75, 78, 79, 80t
photons, 194, 195
photoperiodism in plants, 813–814
photophosphorylation, 202
photoreceptors, 138, 804, 914, 915t, 927–933
  in animals. See compound eyes; eyes (simple); eyespots
  in plants, 138, 804, 814–817
  See also cryptochrome(s); phytochrome(s); rhodopsin(s)
photorespiration: and photosynthesis, 206, 207
photosynthesis, 9, 10, 31, 96, 193–211
  action spectrum, 197, 197
  vs. aerobic respiration, 204t
  aerobic respiration and, 209
  ATP synthesis in, 198, 199, 202–204, 203
  carbon fixation reactions, 199, 199, 204–208, 206t
  chemiosmosis in, 201, 202–204, 203, 206t
  chlorophyll in, 31, 195, 196–198
  in chloroplasts, 95, 96–97
  concentration gradient in, 158
  efficiency reduction, 206
  electron transport in, 198, 200–202, 201, 206t
  environmental benefits, 209
  and gross primary productivity (GPP), 1200, 1215
  light for, 194
  light-dependent reactions, 198–199, 199–204, 199, 206t
  origins, 452–453
  overview of, 194–195, 198–199, 199, 206t
  parenchyma cells in, 713
  photolysis in, 200–201
  photorespiration and, 206, 207
  as redox reactions, 198
  regulation of, 209
  resonance in, 200
  in standing-water ecosystem, 1230
  units (photosystems), 200, 200, 201, 203
  visible light and, 194; action spectrum, 197, 197
photosynthetic protists, 538, 539, 552
  brown algae, 549
  chromalveolates, 544

dinoflagellates, 545
euglenoids, 543
golden algae, 551
green algae, 538, 553
photosystem I (P700), 200, 201, 203
photosystem II (P680), 200, 201, 203
photosystems, 200, 200, 201, 203
phototrophs, 208, 524
phototropins, 804
phototropism, 804, 804
  auxin in, 808
  experiments in, 807–808, 807, 808, 818
Phragmipedium caricinum (lady's slipper), 13
Phthiraptera (order), 668t
phyla (in taxonomy), 11, 483
  See also superphyla
phyletic gradualism model of evolution, 439, 439, 444
PhyloCode, 486
phylogenetic relationships. See evolutionary relationships
phylogenetic species concept, 427–428
phylogenetic systematics. See cladistics
phylogenetic trees, 486–487, 492, 494, 495, 496, 497
  See also cladograms
phylogeny, 488–489
  of animals, 626, 630–637, 637–638
  of chordates, 682–683
  molecular phylogeny, 491, 633–634, 638
  of prokaryotes, 526–527, 528–529t
  of protists, 539
  reconstructing, 489–492, 493–497, 495, 497
  See also evolutionary relationships (phylogenetic relationships)
phylograms, 487
Physalia physalis (Portuguese man-of-war), 644, 644, 645
Physarum polycephalum, 556, 556
Physcomitrella (*patens*), 570, 571, 763
physical barriers to pathogens, 965, 966
physical inactivity
  and cancer, 831
  and cardiovascular disease, 960
physical isolation. See geographic isolation; mechanical isolation
physiological readiness
  for behavior, 1130
  for mating, 1139, 1143
  for migration, 1135
physiological saline, 118
physiology, 822
phytochemicals, 1024, 1028–1029
phytochrome(s), 138, 814–816
Phytophthora infestans, 549
Phytophthora ramorum, 549
phytoplankton
  in flowing-water ecosystems, 1239
  ocean habitats, 1228, 1235, 1239
  ozone and UV radiation, 1260
pia mater, 889, 889
Picea sichensis (Sitka spruce), 1191
picornaviruses, 508t
PID. See pelvic inflammatory disease
pigeons, 1131
pigments, 59
  absorption spectrum, 196, 197
  in chloroplasts, 195–198, 196, 200, 200. See also chlorophyll
  in compound eyes, 928
  in lichens, 618
  melanopsin, 930
  in molds (fungi), 611
  in phototropism, 804
  respiratory pigments, 1003–1004. See also hemoglobin; myoglobin
  See also cryptochrome(s); phytochrome(s); rhodopsin(s)
pigs, 404, 407, 704t
  gene regulation in, 308–309, 308
  replacement organs from, 989
Pikaia, 683
pikas, 704t, 704
Pilbara rocks (Australia), 451–452

protist reproduction, 539
  amoebas, 5, 5, 555
  apicomplexans, 546, 546
  brown algae, 550
  ciliates, 547–548, 547
  diatoms, 549, 549
  golden algae, 551
  green algae, 553–554, 554
  water molds, 548–549, 548
Protista (kingdom-abandoned), 485, 486, 537
protists, 13–14, 93, 485, 537–559
  as aquatic, 538–539
  biological diversity, 538–539, 558
  body plans/types, 538
  cell walls. See under cell walls
  clades, 542t
  classification, 13, 21, 485, 486, 486t, 537, 541
  as endosymbionts. See under endosymbionts
  evolution of, 539–540
  importance, 538
  life cycles, 232, 233; of Chlamydomonas (green algae), 553–554, 554; of Plasmodium, 546; of cellular slime mold, 556–557, 557; water molds, 548–549, 548
  locomotion. See under locomotion
  nutritional modes, 538
  photosynthetic. See photosynthetic protists
  phylogeny, 539
  reproduction. See protist reproduction
  spores. See under spores
  supergroups, 485, 486, 539–540, 541, 542t. See also archaeplastids; chromalveolates; excavates; rhizarians; unikonts
  See also actinopods; algae; alveolates; amoebas; choanoflagellates; diatoms; diplomonads; euglenoids; forams; parabasalids; protozoa; slime molds; stramenopiles; trypanosomes; water molds; and specific protists
proto-oncogenes, 387, 388, 389
protobionts, 449, 449, 463
protofilaments, 101
proton acceptors, 40
proton donors, 40
proton gradients, 123
  across the inner mitochondrial membrane/plasma membrane of prokaryotic cells, 175, 183–184, 183, 184
  across the thylakoid membrane, 201, 202–203
proton pumps
  for active transport, 121–123, 123, 185, 201, 202, 735
  for bacterial flagella, 521
  with contractile vacuoles, 78
protonema (of mosses), 566, 568
protonephridia, 1037, 1037
  in planaria, 649–650
  in rotifers, 660, 660
protons, 27
  atomic number, 27–28
  characteristics, 29t
  in ionic bonds, 35
protoplasm, 82
protoplasmic face (of cell membranes), 112, 129
protostomes, 633, 638, 648–671, 671t
  characters/characteristics, 636t, 671t
  classification, 635, 636t
  cleavage in, 633, 1109
  coelom formation in (schizocoely), 633, 634
  and spiral cleavage, 1109
  See also ecdysozoa; lophotrochozoa
protozoa, 486t, 537
  as endosymbionts, 454
  Tetrahymena, 13
  vacuoles in, 93
  See also protists
proventriculus (in birds), 700
proviruses, 506

proximal convoluted tubules, 1041, 1042, 1042, 1043
  reabsorption of water in, 1045–1046, 1046, 1046–1047, 1048
proximate causes of behavior, 1128, 1135, 1149
Prozac, 875, 906t
PrP protein, 514
Prusiner, Stanley, 513
PSA (prostate-specific antigen), 1082–1083
pseudocoelom, 632–633, 632, 638
  in nematodes, 632, 661, 662
pseudocoelomates, 632–633, 632, 660
pseudocopulation by bees, 788
pseudomonads, 528t
Pseudopodia, 100, 538, 555
pseudostratified epithelium, 823, 825
psilocybin, 620
Psilotum nudum, 574, 577
psychoactive mushrooms, 620
psychological dependence on drugs, 904, 906–907t
psychosocial dwarfism, 1066
PTC (phenylthiocarbamide), 926
Pteridophyta (phylum). See ferns; horsetails
pterosaurs (flying reptiles), 458–459, 459, 694, 695t
  ancestors, 458
  classification, 694
  extinction of, 460
Pterurus glaucas (eastern tiger swallowtail butterfly), 786
Ptilonorhynchus violacens (satin bowerbird), 429, 429, 431
PTSD (Post-Traumatic Stress Disorder), 898
puberty
  in human females, 1085, 1089
  in human males, 1084
Puccinia (graminis), 622, 623
puffballs, 612
pufferfish (Fugu rubripes), 338, 867, 869
pulmonary arteries, 955, 955
pulmonary circulation, 693, 946, 954, 954, 955, 961
pulmonary emphysema, 1009
pulmonary surfactant, 1002
pulmonary valve, 948, 948
pulmonary veins, 955, 955
pulmonate animals, 654
pulp cavity (of tooth), 1017, 1018
pulse, arterial, 950
  See also heart rate
punctuated equilibrium model of evolution, 438–439, 444
Pundamilia (cichlids in Lake Victoria), 436–437, 436, 437, 441
Punnett, Reginald, 243
Punnett square, 243, 248
pupa, 376, 669, 670
  Drosophila pupa, 376, 378
pupfish (Cyprinodon), 432, 432
purines, 68, 68, 267
purple bacteria
  mitochondria as evolved from, 454, 539
  nonsulfur bacteria, 209, 452, 524, 524t
  sulfur bacteria, 452, 524t, 528t
pursuit of prey, 1180
PWS. See Prader–Willi syndrome
pylorus, 1019, 1019
pyramid of biomass, 1199, 1199, 1215
pyramid of energy, 1199–1200, 1200, 1215
pyramid of numbers, 1199, 1215
pyrethrum, 1181
pyridoxine (vitamin B$_6$), 1027t
pyrimidines, 68, 68, 267
Pyrococcus furiosus, 528t, 528
Pyrus communis (pear), 794
pyruvate dehydrogenase, 166, 177
pyruvates
  in aerobic respiration: acetyl CoA formation, 175, 177, 180; glycolysis, 174–175, 175, 176, 179
  in fermentation, 188, 188
  in photosynthesis, 207, 208
Python sebae, 405

pythons: vestigial hind-limbs, 404, 405, 406, 697

quaaludes, 907t
quadrupedalism in anthropoids, 469, 470
quaking aspen (Populus tremuloides), 798
quality of life: biological diversity and, 481–482
Quaternary period, 456t, 461
quaternary structure of proteins/polypeptides, 65–66, 67, 72
queen bee, 1139, 1141
Quercus. See oaks
Quetzalcoatlus, 458–459
quickening, 1120
quorum sensing (by bacteria), 134–135

R (remainder symbol), 49, 50
R factors, 534
R groups
  in amino acids, 61
  in polypeptides, 65, 66
r selection, 1162, 1170
r-selected species, 1162
rabbits, 258–259, 259, 433, 704t, 1023
rabbits foot fern (Polypodium aureum), 575
rabies: cause of, 508, 508t
radial cleavage, 633, 633, 676
radial nervous system, 883
radial symmetry, 630, 631
  pentaradial symmetry, 676, 677
radiation (adaptive). See adaptive radiation
radicle (embryonic root), 762, 791, 791, 797
radio waves, 194, 194
radioactive isotopes: and food chains, 1202
radioactive thymidine, 217
radioisotopes, 29, 398
  decay of, 29, 398–400, 400
  fossil dating with, 400
  medical uses, 29–30
radiolarians, 552
radish (Raphanus sativus), 719
radius (bone), 846–847, 848
radula (of mollusks), 652
raffia palm (Raphia ruffia), 729
rain: acid precipitation, 1247
rain forests: research on, 16
  See also temperate rain forests; tropical rain forests
rain shadow, 1213, 1213, 1216
rainfall. See precipitation
rainwater: pH value, 41
Rana pipiens (leopard frog), 428, 428, 429
Rana ridibanda (frog), 842
Rana sylvatica. See wood frog
Rana temporaria (frog), 1079
random dispersion (of individuals), 1154–1155, 1155, 1170, 1170
random events. See chance
random mating: and genetic equilibrium, 414
ranges (of species), 1237, 1240, 1244, 1257, 1261
Ranvier, nodes of, 862, 862, 871, 872
RAO model (Recent Africa Origin model), 476–477
Raphanus sativus (radish), 719
Raphia ruffia (raffia palm), 729
rapid chromosome mapping, 347
rapid evolution experiments and observations, 407–408, 408
RAS (reticular activating system), 896
Ras pathways, 148, 844
Ras proteins, 148
rat studies: applicability to other organisms, 26
ratites, 699
rats, 704t
  kangaroo rat, 1039, 1189, 1225
  naked mole rat, 1148
  in operant conditioning, 1132–1133
  pheromones and, 1139
  studies applicability to other organisms, 26
ray-finned fishes, 684, 686t, 689–690
rays (fish), 686t, 688, 688
  electro/electromagnetic receptors, 916

rays (in secondary xylem/phloem), 748–750, 749
RBCs. See red blood cells
reabsorption (of glomerular filtrate), 1044–1045
reactants in chemical reactions, 32
reaction centers of chlorophyll, 200, 200
reaction coupling (energy coupling), 158–159, 160
  chemiosmosis and the electron transport chain, 184
  enzymes in, 166
reading frame, 287
realized niche, 1176, 1193
reasoning processes in science, 16
Recent Africa Origin (RAO) model, 476–477
receptacle (of flower), 591, 591, 782, 783
reception (in cell signaling), 136, 136, 137–141
reception (in neural signaling), 861, 912, 913, 914
receptor down-regulation, 138–139, 1057
receptor potentials, 912, 913
receptor up-regulation, 139, 1057
receptor-mediated endocytosis, 125–127, 126
receptors, 135, 136, 138–141, 151–152
  domains, 138
  and enzyme activity, 148
  glutamate receptors, 900, 901
  LDL receptors, 126, 126
  membrane proteins as, 114, 115
  for neurotransmitters, 860, 875, 876
  for plant hormones, 805, 806, 807
  sensory. See sensory receptors
  synthesis of, 138
  See also cell-surface receptors; intracellular receptors; and specific receptors
recessive alleles, 241, 243, 413
  X-linked, 253
recessive disorders/diseases
  autosomal recessive diseases, 358–360, 367
  carriers of, 253–254, 364–365
  X-linked recessive disorder, 361, 366
recessive mutations, 358
recessive traits, 240
  probabilities of, 364–365
reciprocal altruism, 1148
reciprocal translocation between chromosomes, 355, 355
recognition helix, 318, 318
recombinant DNA: formation of, 324, 325
recombinant DNA technology, 323, 324–331, 344
  analysis. See DNA analysis
  applications of, 339–343, 345
  cloning, 324–329
  cutting, 324, 325
  genomics, 335–339
  libraries, 326–328, 327, 344
  PCR technique, 329–331, 330, 344
  restrictions on, 343
  risk assessment, 343, 344
  safety concerns/risks, 343–344, 345
  sequencing. See DNA sequencing
recombinant plasmids, 324, 325, 327, 327
recombinant types (of gametes), 249
recombinant vaccines, 340
recombination (genetic recombination), 246, 249, 522–524, 522, 523
  homologous recombination, 336
  independent assortment and, 245–246
  of linked genes, 250, 250t, 251
  in meiosis, 230, 231
  new proteins from, 298
  and variation, 230, 231
  See also crossing-over; recombinant DNA technology
reconstructing phylogeny/evolutionary relationships, 489–492, 493–497, 495, 497
rectum, 1016, 1023
red algae, 542t, 552–553, 552, 559
  classification, 541, 560
  coralline algae, 553, 646–647, 1234
  as endosymbionts, 544, 551

Scientific Measurement

		Examples
kilo	1000	a kilogram is 1000 grams
centi	0.01	a centimeter is 0.01 meter
milli	0.001	a milliliter is 0.001 liter
micro (μ)	one-millionth	a micrometer is 10^{-6} (one-millionth) of a meter
nano (n)	one-billionth	a nanogram is 10^{-9} (one-billionth) of a gram
pico (p)	one-trillionth	a picogram is 10^{-12} (one-trillionth) of a gram

The relationship between mass and volume of water (at 20°C)
$1\,g = 1\,cm^3 = 1\,mL$

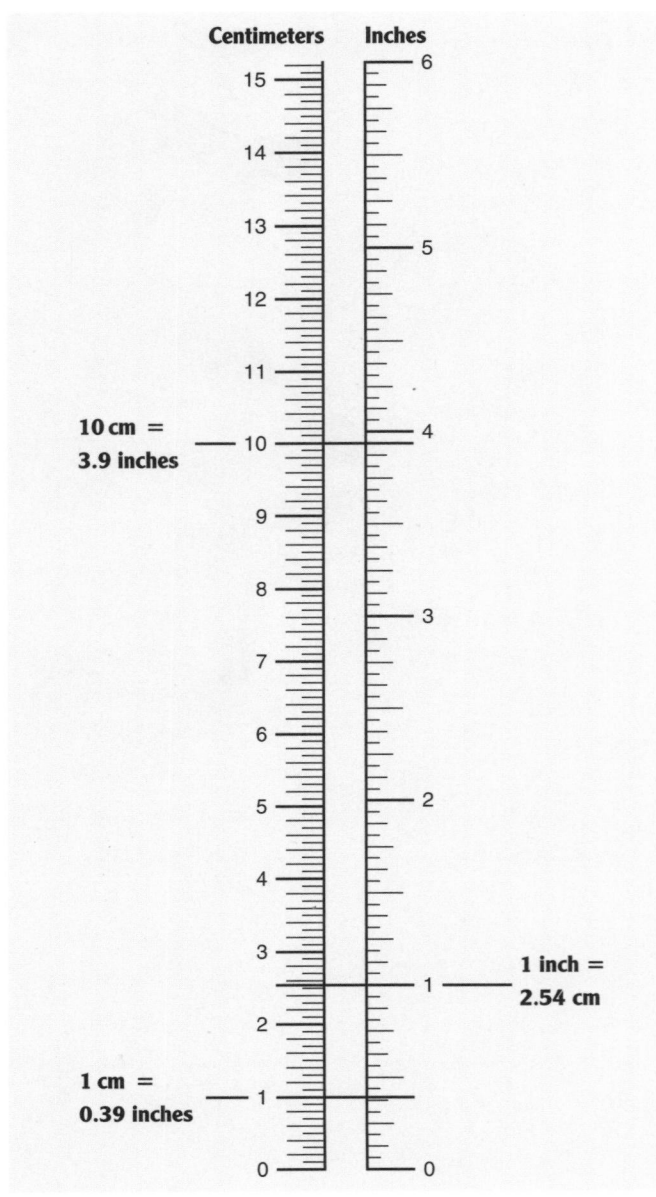

10 cm = 3.9 inches

1 inch = 2.54 cm

1 cm = 0.39 inches

SOME COMMON UNITS OF LENGTH

Unit	Abbreviation	Equivalent
meter	m	approximately 39 in
centimeter	cm	10^{-2} m
millimeter	mm	10^{-3} m
micrometer	μm	10^{-6} m
nanometer	nm	10^{-9} m

Length Conversions

1 in = 2.5 cm	1 mm = 0.039 in
1 ft = 30.48 cm	1 cm = 0.39 in
1 yd = 0.9 m	1 m = 39 in
1 mi = 1.6 km	1 m = 1.094 yd
	1 km = 0.6 mi

To convert	Multiply by	To obtain
inches	2.54	centimeters
feet	30.48	centimeters
centimeters	0.39	inches
millimeters	0.039	inches

STANDARD METRIC UNITS

		Abbreviation
Standard unit of mass	gram	g
Standard unit of length	meter	m
Standard unit of volume	liter	L